P9-AFX-899

Writer's
Market '76

Writer's Market '76

Edited by
Jane Koester and Rose Adkins

WRITER'S DIGEST   CINCINNATI, OHIO 45242

Library of Congress Catalog Card Number 31-20772
ISBN 0-911654-37-2

Published by
Writer's Digest, 9933 Alliance Rd., Cincinnati OH 45242

CONTENTS

Introduction to the 47th Edition

Year-round editorial research makes each edition of the *Writer's Market* increasingly valuable to freelance writers. Since publications classified in different categories often buy material on similar subjects, the use of the Contents and Index pages will prove to be a profitable introduction to this edition.

Every listing in this book was mailed to the person or company that supplied it for verification, and all changes they made have been incorporated into the listings. (Many editors have provided us with telephone numbers, but these are to be used with discretion.) A few magazine and publishing houses go out of business or move after *Writer's Market* is published, but most listings remain correct all year and can be relied on. Freelancers are reminded that, while editors switch jobs frequently, magazine requirements change more gradually because publications continue to reach the same audience for some time after an editor leaves.

Many listings include a final note for freelancers, How To Break In, which gives inside tips for writers, obtained directly from editors of publications. Study the How To Break In information, and consider that along with the editorial requirements given, before writing for the publication.

A listing in this directory does not mean that *Writer's Digest* endorses the market; you must determine for yourself which ones you prefer to work with. We welcome information from you on address and editor shifts, discontinued markets, and dubious editorial business practices. Verified changes or warnings will be published in *Writer's Digest* market columns.

If a publication isn't listed, it is because (1) the publication doesn't actively solicit freelance material, (2) it doesn't pay for material, (3) it has suspended or ceased publication, (4) *Writer's Digest* has received complaints about it and it has failed to answer inquiries satisfactorily.

Consult each monthly issue of *Writer's Digest* for changes occurring in the markets. Using the *Writer's Digest* market information as a supplement to the current edition of *Writer's Market* provides you with the best possible up-to-date market information.

Each market is classified in its single best category. Priorities for classification are as follows: (1) type of market, e.g., consumer magazine, trade journal; (2) audience who reads it, e.g., women, juveniles, sportsmen; and (3) kind of material it buys, e.g., travel hints, cheesecake, regional articles. Headnotes refer you to overlapping categories which include magazines buying similar material.

Individual copyright information is included in each listing. Many publications that "buy all rights" will reassign rights to the author after publication; if they do, their listings indicate this. "Query first" in listings applies to nonfiction only; editors who require queries for fiction say so in their listing. Do not send fiction, poetry, fillers, etc., to an editor who doesn't specifically request that kind of material.

Listings are alphabetized on a word by word basis; for example:

A.D.
AAA Texas Division Texas Motorist
Abingdon Press
Accounting & Business Research
AFI-Atelier Films, Inc.
African Progress
All-Church Press, Inc.
Allen, George & Unwin Ltd.
Allen, J.A., & Co., Ltd.

A letter followed by a period is considered one word; a group of letters without periods (AA) are considered one word; hyphenated compounds are considered one word. Titles containing an & or the abbreviation St. are alphabetized as if the abbreviation were spelled out. Titles beginning with U.S. are also alphabetized as if spelled out. Titles beginning with *Mac* or *Mc* are indexed under "Mac" as though the full form were used.

Abbreviations used in this book are listed below. The Postal Service's two-letter state codes are used in addresses.

A30¢	30 Australian cents	MI	Michigan
b&w	black & white	MN	Minnesota
		MO	Missouri
ms(s)	Manuscript(s)	MS	Mississippi
N.A.	North American	MT	Montana
NZ$	New Zealand dollars	NC	North Carolina
		ND	North Dakota
S.A.E.	self-addressed envelope	NE	Nebraska
S.A.S.E.	self-addressed stamped envelope	NH	New Hampshire
AK	Alaska	NJ	New Jersey
AL	Alabama	NM	New Mexico
AR	Arkansas	NV	Nevada
AZ	Arizona	NY	New York
CA	California	OH	Ohio
CO	Colorado	OK	Oklahoma
CT	Connecticut	OR	Oregon
DC	District of Columbia	PA	Pennsylvania
DE	Delaware	PR	Puerto Rico
FL	Florida	RI	Rhode Island
GA	Georgia	SC	South Carolina
HI	Hawaii	SD	South Dakota
IA	Iowa	TN	Tennessee
ID	Idaho	TX	Texas
IL	Illinois	UT	Utah
IN	Indiana	VA	Virginia
KS	Kansas	VI	Virgin Islands
KY	Kentucky	VT	Vermont
LA	Louisiana	WA	Washington
MA	Massachusetts	WI	Wisconsin
MD	Maryland	WV	West Virginia
ME	Maine	WY	Wyoming

FREELANCE AT WORK

By Hayes B. Jacobs

Any definition of "freelance," whether the word is describing a seamstress, an artist, a photographer or a writer, must embrace the sobering phrase, "not on a regular salary." And there, quite naked, exposed for all the world to see and wonder at, is the reason that genuine, full-time freelance writers are as rare as genuine, full-time ghosts. (Genuine, full-time freelance ghost writers, however, as we shall see in subsequent paragraphs, are, so to say, *something else.*)

Among those rare, full-time freelance writers, of whom there are only a few hundred in the United States, are a fair number who, although they appear to be getting along nicely without a regular salary, are actually undergirded by a small trust fund here, a large parcel of income-producing property there, or, quite frequently, a salaried mate. I know one with a hidden herd of Herefords, and another who rents rooms.

If you're a typical freelance writer, the earnings you produce with your typewriter supplement other, steadier income. Your writing brings in $200 a year (the fledgling freelance); $20,000 a year (the high flyer); $200,000 a year (the superstars); even $2,000,000 a year (yes, it's been done, just as Halley's comet has been sighted).

You probably have some talent, or at least some ability, and a strong desire to see your words in print. To some extent, at least, you've learned to accept frequent rejections, and to trudge confidently on down the writer's lonely road, which is full of detours, pitfalls, and other perils far more numerous than normal people would believe possible.

WRITING – TO BE READ

Whatever milestone you've passed, you've discovered, I hope, that talent, energy, desire, production, and determination are not enough. You must also be a part-time salesman. Why turn out a product that nobody else ever sees, or appreciates? Writing is a communication art; it must "say" something, communicate something to someone before it acquires any sensible reason for its existence. Writing is to be *read*, and the surest way to have your writing read is to have it *published.* (Go on upstairs and write your secret poems if you wish — but if you think they're any good, better leave them tied in neat bundles, protected from mice, as did that closet freelance, Emily Dickinson, who, one should note, was always supported by a loving father.)

It is to help you find someone to publish your writing *now*, while you are yet among us, that this huge compendium called *Writer's Market* is

---

(Hayes B. Jacobs is a New York freelance, whose work has appeared in most of the major magazines. He is the author of Writing and Selling Non-Fiction, *published by* Writer's Digest, *and writes the "New York Market Letter" column for* Writer's Digest *magazine.)*

issued annually. After your stationery store charge account, your typewriter, and your fertile brain, *Writer's Market* is the most indispensable thing in your writing life. It outlines your "sales territory" so that you will not waste precious time, energy, and postage "calling on" customers who have no interest in your product — and customers who have moved away or died. The book's thousands of entries are not the creative handiwork of a group of editor-elves in Cincinnati; they are the closely detailed reports received direct from your potential customers (the editors), telling *you* exactly what they buy, how and when they want it submitted, what and when they pay for it, and what length it should be. Few salesmen out in the real world have access to such up-to-date, bona fide, horse's mouth sales potential data.

Most writers have a few notions about what they want to write. They write it, or perhaps an outline of it, then consult *Writer's Market* to find someone who will buy it. But here let me reveal a big trade secret: a lot of writers sit down and just read *Writer's Market*; they see what the customers want, then write it. In a sense, then, the book can tell you not only where to sell, but what to write. What a fat, jolly, helpful friend of a book!

Smart, practical-minded writers (there *are* some, and almost any writer you're able to name is one of them) recognize that the literary marketplace, like the universe, is an eternal yet ever-changing phenomenon. Magazines go into and out of business, or change hands. Book publishers expand and contract, adding new departments, dropping others. Editors drop dead (too infrequently, some dour and usually unsuccessful writers swear) or move about to graze in greener pastures; they are replaced, demoted, promoted, or just like your Uncle Ed down at the gas company, kicked upstairs. In a single year recently, one major magazine had a succession of three editors, and by the time you read this, the fourth has probably been sent to Personnel for fingerprinting.

Well, you ask, how in tophet can an annual directory like *Writer's Market* keep up with all of those changes? Surprising answer: It can't. Which is why, in addition to studying the newest edition of *Writer's Market*, you must keep up with the monthly market information in the writer's magazines, such as *Writer's Digest*. And even armed with *monthly* reports, plus all the distorted trade gossip you pick up from writer friends, you must expect once in a while to find that while you were awaiting a report on your short story, "Ten Little Chickens," from Miss Addie Foolscap, managing editor of *The National Inhibitor*, of Chicago, Miss Foolscap has left in a huff to become circulation manager of *Western Jam & Jelly*, in Denver, and *The National Inhibitor* has been sold to Inkwell, Inc. of Oosapoosah, Florida, which plans to turn it into a national newsweekly, *Splitsecond*, and that it will no longer use fiction. *Sick-en-ing!*

But don't despair. Fortunately, the percentages are very much with you; the market is mostly stable enough to make *Writer's Market* just what I've called it — indispensable.

Unless you try to use last year's edition, which is not only utterly dispensable but dangerous. Like a time bomb. Call the police and tell them to come get it. Or, you can save up two or three editions, cover them with something flowered, and make a pretty doorstop.

FINDING YOUR MARKET

Whether you write fiction, nonfiction, or poetry, you will do your best work if you write about what interests you most. If you're a magazine writer, the publications you most enjoy reading are usually the ones to aim for in selling your work. But even a glance through *Writer's Market* will show you that there are hundreds of publications you've never seen or heard of, and among them may be some excellent sources of writing income.

Ideally, you'll try to establish yourself with several major markets — magazines that pay top rates. Then, in addition, you'll work for regular contact with the minor markets — those that use shorter pieces, demanding less research and writing time. These markets will also sometimes take material your major markets have turned down.

I don't recommend that anyone *start* with minor markets. It makes little sense to me, esthetically or economically, to "start small." When I quit a steady job to freelance, a well-meaning but rather addled friend said, "Well, I guess you'll just have to tighten your belt." I told her I intended to loosen it. Working steadily for the less demanding, minor publications is, of course, the only thing for those with limited abilities and energies. For others, years of work in the minor leagues affords only a limited chance to test yourself, to see how really good you can be. Suppose Edison had tried only to make a better candle!

It is defeatist thinking, and possibly an indication of a psychological quirk you ought to get rid of, one way or another — and I'm serious — if you sit around thinking, "Oh, there's no point in my trying to sell to a magazine like *Esquire*, or *The New Yorker*, or *Atlantic*. They'd never take anything from *me*. I'll try the little magazines, where I have a better chance." It's like the young man who never asks beautiful, bright, charming girls for a date, for fear of being turned down; he never wins for losing; he goes to the dogs. It's a shame. Unaided by an agent, and without knowing any of the "right people," I made my way into most of the major magazines before any of my work ever appeared in a little magazine. My manuscripts went into the "slushpile," the unsolicited material that inundates editorial offices. It was fished out, read, and bought. The same thing is happening every day to other totally unknown writers. Listen to me! Listen: If your work has made the rounds of all the top markets, and nobody has taken an interest, *then* try the minor markets.

I advise authors of books to follow the same system; try the *major* publishing houses first — as many as twenty if necessary — before sending your book manuscript to the smaller houses.

SELLING SHORT FICTION

Some new writers, I've discovered, need to be reminded that fiction — short stories and novels — describes a world that never existed, but that, except in fantasies like science fiction, *could* exist. Fiction is "made up"; it is a product of the writer's imagination, a projection of his dream world. It is often based on real life; a fictional hero or heroine may resemble someone the writer has known, but important changes are nearly always made — and not just to protect the author from libel action. Real-life experiences usually don't make good fiction; if they are used, they must be transformed, "heightened," lied about, if you will, to make them more dramatic and appealing. Just think of everything you did yesterday. *Everything.* Now, how much of that do you think anyone would ever want to read about? But if you could twist things around a little, and dream up some . . . And you're off, a writer of *fiction.* A liar. A dreamer. A teller of tales. A clever, drama-minded prevaricator.

If you're a beginning prevaricator, you are probably writing short stories, rather than a novel. You love to write short stories, but you've heard they're hard to sell. Don't believe everything you hear. The short story market, let me and this fat book assure you, has not vanished, as the uninformed sometimes glibly remark. It has, however, changed — rather drastically, and particularly since World War II. Some of the mass-circulation magazines that once used large quantities of short fiction have disappeared, but in their place one finds numerous smaller publications that offer fiction to their readers. If your métier is short fiction, then, don't be discouraged; be market-conscious. There are markets for you, plenty of them, and you have only to search them out in the listings that follow.

If you write short fiction, you must be aware that a rather large body of material is published ostensibly as nonfiction, even though it is entirely fiction. I refer, of course, to the many stories contained in the "confession" magazines. Many of these, ironically, have the word "true" right in their titles, but the stories they contain are all made up; pure fiction, created in the minds of fiction writers. One of the country's most successful confession writers once told me that when she began selling consistently while in college, her mother couldn't believe she could come by so much money honorably, and was fearful that her daughter had taken to the streets. Writing confessions may not be for you, but don't turn your nose all the way up. A fair number of writers of "quality" fiction have learned some of their art in this peculiar field. Writing confessions may sound easy — an exercise by and for the feeble-minded, but in its way it is as demanding as many another open to writers. The pay is not high, usually 3¢ to 5¢ a word, so one must produce in quantity in order to realize any substantial monetary reward. Since confession stories are published without by-lines, more than a few writers of quality fiction slyly turn out an occasional confession for extra income. Only their editors know.

SELLING MAGAZINE ARTICLES

We live in an increasingly fact-oriented society, in which everyone's mind is filled with questions: How can I save money on food? How can I repair my own car? Where are the best places to go for inexpensive vacations? How can I tell if my doctor is well qualified? Are face lifts dangerous? What are the best colleges for my children? Are there any really promising cures for cancer? How much Social Security will I receive when I'm 65? Now that every schoolchild knows something about astronauts, aviation, ecology, and many are impressively informed in chemistry, math, and physics, they thirst for even more knowledge and understanding. In the last 25 years, the educational level has risen sharply; people know more, and that makes them want to know still more. More people have traveled; they want to see more of the world, and to know more about it. Everyone seeks facts, and more facts.

The nonfiction writer, as a supplier of facts, as a major source of answers to all the questions in the public's mind, has a greater opportunity than ever before. It's the writer who tells people why they should lose weight, and how to lose it quickly and safely; why their kids misbehave and what to do about it; what cholesterol is; how to invest their money; how to stop smoking; how to start exercising; how to have a happier sex life; how to maintain and repair household equipment; which books are worth reading; which television set is the best buy; which drugs are safe and unsafe.

Every year, more people, and more questions. Jet travel, radio, television and the movies have swept away state and national boundaries; today's citizen is in spirit, if not politically, a world citizen. With an entire world to wonder about, he must do a lot of reading. (He may be a TV addict, but most of what he sees on TV was first written by some writer.) Don't be disheartened when you hear that today's young people are not reading, that their eyes are only on TV or movie screens. Actually they're reading more than any "younger generation" that ever preceded them (check paperback book publishers for the impressive statistics), and moreover, everything they do is being analyzed, written about, by writers.

Do not confuse *articles,* informative pieces usually based on extensive research, with the *personal essay,* in which you express your opinions, or report on some personal experience. Such essays form a small part of the nonfiction market, and are in much less demand than the thoroughly researched "fact piece," or article. Many novice writers become discouraged when, after setting down their views on diet, household management, automobile safety; their opinions on the political scene, religion, sex, or education, find no editors willing to buy their manuscripts. They fail to realize that editors are trying to supply their readers with *facts,* and facts usually come from experts. There's a vast difference between an article on child care written by a pediatrician, an M.D. with 15 years' experience, and that of a young Umapine, Oregon mother who sits down to "tell the world" what a lot she's learned about making granola for her hungry brood.

But if you're determined to be a writer, you need not be a professional to write an authoritative article on child care. As a writer, you can consult child care experts — pediatricians, psychologists, educators — and convey their facts and ideas in your article. Just remember that it's *expertise* that is wanted; if you lack it, you must become a reporter, writing the facts the experts convey to you. You become a fact-gatherer; *your* expertise is in searching out, selecting, and conveying facts.

In many of the nonfiction markets detailed in this book, you will see the phrase, "Query first," or "We prefer queries." This means that you should not submit a finished article to those markets without inquiring. Short features, fillers, humorous sketches, yes; finished, researched articles, no.

A query is simply an inquiry — a letter or an "outline" of the kind of article you have in mind. It is a sales pitch, sent out in advance of the finished product in the hope that the prospective buyer will say, "Yes, send the product." (Actually, what he usually says is more like, "Yes, send it, and we'll be glad to read it — but we can't guarantee we'll buy it.")

Queries accomplish several things. They prevent you from doing a lot of research and writing on something nobody will ever buy. They save the editor time; he can quickly identify a subject as being of interest; if it is, then he can suggest treatment, length, etc.

I hear a few writers objecting to the entire querying process. It takes time, they grouse; you can query only one editor at a time, and that causes delays. I tell them to remember that when an editor prefers queries, it's pointless to try to bludgeon him into *not* preferring queries. He's the customer; he's entitled to buy in the manner *he* chooses. You would not trade long at a store in which, when you asked for carrots, the manager insisted you take rutabagas, instead.

Two kinds of queries are in common use — the "outline" and the letter query. The outline query is not in the form of the outline you were taught to make in English classes. There are no Main Headings, with Roman numerals; no sub-headings numbered 1, 2, 3; no a's, b's, and c's. The outline query merely outlines, summarizes, in a page or two, the article you propose to write. It may be phrased in "outline" language; instead of writing full sentences, you may be elliptical, terse: "Examples would follow, showing applications of this new surgical technique; doctors explain variations, and why each is needed. Pictures available for each technique; all black-and-white, but color could be obtained if necessary."

You may offer an outline query that begins with the actual text of your article. It is typed double-spaced, and looks exactly as if it were the opening of your manuscript text. It gives the "lead," the opening paragraph or two, and several additional paragraphs. Then, switching to single-spacing, you add additional information, couched in the terse, outline language illustrated above. This form of query has the advantage, if you have no publishing credits, of showing the editor something of your writing style.

With a letter query, you merely address the editor, and suggest in a letter the kind of article you have in mind, how you propose to treat the subject, and indicate some of your sources of information.

Both outline and letter queries should contain enough *concrete* information to give the editor a clear idea of the subject and how you would deal with it. Follow all generalized statements with specific facts. Give a few anecdotes. Where possible, offer some quotations from people you will be quoting in the article itself. A sure way to fail with a query is to dawdle along in generalities: "How would you like a lively article on vacationing in the West?" (Where the hell is West? — Nevada, California, Idaho, Colorado? And what is "lively"? Give the essence of your article, so that it can be *seen* at once as lively.) Narrow the subject down, and be specific about what you plan to do with it. Editors get a lot of inane queries ("I'm going to Peru. Would you like a 10,000-word article on Peru?" "My neighbor raises goats and with his fine help I could write you a great goat article."), and reject them with all deliberate speed. Your goal with queries is to convince the editor that you have something new and important to offer; that his magazine should run such an article in the near future, and that you are the ideal person to write it. If you can't be convincing on these three essential points, you're on the wrong track.

If you send an outline query, accompany it with a brief letter, describing your qualifications; include mention of previous publications, professional accomplishments, special circumstances that give you unique qualifications for writing on your subject. If you send a letter query, always include such information, along with the description of your proposed article.

Queries should be offered to one editor at a time. Editors don't like to spend time considering a suggestion, and entering into correspondence about it, only to find that you are selling your article to a competing publication. If your subject is timely, you may add a line: "Since this subject is timely, I would appreciate an early response." A self-addressed stamped envelope (S.A.S.E.) should be enclosed with all queries. Keep a record of where you send queries, with dates of mailing, and responses.

Responses are usually of two kinds. The editor may say "Yes, I want the article you suggest. Send it along." Or he may say, "Yes, I want to see your article, but you will have to write it on speculation." By the latter, he means that he cannot guarantee to buy your article, but is interested enough to look at it, provided you're willing to take the risk of writing it "on spec," only to have the finished piece rejected. If you're a new writer, you will usually be asked to write "on spec," and it is really the only way you can hope to get started.

If you get a "firm assignment" that usually means that there is acute editorial interest, and often — but not always — you will be given a "kill fee," or a "cutoff fee" — a specified amount of money if the article is not finally accepted. If you have any doubt about the basis on which you are undertaking to write an article, by all means inquire, to avoid future misunderstandings and squabbles. Agree, too, on length, purchase price, expense allowances, extra payment, if any, for artwork, and the deadline. If payment is on publication, rather than on acceptance, you should be aware of that. (Payment on publication is a plague in writers' lives, but until it can be wiped out, you'll have to suffer if you do business with those who persist in such an inequitable "I'll pay you when I get around to using your product" policy. I wouldn't write the alphabet for such publications.)

How long should you wait for responses to a query? With major magazines, you should expect a reply in from two weeks to a month. If you are a new, unpublished writer, you must be extra patient. Don't let impatience prompt you to wrathy phone calls, or peppery letters; such intimidations will usually result in a negative report — instantly. But if after two months you've had no reply, write a brief inquiry, giving full information — article subject, date submitted, etc.

When querying, address the appropriate editor by name and title; another reason a directory like this is so valuable. But if you are ever uncertain of an editor's name, you can always just send things to "The Editors"; that is preferable to using the name of an editor who has not been with the publication for seven years.

SELLING PHOTOGRAPHS

Every magazine has an art director, or someone who arranges for "artwork" (photographs, drawings, paintings, diagrams) with which to illustrate articles. You can make a good living as an article writer without ever taking a photograph, although some sophistication in photography is a help to any writer. You may be asked by editors to make picture suggestions. Occasionally you may be asked to work along with a photographer on an assignment.

In some writing fields — notably travel, trade magazine work, and personality features — combining photographic skill with writing can be a tremendous asset. Editors in those fields often buy a picture-story "package," or pay extra for photographs. With a small investment and some practice, you can probably learn to take adequate, if not prize-winning, pictures with which to illustrate your work.

Your librarian can steer you toward helpful books on photography, and your local camera store may have books for sale. You can also learn much from "Selling Pictures With Your Words" by Fred Schnell, in this book. Let me get this word in, though:

Amateurs with cameras often become preoccupied with "things" — the cars, buildings, gadgets, etc., that editors want featured in pictures. Things are important, but readers are people, and they enjoy seeing people in pictures. Study ads for "things," and you'll see what I mean. And another word, about captions: Use some imagination. Don't just make labels for your pictures, such as "Harold Harris in front of his new supermarket," or "Lucille Morgenstern at her desk." You can often work in an interesting fact, one you had no room for in your text, when writing a caption.

PUBLISHING POETRY

It is probably true, as Thomas Hardy said, that "poetry and religion touch each other." It is *certainly* true that poets need a special faith in their art, just as they might have faith in God. If it were not so, there would be little poetry. It is usually written for its own sake, to express truth and understanding; in its highest forms it is "pure" art. And alas! — for pure art there has usually been more admiration than financial reward. If you love poetry, love writing poetry, I urge you to write it, to hope for the best, and to look elsewhere for a means of livelihood.

The object, of course, is to share your poetry, which suggests that you try to have it published. This directory contains a sizable section listing Poetry Publications of many kinds, from those with narrowly defined interests to those accepting poetry of "all types, all lengths; rhymed, unrhymed, metered, unmetered, conventional, experimental, punctuated or not." Poetry editors know what they want, and say so. ("Avoid rhymey birds and trees and bees poetry," declares one. "Come to the point," says another.) Some of these markets pay 2¢ a word, $3 to $15 a poem, $1 a line, etc. Others "pay" with admiration, and copies of their publications.

Many other publications, listed elsewhere in *Writer's Market*, publish poetry — *Mademoiselle, Essence, Atlantic, Harper's*, for example; rates in these markets vary from $2 a line to $25 to $50 a poem.

Nearly all poetry markets favor short poems; those just mentioned rarely run a poem longer than 65 lines, and their typical poems are much shorter — 10 to 15 lines.

Verse — particularly of the light, humorous variety — is also wanted by many magazines, and some newspapers. If you're adept at verse, you may want to explore the many opportunities open to you in the greeting card field. An outline of the types of greeting cards, and a list of editorial requirements, can be found in the Greeting Card Publishers category.

SELLING FILLERS

Many writers supplement their regular writing income by supplying "fillers" — the short features editors find useful to fill out pages. Fees for fillers range from $1 to $150 to $200; most bring $5 to $10. Verse is often used, but fillers usually consist of humorous anecdotes, brief "how-to" pieces, jokes, aphorisms, historical oddities, quizzes, word games, self-tests, etc. Every publication has its favorite kinds of fillers; in addition to consulting *Writer's Market*, you should read several issues of any publication before attempting to supply fillers. Some magazines will pay you for supplying clippings they can reprint as fillers.

A filler manuscript should be typed, double-spaced, on white, 8½x11 paper, with your name and address in an upper corner. The sheet may be sent flat, in a large envelope, or folded into thirds, like a business letter, and mailed in a business-sized envelope. Use a paper clip — not a staple — for filler manuscripts of more than one page. Fold a stamped, self-addressed business envelope into thirds, to enclose if you're sending material to publications that return unwanted fillers. (Some do not, and some do not acknowledge them.) Keep a carbon, and record of dates mailed. When submitting clippings, paste them on an 8½x11 sheet, type the name and date of the source below the clipping, and your name and address in an upper corner. Make a copy of the clipping's contents for your office records — or Xerox the entire sheet after pasting up the clipping.

Some editors buy photographs, or sketches, with captions, for use as fillers. Protect any photographs with cardboard so that they will not become bent. Rough sketches are often acceptable; the magazine's art department will make finished drawings from them. Make a notation on the back of any photograph or sketch, indicating that it is for use with the text of your filler, which you should identify with a title or brief description.

SELLING YOUR BOOK

You've never written a book, but you'd like to write one. Could you sell it? Would any publisher invest the $5,000, or $10,000 or more — often much more — necessary to pay you for the work, and to produce, distribute, advertise and publicize your book? Is that possible — even if you haven't established yourself as a writer, with shorter works, such as short stories or articles?

The answer, of course, is *yes*; or, more accurately, *yes, if* . . .

If you can offer something that a publisher thinks he can profitably sell. Publishing books, some new writers are slow to learn, is a business enterprise, not an activity carried on by beneficent, literary-minded men and women for the betterment of the world. Many book publishers are indeed beneficent and literary-minded, and many want to make the world better. They also have wives and children to feed, and mortgages, car payments, and doctor bills and taxes to worry about. Just like you, they have to make a certain amount of money. They'll gamble, occasionally, in the hope of making more. But day by day, they're a cautious lot, who have learned that it is not usually prudent to spend $10,000 on a project that will net them $323.47.

The book business, though, has always been a somewhat crazy business, which follows its own illogic. Many of its greatest successes have originated with what sensible people would have thought imprudent, foolish investments. Publishers will sometimes accept books that they *know* will lose money, in the hope that the author will eventually produce a best seller.

If, for example, you write an excellent first novel, you stand a good chance of finding a publisher who will publish it, even though he knows that few first novels make money. You can even write three novels, and sell the third to the same publisher who lost money on the first two. With your fourth and fifth money loser, however, your luck will probably fail. People sometimes recover from craziness.

If you yearn to see your name on a book, you'll have a much better chance of publication if the book is nonfiction. And if you even glance at best-seller lists, you're aware that certain kinds of nonfiction have more appeal than others — self-help, with all its ramifications, is one of the leaders. If your book looks as if it would help people look better, eat better, feel better, acquire more money, have better sex lives; if it reassures or consoles them as they face the threats life presents, including the ultimate threat of death; if it offers practical, workable solutions to the thousand-and-one problems of living; if it illuminates some of life's mysteries; if it exposes secrets, reveals scandals, describes corruption in high places, sets history's records straight; if it provides escape and refreshment from life's woes, then you're probably on the right track. To become the author of a successful nonfiction book, you must discover what people *need to know*, or think they need to know, and then tell them — interestingly, in a way that will make their learning process compellingly worthwhile, and preferably pleasant.

Well, fine, you say; but doesn't all that assume that you have some specialized knowledge? You're not an M.D., a psychiatrist with extensive experience in helping people solve their sex problems, and, in fact, you have a sex problem or two, yourself. You haven't spent forty years in the investment business, and you even have trouble balancing your checkbook. You don't *know* any secrets to reveal. Could you still write a successful book that would teach people what they need to know? Yes, if you can work as a reporter or a research scholar works; go to the experts in the field, and write down what they tell you, so that readers can understand it. Through reading, interviewing, pondering, you can perhaps become expert enough to produce a useful book. If you're a good writer, you can possibly join forces with one or more experts, and collaboratively produce a good book. (That path of collaboration, however, is strewn with broken friendships, horrendous fracases and misunderstandings, lawsuits, counter-lawsuits, and other psycho-social debris. Before collaborating with *anyone* beyond the "chat over coffee" stage, get a good lawyer and have a firm understanding, in writing, of who is to do what, who is to share what percentage of profit, subsidiary rights, etc. The same advice applies if you undertake to ghost-write a book for some expert. In either collaborating or ghosting, don't try to avoid legal fees by saying, "But we're good friends; we trust each other." Friends who collaborate even under a clear-cut legal agreement are on a perilous trek, usually with emotion rather than wisdom as a guide.)

Most major nonfiction books are written under contract, drawn up after the author queries a publisher, submitting an outline and some sample chapters. The same is true for some novels. Determine a given publisher's preferences before sending either a query or a completed manuscript. Details on querying book publishers, book contracts, royalties, etc., are given in the preface to the Book Publishers section.

Many new poets and short story writers begin to think about "putting together a book." There's no harm, but a lot of frustration, in trying. The cold fact is that anthologies of serious poetry and short stories, with rare exceptions, have extremely limited sales — even when the author is well known. Many collections of short stories are the result of an established author's, or his or her agent's, having wheedled the publisher into issuing the collection; the contract is sometimes tied to the publication of the author's next novel. The publisher thereby flatters the author's vanity, retains his good will, and keeps him "in the house." A few publishers risk a loss by publishing a limited number of works of poetry; if they are distinctive, and attract favorable critical attention, they add to the house's prestige, and help attract money-making authors.

I've confronted you with some far-from-encouraging facts. Now let me add that you should not let those facts deter you from attempting to get a book of poetry published. Consider how drab the world would be had no publisher ever been allowed to accept, reject, or even look at the poetry of Keats. *Ad astra . . .* and all that.

Meanwhile, back here on earth, poets might do well to band together in groups, and set up their own cooperative publishing houses. With effort, such a venture can be made to work. A group of Minnesota poets set up such a house in 1972, patterning their organization after a Swedish writers' cooperative established in 1969. The U.S. group publishes only the work of Minnesota writers. They'll gladly tell you how they got started, and advise you on setting up a similar organization. You may obtain information by sending a letter, with S.A.S.E., to: Minnesota Writers' Publishing House, 21 Ridge Rd., Morris MN 56267.

THE MARKET FOR PLAYS

Some years ago I sat watching the author of a Broadway play, written and produced nearly thirty years earlier, open her mail. Gleefully, she held up a check. A royalty payment, one of several she receives every year, from amateur productions of her play — which was much less than a resounding hit with its original New York audiences. "It's not making me rich," she said, "but after all these years, it's like finding the money."

Getting a play produced on Broadway, however, is almost as chancy as booking a trip on the next flight to the moon — but every season, a few writers make it. Production costs have frightened away many of the "angels" who put money into Broadway plays, but there are some still fluttering their wings, eagerly; and crouched nearby are producers, reading play scripts, hoping to find that sure-fire hit. Reaching these producers, and those producing Off-Broadway, and Off-Off Broadway, is best accomplished through an agent. (See the section on Authors' Agents for those who handle plays, and screenplays, and the section on Play Producers.)

To start more modestly, you can often get your play produced by local amateur and semi-professional groups, which are proliferating in all sections of the country. And scripts can be offered to the various play publishers. (See listings of Play Publishers.) These people offer flat-rate payments or royalty contracts. It is, of course, wise to try to get a royalty arrangement rather than sell all rights for a single payment — unless the payment is truly substantial.

Whatever direction your play writing efforts take, it will pay you to keep production costs in mind. Large casts, numerous sets, intricate production gimmickry all represent roadblocks to acceptance. Producing a play with a single set, and a small cast, is appealing to both amateur and professional producers.

SELLING TV SCRIPTS

An astonishing number of writers suddenly decide they're going to "break into TV." They sit down and write a drama, or an entire series, bundle up their manuscripts and mail them to CBS or NBC, or even to some sponsor. That's an utter waste of time and energy. Television scripts are marketed solely through agents, and in the section on Authors' Agents you will see the names of those specializing in TV and movie scripts.

Nearly all the TV series you see are produced in California, and the full-time writers on these shows usually live there. By working with an agent, however, it is possible to sell scripts, or sometimes just ideas for scripts, from elsewhere in the country.

Screen and TV writers must take special steps to protect their rights to script properties. The Writers Guild of America West (8955 Beverly Blvd., Los Angeles CA 90048) has a Manuscript Registration Service to assist writers in protecting their material. It is available to non-members as well as members. Information concerning the service, fees, etc., is available from the Guild.

A useful list of all TV shows may be found in the *Ross Reports*, published by Television Index, Inc., 150 Fifth Ave., New York NY 10011. Cost to New York residents is $1.55 per issue, and to all others, $1.45.

"BREAKING IN" TO ANY MARKET

Whatever your specialty as a writer, you should keep in mind the basic principle of salesmanship — providing the "customer" with what *he* wants, when *he* wants it, at a price *he* is willing to pay. It's easy, when one hears of quick, easy fortunes made from best-selling books, to think that the world is just waiting for one's efforts; that all one must do is "type it up," send it off, and wait for the big fat check. The writing life is much more complicated. The successful salesman tries to sense the need for his product, tries to *stimulate* the need (which is what professional writers do with query letters, and sample chapters), then to fill it — with a product so satisfying that the customer will ask for more, and, ideally, pay even more for it.

Sensing, and stimulating needs . . . subtle processes, requiring that one be alert, tuned in, aware of what's going on, and what's likely to go on. Every editor takes a certain pride in sensing, several months in advance, what readers will be wanting to read. You can be helpful to such editors in this prediction process. Get ideas to the editor even before they occur to him, and he'll recognize and reward you as a valuable ally.

You must *study* magazines — regularly. Scrutinize book publishers' lists; read what they are publishing; sense the kinds of things they're buying. If you can acquire that kind of insight, you're in a position to offer things that follow the trend. In some of the entries in this directory, you will find editors' specific suggestions on "how to break in." But whether they offer that counsel or not, the sure way is to discover the kind of thing they're buying, and provide it.

There's another way, too, which many writers overlook. Every editor tries to "do new things," but is often at a loss to decide which new things to do. And if business is good, he is hesitant to change directions. Yet he's sure he can't keep doing the same old thing. Your job is to help him out of his dilemma. Point to a way by which he can institute change with less risk.

Some writers "break in" by contributing only ideas to editors; suggestions for new departments, or columns. Others start with modest contributions of short features, "fillers," or items the magazine's columnists and feature editors can use. A pertinent book review can sometimes be the opening wedge. A watchful eye on what is distinctive about your community or region — an annual festival, a historic landmark, an unusual industry — can lead you to suggest short features, of nationwide interest, that might be overlooked by editors sitting in New York. Sometimes, repeated Letters to the Editor can establish your identity with an editor, who will then think of you when he needs coverage of something going on in your area.

It is possible to acquire a reputation with a magazine even while failing to sell to it. Good, solid contributions, sent in over an extended period, can impress editors with your industry and determination, and tilt a subsequent decision in your favor. ("She's been trying so hard, let's buy this one.") With my first sale to *The New Yorker* came an acceptance letter saying that it was nice to see someone that they'd been "watching" finally come through. They hadn't been watching *me*; they'd been seeing my manuscripts come in, and go out, in quantity, for many months. By a lot of hard work, I'd made them aware of me; aware that I was trying to break in.

I've heard would-be writers say that the best way to break in is to "know someone" — an editor, or his secretary, or someone else close to the editor. Sometimes that can be helpful, but editors are wary of such introductions. I once heard the president of a major publishing house say that one word from him — a recommendation that one of his editors examine a book he'd heard about through friends — was "the kiss of death." The editors resented the implication that someone with "pull" could influence their editorial judgment.

So beware of using "connections," and "pull." What editors want is good manuscripts, and if you have them to offer you needn't "know someone." The best, most useful person a writer can know is himself — to determine what his capabilities are, where his strengths lie, how to prop up his weaknesses.

Doing good work, for which you know there is a need, and becoming sophisticated in the art of marketing it — that is the writer's major strength. Compromising, settling for less than your best work, or aiming for markets that offer no challenge or room for growth, is destructive. If you can't be proud of what you're doing, proud of yourself as a writer, you should be doing something else.

SIDELINES

Anyone with average writing ability can pick up odd jobs, apart from major freelance writing tasks. Yes, even in a recession. I know a freelance who worked as a political speech writer when he was getting started; now he occasionally does a little lobbying. I know another who, having heard that her local radio station was short-handed, picked up part-time work writing commentary for a musical program. Is your bank about to celebrate the anniversary of its founding? Perhaps it could use a booklet, recounting its history, and you could write it, for a nice fee. Many small colleges need public relations help. Churches, lodges, and other organizations sometimes hire outside help to create fund-raising literature. Would your local newspaper use a book review column? A gardening column? Drop in and inquire. I once had a student who wrote a regular gardening column for her small hometown newspaper; that led to a gardening book. Look over the brochures being handed to guests by your local hotels and motels. Are they out-of-date? You could offer to create new ones. Inquire of various community organizations to see if they need help to prepare press releases, advertising and promotion literature.

Here are other sidelines that often fit in well with the freelance writer's life: tutoring school and college students; teaching adult education classes; doing research in your area for other freelance writers; editing and typing theses; proofreading, copy editing, and writing book jacket copy for publishers; working as a local "stringer" for a metropolitan newspaper; assisting shut-ins with correspondence; writing or editing sales literature for manufacturers and distributors; conducting opinion surveys for ad agencies; writing information booklets, which hospitals provide to patients; compiling family genealogies and histories; writing ad copy for realtors; styling and overseeing the production of menus and placemats for hotels and restaurants; answering fan mail for local celebrities; cataloguing for libraries, museums, and historical societies. Wherever there is the slightest need for the written or spoken word, a writer is in demand.

PREPARING MANUSCRIPTS

Writing — good writing — is an art, and any artist worthy of the name takes infinite pains with every detail associated with his work. The physical appearance of your manuscript reflects your taste, your respect for your art, and for the traditions of the profession. It is not enough to write well; your manuscripts must *look* good; they must look professional. By following just a few simple rules, you can enhance the sales possibilities of your writing, preparing manuscripts that gain instant respect in editorial offices. Bad writing, of course, beautifully typed and packaged, has never brought anyone success, but excellent writing, obscured by a sloppily prepared manuscript, has impeded the progress of many a writer.

Here are those rules I referred to: Use *white* heavy-weight bond for all manuscripts. Save money by using the cheapest possible paper for drafts. Splurge on *good* paper, *opaque* paper with some body to it, for manuscripts. Never use ordinary typing paper, which is sometimes deceptively labeled "bond"; it lacks opacity and body. Never use "crinkly" bond, or onion-skin, or the tissue some businesses use for carbon copies. Good bond, 20-pound weight, is usually best. Heavy bond requires more postage but it's worth every extra cent.

Use black (*only* black) typewriter ribbons. When they cease to produce truly black type, throw them out and replace them.

Clean the type of your typewriter. An old toothbrush works fine, but you may need type-cleaning liquid as well. Rubbing alcohol will work, too. Check all "enclosed" letters — the d's, a's, b's, o's, q's, g's, etc.; take a pin and pry out the gunk that accumulates in the enclosures, making an *o* indistinguishable from an *e*, and sending an editor out to the nearest ophthalmologist.

Never use a typewriter with fancy, cursive, script-like type. Sans-serif type is acceptable, but not ideal. Either elite or pica type is all right, but if you're buying a new typewriter, specify pica type; its larger size is easier to read.

Everything, in every manuscript, should be double-spaced. If you have a foreign typewriter, or a small portable whose double spacing is narrower than the standard, you may have to triple-space. Even quoted material, indented on both sides, should be double-spaced.

Use *adequate margins*. If you have pica type, a line-width of 55 spaces will result in adequate side margins. Leave at least 1¼ inches at the top and on the left, and at least 1 inch on the right. The bottom margin may be 1¼ inches, but it looks better if it is 1½ inches.

Why all the fussiness about margins? Beyond the esthetic, there are good, *practical* reasons. When you hold a manuscript, to read it, margins allow room for your thumbs, so they won't cover up the text. And editors need margins in which to write corrections, additions, questions, and instructions to printers and other editors. If you edit your own copy carefully, *you* may need margins. There's still another reason. Reading specialists have found that too long a line of type is fatiguing to the eye. I hope you are convinced.

Indent for all paragraphs. The block form seen in some business correspondence is never suitable for manuscripts. Leave just the regular double-spacing between paragraphs. Indent at least five spaces; eight or ten spaces create a better, less dense-looking page.

Every manuscript should have a title page, which not only identifies it but protects the first page of the text. Use regular white manuscript bond — nothing heavier, nothing fancy! Center the title, which should be in ALL CAPS a little above the middle of the page. Below the title, center the word "By." Below that, center your name, address, and if you wish, your telephone number. If you use a pseudonym, it belongs here. You can type your real name lower on the page, tying the two together with asterisks. Don't enclose the title in quotation marks unless the title itself is a quotation. Don't underscore the title unless it is in a foreign language and should appear in italics.

Some writers include the word-count of the manuscript. I've never felt that necessary; editors can quickly estimate the number of words. If you think there could be some confusion as to whether your manuscript is fiction or nonfiction, you might insert the phrase "A short story" or "An article," centered directly below the title. I put a title page on article queries, and use the phrase "An article query."

Don't "dress up" your title page with asterisks, borders, red type for the title, or any other junk that spells amateurism. New writers seem to feel they must do something special so that their manuscripts will "get attention." Decorated manuscripts get attention, all right; editors spot them at once as the work of an amateur, of someone who — like people loaded with too much jewelry — lack confidence.

The first page of your manuscript should be different from all the others in appearance. Instead of starting the typing at the top of the page, drop down to a point midway on the page to begin the text. Don't repeat the title; just start the regular text.

Number all pages, at the top or bottom of the page; the number is most easily read if centered on the page.

Type your last name in the *extreme* upper left-hand corner of every manuscript page — as close to the edge as you can get it, so it is unobtrusive.

Try to type the same number of lines on every page; some carbon paper comes marked to the edge, to facilitate this, but you can quickly train your eye to tell you the proper number of lines.

Manuscript text should be as nearly perfect as you can make it. Erase errors, and type corrections in neatly. I find *all* error-correcting gadgetry, except an eraser, a nuisance and an unnecessary expense. A good eraser, applied lightly but repeatedly, will expunge errors very well, but if the ribbon is brand new, and the type extremely black, take a piece of ordinary chalk and rub it lightly over the area after using the eraser; that will obliterate any faint mark left on the paper.

When you have finished typing, search for any uncorrected errors. It is permissible to write in a word here and there, or to make a small change with a pen. By all means, write or print legibly, in *full-size* script or letters. Don't try to imitate the typewriter type or you'll cause editorial eyestrain.

On the *next* successive double-spaced line below the last line of your text, center the words "The End." Don't leave a huge gap between the last line of text, and "The End."

If a word should not appear in your text, obliterate it completely with a black pen, and draw an arched guideline over it, to lead the reader's eye on past it.

If you have completed the final typing of a lengthy manuscript, then discover new material that must be included, type an "Insert" page.

Never bind a short story or article manuscript. Don't waste money on glassine folders, brads, binders of any sort.

Never staple a manuscript. Editors despise staples; their work often requires them to separate pages quickly. Use an ordinary paper clip — outsized ones for thick manuscripts.

Type *book manuscripts* exactly as you would shorter material, but for the first page of each chapter, start the text halfway down the page, typing the chapter number (in Roman numerals) and ALL CAPS title, if any, centered just above the beginning of the text. Do not clip chapter pages together. Don't use a binder. Books are usually submitted with the pages stacked in a box (those in which a ream of paper is packaged are excellent), with a simple, typed label (no decorations, no fanciness!) duplicating the information on the title page, pasted on the lid.

Most authors make at least two carbons or photocopies of book manuscripts, and as insurance against fire, theft, or other loss, store one of the copies in "outside" premises, such as a bank safety deposit box, lawyer's office, or friend's house.

PHOTOCOPIED MANUSCRIPTS

I don't know an editor anywhere who does not appreciate receiving *original, typewritten* manuscripts. A photocopy inevitably raises a question in an editor's mind: has the writer made dozens of such copies, and flouting custom, made simultaneous submissions to a number of editors? I dislike working with photocopied manuscripts; in far too many cases, copying machines don't work properly; the first six pages look beautiful, the last thirty pages are barely legible. I'm sure most editors share my dislike. But . . . you'll find some reports in this book from editors who don't. They will accept photocopies, and they say so; if you're photocopy-happy, these are your pals. I urge you not to send a photocopy to any other editors. Nor a carbon copy, *ever,* to *anyone.*

A few — very few — publications are amenable to simultaneous submissions; certain religious publications, for example. Full-length dramatic works are often submitted, in photocopy, to producers. Manuscripts, in such cases, should carry a notation stating that they are being submitted elsewhere.

COVERING LETTERS

Most writers write too many letters, causing editors unnecessary anxiety. The "covering" letter often sent with manuscripts usually need never have been written. What have you to say, really, about a poem, or a short story? "Here is a short story, entitled . . ."? (Your title page says that.) "I hope you'll find it suitable"? (Why else would you have mailed it?) "A stamped, self-addressed envelope is enclosed"? (If you've enclosed one, the editor will see it.) A covering letter is appropriate if you wish to describe your writing credits, or otherwise establish your special qualifications. But remember that editors haven't time to indulge in extensive correspondence with you. They're interested mainly in one thing — good, usable manuscripts.

MAILING MANUSCRIPTS

Article, short story and poetry manuscripts should be mailed flat, not folded. A single poem, or a manuscript of only two or three pages, such as a filler, may be folded in thirds and mailed in business envelopes, but I don't recommend it; heavy bond, when folded, tends to remain that way, so why ask the editor to paw around over manuscripts battling with both hands or an elbow or a foot to keep them open enough to read?

Collate the sheets of your manuscript, stack them with a cardboard on the back, and affix a paper clip in the upper left-hand corner. Fold the self-addressed stamped envelope (S.A.S.E.) and attach it under the cardboard. Insert the "package" in a large manila envelope. Be sure to place your return address on the outside envelope.

Under U.S. Postal Regulation 135.13, manuscripts of any length may be mailed to any point in the United States or its possessions at a special rate. All such material must be marked "Special Fourth Class Rate — Manuscript." This saves you money — but I don't recommend it. Even First Class Mail often moves as if it were hauled by senile, totally blind water buffaloes with arthritis and corns, so why not at least try to speed your work to market? Moreover, all postage expenditures for manuscripts, even those that never sell, are tax deductible, as legitimate business expenses, provided you keep careful records to prove what you've spent. I recommend sending all literary material First Class. Stamp "First Class Mail" on the outer envelope, and also on your S.A.S.E. Consult your Post Office for current rates on all material.

If you use the special Fourth Class rate and enclose a letter, you must add First Class postage and mark the envelope, "First Class Letter Enclosed."

First Class surface rates to Canada are the same as for U.S. mail, but you must not use U.S. postage stamps on return envelopes sent to Canada, or to any other foreign country. Enclose International Reply Coupons, obtainable at the Post Office.

There's usually little point in sending manuscripts Special Delivery, and in some cases, inexplicably, Special Delivery is so unspecial that it actually slows down delivery. (Ask your Congressman why.) But it is wise to insure book manuscripts. Special Delivery and Registered Mail never impress editors, whose mail is usually opened by assistants. If handling a lot of stamps bores you, you may deposit funds with the Post Office and secure a business permit, allowing you to have special "Return Postage Guaranteed" envelopes printed; inquire at your Post Office for details.

WAITING ... HOW LONG?

Most editors try to give prompt attention to manuscripts — even to the unsolicited material with which they are deluged. And that's the truth, despite the discouraging experiences we've all had now and then. Many entries in *Writer's Market* specify the average length of time required for reporting on material. You should add to that the estimated time required for two-way trips by those water buffaloes. When no time is specified, figure from three weeks to two months for the average magazine, up to three months for small, understaffed publications, and two to three months for book publishers.

If you feel a reasonable time has elapsed, and you've had no report, write a letter of inquiry. Don't grumble, or complain, or recite personal troubles such as family illness or mortgage foreclosures. Just *inquire,* politely.

Give *full details* — title, date of submission, etc. If that, and one additional follow-up inquiry produce no result, you might try a phone call. If even that fails, write a letter saying that you are withdrawing the material from the publication's consideration, and submitting it elsewhere. With a copy of such a letter in your files, you are freed of any obligation to the first publisher.

If you feel any publication has mistreated you, been unduly slow or totally delinquent in paying, etc., report, in full detail, to *Writer's Digest* magazine, which regularly investigates, and if the facts warrant, warns other writers about such publications.

REJECTIONS — NOT DEATH CERTIFICATES

If you haven't been in the business long, you may make wrong assumptions when your work is rejected with a little "We regret that ..." slip. A rejection slip may mean only that the editor has just bought something like the piece you submitted, or it may be the kind of thing he never buys. Don't spend a lot of time puzzling over the meaning of rejection slips. Get your manuscript off to another publisher in the next mail. Don't lose confidence in your work. If it wasn't your very best, you never should have sent it out. If it was good enough to try with one editor, it's good enough to try with twenty, or thirty, or even more. Those "top literary agents" you hear about — those super-salespeople — accept rejections as they accept the sunset; it's what happens, every day. They move quickly on to the next prospect.

New writers often expect editors to go into detailed explanations. "At least they could have told me what was *wrong*," they wail. Editors are not working as literary critics, or writing teachers; they are *buyers*, and remodelers and repairers when the product is good but not quite as they want it. They have no time to explain in detail why they aren't buying. Sometimes you may get rejection *letters;* sometimes editors do explain some of their reasons for turning your work down. I've seen writers stare at such letters for days, trying to analyze just what the editor meant. That's a waste of time, too. Usually, the meaning is basically: "I didn't want this manuscript," and it's useless to try to decipher the polite phrases.

What does it mean when an editor scribbles across the bottom of a printed rejection slip: "Sorry. Try us again"? It means: "Sorry. Try us again."

COPYRIGHT

Most new writers worry unduly about copyright. Publishers relieve the writer of most of the problems associated with it. If you sell an article to *McCall's*, it is covered by copyright; the entire contents of the magazine is copyrighted. If later you want to offer the article to a foreign publication, just write to *McCall's* and ask that the copyright be assigned to you. If you publish a book, the publisher will copyright it (or you may copyright it in your own name); you will be protected for 28 years, after which you may renew the copyright for another 28 years. The Authors Guild and others are seeking to have the law changed, to extend protection for the author's lifetime plus 50 years.

Some new writers are afraid that magazines to whom they send their work will steal their ideas, or their material. This has undoubtedly happened, but I've never heard of a case. What editor would even want to be accused of such a shoddy practice? And you should realize that *ideas*, like plain facts, cannot be copyrighted. Also, keep in mind that ideas you express in a query or a manuscript are likely to strike other writers — and editors — at the same time. What could look like theft, then, could well be coincidence. An editor can reject your material, but subsequently buy something quite similar from another writer.

THE "RIGHTS" YOU SELL

You should be aware of what rights you are selling to anyone buying your work. If this isn't made clear to you, inquire before endorsing any check from a publisher. Some publications buy "all rights," which means that they can reprint your material, or sell it to someone else, or make a movie or TV play from it with no further payment to you. (But often, after publication, they will assign certain rights back to you, on request.) Other publishers buy "first serial rights," or "first North American serial rights." "Second serial rights" give a newspaper or magazine the right to print material that has already appeared in some other newspaper or magazine. The term also refers to the sale of an excerpt from a book after the book has been published — even though there may not have been any "first serial" publication.

Suppose you sell something to a publication that is not copyrighted. You may copyright it yourself. Prior to its publication, write to the U.S. Copyright Office, Library of Congress, Washington DC 20559, asking for application forms for a "Contribution to a Periodical." Let the editor know of your plans to do this. Ask the publication to publish the copyright symbol, (a small "C" contained in a circle), the year, and your name along with your contribution. On publication, send two copies of the issue, together with your application, and a $6 fee, to the Copyright Office.

YOUR FREEDOM AS A WRITER

Your freedom as a writer, particularly as an American writer, is something you should take much pride in. It was the freedom of American writers, ingeniously and expertly exercised, that not long ago began to rescue our country from political disaster. Much of the nation's progress, from its beginning, has been made after writers — working freely and without censorship — have pointed the way.

A writer's freedom naturally carries with it tremendous responsibilities. There are penalties for its abuse. One penalty, libel, is far too complex a subject for full discussion here. Briefly, libel is any false statement, written or broadcast, that tends to bring a person into public hatred, contempt, or ridicule; that causes him to be shunned or avoided; or injures him in his business or occupation. In most instances, truth is a complete defense against libel action; if you write only the truth, you are usually on safe ground. If you have any doubts concerning possible libel action, by all means consult an attorney — early, before your work goes beyond your typewriter.

You have another responsibility in exercising your writing freedom. To stay out of trouble, you must respect people's right of privacy. You cannot write just anything about people. The law provides protection to everyone from intrusion on their seclusion or solitude, and into their private affairs; from public disclosure of embarrassing private facts about them; from publicity that places them in a false light; and from appropriation and use, for profit or advantage, of their name and likeness.

But the law gives *much* leeway there; it always considers "the public's right to know." Those who place themselves in the public eye risk the loss of some of their privacy. As a writer, you can, and often should, probe and expose aspects of private lives. But you must be scrupulously truthful. Again — if you have doubts, consult a lawyer.

Among your freedoms is the right to quote material from others' writings. You may quote varying amounts without getting permission, under the "doctrine of fair use." In general, scholars allow quite a lot of their material to be quoted, even without permission; most scholarly works do not compete with each other. "Commercial" authors, however, cannot afford to be so generous. If you have any doubts, write to authors and their publishers for permission to quote. Small portions of text, included in a review or critical essay, are considered "fair use." But in all cases, acknowledgement must be given in your text. You must use special caution in quoting from poems, or song lyrics, since just a few words may constitute a large portion of their text; it's usually wise to secure permission, in writing.

These and other legal questions concerning your work as a writer can often be solved quickly by some self-examination. Are your intentions honest? Are you treating others fairly, and with respect? Are you writing only the truth?

If the answers to those questions are all "Yes," then you are probably not exceeding the bounds of your freedom.

HOW MUCH SHOULD I CHARGE?

Since most magazine editors spell out very clearly what their rates are for articles, stories, etc., the writer doesn't have much to say about setting his own price. It's already determined. But how does the freelancer decide what to charge for various other writing services—especially those jobs he turns up in his own area? His fee depends basically on two things: (1) how much he thinks his time is worth, and (2) how much the client is willing or can afford to pay.

Since the rates paid by advertising agencies, retail stores and other firms who are consistent users of part-time freelance writers vary from city to city, the list which follows can only serve as a rough guideline. The best thing for the freelancer to do is contact other writers, or friends in business who have used part-time freelancers in his area and get some idea of what's been paid for certain kinds of jobs in the past.

Here are some jobs and the rates which have been paid to writers for them.

Advertising copywriting: $3.50 to $7.50 per hour or a "package" price which might be just $25 for a press release or small ad on up to several hundred dollars for a more complex assignment.

Associations, writing for, on miscellaneous projects: $3 to $5 per hour.

As-told-to books: author gets full advance and 50% royalties; subject gets 50% royalties.

Audio cassette scripts: $120 for 20 minutes.

Audiovisual scripts: $1,000 to $1,500 advance against 5 to 10% royalties for 5 to 10 script/visual units.

Biography, writing, for a sponsor: $500 up to $3,000 plus expenses over a 4-year period.

Book manuscript copy editing: $3 to $5 per hour.

Book manuscript rewriting: $500 to $1,000 and up.

Booklets, writing and editing: $500 to $1,000.

Business films: 10% of production cost on films up to $30,000. $150 per day; $20 per hour where % of cost not applicable.

Comedy writing, for night club circuit entertainers: Gags only, $5 to $7. Routines, $100 to $300 a minute. Some new comics try to get 5-minute routines for $100 to $150; but top comics may pay $1,500 for a 5-minute bit from a top writer with credits.

Commercial reports, for business, insurance companies, credit agencies, market research firms: $1.85 to $5 per report.

Company newsletters, "house organs": $50 to $200, 2 to 4 pages.

Conventions, public relations for: $500 to $5,000.

Correspondent, magazine, regional: $5 per hour.

Criticism, art, music, drama, local: free tickets plus $2 to $5.

Editing, freelance book: $5 per hour and up.

Editing a group of religious publications: $75 to $250 per month.

Educational film strips: $1,200.

Educational films, writing: $200 for one reeler (11 minutes of film); $1,000 to $1,500 for 30 minutes.

Educational grant proposals, writing: $50 to $125 per day plus expenses.

Family histories, writing: $200 to $500.

Fiction rewriting: $150 for 10-page short story to $10,000 for complete novel rewrite, under special circumstances.

Folders, announcement, writing: $25 to $350.

Gallup Poll interviewing: $2.50 per hour.

Genealogical research, local: $3 to $5 per hour.

Ghostwriting business speeches, major markets: $500.

Ghostwriting political speeches: $10 to $20 per hour.

Government, local, public information officer: $10 per hour, to $50 to $100 per day.

History, local, lectures: $25 to $100.

House organs, writing and editing: $50 to $200, 2 to 4 pages.

Industrial and business brochures, writing: 4 pages, $120; 8 to 12 pages, $200.

Industrial films: $500 to $1,200, 10-minute reel; 5 to 12% of the production cost of films that run $750 to $1,000 per release minute.

Industrial promotion: $7.50 to $40 per hour.
Industrial slide films: 14% of gross production cost.
Journalism, high school teaching, part-time: % of regular teacher's salary.
Library public relations: $5 to $25 per hour.
Magazine stringing: $5 per hour.
New product releases, writing: $250 plus expenses.
Newspaper ads, writing, for small businesses: $10 for small 1-column ad.
Newspaper column: 80¢ per column inch to $20 per column.
Newspaper stringing: 20¢ to 50¢ per column inch.
Paperback cover copy: $40 to $75.
Pharmacy newsletters: $125 to $300.
Photo-brochures: $700 to $15,000.
Photocomposition on electric typewriter: $6 per hour, 5¢ per line on short jobs.
Political campaign writing: $200 to $250 per week; $25 per page piecework jobs.
Programmed instruction materials, writing: $1,000 to $3,000 per hour of programmed training
    provided. Consulting/editorial fees: $25 per hour; $200 per day, plus expenses, minimum.
Public relations: $125 per day plus expenses.
Publicity writing: $30 per hour; $100 per day.
Radio copywriting: $60 to $165 per week.
Record album cover copy: $75 to $100.
Retail business newsletters: $200 for 4 pages, writing, picture taking, layout and printing
    supervision.
Retainer for fund-raising writing for a foundation: $500 per month.
Retainer for publicity and PR work for an adoption agency: $200 per month.
Retainer for writing for businesses, campaign funds: usually a flat fee but the equivalent of
    $5 to $20 per hour.
Reviews, art, drama, music, for national magazines: $5 to $50.
School public relations: $3.50 to $10 per hour.
Shopping mall promotion: 15% of promotion budget for the mall.
Slide film, single image photo: $75.
Slide presentation for an educational institution: $1,000.
Sports information director, college: $120 to $700 per month.
Syndicated newspaper column, self-promoted: $2 each for weeklies; $5 to $25 per week for
    dailies, based on circulation.
Teaching creative writing, part-time: $15 to $25 per hour of instruction.
Teaching high school journalism, part-time: % of regular teacher's salary.
Teaching home-bound students: $5 per hour.
Technical typing: 50¢ to $1 per page.
Technical typing masters for reproduction: $3 per hour for rough setup then $2 to $4 per
    page or $5 to $6 per hour.
Technical writing: $5 to $12 per hour.
Textbook and Tradebook copy editing: $3.50 to $5 per hour. Occasionally 75¢ per page.
Translation, literary: $25 to $50 per thousand words minimum.
Travel folder: $100.
TV filmed news and features: $15 per film clip.
TV news film still photo: $3 to $5.
TV news story: $15 to $25.

If there are substantial differences in rates in your area for any of these jobs—or
you'd like to add other job categories with which you have personal experience,
please drop a line with the facts to Kirk Polking, Jobs for Writers, care of *Writer's
Market,* 9933 Alliance Road, Cincinnati, Ohio 45242. Your comments will help other
freelancers and future editions of this directory.

SELLING PICTURES WITH YOUR WORDS

by Fred Schnell

The first thing that you should get out of your head as a writer when you start taking pictures to accompany your articles is that you should be doing something artistic. Your job as a writer-with-a-camera is to illustrate your story with sharp, reasonably composed pictures that an editor can use to communicate better with his readers through your story and pictures or to simply make his publication look more appealing by breaking up space. Craftsmanship precedes art for the writer-photographer.

Outside of the ideological mewings-in-the-night magazines, publishing is a business. If you make the business easier or cheaper for an editor by being efficiently professional with the pictures and by saving him the additional expense of hiring someone else to illustrate your prose, he will often show his appreciation with more assignments.

Minimum for publication of a black and white photograph in any publication should be somewhere between $25 and $50 depending upon the circulation. This means you may have to pass some "sales" to lower pay markets. Most pro and major magazines follow the standards set up by ASMP (The Society of Photographers in Communication, 60 E. 42nd St., New York NY 10017). ASMP has a pricing guide for sale you might be interested in purchasing.

If you are going to be a photo pro you should act like one, and professionally packaged and submitted pictures not only create a favorable impression on an editor, they give him the added reassurance that you really seem to know what you're doing.

Most editors today prefer 8x10, double-weight, black and white prints dried either glossy, or dried on a glossy-type paper without the shine. The 35mm transparency is almost universally accepted and even preferred in the major national publications. Where weather and light conditions permit, magazines would prefer that their color be shot on 35mm Kodachrome film and the slowest black and white film that can adequately do the job, although many pros seldom use anything else but Tri-X.

Each print and transparency should have your name, address and telephone number either stamped, written or labeled on it. Every picture unit you submit should be numbered. For example, if you send in ten prints, they should be numbered so that you know how many are returned to you and you can quiz the publication later about anything lost. Who pays for the photo expenses depends upon the arrangement that has been made by you and the publication. Sometimes the magazine will simply give you space

(Additional markets for photography, illustrations, fine art, crafts, designs and cartoons may be found in Artist's Market which is published by Writer's Digest, 9933 Alliance Rd., Cincinnati OH 45242.)

rates for your pictures and expect you to handle the processing and printing expense. At other times, the publication will pay for all film and processing and perhaps even physically do the black and white printing and color processing itself. In either arrangement though, all pictures and negatives belong to you and should be returned sooner or later and paid for if lost, particularly if nothing was used.

There are two ways of captioning prints. One is simply to tape or lightly glue the entire caption to the back of the print. The other, which works better when there is a very complicated caption to describe a complicated picture, is to just attach an inch or so of the top of the caption to the bottom edge of the back of the print and fold the caption around so that the type is facing the photo. The editor can later fold it down and read the caption and refer to the print at the same time.

Whichever way you do it, make sure you don't attach the caption so that it is impossible to remove. If an editor is in a hurry, he may choose not to rewrite the caption, but simply rip it off and send it along its way to the printers. Because you can never tell how things go astray, it's best to also have your name, address and story title on the caption sheet.

As to the content of a caption, it should be a lot like a story and contain as many of the who, what, when, wheres, etc., as possible. It's probable that an editor will rewrite your caption in his own style to fill the space available in the publication. He'll appreciate having the information on the caption without having to dig through the story, possibly under the pressure of deadlines. All this may sound very detailed, but when an editor is sitting at a desk handling hundreds of pictures and stories a day, or week or month, he appreciates thoroughness and thinks favorably of the people who give it to him.

Since you can't write complete caption information on the edge of a transparency, you should place a code number on it that is different from your consecutive count number and key the code number to a caption sheet. For instance, on the 69th transparency you have submitted would be the number 69, your name and address and code number such as, B-2. The editor would then know to look for information under B-2 on the caption sheet, and it is possible that you might have several transparencies coded B-2 because they refer to the same subject. Transparencies should always be protected by individual plastic sleeves and glass-mounted slides should never be sent through the mail because of the problem of breakage and damage.

Pictures should be mailed by putting them in a cardboard sandwich several inches larger than the photos so the edges won't get bent and then slipping that cardboard sandwich into an envelope or wrapping it securely in heavy paper. If you are mailing in an assignment, usually stamped, self-addressed envelopes don't have to be included for the return of the pictures, but many smaller publications simply won't return the material because of the cost of postage if you don't enclose one.

If you send rare or extremely valuable pictures to a publication you should invest in a fiberboard mailing case with canvas straps that photo stores sell in varying sizes. Make sure you point out to the magazine that you would like the material returned in that same case or the empty case returned by itself if the pictures are kept. The cases can literally be reused for years.

The mechanics of photography seem to be the most confusing to writers, but modern technology is making the process of getting clear, well-exposed pictures, literally a snap. In this day of automatic exposure setting cameras and computer controlled strobe lights, which also give you proper exposure, anybody can shoot average pictures for publication. And don't let the ads in magazines about fancy cameras and lenses at fancy prices put you off. For normal publication work, you can almost do as well spending a couple of hundred dollars for photo equipment as you can a thousand dollars.

Although at one time the 2¼x2¼ twin lens reflex was highly regarded for location photography, today practically every journalistic pro uses a 35mm single lens reflex with a few diehards still sticking to the rangefinder cameras like the Leica. Those pros that use their equipment the hardest and have need for special equipment like motors, radio remote controlled cameras, fisheyes and mirror optics, tend to stick to the big three of the 35mm camera line, Nikon, Cannon and Pentax.

These cameras each have their particular feel and benefits, but the most important thing to a writer is that they can be bought and used for huge savings and still be reliable and deliver quality pictures. And there are cheaper new cameras coming out, some automatic, that can be bought for a third of the price of the big three. Also, don't think that by spending a lot of money, you are going to get optics that will make a difference in reproduction. Because of the automation and production of computer-designed lenses today, there isn't a lot of difference between a $100 lens and a $400 lens for general picture taking. For that extra money, you're getting fancy coatings, sturdier mounts and more rugged cameras, but not anything that will show up in most pictures.

The way that new cameras and lenses are jumping up like popcorn today, it's useless to recommend any particular brand because a new and better one might make recommendations obsolete. The best thing for a writer to do is to go to a large camera store, explain his needs, and look particularly at the used equipment. Camera shops seldom have time to check the performance of a camera and a reputable store will readily admit if they don't know how a camera works, why should you, and allow you to return it if the camera or lens is faulty. If the store doesn't allow you a reasonable return time, buy elsewhere.

All high-priced still cameras are sold at discounts of from 20% upwards depending upon the state of the market and the availability of the equipment, so just use the published list price as a bargaining point. As a basic outfit, a writer could make do with a used 35mm single lens, non-automatic camera and an automatic flash and still spend less than $200. As your ability and interest increase, adding a medium wide-angle lens in the 28mm to 35mm bracket to shoot in crowded spaces and a medium telephoto of about 100mm for tight head shots and slightly faraway objects, are good investments. But if your needs are simple, keep the equipment simple.

Processing and printing black and white film is surrounded with mumbo-jumbo. While the mumbo-jumbo isn't that complicated, the writer-photographer should forget about it and turn his black and white film over to a professional lab for processing. Just like a car though, it is nice to know something about what makes photography go and this can easily be learned at an adult education course or two, or from extensive reading. It takes years to become a good darkroom technician. Most writers can better use their time hunting out stories and talking to editors. As for color processing, even the photo pros who like darkroom work usually send their film out to professional labs. I don't mean to slight the satisfaction of working in a darkroom and if it intrigues you, go ahead. Be prepared to spend a lot of time and money for that satisfaction.

The key word in relation to the statements about labs, was, professional. Don't ever trust your film to the local drug store or its modern equivalent, the cut rate processing lab. While there are responsible firms in these areas, they are geared to amateur handling of film and not to the critical standards the pro needs. Check your phone book for a firm that advertises professional processing and give it a try. If you live in an area without a lab, ask your local, full-time professional photographer for the name of a reputable lab in the area or in a neighboring state.

Obviously a writer knows how much reading is important and the writer-photographer should read at least one photo magazine a month to continue his development. Like a writer, he should study the photo needs of his market by looking at back issues of the magazines he is thinking of submitting stories to or has actually received assignments from. It's embarrassingly unprofessional to shoot a "great" picture on an assignment only to find that the magazine used a similar picture or approach a month or two before.

As to basic photographic knowledge to help the beginning writer-photographer, Kodak produces a fine series of pamphlets for 95¢ each called "Here's How" that do a slick job in no-nonsense prose of going from beginning to more complex photography, mostly from the mechanical approach. The series of eight pamphlets is also bound in the book or you can buy any one individually for your area of interest.

Another fine book that will help you develop your vision and ability to guess what editors want is, *Visual Impact in Print*, written by Gerald Hurley and Angus McGougall, published by American Publishers Press, 500 S. Clinton, Chicago IL 60607. Its many visual examples are taken from business magazines and newspapers.

Visual Impact couldn't state the role of the writer-photographer any better when it says that "Communication is best achieved when pictures and words reinforce each other, when they can be made to work in concert."

After mastering the craftsmanship of photography, you can start playing the concertos of communication that will make you big at the editorial box office. That's real music to any writer's ears.

If this is 1977, this edition is out of date. See address in front of book to order latest edition. *Writer's Market* is published annually each fall.

CONSUMER PUBLICATIONS

Alternative Publications

Publications in this section offer writers a forum for expressing anti-establishment or minority ideas and views that wouldn't necessarily be published in the commercial or "establishment" press. Included are a number of "free press" publications that do not pay except in contributor's copies. Writers are reminded that these publications sometimes remain at one address for a limited time or prove unbusinesslike in their reporting on, or returning of, submissions. However, the writer will also find a number of well-established, well-paying markets in this list.

THE ADVOCATE, 2121 South El Camino Real, San Mateo CA 94403. Editor: John Preston. For gay men and women, age 21 to 40; middle-class, college-educated, urban. Newspaper; 64 (10x14) pages. Established in 1968. Every 2 weeks. Circulation: over 50,000. Rights purchased vary with author and material. May buy all rights with the possibility of returning rights to author after publication; second serial (reprint) rights or simultaneous rights. Buys 200 mss a year. Payment on publication. Will send free sample copy to writer on request. Write for copy of guidelines for writers. Will consider photocopied or simultaneous submissions. Reports in 1 month. Query first. Enclose S.A.S.E.
Nonfiction and Photos: "Basically, the emphasis is on the dignity and joy of the gay life style." News articles, interviews, life style features. Major interest in interviews or sketches of gay people whose names can be used, but who are not in "The Movement". Informational, how-to, personal experience, profile, humor, historical, think pieces, photo, reviews of books and records, spot news, successful business operations, new product. Length: open. Pays $10 minimum. Payment for b&w photos purchased without ms or on assignment depends on size of reproduction.

AMAZON QUARTERLY, P.O. Box 434, West Somerville MA 02144. Editors: Laurel Galana and Gina Covina. For lesbian feminists of all ages in all geographic areas; mostly college educated. Quarterly magazine; 72 (8x7) pages. Established in 1972. Circulation: 5,000. All rights are reserved to each individual or artist. Uses 50 mss per year. Payment rates are not set at present. "We have received a grant from CCLM and now divide $250 between the contributors to each issue. That's $1,000 per year for 4 issues." Usually between $40 to $50 for stories and other prose. Will send sample copy to writer for 75¢. Will consider photocopied submissions. Will not consider simultaneous submissions. Reports in 2 months. Submit complete ms. Enclose S.A.S.E.
Nonfiction and Photos: Articles on "lost" lesbians in literature and the arts; women's liberation theory which does not have a heterosexual bent. "We accept no work from men, nor any work with a heterosexual theme. We're especially in need of well-researched essays developing a lesbian-feminist philosophy." Only art photos are used. B&w only; no color. "We are most interested in nonfiction which takes a lesbian/feminist perspective for granted and goes on to explore new territory whether it be in the arts, the sciences, spirituality, whatever. Lesbianism as a topic for discussion is passe. We assume a level of sophistication in our readers that we would hope 7 years of the women's movement has allowed for. Bombast and rhetoric are no longer interesting."
Poetry: "No more lesbian love poems with hackneyed images." Pays $10 to $15. Poetry Editor: Audre Lorde.

BERKELEY BARB, P.O. Box 1247, Berkeley CA 94701. Phone: 415-849-1040. Managing Editor: Jim Schreiber. For readers interested in news of the counterculture and nonsectarian political left. Weekly newspaper; tabloid size, 40 pages. Established in 1965. Circulation: 25,000. Buys all rights, but will reassign rights to author after publication. (Member of the Alternative Press Syndicate. APS members may publish each other's printed material free of charge.) Buys about 1,100 mss a year. Payment on publication. Will send free sample copy to writer on request. Write for copy of guidelines for writers. Will consider photocopied submissions, if assured of first rights. Usually returns rejected material in 2 weeks. Query first or submit complete ms. Enclose S.A.S.E.

Nonfiction and Photos: "Factual articles about the various alternative life styles, movements and politics, especially those of interest to residents of the Bay area. Strictly accurate accounts of persons and events told in a free-wheeling, narrative prose 'coffeehouse rap' style, with as much immediacy and presence as possible. We reject pounds of theoretical opinion pieces and stories of personal revelations each week. And we always have more record and rock concert reviews than we can print." Recently published articles include "Partying With the Poets", showing the interaction of Allen Ginsberg, Charles Bokowski, Lawrence Ferlinghetti, Linda King, booze, and egomania after a Santa Cruz poetry reading; "I Cried at Billy Jack's Trial," in which the writer works as a movie extra and tells how what happens on the set belies the liberating message of the film. Length: 50 to 3,000 words, but 1,000 is the preferred length. Pays 50¢ to 75¢ per column inch (about 1¢ a word). "After 300 column inches or 13 articles are published in *Barb*, rate is 75¢ per column inch." B&w (high contrast) photos purchased with or without accompanying mss. Pays for photos at the following rates: through 12 column inches, $10; 12 through 42 column inches, $15; 42 through 65 column inches, $20; more than 65 column inches, $25. Department Editor: Jim Schreiber, Managing Editor.

Fiction: Short stories from 2,300 to 2,700 words; must be on themes related to the nonfiction articles in the *Barb*.

Poetry: Rarely used, but will consider traditional forms, blank verse, free verse and avant-garde forms. Length: 2 to 500 lines. Pays 50¢ to 75¢ a column inch, with a $5 minimum.

THE BOSTON PHOENIX, 100 Massachusetts Ave., Boston MA 02115. Editor: William Miller. For young, educated middle class and counterculture. Weekly newspaper. Circulation: 200,000. Buys all rights, but will reassign rights to author after publication. Buys 10 short stories and 100 poems a year. Payment on publication. Will send sample copy to writer for $1. Will consider photocopied submissions. Will not consider simultaneous submissions. Reports in 4 to 6 weeks. Submit complete ms. Enclose S.A.S.E.

Nonfiction: "No set theme. Anything well written; people interest. Unsentimental; not corny or folksy; high-quality writing and observation. No humor." Pays $50 to $100.

Fiction: Experimental, mainstream, mystery, satirical; serialized novels. No science fiction. Length: 5,000 words maximum. Pays $50 to $100. Department Editor: Celia Gilbert.

Poetry: Blank verse, free verse, avant-garde forms. Theme open. Length: 4 double-spaced typewritten pages maximum. Pays $10.

BREAKTHROUGH!, 2015 South Broadway, Little Rock AR 72206. Phone: 501-372-4278. Editor: Korra L. Deaver. For "anyone of any age, interested in psychic awareness." Established in 1971. Bimonthly. Buys all rights, but will reassign rights to author after publication. Payment in contributor's copies. Will send a free sample copy to writer on request, if return postage is enclosed. Write for editorial guidelines sheet for writers. Submit only complete ms. Will consider photocopied submissions. Reports within 2 months. Submit seasonal material 3 months in advance. Enclose S.A.S.E.

Nonfiction and Poetry: "*Breakthrough!* is published primarily for the purpose of instruction. 'How-to' articles which explain how one acquires an understanding of, and personal use of, such psychic gifts as clairvoyance, precognition, astral projection, etc., are welcome. These are uncharted paths in the soul's journey through eternity, and an experience which throws light on any breakthrough in these areas will help others to achieve a similar awareness. Most magazines treat the phenomena itself by factual reporting, or interviews with known psychics. We want to instruct others in achieving a similar awareness." Uses informational, how-to, personal experience, inspirational, and think articles. No fiction. Length: less than 5,000 words. Open to all forms of poetry, on themes relating to psychic awareness. Poetry must have an upbeat theme.

BROTHER, A FORUM FOR MEN AGAINST SEXISM, P.O. Box 4387, Berkeley CA 94704. Collective editorship. For a predominantly young, male audience concerned about sexism and sexual oppression; older males and a substantial number of women. "Most of the staff, much of the material, and many of the readers are gay." Quarterly newspaper and newsletter; 16 to 24 (12x16) pages. Established in 1971. Circulation: 3,000 to 4,000. Not copyrighted. Payment in contributor's copies. Will send free sample copy to writer on request. Please include 10¢ in stamp or coin for mailing. Will consider photocopied and simultaneous submissions. Will consider cassette submissions. Reports within 2 months. Query first or submit complete ms. Enclose S.A.S.E.
Nonfiction: "We're relatively unique. There are no other regular men's anti-sexist publications. We print analytical articles and reminiscences around the theme of men struggling with sexism in their own lives. We look for personal treatments, critical of standard male sex role, men and class (economic class relationships and sex roles); men and women (articles on inter-personal relationships). No sexist trash; no anti-woman; no windy, generalized over-views of sex role differences." Length: 1,000 to 1,500 words maximum.
Fiction and Poetry: Experimental and "confession" type stories. All forms of poetry.

COMMUNITIES MAGAZINE, Route 1, Box 191, Oroville CA 95965. For "people currently living or considering living alternative life styles, which would include living cooperatively with like-minded people in rural or urban settings." Magazine about intentional communities published every 2 months. Established in 1972. Circulation: 5,000. Not copyrighted. Payment in contributor's copies. Will send free sample copy on request. Reports on material accepted for publication in 30 days. Returns rejected material in 10 days. Query first or submit complete ms. Enclose S.A.S.E.
Nonfiction: "We would be glad to receive material from writers who would like to see relevant material published. Candid 'what's happening' stories from existing communes; objective info on land buying; communal health and legal problems; theoretical pieces, too." Length: open.

THE COOPERATOR, 17819 Roscoe Blvd., Northridge CA 91324. Editor: Louis K. Acheson, Jr. Published by the International Cooperation Council, a coordinating body of about 175 organizations who "foster the emergence of a new universal person and civilization based upon unity in diversity among all peoples." Semi-annual. Circulation: 1,200 to 1,500. Not copyrighted. Uses 25 mss a year. Pays in contributor's copies. Will send sample copy to writer for 50¢. Will consider cassette submissions. No query required, but "suggest writer read *The Cooperator* first if possible." Reports in 2 months. Enclose S.A.S.E.
Nonfiction, Fiction, Photos, Poetry, and Fillers: "General materials related to our purposes wanted. Need content and style. Top priority is 1,000- to 2,000-word articles that deal with science, art, philosophy, religion, education, human relations or other fields in search of universals." Also wants 300- to 500-word reviews of suitable current books, films, or plays; good poetry up to 40 lines; short humor and quotes; and b&w glossy photos. Uses some fiction of 1,000 to 2,000 words.

THE CRYSTAL WELL, P.O. Box 18351, Philadelphia PA 19120. Editor: Rebecca Judge Weaver. Established in 1964. For "witches, magicians and those interested in witchcraft." Published 6 to 8 times a year. Acquires all rights, but will sometimes reassign rights to author after publication, "on application only." Uses 10 to 17 mss a year. Payment in contributor's copies. Reports on material within 6 weeks. Will send sample copy to writer for $1. Will consider photocopied submissions. Query first or submit complete ms. Enclose S.A.S.E.

Nonfiction and Photos: Articles on "theology, magic, herbal compounding and dispensing; bone and joint healing." Brief, accurate, and factual. How-to and technical book reviews. Length: 100 to 1,500 words. 4x5 b&w photos, with good contrast. Maximum payment of 6 contributor's copies.
Poetry: "Must be religious poetry and meet bardic tests."
How To Break In: "You should be a witch with fair English prose style."

EARTH'S DAUGHTERS, 944 Kensington Ave., Buffalo NY 14215. Editors: Judith Kerman, Janice MacKenzie, Lillian Robinson, Judith Treible. For women and men interested in literature and feminism. Established in 1971. Publication schedule varies from 2 to 4 times a year. Circulation: 1,000. Acquires first North American serial rights. Pays in contributor's copies. Will send sample copy to writer for $1. Will consider clear photocopied submissions and clear carbons. Reports in 10 weeks. Submit complete ms. Enclose S.A.S.E.
Nonfiction and Photos: "Our subject is the experience and creative expression of women. We require a high level of technical skill and artistic intensity; although we work from a left-feminist political position, we are concerned with creative expression rather than propaganda. On rare occasions we publish feminist work by men. We rarely use nonfiction, but might be interested in reviews of work by women for an occasional review issue. Length: 1,000 words maximum. We are generally interested in photos more as free-standing artistic works than as illustrations." Pays in copies only.
Fiction: Feminist fiction of any and all modes. Length: 2,500 words maximum.
Poetry: All modern, contemporary, avant-garde forms. Length: 6 pages maximum.

FALL RISING, Box 81, Halifax, Nova Scotia, Canada. Editor: Frank Hooper. For "those adventuring or thinking of adventuring in alternate life styles." Established in 1973. Bimonthly. Not copyrighted. Buys 60 mss a year. Payment on publication. Will send free sample copy to writer on request. Write for copy of guidelines for writers. Will not consider photocopied submissions. Submit seasonal material (articles attuned to the seasons in nature) 4 months in advance. Reports on material in 4 weeks. Query first or submit complete nonfiction ms; submit complete fiction or poetry ms. Enclose S.A.E. and International Reply Coupons.
Nonfiction and Photos: Articles "exploring alternate life styles; how to get free in a manipulative society; doing more with less; how to do it; how to get it; techniques for alternatives stressing real experiments and projects and achievements; against mediocre compromise, un-life, the rat race; the dehumanizing, the vapid, the loveless. Prose with sinew and substance, in accord with concept of viable alternatives of exploring some of the killing aspects of disease in the larger social fabric. Avoid rhetoric about how terrible everything is and give more specific information on helping to get it together in both mind and action." Regular columns or departments include "Soundings" (interview department); "Survival Tools" (things and ideas that help survival); "Exchange" (available and wanted). Length: "like a woman's skirt— long enough to cover the subject and short enough to be interesting. Don't pad." Pays $50 to $150 for full articles; less for items. 8x10 b&w glossies purchased with or without mss. Captions required. Payment "varies with value to us. Our minimum is $5."
Fiction, Poetry and Fillers: Experimental fiction. Theme "open, but probably will relate to magazine theme." Length: same as for nonfiction. Pays $50 to $150. Avant-garde forms of poetry and free verse. Length: open. Pays $5. Uses newsbreaks, clippings and "helpful ideas" as fillers. Length: open. Pays $2.

FIFTH ESTATE, 4403 Second, Detroit MI 48201. Collective editorship. For a working class audience; 18 to 34. Newspaper; 20 (8x14) pages. Established in 1965. Weekly. Circulation: 15,000. Copyrighted. Buys 100 mss a year. Pays on publication. Will send sample copy to writer for 10¢. Will consider photocopied and simultaneous submissions. Reports in 1 week. Query first or submit complete ms. Enclose S.A.S.E.
Nonfiction and Photos: News articles and features with a leftist/anarchist viewpoint. Must have highly critical and subjective approach. Informational, interview, humor,

expose, personal opinion. Reviews of movies, books, concerts, records. Length: 100 to 10,000 words. Pays $3 to $10. B&w photos purchased with or without ms or on assignment. Pays $3. Captions required.

Fiction: Occasionally buys experimental or humorous fiction. Length: 300 to 1,000 words. Pays $3 to $10.

FOCUS: A JOURNAL FOR GAY WOMEN, Room 323, 419 Boylston St., Boston MA 02116. For gay women of all ages and interests. Published by Daughters of Bilitis, Boston Chapter. Monthly newsletter; 14 (5½x8½) pages. Established in 1970. Circulation: 350. Copyrighted. Payment in contributor's copies. Will send sample copy for 60¢. Will consider photocopied and simultaneous submissions. Reports within 3 months. Query first or submit complete ms. Enclose S.A.S.E.

Nonfiction and Photos: Material of particular interest to gay women: research reports, news, reviews of books, films and plays; personal views, and interviews. Informational, personal experience, profile, humor, historical, think pieces, expose, nostalgia, spot news. A portion of each issue is devoted to New England news and information, including information about the activities of the publisher, Daughters of Bilitis. Length: 4,000 words maximum. B&w photos are used with or without accompanying mss. Captions required.

Fiction: Mainstream, humorous, romance, confession, religious, historical, erotica, fantasy. All must relate to magazine theme.

Poetry and Fillers: Traditional forms of poetry; blank verse, free verse, avant-garde forms, light verse. Uses newsbreaks, clippings, jokes, and short humor as filler material.

GAY LITERATURE, English Department, California State University, Fresno CA 93740. Editor: Dr. Daniel Curzon. For gay readers and tabooless straight people. Magazine; 56 (8½x9½) pages. Established in 1975. Quarterly. Circulation: 1,000. Acquires all rights, but will reassign rights to author after publication. Accepts about 40 mss a year. Payment in contributor's copies. Will send sample copy to writer for $2. Will consider photocopied submissions. Will consider simultaneous submissions if notified. Reports in 1 month. Query first or submit complete ms. Enclose S.A.S.E.

Nonfiction and Photos: "We're demolishing ancient homophobic cruelties through literature in the best sense and use material on universal experiences as lived by gay people. Must be intellectual, but not stodgy." Informational, personal experience, profile, humor, historical, think pieces, personal opinion, literary reviews. Recently published "Dr. Frankel, Where Are You?", an insightful comment on psychiatry. Length: 20 pages maximum. Photos considered.

Fiction: Quality fiction about the gay experience. Experimental or mainstream. Length: 25 pages maximum.

GAY SUNSHINE, A JOURNAL OF GAY LIBERATION, P.O. Box 40397, San Francisco CA 94140. Phone: 415-824-3184. Editor: Winston Leyland. For gay people of all ages throughout North America and abroad. "We especially appeal to people interested in the radical, political and literary aspects of the gay liberation movement." Newspaper. Quarterly; 24 to 28 pages. Established in 1970. Circulation: 10,000. Rights purchased vary with author and material; negotiable. Payment in contributor's copies, or negotiable. Will send sample copy to writer for 50¢. Will consider photocopied submissions. Will not consider simultaneous submissions. Will consider cassette submissions; "interviews only." Reports in 2 to 4 weeks. Submit complete nonfiction mss; query first for short fiction and graphics. Enclose S.A.S.E.

Nonfiction and Photos: Interviews, personal articles, political articles, literary essays. Particularly interested in in-depth interviews with gay people from different backgrounds. "Material should relate to gay people and the gay consciousness. Author should write to us first regarding style, structure, etc." Length: maximum of 10 to 15 double-spaced, typed pages. B&w photos are purchased on assignment. Captions required.

Fiction: Experimental and erotica. Must relate to theme. Length: maximum of 10 to 15 double-spaced, typed pages.

Poetry: Blank verse, free verse, avant-garde forms.

GNOSTICA: News of the Aquarian Frontier, P.O. Box 3383, St. Paul MN 55165. Phone: 612-224-8811. Editor: P.E.I. Bonewits. For educated people interested in astrology, psychic phenomena, witchcraft, alternative religions and sciences, civil liberties and the occult; but not gullible or true believers. Monthly magazine; 48 to 64 pages, tabloid format, 11x16. Established in 1971. Circulation: 20,000. Rights purchased vary with author and material, but usually buys first North American serial rights. "Contributors should state clearly exactly what rights are being offered." Pays within 6 weeks of publication. Will send free sample copy to writer on request. Write for copy of guidelines for writers; enclose S.A.S.E. Will consider photocopied and simultaneous submissions. Query first for nonfiction. Submit only complete ms for all other material. Reports within 2 months. Enclose S.A.S.E.

Nonfiction and Photos: "All articles deal with astrology, the occult, parapsychology and the new sciences, witchcraft and Paganism, herbology, etc. Our contributors must do their homework! Sloppy research, fuzzy thinking or religious biases will bounce a ms faster than anything else. Articles on new psychic research, acupuncture, altered states of consciousness, non-English speaking occultism and witchcraft, history of various occult organizations, implications of current scientific research for the occult, new Pagan organizations, etc." Length: 500 to 5,000 words. Pays 2¢ a word, except by arrangement. Regular columns cover same topics, and run 500 to 600 words. Pays $10 per column. Submit several columns at one time. Photos purchased on assignment only.

Fiction, Poetry, and Fillers: Buys occult fiction (which may be suspense, humorous, historical, etc.) and science fiction based on paranormal phenomena. Length: 1,000 to 9,000 words. Pays 2¢ a word, except by arrangement. Traditional forms of poetry, incantations, medieval and premedieval forms. Length: 1 to 100 lines. Pays 2¢ a word, or $10, whichever is higher. Buys newsbreaks, puzzles (occult crosswords, acrostics), and short humor. Length: 25 to 300 words. Pays 3¢ a word, except by arrangement. Fiction, poetry, and fillers should be sent to Fiction Department, Poetry Department, and Filler Department.

GPU NEWS, Gay Peoples Union, P.O. Box 90530, Milwaukee WI 53202. Editor: Eldon E. Murray. For gay people (both men and women) from all walks of life. News/magazine; 40 (8½x11) pages. Established in 1971. Monthly. Circulation: 1,500. Not copyrighted. Buys about 12 mss a year. Pays on publication. Will send free sample copy to writer on request. Write for copy of guidelines for writers. No photocopied or simultaneous submissions. Reports on material accepted for publication in 1 week. Returns rejected material immediately. Query first. Enclose S.A.S.E.

Nonfiction and Photos: News and feature articles that will appeal to a gay audience. Accepts only gay-oriented material, written from almost any viewpoint. "Remember that our publication is aimed at the general gay reader, not the intellectual or the purient. Women's topics are especially welcome." Informational, how-to, personal experience, interview, profile, inspirational, humor, historical, think pieces, expose, nostalgia, personal opinion, photo, travel, reviews of books, movies, plays; spot news, successful business operations. Recently published "A Canadian Views Gay Liberation", about the contrasts between the U.S. and Canada. Length: open. Pays $15 minimum. Captions are optional for b&w glossies, purchased with or without mss, or on assignment. Pays $5. No color.

Fiction and Poetry: Must relate to theme. All types of fiction. Pays $15. All forms of poetry. Pays $5.

Fillers: Crossword puzzles, recipes. Pays $5.

HIGH TIMES, P.O. Box 386, Cooper Station, New York NY 10003. Editor: Ed Dwyer. For those dedicated to getting high; affluent, educated; interested in life style changes, personal freedom, sex and drugs. Established in 1973. Quarterly. Circulation: 125,000. Buys second serial (reprint) rights. Buys about 100 mss a year. Pays on publication. Will send sample copy to writer for $1. Will consider photocopied or simultaneous submissions. (Writer must advise where other submissions have been made.) Reports very quickly on material accepted for publication. Returns rejected

material immediately. Query useful, but not essential. Enclose S.A.S.E.
Nonfiction and Photos: Articles about drugs and other highs. New drugs, dope dealing, business news, glamor drugs. Nothing on "my drug bust". Brevity and clarity appreciated. Informational, personal experience, profile, interview, humor, historical, expose, nostalgia, personal opinion, photo, travel, successful business operations, new products, merchandising techniques, technical. Length: 3,000 to 5,000 words. Pays $50 to $100. Spot news should be as brief as possible. Medical, legal, book-record reviews. Length: 300 to 1,000 words. Pays $10 to $25. B&w photos purchased with ms; prefers query first for photos.
Fiction and Fillers: Adventure (drug) and erotic fiction. Length: open. Pays $50 to $100. Jokes and short humor bought for filler use. Pays $1 to $5.

JIM'S JOURNAL, Box 1319, Dodge City KS 67801. Editor: James E. Kurtz. For young adult to middle-age readers. All professions. Interested in controversial themes. Established in 1962. Monthly. Circulation: 5,000. Not copyrighted. Payment in contributor's copies. Will send sample copy to writer for 25¢. Will not consider photocopied submissions. Reports on material accepted for publication in 4 weeks. Returns rejected material in 3 to 5 weeks. Query first or submit complete ms. Enclose S.A.S.E.
Nonfiction and Photos: Controversial, underground material, sociology, philosophy, current events, religion, men's liberation, sex. "We honestly invite stimulating material. We want well-written material and we favor the new writer. Be bold, speak out with confidence; no punches pulled. All subjects are carefully read." Informational, personal experience, inspirational, think pieces, personal opinion, expose. Length: 2,500 words maximum. 5x7 or 8x10 b&w photos used with accompanying mss. Captions required.
Fiction: Experimental, mainstream, adventure, erotica, humor, confession, condensed novels. Length: 3,000 words maximum.

THE LADDER, P.O. Box 5025, Washington Station, Reno NV 89503. Editor: Gene Damon. For lesbian and women's liberation audience that is "serious, and much more concerned with reform than revolution." Subject matter includes "any and all material that pertains to the gaining of full human status for all women, including lesbians." Bimonthly. Circulation: 3,900. Acquires one-time use rights, insists on acknowledgement when material is reprinted. Pays in contributor's copies. Will send a sample copy to a writer for $1.25. Query preferred for articles and photos. Reports in 20 days. Enclose S.A.S.E. for return of submissions or reply to queries.
Nonfiction: "Any article dealing with women or lesbians, having to do with women's rights, women's liberation, any civil rights violation that particularly affects women, biographical articles on famous women. No particular slant. Prefer clean, concise style." Length: 1,500 to 5,000 words.
Photos: "Use many, as illustrations for stories and articles." Mostly pictures of women. B&w glossies.
Fiction: "Prefer fiction connected to lesbians in some way, but will accept relevant sensitive portraits of women, especially those that show their limitations in a male-ordered, male-run world. No limitations except no pornography. Can be either sympathetic or not, but must be well-written. Need many short-shorts. Using increasing amount of fiction with future issues." Length: 300 to 5,000 words.
Poetry: "By and about women, all and any women. Probable preference given to lesbian themes but quality is the primary criterion. Using increasing amounts of poetry."
Fillers: Especially needs short humor. Also wants newsbreaks, clippings, jokes, and other fillers.

LIBERA, Eshleman Hall, University of California, Berkeley CA 94720. Collective editorship. For women and anyone interested in women's art and literature. Published twice a year as a feminist journal; 60 pages. Established in 1970. Circulation: 1,000. Copyrighted. Payment in contributor's copies. Will send sample copy to writer for $1. Will consider photocopied but not simultaneous submissions. Reports in 3 months. Submit complete ms. Enclose S.A.S.E.

Nonfiction, Photos and Poetry: Articles written by women. "Emphasis is on movement trends and women's interior life. Problems and life styles of working women and housewives." Length: open. B&w photos are used. Must be under 8x11. Also uses some poetry.

LIBERATION, 339 Lafayette St., New York NY 10012. Collective editorship: Pam Black, David Rosen, Paul Loeb. For readers who share a common sense of radical politics, although not defined along any particular political line. Magazine; 40 (8½x11) pages. Established in 1956. Circulation: 10,000. Acquires all rights, but will reassign rights to author after publication. About half of each issue is from outside contributors. Payment in contributor's copies and a year's subscription. Will send a free sample copy to writer on request. Will consider photocopied submissions. Reports on material accepted for publication in 2 to 3 weeks. Returns rejected material in 4 to 6 weeks. Query first or submit complete ms. Enclose S.A.S.E.
Nonfiction and Photos: "We aren't looking for the same old rhetoric and cliches. We want to break new ground. We'd like to deal with the politics of daily life, such as sports, media bars, sexuality, fashion, housing, and whatever immediate modes of living people wish to explore. We believe that everything is political and accept articles on anything from foreign affairs to psychology, cultural criticism and examination of daily life. We are looking for people to convey a critical sensibility that will challenge the way all of us view our lives and the world." Uses b&w photos. Captions optional.
Fiction and Poetry: Uses all types of fiction and all forms of poetry. "If the politics and content are there (in the broadest sense), then anything is possible."

LOS ANGELES FREE PRESS, 5850 Hollywood Blvd., Los Angeles CA 90028. Editor: Penelope Grenoble. Primarily for Southern Californians, 20 to 40 years old, college education. Weekly newspaper; 28 (14x10) pages. Established in 1964. Circulation: 100,000. Rights purchased vary with author and material. Buys all rights, first serial rights, simultaneous rights. Buys about 1,000 mss a year; mostly local. Pays on publication. Will send sample copy to writer for 25¢. Will consider photocopied submissions. Query first. Enclose S.A.S.E.
Nonfiction and Photos: News; in-depth investigative articles; consumer news; features (entertainment and news-related); public service articles. Liberal viewpoint; thorough investigation and substantiation of statements; organization of thoughts. "Other publications tell you who, what and where; we also tell you why." Of particular interest are articles on the economy; consumer issues. Length: 1,500 words maximum. Pays $20 minimum. Photos purchased with or without accompanying ms, or on assignment. Pays $10 minimum for b&w glossy. Uses no color.

THE LUNATIC FRINGE, P.O. Box 237, South Salem NY 10590. Phone: 914-763-5414. Editor: John H. Coutermash. For "all ages; some are in jails or in other institutions. The rest are students." Quarterly magazine; 36 (6x9½) pages. Established in 1970. Circulation: 600. No payment. "We give copies free of charge to penal and mental institutions all over the world. For this reason, we cannot give even the smallest amount of payment or contributor's copies to the 'free' world." Will send sample copy to writer for $1.25. Will consider photocopied and simultaneous submissions. Reports on material accepted for publication in several weeks. Returns rejected material immediately. Query first for everything but poetry. Enclose S.A.S.E.
Nonfiction: Everything must be penal-oriented. "Black and gallows humor. Social commentary by the antisocial. Personal experience. Expose (penal). Personal opinion and spot news; penal-oriented. Nothing anti-war. We are all aware that war isn't nice. I would like to see more work in areas dealing with the solving of self problems by the particular individual and without the help of mother, God, and the American flag. Problems solved by violence, humor, love, anything. Write as though you were standing before the gates of Hell or Paradise." No do-gooder types of nonfiction; honesty, solid, sad, happiness, love, hate, from birth to death, from heaven to hell. This magazine is for people who talk out of the corner of their mouth; use double negatives and could watch a hanging. Prefers brief length.
Fiction: Humorous (black). Length: brief.

Poetry: "Poetry should be about self. Thoughts, regrets, happiness; times revisited; times ahead. No altruism." Traditional forms, blank verse, free verse, avant-garde forms, light verse, experimental. Length: brief, but will consider all submissions.
Fillers: Short humor. Funny obituaries.

LUNE, Box 91, Bellmore NY 11710. For a young, creative, intelligent audience interested in modern art and culture. Published approximately every 2 months; newsprint magazine; 24 (7x10) pages. Established in 1973. Circulation: 1,500. "We refer all rights to author." Uses 50 to 75 mss a year. Payment in contributor's copies. "We'll negotiate with authors; if a contributor expects to be paid, he or she should mention it." Will send free sample copy to writer on request. Will consider photocopied submissions. Prefers not to see simultaneous submissions. Reports in 4 to 6 weeks. Query first or submit complete ms. Enclose S.A.S.E.
Nonfiction, Fiction and Poetry: "We are a poetry magazine; a literary and art magazine, but at the same time, we're an underground newspaper. We want material with an exciting edge. Good poetry or fiction, a science article that's new and interesting; a controversial political essay. What's important is the writing. Science fiction, psychic phenomena, art and politics, surrealism, science and progress." Experimental and mainstream fiction, artistic erotica, humorous satire and nonconventional religious fiction. Length: open. Poetry in any form or length. Traditional forms, blank verse, free verse, avant-garde forms, light verse.
Fillers: Information on artistic, literary, theatrical, political endeavors always welcome.

THE MATCH!, P.O. Box 3488, Tucson AZ 85722. Editor: F. Woodworth. An anarchist journal for anti-political radicals. 12-page tabloid (11x17). Established in 1969. Monthly. Circulation: 2,500. Not copyrighted. Uses about 50 mss a year. Payment in contributor's copies. Will send free sample copy on request. Will not consider photocopied or simultaneous submissions. Reports on material in 2 weeks. Query first or submit complete ms. Enclose S.A.S.E.
Nonfiction: Political articles and satire. Interviews and personal opinion articles and book reviews. Must be professional and specifically anarchist, not communistic or liberal. Length: 4,000 words maximum.
Fiction: Science fiction must relate to publication's subject matter. Length: 4,000 words maximum.
Poetry: Length and form open, but must relate to subject matter.

THE MOTHER EARTH NEWS, P.O. Box 70, Hendersonville NC 28739. Phone: 704-692-4256. Editor: John Shuttleworth. For "old and young, far right and far left, well educated and not, and everything in between. We're the only publication that recognizes that a New Age of decentralized, grow-your-own, work for yourself, build your own home living is upon us." Magazine published every 2 months; 128 (8½x11) pages. Established in 1970. Circulation: 160,000. "We buy first rights for magazine and any reprint rights we might later make use of. All authors are free to resell anything we buy." Buys about 150 to 200 mss a year. "We often pay on acceptance and then pay something additional on publication. We try to be as generous as we can, to make up for the fact that we're awfully late reporting sometimes." Will send free sample copy to writer on request. Write for copy of guidelines for writers. Will consider photocopied and simultaneous submissions. Query first. Enclose S.A.S.E.
Nonfiction and Photos: How-to-articles. "We especially need home business pieces that detail home businesses that really work. Firsthand reports are always desired on low cost building (especially with natural materials), organic gardening, back to the land, life in small villages and how to make it happen. Emphasis is on how to. Get the facts straight. Write concisely and with great clarity. Make it lively and interesting. Offer hope honestly (you can change your life for the better). Work in the ecology angle. Try to tell people how to live more ecologically sound lives. Also interested in seeing anything on alternative energy systems (wind, water, sun, methane, etc.) that work." Does not want to see anything "trite in the 'I grew an organic garden successfully' vein or anything preachy. Our readers want to know

how to do things themselves, not how someone else takes an ego trip." Recently published articles include "Pennywise Tooth Cleansers," "Make First-Class Profits With a Secondhand Business," "Kitchen Medicine," "Build and Use a Sawdust Stove," "Report From the Ozarks," "Sprouts: Miracle Food for a Nickle a Pound." Length: open. Pays $40 to $500. No additional payment made for b&w photos used with mss.

NEW GUARD, Woodland Rd., Sterling VA 22170. Phone: 703-450-5162. Editor: Mary Fisk. "Mostly for young people under 30 with a substantial number of college students. Virtually all are political conservatives or libertarians." Established in 1962. Monthly. Circulation: 12,000. Buys all rights. Buys 10 mss a year. Payment on publication. Will send free sample copy to writer on request. Will consider photocopied submissions. Submit seasonal material 3 months in advance. Reports on material in 2 weeks. Query first. Enclose S.A.S.E.
Nonfiction: Articles on economics, philosophy, foreign policy and history; book and movie reviews. Articles should have a conservative-libertarian viewpoint; youth-oriented. Length: 2,000 words maximum. "Our payments vary from contributor's copies to $100 an article, depending on quality of the article, qualifications of the author, and our financial condition. Writers should work out payment with us before publication."

NORTHWEST PASSAGE, Box 105, South Bellingham Station, Bellingham WA 98225. Phone: 206-733-9672. Editorship: rotating. For socially conscious persons. Established in 1969. Biweekly. Circulation: 6,000. Not copyrighted. Does not pay. Will send a free sample copy to writer on request. Will consider photocopied submission "if original." Reports in one month. Submit only complete ms. Enclose S.A.S.E.
Nonfiction, Photos, Fiction, Poetry, and Fillers: Publishes "ecological/environmental coverage, particularly of the Northwest; local and regional news, fiction, poetry, reviews, original photography and art. New ideas relating to personal life style are always welcomed." Publishes all types of fiction, nonfiction, and poetry. Length: open. Regular columns are: Cheapos (advice on low-cost living); Eco-Notes: what's being done to and for our environment, Paper Radio: short reports on struggles for liberation, Connexions: free classified personal want ads and information exchange. Length: 250 to 2,500 words, nonfiction; 1,500 to 2,500 words, fiction; 1 to 450 lines, poetry. For b&w and color photos "negative (35mm or 2¼x2¼) required." Uses newsbreaks and imaginative puzzles.

ONTOLOGICAL THOUGHT, P.O. Box 328, Loveland CO 80537. Editor: Robert Moore. For "readers interested in the expressions of the highest qualities of character in everyday living." Monthly. Will send sample copy upon request. Payment in contributor's copies. Query first. Enclose S.A.S.E.
Nonfiction: Each issue centers on a special theme. "We are not a market for commercial writers or for those who aspire to be writers per se. We maintain a high literary standard, but our contributors are not what you call literary people. They are people of intelligence and character, capable of offering stability and balance and a sense of direction to anyone who seeks to express these qualities in their own living. For this reason it is mandatory that potential contributors request and read a free sample copy to acquaint themselves with the unique style and tone of the journal before submitting a ms. Length: 300 to 1,500 words."

ORION MAGAZINE, Lakemont GA 30552. Phone: 404-782-3931. Editor: Roy Eugene Davis. For "that always aware group of people." Magazine published every 2 months; 96 (5¼x8) pages. Established in 1955. Circulation: 2,000. Acquires all rights. Uses 60 or 70 mss a year. Payment in contributor's copies. Will send free sample copy to writer on request. Will consider photocopied and simultaneous submissions. Submit seasonal material 4 months in advance. Reports in 2 weeks. Query first or submit complete ms. Enclose S.A.S.E.
Nonfiction and Photos: "Metaphysical, occult, philosophical, serious matter; not UFO or crank material. Would like to see more philosophy and emphasis on individuality."

Interview, profile, think pieces. Recently published articles include "Yoga for Health," "Talents and Past Life Memories," "Teachings of Ramana Maharishi," "Eat Less to Live Longer." Does not want to see dogmatic, repetitious material stating what's already been said 100 times. Length: open.

Fiction: Experimental fiction. Should have a metaphysical theme. Science fiction and fantasy. Vignettes are preferred.

Poetry: Traditional forms, free verse, avant-garde forms. Metaphysical themes preferred. Length: 20 lines maximum. The "Thought-Forms" column is "usually for the unified presentation of material by a single poet, although, occasionally, an open forum." Length: open.

PAPERS INC., 624 Worcester Ave., Framingham MA 01701. Editor: Douglas Munsell. For the college student and graduate (18 to 35) with appreciation for the oblique angle on life. Magazine; 36 (8½x11) pages. Established in 1974. Every 2 months. Circulation: 10,000. Rights purchased vary with author and material. May buy all rights, but will reassign rights to author after publication; second serial (reprint) rights, or simultaneous rights. Buys 50 to 100 mss a year. Pays on acceptance. Will send sample copy to writer for $1. Write for copy of guidelines for writers. Will consider photocopied and simultaneous submissions. Reports on material in 30 days. Query first or submit complete ms. Enclose S.A.S.E.

Nonfiction and Photos: "Our format allows only brief pieces making one point only, but effectively. No topical pieces." Interview, profile, humor, think pieces, nostalgia, photo articles. Length: 300 to 1,000 words. Pays $5 to $100. Also buys shorter material for the Dreams and/or Interpretation Thereof, and Government Restructuring columns. Length: 600 words, maximum. Pays $25 for column. Pays $3 to $5 for b&w photos suitable for a 133-line screen.

Fiction: "Social comment in a palatable fiction format." Experimental, erotica, science fiction, fantasy, humorous, historical. Serialized novels. Length: 300 to 1,200 words. Pays $5 to $100.

Poetry and Fillers: Blank verse; free verse. No arcane poetry. Length: 5 to 250 words. Pays $5 to $25. Fillers include word and logic puzzles, jokes, short humor, epithets. Length: 25 to 250 words. Pays $5 to $15.

A PILGRIM'S GUIDE TO PLANET EARTH, Box 1080, San Rafael CA 94902. Editor: Parmatma Singh. For readers interested in travel, natural foods, yoga, meditation, religious ways of freeing their personalities; mostly 20- to 30-year-old college graduates and professionals. Guidebook/directory published annually; 300 (5½x8½) pages. Established in 1972. Circulation: 35,000. Rights purchased vary with author and material. Usually buys all rights, but will reassign rights to author after publication. Buys up to 10 mss a year. Payment on publication. Will send sample copy to writer for $4.50. Write for copy of guidelines for writers. Will consider photocopied and simultaneous submissions. Reports in 1 month. Query first. Enclose S.A.S.E.

Nonfiction and Photos: "New Age material: higher consciousness paths, yoga, meditation, growth groups, psychological; natural foods, health, massage, fasting; travel (places not frequently visited); youth, pilgrimages. The change of consciousness on the planet. Travel as a positive life style for spiritual growth. Material should have the spiritual approach and be conscious of the New Age." Informational, how-to, personal experience, profile, inspirational, think pieces. Length: 250 to 2,000 words. Pays $10 to $25. Pays approximately $5 for 6x9 b&w photos purchased without mss. Captions optional.

How To Break In: "Write us first. Don't expect payment for first article."

THE RAG, 2330 Guadalupe, Austin TX 78705. Phone: 512-478-0452. Edited by the Rag Collective. For Austin and Texas residents, primarily. Subject matter includes "political muckraking, poems, alternative living, co-op community news, music, and book reviews." Established in 1966. Weekly. Circulation: 8000. Member of Underground Press Syndicate (copyrighted). No pay, "we all work for the glory, but we'll feed you if you're ever in Austin." Will send a sample copy to a writer for 25¢. Will consider photocopied submissions. "In late August we're usually looking for how-to-survive-at-the-Big-University stuff." Submit seasonal material a week in advance. "We do not report, but if accepted it would appear in a month. We also do not return mss." Do not enclose S.A.S.E. since mss are not returned. Hold original in file and submit photocopy.

Nonfiction and Photos: Freelancer should show "ways for an anticapitalist to survive in a capitalistic society, for a woman to survive and keep her dignity in a sexist society. Our publication practices modified anarchy. No 'culture hero' pieces or other ego flights. More Naderlike assaults on uncritical consumerism." Uses informational, how-to, personal experience, interviews, humor, expose. "We often print half-page or full-page photos—just because they are good photos. B&w only."

Poetry and Fillers: Uses traditional forms, blank verse, free verse, and avant-garde forms. Accepts newsbreaks ("man bites dog, police bite people") and "freak oriented" humor.

SAN FRANCISCO BAY GUARDIAN, 1070 Bryant St., San Francisco CA 94103. Editor: Bruce Brugmann. For "a young liberal to radical, well-educated audience." Established in 1966. Published every two weeks. Circulation: 25,000. Buys all rights, but will reassign them to author after publication. Buys 200 mss a year. Payment on publication. Will consider photocopied submissions. Reports in one month. Query first for nonfiction with sample of published pieces. Enclose S.A.S.E.

Nonfiction and Photos: Publishes "investigative reporting, features, analysis and interpretation, how-to and consumer reviews, and stories must have a San Francisco angle." Freelance material should have a "public interest advocacy journalism approach (on the side of the little guy who gets pushed around by large institutions). More interested in hard investigative pieces. Fewer stories about isolated suffering welfare mothers and other mistreated individuals; should be put in context (with facts) of groups and classes. We would like to see articles on how to survive in the city—in San Francisco." Reviews of 800 to 1,500 words pay $25; short articles of 1,500 to 2,500 words pay $25 to $50; long articles of over 2,500 words pay $50 to $75 and up. Dept. Editor: William Ristow. Photos purchased with or without mss. B&w full negative prints, on 8x10 paper. Pays $10 per published photo, "sometimes $15 for specially assigned shots," $40 to $50 for photo essay. Department Editor: Louis Dunn.

How To Break In: "Working with our summer volunteer projects in investigative reporting, in which we teach the techniques and send new reporters out to do investigations in the Bay Area. Submit applications in mid-Spring each year."

THE SECOND WAVE, Box 344, Cambridge A., Cambridge MA 02139. Editors: Women's Editorial Collective. For women concerned with issues of women's liberation. Quarterly magazine; 44 (8x10) pages. Established in 1971. Circulation: 5,000. Acquires first serial rights. Uses about 20 mss a year. Payment in contributor's copies. Will send sample copy to writer for $1. Will consider photocopied and simultaneous submissions. Reports in 1 to 3 months. Query first or submit complete ms. Enclose S.A.S.E.

Nonfiction and Photos: All material must be related to the theme of women's liberation. "She (the writer) should write only on issues involving women's struggle for liberation, or women's relationships with other women. We do not want work glorifying men, marriage, traditional women's roles, etc. Would like to see articles on the women's liberation movement outside the big cities and in other countries; new issues being dealt with by women, etc." Informational, personal experience, interview, historical and think articles. Length: varies. B&w photos are used with or without accompanying mss. Captions optional.

Fiction and Poetry: Must relate to women's liberation theme. Experimental, mainstream, science fiction, fantasy. Free verse.

SIPAPU, Route 1, Box 216, Winters CA 95694. Editors: Noel Peattie and Dora Biblatz. For "libraries, editors and collectors interested in Third World studies, the counterculture and the underground press." Established in 1970. Semi-annually. Circulation: 500. Buys all rights, but will reassign rights to author after publication (on request). Payment on publication. Will send sample copy to writer for $1. Will consider photocopied submissions. Reports on material in 3 weeks. Query first. Enclose S.A.S.E.

Nonfiction: "Primarily book reviews, interviews, descriptions of special libraries and counterculture magazines and underground papers. We are an underground 'paper' about underground 'papers.' We are interested in personalities publishing dissent, counterculture and Third World material. Informal, clear and cool. We are not interested in blazing manifestos, but rather a concise, honest description of some phase of dissent publishing, or some library collecting in this field, that the writer knows about from the inside." Personal experience, interview, successful library operations. "We usually pay in contributor's copies, but will pay 2¢ per word if payment is required."

SISTERS, 1005 Market St., Suite 404, San Francisco CA 94103. Collective editorship. For lesbian women who are interested in material dealing with their life style, written by women. Published bimonthly by the Daughters of Bilitis; 32 (8x6) pages. Established in 1972. Circulation: 1,000. Rights acquired vary with author and material. "Every issue is put together from contributions received." Payment in contributor's copies. Will consider photocopied submissions. Will not consider simultaneous submissions. Reports on material accepted for publication within 2 months. Returns rejected material within 1 month. Submit complete ms. Enclose S.A.S.E.

Nonfiction and Photos: Articles on such topics as automobile repair; what it's like to be a lesbian; what is going on in various cities within the gay women's movement. "Writers must be female and their work should deal with being a woman in this society. Personal articles are in demand." How-to, personal experience, interview, profile, humor, historical, personal opinion, reviews of anything relevant to lesbians. Length: 1,500 to 6,000 words. Each published writer receives one copy of the issue. Photos are used for covers or with articles.

Fiction: Must be by women and related to theme. Experimental, mainstream, erotica, science fiction, fantasy, humorous, romance. Length: 5,000 to 6,500 words.

Poetry: Will consider anything interesting and unusual. Traditional forms (if otherwise original), blank verse, free verse, avant-garde forms, light verse. Length: 1 to 150 lines.

SUNRISE MAGAZINE, P.O. Box 271, Macomb IL 61455. Phone: 309-837-1307. Editor: Bill Knight. For readers with musical and political interests, especially alternative life styles and institutions, counterculture identifications and experiences. Monthly magazine. Established in 1971. Circulation: 20,000. Rights acquired vary with author and material. May buy all rights but will reassign rights to author after publication. Buys 35 to 60 mss a year. Payment on publication. Will send sample copy to writer for 60¢. Will consider photocopied and simultaneous submissions. Reports on material accepted for publication in 2 to 3 weeks. Returns rejected material in 1 to 2 weeks. Query first for poetry and fiction. Submit complete ms for nonfiction and reviews. Enclose S.A.S.E.

Nonfiction and Photos: "Political, musical, or cultural features; articles, interviews, or investigative news. Reviews of records, concerts, books, films. We attempt to focus primarily on music that has little high paid publicity, similar performers, and serious analyses of the counterculture's development. We also have an interest in innovations in survival, alternative energy sources, etc; in urban areas, as well as rural, new styles in music, new personalities, new experiments in society and culture. We do not necessarily want to see reviews of 'stars' of musical and non-musical media. We look for noncondescending layman language, retaining humor and perspective as related to the counterculture, but author need not keep objectivity. We want and need advocacy, investigative, 'gonzo' journalism." Recently published articles include "Orson Welles," a biographically related critique of Welles' major film contributions; "Cars Are Hard," a humorous nonfiction piece about a drunken pedestrian's experience when hit by a car; "Oil's Well," a two-part in-depth examination of oil companies' windfall profits and their direct correlation to the so-called energy crisis. Feature length: 2,000 to 3,000 words. Pays $20 to $30. 8x10 b&w photos (prints) purchased with or without mss. Pays $5. Photo Department

Editor: Vince Rowe. Reviews: records, books, films. Length: 350 to 550 words. Pays $4 to $9. Reviews Editor: Rick Johnson.
Fiction: Suspense, fantasy and speculative fiction. Length: 2,000 to 3,000 words. Pays $25 to $40. Department Editor: Bill Knight.

UNDERSTANDING MAGAZINE, P.O. Box 206, Merlin OR 97532. Editor: Daniel Fry. Circulation: 750. Not copyrighted. Buys 35 to 40 mss a year. Pays on publication. Will send sample copy to writer for 40¢. Enclose S.A.S.E. for ms return.
Nonfiction and Fillers: Articles that contribute to a better understanding among "all peoples of earth and those not of earth." This may be a social condition, a new idea, or a controversial group. Prefers objective rather than subjective material; some personal ESP experiences. Study publication. "Would like to see more material on UFO sightings, evaluations of the world in which we live." Length: 1,000 words maximum. Pays 1¢ per word. For news clippings of unusual occurrences, pays $1 per clipping.
Poetry: Must express good will and make a positive point. Length: 36 lines maximum. Pays 10¢ per line.

THE UNSPEAKABLE VISIONS OF THE INDIVIDUAL, P.O. Box 439, California PA 15419. Editors: Arthur Winfield Knight and Glee Knight. For adults with general interest leaning toward the literary world. Magazine published tri-annually; 50 to 70 (8½x11) pages. Established in 1971. Circulation: 2,000. Rights purchased vary with author and material. Usually buys all rights, but will reassign rights to author after publication. Buys 30 to 50 mss a year. Will send sample copy to writer for $2. Will not consider photocopied or simultaneous submissions. Reports in 1 month. Submit complete ms. Enclose S.A.S.E.
Nonfiction and Photos: "We have a strong 'beat' emphasis. Our title reflects this purpose. We look for good, competent material, with an individual approach. No biases or taboos toward language and experience." Informational, personal experience, interview, profile, expose, nostalgia, personal opinion; all types of reviews. Length: open. Pays $1 to $50. B&w (8x10) photos are purchased on assignment only. Captions optional. "Photos should reflect the mood and theme of our title." Pays $1 minimum.
3iction: Experimental, mainstream, confession (literary figures). Length: open. Pays $1 minimum.
Poetry: Traditional forms, blank verse, free verse, avant-garde forms. Length: open. Pays $1 minimum.

VECTOR, 83 Sixth St., San Francisco CA 94103. Phone: 415-781-1570. Editor: Richard Piro. For the establishment gay male. Monthly magazine; 48 to 72 pages. Established in 1964. Circulation: 26,000. Not copyrighted. Will send sample copy to writer for $1. Write for copy of guidelines for writers. Will consider photocopied and simultaneous submissions, but must be informed if a simultaneous submission is made. Submit seasonal material (Christmas) 2 months in advance. Reports on material accepted for publication in 2 months. Returns rejected material immediately. Submit complete ms. Enclose S.A.S.E.
Nonfiction and Photos: "Gay consciousness-raising pieces concerning the homosexual experience; political pieces, book reviews, theater/restaurant reviews, humor pieces, good living pieces. Keep in mind that the readership is 90% male homosexual, and that we are not into any forms of pornography." Length: open. Pays $10 to $25. No additional payment for b&w photos used with mss. Captions required.
Fiction: Erotic fiction welcomed. Pornography is not. Rejects fiction that lacks insight and perception. Pays $10 minimum.

WIN MAGAZINE, P.O. Box 547, Rifton NY 12471. Phone: 914-339-4585. Editor: Maris Cakars. For people of all ages concerned about peace and social change. Weekly magazine; 24 (8½x11) pages. Established in 1966. Circulation: 9,000. Not copyrighted. Uses 300 mss a year. Payment in contributor's copies. Will send free sample copy to writer on request. Will consider photocopied and simultaneous submissions. Reports in 1 month. Query first or submit complete ms. Enclose S.A.S.E.

Nonfiction: Material on the movement for peace and justice; building alternatives; analysis of current events from a pacifist perspective; reviews of books relating to these topics. "A positive approach to social change is vital. Otherwise, almost anything goes. We try to take a lighter, more irreverent attitude toward the world's problems. And we need more material on music and other aspects of culture. We do not want to see advice to the government, the movement, people in general, that is not grounded in concrete experience." Informational, how-to, personal experience, interview, profile, historical, think pieces, expose, spot news. Recently published articles include "Inflation and the Military Budget," "The Nixon Pardon and Clemency for War Resisters," "Voices of the Middle East." Length: 1,000 to 2,000 words.

Poetry: Traditional forms, blank verse, free verse and avant-garde forms. Theme: open. Department Editor: Mary Mayo.

How To Break In: "Send us a report from your area which combines news with personal experience; what the police are up to in Seattle, undercover activity in drug circles in Detroit, your experiences with the Indian movement in Wyoming, marching with the farm workers in California, etc."

WITCHCRAFT DIGEST, WICA NEWSLETTER, 153 W. 80 St., Suite 1B, New York NY 10024. Editor: Dr. Leo Louis Martello. For readers from 18 to 80, from psychiatrists to famous psychics, from Ph.D.'s to students, all interested in the pre-Christian pagan religions of the past; establishment people to counterculture types. Annual, 24 to 30 pages, (8½x11). Published by the Witches Anti-Defamation League and Witches Liberation Movement. Established in 1970. Circulation: 3,500. Buys all rights, but will reassign rights to author after publication. Buys 6 to 10 mss a year. Payment on publication; sometimes pays in contributor's copies; by arrangement with author. Will send sample copy to writer for $1.20 (check made out to Dr. Martello). Will consider photocopied and simultaneous submissions. Submit complete ms for nonfiction only. Enclose S.A.S.E.

Nonfiction and Fillers: "Pagan gods and goddesses, origins of popular holidays, new anthropological evidence of mother goddess worship in ancient times, news items on the media which distort the truth about witches, the pagan origins of Christmas, Easter, Resurrection, Atonement, Crucifixion, occult and ESP material related to our interests. Writers should familiarize themselves with the book *Witchcraft: The Old Religion* as to approach. That covers it: A pre-Christian pagan religion devoted to the 'old ways,' nature and earth-oriented, not so much anti- as it is non-Christian. We're the only publication in the U.S. of our kind stressing both witchcraft as a religion and the militant activism of its witch-subscribers-supporters. We don't want articles that confuse true witchcraft with satanism, devil-worship, sex orgies, drugs, black masses, ad nauseum stories about non-initiated self-designated 'pop witches', those with Christian propaganda such as 'I Escaped from Witchcraft', etc. Ugh! Topical subjects we'd like to have covered are the four main witches' Sabbats: Feb. 2, Candlemas or Olmelc, April 30, May Eve, Beltane or Walpurgisnacht; July 31, Lammas or Gule of August; Oct. 31, Halloween or Samhain. Four minor Sabbats are the Solstices, Dec. 22 or Yule; Midsummer, June 21; the Equinoxes March 21 and Sept. 22. Columns are staff written. We pay 1¢ a word; limited market. Also buy newspaper-magazine clippings on witchcraft. Pay is $1 per usable item, first come, first served. None are returned. We prefer articles of 1,000 words, no more than 1,500 words. Pay $10 usually."

WOMEN: A JOURNAL OF LIBERATION, 3028 Greenmount Ave., Baltimore MD 21218. Collective editorship. For women and men who are either active participants in, or interested in, the feminist movement. Quarterly magazine; 72 (8x10) pages. Established in 1969. Circulation: 20,000. Acquires all rights. Uses about 60 mss a year. Payment in contributor's copies. Will send sample copy for $1.25. Will consider photocopied submissions. Reports on material accepted for publication in 5 to 6 months. Returns rejected material in 7 to 8 months. Query first or submit complete ms. Enclose S.A.S.E.

Nonfiction and Photos: One of the oldest of the current feminist publications. Articles are usually related to theme, but welcomes any material that reflects a woman's consciousness. Upcoming themes include: organizing, children, health, aging. Needs more articles by and about third world women; black Chicano, Oriental, etc., as well as articles on ethnic and working class women. Length: 1,000 to 3,000 words. Uses letters and short pieces for "Our Sisters Speak" department. Welcomes photos, drawings, woodcuts, and all other forms of visual artwork by women and of women; especially those related to theme. Photos also used with mss.

Fiction: Open on themes. Length: 4,000 to 5,000 words.

Poetry: Traditional forms, blank verse, free verse, avant-garde forms, light verse. Theme and length are open.

Fillers: Short humor related to theme; not sexist.

WOMEN AND FILM, P.O. Box 4501, Berkeley CA 94704. Editors: Siew Hwa Beh and Saunie Salyer. For all interested in film studies, art, politics. Magazine published 3 times a year; 80 (8½x11) pages. Established in 1972. Circulation: 5,000. Acquires all rights; exceptions negotiable. Will consider photocopied submissions. Will not consider simultaneous submissions. Reports in 2 months. Query first. Enclose S.A.S.E.

Nonfiction: Explorations and analyses of women's role and image in film, TV, video, from a generally feminist-marxist perspective. Informational, personal experience, interview, historical, expose, technical, book reviews, TV reviews. Article length: 300 to 3,000 words. Review length: 200 words. Pays $15 minimum.

Animal Publications

These publications deal with pets, racing and show horses, and other pleasure animals. Magazines about animals bred and raised for food are classified in Farm Publications.

ANIMAL CAVALCADE, 8338 Rosemead Blvd., Pico Rivera CA 90660. Editor: Dr. C. M. Baxter. For animal owners interested in promoting better animal health. Publication of the Animal Health Foundation. Magazine; 32 pages. Special issues: March/April (newborn animals); Summer (skin diseases); Christmas issue. Established in 1969. Every 2 months. Circulation: 30,000. Buys all rights. Buys 15 mss a year, but most of the material is contributed as an assist to the Animal Health Foundation. Pays on publication. Will send sample copy to writer for 60¢. Will consider photocopied or simultaneous submissions. Submit special issue material 3 months in advance. Reports in 30 days. Query first or submit complete ms. Enclose S.A.S.E.

Nonfiction and Photos: This publication is reading material in veterinarians' offices and publishes articles and news relative to animal health. Prefers articles written by veterinarians written in layman's terms. Would like to see factual, educational articles about horses, cows, exotic animals, dogs, cats. No "doggie" material or poems. Could use profiles of veterinarians, think articles for children, animal health reviews. Length: open, but should not be excessive. Pays $15. Needs animal action pictures, especially those involving a veterinarian. Pays $15 for b&w and color.

Fiction and Fillers: Humorous fiction about animals. Length: 2 pages, maximum. Pays $15 maximum. Puzzles about animals, especially horses, dogs, and cats. Newsbreaks and clippings relating to animal health. Pays $15 maximum.

ANIMAL KINGDOM, New York Zoological Park, Bronx NY 10460. Editor: Eugene J. Walter, Jr. For individuals interested in wildlife, zoos, aquariums, and members of zoological societies. Bimonthly. Buys first North American serial rights. Pays on acceptance. Reports in 1 month. Enclose S.A.S.E. for return of submissions.

Nonfiction and Photos: Wildlife articles dealing with animal natural history, conservation, behavior. No pets, domestic animals, or botany. Articles should be scientifically well-grounded but written for a general audience, not scientific journal readers. No poetry, cartoons, or fillers. Length: 1,500 to 3,000 words. Pays $100 to $300. Payment for photos purchased with mss is negotiable.

How To Break In: "It helps to be a working scientist dealing directly with animals in the wild. Or a scientist working in a zoo such as the staff members here at the New York Zoological Society. Most of the authors who send us unsolicited mss are non-scientists who are doing their research in libraries. They're simply working from scientific literature and writing it up for popular consumption. There are a fair number of others who are backyard naturalists, so to speak, and while their observations may be personal, they are not well grounded scientifically. It has nothing to do with whether or not they are good or bad writers. In fact, some of our authors are not specially good writers but they are able to provide us with fresh, original material and new insights into animal behavior and biology. That sort of thing is impossible from someone who is working from books. Hence, I cannot be too encouraging to anyone who lacks field experience."

ANIMAL LOVERS MAGAZINE, P.O. Box 16, Murray Hills NJ 07974. Phone: 201-665-0812. Editor: Mrs. Anita Coffelt. For "pet owners who enjoy reading stories about animals, articles on care, feeding and health, wildlife articles, etc. Sincere animal lovers dedicated to welfare of all animals. Majority are adult." Established in 1969. Quarterly. Circulation: 3,000. Buys all rights, but will reassign rights to author after publication. Pays on acceptance. Will send a sample copy to a writer for 75¢. Write for copy of guidelines for writers; enclose S.A.S.E. Submit only complete ms for fiction and nonfiction. Will consider photocopied submissions. Submit seasonal material 3 months in advance. Reports in 4 to 6 weeks. Enclose S.A.S.E. for return of submissions.

Nonfiction, Photos, and Fiction: "Stories and articles on all members of the animal kingdom, including birds. Majority of material related to cats, dogs, birds. Approximately one story or article per issue on a zoo animal, wildlife, or other animal (horse, hamster, etc.). Articles on preservation of endangered species; articles opposing cruelty to animals, profiles of persons performing extraordinary good deeds for animals, etc. We look for a unique story line. Readers seem to prefer a warm, touching theme . . . or those with a humorous slant . . . human interest qualities." Buys informational, personal experience, interview, humor articles. Length: 600 words maximum. Payment is 1¢ a word. Sharp, clear b&w photos of any size purchased with or without accompanying mss; captions optional. "Animal subjects only—cleverly posed photos will be considered first." Payment is $2 per photo.

How To Break In: "We've given many new writers their first chance at being published. Storylines must be unique and interesting (we're not interested in inconsequential accounts of one's pet). Authors should adhere to word requirement! Superfluous or repetitious data should be avoided! New writers can sell us material if their manuscripts incorporate these and other editorial requirements above."

ANIMALS, Massachusetts Society for the Prevention of Cruelty to Animals, 180 Longwood Ave., Boston MA 02115. Phone: 617-731-2000, Ext. 53. Editor: Richard H. Cowan. For animal lovers, young and old; many well-educated professionals. Monthly magazine; (8½x11), 16 pages. Circulation: 14,000. Buys first North American serial rights. Payment on publication. Will send free sample copy to writer on request. Submit seasonal material 2 months in advance. "Ms will be returned only if accompanied by S.A.S.E." Query preferred. Enclose S.A.S.E.

Nonfiction and Photos: "Non-sensational; no gory photos or 'scare stories.' Stronger cultural focus. We've begun to look at animals in a wider context. The interesting relationship of animals to man in history, art, literature, film and social customs and more, represents a wealth of topics to be explored by talented freelance writers. Our focus is primarily on domesticated animals, though we occasionally publish wildlife material." How-to (building projects for animals), humor (well-written), historical, nostalgia, photo articles. Length: 800 to 2,000 words. Pays 2¢ a word. B&w photos are purchased for $3 to $5 per photo. Captions preferred. Also considers non-Polaroid color photos.

APPALOOSA NEWS, Box 403, Moscow ID 83843. Editor: Don Walker. For people interested in appaloosa horses. Monthly magazine, 180 pages. Established in 1946.

Circulation: 30,000. Not copyrighted. Buys 25 mss a year. Payment on publication. Will send free sample copy to writer on request. Will consider photocopied submissions. Will not consider simultaneous submissions. Submit seasonal material 3 to 6 months in advance. Reports by return mail, if possible. Submit complete ms. Enclose S.A.S.E.

Nonfiction and Photos: Horse related articles. Appaloosa ranches, uses of horses. Length is open. Payment varies, depends on merit, up to $75. Recently published articles include "Carroll Shelby: Winner in a Black Hat," and "James Brolin Stars With Appaloosas." Photos are purchased with accompanying ms with no additional payment. Captions required. B&w photos should be 5x7 or larger; color 35mm minimum. Pays $25 to $75 for color.

CANADA RIDES, 2920 11th St. S.E., Calgary, Alberta, Canada, T2G 3G8. Editor: Mrs. Mary Jo Birrell. For "equine enthusiasts of all ages; horse clubs, ranchers and retired ranchers; city people who are interested in western culture." Established in 1972. Monthly. Circulation: 10,000. Buys all rights but will reassign rights to authors after publication. Buys 60 mss a year. Pays on publication. Will send sample copy for 75¢. Submit complete copy for nonfiction and poetry. Approximate word count on ms should be included. Will consider photocopied submissions. Reports in 1 month. Enclose S.A.E. and International Reply Coupons.

Nonfiction and Photos: "Stories of competitive riders, current or past rodeo champions, western artists, special horse personalities or horse types, and old-time policemen. Anything western, historical and/or horsey such as outstanding cattle spreads, training and breeding stables, and youth groups associated with horses. Although we insist on a professional calibre of writing, the magazine is meant to be informal, warm and personal. This is one of the few Canadian horse magazines that is Canada-wide, rather than provincial. Therefore, the material should be Canadian. We are also interested in informational, how-to, personal experience, interviews, profiles, inspirtional, humor, historical and gymkhana reviews." Length: 1,000 to 3,000 words. Pays 4¢ a word. Photos purchased with ms. Prefers 8x10 b&w. Pays $3.50 per photo, with total of $20 for photos for 1 spread.

Poetry: "We will look at poetry with a western or horsey flavor." Length: open. Pays 25¢ a line.

THE CANADIAN HORSE, 48 Belfield Rd., Rexdale, Ontario, Canada M9W 1G1. Editor: P. G. Jones. For thoroughbred horsemen. Magazine; (8½x11). Established in 1961. Monthly. Circulation: 4,000. Buys all rights. Pays on publication. Query first. Enclose S.A.S.E.

Nonfiction: Material on thoroughbred racing; racing results. Length: 2 pages. Pays $20 per page.

CAT FANCY, 2630 Avon St., Newport Beach CA 92660. Executive Editor: Gene Esquivel. For people who own and/or care about cats as pets. Magazine published every 2 months; 64 (8½x11) pages. Established in 1963. Circulation: 50,000. Rights purchased vary with author and material. Usually buys all rights. Buys 24 mss a year. Pays on publication. Will send sample copy to writer for $1.25. Will not consider photocopied submissions or simultaneous submissions. Submit seasonal material 6 months in advance. Reports in 3 months. Enclose S.A.S.E.

Nonfiction and Photos: Articles about health, grooming and care, etc., of cats. Writer must know subject. No "cute" stories. Informational, how-to, personal experience, interview, profile, historical, think articles and photo articles. Length: 500 to 3,000 words. Pays 3¢ per word. Photos purchased with or without accompanying ms. Pays $10 minimum for 8x10 b&w; $75 minimum for 35mm and 2¼ transparencies.

CATS MAGAZINE, P.O. Box 4106, Pittsburgh PA 15301. Editor: Jean Amelia Laux. For men and women of all ages; cat enthusiasts, vets, geneticists. Monthly magazine. Established in 1945. Circulation: 50,000. Buys first North American serial rights. Buys 50 mss per year. Payment on acceptance. Will send free sample copy to writer on request. Write for copy of guidelines for writers. Will "reluctantly" consider

photocopied submissions. Will not consider simultaneous submissions. Submit seasonal Christmas material 4 to 6 months in advance. Reports within 6 weeks. Enclose S.A.S.E.
Nonfiction and Photos: "Cat health, cat breed articles, articles on the cat in art, literature, history, human culture, cats in the news. Cat pets of popular personalities. In general how cats and cat people are contributing to our society. We're more serious, more scientific, but we do like occasional light or humorous articles portraying cats and humans, however, as they really are. Would like to see something on psychological benefits of cat ownership; how do cat-owning families differ from others? Also movie and book reviews." Length: 800 to 2,500 words. Pays $15 to $75. Recently published articles include "Eight-Pound Therapist," cat used in psychiatric treatment of hospital patients; "Let It Snow!", cats and humans involved in week-long mid-winter power shut-off; "Vet on Wheels," doctor with office in a van. Photos purchased with or without accompanying ms. Captions optional. Pays $15 minimum for 4x5 or larger b&w photos; $100 minimum for color. Prefers 2¼x2¼ minimum, but can use 35mm (transparencies only). "We use color for cover only. Prefer cats as part of scenes rather than stiff portraits."
Fiction and Poetry: Science fiction, fantasy and humorous fiction; cat themes only. Length: 800 to 2,500 words. Pays $15 to $100. Poetry in traditional forms, blank or free verse, avant-garde forms and some light verse; cat themes only. Length: 4 to 64 lines. Pays $10 to $25.

DOG FANCY, 2630 Avon St., Newport Beach CA 92660. Executive Editor: Gene Esquivel. For people who own and/or love dogs. Magazine published every 2 months; 64 (8½x11) pages. Established in 1969. Circulation: 40,000. Buys all rights or first North American serial rights. Buys 24 mss a year. Pays on publication. Will send sample copy to writer for $1.25. Will not consider photocopied or simultaneous submissions. Submit seasonal material 6 months in advance. Reports in 90 days. Enclose S.A.S.E.
Nonfiction and Photos: Articles about dogs. Health, care, etc. Writer should know the subject. Informational, how-to, personal experience, interview, historical, think articles, photo features and technical articles. Length: 500 to 5,000 words. Pays 3¢ a word. Photos purchased with or without accompanying ms. Pays $10 minimum for 8x10 b&w photos; $75 minimum for 35mm or 2¼ transparencies.

THE FLORIDA HORSE, P.O. Box 699, Ocala FL 32670. Editors: Marianne Betancourt and Lauren Marks. For readers interested in thoroughbred horse racing, with the emphasis on Florida-breds. Magazine; 75 pages. Established in 1958. 10 times a year. Circulation: 8,000. Not copyrighted. Buys 20 to 25 mss a year. Payment on publication. Will send free sample copy to writer on request. Will not consider photocopied or simultaneous submissions. Reports on material accepted for publication in 1 month. Returns rejected material in 2 weeks. Query first. Enclose S.A.S.E.
Nonfiction and Photos: "We are the only magazine that exclusively covers Florida thoroughbred racing and breeding. Writers should remember that we are concerned only with the thoroughbred industry or thoroughbred racing and breeding in general, with the major emphasis on Florida. We are especially interested in interviews with well-known racing personalities." Length: 1,500 words minimum. Pays $50 to $100. Recently published articles include "The Gypsy Horse," historical article about the famous race mare, Kincsem; "Where Have All the Racehorses Gone?", an article about racehorses that became hunters.

HORSE AND HORSEMAN, P.O. Box HH, Capistrano Beach CA 92624. Phone: 714-493-2101. Editor: Jack Lewis. For owners of pleasure horses; predominantly female with main interest in show/pleasure riding. Monthly magazine; 74 (8½x11) pages. Established in 1973. Circulation: 89,000. Buys all rights, but will reassign rights to author after publication. Buys 40 to 50 mss a year. Payment on acceptance. Will send free sample copy to writer on request. Write for copy of guidelines for writers. Will not consider photocopied or simultaneous submissions. Submit special material (horse and tack care; veterinary medicine pieces in winter and spring issues)

3 months in advance. Reports within 1 month. Query first or submit complete ms. Enclose S.A.S.E.

Nonfiction and Photos: Training tips, do-it-yourself pieces, grooming and feeding, stable management, tack maintenance, sports, personalities, rodeo and general features of horse-related nature. Emphasis must be on informing, rather than merely entertaining. Aimed primarily at the beginner, but with information for experienced horsemen. Subject matter must have thorough, in-depth appraisal. Interested in more English (hunter/jumper) riding/training copy, plus pieces on driving horses and special horse areas like Tennessee Walkers and other gaited breeds. More factual breed histories. Recently published articles include "First Aid for Horses" (at-home veterinary attention); "The Telltale Teeth" (determining a horse's age by dental exam); "Train This Winter for Spring Shows" (begin halter training now); "Managing a Stallion Station" (stud farm operation); "Jim Brolin: Concerned Appaloosa Breeder" (personality feature). Uses informational, how-to, personal experience, interview, profile, humor, historical, nostalgia, successful business operations, technical articles. Length: 2,000 words minimum. Pays $75 to $150. B&w photos (4x5 and larger) purchased with or without mss. Pays $4 to $10 when purchased without ms. Uses original color transparencies (35mm and larger). Will not consider duplicates. Pays $75 to $100 for cover use. Payment for inside editorial color is negotiated.

HORSE & RIDER, Box 555, Temecula CA 92390. Editor: Ray Rich. For "owners, breeders, and riders of Western type of horse." Buys all rights. Pays on acceptance. No query required. Enclose S.A.S.E. for return of submissions.

Nonfiction and Photos: "Features on training, breeding, feeding, medical advice, general horse care and how-to articles of interest to active horsemen; historical Western articles relating to the horse world. We seldom buy features without photos." Length: 500 to 3,000 words. Pays up to $200 for features with photos; pays $75 for cover chromes; $50 for inside color per chrome.

HORSE LOVER'S NATIONAL MAGAZINE, 651 Brannan St., San Francisco CA 94107. Editor: Lawrence Keenan. For urban horse owners interested in better care and handling of their horses. Bimonthly magazine; 64 to 80 pages. Established in 1936. Circulation: 150,000. Buys first North American serial rights or simultaneous rights. Buys 10 to 15 mss a year. Payment on publication. Will send sample copy to writer for $1. Will consider photocopied and simultaneous submissions. Reports in 2 weeks. Query first. Enclose S.A.S.E.

Nonfiction and Photos: Looks for tightly written articles by someone who knows the subject. Reviews of larger horse shows and rodeos; good features on professional horsemen on the east coast. Does not want to see anything on "me and my love for horses." Uses informational, how-to, interview, profile, personal opinion. Length: open. Pays 3¢ a word. Department Editor: Nancy Nelson. Pays $5 to $10 for b&w photos (5x7 or larger), purchased with or without accompanying mss. Pays $10 to $25 for color transparencies. Captions required.

HORSE, OF COURSE!, Derbyshire Bldg., Temple NH 03084. Phone: 603-654-6126. Editor: Dr. R. A. Greene. For novice horsemen, average age 18 or 19, mostly female readers. "We bridge the gap between horse loving and horse ownership and appeal to beginners." Monthly magazine; 68 pages, (8¼x11¼). Established in 1972. Circulation: 65,000. Rights purchased vary with author and material. Usually buys all rights; but will sometimes reassign rights to author after publication. Buys about 35 to 50 mss per year. Payment on publication. Will send sample copy to writer for $1. Write for copy of guidelines for writers. Submit seasonal material 4 to 6 months in advance. Reports in 90 days. Enclose S.A.S.E.

Nonfiction and Photos: "How-to-do-its about riding and training, interviews, some historical and general interest articles dealing with horses of the 'where to' variety. Prefer illustrated material. Keep it informal. Keep instructional articles basic. Assume the reader knows nothing. We deal strictly with basic material for beginners." Length: 800 to 3,000 words. Pays $10 to $200. Payment averages $20 to $30 per finished page of magazine, including photos. Open to suggestions for columns and regular departments. Length: 600 to 1,000 words. Photos are purchased with accompanying ms with no additional payment. Captions required. Also purchased on assignment. B&w glossies, not less than 4x5. Color transparencies or 4x5 or larger glossy color prints.

Fillers: Interested in horse related puzzles, jokes, and short humor as fillers. Pays $2 to $5.

How To Break In: "Submit a well-written, carefully edited, practical, illustrated manuscript the first time. If photos are included, be sure they will reproduce well. Once we buy one, it's easy to sell us a second."

HORSE PLAY, 50B Ridge Rd., Greenbelt MD 20770. Editor: Carolyn Banks. For performance riders interested in show jumping, foxhunting, combined training. Magazine; 48 (8½x11) pages. Submit foxhunting material September through February. Established in 1973. Monthly. Circulation: 7,500. Buys first North American serial rights. Pays on acceptance. Will send sample copy to writer for $1. Reports in 3 weeks. Query first or submit complete ms. Enclose S.A.S.E.

Nonfiction and Photos: "News coverage of big shows and events. In-depth interviews or how-to articles. Most involve research and are not for beginners. Deal only with English riding. It's important to query on big news events or shows we can't send regulars to." Recently published articles include an in-depth interview with famous rider Chris Collins and "Getting Your Horse Fit", with good specific suggestions. Length: 1,500 to 3,000 words. Pays $50 to $75, but usually $50. Photos purchased with or without ms, or on assignment. Captions required. Action shots preferred. Pays $5 for unsolicited b&w per published photo; when done on assignment, add $40. "Color is assigned (slides only), but will look at samples."

HORSEMAN, THE MAGAZINE OF WESTERN RIDING, 5314 Bingle Rd., Houston TX 77018. Editor: Tex Rogers. For people who own and ride horses for pleasure and competition. Majority own western stock horses and compete in western type horse shows as a hobby. Monthly. "We have four special issues per year, but they're not standard. Subjects may vary from year to year." Established in 1954. Circulation: 172,000. Rights purchased vary with author and material. Buys all rights, first North American serial rights, or second serial (reprint) rights. Buys approximately 80 mss per year. Payment on publication. Will send free sample copy to writer on request. Write for copy of guidelines for writers. Will not consider photocopied submissions. Submit seasonal material 4 months in advance. Reports in 3 weeks. Query first. Enclose S.A.S.E.

Nonfiction, Photos, and Poetry: "How-to articles on horsemanship, training, grooming, exhibiting, nutrition, horsekeeping, mare care and reproduction, horse health, humor and history dealing with horses. We really like articles from professional trainers, or 'as told to' articles by pro horsemen to freelancers. The approach should always be to provide information which will educate and inform readers as to how they can ride, train, keep and enjoy their horses more. Compared to other horse publications, we try to be more professional in our writing and really have meaningful articles in the magazine." Length: 1,000 to 3,000 words. Pays 4¢ a word (one time; 5¢ a word for all rights; 6¢ a word for "as told to" with professional horseman. Photos purchased with accompanying ms with no additional payment. Captions required. Also purchased on assignment. Pays $6 minimum for b&w 8x10 and negs; 35mm or120negs. Ektacolor CPS. "We make prints." Pays $100 for covers; all rights. Buys some traditional forms of poetry. Pays $10 for all rights.

HORSEMEN'S JOURNAL, 6000 Executive Bldg., Suite 317, Rockville MD 20852. Editor: Donald Meredith. For an audience composed entirely of thoroughbred running-horse owners, trainers and breeders. Monthly magazine; standard (8x11), 72 pages. Special issues: May (Kentucky Derby issue); December, July and August (material relating to racehorse breeding and bloodlines); September (material relating to training). Established in 1949. Circulation: 34,000. Rights purchased vary with author and material. Buys all rights, first North American serial rights, and second serial (reprint) rights. Buys "less than 6 unsolicited mss a year, over 50 mss on assignment basis." Payment on publication. Will send sample copy to writer for 75¢. Will not consider photocopied or simultaneous submissions. Submit seasonal material first of month preceding cover date. Reports "as soon as possible." Query first. Enclose S.A.S.E.

Nonfiction and Photos: "Any material which our readership can relate to on a professional level. This includes personality pieces, interviews, how-to articles, veterinary stories and generally material relating to happenings and economics within the racehorse industry." Length: 1,000 to 3,000 words. Pays $30 minimum. 8x10 b&w glossies are purchased with accompanying ms. Captions optional. Pays $7.50 each.

How To Break In: "Because of our monthly deadline and competition from dailies and weeklies, 'current events' pieces are of little use. Material should be incisive, should quote the people involved in their words and should have national import and interest."

NATIONAL HUMANE REVIEW (Official publication of the American Humane Association), P.O. Box 1266, Denver CO 80201. Phone: 303-771-1300. Editor: Eileen F. Schoen. Established in 1913. For children, professionals in the humane field, and others with "an interest in animals and the organized humane movement." Monthly. Circulation: 12,000. Buys first North American serial rights only. Buys 30 to 50 mss a year from freelancers. Write for copy of guidelines for writers. No query required. Submit seasonal material 4 months in advance. Reporting time varies, from "immediate or up to 3 months." Enclose S.A.S.E.

Nonfiction and Fiction: "Primarily, we sell the idea of kindness, rather than a specific organization"; freelance material should "illustrate how kindness achieves more positive results than brutality." Articles can be personal experience, inspirational, or humor pieces. Do not send "articles on local humane societies, individuals who are 'one-man' humane societies, dog training from a 'how-to' approach, pet cemeteries, municipal (dog catcher) articles, editorials on animals. All of these, if used, are staff-written. No submissions on all the pets a family has." Humor, adventure, contemporary animal problems, and animal fiction which should read as nonfiction, so it appears to be an article. Length: 1,000 to 2,000 words, prefer 2,000 words. Pay is 1½¢ a word.

Photos: Vertical pictures of children and animals for cover. Also photo series, humorous or serious, of animals alone or with people. Pays $5 per b&w photo.

Poetry: "Our 'Well Versed' column is very popular with readers since it serves as an emotional outlet for writer's feeling about animals." Uses traditional forms, blank verse, free verse, avant-garde forms, light and humorous verse. No payment.

THE QUARTER HORSE JOURNAL, Box 9105, Amarillo TX 79105. Editor: Audie Rackley. For readers "from all walks of life. Farmers and ranchers, mostly horse owners." Established in 1948. Special issues in April—racing; May—performances; August—youth; September—Western wear; December—stallion issue. Monthly. Circulation: 65,000. Buys all rights. Buys about 24 mss a year. Payment on acceptance. Query first or submit complete ms. Submit seasonal material 2 months in advance. Enclose S.A.S.E.

Nonfiction, Photos, and Fillers: "*The Quarter Horse Journal* is owned by the American Quarter Horse Association and covers all facets of the quarter horse business. Our main purpose is the promotion of the breed and serving our membership." Publishes "current events such as race and show results. Features include outstanding breeders and their successes, personalities, and their contributions to the QH breed. Technical articles related to improvement of the breed welcomed. More technical articles with current research available." Length: 800 to 2,500 words. Pays $25 to $100. Purchases photos with mss. 4x5 or 8x10 b&w glossies. Prefers 2¼x2¼ or 4x5 color transparencies. Payment included with mss. Buys puzzles (horseword).

How To Break In: "Any sincere, talented writer acquainted with the Quarter Horse breed, and who has a background of information, has a chance of getting his material accepted. Unfortunately, very few submit material other than those who have contributed in the past. Material must be related to the industry or tied closely to it. We are always open for suggestions and will discuss editorial matter with those interested."

THE QUARTER HORSE OF THE PACIFIC COAST, P.O. Box 4822, Sacramento CA 95825. Editor: Don Sammons. For breeders, trainers and owners of horses; jockeys, etc. Publication of the Pacific Coast Quarter Horse Association. Magazine; 120 (8½x11) pages. Established in 1945. Monthly. Circulation: 6,200. Pays on acceptance. Will send free sample copy to writer on request. Will consider photocopied and simultaneous submissions. Submit special material (for the November Stallion Issue) 2 months in advance. Reports on material accepted for publication in 2 weeks. Returns rejected material immediately. Submit complete ms. Enclose S.A.S.E.
Nonfiction and Photos: How-to articles on horse subjects. Veterinary advice from qualified individuals, etc. Feature articles on persons associated with the horse industry. No special approach. Prefers diversity as long as it deals with their subject. Does not want to see anything on horse sales or shows. Articles on breeding techniques are used in the November Stallion Issue. Informational, personal experience, interview, profile, humor, historical, think pieces, photo, successful business operations, new product. Recently published "Tax Tips for Horsemen." Length is dependent on subject matter. Pays $50 to $100. Pays $5 for 8x10 b&w glossies purchased with or without mss. Captions required.
Fiction and Fillers: Western and humorous fiction. Pays $50 to $100. "Horsey" crossword puzzles are used as fillers. Pays $20 minimum.

TROPICAL FISH HOBBYIST, 211 W. Sylvania Ave., Neptune City NJ 17753. Editor: Neal Pronek. For tropical fish keepers; mostly male, mostly young. Monthly magazine; 100 (5½x8½) pages. Established in 1952. Circulation: 48,000. Rights purchased vary with author and material. Usually buys all rights, but buys only serial rights in some cases. Buys 50 mss a year. Payment on acceptance. Will send sample copy to writer for $1. Will not consider photocopied or simultaneous submissions. Reports within 1 week. Query first or submit complete ms. Enclose S.A.S.E.
Nonfiction and Photos: "Don't submit material unless you're an experienced keeper of tropical fishes and know what you're talking about. Offer specific advice about caring for and breeding tropicals and related topics. Study the publication before submitting." Informal style preferred. Can use personality profiles of successful aquarium hobbyists, but query first on these. Pays from 1½¢ to 3¢ a word. Pays $5 for b&w glossy photos purchased with or without accompanying mss. No size limitation. Captions optional. Pays $10 for color; 35mm transparency, or larger.

THE WESTERN HORSEMAN, 3850 North Nevada Ave., Colorado Springs CO 80901. Editor: Chuck King. For admirers of stock horses. Monthly. Buys first North American serial rights. Pays on acceptance. Query Chan Bergen, Assistant Editor, before submitting. Reports in 2 to 3 weeks. Enclose S.A.S.E.
Nonfiction and Photos: Dealing with training, handling, feeding, etc., of horses; personalities in the horse world. Pays about $50 for 1,500 words with good b&w photos.

Art Publications

AMERICAN ART REVIEW, P.O. Box 65007, Los Angeles CA 90065. Editor: Martha Hutson. For libraries, museums, professional art historians, artists, collectors; persons interested in American art history heritage. Magazine; 144 (8½x11) pages. Established in 1973. Every 2 months. Special student issue; date varies. Circulation: 10,000. Rights purchased vary with author and material. May buy all rights, but will reassign rights to author after publication; or simultaneous rights. Buys 35 to 40 mss a year. Pays on publication. Will send sample copy to writer for $3.75. Write for copy of guidelines for writers. Will consider photocopied and simultaneous submissions. Submit special issue material 6 months in advance. Reports on material accepted for publication in 2 weeks. Returns rejected material immediately. Query first. Enclose S.A.S.E.

Nonfiction and Photos: Articles must be well-researched and documented, but can be interpretive. Should be highly readable and directed toward art historians/collectors, and concern American art history from the Colonial period to 1950. Would like to see material on American art as an investment; articles about collectors and collections; interpretations of American art history; collecting possibilities. Quality of artists or collectors must be high. Length: 1,500 to 5,000 words. Pays $25 to $150. Student issue uses papers written by undergraduate or graduate art students. Also uses reviews of exhibitions and art books. Length: 1,500 to 3,000 words. Pays $35 to $100. No additional payment for 8x10 b&w glossies or 4x5, 5x7 or 8x10 color transparencies used with mss. Captions required.

THE ART GALLERY, Ivoryton CT 06442. Phone: 203-767-0151. Editor: William C. Bendig. For an art-oriented audience; collectors with an auction and antique interest; museum directors and curators. Established in 1957. Circulation: 30,000. Buys all rights. Payment on publication. Will send free sample copy to writer on request. Reports in 2 weeks. Query first. Enclose S.A.S.E.
Nonfiction: Highly specialized or unique approach required for material on fine arts, antiques, collecting all decorative arts objects plus coins, medals, books, etc. "Current news approach; crisp, clear, concise writing; intelligent, but not stuffy. Normally, everything is commissioned." Length: 1,000 to 4,000 words. Pays $50 to $250.

ART NEWS, 750 Third Ave., New York NY 10017. Editor: Milton Esterow. For persons interested in art. Monthly. Circulation: 38,000. Query first. Enclose S.A.S.E.
Nonfiction: "I'm buying in-depth profiles of people in the art world—artists, curators, dealers. And investigative pieces, including some on antiques. The format is now very flexible to cover personalities, trends, a single painting, and we'll have monthly reports on the art markets." Wants "humanized" art coverage. Length: 800 words; "some major pieces as long as 8,000 words." Pays $75 to $300.
How To Break In: "Reviews of art shows are the traditional way for new writers to break in with us, particularly in the New York area. This can lead to future assignments."

ARTS MAGAZINE, 23 E. 26th St., New York NY 10010. Phone: 212-685-8500. Editor: Richard Martin. A journal of contemporary art, art criticism, and art history, particularly for artists, scholars, museum officials, art teachers and students, and collectors. Established in 1926. Monthly, except July and August. Circulation: 28,500. Buys all rights. Pays on publication. Query first. Study magazine before querying. Enclose S.A.S.E.
Nonfiction and Photos: Art criticism, art analysis, and art history. Topical reference to museum or gallery exhibition preferred. Length: 1,500 to 2,500 words. Pays $100, with opportunity for negotiation. B&w glossies or color transparencies customarily supplied by related museums or galleries.

ARTS MANAGEMENT, 408 West 57th St., New York NY 10019. Phone: 212-245-3850. Editor: A.H. Reiss. For cultural institutions. Five times annually. Circulation: 6,000. Buys all rights. Pays on publication. Mostly staff written. Query first. Reports in several weeks. Enclose S.A.S.E.
Nonfiction: Short articles, 400 to 900 words, tightly written, expository, explaining how art administrators solved problems in publicity, fund raising, and general administration; actual case histories emphasizing the how-to. Also short articles on the economics and sociology of the arts and important trends in the nonprofit cultural field. Must be fact-filled, well-organized and without rhetoric. Payment is 2¢ to 4¢ per word. No photographs or pictures.

DESIGN MAGAZINE, 1100 Waterway Blvd., Indianapolis IN 46202. Editor: Barbara Albert. Established in 1898 for art teachers, students (junior high to college level), artists, home hobbyists and craftpersons. Circulation: 10,000 nationally and in a few foreign countries. Buys all rights unless otherwise specified by author. Buys 60 to 75 mss a year. Pays on publication. Reports on material in 2 months. Enclose S.A.S.E.

Nonfiction and Photos: "Interested in technique or how-to articles for classroom or individual use. All articles should convey a sense of design or art awareness, whether explaining an art technique or craft project. B&w photos or drawings are necessary. *Design Magazine* tries to create an awareness of art in our everyday surroundings. Traditional as well as non-traditional or out-of-the-ordinary ideas are welcome." Pays $20 to $75.

EXHIBIT (incorporating *Revue des Beaux Arts)*, Allied Publications, P.O. Box 23505, Fort Lauderdale FL 33307. Associate Editor: Marie Stilkind. For "customers of art galleries and art supply shops." Bimonthly. Buys North American serial rights only. Pays on acceptance. No queries necessary. Reports on submissions in 2 to 4 weeks. Enclose S.A.S.E. for return of submissions.

Nonfiction and Photos: Articles on current trends, art history and profiles of really famous artists known to the general public. Prefers b&w glossy photos with articles if possible. Length: 500 to 1,000 words. Pays 5¢ an accepted word. $5 a photo.

GLASS ART MAGAZINE, P.O. Box 7527, Oakland CA 94601. Phone: 415-534-2122. Editor: Albert Lewis. For artists working in blown glass, stained glass, conceptual glass, collectors, museum curators, gallery and shop owners, art critics, high school and college students in the arts; general public. Magazine published every 2 months; 48 (11x8½) pages. Established in 1973. Circulation: 11,000. Buys all rights, but will reassign rights to author after publication, on request. Buys over 60 mss a year. Payment on publication. Will send sample copy to writer for $3. Will consider photocopied and simultaneous submissions. Submit seasonal material 3 months in advance. Reports on material accepted for publication in 2 weeks. Returns rejected material in 1 week. Submit complete ms. Query is acceptable, but not required. Enclose S.A.S.E.

Nonfiction and Photos: "Writing should be pointed at university-level comprehension. We want articles of a general nature treating the arts and crafts in the U.S. and abroad (Europe especially). History of crafts (especially glass); psychology of art; urban artist. We'll gladly look at anything dealing with the arts and crafts, especially contemporary glass in the U.S. and Europe (Eastern Europe, too). We confine our main interest to contemporary glass arts, and to subjects touching thereon, viz., the energy crisis. Art-oriented themes, reviews of shows including glass arts. No funky or super-scholarly writing." Interested in articles on alternative fuels for glass melt tanks; alternative furnace and lehr designs utilizing said fuels. Technical articles on physical nature of glass, furnace and lehr design, glass colorants, batch formulas, and so on. Successful business operations (glass blowing or stained glass only). New product (glass oriented only). Articles on summer workshops in glass for the April issue are due before February 1. Articles of year-round glass studies for the June issue are due before April 1. Recently published articles include "Some Thoughts on Stained Glass," "The Role of Artist in Society," "Art and Survival." Pays 4¢ minimum per word. No additional payment is made for 8x10 b&w glossy photos used with mss. Captions required.

Poetry: Avant-garde forms. Prefers those that relate to their theme; otherwise open. Length: open. Pays $5 to $25.

METROPOLITAN MUSEUM OF ART BULLETIN, Metropolitan Museum of Art, Fifth Ave. and 82nd St., New York NY 10028. Editor: Katharine Stoddert. Quarterly. Query first. "Writers contributing must write entirely on speculation. Most of our writers are scholars or have some reputation in the field, and we commission most of our freelance material." Enclose S.A.S.E.

Nonfiction: Publishes museum news, discussion of events and exhibitions, etc. Each issue usually covers a single theme. Writers must be acknowledged experts in their fields. "Our museum experts scrutinize everything very carefully." Length: 750 words; 1,500 to 2,000 words. Pays $75 for short pieces, $150 for longer articles.

NORTHWEST ARTWORLD, Route 1, Bigfork MT 59911. Editor: Les Rickey. For artists, collectors, dealers. Magazine. Special issues include Bronzes (January); Landscapes (June); Women in Western Art (May). Established in 1973. Monthly. Circulation: 11,000. Not copyrighted. Buys 18 mss a year. Pays on publication. Will send a free sample copy to writer on request. Write for copy of guidelines for writers. No photocopied or simultaneous submissions. Submit special issue material 1 month in advance. Reports on material accepted for publication in 2 weeks. Returns rejected material almost immediately. Query first. Enclose S.A.S.E.
Nonfiction and Photos: Articles on western art and that of the Pacific Northwest. Must be tight, terse and telegraphic. No analyses. Emphasis is on biographies of artists. Length: 100 to 1,000 words. Pays 1¢ to 3¢ a word. Buys 4x5 and 5x7 b&w photos with mss. Pays $5 minimum. Color slides (120mm) are also purchased with mss. Pays $25 minimum.
Fillers: Newsbreaks of 100 to 500 words. Pays $5 to $10.

TODAY'S ART, 25 W. 45th St., New York NY 10036. Editor: Ralph Fabri. For "artists (professional and amateur), art teachers, and museums." Monthly. Circulation: 86,000. Buys first rights. Pays on publication. Query first. Enclose S.A.S.E.
Nonfiction and Photos: "Only items referring to art and how-to articles in all fields of art with b&w and some color illustrations. Articles should be easy to follow. Most articles we receive are not sufficiently detailed and a lot have to be rewritten to make them more informative." Length: 400 to 850 words. Pays $25 to $50.
How To Break In: "Every now and then, someone comes up with a good idea, even if no idea can be completely new, of course. But there are many technical and esthetic possibilities in art. Indeed, there's no limit to them. If a writer, young or old, is sure he has something like that, and knows how to present it in an easily comprehensible manner, we are glad to consider the article. But we don't want philosophizing about art, and we do not wish to promote unknown artists."

WESTART, P.O. Box 1396, Auburn CA 95603. Phone: 916-885-3242. Editor: Jean L. Couzens. For practicing artists and craftsmen; art teachers and students; art patrons; gallery-goers. Newspaper published twice a month; 16 to 20 (16x11½) pages. Established in 1962. Circulation: 7,500. Buys all rights, but will reassign rights to author after publication. "We buy little freelance material." Payment on publication. Will send sample copy to writer for 30¢. Will not consider photocopied or simultaneous submissions. Reports within a week or so. Query first or submit complete ms. Enclose S.A.S.E.
Nonfiction and Photos: Emphasis is on current, wide coverage of the art scene; excellent over-view. Publishes news of artists and art activities on the west coast. Not interested in hobbies, personal success stories, or features of a general nature. Recently published articles include "Mosaic for the Blind," "Looking at Landscape," "Abstracts from Nature," and "Writing About Art Writing." Length: 700 to 800 words maximum. Pays 30¢ per column inch for both copy and b&w photos. Captions are optional for photos.

Association, Club, and Fraternal

The following publications exist to publicize—to members, friends, and institutions—the ideals, objectives, projects, and activities of the sponsoring club or organization. Club-financed magazines that carry material not directly related to the group's activities (for example, Manage magazine in the Management and Supervision Trade Journals) are classified by their subject matter in the Consumer, Farm, and Trade Journals sections of this book.

THE AMERICAN LEGION MAGAZINE, 1345 Ave. of Americas, New York NY 10019. Monthly. Circulation: 2.6 million. Reports on most submissions promptly; borderline decisions take time. Buys first North American serial rights. Pays on

acceptance. Include phone number with ms. Enclose S.A.S.E. for ms return.
Nonfiction: Most articles written on order. Some over transom. Writers may query for subject interest, but no assignments to writers unknown to editors. Subjects include national and international affairs, American history, reader self-interest, great military campaigns and battles, major aspects of American life, etc. Length: average of 15 to 20 double-spaced typewritten pages. Pay varies widely with length and worth of work. Research assignments for some skilled reporters. Proven pros only.
Photos: Chiefly on assignment. Very rarely an over-transom photo story or photo clicks.
Poetry and Humor: Limited market for short, light verse, and short, humorous anecdotes, epigrams, jokes, etc. No serious verse. Taboos: old material; bad taste; amateurish work. Short humorous verse: $2.50 per line, minimum $10. Epigrams: $10. Anecdotes: $20.

AUTOMOTIVE BOOSTER OF CALIFORNIA, P.O. Box 765, LaCanada CA 91011. Editor: Don McAnally. For members of Automotive Booster clubs, automotive warehouse distributors and automotive parts jobbers in California. Established in 1967. Monthly. Circulation: 4,000. Not copyrighted. Pays on publication. Submit complete ms. Enclose S.A.S.E.
Nonfiction and Photos: Will look at short articles and pictures about successes of automotive parts outlets in California. Also can use personnel assignments for automotive parts people. Pays $1 per column inch (about 2¢ a word); $5 for b&w photos used with mss.

CIRCLE, 95 Wellesley St., E., Toronto, Ontario, Canada M4Y 1H6. Editor: Corinne Musgrave. For elementary school teachers across Canada. Publication of Canadian Red Cross Society. Newsletter; 6 to 8 pages. Established in 1973. 5 issues annually. Circulation: 14,500. Rights purchased vary with author and material. May buy first serial rights or second serial (reprint) rights. Buys 7 mss a year. Pays on acceptance. Will send free sample copy to writer on request. Write for copy of guidelines for writers. Will consider photocopied and simultaneous submissions. Reports in 1 week. Query first. Enclose S.A.E. and International Reply Coupons.
Nonfiction and Photos: Features must be educational; health, ethics, safety, relief aid methods that can be organized by children; ethnic, cultural information. They should not contain any specific American reference. Specify age of writer. Submissions from children are preferred. Writing should not be too simplistic in style. "Remember that we stress brotherhood of all people. We encourage friendships and concern for fellow people in our communities and throughout the world, regardless of age, religion or political bias." Length: 60 to 800 words. Pays $5 to $60. B&w glossies and color transparencies purchased with or without ms, or on assignment. Pays $5 to $40 for b&w; $10 to $50 for color.
Fiction, Poetry, Fillers: Educational and ethical fiction. Length and payment are the same as for nonfiction. Traditional forms of poetry, relevant verse, free verse, blank verse. Pays $5 minimum. Newsbreaks of issues concerning Red Cross, puzzles about cultural exchange, etc., clippings (Red Cross activities, volunteer agency efforts) used as fillers. Length: 10 to 60 words. Pays $5 to $45.

THE ELKS MAGAZINE, 425 W. Diversey Parkway, Chicago IL 60614. Phone: 312-528-4500. Editor: D.J. Herda. For Elks and their families: "middle-aged, rural Americans." Monthly. Circulation: about 1,500,000. Buys first serial rights. Buys approximately 50 mss a year from freelancers. Pays on acceptance. Returns rejected material within 3 weeks. Acknowledges acceptance of material in 1 month. Always query first. Will not consider photocopied submissions. Submit seasonal material about 4 months in advance. Will send free sample copy to a writer on request. Enclose S.A.S.E.
Nonfiction and Photos: "We purchase 12 lead articles a year, each running about 3,000 words, that vary widely in subject matter from business, money management, and stocks to logging (and in-depth profiles of other industries), CATV and ecology. The only prerequisites here are that the articles be timely, vigorous, and of greatest possible interest to our readers. They should be tightly written and authoritative

(sources usually requested). Writers should be willing to work with the editors whenever rewriting is required. Highest quality b&w photos are appreciated and included in the price of the package. Payment starts around $400 and rises. Back-of-book articles are interesting, informative, or lightly entertaining nonfiction pieces of up to 2,000 words on various subjects of interest to middle America; hunting, fishing, science, medicine, history, etc. Payment ranges from $100 to $300 for back-of-book articles."

Fiction: "Currently seeking high-quality fiction of widest possible appeal to our audience. The genre can be detective, drama, humor, even avant-garde, as long as the writer knows how to handle his craft." Pays $100 to $300.

FUTURE MAGAZINE, P.O. Box 7, Tulsa OK 74102. Publication of the United States Jaycees. Editor: LeRoy Norine. For 18- to 35-year-old young men. Well-educated, affluent, with wide interests. Magazine published every 2 months; 32 pages. Established in 1938. Circulation: 325,000. Buys all rights, but will reassign rights to author after publication. Payment on publication. Will send free sample copy to writer on request. Query first. Enclose S.A.S.E.

Nonfiction: "General editorial features that follow Jaycees programming. VD, crime and corrections, alcohol education, youth, environment, etc. Success stories (usually former or current Jaycees), articles concerning Jaycee chapter projects. Our features are written by assignment only."

INTERNATIONAL RESCUER, International Rescue & First Aid Assn., 5201 Madison Rd., Cincinnati OH 45227. Editor: Patricia Gardner. For members of the association whose main interest is in emergency care. Magazine; 20 to 24 (8½x11) pages. Established in 1956. Bimonthly. Circulation: 4,800. Not copyrighted. Buys about 12 mss a year. Pays on publication. Will send free sample copy to writer on request. Reports on material accepted for publication in 2 months. Returns rejected material in 1 month. Query first or submit complete ms. Enclose S.A.S.E.

Nonfiction and Photos: Feature articles concerning emergency medical care and transportation of the sick and injured. Pays $50 for articles up to 1,500 words; to $100 for feature stories of 2,500 words. Pays $5 for b&w photos; $20 for 4-color transparencies used on cover.

THE KEY MAGAZINE, 144 W. 12th Ave., Denver CO 80204. Publication of the Inter-Community Action Association. Editor: Lou Thomas. For the general public interested in news analysis as well as news reporting. Published 6 times a year. Circulation: 12,000. Buys all rights. Buys about 50 mss a year. Payment on publication. Will send sample copy to writer for 75¢. Mss must be double-spaced, with 55-character line. Reports in 3 to 4 weeks. Enclose S.A.S.E.

Nonfiction and Photos: "News summary materials of events or activities happening (or that have happened) that have national relevance though of local origin. Analysis must be included. Reports on government, culture(s), crime, law, economy, etc. All materials must provide more than one point of view. Seek freelance book, movie, and concert reviews." Buys interviews, profiles, spot news, historical and essay pieces, and photo features. Length: 2,000 to 4,000 words. Pays 1¢ to 3¢ a word. B&w glossies and color transparencies purchased with mss. Pays $5 to $20.

Fillers: Newsbreaks, letters to the editor. Analysis preferably included. Length: 500 to 1,500 words. Pays $5 minimum.

How To Break In: "New writers can best 'break into' our publication by providing fresh approaches to subjects not normally covered by the established news periodicals. Prefer the perspectives of cultural and ethnic groups not represented in the larger publications. Material is selected depending on how well the viewpoint (extremist or conformist) is clearly stated and the position taken is defended."

THE KIWANIS MAGAZINE, 101 E. Erie St., Chicago IL 60611. Executive Editor: David B. Williams. For business and professional men. Published 10 times a year. Buys first North American serial rights. Pays on acceptance. Will send free sample copy on request. Query first. Reports on submission in 2 weeks. Enclose S.A.S.E.

Nonfiction and Photos: Articles about social and civic betterment, business, education, religion, domestic affairs, etc. Emphasis on objectivity, intelligent analysis and thorough research of contemporary problems. Concise writing, absence of cliches, and impartial presentation of controversy required. Length: 1,500 words to 3,000 words. Pays to $300 to $600. "No fiction, personal essays, fillers, or verse of any kind. A light or humorous approach welcomed where subject is appropriate and all other requirements are observed. Detailed queries can save work and submission time. We sometimes accept photos submitted with mss, but we do not pay extra for them; they are considered part of the price of the ms. Our rate for a ms with good photos is higher than for one without."

How To Break In: "We have a new staff and we're trying to do new things. I'm dying to hear from pros with fresh ideas and the rare ability to say a lot in a few words."

THE LION, York and Cermak Roads, Oak Brook IL 60521. Senior Editor: Robert Kleinfelder. For North American members of Lions clubs who by their membership "demonstrate a deep interest in community improvement and service to the less fortunate through volunteer effort." Issued 11 times a year. Circulation: 640,000. Buys all rights. "Do not submit unsolicited articles. All articles are purchased after a query has been submitted and the writer has been instructed on the type of article wanted. A sloppy query will be rejected, no matter how good the story idea may be. We insist on quality." Free sample copy to writer on request. Reports on submissions in 10 days. Pays on acceptance. Submit detailed query. Enclose S.A.S.E.

Nonfiction: Articles in the fields of community betterment and self-improvement. Especially in the market for feature-length stories on unusual and impressive Lions club community service projects. "Except for such taboos as those against partisan politics and liquor in a favorable light, there's really no limitation on acceptable topics—as long as they have appeal and value for an international readership of service-minded men. Prefer solid, anecdotal writing which shows the evidence of thorough research. Lions are positivists, and stories for *The Lion* should reflect this, with emphasis on solutions to dilemmas rather than on the dilemmas themselves." Material must appeal to men of many creeds and political beliefs; must be of general, universal interest; most rejects are on subjects too local or provincial; no connection with a Lions club sponsored activity. Length: 750 to 2,000 words for articles. Always looking for humor articles. Length: up to 100 words. Pays 10¢ per word and up. Recently published articles include "The Misery and Mystery of MS" (describes Multiple Sclerosis and what can be done to help victims), and "The Adoptive Dilemma" (describes how the "right" babies are practically unavailable for adoption).

Photos: Purchased with accompanying mss, with no additional payment. Pays up to $300 for photo features suitable for spread layouts on impressive and unusual Lions Club community service projects (such as photo story on Lion-supported school for retarded children; Lion truck-caravan of furniture, etc., for needy American Indians). 5x7 b&w glossies. Captions required.

THE LOOKOUT, Seaman's Church Institute, 15 State St., New York NY 10004. Editor: Carlyle Windley. "Basic purpose is to engender and sustain interest in the work of the Institute and to encourage monetary gifts in support of its philanthropic work among seamen." Monthly, except combined February-March and July-August issues. Magazine; 20 pages, (6x9). Established in 1909. Buys first North American serial rights. Payment on publication. Will send sample copy to writer on request. Query first. Reports in 1 month. Enclose S.A.S.E.

Nonfiction: Emphasis is on the merchant marine; not Navy, pleasure yachting, power boats, commercial or pleasure fishing, passenger vessels. Buys freelance marine-oriented articles on the old and new, oddities, adventure, factual accounts, unexplained phenomena. Avoid first-person narrations. Length: 200 to 1,000 words. Pays $40 maximum, depending on quality, length, etc.

Photos: Buys vertical format b&w (no color) cover photo on sea-related subjects. Pays $20; lesser amounts for miscellaneous photos used elsewhere in the magazine.

Poetry: Buys small amount of short verse; seafaring-related but not about the sea per se and the cliches about spume, spray, sparkle, etc. Pays $5.

MAIN SHEET, Detroit Yacht Club, Belle Isle, Detroit MI 48207. Editor: Jack Weller-Grenard. Published by Detroit Publication Consultants for "members of the world's largest (membership) yacht club. Median age about 45, but members range from 18 to 81. Mostly college graduates and affluent, solid citizens." Established in 1914. Monthly. Circulation: 3,000. Not copyrighted. Buys 2 or 3 mss a year. Pays on publication. Will send a sample copy to a writer for $1. Submit complete ms. Will not consider photocopied submissions. Submit seasonal material 3 months in advance of issue date. Reports in 2 to 4 weeks. Enclose S.A.S.E. for return of submissions.

Nonfiction and Photos: "A few humorous shorts, a few yachting related articles, but most of the material is generated from within the membership. We discourage freelance submissions because we buy very few, but we will give attention to writers." Buys humor and photo features. Length: 500 to 1,500 words. Pays $15 to $50. Photos purchased with mss; captions required. For 5x5 to 8x10 b&w glossies, pays $5 to $15. For 8x10 color prints of 2¼x2¼ or larger transparencies, pays $25 up. "Photos should be yachting scenes."

NATIONAL 4-H NEWS, 150 N. Wacker Dr., Chicago IL 60606. Editor: Gordon F. Bieberle. For "young to middle-aged adults and older teens (mostly women) who lead 4-H clubs, most with high school, many with college education, whose primary reason for reading us is their interest in working with kids in informal youth education projects, ranging from aerospace to swimming, and almost anything in between." Monthly. Circulation: 100,000. Buys first serial rights. Buys about 48 mss a year. Pays on acceptance. Will send a sample copy to a writer on request. Write for copy of guidelines for writers. Query first. "We are very specialized, and unless a writer has been published in our magazine before, he more than likely doesn't have a clue to what we can use. When query comes about a specific topic, we often can suggest angles that make it usable." Submit seasonal material 6 months to 1 year in advance. Reports in 3 weeks. Enclose S.A.S.E.

Nonfiction: "Education and child psychology from authorities, written in light, easy-to-read fashion with specific suggestions how layman can apply them in volunteer work with youth; how-to-do-it pieces about genuinely new and interesting crafts of any kind; almost anything that tells about kids having fun and learning outside the classroom, including how they became interested, most effective programs, etc., always with enough detail and examples, so reader can repeat project or program with his or her group, merely by reading article. Speak directly to our reader (you) without preaching. Tell him in a conversational text how he might work better with kids to help them have fun and learn at the same time. Use lots of genuine examples (although names and dates not important) to illustrate points. Use contractions when applicable. Write in a concise, interesting way—our readers have other jobs and not a lot of time to spend with us. Will not print stories on 'How this 4-H club made good' or about state or county fair winners." Recently published articles include "Salt-Bead Room Dividers" (how-to photos and short text explaining how to make them), "Cross-Country Skiing" (by experienced sportswoman, tells how to do it, how to begin and equip for it, and relates personal experiences that build reader's enthusiasm for the activity), "Save Your Poinsettia" (short piece tells how to keep plant from year to year and even grow new ones), "Nobody Votes in My Town" (by a real prisoner who has lost the privilege and misses it), and "Preserve Fading History" (tells how to get into gravestone rubbing). Length: 1,700 to 3,400 words. Payment "up to $100, depending on quality and accompanying photos or illustrations."

Photos: "Photos must be genuinely candid, of excellent technical quality and preferably shot 'available light' or in that style; must show young people or adults and young people having fun learning something. Photos are usually purchased with accompanying ms, with no additional payment. Captions required. If we use an excellent single photo, we generally pay $25 and up."

PERSPECTIVE, Box 788, Wheaton IL 60187. Editor: Wilma Garrett. For women lay leaders in the Protestant Pioneer Girls weekday clubs, sponsored by evangelical denominations; mid-thirties; married with several school-age children. Magazine;

32 (8½x11) pages. Publishes special Christmas issue. Established in 1964. Quarterly. Circulation: 18,000. Rights purchased vary with author and material, but usually buys all rights, or first serial or simultaneous rights. Buys 12 to 20 mss a year. Usually pays on acceptance, with payment on publication for certain filler type items. Will send free sample copy to writer on request. Submit complete mss for all types of submissions. No photocopied or simultaneous submissions. Submit seasonal material 7 months in advance. Reports on material accepted for publication in 3 weeks. Reports on material within 2 weeks. Enclose S.A.S.E.

Nonfiction and Photos: Features articles to help leaders "increase skill and effectiveness in club leadership skills, such as craft ideas, Bible study articles, missionary education, and counseling and relationship skill ideas." Also seeking freelance material for Storehouse Column on crafts, activity suggestions, club management, missionary projects, service projects, and outdoor activities. "*Perspective* serves as an official organizational voice for Pioneer Girls, Inc., as well as a leadership tool for club leaders. All work submitted must reflect Scriptural orientation and evangelical viewpoint." Informational, how-to, inspirational, humor, "think" articles, and book reviews on relevant subjects. Length: 500 to 3,000 words for regular features; 200 to 500 words for Storehouse Column. Pays $5 to $40 for regular mss; $5 for Storehouse items.

Fiction and Poetry: Would like to see submissions of religious fictional pieces, and related poetry in traditional and light verse. Length: 500 to 2,000 words for fictional prose, no limit on poetry. Pays same as nonfiction.

Fillers: Also needs religious-text puzzles and short humor items for fillers. Pays $5 on acceptance.

How To Break In: "Submit articles directly related to club work, especially practical in nature, i.e., 'idea' articles for leader self-training in communication; Bible knowledge; teaching skills of all kinds. 'Theory' articles should also contain some practical suggestions for putting concepts, ideas into practice in club setting or in work with girls." Subjects needing coverage in the coming year are: 1) "Working with the exceptional child — rearing disabled, intellectually gifted, stutterer, epileptic, emotionally disturbed, etc. 2) How-to: tell story, use blackboard, help girls memorize, use overhead projector, etc. 3) How can the Christian women and girls in grades 2 to 12 take positive action in the face of specific world and national problems? 4) How can the church and the family work together to transmit Christian values to children?" Recently published articles by freelancers include, "It All Began With a Batch of Pickles . . .", which was inspirational, club-related, and had a missionary thrust; "Help Girls Witness", a topic that readers could relate to, with practical suggestions; and, "The Church & Today's Woman", inductive and woman-oriented. Specific voice to Pioneer Girls clubs, organizational voice as well as leadership tool.

PORTS O' CALL, P.O. Box 530, Santa Rosa CA 95402. Editor: William A. Breniman. Newsbook of the Society of Wireless Pioneers. Society members are mostly early-day wireless "brass-pounders" who sent code signals from ships or manned shore stations handling wireless or radio traffic. Twice yearly. Not copyrighted. Payment on acceptance. Query suggested. Editorial deadlines are May 15 and October 15. Reports on submissions at once. Enclose S.A.S.E.

Nonfiction: Articles about early-day wireless as used in ship-shore and high power operation. Early-day ships, records, etc. "Writers should remember that our members have gone to sea for years and would be critical of material that is not authentic. We are not interested in any aspect of ham radio. We are interested in authentic articles dealing with ships (since about 1910)." Oddities about the sea and weather as it affects shipping. Length: 500 to 2,000 words. Pays 1¢ per word.

Photos: Purchased with mss. Unusual shots of sea or ships. Wireless pioneers. Prefers b&w, "4x5 would be the most preferable size but it really doesn't make too much difference as long as the photos are sharp and the subject interests us." Fine if veloxed, but not necessary. Payment ranges from $2.50 to $10 "according to our appraisal of our interest." Ship photos of various nations, including postcard size, if clear, 25¢ to $1 each. Photo Editor: Dexter S. Bartlett.

Poetry: Ships, marine slant (not military), shipping, weather, wireless. No restrictions. Pays $1 or $2.50 each.

THE ROTARIAN, 1600 Ridge Ave., Evanston IL 60201. Phone: 312-328-0100. Editor: Willmon L. White. For Rotarian business and professional men and their families; for schools, libraries, hospitals, etc. Monthly. Circulation: 461,000. Usually buys all rights. Payment on acceptance. Will send free sample copy and editorial fact sheet to writer on request. Query preferred. Reports in 2 to 4 weeks. Enclose S.A.S.E. with queries and submissions.

Nonfiction: "The field for freelance articles is in the general interest category. These run the gamut from inspirational guidelines for daily living to such weighty concerns as world hunger, peace, and control of environment. Articles should appeal to an international audience and should in some way help Rotarians help other people. An article may increase a reader's understanding of world affairs, thereby making him a better world citizen. It may educate him in civic matters, thus helping him improve his town. It may help him to become a better employer, or a better human being. We carry debates and symposiums, but we are careful to show more than one point of view. We present arguments for effective politics and business ethics, but avoid expose and muckraking. Controversy is welcome if it gets our readers to think but does not offend ethnic or religious groups. In short, the rationale of the organization is one of hope and encouragement and belief in the power of individuals talking together." Length: 2,000 words maximum. Payment varies.

Photos: Purchased with mss or with captions only. Prefers 2¼ square or larger color transparencies, but will consider 35mm also. B&w singles and small assortments. Vertical shots preferred to horizontal. Scenes of international interest. Color cover.

Poetry and Fillers: "Presently overstocked." Pays $1 a line. Pays $10 for brief poems. "We occasionally buy short humor pieces."

How To Break In: "We prefer established writers, but a beginner who has a crisp style, is accurate, and can write with some authority on a subject of international interest has a chance of publication in *The Rotarian.*"

SCOUTING MAGAZINE, North Brunswick NJ 08902. Editor: Walter Babson. For "men and women who are leaders and committeemen supporting Cub Scout Packs, Scout Troops, and Explorer Posts." Bimonthly. Circulation: 1,500,000. Buys about 25 mss a year from freelancers. Pays on acceptance. Will send a free sample copy to a writer on request. Write for a copy of guidelines for writers. Query first with outline of proposed article. Submit seasonal material 6 months in advance. Reports in 2 weeks. Enclose S.A.S.E. for reply to queries.

Nonfiction: "*Scouting Magazine* is for adults. We need scouting success stories, American heritage articles, and information on children, including their educational interests, games, etc." Length: 500 to 1,000 words (some up to 2,000 on assignment). Pays $25 to $75 a magazine page (more for longer assigned stories) for how-to, profiles, inspirational, humor, historical, and photo articles. For the "Worth Retelling" column, we also need "information, humor, and human interest about Scouts and their leaders." Pay is $5 an item.

Photos: Purchased with ms or with captions only. Buys first rights. Photo Editor: Brian Payne.

THE SPIRIT, 601 Market St., St. Genevieve MO 63670. Newsletter of Lindbergh Association. Editor: Bob Hammack. For collectors of Charles A. Lindbergh memorabilia, conservationists, and aviators (many "pioneer"); admirers of Lindbergh with high school to post-graduate backgrounds; ages from 15 to 75. Magazine; 24 (8½x11) pages. Established in 1975. Every 2 months. Circulation: 500 to 1,000. Buys simultaneous rights. Buys all of its material from freelancers. "Writers are eligible for Reader Survey Awards for, 'Best Collector Interest Article', and/or, 'Best Historical Article,' " Pays on publication. Will send sample copy to writer for $1. Will consider photocopied and simultaneous submissions. Reports on material accepted for publication in 1 month. Returns rejected material within 2 weeks. Submit complete mss. Enclose S.A.S.E.

Nonfiction and Photos: This new publication is the first to concern itself with Lindbergh memorabilia, history, research, etc., and seeks anything connected with the "Lone Eagle". "We are especially interested in material dealing with his contributions to archaeology, and his scientific and medical research. If submitting collector material, give sources of supply; if historical, give addresses of museums, displays, individual authors, etc." For this initial year of publication collector-type material, such as medals, postcards, and books with annotated bibliographies, is desirable, as well as historical matter on scientific and conservational material. Also, personal experience, nostalgia, personal opinion, spot and photo news, and book reviews are needed. Length: 250 to 1,000 words. Pays $3 to $10 per ms. When photos are purchased with a ms, they should be the same as the nonfiction article, but photos *are* purchased without accompanying ms with captions required. Pays approximately $5. No color shots. Numismatic, philatelic, and bibliographic items are needed for regular columns; pays $5 per contribution. Length: 500 words.

Poetry: "Would like to see good narrative work regarding the 1927 Trans-Atlantic Flight." Will consider some traditional poetic forms, and blank and free verse. Payment varies.

Fillers: Will use newsbreaks and clippings. Length: 50 to 100 words. Pays $1 per item.

How To Break In: "Do something on Lindbergh's 'advisory role' in either commercial or military aviation. All submitted information must show detailed research."

STEERING WHEEL, P.O. Box 1669, Austin TX 78767. Phone: 512-478-2541. Editor: Kellyn R. Murray. Published by the Texas Motor Transportation Association for transportation management, high school libraries, state agencies, doctors, legislators, mayors, county judges, newspapers. Monthly magazine; 28 pages, (7x10). Established in 1936. Circulation: 7,200. Not copyrighted. Buys about 10 mss a year. Payment on publication. Will send free sample copy to writer on request. Write for copy of editorial guidelines for writers. Submit seasonal holiday material 3 months in advance. Will consider photocopied and simultaneous submissions. Query first. Reports immediately. Enclose S.A.S.E.

Nonfiction and Photos: "Material related to motor transportation in Texas, and other subjects as they relate; highway safety, energy, etc." Buys interviews, profiles, historical, travel, spot news, and coverage of successful business operations. Length: 1,000 to 2,500 words. Pays $15 to $50. Photos purchased with ms. Captions required.

THE TOASTMASTER, 2200 N. Grand Ave., P.O. Box 10400, Santa Ana CA 92711. Editor: Bruce L. Anderson. For toastmasters who recognize their need for self-improvement in communication, especially in oral presentations, and for developing their leadership potential. Many are professionals or are in middle or upper management. Magazine; 32 (8½x11) pages. Established in 1932. Monthly. Circulation: 60,000. Rights purchased vary with author and material. May buy all rights, or first serial rights, or second serial (reprint) rights. Buys 15 to 20 mss a year. Pays on publication. Will send free sample copy to writer on request. Write for copy of guidelines for writers. Will consider photocopied submissions. Reports in 2 weeks. Query first. Enclose S.A.S.E.

Nonfiction and Photos: "We want articles that tell our members how to improve their skills in communication and leadership. Articles on speaking, listening, thinking, leadership and management, meeting planning, etc. The information should be of direct application, with realistic experiences illustrating the principles presented. We prefer not to see theoretical material or over-generalized articles." Informational, how-to, personal experience, interviews. Length: 1,500 to 3,000 words. Pays up to $150. Buys b&w photos and 35mm color transparencies on assignment only. Pays $5 to $15 for b&w; up to $25 for color. Captions required.

V.F.W. MAGAZINE, Broadway at 34th St., Kansas City MO 64111. Phone: 816-561-3420. Editor: James K. Anderson. For members of the Veterans of Foreign Wars, men who served overseas. They range in age from the 20's to veterans of World War I and Spanish-American War veterans. Interests range from sports to national politics. Monthly magazine; 48 pages (8½x11). Established in 1913. Circulation: 1,800,000. Buys all rights. Buys 40 mss a year. Payment on acceptance. Will send sample copy to writer for 50¢. Write for copy of editorial guidelines for writers.

Seasonal material should be submitted 3 months in advance. Query first to "The Editor." Reports in 1 week. Enclose S.A.S.E.

Nonfiction and Photos: "Nonfiction articles on sports, personalities, historical pieces; combat stories in well-defined plot structures. Special emphasis within a subject, special outlook related to veterans. The *V.F.W.* is geared to the man who has served overseas, a distinction that other veterans' organizations do not make." Buys informational, how-to, personal experience, interview, profile, historical, think articles, and travel articles. Length: 1,000 to 1,500 words. Pays 5¢ to 10¢ per word. B&w and color photos purchased with accompanying ms. Captions required. Pays $5 each.

Astrology and Psychic Publications

The following publications regard astrology, psychic phenomena, ESP experiences, and related subjects as sciences or as objects of serious scientific research. Semireligious, occult, mysticism, and supernatural publications are classified in the Alternative category.

AMERICAN ASTROLOGY, 2505 N. Alvernon Way, Tucson AZ 85712. Editor: Joanne S. Clancy. For all ages, all walks of life; college background. Magazine; 116 (9x6) pages. Established in 1933. Monthly. Circulation: 265,000. Buys all rights. Buys 50 to 75 mss a year. Pays on publication. Write for copy of guidelines for writers. No photocopied or simultaneous submissions. Reports in 4 weeks. Submit complete ms. Enclose S.A.S.E.

Nonfiction: Astrological material, often combined with astronomy. More interested in presenting results of research material and data based on time of birth, instead of special Sun sign readings. Source of birth data must be included. Length: 3,500 words. "Payment is made according to the astrological knowledge and expertise of the writer."

ASTROLOGY GUIDE, Sterling's Magazines, Inc., 355 Lexington Ave., New York NY 10017. Phone: 212-391-1400, Ext. 33. Editor: Marsha Kaplan. For a special interest audience involved in astrology, parapsychology and the occult on all levels, from the merely curious to the serious student and practitioner. Monthly magazine; 96 (6½x9½) pages. Established in 1937. Circulation: 49,000. Buys all rights. Buys 120 mss a year. Payment on acceptance. Will send sample copy to writer if available; stock is sometimes low. Will not consider photocopied or simultaneous submissions. Submit seasonal (Christmas, vacation-time, etc.) and special (major astrological events) material 4 to 5 months in advance. Reports in 6 to 8 weeks minimum. Query first or submit complete ms. Enclose S.A.S.E.

Nonfiction: "Mostly astrological articles: Sun-sign, mundane, speculative or research. Slightly more technical for advanced readers, but prefer intelligent popular approach. Emphasis is on use of astrology and the related psychic and occult arts for self betterment in the reader's life. Very interested in buying articles on timely themes in these fields. We accept articles on the psychic and occult as well as astrology. We are more interested in featuring new ideas and new writers than in repeating what has been done in the past. We are attempting to develop a more personal, intimate approach." Would also like to see astrological "portraits" or interviews with current celebrities. Does not want to see articles based only on a knowledge of Sun signs. "They are superficial and boring. Even Sun-sign articles on the traditional themes (health, money, love) should refer (at least in preparation) to other aspects of the birth chart." Length: 2,000 to 3,500 words, but will accept shorter articles. Also uses book reviews and will consider new ideas for new departments. Pays 3¢ a word minimum.

Poetry and Fillers: Poetry is used very rarely but will consider any form that works. Must be related to their theme. Pays minimum of $5. Will consider ideas for puzzles. Short humor and material on astrological experiences and insights are used as fillers. Length: 750 words maximum. Pays 3¢ per word.

ASTROLOGY—YOUR DAILY HOROSCOPE, 600 Third Ave., New York NY 10016. Phone: 212-661-4200. Monthly. Buys all rights. Pays on acceptance. Enclose S.A.S.E.
Nonfiction: Articles on astrology, either popularized or moderately technical. Anxious to attract new writers and can promise a steady market plus a great deal of help from the editor. Knowledge of astrology is necessary. Length: 1,500 to 4,000 words. Pays 2¢ a word, or by arrangement.

BEYOND REALITY MAGAZINE, 303 W. 42nd St., New York NY 10036. Phone: 212-265-1676. Editor: Harry Belil. Primarily for university students interested in astronomy, archaeology, astrology, the occult (the whole range); UFO's, ESP, spiritualism, parapsychology, exploring the unknown. Magazine published every 2 months; 64 (8½x11) pages. Established in 1971. Circulation: 50,000. Buys all rights. Buys 30 to 35 mss a year. Payment on publication. Will send sample copy to writer for $1. Write for copy of guidelines for writers. Will consider photocopied submissions. Will not consider simultaneous submissions. Will consider cassette submissions. Reports in 1 month. Query first or submit complete ms. Enclose S.A.S.E.
Nonfiction and Photos: Interested in articles covering the range of their readers' interests, as well as any new discoveries in parapsychology. How-to, interview, inspirational, historical, think pieces, spot news. Length: 1,000 to 2,000 words. Pays 3¢ per word. No additional payment for b&w photos used with mss.
Fillers: Newsbreaks. Length: 500 words. Pays $10 minimum.
How To Break In: "Show me some pieces you've written and if I like your style, I'll provide you with the subjects to write on. Also looking for current ideas from the campuses, so student writers should give us a try." Lack of research documentation, or re-hashing old material will bring a rejection here.

E.S.P. SHARING DIMENSIONS NEWSPAPER, National Newspapers, Violet Hill AR 72548. Editor: Dr. G. H. Krastman. For any age, interested in E.S.P. Newspaper; 16 pages. Established in 1972. Quarterly. Circulation: 30,000. Buys all rights, but will reassign rights to author after publication. Buys 40 mss a year. Pays on acceptance. Will send free sample copy to writer on request. Will consider photocopied submissions. Reports on material accepted for publication in 30 days. Returns rejected material in 7 days. Submit complete ms. Enclose S.A.S.E.
Nonfiction and Photos: Articles on E.S.P., psychic experiences, psychic's biography. Mail order and moneymaking and moneysaving articles. (Success stories about mail order operator; how-to stories about saving money, by running a business; or how to start a certain business and make a second income. How to do things in business or around the home that save money.) Length: 100 to 2,000 words. Pays 3¢ a word, but 5¢ a word is paid for mss accepted with b&w photos.
Fillers: Newsbreaks, clippings. Pays 3¢ a word, but increases to 5¢ a word when fillers are accepted with photos.

FATE, Clark Publishing Co., 500 Hyacinth Place, Highland Park IL 60035. Editor: Mary Margaret Fuller. Monthly. Buys all rights; occasionally North American serial rights only. Pays on publication. Query first. Reports on submissions in 4 to 8 weeks. Enclose S.A.S.E.
Nonfiction and Fillers: Personal psychic experiences, 300 to 500 words. Pays $10. New frontiers of science, and ancient civilizations, 2,000 to 3,000 words; also parapsychology, occultism, witchcraft, magic, spiritual healing miracles, flying saucers, etc. Must include complete authenticating details. Prefers interesting accounts of single events rather than roundups. Pays minimum of 3¢ per word. Fillers should be fully authenticated. Length: 100 to 300 words.
Photos: Buys good glossy photos with mss or with captions only. Pays $5 to $10.
How To Break In: "We very frequently accept manuscripts from new writers; the majority are individuals' first-person accounts of their own psychic experiences."

HOROSCOPE, 1 Dag Hammarskjold Plaza, 245 E. 47th St., New York NY 10017. Editor: Julia A. Wagner. Monthly magazine; 130 (9½x6½) pages. Established in 1939. Circulation: 300,000. Buys all rights. Buys 75 mss a year. Payment on acceptance.

Will send sample copy to writer for 60¢. Write for copy of guidelines for writers. Will not consider photocopied submissions. Will consider simultaneous submissions. All submissions must be accompanied by a carbon copy. Submit material dealing with major astrological sign changes at least 6 months in advance. Reports in 2 months. Query first or submit complete ms. Enclose S.A.S.E.

Nonfiction: Articles on astrology only. "Love, family, money, employment, and health are our most popular subjects. Must appeal to general readers with some knowledge of astrology. Articles dealing with prevailing conditions are always considered. We will not accept any articles relating to witchcraft." Informational, how-to, profile, inspirational. Recently published articles include "Coping With Emotional Depression," "Earthquake Outlook Through 1977," "Star Guide to Home Decorating," "Astro-Sketch: Lenny Bruce," and "Is Violence in Your Stars?" Length: 3,000 to 4,000 words. Pays 5¢ a word.

Fillers: On astrology only. Length: 25 to 150 words. Submissions must consist of a minimum of 10 fillers. Pays 5¢ a word.

HOROSCOPE GUIDE, 350 Madison Ave., Cresskill NJ 07626. Editor: Jim Hendryx. Monthly. Buys all rights. Pays on acceptance. Will consider photocopied submissions. Reports in about a month. Submit complete ms. Enclose S.A.S.E.

Nonfiction: Anything of good interest to the average astrology buff, preferably not so technical as to require more than basic knowledge of birth sign by reader. Lengths: 1,000 to 5,000 words. Pays 1½¢ per word.

Poetry: 4 to 16 lines on astrology. Pays 50¢ a line.

MOON SIGN BOOK, P.O. Box 3383, St. Paul MN 55165. Editor: Carl Weschcke. For "persons from all walks of life with interests in the occult." Established in 1906. Annual. Circulation: 100,000. Rights purchased vary with author and material. Pays on publication. Query first or submit complete ms. Reports in 8 weeks. Enclose S.A.S.E.

Nonfiction and Photos: "Astrology is the primary subject, but we can use material in any field of the occult, and living in intelligent cooperation with nature. We are a yearly publication dealing with farming, gardening, yearly forecasts for all types of activities, with informative articles on astrology. We try to be educational as well as practical." Length: 3,000 to 10,000 words. Pays 3¢ to 5¢ a word. Photos on assignment.

How To Break In: "The *Moon Sign Book* is a farming and gardening almanac emphasizing astronomical effects on planting, growing, harvesting and using crops to maximum advantage. Since 80% of the book is taken up with tables, we have room for only a few outside articles. Those articles should have something to do with either astrology or gardening (we are also interested in herbs, herbal remedies). Since most freelancers are not astrologers I would suggest that they concentrate on the many aspects of organic gardening or possibly how-to-do features that relate in some way to farming and gardening. Short articles on the occult phenomena (enhancing growth psychically), are also good possibilities for the beginning writer. We are continually looking for astrologers capable of writing 'Sun Sign' predictions for *Moon Sign Book*. Also astrological predictions for weather, stock and commodity markets, news and political developments, etc. We generally stick with one, but we find that quality depends on a variety, and would like to find a few more writers to back us up."

OCCULT, CBS Publications, Popular Magazine Group, a Division of Columbia Broadcasting System, Inc., 600 Third Ave., New York NY 10016. Phone: 212-661-4200. Editor: Anne Keffer. General field of psychic phenomena. Quarterly. Buys all rights. Pays on acceptance. Do not send for sample copy. Query first. Reports in 3 weeks. Enclose S.A.S.E.

Nonfiction: "Occult: ghosts, witchcraft, hauntings, magic, spiritualism, ESP, mediums, astral projection, etc. No fiction. Subject matter is based on documented evidence or substantiated by scientific research." Length: 2,500 to 5,000 words. Payment is $75 to $150.

OCCULT AMERICANA, Box 667, Painesville OH 44077. Editor: Barbara Mraz. For occult history buffs. 18-page mini-mag published every 2 months. Established in 1970. Circulation: 325. Not copyrighted. Occasionally overstocked. Payment on acceptance. Will send free sample copy to writer on request. Will consider photocopied and simultaneous submissions. Reports on material accepted for publication in 2 weeks. Returns rejected material immediately. Query first. Enclose S.A.S.E.

Nonfiction and Photos: Interviews of occult personalities, reports on contemporary occult scenes; historical articles related to American religious history. "We tend to critique the occult scene." Length: 300 to 500 words. Pays $5 to $10. B&w photos are used with mss. No additional payment. Captions required.

POPULAR ASTROLOGY (formerly *Everywoman's Daily Horoscope*), 600 Third Ave., New York NY 10016. Monthly. Buys all rights. Pays on acceptance. Enclose S.A.S.E. for ms return.

Nonfiction: Articles on astrology, either popularized or moderately technical. "We are anxious to attract new writers and can promise a steady market plus a great deal of help from the editor. Knowledge of astrology is necessary." Length: 1,500 to 3,500 words. Pays 2¢ per word, or by arrangement.

PROBE THE UNKNOWN, 5455 Wilshire Blvd., Los Angeles CA 90036. Editor: Henry C. Holcomb. For an audience interested in psychic and paranormal phenomena. Bimonthly magazine; 68 (8½x11) pages. Established in 1971. Circulation: 85,000. Buys all rights. Buys "many" mss a year. Payment on acceptance. Will send free sample copy to writer on request. Will consider photocopied submissions. Reports within 2 weeks. Query first. Enclose S.A.S.E.

Nonfiction and Photos: Articles on psychic phenomena and related fields (UFO's, psychokinesis, clairvoyance, precognition). "We neither accept or deny the presence of psychic phenomena. We merely try to relate the findings of well-qualified personalities in various psychic fields and let our readers determine the worth of these personalities' studies. We approach all subjects from an objective, scientific (whenever possible) viewpoint." Length: 3,000 to 4,000 words. Pays 5¢ to 10¢ a word. Recently published articles include "Life on Mars." Psychic News and Enigmas department uses spot news with photos. Length: 500 to 1,000 words. Pays $5 to $7 for 5x7 or 8x10 b&w glossy photos used with mss or department features.

PSYCHIC, 680 Beach St., Suite 408, San Francisco CA 94109. Editor: James Grayson Bolen; Articles Editor: Alan Vaughan. For general public interested in straightforward, entertaining material on psychic phenomena. Bimonthly. Buys all rights. Payment on acceptance. Query first is mandatory. Reports in 4 to 6 weeks. Enclose S.A.S.E.

Nonfiction and Photos: Documented articles and objective reports on ESP, psychic phenomena and nonoccult, related areas, as well as scientific research and data. See copy of magazine for style. Informative reporting, balance of comments on material, documentation, short bibliography for reader reference, opinion of authorities (both pro and con)—no editorializing. Length: 2,500 to 3,500 words. Pays up to $350. Photos purchased only with mss. Can be b&w glossy prints or any size transparency. Photo Editor: John Larsen.

YOUR PERSONAL ASTROLOGY, Sterling's Magazines, Inc., 355 Lexington Ave., New York NY 10017. Phone: 212-391-1400, Ext. 33. Editor: Marsha Kaplan. For a special interest audience involved in astrology, parapsychology and the occult on all levels, from the merely curious to the serious student and practitioner. Quarterly magazine; 130 (6½x9½) pages. Established in 1940. Circulation: 56,860. Buys 60 mss a year. Payment on acceptance. Will send sample copy to writer if available; stock is sometimes low. Will not consider photocopied or simultaneous submissions. Submit seasonal (Christmas, vacation-time, etc.) and special (major astrological events) material 4 to 5 months in advance. Reports in 6 to 8 weeks minimum. Query first or submit complete ms. Enclose S.A.S.E.

Nonfiction: "Mostly astrological articles: Sun-sign, mundane, speculative or research. Slightly more technical for advanced readers, but prefer intelligent popular approach.

Emphasis is on use of astrology and the related psychic and occult arts for self betterment in the reader's life. Very interested in buying articles on timely themes in these fields. We accept articles on the psychic and occult as well as astrology. We are more interested in featuring new ideas and new writers than in repeating what has been done in the past. We are attempting to develop a more personal, intimate approach." Would also like to see astrological "portraits" or interviews with current celebrities. Does not want to see articles based only on a knowledge of Sun signs. "They are superficial and boring. Even Sun-sign articles on the traditional themes (health, money, love) should refer (at least in preparation) to other aspects of the birth chart." Length: 2,000 to 3,500 words, but will accept shorter articles. Also uses book reviews and will consider new ideas for new departments. Pays 3¢ a word minimum.

Poetry and Fillers: Poetry is used very rarely but will consider any form that works. Must be related to their theme. Pays minimum of $5. Will consider ideas for puzzles. Short humor and material on astrological experiences and insights are used as fillers. Length: 750 words maximum. Pays 3¢ per word.

Automotive and Motorcycle

Publications listed in this section are concerned with the maintenance, operation, performance, racing, and judging of automobiles and motorcycles. Publications that treat vehicles as a means of transportation or shelter instead of as a hobby or sport are classified in the Travel, Camping, and Trailer category. Journals for teamsters, service station operators, and auto dealers will be found in the Auto and Truck classification of the Trade Journals section.

AMA NEWS, Publication of the American Motorcycle Association, Box 141, Westerville OH 43081. Editor: John Yaw. For members of the American Motorcycle Association. Monthly. Rights purchased vary with author and material. Payment on publication. No query required, but all material is accepted on speculation only. Enclose S.A.S.E.

Nonfiction and Photos: As the official publication of the largest motor sports sanctioning body in the world, the editorial scope of *AMA News* is extremely broad, including coverage of professional and amateur motorcycle competition, touring, significant legislation, profiles and interviews with prominent motorcycling personalities and a variety of special features. Road tests and highly technical articles are not published, but how-to pieces will be considered. Material must be exclusive and consistent with programs and policies of the American Motorcycle Association. Material of any length will be considered with longer pieces serialized. Accompanying illustrative material strongly encouraged, especially b&w glossies and color transparencies. Base rates are 2¢ a word; $7.50 per photo and $25 per cover. Higher rates paid where quality merits.

AUTOWEEK AND COMPETITION PRESS, P.O. Box A, Reno NV 89506. Editorial board: Cory Farley, Glenn Howell, Jim MacQueen. Weekly newspaper; 40 pages, (13½x10). Established in 1958. Circulation: 100,000. Rights purchased vary with author and material. May buy one-time or all rights but will reassign rights to author after publication; or first North American serial rights, or simultaneous rights. Buys 110 freelance mss per year. Payment on publication. Will consider photocopied submissions. Reports on material accepted for publication within 1 month. Returns rejected material in 2 to 3 months. Will send sample copy to writer for 50¢. Query first or submit complete ms. Enclose S.A.S.E.

Nonfiction and Photos: "*Autoweek* is the weekly newspaper/magazine of auto racing. Readers share a common interest in every facet of the automobile. Most have a sense of humor, but it ends when newspapers refer to motor sports fans as blood-crazed. Eighty percent of *Autoweek's* editorial content is comprised of race reports, and there is practically no way we will accept one from someone new.

However, we are interested in profiles of people involved with cars, in pieces on old cars, and the atmospherics of the sport. We also need reviews of books about cars. Everything must be related to cars and the people working with them. We are a newspaper, but our writing requirements are for pieces with a magazine style such as *Sports Illustrated*. We would be very interested in stories about people involved with racing, about the social significance of the automobile. We will *not* accept any viewpoint which might be interpreted as negative about either cars or racing. For instance, we will not accept the point of view that racing contributes to the fuel shortage." Uses informational articles, interviews, profiles, humor, historical and think articles; nostalgia, book and film reviews, spot news, new product and technical articles. Length: 500 to 2,500 words, but the maximum length is rarely used. Pays $1.20 per published inch. Photos are purchased with accompanying manuscript with extra payment; without accompanying ms or on assignment. Captions required. Pays $5 per b&w; $10 for b&w used on cover. Color transparencies no smaller than 35mm. Pays $10; $20 for color used on cover. All photos must relate to magazine's theme; racing action considered, though most is done on assignment.
Fiction: Experimental and humorous. Length and payment are the same as for nonfiction.
Fillers: Newsbreaks. Pays $5 to $10.

CAR AND DRIVER, One Park Ave., New York NY 10016. Phone: 212-725-3763. Editor: Stephan Wilkinson. For auto enthusiasts; college educated, professional, median 26 to 28 years of age. Monthly magazine; 124 pages. Established in 1957. Circulation: 725,000. Rights purchased vary with author and material. Buys all rights, first North American serial rights, and second serial (reprint) rights. Buys 4 to 6 mss per year. Payment on acceptance. Submit seasonal material 3 months in advance. Query and include samples of previous work. Reports in 2 months. Enclose S.A.S.E.
Nonfiction and Photos: Nonanecdotal articles about the more sophisticated treatment of autos and motor racing. Exciting, interesting cars. Personalities, past and present in the automotive industry and automotive sports. Treat readers as intellectual equals. Emphasis on people rather than hardware. Informational, how-to, humor, historical, think articles, and nostalgia. Length: 2,000 words. Pays $200 minimum. B&w photos purchased with accompanying mss with no additional payment. Captions required.
How To Break In: "We're looking for outside reviewers for our new book review department, but here as with other pieces, it is best to start off with an interesting query and to stay away from nuts-and-bolts stuff since that will be handled in-house or by an acknowledged expert. Probably the very best way for a new writer to break in with us is with a personal, reasonably hip approach which shows a real intimacy with what we are trying to do. A while back, for instance, we ran a freelance piece on automobiles in Russia, which was the product of an interesting query. We are not like other automotive magazines inasmuch as we try to publish material which could just as well appear in the general magazines. We're not interested in unusual cars. To us the Ford Mustang is infinitely more important than a 1932 Ruxton wicker-seat five-passenger touring car. Good writing and unique angles are the key."

CAR CRAFT, 8490 Sunset Blvd., Los Angeles CA 90069. Phone: 213-657-5100. Editor: John Dianna. For men and women, 18 to 34, automotive oriented. Monthly magazine; 124 pages, 8x11. Established in 1953. Circulation: 300,000. Buys all rights. Buys 6 mss per year. Payment on acceptance. Will not consider photocopied or simultaneous submissions. Reports in 10 days. Query first. Enclose S.A.S.E.
Nonfiction and Photos: Drag racing articles, technical car features, how-to articles, and general car features. Interview, profile, and photo features. Length: open. Pays $100 to $125 per page. Photos are purchased with or without accompanying ms. Captions optional. 8x10 b&w glossy; 2¼ color transparencies. Pays $12.50 for b&w photos; $100 minimum (one page) color. Photo Department Editor: Albert Esparza.

THE CLASSIC CAR, 4581 Boeing, Yorba Linda CA 92686. Editor: William S. Snyder. For the classic car enthusiast, highly specialized in his interest. Uses writing with a "good nonfiction prose style. More interested in clear, factual writing than a lot of 'flash.' " The publication has a "finer focus than general automotive magazines. The reader is extremely knowledgeable to begin with. Accuracy is of utmost importance." Quarterly. Circulation: 5,000. Buys first rights. Buys 4 to 8 mss a year from freelancers. Pays on publication. Query first. Reports in a week to 10 days. Enclose S.A.S.E.

Nonfiction and Photos: Wants "historical articles on various makes and models of classic cars (high quality cars of 1925-1942 vintage), photo articles on classics, restoration how-to articles, interviews, and profiles." Length: 500 to 5,000 words. Pays $25 to $100. 8x10 b&w glossy photos, 4x5 color transparencies. Preferred with captions only. Pays $1 to $5 for b&w; $5 to $25 for color.

CYCLE GUIDE MAGAZINE, 1440 W. Walnut St., Compton CA 90220. Editor: Paul Dean. For motorcycle enthusiasts. Magazine; 96 pages. Established in 1967. Monthly. Circulation: 126,451. Buys all rights. Buys 15 to 20 mss a year. Pays on publication. Will send free sample copy to writer on request. Write for copy of guidelines for writers. No photocopied or simultaneous submissions. Reports in 2 to 4 weeks. Query first or submit complete ms. Enclose S.A.S.E.

Nonfiction and Photos: Material related to motorcycling; technical articles, how-to, personality profiles or interviews in the industry; some touring. Length: open. Pays $50 per published page. Prefers 8x10 b&w glossies, but 5x7 are acceptable. Pays $50 per published page. Pays $75 per published page for color transparencies in any format.

CYCLE NEWS GROUP: CYCLE NEWS EAST, CYCLE NEWS WEST, CYCLE NEWS CENTRAL, Box 498, Long Beach CA 90801. Editor: Charles Clayton. For average motorcycle recreationists. Weekly newspaper. Special issues cover endurance and trail riding, women's angle, motocross, cafe racing, winter riding, etc. Established in 1963. Circulation: 100,000. Buys all rights, but will reassign rights to author after publication. Buys hundreds of mss per year. Payment on publication. Will send sample copy to writer for 50¢. Write for copy of guidelines for writers. Will not consider photocopied or simultaneous submissions. Submit seasonal material 3 months in advance "ideally, but anytime prior is okay." Reports in 1 month. Submit only complete ms. Enclose S.A.S.E.

Nonfiction and Photos: Race reports, history, life style, personality features, interviews, how-to (nuts and bolts), personal experiences with a point. Good writing and photos a must. Interested in people, events, and things. Recently published articles include "Sanity Returns on an Iron Horse," "Motocross Round Table," "How to Win Motocross," "Where to Trail Ride." Length: 1,500 words maximum. Pays 50¢ per column inch, approximately 1¢ per word. B&w and color photos purchased. Pays $2 per column inch for b&w; color payment varies. 2¼ minimum transparencies.

How To Break In: "Observe and report in modern, personal journalism style. Check facts, weed out fluff. Type and double-space with wide margins. Include photos if possible."

CYCLE WORLD, 1499 Monrovia Ave., Newport Beach CA 92663. Editor: Robert Atkinson. For active motorcyclists, "young, affluent, educated, very perceptive." Subject matter includes "road tests (staff-written), features on special bikes, customs, racers, racing events; technical and how-to features involving mechanical modifications." Monthly. Circulation: 197,000. Buys all rights, but will reassign rights to author after publication. Buys 200 to 300 mss a year from freelancers. Payment on publication. Will send sample copy to a writer for 75¢. Write for copy of guidelines for writers. Query first. Submit seasonal material 2½ months in advance. Reports in 4 to 6 weeks. Enclose S.A.S.E.

Nonfiction: Buys informative, well-researched travel stories; technical, theory, and how-to articles; interviews, profiles, humor, spot news, historical pieces, think pieces, new product articles and satire. Taboos include articles about "wives learning to ride; 'my first motorcycle.' " Length: 800 to 5,000 words. Pays $75 to $100 per published page. Columns include Competition, which contains short, local racing stories with photos. Column length: 300 to 400 words. Pays $75 to $100 per published page.

Photos: Purchased with or without ms, or on assignment. Captions optional. Pays $50 for 1 page; $25 to $35 for ½ page. 8x10 b&w glossies, 35mm color transparencies. **Fiction:** Needs mystery, science fiction, and humorous stories. Does not want to see racing fiction or "rhapsodic poetry." Length: 1,500 to 3,000 words. Pays $75 minimum per published page.

DIRT BIKE MAGAZINE, P.O. Box 317, Encino CA 91436. Editor: Chet Heyberger. For young dirt bike riders. Magazine; 100 (8x10) pages. Established in 1971. Monthly. Circulation: 175,000. Buys all rights. Buys about 24 mss a year. Will consider photocopied submissions. No simultaneous submissions. Submit special material 3 months in advance. Reports in about 10 days. Query first. Enclose S.A.S.E.
Nonfiction and Photos: Competition reports outside of southern California of national interest. Light, humorous style, but accurate facts. Informational, how-to, expose, spot news, technical. Length: 1,000 to 8,000 words. Pays 3¢ to 5¢ a word. Hole Shot column uses opinions of general interest. Length: 1,200 to 1,500 words. Payment is the same as for articles. Photos are used in special Crash & Burn issues. Also purchased with or without ms, or on assignment. Pays $5 to $7 for 8x10 b&w glossies. Pays $25 to $50 for 35mm (or larger) transparencies.

DIRT CYCLE, 257 Park Ave., S., New York NY 10010. Editor: Robert Schleicher. For those whose "prime interest is in motorcycle trail riding and off-road racing." Established in 1970. Bimonthly. Circulation: 95,000. Buys all rights. Buys 50 mss a year. Payment on publication. Will send free sample copy to writer on request. Will not consider photocopied submissions. Submit seasonal material 3 months in advance. Reports on submissions in 2 to 4 weeks. Query first. Enclose S.A.S.E.
Nonfiction and Photos: "Road tests. Motorcycle preparation, tuning and hop up. Off-road competition reports. Dirt-riding motorcycle custom-builts. How to ride off-road. Must be experienced riders able to converse in style riders and racers can understand. Friendly, rather than authoritative text, but completely factual. All articles must be photo-illustrated with both color and b&w." Length: 1,000 to 4,000 words. Pays $100 to $225. Pays $7 for 8x10 b&w glossy prints; $25 to $75 per magazine page for 2¼ or larger color transparencies.

DRAG RACING USA, 1420 Prince St., Alexandria VA 22314. Editor: Neil Britt. For drag racing fans, professional racers, manufacturers of speed equipment and car enthusiasts, in general. Magazine; 70 pages. Established in 1963. Monthly. Circulation: 75,000. Buys all rights, but will reassign rights to author after publication. Buys 72 to 96 mss a year. Pays on publication. Will send free sample copy to writer on request. No photocopied or simultaneous submissions. Reports on material accepted for publication in 30 days. Returns rejected material in 60 days. Query first or submit complete ms with photos, charts and artwork. Enclose S.A.S.E.
Nonfiction and Photos: "We are very much interested in personality profiles of racers, both professional and nonprofessional. Auto-related and some technical features are also considered. We tend to stress personality to a much greater extent than most of our competitors. We also stay away from the highly technical articles, cycle articles and van articles. We concentrate on racing and the people. Emphasis may be on an event, a change, a pattern; any related racing topic. There is always room for humorous pieces connected with the sport, and we encourage nostalgic articles, as well as articles on safety, car building, motor building, and technological advances. Informational, how-to, personal experience, interview, profile, humor, historical and personal opinion stories are always welcome. Recently published "On a Clear Day", story of an unknown racer who won the biggest race of the year. Length: 600 to 2,500 words. Pays $75 to $200. Pays $10 for 8x10 b&w glossies purchased without mss or on assignment; $75 to $150 for large format color transparencies of 35mm Kodachrome or 2½ Ektachrome.
Fiction and Fillers: Experimental, adventure, humorous and historical fiction. Length: 400 to 2,500 words. Pays $75 to $150. Newsbreaks, jokes, short humor used as fillers. Pays minimum of $15.

DUNE BUGGIES AND HOT VWS MAGAZINE, P.O. Box 2260, 2930-C Grace Ln., Costa Mesa CA 92626. Editor: Jim Wright. For Volkswagen and dune buggy enthusiasts (18 to 65); college educated, employed, mechanically inclined, sports-minded; almost exclusively male. Magazine; 84 (8½x11-1/8) pages. Established in 1967. Monthly. Circulation: 53,132. Buys first North American serial rights. Buys 100 mss a year. Pays on publication. Will send sample copy to writer for 50¢. No photocopied or simultaneous submissions. Reports in 2 weeks. Submit complete ms. Enclose S.A.S.E.

Nonfiction and Photos: How-to mechanical articles on VWs; new buggy reports, technical mechanical articles; racing events involving dune buggies and/or Volkswagens. Must be informative, well-researched and accurate. Does not use fiction or poems, or anything not relating to VWs and/or dune buggies. Length: 800 to 1,500 words. Pays $45 per published page. Buggin' Around column buys club news items and pays 50¢ per published inch. No additional payment for 8x10 b&w glossies used with mss. Pays $10 for those submitted without ms. Captions required.

EASYRIDERS MAGAZINE, Box 52, Malibu CA 90265. Editor: Lou Kimzey. For "adult men—men who own, or desire to own, expensive custom motorcycles. The individualist—a rugged guy who enjoys riding a chopper and all the good times derived from it." Bimonthly. Circulation: 125,000. Buys first rights. Buys 12 to 20 mss a year. Payment on acceptance. Will send a sample copy to a writer for 25¢. Reports in 2 to 3 weeks. Enclose S.A.S.E. for return of submissions.

Nonfiction, Poetry, and Fillers: "Masculine, candid material of interest to young men. Must be bike-oriented, but can be anything of interest to a rugged young man. It is suggested that everyone read a copy before submitting—it's not *Boy's Life*. Light, easy, conversational writing style wanted, like guys would speak to each other without women being around. Gut level, friendly, man-to-man. Should be bike-oriented or of interest to a guy who rides a bike. *Easyriders* is entirely different from all other motorcycle or chopper magazines in that it stresses the good times surrounding the owning of a motorcycle—it's aimed at the rider and is nontechnical, while the others are nuts and bolts. Not interested in technical motorcycle articles. We carry no articles that preach to the reader, or attempt to tell them what they should or shouldn't do." Buys personal experience, interviews, humor, expose (motorcycle-oriented) articles. Length: 1,000 to 3,000 words. Payment is 5¢ to 10¢ a word, depending on length and use in magazine. "It's the subject matter and how well it's done—not length, that determines amount paid." Traditional, contemporary, avant-garde poetry, light verse. Length: open. Payment is minimum $15. Deptartment Editor: Louis Bosque. Risque joke fillers, short humor. Length: open. Payment: open.

Photos: B&w glossies, 35mm color, 2¼x2¼ color transparencies purchased with mss. "We are only interested in *exclusive* photos of exclusive bikes that have never been published in, or photographed by, a national motorcycle or chopper publication. Bikes should be approved by editorial board before going to expense of shooting. Submit sample photos—Polaroids will do. Send enough samples for editorial board to get good idea of the bike's quality, originality, workmanship, interesting features, coloring." Photo Editor: Pete Chiodo. Payment is $50 to $150 for cover, $75 to $150 for centerspread, $10 for b&w and $35 for color for "In the Wind," $25 up for arty, unusual shots, and $100 to $225 for a complete feature.

Fiction: "Gut level language okay. Any sex scenes, not to be too graphic in detail. Dope may be implied, but not graphically detailed. Must be bike-oriented, but doesn't have to dwell on that fact. Only interested in hard hitting, rugged fiction." Length: 5,000 to 10,000 words. Payment is 5¢ to 10¢ a word, depending on quality, length and use in magazine.

THE ECONOMICAL DRIVER, Box 326, Northport NY 11768. Editor: Mel Shapiro. For car owners who are interested in getting more for their driving dollars. Magazine; 84 (8½x11) pages. Established in 1974. Every 2 months. Circulation: 250,000. Buys all rights. Buys 60 mss per year. Payment on publication. Will send sample copy to writer for 50 cents. Will consider photocopied submissions. No simultaneous submissions. Submit special material 4 to 5 months in advance. Reports on material accepted for publication in 3 weeks. Returns rejected material in 4 weeks. Query first. Enclose S.A.S.E.

Nonfiction and Photos: Articles on anything to do with auto economy. Safety and better driving tips. New products. Maintenance. Informational, how-to, personal experience, interview, profile, humor, travel, spot news. Length: 500 to 3,000 words. Pays $50 to $150. The What's New and Gas Saving Tips departments use material on subjects listed. Length: 700 words. Pays $50 to $60. No additional payment is made for photos submitted with ms.

Fillers: Newsbreaks, clippings, short humor on themes pertinent to economical driving. Length: 50 to 200 words. Pays $5 to $25.

FOUR WHEELER, 6226 Vineland Ave., P.O. Box 978, North Hollywood CA 91603. Editor: Bill Sanders. For 4WD enthusiasts who enjoy reading about races, technical pieces and the newest in 4-wheel-drive equipment and accessories. Most are mechanical/tinkering types and/or racers themselves. Magazine; 90 (11½x8¼) pages. Established in 1956. Monthly. Circulation: 100,000. Buys all rights, but will reassign rights to author after publication. Buys 60 mss a year. Pays on publication. Will send free sample copy to writer on request. No photocopied or simultaneous submissions. Reports in 1 to 2 months. Query first or submit complete ms. Enclose S.A.S.E.

Nonfiction and Photos: Technical pieces. 4-wheel-drive travel articles. Must always emphasize the 4WD angle of the story. Informational, how-to, personal experience. Length: 750 to 1,500 words. Pays $50 to $175. No additional payment for 8x10 b&w glossies purchased with mss. Captions required.

How To Break In: "With good, concise, clean copy that grabs the reader's attention."

MOTOR TREND, 8490 Sunset Blvd., Los Angeles CA 90069. Phone: 213-657-5100. Managing Editor: Tim Taggart. For automotive enthusiasts, backyard mechanics and general interest consumers. Monthly. Circulation: 650,000. Buys all rights, except by negotiation. Tough nut to crack. "Fact-filled query suggested for all freelancers." Reports in 30 days. Enclose S.A.S.E.

Nonfiction: Automotive and related subjects that have national appeal. Emphasis on money-saving ideas for the motorist, high-performance and economy modifications, news tips on new products, pickups, RVs, long-term automotive projects. Packed with facts. Pays $100 per printed page in magazine, or as negotiated.

Photos: Buys photos, particularly of prototype cars in Detroit area. Other automotive matter. 8x10 b&w glossies or transparencies. Pays $25 minimum.

Fillers: Automotive newsbreaks. Any length. Payment open.

MOTORCYCLIST, 8490 Sunset Blvd., Los Angeles CA 90069. Executive Editor: Bob Greene. For male motorcycle enthusiasts. Monthly magazine; 88 pages, (8½x11). Established in 1912. Circulation: 150,000. Rights purchased vary with author and material. Buys all rights; but will sometimes reassign rights to author after publication. Buys 12 to 15 mss per year. Payment on acceptance. Will not consider photocopied or simultaneous submissions. Submit seasonal material 3 months in advance. Query first. Reports in 2 weeks. Enclose S.A.S.E.

Nonfiction and Photos: Technical, how-to-do-it, race reports, and road tests. Pays $100 per published page. Photos purchased with accompanying ms. Captions required. Pays $75 per published page for 8x10 b&w glossies. Pays $100 per published page for 35mm or 2¼ color transparencies.

1001 CUSTOM & ROD IDEAS, Argus Publishers Corporation, 131 Barrington Pl., Los Angeles CA 90049. Phone: 213-476-3004. Editor: Phillip E. Carpenter. For hobbyists who build modified American cars (hot rods); ages 15 to approximately 45, mechanically inclined. Magazine published every two months; 68 pages. Established in 1967. Circulation: 145,000. Rights purchased vary with author and material. Buys all rights or first North American serial rights. Buys 90 mss per year. Payment on publication. Will send free sample copy to writer on request. Write for copy of guidelines for writers. Will not consider simultaneous submissions except to other

Argus magazines. Reports within 2 months. Query first; send sample of copy and photos. Enclose S.A.S.E.

Nonfiction and Photos: "Technical articles on engine building, tuning, installation of performance equipment. Car features on unusual street rods, both early and late models. Read the magazine, pay special attention to quality and type of photos used. We do not accept copy only. Special emphasis on quality photos, how-to articles, no superfluous wordage in copy. We have adequate car features on early street rods from freelancers at present. We don't want rough-looking, dirty cars or technical articles that are written by persons without automotive experience. Our most efficient method of assuring material use is to assign subject matter, or be asked by freelancer about our needs." Recently published articles include "23T From A to Z-Parts I Through III" (step-by-step building of a street roadster) and "Building a Strong Street-Rod Frame," with high quality, detailed photos. Length: 300 to 4,000 words. Pays $40 per page, including photos. Photos purchased with accompanying ms with no additional payment. Captions required. Also purchased without ms or on assignment. Prefers 8x10 b&w glossies (occasionally takes proof sheets with negatives). Pays $10 minimum for b&w photo. Color transparencies; pays $50 minimum.

POPULAR HOT RODDING, Argus Publishers Corp., 131 South Barrington Pl., Los Angeles CA 90049. Phone: 213-476-3004. Editor: Lee Kelley. For automotive enthusiasts. Monthly. Circulation: 260,000. Buys all rights. Pays on publication. Will send a sample copy to a writer on request. Query first. Reports on submissions "as soon as possible." Enclose S.A.S.E.

Nonfiction and Photos: Wants automotive how-to's. Length: open. Pays $50 per printed page. Purchases photos with mss, and with captions only. Uses 8x10 b&w glossies, 2¼x2¼ color transparencies.

PICKUP, VAN & 4WD MAGAZINE (formerly *PV4*), 1499 Monrovia Ave., Newport Beach CA 92663. Editor: Don E. Brown. For vehicle enthusiasts (mostly off-pavement oriented). Magazine; 84 (8½x11) pages. Will look at seasonal material 3 months in advance. Established in 1972. Monthly. Circulation: 75,000. Buys all rights. Buys about 40 mss a year. Pays on publication. Will send free sample copy to writer on request. Write for copy of guidelines for writers. Returns rejected material in 1 month. Reports on accepted material in 45 days. Query first or submit complete ms. Enclose S.A.S.E.

Nonfiction and Photos: Articles relating to pickup trucks, vans and 4-wheel drive vehicles. Subjects include travel, vehicle modifications, helpful hints, customized vehicles that are practical, and do-it-yourself stories. More in-depth technical articles and factual reporting of test vehicles. All product testing is done by staff members. Travel stories without a direct connection with pickups, vans or 4-wheel drives and high quality photos are not wanted. Would like to see more off-pavement articles from the midwest, east and south. Length: 850 to 2,500 words. Pays $50 per printed page (usually 5¢ a word). Photos are purchased with accompanying ms with no additional payment. Also purchased without ms, and on assignment. Captions required. 5x7 or 8x10 b&w; 35mm or 2¼x2¼ color. Pays $12.50 minimum for ¼ page or smaller to $50 for full page.

ROAD & TRACK, 1499 Monrovia Avenue, Newport Beach CA 92663. Editor: Ron Wakefield. For knowledgeable car enthusiasts. Monthly magazine. Buys all rights, but may be reassigned to author after publication. Query first. Reports in 6 weeks. Enclose S.A.S.E.

Nonfiction: "The editor welcomes freelance material, but if the writer is not thoroughly familiar with the kind of material used in the magazine, he is wasting both his time and the magazine's time. *Road & Track* material is highly specialized and that old car story in the files has no chance of being accepted. More serious, comprehensive and in-depth treatment of particular areas of automotive interest." Payment is minimum 12¢ per word but often reaches 20¢ per word.

ROAD RIDER, P.O. Box 678, South Laguna CA 92677. Phone: 714-494-1104. Editor: Roger Hull. "Contrary to what the media would have you believe, we have a well-educated audience (more than 60% with some college) and cut through age groups from late teens to beyond the social security levels. They are active motorcyclists, outdoor lovers and we have more women readers than any other bike publication. We're strictly family style." Monthly magazine; 72 pages minimum, (8½x11). Established in 1969. Circulation: 35,000. Buys all rights, but will reassign to author after publication, on specific request. Buys about 50 mss per year. Payment on publication. Will send free sample copy to a writer on request. "If he'll query us on an idea at the same time requesting sample copy, this permits us to select back issue which may guide him." Will not consider photocopied or simultaneous submissions. "Seasonal material is okay; frequently use such (hypothermia in winter or hot weather riding in summer). Best to check with us in advance." Submit seasonal material 4 months in advance. Reports within 60 days. Query first to R. L. Carpenter, Assistant Editor. Enclose S.A.S.E.

Nonfiction: "Needless to say, we deal with road and street motorcycling; all aspects. We ignore racing, motocross, dirt riding and are for the touring motorcyclist. As such, our interest in the machines is played down; our interest in people is the main thing. Basically we're more about the people who ride motorcycles and tend to avoid the more technical aspects of cycling. Keep it light. We like humor. We don't recommend that a non-cyclist try to write for us. We specialize in road riding. We don't want to hear how one particular make and model of motorcycle is better than anything else on the road. We're doing a series of 'My Favorite Stretch of Road,' usually concerned with a trip of 100 miles or so which is particularly scenic and appealing to road bikers. Length depends, rarely less than 1,000 or over 4,000 words." Pays $25 minimum, "upward depending upon how much fiddling we have to do. Rates increase with subsequent acceptances." Rates for columns (" . . . And Then We Went") start at $10. All testing, product reports, reviews, etc., are staff originated).

Photos: Purchased with accompanying ms with no additional payment. Captions optional, but preferred. Prefers 5x7 b&w glossy; occasionally requests negs. Prefers 2¼ or larger color transparencies, but has used 35mm. Pays $25 for cover (usually assigned).

Fiction and Poetry: "Surprise us!" Cover theme of magazine. Pays $25 minimum for 1,000 to 4,000 words. "We'll look at any poem if it's about bikes." Pays about $20. "We use very little fiction and occasional poetry, but it's gotta be about road cyclists/cycling."

ROAD TEST, 1440 W. Walnut St., Compton CA 90220. Phone: 213-537-0857. Editor: Steve Thompson. For a predominantly male, college-educated, professional audience. Monthly magazine; 80 pages. Established in 1964. Circulation: 80,000. Buys first North American serial rights. Buys about 60 mss a year. Payment on publication. Will send free sample copy to writer on request. Will consider photocopied submissions. Reports in 2 to 8 weeks. Query first or submit complete ms. Enclose S.A.S.E.

Nonfiction and Photos: Automotive subjects, both technical and consumer-oriented. The customer's viewpoint is preferred. Informational, how-to, interview, profile, expose, technical. Recently published articles include "Money and the Automobile" and "That Was the Decade That Wore One Man's View." Length: 1,500 to 2,500 words. Pays 13¢ per word. Photo articles negotiable.

SMALL CARS MAGAZINE, 1420 Prince St., Alexandria VA 22314. Editor: Richard Benyo. For anyone contemplating buying a small car or anyone owning a small car. Magazine; 66 (8½x11) pages. Established in 1973. Monthly. Circulation: 52,000. Buys first serial rights. Buys about 120 mss a year. Pays on publication. Will send sample copy to writer for $1. No photocopied or simultaneous submissions. Reports in 2 weeks. Query first. Enclose S.A.S.E.

Nonfiction and Photos: Articles on experiences with small cars. Pieces on small car development. General auto technology and servicing pieces; road tests, etc. Specifically needs humorous material on small cars, and those on the small car in America. Informational, how-to, personal experience, interview, profile, humor, historical, expose, nostalgia, personal opinion, photo, travel, technical. Recently published "Equalizing the Shifting Load" which dealt with a new auto development.

Length: 800 to 6,000 words. Pays $50 to $250. No additional payment for photos used with mss. Pays $20 for 8x10 b&w glossies purchased without mss when used in conjunction with ms by another author. Captions required.

Fiction: "We would welcome occasional fiction related to small cars. This should be easier than it seems to an imaginative writer." Suspense, adventure and humorous fiction preferred. Length: 800 to 6,000 words. Pays $50 to $250.

Fillers: Jokes and short humor used as fillers. Length: 800 words maximum. Pays $5 to $25.

STOCK CAR RACING MAGAZINE, 1420 Prince St., Alexandria VA 22314. Editor: Richard S. Benyo. For primarily blue collar, ages 18 through 60. Magazine; 82 (8½x11) pages. Established in 1966. Monthly. Circulation: 128,000. Buys first North American serial rights. Buys 80 mss a year. Pays on publication. Will send sample copy to writer for $1. Reports in 2 to 6 weeks. Query first. Enclose S.A.S.E.

Nonfiction and Photos: "Articles on drivers, tracks, promoters, etc., involved with stock car racing. Any style as long as it is good writing. No race reports — we're swamped with them. Would like to see articles about the economy and the local track; the expense of building and supporting a stock car, etc." Interview, profile, humor, historical, expose, nostalgia. Recently published articles include "Big & Still Growing," a progress report on the recent successes at Charlotte Motor Speedway. Length: 1,500 to 6,000 words. Pays $75 to $250. Photos purchased with accompanying ms with no additional payment. Also purchased on assignment. Captions required. 8x10 b&w; color transparencies. Pays $15 for b&w; $100 for color cover; $50 for single page color; $100 for two-page color.

Fiction: "We don't get much fiction; it would have to be properly researched." Length: 1,500 to 10,000 words. Pays $75 to $250.

STREET CHOPPER, 1132 No. Brookhurst, Anaheim CA 92801. Phone: 714-635-9040. Editor: Steve Stillwell. For custom and high-performance motorcycle enthusiasts. Monthly magazine; 84 pages. Established in 1969. Circulation: 100,000. Buys all rights. Buys 25 to 35 mss a year. Payment on acceptance. Will send free sample copy to writer on request. Will not consider photocopied or simultaneous submissions. Reports within 3 months. Query first. Enclose S.A.S.E.

Nonfiction and Photos: Technical-oriented stories dealing with all aspects of motorcycles. "We deal strictly with custom and high-performance motorcycles. No off-road or dirt bikes." Material must be written in laymen's terminology. Greatest interest is in technical stories and how-to articles on motorcycles. Length: open. Pays maximum of $40 per published page. Columns using freelance material include "Checkered Flag" and "Cafe Corner." Length: 2 to 5 double-spaced, typed pages. Pays $40 per published page. Pays $40 to $50 for b&w photos purchased with mss; $75 for color; 2¼ only.

Fillers: Newsbreaks and jokes. Length: 1 to 3 typed, double-spaced pages.

STREET RODDER MAGAZINE, TRM Publications, Inc., 1132 N. Brookhurst, Anaheim CA 92801. Editor: Patrick Ganahl. For the 16- to 50-year-old man (and his family) with an interest in restored/modified old cars. Magazine; 76 (8x11) pages. Established in 1972. Monthly. Circulation: 80,000. Buys all rights, but will reassign rights to author after publication. Buys 25 to 35 mss a year. Payment is usually made on publication, but sometimes, on acceptance. Will send sample copy to writer for $1. Write for copy of guidelines for writers. No photocopied or simultaneous submissions. Reports in 1 month. Query first or submit complete ms. Enclose S.A.S.E.

Nonfiction and Photos: "We need coverage of events and cars that we can't get to. Street rod events (rod runs); how-to technical articles; features on individual street rods. We don't need features on local (Southern California) street rods, events or shops. We stress a straightforward style; accurate and complete details; easy to understand (though not 'simple') technical material. We very seldom accept a story without photos." Recently published an article on the Canadian Street Rod Nationals which had sharp, clear, uncluttered b&w photos; complete coverage; good copy. Length: 250 to 1500 words. Pays $25 to $150. Average payment for 2- to 3-page 5x7, 8x10 b&w feature: $75.

SUPER CHEVY MAGAZINE, Argus Publishers Corporation, 131 Barrington Pl., Los Angeles CA 90049. Editor: Phillip E. Carpenter. For high-performance automotive enthusiasts who build and race their own cars. Magazine published every 2 months; 84 pages. Established in 1973. Circulation: 100,000. Buys first North American serial rights. Buys 90 mss a year. Pays on publication. Will send free sample copy to writer on request. Will not consider photocopied and simultaneous submissions except to other Argus magazines. Reports in 2 months in most cases. Query first or submit complete ms. Enclose S.A.S.E.
Nonfiction and Photos: All articles should be slanted to high-performance-minded individuals. Car features, technical articles dealing with the automobile. New car introductions, new product features, and a few race reports. All cars or pickups must be 100% Chevrolet. Informational, how-to, interview, profiles. Recently published titles include "Performance-Building the Big Block," "Disc Brakes for Early Corvettes." Length: open. Pays $40 per printed page. No additional payment is made for b&w photos (8x10 prints) purchased with mss. Pays $10 to $20 for those purchased separately. Pays $50 to $150 for 2¼x2¼ color transparencies.

SUPER STOCK MAGAZINE, 1420 Prince St., Alexandria VA 22314. Editor: Michael T. Uno. For drag racing and street-oriented high performance auto enthusiasts. Magazine; 82 pages. Established in 1964. Monthly. Circulation: 140,000. Buys first rights. Buys 60 to 75 mss a year. Pays on publication. Will send sample copy to writer for $1. Reports on material accepted for publication immediately. Returns rejected material as soon as possible. Query first or submit complete ms. Enclose S.A.S.E.
Nonfiction and Photos: National race coverage featuring color photography. How-to, detailed technical articles, general technical articles, personality profiles, interviews, car features, etc. Should be fairly high caliber writing (though not necessarily sophisticated) with good photography. Pays $50 a page for text and b&w photos; $75 a page for color photos; $125 for two pages with color photos; $150 for cover photos. Captions required.

YAMAHA HORIZONS, P.O. Box 6600, Buena Park CA 90622. Editor: Gail P. Gellatly. Publication of Yamaha International Corporation. For young and middle aged. Mostly middle and upper middle class. At least high school, most with college education. Family, with both young and teenage children. Motorcycle enthusiasts. Recreation and leisure oriented. Bimonthly magazine; 32 (8½x11) pages. Circulation: 30,000. Not copyrighted. Pays on acceptance. Will send sample copy to writer for $1. Query first. Enclose S.A.S.E.
Nonfiction and Photos: "Articles on or about motorcycle usage. Peripheral articles on recreation, etc. Articles that are nontechnical, general interest. Articles with photos or art stand best chance of acceptance." Informational, how-to, personal experience, interview, profile, humor, historical, think articles, nostalgia, photo, travel, successful business operations and merchandising techniques. Length: 500 to 2,500 words. Pays $25 per article. Features should be accompanied by quality color or b&w photos. Captions required. No extra payment for photos.

Aviation Publications

Publications in this section aim at professional and private pilots, and at aviation enthusiasts in general. Magazines intended for the in-flight passengers of commercial airlines are grouped in a separate In-Flight category. Technical aviation and space journals, and those for airport operators, aircraft dealers, or other aviation businessmen are listed under Aviation and Space in the Trade Journals.

AERO MAGAZINE, Box 1184, Ramona CA 92065. Phone: 714-789-2400. Editor: Marvin Patchen. For "owners of business and pleasure aircraft." Bimonthly. Circulation: 97,000. Buys first rights. Buys about 24 mss a year from freelancers. Pays on publication. Will send a sample copy to a writer for 25¢. Will accept photocopied submissions, if stated on ms that it is not being simultaneously submitted elsewhere. Returns rejected material and acknowledges acceptance of material in 2 to 4 weeks. "Queries are recommended, and if writer is a novice or non-experienced pilot, the ms should be checked over by an experienced pilot before submission." Enclose S.A.S.E.

Nonfiction: Uses "serious articles pertinent to aircraft ownership, including technical, proficient, and profitable utilization of contemporary aircraft." *Aero* is "the only publication that goes strictly to aircraft owners. It does not cover learn-to-fly, historical, nostalgia, agricultural, military, or airline subject matter." Buys how-to's, personal experience articles, interviews, profiles, think pieces, new product and successful business operation coverage, photo stories, and travel pieces. Writer "should realize that all the readers have at least a private license and elementary subjects have no interest for the readers. Reporting should be concise and straightforward." Length: to 2,500 words. Pays $35 to $50 per printed page with photos.

Photos: Purchased with ms. Uses b&w glossies, color transparencies, color prints. Pays $50 for cover; $10 to $35 for inside color.

AIR LINE PILOT, 1625 Massachusetts Avenue, N.W., Washington DC 20036. Phone: 202-797-4176. Editor: C.V. Glines. "Our main readership is composed of airline pilots who are members of the Air Line Pilots Association. Other readers include flying buffs, business aircraft pilots, stewards and stewardesses, and airline industry executives." The editor has the writer's welfare in mind at all times. He has been doing freelance writing himself for a number of years. Monthly. Circulation: 45,000. Buys all rights. Buys about 25 mss a year from freelancers. Pays on publication. Will send a free sample copy on request. Query first. Reports "as soon as decision is made." Enclose S.A.S.E.

Nonfiction: Wants "articles on aircraft safety, aviation history, weather, airline pilots with interesting hobbies and sidelines, air racing, and similar subjects of interest to airline pilots. Especially interested in phase of aviation history dealing with development of airline flying. Qualified writers should ask for a copy. We keep the airline pilot in mind at all times—his interests, desires and his special brand of professionalism. While we treat some subjects lightly, we do not kid around with safety subjects." No aircraft safety articles from "amateurs who know not whereof they speak." Length: 1,000 to 2,500 words. Payment is $75 a printed page.

Photos: B&w glossies purchased with mss. Payment varies. Color transparencies and 35mm color purchased for 4-color covers. Payment is $200.

AIR PROGRESS, Petersen Publishing Co., 8490 Sunset Blvd., Los Angeles CA 90069. Editor: David B. Noland. "For pilots and aspiring pilots and people interested in all aspects of private, commercial, and military aviation." Publishes special issues "on special aviation topics like homebuilt, military, sport, and great aircraft." Monthly. Circulation: 200,000. Buys all rights or first rights. Buys "many" mss each year from freelancers. Pays on acceptance. No query required. Submit seasonal material 3 to 4 months in advance. Returns rejected material and acknowledges acceptance "quickly." Enclose S.A.S.E.

Nonfiction and Photos: Buys mss on aviation subjects: how-to's, interviews, profiles, humor, historical pieces. Primary subject is private flying. "Write well and interestingly." Pays minimum $100 per article or an average of $300 per article. Buys b&w glossies, color transparencies, 35mm color.

THE AOPA PILOT, 7315 Wisconsin Ave., Bethesda MD 20014. Phone: 301-654-0500. Executive Editor: Robert I. Stanfield. For plane owners, pilots, and the complete spectrum of the general aviation industry. Official magazine of the Aircraft Owners and Pilots Association. Monthly. Circulation: 182,000. Pays on acceptance. Reports promptly. Enclose S.A.S.E. for return of submissions.

Nonfiction: Factual articles up to 2,500 words that will inform, educate and entertain flying enthusiasts ranging from the student to the seasoned professional pilot. These pieces should be generously illustrated with good quality photos, diagrams or sketches. Quality and accuracy essential. Topics covered include maintenance, how-to features, new or unusual aircraft or aeronautical equipment, places to fly (travel), governmental policies (local, state or federal) relating to general aviation. Additional features on weather in relation to flying, legal aspects of aviation, flight education, pilot fitness, aviation history and aero clubs are used periodically. Short features of 100 to 300 words written around a single photograph, and strong photo features are always in demand. Payment is up to $300.

Photos: Pays $10 to $25 for each photo or sketch used. Exceptionally good cover color transparencies also purchased.

How To Break In: "Be aviation oriented and study the magazine (available at most airport pilots' lounges). And remember that our audience consists solely of pilots; thus a writer must speak the 'language' and be knowledgeable in the subject area."

AVIATION QUARTERLY, Box 7070, Arlington VA 22207. Publisher and Editor: Brad Bierman. For the serious aviation enthusiast, interested in the history of aviation. Quarterly. Hard-bound volume with four-color illustrations. Established in 1974. Circulation: 5,180. Buys all rights. Buys about 15 to 20 mss a year. Pays on publication. Query first to editorial and production office, Plano, Texas 75074. Phone: 214-423-8516. Enclose S.A.S.E.

Nonfiction and Photos: "We accept only the highest quality articles and photos. Photos with captions must be included or available. Subject matter should be a specific topic within the history of aviation. Writer must have acknowledged experience in his particular field, and must treat his subject in a unique way. Technical articles must also be readable. Nontechnical mss acceptable. It is our intent to make each volume a definitive source of information on a given event, aircraft, person or period within the history of aviation. Preferred length: 4,000 words. Payment varies, depending on subject matter and quality and acceptability of text and photos." Pays $150 to $400 per article.

AVIATION TRAVEL, 6045 Wilson Blvd., Arlington VA 22205. Executive Editor: Michael E. Dunbar. For owners of business and private aircraft; ages 30 to 50; interested in fishing, hunting, boating, photography, gold, sightseeing, beaches, resorts, outdoor and other sports. Offers a substantial market for writers slanting their material to aviation buffs. Editor is a nice guy—a real pro. Bimonthly magazine. Established in 1972. Circulation: 130,000. Buys all rights. Buys about 20 to 30 mss a year. Payment on publication. Will send sample copy to writer for $1. Write for copy of guidelines for writers. Will consider photocopied submissions. Submit seasonal material 3 to 4 months in advance. Query first or submit complete ms. Reports in 2 months. Enclose S.A.S.E.

Nonfiction and Photos: "Short travel articles—where to go, what to see and do. We may feature a general area or special activity, event, or resort which must be accessible by private or business plane. The U.S.A., Canada, Mexico and the Bahamas are preferred. Airport and flight info are helpful, but not required. The style should be light and nontechnical. Stories must be short, informational, and specific enough to be helpful to the traveler. Destinations must be emphasized, rather than flight. Dates, admission, what to take, etc., increase the value of a story. We're the only travel-oriented aviation magazine, featuring places and events accessible by general aviation. We're interested in fly-in wilderness, fishing, hunting, golfing and camping stories at specific locations. Each issue features items of particular interest during the period immediately following." Buys informational articles, how-to's, personal experience articles, interviews, humor, historical articles, photo features, travel pieces, new product articles, and technical articles. Length: 200 to 1,200 words. Pay "varies: about 5¢ per word, depending on subject and quality." Photos purchased with mss or without mss; captions required. Pay "$5 and up, depending on photo, for b&w glossies 5x7 and larger." Pays $5 and up, "depending on photo and use for transparencies only."

CANADIAN WINGS, Box 3278, Station B, Calgary, Alberta T2M 4L8, Canada. Editor: Marg Kobrinsky. For aviation enthusiasts, general aviation, oil and mineral industries; students of aviation. Magazine; 24 (8½x11) pages. Established in 1961. Monthly. Circulation: 25,000. Copyrighted. Buys about 50 mss a year. Pays on publication. Will send free sample copy to writer on request. Write for copy of guidelines for writers. Will consider photocopied and simultaneous submissions. Submit seasonal material 3 months in advance. Reporting time varies. Query first or submit complete ms. Enclose S.A.E. and International Reply Coupons.

Nonfiction and Photos: Technical material on all aspects of aircraft and related equipment. Aviation experiences and techniques; pilot reports on particular aircraft, navigation. In-depth data about flying. Mainly western Canada orientation, although growing into East. Clear, interesting and informative material. Seasonal articles on winter flying and other serious aspects of aviation in the fall and winter; lighter, more entertaining material in spring and summer. Recently published an article on transcendental flying, a whimsical look at turn of the century stunt flyers. Length: open. Pays $50 minimum. No additional payment for photos used with mss. Pays minimum of $15 for those used without mss or on assignment.

Fiction and Fillers: Experimental, mainstream, humorous, historical fiction related to aviation. Length: open. Pays $50 minimum. Newsbreaks, puzzles, clippings, jokes, short humor used as fillers. Pays $10 minimum.

EXXON AIR WORLD, Exxon International Co., Div. of Exxon Corp., 1251 Avenue of the Americas, New York NY 10020. Editor: E.A.C. Wren. For worldwide audience of technical and semitechnical aviation readers. Quarterly. Buys reprint rights. Payment on publication. Query first. Reports "quickly." Enclose S.A.S.E.

Nonfiction and Photos: Uses articles on aviation in action, worldwide; especially the offbeat aviation operation; technical articles. Style should be "unsensational, good 'international' English, informative. accurate." Length 300 to 2,000 words. Must be accompanied with good photos. Pays about 10¢ a word. Photos must be of good quality, interesting subject, striking composition, and adequately captioned. Pays $6 minimum for photos.

GENERAL AVIATION NEWS, P.O. Box 1094, Snyder TX 79549. Phone: 915-573-6318. Editor: M. Gene Dow. For pilots and aircraft owners. Tabloid newspaper; 40 pages. Established in 1950. Published every 2 weeks. Circulation: 30,000. Buys all rights. Buys 50 mss a year. Pays on acceptance. Will send sample copy to writer for 50¢. Write for copy of guidelines for writers. Will consider photocopied submissions. Reports within 1 month. Submit only complete ms. Enclose S.A.S.E.

Nonfiction and Photos: Informative, entertaining, technical, how-to, new products, etc., of general aviation (non-airline, non-military). Knowledgeable aviation articles. Informational, how-to, personal experience, interview, profile, humor, historical, think articles, expose, nostalgia, photo, travel, reviews (aviation books), spot news, successful business operations, new product, merchandising techniques, technical — all on aviation subjects. Any length. Pays $25 for 1,000 words. Pays $15 for 30 column inches for regular columns or departments. Photos purchased with accompanying ms or on assignment. Captions required. Pays $5 for b&w and color.

Fiction: Experimental, suspense, adventure, and humorous fiction on aviation subjects. Pays $25 for 1,000 words.

Poetry and Fillers: Aviation subjects. Pays $15 for poetry. Newsbreaks, clippings, jokes, short humor, and informative filler material. Pays $3.

PLANE & PILOT, Box 1136, Santa Monica CA 90406. Editor: Don Werner. For pilots and plane owners. Magazine; 80 (8½x10½) pages. Established in 1965. Monthly. Circulation: 75,000. Buys all rights. Buys 150 mss a year. Pays on publication. Will send sample copy for $1. No photocopied or simultaneous submissions. Submit seasonal material 6 months in advance. Reports in 3 months. Query first. Enclose S.A.S.E.

Nonfiction and Photos: Almost all articles are from freelance sources. Writer must know aircraft and flying. Seasonal material related to winter, fall, summer and spring weather conditions. Informational, how-to, personal experience, personal opinion, photos, travel. Experiences in owning and flying planes. No cute articles from wives about flying with their husbands. Length: open. Pays $50 to $200. No additional payment for photos used with ms. Captions required.

PRIVATE PILOT, Macro/Comm Corp., 2377 S. El Camino Real, San Clemente CA 92672. Phone: 714-498-1600. Editor: Dennis Shattuck. For owner/pilots of private aircraft, for student pilots and others aspiring to attain additional ratings and experience. Established in 1955. Circulation: 90,000. Buys first North American serial rights. Buys about 60 mss a year. Payment on publication. Will send sample copy to writer for $1.10. Write for copy of guidelines for writers. Will consider photocopied submissions if guaranteed original. Will not consider simultaneous submissions. Reports in 30 days. Query first. Enclose S.A.S.E.

Nonfiction and Photos: Material on techniques of flying, developments in aviation, product and specific airplane test reports, travel by aircraft, development and use of airports. All must be related to general aviation field. "Freelancer must know the subject about which he is writing; use good grammar; know the publication for which he's writing; remember that we try to relate to the middle segment of the business/pleasure flying public. We see too many 'first flight' type of articles. Our market is more sophisticated than that. Most writers do not do enough research on their subject. Would like to see more material on business-related flying, more on people involved in flying." Length: 1,000 to 4,000 words. Pays $75 to $200. Material is also used in the following columns: Business Flying, Homebuilt/Experimental Aircraft, Pilot's Logbook. Length: 1,000 words. Pays $50 to $100. 8x10 b&w glossies purchased with mss or on assignment. Pays $10. Color transparencies of any size are used for the cover. Pays $100.

Black Publications

Black general interest publications are listed in this category. Additional markets for black-oriented material are in the following sections:

Business and Finance Publications, Confession Publications, Juvenile Publications, Literary and Little Publications, Poetry Publications, Politics and World Affairs Publications, Sport and Outdoor Publications, Teen and Young Adult Publications; Theater, Movie, TV and Entertainment Publications; Play Publishers, Book Publishers, Greeting Card Publishers, and Syndicates.

BLACK AMERICA, Fashionable Productions, Inc., 24 West Chelten Ave., Philadelphia PA 19144. Editor: J. Morris Anderson. General interest magazine for blacks. Bimonthly. Buys all rights. Pays on publication. Query first. Enclose S.A.S.E.

Nonfiction: Articles on fashion, social problems, community, education, and other subjects of interest to an adult black audience. Also carries home decorating and cooking features. Length: varies. Pays $25.

Fiction and Poetry: Publishes 1 short story per issue relating to black life. Length: varies. Pays $25. Pays $15 to $25 for poetry.

BLACK TIMES: Voices of the National Community, Box 10246, Palo Alto CA 94303. Editor: Eric Bakalinsky. For mature readers sharing an intimacy with the Black Experience. Tabloid newspaper; 20 (10x14) pages. Established in 1971. Monthly. Circulation: 25,000. Acquires all rights, but will reassign rights to author after publication. Uses 25 mss a year. Pays in contributor's copies. Will send sample copy to writer for $1. Will consider photocopied and simultaneous submissions. Reports in 15 days. Query first or submit complete ms. Enclose S.A.S.E.

Nonfiction and Photos: "Material providing a celebration of Black America for all, aimed at creating awareness of developments in the Black Community. Remember to be aware that however specific your subject, you will be sharing it with a national community." Recently published "Sportin' Life," which had concision, clarity and flow focuses on both the unique and general aspects of Black athletes in America. Length: 500 to 5,000 words. Material for book review column (Read All About It) is also sought. Length: 250 to 1,000 words. B&w photos (5x5 or 8x10) used with both nonfiction and fiction. Captions required.

Fiction, Poetry and Fillers: All types of short fiction, as well as condensed and serialized novels. Length: 500 to 10,000 words. All forms of poetry; 1 to 150 lines. All types of puzzles, as well as jokes and short humor used as fillers. Length: 20 to 250 words.

BLACK WORLD, 1820 South Michigan Ave., Chicago IL 60605. Editor: Hoyt W. Fuller. Special issues: April, drama; May, Pan-African; June, fiction; September, poetry; February, black history. Established in 1942. Monthly. Circulation: 100,000. Rights purchased vary with author and material, but may buy all rights, then reassign them to author after publication. Buys 85 mss a year. Payment on publication. Will send a free sample copy to a writer on request. Will send editorial guidelines sheet to a writer on request. Submit seasonal material 3 to 4 months in advance. Enclose S.A.S.E. for return of submissions.

Nonfiction, Fiction, and Poetry: "Articles, fiction, poems, book reviews dealing with black American, Caribbean, African experiences, with emphasis on cultural and political aspects. Emphasis is on the positive and the constructive; approach problems, issues, situations from black context, with black audience in mind." Buys informational, historical, and book and record reviews. Length: up to 3,900 words. Pays $25 to $150. Fiction should relate to subject matter. Length: up to 3,900 words. Pays $35 to $150. Buys free verse and avant-garde forms of poetry. Should relate to subject matter. Pays $10 to $35.

CORE, 200 W. 135 St., New York NY 10030. Editor: Doris Innis. Publication of the Congress of Racial Equality. Established in 1970. Bimonthly. Circulation: 20,000. Rights acquired vary with author and material. Uses about 60 freelance articles a year. "Most of our articles are donated." Will send free sample copy to writer on request. Will consider photocopied submissions. Submit seasonal material at least 2 months in advance. Query first. Reports within 6 months. Enclose S.A.S.E. for response to queries.

Nonfiction and Photos: "Articles about or related to the black movement, black people's oppression, projected or attempted solutions. Also profiles of Black Movement people. Interviews. Health, food, books, sports. Also interested in travel, fashion, movies or African affairs. The writer's style and emphasis is up to him. We like variety. Of course, it helps if his outlook is black nationalist, but it's not mandatory. We try to make black nationalism (a little understood concept) digestible for the common man as well as the intellectual. Most articles are donated." Length: 500 to 5,000 words. Pays $25 for b&w photos on assignment. Captions optional.

Fiction: Should relate to magazine's theme. Length: 500 to 5,000 words. "Most are donated."

Poetry and Fillers: Free verse and avant-garde forms. Should relate. Length: open. Short humor and anecdotes. Length: 500 to 1,500 words. "Most are donated."

THE CRISIS, 1790 Broadway, New York NY 10019. Phone: 212-245-2100. Editor: Warren Marr, II. Official publication of the NAACP. "Our audience includes government officials, schools and libraries, representative of the leadership group in the black community across the nation, and persons involved in the broad area of human relations." Established in 1910 by W. E. B. Du Bois. Monthly (June/July, August/September issues are combined). Circulation: 100,000. Acquires all rights. "In most situations upon request, we will grant permission to reprint provided proper credit is included." Uses 50 freelance mss a year. "Our payment to writers at this time is in contributor's copies only." Submit complete ms. Reports on material within a month. Enclose S.A.S.E.

Nonfiction: "Articles dealing with civil rights and general welfare of Negroes and other minorities." Informational, interview, profile, historical, think pieces, exposes. Length: 3,000 words maximum.

Fiction: Short stories with a racial theme.

Poetry: Traditional forms, blank verse and free verse. Should relate to magazine's theme. Length: 40 lines maximum.

How To Break In: "What we don't get and would appreciate is material dealing with Blacks in the arts and sciences. And that means all the arts — performing, graphic, etc. We haven't had any material on Blacks in the classical music area, for instance. When dealing with other minorities, stick to material that is applicable across the board — to minorities in general. For example, how does the struggle of a Puerto Rican writer relate to the struggle of all third world writers?" Examples of some people whom the editor would like to see profiled are the late Percy Julian (medical science); Leontyne Price and other black performers at the Met; Alvin Ailey, the dancer. Unprofessional writing, however, will quickly turn this editor off.

EBONY MAGAZINE, 820 S. Michigan Ave., Chicago IL 60605. Editor: John H. Johnson. Address mss to Charles L. Sanders, Managing Editor. For black readers of the U.S., Africa, and the Caribbean. Monthly. Circulation: 1,300,000. Buys all rights. Buys about 20 mss a year from freelancers. Pays on publication. Submit seasonal material 2 months in advance. Query first. Usually reports in less than 30 days, but this varies. Enclose S.A.S.E.
Nonfiction: Achievement and human interest stories about, or of concern to, black readers. Photo essays, interviews, think pieces, profiles, humor, inspirational and historical pieces are bought. Length: 2,500 words minimum. Pays $150 and up.
Photos: Purchased with mss, and with captions only. Buys 8x10 glossies, color transparencies, 35mm color. Submit negatives and contacts when possible. Photo stories. Pays $150 and up.

JET, 820 S. Michigan Ave., Chicago IL 60605. Editor: John H. Johnson. For black readers interested in current news and trends. Weekly. Circulation: 500,000. Study magazine before submitting. Enclose S.A.S.E. for return of submissions.
Nonfiction and Photos: Articles on topics of current, timely interest to black readers. News items and features: religion, education, African affairs, civil rights, politics, entertainment. Buys informational articles, interviews, profiles, spot news, photo pieces, and personal experience articles. Length: varies. Payment to be negotiated.

PENNSYLVANIA BLACK OBSERVER, P.O. Box 72, Reading PA 19603. Editor: J. Murphy. For black audience. Established in 1972. Quarterly. Buys all rights. Payment on publication. Will send sample copy to writer for $1. Reports in 30 days. Enclose S.A.S.E.
Nonfiction, Photos, and Poetry: Articles, poetry, photos relating to black people. "We prefer short articles." Personal experience, interview, profile, humor, personal opinion, photo, and travel articles. Length: 1,000 to 1,500 words. Pays $10, $15, $25, depending on value of article. B&w photos purchased with accompanying ms with no additional payment. Captions required. Blank verse, free verse, and avant-garde forms of poetry, not too long. Pays $5 minimum for poetry.

SEPIA, 75 E. Wacker Dr., Chicago, IL 60601. Editor: Ben Burns. For "black readers of all age groups and interests." Monthly. Circulation: 100,000. Buys all rights. Buys about 75 mss a year from freelancers. Pays on acceptance. Will send a sample copy to a writer for 75¢. Will consider photocopied submissions. Submit seasonal material 3 months in advance. Reports in 1 week. Query first. Enclose S.A.S.E.
Nonfiction and Photos: "We are in the market for well-written, provocative, factual articles on the role of black Americans in all phases of American life. We look for a good writing style, no different from any popularly written publication. We are constantly in need of articles with current news value, but strictly projected for future publication. In this respect, we specifically look for queries on events that will be in the news when our magazine reaches its readers. Articles may be on interesting personalities, entertainers, sports figures, human interest or controversial topics. We will consider any subject if it has good reader appeal for a black audience. It cannot be overemphasized that contributors should study recent issues for general content and style." Buys interviews, profiles, historical articles, exposes, coverage of successful business operations, photo essays. Length: 1,500 to 3,000 words. Pays $100 to $250. Photos are purchased with mss. B&w glossies, color transparencies.

Business and Finance Publications

National and regional publications of general interest to businessmen are listed here. Those in the National grouping cover national business trends, and include some material on the general theory and practice of business and financial management. Those in the Regional grouping report on the business climate of specific regions.

Magazines that use material on national business trends and the general theory and practice of business and financial management, but which have a technical, professional slant, are classified in the Trade Journals section, under the Business Management, Finance, Industrial Management, or Management and Supervision categories.

National

AFRICAN BUSINESS REVIEW, c/o Bisco International, Inc., Suite 1500, 2 Penn Plaza, New York NY 10001. Editor: Ganny D. Awobajo. For businessmen in the U.S. and Africa concerned with Africa, African diplomats, departments of business, U.S. and African universities. Publishes material on African economic relations with the rest of the world; ups and downs of African business; business opportunities, new development projects, etc. Established in 1973. Monthly. Circulation: 5,000. Rights purchased vary with author and material; usually buys all rights, but will reassign rights to author after publication. Buys 150 to 200 mss a year. Payment on publication. Will send free sample copy to a writer on request. Write for copy of guidelines for writers. Will consider photocopied submissions. Reports on material accepted for publication upon acceptance. Returns rejected material in 2 to 3 weeks. Submit complete ms. Enclose S.A.S.E.
Nonfiction: Serious, business-oriented articles, bearing in mind the current state of world business. Articles on African economic relations with U.S., Europe, European Economic Community, Japan, economic cooperations among African states, world bank, etc. Length: 1,000 words. Pays $50. Department Editor: G. D. Awobajo.

BARRON'S NATIONAL BUSINESS AND FINANCIAL WEEKLY, 22 Cortlandt St., New York NY 10007. Editor: Robert M. Bleiberg. For business and investment people. Weekly. Will send free sample copy to a writer on request. Buys all rights. Pays on publication. Enclose S.A.S.E.
Nonfiction: Articles about various industries with investment point of view; shorter articles on particular companies, their past performance and future prospects as related to industry trends for "News and Views" column. Length: 2,000 words or more. Pays $200 to $500 for articles; $100 and up for "News and Views" material. Articles considered on speculation only.
How To Break In: "News and Views might be a good way, but the key thing to remember here is these pieces must be fully researched and thoroughly documented."

BLACK BUSINESS DIGEST, 3133 N. Broad St., Philadelphia PA 19132. Editor: Vincent A. Capozzi. For "the academic world and the educated layman, both black and white. We are heavily subscribed to by institutions of higher learning." Monthly. Pays on acceptance. Submit complete ms for nonfiction. Will consider photocopied submissions. Reports in 6 weeks. Enclose S.A.S.E.
Nonfiction: "We are a magazine concerned with minority economics. Articles range from black manufacturing through to politics insofar as the political scene affects minority economics. Occasionally articles on travel, the medical profession, and community development groups are accepted. Avoid the usual magazine formula story and opinionated pieces which cannot be substantiated. Facts and figures are required to back up contentions. Both black and white authors are represented. Our theme is 'black and white economic cooperation.' Do not send articles which go overboard in condemning white racism; pieces which, while making various charges, have not an authoritative document to back up the contentions." Length: 750 to 2,500 words. Payment negotiable.

BLACK ENTERPRISE, 295 Madison Ave., New York NY 10017. Managing Editor: Robert J. Imbriano. For black executives, professionals, and independent businessmen. Monthly. Established in 1970. Circulation: 185,000. Rights purchased vary with author and material. Buys 20 to 30 mss per year. Payment on acceptance. Will send free sample copy to writer on request. Will consider photocopied submissions. Will not consider simultaneous submissions. Reports in 6 to 8 weeks. Query first. Enclose S.A.S.E.
Nonfiction: Informational articles addressed to business and business-related interests of audience. Stress is on black perspective and economic framework. Unique, exclusive focus on black economic interests. Informational, how-to, personal experience, interview, profile, think articles, and successful business operations. Recently published articles include "A New Breed of Hotelmen" (realistic, well-integrated treatment of real life achievements of many black executives). Length: 1,500 words minimum. Pays up to $500 maximum.

BUSINESS TODAY, Green Hall Annex, Princeton University, Princeton NJ 08540. Editor: Whitney Landon. For college students with business interests. Magazine; 32 pages. Established in 1968. Three times a year. Circulation: 20,000. Buys all rights, but will reassign rights to author after publication. Buys 1 or 2 mss a year. Pays on publication. Will send free sample copy to writer on request. Will consider photocopied and simultaneous submissions. Submit special issue material 3 months in advance. Reports on material accepted for publication in 2 weeks. Returns rejected material immediately, if requested. Query first or submit complete ms. Enclose S.A.S.E.
Nonfiction and Photos: Published by students, using general subject matter on topics relating to business, human interest articles; student business relations. Nothing on the theme of social responsibility. Special issues include multinationals, government regulation of business and career surveys. Length: open. Pays $10 minimum. B&w photos purchased with or without mss. Pays $10 minimum.

BUSINESS WEEK, 1221 Avenue of the Americas, New York NY 10020. Does not solicit freelance material. "There are cases, however, where specific story assignments are given to non-staff writers, if they are particularly well suited to provide copy for our weekly Personal Business column and the monthly Personal Business supplement. If you have a particularly apt idea for the column or the supplement, check with the editors first. We never take anything 'over the transom.' "

THE CAPITALIST REPORTER, 150 Fifth Ave., New York NY 10011. Editor: Patrick H. W. Garrard. Established in 1971. Every 2 months. Circulation: 120,000. Buys all rights. Buys about 100 mss a year. Payment on publication. Will send free sample copy to writer on request. Write for copy of guidelines for writers. Reports promptly. Query first. Queries should be addressed to Richard Berman, Executive Editor. Enclose S.A.S.E.
Nonfiction and Photos: "We give specific how-to information; names and addresses. Also, we believe writing and reading about money can be fun. We stay away from the drab reportage about corporate doings featured elsewhere. We concentrate on individual exploits. We use popular financial stories of particular interest to the entrepreneur." Personal experience, interview, profile, inspirational, humor, expose, successful business operations. Length: 3,000 words maximum. Pays $300 per article; average of 10¢ a word. Photos purchased on assignment.

EXCHANGE, published by the New York Stock Exchange, 11 Wall St., New York, NY 10005. Editor: Edward Kulkosky. For present and potential investors. Monthly. Buys all rights, unless otherwise negotiated. Pays on acceptance. Query first. Enclose S.A.S.E.
Nonfiction: "Articles must have current interest. Investors must be able to relate indirectly and directly. We do profiles of industries, also timely pieces on trends in business, investment, finance, economics and government." Pays up to $350 for standard pieces up to 1,800 words.

FINANCE, 5 East 75 St., New York NY 10021. Editor-in-Chief: H. L. Silberman; Editor: B. K. Thurlow. For corporate executives, upper echelon; weighted toward institutions (banks, trusts, etc.) and investment firms; also general business and commerce. Monthly, 64 pages, newsmag size. Established in 1940. Circulation: 55,000. Buys all rights. Buys 50 mss per year. Pays on publication. Will send free sample copy to writer on request, "if writer interests us." Write for copy of guidelines for writers. Will not consider photocopied or simultaneous submissions. Reports at once. Query first, in every case. Completed mss on assignment only. Enclose S.A.S.E.
Nonfiction and Photos: "Fairly sophisticated articles on business and finance. Occasional picture-text features of general interest to businessman/financier audience. Get in touch with us first: assignments may vary in this regard. *Finance* has traditionally been banking (both commercial and investment) oriented.. But increasingly, we have broadened our scope to embrace a wide range of subjects of interest to our readers. New addition: a column called 'The Good Things in Life Besides Money,' that focuses on their personal interests; recent columns dealt with wines, Persian rugs, pipe tobacco etc. (about 1,000 words and queries invited). Our special areas of interest are investment management, notably by bank trust departments, and international trends." Recently published articles include: "Prospering Persia: Modern Mecca," "U.S. Banking Overseas: A Reappraisal," "Confessions of a Personal Trust Officer," and "Leasing Abroad: The New Frontier." Generally pays $150 for 1,000 words; $200 for 2,000 words; $500 for lead or cover piece of 3,000 words. Premium at their discretion for more complicated pieces involving numerous sources. All pay rates for assignment basis only. Photos are purchased on assignment only.

FORBES, 60 Fifth Ave., New York NY 10011. "We do not buy freelance material." But, on occasion, when a writer of some standing (or whose work is at least known to them) is going abroad or into an area where they don't have regular staff or stringer coverage, they have given assignments or sometimes helped on travel expenses.

FORTUNE, 1271 Ave. of the Americas, New York NY 10020. Staff-written, but they do buy a few freelance articles (by Irwin Ross, for example) and pay extremely well for them.

INVESTMENT & BUSINESS OPPORTUNITY NEWS, P.O. Box 610097, North Miami FL 33161. Editor: Edward J. Foley. For people interested in investment and business opportunities. Newspaper. Established in 1974. Monthly. Circulation: over 50,000. Buys all rights, but will reassign rights to author after publication. Buys about 10 mss a year. Pays on publication. Will send free sample copy to writer on request. Will consider photocopied submissions. No simultaneous submissions. Reports on material accepted for publication in 30 days. Does not return unsolicited material which is rejected. Query first. Enclose S.A.S.E.
Nonfiction and Photos: Business and financial articles. New ideas for money-making opportunities. Articles should tie in with current market conditions and should be preceded with an outline and query. Avoid emphasis on "old" times. Informational, spot news, successful business operations, new product. Length: 1,000 to 3,000 words. Pays 2¢ a word. $5 for b&w glossies purchased with mss. Captions required.

MBA, 555 Madison Ave., New York NY 10022. Editor: Joseph Poindexter. For graduates of business schools and graduate business school students and faculty. "They are the future executives of the nation's largest corporations, heads of their own companies, administrators in public organizations." Monthly magazine; 72 to 84 pages. Established in 1967. Circulation: 90,000. Buys all rights, but will reassign rights to author after publication. Buys 40 to 50 mss a year. Payment on publication. Will send free sample copy to writer on request. Write for copy of guidelines for writers. Reports in 2 weeks. Query first. Enclose S.A.S.E.
Nonfiction and Photos: "Original expository articles on the directions of U.S. and world business. Reportage on the role of the young executive in today's society. Articles tracing the effects of social dynamics on the life style of the young executive.

Articles on significant developments in business, and public sector management. Career guidance articles." Personal experience, interview, profile, expose. Length: 1,500 to 4,000 words. Pays 8¢ to 12¢ per word. Recent articles include "Asleep on the Beat: Why the Newswires Don't Cover Business." Departments use news and analysis of compensation trends for young executives. Length: 1,000 words. Pays 8¢ to 12¢ per word. Photos are purchased on assignment.

MONEY, Time-Life Building, Rockefeller Center, New York NY 10020. Managing Editor: William Simon Rukeyser. "For the middle to upper middle income, sophisticated, well-educated reader. We picture our readers as neither insiders or idiots." Established in 1972. "Commissioned articles only."

MONEY STRATEGIES, Alexander Hamilton Institute, 605 Third Ave., New York NY 10016. Editor: Joseph R. Tigue. For high level management. Newsletter published every 2 weeks. Established in 1909. Buys all rights. Pays on acceptance. Will send free sample copy to writer on request. Query first. Enclose S.A.S.E.
Nonfiction: Ways to save and invest money; management articles; value analyses; management by objectives; job enrichment; ways to higher productivity, etc.; marketing articles; self-help and inspirational articles. Pithy, newsletter style of writing. No puffery. Solid copy with concrete examples. Tries to explain new management techniques with examples of how companies are actually putting them into effect. Length: 1,000 words average. Pays 15¢ per word.

WALL STREET REPORTS, 120 Wall St., New York NY 10005. Editor: Richard A. Holman. For persons interested in stocks and the stock market. Established in 1967. Monthly. Circulation: over 35,000. Query first. Study magazine before querying. Enclose S.A.S.E.
Nonfiction: Buys articles from market experts which will better inform investors and persons interested in investments. Length and payment to be negotiated.

WHAT'S NEW IN TRAINING MANAGEMENT & MOTIVATION, 134 North 13th St., Philadelphia PA 19107. Editor: Judy Gilbert. For training department administrators and managers in industrial and non-industrial organizations. Magazine; 55 (8½x11) pages. Established in 1974. 3 issues a year. Circulation: 30,000. Not copyrighted. Pays on acceptance. Will send free sample copy to a writer on request. Will consider photocopied and simultaneous submissions. Reports on material accepted for publication in 2 weeks. Returns rejected material in 6 weeks. Enclose S.A.S.E.
Nonfiction and Photos: Features informational articles on training programs and purchasing techniques, new training materials, and management techniques as applicable to training managers. "We rely more heavily on editorial features than other publications in this field." Informational, how-to, personal experience, interview, profile, spot news, successful business operations, and new product articles. Length: 250 to 3,000 words. Pays $25 per printed page. Photos desired.

Regional

ALASKA CONSTRUCTION AND OIL, 109 W. Mercer St., Seattle WA 98119. Phone: 206-285-2050. Executive Editor: Roscoe Laing. Associate Editor: Norm Bolotin. For "management in Alaska's fields of construction, oil development, timber, mining, transportation." Special issues: January, Annual Forecast and Review; July, Equipment Directory. Monthly. Circulation: about 8,000. Buys first rights. Buys 35 to 40 mss a year. Pays on publication. Query first. Reports in 2 months. Enclose S.A.S.E.
Nonfiction and Photos: "Anything related to the development of the state of Alaska—except tourism and fisheries." Writer should "get 'inside' the subject. We're not interested in puff, editorial elevation of our advertisers, etc. No newspaper style." Buys interviews, profiles, photo essays, coverage of successful business operations. Length: 500 to 2,000 words. Pays $30 per typeset page. Photos purchased with mss. Color transparencies, b&w glossies. Pays $10 for b&w.

How To Break In: "Alaska is a growing state and a genuine writer's market. Good (well-written) and interesting pieces on construction methods, oil and timber activities, etc., are always of interest, and there's enough happening there that many good stories never get written. Same with accompanying photography."

AUSTIN MAGAZINE, Austin Chamber of Commerce, P.O. Box 1967, Austin TX 78767. Editor: Ann Marett. A business and community magazine dedicated to telling the story of Austin and its people to Chamber of Commerce members. Magazine published monthly by the Chamber; 48 to 64 pages, 8½x11. Established in 1960. Circulation: 5,000. Not copyrighted. Will send sample copy to writer for $1. Will consider original mss only. Reports in 1 month. Enclose S.A.S.E.
Nonfiction and Photos: Articles should deal with interesting businesses or organizations around town with emphasis on Chamber of Commerce members. Articles are also accepted on Austin's entertainment scene. Length: 1,000 to 2,000 words. Pays 2½¢ per word. B&w photos are purchased with mss.

CANADIAN BUSINESS MAGAZINE, 1080 Beaver Hall Hill, Montreal, H2Z 1T2, Quebec, Canada. Editor: Robin Schiele. For senior and middle management men in business and industry in late 40s or early 50s, usually educated to at least bachelor degree level. We also have significant readership among business students and university and government people. Monthly magazine. Established in 1927. Circulation: 45,000. Buys first Canadian serial rights. Buys second serial (reprint) rights, on occasion. Buys 60 to 80 mss per year. Payment on acceptance. Will send free sample copy to writer on request. Will consider photocopied submissions. Simultaneous submissions, "if so indicated." Reports within 8 weeks. Query first. Enclose S.A.S.E.
Nonfiction and Photos: Subjects pertaining directly to Canadian business, including the economic performance of the nation, a region, an industry, or a company; finance; corporate management, investments; trade relations; personnel; government action, particularly planned or newly passed legislation; how-to stories helpful to the reader in his capacity as businessman. Non-academic style, written with a complete familiarity with the Canadian scene (and how it differs from the American). Length: 1,000 to 2,500 words. Pays $100 minimum. Photos purchased with accompanying ms with no additional payment. Captions optional.

COMMERCE MAGAZINE, 130 S. Michigan Ave., Chicago IL 60603. Phone: 312-786-0111. Editor: Gordon A. Moon II. For top businessmen and industrial leaders in greater Chicago area. Also sent to chairmen of and presidents of Fortune 500 firms throughout United States. Monthly magazine; varies from 100 to 400 pages, (8¼x11¼). Established in 1904. Circulation: 12,000. Buys all rights, but will reassign rights to author after publication. Buys 30 to 40 mss per year. Pays on acceptance. Will send sample copy to writer for $1. Query first. Enclose S.A.S.E.
Nonfiction: Business articles and pieces of general interest to top business executives. "We select our freelancers and assign topics. Many of our writers are from local newspapers. Considerable freelance material is used but almost exclusively on assignment from Chicago area specialists within a particular business sector." Pays 4¢ to 8¢ a word.

THE FINANCIAL POST, 481 University Ave., Toronto, Ontario, Canada. Managing Editor: Neville Nankivell. National weekly newpaper on business, investments, and public affairs. Published weekly. Circulation: 150,000. Buys first Canadian rights. Query essential.
Nonfiction: "Business and personal finance topics geared specifically to management and investors, and written from a Canadian point of view for a Canadian audience. Limited freelance market." Length and payment depend on subject and quality; payment begins at 10¢ per word.

FLORIDA TREND MAGAZINE, Box 2350, Tampa FL 33601. Editor: Walker Roberts. For business, industrial and financial executives with Florida interests. Monthly. Circulation: 38,000. Buys all rights, but will reassign rights to author after

publication. Pays on publication. Query first. Reports immediately. Enclose S.A.S.E.
Nonfiction: Articles on successful people or ventures with emphasis on how it was done, in the state of Florida only. Also items relating to general Florida news and financial news. Length: 500 to 2,000 words. Pays $1 per inch for shorts, $50 and up for profiles, $100 to $200 for major research stories.

HOUSTON BUSINESS JOURNAL, 5314 Bingle Road, Houston TX 77018. Phone: 713-688-8811. Editor: Mike Weingart. For "businessmen, investors, management; 25 to 60 years old, generally college graduates." Weekly. Circulation: 10,000. Buys all rights. Buys about 50 mss per year. Pays on publication. Will send a sample copy to a writer on request. Submit seasonal material 1 month in advance. Reports in 2 weeks. Query first. Enclose S.A.S.E.
Nonfiction: "Exclusively about business and it must have specific applications or examples about Houston business. Everything is localized. We publish some special issues, generally to coincide with a meeting or convention, such as a special section on the American Bankers Association convention, or the National Homebuilders Association convention." Buys how-to's, personal experience articles, interviews, profiles, coverage of successful business operations, think pieces, and articles on merchandising techniques. Length: 300 to 1,500 words. Pays $1.50 per column inch.
How To Break In: "Probably the best way for someone to sell us copy is anytime a Houston-based company is doing something of business news significance in their hometown. It might be a meeting before a group of local analysts or it might be the opening of a major facility. We have a correspondent in Bonn who keeps up with the list of Houston-based companies and whenever one of them is in the news there, she goes ahead with an interview with the top executives."

INDIANA MAGAZINE, 1100 Waterway Blvd., Indianapolis IN 46202. Editor: Phyllis L. Thom. For "the business executive (presidents, vice presidents, managers, purchasing agents) in Indiana." Established in 1955. Monthly. Circulation: 8,500. Rights purchased vary with author and material, but may buy first or second serial rights. Buys 12 to 15 mss a year. Payment on publication. Will send a sample copy to a writer for 25¢. Submit seasonal material 2 months in advance. Query first required. Reports in 1 month. Enclose S.A.S.E.
Nonfiction: "Business oriented features of interest to Indiana businessmen. One-half of the magazine contains articles of general business interest, and one-half features a specific segment of business and industry each month such as construction in Indiana." Buys think, successful business operations, and merchandising technique articles. Length: 500 words. Pays $25 to $75. Department Editor: E. A. Kieta.

INVESTOR MAGAZINE, 611 N. Broadway St., Milwaukee WI 53202. Editor: Don Adams. For Wisconsin business and professional people. Monthly. Established in 1970. Circulation: 21,000. Buys all rights but will reassign rights to author after publication. Buys 10 to 20 mss per year. Payment on publication. Will send free sample copy to writer on request. Write for copy of guidelines for writers. Will consider photocopied submissions. Reports in 1 month. Query first. Enclose S.A.S.E.
Nonfiction and Photos: Articles of interest to Wisconsin business persons. "We are interested only in Wisconsin writers who may have specialized knowledge of state business and availability for personal consultation with editor." Length: 1,200 to 3,500 words. Pays $35 to $400. 8x10 b&w photos purchased with ms or on assignment. Captions optional. Pays $25 to $60 for color transparencies.
How To Break In: "Send resume and samples. Wisconsin-based writers only are suitable for our needs."

NEW ENGLANDER MAGAZINE, Dublin NH 03444. Editor: Bradford W. Ketchum, Jr. For business, industrial, and professional management in the six New England states. Monthly. Buys all rights. Payment on acceptance. Will send free sample copy to New England-based writers only. Reports promptly. Enclose S.A.S.E.
Nonfiction and Photos: Articles must have New England business angle and interest. Will consider either ideas or finished articles. Length: 1,000 to 4,000 words. Pays $150 to $350 per article. B&w 5x7 or 8x10 glossy photos purchased with ms or

with captions only. 2¼x2¼ or 4x5 color transparency used for cover only. "Pay higher flat fee to freelance writer when suitable photos are included; $100 minimum for cover. Do not, however, pay separate photo fee to writers."

NEW NORFOLK, P.O. Box 327, Norfolk VA 23501. Editor: Susan S. Phillips. For members of Norfolk Chamber of Commerce, top executives in Norfolk firms. Magazine; 48 pages. Established in 1943. Monthly. Circulation: 5,000. Not copyrighted. Buys about 24 mss a year. Pays on publication. Will send sample copy to writer for $1. Will consider photocopied and simultaneous submissions. Reports in 2 to 3 weeks. Query first or submit complete ms. Enslose S.A.S.E
Nonfiction: Articles dealing with business and industry in Norfolk, Virginia, and surrounding area of southeastern Virginia (Tidewater area only). Profiles, successful business operations, new product, merchandising techniques, book reviews. Length: 500 to 1,500 words. Pays $25 to $100.

REALTY & INVESTMENT, 929 Fee Fee Rd., Suite 200A, Maryland Heights MO 63043. Phone: 314-878-4260. Managing Editor: Rob Nagel. For St. Louis businessmen and professional leaders, including doctors, lawyers, certified public accountants, architects, engineers, bankers, brokers. Published bimonthly. Circulation: 15,000. Buys all rights. Pays within 30 days of publication. Will send free sample copy to writer on request. Submit seasonal material 2 months in advance. Reports within 1 month. Query first. Enclose S.A.S.E.
Nonfiction: Stories of general interest to businessmen with emphasis on St. Louis business and finance. Interested in material on financial issues, the stock market and problems that examine the major social, economic and political crises that affect St. Louis and the nation. Recently published articles include "Apartments: For Rent and Leisure," "Condominiums: For Sale and Savings," "Singles: Courted by St. Louis Business, An Affair of Love and Money." Regular departments include: transportation, leisure, investment, management, personal investment, environment, design, building, financing and taxes. Length: open. Pays $100 to $300 and up, depending on subject.

SAN DIEGO BUSINESS FORUM, P.O. Box 80964, San Diego CA 92138. Editor: Igor Lobanov. For middle and upper management levels of business and industry, plus a large segment of the professional population (doctors, dentists, attorneys) who are interested in investment opportunities. Magazine; 64 (8½x11) pages. Established in 1971. Monthly. Circulation: 11,000. Buys first North American serial rights. Buys 60 to 70 mss a year. Usually pays on publication, but in some cases, on acceptance. Will send sample copy to writer for $1. Will consider photocopied submissions. No simultaneous submissions. Reports in 45 days. Query first or submit complete ms. Enclose S.A.S.E.
Nonfiction: Articles of interest to local business executives and professional men. Material which affects their income or life style. Avoid theme/string of quotes/conclusion formula. Articles must move forward swiftly and have tight, coherent construction. How-to, interview, profile, successful business operations, merchandising techniques. Length: 300 to 2,500 words. Pays $25 to $150.
How To Break In: "Submit either query or finished manuscript on speculation. We use very little material that is not concerned with business in San Diego County in some way. Even general industry problems and self-help material, though broad in scope, must be tied in to some San Diego people or firms."

THE SOUTH MAGAZINE, P.O. Box 2350, Tampa FL 33601. Phone: 813-251-1081. Editor: Roy B. Bain. For chief executive officers of businesses, business leaders, community and government leaders; those interested in the business and economy of the South; decisionmakers and others with an interest in and a stake in the future of the region. Regional business publication; 60 to 80 (8¼x11) pages. Established in 1974. Published every 2 months. Circulation: 45,000. Buys first North American serial rights. Buys 25 to 50 mss a year. Pays on publication. Will send sample copy to writer for $1. Write for copy of guidelines for writers. Reports within 2 months. Query first. Enclose S.A.S.E.

Nonfiction and Photos: Business and economic trends, industry stories affecting the South, profiles, articles on urban growth patterns and problems, major restorations (example, Atlanta's Inman Park or Underground Atlanta), articles with government/agency interplay with community or business patterns, education articles. Length: 300 to 2,000 words. Pays $75 to $250. Photos purchased with or without accompanying ms. Captions required. 5x7 or 8x10 b&w glossies; high contrast. High quality, sharp color, 35mm or 2¼x2¼ transparencies. "Payment depends on pre-arrangements at our discretion."

Child Care and Parental Guidance Publications

The following publications are concerned with child care and parental guidance. Other categories that include markets that buy items about child care for special columns and features are: Confession, Religious, and Women's in Consumer Publications; Education Journals in Trade Journals.

AMERICAN BABY, 575 Lexington Ave., New York NY 10021. Phone: 212-752-0775. Editor: Judith Nolte. For "expectant mothers (from sixth month of pregnancy) and new mothers (until 4 months after baby's birth)." Special issues include early learning and preschool education (August); travel (May). Monthly. Circulation: 1,500,000. Buys first serial rights. Buys about 50 mss a year. Pays on publication; sometimes pays on acceptance. Will send a sample copy to a writer on request. Submit seasonal material 3 months in advance. Reports in 2 weeks. Enclose S.A.S.E.
Nonfiction: Articles on "pre- and post-natal care and health and humorous features on parenthood." Uses features on "early learning, physical, psychological, and mental development of new baby." Writing style should be "clear, not condescending." Would prefer not to see articles on "breastfeeding and natural childbirth." Buys how-to's, personal experience and inspirational articles, interviews, profiles, historical and think pieces, new product and travel articles. Length: 500 to 2,000 words. Pays $25 to $200.
How To Break In: "For writers to get started, they should submit a manuscript on a topic which interests *them,* and, of course, our readership. Creating a new column idea would be fine, or interviewing some authority in a field. I suggest the interview as a good way for the beginner because he can do research, learn to ask questions, and get some writing and editing experience all at the same time, and the work won't be too complicated. I do believe, however, that a good beginner needs knowledge of English and a lot of drive."

BABY CARE, 52 Vanderbilt Ave., New York NY 10017. Editor: Maja Bernath. Managing Editor: Evelyn Podsiadlo. For "mothers of babies from birth through the first year." Quarterly. Circulation: 500,000. Rights purchased vary with author and material. May buy all rights, first North American serial rights, and second serial rights. Payment on acceptance. Will send a free sample copy to a writer on request. Will send editorial guidelines sheet to a writer on request. Submit seasonal material 5 to 6 months in advance. Reports in 1 to 4 weeks. Enclose S.A.S.E.
Nonfiction: Feature articles "include basic infant care (bathing, feeding, common illness, safety); emotional and physical development; how-to's; effect of new baby on family relations; seasonal topics (travel, summer or winter care). Shorter features with a humorous, narrative or reflective approach. Articles can be first-person accounts by mothers and fathers, but prefer medical subject to be written by M.D.'s and R.N.'s or writer who can work well with doctors." Worthy material is used to aid mothers of the very young child. Buys informational, how-to, personal experience, inspirational, humor, nostalgia and travel. Length: 1,000 to 1,800 words. Pays $50 to $125; and slightly higher to professionals such as M.D.'s. Regular columns that seek freelance material are: "Family Corner" — shorter anecdotes about life with

the new baby. Pays $10. "Focus on You" — 500-word mss focusing on a mother's feelings, personal interests or family relationships in regard to the baby. Pays $25. **Poetry:** Uses poetry occasionally; all forms. Length: 4 to 24 lines. Pays $5 to $10. Should relate to subject matter.

BABY TALK, 66 E. 34th St., New York NY 10016. Editor: Eve Hammerschmidt. For new and expectant mothers interested in articles on child development, baby care and homemaking. Monthly. Established in 1934. Circulation: over 1 million. Buys first North American serial rights. Buys 100 to 150 mss a year. Payment on acceptance. Will send free sample copy to writer on request. Submit only complete ms. Enclose S.A.S.E.
Nonfiction and Photos: "Articles on all phases of baby care. Also true, unpublished accounts of pregnancy, life with baby or young children. Write simple, true experience articles, not too lengthy. We have special features (Your Opinions; Life With Baby) especially designed for reader-written mss." Informational, how-to, personal experience, inspirational, humor, think articles, personal opinion, photo, travel (with babies), and new product articles. Length: open. Pays $20 to $50, and occasionally more. Department Editor: Patricia Irons. B&w and color photos are sometimes purchased with or without ms. Captions optional. Payment varies.

EXCEPTIONAL PARENT, P.O. Box 101, Back Bay Annex, Boston MA 02117. Phone: 617-267-5470. Editors: Dr. Stanley D. Klein, Dr. Lewis B. Klebanoff, Dr. Maxwell J. Schleifer. Magazine provides practical guidance for parents and professionals concerned with the care of children with disabilities (physical disabilities, emotional problems, mental retardation, learning disabilities, perceptual disabilities, deafness, blindness, chronic illness, etc.). Bimonthly. Circulation: 11,000. Buys all rights. Buys about 20 mss a year. Pays on publication. Will send sample copy to writer for $2. Send query with outline. Reports in 4 months. Enclose S.A.S.E.
Nonfiction and Photos: "The general intent of the magazine is to provide practical guidance for the parents and professionals concerned with the care of children with disabilities. We print articles covering every conceivable subject within this area, including legal issues, tax information, recreation programs, parent groups, etc. This is a consumer publication within a very specialized market. That we provide practical guidance cannot be stressed too strongly. Articles should be jargon-free. Articles within special areas are checked by an advisory board in the medical and allied professions. There is no other magazine of this type." Buys how-to's, personal experience articles. Length: 800 to 3,000 words. Pays 5¢ a word. Photos accompanied by signed releases are of interest.

EXPECTING, 52 Vanderbilt Ave., New York NY 10017. Editor: Mrs. Maja Bernath. Managing Editor: Evelyn Podsiadlo. Issued quarterly for expectant mothers. Buys all rights. Pays on acceptance. Reports in 2 to 4 weeks after receipt of ms. Enclose S.A.S.E.
Nonfiction: Prenatal development, layette and nursery planning, budgeting, diet, health, fashions, husband-wife relationships, naming the baby, minor discomforts, childbirth, expectant fathers, working while pregnant, etc. Length: 800 to 1,600 words. Pays $50 to $125 for feature articles, somewhat more for specialists.
Fillers: Short humor and interesting or unusual happenings during pregnancy or at the hospital; maximum 100 words, $10 on publication; submissions to "Happenings" are not returned. Other fillers pay up to $40.

HOME LIFE, 127 Ninth Ave., N., Nashville TN 37234. Phone: 615-254-5461. For Christian families. Issued monthly. Buys all rights or North American serial rights. Pays on acceptance. Will send sample copy to writer on request. Write for copy of guidelines for writers. Reports within 30 days. Enclose S.A.S.E.
Nonfiction: "Articles must have a theoretical approach to family problems; experience and human insight into family life subjects. We need material addressed to parents on the growth of children — emotional, intellectual, spiritual, physical. Also human interest content on the family development tasks — marriage, first child, growing children, children leaving home, empty nest. We emphasize strongly personal

experience/human interest approach." Length: 750 to 2,000 words. Pays 2½¢ a word.
Fiction: Short stories of interest to parent and family groups, written from a Christian viewpoint. Length: up to 2,000 words. Pays 2½¢ per word.
Poetry: Inspirational or family slant. 8 to 12 lines. Pays $2.50 minimum.
How To Break In: "We much prefer that a writer write about the area in which he is an expert: himself and his family. Readers much prefer to learn through the vicarious experience. We believe most readers learn through the family experience of other people." One of the keys to *Home Life*'s success is its unique editorial philosophy. Rather than editorializing or philosophizing about family life needs, *Home Life* prefers to let people who have experienced these needs tell their own stories. People like to read about other people and the real-life joys and needs which they have experienced in their own families. The "I" dimension is what *Home Life* strives for.

MOTHER'S MANUAL, 176 Cleveland Drive, Croton-on-Hudson NY 10520. Editor: Beth Waterfall. Bimonthly. Buys all rights unless otherwise specified. Will send sample copy to a writer for 50¢. Payment on publication. Christmas issue deadline: June 1; Summer deadline: Jan. 1; Fall deadline: March 1. Reports on submissions in 6 weeks. Enclose S.A.S.E.
Nonfiction: Articles of broad interest to pregnant women, new mothers and mothers of children through age 6. Always interested in new research going on medically or in the fields of education, child psychology and child behavior in articles written by authorities; well-written articles by mothers who have something to say about family life, child rearing, working mothers, the role of the father. Authoritative material in this field or work where research has been done. Not interested in first-person experiences on childbirth or stories that should be written by authorities in special fields and are not. Read the magazine first. Buys informational articles, how-to's, personal experience articles, interviews and think pieces. Length: 250 to 2,000 words. Pays $200 maximum.

PARENTS' MAGAZINE, 52 Vanderbilt Ave., New York NY 10017. Editor: Genevieve Millet Landau. Special issues: September (Education); November (Health). Monthly. Circulation: 2,150,000. Usually buys all rights; sometimes buys North American serial rights only. Pays on acceptance. Will send free sample copy to a writer on request. Reports on submission in 3 weeks. Query first; enclose outline and sample opening. Enclose S.A.S.E.
Nonfiction: "We are interested in well-documented articles on the problems and success of preschool, school-age, and adolescent children — and their parents; good, practical guides to the routines of baby care; articles which offer professional insights into family and marriage relationships; reports of new trends and significant research findings in education and in mental and physical health; articles encouraging informed citizen action on matters of social concern. We prefer a warm, colloquial style of writing, one which avoids the extremes of either slanginess or technical jargon. Anecdotes and examples should be used to illustrate points which can then be summed up by straight exposition." Length: up to 2,500 words. Payment varies, starting from a base of $250.
Fillers: Anecdotes for "Family Clinic," illustrative of parental problem solving with children and teenagers. Pays $10.

YOUR BABY (service section of *Modern Romances* magazine), *Modern Romances*, 1 Dag Hammarskjold Plaza, New York NY 10017. Buys all rights. Pays on acceptance. Reports in 1 month. Enclose S.A.S.E.
Nonfiction: Uses warmly written, genuinely helpful articles of interest to mothers of children from birth to three years of age, dealing authoritatively with pregnancy problems, child health, child care and training. Should open with an illustrative incident. Editors recommend you study this market before trying to write for it. Length: about 1,000 words. Pays $100. Submissions should be addressed to Service Director, *Modern Romances*. "We continuously receive letters addressed to Your Baby. There is no magazine called Your Baby. This is simply a department within *Modern Romances* magazine."

College, University, and Alumni

The following publications are intended for students, graduates, and friends of the institution. Publications for college students in general are found in the Teen and Young Adult category.

ALCALDE, P.O. Box 7278, Austin TX 78712. Editor: Jack Maguire. The University of Texas at Austin Alumni Magazine for ex-students from the University of Texas with interests in travel, arts, theatre, sports, education; any aspect of life. Magazine; 48 to 56 pages. Established in 1913. Every 2 months. Circulation: 27,000. Not copyrighted. Buys 10 to 15 mss a year. Pays on acceptance. Will consider photocopied submissions. No simultaneous submissions. Reports on material accepted for publication in time to meet their deadline. Returns rejected material immediately. Query first. Enclose S.A.S.E.

Nonfiction and Photos: Articles must be connected with the University of Texas in some way and feature its interests, purposes, history, etc. Informational, personal experience, interview, profile, humor, historical, nostalgia, photo, travel. Length: 500 to 2,000 words; 1,000 words preferred. Pays 4¢ a word. Additional payment for 8x10 b&w glossies used with ms if requested in advance. Captions optional.

THE ALUMNI JOURNAL, 1832 Michigan Ave., Los Angeles CA 90033. Phone: 213-262-2173. Editor: Audrey du Chemin. For graduates of Loma Linda University School of Medicine, medical colleagues, medical students, families of graduates, etc. All medically oriented readers. Magazine published every 2 months; 40 to 44 (8½x11) pages. Established in 1931. Circulation: 5,000. Not copyrighted. Buys 2 or 3 mss a year. Payment on publication. Will send free sample copy to writer on request. Submit special material 3 months in advance of issue date. Special issues include Convention issue, January and February; Mission issue, July and August; Directory issue, November. Query first. Returns rejected material in 1 month. Enclose S.A.S.E.

Nonfiction and Photos: Buys primarily news and features about alumni, the Alumni Association and the school. A few features on medical projects, research, history, particularly in which alumni or faculty of LLU are or were involved." Length: 1,000 to 3,000 words. Pays $10 to $50. Buys b&w glossy photos with accompanying mss. Captions required. No additional payment for photos.

How To Break In: "We do like a query first, and nonfiction should be news and features about alumni. Of special interest are articles about alumni doing interesting research in other countries. For example, we recently published articles about medical work in Western Africa and Afghanistan. These were of special interest to our readers, and quite informative, well-researched."

Comic Book Publications

GOLD KEY COMICS, 850 Third Ave., New York NY 10022. Editor: Wallace I. Green. For children, ages 6 to 15. "Most titles are issued every 2 months or quarterly." Circulation: 150,000 to 250,000. Buys all rights. Payment on acceptance. Enclose S.A.S.E.

Comics: "Our main product is comic books; 65 titles. We publish our own animated and adventure titles as well as licensed animated and adventure properties; e.g., Bugs Bunny, Heckle and Jeckle. I would prefer that potential authors *do not write us just to inquire* as to whether or not we are interested and what kind of material to submit. I suggest the following procedure: Buy copies of our various comics, particularly those you think you can write. If you don't know which ones suit you, you can determine that after reading them. Become familiar with the characters and the kinds of stories we use in particular titles. Write a number of story synopses (keep them brief, please) aimed for particular publications. At the same time, let us know whether you have had any experience writing comics so we'll know how much instruction to give you about the form to follow when writing a script. This last applies only if we like the synopses. We prefer to deal personally with authors, rather than through the mails. But I'd rather anyone who is interested send in his first synopses. We can meet personally later if it seems worthwhile. Our manuscript rate is $10 per page (mss are written page for page with the printed comic). Since we have several writers who produce stories on a more or less regular basis, I do not want to sound overly encouraging. But ours is not a closed shop. There's always room for someone with original and imaginative ideas who can turn them into sound, workable scripts."

MARVEL COMICS GROUP, *Crazy Magazine,* 575 Madison Ave., New York NY 10022. Editor: Marvin Wolfman. For ages 12 to 18 and over. Also college oriented to a minor degree. Interests are varied. Humor magazine (52 pages) published 7 times a year. Established in 1973. Buys all rights. Payment on acceptance. Query first or submit complete ms. Prefers outline first, along with samples of past work. Enclose S.A.S.E.
Fiction: "Satires, short comedy illustrated stories. Parody of TV/movies/books/magazines. Satirical look at what is happening today to be done in illustrated style. Submit outline of idea, and samples of past work. Attempt at more current material. Not typical article like *Crazy* looks at diseases. Far too many writers use the same themes *Mad* uses. Anything that could appear in *Mad* is not what we want." Experimental fiction. Recently published "Kaspar, the Dead Baby," and "Hot-Rods to the Gods." Length: 2 to 6 pages of script. Pays $25 minimum per page.

If this is 1977, this edition is out of date. See address in front of book to order latest edition. *Writer's Market* is published annually each fall.

Confession Publications

Marketing Tip: Confession magazines may use psychic phenomena and supernatural stories, even though some use them very rarely. These stories should not be in the realm of fantasy; they must be plausible. Male-narrator or humorous stories might be another type they'll consider. Suspense crime yarns are always well received if the confessional tone is preserved. Courtroom stories and mental health problems are usually sure sales. It might be wise to query the confession editor first about these out-of-the ordinary stories.

BRONZE THRILLS, 1220 Harding St., Ft. Worth TX 76102. Editor: Mrs. Edna K. Turner. Monthly magazine; 96 pages. Established in 1957. Circulation: 80,000. Buys all rights. Buys 60 mss a year. Payment on acceptance. Will send free sample copy to writer on request. Write for copy of guidelines for writers. Reports in 90 days. Submit complete ms. Enclose S.A.S.E.
Fiction: All material must relate to blacks. Romance or confession; black-oriented. Particularly interested in occult themes or those concerned with UFO's or mental illness. Does not want to see anything dealing with pregnancy, venereal disease, virginal girls getting pregnant after "first mistake" or old woman/young man love affairs unless the story has an unusual angle. Length: 4,000 to 6,000 words. Pays $30.
Photos: B&w and color photos are purchased on assignment. 8x10 b&w glossies. 2¼x2¼ or 4x5 color transparencies. Pays $35 for b&w; $50 for color.

COMPLETE WOMEN'S GROUP: MY ROMANCE, INTIMATE SECRETS, INTIMATE ROMANCES, TRUE SECRETS, SECRET STORY, MY CONFESSION, Magazine Management, 575 Madison Ave., New York NY 10022. Editorial Director: Cara Sherman. For "women between the ages of 16 and 30." Eight times a year, except for *True Secrets* and *My Romance*, which are monthly, and *Intimate Secrets* and *Intimate Romances*, which are bimonthly. Circulation: 170,000 average per issue. Buys all rights. Buys about 150 mss a year. Payment on acceptance. Will send editorial guidelines sheet to a writer on request. Submissions addressed to individual publications in this listing will be considered by all of the publications in this group. Reports in 4 to 6 weeks. Enclose S.A.S.E.
Nonfiction: "Though we do not purchase much nonfiction, if the subject is of interest, relevance, and handled appropriately for our readership, we will consider nonfiction for publication." Length: 3,000 to 5,000 words. Pays $125 to $150.
Fiction: "We look for tender love stories, touching baby stories, and stories dealing with identifiable marital problems, particularly sexual. We are interested in realistic teen stories, male-narrated stories, and tales with supernatural overtones. Stories should be written in the first person, preferably female. They should deal with a romantic or emotional problem that is identifiable and realistically portrays how the narrator copes with her conflict and resolves it. Using a conversational tone, the story is an open, honest confession of her distress, how it affects those close to her, how she works it out. We reject stories based on hackneyed themes and outdated attitudes. In our contemporary society, stories condemning premarital sexual experience, abortion, those that preach chastity, etc., are unsuitable for our needs." Length: 1,500 to 6,000 words. Pays $75 to $150.

INTIMATE STORY, 575 Madison Ave., New York NY 10022. Phone: 212-759-9704. Editor: Jane Bernstein. Fair-dealing editor. For women, ages 12 to 50, mostly in rural or suburban areas. Monthly magazine, 90 pages. Circulation: 170,000. Buys all rights. Buys 120 mss per year. Payment on acceptance. Reports in 5 weeks. Submit only complete ms. Enclose S.A.S.E.

Fiction: "I always need good confession stories written from either a male or female point of view. Themes of interest include most any social or sexual situation. The characters in the story should be believable and the plot must be developed fully and resolved in a satisfying manner. I look for warmth, honesty and originality." Length: 1,500 to 7,000 words. Pays 3¢ a word to maximum of $180 per story.

How To Break In: "Too often writers submit stories that are too much 'idea' and too little emotion. Stories must be sincere, well-plotted and resolved in a satisfying manner, or they will be quickly rejected."

LOPEZ ROMANCE GROUP: UNCENSORED CONFESSIONS, REAL ROMANCES, REAL STORY, 21 W. 26th St., New York NY 10010. Phone: 212-689-3933. Editor: Ardis Sandel. Monthly magazines. Reports on submissions in 4 to 6 weeks; sometimes slower. Buys all rights. Buys about 600 mss a year. Payment on publication. Submissions addressed to individual publications in this listing will be considered by all of the publications. Enclose S.A.S.E.

Nonfiction: Articles dealing with sexual problems of interest to both married women and single girls. Length: up to 2,000 words. Pays up to $75.

Fiction: First-person confession stories; no racial stories. "Stories must be sexy, fresh, realistic, well-plotted, with good characterization and convincing motivation. Sexy passages and dialogue are okay. Need teen-age, courtship, and young-married stories." The editor reports the problem with most beginners' mss here is that the subject matter is too usual, without a different twist or angle to make the story usable. Lengths from short-shorts up to 7,500 words. Pays up to $150 depending on length.

MODERN ROMANCES, 1 Dag Hammarskjold Plaza, New York NY 10017. Editor: Rita Brenig. For blue collar class women. Monthly. Buys all rights. Payment on acceptance. Reports on submissions within 6 weeks. Rejects are accompanied by individual critiques designed to help writers in preparing future submissions. Although only a few lines in length, these point out the basic flaw or flaws of the story. The critiques often help writers revise a reject into a salable ms. Enclose S.A.S.E.

Fiction: "First-person confession stories. Feminine narrator preferred, but masculine not taboo; in either case, narrator should belong to the working class and be someone a reader will like and root for. Narrator should also be believable, memorable, and someone reader can identify with. We like stories to have strong conflicts, good dialogue, and dramatic tension. A sense of reality is important. Write about what's happening right now." Length: 7,000 words maximum. Pays 5¢ a word.

How To Break In: "Read several issues of *Modern Romances*. Perhaps you might start to plan your story by thinking of real people, real situations, and backgrounds you are familiar with. Add (or change or omit) the appropriate character traits, plot twists, details, etc., so the story becomes sharp and clear, dramatic, warm. Use a maximum of dialogue and action, and a minimum of passive narration. Avoid flashbacks."

PERSONAL ROMANCES, 575 Madison Ave., New York NY 10022. Editor: Johanna Roman Smith. Monthly. Buys all rights. Pays on acceptance. Reports on submissions in 4 to 6 weeks. Enclose S.A.S.E.

Fiction: First-person stories told in strong up-to-date terms by young marrieds, singles, and teens revealing their emotional, sexual, and family conflicts and their search to resolve personal problems. Blue collar, white collar group identification. Length: 2,000 to 6,000 words. Top pay is up to $175. "However, payment is also based on merit as well as length; therefore we sometimes pay more for a short piece."

REAL CONFESSIONS, MODERN LOVE CONFESSIONS, MY DIARY, STARTLING CONFESSIONS, Sterling Library Inc., 261 Fifth Ave., New York NY 10016. For female readers. Monthly. Submissions addressed to individual publications in this listing will be considered by both magazines. Established in 1957 and 1962. Circulation: 300,000. Buys all rights. Buys 200 mss per year. Payment on acceptance. Will send sample copy to writer for 25c, to cover cost of handling. Write for copy of guidelines for writers. Will not consider photocopied or simultaneous submissions. Submit seasonal material 5 months in advance. Reports within 8 weeks. Submit only complete ms. Enclose S.A.S.E.

Fiction: "First-person stories only, usually by female narrators, revolving around some romantic theme or an especially interesting human relationship. Almost any aspect of human experience, can be acceptable. We urge anyone who would write for us to study our publications carefully to understand our accustomed style. We require stories with action-packed plots, lots of dialogue, very simple language, very colloquial style. Prefer a likeable narrator who shapes her own destiny, resolves her conflicts and grows emotionally, by the time the story ends. Plots must be realistic, believable, and backgrounds should be authentic. Prefer an upbeat ending. We get too many stories about drunken parents, auto accidents, adulterous situations, lecherous stepfathers, husbands unmasked as homosexuals, to name a few recurring plots. We prefer not to see predictable plots. Suspense helps sell a story. The obvious 'decent good guy' versus 'dashing bad boy' plots are overdone. We prefer timely, fresh ideas or universal ideas with a new twist. Length: 4,000 to 8,000 words; or 1,000 to 3,000 for shorts. We pay in the area of 3¢ a word. We do not think in terms of minimum or maximum."

Photos: Cover material only. Women and girls. Photo Editor: David Esbin.

Consumer Service and Business Opportunity Publications

Magazines in this classification are edited for individuals who don't necessarily have a lot of money, but who want maximum return on what they do have—either in goods purchased or in earnings from investment in a small business of their own. Publications for business executives are listed under Business and Finance. Those on how to run specific businesses are classified in Trade, Technical, and Professional Journals.

BUYWAYS, 1000 Sunset Ridge Rd., Northbrook IL 60062. Editor: Anne Springhorn. For members of NACT, Inc.; National Association of Consumers and Travelers, United Farmers Association, United Builders Association, and American Small Business Association. Association members are middle income, high school graduates. They joined their association to save money on a variety of products (for example, new cars, pharmaceuticals, motels, group travel, car rental, appliances, etc.). Quarterly magazine; 32 (8½x11) pages. Established in 1972. Circulation: 126,000. Buys first North American serial rights. Buys 12 to 16 mss a year. Payment on acceptance. Will send free sample copy to writer on request. Will consider photocopied and simultaneous submissions. Query first. Reports in 3 weeks. Enclose S.A.S.E.

Nonfiction and Photos: "Consumer-oriented articles on how to save, how to buy wisely (money and management); travel articles (domestic and foreign). Emphasis on wise buying for home and travel. Looking for well-researched articles. We prefer third-person to first-person articles. We like articles on regionalized weekend travel, recommended restaurants on regional or specialty basis." Informational, how-to, personal experience, interview, profile, humor, historical, photo, travel, successful business operations, and new product articles. Length: 500 to 2,500 words. Pays 10¢ to 20¢ per word. Color transparencies purchased with or without ms, or on assignment. Captions optional. Payment depends on size and use.

How To Break In: "Query first. Send samples of published work. We prefer xerox copies for our files."

THE CONSUMER GAZETTE, 466 Lexington Ave., New York NY 10017. Editor: Bill Wolf. For homemakers. Established in 1973. Every 2 months. Circulation:

1,000,000. Rights purchased vary with author and material. May buy all rights; but will sometimes reassign rights to author after publication; or first serial rights. Buys 20 to 30 mss a year. Will send sample copy to writer for $1. Will consider photocopied submissions. Submit seasonal material 4 months in advance. Reports in 3 weeks. Submit complete ms. Enclose S.A.S.E.

Nonfiction and Photos: Articles on consumerism: how to get the most for your money, quality information such as *Family Circle*-type features. How to avoid gyps and frauds. Exposes of kinds of fraudulent operations. Informational and personal experience or consumerism trends in particular areas. Prefers articles that revolve around seasons; for example, toys for the Christmas issue; travel for sharp consumers; home economics money savers; making things; fashion. Length: usually 800 to 1,500 words average. Pays up to $200. Buys b&w photos with or without mss. Captions required. Pays minimum of $15 for separate photo purchases.

How To Break In: "One way for the new writer to break in is with an expertise in some field that can provide us with a good how-to article. Tips on beauty and fashion from the point of view of something that looks expensive but isn't. Or, 20 ways to save money redoing your house. Something that works for you and is new in some way. We find that the list approach — 20 methods of, 75 ways to — is the most effective, especially for new writers. If you can do good photographic work, that's a real plus, as we prefer illustrated how-to's and the written material can be short. Another angle might be personal experience with consumer fraud, particularly something with general educational value. We are also looking for more recipe-oriented articles (you might try a regional approach here), material on travel and leisure, education, insurance, banking. One way for the older writer to break in would be to send us a piece on what he learned from living through the last depression, how that has paid off today."

CONSUMER REPORTS, 256 Washington St., Mt. Vernon NY 10550. Editor: Irwin Landau. Staff-written.

CONSUMERS DIGEST, 6316 N. Lincoln, Chicago IL 60659. Editor: Arthur Darack. For high school and college educated do-it-yourselfers. Magazine, published every 2 months; 32 (8½x11) pages. Established in 1958. Circulation: 275,000. Buys all rights. Buys 15 to 20 mss a year. Payment on acceptance. Will send sample copy to writer for 50¢. Query first. Enclose S.A.S.E.

Nonfiction: Material on investments, self help, products and services, health and food, best buys, analysis of cars, appliances, etc. Also how-to's on car, appliance and house repair. Approach is systematic with mass appeal. Not interested in exposes, but will consider material on successful business operations and merchandising techniques and for legal and medical columns. Article length: 1,000 words minimum. Column length: 3,000 words. Pays 5¢ a word.

CONSUMERS' RESEARCH MAGAZINE, Washington NJ 07882. Editor: F.J. Schlink. Monthly. Copyrighted. Limited amount of freelance material used. Query first. Enclose S.A.S.E.

Nonfiction and Photos: Articles of practical interest to ultimate consumers concerned with tests and expert judgment of goods and services which they buy. Must be accurate and careful statements, well-supported by chemical, engineering, scientific, medical, or other expert or professional knowledge of subject. Pays approximately 2¢ per word. Buys b&w glossies with mss only. Pays $5 minimum. "Photos are accepted only if they are clearly relevant to the article being published."

COST-CUTTING FOR BUSINESS, 200-04 58th Ave., Bayside NY 11364. Editor: Jim Atkins. For businessmen who have 50 or fewer employees. Newsletter. Established in 1974. Every 2 weeks. Circulation: 3,000. Buys first North American serial rights. Buys 100 mss a year. Pays on acceptance. Will send free sample copy to writer on request. Write for copy of guidelines for writers. Reports on material accepted for publication in 3 weeks. Returns rejected material in 1 week. Submit complete ms. Enclose S.A.S.E.

Nonfiction: Material of interest to the small businessman (recordkeeping, shoplifting, etc.). Material must be simple. Writer must understand trade publications and their purpose. Length: 100 to 200 words. Pays $10 to $40.

FDA CONSUMER, 5600 Fishers Lane, Rockville MD 20852. Editor: Ellis Rottman. For "all consumers of products regulated by the Food and Drug Administration." A Federal Government publication. Magazine, 40 pages. Established in 1967. Monthly. December/January and July/August issues combined. Circulation: 20,000. Not copyrighted. "All purchases automatically become part of public domain." Buys 4 to 5 freelance mss a year, by contract only. Payment on publication. "Actual payment processed by General Services Administration acting upon notice by editor that terms of contract have been fulfilled." Query first. "We cannot be responsible for any work by writer not agreed upon by prior contract." Enclose S.A.S.E.

Nonfiction and Photos: "Articles of an educational nature concerning purchase and use of FDA regulated products and specific FDA programs and actions to protect the consumer's health and pocketbook. Authoritative and official agency viewpoints emanating from agency policy and actions in administrating the Food, Drug and Cosmetic Act and a number of other statutes. All articles subject to clearance by the appropriate FDA experts as well as the editor. The magazine speaks for the Federal Government only. Articles based on facts and FDA policy only. We cannot consider any unsolicited material. All articles based on prior arrangement by contract. The nature and subject matter and clearances required are so exacting that it is difficult to get an article produced by a writer working outside the Washington DC metropolitan area." Length: average, 2,000 words. Pays $500. B&w photos are purchased on assignment only.

INCOME OPPORTUNITIES, 229 Park Ave., South, New York NY 10003. Editor: Joseph V. Daffron. Managing Editor: Edward Galligan. For all who are seeking business opportunities, full- or part-time. Monthly magazine; (8½x11). Established in 1956. Buys all rights. Buys 100 mss per year. Will send sample copy to writer for $1. Will not consider photocopied or simultaneous submissions. Two special directory issues contain articles on selling techniques, mail order, import/export, franchising and business ideas. Reports in 2 weeks. Query first. Enclose S.A.S.E.

Nonfiction and Photos: Regularly covered are such subjects as mail order, direct selling, franchising, party plans, selling techniques and the marketing of handcrafted or homecrafted products. Wanted are ideas for the aspiring entrepeneur; examples of successful business methods that might be duplicated. No material that is purely inspirational. "Payment rates vary according to length and quality of the submission from a minimum of $50 for a short of a maximum of 800 words, to $200 for a major article of 2,000 to 3,000 words. Illustrations are considered part of the manuscript purchase."

How To Break In: "Study recent issues of the magazine. Best bets for newcomers: Interview-based report on a successful small business venture."

MEDIA & CONSUMER, P.O. Box 850, Norwalk CT 06852. Phone: 203-972-0441. Editor: Francis Pollock. For consumer writers and editors, print and broadcast; advertising, marketing, public relations and business leaders; consumer-affairs officials in government; educators and students; and concerned consumers. Monthly newsletter. Established in 1972. Circulation: 15,000. Buys all rights. Buys 24 mss per year. Payment on publication· Will send free sample copy to writer on request. Submit seasonal material 2 months in advance. Query first. Enclose S.A.S.E.

Nonfiction and Photos: "Reprints of outstanding consumer stories and commentary. Original investigative articles on consumer affairs coverage and the pressures interfering with such coverage. Seeing one or two issues should best convey our approach. Last year, we called ourselves a journalism review, but we are now putting more emphasis on the consumer and what he can do to protect himself. Our combination of material, we believe, is unique." Informational, how-to, and expose. Length: 500 to 2,500 words. Pays $35 to $100. Photos purchased on assignment.

How To Break In: "If you have a story on the issues we're interested in—advertiser pressure, or something new in consumer activism, say—send us a query."

MONEYTREE NEWSLETTER, 417 Water St., Task Bldg., Kerrville TX 78028. Editor: Marshall Sideman. Pays on acceptance. Send large S.A.S.E. for sample copy. **Fillers:** "Items dealing with money. How to invest it, make it grow rapidly, how to get big savings—these have the best chance of acceptance. Our readers want to get rich, or if wealthy already, stay rich." Also uses capsule articles on health, self-help, vocational training, practical science, money-making opportunities, etc. Also capsulized write-ups about free publications, product samples, items of value, etc. And wants condensed summaries of consumer aids and important protective actions by FTC, FDA, Agriculture Dept., HEW, etc. All submissions must be documented by author. Length: 10 to 60 words. Payment is $5.

SMALL BUSINESS DIGEST, P.O. Box 839, Long Beach NY 11561. Editor: A. Costar. For mail order opportunity seekers. Quarterly. Circulation: 17,600. Not copyrighted. Pays on acceptance. Will send a sample copy to a writer for $1.00. Reports in 1 week. Enclose S.A.S.E.
Nonfiction: Uses articles on mail order opportunities, sources of supply, and honest ideas or plans for earning money at home, by mail, etc. Pays $1 per source of supply. For example, where to get 12% interest on your money (source), or where to get no interest loan up to $500 by mail (source).
How To Break In: "Alert writers who can ferret out tested money-making ventures which the average part-time operator has developed, will find *Small Business Digest* a ready market. The part-time project may deal with hobbies, mail-selling, or almost any worthwhile venture."

Detective and Crime Publications

Publications listed in this section provide markets for nonfiction accounts of true crimes. Markets for criminal fiction (mysteries) are listed in Mystery Publications.

CONFIDENTIAL DETECTIVE, CRIME DETECTIVE CASES, 235 Park Avenue, South, New York NY 10003. Editor: B.R. Ampolsk. Bimonthly. Buys all rights. Pays on acceptance. Query preferred. Enclose S.A.S.E.
Nonfiction and Photos: True crime stories. Material must be documented with newsclips. Length: 2,500 to 5,000 words. Pays up to $125 per story. Photos purchased with mss or captions only. Pays up to $15 each.

DETECTIVE FILES GROUP: DETECTIVE FILES, HEADQUARTERS DETECTIVE, DETECTIVE CASES, DETECTIVE DRAGNET, Globe Communications Corp., 1440 St. Catherine St. W., Montreal 107, Quebec, Canada. Editor: Dominick Merle. Monthly. Buys first North American rights. Enclose S.A.E. and International Reply Coupons.
Nonfiction and Photos: "We're looking for current, sensational crimes detailing police investigation and culminating in an arrest. Rarely use anything short of murder. No open-and-shut cases; no unsolved crimes. Main market is U.S. Send either queries or completed mss and photos. There is steady income here for those who deliver." Length: 2,500 to 5,000 words. Pays $100 to $200.

FRONT PAGE DETECTIVE, INSIDE DETECTIVE, 1 Dag Hammarskjold Plaza, New York NY 10017. Editor: James W. Bowser. Monthly. Buys North American serial rights only. Pays on acceptance. Will consider photocopied submissions. Reports on submissions in 10 days. Query first. Enclose S.A.S.E.
Nonfiction: Articles on current crime; must have plenty of drama, action, good police deduction. Lengths: 3,500 to 4,500 words. Pays $200 to $300. Prefers query; however, if querying on current crime, be prepared to deliver ms fast. Good available photos can help sell a ms. Murder stories with photos (who did what to whom and when, and how good the investigation was). Short pieces on some new trend in law enforcement or a new type of crime.

Photos: Purchased with mss or with captions only. Must have crime theme. 8x10 or 5x7 glossies preferred. No color. Pays $10 to $20 for singles; $100 to $125 for photo series. Requires model releases if posed.

MASTER DETECTIVE, 235 Park Avenue South, New York NY 10003. Editor: Albert P. Govoni. For crime buffs, armchair detectives. Established in 1929. Monthly. Circulation: 125,000. Buys all rights. Buys about 125 mss a year. Payment on acceptance. Will send a sample copy to a writer for 50¢. Will send editorial guidelines sheet to a writer on request. Query first required; "we will guide." Reports in 1 week. Enclose S.A.S.E.

Nonfiction and Photos: Subject matter is "crime only. No shorts." Length: 5,000 to 6,000 words. Pays a flat $200. Address to Managing Editor. Photos purchased with or without mss. Wants quality and drama in 8x10 b&w glossies. Pays $12.50.

How To Break In: "This is not a market for the amateur. We buy short pieces only rarely. Most shorts which appear in the magazine are staff-written. We are always interested in competent new writers, but we prefer them to be experienced newspapermen who have a basic understanding of the legal problems inherent in our material, and how to cope with same in their copy. Ideally, the new writer should be a reporter or desk man who has worked on the local case he's trying to sell us, a man with established contacts and rapport with the law enforcement people involved. How does he sell us his first story? A query is a must, and it should be brief but comprehensive and explicit, incorporating these points: locale of crime, date, names of victim and suspect, current status of case (has suspect been indicted, bound over for trial, trial date set or pending), amount of detective work required for solution of case; also we want to know about the art situation: are photos available, and how many? Writer should enclose his phone number. If we're interested, we'll very likely call him and discuss his story, suggesting guidelines for treatment. We are always ready to work hard to develop a promising writer, and many of our most reliable veterans began with us exactly as outlined above. Some have gone on to write several books."

OFFICIAL DETECTIVE STORIES, 235 Park Avenue South, New York NY 10003. Editor: A. P. Govoni. Monthly. Buys all rights. Pays on acceptance. Query mandatory. Reports in one week. Enclose S.A.S.E.

Nonfiction and Photos: True, current stories of crime detection. Length: 5,000 to 6,000 words. Study magazine to see exactly what is wanted. Pays $200. Photos purchased to illustrate stories. Prefers 8x10 glossies, professionally finished. Needs complete caption information and identification for all photos. Pays $12.50 per print used.

STARTLING DETECTIVE, TRUE POLICE CASES, 1440 St. Catherine St. West, Montreal, Que., Canada. Editor: Dominick A. Merle. Bimonthly. Buys all rights. Pays on acceptance. Reports in one week. Enclose S.A.E. and International Reply Coupons for return of submissions.

Nonfiction: "We are constantly in need of current crime cases; we seek those accounts which cover the very latest murder, kidnapping, bank robbery, etc. We find that the best approach in the writing of fact-detective stories is the unfolding of the action in chronological sequence: the finding of the body, the arrival of the police at the scene, their search for clues, the questioning of witnesses, the running down of suspects—and ending with some clever deduction which leads to the apprehension of the chief suspect. The best stories are those in which the culprit's identity is not known to the police for more than 24 hours; this allows for the running down of false clues and suspects. When the killer's identity is known immediately, there is, of course, no possibility for suspense, mystery or detective work. These are what we call 'open-and-shut' cases and should be avoided. We do not seek straight articles on crime subjects." Send query or completed ms and photos. Length: 3,000 to 7,000 words. Pays $100 to $200; more for "blockbusters."

How To Break In: "First, read a few issues of the magazines to become familiar with the style. Second, when you spot a mysterious murder in your area, clip all newspaper accounts, talk to detectives after an arrest is made, to gather more details;

talk to anyone else who might have some information to offer. Third, query me about the story or write it on speculation. Stay away from unsolved cases or 'oldies'. I'm also more receptive to cases which have not attracted national exposure. I'm constantly seeking more stories and new writers."

TRUE DETECTIVE, 235 Park Avenue South, New York NY 10003. Editor: A.P. Govoni. Managing Editor: Walter Jackson. Monthly for armchair detectives, both male and female. Will send sample copy for 50¢. Reports in one week. Buys all rights. Pays on acceptance. No fiction or poetry. Query mandatory. Enclose S.A.S.E.
Nonfiction: Accurate, timely stories of true crimes, preferably murder, with photos of principals, etc. Must be written with strong characterization, motivation, detective work, suspense. Published upon indictment, also stories after trial. Police image must be good. Length: 5,000 to 6,000 words. Pays $200.

Education Publications

Magazines in these listings approach the subject of education with the interests of parents and the general public in mind. Journals for professional educators and teachers are included under Education in the Trade Journals section.

AMERICAN EDUCATION, U.S. Office of Education, 400 Maryland Ave., S.W., Washington DC 20202. Phone: 202-245-8907. Editor: Leroy V. Goodman. For educators and lay readers with a special interest in the field of education. Monthly except combined January-February, August-September issues. Not copyrighted. Payment on acceptance. Query before submitting material. Reports in 2 weeks. Enclose S.A.S.E.
Nonfiction: "Articles that describe specific federally supported programs and projects of proven effectiveness and include helpful information on how they may serve as models for other schools or school districts." Brisk, bright writing desired; full of facts, people, and anecdotes. Length: 2,500 words average. Payment varies with circumstances; average is $300.

AMERICAN TEACHER, 1012 14th St., Washington DC 20005. Editor: Dave Elsila. For "members of the American Federation of Teachers, AFL-CIO, and other classroom teachers." Monthly except July and August. Buys first North American serial rights; will buy simultaneous rights. Pays on publication. Will send a sample copy to a writer on request. Prefers query first. Reports in 4 months. Enclose S.A.S.E.
Nonfiction and Photos: "We want material directly concerned with our primary interests: educational innovation, academic freedom, the teacher union movement, better schools and educational methods, legislation concerning teachers, etc. Pays $25 to $70. Photos purchased with and without mss; captions required. "Stock photos of classroom scenes." Subjects must be in range of subject interest. No specific size. Pays $15.

CHANGE MAGAZINE, NBW Tower, New Rochelle NY 10801. Phone: 914-235-8700. Editor: George W. Bonham. For college faculty and administrators as well as others interested in higher education. Monthly. Circulation: 30,000. Buys all rights. Buys about 150 mss a year. Pays on publication. Will send sample copy to writer on request. Reports in 1 month. Query first. "It's best to send some writing samples with all queries." Enclose S.A.S.E.
Nonfiction: As the leading magazine of higher education, *Change* seeks writers who can produce lively, timely articles on problems, movements, institutions, and people in the world of higher education. *Change* is not a scholarly journal and relies on journalists rather than academics for much of its material. New writers are welcome. Length: 2,000 to 5,000 words. Pays $100 to $350 for major articles.
How To Break In: "Most of the unsolicited material we accept is for the Viewpoint section — opinion pieces of about 1,000 words. Another good section to aim for

is Reports, of which there are four each issue. They are almost invariably handled by freelancers and journalists, not by professional educators. The Reports can be best described as newsbriefs which have been expanded to 1,500 or 2,000 words and cover almost any area of education from a new program at a major university to developments in the textbook industry. Material for either of these sections would be a good introduction for the new writer. We do have trouble getting material on community colleges, so that may be a particularly good area to break in. However, we expect to see some research on general trends and not just what is happening at one school. In our Practically Speaking section we are short on good new ideas for things like 'The Best Way to Finance Your Sabbatical' or 'How to Start a Food Co-op.' We also have a Dialogue column each month for which there is no pay. Check the previous issue for the subject to be covered."

DAY CARE AND EARLY EDUCATION, 72 Fifth Ave., New York NY 10011. Editor: Joseph Michalak. For those interested in early childhood education, concerned parents, those administrators and businessmen involved in day care. Magazine published 5 times a year. 48 to 64 pages. Established in 1973. Circulation: 12,000. Rights purchased vary with author and material. Buys all rights, but will sometimes reassign rights to author after publication; buys first North American serial rights, first serial rights, second serial (reprint) rights, simultaneous rights. Buys 35 mss a year. Payment on publication. Submit seasonal material 4 months in advance. Query first. Reports in 2 months. Enclose S.A.S.E.
Nonfiction and Photos: "Articles dealing with early childhood education, day care funding, materials and services, etc. Practical orientation, emphasizing how to overcome obstacles in day care services, also tips for teachers, new ideas for preschool classrooms, unusual and inventive ideas in the field. Write with sprightly style, nontechnical language, or at least technical terms defined after first usage. We appreciate inventiveness and wit." Payment usually in the area of $150 to $200 for 10-page article. Photos used with accompanying ms with no additional payment.

Food and Drink Publications

Magazines classified here aim at individuals who are interested in and appreciate fine wines and fine foods. Journals aimed at food processors, manufacturers, and retailers will be found in the Trade Journals.

BON APPETIT MAGAZINE (incorporating *Bon Voyage*), 4700 Belleview, Kansas City MO 64112. Editor: M. Frank Jones. For "men who enjoy wine, travel, gourmet restaurants, entertaining; for women who are strong on recipes, entertaining ideas, menus, new products, etc." Magazine published every 2 months; 72 (8½x11¼) pages. Established in 1949. Circulation: 450,000. Rights purchased vary with author and material. May buy all rights; but will sometimes reassign rights to author after publication; or first North American serial rights. Buys 6 to 12 mss a year. Payment on acceptance. Will send sample copy to writer for 70¢. Write for copy of guidelines for writers. Submit seasonal material for November-December holiday issue and September-October wine issue 3 months in advance. Reports on material accepted for publication in 60 days. Returns rejected material in 30 days if accompanied by S.A.S.E.; otherwise destroyed. Submit complete ms. Enclose S.A.S.E.
Nonfiction and Photos: Informational, how-to, historical, travel. Material for "Those Entertaining People" tells and shows how others entertain. "Tools of the Trade" gives detailed information on equipment for the kitchen or bar. "Bon Appetit on Tour" is a personalized travel feature (with photos). "Study magazine for style. Emphasis is on intelligent writing, fairly light and contemporary. Nothing too heavy or esoteric. Most wine articles are staff written. Must be expert." Length: 850 to 1,500 words. Pays 10¢ per word. Pays $10 for b&w photos used with mss; $20 to $25 for color. 35mm slides or 4½x4½ transparencies. Must be of professional quality. Captions are required. Recently published articles include "New England's Vintage

Inns," "My Search for the Perfect Moussaka," "Eating, Drinking, & Cruising on the Thames."

CHOMP, Boston's Food and Dining Magazine, 161 Elm St., Somerville MA 02144. Editor: Phil Blampied. For young professionals; people who enjoy dining out, but without pretensions. Many people on limited budgets, as say, college graduate students. Tabloid newsprint magazine; 24 pages. Established in 1974. Monthly. Circulation: 18,000. Not copyrighted. Buys about 50 mss a year. Pays on acceptance. Will send free sample copy to writer on request. Will consider photocopied and simultaneous submissions. Query first. Reports in 2 weeks. Enclose S.A.S.E.

Nonfiction and Photos: "News and feature material on food, restaurants, food-related consumer news, government involvement in food, consumer view of farming and food biz, etc. Style should be factual, but not dry. Other food and dining-out magazines are for wealthy, stuffy, well-traveled types. We don't expect our readers to eat caviar. Also, other mags are light feature and travel-oriented. We deal with news and political issues of food. Please, no restaurant reviews. Also, no mock-Calvin Trillin witty traveling gourmet stuff. We'd like to see something about the Federal Food and Drug Administration and its role in food. Any large food company and how it operates." Recently published articles include "Gulk!," choking in restaurants is a problem, but are gadgets the answer; a newsy, well-researched piece with new angle on old topic. Personal experience, interview, expose, spot news. Length: 500 to 2,500 words. Pays $15 for informational articles; $25 for how-to. Pays $10 to $25. Photos purchased with accompanying ms. Pays $10 to $15 for b&w. Photo Editor: Ken Kobre.

GOURMET, 777 Third Ave., New York NY 10017. Phone: 212-754-1500. Managing Editor: Miss Gail Zweigenthal. For moneyed, educated, traveled, food-wise men and women. Monthly. Purchases copyright, but grants book reprint rights with credit. Pays on acceptance. Suggests a study of several issues to understand type of material required. Reports within 2 months. Query first. "We prefer published writers, so if you haven't written for us before, you should enclose some samples of previous work." Enclose S.A.S.E.

Nonfiction: Uses articles on subjects related to food and wine—travel, adventure, reminiscence, fishing and hunting experiences. Prefers personal experiences to researched material. Recipes included as necessary. Not interested in nutrition, dieting, penny-saving, or bizarre foods, or in interviews with chefs or food experts, or in reports of food contests, festivals, or wine tastings. Buys recipes only as part of an article with interesting material to introduce them and make them appealing. "Gourmet Holidays" written by staff contributors only. The same is true for material including specific hotel or restaurant recommendations. Sophisticated, light, nontechnical. Length: 2,500 to 3,000 words. Current needs include American regional pieces (no restaurants) and European material. Pays $500 minimum.

Poetry and Verse: Light, sophisticated with food or drink slant. Pays $50 minimum.

How To Break In: "Personal reminiscences are the easiest way to break in, since we tend to use staff writers when recommending hotels or restaurants. Our biggest problem with freelancers is that they are not familiar with our style or that they fail to treat their material with enough sophistication or depth. We don't want pieces which sound like press releases or which simply describe what's there. We like to really cover a subject and literary value is important. We'd very much like to see more regional American material. It seems to be much easier to get people traipsing around Europe."

VINTAGE MAGAZINE, 245 E. 25th St., New York NY 10014. Editor/Publisher: Philip Seldon. For a "broad-based audience of wine drinkers, ranging from the wealthy and sophisticated expert to the novice with a desire to become interested in wine. These are middle income families and above; generally college-educated." Monthly. Circulation: 100,000. Buys all rights. Pays on publication. Will send a sample copy to a writer for $1. Submit seasonal material 2 months in advance. Reports in 3 months. Enclose S.A.S.E.

Nonfiction: "Subject matter includes features on wine mainly written by wine experts, although travel pieces and human interest stories can be written by nonexperts. All editorial material should have a wide emphasis. There is no other publication treating this subject matter in depth for the consumer. Do not send compilations from wine books. Stress gourmet interests." Length: 900 to 3,000 words. Pays $100 to $200; "more for big names."

Photos: Purchased with mss; with captions only. B&w glossies, color transparencies, 35mm color. Rate of payment "open."

Fiction: Mystery, humorous, adventure related to subject matter of *Vintage*. Length: to 2,000 words. Pays $100 to $200; "more for big names."

Poetry and Fillers: Contemporary poetry. Puzzles, jokes, short humor.

WINE NOW, 575 West End Ave., New York NY 10024. Editor: Richard Figiel. For "anyone interested enough in wine to pick up a copy of a wine magazine given out gratis in wine shops; may be novices or knowledgeable." Magazine; 32 (8½x11) pages. Established in 1972. Every 2 months. Circulation: 475,000. Not copyrighted. Buys 24 mss a year. Payment on publication. Will send free sample copy to writer on request. Write for copy of guidelines for writers. Will consider photocopied and simultaneous submissions. Reports in approximately 1 to 2 months. Query first. Enclose S.A.S.E.

Nonfiction and Photos: Articles related to wine — by variety, region, type, country, descriptions of the wines themselves and how to buy them more intelligently and economically and enjoy them more. "Also, subjects tangentially related to wine — use your imagination. Write to intelligent readers who do not necessarily have extensive knowledge and experience of wine. No 'primer' copy and no connoisseur copy. Less focus on the great and expensive wines. No home-wine-making articles. Nothing on individual wineries or wine firms." Recently published articles include "Japan's Timeless Sake" and "Try These for Openers" (aperitifs). Length: 1,000 to 2,500 words. Pays $25 to $150. Faces in Wine column uses interview/profiles of prominent winemakers; Cheesejournal column uses short material on cheese and wine. Column length: 1,000 words. Pays $25 to $50. B&w photos purchased with or without ms or on assignment. Glossies, at least 3x5. Pays $10 to $40. Pays $10 to $175 for color transparencies or quality print.

Poetry: Must relate to subject matter. Traditional forms, blank verse, free verse, avant-garde forms, light verse. Payment is flexible, but begins at $1 a line.

WINE WORLD MAGAZINE, 15101 Keswick St., Van Nuys CA 91405. Editor: Jerry Vonne. For the wine loving public (adults of all ages) who wish to learn more about wine. Magazine published every 2 months; 56 (8½x11) pages. Established in 1971. Buys first North American serial rights. Buys about 72 mss a year. Payment on publication. Will send sample copy to writer on request. Write for copy of guidelines for writers. Will not consider photocopied submissions. Will consider simultaneous submissions, "if spelled out." Reports in 30 days. Query first. Enclose S.A.S.E.

Nonfiction and Photos: "Wine-oriented material written with an in-depth knowledge of the subject, designed to meet the needs of the novice and connoisseur alike. Wine technology advancements, wine history, profiles of vintners the world over. Educational articles only. No first-person accounts. Must be objective, informative reporting on economic trends, new technological developments in vinification, vine hybridizing, and vineyard care. New wineries and new marketing trends. We restrict our editorial content to wine, and wine-oriented material. No restaurant or food articles accepted. No more basic wine information. No articles from instant wine experts. Authors must be qualified in this highly technical field." Length: 750 to 2,000 words. Pays $75 to $250. Pays $10 to $15 for 5x7 or 8x10 b&w photos used with mss; $25 to $50 for 2½x2½ or 35mm color transparencies used with mss. Captions required.

WOMEN'S CIRCLE HOME COOKING, Box 338, Chester MA 01011. Editor: Barbara Hall Pedersen. For women (and some men) of all ages who really enjoy cooking. "Our readers collect and exchange recipes. They are neither food faddists nor gourmets, but practical women and men trying to serve attractive and nutritious meals. Many work full-time, and most are on limited budgets." Magazine; 72 (5x7¼) pages. Monthly. Circulation: 160,000. Buys all rights, but will reassign rights to author after publication. Buys about 50 mss a year. Pays on publication. Will send sample copy to writer for S.A.S.E. Holiday food articles, are always welcome, especially if accompanied by photos, and should be submitted 6 months in advance. Submit complete ms. Reports in 1 to 6 weeks. Enclose S.A.S.E.

Nonfiction and Photos: "We like a little humor with our food, for the sake of the digestion. Keep articles light. Humorous personal experience pieces. Stress economy and efficiency. Remember that at least half our readers must cook after working a full-time job. Draw on personal experience to write an informative article on some aspect of cooking. We're a reader participation magazine. We don't go in for fad diets, or strange combinations of food which claim to cure anything. We'll go a little heavy on historical pieces, because of the bicentennial." Informational, how-to, inspirational, historical, expose, nostalgia, photo, and travel also considered. Length: 50 to 1,000 words. Pays 2¢ to 5¢ per word. Columns and regular features by arrangement. Photos purchased with ms or on assignment. Captions optional. 4x5 b&w, sharp, glossy. 2¼ color, but prefers 4x5. Pays $5 for b&w, $20 or more for color, by arrangement. Photo Department Editor: Karen P. Sherrer.

Fiction, Poetry, and Fillers: Humorous fiction, related to cooking and foods. Length: 1,200 words maximum. Pays 2¢ to 5¢ per word. Light verse related to cooking and foods. Length: 30 lines maximum. No payment. Short humorous fillers, 100 words maximum. Pays 2¢ to 5¢ per word.

General Interest Publications

Publications classified here are edited for national, general audiences and carry articles on any subject of interest to a broad spectrum of people. Other markets for general interest material will be found in the Black, Men's, Newspapers and Weekly Magazine Section, Regional, and Women's classifications in the Consumer section.

ACCENT, 1720 Washington Blvd., P.O. Box 2315, Ogden UT 84404. Phone: 801-393-0107 or 801-393-0802. Editor: Helen S. Crane. For "a wide segment, from the young couple to the retired one." Established in 1968. Monthly. Circulation: 350,000. Rights purchased vary with author and material. Buys 10 to 12 mss a year. Pays on acceptance. Will send a sample copy to a writer on request. Will consider photocopied submissions. Submit seasonal material at least 6 months in advance. Query first. Enclose S.A.S.E. for reply to queries and return of submissions.

Nonfiction and Photos: "The large majority of our articles are written on assignment by professional writers knowledgeable in their fields. We do, however, consider interest-capturing, short features from freelancers. Since our emphasis is on pictures, and our copy space very limited, we require concise, informative, yet lively writing that covers a lot in a few words. We want pieces of lasting general interest suitable for the family. We do not need rambling experience pieces, preachy pieces, or ecology features; nor do we want holiday material. We use a few travel vignettes about exciting yet well-known spots and pieces showing glimpses of life and unusual activities. Writing should be in a fresh, sparkling style." Pays about 5¢ per word. Photos purchased with mss; captions required. "For the most part, we prefer views without people, particularly if they tend to date the views. If people are present, they should be actively engaged in interesting ways. Subjects must be eyecatching and colors sharp." For "at least 5x7" b&w glossies, pays $10 to $15. For color transparencies ("some 35mm, prefer larger"), pays $25 minimum ("more for larger views or covers").

THE ATLANTIC MONTHLY, 8 Arlington St., Boston MA 02116. Phone: 617-536-9500. Editor-in-Chief: Robert Manning. For a professional, academic audience. Monthly. Circulation: 325,000. Buys first North American serial rights. Pays on acceptance. Will send a sample copy to a writer for $1. Reports in 2 weeks to several months. Enclose S.A.S.E. for return of submissions.

Nonfiction: "We prefer not to formulate specifications about the desired content of *The Atlantic* and suggest that would-be contributors examine back issues to form their own judgment of what is suitable." Length: 2,000 to 5,000 words. Rates vary from $100 per magazine page base rate. Author should include summary of his qualifications for treating subject.

Fiction: Short stories by unestablished writers, published as Atlantic "Firsts" are a steady feature. Two prizes of $750 and $250 are awarded to the best of these when a sufficient number of stories are published. Candidates should so label their submissions and list their previous publications, if any, as authors whose stories have appeared in magazines of national circulation are not considered eligible. Will also consider stories by established writers in lengths ranging from 2,700 to 7,500 words. Payment depends on length, but also on quality and author.

Poetry: Uses three to five poems an issue. These must be of high literary distinction in both light and serious poetry. Interested in young poets. Base rate for poetry is $2 per line.

CARTE BLANCHE MAGAZINE, Carte Blanche Corp., 3460 Wilshire Blvd., Los Angeles CA 90010. Phone: 213-381-1927. Editor: J. Walter Flynn. For "professional men and women and their families, with interests relating to our travel, dining and entertainment format." Magazine published every 2 months; 60 to 70 pages. Established in 1964. Circulation: 535,000. Buys all rights. Buys 15 to 25 mss a year. Payment on acceptance. Will send free sample copy to writer on request. Write for copy of guidelines for writers. Will consider photocopied submissions. Will not consider simultaneous submissions. Reports as soon as possible. Query first or submit complete ms. Enclose S.A.S.E.

Nonfiction and Photos: "Articles relating to our travel, dining and entertainment theme; e.g., travel articles, food features (preferably with recipes); stories on hobbies or crafts, etc. We strive for the dramatic and unusual, and we seek original approaches and good ideas. We do not want to see travel articles on places that have been 'done to death.' However, popular areas may be approached from an unusual angle." Length: 1,200 to 1,500 words. Pays approximately $100 for every 400 words. "We lean heavily on good color photos; 35mm minimum."

CHANGING TIMES, The Kiplinger Service for Families, 1729 H St., N.W., Washington DC 20006. Editor: Sidney Sulkin. For general, adult audience interested in personal finance, family money management and personal advancement. Established in 1947. Monthly. Circulation: 1,500,000. Buys all rights. Pays on acceptance. Reports in 30 days. Enclose S.A.S.E.

Items: "Original topical quips and epigrams for our monthly humor feature, 'Notes on These Changing Times.' All other material is staff-written." Pays $10. "Don't waste your postage or our time by sending article queries or manuscripts."

COMMENTARY, 165 East 56th St., New York NY 10022. Editor: Norman Podhoretz. Monthly magazine, 96 pages. Established in 1945. Circulation: 60,000. Buys all rights. "All of our material is done freelance, though much of it is commissioned." Payment on publication. Query first, or submit complete ms. Reports in 4 weeks. Enclose S.A.S.E.

Nonfiction and Fiction: Thoughtful essays on political, social, theological, and cultural themes; general, as well as with special Jewish content. Informational, historical, and think articles. Length: 3,000 to 7,000 words. Pays approximately $30 a page. Nonfiction Editor: Maier Deshell. Uses some mainstream fiction. Length: flexible. Fiction Editor: Marion Magid.

How To Break In: "We're hungry for material in every field, especially good fiction (which we don't see enough of anywhere). Of all the so-called 'highbrow' magazines, we publish more new people than almost anybody. Book reviews are a good way to start. We've found that it gives us an opportunity to assess the new writer without undertaking a major project. Book reviews should be about 1,500 words; on most subjects with obvious exceptions like gothic novels and cookbooks. Query first. If we like what we see, there will be more assignments. Also don't assume it's mostly Jewish-oriented material. That accounts for only about 15 to 20 percent of our writing in the course of a year."

CORONET, Challenge Publications, Inc., 7950 Deering Ave., Canoga Park CA 91304. Publisher: Edwin A Schnepf. Editor: Catherine Nixon Cooke. For general interest readership, focusing predominantly on personalities end entertainment. Established in 1936. Monthly magazine. Circulation: 500,000. Buys all rights. Buys 120 mss a year. Pays on publication. Query first. Enclose S.A.S.E.
Nonfiction, Photos, and Fillers: General subject matter consists of nonfiction articles on latest health discoveries, personality profiles and celebrity interviews, self-improvement and beauty, family life, news and new ideas, social problems, and travel. Length: 1,200 to 1,500 words. Pays $125 to $150 per article or 10¢ per word. Buys b&w and 35mm or 2¼ color photos. Pays $25 for b&w and $50 for color. Buys puzzles and brainteasers.

COUNTRY CLUBBER MAGAZINE, Club Publications, Inc., 3110 Maple Dr., Suite 402, Atlanta GA 30305. Publisher: Richard Williams; Editor: Martha Frances Brown. For members of country clubs in the metropolitan South, especially interested in recreation, pleasant living, travel. Monthly magazine; 50 (8½x11) pages. Established in 1972. Circulation: 27,000. Buys all rights, but will reassign rights to author after publication. Buys 60 to 100 mss a year. Payment on publication. Will send sample copy to writer for 75¢. Submit seasonal material 3 months in advance. Reports on material accepted for publication in 60 days. Returns rejected material in 3 months. Query first or submit complete ms. Enclose S.A.S.E.
Nonfiction and Photos: "We use instructional and general articles on golf, tennis, swimming, boating, fishing, good foods, gourmet cooking, travel, entertaining, gardening (slanted to the South); business (general, personalities or firms). We are a family-oriented magazine, going only to country club members. Keep in mind that golf is our primary interest, although we cover many other subjects. Travel articles should mention golf and tennis facilities, etc. We are not interested in elementary instructional articles or stories which have no tie to country club living." Recent articles include "How the Pros Can Lower Your Handicap," "Games Tennis Players Play" (what you tell about yourself by the way you play tennis), "The Doctor Doesn't Always Know Best" (IRS and medical deductions). Length: 1,000 to 2,000 words. Pays 5¢ to 7¢ per word. Payment is the same for shorter material for the Bon Appetit (cooking) column. Length: 1,000 words. Pays $5 per 5x7 b&w glossy print purchased with ms. Pays minimum of $10 for 35mm slides, or color prints or transparencies. Captions required. "We can use good golf photographs for instructional material."
Fillers: Jokes, short humor. Pays $5 minimum. Department Editor: Deborah Hardin.

FACES, Faces Publications, Box 98901, Seattle WA 98166. Editor: Cliff Hollenbeck. For an affluent audience of mixed ages, well-educated and very well-traveled. Worldwide circulation. Established in 1974. Monthly. Circulation: 500,000. Buys first and one-time rights for 6 months. Less than half of material published is freelance. Payment on publication, or within 30 days of acceptance. Will send free sample copy and guidelines for writers to serious contributors. Will consider photocopied submissions. Submit seasonal material 4 months in advance. Reports in 30 days. Prefers to be queried before submission of material. Enclose S.A.S.E.
Nonfiction and Photos: "We publish well-illustrated articles on general interest subjects of people, travel, recreation, and unusual interest ideas. Visual 'Look' style preferred. All materials must be people-oriented and relate to what people do. As the name indicates, we are faces of people and places. Avoid the hard news approach. Use a light, enjoyable style. Avoid poverty and pornography. Our emphasis is on good writing on people and their locations. Unusual travel, unusual life style of individuals; unusual and usual recreations in a variety of locations." Length: 10,000 words, maximum. Pays $25 to $500; more on assignments. In photos, only color is used; 35mm and up. Positive or negative. Pays $25 to $500 for a series; more

on assignment. Color photos must be top quality and creative. Captions required.
Fillers: Pays up to $200 for 1,500- to 2,000-word and picture fillers on their stated themes.

FORD TIMES, Ford Motor Company, The American Road, Dearborn MI 48121. Managing Editor: William E. Pauli. "Family magazine designed to attract all ages." Monthly. Circulation: 2,000,000. Buys first serial rights. Buys about 125 mss a year. Pays on acceptance. Will send a sample copy to a writer on request. Write for copy of guidelines for writers. Query first. Submit seasonal material 6 months in advance. Reports in 2 to 4 weeks. Enclose S.A.S.E.
Nonfiction, Fiction and Photos: "Almost anything relating to American life, both past and present, that is in good taste and leans toward the cheerful and optimistic. Topics include motor travel, sports, fashion, where and what to eat along the road, vacation ideas, reminiscences, big cities and small towns, the arts, Americana, nostalgia, the outdoors. We strive to be colorful, lively and engaging. We are particularly attracted to material that presents humor, anecdote, first-person discourse, intelligent observation and, in all cases, superior writing. We are committed to originality and try as much as possible to avoid subjects that have appeared in other publications and in our own. However, a fresh point of view and/or exceptional literary ability with respect to an old subject will be welcomed." Length: 1,500 words maximum. Pays $250 and up for full-length stories. "We prefer to have a suitable ms in hand before considering photos or illustration. Speculative submission of good quality color transparencies and b&w photos is welcomed. We want bright, lively photos showing people in happy circumstances. Writers may send snapshots, postcards, brochures, etc., if they wish."

GOOD READING, Henry F. Henrichs Publications, Litchfield IL 62056. Phone: 217-324-2322. Editor: Mrs. Monta Crane. Monthly. Not copyrighted. Buys 50 to 75 mss a year. Pays on acceptance. Will send a sample copy to a writer for 30¢. No query required. Submit seasonal material 4 months in advance. Reports in 1 to 2 months. Enclose S.A.S.E.
Nonfiction and Photos: Articles on "current or factual subjects, slanted to readers in the busy, modern world, and articles based on incidents related to business, personal experiences that reveal the elements of success in human relationships. All material must be clean and wholesome and acceptable to all ages. Material should be uplifting, and non-controversial." Length: 1,000 words maximum; "preferably shorter." Pays $5 to $30. B&w glossies purchased with mss "occasionally."

GREEN'S MAGAZINE, Box 313, Detroit MI 48231. Editor: David Green. For a general audience; the more sentient, literate levels. Quarterly magazine; 72 pages. Established in 1972. Circulation: 1,500. Buys first North American serial rights. Buys 32 to 40 mss a year. Payment on publication. Will send sample copy to writer for $1.25. Will not consider photocopied or simultaneous submissions. Reports in 6 weeks. Submit complete mss. Enclose S.A.S.E.
Fiction: Mainstream, suspense, humorous. must have depth of characterization, a realistic range in conflict areas. Avoid housewife, student, businessmen problems that remain "so what" in solution. Length: 1,000 to 3,500 words. Pays $10 to $25.
Poetry: Haiku, blank verse, free verse. Length: about 36 lines. Pays $3.

GRIT, 208 W. Third St., Williamsport PA 17701. Phone: 717-326-1771. Editor: Terry L. Ziegler. For "residents of all ages in small-town and rural America who are interested in people and generally take a positive view of life." National weekly tabloid newspaper; 44 pages. Established in 1882. Circulation: 1,300,000. Rights purchased vary with author and material. May buy first North American serial rights or second serial (reprint) rights. Buys 800 to 1,000 mss a year. Payment on acceptance, except for reader-participation features, which are paid for on publication. Will send free sample copy to writer on request. Write for copy of guidelines for writers. Will not consider photocopied or simultaneous material. Submit seasonal material 2 to 4 months in advance. Reports on material accepted for publication within 6 weeks. Returns rejected material in 3 weeks. Query first or submit complete ms. Enclose S.A.S.E.

Nonfiction and Photos: "Largely feature-type articles dealing with personalities in such a way that they contribute to our editorial purpose of seeking to inform, entertain, teach highest moral and social principles, improve thought and inspire achievement. Inspiring stories of personal courage and devotion. Stories about individuals and groups who are making an important contribution to their neighbors, community, or American way of life. Stories that demonstrate the power of free enterprise as a desirable and vital aspect of life in America. We prefer not to see stories promoting alcoholic beverages, immoral behavior, narcotics, unpatriotic acts. Annually, we are on the lookout for good Easter, Christmas and other major holiday features. They should show some person or group involved in an unusual and/or uplifting way. We lean heavily toward human interest, whatever the subject. Writing should be simple and down-to-earth. Get to the point quickly, and it is essential that the emphasis be on people rather than things, and to report things and ideas through people rather than abstractly." Recent articles include "Florida Sight-Seeing by Shanty Boat," (about a five-day houseboat cruise available to tourists in southwestern Florida), "Dad in the Delivery Room," (about a husband being present at the birth of his daughter, written by the father), "Bagging Game on Film," (advising camera buffs how to go about getting good wildlife shots), and "The 'Reel' Santa Claus," (about a Missourian who collects and repairs old fishing rods and reels to give to would-be boy anglers). Length: 300 to 1,000 words. Pays minimum of 5¢ per word for original material. Shorter material (600 to 800 words) is used in the following departments: Odd, Strange and Curious; Hobby Hodgepodge; Show Biz Spotlight. Pays 5¢ a word for original material; 2¢ a word for reprint material. Pays $10 for 8x10 b&w glossy prints purchased with mss; $15, with captions only. Pays $35 for 4x5 color transparencies purchased with ms; $40, with captions only. Must be related to publication's theme. Feature Editor: Kenneth D. Loss.

Fiction: Buys only reprint material. Western, romance. Pays 2¢ a word. Department Editor: Mrs. Fran Noll.

Poetry: Traditional forms, light verse. Length: 32 lines maximum. Pays $4 for 4 lines and under, plus 25¢ a line for each additional line.

Fillers: Puzzles. Pays 5¢ a word for original work.

HARPER'S MAGAZINE, 2 Park Ave., Room 1809, New York NY 10016. Phone: 212-686-8710. Editor: Lewis H. Lapham. For well-educated, socially concerned, widely read men and women and college students who are active in community and political affairs. Monthly. Circulation: 325,000. Rights purchased vary with author and material. Buys all rights, but will reassign rights to author after publication; first North American serial rights; first serial rights; second serial (reprint) rights. Buys approximately 12 non-agented, non-commissioned, non-book-excerpted mss a year. Pays on acceptance. Will send a sample copy to a writer for $1. Will look only at material submitted through agents or which is the result of a query. Reports in 2 to 3 weeks. Enclose S.A.S.E. with all queries and submissions.

Nonfiction: "For writers working with agents or who will query first only, our requirements are: Public affairs, literary, international and local reporting, humor." Also buys exposes, think pieces, and profiles. Length: 1,500 to 6,000 words. Pays $200 to $1,500.

Photos: Occasionally purchased with mss. Others by assignment. Pays $35 to $400. Department Editor: Sheila Berger.

Fiction: On contemporary life and its problems. Also buys humorous stories. Length: 1,000 to 5,000 words. Pays $300 to $500.

Poetry: 60 lines and under. Pays $2 per line.

How To Break In: "Personal, impassioned essays are published in our 'Commentary' department. Length should be 200 to 1,000 words. Token payment only."

HARPER'S WEEKLY, Harper's Magazine Co., (Division of Minneapolis Star and Tribune Co., Inc.), 2 Park Ave., New York NY 10016. Editor: Tony Jones. Tabloid. Re-established in 1974. Weekly (except weeks of 1/3, 4/4, 7/11, 9/5). Buys all rights. Pays on publication. Submit complete ms. Enclose S.A.S.E.

Nonfiction and Fillers: "As I said in the first issue of the revitalized *Harper's Weekly* (and have reminded readers in each successive issue), we welcome dispatches from our readers, especially on subjects of topical interest. Ideally, contributions will be short, personal, and anchored to a specific event, situation, or experience. Correspondence must include the writer's name, address, and telephone number. Because of the volume of mail, contributions will not be returned, although we will do our best to acknowledge receipt of all material submitted. We regret that we cannot accept poetry. We reserve the right to abridge or edit contributions for space. While we attempt to verify all matters of fact that we print, we also admit limitations of time and staff. Individual correspondents will be held liable for the accuracy and fairness of their contributions. We pay $15 apiece for items in 'Running Commentary'. A $10 fee is paid when we publish clippings, quotes or other research material (please include sources) submitted by readers."

HOLIDAY, 1100 Waterway Blvd., Indianapolis IN 46202. Phone: 317-634-1100. Managing Editor: Kathryn Klassen. For a mature audience, travel and leisure oriented. Pays on publication. Rights purchased vary with author and material. Write for editorial guidelines. Send query or complete ms (by certified mail if acknowledgement of receipt is desired). Submit seasonal material 4 months in advance. Enclose S.A.S.E.

Nonfiction: "Articles on a wide range of subjects related to travel or free-time activities: regions, communities, resorts (foreign and domestic); cultural and historical places and events; sports and hobbies; entertainment; shopping; food, drink, restaurants; personalities; humor; service articles concerning travel facilities and accessories; vacation houses. Prefer accompanying photos or information on illustrative material." Length: 1,000 to 2,000 words. Payment varies according to length, quality, need; from $5 for fillers to $1,200 for a feature article.

Photos: Technically perfect, well-composed color transparencies, 35mm or larger (or b&w prints) on subjects related to article needs. Specific subjects only, with caption notes. No general scenics. Prefers photos with interesting people, well-known personalities. Payment per photo ranges from $35 to $300 depending on size, quality, usage. Address stock lists and samples (may be duplicates) to Carol Bucheri, Art Director.

How To Break In: "Study back issues. Current needs are for more personality-oriented material, humor, and sharp, upbeat 900- to 1,400-word shorts on fresh, unusual subjects. Avoid first-person travelogues. At *Holiday*, we assume that most people have already been there and so look for something new or for an unusual slant on the familiar. Rarely will we use a piece on a single inn, festival, event. A broader outlook is generally of greater significance and interest; for example, explore trends in amusement parks across the country (with specific examples) rather than report on Disneyland. Recent article ideas we've liked: a personality/art piece on Peggy Guggenheim, an article on vodka by Nathaniel Benchley, and Wallace Stegner's short regional America mood piece on Utah."

HORIZON, 1221 Avenue of the Americas, New York NY 10020. Managing Editor: James F. Fixx. Quarterly. Copyrighted. Circulation: 105,000. Pays on acceptance. Reports within 4 weeks. Enclose S.A.S.E. for ms return.

Nonfiction: History, the arts, archaeology, letters, biography, with emphasis on extremely high-quality writing. Length: 3,000 to 5,000 words. Payment: depends on material; $100 minimum.

IN THE KNOW, Lexington Library, Inc., 355 Lexington Ave., New York NY 10017. Executive Editor: James Spada. Editor: M. B. Shestack. For middle America. Magazine; 64 (8½x11) pages. Established in 1975. Monthly. Circulation: 500,000. Buys all rights. Buys about 200 mss a year. Pays on acceptance. No photocopied submissions. Will consider simultaneous submissions. Reports on material accepted for publication in 60 days. Returns rejected material in 2 to 3 weeks. Query first or submit complete ms. Enclose S.A.S.E.

Nonfiction and Photos: Articles on people in the news; celebrities. Short, succinct, with interview quotes. Background and insight into the subject, so reader will be "in the know". Informational, personal experience, interview, profile, nostalgia, spot news. Recently published "Charley Pride Playing Baseball" which combined two interests. It dealt with a celebrity and was based on an interview (plus exclusive photos). Length: 150 to 750 words. Pays $50 to $200. Pays $25 for 8x10 b&w glossies purchased with or without mss or on assignment. Must be of excellent quality.

INSURANCE MAGAZINE, Allied Publications Inc., P.O. Box 23505, Fort Lauderdale FL 33307. Associate Editor: Louise Hinton. For "the general public, all ages." Bimonthly. Buys North American serial rights only. Pays on acceptance. No query necessary. Reports in 2 to 4 weeks. Enclose S.A.S.E. with all mss.
Nonfiction and Photos: Wants how-to, inspirational, humor, and travel articles. Length: 500 to 1,000 words. Payment is 5¢ a word, and $5 for photos purchased with mss.

LIBERTY, THEN AND NOW, Liberty Library Corp., 250 W. 57th St., New York NY 10019. Editor: James Palmer. Published 4 times a year. No new material used; only reprints from original *Liberty* published between 1924 and 1950.
Nonfiction and Fiction: This publication recreates the "Good Old Days" of the 20's, 30's, 40's in articles and fiction. Has used reprints of original works by H. L. Mencken and W. C. Fields, by George Bernard Shaw and Ben Hecht, as well as hundreds of others, plus new articles that make it *Liberty, Then and Now.* The majority of the material consists of reprints from the original *Liberty.* Some are re-edited for today's readers. Pays $100 to $150.

LITHOPINION, 113 University Pl., New York NY 10003. Phone: 212-254-5404. Editor: Edward Swayduck; Managing Editor: Robert Hallock. Graphic arts and public affairs journal. For more than 10,000 members of Local One, Amalgamated Lithographers of America, and also lithographic employers and more than 20,000 editors, art directors, opinion makers, librarians, teachers, politicians, etc. Quarterly magazine; 80 (9x12) pages. Established in 1965. Circulation: 20,000. Buys first North American serial rights. Buys 32 mss a year. Payment on acceptance, or "within 2 weeks after acceptance." Will send sample copy to writer for $5. Write for copy of guidelines for writers. Query first to Jim Hoffman, Editorial Consultant. Submit only complete ms for humor or satire. Reports in 1 month. Enclose S.A.S.E.
Nonfiction: "We want personality profiles and interviews, historical articles (contemporary and otherwise), examination of the current cultural and social scene, political and sociological commentary, humor with bite and relevance, exposes, and nostalgia. Articles that 'show' the reader through anecdotes, dramatization, dialogue, etc., rather than those that 'tell' the reader dryly or didactically. We dislike writing that sounds like speeches, sermons, academic dissertations, term papers and essays. We feel an article may be for *Lithopinion* if it's on a par with the best stuff that appears in *The New York Times Sunday Magazine, Harper's, The Atlantic Monthly, The Nation,* and *The New Republic.* We strive to produce a journal devoted to experimentation in the arts that are graphic, elucidation of significant patterns in public affairs and examination of social and cultural change." Length: 2,500 to 5,000 words. Pays $750.
How To Break In: "Query us in advance; a paragraph or two is sufficient. We're short on editorial woman-man power, so we don't have the time to consider unsolicited mss. The exception is humorous and satiric articles; we don't assign them (who knows ahead of time what's funny?) but we do welcome them, in completed form — on speculation, of course. With a very small staff and a very high set of editorial standards, we can't afford the luxury of considering queries from neophytes. Our writers are tried-and-true professionals with top credits and extensive experience. Until the beginner has published extensively in other national magazines, he or she should not query us."

LIVELY WORLD, The Magazine of Marriott, c/o Caldwell Communications, Inc., 747 Third Ave., New York NY 10017. Phone: 212-371-6666. Editor: Robert H. Spencer. For upper income businessmen. Quarterly magazine; 32 pages. Established in 1974. Circulation: 250,000. Rights purchased vary with author and material. Usually buys all rights, but will reassign rights to author after publication. Buys over 25 mss a year. Occasionally gets overstocked. Payment on acceptance or sometimes on publication. Will send free sample copy to writer on request. Write for copy of editorial guidelines for writers. Query first or submit complete ms. Reports within 3 months. Enclose S.A.S.E.

Nonfiction and Photos: *Lively World* is issued through Marriott hotels (in-room), cruise ships, charter flights and prime-customer mailing and stockholders. It's a magazine about, and for, active people. Its editorial uniqueness is purposed at conveying to the reader those motivations, sensitivities, attitudes of the active mind on a variety of personalized subjects. On the other hand, first-person style in writing is generally not acceptable; reporting on attitudes of others is. Each issue will contain at least one feature relating to a Marriott destination area. Here, the editorial focus should be on what's socially relevant, timely and provocative in terms such as cultural aspects, creative personalities, newsworthy developments, conservation, etc. The articles should be different from the usual 'here and there' travel article — by adopting a people-related focus and by touching on history, ecology, business or social issues, for instance. Every issue will also have one article on sports and leisure, along with one on food. Regular articles on business, economy, personal finance subjects, along with personality profiles — short and long. There will be an occasional use of sophisticated humor. We prefer to assign articles, but will sometimes accept unsolicited ms." Length: 800 to 3,000 words, with the more desired length being on the side of brevity. "First-rate short essays are our top need. Photos may accompany ms if they aid in the presentation. Photo stories with minimal copy are occasionally used. Most photos are color, and color transparencies are preferable. And, because we want active-people shots, photo releases are desirable." Pays $50 to $400.

How To Break In: "Every article must touch on some 'lively' aspect, ideas, thoughts."

MACLEAN'S, 481 University Ave., Toronto, Ont., Canada M5W 1A7. Editor: Peter C. Newman. For general interest audience. Monthly. Circulation: 750,000. Buys first North American rights. Pays on publication. "Query with 200- or 300-word outline before sending any material." Submit seasonal material 4 months in advance. Reports in 1 month. Enclose S.A.E. and International Reply Coupons.

Nonfiction: "Audience is Canadian and for this reason most of our articles are on Canadian subjects. We want articles on people, places, politics, business, science, medicine, education, entertainment, adventure, sport, social problems and many other things. We don't want articles that are superficial, poorly researched, badly organized, biased, exaggerated or too breathless." Length: 1,500 to 4,000 words. Pays $300 to $1,000.

Photos: Interested primarily in Canadian subjects. Buys b&w glossies, color transparencies, 35mm color. Pays "$100 to $200 per page." Director of Graphics: Paul Galer.

MIDNIGHT, *Globe Newspapers,* 1440 St. Catherine St., W., Montreal, Quebec, Canada. Editor: Joan LeBlanc. For everyone in a family over 18. *Midnight* readers are the same people you meet on the street, and in supermarket lines, the average hard-working American who finds easily digestible tabloid news the best way for his information. Weekly national tabloid newspaper. Established in 1956. Circulation: 1,000,000. Not copyrighted. Buys more than 1,000 mss a year. Payment on acceptance. "Writers should advise us of specializations on any submission so that we may contact them if special issue or feature is planned." Submit special material 2 months in advance. Submit only complete ms. Reports within 1 week. Enclose S.A.S.E.

Nonfiction, Photos, and Fillers: "Sex and violence are taboo. We want upbeat human interest material, of interest to a national audience. Stories where fate plays a major role are always good. Always interested in features on well-known personalities, offbeat people, places, events and activities. Current issue is best guide. Stories are best that don't grow stale quickly. No padding. Grab the reader in the first line or paragraph. Tell the story, make the point and get out with a nice, snappy ending. Don't dazzle us with your footwork. Just tell the story. We don't require queries if the material is professionally written and presented. And we are always happy to bring a new freelancer or stringer into our fold. No cliques here. If you've got talent, and the right material—you're in. Remember—we are serving a family audience. All material must be in good taste. If it's been written up in a major newspaper or magazine, we already know about it." Buys informational, how-to, personal experience, interview, profile, inspirational, humor, historical, expose, nostalgia, photo, spot news, and new product articles. Length: 1,000 words maximum; average 500 to 800 words. Pays $50 to $300. Photos are purchased with or without ms, and on assignment. Captions are required. Pays $25 minimum for 8x10 b&w glossies. "Competitive payment on exclusives." Photo Editor: Tom Pigeon. Buys puzzles, quizzes, and short humor.

How To Break In: "*Midnight* is constantly looking for human interest subject material from throughout the United States and much of the best comes from America's smaller cities and villages, not necessarily from the larger urban areas. Therefore, we are likely to be more responsive to an article from a new writer than many other publications. This, of course, is equally true of photographs. A major mistake of new writers is that they have failed to determine the type and style of our content and in the ever-changing tabloid field, this is a most important consideration. It is also wise to keep in mind that what is of interest to you or to the people in your area may not be of equal interest to a national readership. Determine the limits of interest first. And, importantly, the material you send us must be such that it won't be 'stale' by the time it reaches the readers."

MODERN LIVING, Allied Publications, Inc., P.O. Box 23505, Fort Lauderdale FL 33307. Associate Editor: Louise Hinton. For "the average homeowner." Bimonthly. Buys North American serial rights only. Pays on acceptance. No query necessary. Reports in 2 to 4 weeks. Enclose S.A.S.E. with all submissions.

Nonfiction and Photos: Articles on "home, family, children, teenagers, travel, hobbies, pets, decorating, sports." Buys how-to's, inspirational articles, profiles, humor, spot news, historical and think pieces, travel articles. Length: 500 to 1,000 words. Pays 5¢ per accepted word. Pays $5 for photos purchased with mss.

MODERN PEOPLE NEWSWEEKLY, 11058 W. Addison St., Franklin Park IL 60131. Editor: Tony Richards. For men and women in all walks of life who are interested in the contemporary world around them. Weekly tabloid newspaper; 32 pages. Established in 1972. Circulation: 300,000. Buys all rights, except in cases of special negotiation. Buys 1,000 mss a year. Payment on acceptance. Will send free sample copy to writer on request. Write for copy of guidelines for writers. Query first. "With the exception of fillers, shorts and photo features, we are moving into an almost entirely 'query first' policy." Reports in 2 weeks, sometimes longer. Enclose S.A.S.E.

Nonfiction and Photos: "As you have no doubt noticed, *Modern People* is rapidly changing. While we remain in the tabloid size, graphics and writing style are forging new streams in journalism, and are setting the pace for the publication of the future. Subject matter consists of general interest, personalities; strong, original celebrity interviews and profiles; human interest, consumer protection, medical and scientific developments. Also, short features on local happenings such as 'cliff kite flying in California' and other localized, but general interest pastimes. Features should take a positive attitude even when dealing with a negative subject. We are moving into investigative reporters, but require a query first. We are extremely interested in famous personalities (not necessarily Hollywood personalities), emphasizing the human aspects and the oddities of their lives. Our headlines have often been a week to 2 months ahead of the daily newspapers and we plan to continue this. We're always looking for the 'big story;' significant or highly interesting stories that have not run elsewhere. Avoid topics previously 'done to death' by the news media." Length: 250 to 1,000 words. Prefers 500 to 700 words. Pays $20 to $50. "We prefer articles to be photo-illustrated wherever possible; usually with good, clear action photos rather than head shots. Should be b&w prints (color accepted, if necessary) with enough contrast for good reproduction. 5x7 or larger. Contact sheets accepted for picture selection only. Unpurchased photos are returned." Pays $5 minimum.

Fillers: Buys humorous, offbeat and human interest shorts and unusual news shorts. Length: 50 to 250 words. Also puzzles and tests of similar length. Pays 3¢ a word minimum.

NATIONAL ENQUIRER, Lantana FL 33462. Executive Editor: Brian Wells. For a general audience. Weekly tabloid. Circulation: 3,000,000. Buys first North American rights. Buys 1,000 mss a year. Pays on acceptance. Query first. "No longer accepting unsolicited mss and all spec material will be returned unread." Enclose S.A.S.E.
Nonfiction and Photos: Wants articles of any length on any subject appealing to a mass audience. Requires fresh slant on topical news stories, waste of taxpayers' money by government, the entire field of the occult, how-to articles, rags to riches success stories, medical firsts, scientific breakthroughs, human drama, adventure, personality profiles. "The best way to understanding our requirements is to study the paper." Pays $300 for most completed features; more with photos. "Payments in excess of $500 are not unusual; will pay more for really top, circulation-boosting blockbusters." Uses single or series b&w photos that must be attention-grabbing. Wide range; anything from animal photos to great action photos. "We'll bid against any other magazine for once-in-lifetime photos."

NATIONAL GEOGRAPHIC MAGAZINE, 17th and M Streets, N.W., Washington DC 20036. Phone: 202-296-7500, Ext. 370 (James Cerruti). Editor: Gilbert M. Grosvenor. For members of the National Geographic Society. Monthly. Circulation: 8,900,000. Buys first publication rights with warranty to use the material in National Geographic Society copyrighted publications. Buys 40 to 50 mss a year. Pays on acceptance. Will send a sample copy to a writer for $1.25. Returns rejected material and acknowledges acceptance of material in 2 to 4 weeks. Query first. Writers should study several recent issues of *National Geographic* and send for leaflets "Writing for National Geographic" and "National Geographic Photo Requirements." Enclose S.A.S.E.
Nonfiction and Photos: "First-person narratives, making it easy for the reader to share the author's experience and observations. Writing should include plenty of human-interest incident, authentic direct quotation, and a bit of humor where appropriate. Accuracy is fundamental. Contemporary problems such as those of pollution and ecology are treated on a factual basis. The magazine is especially seeking short American place pieces with a strong regional 'people' flavor. The use of many clear, sharp color photographs in all articles makes lengthy word descriptions unnecessary. Potential writers need not be concerned about submitting photos. These are handled by professional photographers. Hisorical background, in most cases, should be kept to the minimum needed for understanding the present." Length: 8,000 words maximum for major articles. Shorts of 2,000 to 4,000 words "are always needed." Pays from $1,500 to $4,000 (and, in some cases, more) for acceptable articles; from $250 per page for color transparencies. A paragraph of article idea should be submitted to James Cerruti, Senior Assistant Editor. If appealing, he will ask for a one- or two-page outline for further consideration. Photographers are advised to submit a generous selection of photographs with brief, descriptive captions to Mary G. Smith, Assistant Illustrations Editor.
How To Break In: "Send 4 or 5 one-paragraph ideas. If any are promising, author will be asked for a one- to two-page outline. Read the latest issues to see what we want."

THE NATIONAL INFORMER, 11058 W. Addison St., Franklin Park IL 60131. Editor: Jack Steele. Fr "the sophisticated, mature adult, who likes to be informed on topics he usually doesn't find in the daily papers." Weekly. Circulation: 500,000. Buys all rights. Buys about 600 mss a year. Occasionally overstocked. Pays on acceptance. Will send a sample copy to a writer for 25¢. Reports in about 3 weeks. Enclose S.A.S.E.
Nonfiction and Photos: "Our readers like human interest, self-help, and do-it-yourself types of features, particularly if these are sex-oriented. Also, our readers like to be shocked by sex expose features. We're looking for shocking features that expose and titillate. The writer should keep his article fast-paced, informative, and exciting without losing track of his main theme. We don't like slow, plodding features that inform but don't entertain. Our stories need to do both. We do not buy consumer articles or stories with settings in foreign countries." Length: 600 to 1,200 words. Pays 2¢ per word. B&w glossies purchased with mss. Pays $5 to $100.

NATIONAL INSIDER, 2713 N. Pulaski Rd., Chicago IL 60639. Editor: Robert J. Sorren. For a general audience. Weekly newspaper; 20 pages. Established in 1962. Rights purchased vary with author and material. Usually buys all rights but will sometimes reassign rights to author after publication. Buys 500 to 600 mss a year. Payment on acceptance. Will send free sample copy to writer on request. Write for copy of guidelines for writers. Will not consider photocopied or simultaneous submissions. Reports in 2 weeks. Query first. Enclose S.A.S.E.
Nonfiction and Photos: "We are looking for a variety of human interest stories. These generally should be upbeat human interest stories about persons who have overcome handicaps, or beat City Hall, or made millions from a small investment, etc. We're also interested in articles on wasteful government practices, unexplained phenomena, murder mysteries. (The emphasis here must be on the mystery surrounding the crime and good detective work. No gore photos or stories with the emphasis on sex crimes. No fictionalized accounts.) In the past we have published articles relating to sex and sex scandals. We are no longer interested in such material." B&w photos (8x10) purchased with or without mss, or on assignment. Captions required. Payment varies.

NATIONAL POLICE GAZETTE, 520 Fifth Ave., New York NY 10036. Editor: Nat K. Perlow. For persons "between the ages of 20 and 65." Established in 1845. Monthly. Circulation: 200,000. Buys all rights. Buys about 200 mss a year. Pays on publication. Submit seasonal material 3 months in advance. Reports in 1 month. Enclose S.A.S.E.
Nonfiction: In spite of the title of this publication, their primary interests are "sports, general interest articles, latest medical breakthroughs, and profiles of people in the news. Also interested in success stories. We have a keen interest in all features concerning consumer frauds, sports, crime, adventure. We adhere to a hard-hitting formula, being brash instead of subtle. Articles should be anecdotal and written in a light, breezy style." Wants "more sport personality stories based on interviews rather than rehashes from newspaper clips." Buys how-to's, interviews, profiles, inspirational and photo articles, humor, spot news, exposes, new product coverage. Length: 1,000 to 1,500 words. Pays $50 to $150 (5¢ to 10¢ a word).

NATIONAL STAR, 730 Third Ave., New York NY 10017. Editor: James Brady. For every family; all the family—kids, teenagers, young parents and grandparents. Weekly newspaper, 48-page tabloid. Established in 1974. Circulation: 1,000,000. Rights purchased vary with author and material. Buys all rights, but will reassign rights to author after publication; buys first North American serial rights, first serial rights, second serial (reprint) rights. Buys up to 1,000 mss a year. Payment on acceptance. Submit Christmas material 2 months in advance. Query first with brief, one-paragraph outline. Reports "soon as possible." Enclose S.A.S.E.
Nonfiction and Photos: "News stories, features of topical interest, especially on personalities. No fiction or poetry. Be direct, factual, colorful." Informational, how-to, interview, profile, historical, expose, nostalgia, photo, spot news, successful business operations, and new product articles. Not interested in first-person narratives. Length: 100 to 1,500 words. Pays $20 to $1,000. B&w photos purchased with or without ms. Captions required. Pays from $25 to $250.
Fillers: Newsbreaks and puzzles. Address to Steve Dunleavy.

NATIONAL TATTLER, 2717 N. Pulaski Rd., Chicago IL 60639. Editor: Tom Lutz. For a general audience. "If we have a target reader, it is the supermarket shopping housewife, since our publication is sold at supermarket checkout counters." Weekly newspaper; 36 pages. Established in 1964. Circulation: over 1,000,000. Rights purchased vary with author and material. May buy all rights; but will sometimes reassign rights to author after publication; or first North American serial rights. Buys 2,000 to 2,500 mss a year. Payment on acceptance. Will send free sample copy to writer on request. Write for copy of editorial guidelines. Will not consider photocopied or simultaneous submissions. Submit seasonal material, which is used on rare occasions (Christmas and other holidays and certain historical dates) 2 months in advance. Reports in 2 weeks. Query first. Enclose S.A.S.E.

Nonfiction and Photos: "Emphasis is always on human interest. Areas are: celebrities; always with a news peg. We leave the shallow profile interview to the daily press. Volunteers: people helping people. We want articles about individuals who take it on themselves to unselfishly help others. No stories about volunteer organizations. Anti-rat-race: for example, the bank president who drops out to live in a wilderness log cabin. Government waste: stories on government policies or programs that result in scandalous waste of taxpayers' money." Other areas of interest include material dealing with the overcoming of handicaps, rags to riches, unexplained phenomena, medical breakthroughs, world records and the Gee-Whiz Photospot (the unique one-shot photograph that tells its own story with the help of a brief caption line). Except for the photospot feature, length is usually 1,000 to 1,500 words, but some shorter articles are used. Pays $75 to $1,000 and up. "We will bid with any U.S. publication for the blockbuster story." Departments include one on budget saving tips and another on recipes. $5 each is paid for these. Plus various continuing reader participation contests and features for which prizes of $5 to $50 are awarded. Also pays minimum of $15 for story leads that staff develops into articles. B&w photos (8x10) are purchased with or without mss or on assignment. Pays $25 to $75. Captions required. Send to Photo Editor.

NEW TIMES, 1 Park Ave., New York NY 10016. Editor: Jonathan Z. Larsen. For general audience, mostly single, college educated, and in their 30's. News magazine published every 2 weeks; 68 pages. Established in 1973. Circulation: 130,000. Buys first North American serial rights. Buys 24 mss a year. "Guarantee, then full payment on acceptance." Will consider photocopied and simultaneous submissions. Query first or submit complete ms. Reports in 2 to 3 weeks. Enclose S.A.S.E.
Nonfiction and Fillers: "News features, light in style. Fast-paced, individualistic and highly personal coverage of what's happening and why. The news dictates the contents of *New Times*." Buys informational, inspirational, humor, think articles, expose, nostalgia, and spot news. Feature length: 3,000 words. Pays $250 minimum for feature articles. Buys jokes and short humor. Pays $25 minimum. Special "Insider" feature uses short items (500 words). Pays $25.

THE NEW YORKER, 25 W. 43rd St., New York NY 10036. Editor: William Shawn. Weekly. Reports in two weeks. Pays on acceptance. Enclose S.A.S.E.
Nonfiction, Fiction, and Fillers: Single factual pieces run from 3,000 to 10,000 words. Long fact pieces are usually staff-written. So is "Talk of the Town," although ideas for this department are bought. Pays good rates. Uses fiction, both serious and light, from 1,000 to 6,000 words. About 90 percent of the fillers come from contributors with or without taglines (extra pay if the tagline is used).

PAGEANT, P.O. Box 704, 21 Elm St., Rouses Point NY 12979. Editor: Nat K. Perlow. For a general audience. Established in 1945. Monthly magazine. Circulation: 250,000. Buys all rights. Buys 250 mss a year. Payment on publication. Query first. Will read only 1-page queries which include brief outline of articles. No unsolicited mss. Enclose S.A.S.E. with queries.
Nonfiction: General interest articles. Articles about people in the news. Medical breakthroughs. Consumer-oriented features. Offbeat briefs. "We find that many articles submitted to us are rewrites from other magazines. We want a fresh approach, new material and an interesting angle." Informational, how-to, personal experience, interview, profile, inspirational, humor, historical, think pieces, exposes, nostalgia, personal opinion, travel. Length: 1,500 words. Pays $100 to $500.

PEOPLE WEEKLY, Time Inc., Time & Life Bldg., Rockefeller Center, New York NY 10020. Editor: Richard B. Stolley. For a general audience. Established in 1974. Weekly. Circulation: 1,000,000. Rights purchased vary with author and material. Usually buys first North American serial rights with right to syndicate, splitting net proceeds with author 50/50. Payment on acceptance. Query first. Enclose S.A.S.E.
Nonfiction and Photos: "Short pieces on personalities in all fields (sports, politics, religion, the arts, business) centered on individuals of current interest. We deal

exclusively with personality pieces, in all career areas. We accept specific story suggestions only, not manuscripts." Uses question and answer interviews of 1,500 to 2,000 words. Pays $500. Biographies of 2,000 words. Pays $750. Payment for other assigned articles varies with amount of material used. Pays $150 per page for b&w photos purchased with or without mss. Prefers minimum 8x10 from original negatives. Captions required. Photos are also purchased on assignment.

How To Break In: "The new writer is best off aiming for a story on an unknown but extremely interesting person. The little guy out there in the hinterlands that we might overlook and that our stringers might miss. The freelancer in the boondocks is at an advantage here and a success with a story like this will make it easier to approach us with another idea. We like pieces which portray someone who reacts to the trials and tribulations of everyday life in a unique and unusual way — who does something which the rest of us perhaps should, but don't. Famous personalities are mostly handled in-house, but try us if you have a new twist or special access. Remember — we like story suggestions only, so query first."

PURE ENTERTAINMENT, 908 Hibiscus Way, Placentia CA 92670. Publisher: W. L. Shields. Managing Editor: J. Magwood Sullivan. For all ages interested in reading for entertainment. Magazine; 96 (8½x5½) pages. Established in 1975. Quarterly. Circulation: 5,000. Rights purchased vary with author and material. May buy all rights, but sometimes reassigns rights to author after publication; or first North American serial rights; occasionally, first anthology rights. Buys about 50 mss a year. Pays on acceptance. Will send sample copy to writer for 60¢. Write for copy of guidelines for writers. No photocopied or simultaneous submissions. Reports as soon as possible. Submit complete ms. Enclose S.A.S.E.

Fiction: All types suitable to a wide range of ages and interests. Any style; looking for a wide variety. Mainstream, mystery, suspense, adventure, western, science fiction, fantasy, humorous, romance, historical, condensed novels, serialized novels. Length: 7,500 words maximum. Pays $5 minimum.

Poetry and Fillers: Traditional and avant-garde forms of poetry, blank verse, free verse, light verse. Pays $1 to $5. Puzzles of any type and short humor used as fillers. Pays $1 to $5.

READER'S DIGEST, Pleasantville NY 10570. Monthly. Buys all rights to original mss. "Items intended for a particular feature should be directed to the editor in charge of that feature, although the contribution may later be referred to another section of the magazine as seeming more suitable. Manuscripts cannot be acknowledged, and will be returned — usually within eight to 12 weeks — only when return postage accompanies them."

Nonfiction: "*Reader's Digest* is especially interested in receiving the following sorts of material: First Person Articles. An article for this series must be a previously unpublished narrative of an unusual personal experience. It may be dramatic, inspirational or humorous, but it must have a quality of narrative and interest comparable to stories published in this series. Contributions must be typewritten, preferably double-spaced, no longer than 2,500 words. It is requested that documents or photographs not be sent. Payment rate on acceptance: $3,000. Base rate for general articles is $2,000 for first sale. Address to: First Person Editor."

Fillers: "Life in These United States contributions must be true, unpublished stories from one's own experience, revelatory of adult human nature, and providing appealing or humorous sidelights on the American scene. Maximum length: 300 words. Address Life in U.S. Editor. Payment rate on publication: $200. True and unpublished stories are also solicited for Humor in Uniform, Campus Comedy and All in a Day's Work. Maximum length: 300 words. Payment rate on publication: $200. Address Humor in Uniform, Campus Comedy or All in a Day's Work Editor. Toward More Picturesque Speech: The first contributor of each item used in this department is paid $25. Contributions should be dated, and the sources must be given. Address: Picturesque Speech Editor. For items used in Laughter, the Best Medicine, Personal Glimpses, Quotable Quotes, and elsewhere in the magazine, payment is made at the following rates: To the *first* contributor of each item from a published source, $25. For original material, $10 per *Digest* two-column line, with a minimum payment of $25. Address: Excerpts Editor."

READER'S NUTSHELL, Allied Publications, Inc., P.O. Box 23505, Fort Lauderdale FL 33307. Associate Editor: Marie Stilkind. Bimonthly. Buys North American serial rights only. Pays on acceptance. Query not necessary. Reports in 2 to 4 weeks. Enclose S.A.S.E. for return of submissions.
Nonfiction and Photos: "Family magazine for all ages." Wants "humorous articles of general interest." Length: 500 to 1,000 words. Pays 5¢ per accepted word. Pays $5 for photos purchased with mss; b&w glossies.

THE SAMPLE CASE, 632 N. Park St., Columbus OH 43215. Phone: 614-228-3276. Editor: James R. Eggert. For members of the United Commercial Travelers of America, located throughout the U.S. and Canada; 18 years of age and older, with a wide range of interests, educations, and occupations. Established in 1891. Monthly. Rights purchased vary with author and material. Buys all rights, but will reassign rights to author after publication; buys first North American serial rights; first serial rights; second serial (reprint) rights; simultaneous ritghts. Buys 25 to 50 mss a year. Payment on publication. Will send free sample copy to writer on request. Write for copy of guidelines for writers. Will consider photocopied submissions. Submit seasonal material 2 months in advance. Reports in 4 months. Enclose S.A.S.E.
Nonfiction and Photos: "Especially interested in general interest nonfiction. We pay special attention to articles about mental retardation, youth, safety, and cancer." Informational, personal experience, interview, some humor. Length: 500 to 2,000 words. Pays 1½¢ per word. Additional payment for good quality b&w glossies purchased with mss. Captions required.

SATURDAY EVENING POST, 1100 Waterway Blvd., Indianapolis IN 46202. Executive Editor and Publisher: Cory SerVaas. Managing Editor: Fred Birmingham. A family publication for readers interested in travel, food, fiction, personalities, etc. Monthly (except January, June and August) magazine; 140 pages. Established in 1728. Circulation: 800,000. Rights purchased vary with author and material. Usually buys all rights. Buys about 100 mss a year. Payment on publication. Will send sample copy to writer for $1. Reports in 6 to 8 weeks. Query first. Enclose S.A.S.E.
Nonfiction and Photos: Articles of general interest on travel, food, personalities. Lively style with quotations and anecdotes. Strong family orientation; light and positive. Length: 1,500 to 4,500 words. Pays $200 to $1,000. Photos used with or without mss. Captions required.
Fiction: Mystery, suspense, adventure, science fiction, humorous, romance, historical. Length: 2,000 to 5,000 words. Pays $200 to $850.
Poetry and Fillers: Light verse. Short humor. Pays minimum of $10.
How To Break In: "Keenly interested in special topics relating to science, education, government, the arts, personalities with inspirational careers."

SATURDAY REVIEW, 488 Madison Ave., New York NY 10022. Editor: Norman Cousins. "For above average educated audience. Readers travel and read a lot, also like to discuss burning issues of the time — ahead of the time. Great interests in the arts, education, science. Top drawer audience." Biweekly magazine, 72 pages, (8½x11). Established in 1924. Circulation: 550,000. Rights purchased vary with author and material. Buys first North American serial rights. Buys several hundred mss per year. "Sometimes pay on acceptance; most often pay on publication. Depends on author and circumstance." Will send free sample copy to writer on request. Will consider photocopied submissions. Will not consider simultaneous submissions. Submit seasonal material several months in advance. Reports "as quickly as we can — days or weeks at most." Query first. Enclose S.A.S.E.
Nonfiction and Photos: "It is essential that a potential contributor read several issues of *SR* to get an idea of what we publish and how it's put together. We use only nonfiction. Remember that ours is a small but highly literate audience with money and time and education. The level of treatment is very hightoned and above the

obvious – far-sighted, perhaps." Length: probably around, 5,000 words; prefers 3,000. Pays about $200 per page in print. Send queries to Peter Young, Managing Editor. Photos are considered, but inquire first to Judi Adel, Photo Department Editor.
How To Break In: "We are very hard to crack for the new writer because most of our material is done by old hands who have been around forever. Your best shot is probably a book review for the monthly Education Supplement which is six pages long. That's one area where I'm looking for new material and new people. We do very little investigative stuff, but are on the lookout for new ideas, so try a query. Our lead time is six weeks, so think ahead. Also, read the magazine carefully. I get a lot of material which suggests the author is not familiar with *SR*."

SIGNATURE–The Diners' Club Magazine, 260 Madison Ave., New York NY 10016. Phone: 212-689-9020. Managing Editor: Robin Nelson. For Diners' Club members– "businessmen, urban, affluent, traveled, and young." Monthly. Circulation: 800,000. Buys first rights. Buys approximately 75 mss a year. Pays on acceptance. Write for copy of guidelines for writers. Submit seasonal material, including seasonal sports subjects, at least 3 months in advance. Returns rejected material in 2 weeks. Query first. Enclose S.A.S.E.
Nonfiction: "Articles aimed at the immediate areas of interest of our readers–in travel, social issues, personalities, sports, entertainment, food and drink, business, humor. *Signature* runs 5 to 8 nonfiction articles an issue, all by freelancers. Subjects covered in past issues of *Signature* include profiles of writer Gordie Howe, Paul Bocuse, Gladys Heldman and K2 Chief. Articles on secretarial crisis, Wall St. reform, Hallmark, Hershey and New Orleans Superdome. Travel pieces require a raison d'etre, a well-defined approach and angle. Eschew destination or traditional travel piece. Feature articles run 2,500 words maximum and pay $650. Also buy shorter 1,500-word pieces which are a slice of some travel experience and usually written in very personal style. These pay $450. It's important that writer be familiar with our magazine." Contact Josh Eppinger, Executive Editor.
Photos: "Picture stories or support are usually assigned to photographers we have worked with in the past. We rarely ask a writer to handle the photography also. But if he has photos of his subject, we will consider them for use." Pays $50 minimum per photo.

SUNSHINE MAGAZINE, Henry F. Henrichs Publications, Litchfield IL 62056. Phone: 217-324-2322. Editor: Mrs. Monta Crane. For general audience of all ages. Monthly magazine. Established in 1924. Circulation: 100,000. Not copyrighted. Buys 75 to 100 mss per year. Payment on acceptance. Will send sample copy to writer for 40¢. Write for copy of guidelines for writers. Will consider photocopied submissions. Will not consider simultaneous submissions. Submit seasonal material 4 months in advance. Reports in 1 to 3 months. Submit only complete ms. Enclose S.A.S.E.
Nonfiction: "We accept some short articles, but they must be especially interesting or inspirational. *Sunshine Magazine* is not a religious publication, and purely religious material is rarely used. We receive far too much material on the subjects of retirement, adjustment to old age. We use nothing with a sexual emphasis." Length: 250 to 1,200 words. Pays $5 to $30.
Fiction: "Stories must be wholesome, well-written, with clearly defined plots. There should be a purpose for each story, but any moral or lesson should be well-concealed in the plot development. Avoid trite plots that do not hold the reader's interest. A surprising climax is most desirable. Material should be uplifting, and non-controversial." Length: 350 to 1,300 words. Pays $5 to $30.

SWINGERS WORLD, 8060 Melrose Ave., Los Angeles CA 90046. Editors: Carlton Hollander and Elaine Stanton. For "swingers and would-be swingers." Established in 1972. Subject matter must be "swinger oriented." Bimonthly. Buys first North American serial rights. Buys 50 mss a year. Payment on publication. Will send a sample copy to a writer for $1.50. Will send editorial guidelines sheet to a writer on request (enclose S.A.S.E.). Reports in 2 weeks. Query first required. Enclose S.A.S.E.

Nonfiction: "Articles must be pro-swinger. Slick." Length: approximately 2,500 words. Pays about $100.

TOWN AND COUNTRY, 717 Fifth Ave., New York NY 10022. Managing Editor: Jean Barkhorn. For upper-income Americans. Monthly. Not a large market for freelancers. Always query first. Enclose S.A.S.E.
Nonfiction: "We're always trying to find ideas that can be developed into good articles that will make appealing cover lines." Wants provocative and controversial pieces. Length: 1,500 to 2,000 words. Pays $300. Department Editor: Frank Zachary. Also buys shorter pieces for which pay varies. Department Editor: Richard Kagan.

VALLEY LIGHTS, Blackstone Valley Electric Co., P.O. Box 1111, Lincoln RI 02865. Phone: 401-724-7400. Editor: Paul Pinkham. Bimonthly. Circulation: 900. Not copyrighted. Buys about 6 mss a year. Pays on publication. Submit seasonal material 2 months in advance. Reports in 4 to 6 weeks. Enclose S.A.S.E. for return of submissions.
Nonfiction and Photos: How-to's, humor, think pieces, new product coverage, photo and travel articles, safety articles. Length: open. Pays $10 to $40. B&w glossies purchased with mss.

WOODMEN OF THE WORLD MAGAZINE, 1700 Farnam St., Omaha NE 68102. Editor: Leland A. Larson. Published by Woodmen of the World Life Insurance Society for "people of all ages in all walks of life. We have both adult and children readers from all types of American families." Established in 1891. Monthly. Circulation: 400,000. Not copyrighted. Buys "about 20" mss a year. Pays on acceptance. Will send a sample copy to a writer on request. Query first or submit complete ms. Submit seasonal material 3 months in advance of issue date. Reports in 5 weeks. Enclose S.A.S.E. for reply to queries or return of submissions.
Nonfiction: "General interest articles which appeal to the American family — travel, history, art, new products, how-to-do-it, sports, hobbies, food, home decorating, family expenses, etc. Because we are a fraternal benefit society operating under a lodge system, we often carry stories on how a number of people can enjoy social or recreational activities as a group. No special approach required. We want more 'consumer type' articles, inspirational articles, humor, historical articles, think pieces, nostalgia, photo articles." Length: 600 to 2,000 words. Pays $10 minimum, 2¢ a word depending on word count.
Photos: Purchased with or without mss; captions optional "but suggested." Uses 8x10 glossies, 4x5 tranparencies ("and possibly down to 35mm"). Payment "depends on use." For b&w photos, pays $20 for cover, $10 for inside. Color prices vary according to use and quality.
Fiction: Humorous and historical short stories. Length: 600 to 2,000 words. Pays "$10 or 2¢ a word, depending on count."

Health Publications

Nearly every publication is a potential market for an appropriate health article, particularly the General Interest publications.

ACCENT ON LIVING, P.O. Box 700, Bloomington IL 61701. Phone: 309-378-4213. Editor: Raymond C. Cheever. For physically disabled persons and rehabilitation professionals. Quarterly magazine, 96 pages, (5x7). Established in 1956. Circulation: 13,500. Rights purchased vary with author and material. Buys 40 to 60 mss per year. Payment on publication. Will send sample copy to writer for 75¢. Write for copy of guidelines for writers. Will consider photocopied submissions. Will not consider simultaneous submissions. Reports in 2 weeks. Enclose S.A.S.E.
Nonfiction: Articles about seriously disabled people who have overcome great obstacles and are pursuing regular vocational goals. Home business ideas with facts

and figures on how someone confined to their home can run a business and make an average income. Especially interested in new technical aids, assistive devices, devised by an individual or available commercially, such as: bathroom and toilet aids and appliances, clothes and aids for dressing and undressing, aids for eating and drinking, as would be helpful to individuals with limited physical mobility. Intelligent discussion articles concerning the public image of an acceptance or non-acceptance of physically disabled in normal living situations. Articles reporting on lawsuits, demonstrations or protests by handicapped individuals or consumer groups to gain equal rights and opportunities. Length: 200 to 750 words. Pays up to $100 for good articles accompanied by photos.
Photos: B&w photos purchased with accompanying ms. Captions required. Pays $5 to $25.

ALIVE & WELL, Box 8092, Waco TX 76710. Editor: W. R. Spence, M.D. For health educators and the general public. 6 times per year. Average 80 pages, (6x9). Established in 1974. Buys all rights, but will reassign rights to author after publication. Only health news written by physicians; professionals in a branch of medicine or dentistry or a related field. Payment on acceptance. Will send free sample copy to writer on request. Write for copy of guidelines for writers. Will consider photocopied submissions. Will not consider simultaneous submissions. Submit seasonal material 4 months in advance. Reports on material in 2 to 3 weeks. Query first. Enclose S.A.S.E.
Nonfiction and Photos: Positive, constructive, crisp, brief, medically accurate articles dealing with health. Length: 200 to 1,000 words. Pays 5¢ per published word. Pays $5 for b&w photos purchased with accompanying ms. Recently published articles include "Questions Before Marriage," "Who's Afraid of the Croup?," "Exercise After Heart Attacks," and "Another Reason We Need Sleep," all with physician bylines.

BESTWAYS MAGAZINE, 466 Foothill Blvd., La Canada CA 91011. For housewives, students and those with an interest in health and nutrition. Monthly magazine; 64 pages. Established in 1973. Circulation: 115,000. Rights purchased vary with author and material. May buy all rights or simultaneous rights. Buys 100 or more mss a year. Payment on publication. Will send free sample copy to writer on request. Will consider photocopied and simultaneous submissions. Reports on material as soon as possible. Query first or submit complete ms. Enclose S.A.S.E.
Nonfiction and Photos: Articles on vitamins, minerals, exercise, nutrition. Easy to comprehend articles, based on products sold through health food stores. New information or new applications for understanding vitamin and mineral supplementation. Family feeding. Informational, how-to, personal experience, interview, profile, book reviews. Length: 1,600 to 5,000 words. Pays $75 to $150. No additional payment is usually made for b&w photos used with mss, but exceptions are sometimes made. Recently published articles include "Wheat Germ: The Heart of the Grain Issue," "Our Wonderful World of Cheese," "Magic in Your Kitchen (Sprouts)," "Arthritis Can be Prevented and Cured."

FAMILY HEALTH, 545 Madison Ave., New York NY 10022. Managing Editor: Caroline Stevens. For health-minded young parents. Magazine; 66 pages. Special issues: April and November (food and nutrition); October (baby and child care). Established in 1969. Monthly. Circulation: 1,000,000. Rights purchased vary with author and material. May buy all rights but may reassign rights to author after publication; first North American serial rights. Buys most of their articles from freelance writers. Pays on acceptance. Will send sample copy to writer for $1. No photocopied or simultaneous submissions. Submit special issue material 3 months in advance. Reports in 6 weeks. Query first for most nonfiction. Submit complete ms for first-person articles. Enclose S.A.S.E.
Nonfiction: Articles on all aspects of health, both mental and physical; safety, new advances in medicine. Fresh, new approaches essential. No "all about" articles (For example, "All About Mental Health."). Informational, how-to, personal experience, interview, profile, think articles, expose; book reviews. Length: 500 to 3,000 words. Pays $350 to $750.

THE GOOD LIFE, 33 Elm St., Bloomfield NJ 07003. Editor: William L. Florence. For all the family from tykes, to teenagers, to senior citizens. Newsletter/magazine; 48 to 64 pages. Established in 1975. Monthly. Circulation: 50,000. Buys all rights. Buys about 60 mss a year. Pays on acceptance. Will send free sample copy to writer on request. Will consider photocopied submissions. Query first for nonfiction. Reports in 2 to 4 weeks. Enclose S.A.S.E.

Nonfiction, Photos, and Poetry: "All health articles. Articles on all forms of leisure and recreation such as travel, games, etc. What is good for the mind is good for health, etc. Clinical okay, if light and most important, understandable, and not lost in medical terms. Style should be light and upbeat. Not at all interested in heavy tomes. Sex only in the health sense." Recently published articles include "Skinny Dipping: Yes/Sunbathing: No," the title tells the reader everything. Informational, how-to, personal experience, interview, profile, inspirational, humor, historical, think, nostalgia, photo, and travel. Length: 250 to 2,500 words. Pays 10¢ per word. Regular column "Your Body/Shop" uses short paragraphs. Pays $10. Photos purchased without ms or on assignment. Captions optional. Payment negotiable; price on submission. Poetry must relate to health themes. Length: 4 to 40 lines. Pays $15.

HEALTH, American Osteopathic Association, 212 E. Ohio St., Chicago IL 60611. Phone: 312-944-2713. Managing Editor: Mary Anne Klein. For patients of osteopathic physicians. Magazine; 28 pages, 8½x5½. Established in 1955. Published every 2 months. Circulation: 24,000. Buys first serial rights. Pays on acceptance. Will send free sample copy to writer on request. Write for copy of guidelines for writers. Query first. Reports wihtin 6 weeks. Enclose S.A.S.E.

Nonfiction and Photos: "Primarily educational material on health and health-related subjects (ecology, community health, mental health). We do not use first-person or fictional material. We use some feature-type articles on unusual events or situations. Material must be carefully researched (and documented by bibliography to the editor) but must be geared to the layman. We try to gear all material (even though the subject may be concerned with general medicine) to the philosophy of osteopathic medicine. We are especially concerned with preventive medicine, personal health care, nutrition, exercise, etc." Length: 1,200 to 1,500 words. Pays 4¢ per word. B&w photos purchased with ms. Pays $2.50 to $5, depending on quality and originality.

LIFE AND HEALTH, 6856 Eastern Ave., N.W., Washington DC 20012. Editor: Don Hawley. Established in 1884. Monthly. Circulation: 130,000. Buys all rights. Buys 100 to 180 mss a year. Payment on acceptance. Will send editorial guidelines sheet to a writer on request. Will send sample copy to writer for 50¢. Complimentary copies automatically to authors published. No query. Submit seasonal health articles 6 months in advance. Reports on material within two months. Enclose S.A.S.E.

Nonfiction, Photos, Poetry, and Fillers: General subject matter consists of "short, concise articles that simply and clearly present a concept in the field of health. Emphasis on prevention; faddism avoided." Approach should be a "simple, interesting style for laymen. Readability important. Medical jargon avoided. Material should be reliable and include latest findings. We are perhaps more conservative than other magazines in our field. Not seeking sensationalism." Buys informational, interview, some humor. "Greatest single problem is returning articles for proper and thorough documentation. References to other lay journals not acceptable." Regular columns that seek freelance material are "Youth Corner" and "Your Wonderful Body." Length: up to 2,000 words. Pays $50 to $150. Purchases photos with mss. 5x7 or larger b&w glossies. Pays $7.50. Color photos usually by staff. Pays $75. Buys some health-related poetry, minimum of $10. "Can use some in-depth briefs on structure or function such as fingernails, hair, salivary digestion, shivering, etc." Pays $10 to $20.

LISTEN MAGAZINE, 6840 Eastern Ave. N.W., Washington DC 20012. Phone: 202-723-0800. Editor: Francis A. Soper. For teenage audience. *Listen* is used in many high school curriculum classes, in addition to use by professionals; medical personnel, counselors, law enforcement officers, educators, youth workers, etc.

Monthly magazine, 24 pages, (8½x11½). Established in 1948. Circulation: 200,000. Buys all rights. Buys 100 to 200 mss per year. Payment on acceptance. Will send free sample copy to writer on request. Write for copy of guidelines for writers. Will not consider photocopied submissions or simultaneous submissions. Reports within 4 weeks. Query first. Enclose S.A.S.E.

Nonfiction: Specializes in preventive angle, presenting positive alternatives to various drug dependencies. Especially interested in youth-slanted articles or personality interviews encouraging nonalcoholic and nondrug ways of life. Teenage point of view is good. Popularized medical, legal, and educational articles. "We don't want typical alcoholic story/skid-row bum, AA stories." Length: 500 to 1,500 words. Pays 2¢ to 4¢ per word.

Photos: Purchased with or without accompanying ms. Captions required if photos accompany ms; captions optional on general photo submissions. Pays $5 to $10 per b&w (5x7, but 8x10 preferred). Color done mostly on assignment; some general color photos (2x2 transparencies).

Poetry and Fillers: Blank verse and free verse only. No traditional forms. Some inspirational poetry; short poems preferred. Word square/general puzzles are also considered. Pays $5 for poetry. Payment for fillers varies according to length and quality.

How To Break In: "Personal stories are good, especially if they have a unique angle. Other authoritative articles need a fresh approach."

MUSCLE MAGAZINE INTERNATIONAL, 32-A Queen St., W., Brampton, Ontario, Canada. Editor: Robert Kennedy. For 20- to 30-year-old men interested in physical fitness and overall body improvement. Magazine; 116 pages. Established in 1974. Quarterly. Circulation: 110,000. Buys all rights. Buys 80 mss a year. Pays on acceptance. Will send sample copy to writer for $1. No photocopied or simultaneous submissions. Reports in 1 week. Submit complete ms. Enclose S.A.E. and International Reply Coupons.

Nonfiction and Photos: Articles on ideal physical proportions and importance of protein in the diet. Should be helpful and instructional and appeal to young men who want to live life in a vigorous and healthy style. "We do not go in for huge, vein-choked muscles and do not want to see any articles on attaining huge muscle size. We would like to see articles for the physical culturist or an article on fitness testing. We recently published an entirely new and newsy article on an-old time strongman from Canada." Informational, how-to, personal experience, interview, profile, inspirational, humor, historical, expose, nostalgia, personal opinion, photo, spot news, new product, merchandising technique articles. Length: 1,200 to 1,600 words. Pays 6¢ per word. Columns purchasing material include Nutrition Talk (eating ideas for top results) and Shaping Up (improving fitness and stamina). Length: 1,300 words. Pays 6¢ per word. B&w and color photos are purchased with or without ms. Pays $8 for 8x10 glossy exercise photos; $16 for 8x10 b&w posing shots. Pays $100 for color; 2¼x2¼ or larger.

Fillers: Newsbreaks, clippings, puzzles, jokes, short humor. Length: open. Pays $5, minimum.

SWEET 'N LOW, P.O. Box 925, Woodland Hills CA 91365. "A nationally distributed magazine of interest to those whose primary interest is in diet and health." Published every two months. Established in 1972. Circulation: 250,000. Buys all rights. Buys 50 mss per year. Payment on publication. Will send sample copy to writer for $1. Query first. "If no answer in 2 weeks, idea is rejected." Enclose S.A.S.E.

Nonfiction, Fiction, and Photos: Offers low-calorie recipes, the latest in diets, provocative views on diet and health by authorities, coverage of programs at health and diet salons, and interviews with celebrities who have dieted and have succeeded. Photos suitable for publication must accompany ms. Illustrations acceptable. Some way to graphically describe the material is appreciated. An informal, candid approach to diet and health is important. "Our prime audience is women and they are interested in themselves and their children, too. There is no one publication in the field that is specifically devoted to all kinds of diet and which reports to the non-health foods addict about nutrition in an informal, yet informative way. We're open to any new diet or plan, even by local diet salons and teachers. We continue to like medically oriented pieces. We want more controversial subjects covered." Length: prefers 5,000 words. Rates are based on per article basis. Average ranges to $100 per article with photos. Could be more if the article is felt provocative and original enough. "Fiction is also considered, if humorous and with an overall message about health and/or diet."

TODAY'S HEALTH, 535 N. Dearborn St., Chicago IL 60610. Editor: David L. Murray. For "average young American parents, high school age youngsters, adults with high school education." Monthly. Circulation: over 3,000,000. Buys all rights. Pays on acceptance. Will send a sample copy to a writer on request. Query first. "No unsolicited mss." Enclose S.A.S.E.

Nonfiction and Photos: "Looks for family angle wherever possible and covers such subject areas as nutrition, recreation, child development, ecology and other health-related community problems, latest developments in the treatment of diseases. Also looks for fresh insights on improving the ways people interact, health angles on major news events and personalities, and well-documented pieces crusading for better, healthier living. Prefers upbeat approach to stories. Medical articles must be scientifically accurate. Photo stories usually assigned." Buys only one-time rights for photos. Length: 2,500 to 3,000 words. Pays $500 to $1,000. Pays $50 minimum for b&w and $150 for color photos.

How To Break In: "We would first be attracted to a compelling story suggestion; one that we'd ask the writer to build into a substantial outline. We'd get some notion of the writer's style and organizational skills from the outline, and we might also request writing samples to get further insight into the writer's strengths and weaknesses. We do run a short regular feature, '*Today's Health News*,' and contributors would certainly be encouraged to approach us with newsy items turned out with a touch of wit or poignance or some other special quality."

WEIGHT WATCHERS MAGAZINE, 635 Madison Ave., New York NY 10022. Phone: 212-688-4070. Editor: Bernadette Carr. For middle class females, mostly married, with children. Monthly magazine, 68 pages. Established in 1968. Circulation: 660,000. Buys first North American serial rights. Buys 75 to 100 mss per year. Payment on acceptance. Will send sample copy to writer for 75¢. Write for copy of guidelines for writers. Will not consider photocopied or simultaneous submissions. Submit seasonal material 5 months in advance. Reports within 4 weeks. Enclose S.A.S.E.

Nonfiction: General interest articles. Medical articles. Food, fashion, beauty, and success stories are generated in-house. Stay away from weight, diet, exercise and related subjects. "I like to see pieces where authorities are interviewed and quoted." Informational, how-to, humor, think articles, and nostalgia articles. Particularly open to new material on both children and money, but stay away from narrow, personal experience pieces like "How to Have a Garage Sale." Length: 3,000 words maximum. Pay varies, usually $225 to $275.

History Publications

ALASKA JOURNAL, History and Arts of the North, 422 Calhoun Ave., Juneau AK 99801. Phone: 907-586-3165. Editor: R. N. DeArmond. For history students and people interested in Alaska history. Also individuals interested in the art and artists of Alaska. Quarterly magazine, 64 pages, (8½x11). Established in 1970. Circulation: 10,000. Buys first North American serial rights. Buys 30 mss per year. Payment on publication. Will send sample copy to writer for $1. Will consider photocopied submissions. Will not consider simultaneous submissions. Reports in 1 month. Query first. Enclose S.A.S.E.

Nonfiction and Photos: Documented historical articles on Alaska and Yukon territory; articles on Alaska art and artists, with emphasis on color work. Must be familiar with Alaska and its history. Interviews on art only, historical articles, and book reviews. Recently published articles include "The Council City & Solomon River Railroad," "Nancy Stonington, Watercolorist," "Reindeer: Cattle of the Arctic," and "AFL, IWW and Nome: 1905-1908." Length: 500 to 10,000 words. Pays 1¢ to 2¢ per word. Photos purchased with accompanying ms. Captions required. Pays $5 for 5x7 to 8x10 b&w glossy. Color payment by arrangement. 35mm must be Kodachrome II. Photos of works of art only.

AMERICAN HERITAGE, 1221 Avenue of the Americas, New York NY 10020. Phone: 212-997-4056. Editor: Oliver Jensen. Established in 1954. Bimonthly. Circulation: 210,000. Buys all rights. Buys about 20 uncommissioned mss a year. Pays on acceptance. Before submitting, "check our five- and ten-year indexes to see whether we have already treated the subject." Submit seasonal material 8 months in advance. Returns rejected material in 1 month. Acknowledges acceptance of material in 2 months. Query first. Enclose S.A.S.E.
Nonfiction: Wants "historical articles intended for intelligent lay readers rather than professional historians." Emphasis is on authenticity, accuracy, and verve. Style should stress "readability and accuracy." Length: 4,000 to 5,000 words. Pays $350 to $750. Articles Editor: E.M. Halliday.
Fillers: "We occasionally buy shorts and fillers that deal with American history."
How To Break In: "Our needs are such that the criteria for a young, promising writer are unfortunately no different than those for an old hand. Nevertheless, we have over the years published quite a few 'firsts' from young writers whose historical knowledge, research methods, and writing skills meet our standards from the start. Everything depends on the quality of the material. We don't really care whether the author is twenty and unknown, or eighty and famous."

AMERICAN HISTORY ILLUSTRATED, CIVIL WAR TIMES ILLUSTRATED, Box 1831, Harrisburg PA 17105. Phone: 717-234-5091. Editor: Robert H. Fowler. Aimed at general public with an interest in sound, well-researched history. Monthly except March and September. Buys all rights. Pays on acceptance. Will send a sample copy of either for $1. Write for copy of guidelines for writers. Suggestions to freelancers: "Do not bind ms or put it in a folder or such. Simply paperclip it. We prefer a ribbon copy, not a carbon or xerox. No multiple submissions, please. It is best to consult several back issues before submitting any material, in order to see what we have already covered and to get an idea of our editorial preferences. Please include a reading list of materials used in preparing the article." Reports within two weeks. Query first. Enclose S.A.S.E.
Nonfiction: U.S. history, pre-historic to the 1950's, biography, military, social, cultural, political, etc. Also the U.S. in relation to the rest of the world, as in World Wars I and II, diplomacy, The Civil War; military, biography, technological, social, diplomatic, political, etc. Style should be readable and entertaining, but not glib or casual. Slant generally up to the author. Taboos: footnotes, shallow research, extensive quotation. 2,500 to 6,000 words. Pays $50 to $200.
Photos: Buys only occasionally with mss; 8x10 glossies preferred. Does welcome suggestions for illustrations. Address to Frederic Ray, Art Director.

THE AMERICAN WEST, 599 College Ave., Palo Alto CA 94306. Phone: 415-327-4660. Editor: George Pfeiffer, III. For people interested in the history of the West and in modern-day observations about the West. Bimonthly. Circulation: 30,000. Buys all rights. Buys approximately 30 mss a year. Pays within 60 days after acceptance. Will send a sample copy to "an accredited writer" on request. Write for copy of guidelines for writers. Query first. Will consider photocopied submissions. Reports in 3 to 4 weeks. Enclose S.A.S.E.
Nonfiction: "Articles about the West, wilderness, personalities of the old and new West. Our magazine is closest in idea to *American Heritage*, but deals primarily with the West." Prefers historical pieces "with graphics if at all possible." Wants articles that are "well-researched, in-depth, written with a flair. They should cover the subject, but not be too pedantic or studious. Also uses articles on natural history, archaeology, conservation and the environment. No militant articles. Too many pieces

are scantily researched, reminiscences of some long-lost relative, etc. A bibliography listing major sources should be included as an appendix to the article." Length: 2,500 to 4,000 words. Pays $100 to $250. For "Collector's Choice" feature, buys "short, 1,000-word portraits of noteworthy men, places, happenings of the West." Pays $75.

Photos: Purchased with ms. "We prefer captioned photos to be sent with submitted mss. Often seek photos ourselves. B&w or color. Prefer 4x5 transparencies." Also buys photo studies of "scenic wonders of the West." Pays $10 to $50.

How To Break In: "Best bet for us would be our 'Collector's Choice', 1,000-word article with a rare or unusual photo or piece of art. Another possibility is our Book Review Section." Reviews are assigned, but writers may submit their qualifications and special fields of interest if they would like to be included in list of reviewers. Pays from $10 to $40, plus a review copy of the book.

ART AND ARCHAEOLOGY NEWSLETTER, 243 East 39 St., New York NY 10016. Editor: Otto F. Reiss. For people interested in archaeology; educated laymen, educators, some professional archaeologists. Quarterly newsletter, 20 pages, (5½x8½). Established in 1965. Circulation: 1,500. Buys all rights, but will reassign rights to author after publication; buys second serial (reprint) rights. Buys 1 ms per year. Payment on publication. Will send sample copy to writer for $1. Will consider photocopied or simultaneous submissions. Query first. Enclose S.A.S.E.

Nonfiction: "Ancient history, archaeology, new discoveries, new conclusions, new theories. Our approach is similar to the way *Time Magazine* would treat archaeology or ancient history in its science section. A lighter tone, less rigidly academic. Don't avoid mystery, glamor, eroticism. Primarily interested in old world antiquity. Would like intriguing articles on Aztecs, Mayas, Incas, but not travel articles a la *Holiday*. Definitely not interested in Indian arrowheads, Indian pots, kivas, etc." Length: 400 to 2,500 words. Pays $20 to $25 per ms.

Photos: Purchased with accompanying ms with no additional payment. Purchased also without ms for $5 minimum for b&w. Information (data) required for all b&w photos. Will write own captions.

Fiction: Only "time-machine" short stories like Lampedusa's "The Mermaid." Such time-machine short stories are hard to find, because frequently exposition is so space consuming that story turns into a novel. Length: 3,500 words maximum. Pays $20 to $40.

How To Break In: "Spend five years reading books about archaeology and ancient history so that you become something of an expert on the subject. Be prepared to give precise sources, with page and paragraph, for factual statements. Some freelance writers, pretending to submit nonfiction, invent their material. Don't know what is on their mind, perhaps the ambition to be a pocket-size Clifford Irving. Altogether, dealing with freelance people in this field, is more trouble than it is worth. But hope blooms eternal. Perhaps there's another enthusiast who sneaked his way into an Alexander's Tomb."

CANADIAN TREASURE, P.O. Box 3399, Langley, B.C., Canada. Editor: Tom Paterson. For all age groups, with interests in history, treasure, or the great outdoors. Magazine; 72 (6x9) pages. Established in 1973. Quarterly. Circulation: 8,000. Buys first North American serial rights. Buys about 35 mss a year. Pays on publication. Will send free sample copy to writer on request. Will consider photocopied and simultaneous submissions. Reports on material accepted for publication in 6 to 8 weeks. Returns rejected material immediately. Query first or submit complete ms. Enclose S.A.E. and International Reply Coupons.

Nonfiction and Photos: Publishes only historical and treasure articles. Lost, sunken or buried treasure from Canada's provinces and territories, or a state in the U.S. which borders on the Canadian boundary. Bottles, relics, antiques, coin shooting, etc. Historical articles on battles, murders, shipwrecks, etc., (in Canada *only*). Recently published "Battle of Lundy's Lane" about a Canadian-American battle in the War of 1812 and "McLeod's Missing Millions," about lost Canadian treasure. Length: 1,000 to 3,000 words. Pays 1½¢ a word. B&w photos (5x7 or larger) purchased with mss. Pays $3 to $5.

CHICAGO HISTORY, Chicago Historical Society, North Ave. and Clark St., Chicago IL 60614. Editor: Isabel S. Crossner. For members of the Chicago Historical Society, history buffs and libraries. Quarterly magazine; 64 (7½x10¼) pages. Established in 1970. Circulation: 8,000. Usually buys all rights, but may reassign rights to author after publication. Buys 25 mss a year. Payment on acceptance. Will send free sample copy to writer on request. Will consider photocopied submissions. Will not consider simultaneous submissions. Reports on material accepted for publication in 2 to 3 months. Returns rejected material in 1 week. Query first. Enclose S.A.S.E.
Nonfiction: Popular history, well-illustrated. Articles on Chicago and regional history; society, cultural, ethnic, labor; any aspect. Should be well-researched material, nonacademic in style; anecdotal. Would like to see material on Chicago ethnic history by a member of that particular group; and on women's history, labor history, Chicago publications. Length: 4,500 words. Pays $125 to $250. Multiple book reviews on special topics (by a specialist) also used. Length: 1,500 words. Pays $75, plus books.

HISTORICAL REVIEW AND ANTIQUE DIGEST, 605 Merritt St., Nashville TN 37203. For a young adult to retired readership; anyone interested in history and antiques. Magazine; 64 (8½x11) pages. Established in 1972. Quarterly. Circulation: 3,000. Buys all rights. Buys 10 to 12 mss a year. Pays on publication. Will send free sample copy to writer on request. Reports in 8 to 10 weeks. Query first or submit complete ms. Enclose S.A.S.E.
Nonfiction and Photos: Articles on history (people, places and things). Antique articles. including old homes, collections, antique shows, history of antique pieces. "We use a good many pictures with our stories and like historical stories that have not been overworked. We prefer stories from all parts of the country, but we have too many on Tennessee." Recently published articles include "Slave Randal" (about the trial of a Georgia slave), and "Lion of White Hall" (the life of Cassius Clay). Length: 1,500 to 3,500 or 4,000 words. Pays $10 per article or $5 per published page. No additional payment for b&w photos used with ms.

JOURNAL OF AMERICAN HISTORY, Ballantine Hall, Indiana University, Bloomington IN 47401. Editor: Martin Ridge. For professional historians of all ages. Quarterly journal, 350 pages. Established in 1907. Circulation: 12,500. Buys all rights. Buys over 300 mss per year. Payment on acceptance. Reports in 10 to 12 weeks. Submit only complete ms. Enclose S.A.S.E.
Nonfiction: Material dealing with American history; analytical for the audience of professional historians. Length: 900 to 1,500 words. Pays $5 per page.

MANKIND, The Magazine of Popular History, 8060 Melrose Ave., Los Angeles CA 90046. Editor: Alvaro Cardona-Hine. Primarily college graduate reader audience. Bimonthly. Buys North American serial rights only. Buys about 50 mss a year. Pays on publication. Will send sample copy for $1.25. Query first. Enclose S.A.S.E.
Nonfiction: "Queries are preferred and should be extensive enough so the editors may determine where the article is going. We have found that most of the over-the-transom submissions are poorly researched for this market. Assignments are given only to writers who have sold here before or have a reputation in the field of historical writing. We are looking for articles on any aspect of history that can be rendered meaningful and alive and which lends itself to illustration. We would like to emphasize high quality writing together with accurateness and a fresh approach to history. We do not wish to see superficiality, survey generalizations or material of a shocking nature. We see far too many articles on the Civil War and most other aspects of American history." Prefers 5,000 words or less, but occasionally uses longer pieces; on occasion two-parters of 8,000 to 10,000 words. Pays $100 to $500.
Photos: Purchased with mss. Pays $35 per page for b&w. Pays $75 per page for color.
How To Break In: "There are no special departments for the beginner who wants to break in, save 'Guest Column,' which runs usually to 2,000 words and takes current events and compares them to similar happenings in the past. Check the magazine. A new writer can break in only by submitting an article impossible to

turn down. This not only means finding something original in history but treating it our way. Our way is to present material accurately and excitingly. Dry accounts filled with dates, the usual doctorate dissertation, are out, but so are gushy and romanticized accounts. Best way is to read the magazine and submit queries. Warning: we are really overstocked. That is not just a rejection ploy."

MONTANA, The Magazine of Western History, Montana Historical Society, 225 No. Roberts, Helena MT 59601. Phone: 406-449-2694. Editor: Mrs. Vivian Paladin. Quarterly. Circulation: 14,000. Prefers to buy first rights. Pays on acceptance. Will send a sample copy to a writer on request. Write for copy of guidelines for writers. Query first. Reports in 1 month. Enclose S.A.S.E. for reply to queries.

Nonfiction and Photos: "Interested in authentic articles on the history of the American and Canadian West which show original research on significant facets of history rather than the rewriting of standard incidents generally available in print. Evidence of research must accompany articles, either in the form of footnoting or bibliography. Strict historical accuracy is a must for us: we cannot use fictional material, however authentic the background may be. Unless it is very skillfully and authentically employed, contrived dialog is not acceptable." Length: 3,500 to 6,500 words with rare photographs if possible. Photos (b&w) purchased with ms. Pays $40 to $100, "depending on length and quality."

NORTH CAROLINA HISTORICAL REVIEW, 109 E. Jones St., Raleigh NC 27611. Editor: Mrs. Memory F. Mitchell. Quarterly. Buys all publication rights. Will send copy of footnote guide sheets to writer on request. Mss should be double-spaced; footnotes are to be double-spaced at end of article. Send the original and a carbon copy. Reports in 4 to 6 weeks. Enclose S.A.S.E.

Nonfiction and Photos: Scholarly articles relating to North Carolina history in particular, southern history in general. Topics about which relatively little is known or are new in interpretations of familiar subjects. All articles must be based on primary sources and footnoted. Length: 15 to 25 typed pages. Token payment of $10 per article. Likes b&w photos with articles, but no extra payment is made for them.

NORTH SOUTH TRADER, 8020 New Hampshire Ave., Langley Park MD 20783. Editor: Wm. S. Mussenden. For Civil War buffs, historians, collectors, relic hunters, libraries and museums. Magazine; 52 to 68 (8½x11) pages. Established in 1973. Every 2 months. Circulation: 3,000. Rights purchased vary with author and material. Usually buys all rights. Buys 70 mss a year. Pays on acceptance. Will send sample copy to writer for $1. Write for copy of guidelines for writers. Will consider photocopied and simultaneous submissions. Reports within 2 weeks. Query first or submit complete ms. Enclose S.A.S.E.

Nonfiction and Photos: General subject matter deals with battlefield preservation, relic restoration, military artifacts of the Civil War (weapons, accoutrements, uniforms, etc.); historical information on battles, camp sites and famous people of the War Between the States. Prefers a factual or documentary approach to subject matter. Emphasis is on current findings and research related to the places, people, and artifacts of the conflict. Not interested in treasure magazine type articles. Recent articles include one on Civil War plastics, a factual, well-researched article on the little-known role of plastics and hard rubber in the Civil War. Length: 500 to 3,000 words. Pays 2¢ a word. Columns and departments include Relic Restoration, Lost Heritage and Interview. Length: 1,000 to 1,500 words. Pays 2¢ a word. B&w photos are purchased with or without ms. Captions required. Pays $2.

Fillers: Newsbreaks, crossword puzzles, jokes, short humor. Prior query required for these. Pays 2¢ a word.

OLD WEST, FRONTIER TIMES, TRUE WEST, Western Publications, Inc., P.O. Box 3338, Austin TX 78764. Phone: 512-444-3674. Editor: Pat Wagner. Established in 1953. Bimonthly. Circulation: 175,000. Buys first North American serial rights. Payment on acceptance. Will send sample copy to writer for 60¢. Query first. Enclose S.A.S.E.

Nonfiction and Photos: "Factual accounts regarding people, places and events of the frontier West (1850 to 1910). Sources are required. If first-hand account, reminiscences must be accurate as to dates and events. We strive for accounts with an element of action, suspense, heroics and humor. Stories on the better known outlaws, Indians, lawmen, explorers will probably overlap material we have already run." Preferred length: 750 to 4,000 words. Pays 2¢ a word minimum. Buys color cover photos. "We usually buy mss and accompanying photos as a package. All photos are returned after publication."

PERSIMMON HILL, 1700 N.E. 63rd St., Oklahoma City OK 73111. Editor: Dean Krakel. For a Western art and Western history and rodeo oriented audience; historians, artists, ranchers, art galleries, schools, libraries. Publication of the National Cowboy Hall of fame. Established in 1970. Quarterly. Circulation: 20,000. Buys all rights. Buys 20 to 30 mss a year. Pays on publication. Will send a sample copy to writer for $2. Will consider photocopied submissions. No simultaneous submissions. Reporting time on mss accepted for publication varies. Returns rejected material immediately. Submit complete ms. Enclose S.A.S.E.
Nonfiction and Photos: Historical and contemporary articles on famous western figures connected with pioneering the American West, or biographies of such people; stories of Western flora and animal life, famous ranches and early manufacturers. Only thoroughly researched and historically authentic human and horse interest material is considered. May have a humorous approach to subject. Not interested in articles that re-appraise, or in any way put the West and its personalities in an unfavorable light. Length: 2,000 to 3,000 words. Pays a minimum of $150, maximum of $750. B&w glossies or color transparencies purchased with or without ms, or on assignment. Pays according to quality and importance for b&w and color. Suggested captions appreciated.

SEA CLASSICS, 7950 Deering Ave., Canoga Park CA 91304. Phone: 213-887-0550. Editor: Jim Scheetz. For persons "who enjoy in-depth accounts of ships and events at sea." Bimonthly. Circulation: 55,000. Buys first rights. Buys 30 mss a year. Pays on publication. Will send a sample copy and editorial guidelines sheet to a published writer on request. Reports in 3 weeks. Enclose S.A.S.E. for return of submissions.
Nonfiction: "Historical articles dealing with men and ships at sea—from the stately liners to the deadly torpedo boats. Articles should show research and a thorough knowledge of the subject, with new data or fresh approach. A good collection of photographs must support the article. Emphasis is being placed on the liners, research vessels, lumber boats, ice breakers—anything related to the lore of the sea. We recently even included an article on ships appearing on stamps from around the world." Length: 1,000 to 3,500 words. Payment to $150, "depending mostly on photo collection."
Photos: "Photographic content is much more important and is usually the determining factor as to whether or not we can use the article." (Photos emphasize ships as products of the shipbuilder's art, and seldom show people or crews.) B&w and color photos purchased with mss; with captions. "No copyrighted photos or any photos to which rights are held can be accepted unless author has a release."
Fillers: Museum and reunion news items for "Shore Log." Payment with copies when requested.
How To Break In: "We are more than pleased to review, and accept for publication, mss by new writers; however, they must follow our format. It seems many new writers make the mistake of writing a story, then thumbing through *Writer's Market* to see where they might send it without revision. For instance, a writer is wasting his time sending us a ms without photos, no matter how good the article! We provide free sample copies of *Sea Classics* on request. I quickly and willingly send sample copies to writers who show sincere interest in wanting to write for us. Mimeographed requests for sample copies are thrown in the trash. It seems for every hundred freebies I send to writers, I might get two article submissions. A quick glance through the magazine would immediately tell a new writer that photos are a must, and I think that requirement is spelled out quite clearly in our listing. Writers seem to ignore certain guidelines, I suppose with the hopes that their's will be the first exception.

I also expect new writers to follow a certain degree of professionalism; clean, double-spaced, typewritten copy, captions with photos, etc. Why are these things so often ignored? Finally, our readers are avid ship enthusiasts. They quickly spot technical errors in writing. Mss must be thoroughly researched and written with authority, and with as much new information as possible."

VIRGINIA CAVALCADE, Virginia State Library, Richmond VA 23219. Phone: 804-770-2311. Primarily for Virginians and others with an interest in Virginia history. Quarterly magazine; 48 pages. Established in 1951. Circulation: 17,000. Buys all rights. Buys 15 to 20 mss a year. Payment on acceptance. Will send sample copy to writer for 75¢. Write for copy of "Invitation to Authors." Will consider photocopied submissions. Rarely considers simultaneous submissions. Submit seasonal material 15 to 18 months in advance. Reports in 4 weeks to 1 year. Query first. Enclose S.A.S.E.

Nonfiction and Photos: "Readable and factually accurate articles by qualified authors on the personalities, places, and events of Virginia's past are welcomed. Must be directly relevant to some phase of Virginia history. Art, architecture, literature, education, business, technology, and transportation are all acceptable subjects, as well as political and military affairs. We like articles based on thorough, scholarly research and written in a semipopular style. We require footnotes but do not publish them. Authors should avoid contemporary political and social topics, particularly those on which people hold strong and conflicting opinions. Any period from the age of exploration to the mid-twentieth century, and any geographical section or area of the state may be represented. Should deal with subjects that will appeal to a broad readership, rather than to a very restricted group or locality. Originality in either subject matter or approach is essential. Fresh and little known themes are preferred; manuscripts on more familiar subjects should treat them in a new light or rest on new documentary evidence. Authors should query us concerning seasonal material. We publish special issues from time to time. All articles must be suitable for illustration, though it is not necessary that the author provide the pictures. The Library maintains an extensive picture file and can have photographs made of extant subjects when no suitable illustrations can be located. If, however, the author does have pertinent illustrations or knows their location, the editor would appreciate information concerning their availability." Uses 8x10 b&w glossies; color transparencies must be at least 4x5. Length: approximately 2,500 words. Pays $100.

How To Break In: "First, query. Then send a thoroughly researched, well-organized, well-written, fully annotated, interesting article of no more than 15 to 20 pages. Relatively unfamiliar but reasonably significant aspects of Virginia history, based on original research, are preferred. We especially welcome articles from graduate students and professional historians. Authors should avoid a fictionalized or overly popularistic style."

VIRGINIA MAGAZINE OF HISTORY AND BIOGRAPHY, Virginia Historical Society, P.O. Box 7311, Richmond VA 23221. Editor: William M.E. Rachal. Quarterly for serious students of Virginia history. Usually buys all rights. Pays on publication. Reports in one month. Enclose S.A.S.E. for return of submissions.

Nonfiction: Carefully researched and documented articles on Virginia history, and well-edited source material relating to Virginia. Must be dignified, lucid, scholarly. Length: 1,500 to 15,000 words. Appropriate illustrations are used. Pays $2 per printed page.

THE WESTERN PRODUCER, Box 2500, Saskatoon, Sask., S7K 2C4, Canada. Phone: 306-242-7651. Editor: R.H.D. Phillips. For "mainly rural, farm-ranch orient- ed" audience. Circulated in 4 western Canadian provinces. Weekly. Newspaper. Circulation: 150,000. Buys first rights. Pays on acceptance. Reports in 1 month. Enclose S.A.E. and International Reply Coupons for return of submissions.

Nonfiction: Publishes authentic, pioneering western Canadiana, history, memoirs, real experiences. Preferred length not over 2,500 words for short features, longer for serials. Payment varies from 1¢ to 5¢ per word, depending on need and quality.

Photos: Good pioneering photos, Canadian scenic, or seasonal photos accepted. Uses color pix features in addition to b&w. Color transparencies (2¼x2¼) of good quality, all subjects. Pays $5 to $75, depending on use. Query first for photos.
Fiction: Based on western situations (not shooting stories), humorous and otherwise, light love stories. Payment varies from 1¢ to 5¢ a word.
How To Break In: "Bombard the editor with good, lightly written stories tailored to his journal—which means—read the journal first."

Hobby and Craft Publications

Publications in this section are for collectors, do-it-yourselfers, and craft hobbyists. Publications for electronics and radio hobbyists will be found in the Science classification.

ACQUIRE: THE MAGAZINE OF CONTEMPORARY COLLECTIBLES, 170 5th Ave., New York NY 10010. Editor: R. C. Rowe. For collectors, mostly 30 to 65 in age, many rural and suburban, affluent and reasonably well educated. Published 5 times a year. Established in 1973. Circulation: 50,000. Rights purchased vary with author and material. Buys all rights, but will reassign rights to author after publication; first North American serial rights; first serial rights; second serial (reprint) rights; simultaneous rights. Buys 15 to 30 mss a year. "First assignments are always done on a speculative basis." Payment on acceptance. Will send sample copy to writer for $1. Will consider photocopied submissions and simultaneous submissions. Query first, with an outline. Reports within 1 month. Enclose S.A.S.E.
Nonfiction: "Short features about collecting, written in tight, newsy style. We specialize in contemporary (postwar) collectibles. Particularly interested in items affected by scarcity." Informational, how-to, interview, profile, expose, nostalgia. Length: 500 to 2,500 words. Pays $50 to $150. Columns cover stamps, cars, porcelains, glass, western art, and graphics. Length: 750 words. Pays $75.
Photos: B&w and color photos purchased with accompanying ms with no additional payment. Also purchased without ms and on assignment. Captions are required. Wants clear, distinct, full frame image that says something. Pays $10 to $50. Photo Editor: S. Linden.

THE AMERICAN BLADE, P.O. Box 1458, Gretna LA 70053. Editor: William L. Cassidy. For well-educated, professional people, age 25 to 60, interested in cutlery, knives, etc. Magazine; 56 pages (8½x11). Established in 1972. Every two months. Circulation: 75,000. Buys all rights. Buys 50 to 75 mss a year. Payment on publication. Will send sample copy to writer for $1.50. Write for copy of guidelines for writers. Will consider photocopied submissions. Will not consider simultaneous submissions. Reports in 1 to 2 months. Submit complete ms. Enclose S.A.S.E.
Nonfiction and Photos: Main interest is in the history of cutlery. Also uses cutlery collecting tips, material relative to knives, pocketknives, bowie knives, swords, etc. No articles on custom knifemaking or James Bowie. Informational, how-to, interview, profile, historical, personal opinion, technical reviews, spot news, successful business operations, new product, technical. Length: 500 to 2,000 words. Pays $50 to $200. Buys b&w and color photos with or without accompanying ms, or on assignment. Sometimes no additional payment is made for b&w. In other cases, payment for b&w ranges from $3 to $25. 8x10 b&w glossies, no matte, double-weight paper. Pays $100 for 4x5 color transparencies. Captions optional.

AMERICAN COLLECTOR, 13920 Mt. McClellan Blvd., Reno NV 89506. Phone: 702-972-0721. Editor: John F. Maloney. For "collectors of any age; wealthy, well-educated; specialists deeply interested in whatever they collect. Some are investors." Monthly tabloid (newsprint); 40 pages. Established in 1970. Circulation: 60,000. Buys all rights, but will reassign rights to author after publication. Buys about 120 mss a year. Payment on publication. Will send free sample copy to writer on request.

Write for copy of guidelines for writers. Will consider photocopied and simultaneous submissions. Reports in 2 weeks. Query first or submit complete ms. Enclose S.A.S.E.
Nonfiction and Photos: "Articles about private collections, collectors, and collecting, with information on prices, values, trends, availability, fakes, etc. We also buy news and occasional humorous pieces. Most are in-depth features. Make it lively, interesting, even controversial, but no 'antiques are lovely' type stories. Our emphasis is on collecting, rather than history. Keep the tempo lively." Informational, how-to, interview, historical, expose, nostalgia, personal opinion, spot news. Recently published articles include "The Dean of American Bottle Collectors," "Collecting Ambrotypes," "Vintage Autos: Pitfalls on the Road to Profit," "A Guide to Collecting Old Coffee Mills," "Oak Ice Boxes Now Lend Warmth." Length: 2,000 words for features; news up to 500 words. Pays $1.20 per published inch. Pays $5 for b&w photos; $10 for 35mm slide transparencies.
How To Break In: "Send us a well-researched expose on fakes, frauds, swindles, etc. Or, send us an original research piece that turns up new information on a type of antique that is indispensable to those who collect it. (An example of an expose would be our uncovering of 'antique and authentic' Wells Fargo buckles as all being contemporary phonies; an example of new research might be something like 'such-and-such a glass manufacturer made all the glass formerly attributed to so-and-so'."

AMERICANA, 1221 Avenue of the Americas, New York NY 10020. Editor: Michael Durham. For "a very well-educated, mature audience, interested in American history, especially such things as architecture, design, crafts, travel, etc." Established in 1973. Bimonthly. Circulation: 250,000. Buys all rights. Payment on acceptance. Will send sample copy to writer on request. Reports on material in 3 weeks. Query first. Enclose S.A.S.E.
Nonfiction: "Materials of the broadest range of American creation from gardens to cut glass; from collecting Revere silver to automobile hood ornaments. We are interested in anything Americans have created. Our special approach is that, although we are interested in the creative American past, we are a contemporary magazine. The ideal reaction to any story is that the reader will want to and be able to do something about it now; to go to that place, prepare that meal, collect that object, now." Length: 1,500 to 2,500 words. Pays $200 to $300.

THE ANTIQUE TRADER WEEKLY, P.O. Box 1050, Dubuque IA 52001. Editor: Kyle D. Husfloen. For collectors and dealers in antiques and collectibles. Weekly newspaper; 75 to 85 pages. Established in 1957. Circulation: 80,000 to 90,000. Buys all rights, but will reassign rights to author after publication. Buys about 200 mss a year. Payment at end of month following publication. Will send free sample copy to writer on request. Write for copy of guidelines for writers. Will consider photocopied and simultaneous submissions. Submit seasonal material (holidays) 3 to 4 months in advance. Prompt reports. Query first or submit complete ms. Enclose S.A.S.E.
Nonfiction and Photos: "We invite authoritative and well-researched articles on all types of antiques and collectors' items. Submissions should include a liberal number of good b&w photos. We also welcome feature cover stories which are accompanied by a good, clear color negative or transparency which illustrates the feature. The feature should also have several b&w photos. to illustrate the inside text. A color negative of 4x5 is desirable for use as cover photo, but a smaller negative or transparency is sometimes acceptable. We also solicit brief news items concerning antiques and collectibles, related clubs and groups and short notes of interest to antiques hobby." Pays $5 to $35 for feature articles; $35 to $65 for feature cover stories; $5 to $20 for brief news items. "We do not pay for brief information on new shops opening or other material printed as service to the antiques hobby."

ANTIQUES GAZETTE, P.O. Box 776, Merrimack NH 03054. Editor: George Michael. For antique dealers, collectors, buyers, museums. Tabloid newspaper; 36 (11½x17) pages. Established in 1974. Monthly. Circulation: 3,000. Buys all rights, but will reassign rights to author after publication. Buys 48 mss per year. Payment on publication. Will send free sample copy to writer on request. Write for copy of guidelines for writers. Reports immediately. Query first. Enclose S.A.S.E.

Nonfiction and Photos: "We cover New England and serve as a directory of antiquing in these six states. We want 'today' information on the buying, selling, collecting and investing in antiques and art in New England. No articles on the history of antiques." As an example of recently published articles, see "When to Call the FBI," about stealing of antiques. Length: 3 double-spaced, typewritten pages. Pays $15 to $25. No additional payment is made for 5x7 or 8x10 b&w photos used with mss.

THE ANTIQUES JOURNAL, P.O. Box 88128, Dunwoody GA 30338. Editor: John Mebane. For collectors of antiques, art and other collectible objects; antique dealers. Monthly magazine; 68 (8x11) pages. Established in 1946. Circulation: 100,000. Rights purchased vary with author and material. May buy all rights, but will sometimes reassign rights to author after publication. Buys 100 to 150 mss a year. Payment on publication. Will send sample copy to writer for $1. Will not consider photocopied or simultaneous submissions. Submit seasonal material (Christmas) 9 months in advance. Reports in 2 weeks. Query first. Enclose S.A.S.E.

Nonfiction: "Factual, well-researched articles with original material on antiques and other collectible objects. We often focus upon late 19th and early 20th century collectible objects and include the Art Nouveau and Art Deco periods. Many of the traditional antiques have been exhaustively treated, and a freelancer's best bet is to explore a newer area of collecting. Would like to see any new approach to antiques relative to Christmas and other holidays." Informational, interview, historical material. Length: 750 to 2,500 words. Pays $35 to $75. Recently published articles include "Collecting as an Investment," "Stained Glass," and "Big Little Books."

BOAT BUILDER, 229 Park Ave., South, New York NY 10003. Phone: 212-673-1300. Editor: Andrew J. Carra. For "people interested in building their own boats." 2 times a year. Circulation: 50,000. Buys all rights. Buys 6 to 7 mss a year. Pays on acceptance. Reports in 4 weeks. Enclose S.A.S.E.

Nonfiction and Photos: Needs articles that are "step-by-step exposition of how to build different boats, in clear, semitechnical language." New product articles come from manufacturers. Length: 250 to 1,500 words. Payment is $25 to $200. B&w glossy photos with captions are purchased with manuscripts.

COLLECTOR'S WORLD, P.O. Box 919, Kermit TX 79745. Editor: Fred B. Green. For readers interested in collecting and related fields. Monthly. Circulation: 10,000. Buys first North American serial rights. Buys 100 mss a year. Payment on publication. Query first or submit complete ms. Reports in 4 weeks. Enclose S.A.S.E.

Nonfiction and Photos: "Treasure hunting articles on old things wanted by collectors; bottles, relics, antiques, primitives, etc. What collectors are buying; how to find, restore and evaluate and sell them. Lost or missing art treasures, antiques, rare items, etc. Treatment should be objective and informational." Length: 1,500 to 2,000 words. Minimum payment: 10% of published material paid in copies only. Maximum: 3¢ per word. No additional payment for 3x5 or 5x7 b&w photos.

Fillers: On above topics. Length: 300 to 500 words. Minimum payment in copies and byline. Maximum: 3¢ per word.

CRAFT HORIZONS, 44 West 53rd St., New York NY 10019. Editor-in-Chief: Rose Slivka. Bimonthly. Circulation: 33,000. Published by American Crafts Council for professional craftsmen, artists, teachers, architects, designers, decorators, collectors, connoisseurs and the consumer public. Copyrighted. Pays on publication. Will send free sample copy to writer on request. Reports as soon as possible. Query first. Enclose S.A.S.E.

Nonfiction and Photos: 1,000-word articles and accompanying photos on the subject of creative work in ceramics, weaving, stitchery, jewelry, metalwork, woodwork, etc. Discussions of the technology, the materials and the ideas of artists throughout the world working in the above media. Pays $75 to $100 per article. Accompanying photos should be 8x10 b&w glossies. Pays $7.50 per b&w glossy.

CREATIVE CRAFTS, P.O. Box 700, Newton NJ 17860. Editor: Sybil C. Harp. For serious craft hobbyists (mostly mature women). Published 8 times a year plus a Christmas annual; 68 (8x11) pages. Established in 1967. Circulation: about 100,000. Buys all rights. Buys about 60 mss a year. Payment on publication. Will send sample copy to writer for 60¢. Will consider photocopied and simultaneous submissions. Submit special and seasonal material at least 7 months in advance. Reports in 6 weeks. Query first . Enclose S.A.S.E.

Nonfiction and Photos: "How-to articles on all types of crafts. Prefer original craft projects that readers can complete from instructions. Emphasis is on in-depth coverage. Must have clear, instructional style. We do not cover knitting, crocheting or dressmaking. We are always looking for original Christmas ideas for our annual and December issue." Recently published articles include "Patchwork Quilting," "Feather Working," "Twined Basketry." Length: 800 to 2,500 words. Pays $30 to $50 per magazine page. "Going Places" column uses travel articles dealing with special craft shows, fairs, shops, etc. Length: about 1,300 words. Pays $25 per magazine page. "All articles submitted must be illustrated with photos and/or drawings. In cases where photos must be taken professionally, we will give an allowance of up to $35."

DECORATING & CRAFT IDEAS MADE EASY, 1303 Foch, Ft. Worth TX 76107. Editor: Fredrica Daugherty. For women whose main interests are crafts, decorating and sewing. Magazine; 80 (8½x10¾) pages. Established in 1970. Monthly except January and July. Circulation: 650,000. Buys all rights, but will reassign rights to author after publication. Buys 10 mss a year. Pays on publication. Will send free sample copy to writer on request. Write for copy of guidelines for writers. Reports as soon as possible. Query first. Enclose S.A.S.E.

Nonfiction and Photos: Material on craft projects, craft-related travel, sewing projects, needlework projects. Simple, straightforward approach; clear, concise, complete instructions. In crafts, the emphasis must be on what makes the project unique. "We explain a craft project, show it close-up, in a decorative manner and completely explain how a reader can reproduce the project." Length: 600 to 1,000 words, not including instructions. Rate of payment is variable (minimum, $50) and is negotiated with each writer.

EARLY AMERICAN LIFE, Early American Society, P.O. Box 1831, Harrisburg PA 17105. Phone: 717-234-2674. Editor: Robert G. Miner. For "people who are interested in capturing the warmth and beauty of the 1600 to 1850 period and using it in their homes and lives today. They are interested in arts, crafts, travel, restoration, collecting." Magazine published every 2 months; over 100 (8½x11) pages. Established in 1970. Circulation: 240,000. Buys all rights. Buys 50 mss a year. Payment on acceptance. Will send free sample copy to writer on request. Write for copy of guidelines for writers. Will consider photocopied submissions. Will not consider simultaneous submissions. Reports in 1 month. Query first or submit complete ms. Enclose S.A.S.E.

Nonfiction and Photos: "Social history (the story of the people, not epic heroes and battles); crafts such as woodworking and needlepoint; travel to historical sites; country inns; antiques and reproductions; refinishing and restoration; architecture and decorating. We try to entertain as we inform, but always attempt to give the reader something he can do. While we're always on the lookout for good pieces on any of our subjects, the 'travel to historic sites' theme is most frequently submitted. Would like to see more how-to-do-it (well-illustrated) on how real people did something great to their homes." Length: 750 to 4,000 words. Pays $50 to $200. Pays $10 for 5x7 (and up) b&w photos used with mss; minimum of $25 for color. Prefers 2¼ and up, but can work from 35mm.

How To Break In: "Get a feeling for 'today's early Americans', the folks who are visiting flea markets, auctions, junkyards, the antiques shops. They are our readers and they hunger for ideas on how to bring the warmth and beauty of early America into their lives. Then, conceive a new approach to satisfying their related interests in arts, crafts, travel to historic sites, and the story of the people of the 1600 to

1850 period. Write to entertain and inform at the same time, and be prepared to help us with illustrations, or sources for them."

FLEA MARKET QUARTERLY, Box 243, Bend OR 97701. Editor: Annette O'Connell. For flea market owners, dealers and shoppers. All ages, walks of life and educational backgrounds. Magazine (almanac), (8½x11), 50 pages. "Our publication is seasonal; for example, spring, summer, fall, and winter. Established in 1973. Circulation: 5,000. Buys all rights. Buys 20 to 30 mss a year. Payment on acceptance. Will send sample copy to writer for $1. Will consider photocopied submissions. Submit seasonal material 2 months in advance. Submit only complete ms. Reports in 1 month. Enclose S.A.S.E.

Nonfiction and Photos: "Short items of wit; money-making, money-saving tips; recycling ideas; practical ecological news; collecting trends; alternate lifestyle ideas; consumer affairs and health briefs. Use inspirational, optimistic approach, but be frank. There is no other nationwide flea market publication. We particularly like articles giving money-making ideas that require little capital to get started." Informational, how-to, personal experience, interview, profile, inspirational, humor, nostalgia, photo, travel, book reviews, successful business operations, new product, and merchandising techniques. Recent articles include "Flea Market Aura" (tells how shoppers at Houston's Astrohall flea market can buy a picture of their aura from an enterprising flea marketer doing research in Kirilian photography). Pays $20 a published page or $5 to $15 an item. Regular column, "Money Page", pays $5 for money-making ideas. B&w photos are purchased with or without accompanying ms. Captions optional. Pays $5.

Fillers: Newsbreaks and clippings; jokes and short humor. Pays $5 an item.

How To Break In: "Attend a local flea market and find a brief item that would be helpful to our readers."

GEMS AND MINERALS, P.O. Box 687, Mentone CA 92359. Phone: 714-794-1843. Editor: Jack R. Cox. Monthly for the amateur gem cutter, jewelry maker, mineral collector, and rockhounds. Buys first North American serial rights. Payment on publication. Will send free sample copy to writer on request. Write for copy of guidelines for writers. Query first. Reports within a month. Enclose S.A.S.E.

Nonfiction and Photos: Material must have how-to slant. No personality stories. Field trips to mineral or gem collecting localities used; must be accurate and give details so they can be found. Four to eight typed pages plus illustrations preferred, but do not limit if subject is important. Frequently good articles are serialized if too long for one issue. Pays 50¢ per inch for text and pix as published.

How To Break In: "Because we are a specialty magazine, it is difficult for a writer to prepare a suitable story for us unless he is familiar with the subject matter: jewelry making, gem cutting, mineral collecting and display, and fossil collecting. Our readers want accurate instructions on how to do it and where they can collect gemstones and minerals in the field. The majority of our articles are purchased from freelance writers, but most of them are hobbyists (rockhounds) or have technical knowledge on one of the subjects. Infrequently, a freelancer with no knowledge of the subject interviews an expert (gem cutter, jewelry maker, etc.) and gets what this expert tells him down on paper for a good how-to article. However, the problem here is that if the expert neglects to mention all the steps in his process, the writer does not realize it. Then, there is a delay while we check it out. My best advice to a freelance writer is to send for a sample copy of our magazine and author's specification sheet which will tell him what we need. We are interested in helping new writers and try to answer them personally, giving any pointers that we think will be of value to them. Let us emphasize that our readers want how-to and where-to stories. They are not at all interested in personality sketches about one of their fellow hobbyists."

KNIFE DIGEST, P.O. Box 4596, Sather Gate Station, Berkeley CA 94704. Editor: William L. Cassidy. For "an extremely well-educated audience (many professionals) interested in serious sportsmanship and collecting; outdoorsmen." Annual; 320 to 400 (8½x11) pages. Established in 1973. Circulation: 100,000. Buys all rights, but may reassign rights to author after publication. Payment on publication. Will send sample copy to writer for $5.95 plus postage. Write for copy of guidelines for writers, enclosing S.A.S.E. Will consider photocopied and simultaneous submissions. Reporting time varies; can be at least 6 months. Submit complete ms. Enclose S.A.S.E.

Nonfiction and Photos: Articles on military history, knives of the world, development of swords, reports of old manufacture; nostalgia, recollection. "Article should be polished, and complete, for this market. I am really looking for serious historical works, and actively seek book-length mss for guns, knives, archery, locks, etc. Plus illustrative material which is badly needed. Can't use amateur work." Informational, how-to, interview, profile, historical, product reviews, successful business operations, merchandising techniques, technical material. Length: 3,000 words maximum. Pays a varying minimum, but maximum has run to $2,000. "Grindings and Findings" and "The Favorite Edge" departments use shorter material. Payment varies due to content. 8x10 b&w photos purchased with or without accompanying mss, or on assignment. Pays up to $10 for choice material. Pays maximum of $100 for color transparencies; 4x5 or larger. Captions optional. "Our illustrative material is superior. We have a very high standard of quality." Photo Department Editor: Richard Barney.

LAPIDARY JOURNAL, P.O. Box 80937, San Diego CA 92138. Editor: Pansy D. Kraus. For "all ages interested in the lapidary hobby." Established in 1947. Monthly. Circulation: 65,000. Rights purchased vary with author and material. Buys all rights, or first serial rights. Payment on publication. Will send free sample copy to writer on request. Will send editorial guidelines to a writer on request. Will consider photocopied submissions. Query first. Enclose S.A.S.E.

Nonfiction and Photos: Publishes "articles pertaining to gem cutting, gem collecting and jewelry making for the hobbyist." Buys informational, how-to, personal experience, historical, travel, and technical articles. Pays 1¢ a word. Buys good contrast b&w photos. Contact editor for color. Payment varies according to size.

McCALL'S NEEDLEWORK AND CRAFTS MAGAZINE, 230 Park Ave., New York NY 10017. Managing Editor: Eleanor Spencer. Issued semiannually. All rights bought for original designs. Enclose S.A.S.E.

Nonfiction: Accepts the made-up items accompanied by the directions, diagrams, and charts for making them. Preliminary photos may be submitted. Variety of payment depends on items sent in. The range of payment could be from a few dollars to a few hundred dollars.

MAKE IT WITH LEATHER, P.O. Box 1386, Fort Worth TX 76101. Editor: Earl F. Warren. Buys all rights. Bimonthly. Established in 1965. Circulation: 180,000. Buys 60 mss a year. Payment on publication. Will send free sample copy to writer on request. Write for copy of guidelines for writers. Reports on material in 6 to 8 weeks. Enclose S.A.S.E. for return of submissions.

Nonfiction and Photos: "How-to-do-it leathercraft stories illustrated with cutting patterns, carving patterns. First-person approach even though article may be ghosted. Story can be for professional or novice. Strong on details; logical progression on steps; easy to follow how-to-do-it." Length: 2,000 words maximum. Payment starts at $25 to $50 plus $5 to $10 per illustration. "Most articles judged on merit and may range to '$200 plus' per ms. Depends on project and work involved by author." 5x7, or larger, b&w photos of reproduction quality purchased with mss. Captions required. Pays $5 minimum. Color of professional quality is used. Ektachrome slides or sheet film stock. Negs needed with all print film stock. Pays $8.50 minimum. All photos are used to illustrate project on step-by-step basis, and also finished item. "We can do photos in our studio if product sample is sent. No charge, but no payment for photos to writer. Letting us 'do it our way' does help on some marginal story ideas and mss since we can add such things as artist's sketches or drawings to improve the presentation."

Fillers: "Tips and Hints." Short practical hints for doing leathercraft or protecting tools, new ways of doing things, etc. Length: 100 words maximum. Pays $5 minimum.

How To Break In: "There are plenty of leathercraftsmen around who don't feel qualified to write up a project or who don't have the time to do it. Put their ideas and projects down on paper for them and share the payment. We need plenty of small, quick, easy-to-do ideas; things that we can do in one page are in short supply."

MILITARY COLLECTORS NEWS, P.O. Box 7582, Tulsa OK 74105. Editor: Jack Britton. For amateur and advanced collectors of all types of military items. Established in 1967. Monthly. Circulation: 3,200. Buys or acquires all rights. Buys or uses about 12 mss a year. Payment in contributor's copies or cash. "Since we receive many articles from our readers for which no payment other than contributor's copies is made, writers should let us know whether or not payment is expected." Will send sample copy to writer for 25¢. Write for copy of guidelines for writers. Reports in 1 week. Submit complete ms. Enclose S.A.S.E.
Nonfiction and Photos: Articles on the identification of military items (insignia, medals, uniforms, flags, weapons, aircraft, armor), anything that is of a military nature. Covers all periods (Vietnam, Korea, WW I, WW II, Civil War; all earlier periods). Also, military history. Informational, humor, historical, nostalgia. Length: 100 to 2,000 words. Pays 1¢ per word, or 2 to 20 copies of the magazine. "We need photos of WWII, men in uniform, foreign weapons, tanks, etc. (WWI, or earlier). Captions optional. Pays 50¢ to $1, or 2 to 4 copies of the magazine.
Fillers: Clippings, jokes. Length: half page or less. Pays 50¢ to $1, or 2 to 4 copies of the magazine.

MODEL RAILROADER, 1027 N. 7th St., Milwaukee WI 53233. Editor: Linn H. Westcott. For adult hobbyists interested in scale model railroading. Monthly. Buys rights "exclusive in model railroad and rail fan field." Study publication before submitting material. Reports on submissions within four weeks. Query first. Enclose S.A.S.E.
Nonfiction: Wants construction articles on specific model railroad projects (structures, cars, locomotives, scenery, benchwork, etc.). Also photo stories showing model railroads. First-hand knowledge of subject almost always necessary for acceptable slant. Pays base rate of $28 first page, $21 additional pages. (Page is typically 960 words plus 30 sq. in. of illustration, both getting same rate for area.)
Photos: Buys photos with detailed descriptive captions only. Pays $5 and up, depending on size and location. Color: double b&w rate. Full color cover: $84.

NATIONAL ANTIQUES REVIEW, Box 619, Portland ME 04104. Editor: Lillian F. Potter. For museums, libraries, antiques dealers, antiques show promoters, homeowners, individuals (young and old) who are interested in antiquities, restoration and preservation. Monthly magazine; 40 (8½x11) pages. Established in 1969. Circulation: 12,000. Rights purchased vary with author and material. Buys all rights, first North American serial rights, first serial rights. Buys about 150 mss a year. Pays on publication. Will send free sample copy to writer on request. Write for copy of guidelines for writers. Submit seasonal material 2 months in advance. Reports in 1 month. Query first. "Submit qualifications." Enclose S.A.S.E.
Nonfiction and Photos: "Material which relates to antiques' values, both monetary and aesthetic. Informative articles for those who collect and love antiquities. We cover auctions and shows, with pictures and prices. Special features relate to antiques, restorations, histories, visits to special antiques exhibits, etc. We attempt to reach all levels and classes, from priceless museum to lowly flea market finds. Reports are national and international." Recently published articles include "Haiti: Source of Provocative Art," "Samuel Clarke's Utilitarian Fairy Lamps." Length: 900 to 1,200 words. Pays $25. Photos purchased with ms. Captions required. Objects should be clearly visible, sharp, explained in ms. Pays $2 for professional photo, b&w or color; $1 for Polaroids and Instamatics.

NATIONAL HOBBYIST, 805 North First St., McGehee AR 71654. Editor: Winfred D. Farrell. For people looking for a new hobby. Magazine; 8 to 15 (8½x11) pages. Established in 1975. Monthly. Circulation: 2,000. Not copyrighted. Buys 15 mss a year. Pays on publication. Will send sample copy to writer for 10¢. Will consider photocopied submissions. No simultaneous submissions. Reports in 1 to 2 months. Submit complete ms. Enclose S.A.S.E.

Nonfiction and Photos: "Articles to help readers start or improve their hobby. We would like to see some articles about other persons and how they started and how they have progressed. Almost anything that relates to a hobby, but we want some odd ones too, such as beer can collecting or match books, etc. We feature a different hobby each month." Recently published "Numismatics: The Hobby for Everyone". Length: 400 to 1,000 words. Pays $5 to $12. Pays average of $4 for b&w (5x7 or 8x10) b&w glossies purchased with ms or on assignment. Captions required.
Poetry and Fillers: All forms of poetry, but must relate to subject matter. Length: 4 to 12 lines. Pays $1. Word search puzzles, jokes and short humor (related to field) purchased as fillers. Pays 2¢ a word; maximum of $2 per item.

NUMISMATIC SCRAPBOOK MAGAZINE, P.O. Box 150, Sidney OH 45365. Editor: Cortney Coffing. For "coin collectors, mostly specialists in U.S. coins or related numismatic items such as medals, tokens, and paper money. Mostly middle income or high middle income brackets." Monthly. Circulation: 10,500. Buys first rights. Buys 10 mss a year. Pays on publication. Returns rejected material in 2 weeks. Acknowledges acceptance of material in 4 weeks. Query first. Enclose S.A.S.E.
Nonfiction and Photos: "Articles on U.S. coins or related subjects, especially those based on original research or personal experience." Buys personal experience and historical pieces. Length: 250 to 4,000 words. Pays 2¢ per published word with additional allowance for art. Photos purchased with mss. B&w glossies.

THE OLD BOTTLE MAGAZINE, Box 243, Bend OR 97701. Phone: 503-382-6978. Editor: Shirley Asher. For collectors of old bottles, insulators, relics. Monthly. Circulation: 13,000. Buys all rights. Buys 35 mss a year. Pays on acceptance. Will send a sample copy to a writer on reqsest. No query required. Reports in 1 month. Enclose S.A.S.E. for return of submissions.
Nonfiction, Photos, and Fillers: "We are soliciting factual accounts on specific old bottles, canning jars, insulators and relics." Stories of a general nature on these subjects not wanted. "Interviews of collectors are usually not suitable when written by non-collectors. A knowledge of the subject is imperative. Would highly recommend potential contributors study an issue before making submissions. Articles that tie certain old bottles to a historical background are desired." Length: 250 to 2,500 words. Pays $20 per published page. B&w glossies and clippings purchased separately. Pays $5.

POPULAR HANDICRAFT & HOBBIES, Tower Press, Box 338, Chester MA 01011. Editor: Barbara Hall Pedersen. For women with leisure for crafts; some teachers and Brownie leaders. Magazine published every 2 months; 72 (8x11) pages. Established in 1965. Circulation: 100,000. Buys all rights. Buys about 150 mss a year. Payment on publication. Will send free sample copy to writer on request. Write for copy of guidelines for writers. Will not consider photocopied or simultaneous submissions. Submit seasonal material suitable for any of the holidays 6 months in advance. Reports in 2 to 6 weeks. Query first. Enclose S.A.S.E.
Nonfiction and Photos: Projects to make; instructional material having to do with crafts. A few profiles and lots of how-to on a wide range of subjects. "We're slanted to ordinary, every-day people, not slick or sophisticated. We like specific directions for worthwhile projects that use inexpensive, readily available materials. We're fed up with plaques and wall hangings. We'd like to see more useful, and fewer purely decorative, projects." Interested in any foreign or exotic crafts adapted for use with materials available to readers. Old crafts revived. Unusual hobbies. Length: 200 to 2,000 words. Pays 2¢ to 5¢ per word. Also uses reviews of craft books. Length: 1,500 words. Pays $20 to $50. Pays $5 for 4x5 glossy b&w photos purchased with ms. Pays $20 for 4x5 color transparencies purchased with ms; $35, if used on cover. Photo Department Editor: Karen Sherrer.
Fillers: Clippings. Pays 25¢ each.
How To Break In: "Writing a how-to article is a good way, especially so if the writer undertakes the project himself. Second-hand information is usually sketchy. We want precise information, nothing vague. We like a light-hearted approach, and

some humor now and then. Query us first, briefly outlining the project you have in mind."

POSTAL BELL, P.O. Box 2730, Santa Clara CA 95051. Editor: William H. McConnell. For "stamp collectors, whose ages and interests vary widely." Established in 1939. Bimonthly. Circulation: 300. Copyright applied for. "Since this publication is nonprofit, we may pay for an unusual article; most, however, are submitted without pay." Query first. Will consider photocopied submissions. Submit seasonal material 6 to 8 weeks in advance of issue date. Reports in 3 weeks. Enclose S.A.S.E. for reply to queries.
Nonfiction: "Most of the items are stories related to stamps and the nation issuing them. Generally, they relate to the people and culture of Japan. If there is a technical write-up concerning stamp issues, this type of article is always welcome." Length: 500 words. Pays about $10 "if the article is a special one. The contributors are all doing the writing for idea of participating in the creative process. Some of them are professional people in that they are professional research types with the universities; others are pure amateurs, but we all have a great deal of fun with the publication and I am more than interested in having new writers if they are interested in the kind of thing we are doing. I don't always have extra copies of the publication to send out to the would-be writers. It does get expensive when they don't even send S.A.S.E. for a reply, then they don't respond when I do write."

QUILTER'S NEWSLETTER MAGAZINE, Box 394, Wheatridge CO 80033. Editor: Ms. Bonnie Leman. Established in 1968. Monthly. Circulation: 45,000. Buys first or second North American serial rights. Buys about 25 mss a year. Pays on acceptance. Will send free sample copy to writer on request. Will consider photocopied submissions. No simultaneous submissions. Reports in 2 to 3 weeks. Submit complete ms. Enclose S.A.S.E.
Nonfiction, Photos and Fillers: "We are interested in articles, fillers and photos on the subject of quilts and quiltmakers *only*. We are not interested in anything relating to 'Grandma's Scrap Quilts', but could use material about contemporary quilting." Pays 1½¢ a word minimum. Additional payment for photos depends on quality.

RAILROAD MODEL CRAFTSMAN, P.O. Box 700, Newton NJ 07860. Managing Editor: Tony Koester. For "adult model railroad hobbyists, above average, including mature youngsters. All gauges, scales, plus collecting, railfanning." Established in 1933. Monthly. Circulation: 85,000. Buys all rights. Buys 180 to 240 mss a year. Payment on publication. Will send a sample copy to a writer for 75¢. Submit seasonal material six months in advance. Enclose S.A.S.E. for return of submissions.
Nonfiction and Photos: "How-to model railroad features written by persons who did the work. They have to be good. Glossy photos a must. Drawings where required must be to scale, accurately and completely rendered. Some railroad prototype features if of interest to modelers and with modelers' slant. All of our features and articles are written by active model railroaders familiar with the magazine and its requirements. 'Outsiders' don't have the technical know-how to write for us. Non-model railroad writers invariably write up some local hobbyist as 'Joe Doaks has a railroad empire in his basement made all by himself,' treating him as some kind of nut. We do not want the cartoon of little men tying the little girl to model railroad track. We do want topnotch how-to model railroading articles." Purchases photos with and without mss. Captions required. Buys sharp 8x10 glossies and 35mm transparencies. Minimum payment: $1 per column inch of copy ($30 per page); $5 for photos ($1 per diagonal inch of published b&w photos, $3 for color transparencies); $50 for covers (must tie in with feature material in that issue).
How To Break In: "Frankly, there is virtually no chance of making a sale to us unless the author is a very experienced hobbyist in our field. I doubt that a non-model railroad hobbyist has authored a single line of copy for us in the past 40 years, so it's 'hobbyist first, author second' as far as we're concerned. Our material is for the serious hobbyist, not the general public trying to better understand our hobby, as a rule."

RELICS, Western Publications, Inc., P.O. Box 3338, Austin TX 78764. Phone: 512-444-3674. Editor: Pat Wagner. Bimonthly to collectors of Americana. Buys N.A. serial rights and occasionally reprint rights based on where the article originally appeared. Will send sample copy for 35¢. Pays on acceptance. Query appreciated. Reports in 4 to 6 weeks. Enclose S.A.S.E. for reply to queries.

Nonfiction and Photos: General subject matter includes collectibles of any kind except those of museum quality. We are not as much devoted to the coverage of true antiques as to the myriad assortment of nostalgic items. Also pieces pertaining to personal collections if specific information is given, such as current value, how to judge, where to find, how to preserve. Articles must contain useful hints for the collector. Subject preferably American in origin. 2,500 words is tops. Pays 2¢ minimum per word. No mss considered unless accompanied by photos (b&w preferably) or drawings of item. Photos and drawings are returned after publication.

ROCKHOUND, P.O. Box 328, Conroe TX 77301. Editor: John H. Latham. For gem and mineral hobbyists. Magazine published every 2 months; 52 (8½x11) pages. Established in 1971. Circulation: 20,000. Buys all rights, but will reassign rights to author after publication. Buys 75 to 100 mss a year. Payment on acceptance. Will send free sample copy to writer on request. Write for copy of guidelines for writers. Will consider photocopied submissions. Will not consider simultaneous submissions. Reports in 3 to 4 weeks. Submit complete ms. Enclose S.A.S.E.

Nonfiction and Photos: Articles on where and how to find gems and minerals. "We cover only where and how to collect gems and minerals; not the whole lapidary field." Length: 250 to 3,000 words. Pays 2¢ per word. B&w glossies of any size purchased with mss. Captions required. Pays $5. Pays $5 to $35 for color transparencies used on cover.

How To Break In: "Write about collecting sites anywhere in the U.S., except the western states. We receive a glut of mss from the West. We particularly welcome new writers who write about the East, North, South, or Midwest. A bit of research on collecting sites (for gems and minerals) in these parts of the country will really sell us."

SCOTT'S MONTHLY JOURNAL, 10102 F Street, Omaha NE 68127. Editor: William W. Wylie. For stamp collectors. Monthly. Circulation: 28,500. Buys all rights. Pays on publication. Will send a sample copy to a writer on request. Query first. Reports at once. Enclose S.A.S.E.

Nonfiction and Photos: Articles are done on assignment. Lengths, to 1,200 words. Pays $10 per published page. Writer should be an informed stamp collector. Photos purchased to illustrate mss.

How To Break In: "Frankly, I can't feel *Scott's Monthly Journal* offers much to the new writer unless he is an enthusiastic stamp collector whose interest in the hobby and its ramifications is greater than his interest in income from writing. Our readers are rather sophisticated and accurate information means more to them than expressions of enthusiasm for a hobby. Our readers don't have to be 'sold' on the fact that stamp collecting is the best of all human avocations. Would-be contributors should study the journal to get some accurate idea of what we publish."

THE SPINNING WHEEL, Everybodys Press, Inc., Hanover PA 17331. Phone: 717-632-3535. Editor: A. Christian Revi. For antique collectors and dealers. 10 times a year. Pays on publication. Buys exclusive rights unless author wishes some reservations. Enclose S.A.S.E

Nonfiction: Authentic, well-researched material on antiques in any and all collecting areas; home decorating ideas with antiques. Prefers combined scholar-student-amateur appeal. No first-person or family history. Prefers draft or outline first. Requires bibliography with each ms. Quality illustrations. Length: 500 to 1,500 words. Pays minimum $1 per published inch, including pictures.

Photo: Photos and professional line drawings accepted. Photos should be top quality b&w, no smaller than 5x7. If of individual items shown in groups, each should be separated for mechanical expediency. Avoid fancy groupings.

STITCH 'N SEW, Tower Press, Box 338, Chester MA 01011. Editor: Barbara Hall Pedersen. For women of all ages who like to sew. Magazine published every 2 months; 72 pages, (8x11). Established in 1968. Circulation: 200,000. Buys all rights. Buys 50 mss a year. Payment on publication. Will send free sample copy to writer on request. Write for copy of guidelines for writers. Submit holiday crafts, especially Christmas, 6 months in advance. Query first or submit complete ms. Reports in 1 to 6 weeks. Enclose S.A.S.E.
Nonfiction, Photos, and Fillers: "Articles on various facets of needlework; knitting, crocheting, garment construction, embroidery, tatting, gift and toy making, decorative items for the home. Our emphasis is on old-fashioned practicality. Our projects appeal to the woman on a tight budget. We like 'scratch' projects which utilize readily available materials which do not cost much." Length: 1,500 words maximum. Pays $5 to $50. B&w and color photos purchased with accompanying ms. Captions required. Pays $35 for 4x5 color transparency used on cover. Photo Editor: Karen Sherrer. Household hints are purchased for up to $5 each.

TODAY'S COINS, P.O. Box 919, Kermit TX 79745. Editor: Fred B. Green. Semimonthly. Circulation: 25,000. Buys first North American serial rights. Buys 100 mss a year. Payment on publication. Query first or submit complete ms. Reports in 4 weeks. Enclose S.A.S.E.
Nonfiction and Photos: Articles on coins, medals, silver bars, error coins, paper money and other areas of numismatics. Treatment should be objective, informational and factual. Length: 1,000 to 2,000 words. Minimum payment: 75% of freelance paid for in contributor's copies. Maximum: 3¢ per word. Also needs good feature columnists in this area. Uses 3x5 or 5x7 b&w glossy photos.
Fillers: On above topics. Length: 300 to 500 words. Minimum payment in contributor's copies. Maximum: 3¢ per word.

TODAY'S FILM MAKER, 250 Fulton Ave., Hempstead NY 11710. Editor: Barry Tanenbaum. For amateur movie makers and hobbyists. Magazine; 60 pages. Established in 1971. Every 2 months. Circulation: 40,000. Rights purchased vary with author and material. May buy all rights, but will reassign rights to author after publication; first North American serial rights or first serial rights. Buys 25 to 30 mss a year. Pays on publication. Will snd free sample copy to writer on request. Write for copy of guidelines for writers. Will consider photocopied submissions. No simultaneous submissions. Reports in 1 week. Query first. Enclose S.A.S.E.
Nonfiction and Photos: How-to articles; Super 8 film techniques. All material should tell the amateur how to better use his equipment to achieve professional results. Informational, personal experience, interviews, think pieces, personal opinion, reviews. Captions required for photos used with mss. Pays minimum of $35 per published page; $5 for accompanying photos.

TREASURE WORLD, P.O. Box 328, Conroe TX 77301. Editor: John H. Latham. For treasure hunting hobbyists, bottle and relic collectors, amateur prospectors and miners. Magazine published every 2 months; 72 (8½x11) pages. Established in 1969. Circulation: 100,000. Buys all rights but will reassign rights to author after publication. Buys 90 to 100 mss a year. Payment on acceptance. Will send free sample copy to writer on request. Write for copy of guidelines for writers. Will consider photocopied submissions. Will not consider simultaneous submissions. Reports in 3 to 4 weeks. Submit complete ms. Enclose S.A.S.E.
Nonfiction and Photos: Articles about lost mines and buried or sunken treasures. Avoid writing about the more famous treasures and lost mines. Write for a free copy of the November (1973) issue of *Treasure World.* It carries an article on "How to Write for *Treasure World.*" Length: 100 to 3,000 words. Pays 2¢ per word. Pays $5 for b&w glossies (any size) purchased with mss. Captions required. Pays $100 for color transparency used on cover; 35mm minimum.
How To Break In: "Write for our 'Treasure Nuggets' section. Short articles of 100 to 250 words in length. We pay $12.50 for articles used in this section."

TRI-STATE TRADER, 27 N. Jefferson St., Knightstown IN 46148. Editor: Mrs. Elsie Kilmer. For persons interested in antiques, history, restorations, etc. Newspaper; 40 (11x16) pages. Established in 1968. Weekly. Circulation: 27,000. Not copyrighted. Pays on 10th of month following publication. Will send free sample copy to writer on request. Write for copy of guidelines for writers. Submit seasonal (Christmas, Easter, Halloween) material 4 months in advance. Query first. Enclose S.A.S.E.

Nonfiction and Photos: Prefers material that deals with antiques, collectibles, or places of historical interest; restored homes, etc. Chiefly in the North Central and border states. Interested in material on less commonly found antiques, but not museum type pieces; including origin, date of manufacture, unique features; pattern names of glassware; ceramics with dates and origin (including foreign ceramics); trademarks. Much of the material received is too general in content and omits dates, styles, names of firms, etc. Recently published "Russian Bronzes Scarce: Challenge for Collector" (items available, but information limited on subject). Also uses auction reports and nostalgic material related to antiques and collectibles. Length: 1,200 words maximum. Pays $5 to $25. Pays $3 to $5 for b&w photos purchased with or without ms. $2 for Polaroids.

Fillers: Newsbreaks in areas of this newspaper's interests; specific information on subjects of antique and historical interests; used as fillers. Length: 500 words maximum. Pays 25c per published inch.

TRUE TREASURE, P.O. Box 328, Conroe TX 77301. Editor: John H. Latham. For treasure hunting hobbyists, bottle and relic collectors, amateur prospectors and miners. Magazine published every 2 months; 72 (8½x11) pages. Established in 1969. Circulation: 100,000. Buys all rights, but will reassign rights to author after publication. Buys 90 to 100 mss a year. Payment on acceptance. Will send free sample copy to writer on request. Write for copy of guidelines for writers. Will consider photocopied submissions. Will not consider simultaneous submissions. Reports in 3 to 4 weeks. Submit complete ms. Enclose S.A.S.E.

Nonfiction and Photos: Articles about lost mines and buried and sunken treasures. Avoid writing about the more famous treasures and lost mines. Length: 100 to 3,000 words. Pays 2¢ per word. Pays $5 for b&w glossies purchased with mss. Captions required. Pays $100 for color transparencies used on cover; 2¼x2¼ minimum size. "Treasure Nuggets" section uses short articles on publication's theme. Length: 100 to 250 words. Pays $12.50.

WOMAN'S WORLD, Ideal Publishing Corp., 575 Madison Ave., New York NY 10022. Phone: 212-759-9704. Editor: Holly Garrison. For women of all ages and interests. Monthly. Circulation: 300,000. Buys all rights. Will send sample copy to writer for 25¢. Pays on publication. Usually reports within 3 weeks. Query first. Enclose S.A.S.E.

Nonfiction and Photos: "We've changed editorial direction and will now come out concentrating on a single theme each month, rather than on a general range of subjects. Upcoming issues will be devoted mainly to arts and crafts, knitting and crocheting, needlework, gardening, food and other such subjects of interest to women with special emphasis on how they may save money. We stress the personal approach and most how-to's are written by just folks who enclose photos of themselves and their handicraft. Consequently, much of what we buy requires heavy re-writing and the handicraft itself is usually sent here to be photographed. However, we do have some professional writers who find women and their crafts, or whatever, to write about. It would be an especially good idea in our case if a writer first studied our new magazine. Our few regular and general features will be assigned, but we will definitely be buying some mss on the aforementioned subjects." Pays between $50 and $150, depending on length and subject matter; pays more if ms is accompanied by good b&w glossies.

WOMEN'S CIRCLE, Box 428, Seabrook NH 03874. Editor: Marjorie Pearl. For women of all ages. Monthly magazine; 72 pages. Rights purchased vary with author and material. Buys all rights, but sometimes reassigns rights to author after publication. Buys 100 mss a year. Payment on acceptance. Will send sample copy to writer

for 50¢. Will not consider photocopied or simultaneous submissions. Submit seasonal material 7 months in advance. Reports in 1 to 3 months. Query first or submit complete ms. Enclose S.A.S.E.
Nonfiction: How-to articles on hobbies, handicrafts, etc. Also food, recipes, and needlework. Informational approach. Needs Christmas crafts for Christmas annual. Length: open. Pays 3¢ per word.

THE WORKBASKET, 4251 Pennsylvania, Kansas City MO 64111. Editor: Mary Ida Sullivan. Issued monthly. Buys first rights. Pays on acceptance. Query first. Reports within six weeks. Include S.A.S.E. with all queries and submissions.
Nonfiction: Uses articles, 400 to 500 words, which explain how a person or a family has benefited, financially or otherwise, by sewing, needlecraft, etc. Interested in step-by-step directions for making project. Also has a how-to short-stuff section which uses material on hobbies, ideas for pin-money and the like. These are limited to 250 words or under and bring a flat sum of $5. Pays 4¢ a word for articles, plus $5 to $7 for accompanying art.
Photos: 5x7 or 8x10 pix with mss.

WORKBENCH, 4251 Pennsylvania Ave., Kansas City MO 64111. Phone: 816-531-5730. Editor: Jay W. Hedden. For woodworkers, from beginning youngster to retired oldster. Established in 1946. Circulation: 500,000. Buys all rights, but returns all but first magazine rights, on request, after publication. "We work 6 months ahead; buy for a year ahead." Payment on acceptance. Will send free sample copy on request. Write for copy of guidelines for writers. Reports in 10 days. Enclose S.A.S.E.
Nonfiction and Photos: "All material is devoted to the do-it-yourself homeowner and home-shop craftsman. Our consistent contributors are do-it-yourselfers, home-owners, craftsmen. They also know how to use a camera to get sharp black and white photos of projects and operations, and have the ability to make working drawings that are completely and accurately dimensioned. Not finished art, working drawings; our artists redraw everything to fit a particular layout. For the same reason, we do not want 'polished' writing. Everything is rewritten by our editors to fit layout and give the story the *Workbench* slant. We want just the facts; the step-by-step of how you built a project or did an operation. Our editors know home maintenance and are well informed on the latest methods and materials. Don't try to fool us. We also read all of the other do-it-yourself and mechanics magazines. So don't try to sell us the same story you've seen somewhere else. We are happy to work with beginning writers, but very few seem to accept the criticism of an editor." Pays minimum of $100 per published page. Payment for assignments is higher. Covers are 4x5 (or larger) 4-color transparencies that illustrate the lead story. Pays $150 minimum for these.
Fillers: Shop tips with drawing or photo. Pays $10 to $20.
How To Break In: "Always looking for new writers with fresh ideas. Unfortunately, very few would-be writers will accept the criticism of an editor who has been in the business for 20 years. Will work with any new writer, showing him (step by step) how to do a story for us, but he must do it our way."

Home and Garden Publications

THE AMERICAN HOME, 641 Lexington Ave., New York NY 10022. Editor: Margaret E. Happel. For young homemakers. Monthly. Will not consider unsolicited manuscripts, but will review query letters from professional writers. Reports immediately. Enclose S.A.S.E.
Nonfiction: Writers may query, but no unsolicited mss will be read. Editorial focus is on subjects dealing with the home and homemaking: home maintenance, building and remodeling, food, kitchens, home crafts. Before and after experience accomplishments are of interest. Subjects should interest women mainly. Believability, depth of information, and authenticity are a must. The editors want copy and ideas which

will add pleasure to homemaking. Length: 300 to 1,500 words. Payment depends on quantity and quality. Address mss to the Editorial Department or to the department for which it is intended.

Photos: All photography done on commission only.

How To Break In: "Come to us with an unusual skill or specialty. If, for instance, you have a new technique for making dolls, or Christmas decorations, or almost anything in the craft field that our experts would not normally know or hear about, you've got an in. We can forgive a lot in the writing if the idea is really different. It's a narrow door but it is open. If it turns out that you can really write, you may find yourself with future assignments."

APARTMENT LIFE, 1716 Locust, Des Moines IA 50336. Editor: David Jordan. For apartment residents. Magazine, published every 2 months; 108 pages. Established in 1968. Circulation: 450,000. Buys all rights. Buys 60 to 100 mss a year. Payment on acceptance. Will not consider photocopied or simultaneous submissions. Submit seasonal material 5 to 6 months in advance. Reports in 2 months. Query first. Enclose S.A.S.E.

Nonfiction and Photos: "Service material specifically for people who live in apartments. Thorough, factual, informative articles always slanted toward the apartment situation." Informational, how-to, travel. Length: 300 to 1,000 words. Pays $250 to $400. B&w photos and color are purchased with and without accompanying mss, and on assignment. Pays $50 for b&w; $100 for color.

BETTER BUILDING IDEAS, 229 Park Avenue, South, New York NY 10003. Editor: John Lauderdale. For people who are thinking about building a new home or remodeling their present home. Quarterly magazine; 112 pages, (8x10). Established in 1973. Circulation: 50,000. Buys all rights. Buys 15 to 20 mss a year. Payment on acceptance. Will not consider photocopied or simultaneous submissions. Submit seasonal material 4 or 5 months in advance. Reports on material in 1 to 2 weeks. Query first. Enclose S.A.S.E.

Nonfiction and Photos: Articles to help people who are building their own homes better understand various construction techniques, design principles, etc. Some how-to for the weekend handyman who wants to remodel or finish parts of his home. "Give enough detail so that the reader can more intelligently make decisions about building materials, kitchen and bath designs, etc." Length: 2,000 to 3,000 words. Pays $100 to $200. B&w photos purchased with accompanying mss; no additional payment. Captions required.

BETTER HOMES AND GARDENS, 1716 Locust St., Des Moines IA 50336. Phone: 515-284-9011. Editor: James A. Autry. For "middle-and-up income, homeowning and community-concerned families." Monthly. Circulation: 8,000,000. Buys all rights. Pays on acceptance. Query preferred. Submit seasonal material 1 year in advance. Mss should be directed to the department where the story line is strongest. Enclose S.A.S.E.

Nonfiction: "Freelance material is used in areas of travel, health, cars, money management, and home entertainment. Reading the magazine will give the writer the best idea of our style. We do not deal with political subjects or areas not connected with the home, community and family." Pays top rates based on estimated length of published article; $100 to $2,000. Length: 500 to 2,000 words.

Photos: Shot under the direction of the editors. Purchased with mss.

How To Break In: "Follow and study the magazine, to see what we do and how we do it. There are no secrets, after all; it's all there on the printed page. Having studied several issues, the writer should come up with one or several ideas that interest him, and, hopefully, us. We consider freelance contributions in the areas of health, education, cars, money matters, home entertainment, and travel. The next step is to write a good query letter. It needn't be more than a page in length (for each idea), and should include a good stab at a title, a specific angle, and a couple of paragraphs devoted to the main points of the article. This method is not guaranteed to produce a sale, of course; there is no magic formula. But it's still the best way I know to have an idea considered."

FAMILY FOOD GARDEN, P.O. Box 1014, Grass Valley CA 95945. Editor: Elaine McPherson. For gardeners. Magapaper (magazine in newspaper format) published 7 times a year; 24 (9½x13½) pages. Established in 1973. Circulation: 170,000. Buys all rights, but will reassign rights to author upon request. Buys about 50 mss a year. Payment on publication. Will send sample copy to writer on request. Write for copy of guidelines for writers. Will not consider photocopied or simultaneous submissions. Submit seasonal material 3 months in advance. Reports in 3 weeks. Query first or submit complete ms. Enclose S.A.S.E.

Nonfiction and Photos: "Our approach is 'practical' food growing, using chemicals if necessary, but our readers include many organic gardeners. We prefer gardening advice based on personal experience, or sometimes third-person accounts. Not interested in inspirational approach, but in practical, usable advice on all aspects of growing fruit, vegetables and meat. We do not cover flower gardening except very incidentally. We are interested in articles in which the economics of home raising of food are spelled out; exact costs, food budget savings, etc. We do not want recipes, except as inclusions in articles about particular foods. Inspirational gardening articles or very long articles do not have much chance." Recently published articles include: "Basics for Planting Successful Trees," "The Economics of Raising Chickens," "Cabbage Family Rates More Attention," and "Brie Is a Cheese Quite Easy to Make." Length: 300 to 1,200 words. Pays $25 for illustrated articles. No additional payment for b&w and color used with mss. Snapshot size acceptable for b&w; any size color transparencies, but b&w is more often used.

FLOWER AND GARDEN MAGAZINE, 4251 Pennsylvania, Kansas City MO 64111. Editor-in-Chief: Rachel Snyder. For knowledgeable home gardeners. Monthly. Picture magazine. Circulation: 600,000. Buys first rights. Pays on acceptance. Will send a sample copy to a writer on request. Write for copy of guidelines for writers. Query first. Reports in 6 weeks. Enclose S.A.S.E.

Nonfiction: Interested in illustrated articles on how-to-do certain types of gardening, descriptive articles about individual plants. Flower arranging, landscape design, house plants, patio gardening are other aspects covered. "The approach we stress is practical (how-to-do-it, what-to-do-it-with). We try to stress plain talk, clarity, economy of words. We are published in 3 editions: Northern, Southern, Western. Some editorial matter is purchased just for single edition use. Most, however, is used in all editions, so it should be tailored for a national audience. Material for a specific edition should be slanted to that audience only." Length: 1,000 to 1,200 words. Pays 4½¢ a word or more, depending on quality and kind of material.

Photos: Buys photos submitted with mss or with captions only. Pays up to $12.50 for 5x7 or 8x10 b&w's, depending on quality, suitability. Also buys color transparencies, 35mm and larger. Pays $20 to $125 for these, depending on size and use.

How To Break In: "Prospective author needs good grounding in gardening practice and literature. Then offer well-researched and well-written material appropriate to the experience level of our audience. Illustrations help sell the story."

HI-RISE WEEKLY, 75 E. Wacker Dr., Chicago IL 60601. Editor: M. Stehlik. For affluent, involved individuals living in Chicago's high rise buildings (along the lake shore); people concerned with their life style; successful in their careers. Tabloid; 16 to 24 (10x16) pages. Established in 1974. Weekly. Circulation: 20,000. Buys first North American serial rights. Buys 150 to 200 mss a year. Pays on publication. Will send sample copy to writer for 25¢. Write for copy of guidelines for writers. Will consider photocopied or simultaneous submissions. Submit seasonal material 2 months in advance. Reports on rejections or acceptances in 4 weeks. Query first. Enclose S.A.S.E.

Nonfiction and Photos: Publishes 1 to 2 lead articles per issue. Balance is columns which are staff-written. Seeks a lot of reader involvement. Culture, politics, life style (heavy emphasis), how-to. Must be contemporary, or have a contemporary slant. Approach should be very topical. Can be tongue-in-cheek. Needs for seasonal material or mss on special events are difficult to predict unless the article is on assignment. Informational, how-to, personal experience, interview, profile, humor, historical, expose, nostalgia, personal opinion and "think" articles; book, theater and film reviews. Length: 800 to 2,000 words; occasionally longer. Pays 3¢ to 5¢ a word. Recently published material includes "The Sensuous Christmas," a review of unusual gift items; "Theater in Chicago," an interview. No additional payment for photos used with mss.

HI-RISE-LIVING MAGAZINE, 168 Franklin Ave., Hasbrouck Heights NJ 07604. Editor: Mary Sullivan. For tenants of high-rise luxury apartment buildings in the northernmost counties of New Jersey; affluent, sophisticated, cosmopolitan, swinging singles, young marrieds, established executives; very few families. Magazine; 32 to 48 pages. Established in 1972. 10 times a year. January/February and June/July issues are combined. Circulation: 11,500. Rights purchased vary with author and material. May buy first serial rights, second serial (reprint) rights, or simultaneous rights. Buys 10 to 20 mss a year. Pays 30 days after publication. Will send sample copy to writer for $1. Will consider photocopied and simultaneous submissions. Submit seasonal material (sports copy) 3 to 4 months in advance. Reports on material accepted for publication in 2 months. Returns rejected material in 3 weeks. Submit complete ms. Enclose S.A.S.E.

Nonfiction and Photos: Articles pertaining to the life style of the high riser. Typical subjects include art, antiques, audio, career closeups, decorating, entertainment, fashion, gourmet food and wine, health and beauty, indoor gardening, music reviews, sports, travel. Sports copy should be of a seasonal nature, such as a feature on skiing. Would like interesting interviews with celebrities; travel articles; wine articles. Articles should be geared toward the cosmopolitan life style of the high riser. Contains some "home-oriented" material; for example, food, high-rise handyman, etc. No poetry, fiction, or political material. Length: 1,000 to 2,500 words. Pays $10 to $25. No additional payment for 8x10 b&w glossies used with mss.

HORTICULTURE, 300 Massachusetts Ave., Boston MA 02115. Editor: Paul Trachtman. Published by the Massachusetts Horticulture Society. Monthly. "We buy only first and exclusive rights to mss; one time use rights for phtos." Pays after publication. Query first. Reports in 6 weeks. Enclose S.A.S.E.

Nonfiction and Photos: Uses authentic articles from 500 to 1,000 words on plants and gardens, indoors and out, based on actual experience. Study publication. Pays 2¢ to 3¢ per word, more for special features. Photos: color must be accurate tones, transparencies only, preferably not Ektachromes "and accurately identified."

HOUSE AND GARDEN, The Conde Nast Building, 350 Madison Ave., New York NY 10017. Editor-in-Chief: Mary Jane Pool. For homeowners and renters in middle and upper income brackets. Monthly. Circulation: 1,136,444. Buys all rights. Pays on acceptance. Will not send sample copy. "Study magazine before submitting." Reports immediately. Query first and include sample of previous writing. Enclose S.A.S.E.

Nonfiction and Photos: Subjects of interest to "families concerned with their homes. Nothing for young marrieds specifically." Anything to do with the house or gardens and affiliated subjects such as music, art, books, cooking, etc. Length: about 1,500 words. Payment varies. Jerome H. Denner, Assistant Editor, is department editor. Photos purchased with mss only.

How To Break In: "This is a very tough market to break into. We very seldom use unsolicited material, but if anything is going to have a chance of making it here, it should be on a news breaking item. It must be something which has not already been covered in the other major magazines. It must have a new slant. Read the magazine closely for style and avoid things we've already done. We get too many freelancers sending us material on subjects for which the crest of wave has already passed. There's no guarantee that providing a short item (say, for Gardener's Notes, which is mostly staff-written) will be an easier way in, but if you understand our needs and provide something that's really good, there's always a chance. It's best to send a query and a sample of previous writing."

HOUSE BEAUTIFUL, 717 Fifth Ave., New York NY 10022. Editor: Wallace Guenther. For women of all ages. "Women with families are in the majority. Women who are interested in all aspects of modern living and creating a purposeful environment for their families." Monthly magazine; 180 pages. Established in 1896. Circulation: 900,000. Rights purchased vary with author and material. Buys all rights or first North American serial rights. Payment on acceptance. Will send sample copy to writer for $1.50. Will not consider photocopied or simultaneous submissions. Submit seasonal material (entertaining issue in November; personal histories related to remodeling for May and September) 6 to 7 months in advance. Reports in 1 month. Submit complete ms "unless writer has worked with us in the past." Submit articles to Linda B. Downs, Senior Editor. Enclose S.A.S.E.

Nonfiction and Photos: "Because all food and travel material and much of the gardening material we use is prepared by the staff, we are not in the market for articles on these subjects. Other than that, we are interested in almost anything related to the home and modern living, but we avoid health and religious articles. Approach depends on the nature of the subject. We do buy some straight how-to and idea pieces, but even there we look for some expression of insight or relationship to others who might be interested in the same topic. Style and structure are entirely up to the writer. If it works for the story, it will work for us. Crafts are in today, but a lot of people are turning out straight how-to craft stories without realizing that most of those we do use must offer good design as well. Design orientation is very important to us. Others fail to realize that the slice-of-life or humorous features we buy should make a point and not just be a vignette on an amusing or strange incident that happened to that individual. For example, Leonard S. Bernstein is a frequent contributor of lightheartedly styled stories. We don't use little amusing stories with no point or human interest profiles. What I mostly look for from freelancers are slice-of-life stories, but which make a point." Recently published articles include "The Wine Snob Fights Back" about how it's sometimes good to be a wine snob; "The Camera Slave," in which the author writes that he wasn't seeing anything on his trip to Europe because he was always aiming his camera at it; a piece on how to handle weekend guests, planning ahead for food and so forth; and "How's Your CSP?", on common sense. Length: 750 to 2,000 words. Pays $150 to $400. "Shorter material for our Insight section (primarily a straight news/feature type of section) should be sent to John H. Ingersoll, Senior Editor. Anyone who is interested in contributing to this section should look over a couple of copies of *House Beautiful* to see the range of material this encompasses." Length: 700 to 1,500 words. Pays $100 to $300. 8x10 b&w glossies purchased with or without mss, or on assignment. Should be 8x10. High-quality color transparencies are also used. Size: 35mm, 2¼x2¼ or 4x5. Payment varies.

How To Break In: "The Insight section is mostly service oriented and there we recently bought a piece from a woman whom we had never published before on dangerous craft materials. Insight is one place to aim shorter pieces. It's not necessarily an easy way to break in, but it is a way for us to see your work without doing a major manuscript."

HOUSTON HOME & GARDEN, 3133 Buffalo Speedway, P.O. Box 66469, Houston TX 77006. Editor: Don Reynolds. For homeowners with interests in decorating and gardening; middle income and higher; ages of 25 and up. Magazine; 100 (8½x11) pages. Established in 1974. Monthly. Circulation: 17,000. Buys all rights, but will reassign rights to author after publication. Buys about 48 mss a year. Pays on publication. Will send sample copy to writer for $1.50. Will consider photocopied and simultaneous submissions. Submit seasonal material 3 to 4 months in advance. Reports on material accepted for publication in 4 to 6 weeks. Returns rejected material immediately. Query first. Enclose S.A.S.E.

Nonfiction and Photos: Features on individual homes; decorating problems and ideas; lawn care, landscaping, trees, shrubs, flowers, home management; how-to projects; food. All material must have a Houston peg. Easy-going, conversational style, but good feature structure; accuracy, completeness. "We cover only the greater Houston area; people who live here, plants that grow here; shopping information applicable to our local commercial area. We are open on almost any subject that fits our special needs for material of local interest." Informational, how-to, personal experience, interview, humor, historical and think articles. Length: 1,000 to 2,500 words. Pays 5¢ per word. Pays $15 to $25 for b&w glossies purchased with mss. 5x7, or larger. No polaroids. Pays $20 to $50 for 35mm (or larger) color tranparencies.

HOW TO, The Make-It/Fix-It/Grow-It Magazine, 964 North Pennsylvania St., Indianapolis IN 46204. Phone: 317-634-3441. Editor: John Sullivan. For the typical American homeowner family, and not primarily for the man with $1,000 worth of power tools. Quarterly (geared to seasons) magazine; 116 pages (8½x11). Established in 1974. Circulation: 250,000. Buys all rights. Payment on acceptance. Will send free sample copy to writer on request; write for copy of editorial guidelines. Submit seasonal material 6 months in advance. Query first or submit complete ms. Reports within 2 weeks. Enclose S.A.S.E.

Nonfiction, Photos, and Fillers: "Do-it-yourself material. Very detailed instructions and explanations, on a step-by-step basis, in each article. Major editorial material in each issue will be closely tied to the seasonal activities of the reader. Our most immediate need from freelance writers is short back of book features of 1 to 3 pages, and single page and fractional page fillers. This material does not need strong seasonal ties, but should be basic home maintenance stories. Looking for a very wide variety of material, covering everything from plumbing and electrical to the use of hand and power tools, painting and decorating, etc. In short, we want to cover everything inside, outside and all around the house. Articles in the fix-it area are wanted, and our need for make-it type stories is much less at this time. Illustrations are critically important. We want top quality b&w photos, and also use line drawings and sketches." Pays $100 to $150 and up per published page on 1- to 3-page featurettes, and $25 to $50 and up on fractional page and filler-type material. Photos are purchased with or without ms or on assignment. Must be of excellent quality in any format. Captions required. Pays $10 minimum for b&w; 325 minimum for color. Photo Editor: Larry E. Wood.

LEISURE HOME LIVING, 13 Evergreen Rd., Hampton NH 03842. Editor and Publisher: Richard N. Livingstone. For those with an interest in leisure-time activities from building a second home to crafts and gardens (flower and vegetable) with emphasis on do-it-yourself activities. Established in 1970. Semi-annual. Circulation: 20,000. Rights purchased vary with author and material; usually buys all rights. Buys about 5 mss a year. Pays on publication. Will send a sample copy to a writer for $1.50. Submit complete ms. Will consider photocopied submissions. Reports in 1 month. Enclose S.A.S.E.

Nonfiction: "Articles dealing with all aspects of vacation or second home field. These are homes of unusual design and vacation home communities. Material must deal with the northeast area." Buys informational, how-to, and photo articles. Length: 1,000 to 2,000 words. Pays $50 minimum.

Photos: Purchased with or without mss; captions required. Pays $10 minimum.

How To Break In: "We'd like to see material from owners of vacation homes describing their experiences in buying, building or adding on to a second home, or similar articles from non-owners, for our 'First Person' feature."

LEISURE LIVING, 130 Shepard St., Lawrence MA 01843. Editor: Vilma Zuliani. For "active men and women with an interest in tennis, skiing, golfing, fishing and boating. They are very much concerned with the beauty of their home and how to improve it through remodeling, etc." Magazine published every 2 months; 128 (8½x11) pages. Established in 1970. Circulation: 120,000. Rights purchased vary with author and material. May buy all rights, but will sometimes reassign rights to author after publication. Buys 20 mss a year. Payment on publication. Will send sample copy to writer for $1. Will consider photocopied submissions. Submit seasonal material (sports or leisure activities relating to a particular season) 6 months in advance. Reports on material accepted for publication in 6 months. Returns rejected material in 2 months. Query first. Enclose S.A.S.E.

Nonfiction and Photos: How-to articles about home remodeling. In these, the instructions should be described in clear terms, giving thorough information. Articles about sports, especially new or unusual sports. Articles about historic places or events. Length: 250 to 1,000 words. Pays $15 to $75. B&w photos (8x10 glossies) are purchased with or without accompanying ms. When additional payment is made for those purchased with mss, the minimum rate is $10. Also uses 4x5, or larger, color transparencies. Pays minimum of $15 for color.

ORGANIC GARDENING AND FARMING, Rodale Press Publications, 33 E. Minor St., Emmaus PA 18049. Phone: 215-967-5173. Managing Editor: M.C. Goldman. For a readership "ranging the full scope of public now aware and interested in growing plants, vegetables and fruits, as well as concerned about environmental problems." Monthly magazine; 160 to 184 (6x9) pages. Established in 1942. Circulation: 1,000,000. Buys all rights and the right to reuse in other Rodale Press Publications with agreed additional payment. Buys 300 to 350 mss a year. Payment on publication (actually, on preparation for publication). Will send free sample copy to writer on request. Write for copy of guidelines for writers. Reports in 4 to 6 weeks. Query first or submit complete ms. Enclose S.A.S.E.

Nonfiction, Photos and Fillers: "Factual or informative articles or fillers on both backyard gardening and family farming, stressing organic methods. Interested in all crops, soil topics, livestock, indoor gardening, greenhouses; natural foods preparation, storage, etc.; biological pest control; variety breeding, nutrition, recycling, energy conservation; community and club gardening. Strong on specific details, step-by-step how-to, adequate research. Good slant and interesting presentation always help. We do not want to see generalized garden success stories. And some build-it-yourself topics are often repeated. We would like to see material on development, techniques, different approaches to organic methods in producing fruit crops, grains, new and old vegetables; effective composting, soil building, waste recycling, food preparation. Emphasis is on interesting, practical information, presented effectively and accurately." Recently published articles include "The Right Chicken Coop for the Organic Homestead," "A Good Raspberry for Extra Income," and "Three Things I've Learned About Mulch." Length: 1,200 to 2,500 words for features; 100 to 200 words for fillers. B&w and color purchased with mss or on assignment. Enlarged b&w glossy print and/or negative preferred. Pays $10 to $15. 2¼x2¼ (or larger) color transparencies. Pays $75 to $200. Fillers on above topics are also used. Length: 150 to 500 words. Pays $25 to $50.

PERFECT HOME MAGAZINE, 427 6th Ave., S.E., Cedar Rapids IA 52401. Editor: Donna Nicholas Hahn. For "homeowners or others interested in building or improving their homes." Established in 1929. Monthly. Buys all rights. Pays on acceptance. Study magazine carefully before submitting. No seasonal material used. Submit editorial material at least 6 months in advance. Reports "at once." Will send free sample copy to a writer on request. Query first. Enclose S.A.S.E.

Nonfiction: "Ours is a nationally syndicated monthly magazine sponsored in local communities by qualified home builders, real estate companies, home financing institutions, and lumber and building supply dealers. We are primarily a photo magazine that creates a desire for an attractive, comfortable home. We need homebuilding, decorating, and remodeling features, decorating idea photographs, complete home coverage, and plans on homes." No do-it-yourself features. Length: 1 to 3 meaty paragraphs. No set price. "Each month we feature one nationally known guest editor on the theme 'What Home Means to Me.' Check with us before contacting a celebrity since we have had so many of them." Length: 500 to 1,000 words. Pays $50, including copy, photos, signature, and signed release from individual.

Photos: Purchases photos with articles on home building, decorating and remodeling; also purchases photos of interest to homeowners with captions only. Buys either b&w or color; color 3¼x4¼ up. "We return color; keep b&w unless return is requested as soon as issue has been printed. May hold photos 1 year." Photos must be well-styled and of highest professional quality. No models in pictures. Interested in series (for example, several pictures of gates, bay windows, window treatment, fireplaces, etc.). Pays $10 and up.

POOL 'N PATIO, 3923 W. 6th St., Los Angeles CA 90020. Editor: Fay Coupe. Issued twice yearly, in March and June, to residential owners of swimming pools. Buys all rights. Pays on publication. Reports on submissions at once. Enclose S.A.S.E.

Nonfiction and Photos: Articles on how to make pool maintenance easier; technical articles on equipment, unusual use of pools, or unusual pools; human interest or glamour stories on pool owners. Pays 3¢ to 5¢ per word. Length: 500 to 1,500 words. Photos purchased with mss. Pays $5 minimum.

TODAY'S HOMES, 229 Park Ave., S., New York NY 10003. Editor: John Lauderdale. For "people who are planning to build their own home, from initial selection of plans to final construction." Quarterly. Circulation: 60,000. Buys all rights. Buys 15 to 20 mss a year. Will not consider photocopied submissions. Submit seasonal material 4 to 5 months in advance. Reports immediately. Query first. Enclose S.A.S.E.
Nonfiction and Photos: "Articles on planning and designing kitchens and bathrooms; general landscaping; how to select building materials; financial trends applicable to future homeowners (mortgages, insurance, etc.). All articles are slanted to help the layman better understand what is available so that he can more intelligently talk with contractors and get the most for his money. All articles are 'meat and potatoes' stories. Lots of facts translated so that a person outside the building field can understand what would normally be too technical." Length: 2,000 to 3,000 words. Pays $100 to $200. 8x10 b&w glossies purchased with mss. Captions required.
How To Break In: "One way for the newcomer to break in, if he's handy with a camera, is to do a sequence of shots as someone adds a new room or closes in a porch. This could be a shorty — say 700 to 800 words. I really like them and they're hard to come by."

WOMAN TALK MAGAZINE, P.O. Box 356, Blackwood NJ 08012. Editor: Jo P. Italiano. For homemakers of all ages with interests in all areas of homemaking. Published every 2 months; 40 (5½x8½) pages. Established in 1973. Circulation: 1,200. Rights purchased vary with author and material. May buy all rights, but will sometimes reassign rights to author after publication, or second serial (reprint) rights. Buys 50 to 60 mss a year. Payment on publication. Will send sample copy to writer for 50¢. Will consider photocopied submissions. Will not consider simultaneous submissions. Submit seasonal material 3 to 4 months in advance. Reports in 2 to 3 months. Query first or submit complete ms. Enclose S.A.S.E.
Nonfiction and Photos: Articles on goal achievement, interesting women, homemakers, garage sales, gardening, animals, spare-time earning. "We emphasize a person-to-person relationship between our book and the reader and try gently to broaden the horizons of our readers. Our size makes it absolutely necessary that articles be concise. Style is open, but we do prefer a light approach. This does not preclude thoughtful subject matter, but nothing on the sensational side." Informational, how-to, interview, profile, humor, historical. Length: no minimum; 1,200 words maximum. Prefers 400 to 600 words. Pays ½¢ a word. Columns and departments include: Garden Corner, Pet Page, Of Interest to Boys and Girls. Items on needlework of all kinds are always needed. Length: 200 to 400 words. Pays ½¢ a word. Token payment of 25¢ is made for b&w photos used with mss.

Humor Publications

Publications in this category specialize in humor. Other publications that use humor can be found in nearly every category in this book. Some of these have special needs for major humor pieces; some use humor as fillers; many others are simply interested in material that meets their ordinary fiction or nonfiction requirements but has a humorous slant.

APPLE PIE (formerly *Harpoon*), 21 West 26th St., New York NY 10016. Editor: Dennis Lopez. Submissions Editor: Rex Weiner. For readers ages 18 through 30. Bimonthly. Circulation: 90,000. Buys first rights only. Pays on publication. Will send sample copy to writer for $1.50. Query first with sample of your style of humor, and where you've been previously published. Enclose S.A.S.E.

Nonfiction, Fiction, and Parodies: "Comedy, satire, parody, wit, written to and for the enjoyment of the reader. The magazine that dares compete with *National Lampoon.* We cover America, suburbia, affluence, prejudices, politics and government. All material humorous. The style of the humor, the attitude portrayed, is more important than the punchlines. As well as being a highly perceptive writer, you must be a natural high-baller and 60's refugee to make it here. 99% of our material is written by the younger-than-30 set; after all, they know the audience best." Length: shorts (rumors), 50 to 300 words; articles, 2,000 to 3,000 words.

BELCH & FART, Box 635, Tiburon CA 94920. Editor: Marcia Blackman. For young readers with a sense of humor. 36 (8x11) pages. Established in 1974. Every 2 months. Circulation: 10,000. Not copyrighted. Buys 60 mss a year. Payment on publication. Will send sample copy to writer for $2. Will consider photocopied submissions. No simultaneous submissions. Reports on material accepted for publication in 1 month. Returns rejected material immediately. Query first. Enclose S.A.S.E.
Nonfiction: "This is a spoof on *Gourmet Magazine,* using food as a humorous topic. Our profile is probably the same as *Mad Magazine* and *Lampoon.* We use only humorous articles with the emphasis on food, eating, restaurants, cooking, etc. We'd also like to see something on depression cooking and eating." Informational, how-to, personal experience, interview, profile, inspirational, humor, personal opinion, photo, travel, successful business operations, new products, merchandising techniques and reviews of restaurants. As examples of recently published material, see "Musical Food" and "10 Ways to Camouflage Lobster If You're Running a Kosher House". Length: 1,600 to 2,000 words. Pays $50 to $75.

MAD MAGAZINE, 485 Madison Ave., New York NY 10022. Editor: Al Feldstein. Buys all rights. Works almost exclusively with a group of professional, steady contributors. Enclose S.A.S.E.
Nonfiction: "*Mad* deals with that which is most familiar to the most people ... the so-called American scene and well-known international incidents and personages. Satirical article format." Very few unsolicited pieces have been accepted, but they were of exceptional quality. Be sure you are familiar with the magazine before you submit anything. Minimum rate of payment is $160 per page in print.

ORBEN'S CURRENT COMEDY, ORBEN COMEDY FILLERS, 2510 Virginia Ave. N.W., Apt. 701-N, Washington DC 20037. Phone: 202-338-8281. Editor: Robert Orben. For "speakers, toastmasters, businessmen, public relations people, communications professionals." Biweekly; monthly. Buys all rights. Pays at the end of the month for material used in issues published that month. "Material should be typed and submitted on standard size paper. Please leave 3 spaces between each item. Unused material will be returned to the writer within a few days if S.A.S.E. is enclosed. If you do not want the material returned, you should hear from us within 7 weeks if any items have been accepted. We do not send rejection slips. Please do not send us any material that has been sent to other publications. If S.A.S.E. is not enclosed, all material will be destroyed after being considered except for items purchased."
Fillers: "We are looking for funny, performable one-liners, short jokes, and stories that are related to happenings in the news, fads, trends, and topical subjects. The accent is on comedy, not wit. The ultimate criteria is, 'Will this line get a laugh if performed in public?' Material should be written in a conversational style and, if the joke permits it, the inclusion of dialogue is a plus. We are particularly interested in material that can be used by speakers and toastmasters: lines for beginning a speech, ending a speech, acknowledging an introduction, specific occasions, anything that would be of use to a person making a speech. We can use lines to be used at sales meetings, presentations, conventions, seminars, and conferences. Short, sharp comment on business trends, fads, and events is also desirable. Please do not send us material that's primarily written to be read rather than spoken. We have little use for definitions, epigrams, puns, etc. The submissions must be original. If material is sent to us that we find to be copied or rewritten from some other source, we will no longer consider material from the contributor." Pays $3.

SICK MAGAZINE, Pyramid Publications, 919 Third Ave., New York NY 10022. Editor: Paul Laikin. For people who like to laugh. Magazine; 48 (8½x11) pages. Established in 1959. Published every 2 months, plus special issues. Buys all rights. Buys about 100 mss a year. Pays on publication. Submit complete ms. Reports in 2 to 6 weeks. Enclose S.A.S.E.

Nonfiction: Satirical article format for informational, how-to, interview, profile, historical, think articles, expose, nostalgia, personal opinion, travel, spot news, new products, and reviews on media offerings of movies and TV. No specified length. Recently published articles include "Ser-pig-o," a humorous takeoff on a popular motion picture; "Sick Solves the Gasoline Shortage," takeoff on a topical theme; "The Undersea World of Jerque Kooksteau," a satirization of a personality seen often on television. "We pay $35 for every page used in magazine. Sometimes this translates to one or two paragraphs of copy per page."

In-Flight Publications

This list consists of publications read by commercial airline passengers. They use freelance material of general interest such as travel articles, etc., as well as general interest material on aviation.

AIR CALIFORNIA MAGAZINE, Box 21, Corona del Mar CA 92625. Editor: Michael McFadden. For the passengers of Air California, operating between Orange County, San Diego, Ontario and Palm Springs in the south, and San Francisco, Sacramento, San Jose and Oakland in the north. Monthly magazine; 64 (8½x11) pages. Established in 1967. Circulation: 125,000. Buys first North American serial rights. Buys 75 mss a year. Payment on publication. Will send sample copy to writer for $1. Will consider photocopied and simultaneous submissions. Query first on material, especially color photos. Reports on material accepted for publication in "a couple of months." Returns rejected material immediately. Enclose S.A.S.E.

Nonfiction and Photos: Nonfiction only, about California current events, history and the future. "We'll consider and often use serious pieces." Not interested in pieces about wine tasting and how to make money buying silver. Uses some how-to and nostalgic material. Think articles used "only if great." All material must be well-written and not too long. Length: 1,000 to 2,500 words. Pays minimum of $25; $100 with photos or art.

ALOFT, Wickstrom Publishers, Inc., 2701 South Bayshore Dr., Suite 501, Miami FL 33133. Editor: Karl Wickstrom. For National Airlines passengers. Travel-oriented. Offbeat places, things to see and do along NAL route or connecting areas. Designed for light upbeat entertainment. Quarterly. Rights to be negotiated. Pays on publication. Will send sample copy to a writer for 25¢. Will consider photocopied submissions. Reports in 4 to 6 weeks. Query first. Enclose S.A.S.E.

Nonfiction and Photos: Articles on unusual or little-known places rather than national monuments, historical sites, and the usual commercial attractions and travel brochure type of thing. Each issue contains at least one piece by or about a known personality. Gourmet dining (with recipes), a children's activity page, book reviews and fashion, are handled by staff or contributing editors. No controversial or expose articles. Length: 800 to 1,500 words. Pays $150 and up for articles. Query Ms. Pat Pinkerton, Executive Editor. Color transparencies are purchased with mss or captions on travel, sports, adventure. Must be top quality with imaginative approach. No snapshots or Polaroids. Payment negotiated. Photo Editor: Theodore R. Baker.

THE AMERICAN WAY, 633 Third Ave., New York NY 10017. Editor: John Minahan. For businessmen and vacation travelers aboard American Airlines. Monthly. Circulation: 2,000,000. Rights purchased vary with author and material. May buy all rights. Payment on acceptance. Query first. Submit seasonal material 7 months in advance. Reports 4 months prior to an issue. Enclose S.A.S.E. with queries.

Nonfiction: *"The American Way,* in addition to articles on travel, sports, food and the arts, tries to provide its readers stimulating and thought-provoking material that deals with current issues. First off, we like queries rather than actual mss. Also we like writing samples which more or less show a writer's abilities and scope. These will not be returned. We seek out the unusual aspects of both the relatively unknown and the familiar. We are essentially a news magazine, not a travel magazine. We want articles on news events, business, ecology, the environment; art, culture; important historical events." Informational, how-to, interview, profile, humor, historical, think articles, nostalgia, travel, successful business operations and new product articles. Regular columns include: Leisure, This Month, Beard on Food, Crist on Movies. Length: 2,500 words. Pays $200 minimum, $400 maximum.

How To Break In: "Come up with new insights into a major news story well in advance of its breaking (solar energy developments, business techniques, etc.)".

CLIPPER MAGAZINE, East/West Network, Inc., 5900 Wilshire Blvd., #300, Los Angeles CA 90036. Editor: James Clark. For passengers aboard Pan American World Airways. Established in 1949. Monthly. Circulation: 1,000,000. Buys all rights, but will reassign rights to author after publication. Buys 100 mss a year. Pays within 60 days of acceptance. Will send sample copy to writer for $1. Reports on material accepted for publication in 2 weeks or less. Returns rejected material in 1 month or less. Submit complete ms. Enclose S.A.S.E.

Nonfiction and Photos: Articles on travel and business. Length: 1,000 to 2,000 words. Pays $100 to $300. Buys 8x10 b&w glossies and color transparencies (35mm or 4x5) with mss. Pays $25 to $50 for b&w; $50 to $75 for color.

EAST/WEST NETWORK, INC., 5900 Wilshire Blvd., Suite 300, Los Angeles CA 90036. In-flight magazines published by East-West Network include *The California Magazine, Clipper, Flightime, Mainliner, Sky, Sundancer* and the in-room magazine, *Holiday Inn Magazine.* Editorial Director: James C. Clark. In-flight magazines for Allegheny Airlines, Continental Airlines, Delta Air Lines, Hughes Airwest, Ozark Air Lines, Pacific Southwest Airlines, Pan Am and United Airlines. Established in 1968. Monthly. Combined circulation of over 16,000,000. Buys all East-West Network rights. Buys 500 mss a year. Pays within 60 days of acceptance. Will send sample copy to writer for $1. Reports in 1 month. Enclose S.A.S.E.

Nonfiction: "On business, topical subjects, sports, personalities, trends, destinations." Length: 1,000 to 2,500 words. Pays $100 to $500.

LATITUDE/20, 1649 Kapiolani Blvd., #27, Honolulu HI 96814. Editor: Rita Witherwax. For Hawaiian Air passengers; affluent tourists and local people traveling inter-island. Magazine; 36 (8¼x11) pages. Established in 1974. Every 2 months. Circulation: 2,500,000. Not copyrighted. Buys about 30 mss a year. Pays on acceptance. Will send sample copy to writer for $1. Will consider photocopied submissions. No simultaneous submissions. Reports in 1 month. Query first. Enclose S.A.S.E.

Nonfiction and Photos: Primarily interested in Hawaiiana. Practical information and historical facts. Self-improvement articles. Travel-related humor. Ethnic stories are always welcome (Japanese, Chinese, Korean, Filipino, Hawaiian, Samoan, Portuguese). No word pictures of swaying palms and scarlet sunsets. Recently published an article on the Narcissus Festival which had excellent background on the Chinese New Year. Length: 1,000 words maximum. Pays $50 minimum. No additional payment for photos used with mss.

Poetry and Fillers: Must relate to Hawaii or travel. Traditional forms of poetry or light verse. Length: 4 to 20 lines. Pays $5 to $20. Jokes and short humor used as fillers. Length: 2 to 6 lines. Pays $5 to $10.

NORTHLINER, 1999 Shepard Rd., St. Paul MN 55116. Phone 612-647-7296. Editor: James Carney. For businessmen traveling aboard North Central's planes. Established in 1970. Quarterly. Circulation: 90,000. Buys all rights. Buys 8 to 10 mss a year. Payment on acceptance. Will send free sample copy to writer on request. Write for copy of editorial guidelines for writers. Will consider photocopied submissions, "as long as piece has not been previously published." Submit seasonal material

3 to 4 months in advance. Reports within 2 to 3 weeks. Query first or submit complete ms. Enclose S.A.S.E.

Nonfiction: "Short, lively pieces either somehow related to the cities along North Central's route system, or appealing to the traveling businessmen. Writing should be readable rather than academic, clever rather than endlessly descriptive, and tight rather than verbose. No travel stories per se, and very few how-to stories. Very rarely use first-person stories; only acceptable when writer is well enough known to justify first-person approach." Informational, interview, profile, humor, think articles, nostalgia, and successful business operations articles. Length: 900 to 1,500 words. Pays $75 to $250 per story.

Photos: Purchased with accompanying mss and on assignment. Captions required. 35mm or larger color photos. Pays $200 for cover; $50 each for inside originals.

Fillers: Puzzles, jokes, and short humor. Pays $5 to $35.

NORTHWEST EXPERIENCE, 7020 125th S.E., Renton WA 98055. Editor: Troy Bussey. For professional and general public interested in travel and vacation in the Northwestern states of Washington, Oregon, Idaho and Montana. Distributed as in-flight magazine for several regional airlines and paid subscribers. Established in 1972. Quarterly. Circulation: 10,000. Not copyrighted. Will send sample copy to writer for $1. Uses only a limited number of mss per year. Pays on publication. Will consider photocopied submissions. Reports in 30 days. Query first. Enclose S.A.S.E.

Nonfiction and Photos: Travel, sports, outdoor recreation, points of interest, crafts, informational, how-to and nostalgia. Should be written so reader may feel he has experienced or now wishes to experience the activity or area of which the writer has written. Length: 250 to 500 words. Pays $10 to $35 per story. Photos purchased with or without mss. B&w; very seldom uses color. Query first on color photos. Pays from $5 per photo to $50 for photo story.

PASSAGES, 747 Third Ave., New York NY 10017. Phone 212-371-6666. Editor: Richard Stewart. The in-flight magazine for Northwest Orient Airlines. Established in 1970. Monthly. Circulation: 150,000. Rights purchased vary with author and material. Buys all rights, but will reassign rights to author after publication; second serial (reprint) rights; simultaneous rights. Buys 50 mss a year. Payment on publication. Will send free sample copy to writer on request. Write for copy of guidelines for writers. Will consider photocopied submissions. Submit seasonal material 6 months in advance. Reports in 2 to 3 months. Enclose S.A.S.E.

Nonfiction and Photos: "Travel articles with added dimension of social significance, such as ecology, life styles, profiles, business related, sports, science, aviation-related; historical especially, with reference to Northwest destination points. Special need for humor. Writer's own style preferred, with an easy style generally better for informational pieces such as humor. Writers should look to contribute meaning, understanding to reader. Generally seek constructive pieces. Creative, business-related articles along with constructive ones on environment and city improvement. Ski and other sports. Leisure time activities." Length: 1,000 to 3,000 words. Pays $50 to $300, with more payment ($25) made for transparencies bought with mss. Also pays more for assigned work. Color transparencies purchased with mss. Captions optional. Art Director: Ken Hine.

PASTIMES, 4 W. 58th St., Tenth Floor, New York NY 10019. Publisher: Carroll B. Stoianoff. Distributed by Eastern Airlines for "the *New Yorker* reader — top 20% of population in income and education. All travelers, very deep in frequent air travelers, 67% male — average age 40 years. 40% have family income of $25,000 (and over) a year." Monthly. Circulation: 325,000. Rights purchased vary with author and material; may buy all rights (but may reassign rights to author after publication), first North American serial rights, first serial rights, second serial (reprint) rights, or simultaneous rights. Pays on publication. Uses no poetry or fiction. Query first always. Will consider photocopied submissions. Reports in 2 weeks. Enclose S.A.S.E. for reply to queries.

Nonfiction: "Short, intelligent humor or novelty material which will intrigue, hold attention of, and entertain college-educated business and professional people. Must not be overtly or implicitly controversial in any way or rely on shock or satire for its effect. *Pastimes* does not treat general subject matter in the same way as other magazines. It is a bright, relaxed, adult entertainment publication whose primary mission is to interest and amuse intelligent air travelers as a group comprised of intelligent Americans of all persuasions and convictions. We are interested in all topical subjects, but with an original, offbeat, and generally appealing approach rather than the conventional journalistic or didactic approach." Buys interviews, sports articles, profiles, humor, historical articles, think pieces, nostalgia, photo features, travel articles. Length: 1,000 words maximum. Pays $25 to $100.

Photos: Purchased with or without mss or on assignment. 8x10 b&w glossies and 35mm, 2¼ and larger color. Pays $10.

PSA MAGAZINE, 5900 Wilshire Blvd., Suite 300, Los Angeles CA 90036. Editor: Thomas Shess, Jr. Published by East/West Network, Inc., for Pacific Southwest Airlines. For "California businessmen with incomes averaging $20,000 per annum." Established in 1968. Monthly. Circulation: 500,000. Rights purchased vary with author and material. Buys about 40 mss a year. Pays on publication. Will send a sample copy to writer for $1. Reports in 30 days. Query first. Enclose S.A.S.E.

Nonfiction: "California business, restaurants, saloons, cars, travel, sports, construction, fashions. Articles must be by Californians and about California living. Ours is the only statewide publication for high income California businessmen. No articles on air travel, politics, and religion. We'd like to see more articles on California business and businessmen." Buys how-to's, interviews, profiles, humor, historical articles, think pieces, coverage of successful business operations, new product articles, and coverage of merchandising techniques. Length: 1,500 words. Pays $50 to $150. Photos purchased with ms; captions required. For 8x10 b&w glossies, pays $15. For 35mm color, payment "varies, up to $100 for cover."

TWA AMBASSADOR, 1999 Shepard Rd., St. Paul MN 55116. Phone: 612-647-7295. Editor: James Morgan. For TWA passengers; top management executives, professional men and women, and world travelers. Established in 1968. Monthly. Circulation: 321,000. Buys all rights. Pays on acceptance. Will send free sample copy to writer on request. Write for copy of guidelines for writers. Submit seasonal material at least 5 months in advance. Reports on material accepted for publication in 2 weeks to 1 month. Returns rejected material in 3 weeks. Query first. Enclose S.A.S.E.

Nonfiction and Photos: "Most TWA passengers are business oriented, but the airlines serve people of all areas of the world, all strata of society. Keep in mind the international scope of this magazine   avoid subjects of provincial interest unless such subjects are pegs for a more general treatment. Our travel stories must have a specific story angle, preferably from a TWA-route city; we do not use general descriptive pieces about a city or area, or where-to-shop, where-to-eat, what-to-see, broadbrush travel articles. We avoid flight-oriented articles. First-person approach is generally unacceptable. Our goal is to entertain and inform the international reader via an editorial mix consisting of interesting and provocative articles on sports, business, personalities, history, modern living, general human interest topics and foreign and domestic travel." Recently published articles include "New York City: Still the American Dream?" (a survey of the current New York image); "Is There Life on Mars?" (a preview of the 1975-76 NASA flight to Mars, and a discussion of Mars' role in our popular culture); "True Grit: Thomas Hart Benton at 85" (an interview with the crotchety grand old man of American art, published 2 months before his death); "The Cheese Lover's Guide to Europe" (a look at Europe's rich cheese heritage, with appropriate wines and beers suggested). Length: 1,000 to 2,5000 words. Pays $100 to $600 per story; expense arrangements negotiated. Color and b&w photos purchased with accompanying ms; 35mm or larger. Pays $50 inside; $250 cover; $25 b&w.

WESTERN'S WORLD, 141 El Camino, Beverly Hills CA 90212. Phone: 213-273-1990. Editor: Frank M. Hiteshew. Published by Western Airlines for the airline traveler. Established in 1970. 6 times a year. Circulation: 250,000. Buys all rights. Buys 20 to 25 mss a year. Pays on publication. Will consider photocopied submissions. Submit seasonal material 12 months in advance of issue date. Reports in 1 to 3 months. Query first. Enclose S.A.S.E.

Nonfiction: "Articles should relate to travel, dining, or entertainment in the area served by Western Airlines: Hawaii, Minneapolis/St. Paul, Alaska to Mexico, and between. Compared to other airline magazines, *Western's World* strives for a more editorial approach. It's not as promotional-looking; all articles are bylined articles. Some top names in the field." Buys photo features and travel articles. Length: 1,000 to 2,000 words. Pays 10¢ a word.

Photos: Purchased with or without mss or on assignment; captions required. Uses 8x10 b&w glossies, but "rarely." Pays $25. Uses 35mm, 4x5, and larger color transparencies. Pays $25 to $125; "more for cover, subject to negotiation." Tom Medsger, Assistant Editor.

Fiction: Western short stories, fantasy, humor. "Rarely printed because we've seen so few good ones. Should relate to *Western's World.*" Length: 1,000 to 2,000 words. Pays 10¢ a word.

Fillers: "Travel-oriented or brain-teasers." Pays 10¢ per word. Department Editor: Tom Medsger.

Jewish Publications

The publications which follow use material on topics of general interest slanted toward a Jewish readership. Publications using Jewish-oriented religious material are categorized in Religious Publications.

CHAI MAGAZINE, 11 Warren Rd., Baltimore MD 21208. Editor: Jeffrey Pollack. For the well-educated Jewish reader; middle to upper class; 30 to 60 age bracket; full range of interests. Magazine; 64 to 96 (7x10) pages. Established in 1974. Every 2 months. Rights purchased vary with author and material. May buy all rights with the possibility of reassigning rights to author after publication; or first North American serial rights. Buys about 30 mss a year. Pays on acceptance for cover stories; on publication for others. Will send sample copy to writer for 50¢. Will consider photocopied and simultaneous submissions. Submit seasonal material (major Jewish holidays) 2 to 3 months in advance. Reports in 2 to 4 weeks. Query first or submit complete ms. Enclose S.A.S.E.

Nonfiction and Photos: Articles on a full range of Jewish interests; ethnic identity, history, profiles of people, firms, organizations, personal pieces, current events, politics, etc. First-person preferred; an ethnic pride as Jews approach. More interested in ethnic material than religious topics. Recently published a special issue on "Jews in America", which covered Jewish contributions to American society from colonial to modern times. Length: 1,000 to 3,500 words. Pays $125 to $300. B&w glossies (8x10) purchased with or without ms, or on assignment. Pays $20 to $50. Pays $25 to $75 for color transparencies.

Poetry: Traditional forms, blank verse, free verse, light verse. Length: 10 to 100 lines. Pays $5 to $25.

CHRONICLE REVIEW, 2953 Bathurst St., Toronto, Ontario, Canada. Editor: Dr. Arnold Ages. For "exclusively Jewish readers with above average education." Special issues for High Holy Days, Passover issues. Established in 1897. Monthly. Circulation: 9,000. Buys first publication rights only. Buys 30 to 40 mss a year. Payment on publication. Will send free sample copy to writer on request. Submit seasonal material one month in advance. Will consider photocopied submissions. Reports in 2 to 4 weeks. Enclose S.A.E. and International Reply Coupons.

Nonfiction: "We publish think pieces on Jewish-related themes; will also consider biographical profiles of Jewish figures. Our approach is not academic, but journalistic. We are independent of any religious or cultural groups within the larger Jewish community. We get enormous coverage of Israel-oriented articles; we would prefer

North American copy. We would also like material to have Canadian slant." Buys profiles and think articles. Length: 1,000 to 3,000 words. Pays $25 to $100.

How To Break In: "Send in a book review on speculation. Reviews (1,000 to 1,500 words) of nonfiction and fiction books of Jewish interest. I'm always on the lookout for well-written pieces of this nature. Or look at newspaper articles that appear to give promise of a good story. Then probe deeply."

JEWISH CURRENT EVENTS, 430 Keller Avenue, Elmont NY 11003. Editor: S. Deutsch. For Jewish children and adults; distributed in Jewish schools. Biweekly. Pays on publication. No sample copies available. No query required. Reports in 1 week. Enclose S.A.S.E.

Nonfiction: All current event items of Jewish content or interest; news; featurettes; short travel items (non-Israel) relating to Jewish interests or descriptions of Jewish communities or personalities; life in Jewish communities abroad; "prefer items written in news-style format." Length must be short. Pays anywhere from $10 to $300, depending on content, illustrations, length and relevance.

Photos: Purchased with mss. All items of Jewish content or interest. B&w snapshots only. Payment varies.

THE JEWISH DIGEST, 1363 Fairfield Ave., Bridgeport CT 06605. Editor: Bernard Postal. For "urban, well-educated families, interested in topics of Jewish interest." Established in 1955. Monthly. Circulation: 15,000. Buys first North American serial rights. Buys 10 to 20 mss a year. Payment on acceptance. Will send a sample copy to writer for 60¢. Submit seasonal material (Jewish holidays) six months in advance. Will consider photocopied submissions. Reports in 2 weeks. Enclose S.A.S.E.

Nonfiction: Subject matter should be of "Jewish interest. Jewish communities around the world, and personality profiles. Contemporary topics about and relating to Jews in the U.S. and abroad. We would like to see personal experiences, biographic sketches, impressions of the Jewish community here and abroad." Length: 2,000 words. Pays 1¢ to 2¢ a word with $50 maximum.

MIDSTREAM, 515 Park Ave., New York NY 10022. Editor: Joel Carmichael. Monthly. Circulation: 12,000. Buys first rights. Pays on publication. Will send a sample copy to a writer on request. Reports in 2 weeks. Enclose S.A.S.E.

Nonfiction and Fiction: "Articles offering a critical interpretation of the past, searching examination of the present, and affording a medium for independent opinion and creative cultural expression. "Articles on the political and social scene in Israel, on Jews in Russia and the U.S.; generally it helps to have a Zionist orientation. If you're going abroad, we would like to see what you might have to report on a Jewish community abroad." Buys historical and think pieces and fiction, primarily of Jewish and related content. Pays 5¢ to 6¢ minimum per word.

How To Break In: "A book review would be the best way to start. Send us a sample review or a clip, let us know your area of interest, suggest books you would like to review."

THE NATIONAL JEWISH MONTHLY, 1640 Rhode Island, N.W., Washington DC 20036. Editor: Charles Fenyvesi. National B'nai B'rith monthly magazine. Buys North American serial rights. Pays on publication. Enclose S.A.S.E.

Nonfiction: Articles of interest to the Jewish community: economic, demographic, political, social, biographical. Length: 3,000 words maximum. Pays 10¢ per word maximum.

RECONSTRUCTIONIST, 15 W. 86th St., New York NY 10024. Editor: Dr. Ira Eisenstein. A general Jewish religious and cultural magazine. Monthly. Established in 1935. Circulation: 6,000. Buys all rights. Buys 10 mss a year. Payment on publication. Will send free sample copy to writer on request. Query first. Enclose S.A.S.E.

Nonfiction: Publishes literary criticism, reports from Israel and other lands where Jews live, and material of educational or communal interest. Also uses interviews

and features dealing with leading Jewish personalities. Preferred length is 3,000 words and payment is from $15 to $25, made on publication.
Fiction and Poetry: Uses a small amount of poetry and fiction as fillers.

SOUTHERN JEWISH WEEKLY, P.O. Box 3297, Jacksonville FL 32206. Editor: Isadore Moscovitz. For a Jewish audience. Established in 1924. General subject matter is human interest and short stories. Weekly. Circulation: 28,500. Not copyrighted. Buys 15 mss a year. Payment on acceptance. Will send a free sample copy to a writer on request. Will send editorial guidelines sheet on request. Submit seasonal material one month in advance. Reports in 10 days. Enclose S.A.S.E.
Nonfiction and Photos: Approach should be specifically of "Southern Jewish interest." Length: 250 to 500 words. Pays $10 to $25. Buys b&w photos with mss.

WORLD OVER, 426 W. 58th St., New York NY 10019. Editor: Ezekiel Schloss. Buys first serial rights only. Pays on acceptance. Reports within three to four weeks. Query first. Enclose S.A.S.E.
Nonfiction, Photos, and Fiction: Uses material of Jewish interest, past or present for ages 9 to 13 and up. Articles up to 1,200 words; serials of 4,800 words, usually divided into four sections. Fiction should have an ethical or moral slant and be Jewish in content. Length: 600 to 1,200 words. Pays 5¢ a word and up. B&w glossies purchased with mss.

Juvenile Publications

This section of Writer's Market *includes publications for children ages 2 to 12. Magazines for young people 12 to 25 appear in a separate Teen and Young Adult category.*

Most of the following publications are produced by religious groups, and wherever possible, the specific denomination is given. For the writer with a story or article slanted to a specific age group, the sub-index which follows is a quick reference to markets for his story in that age group.

Those editors who are willing to receive simultaneous submissions are indicated. (This is the technique of mailing the same story at the same time to a number of low-paying religious markets of nonoverlapping circulation. In each case, the writer, when making a simultaneous submission, should so advise the editor.) The few mass circulation, nondenominational publications included in this section which have good pay rates are not interested in simultaneous submissions and should not be approached with this technique. Magazines which pay good rates expect, and deserve, the exclusive use of material.

Writers will also note in some of the listings that editors will buy "second rights" to stories. This refers to a story which has been previously published in a magazine and to which the writer has already sold "first rights." Payment is usually less for the re-use of a story than for first-time publication.

Juvenile Publications Classified by Age
Two- to Five-Year Olds: *Children's Playmate, Children's Service Programs, The Friend, Happy Times, Highlights for Children, Humpty Dumpty's Magazine, Jack and Jill, The Kindergartner, Let's Find Out, Nursery Days, Our Little Friend, Quest, Ranger Rick's Nature Magazine, Story Friends.*

Six- to Eight-Year-Olds: *Child Life, Children's Digest, Children's Playcraft, Children's Playmate, Children's Service Programs, Cricket, Crusader, Daisy, Explore, The Friend, Highlights for Children, Humpty Dumpty's Magazine, It's Our World, Jack and Jill,*

Jet Cadet, Let's Find Out, My Jewels, Primary Treasure, Ranger Rick's Nature Magazine, Story Friends, Video-Presse, The Vine, Weekly Bible Reader, Wonder Time, Wow, Young Crusader, Young Judaean.

Nine- to Twelve-Year-Olds: *American Red Cross Youth News, The Beehive, Child Life, Children's Digest, Children's Playcraft, Children's Service Programs, Climb, Cricket, Crusader, Crusader Magazine, Discoveries, Discovery, The Friend, The Good Deeder, Highlights for Children, It's Our World, Jack and Jill, Jet Cadet, My Pleasure, News Explorer, NewsTime, On the Line, Primary Treasure, Quest, Rainbow, Ranger Rick's Nature Magazine, Sprint Magazine, Story Friends, Trails, Video-Presse, The Vine, Wee Wisdom, Young Crusader, Young Judaean, Young Musicians.*

AMERICAN RED CROSS YOUTH NEWS, American National Red Cross, 18th and E Sts., N.W., Washington DC 20006. Editor: Virginia D. Lautz. For elementary school children, mainly grades 4 to 6, ages 9 to 12. Established in 1919. Seven times a year, October through May, excluding January. Circulation: 210,000. Buys first publication rights, serially and otherwise, in English and any other language or medium, including braille and acoustical recording for blind or handicapped children. Right to republish for Red Cross purposes any time, in any language and in any such media. Buys about 8 mss a year. Payment on acceptance. Will send free sample copy to a writer on request. Will send editorial guidelines sheet to a writer on request. Query first for all material. Do not send complete ms. All mss will be returned unread unless query is sent first. Reports in 6 to 8 weeks. Enclose S.A.S.E.
Nonfiction, Photos and Drama: General subject matter consists of informative feature material which would be useful in the elementary curriculum but also interesting and entertaining reading for youngsters at home. Wildlife, ecology, creative dramatics, famous explorers—material that informs and expands the young imagination and world. Also more humorous, innovative treatment of seasonal, traditional topics. Short plays, more games that teach, science experiments, more ways to involve children. Good nonfiction on contemporary topics needed regularly. Since publication is that of Red Cross, also emphasize health, well-being, service, international friendship among children. Length: 1,000 to 1,200 words. Payment varies, but averages $75 to $125. Photos purchased with mss, and on assignment. 8x10 b&w glossies. Payment varies.
Fiction: Buys mystery, suspense, adventure, western, science fiction, fantasy, humorous, and historical fiction. Length: 1,000 to 1,200 words. Payment varies with mss, but averages $50 to $125.

THE BEEHIVE (formerly *Five/Six*), 201 8th Ave., S., Nashville TN 37203. Phone: 615-749-6223. Editor: Miss Martha Wagner. Published monthly in weekly format for children in grades five and six in United Methodist Church schools. Will send free sample copy to a writer on request. Buys all rights. Pays on acceptance. Submit double-spaced copy, 39-character line count. Reports on submissions within three months. Enclose S.A.S.E.
Nonfiction and Photos: Most articles requested by editor from writers. Subject matter relates to or correlates with church school curriculum and interests of children in grades 4, 5 and 6. Should not be overly moralistic or didactic. May provide information to enrich cultural understanding in religion and in relationships with other people. Also well-written biography, not composed from encyclopedias; 200 to 800 words. Pays 3¢ a word. Length: 200 to 800 words. Pays 3¢ a word. Photos purchased with mss. B&w glossies; color transparencies. Pays $1 to $25.
Fiction, Poetry, and Fillers: Modern day life, problems. Unusual historical stories; church history. No slang, references to drinking, or smoking. Might-have-happened Biblical stories. "I am rejecting many manuscripts because of our low budget. Many stories are too long, too unrealistic, or goody-goody." Length: about 800 words. Poetry to 20 lines. Pays 50¢ per line. Puzzles. Pays $5.

CHILD LIFE, P.O. Box 567B, Indianapolis IN 46206. Phone: 317-634-1100. Editor: Jane E. Norris. For children of ages 7 to 11. 10 times a year. Buys all rights unless otherwise specified by author at time of submission. Pays on publication. Submit seasonal material 8 months in advance. Will send sample copy for 50¢. Write for copy of guidelines for writers. Reports in 8 to 10 weeks, but may hold material under consideration for up to 1 year. Enclose S.A.S.E. for return of submissions.

Nonfiction: Present-day science, nature, general information, words, international stories. Little-known anecdotes about famous people, events or accomplishments in which identity is withheld until the end. Length: 1,000 words maximum. Pays about 3¢ per word.

Photos: B&w glossies or color transparencies. Buys photos submitted with mss to illustrate articles. Pays about $2.50 per b&w photo. More for color.

Fiction and Drama: From 600 words for beginner stories to 1,200 for older children. Uses some 2-part serials, about 2,400 words in length. Should be written in realistic, nonmoralizing, nonacademic style. Likes humor or suspense in fiction. No talking, inanimate objects. Pays about 3¢ per word. Also very short, lively plays that can be produced in living room or classroom with minimum of simple props and small casts. Also has a need for urban-oriented stories and stories with ethnic characters, and adventure stories.

Fillers: Puzzles, mazes, tricks and games. Make-its should use materials readily available at home or school and involve a minimum of adult guidance. Explanatory sketches and/or a sample of the finished project should be included if practical. No fixed payment for fillers.

How To Break In: "We welcome new authors. Probably the most important factors are interest level and length of mss. Fiction should be written in a lively style with vivid characters and plenty of action. Fiction should be of interest to children between the ages of 7 and 11 and cannot be longer than 1,200 words. Nonfiction should be short enough to hold interest and should be preferably on lesser-known topics. Complete bibliography or source list must accompany all nonfiction material."

CHILDREN'S DIGEST, 52 Vanderbilt Ave., New York NY 10017. Editor: Elizabeth R. Mattheos. Monthly except June and August, for children ages seven to 12. Buys reprint rights. Pays on publication. Reports in three weeks. Enclose S.A.S.E. for return of submissions.

Nonfiction and Fiction: Accepts only reprint material. Will accept material for readers, ages 7 through 12 only. Stories and articles published in book form only, not in other children's magazines. Will accept activities from other juvenile publications. "We are a reprint magazine. Publishers send us their books on a regular basis. With an editorial staff of one, must limit incoming submissions." Payment varies, according to date of publication, reputation of author, length of article, story, etc. "Although we have commissioned a few pieces such as one on the Bermuda Triangle by the author of the book, we publish almost exclusively reprint material. What I need most is nonfiction, lengths of 1,000 to 2,000 words. Subject areas we've been covering are ecology, current events, science. We're doing a piece now on the new Arab influence and the effects of the enormous amount of money which they now have. I'd like to see more science stories; they are difficult to find. Can be a general article or one based on experiments. No animal stories, please. Just send a tearsheet or the ms."

CHILDREN'S PLAYCRAFT, 52 Vanderbilt Ave., New York NY 10801. Editor: Anita Malnig. Published 10 times a year by Parents' Magazine Enterprises, Inc., as a new magazine of easy-to-make fun activities for boys and girls age 6 to 12. "We are still strictly a reprint magazine."

CHILDREN'S PLAYMATE, 1100 Waterway Blvd., P.O. Box 567B, Indianapolis IN 46206. Phone: 317-634-1100, Ext. 296. Editor: Beth Wood Thomas. For "bright, appreciative children, ages 3 to 8." 10 times a year. Circulation: 250,000. Buys all rights unless otherwise specified at time of submission. Pays on publication. Will send sample copy for 50¢. Write for copy of guidelines for writers. No query. "We do not consider resumes and outlines. Reading the whole ms is the only way to give fair consideration. The editors cannot criticize, offer suggestions, or review unsolicited material that is not accepted." Submit seasonal material 8 months in

advance. Simultaneous submissions not accepted. Reports in 8 to 10 weeks. Sometimes may hold mss for up to 1 year. Enclose S.A.S.E. for return of submissions.
Fiction: Short stories, not over 600 words for beginner readers. No inanimate, talking objects. Humorous stories, unusual plots. Vocabulary suitable for ages 3 to 8. Pays about 3¢ per word.
Nonfiction: Beginning science, not more than 600 words. Monthly "All About...." feature, 300 to 500 words, may be an interesting presentation on animals, people, events, objects, or places. Pays about 3¢ per word.
Poetry: Length: 4 lines minimum. Pays about 25¢ a line; minimum of $5.
Fillers: Puzzles, dot-to-dots, color-ins, mazes, tricks, games, guessing games, and brain teasers. "Attention to special holidays and events is sometimes helpful." Payment varies.

CHILDREN'S SERVICE PROGRAMS, Concordia Publishing House, 3558 S. Jefferson Ave., St. Louis MO 63118. Issued annually by The Lutheran Church—Missouri Synod, for children, aged three through eighth grade. Buys all rights. Receipt of children's worship scripts will be acknowledged immediately, but acceptance or rejection may require up to a year. All mss must be typed, double-spaced on 8½x11 paper. S.A.S.E. must be enclosed for ms return. Write for details.
Nonfiction and Drama: Four 16-page Christmas worship service programs for congregational use published yearly. Children leading the worship and adults joining in singing some of the hymns. Every script should present a worship service emphasizing the Biblical message of the Gospel through which God shares His love and in which His people rejoice. Christmas plays or services requiring elaborate staging or costumes will not be accepted. "We reject programs that require staging and/or costumes; also reject those which lack Gospel." Pays $100, but buys few mss.

CLIMB, Warner Press, 1200 E. Fifth St., Anderson IN 46011. Editor: William A. White. For "ten-year-old boys and girls from across the U.S.A. and Canada." Publishes material "dealing with Christian living and example." Weekly. Circulation: 22,000. Not copyrighted. Buys 225 mss a year. Pays on publication. Will send a sample copy to a writer on request. Write for copy of guidelines for writers. No query required. Will consider photocopied submissions. Submit seasonal material 4 to 5 months in advance. Reports in 2 weeks. Enclose S.A.S.E. for return of submissions.
Nonfiction and Photos: "These stories might deal with current situations of 10- and 11 year-olds who have done something about a problem in their community; current Christian laymen and how they see their job as a Christian; current Christian athletes;" etc. Writer should use a 10-year-old's vocabulary and "lots of dialogue." Buys how-to's, interviews, profiles, think pieces, travel pieces, humor, historical articles, and personal experience nonfiction. Length: 250 to 1,000 words. Pays $7.50 per 1,000 words. B&w glossy photos purchased with mss. Pays $5 to $25; one-time use.
Fiction: "Should challenge and guide readers in the meaning of living a winsome, Christian life." Stories of adventure; also, religious, contemporary problem stories. Length: 800 to 1,200 words. Pays $7.50 per 1,000 words.
Poetry and Fillers: Prefers "readers' poems." Length: 4 to 20 lines. Pays 20¢ per line or $2 per poem. Puzzles, clippings, jokes, short humor used as fillers.

CRICKET, P.O. Box 100, LaSalle IL 61301. Editor: Marianne Carus. For children ages 5 to 12. Monthly magazine; 96 pages. Established in 1973. Rights purchased vary with author and material. May buy all rights, first serial world rights, or second serial (reprint) rights. Buys about 100 mss per year. Usually pays on acceptance. Sample copies of magazine available; $1.25 each. Write for copy of guidelines for writers. Will consider photocopied and simultaneous submissions. Special material should be submitted 9 to 12 months in advance. "We work 1 year in advance of publication." Reports on material accepted for publication in 6 to 8 weeks. Returns rejected material in 6 to 8 weeks. Submit complete ms. Enclose S.A.S.E.
Nonfiction: "We are interested in high-quality material written for children, not

down to children." Biography, science, history, foreign culture, informational, humor, travel. Pays up to 25¢ per word.

Fiction: Realistic and historic fiction; fantasy, myth, legend, folk tale. Does not want to see animal stories or rewritten or retold folk tales that appear in standard story collections and anthologies. Length: 200 to 2,000 words. Pays up to 25¢ per word.

Poetry: Traditional forms, light verse, limericks, nonsense rhymes. Length: 100 lines maximum. Pays up to $3 per line.

Fillers: Short humor, puzzles, songs, crafts, recipes. Length: 200 words maximum. Pays up to 25¢ per word.

CRUSADER, 1548 Poplar Ave., Memphis TN 38104. Phone: 901-272-2461. Editor: Lee Hollaway. For boys ages 6 through 11, who are part of a boys' program in Southern Baptist Churches called Royal Ambassadors. Established in 1970. Monthly. Circulation: 100,000. Rights purchased vary with author and material. May buy first North American serial rights, first serial rights, second serial (reprint) rights, simultaneous rights. Buys 50 to 100 mss a year. Payment on acceptance. Will send free copy to writer on request. Write for copy of guidelines for writers. Will consider photocopied submissions. Submit seasonal material 8 to 10 months in advance. Reports within 3 months. Enclose S.A.S.E.

Nonfiction and Photos: "Articles of general interest to the age group. Articles should often aid the child's interest in the world around him and increase his appreciation for cultures other than his own." Informational, how-to (simple), humor, historical (limited), photo, and travel articles. Nature articles almost always require photos. Length: maximum 1,000 words, but prefers 500. Pays minimum $5, no maximum. Photos are purchased with or without manuscripts, and on assignment. Captions optional. Prefers 5x7 b&w or larger glossy. Pays $5 and up per photo. "Nonfiction photo stories involving boys as well as self-explanatory photos without copy involving boys."

Fiction and Fillers: 12 to 15 short stories are purchased each year. Mainstream, mystery, adventure, humorous, and religious fiction (no sermonizing!). Length: no minimum, maximum 1,200 words. Pays 2½¢ a word. Prefers simple puzzles involving drawing.

CRUSADER MAGAZINE, Box 7244, Grand Rapids MI 49510. Editor: Michael R. McGervey. For boys, age 9 to 14. Magazine; 32 (5½x8½) pages, in cartoon format. Established in 1962. Seven times a year. Circulation: 9,800. Rights purchased vary with author and material. Buys 15 to 20 mss a year. Pays on acceptance. Will send free sample copy to writer on request. Write for copy of guidelines for writers. Will consider photocopied and simultaneous submissions. Submit seasonal material (Christmas, Easter) at least 4 months in advance. Reports on material accepted for publication in 30 days. Returns rejected material in 30 to 60 days. Query first or submit complete ms. Enclose S.A.S.E.

Nonfiction and Photos: Bible discussion topics. Articles about things young boys like (sports, outdoor activities, bike riding, science, crafts, etc.), and the problems they have. Emphasis is on a Christian perspective, but no simplistic moralisms. Material appropriate to Christmas and Easter. Informational, how-to, personal experience, interview, profile, inspirational, humor, think articles. Length: 500 to 1,500 words. Pays 2¢ to 5¢ a word. Pays $5 to $25 for b&w photos purchased with mss.

Fiction and Fillers: Adventure, humorous, religious fiction. Does not want to see stories with predictable happy endings. Length: 500 to 1,500 words. Pays 2¢ to 5¢ a word. Uss short humor and any type of puzzles as fillers. Pays minimum of $10.

DAISY (formerly *Brownie Reader*), 830 Third Ave, New York NY 10022. Editor-in-Chief: Elisabeth Brower. For Brownie Girl Scouts who are in the 6 thorugh 8 age bracket. "We see ourselves as an educational magazine." Buys all rights. 9 issues a year. Payment on publication. Will send free sample copy on request, if adequate postage is enclosed. Will consider photocopied submissions. Submit seasonal material (for special scouting holidays: Juliette Low's birthday, Thinking Day, Girl Scout

Birthday) 6 months in advance. Reports on material acccepted for publication in 6 to 8 weeks. Returns rejected material in 8 to 10 weeks. Query first or submit complete ms. Enclose S.A.S.E.

Nonfiction and Photos: *"Daisy* is used by a Brownie as an extension of her Brownie troop experience, but it also helps her want to try, to do and to discover, all by herself. Brownies are imaginative, creative, young girls striving to learn more about the world around them and how it relates to the life they lead. The writer should remember that Brownies come not only from the suburbs, but also from urban areas, and are of all races and creeds. The writer should also remember that a Brownie's reading vocabulary is limited." Uses articles on nature, science, how-to's, profiles, people in other lands (stressing children, customs and/or folklore), health and safety, places of interest, think pieces. Length: 50 to 500 words. Pays $25 maximum. B&w glossy action photos are preferred. They should include Brownie Girl Scouts or children of that age. Pays about $3. Buys all rights unless otherwise specified by author/photographer at time of submission.

Fiction and Poetry: Light fiction preferred. "It does not have to pertain to Girl Scouting, but can be a general type of children's story. We want to see stories about real children and relationships between people, but not written in a sanctimonious way. We're not preaching to children. We are addressing them as thinking, capable people who simply are not yet thoroughly experienced." Humor or fantasy. Length: 500 words maximum. Pays $25 maximum. Light verse is used. Length and payment vary.

How To Break In: "One way for a writer to break in is to send us a short feature on a young person with whom he is familiar and who has done something extraordinary. It helps if it's a girl and even better if she's a scout. Our readers are interested in what their contemporaries are doing. Other nonfiction possibilities are 'do-you-know-that . . .?' items and scientific subjects. To give you an idea of the kind of thing we like, I read in *The Times* that Mt. Sinai Hospital is using a new computerized eye examination which determines deficiences and the needed corrections in a very short time. They ran a test on school children. This is something which would interest our readers because most of them have had eye tests and very often parents and teachers take a long time to realize that a child is not retarded but has sight problems. We'd want to be able to do a story which tells our readers in a very simplified form how this new testing device works. We've changed the name of the magazine and we're opening it up to girls who are a little older. I'm not using much freelance material right now, not because I wouldn't be happy to, but because it just isn't adequate to our needs. A lot of it is derivative, sentimental, poorly written and much too long."

DISCOVERIES (formerly *Junior Discoveries),* 6401 The Paseo, Kansas City MO 64131. Editor: Sandi Pitcher. For boys and girls 9 to 11. Weekly. Buys first and some second rights. No query required. "No comments can be made on rejected material." Enclose S.A.S.E. for return of submissions.

Nonfiction: Articles on nature, travel, history, crafts, science, Christian faith, biography of Christian leaders, Bible manners and customs, home craft ideas. Should be informal, spicy, and aimed at fourth and fifth grade vocabulary. Sharp photos and artwork help sell features. Length: 400 to 800 words. Pays 2¢ a word.

Photos: Sometimes buys pix submitted with mss. Buys them with captions only if subject has appeal. Send quality photos, 5x7 or larger.

Fiction: Stories with Christian emphasis on high ideals, wholesome social relationships and activities, right choices, Sabbath observance, church loyalty, goodwill, and missions. Informal style. Length: 1,000 to 1,250 words. "Or serials of 2 to 4 parts, average 1,250 words per installment." Pays 2¢ a word.

Poetry: Nature and Christian thoughts or prayers, 4 to 16 lines. Pays 50¢ for each 4 lines.

DISCOVERY, 999 College Ave., Winona Lake IN 46590. Editor: Vera Bethel. For "fourth, fifth, and sixth graders who attend Sunday school." Weekly. Circulation: 14,000. Not copyrighted, "but with masthead notice that all material is property of the author and is not to be used." Pays on acceptance. Buys 300 mss a year.

Will send a sample copy to a writer on request. Submit only complete mss. "We do not read tearsheets. Typed mss only." Accepts simultaneous submissions. Submit seasonal material 3 months in advance. "Especially need seasonal material, no matter when." Reports on material in 1 month. Enclose S.A.S.E. for return of submissions.

Nonfiction and Photos: How-to, personal experience, hobby articles. School and home activities. Informational, historical, and photo articles. Length: 200 to 1,000 words. Pays 2¢ a word. Photos purchased with mss. B&w glossies. Pays $3.50 to $10.

Fiction: All types, but with a Christian philosophy. Fiction should have a lot of action, and have some sort of religious background. Length: 1,000 to 2,000 words. Pays 2¢ a word.

Poetry: Nature poetry. Traditional forms; blank, free, and light verse. Length: 8 to 16 lines. Pays 25¢ a line, $2 minimum.

EXPLORE, Christian Board of Publication, Box 179, St. Louis MO 63166. Editor: Norman Linville. For children in early elementary grades. Established in 1969. Weekly. Circulation: 22,000. Buys first rights. Buys 200 mss a year. Payment on acceptance. Send 25¢ for editorial guidelines and sample copy. Submit seasonal material 6 months in advance. Reports in 30 days. Enclose S.A.S.E.

Nonfiction, Fiction, Fillers and Poetry: How-to articles. Feature articles. Length: 400 words maximum. Short stories. Length: 600 words maximum. Poetry no longer than 12 lines. Illustrated puzzles. Pays 1¢ a word for nonfiction; 25¢ a line for poetry.

THE FRIEND, 50 East North Temple, Salt Lake City UT 84150. Phone: 801-531-2210. Managing Editor: Lucile C. Reading. Appeals to children from age 4 to 12. Publication of the Church of Jesus Christ of Latter-day Saints. Each issue features a different country of the world, its culture, and children. Special issues: Christmas and Easter. Established in 1970. Monthly. Circulation: 170,000. Buys first rights. Payment on acceptance. Sample copy and guidelines for writers will be sent free upon request. Submit only complete ms. Submit seasonal material 6 months in advance. Enclose S.A.S.E. for return of submissions.

Nonfiction: Subjects of current interest, science, nature, pets, sports, foreign countries, and things to make and do. Length: 1,000 words maximum. Pays 3¢ a word and up.

Fiction: Seasonal and holiday stories; stories about other countries and children in them. Wholesome and optimistic; high motive, plot, and action. Also simple, but suspense-filled mysteries. Character-building stories preferred. Length: 1,000 words maximum. Stories for younger children should not exceed 500 words. Pays 3¢ a word and up.

Poetry: Serious or humorous; holiday poetry. Any form. Good poetry, with child appeal. Pays 25¢ a line and up.

How To Break In: "Do you remember how it feels to be a child? Can you write stories that appeal to children ages four to twelve in today's world? We're interested in stories with an international flavor and those that focus on present day problems."

THE GOOD DEEDER, c/o Your Story Hour, Berrien Springs MI 49103. Editor: Shirlee Ingram. For young people, age 10 to 14, who are members of the Good Deeds Club and listeners to Your Story Hour radio program. Established in 1950. Published 10 times a year. Circulation: 12,000. Not copyrighted. Buys 40 mss a year. Pays on publication. Will send sample copy to writer if S.A.S.E. is enclosed. Submit special material for temperance, anti-drug, anti-alcohol, anti-tobacco (March) issues 3 to 5 months in advance. Submit complete ms. Enclose S.A.S.E.

Nonfiction and Photos: Character building stories for kids. "No lost dogs or cats. No windows broken by a baseball followed by the little boy's confession to the cross old lady who forgave him and let him play there every day." Lengths: 500, 750, 1,000 words. Freelance photos are rarely purchased, but pays $8 for 8x10 b&w glossies used on cover; $1 to $3 for inside use.

Fiction: Adventure and Sunday school type religious fiction. Length: 750, 1,000 or 1,500 words. Pays 1¢ to 2¢ per word.

HAPPY TIMES, 3558 Jefferson Ave., St. Louis MO 63118. Phone: 314-664-7000. Editor: Daniel R. Burow. For preschoolers, age 2 to 5. Lutheran publication. Monthly magazine; 16 pages. Established in 1964. Circulation: 70,000. Buys all rights. Buys 15 to 30 mss a year. Payment on acceptance. Will send free sample copy to writer on request. Write for copy of guidelines for writers. Will not consider photocopied submissions. Will consider simultaneous submissions. Submit seasonal material (for all holidays) 12 months in advance. Reports in 2 weeks. Submit complete ms. Enclose S.A.S.E.

Nonfiction and Photos: "We'll consider anything in general, provided it is written on a preschool level. However, we try to avoid 'goodie-goodie' type stories. We also receive an over-abundance of extremely moralizing stories; too many animal stories; too many stories involving grandparents." Uses how-to's, personal experience articles and profiles. Length: open, but prefers one ms page minimum. Pays $5 to $7.50 per ms page. Color transparencies that interest preschoolers or fit a preschool situation are purchased without mss. Pays $15 to $30.

Fiction: Story should relate to themes in Christian education (family living, dealing with fears and conflicts, celebrating life in general and seasons and festivals in particular) without being legalistic or moralistic. Pays $20 to $30 per story (approximately 500 words).

Poetry and Fillers: Poems of any form or length. Pays $5. Puzzles simple enough for preschoolers are used as fillers. Pays $5.

HIGHLIGHTS FOR CHILDREN, 803 Church St., Honesdale PA 18431. Editors: Walter B. Barbe and Caroline C. Myers. For children 2 to 12. 11 times a year. One of the better juvenile markets, but strong competition here. Circulation: approximately 1,000,000. Buys all rights. Pays on acceptance. Write for copy of guidelines for writers. No query. Submit complete ms only. Reports in 2 months. Enclose S.A.S.E.

Nonfiction: Most factual features, including history and science, are written on assignment by persons with rich background and mastery in their respective fields. But contributions always welcomed from new writers, especially science teachers, engineers, scientists, historians, etc., who can interpret to children useful, interesting, and authentic facts, but not of the bizarre or "Ripley" type; also writers who have lived abroad and can interpret well the ways of life, especially of children in other countries, and who don't leave the impression that our ways are always the best. Sports material, biographies, articles about sports of interest to children. Direct, simple style, interesting content, without word embellishment; not rewritten from encyclopedias. State background and qualifications for writing factual articles submitted. Include references or sources of information with first submission. Length: 1,000 words maximum. Pays minimum $50. Also buys original party plans for children 7 to 12, clearly described in 600 to 800 words, including pencil drawings or sample of items to be illustrated. Also, novel but tested ideas in arts and crafts, with clear directions, easily illustrated, preferably with made-up models. Projects must require only salvage material or inexpensive, easy-to-obtain material. Especially desirable if easy enough for early primary grades and appropriate to special seasons and days. Also, fingerplays with lots of action, easy for very young children to grasp and parents to dramatize, step-by-step, with hands and fingers. Avoid wordiness. Pays minimum $30 for party plans; $10 for arts and crafts ideas; $25 for fingerplays.

Fiction: Unusual, wholesome stories appealing to both girls and boys. Vivid, full of action and word-pictures, easy to illustrate. Seeks stories that the child 8 to 12 will eagerly read, and the child 2 to 6 will like to hear when read to him. "We print no stories just to be read aloud; they must serve a two-fold purpose. We encourage authors not to hold themselves to controlled word lists. Especially need humorous stories, but also need winter stories; urban stories; horse stories; and especially some mystery stories void of violence; and stories introducing characters from different ethnic groups; holiday stories devoid of Santa Claus and the Easter Bunny. Avoid suggestion of material reward for upward striving. Moral teaching should be subtle. The main character should preferably overcome difficulties and frustrations through his own efforts. The story should leave a good moral and emotional residue. War, crime, and violence are taboo. Some fanciful stories wanted." Length: 400 to 1,000 words. Pays minimum 5¢ a word.

How To Break In: "We are pleased that many authors of children's literature report that their first published work was in the pages of *Highlights*. It is not our policy to consider fiction on the strength of the reputation of the author. We judge each submission on its own merits. With factual material, however, we do prefer either authorities in their fields or people with first-hand experience. In this manner we can avoid the encyclopedic-type article which merely restates information readily available elsewhere. A beginning writer should first become familiar with the type of material which *Highlights* publishes. We are most eager for the easy-type story for very young readers, but realize that this is probably the most difficult kind of writing. The talking animal kind of story is greatly overworked. A beginning writer should be encouraged to develop first an idea for a story which must involve only a small number of characters and likely a single-incident plot. The story must contain a problem or a dilemma which is clearly understood and presented early. It is then clearly resolved at the end of the story. Description should be held to a minimum. Dialogue is a requirement for it is a means by which children can identify with the characters in the story."

HUMPTY DUMPTY'S MAGAZINE, Parents' Magazine Enterprises, Inc., 52 Vanderbilt Ave., New York NY 10017. Editor: Ruth Craig. For children, 3 to 8 years of age. Magazine published monthly except June and August. Established in 1952. Circulation: 1,250,000. Rights purchased vary with author and material. May buy all rights, but will sometimes reassign rights to author after publication. Buys 25 or more freelance story mss a year. Payment on acceptance. Write for copy of guidelines for writers. No sample copies. Will consider photocopied submissions. Will not consider simultaneous submissions. Submit seasonal material 6 to 8 months in advance. Reports in 2 to 6 weeks. Submit complete ms. Enclose S.A.S.E.

Fiction: "Especially like stories with real-life children and not all suburban types. More urban material about believable children and would like to see some minority stories. One thing that's always anathema to me is the animated inanimate object. Yet I just bought an excellent piece in that genre. I also dislike cliche pieces about sugar girls with dolls at tea parties. Being current and believable is extremely important. We do use some old-fashioned stories — for instance, we just did something on Marsha Mouse, a story adapted from a Rusian folk tale — but real children must be up-to-date. We're cautious about adaptations because we don't want to give our readers something they may have seen before. We have a couple of writers who are specialists in Indian affairs and we use their tales because they haven't appeared anywhere else." Length: 900 to 1,000 words maximum. Pays $50 minimum.

Poetry: Traditional forms, blank verse, free verse, light verse. Length: 4 to 12 lines. Pays $10.

IT'S OUR WORLD, 800 Allegheny Ave., Pittsburgh PA 15233. Editor: Thomas F. Haas. For boys and girls in Catholic elementary schools in the United States, ages 6 to 13. Quarterly. Two-color, four-page (8½x11) newsletter. Established in 1974 by the Holy Childhood Association as a replacement for *Annals of the Holy Childhood*, which is no longer being published. Circulation: 3.1 million. Buys simultaneous rights. Buys 4 or 5 mss a year. Payment on acceptance. Will send free sample copy to writer on request. Write for copy of guidelines for writers. Will consider photocopied and simultaneous submissions. Submit seasonal material 4 months in advance. Reports on material within a month. Submit complete ms. Enclose S.A.S.E.

Nonfiction: "Ours is a publication of mission news for children, dealing with children in other countries, especially those in the developing countries (Third World or mission countries). Stories about children in other countries should show an appreciation for that country's culture, and not give the impression that our culture is better." Interested in current events reports, stories about life in other countries, stories about the legends, culture or customs of various countries (with documentation). Not interested in stories that use animal characters like Sally Squirrel, Charlie Chicken or Oscar Owl. Uses informational, how-to, personal experience, interview, profile, inspirational, humor, adventure, biographical, historical, travel and think articles. Length: 600 to 800 words. Pays minimum of $25.

Fiction: Experimental, mainstream, mystery, suspense, adventure, science fiction, fantasy, humorous, religious and historical fiction. Length: 600 to 800 words. Pays minimum of $25.

Poetry: Traditional forms, light verse and poems written by children. Length: open. Pays $15 to $25.

JACK AND JILL, 1100 Waterway Blvd., Box 567B, Indianapolis IN 46206. Phone: 317-634-1100, Ext. 282. Editor: William Wagner. For children 5 to 12. 10 times a year. Buys all rights. Pays on publication. Will send sample copy to writer for 50¢. Write for copy of guidelines for writers. Submit seasonal material 8 months in advance. Reports in approximately 8 weeks. May hold material seriously being considered for up to 6 months or 1 year. Enclose S.A.S.E.

Nonfiction and Photos: "*Jack and Jill's* primary purpose is to encourage children to read for pleasure. The editors are actively interested in material that will inform and instruct the young reader and challenge his intelligence, but it must first of all be enjoyable reading. Submissions should appeal to both boys and girls." Current needs are for "short factual articles concerned with nature, science, and other aspects of the child's world. Longer, more detailed features: 'My Father (or My Mother) Is a ...'; first-person stories of life in other countries; some historical and biographical articles." Where appropriate, articles should be accompanied by good 35mm color transparencies, when possible. Pays about 3¢ a word. Pays $2.50 for each b&w photo. Pays $5 each for color photo. Using some cover photos; payment for a cover photo is $50 minimum.

Fiction: "May include, but is not limited to, realistic stories, fantasy, adventure—set in the past, present, or future. All stories need plot structure, action, and incident. Humor is highly desirable." Length: 500 to 1,200 words, short stories; 1,200 words per installment, serials of 2 or 3 parts. Pays about 3¢ a word.

Fillers and Drama: "Short plays, puzzles (including varied kinds of word and crossword puzzles), riddles, jokes, songs, poems, games, science projects, and creative construction projects. Instructions for activities should be clearly and simply written and accompanied by models or diagram sketches. We are also in need of projects for our new feature, For Carpenters Only. Projects should be of the type our young readers can construct with little or no help. Be sure to include all necessary information—materials needed, diagrams, etc. Whenever possible, all materials used in projects should be scrap materials that can be readily found around the workshop and home." Payment varies for fillers. Pays about 3¢ per word for drama.

How To Break In: "We have been accused of using the same authors over and over again, not keeping an open mind when it comes to giving new authors a chance. To some extent, perhaps we do lean a little heavier toward veteran authors. But there is a good reason for this. Authors who have been published in *Jack and Jill* over and over again have shown us that they can write the kind of material we are looking for. They obtain *current* issues of the magazine and *study* them to find out our present needs, and they write in a style that is compatible with our current editorial policies. That is the reason we use them over and over; not because they have a special 'in.' We would reject a story by the world's best known author if it didn't fit our needs. After all, our young readers are more interested in reading a good story than they are in reading a good by-line. We are constantly looking for new writers that have told a good story with an interesting slant — a story that is not full of outdated and time-worn expressions. If an author's material meets these requirements, then he stands as good a chance of getting published as anyone."

JET CADET, 8121 Hamilton Ave., Cincinnati OH 45231. Phone: 513-931-4050. Editor: Dana Eynon. For children 8 to 11 years old in Christian Sunday schools. Weekly. Rights purchased vary with author and material. Buys first serial rights or second serial (reprint) rights. Occasionally overstocked. Pays on acceptance. Will send a sample copy to a writer on request. Submit seasonal material 12 months in advance. Reports in 4 to 6 weeks. Enclose S.A.S.E. for return of submissions.

Nonfiction: Articles on hobbies and handicrafts, nature (preferably illustrated), famous people, seasonal subjects, etc. Taboos are liquor, tobacco, murder, guns, swearing, slang, movies, and dancing. Length: 500 to 1,000 words. Pays up to 1½¢ a word.

Fiction: Short stories of heroism, adventure, travel, mystery, animals, biography. True or possible plots stressing clean, wholesome, Christian character-building ideals, but not preachy. Make prayer, church attendance, Christian living a natural part of the story. Length: 900 to 1,200 words; 2,000 words complete length for 2-part stories. Pays up to 1½¢ per word.

Fillers: Bible puzzles and quizzes. Pays up to 1½¢ a word.

How To Break In: "We give the same consideration to a new writer as we do to regular contributors. We just checked our files, and this past year purchased mss from 30 new writers. We look for (1) Christian character-building stories, filled with action and conversation, based on true-to-life situations; (2) articles on a wide range of subjects, filled with accurate facts, and written from a Christian viewpoint. Writers may send for list of themes coming up, and submit stories that correlate with the lesson stressed in a particular issue."

THE KINDERGARTNER, 201 Eighth Ave., S., Nashville TN 37203. Editor: Mrs. Arba O. Herr. For children of kindergarten age. Monthly magazine; 16 (8½x11) pages. Established in 1964. Circulation: 37,000. Buys all rights. Buys about 100 mss a year. Payment on acceptance. Will send free sample copy to writer on request. Write for copy of guidelines for writers. Will not consider photocopied or simultaneous submissions. Submit seasonal material 14 months in advance. Reports on material accepted for publication in 6 weeks. Returns rejected material in 1 to 2 weeks. Query first. Enclose S.A.S.E.

Nonfiction and Photos: All subject matter is planned to complement United Methodist curriculum material. Can use how-to's and simple science discoveries that children can experiment with (weights, measures, shadows, etc.). Games, gift ideas and prayers. Emphasis is on helpfulness and responsibility, including nature, animals or community services, such as doctors, plumbers, etc. "Ask for a set of guidelines which we gladly send on request." Length: 250 to 300 words. Pays 3¢ per word. 8x10 b&w glossies or color transparencies are purchased with or without mss. Both mss and photos need a balance of ethnic groups and sex roles. Payment varies.

Fiction: Experimental, adventure, religious. "In the kindergarten field it's not experimental fiction, but experiential fiction. In the area of bible stories there often is not sufficient dialogue or background to 'make' a story. Therefore, we add experiences typical of the historical period—but not really authentic as to the biblical account. Also, since the child today learns by experience, we often use stories about children whose experiences are typical but at the same time fictitious." Length: 250 to 300 words. Pays 3¢ a word.

Poetry: Free verse. Pays 50¢ per line.

LET'S FIND OUT, Scholastic Magazines, Inc., 50 W. 44th St., New York NY 10036. For children of kindergarten age through fourth grade. Query first. Enclose S.A.S.E.

Fiction: Short stories related to the theme for the entire issue. Pays average of $75.

MY DEVOTIONS, Concordia Publishing House, 3558 S. Jefferson Ave., St. Louis MO 63118. For young Christians, 8 through 12 years of age. Buys little freelance material. Write for guidelines, enclosing 20¢ postage. Material is rejected here because of poor writing, lack of logic, and lack of Lutheran theology. Pays $7.50 per printed devotion.

MY JEWELS, Box 6059, Cleveland OH 44101. Editor: T. T. Musselman. For six-to eight-year-old children attending Christian Sunday schools. A publication of Union Gospel Press. Quarterly in 13 weekly parts. Buys all rights. Buys "very, very few mss; however, we do welcome inquiries from freelance writers who are interested in handling quarterly assignments." Payment on acceptance. Will send free sample copy to writer on request. Write for copy of guidelines for writers. Will not consider photocopied submissions. Submit seasonal material (for all major holidays and seasons) 10 months in advance. Reports on material in 90 days. Query first. Enclose S.A.S.E.

Nonfiction and Photos: "Inspirational Bible study. Biographies of real children are welcome. Should be up-to-date and fresh. All material must have fundamental, evangelical Christian emphasis. Generally handled by assignment, but inquiries are welcome." Length: 400 words. Pays 2¢ a word. B&w photos and color slides are purchased with or without mss, but are not returned. "If the seller wishes to retain his original photographs and slides, he should have duplicates made that can be sold to Union Gospel Press. The duplicates will not be returned."

Fiction: Mainstream and religious fiction with Christian emphasis. Query first about length; usually 450 words. Pays 2¢ a word.

Poetry and Fillers: Traditional forms of poetry. Length: 25 lines. "See and Do" puzzles, mazes, dot-to-dot, riddles. Pays 35¢ a line for poetry. Individual rates for fillers.

MY PLEASURE, Union Gospel Press, Box 6059, Cleveland OH 44101. For children, 9 to 12. Buys exclusive rights. Write for copy of guidelines for writers. Submit complete ms. Enclose S.A.S.E.

Nonfiction and Photos: "All material we select for publication must have an evangelical emphasis. We always have a need for factual stories of the Christian life in action. How-to articles and biographies about Christians whom children can admire and follow. A list of sources must accompany all factual and biographical articles in order for them to be accepted." Length: 900 to 1,200 words. "An article will not be accepted if the words have not been counted. This total should appear in the upper right-hand corner of the first page of the ms." Pays 2¢ per word. "We also purchase slides and photos to accompany articles. We pay $5 for each color slide and $3 for each b&w glossy photo. Purchased photos and slides will not be returned. A detailed letter about our photo and slide policy is available on request."

Fiction: "Stories with a strong emphasis on Christian living. Must have evangelical emphasis." Length: 825 to 1,225 words. Word count must appear on first page of ms. Pays 2¢ per word.

Poetry and Fillers: "Poems should be rich in imagery and figurative language. The theme should be clear, and the rhyme and meter should be consistent with the subject." Length: 16 lines average. Pays 35¢ per line. For fillers, "we consider only puzzles and quizzes that are based on the Bible." Pays $2.50 for short acrostics and beginner puzzles; $3.50 for lengthier glidograms and puzzles; $5 for general crossword puzzles; $7.50 for holiday and special crossword puzzles which are limited to a single topic or area from which to draw clues.

How To Break In: "We need bright, up-to-date material about the Christian life in action. We're looking for current biographies accompanied by photos and slides. Please don't send the same old stories with the names changed!"

NEWS EXPLORER, Scholastic Magazines, Inc., 50 W. 44th St., New York NY 10036. Issued weekly during school year for fourth grade children about nine or 10 years of age. Buys all rights. Pays on acceptance. Will send free sample copy on request. Send only one ms at a time for consideration. Be sure to keep a carbon copy in your file. Do not re-submit the same ms unless a revision is specifically requested. Query first. Enclose S.A.S.E.

Fiction: Humor, classroom setting, boys and girls of today, or of other times, mystery, hobbies, legends, other peoples, adventure, pets. Stories must be well plotted and within the vocabulary range of the average fourth grader. 900 to 1,000 words. Pays minimum $75.

NEWSTIME, Scholastic Magazines, Inc., 50 W. 44th St., New York NY 10036. Weekly for fifth and sixth grade children of 11 and 12 years. Buys all rights. Pays on acceptance. Query first. Enclose S.A.S.E.

Fiction: Tightly written stories with lots of action and lots of dialogue are favored.

Stories with children handling real-life problems and generating understanding of values and differing points of view get special attention. (However, no obvious moralizing or involved psychological problems are used.) The following types, if well-plotted and narrated with incident, are also considered: humor, fantasy, folklore, mystery, adventure, sports, pets, wildlife and nature. (No violence, war, or dating are used.) Presented in a two-page format, the typical story is 1,000 to 1,200 words. One-page stories of 400 to 500 words may also be considered. Two-pagers: $125; one-pager $75.

NURSERY DAYS, The United Methodist Publishing House, 201 8th Ave. S., Nashville TN 37202. Phone: 615-749-6435. Editor: Mrs. Jo Risser. Published weekly for children ages 2, 3, and 4. Buys all rights. Will send free sample copy to a writer on request. Enclose S.A.S.E. for return of submissions.
Nonfiction and Photos: Should cover things of interest to children—church, family, nature, friends, God. Must have religious significance. Deadline 18 months in advance of publication. Photos purchased with mss; prefers 8x10.
Fiction: Short stories relating to child's personal experiences (religious significance on his own age level), 300 words maximum. Pays 2¢ to 4¢ a word.
Poetry: 4 to 8 lines. Pays 50¢ to $1 a line (less for short lines).

ON THE LINE, 616 Walnut Street, Scottdale PA 15683. Phone: 412-887-8500. Editor: Helen Alderfer. For children 10 to 14. Weekly. Buys first rights. Pays on acceptance. Will send a sample copy to a writer on request. Write for copy of guidelines for writers. Reports in 2 weeks. Enclose S.A.S.E. for return of submissions.
Nonfiction and Photos: Designed to increase the child's interest in Christianity, his understanding of the Bible, his identification with the church; human interest sketches of noteworthy children; nature and hobbies. Length: 800 to 1,250 words. Pays up to 3¢ per word; less for simultaneous and second rights. Photos purchased with mss. With captions only. 8x10 semiglossy prints; no color. Especially interested in human interest shots involving youngsters over 9, animals, picture stories. Pays $5 to $10 per photo.
Fiction: Wholesome stories that help readers discover and develop their full potential as persons; that help them take their place beside other peoples of the world as true neighbors; that present the Biblical message in a contemporary, meaningful way; that help children grow in appreciation of the fine arts, especially those that enrich their understanding of Christianity; that sense problem areas of children and provide sympathetic help. Serials to five parts. Pays up to 3¢ per word; 2¢ per word for simultaneous submissions; 1½¢ per word for second rights mss.
Poetry and Fillers: Semi-humorous verse with an unexpected twist often used. Wants some nature verse. Length: 4 to 24 lines. Pays $3.50 to $10. Occasional quizzes and puzzles are used. Pays $4 to $10.

OUR LITTLE FRIEND, PRIMARY TREASURE, Pacific Press Publishing Association, 1350 Villa St., Mountain View CA 94042. Editor: Louis Schutter. Published weekly for youngsters of the Seventh-Day Adventist church. *Our Little Friend* is for children ages 2 to 6; *Primary Treasure*, 7 to 9. Rights purchased vary with author and material. Buys first serial rights (International); second serial (reprint) rights (International). "The payment we make is for one magazine right. In most cases, it is for the first one. But we make payment for second, third right also." Query on serial-length stories. Will accept simultaneous submissions. "We do not purchase material during June, July, and August." Enclose S.A.S.E. for return of submissions or reply to queries.
Nonfiction and Fiction: All stories must be based on fact, written in story form. True to life, character-building stories; written from viewpoint of child and giving emphasis to lessons of life needed for Christian living. True to life is emphasized here more than plot. Nature or science articles, but no fantasy; science must be very simple. All material should be educational or informative and stress moral attitude and religious principle. Honesty, truthfulness, courtesy, health and temper-

ance, along with stories of heroism, adventure, nature and safety are included in the overall planning of the editorial program. *Our Little Friend* uses stories from 700 to 1,000 words. *Primary Treasure*, 900 to 1,500 words. Fictionalized Bible stories are not used. Pays 1¢ per word.

Photos, Poetry, and Fillers: 8x10 glossies for cover. "Photo payment: sliding scale according to quality." Juvenile poetry; up to 12 lines. Puzzles.

QUEST, Box 179, St. Louis MO 63166. Editor: Miss Lee Miller. For children in grades 3 to 6. Weekly. Not copyrighted. Pays on acceptance. Sample copies are sent to writer for 25¢. Write for copy of guidelines for writers before submitting material. Enclose S.A.S.E.
Nonfiction: "Articles on travel, biographies, science or general informational interest. Include sources." Length: 600 words maximum. Pays up to 2¢ per word.
Fiction: "Uses short stories to which children can relate. Emphasis on children learning to identify and clarify values. No fantasy. Avoid preaching and moralizing." Length: 800 to 1,000 words. Pays up to 2¢ a word.
Poetry: "Limited market." Length: 16 lines maximum. Pays 25¢ per line.
Fillers: "Puzzles, illustrated if possible." Payment depends on the content and style. No set minimum. Limited market.

RAINBOW, American Baptist Churches, Valley Forge PA 19481. Editor: Mrs. Gracie McCay. For children in church school classes; grades 3 through 6. Magazine; 8 (5½x8½) pages. Established in 1974. Weekly. Circulation: 10,000. Rights purchased vary with author and material. May buy first North American serial rights, second serial (reprint) rights or simultaneous rights. Buys about 100 mss a year. Pays on acceptance. Will send free sample copy to writer on request. Write for copy of guidelines for writers. Will consider photocopied and simultaneous submissions. Submit seasonal (holiday) material 8 months in advance. Reports as soon as possible, but this may take 6 to 8 months. Query first or submit complete ms. Enclose S.A.S.E.
Nonfiction and Photos: "Biographies and articles on helping children to cope with their everyday life experiences in a Christian manner." Seasonal material for all the holidays. How-to, inspirational, humor, think articles. Recently published articles include "Let's Make Christmas Stockings." Length: 300 to 400 words. Pays 2¢ a word maximum. B&w (5x7 or 8x10) glossies purchased without mss. Pays $7.50 to $10.
Fiction: Adventure, science fiction, humorous, historical Length: 800 to 1,000 words. Pays up to 3¢ a word.

RANGER RICK'S NATURE MAGAZINE, National Wildlife Federation, 1412 Sixteenth St., N.W., Washington DC 20036. Editorial Director: Trudy D. Farrand. For "children from ages 4 to 12, with the greatest concentration in the 7 to 12 age bracket." Monthly, except June and September. Buys all rights. Pays on publication. "Anything written with a specific month in mind should be in our hands at least 8 months before that issue date." Query first. Enclose S.A.S.E.
Nonfiction and Photos: "Articles may be written on any phase of nature, conservation, environmental problems, or natural science. Do not try to humanize wildlife in features. We limit the attributing of human qualities to animals in our regular feature, 'Ranger Rick and His Friends.' The publisher, National Wildlife Federation, discourages wildlife pets because of the possible hazards involved to small children. Therefore, pets of this kind should not be mentioned in your copy." Length: 800 words maximum. Pays from $25 to $250 depending on length. "If photographs are included with your copy, they are paid for separately, depending on how they are used. However, it is not necessary that illustrations accompany material."
Fillers: Games, puzzles, quizzes. Pays $10, but this varies.

SPRINT MAGAZINE, Scholastic Magazines, Inc., 50 W. 44th St., New York NY 10036. For fifth and sixth graders (second grade reading level). Established in 1975. Biweekly. Buys all rights. Pays on acceptance. Reports as soon as possible. Query first. Enclose S.A.S.E.

Fiction and Drama: Subjects for fiction include interpersonal relations (family and friend situations), mystery, science fiction, fantasy, sports, humor, action and adventure. Main need is for story situations familiar to young people, or mysteries, science fiction and fantasy, that starts from a contemporary setting. Length: 300 to 500 words. Pays $75 minimum. Plays must have fast moving plots, lots of action that commands reluctant reader attention from the start. In both areas, these should be easy-reading materials, but should not talk down. Length for plays: 450 to 550 words. Pays $50 minimum.

STORY FRIENDS, Mennonite Publishing House, 616 Walnut Ave., Scottdale PA 15683. For children, 4 to 9 years of age. Editor: Alice Hershberger. Published monthly in weekly parts. Not copyrighted. Payment on acceptance. Will send sample copy to writer on request. Submit seasonal material 6 months in advance. Enclose S.A.S.E.
Nonfiction and Photos: "The over-arching purpose of this publication is to magnify Jesus Christ and His way in terms a child can grasp. Children of this age group are full of questions about God and Jesus, the Bible, prayer, church doctrinal practices. Stories of everyday experiences at home, at church, in school, at play help provide some answers. Of special importance are relationships: patterns of forgiveness, respect, honesty, trust. Prefer short stories; exciting but plausible; spiritual values intrinsic to the story; wide variety of settings and racial backgrounds. Must have spiritual message, but avoid preachiness, and have well-defined spiritual values as an integral part of each story." Length: 150 words. Pays 2¢ to 3¢ per word. Pays $7.50 to $15 for b&w photos purchased with or without ms. Captions optional. Photo Department Editor: Mrs. Jean Bulebush.
Fiction: Suspense, adventure, religious. Should be based on the application of Christian principles on a child's level of understanding. Realistic stories with spiritual value needed for Christmas and Easter. Nothing about Easter bunnies or new clothes, though. Length: 300 to 900 words. Pays 2¢ to 3¢ per word.
Poetry and Fillers: Traditional forms of poetry and free verse. Length: 3 to 12 lines. Pays $2 to $5. Uses crossword puzzles and quizzes.

TRAILS, Pioneer Girls, Box 788, Wheaton IL 60187. Editor: Sara Robertson. Published bimonthly for girls in second through sixth grade. Buys first rights only. Pays on acceptance. Sample copies and writer's packet for $1. Returns within 4 weeks. Enclose S.A.S.E.
Nonfiction and Fillers: Interest articles, nature, history, how-to ideas, crafts, and puzzles. Payment based on material content and length. Usually pays $10 to $40.
Fiction: Need not have strong spiritual emphasis, but should be in keeping with Christian point of view. At least 2 stories used each issue. Length: 1,000 to 2,000 words. Payment based on material content and length. Usually pays $10 to $40.

VIDEO-PRESSE, 3965 est, boul. Henri-Bourassa, Montreal HIH ILI, Que., Canada. Editor: Pierre Guimar. For "French Canadian boys and girls of 8 to 15." Monthly. Circulation: 45,000. Buys all rights. Buys 20 to 30 mss a year. Pays on publication. Will send a sample copy to a writer on request. Reports in 2 weeks. Enclose S.A.S.E.
Nonfiction: "Material with a French Canadian background. The articles have to be written in French, and must appeal to children aged 8 to 15." Buys how-to's, personal experience articles, interviews, profiles, humor, historical articles, photo features, travel pieces. Length: 1,500 to 3,000 words. Pays 3¢ a word.
Photos: B&w glossies, color transparencies; with captions only. Pays $7.50.
Fillers: Puzzles, jokes, short humor.

THE VINE (formerly *Three/Four*), 201 Eighth Ave., S., Nashville TN 37203. Editor: Betty M. Buerki. Publication of The United Methodist Church. For children in grades 3 and 4. Monthly in weekly parts. Buys all rights. Pays on acceptance. Will send a sample copy to a writer on request. Deadlines are 18 months prior to publication date. Reports in 1 month. Enclose S.A.S.E. for return of submissions.
Nonfiction and Photos: Desires articles about science, nature, animals, customs in other countries, and other subjects of interest to readers. Length: approximately

500 words. Pays 4¢ a word. Photos usually purchased with manuscripts only. Uses photo features. Prefers 8x10 glossies. Also uses transparencies.
Fiction: Historical stories should be true to their setting. Stories which make a point about values should not sound moralistic. Also accepts stories written just for fun. Length: 500 to 1,000 words. Writers must know children. Fictionalized Bible stories must be based upon careful research. Pays 3¢ a word.
Poetry: Accepts light verse or religious verse. Pays 50¢ to $1 per line.
Fillers: Puzzles, quizzes, and matching games. Pays 3¢ minimum per word. Pays more for clever arrangements. Puzzles, such as crossword, mazes, etc.; pays $4.50 to $12.50.

WEE WISDOM, Unity Village MO 64065. Editor: Jim Leftwich. Character-building monthly magazine for boys and girls. Designed to help child develop positive self-image and strength to function successfully in tomorrow's world. Free sample copy, editorial policy on request. Buys first North American serial rights only. Pays on acceptance. Enclose S.A.S.E. for return of submissions.
Nonfiction: Entertaining science articles or projects, activities to foster creativity. Pays 3¢ per word minimum.
Fiction: Short and lively stories, education for living without moralizing. "Although entertaining enough to hold the interest of the older child, they should be readable by the third grader. Character-building ideals should be emphasized without preaching. Language should be universal, avoiding the Sunday school image." Length: 500 to 800 words. Pays 3¢ per word minimum.
Poetry: Very limited. Pays 50¢ per line. Prefers short, seasonal or humorous poems. Also buys rhymed prose for "read alouds" and pays $15 up.
Fillers: Pays $3 up for puzzles and games.

WEEKLY BIBLE READER, Standard Publishing, 8121 Hamilton Ave., Cincinnati OH 45231. Phone: 513-931-4050, Ext. 168. Editor: Norma Thurman. For children 6 and 7 years of age. Quarterly in weekly parts; 4 pages. Established in 1965. Circulation: 72,000. Not copyrighted. Buys 75 mss a year. Payment on acceptance. Will send free sample copy to writer on request. Write for copy of guidelines for writers. Will not consider photocopied or simultaneous submissions. Submit seasonal material 18 months in advance. Reports on material accepted for publication in about 6 weeks. Returns rejected material in about 2 weeks. Query first or submit complete ms. Enclose S.A.S.E.
Nonfiction, Photos, Poetry, and Fillers: Religious-oriented material. Stories with morals, fun poems, puzzles and other interesting items. Emphasis is on material that can be read by children themselves. "No fanciful material, superstitions or luck, things that talk, fairies, Easter rabbits, or Santa Claus. We'd like to see material on things children can do to help others; to be pleasing to God, etc." Do not send Bible stories or Buzzy Bee items, as these are staff-written from preplanned outlines. Length for fiction and nonfiction: 300 words maximum. Pays $1 to $10. B&w photos purchased with or without mss. Pays $10. Light verse. Length: 12 lines maximum. Very simple puzzles for this age group. Pays 50¢ to $10.

WONDER TIME, 6401 Paseo, Kansas City MO 64131. Editor: Elizabeth B. Jones. Published weekly by Church of the Nazarene for children ages 6 to 8. Will send free sample copy to a writer on request. Buys first rights. Pays on acceptance. Enclose S.A.S.E. for return of submissions.
Fiction and Poetry: Buys 500- to 750-word stories portraying Christian attitude, without being preachy. Uses stories for special days, stories teaching honesty, truthfulness, helpfulness or other important spiritual truths, and avoiding symbolism. God should be spoken of as our Father Who loves and cares for us: Jesus, as our Lord and Savior. Pays 2¢ a word on acceptance. Uses 8- to 12-line verse which has seasonal or Christian emphasis. Pays 12¼¢ per line and up.

WOW (formerly *Roadrunner*), American Baptist Board of Education and Publication, Valley Forge PA 19481. Editor: Roger Price. A weekly periodical for children 6 to 7 years of age. Buys first North American serial rights. May be slow to report. Enclose S.A.S.E. for ms return.

Nonfiction: Biographies and articles in simple vocabulary, from 200 to 500 words. Pays up to 3¢ per word.

Fiction: Stories of 200 to 500 words in simple vocabulary. Pays up to 3¢ per word.

Poetry and Fillers: Poetry; 12 lines maximum. Puzzles and how-to-do-it projects.

THE YOUNG CRUSADER, 1730 Chicago Ave., Evanston IL 60201. Managing Editor: Michael Vitucci. For children 6 to 12 who are junior members of National WCTU. Monthly. Not copyrighted. Pays on publication. Will send a sample copy to a writer on request. Submit seasonal material 6 months in advance. Reports promptly. Enclose S.A.S.E.

Nonfiction and Fiction: Uses articles on total abstinence, character building, love of animals, Christian citizenship, world friendship. Also science stories. Length: 650 to 800 words. Pays ½¢ per word.

YOUNG JUDAEAN, 817 Broadway, New York NY 10003. Phone: 212-260-4700. Editor: Barbara Gingold. For Jewish kids aged 8 to 13, and members of Young Judaean. Publication of Hadassah Zionist Youth Commission. All material must be on some Jewish theme. Special issues for Jewish/Israeli holidays, or special Jewish themes which vary from year to year; for example, Hassidim, Holocaust, etc. Established in 1916. Monthly (November through June). Circulation: 8,000. Rights purchased vary with author and material. Buys all rights, but will reassign rights to author after publication; buys First North American serial rights; buys first serial rights. Buys 10 to 20 mss a year. Payment in contributor's copies or small token payment. Will send sample copy to writer for 25¢. Prefers complete ms only. Will consider photocopied submissions. Submit seasonal material 4 months in advance. Reports in 2 months. Returns rejected material immediately. Enclose S.A.S.E.

Nonfiction: "Articles about Jewish-American life, Jewish historical and international interest. Israel and Zionist-oriented material. Try to awaken kids' Jewish consciousness by creative approach to Jewish history and religion, ethics and culture, politics and current events." Informational (300 to 800 words), how-to (300 to 500 words), personal experience, interview, humor, historical, think articles, photo, travel, and reviews (books, theater, and movies). Length: 500 to 1,500 words. Pays $5 to $15. "Token payments only, due to miniscule budget."

Photos: Photos purchased with accompanying mss. Captions required. 5x7 maximum. Payment included with fee for article. Illustrations also accepted.

Fiction: Experimental, mainstream, mystery, suspense, adventure, science fiction, fantasy, humorous, religious, and historical fiction. Length: 500 to 1,000 words. Pays $5 to $15. Must be of specific Jewish interest.

Poetry and Fillers: Traditional forms, blank verse, free verse, avant-garde forms, and light verse. Poetry themes must relate to subject matter of magazine. Length: minimum 8 lines. Pays $5 to $15. Newsbreaks, puzzles (all sorts), jokes, and short humor purchased for $5.

How To Break In: "Care about kids and their Jewish education and send us material that will be a creative/enlightening/inspiring addition to that education."

YOUNG MUSICIANS, 127 Ninth Ave., N., Nashville TN 37234. Editor: Jimmy R. Key. For boys and girls age 9 to 11, and their leaders in children's choirs in Southern Baptist churches (and some other churches). Monthly magazine; 52 (7x10½) pages. Established in 1963. Buys all rights. Buys 5 or 6 mss a year. Payment on acceptance. Will send free sample copy to writer on request. Will not consider photocopied or simultaneous submissions. Query first. Enclose S.A.S.E.

Nonfiction: "All material is slanted for use with and by children in church choirs. Music study materials related to study units in *The Music Leader.* Almost all materials are written on assignment." Informational, how-to, historical. Length: 300 to 900 words. Pays approximately 2½¢ per word.

Fiction: Child-centered stories related to church music and music in the home. Length: 600 to 900 words. Pays approximately 2½¢ per word.

Literary and "Little" Publications

Many of the publications in this category do not pay except in contributor's copies. Nonpaying markets are included because they offer the writer a vehicle for expression that often can't be found in the commercial press. Many talented American writers found first publication in magazines like these. Writers are reminded that many "littles" remain at one address for a limited time; others are notoriously unbusinesslike in their reporting on, or returning of submissions. University-affiliated reviews are conscientious about manuscripts but some of these are also slow in replying to queries or returning submissions.

Magazines that specialize in publishing poetry or poetry criticism are found in the Poetry category. Many "little" publications that offer contributors a forum for expression of minority opinions are classified in the listings for Alternative Publications.

AMANUENSIS, POT 1215, University of Kentucky, Lexington KY 40506. Editor: Paul Stephen White. For college students and college educated readers over 18. Semiannual magazine, 48 pages, (7x9). Established in 1971. Circulation: 400. Acquires first North American serial rights. Uses 10 to 15 mss a year. Payment in contributor's copies. Will send sample copy to writer for 50¢. Will consider photocopied and simultaneous submissions. Submit only complete ms. "Submissions arriving in September and January are convenient for us and the writers." Submit seasonal or special material 2 months in advance. Reports within 6 weeks. Enclose S.A.S.E.
Nonfiction and Photos: "Any universal topic. Conciseness is an important factor. It is also best to avoid overworked themes. We offer visual media in addition to literature (photography, sketches, painting and sculpture)." Humor, think articles, expose, photo features, and reviews of any artistic field. Length: 2,500 words maximum.
Fiction and Poetry: Experimental, mystery, suspense, erotica, and humorous fiction up to 2,500 words. Traditional forms, blank and free verse, avant-garde forms, light verse, and all other types of poetry considered. "We don't want love poems." No length limitations.

AMERICAN MERCURY, P.O. Box 1306, Torrance CA 90505. Business Manager and Editorial Associate: La Vonne Furr. Quarterly. Write for copy of guidelines for writers. "All mss must be typed, double-spaced, clean, ready for printer, left margin at least 1½ inches. Break up articles with periodic italicized paragraphs and/or subheads. Authors should submit biographical material to aid editor in preparing a suitable introduction." Enclose S.A.S.E. for return of submissions.
Nonfiction: *Mercury*'s editorial policy is nonpartisan but generally conservative. "It will stress the positive and hopeful aspects of life and Western tradition through reliable and well-written exposes. Articles on fads, dances, narcotics, crime, entertainers are generally unwanted." Wants Americana, nature briefs, humorous comment on everyday life, politics, science, health; particular emphasis on heroic and patriotic themes; satire. "Precede book reviews with a very brief title, then describe book: Title of book in caps, by (name of author), number of pages, publisher, date of publication." Length: 1,000 words maximum for book reviews; 900 to 2,000 words for articles. Payment ranges from one-year complimentary subscription to $50 for unsolicited articles.
Poetry: Poetry is wanted so long as it is not of the "sick," beatnik or meaningless type. "Poetry especially must have a 'positive' and never a negative or hopeless ring to it. Profanity and obscenity are not printed. In all things, a 'victory through right principles' theme is preferred."

AMERICAN NOTES AND QUERIES, Erismus Press, 225 Culpepper, Lexington KY 40502. Book Review Editor: Lee Ash, 31 Alden Rd., New Haven CT 06515. Ten times a year. No payment. Enclose S.A.S.E.

Nonfiction: Historical, artistic, literary, bibliographical, linguistic and folklore matters, scholarly book reviews and reviews of foreign reference books; items of unusual antiquarian interest.

AMERICAN QUARTERLY, Box 1, Logan Hall, University of Pennsylvania, Philadelphia PA 19174. Phone: 215-243-6252. Editor: Dr. Bruce Kuklick. For college professors, teachers, museum directors, researchers, students, college and high school libraries. Readers professionally interested in American studies. Acquires all rights. Does not pay. Reports in 3 to 6 months. Enclose S.A.S.E.
Nonfiction and Photos: Scholarly, interdisciplinary articles on American studies, about twenty pages. August Summer Supplement issue contains annual review of books, articles in American Studies for the current year, dissertation listings, American Studies programs, financial aid, writings on theory of American Studies, membership directory. Occasionally uses photos.

AMERICAN REVIEW, 666 Fifth Avenue, New York NY 10019. Editor: Theodore Solotaroff. For literary and academic audience, but material should appeal to any "common reader." Established in 1967. Published twice a year. Buys North American serial rights only. Pays on acceptance. No query required. Reports in 8 to 10 weeks. Enclose S.A.S.E.
Nonfiction, Fiction, and Poetry: Publishes fine contemporary literature, especially by fairly unknown writers. "We publish a broad range of material and we're not intimidated by the obscene or the very intimate or by very long pieces. We have a lot of space and can go up to 12,000 words on a story, but average length is 4,000 to 6,000 words. We do tend to get a lot more fiction than nonfiction and I'm always on the lookout for good nonfiction. The odds are very tough and I must emphasize that I can only consider writers with first rate craftsmanship and a real command of language and literary form." Pays 6¢ a word. Poetry Editor: Richard Howard.

THE AMERICAN SCHOLAR, 1811 Q St., N.W., Washington DC 20009. Phone: 202-265-3808. Editor: Joseph Epstein. For college educated, mid-20's and older, rather intellectual in orientation and interests. Quarterly magazine, 180 pages, (6¾x9¾). Established in 1932. Circulation: 45,000. Buys all rights, but will reassign rights to author after publication. Buys 20 to 30 mss a year. Payment on publication. Will send sample copy to writer for $1.75. Write for copy of guidelines for writers. Will consider photocopied submissions. Will not consider simultaneous submissions. Reports within 3 weeks. Query first, with samples, if possible. Enclose S.A.S.E.
Nonfiction and Poetry: "The aim of the *Scholar* is to fill the gap between the learned journals and the good magazines for a popular audience. We are interested not so much in the definitive analysis as in the lucid and creative exploration of what is going on in the fields of science, art, religion, politics, and national and foreign affairs. Advances in science particularly interest us." Informational, interview, profile, historical, think articles, and book reviews. Length: 3,500 to 4,000 words. Pays $250 per article and $50 for reviews. Pays $35 to $75 for poetry on any theme.

ANTHELION, P.O. Box 318, Concord CA 94522. Editor: R.W. Whitney. For "a university level readership." Bimonthly. Will send sample copy to writer for $1. Purchases all rights with return of reprint rights upon request. Pays on publication. Reports in 4 to 6 weeks. Authors should include a brief resume and cover letter with submissions. Enclose S.A.S.E.
Nonfiction and Fiction: "Devoted in alternate months to the fields of literature, social and cultural comment, and philosophy. January and July issues are devoted to literary articles and stories. Presently, we are in need of short articles dealing with the 'new' issues of our society. Interviews, reviews and like articles are used to augment our basic copy. We stress that all copy must be verifiable and logical. We seek the new writer with new insights into our modern world. Our pay for articles varies from contributor's copies up to 5¢ a word." Length: 2,500 words maximum.

ANTIOCH REVIEW, P.O. Box 148, Yellow Springs OH 45387. Editor: Paul Bixler. For general, literary and academic audience. Quarterly. Buys all rights. Pays on publication. Reports in 4 to 6 weeks. Enclose S.A.S.E.
Nonfiction: Contemporaneous articles in the humanities and social sciences, politics, economics, literature and all areas of broad intellectual concern. Somewhat scholarly, but never pedantic in style, eschewing all professional jargon. Lively, distinctive prose insisted upon. Length: 2,000 to 8,000 words. Pays $8 per published page.
Fiction: No limitations on style or content. Pays $8 per published page.

ARION, University Professors, Boston University, 270 Bay State Rd., Boston MA 02215. Phone: 617-353-4025. Editors-in-Chief: William Arrowsmith and D. S. Carne-Ross. "Journal of humanities and classics for persons interested in literature of the classical periods of Greece and Rome." Established in 1962. Quarterly journal, 128 pages, (8½x5). Circulation: 1,000. No payment. Acquires all rights, but will reassign rights to author after publication. Will send a sample copy to a writer for $1.75. Query first or submit complete ms. Will consider photocopied submissions. Reports in 6 weeks. Enclose S.A.S.E.
Nonfiction: Uses articles on literature, Greece and Rome. The articles printed are in the form of literary essays. "We deal with the classics as literature, rather than philology." Length: 10 to 40 pages.

ARIZONA QUARTERLY, University of Arizona, Tucson AZ 85721. Editor: Albert F. Gegenheimer. For a university-type audience. Quarterly. "We acquire all rights, but freely give authors permission to reprint. We require editors of anthologies, etc., to obtain permission of authors as well as of ourselves." Payment is in copies and a one-year subscription to the magazine. There are annual awards for the best poem of the year, the best article of the year, the best story of the year and the best book review of the year. Reports in 3 to 4 weeks except during summer. Enclose S.A.S.E.
Nonfiction: "Always interested in articles dealing with the Southwest, but open to articles on any topic of general interest."
Fiction: "Quality" fiction. Southwestern interest preferred, but not essential. Length: normally not over 3,000 words.
Poetry: Uses four or five poems per issue on any serious subject. Prefers short poems; up to 30 lines can be used most readily. The author must have something to say and be equipped to say it.

THE ARK RIVER REVIEW, 911 Lombard St., Philadelphia PA 19147. Editors: Jonathan Katz, A. G. Sobin, Arthur Vogelsang. For "those with an interest in the leading edge of poetry and fiction." Established in 1971. Quarterly. Circulation: 600 to 1,000. Buys first North American serial rights and second serial (reprint) rights. Payment on publication and in contributor's copies. Will send sample copy to writer for $1. Will consider photocopied submissions "only if note attached affirms the ms is not being submitted elsewhere." Reports on material within 6 weeks. Enclose S.A.S.E. for return of submissions.
Fiction and Poetry: "We work with three editors for poetry and fiction, but with a system that does not require a concensus. Thus we hope to be open to a very wide range of material. We would, however, always prefer to take a chance on publishing something that seems really new, rather than taking something highly competent but conventional. Advise writers to read an issue or two before submitting." Experimental and erotic (with redeeming graces) fiction. Length: open. Pays $3 per published page; minimum of $20 per story. Free verse and avant-garde forms of poetry. Length: open. Pays 20¢ a line; minimum payment of $5 per poem.

ART AND LITERARY DIGEST, Madoc-Tweed Art Centre, Tweed, Ontario, Canada. Editor: Roy Cadwell. "Our readers are the public and former students of the Art and Writing Centre. As an educational publication we welcome new writers who have something to say and want to see their name in print and get paid for it." Quarterly. Circulation: 1,000. Not copyrighted. Payment on publication. Will send sample copy for 50¢. Original mss and photocopies are accepted, but not

returned. Unless notified, you may submit elsewhere after 30 days. Enclose S.A.S.E.
Nonfiction and Fiction: How-to articles, inspirational, humorous, travel and personality improvement. "Good writing is essential with integrity and knowledge. Ask
yourself, 'What have I to say?' Slant toward students and alumni. Our readers want
to be informed and, hopefully, learn how to live better." Personal experience articles
and "I was there" type of travel articles are appreciated. Length: 500 words. Pays
$5. "We need digests of articles on art, music, poetry and literary subjects." Pays
1¢ per word.
Fillers: Clippings and short humor. Length: 500 words or less. Pays 1¢ per word.
Poetry: All types. Free verse, light verse, blank verse, traditional and avant-garde.
Length: usually 12 lines, but no limit. Payment in contributor's copies.

ARTS IN SOCIETY, University Extension, The University of Wisconsin, 610
Langdon St., Madison WI 53706. Editor: Edward L. Kamarck. Audience is library
patrons, educators, arts administrators, and members of the general public interested
in the arts. Circulation: 5,000. Buys all rights. Pays on publication. Sample copies
sent to those writers who indicate that they have something to contribute to the
particular focus of upcoming issues. Query first. Reports within six weeks. Enclose
S.A.S.E.
Nonfiction, Photos, and Fiction: In general, four areas are dealt with: teaching and
learning the arts; aesthetics and philosophy; social analysis; and significant examples
of creative expression in a media which may be served by the printing process.
Length: 1,500 to 3,000 words. Pays honorarium. B&w glossy photos used with captions.
Buys fiction "only if illustrative of particular focus of the issue." Pays modest
honorarium.

ASPECT, 66 Rogers Ave., Somerville MA 02144. Editors: Edward J. Hogan, Len
Anderson, Jeff Schwartz, Ellen Schwartz. Primarily for people interested in new
and experimental, as well as traditional and widely accepted writing. Many readers
are themselves involved in the field of writing. Magazine, published every 2 months.
Established in 1969. Circulation: about 300. Acquires first serial rights, but will
reassign to author on request. Payment in 2 contributor's copies. Will send sample
copy to writer for 75¢. Will not consider photocopied submissions. Will consider
simultaneous submissions only if they "are entranced with the work". Submit seasonal
material 120 days in advance. Reports in 4 to 12 weeks. Submit complete ms. Enclose
S.A.S.E.
Nonfiction and Photos: "We are interested in receiving more nonfiction essays on
any topic of general interest. Subjects can include first-person, politics, history,
philosophy and other work of just about any style or point of view. We try to
judge submissions on the basis of how successful they are in what they are trying
to do. Unlike many small literary magazines, we are genuinely open to a wider
variety of approaches. We try to publish work by persons with a wide variety of
proficiency in writing. The only real prerequisite is that the material be of general
interest, or reasonably so." Informational, personal experience, interview, profile,
historical, think pieces, humor, personal opinion, book reviews. Length: 4,000 words
maximum; no minimum. B&w photos are also accepted. Captions optional. Will
also consider reviews of small press books and magazines for the "Small Presses"
department. Length: 250 to 450 words. Department Editor: Edward J. Hogan.
Fiction: Experimental, mainstream, mystery, suspense, adventure, western, science
fiction, fantasy, humorous, historical. Length: 4,000 words maximum; no minimum.
Poetry: Traditional forms, blank and free verse, avant-garde forms. Length: 80 lines
maximum; no minimum. Department Editors: Len Anderson and Jeff Schwartz.

BACHY, Papa Bach Bookstore, 11317 Santa Monica Blvd., Los Angeles CA 90025.
Established in 1972. Semiannual. Circulation: 800. Average number of pages per
issue: 160. Buys first North American serial rights only. Will send sample copy to
writer for $2. Submit complete ms. Will consider photocopied submissions. Reports
within 8 weeks. Enclose S.A.S.E.
Nonfiction, Fiction, Poetry, and Photos: Poetry, fiction, essays, reviews, b&w graphic
art and photos. No length limit, but shorter pieces have a better chance. *"Bachy*

is dedicated to the discovery and publication of neglected or previously unpublished writers and artists of worth. A substantial portion of each issue is reserved for this purpose. The editorial approach is eclectic, choosing the best work received without regard for current fads, cliques or schools."

BALL STATE UNIVERSITY FORUM, Ball State University, Muncie IN 47306. Phone: 317-285-7255. Editors: Merrill Rippy and Frances Mayhew Rippy. For "educated readers interested in nontechnical studies of humanities, fine arts, sciences, social sciences, history, and education." Quarterly. Established in 1959. Acquires all rights, "but author may always reprint at his own request without charge, so long as *Forum* is notified and prior publication in *Forum* is acknowledged." Pays in 5 contributor's copies. Will send a sample copy to a writer on request. Contributors should accompany their entries with a two-sentence description of their academic background or position, their other publications, and their special competence to write on their subject. Contributors submitting multiple copies cut one month from reading time: poems, 7 copies; short stories, 9 copies; plays, 9 copies; articles, 2 copies. Special issues planned on American literature, British literature, education. Reports in 2 weeks to 4 months. Enclose S.A.S.E. for return of submissions.
Nonfiction, Fiction, Drama, and Poetry: Articles that are reasonably original, polished, and of general interest. Length: 50 to 3,000 words. Short stories, one-act plays. Length: 50 to 2,000 words. Uses 5 to 30 poems per issue. Length: 5 to 200 lines.

BLACK SCHOLAR, P.O. Box 908, Sausalito CA 94965. Editor: Robert Chrisman. Mainly for black professionals, educators, and students. Monthly journal of black studies and research, 64 pages, (10x7). Established in 1969. Circulation: 20,000. Acquires all rights. Uses about 60 mss per year. Payment in contributor's copies. Will send free sample copy to writer on request. Write for copy of guidelines for writers. Will consider photocopied submissions. Will consider simultaneous submissions, "but must be so informed." Reports within 2 months. Query first about upcoming topics. Enclose S.A.S.E.
Nonfiction: "We seek essays discussing issues affecting the black community (education, health, economics, psychology, culture, literature, etc.). Essays should be reasoned and well-documented. Each issue is organized around a specific topic: Black education, health, prisons, family, etc. We'd like to see fewer manifestos and impassioned appeals." Informational, interview, profile, historical, think articles, and book and film reviews. Length: 1,500 to 7,000 words.

BLUE CLOUD QUARTERLY, Marvin SD 57251. Phone: 605-432-6151. Editor: Brother Benet Tvedten, O.S.B. Circulation: 2,876. "Copyrights are provided if the authors require them." Payment in contributor's copies. Will send free sample copy to writer on request. Enclose S.A.S.E.
Nonfiction, Fiction and Poetry: Publishes creative writing and other articles by and about the American Indians.

BOOKLETTER, c/o *Harper's Magazine,* 2 Park Ave., New York NY 10016. Phone: 212-686-8710. Editor: Suzanne Mantell. Quarterly. Established in 1974. Newsletter; 16 pages. Query first, with samples of published material. Enclose S.A.S.E.
Nonfiction: Features and essays on both old and new books, and brief book reviews. Some feature articles on publishing personalities, publishing houses, and regional books will be included; these, and the essays, and some of the reviews will be done by freelancers.

BOOKS ABROAD, 1000 Asp, Room 214, University of Oklahoma, Norman OK 73069. Editor: Ivar Ivask. University of Oklahoma holds all rights to materials published in *Books Abroad* unless otherwise noted. Enclose S.A.S.E. for return of submissions.
Nonfiction: Articles (maximum length 3,000 words) concerned with contemporary literature; book reviews of 200 to 300 words on new, important, original works

of a literary nature in any language. All contributions in English. Payment only in offprints (25) of a major article, plus 3 complimentary copies of *Books Abroad.*

BOSTON UNIVERSITY JOURNAL, West Tower Three, 775 Commonwealth Ave., Boston MA 02215. Editor: Paul Kurt Ackermann. For libraries, universities, college educated people. Circulation: 3,000. Buys 30 mss a year. Query first. Reports in 1 month. Enclose S.A.S.E.
Nonfiction, Fiction, and Poetry: "Literary criticism, poetry, scholarly articles on a variety of subjects (must be written clearly, without jargon), a few short stories." No limitations on length. "We also take reviews and b&w art." Pays $10 per printed page; $25 minimum.

BOX 749, Box 749, Old Chelsea Station, New York NY 10011. Phone: 212-989-0519. Editor: David Ferguson. For "people of diverse background, education, income and age—an audience not necessarily above or underground. Such an audience is consistent with our belief that literature (plus art and music) is accessible to and even desired by a larger and more varied portion of society than has generally been acknowledged." Quarterly magazine; 68 (8½x11) pages. Established in 1972. Circulation: 1,000. Acquires all rights, but will reassign rights to author after publication. Uses 50 mss a year. Payment in 2 contributor's copies. Will send sample copy to writer for $2. Will consider photocopied submissions. Will not consider simultaneous submissions. Reports in 2 to 4 months. Submit complete ms. Enclose S.A.S.E.
Fiction, Drama, Music and Poetry: "We publish poetry and fiction of every length and any theme; satire, belles lettres, plays, music and any artwork reproducible by photo-offset. We will consider (and have serialized) long fiction. We will consider full-length plays. We have no particular stylistic or ideological bias."

BULLETIN OF BIBLIOGRAPHY AND MAGAZINE NOTES, F. W. Faxon Company, Inc., Publishing Division, 15 Southwest Park, Westwood MA 02090. Editor: Eleanor Cavanaugh Jones. For college and university professors, undergraduate and graduate students, reference and serials librarians. Quarterly scholarly journal, 44 pages (7x10). Established in 1897. Circulation: 1,800. Not copyrighted, but authors may copyright their own articles. Pays in contributor's copies. Uses about 30 mss a year. Will consider photocopied submissions, but prefers original. Will consider simultaneous submissions. Reports within 10 weeks. Enclose S.A.S.E.
Bibliographies: "We publish bibliographies (primary and/or secondary, annotated or unannotated) on a wide range of topics within the humanities and social sciences. Articles are indexed or abstracted in nine indexes and abstracting journals every year."
How To Break In: "We publish many bibliographies by researchers in specialized fields who find themselves hampered by incomplete or inaccurate bibliographies on particular subjects. Librarians, high school and college teachers, and graduate students often compile checklists for their own use which would be of value to scholars or the general public."

THE CALIFORNIA QUARTERLY, 100 Sproul, University of California, Davis CA 95616. Editor: Elliot Gilbert. "Addressed to an audience of educated, literary and general readers, interested in good writing on a variety of subjects, but emphasis is on poetry and fiction." Quarterly. Usually buys first North American serial rights. Reports in 4 to 6 weeks. Enclose S.A.S.E.
Fiction and Nonfiction: "Short fiction of quality with emphasis on stylistic distinction; contemporary themes, any subject." Experimental, mainstream. Length: 8,000 words. Department Editor: Diane Johnson. Original, critical articles, interviews and book reviews. "We have a certain bias for Western, especially California, material." Length: 8,000 words maximum. Pays $2 per published page.
Poetry: "Original, all types; any subject appropriate for genuine poetic expression; any length suitable to subject." Department Editor: Karl Shapiro. Pays $5 per published page.

CANADIAN FICTION MAGAZINE, P. O. Box 46422, Station G, Vancouver, B.C. V6R 4G7, Canada. Editor: R. W. Stedingh. "A writer's magazine for a literate audience." Established in 1971. Quarterly. Circulation: 1,500. Buys first North American serial rights. Buys 100 to 200 mss a year. Payment on publication. Will send sample copy to writer for $1. Query first for book and film reviews. Submit complete mss for fiction and manifestos. Will consider photocopied submissions, but must be good photocopy. Reports on material in 1 month. Enclose Canadian stamps or International Reply Coupons.

Fiction: "No restrictions on subject matter or theme; however, we don't want anything 'slanted.' We are open to experimental and speculative fiction as well as traditional forms. Matters of style, content and form are author's prerogative. Our emphasis is on the publication of new fiction by relatively unknown writers." In addition to experimental and mainstream fiction, uses self-contained sections of novels in progress. Length: 10,000 words maximum. Pays $3 per printed page.

Nonfiction and Photos: Interviews, expose, personal opinion. Reviews of current books of fiction and movies. Length: 1,000 words. Pays $2 per printed page. "Fiction Forum, which appears whenever suitable material presents itself, usually contains manifestos or controversial discussion of the aesthetics of Canadian fiction." 7x5 b&w photos purchased. Pays minimum of $3.

CANADIAN FORUM, 56 Esplanade St. East, Toronto, Ontario, Canada M5E 1A8. Phone: 416-364-2431. Editor: Michael S. Cross. For students, teachers or professors, and professional people. Monthly magazine, 44 pages, (11x8¾). Established in 1920. Circulation: 10,000. Acquires all rights, but will reassign rights to author after publication. Payment in contributor's copies. Will send sample copy to writer for $1.25. Will consider photocopied submissions. Reports within 1 month. Enclose S.A.E. and International Reply Coupons.

Nonfiction: Mostly Canadian nonfiction, political and literary commentary. Must be intellectual. Preferred subjects are research, politics, sociology, and art. Length: 2,000 to 3,000 words.

Fiction and Poetry: Experimental and mainstream fiction. Length: 2,000 to 3,000 words. Fiction Editor: David Lewis Stein. Also uses traditional forms of poetry, and blank and free verse, avant-garde forms, and light verse. Length: open. Poetry Editor: Tom Marshall.

CANADIAN LITERATURE, University of British Columbia, Vancouver 8, B.C., Canada. Editor: George Woodcock. Quarterly. Circulation: 2,500. No fiction, poetry, fillers or photos. Not copyrighted. Pays on publication. Study publication. Query advisable. Enclose S.A.E. and International Reply Coupons.

Nonfiction: Articles of high quality on Canadian books and writers only. Articles should be scholarly and readable. Length: 2,000 to 5,500 words. Pays $40 to $120 depending on length.

THE CARLETON MISCELLANY, Carleton College, Northfield MN 55057. Phone: 507-645-4431, Ext. 208. Editor: Wayne Carver. "Mostly for academics, writers, and friends and family of the editor. Considerable overlapping of categories here." Published twice a year; magazine, glued and sewn pages, 128 pages, (6x8½). Established in 1960. Circulation: 1,000. Buys first North American serial rights, but will reassign, gladly. Buys 40 or 50 mss per year. Payment on publication. Will send sample copy to writer for $1.50. Will consider "very clear photocopies only." Reports within 6 weeks. "I discourage queries. I have to answer them." Submit complete mss only. Enclose S.A.S.E.

Nonfiction, Fiction, and Poetry: "We amuse ourselves by thinking of *The Carleton Miscellany* as a magazine of general culture, but it comes down to being a lot more literary than I'd like it to be: short stories, poems, reviews, essays on literary subjects. We have a pathological distaste for the usual academic essay of the PMLA sort, though we think it is okay in its place." Uses personal experience, interview, profile, humor, historical, think articles, nostalgia, personal opinion, and general reviews. Length: 1,200 words for reviews, up to 7,000 words for essays. Pays $6 per printed page for reviews; $8 per printed page for other material. A printed page is about

400 words. Publishes experimental, mainstream, science fiction, fantasy, and humorous fiction. Open on theme. Length: up to 7,000 words, "but the 7,000 words would have to be damned good." Pays $8 per printed page. Poetry is also used. Traditional, blank and free verse, avant-garde forms, and light verse. "We have no restrictions as to form. Some prejudices. Anything over 100 lines had better be immortal." Pays $8 per printed page.

CAROLINA QUARTERLY, P. O. Box 1117, Chapel Hill NC 27514. Phone: 919-933-0136. Editor: Jeff Richards. Three issues per year. Reprint rights revert to author on request. Pays on publication, "whenever possible." Reports in 6 to 8 weeks. Submissions should be marked Fiction or Poetry on envelope. Enclose S.A.S.E.
Fiction: "Quality, primary emphasis on stylistic achievement as well as character development and interesting point of view. A place for both the new writer and the professional. Mainly interested in new writers who demonstrate both control of material and sophistication of language. We publish a significant number of unsolicited mss." Pays $3 a printed page. A contest in fiction and poetry for new writers is held annually.
Poetry: "Quality; poems must have original subjects or points of view and demonstrate maturity in technique and in use of language. Popular or conventional verse not wanted." Pays $5 per poem.

CHELSEA, P.O. Box 5880, Grand Central Station, New York NY 10017. Phone: 212-988-2276. Editor: Sonia Raiziss. Acquires first North American serial rights, but sometimes returns rights to author on request. Payment in copies. Enclose S.A.S.E.
Nonfiction, Fiction, and Poetry: "Poetry of high quality; short fiction; occasional nonfiction articles and interviews. Accent on style. Interested in fresh, contemporary translations also."

CHICAGO REVIEW, The University of Chicago, Faculty Exchange, Chicago IL 60637. Editors: Timothy Erwin and Larry Haverkamp. For readers with a serious interest in contemporary literature and the graphic arts. Established in 1946. Quarterly magazine, 200 pages. Circulation: 3,000. Uses 100 to 150 mss a year. Pays in contributor's copies; also offers $100 prizes for fiction and poetry annually. Will send sample copy to writer for $2.45. Reports in 2 months. Enclose S.A.S.E.
Fiction and Poetry: Both experimental works and mainstream literature. Welcomes work by younger and less established writers and poets. Accepts original and in translation. Fiction Editor: Mitchell Marks. Poetry Editor: Roger Gilman.
Nonfiction and Photos: Interviews, reviews and essays are featured, but insightful criticism or commentary in other forms is invited. An issue may devote as many as 75 pages to graphic art and photography. Also uses book reviews and review articles. Graphics Editor: Zeno Sanchez-Ramos.

CHICAGO SUN-TIMES SHOWCASE, 401 N. Wabash Ave., Chicago IL 60611. Editor: Herman Kogan. For avid followers of all the arts—serious and lively. *Showcase* readers are above average of newspaper readers generally. Weekly. Sunday standard-sized section (newspaper), average eight 8-column pages. Established in 1970. Buys all rights. Buys 20 mss a year. Payment on publication, but if publication unduly delayed, payment is made earlier. Will send sample copy to writer for postage. Will consider photocopied submissions. Reports within 1 week. Enclose S.A.S.E.
Nonfiction: "Articles and essays dealing with all the serious and lively arts—movies, theater (pro, semipro, amateur, foreign), filmmakers, painting, sculpture, music (all fields, from classical to rock—we have regular columnists in these fields). Our Book Week columns have from 5 to 10 reviews, mostly assigned. Material has to be very good because we have our own regular staffers who write almost every week. Writing must be tight. No warmed-over stuff of fan magazine type. No high schoolish literary themes." Informational, personal experience, interview, profile, humor, historical, think articles, and personal opinion. Length: 500 to 1,500 words. Pays 5¢ to 10¢ a word. Nonfiction Editor: Herman Kogan. Recently published articles covered Iowa University students helping prisoners publish a magazine; good interviews with Truffaut, Don Siegel; rock and jazz musicians' profiles (with fresh material); reflective essay on Tolkien.

CIMARRON REVIEW, Oklahoma State University, Stillwater OK 74074. Managing Editor: Jeanne Adams Wray. For educated readers, college and university oriented. Quarterly magazine, small and humanistic, 72 pages, (6x9). Established in 1967. Circulation: 1,500. Acquires all rights. Payment in contributor's copies. Will send free sample copy to writer on request. Reports within 5 months. Submit only complete ms. Enclose S.A.S.E.

Nonfiction and Fiction: "Stories, articles, often grouped in specific issues around a theme; such as women, aging, the dignity of work, etc. We are particularly interested in articles that show man triumphant in a polluted, technological world. Contemporary. Grace, lucidity in style; optimistic or positive in outlook. We prefer to do theme issues. No adolescent, adjustment problems in fiction."

THE COLORADO QUARTERLY, Hellems 134, University of Colorado, Boulder CO 80302. Editor: Paul Carter. Acquires all rights. Payment in contributor's copies. Reports in 2 to 3 weeks. Enclose S.A.S.E.

Nonfiction: Articles on a wide range of subjects that concern themselves with regional, national and educational matters, written by specialists, in a nontechnical, nonacademic style. Length: 4,000 to 6,000 words.

Fiction: With plots and believable characters. No esoteric or experimental writing. Length: 3,000 to 5,000 words.

CONFRONTATION MAGAZINE, English Dept., Long Island University, Brooklyn NY 11201. Phone: 212-834-6170. Editor: Martin Tucker. For literate, educated, college graduates. Semi-annual magazine. Established in 1968. Circulation: 2,000. Rights purchased vary with author and material. Buys all rights, but will reassign rights to author after publication; buys first North American serial rights; first serial rights. Buys 50 to 100 mss a year. Payment on publication. Will send sample copy to writer for $1.50. Will consider photocopied submissions and simultaneous submissions. Query first for nonfiction. Submit only complete ms for other material. Reports within 2 months. Enclose S.A.S.E.

Nonfiction and Photos: "Material of all kinds, high literary quality. We're more flexible in our approach, and willing to print, side by side, two opposing views of an issue." Length: varies, but 2,000 words minimum. Pays $10 minimum. Photos purchased with accompanying ms with no additional payment. Photos also purchased on assignment.

Fiction and Poetry: Experimental, mainstream, fantasy, humorous fiction wanted. Theme open. Length: 1,500 to 6,000 words. Pays $25 to $100. Traditional forms of poetry, blank and free verse, and avant-garde forms. Theme open. No length limit. Pays $10 minimum.

CONNECTICUT FIRESIDE & REVIEW OF BOOKS, Box 5293, Hamden CT 06518. Editor: Albert E. Callan. For intelligent, well-educated readers interested in writing. Magazine; 76 (7x9½) pages. Established in 1972. Quarterly. Circulation: 1,500. Acquires all rights, but will reassign rights to author after publication. Pays in contributor's copies. Will send sample copy to writer for 85¢. Will consider photocopied submissions. Reporting time varies. Query first before submitting articles. Submit complete ms for other material. Enclose S.A.S.E.

Nonfiction: Publishes a history article in almost every issue, some general articles and book reviews. "We like material that is cheerful without being trite; thoughtful and well researched." Recently published "Lizzie Borden Case Solved" and "Random Notes of a Quarterly Buff". Length: approximately 200 to 2,000 words.

Fiction: "Our focus on fiction is increasing. We use short stories, but we don't want to see stories about wives who decide not to leave home." Experimental, mystery, suspense, fantasy, humorous, confession and historical fiction. Length: 1,000 to 4,000 words.

Poetry: Traditional and avant-garde forms; blank verse, free verse, light verse. "Prefer 1-page minimum, but have used longer; depends on quality."

CONNECTICUT REVIEW, c/o S.C.S.C., 501 Crescent St., New Haven CT 06515. Phone: 203-397-2101, Ext. 395. Editor: Dr. Bertram D. Sarason. For college professors

and intellectuals. Established in 1965. Biannual. Circulation: 3,000. Rights purchased vary with author and material; usually buys all rights. Uses 4 mss a year. No longer a paying market. Will send free sample copy to writer on request. Will consider photocopied submissions. Reports on material accepted for publication in 4 months. Returns rejected material in 6 months. Submit complete ms. Enclose S.A.S.E.
Nonfiction: Literary criticism, memoirs, by or about significant persons, biography, humor, psychology, sociology, economics. Anything new, e.g., latest trends in writing, in psychology, in political theory. Informational, interview, profile, think pieces. Written in "academic style, but with flair. Author should have humanistic approach and a theme, and reach a generalization." Length: 10,000 words maximum. Does not pay for material.

CONTEMPORARY LITERATURE, Dept. of English, Helen C. White Hall, University of Wisconsin, Madison WI 53706. Editor: L.S. Dembo. Quarterly. "All details should conform to those recommended by the *MLA Style Sheet.*" Does not encourage contributions from freelance writers without academic credentials. Enclose S.A.S.E.
Nonfiction: A scholarly journal which examines various aspects of contemporary literature, from generalizations on current trends and themes, to studies of a writer, his technique, and/or his work, to other specialized treatments of studies in modern literature.

CRITICISM, Wayne State University, Dept. of English, Detroit MI 48202. Editor: Alva Gay. For college and university audience of humanities scholars and teachers. Quarterly. No payment. Reports in 3 months. Enclose S.A.S.E.
Nonfiction: Articles on literature, music, visual arts; no particular critical "school." Style should be clear and to the point. Length: 15 to 20 typewritten pages.

CRITIQUE: STUDIES IN MODERN FICTION, Department of English, Georgia Institute of Technology, Atlanta GA 30332. Editor: James Dean Young. For college and university teachers and students. Established in 1956. Triannual. Circulation: 1,300. Acquires all rights. Pays in contributor's copies. Submit complete ms. Will consider photocopied submissions "rarely." Writers should follow the *MLA Style Sheet.* Reports in 4 to 6 months. Enclose S.A.S.E.
Nonfiction: "Critical essays on writers of contemporary fiction. We prefer essays on writers who are still alive and without great reputations. We only rarely publish essays on well-known, established writers. Currently overworked are essays on the great modern writers: Conrad, James, Joyce, and Faulkner." Uses informational articles and interviews. Length: 4,000 to 8,000 words.

DARK TOWER MAGAZINE, Cleveland State University, University Center, Cleveland OH 44115. Editor: Louise Smerdel. For those interested in literature, poetry, etc. Published 2 times a year (Spring and Fall); 40 (6x9) pages. Established in 1972. Circulation: 700. Copyrighted. Uses 6 mss a year. Pays in copies, or up to $5. Will send free sample copy to writer on request. "Limited supply." Will consider photocopied and simultaneous submissions. Submit no more than 6 poems at one time. Reports within 2 months. Enclose S.A.S.E.
Nonfiction, Photos, Fiction, Drama and Poetry: "We have no thematic restrictions and no structural or stylistic restrictions. Poetry, short stories, literary criticism, and plays. We don't want love poems or personal tragedies, etc. We like creative reviews and criticism." Length: 3,000 words maximum. Pays in copies or up to $5. 8x10 b&w prints are purchased on assignment. Captions optional. Pays $5 plus copies. Experimental, erotica, fantasy, humorous, and prose poems, poetic fiction considered. Length: 3,000 words maximum. Traditional forms of poetry, blank verse, free verse, light verse, or avant-garde forms. Concrete poetry. Pays in copies or up to $5.

DE KALB LITERARY ARTS JOURNAL, 555 N. Indian Creek Dr., Clarkston GA 30021. Phone: 404-294-4203. Editor: William S. Newman. For those interested in poetry, fiction and/or art. Quarterly. Established in 1966. Circulation: 5,000. Acquires first serial rights. Payment in contributor's copies. Will send sample copy to writer for $1.40 (cost plus postage). "Look for announcements of special issues." Seeking

material for National Poets Issue. Submit only complete ms. Reports in 6 to 8 weeks. Enclose S.A.S.E.
Nonfiction, Fiction, Photos, and Poetry: Subject matter is unrestricted. "We consider all types of nonfiction and fiction. Our decisions are based on quality of material.- Traditional, blank verse, free verse, light verse, and avant-garde forms of poetry." B&w photos are used with mss.

DECEMBER MAGAZINE, P.O. Box 274, Western Springs IL 60558. Editor: Curt Johnson. Acquires all rights. Will send sample copy to a writer for $2. Query first for interviews. Pays in 2 contributor's copies. Reports in 5 to 9 weeks. Enclose S.A.S.E.
Nonfiction: Interviews, humorous pieces, movies and political controversies.
Fiction: Chiefly serious fiction. Length: 5,000 words maximum.

DENVER QUARTERLY, University of Denver, Denver CO 80210. Editor: Burton Feldman. For the "general audience for literate articles on culture, literature, etc." Quarterly. Circulation: 800. Buys first rights. Buys 50 to 100 mss a year. Pays on publication. Will send a sample copy to a writer for $2. Reports in 1 month. Enclose S.A.S.E.
Nonfiction, Fiction, and Poetry: "Essays, fiction, poems, book reviews. No special approach, but well-written enough and serious enough for our kind of reader." Length: Not over 8,000 to 10,000 words. Minimum payment is $5 per 350 words for prose, $10 a page ("no matter how many lines on it") for poetry.

DESCANT, Department of English, Texas Christian University, Fort Worth TX 76129. Editor: Betsy Feagan Colquitt. Quarterly. Circulation: 700. Copyrighted. "Permission for republication is always granted." Payment in contributor's copies. Will send sample copy to writer for $1. Will consider photocopied and simultaneous submissions. Reports within 8 weeks. Enclose S.A.S.E.
Nonfiction: Essays dealing with recent literature. Prefers articles that are without the scholarly mechanisms. Literary criticism. Length: 4,000 words maximum.
Fiction: Experimental, mainstream, religious, and historical fiction. Length: 5,000 words maximum; "usually shorter."
Poetry: Traditional forms of poetry, blank verse and free verse, and avant-garde forms. About one-quarter of each issue is devoted to poetry. Length: generally limited to 40 lines, but on occasion uses long poems up to 150 lines.

DRAMA & THEATRE, Department of English, SUNY at Fredonia, Fredonia NY 14063. Editor: Henry F. Salerno. For directors, producers, playwrights, critics, students and teachers of drama and people interested in the theatre. Published 3 times a year; 68-page magazine (8½x11). Established in 1968. Circulation: 1,500. Acquires all rights, but will reassign rights to author after publication. Uses about 30 mss a year. Payment in 10 contributor's copies. Will send free sample copy on request. Will not consider photocopied submissions. Reports on material accepted for publication in 2 to 3 months. Returns rejected material in about 6 weeks. Query first or submit complete ms. Enclose S.A.S.E.
Nonfiction, Drama and Photos: Articles on contemporary drama and theatre; new plays; reviews and interviews; translations of contemporary European drama. Accepts both good literary and theatrical criticism of contemporary drama. Both short and long plays are used in the same issue. Playwrights should use standard play script form. "We get too many so-called 'absurd' plays. We would like to see plays dealing with America's past—remote and recent." Length: 2,500 to 5,000 words. Photos used with accompanying mss.

THE DRAMA REVIEW, 51 West 4th St., New York NY 10012. Phone: 212-598-2597. Editor: Michael Kirby. For students, professors, theatre practitioners, general theatre-going public. Quarterly magazine; 160 (7x10) pages. Established in 1955. Circulation: 15,000. Buys all rights. Buys 5 to 10 mss an issue. Payment on publication. Will send sample copy to writer for $2. Reports on material accepted for publication in 3 months. Returns rejected material in 2 to 3 weeks. Query first. Enclose S.A.S.E.
Nonfiction and Photos: Contemporary and historical material on experimental trends

in the theatre. "Each issue is a special issue. Read current issue to find out what is planned for future issues." Informational, interview, historical, technical material. Length: "as long as article needs to be; no padding." Pays 2¢ per word. Pays $10 per b&w photograph. Captions required.

How To Break In: "We've instituted a new section called Theater Reports which will consist of stories of only about two pages in text on experimental performances around the country. Doing one of these would be the main way for a new writer to draw our attention. What we're after is factual documentation, not criticism. We want to document new trends in the field and we are looking for people who can accurately describe such things as acting style. If the Theater Report worked out for a writer, there is a good chance that we would try that writer with an article later on. Also, we are looking for people we can depend on around the country and even outside the country who can report on experimental trends in their area, so a contributor to Theater Reports could become a regular for us. Again, we want reports on something new in the field, and we're not interested in whether it's good or bad. The writer must watch our magazine so he will know what the upcoming issue themes are. Query first."

EL VIENTO, 348 7th Street, Huntington WV 25701. Editor: William Lloyd Griffin. Established in 1967. Semiannual. "All rights revert to the authors." Pays in contributor's copies. Will consider photocopied submissions. Reports in 6 weeks. Enclose S.A.S.E.
Fiction, Nonfiction, Poetry, and Drama: "We use fiction, nonfiction, poetry, and one-act plays. No taboos except low quality material." Length: 500 to 3,000 words for fiction and nonfiction. El Viento means "the wind" in Spanish. The title was chosen because of its freedom connotation, and they therefore have no taboos, with exception of poor quality material.

EPOCH, A Magazine of Contemporary Literature, 245 Goldwin Smith Hall, Cornell University, Ithaca NY 14850. 3 times yearly. Acquires first serial publication rights. Payment in copies. Reports in 2 months or more. Enclose S.A.S.E. for return of submissions.
Fiction: "Quality. Would like to see more stories which combine a fresh, honest transcription of human experience with power or meaningfulness, but are not adverse to experimental forms." Length: 1,500 to 5,000 words.
Poetry: Approximately 30 to 40 pages each issue devoted to poetry.

EVERYMAN MAGAZINE, 4208½ Whitman Ave., Cleveland OH 44113. Phone: 216-631-1454. Editor: Christopher Franke. For a college literary audience. Annual magazine; 56 (7x10) pages. Established in 1970. Circulation: 500. Rights acquired vary with author and material. May acquire first North American serial rights, second serial (reprint) rights or simultaneous rights. Payment in contributor's copies. Will send free sample copy on request. Will consider photocopied and simultaneous submissions. Query first or submit complete ms. Enclose S.A.S.E.
Nonfiction, Fiction and Poetry: Informational, personal experience, historical articles; think pieces. Length: open. Short, small press reviews. Experimental, erotic, fantasy, humorous, historical and science fiction. Length: open. Traditional forms of poetry; blank verse, free verse, avant-garde forms. Length: open.

FICTION, City College, English Department, 138th St. and Convent Ave., New York NY 10031. Phone: 212-690-8170. Editor: Mark Mirsky. Published by a cooperative of writers. For individual subscribers of all ages; college libraries, bookstores, and college bookstores. Published 3 times a year. Magazine, 28 to 32 pages. Established in 1972. Circulation: 5,000. Acquires all rights, but will reassign rights to author after publication. Payment in contributor's copies only. Will send free sample copy to writer on request. Submit complete ms. Reports as soon as possible, but time "depends on the backlog of material". Enclose S.A.S.E.
Fiction and Photos: "We publish only fiction, up to 3,000 words. There really is no minimum or maximum length, because we edit many pieces. No payment for writers." Photos purchased without accompanying ms. Photo Editor: Inger Grytting.

FICTION INTERNATIONAL, Department of English, St. Lawrence University, Canton NY 13617. Editor: Joe David Bellamy. For "readers interested in the best writing by talented writers working in new forms or working in old forms in especially fruitful new ways; readers interested in contemporary literary developments and possibilities." Semiannual. Circulation: 5,000. Buys all rights (will reassign rights to author after publication), first North American serial rights, first serial rights. Buys 15 fiction, 4 interview, 20 poetry mss a year. Pays on publication. Will send sample copy to a writer for $2. Query first or submit complete ms for interviews; submit only complete ms for fiction or reviews. Prefers not to see photocopied submissions. Reports in 1 to 2 months. Enclose S.A.S.E.
Nonfiction and Photos: "Regularly use interviews with well-known fiction writers." Length: 1,000 to 10,000 words. "Also use book reviews of new fiction, though these are usually assigned." Length: 300 to 500 words. Photos accompanying interviews purchased to illustrate interviews. 8x10 b&w glossies. Payment varies.
Fiction: "Almost no taboos or preconceptions but highly selective. Not an easy market for unsophisticated writers. Especially receptive to innovative forms or rich personal styles. Easily bored by nineteenth-century narratives or predictable, plotridden fictions. Originality and the ability to create living characters are highly desirable qualities." Portions of novels acceptable if reasonably self-contained. Length: no length limitations for fiction but "rarely use short-shorts or mss over 30 pages." Payment is $25 to $150, sometimes higher.

FIRELANDS ARTS REVIEW, Firelands Campus, Huron OH 44839. Phone: 419-433-5560. Editor: Joel D. Rudinger. For general educated audience. Annual magazine, 72 pages, (5½x7½). Established in 1972. Circulation: 1,000. Acquires first serial rights or second serial (reprint) rights. Uses 50 mss a year. Pays in copies. Will send sample copy to writer for $1.25. Will consider photocopied submissions. Submit only complete ms. Accepts mss from October to March of each year. Reports within 8 weeks. Enclose S.A.S.E.
Fiction: "Any style and approach and subject matter as long as the quality is professional and mature. Length: 4,000 words maximum. Will also accept short prose sketches and characterizations sensitive to the human condition. We also need stories that display a sense of humor or clever ironic twist."
Photos: 5x7 or 8x10 b&w's. Any non-cliched subject or style. Unusual perspective, high contrast, experimental materials are of interest as well as fresh approaches to traditional photography.
Poetry: Poems must be original and mature in use of language. Any subject, any theme, any style, any length. High quality and awareness of the art of writing poetry essential.

FLORIDA QUARTERLY, 330 J.W. Reitz Union, University of Florida, Gainesville FL 32601. Editor: Michael Skinner. 3 times a year. Circulation: 1,300. Acquires all rights. Does not pay. Will send sample copy for $1.25. Reports in 6 weeks. Enclose S.A.S.E.
Nonfiction, Fiction and Poetry: Critical, nonpolitical literary essays, including contemporary subjects. Length: 20,000 words. Contemporary fiction; nothing is unacceptable. Length: 15,000 words. Also uses short-shorts or vignettes under 2,000 words. Poetry of any subject matter, style, or length.

FOLKLORE FORUM, 504 North Fess, Bloomington IN 47401. For folklorists, graduate students in the humanities and social sciences. Quarterly magazine; 80 pages, (8½x11). Established in 1968. Circulation: 350. Not copyrighted. Payment in contributor's copies. Will send sample copy to writer for $1. Will consider photocopied and simultaneous submissions. Query first or submit complete ms. Reports within 2 months. Enclose S.A.S.E.
Nonfiction: Articles, bibliographies; book, record, and ethnographic film reviews on topics in folklore. "We encourage short comments and queries. Our objective is to serve as a medium of communication among folklorists. We have a special interest in popular culture and folklore."

FORUM, University of Houston, Cullen Blvd., Houston TX 77004. Editor: William Lee Pryor. Primarily for a sophisticated audience; most of the contributors are university professors. Quarterly. Acquires all rights, but will reassign rights to author after publication. Pays in contributor's copies. "A query letter is a welcome courtesy, although we do not specifically request one." Enclose S.A.S.E.

Nonfiction: "We feature articles in the humanities, fine arts, and the sciences, but we also welcome those bearing on business and technology. Specialized interests involving highly technical or special vocabularies are usually not within our range, however. For articles, we stress the scholarly approach and originality. We recommend use of the Chicago *Manual of Style.* An informal style is not objectionable, but research, if any, should be accurate, thorough, and carefully documented. Our format differs from those publications of a similar orientation in that we attempt to combine scholarship with an appealing, aesthetic setting. We are very much interested in good articles on music, dance, architecture, sculpture, etc., not only for our regular issues, but also for special numbers like recent ones featuring French culture and Renaissance." Length: open.

Photos: "Customarily we have an art section in the magazine devoted to photos of paintings, drawing, sculpture, architecture, etc. Also, we try to illustrate articles, poems, and short stories with photos."

Fiction: "We are open on story themes, and we stress originality. Up to now we have not found it possible to publish condensed or serialized novels."

FOUR QUARTERS, La Salle College, Olney Ave. at 20th St., Philadelphia PA 19141. Editor: John J. Keenan. For college educated audience with literary interest. Quarterly. Circulation: 700. Buys all rights; grants permission to reprint on request. Buys 10 to 12 short stories, 30 to 40 poems, 4 articles a year. Pays on publication. Will send a sample copy to a writer for 50¢. Reports in 4 to 6 weeks. Enclose S.A.S.E.

Nonfiction: "Lively critical articles on particular authors or specific works. Think pieces on history, politics, the arts. Prefer footnotes incorporated. Style must be literate, lively, free of jargon and pedantry." Length: 1,500 to 5,000 words. Payment is up to $25.

Fiction: "Technical mastery gets our attention and respect immediately. We admire writers who use the language with precision, economy, and imagination. But fine writing for its own sake is unsatisfying unless it can lead the reader to some insight into the complexity of the human condition without falling into heavy-handed didacticism." Length: 2,000 to 5,000 words. Pays up to $25.

Poetry: "Quality poetry from 8 to 32 lines. Some shorter ones used for filler without payment." Payment is up to $5.

THE GAR, Box 4793, Austin TX 78765. Phone: 512-453-2556. Editor: Hal Wylie. For those interested in Austin and Texas politics, the counterculture and the arts. Established in 1971. Bimonthly. Payment in contributor's copies. Circulation: 2,000. Copyrighted when necessary for literary materials. Query first. Will consider photocopied submissions. Reports on material in 4 months. Enclose S.A.S.E.

Nonfiction and Photos: Informational, personal experience, interview, profile, humor, historical, expose, personal opinion. Reviews of books, records and the arts. "A lot of political material on local or regional matters; some ecology; occasional general articles and essays. Left of center." Length: 300 to 2,000 words. $20 prize awarded annually. Photos used with or without ms.

Fiction: Experimental, mainstream, erotica, science fiction, fantasy, humorous. $10 prize awarded annually.

Poetry: Traditional forms, free verse, avant-garde forms. $10 prize awarded annually.

GRAFFITI, English Department, Box 418, Lenoir Rhyne College, Hickory NC 28601. Phone: 328-1741, Ext. 211. Editor: Kermit Turner. For writers, college students and faculty. Magazine published twice a year in the spring and fall; 72 (6x9) pages. Established in 1972. Circulation: 250. Acquires first serial rights. All rights return to author after publication. Uses 6 to 8 short story mss a year; about 80 poems. Payment in contributor's copies. Will send sample copy to writer for 50¢. Will not

consider photocopied or simultaneous submissions. Reports on material accepted for publication in 4 months. Returns rejected material in 6 weeks. Submit complete ms. Enclose S.A.S.E.
Nonfiction: Literary reviews of current novels, short story and poetry collections.
Fiction: Short stories; experimental, mainstream. Length: 2,000 to 5,000 words.
Poetry: Traditional forms; free verse. Will consider any length.

THE GREAT LAKES REVIEW, Northeastern Illinois University, Chicago IL 60625. Editors: Gerald Nemanic and Gregory Singleton. Mostly for scholars and academics who are interested in Midwest studies. Semi-annual magazine, 100 pages, (6x9). Established in 1974. Circulation: 500. "We require no rights outside of copyright." Payment in contributor's copies. Write for editorial guidelines for writers. Query first or submit complete ms. Will consider photocopied and simultaneous submissions. Reports in 6 months. Enclose S.A.S.E.
Nonfiction and Poetry: Scholarly articles, bibliographies, interviews, poetry features, personal narratives.

HAIKU MAGAZINE, Box 2702, Paterson NJ 07509. Editor: William J. Higginson. For poets and readers of poems. Quarterly magazine; 40 pages, 5x8. Established in 1967. Circulation: 400. Acquires all rights, but will reassign rights to author after publication. Uses 200 to 300 mss a year. Payment in contributor's copies. Will send sample copy to writer for $2. Write for editorial guidelines. Query first for articles and reviews. Submit complete poetry ms. Reports in 1 month. Enclose S.A.S.E. "Prisoners need not include S.A.S.E.; all other mss received without S.A.S.E. will be thrown away."
Nonfiction and Photos: Articles on poetry, and poetry reviews. Informational, historical, photo features, and poetry reviews. Length: 1,000 to 3,000 words. Some photos and art. Fine art only. Purchased without ms. Prefers no captions.
Poetry: Free verse, avant-garde forms, and concrete poetry. No special theme.

HANGING LOOSE, 231 Wyckoff St., Brooklyn NY 11217. Editors: Dick Lourie, Emmett Jarrett, Ron Schreiber, Robert Hershon. Quarterly. Acquires first serial rights. Payment in copies. Will send sample copy to writer for $1. Reports in 2 to 3 months. Enclose S.A.S.E.
Fiction and Poetry: Experimental fiction. Excellent quality. Length: approximately 3,000 words. "Space for fiction very limited." Fresh, energetic poems of any length.

HAWAII REVIEW, 2465 Campus Rd., University of Hawaii, Honolulu HI 96822. Editor: Christine Cook. For readers 18 and older, interested in literature. Bi-annual; 95 (9x6) pages. Rights purchased vary with author and material. Buys all rights, but will sometimes reassign rights to author after publication; buys first North American serial rights; buys second serial (reprint) rights. Pays on acceptance. Submit only complete ms. Reports in 2 to 3 months. Enclose S.A.S.E.
Nonfiction, Fiction and Poetry: Poetry, prose, reviews. Any subject matter; selection is based on quality. Length is open. Pays $20 to $30 per article or story. Fiction Editor: Susan Foster. Traditional forms of poetry, blank verse, free verse, avant-garde forms, and all other types of poetry. Open on themes. No length limits. Pays $10 per page, with maximum payment of $30 for poetry. Poetry Editor: Jim Long.

HOOSIER CHALLENGER MAGAZINE, 8365 Wicklow Ave., Cincinnati OH 45236. Editor: Claire Emerson. For pro, amateur, and beginner. Quarterly. No payment, but competition for prizes and awards. Will send sample copy for $1.50. Enclose S.A.S.E. for response to queries and return of submissions.
Nonfiction and Photos: Wants intelligent, interesting, unusual articles. "Interested in factual sightings of flying saucers." The "Journey Into the Unknown" department publishes items "dealing with true spiritual experiences." Length: 350 words maximum. B&w photos may accompany mss.
Fiction: "Deliver us from 'over-sex' and profanity in fiction!" Uses short-shorts; any type, but must be in good taste, original, creative. Length: up to 1,000 words. Does not want bad writing and crude expressions woven into stories.

Poetry: Publishes poetry; open to any "types" including satirical verse. Length: 16 lines or less; very few longer ones considered.
Fillers: Epigrams and short philosophical paragraphs, and clean satire.

THE HUDSON REVIEW, 65 E. 55th St., New York NY 10022. Managing Editor: Irene Skolnick. Quarterly. Buys first North American serial rights. Pays on publication. Reports in 6 to 8 weeks. Enclose S.A.S.E. for return of submissions.
Nonfiction, Fiction, and Poetry: Uses "quality fiction up to 10,000 words, articles up to 8,000 words; translations, reviews and poetry." Pays 2½¢ a word for prose, and 50¢ a line for poetry.
How To Break In: "In each issue we publish two omnibus reviews: one might cover 20 books of fiction and the other might be a survey in a nonfiction area. These are always assigned, so the newcomer would be best off trying for the shorter one-book reviews, which run about 1,000 words. If he's successful there, we might eventually assign him one of the omnibus reviews. We take unpublished writers and neither fiction, nonfiction, nor poetry is necessarily an easier route into the magazine. We publish 5 or 6 poems per issue and several essays and stories. One unsolicited piece that sticks out in my memory was an essay on Ezra Pound by someone who at the time was working as a rose-cutter in Maine. We also use review-type essays on theatre and film, which might be another way a writer could break in."

THE HUMANIST, 923 Kensington Ave., Buffalo NY 14215. Phone: 716-837-0306. Editor: Paul Kurtz. For college graduates; humanists with a wide range of interests. Published every two months; 48 to 64 pages, (8½x11). Established in 1973. Circulation: 27,000. Copyrighted. Does not pay. Will send free sample copy to writer on request. Will consider photocopied submissions. Query first. Reports "immediately." Enclose S.A.S.E.
Nonfiction: "General informative articles of an intellectual nature. A thorough treatment of the subject material covered. We're considered to be quite innovative in the types of articles published. Particularly interested in articles about transportation, changing careers in midstream, and euthanasia." Informational, personal experience, historical, think articles, photo features, and book, movie, and TV reviews. Length: 1,000 to 5,000 words. "Occasionally an honorarium is available."

INTER-AMERICAN REVIEW OF BIBLIOGRAPHY, Organization of American States, Washington DC 20006. Editor: Armando Correia Pacheco. For specialists and institutions interested in the culture and bibliography related to the Americas. Quarterly. Copyrighted. Pays on acceptance. Query first. Enclose S.A.S.E.
Nonfiction: Articles, review articles, book reviews, current bibliography in 21 subject fields, notes and news related to the Americas with particular emphasis on the humanities. Pays $50 to $75 per solicited article only.

IRELAND OF THE WELCOMES, 590 Fifth Ave., New York NY 10017. Editor: Elizabeth Healy. "Bulk of material commissioned; freelance material occasionally used." Established in 1952. Bimonthly. Circulation: 40,000. Not generally copyrighted. "Copyright reserved on occasional features." Payment on acceptance for ms; on publication for photos. Will send free sample copy to writer on request. Published in Dublin. The New York address is not an editorial office but an Irish tourist office which handles subscriptions for the magazine. Any editorial queries or requests for the writer's guidelines can also be sent to Elizabeth Healy at P.O. Box 273, Dublin 8, Ireland, for quickest response. Enclose S.A.E. and International Reply Coupons if query is addressed to Dublin; S.A.S.E., if sent to the U.S. office.
Nonfiction and Photos: All stories relate to Ireland and should have some current theme, be it craft, culture, or current events. "Items illuminating Irish culture, tradition, literature, landscape and life style. Humor welcomed. Magazine is designed to widen interest in Ireland and things Irish. Overt propaganda avoided. A personal, anecdotal style preferred. Authority and accuracy important for most themes." Does not want to see anything like "a diary of my vacation in Ireland". Recently published articles include "Discovering the Literature of Ireland"; handwoven Irish silk poplin, tracing its introduction, history, and current production in Cork; and "The Living

Tradition," on authentic Irish folk music. Length: 1,000 to 2,000 words. Payment is by negotiation and begins at $100 for articles, and at $15 for photos. 8x10 b&w glossy photos preferred. Color: transparency or print; not negative. Captions optional. This is a heavily illustrated magazine which depends on high-quality photos and the writer-photographer is at an advantage.

JOHNSONIAN NEWS LETTER, 610 Philosophy Hall, Columbia University, New York NY 10027. Co-editors: James L. Clifford and John H. Middendorf. For scholars, book collectors and all those interested in 18th century English literature. 4 times a year. No payment. Reports immediately. Enclose S.A.S.E.
Nonfiction: Interested in news items, queries, short comments, etc., having to do with 18th century English literature. Must be written in simple style. Length: maximum 500 words.

JOURNAL OF CONTEMPORARY AUTHORS & POETS, Eastwood Library, 140 4th St., Box 444, Brentwood NY 11717. Editor: Eileen Reeds. For those who enjoy serious poetry and thought-provoking essays. All ages; high school students, as well as adults; teachers, librarians. Established in 1973. Quarterly. Circulation: 3,000. Buys first North American serial rights. Payment on publication. Will send sample copy to writer for $3. Write for copy of guidelines for writers. (Return envelope must be enclosed.) Will consider photocopied submissions. Please limit submissions to 2 items and stamped return envelope. Reports on material within 4 weeks. Submit complete ms. Enclose S.A.S.E.
Nonfiction: Most subjects and styles in good taste, with artistic and aesthetic qualities. "Essays must not veer from title and topic, and if they are of a critical nature, must pose a possible solution. A complaint is not an essay." Interested in essays on points of interest that one might visit, whether your hometown or a place the writer traveled to. "Our material is brief, and we feel that the tight writing creates greater impact if properly handled. War, lost love, and devoutly religious themes should be avoided by inexperienced writers, as we invariably receive hackneyed sounding pieces." Informational, how-to, personal experience, profile, inspirational, historical, think pieces, nostalgia, personal opinion, travel. Length: 150 words maximum. Pays ½¢ to 2¢ per word.
Poetry: Traditional forms, blank verse, free verse. Length: 3 to 16 lines. Pays 50¢ to 95¢ per poem. Department Editor: April Scott.

JOURNAL OF MODERN LITERATURE, Temple University, Philadelphia PA 19122. Editor: Maurice Beebe. General subject matter: literary history of the past hundred years—American, British, and world literature in translation. 5 times a year. Buys all rights. Pays on publication. Will send a free sample copy on request. Enclose S.A.S.E.
Nonfiction and Photos: Scholarly articles clearly based on research in social or biographical background, ms revisions, or textual analysis. Except in special numbers, the editors try to avoid top-of-the-head "readings" of individual works of literature. Length: "varies, from notes to full-length monographs." Pays about $100 for full-length articles. Photos purchased with mss.

JOURNAL OF POPULAR CULTURE, University Hall, Bowling Green State University, Bowling Green OH 43402. Phone: 419-372-2610. Editor: Ray B. Browne. For students and adults, interested in popular culture, TV, films, popular literature, sports, music, etc. Quarterly magazine, 256 pages, (6x9). Established in 1967. Circulation: 3,000. Acquires all rights, but will reassign rights to author after publication. Payment in copies. Will send sample copy to writer for $4. Will consider photocopied submissions. Reports within 3 to 6 months. Enclose S.A.S.E.
Nonfiction and Photos: "Critical essays on media, books, poetry, advertising, etc." Informational, interview, historical, think pieces, nostalgia, reviews of books, movies, television. Length: 5,000 words maximum. Payment in contributor's copies (25 reprints). Uses b&w glossies.
Poetry: Avant-garde forms, light verse, popular culture subjects. Length: 100 lines.

JOURNAL 31, Box 2109, San Francisco CA 94126. Editor: David Plumb. For people interested in contemporary trends within the context of literature, art, social political thought, psychology, and drama. Annual. Established in 1972. Circulation: 500. Payment in contributor's copies. Will send sample copy to writer for $1. Reports within 4 weeks. Enclose S.A.S.E. "or ms gets discarded."

Nonfiction and Fiction: "Profiles, excerpts from novels, short stories, film scripts (short), reviews occasionally; only we prefer to use the space for writing. Profiles to 10,000 words, but query first. Fiction to 4,000 words, although we prefer shorter pieces from 50 words on up. No taboos, although we tend to stay away from classical literature. Contemporary language, inner voice, illusion, are all fine."

Poetry: "Prefer free verse and prose poems. We have published long poems (over 100 lines) but they really have to be wired to warrant publication. An editor will constantly weigh one piec against another for space."

Fillers and Photos; Short fictional pieces, humorous or otherwise, from 50 to 150 words. 8x10 b&w glossies with captions. Query first for photos.

KANSAS QUARTERLY, Dept. of English, Kansas State University, Manhattan KS 66502. Phone: 913-532-6716. Editors: Harold W. Schneider and Ben Nyberg. For "adults, mostly academics, and people interested in literature, midwestern history, and art." Established in 1968. Quarterly. Circulation: 1,100. Acquires all rights, but will reassign them to author after publication. Pays in contributor's copies. Will send a sample copy to a writer for $2. Query first for nonfiction. "Follow *MLA Style Sheet* and write for a sophisticated audience." Reports in about 2 to 4 months. Enclose S.A.S.E. for return of submissions or reply to queries.

Nonfiction, Photos, Fiction, and Poetry: Accepts poetry, short stories; art, history and literary criticism on special topics. "We emphasize the history, culture, and life style of the Mid-Plains region. We do not want children's literature, 'slick' material, or special interest material not in keeping with our special numbers." Accepts historical articles on "special topics only." Photos should have captions; 4x6 b&w preferred. Accepts experimental and mainstream fiction. Length: 250 to 10,000 words. Accepts traditional and avant-garde forms of poetry, blank verse, and free verse. Poetry themes open.

KARAMU, English Department, Eastern Illinois University, Charleston IL 61920. Editor: Allen Neff. For literate, university-educated audience. Established in 1967. Annually. Circulation: 300. Acquires first North American serial rights. Uses 25 mss a year. Payment in 2 contributor's copies. Will send sample copy to writer for $1. Submit complete ms. Reports on material in 5 months. Enclose S.A.S.E.

Nonfiction: Articles on contemporary literature. Length: open.

Fiction: Experimental, mainstream. Length: 2,000 to 8,000 words. Dept. Editor: Gordon Jackson.

Poetry: Traditional forms, free verse, avant-garde. "Quality with visual perception or with fresh language." Length: 3 to 80 lines, "but we do publish longer poems." Dept. Editor: Ms. Carol Elder.

KENTUCKY FOLKLORE RECORD, Box U-169, College Heights Station, Western Kentucky University, Bowling Green KY 42101. Phone: 502-745-3111. Editor: Charles S. Guthrie. For libraries and individuals having a professional or personal interest in folklore as a learned discipline. Established in 1955. Quarterly. Circulation: 400. Copyrighted. Acquires all rights. Will grant reprint rights, provided full credit is given to *KFR.* Uses 20 mss a year. Payment in contributor's copies. Will send free sample copy on request. Will not consider photocopied submissions. Follow *MLA Style Sheet.* Usually reports on material in 4 weeks. Query first or submit complete ms. Enclose S.A.S.E.

Nonfiction and Photos: "Our main emphasis is on Kentucky material. Articles dealing primarily with folklife, folk speech, folktales, folksong (songs collected from oral tradition) of Kentucky. Some material pertaining to other areas is used also. Book reviews dealing with recent publications that treat some aspect of folklore. Study an issue of the journal." Also interested in child ballads, folk children's games, nursery rhymes, black folklore, folklore in literature. Not interested in seeing anything pertaining to "Nashville" music. Length: 200 to 2,000 words. B&w photos with good contrast, 8x10 preferred, used with mss. Must relate to the journal's theme.

THE LAKE SUPERIOR REVIEW, Box 724, Ironwood MI 49938. Editors: Faye Pelkola and Cynthia Willoughby. For anyone interested in good literature. Published 3 times a year; 52 (9x6) pages. Established in 1969. Circulation: 750. Acquires first North American serial rights. Uses about 12 short stories a year and 50 to 60 poems a year. Pays in contributor's copies. Will send sample copy for $1.50. Submit only complete ms. Reports in 4 to 8 weeks. Enclose S.A.S.E.
Nonfiction, Fiction, Photos, Drama, and Poetry: "Mostly short fiction and poetry, but we consider essays, nonfiction, and relevant, up-to-date articles and interviews." Nonfiction length: 500 to 3,000 words. B&w photos about 9x6 considered with or without ms. Experimental, mainstream, mystery, erotica, science fiction, fantasy, romance, and humorous fiction. Length: 500 to 3,000 words. All types of poetry.

L'ESPRIT CREATEUR, Box 222, Lawrence KS 66044. Phone: 913-864-3164. Editor: John D. Erickson. Bilingual journal for persons interested in French literature (educators, critics). Quarterly, 95 to 100 pages, (8¾x6). Established in 1961. Circulation: 1,250. Acquires all rights, but will reassign rights to author after publication. Uses about 30 mss a year. Payment in 5 contributor's copies. Will send sample copy to writer for $1.75. Prefers the *MLA Style Sheet* style. "All issues are devoted to special subjects, though we print interviews of French writers or critics and book reviews of critical works that do not correspond to the issue subject. Please note subjects of coming issues, listed in each issue. Submit July 1 for spring issue, Oct. 1 for summer issue, Feb. 1 for fall issue, and April 1 for winter issue." Reports within 3 to 6 months. Query first or submit complete ms. Enclose S.A.S.E.
Nonfiction: "Criticism of French literature centered on a particular theme each issue; interviews with French writers or critics that appear irregularly; book reviews of critical works on French literature. Critical studies of whatever methodological persuasion that observe the primacy of the text. We notice a bit too much emphasis on extra-literary matters and a failure to note the special issues scheduled. Interested in new critical practices in France. We prefer articles that are direct, honest, avoid pedantry, respect the integrity of the literary work and have something intelligent to say." Length: 12 to 15 double-spaced typed pages, or 3,500 to 4,000 words.

THE LITERARY REVIEW, Fairleigh Dickinson University, Rutherford NJ 07070. Editor: Charles Angoff. Quarterly. Copyrighted. "Usually we keep only first rights." Pays in copies. Reports in about 3 months. Enclose S.A.S.E.
Nonfiction, Fiction, and Poetry: Contemporary writing in the field of belles lettres both in the U.S. and abroad. Seeks to encourage literary excellence, and is hospitable both to established writers and young writers of promise. Stresses creative rather than critical writing. No length restrictions.

LITERARY SKETCHES, P.O. Box 711, Williamsburg VA 23185. Editor: Mary Lewis Chapman. For readers with literary interests; all ages. Magazine; 12 (8½x5½) pages. Established in 1961. Monthly. Circulation: 500. Not copyrighted. Buys about 24 mss a year. Pays on publication. Will send free sample copy to writer on request, if a stamped, self-addressed envelope is enclosed. Will consider photocopied and simultaneous submissions. Reports in 1 month. Submit complete ms. Enclose S.A.S.E.
Nonfiction: "We use only interviews of well-known writers and biographical material on past writers. Very informal style; concise. Centennial or bicentennial pieces relating to a writer's birth, death, or famous works are usually interesting. Look up births of literary figures and start from there." Recently published "Writers As Conversationalists" which approached famous writers from a new point of view. Length: 1,000 words maximum. Pays ½¢ per word.

THE LITERARY TABLOID, 38 W. Main St., P.O. Box 198, Bergenfield NJ 07621. Editor: Iris Papazian. For readers interested in all aspects of life and literature. Magazine of tabloid size; 32 (11½x17) pages. Established in 1975. Every 2 months. Circulation: 20,000. Buys all rights, but will reassign rights to author after publication.

Buys about 75 mss a year. Pays on publication. Will send free sample copy to writer on request. Write for copy of guidelines for writers. No photocopied or simultaneous submissions. Reports in 4 to 6 weeks. Query first or submit complete ms. Enclose S.A.S.E.

Nonfiction: "Articles should take fundamental, analytical approach. They must analyze basic ideas and concepts without being esoteric or pedantic. Practically no restrictions on subject matter. But *no* sensationalism. Remember that this is a magazine for 20th Century Renaissance people. Our policy is to avoid sensational and superficial articles." Length: 2,000 to 5,000 words. Pays $50 to $100.

Fiction and Poetry: "Short stories should tell a story. We are open on themes." Length: 5,000 words maximum. Pays $50 to $100. "Poetry should be poetry — not prose in poetic form." Length: 32 lines maximum. Pays $5 to $20.

LONG ISLAND REVIEW, Box 10, Cambria Heights NY 11411. Editors: Stephen Sossaman and Edward Faranda. For those interested in contemporary literature and criticism. Biased only toward the well-crafted and intelligent. Published 3 times a year. Established in 1973. Circulation: 300. Acquires first or second (reprint) serial rights, and all rights returned to author. Payment in contributor's copies. Will consider photocopied submissions. "We're open to new writers, but send a cover letter telling us who you are. We advise writer to see a sample issue first." Will send sample copy to writers for $1. Uses 50 mss a year. Reports in 3 to 4 weeks. Enclose S.A.S.E.

Nonfiction: Literary criticism and articles on literature as craft or as art; any length. Book reviews to about 800 words. Seeks articles for occasional special issues which are announced in the magazine.

Fiction: Experimental or traditional. Length: 3,500 words maximum.

Poetry: Any form, style, or length, but content or message cannot make up for deficiencies in language. Poetry as social criticism, and poetry by Vietnam veterans.

MADRONA, 4332 4th N.E. #3, Seattle WA 98105. Editor: Charles Webb. Associate Editors: J.K. Osborne, Vassilis Zumbaras, John Levy. For readers interested in writing of highest literary quality. Published 3 times a year. 70-page magazine; (7x8½) page size. Established in 1971. Circulation: 500. Acquires all rights, but will reassign rights to author after publication. Uses 150 mss a year. Payment in copies or cash, depending on financial status, grants, etc. Will send sample copy to writer for $1.50. Will consider photocopied submissions. Will not consider simultaneous submissions. Reports on material accepted for publication in 1 month. Returns rejected material in 2 weeks. Submit complete ms. Enclose S.A.S.E.

Nonfiction and Photos: Reviews and essays, generally on literary matters. "We want interesting, lively (as opposed to inert) submissions. We encourage, among other things, intelligent humor." Translations. Reviews. Subject matter is wide open. Length: open. Pays in copies or a minimum of $5. Rate of payment is the same for b&w photos.

Fiction: Open to any genre, but writing must be of highest literary quality. Length: open. Pays in copies or a minimum of $5.

Poetry: All forms, including translations. Special interest in prose poems. Length and themes: open. Pays in contributor's copies or a minimum of $5.

MAGIC LANTERN, Union W302, 2200 E. Kenwood Blvd., Milwaukee WI 53201. Editor: Russell Solem. For university students, faculty and staff; film society officials, educators and film distributors involved in 16mm film programming. Semiannual magazine; 36 (8½x11) pages. Established in 1972. Circulation: 3,000. Acquires first North American serial rights. Payment in contributor's copies. Uses 4 mss per year. Will send free sample copy to writer on request. Will consider photocopied and simultaneous submissions. Reports in 1 month. Query first or submit complete ms. Enclose S.A.S.E.

Nonfiction and Photos: Articles on how to run a film program; booking films, handling films, running films. Technical articles on equipment. Historical pieces on the cinema; capsules on noted directors and important film people. Articles should be geared toward the film professional. "Our readers want to know how they can improve their presentation of films. We are interested in the specific problems connected with this end of the film trade. We are looking for a fresh approach, but no 'fan' material, please." Length: 1,000 to 2,500 words. Would like to see sketches on important film makers and material on film revivals by institutes or museums. Length: 1,000 to 1,500 words. No additional payment is made for b&w photos used with mss. Captions required.

MARK TWAIN JOURNAL, Kirkwood MO 63122. Editor: Cyril Clemens. For those interested in American and English literature. Semiannual. Not copyrighted. Pays in contributor's copies. Reports in 2 weeks. "Queries welcome." Enclose S.A.S.E.
Nonfiction and Poetry: Critical and biographical articles dealing with Mark Twain and other American, English, and foreign authors. Uses some poetry.

THE MASSACHUSETTS REVIEW, Memorial Hall, University of Massachusetts, Amherst MA 01002. Editors: Mary T. Heath and John Hicks. Quarterly. Buys first North American rights. Pays on publication. Reports promptly. Enclose S.A.S.E.
Nonfiction: Articles on literary criticism, public affairs, art, philosophy, music, dance. Average length: 6,500 words. Pays $50.
Fiction: Short stories or chapters from novels when suitable for independent publication. Pays $50.

MERLIN'S MAGIC, 419 91 St., Brooklyn NY 11209. Editor: Merlin F. Teed. Bimonthly. Publication on mimeographed sheets; not copyrighted. Payment in contributor's copy. Reports in 10 days to 2 weeks. Enclose S.A.S.E. for return of submissions.
Nonfiction, Fiction and Poetry: Articles on pertinent subjects of the day; editorials on writing; book reviews. Fiction is limited to short-shorts. Prefers poetry of 20 lines or less, but will consider longer poems.

MICHIANA CREATIVE ARTS REVIEW, Box 284, Route #3, Elkhart IN 46514. Editor: Marla Heim. For high school on up; all persons in northern Indiana and southern Michigan who are interested in the arts — writing, art, ceramics, photography, music. Quarterly magazine; 32 pages, (8½x11½). Established in 1973. Rights always revert to author on publication. No payment. Will send sample copy to writer for $1.25. Will consider photocopied submissions. Query first or submit complete ms. Reports within 3 weeks. Enclose S.A.S.E.
Nonfiction and Photos: "Articles related to the arts—new teaching methods, new and different ways or methods to encourage or enjoy creativity. We are the only publication devoted to the arts in our area. We stick with Indiana-Michigan writers, and hope to encourage participation and involvement here, besides helping writers by giving them a place to showcase their talent. We like how-to articles." Informational, how-to, interview, profile, think articles, photo features, and record and book reviews. Length: 10 typed pages usual maximum. Record reviews for "Wax Impressions" (regular column) should run from 2 to 6 typed pages. Photos accepted with or without ms. "We use photo spreads as a feature for that photographer. Sensitivity photos, new techniques, and unusual photo ideas."
Fiction: Short fiction on any subject. "We are new, and open to ideas." Experimental, mainstream, mystery, suspense, science fiction, humorous fiction. "We will be doing novels in condensed or serialized form on a subsidy basis only." Length: about 3 to 10 typed pages.
Poetry and Fillers: "We use about 20 poems per issue. We see too much rhymed poetry that says the same old thing. We prefer free verse and offbeat poetry." Also traditional forms and avant-garde forms. Shorter poems preferred. Also uses short humor and graffiti as fillers.

MICHIGAN QUARTERLY REVIEW, 3032 Rackham Bldg., University of Michigan, Ann Arbor MI 48104. Editor: Radcliffe Squires. Quarterly. Circulation: 2,000. Buys all rights. Payment on acceptance. Reports in 2 weeks. Enclose S.A.S.E.
Nonfiction: "The magazine will have a much more definitely literary bias under my editorship. But we are still open to general articles. We especially welcome serious

literary criticism." Length: 2,000 to 5,000 words. Payment is 2¢ a word (occasionally $100 to $300).

Fiction and Poetry: "No restrictions on subject matter or language. Experimental fiction welcomed." Length: 2,000 to 5,000 words. Payment is 2¢ a word (occasionally $200 to $300). Pays 50¢ to $1 a line for poetry.

THE MIDWEST QUARTERLY, Kansas State College, Pittsburgh KS 66762. Phone: 316-231-7000. Editor: Rebecca Patterson. For university, state, and big city libraries; students, professors, etc. Quarterly magazine, 120 pages, (6x9). Established in 1959. Circulation: 1,000. Acquires all rights; but will sometimes reassign rights to author after publication. "Our writers are almost exclusively academic personnel. We pay for no material; only in contributor's copies. Will send free sample copy to writer on request. Analytical literary articles for yearly July issue." Submit special material 6 to 9 months in advance. Submit only complete ms. Reports in 2 to 3 months. Enclose S.A.S.E.

Nonfiction and Poetry: "We publish one literary analysis number each July, and the others are a conglomeration of history, social sciences, occasional physical science in nontechnical language. Occasional nontechnical article on music or art. Write scholarly but without heavy documentation. No footnotes. We try to avoid the over-academic note. Length: 2,000 to 4,000 words. We also publish lyric poems, from a quatrain to some 200 to 300 lines."

MISSISSIPPI REVIEW, Box 37, Southern Station, Hattiesburg MS 39401. Phone: 601-266-7180. Editor: Gordon Weaver. For college students, educated general audience, libraries, and writers. Published 3 times a year. Magazine, 100 pages, (6x9). Established in 1972. Circulation: 400. Buys all rights, but will reassign rights to author after publication. Buys 95 mss a year. Payment on publication. Will send sample copy to writer for $1.75. Will consider photocopied submissions. Submit only complete ms. Reports in 2 to 3 months. Enclose S.A.S.E.

Fiction: Literary quality and seriousness; short fiction. "We like to feel we are more open, not committed to any clique, genre, etc." Experimental, mainstream, humorous, and historical fiction. Length: 500 to 5,000 words. Pays $3 per printed page.

Poetry: Traditional forms, blank verse, free verse, and avant-garde forms. Length: 2 to 1,000 lines. Pays $5 per poem.

MODERN FICTION STUDIES, Dept. of English, Purdue University, W. Lafayette IN 47907. Editors: William T. Stafford and Margaret Church. For students and academic critics and teachers of modern fiction in all modern languages. Quarterly magazine, 140 to 160 pages, (6x9½). Established in 1955. Circulation: 4,500. Acquires all rights, but with written stipulated agreement with author permitting him or her to republish anywhere, anytime as long as *MFS* is cited, and splitting 50/50 with him reprints by others of his agreed-to-be-reprinted material. No payment. Reports in 2 to 4 months. "Every other issue is a special issue. See current copy for future topics. Submit material anytime before announced deadline for special issue." Enclose S.A.S.E.

Nonfiction: Interested in critical or scholarly articles on American, British, and Continental fiction since 1880. Length: notes, 500 to 2,500 words; articles, 3,000 to 7,000 words.

MOJO NAVIGATOR(E), 423 S. Humphrey, Oak Park IL 60302. Phone: 312-386-5137. Editor: John Jacob. "Audience is heterogeneous. Interested in poetry, thought, and the arts." Published irregularly; averages 1 issue a year. 50 (5½x8½) pages. Established in 1969. Circulation: 500. Buys, or acquires, all rights, but will reassign rights to author after publication. Buys, or accepts, about 40 poetry mss and fewer nonfiction and fiction mss per year. Payment on publication or in contributor's copies. Will send sample copy to writer for $1. Will consider photocopied submissions. Will not consider simultaneous submissions. Submit special issue material 3 to 4 months in advance. Query first for nonfiction. Submit complete mss for poetry, fiction and short reviews. Enclose S.A.S.E.

Nonfiction: There's a possible interest here in articles on "the explosion of native American writing and publication that's recently developed." Occasionally uses interviews, exposes and poetry reviews. Themes of special issues vary and cannot be predicted. Does not want "cute" writing or religious themes. "A writer should be imaginative and willing to take chances. Nothing is safe here. I'd prefer a writer write for himself, not for me. We are opposed to any notion of thematic unity; the unity appears elsewhere. We publish nothing fanciful. We're serious." Length: 250 words minimum. Pays minimum of $5, or 1 copy of issue.
Fiction: Experimental. Themes open. Length: 100 to 5,000 words. Pays minimum of $5 or 1 copy of issue.
Poetry: Does not want to see traditional poems. Uses free verse, avant-garde forms or projective poems. Length: open, but very long poems are unlikely to be used. Pays $5 to $25 ($50 for special issues) or 1 contributor's copy of issue.

MOVING OUT: FEMINIST LITERARY AND ARTS JOURNAL, Wayne State University, 169 Mackenzie Hall, Detroit MI 48202. Cooperative editorship. For feminists; 18 and older. Journal; 75 (8½x11) pages. Established in 1970. 2 times a year. Circulation: 3,000. Rights acquired vary with author and material. Usually buys all rights, but may reassign rights to author after publication. Payment in contributor's copies. Will send sample copy to writer for $1. Will consider photocopied submissions. No simultaneous submissions. Reports in 4 to 6 months. Query first or submit complete ms. Enclose S.A.S.E.
Nonfiction and Photos: Timely articles (which are not quickly dated) of interest to women. Most contributors are feminists. Emphasis is on women in the arts. Articles/interviews with women artists, musicians, performers. "We've already had quite a few articles on growing up female and others on writers as housewives. We usually are not interested in literary criticism if the book has been out more than a year." Length: 500 to 3,000 words. Pays in copies. B&w photos are used with mss.
Fiction and Poetry: Experimental, mainstream. Serialized novels. Length: 500 to 3,000 words. Traditional and avant-garde forms of poetry. Length: open.

MUNDUS ARTIUM: A Journal of International Literature and the Arts, Ellis Hall, Ohio University, Athens OH 45701. Editor: Rainer Schulte. For all levels except the scholarly, footnote-starved type. Magazine; 160 (6x10) pages. Established in 1967. Semiannual. Circulation: 1,000. Buys all rights, but will reassign rights to author after publication. Buys about 50 mss a year. Pays on publication. Will send sample copy to writer for $3. Write for copy of guidelines for writers. Will consider photocopied submissions. No simultaneous submissions. Reports in 30 days. Submit complete ms. Enclose S.A.S.E.
Nonfiction and Photos: "In articles, we look for people who are able to talk about our non-traditional, conceptual kind of orientation from a broad, esthetic point of view. We like interdisciplinary emphasis. We don't want scholarly articles, kitsch, or social-political material, or descriptive, representational work." Length: open. Pays $15 to $100. Only avant-garde photography is acceptable.
Fiction: Experimental and fantasy. Must be non-traditional and conceptual. Length: open. Pays minimum of $5 per page.
Poetry: Avant-garde forms. Prefers to publish young, outstanding poets from the international and American scene who, as yet, are unrecognized. Pays minimum of $5 per page.
How To Break In: "Since we have a bilingual format, translations of contemporary international poets is a good way. Otherwise, creative work which goes beyond description and regional, national restrictions."

THE MYSTERY READER'S NEWSLETTER, P.O. Box 113, Melrose MA 02176. Editor: Lianne Carlin. For a diversified audience; persons who collect and read mystery fiction. Quarterly newsletter, 60 pages (8½x11). Established in 1967. Circulation: 500. Not copyrighted. Buys about 5 mss a year, "but would like more." Payment on publication. Will send sample copy to writer for $1. Will consider photocopied submissions and simultaneous submissions. Query first. Reports in 2 weeks. Enclose S.A.S.E.

Nonfiction and Photos: "Articles about the genre. No special style, but material must be well-researched. We are about the only publication covering our subject in-depth. Particularly interested in author checklists and interviews." Informational, interview, profile, historical, nostalgia, personal opinion, photo, mystery reviews, and spot news. Length: 500 to 2,000 words. Pays ½¢ per word. Also wants news about authors and new books in the genre. Length: 500 words. Pays $5 per column. B&w photos purchased with or without ms. Pays $1 each.

Poetry and Fillers: Traditional forms of poetry and light verse. Must relate to publication's theme. No length limits. Pays $1 to $2. Newsbreaks, puzzles related to mysteries, and clipping used as fillers. Pays $1 to $2.

NEBULA, 509 Lakeshore Dr., North Bay, Ontario, Canada P1A 2E3. Editor: Ken Stange. For readers interested in literature and the arts; writers. Magazine; 72 (8½x5¼) pages. Established in 1974. Twice a year. Circulation: 500 to 1,000. All rights revert to author. Uses about 20 mss per issue. Pays in contributor's copies. Will send sample copy to writer for $1. No photocopied or simultaneous submissions. Reports in 1 month. Submit complete ms. Enclose S.A.E. and International Reply Coupons.

Nonfiction: Literary criticism, reviews, opinion. Interviews, profiles.

Fiction, Poetry and Fillers: Interested in all forms of fiction and poetry. Open to all genres, but it must be well written. Will be doing thematic issues on "North" and "Canadian Lyric Poetry." Especially interested in formal innovation, i.e., structural innovation. Uses all types of puzzles as fillers, as well as jokes and short humor.

NEGRO AMERICAN LITERATURE FORUM, School of Education, Indiana State University, Terre Haute IN 47809. Editor: Hannah L. Hedrick. For people interested in critical and pedagogical articles on black literature. Quarterly magazine; 32 to 40 (8½x11) pages. Special issues planned: Africa, women, black prison literature, criticism and original works, genre issue, theme issue, single author issue. Established in 1967. Circulation: 700. Acquires all rights, but will reassign rights to author after publication. Payment in contributor's copies. Will send free sample copy to writer on request. Write for copy of guidelines for writers. Will consider photocopied submissions. Will not consider simultaneous submissions. Reports in 2 weeks. Submit complete ms. Enclose S.A.S.E.

Nonfiction and Photos: "Critical and pedagogical articles on black literature. We welcome controversial interpretations that invite an opposing point of view. We suggest consideration of authors and areas that are not frequently investigated. We would like to see critical studies of early Black American literary figures (Frances E. W. Harper, William Wills Brown, Frank J. Webb, Martin R. Delaney); of minor figures of the Harlem Renaissance (Nella Tarson, Ann Spencer, Georgia Johnson, Angelina Grimke, Frank Horns); and of very contemporary authors (those who began publishing in the 1970's). Women authors have been quite neglected (Ann Petry, Paula Marshall, Dorothy West), although Gwendolyn Brooks and Lorraine Hansberry have received a lot of attention. We are more interested in comparative (black/black, black/white, thematic, structural) studies or in thematic or structural analyses than in general studies. Except for minor figures, no biographical information is necessary unless it pertains directly to the theme of the article." Pays $75 for a group of 5 b&w photos of original art by black authors, purchased without accompanying ms. Works by black photographers also accepted.

Fiction and Poetry: Used as filler material. No payment.

THE NEW ENGLAND QUARTERLY, Hubbard Hall, Brunswick ME 04011. Editor: Herbert Brown. For historians and scholars. Established in 1928. Quarterly. Acquires all rights. Does not pay. Usually reports in 4 weeks. Enclose S.A.S.E. for return of submissions.

Nonfiction: Wants scholarly articles on New England life and letters. Length: "essays should be limited to 25 pages, including documentation."

THE NEW INFINITY REVIEW, P.O. Box 412, South Point OH 45680. Phone: 614-377-4182. Editor: James R. Pack. Manuscript Editor: Ron Houchin. For the lovers of new writing with "pizzazz and verve." Quarterly magazine; 44 (5½x8½) pages. Established in 1969. Circulation: 500. Acquires North American serial rights. Pays in contributor's copies. "We feature one writer in every issue." Will send free sample copy to writer on request. Write for copy of guidelines for writers. Will consider photocopied submission, "if readable." All submissions should be accompanied by a brief autobiography, stressing the individual and his/her unique personality, and including current activities and publication credits. Reports within 4 weeks. Enclose S.A.S.E.

Nonfiction and Photos: Essays and articles on literature, drama, motion pictures and art. Articles on psychic phenomena and the occult, myths and legends, and human sociology. Travelogues, personal narratives, personality studies and interviews. Accompanying photos or illustrations are also welcome. Length: 3,000 words maximum.

Fiction: Inclined toward the bizarre, outre, and science fiction. "We publish stories that are mentally exciting." Length: 4,000 words maximum.

Poetry: "Submit 4 to 12 poems to give us a clear perspective of your talent. Traditional forms are acceptable, if void of pedantry, sing-song, and dogma. Free verse, experimental or avant-garde forms welcome with the exception of pointless obscenity. We encourage all poetry approaching the visual. Imagism, nature description, mysticism, humor, and symbolism are also welcome. Translations are acceptable if accompanied with a typed copy of the original poem. No length limit."

How To Break In: "We especially need short reviews, 2 to 4 pages, of strange and/or exciting new movies, books, and record albums. Also good short fiction, 3 to 6 pages, especially humor and satire."

NEW LETTERS, 5346 Charlotte, Kansas City MO 64110. Managing Editor: Robert J. Stewart. For a library and college audience. Magazine: 128 (6x9) pages. Established in 1971. Quarterly. Buys all rights, but will reassign rights to author after publication. Pays on publication. Will send sample copy to writer for $2.50. No photocopied or simultaneous submissions. Reports in 2 weeks to 2 months. Query first or submit complete ms. Enclose S.A.S.E.

Nonfiction and Photos: Interested in expert commentary on contemporary social, political, and cultural subjects (analysis with peculiar insight). Prefers creative writing to scholarship. Literary reviews. Only typed material with a professional appearance. Pays $5 to $20. No additional payment for photos used with ms. Some photos are purchased without ms. Payment for these is minimum of $5.

Fiction and Poetry: Experimental and mainstream fiction of high quality. Length: short. Pays $5 to $20. Traditional and avant-garde forms of poetry. Blank verse and free verse. Pays $5 to $10.

NEW ORLEANS REVIEW, Loyola University, New Orleans LA 70118. Editor: Marcus Smith. For adult, college educated, anyone interested in literature and culture. Quarterly magazine, 96 pages, (9x13). Established in 1968. Circulation: 1,500. Buys all rights, but will reassign rights to author after publication, on request. Buys 200 mss a year. Payment on publication. Will send sample copy to writer for $1.50. Write for copy of editorial guidelines for writers. Will consider photocopied submissions. Query first or submit complete ms. Reports in 2 weeks to 2 months. Enclose S.A.S.E.

Nonfiction: General interest articles. Culture. Avoid too specialized literary analyses. Likes ecology, economics, current political topics. Informational, interview, profile, historical, think articles, personal opinion, and book reviews. Length: 5,000 to 10,000 words. Pays $50. Regular column, "Perspective", multiple book review with unifying topic. Length: 3,000 words. Pays $25. Nonfiction Editor: Peter Cangelosi.

Photos: 8x10 b&w glossies purchased with or without ms. Pays $10.

Fiction and Poetry: High quality fiction, any themes. Experimental and mainstream. Length: 5,000 to 10,000 words. Pays $50. Fiction Editor: Dawson Gaillard. Highest quality poetry. Length: 2 to 100 lines. Pays $10 to $20. Poetry Editor: Francis Sullivan.

NEW WRITERS, 507 Fifth Ave., New York NY 10017. Editors: Constance Glickman and Miriam Easton. For writers, students, educators. Magazine; 96 to 120 pages. Established in 1973. Quarterly. Circulation: 1,000. Buys all rights. Buys about 40 mss a year. Pays on publication. Will send sample copy to writer for $3. Write for copy of guidelines for writers. No photocopied or simultaneous submissions. Submit seasonal material 6 months in advance. Reports in 6 months. Query first for nonfiction; complete ms for fiction and fillers. "Supply brief autobiographical sketch, including educational background in writing; publications, if any. This is helpful, but not required." Enclose S.A.S.E.

Nonfiction and Fillers: Short critiques on stories published in *New Writers.* Length: 400 to 800 words. Pays $10. Short informal paragraphs of interest to the writing community. Pays $1. Also uses articles on writing insights and techniques of writing process, and letters for Open Forum.

Fiction: Quality short stories by student writers. Open on theme. No condensed or serialized novels. Pays $25 to $50.

THE NEW YORK CULTURE REVIEW, 4024 8th Ave., Brooklyn NY 11232. Editor: Daniel M. J. Stokes. Biweekly tabloid newsletter. Established in 1974. Circulation: 2,000. Usually buys first North American serial rights. Pays on publication. Will send sample copy to writer for $1. Write for copy of guidelines for writers. Reports within 1 month. Submit complete ms. Enclose S.A.S.E.

Nonfiction and Photos: Anything that will interest a culturally alive person; publishing, painting, interviews with people in the arts; science, politics, drama, literary criticism, ecology. Informational, profile, historical, think pieces, exposes, personal opinion. Length: 500 to 2,500 words. Pays ½¢ to 5¢ a word. 5x7 or 8x10 b&w glossies. Pays $10 to $25.

Fiction and Poetry: Experimental, avant-garde, science fiction, anything that hits the fiction editor. Length: 500 to 3,000 words. Pays ½¢ to 5¢ a word. No taboos for poetry. Pays 20¢ a line.

THE NEW YORK TIMES BOOK REVIEW, 229 West 43rd St., New York NY 10036. Weekly.

Nonfiction: "Occasional book reviews and essays. Almost all reviewing is done on an assignment basis."

NIMROD, University of Tulsa, 600 South College, Tulsa OK 74104. Editor: Francine Ringold. For professional people interested in good literature and art. Semiannual magazine; 96 (6x9) pages. Established in 1955. Circulation: 1,000. Acquires all rights but will return rights to author on request. Payment in contributor's copies. Will consider photocopied submissions, but they must be very clear. No simultaneous submissions. Reports in 3 to 6 months. Query first or submit complete ms. Enclose S.A.S.E.

Nonfiction: Interviews and essays. Length: open.

Fiction and Poetry: Experimental and mainstream fiction. Traditional forms of poetry; blank verse, free verse and avant-garde forms. "We are interested in quality and vigor. We often do special issues. Writers should watch for announced themes and/or query."

NORTH AMERICAN MENTOR MAGAZINE, 1730 Lincoln Ave., Fennimore WI 53809. Editor: John Westburg. For "amateur and experimental writers, students, teachers, professors, housewives, members of writers' clubs and societies, farmers, professional men and women, etc." Quarterly. Rights acquired vary with author and material; may acquire all rights. Payment in contributor's copies. Will send a sample copy to a writer for $1. Will consider photocopied submissions. Reports in 6 days to 6 months. Enclose S.A.S.E. for return of submissions.

Nonfiction: "Desire writing to be in reasonably good taste; traditional is preferable to the vulgar, but emphasis should be on creativity or scholarship. I know of no other of the small magazine genre that is like this one. We make no claim to being avant-garde, but have been accused of being a rear guard periodical, for we try to follow the general traditions of western civilization (whatever that might be).

Would be interested in readable articles on anthropology, archaeology, American Indians, black or white Africa. Do not want vulgarity or overworked sensationalism. No stuff on riots, protests, drugs, obscenity, or treason. We do not want to discourage a writer's experimental efforts. Let the writer send what he thinks best in his best style." Length: "maximum about 5,000 words."

Photos: "Please make inquiry about photographs in advance. We like to use them if they can be reproduced on multilith offset masters."

Fiction: "Short stories should have a plot, action, significance, and depth of thought, elevating rather than depressing; would be glad to get something on the order of Dickens, Thackeray or Dostoyevsky rather than Malamud, Vidal or Bellow. Sustained wit without sarcasm would be welcome; propaganda pieces unwelcome." Length: up to 5,000 words.

Poetry: Accepts traditional, blank and free verse, avant-garde and light verse. "Poetry from minority cultures." Length: "up to around 1,500 lines."

THE NORTH AMERICAN REVIEW, University of Northern Iowa, Cedar Falls IA 50613. Phone: 319-273-2681. Editor: Robley Wilson, Jr. Quarterly. Circulation: 3,000. Buys all rights for nonfiction and North American serial rights for fiction and poetry. Pays on publication. Will send sample copy for $1. Familiarity with magazine helpful. Reports in 8 to 10 weeks. Query first for nonfiction. Enclose S.A.S.E.

Nonfiction: No restrictions, but most nonfiction is commissioned by magazine. Rate of payment arranged.

Fiction: No restrictions; highest quality only. Length: open. Pays minimum $10 per page.

Poetry: No restrictions; highest quality only. Length: open. Pays 50¢ per line minimum. Dept. Editor: Peter Cooley.

NORTHWEST REVIEW, University of Oregon, Eugene OR 97403. Phone: 503-686-3957. Managing Editor: Michael Strelow. For literate people, high school and up. Strong university following nationally. Northwest emphasis often but not exclusively. Quarterly magazine, 128 pages, (6x9). Established in 1958. Circulation: 450. Buys first North American serial rights. Will send sample copy to writer for $1. Will consider photocopied and simultaneous submissions. Submit only complete ms. Reports within 3 months. Enclose S.A.S.E.

Nonfiction: "Generally by invitation. Reviews, primarily those of first books or those of special interest or small chance of wide circulation. Usually solicited." Nonfiction Editor: Jim Heynen. Pays $6 minimum for nonfiction; book reviews, usually.

Fiction: Experimental, quality literary, and novellas. Fiction Editor: Paul Scotton. Pays $1.50 per page.

Poetry: Traditional forms, blank and free verse, and avant-garde forms. Quality poetry only. Poetry Editor: Jim Heynen.

How To Break In: "It might be wise to query about book reviews to Jim Heynen, poetry and book review editor. We're especially interested in reviewing books out of small publishers and out of the West/Northwest. We try to give coverage to books which are not likely to receive coverage in popular media."

THE OHIO REVIEW, Ellis Hall, Ohio University, Athens OH 45701. Editor: Wayne Dodd. For the general, educated reader. Published 3 times yearly. Established in 1959. Circulation: 1,000. Rights acquired vary with author and material. Acquires all rights or first North American serial rights. Will send sample copy to writer for $2. Submit complete ms. Reports in 6 to 8 weeks. Enclose S.A.S.E.

Nonfiction, Fiction, and Poetry: Buys essays of general intellectual appeal. Seeks writing that is marked by clarity, liveliness, and perspective. Buys excellent fiction. Pays minimum 1¢ a word for nonfiction. Pays minimum $5 a page for poetry.

ONE, The Writer's Magazine of Fiction and Poetry, P.O. Box 1347, New Brunswick NJ 08903. Editor: Paul Freeman. For people who enjoy reading; high school and college students and teachers; men and women interested in good stories and poetry. Magazine; 56 digest-size pages. Established in 1973. Three times a year. Circulation: 500. Acquires first North American serial rights, but reassigns rights on request.

Uses about 15 mss a year. Pays in contributor's copies. Will send sample copy to writer for $1. Write for copy of guidelines for writers. Will consider photocopied submissions. No simultaneous submissions. Reports in 5 weeks. Submit complete ms. Enclose S.A.S.E.

Fiction and Poetry: "We've published science fiction, mysteries, and humor as well as 'straight' literary stories. We look for stories that are honest and emotionally stimulating." Experimental, mainstream, mystery, suspense, adventure, western, erotica, science fiction, fantasy, humorous, romance. Length: 5,000 words maximum. Traditional and avant-garde forms of poetry, blank and free verse. Length: open.

THE OPEN CELL, P.O. Box 5602, San Jose CA 95150. Editor: Milton Loventhal. For an educated audience, with intellectual interests; a large student readership. Published twice a year. Magazine, 8 pages, (11x18). Established in 1969. Circulation: 1,000. Acquires all rights, but will reassign rights to author after publication. Payment in contributor's copies. Will send sample copy to writer for 25¢. Editorial guidelines appear in each issue. Will consider photocopied and simultaneous submissions. Submit only complete ms. Reports in 2 months. Enclose S.A.S.E.

Nonfiction, Fiction, Photos, and Poetry: "We publish essays, short stories, and book reviews of no more than 10 pages in length. We publish poetry, songs, and b&w photos and drawings. Prefer well-crafted work that shows a detailed grasp of the complexities of modern life. Work that bears too much of the imprint of the academy is not of interest to us. We are less bound by academic traditions than other similar publications. We feel that American literary reviews and intellectual journals have by and large ignored the realities of American life and the complexities of American speech patterns." Think articles, personal opinion, and photo features. Length: 10 pages maximum. Nonfiction Editor: Jennifer McDowell. B&w photos purchased without accompanying ms. Captions optional. Experimental, fantasy, and humorous fiction. Length: 10 pages maximum. Fiction Editors: Paula Friedman and Harlan Jones. Traditional forms of poetry, blank verse and free verse, as well as avant-garde forms are considered. Submit no more than 6 poems per issue. Poetry Editor: Daniel Marlin.

OPINION, P.O. Box 1319, Dodge City KS 67801. Editors: Dr. James E. Kurtz and Sue Meyer. For readers from 18 and older; people who have an appetite for invigorating, inspiring, thought-provoking articles. Numerous teachers, clergymen, and professional people. Monthly magazine, 16 (8½x11) pages. Established in 1957. Circulation: 3,700. Not copyrighted. Uses about 38 mss a year. Pays in contributor's copies. Will send sample copy to writer for 30¢. Will consider photocopied submissions and simultaneous submissions. Submit complete ms. Reports in 3 to 5 weeks. Enclose S.A.S.E.

Nonfiction: "We publish articles dealing with social problems, philosophical themes, theological studies. Our articles are on current subjects but inspirational as well. Controversy but not just for the sake of being 'different'. Our writers believe in what they write. Be yourself. Take a deep subject and make it simple—don't write down to people but lift people up to a higher level of understanding. *Opinion* is down to earth. We carry some in-depth essays but for the most part we present to our readers, articles that hit the nail on the head. We are informal but we adhere to the old principles of good writing. Articles on marriage problems are a bit heavy and we prefer to see more material on philosophy and theology. Common sense philosophy. Particularly we want articles on religious adventure; new trends, new happenings." Informational, personal experience, profile, inspirational, historical, think articles, expose, nostalgia, personal opinion, spot news, and new product. Length: 3,000 words maximum.

Photos: Uses 5x7 or 8x10 b&w glossies. Captions optional.

Poetry: Traditional forms, free verse and light verse.

OUT THERE MAGAZINE, 552 25th Ave., San Francisco CA 94121. Editor: Stephen M. H. Braitman. For a literary audience with science fiction interests. Quarterly; 25 (8½x11) pages. Established in 1967. Circulation: 1,000. Acquires first North American serial rights. Uses 4 mss a year. Payment in contributor's copies. Will send sample copy to writer for 75¢. Will consider photocopied and simultaneous submissions. Reports in 1 month. Submit complete ms. Enclose S.A.S.E.

Nonfiction: Informational, interview, humor, historical, nostalgia, personal opinion and book and film reviews. Length: 1,500 words.

Fiction: Science fiction and fantasy; anything above the average of "tameness". Must be quality writing; literature, not pulp. Uses experimental, mainstream, mystery, suspense, adventure, erotica, science fiction, fantasy and humorous fiction. Length: 500 to 2,000 words maximum.

Poetry and Fillers: Traditional forms of poetry, blank verse, free verse, avant-garde forms; light verse. Length: open. Jokes and relevant short humor used as fillers.

THE PARIS REVIEW, 45-39 171 Place, Flushing NY 11358. Editor: George A. Plimpton. Quarterly. Buys all rights. Pays on publication. Address submissions to proper department. Enclose S.A.S.E. for return of submissions.

Fiction: Study publication. No length limit. Pays up to $150. Fiction should be sent to Flushing office. Makes awards of $500 and $250 in annual fiction contest.

Poetry: Study publication. Pays $10 to 25 lines; $15 to 50 lines; $25 to 100 lines; $50 thereafter. Poetry mss must be submitted to Michael Benedikt at 541 E. 72nd St., New York NY 10021.

PARTISAN REVIEW, Rutgers University, New Brunswick NJ 08903. Editor: William Phillips. Buys first rights. Reports in "3 months plus." Enclose S.A.S.E.

Nonfiction, Fiction and Poetry: Buys essays and reviews, as well as short stories. Pays 1½¢ a word. Pays 40¢ a line for poetry.

PEACE & PIECES REVIEW, P. O. Box 99394, San Francisco CA 94109. Editors: Efren Remirez, Maurice Custodio, William Keller, Phyllis Speros, and Todd S. J. Lawson. For multilingual and bilingual writers, artists and photographers. Magazine (8x10). Established in 1973. Quarterly. Circulation: 500 to 5,000. Buys all rights, but will reassign rights to author after publication. Time of payment varies, depending on grants. Will send sample copy to writer for 50¢. Write for copy of guidelines for writers. Will consider photocopied submissions. No simultaneous submissions. Reports in 2 to 5 weeks. Query first. Enclose S.A.S.E.

Nonfiction and Photos: Book reviews, essays, satire, humor. Informational, how-to, interview, profile, think pieces, nostalgia. "We're tired of ranting revolutionary/political writers unless exceptional. We do not like overly sentimental or didactic or religious material. We like funny, gay material or serious, gay work, well done." Length: 500 to 5,000 words. Pays $1 minimum. Grant Information column and poetry column use material of 500 to 2,000 words. Pays $1 minimum. B&w glossies purchased without ms. Prefers 4x4, but up to 8x10 acceptable. Pays $1 minimum.

Fiction: Experimental, science fiction, fantasy, humorous, small amount of erotica. Length: 1,500 to 10,000 words. Pays $1 minimum.

Poetry and Fillers: Traditional forms, blank verse, free verse, avant-garde forms of poetry. Pays $5 to $20. Jokes and short humor used as fillers. Length: 25 to 500 words. Pays $1 minimum.

THE PENNY DREADFUL, c/o The Department of English, Bowling Green State University, Bowling Green OH 43403. Editors: Randy M. Signor and Gordon Anderson. Tabloid format. Established in 1972. Triquarterly. Circulation: 500. "All rights returned to author after publication." Pays in contributor's copies. Will send a sample copy to a writer for 50¢. Reports in 2 weeks. Enclose S.A.S.E. for return of submissions.

Nonfiction, Fiction, Drama and Poetry: The editors encourage submission of poems, fiction, one-act plays, book reviews, interviews, and critical essays. No particular themes. Length: 500 to 3,500 words for fiction and nonfiction; 2 to 120 lines for poetry.

PERFORMING ARTS REVIEW, The Journal of Management and Law of the Arts, 453 Greenwich St., New York NY 10013. Editor: Joseph Taubman. Established in 1970. For lawyers, theater managers, academic libraries in law and arts. Quarterly.

Circulation: 2,200. Acquires primary or secondary U.S. or Canadian rights. Payment in contributor's copies (10 to each author). Will send free sample copy to writer on request. Will consider photocopied submissions. Reports in 2 months. Query first. Enclose S.A.S.E.

Nonfiction: "Articles on theater, law-management, and creativity in the arts. Academic outlook; professional tone. Writer should be experienced in the field of entertainment law or the theater (pro or amateur)." Length: 1,000 to 7,000 words.

THE PERSONALIST, School of Philosophy, University of Southern California, Los Angeles CA 90007. Editor: John Hospers. Quarterly. No honorarium. Follow the *MLA Style Sheet.* Put footnotes at end of article. Reports in approximately 4 months. Enclose S.A.S.E. for return of submissions.

Nonfiction: Uses critical articles pertaining only to the field of philosophy.

PERSPECTIVES, English Department, West Virginia University, Morgantown WV 26506. Phone: 304-293-5022. Editor: Arthur C. Buck. A page of literature, philosophy, and education. Associated with the Charleston *Gazette-Mail State Magazine.* Circulation: 100,000. Appears on a space-available basis, averaging once or twice a month. Buys first rights. Space for freelance material is strictly limited. Pays on publication. No sample copies available. Reports in 1 month. Enclose S.A.S.E.

Nonfiction: Short, informal essays on literature, philosophy, higher education, and linguistics. Interesting, informal style desired. Pays on the average of 2¼¢ per word. Length: 500 to 900 words preferred. Longer articles are occasionally used. Literary satire is sometimes used. Does not use scholarly articles.

Poetry: Length: 30 lines maximum. Any style. No payment.

THE PHOENIX, Morning Star Farm, West Whately, RFD Haydenville MA 01039. Editor: James Cooney. For readers in college, university and public libraries in this country and abroad. Quarterly journal magazine, 224 (5¼x7⅝) pages. Established in 1938. Circulation: 2,500. Acquires all rights, but will reassign rights to author after publication. Uses 30 to 40 mss a year. Payment in contributor's copies and honorary subscriptions. Will send sample copy to writer for $1.50. Write for editorial pamphlet. Will consider photocopied submissions and simultaneous submissions. Reports in 1 month. Enclose S.A.S.E.

Nonfiction, Fiction, and Poetry: "All forms of literature expressing compassion and pity and trust in humanity, resisting injustice and tyranny and seeding reconciliations. The central clue would be Promethean." Mainstream fiction of the human experience, and some serialized novels. Some poetry. No restrictions on length.

PIGIRON, Pigiron Press, P.O. Box 237, Youngstown OH 44501. Phone: 216-744-2258. Editor: Jim Villani. For readers interested in art and literature. Magazine, published 3 times a year; 64 (7x10) pages. Established in 1973. Circulation: 1,500. Acquires all rights, but will reassign rights to author after publication. Payment in contributor's copies. Will send sample copy to writer for $1. Will consider photocopied submissions. Will not consider simultaneous submissions. Reports in 4 to 8 weeks. Submit complete ms. Enclose S.A.S.E.

Nonfiction, Fiction, and Poetry: "Especially concerned with regeneration in the arts as the result of new and established artists maturing and mastering their craft. Equal emphasis on language forms (fiction, poetry, criticism, articles) and design forms (photography, engravings, pen and ink). We treat each issue of our magazine as a work of art in itself, not as another nugatory journal stilting the compositions of the artists we publish. There are no new subjects or themes, but there is a pervasive quality of newness infused in successful works of art. We strive to venerate that newness in the pages of *Pigiron.* Any topic or idea can be evolved into a work of art. We emphasize craft, not theme. Contemporary and experimental forms fare best, but we will publish any form or model if it is flexible and graphic." Length: open.

POCKET POETRY, P.O. Box 70, Key West FL 33040. Editor: Richard Marsh. For poets and anyone with a serious interest in the poetry being published in the

small press publications. Bimonthly; 48 (4¼x7) pages. Established in 1974. Circulation: 1,000. Acquires first serial rights for prose; second serial (reprint) rights for poetry. Uses about 50 mss a year. Pays in contributor's copies. Will send sample copy to writer for 75¢. Authors are invited to send tearsheets or photocopies of published poems. Reports in 1 to 2 months. Query first for reviews. Enclose S.A.S.E.
Nonfiction and Photos: "We use no original poetry. We reprint poetry from recent periodicals and books issued by the independent literary and university presses. Most of our material is sent by the editors and publishers. Brief (to 400 words) reviews, commentary, and dialog are welcome. B&w photos and other illustrations are used for the cover. Inside illustration is usually reprinted from another magazine to accompany a poem or review."

PRAIRIE SCHOONER, Andrews Hall, University of Nebraska, Lincoln NE 68508. Editor: Bernice Slote. Quarterly. Usually acquires all rights, unless author specifies first serial rights only. Payment is in copies of the magazine, offprints, and prizes. Reports usually in a month. Enclose S.A.S.E.
Nonfiction: Uses two or three articles per issue. Subjects of general interest. Seldom prints extremely academic articles. Length: 5,000 words maximum.
Fiction: Uses several stories per issue.
Poetry: Uses 20 to 30 poems in each issue of the magazine. These may be on any subject, in any style. Occasional long poems are used, but the preference is for the shorter length. High quality necessary.

PSYCHOLOGICAL PERSPECTIVES, 595 E. Colorado Blvd., Suite 503, Pasadena CA 91101. Editor: William O. Walcott. Biannual. Reprint rights remain with author. Payment in copies. Enclose S.A.S.E. for return of submissions.
Nonfiction: "Articles in a psychological framework." Length: 5,000 to 7,000 words.
Fiction: Psychological insights preferred. Length: 5,000 to 7,000 words. Dept. Editor: J'nan Sellery, Dept. of Humanities and Social Science, Harvey Mudd College, Claremont CA 91711.
Poetry: Criteria of excellence, clarity, beauty, profundity. Should clearly communicate an experience, with attention to freshness of image and phrase. Length: 40 lines maximum. Dept. Editor: J'nan Sellery, Dept. of Humanities and Social Science, Harvey Mudd College, Claremont CA 91711.

QUARTET, 1119 Neal Pickett Dr., College Station TX 77840. Phone: 813-846-9079. Editor: Richard Hauer Costa. For literate, urban, collegiate audience. Quarterly. Circulation: 1,000. Copyrighted. Acquires first rights only. Reprint rights revert to author provided *Quartet* receives credit line. Uses 100 mss a year. Payment in contributor's copies. Will send a sample copy to a writer for $1. Study recent issues (available at larger colleges, libraries, etc.) before submitting ms. Reports in 6 weeks. Enclose S.A.S.E.
Fiction: Any subject matter, however controversial, provided language is in good taste. Stress the integrity of the individual. "We prefer the well-crafted story but will often accept a sensibly experimental story. We sometimes have to hold stories up to 2 years before they get published in an issue." Length: "up to 6,000 words if quality is exceptional; most comfortable with fiction under 3,500 words but not 500-word anecdotes."

QUEEN'S QUARTERLY, Queen's University, Kingston, Ont., Canada. Editor: J.K. McSweeney. For well-informed readers both within and beyond Canada. Established in 1893. Quarterly. Buys or acquires first North American serial rights. Pays on publication. "Follow the *MLA Style Sheet* in preparing articles." Deadlines: Spring (January 2); Summer (April 1); Autumn (July 1); Winter (October 1). Reports in 3 weeks. Enclose S.A.E. and International Reply Coupons for return of submissions.
Nonfiction: Articles on literary, social, political, economic, educational and other subjects. "Articles must be well considered and show some distinction of presentation, and should be addressed to the intelligent and well-informed general reader, not to the specialist." Length: about 3,000 words. "We no longer pay for nonfiction but provide 50 free offprints."

Fiction: Short stories. Priority to Canadian authors. Length: 2,000 to 4,000 words. Pays $3 a printed page for fiction.
Poetry: "Shorter poems preferred. Priority to Canadian poets." Pays $10 per poem, regardless of length.

THE REMINGTON REVIEW, 505 Westfield Ave., Elizabeth NJ 07208. Editors: Joseph A. Barbato and Dean Maskevich. Published 2 times a year. All rights revert to author upon publication. Reports on material in 2 to 3 months, occasionally longer. Pays in contributor's copies. Enclose S.A.S.E.
Fiction, Poetry, and Photos: "A magazine of new writing and graphics; short stories, poems, parts of novels, and art which, we hope, have a spark of life. We will look at quality fiction and poetry of any school, by new as well as established writers. However, we tend to shy away from work that indicates the contributor has just learned how toes freeze when it gets too cold outside. But if you and your work are alive, by all means let us see something. We want to do what we can to bring promising talent and an appreciative audience together." Fiction length: 1,500 to 10,000 words. Fiction Editor: Joseph A. Barbato. Poetry length should not exceed 100 lines. Poetry Editor: Dean Maskevich. Drawings and photos suitable for b&w, offset reproduction.

RENASCENCE, Essays on Values in Literature, Marquette University, Milwaukee WI 53233. Editor: Dr. John D. McCabe. For college teachers of English, French and theology. Quarterly magazine, 56 (7x10) pages. Established in 1949. Circulation: 675. Acquires all rights. Payment in contributor's copies. Submit only complete ms for literary essays. Reports in 4 to 6 weeks. Enclose S.A.S.E.
Nonfiction: Scholarly and critical articles on literary works of the nineteenth century and, especially, of the twentieth century. Primarily devoted to the study of values in literature. Often invites papers on special topics through announcements in its issues. Length: 2,500 to 5,000 words.

REVISTA/REVIEW INTERAMERICANA, P.O. Box 1293, Hato Rey, Puerto Rico 00919. Editor: John Zebrowski. For "mostly college graduates and people with higher degrees." Established in 1971. Quarterly. Circulation: 2,000. Acquires all rights, "but will pay 50% of money received if reprinted or quoted." Uses 65 to 75 mss a year. Payment in reprints (25) mailed to author. Will send a sample copy to a writer on request. Query first or submit complete ms. Will consider photocopied submissions. Submit seasonal material at least 3 months in advance. Reports in 3 months. Enclose S.A.S.E. for return of submissions or reply to queries.
Nonfiction: "Articles on the level of educated laymen; bilingual. Also book reviews. Multi-disciplinary with preference to Puerto Rican and Caribbean and Latin American themes. Interested in material on ecology and environmental management; modern Puerto Rico; urbanization of Puerto Rico; 25th anniversary of the Commonwealth." Length: maximum 10,000 words.
Photos: B&w glossies, 4x5 minimum. Captions optional. No color.
Fiction and Poetry: "Bilingual; Spanish or English." Experimental, fantasy, humorous and historical fiction. Blank verse, free verse; experimental, traditional and avantgarde forms of poetry.

RIVER BOTTOM, BASEBALL, FLOATING, NICKLE TIMES, 1212 W. 4th Ave., Oshkosh WI 54901. Editor: R.C. Halla. For "all age groups; nonpolitical, past and future conscious; well-educated; artists and artisans." Yearly magazine; 50 (8½x7) pages, plus 3 broadsides. Established in 1973. Not copyrighted. Payment in contributor's copies. Will send sample copy to writer for $1.50. Write for copy of guidelines for writers. Will not consider photocopied submissions. Will consider simultaneous submissions. Reports on material accepted for publication in a minimum of 3 weeks. Returns rejected material in 2 to 3 weeks. Submit complete ms. Enclose S.A.S.E.
Nonfiction: "Any submissions we receive will be considered for all of our publications. *River Bottom* is published annually. The three broadsides are *Floating, Nickle Times* and *Baseball* (which has nothing to do with the sport). Our nonfiction interests are interviews and profiles, as well as reviews of fiction, films and poetry." Length:

500 to 2,000 words. "Although we pay only in contributor's copies, if there is any money left after each year's publishing, there will be prizes given for the best we have received."

Fiction: Experimental, mainstream, science fiction, fantasy. Length: 500 to 2,000 words. Department Editor: Janet Halla.

Poetry: Traditional forms, blank verse, free verse, avant-garde forms, earth poetry. Length: 1 to 50 lines. Department Editor: R. C. Halla.

ROMANCE PHILOLOGY, University of California, Berkeley CA 94720. Editor: Yakov Malkiel, Department of Linguistics. For college and university professors, including graduate students. Quarterly magazine, 120 pages. Established in 1947. Circulation: 1,200. Copyrighted. No payment. Write for copy of editorial guidelines for writers. Query first. Reports within 6 weeks. Enclose S.A.S.E.

Nonfiction: "Scholarly articles, notes, review articles, book reviews, brief reviews, editorial comments, and technical essays. Examine very carefully some of the recent issues." General linguistics, theory of literature, historical grammar; dialectology, textual criticism applied to older romance materials.

RUSSIAN LITERATURE TRIQUARTERLY, 2901 Heatherway, Ann Arbor MI 48014. Editors: Carl R. and Ellendea Proffer. For "readers of material related to Russian literature and art; students, teachers, Russian emigres." Established in 1971. 3 times a year. Circulation: 1,500. Acquires all rights. Uses 40 mss a year. "Most material is printed with payment in copies. When payment is made, the maximum is $200. Some poetry and photographs paid for; depends on name of writer." Will send sample copy for $5. Query first or submit complete ms. Will consider photocopied submissions. Reports on material in 3 weeks. Enclose S.A.S.E.

Nonfiction and Photos: Translations of Russian criticism, bibliographies, parodies, texts and documents from English literature. Critical articles. All in English. Informational, personal experience, interview, historical reviews. Pays maximum of $10 for b&w glossies or negatives. "Only requirement is relation of some kind to Russian art, literature."

THE RUSSIAN REVIEW, Hoover Institution, Stanford CA 94305. Editor: Terence Emmons. Journal; 128 pages. Established in 1942. Quarterly. Circulation: 1,850. Buys all rights, but will reassign rights to author after publication. Buys 2 or 3 mss a year. Pays on acceptance. Will send free sample copy to writer on request. Will consider photocopied submissions. No simultaneous submissions. Reports on material accepted for publication in 4 to 6 weeks. Returns rejected material immediately after decision is made. Query first. Enclose S.A.S.E.

Nonfiction: A forum for work on Russian-American and Soviet-American relations. Uses material of high quality in the fields of Russian history, politics and society, literature and the arts. Personal experience and historical articles. Scholarly reviews. Length: 2,500 to 7,500 words. Pays $50 minimum.

ST. CROIX REVIEW, Box 244, Stillwater MN 55082. Editor: Angus MacDonald. For a wide spectrum from college presidents to students. Published every two months; magazine, 48 (6x9) pages. Established in 1968. Circulation: 3,000. Acquires all rights. Payment in contributor's copies. Will send free sample copy to writer on request. Submit only complete ms. Reports in 2 weeks. Enclose S.A.S.E.

Nonfiction: "Articles must be germane to today's problems." Scholarly but not pedantic articles on religion and/or society for intelligent and concerned American and foreign audience. Must analyze and evaluate current problems in terms of West European intellectual heritage. Editorial viewpoint is classical liberalism. Length: 5,000 words maximum.

SALT LICK, Salt Lick Press, P.O. Box 1064, Quincy IL 62301. Phone: 217-222-1331. Editors: James Haining and Daniel Castelaz. For readers with an interest in new literature and new graphic arts. 68-page magazine with enclosures; published irregularly. Established in 1969. Circulation: 1,200. Acquires all rights. Payment in contributor's copies. Will send sample copy to writer for $1. Will consider photocopied

submissions. Reports within 2 weeks. Submit complete ms. Enclose S.A.S.E.
Nonfiction: Personal experience, interview, personal opinion. Literary reviews.
Fiction and Poetry: Experimental fiction and all forms of poetry. Themes and length open.

SAMISDAT, 1150 Spruce St., Berkeley CA 94707. Editor: Merritt Clifton. "Our audience is anyone we can interest. Mainly hard core literati; teachers, professors, gangsters, professional athletes, girl friends, housewives, publishing representatives, students and street people. Primarily young, primarily educated, and primarily alienated from both New York publishing and the conventional underground." Quarterly magazine; 75 (8½x5½) pages. Established in 1973. Circulation: 500. Not copyrighted. Uses 100 freelance mss a year. Payment in contributor's copies. Will send sample copy to writer for $1. Will not consider photocopied or simultaneous submissions. Reports on material accepted for publication in 1 month, and returns rejected material in 3 weeks, "as a rule, though we do have seasonal pileups delaying us at times." Submit complete ms. Enclose S.A.S.E.
Nonfiction: "Articles do not have to have a Berkeley radical or campus viewpoint. Should cover writing, especially the small press. No unsolicited reviews or interviews, but profiles of our major contributors are welcome. We get tired of juvenile socio-political lampoons. We're not an underground newspaper. Give us maturity. We're non-leftist and nonacademic. Write honestly and naturally. The writer trying to slant work toward us without having seen us is apt to be the first we reject." Length: 500 to 1,500 words, "but more, if we really like it." Payment in contributor's copies. Editor: Robin Michelle Clifton.
Fiction: Experimental, mainstream, suspense, adventure, western, science fiction, fantasy, humorous, romance, historical; serialized novels. "We love any good, short, hard-hitting fiction, with slight bias toward satire. Sharp love stories and realistic depiction of war. Our stylistic masters are Mikail Bulgakov, Ernest Hemingway and D. H. Lawrence. No Henry James. No James Joyce. No pussyfooting, but no porno either. Seems as if the energy crisis, population growth, and the approach of 1984 might provoke more good, speculative fiction." Length: 1,000 to 5,000 words. Department Editor: Tom Suddick.
Poetry: Traditional forms, blank verse, free verse, avant-garde forms, light verse, verse fiction, sonnets. "Poetry preferences are quite distinct. We like depth, but not obscurity. No language trips. Words are for saying things, not sacred entities unto themselves. Emotional impact and intellectual impact should form a solid one/two in fiction and poetry alike." Length: "wide open, within reason." Department Editor: John Coppock.

SAN JOSE STUDIES, San Jose State University, San Jose CA 95192. Editor: Arlene H. Okerlund. For the educated, literate reader. Academic journal; 112 (6x9) pages. Established in 1975. Three times a year; February, May and November. Circulation: 2,000. Acquires all rights, but will reassign rights to author after publication. Uses 30 to 40 mss a year. Pays in contributor's copies. Will send sample copy to writer for $3.50. No photocopied or simultaneous submissions. Reports in 2 to 3 months. Submit complete ms. Enclose S.A.S.E.
Nonfiction and Photos: In-depth, erudite discussions of topics in the arts, humanities, sciences, and social sciences. Review essays of authors. Informational, interview, profile, humor. Photo essays can be free-wheeling. "We receive too few science articles and would like to publish more than we do." Recently published articles on William James and Stanford University; W. E. B. DuBois and the struggle for women's rights; amphetamines and hyperkinetic children. All presented previously unknown information. Length: 5,000 words maximum. Payment consists of 2 copies of the journal.
Fiction and Poetry: Experimental, mainstream, fantasy, humorous, historical and science fiction. Length: 5,000 words maximum. Traditional and avant-garde forms of poetry; blank verse and free verse. Themes and length are open.

SCHOLIA SATYRICA, Department of English, University of South Florida, Tampa FL 33620. Editor: R. D. Wyly. For professors of English in American universities and scholars having an interest in satire. Magazine; 48 (5½x8½) pages. Established in 1975. Quarterly. Acquires first North American serial rights or second serial (reprint) rights. Uses about 48 mss a year. Pays in contributor's copies. Will send sample copy to writer for $1. Will consider photocopied submissions. Reports in 1 month. Submit complete ms. Enclose S.A.S.E.

Nonfiction: Serious, critical articles on the nature of satire itself, and original satire that mocks the scholarly community, its four horsemen, and its sacred cows.

Fiction, Poetry and Fillers: Humorous fiction and erotica. Length: 5,000 words maximum, but prefers shorter material. Satiric blank verse and free verse; avant-garde forms of poetry. Length: 30 lines maximum. Satiric fillers.

SCIMITAR AND SONG, Box 151, Edgewater MD 21037. Editor: Dr. Jean Sterling. Quarterly. Features special issues on ecology, poetry in other countries, and youth's voice. Acquires first rights. Pays in copies. Will send a sample copy to a writer for $2. Query first "for articles." Submit seasonal material "as soon as possible in advance." Reports in 2 to 3 weeks. Enclose S.A.S.E.

Nonfiction and Fiction: Inspirational and historical articles, humor, travel pieces. Fiction desired includes mystery, science fiction, adventure, historical, humorous, contemporary problems, religious, and juvenile. Length is determined by type and content of article or story.

Poetry: Traditional, contemporary, avant-garde, light verse. "No restriction on length. Annual cash prizes and trophies for best published poems."

Fillers: Puzzles, short humor on poets, writers, or poetry. Length: 50 words.

SECOND COMING, P.O. Box 31246, San Francisco CA 94131. Editor: A. D. Winans. Magazine, 72 pages (5½x8½). Published 2 times a year. Established in 1972. Circulation: 1,000. Acquires all rights, but will reassign rights to author after publication. Uses over 100 mss a year. Payment in contributor's copies; $5 token payment for reviews and interviews. Will send sample copy to writer for $1. Will consider photocopied submissions. Will not consider simultaneous submissions. Submit only complete ms. Reports within 4 weeks. Enclose S.A.S.E.

Nonfiction and Photos: "Articles on art and personalities in the arts. Political pieces that are well researched. Study the magazine. Would suggest reading two or more issues before submitting as each issue changes format. Like any magazine, the tone is generated and determined by the likes and dislikes of the editor. I try not to be prejudicial against any school of writing, but let's face it—we're all human and I'd be lying if I said that concrete poetry has much chance with *Second Coming*, when in fact it does not." Interviews, profile, expose, photo, and reviews of personalities in the arts. B&w photos. Artwork and photography also wanted.

Fiction and Poetry: Avant-garde short stories, and poetry of all schools including rhyme. Experimental, science fiction, fantasy, and humorous fiction wanted. Length: 500 to 3,000 words, and occasionally longer. Traditional forms of poetry, blank verse and free verse, avant-garde forms and light verse.

THE SENECA REVIEW, Hobart and William Smith Colleges, Geneva NY 14456 or c/o Ira Sadoff, 718 Jacoby Rd., Xenia OH 45385. Editors: Ira Sadoff, James Crenner. Biannual magazine; 84 (5½x8½) pages. Established in 1970. Circulation: 1,000. Buys all rights, but will reassign rights to author after publication. Buys 100 mss a year. Payment on publication. Will send sample copy to writer for $1.25. Will not consider photocopied or simultaneous submissions. Reports in 4 to 6 weeks. Submit complete ms. Enclose S.A.S.E.

Fiction: Must be of high literary quality. No soap opera type stories. "Writers should see the magazine before submitting." Length: no longer than 25 mss pages. Pays $25.

Poetry: Free verse. Translations of contemporary poetry. No light verse. No rhymed verse. Length: open. Pays $5 per published page.

SEWANEE REVIEW, University of the South, Sewanee TN 37375. Phone: 615-598-5142. Editor: George Core. For audience of "variable ages and locations, mostly college-educated and with interest in literature." Quarterly. Circulation: 3,900. Buys all rights. Pays on publication. Will send a sample copy to a writer for $2.75. Returns rejected material in 2 months. Enclose S.A.S.E. for return of submissions.

Nonfiction and Fiction: Short fiction (but not drama), essays of critical nature on literary subjects (especially modern British and American literature), essay-reviews and reviews (books and reviewers selected by the editors). Payment varies: averages $10 per printed page.

Poetry: Selections of 4 to 6 poems preferred. In general, light verse and translations are not acceptable. Maximum payment is 60¢ per line.

THE SHAKESPEARE NEWSLETTER, University of Illinois at Chicago Circle, English Department, Chicago IL 60680. Editor: Louis Marder. For professors of English and Shakespeare enthusiasts. Published 6 times per academic year. Established in 1951. Circulation: 2,150. Not copyrighted. Payment in contributor's copies. Will send sample copy to writer for 60¢. Will consider photocopied submissions. Will not consider simultaneous submissions. Query first or submit complete ms. "Send the conclusions and I will tell you if I want the facts." Enclose S.A.S.E.

Nonfiction: Solid, original articles. Wants new facts on Shakespeare. Scholarly, yet popular. Length: 1,500 words maximum.

Poetry and Fillers: Occasional poems. No abstract poetry. Shakespeare only; anything that works. Length: 20 lines maximum. Newsbreaks, clippings, jokes, and short humor. Length: 75 words or so.

SHAW REVIEW, S234 Burrowes Bldg., University Park PA 16802. Phone: 814-865-4242. Editor: Stanley Weintraub. For scholars and writers and educators interested in Bernard Shaw and his work, his milieu, etc. Published 3 times a year. Established in 1950. Circulation: 1,000. Acquires all rights, but will reassign rights to author after publication. Payment in contributor's copies. Will consider photocopied submissions. Submit only complete ms. Reports within 2 months. Enclose S.A.S.E.

Nonfiction: "There's no other journal in this very special field. Writers should consult sample copies and find something useful to say about George Bernard Shaw." Length: 5,000 words maximum.

THE SILENT PICTURE, First Media Press, 6 E. 39th St., New York NY 10016. Phone: 212-679-8230. Editor: Anthony Slide. For silent film enthusiasts, film collectors, film teachers, film historians, libraries, museums, film schools. Quarterly magazine; 60 (8x10) pages. Established in 1968. Circulation: 2,000. Acquires all rights. Uses 20 mss a year. Payment in contributor's copies. Will send sample copy to writer for $1. Will consider photocopied and simultaneous submissions. Reports in 2 weeks. Query first. Enclose S.A.S.E.

Nonfiction: Interviews with silent film stars; film reviews; articles about actors, actresses, directors, cameramen, etc. Filmographies; bibliographies. Special interest in interviews with anyone connected with silent films. "We turn down many articles from writers who wish to reminisce about silent films as they remember them. We can only use factual, well-researched and well-written articles that contribute to silent film scholarship." Length: open. Payment is usually made in contributor's copies. "We only pay for exceptional articles."

THE SMALL POND MAGAZINE OF LITERATURE, 10 Overland Dr., Stratford CT 06497. Phone: 203-378-9259. Editor: Napoleon St. Cyr. For "high school students, mostly poets, the rest college and college grad students who read us in college libraries, or in general the literati." Published 3 times a year. 40 pages; (5½x8½). Established in 1964. Circulation: 300. Acquires all rights. Uses about 100 mss a year. Payment in contributor's copies. Will send sample copy to writer for $1. Will consider photocopied submissions. Will not consider simultaneous submissions. Query first or submit complete ms. Reports within 1 month. Enclose S.A.S.E.

Nonfiction, Photos, and Poetry: "About two-thirds poetry, the rest is open to any and all subjects, essays, articles, and stories such as you'd find in *Harper's, Atlantic,* etc. We've had an uncanny knack for discovering talent which has gone on and risen rapidly in the literary field. We don't want anything on the high school and college drug scene, or fiction based on 'love story'. Particularly interested in authoritative inside exposes (not rabid yellow journalism) of some aspect of business, government, international affairs, or even the world of literature and performing arts." Nonfiction length: 2,500 words maximum. Experimental, mainstream, fantasy, historical, and humorous fiction. Length: 200 to 2,500 words. Traditional and avant-garde forms of poetry, blank, free and light verse. Length: 100 lines maximum.

SMALL PRESS REVIEW, P.O. Box 1056, Paradise CA 95969. Editor: Len Fulton. Associate Editor: Ellen Ferber. For "people interested in small presses and magazines, current trends and data; many libraries." Monthly. Circulation: 2,500. "All rights belong to author, but we do copyright the magazine." Accepts 50 to 100 mss a year. Pays on publication. Will send a sample copy to a writer on request. "Query if you're unsure." Reports in 1 to 2 months. Enclose S.A.S.E. for return of submissions or reply to queries.

Nonfiction and Photos: "News, reviews, photos, articles on small magazines and presses and underground papers. Get the facts and know your mind well enough to build your opinion into the article." Uses how-to's, personal experience articles, interviews, profiles, spot news, historical articles, think pieces, photo pieces, and coverage of merchandising techniques. Length: 100 to 500 words. Pays 1¢ to 2¢ a word, "or on arrangement." Uses b&w glossy photos.

THE SMITH, 5 Beekman St., New York NY 10038. Editor: Harry Smith. For students, writers, professors, librarians, others who are interested in literature as art and revolutionary thought. 3 book-size issues, plus supplements. Book format magazine. Established in 1964. Circulation: 2,500. Buys first North American serial rights and second serial (reprint) rights. Buys 200 mss a year. Payment on acceptance. Will send free sample copy to writer on request. Will consider photocopied and simultaneous submissions. Query first for nonfiction. Submit complete ms for fiction and poetry. Reports within 4 weeks. Enclose S.A.S.E.

Nonfiction: Speculative essays. No taboos. Length: 5,000 words or less. Payment is "modest," by arrangement. Dept. Editor: Sidney Bernard.

Fiction and Poetry: Long stories and novellas as well as short-shorts and vignettes of under 2,000 words. Modest payment by arrangement. Fiction Department Editor: Raphael Taliaferro. Has published poems as long as 52 pages. Pays $5 per short poem.

How to Break In: "The only thing I can say about the trend in this office in the use of over-the-transom mss is that the best chance lies in poetry and fiction. We don't tend to encourage new people to do reviews for a couple of reasons — they usually tend to be too formalistic and conventional (in the style of *Saturday Review, The Yale Review,* or *The New York Review*), and besides we have a number of people in the office and outside who have been doing them. Newcomers might want to try their hands at topical essays, perhaps with a polemical stroke, on the aesthetics of literature. But query first. I should point out that we prefer the unknown to the known. It's partly the sense of discovery — that's very important here — and also because we're not that crazy about many of the knowns."

SOUTH AND WEST, 2406 South S St., Ft. Smith AR 72901. Editor: Sue Abbott Boyd. Quarterly. Acquires North American serial rights only. Pays in contributor's copies. Will send sample copy to a writer for $1. Reports in a month. Enclose S.A.S.E.

Nonfiction: Book reviews, scholarly articles on poetry. Length: open.

Fiction: Will use a timely or experimental short story. Can be on "any subject treated with good taste except 'I Love God' themes. We will even consider imaginative God themes, if a new dimension is offered that relates to humanity, the arts, culture, and education." Length: to 2,000 words.

Poetry: "The purpose of the magazine is to encourage new poets as well as give voice to those already established. Emphasis is on modern poetry, expression of new and young thought. This does not, however, mean prejudice against traditional poetry. All types of poems receive equal consideration. We prefer work that is individualistic, that reflects the personality of the writer. No subject is taboo that is handled in good taste. We prefer freshness to merely skillful execution of form. Poetry preferably not exceeding 37 lines, but will not reject a good, long poem."

SOUTH ATLANTIC QUARTERLY, Box 6697, College Station, Durham NC 27708. Editor: Oliver W. Ferguson. For the academic profession. Quarterly. No payment. Proceeds of sale of rights to reprint divided with author. Reports in 6 weeks. Enclose S.A.S.E. for return of submissions.
Nonfiction: Articles on current affairs, literature, history and historiography, art, education, essays on most anything, economics, etc.—a general magazine. No taboos. Length: 2,000 to 5,000 words.

THE SOUTH CAROLINA REVIEW, Department of English, Clemson University, Clemson SC 29631. Editors: R. Calhoun, R. Hill, W. Koon. Established in 1965. Circulation: 500. Acquires all rights, but will reassign rights to author after publication. Uses about 30 mss a year. Payment in contributor's copies. Will send free sample copy to writer on request, if available. Will consider photocopied and simultaneous submissions. Submit seasonal material 3 months in advance. Reports on material accepted for publication within 2 months. Returns rejected material within 1 month. Submit complete ms. Enclose S.A.S.E.
Nonfiction: Critical essays on most literary topics; interviews and book reviews. "For the critical essays, we observe the *MLA Style Sheet.* Otherwise, we have no special requirements, though we find it hard to run pieces over 20 pages of typescript." **Fiction and Poetry:** No restrictions as to category or type.

SOUTH DAKOTA REVIEW, Box 11, University Exchange, Vermillion SD 57069. Phone: 605-677-5220. Editor: John R. Milton. For a university audience and the college educated, although reaches others as well. Quarterly. Acquires North American serial rights and reprint rights. Pays in contributor's copies. Will send sample copy to writer for 50¢. Reports within 4 weeks. Enclose S.A.S.E.
Nonfiction: Prefers, but does not insist upon, Western American literature and history; especially critical studies of western writers. Open to anything on literature, history, culture, travel, the arts, but selection depends on patterns and interests of individual numbers within each volume. Contents should be reasonably scholarly, but style should be informal and readable. All well-written mss will be considered. Length: 6,000 words maximum, but at times has used longer.
Fiction: Western setting preferred (Great Plains, Rockies, Southwest), but receptive to almost anything that is disciplined and original. Quality is more important than subject or setting. No excessive emotions. Rarely uses hunting, fishing, or adolescent narrator or subject studies. Open to paramyth, Jungian treatments, serious themes. Length: 6,000 words maximum, but has used longer at times.
Poetry: Prefers poetry which is disciplined and controlled, though open to any form (tends to prefer traditional free verse). Any length considered, but prefers 10 to 30 lines.

THE SOUTHERN REVIEW, Drawer D, University Station, Baton Rouge LA 70803. Editors: Donald E. Stanford and Lewis P. Simpson. For academic, professional, literary, intellectual audience. Quarterly. Circulation: 3,000. Buys first rights. Pays on publication. Will send sample copy to writer for $1.50. No queries. Reports in 2 to 3 months. Enclose S.A.S.E. for return of submissions.
Nonfiction: Essays; careful attention to craftsmanship and technique and to seriousness of subject matter. "Willing to publish experimental writing if it has a valid artistic purpose. Avoid extremism and sensationalism. Essays exhibit thoughtful and sometimes severe awareness of the necessity of literary standards in our time." Emphasis on contemporary literature, especially Southern culture and history. Minimum number of footnotes. Length: 4,000 to 10,000 words. Pays 3¢ per word minimum.
Fiction and Poetry: Short stories of lasting literary merit, with emphasis on style and technique. Length: 4,000 to 8,000 words. Pays minimum of 3¢ per word. Pays $20 per page for poetry.

SOUTHWEST REVIEW, Southern Methodist University, Dallas TX 75275. Phone: 214-692-2263. Editor: Margaret L. Hartley. For adults, college graduates, literary interests, some interest in the Southwest, but subscribers are from all over America

and some foreign countries. Quarterly magazine; 120 pages, (6x9). Established in 1915. Circulation: 1,000. Buys all rights, but will reassign rights to author after publication. Buys 65 mss a year. Payment on publication. Will send free sample copy to writer on request. Query first for nonfiction. Submit only complete ms for fiction and poetry. Reports within 3 months. Enclose S.A.S.E.
Nonfiction and Photos: "Articles, literary criticism, social and political problems, history (especially Southwestern), folklore (especially Southwestern), the arts, etc. Articles should be appropriate for a literary quarterly; no feature stories. Critical articles should consider a writer's whole body of work, not just one book. History should use new primary sources or a new perspective, not syntheses of old material. We're regional but not provincial." Interviews with writers, historical articles, and book reviews of scholarly nonfiction. Length: 1,500 to 5,000 words. Pays ½¢ a word. Regular columns are Regional Sketchbook (southwestern) and Points of View (excellent personal essays). Uses b&w photos only occasionally for cover.
Fiction: No limitations on subject matter for fiction. No experiences of adolescents—that's overworked. Experimental (not too far out), and mainstream fiction. Length: 1,500 to 5,000 words. Pays ½¢ per word. The John H. McGinnis Memorial Award is made in alternate years for fiction and nonfiction pieces published in *SR*.
Poetry: No limitations on subject matter. "We don't care for most religious and nature poetry." Free verse, avant-garde forms (not too far out), and open to all serious forms of poetry. Length: prefers 18 lines or shorter. Pays $5 per poem.

SPAFASWAP (incorporating *Guardino's Gazette*), 1070 Ahern, LaPuente CA 91746. Phone: 213-962-3910. Editor: Lois J. Long. Published 6 times a year. Circulation: 400. Copyrighted. Uses 300 mss a year. Pays in contributor's copies. Will send sample copy to writer for 50¢. Reports promptly. Enclose S.A.S.E.
Poetry: Traditional forms, free verse, and light verse. No porno. Short, cogent, brittle poetry. No restrictions as to length, but prefers short poems.
Nonfiction and Fiction: Prefers light topics; happy stories. Length: 200 to 300 words.

STAR WEST, P.O. Box 731, Sausalito CA 94965. Editor: Leon Spiro. Semiannual newspaper, with mini-supplements. Established in 1963. Circulation: 5,000. Not copyrighted. Payment in contributor's copies. Will send sample copy to writer for $1. Reports in 2 to 4 weeks. Enclose S.A.S.E.
Nonfiction: Published in 9 languages. Approach should be "dynamic only. Current events, international impact." Inspirational, humor, spot news, think pieces, exposes.
Poetry: Traditional, contemporary, avant-garde, light verse, surrealism. "Poetry that's dynamic, from Black English to haiku." Length: 30 lines maximum.

STONECLOUD, 1906 Parnell Ave., Los Angeles CA 90025. Editor-in-Chief: Dan Ilves. Co-editor: Rick Smith. A journal of literary and artistic effort, the basic purposes of which are genuine communication and human development, thus open to numerous topics. Designed to appeal to public consciousness as well as to professionals in many different areas and to promote an understanding of unity within and between the arts and other fields. Primarily for college students, artists, professionals, and general public community. Established in 1972. Published annually. Circulation: 5,000. Copyrighted but no rights purchased. Payment in contributor's copies. Will send sample copy to writer for $1.50. Will consider photocopied submissions. Submit complete ms. Enclose S.A.S.E.
Nonfiction, Photos, and Graphics: Anything that deals with or reflects "creativity", human development, or toward the expansion of awareness and understanding. Any structure, any style, preferably constructive and of a positive outlook. Personal experience, interview, profile, personal opinion, inspirational, humor. Maximum length: 7,000 words. B&w photos and graphics, no larger than 8½x11 preferred.
Fiction: Experimental, science fiction, fantasy, mystery, suspense, adventure, erotica, humorous, romance. Length: 5,000 words maximum.
Poetry and Fillers: Blank verse, free verse, avant-garde, traditional forms. Maximum length: 500 words. Clippings.
How To Break In: "We prefer to see work aimed at raising the public consciousness to a higher understanding and appreciation of the arts."

STREET CRIES MAGAZINE, Box 210, Old Westbury NY 11568. Editors: Robbie Woliver and Patricia Velazquez. National bi-lingual literary and arts magazine; 100 (8½x5½) pages. "In the past we have had special men's consciousness and women's consciousness issues, and are planning a special Latin issue, prison issue and children's issue." Established in 1972. 3 times a year. Circulation: 5,000. All rights revert to authors/artists. Uses 400 mss a year. Pays in contributor's copies. Will send a sample copy to writer for $2. Will consider photocopied and simultaneous submissions. Reports in 3 months. Submit complete ms. Enclose S.A.S.E.

Nonfiction and Photos: Bilingual publication (English and Spanish) using personal experience, historical, expose, interviews and book reviews. Length: 2,000 words maximum. Accepts only creative photography.

Fiction and Poetry: Experimental, mainstream, erotica, fantasy, and humorous fiction. Length: 2,000 words maximum. All forms of poetry.

STUDIES IN THE TWENTIETH CENTURY, The Whitston Publishing Co., P.O. Box 12, Troy NY 12181. Phone: 518-283-4363. Editor: Stephen Goode. For an exclusively scholarly/critical audience. Subscribers are almost exclusively college and research libraries. Semiannual magazine. 100 (6x9) pages. Established in 1968. Circulation: 350. Acquires all rights, but will reassign rights to author after publication. Payment in 25 offprints plus 3 copies. Submit seasonal material 12 months in advance. Reports in 1 month. Query first or submit complete ms. Enclose S.A.S.E.

Nonfiction: Scholarship and criticism surrounding the movements of the art and literature of the 20th century, especially the philosophy of those movements. "In general, specific themes or detailed analyses of this novel or that poem by a given author are not sought."

SUNDAY CLOTHES, A Magazine of the Arts, Box 66, Hermosa SD 57744. Editor: L. M. Hasselstrom. For well-educated and culturally interested audience. Established in 1972. Quarterly tabloid. Circulation: almost 2,400. Acquires North American serial rights and reprint rights. Uses about 75 mss a year. Payment in 1 contributor's copy. Will send sample copy for $1.10. Will consider photocopied submissions. Submit seasonal material 3 to 4 months in advance. Reports on material in 3 weeks. Submit complete ms. Enclose S.A.S.E.

Nonfiction and Photos: "We want both well-known and unknown writers. Articles by or about artists and writers; interviews, book reviews." Length: up to 6,000 words. 5x7 or 8x10 b&w glossy or matte photos.

Fiction: Experimental, mainstream, fantasy, western, humorous, condensed novels, serialized novels. Length: not over 8,000 words.

Poetry: Traditional forms, short verse, free verse, avant-garde forms and light verse. Length: open.

SUNSTONE REVIEW, P.O. Box 2321, Sante Fe NM 87501. Editors: Sandra Edelman, Wm. Farrington. Editor-in-Chief: Jody Ellis. Established in 1971. Quarterly. Circulation: 500. Acquires all rights, but will give permission to reprint. Payment in contributor's copies. Will send sample copy to writer for $1.50. Reports in 6 weeks. Enclose S.A.S.E.

Nonfiction, Fiction, Poetry, and Photos: "Interested in new writers as well as those well known. Material selected on merit only. Accepts poetry (any form, any length), short fiction, b&w photos, drawings, criticism and short articles."

THOUGHT, The Quarterly of Fordham University, Fordham University Press, Box L, Fordham University, The Bronx NY 10458. Editor: Rev. Joseph E. O'Neill, S.J., Ph.D. Acquires all rights. Payment in copies. Reports within a month. Enclose S.A.S.E.

Nonfiction and Poetry: A review of culture and idea, *Thought* discusses questions of permanent value and contemporaneous interest in every field of learning and culture in a scholarly but not excessively technical way. Articles vary from 5,000 to 10,000 words. Publishes a page or two of poetry in each issue.

TRANSATLANTIC REVIEW, Box 3348, Grand Central Station, New York NY 10017. Editor: Joseph F. McCrindle. For American and English audience. Quarterly.

Established in 1959. Circulation: 3,000. Copyright assigned to author on publication at request. Buys first serial rights. Pays on acceptance "as arranged." Will send a sample copy to a writer for $1.50. Reports in 4 weeks—"sometimes longer with volume." Enclose S.A.S.E. for return of submissions.
Fiction: Short stories of literary quality. Length: 4,500 words maximum.
Nonfiction: Limited to interviews with theatrical and film writers and directors.

TRI-QUARTERLY, University Hall, 101 Northwestern University, Evanston IL 60201. Editor: Charles Newman. 3 times yearly. For an intellectual and literary audience. "Our format is extremely eclectic. The tone and intentions of each issue may vary." Buys first serial rights. Reports on unsolicited mss within eight weeks; solicited mss immediately. Pays on publication. Study publication before submitting mss; enclose S.A.S.E.
Fiction and Photos: No length limits. "We are not committed to the short story as the only publishable form of fiction. Frequently excerpts from longer works tell us more about an author and his work." Payment at $10 per page if possible. Occasionally uses photos.

TWIGS, Box 42, Meta Station, Pikeville KY 41501. Editor: Lillie D. Chaffin. For writers, college students, and university teachers. Biannually. Circulation: 400. Acquires first rights. Accepts 100 or more mss a year. Pays in contributor's copies and prizes. Will send sample copy to writer for $1.50. Reports in 3 to 6 weeks. Enclose S.A.S.E.
Nonfiction: Articles concerning literature. Length: 2,000 to 4,000 words. Nonfiction Editor: Leonard Roberts, Appalachian Studies Center, Pikeville College, Pikeville KY 41501.
Fiction and Poetry: Serious, highest quality material. Length: 2,000 to 4,000 words. Fiction Editor: Leonard Roberts, Appalachian Studies Center, Pikeville College, Pikeville KY 41501. Short, serious, highest quality poetry.

UNICORN: A Miscellaneous Journal, 1153 E. 26 St., Brooklyn NY 11210. Editor: Karen S. Rockow. Established in 1967. Mainly for college and graduate school students and faculty. "Well-educated and sophisticated. Not jaded." Published 3 times a year. Circulation: 700. Acquires all rights, but will reassign rights to author after publication. Uses 15 to 25 freelance mss a year. Pays an honorarium only for nonfiction. Submit complete ms. Generally reports in 3 to 4 weeks, longer over summer, and for poetry and short stories. Will send sample copy to writer for $1. Will consider photocopied submissions. Enclose S.A.S.E. for return of submissions.
Nonfiction and Photos: "*Unicorn* is a community of writers and readers brought together to share their favorite books and topics. Primarily, we publish essays. These range from personal essays to graceful, scholarly papers directed at a general audience. Areas of greatest interest are folklore, popular culture (especially fantasy literature, detective fiction, children's books) and medieval studies, but we will consider mss on any subject. Scholarly and semischolarly papers may include footnotes (use MLA form). The supporting scholarship must be rigorous, but avoid 'intellectualese'. Also have a very offbeat foods column, The Galumphing Gourmet, and publish many reviews, long and short. We are looking for crisp, honest prose and stand committed against pretentiousness. We pay $5 honorarium for each article and essay accepted." B&w glossies, any size. Payment in cost of film plus extra roll and offprints. Optimum length: 2,500 to 5,000 words; 7,500 words maximum, but will break longer articles and consider series.
Fiction: Satire, short stories. Fantasy, detective fiction. Experimental, mainstream, science fiction, humorous fiction. "We publish 1 short story per issue, plus perhaps, a parody or humorous piece." Length: 2,500 words maximum. Payment in copies plus offprints. Dept. Editor: Stuart Silverman.
Poetry: "We are heavily overstocked with poetry at present time. This does not preclude any current acceptances, but does make us more selective. Please limit number of submissions at any one time to 3 poems, unless they are very short. Publication of poetry may be delayed several issues." Traditional forms, blank verse,

free verse, avant-garde forms, light verse and "concrete" poetry. Length: 1 line to 1 single-spaced page. Payment in copies plus offprints. Dept. Editor: Stuart Silverman.

UNIQUEST: THE SEARCH FOR MEANING, First Unitarian Church, 1 Lawson Rd., Berkeley CA 94707. Editor: Joseph Fabry. For writers, artists, and all those interested in small creative groups and encounter groups. Publication of the Uniquest Foundation. Magazine: 44 pages. Established in 1974. Quarterly. Circulation: about 500. Not copyrighted. Uses about 24 mss a year. Payment in contributor's copies. Will send free sample copy to writer on request. Will consider photocopied submissions. Reports in 1 week. Submit complete ms. Enclose S.A.S.E.

Nonfiction: Main field of interest is in material geared toward encounter groups and other forms of small creative groups, such as literary and artistic coteries, but will consider any topic relating to liberal religious values. Currently, seeking material dealing with historic creative groups, such as the Impressionists, the pre-Raphaelite Brotherhood, the Surrealists, etc., with an eye to examining how such groups are structured and how we can learn better ways of organizing our own activities. Distribution is almost exclusively through the book tables of Unitarian-Universalist Churches. Length: 3,000 words maximum.

UNIVERSITY OF TORONTO QUARTERLY, Editorial Department, University of Toronto Press, 63-A St. George St., Toronto, Ontario M5S 1A6, Canada. Editor: W. F. Blissett. For scholars in the humanities in general, but particularly in English. Magazine; 96 pages. Established in 1931. Quarterly. Circulation: 1,900. Buys all rights, but will reassign rights to author after publication. Buys 15 mss a year. Payment on publication. Will send sample copy to writer for $3. Reports on material accepted for publication within 4 months. Returns rejected material promptly. *MLA Style Sheet* must be followed in ms preparation. Submit complete ms. Enclose S.A.E. and International Reply Coupons.

Nonfiction: Scholarly articles on various subjects in the humanities, particularly in English. Length: 5,000 to 6,000 words. Pays $50.

UNIVERSITY OF WINDSOR REVIEW, Windsor, Ontario, Canada. Phone: 519-253-4232. Editor: Eugene McNamara. For "the literate layman, the old common reader." Established in 1965. Biannual. Circulation: 300 plus. Acquires first North American serial rights. Accepts 50 mss a year. Pays in contributor's copies. Will send a sample copy to writer for $1.25 plus postage. Follow *MLA Style Sheet.* Reports in 4 to 6 weeks. Enclose S.A.E. and International Reply Coupons.

Nonfiction and Photos: "We publish articles on literature, history, social science, etc. I think we reflect competently the Canadian intellectual scene, and are equally receptive to contributions from outside the country; I think we are good and are trying to get better. We are receiving too many poems, too many short stories. Everybody in the world is writing them. Too many articles on literature itself. Not enough in the other areas: history, etc." Seeks informational articles. Length: about 6,000 words. For photos, please inquire to Evelyn McLean.

Fiction: Publishes mainstream prose with open attitude toward themes. Length: 2,000 to 6,000 words. Dept. Editor: Alastair MacLeod.

Poetry: Accepts traditional forms, blank verse, free verse, and avant-garde forms. No epics. Dept. Editor: John Ditsky.

If this is 1977, this edition is out of date. See address in front of book to order latest edition. *Writer's Market* is published annually each fall.

UNMUZZLED OX, Box 374, Planetarium Station, New York NY 10024. Editor: Michael Andre. For a highly sophisticated, highly educated audience. Quarterly magazine; 80 (8½x5½) pages. Established in 1971. Circulation: 2,000. Rights purchased vary with author and material. Usually buys first serial rights, but may buy first North American serial rights. Buys 5 mss a year. Payment on acceptance. Will send sample copy to writer for $1. Will consider photocopied submissions. Will not consider simultaneous submissions. Reports on material accepted for publication in 2 months. Returns rejected material within a few days. "Study the magazine and query first." Enclose S.A.S.E.
Nonfiction: Uses material on art and literature and "anything peculiar". Reviews of art and literature are also used. Length: 10 to 10,000 words. Payment ranges from "zero" to $300.
Fiction: Experimental. Erotica. Length: 200 to 10,000 words. Pays "zero" to $300.
Poetry: Free verse and avant-garde forms. Length: open. Pays "up to $200".

VAGABOND, P.O. Box 879, Ellensburg WA 98926. Editor: John Bennett. For "libraries, poets, writers, sensitive and free spirits, minority groups, people of all ages, varied education and with an interest in life ..." Established in 1965. Quarterly. Circulation: 500. Acquires all rights, but will reassign them to author after publication. Uses about 80 mss a year. Payment in contributor's copies. Will send a sample copy for 75¢. Will consider cassette submissions. Query first for nonfiction. Reports in 1 to 2 weeks. Enclose S.A.S.E.
Nonfiction: "I would prefer not to see work that was written with a market in mind. I would like to see material that deals with life and death and all their accoutrements ... joy, laughter, love and hate." Accepts interviews. Length: not more than 5,000 words.
Fiction: Publishes genuine experimental, suspense, adventure, erotica, fantasy, humorous fiction. Length: 5,000 words maximum.

VALLEY VIEWS, P.O. Box 39096, Solon OH 44139. Editor: Nelson P. Bard. For a general audience, people of all ages and all walks of life. Quarterly magazine; 44 pages, (8½x11). Established in 1964. Circulation: 5,000. Copyrighted, but no rights are acquired. The stories remain the property of the author. Uses about 40 stories and 40 poems a year. Payment in contributor's copies. Will send free sample copy to writer on request. Magazine has guidelines printed on its first page. Submit only complete ms. Reports within 6 weeks. Enclose S.A.S.E.
Nonfiction and Photos: "Subject matter is open. Only taboos are slanted articles on racial subjects or soap box articles on politics. Nothing ribald. Nothing very mod. Our magazine is meant to be strictly entertaining, but sometimes informs. No book reviews or lectures. We'd like a few more stories with a regional setting as the background." Length: 3,000 words maximum.
Fiction, Poetry, and Fillers: Mystery, suspense, adventure, western, science fiction, humorous, romance, and historical fiction. Length: 3,000 words maximum. Traditional forms and light verse. "We like poetry to rhyme." Length: prefers shorter poetry. Short humor used as fillers.

THE VILLAGER, 135 Midland Ave., Bronxville NY 10708. Editor: Ruth E. Hilton. Publication of the Bronxville Women's Club. For club members and families; professional people and advertisers. Established in 1925. Monthly, October through June. Circulation: 850. Acquires all rights. Uses 40 mss a year. Pays in copies only. Will send sample copy to writer for 35¢. Submit seasonal material (Fall, Thanksgiving, Winter, Christmas, Easter, Spring) 2 months in advance. Submit only complete ms. Reports within 2 weeks. Enclose S.A.S.E.
Nonfiction, Fiction, and Poetry: Short articles about interesting homes, travel, historic, pertinent subjects, sports, etc. Informational, personal experience, inspirational, humor, historical, nostalgia, travel. Mainstream, mystery, suspense, adventure, humorous, romance, and historical fiction. Length: 900 to 2,500 words. Traditional forms of poetry, blank verse, free verse, avant-garde forms, light verse. Length: 20 lines.

VILTIS (Hope), P.O. Box 1226, Denver CO 80201. Phone: 303-534-2025. Editor: V.F. Beliajus. For teenagers and adults interested in folk dance, folk customs and folklore; all professions and levels of education. Published every two months. Magazine; 40 pages, (12x9). Established in 1942. Circulation: 2,500. Acquires all rights, but will reassign rights to author after publication on request. No payment. Will send free sample copy to writer on request. Query first. Enclose S.A.S.E.
Nonfiction: Uses articles on folklore, legends, customs and nationality backgrounds. Folkish (not too erudite) but informative. Can be any length. Everything must be based on custom.

THE VIRGINIA QUARTERLY REVIEW, 1 West Range, Charlottesville VA 22903. Editor: Charlotte Kohler. Quarterly. Pays on publication. Reports on submissions in 2 weeks. Enclose S.A.S.E. for return of submissions.
Nonfiction: Articles on current problems, economic, historical; literary essays. Length: 3,000 to 6,000 words. Pays $5 for a page of 350 words.
Fiction: Good short stories, conventional or experimental. Length: 2,000 to 7,000 words. Pays $5 for a page of 350 words. Offers prizes for short stories in odd-numbered years.
Poetry: Generally publishes ten pages of poetry in each issue. No length or subject restrictions. Pays 50¢ per line. Offers prizes for poetry in even-numbered years.

WALT WHITMAN REVIEW, Business Office: Wayne State University Press, Detroit MI 48202. Phone: 313-626-6404. Editorial Office: Journalism Program, Speech Communications Department, Oakland University, Rochester MI 48063. Editors: William White and Charles E. Feinberg. For specialists in American literature. Quarterly. Payment in contributor's copies. Wayne State University Press and author share all rights. Reports within a few days. Enclose S.A.S.E. for return of submissions.
Nonfiction: All articles and book reviews, notes and queries should deal with Walt Whitman and his writings. Length: 500 to 6,000 words.

WASCANA REVIEW, English Department, University of Regina, Regina, Sask., Canada. Editor: H.C. Dillow. Published semiannually. Reports in 6 to 8 weeks. Buys all rights. Pays on publication. Enclose S.A.E. and International Reply Coupons.
Nonfiction: Literary criticism of scholarly standard; knowledgeable articles on the theatre, the visual arts and music. Reviews of current books. Art reviews, national and international; query is necessary if there are prints. Length: 2,000 to 6,000 words. Pays $3 per page for criticism articles. Art reviews by arrangement with Editor.
Fiction: "Quality" fiction with an honest, meaningful grasp of human experience. Form is open. Length: 2,000 to 6,000 words. Pays $3 per page.
Poetry: Poetry of high artistic merit: integrity, originality and craftsmanship. Length: 4 to 100 lines. Pays $10 per page.

WAVES, Room 141, Petrie Science Bldg., York University, 4700 Keele St., Downsview, Ontario, Canada L4J 1P2. Editor: Bernice Lever. For university and high school English teachers and readers of literary magazines. Magazine published 3 times a year; 80 (5x8) pages. Established in 1972. Circulation: 1,000. Acquires first North American serial rights. Payment in contributor's copies. Will send sample copy to writer for $1. Will consider photocopied submissions. Will not consider simultaneous submissions. Reports in 6 weeks. Submit complete ms. Enclose S.A.E. and International Reply Coupons.
Nonfiction and Photos: "Intelligent, thorough, unique, humanitarian material. Good quality; yet wide variety of genres and styles. Avoid pornography and carelessness. No 'copies' of Jonathan Livingston Seagull." Uses interviews, essays, literary think pieces and book reviews. Length: 250 to 7,000 words. B&w photos and graphics are used.
Fiction: Experimental, mainstream, fantasy, humorous and science fiction. Length: 500 to 5,000 words.
Poetry and Drama: Free verse and avant-garde forms. Playlets. Length: 2,000 words maximum.

WESTERN HUMANITIES REVIEW, University of Utah, Salt Lake City UT 84112. Phone: 801-581-7438. Editor: Jack Garlington. For educated general readers. Quarterly magazine; 96 pages, (6¾x10). Established in 1947. Circulation: 1,000. Buys first North American serial rights. Buys 8 to 12 mss a year. Payment on acceptance. Will send free sample copy to writer on request. Will consider photocopied and simultaneous submissions. Submit only complete ms. Reports within 6 weeks. Enclose S.A.S.E.

Nonfiction: Authoritative, readable, sophisticated articles on literature, art, philosophy, current events, history, religion, anything in the humanities. Length: about 3,500 words. Interdisciplinary articles encouraged. Departments on film and books. Pays up to $100 for articles; $25 for reviews.

Fiction and Poetry: Pays up to $100 for fiction. Seeks freshness, humor and significance in poetry. No length limits. Pays $35.

THE YALE REVIEW, 1902A Yale Station, New Haven CT 06520. Editor: J.E. Palmer. Managing Editor: Mary Price. Copyrighted. Buys all rights. Pays on publication. Enclose S.A.S.E.

Nonfiction and Fiction: Authoritative discussions of politics, economics, and the arts. Pays $75 per article. Buys quality fiction. Length: 3,000 to 5,000 words. Pays $75 per story.

Men's Publications

ADAM, Publishers Service Inc., 8060 Melrose Ave., Los Angeles CA 90046. Phone: 213-653-8060. Editor: Don Pfeil. For the young adult male. General subject: "Human sexuality in contemporary society." Monthly. Circulation: 500,000. Buys first North American serial rights. Occasionally overstocked. Pays on publication. Will send a sample copy to a writer for $1. Write for guidelines for writers. Reports in 3 to 6 weeks, but occasionally may take longer. Query first on articles. Enclose S.A.S.E.

Nonfiction and Fiction: Sex-oriented articles. Articles and stories must be sophisticated sex and erotic in concept. Prefer slant toward the hip young swinger with mod taste. Length: 1,500 to 3,000 words. Pays $100 to $200.

Photos: All submissions must contain model release including parent's signature if under 21; fact sheet giving information about the model, place or activity being photographed, including all information of help in writing a photo story, and S.A.S.E. Photo payment varies, depending upon amount of space used by photo set.

ALL MAN, MAN'S DELIGHT, Top-Flight Magazines, 13510 Ventura Blvd., Sherman Oaks CA 91423. Editor: Thom Montgomery. For a male audience, ages 21 and older. Monthly. Buys original and second rights. Pays on publication. Material not suitable is rejected the same day it's received. Enclose S.A.S.E.

Nonfiction and Fiction: Anything of interest to men, generally with a male-female slant but not necessarily. Strong narrative hook preferred with a conclusive ending. No strictly lesbian or homosexual yarns. Buys informational, how-to, humor, think articles. Buys mainstream, erotica, science fiction, fantasy, mystery, and humorous fiction. Length: 500 to 2,000 words. Pays 1¢ a word.

ARGOSY, 420 Lexington Ave., New York NY 10017. Editor: Ernest Baxter. For the "adult male, with at least high school education, interested in outdoors, nature, adventure, exploration, camping, hunting, fishing, travel, history, automobiles, sports." Monthly. Circulation: 1,400,000. Rights bought "depend on individual arrangements." Buys 100 mss a year. Payment in 3 weeks; sometimes longer. Reports in 1 month. Query first. Enclose S.A.S.E.

Nonfiction: Articles of personal adventure—humor, offbeat and exotic travel, treasure hunts, unusual outdoor stories—everything of interest to the active, intelligent male except overly sexy material. Must be documented and authentic. "We like to feel that the author was actually on the scene. We don't need anything on the movies or for our regular columns." Length: 2,500 to 3,000 words. Pays $500 to $3,000.

Photos: Major areas for photo stories are outdoor adventure, leisure, and recreation. "Before submitting, photographers should thumb through back issues of *Argosy* to see the type of stories we run." Send color transparencies as well as black and white contact sheets. Pays $100 a page for b&w, $150 for color, and from $500 to $750 for a cover. "But we will pay much more for exceptional material." Photographer is responsible for identifying and explaining his photos. Send pictures; queries cannot describe photos fully. Expenses, if any, must be arranged specifically for each assignment. Picture Editor: Bernie White.

How To Break In: "To break into the pages of *Argosy* for the first time, a new writer would first have to submit a story idea that we like. It could be just two or three paragraphs. And he would also have to include the possibility of good photos. If he's a photographer himself, this would be to his credit. Then, if his story idea is accepted, we would ask him to do the piece on speculation, obviously because we have no idea of how well he can write since, as a beginner, he will have no samples of published stories. In *Argosy* there is no such thing as a small sale; we run only full-length features, no shorts.'"

BLACK KNIGHT MAGAZINE, P. O. Box 8293, Denver CO 80201. Editor: Claiborne J. Williams. For young men (and those who think young); black-oriented. Established in 1974. Bimonthly. Circulation: 20,000. Rights purchased vary with author and material. Usually buys all rights. Submit seasonal material 6 months in advance. Reports in 6 weeks. Query first on interviews; submit complete ms on other material. Enclose S.A.S.E.

Nonfiction: Wants "think-type" articles on timely issues. "We seek no particular style. However, writer must be knowledgeable about the areas covered, for we do look for originality and factual reportage. As to subject matter, we place no restrictions, since we feel the writer should be free to express himself, however controversial the issue may be." Length: 1,500 to 2,500 words. Pays 1¢ to 5¢ a word. Purchases interviews on anyone interesting and newsworthy, with an introduction written by the interviewer. Length: open. Pay varies, depending on depth and quality. "We also need profile articles on men and/or women (individuals or groups) for our 'On The Move' feature. An 8x10 b&w photo of the subject(s) must be included." Length: 300 words. Pays $15.

Fiction: Black-oriented fiction and humorous short stories relating the black experience. A 3x5 b&w photo of the author must accompany both fiction and nonfiction submissions. Fiction length: 1,500 to 2,500 words. Pays 1¢ to 5¢ a word.

Fillers: Jokes are purchased at the rate of $5 each.

BLUEBOOK, MAN'S ILLUSTRATED, 235 Park Ave., S., New York NY 10003. Editor: B.R. Ampolsk. Bimonthly. For "a men's adventure audience." Pays on acceptance. Enclose S.A.S.E. for return of submissions.

Nonfiction and Photos: Accepts only reprint material. True war and adventure stories, heavy on personality development and authentic background. Provocative expose articles. Articles on exotic vacation spots. Pays $100 to $300. Photos with caption material bought at rate of $12.50 each.

CAVALCADE GROUP: CAVALCADE, NIGHT & DAY, CLIMAX, CANDID, SQUIRE, MEN'S CHALLENGE, 7950 Deering Ave., Canoga Park CA 91304. For a male audience, ages 20 to 45. Fiction and articles of interest to men. Established in 1967. Monthly. Circulation: 100,000. Buys all rights, but will reassign rights to author after publication. Buys over 100 mss a year. Payment on publication, or up to 1 month after publication. Will send a copy for $1. Will consider photocopied submissions. Reports in "about a month." Enclose S.A.S.E. for return of submissions.

Nonfiction: Articles that interest a man 20 to 45 years of age who is looking for light entertainment. Informational, personal experience, humor, think, expose, and travel articles. Length: 2,500 to 3,500 words. Pays $50 to $150, including photos.

Fiction: Experimental, mystery, suspense, adventure, western, erotica, science fiction, fantasy, and humorous fiction. Length: 2,500 to 3,500 words. Pays $50 to $75.

Photos: Purchased with accompanying mss only. Captions required. 8x10 preferred. Pays $5 for each b&w. Pays $25 for color transparencies.

CAVALIER, Suite 209, 316 Aragon Ave., Coral Gables FL 33134. Editor: Douglas Allen. For "young males, 18 to 29, 80% college graduates, affluent, intelligent, interested in current events, ecology, sports, adventure, travel, clothing, good fiction." Monthly. Circulation: 250,000. Buys first and second rights. Buys 35 to 40 mss a year. Pays on publication or before. See past issues for general approach to take. Submit seasonal material at least 3 months in advance. Reports in 3 weeks. Query first except on fiction. Enclose S.A.S.E. for return of submissions or reply to query.
Nonfiction and Photos: Personal experience, interviews, humor, historical, think pieces, expose, new product. "Frank—open to dealing with controversial issues." Does not want material on Women's Lib, water sports, hunting, homosexuality, or travel, "unless it's something spectacular or special." Length: 2,800 to 3,500 words. Payment to $300. Photos purchased with mss or with captions. No cheesecake.
Fiction: Mystery, science fiction, humorous, adventure, contemporary problems. Length: 3,000 to 4,000 words. Payment to $300, "higher for special." Department Editor: Mr. Nye Willden.
How To Break In: "Our greatest interest is in originality—new ideas, new approaches; no tired, overdone stories—both feature and fiction. We do not deal in sensationalism but in high-quality pieces. Keep in mind the intelligent 18- to 29-year-old male reader."

DARING MAGAZINE, WILDCAT MAGAZINE, Candar Publishing Co., 235 Park Ave., South, New York NY 10003. Editor: Dan Sontup. For men "with modern outlook on everything that interests men." Every 2 months. Buys all rights. Buys 50 to 75 mss a year. Payment on acceptance, but sometimes delayed. Query first or submit complete ms. Will not consider photocopied submissions. Reports on material in 2 weeks. Enclose S.A.S.E.
Nonfiction and Photos: Articles and features of male interest, including articles of a sexual self-help nature. Study of current issue is recommended. Informational, personal experience, interview, humor, travel. Length: 2,500 to 3,000 words. Pays "up to $125 for regular contributions; more for exceptional articles." 8x10 b&w glossies. 2¼x2¼ color transparencies. Payment for color varies.
Fiction: Mystery, suspense, adventure, science fiction, humorous. Length: 3,500 to 5,000 words. Pays "up to $125; more for exceptional work." Limited use.

DEBONAIR, MAN'S PLEASURE, Top-Flight Magazines, 13510 Ventura Blvd., Sherman Oaks CA 91423. Editor: Rick Talcove. For a male audience, ages 21 and older. Monthly. Buys original and second rights. Pays on publication. Material not suitable is rejected the same day it's received. Enclose S.A.S.E.
Nonfiction and Fiction: Anything of interest to men, generally with a male-female slant but not necessarily. Strong narrative hook preferred with a conclusive ending. No strictly lesbian or homosexual yarns. Buys informational, how-to, humor, think articles. Buys mainstream, erotica, science fiction, fantasy, mystery, and humorous fiction. Length: 500 to 2,000 words. Pays 1¢ a word.

DUDE, GENT, NUGGET, Suite 209, 316 Aragon Ave., Coral Gables FL 33134. Phone: 305-443-2378. Editor: John Fox. "For men 21 to ?; adventure and sex are their interests." Male-oriented subject matter. Every 2 months. Circulation: *Dude* 75,000; *Gent* 100,000; *Nugget* 75,000. *Writer's Market* readers have found these publications very dependable markets. Buys first North American serial rights. Buys about 100 mss a year. Pays on publication. Will send sample copy to a writer for $1. Submit complete ms. Reports on material in 6 to 8 weeks. Returns rejected material in 1 month. Enclose S.A.S.E.
Nonfiction and Photos: "Articles which are male oriented; primarily concerning sex or adventure." Informational, how-to, personal experience, interview, humor, historical, expose, personal opinion and travel. Length: 1,500 to 4,000 words. Pays $100 to $125. Photos purchased with mss.
Fiction: Adventure, erotica, science fiction, humorous. Length: 1,500 to 3,500 words. Pays $100.

ESQUIRE, 488 Madison Ave., New York NY 10022. Editor: Don Erickson. Monthly. Usually buys all rights. Payment on acceptance. Reports in 3 weeks. "We depend chiefly on solicited contributions and material from literary agencies. Unable to accept responsibility for unsolicited material." Query first. Enclose S.A.S.E.

Nonfiction: Articles vary in length, but usually average 4,000 words and rarely run longer than 5,000 words. Articles should be slanted for sophisticated, intelligent readers; however, not highbrow in the restrictive sense. Wide range of subject matter. Rates run roughly between $350 and $1,250, depending on length, quality, etc. Expenses are sometimes allowed, depending on the assignment.

Photos: Art Director Richard Weigand accepts both contacts and 11x14 b&w matte prints. Uses 35mm and larger Ektachrome and Kodachrome color transparencies. Buys all rights. Payment depends on how photo is used, but rates are roughly $25 for single b&w; $100 to $150 for b&w full page; $150 to $200 for full color page. Guarantee on acceptance. Prefers to be queried. Gives assignments and pays some expenses.

Fiction: Gordon Lish, Fiction Editor. "Literary excellence is our only criterion, but we accept only solicited contributions and material from literary agents." Average about 1,000 to 6,000 words. Payment: $350 to $1,500.

FLING, 161 E. Erie St., Chicago IL 60611. Editor-Publisher: Arv Miller. Male audience—21 to 30 years old. Bimonthly. Buys first rights (additional payment if reprinted in Fling Festival annual); first or second rights for photos, with additional payment for reprint use. Pays on acceptance. Reports in 1 week. Query first for nonfiction. Enclose S.A.S.E. for reply to query or return of ms or photographs.

Nonfiction: Subject matter must be directed to adult, male readership. Topics currently needed are: personality profiles from show business (living or dead); male success stories; offbeat, social-scientific-sexual fads; controversial national issues, and in-depth political analysis of youth-oriented interests. Articles should be carefully documented and sparked with accurate quotes. Length: 3,500 to 5,000 words. Pays $125 to $300. For the Fling Report, a regular feature, uses a first-hand investigation of a new sexual phenomenon currently gaining attention in this country. This is not an expose type of piece. It is straight reporting, with one exception: author is involved with the people and events in his report. (Detailed outline is supplied to author upon assignment.) Length: 20 typewritten pages. Pays $150 and up, depending on editing and rewriting necessary. Robert Livingston, Department Editor.

Photos: Magazine buys photo-stories and glamour pinup sets. Send b&w contact sheets, plus 2¼x2¼ or 35mm color transparencies. OK'd contacts are returned for 8x10 glossy enlargements. Study magazine carefully before submitting material. Brief fact sheet on subject or model should be enclosed. Pays $100 to $250 for first rights b&w and color; $75 to $150 for second rights b&w and color. Special photo assignments are sometimes given to freelance photographers upon written query to Editor. Expenses are paid when situation warrants.

Fiction: Short story needs are very specific. Each issue publishes two types of fiction, completely different from each other. Lead fiction is a serious story, examining "the offbeat and far-out relationships between a man and a women." Prefers this type to be a combination of fantasy (in the John Collier tradition) backed up with a great deal of sharp, contemporary dialogue. "The characters should be neurotic within the framework of today's modern society. There must also be a strong element of eroticism, but no clinical or detailed descriptions. Endings should be simple and logical conclusions, rather than trick or gimmicked up." Length: 3,000 to 4,000 words. Payment is $125 to $250, depending on length, importance and editing required. Other fiction should fall into the area of humor or satire. Style must be upbeat, not morbid or ponderous. Some element of sex is necessary, but must be presented within a "happy, fun-type context." Stories should be generally amusing, directed to an adult male audience. Dialogue extremely important. Should be "hip" in the sense of language in current use today. 2,000 to 3,000 words. Pays $100 to $150, depending on length, importance, and editing required. Do not submit science fiction, westerns, mysteries, period pieces, ribald classics, plotless vignettes, stories involving children, animals or ghosts.

FOR MEN ONLY, Magazine Management Co., 575 Madison Ave., New York NY 10022. Editorial Director: Ivan Prashker. Completely freelance. Buys all rights. Pays on acceptance. Reports in 2 weeks. Query first for nonfiction. Enclose S.A.S.E.
Nonfiction: Emphasis here is on fact-adventure stories, contemporary, usually featuring Americans in exotic backgrounds. Writing style should be lean, clean, convincing, with racehorse movement and skillful, believable characterization. "Writers should try to present something new, which perhaps he knows about through his line of work or personal connections. For all our pieces, there has to be a blue collar identification. Recently we ran stories on the new head of the United Mine Workers, an unusual cop, an Army parachutist who has jumped more times than anybody else. You might try to provide us with some excellent artwork or photos. I recently bought a freelance piece on a 1937 racing car and it was the terrific series of drawings that sold me." All story backgrounds should be carefully researched. Preference in adventure material is for stories told in scenes and incidents, rather than factual narrative. Some special categories: combat pieces, profiles of great and heroic living figures, either world-famed or little known. Emphasis should be on the unusual and the out-of-the-ordinary stunt. Bigger-Than-Life Personalities; the main need is for profiles of contemporary people, preferably Americans, occasionally foreigners. Scoundrels, hoaxers, men who have pulled off great swindles, impersonations. Epic disasters; emphasis here is on careful, economical, often heartbreaking description rather than jazzed-up treatments. Behind the News pieces; emphasis on adventure, but with an inside flavor, set against one of the trouble spots of the world. Length is usually 15,000 to 20,000 words. Book-length material runs between 15,000 and 20,000 words. Pays from $275 to $400.
Fiction: No westerns. Adventure settings; tough cops in tight spots, treasure hunters grappling with angry tribesmen, hunters tackling giant anaconda with bow and arrow, and a few involvements with sexy women thrown in carefully but not too explicitly. "I just bought an over-the-transom story about a railroad detective during the thirties. I figure a lot of guys who read this magazine might have been bumming around on trains themselves at that time and have run into a character like this. Actual personal experience is a real plus, though, of course, that's unusual." Length: 3,000 words. Same payment rates as for nonfiction.

GENESIS MAGAZINE, 120 E. 56 St., New York NY 10022. Managing Editor: Michael Minick. Monthly magazine; 120 pages, (8½x11). Established in 1973. Circulation: 600,000. Buys all rights. Submit seasonal material 4 to 5 months in advance. Query first for nonfiction. Submit only complete ms for fiction and pictorials. Reports within 3 weeks. Enclose S.A.S.E.
Nonfiction and Photos: Looking for men's material; political, adventure, humorous. Buys interview, profile, humor, think articles, expose, photo features. Photos are purchased with ms or on assignment. Should include nude sets. Art Director: Susan Cotler.

KNIGHT, Publishers Service Inc., 8060 Melrose Ave., Los Angeles CA 90046. For male adults. Monthly. Buys all rights, but author may ask for and receive all rights other than first North American serial rights after publication. Pays on publication. Query first on articles. Enclose S.A.S.E.
Nonfiction: "Broad variety of subjects of interest to male adults. Sophisticated, sexual slant preferred. Profiles of contemporary personalities; reports on new life styles; latest trends in erotic films, art, theater; photojournalism, coverage of current social movements. Interested in articles in the subjective 'new journalism' style, as well as carefully researched reportage, but all must be erotically oriented. No interest in true adventure pieces or how-to-do-it material." Length: 2,500 to 4,000 words. Pays $50 to $150, based on quality and editorial needs.
Photos: All photo submissions must contain the following: 1) An acceptable release (containing the model's name and signature) for all models used. If the model is under 21 years old (18 if married), the signature of a parent or guardian is required. A sample model release is available on request. 2) A stamped, self-addressed envelope. 3) A fact sheet giving information about the model. 4) Place or activity being

photographed. Include all information that may be of help in writing an interesting text for photo story. Sample fact sheet available on request. Uses b&w photo stories for personality profiles; photo stories covering events, places, or unusual activities, plus special material, such as erotic art, nude theater, etc. Photos bring $15 each when used to illustrate a story. Purchased separately at time issue goes to press. If submitting an entire layout, an effort should be made to capture a model in the midst of various activities; clothed and unclothed shots should be intermingled; interesting settings and backgrounds are essential. "Keep in mind that the model will become a personality if used in the magazine and emphasis should be as much on who she is as what her body looks like. Natural, real girls with whom men can easily identify are most desirable."

Fiction: Always interested in stories of male-female relationships in situations of conflict, crisis, adventure or humorous confusion. Science fiction and fantasy settings are acceptable. Emphasis must be on erotic realism. Offbeat and controversial themes acceptable. Length: 2,500 to 4,000 words. Pays $50 to $150, based on quality and editorial needs.

MALE, 575 Madison Ave., New York NY 10022. Editor: Carl Sifakis. Issued monthly. Pays on acceptance. Query first for both nonfiction and fiction. Enclose S.A.S.E.
Nonfiction: Powerful, dramatic, heroic, true adventures set in exotic backgrounds. Hard-hitting articles, exposes, personality pieces of contemporary interest, with strong male appeal. 5,000 to 7,000 words. Pays $250 to $600.
Fiction and Fillers: Buys a few stories with male appeal. Length: 5,000 words maximum. Pays $5 for short gags which are used as fillers.
How To Break In: "We read all the major papers and magazines searching for new material, so it's hard for a new writer to break in with something he's seen, say, in the *Wall Street Journal*, unless he can not only update the material, but develop a really fresh approach — ask a new question that wasn't even covered in the original piece. Some of our successful freelance pieces have originated with writers who found their idea in a local paper which we don't have access to. This is true, for instance, of some of the UFO and Abominable Snowman articles we've run. Even better is to come up with an idea before it ever reaches the national press — which a freelancer did for us on Boston's 'Combat Zone' where almost anything is allowed sexually by the authorities. We are completely open to new people, but we find that few of them really study the magazine and know what we need. Our readers expect you to show them that what you're writing about is true; you cannot present the titillating facts and leave it at that. You must present the authenticating material and do it in an interesting way. Occasionally a writer will sell us by hitting us with something that we haven't been covering, such as one freelancer who's been selling us gambling stories lately. But that's the exception. It's much wiser to aim for our strengths, because generally there is a good reason when we neglect a certain area. Take sports, for example. Sure, our readers are interested in sports, but that's not why they buy this book and so it's rare that I use a sports piece. A new writer should aim for a nonfiction piece since we use only one fiction piece per issue. Also he would do best to stay away from true adventure stories because it's my experience that they just can't handle it the way we need it. Try sex, sex self-help (written in consultation with a doctor), and general *Reader's Digest*-type stories but with a strong male interest. Right now we're running a lot of recession stuff — but in an upbeat sort of way; where the jobs are available, for example. Of course, six months from now we may be running articles on vacation home frauds."

MAN TO MAN, MR., SIR, 280 Madison Ave., New York NY 10016. Phone: 212-889-0878. Editor: Everett Meyers. 10 times a year. Buys all rights, but usually returns specific rights to author on request. Usually pays on publication. Enclose S.A.S.E.
Nonfiction and Photos: Sharply angled articles that reflect contemporary trends in such subjects as travel, music, sex, new art forms, unusual entertainment, and other activities of interest to men. Length: 2,000 to 5,000 words. Pays $100 and up. Typical payment for article with one or two good b&w photos, $150.

Fiction: "Strong, imaginative stories in modern mood that include man-woman relationships; no one stereotype is demanded. Taboos are against hackneyed plotting and dull writing rather than particular themes or points of view. No rewriting is done in this market, so the original must be mature and professional in execution, as well as fresh in concept." Length: 1,500 to 5,000 words. Pays $75 minimum. **Fillers:** Jokes for male audience. Pays $5.

MODERN MAN MAGAZINE, 8150 N. Central Park, Skokie IL 60076. Phone: 312-675-5602. Editor: Donald Stahl. 80-page monthly. Established in 1952. Circulation: 130,000. Buys all rights. Buys 100 mss per year. Payment on acceptance. Will not consider photocopied or simultaneous submissions. Reports on material in 2 weeks. Submit complete ms. Enclose S.A.S.E.
Nonfiction: Material must have general sex slant. Can be informational, expose, or humorous in its treatment of sex. Length: 2,500 words. Pays $150.

OUI MAGAZINE, 919 North Michigan Ave., Chicago IL 60611. Phone: 312-649-0800. Editor: Nat Lehrman. For young, well-educated, urban-oriented men. Monthly. Established in 1972. Circulation: over 1½ million. Buys all rights. Buys over 100 mss a year. Payment on acceptance. Seasonal material for year-end holidays must be submitted 6 months in advance. Reports within 4 weeks. Query first for nonfiction. Submit only complete ms for fiction and humor. Enclose S.A.S.E.
Nonfiction and Photos: "Articles dealing with subjects of international interest (including travel) as well as pop culture (including entertainment), sex, sports, service, human behavior. Humor and satire are welcome. All material should be characterized by friskiness, irreverence, wit, humor." Informational, interview, profile, humor, nostalgia, photo, travel, and spot news. Length: 5,000 words maximum. Pays $750 to $1,200 for full-length article. Spot news is used for regular column. Openers. Photos (both b&w and color) are purchased without accompanying ms or on assignment. Pays $200 to $400.
Fiction: Experimental, mainstream, mystery, suspense, erotica, science fiction, fantasy, and humorous fiction. Length: 500 to 5,000 words. Pays $500 to $1,200.
Fillers: Newsbreaks, clippings and short humor. Pays $25. Department Editor: Terry Catehpole.

PENTHOUSE, 909 Third Ave., New York NY 10022. Executive Editor: James Goode; Managing Editor: Ken Gouldthorpe. For male audience; upper income bracket, college educated. Established in 1969. Monthly. Circulation: 5,250,000. Buys all rights. Buys 60 to 70 mss a year. Payment on acceptance. Will consider photocopied submissions. Reports in 6 to 8 weeks. Query first. Enclose S.A.S.E.
Nonfiction: Articles on general themes, but not sport or family orientated; money, sex, politics, health, crime, etc. No first person. Male viewpoint only. Length: open. General rates: $250 per 1,000 words. Nonfiction Editor: Peter Bloch.
Fiction: Fiction with some sex content. Experimental, mainstream; mystery, suspense and adventure with erotic flavor; erotica, and science fiction. Length: 3,000 to 6,000 words. Pays $400 and up. Fiction Editor: Gerard Van der Leun.
Photos: Purchased without mss and on assignment. Nude girl sets. Pays $200 minimum for b&w; $250 for color. Spec sheet available from Art Director Joe Brooks.

PIMIENTA MAGAZINE, 1515 N.W. 7th St., Miami FL 331259 Editor: W. Allan Sandler. Audience is "Spanish, male, ages 19 to 50." Monthly. Circulation: 70,000. Copyrighted. Buys about 50 mss a year. Pays on publication. Will send a sample copy to a writer for 50¢. No query required. "Stories may be submitted in English. We will translate." Reports in 1 month. Enclose S.A.S.E. for return of submissions.
Nonfiction, Photos, and Fiction: "Male interest, spicy stories, and adventure." Buys exposes, photo essays, adventure and confession stories. Length: 2,500 to 5,000 words. Pays $25 to $100. Buys b&w glossies. Pays $10.

PIX, Publishers Service Inc., 8060 Melrose Ave., Los Angeles CA 90046. Editor: David Hine. Bimonthly. For the young adult male. Buys first North American serial rights. Pays on publication. Will send sample copy to writer for $1. Write for guidelines for writers. Query first for nonfiction. Reports in 3 to 6 weeks, but may take longer. Enclose S.A.S.E.

Nonfiction and Fiction: Wants hard-hitting fiction with strong sexual slant, ribald humor, articles on erotica, etc. Articles and stories with a very bizarre sexual slant. Humor, too, should be of an erotic, but kinky or far-out nature. The whole spectrum of Krafft-Ebing's treatise on sexuality can be considered in articles and fiction. Pays 3¢ per word minimum.

PLAYBOY, 919 N. Michigan, Chicago IL 60611. Editor-Publisher: Hugh M. Hefner; Exec. Editor: Arthur Kretchmer; Managing Editor: Sheldon Wax. Monthly. Reports in 2 weeks. Buys first rights and others. Enclose S.A.S.E. with mss and queries.

Nonfiction: "Articles should be carefully researched and written with wit and insight; a lucid style is important. Little true adventure or how-to material. Check magazine for subject matter. Pieces on outstanding contemporary men, sports, politics, sociology, business and finance, games, all areas of interest to the urban male." A query is advisable here. Length is about 4,000 to 6,000 words. On acceptance, pays $3,000 for lead article; $2,000 regular. The Playboy interviews run between 8,000 and 15,000 words. After getting an assignment, the freelancer outlines the questions, conducts and edits the interview, and writes the introduction. For an example of what is wanted, see Playboy Interviews: Robert Redford or John Dean. Pays $2,000 on acceptance. Also pays $50 to $250 for idea. Pays more for idea with research which is assigned to a staff writer. If a commissioned article does not meet standards, will pay a turn-down price of $400. Geoffrey Norman, Articles Editor.

Photos: Mark Kauffman, Photography Editor, suggests that all photographers interested in contributing make a thorough study of the photography currently appearing in the magazine. Generally all photography is done on assignment. While much of this is assigned to *Playboy's* staff photographers, approximately 30% of the photography is done by freelancers and *Playboy* is in constant search of creative new talent. Qualified freelancers are encouraged to submit samples of their work and ideas. All assignments made on an all rights basis with payments scaled from $600 per color page; $300 per b&w page; cover, $1,000. Playmate photography for entire project: $6,000. Assignments and submissions handled by Associate Editors Gary Cole and Helga Aktipis, Chicago; Hollis Wayne, New York; Marilyn Grabowski, Los Angeles. Assignments made on a minimum guarantee basis. Film, processing, and other expenses necessitated by assignment honored.

Fiction: Both light and serious fiction. Entertainment pieces are clever, smoothly written stories. Serious fiction must come up to the best contemporary standards in substance, idea, and style. Both, however, should be designed to appeal to the educated, well-informed male reader. General types include comedy, mystery, fantasy, horror, science fiction, adventure, social-realism, "problem," and psychological stories. One special requirement for science fiction is that it deal—in fresh and original ways—with human dilemmas more than technological problems. Fiction on controversial topics is welcome; the only taboo is against formless sketches and excessively subjective writing. *Playboy* has serialized novels by Ian Fleming, Vladimir Nabokov, Graham Greene, Michael Crichton, and Irwin Shaw. Other fiction contributors include Saul Bellow, John Cheever, Bernard Malamud, and P.G. Wodehouse. Fiction lengths are from 2,000 to 10,000 words; occasionally short-shorts of 1,000 to 1,500 words are used. Pays $3,000 for lead story; $2,000 regular; $1,000 short-short. Rates rise for additional acceptances. Rate for Ribald Classics is $400. Unsolicited mss must be accompanied by stamped, self-addressed envelope. Robie Macauley, Fiction Editor.

Fillers: Party Jokes are always welcome. Pays $50 each on publication. Also interesting items for Playboy After Hours, front section (best check it carefully before submission). The After Hours, front section, pays anywhere from $50 for a two-line typographical error to $350 for an original lead item. Subject matter should be humorous, ironic. Has a movie, book, record, theater reviewer, but solicits queries for short (800 words or less) pieces on art, places, people, trips, adventures, experiences, erotica, television—in short, open-ended. Ideas for Playboy Potpourri pay $75 on publication. Query first.

PLAYERS, 8060 Melrose Ave., Los Angeles CA 90046. Phone: 213-653-8060. Editor: Joseph G. Nazel, Jr. For the black male; median age of 21. Monthly magazine; 100 (8⅛x10⅞) pages. Established in 1974. Circulation: 400,000. Rights purchased vary with author and material. May buy all rights but will sometimes reassign rights to author after publication; first North American serial rights, first serial rights or second serial (reprint) rights. Buys 120 mss a year. Payment on publication. Will not consider photocopied or simultaneous submissions. Submit seasonal (sports and travel) material 2 to 6 months in advance. Reports on material in 6 to 8 weeks. Query first on all interviews; submit complete ms for all other material. Enclose S.A.S.E.

Nonfiction and Photos: *"Players* is *Playboy* in basic black."￼ Subject matter should be slanted toward black readership, from a black perspective. Use of street slang and dialect are acceptable in many instances. However, that does not preclude quality in writing. Would like to see more articles involving subjects related to Africa, black politics and business. Informational, interview, profile, humor, expose, nostalgia, personal opinion, sports, travel, reviews of movies, books and records. Length: 1,000 to 5,000 words. Pays 6¢ per word. Photos are purchased on assignment. Send for spec sheet and photo information.

Fiction: The subject area is wide open. Would like to see more action fiction and more sex/love interest fiction. Experimental, adventure, western, erotica, science fiction, fantasy, humorous, historical; serialized novels. Length: 1,000 to 5,000 words. Pays 6¢ a word.

RAMPAGE, 11058 West Addison St., Franklin Park IL 60131. Editor: Jack Tyger. For sophisticated, cosmopolitan adults. Weekly. Circulation: 300,000. Buys all rights. Buys 600 mss a year. Pays on acceptance. Will send a sample copy to a writer for 25¢. Query first or submit complete ms. Enclose S.A.S.E.

Nonfiction and Photos: "Our audience consists of sophisticated, cosmopolitan adult readers who enjoy reading witty, humorous and satirical sex-oriented articles. Our readers also prefer reading shocking expose features. We're always in the market for features on current trends in sex. These features should have a strong humorous or satirical slant. Humorous first-person confession stories are also in order. Writer should know how to put humor, wit and satire to good use in his features. Features must be entertaining. Rather than treating readers as groups of buyers, we try to reach each and every reader on an individual basis." Length: 600 to 1,200 words. Payment is up to 2¢ a word. B&w glossy photos purchased with mss. Payment is $5 to $100.

SAGA, 333 Johnson Ave., Brooklyn NY 11206. Editor: Martin M. Singer. For men ages 17 and up. Monthly. Buys all rights, but will release on request. Pays on acceptance. Reports in 3 to 4 weeks. Query first. Enclose S.A.S.E.

Nonfiction: Articles, first-person adventure, exploration reports—anything of interest to the no-nonsense man. Emphasis has been shifted from the historical subject to the present-day happening, and narrative skill is demanded. Subjects of interest to male audience: war, politics, adventure, hunting, sports, legitimate expose (topical nature), in-depth reports on personalities, travel, crime, treasure (no rehashes, please; current or new information on established trove); science (current developments, but written for laymen). Sex articles, written in good taste; with no pseudo-case histories, based on recent reports. Solid research, from well-known sources, will get careful review. This is a reader's magazine, not a glancer's. Most articles and stories turn on an epic battle of some kind: treasure hunting, man against nature, man against society, man vs. himself, etc. Stresses the 'male triumphant' theme whenever possible. Wants to tell men where to look for buried treasure, how some guy crossed an ocean on a raft, etc. Does not want historical articles on Spanish-American war heroes, etc., or Civil War heroes. World War II is about the most remote history accepted. Editors ask you to query first. Length: 4,000 words. Pays $300 minimum; increase $10 per purchase until permanent plateau of $400; bonus factor thereafter.

Photos: Purchased with mss or captions only. Also buys picture stories. Color very important here. Will look at 35mm; prefers 2¼x2¼. B&w and color. Prefers to see contact sheets, then order 8x10's. Payment varies depending on set and quality;

$350 minimum for picture stories; $150 minimum for cover in color; 4x5 or larger transparencies. Needs b&w or color action stories for men.

How To Break In: "Prefer to look and report on outlines; request that it also cites writer's credentials and projected sources. Narrative flair and accuracy are prerequisites."

STAG MAGAZINE, 575 Madison Ave., New York NY 10022. Editorial Director: Noah Sarlat. Issued monthly. Reports in 2 weeks. Buys all rights. Pays on acceptance. Query first. Enclose S.A.S.E.

Nonfiction: Uses fast, suspenseful, dramatic, true stories. Also uses articles on personalities and crime which run up to 5,000 words. Wants any articles of interest to men. Pays up to $500.

Photos: B&w: singles, illustrations, series. Up to $25 for each article illustration; up to $50 per page for series. Color for covers and cheesecake only.

Fiction: Off-trail fiction bolstered by tense atmosphere and strong sex angle is acceptable, though hero-villain plot is not necessary. 3,000 to 5,000 words. The editor suggests that the inexperienced writer stick to the well-plotted story. Pays up to $300.

How To Break In: "Most of our material is based on successful queries and we read everything that comes in. We have plenty of openings. The best way for a newcomer to break in is with adventure stories, fiction or nonfiction. We're a good market for the freelancer, but unfortunately many of the stories and ideas we get show a lack of familiarity with what we're trying to do. The key thing is to make your story current and based on something newsworthy. When there were a lot of drug busts, we were running a lot of drug bust stories. We also base our stories on current movie themes. At this moment, disaster movies are big and so we are interested in disaster stories. The plots can be the old stuff, but we want to be able to develop the story into an eye-catching, new, newsworthy title. We only do one consumer-oriented piece a month and one sex-fiction piece, so they are more difficult to break into. However, one of our regular freelancers started with a 'true' adventure piece and we have since developed him into an excellent sex-fiction writer. Try to familiarize yourself with our formula and absorb what we want."

THE SWINGER, GEM, 303 W. 42 St., New York NY 10036. Editor: Will Martin. For young men. Bimonthlies. Material submitted will automatically be considered for both publications. Buys all rights or first rights. Buys 85 mss a year. Pays on publication or on assignment of a script to a specific issue. Reports "as soon as we can—depending upon the volume of unsolicited material we receive." Enclose S.A.S.E.

Nonfiction and Fiction: "Articles and fiction with sex-related themes, mainly. Treated straight or satirical or farcical." Also uses light humor and spoofs. Length: 500 to 1,500 words. Payment is $25 to $50.

Photos: B&w glossies. "No specified price."

TOPPER, Top-Flight Magazines, 13510 Ventura Blvd., Sherman Oaks CA 91423. Editor: Charles E. Fritch. For a male audience, all ages. Monthly. Buys original and second rights. Pays "when the blueline is okayed for printing." Material not suitable is generally rejected the same day it's received. Enclose S.A.S.E.

Nonfiction and Fiction: "Anything of interest to men. Male-female slant not required, but we like an interesting story with a conclusive ending." Buys nostalgia, suspense, humor, science fiction, fantasy, ribald tales, mystery, horror, adventure, personality. Length: 500 to 1,500 words. Pays 2¢ a word.

TRUE, Petersen Publishing Co., 8490 Sunset Blvd., Los Angeles CA 90069. Executive Editor: Steve Spence. For "intelligent, thoughtful men." Monthly. Buys all rights, unless negotiated. Pays on acceptance. Query first, with one example of published work. Enclose S.A.S.E.

Nonfiction: Looking for stories dealing with contemporary man-related subjects, in addition to documented, substantiated male topics such as adventure, "macho" personalities, topical news, police and crime, investigative reporting, outdoors (hunting and fishing), machinery (special cars, planes, boats, bikes, etc.); history, nostalgia and other subjects. Stories for *True* must be just that — true. No hackneyed themes or overworked yarns; no mock heroics, no pulp adventure, political axe-grinding or sexual fantasy. Pays up to $1,000 plus for exclusive major features, although payment for each article is negotiated on an individual basis. Also looking for success stories, finance and investment (Money Man column; 1,250 words), medical news, unique sports stories. Payment for 1-page columns or departments begins at $250.

WEEKDAY, 20 N. Wacker Dr., Chicago IL 60606. For the average man. Established in 1953. Circulation: 30,000. Buys all rights. Pays on acceptance. Enclose S.A.S.E.
Nonfiction and Photos: Uses articles slanted toward the average man, with the purpose of increasing his understanding of the business world and helping him be more successful in it. Also uses articles on "How to Get Along With Other People," and articles on meeting everyday problems in real estate, home maintenance, money management, etc. Length: approximately 1,000 words or less. Pays $20 to $50 for these. Uses b&w human interest photos.

Military Publications

Technical and semitechnical publications for military commanders, personnel, and planners, as well as those for military families and civilians interested in Armed Forces activities are listed here. All of these publications require submissions emphasizing military subjects or aspects of military life.

AIR UNIVERSITY REVIEW, United States Air Force, Air University, Maxwell Air Force Base AL 36112. Editor: John H. Scrivner, Jr., Lt. Col., USAF. "For Air Force officers and top-level civilians." Professional military journal. Circulation: 18,500. Not copyrighted. Buys no mss, but gives cash awards on publication. Reports in 6 weeks. Query first. Enclose S.A.S.E.
Nonfiction and Photos: "To stimulate professional thought concerning aerospace doctrines, strategy, policies, plans, programs, concepts, tactics, and related techniques. Footnotes when necessary only. Prefer that the author be the expert. Book reviews are solicited. Not a publicity journal. Narrative style. Also want articles in Spanish and Portuguese for books of readings entitled *Selections From Air University Review.* Photos desired as a supplement to articles, but not necessary. B&w glossies only." Length: 2,500 to 4,000 words. Pays in cash awards up to $100 ("unless written by Federal personnel on duty time").

ARMED FORCES JOURNAL, 1710 Connecticut Ave., N.W., Washington DC 20009. Editor: Benjamin F. Schemmer. For "senior career officers of the U.S. military, defense industry, Congressmen and government officials interested in defense matters, international military and defense industry." Established in 1863. Monthly. Circulation: 17,000. Buys all rights. Buys 15 to 20 mss a year. Pays on publication. Will send a free sample copy to writer on request. Will consider photocopied submissions. Reports in 2 to 4 weeks. Query first. Enclose S.A.S.E.
Nonfiction: Publishes "national and international defense issues: weapons programs, research, personnel programs, international relations (with emphasis on defense aspect). Also profiles on retired military personnel. We do not want broad overviews of a general subject; more interested in detailed analysis of a specific program or situation. Our readers are decisionmakers in defense matters—hence, subject should not be treated too simplistically. Be provocative. We are not afraid to take issue with our own constituency when an independent voice needs to be heard." Buys informational, profile, think articles. Length: 1,000 to 3,000 words. Pays $50 per page.

ARMY MAGAZINE, 1529 18th St., N.W., Washington DC 20036. Phone: 202-483-1800. Editor: L. James Binder. For active military, reserves, retired military, defense-oriented industry, government personnel and their families. Monthly magazine; 64 pages. Established in 1899. Circulation: 90,000. Buys all rights. Buys 90 mss a year. Payment on publication. Will send free sample copy to writer on request. Write for copy of guidelines for writers. Query first. Reports within 6 weeks. Enclose S.A.S.E.
Nonfiction and Photos: "Military subjects; contemporary, historical. While most of our material is of a serious nature, we use as much good humor as we can find, both very short and feature length. We like our articles to get to the point quickly, although we like interesting, attention-getting leads. We are very aware of the 'why' of things and prefer to go deeply into an aspect of a topic rather than carrying a superficial survey type of article which probably already has been done in publications that come out oftener and may have more space. History, specifically well-known history, is overworked. We like new slants within this area, previously unpublished information or material that is little known. Personality profiles in which the writer discovers military types are human and bright are also a drag." Length: 4,000 words maximum. Pays 7¢ to 9¢ per word. Regular columns cover book reviews and editorial opinion. 8x10 b&w glossies and 8x10 color prints or 35mm transparencies purchased with or without ms, or on assignment. Captions required. Pays $5 minimum for b&w; $50 minimum for color. Photo Department Editor: Mrs. Poppy Walker.
Fillers: Uses short humorous fillers. Length: 500 words maximum. Pays $5 to $25.
How To Break In: "We would like to publish more material from writers who do not specialize in military topics and I believe they have much to say to our readers. Gee-whiz approaches and historical pieces recounting events that would obviously be well known to a professional military readership never get very far with us. Best advice: avoid these, query first and tell us what you have published or anything that will give us an idea about your credibility."

AT EASE, Division of Home Missions, Assemblies of God, 1445 Boonville Ave., Springield MO 65802. Editor: Warren McPherson. For servicemen. Magazine; 4 (14x17) pages. Every 2 months. Circulation: 10,000. Buys all rights. "We are quite limited in what we would accept from freelance writers. Everything has to be slanted to Assemblies of God readers." Pays on publication. Will send free sample copy to writer on request. Write for copy of guidelines for writers. "If we can't use a submission and we think another department can, we usually let them see it before replying. Otherwise, as soon as we reject it, we return it." Query first. Enclose S.A.S.E.
Nonfiction and Photos: Materials that will interest servicemen and women. Must have some religious value. Length: 500 to 800 words. Pays minimum of 1½¢ a word. Payment for b&w and color photos subject to author's stated fee and size of picture.

INFANTRY, P.O. Box 2005, Fort Benning GA 31905. Phone: 404-545-2350. Editor: LTC Thomas J. Barham. For young infantry officers. "Over 90% of the readership is military. The reader is interested in current trends in the military (army), new developments, foreign armies and their equipment, solutions to problems encountered in the Army, National Guard and Army Reserve." Bimonthly magazine, 64 pages. Established in 1921. Circulation: 25,000. Not copyrighted. Buys about 100 to 150 mss a year. Payment on publication. U.S. Government employees are ineligible for payment. Will send free sample copy to writer on request. Write for copy of guidelines for writers. Submit only complete ms. Reports in 1 week. Enclose S.A.S.E.
Nonfiction and Photos: "Articles on the organization, weapons, tactics, and equipment of the infantry; any subject of interest to infantrymen. Must be infantry or infantry-related. At least one well-written historical piece used in each issue. No fillers, poems, or humor. 'Famous Infantrymen' is a standing series, a 1-page profile of famous men who served in the infantry. Articles that move, have life and action receive more consideration. Illustrations and photos help sell the product. Individual think pieces used in 'Forum' section, a place for an individual's opinion. *Infantry* is the only magazine in the U.S. that deals specifically with the foot soldier and his problems. Officers and NCO's use *Infantry* as a reference book, especially when new techniques and equipment are introduced. It is the Bible of the infantry. The 'I' stories are

seldom used, but continue to be submitted. Very few articles on Vietnam are published unless they contain a valuable lesson. Freelancers will sell pieces related to 'how to kill a tank', weapons for the infantry, electronic warfare and communications security, camouflage, defensive fortifications, aerial delivery techniques, helicopters and their application, and unique ideas related to building spirit and pride within the infantry." Informational, how-to, personal experience, interview of famous persons, profile, historical, think articles, expose, nostalgia, personal opinion, photo, new product, and technical articles. Send query to Book Review Editor for military book reviews. Length: 1,500 to 3,500 words. Pays 2¢ to 5¢ per word (based on quality of work). Columns include: Famous Infantrymen, Training Tips, How Equipped (foreign armies) Forum. Length: 1,000 to 1,500 words. Pays 2¢ a word. 5x7 or 8x10 b&w photos purchased with accompanying ms with no additional payment. Captions required. $25 paid for good color cover (transparency). Prefers 2¼x2¼ format.

LA VIVANDIERE MAGAZINE, 2634 Bryant Ave., S., Minneapolis MN 55408. Editor: Dennis P. O'Leary. For a history-oriented audience (especially military history); teen through adult. Magazine; 32 (5½x8½) pages. Established in 1973. Quarterly. Circulation: 4,000. Buys all rights, but will reassign rights to author after publication. Pays on publication. Will send sample copy to writer for 50¢. Write for copy of guidelines for writers. No photocopied or simultaneous submissions. Reports in 2 weeks. Query first. Enclose S.A.S.E.
Nonfiction and Photos: Mostly material related to military history; military miniatures and board games. Only well-researched, well-written articles with quality of information as well as quality of writing. "We see too many articles on war game rules which are not well thought out or adaptable to other games. And we would like to see more articles on miniatures and collections." Typical article titles include "Soviet Armour in W.W. II," "3-D Panzerblitz" and "Napoleon's Horseless Soldiers." Length: 1,200 to 2,500 words. Pays 1¢ a word. No additional payment for b&w photos used with mss. Prefers 3x5. B&w glossies are sometimes purchased without ms, or on assignment.
Fiction, Poetry and Fillers: Historical and humorous fiction. Length: 1,200 to 2,500 words. Pays 1¢ a word. All forms of poetry; no longer than 1 page. Pays $5. Jokes and new product items used as fillers. Pays $5.

LADYCOM MAGAZINE: 520 N. Michigan Ave., Chicago IL 60611. Editor: Anne Taubeneck. For military wives who live in the U.S. or overseas. Magazine: 56 to 64 pages. Established in 1969. Every 2 months. Circulation: 300,000. Buys first North American serial rights. Buys about 15 mss a year. Pays on publication. Will send free sample copy to writer on request. Write for copy of guidelines for writers. No photocopied or simultaneous submissions. Submit seasonal (Christmas) material 3 months in advance. Reports on material accepted for publication in 1 week. Returns rejected material in 1 to 2 weeks. Query first. Enclose S.A.S.E.
Nonfiction and Photos: Material must be written for the military wife. Interviews, food, fashion, how-to pieces, personal experience articles, beauty; articles for and about children; travel. Recently published "Bazaaring in Turkey" which featured a military wife shopping in Turkish bazaars. Length varies. Pays $35 to $125. No additional payment for photos used with mss. It Seems to Me column uses pieces written by military wives. Length: 800 to 1,000 words. Pays $50.

LEATHERNECK, P.O. Box 1918, Quantico VA 22134. Phone: 703-640-3171. Managing Editor: Ronald D. Lyons. Usually buys all rights, but will sometimes reassign rights to author under certain circumstances. Pays on acceptance. Query first. Enclose S.A.S.E.
Nonfiction and Photos: Interested in articles covering present-day Marine activities. Photos are mandatory. Not interested in former Marines in politics, sports, etc. *Leatherneck*'s slant today is toward the young Marine. Large percentage of subscribers are parents and dependents of enlisted Marines, consequently material used must be impeccable in taste. Pays $150 up. Length: 2,000 to 3,000 words.
Fiction: "Have temporarily discontinued 'plot' fiction but we are definitely interested in humor pieces with which today's Marine can identify."

Poetry: Poems with Marine themes. Pays $10 each.
How To Break In: "Like most publications, we're interested in young writers. And, if their writing is good, we smile when we sign the check. More than one beginner has 'broken in' with us, and we've watched them go on to bigger and better things. That's happiness. Unhappiness is when we receive manuscripts from young free-lancers—and older ones too—who have not done their homework. The manuscripts come in, and our rejection slips go out. On many of them we pen a note: 'We are sorry to be returning your manuscript, but *Leatherneck* is a magazine published for Marines. Perhaps one of the other service publications would like to see your story about the Navy, Army, Air Force, etc.' Yes, there are opportunities for young freelancers at *Leatherneck*. But they must remember that we are specialized. Our main interest is United States Marines, their problems, their interests and their accomplishments. If a young freelancer thinks he can write professionally about the Marine Corps, without having served in it, he is more than welcome to step up to our firing line. If he can't hit the target, his manuscript will be given a 'Maggie's Drawers' and returned. If he comes anywhere near the 'bull's-eye,' he will be encouraged. Our poetry column (Gyrene Gyngles) is a good opportunity for 'recruits' in the writing field to break in with us. Occasionally we buy short human interest items concerning Marines and their acts of heroism. And, of course, we're always interested in humor pieces, in good taste. You may have seen the Marine Corps' recruiting slogan: 'The Marines are looking for a few good men!' We go along with that. *Leatherneck* is looking for a few good freelancers.'"

MARINE CORPS GAZETTE, Marine Corps Association, Box 1775, MCB, Quantico VA 22134. Editor: Col. Bevan G. Cass, U.S.M.C. (Ret.). May issue is aviation oriented. November issue is historically oriented. Monthly. Circulation: 25,000. Buys all rights. Buys 140 to 160 mss a year. Pays on publication. Will send free sample copy on request. "Will send writer's guide on request." Submit seasonal or special material at least 2 months in advance. Query first. Reports in 30 to 60 days. Enclose S.A.S.E.
Nonfiction: Uses articles up to 5,000 words pertaining to the military profession. Keep copy military, not political. Wants practical articles on military subjects, especially amphibious warfare, close air support and helicopter-borne assault. Also uses any practical article on artillery, communications, leadership, etc. Particularly wanted are articles on relationship of military to civilian government, in-depth coverage of problem areas of the world, Russian and Chinese military strategy and tactics. Also historical articles about Marines are always needed for the November issue, the anniversary of the Marine Corps. Otherwise, historical articles not wanted unless they have a strong application to present day military problems. All offerings are passed on by an editorial board as well as by the editor. Does not want "Sunday supplement" or "gee whiz" material. Pays 3¢ to 6¢ per word.
Photos: Purchased with mss. Pays $5 each. 4x5 glossies preferred.

MILITARY LIFE/MALE CALL, 6 East 43rd St., New York NY 10017. Phone: 212-687-9040. Editor: William H. Lieberson. For the young male overseas in the military. Monthly. Circulation: 400,000. Buys all rights. Pays on acceptance. Will send a sample copy to a writer on request. No query required. Submit seasonal material at least 6 months in advance. Reports very slowly. Enclose S.A.S.E.
Nonfiction, Photos and Fillers: Format has changed so that the articles revolve around servicemen who are either currently in the service or have been in the service and are doing something that would be of interest to other servicemen. The subject areas are limitless. Length: 1,000 to 1,500 words. Pays $75. Anecdotes and sayings sometimes used. Length: 100 to 300 words. B&w glossies and color transparencies (35mm) are purchased with ms. Pays $10 for b&w. Payment for color depends on use.

MILITARY LIVING AND CONSUMER GUIDE, P.O. Box 4010, Arlington VA 22204. Editor: Ann Crawford. For military personnel and their families. Monthly. Circulation: 30,000. Buys first serial rights. "Very few freelance features used last year; mostly staff-written." Pays on publication. Will send a sample copy to a writer

for 25¢ in coin or stamp. "Slow to report due to small staff and workload." Submit complete ms. Enclose S.A.S.E.
Nonfiction and Photos: "Articles on military life in greater Washington DC area. We would especially like recreational features in the Washington DC area. We specialize in passing along morale boosting information about the military installations in the area, with emphasis on the military family—travel pieces about surrounding area, recreation information, etc. We do not want to see depressing pieces, pieces without the military family in mind, personal petty complaints or general information pieces. Prefer 700 words or less, but will consider more for an exceptional feature. We also prefer a finished article rather than a query." Payment is 1¢ to 1½¢ a word. Photos purchased with mss. 8x10 b&w glossies. Payment is $5 for original photos by author.

MILITARY LIVING AND CONSUMER GUIDE'S R&R REPORT, P.O. Box 4010, Arlington VA 22204. Publisher: Mrs. Ann Crawford. For "military consumers worldwide who are members of the Military Living R&R Association." Newsletter. Bimonthly. "Please state when sending submission that it is for the *R&R Report Newsletter* so as not to confuse it with our monthly magazine which has different requirements." Buys first rights, but will consider other rights. Pays on publication. Will send sample issue for 25¢. Enclose S.A.S.E.
Nonfiction: "We use information on little-known military facilities and privileges, discounts around the world and travel information. Items must be short and concise. Stringers wanted around the world. Payment is on an honorarium basis—1¢ to 1½¢ a word."

MILITARY REVIEW, U.S. Army Command and General Staff College, Fort Leavenworth KS 66027. Editor: Col. J. H. Chitty. Professional military journal. Monthly. Total circulation: 21,200 in English, Spanish and Portuguese language editions. Not copyrighted. Pays on publication. Will send free sample copy to a writer on request. Query preferred. Reports on submissions in 2 weeks.
Nonfiction and Photos: Prefers the concise and the direct, expressed in the active voice; precision and clarity of expression to flowery prose; the specific to the general. Wants articles on any subject related to military affairs that is of current interest and significance. Articles dealing with national defense policy, strategy, tactics at the division and higher levels of command, military organization, foreign military and strategic affairs, military history, leadership and professional development. Cite all references. Length: 2,000 to 4,000 words. Payment varies. B&w (8x10) glossies purchased with mss.

NATIONAL GUARDSMAN, 1 Massachusetts Ave., N.W., Washington DC 20001. Phone: 202-347-0341. Editor: Luther L. Walker. For officers and enlisted men of the Army and Air National Guard who will devote a great deal of their own time to serious military training but do not wish to make the Service their lifetime, full-time career. Monthly except August. Circulation: 70,000. Rights negotiable. Buys 10 to 12 mss a year. Pays on publication. Reports "usually, within days." Query first. Enclose S.A.S.E.
Nonfiction and Photos: Military policy, strategy, training, equipment, logistics, personnel policies; tactics, combat lessons learned as they pertain to the Army and Air Force (including Army National Guard and Air National Guard). No history. Material must be strictly accurate from a technical standpoint. Writer must have military knowledge. "It helps if he knows enough about Guard or other reserve forces to orient his piece toward the Guardsman's frame of reference. Style should be easy to read, serious but not pedantic." Does not want exposes. Length: 2,000 to 3,000 words. Payment is 3¢ a word and up, depending on originality, amount of research involved, etc. B&w glossy photos occasionally purchased with mss. Payment is $5 to $10.
Fillers: True military anecdotes (but not timeworn jokes). Length: 50 to 200 words. Payment is $10.

OFF DUTY, 69 Eschersheimer Landstr., 6 Frankfurt/Main, W. Germany. Editorial Director: Thomas C. Lucey. For "U.S. military in Europe and the Pacific. Varies from young bachelor G.I.'s to over-30 and over-40 career men and their wives." Monthly in 3 editions: European, Pacific and West (U.S.). Circulation: 220,000. Buys first rights. Buys 125 to 150 mss a year. Will send a sample copy on request. Query first. Send Pacific and West material to Jim Shaw, *Off Duty,* 645 Madison Ave., New York NY 10022. Submit seasonal queries 5 to 6 months in advance. Reports in 1 month. Enclose S.A.E. and International Reply Coupons.

Nonfiction: "Travel, shopping, art of living, bargains, good values in Europe or Pacific and Alaska-Hawaii-California. Need articles on do-something travel: hunting, fishing, water sports, camping, backpacking, motorcycle trips, etc." Approach should be "practical, specific, anecdotal. Stress what to buy, why; stress where to go, how, why. This is not a dream book." Also uses articles on "travel, folklore, handicrafts, shopping, participation sports, hunting and fishing, and the like." Would prefer not to see "puff copy, newspaper-style travel copy, amateur writing." Length: average 2,000 words. Pays 10¢ per word.

Photos: Purchased with ms; with captions only. B&w glossies. Pays $20; inside color, $40. Color covers negotiated.

OVERSEAS WEEKLY, 401 15th St., Oakland CA 94612. Editor: Linda C. Wheeler. For military personnel varying from the young bachelor GI to the enlisted man and officer. Newspaper (magazine format); 40 pages. Established in 1950. Every 2 weeks. Circulation: 100,000. Usually buys first rights. Buys about 50 to 70 mss a year. Pays on publication. Will send free sample copy to writer on request. Write for copy of guidelines for writers. Will consider photocopied and simultaneous submissions. Submit seasonal material 6 weeks in advance. Reports in 4 to 6 weeks. Query first or submit complete ms. Enclose S.A.S.E.

Nonfiction and Photos: "Since we are biweekly, we need in-depth details. We are not anti-military, so we need both sides of issues. We publish material on unusual crime (courts-martial or court cases involving the military); humorous military incidents, think pieces, new developments at military bases, interviews; features on sports need not be exclusively military. We are interested in where to go, what to do while in service; military goofs to military successes." Recent articles concerned Miss Universe visiting Army hospitals, and others on massage parlors in Baltimore, and VA benefits for Viet vets. Length: 500 to 2,000 words. Pays minimum of 3¢ a word. "Better chance of ms being accepted if accompanied by 8x10 b&w photos."

How To Break In: "Send unusual and creative material. Cover issues regarding military from both sides. Pictures are important in court cases."

PARAMETERS: THE JOURNAL OF THE U.S. ARMY WAR COLLEGE, U.S. Army War College, Carlisle Barracks PA 17013. Phone: 717-245-4943. Editor: Colonel Alfred J. Mock, U.S. Army. For military audience (large percentage of graduate level degrees) interested in national and international security affairs, defense activities and management; also a growing audience among civilian academicians. Biannual. Circulation: 5,800. Not copyrighted. Permission to reprint articles from the journal must be obtained from the Commandant of the U.S. Army War College. Payment on publication. Reports in 2 months. Enclose S.A.S.E.

Nonfiction and Photos: The purpose of *Parameters* is to provide a forum for the expression of mature, professional thought on national and international security affairs, military history, military strategy, military leadership and management, the art and science of land warfare, and other topics of significant and current interest to the U.S. Army and the Department of Defense. Further, it is designed to serve as a vehicle for continuing the education, and thus the professional development, of War College graduates and other military officers and civilians concerned with military affairs. Military implications should be stressed whenever possible. Length: 3,000 to 6,000 words. B&w glossies purchased with mss. Pays $5 per printed page or fraction thereof (to include half-tones, artwork, charts, graphs, maps, etc.) not to exceed $50 per article.

PERIODICAL, P.O. Box W, APO, New York 09829. Editor: Mark H. Magnussen. For historians and old fort buffs. Quarterly magazine, 32 (8¼x6½) pages. Established in 1967. Circulation: 1,200. Buys first North American serial rights. Buys 10 to 15 mss a year. Payment on publication. Will send sample copy to writer for 50¢. Will consider photocopied and simultaneous submissions. Query first or submit complete ms. Reports in 4 weeks. Enclose S.A.S.E.
Nonfiction and Photos: "Articles related to American military posts—the history, preservation, restoration, or memorialization. Factual, with footnotes, written from historian's viewpoint. Particularly interested in place of forts in military policy, and restoration of old forts." Informational, personal experience, historical, nostalgia, photo, travel articles. Length: 300 to 5,000 words. Pays ⅓¢ a word. B&w photos purchased with accompanying ms. Pays "$2 per printed page or proportion thereof."

THE RETIRED OFFICER MAGAZINE, 1625 Eye St., N.W., Washington DC 20006. Phone: 202-331-1111. Editor: Colonel Minter L. Wilson, Jr., USA-Ret. For "officers of the 7 uniformed services and their families." Established in 1945. Monthly. Circulation: 212,000. Rights purchased vary with author and material. May buy all rights or first serial rights. Pays on publication. Will send free sample copy to writer on request. Will consider photocopied submissions "if clean and fresh." Submit seasonal material (holiday stories in which the Armed Services are depicted) at least 3 months in advance. Reports on material accepted for publication within 6 weeks. Returns rejected material in 4 weeks. Submit complete ms. Enclose S.A.S.E.
Nonfiction and Photos: History, humor, cultural, second-career opportunities and current affairs. "Currently topical subjects with particular contextual slant to the military; historical events of military significance; features pertinent to a retired military officer's milieu (second career, caveats in the business world; wives' adjusting, leisure, fascinating hobbies). True military experiences (short) are also useful. Because our audience is derived from all services, we tend to use articles less technical than a single overview publication might publish." Length: 1,000 to 2,500 words. Pays $25 to $250. 8x10 b&w photos (normal halftone). Pays $5. Color photos must be suitable for color separation. Pays $25 if reproduced in color; otherwise, same as b&w. Department Editor: Sandra K. Mullenax.

SEA POWER, 818 Eighteenth St., N.W., Washington DC 20006. Editor: James D. Hessman. Issued monthly by the Navy League of the U.S. for naval personnel and civilians interested in naval and defense matters. Buys all rights. Pays on publication. Will send free sample copy to a writer on request. Reports in 1 to 6 months. Query first. Enclose S.A.S.E.
Nonfiction and Photos: Articles on sea power in general, and the U.S. Navy, the U.S. Marine Corps, merchant marine and naval services and other navies of the world in particular. Should illustrate and expound the importance of the seas and sea power to the U.S. and its allies. Wants timely, clear, nontechnical, lively writing. 500 to 1,500 words. Pays $40 to $200, depending upon length and research involved. Purchases 8x10 glossy photos with mss.

U.S. NAVAL INSTITUTE PROCEEDINGS, U.S. Naval Academy, Annapolis MD 21402. Phone: 301-268-6110. Publisher: Cdr. R.T.E. Bowler, Jr., USN (Ret.); Editor: Clayton R. Barrow, Jr. Monthly for professional Navy audience. Circulation: over 70,000. Reports on submissions in 4 to 6 weeks. Buys all rights. Pays on acceptance. Enclose S.A.S.E.
Nonfiction and Photos: Professional Navy, maritime, Marine Corps subjects. Length: 1,500 to 6,000 words. Pays 4¢ to 6¢ per word as voted by Board of Control. Photos purchased with mss; pays $2 each.
Fillers: Anecdotes with naval or maritime slant. Pays $10.

US MAGAZINE, 6 E. 43rd St., New York NY 10017. Editor: William H. Lieberson. For young military wife and her family. Monthly. Buys all rights. Pays on acceptance. Will send free sample copy to writer on request. Reports are slow (material has to be checked for clearance since it goes into official papers). Query first or submit complete ms. Enclose S.A.S.E.

Nonfiction: "Looking for articles that will appeal to the military wife and family. They should be general enough so that they will interest all three services. As a rule, these women are young with small children." Length: 750 to 1,000 words. Pays $75.

Photos: Purchased with mss; prefers captions but not necessary. Wants b&w glossies and four-color transparencies. Pays minimum of $10 for b&w; $25 minimum for color.

Miscellaneous Publications

AMERICAN ATHEIST MAGAZINE, P.O. Box 2117, Austin TX 78767. Editor: Richard F. O'Hair. For highly educated business and professional people. Monthly; 32 (8½x11) pages. Established in 1963. Circulation: 30,000. Rights purchased vary with author and material. Ms purchased per year range from zero to 60. Payment on publication or in contributor's copies. Will send sample copy to writer for $1, if available. Will consider photocopied and simultaneous submissions. Reporting time varies, depending on volume. Query first or submit complete ms. Enclose S.A.S.E.

Nonfiction: Articles on atheism, agnosticism, humanism, secularism, rationalist, state/church separation, iconoclism, objectivism. Emphasis is on well-researched, intelligent articles, not emotional ones. Nothing on religion and/or its praise. Uses book reviews, interviews, humorous, and informational articles; historical, personal experience, expose, personal opinion. Columns and departments use material on history and economics. Length: open. Pays "market price".

ANDY WARHOL'S INTERVIEW MAGAZINE, 860 Broadway West, New York NY 10003. Phone: 212-533-4700. Editor: Bob Colacello. For those interested in fashion, movies, art and music. Established in 1970. Monthly. Circulation: 82,000. All rights purchased but will negotiate on individual basis. Buys 25 mss a year. Payment on publication. Will send sample copy for $1. Query first. Enclose S.A.S.E.

Nonfiction and Photos: Features exclusive interviews with interesting people in fashion, art, movies, television, music, books, and whatever is happening now. Length: 10,000 words maximum. Pays $25. Prefer 8x10 or larger b&w photos.

How To Break In: "We are interested in interviews with entertainment figures as well as with *entertaining* figures. Usually with famous people with whom I want an interview, I'll assign it to someone I know. So the best way to break in is either with a well-known person to whom you happen to have some kind of access or, more likely, a lesser known *entertaining* person who you can get to yourself. If we like what you do — and I don't know how to describe it; basically what you need is a good interviewing personality rather than writing skill — then I will certainly want to use you in the future and will arrange access for you when it comes to interviewing the more famous types."

CB MAGAZINE, 250 Park Ave., New York NY 10017. Phone: 212-986-6596. Editor: Leo G. Sands. For operators of citizens band two-way radiotelephones for personal and business communications. Established in 1964. Monthly. Circulation: 50,000. Rights purchased vary with author and material. May buy all rights but will sometimes reassign rights to author after publication. Buys 4 mss a year. Payment on publication. Will send sample copy to writer for $1. Will consider photocopied and cassette submissions. Will not consider simultaneous submissions. Reports on material in 30 days. Query first. Enclose S.A.S.E.

Nonfiction and Photos: Case histories of use of citizens band radio in saving lives, etc. Semitechnical articles about equipment installation and repair. "We advocate lawful use of CB radio and oppose hobby type operation which is prohibited by law." Interested in true life stories where CB radio was used to render public service. Not interested in social events concerning CB radio operator clubs. Uses informational, how-to, personal experience articles; expose and technical. Length: 500 to 1,500 words. Pays $15 per published page. B&w photos purchased with accompanying mss; no additional payment.

How To Break In: "Report on a significant incident such as the use of CB radio in a search and rescue operation or at the scene of an accident or disaster. We cannot use material about social and fund raising activities of CB radio users."

COLUMBIA PICTORIAL, Box 184, Kamloops B.C., Canada. Editor: Thelma Carleton. "Not a specialized magazine for one particular group, but a return to the old family journal." Monthly tabloid magazine; 28 pages. Established in 1972. Circulation: 20,000. Buys all rights, but will reassign rights to author after publication. Buys about 120 mss a year. Payment on acceptance. Will send sample copy to writer for 50¢. Write for copy of guidelines for writers. Will not consider photocopied or simultaneous submissions. "We accept multiple submissions. Writers can send as many at one time as they wish, and they do not have to retype mss that have made the rounds to other publications." Submit seasonal material (minimum for Easter and Halloween; larger volume for Christmas) 3 months in advance. Reports on material accepted for publication in 2 weeks. Returns rejected material in 1 week. Established writers may query first. Others are advised to submit complete ms. Enclose S.A.E. and International Reply Coupons.

Nonfiction and Photos: "*Columbia Pictorial* is a return to the old family journal with articles of general interest, plus a complete Home and Fireside section devoted to women and the home. We need religious material for the Church Section and travel-photo features. The main emphasis in newspapers is on tragic news. We do not want any of that type. We do not want articles on abortion, dope, etc. We never use material on unpleasant or controversial topics. We use only material on current subjects that are happy, entertaining and uplifting. Special style of writing should be plain; simple reporting, particularly when the story comes from an interview, which is the type we prefer for the general section. In all cases, we would be looking for a shorter version of the subject." Length: 1,000 to 2,500 words for features. Pays 2¢ per word for material which can be featured even though it may be under 1,000 words. Mini items are used in the forward article section, as well as the women and church section. These should be between 250 words and up to 1,000 words or even over 1,000. Pays 1¢ per word for mini items. B&w photos are purchased with or without mss. 3½x5 up to 8½x11. "We want single photos of children and pets. Please send a caption that matches the expression or action of the subject. Could be a series up to 4 pictures to complete the little episode. A very unusual district happening with short caption." Pays $1 to $5.

Poetry: "The old-fashioned, gentle kind with rhythm and rhyme. Poetry, whether of people, or nature, should bring to the reader an awareness of the love of God and his neighbor." Length: 4 to 24 lines. Pays $1. Department Editor: Heather Spiers.

CREATIVE LIVING, 747 Third Ave., New York NY 10017. Phone: 212-371-6666. Editor: Robert H. Spencer. Published by Northwestern Mutual Life. Established in 1972. Quarterly. Circulation: 200,000. Rights purchased vary with author and material. Usually buys all rights but may reassign rights to author after publication. Buys 40 to 50 mss a year. Occasionally overstocked. Payment on acceptance or on publication. Will send free sample copy to writer on request. Write for copy of guidelines for writers. Prefers items not written in first person. Will not consider photocopied submissions. Submit seasonal sports material 6 months in advance. Reports on material in 2 to 3 months. Query first, with writing sample. Enclose S.A.S.E.

Nonfiction: "We publish *Creative Living* because we think it helps turn people on to themselves. We think it totally conceivable that people who read articles about others living their lives to the hilt might be motivated to think of themselves in a brighter, more creative light. Writers should bone up a bit on what makes the creative process tick. Get behind the facts. Many people lead creative lives. Importantly, we want to know their philosophical basis for living. Stress individuality and use specific examples. Give advice to the reader for gaining greater self-fulfillment. We try to avoid sex and partisan politics." Length: 600 to 2,500 words with greater need for short manuscripts. Pays $50 to $300, sometimes more for complex assignments.

DIVERSION MAGAZINE, P.O. Box 215, Bear Tavern Rd., Titusville NJ 08560. Editor: David Butterfield. For doctors with interests in travel, photography, gardening, fishing, boating. Magazine; 60 pages. Established in 1973. Every 2 months. Circulation: 277,000. Buys first North American serial rights. Buys 35 mss a year. Pays on acceptance. Will send sample copy to writer for $1. Write for copy of guidelines for writers. Will consider photocopied submissions. No simultaneous submissions. Submit seasonal material 3 months in advance for mid-winter issue. Reports in 2 weeks. Query first. Enclose S.A.S.E.

Nonfiction and Photos: Articles on U.S. and North American travel, recreation, hobbies, sports, entertainment, food and drink. Must be informative and contain substantial service information. Reflective essays on the current social and cultural forces redefining our conception of "quality of life." Informational, how-to, personal experience, profile, humor, think pieces, personal opinion. Articles related to holidays are used in mid-winter issue. Recently published "Rocky Mountain Skiing" which successfully combined a vivid and personal account with considerable service information. Length: 1,000 to 3,000 words. Pays $100 to $750. Dr.'s Diversion column uses profiles of doctors with unusual avocations. Collectors' column uses profiles of doctors who are collectors of art, antiques, etc. Column length: 1,500 to 2,000 words. Pays minimum of $100. B&w glossies and color transparencies purchased with or without ms, or on assignment. Pays $50 to $150 a page for b&w; $100 to $200 per page for color. Captions required.

Poetry and Fillers: Humorous, doctor-related light verse. Length: 10 to 20 lines. Pays $10 to $25. Medical or travel-oriented crossword puzzles used as fillers. Length: half-page to full page. Pays $25 to $100.

How To Break In: "Send ideas in query form, along with samples of previously published work."

GOLD!, Western Publications, Inc., P.O. Box 3338, Austin TX 78764. Phone: 512-444-3674. Publisher: Joe Austell Small. For people interested in mining, lost treasure, lost mines, ghost towns. Quarterly; 64 to 72 (8½x11) pages. Established in 1967. Circulation: 150,000. Rights purchased vary with author and material. May buy first North American serial rights or second serial (reprint) rights. Buys 30 to 40 mss a year. Payment on acceptance. Will send sample copy for 60¢. Write for copy of guidelines for writers. Will consider photocopied submissions. Will not consider simultaneous submissions. Reports in 4 to 6 weeks. Query first. Enclose S.A.S.E.

Nonfiction and Photos: True experience, or researched material on experiences of others. "We can also use professionally written articles on current mining activities; laws affecting the treasure hunter or prospector, etc. (These subjects require direct knowledge of the subject.)" Locale not limited to United States. Length: 1,000 to 5,000 words. Pays 2¢ per word minimum. Very clear b&w photos (any size) are purchased with ms as a package. Captions are required. Photos are returned after publication.

INSECT WORLD DIGEST, P.O. Box 108, Rensselaerville NY 12147. Editor: Dr. Ross H. Arnett, Jr. For students, teachers (advanced high school, college, university), amateur and professional entomologists; nature, conservation and ecology groups. Nontechnical articles on insects. Established in 1973. Every 2 months. Circulation: 3,000. Buys first North American serial rights. "Many articles are staff written or rewritten by professional writers." Buys "36 or more mss" a year. Payment on acceptance. Will send sample copy to a writer for $1. Write for copy of editorial guidelines for writers. Will consider photocopied submissions. Submit seasonal material 6 months in advance. Reports on material accepted for publication in 2 months. Returns rejected material in 2 months. "Most material rejected because of technical inaccuracy or too elementary." Query first. Enclose S.A.S.E.

Nonfiction and Photos: "Nontechnical articles on insects, spiders and related organisms; pesticides, study techniques. Popular writing about current research or how to get interested in insect study as a hobby. Do not emphasize danger or weird; spectacular only if spectacular to a professional. Each issue has at least 1 article on insects in relation to environment. Informational, how-to, interview, short humor, historical, think, expose, travel, new product; personal experience if it's right touch, say, collecting experiences in remote areas, etc." Length: up to 3,500 words, except for special feature articles. "We negotiate for articles by contract only. We often use professional rewriters." Usually pays 2¢ a word minimum. Photos purchased with or without accompanying ms. Captions usually required. 5x7 glossy or larger. 35mm transparencies; larger preferred. Pays $5 minimum for b&w; $10 minimum for color. Transparency returned after use.

JOURNAL OF GRAPHOANALYSIS, 325 W. Jackson Blvd., Chicago IL 60606. Editor: V. Peter Ferrara. For audience interested in self-improvement. Monthly. Buys all rights. Pays on acceptance. Reports on submissions in 1 month. Enclose S.A.S.E.
Nonfiction: Self-improvement material helpful for ambitious, alert, mature people. Applied psychology and personality studies, techniques of effective living, etc.; all written from intellectual approach by qualified writers in psychology, counseling and teaching, preferably with degrees. Length: 2,000 words. Pays about 5¢ a word.

MAX, 141 El Camino, Beverly Hills CA 90212. Editor: Frank M. Hiteshew. For big men and tall women. Magazine published 4 times a year. Circulation: 50,000. Buys all rights. Payment on publication. Query first, addressing query to Ann Lapidas, Managing Editor. Enclose S.A.S.E.
Nonfiction: Psychology, fashion, sports and other material related to big and tall men and women. Length: 1,500 to 3,500 words. Pays $100 to $200.

PASSENGER TRAIN JOURNAL, 29 E. Broad St., Hopewell NJ 08525. Managing Editor: Otto Janssen. Established in 1966. For "people who are seriously interested in the maintenance of modern rail passenger service; not 'buffs'." Quarterly. Circulation: 5,200. Not copyrighted. Buys 2 or 3 freelance mss an issue. Payment on publication. Reports on material in 2 to 3 weeks. Will consider photocopied submissions. Query first or submit complete ms. Enclose S.A.S.E.
Nonfiction and Photos: "All our articles are devoted to modern rail passenger service, here and abroad. Must be studious, carefully researched. Any article starting 'Shades of Casey Jones' is summarily rejected. We have nothing to do with freight or nostalgia about steam trains. Prefer not to see anything about model railroading, tourist railroads or personality pieces. Nothing but good, thoroughly researched articles about rail passenger service anywhere in the world." Length: "No limit within reason. Payment ranges from $5 for short, routine pieces to $50 to $75 for good features." 8x10 b&w glossies purchased with or without mss or on assignment. Captions required. Pays $5 for nonassignment photos. No color is used.
How To Break In: "In our rather highly specialized field, there is no substitute for thorough research and tight, pointed writing. Gimmicks may attract our attention initially but they won't make a sale. Much unsolicited freelance material is poorly done and shows that the writer has little understanding of our requirements."

If this is 1977, this edition is out of date. See address in front of book to order latest edition. *Writer's Market* **is published annually each fall.**

PRACTICAL KNOWLEDGE, 325 W. Jackson Blvd., Chicago IL 60606. Editor: V. Peter Ferrara. Bimonthly. A self-advancement magazine for active and involved men and women. Buys all rights, "but we are happy to cooperate with our authors." Pays on acceptance. Reports in 2 to 3 weeks. Enclose S.A.S.E.

Nonfiction and Photos: Uses success stories of famous people, past or present; applied psychology; articles on mental hygiene and personality by qualified writers with proper degrees to make subject matter authoritative. Also human interest stories with an optimistic tone. Up to 5,000 words. Photographs and drawings are used when helpful. Pays a base rate of 5¢ a word; $3 each for illustrations.

QUEST MAGAZINE, 2 St. Clair Ave., W., Toronto, Ontario, Canada M4V 1K6. Editor: Nicholas Steed. For homeowners of $20,000 median income. Magazine; 84 pages. Established in 1972. Every 2 months. Circulation: 675,000. Buys all rights. Buys about 150 mss a year. Pays on acceptance. Will send free sample copy to writer on request. Reports on material accepted for publication in 2 weeks. Returns rejected material in 2 weeks. Query first. Enclose S.A.E. and International Reply Coupons.

Nonfiction and Photos: Only Canadian material. Articles on finance, psychology, sociology and those of general interest. Must emphasize service to provide real benefit to the reader. To increase reader's ability to get along and ahead in today's world, nothing dealing in abstract issues is used. Informational, how-to, personal experience, interview, profile, travel, successful business operations. Length: 1,000 to 5,000 words. Pays $200 to $1,000. Pays minimum of $50 for color photos purchased with mss.

RAIL CLASSICS, 7950 Deering Ave., Canoga Park CA 91304. Editor: Denis Dunning. For adult railroad enthusiasts with a good knowledge of the operation of railroads, and an amazing appetite for rail histories as well as current operations. Magazine; 84 (8½x11) pages. Established in 1971. Monthly. Circulation: 50,000. Buys all rights, but will reassign rights to author after publication. Buys 85 mss a year. Pays on publication. Will send sample copy to writer for $1.50. Write for copy of guidelines for writers. No photocopied or simultaneous submissions. Reports on material accepted for publication in 1 month. Returns rejected material as soon as possible. Submit complete ms. Enclose S.A.S.E.

Nonfiction and Photos: All articles pertain to railroads, for the rail enthusiast. This is not a general interest publication and the writer must have excellent knowledge of railroading. Informational, historical, photo stories. Length: 1,500 to 3,500 words. Pays $50 to $150. Pays $3 for 5x7 (or larger) b&w photos; $20 for color transparencies; any size.

RAILROAD MAGAZINE, 420 Lexington Ave., New York NY 10017. Editor: Freeman Hubbard. "Our magazine has a double-barreled appeal, for railroad men, active or retired; and railfans." Monthly magazine; 64 (8x11) pages. Established in 1906. Circulation: about 35,000. Buys all rights, but will reassign rights to author after publication. Rarely buys second serial (reprint) rights. Buys between 100 and 150 mss a year. Payment on acceptance; occasionally, shortly afterward. Will send free sample copy and guidelines for writers only if the writer is a more or less established writer in the railroad field. A sample copy may be purchased for $1. Query first. Enclose S.A.S.E.

Nonfiction and Photos: "We buy only fact articles dealing with railroads and/or streetcars in the U.S. and/or Canada (past or present), and the employees who help run them. No life stories of old-timers unless they are professional writers, as well as railroaders. We don't want to hear from any writer unless he or she has a specialized knowledge of rail operation or rail lore. Writer should query in advance and prove in first letter that he or she has such a specialized knowledge. We are not interested in articles slanted from the management viewpoint. Furthermore, we like to dramatize railroading with colorful writing, anecdotes, and personalities. We don't want articles on subjects that have been widely publicized in other magazines and/or railroad history books. We don't want routine life stories of colorless railroad men." Would be interested in a story of passenger station train sheds in the U.S. and Canada or a story of the commissary railroad car that the U.S. Bureau of Indian Affairs used to deliver supplies to Indian reservations. Length: 1,500 to 3,500 words. Pays minimum of 5¢ a word, depending on the subject and how well it is handled. Pays $5 to $10 for b&w photos purchased with accompanying mss, and will return photos on request. Any size, if sharply detailed. "Not in the market for photos apart from articles, except that we would pay a good price for a photo of the Jefferson Davis funeral train."

RODEO SPORTS NEWS, 2929 W. 19th Ave., Denver CO 80204. Editor: Arland Calvert. For avid fans of professional rodeo. Tabloid newspaper; 16 to 32 pages. Established in 1952. Annual. Circulation: 29,400. Buys all rights, but will reassign rights to author after publication. Buys 8 to 10 mss a year. Mostly staff-written. Pays on 15th of month following publication. Will send free sample copy to writer on request. Reports in 2 weeks. Query first or submit complete ms. Enclose S.A.S.E.
Nonfiction and Photos: "We are almost completely staff-written, but we do buy freelance articles on individual members of the professional Rodeo Cowboys Association, Inc.; biographical sketches on their rodeo careers. Keep in mind that we are highly specialized." Length: 6 to 7 typewritten, double-spaced pages. Pays minimum of $20. Only 1 color photo purchased annually for cover use. Only 8x10 b&w glossies are considered. Pays $2. Captions required. Recent articles include one about the Rodeo National Finals; a profile of Tom Ferguson, "All Around Champion Cowboy;" an item about Saddle Bronc Champion John McBeth; an item about Bull Riding Champion Don Gay; and in the annual championship edition of *Rodeo Sports News,* a complete rundown on all division champions and awards given.

THE ROSICRUCIAN DIGEST, AMORC, Rosicrucian Park, San Jose CA 95191. Phone: 408-287-9171, Ext. 206. Editor: Robin M. Thompson. Address mss to Editorial Department. Monthly. Buys first rights and the right to reprint. Payment on acceptance. Will send free sample copy to writer on request. Write for a copy of guidelines for writers. Queries accepted but not required. Reports in 3 to 4 weeks. Enclose S.A.S.E.
Nonfiction, Photos, and Fillers: Philosophical and inspirational subjects, art, music, science, education, biographies, historical sketches. Humanitarian, generally uplifting and helpful outlook. Features Mysticism, Science, The Arts. Should appeal to worldwide circulation. Pays 4¢ per word. "We generally only accept photos that come with articles. Pay 2¢ per word for filler material." Recent articles include "I Am Blind But My Dog Can See," the story of the seeing eye; "The Celestial Sanctum, The Economy of Life," a cosmic meeting place for advanced and spiritually developed members of the Rosicrucian Order, the focal point of cosmic radiations of health, peace, happiness, and inner awakening; "Early Egyptian Views on Death," an article that tells how man fears death because he does not understand it, and his ignorance of this natural phenomenon has caused him to resort to sometimes rather strange practices; "Quasars and Earthquake Prediction," a good, sound, scientific article.

SCANDINAVIAN REVIEW, 127 East 73rd St., New York NY 10021. Phone: 212-879-9779. Editor: Erik J. Friis. For Americans interested in Scandinavia. Established in 1913. Quarterly. Circulation: 7,000. Buys all publication rights. Buys 6 mss an issue. Pays on acceptance. Will send a sample copy to a writer for $2.50. Reports in 8 weeks. Enclose S.A.S.E.
Nonfiction and Photos: Wants articles about any phase of life and society in modern Scandinavia, written in a popular fashion. Base articles on research. Length: 2,500 words. Pays $75 maximum. Some photos purchased.
Fiction and Poetry: "Stories are usually written by Scandinavian authors, but stories by Americans, if they have a Scandinavian locale, may be used." Short stories preferred. Pays $75. Buys some poetry; theme open.

SMITHSONIAN MAGAZINE, 900 Jefferson Drive, Washington DC 20560. Editor: Edward K. Thompson. For "associate members of the Smithsonian Institution; 87% with college education." Monthly. Circulation: 800,000. "Our material is automatically copyrighted. In the case of selling second rights *Smithsonian* keeps half, gives the rest to writer. Payment for each article to be negotiated depending on our needs and the article's length and excellence." Pays "first half on assignment or tentative acceptance, remainder on acceptance." Submit seasonal material 3 months in advance. Reports "as soon as possible." Query first. Enclose S.A.S.E.

Nonfiction: "Our mandate from the Smithsonian Institution says we are to be interested in the same things which now interest or should interest the Institution: folk and fine arts, history, natural sciences, hard sciences, etc." Length and payment "to be negotiated."

Photos: Purchased with or without ms and on assignment. Captions required. Pays "$250 a color page, $200 b&w."

SUCCESS UNLIMITED, The Arcade Bldg., 6355 Broadway, Chicago IL 60660. Executive Editor: Arlene Canaday. "Average reader is male, 35 to 40 years of age, with 2 children; works in a professional, sales or managerial capacity; college educated, with a strong motivation to go into business for himself. Enjoys golf, fishing, photography, and gardening." Monthly magazine; 112 pages. Established in 1954. Circulation: 180,000. Rights purchased vary with author and material. May buy all rights, first North American serial rights, first serial rights or second serial (reprint) rights. Buys about 20 mss a year. Occasionally overstocked. Payment on acceptance. Will send free sample copy to writer on request. Write for copy of guidelines for writers. Will consider photocopied submissions. Will not consider simultaneous submissions. Submit seasonal material (Christmas) 4 months in advance. Reports on material accepted for publication in 3 to 4 weeks. Returns rejected material in 1 week. Query first. Enclose S.A.S.E.

Nonfiction and Photos: "Our publication continues to stress the importance of mental attitudes in all areas of endeavor without being preachy about it. If a man gets ahead in this world, we want to know how he did it." Material on self-motivation; profiles of executives, techniques, health, investments (with emphasis on the unusual, rather than just stocks and bond type); occasional in-depth studies in sociological areas such as marriage, family, etc. "We see entirely too many articles dealing with the positive mental attitude theory with very little in the way of concrete examples that a person can relate to. We would like to see new approaches to old themes and material on ideas for making money in inflationary times." Length: 1,000 to 3,000 words. Pays 10¢ a word; $200 maximum. 8x10 or 5x7 b&w glossies or color transparencies used. Pays $10 minimum for b&w; $25 minimum for color. Captions required.

TATTOO, P.O. Box 1397, Smyrna GA 30080. Publisher: Scott Goldenrod. Established in 1972. For "everyone interested in the subject of tattooing." Quarterly. Buys all rights, but will reassign rights to author after publication. Buys 10 to 25 mss a year. Pays on publication. Reports in a few weeks. Will consider photocopied submissions if legible. Will send sample copy to writer for $3. Query first or submit complete ms. Enclose S.A.S.E.

Nonfiction and Photos: "We publish anything related to tattooing. We are especially interested in profiles of artists and articles about clients, life styles, etc., but are not limited to those areas. The writer can do his own thing. If it's dull, we won't use it. If it's really good, we'll pay him more than our base rate." Length: open. Pays 5¢ a word minimum. Pays $10 minimum for photos.

VEGETARIAN TIMES, P. O. Box A3104, Chicago IL 60690. Editor: Paul Obis, Jr. For anyone concerned about the environment, nutrition, and animal welfare; well-educated readers. Newsletter; 24 (8½x11) pages. Established in 1974. Bimonthly. Circulation: 1,000. Rights purchased vary with author and material. Will reassign all rights to author after publication, or will buy first serial or simultaneous rights. Buys 8 mss a year. Pays on publication. Will send sample copy to writer for 50¢. Will consider photocopied and simultaneous submissions. Submit seasonal material 12 to 18 weeks in advance. Reports within 6 weeks. Query first. Enclose S.A.S.E.

Nonfiction and Photos: Features concise articles related to agribusiness, vegetarianism, natural foods, nutrition, animal welfare, and "do-it-yourself" canning, preserving, etc. "We try not to moralize; we are not in the business of selling any contrivances of the 'health' industry. Articles should offer constructive alternative options in addition to stating the problem." No personal pet stories. Informational, how-to, personal experience, interview, profile, historical, expose, personal opinion, successful health food business operations, and restaurant reviews. Recently printed topics from freelancers included, "Veganism", a well-presented, concise, and relevant article, and "Whale Milk", timely material related to world food shortages, and "Corporate Cuisine", a look at American agribusiness. Length: 100 to 2,000 words. Pays 1¢ per word. Will also use 500-word items for regular columns. Pays $5 apiece. Pays $5 total for photos purchased with accompanying ms, "unless otherwise arranged." No color; b&w ferrotype preferred.

How To Break In: "The writing should be of interest to our audience; especially seeking nutritional articles specifically geared to a non-meat diet."

WESTERN TREASURES, 1440 W. Walnut St., Compton CA 90220. Editor: Ray Krupa. For readers who are interested in treasure hunting, exploring ghost towns, abandoned mines, looking for special rocks, minerals, precious stones; and gold prospecting. Magazine; 64 pages. Special issues are published occasionally on gold prospecting, rock hounding; also publishes a ghost town annual. Established in 1966. Published every other month. Circulation: 60,000. Buys all rights. Buys 70 to 75 mss a year. Pays on publication. Will send free sample copy to writer on request. No photocopied or simultaneous submissions. Submit special issue material 6 months in advance. Reports in 2 weeks. Submit complete ms. Enclose S.A.S.E.

Nonfiction and Photos: "We endeavor to publish only true stories on treasure hunting, exploring ghost towns and abandoned mines; looking for special rocks, minerals, precious stones; articles on gold prospecting. Emphasis is on where, when and how. Must be treasure oriented, to which the reader can relate. Pictures with stories are essential. We'd like to see more stories on treasure hunting in the eastern states and treasure hunting experiences relating to the American Revolution and the Civil War." Recently published "Collecting Ghost Towns" and "How to Prospect for Gold." Length: 800 to 3,000 words. Pays 2¢ a word. Also looking for material for the following departments and columns: Treasures in the Headlines, Around the Campfire, Off Road/This & That, Look What They've Found; Minerals, Rocks and Gems. Length: 400 to 1,000 words. Pays 2¢ a word. Pays $5 for 3x5 (or larger) b&w photos purchased with ms; $10 for 35mm color purchased with ms.

Music Publications

AUDIO MAGAZINE, 134 N. 13th St., Philadelphia PA 19107. Editor: Gene Pitts. For men interested in high fidelity components, electronics and music. Magazine; 96 pages. Established in 1947. Monthly. Circulation: 110,000. Buys all rights. Buys about 24 mss a year. Pays on publication. Will send free sample copy to writer on request. Will consider photocopied submissions. No simultaneous submissions. Reports in 3 to 6 weeks. Query recommended, but not required. Enclose S.A.S.E.

Nonfiction and Photos: Articles on hi-fi equipment, design technique, hi-fi history; explanations for beginners and of widely known commercial uses. Pays $35 per published page. No additional payment made for photos used with mss.

BLUEGRASS UNLIMITED, Box 111, Broad Run VA 22014. Editor: Peter V. Kuykendall. For musicians and devotees of bluegrass and old-time country music. Monthly magazine; 36 to 40 pages. Established in 1966. Circulation: 10,000. Buys all rights, but will negotiate for author's use if need arises. Buys 5 to 15 mss a year. Payment on publication. Will send free sample copy to writer on request. Will consider photocopied submissions. Will not consider simultaneous submissions. Reports on material accepted for publication in 30 to 60 days. Returns rejected material within 30 days. Query first or submit complete ms. Enclose S.A.S.E.

Nonfiction and Photos: "Artists' profiles, instrument articles and reviews on related books, records, etc. No specific approach, but must make good reading with informational approach. We do not take many 'fan' style articles." Technical articles and record and book reviews. Length: 500 to 5,000 words. Pays 1½¢ to 2¢ a word. 8x10 b&w glossies purchased with or without mss. Pays $15 per page; $25 per cover.
Fiction and Fillers: Limited use of fiction. When it is published, length is limited to 500 to 1,500 words. Pays 1½¢ to 2¢ per word. Puzzles related to the publication's theme are used as fillers. Length: open. Pays 1½¢ to 2¢ per word.

CREEM, 187 S. Woodward Ave., Suite 211, Birmingham MI 48011. Phone: 313-642-8833. Editor: Juan Uhelszki. Established in 1969. Buys all rights. Pays on publication. Query first. Reports within 2 weeks. Enclose S.A.S.E.
Nonfiction and Photos: Freelance photos and articles, mostly music oriented. "We bill ourselves as America's Only Rock and Roll Magazine." Pays $60 to $75, more for the right story. $15 to $20 for reviews.

FORECAST, 934 Bonifant St., Silver Spring MD 20910. Editor: Brandi Sullivan. Monthly. Circulation: 30,000. Buys all rights. Payment on publication. Will send sample copy to writer for 75¢. Submit seasonal material 3 months in advance. Reports in 3 to 4 weeks. Enclose S.A.S.E.
Nonfiction: Profiles of names in the news in the entertainment world of theater, opera, symphony, art, jazz, rock, dance, ballet. Articles dealing with all aspects of these categories plus FM radio. Length: 600 to 1,200 words. Pays $20 to $75 depending on length and quality of article.

GUITAR PLAYER MAGAZINE, Box 615, 12333 Saratoga-Sunnyvale Rd., Saratoga CA 95070. Phone: 408-446-1105. Editor: Jim Crockett. For persons "interested in guitars and guitarists." 12 times a year. Circulation: 85,000. Buys all rights. Buys 30 to 35 mss a year. Pays on acceptance. Will send a sample copy to a writer on request. Returns rejected material in 1 week. Acknowledges acceptance in 1 week. Query first. Enclose S.A.S.E.
Nonfiction and Photos: Publishes "wide variety of articles pertaining to guitars and guitarists: interviews, guitar craftsmen profiles, how-to features—anything amateur and professional guitarists would find fascinating and/or helpful. On interviews with 'name' performers, be as technical as possible regarding strings, guitars, techniques, etc. We're not a pop culture magazine, but a music magazine." Also buys features on such subjects as a "guitar museum, the role of the guitar in elementary education, personal reminiscences of past greats, technical gadgets and how to work them, analysis of flamenco, etc." Length: open. Pays $25 to $75. Photos purchased with mss. B&w glossies. Pays $15 to $25. Buys 35mm color slides. Pays $50. Buys all rights.

HI-FI STEREO BUYERS' GUIDE, 229 Park Ave., South, New York NY 10003. Editor-in-Chief: Julian S. Martin. Bimonthly magazine whose function is to assist the prospective buyer of high fidelity components in their purchase. Writers are advised to obtain a copy of the magazine and examine it carefully for content. "If you think you can write for us, we suggest you submit to us a precis of the story you would like to write, and await our comments. We pay on impulse before publication." Enclose S.A.S.E.
Nonfiction: "We run a short jazz column and a comprehensive record-review column on classical music. Also, we have a continuing series on opera which takes about 2 pages in the magazine. We don't plan to increase this coverage, nor do we plan to take on additional freelancers to assist us in this area. We are interested in discovering new authors who are familiar with the buying habits of the audiophile and know the current audio marketplace. Average payment is about $200."

HIGH FIDELITY, The Publishing House, State Road, Great Barrington MA 01230. Editor: Leonard Marcus. For well-educated, young, affluent readers, interested in home recording and playback systems (all disc and tape formats) and the program material to play on them. Special issues: March and August, tape; June, speakers; September, new recordings; October, new equipment; December, year's best recordings. Established in 1951. Monthly. Circulation: 260,000. Buys all rights. Buys 12 mss a year. Payment on acceptance. Will consider photocopied submissions, "if they are legible." Submit seasonal material 5 months in advance. Reports in 1 month. Query first or submit complete ms. Enclose S.A.S.E.

Nonfiction: "Material for feature articles is divided between audio equipment and music makers. Audio equipment articles should be backed up with as many technical specifications as possible and appropriate and readily understandable to the lay reader. Music articles should be slanted toward the musician's recording career or recordings of his works or to increase the reader's understanding of music. Articles are sophisticated, detailed, and thoroughly backgrounded." Regular columns include: Speaking of Records, interviews with noted music and recording personalities about their work and favorite recordings; Behind the Scenes, reports of in-progress recording sessions here and abroad. Length: 1,000 to 3,000 words. Pays $150 to $300.

Photos: Purchased with accompanying manuscripts. Captions required. 8x10 b&w glossy payment included in ms payment. Color rarely used; inquire first.

HIGH FIDELITY/MUSICAL AMERICA, The Publishing House, State Road, Great Barrington MA 01230. Editor-in-Chief: Leonard Marcus. Monthly. Established in 1888. Circulation: 20,000. Buys all rights. Pays on publication. Enclose S.A.S.E.

Nonfiction and Photos: Articles, musical and audio, are generally prepared by acknowledged writers and authorities in the field, but does use freelance material. Length: 3,000 words maximum. Pays $25 minimum. New b&w photos of musical personalities, events, etc.

INTERNATIONAL MUSICIAN, 1500 Broadway, New York NY 10036. Editor: J. Martin Emerson. For professional musicians. Monthly. Not copyrighted. Pays on acceptance. Will send a sample copy to a writer on request. Reporting time varies. Query first. Enclose S.A.S.E.

Nonfiction: Articles on prominent instrumental musicians (classical, jazz, rock, or country). Particularly interested in styles of Leonard Feather, Burt Korall, Bill Littleton, John Wilson, etc. Length: 2,000 words. Pays $75 to $125.

LIVING BLUES, P.O. Box 11303, Chicago IL 60611. Phone: 312-227-4144. Editors: Jim and Amy O'Neal. For blues fans and people in the blues business (record companies, agents, disc jockeys, etc.) Bimonthly magazine; 44 to 52 pages. Established in 1970. Circulation: 6,000. Buys all rights, but will reassign rights to author after publication. Buys 20 mss a year. Payment for feature articles and interviews is made on publication. Payment in contributor's copies is made for news and reviews. Will send complimentary sample copy to writer. Write for copy of guidelines for writers. Will consider photocopied submissions. Will not consider simultaneous submissions if submitted to another music publication. Reports on material accepted for publication in 2 to 8 weeks. Returns rejected material in 4 to 12 weeks. Query first or submit complete ms. Enclose S.A.S.E.

Nonfiction and Photos: Articles, interviews, news and reviews on the black American blues tradition, present and past. Personality features on blues artists, both famous and obscure. Looking for in-depth reports on blues activity (artists, clubs, record companies, radio, etc.) in Houston, St. Louis, Mississippi, Indianapolis and other areas. "Many of our articles entail a lot of field research, but we want readable journalistic pieces, rather than research reports. Writers can assume that our readers know the basics of blues and who the major blues performers are. Do not bother sending material on well-known blues singers like B. B. King or Muddy Waters, unless it is very thorough and can present some information that hasn't appeared in dozens of previous articles on such performers. We are also not interested in blues/rock groups. We would like to see new talent discoveries; stories on retired artists, historical pieces; reports/reviews from live performances at blues clubs." Length: 1,000 words minimum for articles; reviews: 200 to 500 words. Pays $10 to $25 for articles and interviews; contributor's copies for reviews and news. Departments use record reviews, book and film reviews. "Live Blues" uses concert/

club reviews; "Blues News" uses material from various cities. Length: 200 to 500 words for reviews; news, minimum of 50 words. Payment for departmental material is in contributor's copies. Pays $2.50 to $5 (more for cover shots) for 4x5 or larger b&w photos. Send positive prints. Captions required. Photos are purchased with or without accompanying mss or on assignment. Must relate to theme.

How To Break In: "Send new information about local blues artists and the blues scenes in various cities, or send thorough interviews/features on important blues personalities. Especially looking for substantial features on contemporary blues artists who are still popular with black audiences."

MUSIC CANADA QUARTERLY, 2585 Drew Rd., Unit 7, Malton, Ontario, Canada. Phone: 416-678-2898. Editor: Bjorn F. Gasmann, Jr. For readers interested in the Canadian and international music scene, films, books, stereo components, musical instruments. Quarterly magazine; 52 to 84 (8x11) pages. Established in 1972. Circulation: 20,000. Buys all rights. Buys 40 mss a year. Payment on publication. Will send sample copy for 50¢ each. Will consider photocopied and simultaneous submissions. Reports on material accepted for publication in 1 week. Returns rejected material immediately. Query first. Enclose S.A.E. and International Reply Coupons.

Nonfiction and Photos: "Anything related to the music scene; rock, folk-rock, jazz, blues, country, classical, etc. Informative, restraint on overworked 'hip' lingo; controversial; good grasp of language, wit, restraint on ecstatic 'hype'. Canadian and international music acts; interviews, resumes, etc. Reports from foreign countries and their current music scene. Country, bluegrass; anything worth knowing about. Prefer not to see poor writing, silly cliches, hysterical raves, repetitious wording, inconsistent style." Length: 200 to 2,000 words. Pays 1¢ to 3¢ per word. No additional payment is made for b&w photos used with mss. Captions optional.

Fillers: Music puzzles, jokes, short humor. Length: 200 to 300 words. Pays 1¢ to 3¢ per word.

PAID MY DUES: JOURNAL OF WOMEN AND MUSIC, P.O. Box 11646, Milwaukee WI 53211. Editors: Dorothy Dean and Lucille Allison. For everyone interested in feminist and women's music; all aspects from technical to herstorical, as well as coverage of the contemporary scene. Magazine; 44 (8½x11) pages. Established in 1974. Circulation: 750. Buys simultaneous rights. Buys about 15 mss per year. Pays on acceptance. Will send sample copy to writer for $1. Write for copy of guidelines for writers. Will consider photocopied submissions. May consider simultaneous submissions. Reports on material accepted for publication in 4 to 6 weeks. Returns rejected material in 8 weeks. Query first. Enclose S.A.S.E.

Nonfiction and Photos: Feminist coverage of music festivals and concerts. In-depth technical articles about instruments, and equipment; herstory on women in music; interviews with contemporary composers and performers. Must have woman-oriented or feminist outlook. Other than that, they look for accuracy and creativity. Also publishes music which can range from complex pieces to short ditties of non-sexist theme. Avoid articles listing the ills of contemporary, sexist music and the sexist music of the 50's. No songs describing the male-oriented culture. No songs of lament. Recently published "The Union Maid", a good article on union women and their music. Article length: 2,000 words, maximum. Pays $1 per ms. B&w photos purchased with or without mss. 2x2, minimum size. Pays $1.

ROCK MAGAZINE, 166 Lexington Ave., (Second Floor), New York NY 10016. Editor: Howard Dando. For "those of college age, often college students whose interests are mainly music (jazz, blues, folk, etc.) and other 'youth culture' subjects." Established in 1969. Bimonthly. Circulation: 118,000. Rights purchased vary with author and material. Buys "approximately 350 to 400 mss a year on assignment; no more than 20 on speculation." Payment made approximately 2 to 3 weeks after publication. Will send free sample copy to writer on request. Write for copy of guidelines for writers. Reports on material within 1 month. Query first for interview and personality pieces; query or submit complete ms for conceptual or idea-oriented stories. Enclose S.A.S.E.

Nonfiction and Photos: "Mainly rock-oriented pieces, either interviews or conceptual pieces, dealing with some phase of music and recording. The more original and unusual the approach, the better. We have no set literary style and encourage writers to develop a distinctive (but intelligible) style of their own. We do, however, prefer a somewhat skeptical or humorous viewpoint, where appropriate. And we have added a new 16-page audio and musical equipment section, and are in the market for writers knowledgeable on the technical aspects but able to relate information on the level of the average consumer." Also uses reviews of records, films and books. Length: 500 to 3,000 words, depending on type of article. Pays $15 to $45. B&w photos, "sharp, bright shots, particularly candids of known musicians." Pays $15; $7.50 for re-use.

ROLLING STONE, 625 Third St., San Francisco CA 94107. Editor: Jann S. Wenner. "Seldom accept freelance material. All our work is assigned or done by our staff."

SONO, 625 President Kennedy Ave., Montreal, Quebec, Canada H3A 1K5. Editor: Paul Saint-Pierre. For amateurs and fanatics of music and of musical instruments. Although this publication is in French, English mss are considered. Quarterly magazine; 50 pages. Established in 1973. Circulation: 15,000. Buys all rights, but will reassign rights to author after publication. Buys 20 mss a year. Payment on acceptance. Reports in 1 week. Query first or submit complete ms. Enclose S.A.E. and International Reply Coupons.

Nonfiction: Interviews with singers, technical articles on quadraphony; on new equipment, trends; reviews of new records, audiolab, etc. Informational, how-to, profile, technical. Length: 600 to 1,200 words. Pays $50 to $150.

STEREO, State Road, Great Barrington, MA 01230. Editor: Norman Eisenberg. For "those interested in quality sound reproduction in the home, including hobbyist in audio, semi-technically minded consumers, music lovers, first time hi-fi buyers, owners of existing stereo systems. Strong college/under 30 readership though not confined to this group." Established in 1960. Quarterly. Circulation: 100,000. Buys all rights, but will reassign them to author after publication in special cases only. Buys about 30 feature article mss a year, others on assignment only. Payment on acceptance. Will send a free sample copy to writer on request. Will consider photocopied submissions. Query first for nonfiction and personalized narrative. Reports in 1 to 2 weeks. Enclose S.A.S.E.

Nonfiction: Articles on hi-fi, stereo, music recordings; behind-the-scenes at studios; surveys of musical forms as related to available recordings; improvement hints for stereo systems, how-it-works pieces; new major developments and trends in audio equipment, interesting installations (pix very desirable here); how-to-buy pieces; current cultural trends related to music and audio. "We like to maintain a pretty free-wheeling approach; we edit for clarity of meaning but we do not want every piece to read as if it were written by the same author. Primary requirements here are accuracy of information, basic interest, and some degree of *au courant* relevancy. Compared to our competition, we tend to be somewhat less 'parochial' in our attitude and treatment. We like to think we have fewer hangups or sacred cows in our subject matter, both technical and musical. We enjoy kidding about our subjects. Our editorial approach may be characterized as irreverent but relevant. For us, the whole 'hi-fi thing' is a blend of the technical and the musical, plus a certain indefinable ingredient that humanizes it all. We would like to see articles on the changing scene in pop music; the new movie music; developments in quadraphonic or four-channel sound; the problems of getting one's hi-fi equipment properly serviced or repaired; experiments with equipment, getting it to sound better." Length: 200 to over 3,000 words. Pays average of 10¢ a word.

Photos and Fillers: "Photos of hi-fi installations are always welcome, but they must be first-rate as photos. Poor lighting and poor focus seem to mar the efforts of most amateurs attempting to shoot indoor scenes." Pays $35 minimum for photos. Also will buy crossword puzzles in which most or many of the words deal with music and/or audio subjects.

Mystery Publications

ALFRED HITCHCOCK'S MYSTERY MAGAZINE, 784 U.S. 1, Suite 6, North Palm Beach FL 33408. Phone: 305-626-5115. Editor: Ernest M. Hutter. For a general audience. Estblished in 1956. Monthly. Buys first North American serial rights and all foreign serial rights. Payment on acceptance. Reports promptly. Submit complete ms. Enclose S.A.S.E.

Fiction: Original and well-written mystery, suspense and crime fiction. No reprints or true crimes. "A 'now' feeling is preferred for every story, both as to plot urgency and today's world. Plausibility counts heavily even in supernatural stories." Length: 1,000 to 10,000 words. Pays 5¢ a word for first North American serial rights, plus 25% additional for all foreign serial rights.

How To Break In: "Think Hitchcock. It's the master's brand of suspense that we want. Generally we like a feeling of contemporary times in our stories. Write tight; write crisp. Avoid using a lot of gore, profanity and explicit sex. It's not needed."

ELLERY QUEEN'S MYSTERY MAGAZINE, 229 Park Avenue South, New York NY 10003. Phone: 212-673-1300. Editor: Ellery Queen. Address mss to Eleanor Sullivan, Managing Editor. Monthly. Circulation: 273,000. Buys first rights. "Authors retain all subsidiary and supplementary rights, including radio and TV. We are also looking for fine reprints providing the author owns and controls the reprint rights." Buys about 160 mss a year. Pays on acceptance. Will consider photocopied submissions, but prefers original. "Do not ask for criticism of stories; we receive too many submissions to make this possible." Returns rejected material and acknowledges acceptance of material within 1 month. "It is not necessary to query us as to subject matter or to write asking for permission to submit the story." Enclose S.A.S.E.

Fiction: "We publish every type of mystery: the suspense story, the psychological study, the deductive puzzle — the gamut of crime and detection, from the realistic (including the 'policeman's lot' and stories of police procedure) to the more imaginative (including 'locked rooms' and 'impossible crimes'). We need tougher stories for our Black Mask section — but we do not want sex, sadism, or sensationalism-for-the-sake-of-sensationalism. We especially are interested in 'first stories' — by authors never before in print." There are "three criteria: quality of writing, originality of plot, and craftsmanship. The most practical way to find out what *EQMM* wants is to read *EQMM*." Also wants detective and crime short stories with sports backgrounds — baseball, football, golf, auto racing — whatever sport the writer is familiar with. "We do not want fact-detective cases or true stories; this is a fiction magazine." Length: 1,500 to 6,000 words. Pays 3¢ to 8¢ per word for original stories.

MIKE SHAYNE MYSTERY MAGAZINE, 8230 Beverly Blvd., Los Angeles CA 90048. Editor: Cylvia Kleinman. Monthly. Buys magazine serial rights only. Pays on acceptance. Reports in 3 weeks. Enclose S.A.S.E.

Fiction: Strong, fast-moving stories. Length: 1,000 to 60,000 words. Pays 1¢ a word and up.

How To Break In: "Study the type of material we use. Know pace of story, type of mystery we buy. Best to send very short material to start, as the new author doesn't handle novelette lengths convincingly."

If this is 1977, this edition is out of date. See address in front of book to order latest edition. *Writer's Market* is published annually each fall.

Nature, Conservation, and Ecology Publications

The magazines classified here are "pure" nature, conservation, and ecology publications —that is, they exist to further the study and preservation of nature and do not publish recreational or travel articles except as they relate to conservation or nature. Other markets for this kind of material will be found in the Regional; Sport and Outdoor; and Travel, Camping, and Trailer categories, although the magazines listed there require that nature or conservation articles be slanted to their specialized subject matter and audience.

AUDUBON, 950 Third Avenue, New York NY 10022. "Not soliciting freelance material; practically all articles done on assignment only. We have a backlog of articles from known writers and contributors. Our issues are planned well in advance of publication and follow a theme."

FORESTS & PEOPLE, P.O. Drawer 5067, Alexandria LA 71301. Editor: John Maddocks. For the forest industry, loggers, tree farmers and forest landowners. This is the Louisiana Forestry Association Magazine. Quarterly tabloid; 48 pages. Established in 1950. Circulation: 19,000. Not copyrighted. Buys 8 to 10 mss a year. Payment on publication. Will send sample copy to writer for $1. Will not consider photocopied submissions. Will consider simultaneous submissions. Submit seasonal material (hunting and outdoor recreation) 1 to 2 months in advance. Reports within 1 month. Query first on forestry articles; submit complete ms for others. Enclose S.A.S.E.
Nonfiction and Photos: Technical forestry articles and forestry news articles, plus lighter feature material related either to trees and forests of Louisiana and southern history; outdoor recreation. Extreme preservationist themes on forests and wildlife are to be avoided, but technical articles on forestry are used. Recent articles include "The Black Forest," "Are Pine Plantations for the Birds?", "Bonsai: Made in U.S.A.", "Faster Growing, Healthier Trees." Length: 1,000 to 2,500 words. Pays $25 to $50. Captions are required for b&w glossies.

FRONTIERS, A Magazine of Natural History, Academy of Natural Sciences, 19th and the Parkway, Philadelphia PA 19103. Editor: Mrs. Vi Dodge. Published four times per year. Circulation: 4,500. Buys first North American serial rights only. Pays on acceptance. Will send a sample copy to writer for $1. Reports on submissions in 2 weeks. Enclose S.A.S.E.
Nonfiction and Photos: Articles on natural science and ecology, written for high school and adult laymen, but scientifically accurate. Length: 1,000 to 2,000 words. Pays $30 to $90. Articles with b&w photos usually given preference. Accuracy, originality, and neatness all weigh heavily. 8x10 b&w photos purchased with mss.

INTERNATIONAL WILDLIFE, 534 N. Broadway, Milwaukee WI 53202. Editor: John Strohm. For persons interested in natural history, outdoor adventure and the environment. Bimonthly. Buys all rights to text; usually one-time rights to photos and art. Payment on acceptance. Query first. "Now assigning most articles but will consider detailed proposals for quality feature material of interest to broad audience." Reports in 2 weeks. Enclose S.A.S.E.
Nonfiction and Photos: Focus on world wildlife, environmental problems and man's relationship to the natural world as reflected in such issues as population control, pollution, resource utilization, food production, etc. Especially interested in articles on animal behavior and other natural history, little-known places, first-person experiences, timely issues. "Payment varies according to value and use of feature articles, but usually begins at $500. Purchase top-quality color and b&w photos; prefer 'packages' of related photos and text, but single shots of exceptional interest

and sequences also considered. Prefer Kodachrome transparencies for color, 8x10 prints for b&w."

LIMNOS, 3750 Nixon Road, Ann Arbor MI 48105. Editor: Jacques LesStrang. For "professional people, concerned with ecological problems of Great Lakes for recreational or conservation purposes. Ages 25 to 50, probably mostly college grads." Established in 1968. Quarterly. Circulation: 10,000. Buys first and second serial rights. Buys 30 to 40 mss a year. Payment on publication. Will send a sample copy to writer for $1. Submit seasonal material 4 to 6 months in advance. Reports in 3 weeks. Query first for nonfiction. Submit complete ms for other material. Enclose S.A.S.E.

Nonfiction, Photos, Poetry, and Fillers: A freelancer must "know what he is talking about. Our magazine is unique in its field." Would not like to see "Lake Erie problems, save-the-animals, save-the-trees type of Sierra Club conservation material." Buys informational, personal experience, interview, profile, historical, think, spot news, and technical articles. Length: 100 to 5,000 words. Purchases photos with or without mss, or on assignment, and captions are optional. Buys 8x10 b&w and 4x5 color. Pays $5 to $25 for b&w and $15 to $100 for color. Poetry is open as to style, but theme should relate to Great Lakes. Pays $5 and up. Filler material of a serious or humorous nature relating to, respectively, water resources and the environment. Length: 50 to 500 words. Pays from $5 to $50, depending on length and use.

THE LIVING WILDERNESS, 1901 Pennsylvania Ave N.W., Washington DC 20006. Phone: 202-293-2732. Editor: Richard C. Olson. For all ages, sharing an interest in the environment and outdoors, specifically wilderness, but by no means exclusively. Quarterly magazine. Established in 1935. Circulation: 80,000. Rights purchased vary with author and material. Buys all rights, but will sometimes reassign rights to author after publication. Buys 12 to 15 mss a year. Payment on publication. Will send free sample copy to writer on request. Query first or submit complete ms. Query first for book reviews. Enclose S.A.S.E.

Nonfiction and Photos: Emphasis on feature articles and book reviews. Read magazine for scope and approach. "We are the primary magazine in the world dealing with wilderness topics." Subjects of particular interest are: the philosophy of wilderness; the role and relevance of wilderness in life and culture. Pays $250 minimum for 2,500 words. Photos purchased with or without accompanying ms. Captions optional. Pays $35 minimum for b&w; $75 minimum for color.

LOUISIANA CONSERVATIONIST, 400 Royal St., Room 126-D, New Orleans LA 70130. Editor: Bob Dennie. For the outdoorsman and his family. Publication of Louisiana Wildlife and Fisheries Commission. Established in 1931. Bimonthly. Circulation: 190,000. Not copyrighted. Payment in contributor's copies. Will send free sample copy to writer on request. Write for copy of guidelines for writers. Will not consider photocopied submissions. Submit seasonal material (for Christmas issue only) 6 months in advance. Returns rejected material in 2 weeks. Reports on mss accepted for publication in 6 to 8 weeks. Query first. "We will look at outlines with query letters." Enclose S.A.S.E.

Nonfiction and Photos: "We use feature-length articles, including how-to's if they are informative and concisely written, of the outdoor variety. We also consider 'offbeat' pieces if they are written to interest a general outdoor audience. Studying the style of the staff writers and published authors in the magazine is the best advice interested writers could get. To be avoided are wordiness, cute tricks, writing with adjectives, and the outmoded 'me and Joe' articles. It is important that a writer be active in the outdoor writing field in order to submit to our magazine." Length: 800 to 2,000 words. Mss should be illustrated with color slides (originals only); 35mm or 2¼x2¼.

NATIONAL PARKS & CONSERVATION MAGAZINE, 1701 18th St., N.W., Washington DC 20009. Editor: Eugenia Horstman Connally. For a mature, high-education audience interested in out-of-doors and environmental matters. Monthly magazine; 32 (8½x11) pages. Established in 1919. Circulation: 50,000. Buys all rights.

Almost all material used is purchased from freelance writers. Payment on acceptance. Will send sample copy to writer for $1.50. Write for copy of guidelines for writers. Submit seasonal material 4 months in advance. Reports on material accepted for publication in 2 weeks. Returns rejected material promptly. Query first. Enclose S.A.S.E.

Nonfiction and Photos: Articles about national parks and monuments, stressing threats confronting them or their particularly unique or significant floral, faunal, geological, or historical features; endangered species of plants or animals and suggestions to save them; protection of natural resources; environmental problems and programs to solve them. Short articles on nature appreciation. Informational, personal experience, think pieces. Length: 1,500 to 2,000 words. Short article length (nature appreciation): 500 to 1,000 words. Pays $75 to $100 for acceptable illustrated articles. No additional payment for b&w and color used with mss, unless selected for cover. Pays $10 to $50 for 8x10 b&w glossies purchased without mss; $25 to $75 for 4x5 color transparencies (some slides) purchased without mss. Captions required. All photos must relate to theme of publication.

How To Break In: "Excellent market for new writers. 'Adventures in the national parks' articles are welcome, particularly those on backcountry hiking, mountain climbing, river running, spelunking. Emphasize conservation and protection of natural resources."

NATIONAL WILDLIFE, 534 N. Broadway, Milwaukee WI 53202. Editor: John Strohm. For persons interested in natural history, outdoor adventure and the environment. Bimonthly. Buys all rights to text; usually one-time rights for photos and art. Payment on acceptance. Reports in 2 weeks. Query first. "Now assigning most articles but will consider detailed proposals for quality feature material of interest to broad audience." Enclose S.A.S.E.

Nonfiction and Photos: "Focus on U.S. environmental problems in general, as well as wildlife in particular, with special emphasis on natural history, wide use of natural resources and some outdoor adventure. Feature material of interest to broad audience, especially on outdoor activities (hiking, climbing, spelunking), first-person experiences, unusual and timely issues. "Payment varies according to value and use of feature articles, but usually begins at $500. We purchase top quality color and b&w photos; prefer 'packages' of related photos and text, but single photos of exceptional interest and sequences also considered. Submit Kodachrome transparencies for color, 8x10 prints for b&w."

NATURAL HISTORY, 79th and Central Park West, New York NY 10024. Editor: Alan Ternes. For "well-educated, ecologically aware audience. Includes many professional people, scientists, scholars." Monthly. Circulation: 350,000. "Copyright on text of articles is held by The American Museum of Natural History." Buys 20 mss a year. Pays on publication. Will send a sample copy to a writer for $1. Submit seasonal material 6 months in advance. Query first or submit complete ms. Enclose S.A.S.E.

Nonfiction: Uses all types of scientific articles except chemistry and physics—emphasis is on the biological sciences and anthropology. Prefers professional scientists as authors. "We always want to see new research findings in almost all the branches of the natural sciences — anthropology, archaeology, zoology, ornithology. We find that it is particularly difficult to get something new in herpetology (amphibians and reptiles) or entomology (insects) and we would like to see material in those fields. We lean heavily toward writers who are scientists or professional science writers. High standards of writing and research. Favor an ecological slant in most of our pieces, but do not generally lobby for causes, environmental or other. Writer should have a deep knowledge of his subject. Then submit original ideas either in query or by ms. Should be able to supply high-quality illustrations." Length: 2,000 to 4,000 words. Payment is "$200 to $600, plus additional payment for photos used."

Photos: Uses some black and white 8x10 glossy photographs; pays up to $50 per page. Much color is used; pays $125 for inside and up to $200 for cover. Photos are purchased for one-time use.

NATURE CANADA, 46 rue Elgin St., Ontario K1S 1X7 Canada. Editor: Dr. Theodore Mosquin. For a general audience; junior high and older, with interests in Canadian environment and nature. Quarterly; 42 pages. Established in 1971. Circulation: 12,000. Buys first serial rights. Buys 25 mss per year, but many of them are solicited. Payment on publication. Will send sample copy to writer for $2.50. Will not consider photocopied or simultaneous submissions. Reports within a month. Query first. "We rely exclusively on solicited material." Enclose S.A.E. and International Reply Coupons.

Nonfiction and Photos: "Material related to nature and environment, wildlife, land use, government policies, citizen's action. Emphasis is on Canadian content. It is favorable to have any article backed up by graphs, charts, maps, photographs." Would be interested in natural history articles on specific animals or plants (Canadian). "We do not want to see intimate personal accounts of canoe trips, walks in the woods, etc." Uses related reviews, informational, how-to, historical and think pieces. Length: 100 to 6,000 words. Pays 3¢ a word. B&w and color photos purchased with or without mss. Pays the following rates for b&w: $20 for full-page; $15 for half-page or smaller; $35 for inside back cover or inside front cover. Color: $100 for front cover; $60 for back cover; $40 for full-page; $30 for half-page; $20 for one-quarter page or smaller. Photo Department Editor: Mrs. Constance Brook.

Poetry and Fillers: Traditional forms, blank verse, free verse, light verse (on related subjects). Length and payment open. Newsbreaks on related subjects are used as fillers. Length: 200 words. Pays 3¢ a word.

PACIFIC DISCOVERY, California Academy of Sciences, Golden Gate Park, San Francisco CA 94118. Phone: 415-221-5100. Editor: Bruce Finson. A journal of nature and culture around the world, read by scientists, naturalists, teachers, students, and others having a keen interest in knowing the natural world more thoroughly. Published 6 times a year by the California Academy of Sciences. Buys first North American serial rights of articles, one-time use of photos. Usually reports within 60 days; publishes accepted articles in 2 to 4 months. Pays on publication. Send query first, with 100-word summary of projected article for review before preparing finished ms. Enclose S.A.S.E.

Nonfiction and Photos: "Subjects of articles include behavior and natural history of animals and plants, ecology, anthropology, geology, paleontology, biogeography, taxonomy, and related topics in the natural sciences. Occasional articles are published on the history of natural science, exploration, astronomy, and archaeology. Types of articles include discussions of individual species or groups of plants and animals that are related to or involved with one another, narratives of scientific expeditions together with detailed discussions of field work and results, reports of biological and geological discoveries and of short-lived phenomena, and explanations of specialized topics in natural science." Length: 1,500 to 3,000 words. Pays $50 per 1,000 words. B&w photos or color slides must accompany all mss or they will not be reviewed. Send 15 to 30 with each ms. Photos should have both scientific and aesthetic interest, be captioned in a few sentences on a separate caption list keyed to the photos and numbered in story sequence. Some photo stories are used. Pays $10 per photo. All slides, negatives, and prints are returned soon after publication.

POLLUTION CONTROL JOURNAL, P.O. Box 533, Denver CO 80202. Phone: 303-222-7737. Managing Editor: Arlene Abady. For "persons of all ages concerned with the environment." Established in 1971. Circulation: 10,000. Quarterly. Buys all rights, but will reassign rights to author after publication. Buys about 40 mss a year. Payment on publication. Will send a sample copy to a writer for 50¢. Will consider photocopied submissions. Reports in 6 to 8 weeks. Query first or submit complete ms. Enclose S.A.S.E.

Nonfiction: "Articles dealing with cause, effect, and solution to ecological problems. Specifically, universal problems on a national and international scale. Issues of the *Journal* have covered strip mining in West Virginia, atomic energy power plants in New York, the endangered turtles of Mexico, classroom environment courses in Texas, an economic study of recycled bottles in Vermont, the 1976 Olympics in Colorado, and the water pollution trends of Jackson Lake, Wyoming. The writer should treat his subject with objectivity." Is currently interested in articles on international pollution problems, educational programs, individual and group action. Length: 1,000 to 4,000 words. Pays $20 to $200.

Photos: Purchased with or without mss; captions required. Maximum payment for any photo, $75.

SNOWY EGRET, 205 S. Ninth St., Williamsburg KY 40769. Phone: 606-549-0850. Editor: Humphrey A. Olsen. For "persons of at least high school age interested in literary, artistic, philosophical, and historical natural history." Semiannual. Circulation: less than 500. Buys first North American serial rights. Buys 30 to 40 mss a year. Pays on publication. Will send sample copy for 50¢. Usually reports in 1 month. Enclose S.A.S.E.

Nonfiction: Subject matter limited to material related to natural history, especially literary, artistic, philosophical, and historical aspects. Criticism, book reviews, essays, biographies. Pays $2 per printed page.

Fiction: "We are interested in considering stories or self-contained portions of novels. All fiction must be natural history or man and nature. The scope is broad enough to include such stories as Hemingway's 'Big Two-Hearted River' and Warren's 'Blackberry Winter.'" Length: maximum 10,000 words. Payment is $2 a printed page. Send mss and books for review to Dr. William T. Hamilton, Dept. of English, Otterbein College, Westerville OH 43081, "but query first, as we have been overstocked on fiction."

Poetry: No length limits. Pays $4 per printed page, minimum of $2. Send poems and poetry books for review to Dr. Hamilton, Literary Editor.

Newspapers and Weekly Magazine Sections

This section includes daily newspapers as well as Saturday and Sunday magazine sections of daily newspapers. They are listed geographically by state headings although some cover wider areas (such as Michiana *which serves both Michigan and Indiana).*

Most of these markets require submissions to be about persons, places, and things in their specific circulation areas. However, some large city and national newspapers that welcome general interest material from nonlocal writers are also included in this list. Newspapers with specialized subject matter or audiences, like The Wall Street Journal *are classified with magazines dealing with the same subject matter or audience.*

A few editors report that some correspondents in their area are attracted to small feature items but let big news stories from their communities slip through their fingers. Freelancers, on the other hand, report that some busy newspaper editors return their submissions without even a rejection slip—or in a few cases, fail to return it at all, even when it's accompanied by a self-addressed envelope. (Since newspaper editors receive many submissions from public relations firms and other individuals who do not expect return of their material, they sometimes automatically toss material they're not interested in publishing. That means a retyping job for the freelancer. It also means you should be wary of sending photographs which are your only copies.)

Arizona

ARIZONA MAGAZINE, 120 E. Van Buren, Phoenix AZ 85016. Editor: Bud DeWald. For "everyone who reads a Sunday newspaper." Weekly; 60 pages. Established in 1953. Circulation: 300,000. Not copyrighted. Buys 250 mss a year. Payment on scheduling. Will send free sample copy on request. Write for copy of guidelines for writers. Will consider photocopied submissions. Will consider simultaneous submissions if exclusive regionally. Reports on material accepted for publication in 2 weeks. Returns rejected material in 1 week. Query first or submit complete ms. Enclose S.A.S.E.

Nonfiction and Photos: "General subjects that have an Arizona connection. Should have a bemused, I-don't-believe-it approach. Nothing is that serious. Should have an abundance of quotes and anecdotes. Would be interested in seeing articles on how to survive in the wide open spaces without gasoline. Historical and travel subjects are being overworked. We don't need someone's therapy." Length: 1,000 to 3,000 words. Pays $50 to $175. B&w and color photos purchased with or without mss or on assignment. Pays $10 to $25 for 8x10 b&w glossies; $15 to $65 for color (35mm or 8x10).

How To Break In: "Find a good personal subject and write about him so the reader will feel he is with the subject. Describe the subject in anecdotes and let him describe himself by his quotes."

California

CALIFORNIA TODAY, 750 Ridder Park Dr., San Jose CA 95131. Editor: Fred Dickey. For a general audience. Weekly newspaper. Circulation: 250,000. Not copyrighted. Buys 50 mss a year. Payment on acceptance. Will send free sample copy to writer on request. Will consider photocopied and simultaneous submissions. Submit seasonal material (skiing, wine, outdoor living) 3 months in advance. Reports on material accepted for publication in 1 week. Returns rejected material immediately. Query first or submit complete ms. Enclose S.A.S.E.

Nonfiction and Photos: A general newspaper requiring that all subjects be related to California and interests in that area. Length: 500 to 3,000 words. Pays $25 to $200. Payment varies for b&w and color photos purchased with or without mss. Captions required.

LOS ANGELES TIMES HOME MAGAZINE, Times Mirror Square, Los Angeles CA 90053. Editor: Carolyn S. Murray. Issued every Sunday. Buys first North American serial rights. Pays on publication. Reports usually in one week. Query first. Enclose S.A.S.E.

Nonfiction: Articles devoted to the home and its environment. Solutions to problems and articles of family interest. No hobby features and only top-flight "how-to-do-it" material. Payment varies.

Photos: Prefers to originate own photography but exception would be made for residential architecture, and here photos must be high-quality 4x5 color transparencies or 8x10 glossy b&w prints. Originals only.

THE SACRAMENTO BEE, P.O. Box 15779, Sacramento CA 95813. Editor: C. K. McClatchy. For a general readership; higher than average education; higher than average interest in politics, government; outdoor-activity oriented. Newspaper; 48 pages. Established in 1857. Daily. Circulation: 170,000 daily; 200,000 Sunday. Not copyrighted. Buys about 200 mss a year. Pays on publication. Will send free sample copy to writer on request. No photocopied submissions. Will consider simultaneous submissions if they are not duplicated in Northern California. Reports in 2 weeks. Query first or submit complete ms. Enclose S.A.S.E.

Nonfiction and Photos: Human interest features, news background. Prefers narrative feature style. Does not want to see sophomoric humor. Will consider interviews, profiles, nostalgic and historical articles; expose; personal experience. Length: 100 to 1,500 words. Pays $20 to $100. Pays up to $30 for material used in children's books column. B&w glossies and color (negatives) purchased with or without mss. Pays $15 to $75 for b&w; $25 to $100 for color. Captions required.

SACRAMENTO UNION WEEKENDER, 301 Capitol Mall, Sacramento CA 95812. Editor: Jackie Peterson. Weekly. Buys "one-time" rights. Buys about 100 mss a year. "We cannot be responsible for return of unsolicited material." Query first. Enclose S.A.S.E.

Nonfiction and Photos: Interested in offbeat, unusual, items of travel, leisure, or general interest. Sometimes buys personality profiles or a first-person piece. "The availability of illustration often dictates my choice. I go back time after time to the few good writers who regularly submit stories to me." Length: "we cannot absorb stories much over 1,200 words." Pays $35 to $50, plus $10 to $15 for b&w, $20 to $25 for each color slide used.

Colorado

CONTEMPORARY MAGAZINE, Sunday supplement to *The Denver Post*, 650 15th St., Denver CO 80201. Editor: Dick Martin. For "young adults to senior citizens (both sexes), aware of today's world." Newspaper format. Buys first rights. Pays on publication. Will send a free sample copy to a writer on request. No query required. "We are being very selective and use a very limited amount of freelance material." Submit seasonal material 3 months in advance. Reporting time varies. Enclose S.A.S.E. for return of submissions.
Nonfiction: "Mostly a family and women's interest magazine." Articles of 500 to 1,500 words. Payment is $50 to $75.

EMPIRE MAGAZINE, *The Denver Post*, P.O. Box 1709, Denver CO 80201. Editor: Carl Skiff. Weekly. Established in 1950. Buys about 250 mss a year. Buys first rights. Payment on acceptance for nonfiction; on publication for photos. Query first. Enclose S.A.S.E.
Nonfiction and Photos: "A rotogravure magazine covering the general scene in our circulation area. We are looking for material of national magazine quality in interest and writing style, but with a strong, regional peg. Our region focuses on Colorado, Wyoming, northern New Mexico, western Kansas and Nebraska. We need solidly researched articles about exciting things, personalities and situations. We also need light humor and reminiscences." Length: 2,500 words maximum. Pays about 5¢ per word. "Photographs can help sell a story." B&w photos are purchased with ms or as singles or series or as picture stories (500 words). Five to 8 photos are used with picture stories. Query first about these. Pays $50 for color transparencies used for cover; $100 for double spread; $25 for singles used inside.

Florida

FLORIDA MAGAZINE, *Sentinel Star*, Box 2833, Orlando FL 32802. Phone: 305-423-4411. Editor: Bill Dunn. Weekly supplement; tabloid, 56 pages. Established in 1952. Circulation: 200,000. Buys first "inside Florida" serial rights. Buys 20 to 30 mss a year. Payment on publication. Will send free sample copy to writer on request. Write for copy of guidelines for writers. Will consider photocopied or simultaneous submissions. Submit only complete ms. Reports in 2 weeks. Enclose S.A.S.E.
Nonfiction: High-interest features about Florida subjects only. "We like perceptive, highly stylized writing, unique slants. We're chiefly staff produced so we must be quite selective. We can use the real offbeat or highly stylized stuff—often first-person —which we otherwise couldn't obtain ourselves."Length: 3,000 words maximum. Pays $50 to $100.
Poetry: Any kind. Prefers shorter lengths. Address Poetry, *Florida Magazine*. Pays $10.

THE FLORIDIAN, Box 1211, St. Petersburg FL 33731. Editor: Anne L. Goldman. For readers primarily interested in Florida life styles. Sunday magazine; 28 to 32 pages. Established in 1967. Weekly. Circulation: over 200,000. Rights purchased vary with author and material. May buy first serial rights, second serial (reprint) rights or simultaneous rights. Buys 100 to 150 mss a year. Pays on acceptance. Will send free sample copy to writer on request. Write for copy of guidelines for writers. Will consider photocopied and simultaneous submissions. Submit seasonal material (Christmas and New Year's) 3 months in advance. Reports in 2 weeks. Query first or submit complete ms. Enclose S.A.S.E.

Nonfiction and Photos: Well-crafted, in-depth features on almost any subject in the state of Florida. Information about consumer problems oriented to the state; general features that have a Florida flavor. Interested in material on inflation and recession; consumerism, particularly in the areas of health; medicine, fresh ecological subjects, social issues of all kinds. No opinion or commentary. "We look for innovative but clear writing. We do not like the once over lightly formula of writing. In-depth research and a lively manuscript, with impact, is our aim. All our stories are hopefully, but not necessarily overtly, *you* oriented. This means that we keep the reader in mind, trying to relate to their needs and interests as times change. For the Christmas and New Year's issues, we must have something new. We avoid tired holiday approaches like the plague." Length: 1,500 to 3,000 words. Pays $75 to $250. Pays minimum of $25 for 8x10 b&w glossies purchased with or without mss or on assignment; or for Ektachrome or Kodachrome color transparencies. Captions required.

MIAMI HERALD TROPIC MAGAZINE, 1 Herald Plaza, Miami FL 33101. Editor: John W. Parkyn. For the population of south Florida. Established in 1967. Weekly. Circulation: 500,000. Rights purchased vary with author and material. Usually buys first Florida rights. Buys 100 mss a year. Payment on publication. Will send free sample copy to writer on request. Will consider photocopied submissions. Reports in 4 to 6 weeks, "frequently much less." Query first or submit complete ms. Enclose S.A.S.E.
Nonfiction: "Well-written, informative and entertaining articles, preferably with some kind of south Florida tie-in. Articles reflecting the genuine interests of people living in our area." Interview, profile, travel, and successful business operations articles also considered. Length: 1,000 to 3,000 words. Pays $100 to $300.
Photos: Purchased with or without accompanying mss. B&w glossies or color transparencies. Pays $50 to $250, depending on quality and number of photos used.

Georgia

THE ATLANTA JOURNAL AND CONSTITUTION MAGAZINE, P.O. Box 4689, Atlanta GA 30302. Editor: Andrew Sparks. Rights purchased vary with author and material, but sometimes releases rights so articles can be sold elsewhere. Special arrangements can be made for articles to be reprinted with permission. Pays on publication. Query first, including short outline of material. Enclose S.A.S.E.
Nonfiction: "Most of our stories are staff written and almost all of them have some local angle." Articles with strong Southern slant, Georgian or Southern background. Best to study magazine. Length: 2,000 words maximum. Payment varies with the number of articles a writer has done and is not on a per word basis.

Illinois

CHICAGO SUN-TIMES' MIDWEST MAGAZINE, 401 N. Wabash, Chicago IL 60611. Editor: Richard Takeuchi. Reports on submissions in 2 weeks. Buys first rights. Pays on publication. Enclose S.A.S.E. with mss and queries.
Nonfiction and Photos: General interest articles, preferably topical, focusing on Chicago or Chicago area. Timeliness is essential for the development of all stories. "No articles on hobbies; no straight narratives." Length: 750 to 2,500 words. Pays $50 to $300. Full color and 8x10 b&w photos purchased as package with mss.

CHICAGO TRIBUNE MAGAZINE, 435 N. Michigan Ave., Chicago IL 60611. Editor: Robert Goldsborough. Not soliciting freelance material. "We have a large oversupply of mss, most of which have come from writers working on assignment. Most of these writers are local writers with whom we have personal contact."

Indiana

MICHIANA, The Sunday Magazine of The South Bend Tribune, Colfax at Lafayette, South Bend IN 46626. Editor: Tom Philipson. For "average daily newspaper readers;

perhaps a little above average since we have more than a dozen colleges and universities in our area." Weekly; 24 pages. Established in 1873. Circulation: 125,000. Rights purchased vary with author and material. May buy first North American serial rights or simultaneous rights providing material offered will be used outside of Indiana and Michigan. Buys 150 to 200 mss a year. Payment on publication. Will consider photocopied submissions if clearly legible. Submit special material for spring and fall travel sections at least 1 month in advance. Reports within a week. Submit complete ms. Enclose S.A.S.E.

Nonfiction and Photos: "Items of general and unusual interest, written in good, clear, simple sentences with logical approach to subject. We like historical material in particular; also some religious material if unusual." Humor, think pieces, travel, photo articles with brief texts. "We avoid all freelance material that supports movements of a political nature. We do not like first-person stories, but use them on occasion. We can use some offbeat stuff if it isn't too far out." Length: 800 to 3,000 words. Payment is $50 to $60 minimum, with increases as deemed suitable. All mss must be accompanied by illustrations or b&w photos or 35mm or larger color transparencies.

THE REPUBLIC, 333 2nd (P.O. Box 10), Columbus IN 47201. Editor: Stu Huffman. For south-central Indiana newspaper readers. Established in 1872. Daily. Circulation: 21,000. Not copyrighted. Acquires first serial rights. Uses 50 to 100 mss a year. Payment on publication. Will send free sample copy to writer on request. Query first or submit complete ms. Will consider photocopied submissions. "Seasonal material sought annually for each season and each holiday. Should arrive 2 weeks in advance." Reports on material in 1 week. Enclose S.A.S.E. for return of submissions or reply to queries.

Nonfiction and Photos: "Saturday 'Week Ender' section open to freelance submissions, but is limited to stories of local and regional interest. Like to find freelance articles about our area to provide readers with information they are not likely to see elsewhere." Coverage desired on Bible Belt reaction to women's rights, new programs in education; efforts by small communities to attract tourists, stories about those attractions, and stories on architectural features in small towns. Length: 500 to 1,500 words. Pays $5 to $50, but payment is based on quality, not length. Photos purchased with accompanying mss, without mss or on assignment. "8x10, but will accept other sizes or negs." Pays $3 to $25. Color transparencies, 35mm to 4x5. Pays $10 to $50. Captions required, with names and addresses.

Poetry: Traditional forms, blank verse, free verse, avant-garde forms, light verse. Length: 4 to 60 lines. No payment. Dept. Editor: Marjorie Sea.

How To Break In: "Through a feature story in our Week Ender section relating the life of one person—especially in south-central Indiana—to a current problem of life. Or with a story relating the architectural development of our 'Athens of the Prairie' to another community's or individual's efforts to upgrade the quality of life in their own area."

Iowa

DES MOINES SUNDAY REGISTER PICTURE MAGAZINE, *Des Moines Register,* 715 Locust St., Des Moines IA 50309. Editor: R. Robert Asbille. For mass newspaper audience, metropolitan and rural. Established in 1950. Weekly. Circulation: 500,000. Buys first serial rights. Buys 30 to 50 mss a year. Payment on publication. Query first preferred. Submit seasonal material 6 to 8 weeks in advance. Enclose S.A.S.E. for reply to queries.

Nonfiction and Photos: "Articles heavily concentrated on Iowa, about what's going on in Iowa; how to survive in the modern world. General interest material. Anything interesting in Iowa, or interesting elsewhere with some kind of tie to Iowans." Length: 2,000 words maximum, but prefers shorter mss. Material must lend itself to strong photographic presentation. If the idea is good, a photographer will be assigned, if writer does not have professional quality photos. Pays $60 to $150. Photos purchased with or without mss. Captions required. Prefers 8x10 b&w glossies. Pays $15 minimum. 35mm or larger transparencies. Pays $60 minimum for cover; $35 for inside use.

How To Break In: "Good local human interest stories should be what a new writer should be looking for. Would suggest you write for free sample copy of magazine. Frequently need short-short articles that will go with one photo. This is a good place for new writer to get that first hit. Our suggestion always is to write about people, not things."

Kentucky

COURIER-JOURNAL AND TIMES MAGAZINE, 525 W. Broadway, Louisville KY 40202. Phone: 502-582-4674. Editor: Geoffrey Vincent. Not soliciting freelance material. "We have a large staff of our own, plus ready access to material in other magazines."

THE VOICE-JEFFERSONIAN, Chenoweth Sq., St. Matthews KY 40207. Phone: 502-895-5436. Editor: Bruce B. VanDusen. For middle and upper income suburban audience. Family readership, but no taboos. Weekly. "No copyright unless the story is super-special and exclusive to us." Will consider cassette submissions. Address all inquiries to the editor. Enclose S.A.S.E.
Nonfiction and Photos: News and Features departments. 300 to 1,500 words on local (East Jefferson County) subjects. "Manuscripts must have a local angle. Writers persistently ignore this fundamental standard." 5x7 b&w glossies. Pays 25¢ to 50¢ per inch; $3.50 to $10 for photos.

Louisiana

SUNDAY ADVOCATE MAGAZINE, Box 588, Baton Rouge LA 70821. Phone: 504-383-1111, Ext. 262. Editor: Charles H. Lindsay. Buys no rights. Pays on publication. Enclose S.A.S.E. for return of submissions.
Nonfiction and Photos: Well-illustrated, short articles; must have local, area or Louisiana angle, in that order of preference. Photos purchased with mss. Rates vary.

Massachusetts

BOSTON GLOBE MAGAZINE, Boston MA 02107. Editor: Robert Levey. Published weekly as a section of the newspaper. Circulation: 630,880. Usually buys first serial rights. Buys about 100 mss a year. Payment on acceptance. Will send free sample copy on request. Will consider photocopied submissions. Reports on material accepted for publication in 3 weeks. Returns rejected material in 2 weeks. Query first or submit complete ms. Enclose S.A.S.E.
Nonfiction and Photos: General interest articles and features. Informational, personal experience, interview, profile, humor, expose, nostalgia. Does not want to see seasonal or holiday themes. Length: 1,000 to 4,500 words. Pays $150 to $300. Pays $150 for b&w photos used with mss. Pays $150 for color used for cover. Prefers 35mm slides.

THE CHRISTIAN SCIENCE MONITOR, 1 Norway St., Boston MA 02115. Phone: 617-262-2300, Ext. 2398. Editor: John Hughes. International newspaper issued daily except Saturdays, Sundays and holidays. Special issues: travel, winter vacation and international travel, summer vacation, autumn vacation, and cruise section. February and September: fashion; May and October: food. Established in 1908. Circulation: 201,000. Buys all rights. Buys about 3,700 mss a year. Payment on acceptance or publication, "depending on department." Submit seasonal material 1 to 2 months in advance. Reports within 4 weeks. Submit only complete ms. Enclose S.A.S.E.
Nonfiction: "In-depth news analysis, features, and essays. Style should be bright but not cute, concise but thoroughly researched. Try to humanize news or feature writing so the reader identifies with it. Avoid sensationalism, crime and disaster. Accent constructive, solution-oriented treatment of subjects. Can use news-in-the-making stories not found elsewhere if subject has sufficient impact on current history (600 to 1,500 words). Feature pages as follows: People, Places, Things page uses colorful human interest material not exceeding 800 words, and humorous anecdotes.

Home Forum page buys essays of 400 to 800 words; education, arts, real estate, travel, women, fashion, furnishings, consumer, environment, and science-technology pages will consider articles not usually more than 800 words appropriate to respective subjects." Pays from $20 to $100. Some areas covered in travel pages include: Swiss, N.E., British, Canadian, Hawaiian, and Caribbean. Features Editor: Robert C. Cowen.

Photos: Purchased with or without mss. Captions required. Pays $10 to $50 depending upon size and where used in paper. Photo Editor: John Young.

Poetry and Fillers: Home Forum uses poetry. Wide variety of subjects and treatment; traditional forms, blank and free verse, but the poetry must be of high quality and proficiency. Short poems preferred. Pays $20 to $40. Crossword puzzles also wanted. Home Forum Editor: Henrietta Buckmaster.

FEATURE PARADE MAGAZINE, *Worcester Sunday Telegram,* 20 Franklin St., Worcester MA 01613. Phone: 617-755-4321. News Editor: Charles F. Mansbach. Sunday supplement. Buys first rights. Payment on acceptance. Enclose S.A.S.E.

Nonfiction and Photos: "The great majority of our articles deal with people, places, events and situations in our central Massachusetts circulation area (Worcester County and surrounding towns). We also use articles about Massachusetts-wide issues and personalities and, on occasion, stories emanating from elsewhere in New England." Pays $50 to $100. B&w photos or color transparencies purchased with mss or separately as photo essays or single photos that can stand alone. Must have strong local angle.

Michigan

FENTON INDEPENDENT, 112 E. Ellen St., Fenton MI 48430. Phone: 313-629-2203. Editor: Robert G. Silbar. Weekly. Newspaper, not a magazine supplement. Buys all rights. Query first. Enclose S.A.S.E.

Nonfiction and Photos: News stories, features, photos of local interest. Wants local material on local people, not generalized articles. Appreciates opinion articles on local topics. All material must have local flavor. Pays 25¢ per column inch.

Montana

THE BILLINGS GAZETTE, Billings MT 59101. Sunday Editor: Kathryn Wright. Weekly. Buys first rights. Pays on publication. Enclose S.A.S.E. with mss and queries.

Nonfiction and Photos: Features stories and photos about circulation area—northern Wyoming and eastern and central Montana—or people from it and now someplace else doing interesting things. Length: 1,000 words plus photos. Pays 25¢ per inch and up depending on quality. $3 to $5 each for action photos.

New Jersey

SOUTH JERSEY LIVING, 1900 Atlantic Ave., Atlantic City NJ 08404. Phone: 609-345-1111. Editor: Paul Learn. For general newspaper audience in South Jersey region. Special issues: some holidays. Established in 1964. Weekly. Circulation: 70,000. Buys all rights, but will reassign rights to author after publication. Buys about 200 mss a year. Payment after publication. Will send free sample copy to writer on request. Write for copy of guidelines. Will consider photocopied submissions. Submit seasonal material 1 month in advance. Reports in 3 months. Also send carbon copy; keep second carbon copy. Enclose S.A.S.E.

Nonfiction: "Articles, profiles, interviews dealing only with South Jersey. Topics run gamut, within limit of family readership: sports, South Jersey history, hobbies, culture, music, art, science. Emphasis is on hotel and resort industries, seashore. Third-person only. No first-person. Want direct quotes, punchlines, emotional highpointing when possible. Especially interested in articles on the following subjects: legalized gambling, lotteries, legalized 'numbers'; ideas to build up seashore resort business." Informational, humor, nostalgia, new product, and technical articles also wanted. Length: 1,000 to 1,500 words. Pays $20 per magazine page for first page; $10 for each succeeding magazine page.

Photos: Purchased with or without accompanying mss. South Jersey angle. Captions required. 8½x11 b&w. Pays $10 for cover; $5 for inside use.

New York

FAMILY WEEKLY, 641 Lexington Ave., New York NY 10022. Editor-in-Chief: Mort Persky. Managing Editor: Reynolds Dodson. No longer accepting unsolicited mss, but will consider queries. Enclose S.A.S.E. for reply to queries.
Nonfiction and Photos: Interested in short, unusual photo items, showing startling b&w pictures and up to 200 words of background text. Pays $25 per item, plus $10 if photo is used.

LI MAGAZINE, *Newsday,* 550 Stewart Ave., Garden City NY 11530. Phone: 516-294-3126. Managing Editor: Stanley Green. For well-educated, affluent suburban readers. Established in 1972. Weekly. Circulation: 366,000. Buys all rights. Payment on publication. Query first. Enclose S.A.S.E. for reply to queries.
Nonfiction and Photos: "Stories must be about Long Island people, places or events." Length: 600 to 2,500 words. Pays $100 to $600. B&w contacts and 35mm transparencies purchased on assignment. Pays up to $100 per page for b&w; $200 per page for color, including cover. Art Director: Cliff Gardiner.

NEW YORK NEWS MAGAZINE, *New York Daily News,* 220 E. 42 St., New York NY 10017. Editor: Richard C. Lemon. For general audience. Weekly. Circulation: over 3 million. Buys first serial rights. Buys about 40 mss a year. Payment on acceptance. Will send free sample copy to a writer on request. Submit seasonal material 2 months in advance. Will consider photocopied submissions. Reports in 4 weeks. Query first. "If you have published before, it is best to include a sample clip." Enclose S.A.S.E.
Nonfiction and Photos: "Interested in all sorts of articles: most interested in human interest stories, articles about people (famous or unknown); least interested in essays and discussion pieces. Continuing need for New York City area subjects. Freelancer should use his own approach to material. Entertainment pieces seem to be over-abundant. We use a number, but they are mostly staff written." Buys informational, personal experience, interview, profile, humor, nostalgia, and photo articles. Length: 600 to 3,000 words. Pays $50 to $750. Photos purchased with or without mss. Captions are required. Specifications for b&w glossies or jumbo contacts: 8x10. Pays $25 for single, $150 for complete picture story. Color specifications: 2½, 4x5 or 35mm transparency. Pays from $35 for single, $200 for set.
How To Break In: "For new writers there are a couple of angles: service pieces are hard to come by. We recently ran a guide to how-to-do-it books for home handy-type people. That was by a guy who had never written for us before. Another place we need material is in food and home furnishings where we run a lot of shorter pieces. That would be one way for us to get to see a new writer's work. The key thing to remember is to start with a suggestion that grabs us and keep your material within screaming distance of New York City."

THE NEW YORK TIMES, 229 W. 43 St., New York NY 10036. Enclose S.A.S.E. for reply to queries or return of mss.
Nonfiction and Photos: *The New York Times Magazine* appears in *The New York Times* on Sunday. "It is a news magazine. We define news in its broadest sense: background of national and international news developments, science, education, family life, social trends and problems, arts and entertainment, personalities, sports, the changing American scene. Freelance contributions are invited. Articles must be timely. They must be based on specific news items, forthcoming events, significant anniversaries, or they must reflect trends. We welcome humor, but here too we insist on news 'pegs.' We do not publish fiction nor do we solicit verse. Our full-length articles run from 3,500 to 5,000 words, and for these we pay $850 on acceptance. ($1,000 after two prior acceptances). Our shorter pieces run from 1,000 to 2,000 words at a rate of $75 per column. There are roughly 400 words in a column. We pay a basic minimum of $50 for photos." Magazine Editor: Lewis Bergman. *Travel*

and Resorts section buys "literate, sophisticated, factual articles, evoking the experience of travel with quotes, anecdotes and even-handed reportage. Authors must be personally familiar with subjects about which they write, free to praise or criticize; under no circumstances will we publish articles growing out of trips in any way subsidized by airlines, hotels or other organizations with direct or indirect interest in the subjects. All submissions are to be considered on speculation; payment upon publication is approximately 10¢ a word; maximum $250 per article; additional $50 for each photo used." *Travel and Resorts* Editor: Robert Stock. *Arts and Leisure* section of *The New York Times* appears on Sunday. Wants "to encourage imaginativeness in terms of form and approach — stressing ideas, issues, trends, investigations, symbolic reporting and stories delving deeply into the creative achievements and processes of artists and entertainers — and seeks to break away from old-fashioned 'human interest' windbaggery." Length: 750 to 2,000 words. Pays $100 to $250 depending on length. Pays $50 for photos. *Arts and Leisure* Editor: William H. Honan.

How To Break In: "The Op Ed page is always looking for new material and publishes many people who have never been published before. We don't get enough personal experience pieces from individuals around the country. And by this I don't mean a piece about your cat getting stuck in a tree or your fascinating aunt or uncle. We want material of universal relevance which people can talk about in a personal way. When writing for the Op Ed page there is no formula and the writing itself does not have to be exceptional. The stuff that works best for us is usually what happens when someone sits down and simply puts his heart on paper. Don't make the mistake of pontificating on the news. We're not looking for more political columnists. Op Ed length runs about 750 words, and pays about $150."

NEWSDAY, 550 Stewart Ave., Garden City NY 11566. Travel Editor: Steve Schatt. For general readership of Sunday Travel Section. Newspaper. Established in 1947. Weekly. Circulation: 400,000. Buys all rights for the New York area only. Buys 100 mss a year. Pays on publication. Will consider photocopied submissions. Simultaneous submissions considered if others are being made outside of New York area. Reports in 4 weeks. Submit complete ms. Enclose S.A.S.E.

Nonfiction and Photos: Travel articles with strong focus and theme for the Sunday Travel Section. Emphasis on accuracy, service, quality writing to convey mood and flavor. Skip diaries; "My first Trip Abroad" pieces or compendiums of activities; downplay first person. Length: 600 to 1,300 words. Pays $50 to $130.

PARADE, *The Sunday Newspaper Magazine,* 733 Third Ave., New York NY 10017. Weekly. Circulation: over 19 million. Buys first North American serial rights. Pays on acceptance. Query first. Enclose S.A.S.E.

Nonfiction: "Interested in features that will inform, educate or entertain a mass circulation domestic audience. Exclusive, news-related articles and photos are required. Subjects may include: well-known personalities, sports, religion, education, community activities, family relations, science and medicine. Articles should be current, factual, authoritative." Length: about 1,500 words. Pays up to $1,000.

Photos: "Photos should have visual impact and be well composed with action-stopping qualities. For the most part, color is used on cover. Transparencies of any size are accepted. Either b&w 8x10 enlargements or contact sheets may be submitted. Accurate caption material must accompany all photos."

How To Break In: "A good way to start out with us is if you have an expertise in some field. For instance, I was speaking to a young writer just the other day who has mainly done work for science publications and textbooks and wants to break into the general field. He's just the kind of person we're looking for. Someone else did a piece for us on the stock market recently. He had expert knowledge in the field and applied it to a general audience. Another thing that would be of advantage to the new writer would be competence with a camera. We are always on the lookout for short features with good illustrations, say 1,000 to 1,500 words. One that we used recently came from a completely unknown person who visited China. He sent us a batch of color and b&w photos and 1,000 words on regimentation in Chinese culture. We made it into the cover story. Then there are our short reports sections: Intelligence Report and Keeping Up With Youth. These are items of about 250 words and provide a good opportunity for us to get to know a new writer. Intelligence Report deals with things like new inventions, new technologies, new acts of government that the reader should be familiar with. Keeping Up With Youth is an ideal slot for someone who is close to campus life and can fill us in briefly on cultural trends and avant-garde directions. Also youth personalities."

Ohio

THE BLADE SUNDAY MAGAZINE, *The Blade,* Toledo OH 43660. Phone: 419-259-6132. Editor: Mike Tressler. For general audience. Circulation: over 200,000. Buys first serial rights. Buys 50 to 60 mss a year. Payment on publication. Will consider photocopied submissions. Reports in 1 to 3 weeks. Query or submit complete ms. Enclose S.A.S.E.

Nonfiction: "General interest articles; personality, life style, leisure, unusual happenings, adventure. Real stories about real people. Emphasis on local (Toledo, northwestern Ohio, southeastern Michigan). Use magazine-style writing; untold stories; quoted dialog and comment." Regular column, "Glimpse," is an entirely local single-page feature. Length: 800 to 2,500 words. Pays $35 to $85.

Photos: Purchased with or without accompanying mss, or occasionally on assignment. Captions required. 8x10 b&w glossies, sharp and unusual. Pays $5 to $7.50. Color slides or 8x10 photos. Pays $10 to $15.

How To Break In: "Breaking in is mostly a matter of submitting well-written material about what's happening today; personal experiences, gutsy dialog, and pertinent point—either locally (for us) or of such a wide interest, it applies anywhere. 'Not breaking in' is submitting roundup articles listing unattributed and unsubstantiated events. No tired old travel pieces or what I call kitchen humor."

COLUMBUS DISPATCH SUNDAY MAGAZINE, 34 South Third St., Columbus OH 43216. Phone: 614-461-5250. Editor: Robert K. Waldron. Buys one-time rights. Payment after publication. Enclose S.A.S.E.

Nonfiction and Photos: Strong Ohio angle is essential in all material. Buys singles, photo series, and illustrated articles. Length: 1,000 to 1,500 words. Pays minimum of 3¢ per word. B&w photos only. Pays $5 per photos. "Pay is flexible, depending on how good the piece is, how much effort has apparently been put into it, etc."

DAYTON LEISURE, *Dayton Daily News,* Fourth and Ludlow Sts., Dayton OH 45401. Phone: 513-223-2112. Editor: Jack M. Osler. Sunday supplement. Circulation: 225,000. Pays on publication. Usually reports within 1 week. Enclose S.A.S.E.

Nonfiction and Photos: Magazine focuses on leisure time activities in Ohio—particularly southwestern Ohio—that are interesting and unusual. Emphasis is on photos supplemented by stories. Up to 1,000 words. Photos should be glossy. "*The Daily News* will evaluate articles on their own merits. Likewise with photos. Average payment per article: $25." Payments vary depending on quality of writing.

THE ENQUIRER MAGAZINE, 617 Vine St., Cincinnati OH 45201. Editor: Sheryl Bills. Weekly; 46 pages. Established originally as the Pictorial Section in 1924. Circulation: 312,000. Not copyrighted. Buys about 150 to 200 mss a year. Pays after publication. Will send free sample copy to writer on request. Write for editorial guidelines. Will consider photocopied and simultaneous submissions. Submit holiday material 2 months in advance. Reports in 2 to 3 weeks. Enclose S.A.S.E.

Nonfiction, Photos, and Fillers: "Primarily interested in local stories about people, places or events of Cincinnati area and Tri-State; also interested in stories of universal appeal and stories of national interest. Prefer factual stories rather than fiction. No short stories or poems. Prefer researched, documented stories told from an objective point of view. Do not like first-person or opinion stories. The most overworked theme is bicentennial material. Anything topical, particularly contemporary issues, will be considered." Informational, how-to, interview, profile, humor, historical, think articles, nostalgia, photo, travel. Length: 500 to 3,000 words. A reader participation column of writer's views on a controversial subject is published regularly. Pays $25 for column. Photos purchased with or without accompanying ms. Captions optional. Prefers 8x11 glossies or contact sheets or color transparencies. Pays $10 for b&w; $20 for color. Photo Editor: Allan Kain. Also buys puzzles, short humor, and quizzes. Length: 100 to 1,000 words.

Oregon

NORTHWEST MAGAZINE, *The Sunday Oregonian,* 1320 S.W. Broadway, Portland OR 97201. Editor: Joseph R. Bianco. For a family type of audience with somewhat higher education level in Oregon than average. Weekly Sunday supplement magazine; 28 to 40 pages. Established in 1965. Circulation: about 400,000. Buys all rights, but will reassign rights to author after publication. Buys 600 to 650 mss a year. Pays in the closest period to the 10th of the month following publication. Will not consider photocopied submissions. Will consider simultaneous submissions. Reports on material accepted for publication in 10 days. Returns rejected material in 2 weeks. Query first or submit complete ms. Enclose S.A.S.E.
Nonfiction and Photos: "Articles of interest to the Northwest. Topical and (sometimes) controversial. Periodically, issue is devoted to a theme. For example, the theme of 'Outdoors' is how-to. How to do the hockey stop in skiing, how to find a remote hiking ridge, etc. Keep Northwest articles short, topical, and of interest to the Northwest. Ecology, environment, and social mores are always subjects of interest. Also, personality profiles of people of interest." Length: 800 to 1,500 words. Pays $40. 8x10 b&w glossies are purchased with mss or on assignment. Captions required. Pays $15.

Pennsylvania

THE PITTSBURGH PRESS, 34 Blvd. of Allies, Pittsburgh PA 15230. Features Editor: William Allan. For general newspaper readers. Established in 1920. Publishes 3 weekly magazines. Circulation: 700,000. Not copyrighted. Buys 25 to 50 mss a year. Pays on publication. Reports in 2 weeks. Submit complete ms. Enclose S.A.S.E.
Nonfiction and Photos: Picture-oriented material for the Roto Magazine; family type stories for Family Magazine. Must be local subjects with good general interest. Informational, how-to, personal experience, profile, inspirational, humor, historical, nostalgia. Pays $25 per published page. No additional payment for b&w photos used with mss.
How To Break In: "Submit good copy."

TODAY, *The Philadelphia Inquirer,* 400 North Broad St., Philadelphia PA 19101. Editor: Scott DeGarmo. "Because we are a metropolitan Sunday newspaper supplement, our readership is largely urban, and we aim for sophisticated or offbeat articles geared to the city. The local writer has the best chance." Circulation: 875,000. Buys first rights only. Buys 125 to 150 mss a year. Pays on publication. "Include phone number with submissions." Submit seasonal material 3 to 4 months in advance. Reports in 3 to 4 weeks. Enclose S.A.S.E. for return of submissions.
Nonfiction and Photos: "We want humor; youth-oriented articles, the offbeat, solid informative articles on how to cope with contemporary problems. Must relate to this city and region. We like stories that give nuggets of information, including dollar figures where appropriate. We like the sophisticated approach—that is, a touch of *New York* magazine. We like stories that help the reader as well as entertain. We do not want, or use, poetry or short stories or personal memoirs." Length: 300 to 3,000 words. Pays $100 minimum. "Photo emphasis is local. We use very little freelance."

Rhode Island

RHODE ISLANDER, *The Providence Journal,* Providence RI 02902. Phone: 401-277-7263. Editor: Douglas Riggs. Sunday magazine section. Circulation: 210,000. Buys first rights. Payment on publication. Will send free sample copy to writer on request. Reports in 2 weeks. Query first or submit complete ms. Enclose S.A.S.E.

Nonfiction and Photos: "Always looking for new writers with real talent. Prefer articles with 'new journalism' flavor (anecdotal, subjective, highly descriptive, thought-provoking, etc.). Rhode Island angle preferred, but not essential." Pays $50 to $200. Photos purchased with mss. Their weekly "Speaking Out" feature uses expressions of opinions on any topic. Length: 1,000 words maximum. Pays $50.

Poetry: "We publish short poems once a month. No restrictions on subject matter or style." Pays $20.

How To Break In: "A phone call or personal visit is better than a query letter. If you have some specific story ideas, you are always welcome. Read the magazine first; sample copies sent on request. Personal contact with writer may mean difference between rejection slip and letter suggesting revisions. But if your stuff is really good, we'll buy it if it comes in by pony express. We're always looking for new talent, especially in southern New England."

Texas

ICONOCLAST, 3507 Cedar Springs, P.O. Box 7013, Dallas TX 75209. Editor: Doug Baker, Jr. For readers interested in the happenings of today on the Dallas scene. Newspaper. Established in 1967. Weekly. Circulation: 6,000. Rights purchased vary with author and material. Buys about 52 mss a year. Pays on publiation. Will send free sample copy to writer on request. Write for copy of guidelines for writers. Will consider photocopied and simultaneous submissions. Reports in 30 days. Query first. Enclose S.A.S.E.

Nonfiction and Photos: News and news features; concise, brief, and to the point. Informational, how-to, personal experience, interview, expose. Length: 300 to 500 words. Pays $10 to $250. Pays $5 for b&w photos purchased without ms or on assignment.

Virginia

NEWPORT NEWS DAILY PRESS INC., TIDEWATER'S NEW DOMINION MAGAZINE SECTION, P.O. Box 746, 7505 Warwick Blvd., Newport News VA 23607. Editor: Howard Goshorn. For a general newspaper readership; shipyard workers, the military. 28-page tabloid in Sunday newspaper. Established in 1896. Circulation: almost 100,000. Not copyrighted. Payment on publication. Will send free sample copy to writer on request. Will consider photocopied submissions. Will consider simultaneous submissions only if other Virginia publications are excluded. Reports in one month. Query first. Enclose S.A.S.E.

Nonfiction and Photos: "This is the only locally edited Sunday magazine in Virginia. We cover topics of wide general interest with some focus on ship-related stories (sailing ships of Chesapeake Bay, for example; ships built in Newport News); Virginia history; railroad stories, particularly with C&O; stories of famous military men once associated with the Virginia Peninsula." Length: tight writing essential. Pays $25 minimum, with photos or art. Captions required. "In fairness, it should be noted that current reproduction quality is not the best and often 'hurts' good photographs."

Washington

PANORAMA MAGAZINE, *The Everett Herald,* Box 930, Everett WA 98203. Phone: 206-259-5151. Editor: Jeanne Metzger. Majority of readers are in Snohomish County, directly north of Seattle. Established in 1973. Weekly. Circulation: 50,000. Buys all rights, but will reassign rights to author after publication. Buys an average of 24 mss a year. Payment on publication "unless mss is to be held for some time." To obtain a sample copy, we "prefer writer address our circulation department." Will consider photocopied submissions. Query first or submit complete ms, but it's "best to make individual contact with editor or write query letter on material to be submitted." Reports within 1 month. Enclose S.A.S.E.

Nonfiction: "We like good picture features, good personal experience pieces, interviews with interesting people, and articles about happenings in the Northwest. In our population area we don't just stay on Northwest subjects. We'll look at anything

that's well-written and has good picture art. We don't really like freelance travel material unless it's offbeat and would be someplace our people might visit." Length: 600 to 1,800 words. Pays $20 to $25 a tabloid page, with pictures.
Photos: Photos are purchased with or without mss, or on assignment. 5x7 or 8x10 b&w glossies, "good quality." Pays $5 to $10. 35mm and larger transparencies, "must be good, bright color." Pays $15 to $20 for cover photo.

THE SEATTLE TIMES MAGAZINE, P.O. Box 70, Seattle WA 98111. Editor: Larry Anderson. For a general audience, above average in education. Sunday newspaper supplement. Circulation: 300,000. Buys first rights only. Buys about 200 mss a year. Pays on publication. Reports in 1 week. Query first or submit complete ms. Enclose S.A.S.E.
Nonfiction: "Looking for Pacific Northwest material, particularly about people. Want worthwhile, interesting people. Need lots of direct quotes." Length: 200 to 1,500 words; can go longer if subject requires it. Pays $40 a page basic rate.

SEATTLE TIMES PICTORIAL, P.O. Box 70, Seattle WA 98111. Editor: Herb Belanger. For a general audience, above average in education. Sunday newspaper supplement. Circulation: 300,000. Buys first rights. Pays on publication. Reports in 1 week. Enclose S.A.S.E.
Nonfiction and Photos: Looking for pictorial essays on regional (Washington, British Columbia) material. Uses b&w photos inside with possible tie-in color (4x5 transparencies) cover. B&w, submit negatives with contact sheets. Text length: 500 to 1,000 words. Pays $30 to $50 for text. Pays $100 for color cover; $20 per page for b&w. Unused negatives and transparencies returned after publication.

SUNDAY MAGAZINE OF THE SPOKESMAN-REVIEW, *The Spokesman-Review,* Spokane WA 99253. Editor: Jack F. Johnson. Readership in eastern Washington, northern Idaho and western Montana. Reports on submissions in one week. Buys one-time rights. Pays on acceptance. Query required. Enclose S.A.S.E. for reply to queries.
Nonfiction: Subject matter of particular interest to Northwest, 1,200 to 2,000 words with photos. Pays $75 minimum.

SUNDAY MAGAZINE, *Tacoma News Tribune,* 1950 S. State St., Tacoma WA 98411. Phone: 206-597-8671. Editor: Dick Kunkle. Sunday supplement. Circulation: 100,000. Pays on publication. Query first. Reports immediately. Enclose S.A.S.E.
Nonfiction and Photos: Articles and photos about Pacific Northwest, particularly the Puget Sound area. Historical, biographical, recreational stories. Pays $35 per printed tabloid page, whether pictures, text or both. Also occasionally buys a color cover transparency for $35. Northwest subjects only.

TOTEM TIDINGS MAGAZINE, *The Daily Olympian,* P.O. Box 407, Olympia WA 98507. Editor: Chris Fruitrich. For newspaper readers. Sunday tabloid; 32 pages. Established in 1974. Weekly. Circulation: 27,000. Not copyrighted. Buys about 35 mss a year. Pays on publication. Will send free sample copy to writer on request if postage is included. Write for copy of guidelines for writers. No photocopied or simultaneous submissions. Reports in 30 days. Query first or submit complete ms. Enclose S.A.S.E.
Nonfiction and Photos: Washington state-oriented articles, preferably from southwestern part of state. Must be bright and fast-paced material. People, places or things — but no first-person articles. Historical, water-oriented and topical pieces dealing with the immediate area. Informational, how-to, interview, profile, humor, historical, nostalgia, travel (but only in the northwest). Length: 1,440 words maximum. Pays $25. Buys color transparencies or b&w (8x10) prints with mss. Pays $3 for both b&w and color.

West Virginia

PANORAMA, *The Morgantown Dominion-Post,* Greer Bldg., Morgantown WV

26505. Sunday supplement issued weekly. Editor: Shelby Young. Rights purchased are negotiable. Pays on publication.

Nonfiction: "While we have considerable material from our regular sources, we are interested in 1,500- to 2,000-word nonfiction about West Virginia places, people, customs and events and about the Appalachian area immediately surrounding the state." Pays $7.50 minimum; usually $30 to $40 range.

STATE MAGAZINE, Sunday Gazette-Mail, 1001 Virginia St., E, Charleston WV 25330. Editor: Harold C. Gadd. For family newspaper readers. Newspaper magazine; (11x14). Established in 1952. Weekly. Circulation: 110,000. Not copyrighted. Buys 150 to 200 mss a year. Pays on publication. Will send sample copy to writer for 25¢. Will consider photocopied submissions. Simultaneous submissions are considered, if not made to other West Virginia newspapers. Submit special issue material by May 1. Reports in 30 to 90 days. Query first or submit complete ms. Enclose S.A.S.E.

Nonfiction and Photos: Emphasis is on West Virginia material; articles and photo essays. "Simple, lucid, tight writing with a logical organization. Writer must want to catch and hold readers' attention in a busy, busy world. We do not want to see material that has obviously been rejected by other publications. We're easy to sell, but not that easy. We would like to see some West Virginia animal profiles slanted to the family hiker, camper or picnicker; or toward youth outdoors." Length: 500 to 1,500 words. Pays $10 to $50. Annually publishes a special issue on West Virginia: Vacationland, in which articles on enjoyable West Virginia vacation locales are used. Length: 500 to 1,000 words. Pays $10 to $50. B&w photos with good contrast, good composition, and sharp focus purchased with or without ms. Pays $5. Ultra-sharp, bright, 35mm (or up to 4x5) color transparencies purchased with or without ms. Pays $20.

How To Break In: "Always query first. Beginning West Virginia writers have best chance. Our freelance policy is designed to encourage them to write about their home state."

Wisconsin

INSIGHT, *The Milwaukee Journal,* Journal Square, Milwaukee WI 53201. Editor: Mike Moore. Sunday magazine. Circulation: 550,000. Reports within 2 weeks. Buys one-time rights. Payment on acceptance. Query preferred. Enclose S.A.S.E.

Nonfiction and Photos: Emphasis on circulation area of Wisconsin and upper Michigan. Length: 2,500 words maximum. Pays $50 to $250 per article. Photos purchased with mss and with captions. Same subject matter as articles. Payment arranged with author or photographer.

RURAL GRAVURE, 2564 Branch St., Middleton WI 53562. Editor: J. C. Curren. For "rural—hometown Midwestern residents." Monthly. Circulation: 650,000. Buys 25 mss a year. Pays on publication. Will send a free sample copy to a writer on request. Submit seasonal material 6 months in advance. Reports "immediately." Enclose S.A.S.E.

Nonfiction: Wants human interest stories and interviews "from Midwest only." Does not want agricultural articles. Length: 1,000 to 3,000 words. Pays $50 to $150.

Photos: B&w glossies purchased with captions only. Pays $15 to $150.

Canada

THE CANADIAN MAGAZINE, The Simpson Tower, 401 Bay St., Toronto M5H 2Y8, Ontario, Canada. Phone: 416-363-7151. Editor: Don Obe. Buys North American serial rights. Pays on acceptance. "We only consider mss written with a very strong Canadian slant." Query first. Enclose S.A.E. and International Reply Coupons.

Nonfiction: Looking for articles of interest to Canadians from coast to coast, on Canadian subjects, written in a lively and informative manner with plenty of human interest. Effective use of anecdotes quite frequently provides this human interest; therefore, use an anecdotal approach to the subject. Articles submitted may cover a wide range of topics—human affairs, religion, science, politics, personalities, humor and sport, hobbies, cookery and fashion. Looking for good literary quality. Strongly recommend an outline letter, of 200 to 300 words, staking out the extent and burden of the article. A green light on the basis of such an outline does not constitute a commitment, but it does mean that they are interested in getting an article on this topic. Length: 1,000 to 2,500 words. Pays up to $250 for short pieces and payment for a full-length article starts at $300. Alan Walker, Managing Editor.

THE ISLANDER MAGAZINE, *The Daily Colonist,* Victoria B.C., Canada. Phone: 604-383-4111. Editor: Alec Merriman. For "just about everyone who lives on Vancouver Island". Weekly; 16 (9x14) pages. Established in 1858. Circulation: 50,000. Not copyrighted. Buys 400 to 500 mss a year. Payment on publication. Will send free sample copy to writer on request. Will not consider simultaneous submissions. Reporting time varies "from a week or two to a year, if it is an article we hope to use." Submit complete ms. Enclose S.A.E. and International Reply Coupons.
Nonfiction and Photos: *"The Islander* is very personally Pacific Northwest, mainly Vancouver Island, and takes a folksy, homespun, almost chatty outlook. We aim at our local market and don't try to compete with the syndicated magazine sections with articles of wide-ranging general interest. We use feature articles about people, places and things, with a Pacific Northwest slant, plus a heavy interest in Northwest history. All material must have the Pacific Northwest angle." Length: 500 to 2,000 words. Pays about $15 per magazine page. Prefers 5x7 or 8x10 b&w glossies, but sometimes uses snapshots. Pays $3 for photos used with ms; $5 for cover use (always a local scene). Captions required.
How To Break In: *"The Islander* leans heavily toward the homespun type of local slant which is an advantage for Pacific Northwest writers. But, a person from this area who is doing something unique or making a success of living elsewhere always makes an acceptable feature. Travel literature is distributed freely by the yard, so a local and different slant must be sought."

WEEKEND MAGAZINE, The Montreal Standard Publishing Company Limited, 231 St. James St. West, Montreal, PQ Canada. Editor: Sheena Paterson. Weekly section of 22 newspapers. Circulation: 1,600,000. Buys first North American rights. Buys 100 mss a year. Pays on acceptance. "All mss and photos sent in are done so on a speculative basis only and should be addressed to the Features Editor or Art Director respectively." Query before submitting material. Enclose S.A.E. and International Reply Coupons with mss and queries.
Nonfiction and Photos: "Articles should have strong Canadian content or be about some person, event or activity of particular interest to Canadians on a national basis. We don't use travel articles or fillers." Length: 1,500 to 2,500 words. Pays $400 to $750. If photos or transparencies are sent in and used in addition to the mss, payment is adjusted accordingly. "Our photographic requirements are for all sizes of color from 35mm up; we prefer color transparencies and b&w prints." Pays from $75 to $200.

Photography Publications

CAMERA 35, Popular Publications, 420 Lexington Ave., New York NY 10017. Phone: 212-586-5050. Editor: Bill Clark. "A very special magazine within a vertical field, directed at thinking photographers." Published 10 times a year. Buys one-time rights. Pays on publication. Enclose S.A.S.E.
Photos: "Photography published in form of portfolios and essays. No taboos for either words or pictures, as long as they fit our needs. To determine needs, study at least 3 recent issues. Good literate writing mandatory. Pay $200 per mini portfolio (2 to 3 pages), $500 per maxi portfolio or essay (4 to 12 pages) b&w or color. Covers, $150. Up to $400 for technical how-to features."

FREELANCE PHOTOGRAPHY, FREELANCE PHOTO NEWS, 4 East State Street, Doylestown PA 18901. Acting Editor: William Cameron. For "amateur and professional photographers, all ages and with various educational backgrounds." Established in 1972 and 1968, respectively. Monthly (FP); every two months (FPN). Circulation: over 25,000. Rights purchased vary with author and material, but may buy all rights. Buys "hundreds" of mss a year. Payment on acceptance or publication. Will send free sample copy to a writer on request. Will send editorial guidelines sheet to a writer on request. "If photographs are to accompany the article, they should be clearly marked with the photographer's name and address, necessary captions or pertinent information must be also clearly available, and if identifiable persons appear in any photo, the proper model release must be attached. Used photos, stories, etc., will not be returned after use unless specifically requested." Reports in two weeks. Query first. Enclose S.A.S.E.

Nonfiction: Interested in articles in the following categories: "A how-to approach toward taking photos or a unique device designed to aid in certain picture situations. It could be with regard to cameras, lighting, studio setup, backdrops, model handling, etc. Included in this could be new darkroom techniques or innovations which would make use of a darkroom more efficient. Aside from the equipment and supporting areas of how-to, an article could be designed from experiences such as 'Promotion sells photos,' 'Linking your camera to a business,' 'A hobby becomes a profitable business,' etc. Unusual experiences which one may have had with a camera or other equipment. Personalities. We'd like to hear about any unique or special happenings by well-known personalities and their involvement in photography. These may be of political figures, TV and movie stars, etc., and their use of cameras and related equipment. Human interest stories. We are interested in stories which illustrate people with unusual or unique job situations and their use of cameras and related equipment. Travel stories. We are not interested in general travel items. They must be geared to a person or group of people and their experience with photography. Articles which inform the reader of how-to or what-to photograph when visiting . . . (city or country) are encouraged and acceptable. Humorous articles are welcome and should be short. These could be of any item which relates to photography, on the lighter side." Also interested in "almost any idea which is photography related." Length: 500 to 5,000 words. Pays $5 to $50.

Photos: " 'The Photo Gallery' is a section of selected photographs submitted by our members and readers at large for display on a space available basis in each issue. Individual photos or a series of photos with captions are considered. Credit line will be given. No payment is usually made for photos appearing in this section. 'Photo Story' is devoted to a series of photographs which would be self-explanatory and contain captions only. A short explanatory paragraph may accompany the series." Photos purchased with and without mss. Captions required. Buys 5x7, but prefers 8x10 b&w glossies. Pays $5 and up.

MODERN PHOTOGRAPHY, 130 E. 59th St., New York NY 10022. Editor: Julia Scully. Monthly. Read by photographers, about half of whom have their own darkrooms. Buys one-time rights. Pays on acceptance. Study copy of magazine before submitting and send in outline before writing script. Enclose S.A.S.E.

Nonfiction: Uses articles on specialized photo techniques; other types of articles are staff-written. Pays $60 per page for text and photographs. Uses either contacts or enlargements; the latter should be 8x10 or 11x14 semi-gloss prints.

Photos: B&w 8x10 or larger prints on glossy dried matte. Uses any type transparency material for color submissions, but they must be 35mm and up in size. $35 minimum for b&w; $100 minimum for color. Please query here before submitting anything.

PHOTOGRAPHIC MAGAZINE, Petersen Publishing Company, 8490 Sunset Blvd., Los Angeles CA 90069. Editor: Paul R. Farber. For all who are interested in photography; all ages. Monthly magazine, 80 pages. Established in 1972. Circulation: 175,000. Rights purchased vary with author and material. Payment on publication. Write for copy of guidelines for writers. Will consider photocopied submissions. Reports in 2 weeks. Query first. Enclose S.A.S.E.

Nonfiction and Photos: "Basically seeking how-to type of article dealing with photography in all areas. Writer should be an authority on his subject and article should be well illustrated with photographs. We seek information that is generally disregarded by other publications in the field—in other words, we cater to the amateur photographer—in picture taking and beginner darkroom." Buys how-to, personal experience, interviews, new product, photos, and travel articles. No restrictions on length, but "must complete subject." Pays $60 per printed page. Pays $35 per black and white, $50 for each color print used.

PHOTOGRAPHY 2001, P.O. Box 318, Concord CA 94522. Editor: William Whitney. For amateur photographers. Quarterly magazine; 72 to 80 (7x10) pages. Established in 1974. Circulation: 20,000. Buys all rights, but will reassign rights to author after publication. Buys 10 to 15 mss a year. Payment on acceptance or upon publication. Will send sample copy to writer for $1. Will consider photocopied and simultaneous submissions. "All submissions must be typed, double-spaced, on only one side of standard 8½x11 paper." Reports in 4 to 6 weeks. Query first or submit complete ms. Enclose S.A.S.E.

Nonfiction and Photos: Uses first-hand material for the interested hobbyist, the freelancer, and the professional. How-to's, money-makers, interviews with successful photographers, informational articles, profiles, think pieces, spot news, new products, merchandising techniques, technical. Should be informal, chatty; filled with data, but not dull. "We want to emphasize the tips and money-making ideas which apply to the up-and-coming new photographer. We do not want to see such themes as 'How I Sold 10 Postcards' or weddings (unless unusual)." Length: 1,500 to 2,500 words. Pays 2¢ to 5¢ per word. 8x10 b&w glossy photographs are purchased with accompanying mss or on assignment. Pays $2 to $5. Pays $25 per color transparency. Captions required. Photo Department Editor: Paul Williams.

Fillers: Newsbreaks, clippings, jokes, short humor. Length: 50 to 250 words. Payment begins in copies of the issue or can go up to $15.

How To Break In: "Emphasize the creative in photography. Creativity is often a personal statement which taps the universal response in the viewer. Photography and articles for our market must emphasize such a statement both in content and in composition."

POPULAR PHOTOGRAPHY, 1 Park Ave., New York NY 10016. Editor: Kenneth Poli. "Mostly for hobby photographers; about 90% are men." Also publishes 6 annuals or one-shots. Monthly. Circulation: 615,000. "Rights purchased vary with author and material, but usually buys one-time if story is author's idea, not ours." Buys 35 to 50 mss a year, "mostly from technical types already known to us." Pays on acceptance. Submit seasonal material 4 months in advance. Reports in 3 to 4 weeks. Query first. Enclose S.A.S.E.

Nonfiction: This magazine is mainly interested in instructional articles on photography that will help photographers improve their work. This includes all aspects of photography, from theory to camera use and darkroom procedures. Utter familiarity with the subject is a prerequisite to acceptance here. It is best to submit article ideas in outline form since features are set up to fit the magazine's visual policies. "Style should be very readable but with plenty of factual data when a technique story is involved. We're not quite as 'hardware' oriented as some magazines. We use many equipment stories, but we give more space to cultural and aesthetic aspects of the hobby than our competition does." Buys how-to's, interviews, profiles, historical articles, new product coverage, photo essays. Length: 500 to 2,000 words. Pays $25 to $400.

Photos: Interested in seeing b&w prints of any type finish that are 8x10 or larger. Also uses any size color transparency. Buys one-time rights except when assigned, then all-time. Pays $25 and up per b&w shot; $50 and up per color shot; $400 for cover. Articles accompanied by pictures are usually bought as a package. Gives few assignments.

Fillers: Uses featurettes that run from 1 to 2 columns to 1-pagers and "Photo Tips," which are short how-to-do-its, illustrated by a single picture. Featurette length should be from 500 to 1,000 words; for the "Photo Tips," less than 100 words or whatever is necessary to give all pertinent information. Pays $25 to $75 for featurettes, depending on use; $10 for illustrated "Photo Tips."

Poetry Publications

This category includes publications that exist to discuss and publish poetry. A few nespapers and other special media using poetry are also included. Many publications in the Literary and Little category are also interested in poetry submissions. Various other poetry markets are listed in other categories throughout the Consumer section.

Many of the markets that follow pay in contributor's copies, prizes or some form of remuneration other than money. We have included such markets because there are limited commercial outlets for poetry and these at least offer the poet some visibility.

Poetry manuscripts should have the poet's name and address typed in the upper left-hand corner. Total number of lines in the poem should appear in the upper right-hand corner. Center the title of the poem 8 to 10 lines from the top of the page. The poem should be typed, double-spaced. The poet's name should again appear at the end of the poem. In the case where the poet submits more than one poem to the editor, each poem should always be typed on a separate sheet of paper. Always enclose S.A.S.E. with poetry submissions.

ADVENTURES IN POETRY, 3915 S. Military Dr., San Antonio TX 78211. Phone: 512-923-8407. Editor: Dr. Stella Woodall. For poets of all ages. Magazine published every 2 months; 30 (8½x5½) pages. Established in 1971. Circulation: "small". Not copyrighted, "but copyright applied for." Uses about 100 mss a year. No payment is made, but $1 is paid for the poem selected to appear on the first page of each issue of the magazine. Will send sample copy to writer for $2. Will consider photocopied, cassette and simultaneous submissions. Submit seasonal material (Easter, autumn, winter, spring) 3 months in advance. Reports in 1 month. Submit complete ms. Enclose S.A.S.E.
Poetry: "Only poems of high moral standards are published. Poems that show the beauty and goodness found in this world. Poems that will help others to be happier and aspire for the greatness of life. Avoid sex and homosexuals, violence, hatred, slams on mothers-in-law, generation gap material." Uses traditional forms, blank verse, free verse and light verse. Publishes poems on loyalty, truth, patriotism, peace, honesty; inspirational and humorous poems. Length: 30 lines maximum. No minimum. "The shorter, the better."

AISLING, 2526 42nd Ave., San Francisco CA 94116. Editor: Paul Shuttleworth. For a college-educated audience interested in Irish and/or American poetry. Established in 1973. Quarterly. Circulation: 300. Acquires all rights, but will reassign rights to author after publication. Uses 60 mss per year. Payment in contributor's copies and subscription. Will send sample copy to writer for $1. Will consider photocopied submissions. Reports on material in 2 weeks. Submit complete ms. Enclose S.A.S.E.
Poetry: Traditional forms, blank verse, free verse, avant-garde forms, light verse. Poems should have clarity, vision, and honesty. "We don't want St. Patrick's Day verse or 'Did your Mother come from Blarney?'." Length: 50 lines maximum.

THE ARCHER, A VERSE QUARTERLY, P.O. Box 9488, North Hollywood CA 91609. Editor: Henry Brown. For an average audience; education above average; most attempting to write as well as enjoying reading verse. Quarterly; 28 pages, (5½x8½). Established in 1951. Circulation: 800. Copyrighted. "All needed rights for book publication, etc., released to writer. We reserve right to make possible use of published material in such fields as broadcast programs, anthologies, etc." Uses

about 200 to 300 mss a year. Payment in contributor's copies. "We cannot guarantee a fast response." Submit complete poetry ms. Enclose S.A.S.E.
Poetry: "Verse. Try to have something original to say and say it in an original way, and as briefly as possible. We have no restrictions as to style or subject matter, but are a bit old-fashioned on matters we may consider in poor taste. We probably take ourselves less seriously than some other publications in the verse field. Our purpose is to give pleasure if possible, and stimulate good writing, if possible." Open on subject matter. Length: 2 to 30 lines, seldom more. "Briefer items have the best chance."

BACHAET, 12 Morris Rd., West Orange NJ 07052. Phone: 201-736-0538. Editor: Geoffrey Jay Palefsky. For "all parts of the population interested in poetry". Issued twice yearly. Established in 1968. Circulation: 500. Not copyrighted. No payment. No free copies. Reports in 1 month. Enclose S.A.S.E.
Poetry: Poems of all types, from 4 to 20 lines. "Looking for a sympathetic editor? We like to help the unpublished. We don't standardize rejection slips."

BARDIC ECHOES, 1036 Emerald Ave., N.E., Grand Rapids MI 49503. Editor: Clarence L. Weaver. Quarterly. Not copyrighted. Payment in contributor's copies. Will send sample copy to writer for 50¢. Reports in 2 months. Limit submissions to no more than 5 poems. Occasionally overstocked." Enclose S.A.S.E.
Poetry: Poetry may be on any subject. Varied style. Length: 40 lines maximum (one full page).

THE BELOIT POETRY JOURNAL, P.O. Box 2, Beloit WI 53511. Editorial Board: Robert H. Glauber, David M. Stocking, Marion Kingston Stocking. Quarterly. Circulation: 1,100. Acquires first serial rights. Accepts approximately 60 mss a year. Payment in 3 contributor's copies. Will send a sample copy to a writer for 50¢. No query required. Reports in 4 months. Enclose S.A.S.E.
Poetry: Uses all types of poetry from the most experimental to the most conservative (with emphasis in each case on quality) and is always on the lookout for interesting new talent. No restrictions as to length or form. One unusual feature is the policy of devoting occasional issues to one long poem or to a special chapbook on one theme.

BITTERROOT, International Poetry Magazine, Blythebourne Station, P.O. Box 51, Brooklyn NY 11219. Editor: Menke Katz. Quarterly. Copyrighted. Payment in 1 contributor's copy. Enclose S.A.S.E.
Poetry: "We need good poetry of all kinds. If we think a poem is very good, we will publish a two-page poem; mostly however, we prefer shorter poems, not longer than one page. We always discourage stereotyped forms."

BROADSIDE SERIES, 12651 Old Mill Pl., Detroit MI 48238. Editor: Dudley Randall. For blacks interested in library poetry collections. Monthly broadside. Established in 1965. Circulation: 500. Buys first North American serial rights. Buys 12 mss a year. Payment on publication. Will send sample copy to writer for 50¢. Reports in 1 month. Enclose S.A.S.E.
Poetry: Black poetry; all forms. Length: 1 page. Pays $10. "Poetry must be of high literary merit as each monthly issue contains only one poem."

CIRCLE, Circle Forum, P.O. Box 176, Portland OR 97207. Editor: Mrs. J. M. Gates. For libraries, schools, and individuals interested in reversible poetry. 16-page quarterly periodical. Established in 1973. Rights revert to respective authors upon publication. Payment in contributor's copies. Will send sample copy to writer for $1. Write for copy of guidelines for writers, enclosing S.A.S.E. Will consider photocopied submissions, but must be unpublished reversible poetry only. Will not consider simultaneous submissions. Submit seasonal material 6 months in advance. Reports in 2 months. Submit complete ms. Enclose S.A.S.E.
Poetry: "*Circle* is dedicated exclusively to poetry that is readable, line by line, either forward or backward. Serious poets may consider development of reversible poetry

regarding general themes or historical themes; historical narratives in reversible poetry are particularly needed. Protest poetry in standard English is welcome. Reversible poetry in traditional or other forms; free of language pollution." Length: 8 lines minimum. No maximum.

CREATIVE MOMENT, Poetry Eastwest Publications, P.O. Box 391, Sumter SC 29150. Editor: Dr. Syed Amanuddin. For "creative writers, poets, and those who are interested in the international scene in contemporary poetry." Established in 1972. Biannual. Circulation: 500. Acquires first serial rights. Payment in contributor's copy. Will send a sample copy to a writer for $1. Will not consider photocopied submissions. Reports in 6 to 8 months. Query first for articles and reviews. Enclose S.A.S.E.

Nonfiction: "We specialize in world poetry written in English and we need intelligent and provocative articles on contemporary English-language poetry of all the regions of the world including Canada, India, Nigeria, Rhodesia, South Africa, and West Indies. Articles should be under 3,000 words with all notes worked into the text. We refuse to read articles with footnotes."

Poetry: "We are interested only in original unpublished poems under 30 lines."

CREATIVE REVIEW, 1718 S. Garrison, Carthage MO 64836. Editor: Glen Coffield. For hobbyists, educated, retired, handicapped, educators. Quarterly mimeographed magazine; 14 to 18 pages. Established in 1961. Not copyrighted. Uses 250 poems a year. Payment in contributor's copies. Will send sample copy to writer for 50¢. Reports within 3 months. Submit complete ms; "one poem to a page (8½x11)." Enclose S.A.S.E.

Poetry: "Poems on creativity, good description, local history, examples of good writing, pictures of life, positive approach, good taste, simple and clear. Good grammar and punctuation, logical structure, understandable to the average reader; interesting beginnings, strong endings, objective imagery, not too abstract. We're perhaps more selective and demanding; more traditional in a knowledgeable sense. We don't want risque, no negativism or tearing down, no difficult typographical experiments, no excess verbosity and repetition, no intellectual snobbery or trite sophistication. No personal frustrations. Not especially interested in the topical, except positive suggestions on current problems." Length: 32 lines maximum. "Quality demands are greater the longer the poem."

DRAGONFLY: A QUARTERLY OF HAIKU, 4102 N.E. 130th Pl., Portland OR 97230. Editor: Lorraine Ellis Harr. Established in 1965. Circulation: over 500. Will reassign all rights to author after publication. No payment. No free copies. Will send sample copy to writer for 75¢. Write for copy of guidelines for writers. Reports in 30 days. "Send only 5 haiku at a time. Use ½ sheet 8½x11. Saves paper and postage. Name and address in upper left-hand corner." Contests and cash awards; student awards each issue. Enclose S.A.S.E.

Nonfiction and Poetry: Haiku poetry only, in the classical/traditional style. Related short articles of 300 words. "We publish a crosscut of all English language haiku as it is being written by today's poets." No long viewpoint articles. No stream-of-consciousness haiku sequences or "pseudo" haiku. No 5-7-5 English language poetry in haiku form.

ENCORE, A QUARTERLY OF VERSE AND POETIC ARTS, 1121 Major Ave., N.W., Albuquerque NM 87107. Phone: 505-344-5615. Editor: Alice Briley. For "anyone interested in poetry from young people in high school to many retired people. Good poetry on any theme." Established in 1966. Quarterly. Circulation: 600. Acquires all rights but will reassign rights to author after publication. Uses 300 mss a year. Occasionally overstocked. Payment in contributor's copies. Will send sample copy to a writer for 25¢. Will consider photocopied submissions "provided the author is free to assign rights to *Encore.* Will require assurance if poem is accepted." Submit seasonal material 6 to 9 months in advance. Reports on material within a month. Submit complete ms. Enclose S.A.S.E.

Nonfiction, Poetry and Photos: "Particularly like poetry which illustrates the magazine's theme that poetry is a performing art. Fresh approach greatly desired. Poetry
by students as well as established poets." Traditional forms, blank verse, free verse,
avant-garde and light verse. Some articles on related subjects. Profiles of poets, poetry
reviews, technical verse writing. Length: open, but "very long articles rarely used."
Prefer no larger than 5x8 b&w glossy photos with good contrast. Pays in contributor's
copies. Also has an annual poetry contest.

EPOS, Crescent City FL 32012. Editor: Evelyn Thorne. For educated people who
read poetry. Quarterly; 36 pages, (6½x10). Established in 1949. Circulation: 500.
Copyrighted. Uses 30 to 35 poems per issue. Payment in contributor's copies. Will
send sample copy to writer for $1. Reports in 1 week. Enclose S.A.S.E.
Poetry: Traditional forms, free verse, and avant-garde forms of poetry. Open on
themes and length.

FOLIO, P.O. Box 31111, Birmingham AL 35222. Editor: Myra Crawford Johnson.
For poets. Magazine published twice a year in the spring and fall; 60 pages.
Established in 1965. Circulation: 600. Acquires all rights, but will reassign rights
to author after publication. Uses 200 (or less) mss a year. Payment in contributor's
copies. Will send sample copy to writer for $1.50. Will consider photocopied
submissions. Will not consider simultaneous submissions. Reports in 8 weeks. Submit
complete ms. Enclose S.A.S.E.
Poetry and Fiction: All forms. Length for fiction: 2,500 words. Poetry length is open.

GRAVIDA, P.O. Box 76, Hartsdale NY 10530. Managing Editor: Lynne Savitt. For
poetry lovers, women supporting a publication run by other women; prisoners, artists,
etc. All ages, interests and educations. Magazine; 26 to 60 (5½x8½) pages. Established
in 1973. Quarterly. Circulation: 500. Copyrighted. Uses about 80 poems a year. Pays
in contributor's copies. Will send sample copy to writer for 75¢. Submissions limited
to 5 typewritten pages; 1 poem per page. Will consider photocopied submissions.
Reports in 6 to 8 weeks. Submit complete ms. Enclose S.A.S.E.
Poetry: "We are not interested in publishing *poets,* but quality poems; vivid, alive,
competent. As long as image and metaphor are fresh, any subject or form is
acceptable." Length: 50 lines maximum.

HAPPINESS HOLDING TANK, P.O. Box 227, Okemos MI 48864. Phone: 517-349-
0552. Editor: Albert Drake. For "poets of various ages, interests; other editors;
students." Triannual magazine; 45 pages, (8½x11). Established in 1970. Circulation:
300 to 500. All rights revert to author automatically. Payment in contributor's copies.
Will send a sample copy to a writer for $1. Reports in 1 to 4 weeks. Not reading
during summer months. Submit complete ms. Enclose S.A.S.E.
Nonfiction and Poetry: Publishes "poems of various kinds, somewhat eclectic—looking for 'excellence.' Essays and articles on modern poetry. Emphasis on younger
but unestablished poets; their work to date. Emphasis on information of various
kinds—to make magazine useful. Interested in printing methods of all kinds." Buys
informational, how-to, and poetry book reviews. Uses all forms of poetry except
light verse. Now doing chapbooks and poetry posters.
How To Break In: "We are eclectic, and have published all kinds of poetry. What
we are looking for is freshness, a lively imagination, the kind of poem that you
remember later. It's a good idea for any writer to read what's being written and
published."

THE HARTFORD COURANT, THIS SINGING WORLD, 285 Broad St., Hartford
CT 06115. Phone: 203-249-6411, Ext. 337. Poetry Editor: Malcolm L. Johnson. For
a general audience. Weekly poetry column in newspaper. Established in 1764.
Circulation: 180,000. Not copyrighted. Uses about 200 poems a year. Payment in
tearsheets. "We are not set up to send free copies." Will consider photocopied
submissions and simultaneous submissions. "Christmas poetry is wanted for the
weekend before Christmas. Seasonal poetry is usually not used out of season." Submit

seasonal poetry 1 month in advance. Reports usually within 2 weeks, unless it is being considered for publication; may take up to 3 months. Submit complete ms. Enclose S.A.S.E.

Poetry: "Any sort of poetry is eligible, but the general readership means that graphically erotic or violent poetry cannot be used. In general, we strive for the same sort of poetry that might be published in a literary magazine. The only guideline would be that the poetry must necessarily be rather short. 50 lines is about the maximum. Seasonal and poet's soul poetry always seems overworked, but creative approaches to these subjects are still welcome. It would be pleasant to receive more light or satirical verse, but these seem difficult genres for many poets." Length: 2 to 50 lines.

HIRAM POETRY REVIEW, P.O. Box 162, Hiram OH 44234. Phone: 216-569-3211. Editor: David Fratus. Published 2 times a year; magazine, 40 pages, (6x9). "Since our chief subscribers are libraries in major cities or libraries of colleges and universities, our audience is highly literate and comprises persons who are actively interested in poetry of high quality." Established in 1967. Circulation: 500. Copyrighted. Acquires all rights, but will reassign rights to author upon written request. Uses approximately 50 poems a year. Payment in 2 contributor's copies plus one year's subscription. Will send free sample copy to writer on request. Reports in 6 weeks. Submit only complete ms. Enclose S.A.S.E.

Poetry: All forms of poetry used. No special emphasis required. "Poems on ecology seem superabundant lately, but we try not to operate on prejudices relating to subjects or themes." Length: open, but we have printed few very long poems.

ICARUS, P.O. Box 8, Riderwood MD 21139. Editor: Margaret Diorio. For readers of poetry. Established in 1973. Quarterly. Circulation: 600. Acquires all rights, but will reassign rights to author after publication. Payment in contributor's copies. Will send sample copy to writer for 75¢. Reports on material in 1 month. Enclose S.A.S.E.

Poetry: Will consider poetry from all schools. Serious poetry, any and all forms. Open on themes. Length: 30 lines or less preferred, but will consider longer poems.

IDEALS, 11315 Watertown Plank Rd., Milwaukee WI 53201. Editor: Maryjane Hooper Tonn. Managing Editor: Lorraine Obst. Payment for poems or articles made at time of publication ($10 and a copy of the issue). Buys one-time rights. Will send sample copy to writer on request. Reports in 2 weeks. Enclose return postage.

Nonfiction, Poetry and Photos: "*Ideals* are books containing clean, wholesome, old-fashioned American ideals, homey philosophy and general inspirational, patriotic, religious, seasonal, family, childhood or nostalgic material. Poems and articles submitted will be carefully reviewed, and such material that we believe will lend itself to use in *Ideals* will be retained in our permanent review files. Such material is carefully reviewed during the preparation of each new book. We cannot definitely guarantee that we will feature the poems or articles which we retain, but we shall make a sincere effort to do so. We assume the privilege of editing retained material where necessary. If, for any reason, you do not want us to enter your material into our review files, kindly advise us when submitting it so that we can promptly return it to you. Please do not send us your original poems or articles. Send only copies. We cannot return your submitted material after it has been entered into our review files. B&w photos should be sharp, clear 8x10 glossies. We pay $20 minimum when purchased for immediate use. We prefer 4x5 or 8x10 color transparencies, for which pay is $100 minimum. 35mm transparencies are accepted, provided they are mounted on a sheet of acetate in groups of at least 20 so they may be easily reviewed."

INTERNATIONAL POETRY REVIEW, 1060 N. Saint Andrews Pl., Hollywood CA 90038. Editor: Henry Picola, Ph.D. For high school students, housewives, college professors, and college students, and businessmen; from 16 years to 88 years. Quarterly magazine, 16 to 24 pages. Established in 1961. Circulation: 6,000. Acquires all rights. Uses about 5 mss a year. No payment. Will send sample copy to writer for $1.

Write for editorial guidelines for writers. "No mss will be read during the summer months. Because of the heavy mail during the winter months, I shall have to hold material for at least 2 months." Query first for poetry accompanied by drawings. Enclose S.A.S.E.

Poetry: "Poems of nature, love, adventure, travel, death, current events. No special style, just be yourself—express yourself as you please but please omit four-letter words." Traditional forms of poetry, blank verse, free verse, avant-garde forms, and light verse. Length: 16 lines.

JEAN'S JOURNAL, Box 15, Kanona NY 14856. Editor: Jean Calkins. For all who enjoy poetry. Quarterly magazine; 70 pages or more, (5½x8½). Established in 1963. Circulation: 450. Copyrighted. Acquires first North American serial rights. No payment. Will send sample copy to writer for 50¢. Write for editorial guidelines for writers (enclose S.A.S.E.). "Each issue is a seasonal issue, and we use material accordingly." Submit seasonal material no more than 6 months in advance. Reports in 2 to 3 weeks. Enclose S.A.S.E.

Nonfiction and Poetry: "Poetry or related articles. Use almost no verse. We like quality poetry, but strive for personal rapport with writers. No trite rhyming; verse." Cash awards and contests. Open on themes. Length: open.

LEMMING, 3551 42nd St., San Diego CA 92105. Editor: Rex Burwell. For young adults, college educated, with literary interests. Established in 1970. Quarterly. Circulation: 200. Acquires all rights, but will reassign rights to author after publication. Payment in contributor's copies. Will send sample copy to writer for 50¢. Reports in 2 weeks. Submit complete ms. Enclose S.A.S.E.

Poetry: Free verse; imagistic. "Freshness of image is very important." Length and theme: open.

THE LITTLE REVIEW, P.O. Box 2321, Huntington WV 25724. Editor: John McKernan. Biannual. Circulation: 1,000. Acquires first rights. No payment. Will send a sample copy to a writer for $1.25. Reports in 1 month. Enclose S.A.S.E. for return of submissions.

Nonfiction and Poetry: "Poetry, translations, critical reviews of contemporary poets, parodies, and satire. We are mainly a poetry magazine."

LOON, P.O. Box 11633, Santa Rosa CA 95406. Editors: D. L. Emblen, Richard Speakes, Richard Welin. For educated readers of any age from 18 up. Magazine published twice a year. Established in 1973. Circulation: 150. Acquires all rights, but will reassign rights to author after publication. Uses 80 poems a year. Payment in contributor's copies. Will send sample copy to writer for $1. Will not consider photocopied or simultaneous submissions. Reports in 2 to 4 weeks. Submit complete ms. Enclose S.A.S.E.

Poetry: Original poems and translations of poems from other languages. No restrictions on form or subject matter. Traditional forms, blank verse, free verse, avant-garde forms, light verse. Prospective contributors are advised to "read a lot of first-rate modern poetry and read a copy of *Loon.*"

THE LYRIC, Bremo Bluff VA 23022. Editors: Ruby Altizer Roberts and John Nixon, Jr. Established in 1921. Quarterly. Circulation: approximately 900. Acquires first North American serial rights. No payment. Reports promptly. Enclose S.A.S.E.

Poetry: "Formal, metrical pieces, preferably rhymed, of not more than 36 lines, stand the best chance here. We want work that is original, yet lucid, and insist on dignity. About equally unimpressed by banality and avant-garde." All published material automatically considered for quarterly and annual cash prizes. Also conducts contest for college undergraduates.

MODERN HAIKU, 260 Vista Marina, San Clemente CA 92672. Editor: Kay Titus Mormino. Readers range from high school age up. "Most are from 20 to 50. Their interests certainly include haiku, art, music, all forms of poetry. Probably most of our readers have attended university. Many are college professors, students, many

are in business or some profession other than teaching. Many are working people."
Quarterly magazine; 48 pages, (8½x5½). Established in 1969. Circulation: 600.
Acquires all rights, but will reassign rights to author after publication. Payment
in copies. Will send sample copy to writer for $2. Write for copy of guidelines
for writers (enclose S.A.S.E.). Reports within 1 month. Submit only complete ms
for poetry. Enclose S.A.S.E.
Nonfiction, Poetry, and Fillers: "Mostly haiku. Also senryu and haibun. Articles
dealing with any aspect of reading or writing the above. Reviews of books on any
of the above. No special requirements or approach, but poetic quality is a must.
We're the only haiku magazine published in North America that publishes haiku
of all schools of thought; *MH* is a showcase for haiku poets from traditional to
experimental. The editors don't play favorites. We would prefer not to see prose
written in 3 lines and called haiku. Line unity, essence of haiku, distinction between
haiku and senryu are of interest." Length: 500 to 3,000 words. Pays in copies.
Department Editor: Robert Spiess. Poetry (haiku and senryu) and fillers (anything
of interest on haiku) should be sent to Kay Titus Mormino. Three prizes are awarded
for poetry published in each issue.

THE MODULARIST REVIEW, Wooden Needle Press, 27 Lee St., Cambridge MA
02139. Editor: R. C. Morse. Established in 1972. Biannual. Circulation: 1,000.
Acquires all rights. Pays in contributor's copies. Will send sample copy to writer
for $1.50. No photocopied or simultaneous submissions. Reports within 3 months.
Query first or submit complete ms. Enclose S.A.S.E.
Poetry and Fiction: "Work submitted must be Modularist; philosophically concerned
with the paraconscious extension of synthesis into modthesis; psychologically concerned with the paraconscious extension of time into four dimensions." Length for
fiction: open, but shorter work preferred. Length for poetry: open.

MUSTANG REVIEW, 212 So. Broadway, Denver CO 80209. Publisher: Karl Edd.
Published twice yearly. Circulation: 500. Acquires first rights. Accepts 80 to 100
mss a year. Payment in copies. Will send a sample copy to a writer for 50¢. Submit
complete ms. Enclose S.A.S.E.
Poetry: Regional grassroots poetry; metaphoric. Length: 14 to 20 lines.

NORTHERN LIGHT (THE FAR POINT), University of Manitoba, 605 Fletcher
Argue Bldg., Winnipeg, Manitoba, Canada R3T 2N2. Editor: George Amabile. For
libraries, university students, writers and those interested in poetry. Magazine of
80 to 100 pages, published twice a year. Established in 1968. Circulation: 1,000.
Acquires all rights. Uses 60 to 75 mss a year. Payment in contributor's copies. Will
send free sample copy on request. Will consider photocopied submissions. Will not
consider simultaneous submissions. Reports in 1 to 4 months. Submit complete ms.
Enclose S.A.E. and International Reply Coupons.
Poetry and Reviews: "We prefer fresh and lucid poetry of the 'whole consciousness';
poetry that is contemporary in style and content (not pop, but contemporary). Should
be written with imagination and intelligence. The poems should transcribe in exact,
lyrical lines the clearest vision possible. We'd like to see the erotic, the mystical,
the surreal (not horror) and poetry of personal relationships and poetry of place.
We don't like long-winded or chatty poems, or any poems that are unclear in diction.
Free verse is preferred. Canadian poems of high quality will get preference over
others of equal quality. We also publish reviews of recent books by Canadian poets."

OINK!, 1225 Greenleaf, Chicago IL 60626. Editors: Paul Hoover and Maxine
Chernoff. Quarterly magazine; 72 pages. Established in 1971. Circulation: 400.
Acquires all rights, but will reassign rights to author after publication. Payment
in contributor's copies. Will send sample copy to writer for $1. Reports on material
accepted for publication in 1 to 2 weeks. Returns rejected material immediately.
Enclose S.A.S.E.
Poetry and Fiction: Avant-garde forms of poetry. Imaginative writing only. Short
fiction; preferably experimental.

OREGONIAN VERSE, c/o *Oregonian*, Portland OR 97201. Editor: Howard McKinley Corning. Poetry column in Sunday edition of newspaper. Payment on tenth of month following publication. Buys first newspaper rights; rights revert to poet after publication. Sometimes overstocked. "We publish only 2 poems a week now, so can use fewer poems." Reports promptly. Enclose S.A.S.E.
Poetry: "Short lyrics of any type preferred. We seek poems of image and meaning, written out of experience, with a fresh use of language. Should be concise, understandable, and professionally written. No sentimental love poems, religious poems, or those in bad taste. Seasonal verse must reach us several weeks in advance." Length: 24 lines maximum. Pays $5.

POEM, P.O. Box 1247, West Station, Huntsville AL 35807. Phone: 205-895-6320. Editor: Robert L. Welker. For adults; well-educated, interested in good poetry. Published 3 times a year; magazine, 65 pages. Established in 1967. Circulation: 500. Acquires all rights, but will reassign rights to author after publication. Uses 200 poems a year. Payment in contributor's copies. Reports within 2 months. Submit complete ms only. Enclose S.A.S.E.
Poetry: "We use nothing but superior quality poetry. Good taste (no pornography for its own sake) and technical proficiency. We give special attention to young and less well-known poets. Do not like poems about poems, poets, and other works of art." Traditional forms, blank verse, free verse, and avant-garde forms. Length and theme: open.

POET LORE, A NATIONAL QUARTERLY OF WORLD POETRY, Editorial Office, 52 Cranbury Road, Westport CT 06880. Phone: 203-227-3833. Editor-in-Chief: John Williams Andrews. Will send sample copy for $1. Payment in copies. Enclose S.A.S.E.
Nonfiction: Can use essays for "Aspects of Modern Poetry" department.
Drama: English language verse plays as space permits.
Poetry: All types, all lengths; rhymed, unrhymed, metered, unmetered, conventional, experimental, punctuated or not. Criteria of excellence, clarity, beauty, profundity.

POETRY, 1228 North Dearborn Pkwy., Chicago IL 60610. Editor: Mr. Daryl Hine. For poets, poetry readers, libraries. Monthly; 64 (5¼x9) pages. Established in 1912. Circulation: 10,000. Buys all rights, but will reassign rights to author after publication. Buys about 500 mss a year. Payment on publication. Will send sample copy to writer for $1.45. Will not consider photocopied or simultaneous submissions. Reports in 4 to 6 weeks. Submit complete ms. Enclose S.A.S.E.
Poetry: "We consistently publish the best poetry being written in English. All forms may be acceptable." Length: open. Pays $1 per line.

POETRY EASTWEST, P.O. Box 391, Sumter SC 29150. Editor: Syed Amanuddin. Published annually. Circulation: about 500. Acquires first serial rights only. Rights revert to author 6 months after publication. Payment of one contributor's copy. Will send sample copy for $1. Reports in six months. Enclose S.A.S.E. with all submissions.
Poetry: Unpublished English poems and translations of contemporary poets of other languages. "We empathize with world poetry movement. We expect poets to emphasize human feeling instead of the cerebral muscle and we look for poetry that dramatizes the poetic experience in terms of fresh image and phrase. We are not interested in poems longer than 30 lines."

POETRY VENTURE, Valkyrie Press, Inc., 8245 26th Ave., N., St. Petersburg FL 33710. Editor: Marjorie Schuck. For poets, writers, scholars. Semiannual magazine; 64 (5¾x8¾) pages. Established in 1968. Circulation: 1,000 to 2,000. Acquires all rights, but will reassign rights to author after publication. Payment in contributor's copies and subscription. Will send sample copy to writer for $1.25. Will consider photocopied submissions. Will not consider simultaneous submissions. Reports on material within 6 months. Query first on poetry essays. Enclose S.A.S.E.

Nonfiction and Poetry: Poetry essays on poetry and/or related topics (the literary scene, contemporary poetry, etc.). Brief articles on individual poets. Commentaries, anthology reviews, poetical analyses. Often features foreign poetry published in both the original and the English translation. Length: 100 to 1,500 words. Traditional forms of poetry, blank verse, free verse, innovative poetry. Length: 112 lines maximum.

POETRY VIEW, 1125 Valley Rd., Menasha WI 54952. Editor: Dorothy Dalton. Published weekly as half-page in *View,* magazine section of the *Appleton Post-Crescent.* Established in 1970. Circulation: 50,000. Not copyrighted. Buys 250 poems per year. Payment on 10th of month following publication. Prefers original submissions; not photocopies. Will not consider simultaneous submissions. Submit seasonal material 2 to 3 months in advance. Reports in 2 to 3 months. Enclose S.A.S.E.
Poetry: Well-written poetry, showing a fresh use of language. No religious poetry or poetry that is overly sentimental. Uses traditional forms, free verse, (lyrics preferred) and light verse. Length: serious poetry, to 24 lines; light verse, 4 to 8 lines. Pays $3 per poem.

QUOIN, 1226 W. Talmage, Springfield MO 65803. Phone: 417-866-5186. Editor: Arlis M. Snyder. Quarterly. Circulation: 500. Not copyrighted. Payment in contributor's copies. Will send a sample copy to a writer for $1. Submit "to within 15 days of month of publication: January, April, July, October." Reporting time varies. Enclose S.A.S.E. for return of submissions.
Poetry: Uses poetry—any and all forms. Writing must be grammatically correct and word usage lexically accurate. Language must be modern, avoiding archaic forms. Metaphysical verse must be consistent with the concept employed. "No maudlin sentimentality." Length: open.

SEVEN, 115 South Hudson, Oklahoma City OK 73102. Editor: James Neill Northe. Published 4 times a year on an irregular basis. Established in 1954. Circulation: 1,000. Buys all rights. Payment on acceptance. Will send sample copy to writer for $1.25. Will not consider photocopied submissions. Will consider simultaneous submissions. Reports on material accepted for publication in 10 days. Returns rejected material immediately. Submit complete ms. Enclose S.A.S.E.
Poetry: "We strive to present only the most sheerly lyrical, poignant and original material possible. Seven poems and 1 reprint are used in each issue. We prefer the classical sonnet over the variations, accenting adherence to the form. Free verse is acceptable, but not as chopped prose. Good ballads are always acceptable. We like titles, punctuation and capitalization where needed. We like well-written and finely expressed spiritual poems, but they must be spiritual (not religious). We prefer the universal approach, rather than the personal. We want lines that communicate; not rambling, disjointed, chopped prose in or out of rhyme, lacking the rhythm and power of free verse." No restrictions as to form or subject. Length: open. Pays $4 per poem.

SOFT PRESS, 1050 Saint David St., Victoria BC, Canada V8S 4Y8. Phone: 604-598-2173. Editor: Robert Sward. For a fairly diverse, younger audience: Canadian students and writers. Published annually; 100-page (6x9) anthology. Established in 1970. Circulation: 300 to 1,000. Rights acquired vary with author and material. Usually acquires all rights, but will reassign rights to author after publication. Payment in contributor's copies. Will send sample copy to writer for $3.50. Will not consider photocopied or simultaneous submissions. Reports in 3 months. Query first with samples of previous work. Enclose S.A.E. and International Reply Coupons.
Poetry: Preference is for freer form poems. Traditional forms, free verse, avant-garde forms, light verse. "No dull poetry in archaic diction."

SOUTHERN POETRY REVIEW, English Department, North Carolina State University, Raleigh NC 27607. Editor: Guy Owen. Circulation: 900. Buys first rights. Payment in contributor's copies. Will send a sample copy to a writer for 50¢. "No mss considered during the summer months." Reports in 1 to 6 weeks. Enclose S.A.S.E.

Poetry: In the modern mode, traditional or experimental. No light verse. Thirty lines or less.

THE SPARROW MAGAZINE, 103 Waldron St., West Lafayette IN 47906. Editors: Felix and Selma Stefanile. For a literary audience of poets, teachers, students, and generally serious and literate persons interested in poetry. Twice a year; 52 pages. Established in 1954. Circulation: about 1,080. Acquires first serial rights. Uses about 25 mss per issue. Payment in contributor's copies. Will send sample copy to writer for 50¢. Will not consider photocopied or simultaneous submissions. Reports in 5 weeks. Submit complete ms. Enclose S.A.S.E.
Nonfiction and Poetry: "Mostly poems, although we have begun to feature the serious essay, usually devoted to a prominent literary figure. A recent essay on Valery discussed the poet's theory, or rather an aspect of his theory, in terms of his own personal practice in everyday life. Our maximum length for essays is 2,000 words. No restrictions on poetry length. We use all and any forms, but we see too many poems fascinated with the author's self, a self neither bright, nor fresh, nor original. We do not pay, but we have a modest prize system of $25 per issue."

SPEAK OUT, P.O. Box 737, Stamford CT 06904. Editor: Agnes D'Ottavio. For "people who write vocationally and avocationally; many new poets; all are concerned citizens." Quarterly magazine; 40 pages. Established in 1972. Circulation: 100 and growing. Acquires all rights. Uses 200 mss a year. Payment in contributor's copies. Will send sample copy to writer for $1. Write for copy of guidelines for writers. Will not consider photocopied submissions. Will not consider simultaneous submissions. Reports in 2 to 6 weeks. Submit complete ms. Enclose S.A.S.E.
Poetry: Topics include "anything that is an unveiling of social and moral injustice, drug abuse, ecology/pollution, poverty, prison reform, justice in the courts." Humane treatment of animals, conditions in mental hospitals, urban renewal, police brutality, etc. No prose; only poetry which has a definite purpose and is not sentimental and self-indulgent. Poets are urged to "come to the point. Don't start a poem and not follow through on the idea. Any form is fine as long as the idea is a complete statement within the poem. Present work clearly and neatly. If incarcerated, note on ms and print clearly." Length: 24 lines maximum.
Photos: B&w photos are sometimes used without ms. Department Editor: Ms. Leonie Haviland.
How To Break In: "Present work clearly and neatly, maintain patience and type mss if possible. If incarcerated, note on ms and print clearly. Always enclose S.A.S.E. If incarcerated and cannot send S.A.S.E., so note on work submitted."

SPRING RAIN PRESS, P.O. Box 15319, Seattle WA 98115. Editor: Karen Sollid. Yearly anthology. 50 to 60 (8½x5) pages. Established in 1971. Circulation: 500. Acquires all rights, but will reassign rights to author after publication. Payment in contributor's copies. Will send sample copy to writer for $3. Write for copy of guidelines for writers, but S.A.S.E. must be enclosed. Will consider photocopied submissions. Will not consider simultaneous submissions. Reports in June each year. Submit complete ms. Enclose S.A.S.E.
Poetry: Traditional forms, blank verse, free verse, avant-garde forms, lyric poetry. "We avoid sentimental poetry." Length: open.

STONE COUNTRY, 20 Lorraine Rd., Madison NJ 07940. Phone: 201-377-3727. Editor: Judy Neeld. For mature and young adults who have a participating interest in all forms of poetry. Magazine, published 3 times a year; 36 (8½x5½) pages. Circulation: 400. Acquires first North American serial rights. Accepts 100 to 150 poems a year. Payment in contributor's copies. Will send sample copy to writer for $1.25 (current issue); $1 (back issue). Reports in 1 month, "more or less". Query first or submit complete ms. Enclose S.A.S.E.
Poetry and Graphics: "We publish poetry and graphics. No thematic or stylistic limitations, but we are unable to publish long narrative poems in full. Overworked approaches include adolescent love, explicit sex, exorcising of personal devil in the first-person singular; use of Anglo-Saxonisms. (Have no objections to these poems,

just not in quantity and usually so badly done.) All themes must be handled maturely and with a search for language, not just the first word that comes to mind or the obvious shocker." Traditional forms, blank verse, free verse, avant-garde forms. Length: 35 lines maximum. No minimum. Graphic work always refers to a specific poem and shares the same page with it. Must be clearly drawn; preferably small (4x4). Larger drawings are used occasionally. Art Editor: Pat McCormick.

UNDER THE MIMOSA TREE, *The Slidell Daily Times,* P.O. Box 490, Slidell LA 70458. Editor: A. Karl Austin. A Sunday poetry column read by a general newspaper audience from Alaska to Florida. Material is used on a one-time basis, all copyrights, future privileges, future rights, belong and remain with individual poet. Uses 4 poems per week. Pays one tearsheet of column. Will consider photocopied and simultaneous submissions. Submit seasonal material 6 weeks ahead of holiday or season. Submit complete ms. Enclose S.A.S.E.
Poetry: "We lean toward all kinds of poetry, including the contemporary scene. No taboos whatsoever except all poems should be in good taste." Traditional forms, blank verse, free verse, avant-garde forms, light verse, all are equally acceptable. Length: 2 to 50 lines.
How To Break In: "Our current aim is to inspire and keep very much alive contemporary poetry and verse as written by you – or your next door neighbor – people with something to communicate to others."

UT REVIEW, University of Tampa, Tampa FL 33606. Editor: Duane Locke. For those who have an interest in the expanded consciousness, immanentism, surrealism, Tibetan mysticism, yoga, etc. Quarterly; 32 pages. Established in 1972. Circulation: 500. Acquires all rights, but will reassign rights to author after publication. Uses 128 poems per year. Payment in contributor's copies. Will send sample copy to writer for 75¢. Will consider photocopied submissions. Reports in 3 weeks. Submit complete ms. Enclose S.A.S.E.
Poetry: "Primarily those presenting the mystical apprehension of nature." Short poems are preferred.

VOICES INTERNATIONAL, 6804 Cloverdale Dr., Little Rock AR 72209. Phone: 501-565-6305. Editors: Clovita Rice and D.H. Thompson. Quarterly. Acquires North American serial rights. Payment in contributor's copy. Reports in 3 weeks. Enclose S.A.S.E.
Poetry and Nonfiction: Quality poetry of all types, showing "purpose and individual expression." Special interest in original poetry with social consciousness and experimental poetry with impact. Must be "people-oriented. Especially interested in encouraging beginning poets who show promise and vitality." Special awards contests. Also uses essays on writing.

WESTERN POETRY, 3253-Q San Amadeo, Laguna Hills CA 92653. Editor: Joseph Rosenzweig. For a well-educated audience with a wide range of interests. Quarterly; 30 to 40 (5½x8½) pages. Established in 1974. Circulation: 200. Acquires first North American serial rights. Uses 120 to 160 mss a year. Payment in 1 contributor's copy. Will send sample copy for $1.25. Reports in 10 days. Submit complete ms. Enclose S.A.S.E.
Poetry: "We accept all types of traditional, contemporary, free form and humorous verse and are not limited as to theme. Contributors are asked to submit at least 3 poems for consideration." Length: 8 to 24 lines, but exceptions are made on very high quality poems. Best of issue awards are also made.

THE WORMWOOD REVIEW, P.O. Box 8840, Stockton CA 95204. Editor: Marvin Malone. Quarterly. Circulation: 700. Acquires all rights, but will reassign rights to author on request. Pays in copies or cash equivalent. Pays on publication. Will send sample copy to writer for $1.50. Reports in 2 to 8 weeks. Enclose S.A.S.E.
Poetry: Modern poetry and prose poems that communicate the temper and depth of the human scene. All styles and schools from ultra avant-garde to classical; no taboos. Especially interested in prose poems or fables. 3 to 500 lines.

YES, Smith Pond Road, R.D. 1, Avoca NY 14809. Phone: 607-566-8355. Editors: Virginia Elson and Beverlee Hughes. Established in 1970. 3 times a year. Circulation: over 300. Reprint allowed if credit given. Accepts about 100 poems a year. Payment in contributor's copies. Will send a sample copy to a writer for $1. Reports in 2 to 4 weeks. Enclose S.A.S.E. for return of submissions.

Poetry: "We are trying to reach a wider and wider group of readers in the belief that poetry does not need to address itself to 'special schools' and that there is room for both tradition and experiment. We do not want the trite, the sentimental, the 'state poet laureate' type of poetry."

Politics and World Affairs Publications

Other categories in Writer's Market *include publications that will also consider articles about politics and world affairs. Some of these categories are Business and Finance, General Interest, and Newspapers and Weekly Magazine Sections.*

AMERICAN OPINION MAGAZINE, Belmont MA 02178. Managing Editor: Scott Stanley, Jr. "A conservative, anti-communist journal of political affairs." Monthly except August. Circulation: 50,000. Buys all rights. Pays on publication. Enclose S.A.S.E.

Nonfiction: Articles on matters of political affairs of a conservative, anti-communist nature. "We favor highly researched, definitive studies of social, economic, political and international problems which are written with verve and originality of style." Length should not exceed 4,000 words nor be less than 3,000. Pays $25 per published page.

AMERICAS, Organization of American States, Washington DC 20006. Managing Editor: Flora L. Phelps. Official organ of Organization of American States. Audience is persons interested in inter-American relations. Editions published in English, Spanish, Portuguese. Monthly. Circulation: 100,000. Buys first publication and reprint rights. Pays on publication. Will send free sample copy on request. Articles received only on speculation. Include cover letter with writer's background. Reports within two months. Not necessary to enclose S.A.S.E.

Nonfiction: Articles of general hemisphere interest on history, art, literature, music, development, travel, etc. Taboos are religious and political themes or articles with non-international slant. Photos required. Length, about 3,000 words. Pays about $75.

CALIFORNIA JOURNAL, 1617 10th St., Sacramento CA 95814. Editor: Ed Salzman. For those with special interest in California state government and politics. Magazine; 40 (8½x11) pages. Established in 1970. Monthly. Circulation: 9,000. Buys all rights. Buys about 75 mss a year. Pays on publication. Will send free sample copy to writer on request. Will consider photocopied submissions. No simultaneous submissions. Returns rejected material very quickly. Query first. Enclose S.A.S.E.

Nonfiction: Articles on subjects within the general area of California state and local government and politics. "We are primarily interested in analysis and interpretation, rather than advocacy at one extreme or facts alone at the other extreme. We feel that environmental issues are overworked and (to a lesser degree) problems of minorities are too." Recently published "Where Women Are Winning", a comprehensive wrapup of an important local government issue. Length: 900 to 6,000 words. Pays $50 per published magazine page.

CURRENT HISTORY, 4225 Main St., Philadelphia PA 19127. Editor: Carol L. Thompson. Monthly. Pays on publication. Reports in one to two weeks. Query preferred. Enclose S.A.S.E.

Nonfiction: Uses articles on current events, chiefly world area studies, stressing their historical, economic, and political background, 3,500 to 4,000 words in length. Academician contributions almost exclusively. Pays an average of $100.

CURRENT WORLD AFFAIRS, P.O. Box 2238, Pasadena CA 91105. Editor: Dr. Marshall Crawshaw. For educators and researchers. Established in 1957. Monthly. Circulation: 5,000. Buys all rights. Buys 10 freelance mss a year. Payment on publication. Query first. Enclose S.A.S.E.

Nonfiction: Political and educational articles. Interview, historical, travel. Pays minimum of $10.

ENCORE AMERICAN & WORLDWIDE NEWS, 515 Madison Ave., New York NY 10022. Editor: Ida Lewis. For "the urban black adult." Established in 1972. Biweekly. Circulation: 100,000. Rights purchased vary with author and material. Buys all rights, but will reassign rights to author after publication. Buys first North American serial rights. Buys over 30 mss a year. Payment arranged after publication. Will send free sample copy to writer on request. Query first. Enclose S.A.S.E.

Nonfiction: News, political analysis, black history; personality pieces; book, movie, theatre, art and music reviews, third world outlook; black perspective. Pays $75 to $350.

How To Break In: "The best way to break in here is with a book review. It should be about 750 to 800 words. Quite a few of our writers have started out that way. Another alternative is with a simple profile, say, about 500 to 600 words. It doesn't have to be a major figure — pick someone who's on the move. Query first for reviews and profiles."

FOREIGN AFFAIRS, 58 E. 68th St., New York NY 10021. Phone: 212-535-3300. Editor: William P. Bundy. For academics, businessmen (national and international), government, educational and cultural readers especially interested in international affairs of a political nature. Established in 1922. Quarterly. Circulation: 75,000. Buys all rights. Buys 45 mss a year. Payment on publication. Will send sample copy to writer for $3. Will consider photocopied submissions. Reports in 2 to 4 weeks. Submit complete ms. Enclose S.A.S.E.

Nonfiction: "Articles dealing with international affairs; political, educational, cultural, philosophical and social sciences. Develop an original idea in depth, with a broad basis on topical subjects. Serious, in-depth, developmental articles with international appeal." Length: 2,500 to 6,000 words. Pays $300.

THE FREEMAN, Irvington-on-Hudson NY 10533. Phone: 914-591-7230. Editor: Paul L. Poirot. For "fairly advanced students of liberty and the layman." Monthly. Buys all rights, including reprint rights. Buys about 44 mss a year. Pays on publication. Enclose S.A.S.E.

Nonfiction: "We want nonfiction clearly analyzing and explaining various aspects of the free market, private enterprise, limited government philosophy, especially as pertains to conditions in the United States. Though a necessary part of the literature of freedom is the exposure of collectivistic cliches and fallacies, our aim is to emphasize and explain the positive case for individual responsibility and choice in a free economy. Especially important, we believe, is the methodology of freedom; self-improvement, offered to others who are interested. We try to avoid name-calling and personality clashes, and find satire of little use as an educational device. Ours is a scholarly analysis of the principle underlying a free market economy." Recently published articles include "Two-Digit Inflation" and "Justice in the Market." Length: not over 3,500 words. Payment is 5¢ a word.

THE NATION, 333 Sixth Ave., New York NY 10014. Editor: Carey McWilliams. Weekly. Query first. Enclose S.A.S.E.

Nonfiction and Poetry: "We welcome all articles dealing with the social scene, particularly if they examine it with a new point of view or expose conditions the rest of the media overlooks. Poetry is also accepted." Length and payment to be negotiated.

How To Break In: "I'm absolutely committed to the idea of getting more material from the boondocks. For instance, a fellow in Denver just sent us a piece we're printing on the firings that are going on at the newspaper there. Right now we're getting stuff at the ratio of about 10 to one from the New York area and I would like to reverse that ratio. If you live somewhere where you think nothing is going on, look again! If you do a piece for us from someplace where we don't have anyone, you could develop into a stringer."

NATIONAL JOURNAL REPORTS, 1730 M St., N.W., Washington DC 20036. Phone: 202-833-8000. Editor: Burt Hoffman. "Very limited need for freelance material because full-time staff produces virtually all of our material."

NATIONAL OBSERVER, 11501 Columbia Pike, Silver Spring MD 20900. No longer in the market for freelance material.

NATIONAL REVIEW, 150 E. 35th St., New York NY 10016. Editor: Wm. F. Buckley, Jr. Issued fortnightly. Buys all rights. Pays on publication. Will send sample copy. Reports in a month. Enclose S.A.S.E.
Nonfiction: Uses articles, 1,000 to 3,500 words, on current events and the arts, which would appeal to a politically conservative audience. Pays about 7½¢ a word. Inquiries about book reviews should be addressed to Mr. George F. Will, 6683 32nd Pl., N.W., Washington DC 20015. Inquiries on movie, play, TV reviews, other cultural happenings, or travel should be addressed to Mr. M. J. Sobran, Jr., 150 E. 35th St., New York, NY 10016.
Poetry: Uses only short, satirical poems of a political nature. Should not run over 30 lines.

THE NEW REPUBLIC—A Weekly Journal of Opinion, 1244 Nineteenth St., N.W., Washington DC 20036. Managing Editor: David Sanford. Buys all rights. Pays on publication. Enclose S.A.S.E.
Nonfiction: This liberal, intellectual publication uses 500- to 2,000-word comments on public affairs and the arts. Pays 8¢ per published word.

NEWSWEEK, 444 Madison Ave., New York NY 10022. Staff-written. Unsolicited mss accepted for "My Turn," a column of personal opinion. Length: 1,100 words maximum.

PRESENT TENSE: THE MAGAZINE OF WORLD JEWISH AFFAIRS, 165 E. 56th St., New York NY 10022. Phone: 212-751-4000. Editor: Murray Polner. For college-educated, Jewish-oriented audience interested in foreign affairs and Jewish life abroad. Quarterly magazine; 80 (8½x11) pages. Established in 1973. Circulation: 25,000. Buys all rights, but will reassign rights to author after publication. Buys 60 mss a year. Payment on acceptance. Will send sample copy to writer for $2.50. Will not consider photocopied or simultaneous submissions. Reports in 4 weeks. Query first. Enclose S.A.S.E.
Nonfiction: Quality reportage of contemporary events (a la *Harper's, Atlantic, New Yorker,* etc.) and well-written memoirs. Personal experience, profiles, essay reviews. Length for essay reviews: 1,500 words maximum. Length for other material: 4,000 words maximum. Pays $150 to $300.

THE PROGRESSIVE, 408 W. Gorham St., Madison WI 53703. Phone: 608-257-4626. Editor: Erwin Knoll. Issued monthly. Buys all rights. Pays on publication. Reports in two weeks. Query first. Enclose S.A.S.E.
Nonfiction: Primarily interested in articles which interpret, from a progressive point of view, domestic and world affairs. Occasional lighter features. Up to 3,000 words. Pays $50 to $150 per ms.

REASON MAGAZINE, Box 6151, Santa Barbara CA 93111. Phone: 805-964-4310. Editor: Robert Poole, Jr. For a readership interested in individual liberty, economic freedom, private enterprise alternatives to government services, protection against inflation and depressions. Monthly; 52 (8½x11) pages. Established in 1968. Circulation: 15,000. Rights purchased vary with author and material. May buy all rights; but will sometimes reassign rights to author after publication; first North American serial rights or first serial rights. Buys 40 mss a year. Payment on publication. Will send sample copy to writer for $1. Write for copy of guidelines for writers. "Manuscripts must be typed, double- or triple-spaced on one side of the page only. The first page (or a cover sheet) should contain an aggregate word count, the author's name and mailing address, and a brief (100- to 200-word) abstract. A short biographical sketch of the author should also be included. Footnotes and other references should be indicated with brackets in the text and should be grouped, in order, at the end of the article." Will consider photocopied submissions. Reports in 3 months. Query first. Enclose S.A.S.E.

Nonfiction and Photos: "*Reason* is specifically a libertarian publication, dealing with social, economic and political problems, and supporting both individual liberty and economic freedom. Articles dealing with the following subject areas are desired: analyses of current issues and problems from a libertarian viewpoint (e.g., education, pollution, victimless crimes, regulatory agencies, foreign policy, etc.). Discussions of social change, i.e., strategy and tactics for moving toward a free society. Discussions of the institutions of a free society and how they would deal with important problems. Articles on self-preservation in the current hostile environment (economic, political, cultural). Lessons from the past, both revisionist history and biographical sketches of noteworthy individuals. Case studies of unique examples of the current application of libertarian/free-market principles." Length: 1,500 to 6,000 words. Pays $25 plus 10 copies of the issue and a 1-year subscription. Book reviews are also used and compensation for these consists of $10 plus a 1-year subscription and 10 copies of the issue containing the review. No additional payment is made for b&w photos. Captions required.

TIME, Rockefeller Center, New York NY 10020. Staff-written.

WASHINGTON MONTHLY, 1028 Connecticut Ave., N.W., Washington DC 20036. Editor: Charles Peters. For "well-educated people interested in politics and government; well-read." Monthly. Circulation: 30,000. Rights purchased depend on author and material. Buys all rights or first rights. Buys about 40 mss a year. Pays on publication. Will send a sample copy to a writer for $1.50. Sometimes does special topical issues. Reports in 2 to 4 weeks. Enclose S.A.S.E.

Nonfiction and Photos: Responsible investigative or evaluative reporting about the U.S. government, business, society, the press, and politics. Length: "average 2,000 to 6,000 words." Pays 5¢ to 10¢ a word. Buys b&w glossies.

WORLD POLITICS, Corwin Hall, Princeton NJ 08540. Editors: Klaus Knorr, Cyril E. Black, Gerald Garvey, Walter F. Murphy, Leon Gordenker. Issued quarterly to academic readers in social sciences. Pays on publication. Buys all rights. Reports in one to six months. Enclose S.A.S.E.

Nonfiction: Uses articles based on original scholarly research on international aspects of the social sciences. Mss should be double-spaced throughout (including footnotes), and have wide margins. Footnotes should be placed at the end of article. Length: 3,000 to 5,000 words. Pays $50 per article.

WORLDVIEW, 170 E. 64th St., New York NY 10021. Phone: 212-838-4120. Managing Editor: Susan Woolfson. For "the informed and concerned reader who insists that discussion of public issues must take place within an ethical framework." Monthly. Buys all rights. Pays on publication. Study the magazine and query first. Enclose S.A.S.E.

Nonfiction: Articles on public issues, religion, international affairs, world politics, and moral imperatives. "The editors believe that any analysis of our present cultural and political problems which ignores the moral dimension is at best incomplete—at worst, misleading. *Worldview* focuses on international affairs, puts the discussion in an ethical framework, and relates ethical judgment to specifically religious traditions." Article length: 2,500 to 5,000 words; "Gray Papers": 300 to 1,000 words; Book reviews: 1,000 words. Payment depends on length and use of material; to be negotiated.

How To Break In: "Probably our most successful unsolicited material are reports from abroad. We also have a 'Gray Paper' section which includes many short takes from 700 to 1,200 words and some items as short as 300 words. Short pieces must be as well written and have the same degree of ethical orientation as the longer ones, but it is one way to break in. Book reviews are also a possibility. If a writer sends some samples of previous work and a list of the types of literature he is interested in, we might try him out with an assignment."

Puzzle Publications

This category includes only those publications devoted entirely to puzzles. The writer will find many additional markets for crosswords, brain teasers, acrostics, etc., by reading the Filler listings throughout the Consumer, Farm, Trade, Technical, and Professional sections of this book. Especially rich in puzzle markets are the Religious, Juvenile, Teen and Young Adult, and General Interest classifications in the Consumer section.

CROSSWORD TIME, TODAY'S CROSSWORDS, CROSSWORD PLEASURE, Donajil Publications, Inc., P.O. Box 152, Whitestone NY 11357. *Crossword Pleasure* and *Crossword Time* bimonthly; *Today's Crosswords*, quarterly. Send single sample only "and inquire from publisher as to particular types of puzzles needed." Request copy of instructions for constructors. Occasionally overstocked. Enclose S.A.S.E.
Puzzles: Fresh, original, informative, quizzes, crossword puzzles only; for family audience. "When constructing new crosswords, make an accurate copy (not a photocopy) of our master diagram. Be sure that black squares and numbers are in exact same places. Send copy only. Hold the masters for future submissions. Put code numbers on top of your diagram copy and also on top of the first sheet of your definitions, along with your name and address. Also state type of puzzle, i.e., Easy, Medium, Stumper, etc. Submit diagram, with answers and numbers on 1 sheet, numbers, definitions, answer words on other, in that order. Keep definitions short—no double definitions. Avoid, if possible, obsolete variants and abbreviations. In 'categorical' puzzles (devoted to special subject), at least 20% of the total words must be related to subject." For fill-ins, "must be 21 squares wide, 18 squares deep. All words of one category. List words alphabetically in each group of 3-letters, 4-letters, etc. No words less than 3 letters, and no single black squares." For diacrostics, "first letters of words, reading downward, must spell out name and/or title of quotation. Quotations must be complete thoughts. Make diagrams 15 squares wide, depth as will." Check puzzles for accuracy before submitting. Pays $2.50 for quizzes, $4 to $10 each for crosswords.
How To Break In: "We have a particular need for Mazewords (word search, find the word). Also fresh, original puzzles for children in 7 to 12 age group. Write for details."

EASY-TIMED CROSSWORD PUZZLES, 575 Madison Ave., New York NY 10022. Editorial Director: Arthur Goodman. Bimonthly. Buys all rights. Pays on acceptance. Query first. Enclose S.A.S.E.
Puzzles: Uses only puzzles size 15x and 13x of easier variety. See current issue for guide. Pays $7 minimum.

OFFICIAL CROSSWORDS, DELL CROSSWORDS, POCKET CROSSWORDS, DELL CROSSWORD ANNUALS, DELL CROSSWORD PUZZLES BOOKS, DELL PUZZLE PUBLICATIONS, 245 East 47 St., New York NY 10017. Editor: Kathleen Rafferty. For "all ages from '8 to 80'—people whose interests are puzzles, both crosswords and variety features." Buys all rights. Enclose S.A.S.E.
Puzzles: "We publish puzzles of all kinds, but the market here is limited to those who are able to construct quality pieces which can compete with the real professionals. See our magazines. They are the best guide for our needs. We publish quality puzzles, which are well-conceived and well edited, with appeal to solvers of all ages and

in about every walk of life. We are the world's leading publishers of puzzle publications and are distributed in many countries around the world in addition to the continental U.S. However, no foreign language puzzles, please! Our market for crosswords and anacrostics is very small, since long-time contributors supply most of the needs in those areas. However, we are always willing to see material of unusual quality, or with a new or original approach. Since most of our publications feature variety puzzles in addition to the usual features, we are especially interested in seeing quizzes, picture features, and new and unusual puzzle features of all kinds. Please do not send us remakes of features we are now using. We are interested only in new ideas. Kriss Krosses are an active market here. However, constructors who wish to enter this field must query us first before submitting any material whatever. Prices vary with the feature, but ours are comparable with the highest in the general puzzle field."

ORIGINAL CROSSWORD, 575 Madison Ave., New York NY 10022. Editorial Director: Arthur Goodman. Bimonthly. Buys all rights. Pays on acceptance. Refer to current issue available on newsstand as guide to type of material wanted. Submissions must be accompanied by self-addressed, stamped envelope for return. **Puzzles:** Original adult crossword puzzles; sizes 15x15 and 13x13; medium and not hard. Same requirements for diagramless, but 15x15 irregular patterns only. Pays $7 to $20.

QUALITY CROSSWORD PUZZLES, FAVORITE CROSSWORD PUZZLES, WORD DETECTIVE, 855 S. Federal Highway, Boca Raton FL 33432. Editor: James L. Quinn. Bimonthly. Reports as soon as possible. Buys all rights. Pays for "articles or assigned material on acceptance, all other on publication." Request requirements sheet before submitting samples; enclose S.A.S.E. Submit seasonal material 6 months in advance. Enclose S.A.S.E.
Puzzles: Buys topical crosswords with a high percentage of theme words, and on offbeat subjects. Avoid all trade names. All material must be typed. "The following types of puzzles are used in our magazines: straight crosswords, topical crosswords (must be 35% topical), double-you-make-it puzzles, diagramless puzzles, alphabetical puzzles, round and rounds, crostics, double plays, cryptograms, cross-additions, skeletons, word quizzes, slidograms, word chains, crossword twins, and crossword triplets. We also use various types of 'filler' material—short puzzles to set on a fraction of a page, consisting of quizzes, brainteasers, conundrums, arithmetic games, off-trail material." For crosswords, use standard sizes: 11x11, 13x13, 15x15, 17x16, 19x19, though "special sizes and novelty shapes are welcomed. To avoid any charge of plagiarism or use of literary material without permission, use only subject matter within the 'public domain.' If novelty or new type of puzzle is submitted, please give complete instructions for solving it." Pays $3 to $25.
Nonfiction: "Articles about words, history of words, people who work with words, items of interest to people who do crossword puzzles." Length: 1,500 words. Pays $50.

WORD QUEST, CROSSWORD AND OTHER PUZZLES, 13510 Ventura Blvd., Sherman Oaks CA 91423. Editor: Joanne Goldstein. For general public, all ages. Magazines; 68 (8⅜x11) pages. Established in 1975. Every two months. Circulation: 173,500. Buys all rights. Pays on publication. Submit only complete constructions. Will not accept photocopied or simultaneous submissions. Returns rejected material in 3 weeks. Enclose S.A.S.E.
Puzzles: This new publication is eager for constructions of puzzles of all types: Crossword, Word Search, Kriss Kross, Diagramless, Cryptograms, Anacrostics, Laddergrams, etc. For inclusion in *Word Quest*, the puzzles must be over 45 words; pays $10 each. Crossword and diagramless puzzle sizes needed are 13x13 ($5 each), 15x15, 18x18 and 21x21 ($10 each). Pays $5 apiece for Kriss Krosses and "all other puzzles."

Regional Publications

General interest publications slanted toward residents of and visitors to a particular city or region are listed below. Since they publish little material that doesn't relate to the area they cover, they represent a limited market for writers who live outside their area. Many buy manuscripts on conservation and the natural wonders of their area; additional markets for such material will be found under the Nature, Conservation. and Ecology, and Sport and Outdoor headings.

Publications that report on the business climate of a region are grouped in the regional division of the Business and Finance category. Newspapers and weekly magazine sections, which also buy material of general interest to area residents, are classified separately under that category heading. Magazines for farm audiences which buy regional general interest material are found in the local division of the General Interest Farming and Rural Life category in the Farm Publications section.

ADIRONDACK LIFE, Willsboro NY 12996. Editor: Lionel A. Atwill. Explores the past, present, and future of the largest wilderness area east of the Mississippi, the 6-million-acre Adirondack Park. Quarterly magazine; 64 pages. Established in 1970. Circulation: 35,000. Buys all rights, but will reassign rights to author after publication. Buys 30 mss a year. Will send free copy to writer on request. Write for copy of editorial guidelines for writers. Submit seasonal material 5 months in advance. Reports within 2 weeks. Query first. Enclose S.A.S.E.
Nonfiction and Photos: "All material must have a connection with the Adirondacks, but beyond that, almost anything goes. We are interested in stories on artists and craftspersons, trips, wildlife, folk tales, natural and man-made phenomena, geography, and unusual personalities." Length: 1,000 to 2,500 words. Pays $25 to $150. Likes photos with articles. 5x7 or larger double-weight b&w, pays $10. 35mm and larger color transparencies pay $30 for one-time repro rights. Uses 6 to 10 scenic shots per issue. Must be taken within the Adirondacks and identified.
How To Break In: "We are highly specialized. Don't send us generalized material such as 'a walk in the woods' or 'driving through the Adirondacks.' We want unique material: 'the last of the Adirondack Panthers', 'iceboating on Lake George', etc."

THE ATLANTIC ADVOCATE, Phoenix Square, Gleaner Bldg., Fredericton, N.B., Canada. Phone: 506-455-6671. Editor-in-Chief: James D. Morrison; Editor: H. P. Wood. Monthly. Circulation: 26,000. Buys North American serial rights. Pays on publication. Will send a sample copy to a writer for 50¢. Editorial deadlines 3 months before publication. Query first. Enclose S.A.E. and International Reply Coupons.
Nonfiction and Photos: "Matters concerning Atlantic Provinces of Canada; subjects of general interest. Current and historical." Length: 1,000 to 2,000 words. Pays 5¢ a word. "Unusual or offbeat b&w photos taken in any of four Atlantic Provinces. Scenic color transparencies considered for covers." Photo payment negotiable; usually supplied with article.
Fiction: Preferably Atlantic Provinces of Canada setting, but other material considered. Length: 1,500 words to 2,000 words. Pays 5¢ a word.
Fillers: Short humor. Pays $2 per column inch.
How To Break In: "We have a need for well-written articles on current problems in the Atlantic Provinces, as well as well-researched articles of a historical nature concerning our (Atlantic) area. We would like writers to submit article ideas. All such correspondence will receive a quick reply."

AUSTIN PEOPLE TODAY (formerly *A.P.T.*), 600 W. 28th, Austin TX 78701. Editor: Peter Kelton. For general Austin public. Established in 1971. Monthly. Circulation: 10,000. Buys all rights. Buys 120 mss a year. Will send free sample copy to writer on request. Query first or submit complete ms. Will consider photocopied submissions. Reports on material in 2 weeks. Enclose S.A.S.E.

Nonfiction: Informational, how-to, politics, expose. "Consumer information; local investigatory news probes; fashion and decorating; what's going on in Austin; fads and kicks. Lead and close should be a knockout. Write with a conversational, personal approach, but not silly or slangy. Walk a line between the over-factual report and the subjective essay. Forget cliche themes. No Austin history. No reworked stories from other media. No personal essays." Length: 800 to 2,500 words. Pays $35 to $50.

BC OUTDOORS, Box 900, Postal Station A, Surrey, B.C., Canada. Phone: 604-574-5211. Editor: Art Downs. Magazine, published every 2 months; 68 (8½x11) pages. Established in 1945. Circulation: 30,000. Buys first North American serial rights. Buys 30 to 40 mss a year. Payment on acceptance. Will send free sample copy to writer on request. Will not consider photocopied submissions. Submit seasonal material 3 months in advance. Reports in 2 to 4 weeks. Query first or submit complete ms. Enclose S.A.E. and International Reply Coupons.

Nonfiction and Photos: Anything of a factual nature about B.C./Yukon, including conservation, history, travel, fishing, camping and wildlife. Must be of general interest. Length: 1,500 to 3,000 words. Pays $40 to $75. 8x10 or 6x9 b&w photos purchased with or without accompanying ms. Pays $5. 35mm color used for covers. Pays $25.

BEND OF THE RIVER MAGAZINE, 108 East Second St., Box 239, Perrysburg OH 43551. Phone: 419-874-7272. Editors: Christine Raizk Alexander and Lee Raizk. For well-educated readers over 40 years of age; interested in history, antiques, etc. Monthly magazine; 24 (9x11) pages. Established in 1972. Circulation: 5,000. Rights purchased vary with author and material. Usually buys all rights, but will reassign rights to author after publication. Buys 50 to 60 mss a year. Payment on publication. Will send free sample copy to writer on request. Will not consider photocopied or simultaneous submissions. Submit seasonal material 2 months in advance; deadline for holiday issue is October 15. Reports in 2 to 3 weeks. Submit complete ms. Enclose S.A.S.E.

Nonfiction and Photos: "We deal heavily in nostalgia, especially related to Ohio history. We are looking for articles about modern day pioneers, doing the unusual. Another prime target is the uplifting feature, spiritual and/or religious sketch or interview. Don't bother sending anything negative; other than that we can appreciate each writer's style. We'd like to see interviews with historical (Ohio) authorities; travel sketches of little known but interesting places in Ohio; grass roots farmers; charismatic people. Nostalgic pieces will be considered for our holiday issue. Our main interest is to give our readers happy thoughts. We strive for material that says 'yes' to life, past and present." Length: open. Pays minimum of $5. Purchases b&w photos with accompanying mss. Pays minimum of $1. Captions required.

How To Break In: "Send us any unusual piece that is either cleverly humorous, divinely inspired or thought provoking. We like articles about heavy historical topics treated in down-to-earth, conversational tones. Contribute a well-written story about a person trying the unique and succeeding, and we'll print it!"

THE BERKELEY MAGAZINE, P. O. Box 237, Berkeley CA 94701. Editor: Richard Clark. For literate, professional people; writers, sophisticated, Bay Area people; ages 35 through 55 years. Magazine; 44 to 60 pages. Established in 1974. Quarterly. Circulation: 5,000. Buys all rights, but will reassign rights to author after publication. Buys 12 to 20 mss a year. Pays 45 days after publication. Will send sample copy to writer for $1. Will consider photocopied and simultaneous submissions. Submit seasonal material 45 days in advance. Query first for articles of non-Berkeley nature. Reports in 1 month. Enclose S.A.S.E.

Nonfiction and Photos: "Articles on or about Berkeley, Northern California; lively, entertaining, well written, or artistic and serious. *Berkeley* is a place for all ideas. Would like to see articles about the well-known writers and artists in Berkeley area." Recently published articles include "Women's Health Conference," a level-headed but highly personal piece of reporting. Length: 1,500 to 2,000 words. Personal experience, interview, profile, humor, historical, think articles and book reviews. Length: 250 to 7,000 words. Regular columns cover theatre, profiles, business scene in Bay Area. Length: 1,000 to 1,500 words. Pays 1½¢ per word. Photos purchased with ms with no additional payment. Also purchased without ms and on assignment. Captions optional. 8x10 b&w; high quality 8x10 color preferred. Pays $30 to $50 for b&w; $50 to $75 for color. Photo Editor: Rob Super.

Fiction and Poetry: Mainstream, mystery, suspense, erotica, fantasy, humorous, confession, historical, and serialized novels. Length: 250 to 7,000 words. Pays 1½¢ maximum per word. Fiction Editor: Samuel Richards. Pays in copies for poetry: traditional forms, blank verse, free verse, light verse. Length: 10 to 50 lines.

BIRMINGHAM MAGAZINE, 1914 Sixth Ave. N., Birmingham AL 35203. Editor: Donald A. Brown. For civic, political, cultural, and business leaders; affluent audience. Monthly. Circulation: 10,000. Buys all rights. Pays on publication. Will send free sample copy on request. Editorial deadlines are 45 days prior to publication. Reports in 2 to 3 weeks. Prefers to see samples of work in advance and usually works by assignment. Query preferred. Enclose S.A.S.E.

Nonfiction: Timely, interpretive, objective articles of Birmingham and the South; progress and problems. Professional, imaginative style, 1,500 to 5,000 words. Pays $75 to $200.

Photos: Purchased with mss. Subject matter, specifications, and payment rate worked out according to the particular story.

BLAIR & KETCHUM'S COUNTRY JOURNAL, P.O. Box 870, Manchester Center VT 05255. Editor: Richard M. Ketchum. For full-time, part-time, or would-be residents of rural New England. Monthly magazine (March through January); special combined issue January and February; 70 (8½x11) pages. Established in 1974. Circulation: 50,000. Rights purchased vary with author and material. May buy all rights; but will sometimes reassign to author after publication; first North American serial rights; first serial rights, second serial (reprint) rights or simultaneous rights. Buys 125 mss a year. Payment on acceptance. Will send sample copy to writer for $1. Will not consider photocopied or simultaneous submissions. Submit seasonal material (on outdoor activities) 3 months in advance. Reports in 3 weeks. Query first. Enclose S.A.S.E.

Nonfiction and Photos: "The key here is 'usefulness'. We're looking for material that tells the reader how to get the most out of rural New England living. Subjects such as 'how to keep your land open,' 'siting a house to take advantage of the weather,' 'what's the right type of community for you and how do you find it?' are examples. Serious reporting of the issues that affect country life; profiles of people doing interesting and unusual things. We're interested in giving more weight to informative material specifically related to country life. We are not interested in nostalgia or history for its own sake, nor are we presently considering poetry or fiction." Informational, how-to, personal experience, interview, humor, historical, think pieces, personal opinion, travel, successful business operations, new product. Length: 250 to 3,000 words. Pays $75 to $500. Pays up to $75 for 4x5 or 8x10 b&w glossy photos purchased with or without mss or on assignment. Captions required. Pays up to $75 for 35mm (or larger) transparencies. Payment for color used on cover is higher.

BUCKS COUNTY PANORAMA MAGAZINE, 33 W. Court St., Doylestown PA 18901. Phone: 215-348-9505. Editor: Ms. Gerry Wallerstein. For readers in the Bucks County/Delaware Valley area. Monthly. Buys all rights, but will reassign subsidiary rights after publication upon request. Pays on acceptance. Will send free sample copy to writer on request. Reports in 2 weeks to 1 month. Query first or submit complete ms. Enclose S.A.S.E.

Nonfiction and Photos: "We are always interested in material related to the Bucks County/Delaware Valley area. Our basic interests are history, nature, ecology, conservation, the arts; people who either live or come from this area doing unique or interesting things. Most columns are staff written, but interested in humorous

or satiric essays." Pays $15. Length: 2,500 words minimum. Pays $25. 8½x11 b&w photos considered with mss. Pays $5.
Fiction and Poetry: Fiction oriented to the Delaware Valley. Length: 1,000 to 3,000 words. Pays $25. Poetry relating to the Delaware Valley is purchased occasionally. Length: 16 lines maximum. Pays $5.

BUFFALO SPREE MAGAZINE, P.O. Box 38, Buffalo NY 14226. Editor: Richard G. Shotell. For "a highly literate readership." Established in 1967. Quarterly. Circulation: 17,000. Buys "first printing rights only." Enclose S.A.S.E.
Nonfiction and Fiction: "Intellectually stimulating essays exploring contemporary social, philosophical, artistic, and environmental concerns. We are not a political magazine. Matters of interest to western New York make up a significant part of what we print." Length: 3,000 words maximum. Pays about $75 for a lead article. "We print fiction, but it must be brilliant." Length: 3,000 words maximum. Pays $75. Department Editor: Gary Goss.
Poetry: "Experimental poetry interests us, provided it is of the highest quality." Pays $15 minimum. Department Editor: Nik Mistler.

CHARLOTTE MAGAZINE (formerly *Charlotte Metrolina Magazine*), 1221 Westinghouse Blvd., P.O. Box 15843, Charlotte NC 28210. Editor: Betty Hill Folts. "Our readers are the upper income, management level group; college graduates living in an urban area. Interested in both spectator and active sports. We are affiliated with the Charlotte Chamber of Commerce and the majority of our subscribers are Chamber of Commerce members." Magazine published every 2 months; 72 (8½x11) pages. Established in 1968. Circulation: 9,000. Rights purchased vary with author and material. May buy all rights, but will reassign rights to author after publication, or first North American serial rights. Buys 60 to 75 mss a year. Payment on publication. Will send free sample copy on request. Write for copy of guidelines for writers. Will not consider photocopied or simultaneous submissions. Reports within 4 weeks. Query first or submit complete ms. Enclose S.A.S.E.
Nonfiction and Photos: "We are a community magazine, which means that we cover subjects and people in this particular area. We are not strictly a business paper, but include books, food, fashion (on occasion). We use business and personality profiles, local in nature; that is, confined for the most part to the Charlotte-Metrolina area. We are interested in stories of people who have left this area and made a success in an unusual way. Local history, the arts, almost any subject, as long as it's tied into Charlotte." Uses informational, profile, humor, historical, think, expose (local), nostalgia, travel (local) and articles on successful local business operations and book reviews. Length: 500 to 3,000 words. Pays $30 to $200. B&w photos and color transparencies are purchased with accompanying mss or on assignment. Pays $5 to $25 for b&w glossies; $10 to $100 for color transparencies. "The keyword for photos is 'localize'."
Fillers: Short humor (local) is also used. Length: 500 to 1,000 words. Pays $5 to $25.

CHICAGO MAGAZINE (formerly *The Chicago Guide*), 500 N. Michigan Ave., Chicago IL 60611. Editor: Allen H. Kelson. For an audience which is "95% from Chicago area; 90% college-trained; upper income; overriding interests in the arts, dining, good life in the city. Most are in 30 to 50 age bracket and well-read and articulate. Generally liberal inclination." Monthly. Circulation: 160,000. Buys first rights. Buys about 50 mss a year. Pays on publication. Will send a sample copy to a writer for $1. Submit seasonal material 3 months in advance. Reports in 2 weeks. Query first. Enclose S.A.S.E.
Nonfiction and Photos: "On themes relating to the quality of life in Chicago ... past, present, future." Writers should have "a general awareness that the readers will be concerned, influential native Chicagoans reading what the writer has to say about their city. We generally publish material too comprehensive for daily newspapers or of too specialized interest for them." Buys personal experience and think pieces, interviews, profiles, humor, spot news, historical articles, exposes. Length:

2,000 to 6,000 words. Pays $100 to $500. Photos purchased with mss. B&w glossies, color transparencies, 35mm color, color prints.
Fiction: Mainstream, fantasy, and humorous fiction. Preferably with Chicago orientation. No word length limits, but "no novels, please". Pays $250 to $500.

CINCINNATI MAGAZINE, Fifth and Race Tower, 120 W. 5th St., Cincinnati OH 45202. Phone: 513-721-3300. Editor: Jean E. Spencer. For generally, upper-income, sophisticated households. Monthly magazine; 64 pages, (8½x11). Established in 1967. Circulation: 15,500. Rights purchased vary with author and material. Usually buys all rights. Buys 60 mss a year. Payment on publication. Will send free sample copy to writer on request. Submit seasonal material 1 year in advance. Will consider photocopied submissions. Reports in 4 weeks. Query first. Enclose S.A.S.E.
Nonfiction: "Anything of interest, with a local angle. Any approach that is local and positive and is not mundane, ponderous, overdone or sick. General humor is greatly overworked. While a lot of it is funny, we can't use it without a local hook to hang it on." Informational, how-to, interview, profile, historical, nostalgia, and successful business operations. Length: 1,500 to 2,000 words. Pays 6¢ per word. Regular column, Queen City History, runs 1,500 words. Pays 6¢ per word.

CLEVELAND MAGAZINE, 1632 Keith Bldg., East 17th St. and Euclid Ave., Cleveland OH 44115. Editor: Michael D. Roberts. For residents of Cleveland. Monthly magazine; 100 pages. Established in 1972. Circulation: 32,000. Buys first North American serial rights. Buys about 75 mss a year. Payment on publication. Will send sample copy to writer for 75¢. Query first. Enclose S.A.S.E.
Nonfiction: Stories dealing with the current events of Cleveland. Profiles of interesting persons from Cleveland. City magazine type stories. Should be up to date and have a hard-hitting approach to personalities or institutions. "We are the only independent, Cleveland-owned publication and we write stories about the city that the newspapers either overlook or avoid." Length: 6,000 words. Pays $75 to $700.

COAST, Box 1347, Myrtle Beach SC 29577. Editor: Dr. S. A. Syme. For tourists to the Grand Strand. Magazine; 180 (5½x8½) pages. Established in 1955. Weekly. Circulation: 17,500. Buys all rights. Buys 5 or 6 mss a year. Pays on acceptance. Will send free sample copy to writer on request. Will consider photocopied and simultaneous submissions. Reports on material accepted for publication in 60 to 90 days. Returns rejected material in 1 week. Query first. Enclose S.A.S.E.
Nonfiction and Photos: "Timely features dealing with coastal activities and events, and an occasional historical article related to the area. Submit an idea before a manuscript. It should be directly related to this coastal area. No vague, general articles." Emphasis is on informational and historical articles. Length: 800 to 1,000 words. Pays $25 to $30. B&w and color photos purchased with mss. Prefers 5x7. Pays $5 to $10 for b&w; $15 to $25 for color.

COAST MAGAZINE, 291 South LaCienega, Beverly Hills CA 90211. Phone: 213-655-9775. Editor: Colman Andrews. For "young, involved Western Americans; college graduates, many of whom have done postgraduate work and are employed in professional, artistic, engineering, technical, educational or managerial work." Monthly. Circulation: 85,000. Buys first North American serial rights. Payment on publication. Write for copy of writer's guidelines. Will send sample copy to writer for $1. Reports in 3 to 5 weeks. Query first. Enclose S.A.S.E.
Nonfiction: "We are edited with the western American and particularly Californian in mind. We want to keep track of the pulse of the West; life styles, arts, politics, ecology, business, education, sports, food, fashion, and so on. Our slant is younger and more tuned in to alternative concepts and institutions. We would rather anticipate trends in art and society rather than merely report on them. We do not want articles particularly on rock music, criticism and personality portraits. Also, we are definitely avoiding fan-type approaches to articles, both in popular music and the other arts." Length: 1,000 to 2,500 words for departments; 2,000 to 3,000 words for feature articles. Pays $75 to $175 per article. Pays $30 to $50 for department material.

COLORADO MAGAZINE, 7190 W. 14th Ave., Denver CO 80215. Managing Editor: James Sample. Published 6 times a year. Circulation: 155,000. Buys all rights for copy and one-time rights for photography. Pays on acceptance. Write for writers' and photographers' guidelines. Reports within 1 month. Enclose S.A.S.E.

Nonfiction: Adventure, action and human interest articles which take place in the present-day Rocky Mountain West (Colorado, Wyoming, Utah, Montana, Idaho and New Mexico only). Articles must convey the unique flavor and experience of life in this region. Also wants historical, adventure-of-the-West articles; no flat or academic accounts. Must bring the Old West alive for the present-day reader and include action, dialog and anecdotes. In addition, uses seasonal outdoor features on skiing, fishing, camping, hiking, hunting, backpacking, jeeping, travel. Desires first-person accounts which convey the unique sense of these activities in the Rocky Mountain West. Photos should accompany mss. Length: 1,500 to 3,000 words. Usually pays 12¢ a word when package includes photos. Also uses "Out-of-the-way-West" featurettes on interesting, offbeat places for tourists and natives to visit. Length: 650 words. Include history, description, anecdotes, photos, maps. Pays $75 for package.

Photos: Photos are purchased with mss. Also approximately 16 color scenics purchased individually for special center section each issue. Attractive views of Western mountains, lakes, streams, ranches, ghost towns, sunsets, flowers, animals, outdoor sports. Minimum size 35mm, though 2¼x2¼ and 4x5 preferred. Pays $75 for one-page scenic and editorial photos, plus bonus for covers and spreads, etc.

THE COMMONWEALTH, 611 E. Franklin St., Richmond VA 23219. Editor: James S. Wamsley. For "high caliber Virginia business, professional, political leaders; educated public at large." Special travel issue (June). Monthly. Circulation: 12,000. Buys all rights. Buys approximately 24 mss a year. Pays on publication. Will "usually" send a sample copy to a writer for 75¢. Submit seasonal material 4 months in advance. Reports in 6 weeks. Query first. Enclose S.A.S.E.

Nonfiction: Any subject of feature quality with specific Virginia interest. No stock material on familiar attractions. Humor; adventure; history; modern, serious subjects, geared for mature readership. "No routine articles on stock attractions of Virginia." Personal experience pieces, interviews, profiles, humor, historical and travel articles, coverage of successful business operations, think pieces, photo essays. Length: 1,200 to 3,000 words. Pays $50 to $100.

Photos: Professional quality, 8x10 glossies purchased with mss.

CUE MAGAZINE, 20 W. 43rd St., New York NY 10036. Editor: Campbell Geeslin. For residents of New York City and the suburbs; unusually high interest in entertainment, the arts, dining out. Magazine; 72 (8x11) pages. Established in 1935. Weekly. Circulation: 300,000. Buys first North American serial rights. Buys 10 to 12 mss a year. Pays on publication. No photocopied or simultaneous submissions. Reports immediately. Query first. Enclose S.A.S.E.

Nonfiction: "This is a service magazine. Articles are always about upcoming events or things that people can do for pleasure. Reviews, listings, interviews with celebrities, articles about places of local interest only." Informational, how-to. Length: 3,000 words maximum. Pays minimum of $100.

D, THE MAGAZINE OF DALLAS, 2902 Carlisle, Dallas TX 75204. Editor: Jim Atkinson. For readers in the Dallas metropolitan area; primarily the middle to upper income group. Magazine; 100 (11x8) pages. Established in 1974. Monthly. Circulation: 37,000. Buys all rights. Buys 10 to 20 mss a year. Pays on publication. Will send sample copy to writer for $1.31. Will consider photocopied and simultaneous submissions. Reports in 1 month. Query first. Enclose S.A.S.E.

Nonfiction and Photos: Articles pertinent to the greater Dallas area, particularly slices of Dallas life that are unique, offbeat, or unknown. Also, solid reportage articles on aspects important to the city's workings; politics, business, arts, etc. Style should be tight, bright, incisive, entertaining. Informational, how-to, profile, historical, expose, nostalgia, travel. Length: 1,500 to 3,000 words. Pays $125 to $250. B&w and color transparencies purchased with ms or on assignment. Pays $20 to $25 for b&w and color.

DELAWARE TODAY, 2401 Pennsylvania Ave., Wilmington DE 19806. Editor: Christopher L. Perry. For Delawareans of above average education and income. Magazine; 68 (8¼x11) pages. Established in 1962. Monthly. Circulation: 8,000. Buys all rights, but will reassign rights to author after publication. Buys about 65 mss a year. Pays on publication. Will send free sample copy to writer on request. Will consider photocopied submissions. No simultaneous submissions. Reports in a month. Query first or submit complete ms. Enclose S.A.S.E.
Nonfiction and Photos: All material must relate to Delaware. Informational, how-to, personal experience, interview, profile, humor, expose, nostalgia. Length: 5,000 words maximum. Pays $35 to $150. Two columns (History, Arts) use material of 1,000 to 1,500 words. Pays $50. B&w glossies are purchased on assignment. Pays $10 to $50. Captions required.

THE DETROITER, 150 Michigan Ave., Detroit MI 48226. Editor: William Hinds. For readers in the Detroit metropolitan and suburban areas. Publication of the Greater Detroit Chamber of Commerce. Magazine; 64 pages. Established in 1973. Monthly. Circulation: 15,000. Buys all rights. Buys 100 to 110 mss a year. Pays on publication. Will send sample copy to writer for $1. Write for copy of guidelines for writers. No photocopied or simultaneous submissions. Reports in 1 month. Query first required. Enclose S.A.S.E.
Nonfiction and Photos: "Subjects for articles should be visible or accessible to the metropolitan Detroit area public. Must have Detroit flavor or slant. Architecture, bridges, people in the performing arts, history, athletic teams, neighborhoods, are all good subjects. In dealing with large institutions, prefers to focus on one timely aspect of the subject." Informational, interview, profile, humor, historical, think pieces, nostalgia, personal opinion, photo. Length: 500 to 3,000 words. Pays $200. B&w photos and color slides purchased with mss or on assignment. Pays minimum of $25.

DOWN EAST MAGAZINE, Camden ME 04843. Editor: Duane Doolittle. 10 times a year. Buys first serial rights. Pays on acceptance. Reports in two weeks. Enclose S.A.S.E.
Nonfiction and Photos: Uses historical and contemporary articles on Maine subjects. Usual feature length is 2,000 to 3,000 words. Pays 3¢ a word average. Buys photos submitted with manuscripts. Maine scenics. 8x10 size is preferred, but smaller size acceptable if sharp. 4x5 color photos preferred. Pays $3 to $5 for b&w, $25 for 4x5 color photos; $15 for smaller transparencies and color prints.
Fillers: Sharply pointed, humorous anecdotes, reflecting Maine character and/or way of life. Pays $5. "I Remember" items, concerning Maine events or people, $5 each with accompanying photo.

THE DRUMMER, 4221 Germantown Ave., Philadelphia PA 19140. Editor: Bob Ingram. Tabloid newspaper; 24 pages. Established in 1967. Weekly. Circulation: 60,000. Rights purchased vary with author and material. Usually buys all rights, but will reassign rights to author after publication. Buys about 50 mss a year. Pays on publication. Will send free sample copy to writer on request. Will consider photocopied submissions. No simultaneous submissions. Reports as soon as possible. Query first. Enclose S.A.S.E.
Nonfiction and Photos: "Articles that, we hope, will either edify or entertain, with a decided emphasis on Philadelphia. This emphasis is most important. We like clarity and brevity and would prefer not to see think pieces." Interview, profile, humor, expose. Length: 750 to 1,000 words. Pays $5 to $50. 8x10 b&w glossies purchased with or without ms. Pays $5 to $10.
Fillers: All types of puzzles. Pays $10.

FIESTA MAGAZINE, 140 N. Federal Hghwy., P.O. Box 820,. Boca Raton, FL 33432. Editor: Paul T. Hutchens. For a Gold Coast of Florida audience; thought leaders and decisionmakers at all levels of business and government. Magazine; 64 to 80 (8½x11) pages. Established in 1970. Monthly. Circulation: 15,000. Buys simultaneous rights provided articles are not submitted to other south Florida periodicals or newspapers. Buys about 130 mss a year. Pays on publication. Will send free sample copy to writer on request. Will consider photocopied and simultaneous submissions. Submit seasonal material 3 months in advance. Reports on material accepted for publication in 60 days. Returns rejected material in 30 days. Submit complete ms. Enclose S.A.S.E.

Nonfiction: "Our general subject matter is regionally oriented to the south Florida area. We prefer articles with historical, cultural, or social slants. They should have a local color approach. Above all, we prefer historical vignettes about events that occurred in our region. Topical subjects are covered by local writers who are close to the south Florida pulse. We are contemplating running a regular feature on life in the future, focusing on what life will be like around the year 2000 A.D. Logical, intelligent projections should stand as the basis for these articles." Length: 750 to 1,500 words. Pays approximately $30 per ms.

FOCUS/MIDWEST, P. O. Box 3086, St. Louis MO 63130. Editor: Charles L. Klotzer. For a liberal audience in Illinois, Missouri and the Midwest. Magazine; 28 to 42 (8½x11) pages. Established in 1962. Every 2 months. Circulation: 7,500. Buys all rights. Pays on publication. Reports in 4 to 6 weeks. Query first. Enclose S.A.S.E.

Nonfiction: Controversial articles; main emphasis on Illinois and Missouri. Facts, interpretation, analyses presenting political, social, cultural and literary issues on the local, regional and national scene of direct interest to the reader in or observer of the Midwest. Informational, interview, profile, think pieces. Length: open. Pays minimum of $25.

Poetry: Blank verse and free verse. Length: open. Pays minimum of $10.

GOLDEN GATE NORTH, P.O. Box 3028, Santa Rosa CA 95403. Editor: Ray Smith. For "educated, concerned people, slightly outdoorsy, most on ecology kick, most settled, with children." Quarterly. Circulation: 10,000. Buys all rights, but exceptions can be arranged. Buys 16 mss a year. Payment on publication. Will send sample copy to a writer for $1. Reports in 6 to 10 weeks. Enclose S.A.S.E.

Nonfiction and Photos: Want "well-documented material on subjects of concern within the region. Each issue, there is one article of regional interest (leaning toward ecology), one of Marin County interest, one of Sonoma County and one interview. Write as a reporter digging deeply into his subject, but get those anecdotes in." Special issues: wine, restaurants, rest and travel. Length: 1,500 words. Pays about 5¢ a word. Buys photos with mss. Pays $10 for b&w glossies. Pays $15 for 35mm color transparencies and color prints.

GULFSHORE LIFE, Gulfshore Publishing Co., Inc., 1039 Fifth Ave., N., Naples FL 33940. Phone: 813-649-9125. Editor: Jean Clarke Denmead. For an upper income audience. Published 6 times a year, November through April. Magazine; 40 to 60 pages. Established in 1970. Circulation: 12,500. Buys all rights, with permission in writing to reproduce. Buys 12 mss a year. Payment on publication. Will not consider photocopied or simultaneous submissions. Submit seasonal material 3 months in advance. Reports on material accepted for publication within 4 months. Returns rejected material as soon as possible. Query first. Enclose S.A.S.E.

Nonfiction: "Basically personal journalism of people, sports, homes, boats; pinpointing all features to seasonal residents, year-round residents and visitors. An 'At Home' personalized feature and one for boat owners appear in each issue. Travel, fishing, environmental articles are also used, but must be tied into personalities." Length: 500 to 1,000 words. Pays $25 to $50.

How To Break In: "Only to be on location: Naples, Marco Island, Ft. Myers, Ft. Myers Beach, Sanibel-Captiva, Whiskey Creek, Punta Gorda Isles."

ILLINOIS ISSUES, Sangamon State University, Springfield IL 62708. Editor: William L. Day. For people in government and concerned citizens. Magazine. Established in 1975. Monthly. Circulation: 1,000. Buys all rights. Buys about 80 mss a year. Pays on publication. Will send free sample copy to writer on request. Write

for copy of guidelines for writers. Reports on material accepted for publication in 30 days. Returns rejected material in 45 days. Query first. Enclose S.A.S.E.
Nonfiction: Articles about Illinois government and public affairs. Emphasize "balance" and use factual approach; avoid advocacy of special viewpoints. Interested in material on controversies in Illinois legislature treated from an all-round viewpoint. Informational, how-to, interview, profile, humor, think pieces, successful business operations, technical. Recently published "Story of a Law: How Assembly Worked Out an Energy Program". Length: 400 to 2,500 words. Pays 5¢ a word minimum.

INDIANAPOLIS MAGAZINE, 320 N. Meridian St., Indianapolis IN 46204. Editor: Craig J. Beardsley. Publication of the Indianapolis Chamber of Commerce for members and others interested in Indianapolis. Established in 1964. Monthly. Not copyrighted. Buys about 50 mss a year. Pays on publication. Will consider photocopied submissions. Seasonal material should be sent 6 months in advance. Reports on material within 10 days. Query first, "but if story is already completed, mail it on in." Enclose S.A.S.E.
Nonfiction and Photos: In-depth features of and about Indianapolis. Also interested in people who once lived in Indianapolis. Controversial articles welcomed, but must have Indianapolis-oriented slant to them. Anything that deals with informational, how-to, personal experience, interview, profile, humor, historical, think pieces, expose, nostalgia, personal opinion, travel, successful business operations, new product, merchandising techniques. Length: 500 to 5,000 words. Pays $100 and as high as $200 for an exceptional article. Editor will make arrangements for photography after ms has been accepted. Uses both b&w and color photos. Pays between $50 and $100.
Fiction and Fillers: Uses very little fiction, unless it's Indianapolis oriented. Short (500 to 1,500 words) humor pieces welcome. Pays $50 to $100.

THE IRON WORKER, Lynchburg Foundry (A Mead Company), P.O. Drawer 411, Lynchburg VA 24505. Phone: 804-847-1724. Editor: Tom Hausman. For Lynchburg Foundry's customers and public in general; generally slanted to upper intellectual group. Quarterly. Circulation: 10,000. Buys first rights and copyrights material. Buys approximately 5 mss a year. Pays on acceptance. Will send a sample copy to writer on request. Submit seasonal material 1 year in advance. Returns rejected material in 6 months. Query first. Enclose S.A.S.E.
Nonfiction: Wants significant Virginia-related articles about American history with national appeal. "Articles submitted must show depth of research on a new or unexplored historical topic. Must be well-written." Prefers action-oriented aticles. Also buys historical articles with human interest, biographies on significant Virginians if previously unexplored, or other historical incidents, topics or personalities which show original research. "Articles should lend themselves to illustrations, preferably drawings, paintings, engravings, etc., of the period rather than pictures of restorations and should be supplied by the author if possible. Prefer not to see articles without strong Virginia tie, articles of strictly local interest or subjects which have already received exhaustive treatment. Cannot use other than well-documented and researched historical articles." Length: 3,500 to 5,000 words. Pays $200 to $600.

JACKSONVILLE MAGAZINE, P.O. Drawer 329, Jacksonville FL 32201. Phone: 904-353-6161. Editor: Tom Ellis III. For civic-minded, concerned community types; sports, business, community oriented interest, films, arts. Florida oriented. Established in 1963. Bimonthly. Circulation: 11,000. Buys all rights. Buys 20 to 25 mss a year. Payment on publication. Will send sample copy to a writer on request. Query first. Submit seasonal material 3 to 6 months in advance. Reports in 3 weeks. Enclose S.A.S.E.
Nonfiction and Photos: Freelancer should write articles "in-depth and well-documented; usually will look at photographs. Writing should be sculptured and keen. Although *Jacksonville Magazine* is published by the Jacksonville area Chamber of Commerce, it is a community magazine." Buys historical, think, photo, travel, successful business operations, and in a broad sense, technical articles. Length: usually 1,500 to 6,000 words, according to subject matter. Pays $150 minimum for 3,000

words. "We accept b&w glossies, good contrast; color transparences." Pays $15 minimum for b&w; color terms to be arranged.

JAPANOPHILE, Box 223, Okemos MI 48864. Editor: Earl R. Snodgrass. For people who have visited Japan or are interested in Japan; all ages. Magazine; 50 (7x10) pages. Established in 1974. Quarterly. Circulation: 800. Rights purchased vary with author and material. Buys all rights, but will reassign rights to author after publication; buys first North American serial rights; second serial (reprint) rights. Buys 50 mss a year. Pays on acceptance. Will send sample copy to writer for $1. Write for copy of guidelines for writers. Will consider photocopied and simultaneous submissions. Submit seasonal material (each issue is built around a season) 4 months in advance. Reports in 2 months. Query preferred, but not required. Enclose S.A.S.E.
Nonfiction and Photos: "Articles that have to do with Japan or Japanese culture. We welcome material about Americans and other non-Japanese who practice a Japanese art in their own country. Hawaii, Los Angeles, and other locations have activity in the Japanese arts as well as Tokyo. Stories must be informed and accurate. We would like more on how Japan retains its culture and tradition while becoming a modern nation." Recently published articles include "Kokeshi: Toy or Treasure," a lively journalistic article about an art form exclusive to Japan; "The King of Love Letters," a lively article about a Tokyo businessman with a different kind of business; "Hachi Becomes a Legend," story behind a statue of a dog in Tokyo. Buys informational, personal experience, interview, profile, inspirational, humor, historical, think articles, nostalgia, personal opinion, photo, travel, book and film reviews, successful business operations. Length: 1,200 words maximum. Pays $5 to $20. Regular columns and features are San Francisco Scene, Tokyo Scene and Profiles of Artists. Length: 1,000 words. Pays $20 maximum. Nonfiction Editor: Robert Cavera. Photos purchased with or without accompanying ms. Captions required. Pays $5 for b&w. Photo Editor: Robert Copland.
Fiction, Poetry, and Fillers: Experimental, mainstream, mystery, adventure, science fiction, humorous, romance, and historical. Themes should relate to Japan. Length: 1,000 to 3,000 words. Pays $20. Fiction Editor: Earl Snodgrass. Traditional forms of poetry; avant-garde forms, and light verse. Should relate to Japan and to a season. Length: 3 to 50 lines. Pays $1 to $10. Poetry Editor: Carol Schumacher. Newsbreaks, puzzles, clippings, short humor. Length: 200 words maximum. Pays $1 to $5. Filler Editor: Earl Snodgrass.

THE KANSAS CITY MAGAZINE, 600 Tenmain Center, 920 Main St., Kansas City MO 64105. Editor: Robert A. Wood. For "high income professional people and businessmen and their families, with a stake in Kansas City. These people are sophisticated movers and doers and require more than a tax bill from their city." Established in 1910. Monthly. Circulation: 14,000. Buys all rights, but will reassign rights to author after publication. Buys about 12 mss a year. Pays on publication. Will send sample copy to writer for 75¢. Will consider photocopied submissions. No simultaneous submissions. Reports in 30 days. Query first required. Enclose S.A.S.E.
Nonfiction and Photos: News, personality profiles, self-help and city interest articles. Informational, how-to, interview, expose. Emphasis is on bright, informed writing and a slant that makes the story especially relevant to Kansas Citians. Recently published an article on a local world-caliber ping pong player. Length: 500 to 2,500 words. Pays $50 to $250. Columns use material of 600 words. Pays $15. No additional payment is made for photos used with mss. Pays $15 for b&w glossies purchased without ms, or on assignment; $25 for color prints or 35mm transparencies purchased without mss or on assignment. Captions required.

LOS ANGELES MAGAZINE, 342 N. Rodeo Dr., Beverly Hills CA 90210. Editor: Geoff Miller. Monthly. Buys first time local rights. Query first. Enclose S.A.S.E.
Nonfiction: Uses articles on how best to live (i.e., the quality of life) in the changing, growing, diverse Los Angeles urban-suburban area; ideas, people, and occasionally places. Writer must have an understanding of contemporary living and doing in Southern California; material must appeal to upper-income, better-educated group

of people. Fields of interest include urban problems, pleasures and cultural opportunities, leisure and trends, candid interviews of topical interest; the arts. Length: 1,000 to 3,000 words. Also uses some satire and humor. Pays 5¢ per word minimum. **Photos:** Buys photographs with mss. B&w should be 8x10. Pays $15 to $35 for single article photos.

MADISON SELECT, 114 N. Carroll St., Madison WI 53703. Editor: E. C. Rankin. For business, civic and social leaders of Madison. Magazine; 20 (8½x11) pages. Established in 1958. Monthly. Circulation: 10,000. Buys all rights, but will reassign rights to author after publication. Buys 10 to 15 mss a year. Pays on publication. Will send sample copy to writer for 50¢. Submit special material (fashion) 2 months in advance. Reports on material accepted for publication 10 days after publication. Returns rejected material immediately. Query first. Enclose S.A.S.E.
Nonfiction and Photos: Human interest material, primarily about Madison and Madisonians. Profile, personal experience, inspirational, humor, expose, travel, successful business operations, new product. Length: 350 to 1,250. Pays 2¢ to 4¢ a word. Also buys material for columns on fashion, arts, travel. Length: 250 to 750 words. Pays $10 to $20. No additional payment for b&w photos used with mss.

MAINE LIFE, RFD 1, Liberty ME 04949. Editor: Dave Olson. For middle age and over, rural, 70% Maine; balance in other states to persons who have either an interest or love for the state of Maine. Monthly tabloid newsprint; 48 pages, (10x15). Established in 1947. Circulation: 30,000. Buys all rights, but will reassign rights to author after publication; buys second serial (reprint) rights. Buys 150 mss a year. Payment on publication. Will send sample copy to writer for 25¢. Will consider photocopied submissions and simultaneous submissions. Special issues cover "Maine outdoors". Submit special or seasonal material 3 months in advance. Reports "as soon as determined". Query first. Enclose S.A.S.E.
Nonfiction and Photos: "Largely historical (Maine), non-controversial 'good-news' type of publication. Slogan is 'For Those Who Love Maine.' Down-to-earth material; more general interest, historical type." Personal experience, interview, profile, inspirational, historical, nostalgia, photo, travel. Length: 500 to 2,500 words. Pays $10 to $35. B&w photos purchased with accompanying ms. Captions required. Pays $3 to $5.

MARYLAND MAGAZINE, 2525 Riva Rd., Annapolis MD 21401. Editor: M. E. Dougherty. Published by the State's Department of Economic and Community Development. Quarterly. Established in 1968. Circulation: 19,500. Buys North American serial rights only. Buys about 30 mss a year. Pays on publication. Editorial deadlines 6 to 12 months in advance. Send S.A.S.E. for sample copy and author's or photographer's guidelines. Query first with outline. Reports in 6 to 8 weeks. Enclose S.A.S.E.
Nonfiction and Photos: Features exclusively places, events, and personages in Maryland. Articles on any facet of life in Maryland except conservation/ecology pieces. Well-researched agricultural, cultural, economic, ethnic, human interest, and travel-in-Maryland features. Also portraits of interesting Marylanders. Length: 600 to 2,000 words. Pays 6¢ a word. Photos purchased with or without mss. Captions required. 8x10 b&w glossies; 35mm or 2¼x2¼ color transparencies. Pays $20 for b&w; $25 for color.

METRO HAMPTON ROADS MAGAZINE, Suite 213, Southern Office Bldg., Norfolk VA 23505. Phone: 804-583-4586. Editor: St. Leger M. Joynes. For well-educated and affluent urban adults. Monthly magazine; 100 pages, (8½x11). Established in 1970. Circulation: 25,000. Rights purchased vary with author and material. Buys all rights, but may reassign rights to author after publication. Buys 150 mss a year. Payment on publication. Will send free sample copy to writer on request. Will consider photocopied submissions, and simultaneous submissions "if not in our market." January issue: Economic Forecast Issue; February issue: Boat Buyers Guide. Submit special issue query 4 months in advance; material 2 months in advance. Reports within 30 days. Query first. Enclose S.A.S.E.

Nonfiction and Photos: "In-depth features on regional issues or trends. A variety of departmental columns including travel, gourmet, fashion, interior design. *Metro* is a city magazine in the tradition of *New York, The Washingtonian, Atlanta, Los Angeles,* etc. Articles should indicate a degree of 'field work', no seat-of-the-pants stuff!" How-to, interview, profile, humor, expose, travel, book reviews. Length: 3,000 to 6,000 words for features; 1,000 to 2,000 words for departments. Pays $50 to $150. Travel, books, humor are covered in regular columns. Length: 1,000 to 2,000 words. Pays $50 to $85. Nonfiction Editor: Sandra Woodward. Photos purchased with ms with no additional payment. Purchased also on assignment. Captions required. Pays $10 to $30 for 8x10 glossies. Pays up to $250 for 4-color covers; 35mm or 2¼x2¼ transparencies. Photo Editor: George Stewart.

MINNESOTAN, 1999 Shepard Rd., St. Paul MN 55116. Phone: 612-647-7304. Editor: Bill Farmer. For Minnesota Federal Savings & Loan depositors. Established in 1973. Quarterly. Circulation: 100,000. Buys all rights, but will usually reassign rights to author after publication. Buys 9 mss a year. Payment on acceptance. Will send free sample copy to writer on request. Write for copy of guidelines for writers. Will consider photocopied submissions if accompanied by statement that it is not a simultaneous submission to other publications. Submit seasonal material 5 months in advance. Reports on ms accepted for publication in 2 to 4 weeks. Returns rejected material in 2 weeks. Query first; most articles that appear in *Minnesotan* are assigned, rather than purchased on spec. Enclose S.A.S.E.
Nonfiction and Photos: "Articles and features about different facets of the State of Minnesota, its history, and some of the people who live there or within 100 miles of the Twin Cities. No special slant required, other than good, readable copy with an attention-grabbing lead." Length: 1,000 to 2,000 words. Pays $100 to $250. Pays $25 for 8x10 b&w photos which are used occasionally (either with or without accompanying ms), but greatest need is for color transparencies. 35mm or larger. Pays $50.

MISSOURI LIFE, 1209 Elmerine Ave., Jefferson City MO 65101. Phone: 314-635-4011. Editor: W. R. Nunn. For readers whose ages range from the upper twenties to retirees; education varies from high school to Ph.D's. Occupations range from farmers to professionals, such as doctors, lawyers, engineers, etc. Bimonthly magazine; 56 (9x12) pages. Established in 1973. Circulation: 11,000. Buys all rights, but will reassign rights to author after publication. Buys 20 mss a year. Payment on publication. Will send sample copy to writer for $1.80. Will consider photocopied and simultaneous submissions. Submit seasonal material 3 months in advance. Reports on material in 3 weeks. Query first or submit complete ms. Enclose S.A.S.E.
Nonfiction and Photos: "Almost any kind of material if it's about Missouri or Missourians. History, travel, recreation, human interest, personality profiles, business, scenic, folklore. The emphasis is on the approach and quality. Because it is a bimonthly, *Missouri Life* must look for the different angle, the human interest, the long-lasting information and appeal, the timelessness of quality and beauty. As an example, see 'Bull Goose of the Ozarks', a colorful, human and informative article about an individual's lasting contribution to state, which appeared in a recent issue." Does not want to see "the stereotyped Ozark hillbilly piece, the travelogue with no feel of the country, the 'social message'." Seasonal material should have a different approach, with a seasonal flavor. Back issues are the best reference. Length: 1,200 to 2,500 words. 8x10 b&w glossy prints and color transparencies purchased with mss. Pays $25 for ms with b&w; $50 for mss with color transparencies; more if exceptional.

MONTANA MAGAZINE, Box 894, Helena MT 59601. Editor: Rick Graetz. For residents of Montana and out of state residents with an interest in Montana. Established in 1970. Quarterly. Not copyrighted. Pays on publication. Will send sample copy to writer for $1. Write for copy of guidelines for writers. Will consider photocopied and simultaneous submissions. Reports in 8 weeks. Query first. Enclose S.A.S.E.

Nonfiction and Photos: Articles on life in Montana; history, recreation. "How-to, where and when type articles." Limited usage of material on Glacier and Yellowstone National Park. Prefers articles on less publicized areas. Informational, profile, think pieces, nostalgia, travel. Length varies. Pays $10 to $25 for short articles with b&w photos; $25 to $100 for longer articles and accompanying b&w photos. Photo size: 5x7 or 8x10.

NASHVILLE!, 5519 Charlotte Ave., Nashville TN 37209. Phone: 615-356-1791. Editor: Charles Turney Stevens. For primarily middle to upper class businessmen, professionals and their families, who live in Nashville-Davidson County and surrounding area. Established in 1972. Monthly. Circulation: 12,000. Buys all rights. Buys 80 mss a year. Payment on acceptance. Will send sample copy to writer for $1.25. Will consider photocopied submissions. Submit seasonal material 3 to 4 months in advance. Reports on material accepted for publication in 3 months. Returns rejected material in 1 month. Submit complete ms. Enclose S.A.S.E.
Nonfiction and Photos: General feature material about or of interest to Middle Tennessee. Informational, interview, profile, historical, expose, nostalgia, photo, travel, successful business operations. Length: 1,200 to 2,400 words. Pays $75 to $100. 5x7 or 8x10 b&w glossy photos purchased with or without accompanying ms or on assignment. Pays $5.50 per print used. Pays $12.50 for color: 35mm or 120.

NEVADA HIGHWAYS AND PARKS MAGAZINE, Carson City NV 89701. Editor: Donald L. Bowers. For travel or vacation-minded people. Quarterly. Buys North American serial rights only. Pays on acceptance. Reports on submissions in 3 to 4 weeks. Query first. Enclose S.A.S.E.
Nonfiction: Nevada-related articles only. Pays 5¢ to 8¢ per word.
Photos: Nevada subject matter only; scenery, tours, activities such as ranching and mining; special events such as rodeos. Photos purchased with either mss or captions only. 4x5 color preferred. Pays $10 to $25 on acceptance for b&w prints; $15 minimum for 4x5 color transparencies.

NEVADA MAGAZINE, Carson City NV 89701. Editor: Donald L. Bowers. For readers interested in Nevada. Official state publication. Established in 1936. Quarterly. Circulation: 60,000. Buys first serial rights. Buys 20 to 25 mss a year. Payment on publication. Query first or submit complete ms. Enclose S.A.S.E.
Nonfiction and Photos: Articles on the Nevada theme: historical, travel, scenic, art, business and industry, etc. Suggest writers study the magazine. Reviews of books on Nevada. Length: 500 to 2,500 words. Pays 5¢ to 8¢ a word. 8x10 b&w glossies on Nevada topics. 4x5 color transparencies on Nevada topics (uses some 2¼).

NEW ALASKAN, Rt. 1, Box 677, Ketchikan AK 99901. Editor: R. W. Pickrell. For residents of southeast Alaska. Tabloid magazine; 28 pages. Established in 1964. Monthly. Circulation: 15,000. Rights purchased vary with author and material. May buy all rights, but will reassign rights to author after publication; or second serial (reprint) rights. Buys about 40 mss a year. Pays on publication. Will send sample copy to writer for 40¢. Will consider photocopied submissions. Reports on material accepted for publication in 60 days. Returns rejected material in 60 to 80 days. Submit complete ms. Enclose S.A.S.E.
Nonfiction and Photos: Feature material about southeast Alaska. Emphasis is on full photo or art coverage of subject. Informational, how-to, personal experience, interview, profile, inspirational, humor, historical, nostalgia, personal opinion, travel, successful business operations, new product. Length: minimum of 1,000 words. Pays 15¢ a word. B&w photos purchased with or without mss. Minimum size: 5x7. Pays $5 per glossy used. Pays $2.50 per negative (120 size preferred). Negatives are returned. Captions required.
Fiction: Historical fiction related to Alaska. Length: open. Pays 1½¢ per word.

NEW ENGLAND GALAXY, Old Sturbridge Village, Sturbridge MA 01565. Editor: Catherine Fennelly. For all ages, people interested in New England history and museums. Quarterly magazine; 60 pages, (5½x7½). Established in 1959. Circulation: 11,500. Rights purchased vary with author and material. Buys all rights, but will occasionally reassign rights to author after publication; buys first North American serial rights. Buys 26 mss a year. Payment on publication. Will send free sample copy to writer on request. Will consider photocopied submissions. Reports within 6 weeks. Query first for nonfiction. Enclose S.A.S.E.

Nonfiction and Photos: "Articles on any aspect of New England history, but not on a specific historic house open to the public. We're aimed at the general public, but emphasize the historical knowledge and accuracy." Biography, social customs, etc. Profile, historical, occasionally nostalgia articles. Length: 2,000 to 3,500 words. Pays $75 to $150. B&w photos purchased with or without ms. 8x10 photos of New England subjects. Pays $10.

Poetry and Fillers: Traditional forms, blank verse, and free verse. New England themes. Length: 6 to 30 lines. Pays $50. Pays $10 for quotes from New England historical sources.

NEW HAMPSHIRE PROFILES, Box 68, Hanover NH 03755. Phone: 603-643-5505. Editor: Peter E. Randall. For persons in all age and income brackets. Monthly. Buys first rights. Buys 40 to 50 mss a year. Pays on publication. Will send a sample copy to a writer for 75¢. "Writers should be very familiar with New Hampshire." Deadlines are 4 months prior to publication. Reports in 1 month. Query first. Enclose S.A.S.E.

Nonfiction: Must be written in a lively readable style and all material must be appropriate to New Hampshire. Buys history, nostalgia, antiques, how-to-do and where-to-find features, personality sketches, contemporary events and activities, conservation, natural history, country living, recreation. Length: 2,500 words maximum. Pays $35 to $100.

Photos: Purchased with mss or captions only. Seeks photo essay treatments of New Hampshire subjects. 8x10 glossies, 35mm transparencies. Now using inside color on a regular basis. Pays $5 minimum for b&w; $25 minimum for color.

NEW HAVEN INFO MAGAZINE, 53 Orange St., New Haven CT 06510. Phone: 203-562-5413. Editor: Sol D. Chain. For those interested in art, music, theatre, recreational activities, etc. Monthly magazine; 40 (6x9) pages. Established in 1952. Circulation: 5,000. Not copyrighted. Buys 20 mss per year. Payment on publication. Will send sample copy to writer for 50¢. Will consider photocopied and simultaneous submissions. Reports on material accepted for publication in 30 days. Returns rejected material in 2 weeks. Query first. Enclose S.A.S.E.

Nonfiction: "Most of our material is on assignment. We publish articles dealing with New Haven area events and people." Personal experience, interview, profile, historical, nostalgia. Length: 350 to 700 words. Pays $10 per page (about 350 words).

NEW JERSEY LIFE, Box 40, Maplewood NJ 07040. Editor: Carlette M. Winslow. For upper income, New Jersey-oriented readers, interested in arts, where to go, issues. Published 10 times a year, no January or July issues. Established in 1931. Circulation: 20,000. Buys first North American serial rights. Buys 10 to 15 mss a year. Payment on publication. Will send sample copy to writer for 70¢. Submit seasonal material 3 to 4 months in advance. Reports within 2 months. Submit only complete ms. Enclose S.A.S.E.

Nonfiction and Photos: Articles geared to New Jersey. Be sure to have material well researched; comprehensive. Culture, history, where to go, what to do. No far-out sensationalism. Informational, historical, photo features. Length: 2,000 to 4,000 words. Pays $25 to $100. Photos (b&w glossies) purchased with ms with no additional payment.

NEW MEXICO MAGAZINE, 113 Washington Ave., Santa Fe NM 87503. Phone: 505-827-3107. Editor: Sheila Tryk. For persons interested in the culture, history, arts, scenery, events and peoples of New Mexico. Monthly. Circulation: 85,000. Buys first rights. Buys approximately 60 mss a year. Pays on acceptance. Will send a

sample copy to a writer for 75¢. Query first. Submit seasonal material 12 months in advance. Reports in 1 to 2 months. Enclose S.A.S.E.
Nonfiction: Subjects include history, camping, travel, hunting, fishing, backpacking, restaurants, art, and resorts, among others. All should have a New Mexico background. No political articles. Purpose is to promote travel and outdoor activities in New Mexico. "Historical articles should contain original research—no rehashing. Articles should be specific—no generalized paeans to the state." No glib, gimmicky "travel guide" writing. Length: 300 to 2,000 words. Pays $10 to $300.
Photos: Almost all photo work done on assignment. No singles. Pays $100 to $300 per assignment.
Poetry: Traditional, contemporary, avant-garde. Length: under 30 lines. Pays in copies. Poetry Editor: Stanley Noyes.

NEW YORK MAGAZINE, 755 2 Ave., New York NY 10017. Phone: 212-986-4600. Editor: Clay Felker. For intelligent readers in the New York area. Circulation: 325,000. Buys all rights. Pays on publication. Query first. Reports in 1 month. Enclose S.A.S.E.
Nonfiction: Articles with ample reportage (not essays) about genuinely new or important aspects of the New York scene. Length: 1,000 to 3,500 words. Pays $250 to $1,000. Send material to Byron Dobell, Editorial Director.

NORTH/NORD, 400 Laurier Ave., West, Ottawa, Ontario, Canada K1A OH4. Phone: 613-995-6207. Editor: Robert F. J. Shannon. For a varied audience, from libraries and educational institutions to businessmen and diplomats, Canadian and international. Special issues on various special subjects in the North. Bimonthly. Established in 1959. Circulation: 6,500. Rights purchased vary with author and material. Buys full rights to publish and permit to be republished. Buys 100 mss a year. Payment on acceptance. Will send free sample copy to writer on request. Write for copy of guidelines for writers. Submit seasonal material 4 months in advance. Submit only complete mss. Enclose S.A.E. and International Reply Coupons.
Nonfiction: "Subjects must pertain to Canada north or other northern areas of the world such as Alaska or Scandinavia. Topics can include resource development (business mining, pipeline, construction and oil and gas industries); history (exploration, archaeology, fur trade); conservation (wilderness, wildlife, national parks, geology); adventure and human interest stories; the arts (folklore, sculpture, print making, etc.); life in the north (housing, transportation, education, communications, health and welfare, government, entertainments); native peoples (customs, life styles, organizations etc.); features on outstanding personalities of the north as well as northern communities." Length: 500 to 2,500 words. Pays $50 to $150.
Photos: Purchased with or without mss. "We use mainly color transparency or print film; some black and white." Pays from $7.50 to $10 for single shot; $20 to $25 for "Face of the North," a photo feature profile of a northern personality. Pays $50 to $75 for cover photo.
Fiction: Fiction should relate to the north. Length: 500 to 2,000 words. Pays $50 to $150.

OLD SEATTLE REVIEW, 5335 Ballard Ave., N.W., Seattle WA 98107. Editor: Duane Dahl. For an upper middle-class audience, with an interest in the area's history. Newspaper; 8 to 12 (11x17) pages. Established in 1974. Monthly. Circulation: 15,000 to 45,000. Rights purchased vary with author and material. May buy all rights, but will occasionally reassign rights to author after publication; or first North American serial rights. Buys about 24 to 30 mss a year. Will send sample copy to writer for 50¢. Write for copy of guidelines for writers. Will consider photocopied submissions, if legible. Will consider simultaneous submissions. Submit seasonal material (Christmas) 3 months in advance. Reports in 2 weeks. Query first. Enclose S.A.S.E.
Nonfiction and Photos: "We are a historical newspaper. Subject matter should relate to the history of the Northwest, particularly Seattle. Especially desirable are never-before-told stories and anecdotes about the people (big and little) who made the Northwest what it is today. Also modern topics relating to historical sites, landmarks,

pioneers, etc. Articles should be geared to a broad audience (not a ponderous history book style). Must be historically accurate, easily readable, but not superficial; generally of a positive nature. Avoid artificial dialogue." Old-fashioned Christmas material — crafts, recipes, traditional celebrations — used in a special holiday edition. Recently published articles include one on a typical Seattle pioneer family. Length: 200 words maximum for anecdotes; 2,000 words maximum for articles. Pays $2.50 for anecdotes; $10 to $30 for articles. 8x10 b&w glossies purchased with mss. Pays $2.50. Captions required.

Poetry and Fillers: Subject matter of poetry is more important than form. Should relate to area. Length: 30 lines maximum. Pays $3 to $10. Uses jokes and historical anecdotes as fillers. Length: 35 to 300 words. Pays $2 to $5.

THE OREGON PEOPLE MAGAZINE, P. O. Box 10145, Portland OR 97210. Editor: Bernerd Park. For middle and upper income Oregonians and people interested in Oregon. Magazine; 64 (8½x11) pages. Established in 1975. Monthly. Circulation: 15,000. Buys all rights, but will reassign rights to author after publication. Buys 85 to 90 mss a year. Pays on publication. Will send free sample copy to writer on request. Write for copy of guidelines for writers. Will consider photocopied submissions. No simultaneous submissions. Reports on material accepted for publication in 1 month. Returns rejected material in 1 week. Query first or submit complete ms. Enclose S.A.S.E.

Nonfiction and Photos: "We are looking for articles on Oregon history, local personalities, Oregon living, fresh view of ethnic groups who have settled in Oregon; consumer interest, nostalgia, modern woman, senior citizen, youth, state travel pieces. We are open to any kind of article as long as it is well-written. We prefer, of course, the Oregon angle, but even that can be waived if someone can show us a piece of good writing. But, we would like to see some serious analytical pieces on the meaning of 'the Oregon experience' viewed against the backdrop of the general decline in the quality of life in other parts of the U.S." Length: 1,500 to 2,500 words. Pays $50 to $400. Columns can use shorter material on the state of the arts in Oregon, or regional anecdotes and news briefs from all parts of the state. Length: 500 to 700 words. Pays $25 to $50. B&w glossies (8x10) are purchased with or without ms, or on assignment. No additional payment for those used with ms. Payment varies for other uses, depending on subject and quality. All photographs should be of people in Oregon settings. Captions required.

Poetry and Fillers: Traditional and avant-garde forms of poetry; blank verse and free verse. Length: 30 lines maximum. Pays 50¢ a line. Clippings, jokes and short humor are used as fillers. Length: 100 words maximum. Pays $10.

ORLANDO-LAND MAGAZINE, Box 2207, Orlando FL 32802. Editor: Edward L. Prizer. For "middle and upper age, middle and upper income, above average education, businessmen, investors, persons moving to Florida from other areas, affluent leisuretime readers, travelers." Established in 1946. Monthly. Circulation: 31,000. Rights purchased vary with author and material. Buys 25 mss a year. Payment on publication. Will send a sample copy to writer for $1. Will consider photocopied submissions. Submit seasonal material 3 months in advance. Reports in 2 to 4 weeks. Query first. Enclose S.A.S.E.

Nonfiction and Photos: General subject matter concerns "articles on central Florida subjects only." Approach "should be a personal experience article, casual and informal. Much of our material is comprised of directly quoted conversations with person interviewed. Always use the 'I' approach. We want nothing outside of central Florida. Seeking highly unusual experiences in Central Florida. Real true-life adventures." Buys informational, how-to, personal experience, interview, profile, humor, historical, think, nostalgia, personal opinion, photo articles. Length: 500 to 5,000 words. Pays 2¢ a word. Dept. Editor: Carole DePinto. Buys 5x7 and 8x10 b&w glossies. Purchased with ms. Captions required. Pays $5 per photo.

OUTDOOR INDIANA, Room 612, State Office Building, Indianapolis IN 46204. Phone: 317-633-4294. Editor: Herbert R. Hill. 10 times a year. Circulation: 30,000. Copyrighted. All material must relate to Indiana. Buys first serial rights. Pays on publication. Reports on submissions in 1 to 4 weeks. Query preferred. Enclose S.A.S.E. **Nonfiction and Photos:** Informative, concise, illustrative, bright articles on Indiana-related topics. No fiction, essays or verse. Length: 1,000 to 2,000 words. Payment by arrangement. Photos of Indiana interest only; purchased with mss or with captions only. B&w photos, 8x10; color transparencies, 2¼x2¼ or larger. Pays up to $10 for b&w; $25 for color; $50 for color cover.

PACIFIC WILDERNESS JOURNAL, P.O. Box 22272, Portland OR 97222. Editor: Frank W. Amato. For readers in the states of Oregon, Washington and California; all ages. 40-page magazine, published every 2 months. Established in 1973. Circulation: 4,000. Buys all rights, but will reassign rights to author after publication. Buys 60 mss a year. Payment on publication. Will send sample copy to writer for 25¢. Write for copy of guidelines for writers. Will consider photocopied and simultaneous submissions. Reports in 3 weeks. Query first or submit complete ms. Enclose S.A.S.E. **Nonfiction and Photos:** Articles on Northwestern wildlife, outdoor sports, history, how-to pieces on outdoor sports; where-to-go material. Must pertain to this region. Informational, how-to, personal experience, interview, historical, travel articles. Length: 500 to 2,500 words. Pays $15 to $50. Mss should be accompanied by 6 b&w photos. No additional payment for b&w.

PACIFICA MAGAZINE, 822 G Street, Arcata CA 95521. Phone: 707-822-3357. Editor: Alann B. Steen. "We've found that *Pacifica* cuts through all ages—the school age child on up, as it's a general magazine in a rather specific area (Northwestern California, Southwestern Oregon)." Monthly magazine, 32 pages, (8½x11). Established in 1971. Circulation: 10,000. Rights purchased vary with author and material. Buys all rights, but will reassign rights to author after publication. Buys 30 to 40 mss a year. Payment on publication. Will send sample copy to writer for 75¢. Write for copy of editorial guidelines for writers. Will consider photocopied submissions. Reports in 2 months. Query first or submit complete ms. Enclose S.A.S.E. **Nonfiction and Photos:** "We lean toward the out-of-doors; more and more toward its appreciation, enjoyment, even toward awareness of its existence. A writer shouldn't take himself too seriously—in other words, stand by for heavy editing, when needed, to fit tone, style, format of magazine. *Pacifica* likes to take even the worst of copy—as long as there is a germ of a story or idea, and as long as the author's ego can stand editing (heavy) or blue penciling. We don't like personal experience articles—when the writer (the person)—is more important than the experience. We like articles to cover hiking, kayaking in Northern (Pacific) California vicinity." Length: 200 to 2,500 words. Pays $5 to $75, depending on quantity and quality. Photos purchased with ms with no additional payment. 5x7 to 11x14 b&w photos preferred. **Fiction and Poetry:** "Would like to see 'tall tales' or light fiction, of any lengths. Traditional forms, blank verse, free verse, and light verse from 4 to 16 lines." Story themes should relate to magazine's subject matter. Poetry theme open. Pays in contributor copies.

PALM BEACH LIFE, Post Office Box 1176, Palm Beach FL 33480. Phone: 305-655-5755. Editor: Kathryn Robinette. "*Palm Beach Life* caters to society (America's oldest society journal) and reflects their interests. Readers are affluent ... usually over 40, well-educated." Special issues on the arts (February), travel (March), and yachting (November), and elegant living, home, family, etc. (September-October). Established in 1906. Monthly with combined September-October issue. Circulation: 12,000. Buys first North American and occasional second rights from non-competitive publication. Payment on acceptance. Will consider photocopied submissions. Submit seasonal material 5 months in advance. Reports in 3 weeks. Query first. Enclose S.A.S.E. **Nonfiction and Photos:** Subject matter involves "articles on fashion, travel, music, art and related fields; subjects that would be of interest to the sophisticated, well-informed reader; especially personality sketches of those in society or those who cater to it. We feature color photos, 'but are crying for good b&w'; also emphasize life in Palm Beach itself. Parties are overdone. Trying to show 'doers' in society." Buys informational, interview, profile, humor, historical, think, photo, and travel articles. Length: 1,000 to 2,500 words. Pays $50 to $125. Purchases photos with and without mss, on assignment. Captions are required. Buys 8x10 b&w glossies at $5 each. Also buys 35mm or 2¼x2¼ transparencies and photo stories. Pay is negotiable.

PHILADELPHIA MAGAZINE, 1500 Walnut St., Philadelphia PA 19102. Editor: Alan Halpern. For cross section of Philadelphians. Monthly magazine; 230 pages, (8¼x11½). Established in 1908. Circulation: 100,000. Rights purchased vary with author and material. Buys all rights; but will sometimes reassign rights to author after publication. Buys first North American serial rights. Buys 50 mss a year. Payment on publication. Will send sample copy to writer for $2. Write for copy of editorial guidelines for writers. Submit seasonal material 3 months in advance. Reports in 1 month. Query first. Enclose S.A.S.E.

Nonfiction and Photos: Reportage—political, sports, personalities, life styles, business, entertainment. Must have Philadelphia area locale. Informational, profile, historical, nostalgia, travel, and successful business operations. Length: 1,200 to 12,000 words. Pays $50 to $500. Photos purchased with accompanying ms with small additional payment for use.

PHOENIX MAGAZINE, 4707 N. 12th St., Phoenix AZ 85014. Editor: Anita J. Welch. For professional, general audience. Monthly magazine. Established in 1966. Circulation: 56,000. Buys all rights, but will reassign rights to author after publication. Buys about 60 mss a year. Payment on publication. Will send sample copy to writer for $1. February issue: Real Estate; March issue: Arizona Lifestyle; August issue: Annual Phoenix Progress Report; June issue: Salute to Summer. Submit special issue material 3 months in advance. Reports in 1 month. Query first or submit complete ms. Enclose S.A.S.E.

Nonfiction and Photos: Predominantly features on some aspect of Phoenix life; urban affairs, arts, life style, etc. Subject should be locally oriented. Informational, how-to, interview, profile, historical, photo, successful local business operations. Length: 1,000 to 3,000 words. Pays $50 to $100, but payment is negotiable. Photos are purchased with ms with no additional payment, or on assignment.

PITTSBURGH RENAISSANCE MAGAZINE, 4802 Fifth Ave., Pittsburgh PA 15213. Editor: Herb Stein. For members of public television station WQED (Pittsburgh). Magazine; 56 pages. Established in 1971. Monthly. Circulation: 35,000. Buys all rights. Buys about 50 mss a year. Pays on publication. Will consider photocopied submissions, if necessary. No simultaneous submissions. Reports on material accepted for publication in 1 month. Returns rejected material as soon as possible. Query first or submit complete ms. Enclose S.A.S.E.

Nonfiction: "We publish articles on public affairs, culture, the arts, history, service, politics, food, business; all related to Pittsburgh and the Western Pennsylvania region. This includes northern West Virginia and eastern Ohio. We look for clarity, interest, humor and accuracy." Informational, how-to, personal experience, interview, profile, humor, historical, think pieces, expose, nostalgia, personal opinion, travel. Recently published "Fire for Profit in Arson City USA" (Pittsburgh is a prime center for arsonists). Length: 1,000 words for columns to 3,500 words for full article. Payment ranges from $50 for a column to $200 for cover story.

ST. LOUISAN, 6306 Clayton Rd., St. Louis MO 63117. Phone: 314-644-2246. Editor: Libby Ferguson. For "those interested in the St. Louis area, recreation issues, etc." Established in 1969. Monthly. Circulation: 20,000. Buys all rights, but will reassign rights to author after publication; buys second serial (reprint) rights. Buys 60 mss a year. Payment on publication. Will send free sample copy to writer on request. Will not consider photocopied submissions. Submit seasonal material 4 months in advance. Reports on material in 2 months. Query first or submit complete ms. Enclose S.A.S.E.

Nonfiction and Photos: "Articles on the city of St. Louis, metro area, arts, recreation media, law, education, politics, timely issues, urban problems/solutions, environment, etc., generally related to St. Louis area. Looking for informative writing of high quality, consistent in style and timely in topic." Informational, how-to, personal experience, interview, profile, humor, historical, think pieces, expose, nostalgia, personal opinion, travel. Length: 1,000 to 5,000 words. Pays $100 to $200. 8x10 b&w glossies purchased on assignment. "Shooting fee plus $10 to $20 per print used. All color on individual basis."

SAN FRANCISCO MAGAZINE, 120 Green St., San Francisco CA 94111. Editor: Milton W. Jones. For Bay area readers interested in travel, foods, arts. Monthly magazine, 80 pages. Established in 1958. Circulation: 30,000. Buys all rights, but will reassign rights to author after publication. Payment on publication. Will send sample copy to writer for $1. October issue: Wine; December issue: articles for Christmas. Submit seasonal material 4 months in advance. Reports "almost immediately." Query first. Enclose S.A.S.E.

Nonfiction and Photos: Articles of interest to San Francisco Bay area readers; northern California information and profiles. Local in theme; more in-depth articles. "I see too many general themes, already done repeatedly. I'd like something new— a new angle on something old." Informational, profile, humor, historical, and travel. Length: varies, but averages 3,000 words. Pays $100 for first published article. Nonfiction Editor: Stephen Peithman. 8x10 b&w photos are purchased with or without mss, for $25, but payment varies. Captions optional. Also buys color transparencies. "We do not encourage freelance photo submissions; usually they are provided by staff photographers or freelance regulars."

SANDLAPPER, The Magazine of South Carolina, P. O. Box 1668, Columbia SC 29202. Editor: Bob W. Rowland. For people living in or coming from South Carolina, interested in history, leisure living, finer things, etc. Magazine; 64 (8½x11) pages. Established in 1968. Monthly. Circulation: 20,000. Buys all rights, but will reassign rights to author after publication. Buys about 150 mss a year. Pays "middle of month after publication." Will send sample copy to writer for $1.25. Write for copy of guidelines for writers. Will consider photocopied submissions. Submit seasonal (Christmas, Thanksgiving, etc.) material 6 months in advance. Reports in 2 to 4 weeks. Query first for nonfiction. Submit complete ms for poetry and fiction. Enclose S.A.S.E.

Nonfiction: Business articles, profiles of citizens, dining out, history pieces, some sports, travel; all pertaining directly to South Carolina. "We concentrate on the state and all material is slanted toward this; our readers don't like controversy, sex, violence, etc. We are looking for bright, scholarly, accurate, documented material for a special bicentennial series on the revolution in South Carolina." Book reviews. Length: 500 to 2,000 words. Pays $25 to $125.

Photos: Purchased with accompanying ms. Captions optional. B&w glossies, no negatives; transparencies or slides preferred. Pays $6 to $8 for b&w; $12 for color, $35 for cover color.

Fiction and Poetry: Mainstream, mystery, adventure, humorous, and historical. Length: 1,000 to 2,000 words. Pays $50 to $125. Traditional forms, blank verse, free verse. Length: 50-line maximum. Pays $10 each. Poetry Editor: Eugene Platt.

THE SENTINEL, Sentinel Publishing Co., 216 W. Jackson Blvd., Chicago IL 60606. Managing Editor: Robert Gale. For Jewish people residing in the Greater Chicago area. News magazine; 40 (10x13½) pages. Established in 1911. Weekly. Circulation: 42,600. Not copyrighted. Pays on publication or on acceptance. Will send free sample copy to writer on request. Will consider photocopied and simultaneous submissions. Submit special material for the Jewish holidays 3 months in advance. Reports on material accepted for publication in 2 weeks. Returns rejected material immediately. Query first or submit complete ms. Enclose S.A.S.E.

Nonfiction and Photos: Feature articles with some local angle. Length: open. Pays minimum of $10. Single column uses local material. Length: 800 words. Pays $10 minimum. No additional payment for b&w photos used with mss.

SOUTH CAROLINA MAGAZINE, Box 89, Columbia SC 29202. Phone: 803-796-9200. Monthly. Buys all rights. Pays on publication. Reports in about 1 week. Will send free sample copy on request. Enclose S.A.S.E.

Nonfiction and Photos: Matters of interest to South Carolinians about state history, places, people, education, art, etc. Length: 500 to 1,000 words. Pays 2¢ a word. Photos purchased with mss. Glossy prints, 8x10 or 5x7. Pays $5.

SOUTH CAROLINA WILDLIFE, P. O. Box 167, Columbia SC 29202. Editor: John Culler. For South Carolinians interested in hunting, fishing, the outdoors. Magazine; 64 (8½x11) pages. Established in 1953. Every 2 months. Circulation: 85,000. Not copyrighted. Buys 10 mss a year. Pays on acceptance. Will send free sample copy to writer on request. Reports in two weeks. Submit complete ms. Enclose S.A.S.E.
Nonfiction and Photos: Articles on outdoor South Carolina with an emphasis on preserving and protecting our natural resources. Length: 800 to 4,000 words. Pays $100 to $500. Pays $15 for b&w glossies purchased with or without ms, or on assignment. Pays $25 for color used inside; $50 for color on back cover; $100, front cover.

SOUTHERN EXPOSURE, P. O. Box 230, Chapel Hill NC 27514. Editor: Bob Hall. For Southerners interested in "left-liberal" political perspective and the South; all ages; well-educated. Magazine; 100 to 230 (8x11) pages. Established in 1973. Quarterly. Circulation: 4,000. Buys all rights. Buys 8 to 10 mss a year. Pays on publication. Will consider photocopied and simultaneous submissions. Submit seasonal material 2 to 3 months in advance. Reports in 1 to 2 months. "Query is appreciated, but not required." Enclose S.A.S.E.
Nonfiction and Photos: "Ours is probably the only publication about the South *not* aimed at business or the upper-class people; it appeals to all segments of the population. *And,* it is used as a resource — sold as a magazine and then as a book — so it rarely becomes dated." Needed are investigative articles about the following subjects as related to the South: women, labor, black people, the economy. Recently published articles from freelancers included, "Agribusiness Gets the Dollar," "South Coast Conspiracy," "Southern Rock 'n Roll," and "Texas Purges Nobel Prize Winner." These analyses went beyond the headlines and the obvious, and the subject matter had not been extensively covered by newspapers or magazines. Informational, interview, profile, historical, think articles, expose, personal opinion, and book reviews. Length: 6,000 words maximum. Pays $50 average per article, $100 maximum. "Very rarely purchase photos, as we have a large number of photographers working for us." 8x10 b&w preferred; no color. Payment negotiable.
Fiction and Poetry: "Fiction should concern the South, i.e., black fiction, growing up Southern, etc." Length: 6,000 words maximum. Pays $5 to $50. All forms of poetry accepted, if they relate to the South, its problems, potential, etc. Length: open. Pays $15 to $25.

SOUTHERN OUTDOORS MAGAZINE, 6300 Westpark, Suite 430, Houston TX 77027. Editor: Charles Coffen. For men in average years; outdoorsmen, well educated. Published every 2 months; 80 pages. Established in 1953. Circulation: 100,000. Buys first North American serial rights. Buys 85 to 100 mss a year. Payment on acceptance. Will send free sample copy to writer on request. Write for copy of editorial guidelines for writers. January/February issue: Boating; July/August issue: Bass Issue; November/December issue: Hunting. Submit special issue material 4 to 6 months in advance. Reports in 2 weeks. Query first. Enclose S.A.S.E.
Nonfiction and Photos: Features on hunting, fishing, boating, camping and travel. How-to, where-to, when-to. Don't send features pertaining to areas other than the South. Photos purchased with ms with no additional payment. Length: 1,800 to 2,000 words. Pays $100 to $125.

THE STATE, P.O. Box 2169, Raleigh NC 27602. Editor: W.B. Wright. Monthly. Buys first rights. Will send a free sample copy on request. Pays on acceptance. Deadlines 1 month in advance of publication date. Enclose S.A.S.E.
Nonfiction and Photos: "General articles about places, people, events, history, general interest in North Carolina. Also reports on business, new developments within the state. Emphasis on travel in North Carolina; (devote features regularly to resorts, travel goals, dining and stopping places)." Will use humor if related to region. Length:

average of 1,000 to 1,200 words. Pays $25 average, $15 minimum. B&w photos purchased with mss. Pays average of $5; minimum of $3.

THE TAMPA TRIBUNE, P. O. Box 191, Tampa FL 33601. Editor: James Clendinen. For a general circulation, newspaper audience. Newspaper; 80 to 160 pages. Established in 1894. Daily. Circulation: 175,000 to 210,000. Not copyrighted, but special stories are copyrighted. Buys several hundred mss a year. Pays 2 to 4 weeks after acceptance. Will consider photocopied submissions. Simultaneous submissions considered (but not if made to nearby publications). Reports on material accepted for publication within a month. Returns rejected material within 2 weeks. Query first or submit complete ms. Enclose S.A.S.E.

Nonfiction and Photos: Articles on travel, history, news events, sports, fashion, profiles, trends, etc. Must have Tampa emphasis or tie-in. Open to any literate style. Informational, how-to, personal experience, interview, humor, think pieces, spot news. Length: 150 to 3,000 words. Pays $15 to $200. Pays $5 to $25 for b&w glossies purchased with or without ms. Pays $15 to $50 for color transparencies purchased with or without ms.

TEXAS METRO MAGAZINE, P.O. Drawer 5566, Arlington TX 76011. Editor: Dr. Dora Dougherty Strother. Executive Editor: S.D. Johnson. General audience. Monthly. Buys all rights. Pays on publication. Will send a sample copy to a writer on request. Submit seasonal material 3 months before publication. Query first. Enclose S.A.S.E.

Nonfiction: General subject matter includes "articles on travel, better living, and investment as it relates to north central Texas, a 10-county area that includes Dallas and Fort Worth." Home living, travel, sports, entertainment, personalities, education, culture, and business related to the general geographic area. Appropriate visuals must accompany articles; i.e., photos, graphs, illustrations. Articles must be aimed generally at a college-level intellect. Must contain facts which can be absorbed by scanning; loose enough to be readable, but meaty. Length: 200 to 1,000 words. Payment varies with the quality of writing and research. There are two sections in which freelance writers writing about Texas, Louisiana, Arkansas, Oklahoma, New Mexico, and Colorado stand a good chance of scoring regularly: The "Metro Travel" section and "Metro Living" section. *Texas Metro* invites attention to the "Recipes of the Southwest" (which includes the aforementioned states) and for which submissions are also solicited.

Photos: "Cover photographs should deal with travel, cooking, gardening, homes, and better living. Payment for cover photos starts at $25. Also will buy striking photos of regional interest which stand alone, sports or scenery, etc. Payment starts at $5."

TEXAS MONTHLY MAGAZINE, P. O. Box 1569, Austin TX 78767. Editor: William Broyles. For Texans (in or out of state) with upper middle class interests. Magazine. Established in 1973. Monthly. Circulation: 100,000. Rights purchased vary with author and material. May buy all rights, with the possibility of reassigning rights to author after publication, or simultaneous rights. Buys very few mss a year. Pays on acceptance. Write for copy of guidelines for writers. Will consider photocopied submissions. Simultaneous submissions will be considered, if notified. Submit seasonal material 4 months in advance. Reports on material accepted for publication in 6 weeks. Returns rejected material in 2 weeks. Query first with approach to and outline of story, plus sources and sampling of work.. Enclose S.A.S.E.

Nonfiction and Photos: Subjects must be of interest to an educated Texas readership. Informational, how-to, personal experience, interview, profile, historical, think pieces, expose, nostalgia. Length: 1,200 to 7,500 words. Pays $100 to $400. Travel, consumer, urban problems and science columns use material of 2,500 words maximum. Pays $100 to $150. Pays $30 for b&w photos purchased with ms.

TEXAS PARADE, P.O. Box 12037, Austin TX 78711. Editor: Kenneth E. Lively. Monthly. Circulation: 50,000. Buys first North American serial rights. Payment on publication. Will send free sample copy to writer on request. Submit seasonal material 6 weeks in advance. Reports in 1 month. Query first or submit complete ms. Enclose S.A.S.E.

Nonfiction and Photos: Articles on people, politics, travel, business, history and sports with a Texas angle. Length: 1,500 to 3,000 words. Pays $125 to $200. B&w and color photos purchased with mss. Captions required. Also Texas-angled photo stories. Pays $10 minimum.

TOWN AND COUNTRY JOURNAL, 101½ Mill St., Coudersport PA 16915. Editor: Geraldine R. Miller. For natives and newcomers of this area. Special double winter issue, January/February. Established in 1972. Monthly. Circulation: 2,000. Not copyrighted. Payment on publication. Will send free sample copy to writer on request. Will consider photocopied submissions. Submit special issue material 3 months in advance. Reports on material accepted for publication in 1 month. Returns rejected material in 2 weeks. Query first or submit complete ms. Enclose S.A.S.E.

Nonfiction and Photos: Articles on the history of the area, local government, nature, real estate, antiques, gardening, subdivision, zoning. May have inspirational or mild ecology theme. Snowmobile and other winter sport material is used for the winter issue; material on fairs is used for the August issue. Other interests include informational, how-to, interviews, profile, nostalgia, merchandising techniques, successful business operations, book reviews. Length: 1,500 to 5,000 words. Pays $5 to $15. 8x10 b&w glossy photos purchased with mss. Pays $5. Captions required.

Poetry: Free verse, light verse. Length: 4 to 20 lines. Pays 50¢ to $1.

TRENTON MAGAZINE, 104 N. Broad St., Trenton NJ 08608. Editor: Lowell Benedict. For primarily business people; well educated, wide ranging interests, and interested in community. Monthly magazine; 50 pages, (8½x11). Established in 1924. Circulation: 10,000. Not copyrighted. Buys about 50 mss a year. Payment on publication. Will send free sample copy to writer on request. Reports within 6 weeks. Query first. Enclose S.A.S.E.

Nonfiction and Photos: "Looking for articles about interesting people in Mercer County area. We're interested in more in-depth look at subject. We have more than enough historical articles submitted." Length: 500 to 2,000 words. Pays $10 to $100, with payment usually being $25 to $50. Photos purchased with ms or on assignment. Captions required. "Photo subjects pretty much the same as theme of magazine subjects. We do use 2-page photo spreads but would like a query first for these. Must be local subjects." Pays $7.50 per 8x10 b&w glossy. Only uses color on cover; assignment only for color.

TULSA MAGAZINE, 616 S. Boston, Tulsa OK 74119. Phone: 918-585-1201. Editor: Larry Silvey. Audience is primarily medium to upper income level Tulsans. Monthly. Circulation: 6,000. Not copyrighted. Pays on publication. Will send sample copy for 25¢. Deadlines are at least 6 weeks prior to publication date, which is normally on the first Thursday of each month. Reports immediately. Query first. Enclose S.A.S.E.

Nonfiction and Photos: Articles must revolve around people or how subject affects people and must have a Tulsa area slant. Style desired is informal and lively. 1,000 to 4,000 words. Payment is negotiable, $50 to $75, depending on length, research. Photos usually taken by staff or on assignment. May be purchased with mss.

UPCOUNTRY, New England's Magazine of Upland Living, 33 Eagle St., Pittsfield MA 01201. Phone: 413-447-7311. Managing Editor: William H. Tague. For people who are interested in the country life of New England. Established in 1973. Tabloid published 12 times a year. Circulation: 90,000. Buys all rights, but will reassign rights to author after publication. Buys 100 to 150 mss a year. Payment on acceptance. "Prefer written or telephone query in advance of sending material, although we consider everything received." Enclose S.A.S.E.

Nonfiction and Photos: "The magazine deals with country living, not as a fantasy, but as a reality. We look for articles on specific topics of current interest to our readership. Quotations, specific examples, etc., are all desirable. Above all, articles

should relate to the region we serve. Articles concerned with moving to and living in the country; coping with country living; rural medicine, taxation, political issues affecting country life; gardening, music, art, theatre, birdwatching, outdoor sports, restaurants, country inns, restorations, preservations, etc. Articles on how to come to terms with our environment. Also articles on city folk moving to the country. How-to articles; homebuilding." Length: 700 to 3,000 words. Pays $30 to $100. B&w negatives or 8x10 print and color transparencies. Payment varies, but pays a minimum of $5 for b&w negatives and prints; $25 to $75 for color transparencies for covers.
Poetry and Fillers: "Must relate to New England rural life." Traditional forms of poetry, blank verse, free verse, light verse. Payment varies but begins at $15. Short humor, clippings. Length: 50 to 200 words. Pays $5 to $20.

UTAH MAGAZINE, 915 S.W. Temple, Salt Lake City UT 84101. Managing Editor: Marlene M. Young. A state magazine for residents of Utah. Established in 1974. Six times a year. Buys first rights. Pays on publication. Will send free sample copy to writer on request. Write for copy of guidelines for writers. Reports on material accepted for publication in 2 to 3 weeks. Returns rejected material in 2 weeks. Submit complete ms. Enclose S.A.S.E.
Nonfiction and Photos: Wide variety of articles on subjects covering life in Utah. Must deal with a scenic attraction; the cultural, recreational, or industrial aspects of Utah; history of the state; personality profiles on residents of Utah. Short subjects are preferred. Length: 100 to 1,000 words. Pays $10 to $25. Pays $5 to $10 for b&w photos purchased with or without mss. Pays $25 for color used on front and back cover. Pays $5 to $15 for color used inside. Prefers 35mm transparencies.

VERMONT LIFE MAGAZINE, 63 Elm St., Montpelier VT 05602. Phone: 802-828-3241. Editor: Brian Vachon. Quarterly. Buys first rights. "Query is essential." Enclose S.A.S.E.
Nonfiction: Wants articles on Vermont, those which portray a typical and, if possible, unique, attractive aspect of the state or people. Style should be literate, clear and concise. Subtle humor favored. Word length averages 1,500 words. Payment averages 10¢ per word.
Photos: Buys photographs with mss and with captions only. Prefers b&w, 8x10 glossies or matte prints, except on assignment. Color submissions must be 4x5 or 35mm transparencies. Buys one-time rights, but often negotiates for re-use rights also. Rates on acceptance; b&w, $10; color, $75 inside, $200 for cover. Gives assignments but not on first trial with photographers. Query first.

VIRGINIA CARDINAL, Box 334, Vienna VA 22180. Editor: Richard H. Weller. Monthly. Buys all rights, "but we grant reprint rights if we get credit." Pays on publication. Query first. "Because of our limited staff, unsolicited mss cannot be handled." Enclose S.A.S.E.
Nonfiction and Photos: "The main circulation of this magazine is in northern Virginia and metropolitan Washington. This area is one of the most affluent and influential in the nation. The magazine reflects the concerns and interests of its readers in the good life. Articles on travel, fashion, sports, gourmet food, books, and history are staff-written. However, freelance writers will find a ready market for feature articles with a fresh and different approach to Virginia's people, places, progress, and problems." Length: 1,500 to 2,500 words. Pays $25 per article. "Articles should be accompanied by photos whenever possible."

THE WASHINGTONIAN MAGAZINE, 1218 Connecticut Ave., N.W., Washington DC 20036. Editor: John A. Limpert. For active, affluent, well-educated audience. Monthly magazine; 200 pages. Established in 1965. Circulation: 60,000. Buys all rights. Buys 75 mss a year. Payment on publication. Will send sample copy to writer for $1.25. Write for copy of guidelines for writers. Will consider photocopied submissions and simultaneous submissions. Reports in 2 weeks. Query first or submit complete ms. Enclose S.A.S.E.
Nonfiction and Photos: *"The Washingtonian* is written for Washingtonians. The subject matter is anything we feel might interest people interested in the mind and

manners of the city. The style, as Wolcott Gibbs said, should be the author's—if he is an author, and if he has a style. The only thing we ask is thoughtfulness and that no subject be treated too reverently. Audience is literate. We assume considerable sophistication about the city, and a sense of humor." Buys how-to's, personal experience, interviews, profiles, humor, coverage of successful business operations, think pieces, and exposes. Length: 1,000 to 7,000 words; average feature, 3,000 words. Pays 7¢ to 10¢ a word. Photos purchased with mss. B&w glossies, color transparencies, 35mm color. Payment is from $15 "for small spot" to $100 "for full page."

Fiction and Poetry: Both must be Washington-oriented. No limitations on length. Pays 7¢ to 10¢ a word for fiction. Department Editor: Jack Limpert. Payment for poetry is negotiable. Poetry Department Editor: Ellen Phillips.

THE WESTERN RESERVE MAGAZINE, Box 243, Garretsville OH 44231. Phone: 216-527-2030. Editor: Mary Folger. For residents of Western Reserve of Ohio; upper middle class; family oriented. Magazine published every 2 months. 52 (8½x11) pages. Established in 1973. Circulation: 10,000. Buys all rights, but will reassign rights to author after publication. Buys 60 mss a year. Payment on publication. For some articles payment is made in contributor's copies. Will send free sample copy to writer on request. Submit material for special events 3 months in advance. Reports in 1 to 2 months. Query first. Enclose S.A.S.E.

Nonfiction and Photos: Material must have regional orientation: historical, what to do, where to go, what to see in the Western Reserve, crafts, collectibles, personalities. Approach should be friendly and informal. "Remember that we are a soft-sell, area-promoting, hometown (but not backwoods) magazine; aware, but not plastic and chrome. And don't try to tell the life story of a famous Western Reserver; give us an in-depth report of one incident." Uses material on "what's going on in the Western Reserve": special events, festivals, bazaars, arts and crafts shows, etc. Length: no minimum; prefers 2,000 maximum. Pays $30 to $50 for articles. No additional payment for b&w photos purchased with mss. Pays $3 to $30 for b&w purchased without ms. Must be professional quality. Captions required.

Fiction: Limited market for humorous or historical fiction with Western Reserve orientation. Length: 300 to 2,000 words. Pays $30 to $50.

Poetry: "Looking for works equal to those of Edgar McCormack, Evan Lodge." Payment consists of $10 and copies of the issue.

Fillers: Short humor. Pays minimum of $10.

WESTWAYS, P.O. Box 2890, Terminal Annex, Los Angeles CA 90051. Phone: 213-746-4410. Executive Editor: N. J. Kockler. Associate Editor: Frances Ring. For "fairly affluent, college-educated, mobile and active Southern California families. Average age of head of household is 42; median income of family is $15,000. Monthly. Buys first rights. Buys approximately 250 mss a year. Pays on acceptance for mss; on publication for most photos. Submit seasonal material at least 4 to 6 months in advance. Reports in 4 to 6 weeks. Query preferred. Enclose S.A.S.E.

Nonfiction: "Informative articles, well-researched and written in fresh, literate, honest style." This publication "covers all states west of the Rockies, including Alaska and Hawaii, western Canada and Mexico. We're willing to consider anything that interprets and illuminates the American West—past or present—for the Western American family. Employ imagination in treating subject. Avoid PR hand-out type style and format, and please know at least something about the magazine." Subjects include "travel, history, modern civic, cultural, and sociological aspects of the West; camping, fishing, natural science, humor, first-person adventure and experience, nostalgia, profiles, and occasional unusual and offbeat pieces. One article a month on foreign travel." Length: 1,000 to 3,000 words. Pays 10¢ a word and up.

Photos: Buys color and b&w photos with or without mss. Prefers 8x10 b&w glossies. Often publishes photo essays. Pays $25 minimum "for each b&w used as illustration;" $25 to $200 per transparency.

Poetry: Publishes 12 to 15 poems a year. Length: up to 24 lines; "occasionally longer." Pays $25.

WISCONSIN TRAILS, P.O. Box 5650, Madison WI 53705. Editor: Jill Weber Dean. For readers interested in natural beauty, history, personalities, recreation, and the arts. Established in 1960. Quarterly. Circulation: 28,000. Rights purchased vary with author and material. "We buy exclusive rights in most cases." Payment on acceptance. Will send free sample copy to writer on request. Write for copy of guidelines for writers. Will consider photocopied submissions. Submit seasonal material 1 year in advance. Reports in 1 month. Query first, or send outline. "A few samples of your work will help us evaluate your ability to develop the idea expressed in your query." Enclose S.A.S.E.

Nonfiction: "Our articles focus on some aspect of Wisconsin life; an interesting site or event, a person or industry, or history and the arts. We do not use first-person essays, (reminiscences are sometimes okay), ecstacies about scenery, or biographies about people who were born in Wisconsin, but made their fortunes elsewhere. No cartoons, crosswords, or fillers. Poetry exclusively on assignment." Length: 1,500 to 3,000 words. Pays $50 to $250, depending on length and quality. For "Where to Go, What to Do" section, pays $15 for 300 words and b&w photo.

Photos: Purchased without mss or on assignment. Captions preferred. B&w photos usually illustrate a given article. Color is mostly scenic. B&w photo of a site, event, etc., for "Where to Go, What to Do" section. Pays $10 each for b&w on publication. Pays $50 for inside color; pays $100 for covers and center spreads. Transparencies; 2¼ by 2¼ or larger are preferred.

WISDOM'S CHILD, 2770 Broadway, New York NY 10025. Phone: 212-866-7920. Editor: Carolyn Jabs. For "residents of the West Side of Manhattan from West 14th to 122nd St. We distribute especially to residences where the average income is over $10,000. Our articles are aimed at young people who like to live in the city." Published every two weeks; 20 to 24 pages, (10x13). Established in 1969. Circulation: 100,000. Buys all rights, but will reassign rights to author after publication. Buys 100 to 124 mss a year. Payment on publication. Will send sample copy to writer for 25¢. Will consider photocopied submissions and simultaneous submissions. "We do yearly issues on Plants, Apartment Improvement, Christmas Holidays and often do seasonal issues (spring fix-up, etc.)." Submit seasonal material 6 weeks in advance. Reports in 1 month. Query first. Enclose S.A.S.E.

Nonfiction and Photos: "We publish stories about all aspects of neighborhood life. We have never published fiction and publish poems only when they are directly related to neighborhood life. Possible subjects for articles include community politics, institutions, education, social trends, habits, stores, anything. Our approach and outlook are specialized enough that I would prefer to explain them to freelancers in person. We are a cross between a neighborhood newspaper and *New York* magazine. We do our feature stories in the style of *New York,* but we tailor them to a neighborhood which is more manageable than the entire city. I rarely purchase unsolicited stories. Writers are advised to send a query on any idea." Length: 450 to 1,500 words. Pays $10 to $100. B&w photos purchased with or without ms, or on assignment. Captions optional. "We are always interested in human interest shots of neighborhood, people, places, activities." Pays up to $40.

Fillers: Newsbreaks (must be local), clippings. Pays to $24.

YANKEE, Main St., Dublin NH 03444. Editor: Judson D. Hale. Monthly. Material relates to New England people, places, things. Usually buys all rights. Pays on acceptance. Will send free sample copy to a writer on request. Reports in 3 weeks. Enclose S.A.S.E.

Nonfiction: About New England and/or New Englanders, past, present or future; interesting people, activities, controversies if of wide interest, especially the unusual in all events; historical, particularly if there is some present-day tie-in. Does not like colloquial style; taboos include "booze, sex, insanity, profanity, dope, etc." Length: 1,500 to 2,500 words. Illustrations help put a feature across. Pays $25 to $400, average $250 to $350, depending on quality, importance, manner of presentation, number of photos, etc.

Photos: Purchased with mss and with identifications only. Current New England seasonal scenics; also unusual old-time photos. Pays $25 on publication or $15 on

acceptance for one-time rights. Color transparencies are often used with articles.
Fiction: Must be placed in New England either by specific location, general reference or simply by New England-type setting; or, if a city, then a New England city, such as Boston. Length: 1,500 to 2,500 words. Pays from $25 to $400; average $300 to $400, depending on quality.
Poetry: Uses modern poetry. Study previous issues to determine type of material desired. Pays $25 per poem. Annual awards are made for poetry appearing in *Yankee* during the calendar year.

YANKEE MAGAZINE'S GUIDE TO NEW ENGLAND (formerly *Yankee Guide to the New England Countryside*), 143 Newbury St., Boston MA 02116. Phone: 617-266-0813. Editor: Georgia Orcutt. For native New Englanders and visitors, all ages and income brackets. Biannual publication; 144 to 160 (8½x11) pages. Established in 1971. Circulation: 135,000. Buys first serial rights. Buys 20 mss a year. Payment on acceptance. Will send sample copy to writer for $1.25. Submit seasonal material (spring/summer; fall/winter) 6 months in advance. Query first with an outline. Enclose S.A.S.E.
Nonfiction and Photos: "We publish unusual features on things to do in New England. We like to show our readers something new each time. Some of our most popular features have been such things as: 'Where to Pick Your Own Strawberries', 'Where to Cut Your Own Christmas Trees', 'Where to Find Waterfalls', etc. We're interested in undiscovered New England places (towns, restaurants, beaches, etc.). Also out-of-the-way places and ideas on how to get there; New England islands. We would prefer not to see ideas on obvious New England attractions such as historic houses or state parks, etc. And we are not interested in subjective reports. We ask that anyone interested in presenting a manuscript, first write in for a copy of our publication. Send $1.25 for this." Length: 300 to 2,000 words. Pays $50 to $200. Pays $10 to $20 for b&w photos (contacts or 8x10 glossies) purchased without accompanying ms or on assignment. Prefers 2¼ color, but will consider 35mm. Pays $100 for full page to $25 for quarter page or smaller. Captions required.

Religious Publications

Educational and inspirational material of interest to a general audience (including students, church members, workers and leaders) within a denomination or religion is the primary interest of publications in this category. Publications intended to assist lay and professional religious workers in teaching and managing church affairs are classified in Church Administration and Ministry in the Trade Journals section. Religious magazines for children and teenagers will be found in the Juvenile, and Teen and Young Adult classifications. Jewish publications whose main concern is with matters of general Jewish interest (rather than religious interest) are listed in the Jewish Publications category.

A.D., 475 Riverside Drive, New York NY 10027. Established in 1972. Published in 2 editions; one for members of the United Presbyterian Church, U.S.A.; one for members of the United Church of Christ. Circulation: 550,000. Usually buys all rights. Always query first to The Editors. Enclose S.A.S.E.
Nonfiction and Fiction: The first half of the magazine contains articles of interest to both Presbyterian and United Church of Christ readers. Every issue carries at least one major piece on some important political or social problem. Length varies. Uses articles expressing individual opinion; personality pieces; news stories that aren't merely of interest within some local parish. Length: 800 to 1,000 words for personality pieces, 400 words for news items, and up to 3,000 words for articles. Pays from $15 to $150 depending on length and quality. Uses fiction with extreme rarity except for a children's story in each issue. Length: 600 to 800 words.

A.M.E. REVIEW, 468 Lincoln Drive, N.W., Atlanta GA 30318. Editor-Manager: William D. Johnson. For the ministerial majority. Quarterly magazine; 68 to 70

(6x9) pages. Established in 1880. Circulation: 5,000. Not copyrighted. Payment on publication. Will send sample copy to writer for $1. Reports in 10 days. Query first or submit complete ms. Enclose S.A.S.E.

Nonfiction and Photos: Uses material on personal experiences and personal achievements of a religious nature; ministerial profiles, human interest articles, pulpit reviews and book reviews (religious and racial). Length: 2,500 words. Pay 10¢ a word. B&w (3x5) photos are purchased with or without accompanying mss. Pays $2.50.

Fiction: Mainstream, fantasy, humorous, religious. Length: open. Pays 8¢ a word.

Poetry: Free verse and light verse for the Poets' Corner. Length: open. Pays $5.

Fillers: Short humor with a religious slant. Pays $2 per line up to 4 lines.

AMERICA, 106 W. 56th St., New York NY 10019. Editor: Donald R. Campion, S.J. Published weekly for adult, educated, largely Roman Catholic audience. Usually buys all rights. Pays on acceptance. Reports in two or three weeks. Write for copy of guidelines for writers. Enclose S.A.S.E.

Nonfiction and Poetry: "We publish a wide variety of material on politics, economics, ecology, and so forth. We are not a parochial publication, but almost all of our pieces make some moral or religious point. We are not interested in purely informational pieces or personal narratives which are self-contained and have no larger moral interest." Articles on literature, current political and social events. Length: 1,500 to 2,000 words. Pays $50 to $75. Poetry length: 10 to 30 lines. Address to Poetry Editor.

AMERICAN REVIEW OF EASTERN ORTHODOXY, Box 390, Dobbs Ferry NY 10522. Phone: 914-693-6777. Editor: Robert Burns, Jr. Principally for clergy, students, seminarians, prominent laity of Eastern Orthodox, Roman Catholic, Espiscopal background. Religious news magazine; 32 (6x8) pages. Established in 1954. Published every 2 months. Circulation: 3,000. Not copyrighted. Buys about 6 mss a year. Pays on acceptance. Will send sample copy to writer for $1. Will consider photocopied and simultaneous submissions. Reports immediately. Submit complete ms. Enclose S.A.S.E.

Nonfiction and Photos: News, short items of religious topical interest. Eastern Orthodox items principally. American view, rather than old country view. Photos and terse descriptive matter dealing with the subject are necessary. News exposes. Informational, interview, historical, and photo articles. Length: 500 to 2,500 words. Pays $10 to $25. Photos purchased with ms with no additional payment. Purchased without accompanying ms for $5 minimum. Captions required. Clear b&w glossies.

ANNALS OF GOOD SAINT ANNE DE BEAUPRE, Basilica of St. Anne, Que., Canada. Phone: 418-827-3254. Editor: Rev. Jean-Claude Nadeau, C.Ss.R. For Catholic families, especially women readers. Monthly. Circulation: 75,000. Buys first North American serial rights. Buys approximately 150 mss a year. Occasionally overstocked. Pays on acceptance. Will send a sample copy to a writer on request. Submit seasonal material 2 months in advance. Reports in 3 weeks. Query first. Enclose S.A.E. and International Reply Coupons.

Nonfiction: "Articles on devotion to St. Anne, major social problems of today, education, ecumenism, family, etc." Interviews, profiles, inspirational and think pieces, humor. Roman Catholic slant. Religious articles of interest to a wide public. Read issues of magazine before submitting. Length: 800 to 1,800 words. Pays 1½¢ to 2¢ per word.

Photos: Purchased with mss and returned after use if requested. Pays $25 to $40 for color transparencies.

Fiction: Limited fiction market. Short stories with strong plot treated in fresh, original manner. Little or no slang. Must not offend Catholic principles or be too goody-goody. Aimed at providing sound Catholic literature for a Catholic family magazine for readers of average education and culture. Writers need not necessarily be Catholic. Length: 1,500 to 1,700 words. Pays $25.

ASPIRE, 1819 E. 14th Ave., Denver CO 80218. Editor: Jeanne Pomranka. For teens and adults: "those who are looking for a way of life that is practical, logical, spiritual, or inspirational." Monthly. Established in 1914. Circulation: 2,900. Copyrighted. Author may use after publication providing credit given *Aspire*. Buys 180 to 190 mss a year. Pays on publication. Will send a sample copy to a writer for a 10¢ stamp. Submit seasonal material 6 to 7 months in advance. Reports in 2 weeks. Enclose S.A.S.E.

Nonfiction: Uses inspirational articles that help to interpret the spiritual meaning of life. Needs are specialized, since this is the organ of the Divine Science teaching. Personal experience, inspirational, think pieces. Also seeks material for "God at Work," a department "written in the form of letters to the editor in which the writer describes how God has worked in his life or around him. 'Teen Talk' includes short articles from teenagers to help other teenagers find meaning in life." Length: 250 to 1,500 words. Pays maximum 1¢ per published word.

Fiction: "Anything that fits in with Divine Science teaching." Length: 250 to 1,000 words. Pays maximum 1¢ per published word.

Poetry: Traditional, contemporary, light verse. "We use very little poetry." Length: average 8 to 16 lines. Pays $2 to $4.

BAPTIST HERALD, 7308 Madison Street, Forest Park IL 60130. Phone: 312-771-8700. Dr. Reinhold J. Kerstan. For "any age from 15 and up, any educational background with mainly religious interests." Established in 1923. Monthly. Circulation: 10,000. Buys all rights. Payment on publication. Occasionally overstocked. Will send a free sample copy to a writer on request. Submit seasonal material 3 to 4 months in advance. Enclose S.A.S.E.

Nonfiction and Fiction: "We want articles of general religious interest. Seeking articles that are precise, concise, and honest. We hold a rather conservative religious line." Buys personal experience, interviews, inspirational, and personal opinion articles. Length: 700 to 2,000 words. Payment is $5 to $10. Buys religious and historical fiction. Length: 700 to 2,000 words. Pays $5 to $10.

BAPTIST LEADER, Valley Forge PA 19481. Editor: Vincie Alessi. For ministers, teachers, and pupils in church schools. Monthly. Buys first rights, or as agreed by author. Pays on acceptance. Will send free sample copy to a writer on request. Read magazine before submitting. Deadlines are seven months prior to date of issue. Reports on submissions in one month. Enclose S.A.S.E.

Nonfiction: Educational topics and social issues. Length: 750 to 1,500 words. Pays 1½ to 3¢ per word.

Photos: Church school settings; church, worship, children's and youth activities and adult activities. Purchased with mss. B&w, 8x10; human interest and seasonal themes. Pays $5 to $10.

BRIGADE LEADER, Box 150, Wheaton IL 60187. Editor: Don Dixon. For men associated with Christian Service Brigade clubs throughout U.S. and Canada. Quarterly magazine; 32 pages, (8½x11). Buys all rights; but will sometimes reassign rights to author after publication; second serial (reprint) rights. Buys 4 mss a year. Payment on acceptance. Will send free sample copy to writer on request. Write for copy of editorial guidelines for writers. Submit seasonal material 4 months in advance. Will consider photocopied submissions. Reports in 2 months. Query first. Enclose S.A.S.E.

Nonfiction and Photos: "Articles about men and things related to them. Relationships in home, church, work. Specifically geared to men with an interest in boys. Besides men dealing with boys' physical, mental, emotional needs–also deals with spiritual needs." Informational, personal experience, inspirational. Length: 800 to 1,200 words. Pays 1¢ minimum a word. Photos purchased with or without ms. Pays $7.50 for b&w. Managing Editor: Paul Heidebrecht.

CALVINIST-CONTACT, P.O. Box 312, Station B, Hamilton, Ontario, Canada. Phone: 416-547-1488. Editor: D. Farenhorst. Christian weekly newspaper. No rights purchased. Enclose S.A.E. and International Reply Coupons.

Nonfiction: "Any material as long as it is suitable for our publication, which has as its aim the practical application of the principles of the Bible as the only true guide in life." Pays 1¢ a word.

CANADIAN CHURCHMAN, 600 Jarvis St., Toronto, Ont. M4Y 2J6, Canada. Editor: Hugh B. McCullum. For a general audience; Anglican Church of Canada; adult, with religio-socio emphasis. Monthly tabloid newspaper; 28 to 32 pages. Established in 1874. Circulation: 280,000. Not copyrighted. Buys 10 to 12 mss a year. Payment on publication. Will send free sample copy to writer on request. Will consider photocopied submissions and simultaneous submissions. Reports in 1 month. Query first. Enclose S.A.E. and International Reply Coupons.

Nonfiction: "Religion, news from churches around the world, social issues, theme editions (native rights, abortion, alcoholism, etc.). Newsy approach; bright features of interest to Canadian churchmen. Prefer rough sketch first; freelance usually on assignment only. Our publication is Anglican-slanted, progressive, heavily socially oriented in presenting topical issues, opinionated columnists." Informational, interview, spot news. Length: 750 to 1,200 words. Pays $35 to $250.

CATHOLIC DIGEST, P.O. Box 3090, St. Paul MN 55101. Editor: Fr. Kenneth Ryan. Monthly. Circulation: 500,000. 95% reprint. Buys Catholic magazine rights. Pays on acceptance. Deadlines 4 to 6 months prior to publication. Reports in 2 weeks. Query first. Enclose S.A.S.E.

Nonfiction: Timely subjects; avoid history, lives of saints, visits to shrines, etc., unless new angle. Articles of general interest in science, health, education, travel, humor, etc., plus articles on current religious developments, parish life, and religious leader profiles. Length: 2,000 to 2,500 words. Pays $75 to $200.

Photos: Purchased with mss; strong family interest—interesting church, parish life abroad, etc. Uses one photo feature per issue. Also uses one color shot for cover each month; prefers subject with religious and timely significance. Can work from contact sheets or good selection of 8x10's. Pays $100 per photo feature.

Fillers: Regular features: "In Our Parish", "People Are Like That", "Hearts Are Trumps", "Flights of Fancy", "The Open Door" (about conversion); "Signs of the Times." Pays from $5 to $50.

CATHOLIC LIFE, 9800 Oakland Ave., Detroit MI 48093. Editor: Robert C. Bayer. For middle-aged Catholics, primarily, who are interested in the missionary aspects of the Catholic Church; particularly the PIME Missionaries. Monthly magazine; 32 pages, (5½x7½). Established in 1954. Circulation: 15,900. Buys first North American serial rights. Buys 20 to 30 mss a year. Payment on publication. Will send free sample copy to writer on request. Write for copy of editorial guidelines for writers. Submit Christmas and Lenten season material 4 months in advance. Reports in 2 weeks. Query first for nonfiction. Submit only complete ms for any fillers which might be appropriate. Enclose S.A.S.E.

Nonfiction and Photos: "Articles dealing primarily with PIME Missionaries and in other missionary subjects covering these countries: Burma, Bangladesh, Africa, Equatorial Brazil, Hong Kong, India, Thailand, Japan, the Philippines. Subjects should not be general, but specifically missionary in flavor. Reportorial style desired, with emphasis on missionary subjects. Much too general material on the Church and articles of controversy we can't use." Informational, interview, profile, and inspirational articles. Length: 800 to 1,500 words. Pays 2¢ per word. B&w photos purchased with ms for $2 each. Must be clear, sharp, and definitely illustrate the material.

Fillers: Religious news of a timeless nature. Pays $5 for each 100-or-more-word filler.

CHICAGO STUDIES, Box 665, Mundelein IL 60060. Phone: 312-566-6401, Ext. 61. Editor: George J. Dyer. For Roman Catholic priests and religious educators. Magazine; 112 pages. Established in 1962. Published 3 times a year. Circulation: 5,500. Buys all rights. Buys 30 mss a year. Pays on acceptance. Will send sample copy to writer for $1. Will consider photocopied submissions. Submit complete ms. Reports within 6 weeks. Enclose S.A.S.E.

Nonfiction: Nontechnical discussion of theological, biblical, ethical topics. Articles aimed at a nontechnical presentation of the contemporary scholarship in those fields. Recently published articles include "Speak of the Devil" (an interesting attempt to correlate biblical and theological data with the mythology of science). Length: 3,000 to 5,000 words. Pays $35 to $100.

CHRIST FOR ALL, REACH OUT, Division of Home Missions, Assemblies of God, 1445 Boonville Ave., Springfield MO 65802. Editor: Ruth Lyon. For members and friends of the Assemblies of God who are interested in Home Missions; young adults through senior citizens. Magazine; 8 (8½x11) pages. *Christ for All* established in 1973; *Reach Out* in 1970. Published every 2 months. Circulation: 35,000. Buys all rights. "Our magazines are quite limited in what we could accept from freelance writers. Most of our work is maintained through contributions of interested churches and friends." Pays on publication. Will send free sample copy to writer on request. Write for copy of guidelines for writers. No photocopied or simultaneous submissions. Submit seasonal material 4 to 6 months in advance. "If we can't use material and we think another department can, we usually let them see it before replying. Otherwise, as soon as we reject it, we return it." Query first. Enclose S.A.S.E.

Nonfiction and Photos: "All material must have some religious value. Home Missions subjects related to ethnic groups, Teen Challenge, chaplaincies, New Church Evangelism. Has to be slanted to and acceptable to members of the Assemblies of God, and the material is restricted to Assemblies of God Home Missions. These magazines are promotional and informative in nature, as well as inspiritional. They exist for the purpose of informing people about our Home Missions ministries and promoting these ministries. Studying the magazines will give the writer a 'feel' of what we need. We would be interested in a story about the outstanding work of some A/G home missionary as seen through the eyes of the writer." Length: 500 to 800 words. Pays 1½¢ a word minimum. B&w and color photos purchased at price set by the contributor. "Must be related to our mission work on Indian reservations, among the deaf or blind; ethnic or minority groups in general. Some pictures can be general, especially scenic or depicting culture or native life.

Fiction: Related to seasonal holidays. Length: 500 to 800 words. Pays minium of 1½¢ a word.

THE CHRISTIAN ATHLETE, Fellowship of Christian Athletes, 812 Traders National Bank Bldg., 1125 Grand Avenue, Kansas City MO 64106. Phone: 816-842-3908. Editor: Gary Warner. For "general audience of all ages interested in athletics, especially as it involves the perspective of the Christian faith. Large segment includes high school, college and professional athletes and coaches." Established in 1959. Monthly. Circulation: 50,000. Buys first rights only. Buys 15 to 25 mss a year. Payment on publication. Will send free sample copy and editorial guidelines to writer on request. Uses sport in season and profiles of athletes. Submit seasonal material four months in advance. Reports in one to two weeks. Enclose S.A.S.E.

Nonfiction: Personal testimonies and profiles. Articles related to athletics and the Christian faith. Heart of magazine is personal profile of athlete or coach with spiritual perspective the center of article. Wants stories "with masculine approach; strong, fast-paced articles and profiles. Articles related to issues in athletics and society. Message and place of Jesus Christ focal point. We're one of the only magazines we know of dealing in two worlds of athletics and Christianity. Not a straight sport magazine or specifically religious publication but one which bridges both worlds. Avoid the trite 'goody-goody' articles. Want the Christian perspective included with a man's warts showing. Don't want the sickeningly sweet Sunday school pap." Uses informational, how-to (sport), personal experience, interview, profile, inspirational, humor, and think articles. Length: 200 to 2,500 words. Pays $10 minimum per article.

Photos: Photos used with mss and on assignment, captions optional. B&w 5x7 or 8x10. Pays $10 minimum for b&w photos. "We can take an excellent sports photo showing emotion, drama, conflict, agony, defeat, joy, etc., and build free verse, Scripture verse, etc., around it."

Poetry and Fillers: Uses free and light verse. Also uses clippings and short humor. No payment for poetry and fillers.

THE CHRISTIAN CENTURY, 407 S. Dearborn St., Chicago IL 60605. Editor: James M. Wall. For church people (lay and clerical) of all faiths. Weekly. Payment on publication. Usually buys all rights. Will consider photocopied submissions. Enclose S.A.S.E.
Nonfiction, Photos, and Poetry: "We consider articles of 2,400 words on all subjects of public concern and controversy to which religion is related." Pays 2¢ a word. Buys b&w glossies. Pays $15 to $35. Prefers short poems. No payment.
How To Break In: "Study back issues as a way of getting on our wavelength. Our weekly ecumenical journal has a strong emphasis on political issues, social problems and international affairs as seen from a liberal religious perspective."

CHRISTIAN HERALD, Chappaqua NY 10514. Phone: 914-769-9000. Editor: Kenneth L. Wilson. Independent, nondenominational family monthly. Established in 1878. Circulation: 300,000. Buys all rights. Buys about 50 to 75 mss a year. Pays on acceptance. Will send sample copy to writer for 75¢. Send S.A.S.E. for copy of guidelines for writers. Will consider photocopied submissions. Submit seasonal material 4 months in advance. Reports on material accepted for publication usually within 8 weeks. Returns rejected material in 4 to 6 weeks. Query first for longer articles. Enclose S.A.S.E.
Nonfiction, Photos, and Poetry: Heavy emphasis upon personal, everyday, art-of-living topics. Articles that tell what is happening in field of religion and what it means to the reader. Subjects of broad general interest in a Christian context. First-person stories with religious, moral, social or inspirational implications. Informational, how-to, personal experience, interview, profile, inspirational, humor, historical, nostalgia, personal opinion and photo. Recently published articles include "Are You Panic-Proof?", "The Mystery of Friendship," "What Became of America's Front Porches?", and "In Defense of Ministers' Wives." Length: 1,000 to 3,000 words. Pays $50 minimum for full-length article. "I Protest" department pays $50. 5x7 or 8x10 b&w photos. Pays $10. Uses several poems an issue. Pays $10 minimum.

CHRISTIAN HERITAGE, Box 176, Hackensack NJ 07602. Editor: Rev. Stuart P. Garver. Published monthly except July and August for Protestant evangelicals with an interest in development inside the Roman Catholic Church. Buys first North American serial rights. Reports promptly as a rule; sometimes needs a month in the summer. Enclose S.A.S.E.
Nonfiction: Prefers readable, nonpedantic treatment of Church-State affairs, both historical and current. Interested in fact-filled and interpretive articles on effect of government policies on organized religion. Also in the market for true stories from lives of former clerics who have gone on to successful careers in other fields. Absolutely rejects all anti-Catholic material. Length: 2,200 to 2,500 words. Pay is $15 to $35.

CHRISTIAN LIFE, Union Gospel Press, Box 6059, Cleveland OH 44101. For adults ages 18 and up. Buys exclusive rights only. "Material purchased cannot later be sold to another publisher." Write for copy of guidelines for writers. Enclose S.A.S.E.
Nonfiction and Photos: "We are interested in true stories, biographies, etc., accompanied with photos and/or slides. Writers should be familiar with sound Sunday school literature. Articles on the Holy Land and the history of Christianity; testimonies, essays, how-to articles; short fillers." Length: 900 to 1,500 words. Pays 2¢ a word.
Fiction: Fiction with strong emphasis on Christian living.
Poetry and Fillers: "We use a limited amount of poetry. Each submission should be rich in imagery and figurative language. Themes should be clear and the rhyme and meter should be consistent with the subject." Length of the poems published varies; 16 lines usually. Pays 35¢ per line for poetry. "We consider only puzzles and quizzes that are based on the Bible." Pays $2.50 to $7.50 per puzzle. Also uses short fillers.

CHRISTIAN LIFE MAGAZINE, Gundersen Dr. and Schmale Rd., Wheaton IL 60187. Editor: Robert Walker. For leadership groups in religious circles. Monthly. Buys all rights. Payment on publication. Reports in 2 weeks to 1 month. Query first for longer articles requiring lengthy research. Enclose S.A.S.E.

Nonfiction and Photos: Devotional and missionary articles, features on Christian organizations, accounts of spiritual aid through Christian witness, church building and remodeling. Sunday school teaching techniques. Christian family life, current events in Christian life, and development of schools and colleges. In all articles, Jesus Christ should be exalted and not individual personalities. It is best to read the magazine first to become familiar with approach (a sample will be sent on request). Major features should be 2,500 to 3,000 words. Shorter articles on how problems were overcome or needs met in areas of Sunday school, church building and management, and family relationships are usually 1,500 to 2,000 words. Pays up to $175 for article and pix on publication. Clear, action photos with articles and news stories at $3 to $5.

Fiction: Well-plotted stories built upon significant problems faced by Christians in their life and walk with the Lord. Should be solved by overt character action. 2,500 to 2,800 words preferred. Pays $50 for short-shorts.

CHRISTIAN LIVING, Mennonite Publishing House, 616 Walnut Ave., Scottdale PA 15683. Editor: J. Lorne Peachey. For Christian families. Monthly. Buys first or second rights. Pays on acceptance. Reports in 2 weeks. Submit complete ms. Enclose S.A.S.E.

Nonfiction and Photos: Articles about Christian family life, parent-child relations, marriage, and family-community relations. Material must address itself to one specific family problem and/or concern and show how that problem/concern may be solved. If about a family activity, it should deal only with one such activity in simple, direct language. All material must relate to the adult members of a family, not the children. Length: 1,000 to 1,500 words. Pays up to $30. No additional payment for b&w photos used with mss.

Fiction and Poetry: Short stories on the same themes as above. Length: 1,000 to 2,000 words. Poems related to theme. Length: 25 lines. Pays up to $30 for fiction; minimum of $5 for poetry.

CHRISTIANITY & CRISIS, 537 West 121 St., New York NY 10027. Editor: Wayne H. Cowan. For professional clergy and laymen; politically liberal; interested in ecology, good government, minorities and the church. Journal of 12 to 16 pages, published every 2 weeks. Established in 1941. Circulation: 10,000. Rights purchased vary with author and material. Usually buys all rights. Buys 5 to 10 mss a year. Payment on publication. Will send free sample copy to writer on request. Will consider photocopied and simultaneous submissions. Reports on material in 3 weeks. Enclose S.A.S.E.

Nonfiction: "Our articles are written in-depth, by well-qualified individuals, most of whom are established figures in their respective fields. We offer comment on contemporary, political and social events occurring in the U.S. and abroad. Articles are factual and of high quality. Anything whimsical, superficial, or politically dogmatic would not be considered." Interested in articles on bio-medical ethics, new community projects; informational articles and book reviews. Length: open. Pays $25 to $50.

How To Break In: "It is difficult for a freelancer to break in here but not impossible. Several authors we now go to on a regular basis came to us unsolicited and we always have a need for fresh material. Book reviews are short (800 to 1,500 words) and may be a good place to start, but you should query first. Another possibility is Viewpoints which also runs short pieces. Here we depend on people with a lot of expertise in their fields to write concise comments on current problems. If you have some real area of authority, this would be a good section to try."

CHRISTIANITY TODAY, 1014 Washington Building, Washington DC 20005. Editor/Publisher: Harold Lindsell. Theologically conservative journal for the clergy and informed laymen. Usually buys all rights. Query first. Enclose S.A.S.E.

Nonfiction: This is a very specialized publication. Do not submit without thoroughly studying the magazine. Most of content is staff-written or done on assignment. Material must be theologically precise, authoritative and highly readable. No biography. Uses essays written from an evangelical (Biblical) Protestant perspective on crucial contemporary issues and indicating the driving relevance of the Christian revelation to the modern scene. Length: 1,500 to 2,000 words. Pays $50 minimum.

CHURCH AND STATE, 8120 Fenton St., Silver Spring MD 20910. Managing Editor: Edd Doerr. Assistant Editor: Albert Menendez. For people with religious liberty and church/state interests. Monthly magazine; 24 pages. Established in 1948. Circulation: 130,000. Buys first North American serial rights. Buys 8 mss a year. Payment on acceptance. Will send free sample copy to writer on request. Submit only complete ms. Enclose S.A.S.E.

Nonfiction and Photos: "Devoted exclusively to news and analysis of problems concerning religious liberty and the interaction of political and religious institutions. We are interested in studies of church-state problems in all countries of the world, and such issues as religious influences in politics and public policy, religious education in public schools, Vatican diplomacy, religious discrimination, etc. We are frankly partisan and vigorously espouse the principle of separation of church and state, full religious liberty and religiously neutral public education." Informational, historical, think articles, expose, personal opinion, and book reviews. Length: 800 to 1,600 words. Pays $25 to $50 per ms. B&w photos purchased with accompanying ms. Captions required. Pay varies.

THE CHURCH HERALD, 630 Myrtle St., N.W., Grand Rapids MI 49504. Editor: Dr. John Stapert. For members and pastors in Reformed Church in America. Publication of the Reformed Church in America. Magazine; 32 (8½x11) pages. Established in 1826. Published every 2 weeks. Circulation: 74,500. Rights purchased vary with author and material. Buys all rights, first serial rights, or second serial (reprint) rights. Buys about 30 mss a year. Pays on acceptance. Will send free sample copy to writer on request. Write for copy of guidelines for writers. Will consider photocopied and simultaneous submissions. Submit material for major Christian holidays 2 months in advance. Reports in less than 2 weeks. Submit complete ms only. Enclose S.A.S.E.

Nonfiction and Photos: "We expect all of our articles to be helpful and constructive, even when a point of view is vigorously presented. Articles on subjects such as Christianity and culture, government and politics, forms of worship, the media, ethics and business relations, responsible parenthood, marriage and divorce, death and dying, challenges on the campus, drug addiction, alcoholism, Christian education, human interest stories within the church, good news of God's blessings, praise, etc. In-depth interviews on religious themes with noted church or national leaders. Articles by or about a well-known and respected Christian doctor, attorney, businessman, teacher, judge, nurse or labor leader, showing how he faces his responsibilities, deals with his problems, and finds a Christian solution, with quotes and anecdotes to illustrate. We are also looking for material that will help us to build a somewhat younger readership, particularly readers in their teens and twenties." Length: 400 to 1,400 words. Pays 2¢ to 3¢ per word. Photos purchased with accompanying ms with no additional payment. Purchased without ms also. Captions optional. Pays $5 to $15 for 8x10 b&w glossy.

Fiction, Poetry, and Fillers: Religious fiction. Length: 400 to 1,400 words. Pays 2¢ to 3¢ per word. Traditional forms of poetry. Length: 30 lines maximum. Pays $5 to $15. Jokes and short humor. Length: about 80 words.

THE CHURCHMAN, 1074 23rd Ave., N., St. Petersburg FL 33704. Editor: Edna Ruth Johnson. For people who think; who care about mankind. Magazine, (8x11). Established in 1804. Monthly, October through March; bimonthly, April through September. Circulation: 10,000. Not copyrighted. Buys about 12 mss a year. Pays on acceptance. Will send free sample copy to writer on request. Will consider photocopied submissions. No simultaneous submissions. Reports within a month. Submit complete ms. Enclose S.A.S.E.

Nonfiction: Sociological, religious and, sometimes, political material. Although founded by Episcopal leadership, this publication is interdenominational, inter-faith, and relevant to today's troubled world. Inspirational, historical, think pieces, expose. Length: 500 to 1,000 words. Pays $10.

COLUMBIA, P.O. Drawer 1670, New Haven CT 06507. Editor: Elmer Von Feldt. For Catholic families; caters particularly to members of the Knights of Columbus. Monthly magazine. Established in 1920. Circulation: 1,200,000. Buys all rights. Buys 50 mss a year. Payment on acceptance. Will send free sample copy to writer on request. Write for copy of guidelines for writers. Submit seasonal material 6 months in advance. Reports in 4 weeks. Query first or submit complete ms. Enclose S.A.S.E.
Nonfiction and Photos: Fact articles directed to the Catholic layman and his family and dealing with current events, social problems, Catholic apostolic activities, education, ecumenism, rearing a family, literature, science, arts, sports and leisure. Length: 1,000 to 3,000 words. Glossy photos (8x10) b&w are required for illustration. Articles without ample illustrative material are not given consideration. Payment ranges from $200 to $400, including photos. Photo stories are also wanted. Pays $15 per photo used and 10¢ per word.
Fiction: Written from a thoroughly Christian viewpoint. Length: 3,000 words maximum. Pays $300 maximum. Humor or satire should be directed to current religious, social or cultural conditions. Pays up to $100 for about 1,000 words.

COMMONWEAL, 232 Madison Ave., New York NY 10016. Editor: James O'Gara. Edited by Roman Catholic laymen. For college-educated audience. Special book and education issues. Biweekly. Circulation: 25,000. Buys 75 mss a year. Pays on acceptance. Will send a sample copy to a writer on request. Submit seasonal material 2 months in advance. Reports in 3 weeks. "A number of our articles come in over-the-transom. I suggest a newcomer either avoid particularly sensitive areas (say, politics) or let us know something about you (your credentials, tearsheets, a paragraph about yourself)." Enclose S.A.S.E.
Nonfiction: "Articles on timely subjects: political, literary, religious." Original, brightly written mss on value-oriented themes. Buys think pieces. Length: 1,000 to 2,500 words. Pays 2¢ a word.
Poetry: Contemporary and avant-garde. Length: maximum 150 lines ("long poems very rarely"). Pays $7.50 to $25. Poetry Editor: John Fandel.

THE COMPANION OF ST. FRANCIS AND ST. ANTHONY, 15 Chestnut Park Rd., Toronto M4W 1W5, Ontario, Canada. Editor: Rev. Leo Linder, OFM Conv. For Catholic families. Monthly magazine; 32 pages (9x6). Circulation: 10,000. Buys first rights. Buys about 100 mss a year. Pays on acceptance or publication. Will send sample copy to writer on request. Write for copy of guidelines for writers. Submit seasonal material 4 months in advance. Reports in 6 to 8 weeks. Query first. Enclose S.A.E. with International Reply coupons.
Nonfiction: Treatment of national and international problems, modern, moral and social issues welcome. Should be Christian in outlook, and slanted toward family reading. Recently published articles include "The Retarded Have Hidden Assets," "What Is True Happiness?", "We Can Accept or Reject Christ," and "Can Money Change People?". Length: 1,200 to 1,500 words. Pays 2¢ per word.
Photos: Purchased with mss, subject matter relating to article. Negatives or glossy photos, 5x7 or 8x10. Payment based on photos used and quality; approximately $2 to $3 per photo, more if suitable for use on cover.
Fiction: Easy reading and interest are primary considerations. While objectively stories should tend toward better Christian living, welcomes the use of humor and satire, and tongue-in-cheek treatment. 1,200 to 1,500 words. Pays 2¢ per word.

THE CONGREGATIONALIST, 801 Bushnell, Beloit WI 53511. Editor: Dr. Louis B. Gerhardt. "This is the publication of the National Association of Congregational Christian Churches. Readers tend to be members of our churches, or generally spiritually oriented people." Monthly magazine; 24 pages (8½x11). Established in 1840. Circulation: 10,000. Rights purchased vary with author and material. Usually buys all rights. Buys 80 to 160 mss a year. Payment on publication. Will send free sample copy to writer on request. Write for copy of editorial guidelines for writers. Submit Thanksgiving, Christmas, Lent and Easter material at least 3 months in advance. Will consider photocopied and simultaneous submissions. Reports in 3 to 4 weeks. Submit only complete ms. Enclose S.A.S.E.

Nonfiction: Articles and miscellaneous features affirming the goodness of man and his spiritual nature. "We accept a wide range of religious views, and welcome views on controversial subjects not generally covered in religious magazines." Length: 300 to 2,500 words. Pays $15 to $50.
Fiction: Experimental, mainstream, religious, and historical fiction on any theme. Length: 300 to 2,500 words. Pays $15 to $50.
Poetry and Fillers: Traditional forms, blank verse, free verse, avant-garde forms, light verse, and religious poetry. Length: 2 lines minimum; no maximum. Pays $5 minimum. Pays $5 to $15 for religious puzzles.

CONTACT, 44 East Franklin Street, Room 302, Huntington IN 46750. Phone: 219-356-2120. Editor: Stanley Peters. Publication of the Church of the United Brethren in Christ. For adult and high school youth audience. Weekly. Circulation: 7,500. Not copyrighted. Will accept material for first use, reprints, and simultaneous submissions. Pays on acceptance. Will send a sample copy to a writer on request. Write for copy of guidelines for writers. Deadlines are 8 months in advance. Reports in 6 to 10 weeks. Submit complete ms. Enclose S.A.S.E.
Nonfiction and Photos: "Biographical sketches of noteworthy living and historical Christians, 'how-to' articles in churches and related organizations; also some on self-improvement, inspirational articles that avoid 'preachiness' and are liberally illustrated with anecdotes." Length: 1,300 to 1,500 words, "nothing longer unless strong enough content to merit division into parts of 1,200 to 1,500 words each." Pays 1¢ per word for first-time use, ¾¢ per word for reprints. Photos purchased with mss; subject matter appropriate to article. B&w glossies. Pays $1 each.
Fiction: Slanted to both youth and adults, or either group. Strongly plotted with a definite resolution which comes as a result of the action. Up to 1,500 words in length. Payment same as for nonfiction.
Poetry: Uses occasional short poems with real messages. Up to 30 lines in length.
Fillers: Newsbreaks and short humor of 50 to 250 words. Same payment as for nonfiction.

THE COVENANT COMPANION, 5101 N. Francisco Ave., Chicago IL 60625. Phone: 312-561-9424. Editor: James R. Hawkinson. "For putting Covenanters in touch with each other and the wider Christian world and promoting our common Christian Mission as a church." Publication of the Evangelical Covenant Church of America. Semimonthly magazine published on the 1st and 15th of each month. Established in the early 1900's. Circulation: 34,000. Rights purchased vary with author and material. May buy all rights; first rights, but will reassign rights to author after publication; second serial (reprint) rights (for lesser fee) or simultaneous rights. Buys 10 to 15 mss a year. Payment on publication. Will send free sample copy to writer on request. Will consider photocopied and simultaneous submissions, provided copyright is clear. Submit seasonal material (Christmas, Easter, Labor Day, Independence Day) 3 months in advance. Usually reports on material accepted for publication 6 weeks before publication. Query first or submit complete ms. Enclose S.A.S.E.
Nonfiction and Photos: "We center on articles of religious interest; subjects relating to Christian life and faith. We prefer pieces submitted from the author's own conviction. Subjects or themes would be determined by the freelancer's convictions concerning what needs doing from his or her point of view." Manuscripts should be typed at 70 characters per line. Length varies from 50 to 60 lines to 110 lines. Pays $10 to $15. B&w photos purchased with or without accompanying mss. Pays $5. Color prints with good contrast are also used. "No color slides, please."

CROSS AND CROWN, 1909 S. Ashland Ave., Chicago IL 60608. Phone: 312-226-0074. Editor: The Very Rev. John J. McDonald, O.P. For all who are genuinely interested in spiritual advancement. Buys all rights, but right to reuse the material is assigned back without charge if credit line is given to *Cross and Crown.* Payment on publication. Query first or submit complete ms. Enclose S.A.S.E.
Nonfiction: Articles that present a serious examination of important truths pertinent to the spiritual life, but placed in the context of today's world. Scriptural, biographical,

doctrinal, liturgical, and ecumenical articles are acceptable. Length: 3,000 to 4,000 words. Pays 1¢ per word.

DAILY BLESSING, P.O. Box 2187, Tulsa OK 74102. Phone: 918-743-6161, Ext. 342. Managing Editor: Billye Morris. Quarterly. Buys all rights. Pays on acceptance. Will send a sample copy to a writer on request. Write for writer's guide. Reports in 2 to 3 months. Enclose S.A.S.E.
Nonfiction: Slanted to make faith in God relevant, meaningful and inspirational in everyday life. "A good meditation includes an illustration, a human experience, anecdote, or example which illustrates the idea presented in the Scripture passage. A good meditation should develop one idea only, with freshness and vitality. Share an experience or idea in a way that blesses the reader and leads him into a spirit of worship. Avoid poetry, controversy, death and war scenes, threadbare illustrations, and overworked themes, criticism of other groups, pious preachments, and quotations from copyrighted sources without permission to quote." Length: 50 characters to a line, 27 lines including title and Scripture verse. Make a thorough study of writers' guide and sample magazine. Pays $5 to $15.
Photos: Scenic, seasonal covers: 4x5 color transparencies or 35mm slides. Pays $35 to $75. Also scenic and mood b&w glossies. Pays $7.50 to $10.

DAILY MEDITATION, P.O. Box 2710, San Antonio TX 78299. Editor: Ruth S. Paterson. Issued bimonthly. Rights purchased vary with author and material. Buys first serial rights when material warrants it, and very occasionally buys reprint material. Freely gives permission to writers to resubmit to others after publication. Payment on acceptance. Will send sample copy to writer on request. Reports within 60 days. Submit complete ms. Enclose S.A.S.E.
Nonfiction: Uses metaphysical teachings, inspirational articles (seasonal articles 6 months in advance), nonsectarian religious articles (emphasis on how to apply principles to reader's life). Length: 750, 1,250 and 1,650 words. (Exact word count must be stated on ms.) Pays ½¢ to 1½¢ a word.
Poetry: Along same lines as above. Length: 16 lines maximum. Pays 14¢ per line.

DAILY WORD, Unity Village MO 64063. Editor: M. Smock. Published by the Unity School of Christianity. A monthly manual of daily studies. Copyrighted. Buys a limited number of short articles and poems. Writer must have an understanding of Unity teachings. Reports in 2 to 3 weeks. Enclose S.A.S.E.
Nonfiction and Poetry: To 1,000 words. Pays 3¢ a word and up. Poetry to 16 lines. Pays 25¢ a line and up.

DECISION MAGAZINE, 1300 Harmon Place, Minneapolis MN 55403. Phone: 612-332-8081. Editor: Dr. Sherwood E. Wirt. Conservative evangelical monthly publication. Buys all rights unless otherwise arranged. Payment on publication. Reports within 2 months. Enclose S.A.S.E.
Nonfiction: Uses little freelance material; best opportunity is in testimony area (1,600 to 2,000 words). Also uses short narratives, 400 to 750 words. "Our function is to present Christ as Savior and Lord to unbelievers and present articles on deeper Christian life for Christian readers. No tangents. Center on Christ in all material." Pays $60 minimum per article.
Poetry: Uses devotional thoughts and short poetry in "Quiet Heart" column. Also has "Editorial Feature" section which uses verse poems, free verse, brief narrative, illustration. No "preaching" or negativism. Positive, Christ-centered. Pays $5 to $25, depending on length of poem and on what page of magazine it appears.
Fillers: Uses fresh quotations from known or unknown individuals, devotional thoughts. Pays $3 per item.

THE DISCIPLE, Box 179, St. Louis MO 63166. Published by Christian Board of Publication of the Christian Church (Disciples of Christ). For ministers and church members, both young and older adults. Weekly. Circulation: 102,000. Buys first rights. Payment on publication. Payment for photos made at end of month of acceptance. Will send a sample copy to a writer for 25¢. Write for copy of guidelines for writers. Will consider photocopied submissions. Submit seasonal material at least 3 months in advance. Reports in several weeks. Enclose S.A.S.E.

Nonfiction: Articles and meditations on religious, historical, inspirational, "how-to-do-it" themes; short pieces. Length: 500 to 800 words. Pays $3 to $7.50. Also uses devotionals of 200 to 500 words for "A Faith for Today" page. Pays $5.

Photos: B&w glossies, 8x10. Occasional b&w glossies, any size, used to illustrate articles. Pays $1 to $5. Pays $5 to $15 when used for covers. No color. Occasionally runs a series, such as religious sculpture, photos of stained glass windows, etc.

Fiction: Occasionally buys short stories. Religious, inspirational, sports, family life or humorous, with not-too-obvious religious or ethical application. Length: 700 to 1,000 words. Pays $10.

Poetry: Uses 3 to 5 poems per issue. All lengths. Themes may be seasonal, historical, religious, occasionally humorous. Pays $1 to $5.

EMMANUEL, 194 E. 76th St., New York NY 10021. Phone: 212-861-1076. Editor: The Rev. Paul J. Bernier, S.S.S. Issued monthly for the Catholic clergy. Rights to be arranged with author. Pays on publication. Enclose S.A.S.E.

Nonfiction: Articles of Catholic (especially priestly) spirituality; can be biographical, historical or critical. Articles on Eucharistic theology, and those which provide a solid scriptural and/or theological foundation for priestly spirituality (prayer, applied spirituality, etc.). Aims at providing today's priest with an adequate theology and philosophy of ministry in today's church. Length: 1,500 to 3,000 words. Usually pays $50.

EMPHASIS ON FAITH & LIVING, 336 Dumfries Ave., Kitchener, Ontario, Canada N2H 2G1. Editor: Dr. Everek R. Storms. Official organ of The Missionary Church. For Church members. Magazine is published twice a month in U.S.A. but serves the Missionary Church in both the U.S. and Canada. Established in 1969. Circulation: 9,000. Not copyrighted. Buys "only a few" mss a year. Will consider photocopied and simultaneous submissions. Uses a limited amount of seasonal material, submitted 3 months in advance. Reports in 1 month. Submit only complete ms. Enclose S.A.S.E.

Nonfiction: Religious articles, presenting the truths of the Bible to appeal to today's readers. "We take the Bible literally and historically. It has no errors, myths, or contradictions. Articles we publish must have this background. No poetry, please. Especially would like articles covering the workings of the Holy Spirit in today's world." Length: approximately 500 words—"not too long". Pays $5 to $10 per ms.

ENGAGE/SOCIAL ACTION, 100 Maryland Ave., N.E., Washington DC 20002. Editor: Allan R. Brockway. For "United Methodist and United Church of Christ clergy and lay people interested in in-depth analysis of social issues, particularly the church's role or involvement in these issues." Established in 1973. Monthly. Circulation: 9,000. Rights purchased vary with author and material. May buy all rights and reassign rights to author after publication. Buys about 30 mss a year. Pays on publication. Will send free sample copy to writer on request. Write for copy of guidelines for writers. Will consider photocopied submissions, but prefers original. Returns rejected material in 1 week. Reports on material accepted for publication in several weeks. Query first or submit complete ms. Enclose S.A.S.E.

Nonfiction and Photos: "This is the social action publication of the United Methodist Church and the United Church of Christ (published by the Board of Church and Society of the United Methodist Church in cooperation with the Council for Christian Social Action of the United Church of Christ). We publish articles relating to current social issues as well as church-related discussions. We do not publish highly technical articles or poetry. Our publication tries to relate social issues to the church—what the church can do, is doing; why the church should be involved. We only accept articles relating to social issues, e.g., war, draft, peace, race relations, welfare, police/community relations, labor, population problems. Reviews of books and music should focus on related subjects." Length: 1,500 words maximum. Pays $35 to $50. 8x10 b&w glossy photos purchased with or without mss. Captions required. Pays $15.

ETERNITY MAGAZINE, 1716 Spruce St., Philadelphia PA 19103. Editor: Russell T. Hitt. For the "religiously conservative layman (rather than the ecclesiastical professional); all points on the spectrum, politically". Monthly; 70 (8x11) pages. Established in 1950. Circulation: 55,000. Buys all rights. Buys very few mss a year. Payment on acceptance. Will send free sample copy to writer on request. Write for copy of guidelines for writers. Will consider photocopied submissions. Submit seasonal material (Christmas, Easter) 3 to 4 months in advance. Reports in 6 to 8 weeks. Submit complete ms. Enclose S.A.S.E.

Nonfiction and Photos: "We seek to be issue-oriented rather than devotional. We look at news trends or events from the perspective of Christian truths which we feel are eternal. Our slant is toward mature Christians who are interested in Bible study and the Biblical emphasis of contemporary developments. Most of our articles are assigned to specific writers who are authorities on various subjects and, consequently, we accept only a very small percentage of freelance mss submitted to us. We are interested primarily in well-written and organized articles on devotional, doctrinal and expository subjects. Occasionally articles dealing with some phase of missionary activity are acceptable. These are enhanced when accompanied by good photographs. We are not opposed to dealing with controversial subjects, especially if they concern important issues which need to be faced courageously. We are not interested in sensational articles which are primarily journalistic. We see too many uninspired expositions of a passage of Scripture; too many pastors' sermons, too many vague, abstract articles that aren't substantiated. The seasonal material that we use for Christmas and Easter must not be trite." Article length: 700 to 2,000 words. Pays $35 to $50. Also uses book essays. These are not reviews, but articles on a genre such as Christian fantasy (Lewis, Tolkien, etc.). Length: 1,000 to 1,200 words. Pays $35 to $50. "The Last Word" uses short, clever or warm pieces to close the magazine. Length: 600 words. Pays $15 to $30.

THE EVANGELICAL BEACON, 1515 E. 66th St., Minneapolis MN 55423. Phone: 612-866-3343. Editor: George Keck. For Evangelical and conservative Protestant audience. Issued biweekly. Buys first rights. Pays on publication. Will send free sample copy to a writer on request. Reports on submissions in 3 to 4 weeks. Enclose S.A.S.E.

Nonfiction and Photos: Devotional material, articles on the church, people and their accomplishments. Recently published articles include "The Search for Noah's Ark," a description of Mt. Ararat expeditions; "Contrasting Conversions," a story of different ways people come to faith; "In the Company of the Vinedresser," how God helped a young mother faced with possible crippling illness. Length: 500 to 1,800 words. Pays ½¢ per word. Photos purchased with captions only. Prefers 8x10's. Pays $3 and up.

EVANGELICAL FRIEND, P.O. Box 232, Newberg OR 97132. Editor: Jack L. Willcuts. Managing Editor: Harlow Ankeny. Audience is conservative Christian families, mainly of the Friends (Quaker) church denomination. Monthly except August. Circulation: 10,700. Not copyrighted. Rarely pays for material. Will send sample copy on request. Reports within one month. Enclose S.A.S.E.

Nonfiction: Varied articles of interest to Christian families. Particularly interested in articles of "how to meet life's crises," meeting human hurts, etc. Write for definite article needs. Most done on assignment. Most articles donated.

Photos: With captions only. Thematic, landscapes, people, illustrations to be used with specific articles. 8x10 glossies preferred. Negatives borrowed if small cropping desired. Pays $5 to $15 for one-time use.

EVANGELICAL RECORDER, 16 Spadina Rd., Toronto, Ontario, Canada, M5R 2S8. Editor: Douglas C. Percy. For clergymen, Church workers, religious folk. Quarterly magazine; 28 (8½x11) pages. Established in 1896. Circulation: 12,500. Not copyrighted. Buys very few mss; "most are contributed." Will send free sample copy to writer on request. Submit seasonal material 4 months in advance. Query first or submit complete ms. Enclose S.A.E. and International Reply Coupons.

Nonfiction: Religious, social, and national material. "We try to maintain a biblical stance even in seemingly non-biblical subjects. Writers would have to be familiar with the Bible. The Christian home, national and personal morality are good subjects." Informational, personal experience, interview, inspirational, humor, think articles, nostalgia, photo, book reviews, and spot news. Length: 600 to 1,500 words.

EVANGELIZING TODAY'S CHILD, P. O. Box 1156, Grand Rapids MI 49501. Director of Periodicals: Rev. Paul W. Bennehoff; Editor: Milt Bryon. Bimonthly. Circulation: 38,000. Interdenominational, international and interracial Christian publication for teachers. Usually buys one-time rights. Pays on acceptance. Will send editorial guide to writer on request. Reports in two months. Enclose S.A.S.E.
Nonfiction: For "Reach and Teach", uses how-to-do-it articles on programs, projects and other topics of interest to Sunday school superintendents, teachers, and leaders of other children's groups. Length: 300 to 1,200 words. Pays 2½¢ per word for first rights.

FAITH AT WORK, 11065 Little Patuxent Pkwy., Columbia MD 21044 Editor: Walden Howard. For clergymen and decisionmaking laymen in a cross section of Christian churches of all denominations (Protestant and Catholic). Established in 1888. Eight times a year. Circulation: 40,000. Buys all rights, but will reassign rights to author after publication. Buys 10 to 12 mss a year. Pays on publication. Will send free sample copy to writer on request. Will consider photocopied submissions. Reports promptly. Query first or submit complete ms. Enclose S.A.S.E.
Nonfiction and Photos: Personal experience articles relating Christian conversion, growth and ministry. Must reflect a particular Christian life style and commitment to Christ lived out in community with others. Length: 1,200 to 2,000 words. Pays $50 to $100. Pays minimum of $10 for b&w glossies used with mss.
How To Break In: "Probably the best way a writer can break in is to keep in mind our audience, since we publish very specialized material for our readers. Of special interest would be first-person experience stories, telling of discoveries made in spiritual growth. Stories that show openness, honesty and caring prevail in a happy, spiritual growth."

FRIAR, Butler NJ 07405. Editor: Father Rudolf Harvey. For families. Established in 1954. 11 times a year. Not copyrighted. Pays on acceptance. Enclose S.A.S.E.
Nonfiction: Uses articles and features on current problems or events; profiles of notable individuals; trends in sociology and education. Length: 1,800 to 3,000 words. Minimum payment of $15.

FRIDAY FORUM (OF THE JEWISH EXPONENT), 226 S. 16th St., Philadelphia PA 19103. Editor: Phyllis Z. Miller. For the Jewish community of Greater Philadelphia. Newspaper supplement. Established in 1971. Monthly. Circulation: 70,000. Usually buys all rights, but will reassign rights to author after publication. Buys about 40 mss a year. Pays on publication. Will send free sample copy to writer on request. Will consider photocopied submissions. No simultaneous submissions. Submit special material 6 months in advance. Reports on material accepted for publication in 2 months. Returns rejected material in 1 month. Query first. Enclose S.A.S.E.
Nonfiction and Photos: "We are interested only in articles of Jewish themes, whether they be historical, thought pieces, Jewish travel sites, photographic essays, or any other piece on a Jewish theme. Topical themes are appreciated." Recently published "The Story of Ruth," an unusually good Holocaust story. Length: 6 to 12 double-spaced pages. Pays $15 minimum. 8x10 b&w glossies purchased on assignment. Captions required.
Poetry: Traditional forms, blank verse, free verse, avant-garde forms, light verse; must relate to theme. Length varies. Pays $5 minimum.

GOOD NEWS, 329 E. Main, Wilmore KY 40390. Editor: Charles W. Keysor. "*Good News* is a voice for Bible-believing Christians within the United Methodist Church. Our subscribers are largely middle-age, middle-income people." Quarterly magazine;

75 (5½x8½) pages. Established in 1967. Circulation: 10,000. Buys "very few" mss a year. Almost all material is contributed (without payment). Will send free sample copy to writer on request. Will consider photocopied and simultaneous submissions. Query first. Enclose S.A.S.E.

Nonfiction: "All of our material is Bible-centered or has to do with religion and the work of the church; the spiritual experience of the Christian, etc." Inspirational, informational, personal experience, interview, think articles, personal opinion. Length: open.

Poetry: Must relate to subject matter. Traditional forms, blank verse, free verse.

GOOD NEWS BROADCASTER, Box 82808, Lincoln NE 68501. Phone: 402-435-2171, Ext. 261. Editor: Theodore H. Epp. Interdenominational magazine for adults from 17 years of age. Monthly. Circulation: 200,000. Buys first rights. Buys approximately 45 mss a year. Pays on acceptance. Will send a sample copy and an author guide sheet to a writer on request. Send all mss to Thomas S. Piper, Managing Editor. Submit seasonal material at least 6 months in advance. Reports in 1 month. Query preferred, but not required. Enclose S.A.S.E.

Nonfiction and Photos: Articles which will help the reader learn and apply Christian biblical principles to his life. From the writer's or the subject's own experience. "Especially looking for true, personal experience 'salvation', 'youth' (17 years and over), 'parents', and 'how to live the Christian life' articles." Nothing dogmatic, or preachy, or sugary sweet, or without biblical basis. Details or statistics should be authentic and verifiable. Style should be conservative but concise. Length: maximum 1,500 words. Pays 3¢ per word, more in special cases. Photos sometimes purchased with mss. Pays $5 to $10, b&w glossies; $25 to $35, color transparencies; $25, 35mm color.

How To Break In: "The basic purpose of the magazine is to present Christ to the lost as Saviour and to promote the spiritual growth of believers, so don't ignore our primary purposes when writing for us. Nonfiction should be biblical and timely; biblical at least in principle. Write about ways to enrich family living, give solutions to people's problems, aids to help Christians live their daily experiences while working or relaxing — on the job, at home, in church, at school, in the community, or on the home or foreign mission field. Communicate spiritual truths in a positive way and without preaching at anyone or dogmatically telling the reader what he has to do. Show a clear progression of thought throughout the article. Use illustrations of your own experiences or of someone else's when God solved a problem similar to the reader's. Be so specific that the meanings and significance will be crystal clear to all readers. We prefer third person articles as a rule."

GOSPEL CARRIER, Pentecostal Church of God of America, P.O. Box 850, Joplin MO 64801. Phone: 417-624-7050. Editor: Marthel Wilson. A Sunday school take-home paper for adults. Quarterly in weekly parts. Buys one-time rights. Also buys second rights and will accept simultaneous submissions. Will send a sample copy to a writer on request. Deadlines for seasonal material are 6 months in advance. Reports in 30 to 45 days. Enclose S.A.S.E.

Nonfiction: "The emphasis here rarely applies to social Christianity. We prefer articles dealing with the deeper Christian commitment. There's a need for human interest articles and special-day and seasonal materials such as Mother's and Father's Day, Thanksgiving, Spring, Winter, etc. Check all bible references carefully, using only King James version unless other version used is specified. Spell out all references in full. Use anecdotes to make your articles more interesting and avoid uninteresting preachments and hackneyed doctrinal expositions. Taboos are tobacco, drinking, dancing." Length: 800 to 1,200 words. Pays ½¢ a word.

Fiction: "Do not add on the spiritual emphasis; make it a logical extension of the story. Avoid miraculous solutions which do not grow out of the story plot. Make your story believable." Religious theme must be basic to the story. 1,000 to 1,800 words. Pays ½¢ per word.

Fillers: "We purchase stories in brief, short personal testimonies, brief sketches from the lives of great Christians." Length: 2 paragraphs to 500 words. Pays $1 minimum. Usually pays ½¢ a word.

GOSPEL HERALD, 616 Walnut Ave., Scottdale PA 15683. Phone: 412-887-7598. Editor: Daniel Hertzler. Issued weekly (50 issues per year) for adult members of the Mennonite Church. Buys first and second rights. Pays on acceptance. Enclose S.A.S.E.
Nonfiction: "Articles used are of a devotional and inspirational nature. Most articles are solicited." Recently published articles include "Service as Lifestyle" and "It's Our World: What Shall We Do About It?". Length: 300 to 1,500 words. Pays minimum of 1½¢ per word.

GUIDEPOSTS MAGAZINE, 747 Third Ave., New York NY 10017. Editorial Director: Arthur Gordon. *Guideposts* is an inspirational monthly magazine for all faiths in which men and women from all walks of life tell how they overcame obstacles, rose above failures, met sorrow, learned to conquer themselves, and became more effective people through the direct application of the religious principles by which they live. Buys all rights, but will reassign rights to author on request, after publication. Enclose S.A.S.E.
Nonfiction and Fillers: Articles and features should be written in simple, anecdotal style with an emphasis on human interest. Recently published articles include "Don't Leave Me" (a housewife learns about love through the needs of a frightened child); "Arrest Jesse Watson!" (how faith helped a sheriff facing an armed fugitive); "A Rose for Mrs. Jolie" (high school girl tells how she solved a bad relationship with a teacher). Short features up to approximately 250 words ($10 to $25) would be considered for such *Guideposts* features as "Fragile Moments," and other short items which appear at the end of major articles. Short mss of approximately 250 to 750 words ($25 to $100) would be considered for such features as "Quiet People" and general one-page stories. Full-length mss, 750 to 1,500 words ($200 to $300). All mss should be typed, double-spaced and accompanied by a stamped, self-addressed envelope. Inspirational newspaper, or magazine clippings often form the basis of articles in *Guideposts,* but it is unable to pay for material of this type and will not return clippings unless the sender specifically asks and encloses postage for return. Annually awards scholarships to high school juniors and seniors.
How To Break In: "The freelancer would have the best chance of breaking in by aiming for a one-page or maybe two-page article. That would be very short, say two-and-a-half pages of typescript, but in a small magazine such things are very welcome. A sensitively written anecdote that could provide us with an additional title is extremely useful. And they are much easier to just sit down and write than to have to go through the process of preparing a query. They should be warm, well-written, intelligent, and upbeat. We like personal narratives that are true and have some universal relevance, but the religious element does not have to be hammered home with a sledge hammer. Address short items to Diana Donohue."

HIGH ADVENTURE, 1445 Boonville Ave., Springfield MO 65802. Editor: Johnnie Barnes. For boys and men. 16 (8½x11) pages. Established in 1971. Quarterly. Circulation: 30,000. Rights purchased vary with author and material. Buys approximately 10 to 12 mss a year. Pays on publication. Will send free sample copy to writer on request. Write for copy of guidelines for writers. "All articles submitted are held in our files. When the decision is made to use an article in a specific issue, then a check will be sent to the author for the article." Query first or submit complete ms. Enclose S.A.S.E.
Nonfiction, Fiction, Photos, and Fillers: Camping articles, nature stories, fiction adventure stories, and jokes. Nature study and campcraft articles about 500 to 600 words. Buys how-to, personal experience, inspirational, humor, and historical articles. Pays $10 per page. Photos purchased on assignment. Adventure and Western fiction wanted. Length: 1,200 words. Puzzles, jokes and short humor used as fillers.

INSIGHT, Box 7244, Grand Rapids MI 49510. Phone: 616-241-5616. Editor: Rev. James C. Lont. For young people; most well-exposed to the Christian faith; intellectual and spiritual levels range from basic to outstanding; vast range of exposure represented. Monthly magazine. Established in 1921. Circulation: 25,000. Not copyrighted. Buys 8 to 10 mss a year. Payment on acceptance. Will send free sample copy to writer on request. Write for copy of guidelines for writers. Seasonal material (having to do with Christmas, summer themes, Thanksgiving, etc.) should be submitted 6 months in advance. Will consider photocopied and simultaneous submissions. Reports in 2 to 3 weeks. Submit complete ms for fiction. Query first or submit complete ms for nonfiction. Enclose S.A.S.E.

Nonfiction and Photos: "Articles that deal biblically with the practical aspects of the Christian life." Personal experience, profile, inspirational, humor. Pays $10 to $35. B&w glossies purchased with or without mss. Captions optional. Pays $10 to $15.

Fiction and Poetry: "Short stories which lead our readers into a better understanding of how their Christian beliefs apply to their daily living." Humorous, science fiction, and religious fiction. Open on story themes. Length: open. Pays $15 to $35. Buys traditional and avant-garde forms of poetry; blank verse, free verse, and light verse. Theme and length: open. Pays $10 to $25.

INTERACTION, 3558 S. Jefferson, St. Louis MO 63118. Co-editors: Mervin Marguardt, Paul Pallmeyer. Monthly. Buys first rights. Will accept simultaneous submission of articles and short stories. Payment on acceptance. Usually reports within 6 weeks. Enclose S.A.S.E.

Nonfiction and Photos: Accepts practical articles that are directed to church school teachers and leaders, as well as articles on various aspects of general education and pieces directed to teachers as persons. Articles should be written in a popular, readable style. Preferred length: 1,000 to 1,500 words. Pays $20 to $50 per article, depending on length and quality. Buys 5x7 or larger b&w photographs with mss for $5 to $10 each.

Fiction: Considered if it makes a point which will aid the church school teacher to gain new perspective of, or insights for, the teaching of the faith. Preferred length: 1,000 to 1,500 words. Pays $20 to $50 per short story.

Poetry: Accepts very little; published only occasionally. Poetry should be short, of a religious nature. Pays $5 to $15.

INTERLIT, David C. Cook Foundation, Elgin IL 60120. Phone: 312-741-2400. Editor: Gladys J. Peterson. For people interested in missionary literature and Christian education, at the graduate level. Established in 1964. Quarterly. Circulation: 6,000. Rights purchased vary with author and material. May buy all rights or second serial rights. Payment on acceptance. Will send free sample copy to a writer on request. Will consider photocopied submissions. Submit seasonal material four months in advance. Each issue is thematic. Reports in two weeks. Query first. Enclose S.A.S.E.

Nonfiction and Photos: Subject matter includes "literature, mass media, and leadership training—how to do it, this is what we did, etc." Buys informational, how-to, personal experience, interview, profile, think, photo, spot news, and technical articles. Length: 500 to 5,000 words. Pays 2¢ to 4¢ a word. Purchases photos with mss only.

JEWISH LIFE, 116 East 27th St., New York NY 10016. Editor: Yaakov Jacobs. For Orthodox Jewish, all ages; mostly college educated. Published under the auspices of the Union of Orthodox Jewish Congregations of America. Quarterly magazine; 60 (5x8) pages. Established in 1933. Circulation: 10,000. Rights purchased vary with author and material. May buy all rights; but will sometimes reassign rights to author after publication. Buys 25 mss a year. Payment on publication. Will send sample copy to writer for $1. Write for copy of guidelines for writers. Will not consider photocopied or simultaneous submissions. Reports on material accepted for publication 1 month before publication. Returns rejected material in 1 month. Query first or submit complete ms. Enclose S.A.S.E.

Nonfiction and Photos: "Anything related to Orthodox Judaism. All articles must reflect Orthodox Jewish outlook and have a clear and direct style. Themes based on current problems in relationship to the Orthodox Jew. We're not interested in what Jewish life was like 50 years ago, but more in translating the relevance of an ancient tradition into the lifestyles of America in the 1970s." Reportorial style pieces on aspects of Orthodox life. Book reviews are also used, but these are usually assigned. Length: 1,000 to 4,000 words. Fifty percent of material is contributed without payment. Payment for other material varies with amount of editing required, but averages 2¢ per word. Photos are purchased on assignment only.

Fiction, Poetry, Fillers: Uses only 1 fiction piece per issue. Experimental, mainstream, fantasy, humorous, religious, historical fiction. Length: 750 to 3,000 words. Traditional forms of poetry, blank verse, free verse, avant-garde forms. Length: 40 lines, maximum. Uses jokes, short humor, anecdotes, real life experiences as fillers. Length: 100 words maximum. Fifty percent of material is contributed without payment. Payment for other material varies with amount of editing required, but averages 2¢ per word.

JEWISH SOCIAL STUDIES, 2929 Broadway, New York NY 10025. Editor: Dr. Sefton D. Temkin. For scholars and students "well read in religious circles." Quarterly. Circulation: 1,200. Buys all rights. Buys 16 mss a year. Pays on publication. Will send a sample copy to a writer for $4. All mss must be footnoted; include all names—first and last; submit 2 copies of mss. Submit seasonal material 2 months in advance. Returns rejected material in 3 months. Acknowledges acceptance of material in 1 week. Enclose S.A.S.E.
Nonfiction: "Sociology and contemporary and historical aspects of Jewish life." Pays $5 per printed page.

LIBERTY, A Magazine of Religious Freedom, 6840 Eastern Ave., N.W., Washington DC 20012. Editor: Roland R. Hegstad. For "responsible citizens interested in community affairs and religious freedom;" professionals. Bimonthly. Circulation: 500,000. Buys first rights. Buys approximately 40 mss a year. Pays on acceptance. Will send a sample copy to a writer on request. Will consider photocopied submissions. Submit seasonal material 6 to 8 months in advance. Reports in 1 week. Query not essential, but helpful. Enclose S.A.S.E.
Nonfiction: "Articles of national and international interest in field of religious liberty, church—state relations. Current events affecting above areas (Sunday law problems, parochial aid problems, religious discrimination by state, etc.). Current events are most important; base articles on current events rather than essay form." Buys how-to's, personal experience and think pieces, interviews, profiles. Length: maximum 2,500 words. Pays $50 to $150.
Photos: "To accompany or illustrate articles." Purchased with mss; with captions only. B&w glossies, color transparencies. Pays $15 to $35. Cover photos to $150.

LIGHT AND LIFE, 999 College Ave., Winona Lake IN 46590. Managing Editor: G. Roger Schoenhals. For cross section of adults, the majority being members of the Free Methodist denomination. Denomination organ of the Free Methodist Church of North America; 20 (8½x11) pages. Published every two weeks (20 per year or 5 per quarter). Established in 1888. Circulation: 22,000. Not copyrighted. Buys 50 mss a year. Payment on publication. Will send free sample copy to writer on request. Submit seasonal articles 4 months in advance. Reports in 2 to 4 weeks. Submit only complete ms. Enclose S.A.S.E.
Nonfiction and Photos: Mostly thematic material which is assigned. Freelance material should be related to what God is doing in and through the Free Methodist Church and articles which express a warm, personal, evangelical point of view. "We prefer first-person accounts. Seasonal material should have clear, warm, Christian viewpoint." Length: 750 to 1,500 words. Pays 2¢ per word. Photos purchased with accompanying ms with no additional payment.
Poetry: Traditonal forms, blank verse and free verse. Length: 30 lines maximum. Pays 25¢ per line, minimum $5.

LIGUORIAN, Liguori MO 63057. Editor: Rev. L. G. Miller. For families with Catholic religious convictions. Monthly. Circulation: 364,000. Not copyrighted. Buys 75 mss a year. Pays on acceptance. Submit seasonal material 4 months in advance. Returns rejected material in 6 to 8 weeks. Enclose S.A.S.E.

Nonfiction and Photos: "Pastoral, practical, and personal approach to the problems and challenges of people today. No travelogue approach or unresearched ventures into controversial areas." Length: 400 to 1,500 words. Pays $35 to $100. Photos purchased with mss; b&w glossies.

THE LITTLE FLOWER MAGAZINE, 2215 Ross Ave., Dallas TX 75201. Editor: Fr. John Michael, O.C.D. For Catholic audience. Published 6 times a year. Established in 1920. Circulation: 34,000. "Copyrighted only upon request." Payment on publication. "Most of our material is donated. Be sure to specify honestly whether or not you just want to pass on an idea to someone, see yourself in print, or expect compensation. If we do pay for an article, we never pay more than 1¢ a word." Will send free sample copy to writer on request. Write for copy of guidelines for writers. Reports in 3 weeks. Enclose S.A.S.E.
Nonfiction: Simple, factual discussions of Christian living, prayer, social action, the thinking of important religious writers. "It is important that factual or doctrinal articles be about a very, very specific topic. We cannot use articles about religion in general. For example, we can always use articles on St. Therese of Lisieux; a good article could be written by referring to a good biography, such as Ida Goerres' *The Hidden Face,* and concentrating on some specific topic, such as Therese's relation to nineteenth century attitudes toward women; her approach to meditation; her relationship to her superior. Since few of our readers are familiar with current religious literature, it is relatively easy to draw material from good works on specific passages in the Bible, on prayer, on current social questions, on the liturgy, etc." Avoid sentimentality and overly personal presentations. Length: 1,250 to 1,700 words.

LIVING MESSAGE, P.O. Box 820, Petrolia, Ontario, NON IRO, Canada. Editor: Rita Baker. For "active, concerned Christians, mainly Canadian Anglican." Publication of the Anglican Church of Canada. Established in 1889. Monthly except July and August. Circulation: 14,000. Not copyrighted. Payment on publication. Will send free sample copy to writer on request. Will consider photocopied submissions. Submit seasonal material 5 months in advance. Reports on material in 3 weeks. Submit complete ms. Enclose S.A.E. and International Reply Coupons.
Fiction, Nonfiction and Photos: "Short stories and articles which give readers an insight into other lives, promote understanding and stimulate action in areas such as community life, concerns of elderly, handicapped, youth, work with children, Christian education, poverty, the 'Third World', etc. Short stories about boys and girls for new feature "Whistle Stop." Length: up to 750 words. Also very short articles, with photos (may be any size b&w), especially about what boys and girls, in groups or individually, are doing to help others. Canadian material preferred for this feature. No sentimentality or moralizing. Readers relate to a warm, personal approach; uncluttered writing. 'Reports' or involved explanatory articles are not wanted. The lead-in must capture the reader's imagination. A feeling of love and optimism is important." Recently published articles include "Breakthrough for Retarded People," "Strength and Spirituality — Indian Style," "Lifeline to Hope" (a Christ-centered program for drug addicts). Length: up to 2,000 words. Pays $5 to $25. 8x10 b&w prints (with article). Pays $5. Fiction length: 1,000 to 1,500 words. Pays $10 to $20.

LOGOS JOURNAL, 185 North Ave., Plainfield NJ 07060. Editor: Howard Earl. For charismatic-evangelical Christians from all walks of life; most are avid readers and are particularly interested in the Holy Spirit. Published every 2 months. Magazine; 64 pages. Established in 1971. Circulation: 100,000. Rights purchased vary with author and material. Buys all rights, but will reassign rights to author after publication; buys first North American serial rights, first serial rights, second serial (reprint) rights with limited fee; rarely simultaneous rights. Buys 12 mss a year. Payment on acceptance if solicited and on publication if not solicited. Will send free sample copy to writer on request. Write for copy of guidelines for writers. Submit seasonal material 3 months in advance. Reports within 10 weeks. Query first or submit complete ms. Enclose S.A.S.E.

Nonfiction: Features to include teaching and current happenings about the charismatic movement (New Testament Christianity); news items and book reviews, selected humor, on New Testament life. Prefer not to receive Bible exposition articles. Personal testimonies of experience with God are the most frequent submission and most frequently rejected—must be well done. The relationship of an active, interested, and living God to a world desperately in need, needs more coverage. Length: 1,200 to 2,500 words for features; 50 to 2,500 for smaller items. Pays $2 per item to 7¢ per word.

Photos: 5x7 or 8x10 b&w glossy or matte purchased with or without ms or on assignment. Captions optional. Payment negotiable.

Fiction: Religious fiction. Length: 1,000 to 3,000 words. Pays 5¢ to 7¢ a word.

Fillers: Newsbreaks, short humor, and inspirational fillers. Length: 25 to 200 words. Pays $2 to $15.

THE LOOKOUT, 8121 Hamilton Ave., Cincinnati OH 45231. Phone: 513-931-4050. Editor: Jay Sheffield. For the adult and young adult of the Sunday morning Bible school. Issued weekly. Buys first rights. Pays on acceptance. Will send free sample copy to a writer on request. Write for copy of guidelines for writers. Reports on submissions within one month. Study publication before submitting material. Enclose S.A.S.E.

Nonfiction: Chiefly methods or news-type articles on phases of educational work of the local church, or articles dealing with personal or family problems of Christian life or work. Length: 1,000 to 1,500 words. Pays $25 to $35.

Photos: Upright glossies, size 8x10. Human interest or scenic shots of exceptionally good composition for cover use. Sharp b&w contrasts. Pays $7.50 to $15.

Fiction: Short-short stories of 1,000 to 1,200 words. To be acceptable, fiction must be characterized by effective storytelling style, interesting quality—capable of catching and holding the reader's interest. Pays up to $35 for short stories.

THE LUTHERAN, 2900 Queen Lane, Philadelphia PA 19129. Phone: 215-848-6800. Editor: Orrin Root. For the adult and young adult of the Sunday morning Bible school. Issued weekly. Buys first rights. Pays on acceptance. Will send free sample copy to a writer on request. Write for copy of guidelines for writers. Enclose S.A.S.E.

Nonfiction: Popularly written material about human concerns with reference to the Christian faith. "We are especially interested in articles in 4 main fields: Christian ideology; personal religious life, social responsibilities; Church at work; human interest stories about people in whom considerable numbers of other people are likely to be interested." Write "primarily to convey information rather than opinions. Every article should be based on a reasonable amount of research or should exploit some source of information not readily available. Most readers are grateful for simplicity of style. Sentences should be straightforward, with a minimum of dependent clauses and prepositional phrases." Length: 500 to 2,000 words. Pays $75 to $200.

Photos: Buys pix submitted with mss. Good 8x10 glossy prints. Pays $10 to $20. Also color for cover use. Pays up to $100.

LUTHERAN FORUM, 155 E. 22nd St., New York NY 10010. Editor: Glenn C. Stone. For church leadership, clerical and lay. Magazine; 40 (8½x11¼) pages. Established in 1967. Quarterly. Circulation: 5,500. Rights purchased vary with author and material. Buys all rights, but will sometimes reassign rights to author after publication; first North American serial rights; first serial rights; second serial (reprint) rights; simultaneous rights. Buys 6 mss a year. Pays on publication. Will send sample copy to writer for 50¢. Will consider photocopied and simultaneous submissions. Returns rejected material at once. Reports on ms accepted for publication in 4 to 6 weeks. Query first or submit complete ms. Enclose S.A.S.E.

Nonfiction: Articles about important issues and actions in the Church and in its internal life and in its cultural/social setting. Payment varies; $10 minimum. Length: 1,000 to 3,000 words. Informational, how-to, personal experience, interview, profile, think articles, expose, personal opinion. Length: 500 to 3,000 words. Pays $10 to $35.

Photos: Purchased with mss or with captions only. Prefers 8x10 prints. Uses more vertical than horizontal format. Pays $5 minimum.

How To Break In: "Send something for our On The Way to the Forum feature. Material for this is usually humorous or offbeat in a gentle way and should have some relation to the life of the Church at some level. Ideal length is 700 to 1,000 words. Payments range from $10 to $20."

THE LUTHERAN JOURNAL, 7317 Cahill Rd., Edina MN 55435. Editor: The Rev. Armin U. Deye. Conservative journal for Lutheran church members middle age and older. Quarterly magazine; 32 pages, (8½x11). Established in 1937. Circulation: 99,000. Not copyrighted. Buys 12 to 15 mss a year. Payment on publication. Will send free sample copy to writer on request. Submit Christmas, Easter, other holiday material 4 months in advance. Will consider photocopied and simultaneous submissions. Reports in 6 weeks. Submit only complete ms. Enclose S.A.S.E.

Nonfiction and Photos: Inspirational, religious, human interest, and historical articles. Interesting or unusual church projects. Informational, how-to, personal experience, interview, humor, think articles. Length: 1,500 maximum; occasionally 2,000 words. Pays 1¢ to 1½¢ a word. B&w and color photos purchased with accompanying ms. Captions required. Payment varies.

Fiction and Poetry: Experimental, mainstream, religious, and historical fiction. Must be suitable for church distribution. Length: 2,000 words maximum. Pays 1¢ to 1½¢ a word. Traditional poetry, blank verse, free verse, related to subject matter of magazine.

THE LUTHERAN STANDARD, 426 S. 5th St., Minneapolis MN 55415. Phone: 612-332-4561. Editor: George H. Muedeking. For family audience. Semimonthly. Buys first rights or multiple rights. Pays on acceptance. Will send free sample copy to a writer on request. Reports on submissions in 3 weeks. Enclose S.A.S.E.

Nonfiction and Photos: Uses human interest, inspirational articles, especially about members of the American Lutheran Church who are practicing their faith in noteworthy ways, or congregations with unusual programs. Also publishes articles that discuss current social issues and problems (crime, draft evasion, etc.) in terms of Christian involvement and solutions. Length: 650 to 1,250 words, with pictures. Pays 2¢ and up per word. Photos used with mss.

Fiction: Tie-in with season of year, such as Christmas, often preferred. Length: limit 1,200 words. Pays 2¢ per word.

Poetry: Uses very little poetry. The shorter the better; 20 lines. Pays $5 per poem.

LUTHERAN WOMEN, 2900 Queen Lane, Philadelphia PA 19129. Editor: Terry Schute. 11 times yearly. Circulation: 45,000. Official magazine for Lutheran Church Women. Acknowledges receipt of manuscript and decides acceptance within two months. Prefers to see mss six months ahead of issue, at beginning of planning stage. Can consider up to three months before issue. (December issue is nearly completed by September 1). Type 70 characters to a line preferably. Buys first rights. Pays on publication. Enclose S.A.S.E.

Nonfiction: Anything of interest to mothers, young or old, professional or other working women, relating to the contemporary expression of Christian faith in daily life, community action, international concerns. Family publication standards. Length: 1,500 to 2,000 words. Some shorter pieces accepted. Pays $30 to $40.

Photos: Purchased with mss or with captions only. Women; family situations; religious art objects; overseas situations related to church. Should be clear, sharp, b&w. Pays $5 each.

Fiction: Should show deepening of insight; story expressing new understanding in faith; story of human courage, self-giving, building up of community. Not to exceed 2,000 words. Pays $30 to $40.

Poetry: Uses very little. "Biggest taboo for us is sentimentality. Obviously we'd be limited to family magazine type contributions regarding range of vocabulary, but we don't want almanac-type poetry." No limit on number of lines. Pays $10 minimum per poem.

THE MARIAN, 4545 W. 63rd St., Chicago IL 60629. Managing Editor: P. P. Cinikas, M.I.C. Published in February, April, June, October, and December. Buys first rights. Pays on publication. Will send free sample copy to a writer on request. Reports on submissions promptly. Enclose S.A.S.E.

Nonfiction: Uses articles on religion, morals, social questions and Christian culture. Length: maximum 1,000 words. Pays 1½¢ minimum per word.

MARIAN HELPERS BULLETIN, Eden Hill, Stockbridge MA 01262. Phone: 413-298-3691. Editor: Bro. Robert M. Doyle, M.I.C. For average Catholics of varying ages with moderate religious views and general education. Quarterly. Established in 1947. Circulation: 750,000. Not copyrighted. Buys 18 to 24 mss a year. Payment on acceptance. Will send free sample copy to writer on request. Reports in 4 to 8 weeks. Submit seasonal material 6 months in advance. Enclose S.A.S.E.

Nonfiction and Photos: "Subject matter is of general interest on devotional, spiritual, moral and social topics. Use a positive, practical, and optimistic approach, without being sophisticated. We would like to see articles on the Blessed Virgin Mary." Buys informational, personal experience, inspirational articles. Length: 300 to 900 words. Pays $15 to $35. Photos are purchased with or without mss; captions optional. Pays $5 to $10 for b&w glossies.

MARRIAGE & FAMILY LIVING, St. Meinrad IN 47577. Phone: 812-357-6649. Editor: John J. McHale. Monthly. Circulation: 60,000. Buys North American serial rights only. Pays on acceptance. Will send sample copy to writer for 10¢. Reports on submissions in 3 to 4 weeks. Enclose S.A.S.E.

Nonfiction: Uses 4 different types of articles: (1) Informative and inspirational articles on all aspects of marriage, especially husband-wife and parent-child relationships. Length: 1,500 to 2,500 words. (2) Personal essays relating amusing incidents that point up the human side of marriage and family life. Length: 1,500 words maximum. (3) Profiles of outstanding couple or couples whose story will be of interest for some special reason, and profiles of individuals who contribute to the betterment of marriage. Length: 1,500 to 2,000 words. (4) Interviews with authorities in the fields of marriage and family (on current problems or new developments). Length: up to 2,500 words. Recently published articles include "The Commune and the Family," "What It Really Means to Be a Father," and "Help for Families in Debt." Pays 5¢ a word.

Photos: Purchased with ms. 8x11 b&w glossies, color transparencies. Pays $125 for 4-color cover photo; $50 for b&w cover photo; $35 for 2-page spread in contents; $30 for one-page in contents; $10 minimum. Photos of couples especially desired. Requires model releases. Department Editor: Ron Fendel.

Fillers: Original jokes, one-liners, and anecdotes for "Two-Ring Circus" feature. Humor arising from parent-child and husband-wife relationships. Length: one-liners or up to 100 words. Submissions for this department cannot be acknowledged or returned. Pays $5 on publication.

MARYKNOLL MAGAZINE, Maryknoll NY 10545. Editor: Rev. Miguel d'Escoto, M.M. For "Maryknoll missionaries and mission workers with major emphasis on the peoples of the developing countries." Pays on acceptance. Will send free sample copy to a writer on request. Query before sending any material. Reports within two weeks. Enclose S.A.S.E.

Nonfiction: "All articles in the magazine must apply in some way to the hopes and aspirations, the culture, the problems and challenges of peoples in Asia, Africa, and Latin America." Length: 1,000 to 1,500 words. Send an outline before submitting material. Average payment: $100.

Photos: Interested in photo stories and in individual b&w and color transparencies. Photo stories in b&w, up to $150; color, up to $200. An individual b&w pays $15; color pays $25. Transparencies returned after use.

THE MENNONITE, 600 Shaftesbury Blvd., Winnipeg, Canada R3P OM4. Editor: Larry Kehler. For a "general readership—age span—15 to 90 years; education—from grade school to Ph.D's; interests—themes dealing with the Christian response to such issues as the family, ethics, war and peace, life style, renewal, etc." Established in 1881. Weekly except in July and August. Circulation: 16,000. Rights purchased vary with author and material. May buy first and second serial rights. Buys 100 to 125 mss a year. Payment on publication. Will send a free sample copy to writer on request. Submit seasonal material three months in advance. Reports in two months. Enclose S.A.E. and International Reply Coupons.

Nonfiction, Photos, Fiction, and Poetry: General subject matter is "articles on Bible study, social and political issues faced by Christians, creative responses to the challenges of 20th century life; some poetry on a variety of subjects; a small amount of fiction. *The Mennonite* is a publication of an historic peace church which pays special attention to ways and means of attempting to resolve conflict at various levels of life—family, community, national and international." Buys personal experience, inspirational, think, and personal opinion articles. Length: 500 to 1,500 words. Pays 1¢ to 2¢ a word. Purchases photos without mss and captions are optional. Pays $5 to $10 for 5x7 or 8x10 b&w glossies. Buys religious fiction. Length: 800 to 1,500 words. Pays 1¢ to 2¢ a word. Buys religious poems in traditional, blank, or free verse. Length: 2 to 40 lines. Pays 25¢ a line.

MENNONITE BRETHREN HERALD, 159 Henderson Hwy., Winnipeg 9, Manitoba, R2L 1L4, Canada. Editor: Harold Jantz. Family publication. Biweekly. Circulation: 9,000. Pays on publication. Not copyrighted. Will send a sample copy for 25¢. Reports within the month. Enclose S.A.E. and International Reply Coupons.

Nonfiction and Photos: Articles with a Christian family orientation; youth directed, Christian faith and life, current issues. 1,500 words. Pays $10 to $30 for accepted ms. Photos purchased with mss; pays $3.

MESSAGE MAGAZINE, Southern Publishing Assn., Box 59, Nashville TN 37202. Editor: W. R. Robinson. Bimonthly; global, and while appealing to all people, emphasizes interests and aspirations of people of color. Buys all rights. Pays on acceptance or publication. Will send free sample copy to a writer on request. Enclose S.A.S.E.

Nonfiction: Material within Judeo-Christian framework of reality. Uses inspiring human interest stories about persons who exemplify faith in God and/or have achieved distinction in the face of great odds. Length: 500 to 800 words. Pays $5 to $25 or more.

Photos: Purchased with mss and with captions only. Photo stories of lasting interest, especially those depicting Negroes or persons in Afro-Asian countries. Pays $7.50 up for b&w; color transparencies up to $100.

Poetry: Quality poetry on religious and nature themes. Length: up to 36 lines. Pays 25¢ per line.

THE MESSENGER OF THE SACRED HEART, 833 Broadview Ave., Toronto, Ont., Canada M4K 2P9. Editor: Rev. F. J. Power, S.J. For "adult Catholics in Canada and the U.S. who are members of the Apostleship of Prayer." Monthly. Circulation: 20,000. Buys first rights. Buys about 12 mss a year. Pays on acceptance. Will send a sample copy to a writer on request. Submit seasonal material 3 months in advance. Reports in 1 month. Enclose S.A.E. and International Reply Coupons.

Nonfiction: "Articles on the Apostleship of Prayer and on all aspects of Christian living"; current events and social problems that have a bearing on Catholic life, family life, Catholic relations with non-Catholics, personal problems, the liturgy, prayer, devotion to the Sacred Heart. Material should be written in a popular, nonpious style. Length: 1,800 to 2,000 words. Pays 2¢ a word. Department Editor: Mary Pujolas.

Fiction: Wants fiction which reflects the lives, problems, preoccupations of reading audience. "Short stories that make their point through plot and characters." Length: 1,800 to 2,000 words. Pays 2¢ a word. Department Editor: Mary Pujolas.

THE MIRACULOUS MEDAL, 475 E. Chelten Ave., Philadelphia PA 19144. Editorial Director: Rev. Donald L. Doyle, C.M. Quarterly. Buys first North American serial rights. Buys articles only on special assignment. Pays on acceptance. Will send free sample copy on request. Normally reports in two days. Query first. Enclose S.A.S.E.

Fiction: Should not be pious or sermon-like. Wants good general fiction—not necessarily religious, but if religion is basic to the story, the writer should be sure of his facts. Only restriction is that subject matter and treatment must not conflict with Catholic teaching and practice. Can use seasonal material. Christmas stories. Length: 2,000 words maximum. Pays 2¢ and up per word. Occasionally uses short-shorts from 750 to 1,250 words.

Poetry: Maximum of 20 lines, preferably about the Virgin Mary or at least with religious slant. Pays 50¢ a line and up.

MOODY MONTHLY, 820 North LaSalle, Chicago IL 60610. Editor: Jerry B. Jenkins. For "Church-oriented Christian families, high school and college graduates, some with Bible school training, special interest in the Bible and in the Protestant evangelical world." Monthly magazine. Circulation: 260,000. Buys all rights. Buys 8 to 12 mss a year. Pays on acceptance. Will send a sample copy to a writer on request. Write for copy of guidelines for writers. Submit seasonal material 4 months in advance. Reports in 2 months. Query first. "Cannot read unsolicited mss." Enclose S.A.S.E.

Nonfiction and Fiction: Wants material which is warm, evangelical and clearly relevant to daily life of the individual Christian. Personal experience articles, devotionals (factual and anecdotal development), solid treatment of contemporary Christian problems, seasonals, and nonpromotional features on Christian organizations and aspects of Christian work; "news of the Christian world, developments in Christian education, personality sketches, Bible exposition, anecdotal material for women, 'How I Did It' stories of Christians in difficult situations." Family department needs "warm, practical material clearly relevant to parents, either fiction or nonfiction." Length: 2,000 to 3,000 words. Pays 5¢ a word.

Photos: B&w glossies; 35mm color. Pays $15 to $100.

Fillers: Newsbreaks, inspirational anecdotes, people-centered stories. Length: 200 to 800 words. Pays 5¢ a word.

NEW CATHOLIC WORLD, 1865 Broadway, New York NY 10023. Managing Editor: Robert J. Heyer. For a "general audience, college educated." Bimonthly. Circulation: 17,000. Buys all rights. Pays on acceptance. Will send free sample copy to writer on request. Submit seasonal material 2 to 3 months in advance. Enclose S.A.S.E.

Nonfiction and Fiction: Each issue is theme oriented. Past themes have included Catholic/Jewish relations, Lent, prayer, fasting and almsgiving, sacraments revisited, religious life of the adolescent, economic justice and Advent. General material concerning issues in religion, literature, politics, etc.; not historical or devotional articles. Also uses humorous and religious fiction. Length: 1,000 to 2,000 words. Pays $60 to $100.

THE NEW ERA, 50 E. North Temple, Salt Lake City UT 84150. Phone: 801-531-2951. Editor: Brian K. Kelly. For young people of The Church of Jesus Christ of Latter-Day Saints (Mormon); their church leaders and teachers. Monthly magazine; 51 pages. Established in 1971. Circulation: 160,000. Buys all rights, but will reassign rights to author after publication. Buys 100 mss a year. Payment on acceptance. Will send sample copy to writer for 35¢. Will consider simultaneous submissions. Submit seasonal material 6 months to a year in advance. Reports in 30 days. Query preferred. Enclose S.A.S.E.

Nonfiction and Photos: "Material that shows how The Church of Jesus Christ of Latter-Day Saints is relevant in the lives of young people today. Must capture the excitement of being a young Latter-Day Saint. Special interest in the experiences of young Latter-Day Saints in other countries. No general library research or formula pieces without the *New Era* slant and feel." Uses informational, how-to, personal experience, interview, profile, inspirational, humor, historical, think pieces, travel, spot news. Length: 150 to 3,000 words. Pays 2¢ to 5¢ a word. Also seeks material for the FYI column (For Your Information) which uses news of young Latter-Day Saints around the world. Uses b&w photos and color transparencies with mss. Payment depends on use in magazine, but begins at $10.

Fiction: Experimental, adventure, science fiction and humorous. Must relate to their young Mormon audience. Pays minimum 3¢ a word.

Poetry: Traditional forms, blank verse, free verse, avant-garde forms, light verse and all other forms. Must relate to their editorial viewpoint. Pays minimum 25¢ a line.

NEW WORLD OUTLOOK, 475 Riverside Dr., Room 1328, New York NY 10027. Editor: Arthur J. Moore, Jr. For United Methodist lay people; not clergy generally. Monthly magazine; 50 pages (9x11¼). Established in 1911. Circulation: 50,000. Buys all rights, but will reassign rights to author after publication; buys first North American serial rights. Buys 15 to 20 mss a year. Payment on publication. Will send free sample copy to writer on request. Write for copy of guidelines for writers. Query first or submit complete ms. Enclose S.A.S.E.

Nonfiction: "Articles about the involvement of the Church around the world, including the U.S., in outreach and social concerns and Christian witness, not solely of one denomination. Write with good magazine style. Facts, actualities important. Quotes. Relate what Christians are doing to meet problems. Specifics. We have too much on New York and other large urban areas. We need more good journalistic efforts from smaller places in U.S. Articles by freelancers in out-of-the-way places in the U.S. are especially welcome." Length: 1,000 to 2,000 words. Usually pays $50 to $150.

NORTH AMERICAN VOICE OF FATIMA, Fatima Shrine, Youngstown NY 14174. Editor: Steven M. Grancini, C.R.S.P. For Roman Catholic readership. Circulation: 19,000. Not copyrighted. Pays on acceptance. Will send free sample copy to a writer on request. Deadlines are the first and 15th of each month. Reports on submissions in two weeks. Enclose S.A.S.E.

Nonfiction, Photos, and Fiction: Inspirational, personal experience, historical and think articles. Religious and historical fiction. Length: 700 words. B&w photos purchased with mss. All material must have a religious slant. Pays 1¢ a word.

Fillers: Religious short humor appropriate to format; study publication. Pays 1¢ a word.

OBLATE WORLD AND VOICE OF HOPE (formerly *OMI Missions*), P.O. Box 96, San Antonio TX 78291. Phone: 512-736-3186. Editor: John A. Hakey, O.M.I. For people interested in the missions and the work of the Oblate Fathers in Texas, Mexico, the Philippines, Latin America, the Orient and the Arctic. Quarterly. Circulation: 50,000. Not copyrighted. Buys very few mss a year. Payment on acceptance. Will send a free sample copy to a writer on request. Will consider photocopied submissions. Submit seasonal material four months in advance. Reports in a month. Enclose S.A.S.E.

Nonfiction and Photos: "We accept stories about the Oblates in the above mentioned missions. Once in a while a very short seasonal story (Christmas or Easter) may be accepted. All material should be sent to the editor." Buys informational, interview, and photo articles. Length: 600 to 1,200 words. Pays 2¢ a word. Purchases photos with mss and captions are optional. B&w only.

OUR FAMILY, Box 249, Battleford, Sask., Canada SOM OEO. Phone: 306-937-2131. Editor: A. James Materi. For the Catholic family. Monthly magazine; 32 pages (8½x11). Established in 1949. Circulation: 9,500. Rights purchased vary with author and material. Buys all rights, but will reassign rights to author after publication; first North American serial rights; first serial rights; second serial (reprint) rights; or simultaneous rights. Buys 100 to 200 mss a year. Payment on acceptance. Will send sample copy to writer for 25c. Write for copy of editorial guidelines for writers. Uses December Christmas material and special September educational material. Submit special and seasonal material 4 months in advance. Will consider photocopied submissions and simultaneous submissions. Reports in 2 to 4 weeks. Query first

or submit complete ms. Enclose S.A.E. and International Reply Coupons.
Nonfiction: Articles should be of an informative nature, written clearly and concisely in an unsophisticated, anecdotal style, with an emphasis on human interest. Especially welcome are challenging, contemporary articles on matters of concern to people as individuals and as families. Uses 5 types of articles: "challenging, contemporary articles on all aspects of marriage and parenthood; informative, anecdotal articles on socio-economic matters as they affect the family and individual members of the family; inspirational articles on the use of recreation and leisure by the family; provocative, hard-hitting articles on religion and its meaning in our lives; instructive articles on socio-political matters that affect the family." Also uses true life articles which reveal deep emotion, such as life crises, problems of adjustment, or spiritual journeys. Length: 1,000 to 3,000 words. "Occasionally will accept longer or shorter articles." Pays to 2¢ a word and up.
Photos: Purchased with ms as package, with extra payment for photos. Should be at least 5x7 b&w glossies. If you submit photos taken by someone else, please enclose statement from them giving you the right to accept payment as agent. Pays $3 to $10. Photos also purchased separately. Pays to $10. Wants photo stories and photo essays on personalities, events, and human/religious themes. Payment by arrangement.
Fiction: Stories that reflect lives, problems and preoccupations of audience. "Anything true to human nature. No sentimentality or moralizing. Stories which are hard-hitting, fast-moving, with a real, woven-in Christian message. For average family reader. Avoid stereotyped 'happy' endings." Length: 1,000 to 3,000 words. Pays to 2¢ a word and up.
Poetry: "Should deal with man in search of himself, for God, for others, for love, for meaning in life, for commitment." Length: 8 to 30 lines. Pays $3 to $10, "depending on length and style."

OUR LADY OF THE SNOWS, National Shrine of Our Lady of the Snows, Belleville IL 62223. Phone: 618-233-2238. Published six times yearly for families, particularly women. Buys first-use rights. Pays on acceptance. Reports in one month. Will accept simultaneous submissions of articles, short stories, and filler items. "We are primarily interested in the short-short, inspirational, religious type of writing." Study publication before submitting. Address mss to Editor. Enclose S.A.S.E.
Nonfiction and Photos: Uses articles that are "religious, both moral and doctrinal, as well as devotional, but written for common folk. No pretension or 'intellectualism': simple language and style, but with something to say." 250 to 500 words. Pays $25 and up. Payment for 8x10 b&w photos submitted with manuscripts begins at $5.
Poetry: Also uses short, meaningful poetry. No payment.

OUR SUNDAY VISITOR, Noll Plaza, Huntington IN 46750. Editor: Richard B. Scheiber. For general Catholic audience. Weekly. Circulation: 400,000. Buys all rights. Buys about 200 mss a year. Pays on acceptance. Will send a sample copy to a writer on request. Submit seasonal material 2 months in advance. Reports in 1 week. Query first. Enclose S.A.S.E.
Nonfiction: Uses articles on Catholic related subjects. Should explain Catholic religious beliefs in articles of human interest, articles applying Catholic principles to current problems, Catholic profiles, etc. Payment varies depending on reputation of author, quality of work and amount of research required. Length: 1,000 to 1,200 words. Minimum payment for major features is $100 and a minimum payment for shorter features is $50 to $75.
Photos: Purchased with mss; with captions only. B&w glossies, color transparencies, 35mm color. Pays $125 for cover photo story, $75 for b&w story; $25 per color photo. $10 per b&w photo.

THE PENTECOSTAL EVANGEL, 1445 Boonville Ave., Springfield MO 65802. Editor: Robert C. Cunningham. Issued weekly, mainly to members of Assemblies of God churches. Write for free sample copy. Submit complete ms. Enclose S.A.S.E.
Nonfiction and Photos: Wants devotional articles on individual's spiritual life, true stories of unusual answers to prayer, personal testimonials of conversion and other

spiritual experiences, articles on home life which convey Christian teaching, seasonal material on Christmas, New Year, Easter, etc. It is important that writers be familiar with doctrinal views of Assemblies of God and with standards for membership in churches of this denomination. Pays 1¢ to 2¢ per word for first rights or all rights. Buys b&w glossy prints (8x10) and color transparencies. Payment varies.
Poetry: Accepts only a small amount of poetry. Payment is up to 40¢ per line.
Fillers: Uses fillers if they have spiritual value; 50 to 150 words.

PENTECOSTAL TESTIMONY, 10 Overlea Blvd., Toronto 17, Ont. M4H 1A5 Canada. Editor: Joy E. Hansell. Monthly. For Church members plus general readership. Established in 1920. Circulation: 15,000. Not copyrighted. Payment on publication. Will send free sample copy to writer on request. Write for copy of editorial guidelines for writers. Submit seasonal material at least 3 months in advance. Query first. Enclose S.A.E. and International Reply Coupons.
Nonfiction: Must be written from Canadian viewpoint. Subjects preferred are contemporary public issues, events on the church calendar (Reformation month, Christmas, Pentecost, etc.) written from conservative theological viewpoint. Pays 1¢ per word for originals. Preferred lengths are 800 to 1,200 words.
Photos: Occasionally buys photographs with mss if they are vital to the article. Also buys b&w photos if they are related to some phase of the main topic of the particular issue. Should be 8x10 b&w prints. Payment is $6 to $10 for cover photos.
Fiction: Might use youth-slanted fiction. Same theological slant, same lengths, same payment as nonfiction.
Poetry: Rarely uses. Pays $2.50 for short poems and sonnets.

PENTECOSTAL YOUTH, P.O. Box 850, Joplin MO 64801. Editor: Aaron M. Wilson. "Primarily edited for youth ages 9 through 17, but is also read by a number of ministers also interested in youth. Leader edition offers program materials and suggestions for youth ministries. Evangelical and Christian in message and approaches." Established in 1956. Monthly. Circulation: 5,000. Buys second serial (reprint) rights and simultaneous rights. Buys 36 to 40 mss a year. Payment on acceptance. Will send free sample copy to a writer on request. Write for copy of guidelines for writers. Will consider photocopied submissions if clear copy. "We particularly need articles and fiction for seasonal issues, but interest must be centered in the age limits of the magazine." Submit seasonal material 60 days in advance. "Usually" reports on material accepted for publication in 30 days. Returns rejected material in 30 days. Submit complete ms. Enclose S.A.S.E.
Nonfiction and Photos: "Character-building articles of interest to youth." Informational, how-to, personal experience, profile, inspirational, short humor, historical, think and short travel articles. "Primarily published for young people of Pentecostal background, and we observe the usual 'holiness' taboos such as tobacco, alcohol, dancing, movies, etc. However, we are not presenting just spiritual or church items. It is intended as a general magazine for Pentecostal youth. Length varies; top is 2,500 words. Normally pay ¼¢ a word; more for special material or specific assignments." Photos purchased with mss. Pays $2 for "routine 8x10 b&w photos; $5 for feature photo. Captions optional. Payment open, but with limited budget."
Fiction, Poetry and Fillers: Humorous and religious fiction. Length: "maximum 2,500, prefer 2,000". Pays ¼¢ a word. Light verse and traditional forms. Length: open. "Payment varies with length." Jokes and puzzles (youth and Bible type). Payment "can vary with material."

PRESBYTERIAN RECORD, 50 Wynford Dr., Don Mills, Ontario, Canada M3C 1J7. Phone: 416-429-0110. Editor: Rev. Dr. DeCourcy H. Rayner. For a church-oriented, family audience. Monthly magazine. Established in 1876. Circulation: 91,000. Not copyrighted. Buys 12 mss a year. Payment on publication. Will send free sample copy to writer on request. Submit seasonal material 3 months in advance. Reports on manuscripts accepted for publication in 2 weeks. Returns rejected material in 4 weeks. Query first. Enclose S.A.E. and International Reply Coupons.

Nonfiction and Photos: Material on religious themes. Check a copy of the magazine for style. Also, personal experience, interview, and inspirational material. Length: 800 to 1,600 words. Pays $20 to $50. Pays $5 to $12 for b&w glossy photos. Captions required. Uses positive color transparencies for the cover. Pays $25.

PRESBYTERIAN SURVEY, 341 Ponce de Leon Avenue, Northeast, Atlanta GA 30308. Phone: 404-875-8921. Editor: John Allen Templeton. For members and ministers of the Presbyterian Church in the U.S. Established in 1910. Monthly. Circulation: 126,000. Rights purchased vary with author and material. Buys 20 to 50 mss a year. Payment on acceptance. Will send sample copy to a writer for 50¢. Usually reports in 4 weeks. Submit seasonal material 4 months in advance. Query first or submit complete ms. Enclose S.A.S.E.

Nonfiction and Photos: Subject matter should be "church-related (Protestant) in content; depth articles with practical theological connotations." Buys inspirational, historical, think, and photo articles with a religious slant. "Pay $25 minimum. No fixed rates; pay more for better copy; more if good art is furnished with ms; seldom buy at the $25 minimum." Buys photos with or without mss, or on assignment, and captions are required. Pays $7.50 minimum for 8x10 b&w.

PURPOSE, 616 Walnut Ave., Scottdale PA 15683. Editor: David E. Hostetler. For adults, young and old, general audience with interests as varied as there are persons. "My particular readership is interested in seeing Christianity work in tough situations and come out on top." Monthly magazine. Established in 1968. Circulation: 20,500. Buys first serial rights; second serial (reprint) rights; simultaneous rights. Buys 200 mss a year. Payment on acceptance. Will send free sample copy to writer on request. Write for editorial guidelines for writers. Submit seasonal material 6 months in advance. Will consider photocopied and simultaneous submissions. Reports within 6 weeks. Submit only complete ms. Enclose S.A.S.E.

Nonfiction and Photos: Inspirational articles from a Christian perspective. "I want material that goes to the core of human problems—morality on all levels, or lack of it in business, politics, religion, sex, and any other area—and shows how Christian answers resolve some of these problems. I don't want glib, sweety-sweet, or civil religion pieces. I want critical stuff with an upbeat. *Purpose* is a story paper and as such wants truth to be conveyed either through quality fiction or through articles that use the best fiction techniques to make them come alive. Our magazine has an accent on Christian discipleship. Basically, this means we think our readers take Christianity seriously and we do not accept a compartmentalized expression of faith. Christianity is to be applied to all of life and we expect our material to show this. We're getting too much self-centered material. By that, I mean many writers see religion as a way of getting their needs met with very little concern for how the other fellow may be affected by their selfishness. I would like to see articles on how people are intelligently and effectively working at some of the great human problems such as overpopulation, food shortages, international understanding, etc., motivated by their faith." Length: 200 to 1,200 words. Pays 1¢ to 3¢ per word. Photos purchased with ms. Captions optional. Pays $5 to $35 for b&w, depending on quality. Normal range is $7.50 to $15. Must be sharp enough for reproduction; prefers prints in all cases. Can use color for halftones at the same rate of payment.

Fiction, Poetry, and Fillers: Humorous, religious, and historical fiction relating the theme of magazine. "Should not be moralistic." Length: 1,750 words maximum. Pays 1¢ to 3¢ per word. Traditional poetry, blank verse, free verse, and light verse. Length: 3 to 12 lines. Pays 25¢ to 50¢ per line. Jokes, short humor, and items up to 400 words. Pays 1¢ minimum per word.

How To Break In: "We are a good market for new writers who combine Christian perceptions with craftsmanship. We are looking for articles which show Christianity slugging it out where people hurt but we want the stories told and presented professionally. Good photography helps place material with us."

QUEEN OF ALL HEARTS, 40 S. Saxon Ave., Bay Shore NY 11706. Editor: James McMillan, S.M.M. For persons "religiously motivated; interested in Catholic Marian spirituality; all ages, apostolically inclined, interested in their spiritual welfare." Bimonthly. Circulation: about 10,000. Not copyrighted. Buys 40 to 50 mss a year. Pays on acceptance. Will send a sample copy to a writer on request. Submit seasonal material 6 months in advance. Reports in 1 month. Submit complete ms. Enclose S.A.S.E.

Nonfiction and Photos: "Religious subjects on art, spirituality, theology, the apostolate, especially with a Marian theme. This is a devotional magazine." Length: 800 to 1,500 words. Pays $15 to $40. Photos purchased with mss. B&w glossies. Payment varies.

Fiction: Religious. Length: 1,000 to 1,800 words. Pays $15 to $40.

Poetry: Contemporary poetry with a Marian theme. Length: 4 to 24 lines. Payment in free subscription.

REVIEW FOR RELIGIOUS, 612 Humboldt Building, 539 N. Grand Blvd., St. Louis MO 63103. Editor: R. F. Smith, S.J. Issued bimonthly for Roman Catholic religious men and women. Pays on publication. Reports in 4 weeks. Enclose S.A.S.E.

Nonfiction, Fiction, and Poetry: Articles on ascetical, liturgical and canonical matters. Length: 2,000 to 10,000 words. Pays $6 a page. Occasionally accepts fiction and poetry on religious subjects. Pays 50¢ per line for poetry.

THE REVIEW OF BOOKS AND RELIGION, Box 86, White River Junction VT 05001. Editors: Kendig Brubaker Cully and Iris V. Cully. For clergy, directors and coordinators of religious education, professors in religion, philosophy, and related fields, lay leaders of all faiths, and general readers, etc. Special sections on children's and gift books. Monthly except December and August. Circulation: 3,000. Most materials used are solicited. Book reviewers are advised to submit their credentials for reviewing and fields of interest. Submit seasonal material 3 months in advance. Reports in 4 to 6 weeks. Query first. Enclose S.A.S.E.

Nonfiction and Poetry: "The bulk of the contents is books in religion and adjacent fields, and there is no pay for reviews, though the reviewer keeps the book provided. Some poetry is used, for which no payment is made except 2 copies of the issue in which it appears. Only sophisticated, urbane poetry dealing with great humane and other religious themes is considered. Occasional articles are commissioned for which payment is made, but only on special occasions and by commissioned request."

ST. ANTHONY MESSENGER, 1615 Republic St., Cincinnati OH 45210. Editor: Rev. Jeremy Harrington, O.F.M. For Catholic family and high school graduate readers. Monthly. Buys first North American serial rights. Pays on acceptance. Will send free sample copy to a writer on request. Write for copy of guidelines for writers. Reports on submissions within 4 weeks. Enclose S.A.S.E.

Nonfiction: Uses human nature as subject matter. Modern society, family, religious, psychological and moral problems and positive suggestions for their solution. Also wants humor. Must be concrete, anecdotal, and be of human interest. No writing down, sentimentalism, or preachiness. Length: 2,500 to 3,500 words. Pays 6¢ per word minimum.

Photos: "We usually do our own work, but are in the market for picture stories on personalities, family and social work features." Uses b&w glossy, 7x10. Requires model releases. Pays $10 and up.

Fiction: Anything true to human nature. No sentimentality or moralizing. Need not be specifically religious. Usually 2,500 to 3,500 words. Also short-shorts. Pays minimum of 6¢ a word, up to $300.

How To Break In: "We receive more opinion articles than we want or can publish, so I would recommend a reporting type article that would interview experts on a topic of deep and personal concern to people or a first-person article in which the writer shares an experience with which others can identify."

SAINTS' HERALD, P.O. Box HH, Independence MO 64055. Editor: Paul A. Wellington. Issued monthly. This is the family magazine of the Reorganized Church of Jesus Christ of Latter Day Saints. Reports in two weeks. Enclose S.A.S.E.

Nonfiction: Wants articles on current religious topics, church members and historical articles of 1,500 words. No payment.
Photos: Pays up to $8 on acceptance for good 8x10 pictures concerning the church.
Fiction: Relating to current religious problems, challenges, trends. Length: 1,500 words.

SANDAL PRINTS, 1820 Mt. Elliott, Detroit MI 48207. Editor: Rev. Allen Gruenke, OFM Capuchin. For people who are interested in the work of the Capuchins. Established in 1952. Circulation: 11,000. Not copyrighted. Payment on acceptance. Will send free sample copy to writer on request. Reports on material accepted for publication in 1 week. Returns rejected material immediately. Query first. Enclose S.A.S.E.
Nonfiction and Photos: Material on the contemporary apostolates and life style of Capuchins (especially in the Midwest). "We do not use any general religious material; no topical subjects or themes accepted." Length: 2,500 words. Pays $25 to $50. Pays $5 per b&w photo.

SCIENCE OF MIND MAGAZINE, 3251 W. 6th St., Los Angeles CA 90020. Phone: 213-388-2181. Editor: Willis H. Kinnear. Monthly. Buys all rights. Pays on publication. Will send free sample copy on request. Reports in six weeks. Enclose S.A.S.E.
Nonfiction: Wants articles on the spiritual aspects of science and philosophy; their relationship to religion; personal experiences of effectiveness of prayer in everyday living. Should be written in language of layman. Slant is toward constructive living by alignment of one's thoughts with the Power of God within one. Length: 1,000 to 1,800 words. Pays approximately 1½¢ per word.
Poetry: Uses poems of four to eight lines. Occasionally uses longer poems as centerspread. Must have spiritual import; imminence of God in creation. Rate varies from $3 to $10.

SCOPE, 426 S. Fifth St., Minneapolis MN 55415. Phone: 612-332-4561, Ext. 397. Editor: Miss Lily M. Gyldenvand. For women of the American Lutheran Church. Monthly. Circulation: 325,000. Buys first rights. Buys 200 to 300 mss a year. Occasionally overstocked. Pays on acceptance. Will send a sample copy to a writer on request. Submit seasonal material 4 to 5 months in advance. Reports in 2 to 3 weeks. Enclose S.A.S.E.
Nonfiction and Photos: "The magazine's primary purpose is to be an educational tool in that it transmits the monthly Bible study material which individual women use in preparation for their group meetings. It contains articles for inspiration and growth, as well as information about the mission and concerns of the church, and material that is geared to seasonal emphases. We are interested in articles that relate to monthly Bible study subject. We also want articles that tell how faith has affected, or can influence, the lives of women or their families. But we do not want preachy articles. We are interested in any subject that touches the home. The possibilities are limitless for good, sharp, stimulating and creative articles." Length: 700 to 1,000 words. Pays $10 to $50. Buys 3x5 or 8x10 b&w photos with mss or with captions only. Pays $7 to $10.
Poetry and Fillers: "We can use interesting, brief, pithy, significant, or clever filler items, but we use very little poetry and are very selective." Pays $5 to $15.

SEEK, Standard Publishing, 8121 Hamilton Ave., Cincinnati OH 45231. Editor: J. David Lang. For young and middle-aged adults who attend church and Bible classes. Sunday School paper; 8 pages. Established in 1970. Quarterly, in weeky issues. Circulation: 60,000. Rights purchased vary with author and material. Prefers first serial rights, but may consider second serial (reprint) rights or simultaneous rights. Buys 100 to 150 mss a year. Pays on acceptance. Will send free sample copy to writer on request. Write for copy of guidelines for writers. No photocopied submissions, but will consider simultaneous submissions in some instances. Submit seasonal (Christmas, Easter, New Year's) material 9 to 12 months in advance. Reports in 30 to 60 days. Query first or submit complete ms. Enclose S.A.S.E.

Nonfiction and Photos: "We look for articles that are warm, inspirational, devotional, of personal or human interest; that deal with controversial matters, timely issues of religious, ethical, or moral nature, or first-person testimonies, true-to-life happenings, vignettes, emotional situations or problems; communication problems, and examples of answered prayer. Article must deliver its point in a convincing manner, but not be patronizing or preachy. Must appeal to either men or women. Must be alive, vibrant, sparkling, and have a title that demands the article to be read. We could use articles of religious theme that relate to the Bicentennial. We will purchase a few articles that deal with faith or trials of blacks or other racial groups. Always need stories of families, marriages, problems on campus, and life testimonies." Recently published articles include "Of Love and Prejudice" which dealt subtly with the prejudice problem. Length: 400 to 1,200 words. Pays 1½¢ to 2¢ a word. B&w photos purchased with or without mss. Pays $7.50 minimum.

Fiction: Religious fiction and religiously slanted historical and humorous fiction. Length: 400 to 1,200 words. Pays 1½¢ to 2¢ a word.

Fillers: Bible crossword puzzles, jumbles and hidden word puzzles are used as fillers. Pays $10 minimum.

THE SIGN, Union City NJ 07087. Phone: 201-867-6400. Editor: Rev. Augustine Paul Hennessy. Monthly. Buys all rights. Will send free sample copy to a writer on request. Reports in three weeks. Enclose S.A.S.E.

Nonfiction and Photos: Uses material of general interest as well as religious material. Wants articles of 1,200 to 3,000 words on social problems, profiles, foreign affairs, human interest. Written in concrete, anecdotal style. Pays $75 to $300. Uses photographs submitted with articles and picture stories.

Fiction: Fiction should have general appeal as well as Catholic interest. Can run up to 3,500 words. Pays $250 to $300.

How To Break In: "Follow the lead of your own enthusiasm. This presupposes some knowledge and depth of feeling. Since *Sign* is geared to the evocation of hope, I remind them that challenges to hope come from areas of their own experience—a complicated home, a changing Church, and a shrinking world. And *Sign* is interested in this kind of material."

SIGNS OF THE TIMES, 1350 Villa, Mountain View CA 94042. Editor: Lawrence Maxwell. Seventh-Day Adventist. For religiously inclined persons of all ages and denominations. Monthly. Buys first rights only. Reports in one week to several months. Enclose S.A.S.E.

Nonfiction: Uses articles of interest to religiously inclined of all denominations. Most material furnished by regular contributors, but freelance submissions carefully read. Sincerity, originality, brevity necessary. Lengths: 700 to 1,800 words.

SISTERS TODAY, St. John's Abbey, Collegeville MN 56321. Editor: Rev. Daniel Durken, O.S.B. "Primarily written and read by religious women of the Roman Catholic Church." Published monthly except July and August. Not copyrighted. Pays on publication. Will send free sample copy on request. Reports promptly. Query first with brief description of article. Enclose S.A.S.E.

Nonfiction: Articles, 1,500 to 3,500 words about the Christian life in general and religious life in particular. Religious renewal, community, prayer, apostolates for Sisters today, the role of religious women in today's world, liturgical and Scriptural commentaries. Pays $5 per printed page. Recently published articles include "Law and Order and Religious Life" (an article on Canon Law for religious).

SOCIAL JUSTICE REVIEW, 3835 Westminister Place, St. Louis MO 63108. Phone: 314-371-1653. Editor: Harvey J. Johnson. Issued monthly except for combination of July-August issues. Not copyrighted; "however special articles within the magazine may be copyrighted, or an occasional special issue has been copyrighted due to author's request." Query first. Enclose S.A.S.E.

Nonfiction: Wants scholarly articles on society's economic, religious, social, intellectual and political problems with the aim of bringing Catholic social thinking to bear upon these problems. 2,000 to 3,000 words. Pays about 1¢ a word.

SPIRITUAL LIFE, 2131 Lincoln Rd., N.E., Washington DC 20002. Phone: 202-832-6622. Editor: Rev. Christopher Latimer, O.C.D. "Largely Catholic, well-educated, serious readers. High percentage are priests and religious, but also some laymen. A few are non-Catholic or non-Christian." Quarterly. Circulation: 14,000. Buys first rights. Buys about 20 mss a year. Pays on acceptance. Will send a sample copy to a writer on request. Write for copy of guidelines for writers. "Brief autobiographical information (present occupation, past occupations, books and articles published, etc.) should accompany article. Follow *A Manual of Style* (University of Chicago)." Reports in 2 weeks. Enclose S.A.S.E.
Nonfiction: Serious articles of contemporary spirituality. Quality articles about man's encounter with God in the present-day world. Language of articles should be college-level. Technical terminology, if used, should be clearly explained. Material should be presented in a positive manner. Sentimental articles or those dealing with specific devotional practices not accepted. "*Spiritual Life* tries to avoid the 'popular,' sentimental approach to religion and to concentrate on a more intellectual approach. We do not want first-person accounts of spiritual experiences (visions, revelations, etc.) nor sentimental treatments of religious devotions." Buys inspirational and think pieces. No fiction or poetry. Length: 3,000 to 5,000 words. Pays $50 minimum. "Four contributor's copies are sent to author on publication of article." Book reviews should be sent to Brother Edward O'Donnell, O.C.D., Carmelite Monastery, P.O. Box 189, Waverly NY 14892.

STANDARD, 6401 The Paseo, Kansas City MO 64131. Editor: Robert D. Troutman. Adult story paper. Copyrighted, Nazarene Publishing House. Weekly. Will accept second rights and simultaneous submissions. Pays on acceptance. Write for copy of guidelines for writers. Reports in about 60 days. Enclose S.A.S.E.
Fiction: "Stories should vividly portray definite Christian emphasis or character-building values, without being preachy. Setting, plot, and action should be realistic." Length: 2,000 to 3,000 words. Pays $20 per 1,000 words.

SUNDAY DIGEST, 850 N. Grove Ave., Elgin IL 60120. Editor: Darlene Petri. Issued weekly for Christian adults. Buys all rights. Pays on acceptance. Will send free sample copy to a writer on request. Write for editorial requirements pamphlet. Reports on submissions in 4 weeks. Enclose S.A.S.E.
Nonfiction and Photos: Needs articles applying the Christian faith to personal and social problems, articles of family interest and on church subjects, personality profiles, practical self-help articles, personal experience articles and inspirational anecdotes. Length: 500 to 1,800 words. "Study our product and our editorial requirements. Have a clear purpose for every article or story—use anecdotes and dialog—support opinions with research." Pays 3¢ per word minimum. Photos purchased only with mss. Pays about $10 each, depending on quality. Negatives requested (b&w). Return of prints cannot be guaranteed.
Fiction: Occasionally uses fiction that is hard-hitting, fast-moving, with a real woven-in, not "tacked on," Christian message. Length: 1,000 to 1,500 words. Pays 3¢ per word minimum.
Poetry: Occasionally used if appropriate to format. Pays 5¢ per word minimum.
Fillers: Anecdotes of inspirational value, jokes and short humor; must be appropriate to format and in good taste. Length: up to 500 words. Pays 5¢ per word minimum.

SUNDAY SCHOOL LESSON ILLUSTRATOR, The Sunday School Board, 127 9th Ave., N., Nashville TN 37234. Editor: William H. Stephens. For members of Sunday School classes that use the International Sunday School Lessons and for adults seeking in-depth Biblical information. Quarterly. Circulation: 50,000. Buys all rights. Buys 25 mss a year. Payment on acceptance. Will not consider photocopied submissions. Submit seasonal material (for Christmas and Easter) 1 year in advance. Reports in 2 weeks. Query first or submit complete ms. Enclose S.A.S.E.
Nonfiction and Photos: Journalistic articles and photo stories researched on Biblical subjects, such as archaeology and sketches of biblical personalities. Material must be written for laymen but research quality must be up-to-date and thorough. Should be written in a contemporary, journalistic style and be based on International Sunday

School Lesson outlines. Pays 2½¢ per word. B&w and color photos purchased with ms or on assignment. Captions required. Pays $7.50 to $10.
Fiction and Poetry: Limited amount of religious fiction. Traditional forms of poetry. Pays 2½¢ a word for fiction; $3 to $20 for poetry, depending on length.

THE SUNDAY SCHOOL TIMES AND GOSPEL HERALD, Union Gospel Press, Box 6059, Cleveland OH 44101. Editor: Rev. John Danilson. For Evangelical Christian families, missionaries; an international readership. Bimonthly. Buys all rights. Buys approximately 175 mss a year. Payment on acceptance. Will send free sample copy to writer on request. Write for copy of guidelines for writers. Submit seasonal material (for all major holidays) 10 months in advance. Returns rejected material within a month. Reports on material accepted for publication in 90 days. Query first or submit complete ms. Enclose S.A.S.E.
Nonfiction and Photos: "Particularly interested in interview type articles about real people and places, i.e., halfway houses, youth group directors, missionaries, etc. Personal experience articles also desired. Evangelical Christian emphasis should be maintained. Subject matter should be relevant to today's Christian. New, fresh topics are desired. Facts and figures must be accurate and verifiable. (List of sources should be supplied.) All articles must be Bible-based according to the King James Version." Length: 1,000 to 2,000 words. Pays 2¢ per word. B&w and color photos are purchased but not returned. Pays $3 for b&w; $5 to $10 for color slides.
Fiction: Must have strong evangelical viewpoint; Bible-based. Length: 1,000 to 2,000 words. Pays 2¢ per word.
Poetry and Fillers: Traditional forms, blank verse, free verse. Must be related to theme. Length: 25 lines. Pays 35¢ a line. Jokes and short humor. Pays 2¢ a word.

THE TEXAS METHODIST/UNITED METHODIST REPORTER, P.O. Box 1076, Dallas TX 75221. Phone: 214-748-6491. Issued weekly for a national readership of United Methodist pastors and laypersons. Not copyrighted. Payment on acceptance. Query first. Enclose S.A.S.E.
Nonfiction and Photos: "We will consider any story that is submitted on the basis of its general appeal to our readership which is almost totally United Methodist. We focus our efforts on the laity, rather than the clergy. Story content should not necessarily be narrowly Methodist, but should be written toward our Methodist audience. Any story which touches the needs and interests of persons as Christians and/or Methodists stands an excellent chance of being accepted for publication. A story about a distinctly Christian response to human need would be looked upon favorably. Writers should submit story ideas for consideration. We do not guarantee use of, or payment for, any story unless specific arrangements are made ahead of time." Recent articles include one on a United Methodist salesman who quit his job to help several human service agencies and the reasons why his faith caused him to make that vocational change; and a former Miss America who now sings her faith in churches and on stage. Pays 3¢ per word. "We encourage the submission of good action photos (5x7 or 8x10 b&w glossies of professional quality) of the person(s) or situation portrayed in the story." Pays $10.

THESE TIMES, Southern Publishing Association, Box 59, Nashville TN 37202. Phone: 615-889-8000. Editor: Kenneth J. Holland. For the general public; adult. Magazine; 36 pages. Established in 1891. Monthly. Circulation: 207,000. Rights purchased vary with author and material. May buy first North American serial rights, second serial (reprint) rights or simultaneous rights. Buys about 50 mss a year. Pays on acceptance. Will send free sample copy to writer on request. Write for copy of guidelines for writers. Will consider photocopied and simultaneous submissions. Will accept cassette submissions. Submit seasonal material 6 months in advance. Reports on material accepted for publication in 2 weeks. Returns rejected material in 1 week. Query first. Enclose S.A.S.E.
Nonfiction and Photos: Material on the relevance of Christianity and everyday life. Inspirational articles. How-to; home and family problems; health. Drugs, alcohol, gambling, abortion, Bible doctrine. Marriage; divorce; country living or city living. "We like the narrative style. Find a person who has solved a problem. Then, tell

how he did it." Recently published "The Executioner (capital punishment) and "The Family Is Where It's At." Length: 250 to 2,500 words. Pays 6¢ to 10¢ a word. B&w and color photos are purchased with or without ms, or on assignment. Pays $20 to $25 for b&w; $75 to $150 for color.

TODAY'S CHRISTIAN MOTHER, 8121 Hamilton Ave., Cincinnati OH 45231. Editor: Mrs. Wilma L. Shaffer. Quarterly. Rights purchased vary with author and material. Buys first North American serial rights and first serial rights. Payment on acceptance. Will send free sample copy to a writer on request. Reports on submissions within one month. Enclose S.A.S.E.
Nonfiction: Devotional and inspirational articles for the family. Also articles concerning the problems and pleasures of parents of preschool children, and Christian child training. Recently published articles include "Cherish Their Differences" (contrast your children; never compare them) and "Know the Motive" (with toddler or teenager, communication counts). Length: 600 to 1,200 words. Also can use some handcraft and activity ideas for preschoolers. Study magazine before submitting. Pays minimum of 1½¢ per word.
How To Break In: "Write about familiar family situations in a refreshingly different way, so that help and inspiration shine through the problems and pleasures of parenthood."

TRIUMPH, 278 Broadview Avenue, Warrenton VA 22186. Editor: Michael Lawrence. For "traditional Catholics, ages 18 and up with college education." Established in 1966. Monthly. Circulation: 10,000. Buys first North American serial rights. Buys 15 mss a year. Payment on publication. Will send a sample copy to a writer for $1. Will consider photocopied submissions. Reports in 1 month. Enclose S.A.S.E.
Nonfiction: General subject matter: "Theological, philosophical, political studies. Commentary on current events from an orthodox Catholic point of view. We are not political conservatives. We transcend the conservative–liberal dialectic. No 'human interest' stories. We would like to see articles on the growing attack on the family." Buys think pieces and movie and book reviews. Length: 1,000 to 3,000 words. Pays 2½¢ a word.

TRUTH ON FIRE!, P.O. Box 223, Postal Station A, Vancouver B.C., Canada V6C 2N3. Editor: Evangelist Wesley H. Wakefield. For British commonwealth residents predominantly. Publication of The Bible Holiness Movement. Every 2 months (usually); 32 (6x9) pages. Established in 1949. Circulation: 1,000 to 2,000. Rights purchased vary with author and material. May buy all rights; but will sometimes reassign rights to author after publication or second serial (reprint) rights. Buys 6 to 15 mss a year. Payment on acceptance. Will send free sample copy to writer on request (as available). Will consider simultaneous submissions. Reports in 2 weeks. Query first or submit complete ms. Enclose S.A.E. and International Reply Coupons.
Nonfiction and Photos: "Evangelical articles; articles dealing with social reforms (pacifism, civil rights, religious liberty); expose articles (present-day slavery, cancer, tobacco, etc.,). first-person testimonies of Christian experience; doctrinal articles from Wesleyan interpretation. Must observe our evangelical taboos. Nothing favoring use of tobacco, alcohol, attendance at dances or theatres; nothing pro-abortion, pro-divorce-remarriage; no hip or slang. Also, we do not accept Calvinistic religious or right-wing political material. Would like to see material on Christian pacifism, anti-semitism, present-day slavery, marijuana research, religious issues in Ireland, and religious articles." Recently published articles include "Bible Speaks to Capital and Labour," "Homosexual; Gay, Queer, or Sin" (views as a sin). "What Is a Protestant?" Length: 300 to 2,500 words (1,000 preferred). Pays $5 to $25. (This varies depending on article and research involved.) Pays $5 to $15 for 5x7 b&w photos purchased with or without mss. "Subjects should conform to our mores of dress (no jewelry, no makeup, no long-haired men, no mini skirts, etc.) except in some news or topical photo."
Fillers: Newsbreaks, quotes. Length: 30 to 100 words. Pays $1 to $2.50.

THE UNITED CHURCH OBSERVER, 85 St. Clair Ave. E., Toronto 7, Ont., Canada. Editor: A.C. Forrest; Associate Editor: Patricia Clarke. For families in the United Church of Canada. 12 times a year. Not copyrighted. Pays on acceptance. Will send a sample copy to a writer for 35¢. Reports in 1 month. Query first. Enclose S.A.E. and International Reply Coupons.
Nonfiction: Wants general interest articles on all subjects of interest to church people. No homiletics. Material must have some church connection. Also deal in international affairs. Bright, journalistic style is necessary. Preferred lengths are 1,000 to 2,500 words. Thorough knowledge of the subject, authority and topnotch writing are looked for. Pays $40 minimum.
Photos: Buys photographs with mss and occasional picture stories. Use both b&w and color; b&w should be 8x10; color, prefers 4x5 transparencies but can work from 2¼x2¼ or 35mm. Payment varies.

UNITED EVANGELICAL ACTION, P.O. Box 28, Wheaton IL 60187. Phone: 312-665-0500. Editor: Tom Johnston. For Evangelical leaders. Quarterly. Circulation: 10,000. Buys all rights. Does not normally use unsolicited material but secures well-documented articles from known authorities on particular topics. Query first. Enclose S.A.S.E.
Nonfiction: "Topics of interest to church leaders—including pastors and laymen—special issues within the evangelical perspective." Length: 1,500 to 2,500 words. Pays 2¢ to 5¢ a word.

UNITY MAGAZINE, Unity Village MO 64065. Editor: James A. Decker. Publication of Unity School of Christianity. Magazine; 66 (7x10) pages. Established in 1889. Monthly. Circulation: 225,000. Rights purchased vary with author and material. May buy first serial rights or second serial (reprint) rights. Buys 200 mss a year. Pays on acceptance. Will send free sample copy to writer on request. Write for copy of guidelines for writers. No photocopied or simultaneous submissions. Submit seasonal material 6 to 8 months in advance. Reports in 2 weeks. Submit complete ms. Enclose S.A.S.E.
Nonfiction and Photos: "Inspirational articles, metaphysical in nature, about individuals who are using Christian principles in their living." Personal experience, interview; nothing of a controversial nature (either politically or religiously). Length: no minimum; 2,000 words maximum. Pays minimum of 2¢ a word. 4x5 or 8x10 color transparencies purchased without mss. Pays $75 each.
Poetry: Traditional forms, blank verse, free verse. Length: 20 lines maximum. Pays 50¢ per line.

THE UPPER ROOM, 1908 Grand Ave., Nashville TN 37203. For "people of all ages and many Christian denominations who have personal daily devotions or family devotions." Established in 1935. Bimonthly. Circulation: 2,500,000. Buys all rights. Buys 365 meditations a year. Payment on publication. Will send a free sample copy to a writer on request. Will send editorial guidelines sheet on request. Enclose S.A.S.E.
Nonfiction: "Subject matter relates to the many facets of the Christian faith. We issue annually a leaflet on writing meditations for *The Upper Room*. This contains many topic areas of general and specific interest. Leaflet is free on request. Space permits development of one major idea per page, accompanied by a meaningful illustration, prayer, and Thought for the Day. Bible text and Bible readings also included. We try to present the merits of the Gospel of Christ and give encouragement in putting the Gospel into practice in everyday life." Length: 250 words. Pays $7 for each meditation used.

VANGUARD: VISION FOR THE SEVENTIES, 229 College St., Toronto, Ontario, Canada M5T 1R4. Estalished in 1970. 6 times a year. Circulation: 2,500. "Copyright is held jointly by author and publisher." Reports in 3 weeks. Query first. Enclose S.A.E. and International Reply Coupons.
Nonfiction: "*Vanguard* does not pay its contributors, but we welcome articles on any range of subjects: politics, economics, education, arts, urban affairs, etc., written from a Christian perspective and contributing to the development of a radical

Christian consciousness and life style. Contributions are reviewed by our editorial committee."

How To Break In: "This is an idea magazine, reaching a highly educated and culturally aware audience. Freelance writers who are not recognized experts in a field should query the editor for assignments. A summary of writer's educational and journalistic background should accompany all queries."

VISIONS, Our Sunday Visitor, Noll Plaza, Huntington IN 46750. Editor: Robert P. Lockwood. For Catholic junior high school (age 11 to 14) students of above average intelligence. Magazine; 12 (8½x11) pages. Estalished in 1974. 27 weeks during the school year. Circulation: 29,000. Buys all rights. Buys about 30 to 40 mss a year. Pays on publication. Will send free sample copy to writer on request. No photocopied or simultaneous submissions. Reports in 3 weeks. Query first or submit complete ms. Enclose S.A.S.E.

Nonfiction and Photos: "We are a Catholic religious publication, and we do want religious articles. But our major goal is to entertain as well as educate, so we will also accept some general interest pieces. Naturally, a Catholic outlook is helpful, but on our general interest articles, there is no need for a trumped-up religious theme. And absolutely *no* sermons." Informational, profile, humor, interview, historical, think pieces. Recently published articles on dinosaurs and the search for Noah's Ark. Length: 200 to 750 words. Pays $30 minimum; $65 for mss with 8x10 b&w photos. Pays $75 to $100 for 4-color photo story. Photos can be inspirational. Nature or Biblical themes acceptable for 4-color spreads.

VISTA, Wesleyan Publishing House, Box 2000, Marion IN 46952. Address submissions to Editor of Sunday School Magazines. Publication of the Wesleyan Church. For adults. Weekly. Circulation: 63,000. Not copyrighted. "Along with mss for first use, we also accept simultaneous submissions, second rights, and reprint rights. It is the writer's obligation to secure clearance from the original publisher for any reprint rights." Pays on acceptance. Will send a sample copy to a writer on request. Editorial deadlines are 9 months in advance of publication. Reports in 6 weeks. Enclose S.A.S.E.

Nonfiction and Poetry: Devotional, biographical, and informational articles with inspirational, religious, moral, or educational values. Favorable toward emphasis on: "New Testament standard of living as applied to our day; soul-winning (evangelism); proper Sunday observance; Christian youth in action; Christian education in the home, the church and the college; good will to others; worldwide missions; clean living, high ideals, and temperance; wholesome social relationships. Disapprove of liquor, tobacco, theaters, dancing. Mss are judged on the basis of human interest, ability to hold reader's attention, vivid characterizations, thoughtful analysis of problems, vital character message, expressive English, correct punctuation, proper diction. Know where you are going and get there." Length: 500 to 1,500 words. Pays 2¢ a word for quality material. Also uses verse. Length: 4 to 16 lines. Pays 25¢ a line.

Photos: Purchased with mss. 5x7 or 8x11 b&w glossies; portraying action, seasonal emphasis or scenic value. Various reader age-groups should be considered. Pays $1 to $2.50 depending upon utility.

Fiction: Stories should have definite Christian emphasis and character-building values, without being preachy. Setting, plot and action should be realistic. Length: 2,000 to 2,500 words; also short-shorts and vignettes. Pays 2¢ a word for quality material.

THE WAR CRY, The Official Organ of the Salvation Army, 546 Avenue of the Americas, New York NY 10011. Editor: Lt. Col. William Burrows. For "persons with evangelical Christian background; members and friends of the Salvation Army; the 'man in the street'." Weekly. Circulation: 290,000. Buys all rights. Buys approximately 200 mss a year. Pays on acceptance. Will send a sample copy to a writer on request. Submit seasonal material for Christmas and Easter issues at any time. "Christmas and Easter issues are four-color. Rate of payment for material used in these issues is considerably higher than for weekly issue material." Reports in 1 month. Enclose S.A.S.E.

Nonfiction: Inspirational and informational articles with a strong evangelical Christian slant, but not preachy. Prefers an anecdotal lead. In addition to general articles, needs articles slanted toward most of the holidays, including Mother's Day, Father's Day, Columbus Day, Washington's and Lincoln's birthdays, etc. Length: 1,000 to 1,800 words. Pays $15 to $35.

Photos: Occasionally buys pix submitted with mss, but seldom with captions only. B&w glossies. Pays $5 to $10.

Fiction: Prefers complete-in-one-issue stories. Stories should run 1,500 to 2,000 words and have a strong Christian slant. May have Salvation Army background, but this is not necessary and may be detrimental if not authentic. Can have modern or Biblical setting, but must not run contrary to Scriptural account. Principal Bible characters ordinarily should not be protagonists. Pays $30 to $40.

Poetry: Religious or nature poems. Uses very little poetry "except on Christmas and Easter themes." Length: 4 to 24 lines. Pays $2.50 to $15.

Fillers: Inspirational and informative items with a strong Christian slant. 1¢ to 2¢ per word.

WORLD ENCOUNTER, 2900 Queen Lane, Philadelphia PA 19129. Acting Editor: Rev. William A. Dudde. For members of the Lutheran Church in America who have more than average interest in, and understanding of, the overseas mission of the Lutheran Church and current human social concerns in other parts of the world. Magazine published every 2 months; 32 (8½x11) pages. Established in 1963. Circulation: 8,000. Buys all rights, but will reassign rights to author after publication. Buys 10 mss a year. Payment on publication. Will send free sample copy to writer on request. Will consider photocopied, cassette and simultaneous submissions, if information is supplied on other markets being approached. Reports in 1 month. Query first or submit complete ms. Enclose S.A.S.E.

Nonfiction and Photos: "This is a religious and educational publication using human interest features and think pieces relating to the Christian world mission and world community. Race relations in southern Africa; freedom movements in Portuguese colonies; social and political ferment in Latin America; resurgence of Oriental religions. Simple travelogues are not useful to us. Prospective writers should inquire as to the countries and topics of particular interest to our constituents. Material must be written in a popular style but the content must be more than superficial. It must be theologically, sociologically and anthropologically sound. We try to maintain a balance between gospel proclamation and concern for human and social development. We focus on what is happening in Lutheran groups. Our standards of content quality and writing are very high." Length: 500 to 1,800 words. Pays $15 to $100. B&w photos are purchased with or without accompanying mss or on assignment. Pays $10 to $20. Captions required.

How To Break In: "Contact Lutheran missionaries in some overseas country and work out an article treatment with them."

WORLD MISSION JOURNAL, 1548 Poplar Ave., Memphis TN 38104. Editor: Jim Newton. For ages 18 and up; conservative; high school education. Subject matter is slanted toward men and missions. Monthly tabloid format. Circulation: 75,000. Buys first North American serial rights. Buys 15 mss a year. Payment on acceptance. Will send free sample copy to writer on request. Write for editorial guidelines for writers. Will consider photocopied submissions. Reports in 2 weeks. Enclose S.A.S.E.

Nonfiction and Photos: Buys informational articles, especially features on Baptist laymen in missions. Length: 500 to 1,600 words. Pays 2½¢ a word. Buys photos with mss. Captions required. Pays $10 for 8x10 or 5x7 b&w glossies.

WORSHIP, St. John's Abbey, Collegeville MN 56321. Phone: 612-363-3765. Editor: Rev. Aelred Tegels, O.S.B. "For readers concerned with the problems of liturgical renewal. The readership is largely Roman Catholic with a growing percentage of readers from the other Christian churches." Monthly, except for July and August. Buys all rights. Pays on publication. Reports in two to three weeks. Enclose S.A.S.E.

Nonfiction: "*Worship* magazine is engaged in an ongoing study of both the theoretic and the pastoral dimensions of liturgy. It examines the historical traditions of worship in their doctrinal context, the experience of worship in the various Christian churches, the finding of contemporary theology, psychology, communications, cultural anthropology, and sociology in so far as these have a bearing on public worship. Since the Second Vatican Council, *Worship* magazine has been fully ecumenical in its editorial board and policies as well as in its contributors and contents. Study a recent issue." Length: 3,000 to 5,000 words. Pays 1¢ to 2¢ a word.

Retirement Publications

DYNAMIC MATURITY, 1909 K St., N.W., Washington DC 20049. Editor: Richard C. Davids. "DM is the official publication of AIM-Action for Independent Maturity. AIM members are the 50 to 65 age bracket, pre-retirees." Established in 1966. Bimonthly. Circulation: 116,000. Rights purchased vary with author and material. May buy all rights with the possibility of reassigning rights to author after publication; or first serial rights, or second serial (reprint) rights. Buys 60 mss a year. Payment on acceptance. Will send a free sample copy to a writer on request. Submit seasonal material 4 months in advance. Reports in 1 week. Query first or submit complete ms. Enclose S.A.S.E.
Nonfiction and Photos: General subject matter is "health for middle years, pre-retirement planning, second careers, well-developed hobbies, 'people in action' with useful activities, exciting use of leisure, financial preparation for retirement. We like the 'you' approach, nonpreachy, use of lively examples. We try to slant everything toward our age group, 50 to 65. We do not want pieces about individuals long retired. Prefer not seeing poetry, 'inspirational' preachments." Buys how-to, personal experience, profile, humor, nostalgia, travel articles. Length: 1,000 to 2,500 words. Pays 10¢ a word minimum, up to $400 per article. Photos purchased with and without mss for covers. Captions required. Pays $15 minimum for professional quality b&w (5x7, 8x10). Pays $25 minimum for professional quality color photos (35mm or 2¼x2¼ transparencies).

MATURE YEARS, 201 Eighth Ave., S., Nashville TN 37202. Editor: Mrs. Daisy D. Warren. For retired persons and those facing retirement; persons seeking help on how to handle problems and privileges of retirement. Established in 1954. Quarterly. Rights purchased vary with author and material; usually buys all rights. Buys about 50 mss a year. Payment on acceptance. Write for copy of guidelines for writers. Submit seasonal material 1 year in advance. Reports within 6 weeks. Submit complete ms. Enclose S.A.S.E.
Nonfiction, Fiction and Photos: "*Mature Years* is different from the secular press in that we like material with Christian and church orientation. Usually we prefer materials that have a happy, healthy outlook regarding aging, although advocacy (for older adults) articles are at times used. Each issue is developed on a specific theme and the majority of theme-related articles are solicited. However, many freelance materials are used. Articles dealing with all aspects of preretirement and retirement living. Short stories and leisure-time hobbies related to specific seasons. Examples of how older persons are helping others. Writing should be of interest to older adults, with Christian emphasis, though not preachy and moralizing. No poking fun or mushy, sentimental articles. We treat retirement from the religious viewpoint. How-to, humor and travel also considered." Length for nonfiction: 1,200 to 2,000 words. Pays 3¢ to 4¢ per word. 8x10 b&w glossies purchased with ms or on assignment. Payment varies. "We buy fiction for adults. Humor is preferred. Please, no children's stories and no stories about depressed, ailing situations of older adults." Length: 1,000 to 2,000 words. Pays 3¢ to 4¢ per word.

MODERN MATURITY, 215 Long Beach Blvd., Long Beach CA 90801. Phone: 213-432-5781. Editor: Hubert Pryor. Publication of the American Association of Retired Persons. For retirees. Bimonthly. Buys all rights. Pays on acceptance. Will send a sample copy to a writer on request. Reports in 2 weeks. Enclose S.A.S.E.

Nonfiction and Fiction: Service pieces for the retiree relating to income, hobbies, health, living; Americana, nostalgia, reminiscence, personality pieces, inspirational articles, current trends—anything of interest to the older American who wants to be "with it." "Especially can use thoughtful interviews with world figures in their older years, sensitive picture essays on how older people live, outspoken pronouncements by noted persons on matters concerning aging and/or retirement. Also in market for Christmas and other holiday material." Buys fiction occasionally. Length: 1,000 to 1,500 words, nonfiction; 1,500 words maximum, fiction. Pays $100 to $500.

Photos: "Special consideration for picture stories, photographic portfolios, etc." Photos must be professional quality only. Pays $25 and up per photo; much more for color and covers.

Fillers: Puzzles, jokes, short humor. Pays $5 and up.

NRTA JOURNAL, 215 Long Beach Blvd., Long Beach CA 90801. Phone: 213-432-5781. Editor: Hubert Pryor. Publication of the National Retired Teachers Association. For retired teachers. Bimonthly. Buys all rights. Pays on acceptance. Will send a sample copy to a writer on request. Reports in 2 weeks. Enclose S.A.S.E.

Nonfiction and Fiction: Service pieces for the retired teacher relating to income, health, hobbies, living; Americana, nostalgia, reminiscence, personality pieces, inspirational articles, current trends. "Also in market for pieces on cultural leaders, cultural subjects and Christmas and holiday material." Buys fiction occasionally. Length: 1,000 to 1,500 words for nonfiction; 1,500 words maximum for fiction. Pays $100 to $500.

Photos: "Special consideration for picture stories, photographic portfolios, etc." Pays $25 and up each; much more for color and covers.

Fillers: Puzzles, jokes, short humor. Pays $5 and up.

RETIREMENT LIVING, 150 E. 58 St., New York NY 10022. Phone: 212-593-2100. Editor: Roy Hemming. Associate Editor: Helen Alpert. "For pre-retirees (age 55 up) and retirees. Readers are alert, active, forward-looking, interested in all aspects of meaningful living in the middle and later years." Monthly. Buys all rights. Pays on acceptance. Will send a sample copy for 75¢ and 18¢ postage. Write for copy of guidelines for writers (enclose S.A.S.E.). Submit seasonal and holiday material 6 months in advance. Reports in 2 to 3 weeks. Queries helpful, but will look at complete ms. "Manuscripts must be accompanied by S.A.S.E.; otherwise not returned."

Nonfiction and Photos: "We like factual personal experiences, humor, income ideas, money management, self-fulfillment; articles with a strong service value or how-to with names and sources for reader follow-up." Unusual travel stories only. Length: 800 to 1,500 words. Pays $75 to $150 an article. "We reserve all rights to edit and rewrite to suit our distinct style and space requirements. Photos and color slides must be of professional quality." Pays $25 and up.

How To Break In: "Profile a well-known or dynamic person in your community whose retirement or retirement plans can be instructive to our readers."

Science Publications

Publications classified here aim at laymen interested in technical and scientific developments and discoveries, applied science, and technical or scientific hobbies. Journals for professional scientists, engineers, repairmen, etc., will be found in Trade Journals.

ASTRONOMY MAGAZINE, 757 N. Broadway, Suite 204, Milwaukee WI 53202. Phone: 414-276-2689. Managing Editor: Ms. Frances Weaver. For laymen interested in astronomy. Monthly magazine; 64 pages. Established in 1973. Circulation: 40,000. Rights purchased vary with author and material. Buys first North American serial rights; second serial (reprint) rights; or simultaneous rights "for book chapter(s) only." Buys 50 mss a year. "Few are unsolicited. Most are commissioned." Payment on publication. Will send sample copy to writer for $1. Reports in 4 to 6 weeks. Query first. Enclose S.A.S.E.

Nonfiction and Photos: "Popular level science articles on astronomy, spaceflight, life in space, etc. Use documentary style, with accompanying photos. We're less technical than other publications. We don't accept material on astrology or the Bible. Most articles are commissioned to established science writers." Buys informational, how-to, photo, and technical articles. Length: 3,000 words maximum. Pays 4¢ to 6¢ a word. B&w photos and color photos purchased with or without ms. Captions optional. Photos must be of astronomers or astronomical subjects. Pays $7.50 for b&w; $10 minimum for color.

BIG COUNTRY 10-5 NEWS, P.O. Box 12181, Denver CO 80212. Phone: 303-455-5414. Editor: Rose Harper. For "ages 14 to 99, generally users of two-way radios known as Citizens Band. (Do not confuse with hams—amateur radio operators). All education levels. Interested in human beings in the same field or related fields and in the unusual aspects of CB radio (not too heavy on technical details)." Established in 1970. Monthly. Circulation: 5,000. Buys all rights, but will reassign them to author after publication upon written request. Retains first book publication rights. Payment on acceptance. Will send sample copy to writer for a 10¢ stamp. Send for editorial guidelines before submission (enclose S.A.S.E.). Reports in 2 months. Enclose S.A.S.E. for return of submissions.

Nonfiction and Photos: Publishes "material affecting users of CB radio. Possible subjects: Just how well do items in the Federal Register register with the average citizen? Who has influenced making of rules and regulations (Part 95 of FCC Rules and Regulations). List price—is this an advertising fraud? What sunlight, heat, cold (or any other such things) do to your CB rig. Articles only at present time." Freelancer should write with "short words, clear meanings, accuracy of facts. Don't fake the peculiar vocabulary, please, as it takes a CBer to do this. Emphasis on the worth of human beings to themselves, to others. We don't mind spice, but will not accept filth: *There is a great difference.* We are unique in our field and have created an opinion impact far beyond our size—something that should be cause for astonishment because we seldom feature VIP's (called Vicious Influence Peddlers in our field) but rather we feature 'you, me, the guy, the gal from everyday life' against a background of CB radio. We use 'handles,' or full legal names for people we feature. We are fair to the 'legals' and 'illegals' using CB radio; both have fair and valid points to make. We do not want to see cutesy stuff. Corn is ok, if it is interesting corn. No preaching, no moralizing. No standing on a pedestal and looking down at the reader. New product material accepted. Articles wanted on legal rights denied the average citizen by our government agencies; progress in the actual structure and use of CB radio in developments in electronics that are of medical benefit (the pacemakers for heart patients are an example of this)." Book reviews (all types). Length: 500 to 1,000 words. Pays 1¢ a word. Purchases photos with and without mss and captions required. B&w snapshots. Pays $1.

Poetry: Regular poetry columns. "Poetry that touches the heart, no matter what subject." Accepts all forms of poetry. Submit no more than 2 or 3 poems at one time. Length: 4 to 16 lines. Pays $1 to $3.

ELEMENTARY ELECTRONICS, 229 Park Avenue South, New York NY 10003. Phone: 212-673-1300. Editor-in-Chief: Julian S. Martin. For electronics hobbyists, amateur radio operators, shortwave listeners, CB radio operators. Magazine; every 2 months; 96 pages. Established in 1950. Circulation: 250,000. Buys all rights. Buys 350 mss a year. Payment on acceptance. Will send sample copy to writer on request. Will not consider photocopied or simultaneous submissions. Reports on material accepted for publication in 2 to 4 weeks. Returns rejected material as soon as rejected. Query first. Enclose S.A.S.E.

Nonfiction and Photos: Construction articles are most needed; also, theory and feature articles related to hobby electronics. How-to and technical articles. The writer should read our book and decide whether he can be of service to us; and then send us a precis of the story he wishes to submit." Length: as required to tell the story. Pays $150 to $250. No additional payment for photos used with mss.

How To Break In: "I would make three suggestions. First, how-to pieces are always winners. The same goes for construction projects. But they must be to fulfill some need, not just for the sake of selling. Finally, installation stories are very good — something that you buy and where the installation takes some degree of know-how that can be illustrated with step-by-step photos. The author will have to take the photos as he does the job. Theory pieces are tougher — you have to really know us and sense our needs and the sorts of things our readers want to learn about. Feeling and timing are key. We are about 98% freelance and most of our material originates in queries. Please read the magazine first!"

FREY SCIENTIFIC COMPANY CATALOG, 465 South Diamond St., Mansfield OH 44903. Published annually. Buys all rights. Buys 50 to 75 rhymes a year. Pays "on acceptance, between October 1 and February 1. Rhymes that arrive after the latter date are held and paid for about November 1, the start of our next publication season." Enclose S.A.S.E.

Poetry: "We use humorous quatrains and limericks in our annual school science materials catalog, which is sent to every high school and college in the U.S. Each rhyme—limerick, quatrain, or couplet—is matched as best as possible to the appropriate section of our catalog. Rhymes pertaining to physics are included in the physics section, biology in the biology section, chemistry in the chemistry section, earth science to earth science, etc." Interested in buying material from writers "who can combine, in a single rhyme, our requirements of proper rhyme construction, distinct scientific reference, and humor. Generally, we will waive any of the three requirements if the rhyme is strong in the other two." Pays $5 per rhyme.

HAM RADIO MAGAZINE, Greenville NH 03048. Phone: 603-878-1441. Editor: James R. Fisk. For amateur radio licensees and electronics experimenters. Special May issue: antenna. Established in 1968. Monthly. Circulation: 45,000. Buys all rights. Buys 20 mss a month. Payment on acceptance. Will send free sample copy to writer on request. Write for copy of guidelines for writers. Submit special issue material 6 months in advance. Reports in 1 month. Query helpful, but not essential. Enclose S.A.S.E.

Nonfiction and Photos: "Technical and home construction articles pertaining to amateur radio. Stress is placed on new development. Technical articles of interest to the radio amateur, or home construction articles pertaining to amateur radio equipment." Length: 500 to 5,000 words. Pays approximately $16 per magazine page. Sharp, clear glossy prints (4x5 to 8x10) purchased with accompanying mss. "Don't wish to see any fiction or operating news."

MECHANIX ILLUSTRATED, 1515 Broadway, New York NY 10036. Phone: 212-869-3000. Editor: Robert G. Beason. Recreation Editor: Bill D. Miller. Home and Shop Editor: Burt Murphy. Managing Editor: Arthur J. Maher. Special issues include boating (spring), new cars (October). Monthly magazine; 106 (8⅛x10⅞) pages. Buys all rights except for picture sets. Pays on acceptance. Write for copy of guidelines for writers. Reports promptly. Query first. Enclose S.A.S.E.

Nonfiction: Feature articles about science, inventions, novel boats, planes, cars, electronics, recreational vehicles, weapons, health, money management, unusual occupations, usually with mechanical or scientific peg, but not too technical. Recently published articles include "A Sneak Preview of the '77 Cars" and "12 Ways to Save on Heating Fuel." Length: 1,500 words. Pays $400 minimum. Also uses home workshop projects, kinks, etc., for Home and Shop section. Pays $75 to $500, and higher in exceptional circumstances. "We offer a varied market for all types of do-it-yourself material, ranging from simple tips on easier ways to do things to

major construction projects. Boatbuilding, furniture construction, painting, photography, electronics, gardening, astronomy, concrete and masonry work or any type of building construction or repair are just a few of the subjects that interest." Pays minimum of $15 for a tip submitted on a postcard without an illustration. Pays $20 to $25 for an illustrated and captioned tip.
Photos: Photos should accompany mss. Pays $400 and up for transparencies of interesting mechanical or scientific subjects accepted for cover; prefers 4x5, but 2¼ square is acceptable. Inside color: $300 for one page, $500 for two, $700 for three, etc. Pays $30 for single (b&w) feature photos involving new developments, etc., in the field, Home and Shop tips illustrated with one photo, $25. Captions are required. B&w picture sets, up to $350. Requires model releases.
Fillers: Pays $75 for half-page fillers.
How To Break In: "If you're planning some kind of home improvement and can write, you might consider doing a piece on it for us. Good how-to articles on home improvement are always difficult to come by. Aside from that, no particular part of the book is easier to break into than another because we simply don't care whether you've been around or been published here before. We don't care who you are or whether you have any credentials — we're in the market for good journalism and if it's convincing, we buy it."

OCEANS, 3131 Fillmore St., San Francisco CA 94123. Editor: Don Greame Kelley. For the alert, involved, and mobile. Established in 1969. Bimonthly. Circulation: 50,000. Pays on publication. Buys 40 to 50 mss a year. Will send free sample copy to writer on request. Write for copy of guidelines for writers. Will consider photocopied submissions. Reports in 2 to 3 months. Query first. Enclose S.A.S.E.
Nonfiction and Photos: "Want articles on the worldwide realm of salt water: marine life (biology and ecology), oceanography, man-sea history, geography, undersea exploration and study, voyages, ships, coastal areas including environmental problems, seaports and shipping, transocean aviation, islands, food-fishing and aquaculture (mariculture), peoples of the sea including anthropological materials. Freelancer should be simple, direct, factual, very readable (avoid dullness and pedantry, make it lively and interesting but not cute, flip, or tongue-in-cheek; avoid purple prose). Careful research, good structuring, no padding. Our magazine is more serious than the common run of diving mags; less technical than *Scientific American.* We do not want articles on scuba; adventuring, travel tend to be overworked. Prefer no sport fishing, boating, surfing, other purely sport-type matter. Diving okay if serious in purpose, unusual in results or story angle. We want articles on rarely visited islands, ports, or shores which have great intrinsic interest, but not treated in purely travelogue style. Can use more on sea birds, port cities, sea-based peoples." Buys informational, how to (limited), personal experience, a few interviews, a few profiles, historical, photo, travel (not pure, per se) and limited technical articles. Length: 1,000 to 4,000 words. Pays $60 per page copy or photos. Purchases photos with mss; sometimes separately. Captions required. Prefers 8x10 b&w glossy. Buys color transparencies, original, 35mm and up. Pays $150 for cover.

POPULAR ELECTRONICS, 1 Park Ave., New York NY 10016. Phone: 212-725-3566. Editor: Arthur P. Salsberg. For electronics hobbyists, hi-fi buffs, TV service, CB'ers, hams. Monthly. Established in 1954. Circulation: 371,000. Buys all rights. Buys about 150 mss a year. Pays on acceptance. Will send sample copy to writer for 75¢. Write for copy of guidelines for writers. Will not consider photocopied or simultaneous submissions. Reports in 2 weeks. Query first. Enclose S.A.S.E.
Nonfiction and Photos: "State-of-the-art reports, tutorial articles, construction projects, etc. The writer must know what he's talking about and not depend on 'hand-out' literature from a few manufacturers or research laboratories. The writer must always bear in mind that the reader has some knowledge of electronics." Informational, how-to, and technical articles. Length: 500 to 3,000 words. Pays $50 to $100 per published page with photo illustration. B&w glossies preferred.
Fillers: Tips and techniques. Length: 25 to 250 words. Pays $2 to $20.

POPULAR MECHANICS, 224 W. 57th St., New York NY 10019. Editor: Jim Liston.

Executive Editor: Sheldon Gallager. Editor: John A. Linkletter; Managing Editor: Daniel C. Fales. Home and Shop Editor: Wayne Leckey. Buys all rights. Pays promptly. Query first. Enclose S.A.S.E.

Nonfiction: Exciting male interest articles with strong science, exploration and adventure emphasis. Looking for reporting on new and unusual developments. The writer should be specific about what makes it new, different, better, cheaper, etc. "We are always looking for fresh ideas in home maintenance, shop technique, and crafts, for project pieces used in the back part of the book. The front of the book uses articles in technology and general science, but writers in that area should have background in science." Lengths: 300 to 2,000 words. Pays $300 to $500 and up.

Photos: Dramatic photos are most important, and they should show people and things in action. Occasionally buys picture stories with short text block and picture captions. The photos must tell the story without much explanation. Topnotch photos are a must with Craft Section articles. Can also use remodeling of homes, rooms and outdoor structures. Pays $25 minimum.

Fillers: How-to-do-it articles on craft projects and shop work well-illustrated with photos and drawings. The writer must provide the drawings, diagrams, cutaways, and/or photos that would be appropriate to the piece. Finished drawings suitable for publication are not necessary; rough but accurate pencil drawings are adequate for artist's copy. Pays $15.

How To Break In: "We are interested in developing more regular freelance correspondents in the West, Far West, and particularly in the South. We don't have anyone in Texas right now. This presents a good opportunity for someone from those areas to break in."

POPULAR SCIENCE MONTHLY, 380 Madison Ave., New York NY 10017. Phone: 212-687-3000. Editor: Hubert P. Luckett. For the well-educated adult male, interested in science, technology, new products. Monthly magazine; 175 pages. Established in 1872. Circulation: 1,725,000. Buys all rights. Buys several hundred mss a year. Payment on acceptance. Write for copy of guidelines for writers. Will not consider photocopied or simultaneous submissions. Submit seasonal material 3 to 4 months in advance. Reports in 2 to 3 weeks. Query first. Enclose S.A.S.E.

Nonfiction and Photos: "*Popular Science Monthly* is a man's magazine devoted to exploring (and explaining) to a nontechnical but knowledgeable readership the technical world around us. We are a 'thing'-oriented publication: things that fly or travel down a turnpike, or go on or under the sea, or cut wood, or reproduce music, or build buildings, or make pictures, or mow lawns. We are especially focused on the new, the ingenious, and the useful. We are consumer oriented and are interested in any product that adds to a man's enjoyment of his home, yard, car, boat, workshop, outdoor recreation. Some of our 'articles' are only a picture and caption long. Some are a page long. Some occupy 4 or more pages. Contributors should be as alert to the possibility of selling us pictures and short features as they are to major articles. Freelancers should study the magazine to see what we want and avoid irrelevant submissions." Length: 2,000 words maximum. Pays a minimum of about $150 a published page. Prefers 8x10 b&w glossies. Pays $20.

Fillers: Uses shortcuts and tips for homeowners, home craftsmen, car owners, mechanics and machinists.

How To Break In: "Probably the easiest way to break in here is by covering a news story in science and technology that we haven't heard about yet. We need people to be acting as bird-dogs for us out there and we are willing to give the most leeway on these performances. What impresses us the most in a freelance piece — when we're thinking about uncovering a good contributor for the future — is the kind of illustrations the writer supplies. Too many of them kiss off the problem of illustrations. Nothing impresses us more than knowing that the writer can take or acquire good photos to accompany his piece. We probably buy the most freelance material in the do-it-yourself and home improvement areas."

RADIO-ELECTRONICS, 200 Park Ave. S., New York NY 10003. Editor: Larry Steckler. For electronics professionals and hobbyists. Monthly. Circulation: 164,000.

Buys all rights. Pays on acceptance. Send for "Guide to Writing." Reports on submissions in 2 weeks. Enclose S.A.S.E.

Nonfiction: Interesting technical stories on electronics, TV and radio, written from viewpoint of the TV service technician, serious experimenter, or layman with technical interests. Construction (how-to-build-it) articles used heavily. Unique projects bring top dollars. Cost of project limited only by what item will do. Emphasis on "how it works, and why." Much of material illustrated with schematic diagrams and pictures provided by author. Pays about $60 to $100 per magazine page.

Photos: Purchased with mss. Model releases required. Payment included in article price. 8x10 glossy.

How To Break In: "The simplest way to come in would be with an equipment report. Some of this is done in-house, but most of it comes from outsiders. Queries aren't necessary; just send the article, five or six typewritten pages."

SCIENCE DIGEST, 224 W. 57th St., New York NY 10019. Managing Editor: Dick Terisi. Science monthly "covering news, trends and developments in all of the disciplines," for readers of all ages. Circulation: 154,000. Buys all rights. Buys 80 to 100 mss a year. Pays on acceptance. Will send a sample copy to a writer for 75¢. Submit seasonal material 3 months in advance. Returns rejected material in 2 to 4 weeks. Query first. Enclose S.A.S.E.

Nonfiction and Photos: Authoritative pieces on any of the sciences. Illustrations are important, and should include diagrams wherever possible, and regular photo illustrations. Occasional social science and medical science articles. Read magazine before querying. "Emphasis on accuracy, interesting material, broad coverage across the disciplines." Buys personal experience articles "from experts only." Occasionally buys science oriented think pieces, exposes, travel articles. Length: 1,000 to 2,000 words. Pays $50 to $350. Photos purchased with mss or with captions only. 5x7 or larger glossies. Accepts most sizes of 4-color transparencies for cover illustration.

Fillers: Newsbreaks. Pays $10 minimum. Department Editor: Douglas Colligan.

How To Break In: "Most people that we have taken on here out of the blue have sold us on a good idea. It should be something that's current, and the newcomer is in a good position if he has access or knowledge of some little thing that's going on — a study at a university near him, for example — that we may not have heard or seen much about. No more animal stories. Short takes are all staff-written. Query first on everything."

SCIENCE NEWS, 1719 N Street, N.W., Washington DC 20036. Editor: Kendrick Frazier. Mostly staff-written. "We'll occasionally use a submitted article from an established science writer who we know and who is familiar with *Science News,* but such occasions are rare. We also occasionally are in the market for prepublication excerpts from books, especially those involving a thoughtful, humanistic approach toward science, by noted scientists of established reputation, but again that is very seldom. We are principally staff-written for two reasons: (1) Being a weekly newsmagazine, we work very close to deadline. Communications and coordination are crucial. Everything must note what we've previously reported on the same subject and then add what's new. (2) Quality control. We have really gotten burned in the past by freelance articles that were factually inaccurate."

SCIENTIFIC AMERICAN, 415 Madison Ave., New York NY 10017. Articles by professional scientists only.

73 MAGAZINE, Peterborough NH 03458. Phone: 603-924-3873. Publisher: Wayne Green. For amateur radio operators and experimenters. Monthly. Buys all rights. Pays on acceptance. Reports on submissions within a few weeks. Query first. Enclose S.A.S.E.

Nonfiction and Photos: Articles on anything of interest to radio amateurs—construction projects, theory, activities, etc. Pays approximately $20 per page. Photos purchased with ms as illustrations.

Science Fiction, Speculative Fiction and Fantasy Publications

ALGOL: A MAGAZINE ABOUT SCIENCE FICTION, P.O. Box 4175, New York NY 10017. Phone: 212-953-0950. Editor: Andrew Porter. For science fiction readers and writers interested in the behind-the-scenes workings of the SF field. Twice annually; 52 to 60 (8½x11) pages. Established in 1963. Circulation: 4,000. Rights purchased vary with author and material. Buys first worldwide serial rights or second serial (reprint) rights. Buys 5 to 10 mss year. Payment on publication. Will send sample copy to writer for $1. Will consider photocopied submissions. Will not consider simultaneous submissions. Reports in 1 to 3 weeks. Query first. Enclose S.A.S.E.

Nonfiction and Photos: Articles on science fiction. Interviews with authors and editors. "Our outlook is generally that of the professional explaining to the interested party; not talking down, but a two-way exchange between equals." No topical items, but does use personal experience, interviews and think pieces. Length: 1,000 to 10,000 words. Pays 1¢ per word. Payment for 5x7 or 8x10 b&w photos varies; purchased on assignment only. Captions optional. Also buys artwork; first publication or second serial rights.

ANALOG SCIENCE FICTION & SCIENCE FACT, 350 Madison Ave., New York NY 10017. Editor: Ben Bova. For general future-minded audience. Monthly. Buys all English serial rights. Pays on acceptance. Reports within 3 to 4 weeks. Query first. Enclose S.A.S.E.

Fiction: Stories of the future told for adults interested in science and technology; central theme usually interaction of strong characters with science or technology-based problems. Length: 3,000 to 60,000 words. Serials only on consultation with Editor. Pays 3¢ to 4¢ a word for novelettes and novels, 5¢ a word for shorts under 7,500 words.

Nonfiction and Photos: Needs illustrated technical articles. Length: 5,000 words. Pays 5¢ a word. Buys photos with mss only. Pays $5 each.

ETERNITY SF, P.O. Box 193, Sandy Springs SC 29677. Editor: Stephen Gregg. For readers interested in science fiction and most other media. Magazine published approximately twice a year. Established in 1972. Circulation: 800. Buys first North American serial rights. Buys about 40 mss a year. Payment on acceptance. Will send sample copy to writer for $1. Will consider photocopied submissions. Will not consider simultaneous submissions. Reports in 1 to 2 weeks. Query before submitting articles or interviews. Submit complete ms for balance of material. Enclose S.A.S.E.

Nonfiction: Interviews, book reviews; profile, personal opinion. Publication reviews (mostly avant-garde or science fiction). Length: 4,000 words maximum for articles; 1,000 words maximum for reviews. Pays ½¢ a word. Recently published articles include "Science Fiction Poetry: Toward a Definition."

Fiction: "Especially interested in fiction that challenges the reader at the same time as it entertains. Vignettes which depend on 'surprise' endings, end-of-the-world stories, and tales of galactic conquest have been overworked in the field and are generally rejected, although there have been exceptions for superior stories." Science fiction, fantasy, experimental. Length: 1,000 to 10,000 words. Pays 1¢ a word.

Poetry: "We are occasionally overstocked with poetry submissions. Traditional and avant-garde forms and blank and free verse are all fine, but we do want to see serious work; nothing trivial." Length: open. Pays 10¢ a line.

FANTASY & TERROR, Box 89517, Zenith WA 98188. Editor: Jessica Amanda. "Readers are generally of a high intellect to grasp fantasy's complexity." Bimonthly.

Established in 1973. Circulation: 2,000. Buys all rights, but will reassign rights to author after publication. Buys over 50 mss a year. Payment on acceptance. Will send sample copy to writer for $1.50. No carbon copies or photocopies. Reports on material accepted for publication within 30 days. Returns rejected material in 10 days. Submit complete ms. Enclose S.A.S.E.

Fiction: Publishes a wider variety of fantasy-oriented material than other fantasy publication. Any kind of fantasy will be considered, except science fiction. Epic, heroic and hardcore fantasy especially desired. "Fantasy, and the horror sub-genre in particular, suffers an outlandish number of overworked cliches, all of which should be avoided. Vampires, pacts with devils, magic mirrors, haunted houses, ad infinitum, simply won't sell here." Length: 2,000 to 15,000 words. Pays ½¢ per word and up, maximum $100 per story.

GALAXY (incorporating *Worlds of If*), 235 E. 45th St., New York NY 10017. Editor: James Baen. For "young, science-oriented, high I.Q. types." Monthly magazine; digest size. Established in 1950. Circulation: 65,000. Buys first serial rights. Buys 125 mss a year. Payment on publication. Write for copy of guidelines for writers. Will consider photocopied and simultaneous submissions. Reports in 1 month. Submit complete ms. Enclose S.A.S.E.

Nonfiction: Informational and think pieces. Length: open. Pays 2¢ to 3½¢ per word.

Fiction: "Science fiction. Characters, plots and context of stories transcend present reality in a plausible manner, preferably conjectured according to known scientific principles. Writers should be familiar with our magazine format and with other science fiction publications, and have a general knowledge of the SF field. We like to strike a more hopeful note, so have a prejudice against 'end of the world is at hand' material. We always welcome stories based on present scientific research." Length: 30,000 words maximum. Pays 2¢ to 3½¢ per word.

How To Break In: "We try to publish one story in each issue by a writer previously unpublished in the science fiction field. So for the brand new writer, it's not to his disadvantage to mention that he's a beginner. We're looking for standard literary forms. Adventure, literary merit, and good new ideas are essential. We want to see plot, and are definitely not interested in literary experimentation, especially not vintage 1930 literary experimentation. Also, don't use the word 'sci-fi'. That might be appropriate for *Time Magazine,* but not for us. 'SF' or 'science fiction' is what we prefer."

THE INTERPLANETARY NOOSE, 1313 Kirts Rd., #89, Troy MI 48084. Editor: Don Williams. For science fiction novices. Magazine; 64 to 84 pages. Established in 1974. Circulation: 20,000. Rights purchased vary with author and material. May buy all rights, but may reassign rights to author after publication; or first North American rights, or second serial (reprint) rights. Buys over 100 mss per year. Half of the payment is made on acceptance; the balance on publication. Will send sample copy to a writer for $1. Write for copy of guidelines for writers. Will consider photocopied and simultaneous submissions. Returns rejected material in 30 days. Submit complete ms. Enclose S.A.S.E.

Fiction: Main interest is in good, well-written science fiction. "Top-notch science fiction and horror only. Some fantasy and sword and sorcery acceptable. Must be logically constructed and easy to follow. No free form verse or experimental garbage; just good solid fiction. We like things by Heinlein, Azimov, Lovecraft, Clark Ashton-Smith, Robert Bloch and Robert E. Howard." Length: 3,500 words maximum. Pays up to 5¢ a word for all rights; up to 3¢ a word for first serial rights.

Nonfiction: Satire. "Write for the high school and college reader. We respect no sacred cows. Feel free to slander and smear. Rock stars, dope, religion, politics; anything. Must be top-notch, biting, irreverent and hysterically funny. We'll also buy unusual interviews with groups and performers of national significance; articles as well as features on the music business. All local material must be restricted to the Ann Arbor, Detroit metropolitan area." Pays up to 5¢ a word for all rights; up to 3¢ a word for first serial rights. Also buys top quality horror-science fiction comic strips; adventure or satire. No less than one full page; no more than 12 pages.

Prefers strips of approximately 8 pages. All comic strips must be complete and lettered. Pays up to $35 per page, or will negotiate price predicted on quality.

WEIRDBOOK, P.O. Box 35, Amherst Branch, Buffalo NY 14226. Editor: W. Paul Ganley. For readers interested in supernatural horror; in fantasy; in sword and sorcery tales. Magazine; 32 (8½x11) pages. Established in 1968. Semi-annual. Circulation: 350. Buys first North American serial rights and right to reprint as part of the entire issue. Buys 10 to 15 mss a year. Pays on publication. Will send a sample copy to writer for $1. No simultaneous submissions, but will consider photocopied submissions, if legible. Reports in 6 weeks. Submit complete ms. Enclose S.A.S.E.
Fiction: "Horror should be based on supernatural rather than psychological elements; no sex or sadism. No science fiction. We insist on a very literate style. We do not specialize in sword and sorcery. Lovecraftian horror, or Dunsanian fantasy, but try to preserve a balance among such elements. Remember that it's not easy to write weird fiction without reading extensively in the fields." Length: 1,500 words maximum. Pays minimum of $1 per published page.

WHISPERS, 5508 Dodge Dr., Fayetteville NC 28303. Editor: Dr. Stuart David Schiff. For intelligent adults with an interest in literate horror, terror, fantasy, sword and sorcery. Many readers collect first edition books and the like in these fields. Magazine; 64 (5x8½) pages. Established in 1973. An approximate quarterly schedule. Circulation: 1,600. Buys first North American serial rights only. Buys 15 to 20 mss a year. Pays half of fee on acceptance; balance on publication. Will consider photocopied submissions. No simultaneous submissions. Reports in 4 to 6 weeks. Submit complete ms. Enclose S.A.S.E.
Fiction: Stories of fantasy, terror, horror, sword and sorcery. Does not want to see science fiction. No rocket ships, futuristic societies, bug-eyed monsters or the like. Authors whose work is most related to their needs include H. P. Lovecraft, Lord Dunsany, Edgar Allan Poe, Algernon Blackwood, Robert Bloch, Fritz Leiber, Ray Bradbury, and Clark Ashton-Smith. Length: 500 to 8,000 words. Pays 1¢ a word.

Social Science Publications

AIM MAGAZINE, P.O. Box 20554, Chicago IL 60620. Editor: Ruth Apilado. For high school and college students and the general public. Bimonthly; 50 (8½x11) pages. Established in 1973. Circulation: 4,000. Not copyrighted. Payment on publication. Will send sample copy to writer for 50¢. Write for copy of guidelines for writers. Will consider photocopied and simultaneous submissions. Submit seasonal material 3 months in advance. Reports in 1 week. Query first or submit complete ms. Enclose S.A.S.E.
Nonfiction and Photos: Uses material of social significance; "down-to-earth gut." Interested in articles on drug addiction and its ills. Personal experience, inspirational, humor, think pieces, personal opinion. Length: 800 words. Pays $10 to $50. Columns and departments use shorter material (150 words). Pays $20. Uses b&w photographs that promote racial harmony. No additional payment is made for photos used with mss.
Fiction: Mainstream. Length: 200 to 800 words. Pays $20 to $50.
Poetry: Traditional forms, blank verse, free verse. Length: 10 to 40 lines. Pays $10 to $25.
Fillers: Jokes of 50 to 100 words. Pays $5 to $15.

THE DIGEST, P.O. Box 20140, Philadelphia PA 19145. Phone: 215-735-3482. Editor: Audrey Canada. For upper middle-class, hip, sophisticated, uninhibited couples and singles; professional types. Established in 1971. Circulation: 35,000. Buys all rights. Pays on publication. Will send free sample copy to writer on request. Will consider photocopied submissions. Reports in 30 days. Query first or submit complete ms. Enclose S.A.S.E.

Nonfiction: "Interested in intellectual articles relating to the love culture of swinging, and sexual-oriented articles that inform, particularly on the psychology of sex. We believe that sex is the ultimate communication between people of high principles. We prefer the humanistic approach as distinguished from the sexist approach. We are not interested in so-called pornography or cheap, tawdry sex articles. Subject matter can range wide and far and cover science, medicine, morality, life styles, provocative sexual subjects such as incest, bi-sexuality, etc." Length: open. Pays $25 to $250.

Fiction: Erotica, fantasy, humor, serialized novels, but sophistication and good taste is the order of the day. Pays $25 minimum.

Poetry and Fillers: Avant-garde forms. Jokes and short humor. Pays $5 each.

HUMAN BEHAVIOR, 12031 Wilshire Blvd., Los Angeles CA 90025. Editor: Marshall Lumsden. For a "college educated audience, interested in social, especially behavioral, sciences; all ages." Established in 1972. Monthly. Circulation: 100,000. Buys first North American serial rights. Buys about 50 mss a year. Payment on acceptance. Will send free sample copy to a writer on request. Will consider photocopied submissions. Reports in 30 to 45 days. Query first. Enclose S.A.S.E.

Nonfiction and Photos: Subject matter consists of nonfiction on social sciences and profiles of prominent social scientists. Length: 1,500 to 4,500 words. Pays $200 to $500. Buys photos with or without mss. Pays $25 per b&w photo. Accepts size 5x7 and up. Pays $50 per color photo; size 35mm and up. Accepts color transparencies.

NEW THOUGHT, 6922 Hollywood Blvd., #706, Hollywood CA 90028. Phone: 213-464-8361. Editor: Blaine C. Mays; Managing Editor: Surinder M. Bhatia. For people wishing to gain greater self-awareness through inner growth and expansion; those who recognize their spiritual, intellectual, and emotional potentials. Quarterly magazine; 96 (6x9) pages. Established in 1915. Circulation: 15,000. Buys all rights. Buys 30 to 40 mss a year. Pays on publication. Will send sample copy and editorial guidelines to writers for $1. Submit complete ms only after receiving editorial guidelines. Reports within 6 weeks. Enclose S.A.S.E.

Nonfiction: "Each issue deals with one theme, covering it in articles written from a psychological, philosophical, or spiritual point of view. Future themes will be creativity, marriage and the family, ecology, man and religion, reincarnation, meditation. The approach should be as concrete and scientific as possible (without going into statistics), avoiding abstract theory and generalizations. Writing should be clear, direct, and constructive. Our publication is constantly looking for new interpretations of constructive ideas rather than sticking to orthodox religious dogmas. Material should not be heavily bible oriented. We want to branch out, considering ideas from a more practical point of view, reflecting the present world, rather than the past." Length: 1,000 to 1,300 words. Pays 2½¢ per word; $25 to $40 per article.

Poetry and Fillers: Traditional forms, blank and free verse. Pays $10 per poem. Pays $5 for constructive fillers (up to 25 words). Send poetry and fillers to Managing Editor Surinder M. Bhatia.

PARAPSYCHOLOGY REVIEW, 29 W. 57th St., New York NY 10019. Editor: Betty Shapin. For a good cross section of the population; considerable formal education; scientific and cultural interests. Established in 1953. Every 2 months. Circulation: 3,000. Buys all rights, but will reassign rights to author after publication. Buys 5 to 10 mss a year. Pays on acceptance. Will send sample copy to writer for 85¢. Reports in 1 to 2 weeks. Query first or submit complete ms. Enclose S.A.S.E.

Nonfiction: Articles, news items, book reviews in this general subject area. Must approach psychical research in scientific, experimental fashion. Length: open. Pays $25 minimum.

PERSONAL GROWTH, P.O. Box 1254, Berkeley CA 94701. Phone: 415-548-1004. Editor: James Elliott. For psychologists and well-informed laymen. Most of them have been to (or led) one or more encounter groups. Monthly magazine; 24 pages, (7x8½). Established in 1964. Circulation: 5,000. Buys all rights, but will reassign rights to author after publication. Buys 12 mss a year. Payment on acceptance. Will send sample copy to writer for 20¢ in postage. Write for copy of guidelines for writers. Will consider photocopied, cassette, and simultaneous submissions. Reports in 2 to 3 weeks. Query first. Enclose S.A.S.E.

Nonfiction: "Anything on personal growth; the human potential movement, psychotherapy, humanistic psychology, etc. Use simple, informal language (not abstract journalese); material should be heavily researched with plenty of examples. We're like *Psychology Today* but with emphasis on personal growth. Taboos are personal accounts of group experiences; articles about the power of positive thinking; articles on 'how religion helped me.' Particularly interested in new psychotherapies—also little-known ideas of such famous psychotherapists as Freud, Jung, and Adler—guided imagery and fantasy." Informational, how-to, interview. Length: 200 to 5,000 words. Pays $15 to $200.

PSYCHOLOGY TODAY, 1 Park Ave., New York NY 10016. Phone: 714-453-5000. For social scientists and intelligent laymen concerned with society and individual behavior. Monthly. Buys all rights. Each ms will be edited by staff and returned to author prior to publication for comments and approval. Author should retain a copy. Reports within 1 month. Address all queries to Articles Editor. Enclose S.A.S.E.

Nonfiction: Most mss written by scholars in various fields. Primary purpose is to provide the nonspecialist with accurate and readable information about society and behavior. Technical and specialized vocabularies should be avoided except in cases where familiar expressions cannot serve as adequate equivalents. Technical expressions, when necessary, should be defined carefully for the nonexpert. References to technical literature should not be cited within article, but 10 to 12 general readings should be listed at end. Suggested length: 3,000 words. Payment is $500.

SEXOLOGY, 200 Park Ave., S., New York NY 10003. Editor: Martin Sage. For a lower middle-class, adult audience. Monthly magazine; 70 pages. Established in 1933. Circulation: 200,000. Rights purchased vary with author and material. May buy all rights, first serial rights, or second serial (reprint) rights. Buys about 150 mss a year. Payment on acceptance. Sample copy will be sent to any writer sending a query, if the query is accepted. Write for copy of guidelines for writers. Will consider photocopied submissions. Will not consider simultaneous submissions. Reports on material accepted for publication within 3 weeks. Returns rejected material in 3 weeks. Query first, with outline. Enclose S.A.S.E.

Nonfiction: "We are striving to bring to the public information which will help the individuals 'come to grips' with their sexual natures. We regularly cover these nonfiction themes: How-to, which covers specific advice on how to perform sexual acts and promote sexual compatibility; physical sexual problems; timely topics that reflect today's sexual activity; recent scientific developments; historical or cultural reports on sex; psychological areas. In short, all aspects of sex we can cover in good taste. We attempt to publish information rather than sensational articles on the subject of sex. Since the subject itself is a bit sensational, this is sometimes a fine line. But any valid attempt to bring information to our public is reviewed." Length: 1,800 words. Pays $150.

SINGLE LIFE, 225 Kearny St., Suite 200, San Francisco CA 94108. For singles in California. Editorial Director: Al Pellegrini. Established in 1970. Monthly. Copyrighted. Buys all rights but will reassign rights to author after publication. Payment on publication. Seasonal material must be submitted 4 months in advance. Submit complete ms. Enclose S.A.S.E.

Nonfiction and Photos: "Content of publication is light with humor important. All articles must have a positive approach to being single. No 'hate' or 'swinger' type articles will be considered. Interviews with prominent single persons; light humor, general travel articles, sports and think pieces." Length: 600 to 1,000 words, but prefers lengths of 750 to 1,000 words. Pays 2¢ a word; $5 per accompanying photo. "Signed release for everyone who can be identified must accompany all photos."

SWINGLE, Editorial Supply House, Inc., 210 E. 35th St., New York NY 10016. Editorial Director: Christopher Watson. For young couples, both leading a "singles" life and living together; age 20 to 30, active and sexually adventurous. Monthly magazine; 100 (8½x11) pages. Established in 1973. Circulation: 250,000. Buys first North American serial rights. Buys 50 mss a year. Payment on publication. Will send free sample copy on request. Will not consider photocopied submissions. Will consider simultaneous submissions. Reports in 2 to 4 weeks. Submit manuscript or introductory paragraphs, or general outline, with some writing sample. Enclose S.A.S.E.

Nonfiction and Photos: "Articles aimed at single guys and girls living together or sharing an apartment or house; emphasis on how to meet new people, how to share in the resultant relationship." Articles should be aimed specifically at audience (as opposed to general interest). Informational, how-to, personal experience, interview, profile, personal opinion, travel, spot news, successful business operations. Length: 1,500 to 3,000 words. Pays 4¢ a word. The following departments also use freelance material: "Finances: Who Pays for What?", "Sharing: Who Cooks, Cleans?", and calendars of swingle events in different cities. Length:1,000 words. Pays $50. Department Editor: Lynn Fallon. Pays $10 to $15 for b&w photos purchased with or without ms. Prefers to see contact sheets. Pays $30 to $35 for color; any size chromes. Photo interest is "primarily in couples (nude, semi-nude, occasionally dressed) in 'situation' scenes (doing something rather than just posing)." Photo Department Editor: Lindy Urban.

Fiction: Experimental, erotica, fantasy, humorous, confession. All must relate to theme. Length: 2,000 to 3,500 words. Pays $100 to $150.

Fillers: Newsbreaks and puzzles for swingles. Length: open. Pays minimum of $25.

Sport and Outdoor Publications

The publications listed in this category are intended for active sportsmen, sports fans, or both. They buy material on how to practice and enjoy both team and individual sports, material on conservation of streams and forests, and articles reporting on and analyzing professional sports.

Writers will note that several of the editors mention that they do not wish to see "Me 'n Joe" stories. These are detailed accounts of one hunting/fishing trip taken by the author and a buddy—starting with the friends' awakening at dawn and ending with their return home, "tired but happy."

For the convenience of writers who specialize in one or two areas of sport and outdoor writing, the publications are subcategorized by the sport or subject matter they emphasize. Publications in related categories (for example, Hunting and Fishing; Archery and Bowhunting) often buy similar material (in this case articles on bow and arrow hunting). Consequently, writers should read through this entire Sport and Outdoor category to become familiar with the subcategories and note down the ones that contain markets for their own type of writing.

Publications concerned with horse breeding, hunting dogs, or the use of other animals in sport are classified in the Animal category. Publications dealing with automobile or motorcycle racing will be found in the Automotive and Motorcycle category. Outdoor publications that exist to further the preservation of nature, placing only secondary emphasis on preserving nature as a setting for sport, are listed in the Nature, Conservation, and Ecology category. Newspapers and Magazine Sections, as well as Regional magazines are frequently interested in conservation or sports material with a local angle. Camping publications are classified in the Travel, Camping, and Trailer category.

Archery and Bowhunting

ARCHERY WORLD, 534 N. Broadway, Milwaukee WI 53202. Phone: 414-276-6600. Editor: Glenn Helgeland. For "archers—average education, hunters and target archers, experts to beginners." Subject matter is the "entire scope of archery—hunting, bowfishing, indoor target, outdoor target, field." Bimonthly. Circulation: 65,000. Buys first serial rights. Buys 30 to 35 mss a year. Pays on acceptance "or as near to it as possible." Will send a free sample copy to a writer on request. Tries to report in 2 weeks. Query first. Enclose S.A.S.E.

Nonfiction: "Get a free sample and study it. Try, in ms, to entertain archer and show him how to enjoy his sport more and be better at it." Wants how-to, semitechnical, and hunting where-to and how-to articles. "Looking for more good technical stories and short how-to pieces." Also uses profiles and some humor. Length: 1,000 to 2,200 words. Payment is $50 to $150.

Photos: B&w glossies purchased with mss and with captions. "Like to see proofsheets and negs with submitted stories. We make own cropping and enlargements." Color transparencies purchased for front cover only. Will look at color prints "if that's the only photo available." Pays $5 minimum for b&w; $50 minimum for color.

BOW AND ARROW, P.O. Box HH/37249 Camino Capistrano, Capistrano Beach CA 92624. Editor: Chuck Tyler. For archery competitors and bowhunters. Bimonthly. Buys all rights, "but will relinquish all but first American serial rights on written request of author." Pays on acceptance. Will send free sample copy to a writer on request. Reports on submissions in six weeks. Study publication. Author must have some knowledge of archery terms. Query first. Enclose S.A.S.E.

Nonfiction: Articles: bowhunting, major archery tournaments, techniques used by champs, how to make your own tackle, and off-trail hunting tales. Likes a touch of humor in articles. Also uses one technical article per issue. Length: 1,500 to 2,500 words. Pays $35 to $150.

Photos: Purchased as package with mss; 5x7 minimum or submit contacts with negatives (returned to photographer). Pays $75 for cover chromes, 2¼ square, minimum.

BOWHUNTER MAGAZINE, P.O. Box 5377, Fort Wayne IN 46805. Phone: 219-432-5772. Editor: M. R. James. For readers of all ages, background and experience. All share two common passions—hunting with the bow and arrow and a love of the great outdoors. Magazine published every 2 months; 56 pages, (8½x11). Established in 1971. Circulation: 70,000. Buys all rights, but will reassign rights to author after publication. Buys 55 mss a year. Payment on acceptance sometimes; usually on publication. Will send free sample copy to writer on request. Will consider photocopied submissions. "We publish a special deer hunting issue each August and usually have a bowfishing issue each spring. Submit seasonal material 6 months in advance." Reports within 4 weeks. Query first or submit complete ms. Enclose S.A.S.E.

Nonfiction, Photos and Fillers: "Our articles are written for, by and about bowhunters. Most material deals with big or small game hunting; however, some technical material on equipment and a few personality profiles are used. We demand that writers inform as well as entertain our readers. Woven into each article should be where-to-go and how-to-do-it material. Writers should anticipate readers' questions and answer them within the article (e.g., costs involved, services of guides or outfitters, season dates, equipment used, etc.). Our publication is called 'The Magazine for the Hunting Archer' with good reason; we use no target or field archery material. Conservation articles have a chance of selling if bowhunters can relate to them. We suggest writers study our magazine. Most articles are first-person accounts and we have no formula we prefer. In fact, we encourage writers 'to be themselves' instead of trying to copy another writer's style. We don't attempt to cover the sport of archery, only bowhunting. We use no field, target, tournament, indoor archery material of any kind. We're presently overstocked with deer and bear hunting articles. We'd like to see more material from distaff bowhunters. We'd be interested in what bowhunters and their state-local-national groups are doing to combat the anti-hunting movement." Informational, how-to personal experience, interview, profile, humor, historical, think articles, expose, personal opinion, spot news, new product, and technical articles. Length: 200 to 5,000 words. Pays $20 to $125. Photos purchased with accompanying ms with no additional payment. Also purchased without ms. Captions optional. Pays $10 to $20 for 5x7 b&w prints; $50 for 35mm or 2¼x2¼ color. Photo Department Editor: Steve Doucette. Also purchases newsbreaks of 50 to 500 words for $5 to $25. Filler Department Editor: Don Clark.

Basketball

BASKETBALL DIGEST, Century Publishing Co., 1020 Church St., Evanston IL 602201. Editor: Michael K. Herbert. For basketball enthusiasts. Established in 1973. Digest size magazine; 100 (5¼x7½) pages. Established in 1973. Monthly during season; 6 times a year. Circulation: 200,000. Buys all rights. Buys about 12 mss a year. Pays on publication. Will send sample copy to writer for $1. Reports in 2 to 4 weeks. Submit only complete ms. Enclose S.A.S.E.
Nonfiction and Photos: Articles on aspects of NBA and ABA professional basketball, profiles of players and coaches, studies of teams, current statistics. Buys interviews, historical, informational, how-to, personal experience, humor, think, nostalgia and technical articles. "We are looking for fresh, original, unusual story angles — perhaps a new look at a certain statistic, or a humorous event told through a player's eyes. The only opportunity for freelance contribution is an article that is timely, unusual or original in approach." Length: 500 to 2,000 words. Pays approximately $75. Photos of players in action; headshots. Pays $10 per shot for 8x10 b&w glossies; $75 for color cover (35mm mounted transparencies); $25 for inside cover color (35mm mounted transparencies).

BASKETBALL WEEKLY, 19830 Mack Avenue, Grosse Point MI 48236. Publisher: Roger Stanton. 18 issues during season, November to April. Circulation: 30,000. Buys all rights. Pays on publication. For free sample copy, send a large S.A.S.E. Reports in 2 weeks. Also include S.A.S.E. with submissions and queries.
Nonfiction, Photos and Fillers: Current stories on teams and personalities in college and pro basketball. Length: 800 to 1,000 words. Payment is $30 to $50. 8x10 b&w glossy photos purchased with mss. Also uses newsbreaks.

HOOP, Professional Sports Publications, 310 Madison Ave., New York NY 10017. Editor: Larry Bortstein. 32-page color insert that is folded into the local magazines of each of the NBA teams. Buys all rights, but will reassign rights to author after publication, if author so requests. "For the most part, assignments are being made to newspapermen and columnists on the pro basketball beat around the country." Will send sample copy to writer for $1. Reports within 1 week. Enclose S.A.S.E.
Nonfiction: Features on NBA players, officials, personalities connected with league. The NBA, founded in 1946-47, is the older of the two established professional basketball leagues. Length: 800 to 900 words. Pays $50 per article.
How To Break In: "The best way for a freelancer to break in is to aim something for the local team section. That can be anything from articles about the players or about their wives to unusual off-court activities. I recently got a piece from a young woman in Buffalo on her reactions as a fan of the Braves. I forwarded it to the Braves' P.R. guy and he decided to use it. The best way to handle this, is to send material directly to the P.R. person for the local team. They have to approve anything that we do on that particular team and if they like it, they forward it to me. They're always looking for new material — otherwise they have to crank it all out themselves."

Bicycling

BICYCLING, P.O. Box 3330, San Rafael CA 94901. Editor: Gail Heilman. Monthly. Buys all rights. Payment on publication. Will send free sample copy to writer on request. Write for copy of guidelines for writers. Enclose S.A.S.E.
Nonfiction: "Articles on the many exciting and unique aspects of bicycling are always

in demand. We need coverage on technical subjects: new products and product evaluations, choosing equipment, maintenance; touring: where to go and how to get there, touring equipment; racing: who, where, why; health: how to get in shape for bicycling and how bicycling helps to keep you in shape; commuting; bikecology; history; news; special events." Length: 1,000 to 3,500 words. Pays $1 per column inch minimum. Each column is 2¼".

Photos: "B&w photos are welcome if accompanied by ms; prefer 8x10 b&w glossy. 35mm or 2¼ color transparencies unaccompanied by ms may be considered for covers. Interesting color covers are always in demand." Pays $7.50 for b&w; $50 for color covers.

Fiction: May be humor, suspense or adventure about adult bicycle travel. Length: 1,000 to 3,500 words. Pays $1 per column inch.

BIKE WORLD, P.O. Box 366, Mountain View CA 94040. Editor: George Beinhorn. For bicyclists aged 5 to 80 interested in training, technical subjects, sophisticated touring stories at the nonbeginner level. Monthly magazine; 50 (8½x11) pages. Established in 1972. Circulation: 16,000. Not copyrighted. Buys 125 mss a year. Payment on publication. Will send free sample copy to writer on request. Will consider photocopied submissions. Will not consider simultaneous submissions. Will consider cassette submissions; interviews only. Submit seasonal material (winter, summer and spring tours; training in winter; riding the rollers, etc.) 2 months in advance. Reports immediately. Query first or submit complete ms. Enclose S.A.S.E.

Nonfiction and Photos: Technical and touring material; physiology and race topics. "All material must be at a level beyond the beginning 'how-to'." Must be tightly written and avoid the "joys of cycling" approach. Tour stories should make the reader feel he would have a good time. Avoid chronological accounts of events that don't involve the reader. "We are more into athletics than ecology or 'romantic bikeology'." Does not want to see material on "how I bought my first 10-speed, or the Rutabaga Canners annual road race, or a peanut butter and flat tire account of a tour to Michigan's world famous glacial moraines." Would like to see material on tours that turn others on without trying to; technical articles that people can use. How to train and tour, etc. Anything of interest to cyclists who enjoy the sport. Length: open. Pays $5 to $100. Pays more if quality deserves it. B&w photos are purchased with or without accompanying mss or on assignment. Pays $2.50 for 5x7 or larger; $2 if they develop negatives. Must have snappy contrast and be in focus. Captions required. Pays $40 for color slides used for cover. Ektachrome-X or K-II with intensity of action, mood, scenery, etc.

Fiction: Mainstream, adventure, fantasy, humorous, historical. Must relate to theme. Length: open. Pays $5 to $100.

Fillers: Short humor. News bits, technical tips. Length: 25 to 300 words. Pays $5 to $10.

BIKER/HIKER, P.O. Box 919, Kermit TX 79745. Editor: Fred B. Green. For readers interested in hiking, biking, ecology. Monthly. Circulation: 10,000. Buys first North American serial rights. Buys 100 mss a year. Payment on publication. Payment in copies for 20% of published material. Reports in 4 weeks. Query first or submit complete ms. Enclose S.A.S.E.

Nonfiction and Photos: Articles on bicycling and related fields such as racing, safety, clubs, etc. Hiking and related fields such as backpacking, camping. Ecology and related fields such as the energy crisis and recycling. Treatment should be objective and informational. Length: 1,000 to 2,000 words. Minimum payment in copies and byline. Maximum: 3¢ per word. No additional payment for 3x5 or 5x7 b&w glossy photos. Also looking for good feature columnists in the above areas.

Fillers: On above topics. Length: 300 to 500 words. Minimum payment in copies. Maximum: 3¢ per word.

Boating

AMERICAN BOATING, Box A, Reno NV 89506. Editor: Jon Thompson. For "boating enthusiasts in the 13 Western states." Established in 1971. Monthly.

Circulation: 50,000. Buys first serial rights. Buys 26 mss a year. Payment on publication. Reports within 1 month. Query first or submit complete ms. Enclose S.A.S.E.

Nonfiction and Photos: General subject matter is "specific boating stories and general interest pieces. We are particularly interested in well-written stories and are looking for offbeat or different subjects, preferably with art. We try to cover the complete boating field as well as feature stories that appeal to all boatmen. We are interested in all types of articles." Length: up to 2,500 words. Pays $1.20 per published inch and more if agreed to by author and publisher. Department Editor: Matilde Arias. Buys photos with and without mss, on assignment, captions required. Pays $5 per 8x10 b&w glossy print used. Pays $10 for each color transparency used. Double for cover. Department Editor: Jerry Stinson.

BAY & DELTA YACHTSMAN, 2019 Clement Ave., Alameda CA 94501. Phone: 415-865-7500. Editor: H. McBurney. For pleasure boaters and water sport enthusiasts of all kinds. Established in 1965. Monthly. Circulation: 17,000. Rights purchased vary with author and material. Usually buys all rights. Buys about 260 mss a year. Payment on publication. Will send free sample copy on request. Will consider photocopied submissions. Reports on material in 2 to 3 weeks. Query first or submit complete ms. Enclose S.A.S.E.

Nonfiction and Photos: "Virtually all aspects of pleasure boating and water sports that are of general interest. How-to-do-it and knowledgeable technical articles; first-person cruising or adventure. Small and large sail; small and large power; fishing, skiing, racing (not race results), skin and scuba diving. Must be knowledgeable about area covered." Length: 1,000 to 2,000 words for general interest features and adventures; 500 to 1,000 words for technical and how-to articles. Payment varies "but minimum of 75¢ per published column inch; with our columns, this runs between 2¢ and 2½¢ per word." Pays $3 for 5x7 b&w (or larger) photos. Captions required.

Fiction: Humorous adventure. Length: 3,000 words maximum. Pays minimum of 75¢ per published column inch.

Fillers: Short humor. Pays minimum of 75¢ per published column inch.

BETTER BOATING, 120 Barbados Blvd., Scarborough, Ontario, Canada M1J 1L2. Editor: Jim Punfield. For boating enthusiasts across Canada. Magazine; 60 pages. Established in 1964. Monthly. Circulation: 25,000. Buys first North American serial rights. Buys 50 to 60 mss a year. Pays on acceptance. Will send free sample copy to writer on request. No photocopied submissions, but will consider simultaneous submissions. Reports in 2 weeks. Query first. Enclose S.A.E. and International Reply Coupons.

Nonfiction: "Editorial serves the common interests of all boaters, yet caters to the special concerns of those who boat under power or sail for pleasure or in competition. We use cruise stories, product stories, adventure stories that are boating oriented; instruction articles on boating." Recently published "Escape!" (across the Atlantic in a 30-foot trimaran). Length: 1,000 to 2,500 words. Pays 10¢ a word.

Fiction: Mystery, adventure, fantasy, humorous fiction related to boating. Length: 1,500 to 2,500 words. Pays 10¢ a word.

BOATING, 1 Park Ave., New York NY 10016. Phone: 212-725-3970. Editor: Richard L. Rath. For sail and powerboat enthusiasts, informed boatmen, not beginners. Publishes special Boat Show issue in January; Fall show issue in October; annual maintenance issue in April. Monthly. Circulation: 230,000. Buys first periodical rights or all rights. Buys 130 mss a year. Pays on acceptance. Will send a sample copy to a writer for $1. Submit seasonal material 6 to 8 months in advance. Reports in 2 months. Query first. Enclose S.A.S.E.

Nonfiction: Uses articles about cruises in powerboats or sailboats with b&w or color photos, that offer more than usual interest; how-to-do-it pieces illustrated with good b&w photos; piloting articles, seamanship, etc.; new developments in boating; profiles of well-known boating people. The editor advises, "Don't talk down to the reader. Use little fantasy, emphasize the practical aspects of the subject." Length: 300 to 3,000 words. Payment is $25 to $350, and varies according to subject and writer's skill. Regular department "Able Seaman" uses expertise on boat operation and handling; about 1,100 to 1,500 words; pays $100 to $150 per piece.

Photos: Buys photos submitted with mss and with captions only. 8x10 preferred, b&w. Interested in photos of happenings of interest to a national boating audience. Pays $20 to $25 each. Also buys color transparencies for both cover and interior use, 2¼x2¼ negative or larger preferred. Pays $100 to $300 for one-time usage, "but not for anything that has previously appeared in a boating publication." Creative Director: Bud Loader.

Fillers: Uses short items pertaining to boating that have an unusual quality of historical interest, timeliness, or instruction. Pays $50 to $100.

How To Break In: "From a time-invested standpoint, it would make sense for the beginning writer to try a short filler subject for us, rather than to go for the jackpot. Unless, of course, he has a great story or article that will sell itself. Acceptability of a piece for our magazine hinges at least as much on the quality of the writing as it does on the subject matter. One man will take a trip around the world and produce bilge water for a manuscript; another, like E. B. White, will row across Central Park Lake and make it a great adventure in the human experience. There's no substitute for talent."

MOTOR BOATING AND SAILING, 224 W. 57th St., New York NY 10019. Editor: Peter R. Smyth. Buys all rights or North American serial rights. Payment on acceptance. Reports within 2 weeks. Query first. Enclose S.A.S.E.

Nonfiction and Photos: Articles on all areas of boating and allied water sports. Should be accompanied by photos. Length: 3,000 words maximum. Pays $150 to $500. Photos purchased with mss or with captions only, with no additional payment. Pays $300 for covers. 8x10 b&w glossies and 2¼ square or 35mm transparencies for color cover.

How To Break In: "The most practical short takes that a freelancer can come at us with are how-to's. How to build something aboard your boat; how to use some device that would normally be for on-shore use; maintenance; repair. We need a lot of these things because we use five or six printed pages of them in each issue. They can range anywhere from three sentences and a photo to 750 or 1,000 words and two or three photos. No query necessary. Someone who breaks in with a few how-to items might very well get more assignments from us, especially if he shows some expertise in a particular field; say, if you're good in electronics. Let us know where your expertise lies. Book reviews might be a good angle too, if you have some experience in the marine field. Query first. We like personal experience pieces very much, but a problem we frequently run into with them is that the author goes to a great deal of trouble writing something which is terribly similar to something we've just done a few months ago, so query first on these. We are especially interested in personal experience pieces that take place away from the Northeast and Florida. You have an excellent chance of breaking in if you can provide us with something from the West Coast or the Great Lakes — this will be an on-going need."

MOTORBOAT MAGAZINE, 38 Commercial Wharf, Boston MA 02110. Phone: 617-227-0888. Editor-in-Chief: Hugh D. Whall. For owners of powerboats (18' long and over) and their families whose interests are fishing, cruising, boat maintenance, new marine technology, the marine environment, on-the-water life styles. Established in 1973. Every 2 months. Rights purchased vary with author and material. Usually buys all rights or first North American serial rights. Buys 8 to 10 mss per issue. Payment on acceptance. Will send free sample copy to writer on request. Will consider photocopied submissions. Will not consider simultaneous submissions. Submit seasonal material 3 months in advance. Reports on material in 4 weeks. Query first, with samples of past work. Enclose S.A.S.E.

Nonfiction and Photos: "Anything within the interests of fishing, cruising, boat maintenance, new marine technology, the marine environment or on-the-water life styles. Good semitechnical pieces on marine biology, life styles as specified above, and cruise/travel pieces about interesting places on the water that are written with wit and style. We are also interested in humor." Seasonal material desired includes boat building and how-to (winter); northern cruising (spring and summer); southern cruising (fall and winter). Length: 1,500 to 3,000 words. Pays a minimum of $150. Prefers mss accompanied by fine color photos. Pays $500 for text and color photos. Captions required.

OUTDOORS, Outdoors Building, Columbia MO 65201. Phone: 314-449-3119. Editor: Lee Cullimore. Published by Mercury Marine for "boaters and water sport enthusiasts." Monthly. Buys first serial rights. Pays "about 1 month prior to publication." Will send a sample copy to a writer on request. Write for copy of guidelines for writers. Reports in 2 weeks. Query first. Enclose S.A.S.E.
Nonfiction and Photos: "*Outdoors* seeks to encourage readers to spend more leisure time enjoying family recreation in outdoor living; to describe new things to do, new places to visit, and new wonders to see. It strives to stimulate the imagination and provide helpful information that will enable more people to realize and share in the benefit of our natural resources. Subject matter accepted for publication in *Outdoors* principally emphasizes boating and closely allied themes, such as cruising, water skiing, boating tips, workshop features, camping by boat, trailering, fishing, personalities, nature, outdoor health, outdoor cooking, waterway restaurants, area profiles, historical subjects, and outdoor fashions. Writing must be extremely tight and thoroughly researched. Preference is given to informative mss presented in an objective manner. The first-person approach is not recommended. Boat racing material is not accepted. Editorial mention of the Mercury name in articles is not permitted; stories concerned with products are staff-written. While a product tie-in is essential in boating stories, other subjects may not have this requirement. Please avoid being overly patronizing in this respect." Length: 1,200 words maximum. "Articles are purchased as a package. As a rule of thumb, rates are about $25 per published page for photo spreads. We do not count words in determining amount. The average article runs $100 to $125. All articles must be accompanied by 8x10 b&w professional quality prints; these are purchased with the ms. Color transparencies (2¼x2¼ minimum size preferred) may be submitted for consideration with the article. Rates for color range from $15 to $25 each, depending on content and quality."

POWERBOAT MAGAZINE, 15917 Strathern St., Van Nuys CA 91406. Editor: Bob Brown. For performance-conscious boating enthusiasts. January, Boat show issue; March, Jet drive issue; June, Water ski issue; October, Outboard issue; November, Stern Drive issue. Monthly. Circulation: 50,000. Buys all rights or one-time North American serial rights. Pays on publication. Will send free sample copy on request. Reports in 2 weeks. Query required. Enclose S.A.S.E.
Nonfiction and Photos: Uses articles about power boats and water skiing that offer special interest to performance-minded boaters, how-to-do-it pieces with good b&w pictures, developments in boating, profiles on well-known boating and skiing individuals, competition coverage of national and major events. Length: 1,500 to 2,000 words. Pays $100 to $150 per article. Photos purchased with mss. Prefers b&w 8x10. 2¼x2¼ color transparency preferred for cover; top quality vertical 35mm considered. Pays $50 to $100 for one-time use.

RUDDER MAGAZINE, 1515 Broadway, New York NY 10036. Editor: Martin Luray. For boat owners. Established in 1895. Monthly. Circulation: 147,000. Buys all rights. Buys 60 mss a year. Payment on acceptance. Will consider photocopied submissions. Submit seasonal material 6 months in advance. Reports in 1 to 4 weeks. Query first, with outline. Enclose S.A.S.E.
Nonfiction and Photos: Subject matter consists of articles on boats and boating. "We want articles from which the boat owner can derive a great deal of information about navigation, electronics, maintenance and the like." Length: 2,000 to 3,000 words. Pays $50 to $300. Photos purchased with or without mss, on assignment, and captions required. Specifications are "verticals for cover" (color). Pays $300.
Fillers: Buys fillers related to boating. Length: 500 to 1,000 words. Pays $50 to $100.
How To Break In: "The most likely area for a new freelancer to break in would be with a piece on a cruise that has some particular significance — because our editors can't be everywhere at once. The author should send in a query first with a precis of what went on and what he or she intends to do. If this sort of piece

is handled successfully, future assignments are likely, especially if the author lives in an area where we don't normally get to."

SAIL, 38 Commercial Wharf, Boston MA 02110. Phone: 617-227-0888. Editor: Keith Taylor. For audience that is "strictly sailors, average age 35, better than average education." Special issues: "Cruising issues, fitting-out issues, special race issues (e.g., America's Cup), boat show issues." Monthly. Buys first North American serial rights. Buys 100 mss a year. Pays on publication. Will send a free sample copy to a writer on request. Submit seasonal or special material at least 3 months in advance. Returns rejected material in 2 weeks. Acknowledges acceptance of material in 1 month. Enclose S.A.S.E.

Nonfiction: Wants "articles on sailing: technical, techniques, and feature stories." Interested in how-to, personal experience, profiles, historical, new product, and photo articles. "Generally emphasize the excitement of sail and the human, personal aspect." Length: 1,000 to 2,000 words. Payment is $50 to $300.

Photos: B&w glossies purchased with mss. Payment is $10 to $25. Color transparencies purchased. Payment is $35 to $200, $300 for covers.

SAILING MAGAZINE, 125 East Main St., Port Washington WI 53074. Phone: 414-284-2626. Editor: William F. Schanen III. For readers mostly between ages of 35 and 44, some professionals. About half of them own their own sailboat. Monthly magazine; 64 pages, (11x17). Established in 1966. Circulation: 24,000. Not copyrighted. Buys 6 mss a year. Payment on publication. Will send sample copy to writer for $1.25. Write for copy of guidelines for writers. Will consider photocopied and simultaneous submissions. Reports within 1 month. Query first or submit complete ms. Enclose S.A.S.E.

Nonfiction and Photos: "Experiences of sailing whether cruising, racing or learning. We require no special style. We're devoted exclusively to sailing and sailboat enthusiasts, and particularly interested in articles about the trend toward cruising in the sailing world." Informational, personal experience, profile, historical, travel, and book reviews. Length: open. Pays $25 minimum. B&w photos purchased with or without accompanying ms. Captions required. Pays $10 for each 8x10 b&w glossy used; also flat fee for series. Photo Department Editor: Micca Leffingwell Hutchins.

SEA, Suite 200, 2706 Harbor Blvd., Costa Mesa CA 92626. Phone: 714-556-7840. Editor: Chris Caswell. For Western boat owners, power and sail, cruising and racing. Monthly. Buys first serial rights. Buys 30 mss a year. Pays on publication. Will send a free sample copy to a writer on request. Submit seasonal material 6 months in advance. Reports in 30 days. Enclose S.A.S.E.

Nonfiction: "Freelance material mainly is cruising type stories, places to visit with a boat; in market for good technical articles from writers with credentials in the technical area they are writing about." Travel articles should be "within reasonable range of readership area." Length: 600 to 3,600 words. Payment is $50 to $250.

Photos: B&w glossies and 2¼x2¼ or larger color transparencies purchased with mss or with captions only. Payment is $10 to $150.

WATERSPORT, 534 N. Broadway, Milwaukee WI 53202. Phone: 414-276-6600. Editor: Glenn Helgeland. For "family boatmen who like to cruise, water ski and fish." Sponsored by the Boat Owners Council of America. Established in 1966. Six times yearly. Circulation: 100,000. Buys first North American serial rights. Buys 18 to 24 mss a year. Payment "as close to acceptance as possible." Will send free sample copy to writer on request. Write for copy of guidelines for writers. Will not consider photocopied submissions. Submit seasonal material 3 months in advance. Reports on material in 3 weeks. Query first. Enclose S.A.S.E.

Nonfiction and Photos: "Articles on boating; preferably with outboards, but also canoeing, sailing and bigger power. Also features about interesting people (may be oddballs) and events in boating. Not much lone wolf adventure boating. Have people in the story doing and experiencing and enjoying. Don't want itinerary reports, or stories about the great boating opportunities of one specific lake, unless there's a great story peg." Length: 250 to 2,200 words. Pays $50 to $400. 8x10 b&w glossy photos purchased with or without mss or on assignment. Pays $10 to $25; "package price negotiated." Any size color. Pays $35 to $100.

YACHTING, Yachting Publishing Corp., 50 West 44th Street, New York NY 10036. Editor: William W. Robinson. For yachtsmen interested in powerboats and sailboats. Monthly. Circulation: 128,000. Buys North American serial rights only. Reports on submissions in 3 weeks. Enclose S.A.S.E.
Nonfiction and Photos: Nuts-and-bolts articles on all phases of yachting; good technical pieces on motors, electronics, and sailing gear. "We're overloaded with cruising articles — everyone seems to be going around Cape Horn in a bathtub." Length: 3,000 words maximum. Pays 6¢ per word. Article should be accompanied by 6 to 8 photos. Pays $15 each for b&w photos, "more for color when used." Will accept a story without photos, if story is outstanding.

Bowling and Billiards

BOWLERS JOURNAL, Suite 214, 1825 N. Lincoln Plaza, Chicago IL 60614. Phone: 312-787-6386. Editor: Mort Luby. For "bowling fans of all ages." Established in 1913. Monthly. Circulation: 17,000. Buys first North American serial rights. Buys 50 mss a year. Payment on publication. Will send free sample copy to a writer on request. Query first. Enclose S.A.S.E
Nonfiction and Photos: General subject matter is "profile of bowling and billiard pros. Stories about tournaments, and unusual characters in bowling or billiards." Seeks "offbeat material" and does not want articles on handicapped bowlers or "how to bowl" articles, unless they appeal to the high-average bowler. Buys interviews, profiles, and articles on successful business operations. Length: 1,000 to 2,000 words. Payment: $50 to $75. Buys 8x10 b&w glossies with mss. Captions required. Pays $10 to $20.

BOWLING, 5301 S. 76 St., Greendale WI 53219. Phone: 414-421-6400. Ext. 232. Editor: Edward J. Baur. Official publication of the American Bowling Congress. Monthly. Established in 1934. Rights purchased vary with author and material. Usually buys all rights. Pays on publication. Reports within 30 days. Enclose S.A.S.E. for return of submissions.
Nonfiction and Photos: "This is a specialized field and the average writer attempting the subject of bowling should be well-informed. However, anyone is free to submit material for approval." Wants articles about unusual ABC leagues and tournaments, personalities, etc., featuring male bowlers. Length: 500 to 1,200 words. Pays $25 to $100 per article. $10 to $15 per photo.
How To Break In: "Submit feature material on bowlers, generally amateurs competing in local leagues, or special events involving the game of bowling. Should have connection with ABC membership."

THE WOMAN BOWLER, 5301 S. 76 St., Greendale WI 53219. Phone: 414-421-9000. Editor: Mrs. Helen Latham. For "women bowlers, ages 8 to 90; people bowling in sanctioned leagues and tournaments; news media; trade groups, manufacturers, etc." Monthly; May-June, July-August issues combined. Circulation: 117,000. Buys all rights. Buys about 25 mss a year. Pays on acceptance. Will send a sample copy to a writer on request. Submit seasonal material 2 months in advance. Reports in 1 month. Query first. Most articles done on assignment by professional writers. Enclose S.A.S.E.
Nonfiction and Photos: Articles on "women's bowling, competitive or administrative." Does not want articles on "senior citizens and handicapped bowling." Buys interviews, profiles, spot news, historical pieces of national significance. Pays $15 to $50. Photos purchased with mss. B&w glossies. Pays $5 to $10.
Fillers: Puzzles. Pays $15 to $50.

Boxing

TOMMY KAY'S BOXING GUIDE, P.O. Box 642, Scottsdale AZ 85252. Phone:

602-838-8427. Editor: Tommy Kay. For boxing fans. Every 2 months (8½x11, 64 pages). Established in 1974. Circulation: 96,000. Buys all rights, but will reassign rights to author after publication. Buys approximately 6 mss per year. Payment on publication. Will send sample copy to writer for 75¢. Will consider photocopied submissions. Reports on material accepted for publication in 6 to 8 weeks. Returns rejected material in 2 weeks. Query first or submit complete ms. Enclose S.A.S.E.

Nonfiction and Photos: Profile articles on top fighters in all divisions, plus in-depth pieces on retired or old-time boxing greats. "Don't send dated pieces; we're a magazine, not a newspaper." Profile the subjects with no blow-by-blow accounts. Informational articles, personal experience, interviews, profiles, humor; historical and nostalgic articles. Length: 1,000 to 3,000 words. Pays $20 to $50. Heavy on photo coverage. No story accepted without photos, but no extra payment is made. 5x7, or larger, b&w glossies. Captions required. Pays $3 to $5 for photos purchased without accompanying ms. Good action closeups for covers. 2¼x2¼ color transparencies. Pays $50 to $75 for covers.

Football

ALL SOUTH CAROLINA FOOTBALL ANNUAL, P.O. Box 3, Columbia SC 29202. Phone: 803-796-9200. Editor: Sidney L. Wise. Associate Editor: Ralph Shealy. Issued annually, August 1. Buys first rights. Pays on publication. Deadline for material each year is 10 weeks preceding publication date. Query first. Enclose S.A.S.E.

Nonfiction and Photos: Material must be about South Carolina high school and college football teams, players and coaches. Pays 2¢ minimum a word. Buys photos with ms. Captions required. 5x7 or 8x10 b&w glossies; 4x5 or 35mm color transparencies. Uses color on cover only. Pays $5 minimum for b&w; $10 minimum for color.

FOOTBALL DIGEST, Century Publishing Co., 1020 Church St., Evanston IL 60201. Editor: Michael K. Herbert. For football enthusiasts. Digest size magazine; 100 (5¼x7½) pages. Established in 1971. Monthly. Circulation: 250,000. Buys all rights. Buys 20 mss a year. Pays on publication. Will send sample copy to writer for $1. Reports in 2 to 4 weeks. Submit only complete ms. Enclose S.A.S.E.

Nonfiction and Photos: Articles on aspects of NFL and WFL professional football, profiles of players and coaches, studies of teams, current statistics. Buys interviews, profiles, historical, informational, how-to, personal experience, humor, think, nostalgic and technical articles. "We are looking for fresh, original, unusual story angles – perhaps a new way of looking at a certain statistic, or a humorous event told through a player's eyes. The only opportunity for a freelance contribution is an article that is timely, unusual or original in approach." Length: 500 to 2,000 words. Pays approximately $75. Buys photos of players in action, headshots. Pays $10 per shot for 8x10 b&w glossies; $75 for color cover and $25 for inside color (35mm mounted transparencies).

FOOTBALL NEWS, 19830 Mack Ave., Grosse Pointe MI 48236. Editor: Roger Stanton. For avid grid fans. Weekly tabloid published during football season; 20 pages. Established in 1939. Circulation: 100,000. Not copyrighted. Buys 12 to 15 mss a year. Payment on publication. Will send sample copy to writer for 25¢. Reports in 1 month. Query first. Enclose S.A.S.E.

Nonfiction: Articles on players, officials, coaches, past and present, with fresh approach. Highly informative, concise, positive approach. Interested in profiles of former punt, pass and kick players who have made the pros. Interview, profile, historical, think articles, and exposes. Length: 800 to 1,000 words. Pays $30 to $50 per ms.

PRO!, Suite 1103, 10880 Wilshire Blvd., Los Angeles CA 90024. Official magazine of the National Football League. Editor: John Wiebusch. For persons who attend NFL games; middle income and higher; ages 25 to 50; most are season ticket-holders. Stadium magazine; 68 pages ("national insert"), averages 100 to 160 locally. Established in 1970. Publishes 4 preseason editions, 7 regular season editions, and 4 postseason editions. Circulation: 4,000,000. Buys all rights. Buys 50 to 60 mss a year. Pays on acceptance. Will send a sample copy to writer on request. Will not consider photocopied submissions; "prefer originals." Does not seek material that "might be dated by some event of the coming NFL season." All articles for the coming year must be submitted by April 1. Reports on material accepted for publication in 60 days. Returns rejected material in 90 days. Query first, or submit a complete ms. Enclose S.A.S.E.

Nonfiction and Photos: Features the "people and events of the colorful past and present of professional football. As the only such magazine in the market and sold in NFL stadiums, we write from the 'inside' of the game. We dislike the breezy, short-paragraph style of newspaper sportswriting and prefer authors to develop thoughts and themes fully." Stories have a wide range of approaches — interview, profile, humor, historical, technical football articles, nostalgia, and personal opinion pieces. Length: 2,000 to 4,500 words. Pays $250 minimum per ms. Pays for photos accompanying mss; however, "an ample library of pro football photos on our premises makes publication of unsolicited photos unlikely. But authors may submit them and a fee may be negotiated if the photos are published." Photo Editor: David Boss.

Fiction and Poetry: "We seek more fiction, especially in the areas of fantasy, humor and experimental forms." Length: 2,000 to 4,500 words. Pays $250 minimum. Free verse poetry submissions also needed.

How To Break In: "A writer wholly unknown to us would draw attention with an unusual story angle, one revealing a heretofore unseen side of the game, told in an entertaining fashion."

SPORTS FOCUS, P.O. Box 488, 17100 W. Capitol Dr., Brookfield WI 53005. Editor: Bruce J. Schroeder. For football fans, ages 15 to 50; most are college graduates. Magazine and newsletter (8½x11). Established in 1965. Every 2 weeks. Circulation: 350,000. Rights purchased vary with author and material. Usually buys all rights. Buys about 25 mss a year. Pays on publication. Reports immediately. Query first or submit complete ms. Enclose S.A.S.E.

Nonfiction and Photos: Articles on anything relating to football. Pays minimum of $25. B&w photos purchased with or without ms. Pays minimum of $5.

Gambling

GAMBLERS WORLD, 527 Madison Ave., New York NY 10022. Editor: Lawrence Bernard. For "adults interested in all aspects of recreational gambling." Established in 1972. Bimonthly. Circulation: 100,000. Rights purchased vary with author and material. May buy all rights, but will reassign rights to author after publication, or first North American serial rights, first or second serial rights or simultaneous rights. Payment on acceptance. Will send sample copy to writer for $1.25. Will consider photocopied submissions. Submit seasonal material 4 to 6 months in advance. Query first. Enclose S.A.S.E.

Nonfiction and Photos: Articles must be knowledgeable on the gambling topic covered. Informational, how-to, personal experience, interview, profile, humor, think pieces, exposes. Length: 100 to 5,000 words. Payment depends on subject matter, quality of writing and length of article. Pays minimum 5¢ per word. Photos purchased with mss or on assignment. Pays $25 minimum per photo. Captions required.

GAMBLING QUARTERLY, Box 412, Station F, Toronto, Ontario, Canada. Editor: Donald W. Valliere. For gamblers of all ages, both sexes, throughout the United States and Canada. Quarterly magazine, 64 to 80 pages. Established in 1974. Circulation: 100,000. Buys all rights. Buys 16 mss a year. Payment on acceptance. Will send free sample copy to writer on request. Query first or submit complete ms. Reports "as soon as possible." Enclose S.A.E. and International Reply Coupons.

Nonfiction and Photos: "Articles on how to gamble, sketches on successful gamblers, latest developments on gambling, interviews and photo stories. Writers must be well acquainted with subject. Readers recognize ill-informed writing. We use more in-depth articles." Buys informational, how-to, personal experience, interview, profile, historical, think articles, expose, nostalgia, personal opinion articles. Recent articles include "Everything You Need to Know About Low Ball Poker." Length: 1,500 to 3,000 words. Pays 6¢ per word. Photos purchased with ms. Captions optional. Pays $10 for b&w; $20 for color.

General Sports Interest

AAU NEWS, AMATEUR ATHLETE YEARBOOK, 3400 West 86th Street, Indianapolis IN 46268. Editor: J. Richard Cassin. For "AAU members and others interested in amateur sports (track & field, swimming, boxing, wrestling, basketball, etc.), school and college coaches and athletic directors; members of sports press and media." Established in 1925. Monthly, plus yearbook. Circulation: 14,000. Pays on publication. Will send free sample copy to a writer on request. Will consider photocopied submissions. Reports immediately. Enclose S.A.S.E.
Nonfiction and Photos: General subject matter is "profiles of top amateur athletes and athletic volunteers or leaders. Reports on AAU championships, previews of coming seasons, etc." Writer should "emphasize contribution to amateur sport in USA. We would like to see features on unusual sports programs and the volunteers who do so much for the youth they help get involved in AAU activity." Buys interviews, profiles, photo, sport book reviews, and spot news articles. Seeks photos of champions as soon as completed. One or two for features; as available for post event coverage. Length: up to 1,000 words. Pays from $10 to $50. Color photos only on assignment. Pays $1 to $25.

LETTERMAN MAGAZINE, 11 S. Second St., St. Charles IL 60174. Phone: 312-377-1120. Editor: Paul Nyberg. Managing Editor: David Mathieu. "*Letterman* is America's only national high school sports magazine. It is the only publication written specifically for the 14- to 18-year-old male age group. Subscribers are members of interscholastic teams." Monthly. Circulation: 200,000. Buys all rights. Buys about 50 mss a year. Pays on publication. Will send a sample copy to a writer for 50¢. Submit seasonal material 2 to 3 months in advance. Reports in 1 month. Query first. Enclose S.A.S.E.
Nonfiction and Photos: "*Letterman* is filled with basically 2 kinds of material: (1) feature articles on outstanding high school athletes. These articles are personality sketches and explain why a boy has achieved both as an athlete and academically, socially, etc. (2) instructional or training material to help boys develop in areas of skills and attitudes." Style should be "simple, straightforward, and never cute. *Letterman* is written for participants. And since our focus is on the high school sports scene, rather than the college and professional sports scene, there are no ready-made heroes. We have to create our own." Buys how-to's, personal experience and inspirational pieces, interviews, profiles, humor, spot news, historical articles, and coverage of new products. Length: 500 to 3,000 words. Pays 3¢ to 10¢ per word. Photos purchased with mss; with captions only. B&w glossies, color transparencies. Pays $10 to $50.

LOUISIANA WOODS & WATER, 4033 Veterans Blvd., Metairie LA 70002. For primarily male audience, ages 16 to 60 years, who range in the skilled to professional bracket. All have a keen interest in the outdoor life, outdoor recreation, hunting, fishing, camping, boating, and conservation. Monthly magazine, 68 to 84 pages. Established in 1973. Circulation: 60,000. Buys first North American serial rights. Buys 200 to 250 mss a year. Payment on publication. Will send free sample copy to writer on request. Write for copy of editorial guidelines for writers. Reports in 10 days. Query first. When query is approved, submit complete ms with photos. "We never buy ms without photos or illustrations." Enclose S.A.S.E.
Nonfiction and Photos: "We are particularly receptive to how-to pieces, better methods, and more interesting ways to hunt, fish, camp, etc. Of course, all material must be Louisiana oriented (no moose on mountains), and writers should study back issues for style and familiarization. We use no poetry at all, no fillers, and no me and Joe's. Studying the magazine is always the best approach. We enjoy success because we don't waste the reader's time by putting the recreation we suggest

and cover out of his immediate reach. We are published for Louisiana, and we stay in Louisiana. No articles about salmon fishing in Alaska are used. That's out of the reader's reach! I've had it with ecology pieces. Most are written on emotion, rather than on research. We cover ecology and environmental issues in depth, but we have several learned conservation writers doing this now. Anything other than the straight, overworked, outdated, lets-go-hunting-and-fishing stuff would be welcomed. Whatever is submitted must have a new slant, a new twist!" Length: 500 to 2,500 words. Pays $20 to $150 per ms, depending on quality. B&w and color photos are purchased with accompanying ms with no additional payment, or purchased on assignment. Captions required. 8x10 b&w preferred, but no smaller than 5x7. Transparencies or C-prints only for color. Pays $2 to $8 for b&w; $5 to $25 inside color; $25 to $100 covers.

OUTDOOR CANADA, Suite 201, 181 Eglinton Ave., E., Toronto, Ontario M2J 1X3, Canada. Editor: Sheila Kaighin. For anyone interested in the Canadian outdoors, including armchair sports people and white water canoeists. A family magazine for readers aged 8 to 80. Magazine; 64 to 80 (8¼x11) pages. Established in 1973. Every 2 months. Circulation: 46,000. Rights purchased vary with author and material. May buy all rights or first North American serial rights. Buys about 50 mss a year. Pays on publication. Will send sample copy to writer for $1. Will consider photocopied submissions. No simultaneous submissions. reports on material accepted for publication in 2 months. Returns rejected material within 3 weeks. Query first. Enclose S.A.E. and International Reply Coupons.
Nonfiction and Photos: "Ours is a family magazine, as opposed to a male-oriented magazine. We want a positive approach toward the outdoors. Writers must have a thorough knowledge of the Canadian outdoors, since ours is a totally Canadian publication." Informational, how-to, personal experience, humor, photo articles. Length: 600 to 3,000 words. Pays $25 to $100. Color transparencies or 8x10 b&w glossies are purchased with or without mss. Pays $10. Captions required.

OUTDOOR JOURNAL, 303 Goldstream Ave., Victoria, B.C. Canada. Editor: Mark Hume. For the outdoor recreationalist; men and women from both professional and blue collar positions, who in their spare time are hunters, fishermen, hikers, mountain climbers, bird watchers, etc. Tabloid newspaper; 16 pages. Established in 1974. Weekly. Circulation: 10,000. Buys all rights, but will reassign rights to author after publication. Buys 8 to 10 mss a year. Pays on acceptance. Will send a free sample copy to writer on request. Reports on material accepted for publication in 1 week. Returns rejected material as soon as possible. Submit complete ms. Enclose S.A.E. and International Reply Coupons.
Nonfiction and Photos: "We're concerned only with articles centered in the province of British Columbia. Main thrust is news and educational articles in the fields of outdoor recreation. We also publish features on hunting, hiking, etc., in the form of personal accounts of an expedition, as well as profiles of notable outdoorsmen and recreationalists. No limitations on style other than those imposed by the subject data to be covered. Although each season has its related outdoor activities, this does not preclude articles which might explain (for instance) what the camper can do during the cold winter months." Recently published articles include "Early Season Cutthroat", an informative, educational, colorful, personal experience feature. Length: 200 to 1,500 words. Pays 25¢ per column inch (about 1¢ a word). B&w and color photos purchased with or witdut mss. 4x5 is the preferred size. Color is reproduced in b&w. Pays $3 for inside use; $5 for cover use.

RX SPORTS AND TRAVEL, Rx Golf and Travel, Inc., 447 S. Main St., Hillsboro IL 62049. Phone: 217-532-6172. Editor: Harry Luecke. For physicians. Monthly. Circulation: 205,000. Buys all rights. Pays on acceptance. Reports on submissions within 8 weeks "when possible." No unsolicited material. Query first. Enclose S.A.S.E.
Nonfiction: Articles on sports, recreation, leisure, and travel of interest to physicians. Articles on golf, tennis, hunting, fishing, boating, shooting and all other major participant sports and on travel. Style is in the *Sports Illustrated-Holiday-New Yorker*

genre. Slant is toward physicians, but any mention of technical, medical or related subjects is strictly taboo. Aim is to entertain readers and inform them of places to go and things to do on vacation and during their leisure hours. Normal minimum is 2,000 words; maximum 3,000 words. Pays $350 maximum. "Freelance work solicited."

Photos: Purchased with mss; physicians participating in golf, tennis, fishing and other sports. Photos must have some action. No "family album" shots used. Photos are desirable but not necessary to support editorial. Photos submitted with mss may be b&w glossies or color transparencies. "We do not purchase photos separately, but include the photos under the price of a combination photo/story."

SPORT, 641 Lexington Ave., New York NY 10022. Phone: 212-935-4758. Editor: Dick Schaap. Monthly. For male spectator sport enthusiasts, ages 28 to 35. Buys all rights. Payment is made on acceptance. Reports within 20 days. Query preferred. Enclose S.A.S.E. for reply to queries.

Nonfiction: "Most of our article ideas originate with the editors, therefore we need original, unusual sports ideas. It is no good to query us on a profile of an athlete; chances are, we have thought of doing him. But if you were to write us suggesting an unusual angle on the athlete, perhaps even a byline, we would definitely be interested. Our regular departments are mostly staff-written." Pays $350 to $1,000; $25 to $50 for acceptable shorts.

Photos: Generally assigned separate from mss. Pays $25 for b&w; $100 page rate for color or $25 plus $150 day rate on assignment; $500 for cover.

SPORTING NEWS, 1212 N. Lindbergh Blvd., St. Louis MO 63166. "We do not actively solicit freelance material."

SPORTS ILLUSTRATED, Time & Life Bldg., Rockefeller Center, New York NY 10020. Outside Text Editor: Pat Ryan. Primarily staff-written, with small but steady amount of outside material. Weekly. Reports in 1 week. Pays on acceptance. Buys all rights or North American serial rights. Enclose S.A.S.E.

Nonfiction: Material falls into two general categories: regional (text that runs in editorial space accompanying regional advertising pages) and long text. Runs a great deal of regional advertising and, as a result, considerable text in that section of the magazine. Regional text does not have a geographical connotation; it can be any sort of short feature (600 to 2,500 words): historical, humor, reminiscence, personality, opinion, first-person, but it must deal with some aspect of sport, however slight. Long text (2,000 to 5,000 words) also must have sporting connection, however tenuous; should be major personality, personal reminiscence, knowing look into a significant aspect of a sporting subject, but long text should be written for broad appeal, so that readers without special knowledge will appreciate the piece. Wants quality writing. Pays $250 minimum for regional pieces, $750 minimum for long text. Smaller payments are made for material used in special sections or departments.

Photos: "Do not care to see photos until story is purchased."

How To Break In: "One possibility would be an item for the section, As I Saw It. These can be as short as 950 words; can be a personal experience or a happening in sports which occurred prior to the inception of the magazine in 1954."

SPORTS TODAY, 919 Third Ave., New York NY 10022. Editorial Director: Phil Hirsch. Managing Editor: Herb Gluck. For male sport enthusiasts. Bimonthly. Buys all rights. Pays on acceptance. Will send a sample copy to a writer for 60¢. Reports in 1 to 3 weeks. Enclose S.A.S.E.

Nonfiction and Photos: Major emphasis is on the main spectator sports of baseball, basketball, football, hockey. Also covers golf, horseracing, etc. Wants dramatic material. Length: 1,500 to 4,000 words. Pays $200. Buys Kodachrome photos for front cover. Pays $150 for cover.

SPORTSHELF NEWS, P.O. Box 634, New Rochelle NY 10802. Editor: Irma Ganz. For "all ages interested in sports." Established in 1949. Bimonthly. Circulation: 150,000. Pays on acceptance. Query first required. Enclose S.A.S.E.
Nonfiction: Subject matter is exclusively sports. Buys how-to articles. Payment varies, "averages about $50 for 1,000 words."

THE SPORTSWOMAN, P.O. Box 2611, Culver City CA 90230. Editor: Marlene Jensen. For "women, age 16 to 66. Many teach physical education. Most are actively involved in sports and have feminist leanings." Established in 1973. Monthly. Circulation: 17,000. Rights purchased vary with author and material. May buy all rights; or second serial (reprint) rights. Buys approximately 50 mss a year. Payment on publication. Will send sample copy to writer for 75 cents. Will consider photocopied submissions. Submit seasonal material 2 months in advance. "We feature golf and tennis each issue, but other sports in their season." Reports on material in 2 weeks. Query first or submit complete ms. Enclose S.A.S.E.
Nonfiction and Photos: "Profiles on top sportswomen. Interviews. Investigative journalism on discrimination and ways to beat it. Reports on unusual sports. Approach subject through the eyes of the sportswoman being discussed or interviewed." Length: 6 to 10 double-spaced, typewritten pages. Pays $50 to $100. B&w photos (8x10) purchased with ms. Occasionally purchased on assignment. Pays $25 for 2 to 3 pictures.

Golf

CAROLINA GOLFER, P.O. Box 3, Columbia SC 29202. Phone: 803-796-9200. Editor: Sydney L. Wise. Associate Editor: Ralph Shealy. Bimonthly. Buys first rights. Payment on publication. Will send free sample copy to a writer on request. Reports in 3 to 8 weeks. Enclose S.A.S.E.
Nonfiction and Photos: Articles on golf and golfers, clubs, courses, tournaments, only in the Carolinas. Stories on the various courses should be done "in the manner that would give the reader a basic idea of what each course is like." Length: 1,200 to 1,500 words. Pays according to quality of ms; 2¢ minimum per word. Buys photos with mss. 5x7 or 8x10 b&w glossies. Color should be 4x5 or 35mm transparencies. Pays $5 minimum for b&w; $25 for color transparencies used for cover.

COUNTRY CLUB GOLFER, 2171 Campus Drive, Irvine CA 92664. Editor: Edward F. Pazdur. For country club members and club golfers: professional, affluent, college-educated. Magazine: 62 pages. Established in 1972. Monthly. Circulation: 55,000. Buys all rights, but will reassign rights to author after publication. Buys about 6 mss a year. Pays on publication. Will send sample copy to writer for $1. Write for copy of guidelines for writers. Will consider photocopied and simultaneous submissions. Reports in 10 days. Query first or submit complete ms. Enclose S.A.S.E.
Nonfiction and Photos: Editorial material is confined to country club activities: primarily, golf. Anything reflecting country club life styles will be considered; golfing or social activities, etc. No specific style, but prefers informative articles slanted toward the more mature, affluent golfer. Informative features on fashions for country clubs, as well as how to entertain, give parties, etc., might be considered. Recently published "Why Your Country Club Should Give Up Its Tax-Exempt Status". Length: open. Pays minimum of $75. No additional payment for b&w glossies or 35mm transparencies purchased with mss. Captions required.
Poetry: Traditional and avant-garde forms of poetry; must be golf-related. Length: 8 to 16 lines. Pays $10 to $25.
How To Break In: "We frequently need to assign writers abroad to write a feature on golfing resorts. For European assignments, writer must also play golf, and be an experienced photographer."

FORE, 3740 Cahuenga Blvd., North Hollywood CA 91604. Editor: Will Hertzberg. Mailed quarterly to the 65,000 members of the Southern California Golf Association. Submit complete ms. Reports in 2 weeks. Enclose S.A.S.E.

Nonfiction and Photos: "Although we do not use a great deal of freelance material, and our rate of payment is low, we are always interested in seeing editorial and photographic material of interest to Southern California golfers. Edited primarily for amateurs, but can always use strong personality profiles and features on professionals as well. Other areas covered include resort/travel with a golf orientation, new equipment, instruction, rules, handicapping, professional and amateur tournament coverage, etc. Rates vary but usually run about $50 per article (1,000 words up), with high quality b&w photos bringing $15 each. Pay more for color."

GOLF CANADA, 56 The Esplanade, Suite 404, Toronto, Ontario M5E 1A8, Canada. Phone: 416-864-9020. Editor: Michael C. Bartlett. For a private and public course audience; Canadian golfers. Published 7 times a year, April to October. Circulation: 85,000. Produces official Canadian Open and Peter Jackson Ladies Classic tournament programs. Buys Canadian and/or North American rights, depending on story. Pays on publication. Reports in 3 weeks. Query first. Enclose S.A.S.E.
Nonfiction and Photos: Chief focus is on the Canadian golf scene, but also includes material on major players and golf events anywhere in the world. Subject matter includes personality features, brief profiles, technical discussions of equipment, instruction, opinion pieces, taped interviews, golf travel and resorts, historical articles. Length: 300 to 2,500 words. Pays $35 to $200. Purchases b&w photos and color transparencies. Pays $25 to $100.
Poetry and Fillers: Light verse; puzzles, jokes and short humor. Length: 2 to 20 lines: 25 to 100 words. Pays $2 to $10 for poetry; $2 to $5 for fillers.

GOLF DIGEST, 297 Westport Ave., Norwalk CT 06856. Editor: Nick Seitz. Monthly publication of *The New York Times.* Circulation: 650,000. Buys all rights. Pays promptly on acceptance. Reports within three weeks. Query first. Enclose S.A.S.E.
Nonfiction: Uses mainly instruction and how-to material, but also features on prominent and unusual golf personalities or events, but prefers initial query. Historical nonfiction pertaining to golf is also good. Up to 2,500 words. Main need is for shorter lengths. Pays a minimum of 20¢ a word (as edited).
Photos: 8x10 b&w glossies for inside use. Payment is $15 and more. Also uses color transparencies. Payment is up to $200. Preferred subjects are nationally known golfers, pro or amateur and other golf scenes.
Fillers: "We are interested in short, humorous fillers and jokes pertaining to the sport and pay a minimum of $10 per item." All filler submissions should be addressed to the attention of Kathy Jonah, Assistant Editor.

GOLF GUIDE, 631 Wilshire Blvd., Santa Monica CA 90406. Editor: D.N. Werner. "For a golfing audience—fans and players of all ages." Established in 1969. Bimonthly. Circulation: 110,000. Buys first North American serial rights. Buys 200 mss a year. Payment on publication. Will send free sample copy to a writer on request. Will send editorial guidelines sheet to a writer on request. Will consider photocopied submissions. Submit seasonal material 3 months in advance. Reports in 2 weeks. Query first. Enclose S.A.S.E.
Nonfiction and Photos: General subject matter is "heavy on instructional articles aimed at the handicap golfer. Freelance material welcome, but must be expertly written and concern instruction. Articles should be based on the thoughts of authorities in the field—professionals on the tour or golf instructors. Writer should have a rather thorough knowledge of golf to be able to get the right material." Length: 1,500 to 2,000 words. Pays $50 to $300. Purchases photos with ms and on assignment. Captions optional. Pays $10 to $25 for 8x10 glossies. Pays up to $100 for 35mm color.

GOLF JOURNAL, Chilton Co., Chilton Way, Radnor PA 19089. Editor: Joe Schwendeman. For golfers of all ages and both sexes. Official publication of the U.S. Golf Association. Magazine: 54 pages. Established in 1948. 10 times a year. Circulation: 50,000. Buys all rights. Buys about 30 mss a year. Payment on publication. Will send sample copy to writer for 75¢. Will not consider photocopied or simultaneous submissions. Reports in 2 weeks. Query first. Enclose S.A.S.E.

Nonfiction and Photos: "As the official publication of the United States Golf Association, our magazine is strong on decisions on the rules of golf, USGA championships, history of the game, and on service articles directed to the club golfer. All facets of golf, its history, courses, and clubs. Instructions. Humor." Length: 500 to 2,000 words. Pays maximum of $300. Pays a minimum of $15 for b&w photos. Captions required.

GOLF MAGAZINE, 380 Madison Ave., New York NY 10017. Phone: 212-687-3000. Editor: John M. Ross. For recreational golfers. Monthly. Buys all rights. Pays on acceptance. Reports in three weeks. Most material done on assignment. Query first. Enclose S.A.S.E.
Nonfiction: Must entertain, instruct or inform the average golfer. Will not accept such things as "My First Day on the Golf Course," or "How I Took Up Golf and Drove My Husband Insane." Length: 1,000 to 2,000 words. Pays from $250 to $500.
Fiction: Golf-oriented short stories. Pays $350 to $500. Length: 2,000 words maximum.
Photos: Purchased with mss or with caption only. Pays $25 for b&w, $50 for color. Send b&w negatives & contact sheet. Send color in transparency form.
Fillers: Short humor. Pays $5 minimum for fillers.
How To Break In: "Every so often we have the happy experience of running into a golf addict who can also write well. His best chance is to aim for a light piece which is not too long and is focused on a personality or is genuinely funny. Anything very technical that would require a consummate knowledge of golf, we would rather assign ourselves. But if you are successful with something light and not too long (say 2,500 words), we might use you for something heavier later. One recent over-the-transom piece we used was a how-to home practice piece. The author had obviously made himself a real authority on the subject through personal experience. Probably the easiest way to break in would be for our Golf Reports section in which we run short (250 words) items on interesting golf feats, events, and so forth. If you send us something like that, about an important event in your area, it is an easy way for us to get acquainted."

INSIDE GOLF, 3100 Riverside Dr., Los Angeles CA 90027. Editor: Mike Doherty. For "golfers and fans." Quarterly. Circulation: 100,000. Buys all rights or North American serial rights. Pays on publication. Reports in 2 weeks. Query first. Enclose S.A.S.E.
Nonfiction: Wants "personality features on golf stars aimed to the knowledgeable fan." Length: open. Payment is "usually $125 to $150 if pictures are included."
Photos: Purchased with mss and with captions only. Wants "golf pro tournament coverage, golf stars' facials or action, other interesting golf material." Payment is $10 for b&w, "up to $150 for color."

Guns

THE AMERICAN SHOTGUNNER, P.O. Box 3351, Reno NV 89505. Editor: Bob Thruston. Tabloid magazine; 32 pages. Established in 1973. Monthly. Circulation: 65,000. Buys all rights. Buys 24 to 50 mss a year. Pays on publication. Will send free sample copy to writer on request. Write for copy of guidelines for writers. Submit special material (hunting) 3 to 4 months in advance. Reports on material accepted for publication in 30 days. Returns rejected material immediately. Submit complete ms. Enclose S.A.S.E.
Nonfiction and Photos: All aspects of shotgunning, trap and skeet shooting and hunting, reloading; shooting clothing, shooting equipment and recreational vehicles. Emphasis is on the how-to and instructional approach. "We give the sportsman actual material that will help him to improve his game, fill his limit, or build that duck blind, etc. Hunting articles are used in all issues, year round." Length: open. Pays $75 to $250. No additional payment for photos used with mss.
Fillers: Tips on hunting, shooting and outdoor themes; short humor. Pays minimum of $10.

BLACK POWDER TIMES, P.O. Box 842, Mount Vernon WA 98273. Editor: Fred Holder. For people interested in shooting and collecting black powder guns, primarily of the muzzle-loading variety. Tabloid newspaper; 12 pages. Established in 1974. Monthly. Not copyrighted. Pays on publication. Will send sample copy to writer for 50¢. Will consider photocopied and simultaneous submissions. Reports on material accepted for publication in 2 to 4 weeks. Returns rejected material in 2 weeks. Query first. Enclose S.A.S.E.

Nonfiction: Articles on gunsmiths who make black powder guns, on shoots, on muzzle-loading gun clubs, on guns of the black powder vintage, and anything related to the sport of black powder shooting and hunting. Emphasis is on good writing and reporting. As an example of recently published material, see "Guardian of the Gate." Informational, how-to, personal experience, interview, profile, historical articles and book reviews. Length: 500 to 2,000 words. Pays 2¢ a word.

Fillers: Clippings; 500 to 2,000 words. Pays ½¢ a word.

GUN WEEK, 119 East Court Street, P.O. Box 150, Sidney OH 45365. Acting Editor: J. O. Amos. For "outdoor sportsmen with a particular interest in firearms collecting, hunting and target shooting. Above average in income and education." Established in 1966. Weekly newspaper. Circulation: 36,000. Buys first North American serial rights. Buys about 35 to 40 mss a year, excluding regular columns. Payment on publication, but special material paid on acceptance. Will send free sample copy to a writer on request. Will consider photocopied submissions, "if sharp and legible." Reports in 2 to 4 weeks. Enclose S.A.S.E.

Nonfiction and Photos: General subject matter includes "any subject relating to lawful firearms ownership and use. Major portion is devoted to legislative activity relating to firearms ownership; reports of shooting competitions; test reports on new products; how-to articles. Original research on firearms preferred. Need factual reports on activity of sportsmen groups fighting anti-gun legislation at local or state levels, and reports on how non-shooters are being turned into shooters. Also will look at test reports, instruction articles and history pieces about small arms. *Gun Week* is the only weekly newspaper covering the shooting sports. Writer should strive for hard-hitting newspaper style. We emphasize news element, while magazines in our field stress narrative accounts of hunting trips, ballistic tests, etc. Because of our technical nature, we receive little material from freelancers. Would welcome more—if it is technically accurate and writer comes up with new slant. Promotion of shooting (any type, trap, skeet, rifle, pistol) as a wholesome family sport is approach we are looking for." Buys informational, how-to, personal experience, interview, profile, humor, historical, spot news, new product, and technical articles. Length: 300 to 1,000 words. Pays 1¢ to 1¼¢ per word with a $35 maximum. Purchases photos with mss, captions required. Pays $3 to $5 for sharp, clear, 5x7, 8x10 b&w glossies.

Fillers: Buys newsbreaks. Length: 100 to 250 words. Pays $2 to $5.

GUN WORLD, Box HH, 34249 Camino Capistrano, Capistrano Beach CA 92624. Editorial Director: Jack Lewis. For ages that "range from mid-twenties to mid-sixties; many professional types who are interested in relaxation of hunting and shooting." Established in 1960. Monthly. Circulation: 129,000. Buys all rights but will reassign them to author after publication. Buys "50 or so" mss a year. Payment on acceptance. Will send a free sample copy to a writer on request. Will not consider photocopied submissions. Submit seasonal material 4 months in advance. Reports in six weeks, perhaps longer. Enclose S.A.S.E.

Nonfiction and Photos: General subject matter consists of "well-rounded articles—not by amateurs—on shooting techniques, with anecdotes; hunting stories with tips and knowledge integrated. No poems or fiction. We like broad humor in our articles, so long as it does not reflect upon firearms safety. Most arms magazines are pretty deadly and we feel shooting can be fun. Too much material aimed at pro-gun people. Most of this is staff-written and most shooters don't have to be told of their rights under the Constitution. We want articles on new development; off-track inventions, novel military uses of arms; do-it-yourself projects in this field." Buys informational, how-to, personal experience, and nostalgia articles. Pays $200 maximum. Purchases photos with mss and caption required. Wants 5x7 b&w.

GUNS AND AMMO, 8490 Sunset Blvd., Los Angeles CA 90069. Editor: Howard French. For "hunters and shooters," average 30 years old, college educated. Monthly. Circulation: 250,000. Buys all rights. Buys 100 mss a year. Pays on publication. Reports in 30 days. Enclose S.A.S.E.

Nonfiction: "We are especially interested in articles of a technical nature directly related to guns, reloading, target shooting, gunsmithing and associated shooting activities. Articles of a more general nature on hunting should be specifically keyed to the gun. No fiction. *Guns and Ammo* reserves the right to edit any accepted ms." Length: 2,000 to 2,500 words. Pays 5¢ and up per word.

Photos: Submit "lots of high quality photos" with all mss. "Probably more mss are rejected for poor illustrations than any other reason. Ideally, b&w photos should be submitted on 8x10-inch single-weight glossy paper. All illustrations should be completely captioned. Mss submitted without illustrations will almost certainly be rejected." Pays $5 per photo. "Limited use of four-color art; must be transparencies, preferably 4x5. 2¼x2¼ is acceptable." Pays $15.

GUNS MAGAZINE, 8150 N. Central Park Avenue, Skokie IL 60076. Editor: J. Rakusan. Monthly for firearms enthusiasts. Buys all rights. Buys 150 mss a year. Pays on publication. Will send free sample copy to a writer on request. Reports on submissions as soon as possible. Enclose S.A.S.E.

Nonfiction and Photos: Informative articles about guns and shooting; reports on new or unusual guns, cartridges, or pieces of shooting equipment; how to shoot for better results at game or targets, etc. Also occasional historical or personality pieces of western, war, or collector interest. Length: up to 3,500 words. Pays $75 to $175. Study magazine before submitting ms. "Articles should be factual, technical, and easy-to-read." Pictures are a must but submit contact sheets for initial selection. "We do not buy separate b&w photos—they should be supplied with the ms. We do buy color transparencies no smaller than 2¼x2¼ for use in our color section and covers—payment for covers is $100 while inside color is $50 a published page."

HANDLOADER MAGAZINE, P.O. Box 3030, Prescott, AZ 86301. Editor: Neal Knox. Bimonthly for gun enthusiasts who reload their ammunition. Buys first North American serial rights only. Pays on publication. Reports in two weeks. Query with outline required. Enclose S.A.S.E.

Nonfiction and Photos: Fresh, informative, knowledgeable, technical articles on handloading ammunition. Style: serious and simple. Length: 1,500 to 3,000 words. Pays $75 to $200, including photos (8x10 glossies preferred) and/or illustrations.

THE RIFLE MAGAZINE, P.O. Box 3030, Prescott AZ 86301. Editor: Neal Knox. Bimonthly. For advanced rifle enthusiasts. Pays on publication. Buys North American serial rights. Reports in 30 days. "A detailed query will help, and is preferred." Enclose S.A.S.E.

Nonfiction and Photos: Articles must be fresh and of a quality and style to enlighten rather than entertain knowledgeable gun enthusiasts. "We are interested in seeing new bylines and new ideas, but if a writer doesn't have a solid knowledge of firearms and ballistics, he's wasting his time and ours to submit." Length: 1,500 to 3,000 words. Pays $75 to $200. Photos should accompany ms. Buys ms and photos as a package.

SHOOTING TIMES, News Plaza, Peoria IL 61601. Executive Editor: Alex Bartimo. "The average *Shooting Times* reader is 29 years old. He has an above average education and income. He is probably a semiskilled or skilled or professional worker who has an avid interest in firearms and the shooting sports." Special reloading issue in February; handgun issue in March. Monthly. Circulation: 134,000. Buys all rights. Buys 85 to 90 mss a year. Pays on acceptance. Will send a free sample copy to a writer on request. Submit seasonal or special material 4 or 5 months in advance. Reports in 4 to 5 weeks. Query first. Enclose S.A.S.E.

Nonfiction and Photos: "Presents a well-balanced content ranging from nontechnical through semitechnical to technical stories covering major shooting sports activities—handguns, rifles, shotguns, cartridge reloading, muzzle loading, gunsmithing, how-to's, and hunting, with a major emphasis on handguns. Hunting stories must be 'gunny' with the firearm(s) and ammunition dominating the story and serving as the means to an end. Articles may run from 1,000 to 2,000 words and must be accompanied by 10 to 12 b&w glossies, 8x10, including 1 or 2 'lead' pictures." Payment is $150 to $300.

Horse Racing

AMERICAN TURF MONTHLY, 505 8th Avenue, New York NY 10018. Editor: Howard Rowe. For "horse racing bettors." Buys 50 to 100 mss a year. Enclose S.A.S.E. **Nonfiction:** General subject matter is "articles, systems and material treating horse racing." Approach should be "how to successfully wager on racing. It is the only publication in the country devoted exclusively to the horse bettor. We have a staff capable of covering every facet aside from system articles." Length: 1,500 to 3,000 words. Pays $35 minimum.

THE BACKSTRETCH, 19363 James Couzens Highway, Detroit MI 48235. Editor: Ruth A. LeGrove. For thoroughbred horse trainers, owners, breeders, farm managers, track personnel, jockeys, grooms and racing fans which span the age range from very young to very old. Publication of United Thoroughbred Trainers of America, Inc. Quarterly magazine, approximately 92 pages. Established in 1962. Circulation: 20,000. Rights purchased vary with author and material. Payment on publication. Will send sample copy to writer for 50¢. Will not consider photocopied submissions. Will consider simultaneous submissions. Reporting time varies, but returns rejected material immediately. Submit only complete ms. Enclose S.A.S.E.
Nonfiction: "Mostly general information. No fiction. Articles deal with biographical material on trainers, owners, jockeys, horses and their careers, historical track articles, etc. Unless his material is related to thoroughbreds and thoroughbred racing, he should not submit it. Otherwise, send on speculation. Payment is made after material is used. If not suitable, it is returned immediately. We feel we have more readable material in *The Backstretch*, and we vary our articles sufficiently to give the reader a variety of reading. Articles of a historical nature or those not depending on publication by a certain date are preferable. No special length requirements. Payment depends on material."

TURF AND SPORT DIGEST, 511 Oakland Avenue, Baltimore MD 21212. Phone: 301-323-0300. Editor: Les Woodcock. For "horse racing enthusiasts of all sorts. Range from very rich to the guy who shouldn't be betting the rent money. Range broad for all other categories. All people associated with the sport." Established in 1924. Monthly. Circulation: 50,000. Buys all rights, but will reassign them to author after publication. Buys about 70 mss a year. Payment on publication. Will consider photocopied submissions, "if legible and clear." Submit seasonal material 3 months in advance. Reports within 3 weeks. Query first. Enclose S.A.S.E.
Nonfiction and Photos: Subject matter includes "personality pieces on jockeys, trainers, horses; news of tracks and industry; historical sketches; handicapping system; anything of interest in the racing world. Constructive criticism, etc. Not interested in breeding." Freelancer should "send a one- or two-paragraph outline of story he is proposing. I want two things: good writing—if profile, get inside the subject and don't be superficial—and solid facts and information. Emphasis on good writing. This is the only horse racing magazine covering the whole sport nationwide. Others specialize in an area or are pointed toward the breeding end of the business. There is always a receptive ear to a penetrating personality profile of someone in the news." Buys interviews; profile, historical, nostalgia articles. Length: 1,500 to 3,000 words. Pays $40 to $100. Purchases photos on assignment but is "interested in good, different, exciting 4-color photos as possible cover or inside material." Payment varies. Pays $100 for color cover.
Fillers: Pays $15 for crossword puzzles.

Hunting and Fishing

ALASKA HUNTING AND FISHING TALES, Box 4-EEE, Anchorage AK 99509. Annually. Buys first North American serial rights. Pays on publication. Reports in 1 month. Enclose S.A.S.E.
Nonfiction and Photos: True first-person hunting, fishing, or adventure stories from Alaska or adjacent Canada. "Material must have an Alaskan setting, and the general requirements in fact are the same as for *Alaska* magazine." Length: maximum 5,000 words; prefers 2,000 to 3,000 words. "Good photos are a must." Pays $25 to $100.

ALASKA MAGAZINE, Box 4-EEE, Anchorage AK 99509. Phone: 907-277-4416. Editor: Robert A. Henning. For wide range of persons interested in Alaska and the North. Wide range of ages. Latest survey shows majority are college-educated and middle income. Monthly magazine; 79 pages, (8½x11). Established in 1935. Circulation: 167,000. Rights purchased vary with author and material. Buys all rights; buys first North American serial rights; buys first serial rights. Payment on publication. Will send sample copy to writer for $1. Submit only complete ms. Enclose S.A.S.E.
Nonfiction and Photos: "Articles about the life and events in Alaska, Yukon, northern B.C. Material should be based on writer's actual experience in the North." Buys informational, how-to, personal experience, interview, humor, historical, photo, travel articles. Length: 100 to 3,000 words. Pays $10 to $100. 8x10 b&w photos purchased with ms with no additional payment. Also purchased without ms. 8x10 b&w glossies or Ektachrome and Kodachrome, color prints, 35mm. Pays $5 minimum. "Photos should accompany all mss." Department Editor: Ed Fortier, Executive Editor.

AMERICAN FIELD, 222 W. Adams St., Chicago IL 60606. Editor: William F. Brown. Issued weekly. Buys first publication rights. Payment made on acceptance. Will send sample copy on request. Reports usually within 10 days. Enclose S.A.S.E.
Nonfiction and Photos: Always interested in factual articles on breeding, rearing, development and training of hunting dogs, how-to-do-it material written to appeal to upland bird hunters, sporting dog owners, field trialers, etc. Also wants stories and articles about hunting trips in quest of upland game birds. Length: 1,000 to 2,500 words. Pays $50 to $200. Uses photos submitted with manuscripts if they are suitable and also photos submitted with captions only. Pays $5 minimum for b&w.
Fillers: Infrequently uses some 100- to 250-word fillers. Pays $5 minimum.

THE AMERICAN HUNTER, 1600 Rhode Island Ave., N.W., Washington DC 20036. Editor: Ken Warner. For sport hunters who are members of the National Rifle Association; all ages, all political persuasions, all economic levels. The best new market to come along in years. Editors are subject matter experts, so authors must be also. Established in 1973. Circulation: over 100,000. Buys first North American serial rights "and the right to reprint our presentation." Buys 200 mss a year. Payment on acceptance. Will send free sample copy to writer on request. Write for copy of guidelines for writers. Would prefer not to see photocopied submissions or simultaneous submissions. Reports in 1 to 3 weeks. Query first or submit complete ms. Enclose S.A.S.E.
Nonfiction and Photos: "Factual material on all phases of sport hunting and game animals and their habitats. Good angles and depth writing are essential. You have to *know* to write successfully here." Not interested in material on fishermen, campers or ecology freaks. Length: open. Pays $25 to $900. No additional payment made for photos used with mss. Pays $10 to $25 for b&w photos purchased without accompanying mss. Pays $20 to $100 for color.

THE AMERICAN RIFLEMAN, 1600 Rhode Island Ave., N.W., Washington DC 20036. Editor: Ashley Halsey, Jr. Monthly. Official journal of National Rifle Association of America. Buys first North American serial rights, including publication in this magazine, or any of the official publications of the National Rifle Association.

Residuary rights will be returned after publication upon request of the author. Pays on acceptance. Will send free sample copy on request. Reports in one to four weeks. Enclose S.A.S.E.

Nonfiction: Factual articles on hunting, target shooting, shotgunning, conservation, firearms repairs and oddities accepted from qualified freelancers. No semifictional or "me and Joe" type of yarns, but articles should be informative and interesting. Will not consider anything that "winks" at lawbreaking, or delineates practices that are inimical to the best interests of gun ownership, shooting, or good citizenship. Articles should run from one to four magazine pages. Pays about $75 to $600.

Photos: Full-color transparencies for possible use on cover and inside. Photo articles that run one to two magazine pages. Pays $35 minimum for inside photo; $75 minimum for cover; payment for groups of photos is negotiable.

CAROLINA SPORTSMAN, Box 2581, Charlotte NC 28201. Editor: Sidney L. Wise; Associate Editor: Ralph Shealy. Bimonthly. Buys all rights. Pays on publication. Will send free sample copy to a writer on request. Reports on submissions in 3 to 8 weeks. Enclose S.A.S.E.

Nonfiction and Photos: Sports stories in quick-moving, vivid, on-the-spot style, dealing with hunting, fishing, camping, backpacking, conservation and other outdoor activities in the Carolinas. Length: 600 to 2,000 words. Pays 1¢ and up per word, depending on ms. B&w glossy photos and color transparencies are purchased with mss, with no additional payment.

Fillers: Sport topics. Length: 25 to 50 words. Pays $5 minimum.

FIELD AND STREAM, 383 Madison Ave., New York NY 10017. Phone: 212-688-9100. Editor: Jack Samson. Monthly. One of the top 3 outdoor publications. Buys all rights. Reports in 6 weeks. Margaret Nichols, Assistant Managing Editor, is great in helping writers perfect their manuscripts. Query first. Enclose S.A.S.E.

Nonfiction and Photos: "This is a broad-based outdoor service magazine. Editorial content ranges from very basic how-to stories that tell either in pictures or words how an outdoor technique is done or device made. Articles of penetrating depth about national conservation, game management, resource management, and recreation development problems. Hunting, fishing, camping, backpacking, nature, outdoor, photography, equipment, wild game and fish recipes, and other activities allied to the outdoors. The 'me and Joe' story is about dead, with minor exceptions. Both where-to and how-to articles should be well-illustrated." Prefers color to b&w. Submit outline first with photos. Length, 2,500 words. Payment varies depending upon the name of the author, quality of work, importance of the article. Pays 18¢ per word and up. Usually buys photos with mss. When purchased separately, pays $150 and up for color. Good market for color covers, as Samson has gone to using transparencies for covers, but must have impact.

Fillers: Buys "how it's done" fillers of 500 to 1,000 words. Must be unusual or helpful subjects. Payment is $250.

FISH AND GAME SPORTSMAN, P.O. Box 1654, Regina, Sask., Canada S4P 3C4. Phone: 306-523-8384. Editor: J. B. (Red) Wilkinson. For fishermen, hunters, campers and others interested in outdoor recreation. "Please note that our coverage area is Alberta and Saskatchewan." Quarterly magazine; 64 to 112 pages, (8½x11). Established in 1968. Circulation: 13,000. Rights purchased vary with author and material. May buy first North American serial rights or second serial (reprint) rights. Buys about 50 mss a year. Payment on publication, or within a 3-month maximum period. Will send sample copy to writer for $1. Write for copy of editorial guidelines. "We try to include as much information on all subjects in each edition. Therefore, we usually publish fishing articles in our winter magazine along with a variety of winter stories. If material is dated, we would like to receive articles 4 months in advance of our publication date." Will consider photocopied submissions. Reports in 4 weeks. Submit only complete ms. Enclose S.A.E. and International Reply Coupons.

Nonfiction and Photos: "It is necessary that all articles can identify with our coverage area of Alberta and Saskatchewan. We are interested in mss from writers who have experienced an interesting fishing, hunting, camping or other outdoor experience. We also publish how-to and other informational pieces as long as they can relate to our coverage area. Too many writers fill their mss with glossy terms, long words, and colorful writing, yet do not give information of a knowledgeable nature on their particular trip or outdoor experience. We don't want to see material on the fluffy clouds and twinkling stars. Instead write about the terrain, the people involved in the trip, and other data closely associated with the particular subject in a factual, straightforward manner. We are very short of camping articles and how-to pieces on snowmobiling, including mechanical information. We generally have sufficient fishing and hunting data. I would be very interested in hearing from writers who are experienced campers and snowmobilers." Length: 1,500 to 3,000 words. Pays $40 to $150. Photos purchased with ms with no additional payment. Also purchased without ms. Pays $7 per 5x7 to 8x10 b&w print; pays $50 for 35mm minimum transparencies.

FISHING AND HUNTING NEWS, 511 Eastlake Ave., E., Seattle WA 98109. Managing Editor: Ken McDonald. For "active fishermen and hunters of all ages with the need to know how-when-where of local activity." Weekly; newspaper type of publication. Circulation 120,000. Not copyrighted. Buys 4 to 5 mss a year. Pays on publication. Will send a free sample copy to a writer on request. Submit seasonal material 1 month in advance. Reports in 10 days. Query first. Enclose S.A.S.E.
Nonfiction: Spot news reports of hunting and fishing conditions in Washington, Oregon, Idaho, Montana, California, Utah, Colorado, and Wyoming. Wants "hunting and fishing opportunity stories—prefer upcoming events." Stories must include "all facts needed for reader to participate in the activity—detailed guidelines." Length: 200 to 3,000 words. Payment is $4 a column (2¼x16). Would consider freelance material for a possible column on recreational vehicles.
Photos: Buys single pix with caption or pix with mss. Needs specific hunting and fishing conditions and catches. Pays $2.50 to $5 each. Buys either 2¼x2¼ or 4x5 transparencies for covers. Pays up to $25.

FISHING WORLD, 51 Atlantic Ave., Floral Park NY 11001. Editor: Keith Gardner. Editors are subject matter experts. A "fact error" is deadly here. Bimonthly. Circulation: 200,000. Buys first North American serial rights only. Pays on acceptance. Will send a free sample copy to a writer on request. Will consider photocopied submissions. Reports in 2 weeks. Query first. Enclose S.A.S.E.
Nonfiction and Photos: "Most of our articles range from 1,500 to 3,000 words with 2,000 words usually preferred. A good selection of action photos should accompany each submission. Subject matter can range from a hot fishing site to tackle and techniques, from tips on taking individual species to a story on one lake or an entire region, either freshwater or salt. However, how-to is definitely preferred over where-to, and a strong biological slant is best of all. Where-to articles, especially if they describe foreign fishing, should be accompanied by sidebars covering how to make reservations and arrange transportation, how to get there, where to stay. Angling methods should be developed in clear detail, with accurate and useful information about tackle and boats. Anecdotes should be pertinent and brief. Our readers are dedicated fishermen who want to improve their sport, not listen to yarnspinning. They are also family men, and if women and children took part in the experiences you are describing, don't hide that fact. Depending on article length, suitability of photographs and other factors, payment is up to $200 for feature articles accompanied by b&w and color transparencies. Color transparencies selected for cover use pay an additional $100."

THE FLYFISHER, 4500 Beach Drive Southwest, Seattle WA 98116. Editor: Steve Raymond. Official publication of the Federation of Fly Fishermen. For "a highly sophisticated audience of expert anglers." Quarterly. Circulation includes FFF members and member clubs. Usually buys first rights. Pays on acceptance for solicited material. Pays on publication for unsolicited material. Subscribes to code of standards adopted by Outdoor Writers Association of America. Write for "notes to contributors." Reports in two to four weeks. Query preferred. Enclose S.A.S.E.

Nonfiction, Photos, and Fiction: "Fly fishing, conservation as it relates to fly fishing, how-to pieces, articles on places, methods and persons related to fly fishing. Also historical and personality pieces." Length: 2,000 words preferred, but some flexibility. Pays up to $150 and sometimes higher. Photos purchased with mss and captions only. B&w glossies, 8x10 preferred, 5x7 acceptable. Will not use photos of dead fish. Pays $5 and up. Pays up to $100 for covers. Fiction with same general subject matter as nonfiction, plus some humor. Length: 1,500 to 2,000 words. Pays up to $100; sometimes higher.

FUR-FISH-GAME, 2878 E. Main, Columbus OH 43209. Editor: A. R. Harding. For outdoorsmen of all ages, interested in fishing, hunting, camping, woodcraft, trapping. Magazine; 64 (8½x11) pages. Established in 1925. Monthly. Circulation: 160,000. Rights purchased vary with author and material. May buy all rights with the possibility of reassigning rights to author after publication; first serial rights or second serial (reprint) rights. Buys 150 mss a year. Pays on acceptance. Will send sample copy to writer for 25¢. Write for copy of guidelines for writers. Will consider photocopied submissions. No simultaneous submissions. Reports in 4 weeks. Submit complete ms. Enclose S.A.S.E.

Nonfiction and Photos: Articles on outdoor-related subjects. Articles on hunting, fishing, trapping, camping, boating, conservation. Must be down-to-earth, informative and instructive. Informational, how-to, personal experience, inspirational, historical, nostalgia, personal opinion, travel, new product, technical. Length: 2,000 to 3,000 words. Pays $50 to $75. Also buys shorter articles for Gun Rack, Fishing, Dog and Trapping departments. Length: 1,000 to 2,000 words. Pays $20 to $30. No additional payment for 8x10 b&w glossies used with ms.

GREAT LAKES SPORTSMAN, NEW ENGLAND SPORTSMAN, Sportsman Publications, 26555 Evergreen, Suite 410, Southfield MI 48076. Phone: 313-355-1270. Editorial Director: James A. Frahm. Excellent, slick magazine. For families with outdoor recreational interests proven by their purchases of major recreational equipment such as boats, snowmobiles, motor homes, and trailers. Broad range of ages and educational levels. All like the outdoors and are concerned with ecology, the environment and wildlife preservation. Magazines published every 2 months; 48 to 80 pages. *Great Lakes Sportsman* established in 1970. *New England Sportsman* established in 1974. *Great Lakes Sportsman* circulation: 150,000. *New England Sportsman* circulation: 75,000. Buys all rights. Buys 60 to 90 mss a year. Payment on publication. Will send free sample copy to writer on request. Submit seasonal material 1 month in advance. Reports within 40 days. Query first. Enclose S.A.S.E.

Nonfiction and Photos: "All articles should be of some service to the reader by telling him how to become more expert in his activity, where to go and what to do in the Great Lakes and New England areas; how to modify or upgrade his equipment, how to get greater value for his recreational dollar. Articles should identify with place or activity. Articles must tell the reader something besides the fact that the writer had a great time fishing, hunting, or riding a trail bike. Tell about equipment, places, or techniques. Buy how-to's, where-to's, personal experience and historical coverage which is part of location articles. Our stories and articles are not 'adventure' stories. We deal in 'where to go and what to do.' We are interested in travel and ecology articles." Length: 600 to 2,500 words. Pays $75 to $225. Columns cover snowmobiling, fishing, rv travel, shooting sports, camping, ecology, boating. Column length: 600 to 1,000 words. Pays $75. Photos purchased with accompanying ms with no additional payment. Purchased without ms also. Pays $50 for vertical color.

ILLINOIS WILDLIFE, P.O. Box 116—13005 S. Western Ave., Blue Island IL 60406. Phone: 312-388-3995. Editor: Ace Extrom. For conservationists and sportsmen. "Tabloid newspaper utilizing newspaper format instead of magazine type articles." Monthly. Circulation: 35,000. Buys one-time rights. Pays on acceptance. Will send a sample copy to a writer for 25¢. Reports in 2 weeks. Enclose S.A.S.E.

Nonfiction and Photos: Want "material aimed at conserving and restoring our natural resources." How-to, humor, photo articles. Length: "maximum 2,000 words, prefer 1,000-word articles." Pays 1¢ per word. B&w glossies. Prefers 5x7. Pays $5.

MARYLAND CONSERVATIONIST, Tawes State Office Building B-3, Annapolis MD 21401. Editor: Raymond Krasnick. For "outdoorsmen, between 10 and 100 years of age." Bimonthly. Circulation: 8,000. Not copyrighted. Buys 20 to 30 mss a year. Pays on publication. Will send a free sample copy to a writer on request. Reports within 30 days. Query first. Enclose S.A.S.E.
Nonfiction: "Subjects dealing strictly with the outdoor life in Maryland. Nontechnical in content and in the first or third person in style." How-to, personal experience, humor, photo, travel articles. Overstocked with material on pollution and Maryland ecology. Length: 1,000 to 1,500 words. Payment is 5¢ a word.
Photos: 8x10 b&w glossies purchased with mss. Payment is $15 a photo. $10 per b&w photo appearing in photo essay. Color transparencies and 35mm color purchased for covers. Payment is $35.

MICHIGAN OUT-OF-DOORS, 2101 Wood St., Box 2235, Lansing MI 48911. Phone: 517-371-1041. Editor: James V. Stabile. For hunters, fishermen, other conservationists and people who enjoy the outdoors and are concerned about natural resources. Monthly. Established in 1947. Circulation: 125,000. Buys about 50 mss a year. Pays on publication. Will send sample copy to writer for 25¢. Write for copy of guidelines for writers. Submit seasonal material at least 3 months in advance. Query first. Reports within 30 days. Enclose S.A.S.E.
Nonfiction and Photos: "We prefer Michigan feature stories aimed toward, but not limited to, hunters, fishermen, campers, and others interested in outdoor recreation and conservation of natural resources. We cover the broad environmental spectrum, with emphasis on conservation and activities that affect our readers. Fishing and hunting features should be illustrated with photos and contain how-to information. Environmental stories should be thoroughly documented. We use no poetry or fiction." Length: 1,200 to 2,500 words for features. Pays $50 to $100 for features; less than $50 for shorter pieces. Pays $25 to $50 for 35mm or larger transparencies for covers.

OUTDOOR LIFE, 380 Madison Ave., New York NY 10017. Editor: Chet Fish. For the active sportsman and his family, interested in fishing and hunting and closely related subjects, such as camping, boating and conservation. Buys first North American serial rights. Pays on acceptance. Query first. Enclose S.A.S.E.
Nonfiction and Photos: "What we publish is your best guide to the kinds of material we seek. Whatever the subject, you must present it in a way that is interesting and honest. In addition to regular feature material, we are also interested in combinations of photos and text for self-contained 1-, 2-, or 4-page spreads. Do you have something to offer the reader that will help him or her? Just exactly how do you think it will help? How would you present it? Photos should be fresh, no more than 1 year old by ideal publication date, and author should appear in some of his own pictures. Material should provide nuts and bolts information so that readers can do likewise. B&w photos should be professional quality 8x10 glossies. Color photos should be original positive transparencies and 35mm or larger. Comprehensive captions are required." Pays $350 minimum for 3,000 words, including b&w photos.
How To Break In: "We are the only magazine of the big three outdoor sports publications with regional sections and that's probably the best in for a writer who is new to us. Check the magazine for one of the six regional editors who would be responsible for material from your area and suggest an item to him. Our regional news pieces cover things from hunting and fishing news to conservation topics to new record fish to the new head of a parks or wildlife agency. The writer has to know the magazine and the subject well and even then it is not easy to break in with us. However, we are running more news these days and fewer features, so this is one possibility. You have an advantage if you can provide us with quality photos to accompany the story. These pieces might range from 300 to 1,000 words.

We also like spectacular personal experience pieces and we will even assign a staff guy to help with the writing if the experience really interests us."

THE OUTDOOR PRESS, North 2012 Ruby St., Spokane WA 99207. Editor: Fred Peterson. For sportsmen; hunters, fishermen, RV enthusiasts. Tabloid newspaper; 16 pages. Established in 1966. Weekly. Circulation: 125,000. Rights purchased vary with author and material. Usually buys first North American serial rights. Buys about 63 mss a year. Pays on acceptance. Will send sample copy to writer for 25¢. Will consider photocopied and simultaneous submissions. Submit special issue material (Snowmobile, December; Boating, February and October; Fishing, April; Camping, May; Steelheads, December) 1 month in advance. Reports on material accepted for publication in 2 weeks. Returns rejected material in 2 weeks. Query first or submit complete ms. Enclose S.A.S.E.

Nonfiction and Photos: How-to-do-it stories; technical in detail. Would like to see material on Indian fishing rights conflicts, crabs, clams, salmon, fly fishing. Does not want anything on ecology. Recently published "Biggest Salmon Are Easy". Length: 750 to 4,000 words. Pays $20 to $750. Also looking for material for their columns on guns, dogs, camping, RV's, fishing. Length: 1,000 words. Pays $5 to $200. B&w photos (5x7 or larger) purchased with or without ms, or on assignment. Pays $10 to $200. Captions required.

Fiction and Fillers: Experimental, suspense, western, erotic, confession, religious fiction. Story themes are open. Length: 500 to 6,000 words. Pays $50 to $1,000. Newsbreaks, puzzles (analog), jokes, used as fillers. Length: 10 to 400 words. Pays 50¢ to $50.

OUTDOORS TODAY, Outdoors Today, Inc., 1105 Francis Place, St. Louis MO 63117. Editor: Allen Baker. For outdoorsmen; hunters, fishermen, campers, boaters. Newspaper tabloid; 16 pages. Established in 1970. Weekly. Circulation: 90,000. Buys all rights, but will reassign rights to author after publication. Buys over 200 mss a year. Pays on 10th of month following publication. Will send free sample copy to writer on request. Will consider photocopied and simultaneous submissions. Submit seasonal material 30 days in advance. Reports on material accepted for publication in 30 to 60 days. Returns rejected material immediately. Submit complete ms. Enclose S.A.S.E.

Nonfiction and Photos: Outdoor-oriented material dealing with central U.S. News, rather than armchair adventure. Emphasis on area news, i.e., opening of smallmouth season in Missouri; county-by-county report on pheasant concentration in South Dakota, etc. No "me and Sam went fishing and caught, etc." material. Informational, how-to, personal experience, interview, profile, inspirational, humor, historical, think pieces, expose, nostalgia, personal opinion, photo, travel, spot news, successful business operations, new product, merchandising techniques, technical. Length: 200 to 700 words. Pays $10 to $100. No additional payment for photos used with mss.

How To Break In: "Deal with news, and keep it short."

PENNSYLVANIA ANGLER, P.O. Box 1673, Harrisburg PA 17120. Editor: J.F. Yoder. For Pennsylvania fishermen and boaters, both resident and visiting; all ages and educational levels, with water-oriented recreational interests. Fishing and boating experiences in Pennsylvania. Special boating issue in July. Established in 1932. Monthly. Circulation: 45,000. Buys all rights. Buys 60 to 70 mss a year. Payment on acceptance. Will send free sample copy to writer on request. Write for copy of guidelines for writers. Submit seasonal material 6 months in advance. Reports in 2 to 4 weeks. Query best, but not mandatory. Enclose S.A.S.E.

Nonfiction, Photos, and Fillers: "Fishing and boating in Pennsylvania. How-to, but more where-to articles are needed to make readers want to do the same things. New methods, new areas, new slants. Only the most unusual treatment on trout fishing will be considered. Avoid verbosity; cover one subject, one location, one style, one theme; no endless rambling. 3 to 5 pages of double-spaced copy with 5 to 10 good 8x10 b&w glossies have one foot in the winner's circle. We're the official fishing and boating magazine of the Commonwealth of Pennsylvania. Mss should not be condemnatory except for official policy or action. We'd like to see more photo spreads. We need especially good boating mss and photos for July issue. Length: 200 to 1,500 words. Material purchased on a per page basis rather than per word or per photo. Payment from $25 to $125 for ms and photos. Good market for Pennsylvania action photos without mss. B&w photos for inside; pays $10 to $35. Covers, prefer 2¼ up; pays to $150. Filler material on related subjects also considered."

PENNSYLVANIA GAME NEWS, P.O. Box 1567, Harrisburg PA 17120. Editor: Bob Bell. Monthly. Circulation: 220,000. Buys all rights; reprint rights usually granted on request. Pays on acceptance. Will send free sample copy to a writer on request. Study magazine before submitting. Reports in 3 to 4 weeks. Query preferred. Enclose S.A.S.E.
Nonfiction: For all outdoorsmen except fishermen—hunting, camping, trapping, natural history. Regular columns on guns, archery, camping, outdoor women. No "winking" at law violators; this is Game Commission publication. Length: 2,500 words maximum except in unusual circumstances. Pays 3¢ per word minimum.
Photos: Purchased with mss and occasionally with captions only. B&w glossy, 5x7 or 8x10, professional quality. Pays $5 to $20.

SALMON TROUT STEELHEADER, P.O. Box 02112, Portland OR 97202. Editor: Frank W. Amato. For sport fishermen in Oregon, Washington, and California. Bimonthly. Buys first serial rights. Pays on publication. Will send free sample copy on request. Reports in 2 weeks. Query first. Enclose S.A.S.E.
Nonfiction and Photos: Articles on fishing for trout, salmon, and steelhead. How-to's and where-to's. Length: 1,000 to 2,500 words. B&w photos purchased with mss. Pays $10 to $50.

SALT WATER SPORTSMAN, 10 High St., Boston MA 02110. Editor: Frank Woolner. Monthly. Probably the best salt water publication on the market. Editorial honesty and integrity unsurpassed. Circulation: 100,000. Buys first American rights only. Pays on acceptance. Will send sample copy to a writer on request. Reports on submissions within one month. Enclose S.A.S.E.
Nonfiction: Fact-feature articles, picture stories dealing with salt water sport fishing in North America, the Caribbean, Central America, South America and Hawaii. "Writers must be well-informed. We prefer to rewrite an exceptional article by a well-informed fisherman, rather than buy a polished piece by a professional journalist who doesn't know his angling. No 'blood and thunder' adventure, or romantic reminiscences. Readers are modern, scientific anglers: they want facts and up-to-date information presented in a readable manner. If there is any slant, it is emphasis on the how-to of sport fishing. Fishing tournaments are not covered by *Salt Water Sportsman*; therefore, articles dealing with contests are unlikely to be accepted. The only exception would be a tournament which serves the public as a whole, rather than the needs of area promotion. We do not use editorial advertising. A popular lure or tackle combination should be described, rather than identified by trade name. Charter boat captains, boats, airlines, guides, etc., may be named, but promotion for the pure sake of promotion will be deleted." Length: feature material, 3,000 words. Photos must accompany articles. Pays a minimum of 5¢ per word for copy.
Photos: Purchased with mss. Should be 8x10 enlargements on single-weight or double-weight paper. "Sometimes we are able to illustrate an article from our own files, and there are occasions when we will arrange artwork to illustrate—but accompanying photos always help to sell a manuscript. Photos should never show a great number of dead fish, because our readers are sensitive to slaughter. Pictures should, wherever possible, tell the story of the article. Action photos showing jumping fish, anglers playing, beaching, gaffing or boating fish are always in demand." Buys color photos for cover use; transparencies in the 2¼x2¼ or larger frame sizes preferred, but will consider 35mm and Kodacolor prints. Pays $200 for one-zime use of a four-color transparency for cover.

SOUTHERN ANGLER'S GUIDE, SOUTHERN HUNTER'S GUIDE, P.O. Box 2188, Hot Springs AR 71901. Editor: Don J. Fuelsch. Covers the northern scene on hunting and fishing completely. Today, the magazine has become a massive tome of excellent data. Buys all rights. Issued annually. Query first. Enclose S.A.S.E. for response to queries.

Nonfiction: Hunting, fishing, boating, camping articles. Articles that have been thoroughly researched. Condensed in digest styyle. Complete how-to-do-it rundown on tricks and techniques used in taking various species of fresh and salt water fish and game found in the southern states. Interested in new and talented writers with thorough knowledge of their subject. Not interested in first person or "me and Joe" pieces. Length is flexible, 750 and 1,800 words preferred, although may run as high as 3,000 words. Pays 5¢ to 30¢ a word.

Photos: Buys photographs with mss or with captions only. Fishing or hunting subjects in southern setting. No Rocky Mountain backgrounds. B&w only—5x7 or 8x10 glossies.

SPORTS AFIELD, With Rod & Gun, 250 West 55 St., New York NY 10019. Editor: Lamar Underwood. For people of all ages whose interests are centered around the out-of-doors (hunting and fishing especially) and related subjects. One of the top 3 best outdoor publications. Monthly magazine, 175 pages. Established in 1887. Circulation: 1,450,000. Buys first North American serial rights. Buys 90 mss a year. Payment on acceptance. Will send free sample copy to writer on request. Write for copy of editorial guidelines. Will consider photocopied and simultaneous submissions. "Our magazine is very seasonal and material submitted should be in accordance. Fishing in spring and summer; hunting in the fall; camping in summer and fall." Submit seasonal material 3 months in advance. Reports within 30 days. Query first or submit complete ms. Enclose S.A.S.E.

Nonfiction and Photo: "Informative how-to articles, and dramatic personal experiences with good photos on hunting, fishing, camping, boating and related subjects such as conservation and travel. Use informative approach. More how-to, more information, less 'true-life' adventure. General hunting/fishing yarns are overworked. Our readers are interested in becoming more proficient at their sport. We want brief, concise, how-to pieces." Buys how-to, personal experience, interview, nostalgia, and travel. Length: 500 to 2,000 words. Pays $600 or more, depending on length and quality. Photos purchased with or without ms. Pays $25 minimum for 8x10 b&w glossies. Pays $50 minimum for 2¼ or larger transparencies; 35mm acceptable.

Fillers: Clippings. Mainly how-to-do-it tips on outdoor topics with photos or drawings. Length: self-contained 1 or 2 pages. Payment depends on length. Regular column, Almanac, pays $10 and up depending on length, for newsworthy, unusual or how-to nature items.

THE TEXAS FISHERMAN, Voice of the Lone Star Angler, Cordovan Corporation, 5314 Bingle, Houston TX 77018. Editor: Steve Hodges. For freshwater and saltwater fishermen in Texas. Monthly tabloid; 40 (10½x14) pages. Established in 1973. Circulation: 15,000. Rights purchased vary with author and material. Usually buys second serial (reprint) rights. Buys 6 to 8 mss per month. Payment on publication. Will send free sample copy to writer on request. Write for copy of guidelines for writers. Will not consider photocopied submissions. Will consider simultaneous submissions. Reports in 4 weeks. Query first. Enclose S.A.S.E.

Nonfiction and Photos: General how-to, where-to, features on all phases of fishing in Texas. Strong slant on informative pieces. Strong writing. Good saltwater stories (Texas only). Length: 2,000 to 3,000 words, prefers 2,500. Pays $35 to $100 depending on length and quality of writing and photos. Mss must include 8 to 10 good action b&w photos or illustrations.

Fillers: Short how-to items. Pays $25.

TROUT, 4260 East Evans, Denver CO 80222. Editor: Alvin R. Grove. Publication of Trout Unlimited, a conservation organization whose primary concern relates to the cold-water fishery. "We are in fact concerned about trout and its management, but in a sense trout are considered as indicators of water quality. Concerns include land management related to ground-water retention, run off of water, snow-pack retention, water pollution, water quality in both streams and lakes, a concern about anadromous fish and such problems as dams, super nitrogen saturation, etc. In some respects Trout Unlimited is like Ducks Unlimited but reflects a larger concern with the environnment as is evidenced by Sierra Club, National Wildlife Federation, etc." For conservationists with an interest in cold water fishing, trout fishing, fly tying, etc. Circulation: 22,000. Not copyrighted. Buys 25 mss a year. Payment on acceptance. Will send free sample copy to writer on request. Write for copy of editorial guidelines. Will not consider photocopied submissions. Submit seasonal material (fly tying, winter; salmon fishing, summer) 3 to 4 months in advance. Returns rejected material in 1 or 2 months. Reports on material accepted for publication within 6 months. Query first or submit complete ms. Enclose S.A.S.E.

Nonfiction and Photos: Articles on trout angling; semiscientific articles on fish management, the environment. Educational approach; conversion of scientific information to popular report. Not interested in the typical "Joe and me" stories or photos of dead fish. Length: 900 to 2,500 words. Pays $35 to $100. Prefers sharp 8x10 b&w photos with or without mss. Captions required. Pays $5 when purchased with mss; $25 for cover.

TURKEY CALL, P.O. Box 218, Falcon Dr., Lexington SC 29072. Editor: John Culler. For all turkey hunters; most hunt other species such as deer and small game, and also are fishermen. Magazine; 24 to 40 pages. Established in 1972. Quarterly. Circulation: 10,000. Buys all rights. Buys 20 mss a year. Pays on acceptance. Will send free sample copy to writer on request. No photocopied or simultaneous submissions. Reports in 3 weeks. Query first or submit complete ms. Enclose S.A.S.E.

Nonfiction and Photos: Articles related to the management of the wild turkey, with an occasional hunting piece. Most stories are on some aspect of management. It is best to write for a copy of the magazine to see how articles are written. Length: 1,500 to 3,000 words. Pays $150 to $300. No additional payment for b&w photos submitted with ms. Captions required.

VIRGINIA WILDLIFE, P.O. Box 11104, Richmond VA 23230. Phone: 804-786-4974. Editor: Harry L. Gillam. Monthly. Slick publication, but uses only Virginia material. For sportsmen, outdoor enthusiasts. Pays on acceptance. Buys first North American serial rights, second serial rights or reprint rights. Will send sample copy on request. Query first. Enclose S.A.S.E.

Nonfiction: Uses factual hunting and fishing stories, especially those set in Virginia. Boating and gunning with safety slant. Conservation projects. Conservation education. New ways of enjoying the outdoors. Factual articles with photos on conservation issue facing Virginians. Especially needs power boating articles. Slant should be to enjoy the outdoors and do what you can to improve it and keep it enjoyable. Material must be applicable to Virginia, sound from a scientific basis, accurate and easy to read. Length: prefers 800 to 1,500 words. Pays 1½¢ to 2¢ per word.

Photos: Buys photos with mss and with captions only. Should be 8x10 glossies. Pays $35 to $40 for 4x5 color transparencies for cover.

WESTERN OUTDOORS, 3939 Birch St., Newport Beach CA 92660. Editor: Burt I. Twilegar. Monthly. Buys first serial rights only. Payment on publication. Reports within 2 to 4 weeks. Query first or submit complete ms. Enclose S.A.S.E.

Nonfiction and Photos: "Where-to-go material on western fishing, hunting, boating, camping, travel, and allied subjects. Articles should deal with 11 continental western states as well as with Western Canada, Baja, Mexico, Hawaii and Alaska. Most material is assigned. Primary requirement is accurate, dependable information on the places not well known. Completed mss accompanied with 8x10 b&w glossy photos are recommended. Articles range from 1 to 4 pages in magazine, with payment averaging $35 per page. Photos and ms are considered a package deal."

WESTERN WASHINGTON FISHING HOLES, P.O. Box 71, Snohomish WA 98290. Editors: Milt Keizer, John Thomas, Terry Sheeley. For fishermen (8 to 80): beginning, competent and veteran anglers interested in better fishing and more enjoyment of the sport. Magazine; 44 to 60 (8½x11) pages. Established in 1974. Every 2 months. Circulation: 10,000. Buys first North American serial rights. Buys

10 to 15 mss a year. Pays on publication. Will send free sample copy to writer on request. Will consider photocopied submissions. No simultaneous submissions. Submit seasonal material 2 months in advance. Reports in 3 weeks. Query first. Send previously published work sample and one- to two-paragraph outline of suggested article.

Nonfiction and Photos: "Detailed maps and articles that 'pick apart' specific angling spots in lakes, salt water and rivers to help fishermen find and catch fish. Must follow our style, with special emphasis on the place, method and detailed mapping of the water. Since we provide an in-depth, how-to approach to specific fishing locations, we want the descriptions of such to match rock for rock, and leaning tree for leaning tree. When anglers seek out the area, these details must be accurate. How-to articles must be applicable to improving fishing tactics, care for tackle, preparing catches for eating; mounting, or making tackle and lures. We would like to see material covering winter steelheading on the Olympic Peninsula, as well as Hood Canal and Strait or Juan de Fuca salmon fishing." Recently published articles on the Toutle River and the Washougal River. Length: 800 to 1,200 words. Pays $40 to $60. No additional payment for b&w photos used with mss. Captions required. Occasionally purchases color for the cover. Payment is by arrangement with the photographer.

Fillers: Fishing how-to. Length: 200 to 600 words. Pays 50¢ per two-and-a-half column inch.

Martial Arts

THE AMERICAN JUDOMAN, 4944 Date Avenue, Sacramento CA 95841. Editor: Philip S. Porter. "60% of our audience is below 16 years of age. The rest young adult judo athletes and about 2,000 judo club instructors." Special issues on Olympic reports and international reports on judo. Established in 1960. Bimonthly. Circulation: 30,000. Buys all rights. Buys about 15 to 25 mss a year. Payment on publication. Will send a sample copy to a writer for $1. Will consider photocopied submissions. Submit seasonal material 3 months in advance. Reports in 2 weeks. Enclose S.A.S.E. for return of submissions.

Nonfiction and Photos: General subject matter is "nonfiction technical and feature material on judo. Human interest on judo. Fiction on oriental martial arts." Approach should be "anything related to judo. Self-defense, today's youth, including humor. Ours is the only publication covering only judo. It is much more authoritative than any other martial arts magazine. Technical material must be sound. Special training or growth stories on local clubs are welcome." Buys personal experience, interview, profile, humor, nostalgia, personal opinion, travel (judo) and technical articles. No limit on length. Payment judged on review. Photos purchased with or without mss. Does not want "low quality photos or posed 'action shots.' " Captions optional. 8x10 b&w glossies. Pays $5 to $25.

BLACK BELT MAGAZINE, Rainbow Publications, Inc., 1845 West Empire Ave., Burbank CA 91504. Editor: Rick Shively. For men, women and children; laymen as well as practitioners of the martial arts. Majority are between the ages of 17 and 35. Monthly. Circulation: 71,000. Buys all rights. Payment on publication. Will send free sample copy to writer on request. Will consider photocopied submissions. Reports in 2 to 4 weeks. Query first, in detail, and include samples of previous work. Enclose S.A.S.E.

Nonfiction, Photos, and Fillers: General subject matter is martial arts (karate, kung-fu, judo, aikido, etc.). "Looking for personality and topical features with a strong central theme. We prefer to map out each story with the writer before he gets into it. Current needs include stories that especially show how the martial arts may contribute to the good of mankind." Length: 1,500 to 2,500 words. B&w photos and color photos desirable. B&w must be 5x7 or 8x10. Captions required. Color transparencies. Pays 4¢ to 10¢ per word for copy, $4 to $7 each for photos. Also buys news items for BB Times and event coverage for World Wide Tourneys. Length: 100 to 1,000 words. Photos desirable.

Fiction: Buys historical or contemporary fiction. Length: 1,500 to 2,500 words.

FIGHTING STARS, Rainbow Publications, Inc., 1845 West Empire Ave., Burbank CA 91504. Publisher: Dick Hennessy. For enthusiasts in self-defense who attend films, spectator sports, spectacles of martial arts exhibits, 66-page (9x11) magazine published every 2 months. Established in 1973. Circulation: 90,000. Buys all rights. Buys 60 mss a year. Payment on acceptance. Will send free sample copy to writer on request. Will consider photocopied submissions. Will not consider simultaneous submissions. Reports within 30 days. Query first. Enclose S.A.S.E.
Nonfiction and Photos: "Profiles of celebrities in martial arts. How martial arts affected their careers, and how their careers complemented the martial arts. Biographical data, details of daily life, plus good profile of the core of subject's existence. No gossip items. Substantiate all stories with fresh interviews and ample quotes. Reviews of martial arts films, spectacles, TV shows, and celebrity tournaments. All material should have strong lead, in-depth approach to what makes subject unique. Use active voice, present tense, clean copy, well-structured story, forceful conclusion." Couple celebrity material with martial arts; deal with both in depth. No puffery. No gossip items. Substantiate all stories with fresh interviews, ample quotes. Would like to see biographies of celebrities in the martial arts, as well as coverage of martial arts films spectacles, TV shows, and celebrity tournaments. Also uses informational, personal experience, interviews, humor, historical, nostalgia, spot news, technical articles and those on successful business operations. Length: 3,000 to 4,000 words. Pays 4c to 10c per word. Pays $10 to $15 for b&w (5x7 or 8x10) glossy photos purchased with or without accompanying ms. Also purchases color transparencies of any size. Pays up to $100 for cover color. Pays $30 to $50 per shot inside color.

KARATE ILLUSTRATED, Rainbow Publications, Inc., 1845 West Empire Ave., Burbank CA 91504. Editor: Rick Shively. For teens and adults heavily involved in karate and kung-fu. Large percentage middle years and in the professions; pursuing martial arts studies and self-defense courses. General public interest in sports. Concentrates on self-defense, oriental martial arts in U.S. Monthly magazine; 66 pages (9x11). Established in 1969. Circulation: 57,000. Buys all rights. Buys 60 features a year and 150 news items on martial arts. Payment on acceptance. Will send free sample copy to writer on request. Will consider photocopied submissions. Reports within 30 days. Query first or submit complete ms. Enclose S.A.S.E.
Nonfiction, Photos and Fiction: "In-depth articles profiling oriental sensei who have succeeded in the martial arts in this country. Top competitors in the martial arts. Techniques, styles and schools of martial arts competition and training. Tournaments. Articles should have a strong beginning; well structured story. Beguiling windup. Clean copy. Present tense, active voice. Avoid the sweetness and light approach. Tell it like it is." Buys informational, how-to, personal experience, interview, profile, historical, think articles, expose, photo, spot news, successful business operations, and technical articles. Length: 1,500 to 2,500 words. Pays 4¢ to 10¢ per word. Buys 5x7 or 8x10 b&w or color transparencies. Historical or contemporary fiction dealing with the martial arts. Length: 1,500 to 2,500 words.

OFFICIAL KARATE, 351 West 54th St., New York NY 10019. Editor: Al Weiss. For karatemen or those interested in the martial arts. Established in 1968. Monthly. Circulation: 100,000. Rights purchased vary with author and material; generally, first publication rights. Buys 60 to 70 mss a year. Payment on publication. Will send free sample copy to writer on request. Will consider photocopied submissions. Reports on material accepted for publication in 1 month. Returns rejected material within 2 weeks. Query first or submit complete ms. Enclose S.A.S.E.
Nonfiction and Photos: "Biographical material on leading and upcoming karateka, tournament coverage, controversial subjects on the art ('Does Karate Teach Hate?', 'Should the Government Control Karate?', etc.) We cover the 'little man' in the arts rather than devote all space to established leaders or champions; people and happenings in our-of-the-way areas along with our regular material. We are only interested in recognized styles. Too often, we receive material on invented techniques or about people with questionable credentials." Informational, how-to, interview, profile, spot news. Length: 1,000 to 3,000 words. Pays $50 to $150. B&w contacts or prints. Pays $5.

Miscellaneous

AUTO RACING DIGEST, Century Publishing Co., 1020 Church St., Evanston IL 60201. Editor: Michael K. Herbert. For auto racing enthusiasts. Digest size magazine; 68 (5¼x7½) pages. Established in 1973. Every 2 months. Circulation: 80,000. Buys all rights. Buys about 15 mss a year. Pays on publication. Will send sample copy to writer for $1. Reports in 2 to 4 weeks. Submit only complete ms. Enclose S.A.S.E.
Nonfiction and Photos: Articles on aspects of USAC, NASCAR, SCCA and IMSA racing as well as some drag racing; drivers and cars; on-the-track happenings. "Stay with the racing and strategy. We are not interested in opinions of writers, or stories written without talking to the principals involved." Profiles of drivers, mechanics, studies of teams, statistics. Buys interviews, profiles, historical, informational, how-to, personal experience, humor, think, nostalgia, and technical articles. "We are looking for fresh, original, unusual humorous events through the driver's eyes. The only opportunity for freelance contribution is an article that is timely, unusual or original in approach." Length: 500 to 2,000 words. Pays approximately $75. Departments are staff-written. Buys photos of drivers in action, cars, headshots. Pays $10 for each shot for 8x10 b&w glossies; $75 for color cover (35mm mounted transparencies); $25 for color inside (35mm mounted transparencies).

BACKPACKER, 28 W. 44 St., New York NY 10036. Editor: William Kemsley, Jr. For backpackers—people who hike and stay out overnight. They are enthusiastic about nature and wildlife; usually conservationists, as well. All ages, but most are college educated, highly sophisticated people, usually professional or business executives or entrepreneurs. Bimonthly magazine (8¼x11, 100 pages). Established in 1973. Circulation: 100,000. Buys all rights. Almost all material is freelance (about 50 to 60 pieces). Payment on acceptance, or within 90 days. Will send sample copy to writer for $2.50. Write for copy of guidelines for writers. Will not consider photocopied submissions. Submit seasonal material a year in advance. Tries to report on material accepted for publication within 2 or 3 weeks. Returns rejected material immediately. Query first. Send complete poetry ms. Enclose S.A.S.E.
Nonfiction and Photos: "It's best to see our publication first; a waste of time to query or submit material unless you are a backpacker, hiker, or cross country skier. We're a high-quality publication, and we demand excellence. It is foolish for anyone who is not fanatically interested in this subject to submit to us. Almost without exception, we do not accept material from non-backpackers. And the material must not violate the new 'backcountry ethic' with regard to such things as campfires, ditching tents, and other old woodsmen's practices that are now taboo in the wilderness because of the increased numbers using the wilderness. We regard backpacking itself as an attitude rather than merely an activity. It is a question of whether we are willing to set aside, for the time being, all the paraphernalia of the electronic-gasoline world of everyday life, of going back to nature as unencumbered as possible. Features don't have to be about exotic areas. We'd just as soon have a piece about Harriman Park NY, as some place in Montana. Your chance of selling a feature piece to any outdoor magazine increases 500% if you can take good color photographs of people doing things. We publish adventure stories about hikes that people have taken in many parts of the world. We have mountain profiles in which the geologic, historical and climbing aspects of the mountain are described. Also, we feature an 'Elder of the Tribe' in each issue, such as John Burroughs or John Wesley Powell." Also uses scientific subjects of interest to backpackers. "But don't show us any 'how to get started' pieces or how it was on your first hike. Nor do we want any guide book type pieces on where to go." Especially needs articles about family weekend hiking close to home. Length: usually 1,500 to 3,000 words, but this varies. Pays $25 to $200. Also uses book reviews. Material is also sought for the "Care & Repair of Equipment" column. Length: 1,000 to 1,500 words. Pays $50 to $75, 8x10 b&w photos purchased with accompanying ms with extra payment. Pays $25 to $50. $100 per page paid for color transparencies. Both color and b&w must relate to magazine's theme.
Poetry: Traditional forms and light verse but must relate to the outdoors, preferably backpacking. Currently needs good short poems. Pays $10 to $25.

How To Break In: "The Right Time section uses 500 to 800 words on conservation issues affecting backpacking (such as the threat to dam the Grand Canyon, off-road vehicles in Allegheny Forest). We need a description of what the issue is, what kind of action the reader can take, and where he can write for further information. Surprisingly, we have a hard time getting material for this section."

HOCKEY ILLUSTRATED, 333 Johnson Ave., Brooklyn NY 11206. Editor: Jim McNally. For young men and women interested in hockey. Established in 1960. Published 7 times a year. Circulation: 140,000. Buys all rights, but will reassign rights to author after publication. Buys 65 mss a year. Payment on acceptance. Will not consider photocopied submissions. Submit seasonal material 3 months in advance. Reports immediately on material accepted for publication. Returns rejected material in 1 month. Query first. Enclose S.A.S.E.
Nonfiction and Photos: Controversial hockey pieces, player profiles, in-depth interviews, humor; informational, personal experience, historical, expose, personal opinion. Length: 1,500 to 2,000 words. Pays $100 to $150. Pays $10 for 8x10 glossy b&w purchased with ms, without ms or on assignment. Captions required. Color: pays $150 for cover; $50 to $75 for inside use for 35mm with available light.
Fiction: Fantasy, humorous, historical. Length: 500 to 1,000 words. Pays $50 to $75.
How To Break In: "We have a new department called The Man Behind the Player, which is, of course, the player himself, but viewed from some interesting off-the-court aspect of his life. The idea is that he's not all ice and skates and sticks and putts. Recent pieces we've done have been about physical ailments the fans would not know about, religious devotion, a player who preferred to play LaCrosse. These are only 360 words each and I want to run four an issue, so it's an ideal slot for a newcomer. A brief query, just a note really, on the guy and what the special angle is, will be enough. We pay approximately $25 for each item. Another opportunity for the new writer is our news item department, Off the Ice. We use lots of little bits and pieces here for which there is no pay. But I'll be grateful and willing to work with a writer who comes in this way."

RUNNER'S WORLD MAGAZINE, P.O. Box 366, Mountain View CA 94040. Editor: Joe Henderson. For "active runners or running coaches and avid followers of the sport." Established in 1966. Monthly. Circulation: 28,000. Buys all rights, but will reassign rights to author after publication. Buys 100 or more mss a year. Payment on publication. Will send free sample copy to writer on request. Write for copy of guidelines for writers. Will consider photocopied submissions. Submit seasonal material 1 month in advance "but assignment should be confirmed 2 to 3 months in advance." Reports on submissions within 2 days. Query first. Enclose S.A.S.E.
Nonfiction and Photos: "We're looking for material with substance and value to readers. They don't buy the magazine primarily to be entertained, but rather to learn. It's more important what writers have to say than how stylishly they say it. This is an 'insider's' publication and few nonrunners write for us. The bulk of the magazine is personality and practical how-to features. Special emphasis is given to new research findings and techniques, written in simple, straightforward style." Length: 500 to 3,000 words. Pays $10 to $40 per published page in the magazine (500 to 1,000 words per page depending on illustrations). 8x10 b&w glossies purchased with or without ms, or on assignment. Pays $3.50 to $4.50. 35mm or 2¼x2¼ slide or larger for color cover use. Pays $50.

SIGNPOST MAGAZINE, 16812 36 Ave., W., Lynnwood WA 98036. Editor: Louise B. Marshall. About hiking, backpacking, and other non-motorized outdoor activities in the Pacific Northwest and British Columbia. Established in 1966. Bimonthly. Rights purchased vary; will consider any rights offered by author. Buys 15 mss a year. Payment on publication. Will send free sample copy to writer on request. Will consider photocopied submissions. Reports in 3 weeks. Query first or submit complete ms. Enclose S.A.S.E.
Nonfiction and Photos: Topics can include: hiking, climbing, backpacking, small boating, lake and stream fishing, snow touring, bicycling, caving and crafts, collecting,

nature, photography, legislation, management problems, Indian lore, astronomy, edibles, music, making equipment, wilderness ethics and teaching outdoor skills." Length: open. Pays $5 to $50. B&w photos are purchased with or without mss. Pays $5 for inside use; $25 for cover.
Fiction and Poetry: Must be related to magazine's theme. Pays $5 to $50 for fiction. Pays $5 minimum for poetry.
Fillers: Puzzles; jokes, short humor; essays, games. Must be related to magazine's theme. Length: open. Pays $5 minimum.

STRENGTH & HEALTH MAGAZINE, P.O. Box 1707, York PA 17405. Phone: 717-848-1541. Editor: Robert Dennis. For a "sports-oriented audience, mainly interested in weightlifting and weight training." Established in 1932. Bimonthly. Circulation: 100,000. Buys all rights, but will reassign rights to author after publication. Payment on publication. Will send free sample copy to writer on request. Will not consider photocopied submissions. Submit seasonal material (for baseball and football seasons) 4 to 5 months in advance. Reports on material within 1 week. Submit complete ms. Enclose S.A.S.E.
Nonfiction and Photos: Sports (mainly weightlifting), exercise, general health and nutrition articles. International events in wrestling, cycling, gymnastics, fencing, karate; Russia vs. U.S.A. tournaments. "Need more originality." Length: 1,000 to 5,000 words. Pays $50 to $100. 5x7 b&w glossy prints purchased with or without mss. Captions required. Pays $5 to $10. Color transparencies for cover use only. Pays $50 to $100.
Fiction: "Related to theme, but open also." Length: 1,000 to 5,000 words. Pays $50 to $100.

TRACK & FIELD NEWS, Box 296, Los Altos CA 94022. Managing Editor: Garry Hill. For anyone interested in the sport of track and field. Magazine; 64 (8x10) pages. Established in 1947. Irregular monthly; 9 times first half of year. Circulation: 20,000. Not copyrighted. Buys 10 to 20 mss a year. Pays on publication. Will send free sample copy to writer on request. Will consider photocopied submissions and (if advised) simultaneous submissions. Reports on material accepted for publication in 10 days. Returns rejected material as soon as possible, if requested. Query first. Enclose S.A.S.E.
Nonfiction and Photos: Generally, news-oriented material (current track news), with features angled to those who are making the news and current issues. Knowledge of the sport is almost mandatory. "We are very factually oriented and have an audience that is composed of the cognoscenti. Be realistic. Tell it like it is." Informational, how-to, personal experience, interview, profile, historical, think pieces, personal opinion, technical articles. Length: 500 to 4,000 words. Pays minimum of $10 per published page. B&w (8x10) glossies purchased without ms. Pays $3 to $10. Captions required.

Mountaineering

CLIMBING MAGAZINE, Box E, 310 Main Street, Aspen CO 81611. Phone: 303-925-3414. Editor: Michael Kennedy. For "mountaineers of the U.S. and Canada." Published 6 times a year. Established in 1970. Circulation: 3,000. Rights purchased vary with author and material. Buys 48 mss a year. Payment on publication. Will send free sample copy to a writer on request. Will consider photocopied submissions. Reports in 2 weeks. Query first or submit complete ms. Enclose S.A.S.E.
Nonfiction and Photos: General subject matter concerns "technical rockclimbing, mountaineering, and ski touring. Articles can be highly technical—our audience is select. Articles with general appeal also sought with a conservationist slant. We try to be a forum for all mountaineers. We would like to see articles on rock preservation, women in climbing, and attitudes toward mechanization of mountaineering." Buys informational, how-to, personal experience, interviews, profile, inspirational, humor, historical, think, personal opinion, photo, travel, mountaineering book reviews, spot news, new product and technical articles. "Regular column that seeks freelance

material is called 'Routes and Rocks,' which consists of personal accounts of climbs." Length: 500 to 4,000 words. Pays about $4 to $45, according to length. Photos purchased with or without mss, on assignment, and captions are optional. Pays minimum of $5 per 8x10 (but accepts all sizes) b&w glossies. Pays $30 for color cover only. Prefers 10x12 transparencies. Should relate to subject matter.

Fiction: Buys experimental, mainstream, adventure, humorous, historical, condensed novels, and serialized novels. Length: 1,000 to 3,000 words. Pays $5 minimum.

Poetry: Buys traditional and avant-garde forms, and free, blank, and light verse. Pays $5 minimum.

MOUNTAIN GAZETTE, 2025 York St., Denver CO 80205. Phone: 303-388-0974. Editor: Mike Moore. For mountain lovers, mountaineers, backpackers, skiers, environmentalists. "The magazine is written in a modern, fresh style—though we consider our readership to be literate men and women of all ages who are involved with or concerned about the environment." Monthly magazine; 36 pages, (9x14). Established in 1966. Circulation: 10,000. Rights purchased vary with author and material. Buys all rights, but will reassign rights to author after publication; buys first North American serial rights; second serial (reprint) rights. Buys 40 to 60 mss a year. Payment on acceptance. Will send free sample copy to writer on request. Write for copy of guidelines for writers. "We'll also send an advance multiple choice Rejection Slip, giving the writer an even better idea of what *not* to do. We make a seasonal shift from skiing, ski touring and winter mountaineering in winter to rock climbing, river running and backpacking in summer." Submit seasonal material 3 months in advance. Will consider photocopied submissions. Reports in 15 to 30 days. Query first or submit complete ms. Enclose S.A.S.E.

Nonfiction: "Articles dealing with the mountains; mountaineering pieces; travel (especially to remote regions of the world); skiing; hiking; river running, etc. Also well-considered environmental pieces as they pertain to the mountains. Architecture, politics, land use. We look for good writing—even the experimental. We like stylists. We are a writer's publication, in that we offer a fairly open-ended forum for writers with something original to say in this field. We're perhaps more open, irreverent, and critical than other publications in this field. We cross many lines—climbing and skiing, for instance. We are not as technically oriented as other publications dealing with the same subjects. We tend toward the literary, the expose, the consumer-oriented. We do not like to see the typical ski resort travel pieces, the usual mountainclimbing route description or the tired old walk down the nature trail." Buys informational, how-to, personal experience, interview, profile, humor, historical, think articles, expose, nostalgia, personal opinion, photos, travel; book, film and equipment reviews; spot news, and technical articles. Length: generally 500 to 8,000 words, but accepts longer mss on occasion. Pays $50 to $250. Short items are used in Mountain Notebook columns. Length: 50 to 300 words. Pays $10 to $25. Photos purchased with or without ms. Captions optional. Pays $10 to $25 for 8x10 b&w photos; $25 to $50 for front or back cover photo. "We will publish artistic photography, if it is very generally related to mountains, exotic travel, even interesting city works to counterpoint the subject of the magazine."

Fiction: All kinds, but definitely must have theme relating to subject matter of magazine. Length: 500 to 8,000 words. Pays $50 minimum.

Poetry: Traditional forms, free verse, and avant-garde forms. Must relate to magazine's subject matter. Length: 10 to 60 lines. Pays $1 per line.

Fillers: Newsbreaks of 50 to 300 words. Pays $10 minimum.

OFF BELAY, 12416 169th Ave., S.E., Renton WA 98055. Phone: 206-226-2613. Editor: Ray Smutek. For the average weekend mountaineer/mountain climber. Established in 1972. Bimonthly. Circulation: 7,000. Buys one-time reproduction rights. Buys 6 feature mss a year; 30 for departments. Payment on publication. Will send sample copy to writer for $1. Will consider photocopied submissions. Submit seasonal (winter-related) material 4 to 6 months in advance. Reports on material in 60 days. Query first. Enclose S.A.S.E.

Nonfiction and Photos: "Features are major articles on a climbing area or especially comprehensive treatments of mountain-related subjects. The objective is to increase the reader's enjoyment, understanding and skills, rather than glorify the exploits of the writer. Articles should assume that the reader has not been to the area or has only a basic knowledge of the subject." No lengthy first-person adventure accounts. Departments which use freelance material include: "History," "Mountain Medicine," "Science," "Equipment Data," "On Technique," "Flora-Fauna." Pays $5 to $25 for departments; $25 to $75 for features. B&w matte dried glossies (5x7 minimum). Pays $2 to $5. Transparencies and negatives pay $1. First-time photo contributors are paid in a subscription.

Fillers: Newsbreaks, short humor, accident reports, expeditions. Length: to 1 full page, as published. Pays maximum of $10. Subscription to first-time contributors.

Skiing and Snow Sports

ALL ABOUT SNOWMOBILES (formerly *Popular Snowmobiling)*, 131 Barrington Pl., Los Angeles CA 90049. Editor: Robert Schleicher. For "ages 25 to 35 male snowmobilers." Established in 1970. Biannual. Circulation: 100,000. Rights purchased vary with author and material, but may buy all rights and then reassign them to author after publication. Buys 10 to 15 mss a year. Will consider photocopied submissions. Submit seasonal material 2 months in advance. Reports in 1 week. Query first. Enclose S.A.S.E.

Nonfiction and Photos: General subject matter consists of "how-to technique on tune-ups, outdoor on snowmobiles, trail riding, camping, and racing. We do not want to see articles on small town race coverage. We do want articles on snowmobile trips, adventures, and safety; community actions pro and con snowmobiles." Buys informational, how-to, personal experience, photo, travel, new product, and technical articles. Length: 2,500 to 3,000 words. Pays $120 to $200, including photos. Photos purchased with or without mss, and on assignment. Captions required. Pays $10 per b&w 8x10 glossy. Pays $100 for color cover. 2¼x2¼ transparencies.

Fillers: Buys short humor relating to snowmobiling. Length: 1 to 3 columns. Pays up to $40.

INVITATION TO SNOWMOBILING, 1500 E. 79th St., Minneapolis MN 55420. Editor: John Ehlert; Managing Editor: Tom Britz. Primarily directed at first-time snowmobilers plus enthusiastic snowmobilers. Established in 1969. Annual. Circulation: 100,000. Rights purchased vary with author and material. May buy all rights, or may buy first North American serial rights. Payment on publication. Will send a sample copy to a writer for $1.50. All material must be submitted between January and June. Reports in 1 month. Enclose S.A.S.E.

Nonfiction and Photos: General subject matter consists of "articles to entertain or educate those getting involved and already involved with snowmobiles. Product tests, well-photographed adventure stories and the like. Technical information of good quality." Freelancer "should know snowmobiles, snowmobilers or special subject (camping, survival, etc.) related to snowmobiles; should be an expert in his field, and/or know snowmobiles inside-out. Use only top-quality work; do not publish press releases or manufacturer-written articles. We don't want articles on 'My First Ride in a Snowmobile,' or safety first." Buys informational, how-to, personal experience, interview, profile, humor, historical, expose, nostalgia, photo, and technical articles. Pays $100 to $500 per ms. "We usually assign photographer on speculation if we have not used him before only if it fits current editorial format. Photos seldom purchased with mss." Send top-quality b&w contact sheets. Pays $10 minimum per b&w photo used. Top-quality slides for color. Pays $15 to $100 depending on use.

NORDIC WORLD MAGAZINE, P.O. Box 366, Mountain View CA 94040. Publisher: Bob Anderson. For people interested and involved in Nordic skiing, primarily cross-country skiing. Every 2 months. Not copyrighted. Buys 60 to 75 mss a year. Pays on publication. Reports in 1 week. Query first or submit complete ms. Enclose S.A.S.E.

Nonfiction: Practical articles on skiing technique and equipment; major race reporting, personality features, personal experience. Nordic skiing articles, and those on ski jumping, snowshoeing, ski mountaineering, ski camping, ski orienteering; stories on training for Nordic skiing. All material must reflect a knowledge of the sport of Nordic skiing on the part of the writer. Length: open. Pays $5 minimum.

NORTHWEST SKIER, 903 N.E. 45th St., Seattle WA 98105. Phone: 206-634-3620. Editor: Robert B. Hinz. Biweekly. Circulation: 15,000. Not copyrighted. Pays on publication. Will send sample copy to writer for 50¢. Reports on submissions immediately. Enclose S.A.S.E. for return of submissions.

Nonfiction: Well-written articles of interest to winter sports participants in the Pacific Northwest and Western Canada, or pieces of a general scope which would interest all of the winter sporting public. Character studies, unusual incidents, slants and perspectives. All aspects of winter sports covered in magazine; not just skiing. Must be authoritative, readable and convincingly thorough. Humor accepted. "Politics are open, along 'speaking out' lines. If you're contemplating a European trip or one to some other unusual recreation area, you might query to see what current needs are. When submitting article, consider pictures to supplement your text." Recently published articles included "The Wilderness: Just How Wild Should It Be?," a think piece about progressive use of America's wilderness; "Affordable Ski Vacations: Getting the Most for Your Money," a how-to piece. Length: 250 words and up. Pays $10 minimum per article.

Photos: Purchased both with mss and with captions only. Wants strong graphics of winter sports scene. Doesn't want posed shots. 8x10 glossies, both b&w and color. Furnish separations. Pays $2 minimum per photo.

Fiction: Uses very little and use depends on quality and uniqueness. Will use humorous fiction and short-shorts. Length: 250 words and up. Pays 50¢ per column inch.

POWDER MAGAZINE, Powder Magazine, Inc., P.O. Box 30753, Seattle WA 98103. Editors: Dave and Jake Moe. Magazine; 48 to 64 pages. Established in 1972. Four times a year; September through December. Circulation: 100,000. Rights purchased vary with author and material. May buy all rights, but will reassign rights to author after publication; or first North American serial rights; or simultaneous rights. Buys 15 to 20 mss a year. Pays on acceptance. Will send sample copy to writer for 50¢. Write for copy of guidelines for writers. No photocopied submissions. Will consider simultaneous submissions. Submit material by mid-June for following winter. Reports on material accepted for publication in 6 weeks. Returns rejected material in 3 weeks. Query preferred. Enclose S.A.S.E.

Nonfiction and Photos: "We want material by or about people who reach out, both into the mountains and themselves, looking for the limits of the ski experience. Avoid classical technique problems, specific equipment tests, and travel guides. We try to emphasize the quality of the ski experience, rather than its mechanics, logistics or commercial aspects." Length: 500 to 1,500 words. Pays $25 to $100. B&w and color transparencies purchased with or without mss or on assignment. Pays $5 to $25 for 8x10 b&w glossies; up to $50 for 35mm or larger transparencies.

Fiction and Poetry: Experimental, mainstream, adventure and humorous fiction. Must relate to subject matter. Length: open. Pays $10 to $50. Traditional and avant-garde forms of poetry; blank verse, free verse and light verse. Length: 10 lines or less. Pays $5 to $25.

SKATING MAGAZINE, Sears Crescent, Suite 500, City Hall Plaza, Boston MA 02108. Editor: Barbara R. Boucher. For a "family audience—generally members of clubs in the U.S. Figure Skating Association. Majority of family heads probably attended college—the sport is very costly; therefore, most are professional people." Established in 1923. Monthly (8 times a year). Circulation: 25,000. Buys all rights. Buys an average of 25 mss a year. Payment on publication. Will send sample copy to a writer on request. Submit seasonal material 6 weeks in advance. Reports in 2 to 8 weeks. Enclose S.A.S.E.

Nonfiction: General subject matter concerns the "sport of international figure skating, emphasis on national events: competitions, interviews with skating personalities, controversies in the skating world, histories, book reviews, innovations in techniques and equipment, club news, and personal experiences. Any theme that is in some way related to amateur figure skating could potentially be accepted. Approach is up to the author's discretion. Other magazines on skating internationally are generally less comprehensive in scope, more local in orientation, and only cover competitions—not other aspects of the sport. Articles on skating matches. We would like to see articles on the following topics: innovations in skating music; politics of ice rinks; the isolation of a child's life devoted to one sport; profiles of foreign skaters. Most feature articles deal with figure skating personalities, but other topics are most welcome. For example, researched pieces on new developments in skate, blade or ice rink technology are especially good. Features on local skating groups in your area may also prove interesting. We also like to receive personal experience or humorous stories." Buys informational, how-to, interview, profiles, historical, think, personal opinion, photo, travel to competition venues, reviews of skating books, and technical articles. Length: 800 to 1,500 words. Pays $25 per article.

Photos: Buys photos with or without mss, on assignment. Captions optional. Pays $5 per 8x10 or 5x7 b&w glossy used. Photo Editor: Bruce A. Boucher.

SKI, 380 Madison Ave., New York NY 10017. Phone: 212-687-3000. Editor: Richard Needham. 7 times a year, September through March. Buys first-time rights in most cases. Pays on publication. Reports within 1 month. Enclose S.A.S.E.

Nonfiction: Prefers articles of general interest to skiers, travel, adventure, how-to, budget savers, technique, equipment, unusual people, places or events that reader can identify with. Must be authoritative, knowledgeably written, in easy, informative language and have a professional flair. Cater to middle to upper income bracket readers who are college graduates, wide travelers. Length: 1,500 to 2,000 words. Pays $100 to $250.

Fiction: Fiction is seldom used, unless it is very unusual. Pays $100 to $250.

Photos: Buys photos submitted with manuscripts and with captions only. Good action shots in color for covers. Pays minimum $150. B&w photos. Pays $25 each; minimum $150 for photo stories. (Query first on these.) Color shots. Pays $50 each; $100 per page.

How To Break In: "We're putting out a *1977 Guide to Cross Country Skiing* for which we will be needing individual text and photo stories on cross-country ski touring and centers. We're looking for 1,000 to 2,000 words on a particular tour and it's an excellent way for us to get acquainted with new writers. Could lead to assignments for *Ski.* Photos are essential. Another possibility is our monthly column, Ski People, which runs 300- to 400-word items on unusual people who ski and have made some contribution to the sport."

SKIING, 1 Park Ave., New York NY 10016. Editor: Al Greenberg. 7 issues, monthly, September to March. Buys all rights. Pays on acceptance. Submit complete ms. Enclose S.A.S.E.

Nonfiction: This magazine is in the market for any material of interest to skiers. Readership varies from teenagers to businessmen, and material used must appeal to and please the confirmed skier. No cross-country and mountaineering personal-experience pieces. Much of the copy is staff-prepared, but many articles and features are purchased freelance, provided the writing is fast-paced, concise, and knowledgeable. Writer must have a good working knowledge of skiing. Good humor and satire also needed. Pays 10¢ minimum a word.

Fillers: For Skiing Scene; light news of skiers. Length: 50 to 300 words. Pays $5 to $50.

How To Break In: "I'm discouraging queries because they don't tell me enough about the writer. I want to see a full-length ms. I recently got a piece from a freelancer which I couldn't use, but his writing was so good I turned around and gave him three assignments. We're looking for articles that cover any phase of skiing from a description of a ski area to personalities. A good way for a new writer to break in is with a short item (500 to 750 words) on a ski personality, not necessarily someone who's famous, but perhaps a real character. Other personality pieces can go to 2,500 words. Another good way to break in is with short items for Skiing Scene — news items, human interest material, which can range from a few lines to a full page (750 words). We do have a need for this short material and it's hard to come by. It's also a good way for me to see a writer's work."

SNOTRACK, 534 N. Broadway, Milwaukee WI 53202. Editor: Bill Vint. "The official publication of the U.S. Snowmobile Association, published for anyone who snowmobiles or is interested in snowmobiling. Their interests are mainly racing, but they have recreational interests too. *SnoTrack* will retain its established format, but will probably expand its recreational snowmobiling coverage because of the addition of *Sno-mobile Times* readers." 6 times a year, during winter months only. Buys first serial rights. Pays on acceptance. Submit seasonal material at least 3 months in advance. Query first. "Submit photos with a query, if photos exist already, or send samples of work." Enclose S.A.S.E.

Nonfiction and Photos: "Interesting photo-article packages on all types of snowmobiling activities, how-to-do-it material, unusual or outstanding race events, rallies, trail rides, family activities, unforgettable personalities, humor; how-to, where-to, technical info on snowmobile maintenance, behind-the-scenes-at-the-races, spot news, interviews, profiles, travel articles. The approach should be concise and clear. We don't want stories without publishable photos." Length: 1,500 words maximum. Pays $50 to $250. Photos purchased with mss; with captions only. Pays $15 to $25 for b&w glossies. Color transparencies, 35mm color. Pays $100 for color transparency for cover.

Fillers: Newsbreaks. Pays $5 to $10.

SNOW GOER, 1999 Shepard Rd., St. Paul MN 55116. Phone: 612-437-2536. Editor: Don Rankin. For snowmobilers. Published monthly September through January. Magazine, 60 to 104 pages. Established in 1968. Circulation: 500,000. Buys all rights. Payment on acceptance. Will send free sample copy to writer on request. Will consider photocopied and simultaneous submissions. Racing annual in November each year. Submit special issue material 4 months in advance. Reports within 2 weeks. Query first or submit complete ms. Enclose S.A.S.E.

Nonfiction and Photos: Features on snowmobiling with strong secondary story angle, such as ice fishing, mountain climbing, snow camping, conservation, rescue. Also uses about 25% mechanical how-to stories, plus features relating to man out-of-doors in winter. " 'Me and Joe' articles have to be quite unique for this audience." Length: 5,000 words maximum. Pays $100 to $400. Photos purchased with mss and with captions to illustrate feature articles. 5x7 or larger b&w; 35mm color. Payment usually included in package price for feature.

SNOW SPORTS, 1500 E. 79th St., Minneapolis MN 55420. Editor: Henry Fiola. For snowmobile owners, outdoor oriented, families. Magazine, 64 to 80 pages. Established in 1970. Published 5 times a year, September to January. Circulation: 500,000. Buys all rights, but will reassign rights to author after publication. Pays on publication. Will consider photocopied submissions. Submit only complete ms. Submit seasonal material 5 to 6 months in advance. Reports in 1 to 2 months. Enclose S.A.S.E.

Nonfiction, Photos, and Fiction: Articles about places to go snowmobiling, things to do on a snowmobile, personalities. No "how fast it's grown" or "how I took my first ride and what happened." How-to, personal experience, photo, travel articles. Length: 1,500 to 2,000 words. Pays $75 to $125, including photos. Photos purchased with ms with no additional payment. Purchased without ms, as part of photo feature. Captions optional. 4x5 or larger b&w; 35mm, 2¼, 4x5, 8x10 color. Pays $50 to $75 for b&w; $75 to $125 for color photo feature. Adventure fiction. Length: 1,500 to 2,000 words. Pays $75 minimum.

SNOWMOBILE INTERNATIONAL, 7400 N. Waukegan Rd., Niles IL 60648. Editor: Paul Hertzberg. 6 times yearly; 80-page magazine. Established in 1972. Circulation: 125,000. Not copyrighted. Buys 6 mss a year. Payment on publication. Will send free sample copy to writer on request. Will consider photocopied and simultaneous submissions. Submit seasonal material for the winter issues 2 to 3 months in advance. Reports in 3 days. Query first or submit complete ms. Enclose S.A.S.E.

Nonfiction: Travel and trail features. Technical articles. Articles on safety, the environment, the energy situation, racing and personalities. All must be in-depth articles. How-to, personal experience, interview, think pieces, expose, nostalgia. Length: 1,000 to 7,500 words. Pays minimum of $100.

Fiction: Humorous, fantasy and science fiction. Must relate to theme. Length: open. Pays minimum of $100.

SNOWMOBILE WEST, 445 N. Capital Ave., P.O. Box 981, Idaho Falls ID 83401. Editor: Darryl W. Harris. For owners of snowmobiles; all ages. Magazine; 48 (8½x11) pages. Established in 1974. Four times during winter. Circulation: 5,500. Buys first North American serial rights. Buys 10 mss a year. Pays on publication. Will send free sample copy to writer on request. Write for copy of guidelines for writers. Submit material for March racing wrap-up 2 months in advance. Reports in 2 months. Query first. Enclose S.A.S.E.

Nonfiction and Photos: Articles about trail riding in the Western U.S.A. Informational, how-to, personal experience, interview, profile, travel. Length: 500 to 2,000 words. Pays 3¢ a word. B&w (5x7 or 8x10) glossies and color transparencies (35mm or larger) purchased with mss. Pays $5 for b&w; $10 for color.

STUDENT SKIER, 233 N. Pleasant St., Amherst MA 01002. Editor: David H. Lyman. (Mss are to be mailed to him at Rockport ME 04856.) For college students; outdoor and sports-minded. Tabloid magazine; 32 (10x15) pages. Established in 1970. Annually. Circulation: 250,000 in fall; 50,000 in winter. Not copyrighted. Buys about 12 mss a year. Pays on publication. Will send free sample copy to writer on request. Write for copy of guidelines for writers. Will consider photocopied and simultaneous submissions. Query first. Enclose S.A.S.E.

Nonfiction and Photos: First-person accounts of traveling to ski resorts; opinion, essays, humorous incidents surrounding skiing or winter sports. Youthful approach required. Nothing on "my first day on skis" or "my opinion on learning how to ski." Recently published, "Confessions of a Streaker" and "Personal Reflection of Waterville Valley." Informational, personal experience, interview, profile, humor, personal opinion. Length: 1,000 to 3,000 words. Pays $50. Purchases 8x10 b&w glossies with or without ms, or on assignment. Pays $10 to $25. Pays $50 for 35mm color transparencies used on cover.

Soccer

SOCCER AMERICA MAGAZINE, P.O. Box 9393, Berkeley CA 94709. Publisher: Clay Berling. For soccer fans, players, coaches and officials. Weekly magazine;20 (8x10) pages. Established in 1971. Circulation: 3,500. Rights purchased vary with author and material. Usually buys all rights. Buys 40 to 60 mss a year. Payment on publication. Will send sample copy to writer for 35¢. Write for copy of guidelines for writers. Will accept simultaneous submissions only if advised of the identity of the other publication receiving it. Reports in 2 weeks. Query first or submit complete ms. Enclose S.A.S.E.

Nonfiction and Photos: Up-to-date news on soccer across the continent and human interest feature stories. "Creative approaches welcome, along with humor and unique interest material having to do with the game of soccer. Must appeal to a majority of a nationwide audience. We treat all areas of soccer, from professional to amateur to youth play. Material of local interest is welcome, but played down. Technical material is solicited." Informational, how-to, personal experience, interview, humor, historical, expose, personal opinion, spot news, new product and reviews of books and films. Length: 200 to 800 words. Articles under 1,000 words receive first consideration. Pays approximately 1¢ a word (50¢ an inch). B&w and color photos (5x7 or 8x10) purchased with or without accompanying mss. Stress is on action photos. Pays $5; $15 for cover. Captions required.

Fillers: Soccer quiz puzzles; jokes, short humor. Length: 20 to 100 words. Pays 50¢ an inch.

SOCCER WORLD, Box 366, Mountain View CA 94040. Editor: Ian Jackson. For U.S. soccer enthusiasts, including players, coaches, and referees. Predominantly high school players and adult coaches. Magazine; 32 pages. Established in 1974. Every 2 months. Circulation: 12,000. Buys all rights, but will reassign rights to author after publication. Buys 75 mss a year. Payment on publication. Will send free sample copy to writer on request. Write for copy of guidelines for writers. Will consider photocopied submissions. No simultaneous submissions. Reports on material accepted for publication within 2 months. Returns rejected material as soon as required. Query first. Enclose S.A.S.E.

Nonfiction and Photos: "Articles are primarily of the how-to variety, but we usually include a personality feature with each issue. The foremost consideration is always practical value, i.e., Can a player, coach, or referee improve his performance through the information presented? We are interested in anything on soccer skills and techniques." Recently published articles include "Beating the Best" and "Three Teams on the Field." Also uses reviews of soccer books. Length: 1,000 words. Pays $10 to $25 per published page. Pays $2.50 to $15 for 5x7 (or larger) b&w glossies; snappy contrast. Pays $40 for 35mm (or larger) color transparencies for cover use. Must be high impact and vertical format.

Swimming and Diving

AQUATIC WORLD MAGAZINE, World Publications, P.O. Box 366, Mountain View CA 94040. Editor: Bob Anderson. "Readership varies; most are active swimmers, coaches or parents; includes age groups of 10 years to 40 plus. We don't try to aim for the lower ages specifically. Most are in high school or college. Most are in competitive swimming." 32- to 40-page magazine, published every 2 months. Established in 1973. Circulation: 10,000. Rights purchased vary with author and material; usually buys first serial rights. Buys about 50 to 55 mss a year. Most of the magazine is composed of freelance material. Payment on publication. Will send free sample copy to writer on request. Will consider photocopied submissions. Will consider simultaneous submissions. Reports on material accepted for publication within 2 weeks. Returns rejected material within 1 month. Query first, or submit complete ms. Enclose S.A.S.E.

Nonfiction and Photos: "Main emphasis is in getting behind the times and discovering the how's and why's of outstanding performances and meeting the swimmers themselves; personal outlook, interests, goals, etc., beyond their in-pool performances. In each issue, we try to include: 1) Interview (with a major swimmer or diver). 2) Personality feature. 3) Training article (weight training, diet, flexibility, etc.). 4) Technical article of the how-to type. 5) Club or team focus. 6) International aquatics (feature swimming, diving and water polo of a foreign country). 7) Profiles of up and coming swimmers. 8) News. 9) Unusual aquatics (ocean swimming, etc.). We'd prefer that the article be written from a participant's viewpoint; i.e., swimmers or coaches writing for swimmers and coaches; personal style." Main interest currently is in international aquatics; reflections on own swimming experience; news of major meets; training and technique; people (interviews, profiles, etc.). Length: open. Pays $5 to $30 per published page. Columns and departments seeking material include: "Coming Events" (upcoming meets); "Racing Highlights" (meet results); "Profiles" (training of upcoming swimmers). Questionnaire for "Profiles" must be obtained from *Aquatic World* office. Length: 250 words minimum. Pays $5 per published page. Payment will be adjusted for shorter lengths. Photos are purchased with accompanying ms with additional payment and without accompanying manuscript. Please identify all persons in pictures. 5x7 or 8x10 b&w prints only. Pays $4 per photo; more, if used for cover. Photos must relate to magazine theme; can also be "mood" shots or shots of swimmers in competition. Photo Department Editor: Diana Yee.

Fillers: Newsbreaks and short, feature type articles. Length: approximately 250 words. Pays $5 minimum.

SKIN DIVER, 8490 Sunset Blvd., Los Angeles CA 90069. Editor: Jack McKenney. Circulation: 129,700. Buys only one-time rights. Pays on publication. Acknowledges material immediately. All model releases and author's grant must be submitted with mss. Manuscripts reviewed are either returned to the author or tentatively scheduled for future issue. Time for review varies. Mss considered "accepted" when published; all material held on "tentatively scheduled" basis subject to change or rejection up to time of printing. Submit complete ms. Enclose S.A.S.E.

Nonfiction and Photos: Stories and articles directly related to skin diving activities, equipment or personalities. Features and articles equally divided into following categories: adventure, equipment, underwater photography, wrecks, treasure, spearfishing, undersea science, travel, marine life, boating, do-it-yourself, technique and archaeology. Length: 1,000 to 2,000 words, well illustrated by photos; b&w at ratio of 3:1 to color. Pays $35 per printed page. Photos purchased with mss; b&w 8x10 glossies; color: 35mm, 2¼x2¼, or 4x5 transparencies; do not submit color prints or negatives. All photos must be captioned; marked with name and address. Pays $35 per published page for inside photos; $100 for cover photos.

SURFER, P.O. Box 1028, Dana Point CA 92629. Phone: 714-496-5922. Editor: Kurt Ledterman. For late teens and young adults. Slant is toward the contemporary, fast-moving and hard core enthusiasts in the sport of surfing. Bimonthly. Buys North American serial rights only. Payment on publication. Will send free sample copy to a writer on request. Reports on submissions in 2 weeks. Enclose S.A.S.E.

Nonfiction: "We use anything about surfing if interesting and authoritative. Must be written from an expert's viewpoint. We're looking for good comprehensive articles on any surfing spot—especially surfing in faraway foreign lands." Length: open. Pays 6¢ to 10¢ per word.

Photos: Buys photos with mss or with captions only. Likes 8x10 glossy b&w proofsheets with negatives. Also uses expert color 35mm and 2¼ slides carefully wrapped. Pays $10 to $50; sometimes up to $100 for the slides. No color prints.

Fiction: "Looking for good plot, ideally with the surfing theme. Must have a connection with surfing, but not necessarily about surfing. Avoid death, injury in the water. No sharks, for example, unless they really have a necessary role in the story. Must be written from an expert's viewpoint." Length: 1,500 to 3,000 words. Also looking for bright short-short fiction with good plot twist. 500 words. Wants good humor. Pays 2¢ to 10¢ per word.

Fillers: See "Pipeline" column on surfing activities for an example of fillers needed. Also uses short humor and short news items about surfing around the world. Pays $5 minimum.

SWIMMING WORLD, 8622 Bellanca Ave., Los Angeles CA 90045. Editor: Albert Schoenfield. For "competitors (12 to 21), plus their coaches, parents, and those who are involved in the conduct of the sport." Monthly. Circulation: 25,000. Buys all rights. Buys 12 to 20 mss a year. Payment on publication. Will send free sample copy on request. Reports in 1 to 2 months. Query first. Enclose S.A.S.E.

Nonfiction: Articles of interest to competitive swimmers, divers and water poloists, their parents and coaches. Can deal with diet, body conditioning, medicine, as it applies to competitive swimming. Nutrition, stroke and diving techniques, developments in pool purification. Must be authoritative. Does not want results of competitions. Length: 1,500 words maximum. Pays up to $25.

Photos: Photos purchased with mss. Does not pay extra for photos with mss. 8x10 b&w only. Also photos with captions. Pays $2 to $3.

Poetry: Uses verse about swimming. Payment depends on length of poem; usually $3 minimum.

THE WATER SKIER, 7th Street and Avenue G, S.W., Winter Haven FL 33880. Editor: Thomas C. Hardman. 7 times per year. Circulation: 12,500. Buys North American serial rights only. Buys limited amount of freelance material. Pays on acceptance. Will send free sample copy to a writer on request. Reports on submissions within 10 days. Enclose S.A.S.E.

Nonfiction and Photos: Occasionally buys exceptionally offbeat, unusual text/photo features on the sport of water skiing. Pays $25 and up per article.

WATERSPORT, 534 N. Broadway, Milwaukee WI 53202. Editor: Glenn Helgeland. Published 6 times a year. For "middle-class, middle-income outboard boating families who like to cruise, fish, and water ski—but also enjoy most other aspects of water sports." Circulation: 25,000. Buys first serial rights. Buys about 40 mss a year. Pays on acceptance, or as close to acceptance as possible. Will send a free sample copy to writer on request. "Get a sample copy and study it before writing a word (other than the letter asking for the sample)." Submit seasonal material 3 months in advance. Reports in 3 weeks on mss. "Photos take longer because usually we don't make final selection until close to deadline." Query first. Enclose S.A.S.E.

Nonfiction: "Emphasize action opportunities for boatmen. Story subject should be of as much interest as possible to broad audience—places, unique recreation ideas, photo essays. Much emphasis on good photos. We avoid 'nuts-and-bolts' stories. We don't use stories about one lake or river. Seldom use personality stories." Length: 500 to 2,000 words. Payment is "$50 to $400 (for stories with photos)."

Photos: Purchased as package with mss and individually. Prefers color transparencies, but will use color prints, 35mm color, and 8x10 b&w glossies with mss. "We are using more b&w photos than previously." Payment for individual color transparencies is $35 to $75 ($100 for front cover).

Tennis

TENNIS, 297 Westport Ave., Norwalk CT 06856. Publisher: Asher J. Birnbaum. Managing Editor: Shepherd Campbell. For persons who play or are interested in playing racquet sports (tennis, badminton, table tennis, and the like), coaches of players, managers of country clubs and tennis facilities, and professionals. Established in 1965. Monthly. Circulation: 225,000. Buys all rights. Pays on publication. Study a recent issue of the magazine and query first. Enclose S.A.S.E.

Nonfiction and Photos: Emphasis on instructional and reader service articles, but also seeks lively, well-researched features on personalities and other aspects of the game. Length varies. Pays $25 to $100 per article; $15 to $50 per 8x10 b&w glossy or color transparency.

TENNIS ILLUSTRATED, 630 Shatto Pl., Los Angeles, CA 90005. Phone: 213-380-6151. Publisher: Doug Middleton. For "beginning, intermediate, and advanced tennis enthusiasts; amateur and professional tennis players; fans of the game and tennis playing families at all levels of skill." Established in 1967. Monthly. Circulation: 50,000. Rights purchased vary with author and material. Usually buys first rights. Buys about 25 mss a year. Pays on publication. Will send a sample copy to a writer "if he seems a serious prospect." Reports in 30 days.

Nonfiction: "*Tennis Illustrated* speaks the language of the active tennis player. Practical, entertaining, edited to attract novice and former players to actively engage in tennis as an interesting and healthful pastime. Regular features include advice for the consumer concerning equipment and accessory selection; the latest in tennis apparel and fashion; new products, instruction, tennis resorts, camps, clinics, news of general interest to tennis players everywhere; tennis humor; book and film reviews, shopper items, and question-and-answer columns. Playing instruction, strategy, and tactics are emphasized through instructional feature articles and illustrated 'winning points' tips from teaching professionals throughout the world. Stress reader involvement. Writers should have a flair for sports writing. Pieces should have action and strong human interest. Writer should not assume that reader knows tennis terminology and organizations—explain all terms, places, and events mentioned in the article. Our publication has a more general, mass audience than existing tennis publications. We do not cater to the upper class 'tennis set.' We aim the book at readers who are discovering the sport. We have all the material we can use on Wimbledon, Forest Hills, movie stars playing tennis, Stan Smith, and Chris Evert. We're interested in material on inner city tennis programs and developing junior players." Seeks

material for tennis humor, instructional, human interest anecdotes, travel and fashion. Length: 250 to 1,500 words. Pays 10¢ a word.
Photos: Purchased with or without mss or on assignment; captions required. Uses 8x10 b&w glossy prints or contact sheets and negatives, "upon prior assignment arrangements." Uses 35mm color slides; "larger format acceptable and preferred for covers." Pays up to $25 per b&w photo, up to $60 per color photo.
Fiction: "Will consider fiction dealing with tennis." Length: 500 to 1,500 words. Pays 10¢ a word.

TENNIS USA, Chilton Co., Chilton Way, Radnor PA 19089. Official publication of the United States Tennis Association for members and those with a serious interest in the sport. Editor: Bob Gillen. Established in 1937. Monthly. Circulation: 60,000. Buys all rights. Pays on acceptance. Will send free sample copy to writer on request. Query first. Enclose S.A.S.E.
Nonfiction and Photos: Features and news stories on tennis events and personalities; instructional articles on how to improve skills; testing and review articles on new equipment, court construction and other technical aspects of the sport; fashion and travel features. Pays $100 to $250.

WORLD TENNIS, 383 Madison Ave., New York NY 10017. Editor: Ron Bookman. Buys all rights. Reports in 1 to 2 weeks. No need to query on interviews or timely pieces. Otherwise a query is essential. Enclose S.A.S.E.
Nonfiction: Player features, tournament reports, instruction, some humor. "Interested in travel pieces which focus on a tennis resort. The writing and the tennis technical material must be very strong and there has to be a real tennis connection. Interested in strong pieces on tennis places we haven't covered. If a writer can develop a unique angle, we'd like player profiles and interviews. One freelance piece we recently published focused on how much it cost a family to get their junior tennis playing daughter a ranking."
How To Break In: "An area which the newcomer might try is something in the realm of the offbeat. We recently got something on tennis in Singapore and Nepal, for instance. But again the tennis connection has to be strong. We don't need news items or gossipy shorts since that's handled in-house."

Wrestling

WRESTLING GUIDE, THE BIG BOOK OF WRESTLING, 5202 Casa Blanca Rd., Scottsdale AZ 85253. Editor: Tommy Kay. Established in 1966. "The magazines are semimonthly, so we put out one 64-page wrestling magazine each month." Circulation: 95,000. Buys all rights, but will reassign rights to author after publication. Buys 120 mss a year. Payment made 4 months prior to publication. Will send sample copy to writer for 60¢. Write for copy of guidelines for writers. Will consider photocopied submissions. Submit seasonal material 3 months in advance. Reports on material within 4 weeks. "If you've never sold to us in the past, submit complete article and sample photos. Experienced, query first." Enclose S.A.S.E.
Nonfiction and Photos: "Profile articles or interviews with top professional stars; picture stories of 8 to 12 action photos plus captions and descriptions of where and how taken; fan club profiles—backgrounding the founding, officers and activities of wrestling fan clubs; general interest wrestling articles. Be sure to read recent issues. We stress approval of scientific wrestling styles over rowdy, illegal, blood 'n guts tactics, and we feature occasional profiles on amateur stars." Length: 800 to 3,000 words. Pays $15 to $35. 5x7 or 8x10 b&w glossies purchased with mss (occasionally without ms). Pays $3 to $5 for those purchased separately. 35mm or 2¼x2¼ color transparencies used for cover. Pays $50 to $75.
Fillers: Also seeking freelance material for "Fightin' Fotos," "Scrapbook of Action Photos" and sports crossword puzzles. Pays $10 for sports crosswords.

Teen and Young Adult Publications

The publications in this category are for young people aged 12 to 26. Publications aimed at 2- to 12-year-olds are classified in the Juvenile category.

ALIVE! FOR YOUNG TEENS, P.O. Box 179, St. Louis MO 63166. Phone: 314-371-6900. Editor: Darrell Faires. A publication of the Christian Church (Disciples of Christ) for youth in junior high school. Monthly. Circulation: 19,000. Not copyrighted. Payment on acceptance. Will send sample copy to writer for 25¢. Submit seasonal material 9 months in advance. "Youth will be strongly encouraged to be 'co-creators' of the magazine by their contribution of articles, poems, etc." Reports usually within 2 weeks. Enclose S.A.S.E.

Nonfiction: "We seek to affirm and celebrate the aliveness of young teens, and to call them to new 'alive-ability.' We seek to stimulate the thinkings, feelings and doings of youth so that they come alive to the creative possibilities of themselves and their world. Emphasis on first-person articles, articles about outstanding youth, or youth programs, projects and activities (with photos)." Length: 1,500 words maximum. Pays 2¢ a word.

Photos: 8x10 b&w glossies preferred; mostly of youth (preferably junior high age) and youth activities. Pays $5 to $10.

Fiction: Should be related to real life issues of young teens. "We don't like fiction which is too moralistic or preachy; characters who do not come across as real, believable, contemporary persons." Length: 1,500 to 2,000 words. Pays 2¢ per word.

Poetry: Personal insight, affirmation and humorous verse. 16 lines maximum. Pays 25¢ per line.

Fillers: Short humor and puzzles pay 2¢ per word or $3 to $10 per item.

AMERICAN GIRL MAGAZINE, 830 Third Ave., New York NY 10022. Editor: Cleo Mitchell Paturis. For young teens, about 14, 15 years old. Monthly magazine, 52 pages. Established in 1924. Circulation: 800,000. Buys all rights. Buys 50 mss a year. Payment on acceptance. Will send free sample copy to writer on request. Write for copy of editorial guidelines for writers. Submit seasonal material 4 months in advance. Will consider photocopied submissions. Reports in 2 weeks. Query first. Enclose S.A.S.E.

Nonfiction: "We like articles about teens or subjects that teens would be interested in. Writer should query us first." Length: 500 to 1,200 words. Pays $75 to $150.

Fiction: Mainstream, mystery, and adventure fiction. Length: 800 to 1,200 words. Pays $75 to $125.

How To Break In: "This is a very tight market now, money is low, and I'm using all the freebies I can get. Any writer who's trying to make it in this tight economy should think to herself/himself whether the story she/he is about to send me might be available to me through some other channel — free. Writers outside of New York query me all the time on material I can get through the Girl Scout organization PR people free. An example would be a 15-year-old scout in Denver who's just won an extraordinary award. Don't waste your time on material like that. On the other hand, a woman in California just sent me a story about a 21-year-old who just became the state's first female forest ranger. That's perfect. How could I know about such a thing? I'm still buying several freelance pieces per issue, but you've got to provide me with something that I wouldn't have any way of knowing about and that wouldn't be available to me for free through some other source."

AMERICAN NEWSPAPER CARRIER, American Newspaper Boy Press, 915 Carolina Ave., N.W., Winston-Salem NC 27101. Editor: Charles F. Moester. Buys all rights. Pays on acceptance. Will send list of requirements on request. Reports in 10 days. Enclose S.A.S.E.

Fiction: Uses a limited amount of short fiction, 1,500 to 2,000 words. It is preferable, but not required, that the stories be written around newspaper carrier characters. Before writing this type of fiction for this market, the author should consult a newspaper circulation manager and learn something of the system under which the independent "little merchant" route carriers operate generally the country over. Stories featuring carrier contests, prize awards, etc., are not acceptable. Humor and mystery are good. Stories are bought with the understanding that *American Newspaper Carrier* has the privilege of reprinting and supplying the material to other newspaper carrier publications in the U.S., and such permission should accompany all mss submitted. Pays $15 and up for stories.

THE BLACK COLLEGIAN, 3217 Melpomene Ave., New Orleans LA 70125. Phone: 504-522-2372. Managing Editor: Kalamu Ya Salaam. For black college students and recent graduates with an interest in black cultural awareness, sports, fashion, news, personalities, history, trends, current events, and job opportunities. Published bimonthly during school year; 60-page magazine. Established in 1970. Circulation: 85,000. Rights purchased vary with author and material. Usually buys first North American serial rights. Buys 15 mss a year. Payment on publication. Will send free sample copy to writer on request. Write for copy of guidelines for writers. Will consider photocopied submissions. Will not consider simultaneous submissions. Submit special material (Career Issue in September; Travel Issue in March) 2 months in advance. Returns rejected material in 1 month. Query first. Enclose S.A.S.E.
Nonfiction and Photos: Material on careers, sports, fashion, black history, news analysis. Articles on problems and opportunities confronting black college students and recent graduates. Informational, personal experience, profile, inspirational, humor, think pieces, nostalgia, personal opinion, travel. Length: 1,000 to 3,000 words. Pays $20 to $50. Department and column material includes book and record reviews, how-to, interviews, historical, expose. Length: 2,000 words. Pays $20. B&w photos or color transparencies purchased with or without mss. 5x7 preferred. Pays $5 for b&w; $10 to $50 for color.

BOYS' LIFE, Boy Scouts of America, National Headquarters, Route 1, North Brunswick NJ 08902. Editor: Robert E. Hood. For boys 8 to 19. Magazine; 8-5/16 x 11. Monthly. Circulation: over 2,000,000. Buys all rights. Buys 25 to 35 mss a year. Pays on acceptance. Will send free sample copy to writer on request. Material dealing with specific season or fixed calendar date should be submitted 6 months to 1 year in advance. Reports within 6 weeks. Send queries and mss to Articles Editor. Enclose S.A.S.E.
Nonfiction and Photos: Articles on practically any subject. The average boy has multiple hobbies and interests, which can be used as topics for feature articles. When possible, photos should be submitted with ms. Length: 500 to 1,500 words. "We are a big market for short features, most of them one-half page in length, from 500 to 600 words. We also use many photo-features showing how-to in crafts, hobbies, sports and other boy-interest skills such as model-making, fishing, science, nature, pets and camping. Photo-features should have an adequate selection of b&w prints with crisp, clearly written copy. Payment for full-length features is $350 minimum; short features, $150 to $250 depending on quality. Photo rates are A.S.M.P. and up, depending on the photographer's reputation and the difficulty of the assignment.
Fiction: Interesting plot, sound characterization, conflict, action or humor or suspense, and good, literate writing. "Most of the stories we publish deal with boys in their teens, but main characters may be men of any age when the story situation demands. Stories must be technically correct as far as sports rules, historical dates, natural and science phenomena, and similar allusions are concerned. Stories should run from about 3,000 words down to 2,500 words, or shorter. We prefer the O. Henry type or the kind once popular in *Liberty Magazine,* in a length which can be contained, with illustration, on a two-page spread." Pays $150 minimum.

CAMPUS, 42 Mercer St., Toronto, Ontario, Canada M5V 1H3. Editor: Susan Pearce. For students of universities, colleges and high schools. Magazine; 40 (8x11) pages.

Established in 1968. Every 2 months. Circulation: 12,500. Copyrighted. Pays on acceptance. Will send free sample copy to writer on request. Will consider photocopied submissions. No simultaneous submissions. Reports on material accepted for publication in 2 weeks. Returns rejected material immediately. Query first or submit complete ms. Enclose S.A.E. and International Reply Coupons.

Nonfiction: Articles should be geared to students' needs and interests. Should be useful, but interesting. Career information, travel, entertainment, information on stock markets, insurance, etc. Informational, how-to, personal experience, interview, profile, humor, think pieces, personal opinion. Reviews of books and music. Length: 500 to 1,500 words. Pays $30 to $60.

CAMPUS AMBASSADOR MAGAZINE (CAM), 1445 Boonville Ave., Springfield MO 65802. Editor: Dave Gable. For students on secular campuses only. Published by Christ's Ambassadors Department, Assemblies of God. Published 6 times a year (October, November, January through April); magazine, 16 pages, (7x10). Circulation: 12,000. Buys all rights, but will reassign rights to author after publication. Buys 6 mss a year. Payment on acceptance or on publication. "It varies according to type of material." Will send free sample copy to writer on request. Submit Christmas and Easter material 6 months in advance. Will consider photocopied submissions. Reports in several weeks. Enclose S.A.S.E.

Nonfiction: College-age slanted, religious nonfiction on personal evangelism, missions, Bible doctrines, Christianity and the sciences, devotional material. 400 to 1,200 words. Pays ½¢ to 1½¢ per word.

Photos: Purchased with mss. Prefers 5x7 b&w glossy. Payment varies according to quality and use.

Poetry: Must have spiritual significance and collegiate relevance. Length: 50 lines maximum. Pays 20¢ per line.

CAMPUS LIFE MAGAZINE, Box 419, Wheaton IL 60187. Phone: 312-668-6600. Editor: Philip Yancey. For high school to college-age students with a wide range of interests. Magazine; 96 (8¼x11¼) pages. Established in 1946. Monthly except in summer when only 2 issues are published. Circulation: 150,000. Rights purchased vary with author and material. Buys first serial rights, second serial (reprint) rights, or simultaneous rights. Buys 5 to 25 mss a year. Most articles are staff-written or assigned. Pays on publication. Will send free sample copy to writer on request. Write for copy of guidelines for writers. Will consider photocopied and simultaneous submissions. Submit college-related articles (for in-coming students) 3 to 4 months in advance. Reports in 2 to 3 weeks. Enclose S.A.S.E.

Nonfiction and Photos: "Humor, different kinds of sports (unusual). All non-humorous writing should reflect some aspect of Christian experience or world-view. One kind of story is particularly effective for us: a dramatic incident from the life of the writer or friend. We're evangelical Christian, youth-oriented." Recently published articles include "Stuck With Life," true story of paraplegic who considered euthanasia (gripping); "Committing Mozart in Public," street musicians in San Francisco (great photos and unusual story angle). Informational, personal experience, inspirational, humor, think articles, photo; book and movie reviews. Length: 100 to 10,000 words. Usually pays $35 to $150, but payment depends on length and how the article is used. Regular columns include: Etc. (kooky facts) and Doubletake (kooky photos with humorous captions). Length: 10 to 50 words. Pays $10 to $50. Photos purchased with or without ms, or on assignment. Captions optional. Pays $20 for b&w; $40 to $60 for color; $100 for cover shot.

Fiction and Poetry: Humorous and religious fiction. Length: 100 to 10,000 words. Pays $10 minimum. Traditional forms of poetry, blank verse, free verse, avant-garde forms, light verse, all types. Length: 1 to 100 lines. Pays $10 to $50.

CAMPUS NEWS, P.O. Box 318, Concord CA 94522. Editor: R. W. Whitney. A biweekly newspaper aimed at the university student. Established in 1971. Circulation: 25,000. Rights purchased vary with author and material. May buy all rights, but may reassign rights to author after publication. May buy first North American serial rights, first serial rights, second serial (reprint) rights or simultaneous rights. Buys

30 to 40 mss a year. Payment on publication. Will send sample copy to writer for 25¢. Will consider photocopied submissions. Submit seasonal material 4 months in advance. Reports on material in 2 to 4 weeks. Query first for columns, reviews and fiction. Submit complete ms for nonfiction. Enclose S.A.S.E.

Nonfiction and Photos: "Reviews of records and films, how-to articles, columns and articles telling of activities or happenings of interest to the college student. Concerts and events such as film festivals, summer activities; travel. Approach should be casual, open, pointed. We do not want to see the radical diatribe type of article. We prefer exposes to be tempered with fact and logic." Length: 200 to 1,500 words. Pays 25¢ to 60¢ per column inch. Department Editor: Paul R. Williams. 8x10 b&w glossy photos purchased with or without mss. Captions required. Pays $2. Department Editor: R. W. Whitney.

Fiction: Experimental, mainstream. Length: 500 to 1,500 words. Pays 10¢ to 60¢ per column inch. Department Editor: R. W. Whitney.

Poetry and Fillers: Traditional forms, blank verse, light verse, free verse, avant-garde forms. Length: 24 lines maximum. Newsbreaks, puzzles, jokes, short humor. Length: 200 words maximum. Pays 10¢ to 60¢ per column inch. Poetry Department Editor: Paul R. Williams. Fillers Department Editor: R. W. Whitney.

CATALYST, P.O. Box 179, St. Louis MO 63166. Editor: Jerry O'Malley. For senior high school youth, usually attending Disciple of Christ churches. Monthly magazine; 32 pages. Not copyrighted. Buys about 10 mss per week, including poetry. Will send sample copy to writer for 25¢. Enclose S.A.S.E.

Nonfiction: "We try to lean more toward humor and satire. Articles should include some aspects of religion or of social issues or what high school youth are doing in these areas. Articles concerning prisons and prisoners. Articles concerning death. In all phases of the magazine, humor, especially satire that means something, will be appreciated." Length: 1,000 words. Pays 2¢ per word.

Photos: Purchased with accompanying ms. Some abstract and scenery photos, but desire especially photos of teenagers (all colors, shapes, and sizes) doing what today's teenagers do. 8x10 preferred, but will accept any size of good b&w photos. State your asking price. "Usually pay $7.50; sometimes less. Always less per photos in a photo feature or with articles. This payment depends on quality of photo."

Fiction: "Any subject that interests a sincere, intelligent, sensitive high schooler interests us." Experimental, science fiction, humorous, religious. Length: 1,000 to 1,200 words. Pays 2¢ per word.

Poetry: "Poetry topics same as topics included above. Seasonal poetry is also used. We query you concerning payment of exceptionally long poems. We prefer 16 lines or less." Usually pays 15¢ per line minimum.

CHRISTIAN ADVENTURER, P.O. Box 850, Joplin MO 64801. Editor: Mrs. Marthel Wilson. General religious for those 13 through 19 years of age. Quarterly in weekly parts. Circulation: 5,000. Buys second serial (reprint) rights and simultaneous rights. Buys 115 mss a year. Quarterly pay periods. Will send free sample copy to writer on request. Write for copy of guidelines for writers. Will consider photocopied submissions. Submit seasonal material 9 months in advance. Reports on material accepted for publication in 2 months. Returns rejected material in 1 month. Submit complete ms. Enclose S.A.S.E.

Nonfiction: "We use only material which takes the fundamental Christian point of view." Informational, personal experience, interview, inspirational, historical, think pieces, nostalgia. Length: 1,500 words maximum; 1 paragraph minimum. Pays ½¢ a word.

Fiction: Only religious. Preferred length: 1,500 words. Pays ½¢ a word.

Fillers: Religious puzzles and items of personal experience. Length: 1 paragraph to 500 words. Pays ½¢ a word.

CIRCLE K MAGAZINE, 101 E. Erie St., Chicago IL 60611. Executive Editor: Carl L. Stack. Organizational publication of Circle K International, collegiate organization of Kiwanis International. For co-ed collegians, service oriented, young, involved. Published 5 times a year; magazine, 16 pages, (8x11). Circulation: 15,000. Not copyrighted. Buys 10 mss a year, but this varies. Payment on acceptance. Will send free sample copy to writer on request. Submit seasonal material 2 months in advance. Will consider cassette submissions. Reports within 3 weeks. Submit complete ms with short cover letter. Enclose S.A.S.E.

Nonfiction: "Authoritative, well-researched, quality nonfiction. General interest articles for college students; attitudes and opinions, groups and leadership dynamics, social/political issues, ecology, drugs. Offbeat humor. Service activities like Vista, Peace Corps, etc. Approach should be young and alive, addressing outstanding, dedicated students. To the point. Substantial, informative. Altruism, service to community. Particularly interested in articles on ecology, health, and other material geared to service programs of involved students." Informational, how-to, personal experience, interview, profile, humor, historical, think articles, nostalgia, personal opinion, photo, and travel articles. Length: 800 to 2,500 words. Pays 3¢ a word minimum.

Photos: B&w clear glossies purchased with accompanying ms. Also purchased without ms; payment varies.

CO-ED, Scholastic Magazines, Inc., 50 W. 44th St., New York NY 10036. For girls ages 14 to 18. Monthly. Buys all rights. Pays on acceptance. Will send free sample copy on request. Query first. Enclose S.A.S.E.

Fiction: "Stories dealing with problems of contemporary teenagers. Emphasis on personal growth of one or more characters as they confront problems with friendships, dating, family, social prejudice. Suggested themes: finding identity, reconciling reality and fantasy, making appropriate life decisions. Try for well-rounded characters and strong, logical plots. Avoid stereotyped characters and cliched, fluffy romances. If girls with conventional 'feminine' interests are portrayed, they should nonetheless be interesting, active and realistic people. Humor is welcome; so are sports and adventure stories in colorful local or foreign settings." Length: 5,000 words maximum. Pays $150 minimum.

CONQUEST, 6401 The Paseo, Kansas City MO 64131. Editor: Dan Ketchum. Teens' magazine with a point of view that attempts to mold as well as reflect the junior and senior high school Christian teen, sponsored by the youth organization of the Church of the Nazarene. Monthly. Pays on acceptance. Accepts simultaneous submissions. Buys second rights. Will send free sample copy and Editorial Specifications sheet on request. Reports on submissions in 6 weeks. Enclose S.A.S.E.

Nonfiction: Helpful articles in the area of developing the Christian life; first person, "this is how I did it" stories about Christian witness. Length: up to 2,500 words. Articles must be theologically acceptable and make the reader want to turn over the page to continue reading. Should not be morbid or contain excessive moralizing. Looking for fresh approach to basic themes. The writer should identify himself with the situation but not use the pronoun "I" to do it. Also go easy on "you" (unless the second approach is desired). The moral or application should not be too obvious. Also needs articles dealing with doctrinal subjects, written for the young reader. Pays a minimum of 1½¢ per word. Works six months ahead of publication.

Photos: 8x10 b&w glossies of teens in action. Payment is $7.50 and up. Also considers photo spreads and essays. Uses one color transparency per month for cover.

Fiction: "Adventure, school, and church-oriented. No sermonizing." Length: 2,500 words maximum. Payment is a minimum of 2¢ a word.

DASH, Box 150, Wheaton IL 60187. Editor: Don Dixon. For boys 8 to 11 years of age. Most subscribers are in a Christian Service Brigade program. Monthly magazine; 32 pages. Established in 1972. Circulation: 32,000. Rights purchased vary with author and material. Usually buys all rights, but will sometimes reassign rights to author after publication. Buys 5 mss a year. Payment on publication. Will send free sample copy to writer on request. Write for copy of guidelines for writers. Will consider photocopied and simultaneous submissions. Submit seasonal material 4 months in advance. Reports on material accepted for publication as soon as possible. Returns rejected material in 4 weeks. Query first. Enclose S.A.S.E.

Nonfiction and Photos: "Our emphasis is on boys and how their belief in Jesus Christ works in their everyday life." Uses short articles about boys of this age; problems they encounter. Material on crafts and games. Interview, profile. Length: 1,000 to 1,500 words. Pays $30 to $60. Pays $7.50 for 8x10 b&w photos purchased with ms. Captions required.

Fiction: Religious. Length: 1,000 to 1,500 words. Pays $20 to $60.

ENCOUNTER, Wesleyan Publishing House, Box 2000, Marion IN 46952. Address submissions to Editor of Sunday School Magazines. For senior teens, ages 15 to 18. Weekly. Special issues for all religious and national holidays. Not copyrighted. Pays on acceptance. Will send a free sample copy to a writer on request. Submit special material 9 months in advance. Reports in 6 weeks. Enclose S.A.S.E.

Nonfiction: "Features of youth involvement in religious and social activity, travel, youth of other countries, history, biographies including people of all races, informational articles of educational, religious, or cultural value. Avoid implied approval of liquor, tobacco, theatres, and dancing." Length: 200 to 1,000 words. Payment is "2¢ a word for quality material."

Fiction: Stories with definite Christian emphasis and character-building values, without being preachy. Setting, plot, and action should be realistic. Length: 1,000 to 2,000 words. Serials should be no longer than 8 chapters, about 1,800 words per chapter. Payment is "2¢ a word for quality material."

Photos: 5x7 and 8x11 b&w glossies purchased with mss. Portraying action or the teenage world, or with seasonal emphasis. Payment is $1 to $10 depending on utility and quality.

Poetry: Religious and/or seasonal, expressing action, imagery. Length: 4 to 16 lines. Payment is 25¢ a line.

ETC., 6401 The Paseo, Kansas City MO 64131. Editor: J. Paul Turner. Published by the Church of the Nazarene. For the "18- to 24-year-old student, young professional, and serviceman." Monthly. Circulation: 18,000. Buys first rights or second rights. Buys approximately 50 mss a year. Pays on acceptance. Will send a sample copy to a writer on request. Submit seasonal material 6 months in advance. Enclose S.A.S.E.

Nonfiction: "Helpful articles in the area of developing the Christian life, how the Christian meets his world." Writer's style should be "evangelical in emphasis; material should have a real 'bite' in it." Wesleyan doctrine. Buys interviews, profiles, inspirational and think pieces, humor, photo essays. Length: 2,500 words maximum. Pays minimum 1½¢ a word.

Photos: B&w glossies. Pays $5 to $15. Interested in photo spreads and photo essays.

EVANGEL, 999 College Ave., Winona Lake IN 46590. Editor: Vera Bethel. Methodist weekly publication for young people of college age and young adults. Not copyrighted. Pays on acceptance. Will send free sample copy on request. Write for copy of guidelines for writers. Reports within a month. Enclose S.A.S.E.

Nonfiction: Any religious, moral or ethical problems which confront today's young Christians; racial issues, responsibility toward minority groups such as migrants or the Appalachian poor whites, almost any of these social problems which pose some sort of moral decision or responsibility. Pays 2¢ a word for articles, 300 to 1,000 words. Also uses human interest articles, 1,000 words.

Fiction: Dealing with the Christian answer to contemporary problems, including the racial problem. Stories should have a specific moral or religious message, but not an obvious one. Preferably written from the young person's viewpoint, but not necessarily from the viewpoint of a Christian. Length: 1,800 to 2,000 words. Pays 2¢ a word. Also uses short-shorts.

Photos: Pays $1 to $10 for photos submitted with mss. Can be 3x5, 6x8, or 8x10.

Poetry: From four lines to 25. Religion, nature, personal attitudes. Pays 25¢ per line.

Fillers: Short devotional articles, 100 to 500 words; anecdotal or straight exposition. Fresh, pointed, without trite expressions. Pays $5 minimum.

EVENT, 127 9th Ave., N., Nashville TN 37203. Editor: Linda Lawson. Issued monthly for Southern Baptist youth, ages 12 to 17. Circulation: 225,000. Buys all rights, first rights, and simultaneous submissions provided other publications are listed. Pays on acceptance. Will send free sample copy to a writer on request. "Profanity and moral problems such as smoking, petting, and drinking as natural or acceptable behavior are taboo." Mss should be double-spaced and include approximate number of words, rights for sale, and Social Security number of the author. Deadline for seasonal material one year in advance of publication. Reports within three to four weeks. Query helpful, but not required. Enclose S.A.S.E.

Nonfiction and Photos: Stories of achievement by high school youth, photo stories of places and persons interesting to youth, sports and sports figures, do-it-yourself and self-development features, vocational information, dating skills, science, human relations, preparation for college, citizenship, travel (limited amount), hobbies (especially for boys). Wants up-to-date subjects, given fresh treatment. Length: 750 to 1,500 words. Pays 2½¢ per word (all rights); 1¼¢ per word (one right). Photos purchased with mss only. No specific size, although 8x10 preferred. Main requirement is that photos be sharp and clear and fit article. No color. Pays $5 to $10.

Fiction: Occasionally buys boy-girl or sports stories with a come-to-realize theme or a situation where a young person faces a problem reflecting the needs of high school youth. Length: 1,500 to 3,000 words. Pays 2½¢ per word (all rights); 1¼¢ per word (one right).

Poetry: Short poems; humorous, devotional, nature, self-understanding. Length: 4 to 20 lines. Only poems of unusual merit above this length. Pays 35¢ to 50¢ per line.

Fillers: 300 to 500 words on devotional, personality, or humorous subjects. Pays 2½¢ per word. Also general information, puzzles and quizzes. Pays $5 to $10.

EXPLORING, Boy Scouts of America, Rte. #1, North Brunswick NJ 08902. Editor: Dick Pryce. Executive Editor: Annette Stec. For "ages 15 to 20. Grade school, high school, some college. Interests are general and wide—indoor, outdoor, career, education, sports, cars, planes, psychology, etc." Published 6 times a year. Buys all rights. Buys about 40 mss a year. Pays on acceptance. Will send a free sample copy to a writer on request. Submit seasonal material 6 months in advance. Reports in 4 weeks. Query first. Enclose S.A.S.E.

Nonfiction: "Subjects: careers, colleges, exploring, travel, music, contemporary youth activities, sports." Interested in how-to, personal experience, interviews, profiles, humor, think pieces, and photo articles. Consider the ages and education of our readers, yet realize we're not a 'far out' youth magazine. No sex; no particularly controversial themes; nothing below the age-level interest." Length: 900 to 2,500 words. Payment is $150 to $500. "Looking for talented young writers."

Photos: Payment is $250 for cover, $150 a page for inside color, $100 a page for b&w. Purchases one-time use rights for general interest; all rights for assigned articles. Department Editor: Brian Payne.

FACE-TO-FACE, 201 Eighth Ave. South, Nashville TN 37202. Phone: 615-749-6219. Editor: Sharilyn S. Adair. For United Methodist young people, ages 15 to 18 inclusive. Published by the Editorial Division of the General Board of Discipleship of The United Methodist Church. Quarterly magazine; 48 pages. Each issue is a theme issue. Established in 1968. Circulation: 30,000. Rights purchased vary with author and material. Buys first North American serial rights, first serial rights, or simultaneous rights. Buys about 8 mss a year. Payment on acceptance. Will send free sample copy to writer on request. Submit Christmas, Easter and summertime material 8 to 9 months in advance. Reports in 1 to 2 months. Query first, if you prefer, by outlining any article or story ideas. Enclose S.A.S.E.

Nonfiction: "Our purpose is to speak to young person's concerns about their faith, their purpose in life, their personal relationships, goals, and feelings. Articles and features (with photos) should be subjects of major interest and concern to high school young people. These include dating, marriage, home and family life, school, extracurricular activities, vocations, etc. Satires, lampoons, related to the theme of an issue are also used." Length: 1,800 words maximum. Pays 3¢ a word minimum.

Photos: Uses 8x10 b&w glossies with high impact and good contrast. Pays $15 for one-time use of b&w. "We buy stock photos and those especially taken to illustrate articles."
Fiction: Must deal with major problems and concerns of older teens—such as finding one's own identity, dealing with family and peer-group pressures, and so forth. No straight moral fiction or stories with pat answers or easy solutions used. Prefer unresolved endings. Story must fit theme of issue. No serials. Length: 2,500 to 3,000 words. Pays 3¢ per word.
Poetry: Related to the theme of an issue. Free verse, blank verse, traditional and avant-garde forms. Length: 10 to 150 lines. Pays 25¢ per line.

FLIP MAGAZINE, 34 West Putnam Ave., Greenwich CT 06830. Editor: Barbara Benson. Issued monthly to teenage girls, ages 11 to 17. Pays on publication. Buys all rights. Reports in three weeks. Query first and state credentials and interest in the field. Address queries to Barbi Sardinas, Managing Editor. Enclose S.A.S.E.
Nonfiction: Wants medium-length, exclusive, accurate articles on the pop scene as viewed by teenage girls. Usually based on interviews with top pop personalities. Breezy, intimate, but honest and candid style. Teen pop recording stars and TV personalities emphasized. Pays $50 and up.
Photos: With mss or with captions only. Any size; popular music and TV personalities of teen interest. Purchases all photo rights. Price negotiable, depending on exclusivity, quality and quantity. Direct photo queries to Hank Azzato, Art Director.

FOR TEENS ONLY, 235 Park Avenue, South, New York NY 10003. Editor: B.J. Lange. For "young teenage girls, aged 10 to 16, from all parts of the country." Quarterly. Buys all rights. Buys 28 to 30 mss a year. Pays on acceptance. Submit seasonal material 3 to 4 months in advance. Reports in 1 month. Enclose S.A.S.E.
Fiction: "Themes are predominantly boy-girl, but we can use friendship, family, growing up, etc.,—anything that relates to a teenage girl's life. Can use mystery and contemporary problem stories. Stories should not be written down to the reader—situations and especially dialog must be realistic. Fiction should be generally geared to the season in which it will be appearing (no school settings in the summer, for example), but we do not zero in on specific holidays." Length: 1,500 to 4,000 words. Payment is $50.

FREEWAY, Scripture Press, 1825 College Ave., Wheaton IL 60187. Publication Editor: Anne Harrington. For "Christian high school and college Sunday school class kids." Established in 1943. Weekly. Circulation: 100,000. Buys all rights, "but passes along reprint fees to author, when material is picked up after publication." Buys 100 mss a year. Will send free sample copy to a writer on request. Write for copy of guidelines for writers. Will not considered photocopied submissions. Reports on material accepted for publication in 6 weeks. Returns rejected material in 3 weeks. Query first or submit complete ms. Enclose S.A.S.E.
Nonfiction and Photos: "Mostly person-centered nonfiction with photos. Subject must have had specific encounter with Christ. Direct tie-in to faith in Christ. No simply religious or moral stories; subjects must be specifically Christ-centered. Christian message must be woven naturally into a good, true, dramatic, human interest story. Current interest is in the occult, Satanism, witchcraft and battles by Christians against grief, tragedy, danger, etc." Thought articles on Biblical themes. Length: 500 to 1,500 words. Pays up to $75. Pays $15 maximum for 5x7 and 8x10 b&w photos.
Fiction: Same themes, lengths and rate of payment as nonfiction.

HICALL, Gospel Publishing House, 1445 Boonville Ave., Springfield MO 65802. Editor: James E. Erdmann. For Church-oriented teenagers, 12 to 19 years. Weekly Sunday School take-home paper; 8 pages, (5½x8½). Established in 1942. Circulation: 165,000. Not copyrighted. Buys 125 mss a year. Payment on acceptance. Will send free sample copy to writer on request. Write for copy of "Writing for Assemblies of God Publications. We use seasonal material for New Year's, Easter, Mother's Day, Father's Day, July 4th, Thanksgiving, and Christmas." Submit seasonal material

1 year in advance. Will consider photocopied submissions and simultaneous submissions. Reports within 1 month. Submit only complete ms. Enclose S.A.S.E.

Nonfiction: "Articles stressing to the reader Bible principles for everyday living. We stress a personal everyday relationship with Christ in our stories and articles in addition to just good moral living. Human interest, geographical, missionary, nature and scientific articles, or any other topics interesting to teenagers, with emphasis on 15- to 17-year-olds. Articles should have evangelical emphasis, but should not be preachy or have tacked-on moral. Length of 500 to 700 words with 1,000 words maximum. Pays 1¢ to 2¢ per word.

Photos: Purchased with or without ms. Captions required. Teens in everyday activity scenes. Size is not as important as subject matter and clarity of picture. Must be suitable for offset printing. 4x5 or 8x10 b&w. Pays $5 for clear b&w glossies; $10 for transparencies.

Fiction: Stories, 1,200 to 1,800 words, on any subject interesting to teenagers. Strong evangelical emphasis, but not preachiness, should be inherent part of story. Good plots wanted in which main character solves his problems through putting Biblical principles and Christian values into action. Stories of two, three, and four parts considered. Each should be accompanied by synopsis. Pays 1¢ to 2¢ per word.

Poetry and Fillers: Traditional forms, free verse, light verse. Theme: open. Length: 8 to 20 lines. Pays 20¢ per line, $1 minimum. Clippings and short humor also wanted. Must have definite relationship to teenagers' spiritual life. Length: 500 words maximum; 1 to 3 column inches. Pays 75¢ per column inch.

HIGH, 1233 Central, Evanston IL 60201. Editor: David Olson. For teenage churchgoers (evangelical churches) of various denominations. Established in 1959. Quarterly issues of 3 monthly parts. Buys all rights. Buys 100 mss a year. Payment on acceptance. Will send sample copies (plus information packet) to writer on request. Submit seasonal material 9 to 15 months in advance. Must be issue-related. Reports on material in 2 to 3 months. Query first. Enclose S.A.S.E.

Nonfiction: "Articles that help readers live the Christian life in their own world and understand what commitment to Christ means. All aspects of daily life on which Christianity has a basic bearing. Evangelical, contemporary and teen-related." Informational, how-to, personal experience, interview, inspirational, humor. Pays minimum of 4¢ per word. Length: 1,000 words maximum; shorter preferred.

HIS, 5206 Main St., Downers Grove IL 60515. Phone: 312-964-5700. Editor: Stephen Board. Issued monthly from October to June for collegiate students, faculty administrators, and graduate students belonging to the evangelical Christian faith. Buys all rights. Payment on acceptance. Reports within 10 days, or as work permits. Enclose S.A.S.E.

Nonfiction: Articles dealing with practical aspects of Christian living on campus, relating contemporary issues to Biblical principles. Should show relationships between Christianity and various fields of study, Christian doctrine, and missions. Mss up to 1,500 words. Pays 1¢ a word. Reports in 3 months.

Photos and Poetry: Uses b&w singles. Pays $10 per photo. Also uses photo series in which $6 per photo is paid. No color. Rarely accepts illustrated articles. Photos should be original and creative. Poetry occasionally bought. Pays $5 to $10.

JUNIOR BOWLER, 5301 S. 76th St., Greendale WI 53129. Phone: 414-421-6400. Official publication of American Junior Bowling Congress. Editor: Marilyn Jeppesen. For boys and girls ages 21 and under. Established in 1946 as *Prep Pin Patter*; in 1964 as *Junior Bowler*. Monthly, November through April. Circulation: 89,000. Buys all rights. Pays on publication. Reports within 10 days. Query first. Enclose S.A.S.E.

Nonfiction and Photos: Subject matter of articles must be based on tenpin bowling and activities connected with American Junior Bowling Congress only. Audience includes youngsters down to 6 years of age, but material should feature the teenage group. Length: 500 to 800 words. Accompanying photos or art preferred. Pays $30 to $100 per article. Photos should be 8x10 b&w glossies related to subject matter. Pays $5 minimum.

KEYNOTER MAGAZINE, 101 E. Erie St., Chicago IL 60611. Executive Editor: Carl L. Stack. An organizational publication of Key Club International. For high school males, 15 to 18, members of Key Club, a Kiwanis International sponsored youth organization; service oriented. Published 7 times a year; magazine, 16 pages, (8x11). Circulation: 95,000. Not copyrighted. Buys less than 15 mss a year. Payment on acceptance. Will send free sample copy to writer on request. Submit seasonal material 2 months in advance. Reports in 3 weeks. Query first. Enclose S.A.S.E.

Nonfiction and Photos: "Topical material directed to mature young men. Current social concerns, leadership, humor, etc. Use a young, alive approach, addressing outstanding, dedicated students. To the point. Substantial, informative. Community service. Buys informational, how-to, personal experience, interview, profile, humor, historical, think articles, nostalgia, personal opinion, and photo features. Length: 800 to 2,500 words. Payment varies, but usually 8¢ a word maximum. B&w clear glossies purchased with accompanying ms. Purchased also without ms. Pays 3¢ a word minimum.

LIVE, 1445 Boonville Ave., Springfield MO 65802. Editor: Gary L. Leggett. For young people and adults in Assemblies of God Sunday Schools. Weekly. Special issues during Easter, Thanksgiving, and Christmas use articles of a devotional nature. Circulation: 225,000. Not copyrighted. Buys about 100 mss a year. Payment on acceptance. Will send free sample copy to writer on request. Write for copy of editorial guidelines for writers. Submit seasonal material 12 months in advance. Reports on material within 6 weeks. Enclose S.A.S.E.

Nonfiction and Photos: "Articles with reader appeal, emphasizing some phase of Christian living, presented in a down-to-earth manner. Biography or missionary material using fiction techniques. Historical, scientific or nature material with a spiritual lesson. Be accurate in detail and factual material. Writing for Christian publications is a ministry. The spiritual emphasis must be an integral part of your material." Length: 1,000 words maximum. Pays 1¢ to 2¢ a word, according to the value of the material and the amount of editorial work necessary. Color photos or slides purchased with mss, or on assignment. Pay open.

Fiction: "Present believable characters working out their problems according to Bible principles; in other words, present Christianity in action, without being preachy. We use very few serials, but we will consider four- to six-part stories if each part conforms to average word length for short stories. Each part must contain a spiritual emphasis and have enough suspense to carry the reader's interest from one week to the next. Stories should be true to life, but not what we would feel is bad to set before the reader as a pattern for living. Stories should not put parents, teachers, ministers or other Christian workers in a bad light. Setting, plot and action should be realistic, with strong motivation. Characterize so that the people will live in your story. Construct your plot carefully so that each incident moves naturally and sensibly toward crisis and conclusion. An element of conflict is necessary in fiction. Short stories should be written from one viewpoint only." Length: 1,200 to 2,000 words. Pays 1¢ to 2¢ per word.

Poetry: Buys traditional, free, and blank verse. Length: 12 to 20 lines. Pays 20¢ per line.

Fillers: Brief, purposeful, usually containing an anecdote, and always with a strong evangelical emphasis.

THE MODERN WOODMEN, 1701 First Ave., Rock Island IL 61201. Editor: Robert E. Frank. For members of Modern Woodmen of America, a fraternal insurance society. Magazine published every 2 months; 24 to 32 pages. Established in 1883. Circulation: 325,000. Not copyrighted. Payment on acceptance. Will send free sample copy to writer on request. Write for copy of editorial guidelines for writers. "We need materials on heroes and heroines of American Revolution." Submit material 4 months in advance. Will consider photocopied and simultaneous submissions. Reports in 3 to 4 weeks. Submit only complete ms. Enclose S.A.S.E.

Nonfiction, Fiction, Photos, and Poetry: "Nonfiction may be either for children or adults. Fiction should be slanted toward children up to age 16. Our audience is broad and diverse. We want clear, educational, inspirational articles for children and young people. We don't want religious material, teen romances, teen adventure stories." Buys informational, how-to, historical, and technical articles. Length: 1,500 to 2,000 words. Pays $35 per ms. Mainstream, and historical fiction. Length: 1,500 to 2,500 words. Pays $35. B&w photos purchased with ms. Captions optional. Prefers vertical, b&w glossy photos for cover use. Payment varies with quality and need. "Narrative poetry is all we use; we are not in the market for short poems as fillers and we do not have a poet's page. Pay $35 minimum, since we only buy poetry that can be given a full-page treatment."

MY DELIGHT, Union Gospel Press, Box 6059, Cleveland OH 44101. For teenagers 13 through 17. Nondenominational fundamental, evangelical Christian magazine. Buys exclusive rights only. Pays within 90 days of acceptance. Will send free sample copy to writer on request. Write for copy of guidelines for writers. Reports within 3 months. Enclose S.A.S.E.

Nonfiction and Photos: Biographies about Christians whom young people can admire and follow; how-to articles. Length: 1,000 to 1,500 words. Payment varies; usually 2¢ per word. Also purchase slides and photos to accompany articles. Pays $5 for each color slide and $3 for each b&w glossy.

Fiction: Must have strong emphasis on Christian living; true-life stories with moral emphasis; no slang. Length: 1,000 to 1,500 words. Also uses shorts of approximately 300 words. Payment varies; but usually 2¢ per word.

Poetry and Fillers: "We use a limited amount of poetry. Each submission should be rich in imagery and figurative language. The theme should be clear, and rhyme and meter should be consistent with the subject." Length: average 16 lines. Pays 35¢ per line. Also uses short fillers, puzzles, and quizzes, based on the Bible. Pays $2.50 minimum.

How To Break In: "Give us something fresh but maintaining an evangelical emphasis. True stories with photos or slides are what we look for most, but please footnote all facts, or supply a complete bibliography. All direct quotations must have accompanying sources."

PENTECOSTAL YOUTH, P. O. Box 850, Joplin MO 64801. Phone: 417-624-7050. Editor: Andrew Shetley. Primarily edited for teenagers, but also read by a number of ministers and other adults interested in youth. Contains program materials and suggestions for successful youth ministry. Evangelical and Christian in message and approach. Established in 1956. Monthly. Circulation: 2,000. Buys second serial (reprint) rights and simultaneous rights. Pays on publication. Sample copy and guidelines for writers sent on request when accompanied with 9x12 self-addressed envelope. Submit complete ms. "We prefer photocopied submissions, so writer doesn't worry so much about slow reply." Rejected material returned within 1 month. Material not returned in that time is held for later publication. Enclose S.A.S.E.

Nonfiction and Photos: "Character-building articles of interest to youth. Informational, how-to, personal experience, profile, inspirational, short humor, historical, think, and short travel stories. Primarily published for young people of Holiness background, thus we observe the usual taboos such as tobacco, alcohol, dancing, movies, drugs, immorality, etc. However, we are not presenting just spiritual or church-related items. It is intended as a general magazine for Pentecostal teenagers." Length: 2,500 words maximum (author should give approximate word count on ms). Usually pays ½¢ a word; more for special articles. Photos purchased with ms. Pays $2 for routine b&w photos; $5 for feature photo.

Fiction, Poetry, and Fillers: Humorous and religious fiction. Length: 2,500 maximum; 2,000 preferred. Pays ½¢ a word. Any style poetry, length open. Youth and bible type jokes and puzzles. Payment at discretion of editor, according to use.

PROBE, 1548 Poplar Ave., Memphis TN 38104. Phone: 901-272-2461. Editor: Mike Davis. Baptist publication. Monthly for boys ages 12 to 17. Usually buys first rights. Will accept simultaneous submissions if there is no conflict in market. Payment on acceptance. Will send a free sample copy to a writer on request. Submit seasonal material at least 5 months in advance. Reports in three weeks. Enclose S.A.S.E.

Nonfiction and Photos: Any subject of special interest to boys in this age group. Buys how-to's, humor, interviews with prominent people, profiles, inspirational and historical articles, sports, outdoors, think pieces, missions, travel. Length: 1,200 words maximum, and shorter lengths preferred. Pays 2½¢ a word. B&w photos (5x7 or larger) purchased with mss and with captions only. Pays $10.

Fiction: Stories, especially mission, adventure, and seasonal, with "boy appeal." 1,200 words maximum. Pays 2½¢ per word. Prefers stories that aren't preachy; that are interesting and exciting, but aren't corny, and that have some conflict in the plot but aren't artificial or strained. Limited need. "Uses very little fiction."

REACHOUT, Light and Life Press, Winona Lake IN 46590. Editor: Vera Bethel. For "young teens, 12, 13, and 14-year-olds." Weekly. Circulation: 35,000. Not copyrighted. Buys 250 mss a year. Pays on acceptance. Will send a free sample copy to a writer on request. Submit seasonal or holiday material 3 months in advance. Reports in 1 month. Enclose S.A.S.E.

Nonfiction and Photos: Wants articles with photos on youth projects and hobbies. Can be how-to, personal experience, inspirational, or think pieces. Length: 500 to 1,000 words. Payment is 2¢ a word. B&w glossy photos purchased with mss, 8x10 preferred. Payment is $3.50 to $10.

Fiction: "We want stories with a Christian orientation; not secular in tone but definitely not pious; fast-paced and contemporary in style. Stories should involve junior-high interests which center largely around school activities and hobbies." Length: 1,500 to 2,000 words. Payment is 2¢ a word.

Poetry: Payment is 25¢ a line for nature and devotional poetry.

REFLECTION, Pioneer Girls, Box 788, Wheaton IL 60187. Phone: 312-293-1600. Editor: Sara Anne Robertson. Published bimonthly for girls in junior high and senior high school. Buys first and (at times) all rights. Pays on acceptance. Sample copies and writer's packet for $1. Reports in six weeks. Query to Article Editor for nonfiction. Enclose S.A.S.E.

Nonfiction: Inspirational articles should indicate practical relevance of Christianity to problems facing age group. Other nonfiction articles range from humorous to informative (careers, hobbies, how-to, recipes, etc.). Pays $10 to $30 or approximately 2¢ a word.

Photos: Pays $10 for inside use; $25 for cover use. B&w photos only.

Fiction: Timely and honest stories of 1,000 to 2,500 words. Need not have strong spiritual emphasis but should be in keeping with Christian point of view. At least one story used every month. Pays $20 to $40 or approximately 2¢ a word. Address to Fiction Editor.

Fillers: Uses puzzles and games. Pays $20 to $30 or probably 2¢ a word, per item.

SCHOLASTIC SCOPE, Scholastic Magazines, Inc., 50 W. 44th St., New York NY 10036. Circulation: 1,300,000. Buys all rights. Issued weekly. 4th to 6th grade reading level; 15 to 18 age level. Reports within 4 to 6 weeks. Query first. Enclose S.A.S.E.

Nonfiction and Photos: Articles about teenagers who have accomplished something against great odds, overcome obstacles, performed heroically, or simply done something out of the ordinary. Prefers articles about people outside New York area. Length: 400 to 1,200 words. Payment is $50 per magazine page. Photos purchased with articles. Pays $25 for every photo used.

Fiction and Drama: Problems of contemporary teenagers (drugs, prejudice, runaways, failure in school, family problems, etc.); relationships between people (inter-racial, adult-teenage, employer-employee, etc.) in family, job, and school situations. Strive for directness, realism, and action, perhaps carried through dialogue rather than exposition. Try for depth of characterization in at least one character. Avoid too many coincidences and random happenings. Although action stories are wanted, it's not a market for crime fiction. Looking for material about American Indian, Chicano, Mexican-American, Puerto Rican, and Black experiences among others. Occasionally uses mysteries and science fiction. Length: 400 to 1,200 words. Uses plays up to 3,000 words. Pays $150 minimum, except for short-shorts. Pays $100 for 500 to 600 words.

SCHOLASTIC SEARCH, Scholastic Magazines, Inc., 50 West 44th St., New York NY 10036. For 4th to 6th grade reading level; 14 to 17 age level. "Since our needs are subject to change, a careful study of the magazine will help authors." Occasionally overstocked with material. Query first. Enclose S.A.S.E.

Nonfiction, Drama, and Photos: Nonfiction about relationships between people (inter-racial, intercultural, adult-teenage, employer-employee, etc.) in family, job and school situations. Interested in three kinds of nonfiction articles with photos. (1) Personal interviews with fairly young people who have jobs that do not require a college education and are not closed to members of minority groups; include job requirements, advantages and disadvantages, pay, opportunities for advancement, where to write for further information in this field, etc. (2) Articles with photos about teenagers who are doing something or have accomplished something unusual or interesting. (3) World cultures articles and photos that tell a story about specific people or groups in different parts of the world. Length: 400 to 1,200 words. Pays $150 minimum. Also uses historical plays up to 3,000 words.

SCHOLASTIC VOICE, Scholastic Magazines, Inc., 50 W. 44th St., New York NY 10036. For high school students ages 14 to 17. Established in 1946. Circulation: 450,000. Buys all rights. Reports within 4 to 6 weeks. Query first. Enclose S.A.S.E.

Fiction and Drama: Uses stories and plays strong on plot and characterization and dealing with problems of interest to teenagers. Steer clear of teenage stereotypes. Good subjects are boy-girl situations (but avoid formula stories about puppy love), school situations, adventure, mystery, science fiction, family situations, sports. Problems that confront teenagers, like finding one's own identity, setting standards of conduct, reconciling ideals and reality, bridging the generation gap, etc., are good. Plays should be suitable for both concert presentation (reading aloud without acting out) and stage presentation. Avoid over-subtlety but try to include situations and ideas that provoke thought and discussion. Length: 1,500 to 3,000 words; also short-shorts of 500 to 1,000 words. Pays $150 minimum, except for short-shorts. Pays $100 for 500 to 600 words.

SEVENTEEN, 320 Park Ave., New York NY 10022. Managing Editor: Ray Robinson. Monthly. Circulation: 1,550,000. Buys all rights for nonfiction and poetry. Buys first rights on fiction. Pays on acceptance. Reports in about 2 weeks. Enclose S.A.S.E.

Nonfiction and Photos: Articles and features of general interest to young women who are concerned with the development of their own lives and the problems of the world around them; strong emphasis on topicality and helpfulness. Send brief outline and query, summing up basic idea of article. Also like to receive articles and features on speculation. Length: 2,000 to 3,000 words. Pays $100 to $500 for articles written by teenagers but more to established adult freelancers. Articles are commissioned after outlines are submitted and approved. Fees for commissioned articles generally range from $500 to $1,350. Photos usually by assignment only. Pamela Hoffman, Art Director.

Fiction: Babette Rosmond, Fiction Editor. Top-quality stories featuring teenagers—the problems, concerns, and preoccupations of adolescence, which will have recognition and identification value for readers. Does not want "typical teenage" stories, but high literary quality. Avoid oversophisticated material; unhappy endings acceptable if emotional impact is sufficient. Humorous stories that do not condescend to or caricature young people are welcome. Best lengths are 2,500 to 8,000 words. Occasionally accepts 2- or 3-part stories such as mysteries and science fiction with adolescent protagonist and theme. Pays $50 to $300. Conducts an annual short story contest.

Poetry: By teenagers only. Pays $5 to $25.

How To Break In: "The best way for beginning teenage writers to crack the *Seventeen* lineup is for them to contribute suggestions and short pieces to the Free-For-All column, a literary format which lends itself to just about every kind of writing: profiles, puzzles, essays, exposes, reportage, and book reviews."

STRAIGHT, 8121 Hamilton Ave., Cincinnati OH 45231. Phone: 513-931-4050. Editor: Judy Trotter. Weekly for teenagers; primarily distributed through Christian Sunday schools. Buys first rights. Pays on acceptance. Will send free sample copy to a writer on request. Reports on submissions in 2 to 4 weeks. Query not necessary. Deadline for seasonal material 12 months before publication date. Include Social Security number on ms. Enclose S.A.S.E.

Nonfiction: Christian approach to current events and teen problems. Articles on teen activities, Bible study. Christian sportsmen, missions, group projects, etc. Length: 1,000 to 1,200 words.

Fiction: Must be well written, and believable. Main characters should be teens who cope with problems by using Christian principles. Must appeal to teenagers and have interesting, well-constructed plots. Stories should have character-building elements without being preachy. Main characters should be teenagers. Need stories to correlate with International Sunday School Lesson Outline. Payment to $35.

Poetry: Teen-written only. Should be submitted to Straight Pens Club. Author must include date of birth. Social Security number and S.A.S.E. Rate of payment determined by quality.

THE STUDENT, 127 Ninth Ave. N., Nashville TN 37234. Editor: Norman L. Bowman. Publication of National Student Ministries of the Southern Baptist Convention. For college students; focusing on freshman and sophomore level. Published 9 times during the school year. Circulation: 25,000. Buys all rights. Will buy first rights on request. Payment on acceptance. Will send sample copy to writer on request. Mss should be double spaced on white paper with 70-space line, 25 lines per page. Prefers complete ms rather than query. Reports usually in 6 weeks. Enclose S.A.S.E.

Nonfiction: Contemporary questions, problems, and issues facing college students viewed from a Christian perspective. The need to develop high moral and ethical values. The struggle for integrity in self-concept and the need to cultivate interpersonal relationships directed by Christian love. Length: 1,500 to 1,800 words. Satire and parody on college life, humorous episodes; emphasize clean fun and the ability to grow and be uplifted through humor. Length: 1,500 words maximum. Pays 2½¢ a word after editing with reserved right to edit accepted material.

Poetry: Related to student interests and needs. Length: 30 lines maximum. Pays approximately 35¢ per line.

TEEN MAGAZINE, 8831 Sunset Blvd., Hollywood CA 90069. Editorial Director: Robert MacLeod; Editor: Roxie Camron. For teenage girls. Monthly magazine; 100 pages. Established in 1957. Circulation: 864,000. Buys all rights. Predominantly staff written. Payment on acceptance. Will send sample copy to writer for 75¢. Submit seasonal material 4 months in advance. Will consider photocopied and simultaneous submissions. Reports in 2 weeks. Enclose S.A.S.E.

Nonfiction: Articles on self-improvement in personality and social areas, with light, anecdotal, nonpreachy approach. Contemporary life style features. Controversial problems. Greatest editorial need: full-length features for sex and dating series. Length: 1,200 to 2,400 words. Payment up to $200, depending on quality. Feature Editor: Kathy McCoy.

Photos: Purchased with mss only. 5x7 and 8x10 glossy prints of high quality. *Teen* considers photos part of the package when submitted with special features-personality profiles. Rate on needed buyouts $12.50 each. Color for the most part is shot locally under the direction of Barbara Gilbert, Art Director.

Fiction: Stories up to 3,500 words dealing specifically with teenagers—variety in setting, believable plots, romance and humor wanted. Pays $150. Fiction Editor: Daina Hulet.

TEENS TODAY, 6401 The Paseo, Kansas City MO 64131. Phone: 816-333-7000, Ext. 294. A Wesleyan/Conservative market. Editor: Roy F. Lynn. For 10th, 11th and 12th graders. Published weekly. Buys one-time or all rights. Buys 150 to 200 mss a year. Pays on acceptance. Will send free sample copy to writer on request. Write for copy of guidelines for writers. Seasonal deadlines are 10 months prior to publication date. Reports within 6 to 8 weeks. Enclose S.A.S.E.

Nonfiction, Fiction, and Poetry: Articles on contemporary teen problems from a Christian perspective (Wesleyan/Conservative). Poetry accepted with discretion. Stories must be realistic, contemporary, and must use the best writing techniques. Please send your sticky-sweet moralizing pieces elsewhere. Article length: 1,500 words maximum. Fiction length: 2,500 words maximum. Pays 2¢ per word for stories and articles; up to 25¢ per line for poetry. Pays $1 minimum for each poem.

TIGER BEAT MAGAZINE, 7060 Hollywood Blvd., #800, Hollywood CA 90028. Editor: Sharon Lee. For young teenage girls and subteens. Median age: 13. Monthly magazine: 84 (8½x11) pages. Established in 1960. Circulation: 500,000. Buys all rights. Buys 10 mss per year. Payment on acceptance. Will send free sample copy to writer on request. Reports on material accepted for publication in 3 weeks. Returns rejected material immediately. Query first. Enclose S.A.S.E.
Nonfiction and Photos: Stories about young entertainers; their lives, what they do, their interests. Quality writing expected, but must be written simply; romanticized, and capable of being understood by subteens. Length: depends on feature. Pays $50 to $100. Pays $15 for b&w photos used with mss: captions optional. $50 for color used inside; $75 for cover. 35mm slides preferred.

VENTURE MAGAZINE, Box 150, Wheaton IL 60187. Editor: Don Dixon. Publication of Christian Service Brigade. For young men 12 to 18 years of age. Most participate in a Christian Service Brigade program at a local evangelical church. Monthly magazine; 32 pages. Established in 1959. Circulation: 32,000. Rights purchased vary with author and material. Buys all rights, but will sometimes reassign rights to author after publication. Buys 5 mss a year. Payment on publication. Will send free sample copy to writer on request. Write for copy of guidelines for writers. Submit seasonal material 4 months in advance. Will consider photocopied and simultaneous submissions. Reports within 4 weeks. Query first. Enclose S.A.S.E.
Nonfiction, Fiction and Photos: "Articles with emphasis on sports. Well-known participants with a faith in Jesus Christ. Short stories about problems and how they were resolved. Religious fiction. Our emphasis is on boys and young men. How their belief in Jesus Christ works into their everyday life." Interviews and profiles. Length: 1,000 to 1,500 words. Pays $20 to $60. 8x10 b&w photos purchased with ms. Captions required. Pays $7.50.

WIND, The Wesleyan Church, Box 2000, Marion IN 46952. Phone: 317-674-3301, Ext. 48. Executive Editor: David Keith. Student Editor: Rita Wright. For young teen through college age readers. Monthly newspaper; 8 (11x17) pages. Circulation: 8,000. Buys first rights or second (serial) reprint rights. Buys 45 to 50 mss a year. Payment on publication. Will send free sample copy to writer on request. Write for copy of guidelines for writers. Will consider photocopied and simultaneous submissions. Submit seasonal material at least 3 months in advance. Reports in 10 days to 2 weeks; "possibly longer." Query first or submit complete ms. Enclose S.A.S.E.
Nonfiction: "Our publication attempts to promote Bible study, personal piety and aggressive evangelism. We attempt to appeal not only to youth within the church, but also to unchurched youth. We publish short, inspirational articles, full-length articles and features. Themes may include spiritual life, personal problems or areas of concern; personality and character development, relationships with others; moral issues such as drugs, etc.; seasonal, historical and informative articles." Length: 1,000 words maximum. Pays 2¢ a word for first rights; 1¢ a word for second rights.
Fiction: Religious short stories. "We do not use a great amount of fiction, but will occasionally print a piece that fits a theme. Please, no 'easy way out' endings. Be realistic. Even problems that are solved can leave a scar. Sometimes a problem is never solved, but is for the purpose of teaching a lesson. Be honest." Length: 1,000 words maximum. Pays 2¢ a word for first rights; 1¢ a word for second rights.
Poetry: Related to theme. Pays 25¢ a line.

WITH, Mennonite Publishing House, 616 Walnut Ave., Scottdale PA 15683. Editor: Richard A. Kauffman. For senior high school students. Established in 1968. Rights purchased vary with author and material. May buy first rights or second serial (reprint) rights. Submit complete ms. Enclose S.A.S.E.

Nonfiction and Photos: Articles dealing with any subject of interest to high school youth. Idea/think pieces, attempting to get readers to do serious thinking on all types of subjects. Personality/personal experience articles, about real people in real life situations. Christianity in action, outlining what churches and youth groups are doing to fulfill their mission in the world. Guidance, with practical pointers and ideas on vocational, marital, devotional, and educational problems. The contemporary world, delving into the society, its problems, discoveries, and joys. Glossy photos for article illustration are also accepted. Pays 3¢ a word.

Fiction: Stories of young people involved in being obedient to Christ in their lives. These should raise a problem and help the reader to find its solution. All mss should be written in adult language, have plenty of anecdotes and get somewhere fast. Pays 3¢ a word.

Poetry: Should deal with youth in relation to their world. Should be short. Preferred length: 50 lines maximum. Pays $5 to $15.

WORKING FOR BOYS, 601 Winchester St., Newton Highlands MA 02161. Editor: Brother Jerome, C.F.X. For junior high, parents, grandparents (the latter because the magazine goes back to 1884). Quarterly magazine; 28 pages. Established in 1884. Circulation: 26,750. Not copyrighted. Buys 50 mss a year. Payment on acceptance. Will send free sample copy to writer on request. Submit special material (Christmas, Easter, sports, vacation time) 6 months in advance. Reports in 1 week. Submit only complete ms. Enclose S.A.S.E.

Nonfiction and Photos: "Conservative, not necessarily religious, articles. Seasonal mostly (Christmas, Easter, etc.). Cheerful, successful outlook suitable for early teenagers. Maybe we are on the 'square' side, favoring the traditional regarding youth manners: generosity to others, respect for older people, patriotism, etc. Animal articles and tales are numerous, but an occasional good dog or horse story is okay. We like to cover seasonal sports." Buys informational, how-to, personal experience, historical and travel. Length: 500 to 1,000 words. Pays 3¢ a word. 6x6 b&w glossies purchased with ms for $10 each. "Photo purchases are very rare. Usually staff provides these."

Fiction: Mainstream, adventure, religious, and historical fiction. Theme: open. Length: 500 to 1,000 words. Pays 3¢ a word.

YOUNG AMBASSADOR, Box 82808, Lincoln NE 68501. Phone: 402-435-2171. Managing Editor: Robert H. Sink. For early teens. Monthly magazine; 40 pages, (8¼x11). Established in 1946. Circulation: 88,000. Buys all rights, but will reassign rights to author after publication. Buys 40 mss a year. Payment on acceptance. Will send free sample copy to writer on request. Write for copy of guidelines for writers. Reports in 3 weeks. Query first or submit complete ms. Enclose S.A.S.E.

Nonfiction: "Material that covers social, spiritual and emotional needs of teenagers. Interviews with teens who are demonstrating their faith in Christ in some unusual way. Biographical articles about teens who have overcome obstacles in their lives. Prefer not to see 'preachy' stories." Informational, how-to, personal experience, interview, inspirational, historical, and photo features. Length: 500 to 2,000 words. Pays 3¢ per word maximum. Regular column, Teen Scene, uses activities of church or school youth groups, prayer groups, Bible Study groups, or individual youth projects. Length: 2,000 words maximum. Pays 3¢ per word maximum.

Fiction: "Stories of interest to early teenagers with strong, well-developed plot and a definite spiritual tone, but not preachy. Seasonal stories needed. Should have a realistic, contemporary setting and offer answers to the problems teens are facing." Experimental, mystery, suspense, adventure, religious, and historical fiction. Theme: open. Length: 500 to 2,000 words. Pays 3¢ a word maximum.

YOUNG MISS, 52 Vanderbilt Ave., New York NY 10017. Phone: 212-685-4400. Editor: Rubie Saunders. Monthly, except June and August, for girls 10 to 14. Buys all rights. Pays on acceptance. Will send editorial requirement sheet to a writer, if S.A.S.E. is enclosed with request. Reports on submissions in 3 to 4 weeks. All mss must be typed, double-spaced. Enclose S.A.S.E.

Nonfiction: No food, fashion or beauty articles are wanted, but practically everything else goes. Hobbies, unusual projects, self-improvement (getting along with parents, brothers, etc.); how-to articles on all possible subjects. Length: about 1,500 words. Pays $50 minimum. Do not submit illustrations. Rough sketches may accompany a how-to article.

Fiction: "All fiction should be aimed at girls 10 to 14, with the emphasis on the late 12- to 14-year olds. Stories may be set in any locale or time—urban, western, foreign, past, contemporary, or future. Boys may be involved, even in a romantic way, as long as it is tastefully done. Mystery and adventure stories are also welcomed. Stories of today are particularly desirable. Especially interested in fiction with an urban setting dealing with the *real* problems today's young teens face. Overstocked on stories about middle income, small town girls who seem to have no problems greater than getting a date for a school dance or adjusting to a new neighborhood." Length: 2,000 to 2,300 words. Strongly plotted novelettes up to 6,500 words. Pays $50 minimum.

Fillers: Crossword puzzles and short quizzes on general information and personality subjects. Pays $10 to $25. Occasionally uses how-to fillers; currently overstocked on these.

YOUNG WORLD, Box 567B, Indianapolis IN 46206. Phone: 317-634-1100. Editor: Johanna Bradley. For young people 10 to 14 years old. Monthly, except June/July and August/September. Buys all rights. Pays on publication. Will send sample copy to writer for 50¢. Write for copy of guidelines for writers. Submit seasonal material at least 8 months in advance. Minimum reporting time is 10 to 12 weeks. Enclose S.A.S.E.

Nonfiction and Photos: Historical, scientific, contemporary articles, and articles dealing with community involvement. "We are particularly interested in articles about young people doing things: community projects, sports, business enterprises. Also good are informational, how-to, interview, profile, and humorous articles and photo features. We are always interested in contemporary craft projects with clear directions and photos of the finished product. Articles based on interviews with sports or entertainment personalities or teenagers who have accomplished significant things are welcome." Length: 900 words maximum. Pays approximately 3¢ a word. Photos are purchased with accompanying ms. Captions required. Pays $2.50 for each b&w; $5 for color.

Fiction: Adventure, mystery, humor, realism, suspense, westerns, science fiction, romance, and historical fiction. Length: 2,000 words maximum; slightly shorter preferred. Limited number of two-part suspense stories accepted; total word limit 3,500 words. Pays about 3¢ a word.

Poetry: Humorous poetry for young teenagers. traditional forms, blank and free verse, and light verse. Theme is open. No length limits. No fixed rate of payment.

Puzzles: All types desired; math or word. Should be difficult enough for this age group. No fixed rate of payment.

YOUTH ALIVE, 1445 Boonville Ave., Springfield MO 65802. Editor: Al Ferguson. "Official youth organ of the Assemblies of God, slanted primarily to late teens." Monthly. Circulation: 36,000. Buys all rights unless specified, but "we are interested in multiple submissions, second rights, and other reprints." Pays on acceptance. Will send a free sample copy to a writer on request. Reports in 6 weeks. Enclose S.A.S.E.

Nonfiction, Photos, and Poetry: "Purpose is to provide news of the Pentecostal youth scene, to inspire to Christlike living, and to be used as a witnessing tool. We can use photo features, photos, interviews, forums, biographical features, reports on outstanding Christian youth, how-to-do-it features, satire, humor, allegory, anecdotes, poems, news, motivational articles, testimonies, seasonal material, personal experiences. Avoid cliches, unexplained theological terms, sermonizing, and 'talking down' to youth. Read *Youth Alive* to get our style, but don't be afraid to submit something different if you think we might like it." Length of articles: 300 to 1,200 words. Payment is 2½¢ a word, slightly higher for assigned articles. Teen-slanted human interest photos purchased with mss or with captions. 8x10 b&w glossies or color transparencies. Payment is $10 to $25. Payment for poetry is 20¢ a line.

YOUTH IN ACTION, 901 College, Winona Lake IN 46590. Phone: 219-267-7621. Wesleyan Arminian theology. Editor: Vanetta Brandt. For teens, college students, servicemen, pastors, youth leaders, and other interested adults. Nine issues a year; 16 (8½x11) pages. Established in 1956. Circulation: 5,000. Not copyrighted. Buys 10 to 15 mss a year. Pays on publication. Will send free sample copy to writer on request. Write for copy of guidelines for writers. Will consider photocopied submissions. Reports in 4 weeks. Enclose S.A.S.E.
Nonfiction: Articles reporting news and activities of denominational youth activities, outstanding achievements, awards, and honors. Also general articles of interest to teens; spiritually uplifting. Articles designed to help in Christian growth, conduct, witness (Wesleyan Arminian theology). Informative articles or religious Christian attitude toward current topics. Personal experience, interview, inspirational, humor. Length: 500 to 1,500 words. Pays 1½¢ a word.
Photos: Purchased with or without ms. Captions required. 5x7 or 8x10 b&w glossies. Pays $5 to $10. Pays $40 for color slides.
Fiction, Poetry, and Fillers: Stories should be significant while entertaining the reader. Length: 750 to 1,500 words. Pays 1½¢ a word. Blank verse, free verse. Pays 1½¢ a word; $5 minimum. Jokes and short humor. Pays $5 to $10.

Theater, Movie, TV, and Entertainment Publications

For those publications whose emphasis is on music and musicians, see the section on Music Publications. Nonpaying markets for similar material are listed in the Literary and "Little" Publications category.

AFTER DARK, 10 Columbus Circle, New York NY 10019. Phone: 212-977-9770. Editor: William Como. For an audience "20 to 55 years old." Monthly. Circulation: 121,000. Buys first rights. Buys about 30 mss a year. Pays on publication. Will send a sample copy to a writer for $1.25. Submit seasonal material 4 months in advance. Reports in 3 to 4 weeks. Query first, including copies of previously published work. Enclose S.A.S.E.
Nonfiction and Photos: Articles on "every area of entertainment—films, TV, theater, nightclubs, books, records." Length: 2,500 to 3,000 words. Pays $75 to $150. Photos with captions only. B&w glossies, color transparencies. Pays $20 to $50.
How To Break In: "The best way to crack *After Dark* is by doing a piece on some new trend in the entertainment world. We have people in most of the important cities, but we rely on freelancers to send us material from out-of-the-way places where new things are developing. Some of our contributing editors started out that way. Query first."

AFTERNOON TV, 185 Madison Ave., New York NY 10016. Monthly. For soap opera viewers. Reports at once. Enclose S.A.S.E.
Nonfiction and Photos: Interviews with afternoon TV stars. Pays $50 for a four-page story; $100 for eight-page story. Minimum length: 4 typewritten pages. Photos purchased with mss. Pays up to $15 per photo.
How To Break In: "We're a very tough market to break into. Everything we do is interviews with daytime TV performers which makes us a market as specialized as *Popular Mechanics*. If a writer has some credits elsewhere and has done personality pieces before, the best way to break in here would be with a story about a lesser star in one of the New York soaps. We have a West Coast editor and a regular staff of writers out there, and besides, New York has ten soaps while there are only three in California. The interview doesn't have to be with a performer we've never interviewed before, but it should have some new angle."

BLACK STARS, 820 South Michigan Ave., Chicago IL 60605. Editor: Ariel Perry Strong. For young housewives, teenagers, and persons who are interested in the private lives of entertainers. Established in 1971. Monthly. Circulation: 300,000. Buys all rights. Buys 72 mss a year. Payment on publication. Will send free sample copy to writer on request. Query first. Enclose S.A.S.E.

Nonfiction and Photos: "Only articles pertaining to entertainers. Biographies, movie reviews, television reviews and record reviews. We deal only with black entertainers. B&w photos should accompany articles." Length: 2,000 to 4,000 words. Pays $100 to $200.

CANADIAN THEATRE REVIEW, Room 222, Administrative Studies Bldg., York University, 4700 Keele St., Downsview, Ontario M3J 1P3, Canada. Phone: 416-667-3249. Editor: Don Rubin. For critics, actors, educators, audiences. Quarterly magazine; 152 (6x9) pages. Established in 1973. Circulation: 2,500. Buys all rights, but will reassign rights to author after publication. Buys 80 mss a year. Payment on publication. Will send sample copy to writer for $2.50. Submit seasonal or special material 7 weeks in advance. Reports within 3 weeks. Query first, send an outline of article, or submit complete ms. Enclose S.A.E. and International Reply Coupons.

Nonfiction and Photos: Essays relating to the theatre. Reviews. Canadian orientation. "We're the only publication covering Canadian theatre." Also uses historical documentation relating to the Canadian theatre as it existed in the past and regional essays by leading members of the theatrical community. Length: 1,000 to 5,000 words. Pays $25 to $100. Regular features are Carte Blanche (free-form essays) and a playscript. Pays $35 for Carte Blanche and $100 for playscript. B&w photos (5x7 or larger) are purchased without ms or on assignment. Captions required. Pays $5 for each photo used.

Drama: Pays $100 for 3-act plays of interest to Canadians.

CASTLE OF FRANKENSTEIN, c/o Gothic Castle, 509 Fifth Ave., New York NY 10017. Editor: Calvin Thomas Beck. For "those interested in films pertaining to fantasy, horror and science fiction. Also in comic books and science fantasy books." Established in 1961. Bimonthly. Circulation: 110,000. Buys second serial (reprint) rights. Buys 90 to 115 mss a year. Payment on acceptance. Will send sample copy to a writer for 50¢ and S.A.S.E. Will consider photocopied submissions "only if original is lost." Reports on material accepted for publication in 2 to 4 weeks. Returns rejected material in 1 to 3 weeks. Submit complete ms. Enclose S.A.S.E.

Nonfiction and Photos: "About 75% of each issue is devoted to essays on fantasy-horror films, their directors, stars, writers, etc. Also, histories of the genre (especially interviews) and reviews are accepted. It's preferable if writer knows and likes fantasy and horror films, whether in theater or TV program form. We're tired of stuff only on Karloff, Lugosi and other oldtimers, unless someone has something new to say or an entirely fresh slant." Pays ¾¢ to 3¢ per word, "depending on quality and importance of ms." Pays $1 to $4 for film reviews. "We prefer photos (pertaining to an article-review) accompanying mss, though lack of them will not ruin chances of acceptance, especially when the material is good." Pays $1 to $3 per photo.

Fillers: Newsbreaks ("no free studio releases, please!"). Pays $1 to $3; "depends on uniqueness." Pays 50¢ to $2.50 for clippings.

DANCE MAGAZINE, 10 Columbus Circle, New York NY 10019. Phone: 212-977-9770. Editor: William Como. Monthly. For the dance profession and members of the public interested in the art of dance. Buys all rights. Pays on publication. Will send sample copy to writer for $1.50. Query suggested. Enclose S.A.S.E.

Nonfiction: Personalities, knowledgeable comment, news. Length: 2,500 to 3,000 words. Pays $25 to $50.

Photos: Purchased with articles or with captions only. Pays $5 to $10.

How To Break In: "Do a piece about a local company that's not too well known but growing; or a particular school that is doing well which we may not have heard about; or a local dancer who you feel will be gaining national recognition. Query first."

DRAMATICS MAGAZINE, Box E, College Hill Station, Cincinnati OH 45224. Phone: 513-541-7379. Published by The International Thespian Society. Editor: Thomas A. Barker; Associate Editor: Doug Finney. An educational magazine for students, teachers, and directors of theatre arts. Established in 1929. Published bimonthly in September, November, January, March and May. Circulation: 50,000. Buys first serial rights. Pays on acceptance. Will send free sample copy to writer on request. Prefers complete ms, but will respond to query letters. Abstracts, by assignment or request only. Include a short biographical sketch and your past involvement in theatre arts, as well as your journalistic experience. Reports in 3 months (or notifies authors if a longer period is needed for review), and generally prints all accepted material within 3 months of acceptance, except during summer months. Enclose S.A.S.E.

Nonfiction: Exciting and crisply written articles on any phase of all of the performing arts. Avoid pedagogics. Articles based on any phase of play production, worldwide theatre innovations, acting, directing, dance, mime, touring theatres, repertory companies, children's theatre, psycho-drama, film, television, dance, puppetry, religious drama, black theatre, the unique script or production, the usual script or production uniquely created, any of the technical areas, history of theatre, personality pieces, interviews, questions and answers with noted theatre creators. Length: 2,000 to 2,500 words. Pays $15 to $40. 5x7 or 8x10 b&w photos used with ms, with no additional payment.

Drama: "We print one short one-act play each issue. Subject matter must be suitable for high school production, run about 30 minutes when produced, and must never have been published before. We discourage the unsolicited submission of one-act scripts, since most of the plays we publish yearly are award winners from one of the divisions of Playwright's Competition. For complete information on Dramatics Magazine's Playwright's Competition (with more than $500 in cash awards, as well as probable publication in *Dramatics*) request a copy of the Competition's Awards and Specifications (Form 77-R-12-74). All plays published in *Dramatics* become the property of The International Thespian Society, unless copyrighted by the author before publication. Competition submissions are accepted yearly from January 1 to May 1. Winners are announced each autumn.

Fiction: "We publish 3 to 5 three-part to eight-part series each year. A query is necessary before submission of a series. We suggest a query, with outline and summary be submitted before work on series continues. We may ask for the first part, before acceptance. Occasionally authors may be asked to extend a long piece into a series. Series are usually by assignment only, and assignments are to seasoned authors who have contributed previous material to us, or have an adequate portfolio of published clips. Payment for series varies."

FILM COMMENT, 1865 Broadway, New York NY 10023. Editor: Richard Corliss. For film students, teachers and scholars. Has select group of writers which usually fills its needs. Query before sending mss. Enclose S.A.S.E.

FILM QUARTERLY, University of California Press, Berkeley CA 94720. Phone: 415-642-6333. Editor: Ernest Callenbach. Issued quarterly. Buys all rights. Pays on publication. Query first. Enclose S.A.S.E.

Nonfiction: Articles on style and structure in films, articles analyzing the work of important directors, historical articles on development of the film as art, reviews of current films and detailed analyses of classics, book reviews of film books. No restrictions on length. Must be familiar with the past and present of the art; must be competently, although not necessarily breezily, written; must deal with important problems of the art. Payment is about 1½¢ per word.

INSPIRATIONAL RADIO/TV PROGRAM GUIDE, 30W406 Roosevelt Rd., West Chicago IL 60185. For listeners to Christian radio and television programs. Feature magazine with listings of local Christian programming. Quarterly; 32-page national shell and 32-page local insert. Established in 1973. Circulation: 100,000. Rights purchased vary with author and material. Usually buys all rights, but will reassign rights to author after publication. Buys 10 mss a year. Payment within 30 days of acceptance. Will send free sample copy to writer on request. Will consider photocopied submissions, but only if guaranteed not to be simultaneous submissions. Submit seasonal material (Christmas, Thanksgiving, Easter) 4 months in advance. Reports on material accepted for publication in 30 days. Returns rejected material in 5 days. Query first or submit complete ms. Enclose S.A.S.E.

Nonfiction and Photos: "We have a national shell which is the same in each of 12 cities, but each city has its own custom packaged insert listing all Christian programming from every station. We like behind-the-scenes stuff on personalities. Not the usual life story or hero worship type of thing. Must be something unique. Get the subject's views on how his faith relates to current issues, etc. Personality features on Christian recording artists, actors, radio and TV celebrities. We want entertaining features on people whose lives and views communicate, not some freelancer's ideas on how to live the Christian life. No sermons, exhortations, etc. Holiday pieces are good." Length: 800 to 2,000 words. Pays $100 to $225. Pays $15 to $25 for b&w photos purchased with mss. Minimum 5x7; clean and sharp. Pays $25 to $40 for color transparencies. Photos may also be purchased on assignment. Captions optional.

Fiction: Will buy one piece of religious fiction per year. Must relate to subject matter. Length: 1,000 to 1,500 words. Pays 10¢ per word.

MODERN MOVIES' HOLLYWOOD EXPOSED, Magazine Management Co., 575 Madison Ave., New York NY 10022. Editor: Sherry Romeo. Magazine; 72 (8½x11) pages. Monthly. Circulation: 250,000. Buys all rights. "All material is freelance, but the majority is on assignment, not on speculation, but would be interested in people contacting us who have access to stars for assignments." Pays on acceptance. Submit seasonal material 12 weeks in advance. Reports in 4 to 6 weeks. Query first; new writers should send sample of writing. Enclose S.A.S.E.

Nonfiction and Photos: "We have interviews with stars, gossip columns, articles; we have a chattier style, a *New York Magazine* style. We don't want articles copied from other sources; no how-to stuff." Pays $50 minimum. Photos purchased with or without ms, or on assignment. Captions optional. Pays $15 minimum for b&w photos.

MODERN SCREEN MAGAZINE, 1 Dag Hammarskjold Plaza, New York NY 10017. Editor: Joan Thursh. Monthly. No fiction or verse. Buys first serial rights. Payment on acceptance. Will consider photocopied submissions. Reports in two weeks. Will send sample copy on request. Query first. Enclose S.A.S.E.

Nonfiction: Uses true articles on movie stars, TV stars, show business personalities and figures who attract world attention. Length: up to 2,000 words. Pays a minimum of $200.

Photos: Buys singles and photo series in b&w and color. Buys pix submitted with mss. Uses contacts up to 8x10. Pays $20 and up.

How To Break In: "We're starting a new section which will contain something along the lines of news briefs — but briefs which are heavily slanted toward a specific personality and which will hold up two-and-a-half to three months after they're published. It would be a good way to break in since we have been tending to stick with the people we know for features. The best way to describe these briefs would be to say they will be like little features, but about people or incidents that can't really be blown up into a full-length story. Interesting information about less important people. But it should be written with a feature story slant. Otherwise if you feel you have a good interview or a good contact, write and tell me what you've got. No need to query for the briefs."

MOTION PICTURE, Macfadden-Bartell Corp., 205 E. 42nd St., New York NY 10017. Editor: Patricia Sellers. Audience is "female high school graduates, 20 to 70 years old." Monthly. Buys all rights. Buys approximately 140 mss a year. Pays on publication. Submit seasonal material 3 months in advance. Reports in 1 week. Query first. Enclose S.A.S.E.

Nonfiction: Uses short, interesting stories about top Hollywood stars; sharply angled. These can vary from personality profiles to timely, newsworthy stories, or stories involving the basic emotions and slanted for self-help. "We specialize in 'camera-closeups'." Buys interviews, profiles, exposes. Length: 2,500 to 4,000 words. Pays $200 minimum for full-length articles. Pays less for self-contained features.

Photos: Wants top-rate black and white; color photography (any size). Pays $25 minimum for b&w; $200 for full-page color.

MOVIE LIFE, 575 Madison Ave., New York NY 10022. Editor: Seli Grove. "Basically, for women, from 9 to 90, interested in peeking at the private lives of entertainment stars." Established in 1938. Monthly. Circulation: 225,000. Buys all rights. Buys about 150 mss a year. Payment on publication. Will not consider photocopied or simultaneous submissions. Reports on material in 3 to 6 weeks. Query first. Enclose S.A.S.E.

Nonfiction and Photos: Feature articles on well-known movie and television personalities. Interviews. Length: 1,500 to 2,000 words. Pays $125 to $200. 8x10 b&w photos purchased with accompanying mss for $25, or without extra payment, depending on the article and photos.

How To Break In: "Let's suppose Elvis comes to town. Check with the local paper to find out who is handling publicity for him. Then see if you can arrange an interview. Also, please get a letter from the press person acknowledging that such an interview actually took place. I'm afraid to say, we sometimes get accounts of meetings which never happened, so we do have to check. You should read our magazine and become familiar with the style. We like first-person accounts and can help out with the style if the facts are good. Our stories tend to be very personal — more visceral then intellectual. Don't be blunted by what you think I might not like. And don't overlook doing some library research for some interesting background on your subjects."

MOVIE MIRROR, TV PICTURE LIFE, PHOTO SCREEN, 355 Lexington Ave., New York NY 10017. Editor of *Movie Mirror:* Joan Goldstein. Editor of *TV Picture Life:* Lyla Aubry. Editor of *Photo Screen:* Madeline Eller. Monthlies. Buys 10 to 12 mss a month. Pays on acceptance. Submit complete ms. Reports promptly. Enclose S.A.S.E.

Nonfiction: "The most desired sort of story is the fresh and strongly angled, dramatically told article about the private life of a leading motion picture or television star. Categories of stories popular with readers (they've changed little over the years): romantic love, weddings, married life, babies, parent/child relationships, religion, health, extra-marital affairs, divorces, dangerous moments survived, feuds. The major difference in fan mag writing then and now is the increased frankness permissible in today's articles. When many stars talk forthrightly about living together without marriage, bearing children out of wedlock, personal sexual inclinations, etc., fan magazine editors have little choice but to go along with contemporary trends. The object, no matter the category of article, is to tell the reader something she did not already know about a favorite performer, preferably something dramatic, provocative, personal. Our readers are female (over 90% of them), youngish (under 45), and often are wives or daughters of bluecollar workers. It is our purpose to bring a bit of vicarious excitement and glamour to these readers whose own lives may not be abundantly supplied with same. Stars they want to read about now are: (TV) Dean Martin, Mary Tyler Moore, Redd Foxx, Carol Burnett, Sonny Bono, Cher, Peter Falk, William Conrad, and the leads of 'All In The Family,' 'The Waltons,' 'M*A*S*H,' and 'Maude'; (Movies) Elvis Presley, Liz Taylor, Barbara Streisand, Liza Minnelli, Paul Newman, Steve McQueen, John Wayne, Robert Redford. While most of our manuscripts are written by top magazine and newspaper writers in Hollywood and New York, we have an open-door policy. Any writer able to meet our specific editorial needs will get a 'read' here. Until we know your work, however, we would have to see completed manuscripts rather than outlines. Writers outside the two show biz meccas might keep in mind that we are particularly interested in hometown stories on contemporary celebrities. Average length for articles is 2,000 words. Pay starts at $200, going considerably higher for genuine scoops."

MOVIE STARS, 575 Madison Avenue, New York NY 10022. Editor: Ann Hamilton. For housewives "ages 22 to 44 with a high school education." Established in 1935. Buys all rights. Buys 100 mss a year. Payment on publication. Query required. Enclose S.A.S.E.

Nonfiction and Photos: General subject matter consists of "articles on movies and television personalities." Pays $150 for a 7- to 8-page article. Pays $25 per b&w photo.

How To Break In: "There are two good ways to break in. One is to come up with a cover-line idea we can use on a particular celebrity. Suggest it to us before starting the piece. The other is to have access to a celebrity personality with whom you can do a personal interview. Query first and try to include some personal information about yourself — a resume is good. When you're doing a piece for us, check with me after you've done the interview so we can agree on the right angle to take with the piece."

MOVIE WORLD, Magazine Management Fan Magazines, 575 Madison Avenue, New York NY 10022. Editor: Jan Mussachio. Fan magazine covering TV and movie fields. Monthly. Buys all rights. Pays on acceptance. Query first on angle and title on unassigned material. Enclose S.A.S.E.

Nonfiction and Photos: "News stories concerning top TV and movie personalities may be submitted in interview or third-person format, although the interview preferred. Articles with melodramatic, emotional impact are acceptable, but writing must be clear, witty, and fresh in its approach. Mss should be gossipy and fact-filled and aimed toward working class adults." Length: 1,500 to 2,500 words. Pays up to $200 for exclusive interviews. Pays up to $35 for b&w and up to $1,000 for color used for cover material.

PERFORMING ARTS IN CANADA, 52 Avenue Rd., Toronto, Ont., Canada. Phone: 416-921-2601. Chairman, Editorial Advisory Board: Arnold Edinborough. For "well-educated persons between 25 and 45 with special interest in theater, music, dance." Quarterly. Circulation: 30,000. Buys first rights. Buys 30 to 40 mss a year. Pays 2 weeks following publication. Will send a sample copy to a writer for 50¢. Reports in 3 to 6 weeks. Query first. Enclose S.A.E. and International Reply Coupons.

Nonfiction: "Articles covering Canadian performing arts." Material for department "What's Going On." Length: 200 to 1,200 words. Pays $20 to $75.

PHOTOPLAY, 205 East 42nd St., New York NY 10017. Editor: Lynne Dorsey. For women, ages 18 to 50. Monthly. Buys all rights. Pays on acceptance. Will send a sample copy to a writer on request. Reports in 2 weeks. Query first. Enclose S.A.S.E.

Nonfiction and Photos: Uses strongly angled stories on "stars"—in all entertainment media, all walks of life—that would appeal to women of all ages. Pays $200 minimum. Buys pix of "stars" with or without ms. Payment varies with pix subject and exclusivity. Pays $25 minimum for b&w; $150 minimum for color.

PLAYBILL MAGAZINE, 151 E. 50th, New York NY 10022. Issued monthly; free to theatregoers. Buys first and second U.S. magazine rights. Enclose S.A.S.E.

Nonfiction: The major emphasis is on current theatre and theatre people. On occasion, buys humor or travel pieces if offbeat. Wants sophisticated, informative prose that makes judgments and shows style. Uses unusual interviews, although most of these are staff written. Style should be worldly and literate without being pretentious or arch; runs closer to *Harper's* or *New Yorker* than to *Partisan Review*. Wants interesting information, adult analysis, written in a genuine, personal style. Humor is also welcome. Between 1,000 and 2,500 words for articles. Pays $100 to $300 each.

How To Break In: "We're difficult to break into and most of our stuff is assigned. We don't take any theater pieces relating to theater outside New York. We also have stuff on boutiquing, fashions, men's wear, women's wear. The best way for a newcomer to break in is with a short humorous or satirical piece — no more than 1,500 words. A number of people have come in that way and some of them have subsequently received assignments from us."

PRE-VUE, P.O. Box 20768, Billings MT 59102. Editor-Publisher: Virginia Hansen. "We are the cable-TV guide for southern Montana; our audience is as diverse as people who subscribe to cable TV." Weekly magazine; 32 to 40 pages. Established in 1969. Circulation: 15,000. Not copyrighted. Buys about 40 feature-length articles a year; 12 or so shorts, and 100 pieces of light, short verse. Payment on publication. Will send free sample copy to writer on request. Will consider photocopied submissions, if they are legible. Will consider simultaneous submissions, but prefers the first look. Submit seasonal material (any holiday, but with a regional tie-in) 2 months in advance. Reports in 2 to 6 weeks. Query first. Submit complete poetry mss. Enclose S.A.S.E.

Nonfiction and Photos: "Subject matter is general, but must relate in some way to television or our reading area (southern Montana). Lead articles must be of as much interest to a reader in Missoula (western Montana) as they are to a reader in Miles City (eastern Montana). We also use articles on history, the arts, sports, profiles, etc. Since we are the only cable-TV and entertainment guide in a weekly magazine format in our area, a prospective contributor might do well to read back issues. We would like articles to have a beginning, middle and end; in other words, popular magazine style, heavy on the hooker lead. We're interested in holidays and special events in our reading area." Informational, how-to, personal experience, interview, profile, inspirational, humor, historical, think pieces, nostalgia, travel, TV or book reviews, spot news, successful business operations, new product. Feature length: 700 to 1,200 words. Shorts: 50 to 500 words. Pays minimum of 2¢ per word. 8x10 (sometimes smaller) b&w photos purchased with mss or on assignment. Pays $3 to $6. Captions required. Department Editor: Virginia Hansen.

Poetry: Traditional forms, blank verse, free verse, light verse. Length: 2 to 8 lines. Pays $2.

Fillers: Short humor, local history and oddities. Length: 50 to 500 words. Pays minimum of 1¢ per word.

SCREEN AND TV ALBUM, Ideal Publishing Corp., 575 Madison Ave., New York NY 10022. Editor: Seli Groves. Entertainment news magazine published every 2 months. Audience ranges from sub-teens to mature people in their 60's and "we try to fill the magazine with personalities appealing to these various ages." Buys all rights. Buys 4 to 6 mss a year. Pays on publication. Will send sample copy to writer for 75¢. Query first. Reports within 10 days. Enclose S.A.S.E.

Nonfiction and Photos: Stories concerning popular personalities of film, TV and recording industries must be of human interest, concerned with some personal, not professional, aspect of personality's life. "Give me your ideas on a story, plus your sources for same. Interviews (caution) will be checked through from this end with the personality before any such article is purchased. Check the new TV shows, the new films, and write about them." Recently published articles include "Cher and the Baby Sonny Won't Let Her Keep" (this refers to an item, since withdrawn by Sonny Bono, concerning a possible custody suit for their daughter; writer submitted idea at right time.) Interview and photo articles. Length: 1,000 to 3,500 words. "Payments arranged per article prior to transfer of material from writer to editor. I will quote price or discuss asked-for payment." Please query Ms. Sheila Steinach on any photo submission.

How To Break In: "One thing you might try to do is take a look at the second banana on a hit TV show and see what he's doing. We're interested in new personal angles — perhaps he was adopted and is willing to talk about it. We're using longer pieces now and more photos. The main thing a freelancer has to prove to me is that he is dependable, can meet deadlines, can take positive editorial criticism, and is accurate."

SCREEN STARS, Magazine Management Fan Magazines, 575 Madison Avenue, New York NY 10022. Editor: Adrienne Baker. Monthly. Buys all rights. Payment on acceptance. Query first on angle and title on unassigned material. Enclose S.A.S.E.

Nonfiction and Photos: "Fan magazine covering TV and movie fields. News stories concerning top TV and movie personalities may be submitted in third-person format, although the interview is preferred. Articles must contain new material. Stories with melodramatic, emotional impact are acceptable, but writing must be clear, witty, and fresh in its approach. Mss should be gossipy and fact-filled and aimed toward working class young adults." Length: 1,500 to 2,500 words. Pays $100; up to $200 for exclusive interviews. Pays up to $35 for b&w and up to $1,000 for color used for cover.

SCREEN STORIES, 575 Madison Ave., New York NY 10022. For women, ages 21 to 50. Monthly. Circulation: 150,000. Buys approximately 100 mss a year. Pays on publication. Will send a sample copy to a writer for 50¢. Submit seasonal material 4 months in advance. Query first. Enclose S.A.S.E.
Nonfiction: "Movie condensations and stories about the personal lives of the stars. We feature full-length movies and nostalgic articles on past stars and films." Buys interviews, personal experience articles. Pays $75 to $300.

SQUARE DANCE, P.O. Box 788, Sandusky OH 44870. Editors: Stan and Cathie Burdick. For square dancers and callers. Special issues include vacations (April) and fashions (July). Monthly. Circulation: 15,000. Buys all rights. Pays on publication. Will send a sample copy to a writer on request. Submit seasonal material 2 to 3 months in advance. Reports in 1 week. Enclose S.A.S.E.
Nonfiction and Photos: Articles about "dancing, leadership and teaching techniques, organizing and conducting clubs, positive attitudes." Buys how-to's, personal experience and inspirational pieces, interviews, profiles, humor, spot news, think pieces, historical and travel articles, photo essays. Length: 600 to 800 words. Pays 50¢ a column inch (usually averages out to about 1¢ a word). Purchases photos with mss or with captions only. B&w glossy, any size. Pay rate based on $5 per page.
Fiction: Would like a good story related to square dancing. Buys humorous, historical, and contemporary problem stories. Length: 800 to 1,000 words. Pays 50¢ a column inch (usually averages out to about 1¢ a word).
Poetry and Fillers: Light verse. Pays 50¢ a column inch (usually averages out to about 1¢ a word). Puzzles are used as fillers.

TAKE ONE, Box 1778, Station B., Montreal H3B 3L3. Que., Canada. Phone: 514-843-7733. Editorial Director: Joe Medjuck. Editor: Peter Lebensold. For anyone interested in films in modern society. Not a fan magazine. Bimonthly. Circulation: 25,000. Buys North American serial rights. Pays on publication. Will send free sample copy on request. Reports in 3 weeks. Query preferred. Enclose S.A.E. and International Reply Coupons.
Nonfiction and Photos: Interviews, articles, photo stories, reviews. Anything having to do with film. Articles on directors, actors, etc. On new or classic films, on aspects of the industry, current or historical, on aesthetic developments. Anything of interest in this broad area of the communication arts. No taboos at all. Style should be lively, informed and opinionated rather than "newspaperese." Length: 700 to 5,000 words; 1,000 words maximum, reviews. Pays about 2¢ per word. Purchases photos with mss. Events, people in film and/or TV. 8x10 b&w glossy. Pays $5 minimum for photos, but tries to get most photos free from film distributors.
Fiction: Very rarely buys fiction. Query first. Maximum 5,000 words. Also uses short-shorts under 2,000 words. Must deal with some aspect of film. No taboos. Pays about 1¢ per word.
Poetry: Rarely published. Must deal with some aspect of film. No taboos. Pays $10 minimum.
Fillers: Puzzles. Must deal with some aspect of film or TV. Pays $10 minimum.
How To Break In: "Most writers who have been published in our magazine started out by sending us a review, interview or article on some subject (a film, a filmmaker) about which they cared passionately and (more often than not) had — as a result of that caring — a particular degree of expertise. Often they just happened to be in the right place at the right time (where a film was being made, where a filmmaker was making a public appearance or near where one lived)."

TV & MOVIE SCREEN, 355 Lexington Ave., New York NY 10017. Editor: Roseann C. Hirsch. For people interested in television and show business personalities.

Magazine; 74 pages. Monthly. Circulation: 500,000. Rights purchased vary with author and material. Usually buys all rights. Buys 100 mss a year. Pays on acceptance. Query first. Reports immediately. Enclose S.A.S.E.

Nonfiction and Photos: Celebrity interviews and angle stories; profile articles. Punchy, enticing and truthful. Recently published articles include "Elvis Blamed in Bedroom Scandal!" (true story of girls trying to break into Elvis' bedroom). Length: 1,000 to 1,500 words. Pays $150 to $200. Photos of celebrities purchased without ms or on assignment. Pays $25 each.

TV DAWN TO DUSK, 575 Madison Ave., New York NY 10022. Editor: Jean Thomas. For daytime television viewers. Established in 1970. Monthly. Circulation: over 200,000. Buys all rights. Pays on publication. Study magazine and query first. Enclose S.A.S.E.

Nonfiction: Personality pieces with daytime TV stars of serials and quiz shows; main emphasis is on serial stars. Also interested in some women's interest material. Buys interviews, personality pieces, round-up articles, how-to's, profiles, and personal experience articles related to daytime TV only. Length: approximately 6 pages. Pays $150 minimum.

How To Break In: "The key thing for breaking in here is to have access to one of the daytime TV personalities. Perhaps you're an old childhood friend, classmate, or you once worked together. Try to choose a character whose story line is evolving into a bigger and more important role. But query first; don't waste your time doing a story on a character who will be going off the show soon. For writers who don't have this kind of access, the best bet is a career retrospective of one of the major characters who has been on for years. You'll need to check a library for clippings."

TV GUIDE, Radnor PA 19087. Executive Editor: Alexander Joseph. Published weekly. Study publication. Query first (with outline) to Andrew Mills, Assistant Managing Editor. Enclose S.A.S.E.

Nonfiction: Wants offbeat articles about TV people and shows. This magazine is not interested in fan material. Also wants stories on the newest trends of television, but they must be written in layman's language. Length: 200 to 2,000 words. Pays $250 minimum.

Photos: Uses professional high-quality photos, normally shot on assignment, by photographers chosen by *TV Guide*. Prefers color. Pays $150 day rate against page rates—$250 for 2 pages or less.

TV RADIO MIRROR, 205 East 42nd St., New York NY 10017. Editor: Patricia Canole. For women of all ages. Pays on acceptance. Reports immediately. Query first. Enclose S.A.S.E.

Nonfiction and Photos: "As the largest 'fan' magazine in the TV field (and radio to a lesser extent), we publish each month 12 or so personal articles about the private lives of television's most popular performers, i.e., stars of such shows as 'M*A*S*H,' 'Rhoda,' 'Maude,' 'All in the Family,' etc., as well as many of the daytime television dramas. Love, marriage, family life, religion, these are the broad human-interest areas which produce the stories preferred by *TVRM*. Except for standard staff-written features, all stories are from freelancers, usually based in Hollywood or New York. But we are a wide-open market to any writer who can meet our requirements. It is possible that a writer who lives, for example, in the home town of a major TV star could click at *TV Radio Mirror* by doing an in-depth 'home-town report' on this celebrity, derived from interviews with his former teachers, friends, employers, family members, etc." Length: prefers 2,000 to 3,000 words. Pays 10¢ a word and up. Photos are bought from top-quality freelance photographers.

TV RADIO TALK, 575 Madison Ave., New York, NY 10022. Monthly. Buys first rights. 100% freelance. Reports in three weeks. Query first. Enclose S.A.S.E.

Nonfiction and Photos: "Uses interview and third person stories on TV stars, movie stars, record personalities and others who are famous. The stories should be factual. We do not print fiction. We like stories that are fresh and exclusive. There should be conflict in any story suggestion. The slant is usually for the star. The writing should fit the subject; if a love story, tender; if a scoop, exciting." Length: up to 2,000 words. Pays minimum of $300 on acceptance; pays higher for top stories. Pays $20 up for photos; any size.

TV SHOWPEOPLE, 180 Madison Ave., Suite 1103, New York NY 10016. Editor: David Houston. For TV enthusiasts who want background information on personalities, background people (producers, directors, writers, etc.) Magazine; 66 (8½x11) pages. Established in 1975. Monthly. Circulation: 400,000. Buys all rights. Buys about 100 mss a year. Pays on publication. Will send sample copy to writer for $1. Write for copy of guidelines for writers. No photocopied or simultaneous submissions. Reports on material accepted for publication in 1 month. Returns rejected material immediately. Query first. Enclose S.A.S.E.

Nonfiction and Photos: Interviews with top TV personalities. Articles on how shows are written, produced, taped or filmed. Occasional articles on new trends in entertainment (heavily researched); censorship, and the like. Occasional articles on the making of commercials. Material must be entertaining; must be benevolent even if critical of TV fare. Uses interviews, profiles, spot news and nostalgic articles (if related to TV). Interviews must, while not prying into unwelcome areas, be perceptive and yield a good picture of the personality's personality, character, ideas and life style. It is important to remember that this is *not* a fan magazine. Writer's manual available on request. Length: 1,000 to 2,000 words. Pays $100 to $200. The Local Scene column uses short pieces on popular local TV shows or personalities. Length: 500 words. Pays $40. Payment ranges from $10 for a single shot to $100 for a roll of color and a roll of b&w. Such photo series should yield a wide variety of poses and candids and "environment" long shots. Photo guidelines available on request.

How To Break In: "Show us previously published material that looks like our kind of writing. Live in Los Angeles or New York. Have ideas for original approaches to subject matter. Query first."

TV STAR PARADE, 575 Madison Avenue, New York NY 10022. Phone: 212-759-9704, Ext. 18. Editor: Kathy Loy. For "females, 13 to 60 years old, interested in private lives of TV and soap opera stars." Monthly. Circulation: 400,000. Buys all rights. Payment on publication. Submit seasonal material 2 months in advance. Reports in 2 to 3 weeks. Query first required with basic outline of proposed feature. Enclose S.A.S.E.

Nonfiction and Photos: General subject matter consists of interviews, "backstage stories," romance, etc. Approach should be a "chatty style with special attention to dialog, quotes from the stars. We like to use as many real interviews as possible. We never publish made up quotes or interviews. We do not want angles that have been dredged up time and again just to fill space. Interested in timely material." Buys informational, personal experience, interviews, profile, nostalgia, photo articles. "I would appreciate new ideas for columns." Length: "5 to 7 typewritten pages." Pays $150 to $200. Photos are purchased without mss and on assignment. Captions are optional. Wants candid b&w. Pays $25 per photo on publication.

WEEKDAY TV, Ideal Publishing Corp., 575 Madison Ave., New York NY 10022. Phone: 212-759-9704. Editor: Kathy Loy. Bimonthly. Buys all rights. Payment on publication. Will send free sample copy to writer on request. Query first. Enclose S.A.S.E.

Nonfiction: "Features daytime television stars. Soap opera stars and game show hosts are the subjects of most of the articles. Also use behind the scenes type articles and plot synopses of the soap operas from time to time. All story submissions must be the result of interviews, not articles written from clips and previously published information." Pays $100 to $200, depending on length and quality of article.

How To Break In: "Interview soap stars, then query us with your story ideas. Keeping up with the soap opera plots and cast changes is mandatory. Avid soap watchers are needed to write plot synopses and nostalgia pieces. The new writer might try us with a puzzle or game based on daytime celebrities or show characters."

WESTSCENE, P.O. Box 125, Loomis CA 95650. Phone: 916-652-7939. Editor: Charles F. Slater. For a highly educated audience with a keen interest in the performing arts. "Many subscribers are actors, directors, producers, dancers and singers, as well as those who are primarily devotees." Monthly tabloid newspaper; 12 to 16 pages. Established in 1974. Circulation: 1,800. Not copyrighted. Buys about 10 mss a month. Payment on publication. Will send free sample copy to writer on request. Will not consider photocopied or simultaneous submissions. Reports immediately. Query first or submit complete ms. Enclose S.A.S.E.

Nonfiction and Photos: "Criticism in dramatic art, ballet and opera; problem/solutions in producing for a live audience; technical innovations in the theatre; theatre history of the West; book reviews concerning the theatre, opera, ballet; features on individuals, especially those with unique accomplishments and potential who have not been discovered. Avoid pomposity and pedagese; (but not appropriate technical vocabulary); be brief, lucid and lively. We are pro-living theatre and welcome contributions that point out the cultural contribution of this art form. Our emphasis is on news of West Coast theatre with focus on little, civic, college and community production, although professional theatre is not ignored." Length: 500 to 1,500 words, occasionally to 2,000 words. Pays 15¢ per column inch plus 1-year free subscription. Pays $2 for b&w captioned photos purchased with or without mss.

Travel, Camping, and Trailer Publications

Publications in this category tell campers and tourists where to go, where to stay, how to get there, how to camp, or how to select a good vehicle for travel or shelter. Publications that buy how-to camping and travel material with a conservation angle are listed in the Nature, Conservation, and Ecology classification. Newspapers and Weekly Magazine Sections, as well as Regional Publications, are frequently interested in travel and camping material with a local angle. Hunting and fishing and outdoor publications that buy camping how-to's will be found in the Sport and Outdoor category. Publications dealing with automobiles or other vehicles maintained for sport or as a hobby will be found in the Automotive and Motorcycle category. Many publications in the In-Flight category are also in the market for travel articles and photos.

AWAY, 888 Worcester St., Wellesley MA 02181. Editor: Gerard J. Gagnon. For "members of the ALA Auto & Travel Club, interested in their autos and in travel. Ages range from approximately 20 to 65. They live primarily in New England." Slanted to seasons. Quarterly. Circulation: 240,000. Buys first serial rights. Pays on acceptance. Will send a sample copy to a writer on request. Submit seasonal material 6 months in advance. Reports "as soon as possible." Although a query is not mandatory, it may be advisable for many articles. Enclose S.A.S.E. for return of submissions or reply to queries.

Nonfiction and Photos: Articles on "travel, tourist attractions, safety, history, etc., preferably with a New England angle. Also, car care tips and related subjects." Would like a "positive feel to all pieces, but not the Chamber of Commerce approach." Buys both general seasonal travel and specific travel articles, for example, travel-related articles (photo hints, etc); outdoor activities; for example, gravestone rubbing, snow sculpturing; historical articles linked to places to visit; humor with a point, photo essays. Recently published articles include "Cape Cod's Winter Season" and "Basketball's National Shrine." "Would like to see more nonseasonally oriented material. Most material now submitted seems suitable only for our summer issue. Avoid pieces on hunting and about New England's most publicized attractions, such as Old Sturbridge Village and Mystic Seaport." Length: 800 to 1,500 words. "preferably 1,000 to 1,200." Pays approximately 10¢ per word. Photos purchased with mss; with captions only. B&w glossies. Pays $5 to $10 per b&w photo, payment on publication based upon which photos are used. Seasonally oriented cover photos pay higher; payment negotiable.

Fiction: Humor. "Should have a point and, perhaps, a New England flavor, angle or slant." Length: 500 to 800 words. Pays $50 to $80.

How To Break In: "New writers stand the same chance as experienced writers in getting published in *Away*. If the need, the quality, the content, the approach, and the timeliness are there, we buy the piece, regardless of whether it's the writer's first sale or the writer's 1000th sale. It should be emphasized that all writers would be wise to learn their market before sending material to *Away* or any other publication."

THE CAMPFIRE CHATTER, Box 248, Littleton MA 01460. Editor: Bryant "Red" Chaplin. For family audience, active family campers (RV and canvas); all outdoor interests. Format alternates; magazine and tabloid. Established in 1957. Monthly. Circulation: 14,000. Buys all rights, but will reassign rights to author after publication, "on request prior to purchase. Most material is staff-written." Pays on acceptance. Will send sample copy to writer for $1 plus S.A.S.E., which includes copy of each format and guidelines for writers. Submit seasonal material 6 months in advance. Reports in 1 to 2 months. Query first. Enclose S.A.S.E.

Nonfiction and Photos: "Articles must be about family camping or outdoor recreational activities for which family camping provides the means to the end. All material should be written to help the reader enjoy the experience written about. Travel, camping-related sports, how-to of RV use and tenting; helpful and interesting. We do buy equipment pieces, but don't stress it. We provide an escape for our readers from topical themes. If they want to be unhappy, let them read the daily paper and watch the boob tube." Informational, how-to, personal experience (but no first camping trip sagas), humor (camping), historical, think articles, nostalgia, travel, and technical (camping) articles. Length: 200 to 2,500 words, but prefers 1,500 to 2,000 words. Pays 2¢ per word on speculation, 3¢ per word on assignment, 15% bonus on how-to material. Cooking column accepts recipes and campground column accepts short reports on good campgrounds. No payment for either. Photos purchased with ms. Captions required. Any size b&w; 8x10 for cover shots, preferably verticals. Pays $2 minimum; $15 for cover shots; $1 for publicity release photos obtained by the author.

CAMPING & TRAILERING GUIDE, Rt. 1, Box 780, Quincy CA 95971. Phone: 916-283-0666. Editor-in-Chief and Publisher: Geo. S. Wells. Editor: Bill Shepard. "Our audience is made up of family campers ranging from young marrieds to retirees. Median age is mid-30's. All types of family camping." Established in 1959. Circulation: 90,000. Buys all rights, but will reassign rights to author after publication. Buys 30 to 45 mss a year. Payment on publication. Will send sample copy and guidelines for writers for 25¢ in coins or stamps. Will consider photocopied submissions. Submit seasonal material "4 months prior to cover date." Reports on material accepted for publication within 1 month. Returns rejected material within 1 month. Query first, describing article content and include first paragraph sample. Enclose S.A.S.E.

Nonfiction and Photos: "Articles on any phase of family camping and the whole range of equipment from backpacking gear through tents, tent-trailers, travel trailers, pick-up campers, van campers and motor homes. Family recreational vehicle-travel stories get the most space and this is also the category in which we are most likely to be overstocked. An out-of-the-way camping spot or an original treatment always gets close attention. Other welcome subjects include articles about how to build camping equipment, wilderness camping, foreign camping and many peripheral activities such as canoeing, small boat camping, cycling, nature photography and so on. First-person style and first-hand experience are preferred. Especially in demand at present are short articles (300 to 500 words and 2 or 3 b&w photos) about favorite or unusual campgrounds. Short how-to articles on almost any subject applicable to family campers. Article payment is $40 to $75; $25 for short-shorts."

Fillers: Camping tips. Length: 25 to 250 words. Pays $2.50 to $10.

CAMPING JOURNAL, Davis Publications, Inc., 229 Park Ave. S., New York NY 10003. Editor: Andrew J. Carra. For suburbanite couples, in their thirties, with 2 children; they own one type of recreational vehicle or another, or at least a tent; go camping during their vacations and on several weekends through the year. Established in 1962. Monthly. Circulation: 280,000. Buys all rights, but may reassign rights after publication. Buys 150 mss a year. Payment on acceptance. Write for copy of guidelines for writers. Reports in 5 weeks. Query first "one year in advance." Enclose S.A.S.E.

Nonfiction and Photos: "Travel articles, with information included in each article to show where the nearest camping facilities to that attraction may be; how they are equipped; how-to articles, involving basic camping skills, including recreational vehicle-type camping skills as well as backpacking skills; product round-up articles, which are not test reports, but rather general reports on the capabilities of the equipment and its cost. Write concisely, and never repeat yourself. Avoid the vernacular of the 'old-time' camper, because most campers today have never heard of many of those terms. Especially avoid colloquialisms. Intelligent, rather than folksy. Especially interested in new developments in campgrounds, new products, new ways to solve old problems, new insights into some of the more popular places that everyone seems to enjoy going back to every year. Any skills or adventure articles must be set in the context of a family camping situation. This means there must be something in the article that a child can relate to as well as his parents. Regular columns are presently assigned, but if a freelancer wants to offer his services in competition with an existing contributor, he is welcome to try." Length: 750 to 2,000 words. Pays $100 to $250. B&w photos and 4/c (35mm or larger transparencies) are purchased with mss. Captions required. "First-rate quality only." Nonfiction and Photo Dept. Editor: Martin Hanft.

Fillers: Short humor. Length: 750 words. Pays $50 to $150. Dept. Editor: Martin Hanft.

CARIBBEAN WORLD COMMUNICATIONS, INC., Suite 312, 1519 Ponce de Leon Ave., Santurce PR 00909. Editor: Al Dinhofer. Produces Sunday Travel section for *The San Juan Star.* Circulation: 65,000. Buys one-time rights. Buys approximately 10 to 15 mss a year. Pays on publication. Reports in 2 to 4 weeks. Enclose S.A.S.E.

Nonfiction and Photos: "Travel features of interest to the local market, with special interest in other areas convenient to this one—United States, Latin America, Mexico, Caribbean, Europe—especially Spanish-speaking areas." Photos purchased with mss. Length: 1,000 to 1,500 words. Pays approximately $15.

CHEVRON USA, P.O. Box 6227, San Jose CA 95150. Editor: Marian May. For members of the Chevron Travel Club. Quarterly. Buys North American serial rights. Pays within 60 days of acceptance. Will send a sample copy to a writer on request. Reports in 4 to 6 weeks. Prefers mss on speculation. Enclose S.A.S.E.

Nonfiction: Travel in western, eastern and southern U.S. — close-to-home trips or areas readily accessible by plane, train, bus. Historical emphasis — famous trails, towns, landmarks. Pictorials with nature and environmental themes. Family activities — sports, handcrafts. Each piece should have specific slant — tied to season, unusual aspect. In general, prefers specific subjects well-detailed rather than sketchy. Length: 500 to 1,500 words. Pays 15¢ a word and up. "But we'd rather settle on a package price."

Photos: Purchased with mss. Subject matter same as nonfiction. No empty scenics. Majority of photos must have active people in them, doing things or driving or touring or hiking. Prefers 2¼ square or 4x5 top quality 35mm. Pays $125 full page for color, minimum $50. For b&w, pays $50 full page, $35 minimum.

Fillers: Anecdotal material. Must be about travel, personal experiences. Length: about 200 to 250 words. Pays $25 each.

DISCOVERY MAGAZINE, Allstate Plaza, Northbrook IL 60062. Editor: Alan Rosenthal. For motor club members; mobile familes with above average income. "All issues pegged to season." Established in 1961. Quarterly. Circulation: 840,000. Buys first North American serial rights. Buys 40 mss a year. Payment on acceptance. Will send free sample copy to writer on request. Write for copy of guidelines for writers. Submit seasonal material 8 to 12 months in advance. Reports in 3 weeks. Query first. Enclose S.A.S.E.

Nonfiction and Photos: "Primarily travel subjects. Also automotive and safety. First-person narrative approach for most travel articles. Short pieces on restaurants must include recipes from the establishment." Travel articles and photos often are purchased as a package. Rates depend on how the photos are used. Color transparencies (35mm or larger) are preferred. Photos should show people doing things; captions required. Send transparencies by registered mail, with plenty of cardboard protection. Buys one-time rights for photography. Color photos are returned after use. Recently published articles include "Winter With Currier & Ives" (does the classic New England winter pictured by the renowned printmakers still exist today?) and "Abracadabra: Magic Is Everywhere" (audiences throughout the nation find that it's still fun to be fooled, as the crafty art of conjuring stages a clever comeback). Length: 1,000 to 2,500 words. "Rates vary, depending on type of article, ranging from $150 to $400 for full-length features." Photos purchased with accompanying mss; captions required. Photos also purchased on assignment.

Fillers: True, humorous travel anecdotes. Length: 50 to 150 words. Pays $10.

FAMILY HOUSEBOATING, 23945 Craftsman Rd., Calabasas CA 91302. Editor: Bill Estes. For owners and prospective buyers of houseboats. Bimonthly. Circulation: 50,000. Buys all rights. Pays on publication. Will send free sample copy on request. Reports in three weeks. Query desirable. Enclose S.A.S.E.

Nonfiction and Photos: Interested in articles of interest to houseboat owners and prospective buyers, including how-to pieces, personalities, houseboating waterways, technical and maintenance articles. Length: to 2,000 words. Pays $50 to $125, including photos.

HANDBOOK AND DIRECTORY FOR CAMPERS, 1999 Shepard Rd., St. Paul MN 55116. Phone: 612-647-7402. Editor: Richard L. Smith. For families whose members range in age from infancy to past retirement, and whose leisure interests are aimed primarily at outdoor recreation and travel with recreational vehicles providing the means to enjoyment of this new life style. Established in 1971. Annual. Circulation: 1,650,000. Buys all rights, but will reassign rights to author after publication. Buys 6 to 12 mss a year. Payment on acceptance. Will send free sample copy to writer on request. Write for copy of guidelines for writers. Will consider photocopied submissions. Reports in 30 days. Query first. Enclose S.A.S.E.

Nonfiction: "General articles on outdoor living and travel including how to prepare for trip and ways to gain more enjoyment from the going, staying, and coming home portions of it. In all cases, emphasis should be on the positive, fun aspects of travel and camping, not on the problems sometimes encountered. Writing should be readable rather than academic, clever rather than endlessly descriptive, tight rather than verbose. A good lead is considered essential. First-person articles and stories about personal experiences are not acceptable. We try to emphasize that camping is not only fun in itself, but is the means to all kinds of peripheral activities not normally available to the average family. Editorial slant is consistently on the enjoyment aspects of the experience." Informational, how-to, profile, humor, historical, nostalgia, photo, and travel articles. Length: 700 to 1,500 words. Pays $75 to $275.

Photos: Purchased with accompanying mss or on assignment. Captions optional. Uses color; 35mm and larger. Pays $200 for cover; $50 each for inside use.

THE LUFKIN LINE, Lufkin Industries, Inc., P.O. Box 849, Lufkin TX 75901. Editor: Miss Virginia R. Allen. For men in oil and commercial and marine gear industries; readers mostly degreed engineers. Each issue devoted to different areas where division offices located; that is, West Coast, Canada, Mid-Continent, Rocky Mountain, Texas, Gulf Coast, International. Established in 1924. Quarterly. Circulation: 12,000. Not copyrighted. Buys 4 to 8 mss a year. Payment on acceptance. Will send free sample copy to writer on request. Write for copy of guidelines for writers. Will consider photocopied submissions. Submit seasonal material 3 to 4 months in advance. Reports in 1 month. Query first for travel articles. Enclose S.A.S.E.

Nonfiction and Photos: "Travel articles. Subjects dealing with western U.S. and Canada, and (rarely) foreign travel subjects. Recently published articles include "Atlanta — Gracious and Vivacious" and "Houston Has Something for Everyone." Product articles staff written. Length: 1,000 to 1,200 words. Pays $50 per ms with illustrating photos. Color transparencies of seasonal subjects are purchased for inside front cover; pays $30. Illustrations for travel articles may be color prints or transparencies. No b&w photos are purchased. Color photos for travel articles may be secured from state tourist or development commissions.

THE MIDWEST MOTORIST, 3917 Lindell Blvd., St. Louis MO 63108. Editor: Martin Quigley. For "the typical rural type to the best educated in the Midwest." Publication of The Auto Club of Missouri. Bimonthly. Circulation: 275,000. Not copyrighted. Payment on acceptance. Will send free sample copy to writer on request. Reports in 2 to 6 weeks. Query first. Enclose S.A.S.E.
Nonfiction and Photos: "Features of interest to our motoring public. Articles cover important auto-oriented consumer issues as well as travel and auto interest pieces. We seek serious, well-documented consumer and ecology pieces, and are also interested in lighter material, focusing on unusual places to visit." Buys occasional interviews, travel-related humor, think pieces, photo essays. Length: about 1,200 words. Pays $50 to $200. B&w glossy photos purchased with mss. No color.

MINNESOTA AAA MOTORIST, Minnesota State Automobile Association, 7 Travelers Trail, Burnsville MN 55337. Editor: Ron D. Johnson. For professional people, educated farmers and businessmen and women interested in travel. Monthly magazine. Established in 1957. Circulation: 250,000. Buys first North American serial rights. Buys 20 to 30 mss a year. Payment on acceptance. Will send free sample copy to writer on request. Write for copy of guidelines for writers. Reports in 3 weeks. Submit complete ms. Enclose S.A.S.E.
Nonfiction and Photos: "Nonfiction articles on domestic and foreign travel, motoring, car care, which are well written and interesting. We have our own auto consultant for articles on automobile safety." Wants "well-written, interesting articles on places throughout the world, where our readers would like to go. We receive too many freelance articles on Florida." Submissions should "be readable and entertain and educate our readers." Buys how-to's, personal experience articles, interviews, humor, historical and travel articles, photo essays. Length: 800 to 1,200 words. Pays $150 minimum. Good b&w, 8x10, glossy photos purchased with mss. Pays $15 per photo.

MOBILE LIVING, P.O. Box 1418, Sarasota FL 33578. Editor: Frances Neel. Bimonthly. Buys first rights only. Pays on publication. Will send a free sample copy to a writer on request. Reports on submissions within 1 month. Enclose S.A.S.E.
Nonfiction: Articles on recreational vehicle experiences and travel via recreational vehicles. In travel articles, include names of parks to stay at while seeing the sights, etc. Hobbies involving recreational vehicles and how-to-do-it articles that apply to a general audience also wanted. Length: 1,500 words maximum. Pays 1¢ per word.
Photos: With captions and illustrating articles. B&w glossies only. Returned after use. Pays $3 each.

MOTOR CLUB NEWS, 5011 Capitol Ave., Omaha NE 68132. Editor: Barc Wade. For members of the Cornhusker Motor Club, an organization of car owners interested in travel, recreation, car care, consumer-connected problems. Magazine; 32 (8½x11) pages. Established in 1932. Every 6 weeks. Circulation: 80,000. Buys all rights, but will reassign rights to author after publication. Buys 12 to 15 mss a year. Pays on acceptance. Will send free sample copy to writer on request. Write for copy of guidelines for writers. Will consider photocopied submissions. Simultaneous submissions acceptable if notified. Reports in 2 weeks. Query first. Enclose S.A.S.E.
Nonfiction and Photos: Travel articles and those on car care. Car-related material. Approach should be very personal; based on personal experiences with reader's interests in mind, including costs of hotels, restaurants, etc. Thorough study of past issues is recommended so that the writer is familiar with style and types of articles

used. Length: 500 to 2,200 words. Pays 7¢ a word; $150 maximum. Exceptionally sharp b&w photos purchased with mss. Pays $5.

MOTOR NEWS, Auto Club Drive, Dearborn MI 48126. Phone: 313-336-1500. Travel Editor: Len Barnes. For travelers to all parts of the world. Special issues include Florida and the Caribbean (December); Outdoors and Camping (February); the Western United States (April); Michigan (May). Monthly. Buys first serial rights. Occasionally overstocked. "We like, but do not insist, on exclusive pictures." Pays on acceptance. Deadlines are 3 months before publication. "Therefore an article on a timely event or area that can be visited only at a certain time must be received well in advance of its intended publication. In some cases, we will hold an article in our files until it becomes timely." Reports in 3 weeks. Query first. Enclose S.A.S.E.
Nonfiction and Photos: Articles about "offbeat or well-known tourist objectives in the U.S." Likes material that describes these areas colorfully, yet which avoids travel writing cliches. "In addition to descriptions of things to see and do, articles should contain accurate, current information on costs the traveler would encounter on his trip. Items such as lodging, meal and entertainment expenses should be included, not in the form of a balance sheet but as an integral part of the article. Tips on what to pack and wear and other trip-planning features should be included." Besides straight travel articles, also interested in "things to do"—subjects concerning camping, hunting, fishing, boating and special events. "Always in the market for pieces about Michigan and like an article to have a Michigan slant if possible." Length: 800 to 1,200 words. Pays between $75 and $200. Requires four or five 8x10, b&w glossies with each article of the above-mentioned length. Pays, with 4 or 5 b&w photos, from $100 and $175, and sometimes higher for special subjects.

MOTORHOME LIFE & CAMPER COACHMAN, Trailer Life Publishing Co., Inc., 23945 Craftsman Rd., Calabasas CA 91302. Editor: Bill Estes. For owners and prospective buyers of motorhomes, mini-motorhomes, campers, camping-converted vans. Established in 1962. Published every 2 months. Circulation: 125,000. Buys all rights. Buys about 50 mss a year. Pays on publication. Will send sample copy to writer for $1. Write for copy of guidelines for writers. Submit seasonal material 3 months in advance. Reports in 1 month. Enclose S.A.S.E.
Nonfiction and Photos: "Articles which tell the owner of a self-propelled RV about interesting places to travel, interesting things to do. Do-it-yourself improvements to chassis or coach are heavily emphasized. Human interest and variety articles sought as well. All material must be tailored specifically for our audience. We cover only self-propelled recreational vehicles – no trailers." Informational, personal experience, humor, historical, personal opinion, travel, new product, and technical articles. Length: 2,500 maximum. Pays $50 to $125. Photos purchased with accompanying ms with no additional payment.

NATIONAL MOTORIST, 65 Battery Street, San Francisco CA 94111. Editor: Jim Donaldson. For California motorists who are members of the National Automobile Club. Every other month starting from January 1. Usually buys first publication rights. Query first or submit complete ms. Enclose S.A.S.E.
Nonfiction: Stories about anything that would be of interest to the average motorist who lives in California and does most of his motoring along the Pacific Slope and some of it in the other western states. Stories about car care, techniques for motor travel, interesting places to visit, people and events in western history that help illuminate the current scene; interesting outdoor activities and hobbies in which the reader can directly or vicariously participate; wildlife, hunting, fishing; all are possible stories. Prefers writing in the second or third person. Length: around 500 words or around 1,100 words. Pays 10¢ per word minimum.
Photos: Buys pictures submitted with mss; doesn't buy pictures submitted with captions only. Likes 8x10 b&w glossies, sharp, crisp, and dramatic. Uses some color. Pays $15 and up per b&w picture; $25 and up per color transparency.

How To Break In: "Just send us a query or a complete ms. We're usually on the lookout for good stories."

NORTHEAST OUTDOORS, 95 North Main St., Waterbury CT 06702. Phone: 203-757-8731. Editor: John Florian. Monthly. Circulation: 20,000. Buys all rights. Pays on publication. Will send free sample copy to writer on request. "Queries are not required, but are useful for our planning and to avoid possible duplication of subject matter. If you have any questions, or wish to cover some event live and ask about it first, please feel free to contact the editor." Deadlines are on the 10th of the month preceding publication. Reports in 15 to 30 days. Enclose S.A.S.E.

Nonfiction and Photos: Interested in articles and photos that pertain to outdoor activities in the Northeast. Recreational vehicle tips, maintenance and care are prime topics, along with first-person travel experiences in the Northeast while camping. "While the primary focus is on camping, we carry some related articles on outdoor topics like skiing, nature, hiking, fishing, canoeing, etc. In each issue we publish a 'Favorite Trip' experience, submitted by a reader, relating to a favorite camping experience, usually in the Northeast. Payment for this is $20 and writing quality need not be professional. Our pay rate is flexible, but generally runs from $20 for short, simple articles, $30 to $40 for features without photos, and up to $60 for features accompanied by 2 or more photos. Features should be from 300 to 1,000 words. Premium rates are paid on the basis of quality, not length. For photos alone we pay $7.50 for each 8x10 b&w print we use. Photo layouts bring $40."

OHIO MOTORIST, 6000 S. Marginal Rd., Cleveland OH 44103. Editor: A. K. Murway, Jr. For AAA members in 5 northeast Ohio counties. Established in 1909. Monthly. Circulation: 180,000. Buys one-time publication rights. Buys 30 mss a year. Payment on acceptance. Will send free sample copy to writer on request. Submit seasonal material 2 months prior to season. Reports in 2 weeks. Submit complete ms. Enclose S.A.S.E.

Nonfiction and Photos: "Travel, including foreign; automotive, highways, etc.; motoring laws and safety. No particular approach beyond brevity and newspaper journalistic treatment. Articles for travel seasons." Needs fuel crisis material. Length: 2,000 words maximum. Pays $25 to $75 per article including b&w photos. 8x10 b&w photos preferred. Purchased with accompanying mss. Captions required. Pays $8 to $20 for singles, although "rarely" purchases singles.

Poetry: Light verse. Length: 4 to 6 lines. Pays $6 to $8.

POINTS, 465 W. Milwaukee, Detroit MI 48202. Editor: Robert A. Sumpter. Bimonthly. Buys all rights. "Purchased material becomes property of General Motors." Query before making submission, as articles are generally set for the year ahead. When OK'd for submission (with good color transparencies, any size) submit as soon before deadlines as possible. Deadline for copy and photos is 6 months before date of issue. Deadline for September issue is March 1; for November issue, May 1; for January issue, July 1; for March issue, September 1; for May issue, November 1; for July issue, January 1. Enclose S.A.S.E.

Nonfiction: Articles should involve the how and why of hobbies, sports, and other subjects relating to travel. Family action, all types of camping and family outdoor activities in season or year 'round. Stress the how and why and unusual, little known aspects. Travel-related hobbies such as collecting rocks, desert treasures, beachcombing. Man- and woman-action, such as specific techniques of fishing, mountain climbing, scuba diving. How-to and equipment suggestions for beginner to the practicing enthusiast. Arts and crafts, such as stained glass from travel finds, leathercraft from hunting hides, on-site art such as landscape painting. Also parent-children feature such as teaching how to find way with and without compass, canoeing, archery, identifying wildlife by tracks. Action subjects should be able to be done anywhere, or in a broad area, mountains, plains, oceans and gulf, fresh waters, desert, etc. A particular place may be used as a focal point only to show "how it was done" and "why", and equipment and preparation suggestions. Other areas and sources of information should be telescoped into a paragraph or two. Prefers active prose, good presentation of how-to aspects from beginning stage to advanced. Photos should include how-to illustrations, results, and human interest on-site shot. Length: from 600 to 800 words. For single-page feature with color photos, pays to $150, $100 if color transparencies submitted with ms cannot be used. For two-page story with color photos, pays to $300. $200 without photos. For three-page feature with photos pays $400; without photos $300. This size seldom used.

Photos: Purchased with mss. See nonfiction above. Also pays to $150 for transparency for cover. Wherever natural to article, a GMC truck or recreational vehicle should be shown. "All competitive makes will render photo useless."

RELAX, The Travel & Recreation Magazine for Physicians, 136-138 N. Montezuma, Prescott AZ 86301. Editor: Helen Martin. For active physicians throughout the country. Magazine; 36 to 64 (8x11) pages. Established in 1972. Monthly. Circulation: 100,000. Buys all rights, but will reassign rights to author after publication. Buys 40 to 65 mss a year. Pays on publication. Will send free sample copy to writer on request. Write for copy of guidelines for writers, enclosing S.A.S.E. No photocopied or simultaneous submissions. Reports on material accepted for publication in 3 months. Returns rejected material in 2 months. Query first. Enclose S.A.S.E.

Nonfiction and Photos: "As a leisure-time publication, we want articles involving doctors; hobbies they enjoy, sports for participation, recreational ideas, and travel articles. Fishing, boating, golf, flying, tennis, automotive; recreational vehicles. Almost everything we use tells about a potential activity for our doctor/readers. Articles should give the reader a respite from the pressures of an active practice and should, whenever possible, include a doctor or a doctor's reactions to the subject. Although our material is slanted toward doctors, we use *no* medical material. No 'my hospital experience' material, no matter how humorous the writer may think it is." Recently published "Skiing Switzerland" an article which combined travel with activity. Length: 1,000 to 2,000 words. Pays $100 to $350. Sharp b&w glossies or 35mm or 2¼x2¼ color transparencies used with mss. No additional payment. Identifying captions required.

RV VAN WORLD, 16200 Ventura Blvd., Encino CA 91416. Editor: E. Pierce. For recreational van owners, campers, travelers. Established in 1973. Monthly. Circulation: 80,000. Buys all rights. Buys 15 to 30 mss a year. Payment on publication. Will send free sample copy to writer on request. Write for copy of guidelines for writers. Submit seasonal material at least 4 months in advance. (Winter camping and winter RV material needed in midsummer.) Reports on material in 1 week. Query first. Enclose S.A.S.E.

Nonfiction and Photos: Travel articles (exclusive of Southwest). How-to articles related to RV repair or maintenance. Semitechnical articles related to RVs. "Fairly breezy style while keeping in mind our audience. Any technical material must be accurate." Personal experience, humor, informational. Length: 1,800 to 2,000 words. Pays $40 per printed page in magazine (with 50 percent photos). Can use negatives and contact sheet; crisp focus, uncluttered background. Captions on separate sheet(s) keyed to numbers on photos. No extra payment for b&w. Color transparencies; 35mm or larger. Pays "$25 extra for color lead."

SEA BOATING ALMANAC, Box Q, Ventura CA 93001. A CBS Consumer Publication. Phone: 805-644-6043. Editor: William Berssen. For "boat owners in the Pacific Southwest." Established in 1965. Published in three editions to cover the Pacific coast. Circulation: 36,000. Buys all rights. Buys 12 mss a year. Payment on publication. Will send a sample copy to a writer for $5.25. Submit seasonal material 3 to 6 months in advance. Reports in 4 weeks. Query first. Enclose S.A.S.E.

Nonfiction and Photos: "This is a cruising guide, published annually in 3 editions, covering all of the navigable waters in the Pacific coast. Though we are almost entirely staff-produced, we would be interested in well-written articles on cruising and trailer-boating along the Pacific coast and in the navigable lakes and rivers of the western states from Baja California to Alaska inclusive." Pays $50 minimum. Pays $5 for 8x10 b&w glossies.

SUNBOUND MAGAZINE, Caldwell Communications, 747 Third Ave., New York NY 10017. Editor: Robert H. Spencer. For an estimated 200,000 readers who are traveling from Virginia or Kentucky to Florida; an intelligent audience with a wide range of interests. Magazine; 8x11. Established in 1975. Quarterly. Circulation:

200,000. Rights purchased vary with author and material. Buys all rights, but will sometimes reassign rights to author after publication; first serial rights; second serial (reprint) rights. Buys about 25 mss a year. Pays on acceptance. Will send free sample copy to writer on request. Write for copy of guidelines for writers. Reports in 2 to 6 weeks. Enclose S.A.S.E.

Nonfiction, Fiction, and Photos: Heavily weighted to articles in Florida area. Want thoughtfully developed theme. Travel articles plus more general pieces on food, the arts, sports and interesting life styles, especially if they relate to train destination area. Occasional humor. Business, sports and humor are hard to find well-written. Informational, interview, profile, historical, think articles, travel, successful business operations, and new product. Length: 1,000 to 1,500 words. Pays $50 to $400, but usually $100 to $200. Photos purchased with or without ms. Art Director: Ken Hine. Also buys humorous fiction. Length: 700 to 1,000 words.

TRAILER LIFE, 23945 Craftsman Road, Calabasas CA 91302. Editor: Art Rouse. Monthly. For owners and potential buyers of trailers, campers and motor homes. No manuscripts or photos will be returned unless accompanied by a stamped, self-addressed envelope. Buys all rights. Pays on publication, which may be many months after acceptance. Will send sample copy on request. Reports within 3 weeks. Enclose S.A.S.E.

Nonfiction: Uses articles about the art of using a trailer, camper or motor home, and the problems involved. Length: up to 1,500 words. Also uses how-to-do-it articles with step-by-step photos a necessity. Length: no more than 800 words. Combine as many operations in each photo or drawing as possible. Personal experience stories must be truly interesting. Merely living in or traveling by trailer is not enough. Uses travel articles with 3 to 6 good 8x10 glossy prints on trips that are inexpensive or unusual into areas which are accessible by a travel trailer or pickup camper. Length: 1,000 to 1,500 words. Also uses short travel pieces, with a couple of photos, of interesting places off the established routes. Length: 100 to 250 words. Allied interest articles are one of main interests—things that trailerists (people traveling in trailers) do or would like to do—boating, hiking, fishing, spelunking hobbies. When writing about allied sports or activities, a definite tie-in with travel trailers, motor homes or pickup campers is essential; the articles must be linked to the extent that you tell readers how their trailers fit into the sport, and where they can park while there. All travel articles should include basic information on trailer parking facilities in the areas, costs, locations, and time of year, etc. Payment varies, "based on the quality of the material submitted and how it's used, but $100 to $150 per article is present rate."

Photos: "We occasionally buy separate photos or cover shots, but most of these are shot on assignment. A good selection of photos must accompany all articles, but we will occasionally run a photo story by itself. Photos should be 8x10 glossy. Prints should be numbered and the photographer identified on the back, with numbers corresponding to a caption sheet. Photos should show action, not static poses, and should be as close up as the subject matter will allow."

TRAILER TRAVEL, Woodall Publishing Co., 500 Hyacinth Place, Highland Park IL 60035. Editor: Jerry Pinkham. For older couples and families with older children. Their interests are camping and traveling thoughout North America in recreation vehicles. Magazine; 125 pages. Established in 1936. Monthly. Circulation: 220,000. Rights purchased vary with author and material. Usually buys all rights, but may reassign rights to author after publication. Buys about 150 mss a year. Pays on acceptance. Will send free sample copy to writer on request. Write for copy of guidelines for writers. No photocopied or simultaneous submissions. Reports on material accepted for publication in 2 weeks. Returns rejected material in 1 week. Query first for all material except fillers. Enclose S.A.S.E.

Nonfiction and Photos: Travel articles slanted to vacation trips and areas that RV owners would like to see. General RV-related articles; insurance, storage, equipment, decorating, improvement ideas, new camping and traveling ideas, money-saving tips, RV life style stories, etc. "We try to present articles that are highly informative, useful, and inspirational in order to heighten our readers' knowledge and enthusiasm for their RV hobby. Our writing style is aimed at being enthusiastic, light, enjoyable, and easy to read and understand. Definitely not verbose; concise without being cryptic. Always slant material straight at an RVer's interest area. Most writers consistently try to break into the travel area and that's the most crowded basket of material we see. We prefer to see writers concentrate on innovative topics relating to RV's. No Bicentennial material — we're flooded already." Length: 1,500 to 3,000 words. Pays about 10¢ a word. No additional payment for photos used with mss. Captions required. Pays $100 for material used in RV Improvement Ideas column. **Fillers:** Newsbreaks, puzzles of the quiz type, clippings, used as fillers. Pays about 10¢ a word.

How To Break In: "We are not a book for the novice recreation vehicle owner, but we always welcome hearing from writers who can supply fresh and progressive ideas to the accomplished RV camper and traveler, be he a full-timer or a weekend camper."

TRAVEL AND LEISURE, 61 W. 51st St., New York NY 10019. Editor-in-Chief: Caskie Stinnett. Monthly. Circulation: 2,500,000. Buys first North American serial rights. Pays on acceptance. Reports in 1 week. Query first. Enclose S.A.S.E.

Nonfiction and Photos: Uses articles on travel and vacation places, food, wine, shopping, sports. Most articles are assigned. Recently published articles include "Where the Swedish Girls Go." It's Gotland, in the Baltic Sea and it has some of Europe's finest beaches; "Granada: City of the Alhambra," a distinguished writer finds there is more to the city than its Moorish landmark; "The Roman's Rome: Noisy Trastevere," this raucous city within a city has the sharpest flavor of Italy. Length: 1,000 to 3,000 words. Pays $500 to $3,000.

Photos: Makes assignments to photographers. Pays expenses.

How To Break In: "New writers might try to get something in one of our regional editions (East, West, South, and Midwest). They don't pay as much as our national articles, but it might be a good way to start. We use a lot of these pieces and they need be no more than 500 to 800 words, 1,000 tops. They cover any number of possibilities from traveling a river in a certain state to unusual new attractions. Recent examples include the South Street Seaport in New York City, Cooperstown, the Theme Parks in Texas, and Chicago's John Hancock Center."

TRAVELORE REPORT, 225 S. 15th St., Philadelphia PA 19102. Editor: Ted Barkus. For affluent travelers; businessmen, retirees, well educated; interested in specific tips, tours, and value opportunities in travel. Monthly newsletter; 4 pages, (8½x11). Established in 1972. Circulation: 10,000. Buys all rights, but will reassign rights to author after publication. Buys 25 to 50 mss a year. Payment on publication. Will send sample copy to writer for $1. Submit seasonal material 2 months in advance. Enclose S.A.S.E.

Nonfiction and Fillers: "Brief insights (25 to 200 words) with facts, prices, names of hotels and restaurants, etc., on offbeat subjects of interest to people going places. What to do, what not to do. Supply information. We will rewrite if acceptable. We're candid—we tell it like it is with no sugar coating. Avoid telling us about places in United States or abroad without specific recommendations (hotel name, how much, why, how long, etc.)." Pays $5.

TRIP AND TOUR, Allied Publications, Inc., P.O. Box 23505, Fort Launderdale FL 33307. Associate Editor: Marie Stilkind. For customers of travel agents. Bimonthly. Buys North American serial rights. Pays on acceptance. Reports in 2 to 4 weeks. Enclose S.A.S.E. for return of submissions.

Nonfiction and Photos: "Travel articles and photos on places outside the continental U.S.A." Buys humor and travel pieces. Length: 500 to 1,000 words. Pays 5¢ per accepted word. Pays $5 for photos purchased with mss.

VAGABONDING, P.O. Box 20095, Oklahoma City OK 73120. Editor: Joe Williams. For anyone interested in off-the-beaten-path travel by means of camping, van camping, hitchhiking, expeditions, trekking, voyaging, etc.; age group 18 to 70; college educated. Magazine; 24 (8½x11) pages. Established in 1974. Bimonthly. Circulation:

1,000 (based on 1st issue, May, 1974). In process of becoming copyrighted. Buys 30 mss a year. Pays on publication. Will send sample copy to writer for 50¢, and editorial guidelines sheet on request. Will consider photocopied and simultaneous submissions. Submit seasonal travel articles 1 to 2 months in advance. Reports within 1 week. Query first, "so we can throw out some ideas before completion of article, or send in your copy." Enclose S.A.S.E.

Nonfiction and Photos: Features articles *only* relating to "new out-of-the-way places and travel, or out-of-the-way things to do. More concerned about inexpensive travel and leading a nomadic life, articles about how to get there, costs, transport, sights, etc." Recently published features by freelancers included: "All About Freightering," a good factual article telling the ins and outs of freighters and how to go about getting information on them, and, "Getting Back to the Outback," Australian article that is interesting reading due to the author's style and his experiences working in a talc mine, and "Backpacking Across Asia," about experiences while hitchhiking around the world. *"Vagabonding* is interested in what is out there in the world to experience, how to go about it, where and when to do it cheaply and have fun in the process. Also needs material relating to travel such as how to get jobs overseas, transportation information and equipment reviews." Informational, how-to, personal experience, interview, humor, historical, all-photo travel, spot news, reviews of relevant books, and new vehicle and equipment products reviews. No length specifications. Pays $10 minimum; "If the work is good and is in the 8,000 to 9,000 word range, we will pay up to $50." Also seeking material to form equipment and vehicle review columns. Length: 2,000 words. Will pay "$10 to $50 depending on subject and quality."

How To Break In: "Write us giving an idea for an article. We'll bend over backwards trying to help the person develop it. *Vagabonding* is a good place for a fledgling young writer/beginner to break into print. As long as his/her material flows, reads well, and has a story to tell about off-the-beaten-path travel is all that matters."

WANDERLUST, P.O. Box 3338, Austin TX 78764. Editor: Joe Austell Small. "Primarily our readers are adult men and women who are interested in adventure, travel, the world's peoples, danger and personal ingenuity." Quarterly magazine; 64 (8⅛x10⅞) pages. Established in 1971. Circulation: 150,000. Rights purchased vary with author and material. May buy first North American serial rights or second serial (reprint) rights. Buys 60 mss a year. Payment on acceptance. Will send free sample copy on request. Write for copy of guidelines for writers. Will consider. photocopied submissions. Will not consider simultaneous submissions. Reports in 4 to 6 weeks. Query first. Enclose S.A.S.E.

Nonfiction and Photos: "We concentrate on 'swashbuckling,' true, action articles rather than the travelogue type. Accounts of actual experiences in distant lands which were unusual, suspenseful or dramatic in some way. Since these are firsthand accounts, or based on interviews with actual participants, we can only suggest that the emphasis is on adventurous happenings, not 'trips.' We are not encouraging war experiences where military action is concerned. Also, we use only four accounts with a U.S. locale in each issue." Length: roughly 1,000 to 5,000 words; 2,000 to 3,000 preferred. Pays from $50 for a short article (without photos) to $150 for longer articles with good photographs. No additional payment for b&w photos (any size); quality important. Photos are returned after publication.

WESTINDIES NEWSLETTER, 1519 Ponce de Leon Avenue, Suite 312, Santurce PR 00909. Editor: Al Dinhofer. For "travelers who are interested in the Caribbean area and seek current, unvarnished information that will facilitate travel, save them money, and take them to where it's happening." Monthly. Buys one-time rights. Payment on publication. Will send free sample copy to writer on request. Submit seasonal material 2 months in advance. Query first. Enclose S.A.S.E.

Nonfiction: "Our monthly newsletter covers all activities, good buys, festivals, complaints, opinions, comments, tips, suggestions, etc. All must be current, accurate and in telegraphic style." Buys 3 to 6 "special reports of 500 words, also news notes of some dozen sentences in newsletter." Pays 50¢ per typewritten line.

WILDERNESS CAMPING, 1597 Union St., Schenectady NY 12309. Phone: 518-374-2533. Editor: Harry N. Roberts. For self-propelled wilderness travelers; hikers, canoeists, ski tourers, snowshoers, mountaineers, kayakers and bicyclists. Published every 2 months; 64 (8½x10½) pages. Established in 1971. Circulation: 55,000. Buys first North American serial rights. Occasionally overstocked. Payment on publication. Will send sample copy to writer for $1. Write for copy of guidelines for writers. Will consider photocopied submissions. Will not consider simultaneous submissions. Submit seasonal material at least 4 months in advance. Reports as soon as possible. Query first or submit complete ms. Enclose S.A.S.E.

Nonfiction and Photos: How-to, where-to, what to take. Personal narratives. Not limited to the U.S. Topic should be treated honestly and vividly. "We could use more bicycle touring articles, both route-oriented, how-to-oriented and equipment-oriented." Profile, historical, nostalgia, personal opinion, technical. Length: 250 to 9,000 words. Pays $50 to $150. 5x7 or 8x10 b&w glossy photos purchased with or without mss. Pays minimum of $7.50. Captions optional. Pays minimum of $10 for color; $100 for covers. Must be at least 35mm transparencies.

Poetry: "Mainly interested in poetry related to subject matter; no set style." Length: open. Pays minimum of $10.

WISCONSIN AAA MOTOR NEWS, 433 West Washington Ave., Madison WI 53703. Phone: 608-257-0711. Editor: Hugh P. (Mickey) McLinden. Aimed at audience of domestic and foreign motorist-travelers. Monthly. Circulation: 211,000. Buys all rights. Pays on publication. Reports immediately. Enclose S.A.S.E. for return of submissions.

Nonfictin and Photos: Domestic and foreign travel; motoring, safety, highways, new motoring products. Length: 500 words maximum. Pays $25 minimum. Photos purchased with mss or with captions only. B&w glossy. Pays $10 minimum.

Union Publications

BOOT & SHOE WORKERS JOURNAL, 1265 Boylston St., Boston MA 02215. Editor: William N. Scanlan. Published by the Boot and Shoe Workers Union, AFL-CIO for "members of the union in the shoe industry. Aged from 18 to 70; men and women; skilled and unskilled." Established in 1896. Bimonthly. Circulation: 40,000. Not copyrighted. Pays on publication. Will send a sample copy to a writer on request. Will consider photocopied submissions. Reports in 2 weeks. Enclose S.A.S.E. for return of submissions.

Nonfiction: "Our members are interested in the advantages of union membership in matters of wages, fringes, human dignity and in achievements through membership. We publish articles on personal success in putting kids through school, overcoming employment handicaps, community achievements of union, etc. We like true case histories of dignity gained through union membership, community betterment created by labor-management cooperation, community contributions by union in place of antagonism arising from misunderstanding. Our readers actually strive for these results and want to know that such results are not beyond reach. We have been getting material slanted to retail and manufacturing interest; we want shop-oriented viewpoints by workers or writers who have been through the factory work scene. We are interested in stories of one-industry town whose shoe factory has been forced to close because of foreign shoe imports and the workers' stories of the effects of the closing." Also seeks material for the "Who Needs a Union?" department, which "uses stories of successful grievance processing, winning back wages for aggrieved workers, getting job reinstatement for unfairly fired worker, etc." Length: 250 to 1,500 words. Pays $10 to $35, "more in special cases."

Photos: Purchased with or without mss; captions optional. "Photo subjects should generally be the same as nonfiction, but ironic or unusual shots around which we can write a pro union story are okay." For 2¼x3¼ b&w glossy, pays $5.

UNION NEWS, P.O. Box 2812, Denver CO 80201. Phone: 303-266-0811. Editor: E. Paul Harding. Official publication of Oil, Chemical and Atomic Workers International Union. For union members. Monthly tabloid newspaper; 12 pages. Established in 1944. Circulation: 175,000. Not copyrighted. Payment on publication. Will send free sample copy to writer on request. Reports on material accepted for publication in 30 days. Returns rejected material in 10 days. Query first. Enclose S.A.S.E.
Nonfiction and Photos: Labor union materials, political subjects and consumer interest articles. Interview, profile, think pieces and exposes. Most material is done on assignment. Length: 2,000 to 6,000 words. Pays $100 to $200. No additional payment is made for 8x10 b&w glossy photos used with mss. Captions required.

UTU NEWS, (formerly *United Transportation Union News*), 14600 Detroit Ave., Cleveland OH 44107. Published by the United Transportation Union for members. Editor: Jim Turner. Weekly. Not copyrighted. Photos only. Pays on publication. Reports at once. Enclose S.A.S.E. for return of photos.
Photos: Current news shots of railroad or bus accidents, especially when employees are killed or injured. Prefers 8x10 b&w glossies. Pays $15 minimum.

Women's Publications

The publications listed in this category specialize in material of interest to women. Other publications which occasionally use material slanted to women's interests can be found in the following categories: Alternative, Child Care and Parental Guidance; Confession, Education, Farm, Food and Drink; Hobby and Craft; Home and Garden; Religious, and Sport and Outdoor publications.

AAUW JOURNAL, 2401 Virginia Ave. N.W., Washington DC 20037. Publication of American Association of University Women. Editors: Jean Fox and Pat Kresge. For women of all ages who have at least a B.A. degree. Published five times annually as a newspaper; twice as a magazine; 12 to 16 pages, newspaper; 48 pages, magazine. Circulation: 185,000. Buys first serial rights. Buys about 10 mss a year, but this varies. Pays on publication. Will send sample copy to writer for $1. Will consider photocopied and simultaneous submissions. Will consider cassette submissions. Reports in 3 to 6 weeks. Query first; "send sample of work first." Enclose S.A.S.E.
Nonfiction and Photos: "Material used in our journal is usually related to broad themes which AAUW is concerned with. For the next two years, these concerns include world pluralism, the human encounter, economic facts of life, living with less, the 21st century, deciding now, society and the individual. No special style or approach necessary. Emphasis on women and their efforts to improve society. B&w photos are purchased on assignment. Captions optional. Pay is minimal since we are a nonprofit organization." Pays $100 maximum.

BRANCHING OUT, Canadian Magazine for Women, P.O. Box 4098, Edmonton, Alberta, Canada T6E 4T1. Editor: Sharon Batt. For Canadian women; feminist, but not heavily radical, with literary interests, general political, historical, artistic and philosophical interests. Magazine; 48 (8½x11) pages. Christmas, summer holiday, etc., material, but no special theme issues. Established in 1973. Published every 2 months. Circulation: 4,000. Buys first North American serial rights. "Contributors may sell second rights to their work elsewhere." Buys 120 mss a year. Pays on publication. Will send sample copy to writer for $1. Write for copy of guidelines for writers. Will consider photocopied submissions. Submit seasonal material 4 months in advance. Reports in 3 to 4 months. Query first suggested for nonfiction. Enclose S.A.E. and International Reply Coupons.
Nonfiction: "Feminist, high literary quality; also general interest material and not necessarily feminist. We don't publish anything that is anti-feminist. Avoid rambling,

loosely constructed, highly personal reactions to feminist issues. Take a new or more subtle approach to feminist questions; don't rework the same hackneyed questions (abortion, for example) in the same old way. Interested in material about International Women's Year: women in other countries, life styles, problems." Recently published articles include "The Brazilian Woman as Writer" (good photos, clear style, unusual subject) and "Winning in the Sierras" (touches a female problem from a different angle, women working in gambling casinos). Length: 500 to 5,000 words. Pays $5 minimum for first contribution; $7.50 for second. Regular departments: Both Sides Now (1,000 to 2,000 words); opinion. Here and There (50 to 350 words); notices. Women in Business (1,000 to 2,500 words). Reviews (350 to 1,500 words). Pays $5 minimum.

Photos: Purchased with ms with no additional payment. Captions optional. Purchased without ms or on assignment also. Pays $5 each for art photos. 8x10 developed b&w, not negs. Photos should be women and female problems dealt with as art. Also photo essays on topics of general interest. Photo Department Editor: Alice Baumann-Rondez.

Fiction: Experimental, mainstream. No western, romance or confession. Fiction must be good; not sentimental; tightly constructed, high quality writing. Length: 1,000 to 5,000 words. Pays $5 minimum. Fiction Editor: Karen Lawrence.

Poetry: "We consider sets of poems up to about 8, as a unit. High artistic quality. Not interested in sentimental pieces." Length: open. Pays $5 minimum. Poetry Editor: Karen Lawrence.

BRIDE'S MAGAZINE, The Conde Nast Bldg., 350 Madison Ave., New York NY 10017. Phone: 212-692-5032. Editor: Barbara Donovan Tober. A very attractive publication for the first-time bride in her early twenties, her family and friends, the groom and his family. Magazine published 6 times a year. Established in 1934. Circulation: 300,000. Buys all rights. Buys about 25 mss a year. Payment on acceptance. Write for copy of editorial guidelines for writers. Reports within 6 weeks. Query first or submit complete ms. Enclose S.A.S.E.

Nonfiction: "We want articles on current psychological or sociological topics closely linked to marriage today. Keep in mind contemporary reappraisals of marriage roles but remember that each couple deserves the freedom to choose their life styles. Topics should be well-defined; material well-organized with a bright introduction and optimistic conclusion. Include interviews with authorities and/or young couples. First- or second-person narrative, roundtable, or quiz. Our primary concern is to help the bride with both her wedding and her marriage." Length: 1,500 to 2,500 words. Pays $200 to $500. Articles Editor: Peyton Bailey.

How To Break In: "Send us a well-written article that is both easy to read and offers real help for the bride as she adjusts to her new role. Nothing on wedding and reception planning, or etiquette, as these are written by staff."

CHATELAINE, 481 University Ave., Toronto M5W 1A7, Canada. Phone: 416-595-1811. Editor: Doris McCubbin Anderson. Managing Editor: Jean Y. Wright. For "Canadian women, from age 20 up, mainly homemakers, with or without outside jobs." Monthly. Buys first world serial rights in English and French (the latter to cover possible use in *Chatelaine's* sister French-language edition, edited in Montreal for French Canada). Pays on acceptance. Reports in 2 to 4 weeks. Query first. Enclose S.A.E. and International Reply Coupons.

Nonfiction: Articles examining all and any facets of Canadian life especially as they concern or interest Canadian women. Uses material on medical subjects; education. Also full-length personal experience stories with deep emotional impact. Subjects outside Canada need some Canadian tie-in. For all serious articles, deep, accurate, thorough research and rich detail are required. A shallow once-over-lightly treatment will not do for *Chatelaine*. Length: 2,000 to 3,600 words for full-length major pieces; 1,000 words minimum for minor or humorous pieces. Pays minimum $600 for a major research article.

Fiction: Settings should be Canadian if at all possible. In demand are romance; mystery or suspense; down-to-earth, human stories with real character impact. Also new emphasis is being placed on superior adult fiction. Preferably, the central character should be a woman. Very little demand for stories where the central character is a child (though children can be important secondary characters), or animal stories. Length: 3,000 to 4,000 words preferred, though this can vary depending on the story. No short-shorts. Payment starts at $400. Send fiction manuscripts to Miss Almeda Glassey, Fiction Editor.

How To Break In: "Query us with a page or two of outline on a specific article idea and with a specific angle. Probably a personal experience story, if the experience is dramatic and different enough, would be a good entree. We usually find that readers can provide one such story from their lifetime although they do not then move on to become writers."

COSMOPOLITAN, 224 West 57th St., New York NY 10019. Editor: Helen Gurley Brown. Managing Editor: Walter Meade. For career women, ages 18 to 34. Monthly. Circulation: 1,800,000. Buys all rights. Pays on acceptance. Not interested in receiving unsolicited manuscripts or queries, as editorial staff hasn't time to read them. All material is assigned to established, known professional writers who sell regularly to top national markets, or is commissioned through literary agents.

Nonfiction and Photos: Not interested in unsolicited manuscripts or queries; for agents and top professional writers, requirements are as follows: "We want pieces that tell a hip, attractive, 18- to 34-year-old, intelligent, good-citizen girl how to have a more rewarding life—'how-to' pieces, self-improvement pieces as well as articles which deal with more serious matters. We'd be interested in articles on careers, part-time jobs, diets, food, fashion, men, the entertainment world, emotions, money, medicine and psychology, and fabulous characters. We don't want very many cosmic pieces—about space, war on poverty, civil rights, etc." Uses some first-person stories. Logical, interesting, authoritative writing is a must, as is a feminist consciousness. Length: 1,200 to 1,500 words; 3,000 to 4,000 words. Pays $200 to $500 for short pieces, $750 to $1,500 for longer articles. Photos purchased on assignment only.

Fiction: Not interested in unsolicited manuscripts; for agents and top professional writers, requirements are as follows: "Good plotting and excellent writing are important. We want short stories dealing with adult subject matter which would interest a sophisticated audience, primarily female, 18 to 34. We prefer serious quality fiction or light tongue-in-cheek stories on any subject, done in good taste. We love stories dealing with contemporary man-woman relationships. Short-shorts are okay but we prefer them to have snap or 'trick' endings. The formula story, the soap opera, skimpy mood pieces or character sketches are not for us." Length: short-shorts, 1,500 to 3,000 words; short stories, 4,000 to 6,000 words; condensed novels and novel excerpts. "We also use murder or suspense stories of about 25,000 to 30,000 words dealing with the upper class stratum of American living. A foreign background is acceptable, but the chief characters should be American." Has published the work of Agatha Christie, Joyce Carol Oates, Evan Hunter, and other established writers. Pays about $1,000 and up for short stories and novel excerpts, $4,500 and up for condensed novels. Fiction Editor: Harris Dienstfrey.

ESSENCE, 300 E. 42nd St., New York NY 10017. Editor-in-Chief: Marcia Gillespie. For black women, age 18 to 34. Monthly. Circulation: 350,000. A publication that lives up to its image—nice pay, nice magazine. Buys first North American serial rights. Payment after publication. Will send sample copy to writer for $1. Will consider photocopied submissions. Reports in 4 to 6 weeks. Query first for nonfiction. "We like to see a sampling of the writer's work with queries. Queries should have well-developed ideas." Enclose S.A.S.E.

Nonfiction and Photos: "First-time authors must submit on speculation. Subjects that I am most interested in are as follows: life styles, family health, day care, education, women's health, money savers, budgets, people pieces that go beyond facades; new trends, politics, sex, religion, consumer affairs, shopping guides, careers, the arts, entertainment personality pieces; other black interest pieces." Length: 1,500 to 3,000 words. All mss must be typed and double-spaced. Pays $150 to $400. Photos purchased with or without mss. Black themes. Payment varies.

Fiction: High-quality stories with black themes. Some short-shorts. Length: 3,000 words maximum. Pays $150 to $300. Department Editor: Sharyn Skeeter.

Poetry: No limitations on subject matter, but must be of high quality. Length: 65 lines maximum. Pays $25 to $50.

How To Break In: "A new writer might aim for one of our departments that takes shorter pieces. 'Essence Woman,' for instance, runs anywhere from one to six profiles each month. 'Bring It Down Front' runs pieces of 1,500 to 2,000 words in which the writer analyzes a topic of special importance from his own viewpoint. In a recent issue a writer argued that packaging is inherently racist. A piece for either of these departments would give us the opportunity to see a writer's work."

FAMILY CIRCLE MAGAZINE, 488 Madison Ave., New York NY 10022. Editor: Arthur Hettich. For women/homemakers. An excellent consumer-pitch publication. Fine articles, family oriented as one would expect. Excellent decorating features, often within reach of most readers. Monthly. Usually buys all rights. Pays on acceptance. Will send a sample copy to a writer for 35¢. Reports in 6 weeks. Query first. "We like to see a strong query on something unusual or humorous, and are especially interested in people with credentials — economic, medical, or education." Enclose S.A.S.E.

Nonfiction: Women's interest subjects such as family and social relationships, children, humor, physical and mental health, leisure-time activities, self-improvement, popular culture, travel. Service articles, particularly dealing with the inflation and recession. For travel, interested mainly in local material, no foreign or extensive travel. "We look for human stories, told in terms of people. We like them to be down-to-earth and unacademic." Length: 1,000 to 2,500 words. Pays $250 to $2,500.

Fiction: Occasionally uses fiction relating to women. Buys short stories, short-shorts, vignettes. Length: 2,000 to 2,500 words. Payment negotiable. Minimum payment for full-length story is $500.

Fillers: Short, women's service type or family oriented. Short humor, how-to, or inspirational. 500 words. Pays $100 and up.

FARM WIFE NEWS, 733 N. Van Buren, Milwaukee WI 53202. Editor: Carol Haiar. For farm and ranch women of all ages; nationwide. Established in 1970. Circulation: 150,000. Not copyrighted. Buys over 400 mss a year. Payment on publication. Will send free sample copy to writer on request. Write for copy of guidelines for writers. Will consider photocopied submissions. Submit seasonal material 4 to 6 months in advance. Reports in 1 month. Query first or submit complete ms. Enclose S.A.S.E.

Nonfiction and Photos: "We are always looking for good freelance material. Our prime consideration is that it is farm-oriented, focusing on a farm woman or a subject that would appeal especially to her." Uses a wide variety of material: articles on vacations, daily life, sewing, gardening, decorating, outstanding farm women, etc. Topic should always be approached from a rural woman's point of view. Informational, how-to, personal experience, interview, profile, inspirational, humor, think pieces, nostalgia, personal opinion, travel, successful business operations. Length: 1,200 words maximum. Departments and columns which also use material are: A Day in Our Lives, Our Favorite Vacation, Besides Farming, Farm Woman on the Go, Country Crafts, Sewing and Needlecraft, Gardening, Decorating, I Remember When, Farm Nature Stories. Pays $20 to $100. B&w photos are purchased with or without accompanying mss. Color slides and transparencies are also used. They look for scenic color photos which show the good life on the farm. Captions required. Payment depends on use, but begins at $10 for b&w photos; at $25 for color slides or transparencies.

Fiction: Mainstream, humorous. Themes should relate to subject matter. Length: 2,000 words maximum. Pays $40 to $70.

Poetry: Traditional forms and light verse. Length: open. Pays $15 for most poetry; more for long pieces. Must relate to subject matter.

Fillers: Word puzzles and short humor. Pays $15 to $30.

THE FEMINIST ART JOURNAL, 41 Montgomery Pl., Brooklyn NY 11215. Editor: Cindy Nemser. For anyone interested in the arts; women, particularly. Journal: 40

(8¼x11) pages. Established in 1972. Quarterly. Circulation: 10,000. Buys all rights, but will reassign rights to author after publication. Buys about 50 mss a year. Pays on publication. Will send sample copy to writer for $1.25. Will consider photocopied submissions. No simultaneous submissions. Reports in 2 to 3 weeks. Query first or submit complete ms. Enclose S.A.S.E.

Nonfiction and Photos: Anything dealing with the visual or performing arts; literary criticism, book reviews; interviews. Emphasis is on feminist orientation. Women's history in the arts; current feminist or women artists' events. Must be clear and concise with a feminist or humanist slant. Length: 300 to 6,000 words. Pays $10 to $25. No additional payment made for b&w photos used with ms. Captions required.

GLAMOUR, 350 Madison Ave., New York NY 10017. Phone: 212-692-5500. Editor-in-Chief: Ruth Whitney; Managing Editor: Phyllis Starr Wilson. Fine magazine for self-improvement and fashion. Monthly. "From a freelance writer we buy first North American serial rights. For our columns we often hold all rights or first North American serial rights." Query first. Enclose S.A.S.E.

Nonfiction: Fashion, beauty, decorating and entertaining, travel are staff-written, but there is a need for current interest articles; helpful, informative material, humorous or serious, on all aspects of a young woman's life (18 to 35 years old); medicine, mental health, social, economic and emotional problems. Freelancers might study the magazine for style, approach. Length: 2,000 to 3,000 words. Short pieces bring $300 to $500. Pays $750 minimum for regular article.

GOOD HOUSEKEEPING, 959 Eighth Ave., New York NY 10019. Editor: John Mack Carter. Issued monthly. Rights purchased vary with author and material, but usually buys all rights. Query with an informal letter first. Outlines must pinpoint the idea specifically. Enclose S.A.S.E.

Nonfiction: Elizabeth Pope Frank, Articles Editor; Robert Liles, Features Editor; Timothy Mulligan, Editor for "The Better Way." Three categories for nonfiction: 1. General articles on subjects of topicality and consequence that concern readers in a meaningful way. This might be anything from a report on a current controversial problem or a vexing social issue to a dramatic personal narrative dealing with unusual experiences of average families. Most writers miss the boat because of lack of impact, warmth and dramatic appeal with which the average housewife can identify. Material must be accurate, honest, bright, comprehensive and imaginatively presented. Depth reporting is a must. Most articles run between 1,200 and 5,000 words. Rates range from $500 for short features to $5,000 for important articles. 2. Short features include small pieces on big celebrities. These miniatures never attempt to tell everything about anyone, but try to explore some single and interesting angle of the subject's life or point of view. Prefer subjects whose names are well-established. Also interested in short narratives and humor. 3. Material for "The Better Way": This is the special information section of the magazine. Since it must fit a stylized format, they don't buy a finished article—just ideas and, on occasion, depth research on a subject of practical interest to housewives. Pays $25 to $50 for ideas and up to $350 for research assignments.

Fiction: Naome Lewis, Fiction Editor. Must portray problems which offer a strong element of reader identification. Characterization and thought content count more than plot, but also look for stories which contain practical and believable solutions offered in dramatic contexts. Average length is 4,000 words. Novelettes, book excerpts, condensations and serials also used. Payment starts at $1,000 for short-shorts.

Poetry: Usually overstocked in light verse category. Address serious poetry (preferably short) to Leonhard Dowty. Pays $25 and up for verse on basis of $5 a line.

Fillers: Submit to Robert Liles. Humorous short-short prose for "Light Housekeeping" feature needed. Payment $25 to $100. Buys epigrams, short humor.

HADASSAH MAGAZINE, 65 E. 52nd St., New York NY 10022. Editorial Director: Mrs. Roslyn K. Brecher. Executive Editor: Jesse Zel Lurie. For members of Hadassah. Monthly, except July and August. Circulation: 325,000. Buys U.S. publication rights. Pays on publication. Reports in 6 weeks. Enclose S.A.S.E.

Nonfiction: Primarily concerned with Israeli, the American Jewish community and American civic affairs. Length: 1,500 to 3,000 words. Pays 10¢ a word.
Photos: "We buy photos only to illustrate articles, with the exception of outstanding color from Israel which we use on our covers. We pay $100 and up for suitable color photo."
Fiction: Short stories with strong plots and positive Jewish values. Length: 3,000 words maximum. Pays 10¢ a word.
How To Break In: "We read all freelance material that comes in and we don't go by name, so total unknowns have an excellent chance. If you're in the education field, you have an advantage as we are looking for good material on the problems of Jewish education. Also, for the Bicentennial era, we will be especially receptive to new material on Jewish history — from any period."

HARLEQUIN, 240 Duncan Mill Rd., Suite 605, Don Mills, Ontario, Canada M3B 1Z4. Editor: Mrs. Beth McGregor. For women (age 29 to 65) in the home and at work. Magazine: 70 to 80 (8x11) pages. Established in 1973. Monthly. Circulation: 75,000. Rights purchased vary with author and material. May buy all rights, first North American serial rights, or second serial (reprint) rights. Buys about 35 to 45 mss a year. Pays on acceptance. Reports in 2 to 3 weeks. Query first with a brief outline. Enclose S.A.E. and International Reply Coupons.
Nonfiction: Specialized women's interest feature articles; cooking, inspirational, personal experience, informational, profile, historical. Material on the happy side, with an upbeat note; triumph over personal problems; travel with a woman's point of view. Clean, wholesome reading. Length: 1,000 to 3,500 words. Pays $50 to $150.
Fiction: Romantic, with a happy ending. Length: 1,000 to 4,500 words. Pays $50 to $125.

HARPER'S BAZAAR, 717 Fifth Ave., New York NY 10022. Editor-in-Chief: Anthony Mazzola. For "women, late 20's and above, middle income and above, sophisticated and aware, with at least 2 years of college. Most combine families, professions, travel, often more than one home. They are active and concerned over what's happening in the arts, their communities, the world." Monthly. Rights purchased vary with author and material. May buy first North American serial rights. No unsolicited mss. Query first. Enclose S.A.S.E.
Nonfiction and Photos: "We publish whatever is important to an intelligent, modern woman. Fashion questions plus beauty and health—how the changing world affects her family and herself; how she can affect it; how others are trying to do so; changing life pattern and so forth. Query us first."

LADIES' HOME JOURNAL, 641 Lexington Ave., New York NY 10022. Editor: Lenore Hershey. Buys all rights. Pays on acceptance. Issued monthly. Query first for nonfiction; send complete ms for fiction. Enclose S.A.S.E.
Nonfiction and Fiction: "Articles that talk to readers as women, that deal with the accomplishments and feelings of real people, that aren't self-conscious about being emotional, that tell in 2,000 words a story so compelling that the reader would finish it even at 10,000 words. Send query to David Sendler, Articles Editor." Short stories on life and love. Length: 1,000 to 4,000 words. Phyllis Levy, Fiction Editor. Payment varies according to length and quality of manuscript, but usually begins at $1,500; $500 for regionals.

LADY'S CIRCLE MAGAZINE, Lopez Publications, Inc., 21 West 26th St., New York NY 10010. Editor: Evan Barbara Frances. For homemakers. An honest magazine trying and succeeding to be what it is to the people it appeals to. Monthly. Buys all rights. Pays on publication. Will send a sample copy to a writer for 35¢. Will consider photocopied submissions. Reporting time varies from 1 week to 3 months. Query first, with brief outline. Enclose S.A.S.E.
Nonfiction and Photos: Particularly likes first-person or as-told-to pieces about health and doing good. Also how homemakers and mothers make money at home. Hobbies and crafts. Also articles on baby care, home management, gardening, as well as

problems of the homemaker. Articles must be written on specific subjects and must be thoroughly researched and based on sound authority. Length: 2,500 words. Pays $125. Pays $15 for good b&w photos accompanying articles.

McCALL'S, 230 Park Ave., New York NY 10017. Editor: Robert Stein. "Study recent issues." Monthly. Circulation: 6,800,000. Buys North American serial rights. Pays on acceptance. "All mss must be submitted on speculation and *McCall's* accepts no responsibility for unsolicited mss." Reports in 4 to 6 weeks. Query first. Enclose S.A.S.E.

Nonfiction: Miss Helen Markel, Editor. No subject of wide public or personal interest is out of bounds for *McCall's* so long as it is appropriately treated. The editors are seeking meaningful stories of personal experience. They are on the lookout for new research that will provide the basis for penetrating articles on the ethical, physical, material and social problems concerning readers. They are most receptive to humor and belles lettres. *McCall's* buys between 200 and 300 articles a year, many in the 1,000- to 1,500-word length. Miss Lisel Eisenheimer is Editor of Nonfiction Books from which *McCall's* frequently publishes excerpts. These are on subjects of interest to women: biography, memoirs, reportage, etc. Address queries for "Right Now" column to Jean Pascoe. Subjects can be education, medicine, ecology, women doing interesting things, women's liberation, any timely subject. Length: 300 to 500 words. Payment is up to $300. The magazine is not in the market for new columns. Almost all features on food, household equipment and management, fashion, beauty, building and decorating are staff-written.

Fiction: Mrs. Helen DelMonte, Editor. "Again the editors would remind writers of the contemporary woman's taste and intelligence. Most of all, fiction can awaken a reader's sense of identity, deepen her understanding of herself and others, refresh her with a laugh at herself, etc. *McCall's* looks for stories which will have meaning for an adult reader of some literary sensitivity. *McCall's* principal interest is in short stories; but fiction of all lengths is considered." Length: about 4,000 words. Length for short-shorts: about 2,000 words. Payment begins at $1,250.

How To Break In: "Your best bet is our monthly newsletter section, Right Now. It's an eight-page section and we buy a lot of freelance material for it, much of that from beginning writers. Some people have gone on from Right Now to do feature material for us. We use 500- to 700-word items in Right Now, many of them how-to's or with a practical intent of some kind. We pay $200 to $250. The stories must have a certain immediacy to suburban housewives in their thirties and forties. New trends, new developments, new ideas. Some recent Right Now items include a new birth control drug that lasts three months, where the jobs are, how to adopt a foreign child, scholarships for older women, children using math calculators in class, growing vegetables on your window sill. Each idea must have a fresh approach."

MADEMOISELLE, 350 Madison Ave., New York NY 10017. Editor-in-Chief: Edith Raymond Locke. Directed to college-educated women between the ages of 18 to 25. Circulation: 807,352. Reports on submissions in 3 to 4 weeks. Buys first North American serial rights. Pays on acceptance. Prefers written query plus samples of work, published or unpublished. Enclose S.A.S.E.

Nonfiction: Particular concentration on articles of interest to the intelligent young woman that concern the arts, education, careers, European travel, current sociological and political problems. Articles should be well-researched and of good quality. Prefers not to receive profile articles of individuals or personal reminiscences. Length: "Opinion" essay column, 1,300 words; articles, 1,500 to 6,000 words. Pays $300 for "Opinion" essay column; articles $350 to $850. Managing Editor: Mary Cantwell.

Photos: Commissioned work assigned according to needs. Photos of fashion, beauty, travel; career and college shots of interest to accompany articles. Payment ranges from no-charge to an agreed rate of payment per shot, job series, or page rate. Art Director: Roger W. Schoening. Buys all rights. Pays on publication for photos.

Fiction: High-quality fiction by both name writers and unknowns. Length: 2,500 to 6,500 words. Pays $300 and up. Uses short-shorts on occasion. "We are particularly interested in encouraging young talent, and with this aim in mind, we conduct a college fiction contest each year, open to men and women undergraduates. A $500 prize is awarded for each of the two winning stories which are published in our August issue. However, our encouragement of unknown talent is not limited to college students or youth. We are not interested in formula stories, and subject matter need not be confined to a specific age or theme." Fiction Editor: Mrs. Ellen A. Stoianoff. Annually awards two prizes for short stories.

Poetry: Must be of very high literary quality, under 65 lines. Pays $25 minimum. Address ms to Mrs. Ellen A. Stoianoff. Annually awards two prizes for poetry.

MODERN BRIDE, 1 Park Ave., New York NY 10016. Executive Editor: Cele G. Lalli. An exquisite magazine with limited subject matter. Bimonthly. Buys all rights. Pays on acceptance. Reports in 2 weeks. Enclose S.A.S.E.

Nonfiction: Uses articles of interest to brides-to-be. "We prefer articles on etiquette, marriage, planning a home, and travel from honeymoon point of view. *Modern Bride* is divided into three sections: the first deals with wedding dresses; the second with home furnishings; the third with travel. We buy articles for all three; we edit everything, but don't rewrite without permission." Length: about 2,000 words. Payment is about $150 and up.

Poetry: Buys some poetry pertaining to love and marriage. Pays $15 to $25 for average short poem.

MS. MAGAZINE, 370 Lexington Ave., New York NY 10017. Editor-in-Chief and Publisher: Patricia Carbine. Editor: Gloria Steinem. For "women predominantly; varying ages, backgrounds, but committed to exploring new life styles and changes in their roles and society." Established in 1972. Monthly. Circulation: over 400,000. Rights purchased vary with author and material. Pays on acceptance. Will consider photocopied submissions. Submit seasonal material at least 3 months in advance. Reports in 2 to 3 weeks. Query first for nonfiction only, "with ideas and outline, and include samples of previous work." Address to Query Editor. Submit complete ms for fiction. Enclose S.A.S.E.

Nonfiction: "Articles, features on the arts, women's minds, women's bodies that relate to exploring new life styles for women and changes in their roles and society. We are a how-to magazine—how a woman may gain control of her life. We are hoping to change the status quo—to treat women as human beings, and not to insult their personhood with down-putting editorializing or insensitive advertising. We encourage women to live their lives as unique people, not role players. We would like more input on what women are doing politically in their communities." Buys informational articles, how-to's, personal experience articles, interviews, profiles, inspirational articles, humor, historical articles, think articles, exposes, personal opinion pieces, photo articles, new product articles, coverage of successful business operations, and art, book, and film reviews. Length varies. Pays $100 to $500. Send to Manuscript Editor.

Photos: Purchased with mss, without mss, or on assignment. Payment "depends on usage." Address to Art Department.

Fiction, Poetry and Fillers: Personal experience, fantasy, humorous, historical; condensed novels, serialized novels. Length: 3,000 words maximum. Pays up to $500. Address to Fiction Editor. Traditional forms, blank verse, free verse, avant-garde forms and light verse, relating to magazine subject matter. Address to Poetry Editor. "We accept nonfiction filler length material only for the Gazette section of the magazine; news from all over." Length: filler length to 3,000 words maximum. Pays up to $500. Address to Nonfiction Editor.

How To Break In: "The Gazette section which features short news items is the easiest way to get published here. We use a lot of material from all over the country on politics, the women's movement, human interest material, women profiles. Regional material from outside New York stands the best chance, but nothing is a sure bet. We get a lot of material we can't use from people who don't understand the kind of orientation we seek. One recent successful profile was on an older woman who had developed a continuing education program. It is possible to move from the Gazette to do other work for *Ms.*"

NATIONAL BUSINESS WOMAN, 2012 Massachusetts Ave. N.W., Washington DC 20036. Phone: 202-293-1100. Editor: Lola S. Tilden. For "all mature, educated, employed women." Established in 1919. 11 times a year. Buys all rights and second serial rights. Buys 10 or 12 mss a year. Payment on acceptance. Will send a sample copy to a writer for $1. Will consider photocopied submissions. Reports on rejected material immediately. Enclose S.A.S.E.

Nonfiction: "Originality preferred. Written specifically for members of the National Federation of Business and Professional Women's Clubs, Inc. No fiction or poems." Buys informational, think, and successful business operations articles. Length: 1,000 to 1,200 words. Pays $10 to $35.

NEW WOMAN, P.O. Box 24202, Fort Lauderdale FL 33307. Associate Editor: Wendy Danforth. For "thinking women of all ages, puberty through bifocals; beauty and brains concern them." Monthly. Buys all rights. Pays on publication. Query first essential. Do not submit complete ms. Enclose S.A.S.E.

Nonfiction: "Everything of interest to the self-starting, self-actualizing, career-minded Renaissance woman. The style should be assured, with flair, humor, warmth, sparkle, wit; the outlook should be refined; antitraditional sexist roles. The status and image of women are particularly important to us. Our readers meet men on a parity basis; she's the new woman, he's the new man. No more interviews in question-and-answer format — we'd like more charm." Buys how-to's, interviews, profiles, personal experience articles, inspirational and think pieces, humor, coverage of successful business operations, exposes, travel features, articles on "psychology, sexology, and politics." Seeks material for departments on "child-rearing; finance; the problems of separated, divorced, or widowed new women; new marriage styles." Length: 500 to 3,000 words. "Payment depends on article."

NEWS LADY, *Chicago Daily News,* 401 N. Wabash, Chicago IL 60611. A column for women. Buys first North American rights. Occasionally overstocked. Pays on publication. Reports in 3 weeks, "sometimes longer." Enclose S.A.S.E.

Nonfiction: Essays on topics of interest to women. "We prefer essays from women in the *Daily News* trading zone (Illinois, southern Wisconsin, northern Indiana), but we will accept particularly good essays from all over the U.S. Food, farm, garden, and pet essays are not especially liked, but we have made exceptions. We are trying to get essays with a greater degree of sophistication about women's lib, consumerism, and social problems. We're interested in humor, especially family humor. Please, no reporting or didactic essays." Length: 500 to 600 words. Pays $25 savings bond.

PLAYGIRL MAGAZINE, 1801 Century Park East, Los Angeles CA 90067. Phone: 213-553-8006. Editor-in-Chief: Marin Scott Milam. For an aware, young, contemporary female audience of all ages, today's multi-faceted women in all occupations, who are interested in a wide range of subjects. Monthly magazine; 136 pages. Established in 1973. Circulation: 2,100,000. Rights purchased vary with author and material. May buy all rights or first North American serial rights. Buys about 120 mss a year. Payment on acceptance. Will send sample copy to writer for $1.25. Will consider photocopied submissions. Will not consider simultaneous submissions. Submit seasonal material for all of the traditional holidays 4 months in advance. Reports in 1 month. Query first for nonfiction. Submit complete ms for fiction. Enclose S.A.S.E.

Nonfiction and Photos: "*Playgirl* does not believe in limiting women's horizons, as most women's magazines do. We use material on any area of concern to women, but not just the traditional areas of home and children. Must be totally professional. We are most concerned with literary quality and slant. Articles must be well-researched and tightly written and must demonstrate a respect for the intelligence of our readers." Uses informational, how-to, personal experience, interview, profile, think pieces, nostalgia, travel and career articles. Length: 2,000 words minimum. Pays minimum of $300. B&w and color photos are purchased on assignment only. Art Director: Robert Carpentier.

Fiction: "Stories may be sexually oriented, but not salacious. Female characters should be three-dimensional and portrayed realistically." Experimental, mainstream, mystery, suspense, erotica, fantasy, humorous, romance, excerpts from novels. Length: 1,000 to 7,500 words. Pays $300 to $1,000.

REDBOOK MAGAZINE, 230 Park Ave., New York NY 10017. Issued monthly. Buys first North American rights. Reports in 2 to 3 weeks. A freelancer's dream. Receptive, honest, sincere. The editors will even violate the magazine's editorial rules if you have something that makes them care enough. Pays top rates, on acceptance. Enclose S.A.S.E.
Nonfiction: Robert J. Levin, Articles Editor. Articles relevant to the magazine's readers, who are young women in the 18- to 34-year-old group. Especially interested in submissions for "Young Mother's Story" and "Young Woman's Story" features. "If you have had some experience in your family, social or marital life that you feel may be particularly interesting and helpful to other young mothers or young women, we would be interested in seeing your story. Please don't hesitate to send it because you think your spelling or punctuation may be a bit rusty; we don't judge these stories on the basis of technicalities and we do make minor editing changes. For each 1,000 to 2,000 words accepted for publication, we pay $500. Mss accompanied by a stamped, self-addressed envelope, must be signed (although name will be withheld on request), and mailed to: Young Mother's Story or Young Woman's Story, c/o *Redbook Magazine.* Stories do not have to be typed, but we appreciate it when they are legibly written." Length: articles, 3,500 to 4,500 words; short articles, 2,000 to 2,500 words.
Fiction: Anne Mollegen Smith, Fiction Editor. Uses a great variety of types of fiction, with contemporary stories appealing especially to women in demand. Short stories of 3,500 to 5,000 words are always needed. Also short-shorts of 1,400 to 1,600 words. Payment for short-shorts begins at $750, and at $1,000 for short stories.
How To Break In: "It is very difficult to break into the nonfiction section, although two columns — Young Mothers and To Be a Woman — which publish short personal experience pieces (1,000 to 1,500 words) do depend on freelancers. Recent articles were about a woman who gained an insight about herself on a mountain climbing trip with her husband and on how a family coped after their child had been raped. One recent successful feature freelance piece was on Elizabeth Taylor's granddaughter — which suggests our desire for a new slant on a popular name. Our situation for the fiction department is quite different. We buy a quarter of our short stories cold from writers whose articles come in brown envelopes in the mail. Another 40% are repeats from writers who were originally unsolicited and less than half are from agented writers. We buy about 50 stories a year. This is clearly the best way to break into *Redbook* and we even sometimes ask successful fiction people to do a nonfiction piece, say, essay for our Christmas issue. Most of the stories we're proud of — the fresh material which gives *Redbook* fiction its distinctiveness — are from people we've discovered through the unsolicited mail. So when we open each brown envelope, it is with a great deal of hope. We read everything that comes in and try to give a reading the day it arrives. Still the odds are very difficult, since we do get a great deal of submissions. The short-shorts (8½ pages or even shorter) have the very best chance."

SPHERE MAGAZINE, 500 N. Michigan Ave., Chicago IL 60611. Editor: Joan Leonard. Monthly. Study several issues of the publication and query first. Enclose S.A.S.E. Unsolicited mss not accepted.

TODAYS FAMILY, P. O. Box 31467, Dallas TX 75231. Editor: Sherry Gish. For middle-class families, 35 to 55 age bracket. Buys first North American serial rights. Pays the 28th of the month of issue. Will send sample copy to writer for 25¢. Reports promptly. Query first. Enclose S.A.S.E.
Nonfiction and Photos: Family fun, creative crafts, what's new and how it applies to readers; personal relationships, homes, finances, health. No household humor. Fashion, needlecraft, travel, food, flea market, home maintenance are staff written. Recently published articles include "Ginseng's Powers: Magical or Mythical," "If You Can't Sleep With Your Spouse," "First Aid for the Doctor Shortage" (physician's

assistants), "New Safety Colors," "Plant Dig" (in Georgia). Maximum length: 2,000 words. Pays up to $50. Articles on meaningful personal experiences for Life-Paths feature are limited to 2,000 words. Pays up to $25. B&w glossies are purchased with mss, with no additional payment.

Fiction: General family appeal with adult main characters. Length: 3,000 words maximum; shorter lengths preferred. Pays $50.

VIVA, 909 Third Ave., New York NY 10022. For predominantly female audience between 18 and 27. Monthly. Pays within 30 days following publication. Usually reports in 2 to 6 weeks. Submit complete ms. Enclose S.A.S.E.

Fiction: Experimental, mainstream, suspense, adventure, erotica, humorous and science fiction. Writers must consider the nature of the magazine before submitting material. Should have strong narrative structure. Avoid mediocrity and the cliche. Length: 1,000 to 4,000 words. Pays about 25¢ per word. Fiction Editor: Gerard Van Der Leun.

VOGUE, 350 Madison Ave., New York NY 10017. Editor: Grace Mirabella. Issued monthly. For highly intelligent women. Query first. Enclose S.A.S.E.

Nonfiction: Uses articles and ideas for features, 2,000 to 2,500 words. Fashion articles are staff-written. Material must be of high literary quality, contain good information. Pays $300 and up, on acceptance. Kate Lloyd, Associate Editor.

W, *Women's Wear Daily*, 7 East 12th St., New York NY 10003. Completely staff-written newspaper.

THE WOMAN, 235 Park Ave. South, New York NY 10003. Editor: Diana Lurvey. For women who are now or have once been married. They may or may not work outside the home, but their main interest is in home and family. Published every two months. Digest-sized magazine, 146 pages. Established in 1965. Circulation: 250,000. Buys all rights, but will reassign rights to author after publication. Buys 90 mss a year. Payment on acceptance. Will send sample copy to writer for 50¢. Submit seasonal material 6 months in advance. Reports in 2 weeks. Query first or submit complete ms. Enclose S.A.S.E.

Nonfiction: "We are looking for material which will enrich our readers' lives. Help them to be healthier, happier, have better marriages, manage their children better, cope with aged parents, save money, etc. Poorly written money-saving articles won't make it here, and we do not publish anything to do with abnormal sex." Informational, how-to, personal experience, interview, profile, inspirational, think articles, expose, nostalgia, personal opinion. Length: open. Pays $50.

WOMAN'S DAY, 1515 Broadway, New York NY 10036. Editor: Geraldine Rhoads. Monthly. Fine consumer-oriented magazine. Different enough from others to stand on its own. Excellent taste, instructions for making many things—clothes, toys, furniture, etc., within range of average woman. "Homier" in tone, and very well done. Circulation: over 8,000,000. Buys first and second North American serial rights. Pays on acceptance. Reports within 2 weeks on queries; longer on mss. Submit detailed queries first to Rebecca Greer, Articles Editor. Enclose S.A.S.E.

Nonfiction: Uses articles on all subjects of interest to women—marriage, family life, child rearing, education, homemaking, money management, travel, family health, and leisure activities. Also interested in fresh, dramatic narratives of women's lives and concerns. Length: 500 to 3,000 words, depending on material. Payment varies depending on length, whether it's for regional or national use, etc.

Fiction: Uses little fiction; high-quality, genuine human interest romance and humor, in lengths between 1,500 and 3,000 words. Payment varies. "We pay any writer's established rate, however." Dept. Editor: Eileen Herbert Jordan.

Fillers: Brief (500 words maximum), factual articles on contemporary life, community projects, unusual activities are used—condensed, sprightly, and unbylined—in "It's All in a Woman's Day" section. "Neighbors" column also pays $25 for each letter and $5 for each brief practical suggestion on homemaking or child rearing. Address to the editor of the appropriate section.

WOMEN IN BUSINESS, 9100 Ward Parkway, Kansas City MO 64114. Phone: 816-361-6621. Editor: Shelley K. Mayer. For "businesswomen in various professional, technical, and service fields." Established in 1949. 9 times a year; combined issues in March/April, July/August, November/December. Special issues include citizenship issue (February) and travel issue (March/April). Buys all rights. Buys about 20 mss a year. Pays on acceptance. Will send a sample copy to a writer on request. Write for copy of guidelines for writers. Query first or submit complete ms. Will consider photocopied submissions. Reports in 4 to 6 weeks. Enclose S.A.S.E.

Nonfiction: "Our policy prohibits acceptance of articles about women who are not members of the American Business Women's Association (ABWA). Subjects relating to all aspects of business; educational topics (retirement planning, how to handle your money), guides for working women; emphasis on new office techniques, products, careers, etc. All material is carefully developed to interest the working woman—all levels of business." Interested in material on "fashions for businesswomen (fall and spring), how a woman can best advance in business, employment areas that offer financial benefits to women." Buys informational articles, how-to's, profiles, think pieces, travel articles, new product articles, and articles on merchandising techniques. Will not accept articles about individual success stories. Length: 1,500 words maximum. Pays 3¢ to 5¢ a word.

Photos: Purchased with mss, without mss; captions required. Uses 8x10 b&w glossies. Pays $20 for photos accompanying articles. Pays $35 for cover photo.

WOMEN'S ALMANAC, Armitage Press, Inc., 1430 Massachusetts Ave., Cambridge MA 02138. Phone: 617-492-0999. Editor: Ryan A. Kuhn. For "women interested in the rapidly evolving national events which affect their lives in a practical way." Material that is vital, unusual, extremely usable. Not just for entertainment; very informative. Established in 1973. Semiannual. Circulation: 100,000. Buys all rights. Buys 80 mss a year. Payment on publication. Will send sample copy to writer for $1.30. Write for copy of guidelines for writers. Will consider photocopied submissions. Submit material at least 2 months in advance of publication dates (2/15; 5/15; 8/15; 11/15). Reports 2 weeks after receipt. Query first. Enclose S.A.S.E.

Nonfiction: "Articles that are concise, readable and professional; spanning common knowledge on the subject while offering the latest (and, perhaps unusual) developments in the field. Our emphasis is upon, above all, the practical use our readers may find in the articles. Straightforward. Many advances and developments occurring in areas of concern to women have not been effectively 'translated' into immediately usable information. For instance, what consumer frauds are directed specifically against women? What makes a good day care center? What are the chances of increased employer day care? The *Almanac* is an answer magazine. All ideas are welcomed. National events inspire much of our content." Departments seeking freelance material include: "Law and Women," "Employment," "Adult Education," "Health," "Law and Children," "Child Education," "Finances," "Consumerism." Length: 1,500 to 2,500 words. Pays approximately 5¢ per word, depending on quality.

If this is 1977, this edition is out of date. See address in front of book to order latest edition. *Writer's Market* is published annually each fall.

Company Publications

Material for these company publications must perform a useful business service for the company. Other company publications whose subject matter is not directly product-related or primarily employee-directed are listed in various categories in Consumer Publications, as well as in Trade, Technical and Professional Journals. Association, Club and Fraternal; College, University and Alumni; Union and In-Flight Publications are categorized under those chapter headings.

ACF HORIZONS, ACF Industries, 750 Third Ave., New York NY 10017. Phone: 212-986-8600. Editor: Orlan J. Fox. For "employees and the public." Quarterly. Circulation: 18,000. Buys "non-exclusive" rights. Pays on publication. Will send a sample copy to a writer on request. Query first. Reports in 1 month. Enclose S.A.S.E.
Nonfiction, Photos, and Fillers: "Articles related to the products and operations of the divisions of ACF Industries: railroad equipment, automotive fuel systems, valves and fittings. Material must have ACF tie-in." Length: "the shorter the better." Pays $5 minimum. Buys 8x10 single-weight b&w glossies.

BAROID NEWS BULLETIN, P.O. Box 1675, Houston TX 77001. Phone: 713-524-6381. Editor: Marvin L. Brown. Publication of the Baroid Division of N L Industries, Inc. "The market we primarily serve are employees of the petroleum industry worldwide." Established in 1941. Quarterly. Circulation: 18,000. Buys North American rights, but will reassign rights to author after publication. Buys 15 to 20 manuscripts a year, "but we could buy more." Pays on acceptance. Will send free sample copy to writer on request. Reports on material in 3 weeks. Submit complete ms. Enclose S.A.S.E.
Nonfiction and Photos: "We prefer articles of the prose feature story type. Travel, the Old West or Civil War, historical material, and humor are good topics. But we will print anything that is quality, especially if it is oil field oriented (but they don't have to be). Each quarterly publication includes feature articles and art plus technical articles written by our employees. Informational, humor, historical, nostalgia, travel, and pro-free enterprise articles are other examples." Recently published articles include "Baseball's Best Brawls"; "Abe (Lincoln) Loved a Good Fight"; and "Red China's Oil". Length: 1,000 to 3,000 words. Pays 3¢ to 10¢ per word. B&w glossies or color transparencies purchased with ms.
Fiction: Should be related to oil field. Also buys suspense, adventure, western, humorous, historical, pro-America. Length: 1,000 to 3,000 words. Pays 3¢ to 10¢ per word.
Poetry: Should relate to oil field. Traditional, blank verse, free verse and light verse. Length: not over 2 typewritten pages. Pays minimum of 3¢ per word; maximum depends on quality.
Fillers: "Our 'Cerebrations' column uses 3 or 4 math or logical problems per issue. These are petroleum-related puzzles." Length: open. Pays minimum of 3¢ per word.

THE BEAVER, 77 Main St., Winnipeg, MB, Canada. Editor: Helen Burgess. Publication of Hudson's Bay Company for "mature students and adults". Established in 1920. Quarterly. Circulation: 40,000. Buys all rights. Buys about 30 mss a year. Pays on acceptance. Will send a sample copy to a writer on request. Submit seasonal material at least 6 months in advance. Reports in 2 weeks. "Content is quite specialized; suggest query first." Enclose S.A.E. and International Reply Coupons.
Nonfiction and Photos: "Well-illustrated, authentic articles on life in the Arctic and areas of early Hudson's Bay Company activities; historical and present-day fur trade, nature subjects, Indians, and Eskimos. Accurate information must be presented in a readable way. No more articles on Arctic canoe trips." Buys informational articles, personal experience pieces, profiles, and historical articles. Length: 1,000 to 4,000 words. Pays minimum 5¢ a word. Photos purchased with mss; captions required. Pays minimum $5 for 8x10 b&w glossies. Pays minimum $10 for 35mm or 4¼x4¼ color slides.

BUSINESS ON WHEELS, P.O. Box 13208, Phoenix AZ 85002. Phone: 602-257-1062. Editor: Frederick H. Kling. "External house organ of Goodyear Tire and Rubber Company for distribution to owners and operators of truck fleets, both common carrier trucking systems and trucks used in connection with businesses of various types." Quarterly. Not copyrighted. Pays on acceptance. "Stories on assignment only. We like to choose our own subjects for case history stories." Query first. Enclose S.A.S.E.

Nonfiction and Photos: "Freelance writers and photographers (especially writer-photographer teams or individuals) are invited to send in their qualifications for assignment of articles on truck-fleet operators in their territory. Payment from $250 to $300, plus expenses, for complete editorial-photographic coverage, additional for color, if used."

THE CARAVANNER, 15939 Piuma Ave., Cerritos CA 90701. Contact: Frank Quattrocchi, Guerin, Johnstone, Gage Inc., 600 S. Commonwealth Ave., Los Angeles CA 90005. For persons in the 50 to 60 year age class; retired or semi-retired who have expressed a definite interest in the Airstream make of travel trailer. Publication of Airstream, a Division of Beatrice Foods Co., Chicago IL. Newspaper; 8 pages, 11¼x16¼. Established in 1954. Circulation: 450,000. Not copyrighted. Pays on acceptance; "writer has to fill out and return an invoice." Will send free sample copy to writer on request. Write for copy of guidelines for writers. Will consider photocopied submissions. "We like seasonal stories but rarely get them." Submit seasonal material 3 months prior to season. Returns rejected material in 1 to 2 weeks. Reports on material in 3 to 4 weeks "unless I'm on vacation. Query is not required, but is useful." Enclose S.A.S.E.

Nonfiction: "Interesting uses of the Airstream make of travel trailers. Material must be entirely factual and not exaggerated, but upbeat. Writer must know what we usually print in our pages. We're really looking for truth; sharp analysis. The recreational vehicle, of which a travel trailer is one kind, has really encouraged or engendered a new life style in modern America — I'd like to see that examined." Personal experience, interview, nostalgia, travel, and successful business operations. Length: 500 to 2,000 words. Usually pays $50 to $150 or so. "We generally pay $75 for 1,000 to 1,500 words with 3 photos, but I'm glad to give a bonus here and there for better material."

Photos: Purchased with accompanying ms with no additional payment. Photos generally required with ms. Pays $5 minimum if photos are exceptional, and without accompanying ms. 5x7 b&w, but no Polaroid. Captions required.

C-B MANIFOLD, Cooper-Bessemer Co., N. Sandusky St., Mt. Vernon OH 43050. Phone: 614-397-0121, Ext. 2420. Editor: Carl G. Mueller. For company employees. Bimonthly. Not copyrighted. Pays on acceptance. Query first. Reports in 2 weeks. Enclose S.A.S.E.

Nonfiction and Photos: "Thoroughly researched articles on Cooper-Bessemer equipment." Length: 500 words. Pays $35 to $50. B&w photos purchased with or without ms. Captions required. Pays $10 to $15.

CHANNELS OF BUSINESS COMMUNICATION, Northwestern Bell Telephone Co., 100 S. 19th St., Omaha NE 68102. Phone: 402-422-2873. Editor: G.T. Metcalf. For "top level executives." Quarterly. Circulation: 50,000. Buys first North American serial rights. Reports in 1 month. Query first. Enclose S.A.S.E.

Nonfiction: "Articles on new developments and techniques in business communications, such as WATS, data transmission, time-shared computers, industrial television, etc. Also occasional general interest features on sports, hobbies, personalities, events, and points of interest in Iowa, Minnesota, Nebraska, North Dakota, and South Dakota. Material is drawn almost exclusively from this five-state area. Writers who do not either live or travel frequently in this part of the country have small chance of coming up with the type of material we seek. Writing must be good and tight." Length: 500 to 1,000 words. Pays $150 minimum.

CIBA-GEIGY JOURNAL, 4002 Basel, Switzerland. Editor: Stanley Hubbard. For "employees, mainly staff and scientific-technical, of Ciba-Geigy, together with 'opinion leaders,' customers, educational institutions, etc., in most English-speaking countries." Established in 1971. Circulation: 27,000. Rights purchased vary with author and material; may buy all rights, but will reassign rights to author after publication. Buys 4 to 6 mss a year. Pays on publication. Will send a sample copy to a writer on request. Will consider photocopied submissions. Submit seasonal material 5 months in advance. Reports in 4 weeks. Query first. Enclose S.A.E. and International Reply Coupons.

Nonfiction and Photos: "Popularized scientific and technical presentations, international cooperation subjects, regional and historical contributions related to group activities, human interest — if possible, with product or operational tie-in. The approach should be literate; no writing down. The internationalism of our company is the basic determining factor — we are interpreting from continent to continent rather than talking to a homogeneous, neatly defined readership." Buys informational articles, humor, historical articles, think pieces, nostalgia, photo features, travel articles, and technical articles. Length: 500 to 3,000 words. Pays minimum of $50. Photos purchased with mss; captions required. For b&w, pays $10. For color ("if prints, only first quality"), pays $10 to $20.

THE COMPASS, Mobil Sales and Supply Corp., 150 E. 42nd St., New York NY 10017. Editor: R.G. MacKenzie. For "international marine interest." Established in 1920. Quarterly. Buys first serial rights. Pays on acceptance. Will consider photocopied submissions. Reports in 1 week. Query first. Enclose S.A.S.E.
Nonfiction and Photos: "Various marine or maritime subjects, with particular emphasis on history, origin, and scientific developments." Length: 2,000 to 4,000 words. Pays $100 to $250. Photos purchased with accompanying ms, with no additional payment. Must be on marine subjects. B&w glossies, any size; color, 2¼x2¼ or larger.
Fiction: "Sea stories, particularly about windship days." Length: 2,000 to 4,000 words. Pays $100 to $250.

CORVETTE NEWS, Room 316, 465 W. Milwaukee, Detroit MI 48202. For Corvette owners worldwide. Bimonthly. Circulation: 170,000. Buys all rights. Pays on acceptance. Write for sample copy and editorial guidelines. Query first. Enclose S.A.S.E.
Nonfiction and Photos: "Articles must be of interest to this audience. Subjects considered include: (1) Technical articles dealing with engines, paint, body work, suspension, parts searches, etc. (2) Competition, 'Vettes vs. 'Vettes, or 'Vettes vs. others. (3) Profiles of Corvette owners/drivers. (4) General interest articles, such as the unusual history of a particular early model Corvette, and perhaps its restoration; one owner's do-it-yourself engine repair procedures, maintenance procedures; Corvettes in unusual service; hobbies involving Corvettes; sports involving Corvettes. (5) Road hunts. (6) Special Corvette events such as races, drags, rallies, concourse, gymkhanas, slaloms. (7) Corvette club activities." Length: 800 to 2,400 words. Pays $50 to $500, including photos illustrating article. Color transparencies or b&w negatives preferred. Pays additional fee of $35 for cover shot which is usually selected from photos furnished with article used in that issue.

DUNCAN REGISTER, Duncan Electric Co., Box 180, Lafayette IN 47902. For "electric utility industry," customers of Duncan Electric Co. Quarterly. Not copyrighted. Pays on acceptance. "Address queries to the Editor." Enclose S.A.S.E.
Photos: "Scenic photos only, suitable for a magazine cover." 4x5 vertical or 2¼x2¼ color transparencies. Pays $45 to $55 per transparency. "We buy only photos for covers. We are not interested in outside-written articles."

THE EDUCATIONAL FOCUS (formerly *Bausch & Lomb Focus*), Optics Center SOPD Division, Bausch & Lomb, 1400 N. Goodman St., Rochester NY 14602. Editor: R. I. Fiester. For "high school and college science teachers and professors, laboratory and engineering personnel in industry and government, hospitals, school libraries, and Bausch and Lomb dealers and salesmen." Established in 1929. Annual. Circulation: 25,000. Buys all rights. Pays "within 2 weeks following acceptance." Will send a sample copy to a writer on request. Write for copy of guidelines for writers. Reports in 2 weeks. Enclose S.A.S.E. for return of submissions.

Nonfiction and Photos: "We are primarily interested in articles dealing with new or unusual uses of scientific optical equipment, new approaches to teaching, or interesting adaptations and accessories devised for use with such equipment. Obviously, we prefer that the story be concerned with Bausch and Lomb equipment, but we will not reject an article simply because it makes a reference to the use of competitive optical equipment. Serious consideration will be given to any article that advances the cause of science in any area — in schools, industry, hospitals, research labs, etc. — whether or not scientific optical equipment is used (although, obviously, that is preferred). How-to stories describing the construction of scientific optical equipment by students are very much to our liking. Such articles should be accompanied by drawings and photographs so that another student can easily duplicate the equipment from information contained in the article. We do not buy highly technical articles delineating unsupported scientific theories. No articles that 'run down' competitive optical equipment, even if unnamed." Length: 1,500 to 3,000 words. Pays "3¢ per word as published. We do pay more for articles, depending on the type of material, ease of bringing it to finished form, etc." Photos purchased with mss. "A picture story is particularly appealing to us." Uses b&w for inside use, color for cover "if it illustrates a point about an inside article." Pays $5 minimum per photo. "When we give the author permission to have photos taken, we pay the photographer's fee, including the cost of prints, without further reimbursement to the author."

THE ENTHUSIAST, 3700 W. Juneau, Milwaukee WI 53208. Phone: 414-342-4680. Editor: T.C. Bolfert. Published by Harley-Davidson Motor Co., Inc. for "motorcycle riders of all ages, education, and professions." Established in 1920. Bimonthly. Circulation: 150,000. Not copyrighted. Pays on publication. Will send a sample copy to a writer on request. Write for copy of guidelines for writers. Will consider photocopied submissions. Submit seasonal material 2 months in advance. Reports in 2 to 4 weeks. Query first or submit complete ms. Enclose S.A.S.E.
Nonfiction and Photos: "Stories on motorcycling or snowmobiling—humor, technical, racing, touring, adventures, competitive events. All articles should feature Harley-Davidson products and not mention competitive products. We do not want stories concerning sex, violence, or anything harmful to the image of motorcycling. We use travel stories featuring Harley-Davidson motorcycles, which must be illustrated with good quality photos of the motorcycle and travelers with scenic background taken on the trip. Also needed are stories of off-road usage, e.g., scrambles, racing, motocross, trail riding, or any other unusual usage. We use snowmobile stories in fall and winter." Informational articles, how-to's, personal experience articles, interviews, profiles, inspirational pieces, humor, historical articles, photo features, travel articles, and technical articles. Length: 3,000 words. Pays 5¢ "per published word, or as previously agreed upon." Photos purchased with mss and without mss; captions optional. Uses "quality b&w or color 4x5 prints or larger." Pays $7.50 to $15.
Fiction: "Good short stories with the image of clean motorcycling fun. No black leather jacket emphasis." Buys adventure and humorous stories. Length: 3,000 words maximum. Pays 5¢ "per published word, or as previously agreed upon."
Fillers: Jokes, short humor. Length: open. Pays $15.

FORD TRUCK TIMES, 420 Lexington Ave., New York NY 10017. Phone: 212-686-7000. Ask for Warren Weith or Mrs. Sue Holden. Editor: Warren Weith. For "truck owners." A promotional publication for Ford Motor Company handled through J. Walter Thompson Advertising Company. Quarterly. Circulation: over 3 million. Not copyrighted. Pays on publication. Will send a sample copy to a writer on request. Query preferable. Will consider photocopied submissions. Enclose S.A.S.E.
Nonfiction and Photos: "General interest articles (sports, adventure, recreation, hobby) with a Ford truck tie-in; success stories about people who employ Ford trucks in connection with truck operation and ownership; unusual uses of Ford trucks; truck body modifications (customizer innovations) relating to Ford trucks; truck-connected business promotion ideas; general information of a lively nature which would concern truck operators (such as safety, taxes, depreciation)." Types of Ford trucks considered for a story are Pickups, SuperCabs, Vans, Broncos,

Rancheros. Releases are required for authorship and from persons appearing in photos. Length: 1,500 to 2,000 words. "We now only accept full-length features." Pays $250 to $600 depending on quality of photos and story content. Prefers 35mm, 2¼x2¼ or larger color transparencies. "The cover photo is usually selected from photos illustrating one of the features of a given issue." For cover photo, pays $100 maximum.

GOING PLACES, 65 Broadway, New York NY 10006. Editor: Barbara Ross. For American Express Company employees and employees of American Express Company subsidiaries. Bimonthly. Not copyrighted. Pays on acceptance. Will send a sample copy to a writer on request. Query first. Enclose S.A.S.E.
Nonfiction and Photos: Does not purchase freelance mss, but sometimes makes assignments for company-oriented articles outside New York. Also occasionally makes assignments for company-oriented b&w photos.

GOULDS PUMPS INDUSTRIAL NEWS, 240 Fall St., Seneca Falls NY 13148. Editor: D.P. Beehler. Published by Goulds Pumps, Inc. for "industrial engineers, maintenance people, designers, purchasing agents for chemical process, paper, marine, mining, utility, municipal industries." Established in 1937. Bimonthly. Circulation: 15,000. Not copyrighted. Write for copy of guidelines for writers. Query first. Enclose S.A.S.E.
Nonfiction and Photos: "Case histories, industrial pump related human interest: old replaces new, solves the problem, out-of-the-ordinary application, assisting in scientific breakthrough, used in state-of-the art service, etc." Buys humor, historical articles, coverage of successful business operations, and technical articles. Length: maximum 700 words. Pays $25 to $50 per article. Photos purchased with or without mss.

HARVEST, Campbell Soup Company, Campbell Place, Camden NJ 08101. Editor: Dan H. Dolack. For Campbell Soup Company employees. Quarterly. Circulation: 30,000. Buys all rights "only to copy and photos; will return photos to the writer after publication on request, but some time may elapse between acceptance and publication." Pays on acceptance. Will send a sample copy to a writer on request. Write for copy of guidelines for writers. Reports in 2 to 8 weeks. Query first. Enclose S.A.S.E.
Nonfiction and Photos: "Vocabulary is simple, sentence structure uncomplicated, but done well enough that the literate person would consider it readable. We want an easy-to-read flow. Read a sample copy to get the feel of the style. Articles can often be helped by some fiction techniques, good dialog, setting the scene to give atmosphere, a bit of action. We do not want our stories overwritten, the 'literary' story doesn't have a chance. If an article has a strong company tie-in (such as showing a Campbell, Swanson, Pepperidge Farm, Bounty, or other Campbell Soup Company product in use in a natural — not contrived — way), it stands a better chance of acceptance. We seldom buy articles that do not relate to Campbell Soup Company or to food or nutrition. We do not buy recipes." Length: 500 to 1,500 words. Pays 10¢ per word. Color photos purchased with mss. "Photo standards are high; good transparencies (35mm or 2¼x2¼) stand the best chance of acceptance. Photos with mss must tell the story, not just accompany it. We prefer candid, available-light photography, and are not interested in run-of-the-mill flash photography. Photos accepted for publication become the property of Campbell Soup Company; extras returned on request." Pays $30 to $50 per transparency.

HOBART WELDWORLD, Hobart Brothers Co., Troy OH 45273. Phone: 513-339-6509. Editor: Daniel Lea. For "men and women with engineering degrees or technical education who are practicing a technical profession related to welding fabrication or who have moved into manufacturing management posts." Established in 1941. Quarterly. Circulation: 50,000. Usually buys first rights only. Buys "a few" mss a year. Pays on publication. Will send a sample copy to a writer on request. Will consider photocopied submissions. Reports in 1 month. Query first or submit complete ms. Enclose S.A.S.E.

Nonfiction and Photos: "Technical articles on arc welding applications. The writer should submit items only about exotic or unusual applications, give full technical information, and describe the benefits of equipment or process for the application as compared with other welding methods. Give figures, if possible. Unless a specific product benefit is involved, we worry about the application and let the product references come as they may. We're interested in coverage of big construction projects, in which welding plays a major part." Length: 300 to 1,000 words. Pays $25 minimum. Photos purchased with mss; captions required. Buys color negatives or transparencies, only. Pays $20 minimum each.

How To Break In: "We are trying to upgrade our photos as to artistic quality, impact, and information value, and will be impressed by submissions which help do this."

IMPERIAL OIL FLEET NEWS, 111 St. Clair Ave., W., Toronto M5W 1K3 Ont., Canada. Phone: 416-924-9111, Ext. 509. Editor: G. R. McKean. For "seamen of Imperial Oil tankers." Quarterly. Not copyrighted. Pays on publication. Reports immediately. Enclose S.A.E. and International Reply Coupons for return of submissions.

Nonfiction and Photos: "Sea-flavored stories written to interest the seamen of the Imperial tanker fleet." Length: 1,500 words maximum. Pays $25 per story, $40 "when illustrations are included." B&w photos are purchased with or without accompanying ms; captions required.

INDUSTRIAL PROGRESS, P.O. Box 13208, Phoenix AZ 85002. Phone: 602-257-1062. Editor: Frederick H. Kling. External house organ of Goodyear Tire and Rubber Company, for "executives, management, and professional men (designers, engineers, etc.) in all types of industry." Bimonthly. Not copyrighted. Pays on acceptance. Enclose S.A.S.E. for return of submissions.

Nonfiction and Photos: Male-interest features: hobbies, sports, novelty, mechanical, do-it-yourself, personalities, adventure, etc. Must be strongly photographic. Some color features used. Pays from $25 to $35 for a single photo caption item to $150 for full-length features (up to 1,000 words) with 4 or 5 b&w photos; more for full-length color features.

INLAND, 30 W. Monroe St., Chicago IL 60603. Phone: 312-692-2448. Managing Editor: Sheldon A. Mix. External publication of Inland Steel Company. Mainly for businessmen and their families. Ages vary; range probably 25 through 65. College educated. Interested in Middle West, in history and sports, in being entertained as well as in being given something to think about. Quarterly magazine; 24 (11¼x8½) pages. Established in 1953. Circulation: 12,000. Buys first North American serial rights. Buys 8 to 10 mss a year. Payment on acceptance. Will send free sample copy to writer on request. Reports in 2 to 4 weeks. "Writers unknown to us are better off sending completed mss. We hesitate to ask unknown writers to prepare articles based on queries." Enclose S.A.S.E.

Nonfiction: Articles, essays, humorous commentaries, pictorial essays. "We like well-done individuality. Half of each issue deals with staff-written steel subjects; half with widely ranging nonsteel matter. Articles and essays related somehow to Midwest (basically Illinois, Wisconsin, Minnesota, Michigan, Missouri, Iowa, Indiana, Ohio) in such subject areas as history, folklore, sports, humor, the seasons, current scene generally; nostalgia and reminiscence if appeal is broad enough. But subject less important than treatment. Encourage individuality, thoughtful writing, fresh ideas, and approaches. Please don't send slight, rehashed historical pieces or any articles of purely local interest." Personal experience, profile, inspirational, humor, historical, think articles, nostalgia, personal opinion, photo articles. Recent articles include "Warren G. Harding: A Half-Century Later;" "Portrait of a Tradition" (about Notre Dame football); the story behind an unusual last will and testament written by an Illinois man. Length: 1,200 to 5,000, but this may vary. Pays $200 (if article is short and needs considerable editing or rewriting) to $500.

Photos: Purchased with or without mss. Captions required. "Payment for pictorial essay same as for text feature."

Fiction: Mainstream or humorous. "Don't run fiction regularly; must have Midwest themes." Length: open. Pays $300 minimum.

NEWS OF THE ENGINEERING DEPARTMENT, Louviers Building, E. I. Du Pont de Nemours & Co., Inc., Wilmington DE 19898. Editor: Michael R. Tyler. For employees. Monthly. Buys one-time rights. Pays on publication. Will send a sample copy to a writer on request. Will consider photocopied submissions. Reports in 2 weeks. Query first. Enclose S.A.S.E.

Nonfiction and Photos: "General items with Du Pont engineering department tie-in; engineering accomplishments of the company." Length: 2,000 words maximum. Pays $50 to $250. 8x10 b&w glossies purchased with mss and with captions only.

ONAN NEWS, ONAN DISTRIBUTOR NEWS, 1400 73rd Ave. N.E., Minneapolis MN 55432. Phone: 612-786-6322. Editor: Patricia Halsten. For "Onan employees, distributors, dealers, and customers." Monthly *(Onan News);* bimonthly *(Onan Distributor News).* Circulation: 8,000. Not copyrighted. Buys about 12 mss a year. Pays on acceptance. Will send a sample copy to a writer on request. Will not consider photocopied submissions. Reports on material accepted for publication in 30 days. Returns rejected material in 15 days. Query first. Enclose S.A.S.E.

Nonfiction and Photos: "Application stories on Onan products and feature stories on Onan employees, distributors, and dealers. The story should be readable, informative, and interesting. It should be able to stand alone, and the mention of Onan products should not necessarily be important to the story line. We do not want material on recreational vehicles — our marketing emphasis has shifted." Length: "about 1,000 words, but we will look at anything on the subject, no matter how short. And if it takes 5,000 well-chosen words to put a message across, we'll consider that, too. Remuneration depends on so many things other than the number of words: difficulty in obtaining the material, accompanying photographs (we prefer contact sheets and require negatives — b&w with captions only), quality of article, timeliness, and degree of importance of theme to our audience. Our normal pay for a four-page typed article accompanied by 8 to 12 b&w negatives is $150. This includes expenses, unless an additional allowance is authorized in advance by the editor."

OUR SUN, Sun Oil Co., 1608 Walnut St., Philadelphia PA 19103. For "local, state, and national government officials; community leaders; news and financial communicators; educators, shareholders, customers, and employees of Sun Oil Company." Established in 1923. Published three times a year. Circulation: 80,000. Not copyrighted. Buys 1 or 2 articles a year. "Most are staff written." Pays on acceptance. Will send a sample copy to a writer on request. Reports in 3 to 6 weeks. Query first. Enclose S.A.S.E.

Nonfiction: "Articles only. Subject matter should be related to Sun Oil Company, oil industry, or national energy situation. Articles should be directed toward a general audience. Style: magazine feature. Approach: nontechnical. Travel themes are currently being overworked." Buys informational articles, interviews, profiles, historical articles, think pieces, coverage of successful business operations. Length: 1,000 to 3,000 words. Pays $300 to $800.

Photos: Purchased on assignment; captions optional. "We do not buy photos on spec." Pays $100 to $400 a day for photographic assignments.

PGW NEWS, Philadelphia Gas Works, 1800 N. 9th St., Philadelphia PA 19122. Phone: 215-796-1260. Editor: William B. Hall. For "company employees, retirees, suppliers, other gas companies in U.S. and abroad, government officials in Pennsylvania." Monthly. Circulation: 5,000. Not copyrighted. Pays on acceptance. Will send a sample copy to a writer on request. Submit seasonal material 3 to 4 months in advance. Reports in 1 to 2 months. Enclose S.A.S.E. for return of submissions.

Nonfiction: "Material that is related to employees or that could be employee-directed. We put considerable stress on personality features. Nothing from extremist sources will be considered. We are straight and middle-of-the-road in our presentation." Buys how-to's, patriotic pieces, inspirational and some travel articles and think pieces. Length: 1,000 words. Pays $25 minimum.

Photos: B&w glossies. Pays $10 minimum.

ROSEBURG WOODSMAN, 1220 S. W. Morrison St., Portland OR 97205. Publication of Roseburg Lumber Company. Editor: Rodger Dwight. For wholesale and retail lumber dealers and other buyers of forest products, such as furniture manufacturers and paper products companies. Magazine; 8 pages, (8¼x11). Publishes a special Christmas issue. Established in 1955. Monthly. Circulation: 10,000. Buys all rights, but will reassign rights to author after publication. Buys approximately 20 mss per year. Pays on publication. Will send free sample copy to a writer on request, as well as editorial guidelines sheet. Will not consider photocopied or simultaneous submissions. Submit seasonal material 3 months in advance. Reports on material accepted for publication in 1 week. Returns rejected material immediately. Query first, or submit complete mss. Enclose S.A.S.E.
Nonfiction and Photos: Features on the "residential, commercial and industrial applications of Roseburg's wood products, such as lumber, plywood, prefinished wall paneling, and flakeboard — vinyl-laminated and printed." Informational, how-to, interview, profile, new products, technical and merchandising techniques articles. Length: 500 to 1,000 words. Pays 10¢ per word. Pays $10 per b&w glossies purchased with mss; 8x10. Pays $25 to $50 per color transparency or print.
How To Break In: "We seek the short story approach in our mss, showing successful applications of our wood products."

RURALITE, P.O. Box 1731, Portland OR 97207. Phone: 503-223-7395. Editor: Aaron C. Jones. For "rural people served by our member utilities in Oregon, Washington, Idaho, Nevada and Alaska." Established in 1953. Monthly. Circulation: 120,000. Buys first North American serial rights. Buys 300 mss a year. Payment on acceptance. Will send free sample copy to Northwest writers on request. Will consider photocopied submissions. Submit seasonal material 3 months in advance. Reports on material in 15 days. Query first. Enclose S.A.S.E.
Nonfiction and Photos: "Human interest stories about member-owners of the public utilities that send *Ruralite* to their members. Articles that offer good advice to rural people; how to repair or how to live more safely, etc. Must have some connection with utility or members of utility." How-to, inspirational, new product. Length: 250 to 2,500 words. Pays $25 to $100. B&w photos purchased with accompanying mss or without ms. Captions required. Pays $7.50.

SAFECO AGENT, Safeco Insurance, Safeco Plaza, Seattle WA 98185. Editor: Bob Sincock; Managing Editor: Jack C. High. For independent insurance agents, multiline, highly professional; must compete for their favor with other insurance companies they represent, so content is nearly all Safeco-oriented. Established in 1923. Bimonthly. Circulation: 15,000. Copyrighted. Buys 4 to 8 mss a year. "Depends on availability of qualified writer to handle assignment in specific geographical area." Payment on acceptance. Will send free sample copy to writer on request. Reports in 2 weeks. Query first. Enclose S.A.S.E.
Nonfiction: "Interested in articles by assignment only. Agent success articles. Case histories, profiles, interviews. How to prospect, sell insurance, develop accounts. Agency management. All articles related to Safeco products, policies and procedures. Emphasize agent's success as a Safeco representative. Give testimonials." Informational, how-to, personal experience, interview, profile, inspirational, successful business operations, merchandising techniques and technical. Length: 600 to 1,600 words. Pays to $200 or thereabouts.
Photos: Pays $10 minimum for b&w glossy stock photos. Photos by assignment are negotiated.

SINGER LIGHT, 30 Rockefeller Plaza, New York NY 10020. Editor: Joan Moschello. For Singer employees. Circulation: 80,000. Usually buys all rights. Pays on acceptance. Will send a sample copy to a writer on request. "It's best to query on major articles." Enclose S.A.S.E.
Nonfiction and Photos: "News items and feature articles with a Singer products or Singer employee tie-in. Stories should be illustrated with photos." Length: 1,500 words maximum. Pays 10¢ a word for news items of 200 words maximum. Pays $50 to $250 for features, "depending on length, scope, and quality." Photos purchased

with mss. Buys picture stories with a Singer product or Singer employee tie-in. "We prefer the available light approach wherever practical." Send b&w contact sheets or 8x10 glossies; "no color." Model releases required. Pays $50 to $250 for picture stories, "depending on number of pictures, scope, and quality." Pays $10 to $25 for single photos with captions, "depending on importance or originality."

SMALL WORLD, Volkswagen of America, 818 Sylvan Ave., Englewood Cliffs NJ 07632. Editor: Burton Unger. For "Volkswagen owners in the United States," 5 times a year. Buys all rights. Payment on acceptance. Write for copy of guidelines for writers. Reports in 1 month. "If you have a long feature possibility in mind, please query first. Though queries should be no longer than 2 pages, they ought to include a working title, a short, general summary of the article, and an outline of the specific points to be covered. Where possible, please include a sample of the photography available. We strongly advise writers to read at least 2 past issues before working on a story." Enclose S.A.S.E.

Nonfiction and Photos: "Interesting stories on people using Volkswagens; useful owner modifications of the vehicle; travel pieces with the emphasis on people, not places; Volkswagenmania stories, personality pieces, inspirational and true adventure articles. VW arts and crafts, etc. The style should be light. All stories must have a VW tie-in. Our approach is subtle, however, and we try to avoid obvious product puffery, since *Small World* is not an advertising medium. We prefer a first-person, people-oriented handling. Length: 1,500 words maximum; shorter pieces, some as short as 450 words, often receive closer attention." Pays $100 per printed page for photographs and text; otherwise, a portion of that amount, depending on the space allotted. Most stories go 2 pages; some run 3 or 4. Photos purchased with ms; captions required. "We prefer color transparencies, particularly 35mm slides. All photos should carry the photographer's name and address. If the photographer is not the author, both names should appear on the first page of the text. Where possible, we would like a selection of at least 40 transparencies. It is recommended that at least one show the principal character or author; another, all or a recognizable portion of a VW in the locale of the story. Quality photography can often sell a story that might be otherwise rejected. Every picture should be identified or explained." Model releases required. Pays $250 for cover photo.

Fillers: "Short, humorous anecdotes about Volkswagens." Pays $15.

TEXACO TEMPO, 90 Wynford Dr., Don Mills, Ontario, M3C 1K5, Canada. Editor: Robert Cameron. Published by Texaco Canada Ltd. for "employees, shareholders, plant-community leaders, the press." Established in 1959. Quarterly. Circulation: 6,500. Not copyrighted. Buys about 10 mss a year. Pays on acceptance. Will send a sample copy to a writer on request. Write for copy of guidelines for writers. Will consider photocopied submissions. Reports in 2 weeks. Query first. Address to "Public Relations Dept." Enclose S.A.E. and International Reply Coupons.

Nonfiction and Photos: "Related to Canadian oil industry and particularly to activities of this company, a fully integrated oil company which explores for crude oil, drills for it, transports it, refines it, transports the products, and sells them at wholesale and retail. The publication tries to meet external and internal readership needs. No articles on cute little local tourist interest sights or happenings which people might drive 25 miles to see, but not 250 or 2,500 miles." Buys informational articles, how-to's, personal experience articles, profiles, humor, historical articles, nostalgia, travel pieces, and coverage of successful business operations. Length: 800 to 2,000 words. Pays $100 to $200. B&w (5x7 upwards) glossy photos purchased with mss with no additional payment. Captions required.

UNIROYAL WORLD, Oxford Management and Research Center, Middlebury CT 06749. Editor: Renee Follett. Published by Uniroyal, Inc. for "wage and salary employees, all ages and educations; they are plant, office, and management employees." Established in 1964. 8 times a year. Circulation: 65,000. Not copyrighted. Pays on acceptance. Will send a sample copy to a writer on request. Will consider photocopied submissions. Reports in 3 weeks. Enclose S.A.S.E.

Nonfiction and Photos: "This publication deals primarily with Uniroyal — its people, places and products. We publish general information dealing with specific aspects of Uniroyal and the rubber industry. Articles must relate to Uniroyal employees." Buys informational articles, how-to's, personal experience articles, interviews, profiles, humor, think articles, coverage of successful business operations and merchandising techniques. Length: 600 to 1,200 words. Pays $50 to $200. 8x10 b&w glossies purchased with mss; captions required. Pays $20 per photo.

VICKERS VOICE, Box 2240, Wichita KS 67201. Editor: Derald Linn. For employees of Vickers Petroleum Corp. Quarterly magazine; 16 pages. Circulation: 2,000. Not copyrighted. Payment on publication. Will send free sample copy to writer on request. Query first or submit complete ms. Enclose S.A.S.E.
Nonfiction and Photos: Articles about activities of the company, its parent company, and its subsidiaries. Articles showing, by example, how a service station owner or manager can make more money from an existing outlet; travel articles. Length: 500 to 1,000 words. Pays $15 to $25. Photos purchased with or without mss or on assignment. Captions required. Pays $10 for 8x10 b&w glossies.

FARM PUBLICATIONS

Crops and Soil Management

The publications in this category limit themselves to advising farmers on techniques for raising food from the soil and on cultivating the soil effectively. Other magazines that buy material on the raising of crops and soil management will be found in the General Interest Farming and Rural Life classification.

COTTON FARMING MAGAZINE, Little Publications, 3637 Park Ave., Memphis TN 38111. Phone: 901-327-4168. Editor: Tom Griffin. Buys all rights. Pays on publication. Will send a free sample copy and outline of requirements to a writer on request. Reports in approximately 3 to 6 weeks. Enclose S.A.S.E. for return of submissions.
Nonfiction and Photos: Continually looking for material on large-acreage cotton farmers (200 acres or more). Likes stories on one phase of a grower's production such as his weed control program, insect control, landforming work, or how he achieves higher than average yields. Length: 1,000 to 1,200 words with at least 3 in-the-field photos. Payment is 10¢ a word.

CRANBERRIES MAGAZINE, Box J, R-55 Summer St., Kingston MA 02364. Phone: 617-585-6561. Editor: Mrs. Jane B. Presler. For "cranberry growers—older audience—interested in growing good crops—most have high school education—some college." Monthly. Circulation: 1,000. Buys first rights. Buys 2 to 3 mss a year. Pays on publication. Will send a free sample copy to a writer on request. Query first. Reports in 2 to 3 weeks. Enclose S.A.S.E.
Nonfiction and Photos: Wants "personal profiles of cranberry growers—new techniques of growing. We reject material that isn't pertinent enough to merit the cost. We need specific grower profiles, unique material that will be informative and helpful to cranberry growers. We have to reject general interest material, scenery-type photos, etc." Payment is "none to $20." 5x7 b&w glossy photos purchased with mss. Payment is $5.

CROPS AND SOILS MAGAZINE, 677 South Segoe Rd., Madison WI 53711. Editor: William R. Luellen. For the modern farmer and his advisors (agribusiness, county extension personnel, vo-ag, as well as industrial, extension, and research agronomists with this clientele). 9 times a year. Buys all rights for articles. Buys one-time rights

for photos. Pays on publication. Reports in 1 month. Query first. Enclose S.A.S.E.
Nonfiction and Photos: Articles about current research and articles reviewed for accuracy by USDA or state college workers have best chance for acceptance. "We use scientifically proven research that has practical value. Nothing else!" Interested in material dealing with new or unusual field crops, seed production methods, new cultivation practices, new harvesting methods, irrigation and drainage practices, tillage, weed and insect control. These can be short items of a few paragraphs up to illustrated features of 1,000 to 1,500 words. Pays 2¢ to 4¢ a word.

THE FLUE-CURED TOBACCO FARMER, 559 Jones Franklin Rd., Suite 150, Raleigh NC 27606. Editor: Carl P. Johnson. For farmers who produce 4 or more acres of flue-cured tobacco. Magazine; 40 pages. Established in 1964. Eight times a year. Circulation: 45,500. Buys all rights, but will reassign rights to author after publication. Buys 24 mss a year. Pays on publication. Will send free sample copy to writer on request. Reports immediately. Query first. Enclose S.A.S.E.
Nonfiction and Photos: Production and industry-related articles. Emphasis is on a knowledge of the industry and the ability to write specifically for it. All material must be in-depth and be up to date on all industry activities. Informational, how-to, personal experience, interview, profile, personal opinion, successful business operations. Length: open. Pays $2 per column inch. B&w glossies (5x7) purchased with mss. Pays $10. Captions required.

THE PEANUT FARMER, 559 Jones Franklin Rd., Suite 150, Raleigh NC 27606. Editor: Carl P. Johnson. For peanut farmers with 15 or more acres of peanuts. Magazine; 32 pages. Established in 1965. Eight times a year. Circulation: 28,500. Buys all rights, but will reassign rights to author after publication. Buys about 24 mss a year. Pays on publication. Will send free sample copy to writer on request. Reports immediately. Query first or submit complete ms. Enclose S.A.S.E.
Nonfiction and Photos: Production and industry-related articles. Must be in-depth and up to date on all industry activities. Informational, how-to, personal experience, interview, profile, personal opinion, successful business operations. Length: open. Pays $2 a column inch. Pays $10 for 5x7 b&w glossies purchased with mss. Captions required.

POTATO GROWER (OF IDAHO), P.O. Box 981, Idaho Falls ID 83401. Editor: D. Brent Clement. For potato growers, packers, shippers, buyers, processors, university personnel associated with agriculture interested in the production and successful marketing of potatoes. Magazine; 32 to 40 pages. Established in 1972. Monthly. Circulation: 14,000. Buys first North American serial rights. Buys 10 to 12 mss a year. Pays on publication. Will send free sample copy to writer on request. No photocopied submissions. Will consider simultaneous submissions. Submit material for special issues (irrigation and potato storage) 6 weeks before publication. Reports on material accepted for publication immediately. Returns rejected material in 2 weeks. Query first. Enclose S.A.S.E.
Nonfiction and Photos: Editorial coverage includes all phases of potato growing, shipping, packaging, planting, fertilizing, frost protection, insect and disease control, weed control, harvesting, storage and marketing methods. Human interest stories on potato growers, research related to potatoes and other subjects of interest to potato growers also considered. Basic interest is in the western U.S. potato producing areas. May consider an occasional feature story on what's happening in specific potato producing areas; growth, new development, marketing problems, etc. Assigned articles only. Length: 2,500 words maximum. Pays 1¢ to 3¢ a word. Pays $5 for 5x7 or 8x10 b&w glossies purchased with or without ms; $15 to $25 for color. No high-speed film. Captions required.
Fillers: Short humor related to subject matter. Pays $5 to $10.

RICE FARMING MAGAZINE, Little Publications, 3637 Park Ave., Memphis TN 38111. Editor: Tom Griffin. Buys all rights. Pays on publication. Will send a free sample copy and outline of requirements to a writer on request. Reports in approximately 3 to 6 weeks. Enclose S.A.S.E. for return of submissions.

Nonfiction and Photos: Continually looking for material on large acreage rice farmers (200 acres or more). Stories on one phase of grower's production such as his weed control program, insect control, landforming work, or how he achieves higher than average yields. Include at least 3 in-the-field photos. Length: 1,000 to 1,200 words. Payment is 10¢ a word.

THE RICE JOURNAL, P.O. Box 14260, Washington DC 20044. Editor: C. B. Morrison. For readers interested in rice and rice farming and marketing. Magazine; 40 to 120 (8½x11) pages. Established in 1897. Monthly. Circulation: 10,000. Buys all rights, but will reassign rights to author after publication. Buys about 12 mss a year. Pays on publication. Reports in 10 days. Query first. Enclose S.A.S.E.
Nonfiction and Photos: Informational, profile, humor and travel; related to rice industry. Articles on duck hunting. Length: open. Pays minimum of $40 for articles, less for fillers. B&w photos and color transparencies purchased without mss. Pays $25 for b&w; $50 for color.

SOYBEAN DIGEST, Hudson IA 50643. Editor: Carol Koch. For American Soybean Association members. 13 issues a year. Not copyrighted. Will send a free sample copy to a writer on request. Query first. Enclose S.A.S.E.
Nonfiction and Photos: Bulk of editorial material is staff-written, but uses good articles on phases of soybean production and usage and personalities when they have a real message for the industry. "We publish articles according to the soybean grower's year. For example, Soybean Outlook (December issue), Herbicides (February issue), etc." Length should be up to 2,000 words. Pays $50 minimum. Occasionally uses 8x10 b&w glossies or color. No additional payment for photos used.

THE SUGARBEET, Box 1520, Ogden UT 84402. Editor: A. L. Hanline. Publication of The Amalgamated Sugar Company. For readership "strongly involved in beet sugar industry." Established in 1937. Quarterly. Circulation: 6,500. Not copyrighted. Payment on publication. Will send free sample copy to writer on request. Query first. Enclose S.A.S.E.
Nonfiction and Photos: "Articles dealing with the growing and harvesting of sugar beets; namely, seedbed preparation, fumigating, fertilizing, planting, weed and insect control, fungus control, irrigating, cultivating, mechanical thinning, harvesting; college research in these areas also desired. Should be tight, direct exposition written to the growers, not research personnel. Each issue is devoted to a specific phase of growing sugar beets during that time of the year." How-to, interview, technical, successful business operations with ample photos. Length: 750 to 2,000 words. Pays $25 to $50. 8x10 b&w glossies purchased with mss. No additional payment. Captions required.

VEGETABLE GROWERS MESSENGER, Caroline Publishing Co., Preston MD 21655. Editor: Max Chambers. For commercial vegetable growers and marketers. Bimonthly. Buys all rights. Pays on publication. Reports promptly. Query preferred. Enclose S.A.S.E.
Nonfiction: Uses articles about vegetable production, harvesting, marketing, and packaging aimed at commercial growers only. Pays 3½¢ a word.
Photos: Pays $5 for 4x5, 5x7, and 8x10 b&w glossies.

Dairy Farming

Publications for dairymen are classified here. Publications for farmers who raise animals for meat, wool, or hides are included in the Livestock category. Other magazines that buy material on dairy herds will be found in the General Interest Farming and Rural Life classification. Journals for dairy products retailers will be found under Dairy Products in the Trade Journals section.

DAIRY GOAT JOURNAL, P.O. Box 1908, Scottsdale AR 85252. Editor: Kent Leach. Monthly for breeders and raisers of dairy goats. Generally buys exclusive rights. Pays on acceptance. Sample copy will be sent on request. Reports in ten days. Query first. Enclose S.A.S.E.

Nonfiction and Photos: Uses articles, items, and photos that deal with dairy goats, and the people who raise them. Goat dairies and shows. How-to-do-it articles up to 1,000 words. Pays 5¢ a word. Also buys 8x10 b&w photos for $1 to $15.

DAIRY HERD MANAGEMENT, P.O. Box 67, Minneapolis MN 55440. Editor: George Ashfield. For professional dairymen. Monthly. Established in 1966. Circulation: 55,000. Not copyrighted. Buys 20 to 25 mss a year. Payment on acceptance. Will send free sample copy to writer on request. Write for copy of guidelines for writers. Special emphasis issues are February (milking and milk handling), April (waste management), June (dairy health), and November (nutrition). Submit special material 2 months in advance. Reports in 2 to 4 weeks. Query first. Enclose S.A.S.E.

Nonfiction and Photos: Interested in all aspects of dairy herd management, including feeding, milking, herd health, breeding and waste management. Articles include producer technique features as well as scientific research results. Informational, how-to, interview, profile articles. Length: 2,000 to 2,500 words. Pays $40 to $200. Photos purchased with ms. B&w photos get no additional payment. Color payment is negotiated.

THE DAIRYMAN, P.O. Box 819, Corona CA 91720. Editor: Dolores Davis Miller. For large herd dairy farmers. Monthly. Buys reprint rights. Pays on publication. Will send a sample copy to a writer on request. Reports in 3 weeks. Enclose S.A.S.E.

Nonfiction and Photos: Uses articles on anything related to dairy farming, preferably anything new and different or substantially unique in operation, for U.S. subjects. Acceptance of foreign dairy farming stories based on potential interest of readers. Pays $1 per printed inch. Buys photos with or without mss. Pays $5 each.

DAIRYMAN'S DIGEST (Southern Region Edition), P.O. Box 809, Arlington TX 76010. Editor: Phil Porter. For commercial dairy farmers and their families, throughout the central U.S., with interests in dairy production and marketing. Magazine; 32 (8½x11) pages. Established in 1969. Monthly. Circulation: 9,000. Not copyrighted. Buys about 34 mss a year. Pays on publication. Will send free sample copy to writer on request. Reports in 3 weeks. Query first. Enclose S.A.S.E.

Nonfiction and Photos: Emphasis on dairy production and marketing. Buys articles of general interest to farm families, especially dairy-oriented. Seeks unusual accomplishments and satisfactions resulting from determination and persistence. Must be positive and credible. Needs newsbreaks, fresh ideas, profile, personal experience articles. Buys some historical, inspirational or nostalgia. Also articles of interest to farm wives; patriotic, family; any subject. Length: 50 to 1,500 words. Pay varies from $10 to $125 per article, plus additional amount for photos, depending on quality.

General Interest Farming and Rural Life

The publications listed here aim at farm families or farmers in general and contain material on sophisticated agricultural and business techniques. Magazines that specialize in the raising of crops will be found in the Crops and Soil Management classification; publications exclusively for dairymen are included under Dairy Farming; publications that deal exclusively with livestock raising are classified in the Livestock category; magazines for poultry farmers are grouped under the Poultry classification. Magazines that aim at farm suppliers are grouped under Agricultural Equipment and Supplies in the Trade Journals section.

National

AGRI FINANCE, Suite G, 5520 Touhy Ave., Skokie IL 60076. Editor: Ted A. Priebe. For "agricultural specialists and loan officers of banks and other lending institutions that deal with farmers and allied businesses." Established in 1959. Bimonthly. Circulation: 15,000. Buys all rights. Buys 25 to 30 mss a year. Payment on publication. Will send free sample copy to a writer on request. Will send editorial guidelines sheet to a writer on request. Query first required. Enclose S.A.S.E.
Nonfiction: Articles that "interpret developments in agriculture as they affect the flow of loanable funds into agricultural businesses and enterprises." Pays $100 minimum.

AGWAY COOPERATOR, Box 1333, Syracuse NY 13201. Editor: James E. Hurley. For farmers. Monthly. Pays on acceptance. Usually reports in 1 week. Enclose S.A.S.E. for return of submissions.
Nonfiction: Should deal with topics of farm or rural interest. Length: 1,200 words maximum. Payment is $50 to $100, usually including photos.
Photos: Payment is $5 to $15 for photos purchased singly.

THE AMERICAN FARMER, 225 Touhy Ave., Park Ridge IL 60068. Photo and Copy Editor: Herb Kinnear. For "all ages of farmers and ranchers in all states except Alaska. All are members of Farm Bureau." Established in 1925. 9 times a year. Circulation: 2,400,000. Query first. Enclose S.A.S.E.
Nonfiction and Photos: Subject matter consists of short articles of general agricultural interest, especially how farm families solve their economic, social and environmental problems. "We do not use how-to production articles but concentrate on economic issues that affect farmers' day-to-day management decisions. Query with a definite plan and idea in mind. Our publication covers the business aspect of agriculture stressing new agricultural developments as they affect farmers, developments in nonagricultural subjects that affect agriculture; exports and imports that affect farmers and their management decisions; farm product utilization and utilization research and marketing of products from the farmer's viewpoint." Length: 700 words maximum. Payment varies. Must have illustrative material. Only highest quality 8x10 b&w photos or 2¼ color transparencies or larger considered. Pay for photos varies according to use.

BIG FARMER, 131 Lincoln Hwy., Frankfort IL 60423. Phone: 815-469-2163. Editor: Bob Moraczewski. Published 9 times a year. Buys first rights. Pays on acceptance. Will consider cassette submissions. Query first. Enclose S.A.S.E.
Nonfiction: Articles to help readers improve management skills of large-scale farms. Particularly interested in articles on money and business management as related to the operation of modern farms. No fiction, verse, or poetry. Length: 1,000 to 1,500 words. Pays $50 to $350.
Photos: Livestock color, dramatic large-scale farming situations to illustrate general features. Photographic quality requirements very high. Pays $20 for b&w; $50 or more for color, one-time use inside.

CAPPER'S WEEKLY, 616 Jefferson St., Topeka KS 66607. Editor: Dorothy Harvey. For Midwestern residents, especially for farmers and persons living in small towns. Established in 1879. Weekly tabloid newspaper. Circulation: over 460,000. Not copyrighted. Submit seasonal material 8 to 10 weeks in advance. Query first. Enclose S.A.S.E.
Nonfiction and Poetry: Emphasis on human interest material that appeals to readership. Uses material, including poetry, for "In the Heart of the Home," "Open Session," and general news briefs. Length: open. Payment for nonfiction "depends on quality and length of article." Pays $2 minimum for 4-line poem.
Fiction: Publishes novels in serialized form. Payment "depends on quality and length."

FARM JOURNAL, Washington Square, Philadelphia PA 19105. Editor: Lane

Palmer. Many separate editions for different parts of the U.S. Material bought for one or more editions depending upon where it fits. Buys first rights. Payment made on acceptance and is the same regardless of editions in which the piece is used. Query before submitting material. Enclose S.A.S.E.

Nonfiction: Timeliness and seasonableness are very important. Material must be highly practical and should be helpful to as many farmers as possible. Farmers' experiences may apply to any phase of farming and animal raising, as well as to the farmhouse and the community. Technical material must be accurate. Pays $25 minimum.

Photos: Much in demand either separately or with short how-to material in picture stories and as illustrations for articles. Warm human interest pix for covers—activities on modern farms. For inside use, shots of homemade and handy ideas to get work done easier and faster, farm news photos, and pictures of children on the farm. In b&w, 8x10 glossies are preferred; color submissions should be 2¼x2¼ for the cover, and 35mm for inside use. Pays $50 and up for b&w shot; $75 and up for color.

FREE PRESS WEEKLY REPORT ON FARMING, 300 Carlton St., Winnipeg, Manitoba, Canada R3C 3C1. Editor: Bruce P. McDonald. For farmers and other agriculturists of all ages, etc., with majority in the above average income groups and a growing tendency to graduates in agriculture. Weekly. Established in 1880. Circulation:300,000. Buys first serial rights. Buys 25 mss a year. Payment on publication. Articles for spring planting time, late summer and fall harvest should be submitted 2 months in advance. Will consider photocopied submissions. Submit only complete ms. Enclose S.A.E. and International Reply Coupons.

Nonfiction and Photos: "We want articles with practical application in agriculture, with emphasis on good, profitable business. Approach farming as a business and an interesting way of life." How-to, personal experience, interview, photo, successful business operations, new product, and technical articles. Length: 200 to 2,000 words. Pays 50¢ per printed column inch. Color slides (positives) and 5x7 or 8x10 b&w glossies purchased with ms. Pays $3 each. Captions required.

Fiction: "The only fiction we publish consists of short novels, condensed and run as serials." Pays approximately $100 minimum for five-parter.

How To Break In: "Since we're a weekly, our slant is more timely and vital than the monthly magazine approach. Emphasis is on current issues, policy changes and effects."

THE FURROW, Deere & Co., John Deere Rd., Moline IL 61265. North American Editor: George R. Sollenberger. For upper-income farm families. Seven times yearly. Buys international rights. Pays on acceptance. Will send a sample copy to a writer on request. No query required. Reports in 2 weeks. Enclose S.A.S.E.

Nonfiction and Photos: Uses short articles aimed specifically at upper-income farm audience, with emphasis on semitechnical features describing or analyzing new developments in production and marketing of crops and livestock. Writing must be top quality professional work. Rarely buys from freelancers not thoroughly familiar with agricultural technology. Length: 1,500 words maximum. Color negatives or transparencies, including 35mm, purchased only with mss. "Minimum payment for an unillustrated one-page article is $75. For a one-page color story, $125. These are for articles that can be used in one of our 10 regional editions. Almost all freelance articles we buy are of broad enough interest to go in several regional editions, and thus they are worth more. In other words, we hardly ever buy anything at minimum rates."

THE NATIONAL FUTURE FARMER, Box 15130, Alexandria VA 22309. Phone: 703-360-3600. Editor: Wilson Carnes. For youth, 14 to 21 years old, studying vocational agriculture (agribusiness) in high school, members of Future Farmers of America (FFA). Bimonthly. Buys all rights unless otherwise arranged. Pays on acceptance. Will send a sample copy to a writer on request. Reports in 2 weeks. Enclose S.A.S.E.

Nonfiction: "Most articles are staff-written, but purchase a few" in three major categories: 1. The FFA: Articles about present and former members who have made

unusual or outstanding accomplishments, provided they would be of interest nationally or have inspirational value. These could be success stories on their farming programs, leadership activities, and other worthwhile endeavors. Local chapter or group activities are appropriate if they are unusual or different and contain ideas or suggestions other chapters might use. 2. Agriculture: "Articles must appeal to a variety of interests and involve young people who are getting established in farming, ranching, or other careers in agribusiness. Articles on management, financing, and other ways of developing an adequate resource base for a career in agriculture are particularly appealing. Articles on technology are considered when they are not too specialized and are translated into an easy-to-read form. Some how-to material for the age group is also considered." 3. General interest: Well-written articles which help the reader broaden his education, tips and suggestions for choosing and preparing for a vocation, hobbies, sports and recreation, social and personality improvement. Shorter articles preferred, concisely written and well illustrated. Maximum length: 1,000 words. Pays up to 4¢ a word for well-written articles.
Photos: 8x10 b&w photos and 4x5 color transparencies of FFA scenes wanted. Pays up to $7.50 for b&w, up to $100 for color transparencies for cover; $50 for calendar photo; uses 12 per year.

THE PROGRESSIVE FARMER, 820 Shades Creek Pkwy., Box 2581, Birmingham AL 35209. Buys first publication rights. Will send sample copy for 40¢. Will consider photocopied submissions if not simultaneously submitted elsewhere. Reports in 1 month. Query essential. Send to Editorial Director. Enclose S.A.S.E.
Nonfiction and Photos: Buys articles dealing with personal experiences in farming; how-to-do-it articles from the South. Style should be easy-to-read, farm-oriented writing. Also wants freelance material for regular columns Handy Devices (farm), and Jokes. Pays $15 a column and up. 8x10 b&w glossy photos purchased with mss. Pays $10 a photo and up.

SUCCESSFUL FARMING, 1716 Locust St., Des Moines IA 50336. Phone: 515-284-9204. Editor: Dick Hanson. For top farmers. 12 times a year. Buys all rights. Pays on acceptance. Will consider photocopied submissions. Query first. Enclose S.A.S.E.
Nonfiction: "Most of our material is too limited and unfamiliar for freelance writers—except for the few who specialize in agriculture, have a farm background and a modern agricultural education." Length: about 1,500 words maximum. Pays on basis of space used, $10 to $300.
Photos: Ralph Figg, Art Director, prefers 8x10 b&w glossies to contacts; color should be 2¼x2¼, 4x5 or 8x10. Buys exclusive rights and pays $20 for b&w, more for color. Assignments are given, and sometimes a guarantee, provided the editors can be sure the photography will be acceptable. Pays for meals, phone, lodging.

Local

AGROLOGIST, Agricultural Institute of Canada, 151 Slater St., Suite 907, Ottawa, Ontario, Canada K1P 5H4. Managing Editor: W. E. Henderson. For professionals in agriculture: scientists, researchers, economists, teachers, extension workers; most are members of the Agricultural Institute of Canada. Magazine; 40 pages. Established in 1934. Quarterly. Circulation: 6,500. Not copyrighted. Buys 1 or 2 mss a year. Pays on acceptance; occasionally in contributor's copies. Will send free sample copy to writer on request. No photocopied submissions but will consider simultaneous submissions, if so identified. Reports in 1 to 2 weeks. Query first or submit complete ms. Enclose S.A.E. and International Reply Coupons.
Nonfiction and Photos: Articles on subjects of interest to a wide range of disciplines within agriculture, such as results and applications of new research, economic implications, international agricultural trends, overviews, transportation, education, marketing, etc. Highly technical and specialized material presented as much as possible in layman's language. Main interest is not in new facts, but in the interpretation and implication of facts and situations. "We don't publish 'as is' technical papers (such as those prepared for symposia) or scientific journal material. But we will look at it. If the information is of interest, we could suggest how it

might be rewritten for our use. We are particularly interested in articles that highlight how some action of agriculture is affecting nonagriculture areas; e.g., ecology topics, food crisis, etc." Recently published "The Inside Story," which dealt with conditions of work for a farm laborer in Canada. Length: 500 to 2,500 words. Most articles are not paid for; those that are average $100 for 1,500 words. No additional payment for b&w photos used with mss. Pays $5 to $15 for 8x10 b&w glossies purchased without mss or on assignment.

AMERICAN AGRICULTURALIST AND THE RURAL NEW YORKER, P.O. Box 370, Ithaca NY 14850. Editor: Gordon Conklin. Monthly. Not copyrighted. Buys all rights. Pays on acceptance. Will send a free sample copy to a writer on request. Reports immediately. Enclose S.A.S.E. for return of submissions.
Nonfiction and Photos: Short articles on farm subjects of general interest to farm and suburban dwellers. Pays 2¢ to 3¢ a word. Photos purchased with mss and with captions only. Pays $5.

BUCKEYE FARM NEWS, 245 N. High St., Columbus OH 43216. Phone: 614-225-8905. Editor: S.C. Cashman. For a rural audience, "mostly farmers with a high school education or better, 21 to 75 years of age." Established in 1922. Monthly. Circulation: 70,000. Buys all rights, but will reassign rights to author after publication; buys first serial rights in the state of Ohio. Buys 12 to 20 mss a year. Pays on publication. Will send a sample copy to a writer on request. Submit seasonal material at least 36 days in advance of issue date. Will consider photocopied submissions. Reports in 2 to 4 weeks. Query first or submit complete ms. Enclose S.A.S.E.
Nonfiction and Photos: "Articles on agri-marketing, human interest, public affairs material of interest to rural people, farm organization news, etc. Articles must show the value of something to the farm reader or the members of his family. We do not use a lot of material dealing with agri-production, and do not use short stories dealing with farm people. We'd like to see material on farm politics, farm programs, exports and imports, and environmental matters. Material related to the interests and concerns of Ohio people has priority." Buys how-to's, informational articles, personal experience articles, interviews, inspirational articles, and coverage of successful business operations. Length: 400 to 3,000 words. Pays $25 to $100. Photos with captions purchased with mss.

CAROLINA COOPERATOR, 125 E. Davie, Raleigh NC 27601. Editor: Robert J. Wachs. For Carolina farmers. Monthly. Buys all rights. Not many freelance articles bought. Pays on acceptance. Will send a free sample copy to a writer on request. Reports as soon as possible. Enclose S.A.S.E. for return of submissions.
Nonfiction: Interested only in material related to Carolina agriculture, rural living, and farmer co-ops. Length: 1,200 words maximum. Payment is $15 to $35.

COUNTRY LIVING MAGAZINE, 6677 Busch Blvd., Columbus OH 43229. Phone: 614-268-3579. Managing Editor: Marcus T. Orr. For member-consumers of electric cooperatives throughout rural Ohio. 32-page publication in 23 editions. Monthly. Circulation: 148,000. Not copyrighted. Pays on acceptance. Will send free sample copy to writer on request. Usually reports within 3 months. Enclose S.A.S.E.
Nonfiction: New ideas, applications and shortcuts for home and farm, preferably related to use of electricity. Hobbies, crafts, informative, leisure-time interests directed to rural Midcentral U.S. people. Length: 500 words maximum. Pays 3¢ minimum per word.
Photos: Human interest; homemade and handy electric power use applications. B&w glossies, any size, purchased with mss or with captions only. Pays about $7.50 each. Occasionally buys color transparency or color print for cover. Pays $25 minimum for one-time use; photos returned. Prefers good rural Midwest scenics; activity that is seasonal.
Fiction: Only vignettes (rural related) of 750 words or less. Prefers seasonal, nostalgia, humor. Pays 3¢ minimum per word.
Poetry: Seldom used. Sometimes buys 13 lines or less related to above subjects. Pays 50¢ minimum a line.

THE DAKOTA FARMER, P.O. Box 910, Aberdeen SD 57401. Phone: 605-225-5170. Editor: Joe Isakson. For farmers and families in North and South Dakota. "All have agriculturally related occupations and interests." Special issues include Beef issue (August). Monthly. Circulation: 84,000. Rights bought "depend on story and author. We are flexible." Buys 25 to 30 mss a year. Pays on publication. Will send a sample copy to a writer on request. Submit seasonal material 3 to 4 months in advance. Returns rejected material in approximately 15 days. Query first. Enclose S.A.S.E.

Nonfiction: "Human interest features of Dakota farm people, history, or events. Keep in mind we write for Dakotans. Stories should be geared to that audience. Articles should be objective. We take sides on controversial issues on our editorial page only." Buys how-to's, personal experience stories, interviews, new product articles, photo essays, historical and travel pieces, and successful business operation coverage. Length: 500 to 2,000 words. Pays 4¢ per published word; 3¢ and 4¢ per published word in home section.

Photos: Purchased with mss. With captions only. B&w glossies, color transparencies. Pays $50 or more for cover photos.

Poetry: Buys traditional and contemporary poetry and light verse. Length: 5 to 15 lines. Pays $5 to $8 per poem. Poetry Editor: Karen Buechler.

FARM AND COUNTRY, 30 Bloor St., W., Toronto, Ontario M4W 1AE Canada. Editor: John Phillips. News Editor: Michael Sage. For Ontario farmers. Tabloid newspaper; 40 pages. Established in 1894. 19 times a year. Circulation: 86,000. Buys all rights, but will reassign rights to author after publication. Buys 120 mss a year. Payment on publication. Write for copy of guidelines for writers. Will consider photocopied submissions. Submit seasonal material 4 weeks in advance. Reports in 1 week. Query first. Enclose S.A.E. and International Reply Coupons.

Nonfiction and Photos: Informational articles on farm business, how-to-do-it around the farm; practical application of agricultural research. "Keep to the subject. We like crisp, short sentences, an original approach, simple style. Nothing folksy or homespun." Length: 250 to 600 words. Pays $2 to $4 per 37 words. Buys 5x7 glossies with mss. Pays $8. Captions required.

FARMFUTURES, 534 N. Broadway, Milwaukee WI 53202. Editor: Royal Fraedrich. For high income farmers. Magazine; 32 (8½x11) pages. Established in 1973. Monthly. Circulation: 30,000. Buys all rights. Buys 60 to 100 mss a year. Pays on publication. Will send free sample copy to writer on request. No photocopied or simultaneous submissions. Reports on material accepted for publication in 30 days. Returns rejected material in 2 weeks. Query first. Enclose S.A.S.E.

Nonfiction and Photos: "Ours is the only national farm magazine devoted exclusively to marketing and the financial management side of farming. We are looking for case histories of successful use of commodity futures markets by farm operators. Major articles deal with marketing and financial strategies of high income farmers. Major commodity interests include corn, cattle, hogs, soybeans, wheat, cotton, and other grains. Market material must be current; thus, must be written within 2 to 3 weeks of publication." Interviews, profiles, personal experience and successful business operation articles pertaining to agricultural commodity markets. Length: 1,000 to 2,000 words. Pays $50 to $250. No additional payment for b&w photos used with mss.

FARMLAND NEWS, P.O. Box 7305, Kansas City MO 64116. Editor: Frank C. Whitsitt. For rural members of farmer co-ops. Tabloid newspaper; 24 pages. Established in 1932. Not copyrighted. Buys 25 to 35 mss a year. Will send free sample copy to writer on request. No photocopied or simultaneous submissions. Submit seasonal material (Christmas, Thanksgiving, Easter) 6 months in advance. Reports on material accepted for publication in 1 to 2 weeks. Returns rejected material in a few days. Query first. Enclose S.A.S.E.

Nonfiction: "We try to personalize and humanize stories of broad significance. We use features of interest to our rural audience, as well as holiday-slanted material (Christmas, Thanksgiving, Easter)." Length: open. Pays $20 to $100.

FLORIDA GROWER & RANCHER, 559 Jones Franklin Rd., Suite 150, Raleigh NC 27606. Editor: Carl P. Johnson. For citrus grove managers and production managers; vegetable growers and managers. Magazine; 24 pages. Established in 1912. Monthly except for combined June/July issue. Circulation: 12,000. Buys all rights, but will reassign rights to author after publication. Buys about 40 mss a year. Pays on acceptance. Will send free sample copy to writer on request. Reports on material immediately. Query first or submit complete ms. Enclose S.A.S.E.
Nonfiction and Photos: Articles on production and industry-related topics. In-depth and up to date. Writer must know the market and write specifically for it. Informational, how-to, personal experience, interview, profile, personal opinion, successful business operations. Length: open. Pays $2 a column inch. Pays $10 for 5x7 b&w glossies used with mss. Captions required.

FLORIDAGRICULTURE, P.O. Box 730, Gainesville FL 32602. Editor: Tom Millsaps. For members of the Florida Farm Bureau Federation. Magazine; 32 pages. Established in 1941. Monthly. Circulation: 63,000. Not copyrighted. Buys about 12 mss a year. Pays on publication. Will send free sample copy to writer, if postage is enclosed with request. Will consider photocopied and simultaneous submissions. Submit seasonal material (Christmas and Thanksgiving) 3 months in advance. Reports on material accepted for publication in 4 to 6 weeks. Returns rejected material in 2 to 4 weeks. Submit complete ms. Enclose S.A.S.E.
Nonfiction and Photos: "We cover the broad spectrum of Florida farming and use articles of general interest to Florida farmers. We can't stress the word 'Florida' enough. The outlook is always toward the Florida farmer. The Federation serves all farmers, not specialized interests. Our theme is 'The Voice of Agriculture'. Articles on the economic problems facing the farmer and how he can best meet them would be of interest. And remember, understand your subject matter thoroughly because the farmer will. We like crisp, provocative writing. Don't make it so folksy as to appear to be writing down to your reader. Please, no stories on why the farmer isn't to blame for high food prices. And, no stories on part-time farmers, or on people who have moved from the big city to get back to rural life." Length: 500 to 1,500 words. Pays $50 to $250, depending on length and content. No additional payment for b&w photos used with mss. But b&w photo essays of Florida farm scenes will be considered. Payment negotiable.

GEORGIA FARMER, 500 Plasamour Dr., P.O. Box 13755, Atlanta GA 30324. Phone: 404-876-1800. Editor: Elmo Hester. For commercial farmers of Georgia. Monthly. Not copyrighted. Pays on publication. Reports immediately. Query helps, but must have meat in it. Enclose S.A.S.E.
Nonfiction and Photos: Concise how-to and success farm stories localized to Georgia. Subject can vary anywhere within the areas of interest to farm readers or agribusiness readers. Length: 1,200 words maximum. Payment is $5 to $50. Photos are occasionally bought with mss; payment included in price of article. Any size; color used.

MICHIGAN FARMER, 4415 N. Grand River Ave., Lansing MI 48906. Phone: 517-372-5254. Editor: Dayton Matlick. Semimonthly. Buys first North American rights. Pays on acceptance. Reports in 1 month. Query first. Enclose S.A.S.E.
Nonfiction: Uses articles of interest and value to Michigan farmers, which discuss Michigan agriculture and the people involved in it. "These are fairly technical. Also articles for home section about Michigan farm housewives and what they are doing. Although articles are technical, lucid easy-to-understand writing is desired. Length depends on topic." Rates are 2¢ a word minimum; special stories bring higher rates.
Photos: Buys some b&w singles; also a few color transparencies, for cover use. Pays $2 to $5 each for b&w, depending on quality. Pays $50 for selected cover transparencies of identifiable Michigan farm or rural scenes.

OKLAHOMA RANCH AND FARM WORLD, Box 1770, Tulsa OK 74102. Phone: 918-583-2161, Ext. 230. Editor: Herb Karner. For a rural, urban, and suburban readership. Monthly. Buys first serial rights. Pays on publication. Query first. Enclose S.A.S.E.

Nonfiction and Photos: Wants farm and ranch success stories; also suburban living, homemaking, youth, 4-H, and F.F.A. Effective photo illustrations necessary. Preferred length: 700 to 800 words. Pays $7.50 a column, sometimes more for exceptional copy. Photos purchased with mss and occasionally with captions only. Prefers b&w glossies, at least 5x7. Pays $3.50 each.

RURAL ELECTRIC MISSOURIAN, 2722 E. McCarty St., Jefferson City MO 65101. Phone: 314-635-6857. Editor: Don Yoest. For rural readers (farm and nonfarm). Monthly. Not copyrighted. Buys exclusive Missouri first rights. Pays on acceptance. Usually reports in 30 to 90 days. Query first. Enclose S.A.S.E.
Nonfiction: Buys articles on electrical equipment—new applications in home, farm, shop, business, or cooperative business. Also uses human interest material, preferably with a humorous rural flavor. Length: 500 to 1,000 words. Payment varies and is negotiated; minimum $10.
Photos: 8x10 b&w glossies occasionally purchased either with mss or with captions only. Payment varies; minimum $5 a photo.
Poetry: "Short, human interest, rural items needed." Pays $5.

SOUTH CAROLINA FARMER-GROWER, 500 Plasamour Dr., P.O. Box 13755, Atlanta GA 30324. Phone: 404-876-1800. Editor: Elmo Hester. For commercial farmers of South Carolina. Monthly. Not copyrighted. Pays on publication. Reports immediately. Query helps, but must have meat in it. Enclose S.A.S.E.
Nonfiction and Photos: Wants concise how-to and success farm stories localized to South Carolina. Subject can vary anywhere within the areas of interest to farm readers or agribusiness readers. Length: 1,200 words maximum. B&w or color photos, any size, occasionally bought with mss. Payment (including photos) is $5 to $50.

WALLACES FARMER, 1912 Grand Ave., Des Moines IA 50305. Phone: 515-243-6181. Editor: Monte N. Sesker. For Iowa farmers and their families. Semimonthly. Buys Midwest States rights (Nebraska, Minnesota, Wisconsin, Illinois, Missouri, South Dakota, and Iowa). Pays on acceptance. Reports in 2 weeks. Enclose S.A.S.E. for return of submissions.
Nonfiction and Photos: Occasional short feature articles about Iowa farming accompanied by photos. Payment varies. Length: 500 to 750 words. Pays about $50. Photos purchased with or without mss. Should be taken on Iowa farms. Pays $7 to $15 for 8x10 b&w; $50 to $100 for 4x5, 2¼x2¼ color transparencies. See recent issue covers for examples.

WISCONSIN AGRICULTURIST, 2536 Golf Ave., Racine WI 53404. Editor: Ralph S. Yohe. For Wisconsin farmers. Bimonthly. Buys first rights. Reports in 2 weeks. Enclose S.A.S.E. for return of submissions.
Nonfiction: Articles containing how-to-do-it information useful to Wisconsin farmers. Also uses feature-type material about Wisconsin farmers. Short sentences, simple words, short paragraphs. Stories should run at least three typed, double-spaced pages. Pays $40 and up.
Photos: Wants photos of farm operations, preferably Wisconsin scene with identifiable farmer. Buys some how-to-do-it photo series of farm interest. Pays $5 to $10 a photo for 8x10 b&w glossies; pays $50 to $100 for all rights to 2¼x2¼ or larger color transparencies.

Livestock

Publications in this section are for farmers who raise cattle, sheep, or hogs for meat, wool, or hides. Publications for farmers who raise other animals are listed in the Miscellaneous category; also many magazines in the General Interest Farming and Rural Interest classification buy material on raising livestock. Magazines for dairymen are included under Dairy Farming. Publications dealing with raising horses, pets, or other pleasure animals will be found under Animal in the Consumer Publications section.

AMERICAN HEREFORD JOURNAL, 715 Hereford Dr., Kansas City MO 64105. Editor: Bob Day. Monthly. Buys first North American serial rights. Pays on publication. Reports in 30 days. Always query first. Enclose S.A.S.E.
Nonfiction and Photos: Breeding, feeding, and marketing of purebred and commercial Herefords, with accent on well-substantiated facts; success-type story of a Hereford cattleman and how he did it. Length: 1,000 to 1,500 words. Pays average of 2½¢ to 3¢ a word. Buys 5x7 b&w glossy photos for use with articles. Pays $3 each.

ARKANSAS CATTLE BUSINESS, 208 Wallace Bldg., Little Rock AR 72201. Phone: 501-372-3197. Editor: Mary Hinkle. For beef cattlemen. Not copyrighted. Buys 2 to 3 mss a year. Pays on acceptance. Will send a free sample copy to a writer on request. Reports in 2 weeks. Query first. Enclose S.A.S.E.
Nonfiction and Photos: Articles related to beef cattle production and allied interests, with an Arkansas slant. Could also use historical articles on Arkansas. Length: 1,000 to 2,000 words. Pays 2¢ a word maximum. Photos purchased with mss. Payment varies.

BEEF, 1999 Shepard Rd., St. Paul MN 55116. Phone: 612-647-7374. Editor: Paul D. Andre. For cattle feeders whose production will range from 50 head to 500,000 head annually. Monthly. Established in 1964. Circulation: 65,000. Not copyrighted. Buys 6 to 10 mss a year. Payment on acceptance. Will send free sample copy to writer on request. Write for copy of guidelines for writers. Reports within 1 month. Query first or submit complete ms. Enclose S.A.S.E.
Nonfiction and Photos: "Only material related to cattle feeding. Know the cattle feeding field and write concisely and in-depth. Research in the field, actual on-the-scene features describing how feeding operations are conducted." Informational, how-to, personal experience, photo, new product articles. Length: open. Pays $25 to $200. Photos purchased with accompanying ms with no additional payment. Captions required. Also purchased without ms. Pays $25 for 8x10 b&w glossy; up to $100 for 35mm or larger color.

BIG FARMER CATTLE, DAIRY AND HOG GUIDES, 131 Lincoln Highway, Frankfort IL 60423. Phone: 815-469-2163. Editor: Greg Northcutt. "To qualify for this controlled circulation publication, the reader must gross $20,000-plus annually." Established in 1970. Monthly, except June, July and December. Circulation: 100,000. Rights purchased vary with author and material; may buy all rights, but will reassign rights to author after publication. Pays on acceptance. Will send a sample copy to a writer on request. Will not consider photocopied submissions. Will consider cassette submissions. "We prefer articles typed at 37 characters wide and no longer than 6 typewritten pages." Submit seasonal material 3 months in advance. Reports in 1 month. Query first or submit complete ms. Enclose S.A.S.E.
Nonfiction and Photos: "Management articles must be on specific areas; not general features about an operator's operation. Articles must be to the point and acceptable for livestock producers across the country. We'd like to see articles on marketing strategies." Buys informational and how-to articles, interviews, and coverage of successful business operations. Length: 2,000 words maximum. Pays $100 minimum.

Captioned photos purchased with and without mss. Pays $15 for 8x10 or 5x7 glossy prints "if not submitted with ms." Pays $25 minimum for color transparencies "from 35mm and up."

CATTLEMEN, The Beef Magazine, 1760 Ellice Ave., Winnipeg, Manitoba, R3H OB6, Canada. Phone: 204-774-1861. Editor: Harold Dodds. For Canadian beef producers. Monthly magazine. Special issue on animal health in September (deadline, August 10); forage issue in May (deadline, April 10). Buys North American serial rights only. Pays on acceptance. Will send a sample copy for 25¢. Reports in 2 weeks. Always query first. Enclose S.A.E. and International Reply Coupons.
Nonfiction: Industry articles, particularly those on raising and feeding beef in Canada. Also how-to-do-it and success stories with good management slant. Writer must be informed. Uses an occasional historical item. Pays up to $150 for industry and historical articles, more for special assignments.
Photos: Canadian shots only, purchased with mss and for cover. B&w and color for cover. Pays up to $10 for b&w; up to $75 for color.

FEEDLOT MANAGEMENT, P.O. Box 67, Minneapolis MN 55440. Editor: Fred E. Tunks. For agri-businessmen who feed cattle and/or sheep for slaughter. Special issues include waste management (May); feeder cattle (September); nutrition (November). Monthly. Circulation: 20,000. Not copyrighted. Pays on acceptance. Will send a free sample copy to a writer on request. Reports in 1 to 5 weeks. Query first. Enclose S.A.S.E.
Nonfiction: Wants detailed, thorough material relating to cattle or lamb feeding and related subject areas—waste management, nutrition, marketing and processing, feeding, animal health. "Write for a copy of the magazine. Writers should know something about the industry in order to get the information that's important. We can accept highly technical articles, but there's no room for simple cursory articles. Feature articles on feedlots should include photos." No length restriction. Pays $30 to $200.
Photos and Fillers: 8x10 and 5x7 b&w glossies purchased with mss and with captions only. Pays 50¢ an inch for newsbreaks and clippings.

HOG FARM MANAGEMENT, Box 67, Minneapolis MN 55440. Phone: 612-374-5200. Editor: Gene Johnston. For "large-scale hog producers who make raising hogs their primary business. Average age: 43.5. Average education: 12.5 years. Average investment: $174,000. Average acres farmed: 558.2." Special issue in July seeks farrowing-related material for a farrowing issue. Established in 1964. Monthly. Circulation: 46,000. Not copyrighted. Buys 12 to 15 mss a year. Payment on acceptance. Will send a sample copy to a writer for $1. Will send editorial guidelines sheet to a writer on request. Will consider photocopied submissions. Submit seasonal material 3 to 4 months in advance. Reports in 2 to 4 weeks. Query first. Enclose S.A.S.E.
Nonfiction and Photos: General subject matter consists of "management-oriented articles on problems and situations encountered by readers. Subjects include marketing, management, nutrition, disease, waste management, buildings and equipment, accounting and recordkeeping." Articles on a hog producer's operation should focus on one unique aspect or angle, and not give a general description of the producer's entire operation. Controversial articles OK, as are industry articles (trends) and round-ups on new developments. Edited for the largest, most business-like producers. More semitechnical and in-depth management information. Prefers not to see articles describing a producer's entire operation, written very general and shallow. Looks for articles that focus on only one subject. Buys informational, how-to, personal experience, interview, profile, think, personal opinion, photo, spot news, successful business operations, new product, merchandising techniques, and technical articles. Regular columns that seek freelance material are "Swine Research Review," "Industrial Bulletins," and "Crop Management." Length: up to 2,000 words. Pays $75 to $200 "for maximum feature article." Buys 5x7 or 8x10 b&w glossies. Also buys color transparencies that are at least 2¼x2¼. Must relate to subject matter. Pays $10 to $20 per each b&w photo. Pays $25 to $50 for color photos.

IBIA NEWS, 123 Airport Rd., Ames IA 50010. Editor: Jim Glenn. Published by the Iowa Beef Improvement Association. For cow-calf producers (farmers) in the Corn Belt states. Tabloid style magazine; 24 (11½x17) pages. Established in 1968. Monthly. Circulation: 45,000. Not copyrighted. Pays on acceptance. Will send free sample copy to writer on request. Will consider photocopied and simultaneous submissions. Returns rejected material immediately. Query first or submit complete ms. Enclose S.A.S.E.

Nonfiction and Photos: "Our only interest is genetic improvement of beef cattle and updated cattle raising procedures. Success stories on beef cattle producers (not feeders) who participate in a program of performance testing. Articles on new equipment, products or procedures applicable to cow-calf operations. We prefer a conservative, typical Midwest farm approach." Interview, profile, successful business operations and technical articles. Length: 1,000 to 1,500 words. Pays $40 to $100. Photos are purchased with mss or on assignment. No additional payment is made for those purchased with mss.

THE KANSAS STOCKMAN, 2044 Fillmore, Topeka KS 66604. Editor: Rich Wilcke. For cattle producers and feeders. Established in 1916. Monthly. Circulation: 6,500. Not copyrighted. Payment on publication. Will send sample copy to writer for 50¢. Will consider photocopied submissions. Submit seasonal material 2 months in advance. Premier Producer Issue (May), Cattle Feeder Issue (July), Marketing Issue (September). Reports on material in 2 months. Submit complete ms. Enclose S.A.S.E.

Nonfiction and Photos: Material on "how-to issues of importance to cattlemen; production management articles. Human interest, humor, Kansas cattle industry history, Kansas ranchers or ranches. Writer ought to understand the cattle business." Length: 500 to 1,200 words. Pays 2¢ per word. "We welcome b&w photos and pay $5 for them. Color photos are considered only if an inquiry is made first." Recently published articles include "Exposing Some of the Myths of Marketing;" "Is Inflation Here to Stay?"; "Good Record-Keeping Is Essential"; "The Cow Business Game" (humor).

NATIONAL LIVESTOCK PRODUCER, 733 N. Van Buren, Milwaukee WI 53202. Editor: Frank Lessiter. For beef and hog producers who farm and ranch. Monthly, 48 pages. Established in 1922. Circulation: 240,000. Buys all rights. Buys 30 mss a year. Payment on acceptance. Will send free sample copy to writer on request. Will consider photocopied submissions. Will not consider simultaneous submissions. Seasonal material should be submitted 2 months in advance. Reports promptly. Query first. Enclose S.A.S.E.

Nonfiction and Photos: "Production and management articles on beef cattle and swine and feed crops that support this type of livestock. We prefer tighter, management-oriented writing. Material on high food costs, the energy crisis; how to improve your management. No single farmer or rancher case histories (these are being overworked)." Length: 350 to 1,200 words. Pays $50 to $350. No additional payment for 5x7 or 8x10 sharp, clean b&w glossy photos. Sharp, good quality color purchased on assignment.

NATIONAL WOOL GROWER, 600 Crandall Bldg., Salt Lake City UT 84101. Phone: 801-363-4484. Associate Editor: Vern Newbold. Not copyrighted. A very limited market. Best to query first here. Reports in 4 to 5 days. Enclose S.A.S.E.

Nonfiction: Material of interest to sheepmen. Length: 2,000 words. Pays 1¢ per word for material used.

NEW MEXICO STOCKMAN, P.O. Box 7127, Albuquerque NM 87104. Editor: Chuck Stocks. For ranchers in the southwest (and their families). Primary interests are in cattle and sheep management, purebred livestock news, shows; show and race horse features, and government action affecting agriculture. Magazine; 70 to 95 pages. Established in 1935. Monthly. Circulation: 10,750. Not copyrighted. Buys about 12 mss a year. Pays on publication. Will send free sample copy to writer on request. Write for copy of guidelines for writers. Will consider photocopied and simultaneous submissions. Reports on material accepted for publication on first of month prior to publication. Returns rejected material on 30th of month of publication. Query first. Enclose S.A.S.E.

Nonfiction and Photos: "Factual pieces on people and events which interpret the facts in terms that are identifiable by people who have lived and worked on the ranch. Try to keep it straightforward and not too flowery. Articles should reflect a familiarity with the technical and colloquial vocabulary used in the livestock industry. Subjects dealing with management and business practices used by successful stockmen should be instructive to readers. We are particularly interested in articles that lend themselves to innovative graphic treatment. Articles may also reflect strong opinions if supported by facts. We would also be interested in factual articles on artificial insemination, embryo transplants, importation of European cattle breeds. Personality profiles on New Mexico ranchers of note. Historical articles that relate to the development of the livestock industry in the southwest." Length: 100 to 1,500 words. Pays $5 to $45. Southwest Feedlot Roundup column uses factual gatherings from cattle feedlots in Texas, New Mexico and Arizona; reports of new techniques in feeding cattle and marketing fat cattle. Length: 250 words. Payment varies, but begins at $15. 8x10 b&w glossies purchased without ms or on assignment. Pays $5 to $15. Pays $10 to $25 for 2¼x2¼ color transparencies.

Fiction and Fillers: Humorous fiction must relate to subject matter. Length: 100 to 300 words. Pays $5 to $30. Newsbreaks, clippings, short humor (related to subject matter) used as fillers. Length: 25 to 100 words. Pays $5 to $10.

How To Break In: "Submit a sample of previous work (published or unpublished) along with a letter detailing writer's interest and availability for special assignments."

THE OKLAHOMA COWMAN, 2500 Exchange Ave., Oklahoma City OK 73108. Editor: John McCarroll. For cattle producers and feedlot owners (mostly within Oklahoma) who are members of the Oklahoma Cattlemen's Association and are deeply involved in the actual business of producing and selling beef cattle. Magazine; 40 (8½x11) pages. Established in 1961. Monthly. Circulation: 5,500. Buys all rights, but will reassign rights to author after publication. Buys 2 or 3 mss a year. Pays on publication. Will send sample copy to writer for $1. Will consider photocopied submissions. Simultaneous submissions considered if assured of first publication rights. Submit seasonal material (geared to management practices) 1 month in advance. Reports on material accepted for publication in 2 weeks. Returns rejected material immediately. Query first. Enclose S.A.S.E.

Nonfiction and Photos: "We are exclusively interested in beef cattle and centered around field crops, horses, etc., as they relate directly to cattle production. Mostly reports of state activity in education, extension, etc., to inform the cattleman. Also, regular feature stories on historical significance of Oklahoma's cattle background. All material dealing with management practices should be geared to season. New ideas on more intensive production practices and 'success' stories on Oklahoma cattle people, as well as adaptability of cattle people to the current economic drain on their land, labor and capital. No Wild West fictionalized articles." Length: 500 to 750 words. Pays $10 to $25. "Photos may make the difference in acceptance of articles. They should be an integral part of the subject." No additional payment. Captions required.

POLLED HEREFORD WORLD, #1 Place, 4700 E. 63rd St., Kansas City MO 64130. Phone: 816-333-7731. Editor: Marilyn Sponsler. For "breeders of polled Hereford cattle—about 80% registered breeders, about 5% commercial cattle breeders; remainder are agri-businessmen in related fields." Established in 1947. Monthly. Circulation: 20,000. Not copyrighted. Buys "very few mss at present." Pays on publication. Will send a sample copy to a writer on request. Will consider photocopied submissions. Submit seasonal material "as early as possible; 2 months preferred." Reports in 1 month. Query first for reports of events and activities. Query first or submit complete ms for features. Enclose S.A.S.E. for return of submissions or reply to queries.

Nonfiction: "Features on registered or commercial polled Hereford breeders. Some on related agricultural subjects (pastures, fences, feeds, buildings, etc.). Mostly technical in nature; some human interest. Our readers make their living with cattle, so write for an informed, mature audience." Buys informational articles, how-to's, personal experience articles, interviews, profiles, inspirational articles, humor, historical and think pieces, nostalgia, photo features, coverage of successful business operations, articles on merchandising techniques, and technical articles. Length: "varies with subject and content of feature." Pays about 5¢ a word ("usually about 50¢ a column inch, but can vary with the value of material").

Photos: Purchased with mss, sometimes purchased without mss, or on assignment; captions required. "Only good quality b&w glossy prints accepted; any size. Good color prints or transparencies." Pays $2 for b&w photos, $2 to $25 for color. Pays $25 for color covers.

SIMMENTAL JOURNAL, Box 410, Cody WY 82414. Editor: Lee Myers. For cattle breeders. Tabloid; 16 pages. Established in 1975. Every two weeks. Circulation: 3,000. Buys first serial rights. Buys about 20 mss a year. Pays on publication. Will send free sample copy to writer on request. Will consider photocopied and simultaneous submissions. Reports in 1 month. Query first or submit complete ms. Enclose S.A.S.E.

Nonfiction and Photos: Articles on individual ranches or ranchers. Informational, how-to, personal experience, profile, interview, successful business operations. Length: 1,000 words maximum. Pays $15 minimum. Pays $15 for 8x10 b&w glossy prints purchased with or without ms; $25 for color transparencies or negatives.

SIMMENTAL SHIELD, P.O. Box 511, Lindsborg KS 67456. Editor: Chester Peterson, Jr. Official publication of American Simmental Association. Readers are purebred cattle breeders and/or commercial cattlemen. Monthly; 180 pages. Circulation: 6,500. Buys all rights. Pays on publication. Will send free sample copy to writer on request. February is AI issue; August is herd sire issue; November is brood cow issue. Submit material 3 to 4 months in advance. Reports in 1 week. Query first or submit complete ms. Enclose S.A.S.E.

Nonfiction, Photos, and Fillers: Farmer experience; management articles with emphasis on ideas used and successful management ideas based on cattleman who owns Simmental. Research: new twist to old ideas or application of new techniques to the Simmental or cattle business. Wants articles that detail to reader how to make or save money or pare labor needs. Buys informational, how-to, personal experience, interview, profile, humor, think articles. Rates vary, but equal or exceed those of comparable magazines. Photos purchased with accompanying ms with no additional payment. Interested in cover photos; accepts 35mm if sharp, well-exposed. Also buys puzzles and short humor as filler material.

Miscellaneous

BUFFALO!, Box 822, Rapid City SD 57701. The Organ of the National Buffalo Association. Editor: D.C. Jennings. "Audience is made up of buffalo ranchers throughout the U.S. and Canada and a variety of folks with a common curiosity about the history and present existence of the buffalo." Monthly. Established in 1972. Circulation: about 2,500. Buys all rights, but will reassign rights to author after publication. Buys 10 to 20 mss per year. Payment on acceptance. Will send free sample copy to writer on request. Will consider photocopied submissions. Reports on material accepted for publication in 1 to 2 months, "but if we hold an article longer than 3 weeks, it is done with the author's permission." Returns rejected material immediately. Query is appreciated, but not necessary. Enclose S.A.S.E.

Nonfiction and Photos: All material should relate to buffalo and people who are connected with buffalo in some way: craftwork, raising, training. Historical material is very much sought. Will review anything and everything from past to present dealing with the buffalo and the industry evolving around it. Especially interested in articles about buffalo husbandry. All material should be written for an audience of average intelligence, mainly interested in learning more about buffalo and the buffalo industry.

Not interested in blood and guts stories of buffalo hunting. No "bless the beasts and children" type scenes. "We are devoted to the preservation, not the extinction, of the buffalo. Historical matter will be given more leeway." Length: 600 to 2,000 words. Spot news length: 150 to 250 words. Pays 3¢ to 5¢ per word. B&w photos purchased with accompanying mss; minimum 5x7 glossies. Captions required. Pays $5 to $15.

Fiction: Adventure, western and historical fiction heavily related to the buffalo. "Frontier diaries are a good place to look for historical fiction." Length: 800 to 2,000 words. Pays 3¢ to 5¢ a word.

Fillers: Newsbreaks. Length: 25 to 65 words. Pays 1¢ to 3¢ per word.

GLEANINGS IN BEE CULTURE, 623 West Liberty St., Medina OH 44256. Editor: Lawrence R. Goltz. For beekeepers. Monthly. Buys first North American serial rights. Pays on publication. Reports in 15 to 90 days. Enclose S.A.S.E.

Nonfiction and Photos: Interested in articles giving new ideas on managing bees. Also uses success stories about commercial beekeepers. Length: 3,000 words maximum. Pays $23 a published page. Sharp b&w photos pertaining to honeybees purchased with mss. Can be any size, prints or enlargements, but 4x5 or larger preferred. Pays $3 to $5 a picture.

How To Break In: "Do an interview story on commercial beekeepers who are cooperative enough to furnish accurate, factual information on their operations."

Poultry

The publications listed here specialize in material on poultry farming. Other publications that buy material on poultry will be found in the General Interest Farming and Rural Life classification.

INDUSTRIA AVICOLA (Poultry Industry), Watt Publishing Co., Mt. Morris IL 61054. Phone: 815-734-4171. Editor: Gary Buikema. For "poultry producers (minimum 1,000 hens and/or 20,000 broilers annually and/or 1,000 turkeys annually) who have direct affiliation with the poultry industry in Latin America, Spain and Portugal." Circulation: 12,100. Buys all rights. Pays on acceptance. Will send a free sample copy to a writer on request. Will consider cassette submissions. "Prefer mss written in English." Reports in 10 days. Query first. Enclose S.A.S.E.

Nonfiction and Photos: Specialized publication "for poultry businessmen of Latin America, Spain, Portugal. Printed only in Spanish. Emphasis is to aid in production, processing, and marketing of poultry meat and eggs. Keep readers abreast of developments in research, breeding, disease control, housing, equipment, marketing production and business management. Analytical and trend articles concerning the poultry industry in Latin countries are given preference." Length: up to 1,000 to 1,500 words. Pays $40 to $130 depending on content and quality. Photos are purchased with mss. No size requirements.

POULTRY MEAT, P.O. Box 947, Cullman AL 35055. Phone: 205-734-6800. Editor: Robert E. Caskey. For "large broiler producers, processors, and marketers and for those in management or key positions in the broiler or broiler-related supply business." Special issues include marketing, housing, and convention issues. Monthly. Circulation: 8,500. Not copyrighted. Buys 15 to 25 mss a year. Pays on acceptance. Will send a sample copy to a writer on request. Submit seasonal material 2 months in advance, "but only after a query on the special issues." Reports in 2 weeks. Query first. Enclose S.A.S.E.

Nonfiction: "Articles are designed to aid the broiler industry to do a better job in producing, processing, and marketing the product at a profit. Should be detailed and should be about new ideas and practices. Stories about progressive operations could be done in almost any style as long as the articles are concise and detailed. Business management articles come in floods, and are so general that poultry plant

manager could be changed to hardware store manager. These do not get published."
Buys interviews, coverage of successful business operations and merchandising
techniques. Length: 1,200 to 2,000 words. Pays $30 to $100.

TURKEY WORLD, Mount Morris IL 61054. Editor: Bernard Heffernan. Monthly.
Reports on submissions in two weeks. Buys all rights. Pays on acceptance. Query
first. Enclose S.A.S.E.
Nonfiction and Photos: Clear, concise, simply written, factual articles beamed at
producers, processors and marketers of turkeys and turkey products. Length: 1,200
to 2,000 words. Pays $50 to $100.

If this is 1977, this edition is out of date. See address in front of book to order latest edition. *Writer's Market* is published annually each fall.

TRADE, TECHNICAL, AND PROFESSIONAL JOURNALS

Freelance writers frequently get their start by "breaking into print" in trade journals. These publications sometimes buy articles that are readily researched in urban localities and usually require less of a literary style. There are sometimes a great many trade journals in the same field, but their editorial needs vary. So, it's quite important to read copies of each magazine before you even send the editor a query letter.

In studying trade publications, look for the same vital points that would need investigation in a consumer magazine: audience, article subjects, handling and approach to subjects; style. Most trade journals fall into three audience groups: those for retailers, who are interested in unusual store displays that they can apply to their own store, successful sales campaigns, etc.; those for manufacturers, who want stories on how a plant solved an industry problem related to them, how certain equipment performed in production, etc.; and those for educated, skilled professionals or industry experts. The latter group of trade journals buys technical or scientific articles on systems design; new discoveries in biology, chemistry, or physics that affect the reader's job or product; etc.

Basically, all material a trade journal buys will involve the problems that arise in the trade it covers. *Seaway Review*, for example, will not be interested in material that is not directly related to the St. Lawrence Seaway. There are further limitations on editorial requirements depending on whether a journal goes to everyone interested in the trade (like *Chain Saw Industry and Power Equipment Dealer*) or to some special mix of persons with different but related jobs (like *Mergers & Acquisitions*).

Trade journal articles are frequently handled in straight reporting fashion, describing in plain language what some business or plant did, and illustrated with photos. The information is practical to the extent that it gives the reader an idea or method that worked for someone else and that he may be able to use. Some journals prefer profiles of entire plants, others like discussions limited to one machine. You'll want to do your own exploring of the editors' preferences. Similarly, some journals use more scientific terminology than others.

Because each magazine has its own singular requirements that, once learned, are relatively easy to fill, many trade writers write for only a few editors whom they know well. They regularly suggest articles which will be assigned to them if acceptable and also receive assignments for stories in their territory. Usually the professional will not write an article without a prior go-ahead on a query.

If you're just starting out, you'll want to do a lot of trade journal reading to select your best market and research your story in depth. In fact, you'll start off by giving it more time than it's worth. However, as you talk with individuals in your trades, you'll gain experience that will eventually qualify you to supply the technical journals in your field.

Advertising and Marketing

In this category are journals for professional advertising agency executives, and copywriters, and marketing men. Publications that deal with the advertising and marketing of specific products, such as hardware or clothing, are classified under the name of the product. Journals for salesmen will be found in the Selling and Merchandising category.

ADVERTISING AGE, 740 N. Rush, Chicago IL 60611. Managing Editor: L. E. Doherty. Currently staff-produced.

THE COUNSELOR, NBS Building, Second and Clearview Aves., Trevose PA 19047. Phone: 215-355-5800. Managing Editor: Connie Goldstein. For "the specialty advertising industry." Monthly. Buys first North American serial rights and reprint rights; may buy simultaneous rights. Pays on publication. Reports in 10 days. Enclose S.A.S.E.
Nonfiction and Photos: "Articles on sales management, case histories of specialty programs, interviews with industry suppliers and distributors, other articles of interest to the industry." Length: 2,000 words minimum. Pays $35 to $75. "Illustrative material bought to accompany articles only."

INCENTIVE MARKETING, 633 Third Ave., New York NY 10017. Editor: Murray Elman. For "marketing executives in a wide variety of industries who buy and use premiums or incentives as a definite part of their sales programs." Established in 1905. Monthly. Circulation: 33,000. Rights purchased vary with author and material. Buys 125 to 200 mss a year. Pays on acceptance. Will send a sample copy to a writer on request. Write for copy of guidelines for writers. Query first. Will consider photocopied submissions. Submit seasonal material 3 months in advance. Reports in 1 month. Enclose S.A.S.E.
Nonfiction and Photos: "Marketing profiles and case histories of how companies make use of premiums/incentives to promote their products or services. Articles should include information on strategies, tactics, research, planning, promotion, distribution, and servicing of incentive merchandising techniques. Always write from the point of view of the company using premiums and emphasize the specific results of completed promotions. Articles should never be based on interviews with suppliers. Stress the incentive philosophy in the context of overall marketing strategy. We receive too many case histories on bank promotions." Buys interviews, profiles, travel promotion information, and coverage of successful business operations and merchandising techniques. Length: 1,500 words minimum, "but the longer, the better." Pays $85 to $125. Photos purchased with mss or on assignment.

MAC/WESTERN ADVERTISING, 6565 Sunset Blvd., Los Angeles CA 90028. Editor: Lee Kerry. For "people involved in advertising: media, agencies, and client organizations as well as affiliated businesses." Weekly. Buys all rights. Pays on acceptance. Query first; "articles on assignment." Reports in 1 month. Enclose S.A.S.E.
Nonfiction and Photos: "Advertising in the West. Not particularly interested in success stories. We want articles by experts in advertising, marketing, communications." Length: 1,000 to 1,750 words. Pays $100. Photos purchased with mss.

MAIL ORDER BUSINESS, Box 1047, Welch WV 24801. Editor: Nigel A. Maxey. For personnel of mail order firms, active mail order businessmen and women; persons interested in entering the mail order business. Magazine; 32 (8x11) pages. Established in 1972. Every 2 months. Circulation: 10,000. Buys all rights. Buys 10 to 20 mss a year. Pays on publication. Will send free sample copy to writer on request. Write for copy of guidelines for writers. Will consider photocopied and simultaneous submissions. Reports in 1 month. Query first or submit complete ms. Enclose S.A.S.E.
Nonfiction and Photos: "We are primarily interested in case histories of successful mail order businesses and advertising campaigns. An occasional article on a business

or ad that flopped might be considered, provided some very worthwhile lessons are drawn. We use some advice articles, but most of these are from regular contributors. Material must be factual and contain information which would help the mail order operator increase his business. Many articles submitted deal only with theory as to how to operate a successful mail order business. However, we are interested in material backed up by specific illustrations and facts." Informational, interview, successful business operations, merchandising techniques. Length: 1,000 to 5,000 words. Pays $1 per column inch; this averages about 35 words. No additional payment for b&w photos used with mss.

MARK II, THE SALES AND MARKETING MANAGEMENT MAGAZINE, 109 Railside Rd., Don Mills, Ont., Canada. Editor/Publisher: Harry Weston. For "Canadian marketing, sales management, advertising, and agency executives." Buys first rights. Pays on publication. Will send a sample copy to a writer on request. Reports "in a few days." Enclose S.A.E. and International Reply Coupons.
Nonfiction and Photos: "Case histories, conceptual articles. Innovative; lively style. Should have a Canadian slant. Not a market for beginners." Length: 1,500 to 2,000 words. Pays 5¢ a word. 8x10 b&w glossies purchased with mss. Pays $5.

SALES MANAGEMENT/THE MARKETING MAGAZINE, 633 Third Ave., New York NY 10017. Phone: 212-986-4800. Editor: Robert H. Albert. For sales and marketing and other business executives responsible for the sale and marketing of their products and services. Magazine published twice a month. Established in 1918. Circulation: 43,168. Buys all rights. Buys the occasional outstanding article on selling and marketing; domestic and international. Payment on publication. Will send free sample copy to writer on request. Reports in 1 week. Query first. Enclose S.A.S.E.
Nonfiction: "Articles on the sales and marketing operations of companies, concerning the evaluation of markets for products and services; the planning, packaging, advertising, promotion, distribution and servicing of them, and the management and training of the sales force." Informational, how-to, personal experience, interview, profile, humor, think pieces, expose, spot news, successful business operations, new product, merchandising techniques, technical. Length: 500 to 1,800 words. Pays minimum of $200.

SOUTHWEST ADVERTISING & MARKETING, 5314 Bingle Rd., Houston TX 77018. Editor: Bob Gray. For executives of advertising agencies and corporate ad managers in Texas, Oklahoma, Louisiana, Arkansas and New Mexico; media executives and executives of supplies (printing, litho, and paper plants). Magazine; 40 (7x10) pages. Established in 1946. Monthly. Circulation: 6,000. Buys all rights. Buys about 36 mss per year. Pays on publication. Will send free sample copy to writer on request. No photocopied or simultaneous submissions. Reports in 2 weeks. Query first. Enclose S.A.S.E.
Nonfiction and Photos: How-to articles in advertising and marketing fields, as well as success stories of ad campaigns; new ideas in merchandising; fresh approaches to old selling ideas; how bright people solve their toughest problems in this business. "We emphasize clear, uncomplicated English. This is a sophisticated audience that respects plain language and cannot be snowed. Stick to facts, quotes, and what the writer is absolutely sure of. We always like to see fresh ideas on direct mail shortcuts and merchandising success stories." Informational, interview, profile, think pieces, personal opinion, successful business operations and articles on merchandising techniques are considered. Length: 2,000 words. Pays 7¢ a word. No additional payment for photos used with mss. Captions required.

STIMULUS, 67 Yonge St., Toronto, Ontario, Canada. Editor: Dean Walker. For advertising and marketing executives. 60-page (8x10) magazine published every 2 months. Established in 1966. Circulation: 6,500. Not copyrighted. Buys 15 mss a year. Payment on publication. Will send free sample copy to writer on request. Reports on material accepted for publication in 2 weeks. Returns rejected material in 2 weeks. Query first. Most work is assigned. Enclose S.A.E. and International Reply Coupons.

Nonfiction and Photos: Canadian topics only. Provocative business stories and think pieces. In-depth and offbeat material on the business and craft of advertising. "We have a greater need to be stimulating to our specialized audience." Length: 600 to 3,000 words. Pays $50 to $300. Photos purchased with accompanying mss with no additional payment. Captions required.

VISUAL MERCHANDISING, 407 Gilbert Ave., Cincinnati OH 45202. Editor: David E. Phillips. For "department and specialty store display directors, exhibitor producers, point-of-purchase producers, store planners, and shopping center promotion directors. Market Week issues twice annually." Monthly. Not copyrighted. Pays on publication. Will send a sample copy to a writer for 80¢. Query first with photo sample; "we do use specific freelancers on an assignment basis and would like to have additional capable writers in southern California, Atlanta, Dallas, and Miami." Reports in 1 week. Enclose S.A.S.E.

Nonfiction and Photos: "Articles showing how to better display merchandise in every retail category. Besides merchandise presentation, features are desired on the subjects of national advertiser's showrooms, store-wide and shopping center promotions and sophisticated point-of-purchase displays. Articles showing how national advertisers participate in exhibits, trade shows, expositions, with emphasis on design and construction; articles showing how basic construction materials are employed in professional displays, exhibits, store fixtures, point-of-purchase displays." Length: "should be adequate to comprehensively cover the subject. We also buy articles of 700 words or less, with 2 or 3 photos, on professional displays and exhibits which include a testimonial on the value to the store." Pays $50 to $80. B&w photos purchased with mss or with captions and brief introductory paragraph. Pays $5.

Fillers: Newsbreaks. Pays $5 to $15.

How To Break In: "If not completely knowledgeable about field, interview industry expert with 'quote' story."

Agricultural Equipment and Supplies

CANADIAN FARMING, International Harvester Agricultural Sales, 1190 Blair Road, Burlington, Ontario L7M 1K9. Editor: Dennis S. Hladysh. Published by International Harvester Company of Canada, Limited. Audience ranges from agricultural engineers, students, government agencies, agricultural equipment interest groups, 4H-ers to farmers and dealers. Quarterly magazine; 20 to 24 (8¼x10¾) pages. Established in 1915. Circulation: 150,000. English, 25,000 French. Buys all rights, but will reassign rights to author after publication. Buys about 12 mss a year. Pays on publication. Will send free sample copy to writer on request. Submit seasonal material at least 3 months in advance. Reports within 1 month. Query first with outline of proposed article. Enclose S.A.E. and International Reply Coupons.

Nonfiction and Photos: "Generally, stories are on better farming procedures, machinery management and an occasional safety article or general farm interest story. Prefer stories to deal with people who use International Harvester equipment. We prefer to publish articles on new procedures which have been used by farmers and are of a general successful nature. Minimum tillage, leasing, overbuying, etc. Articles should deal with machinery, planting, harvesting, foraging, etc. Stay away from husbandry or livestock type themes unless machinery has main association." Also uses articles on haying, fall harvest/tillage, winter maintenance, and seasonal articles dealing with better farming and machinery management. Recently published articles include "One-Man Farm" (told how a man ran 265 acres and 60 cows), "Machinery Co-op" (about farmers who pooled resources to save time, money and effort, successfully). Length: 1,000 to 2,000 words. Pays 10¢ per published word. Uses b&w and 35mm or 2¼x2¼ color. Captions optional. Pays a minimum of $15 each for b&w; $35 minimum for color.

CUSTOM APPLICATOR, 3637 Park Ave., Memphis TN 38111. Phone: 901-327-4168. Editor: Tom Griffin. For "firms that sell and custom apply agricultural chemicals." Circulation: 17,000. Buys all rights. Pays on publication. "Query is best.

The editor can help you develop the story line regarding our specific needs." Enclose S.A.S.E.

Nonfiction and Photos: "We are looking for articles on custom application firms telling others how to better perform jobs of chemical application, develop new customers, handle credit, etc. Lack of a good idea or usable information will bring a rejection. If the idea is good and the information is good (developed) we can always run it through a typewriter." Length: 1,000 to 1,200 words "with 3 or 4 b&w glossies." Pays up to $125.

FARM SUPPLIER, Mt. Morris IL 61054. Editor: Ray Bates. Monthly. Buys all rights. Pays on acceptance. Query first. Reports in 1 month. Enclose S.A.S.E.

Nonfiction and Photos: "Articles on retail management and merchandising achievements by retail farm supply outlets and sales and service men. Product news developments now emphasized in departments, shorts, and features." Length: 1,000 to 1,400 words, "plus 3 or 4 original 8x10 glossies." Pays $5 to $25 "for short articles," $50 to $100 for feature articles. Photos purchased with and without mss; captions required. Pays $5 to $15.

Architecture

Publications in this category aim at architects and city planners who concern themselves with the design of buildings and urban environments. Journals for architects that emphasize choice of materials, structural details, and methods of constructing buildings will be found in the Construction and Contracting classification.

ARIZONA ARCHITECT, Drawer 4000-A, Tucson AZ 85717. Editor: Don Kirkland. For architects, engineers, government officials, boards of education. Magazine; 32 (8½x11) pages. Established in 1957. Every 2 months. Circulation: 3,500. Buys all rights. Buys about 6 mss a year. Pays on publication. Will send free sample copy to writer on request. Reports in 2 weeks. Query first. Enclose S.A.S.E.

Nonfiction and Photos: Material by, about, or for architects, with emphasis on architectural and related subjects in Arizona. Informational, profile, historical, think pieces, successful business operations, technical articles. Length: open. Pays $35 to $75. Pays $5 for b&w glossies; 5x8 minimum.

INLAND ARCHITECT, 1800 S. Prairie, Chicago IL 60616. Editor: M. W. Newman. For architects, planners, engineers, people interested in architecture (buffs) or urban affairs. Monthly magazine; 36 (8½11) pages. Established in 1957. Not copyrighted. Buys 24 mss a year. Payment on publication. Will send sample copy to writer for $1. Will not consider photocopied submissions. Will consider simultaneous submissions. Two triple-spaced copies of each submission are required. Reports in 1 month. Query first. Enclose S.A.S.E.

Nonfiction and Photos: "Articles cover appraisal of distinguished buildings, profiles of individual architects and firms, historic buildings and preservation, related education, architectural philosophy, interior design and furnishing, building technology, architectural education, economics of the architectural field, and the business operation of an architect's office. In addition, periodic articles concern such urban matters as city planning, housing, transportation, population shifts, and ecology. The emphasis is regional (Chicago and Illinois) with occasional forays into the greater Midwest. Approach should be one of serious criticism and investigative journalism in journalistic style." Recent articles have included one on research into the effects of light and color on people and another on approval of city planning in Chicago. Length: flexible, but is usually 1,000 to 2,500 words. Pays $50 to $100. B&w glossy photos are purchased with mss; no additional payment. Captions (and identifications) required.

PROGRESSIVE ARCHITECTURE, 600 Summer St., Stamford CT 06904. Editor: John M. Dixon. Monthly. Buys first-time rights for use in architectural press. Pays on publication. Enclose S.A.S.E.

Nonfiction and Photos: "Articles of technical professional interest devoted to architecture and community design and illustrated by photographs and architectural drawings. Also use technical articles, which are prepared by technical authorities and would be beyond the scope of the lay writer. Practically all the material is professional, and most of it is prepared by writers in the field who are approached by the magazine for material." Pays $50 to $250. Buys one-time reproduction rights to b&w and color photos.

Auto and Truck

The journals below aim at automobile and truck dealers, repairmen, or fleet operators. Publications for highway planners and traffic control experts are classified in the Government and Public Service category. Journals for traffic managers and transportation experts (who route goods across the continent) will be found in Transportation.

AUTO MERCHANDISING NEWS, 1188 Main St., Suite 500, Bridgeport CT 06604. Editor: Bob Adams. For buyers and merchandisers at chain auto stores and automotive departments of department stores; and the wholesale distributors serving these volume parts and accessories retailers. Monthly magazine; 100 pages. Established in 1971. Circulation: 19,000. Buys all rights. Payment on publication. Will send free sample copy to writer on request. Will consider simultaneous submissions. Reports quickly on material accepted for publication. Returns rejected material immediately. Query first. Enclose S.A.S.E.
Nonfiction and Photos: News on retailers, wholesalers, companies, merchandising techniques and programs. Informational, how-to, spot news, successful business operations. "Most stories are pegged to some type of news lead. We avoid the more gratuitous features." Length: open. Pays 5¢ a word. Pays minimum of $7.50 for sharp b&w glossy photos and color transparencies. Captions required.

AUTOMOTIVE NEWS, 965 E. Jefferson Ave., Detroit MI 48207. Editor: Robert M. Lienert. For management people in auto making and auto dealing. Weekly. Established in 1925. Circulation: 56,000. Buys all rights. Buys 10 mss a year. Payment on acceptance. Free sample copy to writer on request. Query first. Enclose S.A.S.E.
Nonfiction and Photos: News material valuable to the auto trade. "Current and complete familiarity with the field is essential, so we don't use much freelance material." Articles must be accurate with the emphasis on the how rather than the what. Ideas must be helpful to dealers, and written in a news style. Pays $1 per inch of type (about 50 words). Photos are purchased with mss. No additional payment.

BRAKE AND FRONT END SERVICE, 11 S. Forge St., Akron OH 44304. Phone: 216-535-6117. Editor: John B. Stoner. For "brake, front end, alignment shops (not service stations)." Monthly. Buys all rights. Pays on publication. Query first. Reports "at once." Enclose S.A.S.E.
Nonfiction and Photos: "Specialty shops taking on new ideas such as tune-ups; independent auto diagnosis; new merchandising techniques; growth of business, volume; reasons for growth and success. Expansions, any unusual brake shops." Length: "about 1,000 words." Pays 4¢ to 5¢ a word. B&w glossies purchased with mss. Pays $5.

CANADIAN AUTOMOTIVE TRADE, 481 University Ave., Toronto M5W 1A7, Ont., Canada. Editor: Edward Belitsky. For "automotive wholesale and retail industry." Monthly. Buys first Canadian serial rights. Pays on acceptance. Will send a sample copy to a writer on request. "Query with outline essential." Reports "within reasonable interval." Enclose S.A.E. and International Reply Coupons.
Nonfiction and Photos: "Technical, mechanical, and maintenance articles from knowledgeable sources; how-to articles on automotive service and repair, written for professionals. Must be of interest and value to a purely Canadian audience of technicians. No-nonsense style—facts, crisply told; Canadian angle preferred. Also, features related to business management, training, and customer relations." Length:

1,200 to 1,500 words. Pays 7¢ to 10¢ a word, $65 to $125 for two-page spread. "2 to 4 well-captioned photos" purchased with mss; 8x10 b&w glossies preferred. No color. Pays $5 to $10.

COMMERCIAL CAR JOURNAL, Chilton Way, Radnor PA 19089. Editor: James D. Winsor. Monthly. Buys all rights. Pays on acceptance. "Query first with article outline." Enclose S.A.S.E.
Nonfiction: "Articles and photo features dealing with management, maintenance, and operating phases of truck and bus fleet operations. Material must be somewhat specialized and deal with a specific phase of the operation." Length: open. Pays $50 to $150.
Photos: "Occasionally use separate photos with captions." Pays $5 to $20.

CONOCO TODAY, Box 2197, Houston TX 77001. Editor: John H. Walker. Continental Oil Company. Bimonthly. Copyrighted. Buys all rights. Pays on acceptance. Will send free sample copy on request. Query first. Reports at once. Enclose S.A.S.E.
Nonfiction: Conoco service station operation and wholesale distributor operations, news and ideas. Length: 1,000 words. Pays 7¢ a word.
Photos: Purchased with mss. B&w 8x10, pays $10.

JOBBER NEWS, 109 Vanderhoof Ave., Toronto M4G 252, Ont., Canada. Editor: Sam Dixon. For "parts wholesalers and rebuilders in Canada." Monthly. Not copyrighted. Pays on publication. Query first. Enclose S.A.E. and International Reply Coupons.
Nonfiction: "Management features slanted to auto parts wholesaling are main interest. This is a specialized field and much research is required. Must have authentic Canadian application; rewrites of American applications not wanted." Length: 1,000 words maximum. "The rate of pay, which is a flat fee per feature, is negotiated with the author, and begins at $25."

JOBBER TOPICS, 7300 N. Cicero Ave., Lincolnwood IL 60646. Articles Editor: Jack Creighton. For "automotive parts and supplies wholesalers." Monthly. Buys all rights. Pays on publication. Enclose S.A.S.E.
Nonfiction and Photos: Most editorial is staff written. "Articles with unusual or outstanding automotive jobber procedures, with special emphasis on sales and merchandising: any phase of distribution. Especially interested in merchandising practices and machine shop operation." Length: 2,000 words maximum. Pays 4¢ a word minimum. 5x7 or 8x10 b&w glossies purchased with mss. Pays $5 minimum.

MAGIC CIRCLE, c/o Aitkin-Kynett, 4 Penn Center, Philadelphia PA 19102. For the automobile mechanic in his own shop, in the service station, fleet garage, repair shop or new car dealership. Company publication of the Dana Corporation. Magazine; 20 (8½x11) pages. Established in 1955. Quarterly. Circulation: 80,000. Buys all rights, but will reassign rights to author after publication. Buys 2 or 3 mss a year. Pays on acceptance. A free sample copy will be sent only if a viable query is sent at the same time. Will consider photocopied submissions and may consider simultaneous submissions. Reports in 2 weeks. Query first. Enclose S.A.S.E.
Nonfiction and Photos: "Articles on anything that will make the mechanic a better, more efficient, more profitable mechanic and businessman. We need a light style, but with plenty of detail on techniques and methods. We might be interested in some bicentennial travel material." Informational, how-to, travel, successful business operations, merchandising techniques, technical articles. Length: 500 to 2,000 words. Pays $150 maximum. B&w and color photos are purchased with or without ms. Captions required. Pays $25 for b&w 8x10 glossies; $50 for 2¼x2¼ or 35mm color.

MERCHANDISER, Amoco Oil Company, P.O. Box 6110-A, Chicago IL 60680. Editor: Gerald J. Bayles. For Amoco service station dealers, jobbers. Quarterly. Circulation: 30,000. Buys all rights, but will reassign after publication. Buys 3 or 4 mss a year. Pays on publication. Query recommended. Enclose S.A.S.E.
Nonfiction and Photos: Short, to-the-point, success stories and how-to stories, that

will trigger creative thinking by the reader. Storylines are most often in the merchandising, motivational, and educational areas. Length: 750 words maximum. Payment varies, with minimum of $100. Uses b&w and color photos

MILK HAULER AND FOOD TRANSPORTER, 221 N. La Salle St., Chicago IL 60601. Editor: Douglas D. Sorenson. For "tank truck haulers who pick up milk from dairy farms and transporters who deliver milk to outlying markets." Buys first rights. Pays on acceptance. Query first. Reports in 2 to 3 weeks. Enclose S.A.S.E.
Nonfiction and Photos: "Particularly interested in success stories on transporters whose operation includes the hauling of cheese and other dairy products, liquid sugar, molasses, citrus juice, and other edible foods. Good photos essential. Pay up to $50 an article, $5 each for sharp b&w photos."

MODERN BULK TRANSPORTER, 4801 Montgomery Lane, Washington DC 20014. Phone: 301-654-8802. Editor: Don Sutherland. For "management of companies operating tank motor vehicles which transport liquid or dry bulk commodities." Monthly. Buys first rights only. Pays on acceptance. Will consider photocopied submissions, but "we're prejudiced against them." Enclose S.A.S.E.
Nonfiction and Photos: "Articles covering the tank truck industry; stories concerning a successful for-hire tank truck company, or stories about use of tank trucks for unusual commodities. We especially seek articles on successful operation of tank trucks by oil jobbers or other so-called 'private carriers' who transport their own products. Approach should be about specific tank truck problems solved, unusual methods of operations, spectacular growth of a company, tank truck management techniques, or other subjects of special interest. Simple description of routine operations not acceptable." Length: 1,000 to 3,000 words, "preferably accompanied by pictures." Pays minimum 5¢ a word. Pays minimum $30 per published page "for general articles exclusive in trucking field only (such as maintenance and mechanical subjects)." Pays minimum $25 for reporter assignments—producing fact sheet for rewrite. 8x10, 5x7 glossies purchased with exclusive features. Pays $7.

MODERN TIRE DEALER, Box 5417, 77 N. Miller Rd., Akron OH 44313. Phone: 216-867-4401. Editor: C.S. Slaybaugh. For "independent tire dealers." Monthly. Buys all rights. Pay on publication. Will consider photocopied submissions. Query first. Reports in 1 month. Enclose S.A.S.E.
Nonfiction, Photos, and Fillers: "How TBA dealers sell tires, batteries, and allied services, such as brakes, wheel alignment, shocks, mufflers. The emphasis is on merchandising. We prefer the writer to zero in on some specific area of interest; avoid shotgun approach." Length: 1,500 words. Pays $50 to $100. 8x10, 4x5, 5x7 b&w glossies purchased with mss. Pays $5. Buys 300-word fillers. Pays $5 to $10.

MOTOR, 1790 Broadway, New York NY 10019. Editor: J. Robert Connor. For automobile service and repairshop operators, dealer service managers. Monthly. Buys all rights. Pays on acceptance. Query first. Reports in 1 week. Enclose S.A.S.E.
Nonfiction: Specializes in service and repair of both domestic and foreign cars for professional mechanic. Merchandising, sales promotion and management articles containing ideas that can be adapted by independent garages and service stations. Emphasis on how-to material. Wants stories on wholesalers, jobbers, and interviews with executives for 16-page section in Aftermarket Journal edition. Length: 1,200 to 1,500 words. Pays $75 to $300; sometimes higher for exceptional pieces.
Photos: Purchased with mss or with captions, of interest to readership. 8x10 glossies. Pays $25 for single b&w photo; $400 for cover color photo.

MOTOR VEHICLE INSPECTION NEWS, PAA Service, Inc., P.O. Box 2955, Harrisburg PA 17105. Editor: Richard D. Clemmer. For motor vehicle inspection station network that handles periodic motor vehicle inspection; service stations, garages, new and used car dealers. Magazine; 16 pages. Established in 1974. Every 2 months. Circulation: 16,686. Rights purchased vary with author and material. Usually buys all rights, but will reassign rights to author after publication. Pays on publication. Will send free sample copy to writer on request. Write for copy of guidelines for writers. Will consider photocopied and simultaneous submissions. Reports on material accepted for publication on tenth of month prior to publication. Returns rejected material immediately. Query first. Enclose S.A.S.E.

Nonfiction and Photos: Articles on auto inspection regulations, new products, industry regulations, mechanical tips. General interest articles that improve the mind, as well as those on education, tax tips, etc. Programmed P/R material to mold relationships to develop a positive awareness of the auto business, in particular, and auto aftermarket, in general. Nothing on tips to the consumer. Prefers tips to the independent businessman type of ideas. Material on auto-oriented successful business operations and technical material on the servicing of autos and updating of safety. Length: 1,500 words. Pays minimum of $25 per published page. No additional payment for b&w photos used with mss.

NTDRA DEALER NEWS, 1343 L St., N.W., Washington DC 20005. Editor: Donald L. Thompson. For tire dealers and retreaders. Publication of the National Tire Dealers & Retreaders Association. Weekly magazine; 16 pages. Established in 1935. Circulation: 7,500. Occasionally copyrighted, depending on content. Will send free sample copy on request. Will consider photocopied and simultaneous submissions. Reports immediately. Query first. Enclose S.A.S.E.

Nonfiction: Articles relating to retailing and marketing, with special emphasis on the tire dealer, retreader and small businessman in general. Dealer and consumer comments regarding this industry. Most articles received are of too general interest. Uses informational, technical, how-to, inteview, think pieces and material on successful business operations and merchandising techniques. Pays $150 to $200.

O AND A MARKETING NEWS, P. O. Box 765, LaCanada CA 91011. Editor: Don McAnally. For "service station dealers, garagemen, TBA (tires, batteries, accessories) people, oil company marketing management." Bimonthly. Circulation: 11,000. Not copyrighted. Pays on publication. Query first. Reports in 1 week. Enclose S.A.S.E.

Nonfiction and Photos: "Straight news material; management, service, and merchandising applications; emphasis on news about or affecting markets and marketers within the publication's geographic area of the 7 western states. No restrictions on style or slant." Length: maximum 1,000 words. Pays $1 per column inch (about 2¢ a word). Photos purchased with or without mss; captions required. Pays $5.

OHIO TRUCKING NEWS, Mezzanine Floor, Neil House Hotel, Columbus OH 43215. Editor: Cynthia J. Wilson. Publication of the Ohio Trucking Association. Quarterly. Buys material for exclusive publication only. Pays on publication. Free sample copy on request. Query not required. Reports in 30 days. Enclose S.A.S.E.

Nonfiction: Modern developments in truck transportation, particularly as they apply to Ohio industry and truck operators. Length: 1,500 words. Pays $25 to $50.

Photos: With mss or with captions only. Transportation subjects. Pays $10.

OPEN ROAD, 1015 Florence St., Fort Worth TX 76102. Editor: Chris Lackey. For "professional over-the-road truck drivers of America." Monthly. Buys North American serial rights. Pays on publication. Will send a sample copy to a writer on request. Query first. Reports in 2 to 4 weeks. Enclose S.A.S.E.

Nonfiction and Photos: "Pieces on truck drivers—articles about new model heavy trucks and equipment, acts of heroism, humor, unusual events, special driving articles, advice to other drivers, drivers who do good jobs in community life or civic work, etc." Recently sponsored two special events: selection of an outstanding woman trucker, "Queen of the Road," for 1975; and Truck Drivers Country Music Awards Competition, a national poll among professional truck drivers, picked outstanding artists in 10 country music categories. Length: "prefer 1,000 to 1,500 words, usually." Pays "about 5¢ a word." 5x7 or 8x10 b&w glossies purchased with mss. Pays $5 to $10, depending on quality and newsworthiness, "more for covers."

REFRIGERATED TRANSPORTER, 1602 Harold St., Houston TX 77006. Monthly. Not copyrighted. Pays on publication. Reports in 1 month. Enclose S.A.S.E.

Nonfiction and Photos: "Articles on fleet management and maintenance of vehicles, especially the refrigerated van and the refrigerating unit; shop tips; loading or handling systems, especially for frozen or refrigerated cargo; new equipment specifications; conversions of equipment for better handling or more efficient operations. Prefer articles with illustrations obtained from fleets operating refrigerated trucks or trailers." Pays minimum $45 per page or $2 per inch.
Fillers: Buys newspaper clippings. "Do not rewrite."

SERVICE STATION AND GARAGE MANAGEMENT, 109 Vanderhoof Ave., Suite 101, Toronto, Ont. M4G 2J2, Canada. Editor: Joe Holliday. For "service station operators and garagemen in Canada only." Established in 1956. Monthly. Circulation: 24,000. Buys first Canadian serial rights. Buys 1 or 2 articles a year. Pays on acceptance. Will send a sample copy to a writer for 50¢. Query first. Reports in 2 days. Enclose S.A.E. and International Reply Coupons.
Nonfiction and Photos: "Articles on service station operators in Canada only; those who are doing top merchandising job. Also on specific phases of service station doings: brakes, tune-up, lubrication, etc. Solid business facts and figures; information must have human interest angles. Interested in controversial legislation, trade problems, sales and service promotions, technical data, personnel activities and changes. No general, long-winded material. The approach must be Canadian. The writer must know the trade and must provide facts and figures useful and helpful to readers. The style should be easy, simple, and friendly—not stilted." Length: 1,000 words. Pays 4¢ to 5¢ a word average, "depending on the topic and the author's status." Photos purchased with mss and without mss "if different or novel"; captions required. Pays $5 for 5x7 or 8x10 b&w glossies.

SHOP TALK, P.O. Box 2586, Framingham MA 01701. Editor: Jay A. Kruza. For automotive technicians and managers of proprietary businesses. Magazine published every 2 months; 44 pages, 8½x11. Established in 1966. Circulation: 7,000. Buys all rights, but will reassign rights to author after publication. Will send free sample copy to writer on request. Write for copy of guidelines for writers. Will consider photocopied and simultaneous submissions. Query first. Reports within 4 weeks. Enclose S.A.S.E.
Nonfiction and Photos: "Management and technical articles. Write with colloquial style with 2 or 3 characters conversing about situations or procedures of running a business or handling customers, employees, etc. Articles usually supply other easy-to-get-at reference sources for further information on topic. Personality and historical sketches are overworked at present." Buys informational, personal experience, interview, humor, personal opinion, photo, reviews, spot news, successful business operations, merchandising techniques, and technical articles. Length: 400 to 2,000 words. Pays $20 to $100. Photos purchased with ms. Captions optional. Pays $7.50 for b&w photos up to size 8x10.

SOUTHERN AUTOMOTIVE JOURNAL, 1760 Peachtree Rd., N.W., Atlanta GA 30309. Phone: 404-874-4462. Editor: William F. Vann. For service stations, auto dealers, garages, body shops, fleets, and parts jobbers. Monthly. Buys all rights. Will send a sample copy to a writer for $1. Query first. Enclose S.A.S.E.
Nonfiction and Photos: "Articles of interest to the automotive aftermarket." Length: open. Payment varies. Photos purchased with ms.

SOUTHERN MOTOR CARGO, P. O. Box 4169, Memphis TN 38104. Editor: William H. Raiford. For "trucking management and maintenance personnel of private, contract, and for-hire carriers in 16 southern states (Ala., Ark., Del., Fla., Ga., Ky., La., Md., Miss., N.C., Okla., S.C., Tenn., Tex., Va., and West Va.) and the District of Columbia." Special issues include "ATA Convention," October; "Transportation Graduate Directory," December; "Mid-America Truck Show," March. Monthly. Circulation: 35,000. Buys first rights within circulation area. Pays on publication. Will send a sample copy to a writer on request. "No query necessary." Reports "usually in 2 weeks." Enclose S.A.S.E.

Nonfiction: "How a southern trucker builds a better mousetrap. Factual newspaper style with punch in lead. Don't get flowery. No success stories. Pick one item, i.e., tire maintenance, billing procedure, etc., and show how such-and-such carrier has developed or modified it to better fit his organization. Bring in problems solved by the way he adapted this or that and what way he plans to better his present layout. Find a segment of the business that has been altered or modified due to economics or new information, such as 'due to information gathered by a new IBM process, it has been discovered that an XYZ transmission needs overhauling every 60,000 miles instead of every 35,000 miles, thereby resulting in savings of $$$ over the normal life of this transmission.' Or, 'by incorporating a new method of record keeping, claims on damaged freight have been expedited with a resultant savings in time and money.' Compare the old method with the new, itemize savings, and get quotes from personnel involved. Articles must be built around an outstanding phase of the operation and must be documented and approved by the firm's management prior to publication." Length: 2,500 to 3,500 words. Pays minimum 4¢ a word for "feature material."

Photos: Purchased with cutlines; glossy prints. Pays $5.

SPEED AND CUSTOM DEALER, 11 S. Forge St., Akron OH 44304. Phone: 216-535-6117. Editor: Gary L. Gardner. For speed shop owners, counter salesmen; all heavily involved with high-performance automotives. Monthly magazine; 60 (8½x11) pages. Established in 1966. Circulation: 18,500. Rights purchased vary with author and material. Usually buys all rights, but there are exceptions. Buys 8 to 10 mss a year. Payment on publication. Will consider photocopied submissions. Will not consider simultaneous submissions. Reports in 1 week. Query first or submit complete ms. Enclose S.A.S.E.

Nonfiction and Photos: "Features on successful shops, trade-oriented race coverage, auto show material, product and marketing articles." Each feature must have plenty of factual material to back it up. Articles should be involved in the business of selling high performance. We see too many success stories with not enough facts by writers who know very little about the market and haven't tried to learn." Informational, how-to, interview, nostalgia, merchandising techniques, technical. Recently published articles include "Decal Dilemma: Analysis of Race Sponsorship." Length: 1,000 to 2,500 words. Pays minimum of 4¢ a word. Pays minimum of $6.50 for b&w photos purchased with mss. Captions required.

TIRE REVIEW, 11 S. Forge St., Akron OH 44304. Phone: 216-535-6117. Editor: William Whitney. For "independent tire dealers and retreaders, company stores, tire company executives, some oil company executives." Monthly. Circulation: 34,000. Buys first rights. Buys 6 or 7 mss a year. Pays on publication. Will send a free sample copy to a writer on request. Query first. Reports in 1 week. Enclose S.A.S.E.

Nonfiction and Photos: "Tire industry news, including new product news, research and marketing trends, legislative news, features on independent tire dealers and retreaders, news of trade shows and conventions, tire and related accessory merchandising tips. All articles should be straightforward, concise, information-packed, and not slanted toward any particular manufacturer or brand name. Must have something to do with tires or the tire industry, particularly independent dealers doing brake and front-end services." Length: "no limitations." Pays 3¢ a word. B&w glossies purchased with and without mss. Pays "$5 a photo with story, $8.50 for photos used alone."

TODAY'S TRANSPORT INTERNATIONAL (TRANSPORTE MODERNO), P.O. Box 1256, Stamford CT 06904. Phone: 203-327-9340. Editor: Philip R. Moran. For "vehicle and fleet operators and materials-handling executives in 110 countries of Asia, Africa, Australia, New Zealand, Latin America, the Caribbean, and the Middle East." Bimonthly. Circulation: 41,000. Buys international rights. Buys 15 to 20 mss a year. Pays on acceptance. Will send a sample copy to a writer on request. Query first. Reports in 1 week. Enclose S.A.S.E.

Nonfiction and Photos: "Write for our audience, that is, avoid a U. S.-oriented approach. Our readers mainly are in developing countries." Wants "articles showing new techniques, how-to-do-it approaches, etc., on an administrative plane." Length: 2,000 to 2,500 words. Pays $100 to $150, "for article and accompanying illustrations where applicable (charts, photos, etc.). We translate into Spanish."

WARD'S AUTO WORLD, 28 W. Adams, Detroit MI 48226. Editor: David C. Smith. For automotive industry executives and engineers; top and middle management. Monthly magazine; 80 pages. Established in 1964. Circulation: 50,000. Buys all rights. Buys 5 to 10 mss a year. Payment on publication. Will send free sample copy to writer on request. Write for copy of guidelines for writers. Will not consider photocopied or simultaneous submissions. Will accept cassette submissions. Seasonal material is done only on assignment. Reports on material accepted for publication in 4 weeks. Returns rejected material quickly. Query first. Enclose S.A.S.E.
Nonfiction and Photos: News stories or topical features. "Our entire slant is news." Informational, interview, profile, historical, expose, personal opinion, spot news, successful business operations, new product, merchandising techniques, technical, book reviews. Length: open. Pays $100 to $500. Payment varies for 8x10 b&w photos or 4x5 color. Sometimes no additional payment is made for those purchased with mss. Captions required.

WAREHOUSE DISTRIBUTION, 7300 N. Cicero Ave., Lincolnwood, Chicago IL 60646. Editor: Syd Cowan. For "businessmen in the auto parts distribution field who are doing above one million dollars business per year." 10 times a year. Circulation: 25,000. Buys all rights. Pays on publication. Query first. Most material is staff written. Reports "within a reasonable amount of time." Enclose S.A.S.E.
Nonfiction and Photos: "Business management subjects, limited to the automotive parts distribution field." Length: 1,500 to 2,000 words. Pays 4¢ to 10¢ a word, "based on value to industry and the quality of the article." Photos purchased with and without mss; captions required. Wants "sharp 5x7 prints." Pays maximum $6.

WAREHOUSE DISTRIBUTOR NEWS, 11 S. Forge St., Akron OH 44304. Editor: John B. Stoner. For warehouse distributors and redistributing jobbers of automotive parts and accessories, tools and equipment and supplies (all upper management personnel). Magazine; 60 (7x10) pages. Established in 1967. Monthly. Circulation: 13,000. Rights purchased vary with author and material. May buy all rights or simultaneous rights. Buys about 12 mss a year. Pays on publication. Will send sample copy to writer for $1. Will consider photocopied and simultaneous submissions. Reports at once. Query first. Enclose S.A.S.E.
Nonfiction and Photos: Automotive aftermarket distribution management articles and those on general management, success stories, etc., of interest to the industry. Articles on manufacturers and their distributors. Must be aftermarket-oriented. Each issue centers around a theme, such as rebuilt parts issue, import issue, materials handling issue, etc. Schedule changes yearly based on developments in the industry. Does not want to see freelance material on materials handling, management or product information. Would be interested in merchandising articles; those on EDP startup, and interviews with prominent industry figures. Recently published articles on leasing and hiring/firing. Length: open. Pays 4¢ to 5¢ a word. B&w (5x7) photos purchased with or without ms. Pays $5 to $6. Captions required.

Aviation and Space

In this category are journals for aviation businessmen and airport operators and technical aviation and space journals. Publications for professional and private pilots are classified with the Aviation magazines in the Consumer Publications section.

AIR FACTS MAGAZINE, 110 E. 42 St., New York NY 10017. Editor: Leighton Collins. For pilots and aircraft owners. Established in 1938. Monthly. Circulation: 18,500. Buys all rights. Buys 40 mss a year. Payment on acceptance. Will send sample copy to writer for $1. Write for copy of guidelines for writers. Will not consider photocopied submissions. Submit seasonal material 3 months in advance. Reports on material accepted for publication in 2 months. Returns rejected material in 3 months. Query first or submit complete ms. Enclose S.A.S.E.

Nonfiction and Photos: Travel articles related to aviation. Must be typed, double-spaced, on 8½x11 paper and submitted in duplicate. Must be accompanied by appropriate photographs and 1-page bibliography on author. Length: 10 typed pages or less. Pays $50 to $150 for first article. No additional payment for photos.

BUSINESS AND COMMERCIAL AVIATION, One Park Ave., New York NY 10016. Editor: Archie Trammell. For "pilots and business aircraft operators." Monthly. Circulation: 52,000. Buys all rights. Buys "very little" freelance material. Pays on acceptance. Will send a sample copy to a writer for $1. Query first. Reports "as soon as an evaluation is made." Enclose S.A.S.E.

Nonfiction and Photos: "Our readers are pilots and we have found general articles to be inadequate. Writers with a technical knowledge of aviation would be most suitable." Wants "reports on business aviation operations, pilot reports, etc." Length: "no limits." Pays $100 to $300. B&w photos of aircraft purchased with mss. Pays $15 to $20. Pays $300 for cover color photos. Uses very little freelance photography.

GENERAL AVIATION BUSINESS, P.O. Box 1094, Snyder TX 79549. Phone: 915-573-6318. Editor: M. Gene Dow. For people in business phases of general aviation. Tabloid newspaper; 40 pages. Established in 1973. Monthly. Circulation: 13,000. Buys all rights. Pays on acceptance. Will send sample copy to writer for 50c. Write for copy of guidelines for writers. Will consider photocopied submissions. Reports on material in 1 month. Submit only complete ms. Enclose S.A.S.E.

Nonfiction and Photos: Informative, entertaining, technical, how-to, new products, etc., of general aviation (non-airline, non-military). Knowledgeable aviation articles. All types of articles on aviation subjects. Reviews of aviation books. Pays $25 per 1,000 words. Pays $15 for 30 column inches for regular columns or departments. Photos purchased with accompanying ms or on assignment. Captions required. Pays $5 for b&w and color.

Fiction: Experimental, suspense, adventure, humorous fiction on aviation subjects. Pays $25 per 1,000 words.

Poetry and Fillers: Aviation subjects. Pays $15 for poetry. Newsbreaks, clippings, jokes, short humor and informative items for fillers. Pays $3.

INTERLINE REPORTER, 2 W. 46th St., New York NY 10036. Editor: Eric Friedheim. An inspirational and interesting magazine for airline employees. Buys first serial rights. Query first. Enclose S.A.S.E.

Nonfiction and Photos: Wants nontechnical articles on airline activities; stories should be slanted to the sales, reservations and counter personnel. Articles on offbeat airlines and, most of all, on airline employees—those who lead an adventurous life, have a unique hobby, or have acted above and beyond the call of duty. Personality stories showing how a job has been well done are particularly welcome. Length: up to 1,200 words. Payment is $50 to $75 for articles with photographic illustrations.

JET CARGO NEWS, 5314 Bingle Rd., Houston TX 77018. Phone: 713-688-8811. Editor: Britt Martin. For "traffic and distribution managers, marketing executives, sales executives, and corporate management who use or may sometime use air transportation to ship their company's products." Established in 1968. Monthly. Circulation: 20,333. Buys all rights. Buys 6 to 10 mss a year. Pay on publication. Will send a sample copy to a writer on request. Write for copy of guidelines for writers. Submit complete ms. Will not consider photocopied submissions. Submit seasonal material 2 weeks in advance of issue date. Reports "within a month, if postage is included." Enclose S.A.S.E. for return of submissions.

Nonfiction and Photos: "Air marketing success stories, cargo rate changes, new ideas on packaging and/or sales. The writer's message should be to the shipper, not to or about airlines. We feel the shipper wants to know how an airline can help him, and that he's not particularly interested in the airline's economics. Use a tight, magazine style. The writer must know marketing. We want depth, how-to material. We don't like the 'gee whiz' approach to product marketing by air. We are not particularly interested in rare items moving by air frieght. Rather, we are interested in why a shipper switches from surface to air transportation." Buys informational articles, how-to's, interviews, and coverage of successful business operations. Length: maximum 2,500 words. Pays 5¢ a word. 7x10 b&w glossies purchased with and without mss; captions required. Pays $7.50.

ROTOR & WING, News Plaza, Peoria IL 61601. Editor: Geoff Sutton. For commercial, civil government, and corporate helicopter owners, operators, and pilots. Established in 1967. Bimonthly. Circulation: 24,000. Buys all rights. Payment on acceptance. Will send sample copy to writer on request. Query first and submit proposed lead (200 to 400 words). Reports in 4 weeks. Enclose S.A.S.E.
Nonfiction and Photos: Feature stories dealing with commercial helicopter operators' activities, especially those that are good examples of how one operator may improve his business by learning what others are doing. Directed to commercial helicopter operators and pilots, also civil government and police helicopter owners. Military helicopter coverage is restricted to those programs and aircraft that have, or will have, commercial or civil applications and interest. Length: 2,500 words. Pays $150 to $250. Photos purchased with mss; 8 to 10 b&w glossies required.

Baking

PACIFIC BAKERS NEWS, Route 2, Belfair WA 98528. Phone: 206-275-6421. Publisher: Leo Livingston. Business newsletter for commercial bakeries in the western states. Monthly. Pays on publication. "We don't require S.A.S.E."
Fillers: Uses bakery business reports and news about bakers. Buys only brief "boiled-down news items about bakers and bakeries operating only in Alaska, Hawaii, Pacific Coast and Rocky Mountain states. Welcome clippings. Need monthly news reports and clippings about the baking industry from most western cities (except Seattle and Los Angeles areas). We don't use how-to and think pieces or feature articles." Length: 10 to 200 words. Pays 4¢ a word for clips and news used.
How To Break In: "Send brief news reports or clippings on spot business news about bakers and bakeries in the following western states: California, Arizona, Nevada, New Mexico, Colorado, Utah, Wyoming, Montana, Idaho, Oregon, Washington, Alaska, and Hawaii."

SPECIALTY BAKERS VOICE, 299 Broadway, New York NY 10007. Editor: Irving Walters. For "bakery management." Semimonthly. Not copyrighted. Pays on publication. Query first. Enclose S.A.S.E.
Nonfiction: "Articles geared to the single unit and multi-unit retail bake shop on topics such as merchandising, management techniques, store layout, production, employee-employer relations, bakery sanitation, customer service. Articles must be concise, business-oriented, and must include examples." Length: 1,000 to 1,500 words. Pays 2¢ a word.

Beverages and Bottling

The following journals are for manufacturers, distributors, retailers of soft drinks and alcoholic beverages. Publications for bar and tavern operators and managers of restaurants are classified in the Hotels, Motels, Clubs, Resorts, and Restaurants category.

BEER WHOLESALER, Patio Bldg., 76 S.E. Fifth Ave., Delray Beach FL 33344. Editor: Steve Flanagan. For beer wholesalers. Established in 1968. Quarterly. Circulation: 7,200. Buys all rights. Payment on publication. Query first. Enclose S.A.S.E.
Nonfiction and Photos: "Anything of interest to beer wholesalers; what others are doing, etc." Length: open. Pays 3¢ a word. Pays $5 for each 3x5 (or larger) photo.

BEVERAGE INDUSTRY, 777 Third Ave., New York NY 10017. Editor: Joseph Behrens. For "beverage plant management." Special issues on soft drinks, beer, bottled water, trucks, vending, packaging, materials handling. Biweekly. Buys all rights. Pays on publication. Will send a sample copy to a writer on request. Query first, "outlining proposed treatment." Reports in 10 days. Enclose S.A.S.E.

Nonfiction and Photos: "Beverage plant case histories, detailing manner of operation and specific reasons for success of particular marketing or technological venture; promotional campaigns, special sales efforts, methods of introducing new products, sales training, fleet management, product control, etc. Interesting lead paragraph, then straight facts on operations. Also, quotes from management executives." Length: 1,500 to 2,000 words. Pays minimum of 2¢ "per published word." Photos purchased with mss. "Should be sharp b&w glossies, preferably illustrating some pertinent aspect of the article." Pays $5.

Fillers: "Newsbreaks pertinent to the beverage industry." Will buy newspaper clippings, if information useful.

BEVERAGE WORLD (formerly *Soft Drinks*), 10 Cutter Mill Rd., Great Neck NY 11021. Editor: Paul Mullins. Monthly. Buys all rights. Pays on publication. Will send a sample copy to a writer on request. Query first. Reports in 1 month. Enclose S.A.S.E.

Nonfiction and Photos: "Articles on any subject pertaining to manufacturers of carbonated and non-carbonated soft drinks, wine or beer. Emphasis should be on sales, distribution, merchandising, advertising, and promotion. Historical articles and 'how-to dissertations' are not desired; no shorts, fillers, or rewritten newspaper clippings." Pays "$35 per printed page (about 1,200 words). Illustrations should be supplied where possible." Pays $5 for each photo used.

MICHIGAN BEVERAGE NEWS, 24681 Northwestern Highway, Suite 408, Southfield MI 48075. Editor: C. Ronald Johnston. For "owners of bars, taverns, package liquor stores, hotels, and clubs in Michigan." Semimonthly. Buys exclusive rights to publication in Michigan. Pays on publication. Will send a sample copy to a writer on request. Query first. Reports "immediately." Enclose S.A.S.E.

Nonfiction and Photos: "Feature stories with pictures. Unusual attractions and business-building ideas in use by Michigan liquor licensees. Profit tips, success stories, etc., slanted to the trade, not to the general public. Especially interested in working with freelancers in Grand Rapids, Flint, Kalamazoo, Marquette, Saulte Ste. Marie, and Bay City areas." Length: 500 to 750 words. Pays "50¢ to $1 per column inch." Buys photos of Michigan licensees engaged in business activities. Pays "50¢ per column inch."

MID-CONTINENT BOTTLER, Box 2298, Shawnee Mission, Kansas City MO 66201. Publisher: Floyd E. Sageser. For "soft drink bottlers in the 18-state midwestern area." Bimonthly. Not copyrighted. Pays on acceptance. Will send a sample copy to a writer on request. Reports "immediately." Enclose S.A.S.E.

Nonfiction and Photos: "Items of specific soft drink bottler interest with special emphasis on sales and merchandising techniques. Feature style desired." Length: 2,000 words. Pays $15 to $50. Photos purchased with mss.

MODERN BREWERY AGE, 80 Lincoln Ave., Stamford CT 06902. Editor: Stanley N. Vlantes. For "brewery executives on the technical, administrative, and marketing levels." Bimonthly. Buys North American serial rights. Pays on publication. Query first. Reports "at once." Enclose S.A.S.E.

Nonfiction and Photos: "Technical and business articles of interest to brewers." Length: "no more than 6 or 7 double-spaced typewritten pages." Pays "$35 per printed page (about 3 to 3½ pages double-spaced typewritten ms)." Photos purchased with mss; captions required. Pays $7.50.

SOUTHERN BEVERAGE JOURNAL, P. O. Box 561107, 13225 S. W. 88th Ave., Miami (Kendall) FL 33156. Managing Editor: Raymond G. Feldman. For "operators of package stores, bars, restaurants, hotel lounges, and dining rooms in Florida, Georgia, South Carolina, Texas, Tennessee, Arkansas, Louisiana, Mississippi." Established in 1944. Monthly. Circulation: about 23,000. Buys "exclusive rights for the 8 southern states." Buys about 12 mss a year. Pays on acceptance or on publication. Will send a sample copy to a writer on request. Write for copy of guidelines for writers. Query first. Will "hardly ever" consider photocopied submissions. Reports in "about a week." Enclose S.A.S.E.

Nonfiction and Photos: "How operators of package stores, bars, restaurants, hotels, and dining rooms merchandise—what they do to attract customers, keep them coming back, and how they promote their operations and the products they sell. We are different from other beverage journals because of our regional circulation and because of our emphasis on merchandising and promotion." Length: open. Pays 4¢ to 6¢ a word, "but it really depends on the article itself; sometimes we don't count words, but we pay for value." Photos purchased with mss only. Prefers 8x10 b&w glossies, but will consider 5x7. Pays $5.

WINES & VINES, 703 Market St., San Francisco CA 94103. Editor: Philip Hiaring. For everyone concerned with the wine industry including winemakers, wine merchants, suppliers, consumers, etc. Monthly magazine. Established in 1919. Circulation: 5,500. Rights purchased vary with author and material. May buy first North American serial rights or simultaneous rights. Buys 4 or 5 mss a year. Payment on acceptance. Will send free sample copy to writer on request. Will not consider photocopied or simultaneous submissions. Submit special material (brandy, January; vineyard, February; champagne, June; marketing, September; aperitif/dessert wines, November) 3 months in advance. Reports in 2 weeks. Query first. Enclose S.A.S.E.

Nonfiction and Photos: Articles of interest to the trade. "These could be on grapegrowing in unusual areas; new winemaking techniques; wine marketing, retailing, etc." Interview, historical, spot news, merchandising techniques, technical. Does not want to see stories with a strong consumer orientation as against trade orientation. Author should know the subject matter, i.e., know proper winegrowing/winemaking terminology. Recent articles published include "What Imports Portend." Length: 1,000 to 2,500 words. Pays $25 to $50. Pays $5 to $10 for 4x5 or 8x10 b&w photos purchased with mss. Captions required.

Book and Book Store Trade

CHRISTIAN BOOKSELLER, Gundersen Dr. and Schmale Rd., Wheaton IL 60187. Editor: William T. Bray. For "Christian booksellers." Monthly. Buys all rights. Pays on publication. Will send sample copy to writer on request. Query first. "Writers urged to study magazine before submitting." Reports in 2 weeks. Enclose S.A.S.E.

Nonfiction and Photos: "Success stories, illustrated with glossy photos, about established Christian booksellers. Stories should highlight specific techniques and managerial policy contributing to the success of the store. We use how-they-did-it articles on phases of bookstore administration and management with an anecdotal approach, and articles presenting proven techniques for seasonal or year-round items. These must be based on actual bookstore experience or sound sales techniques. Features focusing on trends in the Christian book and supply trade; short news articles, with photos if possible, reporting significant developments in the bookstore or publishing field; comprehensive reports on successful store layouts, traffic flow, with glossy illustrations or diagrams. Approach articles from a 'how-they-did-it' rather than 'how-to-do-it' point of view." Length: 1,500 to 2,000 words "with 2 or 3 photos." Pays $35 per article. Pays $3 to $5 for photos.

COLLEGE STORE EXECUTIVE, 211 Broadway, Lynbrook NY 11563. Editor: Robert G. Zeig. For "managers, buyers, and business operators of campus stores."

10 times a year. Circulation: 9,500. Buys North American serial rights. Pays on publication. Will send a sample copy to a writer on request. Query first. Reports "immediately." Enclose S.A.S.E.

Nonfiction and Photos: "Descriptions of unusual displays, merchandising techniques, etc., used in a specific 'bookstore' on campus. (We refer to these stores as college stores.) Best source of information is the manager of the store." Length: 1,000 words. Pays 5¢ a word. Photos purchased with mss. Should be "of college stores, expansion, unusual displays, unusual lines being carried in the store, etc. Should be sharp and clear." Pay negotiable, generally $5.

Poetry and Fillers: "Can pertain to any phase of bookselling or retailing to college students." Length: open. Pays 5¢ a word.

PUBLISHERS WEEKLY, 1180 Ave. of the Americas, New York NY 10036. Editor-in-Chief: Arnold W. Ehrlich. Weekly. Buys first North American rights only. Pays on publication. Reports "in several weeks." Enclose S.A.S.E. for return of submissions.

Nonfiction and Photos: "We rarely use unsolicited mss because of the highly specialized audience and their professional interests, but we can sometimes use news items of bookstores or store promotions for books, or stories of book promotion and design." Payment negotiable; generally $50 to $75 per printed page. Photos purchased with and without mss "occasionally."

QUILL & QUIRE, 59 Front St., E., Toronto, Ontario M5E 1B3, Canada. Editor: Fiona Mee. For professional librarians, writers, booksellers, publishers, educators, media people; anyone interested in Canadian books. Newspaper; 32 (11½x17) pages. Established in 1935. Monthly. Circulation: 12,000. Rights purchased vary with author and material. May buy all rights or second serial (reprint) rights. Buys 120 mss a year. Pays on acceptance. Will send free sample copy to writer on request. Reports in 1 week. Query first. Enclose S.A.E. and International Reply Coupons.

Nonfiction and Photos: Interviews, profiles, commentary. Strong emphasis on information. Subject must be of Canadian interest. Length: 1,000 to 2,000 words. Pays $65 to $100. B&w photos purchased with mss. Pays $15.

RELIGIOUS BOOK REVIEW, P.O. Box 296, Williston Park NY 11596. Editor: Charles A. Roth. For booksellers and librarians. Quarterly magazine; 48 (8½x11) pages. Established in 1970. Circulation: 9,500. Buys all rights. Buys 10 mss a year. Payment on acceptance. Will send sample copy to writer on request. Write for copy of guidelines for writers. Will consider photocopied and simultaneous submissions. Reports in 3 weeks. Query first. Enclose S.A.S.E.

Nonfiction: Uses religious book related articles; notes to authors, interviews, surveys. Articles should be of interest to booksellers, librarians, publishers and educators. Survey articles should cover a particular subject, e.g., ecumenism, etc. Interested in material on the future of religious publishing. Informational, how-to, personal experience, profile, historical, think pieces, personal opinion, successful business operations. Length: 1,000 to 2,500 words. Pays $75 to $125.

Brick, Glass, and Ceramics

AMERICAN GLASS REVIEW, 1115 Clifton Ave., Clifton NJ 07013. Editor: Donald Doctorow. For manufacturers, fabricators, and distributors of glass and glass products. Monthly. Pays on publication. Reports in 3 to 4 weeks. Enclose S.A.S.E.

Nonfiction and Photos: "Illustrated articles on uses of glass, application in new buildings, new container uses, products using fiber glass, glass factory operations, etc." Pays $25 per printed page.

AUTO AND FLAT GLASS JOURNAL, 1929 Royce Ave., Beloit WI 53511. Editor: Richard L. Sine. For owners and employees of glass shops. Magazine; 24 (6x9) pages. Established in 1953. Monthly. Circulation: over 3,500. Rights purchased vary with author and material; usually buys all rights. Buys 12 mss a year. Pays on acceptance. Will send sample copy to writer for 50c (plus S.A.S.E. and 7x10 envelope). Will consider photocopied submissions only with guarantee of priority within the trade. Submit seasonal material 3 months in advance. Reports on material accepted for publication in 2 weeks. Returns rejected material in 10 days. Query first or submit complete ms. Enclose S.A.S.E.

Nonfiction and Photos: Self-help pieces and successful shop features. Emphasis is on what another shop owner/manager would gain from what a particularly successful owner/manager has to say. Would like to see something on a catchy, successful way of promoting a shop; offbeat angles within the trade. Holiday-oriented features of substance. No locally oriented stories about kind-hearted persons who made good. Length: 1,000 to 2,000 words. Pays minimum of 3¢ per word. Buys 8x10 b&w photos, with or without ms. Pays $5.

Fillers: Jokes and short humor related to the trade. Length: 100 words minimum. Pays $5.

BRICK AND CLAY RECORD, 5 S. Wabash Ave., Chicago IL 60603. Phone: 312-372-6880. Managing Editor: Phil Jeffers. For "the heavy clay products industry." Monthly. Buys all rights. Pays on publication. Query first. Reports in 15 days. Enclose S.A.S.E.

Nonfiction and Photos: "News concerning personnel changes within companies; news concerning new plants for manufacture of brick, clay pipe, refractories, drain tile, face brick, glazed tile, lightweight clay aggregate products and abrasives; news of new products, expansion, new building." Pays minimum 8¢ "a published line. Photos paid for only when initially requested by editor."

Fillers: "Items should concern only news of brick, clay pipe, refractory, or clay lightweight aggregate plant operations. If news of personnel, should be only of top-level plant personnel. Not interested in items such as patio, motel, or home construction using brick; of weddings or engagements of clay products people, unless major executives; obituaries, unless of major personnel; items concerning floor or wall tile (only structural tile); of plastics, metal, concrete, bakelite, or similar products; items concerning people not directly involved in clay plant operation." Pays $3 "per published 2- or 3-line brief item." Pays minimum $3 for "full-length published news item, depending on value of item and editor's discretion. Payment is only for items published in the magazine. No items sent in can be returned."

CERAMIC INDUSTRY, 5 S. Wabash, Chicago IL 60603. Editor: J. J. Svec. For the ceramics industry; manufacturers of glass, porcelain, enamel, whitewares and electronic/industrial newer ceramics. Magazine; 50 to 60 pages. Established in 1923. Monthly. Circulation: 7,500. Buys all rights. Buys 10 to 12 mss a year (on assignment only). Pays on acceptance. Will send free sample copy to writer on request. Reports immediately. Query first. Enclose S.A.S.E.

Nonfiction and Photos: Semitechnical, informational and how-to material purchased on assignment only. Length: 500 to 1,500 words. Pays $35 per published page. No additional payment for photos used with mss. Captions required.

CERAMIC SCOPE, 6363 Wilshire Blvd., Los Angeles CA 90048. Editor: Mel Fiske. For "ceramic hobby teachers, dealers, and distributors." 10 times a year, plus annual *Ceramic Hobby Industry Guide.* Buys all rights. Pays on acceptance. Query first. Reports "immediately." Enclose S.A.S.E.

Nonfiction and Photos: "Articles on all phases of studio management (such as merchandising, promotion, pricing, credit and collection, recordkeeping, taxes, display, equipment and layout); case histories of actual studio operation; discussion of ceramic business practices and policies; news about traveling teachers, studios, shows, books, ceramic associations; reports on manufacturers' aids, products, services, displays, and literature. We reject poorly written stories that allegedly apply to all fields and actually apply to none." Length: open. Pays 2¢ a word. Photos purchased with mss. "Show interior of ceramic studios, workshops, and classes." Pays $5.

GLASS DIGEST, 15 E. 40th St., New York NY 10016. Phone: 212-685-0785. Editor: Oscar S. Glasberg. Monthly. Buys all rights. Pays on publication "or before, if ms held too long." Will send a sample copy to a writer on request. Reports "as soon as possible." Enclose S.A.S.E. for return of submissions.

Nonfiction and Photos: "Items about firms in glass distribution, personnel, plants, etc. Stories about outstanding jobs accomplished—volume of flat glass, storefronts, curtain walls, auto glass, mirrors, windows (metal), glass doors; special uses and values; who installed it. Stories about successful glass jobbers, dealers, and glazing contractors—their methods, promotion work done, advertising, results." Length: 1,000 to 1,500 words. Pays 5¢ a word, "occasionally more. No interest in bottles, glassware, containers, etc., but leaded and stained glass OK." B&w photos purchased with mss; "8x10 preferred." Pays $5, "occasionally more."

How To Break In: "Find a typical dealer case history about a firm operating in such a successful way that its methods can be duplicated by readers everywhere."

Building Interiors

DECOR, The Magazine of Fine Interior Accessories, 408 Olive, St. Louis MO 63102. Phone: 314-421-5445. Editor: Bill Humberg. For retailers, including individual gallery owners, managers of picture and interior accessory departments of department stores, mirror store owners, home furnishings stores and picture framers. Monthly magazine; 100 (8½x11) pages. Established in 1875. Circulation: 10,000. Buys "rights exclusive to our field". Buys 36 mss a year. Payment on acceptance. Will send free sample copy to writer on request. Write for copy of guidelines for writers. Will not consider photocopied submissions. Will consider simultaneous submissions. Submit special issue material (framing, April; clocks and lamps, June; original art, October; mirrors, November; holiday displays, stories, Christmas) three months in advance. Reports in 1 week. Query first. Enclose S.A.S.E.

Nonfiction and Photos: "How-to articles (how to advertise, how to use display space, how to choose product lines, how to use credit) giving, in essence, new and better ways to show a profit. Most often in the form of single store interviews with a successful store manager. No editorializing by the freelancer, unless he has proper credentials. Our emphasis is on useful material, not merely general interest. How does this businessman keep his customers, get new ones, please the old ones, etc." Length: open. Pays $65 to $125. No additional payment for 5x7 or 8x10 b&w photos used with mss.

DECORATING RETAILER, 9334 Dielman Industrial Dr., St. Louis MO 63132. Editor: John Rogers. For "paint and wallpaper retailers who own or operate independent stores. They are interested in factual, concrete information on how they can improve their businesses." Established in 1964. Monthly. Circulation: 30,000. Buys all rights. Buys about 20 mss a year. Pays on acceptance. Will not consider photocopied submissions. Submit seasonal material 2 months in advance. Reports in 2 weeks. Enclose S.A.S.E.

Nonfiction and Photos: "Articles on the merchandising, display, and sale of paint, wallcoverings, art and craft products, and other allied decorating products. Interested in direct, to-the-point pieces on how retailers can improve their operations. We prefer the interview-type article, telling how one or 2 retailers faced a problem and solved it. Articles should be specific and full of factual, concrete recommendations, preferably coming from other retailers who have had the experience. Quotes, descriptions of stores, displays, promotions, etc., are desirable. No 'abstract' articles on concepts. We want our readers to know how the suggestion has worked for other retailers, how and why it might or might not work for them. No clippings." Buys informational articles, how-to's, personal experience articles, interviews, profiles, coverage of successful business operations, and articles on merchandising techniques. Length: 1,000 to 1,500 words. Pays 5¢ a word. 5x7 b&w photos purchased with mss; captions optional. Pays $7.50.

KITCHEN BUSINESS, 1515 Broadway, New York NY 10036. Editor and Publisher: Patrick Galvin. For "kitchen cabinet and countertop plants, kitchen and bath planning specialists, and kitchen–bath departments of lumber, plumbing, and appliance businesses." Monthly. Buys all rights. Pays on acceptance. Will consider photocopied submissions. Often overstocked. Reports in 1 month. Enclose S.A.S.E.

Nonfiction and Photos: "Factual case histories with illustrative photos on effective selling or management methods; picture tours of outstanding kitchen showrooms of about 1,000 words; articles on management methods for kitchen distributorships which handle a full range of kitchen products; 'how-to' shop stories on kitchen cabinet shops or countertop fabricators, or stories on how they adapt to growth problems." Length: "600 words and 2 photos to 2,000 words and 10 photos." Pays $50 "first published page, minimum $30 each succeeding page, as estimated at the time of acceptance." Photos purchased with mss.

How To Break In: "Just go ahead and do it. Select the best looking kitchen firm in your area, go in and tell the boss you're a writer and want to do a story for *Kitchen Business,* ask him to let you sit down and read an issue or two, interview him on a single how-to-do-it topic, shoot some pictures to illustrate the points in the interview, and take a chance. Include his phone number so I can check with him. If it's good, you'll get paid promptly. If it shows promise, I'll work with you. If it's lousy, you'll get it back. If it's in between, you might not hear for a while because I hate to send them back if they have any value at all. This worked for me through a dozen years of highly successful freelancing. It will work for anyone who has any reporting talent at all."

PROFESSIONAL DECORATING & COATING ACTION, 7223 Lee Hghwy., Falls Church VA 22046. Editor: Heskett K. Darby. For owners of contracting businesses. Publication of the Painting and Decorating Contractors of America, Inc. Magazine; 28 pages. Established in 1938. Monthly. Circulation: 13,000. Copyrighted. Rights negotiable. Buys about 12 mss a year. Pays on acceptance. Will send free sample copy to writer on request. No photocopied or simultaneous submissions. Reports immediately on material accepted for publication. Returns rejected material within 2 weeks. Query first. Enclose S.A.S.E.

Nonfiction and Photos: "We like short pieces that are assisted by good quality illustration photos. Articles dealing with or describing unusual painting and decorating jobs. Solutions to coating problems (as in areas of highly corrosive marine atmospheres); chemical processing plants; descriptions of coating systems; kind of paints involved, equipment, etc. Also systems stories on contractors, business administration. We like a straightforward description of the job or system. Emphasis is on the equipment and materials. We don't want to see the stereotyped article about a company's operations. To be of interest, the story should be about an unusual operation; some unique approach to an industry problem." Recently published "Coating a Tunnel: U.S. Tryout for Canadian System." Length: 1,000 words maximum. Pays 7¢ to 10¢ a word. B&w photos (4½x5 minimum) purchased with or without ms or on assignment. Captions required. Pays $7.50

WALLS AND CEILINGS, 14006 Ventura Blvd., Sherman Oaks CA 91423. Phone: 213-789-8733. Editor: Robert F. Welch. For "contractors involved in lathing and plastering, drywall, acoustics, fireproofing, curtain walls, movable partitions and their mechanics, together with manufacturers, dealers, and architects." Monthly. Circulation: 7,500. Not copyrighted. Buys 25 mss a year. Pays on publication. Will send a sample copy to a writer on request. Query first. Reports in 30 days. Enclose S.A.S.E.

Nonfiction and Photos: "As technical as possible. Should be helpful to professional operator—diagrams, sketches, and detail pictures should illustrate material." Interested in interviews, spot news, successful business operations, new product, merchandising techniques. Length: maximum 1,000 words. Pay "depends upon value to our readers—maximum usually $50 to $75." B&w glossies purchased with and without mss; captions required. Pays $3 to $5.

How To Break In: "Interview a contractor about an unusual job or his principles of business management."

Business Management

The publications listed here are aimed at owners of businesses and top level business executives. They cover business trends and general theory and practice of management. Publications that use similar material but have a less technical or professional slant are listed in Business and Finance in the Consumer Publications section. Journals dealing with banking, investment, and financial management are classified in the Finance category in this section.

Publications dealing with lower level management (including supervisors and office managers) will be found in Management and Supervision. Journals for industrial plant managers are listed under Industrial Management, and also under the names of specific industries such as Machinery and Metal Trade or Plastics. Publications for office supply store operators will be found with the Office Equipment and Supplies Journals.

ADMINISTRATIVE MANAGEMENT, 51 Madison Ave., New York NY 10010. Editor: Walter A. Kleinschrod. For middle to upper level executives responsible for office administration, including communications, personnel, salary and compensation, and clerical functions. Established in 1940. Monthly magazine (88 pages). Circulation: 53,000. Buys all rights or first North American serial rights. Buys 25 mss a year. Payment on publication. Will not consider photocopied or simultaneous submissions. Will send free sample copy to writer on request. Write for copy of guidelines for writers. Reports in 1 month. Query first with an outline. Enclose S.A.S.E.
Nonfiction and Photos: "Material tailored to top, upper and middle managers responsible for office-based functions collectively known as 'administration'. Topics include business systems, personnel management, office environment, trends." Informational articles and think pieces on successful business operations. Length: 1,000 to 2,500 words. Pays $50 to $200. Photos purchased with accompanying ms with no additional payment.

BUSINESS DIGEST OF FLORIDA, P.O. Drawer 23729, Oakland Park FL 33307. Editor: Mary Lathrop. For executives and general managers of business and industry. Established in 1973. Circulation: 7,500. Not copyrighted. Buys 20 mss a year. Pays on publication. Will send free sample copy to writer on request. Will consider photocopied and simultaneous submissions. Reports on material accepted for publication in 3 months. Returns rejected material immediately. Query first or submit complete ms. Enclose S.A.S.E.
Nonfiction: Articles on profits, business management, business psychology, morale, motivation, better methods of operation. Emphasis is on writing about successes and failures from past experiences; analyzing present needs in business; future trends, general problems management and employees are faced with. "Must be adaptable to Florida thinking and ways of functioning, and at the same time generate new ideas and thinking." Recently published "The Morality of Profit", which pointed the way, contrary to news reports, that people are in business for no other reason. Length: 1,200 to 1,500 words. Pays $25 per published page. Shorter material is sought for Business Clinic – Stock Market (trends and good buys); Sexy Business (articles, briefs, geared for female career people; gossip type shorts on employee-management relations). Pays $15.
How To Break In: "The writer must have enough insight into the future and be able to produce an article that covers present day problems constructively."

EXECUTIVE REVIEW, 224 S. Michigan Ave., Chicago IL 60604. Editor: Harold Sabes. For "management of small and middle-sized companies, middle management in larger companies and corporations." Established in 1955. Monthly. Circulation: 25,000. Not copyrighted. Buys about 10 mss a year. Pays on publication. Will send a sample copy to a writer on request. Submit complete ms. Will consider photocopied submissions. Reports in 1 week. Enclose S.A.S.E.
Nonfiction: "Articles are mainly how-to, dealing with business activities from the

reception desk through the office, manufacturing and delivery. We're interested in articles dealing with business activities and with the personal activities of businessmen. *Executive Review* is sold as an external house organ. It is distributed to the customers and prospects of the sponsor-advertiser." Buys informational articles, how-to's, personal experience articles, humor, think articles, coverage of successful business operations, and articles on merchandising techniques. Length: 1,200 to 1,500 words. Pays up to $50 an article.

HARVARD BUSINESS REVIEW, Soldiers Field, Boston MA 02163. Phone: 617-495-6800. Editor: Ralph F. Lewis. For top management in U.S. industry, and in Japan and Western Europe; younger managers who aspire to top management responsibilities; policymaking executives in government, policymakers in noncommercial organizations, and professional people interested in the viewpoint of business management. Published 6 times a year. Buys all rights. Payment on publication. Query first. Reports in 2 to 6 weeks. Enclose S.A.S.E.
Nonfiction: Articles on business trends, techniques and problems. "*Harvard Business Review* seeks to inform executives about what is taking place in management, but it also wants to challenge them and stretch their thinking about the policies they make, how they make them, and how they administer them. It does this by presenting articles that provide in-depth analyses of issues and problems in management and, wherever possible, guidelines for thinking out and working toward resolutions of these issues and problems." Length: 3,000 to 6,000 words. Pays $100.

MARKETING LETTER, Alexander Hamilton Institute, 605 Third Ave., New York NY 10016. Editor: J. M. Jenks. For upper level business and marketing executives. Newsletter; 8 pages. Established in 1974. Monthly. Buys all rights. Buys about 10 mss a year. Pays on acceptance. Will send free sample copy to writer on request. No photocopied or simultaneous submissions. Reports in 2 weeks. Query first. Enclose S.A.S.E.
Nonfiction: Articles on marketing research, advertising, sales management, physical distribution. Prefers the case history approach; clear writing, narrow focus; from top management's point of view. No opinionated editorializing. Uses telephone or in-person interviews. Length: 1,000 to 1,200 words. Pays 15¢ a word.

MAY TRENDS, 111 S. Washington St., Park Ridge IL 60068. Phone: 312-825-8806. Editor: J.J. Coffey, Jr. For chief executives of businesses, trade associations, government bureaus, Better Business Bureaus, educational institutions, newspapers. Publication of George S. May International Company. Magazine published 3 times a year; 28 to 30 pages. Established in 1967. Circulation: 10,000. Buys all rights. Buys 15 to 20 mss a year. Payment on acceptance. Will send free sample copy to writer on request. Reports on material accepted for publication in 1 week. Returns rejected material immediately. Query first or submit complete ms. Enclose S.A.S.E.
Nonfiction: "We prefer articles dealing with problems of specific industries (manufacturers, wholesalers, retailers, service businesses) where contact has been made with key executives whose comments regarding their problems may be quoted." Avoid material on overworked, labor-management relations. Interested in small supermarket success stories vs. the "giants"; automobile dealers coping with existing dull markets; contractors solving cost—inventory problems. Will consider material on successful business operations and merchandising techniques. Length: 1,500 to 3,000 words. Pays $100 to $250.

Church Administration and Ministry

ADULT BIBLE TEACHER, 6401 The Paseo, Kansas City MO 64131. Phone: 816-333-7000. Editor: John B. Nielson. For teachers of adults. Quarterly. Buys first and second rights; will accept simultaneous submissions. Pays on acceptance. Will consider photocopied submissions. Reports in 6 weeks. Enclose S.A.S.E.

Nonfiction: "Articles of interest to teachers of adults and articles relevant to the International Sunday School Lessons." Length: 1,300 words maximum. Pays minimum $20 per 1,000 words. Department Editor: Donald S. Metz.
Photos: Purchased with captions only. Pays minimum $5.
Poetry: Inspirational, seasonal, or lesson-related (Uniform Series) poetry. Length: 24 lines maximum. Pays minimum 25¢ per line.

THE CHAPLAIN, 3900 Wisconsin Ave., N.W., Suite N 200, Washington DC 20016. Editor: Reverend Edward I. Swanson. For ordained clergymen on active duty as military chaplains (all services); retired chaplains. Magazine; 80 (6x9) pages. Established in 1944. Quarterly. Circulation: 6,000. Buys first North American serial rights. Buys about 12 mss a year. Pays on acceptance. Will send free sample copy to writer on request. Write for copy of guidelines for writers. No photocopied or simultaneous submissions. Query first or submit complete ms. Reports in 4 to 6 weeks. Enclose S.A.S.E.
Nonfiction and Photos: Articles on aspects of the military chaplaincy system of the religiously pluralistic nation. "We solicit articles on specific subjects from writers either known or recommended to us. We are using a thematic approach to our journal and, therefore, are able to design the content accordingly." Recently published articles include "The Aging Parent and the Service Family," "Guilt and the Pastoral Counselor," and "The Functions of an ARCOM Chaplain." Length: 3,000 to 4,000 words maximum. Pays 2¢ a word. Pays $5 to $7.50 for 8x10 b&w glossies purchased with mss or on assignment. Captions required.

CHURCH ADMINISTRATION, 127 Ninth Ave., N., Nashville TN 37234. Phone: 615-254-5461, Ext. 363. Editor: George Clark. For Southern Baptist pastors, staff, and volunteer church leaders. Monthly. Buys all rights. Will also consider second rights. Uses limited amount of freelance material. Pays on acceptance. Will send a free sample copy to a writer on request. Write for copy of guidelines for writers. Reports in 1 month. Enclose S.A.S.E. for return of submissions.
Nonfiction and Photos: "How-to-do-it articles dealing with church administration, including church programming, organizing, and staffing, administrative skills, church financing, church food services, church facilities, communication, pastoral ministries, and community needs." Length: 750 to 1,200 words. Pays 2½¢ a word. Pays $7.50 to $10 for 8x10 b&w glossies purchased with mss.
How To Break In: "A beginning writer should first be acquainted with organization and policy of Baptist churches and with the administrative needs of Southern Baptist churches. He should perhaps interview one or several SBC pastors or staff members, find out how they are handling a certain administrative problem such as 'enlisting volunteer workers' or 'sharing the administrative load with church staff or volunteer workers.' I suggest writers compile an article showing how *several* different administrators (or churches) handled the problem, perhaps giving meaningful quotes. Submit the completed manuscript, typed 54 characters to the line, for consideration."

CHURCH MANAGEMENT-THE CLERGY JOURNAL, 212 Commercial Bldg., 115 N. Main St., Mt. Holly NC 28120. Phone: 704-827-9296. Editor: Dr. Norman L. Hersey. For ministers, rabbis and priests. Magazine. Published 10 times a year. Established in 1924. Circulation: 14,500. Rights purchased vary with author and material. Usually buys all rights, but will reassign rights to author after publication. Will consider photocopied submissions. Will not consider simultaneous submissions. Submit seasonal material 4 months in advance. Reports on material accepted for publication in 2 weeks. Returns rejected material in 2 to 4 weeks. Query first. Enclose S.A.S.E.
Nonfiction and Photos: Professional how-to articles slanted to clergymen. Avoid theological emphasis. Interested in coverage of seasonal church services (Christmas, Lent, Easter, vacation schools). Also informational, profile, inspirational, humorous and historical articles; personal opinion. Length: 1,200 words maximum. Pays $2.50 to $25. Pays $1 to $5 for 7x10 b&w glossies purchased with mss. Captions required.

THE EDGE, 6401 The Paseo, Kansas City MO 64131. Editor: Norman J. Brown.

For Church of the Nazarene Sunday School teachers, pastors, Sunday school superintendents, supervisors and workers. Established in 1973. Quarterly. Circulation: 45,000. Buys all rights. Buys about 50 mss a year. Pays on acceptance. Will send free sample copy to writer on request. Write for copy of guidelines for writers. Submit seasonal material 10 months in advance. Reports in 10 to 12 weeks. Query first. Enclose S.A.S.E.

Nonfiction: "The function of the magazine is to provide inspiration, information, promotional ideas, methods, and how-to articles in Christian education. Basic ideas include a true story which motivates, a special project successfully completed by a school, class, or department; an outstanding promotional idea; a human interest story of an outstanding worker; a new way to use an old method; specific accomplishment through the use of Nazarene graded curriculum; how-to articles related specifically to age group methods and materials; articles which help teachers understand pupils; suggestions on local church management and Sunday school administration." Length: 1,000 words maximum. Pays 2¢ a word.

Photos: Used when they tell a story. Very few groups of photos are purchased. 5x7 or larger required. Pays $6 minimum.

Fiction: Considered if it is short and deals with a problem in the field. Length: 1,000 words maximum. Pays 2¢ a word.

HISWAY MAGAZINE, 1445 Boonville Ave., Springfield MO 65802. Editor: Glen Ellard. For "ministers of youth (Christian)." Basic Christianity and Christian activism. Special issues at Christmas and Easter. Established in 1944. Monthly. Circulation: 7,500. Buys all rights, but will reassign rights to author after publication. Buys first North American serial rights, second serial (reprint) rights and simultaneous rights. Buys 20 to 30 mss a year. Payment on acceptance. Will send free sample copy to a writer on request. Will consider photocopied submissions. Submit seasonal material 6 months in advance. Submit only complete ms. Reports in 6 weeks. Enclose S.A.S.E.

Nonfiction: "How-to" articles (e.g., "How to Evangelize Youth Through Music," "How to Study the Bible for Personal Application," "How to Use the Media for the Christian Message"); skits and role-plays; Bible raps, original choruses, Bible verses set to music, posters, ideas for youth services, socials, and fund raising; interviews with successful youth leaders. Avoid cliches (especially religious ones); educational philosophy; youth (or student) centered instead of adult (or teacher) centered; relational approach instead of talking down. Length: 500 to 2,500 words. Pays 3c a word.

KEY TO CHRISTIAN EDUCATION, 8121 Hamilton Ave., Cincinnati OH 45231. Editor: Marjorie Miller. For Sunday school leaders. Quarterly. Not copyrighted. Pays on acceptance. Free sample copy on request. "Study sample for style and editorial requirements before submitting ms." Will consider cassette submissions. Reports in 30 days. Enclose S.A.S.E.

Nonfiction and Photos: How-to articles helpful to teachers, departmental superintendents, youth leaders, Sunday school superintendents, ministers of Christian education. Should not be highly technical. Length: 800 to 1,600 words. Pays $20 to $50. Buys 8x10 b&w photos with mss. Pays $5 to $10. "Tested Ideas" type articles on Sunday school plans that have worked. Length: 50 to 75 words. Pays $5 each.

PASTORAL LIFE, Society of St. Paul, Canfield OH 44406. Editor: Victor L. Viberti, S.S.P. For priests and those interested in pastoral ministry. Monthly. Circulation: 8,600. Buys first rights. Payment on acceptance. Will send sample copy to writer on request. "Queries appreciated before submitting mss. New contributors are expected to accompany their material with a few lines of personal data." Reports in 7 to 10 days. Enclose S.A.S.E.

Nonfiction: "Professional review, principally designed to focus attention on current problems, needs, issues and all important activities related to all phases of pastoral work and life. Avoids merely academic treatments on abstract and too controversial subjects." Length: 2,000 to 3,400 words. Pays 3¢ a word minimum.

SUCCESS, Baptist Publications, P.O. Box 15337, Denver CO 80215. Editor: Mrs. Edith Quinlan. A magazine slanted to Christian education workers. Quarterly. Buys first rights "usually". Pays on publication. Will send a sample copy to a writer on request. Write for copy of guidelines for writers. Query first or submit complete ms. "Enclose short biographical sketch with submission, especially if engaged in Christian education work." Reports "as soon as possible." Enclose S.A.S.E.

Nonfiction and Photos: Gives ideas, helps and information for Sunday School superintendents, teachers and youth workers, with a view to helping them achieve excellence. "Articles may be of a general nature slanted to all Christian education workers, or may be slanted to specific age groups such as preschool, elementary, youth and adult. We are more desirous of receiving articles from people who know Christian education, or workers who have accomplished something worthwhile in Sunday School and/or Training Time, than from trained or experienced writers who do not have such experience. A combination of both, however, would be ideal." Length: 500 to 2,000 words. Pays 2¢ to 3¢ per word, depending on amount of editing required and the value of the article to the total content of the magazine. Photos accompanying articles are helpful. Pays $1 to $10 per photo.

SUNDAY SCHOOL COUNSELOR, 1445 Boonville Ave., Springfield MO 65802. Editor: Sylvia Lee. Monthly. "We will accept simultaneous submissions providing the author advises us of the other publications to which he has sent the ms." Limited amount of freelance material bought. Enclose S.A.S.E. for return of submissions.

Nonfiction and Photos: Interested in news with a Sunday school slant, particularly reports of "this is the way we do it" variety which provide ideas that may be adapted by other Sunday schools. "Be specific; avoid generalities; give enough details for clarity." Length: 1,200 words average. Pays 1¢ to 2¢ a word. Articles may be illustrated with photographs; informal action shots of good quality, rather than posed group pictures. Sketches or photographs may also be included with brief items for teachers and department leaders.

How To Break In: "Send us a clear concise report of a teaching method or technique which the author or another person has successfully used in a Sunday school classroom. Our emphasis is on practical how-to-do-it information, and this is the kind of material we are constantly looking out for."

YOUR CHURCH, 198 Allendale Rd., King of Prussia PA 19406. Phone: 215-265-9400. Editor: Richard L. Critz. For the ministers of America's churches. "We reach 2 out of 3 of them; all faiths; Protestant, Catholic, Jew." Magazine published every 2 months; 56 (8¼x11) pages. Established in 1955. Circulation: 200,000. Buys all rights. Buys 15 to 20 mss a year. Payment on publication. Will send free sample copy to writer on request. Will consider photocopied submissions. No simultaneous submissions. Reports within a month or two. Query first or submit complete ms. Enclose S.A.S.E.

Nonfiction and Photos: "News material for pastors; informative and cogently related to some aspect of being a pastor (counseling, personal finance, administration, building, etc.). No special approach required, but we seldom use liturgical material. We stress the personal, the informal, and avoid the pretentious. Would like to see good material on music, the arts and crafts in the church." Informational, how-to, inspirational, think pieces. Length: 2 to 15 typewritten pages. Pays $25 to $75. No additional payment made for b&w photos.

How To Break In: "The best way is to treat a relevant subject with humor and the personal touch."

Clothing and Knit Goods

HOSIERY AND UNDERWEAR, 757 Third Ave., New York NY 10017. Editor: Trudye Connolly. For hosiery executives; buyers in department stores, supermarket, drug, discount and variety chains; management and personnel in companies manufacturing hosiery and supplies for the industry. Monthly. Circulation: 14,000. Buys all rights. Pays on acceptance. Query first. Reports in 10 days. Enclose S.A.S.E.

Nonfiction and Photos: "Articles needed for split readership; one half of magazine deals with marketing; the distribution and sale of hosiery items. The other half deals with manufacturing, technological developments, production methods, and managerial systems in the mills. Marketing features explore display, selling techniques, advertising, specific merchandising philosophies of various outlets selling hosiery. (General 'store tour' not acceptable.) Manufacturing features explore technology, production, personnel management, trends in hosiery mills and with companies supplying the hosiery industry." Length: 1,000 to 2,000 words. Pays 5¢ a word. $5 to $7 per glossy b&w photo.

TACK'N TOGS MERCHANDISING, P. O. Box 67, Minneapolis MN 55440. Address mss to The Editor. For "retailers of products for horse and rider and Western and English fashion apparel." Established in 1971. Monthly. Circulation: 14,000. Rights purchased vary with author and material; may buy all rights. Buys 25 to 30 mss a year. Pays on acceptance. Will send a sample copy to a writer on request. Write for copy of guidelines for writers. Query first. Enclose S.A.S.E.

Nonfiction and Photos: "Case histories, trends of industry." Buys informational articles, how-to's, personal experience articles, interviews, profiles, personal opinion articles, coverage of successful business operations, new product pieces, and articles on merchandising techniques. Length: open. Pays "up to $100." B&w glossies and color transparencies purchased with mss.

TEENS AND BOYS, 71 W. 35th St., New York NY 10001. Editor: Mrs. Kathie M. Andersen. For "retailers and manufacturers of boys' and young men's apparel (ages 5 to 20)." Monthly. Not copyrighted. Pays on publication. Will send a sample copy to a writer on request. Query first; "on assignment only. Unsolicited mss will not be returned or read." Enclose S.A.S.E.

Nonfiction and Photos: "We are a trade publication, dealing with the boys' and young men's apparel market. The type of story we are interested in deals with exceptional retail stores for these categories. Things to look for: interesting decor, valid merchandising philosophy, great success in a short time, well-established place in the community, etc. All types of stores, from discounters to specialty stores could be subject matter for us." Length: 1,000 to 1,500 words. Pays 5¢ per word. "Photos should be clear and clean. There should be one of the persons interviewed, and one which includes the store's logo (sign). Other photos should be included only if they are noteworthy, i.e., showing something that would be of interest to our readers. Manikin shots (unless a new type of manikin is used) are not interesting." Pays $7.50.

How To Break In: "If someone were trying to write for *Teens and Boys,* I would advise him to first write for a copy of the magazine, as well as a list of questions I have prepared to help anyone who writes for us. Then he should suggest a story idea (an interview with a particularly good retailer). If we approve the idea, then the interview can take place."

WESTERN OUTFITTER, 5314 Bingle Rd., Houston TX 77018. Publication Manager: Tad Mizwa. For "owners or managers of retail stores or store departments which sell western riding supplies, tack, or clothing." Monthly. Buys all rights. Pays on publication. Query first. Enclose S.A.S.E.

Nonfiction and Photos: "Articles covering all phases of merchandising—product information, selling to horsemen, promotional gimmicks used successfully by Western stores. Writer must know merchandising and selling." Length: 1,000 to 3,000 words. Pays 4¢ a word. Photos purchased with mss. Pays $7.50.

Coin-Operated Machines

AMERICAN COIN-OP, 500 N. Dearborn St., Chicago IL 60610. Phone: 312-337-7700. Editor: Bob Harker. For businessmen and businesswomen who own coin-operated laundry and drycleaning stores; operators, distributors and industry leaders. Monthly magazine; 51 (8¼x11¼) pages. Established in 1960. Circulation: 24,000. Rights purchased vary with author and material but are exclusive to the field. Buys 90 mss per year. Payment on publication. Will send sample copy to writer on request. Will not consider photocopied or simultaneous submissions. Reports on material accepted as soon as possible. Returns rejected material immediately. Query first. Enclose S.A.S.E.

Nonfiction and Photos: "We emphasize store operation and management and use features on industry topics: maintenance, store management, customer service, advertising. While it is perhaps an oversimplification to say that a good coin-op feature defines the store in terms of the reader, such an article should describe the store and its operation and especially the outstanding or unique characteristics of the store, that the reader can apply in his own operation. Possible subjects could feature coverage of site, customer service, attendants, security, advertising, fabrics, maintenance, business management. Avoid generalizations about 'a nice new store'. What is different about it? How is it being promoted effectively? Mss should have no-nonsense, businesslike approach and be brief. We avoid the gee-whiz puff piece glorifying the store owner's name or the name of a product, as well as an inappropriate approach, incompetence, generality, unfamiliarity." Uses informational, how-to, interview, profile, think pieces, spot news, successful business operations articles. Length: 500 to 3,000 words. Pays minimum of 3¢ per word. Pays $5 for 8x10 b&w glossy photos purchased with mss. Must be clear and have good contrast.

Fillers: Newsbreaks, clippings. Length: 500 words maximum. Pays 3¢ per word.

How To Break In: "By knowing the field and by being able to send an intelligent query about a coherent ms appropriate to our readership."

COIN LAUNDERER & CLEANER, 525 Somerset Dr., Indianapolis IN 46260. For owners, operators, and managers of coin-operated and self-service laundry and drycleaning establishments. Monthly. Buys all rights. Enclose S.A.S.E.

Nonfiction: "Our requirements are for self-service coin laundry and drycleaning store management articles which specify the promotion, service, or technique used by the store owners; the cost of this technique; and the profit produced by it. Freelance writers must be familiar with coin laundry and drycleaning industry to prepare an article of sufficient management significance." Pays 5¢ per printed word.

COINAMATIC AGE, 60 E. 42nd St., New York NY 10017. Phone 212-682-6330. Editor: C. F. Lee. For operators/owners of coin-operated laundries; dry cleaners. Bimonthly. Buys all rights. Pays on publication. "Queries get same-day attention." Enclose S.A.S.E.

Nonfiction and Photos: "We are currently considering articles on coin-operated laundries, or in combination with drycleaners. Slant should focus on the unusual, but at the same time should stress possible adaptation by other coinamat operators. Particular interest at this time centers on energy conservation methods. We are interested in promotional and advertising techniques; reasons for expansion or additional locations; attached sidelines such as gas stations, restaurants, and other businesses; Main Street vs. shopping center operations; successes in dealing with permanent press garment laundering and cleaning; ironing services; and, primarily, financial success, personal satisfaction, or any other motivation that the owner derives from his business. Give the story punch, details, and applicability to the reader. Include a list of specifications, detailing the number of units (washers, dryers, etc.), the different pound-loads of each machine and the make and model numbers of all of these, as well as any vending machines, change-makers, etc. 3 action photos (preferably a minimum of 6) must accompany each article. At this time, we are especially interested in combined laundry/drycleaning articles. Submitted photos must include an exterior shot of the installation and interior shots showing customers. Where possible, a photo of the owner at work is also desired. If you have a far-out slant, query first." Pays 3¢ to 4¢ a word, depending on need to rewrite. Length: 1,200 to 2,000 words. No "plugola" for manufacturers' products, please. Photos purchased with mss. Pays $12 for 3 photos and $6 for each additional photo.

VENDING TIMES, 211 E. 43rd St., New York NY 10017. Editor: Arthur E. Yohalem. For operators of vending machines. Monthly. Circulation: 13,500. Buys all rights. Pays on publication. Query first; "we will discuss the story requirements with the writer in detail." Enclose S.A.S.E.

Nonfiction and Photos: Feature articles and news stories about vending operations; practical and important aspects of the business. Recently published articles include "ARA World Trade Center Operation Requires Vertical Route Structure;" most vending routes are horizontal — that is, a guy normally stops every five or ten blocks to service his machines. But the World Trade Center is so tall (100 stories) that somebody's complete concession will be on a vertical stretch of 30 floors. Also recently published an article about handling the problems of people breaking into machines. "We are always willing to pay for good material. Primary interest is photo fillers." Pays $5 per photo.

Confectionery and Snack Foods

CANDY AND SNACK INDUSTRY, 777 Third Ave., New York, NY 10017. Phone: 212-838-7778. Editor: Myron Lench. For confectionery and snack manufacturers. Monthly. Buys all rights. Query first. Reports in 2 weeks. Enclose S.A.S.E.

Nonfiction: "Feature articles of interest to large scale candy, cookie, cracker, and other snack manufacturers that deal with activities in the fields of production, packaging (including package design), merchandising; financial news (sales figures, profits, earnings), advertising campaigns in all media, and promotional methods used to increase the sale or distribution of candy and snacks." Length: 1,000 to 1,250 words. Pays 5¢ a word; "special rates on assignments."

Photos: "Good quality glossies with complete and accurate captions, in sizes not smaller than 5x7." Pays $5. Color covers.

Fillers: "Short news stories about the trade and anything related to candy and snacks." Pays 5¢ per word; $1 for clippings.

CANDY MARKETER, 777 Third Ave., New York NY 10017. Phone: 212-838-7778. Editor: Mike Lench. For owners and executives of wholesale and retail businesses. Monthly magazine. Established in 1967. Circulation: 14,000. Buys all rights. Buys 20 mss a year. Payment on acceptance. Will send free sample copy to writer on request. Will consider photocopied submissions. Will not consider simultaneous submissions. Submit seasonal material at least 6 weeks in advance. Reports within 2 weeks. Query first. Enclose S.A.S.E.

Nonfiction, Photos, and Fillers: News and features on the candy trade. "Describe operation, interview candy buyer or merchandise manager; quote liberally. More interested in mass operations, than in unusual little shops." Informational, how-to, interview, profile, spot news, successful business operations, merchandising techniques. Annual issues on Halloween merchandising, Christmas merchandising and Easter merchandising are published in May, June and November (respectively). Length: 1,000 to 2,500 words. Pays 5¢ a word. 5x7 or 8½x11 b&w photos and color transparencies or prints purchased with or without mss. Captions required. Pays $5 for b&w; $15 for color. Pays $1 for each clipping used.

NATIONAL CANDY WHOLESALER, 1430 K St., N.W., Washington DC 20005. Editor: Barbara A. Moskowitz. For people involved in the wholesale candy and tobacco business: owners of distribution companies, salesmen, brokers. These are small businessmen, often in a family-owned company. 76-page magazine published 10 times a year for the candy distribution industry. Established in 1948. Circulation: about 8,000. Buys all rights. Buys 3 to 4 mss a year. Payment on acceptance. Will send free sample copy to writer on request. Will consider photocopied submissions. Will not consider simultaneous submissions. Reports immediately. Query first. Enclose S.A.S.E.

Nonfiction and Photos: Articles based on interviews with candy wholesale companies and occasionally with candy manufacturers. Articles which specifically relate to the management of these kinds of businesses. Not interested in general management tips, either personal or corporate. "We prefer to suggest assignments, since our publication is fairly narrow in scope." Informational, how-to, profile, merchandising techniques. Length: 2,500 to 3,500 words. Pays $75 to $100. "Type of photos required must be discussed with the writer." Pays $50 for minimum of 5 b&w photos (5x7 or 8x10). Captions required.

How To Break In: "Be willing to do interviews with companies we suggest which are located in your area."

Construction and Contracting

AMERICAN ROOFER & BUILDING IMPROVEMENT CONTRACTOR, 915 Burlington, Downers Grove IL 60515. Phone: 312-964-6200. Editor: Johanna C. Gudas. For "business executives heading roofing contractor firms, architects, engineers, specification writers, and others in the construction industry." Established in 1911. Monthly. Circulation: 17,500. Buys all rights, but will reassign rights to author after publication. Buys 10 to 15 mss a year. Pays on publication. Will send a sample copy to a writer on request. Will not consider photocopied submissions. Reports "immediately, as a general rule." Query first. Enclose S.A.S.E.

Nonfiction and Photos: "Industry news, stories on roofing contractors, business management, estimating, unusual roofing jobs, technical material on any aspect of this industry. Articles should always be written from the viewpoint of the roofing contractor or architect, or in relation to his point of view, rather than construction in general. Management articles on accounting, sales, saving time, etc., are the subjects most submitted and overworked. We prefer application data—we're interested in industry solutions to problems in these areas, with job details, contractor facts, and how the job was handled." Buys how-to's ("only if very unusual"), interviews, profiles, humor ("industry only"), photo features, coverage of successful business operations ("must relate to problem solving"), articles on merchandising techniques, and technical articles. Length: 800 to 2,000 words. Pays 2¢ a word. B&w photos purchased with mss; captions required. Pays $10 minimum for photos.

BATIMENT, 625 President Kennedy Ave., Montreal 111, Que., Canada. Phone: 514-845-5141. Editor: Claude Picher. Published in French for "contractors, architects." Established in 1927. Monthly. Circulation: 6,000. Rights purchased vary with author and material. Buys about 25 mss a year. Pays on acceptance. Will send a sample copy to a writer on request. Write for copy of guidelines for writers. Enclose S.A.E. and International Reply Coupons.

Nonfiction: "Articles on new techniques in construction and subjects of interest to builders. Interested in residential, apartment, office, commercial, and industrial buildings—not in public works. Generally, articles written in English are rejected." Length: 500 to 1,000 words. Pays $50 to $75.

BAY STATE BUILDER, 93 Purchase St., Boston MA 02110. Editor: Richard Pozniak. For home builders, land developers, architects, building material manufacturers and suppliers; bankers, landscapers, contractors, real estate investors. Magazine; 30 (8½x11) pages. Established in 1953. Monthly. Circulation: 30,000. Buys all rights. Buys about 12 mss a year. Pays on publication. Will send sample copy to writer for 60¢. Write for copy of guidelines for writers. Will consider photocopied and simultaneous submissions. Reports on material accepted for publication in 1 month. Returns rejected material immediately. Query first, with outline. Enclose S.A.S.E.

Nonfiction and Photos: Anything that relates to the home building industry or related fields. News or general feature format is desirable. Especially interested in articles with a New England or Massachusetts angle. Material about any new developments or innovations in the building profession. Does not want to see anything on the economy and its relationship to the building profession. Informational, how-to, personal experience, interview, profile, think pieces, expose, successful business operations, new product, merchandising techniques, technical. Recently published "The Mini Warehouse Can Put Money in Your Pocket." Length: open. Pays 8¢ a word. No additional payment for b&w or color photos. Captions required.

Fillers: Newsbreaks, clippings, short humor. Pays minimum of $5.

BIG, P.O. Box 13208, Phoenix AZ 85002. Editor: Frederick H. Kling. Published by Goodyear Tire and Rubber Company for "owners, operators, and distributors of big earth-moving equipment, the type used in construction of roads, highways, dams, and in mining. Stories on assignment only." Not copyrighted.

Nonfiction and Photos: "Freelance writers and photographers are invited to send in their qualifications for assignment of articles on construction projects, contractors, equipment distributors in their territory. Payment from $250 to $300, plus expenses, for complete editorial-photographic coverage. Additional payment for color, if used."

CALIFORNIA BUILDER & ENGINEER, 363 El Camino Real, South San Francisco CA 94080. Senior Editor: Mahlon R. Fisher. For "contractors, engineers, machinery distributors for construction industry." Seeks material for water development and market issues. Established in 1894. Biweekly. Circulation: 12,500. Not copyrighted. Buys 30 to 40 mss a year. Pays on publication. Will send a sample copy to a writer on request. Will consider photocopied submissions. Submit seasonal material 2 months in advance. Reports in 2 weeks. Query first. Enclose S.A.S.E.

Nonfiction: "How-to articles: how can a contractor save time or money. Compared to similar publications, we give greater California coverage well within the regional framework." Interested in material on "the highway trust fund." Buys "normally only feature-type articles": how-to articles, interviews, profiles, humor, personal experience articles, photo features, coverage of successful business operations. Length: 1,000 to 5,000 words. Pays "$50 a printed page." Interested in historical stories on construction in 1776; and sketches or drawings of same. Pays $15 each.

Photos: "We prefer 8x10 b&w glossies. By arrangement only."

CONSTRUCTION EQUIPMENT OPERATION AND MAINTENANCE, P.O. Box 1689, Cedar Rapids IA 52406. Phone: 319-366-1597. Editor: C.K. Parks. For users of heavy construction equipment. Bimonthly. Buys all rights. Pays on acceptance. Query first. Reports in 1 month. Enclose S.A.S.E.

Nonfiction and Photos: "Articles on selection, use, operation, or maintenance of construction equipment; articles and features on the construction industry in general; job safety articles." Length: "3 to 4 printed pages." Pays $200. Also buys a limited number of job stories with photos, and feature articles on individual contractors in certain areas of U.S. and Canada. Length varies. Pays $50 to $200.

CONSTRUCTION SPECIFIER, 1150 17th St., N.W., Washington DC 20036. Editor: Thomas A. Cameron. Professional society journal for architects, engineers, specification writers, contractors. Monthly. Circulation: 12,000. Buys all rights. Pays on publication. Will send a sample copy to a writer on request. Deadlines are 45 days preceding publication on the 10th of each month. Reports in 4 to 7 days. Query required. Enclose S.A.S.E.

Nonfiction and Photos: "Articles on building techniques, building products and material." Length: minimum 3,500 words. Pays $150 to $200. Photos "purchased rarely; if purchased, payment included in ms rate." 8x10 glossies.

CONSTRUCTIONEER, 1 Bond St., Chatham NJ 07928. Phone: 201-635-6450. Editor: Ken Hanan. For contractors, distributors, material producers, public works officials, consulting engineers, etc. Established in 1945. Biweekly. Circulation: 18,000. Rights purchased vary with author and material. Buys all rights but will reassign rights to author after publication. Buys 10 to 15 mss a year. Payment on acceptance. Will send a sample copy to writer for $1. Write for copy of guidelines for writers. Query first. Will consider photocopied submissions. Submit seasonal material 2 months in advance. Reports on material accepted for publication in 30 to 60 days. Returns rejected material in 30 days. Enclose S.A.S.E.
Nonfiction and Photos: Construction job stories; new methods studies. Detailed job studies of methods and equipment used; oriented around geographical area of New York, New Jersey, Pennsylvania and Delaware. Winter snow and ice removal and control; winter construction methods. Current themes: public works, profiles, conservation. Length: 1,500 to 1,800 words. Pays $100 to $200. B&w photos purchased with or without accompanying ms or on assignment. Pays $5 to $8.

CONSTRUCTOR MAGAZINE, 1957 E St., N.W., Washington DC 20006. Editor: Richard Bing. Publication of the Association of General Contractors of America for "men in the age range of approximately 25 to 70 (predominantly 40's and 50's), 50% with a college education. Most own or are officers in their own corporations." Established in 1902. Monthly. Circulation: 23,000. Buys all rights, but will reassign rights to author after publication. Buys about 30 mss a year. Pays on publication. Will send a sample copy to a writer for 50¢. Query first or submit complete ms. Reports in 30 days. Enclose S.A.S.E.
Nonfiction: "Feature material dealing with labor, legal, technical, and professional material pertinent to the construction industry and corporate business. We deal only with the management aspect of the construction industry. No articles on computers and computer technology." Buys informational articles, interviews, think pieces, exposes, photo features, coverage of successful business operations, and technical articles. Length: "no minimum or maximum; subject much more important than length." Pays $50 to $300.

ENGINEERING AND CONTRACT RECORD, 1450 Don Mills Road, Don Mills, Ont., Canada M3B 2X7. Phone: 416-445-6641. Editor: Brandon Jones. For contractors in engineered construction and aggregate producers. Established in 1889. Monthly. Circulation: over 18,000. Buys first and second Canadian rights. Buys 12 to 15 mss a year. Pays on publication. Will send free sample copy to writer on request. Query first. Reports in 2 weeks. Enclose S.A.E. and International Reply Coupons.
Nonfiction and Photos: "Job stories. How to build a project quicker, cheaper, better through innovations and unusual methods. Articles on construction methods, technology, equipment, maintenance and management innovations. Management articles. Stories are limited to Canadian projects only." Length: 1,000 to 1,500 words. Pays 10¢ per printed word and $5 per 8x10 printed photo. B&w glossies purchased with mss. 5x7 preferred.

FARM BUILDING NEWS, 733 N. Van Buren, Milwaukee, WI 53202. Editor: John R. Harvey. For farm structure builders and suppliers. 6 times a year. Buys all rights. Pays on acceptance. Will send a free sample copy on request. Query suggested. Deadlines are at least 4 weeks in advance of publication date; prefers 6 to 8 weeks. Reports immediately. Enclose S.A.S.E.
Nonfiction and Photos: Features on farm builders and spot news. Length: 600 to 1,000 words. Pays $150 to $200. Buys color and b&w photos with ms.

JOURNAL OF COMMERCE, 2000 West 12th Ave., Vancouver, B.C., Canada. Editor: A.H.A. Brown. For engineers, architects, contractors, developers and construction industry specialists. Weekly. General business newspaper, tabloid 20 pages, with emphasis on construction. Established in 1911. Circulation: 9,000. Buys all rights. Payment on publication. Query first. Enclose S.A.E. and International Reply Coupons.
Nonfiction and Photos: Specialized technical articles on construction methodology and equipment. Take the approach of writing a newspaper feature, interview, or

report. "Many publications deal with construction projects, etc., but not for an audience that knows the field thoroughly; we go beyond 'daily' style of how much? how big?, etc." Particularly interested in articles about Canadian products being employed in the U.S. construction field. Length: 2,000 words maximum. Pays 5¢ a word. Captioned photos are purchased with accompanying ms. Pays $5 each.

MODERN STEEL CONSTRUCTION, American Institute of Steel Construction, 1221 Avenue of the Americas, New York NY 10020. Editor: Mary Anne Stockwell. For architects and engineers. Quarterly. Not copyrighted. Pays on acceptance. Query first. Enclose S.A.S.E.
Nonfiction and Photos: "Articles with pictures and diagrams, of new steel-framed buildings and bridges. Must show new and imaginative uses of structural steel for buildings and bridges; new designs, new developments." Length: "1 and 2 pages." Pays $100. Photos purchased with mss.

URBAN GROWTH, 854 National Press Bldg., Washington DC 20045. Publisher: Warren Burkett. For all involved in building, developing, financing, controlling urban and rural land or economic developments; heavily oriented to reporting attempts by citizen activist groups to modify or control future use of land and environment. Newsletter; 8 pages. Established in 1973. Every 2 weeks. Circulation: 1,000. Not copyrighted. Buys about 50 mss a year. Pays on publication. Will send sample copy to writer for 50¢. Reports quickly. Query first for special reports of over 1,000 words. Submit complete ms for items under 500 words. Enclose S.A.S.E.
Nonfiction: Activities of planners, developers, public officials, citizens' groups in conflict situations involving use of rural and urban land and space; state/local/national laws controlling growth and development; financing. Likes success stories of builders, officials, planners who resolve conflict with citizens' groups with skill or who fail spectacularly to do so. Prefers terse, pointed, brash, humorous, bright copy that gets right to the point without mincing words. Does not shy away from controversies, convictions, or business failures involving land use and urban growth issues. Every story needs two things: name, telephone number and complete address of a responsible person who can supply additional information; backup newspaper clippings, copies of reports or other documents. Clippings should contain the name of the publication and the date. Writers should not be surprised to find short features and news items rewritten heavily. Interested in coverage of successful attempts by citizens or planners to resolve conflicts over land use; urban developments, roads and highways; water and air pollution controversies. Looks for the new, unique, wry, funny, illogical, offbeat angles. Recently published articles include "Plus—Son of Ramapo" (new twist on plan to limit growth); "Coast Energy Conflict Flares" (California friends of coastal zoning panicked by energy crisis propaganda). Length: 100 to 200 words. Length for special reports: 1,000 to 2,000 words. Pays $1 minimum for roundup items; minimum of $100 for special reports.
How To Break In: "Send stories and backup clips where available. Always include at least one complete address of source so readers can write for more details, publications, reports, court decisions, etc."

WESTERN CONSTRUCTION, 609 Mission St., San Francisco CA 94105. Phone: 415-982-4343. Editor: Gene Sheley. For "heavy constructors and their job supervisors." Monthly. Buys all rights and simultaneous rights. Pays on acceptance. Query first. Enclose S.A.S.E.
Nonfiction and Photos: "Methods articles on street, highway, bridge, tunnel, dam construction in 13 western states. Slant is toward how it was built rather than why." Writers in this field should have a background in civil engineering, heavy machine operation, or writing experience in associated fields such as commercial building construction. Academic training not as important as field experience and firsthand knowledge of the writer's subject. Length: 1,500 to 2,500 words and 6 photos. Pays minimum $40 "per printed magazine page."

WORLD CONSTRUCTION, 666 Fifth Ave., New York NY 10019. Phone: 212-489-4652. Editor: Donald R. Cannon. For "English-speaking engineers, contractors, and government officials in the Eastern hemisphere." Spanish edition for Latin American readers. Monthly. Buys all rights. Pays on publication. Will send a sample copy to a writer on request. Query first. Reports in 1 month. Enclose S.A.S.E.

Nonfiction and Photos: "How-to articles which stress how contractors can do their jobs faster, better, or more economically. Articles are rejected when they tell only what was constructed, but not how it was constructed and why it was constructed in that way." Length: about 1,000 to 6,000 words. Pays $65 "per magazine page, or 4 typed ms pages." Photos purchased with mss; b&w glossies no smaller than 4x5.

How To Break In: "Send something from overseas. We're not distributed in North America, so we're very interested in writers who are living or traveling abroad and who know how to spot an engineering story."

Dairy Products

DAIRY RECORD, 141 East Fourth St., St. Paul MN 55101. Phone: 612-224-5345. Editor: Don Merlin. Monthly. For the dairy processing industry. Not copyrighted. Pays on publication. Enclose S.A.S.E.

Nonfiction: Contributions must be confined to spot news articles and current events dealing with the dairy industry, especially news and news commentary of fluid milk distribution and the manufacturing and processing of dairy products. "Newsclips are okay. Not interested in items dealing with cows, dairy farms, herd management, etc." Pays minimum of 40¢ per column inch.

DAIRY SCOPE, P.O. Box 3330, San Rafael CA 94902. Phone: 415-472-4711. Editor: Sally Taylor. For dairy executives in the western part of the U.S. Buys all rights. Pays on publication. Will send a sample copy to a writer on request. Write for copy of guidelines for writers. Enclose S.A.S.E. for return of submissions.

Nonfiction and Photos: Wants "news stories and photos pertaining to distribution and sales of milk and cream and manufacture and distribution of manufactured dairy products in eleven western states, plus Alaska and Hawaii. Also news stories pertaining to meetings, legal actions and other activities connected with dairy industry in this area, including news of people in industry—promotion, retirements, deaths, etc." Recently published articles include "The Logistics of Plant Moving—Sinton Dairy", describing how cost of a plant move paid for itself with more efficient plant operation. Length: open. Pays 4¢ a word ($2 a column inch). Photos purchased with mss; with captions only. B&w glossies, color transparencies. Pays $5 for b&w photos.

Data Processing

COMPUTER DECISIONS, 50 Essex St., Rochelle Park NJ 07662. Editor: Hesh Wiener. For computer professionals, computer-involved managers in industry, finance, academia, etc. Well-educated, sophisticated, highly paid. Computers trade journal; 64 pages plus supplements. Established in 1969. Monthly. Circulation: 85,000. Buys all rights, "but we have made a few exceptions for fiction and some other special stories." Buys 12 to 24 mss a year. Pays on publication. Will send free sample copy to writer "who has a good background," but send $3 "if you're just looking around." Will consider photocopied submissions. Reports in 4 weeks. Enclose S.A.S.E.

Nonfiction, Fiction, and Poetry: "Mainly serious articles about technology, business practice. Interviews. Informational, technical, think articles. Exposes. Spot news. Fiction with a moral about technology and society. Doggerel (humor). News pieces about computers and their use. Style is unimportant, just so it's readable. We have excellent copy people here. On news, the story should be written so we can cut. Articles should be clear and not stylized. Assertions should be well-supported by facts. We are business-oriented, witty, more interested in the unusual story, somewhat less technical than most. We'll run a good article with a computer peg even if it's not entirely about computers. We're tired of the 'how I installed a yellow computer and saved 50 cents a week' kind of drivel. We want social issues involving computers — welfare, equal employment, privacy. Business analysis done by people with good backgrounds. Investigative stories on computers and crime." Recently published a biography of Lady Lovelace, a pioneer computer programmer in 19th century England, a few fiction pieces, a Lovecraft parody, an essay on the good done by technology, and endless other stories. Length: 300 to 1,000 words for news; 1,000 to 5,000 words for features. Pays 3¢ to 10¢ per word. Mainstream, mystery, science fiction, fantasy, humorous, and historical fiction must have computer theme. Length: 1,000 to 3,000 words. Pays 3¢ to 6¢ per word for one-time rights. Poetry, light verse, should be about computers. Length: 4 to 24 lines. Pays $15 to $50 per poem. Nonfiction, Fiction, and Poetry Editor: Larry Lettieri.

COMPUTER DESIGN, 221 Baker Ave., Concord MA 01742. Editor: John A. Camuso. For digital electronic design engineers. Monthly. Buys all rights and simultaneous rights. Pays on publication. Will send sample copy on request. Query first. Reports in 4 to 8 weeks. Enclose S.A.S.E.
Nonfiction: Publishes engineering articles on the design and application of digital circuits, equipment, and systems used in computing, data processing, control and communications. Pays $30 to $40 per page.

COMPUTERWORLD, 797 Washington St., Newton MA 02160. Editor: E. Drake Lundell, Jr. For management-level computer users, chiefly in the business community, but also in government and education. Established in 1967. Weekly. Circulation: 67,000. Buys all rights, but may reassign rights to author after publication. Buys about 100 mss a year. Pays on publication. Will send free sample copy to writer on request, if request is accompanied by story idea or specific query. Write for copy of guidelines for writers. Will consider photocopied submissions only if exclusive for stated period. No simultaneous submissions. Submit special issue material 2 months in advance. Reports on material accepted for publication in 2 to 4 weeks. Returns rejected material immediately. Query first. Enclose S.A.S.E.
Nonfiction and Photos: Articles on problems in using computers; educating computer people; trends in the industry; new, innovative, interesting uses of computers. "We stress impact on users and need a practical approach. What does a development mean for other computer users? Most important facts first, then in decreasing order of significance. We would be interested in material on factory automation and other areas of computer usage that will impact society in general, and not just businesses. We prefer *not* to see executive appointments or financial results. We occasionally accept innovative material that is oriented to unique seasonal or geographical issues." Length: 250 to 1,200 words. Pays 5¢ to 10¢ a word. B&w (5x7) glossies purchased with ms or on assignment. Captions required. Pays $5 to $10.
Fillers: Newsbreaks, clippings. Length: 50 to 250. Pays 5¢ to 10¢ a word.

CREATIVE COMPUTING, P.O. Box 789-M, Morristown NJ 07960. Editor: David Ahl. For high school and college students, teachers, professors and others interested in computers and technology from a nontechnical viewpoint. Magazine: 48 pages (8½x11). Established in 1974. Bimonthly. Circulation: 12,000. Buys all rights, but will reassign rights to author after publication. Buys 20 to 30 mss a year. Payment on publication. Will send sample copy to writer for $1. Will consider photocopied submissions. Will not consider simultaneous submissions. Reports in 2 to 3 weeks. Query first or submit complete ms. Enclose S.A.S.E.
Nonfiction and Photos: Articles on the role of computers in medical care, law enforcement, education, space exploration, elections, etc. The human interest side of computers and technology. Also games, classroom activities, things to do, and teaching hints. No research articles, unless on layman's level. Length: 500 to 3,000 words. Pays $10 to $300. Recently published articles include "Crime, Cops, Computers" (interesting and current); "Daddy and His Computer" (a humorous and

human approach to machines). 5x7 or 8x10 photos are purchased with mss. Minimum payment of $3. Captions are optional. No color.

Fiction: Stories on runaway computers, robots, computers talking to each other, computers gaining human intelligence, etc. Suspense, adventure, science, fantasy, humorous fiction. Must relate to subject matter. Length varies from 500 to 3,000 for a story for one issue, or up to 10,000 for serials. Pays $10 to $400.

EPIC, 338 Mountain Rd., Union City NJ 07087. Manuscript Editor: Harry Kickey. For "executives of companies with annual sales between $500,000 and $5,000,000." Monthly. Buys all rights. Pays on publication. Will send sample copy to a writer on request. Query first. Reports in 2 weeks. Enclose S.A.S.E.

Nonfiction: "Articles on the use of computers by small companies. Should be written in English rather than computerese. Articles are addressed to nontechnical general executives. No company puffs, but can discuss equipment of manufacturers by name. Articles on comparison of capabilities of competing peripheral equipment, particularly input devices. Heavy use of visuals and illustrating diagrams." Charts purchased with mss. Length: 1,000 to 2,000 words. Pays 5¢ per printed word. Pays $10 for charts "if usable as is," $5 "if they need to be re-rendered."

Photos: Purchased with mss; with captions only. 8x10 glossies. Pays $5.

JOURNAL OF SYSTEMS MANAGEMENT, 24587 Bagley Road, Cleveland OH 44138. Phone: 216-243-6900. Managing Editor: William Ripley. For systems and procedures and administrative people. Monthly. Buys all serial rights. Pays on publication. Will send a free sample copy on request. Query first. Reports as soon as possible. Enclose S.A.S.E.

Nonfiction: Uses articles on case histories, projects on systems, forms control, administrative practices, computer operations. Length: 3,000 to 5,000 words. Maximum payment is $25.

MODERN DATA, P.O. Box 369, Hudson MA 01749. Phone: 617-562-9305. Editor: Alan R. Kaplan. For data processing managers, computer users, and computer systems designers and manufacturers. Established in 1968. Monthly. Circulation: 86,000. Buys all rights but usually shares republication rights with author. Buys very few mss. Payment 30 to 60 days after publication. Will send sample copy to a writer for $1. Will consider photocopied submissions. Query first. Reports in 30 days. Enclose S.A.S.E.

Nonfiction and Photos: "Equipment surveys, application stories; expository articles on general methods and techniques. Will consider short (750 words) articles on social consequences of computer technologies; areas of specialization are mini- and microcomputers and data communications. When we reject freelance material it's because the material is either 'old hat', irrelevant or unsophisticated, or generally contains insufficient substantive, supportive data." Informational, historical, think pieces, reviews of computer equipment, successful business operations, new products and applications. Length: 1,500 words maximum. Pays $25 to $35 per magazine page. "What Hath Babbage Wrought?" department pays $10 for short, humorous, original items. 4x5 or 8x10 b&w photos purchased with mss. Captions optional.

Dental

CAL MAGAZINE, 3737 West 127th St., Chicago IL 60658. Editor: T.G. Baldaccini. Coe Laboratories, manufacturers of dental supplies. For dentists, dental assistants and dental technicians. Established in 1935. Monthly. Circulation: 50,000. Buys all rights, but will reassign to author after publication. Pays on acceptance. Will send free sample copy on request. Submit complete ms only. Reports in 6 weeks. Enclose S.A.S.E.

Nonfiction and Photos: Articles pertaining to or about dentists and dentistry; accomplishments of dentists in other fields. History, art, humor, adventure, unusual achievements, successful business operations, new products, merchandising techniques and technical. Length: 1,500 to 2,000 words. Pays $25 to $100. B&w photos only, 8x10 or 5x7 glossy, purchased with mss or captions only. Pays $25 to $50.

Fiction: "Related in some way to dentistry." Length: 1,500 to 2,000 words. Pays $25 to $100.

Poetry and Fillers: Light verse. "Related to dentistry." Puzzles, short humor. Pays $3 minimum.

DENTAL ECONOMICS, P.O. Box 1260, Tulsa OK 74101. Editor: Richard L. Henn, Jr. For practicing dentists in the U.S., senior dental students, dental auxiliaries and dental suppliers. Established in 1911. Monthly. Circulation: 104,000. Buys first North American serial rights. Buys 75 mss a year. Payment on acceptance when material has been assigned. Payment on publication for unsolicited material. Will send free sample copy to writer on request. Query first or submit complete ms. Reports on material in 4 to 6 weeks. Enclose S.A.S.E.

Nonfiction and Photos: "Practice administration material; patient and personnel relations, taxes, investments, professional image; original 'case history' articles on means of conducting a dental practice more efficiently or more successfully (preferably with a D.D.S. byline). Lively writing style; in-depth coverage. Mss must be oriented to the dental profession and non-clinical in nature." Length: 1,000 to 2,500 words. Pays $25 to $300 "depending on material." B&w glossy photos; contact prints. Captions required.

DENTAL MANAGEMENT, 757 Third Ave., New York NY 10017. Editor: M.J. Goldberg. For practicing dentists. Monthly. Buys all rights. Buys two or three articles per issue. Pays on acceptance. Query first. Enclose S.A.S.E.

Nonfiction and Photos: "No clinical or scientific material. Magazine is directed toward the business side of dentistry—management, collections, patient relations, fees, personal investments and life insurance. Writing should be clear, simple, direct. Like lots of anecdotes, facts and direct conclusions." Pays 5¢ to 15¢ per word, depending on quality and research. Photos purchased with ms. Pays $10.

PROOFS, The Magazine of Dental Sales, Box 1260, Tulsa OK 74101. Phone: 918-582-0065. Editor: Richard Henn. Monthly. Pays on publication. Will send free sample copy on request. Query first. Reports in a week. Enclose S.A.S.E.

Nonfiction: Uses short articles, chiefly on selling to dentists. Must have understanding of dental market. Pays about $20.

TIC MAGAZINE, Box 407, North Chatham NY 12132. Phone: 518-766-3047. Editor: Joseph Strack. For dentists, dental assistants, and oral hygienists. Monthly. Buys first publication rights in the dental field. Pays on acceptance. Reports in 2 weeks. Query first. Enclose S.A.S.E.

Nonfiction: Prefers a simple, almost popular style. Uses articles (with illustrations, if possible) as follows: 1. Lead feature: Dealing with major developments in dentistry of direct, vital interest to all dentists; 2. How-to-do-it pieces: Ways and means of building dental practices, improving professional techniques, managing patients, increasing office efficiency, etc.; 3. Special articles: Ways and means of improving dentist-laboratory relations for mutual advantage, of developing auxiliary dental personnel into an efficient office team, of helping the individual dentist to play a more effective role in alleviating the burden of dental needs in the nation and in his community, etc.; 4. General articles: Concerning any phase of dentistry or dentistry-related subjects of high interest to the average dentist. Recently published articles include "Jewelry-Making, The Number One Hobby for Dentists" (a featured cover article on a hobby made-to-order for dentist skills). Length: 800 to 3,200 words. Pays 4¢ minimum per word.

Photos: Photo stories: four to ten pictures of interesting developments and novel ideas in dentistry. B&w only. Pays $10 minimum per photo.

How To Break In: "We can use fillers of about 300 words or so. They should be pieces of substance on just anything of interest to dentists. A psychoanalyst broke in with us recently with pieces relating to interpretations of patients' problems and attitudes in dentistry. Another writer just broke in with a profile of a dentist working with an Indian tribe. If the material's good, we'll be happy to rewrite."

Department Store, Variety, and Dry Goods

JUVENILE MERCHANDISING, 370 Lexington Ave., New York NY 10011. Phone: 212-532-9290. Editor: Lee Clarke Neumeyer. For buyers and merchandise managers in nursery furniture, wheel goods, preschool toys and related lines, including juvenile specialty shops, department stores, chain stores, discount stores, rated PX's, leading furniture stores with juvenile departments, and resident buying offices. Monthly. Circulation: 11,000. Buys all rights, but will reassign rights to author after publication; buys second serial (reprint) rights. Buys 18 mss a year. Payment on publication. Will send free sample copy to writer on request. Reports in 1 week. Query first. Enclose S.A.S.E.

Nonfiction and Photos: "Stories should emphasize how sales and profits can be increased. How-to articles, merchandising stories, juvenile store coverage, etc. Solid features about a phase of juvenile operation in any of the above-mentioned retail establishments. Not interested in store histories. Mss on successful displays, methods for more efficient management; also technical articles on stock control or credit or mail promotion—how a specific juvenile store uses these, why they were undertaken, what results they brought. Factual material with pertinent quotes, but not folksy. Emphasis on benefits to other retail operations. Illustrated interviews with successful dealers." Length: 1,000 to 1,500 words. Pays $50 to $75.

MILITARY MARKET, 475 School St., S.W., Washington DC 20024. Editor: Jerry McConnell. For military grocery and general merchandise store management and headquarters officials. Monthly magazine; 70 to 100 pages. Established in 1954. Circulation: 13,500. Buys all rights, but will reassign rights to author after publication. Payment on acceptance. Sample copy to writer for $1. Will consider photocopied and simultaneous submissions. Reports in 2 weeks. Query first. Enclose S.A.S.E.

Nonfiction and Photos: "We publish two monthly editions: a 'commissary edition' and an 'exchange edition'. These are separate magazines covering different fields. Material on retail operations, merchandising, store equipment, etc., is used." Informational, how-to, interview, think pieces, spot news, successful business operations, new product and articles on merchandising techniques. Length: open. Pays "$75 per page against 10¢ per word." Pays $10 to $15 for b&w photos purchased with mss or on assignment. $25 to $50 for color. Captions required.

How To Break In: "This is a very specialized field. A freelancer must have a good knowledge of retailing and merchandising, plus knowledge of how exchanges and commissaries work."

SEW BUSINESS, 1271 Avenue of the Americas, New York NY 10020. Editor: Mary Colucci. For retailers of home-sewing merchandise. Monthly. Circulation: 14,000. Not copyrighted. Buys about 100 mss a year. Pays on publication. Will send a sample copy to a writer on request. Query first. Reports in 1 month. Enclose S.A.S.E.

Nonfiction and Photos: Articles on department store or fabric shop operations, including coverage of art needlework, piece goods, patterns, sewing accessories and all other notions. Interviews with buyers—retailers on their department or shop. "Unless they are doing something different or offbeat, something that another retailer could put to good use in his own operation, there is no sense wasting their or your time in doing an interview and story. Best to query editor first to find out if a particular article might be of interest to us." Length: 500 to 1,500 words. Pays $85 minimum. Photos purchased with mss. "Should illustrate important details of the story." Sharp 8x10 b&w glossies. Pays $5.

Fillers: $2.50 for news items less than 100 words. For news item plus photo and caption, pays $7.50.

Drugs, Health Care, and Medical Products

CANADIAN PHARMACEUTICAL JOURNAL, 175 College St., Toronto, Ontario, Canada M5T 1P8. Phone: 416-962-3431. Editor: Arnold V. Raison. For pharmacists ranging in age from 22 to 70; education ranging from 1 year (older) to 4 or 5 years; recent graduates. Monthly magazine of 32 (8½x11¼) pages. Established in 1868. Circulation: 10,000. Rights purchased vary with author and material. Buys 4 or 5 mss a year. Payment on publication. Will send free sample copy to writer on request. Write for copy of guidelines for writers. Will accept cassette submissions. Submit special supplement material 3 months in advance. Reports on material accepted for publication in 1 month. Returns rejected material in 6 weeks. Query first. Enclose S.A.E. and International Reply Coupons.

Nonfiction and Photos: Material relative to pharmacy and pharmacy practice; community, hospital, industrial, governmental, academic. Innovations in pharmacy modernization and patient record systems. Emphasis is on professionalism in pharmacy practice since it is the official organ of the Canadian Pharmaceutical Association and, as such, reflects the thinking and policies of the association. Interested in articles on computerization in pharmacy practice and publishes occasional special supplements on current themes. Informational, how-to, personal experience, interviews, think pieces, spot news, successful business operations, merchandising techniques. Length: 1,000 to 3,000 words. Pays 5¢ per published word. Material for columns or departments on insurance, investment, merchandising ideas. Length: about 1,000 words or less. Payment is contingent on value; usually 5¢ a word. Uses 5x7 b&w glossy photos and 5x7 color. Photos should relate to editorial copy. Captions required. Payment by arrangement.

DRUG TOPICS, 550 Kinderkamack Rd., Oradell NJ 07649. Phone: 201-262-3030. Editor: David W. Sifton. For retail drug stores and wholesalers, manufacturers, and hospital pharmacists. Monthly. Circulation: over 50,000. Buys all rights. Query first. Pays on acceptance. Enclose S.A.S.E.

Nonfiction: News of local, regional, state pharmaceutical associations, legislation affecting operation of drug stores, news of pharmacists in civic and professional activities, etc. Query first on drug store success stories which deal with displays, advertising, promotions, selling techniques. Length: 1,500 words maximum. Pays $5 and up for leads, $25 and up for short articles, $50 to $200 for feature articles, "depending on length and depth."

Photos: May buy photos submitted with mss. May buy news photos with captions only. Pays $20.

HEARING AID JOURNAL, P.O. Box A3945, Chicago IL 60690. Editor: Donald Radcliffe. For retail hearing aid specialists, their consultants, and other professionals in the hearing health field; small business people who fit and sell hearing aids to the public. Magazine; 48 (7x10) pages. Established in 1945. Monthly. Circulation: 8,000. Buys all rights, but will reassign rights to author after publication. Buys very few mss. Pays on acceptance. No photocopied or simultaneous submissions. Reports in 2 to 3 weeks. Query first essential. Enclose S.A.S.E.

Nonfiction and Photos: Articles dealing with hearing aids and other instrumentation for hearing correction. Case histories of hearing aid specialists and their operations. Articles on small business management. Occasionally will assign meeting coverage in writer's area. No consumer-oriented or non-trade material. Length: 750 to 1,000 words. Pays 7¢ a word. B&w glossies purchased with mss; 5x7 preferred. Pays $7.

N.A.R.D. JOURNAL, 1 E. Wacker Dr., Chicago IL 60601. Editor: Louis E. Kazin. Semimonthly. Buys all rights. Query first. Enclose S.A.S.E.

Nonfiction and Photos: Uses success stories about independent retail druggists; novel methods used in promotion of business; community contributions of individual druggists. Length: about 500 words. Pays $50. Occasionally buys 8x10 photos with mss. Pays $25 for photos from professional photographers.

PATIENT AID DIGEST, 2009 Morris Ave., Union NJ 07083. Phone: 201-687-8282. Editorial Director: Albert L. Cassak. For pharmacists who have home health care departments, as well as manufacturers of patient aid products. Bimonthly. Circulation: 11,000. "Articles may not be reprinted without permission." Pays on publication. Will send a sample copy to a writer on request. Query first. Submit seasonal material 3 months in advance. Enclose S.A.S.E.
Nonfiction and Photos: Can range from articles on existing home health care centers to opportunities for proprietors; human interest stories pertaining to home health care. Approach should be "nontechnical." Does not accept articles that are too promotional. Buys interviews, profiles, coverage of successful business operations and merchandising techniques. Length: 1,500 words maximum. Pays $10 to $60. Photos purchased with mss.

TILE AND TILL, Eli Lilly Company, Box 618, Indianapolis IN 46206. Editor: W. F. Pillow. For "druggists all over the country." Bimonthly. Circulation: 84,000. Buys one-time rights. Pays on acceptance. Enclose S.A.S.E. for return of submissions.
Nonfiction and Photos: "This publication covers the professional side of pharmacy. We can use exceptional human interest stories that have a wide appeal and a pharmacy slant. If you cover personality or salesmanship in 300 to 700 words (occasionally to 1,200 words) and toss in a clear picture or two, your story will rate a careful reading." Pays 4¢ to 5¢ a word.

WHOLESALE DRUGS, 1111 E. 54th St., Indianapolis IN 46220. Editor: William F. Funkhouser. Bimonthly. Buys first rights only. Query first. Enclose S.A.S.E.
Nonfiction and Photos: Wants features on presidents and salesmen of Full Line Wholesale Drug Houses throughout the country. No set style, but subject matter should tell about both the man and his company—history, type of operation, etc. Pays $50 for text and pictures.

Education

Publications in this listing are for professional educators, teachers, coaches, and school personnel. Magazines for parents or the general public interested in education topics are classified under Education in the Consumer Publications section.

AMERICAN SCHOOL BOARD JOURNAL, National School Boards Association, State National Bank Plaza, Evanston IL 60201. Phone: 312-869-7730. Editor: James Betchkal. Monthly. Rights purchased vary with author and material. Pays an honorarium. Enclose S.A.S.E.
Nonfiction: "Commentary on the politics of public education below college level. Also articles on problems arising out of organization and administration of city, town, and county school systems, with special emphasis upon administrative work of boards of education and superintendents of schools, and school business managers and problems of financing and school planning." Length: 400 to 800 words.

ARTS AND ACTIVITIES, 8150 N. Central Park Ave., Skokie IL 60076. Phone: 312-675-5602. Managing Editor: Morton Handler. For "art teachers in elementary, junior high, and senior high schools." Monthly, except July and August. Buys all rights. Pays on publication. Will send a sample copy to a writer on request. Reports in 1 month. Enclose S.A.S.E.
Nonfiction and Photos: "Articles for teachers on creative art activities for children in elementary, junior high, and senior high schools, with illustrations such as artwork

or photos of activity in progress. Payment is determined by length and educational value." Pays minimum $30.

BUSINESS EDUCATION WORLD, 1221 Avenue of the Americas, New York NY 10020. Editor: Susan Schrumpf. For "business and office education instructors, classroom teachers, teacher educators and state and local supervisory personnel." 5 times a year. Circulation: 100,000. Buys all rights, but will reassign rights to author after publication. Buys 30 to 40 mss a year. Pays on publication. Will send a sample copy to a writer on request. Write for copy of guidelines for writers. Submit complete ms. Will not consider photocopied submissions. Reports in 6 to 8 weeks. Enclose S.A.S.E.
Nonfiction: "Business, office education, innovative classroom techniques and curricula, professional news, methodology." Interested in freelance material for "Post 12", a column devoted to educators at collegiate and business school levels, and for "Shorthand Research Review". Length: 1,600 to 2,500 words. Recently published articles include "Applying Economic Theory Through Studies of the Business Community" and "How Will Your Stenographic Graduates Measure Up on the Job?". Pays $5 to $50.

CHANGING EDUCATION, 1012 14th St., N.W., Washington DC 20005. Editor: Dave Elsila. For classroom teachers at all levels and in all subject areas. Monthly section of *American Teacher*. Circulation: 525,000. Not copyrighted. Buys 20 mss a year. Payment on publication. Will send free sample copy to writer on request. Will consider photocopied submissions. Reports on material in 4 months. Query first. Enclose S.A.S.E.
Nonfiction and Photos: "Articles on subjects of interest to classroom teachers, especially on topics related to academic freedom, more effective schools, the labor movement, and so on. Our examination of issues is generally from the teacher-union viewpoint." Informational, how-to, personal experience, interview, profile, historical, think articles, expose, personal opinion, reviews of educational books. Length: 1,000 to 2,000 words. Pays $50 to $150. 8x10 b&w glossies. Pays $15 to $30.

CHILDREN'S HOUSE, P.O. Box 111, Caldwell NJ 07006. Editor: Kenneth Edelson. For teachers and parents of young children. Magazine; 32 (8½x11) pages. Established in 1966. Every 2 months. Circulation: 50,000. Buys all rights. Buys 30 to 40 mss a year. Pays on publication. Will send sample copy to writer for $1. Write for copy of guidelines for writers. Will consider photocopied submissions. Reports on material accepted for publication in 3 to 6 months. Returns rejected material immediately. Query first or submit complete ms. Enclose S.A.S.E.
Nonfiction and Photos: Articles on education, open education, Montessori, learning disabilities, atypical children, innovative schools and methods; new medical, psychological experiments. "We're not afraid to tackle controversial topics such as sex education, integration, etc., but we don't want to see personal or family histories." Informational, how-to, profile, think articles. Recently published articles include one on integrated classroom and another on shortcut to communication. Length: 800 to 2,000 words. Pays 2¢ to 5¢ a word. 5x7 or 7x9 b&w glossies purchased on assignment. Pays minimum of $5. Department Editor: Gloria Biamonte.
Fillers: Newsbreaks, clippings. Length: 1 or 2 paragraphs. Pays minimum of $1 per column inch.

CHRISTIAN TEACHER, Box 550, Wheaton IL 60187. Editor: Phil Landrum. For "members of the National Association of Christian Schools. They are mostly grade school teachers; also, high school teachers, principals, board members, parents." Established in 1964. Bimonthly, except during summer. Circulation: 7,000. Not copyrighted. Pays on acceptance "or shortly after." Will send a sample copy to a writer on request. Query first. Reports "quickly." Enclose S.A.S.E.
Nonfiction and Photos: "Educational trends, reports, how-to—mostly informative or inspirational. Our publication deals with education from a Christian point of view." Length for articles: 500 to 2,000 words. Payment: "no set rate; work on assignment only." Photos purchased with and without mss.

EDUCATIONAL RESEARCHER, 1126 16th St., N.W., Washington DC 20036. Director of Publications: P. E. Stivers. For professors of education and social sciences, directors of research in departments of education or school systems, administrators and teachers who wish to keep up with research developments. Monthly magazine; 24 pages. Established in 1972. Circulation: 12,000. Rights purchased vary with author and material. Usually buys all rights, but will reassign rights to author after publication. Buys 6 to 18 mss a year; most are commissioned. Payment on acceptance but topic must be cleared first. Will send free sample copy to writer on request. Write for copy of guidelines for writers. Will consider photocopied submissions. Will consider simultaneous submissions if told where other submission has been made. Reports on material accepted for publication in 4 weeks. Returns rejected material in 8 weeks. Query first. Enclose S.A.S.E.

Nonfiction and Photos: This is a news-feature magazine focusing on the discussion of issues. Uses articles that are analyses or syntheses of scholarly inquiry written in a narrative style. Articles should emphasize interpretations and implications for research and development in education. Also uses essay-reviews of publications dealing with the significance of the work in the field of educational research. Essay-reviews must not be limited to commentary on the contents, structure, thesis or validity of the work. Most classroom subjects are not relevant. Focus needs to be research, rather than practice. Brief commentaries on issues, events, or developments in educational research are also used. Length: 1,800 to 2,500 words. Pays about $200. Prefers 8x10 b&w photos "with an abstract or design look." Pays $25 to $50 for those purchased without ms.

FORECAST MAGAZINE FOR HOME ECONOMICS, 50 W. 44th St., New York NY 10036. Address mss to Gloria Spitz, Editor. For teachers of home economics in junior and senior high schools. Monthly. September through May-June. Buys all rights. Pays on publication. "Query or outline strongly recommended." Reports in 2 months. Enclose S.A.S.E.

Nonfiction and Photos: "Articles of interest to home economics teachers in education, family relations, child development, clothing, textiles, grooming, foods, nutrition, and home management." Length: 1,500 to 3,000 words. Pays average $75, "depending on the author and length." B&w photos accepted with mss.

HOSPITAL/HEALTH CARE TRAINING MEDIA PROFILES, Olympic Media Information, 161 W. 22 St., New York NY 10011. Phone: 212-691-3926. Associate Editor: Marlene Hamerling. For hospital education departments, nursing schools, schools of allied health, paramedical training units, colleges, community colleges, local health organizations. Serial, in loose leaf format, published every 2 months. Established in 1974. Circulation: 1,000 plus. Buys all rights. Buys about 240 mss a year. Payment on publication. Will send free sample copy to writer on request. Write for copy of guidelines for writers. Will not consider photocopied or simultaneous submissions. Reports in 1 month. Query first. Enclose S.A.S.E.

Nonfiction: "Reviews of all kinds of audiovisual media. We are the only existing review publication devoted to evaluation of audiovisual aids for hospital and health training. We have a highly specialized, definite format that must be followed in all cases. Samples should be seen by all means. Our writers should first have a background in health sciences, secondly, some experience with audiovisuals; and third, follow our format precisely. Besides basic biological sciences, we are interested in materials for nursing education, in-service education, continuing education, personnel training, patient education, patient care, medical problems." Pays $5 to $15 per review.

How To Break In: "Contact us and send a resume of your experience in writing for hospital, science, health fields. We will assign audiovisual aids to qualified writers and send them these to review for us. Unsolicited mss not welcome."

INDUSTRIAL EDUCATION, 1 Fawcett Place, Greenwich CT 06830. For administrators and instructors in elementary, secondary, and higher education for industrial arts, vocational, industrial and technical education. Monthly, except July and August and combined May—June issue. Buys all rights. Pays on publication. Write for copy of guidelines for writers. Deadline for Shop Planning Annual is Dec. 29; for Back to School and Projects, July 1. Reports in 5 weeks. Enclose S.A.S.E. for return of submissions.

Nonfiction and Photos: "Articles dealing with the broad aspects of industrial arts, vocational, and technical education as it is taught in our junior and senior high schools, vocational and technical high schools, and junior college. We're interested in analytical articles in relation to such areas as curriculum planning, teacher training, teaching methods, supervision, professional standards, industrial arts or vocational education, industrial practice, relationship of industrial education to industry at the various educational levels, current problems, trends, etc. How-to-do, how-to-teach, how-to-make articles of a very practical nature which will assist the instructor in the laboratory at every level of industrial education. Typical are the 'activities' articles in every instructional area. Also typical is the article which demonstrates to the teacher a new or improved way of doing something or of teaching something or how to utilize special teaching aids or equipment to full advantage—activities which help the teacher do a better job of introducing the industrial world of work to the student." Length: maximum 2,500 words. Pays $25 "per printed page." 8x10 b&w photos purchased with ms.

Fillers: Short hints on some aspect of shop management or teaching techniques. Length: 25 to 250 words.

INSTRUCTOR MAGAZINE, 7 Bank St., Dansville NY 14437. Editor: Dr. Ernest Hilton. For elementary classroom teachers and supervisors. Established in 1891. Monthly except July and August. Circulation: 275,000. Rights purchased vary with author and material. Buys all rights or first serial rights. Payment on acceptance. Will send free sample copy to writer on request. Write for copy of guidelines for writers. Submit complete ms. Submit seasonal material 6 months in advance. Reports on material accepted for publication in 4 months. Returns rejected material in 1 month. Enclose S.A.S.E. for return of submissions.

Nonfiction and Photos: "Professional articles on various aspects of education; ideas and suggestions about effective teaching activities. Descriptive work about a program, emphasizing the specific techniques necessary for teachers to follow. Need seasonal articles on teaching suggestions and art activities. Informational and technical. Interviews." Length: 600 to 1,500 words. "Payment rates vary so much depending upon length, quality, and how the material is to be used. For a one-paragraph idea we may pay as little as $5 and as much as $500 for a long, full-length feature." 8x10 glossies and 4x5 color transparencies purchased with ms.

Fiction, Poetry and Drama: Stories, poems, plays for elementary classroom use. Historicals, real life, holidays. Length: 600 to 1,000 words. Payment varies. Department Editor: Kathryn Eldridge.

LEARNING, 530 University Ave., Palo Alto CA 94301. Managing Editor: Morton Malkofsky. For elementary school teachers. Established in 1972. Monthly. Circulation: 225,000. Buys all rights, but will reassign rights to author after publication. Buys 100 to 150 mss a year. Payment on acceptance. Query first. Will consider photocopied submissions. Reporting time "depends on story." Rejected material is returned in 1 day to 3 weeks. Enclose S.A.S.E.

Nonfiction and Photos: "We publish manuscripts that describe innovative teaching strategies or probe controversial and significant social/political issues related to the professional and classroom interests of preschool to 8th grade teachers. Reports of classroom action and/or documentation of claims should be an integral part of all submitted manuscripts." Length: 300 to 3,000 words. Pays $50 to $500. Photos purchased with accompanying mss or on assignment. Captions required. "Contact sheets and negs."

THE LIVING LIGHT, 1312 Massachusetts Ave., N.W., Washington DC 20005. An interdisciplinary review for "professionals in the field of religious education, primarily Roman Catholics." Established in 1964. Quarterly. Buys all rights but will reassign rights to author after publication. Buys 4 mss a year. Payment on publication. Will send sample copy to writer for $2.50. Submit complete ms. Reports on material in 30 to 60 days. Enclose S.A.S.E.

Nonfiction: Articles that "present development and trends, report on research and encourage critical thinking in the field of religious education and pastoral action. Academic approach." Length: 2,000 to 5,000 words. Pays $40 to $600.

THE MASSACHUSETTS TEACHER, 20 Ashburton Place, Boston MA 02108. Phone: 617-742-7950. Editor: Russell P. Burbank. For Massachusetts educators. Monthly, October through May. Buys all rights. Pays on publication. Query first. Reports in 1 month. Enclose S.A.S.E.

Nonfiction and Photos: "We want provocative education articles, features on classroom innovations that are two steps above the ordinary; well-researched authoritative articles (we check your facts) on items of interest to Massachusetts classroom public school teachers." Pays $25 and up. Occasionally buys photos with mss. Prefers at least 5x7.

MEDIA & METHODS, 134 N. 13th St., Philadelphia PA 19107. Managing Editor: Anthony Prete. For English and social studies teachers who have an abiding interest in humanistic and media-oriented education, plus a core of librarians, media specialists, filmmakers; the cutting edge of educational innovators. Magazine; 56 to 64 (8½x11) pages. Established in 1964. Monthly (September through May). Circulation: 55,000. Rights purchased vary with author and material. May buy all rights or first North American serial rights. About half of each issue is freelance material. Pays on publication. Will send free sample copy to writer on request. Will consider photocopied submissions. No simultaneous submissions. Reports on material in 2 months. Submit complete ms or query first. Enclose S.A.S.E.

Nonfiction: "We are looking for middle school, high school or college educator who has something vital and interesting to say. Subjects include practical how-to articles with broad applicability to our readers, and innovative, challenging, conceptual-type stories that deal with educational change. Our style is breezy and conversational, occasionally offbeat. We make a concentrated effort to be non-sexist; mss filled with 'he', 'him', and 'mankind' (when the gender is unspecified) will pose unnecessary barriers to acceptance. We are a trade journal with a particular subject emphasis (media-oriented English and social studies), philosophical bent (humanistic, personal), and interest area (the practical and innovative)." Length: 2,500 words maximum. Pays $15 to $200.

MOMENTUM, National Catholic Educational Association, 1 Dupont Circle, Suite 350, Washington DC 20036. Phone: 202-293-5954. Editor: Carl Balcerak. For Catholic administrators and teachers, some parents and students, in all levels of education (preschool, elementary, secondary, higher). Quarterly magazine; 56 to 64 (8½x11) pages. Established in 1970. Circulation: 14,500. Buys all rights. Buys 28 to 36 mss per year. Payment on publication. Will send free sample copy to writer on request. Will consider photocopied and simultaneous submissions. Submit special issue material 2 months in advance. Query first. Reports in 2 weeks. Enclose S.A.S.E.

Nonfiction and Photos: "Articles concerned with educational philosophy, psychology, methodology, innovative programs, teacher training, etc. Catholic-oriented material. Book reviews on educational—religious topics. Innovative educational programs; financial and public relations programs, management systems applicable to nonpublic schools. No pious ruminations on pseudoreligious ideas. Also, avoid general topics, such as what's right (wrong) with Catholic education. In most cases, a straightforward, journalistic style with emphasis on practical examples, is preferred. Some scholarly writing, but little in the way of statistical. All material has Catholic orientation, with emphasis on professionalism; not sentimental or hackneyed treatment of religious topics." Length: 2,500 to 3,000 words. Pays 2¢ per word. Pays $5 for b&w glossy photos purchased with mss. Captions required.

NATIONAL ON-CAMPUS REPORT, Lakewood Plaza, Madison WI 53704. Phone: 608-249-2455. Editor: William H. Haight. For education administrators, corporate marketing executives, journalists, directors of youth organizations. Established in

1972. Monthly. Not copyrighted. Buys 100 mss a year. Payment on publication. Will send sample copy to writer for 50¢. Write for copy of guidelines for writers. Will consider photocopied submissions. Reports on material in 1 month. Submit complete ms. Enclose S.A.S.E.

Nonfiction and Fillers: Short, timely articles relating to events and activities of college students. Also buys newsbreaks and clippings related to college students and their activities. Length: 25 to 800 words. Pays 10¢ to 12¢ per word.

NJEA REVIEW, 180 W. State St., Trenton NJ 08608. Editor: George M. Adams. Aimed at entire educational community in New Jersey, from nursery through higher education. Monthly. Circulation: 107,000. Buys all rights. Pays on publication. Does not pay for articles by New Jersey teachers. Will send a sample copy to a writer on request. Write for copy of guidelines for writers. Query required. Enclose S.A.S.E.

Nonfiction: Prefers articles describing successful educational practices to theorizing on "what should be." Articles should be timely, broad enough in scope to appeal to entire profession, well researched, but not too technical and not footnoted. Writing should be imaginative, crisp and unaffected, with use of human interest appeal and humor. Needed are pieces on new trends in education, such as teaching and curriculum experimentation, as well as subject area articles. Articles especially valuable if based on experience in a New Jersey school or college. Length: 500 to 1,000 words. "Our editorial policy for writing for the *NJEA Review* prohibits paying anyone who is eligible for our association membership—which would include any New Jersey teacher. Other writers' fees are based upon negotiations between us and the writer but generally run around $50 for a small feature article."

Photos: B&w photos purchased with captions. Pays $5.

PHI DELTA KAPPAN, 8th & Union Sts., Bloomington IN 47401. Editor: Stanley Elam. For educators, especially those in leadership positions, such as administrators; mid-forties; all hold BA degrees; one-third hold doctorates. Magazine; 72 (8½x11) pages. Established in 1915. Monthly, 10 issues, September through June. Circulation: 107,000. Generally buys all rights, but will sometimes reassign rights to author after publication (this varies with the author and material). Buys 10 to 15 mss a year. Payment on publication. Will send free sample copy to a writer on request. Submit complete ms for nonfiction articles. No photocopied or simultaneous submissions. Reports on material accepted for publication in 1 to 2 months. Returns rejected material within 2 months. Enclose S.A.S.E.

Nonfiction and Photos: Features articles on education, emphasizing policy, trends, both sides of issues, controversial developments. Also, informational, how-to, personal experience, interview, profile, inspirational, humor, think articles, expose. "Our audience is scholarly but hard-headed." Length: 500 to 3,000 words. Pays $25 to $250 per ms. Pays average photographer's rates for b&w photos purchased with mss, but captions are required. Will purchase photos on assignment. Sizes: 8x10 or 5x7 preferred.

How To Break In: "We want research-based, informative material. Analysis, not opinion, is our emphasis. Submit the complete ms."

SCHOLASTIC COACH, 50 W. 44th St., New York NY 10036. Editor: Herman L. Masin. Monthly, except June and July. Buys first rights. Pays on publication. Reports in 10 days. Enclose S.A.S.E.

Nonfiction: This magazine is directed to the coaches and physical education directors in colleges and high schools. Uses authoritative, technical articles on football, basketball, track and field, tennis, baseball, soccer, swimming, and all physical education activities. Length: 1,000 to 2,000 words. Pays $30 per article.

Photos: Single photos used must have dramatic action. Pays $5 to $15 per photo.

SCHOLASTIC TEACHER'S EDITIONS, 50 W. 44th St., New York NY 10036. Phone: 212-867-7700. Editor: Loretta Hunt Marion. For teachers of Grades K to 6 and English social studies and science teachers of grades 7 to 12. Established in 1946. Published weekly during the school year. Circulation: 410,000. Rights purchased vary with author and material. Buy all rights; but sometimes will reassign rights to author after publication, or first North American serial rights. Buys 25 to 30 mss a year. Payment on acceptance. Will send free sample copy to writer on request. Write for copy of guidelines for writers. Will not consider photocopied or simultaneous submissions. Submit seasonal material for summer travel issue for teachers (published in March) 4 to 6 months in advance. Reports in 6 weeks. Query first. Enclose S.A.S.E.

Nonfiction and Photos: New weekly format emphasizes education news. Editor will assign a number of in-depth news features dealing with current trends, issues, and controversies on the national education scene. Payment starts at $50 to $60 and varies according to length of story. Also interested in articles of about 1,000 words on teaching methods or innovative programs, with particular interest in social studies, language arts, science, or classroom management techniques. These "how-to" articles pay $40 to $75 and may be submitted on an unsolicited basis, but query letters are encouraged. "If a single innovative or practical teaching method doesn't have the scope of an article, it might find a place in our Teaching Tips column." Length: 100 to 200 words. Pays minimum of $5. Credit is given to contributors. Pays minimum of $10 for 8x10 b&w glossy photos purchased with mss. Captions are optional.

SCHOOL ARTS MAGAZINE, 72 Printers Bldg., Worcester MA 01608. Editor: George F. Horn. For art and craft teachers and supervisors from grade through high school. Monthly, except July and August. Will send a sample copy to a writer on request. Pays on publication. Reports in 90 days. Enclose S.A.S.E.

Nonfiction and Photos: Articles, with photos, on art and craft activities in schools. Length: 1,000 words. Payment is negotiable but begins at $20 per article.

SCHOOL SHOP, 416 Longshore Dr., Ann Arbor MI 48107. Editor: Lawrence W. Prakken. For "industrial and technical education personnel." Special issue in April deals with varying topics for which mss are solicited. Monthly. Circulation: 45,000. Buys all rights. Pays on publication. Will send a sample copy to a writer on request. Query first: "direct or indirect connection with the field of industrial and/or technical education preferred." Submit mss to Howard Kahn, Managing Editor. Submit seasonal material 3 months in advance. Reports in 2 months. Enclose S.A.S.E.

Nonfiction and Photos: Uses articles pertinent to the various teaching areas in industrial education (woodwork, electronics, drafting, machine shop, graphic arts, computer training, etc.). "Outlook should be on innovation in educational programs, processes, or projects which directly apply to the industrial-technical education area." Buys how-to's, personal experience and think pieces, interviews, humor, coverage of new products. Length: 500 to 2,000 words. Pays $15 to $40. 8x10 photos purchased with ms.

SCIENCE ACTIVITIES, Room 302, 4000 Albermarle St., N.W., Washington DC 20016. Phone: 202-362-6445. Publisher: Cornelius W. Vahle, Jr. Editors: T. L. Stoddard and Jane Powers Weldon. For science teachers (high school, junior high school and college). Published every 2 months. Magazine. 48 pages. Established in 1969. Circulation: 6,500. Buys 30 mss a year. Payment on publication. Will send sample copy to writer for $2. Reports in 30 days. Enclose S.A.S.E.

Nonfiction and Photos: "Articles on creative science projects for the classroom, including experiments, explorations, and projects in every phase of the biological, physical and behavioral sciences." Length: 500 to 2,500 words. Pays $10 per printed page. Photos purchased with ms; no additional payment. Captions required.

TEACHER, One Fawcett Pl., Greenwich CT 06830. Editor: Claudia Cohl. For teachers of kindergarten through junior high grades. Monthly, except July and August. (May–June, combined issue.) Pays on publication. Write for copy of guidelines for writers. Query first "with brief outline of material and note on illustration availability." Enclose S.A.S.E.

Nonfiction, Photos, and Children's Songs: "Articles of current educational interest, accounts of actual uses of new teaching techniques, classroom-tested units of work. Also needed are original children's songs. Articles should be long on fact, short

on preachy material. Historical subjects must be authenticated with sources given."
Length: maximum 2,500 words. Pays 1¢ a word. "Photos may be included as
illustrations or sent separately with captions." Pays minimum $5, depending on size
and usage. Also buys art projects, creative arts and crafts, accompanied by clear
b&w glossies when possible. Pays 1¢ a word.

THE TEACHER PAPER, 2221 N.E. 23rd St., Portland OR 97212. Editors: Robin
and Fred Staab. For classroom teachers. Magazine; 32 (8½x11) pages. Established
in 1968. Copyrighted. "Reprint permission given on request." Buys about 50 mss
a year. Pays on publication. Will send sample copy to writer for $1. Will consider
photocopied submissions. No simultaneous submissions. Reports on material accepted for publication in 5 months. Returns rejected material as soon as possible. Submit
complete ms. Enclose S.A.S.E.
Nonfiction: Only material from classroom teachers is acceptable. Opinion and fact
concerning teaching and public schools. No jargon. Only honest, straight prose. How
to survive in the public schools. Informational, how-to, personal experience, interview,
humor, think pieces, expose, personal opinion; reviews of books, magazines, films,
other media. Length: 2,500 words maximum. Pays 1¢ a word.

TECHNICAL EDUCATION NEWS, 1221 Avenue of the Americas, New York NY
10020. Editor: Mrs. Susan S. Schrumpf. For technical and occupational educators
and those working with training programs in business, industry and the government.
Magazine published periodically during the school year by the Gregg—Community
College Division, McGraw-Hill Book Co. Established in 1941. Circulation: 50,000.
Buys all rights, but will reassign rights to author after publication. Buys 20 mss
a year. Payment on publication. Will send free sample copy to writer on request.
Write for copy of guidelines for writers. Will not consider photocopied or simulta-
neous submissions. Reports in 6 to 8 weeks. Query first or submit complete ms.
Enclose S.A.S.E.
Nonfiction: Articles on technical and occupational education; classroom oriented.
Recently published articles include "Toward a Unified Industrial Education Pro-
gram." Length: 1,600 to 2,500 words. Pays $50.

TODAY'S CATHOLIC TEACHER, 2451 E. River Rd., Suite 200, Dayton OH 45439.
Editor: Ruth A. Matheny. For educators (teachers, administrators, school board
members) and parents interested in the nonpublic school, particularly the Catholic
school. Magazine published 8 times during the school year; 48 to 96 (8¼x11) pages.
Established in 1967. Circulation: 70,000. Not copyrighted. Buys 25 mss a year.
Payment on publication. Will send sample copy to writer for 50¢. Write for copy
of guidelines for writers. Will not consider photocopied or simultaneous submissions.
Submit seasonal material (Christmas, Thanksgiving, Easter—successful programs or
celebrations) 2 to 3 months in advance. Reports on material accepted for publication
in 2 months. Returns rejected material promptly if not to be considered at all. Query
first or submit complete ms. Enclose S.A.S.E.
Nonfiction and Photos: "Informative features describing philosophy, innovative
practices, practical solutions to common problems of Catholic schools. Successful
public relations programs that lead to increased parental and community involvement
in the Catholic school are of special interest. During the 1975-76 school year, will
be interested in reviewing successful Bicentennial-oriented projects in social studies
or language arts in a Catholic school stiuation. Too many of the mss coming to
us are of a too general nature, offering nothing new to inspire readers to thought
or action. At the same time, anything too localized has no place in a national magazine.
Anything that is sound pedagogically is of interest to us, but we prefer that it have
a Catholic or other nonpublic school application. Prefer straightforward, readable,
lively style, as opposed to profound, scholarly approach. First-person reactions and
direct quotations are a 'plus'." Length: 500 to 1,500 words. Pays $15 to $75. No
additional payment is made for b&w photos used with mss.

TODAY'S EDUCATION: NEA JOURNAL, National Education Association, 1201
16th St., N.W., Washington DC 20036. Editor: Dr. Mildred S. Fenner. Copyrighted.

"We buy one-time editorial use of freelance photos." Does not pay for submissions, except photos. No query necessary. Enclose S.A.S.E.

Nonfiction: Articles on teaching methods and practices; human interest, popular style. "We generally accept manuscripts from teachers who are members of the local, state, and national education associations since the magazine belongs to those teachers. However, we occasionally buy mss from freelance writers who are not eligible to be regular members of the National Education Association since they are not teachers. Such writers are, of course, not eligible to be active NEA members and therefore we do not require membership in those cases." Length: 800 to 2,000 words. No payment.

Photos: Buys singles and photo series of school situations and scenes. Requires model releases. 8x10 b&w. Pays $25 for b&w. Photo Editor: Walter Graves.

TRAINING FILM PROFILES, Olympic Media Information, 161 W. 22 St., New York NY 10011. Phone: 212-691-3926. Editor: William A. Starika. For colleges, community colleges, libraries, training directors, manpower specialists, education and training services, career development centers, audiovisual specialists, administrators. Serial in looseleaf format, published every 2 months. Established in 1967. Circulation: 1,000. Buys all rights. Buys 200 to 240 mss a year. Payment on publication. Will send free sample copy to writer on request. Write for copy of guidelines for writers. Will not consider photocopied or simultaneous submissions. Reports on material accepted for publication in 2 months. Returns rejected material in 1 month. Query first. Enclose S.A.S.E.

Nonfiction: "Reviews of instructional films, filmstrips, videotapes and cassettes, sound-slide programs and the like. We have a highly specialized, rigid format that must be followed without exception. Ask us for sample 'Profiles' to see what we mean. Besides job training areas, we are also interested in the areas of values and personal self-development, upward mobility in the world of work, social change, futuristics, management training, problem solving, and adult education." Items thus far published cover employee training, job seeking, human relations, communication skills, management, job orientation, continuing education and similar topics. Pays $5 to $15 per review.

How To Break In: "Contact us first. Unsolicited manuscripts are not wanted. If part of your full-time work is to preview audiovisual materials, you probably can do something for us."

WHAT'S NEW IN HOME ECONOMICS, 41 E. 42nd St., Suite 1220, New York NY 10017. Editor: Mary Bushee Murphy. For "home ec college grads; most are teachers; all ages and levels of experience; broad interest range—virtually anything regarding the practical aspects of family life and education." Established in 1936. 14 times during the school year. Circulation: about 28,000. Buys all rights. Buys "very few" mss a year. Pays on publication "in special cases; otherwise, pays in contributors' copies." Query first. Will consider photocopied submissions. Submit seasonal material 6 months in advance. Enclose S.A.S.E.

Nonfiction and Fiction: "As a rule, we only accept material from home economists. Exceptions are recognized authorities in special areas (for example, an M.D. on a health topic). We're quite interested in short-short stories appropriate for classroom use for junior and senior high and on topics of general interest to teachers. The approach should be straightforward, with an informative orientation. Nonfiction must all be related to home economics, consumer education, etc." Length: 300 to 1,500 words. Pays $25 to $200, "but we rely heavily on the free contributions of our readers."

Electricity

Publications classified here aim at electrical engineers, electrical contractors, and others who build, design, and maintain systems connecting and supplying homes, businesses, and industries with power. Journals dealing with generating and supplying power to users will be found in the Power and Power Plants category. Publications for appliance servicemen and dealers will be found in the Home Furnishings classification.

ELECTRICAL APPARATUS, 400 N. Michigan Ave., Chicago IL 60611. Address Editorial Department. Phone: 312-321-9440. Monthly for electrical apparatus service specialists. Circulation: 20,000. Buys all rights. Pays on acceptance. Will send a sample copy to a writer for $1.25. Query first; uses assigned articles only. Reports in 2 weeks. Enclose S.A.S.E.
Nonfiction: Uses technical and semitechnical illustrated features on specific phases of operation of industrial, electrical apparatus, service firms and in-plant departments; any material directly applicable to maintenance operations. Length: 500 to 2,000 words. Pay "varies, depending on article, but generally runs between $75 and $200."
Photos: Purchased with ms or with captions only. 8x10 or 5x7 glossies that show equipment details or single photos with captions describing an event of interest, people in the industry, meetings of associations. Pays $5 minimum.

ELECTRICAL CONSULTANT, P.O. Box 7800, Atlanta GA 30309. Editor: F. William Payne. For "consulting electrical engineers; both those in private practice and employed by others." Monthly. Buys first rights. "Queries relating to proposed subjects answered promptly." Reports promptly. Enclose S.A.S.E.
Nonfiction: Wants "well-written articles relating to the design and specification of electrical systems for commercial and industrial buildings, institutions, and special projects such as airports, expositions, stadiums, etc. Articles must be based on interviews with consulting electrical engineers." Pays $50 to $75.

ELECTRICAL CONTRACTOR, 7315 Wisconsin Ave., Washington DC 20014. Editor: Larry C. Osius. For electrical contractors. Monthly. Buys first rights, reprint rights, and simultaneous rights. Will send free sample copy on request. Freelance material bought on assignment following query. Usually reports in 1 month. Enclose S.A.S.E.
Nonfiction and Photos: Installation articles showing informative application of new techniques and products. Slant is product and method contributing to better, faster, more economical construction process. Length: "1 column to 4 pages." Pays $60 per printed page, including photos and illustrative material. Photos should be sharp, reproducible glossies, 5x7 and up.

ELECTRICAL CONTRACTOR & MAINTENANCE SUPERVISOR, 481 University Ave., Toronto, Ont., M5W 1A7, Canada. Editor: George McNevin. For "middle-aged men who either run their own businesses or are in fairly responsible management positions. They range from university graduates to those with public school education only." Established in 1952. Monthly. Circulation: 13,000. Rights purchased vary with author and material. "Depending on author's wish, payment is either on acceptance or on publication." Will send a sample copy to a writer on request. Query first. Enclose S.A.E. and International Reply Coupons.
Nonfiction and Photos: "Articles that have some relation to electrical construction or maintenance and business management. The writer should include as much information as possible pertaining to the electrical field. We're not interested in articles that are too general and philosophical. Don't belabor the obvious, particularly on better business management. We're interested in coverage of labor difficulties." Buys informational articles, how-to's, profiles, coverage of successful business operations, new product pieces, and technical articles. Length: "no minimum or maximum." Pays "8¢ a published word or 6¢ a word on submitted mss, unless other arrangements are made." Photos purchased with mss or on assignment; captions optional. Pays "$7 for the first print and $2 for each subsequent print, plus photographer's expenses."

Electronics and Communications

Listed here are publications for electronics engineers, radio and TV broadcasting managers, electronic equipment operators, and builders of electronic communication systems and equipment, including stereos, television sets, and radio-TV broadcasting systems. Journals for professional announcers or communicators will be found under

Journalism; those for electronic appliance retailers will be found in Home Furnishings; publications on computer design and data processing systems will be found in Data Processing. Publications for electronics enthusiasts or stereo hobbyists will be found in Hobby and Craft or in Music in the Consumer Publications section.

BROADCAST ENGINEERING, 1014 Wyandotte, Kansas City MO 64105. Editor: Ron Merrell. For "owners, managers, and top technical people at AM, FM, TV stations, cable TV operators, educational and industrial TV and business communications, as well as recording studios." Established in 1959. Monthly. Circulation: 30,000. Buys all rights, but will reassign rights to author after publication. Buys about 50 mss a year. Pays on acceptance; "for a series, we pay for each part on publication." Will send a sample copy to a writer on request. Write for copy of guidelines for writers. Query first. Will not consider photocopied submissions. Submit seasonal material at least 3 months in advance. Reports in 2 weeks. Enclose S.A.S.E.
Nonfiction and Photos: Wants technical features dealing with design, installation, modification, and maintenance of radio and television broadcast station equipment; interested in features on educational and cable TV systems, other material of interest to communications engineers and technicians, and on self-designed and constructed equipment for use in broadcast and communications fields. "Currently looking for business, industrial, and medical application of video systems. This includes the use of video equipment in varied security systems; and instructional TV how-to's with pictures; articles on overcoming problems. Articles start with the evolution of the problem and resolve with the solution. We use a technical, but not textbook, style. Our publication is mostly how-to and it operates as a forum, talking with readers, not down to them. We reject material when it's far too general, not on target, or not backed by evidence or proof. Some articles and photos need releases and they are seldom included. We're overstocked with build-it-yourself articles, except for our 'Station to Station' column, where we take short-shorts and pay up to $25. We're especially interested now in articles on recording studios and improving facilities and techniques." Length: 1,500 to 2,000 words for features, with drawing and photos, if possible. Pays $75 to $200 for features and $15 to $25 for "Station to Station." Photos purchased with and without mss; captions required. Pays $5 to $10 for b&w, pays $10 to $35 for color (2¼x2¼ color transparencies or larger).
How To Break In: "Offer new solutions to old problems and include pictures of people in action on these problems."

BROADCAST MANAGEMENT/ENGINEERING, 274 Madison Ave., New York NY 10016. Editor: J. Lippke. For general managers, chief engineers, program directors of radio and TV stations. Established in 1964. Monthly. Circulation: 28,000. Buys all rights, but will reassign rights to author after publication. Buys 1 to 3 mss a year. Pays on publication. Reports in 4 weeks. Query first. Enclose S.A.S.E.
Nonfiction: Articles on cost-saving ideas; use of equipment, new programming ideas for serving the public. Tone of all material is professional to professional. "We're interested in the profile or program sound of competitive stations in a market." Length: 1,200 to 3,000 words. Pays $25 to $100. Recently published articles include "Cablecasters' Roundtable," written by a freelancer who attended an out-of-town panel session.

BROADCASTER, 77 River St., Toronto, Ont., M5A 3P2 Canada. Editor: Doug Loney. For the Canadian "communications industry—radio, television, cable, ETV, advertisers, and their agencies." Buys all rights. Pays on acceptance. Will send a sample copy to a writer on request. "Queries and all material will be acknowledged within a month, and I will endeavor to offer constructive criticism where necessary." Enclose International Reply Coupons.
Nonfiction: "We are looking for articles illustrating how the various communicators conduct their business; controversies, inventions, and innovations of broadcast engineers; profiles or interviews on successful men and women; development of program ideas; industry news and technical news in layman's language. Writers should

be familiar with the Canadian scene. No consumer-oriented material." Length: 500 to 3,000 words. Payment is $25 up.

CANADIAN ELECTRONICS ENGINEERING, 481 University Ave., Toronto M5W 1A7, Ont., Canada. Phone: 416-595-1811, Ext. 636. Editor: Cliff Hand. For technically trained users of professional electronics products. Monthly. Buys Canadian serial rights. Pays on acceptance. Will send free sample copy to a writer on request. Will consider cassette submissions. Query first with brief outline of article. Reports in 2 to 4 weeks. Enclose S.A.E. and International Reply Coupons.
Nonfiction: Science and technology involving professional electronic products and techniques. Must have direct relevance to work being done in Canada. Length: maximum about 1,500 words. Pays 5¢ to 8¢ per word depending on importance of subject, amount of research, and ability of writer.
Photos: Purchased with mss. 4x5 to 8x10 b&w glossy prints; must provide useful information on story subject. Pays average professional rates for time required on any particular assignment.

COMMUNICATIONS NEWS, 402 W. Liberty Drive, Wheaton IL 60187. Editor: Bruce Howat. For managers of communications systems. Monthly tabloid magazine; 88 pages. Established in 1964. Circulation: 35,000. Buys all rights. Buys 6 to 8 mss a year. Payment on publication. Will send free sample copy to writer on request. Will consider photocopied submissions. Will not consider simultaneous submissions. Reports on material accepted for publication in 4 weeks. Returns rejected material in 3 weeks. Query first or submit complete ms. Enclose S.A.S.E.
Nonfiction: Case histories of problem-solving for communications systems. Must be terse, factual, helpful. Informational and how-to articles; think pieces. Length: 1,600 words maximum. Pays 3¢ per word.

EDN, 221 Columbus Ave., Boston MA 02116. Phone: 617-536-7780. Editor: Roy W. Forsberg. For electronic design engineers. Semimonthly. Buys all rights. Payment when material is published. Will send free sample copy to writer on request. Reports "immediately." Enclose S.A.S.E.
Nonfiction and Photos: News from the field, concepts, developments, events; articles on microelectronics, design, materials, instrumentation and measurement, packaging, etc. Articles must be original, practical, accurate, pertinent and free of sales promotion. Length: up to 5,000 words, average 1,000 to 1,200 words. Pays flat rate based on quality of article ($30 per printed page); no payment for news, new product or new literature releases. Photos purchased with mss; b&w glossy. Color transparencies or prints.

ELECTRONIC BUYERS' NEWS, 280 Community Dr., Great Neck NY 11021. Editor: James Moran. For buyers in electronics companies. Newspaper; 48 pages. Established in 1972. Circulation: 35,000. Rights purchased vary with author and material. Usually buys first rights. Pays on publication. Will send free sample copy to writer on request. Reports on material accepted for publication in 2 to 3 months. Rejected material is not returned unless requested. Query first. Enclose S.A.S.E.
Nonfiction: "Each issue features a specific theme or electronic component. Articles are usually accepted from companies involved with that component. Other stories are accepted occasionally from authors knowledgeable in that field." All material is aimed directly at the purchasing profession. Length: open. Pays $100 minimum.

ELECTRONIC PACKAGING AND PRODUCTION, 222 W. Adams St., Chicago IL 60606. Editor: Donald J. Levinthal. For engineers and designers involved in electronic equipment prototype design and volume production. Magazine; 175 (8x11) pages. Established in 1960. Circulation: 26,500. Buys all rights. Buys 40 mss a year. Pays on publication. Will send free sample copy to writer on request. Write for copy of guidelines for writers. Will consider photocopied submissions. No simultaneous submissions. Reports in 2 to 3 weeks. Query first. Enclose S.A.S.E.

Nonfiction and Photos: Subject matter to be related to the physical design and production of electronic equipment — PC boards, cooling, artwork generation, microelectronics fabrication, etc. New and interesting techniques in packaging and production. Semiconductor and hybrid design and fabrication; systems packaging techniques. Should be detailed and technical and of benefit to the reader. "We specialize in the physical design and implementation of electronic equipment and are not concerned with electronic circuit design. An initial outline and abstract should be submitted for approval." Prefers not to see lab report style or articles that are sales pitch oriented. Length: 2,000 to 3,000 words. Pays $25 per published page. Columns and departments use news items involving up-to-date happenings in packaging and production, trends, etc. Length: 500 words. Payment to be negotiated. No additional payment for photos used with mss. Captions optional.

How To Break In: "Must be involved in science or engineering and be qualified to write on a given subject. Send outline, abstract and affiliations."

ELECTRONIC SERVICING, 1014 Wyandotte St., Kansas City MO 64105. Editor: C.H. Babcoke. Monthly. Circulation: 65,000. Buys all rights. Pays on acceptance. Will send a free sample copy on request. Write for author's guide before submitting. Query required. Reports in 1 to 3 weeks. Enclose S.A.S.E.

Nonfiction and Photos: Articles and illustrating photos with step-by-step procedures for diagnosing, repairing or installing consumer electronic products. Length: 1,000 to 1,500 words. Pays $125 to $200.

ELECTRONICS, 1221 Avenue of the Americas, New York NY 10019. Editor: Kemp Anderson. Biweekly. Buys all rights. Query first. Reports in 2 weeks. Enclose S.A.S.E.

Nonfiction: Uses copy about research, development, design and production of electronic devices and management of electronic manufacturing firms; articles on "descriptions of new circuit systems, components, design techniques, how specific electronic engineering problems were solved; interesting applications of electronics; step-by-step, how-to design articles; nomographs, charts, tables for solution of repetitive design problems." Length: 1,000 to 3,500 words. $30 per printed page.

ELECTRONICS RETAILING, 645 Stewart Ave., Garden City NY 11590. Editor: Robert R. Mueller. For independent, department, chain and discount stores; buyers of consumer electronics (hi-fi, TV, autosound, calculators, electronic watches, and related products). Tabloid; 24 pages. Established in 1975. Monthly. Circulation: 35,000. Buys all rights, but will reassign rights to author after publication. Buys about 500 mss a year. Pays on publication. Will send free sample copy to writer on request. Write for copy of guidelines for writers. No photocopied or simultaneous submissions. Reports on material accepted for publication in 2 weeks. Returns rejected material immediately. Query first. Enclose S.A.S.E.

Nonfiction and Photos: "We are looking primarily for hard news stories about the retailers in our audience. We prefer a straight news style and more extensive coverage of broader product areas. We will never publish a 'desk' article, unless we solicit it from an industry expert. Unfortunately, many of the freelance articles sent over the transom fall into this category." Interview, expose, spot news, merchandising techniques, technical articles. Length: 100 to 1,500 words. Pays 10¢ a word. B&w photos (5x7 or larger; no Polaroids) should support accompanying ms. Pays $10. Captions required.

How To Break In: "Query first. We have occasional openings for stringers in some parts of the country."

MICROWAVES, 50 Essex St., Rochelle Park NJ 07450. Managing Editor: Richard T. Davis. For microwave engineers and engineering managers. Monthly magazine; 80 to 100 (8x10) pages. Established in 1962. Circulation: 40,000. Buys all rights. Buys 24 to 36 mss a year. Payment on publication. Will send sample copy to writer on request. Write for copy of guidelines for writers. Will consider photocopied submissions. Reports in 3 months. Query first. "Submit outline and send resume of technical writing experience." Enclose S.A.S.E.

Nonfiction: Interested in material on research and development in microwave technology and economic news that affects the industry. Pays $100 per published page (approximately 840 words per published page) plus "25% bonus if you are a second-time author and a 50% bonus if you publish with us 3 times or more." **How To Break In:** "Ask yourself these questions: Does my subject have broad appeal to microwave men? Is my subject timely? Does my information have practical value in design, application or management? If you can explain your design ideas to fellow engineers at your plant, you can be sure you can do the same to readers of *MicroWaves.*"

P. D. CUE, 306 15th St., Des Moines IA 50309. Publisher: Malcolm Freeland. For television station program executives who are in charge of local programming. Magazine published every 2 months; 36 to 48 (7½x10) pages. Established in 1974. Circulation: 1,500. Buys all rights for 6 months. Buys 2 or 3 mss per issue. Payment on acceptance. Will send sample copy to writer for $1. Reports on accepted material in 10 days. Returns rejected material in 1 week. Query first. Enclose S.A.S.E.
Nonfiction and Photos: Unique ideas on local television programs (not network) with cost figures, amount of film used, manpower, audience acceptance, camera techniques, equipment used, amount of time spent planning and producing. Interested in any unique approach to local television programs that are comparatively new on the scene. "Many submissions are just too general. Sound like they have been rewritten from a news clipping." Uses interviews and material on successful business operations and technical aspects of the industry. Length: 1,000 to 1,500 words. Pays $25 to $50. No additional payment is made for b&w (3x5, 5x7 or 8x10) photos used with mss. Captions required.

Engineering and Technology

Publications for electrical engineers are classified under Electricity; journals for electronics engineers are classified with the Electronics and Communications publications.

CANADIAN CONSULTING ENGINEER, 1450 Don Mills Rd., Don Mills, Ontario M3B 2X7, Canada. Managing Editor: Russell B. Noble. For private engineering consultants. Buys exclusive rights preferably; occasionally exclusive to field or country. Payment on publication. Reports in 15 days. Enclose S.A.E. and International Reply Coupons.
Nonfiction: "We serve our readers with articles on how to start, maintain, develop and expand private engineering consultancies. Emphasis is on this management aspect. We are not a how-to magazine. We don't tell our readers how to design a bridge, a high rise, a power station or a sewage plant. Paradoxically, we are interested if the bridge falls down, for engineers are vitally interested in Errors and Omissions claims (much like journalists are about libel suits). We have articles on income tax, legal problems associated with consulting engineering, public relations and interviews with political figures. When we write about subjects like pollution, we write from a conceptual point of view; i.e., how the environmental situation will affect their practices. But because our readers are also concerned citizens, we include material which might interest them from a social, or educational point of view. The word to remember is *conceptual* (new concepts or interesting variations of old ones)." Usually pays $50 to $175, but this is dependent on length and extent of research required.

DETROIT ENGINEER, 18226 Mack, Grosse Pointe MI 48236. Editor: Jack Weller-Grenard. For "members of the Engineering Society of Detroit. They are engineers, architects, and persons in other related fields. The median age is about 51; mostly affluent, with wide-ranging interests." Established in 1945. Monthly. Circulation: 7,000. Rights purchased vary with author and material; may buy all rights, but will reassign rights to author after publication. Buys less than 4 mss a year. Pays on publication. Will send a sample copy to a writer for $1. Submit complete ms. Will not consider photocopied submissions. Submit seasonal material 3 to 4 months in advance. Returns rejected material "usually in 2 weeks." Acknowledges acceptance of material in 4 to 6 weeks. Enclose S.A.S.E.

Nonfiction: *"Detroit Engineer* publishes articles on subjects of regional, southeastern Michigan interest not covered in other publications. We are only interested in the unusual and highly specific technical or man-oriented pieces, such as an expose on the Wankel engine or a new way to harness solar energy—subjects of wide interest within the scientific community." Buys exposes and technical articles. Length: 500 to 2,000 words. Pays $50 to $100.

Photos: Buys 4x5 to 8x10 b&w glossies; "any surface." Pays $5 to $15. Buys 8x10 color prints or larger transparencies for cover use. Pays minimum $25.

ELECTRO-OPTICAL SYSTEMS DESIGN MAGAZINE, Room 900, 222 W. Adams St., Chicago IL 60606. Phone: 312-263-4866. Editor: Robert D. Compton. Monthly. Circulation: 26,000. Buys all rights. Pays on publication. Will send a sample copy to a writer on request. Write for copy of guidelines for writers. Will consider cassette submissions. Query required. Editorial deadlines are on the 5th of the month preceding publication. Enclose S.A.S.E.

Nonfiction and Photos: Articles and photos on lasers, laser systems, and optical systems aimed at electro-optical scientists and engineers. "Each article should serve a reader's need by either stimulating ideas, increasing technical competence, improving design capabilities in the following areas: natural light and radiation sources, artificial light and radiation sources, light modulators, optical components, image detectors, energy detectors, information displays, image processing, information storage and processing, system and subsystem testing, materials, support equipment, and other related areas." Rejects flighty prose, material not written for type of readership, and irrelevant material. Pays $30 per page. Submit 8x10 b&w glossies with ms.

LIGHTING DESIGN & APPLICATION, 345 E. 47th St., New York NY 10017. Editor: Chuck Beardsley. For "lighting designers, architects, consulting engineers, and lighting engineers." Established in 1971. Monthly. Circulation: 17,500. Rights purchased vary with author and material. Buys about 10 mss a year. Pays on acceptance. Query first. Will not consider photocopied submissions. Enclose S.A.S.E.

Nonfiction: "Lighting application, techniques, and trends in all areas, indoors and out. Our publication is the chief source of practical illumination information." Buys informational and think articles. Length: 500 to 2,000 words. Pays $150.

How To Break In: "Interview authorities in the field of illuminating engineering."

NEW ENGINEER, 730 Third Ave., New York NY 10017. Phone: 212-758-5300. For "engineering school students at the graduate and undergraduate levels and young professional engineers, recent graduates, engineers in management." 11 times a year with combined August/September issue. Circulation: 63,000. Buys first rights. Buys 20 to 30 mss a year. Pays on publication. Will send a sample copy to a writer on request. Will consider cassette submissions. Query first with outline or abstract. Submit seasonal material 4 months in advance. Enclose S.A.S.E.

Nonfiction and Photos: Articles on "engineering trends, employment patterns, outlook, profiles of successful engineers, social responsibility, engineering education. Articles should interest young engineers in general. Our publication approaches the engineer as a professional person—as a member of an elite group." Publishes issues on "minority groups and engineering and environment and the engineer." Buys how-to's, personal experience articles, interviews, profiles, humor, coverage of successful business operations, and new product articles. Does not want to see articles that are too technical or with too limited an appeal. Style should be more for consumer readership. Length: 1,500 to 4,000 words. Pays 6¢ to 15¢ a word. B&w glossies, 35mm color, and color transparencies purchased with mss. Payment "usually $20 to $25."

Fiction: Humorous; "engineering related." Length: 1,000 to 2,000 words. Pays 6¢ to 15¢ a word.

Finance

The magazines listed below deal with banking, investment, and financial management. Magazines that use similar material but have a less technical or professional slant are listed in the Consumer Publications under Business and Finance.

BANK SYSTEMS & EQUIPMENT, 1501 Broadway, New York NY 10036. Editor: Alan Richman. For bank and savings and loan association operations executives. Monthly. Circulation: 22,000. Buys all rights. Pays on publication. Query first for style sheet and specific article assignment. Mss should be triple spaced on one side of paper only with wide margin at left-hand side of the page. All illustrations should be captioned. Enclose S.A.S.E.
Nonfiction: Third-person case history articles and interviews as well as material relating to systems, operations and automation. Charts, systems diagrams, artist's renderings of new buildings, etc., may accompany ms and must be suitable for reproduction. Prefers one color only. Length: open. Pays $75 for first published page, $45 for second page, and $40 for succeeding pages.
Photos: 5x7 or 8x10 single-weight glossies. Candids of persons interviewed, views of bank, bank's data center, etc. "We do not pay extra for photos."

BURROUGHS CLEARING HOUSE, Box 418, Detroit MI 48232. Managing Editor: Norman E. Douglas. For bank and financial officers. Monthly. Buys all publication rights. Pays on acceptance. Will send a sample copy on request. Query first on articles longer than 1,800 words. Enclose S.A.S.E.
Nonfiction: Uses reports on what banks and other financial institutions are doing; emphasize usable ideas. "We reject an article if we question its authenticity." Length: 1,000 to 2,000 words; also uses shorter news items. Pays 10¢ a word. Additional payment of $5 for usable illustrations.
Photos: Should be 8x10 glossy b&w. Also buys pix with captions only. Pays $5.

C. G. A. MAGAZINE, Suite #800, 535 Thurlow St., Vancouver, British Columbia V6E 3L2, Canada. Editor: John A. Haskett. Publication of Certified General Acccountants' Association of Canada. For professional (C.G.A.) accountants, financial reporters and editors, politicians, etc. All C.G.A. members have completed a minimum five-year academic program. Magazine; 48 pages. Established in 1967. Every 2 months. Circulation: 25,000. Buys all rights, but will reassign rights to author after publication. Buys 12 to 15 mss a year. Pays on acceptance. Will send free sample copy to writer on request. Write for copy of guidelines for writers. Query first. Reports in 2 to 4 weeks. Enclose S.A.E. and International Reply Coupons.
Nonfiction, Photos, and Fillers: Accounting and financial subjects of interest to highly qualified professional accountants and other financial officers. Majority of them are industrial (i.e., corporation) accountants as opposed to accountants in public practice. All submissions must be relevant to Canadian accounting. All material must be of top professional quality, but at the same time written simply and interestingly. Recently published articles covered how corporation accountants can improve their status, how specific accountants have handled specific accounting problems, how accounting for inflation should be handled. Buys informational, how-to, personal experience, interview, profile, and think articles. Length: 1,500 to 3,000 words. Pays $100 to $200. Regular columns, How I Do It and Accounting Elsewhere, run 500 to 1,500 words. Pays $50 to $100. Nonfiction Editor: Merrilee Davey. Photos purchased with accompanying ms with no additional payment. Captions required. Clippings and jokes (accounting oriented only). Pays $1 minimum.

THE CANADIAN BANKER AND ICB REVIEW, Box 282, Toronto Dominion Centre, Toronto, Ont., Canada. Editor: William Ivens. For bankers and businessmen. Bimonthly. Buys first reproduction rights. Pays on publication. Will send sample copy on request. Query not necessary but desirable. Reports in 6 weeks. Enclose S.A.E. and International Reply Coupons.
Nonfiction and Photos: History of banking in Canada, international agencies, banking biographies, industries, government developments related to finance and business.

legislation. "We generally reject articles that relate only to the U.S. banking system and not to the Canadian banking system." Pays up to $250. Prefers photos with articles.

THE COMMERCIAL AND FINANCIAL CHRONICLE, 110 Wall St., New York NY 10005. Tabloid newspaper; 72 pages. Established in 1839. Weekly. Circulation: 6,000. Not copyrighted. Buys about 10 mss a year. Pays on publication. Will send a free sample copy to writer on request. No photocopied or simultaneous submissions. Reports on material accepted for publication during week of publication. Does not return material unless S.A.S.E. is enclosed. Query first.
Nonfiction and Photos: Articles on various aspects of finance. Informational, how-to, interview, profile, think pieces, expose, personal opinion, successful business operations. Reviews of financial books. Length: open. Pays $200. No additional payment for photos used with mss. Captions required.

COMMODITIES MAGAZINE, 1000 Century Plaza, Columbia MD 21044. Phone: 301-730-5359. Editor: Edgar K. Lofton, Jr. For private, individual futures traders, brokers, exchange members, agri-businessmen; agricultural banks; anyone with an interest in commodities. Monthly magazine; 40 to 48 (8½x11) pages. Established in 1971. Circulation: 16,000. Buys all rights, but will reassign rights to author after publication. Buys 30 to 40 mss a year. Payment on publication. Will send sample copy to writer on request. Write for copy of guidelines for writers. Will consider photocopied submissions. Will not consider simultaneous submissions. Reports on material accepted for publication within 1 month. Returns rejected material within 2 months if accompanied by S.A.S.E. Query first or submit complete ms. Enclose S.A.S.E.
Nonfiction and Photos: Articles analyzing specific commodity futures trading strategies; fundamental and technical analysis of individual commodities and markets; interviews, book reviews, "success" stories; news items. Material on new legislation affecting commodities, trading, any new trading strategy (results must be able to be substantiated); personalities. Does not want to see "homespun" rules for trading and simplistic approaches to the commodities market. Treatment is always in-depth and broad. Informational, how-to, interview, profile, technical. "Articles should be written for a reader who has traded commodities for one year or more; should not talk down or hypothesize. Relatively complex material is acceptable." Length: No maximum or minimum; 2,500 words optimum. Pays 6¢ per word. Pays $15 for glossy print b&w photos. Captions required.

FINANCIAL QUARTERLY, P. O. Box 14451, North Palm Beach FL 33408. Editor: Thomas A. Swirles. For "bank and savings and loan presidents, vice-presidents, etc. We now go to motor credit unions as well." Established in 1969. Quarterly. Circulation: 64,000. Rights purchased vary with author and material. Pays on publication. Will send a sample copy to a writer on request. Submit complete ms. Will consider photocopied submissions. Reports on material accepted for publication "at closing." Returns rejected material in 1 month. Enclose S.A.S.E.
Nonfiction and Photos: "Bank product information, trends in banking, etc." Buys informational articles, how-to's, interviews, and coverage of merchandising techniques. Length: 500 to 750 words. Pays $200 to $500. Photos purchased with mss.

THE INDEPENDENT BANKER, Box 267, Sauk Centre MN 56378. Editor: Bill McDonald. Associate Editor: Al Blair. For bankers. Monthly. Buys all rights. Pays on acceptance. Usually reports in 1 month. Enclose S.A.S.E.
Nonfiction and Photos: Human interest or how-to-do-it articles that will appeal to officers of independent banks in small communities. Avoid articles slanted toward large branch or holding company banks and savings and loans. Length: open. Rate is 5¢ a published word, with $100 maximum payment for any article, regardless of word count. Pays $5 each for 8x10 or 5x7 b&w glossies accepted.

MERGERS & ACQUISITIONS, 1621 Brookside Rd., McLean VA 22101. Editor: Stanley Foster Reed. For presidents and other high corporate personnel, financiers, buyers, stockbrokers, accountants, and related professionals. Quarterly. Buys all rights. Pays 21 days after publication. Will send a free sample copy to a writer on request. Highly recommends query with outline of intended article first. Include 50-word autobiography with mss. Enclose S.A.S.E.

Nonfiction: "Articles on merger and acquisition techniques (taxes, SEC regulations, anti-trust, etc.) or surveys and roundups emphasizing analysis and description of trends and implications thereof. Articles should contain 20 to 60 facts per 1,000 words (names, dates, places, companies, etc.). We reject articles that are badly researched. We can fix bad writing but not bad research. Accurate research is a must and footnote references should be incorporated into text. Avoid 'Company A, Company B' terminology." Length: maximum 10,000 to 15,000 words. Pays $50 to $100 per 1,000 printed words for freelance articles; $200 honorarium or 200 reprints for articles by professional business persons, such as lawyers, investment analysts.

NABW JOURNAL, 9 S. Fairview Ave., Park Ridge IL 60068. Editor: Judy Woodbury. For women officers of commercial banks. Magazine; 32 (8½x11) pages. Established in 1922. Every 2 months. Circulation: 15,000. Buys all rights. Buys 3 to 6 mss a year. Pays on publication. Will send free sample copy to writer on request. Reports in 2 weeks. Query first. Enclose S.A.S.E.

Nonfiction and Photos: General banking topics; problems of women in management; profiles of successful women bank executives. How-to, interview, think articles, personal opinion, successful business operations, merchandising techniques. Length: 500 to 2,000 words. Pays 10¢ a word minimum. B&w photos purchased with ms. Pays $10. Captions required.

PACIFIC BANKER AND BUSINESS, 1 Yesler Way, Seattle WA 98104. Phone: 206-623-1888. Editor: Vernon White. For banking and finance people. Monthly. Buys all rights. Pays on acceptance. Will send sample copy on request. Query first. Reports in 2 weeks. Enclose S.A.S.E.

Nonfiction: Uses features pertaining to finance and business. Length: 1,000 words. Pays $35 to $100.

Fishing

CANADIAN FISHERMAN AND OCEAN SCIENCE, Gardenvale, Que., HOA 1BO, Canada. Phone: 514-457-3250. Editor: Allan Muir. Not copyrighted. Pays on publication. Will send a sample copy to a writer on request. Reports in 1 month. Enclose S.A.E. and International Reply Coupons.

Nonfiction: Articles describing new developments in commercial fisheries and oceanography. Will also consider sketches and controversial articles about Canadian fisheries and oceanological developments. Style should be strictly factual and easy to read. Length: up to 1,000 words. Pays 3¢ to 5¢ per word.

Photos: Buys photos with mss and with captions only. Pays $3 and up.

NATIONAL FISHERMAN, Camden ME 04843. Editor: David R. Getchell. For commercial fishing and boat building readership. Monthly. Buys one-time rights. Pays on acceptance. Will send free sample copy to a writer on request. Data sheets available. Article proposals should be accompanied by sample of work. Reports in 2 to 3 weeks. Enclose S.A.S.E.

Nonfiction: Features and articles pertaining to commercial fishing, boat building and general marine subjects. Prefers informal style, human interest, unpretentious approach. Some technical detail necessary in certain stories. "We frequently run maritime history articles, and all such articles submitted will be carefully reviewed. There's a good chance we will have a special Bicentennial section in our July 1976 edition, and more historical material than usual may be needed. But, query first." Length: maximum 3,000 words. Pays 2¢ per word; more for text and photo package.

Photos: Purchased with mss or with captions. Good quality, size varies. Prefers 5x7

or 8x10 b&w; can use b&w snapshots. Pays $5.
Fillers: Long or short news items pertaining to commercial fishing, boat building and general marine subjects. Pays 2¢ per word.

Florists, Nurserymen, and Landscaping

FLORIST, 900 West Lafayette, Detroit MI 48226. Editor: Frank J. Baccala. For retail and wholesale florists. Monthly. Circulation: 21,000. Buys all rights. Pays on acceptance. Will send a sample copy to a writer on request. No query required. Submit seasonal material 3 months in advance. Reports in 3 weeks. Enclose S.A.S.E.
Nonfiction and Photos: Shop management, sales promotion, developments in flower culture. "No articles that glorify the individual florist." Length: 500 to 1,200 words. Pays 5¢ a word. Photos purchased with mss. B&w glossies, color transparencies. Pays $5 to $30.

FLOWER NEWS, 549 W. Randolph St., Chicago IL 60606. Phone: 312-236-8648. Editor: Barbara Gilbert. Weekly. Not copyrighted. Pays on acceptance. Reports immediately. Enclose S.A.S.E.
Nonfiction: Uses retail advertising, merchandising, how-to articles of interest to retail florists. "We accept articles already researched and complete on subjects having to do with promotional ideas, holiday business, how to set up a flower shop. Also articles of a technical nature. No articles on specific flower shops." Pays $10.

TELEFLORA SPIRIT, 2400 Compton Blvd., Redondo Beach CA 90278. Editor: Jorian Clair. Official publication of Teleflora, Incorporated, for retail florist subscribers to Teleflora's flowers-by-wire service. Positioned as "The Magazine of Professional Flower Shop Management." Monthly. Circulation: 14,000. Buys one-time rights in floral trade magazine field. Pays on publication. Reports in 2 to 3 weeks. Enclose S.A.S.E.
Nonfiction and Photos: Articles dealing with buying and selling profitably, merchandising of product, management, designing, shop remodeling, display techniques, etc. Also, allied interests such as floral wholesalers, growers, tradespeople, gift markets, etc. All articles must be thoroughly researched and professionally relevant. Any florist mentioned must be a Teleflorist. Length: 1,000 to 3,000 words. Pays 8¢ per published word. Photos purchased with mss or with captions only. 8x10 b&w glossies preferred. Captions required. Pays $7.50.

Food Products, Processing, and Service

In this list are journals for food wholesalers, processors, warehousers, caterers, institutional managers, and suppliers of grocery store equipment. Publications for grocery store operators are classified under Groceries. Journals for food vending machine operators will be found under Coin-Operated Machines.

FOOD MANAGEMENT, 757 Third Ave., New York NY 10017. Editor: William B. Patterson. For institutional food service field (schools, colleges, nursing homes, hospitals, contract feeders). Monthly. Circulation: 50,000. Buys all rights. Payment on acceptance. Write for copy of guidelines for writers. Query first. Enclose S.A.S.E.
Nonfiction and Photos: Articles on food management, food purchasing and storage, menu planning, food preparation and cooking, methods of serving, sanitation, employee motivation, security, legislation. Length: 2,000 to 3,000 words. Pays 7¢ per word and up. Strong, action-type 35mm color. Pays $15 for color.
How To Break In: "The easiest way to break in would be with an article for our Case Book department. These are short how-to's which describe how an institution solved a particular problem. For example, we recently ran a Case Book on how one hospital saved $52,000 by going to a one-step assembly line — what they did before, how they came up with the idea and how it was put into effect. 500 to 750 words."

FOOD MARKETER, 2700 Cumberland Pkwy., Suite 500, Atlanta GA 30339. Editor: Beth Souther. For food wholesalers and independent retailers. Publication of the Foodland International Corporation. Magazine; 32 to 48 (8½x11) pages. Monthly. Circulation: 4,000. Buys first serial rights. Buys 15 to 50 mss a year. Will send free sample copy to writer on request. Write for copy of guidelines for writers. Will consider photocopied and simultaneous submissions. Reports on material accepted for publication in 10 days. Returns rejected material immediately. Submit complete ms. Enclose S.A.S.E.

Nonfiction and Photos: Food industry news, trends and innovations. Emphasis is on the food dealer's and distributor's point of view. Informational, how-to, interview, think pieces, successful business operations, merchandising techniques. Recently published "Dollars in the Dairy Case" and "Specialty Shops." Length: 1,000 to 2,500 words. Pays $25 to $150. 8x10 b&w glossies purchased with ms. Pays $5 to $25. Pays $50 for 35mm or 2¼x2¼ color transparencies used on the cover.

KITCHEN PLANNING, 757 Third Ave., New York NY 10017. Editor: Freda Barry. Buys all rights. Pays on acceptance. Query first. Enclose S.A.S.E.

Nonfiction and Photos: How-to, in-depth articles on designing institutional food service—installations based on actual experience of specific operation—with quotes, facts, figures. Length: 1,000 to 1,500 words. Kitchen floor plans must accompany ms. B&w glossies purchased with ms. Pays 7¢ to 10¢ a word. Pays $5 for each photo.

MEAT PLANT MAGAZINE, 10225 Bach Blvd., St. Louis MO 63132. Editor: Albert Todoroff. For meat processors, locker plant operators, freezer provisioners, portion control packers, meat dealers, and food service (food plan) operators. Bimonthly. Pays on acceptance. Reports in 2 weeks. Enclose S.A.S.E. for return of submissions.

Nonfiction, Photos, and Fillers: Buys feature-length articles and shorter subjects pertinent to the field. Length: 1,000 words for features. Pays 1½¢ a word. Pays $3.50 for photos.

PRODUCE NEWS, 6 Harrison St., New York NY 10013. Editor: Walter H. Preston. For "commercial growers and shippers, receivers, and distributors of fresh fruits and vegetables, including chain store produce buyers and merchandisers." Established in 1897. Weekly. Circulation: 5,300. Not copyrighted. Pays on publication. Will send a sample copy to a writer on request. Query first. "Our deadline is Wednesday afternoon before Friday press day each week." Enclose S.A.S.E.

Nonfiction, Fillers and Photos: "News is our principal stock in trade, particularly trends in crop growing, distributing, and marketing. Tell the story clearly, simply, and briefly." Buys informational articles, how-to's, profiles, spot news, coverage of successful business operations, new product pieces, articles on merchandising techniques. Length: "no special length." Pays 50¢ a column inch for original material, 40¢ a column inch for clippings. 8½x11 b&w glossies purchased with ms.

QUICK FROZEN FOODS, 757 Third Ave., New York NY 10017. Phone: 212-754-4335. Associate Publisher and Editor: Sam Martin. Monthly. Buys all rights but will release any rights on request. Pays within 30 days after acceptance. Query first. Guaranteed assignments by special arrangement. Will accept names for file of correspondents who would be given assignments when and if story breaks in their locality. Reports in 30 days. Enclose S.A.S.E.

Nonfiction and Photos: Uses feature articles and short articles on frozen food operations in processing plants, wholesalers' warehouses, chain stores and supermarkets. Good articles on retailing of frozen foods. Can also use articles (all lengths) and photos on frozen foods in any foreign country, whether packer, retailer, distributor, or warehouse level. Pays 2¢ to 3¢ a word. Pays $5 a photo.

Fillers: Pays $1 minimum for clippings.

SNACK FOOD, Harcourt Bldg., Duluth MN 55802. Phone: 218-727-8511. Editor: Jerry L. Hess. For manufacturers of snack foods (potato chips, cookies, crackers, pretzels, corn chips, fabricated chips, snack cakes and pies, frozen snacks and frozen pizza, extruded snacks, toaster pastries, nutmeats). Readers are in management, production, sales, marketing and packaging design. Monthly magazine; (8x11¼) pages. Established in 1912. Circulation: 10,000. Buys all rights. Buys 6 or 8 mss a year. Payment on acceptance. Will send free sample copy to writer on request. Write for copy of guidelines for writers. Submit seasonal material 3 months in advance. Query first. Enclose S.A.S.E.

Nonfiction and Photos: This is a sales and marketing oriented publication which uses case history articles on successful manufacturers. Writers are asked to write the editor about possible leads in their areas. Also uses interviews and profiles. Length: 1,000 to 2,000 words. Pays 5¢ to 7¢ per word. B&w photos are purchased with mss. Pays $5 to $6.

Fur

FUR TRADE JOURNAL, Bewdley, Ont., Canada. Phone: 416-797-2281. Editor: Charles Clay. For fur ranchers in mink, chinchilla, rabbit, nutria; and for all aspects of fur pelt sales, garment manufacture, garment retailing. Monthly. Buys first Canadian rights. Pays on publication. Very little freelance material used. Mostly staff-written. Query first. Reports "immediately." Enclose S.A.E. and International Reply Coupons.

Nonfiction: Articles on anything of practical value and interest to fur ranchers. Length: up to 1,500 words. Pays 2¢ per word.

Photos: Purchased with mss; dealing with fur ranching. Pays $3 to $5.

U.S. FUR RANCHER, 3055 N. Brookfield Rd., Brookfield WI 53005. Publisher: Bruce W. Smith. For mink farmers. Monthly. Buys first world rights. Pays on publication. Will send free sample copy on request "by letter, not postcard. Queries imperative, including names and addresses of proposed interview subjects." Reports "immediately." Enclose S.A.S.E. for return of submissions.

Nonfiction and Photos: "Articles and photos on mink-ranch operations, based on interviews with manager or owner. Not interested in any fur-bearing animals except mink. Opportunities for freelancers traveling to foreign nations in which mink are raised. We reject an article if we find factual errors resulting from carelessness in interviewing and research." Recently published articles include "Dentist by Day, Mink Farmer at Night and on Weekends," "Mink Ranching Problems in the United Kingdom," and "Artificial Lighting Regimen Boosts Kit Production." Length: 1,000 to 2,000 words. Pays $30 to $75 per article, including four contact prints at least 2¼ square.

Gas

BUTANE-PROPANE NEWS, P.O. Box 3027, Arcadia CA 91006. Phone: 213-446-4607. Editor-Publisher: William W. Clark. For LP-gas distributor dealers with bulk storage plants, LP bottled gas dealers and manufacturers of appliances and equipment. Monthly. Buys all rights. Pays on publication. Will send free sample copy on request. Will consider cassette submissions. Query preferred. Reports in 1 week. Enclose S.A.S.E.

Nonfiction: Articles on advertising and promotional programs; plant design, marketing operating techniques and policies; management problems; new, unusual or large usages of LP-gas; how LP-gas marketers are coping with the energy crisis. Completeness of coverage, reporting in depth, emphasis on the why and the how are musts. "Brevity essential but particular angles should be covered pretty thoroughly." Pays $40 per magazine page.

Photos: Purchased with mss. 8x10 desired but not required; can work from negatives. Pays $5.
Fillers: Clippings and newsbreaks pertinent to LPG industry. Clippings regarding competitive fuels (electricity, oil) with relationship that would have impact on LPG industry. Pays $5 minimum for clippings.

GAS APPLIANCE MERCHANDISING, 1 East First St., Duluth MN 55802. Editor: Zane Chastain. For gas appliance dealers, builders, plumbers, contractors, and gas utility personnel. Bimonthly. Buys all rights. Pays on acceptance. Will send free sample copy on request. Write for copy of guidelines for writers. Reports in 1 week. Enclose S.A.S.E.
Nonfiction: "Gas appliance dealer case histories. Articles on gas utility promotions. Marketing trends, displays." Length: 800 to 1,500 words. Pays 5¢ to 6¢ per word.
Photos: Purchased with mss or with captions only. 5x7 glossies. Pays $5 to $7.

LP-GAS, 1 East First St., Duluth MN 55802. Editor: Zane Chastain. For liquefied petroleum gas (propane, 'bottled gas') marketers. Monthly. Buys all rights. Pays on acceptance. Query first. Enclose S.A.S.E.
Nonfiction: Uses dealer and LP-gas utilization articles, "how-to" features on selling, delivery, service, etc. Tersely written, illustrated by photo or line for documentation. Length: maximum 1,500 words. Pays 5¢ a word.
Photos: Pix with mss or captions only not less than 2¼x2¼. Pays $5 to $7.

SOONER LPG TIMES, 2910 N. Walnut, Suite 114-A, Oklahoma City OK 73105. Editor: John E. Orr. For "dealers and suppliers of LP-gas and their employees." Monthly. Not copyrighted. Pays on publication. Reports in 3 weeks. Enclose S.A.S.E.
Nonfiction: "Articles relating to the LP-gas industry, safety, small business practices, and economics; anything of interest to small businessmen." Length: 1,000 to 2,000 words. Pays $10 to $15.

Government and Public Service

Below are journals for individuals who provide governmental services, either in the employ of local, state, or national governments or of franchised utilities. Included are journals for city managers, politicians, civil servants, firemen, policemen, public administrators, urban transit managers, utilities managers, etc.

Publications that emphasize the architectural and building side of city planning and development are classified in Architecture. Publications for lawyers are found in the Law category. Journals for teachers and administrators in the schools are found in Education. Publications for private citizens interested in politics, government, and public affairs are classified with the Politics and World Affairs magazines in the Consumer Publications section.

THE CALIFORNIA HIGHWAY PATROLMAN, 1225 8th St., Suite 150, Sacramento CA 95814. Phone: 916-442-0411. Editor: Joseph L. Richardson. "About half our circulation is made up of California Highway Patrolmen, with remaining subscriptions going to families with children, schools, businesses concerned with traffic safety (trucking companies, etc.), professional offices for waiting rooms." Established in 1937. Monthly. Circulation: 13,000. Buys all rights, but will reassign rights to author after publication. Buys 80 mss a year. Payment on publication. Will send free sample copy to writer on request. Write for copy of guidelines for writers. Submit seasonal material 3 months in advance. Query first or submit complete ms. Reports in 1 month. Enclose S.A.S.E.
Nonfiction and Photos: "Although our name implies that we are a law enforcement magazine, we are not. We are not interested in law enforcement subjects per se, unless they deal with our theme of transportation safety. However, we are expanding our format somewhat to include other types of transportation articles, other than

just traffic safety. Articles on boating, bicycling, motorcycling, snowmobiling and recreational vehicle usage (dirt bikes, dune buggies, motor homes, etc.) will be needed to fill our pages. We will still be using articles on traffic safety (our main theme), driver education, early California (historical topics dealing with early California 49-er days), and travel. Biggest things we are looking for in all of the above are informative, entertaining and illustrated articles (always a big plus on this editor's desk)." Length: 800 to 3,500 words. Pays 2½¢ a word; $2.50 per b&w photo purchased with mss. Captions required.

How To Break In: "We are an excellent prospect for new writers trying to break into print because we are more concerned with the quality and appeal of work being submitted than we are with the writer's record of sales to us or other publications."

CAMPAIGN INSIGHT, Petroleum Bldg., Wichita KS 67202. Phone: 316-265-7421. Editor: Susan Armstrong. For "persons who are politically oriented, who are interested in staying abreast of the latest political techniques." Established in 1969. Every 2 weeks. Circulation: 4,000. Buys first North American serial rights. Buys 50 mss a year. Payment on acceptance. Will send free sample copy to writer on request. Query first. Will consider photocopied submissions. Reports on material in 30 days. Enclose S.A.S.E.

Nonfiction and Photos: "Strictly how-to material. We like profiles on campaigns at all levels—city to the White House—as long as they're liberally laced with specific techniques that lead to the win or loss. No partisan material or philosophy wanted—just the nuts and bolts of good campaigning. We only assign from queries. Any facet of any political technique will get a good hearing from us." Length: 800 to 1,500 words. Pays 5¢ per word. B&w photos; 5x7 minimum. Pays $5 per half-tone.

How To Break In: "Query me with a good idea on a story detailing the 'how to' techniques that won a particular campaign."

FIRE CHIEF MAGAZINE, 625 N. Michigan Ave., Chicago IL 60611. Phone: 312-642-9862. Editor: William Randleman. For chiefs of volunteer and paid fire departments. Buys all rights. Will not consider simultaneous submissions or material offered for second rights. Pays on publication. Reports in 10 days. Enclose S.A.S.E.

Nonfiction: Wants articles on fire department administration, training, or fire-fighting operations. Will accept case histories of major fires, extinguished by either volunteer or paid departments, detailing exactly how the fire department fought the fire and the lessons learned from the experience. "Prefer feature articles to be bylined by a fire chief or other fire service authority." Writing must be simple, clear, and detailed, preferably conversational in style. Pays $1 to $1.50 per column inch.

Photos: Used with mss or with captions only. 4x5 or larger; Polaroid or other small prints of individuals or small subjects accepted. Pays up to $35 for acceptable color photos. Pays nothing for public domain photos, up to $5 for exclusives, $1 for mug shots.

FIRE ENGINEERING, 666 Fifth Ave., New York NY 10019. Editor: James F. Casey. For commissioners, chiefs, senior officers of the paid, volunteer, industrial, and military fire departments and brigades. Buys all rights. Pays on publication. Reports in 3 weeks. Enclose S.A.S.E. for return of submissions.

Nonfiction and Photos: Wants articles on fire suppression, fire prevention, and any other subject that relates to fire service. Length: 750 to 1,500 words. Pays minimum 3¢ a word and up. Good photos with captions always in demand. Particular need for color photos for cover; small print or slide satisfactory for submission, but must always be a vertical or capable of being cropped to vertical. Transparency required if accepted. Pays $75 for color shots used on cover, $15 and up for b&w shots.

FOREIGN SERVICE JOURNAL, 2101 E St., N.W., Washington DC 20037. Phone: 202-338-4045. Editor: Shirley R. Newhall. For Foreign Service officers and others interested in foreign affairs and related subjects. Monthly. Buys first North American rights. Pays on publication. Query first. Enclose S.A.S.E.

Nonfiction: Uses articles on "international relations, internal problems of the State

Department and Foreign Service, informative material on other nations. Much of our material is contributed by those working in the fields we reach. Informed outside contributions are welcomed, however." Length: 2,500 to 4,000 words. Pays 2¢ to 3¢ a word.

MANPOWER, Dept. of Labor PH 10414, Washington DC 20213. Editor: Ellis Rottman. For job training, poverty and education specialists. Monthly. Circulation: 30,000. Not copyrighted. Pays on publication. Will send a free sample copy on request. Query preferred. Enclose S.A.S.E.
Nonfiction: Articles on government and private efforts to solve manpower, training, and education problems, particularly among the disadvantaged. Length: 600 to 4,000 words. "Payment for unsolicited articles used in the magazine is $75 to $100. For articles done by outside writers on assignment, payment is negotiable."

MODERN GOVERNMENT (SERVICIOS PUBLICOS), P.O. Box 1256, Stamford CT 06904. Phone: 203-327-9340. Editor: Philip R. Moran. For government officials, private contractors and executives of public utilities and corporations in Latin America and Spain (Spanish) and Asia, Australasia, Africa, the Middle East and the Caribbean (English). 9 times a year. Circulation: 42,000. Buys international rights. Pays on acceptance. Will send free sample copy on request. Query advised. Reports in 1 week. Enclose S.A.S.E.
Nonfiction and Photos: All material should be of interest to government officials in developing nations. Strong "how to do it" (but not highly technical) angle on infrastructure development, public works, public transportation, public health and environmental sanitation, administrative skills, etc. Avoid strictly U.S. orientation. Publications go only overseas. Articles are bought in English and translated into Spanish. Length: 1,500 to 2,000 words. Pays $100 to $150 for article with up to 6 photos.

NATIONAL POLICE & FIRE JOURNAL, 1100 N.E. 125th St., Miami FL 33161. Editor: Thomas Moore. For law enforcement officers and fire fighters and citizen members from all walks of life. Tabloid newspaper; 12 to 16 pages. Established in 1974. Every 2 months. Circulation: 40,000. Buys all rights. Buys 20 to 50 mss a year. Pays on publication. Will send free sample copy to writer on request. Write for copy of guidelines for writers. Will consider photocopied and simultaneous submissions. Reports on material accepted for publication in 90 to 180 days. Returns rejected material immediately. Submit complete ms. Enclose S.A.S.E.
Nonfiction and Photos: "We cover the entire public safety field and publish facts about police and fire departments. Equipment, ideas, heroism; what is new and what is happening in public safety. Writers must use newspaper style and have pictures available to use with stories. Would like to see more material about volunteer fire departments, their men and services in rescue and fire fighting operations." Recently published articles include "Hostages", a unique study of a new major law enforcement problem. Length: 500 to 2,000 words. Pays $5 to $25. Pays $1 to $5 for clear b&w photos; any size. Photos will not be returned if used. Captions required.

NATION'S CITIES, 1620 Eye St., Washington DC 20006. Managing Editor: Raymond L. Bancroft. For municipal officials, mayors, city managers, councilmen, and department heads. Monthly. Buys first North American serial rights. Pays on acceptance. Will send a sample copy to a writer on request. Query first. Reports in 1 month. Enclose S.A.S.E.
Nonfiction and Photos: Limited budget for freelance material. Wants "articles covering role of city government in improving community development through better administration, new techniques, and cooperation with public and other governments." Prefers mss illustrated with photos or charts and graphs so as to be "quickly meaningful to the harried city executive." Welcomes "pro and con treatment of important subjects and new ideas. We try to run articles which would be of interest to not only city officials in the large metropolitan areas, but also those in smaller and scattered regions. Articles should be fresh, vigorous, active,

and accurate, as well as friendly, lucid, easy-to-read, interesting, and valuable to urban affairs decisionmakers." Length: 750 to 1,250 words. Pays $50 to $100.

PASSENGER TRANSPORT, 1100 17th St. N.W., Washington DC 20036. Editor: Albert Engelken. Published by the American Public Transit Association for those in urban mass transportation. Pays on publication. Very little material bought. Enclose S.A.S.E.
Nonfiction: Uses short, concise articles which can be documented on urban mass transportation. Latest news only. No airline, steamship, intercity bus or railroad news. Pays 40¢ per column inch.
Photos: Sometimes buys photographs with mss and with captions only, but standards are high. 8x10's preferred. No color.

POLICE TIMES MAGAZINE, 1100 N. E. 125th St., N. Miami FL 33161. Editor: Gerald S. Arenberg. For "law enforcement officers; federal, state, county, local, and private security." Monthly. Circulation: 50,000. Buys all rights. Buys 10 to 20 mss a year. Pays on publication. Will send a free sample copy to a writer on request. No query required. Reports "at once." Enclose S.A.S.E.
Nonfiction and Photos: Interested in articles about local police departments all over the nation including Mexico and Canada. In particular, short articles about what the police department is doing, any unusual arrests made, acts of valor of officers in the performance of duties, etc. Also articles on any police subject from prisons to reserve police. "We prefer newspaper style. Short and to the point. Photos and drawings are a big help." Length: 300 to 1,200 words. Payment is $5 to $15—up to $25 in some cases based on 1¢ a word." Uses b&w Polaroid and 8x10 b&w glossies, "if of particular value." Pays $1 for each photo used.

PUBLIC UTILITIES FORTNIGHTLY, Suite 502, 1828 L St. NW., Washington, DC 20036. Editor-in-Chief: Francis X. Welch. For utility executives, regulatory commissions, lawyers, etc. Semimonthly. Pays on publication. "Study our publication." Reports in 3 weeks. Enclose S.A.S.E.
Nonfiction: Length: 2,000 to 3,000 words. Pays $25 to $200.

RESERVE LAW, 2440 Freedom Dr., San Antonio TX 78217. Editor: Otto Vehle. Publication of Reserve Law Officers Association of America. For sheriffs, chiefs of police, other law enforcement officials and their reserve components. Established in 1969. Bimonthly. Circulation: "over 10,000." Not copyrighted. Payment on publication. Will send free sample copy to writer on request. Submit complete ms. Will consider photocopied submissions. Enclose S.A.S.E.
Nonfiction and Photos: "Articles describing police reserve and sheriff reserve organizations and their activities should be informative and interesting. Style should be simple, straightforward, and with a touch of humor when appropriate. We need current features on outstanding contemporary lawmen, both regular officers and reserves." Length: 500 to 2,000 words. "In most cases, ms should be accompanied by high contrast 8x10 b&w action photos, properly identified and captioned." Pays minimum of $10; plus $5 for first photo and $2.50 for additional photos used in same article. Also seeks material for the following columns: "Ichthus," a chaplain's column dealing with Christian law officers (100 to 500 words); "Law-Haw," humorous anecdotes about police work (40 to 60 words); "Fundamentals," basic "how-to's" of law enforcement (100 to 500 words). Payment in contributor's copies or a maximum of $50.
Fiction: "Fictionalized accounts of true police cases involving reserve officers will be accepted if they meet our needs." Length: 200 to 800 words. Pays maximum of $50.
Fillers: Jokes and short humor "of the law enforcement type." Length: 20 to 80 words. Pays maximum of $10.

SEARCH AND RESCUE MAGAZINE, P.O. Box 153, Montrose CA 91020. Editor: Dennis Kelley. For volunteer and paid professionals involved in search and rescue.

Established in 1973. Quarterly. Circulation: 1,800. Buys all rights, but will reassign rights to author after publication. Buys about 10 mss a year. Pays on acceptance. Will send sample copy to writer for $1.25. Reports in 2 weeks. Query first or submit complete ms. Enclose S.A.S.E.

Fiction, Nonfiction and Photos: All material must be related to search and rescue work. Particularly likes photo essays. Pays $25 to $100. No additional payment for b&w photos used with mss. Captions required.

STATE GOVERNMENT ADMINISTRATION, 17915-B Sky Park Blvd., Irvine CA 92707. Editor: David A. Reed. For "top officials, managers, administrators and legislators at the state level in the government of all 50 states." Published 8 times a year. Circulation: 12,600. Buys all rights. Buys 4 or 5 mss a year. Pays on publication. Will send a sample copy to a writer on request. Query first or submit complete ms. Submit seasonal material at least 2 months in advance of issue date. Reports in 4 to 6 weeks. Enclose S.A.S.E.

Nonfiction and Photos: "A great amount of free material comes in from 50 states and PR departments. Innovative methods that states are employing to increase the efficiency of administration, personnel management and training, revenue programs, issues facing states, new methods, procedures, and systems to reduce costs. We are management and administration oriented, as opposed to public works oriented. We are interested in environmental/pollution coverage." Length: 1,000 to 1,500 words. Pays 2¢ a word. 8x10 b&w glossies purchased with mss; captions required. Pays $2.50.

VIRGINIA MUNICIPAL REVIEW, P.O. Box 100, Travelers Bldg., Richmond VA 23201. Editor: Ralph L. Dombrower. For federal, state, city, town and county officials. Monthly magazine; 24 to 32 pages. Established in 1921. Circulation: 11,000. Not copyrighted. Payment on acceptance. Reports in 10 days. Query first. Enclose S.A.S.E.

Nonfiction and Photos: Articles on governmental subjects. Well-researched, informative; current problems. Length: 500 words maximum. Pays 10¢ a word. No additional payment made for b&w photos used with mss.

Groceries

The journals that follow are for owners and operators of retail food stores. Journals for food wholesalers, packers, warehousers, and caterers are classified with the Food Products, Processing, and Service journals. Publications for food vending machine operators are found in the Coin-Operated Machines category.

CONVENIENCE STORE NEWS, 254 W. 31 St., New York NY 10001. Editor: Jesse Stechel. For executives and buyers of convenience store retailing organizations and owners of individual stores. Established in 1969. Biweekly. Circulation: 8,000. Not copyrighted. Payment on publication. Will send free sample copy to writer on request. Enclose S.A.S.E.

Nonfiction and Photos: "News stories on developments in convenience store industry or developments that affect it, such as new laws and regulations; feature articles on successful operations." Pays $2 per column inch. B&w photos. Pays $5.

How To Break In: "The best way for a newcomer to break in would be with a news story from his area. They run an average of several hundred words. News material could be a new advertising campaign, an effective new promotion, the opening of a new store, or the promotion of an executive. Someone who can send us this sort of thing from outside New York can easily develop into a regular correspondent to whom we would assign feature work. We also buy feature stories. We like to see photos, and again, it helps if you're outside the New York area."

DELI NEWS, P.O. Box 706, Hollywood CA 90028. Editor: Michael Scott. For supermarket delicatessen buyers, retail store owners, chain store executives in California. Special issues: May, Dairy; June, Hot Dog; July, Sandwich; Sept., Fall Cheese Festival; Dec., Christmas holidays. Monthly. Circulation: 6,000. Not copyrighted. Pays on acceptance. Will send sample copy to writer for $1. Query not required. Enclose S.A.S.E.

Nonfiction: Delicatessen foods and store operations in California. Success stories. How products are made. Personal profile or company stories. Length: 1,500 words minimum. Pays $15 to $40.

Photos: Purchased with mss or captions only. B&w, clear, sharp, glossy. Pays $5 to $25.

Fiction: Humorous, with some connection or relation to supermarkets or food, preferably refrigerated products. Length: minimum 500 words. Pays $15 to $40.

Poetry: About supermarket deli departments or operators. Pays $5 to $10.

How To Break In: "I occasionally do an industry-wide research article on a deli food item. I tried but was unable to get material for an article on herring, which comes out of the Atlantic. Consumer or industry-executive interviews on various industry subjects are always good. I may do one on what is the best location for a deli within the supermarket. Retailers are always interested in merchandising and promotional ideas—including the pros and cons of various advertising methods, instore displays, couponing, pricing, etc. Product packaging is another important subject. Humorous fiction that is funny, and in some way connected to the food business is always welcome. Every year we need a Christmas feature that deals with foods."

FOODSMAN, 1001 E. Main St., Richmond VA 23219. Phone: 804-644-0731. Editor: Jay Lassiter. For food retailers, wholesalers, distributors. Monthly magazine; 40 to 50 pages. Established in 1939. Circulation: 12,500. Not copyrighted. Payment on publication. Will send free sample copy to writer on request. Query first. Queries handled immediately. Enclose S.A.S.E.

Nonfiction and Photos: "Consumer articles; anything of interest to food people. From attitude surveys, operational studies, general interest articles or photo layouts on store design. Emphasis is on mid-Atlantic region and helpful ideas to be implemented by either food retailers, wholesalers or distributors." Informational, interviews with government officials, profiles, think pieces, training reviews, spot news, successful business operations, new product, merchandising techniques. Length: open. Payment varies.

GROCERY COMMUNICATIONS, P.O. Box 925, Woodland Hills CA 91365. Phone: 213-883-7656. Editor: Steve Curran. For "food retailers in the 11 western states. Their interest: how to make a profit." Established in 1970. Monthly. Circulation: 36,000. Buys all rights. Buys about 20 mss a year. Pays on acceptance. Query first. Submit seasonal material 2 months in advance of issue date. Reports in 2 weeks. Enclose S.A.S.E.

Nonfiction and Photos: "We need short news stories on local operators, food brokers, enterprising retailers, new products given a push in local markets, new departments. Local meetings are covered. The writer should take an informative, objective marketing approach. We are very marketing oriented; we do need stringers in the 11 western states." Length: maximum 5,000 words. Pays $25 to $200. Pays $1 for local news clippings. 5x7 b&w photos purchased with mss; captions required.

PROGRESSIVE GROCER, 708 Third Ave., New York NY 10017. Phone: 212-490-1000. Editor: Edgar B. Walzer. For supermarket operators, managers, buyers; executives in the grocery business. Monthly magazine; 150 pages. Established in 1922. Circulation: 90,000. Rights purchased vary with author and material. May buy all rights, but will reassign rights to author after publication; first North American serial rights; first serial rights; second serial (reprint) rights or simultaneous rights. Buys about 10 mss a year. Payment on acceptance. Will send free sample copy to writer on request. Write for copy of guidelines for writers. Will consider photocopied and simultaneous submissions. Submit seasonal merchandising material (spring, summer, fall, holiday) 3 months in advance. Reports in 2 to 3 weeks. Query first. Enclose S.A.S.E.

Nonfiction and Photos: Articles on supermarket merchandising; success stories; consumer relations pieces; promotional campaigns; personal pieces about people in the business. How grocers manage to relate and communicate with consumers via smart programs that really work. Tight, direct, informal, colorful writing needed. Does not want to see anything about quaint little "mom and pop" stores or "run of mill" stores with nothing more than half-hearted gourmet sections. Length: open. Pays minimum of 5¢ a word. Pays minimum of $15 for b&w glossies; $25 for color. Captions required. Department Editor: Joseph S. Coyle.

TEXAS FOOD MERCHANT, 1701 LaSalle, Waco TX 76705. Editor: Sarah Dudik. For people interested primarily in the food industry. Monthly magazine, 28 pages. Established in 1928. Circulation: 4,000. Rights purchased vary with author and material. Payment on publication. Will send free sample copy to writer on request. Will consider photocopied and simultaneous submissions. Uses material for Christmas, Spring, Easter, Summer, Fall, Thanksgiving. Submit seasonal material 3 months in advance. Submit only complete ms. Reports immediately. Enclose S.A.S.E.
Nonfiction, Photos and Fillers: "Articles about the food industry, personnel, etc. We do use local and state as well as national issues." Informational, how-to, interview, profile, inspirational, humor, think articles, successful business operations, new product, merchandising techniques, and technical articles. No length limits. Pays 2¢ a word; higher for exceptional material. Photos purchased with accompanying ms with no additional payment. Also uses jokes and short humor.

Grooming Products and Services

AMERICAN HAIRDRESSER/SALON OWNER, 100 Park Ave., New York NY 10017. Phone: 212-532-5588. Editor: Irene Frangides. For beauty shop owners and operators. Monthly. Buys all rights. Pays on publication. Reports "6 weeks prior to publication." Enclose S.A.S.E.
Nonfiction: "Technical material; is mainly staff-written." Pays $25 per magazine page.

HAIRSTYLIST, Allied Publications Inc., P.O. Box 23505, Fort Lauderdale FL 33307. Associate Editor: Marie Stilkind. Buys North American serial rights only. Pays on acceptance. Query not necessary. Reports in 2 to 4 weeks. Enclose S.A.S.E.
Nonfiction and Photos: Wants "articles of general interest to the professional beautician." Interested in how-to's, interviews, and profiles. Length: 500 to 1,000 words. Payment is 5¢ a word. Pays $5 for b&w glossy photos of hairstyles.

PROFESSIONAL MEN'S HAIRSTYLIST, 100 Park Ave., New York NY 10017. Editor: Sandra Kosherick. For "men and women serving the men's hairstyling and barbering profession." Monthly. Circulation: 65,000. Rights purchased vary with author and material. Buys 10 to 12 mss a year. Pays on publication. Will send a sample copy to a writer on request. Write for copy of guidelines for writers. Query first. Submit seasonal material 2 months in advance of issue date. Enclose S.A.S.E.
Nonfiction and Photos: "Matter only relating to the hairstyling profession. Material should be technical—written from the viewpoint of professionals. Currently overworked are articles on female barbers or hairstylists and unisex salons. We're interested in articles on new trends in men's hairstyling." Buys informational articles, how-to's, interviews, coverage of successful business operations, articles on merchandising techniques, and technical articles. Length: 750 to 2,500 words. Pays $25 to $75. 8x10 b&w glossies purchased with mss and on assignment. Pays $25.

WOMAN BEAUTIFUL, Allied Publications, Inc., P.O. Box 23505, Fort Lauderdale FL 33307. Associate Editor: Marie Stilkind. For "students at beauty schools and people who go to beauty salons." Buys North American serial rights only. Pays on acceptance. Reports in 2 to 4 weeks. Enclose S.A.S.E. with all submissions.
Nonfiction and Photos: "Articles on hairstyling, beauty, and fashion." Length: 500 to 1,000 words. Pays 5¢ per accepted word. Pays $5 for photos of hairstyles.

Hardware

In this classification are journals for general hardware wholesalers and retailers, locksmiths, and retailers of miscellaneous special hardware items. Journals specializing in the retailing of hardware for a certain trade, such as plumbing or automotive supplies, are classified with the other publications for that trade.

CHAIN SAW AGE, 3435 N.E. Broadway, Portland OR 97232. Editor: Norman W. Raies. For "mostly chain saw dealers (retailers); small businesses—typically small town, typical ages, interests, education." Monthly. Circulation: 10,000. Not copyrighted. Buys "very few" mss a year. Payment on acceptance or publication—"varies." Will send a sample copy to a writer on request. Query first. Will consider photocopied submissions. Enclose S.A.S.E.
Nonfiction and Photos: "Must relate to chain saw use, merchandising, adaptation, manufacture, or display." Buys informational articles, how-to's, personal experience articles, interviews, profiles, inspirational articles, personal opinion articles, photo features, coverage of successful business operations, and articles on merchandising techniques. Length: 500 to 1,000 words. Pays $20 to $50 ("2½¢ a word plus photo fees"). Photos purchased with mss, without mss, or on assignment; captions required. For b&w glossies, pay "varies."

CHAIN SAW INDUSTRY AND POWER EQUIPMENT DEALER, Louisiana Bank Bldg., P.O. Box 1703, Shreveport LA 71166. Phone: 318-222-3062. Editor: O.M. Word. For chain saw and outdoor power equipment dealers. Bimonthly. Buys first rights. Buys 1 or 2 articles per issue. Pays on publication. Will send free sample copy on request. Reports as quickly as possible. Enclose S.A.S.E. for return of submissions.
Nonfiction: Articles on successful or unusual chain saw and other small outdoor power equipment dealers, explaining factors which make them so. Human interest material necessary. Articles on unusual uses or unusual users of these tools. Articles on dealers whose profits have increased through diversification of stock. Information on new markets and accessory items. Slant to help dealers do a better job of merchandising. Reader audience varies from large hardware dealers in major cities to crossroad filling station shops in rural areas. Length: 1,000 to 1,500 words. Pays 3½¢ a word.
Photos: Purchased with mss or with captions. B&w, sharp, action if possible; caption must include identification. Pays $5.

HARDWARE AGE, Chilton Way, Radnor PA 19089. Phone: 215-687-8200. Editor: Jon P. Kinslow. For "manufacturers, wholesalers, and retailers in the hardware/housewares/lawn and garden industry. About half of our circulation is independent hardware retailers, and another significant portion is mass merchandisers." Established in 1857. Monthly. Circulation: 50,000. Buys all rights. Buys about 10 mss a year. Pays on acceptance. Will send a sample copy to a writer for $1. Write for copy of guidelines for writers. Query first or submit complete ms. Will not consider photocopied submissions. Submit seasonal material 3 months in advance. Reports in 3 weeks. Enclose S.A.S.E.
Nonfiction: "Articles relating how hardlines retailers increase sales and profits through better management, merchandising, etc. Generally these articles are built around a specific product category. Field research by our own editorial staff is quite thorough." Does not want to see "the round-up story on a single store which tells how that one store does a good job—usually, a good job on everything! Tell us how one store does one thing well. Better yet, tell us how several stores in different parts of the country do one thing well. We have a strong emphasis on the large volume hardlines outlet. Also, we aim for features that are more in-depth—both in the information and the geographic coverage. We have on occasion covered such non-merchandising subjects as product liability, consumerism, and black employment

in the hardware industry." Length: open. Pays $100 to $125 "for a good piece with text and photos filling three pages." Captioned photos purchased with mss, without mss, or on assignment. "Photo subjects should be the same as nonfiction, and no people in the photos, please." For b&w, submit enlargements or proof sheets and negatives. Pays $10 to $15 per b&w photo, "more for series of related photos." Pays $15 minimum for color. "Prefer proof sheets. We will select for enlargements." Dept. Editor: Chris Kelly, Managing Editor.
Fillers: "Short fillers on management/merchandising." Pays $10 to $15.

HARDWARE MERCHANDISING, 481 University Ave., Toronto 1, Ont., Canada. Editor: Starr Smith. For "hardware retailers and hardware and houseware buyers across Canada." Monthly. Circulation: 8,900. Rights purchased vary with author and material. Buys about 12 mss a year. Pays on acceptance. Will consider cassette submissions. Query first. Enclose S.A.E. and International Reply Coupons.
Nonfiction and Photos: "Any articles demonstrating ways to increase profit for the above audience. The approach must be geared to management improving profit/ image picture in retailing. This is a Canadian book for Canadians." Buys informational articles, how-to's, coverage of successful business operations and merchandising techniques, new product articles, and technical articles. Length: open. Pays 8¢ minimum per word. 8x10 b&w glossies purchased with mss; captions optional.

NORTHERN HARDWARE TRADE, 5901 Brooklyn Blvd., Suite 203, Minneapolis MN 55429. Phone: 612-533-0066. Editor: Edward Gonzales. For "owners, managers of hardware and discount stores and lumber yards and home centers; hardware, sporting good, wholesalers." Special issues include lawn and garden (Jan., Feb.), fishing tackle (March, April), and hunting equipment (June, July). Established in 1971. Monthly. Circulation: 16,500. Not copyrighted. Buys about 12 mss a year. Pays on publication. Will send a sample copy to a writer on request. Query first or submit complete ms. Submit seasonal material 3 months in advance of issue date. Enclose S.A.S.E.
Nonfiction and Photos: "Case histories on successful retail stores." Buys how-to's and articles on successful business operations. Pays 4¢ a word. B&w photos purchased with mss. Pays $5.

OUTDOOR POWER EQUIPMENT, 3339 W. Freeway, P. O. Box 1570, Fort Worth TX 76101. Publisher: Bill Quinn. Established in 1959. Monthly. Circulation: 10,000. Not copyrighted. Pays on publication. Query first. Enclose S.A.S.E.
Nonfiction and Photos: Photo-story of a single outstanding feature on power equipment stores (lawnmower, snowblower, garden tractors, chain saws, tiller, snowmobiles, etc.). Feature can be a good display, interior or exterior; sales tip; service tip; unusual sign; advertising or promotion tip; store layout; demonstrations, etc. Photos must be vertical. One 8x10 photo sufficient. Length: 200 to 300 words. Pays $32.50 to $37.50.

OUTDOOR POWER PRODUCTS/EQUIPEMENT MOTORISE PLEIN AIR, 481 University Ave., Toronto 1, Ont., Canada. Phone: 416-595-1811. Editor: Starr Smith. 8 times a year. Usually buys first North American rights, but it varies. Pays on acceptance or on publication "as per agreement." Will consider cassette submissions. Query first. Enclose S.A.E. and International Reply Coupons.
Nonfiction: "We're interested in any new approach to increase the profitability of an outdoor power products dealer." Material is rejected if not Canadian in content or if it's poor quality. Length: open. Pays 8¢ minimum per word.

SOUTHERN HARDWARE, 1760 Peachtree Rd., N.W., Atlanta GA 30309. Phone: 404-874-4462. Editor: Ralph E. Kirby. For retailers of hardware and allied lines. Established in 1900. Monthly. Circulation: 16,000. Buys all rights. Buys 50 mss a year. Payment on acceptance. Will send free sample copy to writer on request. Write for copy of guidelines for writers. Submit seasonal material 3 to 4 months in advance. Reports on material accepted for publication in 30 days. Returns rejected material immediately. Query first. Enclose S.A.S.E.

Nonfiction and Photos: "Articles dealing with the sales and merchandising activities of specific southern hardware retailers; new home centers and stores serving do-it-yourself customers." Successful business operations; merchandising techniques. Bulletin on special seasonal issues should be requested. Length: 4 double-spaced pages, maximum. Pays $30 to $100. 5x7 or 8x10 b&w photos purchased with or without ms. Captions required. Pays $5 to $20, depending on quality.

Home Furnishings and Appliances

APPLIANCE SERVICE NEWS, 5841 Montrose Ave., Chicago IL 60634. Editor: J. J. Charous. For professional appliance service people from both urban and rural areas whose main interest is the repairing of major and portable appliances. Their jobs consists of either service shop owner, service manager, or service technician. Monthly "newspaper style" publication; 24 pages. Established in 1950. Circulation: 41,350. Buys all rights. Buys about 2 mss per issue. Payment on publication. Will send free sample copy to writer on request. Write for copy of guidelines for writers. Will not consider photocopied submissions. Will consider simultaneous submissions. Reports in about 1 month. Query first. Enclose S.A.S.E.
Nonfiction and Photos: "The types of articles we publish directly relate to the business of repairing appliances. We want articles that affect service and the business it involves. We don't want articles explaining how one can get the most out of salesmen or how to increase sales. We do, however, want articles on how a servicer can better operate his service business and how to increase his service business in his community. Each month, we run a technical article explaining how a specific appliance is repaired. Others inform the service person about how he can improve his business operation. We prefer that the freelancer write in a straightforward, easy-to-understand style about the appliance repair industry. Writing should be crisp and interesting, as well as highly informational. We prefer that articles concern appliance service people, i.e., people who repair refrigerators, ranges, washing machines, toasters, microwave ovens, etc. Electronics, like TV's, radios, etc., are not our territory. We are looking for material on how service people can beat inflation and the recession." Length: open. Pays 5¢ per word. Pays $10 for b&w photos used with mss. Captions required. Department Editor: James J. Hodl.

CASUAL LIVING MAGAZINE, Time & Life Bldg., 1271 Avenue of the Americas, New York NY 10020. Phone: 212-586-2806. Editor: Marvin L. Wilder. For retailers and manufacturers of summer and casual furniture and accessories. Monthly. Circulation: 10,500. Buys all rights. Pays on publication. Query first. Reports in 2 weeks. Enclose S.A.S.E.
Nonfiction: "Articles on how various department stores, discount houses and specialty stores used advertising, promotion and display to improve business. Should be well-written, well-slanted, non-blurb material with good b&w photos." Length: 500 to 1,000 words. Pays $80.
Photos: Anything pertaining to outdoor and casual furniture industry; purchased with mss. Pays $5 each for 8x10's.

CHINA GLASS & TABLEWARE, 1115 Clifton Ave., Clifton NJ 07013. Editor: Donald Doctorow. Monthly. Pays on publication. Query first. Reports within 4 weeks. Enclose S.A.S.E.
Nonfiction and Photos: Interested in articles on department store and specialty shop china, glass, silverware and tableware merchandising ideas; special promotion, display techniques, advertising programs, and retail activities in this field. Length: 1,000 to 2,000 words. Pays $35 a published page. Photos with suitable captions should accompany articles.

CONSUMER ELECTRONICS, 201 E. 42 St., New York NY 10017. Editor: Cathy Ciccolella. Buys first rights. Pays on publication. Query first. Enclose S.A.S.E.
Nonfiction and Photos: Publishes "news stories dealing with successful promotions of home electronics products. New store openings and other news of interest to

retailers of radio, TV, high fidelity, tape and other consumer electronics." Pays 5¢ a word as a basic rate; more with photos.

FLOORING MAGAZINE, 757 Third Ave., New York NY 10017. Editor: Michael Korsonsky. For floor covering retailers, wholesalers, floor covering specifiers, architects, etc. Monthly. Circulation: 20,000. Buys all rights. Buys 10 to 12 mss a year. Payment on acceptance. Will send free sample copy to writer on request. Query first. Reports on material in 2 to 4 weeks. Enclose S.A.S.E.

Nonfiction and Photos: "Merchandising articles, new industry developments, unusual installations of floor coverings, etc. Conversational approach; snappy, interesting leads; plenty of quotes." Informational, how-to, interview, successful business operations, merchandising techniques, technical. Length: 1,500 to 1,800 words. Pays 5¢ to 10¢ a word. 5x7 or 8x10 b&w photos. Pays $5. Color transparencies (when specified). Pays $7.50. Captions required.

FURNITURE & FURNISHINGS, 1450 Don Mills Rd., Don Mills, Ontario, M3B 2X7, Canada. Phone: 416-445-6641. Editor: Ronald H. Shuker. For an audience that includes all associated with making and selling furniture, floorcoverings and fabrics, as well as suppliers in the trade; lamps and accessories manufacturers and dealers; decorators and designers; domestic and contract readers (not consumers). Monthly magazine (tab size); 28 pages. Established in 1910. Circulation: 11,500. Buys first Canadian serial rights. Buys 20 mss a year. Payment on publication. Will send free sample copy to writer on request. Write for copy of editorial guidelines for writers. Will not consider photocopied submissions if they have been made to other Canadian media. Submit special material for Market Previews and Product Reports 2 months in advance. Reports on material accepted for publication in 1 month. Returns rejected material immediately. Query first. Enclose S.A.E. and International Reply Coupons.

Nonfiction and Photos: "The magazine is not news-oriented. Rather, it is more feature-oriented, covering various subjects in depth. Very much a merchandising magazine for home furnishings retailers in Canada. We publish merchandising and retailer success stories; product trends; management articles; promotion/advertising programs. Styles, designs, color trends. Emphasis is on how-to—what others can learn from what others are doing. Writing is tight, semi-aggressive, and interesting. We'd like to see feature reports analyzing the retail situation in various cities and towns in Canada; who are the top retailers in each center and why; or personality profiles of people in this industry. We do not want U.S. or foreign-oriented articles unless they report on trends in styles, designs, colors and materials used in furniture, floorcoverings, fabrics appearing in major trade shows in the U.S. and Europe with photos showing examples of these trends. Must be aimed at Canadian readers." Length: 500 to 2,000 words. Pays up to $250 or more. Pays $10 for b&w photos purchased with mss. Captions required.

FURNITURE DESIGN AND MANUFACTURING, 7373 N. Lincoln Ave., Chicago IL 60646. Editor: Raymond A. Helmers. For furniture manufacturers and designers. Monthly. Usually buys first publication rights. Pays on publication. Query first. Reports in 2 weeks. Enclose S.A.S.E.

Nonfiction and Photos: "Most material is staff-produced. Very, very limited market for freelance writers; then only those with proven technical knowledge." Wants technical and management articles dealing only with the volume mass production of furniture of all kinds—the methods, materials and tools used by modern, progressive plants. Length: 3,000 words. Pay: open. Photos purchased with ms.

GIFT & TABLEWARE REPORTER, 1515 Broadway, New York NY 10036. Phone: 212-764-7317. Editor: Jack McDermott. For "merchants (department store buyers, specialty shop owners) engaged in the resale of giftwares, china and glass, decorative accessories." Biweekly. Circulation: 20,000. Buys all rights. Buys 150 to 200 mss a year. Pays on acceptance. Will send a sample copy to a writer on request. Query first or submit complete ms. Will consider photocopied submissions. Reports "immediately." Enclose S.A.S.E. for return of submissions.

Nonfiction: "New store announcements, retail store success stories. Be brief, be factual, describe a single merchandising gimmick. Our distinguishing factor is conciseness, fast-moving factuality. We are a tabloid format—glossy stock. Descriptions of store interiors are less important than a sales performance. We're interested in articles on aggressive selling tactics." Buys coverage of successful business operations and merchandising techniques. Length: 300 words. Pays "minimum $2.50 for first inch on galley, $1 for each additional inch."

Photos: Purchased with and without mss and on assignment; captions optional. "Individuals are to be identified." For b&w glossies, pays $6.

Fillers: "Newsbreaks on new store openings." Length: 50 to 100 words. Pays "$2.50 for first inch, $1 for each additional inch."

GIFTS & DECORATIVE ACCESSORIES, 51 Madison Ave., New York NY 10010. Phone: 212-689-4411. Editor: Phyllis Sweed. For the "quality gift and decorative accessories retailer, independent store and department store." Established in 1917. Monthly. Circulation: over 26,000. Buys all rights. Buys 10 to 12 mss a year. Payment on publication. Write for copy of guidelines for writers. Submit seasonal material 2 to 3 months *in advance* of the following deadlines: Bridal, February 15 or July 15; Christmas, July 1; resort merchandising, January 15. Reports on material in 3 months. Query first. Enclose S.A.S.E.

Nonfiction and Photos: "Our features deal with all retail phases of the gift industry; dealer case histories (a store problem and how someone solved it); dealer activities (displays, promotions, new stores, enlargements, remodelings); dealer opinions as they relate to the gift store (on matters relating to business policy, industry problems, industry controversies). Stories also deal with subjects of direct interest to gift retailers: style trends, marketing trends, shifts in consumer buying habits, statistical surveys and other 'think piece' subjects. In case histories, be clear with detailed step-by-step descriptions of the 'how' angle. In dealer activity pieces, probe beneath obvious surface things to the 'reasons why'. In opinion articles, offer positive solutions to problems, or at least present both sides. In all stories, remember that nothing works better than short, declarative sentences with an entertaining lilt where possible." Most acceptable are case history stories with good photos. Length: 1,000 to 5,000 words. Pays $25 to $100. 5x7 or 8x10 clear and sharp b&w photos purchased with ms. Pays $7.50. 4x5 transparencies (sharp color prints) or 35mm can be used. Pays $7.50 for 35mm; $15 for 4x5 color transparencies.

LINENS, DOMESTICS AND BATH PRODUCTS, 370 Lexington Ave., New York NY 10017. Editor: Ruth Lyons. For department store, mass merchandiser, specialty store and bath boutique. 6 times a year. Buys all rights. Pays on publication. No photocopied submissions. Reports in 4 to 6 weeks. Query first. Enclose S.A.S.E.

Nonfiction and Photos: Merchandising articles which educate the buyer on sales trends, legislation, industry news, styles; in-depth articles with photos on retail sales outlets for bath products, linens and sheets, towels, bedspreads. Length: 700 to 900 words. Pays $30 a published page ("the average article is 1 to 3 pages long"). Photos purchased with mss. For b&w glossies, pays $5. For Ektachrome color, pays $30.

MART MAGAZINE, Berkshire Common, Pittsfield MA 01201. Editor: Jack Adams. For retailers, distributors, and manufacturers of home appliances and home electronic items. Semimonthly. Circulation: 54,000. Buys exclusive rights in retailing field. "Substantial increase in size of editorial staff has lessened need for freelance material at this time, although will not pass up outstanding stories." Pays on acceptance. Will send free sample copy on request. Special Christmas Merchandising Issue, deadline Sept. 10; Gift Giving Issue, deadline March; Air Conditioning Issue, deadline Jan. 20. Reports in 3 weeks. Query first. Enclose S.A.S.E.

Nonfiction: Articles and case histories showing how retailers successfully merchandise home appliances or home electronic items. Length: 500 to 750 words. Pays $50 to $100.

Photos: Uses photos of good displays, especially Christmas displays. 8x10 glossy preferred; 2¼x2¼ or 4x5 color shots also used. For b&w, pays $10.

NHFA REPORTS, 405 Merchandise Mart, Chicago IL 60654. Editor: Peggy Heaton. For top management of stores specializing in all home furnishings products. Monthly magazine; 80 to 100 pages. Established in 1923. Circulation: 15,000. Buys all rights. Buys 2 to 3 mss a year. Payment on publication. Will send free sample copy to writer on request. Reports immediately. Query first. Enclose S.A.S.E.

Nonfiction and Photos: Articles on managing, merchandising, operating the home furnishings store in all facets from advertising to warehousing. Concise and very factual reporting of new developments or activities within the retail store with explanation of why and how something was accomplished, and results or benefits. "We largely present 'success' stories that give ideas the reader might want to adapt to his own individual operation." Interested in material on special services to consumers, internal cost-cutting measures, traffic-building efforts; how the small store competes with the giants; unusual display techniques or interesting store architecture. Does not want to see straight publicity or "puff" articles about store owners or their operations, with no news value or interest to others on a national basis, or articles that are too general with no specific point. Length: 800 to 2,000 words. Pays 4½¢ per word. 5x7 b&w glossy photos are purchased with or without mss, or on assignment. Pays $5. Captions optional.

RETAILER AND MARKETING NEWS, P.O. Box 57194, Dallas TX 75207. Editor: Michael J. Anderson. For "retail dealers and wholesalers in appliances, television, and furniture." Monthly. Circulation: 10,000. Buys all rights. Buys 3 mss a year. Pays on publication. Will send a free sample copy to a writer on request. No query required. Will consider photocopied submissions. Mss will not be returned unless S.A.S.E. is enclosed.

Nonfiction: "How a retail dealer can make more profit" is the approach. Wants "sales promotion ideas, advertising, sales tips, business builders, and the like, localized to the southwest and particularly to north Texas." Length: 100 to 500 words. Payment is $5 to $20.

Fillers: Newsbreaks, jokes, short humor. Pays $5.

SOUTHWEST FURNITURE NEWS, 4313 N. Central, P.O. Box 64667, Dallas TX 75206. Editor: Cinde Weatherby. For retail home furnishing business people; home furnishings manufacturers, and others in related fields. Magazine; 50 to 100 pages. Established in 1923. Circulation: 10,000. Not copyrighted. Buys 2 mss a year. Pays on publication. Sometimes pays in copies only. Will send a free sample to writer on request. No photocopied or simultaneous submissions. Reports in 2 weeks. Query first. Enclose S.A.S.E.

Nonfiction: Informational articles about selling, construction of furniture, credit, business, freight, and transportation. "Must have honest, well-researched approach. Would like to see something on freight or flammability regulations." Interview, nostalgia, new product, merchandising techniques, technical. Length: 300 to 1,500 words. Pays $50 maximum. Occasionlly pays in copies only.

UPHOLSTERING INDUSTRY MAGAZINE, 600 S. Michigan Ave., Chicago IL 60605. Phone: 312-427-2493. Editor: Dorothy Jerome. For "upholstery manufacturers, custom upholsterers, furniture designers, fabric distributors." Established in 1888. Monthly. Circulation: 16,000. Buys first North American serial rights. Buys about 6 mss a year. Pays on publication. Will send a sample copy to a writer on request. Query first or submit complete ms. Will not consider photocopied submissions. Submit seasonal material 2 months in advance. Reports "at once." Enclose S.A.S.E.

Nonfiction and Photos: "Straightforward articles dealing with technical and mechanical aspects of furniture manufacturing, fabric manufacturing and distribution ... businesslike." Buys informational articles, how-to's, interviews, profiles, exposes, coverage of successful business operations, and operations of upholstering and reupholstering. Length: "sufficient for story." Pays $85. Photos purchased with mss; captions required. For b&w glossies, pays $5.

Hospitals, Nursing, and Nursing Homes

In this listing are journals for nurses; medical and nonmedical nursing home, clinical, and hospital staffs; and laboratory technicians and managers. Journals for physicians in private practice or that publish technical material on new discoveries in medicine will be found in the Medical category.

DOCTORS' NURSE BULLETIN, 9600 Colesville Rd., Silver Spring MD 20901. Editor: Bob Bickford. Quarterly. Occasionally copyrighted. Pays on publication. Reports in a few days. Enclose S.A.S.E.
Nonfiction: Uses articles of interest to the doctor's nurse. Pays from $5 to $50, depending on length and value.
Photos: Buys photographs with mss and with captions only. B&w only. Pays $3 minimum.

HOSPITAL PROGRESS, 1438 S. Grand, St. Louis MO 63104. Phone: 314-773-0646. Editor: Robert J. Stephens. For hospital and nursing home administrators, trustees and department heads. Monthly magazine; 100 (8¼x11¼) pages. Established in 1920. Circulation: 16,000. Buys all rights. Buys no more than 5 mss a year. Payment on publication. Will send sample copy to writer for $1. Will consider photocopied submissions. Will not consider simultaneous submissions. Reports in 3 months. Query first. Enclose S.A.S.E.
Nonfiction and Photos: Items of interest to Catholic institutions, as well as material on business office techniques, flood and disaster stories. Must be written for professionals and community service people. Informational, how-to, think pieces, successful business operations. Length: 1,500 to 3,000 words. Pays $25 per published page. Pays $10 for b&w photos purchased with mss.

HOSPITAL SUPERVISOR'S BULLETIN, 681 Fifth Ave., New York NY 10022. Editor: Phyllis D. Alexander. For hospital supervisors of non-medical areas: clerical, laundry, kitchen, maintenance, etc. Semimonthly. Query first to The Editor. Pays on acceptance. Buys all rights. Enclose S.A.S.E.
Nonfiction: Interview-based articles, quoting by name topnotch hospital supervisors in public and voluntary hospitals who tell what today's problems are in hospital supervision, how they solve these problems, what results they're getting, illustrated by examples from daily hospital life. Emphasis on good methods of "getting things done through others." Problem areas: motivation, communication, self-development, planning, absenteeism and tardiness, job enrichment, goal-setting, supervising the undereducated, training, disciplining, personnel shortages, getting employees to accept change. Wants factual, accurate reporting; no "atmosphere" needed. Length: prefers 2- to 3-page articles; a page has about 450 words. Pays $25 a printed page.

JOURNAL OF PRACTICAL NURSING, 122 E. 42 St., New York NY 10017. Editor: Candace S. Gulko, R.N. For practical nurses, practical nurse educators, registered nurses, hospital and nursing home administrators, and other allied health professionals. Monthly magazine; 32 to 44 pages. Established in 1951. Circulation: 38,000. Buys, or acquires, all rights. Buys, or accepts, 10 to 20 mss a year. Payment, when made, is on publication. Seventy percent of the material is contributed without any payment, except for contributor's copies. Will send free sample copy to writer on request. Write for copy of guidelines for writers. Will not consider photocopied or simultaneous submissions. Reports in 1 month. Query first. Enclose S.A.S.E.
Nonfiction and Photos: "Clinical articles on new developments in treatment, new approaches to patient care, research in medicine, learning approaches, books, nursing experience, human interest. Special emphasis should be on the attitude or approach of the practical nurse." Uses informational, how-to, personal experience, interviews, profiles, inspirational, historical, think, expose and personal opinion and technical

articles. Recently published articles include "Urinary Ostomy in Childhood," and "Guided Tour of an ICN." Length: 800 to 2,000 words. Rate of payment is $10 to $50, but 70% of material is contributed without payment, except for contributor's copies. No additional payment for b&w photos used with mss. Captions required.
Poetry and Fillers: Only accepts poetry occasionally. Traditional, blank verse and free verse. Crossword puzzles. Does not pay for poetry or fillers.

MEDICAL LAB, 750 Third Ave., New York NY 10017. Phone: 212-697-8300. Editor: Margaret Howell. For chief and supervisory medical technologists. Monthly. Buys all rights, "but very liberal about granting reprint and copy permissions." Pays on publication. Will consider cassette submissions. Query first. Reports in 1 week. Enclose S.A.S.E.
Nonfiction and Photos: New medical advances as applied to the clinical laboratory. Straight technical material, operational features, economics in the lab, and how-to features are also invited. Length: maximum 1,500 words. Photos should accompany ms. Pays $25 to $100, plus $5 a photo.

MEDICAL RECORD NEWS, 875 N. Michigan Ave., Suite 1850, John Hancock Building, Chicago IL 60611. Phone: 312-787-2672. Editor: Mary J. Waterstraat. For "persons (of all ages) in hospitals and other health care facilities who are responsible for the medical record department; also edited for hospital administrators, information scientists, medical educators; biostatisticians, insurance representatives, systems analysts, medico-legal authorities, federal and state health officials, medical record students, etc." Established in 1928. Bimonthly. Circulation: 12,000. Buys all rights. Buys 3 or 4 mss a year. Pays on acceptance. Will send a sample copy to a writer for $2. Will consider photocopied submissions. Reports in 2 to 3 weeks. Query first. Enclose S.A.S.E.
Nonfiction: "Articles deal with recording and transcribing systems and equipment, record retention, record retrieval, photocopying, microfilming, and microfiche, analyzing, summarizing, computerizing, and making available patient case histories for medical research. Do not just play up a specific product or manufacturer—if a system is being utilized which is unique or somewhat unusual, tell why and how, etc., then end the article. Use a fresh, intelligent, instructive, informative approach. We are interested in new systems being put to use or recently initiated; articles that are bylined by registered record administrators or accredited record technicians concerning new products or systems." Buys informational articles, how-to's, coverage of successful business operations, and technical articles. Length: 1,200 to 3,500 words. Pays $45 to $125. Department Editor: Marshall Dick.
Photos: Purchased with or without mss or on assignment; captions optional. For 5x7 or 8x10 "sharp, interesting" b&w photos, pays $5 to $10.

NURSING CARE, 75 E. 55th St., New York NY 10022. Phone: 212-688-7110. Editor: Fyat Raines. For licensed practical nurses. 12 times a year. Circulation: 65,000. Buys North American serial rights. Pays on publication. Will send free sample copy on request. Query first. Enclose S.A.S.E.
Nonfiction: Nursing articles geared specifically to licensed practical nurses and their profession. "Some of our popular stories have included a nurse's firsthand account of a patient with ulcerative colitis; a nurse's first experience with a schizophrenic patient; instructional pieces in the fields of psychiatry, obstetrics, pediatrics, and gynecology; articles on continuing education and career opportunities. For instance, in the last category, we ran a series on nurses in doctors' offices, industrial nursing, and nurses working in the home. I'd like more first-person stories from nurse-writers, more on nutrition and more articles from doctors." Length: maximum 2,500 words. Pays $25 minimum per article.

PROFESSIONAL MEDICAL ASSISTANT, One East Wacker Dr., Chicago IL 60601. Editor: Esther A. Strom. "About 95% of our subscribers belong to the American Association of Medical Assistants. They are professional people employed by a doctor of medicine." Established in 1957. Bimonthly. Circulation: 18,000. Rights purchased vary with author and material. Buys about 3 mss a year. Pays on acceptance. Will send a sample copy to a writer on request. Submit complete ms. Will consider photocopied submissions. Reports in 2 weeks. Enclose S.A.S.E.

Nonfiction and Photos: "Articles dealing with clinical, clerical, and administrative procedures in a physician's office. Request our publication to study for the style we require." Buys informational articles, how-to's, and humor. Length: 500 to 2,500 words. Pays $15 to $50. 8x10 b&w glossies purchased with mss; captions required. Pays $20 to $50.

Fillers: Jokes; "crosswords for allied health personnel." Payment $5 to $20.

RN, 496 Kinderkamack Rd., Oradell NJ 07649. Editor: John H. Lavin. For registered nurses, mostly hospital-based but also in physicians' offices, public health, schools, industry. Monthly magazine of 100 pages. Established in 1937. Circulation: 240,000. Buys all rights. Buys 20 to 30 mss a year. Payment on acceptance. Will send free sample copy on request. Write for copy of guidelines for writers. Will not consider photocopied or simultaneous submissions. Reports in 2 to 3 weeks. Query first or submit complete ms. Enclose S.A.S.E.

Nonfiction and Photos: "If you are a nurse who writes, we would like to see your work. Editorial content: diseases, clinical techniques, surgery, therapy, research, equipment, drugs, etc. These should be thoroughly researched and sources cited. Personal anecdotes, experiences, observations based on your relations with doctors, hospitals, and the public. Legal problems, insurance, taxes, income, expenses as they affect nurses. Our style is simple, direct, not preachy. Do include examples, case histories that relate the reader to her own nursing experience. Talk mostly about people, rather than things. Dashes of humor or insight are always welcome. Include photos where feasible." Length: 1,800 words maximum. Pays up to 10¢ per word; $35 minimum for b&w photos.

How To Break In: "Most material we buy is written by R.N.s. A freelancer has to have some technical expertise in our field and understand our audience. His best bet: study the magazine before he tries to write for it."

Hotels, Motels, Clubs, Resorts, Restaurants

Journals which emphasize retailing for bar and beverage operators are classified in the Beverages and Bottling category. For publications slanted to food wholesalers, processors, and caterers, see Food Products, Processing, and Service.

CLUB & FOOD SERVICE, P.O. Box 788, 211 Broadway, Lynbrook NY 11563. Editor: Glenn E. Flood. For men and women who are managers and supervisors of U.S. military clubs and food service operations and Washington policy writers regarding military welfare and recreation; Congressmen, etc. Monthly magazine; 48 pages. Established in 1966. Circulation: 12,000. Buys all rights. Buys 3 mss a year. Payment on acceptance. Will send free copy to writer on request. Write for copy of guidelines for writers. Will not consider simultaneous submissions. Reports in 1 month. Query first or submit complete ms. Enclose S.A.S.E.

Nonfiction and Photos: Interested in new ideas in management; interviews with club and food service leaders; how certain businesses operate; facilities; budget managing; how to increase profits. Informational, how-to, think pieces, spot news, merchandising techniques. Length: 500 to 2,500 words. Pays 5¢ to 10¢ a word. Pays $7.50 for photos purchased with or without accompanying mss. Captions required.

CLUB EXECUTIVE, 1028 Connecticut Ave. N.W., Washington DC 20036. Phone: 202-296-4514. Editor: Paul E. Reece. For military club managers. Monthly. Not copyrighted. Pays on publication. Reports in 2 weeks. Enclose S.A.S.E.

Nonfiction: Articles about food and beverages, design, equipment, promotional ideas, etc. Length: 1,500 to 2,000 words. Pays 4¢ a word.

COMMERCIAL FOODSERVICE ILLUSTRATED, 2177 Ocean St., Marshfield MA 02050. Editor: Dick Howard. For men and women who own and operate restaurants, hotels, clubs; age 25 to 75. Magazine: 48 to 80 pages. Established in 1974. Bimonthly. Circulation: 125,000. Rights purchased vary with author and material. Usually buys all rights, but will reassign rights to author after publication. Buys 30 mss a year. Payment on acceptance. Will send free sample copy to writer on request. Submit seasonal material 2 months in advance. Query first. Enclose S.A.S.E.

Nonfiction and Photos: Business ideas and personality articles relative to restaurant business. Emphasis is on people, rather than organizations. Informational, interview, profile, personal opinion, successful business operations, merchandising techniques. Length: 100 to 1,000 words. Pays $50 to $2,500. No additional payment is made for 8x10 b&w glossies purchased with mss. Payment for photos purchased on assignment is negotiable. Minimum payment of $50.

FOOD EXECUTIVE, 508 IBM Building, Fort Wayne IN 46805. Phone: 219-484-1901. Associate Editor: Christina L. Brasher. For restaurant, hotel, cafeteria owners and managers. Bimonthly. Not copyrighted. Pays on acceptance. Query first. Enclose S.A.S.E.

Nonfiction: Material dealing with restaurant, institutional, industrial, and catering food service (includes government and military) operation and techniques such as cost control, personnel, portion control, layout and design, decor, merchandising. Also new trends in the food service industry, general economic problems, labor situations, training programs for personnel. Must be written for professionals in the field. Length: 500 to 2,000 words. Pays 1½¢ per word.

Photos: "Pertinent photos." Pays $3 to $5.

HOSPITALITY MAGAZINE, 614 Superior Ave., W., Cleveland OH 44113. Editor: Robert Kiener. For motel and hotel operators. Monthly. Buys all rights. Buys very little freelance material. Pays on publication. Query first. Enclose S.A.S.E.

Nonfiction: "This is not a travel magazine. We buy articles that contain ideas other lodging operators have found practical and helpful in lowering costs, saving time, serving the public better." Pays 4¢ a word.

Photos: Purchases captioned photos, 5x7 or larger, of superior ways of doing things in hotel, motel, or resort. Pays $10.

KANSAS RESTAURANT MAGAZINE, 359 South Hydraulic St., Wichita KS 67211. Editor: Neal D. Whitaker. For food service operators. Special issues: Christmas, October Convention, Who's Who in Kansas Food Service, Beef Month, Dairy Month, Wheat Month. Monthly. Circulation: 1,400. Not copyrighted. Pays on publication. Will send sample copy for 50¢. Reports "immediately." Enclose S.A.S.E.

Nonfiction and Photos: Articles on food and food service. Length: 1,000 words maximum. Pays $10. Photos purchased with ms.

MOTEL/MOTOR INN JOURNAL, P.O. Box 769, 306 E. Adams Ave., Temple TX 76501. Editor: Ray Sawyer. For owners, managers, housekeepers, food and beverage managers of motels. Magazine; 50 to 120 pages. Established in 1937. Monthly. Circulation: 28,500. Buys all rights. Buys 20 to 40 mss a year. Pays on acceptance. Will send free sample copy to writer on request. No photocopied or simultaneous submissions. Reports in 2 weeks. Query first. Enclose S.A.S.E.

Nonfiction and Photos: "More interested in solid, meaty articles than in writing style. How-to, nuts-and-bolts articles on what goes into a successful, first-class operation; effective promotion; construction techniques; upgrading and maintenance techniques; other factors that go into a successful motel. How to deal with economic conditions, the energy problem; promotional techniques, operational and management techniques, etc." Length: open. Pays 4¢ a word. 8x10 b&w glossies purchased with mss. Pays $5. Pays $10 for 4x5 color transparencies or prints purchased with mss. Captions required.

NATION'S RESTAURANT NEWS, 2 Park Ave., New York NY 10016. Editor: Michael Steven Schweitzer. National business newspaper for "executives of major restaurant chains and owners of the country's better, more prosperous restaurants." Biweekly. Circulation: 52,000. Buys all rights. Buys "several hundred" mss a year. Pays on acceptance. Will send a free sample copy to a writer on request. Reports in 10 days. Enclose S.A.S.E.

Nonfiction: "News and newsfeatures, in-depth analyses of specific new types of restaurants, mergers and acquisitions, new appointments, commodity reports, personalities. Problem: Most business press stories are mere rehashes of consumer pieces. We must have business insideness. Sometimes a freelancer can provide us with enough peripheral material that we'll buy the piece, then assign it to staff writers for further digging. We'd like to see more humorous submissions." Length: 2,000 words maximum. Pays $5 to $75.

Photos: B&w glossies purchased with mss and captions only. Pays $10 and up.

How To Break In: "Send most wanted material, such as personality profiles, light nonfictional treatment of subjects relating to food service, but no how-to stories."

PIZZA AND PASTA (formerly *A Slice of Pizza*), 23 N. Washington, Suite 201, Ypsilanti MI 48197. Editor: Lynda L. Boone. For pizzeria owners and managers, Italian restaurateurs, and manufacturers and wholesalers in related fields. Publication of North American Pizza Association. Magazine published every 2 months; 58 (8½x11) pages. Established in 1969. Circulation: 24,500. Rights purchased vary with author and material. May buy all rights, but will reassign rights to author after publication; or second serial (reprint) rights. Buys 4 mss a year. Payment on acceptance. Will send free sample copy to writer on request. Will consider photocopied submissions. Reports in 3 weeks. Query first. "We will give consideration to a completed article, but a query first would be helpful, both to the writer and to us." Enclose S.A.S.E.

Nonfiction and Photos: "Articles dealing with the operation of pizzerias and Italian restaurants; decor, customer relations, advertising, community service, management, employee training ... all aspects of running a successful food service establishment. Humor, unless both the slant and content are exceptional, is not used. Interviews with successful owners and operators are used in each issue, but these are not accepted from freelancers. The point of view should be from that of the store owner and operator; generally, an article from the customer's point of view would not be used. A direct and businesslike approach is a necessity with our readers. Style should be easy to read and concise. Don't pad the article to the nth degree in an attempt to camouflage a lack of knowledge of the market. We'd be quite interested in seeing a survey-type article done on what the general public thinks of pizza; specifically, pizza is a very nutritious food, but the public probably doesn't think of it as such. If a freelancer has an inexpensive way of contacting people in various parts of the country, this could be great." Uses informational articles, how-to and those on merchandising techniques. Length: 500 words minimum; 7 double-spaced typed pages, maximum. Pays $15 to $20 for short articles; $35 for feature articles. Photos are not usually needed, but can use 5x7 b&w glossies. Pays $3. "Photos are only purchased if they illustrate a point made in the article; they are not usually needed with the type of article we purchase from freelance writers."

RESORT MANAGEMENT, P.O. Box 4169, Memphis TN 38104. Phone: 901-276-5424. Editor: Allen J. Fagans. For "the owners and/or managing executives of America's largest luxury vacation resorts." Monthly. Buys first rights only. Pays on publication. Will send free sample copy on request. Query first. "Editorial deadline is the 1st of the month; i.e., January material must be received by December 1." Reports in 10 days. Enclose S.A.S.E.

Nonfiction and Photos: "This is not a travel or tourist publication. It is a 'how-to-do-it' or 'how-it-was-done' business journal. Descriptive background of any sort used to illustrate the subject matter must be held to a minimum. Our material helps managers attract, house, feed and provide entertainment for guests and their friends, and bring them back again and again. Any facet of the resort operation could be of interest:

guest activities, remodeling, advertising and promotion, maintenance, food, land-scaping, kitchen, personnel, furnishings, etc. We do not want to see material relating to any facet of commercial hotels, motels, motor courts, fishing and hunting camps, housekeeping or other facilities serving transients. Material submitted must be accurate, to the point, and supported by facts and costs, plus pertinent examples illustrating the subject discussed." Length: 800 to 1,000 words. Pays 60¢ per inch for a 20-em column; 40¢ per inch for a 13-em column. "Photos of the resort and of its manager, and the subject(s) being discussed are a must." Pays $5.

Fillers: Uses clippings related to resorts and resort area organizations only. Promotions: president, general manager, resident manager (including changes from one resort to another). Resort Obituaries: president, owner, general manager. Resort construction: changes, additions, new facilities, etc. New resorts: planned or under construction. Changes in resort ownership. Resort news: factual news concerning specific resorts, resort areas, state tourism development. Not interested in clippings about city hotels, roadside motels, motor inns or chain (franchise) operations. Clippings must be pasted on individual sheets of paper, and addressed to Clipping Editor. Your complete mailing address (typed or printed) must be included, as well as the name of the newspaper or magazine and date of issue. Do not send advertisements or pictures. Clippings will not be returned unless a self-addressed envelope and sufficient postage is enclosed. Pays $1 per clipping used.

Industrial Management

The journals that follow are for industrial plant managers, executives, distributors, and buyers; some industrial management journals are also listed under the names of specific industries, such as Machinery and Metal Trade. Publications for industrial supervisors are listed in Management and Supervision.

AUTOMATION, Penton Plaza, 1111 Chester Ave., Cleveland OH 44114. Phone: 216-696-7000. Editor: Lee D. Miller. The production engineering magazine; interested in concepts, procedures and hardware involving production processes and machines, handling equipment, controls, and manufacturing information handling plus personal and professional development." Established in 1954. Circulation: 90,000. Buys all rights. Buys less than 20 mss a year. Payment on publication. Will send sample copy to writer for $1. Write for copy of guidelines for writers. Query first or submit complete ms. Will consider photocopied submissions. Submit seasonal material 4 months in advance. Reports on material in "about a month." Enclose S.A.S.E.

Nonfiction and Photos: "Feature articles and short items describing new equipment, new components and free new literature related to our readers' interests. Keep the interests and characteristics of our readers in mind. Try to supply illustrations or ideas for good graphics." Length: 3,000 to 5,000 words. Pays average of $25 per printed page. 8x10 b&w glossies; 3x5 or larger transparencies (8x10 prints) purchased with mss. Captions required.

Fiction: Humorous fiction related to subject matter. Length and payment are the same as for nonfiction.

COMPRESSED AIR, 942 Memorial Pkwy., Phillipsburg NJ 08865. Phone: 201-859-2270. Editor: S. M. Parkhill. For "management and upper management men concerned with the production, distribution and utilization of compressed air and other gases in all industries." Established in 1896. Monthly. Circulation: 150,000. Buys all rights, but will reassign rights to author after publication. Buys 18 mss a year. Payment on publication. Will send free sample copy to writer on request. Write for copy of guidelines for writers. Query first. Will consider photocopied submissions. Reports on material in 2 weeks. Enclose S.A.S.E.

Nonfiction and Photos: "Case histories of pneumatic applications; in-depth articles about companies using pneumatics in construction and mining projects. Unusual and unique applications of air power. Must be factually and technically accurate, but in a quasi-technical style. This is not a 'how-to' magazine." Informational, historical, think articles, successful business operations, technical. Recently published articles include "Oneida Silversmiths" (craftsmen and air power combine to produce quality tableware), "Saving Energy in Industrial Plants" (energy conservation is good business practice). Length: open. Pays $10 to $25 per published page. Photos purchased with ms. Captions required.

ENERGY NEWS, P.O. Box 1589, Dallas TX 75221. Editor: Claribel Simpson. For natural gas industry and oil industry executives and management personnel and related industries' management (suppliers, consultants). Newsletter; 4 (8½x11) pages. Established in 1970. Every 2 weeks. Circulation: 500. Buys all rights. Pays on publication. Will send free sample copy to writer on request. Will consider simultaneous and photocopied submissions. Reports in 2 weeks. Submit complete ms. Enclose S.A.S.E.
Nonfiction: Latest news about the industry; discoveries, government regulations, construction projects, new trends, supplies, prices of natural gas. Concise, personal style (as to a certain small group, as opposed to mass media style). Length: 250 words maximum. Pays 10¢ a word.

ENERGY WEEK, P.O. Box 1589, Dallas TX 75221. Editor: Ernestine Adams. For general industry executives who need to know about the energy situation to make decisions, obtain supplies; energy industry executives, suppliers, consultants, etc., to energy industry. Newsletter; 4 (8½x11) pages. Established in 1974. Every 2 months. Circulation: 500. Buys all rights. Pays on publication. Will consider photocopied and simultaneous submissions. Reports in 2 weeks. Submit complete ms. Enclose S.A.S.E.
Nonfiction: News about new trends, the supply situation, prices for all energy items (crude, LPG, natural gas, gasoline, etc.), research of all branches of the energy industry; oil, coal, gas, solar, etc. Must be concise and aimed at general industry (that buys most energy). Length: 250 words maximum. Pays 10¢ a word.

HANDLING AND SHIPPING, 614 Superior Ave. W., Cleveland OH 44113. Phone: 215-696-0300. Executive Editor: John F. Spencer. For operating executives with physical distribution responsibilities in transportation, material handling, warehousing, packaging, and shipping. Monthly. Buys all rights. Pays on publication. "Query first with 50-word description of proposed article." Enclose S.A.S.E.
Nonfiction and Photos: Material on aspects of physical distribution management, with economic emphasis. Informational and successful business operations material. Writer must know the field and the publications in it. Not for amateurs and generalists. Length: 1,500 to 3,000 words. Pays minimum of $30 per published page. No additional payment is made for b&w photos used with mss, but they must be sharp, for good reproduction. No prints from copy negatives. Any size. Color used may be prints or transparencies.

INDUSTRIAL DISTRIBUTION, 16 W. 61st St., New York NY 10023. Phone: 212-765-7290. Editor: George J. Berkwitt. Monthly. Buys all rights. Will consider cassette submissions. Enclose S.A.S.E.
Nonfiction: "Articles aimed at making industrial distributor management, sales and other personnel aware of trends, developments and problems and solutions in their segment of industry. Articles accepted range widely; may cover legislation, sales training, administration, Washington, marketing techniques, case histories, profiles on industry leaders, abstracted speeches — any area that is timely and pertinent and provides readers with interesting informative data. Use either roundups or bylined pieces." Length: 900 words minimum. Pays "flat fee based on value; usually $50 per published page."

INDUSTRIAL DISTRIBUTOR NEWS, 1 West Olney Ave., Philadelphia PA 19120. Managing Editor: Stephen A. Albertini. For industrial distributors, wholesalers of industrial equipment and supplies; business managers and industrial salesmen. Established in 1959. Monthly. Circulation: 31,000. Buys all rights. Buys 5 to 10 mss a year. Payment on publication. Will send free sample copy to writer on request. Reports on material within 6 weeks. "Company policy dictates no bylined articles except when noted by publisher. Therefore, no freelance material used unless assigned through initial query first." Enclose S.A.S.E.

Nonfiction and Photos: "Factual feature material with a slant toward industrial marketing. Case studies of distributors with unusual or unusually successful marketing techniques. Avoid triteness in subject matter. Be sure to relate specifically to industrial distributors." Informational, how-to, interview. Length: 500 to 3,000 words. Pays $50 to $200, including photos. B&w 8x10 or 2¼x2¼ color transparencies.

INDUSTRIAL NEWS *(Southern California Industrial News, North California Electronic News, Northern California Industrial News, Southwest Industrial News, Pacific Northwest Industrial News, Pacific Coast Plastics, Pacific Coast Metals),* P.O. Box 3631, Los Angeles CA 90051. Editor: Larry Liebman. For manufacturing executives and industrial suppliers, as well as technical people (engineers and chemists). Tabloid newspapers. Established in 1948. *Southern California Industrial News* is published weekly. The balance are monthlies. Circulation: over 50,000. Buys simultaneous rights. Payment on publication. Will send free sample copy to writer on request. Will consider photocopied and simultaneous submissions. Reports in 2 weeks. Query first. Enclose S.A.S.E.

Nonfiction and Photos: Hard news, industry oriented. Should pertain to the area of each publication. Should be to the point, not long-winded or overly technical. Not interested in energy crisis stories by instant experts. Does like to see the how-to approach in all industrial situations, without it being a "puff" for a particular producer. Informational, interview, profile, expose, spot news, successful business operations, new products, merchandising techniques. Length: 50 to 100 typewritten lines. Pays $10 to $50. No additional payment for b&w photos used with mss. Captions required.

INDUSTRIAL WORLD, 386 Park Ave., S., New York NY 10016. Phone: 212-689-0120. Editor and Publisher: S. W. Kann. For plant managers abroad. Monthly. Buys first world rights. Pays on publication. Will send a sample copy to a writer on request. Write for copy of guidelines for writers. Query first. Formal outlines not required; paragraph of copy sufficient. Reports in 30 days. Enclose S.A.S.E.

Nonfiction and Photos: "Interested primarily in articles dealing with application of U.S. industrial machinery and know-how abroad. Clear, factual data necessary. Articles of more than passing interest to plant managers on production tools, techniques, unusual installation, new or novel solutions to production problems, etc. Should be slanted for the overseas plant manager." Length: 1,000 to 3,000 words. Pays "$60 for first printed page of article, $40 for each subsequent page." Photos purchased with mss. 5x7 or 8x10 glossies only; must be clean, professional, quality. ("If necessary, we will make prints from author's negatives which will be returned. Photos supplied, however, are usually not returned.")

How To Break In: "Concentrate on the adaptations of industrial know-how in the developing nations. Your best chance of getting an assignment will be if you are planning to travel in one of the less frequently traveled areas and have an idea for a story of this kind. We tend to rely on regular contributors in certain areas and if you plan to stay abroad, you could become a stringer."

MODERN PLANT OPERATION AND MAINTENANCE, 209 Dunn Ave., Stamford CT 06905. Phone: 203-322-7676. Editor: Kenneth V. Jones. For plant engineers and managers. Quarterly. Circulation: 55,000. Buys all rights. Pays on acceptance. Will send sample copy on request. "We reject all unsolicited material unseen, as we are not set up to handle it. All assignments come from us and we can use only the people who truly know the field. Send letter stating qualifications and availability." Enclose S.A.S.E. Do not send query letters.

Nonfiction and Photos: Length: 600 to 1,000 words. Pays $100 to $150.

THE PHILADELPHIA PURCHASOR, 1518 Walnut St., Suite 610, Philadelphia PA 19102. Editor-in-Chief: Howard B. Armstrong, Jr. For buyers of industrial supplies

and equipment, including the materials of manufacture, as well as the maintenance, repair and operating items; and for buyers of office equipment and supplies for banks and other industries. Magazine; 65 (8¼x11¼) pages. Established in 1926. Monthly. Circulation: 4,000. Not copyrighted. Buys 25 to 35 mss a year. Pays on acceptance. Will send free sample copy to writer on request. Write for copy of guidelines for writers. Will consider photocopied and simultaneous submissions. Reports in a month. Query first or submit complete ms. Enclose S.A.S.E.
Nonfiction and Photos: "We use articles on industrial, service and institutional purchasing — *not* consumer. We also use business articles of the kind that would interest purchasing personnel. Ours is a regional magazine covering the middle Atlantic area, and if material takes this into account, it is more effective." Length: 900 to 1,200 words. Pays minimum of $15. No additional payment for b&w photos used with mss.

PURCHASING, 221 Columbus Ave., Boston MA 02116. Editorial Director: Robert Haavind. For purchasing specialists, primarily in manufacturing industries. Semimonthly. Circulation: 72,000. Buys all rights. Buys about 20 mss a year. Payment on publication. Will send free sample copy to writer on request. Submit seasonal material 3 months in advance. Reports in 10 days. Query first. Enclose S.A.S.E.
Nonfiction: Some news items (on price shifts, purchasing problems, etc.) from stringers. Features on better purchasing methods (with real examples), on evaluating or specifying. Items must be generalized and objective. Back up topics with good data, examples, charts, etc. No product pitches. Particularly interested in contract writing, negotiating techniques. Informational, how-to, and spot news. Length: 500 to 1,500 words. Pays $50 to $150.
How To Break In: "Send us a proposal first, or apply as a stringer in your area."

Insurance

BUSINESS INSURANCE, 740 N. Rush Street, Chicago IL 60611. Editor: Stephen D. Gilkenson. For "corporate risk managers, insurance brokers and agents, insurance company executives. Generally middle-aged (40 to 64). Most have college degrees. Interested in insurance, safety, security, consumerism, employee benefits, investments." Special issues on safety, pensions, health and life benefits, international insurance. Biweekly. Circulation: 38,000. Buys all rights. Buys 75 to 100 mss a year. Pays on publication. Submit seasonal or special material 2 months in advance. Reports in 2 weeks. Query required. Enclose S.A.S.E.
Nonfiction: We publish material on corporate insurance and employee benefit programs and related subjects. We take everything from the buyers' point of view, rather than that of the insurance company, broker, or consultant who is selling something. Items on insurance company workings do not interest us. Our special emphasis on corporate risk management and employee benefits administration requires that freelancers discuss with us their proposed articles before going ahead. Length is "subject to discussion with contributor." Payment is $2.50 a column inch.

INSPECTION NEWS, P.O. Box 4081, Atlanta GA 30302. Phone: 404-875-8321. Editor: H. A. McQuade. For "management employees of most American corporations, especially insurance companies. This includes Canada and Mexico. Pass-along readership involves sub-management and non-management people in these firms. Distributed by Retail Credit Co." Quarterly. Circulation: 97,000. Not copyrighted; "we allow customer publications free reprint privileges. Author free to negotiate fee independently, however." Buys 3 to 5 mss a year. Pays on acceptance. Will send a sample copy to a writer on request. Query first: "present idea in paragraph outline form. Accepted queries should result in authors' submitting double-spaced copy, typed 40 characters to the line, 25 lines to the page." Reports in 2 to 3 weeks. Enclose S.A.S.E.

Nonfiction and Photos: "Insurance-related articles — new trends, challenges, and problems facing underwriters, actuaries, claim men, executives, and agents; articles of general interest in a wide range of subjects — the quality of life, ecology, drug and alcohol-related subjects, safe driving, law enforcement, and insurance-related Americana; inspirational articles to help managers and executives do their jobs better. Write with our audience in mind. Only articles of the highest quality will be considered. Especially interested in material written by insurance underwriters, executives, college instructors, and college professors on previously unpublished or updated facets of our area of interest. More than 90% of our readers are customers of Retail Credit or its various affiliates, and they expect to see articles that help them know and understand the business information business." Buys inspirational articles, think pieces about insurance industry needs for business information services, etc. Length: 1,000 to 2,000 words. Pays 1¢ to 2¢ a word, "depending on quality and importance of material, but not less than $25." B&w glossies relating to theme of article purchased with mss; 5x7 or 8x10. Pays $5 to $15. Examples of articles published are: "Snowmobiles—Mortality & Morbidity" (in a far-ranging look at the development and present status of snowmobiles, the author raises some questions that call for thoughtful answers); "Business Fraud—The Problem, The People, The Preventatives" (in a copyrighted excerpt from his book, *Mind Your Own Business*, the author examines dishonesty in business; insurance is important, he says, but you need more).

THE SPECTATOR, Chilton Way, Radnor PA 19087. Phone: 215-687-9198. Managing Editor: Elinor Kinley. For "executives and key brokers in insurance-related fields." Monthly. Buys first publication rights. Query first. Enclose S.A.S.E.
Nonfiction: "In-depth observations relevant to the insurance and financial community, including broad-based statistical studies." Pays $25 minimum. Examples of articles published: One article was about insuring public school districts, explaining how a school district buying its insurance on merit without the intrusion of local poltics, should be approached in the same way as any industrial account. Another article gave a statistical report on the growing importance of aviation insurance, stating the age of the jet, superjet and the SST will bring many underwriting problems to the insurance underwriter and broker. One other article showed the insurance company's role in ghetto enterprise and jobs.

UNITED STATES REVIEW, 617 West Ave., P. O. Box 505, Jenkintown PA 19046. Publisher: Robert R. Dearden IV. Editor: John C. Duncan and Diane L. Miles. For "insurance agents and brokers who are independent agents and all insurance-related industry in the Middle Atlantic region." Established in 1868. Weekly. Circulation: 5,000. Not copyrighted. Buys about 20 mss a year. Pays on publication. Will send a sample copy to a writer for 35¢. Submit seasonal material 3 months in advance. Enclose S.A.S.E.
Nonfiction: Buys coverage of successful business operations and articles on merchandising techniques. Length: open. Pay: open.

Jewelry

AMERICAN JEWELRY MANUFACTURER, 340 Howard Bldg., 155 Westminster St., Providence RI 02903. Editor: Steffan Aletti. For manufacturers of supplies and tools for the jewelry industry; their representatives, wholesalers and agencies. Established in 1956. Monthly. Circulation: 5,000. Buys all rights (with exceptions). Buys 2 to 5 mss a year. Will send free sample copy to writer on request. Write for copy of guidelines for writers. Query first. Will consider photocopied submissions. Submit seasonal material 3 months in advance. Reports on material within a month. Enclose S.A.S.E.
Nonfiction and Photos: "Topical articles on manufacturing; company stories; economics (i.e., rising gold prices). Story must inform or educate the manufacturer. Occasional special issues on timely topics, i.e., gold; occasional issues on specific processes in casting and plating." Informational, how-to, interview, profile, historical,

expose, successful business operations, new product, merchandising techniques, technical. Length: open. Payment "usually around $25." B&w photos purchased with ms. 5x7 minimum.

CANADIAN JEWELLER, The Giftware and Jewellry Magazine, 481 University Ave., Toronto, Ontario, Canada MW5 1A7. Editor: Dennis Mellersh. For retail jewellers. Magazine; 75 pages. Established in 1876. Monthly. Circulation: 4,000. Rights purchased vary with author and material. May buy all rights but will reassign rights to author after publication; or first North American serial rights. Pays on acceptance. Write for copy of guidelines for writers. No photocopied or simultaneous submissions. Reports in 2 weeks. Query first. Enclose S.A.E. and International Reply Coupons.
Nonfiction and Photos: Informative articles which help jewellers buy more effectively. Length: open. Pay 8½¢ a word. B&w photos purchased with mss. Pays minimum of $7.50. "If photography is assigned, the custom is to pay the photographers daily, half-day, or hourly fee and a nominal charge for prints."

JEWELER'S CIRCULAR-KEYSTONE, Chilton Company, Radnor PA 19089. Editor: George Holmes. For "retail jewelers doing over $30,000 annual volume." Monthly. Circulation: 22,000. Buys all rights. Buys 10 or 12 mss a year. Pays on publication. Will send a free sample copy to a writer on request. Query first. Reports "immediately." Enclose S.A.S.E.
Nonfiction and Photos: Wants "how-to-articles, case history approach, which specify how a given jeweler solved a specific problem. No general stories, no stories without a jeweler's name in it, no stories not about a specific jeweler and his business." Length: 1,000 to 2,000 words. Payment is $75 to $100. Also wants "items about promotion or management ideas implemented by a jeweler" for department "Ideas That Pay." Length: 150 to 300 words. Payment is $10 to $15. Buys photos with mss.

MODERN JEWELER, 15 W. 10th St., Kansas City MO 64105. Managing Editor: Dorothy Boicourt. For retail jewelers and watchmakers. Monthly. Pays on acceptance. Will send sample copy only if query interests the editor. Reports in 30 days. Enclose S.A.S.E.
Nonfiction and Photos: "Articles with 3 or 4 photos about retail jewelers—specific jewelers, with names and addresses, and how they have overcome certain business problems, moved merchandise, increased store traffic, etc. Must contain idea adaptable to other jewelry operations; 'how-to' slant. Informal, story telling slant with human interest. We are not interested in articles about how manufacturing jewelers design and make one-of-a-kind jewelry pieces. Our readers are interested in retail selling techniques, not manufacturing processes. Photos must include people (not just store shots) and should help tell the story." Pays average $70 to $90 for article and photos.

THE NORTHWESTERN JEWELER, Washington and Main Sts., Albert Lea MN 56007. Associate Editor: John R. Hayek. Monthly. Not copyrighted. Pays on publication. Enclose S.A.S.E.
Nonfiction and Photos: Uses news stories about jewelers in the Northwest and Upper Midwest and feature news stories about the same group. Also buys retail jeweler "success" stories with the "how-to-do" angle played up, and occasionally a technical story on jewelry or watchmaking. Pictures increase publication chances. Pays 1¢ a published word. Pays $2.50 per photo.

SOUTHERN JEWELER, 75 Third St., N.W., Atlanta GA 30308. Phone: 404-881-6442. Editor: Charles Fram. For southern retail jewelers and watchmakers. Monthly. Not copyrighted. Submit seasonal material by the 15th of the month preceding issue date. Enclose S.A.S.E. for return of submissions.
Nonfiction: Articles relating to southern retail jewelers regarding advertising, management, and merchandising. Buys spot news about southern jewelers and coverage of successful business operations. Prefers *not* to see material concerning jewelers

outside the 14 southern states. Length: open. Pays 1¢ per word.
Photos: Buys b&w glossies. Pays $4.
Fillers: Clippings "on southern retail jewelers and stores." Pays 50¢ "if used."

Journalism

Because many writers are familiar with the journals of the writing profession and might want to submit to them, those that do not pay for contributions are identified in this list. Writers wishing to contribute material to these publications should write the editors for their requirements or query before submitting work. A self-addressed, stamped envelope must accompany all such inquiries.

AMERICAN PRESS, 651 Council Hill Rd., Dundee IL 60118. Editor: Clarence O. Schlaver. "We do not accept freelance material."

ARMED FORCES WRITER, George Washington Station, Alexandria VA 22305. Phone: 301-656-3544. Editor: Col. Frank Martineau. For military and civilian writers and journalists, public relations personnel with membership in Armed Forces Writers League, Inc. Bimonthly. Not copyrighted. Buys about 20 mss a year. Pays on acceptance. Will send free sample copy on request; send self-addressed 9x12 envelope. Query first or submit complete ms. Will consider photocopied submissions. Reports in 30 days. Enclose S.A.S.E.
Nonfiction: Articles on writing or other forms of communications (art, photography, public relations, etc.). Material must have positive educational and professional content (how to write and sell); must be authoritative by reason of author's recognized professional achievement. Buys informational and how-to articles. Occasionally overstocked. Length: 500-word "shorticles"; 800 to 1,500-word features. Pays $5 to $10; "better rate depends on quality, significance or timeliness."
Fillers: "Newsbreaks of interest to writers and artists." Length: 300 words. Pays $2.
How To Break In: "Write a case history of your development as a writer and your first sale, with some connection to the military service."

BLACK WRITERS' NEWS, 4019 S. Vincennes Ave., Chicago IL 60653. Editor: Alice C. Browning. Only accepts material written by members of the Black Writers' Conference.

THE CALIFORNIA PUBLISHER, 6151 W. Century Blvd., Los Angeles CA 90045. Phone: 213-641-8300. Editor: Mrs. Peggy Plendl. Does not pay.

CANADIAN AUTHOR AND BOOKMAN, 8726 116th St., Edmonton 61, Alberta, Canada. Editor: Mary E. Dawe. Does not pay.

THE CATHOLIC JOURNALIST, 432 Park Ave. S., New York NY 10016. "We are no longer buying freelance material."

COLLEGIATE JOURNALIST, School of Journalism, Ohio University, Athens OH 45701. Phone: 614-594-7312. Editor: Prof. J.W. Click. For editors and staff members of college student newspapers, yearbooks, magazines and other student-edited publications; some advisers to these publications. 3 times a year. College student magazine, 16 pages, 8½x11. Established in 1963. Circulation: 1,000. Not copyrighted. Payment in contributor's copies. Will send sample copy to writer for $1. Reports "immediately or up to 6 months." Enclose S.A.S.E.
Nonfiction and Photos: Articles on crucial issues to student editors (legal cases, ethical issues, administrative censorship, case histories, how-to, innovations in editing and printing and occasional material on broad issues of higher education). Aim right at the college student editor and give him information he can benefit from

or practical advice he can use. Keep the ms short; generally no longer than 6 pages. Survey of depth reporting in college newspapers, how newspapers are handling energy and inflation problems, changing enrollments, etc., on their campuses. Length: 200 to 2,000 words. Photos welcome, captions required. No payment.

COLUMBIA JOURNALISM REVIEW, 700 Journalism Building, Columbia University, New York NY 10027. Managing Editor: Kenneth M. Pierce. "We welcome queries concerning the media, as well as subjects covered by the media. All articles are assigned."

CONTENT, 22 Laurier Ave., Toronto, Canada M4X 1S3. Phone: 416-920-6699. Editor: Barrie Zwicker. For working journalists in all media in all parts of Canada, journalism faculty and students, freelance writers, government information officers, public relations and advertising people, and citizens concerned about the performance of the news media. Established in 1970. Circulation: 5,000. Rights purchased vary with author and material; may buy all rights, but will reassign rights to author after publication. Buys about 60 mss a year. Pays on or before publication. Will send free sample copy to writer on request. Write for "Statement of Editorial Policy Regarding Payment to Writers, Photographers and Artists." Will consider cassette submissions. Query first with 100-word outline of suggested article if an established writer. If breaking in, please enclose brief biography biased toward explaining why you are qualified to comment on the territory behind the news. If sending complete ms, submit in triplicate. Enclose S.A.E. and International Reply Coupons.
Nonfiction: "All material deals in one way or another with news media performance. By and large, material should deal with Canadian events, or have distinct relevance in Canada. There is no other journalism review of national stature in Canada. Peripheral and humorous material purchased, to balance the incisive and thoughtful analyses that constitute most of *Content.*" Length for major articles: 2,000 words minimum. Pays $15 to $500.
Photos: Purchased with or without mss. Must be carefully captioned. Prefers b&w glossies. Uses photo spreads, especially photos straight media refused to run. Pays $5 minimum.
Fillers: Examples from the media of silly or superficial news coverage, with acid caption, and explanatory cutline if required. Pays $2 minimum.

EDITOR & PUBLISHER, 850 Third Ave., New York NY 10022. Managing Editor: Jerome H. Walker, Jr. Weekly. Query first. Enclose S.A.S.E.
Nonfiction: Uses newspaper business articles and news items; also newspaper personality features.
Fillers: "Amusing typographical errors found in newspapers." Pays $2.

FEED/BACK, THE JOURNALISM REPORT AND REVIEW, Journalism Department, San Francisco State College, 1600 Holloway, San Francisco CA 94132. Editors: B. H. Liebes, Lynn Ludlow. Managing Editor: David M. Cole. For the working journalist, the journalism student, the journalism professor, and the journalistic layman. Magazine; 40 (8x11) pages. Established in 1974. Quarterly. Circulation: 1,500. Not copyrighted. Pays in subscriptions and copies. Will send free sample copy to writer. Will consider photocopied and simultaneous submissions. Reports on material accepted for publication in 1 month. Returns rejected material in 2 weeks. Query first. Enclose S.A.S.E.
Nonfiction and Photos: In-depth views of journalism in Northern California. Criticism of journalistic trends throughout the country, but with a local angle. Reviews of books concerning journalism. Informational, interview, profile, humor, historical, think pieces, expose, nostalgia, spot news, successful (or unsuccessful) business operations, new product, technical; all must be related to journalism. Recently published "The Anatomy of a Murder Story." Length: 1,000 to 10,000 words. B&w glossies (8x10 or 11x14) used with or without mss. Pays in subscriptions and/or copies, tearsheets for all material.
Poetry: Traditional forms of poetry and light verse. Must relate to journalism. Length: 5 to 50 lines.

FOLIO, 125 Elm St., P.O. Box 696, New Canaan CT 06840. Phone: 203-966-5691. Editor: Howard S. Ravis. For publishing company executives. Bimonthly. Usually buys all rights. Query first. Enclose S.A.S.E.

Nonfiction: "Covers 6 specific areas of interest to executives of magazine publishing companies: management (including finances), sales, circulation and fulfillment, production, editing, and graphics. All material should be written with our audience in mind. Above all, we are a how-to magazine, and every story should have information that can be applied by magazine publishers." Length: 3,500 words maximum; "articles for each of the departments (1 department for each of the areas mentioned above) run to about 1,800 words." No payment.

THE JOURNALISM EDUCATOR, Department of Journalism, University of Nevada, Reno NV 89507. Phone: 702-784-6531. Editor: LaRue W. Gilleland. For journalism professors and a growing number of news executives in the U.S. and Canada. Published by the Association for Education in Journalism. Founded by the American Society of Journalism Administrators. Quarterly. Enclose S.A.S.E.

Nonfiction: Uses articles dealing with problems of administration and improvement of teaching in journalism education at the university level. Maximum length: 2,500 words. Does not pay.

JOURNALISM QUARTERLY, School of Journalism, Ohio University, Athens OH 45701. Phone: 614-594-6710. Editor: Guido H. Stempel, III. For members of Association for Education in Journalism; also, other academicians and journalism practitioners. Established in 1923. Quarterly. Usually acquires all rights. Circulation: 4,000. Write for copy of guidelines for writers. Submit only complete ms "in triplicate." Will consider photocopied submissions. Reports in 4 to 6 months. Enclose S.A.S.E. for return of submissions.

Nonfiction: Research in mass communication. Length: 4,000 words maximum. No payment.

MEDICAL COMMUNICATIONS, School of Journalism, College of Communication, Ohio University, Athens OH 45701. Phone: 614-594-2671. Editor: Byron T. Scott. For medical libraries, members of the American Medical Writers Association, physicians, journal and magazine editors, medical illustrators and pharmaceutical advertising people. Quarterly, 24- to 32-page digest size magazine. Established in 1971. Circulation: over 2,000. Acquires first North American serial rights. Uses 6 to 8 freelance mss per issue. Payment in contributor's copies. Will send sample copy for $1.25. Will not consider photocopied or simultaneous submissions. Submit seasonal or special material 2 to 3 months in advance. Reports on material accepted for publication in 6 weeks. Returns rejected material in 4 weeks. Query first. Enclose S.A.S.E.

Nonfiction and Photos: Articles relating to any aspect of medical communications including inter- and intra-personal writing. May be either philosophic or how-to with the proviso that it must tell the medical communicator something that will enrich his professional goals and achievements. "We are more of a journal than a magazine, but like to take a less formal approach in the hopes of improving an article's readability across the broad range of AMWA membership." Uses fairly serious, straightforward style. Humor accepted, but rarely. Footnotes may be required. Does not want to see anything on "how doctors can't communicate with their patients. We know this, and improving the situation is a major purpose of our organization." Length: 1,500 to 3,000 words. Charts and photos are used with mss, if needed. Payment in copies.

MILITARY MEDIA REVIEW (formerly *The Military Journalist*), DINFOS-PAO, Bldg. 400, Ft. Ben Harrison IN 46216. Editor: David M. Ruff. Pays in copies.

MORE, A Critical Review of the Nation's Media, 750 Third Ave., New York NY 10017. Editor: Richard Pollak. For "both men and women active in media and

readers and viewers interested in how media operates." Monthly. Circulation: 20,000. Rights purchased vary with author and material. Buys all rights, but will reassign them to author after publication. Buys 70 mss a year. Pays on publication. Will send a copy to writer for $1. Query first. Reports promptly. Enclose S.A.S.E.
Nonfiction: Publishes "critical evaluations of the media—print and electronic, over-ground and underground. Heavy emphasis on solid reporting and good writing. Essayists need not apply. With the exception of the generally scholarly *Columbia Journalism Review*, there is no publication doing what we do." Length: "ordinarily 4,000 words." Pays 10¢ a word.

THE PEN WOMAN, 1300 17th St., N.W., Washington DC 20036. Editor: Wilma Burton. For women writers, artists and composers. Magazine published 9 times a year; 32 to 36 (6x9) pages. Established in 1920. Circulation: 6,000. Will send sample copy to writer if S.A.S.E. is enclosed. "We are overstocked from our own members since we are an official publication for NLAPW, an organization of professional writers. Only on occasion do we accept freelance material."

PHILATELIC JOURNALIST, P.O. Box 150, Clinton Corners NY 12514. Phone: 914-266-3150. Editor: Gustav Detjen, Jr. For "journalists, writers, columnists in the field of stamp collecting." Established in 1971. Bimonthly. Circulation: 1,000. Not copyrighted. Pays on publication. Will send a sample copy to a writer on request. Query first. Will consider photocopied submissions. Submit seasonal material 2 months in advance. Reports in 2 weeks. Enclose S.A.S.E.
Nonfiction and Photos: "Articles concerned with the problems of the philatelic journalist, how to publicize and promote stamp collecting, how to improve relations between philatelic writers and publishers and postal administrations. Philatelic journalists, many of them amateurs, are very much interested in receiving greater recognition as journalists. Any criticism should be coupled with suggestions for improvement." Buys profiles and personal opinion articles. Length: 250 to 500 words. Pays $15 to $30. Photos purchased with ms; captions required.
Fillers: Jokes, short humor. Length: 2 to 5 lines. Payment negotiated.

PHOTOLITH, Texas Tech University, P.O. Box 4080, Lubbock TX 79409. Editors: William R. England, Jr., and Kay Dowdy For high school and college publications and journalism students and advisors. Deals with articles of interest for the 15- to 18-year-old group and the teachers. Magazine published monthly during the school year; 8 issues 30 (8½x11) pages. Established in 1950. Circulation: 2,500. Not copyrighted. Uses 50 mss per year. Payment in contributor's copies. Will not consider simultaneous or photocopied submissions. Reports on material accepted for publication in 10 days. Returns rejected material in 2 weeks. Query first or submit complete ms. Enclose S.A.S.E.
Nonfiction: "We feel we provide a more contemporary approach to publication trends and problems. We treat new ideas as innovative approaches that deserve a hearing. We use articles dealing with school/college newspapers and yearbooks. Layout design, journalistic reporting, photography, art, business management. In short, all of the essential elements involved in getting together a successful communications vehicle." Length: 2,500 words. Payment in copies.

PNPA PRESS, 2717 N. Front St., Harrisburg PA 17110. Phone: 717-234-4067. Editor: Ruth E. Kuhn. No payment.

PUBLISHERS' AUXILIARY, 491 National Press Bldg., Washington DC 20004. Editor: Mrs. Beverly Nykwest. For newspaper publishers, general managers, other newspaper executives. Publication of the National Newspaper Association. 24-page newspaper published twice a month. Established in 1865. Circulation: 13,000. Not copyrighted. Payment on publication. Will consider photocopied submissions. Submit special issue material 1 month in advance. Reporting time varies. Returns rejected material immediately. Query first. Enclose S.A.S.E.
Nonfiction and Photos: "We are a newspaper for newspaper people. We use only items that relate to some aspect of newspaper publishing, written in newspaper style.

Since our audience is almost exclusively management people, all material is geared toward management. All work is assigned and is primarily coverage of newspaper organization meetings." Does not want to see features on "old-time" journalists. Is interested in material on newspaper plant design. How-to, interview, profile, successful business operations, new product, merchandising techniques; book reviews. Length: open. Pays $25 to $50. B&w photos purchased on assignment. Pays minimum of $5.

THE QUILL, National Magazine for Journalists, 35 E. Wacker Dr., Chicago IL 60601. Phone: 312-236-6577. Editor: Charles Long. For newspaper personnel, broadcasters, magazine writers and editors, freelance writers, journalism educators and students, public relations and advertising executives and others interested in journalism. Established in 1912. Monthly. Circulation: 27,000. No payment. Rights acquired vary. Will send free sample copy to writer on request. Query first. Enclose S.A.S.E.
Nonfiction: "Articles relating to all aspects of journalism; nuts and bolts type features, freedom of the press articles, profiles of people and places in the media; news items. Regardless of the subject matter, write in a readable style and a structure understandable to a lay audience; nothing that appears like a term paper or thesis."

ST. LOUIS JOURNALISM REVIEW, P.O. Box 3086, St. Louis MO 63130. A critique of St. Louis media, print and broadcasting, by working journalists. Bimonthly. Buys all rights. Enclose S.A.S.E.
Nonfiction: "We might buy material which analyzes, criticizes or reveals information about the local (St. Louis area) media institutions, media personalities, or media trends. Since the entire staff consists of volunteers, we can only offer minimal payment of $20 to freelancers."

SCHOLASTIC EDITOR GRAPHICS/COMMUNICATIONS, 720 Washington Ave., S.E., Suite 205, University of Minnesota, Minneapolis MN 55414. Editor: Jeanne Buckeye. For high school and college journalism students, publications editors, staffs and advisers as well as mass media people. Monthly (Sept.-May with Dec.-Jan. issues combined) magazine; 32 pages, 8½x11. Special issue in April, Summer Workshop issue; articles on summer journalism workshops would be appropriate. Established in 1921. Circulation: 3,000. Buys all rights, but will reassign rights to author after publication. Buys about 30 mss each year. Pays in contributor's copies. Will send free sample copy to writer on request. Query first or submit complete ms for nonfiction. Reports in 2 to 4 weeks. Enclose S.A.S.E.
Nonfiction and Photos: "How-to articles on all phases of publication work, photography, classroom TV and the general field of communications. How to save money setting up a darkroom, make your yearbook layouts exciting with press-on lettering, etc. Style should avoid using first person. Looking for articles that have a lively, exciting approach. Especially interested in articles that suggest interesting illustration possibilities." Informational, how-to, personal experience, profile, photo feature, spot news, successful business operations, new product articles, merchandising techniques, technical; journalism and mass media topics book reviews. Length: 10 to 20 typed, double-spaced pages for articles. Regular columns are Reading Between the Lines (book reviews), Publicity (news releases) and Conglomerata (new product ideas). Length: 2 pages, double-spaced, typed. 8x10 b&w glossies wanted, but will accept smaller if not accompanied by ms. Captions optional. Have occasional use for mod photos.

TODAY'S WRITERS, 725 S. Central Exp., Suite D-11, Richardson TX 75080. Editor: Charles E. Stovall. For creative writers, ranging in ages from 21 to 75. Magazine, 32 pages. Established in 1974. Every 2 months. Circulation: 10,000. Rights purchased vary with author and material. Usually buys all rights. Pays on publication. Will send free sample copy to writer on request. Write for copy of guidelines for writers. Submit seasonal material (holidays, Christmas, July 4th, etc.) 4 to 6 weeks in advance. Query first. Reports in 1 month. Enclose S.A.S.E.
Nonfiction: General material in creative writing field. Write with a style that shows grasp of the field being covered, outreach that is stimulating to the writer seeking

self-improvement. "We try to be a helping hand to writers who are on the way up — though this is not exclusive, it is an ever present need in the field of writing. We want more television writing, more dramatization." How-to, inspirational, humor, think articles, nostalgia, photo, spot news, successful business operations. Recently published articles include "Writing and Record Keeping" (practical), "Pied Piper of the Pros" (human interest article), and "The Stuff Writers Are Made Of." Length: 1,500 to 2,000 words. Pays 5¢ per word. Regular columns cover religious writing, confession, fiction, nonfiction, script writing for plays, movies, radio, TV. Length: 1,500 words.
Photos: Photos purchased with ms with no additional payment. Captions required. Department Editor: Teresa R. Stovall.
Fiction: Mystery, suspense, adventure, western, humorous, and confession. Department Editor: John Bibee.
Poetry and Fillers: Blank verse, free verse, and light verse. Poetry Editor: Jerry Burke. Fillers to 750 words. Pays 5¢ a word. Filler Department Editor: Selma Glasser.

THE WRITER, 8 Arlington St., Boston MA 02116. Editor: A.S. Burack. Monthly. Pays on acceptance. Uses very little freelance material. Enclose S.A.S.E.
Nonfiction: Articles of instruction for writers. Length: about 2,000 words. Pays minimum $25.

WRITER'S DIGEST, 9933 Alliance Rd., Cincinnati OH 45242. Editor: John Brady. For writers. Established in 1919. Monthly. Circulation: 120,000. Buys first magazine rights and book rights. Buys about 50 mss a year. Pays on acceptance. Will send a sample copy to a writer on request. Will consider photocopied submissions. Submit seasonal material at least 3 months in advance of issue date. Reports in 3 weeks. "Query first for in-depth features." Enclose S.A.S.E.
Nonfiction: "Practical instructional features on specific types of writing for the freelance market. In-depth market features on major magazine and book publishing houses; interviews with outstanding writers. Discussions of specialized fields of writing, such as greeting cards, wire service reporting, comedy writing, script writing, new potential freelance markets, etc. Regular columns cover poetry, cartooning, photojournalism, TV, law and the writer, and New York markets. We also publish articles on subjects related to the business aspects of writing for publication." Length: 500 to 3,000 words. Pays 3¢ to 5¢ a word; "more for outstanding pieces."
Photos: "Well-known writers, the New York scene, the writing life; for inside and cover use." B&w only. Pays $15 to $35.
Fillers: Clippings, etc., about well-known writers. Will not be returned. Pays $2 to $5.

WRITER'S YEARBOOK, 9933 Alliance Rd., Cincinnati OH 45242. Editor: John Brady. For writers. Established in 1930. Annual. Buys first magazine and book rights. Buys 20 mss a year. Pays on acceptance. Will send a sample copy to a writer for $2. "Most articles are on assignment, but will look at queries from July to September each year." Will consider photocopied submissions. Enclose S.A.S.E.
Nonfiction: "In-depth reports on magazine and book publisher requirements; articles of instruction on type of writing; exclusive interviews with top writers." Length: 1,000 to 4,000 words. Pays 5¢ a word; "more for outstanding pieces."
Photos: Purchased with and without mss; captions required. "B&w glossies of extremely well-known U.S. writers; New York street scenes. Depending on use, we pay $15 to $35."

Laundry and Dry Cleaning

Some journals in the Coin-Operated Machines category are also in the market for material on laundries and dry cleaning establishments.

AMERICAN DRYCLEANER, 500 N. Dearborn St., Chicago IL 60610. Phone: 312-337-7700. Editor: Paul T. Glaman. For professional drycleaners. Monthly. Circulation: 30,000. Buys all rights. Pays on publication. Will send free sample copy on request. Reports "promptly." Enclose S.A.S.E.
Nonfiction and Photos: Articles on merchandising, diversification, sales programs, personnel management, consumer relations, cost cutting, workflow effectiveness, drycleaning methods. "Articles should help the drycleaner build his business with the most efficient utilization of time, money and effort, inform the drycleaner about current developments within and outside the industry which may affect him and his business, introduce the drycleaner to new concepts and applications which may be of use to him, teach the drycleaner the proper methods of his trade. Tight, crisp writing on significant topics imperative. Eliminate everything that has no direct relationship to the article's theme. Select details which add depth and color to the story. Direct quotes are indispensable." Pays 3¢ to 5¢ per word. Photos purchased with mss; quality 8x10 b&w glossies. Photos should help tell story. No model releases required. Pays $5.

AMERICAN LAUNDRY DIGEST, 500 N. Dearborn St., Chicago IL 60610. Phone: 312-337-7700. Editor: Ben Russell. For management of all types of laundries: family service, industrial, linen supply, diaper service, coin-op and institutional. Monthly. Buys first rights. Pays on publication. Will send free sample copy on request. Write for copy of guidelines for writers. Queries preferred. Reports "promptly." Enclose S.A.S.E.
Nonfiction: "Plant stories or interviews with heads of plants relating to either a single subject or a wide range of subjects, including production, cost-cutting, work-flow, marketing, sales, advertising, labor, etc. In short, articles that will help our readers run their own plants more profitably. We like for writers to explore the whys and why nots as well as the whats and hows." Pays minimum 3¢ a word.
Photos: Purchased with mss or with captions only. Candid action shots. Prefers 8x10 b&w glossy; 5x7 acceptable. Pays $5 minimum.
Fillers: Newsbreaks, clippings. Length: 10 to 300 words. Pays minimum $3.
How To Break In: "A beginning freelancer should: (1) familiarize himself with the magazine; (2) research the field by contacting editors, associations and perhaps his local library, for background information; (3) decide honestly if he can write and wants to write about some of the activities engaged in by industry firms; (4) try to find a story possibility in his locale that would fit in with the editorial approach of our magazine. Then query, suggesting a slant and including a list of questions that he thinks should be asked. Also include a list of suggested photos. Any editor worth his salt will be delighted to work with a beginning writer who goes to this trouble, and he will undoubtedly suggest other questions and, in general, give all the help he can."

INDUSTRIAL LAUNDERER, 1730 M St., N.W., Suite 613, Washington DC 20036. Editor: James L. Trichon. For decisionmakers in the laundry industry. Publication of the Institute of Industrial Launderers, Inc. Magazine; 24 pages. Established in 1949. Monthly. Circulation: over 3,000. Buys all rights, but will reassign rights (with some exceptions) to author after publication. Buys 15 to 20 mss a year. Pays on publication. Will send free sample copy to writer on request. Write for copy of guidelines for writers. No photocopied or simultaneous submissions. Reports in 1 week. Query first. Enclose S.A.S.E.
Nonfiction and Photos: General interest pieces for the industrial laundry industry; labor news, news from Washington; book reviews on publications of interest to

people in this industry. Technical advancements and "people" stories. Informational, personal experience, interview, profile, historical, successful business operations, merchandising techniques. Length: no less than 750 words. Pays minimum of $150. No additional payment for 8x10 b&w glossies used with ms. Pays minimum of $5 for those purchased on assignment. Captions required.

How To Break In: "Send covering letter along with copies of published material."

Law

JURIS DOCTOR MAGAZINE FOR THE NEW LAWYER, 555 Madison Ave., New York NY 10022. Editor: Robert Stuart Nathan. For "young lawyers, ages 25 to 37." 11 times per year. Circulation: 95,000. Buys first rights. Buys 30 mss a year. Pays on publication. Will send a free sample copy to a writer on request. Query first "with 2 short writing samples and an outline." Reports in 5 weeks. Enclose S.A.S.E.

Nonfiction: Wants articles on the legal profession, as well as travel and leisure items. Writer should show a knowledge of law, but should not be overly technical. Willing to research. "Most articles are muckraking pieces about the profession—the organized bar, law schools, new areas of legal practice. We also run book reviews." Interested in how-to, interviews, and profiles. Length: 2,000 to 3,500 words. Book reviews, 900 words. Payment is 10¢ a word. $50 for reviews. Recently published articles include "The Sinking of Title VII," "The Preposterous Case of Vermont Law School," "Rape: Who's on Trial?", and "Is Specialization a Conspiracy?"

Photos: B&w glossies purchased with mss and with captions only. Payment is $25.

LAWYER'S NEWSLETTER, 1180 S. Beverly Dr., Los Angeles CA 90035. Editor: Stephan Z. Katzan. For "attorneys." Monthly. Buys all rights. Pays on publication. Will send a sample copy to a writer on request. Reports in 2 weeks. Enclose S.A.S.E.

Nonfiction: "Our publication's main purpose is to increase the efficiency of attorneys and of law office operations. We are interested in suggestions and ideas for improvement of office operations as well as articles on legal economics." Length: 2,000 words maximum. Pays $100 per article.

STUDENT LAWYER, 1155 E. 60th St., Chicago IL 60637. Editor: David Martin. For law students or young lawyers, interested in social issues with legal emphasis, political material, job markets for lawyers; liberal interest in radical and other discriminatory issues. Publication of Law Student Division, American Bar Association. Magazine; 60 (8½x11) pages. Established in 1972. Monthly, except June, July, and August. Circulation: 25,000. Buys all rights. Buys about 50 mss a year. Pays on publication. Will send a sample copy to writer for 50¢. No photocopied or simultaneous submissions. Reports in 2 weeks. Query first or submit complete ms. Enclose S.A.S.E.

Nonfiction and Photos: "Our articles deal with the law, but since the law permeates all of society, our articles cover most of the major social issues. The articles do not have footnotes and can be personalized, bearing the author's distinctive style. Although we encourage subjective writing, the issue being dealt with should cover the major facts." Interested in articles on law and the rights of women, minorities, aged, children; investigative pieces on abuses of the law or the need for new laws. Recently published, "A Bill of Lefts", a highly personal and humorous piece on a bill of rights for left-handed people; "Those Mother Earth Blues", concerning the recent laws (and lack of them) regarding strip mining. Length: 1,000 to 3,000 words. Pays $25 to $75. Pieces of 1,000 words are bought for the Pro Se column (a column of opinion) and the To Read column (book reviews). Pays $25. B&w photos (8x10) purchased with or without ms or on assignment. Pays $35. Pays $50 for color slides or transparencies. Captions optional. Photo Editor: J. J. Podell.

Fiction: Mainstream and humorous stories of 1,000 to 3,000 words are sought. Pays $25 to $75.

Leather Goods

MASTER SHOE REBUILDER MAGAZINE, 15 Stonybrook Dr., Levittown PA 19055. Editor: Harold Lefcourt. For shoe repair shop owners. Magazine; 16 (7¼x10) pages. Established in 1942. Monthly. Circulation: 2,500. Buys all rights. Buys 20 to 30 mss a year. Pays on publication. Will send free sample copy to writer on request. Will consider photocopied and simultaneous submissions. Reports on material accepted for publication in 60 days. Returns rejected material immediately. Submit complete ms. Enclose S.A.S.E.
Nonfiction and Photos: Technical, small business information, customer relations articles. Simple writing. Informational, how-to, personal experience, profile, nostalgia, photo, travel, successful business operations, new product, merchandising techniques. Recently published an article on shoe repair training in the Philadelphia school system. Pays $10 to $65. Interviews with shoe repair shop owners and their success stories. Pays $25 to $40. No additional payment for b&w photos used with ms. Captions required. Pays $7.50 for photos purchased without mss.

Library Science

AMERICAN LIBRARIES, 50 E. Huron St., Chicago IL 60611. Phone: 312-944-6780. Editor: Arthur Plotnik. For librarians. "A highly literate audience. They are for the most part practicing professionals with high public contact and involvement interest." 11 times a year. Circulation: 35,000. Buys first North American serial rights. Will consider photocopied submissions if not being considered elsewhere at time of submission. Submit seasonal material 9 months in advance. Reports within 12 weeks. Enclose S.A.S.E.
Nonfiction, Photos, and Fillers: "Material reflecting the special and current interests of the library profession. Non-librarians should browse recent journals in the field, available on request in medium-sized and large libraries everywhere. Topic and/or approach must be fresh, vital, or highly entertaining. Stereotyped stories about old maids, overdue books, fines, etc., are unacceptable. Our first concern is with the American Library Association's activities, and how they relate to the 35,000 reader/ members. Tough for an outsider to write on this topic, but not to supplement it with short, offbeat library stories and features. Will look at all good b&w, natural light photos of library situations, and at color transparencies for possible cover use." Pays $5 to $150 for fillers and articles. Pays $5 to $50 for photos.
How To Break In: "With a sparkling, 300-word report on a true, offbeat library event, or with an exciting photo and caption."

FORECAST, The Baker & Taylor Co., 1515 Broadway, New York NY 10036. Editor: Rohest McCord. For public, school and special librarians nationwide. Magazine; 96 pages. Established in 1975. Published 8 times a year. Circulation: 40,000. Rights purchased vary with author and material. Buys all rights, but will sometimes reassign rights to author after publication. Buys 100 mss a year. Pays on acceptance. Will send free sample copy to writer on request. Write for copy of guidelines for writers. Will consider photocopied and simultaneous submissions. Submit only complete ms. Reports in 1 month. Enclose S.A.S.E.
Nonfiction and Photos: "Articles related to the book and information field and of special interest to librarians. Submit mss that cover topics of interest to librarians poorly covered in other publications. Articles about small presses, effect of economy on public libraries, how-to articles in library techniques (innovative), impact of technology on libraries, innovative library programs, library schools, are librarians adequately prepared?, etc." Recently published articles include "Bestsellers," "And

Then You Can Go Home," "A Few Words About Trout Fishing," "The Library as a Community Service," "The Library of the Future." Length: 1,500 to 3,500 words. Pays $75 to $250. Photos purchased with ms with no additional payment. Captions optional. Additional payment if photos are assigned.
Fiction and Fillers: Serialized novels, two installments at most. Must be "name" author or unusual work. Payment negotiable. Pays $20 to $75 for puzzles and jokes used as fillers.

THE HORN BOOK MAGAZINE, 585 Boylston St., Boston MA 02116. Editor: Ethel Heins. For librarians, teachers, parents, authors, illustrators, publishers. Bimonthly. Circulation: 27,500. Buys all rights, "subject to author's wishes." Buys 24 mss a year. Pays on publication. Will send a free sample copy to a writer on request. No query required. Reports in 3 months. Enclose S.A.S.E.
Nonfiction: Uses four or five articles per issue about children's books or children's pleasure reading, both in this country and others. Material must have originality and the ability to give inspiration to those working with children and books. Does not want articles on techniques of reading or articles aimed at the education market. Recently published articles include "Filming 'Zlateh the Goat' ", "As Far As You Can Bear to See: Excellence in Children's Literature" and "The Making of a Literary Reader." Read the magazine before submitting. "It is a literary magazine. Good writing required as well as suitable subject." Length: 3,000 words maximum. Pays "$20 a page."

LIBRARY JOURNAL, 1180 Avenue of the Americas, New York NY 10036. Editor: John N. Berry III. For librarians (academic, public, special, school). 115-page (8½x11) magazine published every 2 weeks. Established in 1876. Circulation: 40,000. Buys all rights. Buys 50 to 100 mss a year (mostly from professionals in the field). Payment on publication. Submit complete ms. Enclose S.A.S.E.
Nonfiction and Photos: Professional articles on criticism, censorship, professional concerns, library activities, historical articles and spot news. Outlook should be from librarian's point of view. Length: 1,500 to 2,000 words. Pays $50 to $250. Payment for b&w glossy photos purchased without accompanying mss is $25. Must be at least 5x7. Captions required.

MEDIA: LIBRARY SERVICES JOURNAL, 127 Ninth Avenue, North, Nashville TN 37234. Phone: 615-254-5461, Ext. 471. Editor: Wayne E. Todd. For "adult leaders in church organizations and people interested in library work, especially church library work." Quarterly. Circulation: 20,000. Buys all rights. Pays on acceptance. Will send a free sample copy to a writer on request. Query first. Enclose S.A.S.E.
Nonfiction: "Articles related to media, especially that relate to church libraries, audiovisuals available. The materials should definitely be practical for church library staffs or stories related to the use of media with persons." Interested in how-to, personal experience, inspirational. No length limitations. Payment is 2½¢ a word.

MICROFORM REVIEW, P.O. Box 1297, Weston CT 06880. Editor: Allen B. Veaner. For "librarians and educators at the college and university level." Established in 1972. Quarterly. Circulation: over 1,000. Rights purchased vary with author and material; may buy all rights. Buys "a few" mss a year. Pays on acceptance. Will send free sample copy to a writer on request. Write for copy of guidelines for writers. Query first. Will consider photocopied submissions. Reports in 3 weeks. Enclose S.A.S.E.
Nonfiction and Photos: "Articles dealing with micropublications, libraries and research using micropublications. We're interested in problems libraries have using microforms and the solutions to those problems." Buys informational articles, how-to's, personal experience articles, interviews, profiles, historical articles, reviews of micropublications, coverage of successful business operations, new product articles, articles on merchandising techniques, and technical articles. Length: 2,000 to 8,000 words. Pays $20 to $50. Photos purchased with and without mss; captions required.

THE PAMPHLETEER MONTHLY, 55 E. 86 St., New York NY 10028. Editor: William Frederick. A review source for all paper-covered materials: from single-page leaflets to booklets up to 120 pages. For the library trade; buying guide for public, college, university and special libraries; book review source. Magazine; 48 (6x9) pages. Established in 1940. Monthly except July/August. Circulation: 6,000. Buys all rights. Pays on acceptance. Query first. Send in a resume and clips of previous reviews or published writing. Enclose S.A.S.E.
Nonfiction: Book reviews on assignment only. Length: 50 words, average. Pays $1. (Usually, 50 to 100 assigned reviews at a time.)

SCHOOL LIBRARY JOURNAL, 1180 Avenue of the Americas, New York NY 10036. Phone: 212-764-5202. Editor: Lillian N. Gerhardt. For librarians in schools and public libraries. 88-page (8x11) magazine published monthly from September to May. Established in 1954. Circulation: 30,000. Buys all rights. Buys about 6 mss a year. Payment on publication. Will not consider photocopied or simultaneous submissions. Reports on material in 3 months. Enclose S.A.S.E.
Nonfiction: Articles on library services, local censorship problems, how-to articles on programs that use books or films. Informational, personal experience, interview, expose, successful business operations. "Interested in history articles on the establishment/development of children's and young adult services in schools and public libraries." Length: 2,500 to 3,000 words. Pays $100.

WILSON LIBRARY BULLETIN, 950 University Ave., Bronx NY 10452. Phone: 212-588-8400. Editor: William R. Eshelman; Assistant Editor: Harriet Rosenfeld. For professional librarians and those interested in the book and library worlds. Monthly, September through June. Circulation: 33,000. Buys North American serial rights only. Pays on publication. Sample copies may be seen on request in most libraries. "Ms must be original copy, double spaced; additional Xerox copy or carbon is appreciated. Deadlines are a minimum 2 months before publication." Reports in 2 to 8 weeks. Enclose S.A.S.E. for return of submissions.
Nonfiction: Uses articles "of interest to librarians throughout the nation and around the world. Style must be lively, readable and sophisticated, with appeal to modern professionals; facts must be thoroughly researched. Subjects range from the political to the comic in the world of media and libraries, with an emphasis on the human as well as the technical aspects of any story. No condescension: no library stereotypes." Recently published articles include "What's Slowing Down the 8mm Revolution?", "Napoleon's Great Librarians," and "Junior Books for Senior People." Length: 3,000 to 6,000 words. Pays about $50 to $150, "depending on the substance of article and its importance to readers."
How To Break In: "With a first rate b&w photo and caption information on a library, library service, or librarian that departs completely from all stereotypes and the commonplace. Note: Libraries have changed! You'd better first discover what is now commonplace."

Lumber and Woodworking

THE BRITISH COLUMBIA LUMBERMAN, 2000 West 12th Ave., Vancouver 9, B.C., Canada. Editor: Brian Martin. For forest industries (logging, sawmilling, plywood, marine and forest management). Monthly. Buys first rights. Pays on publication. Send resume, query, and topic outline first. Each issue has a specific theme. For example, sawmill trends, marine review, etc. Reports in 2 weeks. Enclose S.A.E. and International Reply Coupons.
Nonfiction: In-depth research articles on new developments, theories, practical applications, new methods, equipment usage and performance, etc., in the industry. Must be specific and accurate; especially applicable to forestry in British Columbia. Length: maximum 1,500 words. Pays 5¢ a word.

Photos: Purchased with mss or with captions only. B&w glossy; minimum 4x5 (8x10 preferred). Pays $5.

CANADIAN FOREST INDUSTRIES, 1450 Don Mills Rd., Don Mills, Ont., M3B 2X7, Canada. Editor: Rick Letkeman. Monthly. Buys all rights. Will consider cassette submissions. Reports within 1 month. Query first. Enclose S.A.E. and International Reply Coupons.

Nonfiction: Uses "articles concerning industry topics, especially how-to articles that help businessmen in the forest industries. All articles should take the form of detailed reports of new methods, techniques and cost-cutting practices that are being successfully used anywhere in Canada, together with descriptions of new machinery and equipment that is improving efficiency and utilization of wood. It is very important that accurate descriptions of machinery (make, model, etc.) be always included and any details of costs, etc., in actual dollars and cents can make the difference between a below-average article and an exceptional one." Length: 1,200 to 2,500 words. Pays 10¢ a word, more with photos.

Photos: Buys photos with mss, sometimes with captions only. Should be 8x10, b&w glossies or negatives. Pays $10 minimum.

NATIONAL HARDWOOD MAGAZINE, P.O. Box 18436, Memphis TN 38118. Phone: 901-362-1700. Editor: Floyd Keith. For "hardwood lumber mills and furniture manufacturers; their education varies, as do their interests." Established in 1927. Monthly. Circulation: 5,000. Buys all rights. Buys 12 to 24 mss per year. Pays on acceptance. Will send a sample copy to a writer on request. Write for copy of guidelines for writers. Query first. Will not consider photocopied submissions. Returns rejected material "usually right away." Reports on ms accepted for publication "usually within 3 to 4 months." Enclose S.A.S.E.

Nonfiction and Photos: "Furniture plant stories on those using large amounts of hardwood lumber; also, other plants that use hardwoods: casket firms, etc. We're the only publication dealing exclusively with hardwood lumber producers and users." Each plant story should include the following: Name of company and location, names of officers and plant manager, products manufactured, size of plant, number of employees, average number of hours per week the plant runs, sales force. (Do they have their own? Where's the sales office located? Where are the showrooms?). Complete descriptions of outstanding features or production ideas (how they work; what has been accomplished since their installation, etc.) Quantities, grades, thicknesses of lumber purchased annually; kinds of dimension used and for what purpose. Species of veneer purchased and for what purpose. Make of dry kilns, number, their capacity and moisture content of the lumber dried. Size of lumberyard and average inventory carried. History of the company and its growth; future plans. Dollar value of plant. Description of the flow of material through the plant from the back door to the front (lumberyard to the shipment of the finished product). In human interest articles, look for the following: An unusual request from a customer which the company fulfilled. The struggles the infant company went through to get established. The life of the man behind the company; how he got started in the business, etc. Has the company a unique record or reputation throughout the industry? What is it and how did it come about? 5x7 (or smaller) b&w glossies purchased with mss; captions required. Usually pays $125 for complete story and photographs.

PLYWOOD AND PANEL MAGAZINE, P.O. Box 567B, Indianapolis IN 46206. Phone: 317-634-1100. Editor: James F. Burrell. For manufacturers and industrial fabricators of plywood and veneer and particleboard. Monthly. Buys all rights. Pays on publication. Enclose S.A.S.E.

Nonfiction: "Factual and accurate articles concerning unusual techniques or aspects in the manufacturing or processing of veneer, plywood, particleboard, hardboard; detailing successful and/or unusual marketing techniques for wood panel products;

or concerning important or unusual industrial end-uses of these materials in the production of consumer goods." Length: maximum 1,000 words. Pays maximum 5¢ a word.
Photos: Of good quality and directly pertinent to editorial needs. Action photos; no catalog shots. No in-plant photos of machinery not operating or not manned in natural fashion. Must be completely captioned; 5x7 b&w or larger preferred. Pays up to $5 per photo.

WOOD & WOOD PRODUCTS, 300 W. Adams St., Chicago IL 60606. Editor: James D. Saul. "For management and operating executives of all types wood product manufacturers normally employing minimum of 20 persons." Monthly. Circulation: 30,000. Buys first rights. Pays on acceptance. Will send fact sheet on request. "Detailed query imperative." Reports in 2 to 4 weeks. Enclose S.A.S.E.
Nonfiction: "Semitechnical to technical articles, manufacturing process descriptions, safety, management. Prefer an in-depth treatment of how one company solved one or more problems. No handicraft, forestry or logging articles. Must be entirely factual and accurate. Photos essential." Length: 1,500 words maximum. Pays $100 and up for feature articles, based on merit, not length. Need list of suppliers of machinery, equipment and material, and flow diagram of operation.
Photos: Purchased with mss. "Must have complete descriptive captions; flow diagram. Photos of employees and machinery in natural operating positions. No mug shots, no catalog shots wanted. Any size negative from 35mm up; prints 5x7 or 8x10." Color only on assignment.

WOODWORKING & FURNITURE DIGEST, Hitchcock Bldg., Wheaton IL 60187. Editor: Richard D. Rea. For industrial manufacturers whose products employ wood as a basic raw material. Monthly. Buys all rights. Pays on publication. Will send free sample copy to serious freelancer on request. Query first. Reports in 10 days. Will sometimes hold ms for further evaluation up to 2 months, if it, at first, appears to have possibilities. Enclose S.A.S.E.
Nonfiction and Photos: "Articles on woodworking and furniture manufacturing with emphasis on management concepts, applications for primary raw materials (including plastics, if involved with wood), technology of remanufacturing methods and machines, and news of broad industry interest. Articles should focus on cost reduction, labor efficiency, product improvement, and profit. No handcraft, do-it-yourself or small custom shopwork. Present theme, or why reader can benefit, in first paragraph. Cover 'feeds and speeds' thoroughly to include operating data and engineering reasons why. Leave reader with something to do or think. Avoid mechanically handled case histories and plant tours which do not include management/engineering reasons." Photos, charts and diagrams which tell what cannot be told in words should be included. "We like a balance between technical information and action photos." Length: "no length limit, but stop before you run out of gas!" Pays $35 to $50 per published page. Photos purchased with mss. Good technical quality and perception of subject shown. No posed views. Prefers candid action or tight closeups. Full-color cover photo must be story-related.

Machinery and Metal Trade

ASSEMBLY ENGINEERING, Hitchcock Publishing Co., Wheaton IL 60187. Editor: Robert T. Kelly. For design and manufacturing engineers and production personnel concerned with assembly problems in manufacturing plants. Monthly. Buys first publication rights. Pays on publication. Sample copy will be sent on request. "Query first on leads or ideas. We report on ms decision as soon as review is completed and provide edited proofs for checking by author, prior to publication." Enclose S.A.S.E.
Nonfiction and Photos: Wants features on design, engineering and production practices for the assembly of manufactured products. Material should be submitted

on "exclusive rights" basis and, preferably, should be written in the third person. Subject areas include selection, specification, and application of fasteners, mounting hardware, electrical connectors, wiring, hydraulic and pneumatic fittings, seals and gaskets, adhesives, joining methods (soldering, welding, brazing, etc.), and assembly equipment; specification of fits and tolerances; joint design; design and shop assembly standards; time and motion study (assembly line); quality control in assembly; layout and balancing of assembly lines; assembly tool and jig design; programming assembly line operations; working conditions, incentives, labor costs, and union relations as they relate to assembly line operators; hiring and training of assembly line personnel; supervisory practices for the assembly line. Also looking for news items on assembly-related subjects, and for unique or unusual "ideas" on assembly components, equipment, processes, practices and methods. Requires good quality photos or sketches, usually close-ups of specific details. Pays $30 per published page.

AUTOMATIC MACHINING, 65 Broad St., Rochester NY 14614. Editor: Donald E. Wood. For metalworking technical management. Buys all rights. Query first. Enclose S.A.S.E.
Nonfiction: "This is not a market for the average freelancer. Articles deal in depth with specific job operations on automatic screw machines, chucking machines, high production metal turning lathes and cold heading machines. Part prints, tooling layouts always required, plus written agreement of source to publish the material. Without personal background in operation of this type of equipment, freelancers are wasting time." Length: "no limit." Pays $20 per printed page.

CANADIAN MACHINERY AND METALWORKING, 481 University Ave., Toronto M5W 1A7, Ont., Canada. Editor: A. Whitney. Monthly. Buys first Canadian rights. Pays on publication. Will consider cassette submissions. Query first. Enclose S.A.E. and International Reply Coupons.
Nonfiction: Technical and semitechnical articles dealing with metalworking operations in Canada and in the U.S., if of particular interest. Accuracy and service appeal to readers is a must. Pays minimum 7¢ a word.
Photos: Purchased with mss and with captions only. "Color for covers only." Pays $5 minimum for b&w features, $50 for color covers.

CUTTING TOOL ENGINEERING, P.O. Box 937, Wheaton IL 60187. Editor: N.D. O'Daniell. For metalworking industry executives and engineers concerned with design, function, and application of metal cutting tools. Monthly. Circulation: 25,000. Buys all rights. Pays on publication. Will send free sample copy on request. Query required. Enclose S.A.S.E.
Nonfiction: "Intelligently written articles on specific applications of all types of metal cutting tools—mills, drills, reamers, etc. Articles must contain all information related to the operation, such as feeds and speeds, materials machined, etc. Should be tersely written, in-depth treatment. In the Annual Diamond Directory, published in July, we cover the use of diamond cutting tools and diamond grinding wheels." Length: 1,000 to 2,500 words. Pays "$35 per published page, or about 5¢ a published word."
Photos: Purchased with mss. 8x10 b&w glossies. No Polaroids.

FOUNDRY MAGAZINE, Penton Plaza, Cleveland OH 44114. Phone: 216-696-7000. Editor: J. C. Miske. Monthly. Reports in 2 weeks. Enclose S.A.S.E.
Nonfiction and Photos: Uses articles describing operating practice in foundries written to interest companies producing metal castings. Length: maximum 3,000 words. Pays $35 a printed page. Uses illustrative 8x10 photographs with articles.

INDUSTRIAL FINISHING, Hitchcock Building, Wheaton IL 60187. Editor: Matt Heuertz. Monthly. Circulation: 35,000. Buys first rights. Buys 3 or 4 mss a year. Pays on acceptance. Will send a free sample copy to a writer on request. Query first. Enclose S.A.S.E.
Nonfiction and Photos: Wants "technical articles on finishing operations for oem products." Style should be "direct and to the point." Photos purchased with mss, "as part of the complete package which we purchase at $100 to $150."

INDUSTRIAL MACHINERY NEWS, P.O. Box 727, Dearborn MI 48121. Editor: Lucky D. Slate. For "metalworking manufacturing managers and engineers who plan and select methods of manufacturing design equipment for manufacturers, or create or refine manufacturing techniques and work in metalworking plants." Established in 1952. Monthly. Circulation: 65,000. Buys all rights. Pays on publication. Will send a sample copy to a writer for $1. Write for copy of guidelines for writers. Will consider photocopied submissions. Query first or submit complete ms. Repoits in 1 to 3 months. Enclose S.A.S.E.

Nonfiction and Photos: Articles on "metal removal, metal forming, assembly, finishing, inspection, application of machine tools, technology, measuring, gauging equipment, small cutting tools, tooling accessories, materials handling in metal-working plants, safety programs. We give our publication a newspaper feel—fast reading with lots of action or human interest photos." Buys how-to's. Pays $25 minimum. Length: open. Photos purchased with mss; captions required. Pays $5 minimum.

Fillers: Newsbreaks, puzzles, jokes, short humor. Pays $5 minimum.

How To Break In: "Stories on old machine tools—how they're holding up and how they're being used."

METALWORKING, 297 Old Kingston Rd., West Hill, Ont., Canada. Editor: Don Quick. Buys first publication rights. Query first. Enclose S.A.E. and International Reply Coupons.

Nonfiction and Photos: "Articles with illustrations on machine production and management techniques in Canada. Magazine readership covers management, production, engineering, and purchasing functions of all industry wherever any metal is worked. Submission should detail a manufacturing process involving metal; report on metallurgical discoveries having a manufacturing management relation to production." Material with a Canadian plant angle only. Length: 600 to 1,500 words. Pays 2¢ to 5¢ a word, "depending on quality."

MODERN MACHINE SHOP, 600 Main St., Cincinnati OH 45202. Editor: Fred W. Vogel. Monthly. Pays 30 days following acceptance. Query first. Reports in 5 days. Enclose S.A.S.E.

Nonfiction: Uses articles dealing with all phases of metal manufacturing and machine shop work, with photos. Length: 1,500 to 2,000 words. Pays current market rate.

ORNAMENTAL METAL FABRICATOR, Suite 106, 443 E. Paces Ferry Rd. N.E., Atlanta GA 30305. Editor: Blanche Blackwell. For fabricators of ornamental metal who are interested in their businesses and families, their community and nation. Most are owners of small businesses employing an estimated average of 10 persons, usually including family members. Official publication of the National Ornamental Manufacturers Association. Magazine published every 2 months; 24 pages. Established in 1958. Circulation: 5,500. Not copyrighted. Buys 6 mss a year. Payment on acceptance. Will send free sample copy to writer on request. Will not consider photocopied or simultaneous submissions. Submit seasonal material 2 months in advance. Reports immediately. Query first. Enclose S.A.S.E.

Nonfiction and Photos: "Our publication deals solely with fabrication of ornamental metal, a more creative and aesthetic aspect of the metals construction industry. Special emphasis on ornamental metal trade. How-to articles that will help our readers improve their businesses. Articles on use and history of ornamental metal; on better operation of the business; on technical aspects. News about the association and its individual members and about 6 regional chapters affiliated with the national association. Articles on the effects of steel shortage on ornamental metal fabricator and how a typical firm is handling the problem; the search for qualified employees; successful prepaint treatments and finishes." Prefers not to see "character study" articles. Length: 1,000 to 5,000 words. Pays 3¢ per word. B&w glossy photos purchased with accompanying mss. Pays $4. Color is not accepted.

POWER TRANSMISSION DESIGN, 614 Superior Ave. West, Cleveland OH 44113. Phone: 216-696-0300. Editor: Tom Hughes. For design engineers and persons who buy, operate, and maintain motors, drives, bearings, and related controls. Monthly. Circulation: 46,500. Buys all rights, but may reassign rights to author after publication. Pays on acceptance. Reports in 3 weeks. Enclose S.A.S.E.

Nonfiction and Photos: "The article should answer these questions: What does the machine do? What loads and load changes, speed and speed changes, does the operation impose upon the drive system? What drive system do you use and why? What were the alternatives, and why did you reject them? How did the operating environment affect the selection of motors, drives, bearings, and controls? How is the machine designed for easy maintenance? What are the sizes and capacities of the motors, drives, bearings, and controls? How does the drive system design make the machine superior to competitive machines? To previous models of your manufacture? What specific advances in motors, drives, bearings, and controls have led to improvements in machines like this one? What further advances would you like to see? Accompany your write-up with a photo of the machine and close-ups of the drive system and schematic drawings and blueprints, if necessary." Length: 600 to 6,000 words; "anything longer we'll break up and serialize." Pays $25 "per published magazine page (about 600 words to a page)."

PRODUCTION, Box 101, Bloomfield Hills MI 48013. Editor: Robert F. Huber. For "managers of manufacturing." Monthly. Circulation: 80,000. Buys all rights. Buys "a few" mss a year. Pays on acceptance. Query first. Enclose S.A.S.E.
Nonfiction and Photos: "Trends, developments, and applications in manufacturing." Length: open. Pays $50 to $350. Photos purchased with mss; captions required.

PRODUCTS FINISHING, 600 Main St., Cincinnati OH 45202. Editor: Gerard H. Poll, Jr. Monthly. Buys all rights. Pays within 30 days after acceptance. Reports in 1 week. Enclose S.A.S.E. for return of submissions.
Nonfiction: Uses "material devoted to the finishing of metal and plastic products. This includes the cleaning, plating, polishing and painting of metal and plastic products of all kinds. Articles can be technical and must be practical. Technical articles should be on processes and methods. Particular attention given to articles describing novel approaches used by product finishers to control air and water pollution, and finishing techniques that reduce costs." Pays 8¢ minimum per word.
Photos: Wants photographs dealing with finishing methods or processes. Pays $10 minimum for each photo used.

STEEL FACTS, 1000 16th St., N.W., Washington DC 20036. Editor: Thomas D. Patrick. For "opinion leaders; all ages and professions." Established in 1933. Quarterly. Circulation: 140,000. Not copyrighted. Buys 4 to 6 mss a year. Payment on acceptance. Will send free sample copy to writer on request. Query first. Enclose S.A.S.E.
Nonfiction and Photos: Articles on the environmental, energy, economics, international trade, new technology aspects of the steel industry. "No product articles." Interviews, think pieces, technical. Length: 50 to 2,000 words. Pays $25 to $400. Photos purchased with or without accompanying ms or on assignment. Proofsheets and negatives. Color transparencies. Pays $15 to $100. Captions required. Freelance articles on assignment only. Recent articles were about the Russian steel industry, nuclear energy, inflation and profits, recycling, and railroads.

33 MAGAZINE, McGraw-Hill Bldg., 1221 Avenue of the Americas, New York NY 10020. Editor: Joseph L. Mazel. For "operating managers (from turn foreman on up), engineers, metallurgical and chemical specialists, and corporate officials in the steelmaking industry. Work areas for these readers range from blast furnace and coke ovens into and through the steel works and rolling mills. *33*'s readers also work in nonferrous industries." Monthly. Buys all rights. Pays on publication. Will send free sample copy on request. Query required. Reports in 3 weeks. Enclose S.A.S.E.
Nonfiction and Photos: Case histories of primary metals producing equipment in use, such as smelting, blast furnace, steelmaking, rolling. "Broadly speaking, *33*

Magazine concentrates its editorial efforts in the areas of technique (what's being done and how it's being done), technology (new developments), and equipment (what's being used). Your article should include a detailed explanation (who, what, why, where, and how) and the significance (what it means to operating manager, engineer, or industry) of the techniques, technology or equipment being written about. In addition, your readers will want to know of the problems you experienced during the planning, developing, implementing, and operating phases. And, it would be especially beneficial to tell of the steps you took to solve the problems or roadblocks encountered. You should also include all cost data relating to implementation, operation, maintenance, etc., wherever possible. Benefits (cost savings; improved manpower utilization; reduced cycle time; increased quality; etc.) should be cited to gauge the effectiveness of the subject being discussed. The highlight of any article is its illustrative material. This can take the form of photographs, drawings, tables, charts, graphs, etc. Your type of illustration should support and reinforce the text material. It should not just be an added, unrelated item. Each element of illustrative material should be identified and contain a short description of exactly what is being presented." Pays $35 per published page. Minimum 5x7 b&w glossies purchased with mss.

THE WELDING DISTRIBUTOR, Box 128, Morton Grove IL 60053. Editor: Donald Jefferson. For wholesale and retail distributors of welding equipment and safety supplies and their sales staffs. Bimonthly. Buys all rights. Pays on publication. Enclose S.A.S.E. for return of submissions.
Nonfiction: Categories of editorial coverage are: management, process/product knowledge, profiles, selling and safety. Pays 2¢ a word.

Maintenance and Safety

MAINTENANCE SUPPLIES, 101 W. 31 St., New York NY 10001. Editorial Director: John Vollmuth. For distributors of sanitary supplies. Monthly. Circulation: 10,000. Not copyrighted. Payment on publication. Will send free sample copy to writer on request. Submit complete ms. Reports "as soon as possible." Enclose S.A.S.E.
Nonfiction and Photos: All news stories are staff-written. "Articles pointing out trends in the sanitary supply fields; stories about distributors, possible markets and merchandising. We expect a writer to turn out an article about some aspect of the sanitary supply field for readers who sell the products of this industry. General sales articles are sometimes accepted, but stories geared to the specific industry are much preferred." Length: 1,500 words. Pays $90. 8x10 b&w photos purchased with accompanying ms. Captions required.
How To Break In: "Probably the best way to break in would be with a story on the cleaning of an unusual establishment. For instance, we've had stories on cleaning the World Trade Center, cleaning Rockefeller Center, and cleaning Trinity Church. Should be done from the point of view of what supplies were used. Another good type of piece is the profile of someone in the field, such as a distributor of janitorial supplies. It would ideally be a good, sound company with a plant that lends itself to photos, and it would help if they also have some unusual procedures or selling techniques."

OCCUPATIONAL HAZARDS, 614 Superior Ave. W., Cleveland OH 44113. Editor: Peter J. Sheridan. "Distributed by function to middle management officials in industry who have the responsibility for accident prevention, occupational health, plant fire protection, and plant security programs. Job titles on our list include: safety directors, industrial hygienists, fire protection engineers, plant security managers, and medical directors." Monthly. Buys first rights in field. Pays on publication. Reports in 30 days. Enclose S.A.S.E.
Nonfiction: "Articles on industrial health, safety, security and fire protection. Specific facts and figures must be cited. No material on farm, home, or traffic safety. All material accepted subject to sharp editing to conform to publisher's distilled writing

style. Illustrations preferred but not essential. Work is rejected when story is not targeted to professional concerns of our readers, but rather is addressed to the world at large." Length: 300 to 2,000 words. Pays minimum 3¢ a word.

Photos: Accepts 4x5, 5x7 and 8x10 photos with mss. Pays $5.

SDM: SECURITY DISTRIBUTING & MARKETING, 2639 S. La Cienega Blvd., Los Angeles CA 90034. Editor: Robert J. Bargert. For security products dealers, distributors, manufacturers; electrical and electronics engineering background; technically oriented. Magazine; 80 to 96 pages; 8½x11. Buys all rights. Buys 10 to 12 mss a year. Pays on publication. Will send free sample copy to writer on request. Submit complete ms. Submit special or seasonal material 3 months in advance. Reports in 1 week. Enclose S.A.S.E.

Nonfiction and Photos: News stories, case history success stories, how-to stories (how to advertise and promote, etc.). Length: 1,500 to 5,000 words. Pays $45 per printed page. Photos purchased with accompanying ms. Captions required. Pays $7.50 for b&w; $15 for color.

How To Break In: "New writers should obtain some working knowledge of the security products field. Interested in obtaining stories about dealers who installed burglar alarms that worked when needed. Can be obtained from news stories in papers and followed up with personal interview with dealer."

Management and Supervision

This category includes trade journals for lower level business and industrial managers, including supervisors and office managers. Journals for business executives and owners are classified under Business Management. Those for industrial plant managers are listed in Industrial Management.

THE BUSINESS QUARTERLY, School of Business Administration, University of Western Ontario, London, Ontario N6A 3K7, Canada. Editor: Doreen Sanders. For persons in upper and middle management, university education, interested in continuing and updating their management education. Established in 1933. Quarterly. Circulation: 7,100. Buys all rights. Buys 35 mss a year. Payment on publication. Reports in 3 months. Query first with brief outline of article. Enclose S.A.E. and International Reply Coupons.

Nonfiction: Articles pertaining to all aspects of management development. Must have depth. "Think" articles and those on successful business operations. Length: 2,000 to 5,000 words. Pays $100.

CALIFORNIA INDUSTRY, 609 Mission St., San Francisco CA 94105. Editor: Gary Hanauer. For corporation chiefs, company presidents, top-line executives, foremen, plant managers, plant engineers, material handlers, production line chiefs, purchasing agents, sales managers, and others involved in the purchase or approval of new equipment and supplies in California, Oregon, Washington, Arizona, and Hawaii. Magazine; 36 to 60 (8x11) pages. Established in 1925. Published 10 times a year. Circulation: 17,300. Rights purchased vary with author and material. Usually buys all rights, but may buy simultaneous rights. Buys 25 to 40 mss a year. Pays on publication. Will send free sample copy to writer on request. Will consider photocopied and simultaneous submissions. Reports in 3 to 10 days. Query first. Enclose S.A.S.E.

Nonfiction and Photos: "Basic themes for purchased articles include the latest in how-to industrial information, spanning a wide range of horizontal interests: plant engineering, production, material handling, management, hiring, training, recruitment, saving energy, controlling plant pollution, etc. Material is focused on actual case histories in our five reader states. Generally, we'll be looking for more articles on pollution control, safety, conveying, the use of racks, other material handling subjects, worker protection devices, and anything in the 'unique' category. For example, we've run an article on a plant that's allowing its workers to build a victory garden in space next to the building. Another one told about the operation of industrial cafeterias." Length: 750 to 1,000 words. Pays $50 to $75; occasionally to $150.

CONSTRUCTION FOREMAN'S & SUPERVISOR'S LETTER, 24 Rope Ferry Rd., Waterford CT 06385. Editor: Harry Hintlian. For company supervisors involved in all phases of construction. Established in 1965. Semimonthly. Circulation: 9,000. Buys all rights. Buys 4 to 6 mss per issue. Pays on acceptance. Will send free sample copy to writer on request. Write for copy of guidelines for writers. Reports in 3 weeks. Query first or submit complete ms. Enclose S.A.S.E.

Nonfiction and Photos: Interviews with supervisors whose performance is above average. Does not want to see anything outside of their field of interest. Length: 200 to 800 words. Pays 7¢ per edited word; $5 for "mug shot" photos. Captions required.

THE FOREMAN'S LETTER, National Foremen's Institute, 24 Rope Ferry Rd., Waterford CT 06385. Editor: Frank Berkowitz. For industrial supervisors. Semimonthly. Buys all rights. Pays on acceptance. "Query preferred only if out-of-pocket expenses may be involved." Interested in regular stringers (freelance) on area exclusive basis. Enclose S.A.S.E.

Nonfiction: Interested primarily in direct interviews with industrial (including construction and public utilities companies) foremen in the U.S. and Canada, written in newspaper feature or magazine article style, with concise, uncluttered, non-repetitive prose as an essential. Subject matter would be the interviewee's techniques for managing people, bolstered by illustrations out of the interviewee's own job experiences. Slant would be toward informing readers how their most effective contemporaries function, free of editorial comment. "Our aim is to offer information which, hopefully, readers may apply to their own professional self-improvement." Length: maximum 750 words. Pays 7¢ to 8½¢ a word "after editing."

Photos: Buys photos submitted with mss. "Captions needed for identification only." Head and shoulders, any size b&w glossy from 2x3 up. Pays $5.

INSTITUTIONAL PRODUCT NEWS, 221 N. LaSalle, Suite 748, Chicago IL 60601. Editor: Laurel Kennedy. For administrators of large hospitals, school systems, universities, nursing homes, hotel/motel chains, auditoriums, restaurants. Magazine; 40 tabloid pages. Established in 1973. Monthly. Circulation: 88,000. Buys all rights, but will reassign rights to author after publication. Buys about 52 mss a year. Pays on publication. Will send free sample copy to writer on request. Write for copy of guidelines for writers. Will consider photocopied and simultaneous submissions. Reports in 1 month. Query first or submit complete ms. Enclose S.A.S.E.

Nonfiction: Anything of interest horizontally to the institutional market. Architecture, environmental products, office theory and management techniques; security installations, furnishings articles; laundry management ideas; maintenance systems. Interesting office equipment or management theory applications. Refurbishing stories from an architectural or furnishings slant. Stories of different sanitation and maintenance systems. Stress laid on management ideas and techniques; installations. Writers are advised to call first for editorial directions. The first-person writing approach is to be avoided. Keep in mind the broad market segment reading the article; make article appeal to all elements. Length: 2,000 to 4,000 words. Pays maximum of $50 per published page.

How To Break In: "If in area, call and make an appointment, and bring in writing samples. If not in area, send writing samples and outline of article idea; follow up with phone call."

LE BUREAU, 625 President Kennedy, Montreal H3A 1K5, Que., Canada. Editor: Paul Saint-Pierre. For "office executives." Established in 1965. 6 times per year. Circulation: 7,500. Buys all rights, but will reassign rights to author after publication. Buys about 10 mss a year. Pays on acceptance. Will send a sample copy to a writer on request. Query first or submit complete ms. Submit seasonal material "between

1 and 2 months" of issue date. Enclose S.A.E. and International Reply Coupons for return of submissions.

Nonfiction and Photos: "Our publication is published in the French language. We use case histories on new office systems, applications of new equipment, articles on personnel problems. Material should be exclusive and above-average quality." Buys personal experience articles, interviews, think pieces, coverage of successful business operations, and new product articles. Length: 500 to 1,000 words. Pays $50. B&w glossies purchased with mss. Pays $5.

MANAGE, 2210 Arbor Blvd., Dayton OH 45439. "Official publication of the National Management Association. Most readers are members of company or city chapters of this organization. They are primarily middle management, first line supervisors, or scientific-technical managers." Established in 1925. Bimonthly. Circulation: 70,000. Buys first North American serial rights "with reprint privileges," or "sometimes" second serial or simultaneous rights. Buys about 24 mss a year. Pays on acceptance. Will send a sample copy to a writer on request. Write for copy of guidelines for writers. Query first or submit complete ms for nonfiction, quizzes, puzzles. Submit complete ms for short humor. Address mss to Managing Editor. Will consider photocopied submissions. Returns rejected material in 2 weeks. Reports on mss accepted for publication in 1 month. Enclose S.A.S.E.

Nonfiction and Photos: "Content shows how to advance the management abilities and status of our readers. Most articles concern 1 or more of the following categories: communications, economics and cost reduction, executive abilities, health and safety, labor-human relations, leadership and motivation, professionalism. Articles must be practical and tell the manager how to apply the information to his job. Be specific and back up statements with facts and, where possible, charts and illustrations. Include pertinent anecdotes and examples. In general, we want lively, interesting articles of immediate value to our readers. *Manage* also contains articles dealing with NMA's clubs, activities, and members, but these are staff-written. We do not want academic reports, essays, personal opinion pieces, overt promotions, or 'how my company did this.'" Buys informational articles, how-to's, interviews, humor "relating to management," think articles, coverage of successful business practices. Length: 600 to 2,500 words for articles; under 500 words for humor. Pays 3¢ to 5¢ a word. 8x10 or 5x7 b&w glossies purchased with mss, captions required. "No mug shots." Pays $5 for inside use, $15 if used for cover.

Poetry: "Not published previously, but light verse relating to management might be considered." Length: 2 to 4 lines. Pays $5.

Fillers: Puzzles, quizzes "in same areas as nonfiction." Pays $2 to $5, "depending on length and quality."

MANAGEMENT DIGEST, Allied Publications, Inc., P.O. Box 23505, Fort Lauderdale FL 33307. Associate Editor: Louise Hinton. Buys first North American serial rights. Pays on acceptance. Reports in 2 to 4 weeks. Enclose S.A.S.E.

Nonfiction and Photos: "Articles of interest to executive management personnel." Buys interviews, profiles, inspirational articles, humor, spot news, coverage of successful business operations, think pieces, photo features, and articles on merchandising techniques. Length: 500 to 1,000 words. Pays 5¢ a word. B&w glossies purchased with mss. Pays $5.

MODERN BUSINESS REPORTS, Alexander Institute, 605 Third Ave., New York NY 10016. Editor: J. M. Jenks. For management and business methods personnel. Newsletter; 8 pages. Established in 1972. Monthly. Buys all rights. Buys 25 mss a year. Pays on acceptance. Will send free sample copy to writer on request. No photocopied or simultaneous submissions. Reports in 2 weeks. Query first. Enclose S.A.S.E.

Nonfiction: Articles on management methods and practices, management by objectives, cost reduction methods, administration. All material must give readers a piece of information on a mangement or business practice that can be used or put to use in a company. Would be interested in material on transcendental meditation in business and transactional analysis in business. Length: 1,000 to 1,500 words. Pays 15¢ a word.

OFFICE SUPERVISOR'S BULLETIN, Bureau of Business Practice, 681 Fifth Ave., New York NY 10022. Phone: 212-758-8210. For first and second line office supervisors. Semimonthly. Buys all rights. Pays on acceptance. Will send a free sample copy to a writer on request. Query first. Address mss to the Editor. Reports in 1 week. Enclose S.A.S.E.
Nonfiction: "Emphasis is on good methods of getting things done through others. Articles give practical how-to tips to help office supervisors increase productivity, cut absenteeism and tardiness, raise morale, cut costs, and generally do their jobs better. From freelancers, we need interview-based articles quoting, by name, top-notch (but lower level) office supervisors in industry, business and government. You should ask interviewees to pinpoint current problems in supervision, discuss how they're solving these problems in their company, what results they're getting. Illustrate with real examples from daily office life. We're interested only in 'people problems' common to all offices, not systems or machinery problems. Sample subjects: Planning, training, disciplining, listening, motivating, evaluating performance, counseling getting along with the boss, reducing errors, enriching jobs, controlling costs, affirmative action, upward and downward communication. For current subjects, keep yourself informed by checking lists of seminars offered by universities, American Management Association, chambers of commerce, and by regularly checking management publications. If you're serious about writing in this field, spend some time in the library reading about management. We do not give assignments. You must find interviewees yourself. For leads, look for stories about successful new methods or training programs in: financial pages of your local paper, house organs (ask friends for their company publications), announcements of business seminars. Please don't interview management consultants or professors. But you can ask them what companies are doing great things in supervision. If you have a subject in mind, contact the public relations department of a likely company. Utilities, banks, insurance companies, any firms with lots of paperwork are good prospects. To stay on target as you write and interview, keep saying to yourself: 'How is this important to the lower level office supervisor?' Avoid topics he has no control over (changing company salary policies, moving to another location, buying computers). Keep in mind the problem/solution/result format. Don't talk down to readers; they know more than you do about supervising." Recently published articles include "Learn the Art of Saying 'No'," "How to Let Workers Know You Really Care," and "Skillful Listening Prevents Discontent." Length: 900 to 1,350 words. Pays $35 per published page (about 450 words). Prefers 2- to 3-page articles.

SUPERVISION, 424 N. 3rd Street, Burlington IA 52601. Phone: 319-752-5415. Editor: G.B. McKee. For foremen, personnel managers, supervisors, and department heads. Monthly. Buys all rights. Pays on publication. Sample copy sent on request. Query first. Reports in 10 days. Enclose S.A.S.E.
Nonfiction and Photos: Wants "how-to articles dealing with manufacturing plant situations relating to improving production, cutting costs, handling grievances, eliminating waste, building morale. Case study situations preferred, showing how a specific problem was overcome and what benefits resulted. Clear style wanted; article must contain practical information." Length: 1,500 to 2,000 words. Payment is 2¢ a word. Occasionally buys b&w photos with mss. Payment is $5.

TRAINING, The Magazine of Manpower and Management Development, One Park Ave., New York NY 10036. Phone: 212-725-3949. Editor: Harold Littledale. For people who train other people in business and industry; government and the military; in hospitals; educational and social service agencies. Monthly. Rights purchased vary with author and material. Usually buys all rights, but will buy first North American serial rights. Pays on acceptance. Will consider photocopied submissions. Submit seasonal material 3 months in advance. Reports in 4 weeks. Query first for all material. Enclose S.A.S.E.

Nonfiction and Photos: "We seek information on the management and techniques of employee training. Material should discuss a specific training problem; why the problem existed; how it was solved, the alternative solutions, etc. Should furnish enough data for readers to make an independent judgment about the appropriateness of the solution to the problem. Articles are written from the viewpoint of a practitioner for other practitioners. No 'gee whiz' approach which might be suitable for general-audience magazines. We want names and specific details of all techniques and processes used." Pays $30 per printed page. No extra payment for photos.

UTILITY SUPERVISION, National Foremen's Institute, 24 Rope Ferry Rd., Waterford CT 06385. Phone: 203-442-4365. Editor: Frank Berkowitz. For "first-line supervisors for public utilities companies (electric & gas companies, water companies, sewerage departments, municipal mass transportation, etc.)" Semimonthly. Buys all rights; buys first rights for photos. Buys 100 mss a year. Pays on acceptance. Will send a free sample copy to a writer on request. Query first. Reports in 2 weeks. Enclose S.A.S.E.
Nonfiction and Photos: Wants "interviews with working supervisors, dealing with techniques they utilize in directing employees." Approach should be "tightly written, unrepetitious, newspaper or magazine feature-style, free of any editorializing, free of irrelevancies." Does not want think pieces. "We rely almost exclusively on the direct interview." Length: 800 words maximum. Payment is 7¢ a word minimum, "as edited." B&w glossy "head and shoulders" photos purchased with mss. Payment is $5.

Marine Industries and Water Navigation

In this list are journals for seamen, boatbuilders, navigators, boat dealers, and others interested in water as a means of travel or shipping. Journals for commercial fishermen are classified with Fishing journals. Publications for scientists studying the ocean will be found under Oceanography.

AMERICAN SHIPPER, (formerly *Florida Journal of Commerce/Seafarer*). Box 4728, Jacksonville FL 32201. Editor: David A. Howard. For businessmen in shipping, transportation and foreign trade. Monthly magazine; 32 pages. Established in 1958. Circulation: 12,000. Not copyrighted. Buys 36 mss a year. Pays on acceptance. Will send free sample copy to writer on request. Reports within 1 month. Enclose S.A.S.E.
Nonfiction and Photos: "In-depth features. Analytical pieces (based on original data or research). Port finances. Other transportation and export items (in-depth) with solid figures. News approach, basically. No 'old salt' human interest." Length: "depends on need of subject." Pays $100 to $150. Photos purchased with accompanying ms with no additional payment. Captions required.

THE BOATING INDUSTRY, 205 E. 42nd St., New York NY 10017. Editor: Charles A. Jones. For "boating retailers and distributors." Established in 1929. Monthly. Circulation: 26,000. Buys all rights, but will reassign rights to author after publication. Buys 10 to 15 mss a year. Pays on publication. Will send a free sample copy to a writer on request. "Best practice is to check with editor first on story ideas for go-ahead." Submit seasonal material 3 to 4 months in advance of issue date. Returns rejected material in 2 months. Acknowledges acceptance of material in 1 month. Enclose S.A.S.E.
Nonfiction and Photos: Uses "boat dealer success stories." Pays 7¢ to 10¢ a word. B&w glossy photos purchased with mss. Payment for photos is $5 to $35 for covers.

MARINE ENGINEERING LOG, 350 Broadway, New York NY 10013. Phone: 212-966-7700. Editor: Robert Ware. For shipbuilding and ship repair companies; ship operating companies, owners, agents and brokers; naval architects and marine engineers; other readers associated with the marine field. Monthly except June, when publication is semimonthly. Buys exclusive rights "unless specific arrangements are

made to the contrary." Pays on publication. Reports "immediately." Enclose S.A.S.E.
Nonfiction and Photos: Wants "articles of a technical or semitechnical nature on all aspects of shipbuilding and ship operation." Length: 500 to 4,000 words, "depending on the subject." Pays 5¢ per published word. Pays $5 per 8x10 glossy photo purchased with ms.

SEAWAY REVIEW, 3750 Nixon Rd., Ann Arbor MI 48105. Editor: Jacques LesStrang. Professional journal dealing with the St. Lawrence Seaway, Great Lakes, Lake ports and shipping. Quarterly. Buys North American serial rights. Pays on acceptance. Sample copy available for $1. "Query first on features as these are usually assigned to experts in their respective fields. From time to time will have assignments for writers in the states covered by the journal and will keep on file the names of qualified writers in these areas. Writers should support their listings with either credits or samples of their work. Deadlines fall on the 10th of the months preceding April, July, Oct. and Jan." Reports in two weeks. Enclose S.A.S.E.
Nonfiction: Articles of a professional nature relating to Great Lakes shipping, the economics of the eight states which comprise the Seaway region (Minnesota, Ohio, Wisconsin, Michigan, New York, Pennsylvania, Indiana and Illinois), port operation, the Seaway's role in state economic development, etc. Length: 1,000 to 1,500 words, short features; minimum 3,000 words, articles. "Payment varies with the knowledgeability of the author and the value of the subject matter; up to $250."
Photos: Purchased both with mss and with captions only. 8x10 glossy b&w or 4x5 Ektachrome on Lake shipping or port activity, if newsworthy. Pays $25 per accepted b&w photo, and "$100 for color—scenic as well as news photos."
Fillers: Uses spot news items relating to Lake ports. Length: 50 to 500 words. Pays $5 to $50.

THE WORK BOAT, P.O. Box 52288, New Orleans LA 70152. Phone: 504-525-7387. Managing Editor: Philip C. Sperier. Monthly. Buys first rights. Pays on publication. Query first. Reports in 2 week. Enclose S.A.S.E.
Nonfiction and Photos: "Articles on waterways, river terminals, barge line operations, work boat construction and design, barges, dredges, tugs. Best bet for freelancers: One-angle article showing in detail how a barge line, tug operator or dredging firm solves a problem of either mechanical or operational nature. This market is semitechnical and rather exacting. Such articles must be specific, containing firm name, location, officials of company, major equipment involved, by name, model, power, capacity and manufacturer; with b&w photos." Length: 1,000 to 5,000 words. Pays $90 minimum. 5x5 or 5x7 b&w; 4x5 color prints only. No additional payment for photos.

Medical

Publications that are aimed at private physicians or which publish technical material on new discoveries in medicine are classified here. Journals for nurses, laboratory technicians, hospital resident physicians, and other medical workers will be found with the Hospitals, Nursing, and Nursing Homes journals. Publications for druggists and drug wholesalers and retailers are grouped with the Drugs, Health Care, and Medical Products journals.

AMERICAN FAMILY PHYSICIAN, 1740 W. 92nd St., Kansas City MO 64114. Phone: 816-333-9700. Publisher: Walter H. Kemp. Monthly. Circulation: 126,000. Buys all rights. Pays on publication. "Most articles are assigned." Query first. Reports in 2 weeks. Enclose S.A.S.E.
Nonfiction: Interested only in clinical articles. Length: 2,500 words. Pays $50 to $200.

AUDECIBEL, Journal of the National Hearing Aid Society, 20361 Middlebelt, Livonia MI 48152. Editor: Anthony DiRocco. For "otologists, hearing aid specialists, educators of the deaf and hard of hearing, audiologists, and others interested in hearing and audiology." Established in 1951. Quarterly. Circulation: 12,600. Buys all rights. "A very limited freelance market. Most articles submitted are from authorities in the field who publish for professional recognition, without fee." Pays on publication. Will send a sample copy to a writer on request. Write for copy of guidelines for writers. Query first or submit complete ms. Enclose S.A.S.E. for return of submissions.

Nonfiction and Photos: "Purpose of the magazine is to bring to the otologist, the clinical audiologist, the hearing aid audiologist and others interested in the field, authoritative articles and data concerned with research, techniques, education and new developments in the field of hearing and hearing aids. In general, *Audecibel's* editorial policy emphasizes a professional and technical approach rather than a sales and merchandising approach. Seven types of articles are used: technical articles dealing with hearing aids themselves; technical articles dealing with fitting hearing aids; case histories of unusual fittings; technical articles dealing with sound, acoustics, etc.; psychology of hearing loss; medical and physiological aspects; professional standards and ethics. We are not interested in human interest stories, but only in carefully researched and documented material." Length: 200 to 2,000 words; "will consider longer articles if content is good. No set rate of payment." Photos purchased with mss; captions optional. Pays $3 to $5.

How To Break In: "Before you submit an article, it's a good idea to send a query. Let us know what your idea is. It may be that we're overstocked with the type of article you want to write. Or, it may be that it's just what we need, and we may be able to give you some information from our files, or suggestions of names of people to contact."

CANADIAN DOCTOR, 310 Victoria Ave., Montreal, P.Q., Canada H32 ZN1. Phone: 514-487-2302. Editor: David Elkins. For all Canadian physicians. Monthly magazine; 125 (8x10) pages. Established in 1973. Circulation: 30,000. Buys all rights, but will reassign rights to author after publication. Buys 50 mss a year. Payment on publication. Will send sample copy to writer for $2. Guidelines for writers are sent only after a story idea has been accepted. Will consider photocopied submissions. Will not consider simultaneous submissions. Reports in 2 weeks. Query first. Enclose S.A.E. and International Reply Coupons.

Nonfiction and Photos: Articles concerning financial planning for Canadian physicians; practice management, professional relations. Some travel and retirement material. Tax and estate planning would be of interest, as well as informational articles. All material must be "informal and anecdotal, but with authority. Freelancers should really know the subject. Unassigned articles usually miss the specialized tone we use with our audience. We reject material when the subject is too general." Length: 2,000 words maximum. Pays 5¢ to 10¢ a word. Also looking for shorter material for the Canadian Real Estate column. Length: 1,000 to 1,500 words. Pays $100. Department Editor: Irwin Stephen. Pays $15 for 8x10 b&w photos purchased with mss. $25 for color transparencies used with mss. Captions required.

Fillers: Jokes. Length: 100 words. Pays $5.

MEDICAL DIMENSIONS, 555 Madison Ave., New York NY 10022. Phone: 212-758-5300. Editor: Gila Berkowitz. For young doctors; age range, 22 to 39. Established in 1972. Circulation: 60,000. Rights purchased vary with author and material. Usually buys first North American serial rights. Buys 60 to 80 mss a year. Payment on acceptance. Will send free sample copy to writer on request. Will consider photocopied submissions. Will not consider simultaneous submissions. Reports on material accepted for publication in 2 to 3 weeks. Returns rejected material in 1 week. Query first or submit complete ms. Enclose S.A.S.E.

Nonfiction: Articles on practical medicine; narratives on experiences in the profession; humor in medicine. Anecdotal information is always helpful. "We stay clear of journal medical science. We publish what the young doctor is interested in, in the practical rather than the didactic side of medicine." Interested in material on the following topics: Why do patients switch doctors? Which medical reference books are best? How does a lawyer choose a doctor for a case?" Length: 500 to 3,000 words. Pays $25 to $500.

MEDICAL OPINION, 575 Madison Ave., New York NY 10022. Editor: Genell Subak-sharpe. For physicians primarily in private practice. Monthly. Circulation: 170,000. Buys all rights. Buys 30 to 55 mss a year. Payment on acceptance. Query first. Reports in 4 to 6 weeks. Enclose S.A.S.E.
Nonfiction: "Interested in articles written by physicians which are reflective and informative on specific aspects of modern medical practice. Topics may run from the clinical to philosophical to political. We are not a news magazine. We do not feature products or immediate breakthroughs, but rather subjects and therapeutic areas that have been at least partially exposed to our audience. An occasional humorous or historical article is acceptable, but must have very strong roots in some areas of medicine. No fiction, poetry or 'cute pieces'. All articles should offer a clearly defined opinion. Style is not technical, but follows the more lively consumer magazine style. Be careful not to oversimplify or to confuse medical terms with clear writing." Length: 1,500 to 2,500 words. Pays $150 to $250.

THE MEDICAL POST, 481 University Ave., Toronto 1, Ont., Canada. Editor: Earl Damude. For the medical profession. Semimonthly. Will send sample copy to medical writers only. Send query first to John Shaughnessy, Managing Editor. Buys first North American serial rights. Pays on publication. Enclose S.A.E. and International Reply Coupons.
Nonfiction: Uses "newsy, factual reports of medical developments, technical advances, professional appointments. Must be aimed at professional audience, and not written in 'popular medical' style." Length: 300 to 800 words. Pays 9¢ a word.
Photos: Uses photos with mss or captions only, of medical interest; pays $5 up.

THE NEW PHYSICIAN, 1400 Hicks Rd., Rolling Meadows IL 60008. Editor: Terrence S. Carden, Jr., M.D. For medical students, interns and residents. Magazine; 72 (8½x11) pages. Established in 1952. Monthly. Circulation: 78,000. Buys all rights. Buys 6 to 12 mss a year. Pays on publication. Will send free sample copy to writer on request. No photocopied submissions. Will consider simultaneous submissions. Reports on material accepted for publication in 4 to 6 weeks. Returns rejected material immediately. Query first. Enclose S.A.S.E.
Nonfiction and Photos: "Articles on social, political, economic issues in medicine/ medical education. Our readers need more than a superficial simplistic look into issues that affect them. We want skeptical, accurate, professional contributors to do well-researched, comprehensive reports, and offer new perspectives on health care problems." Not interested in material on "my operation," or encounters with physicians, or personal experiences as physician's patient. Occasionally publishes special topic issues, such as those on emergency care and foreign medical graduates. Recently published a freelance article on a housestaff peer review group in California. Informational articles, interviews, and exposes are sought. Length: 500 to 2,500 words. Pays $25 to $250. Pays $10 to $25 for b&w photos used with mss. Captions required.

OSTEOPATHIC PHYSICIAN, Box 253, North Madison OH 44057. Publication and official office: 733 Third Ave., New York NY 10017. Editor: Dr. J. Dudley Chapman. For osteopathic physicians and students with 4 years of college and 4 years of medical school and internship, as a minimum; specialists have an additional 4 years. The major portion of the audience are general or family physicians. Some 2,000 doctors of medicine also receive this publication. Established in 1933. Circulation: 18,000. Rights purchased vary with author and material. Usually buys all rights, but will reassign rights to author after publication. Buys 25 mss a year. Payment on publication. Will send sample copy to writer for $1. Will consider photocopied submissions. Submit special issue (December) material 4 months in advance. Reports on material accepted for publication in 21 days. Returns rejected material in 30 days. Query first or submit complete ms. Enclose S.A.S.E.

Nonfiction and Photos: "This is a journal dedicated to the psychological, philosophical and social aspects of medicine as they relate to the physician in private practice. There is a special emphasis on the role of human sexuality in the series, as well as other family life topics." Prefers material on social changes that affect practice of medicine, philosophical issues directed toward doctors; marital and social issues affecting health and medicine; occasional political matters affecting health care, and the third party matter. A special issue is published in December on the personal life of physicians: hobbies, travel, aesthetics, recreation. Prefers that the opening paragraph of all manuscripts define the topic and problem to be discussed. Likes individual style and variation that deliver the message. Dislikes stylized, formal writing. Does not want to see material on medical economics and business management. Current interest is in articles on the future of marriage, the government's influence on the rising cost of medicine, the organization's defense and hiding of bad medicine. Maximum length is 10 double-spaced pages with wide margins. Pays $50 to $125.

Poetry: Free verse and avant-garde forms. "We do publish poetry, but in theme with all of our material; not poetry for poetry's sake but poetry with a message and meaning. We limit poetry very restrictively." Maximum length of 54 lines. Pays up to $100.

PHYSICIAN'S MANAGEMENT, 757 Third Ave., New York NY 10017. Phone: 212-754-2135, Tuesday and Thursday mornings only. Editor: Gene Balliett. For physicians in private practice. Monthly magazine. Established in 1960. Circulation: 200,000. Rights purchased vary with author and material. May buy all rights, but will reassign rights to author after publication; all rights; first serial rights or second serial (reprint) rights. Buys about 70 mss a year. Payment on acceptance. Will send sample copy to writer for $2. (Request must be sent to the Circulation department of Harcourt, Brace, Jovanovich, 1 East First St., Duluth MN 55802.) Will consider photocopied and simultaneous submissions. Reports on material in 2 to 4 weeks. Query first. Enclose S.A.S.E.

Nonfiction and Photos: Articles and occasional roundtable discussions. Possible subjects are office management, investing, personal finances, the significance of socio-economic news, personnel administration; advice on making, spending, and saving money, with some very occasional attention to travel. "We generally follow *New York Times* style, and we're very heavy on service benefit. We're not much for gee-whiz pieces. We're not terribly big on far-out investing ideas. The New York Stock Exchange is scary enough for most of our readers. That's not to say that we never run articles on investing in coins or diamonds or the like. We just don't like to repeat any such piece more often than once every 3 or 4 years. I'd love to see 'Great Train Rides of the World' or 'Great South American Vacation Cities'." Length: 400 to 2,000 words. Pays 5¢ to 20¢ a word. Pays $25 to $75 for b&w photos purchased with or without mss. "Submit negatives and contact or wallet prints. We'll return all." Prefers color slides, but will accept negatives. Pays $75 to $150.

PRACTICAL PSYCHOLOGY FOR PHYSICIANS, 757 Third Ave., New York NY 10017. Phone: 212-754-4342. Editor: Robert McCrie. For general practitioners, internists, family physicians, osteopaths. Monthly magazine; 76 pages. Established in 1972. Purchased by Harcourt, Brace, Jovanovich Publications, Inc. in 1973. Circulation: 105,000. Rights purchased vary with author and material. May buy all rights; but will sometimes reassign rights to author after publication; first North American serial rights or second serial (reprint) rights. Buys 2 mss per issue. Payment on publication. Will send free sample copy to writer on request. Write for copy of guidelines for writers. Will consider cassette submissions. Query first, giving specific information about the story idea. Enclose S.A.S.E.

Nonfiction and Photos: Articles with a useful or practical orientation from the behavioral sciences of general interest and value to practicing physicians. Articles should be in nontechnical language. Use 2 or more authorities in each completed article. "This is the only publication concerned with the behavioral sciences going to primary care physicians. All articles should be timely and useful and not repeated themes covered in other publications reaching general physicians." Informational, interview, think pieces. Length: 1,500 to 2,000 words. Pays 5¢ to 15¢ per word. B&w and color photos used with mss. "Generally, photos will be an integral part of the article and can be taken by the article editor/writer." Captions optional.

PRIVATE PRACTICE, 3035 N.W. 63rd, Suite 299, Oklahoma City OK 73116. Editor: Llewellyn H. Rockwell, Jr. For "medical doctors in private practice." Monthly. Buys first North American serial rights. Pays on acceptance. Query first. Enclose S.A.S.E. **Nonfiction and Photos:** "Articles which indicate importance of maintaining freedom of medical practice or which detail outside interferences in the practice of medicine, including research, hospital operation, drug manufacture, etc. Straight reporting style. No cliches, no scare words such as 'socialists,' etc. No flowery phrases to cover up poor reporting. Stories must be actual, factual, precise, correct. Copy should be lively and easy-to-read. Also publish historical, offbeat, and humorous articles of medical interest." Length: up to 2,500 words. Pays "usual minimum $150." Photos purchased with mss only. B&w glossies, 8x10. Payment "depends on quality, relevancy of material, etc."

SURGICAL BUSINESS, 2009 Morris Ave., Union NJ 07083. Editor: Adrian Comper. For medical/surgical dealers and dealer/salesmen. Magazine; 92 pages. Established in 1938. Monthly. Circulation: 6,800. Buys exclusive industry rights. Buys 5 to 10 mss a year. Pays on publication. Will send free sample copy to writer on request. Write for copy of guidelines for writers. Will consider photocopied and simultaneous submissions. Reports in 3 months. Query first or submit complete ms. Enclose S.A.S.E. **Nonfiction:** "We publish feature-length articles dealing with manufacturers within the industry, as well as meeting coverage and general information within the industry. We do not desire promotional material about a company or product. Mss should be objective and to the point." Recently published "Medical Device Legislation: Challenge and Opportunity," an explanation of legislation important to manufacturers and dealers. Length: open. Pays 5c a word.

Milling, Feed, and Grain

FEED INDUSTRY REVIEW, 3055 N. Brookfield Rd., Brookfield WI 53005. Publisher: Bruce W. Smith. For manufacturers of livestock and poultry feed. Quarterly. Circulation: 8,000. Buys all rights. Pays on publication. Will send a free sample copy on receipt of letter only, no postcards. Query preferred. Reports in one week. Enclose S.A.S.E.
Nonfiction: "Profile articles on progressive feed manufacturing operations, including data on plant layout and equipment, research, and distribution. This is a market for factual reporters, not creative writers. Market extremely limited; queries imperative prior to submitting completed articles." Length: 1,500 to 2,200 words. Pays $20 to $75.
Photos: Usually buys only with mss, occasional exceptions. Subject matter should be agribusiness, plants, or other physical facilities. Wants b&w glossies, horizontal prints. Pays $7 to $10.

THE WHEAT SCOOP, 606 25th St. North, P.O. Box 2663, Great Falls MT 59403. Editor: Ray Fenton. 8 times a year. Not copyrighted. Query first. "Very little freelance material purchased." Enclose S.A.S.E.
Nonfiction: Uses "articles on grain research, freight rates, fertilizers, domestic markets and foreign markets as they pertain to Montana. Clarity and precision necessary. Authenticity, definite Montana tie-in are musts." Length: 100 to 1,000 words. Payment negotiated.
Photos: Buys photos with mss and with captions only. Particularly needs art wheat photos, from seeding to harvesting, b&w or color; unusual or art type.

Mining and Minerals

AMERICAN GOLD NEWS, P.O. Box 457, Ione CA 95640. Editor: Cecil L. Helms. For anyone interested in gold, gold mining, gold companies, gold stocks, gold history, gold coins, the future of gold in our economy. Tabloid newspaper; 16 pages. Established in 1933. Monthly. Circulation: 3,500. Not copyrighted. Pays on publication. Will send free sample copy to writer on request. Write for copy of guidelines for writers. No photocopied or simultaneous submissions. Submit seasonal material (relating to seasonal times in mining country) 2 months in advance. Reports on material accepted for publication in 2 weeks. Returns rejected material in 2 weeks. Query first or submit complete ms. Enclose S.A.S.E.

Nonfiction and Photos: "This is not a literary publication. We want information on any subject pertaining to gold told in the most simple, direct, and interesting way. How to build gold mining equipment. History of mines (with pix). History of gold throughout U.S. Panning and travel in the gold country. Picture stories of mines, mining towns, mining country. Recently published "Plumas-Eureka Mine," a good history of an early 19th century mine. Length: 500 to 2,000 words. Pays $10 to $25. B&w photos purchased with or without ms. Must be sharp, if not old, historical photos. Pays $2.50 to $25. Captions required.

Fiction and Poetry: Western, adventure, humorous fiction related to gold mining. Length: 500 to 2,000 words. Pays $10 to $25. Traditional forms of poetry; light verse. Should relate to mining country, or people. Length: short. Pays $5 to $10.

COAL AGE, 1221 Avenue of the Americas, New York NY 10021. Phone: 212-997-2457. Editor: Harold Davis. For supervisors, engineers and executives in coal mining. Monthly. Circulation: 16,000. Buys all rights. Pays on publication. Reports in two to three weeks. Enclose S.A.S.E.

Nonfiction: Uses some technical (operating type) articles; some how-to pieces on equipment maintenance. Pays $35 per page. "More honorarium than payment."

Miscellaneous

AMERICAN CANDLEMAKER, P.O. Box 22227, San Diego CA 92122. Phone: 714-755-1410. Editor: A. Paul Theil. For "high school age through retirees who engage in candlemaking, either as a hobby or a semiprofessional endeavor. Usually have accompanying interest in allied crafts." Monthly magazine; 12 (8½x11) pages. Established in 1972. Circulation: 1,000. Buys first rights. Payment is usually made 2 weeks after acceptance. Will send sample copy to writer for 70¢. Will not consider photocopied or simultaneous submissions. Submit seasonal material (Easter, Thanksgiving, Christmas) at least 3 months in advance. Reports in 2 weeks. Submit complete ms. Enclose S.A.S.E.

Nonfiction and Photos: "All phases of material directly related to candlecrafting, either in the creation of the candle, decoration, techniques; the how-to. The latter is tested, however, before we publish it to assure accuracy. Writer may use his own approach, but nothing 'far out.' Special emphasis is helpful, of course, since we receive large numbers of manuscripts from reputable, professional candlemakers." Uses informational, how-to, historical, successful business operations, new product, merchandising techniques and technical material. Especially interested in material on the use of candles for all occasions in foreign lands. Length: no minimum; 1,500 words maximum. Pays 2½¢ per word. B&w photos (4x5) are used with mss. No additional payment.

THE ANTIQUES DEALER, 1115 Clifton Ave., Clifton NJ 07013. Phone: 201-779-1600 or 212-947-9270. Editor: Stella Hall. For antiques dealers. Monthly magazine. Established in 1949. Circulation: 20,000. Buys all rights. Buys 40 mss a year. Payment on publication. Will send free sample copy to writer on request. Will consider photocopied submissions "if clear". Enclose S.A.S.E.

Nonfiction: "We are interested in articles on the Bicentennial directly related to the antiques dealers across the country; for example, ways for them to tie-in with promotions, ways to help them sell antiques, general marketing help, that sort of thing." Only articles of interest to dealers; may be tutorial if by authority in one specific field; otherwise of broad general interest to all dealers. Glass, china, porcelain, furniture, oriental, Americana, shows. News of youth market, antique imports from Sweden, Camaroon, Columbia, Burma, New Zealand, Canada, Phillipines, Egypt. Length: no minimum; maximum 2-part article, about 7,000 words; 3,500 words if one-part. Pays $30 a page for features; $1.50 for few sentence obit. Columns cover Trade News; anything from a couple of sentences to about 200 words, with photo or two. Usually pays just $1.50 if very short.

Photos: Purchased with or without accompanying mss, or on assignment. Pays $5 per b&w, no smaller than 5x7 (glossy).

Fillers: Suitable for professional dealers; any type of fillers. Length: 300 to 400 words. Pays approximately $15 for half-page.

How To Break In: "Submit 'hard news'—brief one-paragraph items are used in Trade News column. Also, for feature articles, knowledge of antiques and/or antiques business more important than writing ability. Photos always help sell a ms."

APA MONITOR, 1200 17th St., N.W., Washington DC 20036. Editor: Sharland Trotter. For psychologists, interested in behaviorial science and mental health. Newspaper; 32 (11x16) pages. Established in 1970. Monthly. Circulation: 45,000. Buys all rights. Buys about 5 mss a year. Pays on publication. Will send free sample copy to writer on request. Will not consider photocopied and simultaneous submissions. Reports on material accepted for publication in 2 weeks. Returns rejected material in 1 month. Query first. Enclose S.A.S.E.

Nonfiction and Photos: News and features about psychology and political, social, economic developments that affect psychology; APA (American Psychological Association) affairs. "We put more emphasis on organizational and political aspects of psychology as a profession; less on interpretation of scientific findings to the public. Keep in mind that the reader is probably better informed about the substantive science and practice of psychology than the writer." Informational, interview, profile, humor, historical, think articles, expose, new product, photo. Length: 300 to 1,000 words. Pays 10¢ per word. Pays $15 for b&w photos (5x7) purchased with or without ms, or on assignment. Photo Editor: Jules Asher.

BRUSHWARE, 330 Main St., Madison NJ 07940. Phone: 201-766-0835. Editor: C.D. Baldwin. For manufacturers and suppliers in the brush, broom, mop, and roller industries. Quarterly. Circulation: 1,500. Copyrighted; "rights remain with author." Pays on publication. Reports in 30 days. Query first. Enclose S.A.S.E.

Nonfiction and Photos: Length: 800 to 1,000 words. Pays 4¢ per word. Photos purchased with mss.

How To Break In: "Inquire first with subject idea, illustrations etc., in mind. We need brush company profile articles. We reject material when the writer doesn't follow instructions about brush articles only. One wanted to write something about chimney sweeps! No good."

CHANNELS, National Public Relations Council, 815 Second Ave., New York NY 10017. Editor: Don Bates. For communications specialists, writers, public relations and public affairs pros, administrators, executives in agencies and organizations, including business firms serving the needs of people in health, social welfare, community service. Newsletter. Established in 1922. Every 2 weeks. Circulation: 7,000. Not copyrighted. Buys 6 to 12 mss a year. Pays on publication. Will send sample copy to writer for 50¢. Will consider photocopied and simultaneous submissions. Reports in 10 days. Query first. Enclose S.A.S.E.

Nonfiction and Photos: News on communications in health, social welfare and community service. Also brief notes on public service contributions by national and local media. Short features on communications case studies. How-to of effective print and audiovisual techniques. Notes on trends, issues, events affecting communicators helping people. Dilemmas of effective communications in health, social welfare, community service, i.e., how to communicate well, get a response, and meet a need without causing controversy, and without promising more than can be delivered. Recently published "Ten Ways to Use Videotape in Public Relations." Length: 100 to 1,000 words. Pays $10 to $50. Communications Forum column length: 600 to 1,000 words. Pays $30 to $50. Pays $10 for 8x10 glossies used with mss. Captions required.

How To Break In: "Query first and send xerox or sample of published writing that indicates style, as well as understanding of communications' needs and problems in people-helping and public service efforts. If we give you a go-ahead, write an article, with solid facts and opinion, on subjects of interest to our readers. A first usually means a second. But, query first."

DRESSAGE, The National Magazine, P.O. Box 2460, Cleveland OH 44112. Editor: Ivan I. Bezugloff, Jr. For readers interested in classical horsemanship and/or combined training. Magazine; 32 to 40 (8½x11) pages. Established in 1971. Monthly. Circulation: 3,000. Buys first North American serial rights. Buys about 40 mss a year. Pays on publication. Will send free sample copy to writer on request. No photocopied or simultaneous submissions. Reports in 14 days. Query first or submit complete ms. Enclose S.A.S.E.

Nonfiction: Educational materials on training horses and riders in using the principles of dressage (classical horsemanship). Length: open. Pays 10¢ per published line.

Fiction: Humorous, equestrian fiction, particularly amusing and entertaining short stories. Must be related to dressage. Length: 700 to 1,200 words. Pays $21 to $36.

EMERGENCY PRODUCT NEWS, GHP Publications, P.O. Box 926, Encinitas CA 92024. Phone: 714-753-6475. Editor: Linda Piskorski and Wendy Herold. For emergency medical technicians, ambulance companies, industrial plants, colleges and universities, hospitals, military bases and government institutions, rescue squads, police departments, fire departments, physicians and nurses, civil defense workers, national parks, etc. Magazine (72 pages) published every 2 months. Established in 1969. Circulation: 92,000. Buys first North American serial right. Buys about 15 to 20 mss a year. Pays on publication. Will send free sample copy to writer on request. Will consider photocopied submissions. Reports in 30 days. Query first. Enclose S.A.S.E.

Nonfiction and Photos: "Articles dealing with emergency care and transportation of the sick and injured; techniques in treatment, first aid techniques, new products, organizational structure on care institutions, human interest, interesting or amusing rescue situations. Writer must be knowledgeable in the field. Material must be technically sound and related to the emergency medical field. Emphasis is on first aid treatment or emergency medical transportation and medical specialists." Recent articles include "The EMT in Training," "Legal Responsibilities of the EMT," and "The Blaze in the Firehouse." Length: open. Pays $25 to $150. B&w photos purchased with or without ms. Pays $10. Captions required with appropriate identifications. "Also accept color transparencies for use on cover. Pay $75 for cover photo. Illustrations and line drawings are acceptable when accompanied by ms."

HOUSEHOLD AND PERSONAL PRODUCTS INDUSTRY, 4 Second Ave., Denville NJ 07834. Editor: Hamilton C. Carson. For "manufacturers of soaps, detergents, cosmetics and toiletries, waxes and polishes, insecticides, and aerosols." Established in 1964. Monthly. Circulation: 12,000. Not copyrighted. Buys 3 to 4 mss a year, "but would buy more if slanted to our needs." Pays on publication. Will send a sample copy to a writer on request. Query first. Will consider photocopied submissions. Submit seasonal material 2 months in advance. Enclose S.A.S.E.

Nonfiction and Photos: "Technical and semitechnical articles on manufacturing, distribution, marketing, new products, plant stories, etc., of the industries served. Some knowledge of the field is essential in writing for us." Buys informational articles, interviews, photo features, spot news, coverage of successful business operations, new product articles, coverage of merchandising techniques, and technical articles. Length: 500 to 2,000 words. Pays $5 to $125. 5x7 or 8x10 b&w glossies purchased with mss. Pays $3 to $5.

MEETINGS & EXPOSITIONS, 10 E. 39th St., New York NY 10016. Phone: 212-689-2809. Managing Editor: Peggy Herman. For corporate and trade association meeting planners, exhibit managers and incentive travel program managers. Quarterly magazine; 100 (8½x11) pages. Established in 1972. Circulation: 38,000. Rights purchased vary with author and material. May buy all rights, first serial rights or second serial (reprint) rights. Buys 5 to 8 mss a year. Payment is usually made on acceptance, but payment for filler material is sometimes made on publication. Will consider photocopied or simultaneous submissions. Reports quickly. Query first. Enclose S.A.S.E.
Nonfiction: "We need well-written, informative articles on all aspects of meeting planning. Short, snappy articles, rather than tomes. We assume a certain competence in our area of specialization on the part of our readers. Articles dealing with meeting planning, expositions and incentive travel. We are especially seeking humorous material about meetings and/or trade shows." How-to, interview, profile, humor, think pieces, successful business operations. Length: 1,200 words maximum. Pays $100.

MILLIMETER MAGAZINE, 139 E. 43rd St., New York NY 10017. Publishers: William Blake, George Cooper and Monte Stettin. Editors: Robert Avrech and Larry Gross. For advertising people, as well as filmmakers, technicians, writers, animators, directors, sound men, students. "We're paying equal attention to business, craft, and art with a special emphasis on the personalities involved." Monthly, 52 (8½x11) pages. Established in 1973. Circulation: 10,000. Buys all rights but will reassign rights to author after publication. Buys 30 mss a year. Pays on publication. Will send sample copy to writer for $1. Will consider photocopied and simultaneous submissions. Submit special material (some issues are built around a particular theme: TV, animation, advertising, etc.) 3 months in advance. Reports within 5 weeks. Qiery first. Enclose S.A.S.E.
Nonfiction: Emphasis on off-camera personalities or new developments and trends in the film industry, advertising, cable TV, video tape or animation. Interested in articles pertaining to the history of motion pictures, videotapes, and the related technology. "We like to think of ourselves as having a style similar to *New York* magazine but our range includes all the major film-making centers around the country and in Europe. We encourage queries and make quick decision on all articles." Informational, personal experience, interview, profile. Length: 800 to 2,000 words. Pays $50 to $100 per mss. Recent articles include "Interview with Al Ruddy;" a detailed discussion of the making of *The Godfather* and *The Longest Yard*; a long, well-researched piece on the issues involved in understanding feature distribution; and a fascinating piece of reportage dealing with on-location problems faced by commercials directors.

MODEL NEWS OF HOUSTON, Box 13447, Houston TX 77019. Editor: K. White. For "models, agents, clients." Established in 1971. Monthly. Circulation: 500. Pays on acceptance. Query first for all material. Submit seasonal material 2 months in advance of issue date. Enclose S.A.S.E.
Nonfiction and Photos: "Relates to modeling techniques, training, shows." Buys informational articles, how-to's, photo features, new product articles, and coverage of merchandising techniques. Length: 300 to 1,000 words. Pays 1¢ to 2¢ a word. No additional payment for b&w glossies purchased with mss.

PROBLEMS OF COMMUNISM, IPS/MC, U.S. Information Agency, 1776 Pennsylvania Ave., N.W., Washington DC 20547. Phone: 202-632-5119. Editor: Paul A. Smith, Jr. For scholars and decisionmakers in all countries of the world with higher education and a serious interest in foreign area studies and international relations. Established in 1952. Circulation: 35,000. Not copyrighted. Buys 60 to 70 mss a year.

Payment on acceptance. Will send free sample copy to writer on request. Will consider photocopied submissions. Reports on material accepted for publication in 3 months. Returns rejected material in 3 months. Query first or submit complete ms. Enclose S.A.S.E.

Nonfiction and Photos: "*Problems of Communism* is one of a very few journals devoted to objective, dispassionate discourse on a highly unobjective, passionately debated phenomenon: communism. It is maintained as a forum in which qualified observers can contribute to a clearer understanding of the sources, nature and direction of change in the areas of its interest. It has no special emphasis or outlook and represents no partisan point of view. Standards of style are those appropriate to the field of international scholarship and journalism. We use intellectually rigorous studies of East-West relations, and/or related political, economic, social and strategic trends in the USSR, China and their associated states and movements. Length is usually 5,000 words. Essay reviews of 1,500 words cover new books offering significant information and analysis. Emphasis throughout *Problems of Communism* is on original research, reliability of sources and perceptive insights. We do not publish political or other forms of advocacy or apologetics for particular forms of belief." Pays $350 for articles; $150 for essay reviews. Pays $25 for b&w glossies.

SANITARY MAINTENANCE, 407 E. Michigan St., Milwaukee WI 53201. Phone: 414-271-4105. Managing Editor: Donald Mulligan. For distributors of equipment in the sanitary supply industry. Established in 1943. Monthly. Circulation, 11,300. Buys all rights. Buys 20 mss a year. Payment on publication. Will send free sample copy to writer on request. Write for copy of guidelines for writers. Will consider cassette submissions. Reports in 6 weeks. Query first or submit complete ms. Enclose S.A.S.E.

Nonfiction and Photos: "*Sanitary Maintenance* publishes a variety of articles on methods of sanitation and cleaning (along with products), salesmanship in the field, sanitation association news, contract cleaning methods, contract services, transportation, outlooks on the financial world and related general news. Style may vary as does the subject matter, as long as it considers the audience." Informational, product reviews. Successful business operations. Length: open. Pays about $100 per article. No additional payment for b&w glossies.

SOLAR ENERGY DIGEST, P.O. Box 17776, San Diego CA 92117. Editor: William B. Edmondson. This is the Solar Energy Conversion Newsletter for scientists, engineers, technicians, executives, environmentalists, ecologists, and "ordinary garden variety solar energy buffs". Established in 1973. Monthly. Buys all rights, but will reassign rights to author after publication. Buys 20 to 25 mss a year. Payment on publication. Will send sample copy to writer for $1. Will not consider photocopied submissions. Returns rejected material within 2 weeks. Reports on material accepted for publication in 2 to 4 weeks. Query first or submit complete ms. Enclose S.A.S.E.

Nonfiction: "Short abstracts of the many direct and indirect ways in which solar energy is being put to work all over the world to help relieve the energy/pollution crisis. Use the newspaper approach, but condense, condense and condense." How-to, interview, successful business operations, new products, merchandising techniques, technical; reviews of books on solar energy. Length: 100 to 500 words. Pays 1¢ to 3¢ per word.

TOBACCO REPORTER, 424 Commercial Square, Cincinnati OH 45202. Editor: F. Lee Stegemeyer. For tobacco growers, processors, warehousemen, exporters, importers, manufacturers and distributors of cigars, cigarettes, and tobacco products. Monthly. Buys all rights. Pays on publication. Enclose S.A.S.E.

Nonfiction and Photos: Uses original material on request only. Pays approximately 2½¢ a word. Pays $3 for photos purchased with mss.

Fillers: Wants clippings on new tobacco product brands, local tobacco distributors, smoking and health, and the following relating to tobacco and tobacco products: job promotions, obituaries, honors, equipment, etc. Pays minimum 25¢ a clipping on use only.

WOMAN COACH MAGAZINE, P.O. Box 93, Cochituate Station, Wayland MA 01778. Editor: John S. O'Neill. For women actively engaged in the coaching or administration of girls' interscholastic or women's intercollegiate athletics. Magazine; 40 (8½x11) pages. Estblished in 1975. Every 2 months except July-August. Circulation: 13,500. Buys all rights, but will reassign rights to author after publication. Buys 50 mss a year. Pays on publication. Will send free sample copy to writer on request. Write for copy of guidelines for writers. Will consider photocopied submissions. No simultaneous submissions. Submit coaching features 2 to 3 months prior to their playing season. Reports in 2 to 3 weeks. Query first. Enclose S.A.S.E.

Nonfiction and Photos: Feature articles dealing with the techniques and strategies of coaching seasonal sports for high school girls and college women. These must be written by or obtained through interviews with recogized expert coaches. All material must be slanted toward the woman coach, not the woman athlete or the general female consumer. The slant should be positive and constructive, offering readers positive examples and practical solutions to problems facing schoolgirl sports today; informative, how-to, interviews, and successful operation profile pieces are needed most. Recently published "The Prairie View A&M Regimen for the 440-Yard Dash." Length: 800 to 2,500 words. Pays 5¢ per word. B&w glossy (8x10 or 5x7) prints and color transparencies (8x10 or 4x5 chromes preferred; 70mm or 35mm acceptable) purchased with or without ms. Pays $25 maximum for b&w; $100 maximum for color.

Poetry and Fillers: Traditional forms of poetry, blank verse, free verse, light verse; related to theme. Length: 50 lines maximum. Pays $25 maximum. Pays 25¢ for related newsbreaks and clippings.

How To Break In: "Submit a well-written interview with a highly successful woman coach, or a good profile of a successful girls' or women's athletic program."

Music

THE CHURCH MUSICIAN, 127 Ninth Ave. N., Nashville TN 37234. Editor: William Anderson. Southern Baptist publication. For Southern Baptist church music leaders. Monthly. Circulation: 20,000. Buys all rights. Pays on acceptance. Will send a sample copy to a writer on request. Will consider cassette submissions. No query required. Reports in 2 months. Enclose S.A.S.E.

Nonfiction: Leadership and how-to features, success stories, articles on Protestant church music. "Many articles lack a personal touch (music history, for example), and are rejected. Others have too much sentiment or are badly written." Length: maximum 1,300 words. Pays up to 2½¢ a word.

Photos: Purchased with mss; related to mss content only.

Fiction: Inspiration, guidance, motivation, morality with Protestant church music slant. Length: to 1,300 words. Pays up to 2½¢ a word.

Poetry: Church music slant, inspirational. Length: 8 to 24 lines. Pays $5 to $10.

Fillers: Puzzles, short humor. Church music slant. Pays $3 to $5.

How To Break In: "I'd advise a beginning writer to write about his or her experience with some aspect of church music; the social, musical, and spiritual benefits from singing in a choir; a success story about their instrumental group; a testimonial about how they were enlisted in a choir—especially if they were not inclined to be enlisted at first. A writer might speak to hymn singers—what turns them on and what doesn't. Some might include how music has helped them to talk about Jesus as well as sing about Him. We would prefer most of these experiences be related to the church, of course, although we include many articles by freelance writers whose affiliation is other than Baptist. We are delighted to receive their manuscripts, to be sure. A writer might relate his experience with a choir of blind or deaf members. Some people receive benefits from working with unusual children—retarded, or culturally deprived, emotionally unstable, and so forth. Photographs are valuable here."

CLAVIER, 1418 Lake Street, Evanston IL 60204. Editor: Mrs. Dorothy Packard. 9 times a year. Buys all rights. Pays on publication. Sample copy will be sent on request. "Suggest query to avoid duplication." Reports in 2 weeks on very good or very bad mss, "quite slow on the in-betweens." Enclose S.A.S.E.

Nonfiction and Photos: Wants "articles aimed at teachers of piano and organ. Must be written from thoroughly professional point of view. Avoid, however, the thesis-style subject matter and pedantic style generally found in scholarly journals. We like fresh writing, practical approach. We can use interviews with concert pianists and organists. An interview should not be solely a personality story, but should focus on a subject of interest to musicians. Any word length. Photos may accompany ms." Pays $15 to $18 per printed page.

HIGH FIDELITY TRADE NEWS, 25 W. 45th St., New York NY 10036. Editor: J. Bryan Stanton. For "retailers, salesmen, manufacturers, and representatives involved in the high fidelity/home entertainment market." Established in 1956. Monthly. Circulation: 17,500. Buys all rights. Buys about 36 to 50 mss a year. Pays on acceptance. Will send a sample copy to a writer on request. Query first; "all work by assignment only." Enclose S.A.S.E.

Nonfiction: "Dealer profiles, specific articles on merchandising of high fidelity products, market surveys, sales trends, etc." Length: "open." Pay varies "as to type of article and experience of writer."

How To Break In: "We prefer to rely on our own resources for developing story ideas. Let us know about your willingness to work and submit, if possible, some samples of previous work. Even if you're a new writer, we're still likely to try you out, especially if you know the business or live in a market area where we need coverage. Articles on merchandising, product reports, and dealer profiles."

THE INSTRUMENTALIST, 1418 Lake St., Evanston IL 60204. Editor: Kenneth L. Neidig. For instrumental music educators. Established in 1946. Monthly except in July. Circulation: 18,700. Buys all rights. Liberal permission to reprint. Buys 200 mss a year. Payment on publication. Will send sample copy to writer for $1 postpaid. Will consider photocopied submissions. Submit seasonal material 3 months in advance. Summer Camps, Clinics, Workshops (March); Nostalgia/History (June); Back to School (September); Music Ind. (August). Query first. Reports on material accepted for publication within 4 months. Returns rejected material within 3 months. Enclose S.A.S.E.

Nonfiction and Photos: "Practical information of immediate use to instrumentalists. Not articles 'about music and musicians,' but articles by musicians who are sharing knowledge, techniques, experience. 'In-service education.' Professional help for instrumentalists in the form of instrumental clinics, how-to articles, new trends, practical philosophy. Most contributions are from professionals in the field." Interpretive photojournalism. Length: open. Pays $10 to $100, plus 3 contributor's copies. Quality b&w prints. Pays $5. Color: 35mm and up. Pays $25.

How To Break In: "With a topic of immediate practical application to the work of the school band/orchestra director—clear, concise, lacking in 'educationese'."

MUSIC JOURNAL, 370 Lexington Ave., New York NY 10017. Editor: Robert Cumming. For music educators and dealers; teachers, students and professionals, music lovers, in general. 50-page magazine published 10 times a year; monthly, September through May, plus summer and winter annuals. Established in 1943. Circulation: 32,670. Rights purchased vary with author and material. Usually buys first North American serial rights. Buys 30 to 35 mss a year. Payment on publication. Will send sample copy to writer for 50¢. Will not consider photocopied or simultaneous submissions. Submit special issue material (folk, country/western, rock, jazz) 3 months in advance. Reports on material accepted for publication in 3 weeks. Returns rejected material immediately. Query first or submit complete ms. Enclose S.A.S.E.

Nonfiction and Photos: "We embrace all musical subject areas, exploring the many mansions of the composer, conductor, performer, private teacher, student, educator, artist, manager and the average music lover." Does not solicit material on the opera. Uses informational articles, personal experience, inspirational, humorous, historical and nostalgic articles, as well as those dealing with personal opinion, spot news, successful business operations, new products, merchandising techniques, technical. Length: 500 to 1,200 words. Pays $25 to $50. No additional payment is made for photos used with mss.

Poetry: Traditional forms, blank verse, free verse, avant-garde forms, light verse. Must relate to music. Length: open. Pays $5.

How To Break In: "Stories of special interest to instrumentalists are the hardest to come by and would be the best way to break in. Some examples are 'How to Buy a French Horn,' 'The History of the Oboe,' 'Adolphe Sax, the Inventor of the Saxophone.' Otherwise, the key thing to keep in mind is that we are trying to be timely. We'd like more articles for music educators, too. We're trying to offset the illiteracy promoted by the boob-tube."

MUSIC MINISTRY, 201 Eighth Ave. S., Nashville TN 37202. Editor: H. Myron Braun. Affiliated with United Methodist Church. For church musicians, pastors, educators. Monthly. Circulation: 13,000. Buys all rights; occasionally buys first rights only. Buys 20 to 25 mss a year. Pays on acceptance. Will send a sample copy to a writer on request. No query required. Submit seasonal material 7 to 8 months in advance. Reports in 2 to 3 months. Enclose S.A.S.E.

Nonfiction: Articles that deal with philosophy, history, and practice of music in the life of the organized church. Pays 2¢ to 2½¢ per word minimum.

Photos: Purchased with mss, 8x10. Pays $7.50.

Fiction: Very limited use of short-shorts that illustrate "right attitudes or practices" with regard to music and its relationship to life. Pays 2¢ to 2½¢ per word minimum.

Poetry: Very limited use. Traditional and contemporary forms; subjects of seasonal, music, worship, theological concerns. Pays 50¢ per line minimum.

MUSIC TRADES, 80 West St., P.O. Box 432, Englewood NJ 07631. Phone: 201-871-1965. Editor: John F. Majeski, Jr. For "music store owners and salesmen; manufacturers of pianos, organs, band instruments, guitars, etc." Monthly. Circulation: 7,000. Copyrighted, "but rights remain with author." Pays on publication. Enclose S.A.S.E. for return of submissions.

Nonfiction and Photos: Uses news and features on the musical instrument business. Also uses case history articles with photos, dealing specifically with musical instrument merchandising, not including record or hi-fi shops. No limit on length. Payment negotiable, minimum $1.

Fillers: Clippings of obituaries of music store people. Music store openings. Pays $1 minimum.

MUSICAL MERCHANDISE REVIEW, Peacock Business Press, 200 S. Prospect Ave., Park Ridge IL 60068. Phone: 312-823-3145. Editor: John Metcalfe. For musical instrument and accessory dealers and retailers, wholesalers and distributors, importers, exporters, manufacturers of all types of musical instruments and their accessories, related electronic sound equipment, general musical accessories, musical publications and teaching aids. (Readership does not include those specifically and totally involved in the tape and recordings or audio and video equipment consumer markets.) Established in 1879. Monthly. Circulation: about 8,000. Buys all rights, but will reassign rights to author after publication. Buys 12 mss a year. Payment on publication. Will send free sample copy to writer on request. Write for copy of guidelines for writers. Will not consider photocopied submissions. Submit seasonal oaterial 3 months in advance. Reports on material in 3 weeks. Query first. Enclose S.A.S.E.

Nonfiction and Photos: Articles and features should be slanted to the dealer's interest and edification (success stories, innovation, unusual background or methods; tips on store layout, advertising, promotion; student training facilities, involvement with local education, community, municipality; merchandising techniques, salesmanship, services). Length: 1,500 words. Pays 3¢ per word. 5x7 b&w glossy photos should illustrate main points. Six photos are preferred with each ms. Pays $3 each. Special articles of general musical interest or curiosity will also be considered. Pays minimum of 3¢ per word.

Fillers: News of store openings, personnel promotion, deaths; some slanted puzzles, verse. Pays minimum of $5.

THE MUSICAL NEWSLETTER, 654 Madison Ave., Suite 1703, New York NY 10021. Editor: Patrick J. Smith. For "amateur and professional music lovers who wish to know more about music and be given more specific information." Established in 1971. Quarterly. Circulation: 600. Rights purchased vary with author and material; may buy first serial rights in English or second serial rights. Pays on acceptance. Will send a sample copy to a writer for $1. Query first for nonfiction, "giving list of subjects of possible interest and outlines, if possible." Will consider photocopied submissions. Enclose S.A.S.E.
Nonfiction: "Articles on music and the musical scene today. The bulk of articles are on 'classical' music, but we also publish articles on jazz and pop. Articles need not pertain to music directly, such as socio-economic articles on performing entities. As the level of our publication is between the musicological quarterly and the record review magazine, what we want is readable material which contains hard-core information. We stress quality. We are always happy to examine freelance material on any aspect of music, from articles on composers' works to philosophical articles on music or reportorial articles on performing organizations. We discourage reviews of performances and interviews, which we feel are adequately covered elsewhere." Length: 3,000 words maximum. Pays 10¢ a word.

OPERA NEWS, 1865 Broadway, New York NY 10023. Editor: Robert Jacobson. For all people interested in opera; opera singers, opera management people, administrative people in opera, opera publicity people, artists' agents; people in the trade and interested laymen. Magazine; 32 to 72 pages. Established in 1933. Weekly. (Monthly in summer.) Circulation: 73,376. Copyrighted. Pays on publication. Will send sample copy to writer for 75¢. Query first. Enclose S.A.S.E.
Nonfiction and Photos: Most articles are commissioned in advance. In summer, uses articles of various interests on opera; in the fall and winter, articles that relate to the weekly broadcasts. Emphasis is on high quality in writing and an intellectual interest in the opera-oriented public. Informational, how-to, personal experience, interview, profile, humor, historical, think pieces, personal opinion; opera reviews. Length: 300 words maximum. Pays 10¢ per word for features; 8¢ a word for reviews. Pays minimum of $25 for photos purchased on assignment. Captions required.

SOUTHWESTERN MUSICIAN, P.O. Box 9908, Houston TX 77015. Editor: J.F. Lenzo. For music teachers. Monthly (August through May). Buys all rights. Pays on acceptance. Reports in 30 days. Enclose S.A.S.E.
Nonfiction: Wants "professionally slanted articles of interest to public school music teachers." Pays $25 to $50.

Oceanography

The journals below are intended primarily for scientists who are studying the ocean. Publications for ocean fishermen will be found under Fishing. Those for persons interested in water and the ocean as a means of travel or shipping are listed with the Marine Industries and Water Navigation journals.

OCEAN INDUSTRY, Box 2608, Houston TX 77001. Editor: Donald M. Taylor. For ocean-oriented technical personnel. Monthly. Circulation: 34,000. Buys all rights. Pays on acceptance. Will send free sample copy on request. Query required. Reports in 1 month. Enclose S.A.S.E.
Nonfiction: New developments relating to industry in ocean. No historical material; nothing that begins, "Over 70% of the earth is covered with water..." Length: 500 to 3,000 words. Pays "$30 to $50 per published page, or $1 per inch for short world report items."

Photos: Purchased with mss. "New ideas; new developments relating to industry in the ocean."

SEA FRONTIERS, 3979 Rickenbacker Causeway, Virginia Key, Miami FL 33149. Editor: F. G. W. Smith. For "members of the International Oceanographic Foundation. People with an interest in the sea; professional people for the most part; people in executive positions and students." Established in 1954. Bimonthly. Circulation: 70,000. Buys all rights. Buys 20 to 25 mss a year. Payment on publication. Will send free sample copy to writer on request. Write for copy of guidelines for writers. Query first. Will consider photocopied submissions "if very clear." Reports on material within 6 weeks. Enclose S.A.S.E.

Nonfiction and Photos: "Articles (with illustrations) covering explorations, discoveries or advances in our knowledge of the marine sciences, or describing the activities of oceanographic laboratories or expeditions to any part of the world. Emphasis should be on research and discoveries rather than personalities involved." Length: 500 to 3,000 words. Pays 5¢ to 8¢ a word. 8x10 b&w glossy prints and 35mm (or larger) color transparencies purchased with ms. Pays $25 for color used on front and back cover. Pays $15 for color used on inside covers.

How To Break In: "The best way for a beginning writer to break into *Sea Frontiers* would be to study our style, query us concerning a subject and then submit a short article, with photographs. Before being submitted, the manuscript should be checked by a scientist doing work in the area with which the manuscript is concerned. The writer should also be sure that his sources are authoritative and up to date."

Office Equipment and Supplies

GEYER'S DEALER TOPICS, 51 Madison Avenue, New York NY 10010. Editor: Neil Loynachan. For individual office equipment and stationery dealers, and special purchasers for store departments handling stationery and office equipment. Monthly. Buys all rights. Pays on acceptance. Query first. Reports "immediately." Enclose S.A.S.E.

Nonfiction and Photos: Articles on merchandising and sales promotion; programs of stationery and office equipment dealers. Problem-solving articles relating to retailers of office supplies, social stationery items, gifts (if the retailer also handles commercial supplies), office furniture and equipment and office machines. Minimum payment, $35, but quality of article is real determinant. Length: 300 to 1,000 words. B&w glossies are purchased with accompanying ms with no additional payment.

OFFICE PRODUCTS, Hitchcock Building, Wheaton IL 60187. Phone: 312-665-1000. Editorial Director: Thomas J. Trafals. For "independent dealers who sell all types of office products—office machines, office furniture, and office supplies." Established in 1904. Monthly. Circulation: 24,000. Buys all rights, but will reassign rights to author after publication. Pays on acceptance. Query first on any long articles. Article deadlines are the 1st of the third month preceding date of issue. News deadlines are the 1st of each month. Will consider photocopied submissions. Reports in 3 to 4 weeks. Enclose S.A.S.E.

Nonfiction: "We're interested in anything that will improve an office product dealer's methods of doing business. Some emphasis on selling and promotion, but interested in all phases of dealer operations. Also news of the field—new stores, expansions, remodelings of OP dealerships." Length: "that which tells the story, and no more or less." Pays $25 to $150 "based on quality of article."

Photos: Purchased with and without mss. "Some news photos. Also, photos of new stores, promotions, etc., but we're not actively looking for these now." Pays $10.

OFFICE WORLD NEWS, 645 Stewart Ave., Garden City NY 11530. Editor: Robert P. Mueller. For independent office products dealers. Monthly; 24 to 60 tabloid pages. Established in 1972. Circulation: 16,000. Buys all rights. Payment on publication. Will send free sample copy to writer on request. Will not consider photocopied or simultaneous submissions. Reports on material accepted for publication in 2 weeks. Returns rejected material immediately (if requested and S.A.S.E. is enclosed). Query first. Enclose S.A.S.E.

Nonfiction and Photos: "Most freelance material is written on assignment or following queries by our freelance 'stringers'. There are occasional openings in some parts of the country for experienced newswriters. Our published material consists of news and news-related features. Straight news reporting, with emphasis on the effect on office product dealers. No textbook management articles will be accepted." Uses interviews, personal opinion, spot news and new product material. "We try to limit our content to hard news." Length: 100 to 500 words. Pays 10¢ per word. B&w and color photos are purchased with mss or on assignment. $10 for 5x7 (minimum) b&w; $15 for 4x5 color transparencies, but will consider slides and 5x7 or 8x10 prints. Department Editor: Geri Hanna.

How To Break In: "Will consider any experienced newswriter for stringer assignments, except in New York metropolitan area."

SOUTHERN STATIONER AND OFFICE OUTFITTER, 75 Third St. N.W., Atlanta GA 30308. Editor: Earl Lines, Jr. For retailers of office products in the Southeast and Southwest. Monthly. Not copyrighted. Pays on publication. Will send free sample copy on request. Query required. Reports promptly. Enclose S.A.S.E.

Nonfiction: Can use articles about retailers in the Southeast and Southwest regarding problems solved concerning store layout, inventory, personnel, etc. "We want articles giving in-depth treatment of a single aspect of a dealer's operation rather than superficial treatment of a number of aspects." Must be approved by subject. Length: 1,000 to 1,400 words. Pays 2¢ to 4¢ a word.

Photos: Purchased with mss. Pays $5.

Optical

OPTICAL JOURNAL AND REVIEW OF OPTOMETRY, 203 King of Prussia Road, Radnor PA 19087. Phone: 215-687-9590. Editor: Christine M. Kelly. Semimonthly. Buys exclusive rights in the field. Pays on publication. Enclose S.A.S.E.

Nonfiction: Uses technical articles, authoritatively written, of optometry, and ophthalmic optics. News and activities of optometrists, opticians, and optical manufacturers, importers, and wholesalers. "We don't like articles that are too general, that can apply to any field; padding." Pays 60¢ per printed inch minimum.

Photos: Photos may be singles or to illustrate articles; b&w only. Pays $5.

RXO JOURNAL OF OPTICIANRY, 1250 Connecticut Ave., N.W., Washington DC 20036. Managing Editor: Robert E. Levine. For opticians interested in marketing ideas, fashion, and health legislation. Monthly magazine; 36 pages, 7¼x10⅛. Established in 1948. Circulation: 5,500. Buys all rights, but will reassign rights to author after publication. Payment on publication. Will send free sample copy to writer on request. Write for copy of editorial guidelines for writers. Query first. Enclose S.A.S.E.

Nonfiction and Photos: "Technical articles, news articles about new developments in any area of opticianry, fashion in eyewear, interpretive articles about certification and other interests to the allied health professional. We are writing to a businessman audience. Must be familiar with professional retail dispensing opticianry. We appeal to the managerial rather than merely the dispenser. Particularly interested in impact of National Health Insurance on the vision care market." Informational, how-to, interview, profile, think articles, photo, successful business operations, new product, merchandising techniques, and technical articles. Length: 1,500 word minimum. Pays 5¢ per word. Photos purchased with accompanying ms. Captions required. Must show dispensing opticians at work. Pays $20 for b&w; $30 for color.

Packing, Canning, and Packaging

Journals in this category are for packaging engineers and others concerned with new methods of packing, canning, and packaging foods in general. Other publications that buy similar material will be found under the Food Products, Processing, and Service heading.

FOOD AND DRUG PACKAGING, 777 Third Ave., New York NY 10017. Editor: Ben Miyares. For packaging decisionmakers in food, drug, cosmetic firms. Established in 1959. Biweekly. Circulation: 45,000. Rights purchased vary with author and material. Pays on acceptance. "Queries only." Enclose S.A.S.E.
Nonfiction and Photos: "Looking for news stories about local and state (not federal) packaging legislation, and its impact on the marketplace. Newspaper style." Length: 1,000 to 2,500 words; usually 500 to 750 words. Payments vary; usually 5¢ a word. Photos purchased with mss. 5x7 glossies preferred. Pays $5.
How To Break In: "1) Get details on local packaging legislation's impact on marketplace/sales/consumer/retailer reaction, etc. 2) Keep an eye open for *new* packages. Query when you think you've got one. New packages move into test markets every day, so if you don't see anything new this week, try again next week. Buy it; describe it briefly in a query."

MODERN PACKAGING, 205 East 42nd St., New York NY 10017. Phone: 212-573-8107. Editor: Thomas M. Jones. For product manufacturers who package or have contract-packaged their product lines; suppliers of packaging materials and equipment. Established in 1927. Monthly including annual encyclopedia. Circulation: 46,000 domestic; 6,000 foreign. Buys all rights. "Very little freelance material bought; mostly on assignment." Payment on publication. Will send free sample copy to writer on request. Write for copy of editorial guidelines (technical/engineering only). Query first, with brief description of subject and available illustration. Reports "immediately." Enclose S.A.S.E.
Nonfiction: "Trend reports, how-to, news, engineering and technical reports." Length: open. Pays $30 per printed page.

PACKING AND SHIPPING, 437 E. Fifth St., Plainfield NJ 07060. Editor: C.M. Bonnell, Jr. For "packaging engineers, traffic managers, shipping managers, and others interested in physical distribution, industrial packaging and shipping." 9 times a year. Buys all rights. Pays on publication. A sample copy will be sent on request. Query first. Reports "promptly." Enclose S.A.S.E.
Nonfiction: Packing, handling and physical distribution procedure by land, sea and air as related to large company operations. Length: 1,000 words. Pays ½¢ to 1¢ a word.
Photos: Uses photographs of new products. Pays $1 each for size 5x7.

WESTERN MATERIAL HANDLING/PACKAGING/SHIPPING, 606 N. Larchmont Blvd., Los Angeles CA 90004. Phone: 213-461-2761. Editor: Jack Gibson. For persons responsible for material handling, packaging, shipping applications in western industrial, manufacturing and warehousing operations. Magazine published every 2 months; 48 (8½x11) pages. Established in 1957. Circulation: 16,000. Buys all rights, but will reassign rights to author after publication. Buys 10 mss a year. Payment on publication. Will send sample copy to writer for $2. Will not consider photocopied or simultaneous submissions. Reports on material accepted for publication in 1 month. Returns rejected material immediately. Query first or submit complete ms. Enclose S.A.S.E.
Nonfiction and Photos: Case histories of applications by western firms showing new techniques, systems, equipment or products in use and the results (reduced costs, faster production, less labor, more efficiency, etc.). Approach should be from the

standpoint of a company's solution to a problem in an area related to magazine's editorial scope. All stories are based on western firms. Length: 350 to 2,000 words. Pays $40 per published page. No additional payment for b&w photos used with mss. Captions required.

Paint

Additional journals that buy material on paint, wallpaper, floor covering, and decorating products stores are listed under Building Interiors.

AMERICAN PAINT & COATINGS JOURNAL, 2911 Washington Ave., St. Louis MO 63103. Phone: 314-534-0301. Editor: Fred Schulenberg. For coatings (paint, varnish, lacquer, etc.) manufacturers; their raw material and equipment suppliers; chemists, salesmen, educators. Weekly magazine; 90 (5¾x8) pages. Established in 1916. Circulation: 7,900. Copyrighted. Payment on publication. Will send free sample copy to writer on request. Submit special theme material 1 month in advance. Reports promptly. Query first or submit complete ms. Enclose S.A.S.E.
Nonfiction and Photos: "Ours is largely a news journal, using news of the industry and features, technical papers and obituaries. Would like to see material on innovations by industry to counter government regulations on material shortages." Profile, historical, spot news, successful business operations, new product. Special theme issues are published periodically. Writer should query editor. Pays $3 to $5 for 5x7 b&w photos purchased with or without accompanying ms. Color is on assignment only.

AMERICAN PAINT & COATINGS JOURNAL CONVENTION DAILY, 2911 Washington Ave., St. Louis MO 63103. Editor: Fred Schulenberg. For manufacturers of coatings (paints, etc.); suppliers of materials and equipment for coatings producers; educators. Magazine. Established in 1916. Daily during paint association convention held 5 times a year. Circulation: 6,500. Buys all rights. Query first. Reports in 3 weeks. Enclose S.A.S.E.
Nonfiction and Photos: News of companies and people; illustrated features; plant expansions; new product items. Informational, interview, profile, photo, spot news, successful business operations, merchandising techniques, and technical articles. Length: 300 words (news items); 1,200 words (features). Pays 4¢ per word for short items; usually $20 to $30 for features; more for assigned work. Photos purchased with accompanying ms. Captions required. B&w glossies; at least 4x5". Pays $4 each. Query for color.

AMERICAN PAINT AND WALLCOVERINGS DEALER, 2911 Washington Ave., St. Louis MO 63103. Editor: Clark Rowley. Monthly. Buys first North American serial rights. Pays on publication. Sample copy will be sent on request. Write for copy of guidelines for writers. Reports in 3 weeks. Enclose S.A.S.E.
Nonfiction and Photos: Interested in articles that tell how paint and wallpaper, hardware, lumber and building supply dealers have built their decorating products businesses or have sold specific classes of merchandise such as: Paints, alkyd finishes, latex paints, masonry and specialty paints, enamels, wood finishes; wallpaper and fabrics, scenics, photomurals, metallic papers; rental equipment such as floor sanders and edgers, steamers; window shades and venetian blinds; spray guns and equipment; artist's materials, crafts, toys, ladders, floor tile, linoleum, carpeting, unfinished furniture and window glass. Also wants articles about remodeled or new stores, advertising and promotional programs, window displays, etc. Don't include "names of manufacturers and their brands. Identify products by generic names." Do include "the full name and address of the store and the name of the owner or manager who was interviewed." Pictures are a necessity. Pays 2¢ to 3¢ a word for text, $5 to $6 for photos.

AMERICAN PAINTING CONTRACTOR, 2911 Washington Ave., St. Louis MO 63102. Phone: 314-534-0301. Editor: E. L. Below. For professional painting contractors, architects, industrial maintenance engineers; operators of hotels, motels, government buildings and military districts, public and institutional buildings. Monthly magazine; "pocket size"; 80 to 100 pages. Established in 1924. Circulation: 35,000. Buys all rights, but will reassign rights to author after publication. Buys about 50 mss a year. Payment on publication. Will send free sample copy to writer on request. Will not consider photocopied or simultaneous submissions. Reports in 30 to 45 days. Query first or submit complete ms. Enclose S.A.S.E.

Nonfiction and Photos: Material on "large-scale painting and decorating projects with special applications or problem-solving challenges for contractors; general operations of a contracting business; public relations concepts for painting contractors. Positively no do-it-yourself. This magazine is for 'pro's' only. Must have top journalism approach in style. In-depth stories on a professional level, requiring knowledge of field or research. Should be well-written and detailed (for painting contractors); exactly how things were done, in what order, what was used, problems encountered, etc. Stories with different angles, different problems, will be successful if the other requirements are met." Informational, how-to, interview, profile, think pieces; spot news, successful business operations, merchandising techniques, technical; new product (if related). Length: 1,500 to 2,000 words. Pays 5¢ to 8¢ per word. Pays $5 for 8x10 b&w glossy photos; $7 for color slides or negatives, when purchased with mss. Captions required.

How To Break In: "Mandatory to study field and understand mechanics of large painting projects or top grade residential decorating (painting or paperhanging)."

CANADIAN PAINT AND FINISHING MAGAZINE, 481 University Ave., Toronto 2, Ont., Canada M5W 1A7. Phone: 416-595-1811. Editor: W. H. Lurz. Monthly. Buys first North American serial rights. Pays on acceptance for mss, on publication for photos. Query first. Reports in 1 week. Enclose S.A.E. and International Reply Coupons.

Nonfiction and Photos: "Semitechnical and news articles on paint manufacturing, industrial finishing techniques, new developments. Also interested in electroplating. Mostly Canadian material required." Accompanied by photos. Length: 800 to 1,500 words. Pays minimum 5¢ a word. Pays $5 for 8x10 b&w glossies.

WESTERN PAINT REVIEW, 1833 W. 8th St., Suite 206, Los Angeles CA 90057. Phone: 213-483-7727. Editor: Ernest C. Ansley. For painting and decorating contractors, retail paint dealers and paint manufacturers. Established in 1920. Monthly. Circulation: 18,000. Buys first North American serial rights. Buys 25 to 30 mss a year. Payment on publication. Query first. Will consider photocopied submissions. Submit seasonal material 2 months in advance. Reports on material within 3 weeks. Enclose S.A.S.E.

Nonfiction and Photos: Articles on successful business operations, merchandising techniques. Technical articles. Length: 500 to 3,000 words. Pays 4¢ a word minimum. 4x5 minimum glossy b&w photos purchased with ms. Captions required. Pays $4.

Paper

FORET ET PAPIER, 625 President Kennedy Ave., Montreal, Quebec, Canada H3A 1K5. For engineers, technicians, foremen engaged in papermaking, research, forestry. Editor: Paul Saint-Pierre, C. Adm. Magazine; 56 (8½x11) pages. Established in 1975. Quarterly. Circulation: 6,000. Buys all rights, but will reassign rights to author after publication. Buys about 12 mss a year. Pays on acceptance. Will send free sample copy to writer on request. Will consider photocopied submissions. Reports in 1 week. Submit complete ms. Enclose S.A.E. and International Reply Coupons.

Nonfiction and Photos: Technical articles on new processes, new equipment. Reviews of conventions, how-to, personal experience, new product and technical articles, and those based on personal experience in the industry. Length: 500 to 1,200 words. Pays 5¢ to 10¢ a word. Glossy prints (5x7 or larger) purchased with ms. Captions required. Pays minimum of $10.

PAPERBOARD PACKAGING, 777 Third Ave., New York NY 10017. Editor: Joel J. Shulman. For "managers, supervisors, and technical personnel who operate corrugated box manufacturing and folding cartons converting companies and plants." Established in 1916. Monthly. Circulation: 8,200. Buys all rights. Pays on publication. Will send a sample copy to a writer on request. Query first. Will consider photocopied submissions. Submit seasonal material 3 months in advance. Enclose S.A.S.E.
Nonfiction and Photos: "Application articles, installation stories, etc. Contact the editor first to establish the approach desired for the article. Especially interested in packaging systems using composite materials, including paper and other materials." Buys technical articles. Length: open. Pays "$50 per printed page (about 1,000 words to a page), including photos. We do not pay for commercially oriented material. We do pay for material if it is not designed to generate business for someone in our field. Will not pay photography costs, but will pay cost of photo reproductions for article."

SOUTHERN PULP AND PAPER MANUFACTURER, 75 Third St., N.W., Atlanta GA 30308. Editor: Gary W. Johnston. For "those actively associated with a pulp and/or paper manufacturing or converting operation." Monthly. Pays after publication. Reports in 2 weeks. Enclose S.A.S.E.
Nonfiction and Photos: Production, new methods, processing, and new mill or mill expansion stories written to interest pulp and paper companies' personnel. Length: up to 2,000 words. Pays 35¢ per column inch or more, depending upon importance of subject matter and quality of material. Pays $2 per photo.

Petroleum

EM REPORT, P.O. Box 1589, Dallas TX 75221. Editor: Ernestine Adams. For executives and technical managers in the oil and gas industries. Monthly. Buys all rights. Pays on publication. Reports immediately. Enclose S.A.S.E.
Nonfiction: Articles about management and economics in petroleum and natural gas industries. Inside news stories on energy. Payment varies; usually 5¢ per word.

FUEL OIL NEWS, 309 Bloomfield Ave., Caldwell NJ 07006. Editor: T. R. Byrley. For retail fuel oil dealers and installers of all heating equipment. Monthly magazine; 48 to 64 (8¼x11¼) pages. Established in 1935. Circulation: 15,000. Buys all rights. Buys 35 to 50 mss a year "but mostly from established writers, who know something about our business". Payment on publication. Will send free sample copy to writer on request. Write for copy of guidelines for writers. Reports in 10 days. Query first. Enclose S.A.S.E.
Nonfiction: Interviews with selected dealers; descriptions of unusual installations. "If the writer is in a market not already covered, we supply an interview questionnaire which will produce the story, if there is one." Length: open. Pays $35 to $50 per published page, depending on material.

FUELOIL AND OIL HEAT, 200 Commerce Rd., Cedar Grove NJ 07009. Feature Editor: M. F. Hundley. For distributors of fueloil, heating equipment dealers. Monthly. Buys first rights. Pays on publication. Reports in 2 weeks. Enclose S.A.S.E.
Nonfiction: Management articles dealing with fueloil distribution and equipment selling. Length: up to 2,500 words. Pays $25 to $35 a printed page.

HUGHES RIGWAY, Hughes Tool Co., P.O. Box 2539, Houston TX 77001. Editor: Tom Haynes. For men in the oilfield. Age varies (21 to 65). Quarterly magazine; 24 (8x11) pages. Established in 1963. Circulation: 15,000. Buys first North American serial rights. Buys about 3 mss a year. Payment on acceptance. Will send free sample copy to writer on request. Write for copy of guidelines for writers. Will consider photocopied submissions. Query first or submit complete ms. Reports within 1 month. Enclose S.A.S.E.
Nonfiction and Photos: "Character-revealing historical narratives about little-known incidents, heroes, or facts, particularly those which contradict conventional concepts. Also, topical reportorial features about people in oil or drillling. Must be thoroughly documented." Length: 2,000 to 2,500 words. Pays 10¢ a word. Photos purchased with mss. Pays a flat rate of $50 per printed page for features and articles with good photographs or for picture stories.
Fiction: "Top-quality fiction in oilfield settings." Length: 2,000 to 2,500 words. Pays 10¢ a word.

HYDROCARBON PROCESSING, P.O. Box 2608, Houston TX 77001. Editor: Frank L. Evans. For personnel in oil refining, gas, petrochemical processing or hydrocarbon processing industries, including engineering, operation, management phases. Special issues: January, Maintenance; April, Natural Gas Processing; September, Refining Processes; November, Petrochemical Processes. Monthly. Buys all rights. Write for copy of guidelines for writers. Enclose S.A.S.E.
Nonfiction: Wants technical manuscripts on engineering and operations in the industry which will be of help to personnel. Also nontechnical articles on management, safety and industrial relations that will help technical men become managers. Length: open, "but do not waste words." Pays about $25 per printed page.
Photos: Buys photos as part of nonfiction package; and infrequently, with captions only. Prefers 8x10 but can use 5x7 or even smaller if extremely sharp.
How To Break In: "Articles must all pass a rigid evaluation of their reader appeal, accuracy and overall merit. Reader interest determines an article's value. We covet articles that will be of real job value to subscribers. Before writing—ask to see our Author's Handbook. You may save time and effort by writing a letter, and outline briefly what you have in mind. If your article will or won't meet our needs, we will tell you promptly."

IMPERIAL OIL REVIEW, 111 St. Clair Ave. W., Toronto, Ont. M5W 1K3, Canada. Editor: Kenneth Bagnell. Bimonthly. Buys all rights. Payment on acceptance. Will send a sample copy to a writer on request. Query first. Reports in 1 week. Enclose S.A.E. and International Reply Coupons.
Nonfiction: "Subject matter is general, but we like material that can be tied in to the oil industry. Articles specifically about the oil industry are generally staff written. Material must be Canadian." Length: 2,500 words maximum. Pays $300 minimum.

NATIONAL PETROLEUM NEWS, 1221 Avenue of the Americas, New York NY 10020. Editor: Frank Breese. For businessmen who make their living in the oil marketing industry, either as company employees or through their own business operations. Monthly magazine; 90 pages. Established in 1909. Circulation: 20,000. Rights purchased vary with author and material. Usually buys all rights. Buys 2 mss a year. Payment on acceptance if done on assignment. Payment on publication for unsolicited material. Query first. Enclose S.A.S.E.
Nonfiction and Photos: Material related directly to developments and issues in the oil marketing industry and "how-to" and "what-with" case studies. Informational; successful business operations. Length: 2,000 words maximum. Pays $60 per printed page. Payment for b&w photos "depends upon advance understanding". Department Editor: Carolyn DeWitt.

OFFSHORE, P.O. Box 1941, Houston TX 77001. Phone: 713-621-9720. Editor: Robert G. Burke. For companies involved in drilling, producing, exploration, pipelining, in the oil and gas industry; engineering-construction, shipbuilding, oceanography, underwater mining, marine services, oilwell services, equipment manufacturers and supply companies. June 20 is Annual Drilling and Production Issue. Major offshore oil areas of the world are reviewed. Established in 1954. Monthly. Circulation: 16,000. Buys first North American serial rights. Buys 15 to 20 mss a year. Pays on publication. Query required. Reports in 2 to 4 weeks. Enclose S.A.S.E.

Nonfiction and Photos: Informative, explanatory material on how a project was accomplished. Aim at the working engineer, middle management, workmen, and persons interested in commercial offshore projects and commercial oceanography. Buys informational articles, personal experience articles, interviews, profiles, and spot news. Length: 500 to 3,500 words. Pays $1 per column inch. Photos purchased with mss.

OILWEEK, 918 6th Ave., S.W., #200, Calgary, Alberta, Canada T2P 0V5. Editor: Vic Humphreys. For senior management, engineers, etc., in the energy industries. Magazine; 36 to 50 pages. Established in 1948. Weekly. Circulation: 11,000. Rights purchased vary with author and material. Usually buys all rights. Pays on publication. Will send free sample copy to writer on request. Write for copy of guidelines for writers. Reports on material accepted for publication in 2 weeks. Returns rejected material in 2 weeks. Query first. Enclose S.A.E. and International Reply Coupons.

Nonfiction: News or semitechnical articles which have a Canadian content or Canadian application, directed toward the petroleum, or in some instances, energy field. Recently published "Canadian Company Makes Inroads With Digital Services for the Oilfield." Length: 1,500 words maximum. Pays 10¢ a word minimum.

PETROLEUM ENGINEER INTERNATIONAL, PIPELINE & GAS JOURNAL, P.O. Box 1589, Dallas TX 75221. Monthly. Buys all rights. Query first. Enclose S.A.S.E.

Nonfiction and Photos: "Technical and semitechnical articles about the petroleum industry, but not about the marketing of oil. Must concern methods in drilling, production, pipeline construction and operation and gas distribution. Knowledge of the oil industry is essential. Pictures and illustrations help." Length: 2 to 10 typed pages. Pays $35 to $250.

PETROLEUM INDEPENDENT, 1101 Sixteenth St., N.W., Washington DC 20036. Phone: 202-466-8240. Editor: Robert Gouldy. For "independent petroleum drillers, operators, producers, bankers, and congressmen." Bimonthly. Circulation: about 12,500. Buys first rights. Buys about 20 mss a year. Guaranteed payment on acceptance. Sample copy to a writer on request. Query first. Reports promptly. Enclose S.A.S.E.

Nonfiction: "Anything of political or economic interest to our audience. Most material solicited from experts in their fields. Will consider any unusual, interesting oil drilling/producing events. We frequently print articles about towns with a strong petroleum background or round-up stories describing a particularly active exploration area. Not wanted are articles on foreign production, refining, marketing, and other segments of the industry, each of which has its own magazine." Buys how-to's, interviews, and profiles; occasionally, historical and photo articles. Ironic and/or unusual situations regarding energy shortages (oil, gas) in particular areas. Length: maximum 2,500 words. Pays $50 to $75 per magazine page. Always negotiable.

Photos: Purchased with mss; with captions only. B&w glossies, color transparencies, color prints. Pays $5 to $25 for photos not accompanying mss.

Fiction: "Rarely bought, but will consider it if well-done and slanted toward petroleum politics or economics." Length: maximum 2,500 words. Pays $50 to $75 per magazine page. Always negotiable.

PETROLEUM MARKETER, 636 First Ave., West Haven CT 06516. Editor: Kevin Chase. For "independent oil jobbers, major oil company operations and management personnel, and petroleum equipment distributors." Bimonthly. Circulation: 20,000. Buys North American serial rights. Pays on publication. Will send a sample copy to a writer on request. Query first. Reports "within 3 days of receipt." Enclose S.A.S.E.

Nonfiction and Photos: "Success stories on how an oil jobber did something;

interpretive marketing stories on local or regional basis. We want straightforward, honest reporting. Treat the subject matter with dignity." Length: 1,200 to 1,500 words. Pays "$35 per printed page." Photos purchased with and without mss; captions required. "Glossies for reproduction by engraving; subject matter decided after consultation." Pays $5.

PETROLEUM TODAY, 1801 K St., N.W., Washington DC 20006. Phone: 202-833-5778. Editor: Cynthia Riggs Stoertz. For "mostly men, in their early fifties; what we call opinion leaders; may be clergymen, legislators, newspapermen, club leaders, professors; but few oil industry people." Established in 1959. Published 3 times a year. Circulation: 110,000. Not copyrighted. Buys 8 to 10 mss a year. Payment on publication. Will send free sample copy to writer on request. Query first. Reports on material in 2 to 6 weeks. Enclose S.A.S.E.
Nonfiction and Photos: "Articles on issues that currently face the petroleum industry on the energy crisis, marine drilling, the environment, taxation, the Alaska pipeline, offshore drilling, consumerism, coastal zone management. Also like to use a few short, light articles; oil-related." Informational, personal experience, interview, profile, think pieces. Length: open. Pays $200 to $750. 8x10 b&w glossy photos purchased with or without accompanying mss, or on assignment. Captions required. Pays $25. 35mm (or larger) color transparencies. Pays $50 a quarter page; $250 for cover. Must be petroleum-related.

PIPE LINE INDUSTRY, P.O. Box 2608, Houston TX 77001. Editor: Don Lambert. For gas and oil pipeline and distribution industry. Monthly. Circulation: about 22,000. Buys all rights. Pays on publication. Will send free sample copy to a writer on request. Query preferred; include outline indicating approach, depth, and probable photos or other illustrations to be submitted. Reports in 10 days. Enclose S.A.S.E.
Nonfiction: Short technical features; ideas for doing a job easier, cheaper, and safer; operating hints, etc. Length: "varies." Pays $25 per page; higher rates upon advance agreement. Gas and Engineering Editor: Carrington Mason; Associate Editor-Construction: Dave Deason.
Photos: Purchased with mss; construction and operations of facilities in the gas and pipeline industry. 8x10 glossies preferred. Payment depends on space and manner in which photo is used.

PIPELINE CONSTRUCTION, 3314 Mercer St., Houston TX 77027. Editor: William Quarles. For pipeline and utility contractors. Established in 1945. Circulation: 13,000. Buys all rights but will reassign rights to author after publication. Pays on acceptance. Will send free sample copy to writer on request. Write for copy of guidelines for writers. Query first. Enclose S.A.S.E.
Nonfiction: Feature articles on pipeline jobs, oil, gas, water, sewer pipelines. Job description, equipment, personnel, unusual features of projects. Length: 600 to 2,000 words. Pays $35 per published page.

Pets

Listed here are publications for professionals in the pet industry; wholesalers, manufacturers, suppliers, retailers, owners of pet specialty stores, pet groomers. Also aquarium retailers, distributors, manufacturers and those interested in the fish industry.

AQUARIUM INDUSTRY, Toadtown, Magalia CA 95954. Editor: Robert Behme. For aquarium retailers, distributors, manufacturers. Tabloid newspaper published 12 times a year; 16 (9x13½) pages. Established in 1973. Circulation: 12,400. Not copyrighted. Buys 2 to 4 mss per issue. Payment within 30 days of acceptance. Will send free sample copy to writer on request. Will not consider photocopied or simultaneous submissions. Reports in 10 days. Query first. Enclose S.A.S.E.
Nonfiction: News-oriented shorts; how-to features. Interviews with retailers on ways to improve stores, sales, etc. Material must be "most concise piece possible. No

fat. No (or very few) superlatives. Facts and description when important to the story." Interested in retailer and distributor stories, personnel changes, new shops opening up, etc. Length: 700 to 1,000 words. Pays $30 to $50. Also open to column ideas from those who know fish and the fish business.

FROM THE KENNELS, P.O. Box 1369, Vancouver WA 98660. Editor: J.C. Perkins. For owners of purebred dogs. Tabloid newspaper; 16 pages. Established in 1970. Twice a month. Circulation: 5,000. Not copyrighted. Buys few mss a year. Will send free sample copy to writer on request. Write for copy of guidelines for writers. Will consider photocopied and simultaneous submissions. Reports in 10 days. Query first. Enclose S.A.S.E.
Nonfiction: Articles must concern purebred dogs and their owners. Expose, personal opinion articles. "If the article has merit, we will be willing to pay. Author should suggest the amount desired in initial correspondence with us. If we do not agree with that estimate, we will return the submission."

PET AGE, 2561 North Clark St., Chicago IL 60614. Editor: Richard L. Shotke. For "professionals in the pet industry: wholesalers, manufacturers, suppliers, retailers, etc." Monthly. Circulation: 21,000. Buys all rights. Buys 25 to 35 mss a year. Pays on acceptance. Will send a sample copy to a writer on request; "postage must accompany request." Query first "with an outline of the specific slant or peg suggested." Submit seasonal material at least 3 to 4 months in advance. Reports in 1 month. Enclose S.A.S.E.
Nonfiction and Photos: "Features which describe innovative approaches, success stories, how-to's, etc., for pet industry personnel on subjects such as pet shop advertising, creating pet promotion projects, pet salesmanship, shop design, use of products, etc. Concentrate on features which provide specific practical methods of improving merchandising. No visits to local pet shops unless particularly innovative, with unusual success story in some phase. No interest in cute stories or poetry or other consumer-oriented material." Buys how-to's, coverage of successful business operations, new product coverage, articles on pet merchandising techniques. Length: 250 to 2,500 words. Pays $5 to $40. Photos purchased with mss; captions required. Pays $2 to $10.
How To Break In: "Submit a query about writing up and photographing a retail pet shop which has had success in using unusual or unique approaches to sales promotions, operations which have produced successful results."

THE PET DEALER, 225 W. 34 St., New York NY 10001. Phone: 212-279-0800. Editor: Fred Rackmil. For owners of pet specialty stores, departments and dog groomers. Monthly magazine, 100 (8½x11) pages. Established in 1950. Circulation: 7,800. Buys 12 mss a year. Buy all rights. Payment on acceptance, when length is determined. Will send free sample copy on request. Write for copy of guidelines for writers. Will not consider photocopied or simultaneous submissions. Reports on material in 10 days. Query first or submit complete ms. Enclose S.A.S.E.
Nonfiction and Photos: Success stories about pet shops, and occasional stories about distributors and jobbers in the pet field. Articles about merchandising trends and innovations. Stories about pets themselves are of no possible interest. Length: 1,500 words maximum. Pays $25 per printed page. Photos (no smaller than 5x7) or negatives, are purchased with mss, with no additional payment. Captions required.
Fillers: Buys occasional newspaper clippings if they relate specifically to operation or news of pet stores. Pays minimum of $50.
How To Break In: "We're interested in store profiles outside the New York area. Photos are of key importance. Good photos and lots of them can sell an otherwise inadequate piece. The story we can always fix up, but we can't run out and take the photos. The best thing to do is send a sample of your work and some story proposals. Even if your proposals are not that strong, we still might want to use you on one of our own ideas. Articles focus on new techniques in merchandising or promotion, or on someone with a special new sideline — like the guy in New York who makes house calls for sick fish."

PET MASS MARKETING, 1 East First St., Duluth MN 55802. Phone: 218-727-8511. Managing Editor: Terry Kreeger. For pet supply buyers for mass markets. Every 2 months. 80-page magazine (9x12). Established in 1973. Circulation: 12,500. Buys all rights. Buys 6 to 12 mss a year. Payment on acceptance. Will send free sample copy to writer on request. Will not consider photocopied or simultaneous submissions. Will consider cassette submissions. Reports on material in 30 days. Query first or submit complete ms. Enclose S.A.S.E.

Nonfiction and Photos: Style and subject of articles must be of interest to this specialized market (buyers of pet supplies and pet foods for supermarkets, department, discount, variety, drug, auto and hardware stores). Profiles on pet departments of major mass marketers; comparisons of methods; statistical analysis; trends, industry news, unique promotions or departments. Length: 750 words minimum. No maximum. Pays 5¢ per word. Pays $6 to $7.50 for b&w photos; $12.50 to $15 for color slides. $45 for cover. Photos are purchased with or without mss, or on assignment. Captions required.

PETS/SUPPLIES/MARKETING, 1 E. First St., Duluth MN 55802. Editor: Paul A. Setzer. For owners and/or managers of retail pet operations, grooming shops or kennels; rack jobbers, wholesalers and manufacturers of pet products. Monthly magazine; 90 to 100 (9x12) pages. Established in 1946. Circulation: 14,000. Buys all rights. Buys 55 to 60 mss a year. Payment on acceptance. Will send free sample copy to writer on request. Write for copy of guidelines for writers. Will not consider photocopied or simultaneous submissions. Submit material for special issues 2 to 3 months in advance. Special issues vary from year to year and this information is available upon request or specific assignment. Reports on material accepted for publication within a month. Returns rejected material in 1 to 2 weeks. Query first. Enclose S.A.S.E.

Nonfiction and Photos: "We are well known for our statistical reviews of the pet industry as a whole. We use profiles of 'successful' pet shops, grooming salons, etc. General business and/or merchandising articles. Retailing 'tips', business how-to's; items of interest to the typical pet shop retailer. We are interested in good examples of successful pet retail shops with ideas that the average retailer can incorporate. We usually have special issues devoted to the saltwater industry, grooming, aquariums, merchandising of products, outdoor pools and ponds, terrariums, small animals and a special Christmas issue. We do not want to see articles on 'the pet shop down the street'. Only good, well-established pet shops merit our coverage. We also do not want articles on the family pet, since we are not a consumer magazine." Length: 2,000 to 3,000 words. Pays 5¢ per word. Short features are also used on news and tips on grooming; pet foods, events, birds, unusual animals. Length: 500 words maximum. Pays $50 to $100. Purchases b&w and color photos with mss or on assignment. A few are purchased without mss. Prefers 8x10 b&w glossies but will accept 5x7 and contact sheets. Pays $6 to $7.50. Prefers 2¼x2¼ color transparencies, but will accept 35mm. Pays $12.50 to $15; $30 to $40 for cover shot. Captions required. Department Editor: Pamela Martodam.

Fillers: Newsbreaks, clippings, jokes. Length: 100 words maximum. Pays 5¢ per word. Department Editor: Barbara Treleven.

Photography

AMERICAN CINEMATOGRAPHER, 1782 N. Orange Dr., Hollywood CA 90028. Editor: Herb A. Lightman. For motion picture directors of photography and film production personnel. Monthly. Buys all rights. Query first. Enclose S.A.S.E.

Nonfiction and Photos: Uses articles dealing with the photography and allied technology of motion pictures in all fields of film production. Treatment must be technical or semitechnical, describing unusual problems encountered and how solved, with substantial emphasis on the equipment and mechanical techniques used. Length: 1,500 to 2,500 words. Pays up to $75. Photos purchased with ms.

BUSINESS SCREEN, 757 Third Ave., New York NY 10017. Editor: Bob Seymour. For sponsors, producers and users of business, commercial advertising and industrial motion pictures, slidefilms and related audiovisual media. Bimonthly. Buys all rights. Pays on publication. Query first. Reports in 2 weeks. Enclose S.A.S.E.

Nonfiction: "Short articles on successful application of these 'tools' in industry and commerce, but only when approved by submission of advance query to publisher's office. Technical articles on film production techniques, with or without illustrations, science film data and interesting featurettes about application or utilization of films in community, industry, etc., also welcomed." Pays up to 5¢ a word.

INDUSTRIAL PHOTOGRAPHY, 750 Third Ave., New York NY 10017. Editor: Natalie Canavor. For professional photography specialists who fulfill the visual communications needs of business, industry, government, science, medical and other organizations. Magazine; 64 (8½x11) pages. Established in 1951. Monthly. Circulation: 40,000. Rights purchased vary with author and material. May buy all rights, but occasionally will reassign rights to author after publication; or first North American serial rights. Buys 25 mss a year. Pays on publication. Will send free sample copy to writer on request. Will consider photocopied submissions. No simultaneous submissions. Reports in 4 weeks. Query first or submit complete ms. Enclose S.A.S.E.

Nonfiction and Photos: Features describing ideas, applications and techniques for all types of still photography, motion pictures, audiovisuals, industrial video. Material is balanced from how-to articles to discussion of visual communication trends. "Freelancer should write only about subjects he is fully qualified to handle from a strictly professional orientation. Will specify needs in personal letter providing contributor describes his general qualifications." Informational, how-to, interview, profile, think articles, technical pieces and coverage of successful photo department operations. Length: 750 to 3,000 words. Pays $50 to $275. Good b&w prints (minimum 5x7) and color transparencies (35mm minimum) or good color prints should amply illustrate articles. No additional payment. "We also like to see outstanding examples of a photographer's work."

How To Break In: "Suggest a specific story idea — subject, event, person to interview, etc. — with outline of author's qualifications to handle the subject or subjects."

PHOTOJOURNALIST, P.O. Box 1466, Columbus MS 39701. Editor: Dr. Richard H. Logan. For amateur and some professional photographers, photojournalists, article writers. Some youngsters, some retirees. Newsletter published 10 times yearly; 4 sheets (8½x11). Established in 1968. Acquires first rights only. Uses 14 mss a year. Payment in photography or writers' books. Will send 2 sample copies to writer for 25¢. Write for copy of guidelines for writers. Will not consider photocopied or simultaneous submissions. Reports in 2 weeks. Query first or submit complete ms. Enclose S.A.S.E.

Nonfiction: Short articles by or about photojournalists who have succeeded by applying the tips or ideas recommended. Must be factual and proven successful. Interested in material on how to get ideas; how retired people can make money in photography or photojournalism; how to cope with the energy crisis. No general pieces. They must be specific and helpful. Uses informational, how-to, personal experience, interview (if well-handled), successful business operations, merchandising techniques and technical material if simply presented. Length: 1 to 2 pages, double-spaced. Pays "$15 to $25 worth of photo books we have in stock for longer and unusual items; $5 worth of photo books we have in stock for short items."

How To Break In: "Submit a good, tightly written, short article, giving practical help on photography or photojournalism that our readers can use to increase their freelance income."

PHOTOMETHODS, One Park Ave., New York NY 10016. Editor: Fred Schmidt. For those who use imaging in their work, including full-time corporate and independent photographers and functional photographers (those who use imaging, not full-time photographers). Magazine; 60 pages, 8x11. Established in 1957. Monthly. Circulation: 50,000. Buys all rights. Buys about 30 mss a year. Pays on publication.

Will send free sample copy to writer on request. Query first. If possible, include samples of work, or list of recent published articles. Reports in 1 to 3 months. Enclose S.A.S.E.

Nonfiction and Photos: "Application stories in: film, still, audiovisual, video, micro graphics, graphic reproduction, processing. Each in three levels: basic, intermediate, advanced. Make technical information interesting; still provide reader with what he wants and needs. Style should be clear, concise, simple sentences; clean style. We don't want puff pieces for products or persons. Special interest themes might cover anything new in imaging, perhaps esoteric now, but with possible future use." Informational, how-to, personal experience, interview, and technical articles. Length: 850 to 3,000 words. Pays $75 minimum. Photos purchased with accompanying ms with no additional payment. Captions required.

THE PROFESSIONAL PHOTOGRAPHER, 1090 Executive Way, Des Plaines IL 60018. Editor: Donald L. Wiley. For practicing professional photographers. Magazine; 120 pages, 8½x 11. Established in 1907. Monthly. Circulation: 26,000. Rights purchased vary with author and material. Usually buys all rights, but will sometimes reassign rights to author after publication. Buys 3 to 6 mss a year. Pays on publication. Will send sample copy to writer for $1.50. Write for copy of guidelines for writers. Will consider photocopied submissions. Query first. Submit seasonal material 6 months in advance. Reports in 2 weeks. Enclose S.A.S.E.

Nonfiction and Photos: How-to, case histories of successful studios, business methods. Pays $15 to $50. Photos purchased with accompanying ms with no additional payment. Captions required.

THE RANGEFINDER MAGAZINE, P.O. Box 66925, Los Angeles CA 90066. Editor: Janet Marshall Victor. For career photographers. Established in 1952. Monthly. Circulation: 40,000. Buys first serial rights. Buys about 20 mss a year. Pays on publication. Will send a sample copy to a writer for $1. Write for copy of guidelines for writers. Query first "for major features; no query required on secondary material." Will consider photocopied submissions "if legible." Reports in 2 weeks. Enclose S.A.S.E.

Nonfiction and Photos: "Feature material is judged on the basis of the real benefit to professional photographers. Does it help them improve their status, either quality-wise or business-wise? No biographies, please. Please let us see what you have. We are always interested in new material. If you wish to be paid for the article, be sure to indicate by stating on the manuscript the words, 'Your usual rates'. Otherwise it will be assumed that the material is contributed at no cost to us by one of our readers who wishes to share his knowledge with his fellow photographers." Recently published articles include "Why the Print Doesn't Match the Transparency", "Survival in School Photography", and "One Mind's Eye: Arnold Newman in Retrospect". Length: 1,000 to 2,000 words. Pays $18 to $24 per published page (including illustrations). Uses 8x10 matte or glossy b&w photos. Uses color.

Plastics

CANADIAN PLASTICS, 1450 Don Mills Rd., Don Mills, Ont., Canada. Phone: 416-445-6641. Editor: Antony Anden. For management people in the plastics industry. Monthly. Buys first rights. Pays on publication. Query first. Reports in 2 to 4 weeks. Enclose S.A.E. and International Reply Coupons.

Nonfiction: Accurate technical writing. Accuracy is more important than style. "We reject some freelance material because of lack of Canadian relevance; we like to publish articles that are meaningful to the reader; something he can use for his benefit as a businessman." Pays 7¢ a word.

Photos: Buys photos submitted with ms. Pays $5.

Fillers: Buys newsbreaks. Pays $5 for news items; $15 for longer features.

PLASTICS TECHNOLOGY, 633 3rd Ave., New York NY 10017. Phone: 212-986-4800. Editor: Malcolm W. Riley. For plastic processors. Circulation: 40,000. Buys all rights. Pays on publication. Will send free sample copy on request. Query preferred. Reports in 2 weeks. Enclose S.A.S.E.
Nonfiction and Photos: Articles on plastics processing. Length: "no limits." Pays $30 to $35 per published page. Photos and all artwork purchased with ms, with no additional payment.

Plumbing, Heating, Air Conditioning, and Refrigeration

Publications for fuel oil dealers who also install heating equipment are classified with the Petroleum journals.

CONTRACTOR MAGAZINE, Berkshire Common, Pittsfield MA 01201. Editor: Seth Shepard. For mechanical contractors, wholesalers, engineers. Newspaper; 70 (11x15) pages. Established in 1954. Every two weeks. Circulation: 38,000. Not copyrighted. Buys 30 mss a year. Pays on publication. Will send sample copy to writer for $1.50. Write for copy of guidelines for writers. Will consider photocopied submissions. No simultaneous submissions. Reports in 1 month. Query first or submit complete ms. Enclose S.A.S.E.
Nonfiction and Photos: Articles on materials, crafts, policies, business methods of the air conditioning, heating, plumbing industry. "All presentation styles are employed, depending on the topic being covered: news, interpretive reports, how-to, etc." Informational, interview, profile, think articles, expose, spot news, successful business operations, merchandising techniques, technical. Pays $150 maximum. 5x7 b&w glossies purchased with or without ms. Pays $5. Captions required.

DE/JOURNAL, 450 E. Ohio St., Chicago IL 60611. Editor: Stephen J. Shafer. For independent businessmen who sell and install plumbing, heating, air conditioning, process piping systems. Established in 1889. Monthly. Circulation: 45,000. Rights purchased vary with author and material. May buy all rights or usually will reassign rights to author after publication. Buys 30 mss a year. Payment on publication. Will send sample copy to writer for $2. Will consider photocopied and simultaneous submissions. Reports in 1 month. Query first or submit complete ms. Enclose S.A.S.E.
Nonfiction and Photos: "Only management and technical articles, pertaining to industry. Familiarity with industry described most important. Emphasis is on management." Interview, successful business operations, merchandising techniques, technical. Payment varies with quality, but the usual rate is $25 per published page. B&w photos.

ELECTRIC HEAT, 400 N. Michigan Ave., Chicago IL 60611. For "heating contractors, electric utility heating specialists, builders, architects, consulting engineers." Established in 1955. Bimonthly. Circulation: 11,000. Buys all rights. Pays on acceptance. Will send a sample copy to a writer for $1. Query first. Reports in 2 to 3 weeks. Enclose S.A.S.E.
Nonfiction and Photos: "Specific case histories of ways and means of selling or installing electric heating equipment, components and accessories for electric heating. Illustrated articles of new and converted electrically heated industrial, commercial, and residential buildings." Length: 750 to 1,500 words. Pays $75 to $200. 8x10 or 5x7 b&w glossies purchased with mss. Pays minimum $5.

EXPORT, 386 Park Ave., S., New York NY 10016. Editor: M. Downing. For importers and distributors in 165 countries who handle hardware, air conditioning and refrigeration equipment and related consumer hardlines. Magazine; 60 to 80 pages. Established in 1877. Every 2 months. Circulation: 38,500. Buys first serial rights. Buys about 10 mss a year. Pays on acceptance. Reports in 1 month. Query first. Enclose S.A.S.E.

Nonfiction: News stories of products and merchandising of air conditioning and refrigeration equipment, hardware and related consumer hardlines. Informational, how-to, interview, profile, successful business operations. Length: 1,000 to 3,000 words. Pays 10¢ a word, maximum.

How To Break In: "One of the best ways to break in here is with a story originating outside the U.S. or Canada. Two recent examples are 'LAIRCO: It All Started with Apples,' about an air conditioning equipment manufacturer in Beirut; and 'Shoppers Adjust to Changing Economy,' about the Japanese market and distribution system — both from freelancers. Our major interest is in new products and new developments — but they must be available and valuable to overseas buyers. We also like company profile stories. A key thing we look for in writers is some kind of expertise in our field. Departments and news stories are staff written."

HEATING/PIPING/AIR CONDITIONING, Two Illinois Center, Chicago IL 60601. Phone: 312-565-1282. Editor: Robert T. Korte. Monthly. Buys all rights. Pays on publication. Query first. Reports in 2 weeks. Enclose S.A.S.E.

Nonfiction: Uses engineering and technical articles covering design, installation, operation, maintenance, etc., of heating, piping and air conditioning systems in industrial plants and large buildings. Length: 3,000 to 4,000 words maximum. Pays $30 per printed page.

HEATING, PLUMBING, AIR CONDITIONING, 1450 Don Mills Rd., Don Mills, Ont., Canada. Editor: Nick Hancock. For mechanical contractors; plumbers; warm air heating, refrigeration and air conditioning contractors; wholesalers; architects; consulting and mechanical engineers who are in key management or specifying positions in the plumbing, heating, air conditioning and refrigeration industries in Canada. Monthly. Circulation: 13,500. Buys North American serial rights only. Pays on publication. Will send free sample copy to a writer on request. Reports in 1 to 2 months. Enclose S.A.E. and International Reply Coupons.

Nonfiction and Photos: News, technical, business management and "how-to" articles which will inform, educate and motivate readers who design, manufacture, install, service, maintain or supply fuel to all mechanical components and systems in residential, commercial, institutional and industrial installations across Canada. Length: 1,000 to 1,500 words. Pays 6¢ per word. Photos purchased with mss. Prefers 5x7 or 8x10 glossies.

ILLINOIS MASTER PLUMBER, 140 S. Dearborn St., Chicago IL 60603. Editor: J.E. Fitzgerald, Jr. For members of plumbing and heating, cooling trade, architects, engineers, union officials, manufacturers and wholesalers in industry. Monthly. Buys all rights. Pays on publication. Will send free sample copy to a writer on request. Reports in 30 days. Enclose S.A.S.E.

Nonfiction: Articles on tax problems, accounting, service; humorous articles. Subjects of interest to readers in the plumbing, heating and cooling trade. Length: 1,200 words. Pays $1.50 per 100 words.

IOWA PLUMBING, HEATING, COOLING CONTRACTOR, Box 56, Boone IA 50036. Editor: R. G. Canier. For those in the plumbing-heating-cooling contracting industry plus state procurement authorities. Monthly. Circulation: 1,100. Not copyrighted. Pays on publication. Will send sample copy to a writer on request. "Study publication." Enclose S.A.S.E. for return of submissions.

Nonfiction, Photos, and Fiction: Articles on development, engineering problems and improvements in general covering new equipment, new materials, legal review, state news, national news; other topics. Photos and fiction appropriate to format. Pays 2½¢ a word; $5 each for photos.

MOBILE AIR CONDITIONING, 6116 N. Central Pkwy., Dallas TX 75206. Phone: 214-361-7014. Editor: L. T. Merrill. For manufacturers of air conditioners, parts;

distributors and dealers. Monthly magazine, 20 to 40 (8½x11) pages. Established in 1970. Circulation: over 4,000. Buys all rights, but will reassign rights to author after publication. Payment on acceptance. Will send free sample copy to writer on request. Will consider photocopied submissions. Will not consider simultaneous submissions. Submit seasonal material on the first of the preceding month. Returns rejected material immediately. Query first. Enclose S.A.S.E.

Nonfiction and Photos: "Basically, 10 issues a year deal with specific application areas of mobile type air conditioners for autos, trucks, recreational vehicles, farm and construction vehicles, boats, aircraft, parts and tools. Subject matter would have to be related. Industry sales information. How-to stories. Service tips and use of tools, etc. Material should be analytical, factual, with some humor." Informational, interview, think pieces, successful business operations, merchandising techniques, technical. Length: 500 to 2,200 words. Pays $1.50 per column inch. Pays $5 for b&w photos accepted with mss. Captions required.

SNIPS MAGAZINE, 407 Mannheim Rd., Bellwood IL 60104. Phone: 312-544-3870. Editor: Nick Carter. For sheet metal, warm air heating, ventilating, air conditioning, and roofing contractors. Monthly. Buys all rights. "Write for detailed list of requirements before submitting any work." Enclose S.A.S.E.

Nonfiction: Material should deal with information about contractors who do sheet metal, warm air heating, air conditioning, ventilation and roofing work; also about successful advertising campaigns conducted by these contractors and the results. Length: "prefers stories to run less than 1,000 words unless on special assignment." Pays 2¢ each for first 500 words, 1¢ each for additional words.

Photos: Pays $2 each for small snapshot pictures, $4 each for usable 8x10 pictures.

Power and Power Plants

Publications in this listing aim at company managers, engineers, and others involved in generating and supplying power for businesses, homes, and industries. Journals for electrical engineers who design, maintain, and install systems connecting users with sources of power are classified under the heading Electricity.

DIESEL AND GAS TURBINE PROGRESS, P.O. Box 7406, 11225 West Blue Mound Rd., Milwaukee WI 53213. Editor: Bruce W. Wadman. For engineers, purchasers, and users of diesel and natural gas engines and gas turbines. Monthly. Pays on acceptance. Will send free sample copy to a writer on request. "Query with brief details about engine system and location. Send queries to Tony Alberte, Managing Editor." Reports in 4 weeks. Enclose S.A.S.E.

Nonfiction and Photos: Illustrated on-the-job articles detailing trend-setting application of diesel, gas (not gasoline) engines, gas turbine engines in industrial and commercial service. Material must thoroughly describe installation of the prime mover and auxiliary equipment, special system requirements, and controls. Articles must be slanted to the viewpoint of the user. Length: 2,500 words. Pays $65 and up per page.

ELECTRIC LIGHT AND POWER, Cahners Building, 221 Columbus Ave., Boston MA 02116. Editorial Director: Robert A. Lincicome. 2 editions (Energy/Generation and Transmission/Distribution) for electric utility engineers, engineering management and electric utility general top management. Monthly. Buys all rights. Pays on publication. Will send free sample copies to a writer on request. "Query not required, but recommended." Reports in 1 week. Enclose S.A.S.E.

Nonfiction and Photos: Engineering application articles, management subjects, electric utility system design, construction and operation, sales, etc. Articles may be case histories, problem-solutions, general roundups, state-of-the-art, etc. Must be technically oriented to industry. Length: 500 to 3,000 words. Pays $35 first published page, $25 second published page, $15 third published page, $10 fourth and succeeding pages. Photos purchased with mss as package; no separate photos accepted. Prefers 8x10 glossy prints, b&w; color transparencies, 2¼x2¼ or larger.

POWER ENGINEERING, 1301 S. Grove Ave., Barrington IL 60010. Phone: 312-381-1840. Editor: John Papamarcos. Monthly. Buys first rights. "Must query first." Enclose S.A.S.E.
Nonfiction and Photos: Articles on electric power field design, construction, and operation. Length: 500 to 1,500 words. Pays $80 to $200, "depending on published length." Uses 8x10 glossies with mss.
How To Break In: "We do not encourage freelance writers in general. We do review anything that is sent to us, but will generally accept articles only from people who are involved in the power field in some way and can write to interest engineers and management in the field."

PUBLIC POWER, 2600 Virginia Ave., N.W., Washington DC 20037. Phone: 202-333-9200. Editor: Ron Ross. Established in 1943. Bimonthly. Not copyrighted. Pays on publication. Query first. Enclose S.A.S.E.
Nonfiction: News and features on municipal and other local publicly owned electric systems. Pays $10 to $60.
Photos: Pays $3 each for 8x10 glossy prints.

RURAL ELECTRIFICATION, 2000 Florida Ave., N.W., Washington DC 20009. Editor: J. C. Brown, Jr. For managers and boards of directors of rural electric systems. Monthly. Buys all rights or reprint rights. Pays on acceptance. Will send sample copy on request. Query first. Reports in one month. Enclose S.A.S.E.
Nonfiction: Uses articles on the activities of rural electric systems which are unusual in themselves or of unusually great importance to other rural electric systems across the country. Length: "open." Pay "negotiable, but usually in $50 to $250 range."
Photos: Uses photos with or without mss, on the same subject matter as the articles; 8x10 glossies. Pays $5 for b&w; $10 for color.

Printing

AMERICAN INK MAKER, 101 W. 31st St., New York NY 10001. Editor: John Vollmuth. For those in managerial and technical positions in the printing ink and pigment industries. Monthly. Circulation: 3,300. Buys all rights. Pays on acceptance. Will send free sample copy to a writer on request. Query first. Reports "immediately." Enclose S.A.S.E.
Nonfiction and Photos: Articles on new products for printing inks and pigment producers; articles on companies in these fields. Length: 1,200 words. Pays 3¢ per word. Pays $5 per b&w photo (unless on assignment, in which case payment is negotiated).
Fillers: Newsbreaks, clippings, short humor on ink and pigment industries. Pays $1 minimum.

GRAPHIC ARTS MONTHLY, 7373 N. Lincoln Ave., Chicago IL 60646. Phone: 312-267-4260. Editor: Dr. Paul J. Hartsuch. Monthly. Buys all rights. Pays on acceptance. Query first. Reports in 30 days. Enclose S.A.S.E.
Nonfiction and Photos: Uses articles of interest to management, production executives, and craftsmen in printing and allied plants. Recently published articles include "Electronics in the Newsroom," "Developments in Sheetfed Offset Inks," and "Demand Increases for Foreign Language Type." Length: maximum 2,500 words. Pays average of $100. Photos purchased with mss.

GRAPHIC ARTS SUPPLIER NEWS, 134 North 13th St., Philadelphia PA 19107. Phone: 215-564-5170. Editor: Peggy Bicknell. For dealers, salesmen, and manufacturers of printing equipment and supplies. 6 times a year. Buys first publication rights. Query preferred. Reports in 2 months. Enclose S.A.S.E.

Nonfiction: Feature articles with heavy emphasis on sales, marketing, profiles and promotion techniques, and some news related to graphic arts supply. Pays 4¢ per word; assignments: flat fee of $100 with photos.
Photos: On assignment only; payment varies with assignment.

THE INLAND PRINTER/AMERICAN LITHOGRAPHER, 300 W. Adams St., Chicago IL 60606. Editor: Richard H. Green. For qualified personnel active in any phase of the graphic arts industry. Established in 1883. Monthly. Circulation: 59,000. Buys all rights, unless otherwise specified in writing at time of purchase. Pays on publication. Free sample copy to a writer on request. Query first. Submit seasonal material 2 months in advance. "Study publication before writing." Enclose S.A.S.E.
Nonfiction: Articles on management; technical subjects with illustrations with direct bearing on graphic arts industry. Length: 1,500 to 3,000 words. Pays $50 to $200.
Photos: Purchased with mss; also news shots of graphic arts occurrences. 5x7 or 8x10 glossy. Pays $5 to $10.
Fillers: Newsbreaks, clippings, short humor; must relate to printing industry. Length: 100 to 250 words. Pays $10 minimum.

MID-ATLANTIC GRAPHIC ARTS REVIEW, 1010 Arch St., Philadelphia PA 19107. Editor: Robert W. Hardy. For "printers, print shops, in-plant printing manufacturers, etc." Special issues include Book Printing (May), Key Personalities (July or August), Lithography (September), Directory (December). Monthly. Circulation: over 5,000. Buys all rights. Buys 4 or 5 mss a year. Pays on publication. Will send a sample copy to a writer on request. Query first. Submit seasonal material 2 to 3 months in advance. Reports in 10 days. Enclose S.A.S.E.
Nonfiction: Articles should be on local printing, the needs of printing buyers, profiles on management of local printers (Eastern Pennsylvania, New Jersey, Delaware, Maryland, Northern Virginia, Washington, DC) and marketing. "Style should be in-depth and detailed, but give the human interest approach. The informal approach is favored." Interested in seeing material on the following subjects: Survival amid financial crises; coping with shortages (paper, alcohol, other materials); success amid disaster. Does not want to see any material on the use of a product. Length: 50 to 5,000 words. Pays 4¢ a word.
Photos: Purchased with mss. B&w glossies. Pays $5.
Fillers: Newsbreaks. Length: 200 words maximum. Pays 4¢ a word.

MODERN LITHOGRAPHY, 8150 Central Park Ave., Skokie IL 60076. Editor: Jerome Rakusan. For "management, supervisors, employees of lithographic plants." Established in 1935. Monthly. Circulation: 16,000. Buys first North American rights. Buys 15 to 20 mss a year. Pays on publication. Will send a sample copy to a writer on request. Submit complete ms. Will not consider photocopied submissions. Submit seasonal material at least 3 months in advance. Reports in 2 to 3 weeks. Enclose S.A.S.E.
Nonfiction and Photos: "Technical articles on new developments in lithography; success stories of litho plants and manufacturers. Concentrate on material of interest to our readers within the story structure. We specialize in only the lithographic segment of the printing industry, so we cover details in greater depth." Buys informational articles, interviews, historical articles, coverage of successful business operations, and technical articles. Length: 500 to 1,000 words. Pays 3¢ to 4¢ a word. 8x10 b&w glossies purchased with mss; captions required.

NEWSPAPER PRODUCTION, 19 Church St., P.O. Box 417, Berea OH 44017. Editor: Rodney G. Brower. For production management and top management at weekly and daily newspapers. Magazine; 64 (8¼x11¼) pages. Established in 1972. Monthly. Circulation: 16,000. Buys all rights. Pays on acceptance. Will send free sample copy to writer on request. Will consider photocopied submissions. No simultaneous submissions. Submit special material (for March plant planning and improvement issue) 3 months in advance. Reports on material accepted for publication in several weeks. Returns rejected material in 1 month. Query first. Enclose S.A.S.E.

Nonfiction: Articles dealing with technical aspects of newspaper production. Length: about 7 double-spaced, typed pages. Payment depends on quality and content; begins at $35.

PLAN AND PRINT, 10116 Franklin Ave., Franklin Park IL 60131. Phone: 312-671-5356. Editor: James C. Vebeck. For blue print, photocopy, offset, microfilm, diazo and allied reproduction firms; dealers in architects', engineers', and draftsmen's supplies and equipment; in-plant reproduction department supervisors, and design and drafting specialists. Monthly; except bimonthly July/August and December/January. Circulation: 19,000. Buys all rights. Pays on acceptance. Will send a sample copy to a writer on request. Query preferred. Reports in 2 weeks. Enclose S.A.S.E.
Nonfiction: Wants features on commercial reproduction companies and in-plant reproduction departments, on a specific theme such as offset, microfilm, diazo; the promotion of these services, solving of problems with regard to these services; technical articles on techniques involved in reproduction work, and how commercial reproduction companies work with the captive in-plant reproduction departments; articles relating to areas of design and drafting. Do not send articles on "how a company grew from 2 employees to 500, etc." Pays $20 to $100. Photos purchased with mss; b&w glossies. Pays $5 to $10.
Poetry: Uses humorous verse related to reproduction industry, design, and drafting. Length: 4 to 12 lines. Pays $5 to $7.50, depending upon length and quality.
Fillers: Epigrams, anecdotes, and short humor on the above topics. Pays $5.

PRINTING IMPRESSIONS, 134 N. 13th St., Philadelphia PA 19107. Editor: James F. Burns, Jr. For production people who also sell and manage. "Write for journeyman-level production people when discussing processes and procedures; in management discussions, address problems on college-level basis." Monthly tabloid size magazine; 100 (11x16) pages. Established in 1958. Circulation: 70,000. Buys all rights. Buys 2 or 3 mss a year. Payment on publication. Will consider photocopied submissions, if legible enough. Will not consider simultaneous submissions. Reports within a month or so. Query first. Enclose S.A.S.E.
Nonfiction and Photos: Personal experience, interview, profile, successful business operations. "Ask for an assignment after 1) outlining topic and suggesting reason for merit; 2) supply sample of work you've done; 3) mention payment expected. Only expository writing wanted. Chances of hitting with a speculative article are 100 to 1." Length: 1,000 to 2,000 words. Pays 4¢ a word. Pays $10 for b&w photos published with mss. Captions required.

PRINTING MANAGEMENT MAGAZINE, 106 Benton Rd., Paramus NJ 07652. Phone: 201-265-5027. Editor: Jeremiah E. Flynn. For management executives in the printing business who function as company owners, general managers, vice-presidents, plant managers, production managers, superintendents and mechanical department foremen in commercial, magazine, and private plants, including engraving and electrotype plants. Monthly. Buys all rights "within the industry. A query is appreciated before submission." Reports in 2 weeks. Enclose S.A.S.E.
Nonfiction: Articles must be of value to management. Length: around 1,500 words, although it varies depending on value of subject. Pays $35 to $50 per printed page.

PRINTING SALESMAN'S HERALD, Champion Papers, a division of Champion International, 245 Park Avenue, New York NY 10017. Editor: Michael Corey. For printing, graphic arts industries. Bimonthly. Buys all rights. Pays on acceptance. Reports in 1 to 4 weeks. Enclose S.A.S.E.
Nonfiction: Articles on salesmanship as applicable to the selling of printing; technical pieces relating to printing production; sales incentive material as seen from both sides of the desk. Material must be valid to the publication's audience and well-written. Pays $50 if material is worth developing but needs rewriting; $75 to $100 if copy is meaty and well-written.

SCREEN PRINTING, 407 Gilbert Ave., Cincinnati OH 45202. Editor: Arnold Z. Brav. For the screen printing industry, including screen printers (commercial, industrial and captive shops), suppliers and manufacturers, ad agencies and allied professions. Monthly magazine; 64 to 68 pages. Established in 1953. Circulation: 7,000. Rights purchased vary with author and material. Buys all rights, but may reassign rights to author after publication. Payment on publication. Will send free sample copy to writer on request. Write for copy of guidelines for writers. Will not consider photocopied submissions. Will consider simultaneous submissions. Reporting time varies for material accepted for publication. Returns rejected material immediately. Query first. Enclose S.A.S.E.

Nonfiction and Photos: "Since the screen printing industry covers a broad range of applications and overlaps other fields in the graphic arts, it's necessary that articles be of a significant contribution, preferably to a specific area of screen printing. Subject matter is fairly open, with preference given to articles on administration or technology; trends and developments. We try to give a good sampling of technical articles, business and management articles; articles about unique operations. We also publish special features and issues on important subjects, such as material shortages, new markets and new technology breakthroughs. While most of our material is nitty-gritty, we appreciate a writer who can take an essentially dull subject and encourage the reader to read on through concise, factual, flairful and creative, expressive writing. Interviews are published after consultation with and guidance from the editor." Interested in stories on unique approaches by some shops on how to lick the problems created by the petroleum shortage (the industry relies heavily on petrol products). Length: 1,500 to 2,000 words. Pays minimum of $60 for major features; minimum of $50 for minor features; minimum of $35 for back of book articles. Pays $15 for photos used on cover; b&w only. Published material becomes the property of the magazine.

SOUTHERN PRINTER & LITHOGRAPHER, 75 Third St., N.W., Atlanta GA 30308. Editor: Charles Fram. For commercial printing plant management in the 14 southern states. Established in 1924. Monthly. Circulation: 3,000. Not copyrighted. Payment on publication. Write for copy of guidelines for writers. Query first. Will consider photocopied submissions. Reporting time on submissions varies. Enclose S.A.S.E.

Nonfiction and Photos: Feature articles on commercial printing plants in the 14 southern states and their personnel. Length: 1,000 to 1,500 words. Pays 1¢ a word. B&w photos. Pays $4.

Railroad

THE SIGNALMAN'S JOURNAL, 601 West Golf Rd., Mt. Prospect IL 60056. Phone: 312-439-3732. Editor: Robert W. McKnight. Monthly. Buys first rights. Query first. Reports in 3 weeks. Enclose S.A.S.E.

Nonfiction: Can use articles on new installations of railroad signal systems, but they must be technically correct and include drawings and photos. "We do not want general newspaper type writing, and will reject material that is not of technical quality." Length: 3,000 to 4,000 words. Pays $10 per printed page, and up.

Photos: Photographs dealing with railroad signaling. Pays $5.

Real Estate

AREA DEVELOPMENT, 114 East 32nd St., New York NY 10016. Phone: 212-532-4360. Editor: Albert H. Jaeggin. For chief executives of nation's leading firms faced with problems of finding new sites, building new plants or relocating existing facilities. Monthly. Buys all rights, reprint rights, and possibly simultaneous rights. Query first. Enclose S.A.S.E.

Nonfiction: Wants articles on all subjects related to facility planning, including: finding new sites, building new plants and/or expanding and relocating existing facilities; community and employee relations; political climate; transportation, recreational and educational facilities; financing; insurance; plant design and layout; safety factors; water and air pollution controls; case histories of companies which have moved or built new plants. Must be accurate, objective (no puffery) and useful to executives. Must avoid discussions of merits or disadvantages of any particular community, state or area. Also carries news items on activities, people, areas, books on facility planning, based on releases. Pays $40 per printed page.
Photos: Buys glossy photos. Pays $40 per page.

COMMUNITY DEVELOPMENT DIGEST, Community Development Services, Inc., 1319 F St. N.W., Washington DC 20004. Phone: 202-638-6113. Editor: Ash Gerecht. For housing and community development professionals. 18-page (8½x11) newsletter published twice a month. Established in 1965. Not copyrighted. Uses about 1,400 clippings a year. Payment on publication. Write for copy of guidelines for writers. Reports in 1 month. Query first. Enclose S.A.S.E.
Fillers: Uses contributions of newspaper clippings on housing and community development; substantive actions and litigations, that would be of interest to housing and community development professionals beyond immediate area. "We reject material when the territory has already been covered; material not of interest to our needs." Particularly wants regular contributors for multistate region, or at least a full state. Pays $1.10 for each clipping used in steady arrangement, $2 for specials.

PROPERTIES MAGAZINE, 4900 Euclid Ave., Cleveland OH 44103. Editor: Gene Bluhm. Monthly. Buys all rights. Pays on publication. Query first. Enclose S.A.S.E.
Nonfiction and Photos: Wants articles of real estate and construction news value. Interested primarily in articles relating to Northeastern Ohio. Length: up to 700 words. Pays $25 minimum. Buys photographs with mss, 8x10 preferred.

SHOPPING CENTER WORLD, 461 Eighth Ave., New York NY 10001. Phone: 212-239-6222. Editor: Davis Crippen. For executives in or servicing the shopping center industry. Monthly magazine; 75 (8¼x11¼) pages. Established in 1972. Circulation: 16,000. Buys all rights. Buys about 10 mss a year. Payment on publication. Will send free sample copy to writer on request. Write for copy of guidelines for writers. Will consider cassette submissions. Reports in 2 weeks. Query first. Enclose S.A.S.E.
Nonfiction and Photos: Articles on innovations in the industry, and on trends such as energy use; environmental effects on centers, etc. Recently published articles include "Canadian Law Conference," "Center in Arctic Cold." Length: 1,000 to 2,500 words. Pays $50 to $200. No additional payment made for b&w photos used with mss.
Fillers: Newsbreaks: Length: Under 100 words. Pays $5 to $25. Department Editor: Eric Peterson.

Recreation Park and Campground Management

CAMPGROUND AND RV PARK MANAGEMENT, P.O. Box 1014, Grass Valley CA 95945. Editor: Bob Behme. 8 times a year. Circulation: 14,000. Buys all rights. Pays on publication. Will send a free sample copy on request. "Best to query first." Reports in 1 month. Enclose S.A.S.E.
Nonfiction and Photos: Success stories and management information articles for owners of campgrounds and recreation vehicle parks. News stories about campgrounds, campground associations, campground chains and any other subjects helpful or of interest to a campground operator. Also uses features about such subjects

as a specialized bookkeeping system for campground operations, an interesting traffic circulation system, an advertising and promotion program that has worked well for a campground, an efficient trash collection system. Successful operation of coin-operated dispensing machines, successful efforts by a campground owner in bringing in extra income through such means as stores, charge showers, swimming fees, etc. Use newspaper style reporting for news items and newspaper feature style for articles. Length: 500 to 700 words, news stories; 300 to 1,200 words, features. Pays $20 to $50. "B&w photos should accompany articles whenever practicable."
Fillers: Pays $2 to $5 for ideas which eventually appear as stories written by staff or another writer; $5 to $10 for newsbreaks of one paragraph to a page.

PARK MAINTENANCE, P.O. Box 409, Appleton WI 54911. Phone: 414-733-2301. Editor: Erik L. Madisen, Jr. For administrators of areas with large grounds mainte-nance and outdoor recreation facilities. Special issues include March, Swimming Pool and Beach; July, Turf Research and Irrigation Annual; October, Buyer's Guide issue. Established in 1948. Monthly. Circulation: 17,000. Buys all rights. Buys 4 or 5 mss a year. Pays on acceptance. Will send a sample copy to a writer on request. Write for copy of guidelines for writers. Query first. "Outline material and source in letter, and include S.A.S.E." Will consider photocopied submissions "if exclusive to us." Deadlines are the first of the month preceding publication. Reports in 2 weeks.
Nonfiction: How-to, case history, technical or scientific articles dealing with mainte-nance of turf and facilities in parks, forestry, golf courses, campuses. These may be new or unique ideas adopted by park systems for greater use or more efficient and economical operation. Also, methods of dealing with administrative, financial, personnel and other problems; new phases of landscape architecture and building design. Buys how-to's and interviews. Length: up to 1,000 words. Pays 2¢ a word.
Photos: Purchased with mss if applicable; 8x10 or 5x7 b&w glossies. "Captions required." Pays minimum of $2 each; $5 for front cover.

TOURIST ATTRACTIONS AND PARKS, Bldg. #30, 20-21 Wagaraw Rd., Fair Lawn NJ 07410. Phone: 201-797-2522. Editor: Martin Dowd. For owners and managers of theme parks, amusement parks, national and state parks, zoos, etc. Published 2 times a year; magazine, 52 pages, 8½x11. Established in 1972. Circulation: 6,500. Buys first North American serial rights. Buys 3 or 4 mss a year. Payment on acceptance. Will send free sample copy to writer on request. Query first or submit complete ms. Reports in 2 weeks. Enclose S.A.S.E.
Nonfiction, Photos, and Fillers: "Articles on the science of managing a tourist attraction. How to increase the number of visitors, how to handle crowds best, how to train people to handle crowds, operate rides, feed large masses of tourists. We prefer articles about how a specific manager has solved a specific problem in the operation of a tourist attraction. Prefer quotes, specific examples. We'd like to see articles about attractions preparing for bicentennial celebration." Informational, how-to, personal experience, interview, profile, and successful business operations and technical articles. Length: 500 to 2,000 words. Pays 4¢ minimum a word. Regular columns use items on advertising, promotion, training, maintenance, rides, food. Length: 500 to 1,500 words. Pays 4¢ minimum per word, plus $10 for each photo used. 8x10 or 5x7 b&w photos purchased with mss for $10. Captions optional. Pays 80¢ a printed inch for clippings.

Secretarial

MODERN SECRETARY, Allied Publications, P.O. Box 23505, Fort Lauderdale FL 33307. Associate Editor: Marie Stilkind. Monthly. Buys North American serial rights only. Pays on acceptance. Query not necessary. Reports in 2 to 4 weeks. Enclose S.A.S.E.
Nonfiction and Photos: "Office tips, articles and photos about secretaries. Also articles about secretaries to famous personalities, or other material of interest to secretaries."

Length: 500 to 1,000 words. Payment is 5¢ a word, and $5 for b&w glossy photos purchased with mss.

TODAY'S SECRETARY, 1221 Avenue of the Americas, New York NY 10020. Editor: Lauren Bahr. For students (mostly female, age 16 to 21) training for careers in the business world. Magazine; 32 pages. Established in 1898. Monthly. Circulation: 80,000. Buys all rights. Buys about 40 mss a year. Pays on acceptance. Will send free sample copy to writer on request. Write for copy of guidelines for writers. Will consider photocopied submissions. No simultaneous submissions. Query first for articles; submit complete ms for fiction. Enclose S.A.S.E.

Nonfiction: Articles on business trends, secretarial procedure; articles of general interest to young women (communications, human relations; beauty and fashion). Should be informational in nature. An imaginative manner of presentation is encouraged with emphasis away from factual, textbooklike approach. Material must have professional slant, reaching for the informed, contemporary, young businesswoman. Length: 800 words minimum. Pays $75 to $150. Columns are staff written, but new ideas for columns are always welcome.

Fiction: Any good story line acceptable. Length: 800 to 900 words. Pays $35.

How To Break In: "The best way to break in would be with a piece for our one-page humor section or with a short piece of fiction (800 words). Keep in mind that our audience is mostly women, age 16 to 22, in high school or business school. Also, the stories shouldn't be too heavy — we print them in shorthand as a skills exercise for our readers. Other good freelance possibilities include profiles of secretaries with unusual job responsibilities or in an unusual field, and secretarial procedure stories — tips on filing, making travel arrangements for your boss, etc."

Selling and Merchandising

In this category are journals for salesmen and merchandisers who publish general material on how to sell products successfully. Journals in nearly every other category of this Trade Journal section will also buy this kind of material if it is slanted to the specialized product or industry they deal with, such as clothing or petroleum. Publications for professional advertising and marketing men will be found under Advertising and Marketing Journals.

AGENCY SALES MAGAZINE, Manufacturers' Agents National Association, 3130 Wilshire Blvd., Ste. 309, Los Angeles CA 90010. Editor: Gayle L. Hall. For independent sales representatives and corporate sales offices. Monthly magazine; 36 (8½x11) pages. Established in 1950. Circulation: 11,000. Buys all rights. Pays on publication. Will send free sample copy to writer on request. Will consider photocopied and simultaneous submissions. Reports within 2 months. Query first. Enclose S.A.S.E.

Nonfiction and Photos: "Articles on independent sales representatives, their suppliers and customers, and their operations. Must be on the subject of independent selling from the agent's point of view." Informational, how-to, personal experience, interview, profile, successful business operations and techniques. Length: 500 to 2,500 words. Pays $50 to $100. B&w photos purchased with accompanying ms with no additional payment. Captions required.

AMERICAN FIREARMS INDUSTRY, 70001 N. Clark St., Chicago IL 60626. Editor: Andrew Molchan. For retailers of firearms and accessories. Monthly magazine; 48 (8½x11) pages. Established in 1972. Circulation: 20,000. Buys all rights, but will reassign rights to author after publication. Buys 12 mss a year. Payment on publication. Will send free sample copy to writer on request. Write for copy of guidelines for writers. Will consider photocopied and simultaneous submissions. Will consider cassette submissions. Reports on material accepted for publication in 2 weeks. Returns rejected material in 1 month. Query first. Enclose S.A.S.E.

Nonfiction and Photos: "We need sales articles: how to display, customer relations, local advertising tips, local operations, legal, etc. Better retailing and marketing articles, as well as those on dealer liability and how to become a better retailer." Informational, how-to, interview, profile, think pieces, merchandising techniques, successful business operations. Length: 1,200 to 2,400 words. Pays $60 to $120. Material for specific industry columns is also sought. Length: 1,200 words. Pays $60. No additional payment for b&w glossy photos that are purchased with accompanying mss. Captions required.

ARMY/NAVY STORE AND OUTDOOR MERCHANDISER, 225 W. 34 St., New York NY 10001. Editor: Georgette Manla. For the owners of army/navy surplus and outdoor goods stores. Established in 1947. Circulation: 3,000. Buys all rights. Buys 30 mss a year. Pays on publication. Will send free sample copy to writer on request. Will consider cassette submissions. Query preferred, "but not mandatory." Enclose S.A.S.E.
Nonfiction and Photos: Articles on the methods stores use to promote items; especially on how army/navy items have become fashion items, and the problems attendant to catering to this new customer. Sources of supply, how they promote, including windows, newspapers, etc. "If the guy wants to tell his life story, listen and take notes. Use simple words. Stick to a single subject, if possible. Find out how the man makes money and tell us. The true 'success' story is the most frequently submitted and the most dreadful; yet nothing is of more interest if it is done well. No one truly wishes to tell you how he earns money." Length: open. Pays $25 to $75. No additional payment for 5x7 photos or negatives.

CAMPGROUND MERCHANDISING, 20-21 Wagaraw Rd., Bldg. #30, Fair Lawn NJ 07410. Editor: Martin Dowd. For owners and managers of recreation vehicle campgrounds who sell merchandise or equipment to people who vacation in recreation vehicles. Magazine published 3 times a year; 56 (5½x8½) pages. Established in 1972. Circulation: 6,500. Buys first North American serial rights. Buys 5 mss a year. Payment on acceptance. Free sample copy to writer on request. Will not consider photocopied or simultaneous submissions. Submit seasonal material 3 months in advance. Reports in 2 weeks. Query first or submit complete ms. Enclose S.A.S.E.
Nonfiction and Photos: "We specialize in RV campgrounds that resell equipment or merchandise to RV'ers who are visiting the RV campground. We use articles about how to best operate a recreation vehicle campground. The best approach is to interview managers of recreation vehicle campgrounds about their operations. Not interested in RV campgrounds selling bread, milk, ice cream. Main interest is in their sales of equipment or merchandise wanted only by RV'ers, and how the resale of merchandise and equipment in an RV campground made it profitable." Informational, how-to, personal experience, interview, successful business operations, merchandising techniques. Length: 800 to 1,500 words. Pays about 4¢ a word. Prefers 8x10 b&w glossies, but can use 5x7. Pays $10 for each one used with ms. No color. Captions optional.
Fillers: Clippings are purchased only if newsworthy. Pays 80¢ per inch used.

CHAIN STORE AGE, GENERAL MERCHANDISE EDITION, 2 Park Ave., New York NY 10016. Editor: Walter J. Schruntek. For major chain store executives, field and store management personnel in the general merchandise chain field. Established in 1925. Monthly. Circulation: 33,500. Buys all rights. Purchases of mss are limited to special needs and commitments: "12 columns in fashions (from London), 12-plus pages of government news from Washington." Pays on publication. Will send free sample copy to writer on request. Reports in 2 weeks. Submit complete ms. Enclose S.A.S.E.
Nonfiction: Retail-related news across a wide band of merchandise categories (housewares, home sewing, toys, stationery, fashionwear, etc.). News about companies, promotions, people-on-the-move. Sharp, to the point, strong on facts. Subjects that are on the tip of chain retailers' minds about their business. How chain retailers are coping with traffic fall-off by tightening productivity screws in day-to-day

operations. "We have one defiinite 'no-no' — sloppy copy that is not proofread." Length: 250 to 300 words. Pays minimum of $10 per page.

HEALTH FOODS BUSINESS, 225 W. 34th St., New York NY 10001. Editor: Georgette Manla. For owners of health food specialty stores and the persons who sell such products in these stores. Monthly magazine; 100 (8½x11) pages. Established in 1953. Circulation: 4,380. Buys all rights. Buys 24 mss a year. Payment on publication. Will send free sample copy to writer on request. Will not consider photocopied or simultaneous submissions. Will consider cassette submissions. Reports on material in 10 days. Query first or submit complete ms. Enclose S.A.S.E.

Nonfiction and Photos: Success stories about health foods shops; merchandising of specific health or natural foods; co-op buying or advertising; effect of local laws on business; categories of foods sold most successfully; tips on selling books. Interviews and articles on successful business operations and merchandising techniques. Stories about use of health foods themselves. Pays $25 per published page. B&w photos purchased with mss, with no additional payment. No smaller than 5x7, or negatives. Captions required.

MASS RETAILING MERCHANDISER, 222 W. Adams, Chicago IL 60606. Managing Editor: Stuart D. Strand. For chain store presidents, board chairmen, departmental buyers, merchandising managers, group merchandising managers, store managers. Magazine; 48 to 80 pages. Established in 1932. Monthly. Circulation: 35,851. Buys all rights, but will reassign rights to author after publication. Buys 36 to 50 mss a year. Pays on publication. Will send a free sample copy to writer on request. Write for copy of guidelines for writers. Material required 40 days prior to publication date. Returns rejected material immediately. Query first or submit complete ms. Enclose S.A.S.E.

Nonfiction: Reports from chain store buyers on products they purchased, prices paid, markups, margins; how products are advertised, and displayed. Informational, how-to, telephone interviews, spot news, successful business operations, merchandising techniques. Length: 1,500 words. Pays $150 to $250.

NON-FOODS MERCHANDISING, 124 E. 40th St., New York NY 10016. Editor: Bill Hogue. For buyers of general merchandise, health and beauty aids for sale through supermarkets. Established in 1955. Monthly. Circulation: 15,000. Buys all rights. Pays on publication. Will send a sample copy to writer on request if 9x12 S.A.S.E. is enclosed with 20¢ postage. No photocopied or simultaneous submissions. Reports in 2 weeks. Query first. Enclose S.A.S.E.

Nonfiction and Photos: "In the industry we serve, people expect to read material in our magazine that will increase their business success. We provide information and ideas by example, through surveys, and in-depth studies. We use articles (always with photos) about successful concepts in our industry. In-depth studies of one company's operations, for example, or interviews with outstanding people in the business, with some familiarity with the jargon of the trade. Writer must have thorough knowledge of the industry." Length: 1,000 to 3,500 words. Pays 3¢ a word minimum; minimum of $5 for photos used with mss. Captions required.

SALESMAN'S OPPORTUNITY MAGAZINE, 1460 John Hancock Center, Chicago IL 60611. Phone: 312-337-3350. Editor: Jack Weissman. For "people who are eager to increase their incomes by selling or through an independent business of their own." Established in 1923. Monthly. Buys all rights. Buys about 50 mss a year. Payment on publication. Will send free sample copy to writer on request. Write for copy of guidelines for writers. Submit complete ms. Will consider photocopied submissions, but must have exclusive rights to any article. Enclose S.A.S.E.

Nonfiction: "Our editorial content consists of articles dealing with sales techniques, sales psychology and general self-improvement topics that are inspirational in character." Should be tightly written, very specific. "We prefer case history type articles which show our readers how to do the same things that have helped others succeed in the direct selling industry. We are particularly interested in articles about successful women in the direct selling door-to-door field, particularly for our annual women's issue which is published each August." Length: 250 words for column features; maximum of 1,000 words for full-length articles. Pays $20 to $35.

SOLUTION, 1 Jake Brown Road, Old Bridge NJ 08857. Editor: George S. Bahue. Published by Blonder-Tongue Laboratories for television service technicians. Buys all rights. Pays on publication. Will send a sample copy to a writer on request. Will consider photocopied submissions. Reports in 2 weeks. Enclose S.A.S.E.
Nonfiction and Photos: "General information on TV distribution system servicing; other related information of interest to service technicians, particularly the merchandising aspects of the business." Length: 1,000 words. Pays $200 to $300. Photos purchased with mss.

SPECIALTY FOOD MERCHANDISING, 29 Park Ave., Manhasset NY 11030. Editor: Saul Tarter. For "professional buyers of specialty foods representing such outlets as department stores, gourmet food stores, cheese shops, supermarket chains, variety chains, discount stores." Established in 1971. Monthly. Circulation: 7,700. Buys all rights. Buys 18 to 24 mss a year. Payment on publication. Will send free sample copy to writer on request. Editorial guidelines sent to writer with first assignment. Query first. Reports in 10 days. Enclose S.A.S.E.
Nonfiction and Photos: Merchandising stories on unusual or outstanding successful distributor/retail firms within the quality food field. "Advise if writer is particularly knowledgeable in the field or in any related field (i.e., supermarket merchandising) and if he has professional ability with a camera. Will provide specific assignment, arranging beforehand for necessary interview with subject firm." Length: Up to 2,000 words, with 5 to 8 photos. Pays 6¢ per word. 5x7 or 8x10 b&w photos. Pays $6. 2x2 color mount or 2x2 transparencies, unmounted. Pays $20.

SPECIALTY SALESMAN AND BUSINESS OPPORTUNITIES MAGAZINE, 307 N. Michigan Ave., Chicago IL 60601. Editor: Jane Bjoraas. For salesmen selling "direct." Monthly. Buys all rights. Pays on acceptance. Will send free sample copy to a writer on request. Reports in 4 weeks. Enclose S.A.S.E.
Nonfiction and Photos: Articles about people involved in direct selling. Subject matter may fall into these three categories: stories of successful direct salesmen; advice by men and women who have successfully sold, and inspirational or motivational articles. Likes good photos to illustrate stories. Length: 500 to 1,500 words. Pays 3¢ per word; extra for photos. Photos purchased with mss. Pays $5.

THE WHOLESALER, 110 N. York Rd., Elmhurst IL 60126. Editor: Laurence M. Grinnell. For owners or managers of wholesale plumbing, heating, air conditioning and refrigeration firms. Tabloid magazine; 60 to 80 pages. Established in 1946. Monthly. Circulation: 20,000. Buys first North American serial rights. Pays on acceptance. No photocopied or simultaneous submissions. Reports in 3 to 5 weeks. Query first. Enclose S.A.S.E.
Nonfiction and Photos: "We are now opening our magazine to occasional purchases from freelancers. Our only interest is in stories about wholesalers who have been particularly successful in one particular area of business: Use of EDP, inventory control, collections, warehousing, etc. It must be something a little out of the ordinary. Our readers should be able to read these stories and apply the information to their own business operation. Remember, we do not use general profiles of wholesalers. They must do some specific thing well." Length: 1,000 to 3,000 words. Pays 3¢ to 7¢ a word. No additional payment for b&w photos used with mss. Captions required.

Show People and Amusements

AMUSEMENT BUSINESS, 1717 West End Ave., Nashville TN 37203. Managing Editor: Tom Powell. For managers of mass entertainment facilities such as auditoriums, arenas, fairs, amusement parks, theatres, miniature golf courses and other leisure time attractions. Established in 1894. Weekly. Circulation: over 15,500. Buys all rights. Buys over 25 mss a year. Payment on publication. Will send free sample copy on request. Write for copy of guidelines for writers. Submit seasonal material 3 to 4 months in advance. Reports on material in a month or 6 weeks. Query first. Enclose S.A.S.E.

Nonfiction and Photos: News reports and in-depth instructional articles. Check with editor in advance on each subject; prefers not to see anything glorifying single product. Interested in articles on the effect of gas shortage on leisure time; Wall Street view of leisure time field, particularly amusements; financial analysis of pro sports franchises. Also publishes special booking guides, annual directories for fair, exhibition and auditorium fields, as well as instructional stories for ice skating/hockey field. Informational, how-to, interview, profile, think articles, nostalgia, spot news, successful business operations, new products, merchandising techniques. Pays minimum of $1 per published inch per 11 to 13 pica column. Prefers 8x10 b&w photos. Pays $5.

THE BILLBOARD, 9000 Sunset Blvd., Los Angeles CA 90069. Editor-in-Chief and Publisher: Lee Zhito. News Editor: Eliot Tiegel. Special Issues Editor: Earl Paige. (All Los Angeles). Jukebox Programming Editor: Ann Dustin (Chicago). Record Review Editor: Bob Kirsch; Talent Editor: Nat Freedland; Marketing News Editor: John Sippel; Radio/TV Editor: Claude Hall; Country Music Editor: Bill Williams (Nashville); classical and International News Editor: Bob Sobel (New York). Weekly. Buys all rights. Payment on publication. "Send us suggested story idea. We will get back to writer with either turndown or okay, and some ideas for furnishing story." Enclose S.A.S.E.

Nonfiction: "Correspondents are appointed to send in spot amusement news covering phonograph record programming by broadcasters and music machine operators; record merchandising by retail dealer. We are extremely interested in blank tape, and tape playback, and record hardware stores." Length: short. Pays 25¢ to $1 per published inch; $5 per published photo.

G-STRING BEAT, Box 2207, Peabody MA 01960. Editor: Rita Atlanta. Established in 1973. "The magazine of modern burlesque." Quarterly. Circulation: 20,000. Buys all rights. Buys 25 to 30 mss a year. Payment on publication. "There is roughly a 12-week deadline on all material." Returns rejected material immediately. Reports on material accepted for publication in 1 month. Will send sample copy to writer for $2. Will not consider photocopied submissions. Query for nonfiction; send complete fiction ms. Enclose S.A.S.E.

Nonfiction and Photos: "Everything must be related to burlesque: the beautiful girls, baggy pants comics and red hot music. Newsy profiles on all aspects of the business provided they are not puffs. Profiles must have an in-depth quality to make the subject come alive and human. A simple, direct news style, with a fact in every sentence. The aim of each article should be to improve the image of burlesque as an entertainment form. Performers are human with human hopes and fears. This must come alive in each article and give the reader the feeling of knowing the subject. Will not consider anything that downgrades the business of burlesque." Length: 2,000 words maximum. Pays 2¢ a word, "but payment will vary according to quality." Gossip column pays $1 per paragraph used for good interviews; short as possible. 8x10 b&w photos, but "we have a file of more than 5,000 theatrical photos and, in all probability, we have photo of subject on file." Pays $15.

Fiction: "Interested in seeing completed ms for murder-mystery stories related to burlesque. Will buy one fiction piece an issue." Length: 2,000 words. Pays 2¢ a word. Dept. Editor: John Bane.

VARIETY, 154 W. 46th St., New York NY 10036. Executive Editor: Syd Silverman. Does not buy freelance material.

Sport Trade

AMERICAN BICYCLIST AND MOTORCYCLIST, 461 Eighth Ave., New York NY 10001. Phone: 212-563-3430. Editor: Stan Gottlieb. For bicycle sales and service shops. Established in 1879. Monthly. Circulation: 7,854. Buys all rights. Pays on publication. Query first. Reports within 10 days. Enclose S.A.S.E.
Nonfiction and Photos: Typical story describes (very specifically) unique traffic-builder or merchandising idea used with success by an actual dealer. Emphasis is on showing other dealers how they can follow a similar pattern and increase their business. Articles may also be based entirely on repair shop operation, depicting efficient and profitable service systems and methods. Length: 1,800 to 2,500 words. Pays 3¢ a word, plus bonus for excellent manuscript. Relevant b&w photos illustrating principal points in article purchased with ms. 5x7 minimum. No transparencies. Pays $5 per photo.
Fillers: Short items on repair shop hints for workbench page. Length: 50 words maximum. Payment varies.

THE APBA JOURNAL, 415 Cotswold Ln., Wynnewood PA 19096. Editor: Benjamin L. Weiser. For an extremely varied audience; all with dedicated interest in the APBA/sports games; median age of 28; moderate income. Established in 1967. Monthly. Circulation: 2,000. Rights purchased vary with author and material. May buy all rights, first serial rights, or second serial (reprint) rights. Accepts a limited number of freelance mss. Payment on acceptance. Will send sample copy to writer for 50¢. Will consider photocopied submissions. Will consider cassette submissions; taped interviews. Submit seasonal material 3 months in advance. Reports on material in 2 weeks. Query first. Enclose S.A.S.E.
Nonfiction and Photos: Research/analysis features on APBA sports games, especially baseball. Personality type articles, personal experience, game results, regular columnists, etc. Looking for more articles specifically on research into sports history relevant to the table sports world of APBA games. "Material is accepted all year round, though we stress baseball January through August; golf, football, horse racing, and basketball August through January." Departments seeking material include "AJ Focus" on personalities, oddities, newsworthy events, etc.; "APBA Scene", brief tidbits on personalities, etc. "Q/A Forum", questions and answers; "Front Page Feature", in-depth research/analysis. Length for Focus and Front Page Feature: 650 words maximum. Pays 1¢ to 3¢ a word. No payment for APBA Scene or Q/A Forum. Photos are purchased only on assignment and a query is required for photographic assignments.
Fillers: Relevant newsbreaks and clippings. No payment.

BICYCLE DEALER SHOWCASE, 2070 Business Center Dr., Suite 125, Irvine CA 92664. Editor: Steve Ready. For bicycle dealers and distributors. Magazine: 48 pages. Established in 1972. Monthly. Circulation: 9,000. Buys all rights. Buys about 12 mss a year. Pays on publication. Will send free sample copy on request. Write for copy of guidelines for writers. Submit seasonal material 2 months in advance. Reports on material in 3 to 4 weeks. Query first or submit complete ms. Enclose S.A.S.E.
Nonfiction and Photos: Articles dealing with marketing bicycle products; financing, better management techniques, current trends, as related to bicycle equipment or selling. Material must be fairly straightforward, with a slant toward economic factors or marketing techniques. Informational, how-to, interview, profile, humor, successful business operations, merchandising techniques, technical. Length: 1,000 to 1,500 words. Pays $35 to $50. 8x10 b&w glossies purchased with mss. Pays $5 for each published b&w photo.

BICYCLE JOURNAL, 3339 W. Freeway, Fort Worth TX 76101. Publisher: Bill Quinn. Established in 1947. Monthly. Circulation: 7,500. Not copyrighted. Pays on publication. Enclose S.A.S.E. for return of submissions.
Nonfiction, Photos and Fillers: Wants stories only about dealers who service what they sell. Stories of a single outstanding feature of bike store, such as a good display, interior or exterior; sales tip; service tip; unusual sign; advertising or promotion tip; store layout, etc. Photo must be vertical. One 8x10 photo is sufficient. Length: 200 to 300 words. Pays to $37.50.

GOLF SHOP OPERATIONS, 297 Westport Ave., Norwalk CT 06856. Phone: 203-847-5811. Editor: James McAfee. For golf professionals at public and private courses, resorts, driving ranges. Magazine (40 pages) published 6 times a year. Established in 1963. Circulation: 10,700. Not copyrighted. Buys 12 mss a year. Payment on publication. Free sample copy on request. Write for copy of guidelines for writers. Will consider photocopied submissions. Will not consider simultaneous submissions. Submit seasonal material (for Christmas and other holiday sales) 3 months in advance. Reports in 3 weeks. Query first or submit complete ms. Enclose S.A.S.E.
Nonfiction and Photos: "We emphasize improving the golf professional's knowledge of his profession. Articles should describe how pros are buying, promoting, merchandising and displaying wares in their shops that might be of practical value to fellow professionals. Must be aimed only at the pro audience. We would be interested in seeing material on how certain pros are fighting the discount store competition." How-to, profile, successful business operations, merchandising techniques. Pays $50 to $100. Pays $10 for b&w photos purchased with or without mss. Captions required.
Fillers: Newsbreaks. Length: 50 to 150 words. Pays $10 to $25.

GOLFDOM, 9800 Detroit Ave., Cleveland OH 44102. Assistant Editors: Bob Earley, Nick Romano. For the golf industry; golf club pros, course superintendents, club managers, owners of golf courses. Publication of the Harvest Publishing Co. Magazine; 80 pages. Established in 1932. Monthly. Circulation: 32,000. Buys all rights. Buys 12 to 15 mss a year. Pays on acceptance. Will send free sample copy to writer on request. Will consider photocopied and simultaneous submissions. Reports at once. Query first. Enclose S.A.S.E.
Nonfiction and Photos: "Our magazine is *not* designed to improve a person's golf game. We publish articles designed to inform our audience about news of the industry and to help them run their course more efficiently. We'd like to see something on any new techniques a course superintendent has used to treat his turf; how a pro designed a new lesson structure to get more members involved at his club; a special promotion a club manager used to get a particular event rolling at his course." Recently published articles include one on how a pro set up his new pro shop and another on how a superintendent toughened up his course. Informational, how-to, personal experience, interview, profile, successful business operations, merchandising techniques. Length: 750 to 2,000 words. Pays $100 to $150. No additional payment for 5x7 or 8x10 b&w glossies used with mss.

KENDALL SPORTS TRAIL, The Kendall Company, Sports Division, 20 Walnut St., Wellesley Hills MA 02181. Editor: J.S. O'Neill. For "high school and college athletic directors, coaches, trainers, team physicians and student trainers, amateur and youth league coaches, pro team trainers, sporting goods buyers and dealers." Bimonthly. Circulation: 70,000. Buys first North American serial rights. Payment on publication. Will send a sample copy to a writer on request. Will consider photocopied submissions. Deadlines are November 1 (January-February issue), January 1 (March-April issue), March 1 (May-June issue), July 1 (September-October issue), September 1 (November-December issue). Query first. Reports in 1 month. Enclose S.A.S.E.
Nonfiction: "Subject matter includes all phases of athletic department and sports management, including game and personnel management, equipment purchasing and maintenance, athletic department finance and budget administration, athletic injury management and sports medicine, legal aspects of athletic administration,

coaching psychology, sociology of sports, sports sciences, and current problems in coaching and athletic department administration." Length: 2,500 words maximum. Pays 5¢ a word.

Photos: "Photos to illustrate features on all aspects of school athletic administration. School sports action scenes. Photos of exemplary athletic training room plants and of training room techniques. Prefer dramatic verticals, but we can fit equally dramatic horizontals into our layouts. No negative approaches. No controversial personalities. B&w glossies, 8x10 or 5x7; color transparencies, 4x5, 35mm or 70mm. Pays $5 to $25 a photo for b&w; $50 to $70 a photo for color.

MOTORCYCLE DEALER NEWS, P.O. Box 2830, Newport Beach CA 92663. Editor: John Rossman. For motorcycle dealers and key personnel of the industry. Monthly. Buys first serial rights. Payment on publication. Will send free sample copy to writer on request. Write for copy of guidelines for writers. Query first. Reports in 4 weeks. Enclose S.A.S.E.

Nonfiction and Photos: "Looking for articles that examine problems of dealers and offer a solution. These dealer articles are not a history of the business, but one unique aspect of the store and its attempt to hurdle an obstacle that may aid other dealers in a similar situation. This is not to be a success story, but rather a fresh look at tackling problems within the industry. Tips for dealers on selling merchandise, creating new displays and improving basic business knowledge are also needed. In-depth articles regarding liability insurance, warranty, land usage, noise pollution and advertising have been handled recently. Usually, in-depth articles about current problems are staff written. However, do not hesitate to query. We do not use articles of a general or unspecific nature. Concrete examples are a must. Photos help sell the article." Length: 750 to 2,500 words. Pays $50 to $100. 8x10 b&w glossy photos purchased with mss or with captions only. Modern stores, dealer awards, etc. Minimum payment for photo not accompanied by ms is $5.

MOTORCYCLE INDUSTRY NEWS, 6226 Vineland Ave., P.O. Box 978, North Hollywood CA 91603. Phone: 213-877-1195. Editor: Carol Sims Ashworth. For motorcycle retail dealers, manufacturers and distributors of motorcycles and accessories, and key industry personnel. Monthly magazine; 64-page tabloid. January issue is devoted to motorcycle accessory trade; June issue, retail marketing. Established in 1972. Circulation: 15,000. Buys first serial rights. Buys 100 mss a year. Payment on publication. Will send free sample copy to writer on request. Will not consider photocopied or simultaneous submissions. Submit material for special issues 3 months in advance. Reports as soon as possible. Submit complete ms. Enclose S.A.S.E.

Nonfiction and Photos: "Manufacturer, distributor, and dealer profiles; features related to business management, retail marketing and advertising techniques, training, and customer relations. Particularly interested in success stories, seasonal displays, relationship of motorcycles to other industries. Current and complete familiarity with the field is essential, as are good photos. Must be lively, informative and knowledgeable. Should take a positive approach to methods of building a successful retail motorcycle business and be based on in-depth reporting on marketing conditions." Does not want to see dealer profiles that do not have strong themes in retail merchandising. Informational, successful business operations, merchandising techniques, technical. Length: 1,000 to 2,000 words. Pays 5¢ a word; maximum of $175. No additional payment is made for photos used with mss. Captions required.

NATIONAL BOWLERS JOURNAL AND BILLIARD REVUE, 875 N. Michigan Ave., Ste. 3734, Chicago IL 60611. Editor: Mort Luby, Jr. For proprietors of bowling centers, dealers and distributors of bowling and billiard equipment. Also for professional bowlers and billiard players. Monthly. Circulation: 17,000. Buys first rights. Buys 20 to 30 mss a year. Pays on publication. Will send a free sample copy to a writer on request. Query editor first. Reports in 2 to 3 weeks. Enclose S.A.S.E.

Nonfiction and Photos: Uses illustrated articles about successful bowling and billiard room proprietors who have used unusual promotions to build business, profiles of interesting industry personalities (including bowlers and billiard players), and coverage of major competitive events, both bowling and billiards. "We publish some controversial matter, seek out outspoken personalities." Length: 1,500 to 2,500 words. Pays $50 to $75. Photos purchased with mss. B&w glossies. Pays $10.

POOL NEWS, 3923 W. 6th St., Los Angeles CA 90020. Editor: Fay Coupe. For pool trade; pool builders, service firms, retail stores and distributors. Established in 1961. Twice a month. Circulation: 10,000. Buys all rights but will reassign rights to author after publication. Buys 300 mss a year. Payment on acceptance. Query first or submit complete ms. Will consider photocopied submissions. Returns rejected material immediately. Reports on material accepted for publication in 1 month. Enclose S.A.S.E. for reply to queries or return of submissions.
Nonfiction and Photos: Stories on the swimming pool industry. Pays 5¢ a word. B&w photos purchased with mss. Captions required.

RVR, RECREATIONAL VEHICLE RETAILER, 23945 Craftsman Rd., Calabasas CA 91302. Editorial Director: Denis Rouse. For men and women of the RV industry, primarily those involved in the sale of trailers, motorhomes, pickup campers, to the public. Also, owners and operators of trailer supply stores, plus manufacturers and executives of the RV industry nationwide and in Canada. Magazine; 100 pages, 8¼x11. Established in 1972. Monthly. Circulation: 28,000. Buys all rights. Buys 100 to 150 mss a year. Pays on publication. Will send free sample copy to writer on request. Write for copy of guidelines for writers. Reports on material in 3 weeks. Query first or submit complete ms. Enclose S.A.S.E.
Nonfiction and Photos: "Stories that show trends in the industry; success stories of particular dealerships throughout the country; news stories on new products; accessories (news section); how to sell; how to increase profits, be a better business-man. Interested in broadbased, general interest material of use to all RV retailers, rather than mere trade reporting." Informational, how-to, personal experience, interview, profile, humor, think articles, successful business operations, and merchandising techniques. Length: 1,000 to 2,000 words. Pays $50 to $125. Shorter items for regular columns or departments run 800 words. Pays $50 to $75. Photos purchased with accompanying ms with no additional payment. Captions required.
Fillers: Dealer/industry items from over the country; newsbreaks. Length: 100 to 200 words. Pays $5 for item, with photo. Department Editor: Alice M. Robinson, Managing Editor.

SELLING SPORTING GOODS, 717 N. Michigan Ave., Chicago IL 60111. Phone: 312-944-0205. Editor: Thomas B. Doyle. For owners and managers of retail sporting goods stores. Established in 1945. Monthly. Circulation: 16,000. Buys all rights. Buys 12 mss a year. Pays on acceptance. Will send free sample copy to writer on request. Submit seasonal material 3 months in advance. Enclose S.A.S.E.
Nonfiction and Photos: Articles on "full-line and specialty sporting goods stores. Buys informational articles, how-to's; articles on retail sporting goods advertising, promotions, in-store clinics/workshops; employee hiring and training; merchandising techniques. Articles related to the retailing of particular sports products are the most desired." Length: 750 to 1,000 words. Pays 5¢ to 8¢ a word. B&w glossy photos purchased with or without accompanying ms. 5x7 minimum. Captions required. Color transparencies. Pays $75 to $100 for cover transparency.
How To Break In: "Practice photography! Most stories, no matter how good, are useless without quality photos. They can be submitted as contact sheets with negatives to hold down writers' cost."

THE SHOOTING INDUSTRY, 8150 N. Central Park Blvd., Skokie IL 60076. Phone: 312-675-5602. Editor: J. Rakusan. For manufacturers, dealers, sales representatives of archery and shooting equipment. 12 times a year. Buys all rights. Buys about 135 mss a year. Pays on publication. Will send free sample copy to a writer on request. Query first. Reports in 2 to 3 weeks. Enclose S.A.S.E.
Nonfiction and Photos: Articles that tell "secrets of my success" based on experience of individual gun dealers; articles of advice to help dealers sell more guns and shooting equipment. Also, articles about and of interest to manufacturers and top

manufacturers' executives. Length: up to 3,000 words. Pays $50 to $150. Photos essential; b&w glossies. Purchased with ms.

SKI AREA MANAGEMENT, Box 242, North Salem NY 10560. Editor: David Rowan. For ski area managers. Quarterly. Circulation: 6,000. Buys all rights. Buys about 10 mss a year. Pays on publication. Will send a sample copy to a writer on request. Query first. Reports immediately. Enclose S.A.S.E.
Nonfiction and Photos: "Articles on restaurant management, slope grooming, lift maintenance, lift construction, ski schools, snowmaking, marketing, insurance." Length: 1,000 to 5,000 words. Pays $50 to $200. B&w glossies purchased with mss.

SKI BUSINESS, 380 Madison Ave., New York NY 10017. Editor: Evan Cooper. For ski retailers and instructors. Monthly newspaper; 24 pages. Established in 1960. Circulation: 15,000. Payment on publication. Will send free sample copy to writer on request. Write for copy of guidelines for writers. Will consider photocopied submissions. Will not consider simultaneous submissions. Reports immediately. Query first or submit complete ms. Enclose S.A.S.E.
Nonfiction and Photos: Stories on retail operations, service, repair, teaching techniques; profiles on ski industry executives; promotion and advertising tips. Material must be slanted to a retail audience. Interested in articles on how retailers are coping with the energy crisis. Does not want to see general stories that lack specifics; i.e., volume, advertising budget, turnover, size of store. Length depends on topic. Payment depends on topic and length of ms. "We are a trade paper and, therefore, our rates are low." Photos are purchased with ms.

SKIING TRADE NEWS, One Park Ave., New York NY 10016. Editor: William Grout. For ski shop owners. Semiannual magazine; 150 pages. Established in 1964. Circulation: about 5,000. Buys first North American serial rights. Buys 10 mss a year. Payment on acceptance. Reports on material accepted for publication in 30 days. Returns rejected material in 30 days. Query first. Enclose S.A.S.E.
Nonfiction: Factual how-to or success articles about buying at the ski trade shows, merchandising ski equipment, keeping control of inventory, etc. Length: 2,000 words. Pays 10¢ a word.
How To Break In: "Find a ski shop that is a success, one that does something (merchandising, etc.) differently and makes money at it. Research the reasons for the shop's success and query."

THE SPORTING GOODS DEALER, 1212 North Lindbergh Blvd., St. Louis MO 63166. Phone: 314-997-7111. Editor: C. C. Johnson Spink. For members of the sporting goods trade; retailers, manufacturers, wholesalers, representatives. Monthly magazine. Established in 1899. Circulation: 15,450. Buys second serial (reprint) rights. Buys about 15 mss a year. Payment on publication. Will send free sample copy to writer on request. Write for copy of guidelines for writers. Will not consider photocopied or simultaneous submissions. Query first. Enclose S.A.S.E.
Nonfiction and Photos: "Articles about specific sporting goods retail stores, their promotions, display techniques, sales ideas, merchandising, timely news of key personnel; expansions, new stores, deaths—all in the sporting goods trade. Specific details on how specific successful sporting goods stores operate. What specific retail sporting goods stores are doing that is new and different. We would also be interested in features dealing with stores doing an outstanding job on baseball retailing, fishing, golf, tennis, firearms/hunting. Query first on these." Successful business operations, merchandising techniques. Length: open. Pays $2 per 100 published words. Also looking for material for the following columns: Terse Tales of the Trade; Selling Slants; Open for Business (new retail sporting goods stores or sporting goods departments). All material must relate to specific sporting goods stores by name, city, and state; general information is not accepted. Pays minimum of $3.50 for sharp and clear b&w photos; size not important. These are purchased with or without mss.
Fillers: Clippings. These must relate directly to the sporting goods industry. Pays 2¢ per published word.

SPORTS MERCHANDISER, 1760 Peachtree Rd., N.W., Atlanta GA 30309. Editorial Director: Ralph E. Kirby. For "retailers of sporting goods in all categories; wholesalers, manufacturers, sales personnel in all industry categories." Established in 1969. Monthly. Circulation: 23,000. Buys all rights. Payment on acceptance. Will send free sample copy to writer on request. Write for copy of guidelines for writers. Submit seasonal material 3 to 4 months in advance. "Writer should request bulletin on special issues." Query first. Enclose S.A.S.E.

Nonfiction and Photos: "Articles purchased are those dealing with the sales, promotional and merchandising activities of retailers of sporting goods: independent stores, department stores, mass merchandisers, specialty stores. The techniques of successful business operations; procedures, innovations, campaigns, etc." Length: 5 double-spaced pages, maximum. Pays $50 to $100 and up depending on quality. 5x7 or 8x10 b&w photos purchased with or without accompanying ms. Captions required. Pays $10 to $25.

SWIMMING POOL WEEKLY/SWIMMING POOL AGE, P.O. Box 11299, Fort Lauderdale FL 33306. Managing Editor: Dave Kaiser. For "swimming pool dealers, distributors, manufacturers, and those in fields related to above-ground pools." Established in 1971. Biweekly. Circulation: 15,000. Rights purchased vary with author and material; may buy all rights, but will reassign rights to author after publication. Buys about 100 mss a year. Pays on publication. Will send a sample copy to a writer on request; enclose S.A.S.E. Query first "always." Will not consider photocopied submissions. Submit seasonal material 2 months in advance. Reports in 1 week. Enclose S.A.S.E.

Nonfiction: "Articles on any aspect of the pool industry—from marketing to learn-to-swim programs. Always interested in unique merchandising techniques, dealer success stories, or new uses for pools." For annual edition, buys features "describing new techniques, facilities, and advances in pool technology." Length: maximum 500 words. Pays 3¢ to 6¢ a word, $20 per article.

Photos: Purchased with mss or as photo stories. "Pictures of unique store displays or merchandising layouts welcome." 5x7 or 8x10 glossies. Pays $5.

Fillers: Newsbreaks, clippings. Length: 50 to 100 words. Pays $5.

TENNIS INDUSTRY, 915 N.E. 125 St., Suite 2-C, No. Miami FL 33161. Editor: Michael Keighley. For "those responsible for the management of tennis clubs and related tennis operations." Established in 1972. Monthly, Dec./Jan. through November. Circulation: 14,000. Buys all rights. Buys 10 to 15 mss a year. Payment on publication. Will send free sample copy to writer on request. Query first. Will consider photocopied submissions. Reports on material within 2 months. Enclose S.A.S.E.

Nonfiction and Photos: "Articles on the business aspects of tennis with emphasis on the financial. Latest information about tennis products, new court surfaces, recreational center planning, the effect of tennis facilities on hotel occupancy; the costs of creating and operating tennis complexes at schools, in cities and at resorts and country clubs." Length: 900 to 1,500 words. Pays 5¢ a word. 8x10 b&w, 35mm color purchased with ms.

Stone and Quarry Products

ASBESTOS, 131 North York Road (P.O. Box 471), Willow Grove PA 19090. Editor: Mrs. Doris M. Fagan. For the vertical asbestos industry. Monthly. Copyrighted. Pays on publication. Will send free sample copy to a writer on request. Query first. Enclose S.A.S.E.

Nonfiction: "Interested only in items concerning some phase of the international asbestos industry, i.e., new asbestos mines and mills, progress reports on asbestos mines and mills, new or improved techniques in processing asbestos fiber and the manufacture of asbestos-based products, personnel changes and expansions within

asbestos firms, asbestos vs. industrial and public health (including techniques to control the emanation of asbestos dust), findings from research into new uses for asbestos (including utilization of the fiber as a reinforcement to improve the effectiveness of plastics, synthetics, and composite materials), improvements in already existing asbestos-based products, etc. We are not interested in news of the asbestos workers union or in advertisements. We make little use of photographs or other graphics." Length: 500 to 3,000 words. Pays 1¢ to 1½¢ per word "as the article appears in the journal."
Fillers: Newsbreaks and clippings related to asbestos industry. Length: maximum 500 words. Pays 1¢ a word, "as published in *Asbestos*".

CONCRETE CONSTRUCTION MAGAZINE, P.O. Box 555, Elmhurst IL 60126. Editor: William H. Kuenning. For general and concrete contractors, architects, engineers, concrete producers, cement manufacturers, distributors and dealers in construction equipment, testing labs. Monthly magazine; 48 to 56 (8½x11) pages. Established in 1956. Circulation: 85,000. Buys all rights. Buys 50 mss a year. Payment on acceptance. Will send free sample copy to writer on request. Write for copy of guidelines for writers. Will consider photocopied and simultaneous submissions. Reports on material accepted for publication in an indefinite time. Returns rejected material in 1 to 2 months. Submit complete ms. Enclose S.A.S.E.
Nonfiction and Photos: "Our magazine has one topic to discuss: cast-in-place (site cast) concrete. Our articles deal with tools, techniques and materials which result in better handling, better placing, and ultimately an improved final product. We are particularly firm about not using proprietary names in any of our articles. Manufacturers and products are never mentioned; only the processes or techniques that might be of help to the concrete contractor, the architect or the engineer dealing with the material. We do use 'bingo cards' which accomplish the purpose of relaying reader interest to manufacturers, but without cluttering up the articles themselves with a lot of name dropping." Length: 300 to 3,000 words. Pays 7¢ per published word. Pays $10 for b&w glossy photos and color used with mss. Photos are used only as part of a completed ms.

MONUMENTAL NEWS REVIEW, P.O. Box 523, Olean NY 14760. For monument dealers throughout the world. Magazine; 52 pages. Established in 1895. Monthly. Circulation: 3,300. Not copyrighted. Pays on acceptance. Will send free sample copy to writer on request. Submit complete ms. Enclose S.A.S.E.
Nonfiction and Photos: Anything of interest to monument manufacturers and dealers. Cemetery news, civic memorials; granite and marble quarrying. Inspirational, historical, new product, merchandising techniques, technical. Recently published "Cemetery Problems Are Your Business". Length: 200 to 600 words. Pays 10¢ a word. Pays minimum of $20 for b&w photos; minimum of $10 for color.

ROCK PRODUCTS, 300 W. Adams St., Chicago IL 60606. Phone: 312-726-2802. Editor: Sidney Levine. For nonmetallic minerals mining producers. Monthly. Buys all rights. Pays on publication. Query first. Reports within 4 weeks. Enclose S.A.S.E.
Nonfiction and Photos: "Covers the construction minerals segment of the non-metallic (industrial) minerals industry. Uses articles on quarrying, mining, and processing of portland cement, lime, gypsum, sand and gravel, crushed stone, slag, and expanded clay and shale. Other non-metallic metals covered include dimension stone, asbestos, diatomite, expanded flyash, vermiculite, perlite. Equipment and its applications are emphasized in the operating and technical coverage. Feature articles describe complete plant operations, design and planning, company profiles, marketing, and management techniques." Length: open. $35 per published page.
How To Break In: "Articles for *Rock Products* are prepared by specialists or authorities in their particular field. For the beginning writer, an engineering or technical background is a major prerequisite. For 'professional' freelancers, I suggest what the pro already knows: 'Study the book.'"

Textile

AMERICA'S TEXTILE REPORTER/BULLETIN, P.O. Box 88, Greenville SC 29601. Editor: Laurens Irby. For "officials and operating executives of manufacturing corporations and plants in the basic textile yarn and fabric industry." Established in 1878. Monthly. Circulation: 22,000. Not copyrighted. Buys "very few" mss a year. Pays on publication. Will send a sample copy to a writer for $1. Write for copy of guidelines for writers "only if background is suitable." Query first. "It is extremely difficult for non-textile industry freelancers to write for us." Enclose S.A.S.E.
Nonfiction: "Technical and business articles about the textile industry." Length: open. Pays $25 to $50 per printed page.

FIBRE AND FABRIC, P.O. Box 401, Acton MA 01720. Editor: Vincent A. Paradis. For textile executives. Monthly. Buys all rights. Pays on acceptance. "Query saves time." Reports in 10 days. Enclose S.A.S.E.
Nonfiction: Articles on textile manufacturing slanted to the production or management executive. Also first-person accounts of practical solutions to production problems in the card, spin, weave, dye, and finish rooms of textile manufacturers. Length: 1,500 to 3,000 words. Pays 2¢ to 5¢ per word.

SOUTHERN TEXTILE NEWS, Box 1569, Charlotte NC 28201. Editor: Ernest E. Elkins. For textile and apparel industries. Weekly. Circulation: approximately 7,800. Not copyrighted. Pays on publication. Will send free sample copy on request. Query first. Reports within 1 week. Enclose S.A.S.E.
Nonfiction: Articles and features on industry and textile industry-oriented personalities. Must have textile tie-ins. Length: up to 2,000 words. Pays minimum 35¢ per column inch.
Photos: Uses 8x10 photos related to textile industry; good contrast and quality. Pays up to $5 for good photos.

TEXTILE WORLD, 1175 Peachtree St., N.E., Atlanta GA 30361. Editor-in-Chief: Laurence A. Christiansen. Monthly. Buys all rights. Pays on acceptance. Enclose S.A.S.E.
Nonfiction and Photos: Uses articles covering textile management methods, manufacturing and marketing techniques, new equipment, details about new and modernized mills, etc., but avoids elementary, historical, or generally well-known material. Pays $25 minimum per page. Photos purchased with accompanying ms with no additional payment, or purchased on assignment.

Toy, Novelty, and Hobby

PROFITABLE CRAFT MERCHANDISING, News Plaza, Peoria IL 61601. Phone: 309-682-6626. Editor: Ellen M. Dahlquist. For craft retailers. Monthly magazine; 80 (8½x11) pages. Circulation: 12,500. Buys all rights. Buys 60 to 75 mss a year. Payment on acceptance. Will send free sample copy to writer on request. Write for copy of guidelines for writers. Will not accept photocopied submissions. Will consider simultaneous submissions only if not submitted to a competitive publication. Submit seasonal material for Christmas merchandising issue, which is published in August, 4 months in advance. Reports in 4 weeks. Query first. Enclose S.A.S.E.
Nonfiction and Photos: Articles on store management techniques. Craft retailer success stories. Coverage of news events such as trade shows and conventions and better consumer shows that have heavy retailer participation. Store management oriented articles. Does not want to see interviews of craft retailers. "Keep in mind that the primary purpose of *Profitable Craft Merchandising* is to tell the retailer

how to make money." Informational, how-to, personal experience, spot news, new product, successful business operations, and merchandising techniques. Length: 1,000 to 2,500 words. Pays $45 to $250. 4 to 10 good quality 8x10 or 5x7 b&w glossy photos are usually used with mss. No additional payment. Captions required. Color photos are not used unless especially requested.

SOUVENIRS AND NOVELTIES, Bldg. 30, 20-21 Wagaraw Rd., Fair Lawn NJ 07410. Phone: 201-797-2522. Editor: Martin Dowd. For "owners and managers of tourist attractions and souvenir shops who buy and sell souvenirs and novelties at resorts, parks, museums, airports, etc." Special issues include parks, museums, attractions (April), tourist travel terminals shops (June), free attractions (December). Established in 1962. Bimonthly. Circulation: 6,500. Buys first North American serial rights. Buys about 15 mss a year. Pays on acceptance. Will send a sample copy to a writer on request. Write for copy of guidelines for writers. Query first or submit complete ms. Will consider photocopied submissions. Submit seasonal material 3 months in advance of issue date "if possible." Reports in 1 week. Enclose S.A.S.E.
Nonfiction and Photos: "Articles about how to buy and sell souvenirs and novelties. How to manage a souvenir or novelty shop. How to handle inventory, pilferage, prices, etc. The writer should interview managers and owners and report on what they say about how to sell and buy souvenirs and novelties. How to display merchandise, how to train employees, etc. We specialize in a narrow field of merchandising for tourists, generally. I am not really interested in travel articles." Buys informational articles, how-to's, interviews, and coverage of successful business operations. Length: 500 to 1,500 words. Pays minimum $1 per column inch. Photos purchased with ms; captions required. For 8x10 or 5x7 b&w glossies, pays $5 "for amateur photos" and $10 "for professional photos. Will pay for photos even if supplied by the park or attraction or museum, as long as we use them and the writer obtains them."
Fillers: Clippings. "Must be about souvenir or novelty business, or don't bother to send them, please. We pay 80¢ a published inch if we use the clipping."

THE STAMP WHOLESALER, P.O. Box 529, Burlington VT 05401. Editor: Lucius Jackson. For small-time independent businessmen; many are part-time and/or retired from other work. Published 21 times a year; 68 (8½x11) pages. Established in 1936. Circulation: 9,700. Buys all rights. Buys 40 mss a year. Payment on acceptance. Will send free sample copy to writer on request. Will not consider photocopied or simultaneous submissions. Reports on material accepted for publication in 1 day to 1 year. Returns rejected material when decision is reached. Submit complete ms. Enclose S.A.S.E.
Nonfiction and Photos: How-to information on how to deal more profitably in postage stamps for collections. Emphasis on merchandising techniques and how to make money. Does not want to see any so-called "humor" items from nonprofessionals. Length: 1,500 to 2,000 words. Pays 3¢ per word, minimum. B&w photos (6x9) purchased with or without mss, or on assignment. Captions required. Pays $5 minimum.

TOY & HOBBY WORLD, 124 E. 40th St., New York NY 10016. For everyone in the toy and hobby industry from manufacturer to retailer. Magazine, published twice a month. Established in 1961. Circulation: 16,500. Not copyrighted. Buys 5 mss a year. Payment on publication. Will send sample copy to writer for 50¢. Will consider photocopied submissions. Will not consider simultaneous submissions. Returns rejected material when requested. Query first. Enclose S.A.S.E.
Nonfiction and Photos: Merchandising and news. Informational, how-to, new product. Technical articles for manufacturers; features about wholesalers, retailers, chains, department stores, discount houses, etc., concerned with their toy operations. Prefers stories on toy wholesalers or retailers who have unusual success with unusual methods. Also interested in especially successful toy departments in drug stores, supermarkets, hardware stores, gas stations, etc. No interest in mere histories of run-of-the-mill operators. Use a news style. Length: 1,000 to 3,000 words. Pays 4¢ a word. Buys

8x10 b&w photos with mss and with captions only. Must be glossy on singleweight paper. No color. Pays $6 plus word rate. Prefers captions.

Trailers

MOBILE HOME MERCHANDISER, 300 W. Adams St., Chicago IL 60606. Editor: James M. Mack. For mobile home dealers, mobile home park operators and developers. Monthly magazine; 110 pages. Established in 1952. Circulation: 20,500. Buys all rights. Buys 6 mss a year. Payment on publication. Will send free sample copy to writer on request. Write for copy of guidelines for writers. Will consider photocopied submissions. Will not consider simultaneous submissions. Reports on material accepted for publication within 4 weeks. Returns rejected material immediately. Query first or submit complete ms. Enclose S.A.S.E.
Nonfiction and Photos: "Article emphasis is on merchandising/sales techniques. How-to articles. Factual accounts of dealer's operation. Must have in-depth treatment and offer clear, concise reporting of the subject, and essential details for readers' understanding and possible emulation. Dispense with detailed biography of dealer or his business." Material on successful business operations is also used. Length: open. Pays $35 per published page including photos. Captions are required for 5x7 or larger b&w photos.

MOBILE-MODULAR HOUSING DEALER MAGAZINE, 6229 Northwest Highway, Chicago IL 60631. Phone: 312-774-2525. Editor: James Kennedy. For dealers, manufacturers and suppliers concerned with the industry. Monthly magazine; 130 (8¼x11¼) pages. Established in 1949. Circulation: 19,000. Buys all rights, but will reassign rights to author after publication. Payment on publication. Will send free sample copy to writer on request. Write for copy of guidelines for writers. Reports as soon as possible. Query first. Enclose S.A.S.E.
Nonfiction and Photos: "Dealer success stories; in-depth techniques in dealership operations; service articles; financing, features; dealer/manufacturer relationships. Every article should be dealer oriented, pointed to the dealer for the benefit of the dealer. Focus on some one or two aspects of the dealer operation largely responsible for the company's success. A general overall description of the dealership is necessary for a well-rounded story, but an important aspect of the firm's operation should be developed, such as merchandising the product, unique inventory control; before and after sales service; financing procedures; salesmen programs, accessories and parts success." Also uses warrantee features, material on manufacturers and dealer franchise agreements; consumerism and service articles. Length: 500 to 2,000 words. Pays $2 per column inch (13 picas wide). 7x10 b&w glossy photos purchased with mss or on assignment. Pays $7. Captions required.

TRAILER/BODY BUILDERS, 1602 Harold St., Houston TX 77006. Editor: Paul Schenck. For the manufacturers and builders of truck trailers, truck bodies, truck tanks, vans, cargo containers, plus the truck equipment distributors. Monthly. Not copyrighted. Pays on publication. Will send free sample copy to a writer on request. Reports in 30 days. Enclose S.A.S.E.
Nonfiction: "Material on manufacturers of truck trailers, and truck bodies, school bus bodies, also their sales distributors. These also go under the names of semitrailer manufacturing, custom body builders, trailer sales branch, or truck equipment distributor. No travel trailers, house trailers, mobile homes, or tire companies, transmission people or other suppliers, unless it directly affects truck body or truck trailer. Need shop hints and how-to features. Many stories describe how a certain special truck body or truck trailer is built." Pays $2 per inch or $40 per page.
Photos: Buys photos appropriate to format. Study publication. Pays $10.
Fillers: "New products and newspaper clippings appropriate to format. Do not rewrite clippings." Pays $1.50 per inch or better on news items.

Transportation

These journals aim at traffic managers and transportation experts (who route goods across the continent). Publications for automobile and truck dealers, repairmen, or fleet operators are classified in the Auto and Truck category. Journals for highway planners and traffic control experts are in the Government and Public Service listing.

CANADIAN TRANSPORTATION AND DISTRIBUTION MANAGEMENT, 1450 Don Mills Rd., Don Mills, Ontario M3B 2X7, Canada. Editor: Douglas W. Seip. For "industrial traffic managers and rail, road, air, marine, and transit carriers." Monthly. Buys all rights. Pays on publication. Will send a sample copy to a writer on request. Reports in 6 weeks. Enclose S.A.E. and International Reply Coupons.
Nonfiction and Photos: "This publication covers the complete spectrum of innovations in transport service and equipment related to the Canadian scene. Of particular interest are stories describing how shippers and carriers work together to mutual advantage. Field is changing rapidly due to technological change, world competition, etc., and cooperation between shippers and carrier is being forced by these conditions. All of this is reflected in our editorial content." Length: 1,000 to 3,000 words. Pays 5¢ a word minimum. 8x10 b&w photos purchased with mss. Pays $6.

DEFENSE TRANSPORTATION JOURNAL, 1612 K St., N.W., Washington DC 20006. Publisher and Editor: Gerald W. Collins. For "transportation executives and managers of all ages and military transportation officers. Generally educated with college degree." Established in 1945. Bimonthly. Circulation: 13,000. Rights purchased vary with author and material; may buy all rights, but may reassign rights to author after publication. Buys 5 to 10 mss a year. Pays on acceptance. Will send a sample copy to a writer on request. Write for copy of guidelines for writers. Submit seasonal material 2 to 3 months in advance. Reports in 2 to 3 weeks. Enclose S.A.S.E.
Nonfiction: "Articles on transportation, distribution, and traffic management in the U.S. and abroad. This publication emphasizes transportation as it relates to defense and emergency requirements." Buys informational and personal experience articles. Length: 2,500 words. Pays $100.
How To Break In: "Study the magazine very carefully, perhaps even discuss the editorial goals with the editor, and then come up with creative ideas or a new approach to an old idea, that would be valuable to the magazine. Whether it be a new column, a research article or new ideas along other lines, I believe a fresh, imaginative view is the most helpful to an editor."

HIGHWAY USER QUARTERLY, 1776 Massachusetts Ave., N.W., Washington DC 20036. Editor: William R. Talbott. For highway officials, educators, transportation executives, engineers, legislators. Quarterly magazine. Established in 1932. Circulation: 13,700. Buys all rights. Buys 3 to 4 mss a year. Payment on acceptance. Will send free sample copy to writer on request. Will consider photocopied submissions. Will not consider simultaneous submissions. Reports in several weeks. Query first or submit complete mss. Enclose S.A.S.E.
Nonfiction and Photos: Articles on various aspects of transportation problems written in a thoughtful, readable style. Subject must be well researched. Articles on highway finance and aspects of highway safety. Length: about 3,000 words. Pays $250. No additional payment made for b&w photos used with mss. In some cases, an additional payment of $25 is made.

Travel

PACIFIC TRAVEL NEWS, 274 Brannan St., San Francisco CA 94107. Editor: Shirley Fockler. For travel trade—travel agencies, transportation companies. Monthly. Buys one-time rights for travel trade publications. Pays on publication unless material is for future use; then on acceptance. Will send sample copy on request. All material purchased on assignment following specific outline. Query about assignment. "Do not send unsolicited mss or transparencies." Reports in 1 to 3 weeks. Enclose S.A.S.E.

Nonfiction: Writer must be based in a country in coverage area of the Pacific from Hawaii west to India, south to Australia and New Zealand. "We are not interested in how-to articles, such as how to sell, decorate your windows, keep your staff happy, cut costs." Pays $200 maximum.

Photos: Purchased with mss or captions only. Related to travel attractions, activities within Pacific area. Sometimes general travel-type photos, other times specific photos related to hotels, tours, tour equipment, etc. Buys mainly b&w glossy, 5x7 or larger. Also buys about 18 color transparencies a year, 35mm top quality. Pays up to $10 for b&w; up to $50 for inside color; $75 for color used on cover.

THE STAR SERVICE INC., Sloane Agency Travel Reports, P.O. Box 6156, Ft. Lauderdale FL 33310. Phone: 305-472-8794. Editor: Robert D. Sloane. Editorial manual sold to travel agencies on subscription basis. Buys all rights. Buys about 2,000 reports a year. Pays on publication. Write for instruction sheet and sample report form. Query first. Initial reports sent by a new correspondent will be examined for competence and criticized as necessary upon receipt, but once established, a correspondent's submissions will not usually be acknowledged until payment is forwarded, which can often be several months, depending on immediate editorial needs. Enclose S.A.S.E.

Nonfiction: "Objective, critical evaluations of worldwide hotels suitable for North Americans, based on inspections. Forms can be provided to correspondents so no special writing style is required, only perceptiveness, experience, and judgment in travel. No commercial gimmick—no advertising or payment for listings in publication is accepted." With query, writer should "outline experience in travel and forthcoming travel plans, time available for inspections. Leading travel agents throughout the world subscribe to Star Service. No credit or byline is given correspondents due to delicate subject matter often involving negative criticism of hotels. We would like to emphasize the importance of reports being based on current experience and the importance of reporting on a substantial volume of hotels, not just isolated stops (since staying in hotel is not a requisite) in order that work be profitable for both publisher and writer. Experience in travel writing is desirable." Length: "up to 200 words, if submitted in paragraph form; varies if submitted on printed inspection form." Pays $5 per report used. "Guarantees of acceptance of set numbers of reports may be made on establishment of correspondent's ability and reliability (up to about $250, usually), but always on prior arrangement."

TRAVEL/AGE WEST, 582 Market St., San Francisco CA 94104. Phone: 415-781-8353. Managing Editor: Donald C. Langley. For travel agency sales staffs. Established in 1969. Weekly. Circulation: 13,000. Rights purchased vary with author and material. May buy second serial (reprint) rights. Buys 12 mss a year. Payment on publication. Will send free sample copy to writer on request. Will consider photocopied submissions. Submit seasonal material at least 2 months in advance. (Pacific issue in late winter; cruise issues in late winter and late summer; travel agent convention issue in fall). Reports on material in 3 weeks. Query first or submit complete ms. Enclose S.A.S.E.

Nonfiction and Photos: "We accept a limited amount of material on 'how to sell' or 'how to promote', but most of the freelance material we buy concerns destinations to which our agent/readers might be sending their clients. The writer must remember that the reader will not be taking the trip himself, but will be selling it to others. Therefore, the 'you' element cannot be used. Don't waste time on describing do-it-yourself travel; our readers' jobs are to take that aspect out of travel. They need to know prices and addresses. We carefully avoid a promotional tone." Length: 500 to 1,000 words. Pays $1.50 per column inch ("with 10-point type and unjustified columns, stories tend to measure long"). B&w photos purchased with mss. Captions required. Pays $1.50 per column inch.

How To Break In: "It would help if writers would write from a consumer, rather than a trade, point of view. Also to remember they are writing for a newspaper, not a guide book."

THE TRAVEL AGENT, 2 W. 46th St., New York NY 10036. Editor: Eric Friedheim. For "travel agencies and travel industry executives." Established in 1929. Semiweekly. Circulation: 18,000. Not copyrighted. Pays on acceptance. Query first. Reports "immediately." Enclose S.A.S.E.
Nonfiction and Photos: Uses trade features slanted to travel agents, sales and marketing people, and executives of transportation companies such as airlines, ship lines, etc. History-related articles on tourism, with illustrations. No travelogues such as those appearing in newspapers and consumer publications. Articles should show how agent and carriers can sell more travel to the public. Length: up to 2,000 words. Pays $50 to $100. Photos purchased with ms.

TRAVELSCENE MAGAZINE, 888 Seventh Ave., New York NY 10011. Managing Editor: Baran S. Rosen. For three diverse audiences: airline reservationists, travel agents, and corporate travel planners. Magazine; 60 (8½x11) pages. Established in 1965. Monthly. Circulation: 97,000. Buys all rights. Buys 30 to 40 mss a year. Payment usually made on acceptance. Will send free sample copy to writer or request. Will consider photocopied and simultaneous submissions. Submit special issue material 5 months in advance. Reports in 2 to 6 weeks. Query first. Enclose S.A.S.E.
Nonfiction and Photos: "We are the largest of any travel industry publication and publish articles which help our audience do a better job of planning travel as well as to give them a better understanding of their field of work. We don't want stories from non-writers about their family trip to Oshkosh. Any destination pieces must be insightful, not a mere listing of sights." Would also be interested in seeing articles on successful travel business operations. Recently published articles on where to find bargains in Europe; a new program by the Irish Tourist Board for travel agents; and one on Pan Am's new global car rental system. Length: 2,000 to 3,000 words. Pays $75 to $200. B&w and color photos purchased with or without ms, or on assignment. Pays $5 to $10.
Fillers: Jokes related to travel. Length: 25 to 100 words. Pays $10 to $20.
How To Break In: "Writer should submit past samples of work, an outline of proposal(s), and include S.A.S.E. and phone number. Getting a first assignment may not be too difficult, if the writer can write. We are looking for and need good writers. If stories are submitted, they must be an average of 8 to 12 pages, double spaced; 13 to 15 maximum."

Veterinary

CANINE PRACTICE JOURNAL, FELINE PRACTICE JOURNAL, Veterinary Practice Publishing Co., P.O. Box 4506, Santa Barbara CA 93103. Editor: Dr. Anna P. Gilbride. For graduate veterinarians working primarily in small animal practice, or in mixed practices (large and small) which do a substantial volume of dog and cat practice. Published every two months; magazines, 52 pages, 7x10. *Feline Practice Journal* established in 1971. Circulation: 5,300. *Canine Practice Journal* established in 1974. Circulation: 3,000. Rights purchased vary with author and material. Buys all rights, but will reassign rights to author after publication. Buys second serial (reprint) rights. "Strictly technical medical and surgical content written so far exclusively by graduate veterinarians." Payment on publication. Will send sample copy to writer free, on request, if an apparently legitimate author in this field.Write for copy of editorial guidelines for writers. Will consider photocopied submissions. Query first. Reports within 2 weeks. Enclose S.A.S.E.
Nonfiction and Photos: "Strictly technical medical and surgical articles for veterinarians, by veterinarians. One of our magazines deals exclusively with feline (cat) medicine and surgery; the other, with canine (dog) medicine and surgery. Writer would first have to be a veterinarian, or a scientist in one of the life sciences fields

(for example, biology, nutrition, zoology). We send an author's guide on request. Our journals are specifically vertical magazines in a field heretofore served by horizontal magazines. That is, we publish single-species journals, the others publish multi-species journals." Length: 300 to 5,000 words. Pays $10 per published page, plus $5 for illustrations or photos. 4x5 to 8x10 b&w matte or glossy. 35mm or 4x5 color transparencies or negative. Pays $5 each.

How To Break In: "We urge you to submit material that is of practical value to the clinician in everyday practice. Present your ideas and experiences as though you were discussing them person-to-person with a colleague. Describe the situation and action concisely, in a direct manner, eliminating extraneous material as much as possible. Remember, you are helping fellow professionals — give them all the information, but don't confuse the issue with unrelated material."

NORDEN NEWS, Norden Laboratories, 601 W. Cornhusker Highway, Lincoln NE 68521. Editor: Patricia Pike. For "doctors of veterinary medicine (clinicians, instructors in schools of veterinary medicine) and juniors and seniors in colleges of veterinary medicine." Established in 1929. Quarterly. Circulation: 15,000. Rights purchased vary with author and material. Will buy all rights, first North American serial rights, or second serial (reprint) rights. Buys 4 to 6 mss per year. Pays on publication. Will send a free sample copy to a writer on request. Will consider cassette submissions. Query first or submit complete ms. Submit seasonal material 3 to 4 months in advance. Reports in 1 month. Enclose S.A.S.E.

Nonfiction and Photos: "Technical articles, particularly in the area of diagnosis and treatment of diseases of animals; business-oriented articles relevant to practice management; feature articles about a veterinarian with an unusual approach to the practice of veterinary medicine, unique hobby or role in community activities. Avoid generalities. Articles should include specific details; many rejected because they are either not technical enough, or subject is unique to the laymen, but ordinary to other vets. Attempt to maintain a smoother, easier reading style. We prefer mss 3 to 4 pages long. We are currently paying $100 for ms, plus $7.50 for photos. $50 for 1-page articles. 8x10 or 5x7 b&w glossies are acceptable." Purchased with or without mss, or on assignment. Captions optional. Color transparencies or prints. Payment depends on use; $7.50 for article illustrations. "We are interested in unusual photos of animals which could be used as title page illustrations, or used with an ad. Of special interest: cats, dogs, feeder cattle, and horses."

VETERINARY ECONOMICS MAGAZINE, 2728 Euclid Ave., Cleveland OH 44115. Editorial Director: John D. Velardo. For all practicing veterinarians in the U.S. Monthly. Buys exclusive rights in the field. Pays on publication. Enclose S.A.S.E.

Nonfiction and Photos: Uses case histories telling about good business practices on the part of veterinarians. Also, articles about financial problems, investments, insurance and similar subjects of particular interest to professional men. Pays $15 to $25 per printed page depending on worth. Pays maximum $100. Photos purchased with ms. Pays $7.50.

VETERINARY MEDICINE/SMALL ANIMAL CLINICIAN, 144 North Nettleton Ave., Bonner Springs KS 66012. Phone: 913-422-5010. Editor: Dr. C.M. Cooper. For graduate veterinarians, research, libraries, schools, government agencies and other organizations employing veterinarians. Monthly. Circulation: 14,280. Buys North American serial rights. Occasionally overstocked with business/investment type mss. Pays on publication. Reports in 2 weeks. Enclose S.A.S.E.

Nonfiction: Accepts only articles dealing with medical case histories, practice management, business, taxes, insurance, investments, etc. Length: 1,500 to 2,500 words. Pays $15 per printed page. Dept. Editor: Ray E. Ottinger, Jr.

How To Break In: "Write up clinical reports for local veterinarians. We prefer to carry veterinarian as author."

Water Supply and Sewage Disposal

GROUND WATER AGE, 110 N. York Rd., Elmhurst IL 60126. Phone: 312-833-6540. Editor: Gene Adams. For water well drilling contractors and water well drilling business owners. Established in 1965. Monthly. Circulation: 15,000. Rights purchased vary with author and material. Buys all rights but will reassign rights to author after publication. Buys first North American serial rights, first serial rights (reprint) and simultaneous rights. Buys 12 to 18 mss a year. Payment on acceptance. Will send free sample copy to writer on request. Query first. Will consider photocopied submissions. Submit seasonal material 3 to 6 months in advance. Reports on material within 2 weeks. Enclose S.A.S.E.
Nonfiction and Photos: Technical articles on business operation. Informational, how-to, interview, historical, merchandising techniques. Length: open. Pays 4¢ to 8¢ a word. B&w photos. Minimum 4x5. Prefers 8x10. Pays $5 to $15. Purchased with accompanying ms. Captions required. Pays $25 to $75 for color.

WATER AND SEWAGE WORKS, 434 S. Wabash, Chicago IL 60605. Editors: Frank Reid and Joe Ziemba. For technicians in water and waste-water field. Monthly. Buys all rights. Pays on publication. Write for copy of guidelines for writers. Query preferred. Reports in 2 weeks. Enclose S.A.S.E.
Nonfiction and Photos: Wants articles such as "Cost of Trickling Filter Recirculation," "Manganese Removal From Water Supplies," and "How to Help Small Businesses Get Pollution Loans" which appeared in recent issues. Length: 2,500 words. Pays $25 per printed page. Photos purchased with mss, with no additional payment.

WATER WELL JOURNAL, P.O. Box 29168, Columbus OH 43229. Editor: Anita Stanley. For "water well drillers, manufacturers, and suppliers of water well equipment, geologists, engineers, and other technical people in the ground water field." Established in 1949. Monthly. Circulation: about 16,000. Buys all rights, but will reassign rights to author after publication. Buys about 12 mss a year. Pays on publication. Will send a sample copy to a writer on request. Will consider photocopied submissions. Submit seasonal material 2 to 3 months in advance of issue date. Reports in 1 month. Query first. Enclose S.A.S.E.
Nonfiction and Photos: "Articles of special interest to water well contractors, including business and legal angles, humorous instances; some historical interest, some technical articles. News items of national interest. Simple, readable style." Buys informational articles, how-to's, personal experience articles, interviews, profiles, humor, historical articles, nostalgia, coverage of successful business operations, and technical articles. Length: 500 to 2,000 words. Pays "up to $25 per page of printed matter. There are 600 to 1,000 words per page. Minimum 2¢ a word." B&w photos purchased with mss; captions required. Pays $4 for single photo, $3 for each additional photo in set.

If this is 1977, this edition is out of date. See address in front of book to order latest edition. *Writer's Market* is published annually each fall.

BOOK PUBLISHERS

Last year, there were almost 40,000 books published. This year, will one of them be yours? There are several special angles that must be kept in mind about the book publishing field and they should be considered before you send your finished book manuscript to a publisher.

A carbon copy of your book manuscript must be kept in your files. Even though your manuscript may have been sent by registered mail, the publisher will not foot the bill for the cost of retyping your manuscript if it is lost. It is essential, therefore, that a carbon copy of your book manuscript be retained in your files.

Do not bind or staple a manuscript. Always enclose return postage and a self-addressed envelope (S.A.E.)

What you have to say belongs in the book. Any matter enclosed in a covering letter that is not specifically important cannot help you. A covering letter should list your previously published works *only* if of some importance and issued by a respected publisher.

There is a fairly wide range of time in which publishers report to authors concerning their book manuscript submissions. The best you can expect is three weeks from the time you mail the manuscript. If you get a decision within a month after mailing, you are lucky. Seven weeks is average. Three months is not unusual. After that length of time, send a brief query, enclosing a stamped, self-addressed envelope.

What rights? Since you are selling a book, the logical thing is to offer "book rights only." If you are a beginner, you are in a tough bargaining position regarding movie, syndicate, paperback and book club rights. But try to hold on to as many of these rights as possible. You cannot copyright a book manuscript until it is actually printed; and then the publisher usually does it in your name. No specific rights are typed in on the title page of your manuscript. The rights you are asked to sell will be contained in the book contract.

CONTRACTS AND ROYALTIES

Many publishers offer a writer an advance against royalties to be paid on sales. The size of the advance varies with the subject matter of the book, the publisher's evaluation of its sales potential, your reputation as a writer and your or your agent's success in negotiating with the publisher. An advance on a juvenile might be only $500, while very successful authors may receive several hundred thousand dollars as an advance against royalties on a multiple-book contract. However, some rental library book publishers pay as little as $250 total outright fee for a book, as do some racy fiction paperback publishers.

Generally speaking, trade books—the kind that are sold in book stores: novels, nonfiction books, etc.—have a standard minimum royalty payment of 10% on the first 5,000 or 10,000 copies, 12½% on the next several thousand copies, and 15% thereafter. This percentage is based on the retail price of the book. For subsidiary rights, first book authors are usually offered 50% of what the publisher receives for paperback and book club rights; 90% on movie and TV sales. For paperback originals, the standard minimum royalty is 4% on the first 150,000 copies and 6% thereafter.

In the textbook field, college textbooks have a royalty based anywhere between 8% and 12% of the net price the publisher receives. Although a book is listed at $6, for example, no one pays $6 for the book since the school is given a bulk order price. The author receives his royalty then, based on the net amount of money that the publisher has received for his book. In the case of elementary and secondary school textbooks, the author's royalty will be much less—3% to 5%, based on the amount of illustration cost and staff work the publisher has had to prepare this textbook for purchase by schools.

In the case of juveniles, two situations obtain. On some picture books, the royalties range between 10% and 15%, with author and illustrator getting 5% to 7½% each. In other cases, the author gets the full royalty and the illustrator is paid a flat fee by the publisher.

Who makes money on a first novel? Nobody. Once in a while lightning will strike and a first novel will sell 50,000 copies or more.

Is it worth it? A novel teaches you a great deal. It builds up a profitable audience for your later books. It gives you prestige if you get good reviews. Book publishers are willing to gamble because the "names" of today were the unknown first novelists of ten and fifteen years ago.

MARKETING YOUR FIRST NOVEL

The easiest way to dispense with all thought and trouble of marketing is to ship the novel off to an agent. But asking an agent to handle a first novel without the payment of any fee is rather presumptuous. A first novel generally sells from 500 to 2,000 copies and if the author receives a royalty of 10% of the retail price of $4.50, he will receive a gross of up to $900. This means the agent gets a gross of $90 (10% of author's gross). That's not bad for the agent. All he has to do is call up the publisher, send over the novel, collect $900, and send the author $810. Would that it were so!

First, the agent must, in fact, read the novel to determine the publishers to whom he should send it. Second, if it is a first novel the agent may find passages that can be cut, chapters than can be improved and dialog that can be shortened. This often necessitates returning the novel to the author and dictating several pages of comment.

After the agent sends the novel to the publisher, he makes a note on his calendar to follow up the publisher in thirty days. He must also keep his eyes open for some sort of sales channels which will particularly justify the publisher's purchase of the book. If the first, second and third publishers do not buy the book, the agent then must proceed to send it to the fourth, fifth and sixth publishers.

That's why an agent is not too anxious to handle a first novel on a 10% commission basis without an advance fee. Further, even with the fee for handling, a first novel is not a profitable proposition. The only excuse for an agent's being willing to handle it is that he feels, along with the publisher who buys it, that the author will be able to produce subsequent novels which will find an increasingly larger market.

The author may want to market his first novel himself. How?

The traditional way is to bundle the novel off to some publisher who includes in his current catalog a book or books somewhat similar in their sales appeal to your own. Certainly, you would not send a first novel in the detective field to a publisher who issues only juveniles; and you would not send a juvenile novel a publisher who issues only Bibles. This is fundamental, but unhappily, not all authors examine the publisher's current catalog before sending the novel off. You can examine the publisher's current catalog at any large book store, at your local library, or by simply writing the publisher and asking for his current catalog. (Information about the availability of a catalog appears in each of the following listings.)

THE OUTLINE AND SAMPLE CHAPTER METHOD

A somewhat different procedure from the foregoing is followed by a good many professionals to save postage and speed up results. This method is preferred by most of the publishers in the following listings.

Type a synopsis of your novel (or nonfiction book) in one or two pages. Attach with this synopsis the first two or three chapters of your book, and, in addition, one other chapter which you believe to be well-written, dramatic, and with some sort of a sales hook that a copy writer can use when he writes the ads on your book to go to the consumer and trade press. This package containing, at the most, four chapters and a brief synopsis of the novel, should go to the editor of the publishing house which you believe is now in the field in which your book is located—that is, juvenile, western, detective, light love, etc. Enclose a letter stating as briefly as possible that you are working on a book and here is a sample of what you have, and would the publisher like to see more? If he expresses interest, send him the works; if he does not, your material will be returned in the self-addressed, stamped envelope (S.A.S.E.) you enclosed with the manuscript. You are able to circulate ten publishers in ten months, whereas if you send your entire book, you would be lucky to reach four publishers in ten months. In addition, your book will not get shopworn.

Only publishers who offer a royalty contract are included in these listings. Firms that specialize in subsidy publishing are listed at the end of this section.

ABBEY PRESS, St. Meinrad IN 47577. Editor: John J. McHale. Publishes hardcover and paperback originals, reprints, and anthologies. "Royalty schedule variable; usually 7% of retail price with reasonable advance." Usual advance is $300, but average varies, depending on author's reputation and nature of book. Published 10 titles last year. Will send a catalog to a writer on request. Send query with outline and sample chapter. Reports in 3 weeks. Enclose return postage.
Nonfiction: "Primarily books of general religious interest, but we will be happy to consider queries on other areas, especially marriage and family."

ABELARD-SCHUMAN, LTD., 666 Fifth Ave., New York NY 10019. Phone: 212-489-2200. Senior Editor: Frances Schwartz. Publishes hardcover and paperback originals and translations. Offers standard royalty contract. Published 28 titles last year. Query first. Reports in 4 to 6 weeks. Enclose return postage.

General: Publishes fiction, nonfiction, science, biography, garden, cookbooks, children's books.

ABINGDON PRESS, 201 Eighth Ave. S., Nashville TN 37203. Senior Editor: Emory S. Bucke; College Editor: Pierce S. Ellis, Jr.; Editor of Religious Books: Paul M. Petit; Editor of General Books: Robert J. Hill, Jr.; Juvenile Editor, Nashville: Ernestine Calhoun; Editor of Fine Arts: Richard Loller; Editor of Research Projects: Jean Hager. Payment in royalties. No advance. Published 90 titles last year. Write for guide to preparation of mss. Query first. Reports in 1 month. Enclose return postage.
Nonfiction, Juveniles, and Textbooks: Publishes religious (United Methodist), children's and general books (biography, philosophy, art, music, religion), and college texts. Wants books on marriage, the family, Americana, recreation, and social concerns. Length: 200 pages.

ACADEMIC PRESS, INC., 111 Fifth Ave., New York NY 10003. Editorial Vice-President: James Barsky. Royalty varies. Published 385 titles last year. Will send copy of current catalog to a writer on request. Submit outline, preface and sample chapter. Reports in 1 month. Enclose return postage.
Science: Specializes in scientific, technical and medical works. Textbooks and reference works in natural, behavioral-social sciences at college and research levels.

ACE BOOKS, 1120 Avenue of the Americas, New York NY 10036. Publishes paperback originals and reprints. "All royalty terms depend on material. Standard advances against standard royalty contracts, varying with the quality and nature of the material." Published 240 titles last year. Will send a catalog to a writer on request. Will consider photocopied submissions "if clearly readable." Query first. Address all queries to Evelyn B. Grippo, Vice-President, Editorial. "Include a 1-page or less synopsis of the plot. The editor can then tell quickly if story line is suitable for publication." Reports in 6 weeks. Enclose return postage.
Fiction: "Gothic suspense, mysteries, science fiction, westerns, war novels, nurse novels, modern novels, historicals, double westerns, double science fiction." Length: 55,000 words minimum, "except for doubles." Wants "no short story collections or anthologies."
Nonfiction: "Occult, puzzle books, contemporary problems, nostalgia. No books of limited local interest." Length: 55,000 words minimum.

ACTIVA PRODUCTS, INC., 582 Market St., Suite 1908, San Francisco CA 94104. Editor-in-Chief: Gregory Frazier. Publishes paperback originals and reprints. Royalty is negotiable, but generally runs 6% of net selling price, with $500 advance against earned royalties. Titles published last year: 2. Since books are designed for the craft market, they are generally not sold in the book trade, but are sold to craft, hobby and toy wholesalers, who in turn sell to retail outlets. Will send catalog to writer on request. Query first. If acceptable, will request outline and sample chapters. Queries should be addressed to Gregory Frazier, and accompanied by S.A.S.E. Reports on mss accepted for publication in 3 to 4 weeks. Returns rejected material in 1 week.
Hobbies and Crafts: "We are interested in receiving queries about manuscripts dealing with all aspects of adult crafts and hobbies. We serve a definite market, and are only interested in craft and hobby type how-to books. Some examples are mold-making and casting crafts; needle crafts; jewelry crafts; papier-mache, decoupage; flower crafts; ceramics; stained glass; shell craft, tole painting, enameling, quilting. The writer should be acquainted with all aspects of the particular craft, and be able to explain it lucidly to others, particularly the novice. An ability to photograph the various stages of the craft is extremely helpful, but not mandatory. The writer should be able to produce made-up pieces of the craft. In short, should be professional. We stress quality both in format and content." Current titles include: *Adventures in Celluclay* and *Flower Drying Art.* Word length varies with subject matter.

ADDISONIAN PRESS AND YOUNG SCOTT BOOKS, Juvenile Division of Addison-Wesley Publishing Co., Inc., Reading MA 01867. Editor-in-Chief: Ray Broekel. Publishes hardcover originals. Contracts "vary." Advance is negotiable. Published 21 titles last year. Will send a catalog to a writer on request. Send complete ms for fiction; send outline and sample chapter for nonfiction. Reports in 2 to 3 weeks. Enclose return postage.
Juveniles: Publishes picture books and nonfiction for 4- to 16-year olds.

ADVANCE HOUSE PUBLISHERS, P.O. Box 334, Ardmore PA 19003. Manager: S.N. Davis. Publishes paperback originals. Offers 7½% royalty contract. Published 2 titles last year. "We promote sales through direct mail bulletins. We never advertise. Book dealers sell about ⅓ of our work." Query first for law, science, and business; send outline and 1 sample chapter with outline of chapter headings. Will consider photocopied submissions. Enclose return postage.
Business, Law, Scientific, and Technical: "We publish books in 3 fields: science, law and patents, and business. Our books are specific and are directed to selected audiences. The writer should take a serious approach, based on research or experience."

ADVANCED LEARNING CONCEPTS, INC., 211 W. Wisconsin Ave., Milwaukee WI 53203. Editor-in-Chief: Richard W. Weening. Publishes hardcover and paperback originals. Royalty contract; either at a straight rate, or a fee plus royalties. Advance varies; usually 50% of the contract fee. Titles published last year: 25. Books marketed nationally and internationally by Children's Press and Follett Publishing Co. Will send editorial guidelines to writer on request. Query first for nonfiction. Submit outline and sample chapters for fiction. Will consider photocopied submissions. Returns rejected material in 2 to 3 weeks. Enclose return postage.
Education: Specializes in the development and publication of curriculum and supplementary reading, social studies, math, science, and language arts programs for primary, elementary, and secondary students; early childhood educational programs. "We commission mss and, prior to actual writing, prepare guidelines for the author to follow when doing a ms. Our books are different in subject matter. An early series was on moods and emotions for use by a classroom teacher. Our materials are based on careful research and consultation with university researchers, child psychologists, and a graphic consulting firm with an educational research background. We are publishing a series of books on current sports personalities (for the primary grades), a series of how-to books (ages 6 to 9) and a series of books on moods and emotions for elementary students (grades 4 to 6). We will need good authors for all these projects. If we commission an author, mss should be consistent with the University of Chicago *Manual of Style.* Length will vary with project." Recently completed the Venture Series, a group of 6 books on sports for low-motivated high school students.

AERO PUBLISHERS, INC., 329 Aviation Road, Fallbrook CA 92028. Editor-in-Chief: L. W. Reithmaier. Offers 10% royalty contract. No advance. Published 8 titles last year. Submit chapter outline and sample chapters. Reports in 3 months. Enclose return postage.
Aviation and Science: General science nonfiction: books dealing with aviation and space. Length: 50,000 to 100,000 words. Current titles include *L-1011 and The Lockheed Story* (Ingells), *Aviation and Space Dictionary* (Gentle and Reithmaier), and *Hero Next Door* (Burnham).

ALASKA NORTHWEST PUBLISHING CO., Box 4-EEE, Anchorage AK 99509. Editor: Robert A. Henning. Publishes hardcover and paperback originals. "Contracts vary, depending upon how much editing is necessary. Everybody gets 10% of gross, which averages around 8% because direct mail retail sales are high. Pros may get a flat fee in addition, to increase the percentage. Advances may be paid when ms is completed." Published 12 titles last year. Free catalog to writer on request. "Rejections are made promptly, unless we have 3 or 4 possibilities in the same general field and it's a matter of which one gets the decision. That could take 3 months." Send queries and unsolicited mss to Byron Fish, Book Editor. Enclose return postage.

General Nonfiction: "Alaska, Northern B.C., Yukon, and Northwest territories are subject areas. Emphasis on life in the last frontier, history, outdoor subjects such as hunting and fishing. Writer must be familiar with the North first-hand, from more knowledge than can be gained as a tourist. We listen to any ideas. For example, we recently did a book of woodprints." Art, nature, history, sports, hobbies, recreation, pets, and travel. Length: open. Current titles include *Handloggers* (Alaskana), *Alaskan Igloo Tales* (history), *At Home With the High Ones* (nature), *Richard Harrington's Yukon* (travel), *Alaska Fishing Guide* (sports).

ALDINE PUBLISHING COMPANY (formerly Aldine-Atherton, Inc.), 529 S. Wabash Ave., Chicago IL 60605. Managing Editor: Georganne Marsh. Publishes hardcover originals. Royalty schedule varies. Published 30 titles last year. Query first. Enclose return postage.

Textbooks: Publishes high school and college textbooks.

ALLIANCE PRESS (LONDON) LTD., P.O. Box 593, Times Square Station, New York NY 10036. Affiliate of Diplomatic Press, Inc. Pays 10% of net price. Send query letter with outline and sample chapters to the Editor. Reports in 2 months. Enclose return postage.

Fiction and Nonfiction: Publishes books in every field of human interest—adult fiction, juvenile, history, biography, science, philosophy, the arts, religion and general nonfiction. Length requirements: 65,000 to 125,000 words.

ALLYN & BACON, 470 Atlantic Ave., Boston MA 02110. Publishes hardcover originals. Royalties vary. Query first. Enclose return postage.

Textbooks: Texts for elementary and high schools and colleges.

AMERICAN ASTRONAUTICAL SOCIETY, P.O. Box 746, Tarzana CA 91356. Editor: H. Jacobs. Publishes hardcover originals. Offers 10% royalty contract, or "by arrangement. Advance by arrangement." Published 5 titles last year. Reports in 30 days. Enclose return postage.

Reference, Monograph, History and Technical: Monographs in the field of astronautics but also covering the application of aerospace technology to earth problems. Will consider books only in excess of 100 pages. Historical books or reference books also considered. Books are directed to the specialist or technically oriented layman for use in research establishments, libraries; public, college, or special college-level style. "All our books must relate to astronautics, space sciences and disciplines, and their applications. We have 2 series: Advances in the Astronautical Sciences and Science and Technology." Length: 100 to 600 pages.

AMERICAN CLASSICAL COLLEGE PRESS, P.O. Box 4526, Albuquerque NM 87106. Editor-in-Chief: Leslie Dean. Pays a flat sum plus royalties of 10-15%. Published 14 titles last year. Prefers queries. Enclose return postage.

Nonfiction: Publishes history, biography, scientific phenomena, and philosophy books. Also economics, Wall Street and the stock market. Mss should be short, to the point, informative, and practical. Length: 20,000 to 40,000 words. Publishes The Science of Man Research Books series.

THE AMERICAN WEST PUBLISHING COMPANY, 599 College Ave., Palo Alto CA 94306. Editor of Books: Patricia Kollings. Publishes originals only. Payment on royalty basis. Advances are negotiated. Published 6 titles last year. Submit query with outline, sample chapter and sample illustrations (if applicable) before submitting complete ms. Reports in 2 months. Enclose return postage.

History, Biography, Natural History, and Ecology: Emphasis on the trans-Mississippi West. Standards of writing style and historical and scientific scholarship are extremely high; exceptional in terms of literary merit and scholarship. No fiction or poetry. Especially interested in pictorial history and picture/text combinations on natural history subjects. Length: 150,000 words maximum for standard works; 70,000 for pictorial works. Current titles inlcude *Anasazi, Mark Twain's Mississippi,* and *Ghost Trails.*

THE W. H. ANDERSON CO., 646 Main St., Cincinnati OH 45201. Managing Editor: Jean C. Martin. Offers royalty contract. Send outlines and sample chapters. Reports in 6 weeks. Enclose return postage.
Nonfiction: Mss dealing with law; criminal justice and corrections; public administration.

ARCHITECTURAL BOOK PUBLISHING CO., INC., 10 E. 40th St., New York NY 10016. Editor: Walter Frese. Royalty is percentage of retail price. Prefers queries, outlines and sample chapters. Reports in 2 weeks. Enclose return postage.
Architecture and Industrial Arts: Publishes architecture, decoration, and reference books on city planning and industrial arts. Also interested in history, biography, and science of architecture and decoration.

ARCO PUBLISHING CO., INC., 219 Park Ave. S., New York NY 10003. Editor-in-Chief: David Goodnough; Education Editor: Edward Turner. Publishes hardcover and paperback originals and reprints. Offers standard 10-12½-15% royalty contract; average advance is $1,000. Published about 100 titles last year. Query first. Will consider photocopied submissions. Reports in 4 to 6 weeks. Enclose return postage.
General Nonfiction: Books on all subjects—history, biography, science, the arts (with emphasis on the do-it-yourself approach, instructions, etc.) Interested in educational books, programmed learning, etc. Also study guides, laws for the layman, sports, self-improvement, hobbies, English language, reference, health, antiques. Especially interested in mss on "health and nutrition, sports, and horses." No humor. Length: 60,000 words and up. Recent titles include: *The Basic Book of Antiques* (Michael), *America's Historic Villages and Restorations* (Haas).

ARTISTS & WRITERS PUBLICATIONS, P.O. Box 3692, San Rafael CA 94901. Editorial Director: Doreen Nagle. Publishes paperback originals. Standard minimum book contract of 10-12½-15%. Advances are worked out individually. Published 1 title last year. Submit 2 chapters plus full outline. "If a manuscript strikes us as salable, we will try to sell it via premium/sales incentive marketing—books purchased by manufacturers, etc., that can be offered to their customers." Reports in 6 weeks. Enclose return postage.
General Nonfiction: "We do not want to become a one-style house, but there are certain things we will not publish poetry of any sort and basic cookbooks are among them. Anything with an unusual slant will be considered. Since we are now doing premium/incentive books, we do get orders for all types of manuscripts, but we do not see fiction books in our near future. Want books that are not only informative, but are written in a chatty style utilizing a story format. We will not publish a basic book on anything—especially cooking. We will publish, however, a basic easy-to-use guide for the handyman if it has not been done before and if there is a proven need for it. Aside from books that are requested by our clients, would like to do other unusual cookbooks written by people who have well researched the field: wine, cheese, etc. The type of cookbooks we would like to do must be enjoyed by every member of the house, not just the cook." Other areas of publishing interest include: business, juveniles, reference, self-help and how-to, sports, hobbies, recreation and pets. Length: open.

ASSOCIATED PUBLISHERS' GUIDANCE PUBLICATIONS CENTER, 355 State St., Los Altos CA 94022. Editor: George Pfeil. Publishes paperback originals. "Offer standard minimum book contract, but there could be special cases, different from this arrangement. We might give more to an author who can provide competent artwork, less if he uses our resources for basic material. We have not made a practice of giving advances." Published 3 titles last year. Submit outline and sample chapters, or submit complete ms. Will consider photocopied submissions. Reports in 30 days. Enclose return postage.

Education: "In addition to bibliographies, which we develop and publish ourselves, we are interested in most kinds of guidance materials. We distribute these from many sources; but would consider publication of books and pamphlets suitable for high school students, but only in the field of guidance, including occupational information, college entrance and orientation, and personal and social problems. We are less concerned with a single title than a group of related titles or a series of publications which may be developed over a period of time. We would like a series of career materials which can be produced and sold inexpensively for junior and senior high school students, with or without tape and/or filmstrip materials correlated with them. We would like materials relating to the *Dictionary of Occupational Titles* for student use; a first class student study guide or a series for different levels to and including college freshmen; a series of social dramas for junior and senior high school use; a series of pamphlets on occupations, individually and/or in groups. Although we sell to counselors, most of our own materials are aimed at seventh- to twelfth-grade students and those constitute our main market. The vocabulary level usually should be that of average students in the seventh to tenth grades. We prefer not to publish large volumes; stay away from textbooks for school subjects where there are already many books; do not reach markets below or above high school except for additional sales beyond our primary market; do not sell to bookstores, though some buy from us; do not sell to school and public libraries. We are planning a series of occupational pamphlets, a filing system on American colleges. Someone knowledgeable in labor statistics, employment problems, etc., could do the first one; someone familiar with materials on college entrance could do the latter. Interested in publishing about the energy problem and economic conditions in terms of occupations and their impact on the growth or decline of industries over a long range of time. Definitely not interested in poetry, fiction, and pseudo-scientific material. Books published in following categories only: Economics, Self-help and How-to, Sociology, and Guidance. No strict length requirements."

ASSOCIATION PRESS, 291 Broadway, New York NY 10007. Managing Editor: Robert Roy Wright. Publishes hardcover and paperback originals. Pays 5% royalty for paperbacks; 10% for hardcover. Advance varies, depending on author's reputation and nature of book. Published 30 titles last year. Prefers query with outline and sample chapter. Will consider photocopied submissions. Reports in 5 weeks. Enclose return postage.
General Nonfiction, Education, Religion, Sociology, and Sports: Publishes general nonfiction, religion, youth leadership, youth problems, recreation, sports, national and international affairs, physical fitness, marriage and sex, crafts and hobbies, social work and human relations. "Word length is a function of the subject matter and market of each book;" ranges from 40,000 words up.

ATHENEUM PUBLISHERS, 122 E. 42nd St., New York NY 10017. Editor-in-Chief: Herman Gollob. Published 28 titles last year. For unsolicited mss prefer query, outline, or sample chapter. Submit complete ms for juveniles. All freelance submissions with the exception of juveniles, should be addressed to "The Editors." Reports in 4 weeks. Enclose return postage.
General Fiction and Nonfiction: Publishes adult fiction, history, biography, science (for the layman), philosophy, the arts and general nonfiction. Length: over 40,000 words.
Juveniles: Juvenile nonfiction books for ages 3 to 18. Length: open. Picture books for ages 3 to 8. "No special needs; we publish whatever comes in that interests us. No bad animal fantasy." Dept. Editor: Miss Jean Karl. Margaret K. McElderry Books: Fiction and nonfiction preschool through 18. Interested in anything of quality. Editor: Margaret K. McElderry.

ATHLETIC PRESS, P.O. Box 2314-D, Pasadena CA 91105. Editor-in-Chief: Donald Duke. Publishes paperback originals. Royalty contract "varies, from 5% to 10%, depending on editing required for publication. No advances." Published 3 titles last year. Will send a catalog to a writer on request. Query first. Reports in 2 weeks. Enclose return postage.

Sports: "Athletic training manuals with exercises, diet, etc., for participant improvement in sports of track and field, wrestling, football, etc. Our books are published for the participant—not the coach." Length: open. Dept. Editor: Kevin Ohlson. Current titles include *Physical Conditioning*.

ATLANTIC MONTHLY PRESS, 8 Arlington St., Boston MA 02116. Director: Peter Davison; Associate Director: Upton Birnie Brady; Editor of Children's Books: Emilie McLeod. "Advance and royalties depend on the nature of the book, the stature of the author, and the subject matter." Query letters welcomed. Mss preferred, but outlines and chapters are acceptable. Send outline and sample chapters for juvenile nonfiction; send complete ms for juvenile picture books. Enclose return postage.

General Fiction and Nonfiction: Publishes, in association with Little, Brown and Company, fiction, general nonfiction, juveniles, biography, autobiography, science, philosophy, the arts, belles lettres, history, world affairs and poetry. Length: 50,000 to 200,000 words. For juvenile picture books for children 4 to 8, looks for "literary quality and originality."

AUGSBURG PUBLISHING HOUSE, 426 S. Fifth St., Minneapolis MN 55415. Director, Book Dept.: Roland Seboldt. Payment in royalties on larger books; purchases short books outright. Published 40 titles last year. Prefers queries, outlines and sample chapters. Reports in 1 month. Enclose return postage.

Fiction, Nonfiction, Juveniles, Poetry, and Religion: Publishes primarily religious books. Also nonfiction and fiction, juveniles, and some poetry. Specializes in Christmas literature; publishes "Christmas," an American Annual of Christmas Literature and Art. Length: "varied." Juveniles are usually short.

AURORA PUBLISHERS, INC., 118 16th Ave. S., Nashville TN 37203. Publisher: Dominic de Lorenzo. Publishes hardcover and paperback originals and reprints. Offers standard royalty contract. Usual advance is $500 to $1,000 but this varies, depending on author's reputation and nature of book. Published 10 titles last year. Query first or submit outline and sample chapters. Reports on material within 4 to 6 weeks. Enclose return postage.

General Fiction and Nonfiction: Science fiction, sociology, law, art, how to, religious philosophy, history, cookbooks. Current titles include *Christ's Mass* (Kershaw) and *The Moths & Violets of Vito and Me* (Mason/Mahan).

Academic: Casebooks on literary works and authors.

Juveniles: Preschool through young adult. Books which foster positive self-image. Editors: Shirley George, Carolyn Aylor.

AVIATION BOOK COMPANY, 555 West Glenoaks Blvd., P.O. Box 4187, Glendale CA 91202. Editor: Walter P. Winner. Specialty publisher. Publishes hardcover and paperback originals and reprints. No advance. Published 8 titles last year. Will send a catalog to a writer on request. Query with outline. Reports in 2 months. Enclose return postage.

Nonfiction: Aviation books, primarily of a technical nature and pertaining to pilot training. Young adult level and up. Also aeronautical history.

AVON BOOKS, 959 Eighth Ave., New York NY 10019. Editor-in-Chief: Peter M. Mayer. Executive Editor: Robert Wyatt. Publishes originals and reprints. Minimum royalties: 4% of retail price for first 150,000 copies, 6% thereafter; "frequently higher. Minimum payment is $1,250, but have paid over $100,000 for original mss. Usual advance is $3,500." Published 325 titles last year. Send query for nonfiction and fiction. "For science fiction, contact Bill Van Assen. For juveniles, contact Nancy Coffey, Senior Editor." Current catalog available on request. Reports in 4 to 6 weeks. Enclose return postage.

General Fiction and Nonfiction: Adult fiction, general nonfiction including biography

and juveniles. Interested in original contemporary novels set in America or with American characters. Particularly interested in published authors, especially science fiction. Length: 50,000 to 150,000 words. General nonfiction with the popular touch. Recent titles include *Watership Down, The Wildest Heart.*
Juveniles: Books of interest to ages 7 to 14 and biographies about present-day public figures, personality books, etc. Length: 30,000 to 50,000 words.

AWARD BOOKS, Division of Universal Publishing and Distributing Corp., 235 E. 45th St., New York NY 10017. Editorial Director: Agnes Birnbaum. Publishes paperback originals and reprints. Payment rates vary. Usual advance is $2,000. Royalties 4% and 6%. Published 132 titles last year. Submit outline and sample chapters. Will consider photocopied submissions. Enclose return postage.
Fiction: Action and adventure (especially espionage, combat, western); mysteries, gothics, science fiction, romance, TV and movie tie-ins.
Nonfiction: Topics of current interest; biographies, health and nutrition, sports, games, how-to books. Length: approximately 60,000 words.

BAKER BOOK HOUSE, 1019 Wealthy St., Grand Rapids MI 49506. Publishes originals and reprints. Royalty schedule: 10% on case bound and 5% on paperbacks with escalation clause, except for 150 copies for promotional purposes. Published 175 titles last year. Query first with outline and sample chapter to Dan Van't Kerkhoff. Will send catalog on request. Reports in 4 to 6 weeks. Enclose return postage.
Religion: Religious juveniles, devotions, Bible study aids, reference, and gift books.

BALE BOOKS, Box 50, Sioux Falls SD 57101. Editor-in-Chief: Don Bale, Jr. Publishes hardcover and paperback originals and reprints. Offers standard 10-12½-15% royalty contract; "no advances." Sometimes purchases mss outright for $500. Published 3 titles last year. "Most books are sold through publicity and ads in the coin newspapers." Will send a book list to writers who send S.A.S.E. Will consider photocopied submissions. "Send ms by registered or certified mail. Be sure copy of ms is retained." Reports usually within several months. Enclose return postage.
Nonfiction and Fiction: "Our specialty is coin and stock market investment books; especially coin investment books and coin price guides. We are open to any new ideas in the area of numismatics. The writer should write for a teenage through adult level. Lead the reader by the hand like a teacher, building chapter by chapter. Our books sometimes have a light, humorous treatment, but not necessarily."

BALLANTINE BOOKS, INC., 201 E. 50th St., New York NY 10022. Publishes hardcover and paperback originals and reprints. Royalty contract varies. Published 300 titles last year; about ⅓ were originals. Query first. Enclose return postage.
General: General fiction and nonfiction, with a special interest in the environment and ecology. Also publishes gift books.

BANTAM BOOKS, INC., 666 Fifth Ave., New York NY 10019. Senior Vice President and Editorial Director: Marc H. Jaffe; Assoc. Editorial Director: Allan Barnard; Executive Editor: Grace Bechtold. Principally reprint. "Query first always. No longer accept unsolicited mss. Mss will be returned unread unless they are sent at our request." Published 406 titles last year. "Will consider, in special cases, mss, both fiction and nonfiction, which are aimed specifically at our market, but query first." Current catalog available on request. Reports in 1 month. Enclose return postage.
General Fiction and Nonfiction: Publishes adult fiction and general nonfiction education titles. Length: 75,000 to 100,000 words. Current titles include *Jaws; You Can Profit From a Monetary Crisis.*

BARCLAY HOUSE, 21322 Lassen Ave., Chatsworth CA 91311. Editor: George Karnaookh. Publishes paperback originals. Offers contract for outright purchase or for an advance against royalties, depending on the potential of the material. Average advance is $1,000. Published 72 titles last year. Will send a catalog to writer on request. Send outline and sample chapter. Reports within 4 weeks. Enclose return postage.

Nonfiction: Interested in seeing material dealing with human sexual behavior as well as with nonsexual behavior that hinges on the dynamics of violence. The presentation for the first genre may be in case history form or in straight expository narrative style, but should in both instances include authoritative commentary by the author that draws upon established psychiatric, psychological and sociological sources. The slant, style, and emphasis of books may be best gathered from copies of current titles. Length: 45,000 to 55,000 words.

Fiction: High quality, well-plotted adult novels with contemporary characters, settings and problems. Length: 45,000 to 55,000 words.

BARLENMIR HOUSE PUBLISHERS, 413 City Island Ave., New York NY 10064. Publishes hardcover and paperback originals. Offers standard royalties. Advance varies. Published 12 titles last year. Query first to Editor-in-Chief "with samples of work, brief biography, and S.A.S.E. No unsolicited mss are invited."

Fiction and Nonfiction: No adherence to special schools of writing, age, or ethnic group. Acceptance based solely on original and quality work. For Gallery Series, wants "fine, quality books and discovery literature. Themes range from narrative writing on the American Indian, cosmic and visionary philosophy, health, psychology, how-to, found poems, TV, wrestlers, in diverse free forms, ranging from surreal to real via explosive, original work." Length: approximately 50,000 words for fiction and nonfiction; 80 to 250 ms pages for art, applied art, music; 50 to 80 ms pages for poetry.

A.S. BARNES AND CO., INC., Cranbury NJ 08512. Editor: Miss Dena Rogin. Publishes hardcover and paperback originals and reprints; occasionally publishes translations and anthologies. Contract negotiable: "each contract considered on its own merits." Advance varies, depending on author's reputation and nature of book. Published 100 titles last year. Will send a catalog to a writer on request. Query first. Reports as soon as possible. Enclose return postage.

General Nonfiction: "General nonfiction with special emphasis on history, art, cinema, antiques, sports, and crafts."

BARRE PUBLISHERS, Valley Rd., Barre MA 01005. Editor-in-Chief: Ronald P. Johnson. Publishes hardcover and paperback originals. Offers standard minimum book contract of 10-12½-15%. "We offer few advances." Published 20 titles last year. Will send free catalog to writer on request. Will consider photocopied submissions. Submit outline and sample chapters or complete ms. Reports in 4 weeks. Enclose return postage.

General Nonfiction and Poetry: "We specialize in fine craftsmanship and design. History, Americana, art, travel, photo essays, poetry, New Englandiana, cookbooks, cooking and foods, nature, photography, self-help and how-to, sports, hobbies, recreation and pets. No length requirements; no restrictions for style, outlook, or structure. Our emphasis on quality of manufacture sets our books apart from the average publications. Particularly interested in folk art and crafts." Current titles include *Successful Craftsman.*

BEAU LAC PUBLISHERS, Box 248, Chuluota FL 32766. Publishes hardcover and paperback originals. Query first. Enclose S.A.S.E.

Nonfiction: "Military subjects. Specialist in the social side of service life." Current titles include *Military Weddings and the Military Ball* (Gross & Tomlinson).

BEEKMAN PUBLISHERS, INC., 53 Park Pl., New York NY 10007. Editor-in-Chief: Stuart A Ober. Publishes hardcover originals and reprints. Royalty schedule: 10%. Published 47 titles last year. Will send catalog to writer on request. Submit complete ms. Will consider photocopied submissions. Reports in 1 month. Enclose return postage.

General Nonfiction and Fiction: Specializes in business and economic titles, but welcomes manuscripts on all nonfiction subjects. Special interest in investigative journalism and Americana on the '76 theme. Mainstream fiction.

CHAS. A. BENNETT CO., INC., 809 West Detweiller Dr., Peoria IL 61614. Editor: Michael Kenny. Payment is on royalty basis. Published 8 titles last year. Reports in 2 months. Enclose return postage with ms.
Textbooks: Particularly interested in high school textbook mss on industrial education and home economics. Recently published titles include *Food Service Careers* (Cornelius), *Technology of Industrial Materials* (Kazanas).

BETHANY PRESS, Book Division of Christian Board of Education, P.O. Box 179, St. Louis MO 63166. Editor-in-Chief: Sherman H. Hanson. Publishes hardcover and paperback originals. Standard 10% royalty contract. Published 7 titles last year. Query first. Will not consider photocopied submissions. Reports in 30 days. Enclose return postage.
Nonfiction: Books dealing with Christian experience, church life and programming, Christian education, Bible reading and interpretation. Writer should offer clear prose, readable by lay persons, speaking to their concerns as Christians and churchmen or churchwomen. Recent titles include *The Church Library: Tips and Tools; Sermons From Hell; Help for the Distressed.*

BINFORD & MORT, PUBLISHERS, 2536 S.E. 11th Ave., Portland OR 97202. Editor-in-Chief: L.K. Phillips. Publishes hardcover and paperback originals and reprints. Offers standard 10-12½-15% royalty contract. Usual advance is $500, but average varies, depending on author's reputation and nature of the book. Published 21 titles last year. Writer should "query us first regarding his ms. We prefer complete mss, but will consider partially finished ones." Will consider photocopied submissions. Reports in 6 to 12 weeks. Enclose return postage.
Nonfiction and Fiction: "Books about the Pacific Northwest—historical, scientific, travel, biography, Northwest Americana, geological, archaeological, botanical, marine, etc. Our emphasis is on nonfiction or on strongly historical fiction. Length should be around 60,000 words, but type of ms will determine length in many cases. We are always interested in new material on this region." Recent titles include *Oregon River Tours* (Garren); *Eliza R. Barchus, The Oregon Artist* (Barchus); *Trail to North Star Gold* (Martinsen); *Lost Mines and Treasures of the Pacific Northwest* (Hult); *Black Sand and Gold* (Martinsen).

JOHN F. BLAIR, PUBLISHER, 1406 Plaza Dr., Winston-Salem NC 27103. Editor-in-Chief: John F. Blair. Publishes hardcover originals; occasionally paperbacks and reprints. Royalty to be negotiated. Published 7 titles last year. Will send a catalog on request. Submit complete ms. Reports in 6 weeks; "authors urged to inquire if they have not received an answer within that time." Enclose return postage.
General Fiction, Nonfiction, Juveniles, and Poetry: Adult fiction, juvenile, history, biography, philosophy, the arts, religion, general nonfiction and occasionally poetry. In juveniles, preference given to books for ages 10 through 14 and up; in history and biography, preference given to books having some bearing on the southeastern United States. Does not want anything very technical in philosophy nor very expensive art books. First volumes of poetry should be about 64 pages, complete. No length limits for juveniles. Other mss may be 140 pages or more. Recent titles include *A Wet Butt and a Hungry Gut, Blackbeard the Pirate* (autobiography and biography); *Teach's Light, Jill and The Nutcracker Ballet* (juveniles); *Poetics South, Step Carefully in Night Grass* (poetry); *A Spiritual Divorce* (short stories).

BLAKISTON COLLEGE BOOKS, McGraw-Hill Book Co., 1221 Avenue of the Americas, New York NY 10020. Editor-in-Chief: Joseph J. Brehm. Pays on royalty basis. Published 20 titles last year. Enclose return postage with ms.
Textbooks: Publishes textbooks, major reference books and audiovisual materials in the fields of medicine, dentistry, nursing, and allied health.

THE BOBBS-MERRILL CO., INC., Continuing Education & College Department, 4300 W. 62nd St., Indianapolis IN 46268. Editorial Director: Thomas D. Wittenberg. "Queries are acceptable, but do not send complete manuscripts." Enclose S.A.S.E.

Nonfiction: "We are interested in the following disciplines: Behavioral Sciences, Humanities, Vocational and Technical Books."

THE BOBBS-MERRILL CO., INC., 4 W. 58th St., New York NY 10019. Editor-in-Chief: Eugene Rachlis. Publishes hardcover originals. Offers standard 10-12½-15% royalty contract. Advances vary, depending on author's reputation and nature of book. Published about 90 titles last year. Query first. Address all mail to J. J. Fleckner. No unsolicited mss. Reports in 4 to 6 weeks. Enclose return postage.
General Fiction, General Nonfiction, and Juveniles: Publishes American and foreign novels, suspense, science fiction, film, politics, history, and current events, biography/autobiography. Sorry, no poetry.

THE BOND WHEELWRIGHT COMPANY, Freeport ME 04032. Editor: Thea Wheelwright. Offers 10% royalty contract. No advance. Published 5 titles last year. Query first. Enclose return postage.
Nonfiction: "We are interested in nonfiction only—books that have a regional interest or specialized subject matter (if the writer is an authority), or how-to-do-it books. Length can vary from 50,000 words up, or start at less if there are a lot of illustrations (b&w only)."

BOOKS FOR BETTER LIVING, 21322 Lassen St., Chatsworth CA 91322. Editor: Hedy White. Publishes paperback originals and reprints. Offers standard paperback royalties against an advance that depends on project. Published 25 titles last year. Books aimed at general interest, mass market audiences. Submit outline and sample chapters or query letter. Enclose return postage.
General Nonfiction and Reference: Money, health, nutrition, business, psychology, the occult, women's interest, self-improvement, etc. Length: 50,000 words minimum.

THE BOREALIS PRESS LIMITED, 9 Ashburn Dr., Ottawa, Ontario K2E 6N4, Canada. Editor: W. Glenn Clever. Publishes paperback originals and reprints. Offers 5% maximum, for all rights. No advance offered. Published 10 titles last year. Will send free catalog to writer on request. Submit outline and sample chapters for nonfiction; submit complete ms for poetry and criticism. Will consider photocopied submissions. Reports within 6 months. Enclose S.A.E. and International Reply Coupons.
Nonfiction, Fiction, Juveniles, Biography and Poetry: "Book-length mss of poetry, essays, literary criticism, history, general topics. Biography and children's fiction. No special requirements except that we are interested more in conservative attitudes than in extremes. We publish only Canadian material. We do not want to see work supercharged with sex, violence, or other sensationalism." Length: 60 to 64 pages, not exceeding 25 lines per page.

THOMAS BOUREGY AND CO., INC., 22 E. 60th St., New York NY 10022. Editor: Ms. Ellen LaBarbera. Offers $300 advance on publication date; 10% of retail price on all copies after the original printing of 3,000, to which the $300 applies. Published 60 titles last year. Query first. Reports in 1 month. Enclose return postage.
Fiction: For teenagers and young adults. Publishes romances, nurse and career stories, westerns and gothic novels. Sensationalist elements should be avoided. Length: 50,000 words. Also publishes Airmont Classics Series.

R.R. BOWKER CO., 1180 Avenue of the Americas, New York NY 10036. Editor-in-Chief: Pauline A. Cianciolo; Acquisitions Editor: Patricia G. Schuman; Marketplaces Editor: Jack A. Neal; Directories Editor: Olga S. Weber. Royalty basis by contract arrangement. Published 66 titles last year. Query first. Reports in 2 to 4 weeks. Enclose return postage.
Book Trade and Reference: Publishes books for the book trade and library field, reference books, and bibliographies.

BOWLING GREEN UNIVERSITY POPULAR PRESS, 101 University Hall, Bowling Green State University, Bowling Green OH 43403. Editor: Ray B. Browne.

Publishes hardcover and paperback originals. Offers 10% royalties; no advance. Published 10 titles last year. Will send a catalog to a writer on request. Send complete ms. "Follow MLA style manual." Enclose return postage.

Nonfiction: "Popular culture books generally. We print for the academic community interested in popular culture and popular media." Interested in nonfiction mss on "science fiction, folklore, black culture." Will consider any book-length mss.

BOWMAR, 622 Rodier Dr., Glendale CA 91201. Editor-in-Chief: Karle Lindstrom. Publishes hardcover and paperback originals. Offers standard minimum book contract of 10-12½-15%. Books marketed by direct national sales force. Published 79 titles last year. Query first. "Formal detailed proposal preferred over completed final mss." Catalog available on request. Will consider photocopied submissions. Reports in 1 month. Enclose return postage.

Textbooks: "Special emphasis on early childhood materials. Must be geared to classroom use, textbooks, supplementary reading; writer must be acquainted with latest educational philosophy." Published Monster Books, a series of 12 softcover books; text is taken from children's sentence patterns, written by children, compiled by authors; appropriate for discussion, language development, creative writing and reading. Material must be typed. Current series is ABC Serendipity Series by Albert G. Miller.

BRANDON BOOKS, 21322 Lassen St., Chatsworth CA 91311. Senior Editor: Larry T. Shaw. Publishes paperback originals. "Payment varies according to quality. Standard paperback royalties; $1,000 minimum. In the past, we bought more books for an outright fee, but are now writing more royalty contracts." Usual advance is $1,000, but this varies, depending on author's reputation, and nature of book. Published 78 titles last year. Prefers a query with outline and three sample chapters. "Before submitting, check our latest releases at newsstands or bookstores in order to understand our market requirements." Enclose return postage.

Fiction: Fiction of mass-market appeal, strong male interest and frankly adult in treatment. Novels should be strong on plot, characterization and motivation. Length: 60,000 words and up.

CHARLES T. BRANFORD CO., 28 Union St., Newton Centre MA 02159. Editor: Mrs. Leo L. Jacobs. Pays on royalty basis (10% on retail price when sold at regular discount). Published 29 titles last year. Query before submitting. Reports in 45 days. Enclose return postage.

General Nonfiction: Publishes general nonfiction and books on arts, crafts, natural history, needlework, dolls, antiques, sports, gardening. Current titles include *Canvas Work* (Gray); *Creative Thread Design* (Morris); *Ideas for Patchwork* (Ives); *Technique of Macrame* (Burleson).

GEORGE BRAZILLER, INC., 1 Park Ave., New York NY 10016. Offers standard 10-12½-15% royalty contract. Advance varies, depending on author's reputation and nature of book. Published 28 titles last year. Prefers completed mss. Reports in 6 weeks. Enclose return postage.

General Fiction and Nonfiction: Publishes fiction and nonfiction; literature, art, philosophy, history, science. Length: 70,000 to 90,000 words.

BREVET PRESS, P.O. Box 178, Sioux Falls SD 57101. Publishes hardcover and paperback originals and reprints. Offers standard royalty contract. "We will also, at times, offer a flat rate contract." Published 6 titles last year. Books distributed through book stores and directly to individuals through the mail. "We include extensive advertising and emphasize our books' comprehensiveness, easy reference and readability." Will send a listing and description of books published on request. Query first. Will consider photocopied submissions. Enclose S.A.S.E.

General Nonfiction: "Our books are confined to nonfiction on business management and national, state and local histories. However, in the future, we will be expanding into a wider variety of subjects. We need manuscripts that appeal to the general public. They should be easily read and understood by the man on the street and organized, if necessary, for easy reference. At this time, submitted work should be confined to those on business management and state and local history." Recent titles include *Brevet's Historical Markers & Sites* (state history); *Custer's Prelude to Glory* (General Custer's 1874 expedition into the Black Hills); *Flight of Eagles* (The American Kosciuszko Squadron fighting for Poland during the Polish-Russian War of 1919-20).

WILLIAM C. BROWN CO., PUBLISHERS, 2460 Kerper Blvd., Dubuque IA 52001. Executive Editor: Richard C. Crews. Royalties vary. Query first. Enclose return postage.
Textbooks: College textbooks.

BUTTERWORTHS, 161 Ash St., Reading MA 01867. Phone: 617-944-3323. Chief Executive: Dennis D. Beech. Sliding scale royalty. Flexible advance. Published 75 titles last year. Current catalog available on request. Prefers query with outline and sample chapters. Reports in 2 to 4 weeks. Enclose return postage.
Nonfiction: Publishes legal, medical and other health sciences books of any length.

CAMARO PUBLISHING COMPANY, P.O. Box 90430, Los Angeles CA 90009. Editor-in-Chief: Garth W. Bishop. Publishes paperback originals. "Every contract is different. Many books are bought outright." Published 5 titles last year. Query first. Enclose return postage.
Nonfiction: Books on travel, food, wine. Recently published *Los Angeles on Foot.*

CAROLRHODA BOOKS INC., 241 First Ave. N., Minneapolis MN 55401. Publishes hardcover and paperback originals. "No definite royalty or payment policy. Each situation differs." Will send catalog and author guidelines flier to writer on request. Send complete ms, with or without art, to Rebecca Poole, General Manager. Reports within 3 months. Number of titles published last year: 6. Enclose return postage.
Juveniles: Specializes in fiction picture storybooks for children. No seasonal or religious material. Length: no more than 10 ms pages, double spaced.

JAMES F. CARR BOOKS, 227 E. 81st St., New York NY 10028. Editor-in-Chief: James F. Carr. Publishes hardcover originals and reprints. Royalty schedule varies. Published 1 title last year. Query first. Enclose return postage.
Art: Books in the area of American art history. Currently compiling a multi-volume biographical dictionary of artists in North America. Always interested in biographical work on American artists. Length is flexible.

THE CAXTON PRINTERS, LTD., P.O. Box 700, Caldwell ID 83605. Publisher: Gordon Gipson. Pays royalties of 10%. Usual advance is $500 on paperbacks; minimum of $1,000 on hardcovers. Published 10 titles last year. Catalog available on request. Query before submitting ms. Publisher does not pass on excerpts or synopses, only complete mss. Reports in 4 to 6 weeks. Enclose return postage.
Americana and Politics: Publishes adult books of nonfiction western Americana or of conservative political nature. No fiction, scientific mss. Length: 40,000 words and up. Recent titles include *Timber Country; Logging in the Great Northwest; Running Her Easting Down* (story of the Cutty Sark and other great China Clippers); *The Story of Crater Lake National Park* (illustrated in b&w with early day and current photos).

CELESTIAL ARTS, 231 Adrian Rd., Millbrae CA 94030. Vice-President and General Manager: Jean Louis Brindamour. Publishes paperback originals. Offers standard royalty contract. No advance. "We market worldwide through gift and card shops as well as through retail and wholesale book accounts." Published 40 titles last year. Query first, with outline and sample chapters. Include descriptions or examples of artwork and photos. Will consider photocopied submissions. Reports within 6 weeks. Enclose return postage.
General Nonfiction: Awareness/sensitivity poetry and philosophy utilizing illustrative photography and/or original artwork; instructional, introductory level texts on various

subjects of unique interest or uniquely approached subjects of general interest; occult, health and nutrition, cookbooks, religious and inspirational, biographies, how-to, popular psychology. Current titles include *The Human Dynamo* (Holzer) and *Wells Fargo: The Legend* (Robertson).

CHAIN STORE PUBLISHING CORP., 2 Park Ave., New York NY 10016. Publishing Director: Richard J. Staron. Publishes hardcover and paperback originals. Standard minimum book contract considered individually. No advance. Books marketed through house ads and direct mail. Published 5 titles last year. Will send catalog to writer on request. Write for copy of guidelines for writers. Query first or submit outline and sample chapters. Will consider photocopied submissions. Reports on accepted material in 2 months. Immediate reports on rejected material. Enclose return postage.
Business: "Reference, guideline or how-to books dealing with all aspects of management, administration and planning in mass retailing, including supermarket, drug store, variety and general merchandise, retailing, discount and restaurant fields. Books aimed at store management, regional management and/or top management. Length: 125 to 400 pages. Also paperbacks on topical problems and issues in the same retail fields. Length: 128 to 150 pages. Training manuals for all levels of employees in the same fields. Length: 90 to 160 pages. Mss should be practical and factual, giving concrete suggestions. Follow Chicago *Manual of Style.*" Recent titles include *Planning and Operating a Successful Food Service Operation* (Kahrl) and *Security Control: Internal Theft* (Curtis).

CHARTERHOUSE BOOKS INCORPORATED, 750 Third Ave., New York NY 10017. Editor-in-Chief: Carol Eisen Rinzleo. Publishes hardcover fiction and nonfiction. Offers standard royalty contract. Distributes books through David McKay Co., Inc. Published 20 titles last year. Will send catalog to a writer on request. Query first or submit outline and sample chapters for nonfiction; submit outline and sample chapters for other material. Will consider clean photocopied submissions. Reports in 3 to 4 weeks. Enclose return postage.
General Nonfiction and Fiction: "We publish general trade books, with emphasis on quality fiction and works of social interest, especially in the political, historical, and economic fields; also a strong interest in biography. We're not aiming at any special audience. We want anything really good of its kind. We don't want custom-tailored books, but works that grow out of a strong impulse on the writer's end. We're looking especially for nonfiction that has an on-going life, both in backlist sales of hardcover editions and a quality paperback edition." Length varies between 40,000 and 120,000 words.

CHATEAU PUBLISHING, INC., P.O. Box 20432, Herndon Station, Orlando FL 32814. Editor-in-Chief: Marcia Roen. Publishes hardcover and paperback originals. Standard minimum book contract of 10-12½-15%. Advance varies. Published 3 titles last year. Will consider photocopied submissions. Query first. Enclose return postage.
General Nonfiction, Biography, Cookbooks, Hobbies, and Sports: Biography, book trade, cookbooks, humor, law, self-help and how-to, sports, hobbies, recreation and pets; criminology. Recent titles include *The Greatest Diet in the World* and *You're on the Air With Mike Miller.*

CHILDRENS PRESS, 1224 W. Van Buren Ave., Chicago IL 60607. Managing Editor: Joan Downing. "Outright purchase, or $500 advance against 10¢ to 20¢ per book, for juvenile picture books. Outright purchase only for juvenile nonfiction books." Send outline with sample chapters or complete ms for juvenile nonfiction; send complete ms for picture books. Do not send finished artwork with ms. Reports in 3 to 6 weeks. Enclose return postage.
Juveniles: Publishes only children's books. Nonfiction, curriculum-oriented material for supplementary use in elementary classrooms, and easy picture books for beginners. For juvenile nonfiction, wants easy-to-read curriculum-oriented books. Unusual social studies for grades 2 to 5. Length: 50 to 2,000 words. For picture books, needs are very broad, but no fantasy or rhyme. Picture books should be geared to kindergarten

to grade 3. Length: 50 to 1,000 words. Current titles include *Heroes, Events, and Cities of the Revolution* (Lee); *Enchantment of Africa* (Carpenter); *Blue Bug's Beach Party* (Poulet); *Rackety That Very Special Rabbit* (Friskey); *The Story of Fort Sumter* (Burney); *Welcome to the World Books* (Friskey).

CHILTON BOOK COMPANY, 201 King of Prussia Rd., Radnor PA 19089. Editor-in-Chief: John Kelly. Senior Editor, Trade Books: Benton Arnovitz; Senior Editor, Arts & Crafts: Crissie Lossing; Senior Editor, Automotive: Paul Driscoll. Publishes hardcover and paperback originals and paperback reprints. Offers standard royalty contract; advance is negotiable. Published 99 titles last year. Query first with outline and sample chapter. Reports in 2 to 8 weeks. Enclose return postage.
General Nonfiction: How-to, biography, history, popular music, games (chess) and recreation, nature, sports, popular psychology, popular science, travel, sociology and religion, current events, reference, business, occult, arts and crafts, and automotive. No fiction, juveniles, or poetry. Minimum length: arts and crafts, 35,000 words; all other categories, 50,000 words. Many of the general trade titles have a utilitarian aspect and are aimed at a college age through 30s market. Current titles include: *The Rise of Japanese Baseball Power* (Obojski); *The Story of The Jewish Defense League* (Kahane); *Build Your Own Greenhouse* (Neal); *Why Did You Do That?* (Torrey); *Cooking Crystal Craft* (Heller).

CHRONICLE BOOKS, 870 Market St., San Francisco CA 94102. A division of the Chronicle Publishing Co., publisher of *The San Francisco Chronicle.* Editor: Phelps Dewey. Publishes hardcover and paperback originals, reprints, and anthologies. Offers standard royalty contract. No advance. Published 12 titles last year. Send query with outline and sample chapter. "We prefer outline and sample chapter to complete ms." Reports in 1 month. Enclose return postage.
General Nonfiction: Current titles are in the fields of animals, architecture, conservation, food, history, the outdoors, sports, travel. Length: 60,000 to 100,000 words.

CITADEL PRESS, 120 Enterprise Ave., Secaucus NJ 07094. Editor-in-Chief: Allan J. Wilson. Publishes hardcover and paperback originals; paperback reprints. Offers standard minimum book contract of 10-12½-15%. Published 65 titles last year. Will send a catalog to writer for $1. Will consider photocopied submissions. Query first or submit outline and sample chapters. Reports in 6 weeks to 3 months. Enclose return postage.
Nonfiction and Fiction: Americana, biography, history, filmography, occult, black studies. Highly selective, offbeat, sensational fiction. Not interested in mss dealing with religion, poetry, theater, or current politics. Length: 70,000 words minimum. Recent titles include *The Girls of Nevada* and *The Films of Rita Hayworth.*

CLARKE, IRWIN & CO., LTD., 791 St. Clair Ave. W., Toronto, Ont., Canada, M6C 1B8. Publishes originals and reprints in hardcover and paperback. Royalty schedule varies. Published 22 titles last year. Will send catalog to writer on request. Send outline plus sample chapter, or completed mss. Reports in 8 weeks. Enclose S.A.E. and International Reply Coupons.
Fiction, Nonfiction, and Poetry: General nonfiction, biography, belles lettres, fiction, 60,000 words and up; short story, poetry collections. Particularly interested in Canadian subjects. Poetry mss should contain at least 64 poems. If an author has illustrations to accompany his ms, list them, but submit only 2 or 3 samples with ms. Current titles include *Crafts Canada* (Abrahamson), and *Lovers & Others* (Sutton).

CLIFF'S NOTES, INC., Box 80728, Lincoln NE 68501. Editor: Harry Kaste. Publishes paperback originals. Outright purchase, with full payment upon acceptance of ms. Published 13 titles last year. Current catalog available on request. Query. Contributors must be experienced teachers with appropriate special interests; usually have Ph.D. degree. Reports in 4 weeks. Enclose return postage.
Nonfiction: Publishes paperback study aids on literary classics and works of ideas for high school and college students. Length: 35,000 to 50,000 words. Currently

emphasizing new series of subject matter course outlines with compensation to be on royalty basis. Also occasional trade or textbooks of special merit.

COLGATE UNIVERSITY PRESS, Hamilton NY 13346. Editor-in-Chief: R. L. Blackmore. Publishes hardcover originals, reprints, and an annual journal about the Powys family of writers and their circle. No other subjects at this time. Offers standard royalty contract; "rarely an advance." Published 3 titles last year. Will send a catalog to a writer on request. Query first. Will consider photocopied submissions. Reports in 1 month. Enclose return postage.
Biography: "Books by or about the Powyses: John Cowper Powys, T. F. Powys, Llewelyn Powys. Our audience is general and scholarly." Length: open. Current titles include these books by John Cowper Powys: *Obstinate Cymric, Dostoievsky, The Inmates, Two & Two, Real Wraiths.*

COLLIER-MACMILLAN CANADA, LTD., 1125 B Leslie St., Don Mills, Ont., Canada. Publishes both originals and reprints in hardcover and paperback. Advance varies, depending on author's reputation and nature of book. Published 35 titles last year. Always query. Reports in 6 weeks. Enclose S.A.E. and International Reply Coupons.
General Nonfiction: "Topical subjects of special interest to Canadians; how-to books."
Textbooks: Recently inaugurated a strong emphasis on school and college text publication. History, geography, science, economics, and social studies: mainly texts conforming to Canadian curricular requirements. Also resource books, either paperback or pamphlet for senior elementary and high schools. Length: open.

COLORADO ASSOCIATED UNIVERSITY PRESS, University of Colorado, 1424 Fifteenth St., Boulder CO 80302. Editor: Margaret C. Shipley. Publishes hardcover and paperback originals. Offer standard 10-12½-15% royalty contract; "no advances." Published 9 titles last year. Will send a catalog to a writer on request. Query first. Will consider photocopied submissions "if not sent simultaneously to another publisher." Reports in 3 months. Enclose return postage.
Nonfiction: "Scholarly and regional." Length: 250 to 500 ms pages. Current titles include *Charles Dickens Sketches* (literary scholarship) and *The New West* (photographic essay).

COLUMBIA UNIVERSITY PRESS, 562 W. 113th St., New York NY 10025. Editor-in-Chief: John D. Moore. Publishes hardcover and paperback originals. Royalty contract to be negotiated. Published 102 titles last year. Query first. Enclose return postage.
Nonfiction: "General interest nonfiction of scholarly value."
Scholarly: Books in the fields of literature, philosophy, fine arts, Oriental studies, history, social sciences, science, law.

CONCORDIA PUBLISHING HOUSE, 3558 S. Jefferson Ave., St. Louis Mo. 63118. Pays royalty on retail price; outright purchase in some cases. Current catalog available on request. Published 40 titles last year. Send outline and sample chapter for nonfiction; complete mss for fiction. Reports in 3 months. Enclose return postage.
Religion, Juveniles, and Fiction: Publishes Protestant, general religious, theological books and periodicals; music works, juvenile picture and beginner books and adult fiction. "As a religious publisher, we look for mss that deal with Bible stories, Bible history, Christian missions; and mss that deal with ways that readers can apply Christian beliefs and principles to daily living. Any ms that deals specifically with theology and/or doctrine should conform to the tenets of the Lutheran Church-Missouri Synod. We suggest that, if authors have any doubt about their submissions in light of what kind of mss we want, they first correspond with us."

CONSTRUCTION PUBLISHING CO., INC., 2 Park Avenue, New York NY 10016. Editor-in-Chief: William H. Edgerton. Publishes originals and reprints in both hardcover and paperback. Offers "negotiable" royalty. Published 8 titles last year.

Markets by direct mail only. Will send catalog to a writer on request. Query first, or submit outline and sample chapters or complete ms. Will consider photocopied submissions. Reports in 1 to 2 weeks. Enclose return postage.

Technical: "Anticipated titles will cover the subject areas of construction management, value engineering, computer applications in design and construction, management of the professional design firm, minority group contractors, and trade-by-trade estimating handbooks. In addition the firm will publish pricing books in other subject areas overlapping construction such as coverage of machinery and equipment prices. Subject should be construction related."

DAVID C. COOK PUBLISHING CO., 850 N. Grove Ave., Elgin IL 60120. Editor-in-Chief: David C. Cook III. Publishes paperback originals and reprints. Offers 6% of retail price up to 150,000; then 8%. Average advance is $1,000. Write for editorial guidelines sheet. Will consider photocopied submissions. Submit outline and sample chapters or query to Mrs. Isabel Erickson, New Products Editor. "Type double-spaced; retain a copy yourself." Reports in 8 weeks. Enclose return postage.

Religion: "We are interested in paperback books for children, young adults, and adults; true experience with Christian application; fiction (especially children's); Christian education topics; how-to-do-it type instructions. We're planning Church/family in action series; Christian Education Series; and Church Heritage Series. We'd like mss about Christian family life; Christian apologetics on a popular level; books dealing with world and social issues that admit Christian conclusions. Our audience is mainly Evangelical church people, but we also sell paperbacks to mass market." Adult Trade Fiction Editor: Isabel Erickson; Art Editor: Ed Elsner; Juveniles and Religion Editor: Timothy Udd.

CORAL REEF PUBLICATIONS, INC., 1127 S. Patrick Dr., Satellite Beach FL 32937. Editor-in-Chief: John C. Roach, Jr. Publishes hardcover originals. Offers standard minimum book contract of 10-12½-15%. Negotiable advance depends on author and material, but usually $1,000. Published 1 title last year. Submit outline and sample chapters or complete ms. Will send free catalog to writer on request. Will consider photocopied submissions. Use Chicago *Manual of Style.* Reports within 2 months. Enclose return postage.

General Nonfiction: Military history, history, film history, biographies, autobiographies. Factual information pertaining to subject written about. Length: 60,000 words minimum. Planning the following series: American Film History, American Military History.

Fiction: All fiction paperback originals will appear under the Neptune Books logo, a division of Coral Reef Publications, Inc. Length: 40,000 words and up. Will look at all fiction. Current titles include *The U-237 in the Devil's Triangle.*

CORDOVAN CORPORATION, 5314 Bingle Rd., Houston TX 77018. Editor-in-Chief: Bob Gray. Publishes hardcover and paperback originals and reprints under the Cordovan Press, Horseman Books, and Fisherman Books imprints. Offers standard minimum book contract of 10-12½-15%. Published 7 titles last year. Marketed heavily by direct mail and through various consumer and trade periodicals. Will send editorial guidelines sheet to writer on request. Will consider photocopied submissions. Query first or submit outline and sample chapters. Reports in 1 month. Enclose return postage.

Nonfiction: Cordovan Press, a trade book division, seeks books on Texas history for the history buff interested in Texana. Horseman Books are practical, how-to books on horse training, grooming, feeding, showing, riding, etc., either by experts in the field or 'as told to' a writer by an expert. Fisherman Books are how-to, where-to, when-to books on fishing in Texas and/or the Southwest. Author must be noted expert in fishing, or be retelling what a noted expert told him. "The emphasis is on plain language in all of these lines. Short sentences. Make the verbs sing the song. Pungent quotes. Don't try to snow the readers; they are too sharp and already know most of the score in all areas. Use humor when it isn't forced." Length: 150 ms pages. Recent titles include *Texas: 1874; Applied Horse Psychology; Fishing the Bays of Texas.*

CORNELL MARITIME PRESS, INC., Box 109, Cambridge MD 21613. Publisher: Robert F. Cornell. Hardcover and quality paperbacks, both originals and reprints. Payment is on regular trade publishers' royalty basis: 10% for first 5,000 copies, 12½% for second 5,000 copies, 15% on all additional. Revised editions revert to original royalty schedule. Published 9 titles last year. Will send catalog on request. Send queries first, accompanied by writing samples and outlines of book ideas. Reports in 2 to 4 weeks. Enclose return postage.
Marine: Nonfiction relating to marine subjects, highly technical; manuals; how-to books on any maritime subject. Current titles include *Export/Import Traffic Management, Advanced First Aid Afloat.*

R.D. CORTINA CO., INC., 136 W. 52nd St., New York NY 10019. General Editor: MacDonald Brown. Pays on a fee and a royalty basis. Published 32 titles last year. Do not send unsolicited mss; send outline and sample chapter. Reports in 2 months or less. Enclose return postage.
Textbooks: Publishes language teaching textbooks for self-study and school; also publishes language teaching phonograph records and tapes. Materials of special ESL interest. Word length varies.

COWARD, McCANN & GEOGHEGAN, 200 Madison Ave., New York NY 10016. President and Editor-in-Chief: John J. Geoghegan. Pays on a royalty basis. For juveniles, offers 5% to 10% royalties; for juvenile nonfiction, advance is $500 to $3,000. Unsolicited mss will be returned unread. Query the editor, who will advise whether to submit ms. Enclose return postage.
General Fiction and Nonfiction: Publishes novels, including mysteries (no westerns or light or salacious love stories); outstanding nonfiction of all kinds; religious, history, biography (particularly on American figures). Also interested in humor. All should have general appeal. Length: 60,000 words and up.
Juveniles: "We will look at anything. Our needs vary considerably. Want picture books for ages 4 to 12. Want nonfiction for ages 4 and up."

CRAFTSMAN BOOK COMPANY OF AMERICA, 542 Stevens Ave., Solana Beach CA 92075. Editor-in-Chief: Gary Moselle. Publishes paperback originals. Royalty of 12½ to 15% of gross revenues, regardless of quantity sold. Published 8 titles last year. "About 75% of our sales are directly to the consumer and since royalties are based on gross revenues, the actual revenue realized is maximized." Will send free catalog to writer on request. Will consider photocopied submissions. Submit outline and sample chapters. Reports in 2 weeks. Enclose return postage.
Technical: "We publish technical books and are aggressively looking for queries and outlines on manuscripts related to construction, carpentry, masonry, plumbing, civil engineering, building estimating, chemical engineering and petroleum technology. Our books are written as practical references for professionals in their respective fields and each book should be written to answer practical questions and solve typical problems. Emphasis is on charts, graphs, illustrations, displays and tables of information. We are producing a series on how to become a successful construction contractor, construction estimator, civil engineer, etc. We can use practical, descriptive information. We don't want to see reprints of magazine articles and isolated essays which do not have the breadth or scope to warrant consideration for publication." Recent titles include *Work Items for Construction Estimating.*

CRAIN BOOKS, 740 Rush St., Chicago IL 60611. Editor-in-Chief: Melvin J. Brisk. Publishes hardcover and paperback originals and reprints. Standard minimum book contract, but there are variations depending on the salability of the book. Published 6 titles last year. Marketed by direct mail and distribution through bookstores. Will send free catalog to writer on request. Will consider photocopied submissions. Query first, with outline and sample chapters. Reports on material accepted for publication in 3 months. Returns rejected material immediately. Enclose return postage.
Business: "We prefer practical, how-to, problem-solving books for both the professional business and college market, since we publish in both areas. Books aimed at the professional businessman should offer something distinctive, either designed

to increase profits of company or expertise of executives. Business, marketing, communications, automotive, insurance, graphic arts books. We try to stay away from topical themes or current subjects that do not stand the test of time. We do not want books such as 'How I Made $1,000,000 in the Stock Market.' Too often, these get-rich-quick titles do not measure up." Recent titles include *Successful Direct Marketing Methods* (Stone), a comprehensive work on direct response techniques.

CRANE, RUSSAK & COMPANY, INC., 347 Madison Ave., New York NY 10017. Editor-in-Chief: Ben Russak. Publishes hardcover originals. On monographs, offers no royalty for first 1,000 copies sold, 7% on the second 1,000 copies, and 10% on all copies sold after the first 2,000. No advances. "We promote our books by direct mail to the exact market for which each book is intended." Submit outline and sample chapters. Reports in 1 month. Enclose return postage.
Technical and Reference: "We publish scientific and scholarly works at the graduate and reference level: postgraduate textbooks and reference books for scholars and research workers. Our publications also appeal to members of professional societies. We'd like to see manuscripts on large-scale systems analysis in relation to solution of large-scale social problems. But do not send any popular material or matter which is intended for sale to the general public." Length: 60,000 to 120,000 words.

CREATION HOUSE, INC., 499 Gundersen Dr., Carol Stream IL 60187. Editor: Marjorie Jantzen. Publishes hardcover and paperback originals. Offers standard royalty contract. Published 15 titles last year. Will send a catalog to a writer on request. Send query with outline and sample chapter. Follow Chicago *Manual of Style.* Reports in 1 to 2 months. Enclose return postage.
Religion and Philosophy: "We publish exclusively evangelical Christian literature, primarily mss dealing with contemporary issues or subjects of interest to a wide spectrum of readers of religious books. This would include social problems, personal ethics, biography, autobiography, devotional, some religious fiction, and studies of the Bible in general. We publish mostly popular type books although we do have a few of a more scholarly nature." Curent titles include *Finger Lickin' Good* (Sanders), *What's a Nice Person Like You Doing Sick?* (Parker), *A School for Peter* (Matson).

CRESTLINE PUBLISHING CO., Box 48, Glen Ellyn IL 60137. Editor-in-Chief: George H. Dammann. Publishes hardcover automotive books. Usually offers 10% royalty. Negotiable advance. Published 2 titles last year. Will send free catalog to writer on request. Query first. Reports within 1 month. Enclose return postage.
History: "100% keyed to the serious automotive buff, primarily antique auto enthusiasts of all ages who want quality pictorial reference works on automotive history. We publish highly specialized automotive histories, both on a marque (make) basis, such as the complete history of Chevrolet, Ford, Buick, etc., or on a type basis, such as funeral cars, fire engines, etc. Since we are so highly specialized, a writer would have to work under our direction, starting with query, and following through from there. A writer must have a thorough knowledge of the subject he wants to write about, be able to produce sufficient material to 'fill the book' and be able to write. Crestline uses a definite pictorial format from which it will not vary. Each book contains 1,500 to 2,000 photos, with the major portion of the story told via captions. We don't want any collections of old ads, reprints of shop manuals for old auto books, and no textual works. Our books are strictly photo stories." Current titles include *70 Years of Chrysler* (automotive series).

CRITERION BOOKS, 666 Fifth Ave., New York NY 10019. Phone: 212-489-2200. Senior Editor: Frances Schwartz. Publishes hardcover originals. Offers standard royalty agreements and advances. Published 5 titles last year. Catalog available from Publicity Dept. Query first. Reports in 8 weeks. Enclose return postage.
Fiction: Quality fiction, both historical and contemporary, including science fiction, mysteries, adventure stories.
Nonfiction: Select authoritative nonfiction, including crafts books and how-to's.

Juveniles: Juveniles for ages 9 through 14 and up. Prefers 20,000 words for younger groups, 25,000 to 35,000 for junior and senior high level mss.

THOMAS Y. CROWELL CO., 666 Fifth Ave., New York NY 10019. Senior Editor: Frances Schwartz. Editor-in-Chief, Trade and Reference Dept.: Paul Fargis. Send trade submissions to Priscilla Logue. Reference Editor for submissions: Pat Barrett. Offers standard 10-12½-15% royalty contract. Published 180 titles last year. Query first. Reports in 1 to 2 months. Enclose unglued return postage.
Nonfiction, Juveniles, and Textbooks: "Trade and reference books, children's books, college and secondary school reference books. Interested in general books of an informational nature."

CROWN PUBLISHERS, 419 Park Ave., S., New York NY 10016. Editor-in-Chief: Herbert Michelman. Contracts offered on basis of stature of writer, outline, subject and sample material. For juveniles, offers "10% against catalog retail price on books for older children; for picture books, 5% of the catalog retail price to the author and 5% to the artist. However, royalty scales may vary. Advance varies, depending on author's reputation and nature of book." Published 225 titles last year. Will send catalog on request. Prefers queries. Send complete ms for juvenile picture books. Address mss to department editor. Reports in 2 to 6 weeks. Enclose return postage.
General Fiction and Nonfiction: General fiction and nonfiction; pictorial histories, popular biography, science, books on decorative arts and antiques, crafts; some on music, drama and painting. Current titles include *Kovel's Complete Antiques Price List, Fascinating World of the Sea, Fun With Growing Herbs Indoors.* Senior Editors: Millen Brand, David McDowell; Special Projects: Brandt Aymar; Collector's Books: Kay Pinney; Science: Paul Nadan.
Juveniles: For juvenile nonfiction for all ages, wants "contemporary issues of a social and political nature. Length depends on the book." Picture books for preschoolers to children 7 years old "should be approached in terms of telling a good story. Length depends on the book." Children's Books Editor: Norma Jean Sawicki.

CUSTOMBOOK, INCORPORATED, The Custom Bldg., South Hackensack NJ 07606. A new opportunity for writer-reporters has been developed by Custombook, Inc., nationwide publishers of color editions for churches. "These limited editions are published in conjunction with special occasions such as anniversaries, construction, renovations or for general education. As a result of major technical breakthroughs, such limited color editions are now practical for the first time. The books feature full-color photographs and the story of each church, its history, stained glass, symbolism, services, and organizations. Writers are being sought in most regions of the country to work. Recommendations are being sought from talented writers as to which churches would be the best subject for their initial Custombook. Older churches with major anniversaries (10th, 25th, 50th, 100th), new construction, or renovations (church, religious school, or convent), would be good subjects. The company will then contact the churches recommended by writers. $50 will be paid to any individual whose recommendation of a church eventually results in a Custombook. The organization will at the same time evaluate previous written efforts of this individual. If their editorial staff engages the writer to prepare the ms for the book, and the writer completes the ms himself, he will be paid $200 for his initial effort. Additional assignments may then follow from our own sources or from additional recommendations by the writer." Further details on the program are available from Mrs. Joan Curtis, Editor, at the above address.

DARTNELL CORPORATION, 4660 North Ravenswood Ave., Chicago IL 60640. Editorial Director: John Steinbrink. Publishes manuals, reports, hardcovers. Royalties: sliding scale. Published 12 titles last year. Send outline and sample chapter. Reports in 4 weeks. Enclose return postage.
Business: Interested in new material on business skills and techniques in management, supervision, administration, advertising sales, etc. Current titles include *Job Enrichment Programs* (business management) and *How to Make Sales Meetings Come Alive* (sales/marketing).

DASEIN-JUPITER HAMMON PUBLISHERS, G.P.O. Box 2121, New York NY 10001. Editor-in-Chief: A. Rini. Offers standard royalty contract. Published 15 titles last year. Query first. Reports in 90 days. Enclose return postage.
Nonfiction and Fiction: Trade books.

DAUGHTERS, INC., Plainfield VT 05677. Publishes paperback originals. Royalty contract starts at 15% with graduated increases to 20%. All advances are $1,000. Published 8 titles last year. Will send catalog to writer on request. Will consider photocopied submissions. Submit complete ms. Reports in 2 months. Enclose return postage.
Fiction: "We only consider novels. Full-length feminist novels."

DAVIS PUBLICATIONS, INC., 50 Portland St., Worcester MA 01608. Published 10 titles last year. Write for copy of guidelines for authors. Submit complete ms. Enclose return postage.
Art and Reference: Publishes art and craft books. "Keep in mind the reader for whom the book is written. For example, if a book is written for the teacher, avoid shifting from addressing the teacher to addressing the student. Include illustrations with text. All illustrations should be collated separately from the text, but keyed to the text. Photos should be good quality original prints. Well-selected illustrations can explain, amplify, and enhance the text. It is desirable for the author's selection of illustrations to include some extras. These may be marked 'optional.' The author should not attempt to lay out specific pages. Poorly selected illustrations or too many competing illustrations in a short space can mar a book. For instance, if you are planning a 125- to 150-page book and you have over 300 photos (more than 2 photos per page, average), you probably have too many."

DAW BOOKS, INC., 1301 Avenue of the Americas, New York NY 10019. Editor: Donald A. Wollheim. Publishes paperback originals and reprints. Standard paperback book contract with advances starting at $1,500. Published 59 titles last year. Books are distributed nationally and internationally by The New American Library. Submit complete ms. Will not consider photocopied submissions. Reports in 4 to 8 weeks. Enclose return postage with ms.
Fiction: "Science fiction only, 5 titles a month. About 70% are original works. Mainly novels with occasional collections of the short stories of one author (name authors only). Space flight, future adventure, scientific discovery, unusual concepts, and all the vast range of s-f conceptions will be found in our works. We prefer good narrative presentation without stress on innovations, avant-garde stunts, etc." Length: 55,000 to 75,000 words.

THE JOHN DAY COMPANY, INC., 666 Fifth Ave., New York NY 10019. Phone: 212-489-2200. Senior Editor: Frances Schwartz. Publishes hardcover originals. Royalty schedule varies. Will send a catalog to writer on request. Query first. Reports in 4 to 7 weeks. Enclose return postage.
General: Publishes adult fiction, juveniles, history, biography, science, and books on the arts. "Adult fiction is not a large field for us; we have never published anything approaching 'pulp' fiction, so we have a rather high general standard of excellence in this field's requirements. Our juvenile books are primarily of an educational-supplementary materials nature, or story books which are unique; 'classic' enough to merit special attention."

DELL PUBLISHING CO., INC. (including Delacorte Press), 245 E. 47th St., New York NY 10017. Book Division. Publishes hardcover and paperback originals and reprints. Standard royalty schedule. Published 416 titles last year. Query first always. "Mss that arrive without a preceding query answered in the affirmative by a member of our staff will have to be returned unread. On fiction queries, we would like to know what sort of book the author has written or proposes to write—whether straight novel, romance-suspense, mystery, historical, or Gothic. A paragraph further describing the story would also be helpful." Send complete ms for juveniles. Reports in 8 to 10 weeks. Enclose return postage.

General Fiction and Nonfiction: Publishes adult fiction; general nonfiction including philosophy, biography, history, religion, science, the arts; juvenile.

Juveniles: Delacorte Press children's books: poetry, history, sports and science for ages 12 and over; history, social science and fiction for intermediate level; picture books for the very young. Length: 30,000 to 50,000 words for ages 12 to 16. Juvenile Editor: Ronald Buehl.

T.S. DENISON AND COMPANY, INC., 5100 W. 82nd St., Minneapolis MN 55437. Editor: Lawrence M. Brings. Publishes hardcover and paperback originals. "Flat rate royalty per thousand copies sold. Some mss purchased outright. No advance." Will send a catalog to a writer on request. Submit complete ms. Will not consider photocopied submissions. Enclose return postage.

Education and Juveniles: Juveniles: 300 to 1,500 words, Early Childhood Series, controlled vocabulary; Primary and Upper Grades, coordinated with units of classroom study. Biography: Men of Achievement Series, on assignment only. From 200 to 400 standard page length. Subject must give consent and agree to approve the finished ms. Also science books for elementary and high school classroom use. Length varies. Publishes all types of aids for teachers, particularly in elementary grades.

DENLINGER'S PUBLISHERS, P.O. Box 76, Fairfax VA 22030. Editor-in-Chief: Mrs. R. Annabel Rathman. Royalty varies, depending upon type of ms; averages 10%. Specific information given upon receipt of query indicating type of projected ms. No advance. Published 6 titles last year. Reports in 3 months. Enclose return postage.

Fiction and Nonfiction: Publishes fiction, nonfiction, general publications, books on dog breeds (not dog stories). Length varies, depending upon type of publication.

THE DIAL PRESS, INC., 1 Dag Hammarskjold Plaza, New York NY 10017. Editor-in-Chief: Richard Marek. Pays on a royalty basis. Usual advance is $1,500 minimum, depending on author's reputation and nature of book. Published 70 titles last year. Query first. Reports in 6 weeks or sooner. Enclose return postage.

General Fiction and Nonfiction: "No definite rule governing types of material published." Length: 65,000 words minimum.

Juveniles: Editor of Children's Books: Phyllis Fogelman.

DIANA PRESS, INC., 12 W. 25th St., Baltimore MD 21218. Editors: Casey Czanik, Nancy Myron, Coletta Reid. Publishes paperback originals and reprints. Offers standard minimum book contract of 10-12½-15%. Average advance is $1,000. Published 5 titles last year. "We sell most of our books to women's bookstores, alternative bookstores, university bookstores and women's studies classes. We do a very lively direct mail-order business for women in remote areas." Will send free catalog and editorial guidelines to writer on request, if S.A.S.E. is enclosed. Will consider photocopied submissions. Query first. Enclose return postage.

Fiction, Nonfiction, Juveniles, Poetry: "We are a feminist publishing house. We publish books by women only. We publish poetry, children's books, nonfiction, fiction and many article anthologies. We are interested in works that aid in building an independent women's culture and consciousness. We don't want to see poetry that is self-indulgent and undisciplined. We welcome mss from black and third world women, working class women and lesbians. Books should be aimed toward women and build women's sense of self, understanding of oppression, or offer possibilities for change. We are interested in practical works for women in areas that they are discriminated against; e.g., how to become an electrician, etc. We specialize in nonfiction, essay type material." Length: 80,000 words maximum. Recent titles include *Class and Feminism, Lesbianism and the Women's Movement.*

THE DIETZ PRESS, INC., 109 E. Cary St., Richmond VA 23219. Editor: August

Dietz, III. Requires preliminary letter stating the subject and briefly outlining the material. Enclose return postage.
Nonfiction: Publishes biography, books of an historical nature, Americana, unusual cook and hostess books. Length: 40,000 to 50,000 words. No poetry.

DILLON PRESS, 500 S. 3rd St., Minneapolis MN 55415. Editor-in-Chief: Mrs. Uva Dillon. Publishes hardcover originals. Contract and royalty schedule to be negotiated. No advance. Published 20 titles last year. Will send catalog to writer on request. Queries and/or mss encouraged for both trade and educational juvenile categories. Queries encouraged in the area of general nonfiction, adult. Will consider photocopied submissions. Reports in 6 weeks. Enclose return postage.
Juveniles: Interested in the areas of science fiction, ghost or mystery stories, nostalgia. Also true life adventure stories (not necessarily biographical, just realistic), about children of today or from earlier days. For ages 10 to 14; average length 30,000 words. Also interested in retellings of folk tales and legends from this country and around the world, for ages 6 to 9; will consider individual titles as well as collections.
General Nonfiction: Adult. Specifically, we need mss for our "Ethnic" series. Each of these books describes old country customs and traditions, to acquaint readers with the ethnic roots of Americans. Average length: 65,000 words.

DIMENSION BOOKS, INC., P.O. Box 811, Denville NJ 07834. Regular royalty schedule. Advance is negotiable. Titles published last year: 39. Current catalog available if S.A.S.E. is enclosed. Send query first to editorial office. Address mss to Thomas P. Coffey. Reports in 1 week on requested mss. Enclose return postage.
General Nonfiction: Publishes general nonfiction including religion, principally Roman Catholic. Also psychology and music. Length: 40,000 words and over. Recent titles include *Breadth of the Mystic* (Maloney), *Spirituality and the Gentle Life* (van Kaam).

DIPLOMATIC PRESS, INC., Address all communications to: P.O. Box 593, Times Square Station, New York NY 10036. Royalty schedule: 10% off published price. Reports in 6 months. All subsidiary companies of Diplomatic Press consider mss at the New York headquarters only. Wants mss only from professional or skilled, if not established, writers. "Unsolicited mss must be accompanied by self-addressed and stamped envelopes or label. Otherwise they are not returned."
General Nonfiction, Fiction, and Textbooks: General adult nonfiction and fiction. Textbook publisher to different universities and colleges. Considers publications in French, German, Italian and Spanish languages if they are of scholastic or universal appeal. Length: 50,000 to 75,000 words.

DODD, MEAD & CO., 79 Madison Ave., New York, NY 10016. Executive Editor: Allen T. Klots, Jr. Royalty basis: 10% to 15%. Advances vary, depending on the sales potential of the book. A contract for nonfiction books is offered on the basis of a query, a suggested outline and a sample chapter. Write for permission before sending mss. Published 150 titles last year. Adult fiction, history, philosophy, the arts, and religion should be addressed to Editorial Department. Reports in 1 month. Enclose return postage.
General Fiction and Nonfiction: Publishes book-length mss, 70,000 to 100,000 words. Fiction and nonfiction of high quality, mysteries and romantic novels of suspense, biography, popular science, travel, yachting, music, and other arts. Very rarely buys photographs or poetry.
Juveniles: Length: 1,500 to 75,000 words. Children's Books Editor: Mrs. Joe Ann Daly.

DOUBLEDAY & CO., INC., 245 Park Ave., New York NY 10017. Managing Editor: Pyke Johnson, Jr. Publishes hardcover and paperback originals; publishes paperback reprints under Anchor, Dolphin and Image imprints. Offers standard 10-12½-15% royalty contract. Advance varies. Reports in 1 month. Special submission requirements outlined below. Enclose return postage.
Nonfiction and Fiction: "Doubleday has had to institute a new policy concerning

the handling of manuscripts. We are returning unopened and unread all complete manuscripts, accompanied by a form telling how we would like submissions made. However, in 3 areas, we will accept complete manuscripts: Mysteries, science fiction and westerns. These mss should be addressed to the appropriate editor (for example, Science Fiction Editor) and not just to Doubleday."

DOUBLEDAY CANADA LTD., 105 Bond St., Toronto 2, Ont., Canada. Managing Editor: Betty J. Corson. Publishes hardcover originals. Offers standard royalty contract. Advance varies. Published 12 titles last year. Will send a catalog to a writer on request. Send query, outline and sample chapters. Reports in 1 to 2 months. Enclose return postage.
General Nonfiction and Fiction, and Juveniles: "We publish trade books of all sorts that are either about Canada or written by Canadian residents." Recent titles include: *Tribal Justice* (Blaise), *Six War Years* (Broadfoot), and *The Burden of Adrian Knowle* (Fry). Lengths: 60,000 to 100,000 words for nonfiction; 55,000 to 90,000 words for fiction; open for juveniles.

J. J. DOUGLAS LTD., 132 Philip Ave., North Vancouver, B.C., Canada V7P 2V6. Editor-in-Chief: Marilyn Sacks. Publishes hardcover and paperback originals and reprints. Offers standard contract; 8% on paperback editions. Average advance is $300. Published 14 titles last year. "Associated with David & Charles, large British Commonwealth publisher of nonfiction, practical books." Will send free catalog to writer on request. Query first with outline and sample chapters. Send history of writing credits. Will consider photocopied submissions. Reports in 4 to 8 weeks. Enclose S.A.E. and International Reply Coupons.
Nonfiction, Fiction, and Juveniles: "Emphasis on how-to-do-it books, Canadian history, reference, guides and particularly subjects of Pacific Northwest interest. Ms should be authoritative but presented simply. We edit jargon and repetition heavily. Tough editing; excellent graphics; careful design. Also interested in sailing and crafts books. Interests are also in mainstream fiction, crafts, cooking and foods, self-help, juveniles, nature, sports, hobbies, recreation and pets." Length: 30,000 to 100,000 words.

DOW JONES-IRWIN, INC., 1818 Ridge Rd., Homewood IL 60430. Publishes originals only. Royalty schedule 10% of net. Advance negotiable. Published 25 titles last year. Send completed mss to the attention of Editorial Director. Enclose return postage with mss.
Nonfiction: Business and industrial subjects.

DRAKE PUBLISHERS, INC., 381 Park Ave. S., New York NY 10016. Publisher: Lawrence Gadd. Managing Editor: Douglas Corcoran. Publishes hardcover and paperback originals and reprints. Offers standard 10-12½-15% royalty contract; "all advances are arranged individually." Published over 100 titles last year. Query with sample chapters and outline. Ms must be typewritten on 8½x11 bond paper and should be presented with a carbon or a Xerox. Will consider photocopied submissions. Reports in 30 days. Enclose return postage with ms.
General Nonfiction, Cookbooks, Self-Help and How-To, and Hobbies: "Publishes general nonfiction books, including woodworking, craft and how-to books, cookbooks, travel guides, etc. Gardening, film, television, quiz books, hobbies, games, business, history, music, etc. The books are geared in general to home craftsmen or home repairmen, although our books are often used, and praised by professionals. We are flexible about length, but prefer our books to be at least 132 pages long. Craft books of any sort should be characterized by conciseness and clarity of presentation—step-by-step instructions, diagrams when necessary, and photos are most desirable. Drake books are noted for their thoroughness and for the excellence of the directions found in them. Clarity, objectivity and in-depth research are paramount. New lines include film biographies, exercise, and biographies of world leaders." Length: 50,000 to 90,000 words. Current titles include *Vincent Price Unmasked* (Parish) and *Ernie Kovacs* (Walley).

DRAMA BOOK SPECIALISTS/PUBLISHERS, 150 West 52nd St., New York NY 10019. Publishes hardcover and paperback originals. Royalties usually 10%. Advance varies. Published 20 titles last year. Send query only to Ralph Pine. Do not send complete mss. Reports in 4 to 8 weeks. Enclose S.A.S.E.
Drama: "Theatrical history, texts, film, and books dealing with the performing arts."

DROKE HOUSE/HALLUX, INC., P.O. Box 2027, Anderson SC 29621. Editor: S. G. Hall. Publishes hardcover originals. Offers standard royalty contract with small advances. Published 9 titles last year. Will send a catalog to a writer on request. Send outline and sample chapter. Reports in 6 to 8 weeks. Enclose return postage.
General: "National book publishers—fiction and nonfiction books of all types, from novels to the occult to inspiration, self-help, etc." Length: 30,000 to 120,000 words.

DUNELLEN PUBLISHING CO. INC., 386 Park Ave., S., New York NY 10016. Acquisitions Editor: Robert Nicholas. Publishes hardcover originals. "Our royalty rate is 7½-10-12½%. We do not issue any advance to authors." Publishes 15 to 20 titles a year. "Our distribution is mainly in the academic fields and the libraries, not so much to the general public bookstores." Submit outline and sample chapters. "We send out an authors' guide to anyone preparing a manuscript." Will consider photocopied submissions. Reports in 2 to 3 weeks. Enclose return postage.
General Nonfiction: "We deal mainly in the social sciences. Subjects include the legal field, economics, international politics, urban affairs, etc.; occasionally books in the experimental and theoretical psychology field; black studies. We prefer original studies, which have been well researched, with a scholarly approach. We plan to start an empirical studies line as opposed to the more theoretical University Press of Cambridge Series. We would prefer not to see any more books on either World War II or the Vietnam War." Other publishing interests include business, law, public administration, education, multimedia material, sociology, urban and environmental, labor and diplomacy. Prefers mss under 300 typewritten pages. Recent titles include: *Health Services for Tomorrow* (Burns), *Educational Alternatives for Colonized People* (Williams).

DUQUESNE UNIVERSITY PRESS, Pittsburgh PA 15219. Royalty schedule is 10%. No advance. Query first. Reports in 6 months or less. Enclose return postage.
Nonfiction: Scholarly books on philosophy and philology and psychology. Length: open. Current titles include *Persistent Problems of Psychology* (MacLeod), *Sense and Significance* (Ihde).

E.P. DUTTON AND CO., INC., 201 Park Ave. S., New York NY 10003. Editor-in-Chief, adult publications: T. B. Congdon. Juvenile Department: Ann Durell. Dutton Paperback: Cyril Nelson. Staple: Marian Skedgell. Pays by advances and royalties. Published 130 titles last year. Queries welcomed for nonfiction of high quality on almost any subject for the general reader. Before sending mss, query with outline and sample chapters. Enclose return postage.
General Fiction and Nonfiction: Publishes novels of permanent literary value; mystery, nonfiction, religious, travel, fine arts, biography, memoirs, belles lettres, history, science, psychology, translations, and quality paperbacks.
Juveniles: "We're finding some of our most successful children's books in the unsolicited ms pile."

DUXBURY PRESS (Division of Wadsworth Publishing Co.), 6 Bound Brook Court, North Scituate MA 02060. Publishes hardcover and paperback originals. Contract varies "depending on number of authors involved and degree of involvement. Usually offers 10 to 15% with advance arrangements on a limited basis." Published 23 titles last year. Submit outline, publishing rationale, and sample chapter. Uses Chicago *Manual of Style.* Enclose return postage.
General Nonfiction: "Social science and quantitative methods college texts. Also geography, environmental studies, and interdisciplinary studies; economics, history, politics, sociology, criminal justice, vocational education, and sex education. Some books in these areas of a semi-trade nature as well. Emphasis on pedagogy and

quality of thought. Authors mostly Ph.Ds but some work in collaboration with professional writers, researchers, etc., whom we hire. Emphasis on new and exciting approaches to knowledge in these areas; novel formats and varying lengths. We accept a wide latitude of styles, outlooks and structures, as long as each is accompanied by a detailed and thorough rationale and is the embodiment of a responsible trend in the academic field." Length: 50,000 to 200,000 words. Recent titles include: *Politics for Human Beings* (Isaak/Hummel), *Ecology* (Levine et al), *Community Health Nursing: Patterns and Practice* (Archer/Fleshman).

LES EDITIONS DE L'ETOILE, 325-327 Mont-Royal Est., Montreal H2T 1P8, PQ, Canada (formerly John Desgranges). Offers 10% royalty contract. No advance. Enclose S.A.E. and International Reply Coupons for return of submissions.
General Fiction and Nonfiction: General publisher of all types of books in French language only.

ELK GROVE BOOKS, P.O. Box 1637, Whittier CA 90609. Division of Childrens Press, 1224 W. Van Buren St., Chicago IL 60607. Editor: Ruth Radlauer. Publishes hardcover originals. "Outright purchase and some contracts without escalation and with split with illustrator." No advance. Published 10 titles last year. "Emphasis on school and library distribution." Write to Childrens Press for catalog. Query first, with one page sample of text, giving subject, length, and age level. Reports in 6 weeks to 6 months. Enclose return postage.
Juveniles: "Hardcover books geared to supplement curriculum subjects and for reading instruction, especially for reluctant, slow-starting, and beginning readers. Easy-read, how-to (grade 2), and fiction for middle grades (about 10,000 words). Writers must have an up-to-date understanding of today's child who is surrounded by stimuli that are much more fun (sometimes) than reading. Forget your grandchild, your own child, but look at and listen to their friends, the kids in the park, the ones you dislike as well as the ones you like. Grab him and make him want to read what you write. It's also good to think 'format'. Design it in your head to fit a 32, 48, or 64 page book. Also think in terms of expense of production. We're especially interested in seeing sports, how-to for early grades. We do not publish picture stories as such. And no cute and charming stories about personified animals." Current titles include *You Can Make Good Things to Eat* (Bayles) and *Cowboy on Ice* (Maxwell).

ETC PUBLICATIONS, 18512 Pierce Terrace, Homewood IL 60430. Editor-in-Chief: Richard W. Hostrop. Publishes originals in both hardcover and paperback. Nonfiction only. Standard minimum book contract. "Rarely are advances given, but exceptions of up to $1,200 are occasionally made, depending on author's reputation and nature of book." Published 12 titles last year. Will send a catalog to a writer on request. "Submit completed work along with vita. Prefer three authoritative 'testimonials' to accompany manuscript." Will consider photocopied submissions of good quality. Reports in 1 month. Enclose return postage.
Education: "We publish material on all subjects at all levels in the fields of education, educational technology, and educational communications. Mss must be geared to reach a wide number of professional educators, on significant topics." Length: 50,000 to 150,000 words. Recent titles include *The Young Russians* (Geyer) and *The Early School Years Read Aloud Program* (Whitehead).

M. EVANS AND COMPANY, INC., 216 E. 49 St., New York NY 10017. Editor-in-Chief: Herbert M. Katz. Publishes hardcover originals. Royalty schedule to be negotiated. Publishes 30 books a year. Query first. Will consider photocopied submissions. No mss should be sent unsolicited. A letter of inquiry is essential. Reports on rejected material in 6 to 8 weeks. Reporting time on accepted material varies. Enclose return postage.
General Fiction and Nonfiction: "We publish a general trade list of adult fiction and nonfiction, cookbooks and semi-reference works. The emphasis is on selectivity since we publish only 30 books a year. Our fiction list represents an attempt to combine quality with commercial potential. Our most successful nonfiction titles

have been related to the behavioral sciences. No limitation on subject. A writer should clearly indicate what his book is all about, frequently the task the writer performs least well. His credentials, although important, mean less than his ability to convince this company that he understands his subject and that he has the ability to communicate a message worth hearing." Recent titles include: *Too Much* (Westlake), *Meeting at Potsdam* (Mee), *The Cosmopolitan Girl* (Drexler).
Juveniles: "We are always in the market for a new juvenile series, particularly in the sciences at the younger age levels." Length: open.

F & W PUBLISHING CORP., 9933 Alliance Rd., Cincinnati OH 45242. Editor-in-Chief: Richard Rosenthal. Publishes hardcover originals. Offers 10% royalty contract. Usual advance is $1,000 to $2,000. Published 5 titles last year. Query first. Reports in 2 weeks. Enclose return postage.
Nonfiction: Books must relate to the craft of writing. Representative titles include *Writing and Selling Nonfiction, One Way to Write Your Novel, Writing for Children and Teenagers.*

FAIRCHILD BOOKS & VISUALS, Book Division, 7 East 12th St., New York NY 10003. Manager: Ed Gold. Publishes hardcover and paperback originals. Offers standard minimum book contract. No advance. Pays 10% of net sales distributed twice annually. Published 12 titles last year. Will consider photocopied submissions. Will send free catalog to writer on request. Query first, giving subject matter and brief outline. Enclose return postage.
Business and Textbooks: Publishes business books and textbooks relating to fashion, electronics, marketing, retailing, career education, advertising, home economics, and management. Length: open. Current titles include *Fabric Science* and *Dictionary of Fashion.*

FAIRLEIGH DICKINSON UNIVERSITY PRESS, Rutherford NJ 07070. Editor: Charles Angoff. Royalty by arrangement. Usually offers no advance. Published 25 titles last year. Reports within 6 months. Enclose return postage with ms.
Nonfiction: "Only works of the highest scholarship; real contributions to their fields." Length: open.

FAMILY LAW PUBLICATIONS, 838 N. Harlem Ave., River Forest IL 60305. Editor: N.C. Kohut. Publishes hardcover and paperback originals. Offers standard 10-12½-15% royalty contract. Published 1 title last year. Query first with outline and sample chapters for nonfiction. Enclose return postage.
Law: "Socio-legal books on marriage and divorce. Interested in books on divorce reform." Length: 2,500 to 7,500 words.
Sociology: "Serious books on upgrading family life, including research studies."

FAR EASTERN RESEARCH AND PUBLICATIONS CENTER, P.O. Box 31151, Washington DC 20031. Publishes hardcover and paperback originals and reprints. "Royalty is based on the standard rate or outright purchase. Pays up to $2,000 advance against standard royalties." Submit a synopsis or table of contents with sample chapter, along with biographical sketches, to editor-in-chief. Reports in 2 months. Enclose return postage with ms—"enough postage to cover registered mail for return of submissions."
Nonfiction: Subject emphasis: reference materials on the Far East, especially on the Chinese, Japanese, and Korean people. All lengths.

FARNSWORTH PUBLISHING CO., INC., 78 Randall Ave., Rockville Centre NY 11570. President: Lee Rosler. Publishes hardcover originals. "Standard royalty applies, but 5% is payable on mail order sales." Published 12 titles last year. Will send a catalog to a writer on request. Send query. Reports in 1 to 5 weeks. Enclose return postage.
General Nonfiction and Business and Professional: "Our books generally fall into 2 categories: 1. Books which appeal to executives, lawyers, accountants, and life underwriters. Subject matter may vary from selling techniques, estate planning,

taxation, money management, etc. 2. Books which appeal to the general populace which are marketable by direct mail and mail order, in addition to book store sales."

FARRAR, STRAUS AND GIROUX, INC. (including Hill and Wang), 19 Union Square West, New York NY 10003. Editor-in-Chief: Aaron Asher. Variable advance and royalty arrangements. Published 150 titles last year. Prefers queries. Enclose S.A.S.E.
General Fiction, Nonfiction and Juveniles: Publishes general fiction, nonfiction and juveniles. New emphasis on nonfiction, primarily biography. Publishes Noonday paperbacks, scholarly reprints under Octagon Books imprint (Henry Schlanger, Editor), and Hill and Wang books (Arthur W. Wang, Editor). Juveniles Editor: Clare Costello.

FAWCETT PUBLICATIONS, INC./GOLD MEDAL BOOKS, 1515 Broadway, New York NY 10036. Publishes paperback originals only. Advances and royalties are flexible and competitive. Address query first to the editors before submitting ms. Reports in 3 to 8 weeks. Enclose return postage.
Nonfiction and Fiction: Seeks books of broad, mass-market appeal.

F. W. FAXON COMPANY, INC., 15 Southwest Park, Westwood MA 02090. Editor-in-Chief: Albert H. Davis, Jr. Publishes hardcover originals. Offers 10% of sales net price for each book sold, payable at the end of each fiscal year. No advance. Books are marketed through advertising, mail campaigns, book reviews, and library conventions. Will send catalog to writer on request. Mss must be original copy, double-spaced, and must be accompanied by a copy. They should contain reference material useful to library users throughout the world. Query first. Enclose S.A.S.E.
Reference: "We publish library reference books. These are primarily indexes but we would also consider bibliographies and other material useful to library users. We would be interested in publishing indexes on topics of current interest which have not been indexed previously." Current titles are *Index to Fairy Tales, Index to Handicrafts, Classified List of Periodicals for the College Library.*

FREDERICK FELL PUBLISHERS, INC., 386 Park Ave. S., New York NY 10016. Editor-in-Chief: Frederick V. Fell. Publishes hardcover and paperback originals and reprints. "All of our contractual agreements with our authors are flexible. Advance is negotiable." Published 30 titles last year. Will send free catalog to writer on request. Write for copy of author's guidelines. Will consider photocopied submissions. Query first. Address all editorial correspondence to Charles G. Nurnberg, Editor. Reports within 4 weeks. Enclose S.A.S.E.
General Nonfiction: "We are always looking for new material for our Fell's Guide Series: how-to, handicrafts and hobbies, Americana, cuisine, popular science, travel, sports, vocational and recreational activities; Fell's Business & Financial Bookshelf: nontechnical books for the reader who wants to get ahead in business, start his or her own venture (our most successful titles in this series proposed new, unusual and lucrative ways to go about this), management of employees, time and money for the entrepreneur and the top executive; Fell's Better Health Series: nutritional and dietary works, particularly those dealing with specific ailments — obesity, diabetes, backache, arthritis — motivational, self-help, psychology and parapsychology — all phases of mental and physical health. We prefer that these be written by a recognized authority in the field. We are on the lookout, too, for top-quality material in the areas of biography, topical nonfiction, lifestyles, the good life, the outdoors, the environment, the society — in short, anything of exceptional interest and quality dealing with modern living. Our titles are directed toward the general literate reader. We like our incoming material to be crisp and clean, comprehensive when the subject calls for it, not unnecessarily obscure or unconventional in style, tightly structured, unified, and professional. Also interested in ecology, the society in transition, the crises (global and personal) which confront us all; the threat to freedom and self-expression, the question of values in the times in which we live, man's proclivity for self-destructiveness and the varying solutions to and diversions from these (please no exposes or manifestos). Virtually all topical issues and trends are of interest to

us. Length: 60,000 words minimum, no maximum; flexible. We are not interested in books with religious themes, memoirs (except, of course, something in the order of *Pentimento* or *Cosell*), poetry, or juveniles."

Fiction: "Although we publish very little adult fiction, we are on the lookout for unusual, controversial, high-quality mss. Queries or outlines and sample chapters should be sent to Charles G. Nurnberg, Editor."

Business: "In Fell's Business Book Shelf, we publish books on all aspects of business: Success in leadership, management, financial growth, investments, and experiences in the business world. Material in those categories should be sent to Charles G. Nurnberg, Editor."

Health: "Books for Fell's Better Health Series should deal with both physical and mental health and well-being. Query Charles G. Nurnberg, Editor."

FIELDING PUBLICATIONS, INC., 105 Madison Ave., New York NY 10016. Editor: Eunice Riedel. Published 10 titles last year. Send outline and sample chapter. Reports in 3 weeks. Enclose return postage.

Travel: Interested in general nonfiction books in the field of travel. Minimum length: 60,000 words.

FILTER PRESS, Box 5, Palmer Lake CO 80133. General Editor: G.L. Campbell; Cookery Editor: L.W. Campbell. Publishes paperback originals or reprints. Pays 10% net sales. No advance. Published 8 titles last year. Will send a catalog to a writer on request. Query with outline. Will consider photocopied submissions "if legible." Reports on query in 1 week; on solicited mss in about 3 weeks. Enclose return postage.

Americana: Western Americana. Books on Western motif. Also publishes Western history books about Indians, early explorations, ghost towns, national parks. Length: 5,000 to 20,000 words (48 to 68 illustrated pages). "We have built our Wild and Woolly West series around reprints of 19th century travel materials, using the antique wood engravings as well as other illustrations to preserve the Victorian atmosphere which is so much a part of the Old West. Indians, miners, bad guys, explorers, and other residents of the Old West are suitable material. While a casual, humorous, or light style is acceptable, the subject should be treated with whatever respect it merits. Writing should be competent. Research should be accurate. We prefer to avoid footnotes except where the ideas cannot be placed in the narrative. A bibliography may be desirable in many cases, but it is not essential. We will do more on American Indians. Too many people are finding notes or diaries written by Uncle Charlie; these are coming to us with little or no added work on them, and nothing to relate them to the past or present. Too many are working on Jesse James-buried treasure sorts of things, with nothing really new. Because we are small, we are not the publisher for a book that should be aimed at the mass market." Length: 5,000 to 20,000 words (48 to 68 pages).

Nonfiction: "We departed from the Wild and Woolly West series to some extent in publishing *In Case I'm Found Unconscious*, a nontechnical medical book for the diabetic and his family. We will do other non-Western books whenever they appeal to us." Interested in cookbooks, history, medicine, western pioneer, scientific, self-help and how-to, hobbies, recreation, technical, textbooks, and travel.

FINANCIAL TECHNOLOGY LIMITED, 23 River Rd., North Arlington NJ 07032. Editor-in-Chief: M. Willis McConahy. Publishes hardcover and paperback originals and reprints. Usually offers standard minimum book contract, but arrangements are negotiable. Published 6 titles last year. Books marketed through extensive magazine and direct mail advertising. Will send free catalog to writer on request. Submit complete ms. Will consider photocopied submissions. Reports in 3 weeks. Enclose return postage.

Business and Finance: "Books on business, finance, taxes, etc. Economics, law, reference, self-help and how-to. We specialize in pamphlets and short run publications, although we will consider longer material in the same general subject areas. No wishy-washy 'isn't it great to have your own business?' type of books. And, no purely inspirational business books." Length is very flexible; anything from a pamphlet, on up. Recent titles include *Tax Havens—What They Are and How They Work*, a short guide to forming companies and trusts in countries that have low taxes, or no taxes.

FIRST MEDIA PRESS, 6 East 39th St., New York NY 10016. Editor-in-Chief: Patrick Montgomery. Publishes paperback originals. Offers standard minimum book contract of 10-12½-15%. No advance. Published 1 title last year. Will send free catalog to writer on request. Query first. Will consider photocopied submissions. Reports in 1 month. Enclose S.A.S.E.
Nonfiction: Publishes books on the cinema. Well-researched monographs and books with limited appeal. "We require well-researched, in-depth material that can be taken seriously. We're not really equipped for mass market publishing." Length: open.

FITZHENRY & WHITESIDE, LIMITED, 150 Lesmill Rd., Don Mills, Ontario, Canada. Editor-in-Chief: Robert Read. Publishes hardcover and paperback originals and reprints. Chiefly educational materials. Royalty contract "varied." Advance negotiable. Published 30 titles last year. Submit outline and sample chapters. Will consider photocopied submissions. Reports on material accepted for publication in 1 month. Returns rejected material within 2 months. Enclose return postage.
General Nonfiction, Drama and Poetry: "Especially interested in topics of interest to Canadians." Biography; business; cookbooks, cooking and foods; history; medicine and psychiatry; nature; politics. Canadian plays and poetry are also of interest. Length: open.
Textbooks: Elementary and secondary school textbooks in social studies and reading, science and math.

FLEET PRESS CORPORATION, 160 Fifth Ave., New York NY 10010. Editor: Susan Nueckel. Publishes hardcover and paperback originals and reprints. Royalty schedule "varies." Advance "varies." Published 27 titles last year. Will send a catalog to a writer on request. Send query and outline. Reports in 6 weeks. Enclose return postage with ms. Will not evaluate unsolicited mss.
General Nonfiction: "History, biography, arts, religion, general nonfiction, sports." Length: 45,000 words.
Juveniles: Nonfiction only. Stress on social studies and minority subjects; for ages 8 to 15. Length: 25,000 words.

FORTRESS PRESS, 2900 Queen Lane, Philadelphia PA 19129. Senior Editor and Director: Norman A. Hjelm. Publishes hardcover and paperback originals. Offers 7% to 8½% paperback royalties; offers 10% hardcover royalty. Advances are negotiable, depending on author's reputation and nature of book. Published about 60 titles last year. Will send a catalog to a writer on request. Query first. "Use *Chicago Manual of Style*." Reports in 2 months. Enclose return postage.
Religion and Philosophy: "Fortress Press is a major publisher of general religious and theological books. Our academic listing — books in the field of Biblical studies, systematic theology, ethics, church history, etc. — is extensive and well known. The major portion of published titles, however, is for a more general reading audience — laity and clergy of all denominations. Book length varies, from 27,500 to 125,000 words. Books should be readable in style (for 'general religious' books, the reading level should be from ninth to twelfth grades, according to the Fogg Standard); academic books must be in proper scholarly form (apparatus, etc.) and must reflect awareness of current theological trends and methods. We have high standards of editing, a willingness to use visual materials other than print, and a serious religious commitment without denominational or confessional limitations. New series in the area of pastoral counseling. Mss must be devoted to specific areas — e.g., counseling the drug addict, alcoholic, divorced person, etc. They should be concrete and designed to help clergy in the development of counseling ministries. In books for the lay person, we would like to see coverage of the crisis of authority in American society; new forms of viable parish life for American churches, the question of law and freedom, books for creative worship, books of value for senior citizens. No standard

'daily devotions' or unsolicited sermons." Recent titles include *Hermeneia: A Critical and Historical Commentary on the Bible; Creative Pastoral Counseling and Care* (10-volume series edited by Howard Clinebell); *Speaking in Parables* (TeSelle); *Healing: A Spiritual Adventure* (Peterman); *Women in a Strange Land* (Fischer); *The Best Is Yet to Be: Reflections on Growing Old* (Rommel, illustrated).

FRANCISCAN HERALD PRESS, 1434 West 51st St., Chicago IL 60609. Editor: Rev. Mark Hegener, O.F.M. "Royalty schedule — 10% and up with volume. Advance: depending on nature and length of ms." Published 24 titles last year. Send query and outline. Use University of Chicago *Manual of Style.* Reports in 30 days. Enclose return postage.
Religion: "A Catholic publishing house with a wide range of interests in theology, sociology, culture, art and literature, reflecting, interpreting, directing the socio-religious and cultural aspects of our times." Synthesis Series of booklets (10,000 word maximum) in the field of religion and psychology. Church history, biography and specialized publications on history, purpose and personages of the Franciscan Order. Lengths run from 5,000 to 60,000 words.

THE FREE PRESS, a Division of the Macmillan Publishing Co., Inc., 866 Third Ave., New York NY 10022. President: Edward W. Barry. Editor-in-Chief: Charles E. Smith. Royalty schedule varies. Published 75 titles last year. Send sample chapter, outline, and query letter before submitting mss. Reports in 3 weeks. Enclose return postage.
Nonfiction and Textbooks: Publishes college texts and adult educational nonfiction in the social sciences and humanities.

GENERAL AVIATION PRESS, P.O. Box 916, Snyder TX 79549. Editor-in-Chief: M. Gene Dow. Publishes hardcover and paperback originals. Offers standard book contract of 10-12½-15%. Advance is negotiated. Published 3 titles last year. Books are marketed through aviation publications. Will consider photocopied submissions. Reports in 1 month. Submit outline and sample chapters or complete ms. Enclose return postage.
Aviation: Subjects pertain strictly to general aviation; non-airline, non-military. How-to, biographies of well-known aviators, safety, organizations, etc. Almost any subject related to private and business aircraft and flying. Must be written with knowledge of aircraft and pilots. Recent titles include *How to Fly an Aeroplane* and *Weather Flying.*

C. R. GIBSON CO., 39 Knight St., Norwalk CT 06856. Director of Publication: M. Murphy. Publishes gift brochures in both hardcover originals and anthologies. Offers fixed royalty rate per copy sold. Advance varies according to formats; minimum of $750 to $1,000. Query first, with outline and sample chapters. Reports in 4 to 8 weeks. Enclose return postage.
Gift Books: Arts and crafts; Christian books for inspirational outlets. Recent titles include *The Beauty of Birds* (Dunn).

GINN AND COMPANY, 191 Spring St., Lexington MA 02173. Editor-in-Chief: Richard Morgan. Royalty schedule: from 10% of net on a secondary book to 6% on elementary materials. Published 240 titles last year. Sample chapters, complete or partially complete mss will be considered. Reports in 2 to 6 weeks. Enclose return postage.
Textbooks: Publishers of textbooks and instructional materials for elementary and secondary schools.

GOLDEN PRESS (Western Publishing Co.), 850 Third Ave., New York NY 10022. Editorial Director: Jack B. Long. Submit all material to: Bruce Butterfield, Assistant to Editorial Director. Publishes hardcover and paperback originals and reprints. "Our royalty rates vary with each title. Advance varies." Write for copy of guidelines to authors. Submit complete ms. Will consider photocopied submissions. Reports in 3 months. Enclose return postage.

Juveniles and General: "The juvenile books that originate in our New York office cost over $1 and are written for ages of 2 to 12 and up. We do not publish fiction for teens. We publish large picture books for the very young and nonfiction books for upper elementary and junior high school readers. We strongly recommend that writers study our publications thoroughly before submitting material."

GOLDEN WEST BOOKS, P.O. Box 8136, San Marino CA 91108. Publisher: Donald Duke. Royalty schedule: 5%-10%, depending on work. No advance. Published 4 titles last year. Send outline or sample chapter. Reports in 2 weeks. Enclose return postage.
Nonfiction: "We are concerned only with transportation history: railroads, steamships, transportation Americana." Length: open.

GRAY'S PUBLISHING LTD., Box 2160, Sidney, BC, Canada. Editor: Gray Campbell. Publishes hardcover and paperback originals. Offers standard royalty contract. No advance. Published 8 titles last year. Will send a catalog to a writer on request. Query first with outline. Reports in 6 to 10 weeks. Enclose S.A.E. and International Reply Coupons.
Nonfiction: Wants "nonfiction, Canadiana" geared to high-school age audience, adults. Length: 60,000 to 120,000 words. Current titles include *Doukhobor Daze, There Is My People Sleeping; Wild Flowers Field Guides; Ice With Everything* (Tilman); *Canaries on the Clothes Line* (McKeever).

GREEN NOTE MUSIC PUBLICATIONS, P.O. Box 4187, Berkeley CA 94704. Editor-in-Chief: Straw Dog. Publishes paperback originals. Advance and royalty contracts vary according to individual situations. Published 2 titles last year. Will send free catalog to writer on request. Submit complete ms. Will not consider photocopied submissions. Reporting time "varies with workload." Enclose S.A.E. and return postage.
Music: Music instruction, and music information books, dealing with contemporary popular music idioms (jazz, rock, blues, etc.). Material should be clearly and simply presented, and should have immediate, practical application. Uninterested in theorizing, or in a "preparatory" approach (involving scales, exercises, etc.). "Our books differ in quality and usefulness. Most of our titles are accompanied by recorded soundsheets (music, we believe, being an aural, rather than a visual, art)."

STEPHEN GREENE PRESS, P.O. Box 1000, Brattleboro VT 05301. Standard royalty basis. Published 17 titles last year. Will send a catalog on request. Address all queries to Orion M. Barber, Managing Editor; outlines with sample chapters in all cases. Reports in 45 days. Enclose return postage.
General Nonfiction: Publishes general adult nonfiction: Americana, regional (New England) literature, biography, sports (especially horse and individual sports like cross-country skiing, snowshoeing), humor, railroads, cooking, aviation, nature and environment, how-to, self-reliance. Must meet high literary standards. Recent titles include *Farm Town; Beasts in Heraldry; Goodbye Lizzie Borden; I Remember Cape Cod; Sprouts to Grow and Eat.*

If this is 1977, this edition is out of date. See address in front of book to order latest edition. *Writer's Market* is published annually each fall.

GREENLEAF CLASSICS, INC., P.O. Box 20194, San Diego CA 92120. Original novels only. Outright purchase with payment on acceptance. "Payment varies according to quality of book, and how closely the work conforms to our requirements." Published over 300 titles last year. Submit outline and first 3 chapters. Reports in 2 to 3 weeks. Enclose S.A.S.E.
Erotica: Publishes erotic fiction. "All stories must have a strong sexual theme. All plots are structured so that characters must get involved in erotic situations. Too many stories are lacking the basics (plot, characterization and a sexual theme) of a good erotic novel." Preferred length: 40,000 to 50,000 words. Recent titles include *Go Down; Naked; The Nymph Nurse; Hungry Spouse; Teaser Wife.*

GREENWICH PRESS, 335 Bleecker St., New York NY 10014. Editor: Anton Hardt. Publishes hardcover originals and reprints. Query first. Enclose return postage.
Nonfiction: "Books only on the subject of antiques and possibly allied fields."

GREGG DIVISION, McGraw-Hill Book Co., 1221 Ave. of the Americas, New York NY 10020. General Manager: Charles B. Harrington. Publishes hardcover originals. "Contracts negotiable; no advances." Query first. "We accept very few unsolicited mss." Reports in 1 to 2 months. Enclose return postage with query.
Textbooks: "Textbooks and related instructional materials for the career education market." Publishes books on typewriting, office education, shorthand, accounting and data processing, distributing and marketing, trade and industrial education, health and consumer education.

GRIFFIN HOUSE PUBLISHERS, 455 King Street West, Toronto, Ontario, Canada. Publishes hardcover and paperback originals. Offers standard royalty contract. Small advance. Published 7 titles last year. Will send a catalog to a writer on request. Send complete ms. Enclose S.A.E. and International Reply Coupons.
General Fiction, General Nonfiction, History and Biography: Interested in general interest and Canadiana books.

GROSSET AND DUNLAP, INC., (including Tempo Teenage Paperbacks and Universal Library), 51 Madison Ave., New York NY 10010. Editor-in-Chief: Robert Markel. Publishes hardcover and paperback originals and reprints, as well as a "very few" translations, and anthologies "on occasion." Royalty and advance terms generally vary. Published "close to 400" titles last year. Will send a catalog to a writer on request. Send query letter, outline, or sample chapter only; do not send complete ms. "We do not accept unsolicited manuscripts." Reports in 3 to 5 weeks. Enclose return postage with query.
General Fiction: "Very seldom — usually only via literary agent."
General Nonfiction and Reference: "No limits—anything and everything that would interest the 'average' American reader: sports, health, ecology, etc." Interested in history, science, religion, biography, the arts, and literature. Favors writers with strong experience and good credits.
Juveniles and Teen: Editor-in-Chief, Children's Picture Books: Doris Duenewald.

GROSSMAN PUBLISHERS, 625 Madison Ave., New York NY 10022. Editor-in-Chief: Daniel Okrent. Publishes hardcover and paperback originals and paperback reprints. Royalty contract and advance vary. Published 30 titles last year. Will send catalog to writer on request. Query first. Reports in 4 weeks. Enclose return postage.
General Trade Books: Fiction, cookbooks, cooking and foods; history, photography, poetry, sociology.

GUITAR PLAYER PRODUCTIONS, P.O. Box 615, Saratoga CA 95070. Editor-in-Chief: Eric Kriss. Publishes hardcover and paperback originals and reprints. Offers a contract with 10% standard royalty, but with a few features common to music trade agreements. Advance varies from $500 to $1,000, depending on artist's stature, etc. Published 3 titles last year. Marketed through the book trade, music stores and dealers and direct mail. Editorial guidelines available on request. Query first, or submit outline and sample chapters, or complete ms. Reports in 2 weeks. Enclose return postage.

Music: Instructional music books for guitarists of all styles. Technical books on quitar repair, electronics for musicians, etc. Instructional booklets to accompany recordings. "We do not publish general method or theory books, but concentrate on individual styles and artists. We aim for the intermediate/advanced musician. We want clear, well-written prose; in-depth knowledge of subject. Strong historical and musical foundation; no personal opinion (except in special circumstances). No general method or theory books. We don't need titles like 'Finger-Pickin-Guitar' or 'Easy Chords for Guitar'. Mss must be typed in standard style. Music notation and tablature in pencil only. Photos must be properly marked." Recent titles include *Rock Guitarists* and *In Session With Herb Ellis*.

GULF PUBLISHING COMPANY, P.O. Box 2608, 3301 Allen Parkway, Houston TX 77001. Editor: Clayton A. Umbach, Jr. Publishes hardcover originals. Royalty schedule: 8%-15%. "Generally we do not have any advance." Published 16 titles last year. Will send a catalog to a writer on request. Write for copy of *Author's Handbook* ($2) for details on proper ms submission. Send query with outline. Reports in 6 to 8 weeks. Enclose return postage.

General Nonfiction, Technical and Scientific, Business, and Textbooks: "Scientific, technical, college texts, management, training, self-help. We attempt to reach untapped technical, training, and managerial markets."

H.P. BOOKS, P.O. Box 5367, Tucson AZ 85703. Editorial Coordinator: Carl Shipman. Publishes paperback originals and reprints. Royalty schedule "varies with title and distribution requirements. We rarely offer an advance and do not believe in 'front money' per se. We use our own contract. This is worked out with author when written." Published 4 titles last year. Will send a catalog to a writer on request. Send query and outline and return postage. "No mss without prior correspondence to determine whether there is a fit."

Hobbies: "General how-to titles related to hobbies and leisure-time activities, especially automotive, motorcycling, art and craft, photography, gardening, landscaping, cooking, etc. Our books are heavily illustrated and copy-only books are not being solicited."

HAESSNER PUBLISHING, INC., Drawer B, Newfoundland NJ 07435. Editor: Walter R. Haessner. Publishes hardcover originals. Offers standard 10-12½-15% royalty contract. Advance varies. Published 12 titles last year. Will send a catalog to a writer on request. Query first with outline and sample chapters for nonfiction. Will consider photocopied submissions "sometimes. Follow Ayer Style Book. Pica type preferred; 60 character count per line, 25 lines deep." Reports on ms accepted for publication in 6 weeks. Returns rejected material in 4 weeks. Enclose return postage.

Nonfiction: Transportation (antiques, motorsports, boating, aircraft, war tanks, how-to-do-it). Travel, sports, art, reference.

HARCOURT BRACE JOVANOVICH, INC., 757 Third Ave., New York NY 10017. Director of Trade: Kathy Robbins. Publishes hardcover originals and paperback reprints. Published 69 trade adult books, 15 juveniles, and 37 paperbacks last year. Query first or send sample chapters for nonfiction manuscripts. Submit complete fiction ms. Enclose return postage.

Juveniles: Barbara Lucas, Editor. Fiction and nonfiction mss for beginning readers through the young teenager. Length: 5,000 words to 60,000 words. "We will be doing more nonfiction than fiction. Fiction must be of exceptional quality. Our lists will probably contain fewer picture books, translations, and imports."

General Fiction and Nonfiction: For adults. Length: 60,000 words and up.

HARIAN PUBLICATIONS, 1000 Prince St., Greenlawn NY 11740. Editor: Frederic Tyarks. Advances paid on royalties. Published 8 titles last year. Will send copy of current catalog on request. Query first. Reports in 1 week. Enclose S.A.S.E.

Nonfiction: Books on travel, retirement, investments, and health. Length: 50,000 words minimum for completed mss.

HARPER & ROW, PUBLISHERS, INC., (including Torchbooks, Colophon, and Perennial Library, and Barnes & Noble), 10 E. 53rd St., New York NY 10022. Publishes hardcover and paperback originals and reprints. Royalty schedule subject to negotiation, but generally 10% to 5,000; 12½% to 10,000; 15% thereafter. Query letters, sample chapters and outlines preferred. For fiction, prefers completed ms. Address General Trade Dept. for fiction and nonfiction. Address Children's Book Dept. for juveniles. Reports in 4 to 6 weeks. Enclose return postage.

General Fiction and Nonfiction: Publishes books between 40,000 and 200,000 words in the following departments: college, elementary and high school, mail order, medical, nature and outdoor, religious, social and economic, and trade. Trade books can cover any subject of general interest, fiction or nonfiction, rather than specialized or scholarly works.

Juveniles: Ellen Rudin, Juvenile Editor.

Textbooks: Publishes elementary and high school textbooks. Address Ray Sluss, Publisher, El-Hi Division, 2500 Crawford Ave., Evanston IL 60201. College textbooks. Address College Dept. Harper & Row, 10 E. 53rd St., New York NY 10022. Junior college textbooks. Address Canfield Press, 850 Montgomery St., San Francisco CA 94133.

HARVARD UNIVERSITY PRESS, 79 Garden St., Cambridge MA 02138. Director: Arthur J. Rosenthal. Published 109 titles last year. Prefers queries with outlines. Enclose return postage.

General Nonfiction: Publishes general nonfiction including history, science, religion, philosophy and the arts. Publishes books of scholarly research directed toward a scholarly audience.

HARVEST HOUSE, LTD., PUBLISHERS, 4795 St. Catherine St. W., Montreal, P. Q., Canada, H3Z 2B9. Editor: Maynard Gertler. Publishes hardcover and paperback originals, reprints, and translations. Royalty schedule varies between 6% and 12%. Published 16 titles last year. Prefers completed ms. Reports in 6 weeks. Enclose S.A.E. and International Reply Coupons.

Nonfiction: History, biography, philosophy, science, social sciences, education, public affairs, and general nonfiction. "We prefer nonfiction to fiction and deal with mss concerning Canadian and general world interest." Minimum length is 35,000 words.

HARVEY HOUSE, INC., 20 Waterside Plaza, New York NY 10010. Editor: Mrs. Jeanne Gardner. Publishes hardcover originals. Royalty and advance varies. Published 10 titles last year. Will send catalog to a writer on request. Query first or submit complete ms. Reports in 3 to 12 weeks. Enclose return postage.

Juveniles: "Children's books primarily — fiction and nonfiction. Strong interest in subject matter that supplements science and social studies curriculums in elementary and junior high schools." Story of Science series geared to grades 5 to 8; Science Parade series, grades 2 to 6. Length for juvenile nonfiction books: 5,000 to 35,000 words maximum. Wants easy-to-read books for K-3 and 2-5. Some categories in which titles were published last year include fiction, science, biography, sports, cookbooks (juvenile), easy-to-read, history. Recent titles include *Illustrated Football Dictionary for Young People* (Olgin); *Coal: Energy & Crisis* (Chaffin).

HASTINGS HOUSE PUBLISHERS, INC., 10 E. 40th St., New York NY 10016. Editor: Walter Frese. Editor of Graphic Arts, Communication Arts (Radio, TV, Printing): Russell F. Neale. Editor of Children's Department: Judy Donnelly. Offers 10% minimum royalty contract. Published 89 titles last year. Query first, "describing ms." Reports in 4 weeks. Enclose return postage.

Nonfiction: Publishes general nonfiction, biography, history, the graphic arts, architecture and decoration.

HAYDEN BOOK COMPANY, INC., 50 Essex St., Rochelle Park NJ 07662. Editorial Director: S.W. Cook. Advance and royalty arrangements vary; generally 10% to 15% of net. Published 51 titles last year. Will send a catalog to a writer on request. All book proposals should include complete outline, preface and two representative chapters. Reports in 6 weeks. Enclose return postage.

Technical: Publishes technician-level and engineering texts and references in many subject areas (emphasis on electronics); texts and references for hotel, restaurant and institution management and other personnel (emphasis on management, food preparation, handling). Recent titles: *Dial 911; Understanding Electronic Switching Systems.*

Textbooks: Texts, references, and visual aids for junior and senior high schools, technical institutes and community colleges in English, computer sciences, mathematics, social studies and other subject areas. Recent titles: *Moviemaking Illustrated; Programming Proverbs.*

Education: "Books on education and other subjects of interest to teachers, college faculty, students, general public."

D.C. HEATH & CO., 125 Spring St., Lexington MA 02173. Editors: Economics and Math: Irving Rockwood; History & Political Science: Joe Hodger; Education & Sociology: Lane Akers; Science & Psychology: Jeff Holtmeier; Modern Languages: Stan Galek; Technical: Michael McCarroll. General Manager, College Division: John T. Harney. Publishes hardcover and paperback originals. Offers standard royalty rates for textbooks. Advance is negotiated. Published about 150 titles last year. Will send a catalog to a writer on request. Query first. Returns rejected material in 2 weeks. "Finished mss accepted are published within 1 year." Enclose return postage.

Textbooks: "Texts at the college level in sociology, psychology, history, political science, chemistry, math, physical science, economics, education, modern language, and English." Length varies.

HEIDELBERG PUBLISHERS, INC., 3707 Kerbey Lane, Austin TX 78731. Editor-in-Chief: David L. Lindsey. Publishes hardcover originals. Offers standard minimum book contract. Advance varies. Published 4 titles last year. Query first or submit complete ms. Will consider photocopied submissions. Enclose return postage and S.A.E.

General Fiction and Nonfiction: "We are a general interest publisher and willing to see works of fiction (no short stories), nonfiction, biography, book trade, history, philosophy, photography, and travel." Current titles include *Food Reform: Our Desperate Need,* a well-researched expose of the inadequacies of the American diet and such a diet's definite contribution to cancer, heart disease, diabetes, and other degenerative diseases; *Carrasco!,* a book of investigation reporting on a Mexican dope running organization operating back and forth across the Mexican border from Texas.

HELLRIC CHAPBOOK SERIES, 39 Eliot St., Jamaica Plain MA 02130. Editor: Ottone M. Riccio. "Mostly works by 1 author, but at times anthologies, memorial volumes, etc." Buys first North American rights only on material used in anthologies. Pays in "copies plus royalties on copies sold on chapbooks by one author; copies on anthologies." Printing run is 500 copies. Publishes 3 to 6 titles a year. Query first for nonfiction except humor; send complete ms for humor, poetry, fiction, plays. Reports in 2 to 4 weeks. Enclose return postage.

General: "No restrictions on subjects, form, etc. Prefer avant-garde and experimental. Looking for collections of poems, short stories, plays, novellas, etc. We're interested in material that makes something happen in the reader's mind and emotional apparatus. We try to search out the promising but unestablished writers. We'll look at anything because we're more interested in how the writer writes than what he writes about — though he should write about something." Length: fiction, 20 to 80 pages (250 words a page); nonfiction, 20 to 40 pages; poetry, at least 20 pages. For Pyramid Pamphlet series, uses poetry of 12 to 20 pages. The Chapbook series is behind schedule temporarily.

HENDRICKS HOUSE, INC., 103 Park Ave., New York NY 10017. Editorial Office: Putney VT 05346. Editor: Walter Hendricks. Publishes hardcover originals and hardcover and paperback reprints. Published 5 titles last year. Will send a catalog to a writer on request. Submit complete ms. Will consider photocopied submissions. Reports in 1 month. Enclose return postage with ms.
Nonfiction: "Mainly educational." Publishes Americana, biography, history, philosophy, reference, and textbooks.

HERALD HOUSE, Drawer HH, 3225 S. Noland Rd., Independence MO 64055. Editor-in-Chief: Paul A. Wellington. Publishes hardcover originals. Standard royalty contract. Usual advance is $500, but this varies, depending on author's reputation and nature of book. Published 20 titles last year. Will send free catalog to writer on request. Query first. Reports in 2 months. Enclose return postage.
Religion: Publishes religious books for adults and children. Fiction, poetry, doctrinal texts, history, etc. All books must be relevant to the Reorganized Church of Jesus Christ of Latter-Day Saints. Length: 30,000 to 60,000 words.

HOLIDAY HOUSE, INC., 18 E. 56th St., New York NY 10022. Editor: Margery Cuyler. Published 18 titles last year. Reports in 4 to 6 weeks. Enclose return postage.
Juveniles: Publishes children's books only — fiction and nonfiction, for preschool through teenage boys and girls.

HOLLOWAY HOUSE PUBLISHING CO., 8060 Melrose Ave., Los Angeles CA 90046. Editor: Charles D. Anderson. Publishes originals, reprints and translations. "Our payment is comparable to that of all paperback book publishers. We promote heavily, giving each book individual attention. Prefer queries on all submissions. But mss and partials may be submitted provided they are accompanied by an outline covering all salient points. We try to report in 2 weeks if rejected and in 2 months if interested, but this is subject to the volume of mss received. We do not publish poetry, short stories or plays." Published 24 titles last year. Enclose S.A.S.E. with queries or submissions.
Nonfiction: "We're looking for extraordinary works on all subjects of enduring interest which have something to say and which say it well. Prefer 50,000 to 100,000 words. You must query first and all queries or mss must be accompanied by a brief synopsis of the work." Current titles include *How to Play and Win at Gin Rummy* and *Outlaws of the Old West.*
Fiction: "We're looking for general novels." Also particularly interested in realistic, contemporary novels of the Black Experience. "We are not in the market for sex books."

A.J. HOLMAN COMPANY, East Washington Square, Philadelphia PA 19105. Editor: Dr. Russell T. Hitt. Publishes hardcover originals. "Generally, we stick to the standard royalty contract." Published 8 titles last year. Will send a catalog to a writer on request. Submit outline and sample chapters or complete ms. Will consider photocopied submissions "for outlines only." Reports on ms accepted for publication in 30 to 60 days. Returns rejected material in about 6 weeks. Enclose return postage.
Religion: "We are the religious division of the J.B. Lippincott Company. The type of book we are most interested in is written for the man on the street and not necessarily for the theologian. Interested in books on current subjects as they relate to the religious aspects of life, biographies, how-to-do-it books, etc. Most books we publish are in the 128- to 156-page length. Our primary market is the conservative religious layman rather than the minister/educator. This should be given the greatest consideration. Many writers write over the heads of this audience when approaching a religious subject." Interested in material on "how a person's life has been changed by faith in God."

HOLT, RINEHART AND WINSTON OF CANADA, LTD., 55 Horner Ave., Toronto 18, Ontario, Canada. Director, Research and Product Development: J.C. Mainprize. Publishes hardcover and paperback originals and anthologies. Offers standard royalty contract. "Advance depends on material. Flat fee only in anthologies." Published

60 titles last year. Will send a catalog to a writer on request. Send query with outline and sample chapter for nonfiction and textbooks. Reports in 1 to 3 months. Enclose Canadian postage or International Reply Coupons.

General Nonfiction: "Canadian authors preferred." Buys business and professional, arts, history and biography.

Textbooks: "All fields—elementary, secondary, and college levels. Must be by Canadians or dealing specifically with Canadian materials."

HOOVER INSTITUTION PRESS, Stanford University, Stanford CA 94305. Usually offers 10% royalty. Prefers outline first. Should be addressed to Secretary, Publications Committee. Reports in 6 to 10 weeks. Enclose return postage.

Economics, History, and Political Science: History and political science, primarily 20th century, concerning political, social or economic change; documentaries, studies, or bibliographies relating to 20th century political, social or economic change. New series in domestic economic problems. Length: 40,000 words minimum.

HOPKINSON & BLAKE, 329 Fifth Ave., New York NY 10016. Editor-in-Chief: Len Karlin. Publishes clothbound and paperback originals. Offers standard 10-12½% royalty contract; average advance $1,000. Published 6 titles last year. Will consider photocopied submissions. Query first. Reports in 2 weeks. Enclose return postage.

Nonfiction: Mainly for college market. "We plan to continue to publish books on motion pictures. Also going into social sciences." Recent titles include *Lorentz on Film* (Lorentz); *Women Who Make Movies* (Smith); *Soundtrack: The Music of the Movies* (Evans).

HORIZON PRESS, 156 Fifth Ave., New York NY 10010. Prefers complete ms. Royalty schedule standard scale from 10% to 15%. Published 26 titles last year. Will send catalog. Reports in 4 weeks. Enclose return postage with ms.

Nonfiction: History, science, biography, the arts, general. Length: 40,000 words and up.

HOUGHTON MIFFLIN CO., 2 Park St., Boston MA 02107. Editor-in-Chief: Austin G. Olney. Publishes hardcover and paperback originals and reprints. Pays by royalty contract. Published 466 titles last year. Queries welcomed on basis of at least 50 mss pages plus an outline. Reports within 1 month. Enclose return postage with query and outline.

General: Publishes general literature, fiction, biography, autobiography, history. Length: 25,000 words minimum; 70,000 to 140,000 words for biographies. Poetry; children's books. Also publishes paperbacks, including Sentry Editions, which are reprints of titles of permanent interest in a soft-backed edition. Recent titles include *Dog Soldiers* (Stone); *Uphill* (McGovern and Hoyt).

Textbooks: Elementary, secondary, and college textbooks.

HOUSE OF COLLECTIBLES, INC., P.O. Box D, Florence AL 35630. Publisher: Joel R. Anderson. Publishes hardcover and paperback originals. Royalty is based on the stature of the author, the subject and the ms. Average advance is $1,000. Published 15 titles last year. Complete distribution and marketing range in all fields with heavy coverage on the collectible markets. Will send catalog to writer on request. Submit outline and sample chapters. Will consider photocopied submissions. Mss must be typed, double spaced with sample illustrations, when necessary. Reports within 2 months. Enclose return postage.

Nonfiction: "On the subject of collectibles (antiques, numismatics, philatelics) and how-to-do books. We prefer an author who knows his or her subject thoroughly. Style and general format are left entirely to the author. Any special treatment or emphasis is a matter of decision for the author." Interested in mss on Indian collectibles, bicentennial collectibles, gold coin collectibles, knife collectibles. Current titles include *Official Guide to Silver & Silverplate; Official Guide to Antiques & Curios; Official Guide to Bottles; Old & New; Official Guide to Comic Books; Official Black Book of U.S. Coins; Official Guide of U.S. Paper Money.*

HOWELL-NORTH BOOKS, 1050 Parker St., Berkeley CA 94710. President: Mrs. Morgan North. Publishes hardcover and paperback originals. Pays 10% of retail price; no advance. Published 5 titles last year. Current catalog available. Send query, outline and sample chapter. Reports in 10 weeks. Enclose return postage.
Nonfiction: Publishes railroadiana, works on transportation, steamboating, mining, California, marine nonfiction pictorials, histories, Americana, and especially influence of the west. Length: 30,000 words minimum. Recent titles include *Los Angeles: Epic of a City* (Bowman); *The Last Whistle: Ocean Shore Railroad* (Wagner).

HUBBARD PRESS, Publishers of Donohue/Hampton Books, P.O. Box 442, 2855 Shermer Road, Northbrook IL 60062. Editor: Eleanor McConnell. Published 5 titles last year. Query before sending mss. Enclose return postage.
Juveniles and Science: Publishes juvenile books and science publications. Fiction, picture books, science, nature, nursery rhymes.

HURTIG PUBLISHERS, 10560 105 St., Edmonton, Alta., Canada. Editor: Jan Walter. Publishes hardcover and paperback originals and reprints. Usual advance is $1,000, but this varies, depending on author's reputation and nature of book. "Royalties start at 10%." Published 9 titles last year. Will send a catalog to a writer on request. Query first. Reports in 6 weeks. Enclose S.A.E. and International Reply Coupons.
Nonfiction: "Interested in topical Canadian nonfiction of a political or social comment nature, also Canadian history and biography." Length: 50,000 to 200,000 words. Recent titles include *Colimbo's Canadian Quotations* (reference/literature); *Tales From the Smokehouse* (legends/literature).

INDEPENDENCE PRESS, Drawer HH, 3225 So. Noland Rd., Independence MO 64055. Editor-in-Chief: Paul A. Wellington. Publishes hardcover originals. Offers standard minimum book contract of 10-12½-15%. "Variation on the standard contract depends on author's reputation and nature of book." Advance is $500. Published 6 titles last year. Will send free catalog to writer on request. Submit outline and sample chapters for nonfiction to Book Editor. Submit complete ms for fiction and self-help nonfiction. "We use the Chicago *Manual of Style*." Reports within 6 weeks. Enclose S.A.E. and return postage.
General Nonfiction, Fiction and Juveniles: "We are interested in mss which develop character and self-appreciation, which deal with positive solutions to problems and exhibit a realistic approach to life situations. They should be lively, imaginative, and innovative. Those of a historical nature should be carefully researched but have a strong story line with believable characters and vivid descriptions. We prefer clean language acceptable for school and family use. We appreciate accuracy in research of culture, dress, language peculiarities of the period, etc. We would like to have books, especially children's literature, dealing with minority groups, sound psychological principles, anti-sexist approach to today's world. We've published a number of books about Missouri and/or midwest history. We're saturated currently on these subjects." Adult Trade Fiction, Americana, History, Humor, Juveniles, Library, Poetry, Self-help & How-to, and Autobiography/Biography Editor: Jean Hurshman. Religion Editor: Paul A. Wellington.

INDIANA UNIVERSITY PRESS, 10th and Morton Sts., Bloomington IN 47401. Editorial Director: John Gallman. Publishes hardcover originals and paperback reprints. Normally pays 10% royalty. Published 57 titles last year. Queries should include as much descriptive material as is necessary to convey scope and market appeal of ms. Reports on rejections in 6 weeks or less; on acceptances, in 3 months. Enclose return postage.
Nonfiction: Scholarly books on humanities, public policy, film, music, linguistics, social science; regional materials, serious nonfiction for the general reader.

INTERNATIONAL MARINE PUBLISHING COMPANY, 21 Elm St., Camden ME 04843. Editor: Peter Spectre. Publishes hardcover and paperback originals and reprints. "Standard royalties, with advances." Published 10 titles last year. Will send a catalog to a writer on request. "Material in all stages welcome. Query invited, but not necessary." Reports in 4 weeks. Enclose return postage with ms.

Marine Nonfiction: "Marine nonfiction only — but a wide range of subjects within that category: fishing, boatbuilding, yachting, sea ecology and conservation, maritime history, cruising, true sea adventure, etc. — anything to do with boats, lakes, rivers, seas, and the people who do things on them, commercially or for pleasure. No word length requirements. Pictorial books with short texts are as welcome as 60,000-word mss." Current leading titles include *Charlie York: Maine Coast Fisherman* (Clifford); *Cape Cod Fisherman* (Schwind); *Successful Bluefishing* (Lyman); *Self-Steering for Sailing Craft* (Letcher).

INTERNATIONAL WEALTH SUCCESS, Box 186, Merrick NY 11566. Editor: Tyler G. Hicks. Offers royalty schedule of 10% of list price. Usual advance is $1,000, but this varies, depending on author's reputation and nature of book. Published 12 titles last year. Query first. Will consider photocopied submissions. Reports in 4 weeks. Enclose return postage.

Self-Help and How-to: "Techniques, methods, sources for building wealth. Highly personal, how-to-do-it with plenty of case histories. Books are aimed at the wealth builder and are highly sympathetic to his problems." Financing, business success, venture capital, etc. Length 60,000 to 70,000 words. Current titles include *Business Capital Sources: Small Business Investment Handbook; How to Make a Fortune as a Licensing Agent.*

THE INTERSTATE PRINTERS AND PUBLISHERS, INC., 19-26 N. Jackson St., Danville IL 61832. Editorial and Marketing Manager: Paul A. Sims. Royalty schedule varies; however, it is usually 10% of wholesale price. Published 48 titles last year. Will send a current catalog to a writer on request. Prefers queries, outlines, or sample chapters. Reports in 30 to 60 days. Enclose return postage.

Textbooks: Publishes textbooks primarily, in agriculture, industrial arts, home economics, athletics, and special education. Preferred word length varies according to content covered. Recent titles include *Ezra Taft Benson and the Politics of Agriculture* (Schapsmeier and Schapsmeier); *Law and the North Carolina Teacher* (Smith).

INTER-VARSITY PRESS, Box F, Downers Grove IL 60515. Editor: Dr. James W. Sire. Publishes hardcover and paperback originals, reprints, translations, and anthologies. Royalty schedule "varies with the ms and the author." Published 28 titles last year. Will send a catalog to a writer on request. Send outline and sample chapter. Reports in 16 weeks. Enclose return postage.

Religion and Philosophy and Textbooks: "Publishes books geared to the presentation of Biblical Christianity in its various relations to personal life, art, literature, sociology, philosophy, history, etc.; college, university, and seminary-level textbooks on any subject within the general religious field. The audience for which the books are published is composed primarily of university students and graduates. The stylistic treatment varies from topic to topic and from fairly simplified popularization for college freshmen to extremely scholarly works primarily designed to be read by scholars." Current leading titles include *No Little People* (Schaeffer); *How to Understand Your Bible* (Sterrett).

THE JOHNS HOPKINS UNIVERSITY PRESS, Baltimore MD 21218. Editor-in-Chief: Michael A. Aronson. Publishes mostly clothbound originals and paperback reprints; some paperback originals. Payment varies; contract negotiated with author. Prompt report, usually 8 weeks. Published 75 books last year. Prefers query letter first. Enclose S.A.S.E.

Nonfiction: Publishes scholarly books and nonfiction for the intelligent reader; biomedical sciences, history, literary criticism, psychology, education, international affairs, and economics. Length: 40,000 words minimum.

JONATHAN DAVID PUBLISHERS, 68-22 Eliot Ave., Middle Village NY 11379. General Editor: Alfred J. Kolatch. Publishes hardcover and paperback originals.

Offers standard 10-12½-15% royalty contract; "advances according to credentials." Published 25 titles last year. Will send a catalog to a writer on request. Send query with detailed outline and sample chapter. Reports in 2 to 4 weeks. Enclose return postage.

General Nonfiction: "General nonfiction for adults. Because we are new in the general book field, we feel that we can give the author a more personal relationship than he ordinarily would receive. Our titles must have a mass audience potential. We're always open to solid ideas. We generally recruit our top authors, but we are interested in hearing from able writers with nonfiction book ideas." Recent titles include *Cars of the Stars; Miracles in Medicine.* Also publishes reference books.

JUDSON PRESS, Valley Forge PA 19481. Managing Editor: Harold L. Twiss. Publishes hardcover and paperback originals. Generally 10% royalty on first 7,500 copies; 12½% on next 7,500; 15% above 15,000. "Payment of an advance depends on author's reputation and nature of book." Published 31 titles last year. Catalog available on request. Prefers a query letter accompanied by outline and sample chapter. Reports in 3 months. Enclose return postage.

Religion: Adult religious nonfiction of 30,000 to 200,000 words.

WILLIAM KAUFMANN, INC., One First St., Los Altos CA 94022. Editor-in-Chief: William Kaufmann. Publishes hardcover and paperback originals. "Generally offers standard minimum book contract of 10-12½-15%, but "special requirements of book may call for lower royalties." No advance. Published 4 titles last year. Query first. Reports within a few weeks. Enclose S.A.S.E.

Education: Main interests are academic trade books; that is, general interest books that are developed by professional teachers or by well-known writers, and are aimed at readers with good high school or even college education. Prefer books suitable for use as supplemental reading or basic adoption for forward-looking courses; but not particularly interested in conventional textbooks. Good writing, high quality (accuracy and depth), originality, are major qualities sought. Should be for literate, issue or problem oriented audiences, and have staying power (not too ephemeral, trendy, etc.). Originality in approach, format, organization, and illustration." Adult trade fiction, economics, environmental, law, politics, regional planning, and scientific areas (psychology and human biology) of interest also. Current titles include *Jonah's Dream: A Meditation on Fishing* (Berlin); *Sport in Classic Times* (Butler); *Pain Control Through Hypnosis and Suggestion* (Hilgard); *Stalking the Wild Taboo* (Hardin); *Should Trees Have Standing?* (Stone).

KEATS PUBLISHING, INC., 212 Elm St., P.O. Box 876, New Canaan CT 06840. Editor: A. Keats. Publishes hardcover and paperback originals and reprints. Offers standard 10-12½-15% royalty contract. Advance varies. Published 23 titles last year. Will send a catalog to a writer on request. Query first with outline and sample chapter. Reports in 2 months. Enclose return postage.

Nonfiction: "Natural health, special interest; industry-subsidy. Also, mss with promotion and premium potential. In natural health, anything having to do with the current interest in ecology, natural health cookbooks, diet books, organic gardening, etc." Length: open.

Religion: "Largely in the conservative Protestant field."

KENT STATE UNIVERSITY PRESS, Kent State University, Kent OH 44242. Director: Paul H. Rohmann. Publishes hardcover originals. Standard minimum book contract; rarely gives an advance. Published 8 titles last year. Will send a catalog to a writer on request. "Please always write a letter of inquiry before submitting mss. We can publish only a limited number of titles each year and can frequently tell in advance whether or not we would be interested in a particular ms. This practice saves both our time and that of the author, not to mention postage costs." Reports in 10 weeks. Enclose return postage.

Nonfiction: Especially interested in "scholarly works in history of high quality, particularly any titles of regional interest for Ohio. Also will consider scholarly biographies, social sciences, scientific research, the arts, and general nonfiction."

DALE STUART KING, PUBLISHER, 2002 N. Tucson Blvd., Tucson AZ 85716. Publishes hardcover and paperback originals. Royalty schedule: usually 12% of gross sales. Catalog available on request. Send query first, then outline and sample chapter. Reports in less than 30 days. Enclose return postage.
Nonfiction: Publishes specialized history, biography, science, and general nonfiction on the Southwest only. Length: around 60,000 words.

KIRKLEY PRESS, INC., P.O. Box 200, Timonium MD 21093. Editor: Alan Dugdale. Publishes paperback 16-page booklets. "We buy mss outright and pay upon acceptance. Payment (total) varies between $200 and $300, depending on subject and strength with which written. Sample of our material sent on request." Send complete ms. "Try to answer in 2 weeks." Enclose return postage.
Business: "We publish small booklets which are sold to businesses for distribution to the employee. They attempt to stimulate or motivate the employee to improve work habits. Basically they are pep talks for the employee. We need writers who are so close to the problems of present-day employee attitudes that they can take one of those problems and write about it in a warm, human, understanding, personal style and language that will appeal to the employee and which the employer will find to his advantage to distribute to the employees." Length: 2,400 to 2,600 words.

ALFRED A. KNOPF, INC., 201 East 50th St., New York NY 10022. Senior Editor: Ashbel Green. Payment is on royalty basis. Published 152 titles last year. Send query letter for nonfiction; query letter or complete mss for fiction. No unsolicited poetry manuscripts. Will consider photocopied submissions. Reports in 2 to 4 weeks. Enclose self-addressed, stamped envelope.
Fiction: Publishes book-length fiction of literary merit by known or unknown writers. Length: 30,000 to 150,000 words.
Nonfiction: Book-length nonfiction, including books of scholarly merit on special subjects. Preferred length: 40,000 to 150,000 words. A good nonfiction writer should be able to follow the latest scholarship in any field of human knowledge, and fill in the abstractions of scholarship for the benefit of the general reader by means of good, concrete, sensory reporting.
Juveniles: No minimum length requirement. Juvenile Editor: Pat Ross.

JOHN KNOX PRESS, 341 Ponce de Leon Avenue, N.E., Atlanta GA 30308. Editor: Dr. Richard A. Ray. Publishes hardcover and paperback originals, reprints, and translations. Payment by royalty. Published 24 titles last year. Will send a catalog to writer on request. Send query with personal vita, outline, and sample chapter. "It would be helpful if the author's covering letter includes a brief description of book's potential market and uniqueness in the field." Ms should be double-spaced, 60 characters to a line, 25 lines per page. Conform to *A Manual of Style* (12th edition), The University of Chicago Press. Reports in 3 months. Enclose return postage.
Religion and Philosophy: "We are looking for books dealing with personal faith; family and interpersonal relationships; inspiration; Biblical and theological scholarship; and the relation of religion to social, cultural, ethical, or aesthetic concerns. The audience varies with the book." Length: 15,000 to 60,000 words.

LANTERN PRESS, INC., 354 Hussey Rd., Mount Vernon NY 10552. Payment is on royalty basis, or outright purchase, if preferred. Usual advance is $250 on signing, $250 on publication. Titles published last year: 5. No mss should be sent unless authorized. Query first. Reports in 3 to 4 weeks. Enclose return postage.
Nonfiction: Publishes adult nonfiction, self-help, mail-order books. Length: 2,000 to 30,000 words.
Juveniles: Especially interested in juveniles for all ages. Juvenile Editor: J.R. Furman.

SEYMOUR LAWRENCE, INC., 90 Beacon St., Boston MA 02108. Publisher: Seymour Lawrence. Editor: Merloyd Lawrence. Publishes hardcover originals. Seymour Lawrence books are published in association with the Delacorte Press. Royalty

schedule: 10% to 5,000 copies; 12½% to 10,000; 15% thereafter on adult hardcover books; 10% on children's books. Published 12 titles last year. Send outline and sample chapters. Enclose return postage.
Nonfiction, Fiction, Juveniles: Child care and development books for the general reader; no textbooks. Adult fiction. Juvenile fiction and picture books. Recent titles include *Starting Over* (Wakefield); *Toddlers and Parents* (Brazelton).

LAWYERS AND JUDGES PUBLISHING CO., 817 E. Broadway, P.O. Box 6081, Tucson AZ 85733. Editor-in-Chief: Ronald H. Weintraub. Publishes paperback originals. "We negotiate each title separately." No advance. Published 5 titles last year. Will send catalog to writer for 25¢. Will consider photocopied submissions. Query first. Reports in 10 days. Enclose S.A.S.E.
Business and Law: Question and answer booklets about the law for laymen. Case organizers for lawyers and their secretaries. How-to books for lawyers and accountants. Question and answer format desired. "Lawyers purchase question and answer booklets to give to their clients at no charge, in order to reduce office time needed to educate the client. How-to books stress practical aspects of complying with the hundreds of different federal government forms. We're planning more Practical Guides, and taxes and government regulations are good themes also."

LEARNING TRENDS, 175 Fifth Ave., New York NY 10010. Editor-in-Chief: David A. Katz. Publishes hardcover and paperback originals. Contract and advance "subject to negotiation; usual advance is $1,000." Published 24 titles last year. Will send a catalog to a writer on request. Submit outline and sample chapters. Will consider photocopied submissions. Reports in 6 weeks. Enclose return postage.
Textbooks: "Textbooks, grades K to 12; emphasis on slow learner material. Especially interested in career education, and other areas lending themselves to a high interest, low reading level approach. Other media besides print welcome. Short chapters and study aids recommended. Interested in relevant, original materials in social studies, language arts, science, mathematics, and other fields represented in school curricula. The high conceptual level and slow learner approach is recommended."

LENOX HILL PRESS, 419 Park Ave. S., New York NY 10016. Editor: Alice Sachs. Pays $150 for westerns, $250 for romances. Books published last year: 72. Address query letters to Phyllis Fleiss, Editorial Department; entire mss when possible. Reports in 6 weeks. Enclose return postage.
Fiction: Publishes sweet romances, gothics, old-time western yarns. Prefers 55,000 to 60,000 word lengths.

LERNER PUBLICATIONS CO., 241 First Ave. N., Minneapolis MN 55401. Published 35 titles last year. Current catalog and brochure listing author guidelines available on request. Query unnecessary; prefers complete ms. Send ms to Jennifer Martin. Will consider photocopied submissions. Reports within 3 months. Enclose return postage with ms.
Juveniles: Publishes fiction and educational books for children from preschool through high school, including books in the following subject areas: K-3 reading and language arts, remedial reading, art appreciation, music, mathematics, science, social science, family living and medical topics, career education, sports, science fiction, picture storybooks.

LESTER AND ORPEN LIMITED, PUBLISHERS, 42 Charles St. E., 8th floor, Toronto, Ontario M4Y 1T4, Canada. Phone: 416-961-1812. Editor-in-Chief: Malcolm Lester. Publishes hardcover and paperback originals and reprints. Offers standard minimum book contract of 10-12½-15%. No advance. Published 9 titles last year. Will send free catalog on request. Query first with outline and one sample chapter showing style and treatment. Submit complete ms only if writer has been published before. Will consider photocopied submissions. Reports in 6 weeks. Enclose S.A.E. and International Reply Coupons.
General Fiction, General Nonfiction, Juveniles and Drama: "Our basic philosophy of publishing only carefully selected books is stronger than ever; each and every

title reflects a uniqueness in concept, careful and imaginative editing and design, and powerful and creative promotion. Our philosophy is that the book should be as long or as short as the subject warrants." Publishes adult trade fiction, Americana, biography, sociology, philosophy, book trade, cookbooks (cooking and food), erotic, foreign language, juveniles, plays, religion, and scientific works. Current titles include *Candy, Chocolate, Ice Cream, and How to Lick 'em!* by Sandy Sprung (health/diet); *Some Camel, Some Needle* by Arnold Edinborough (religion/humanism).

LIBRA PUBLISHERS, INC., 391 Willets Rd., P.O. Box 165, Roslyn Hts., L.I. NY 11577. Pays royalties of 10% and up. No advance. Published 10 titles last year. Wants queries with outlines and sample chapters. Send inquiries to Editor-in-Chief. Reports in 2 weeks. Enclose return postage.
Nonfiction: Books on history, biography, science, behavioral sciences, philosophy, religion, psychology, psychiatry. All nonfiction subjects considered. No word length requirements.
Fiction and Poetry: Some books of fiction and poetry.

LIBRARIES UNLIMITED, INC., P.O. Box 263, Littleton CO 80120. Editor-in-Chief: Bohdan S. Wynar. Acquisition Editor: Richard Gray. Publishes hardcover and paperback originals. Offers standard 10-12½-15% royalty contract. No advance. Published 25 titles last year. Will send a catalog to a writer on request. Send complete ms. Follow Chicago *Manual of Style.* Will consider photocopied submissions. Reports in 1 to 3 months. Enclose return postage with ms.
Library and Reference: Reference books (no multivolume sets) on all subjects of interest to public, school and university libraries.
Textbooks: Publishes textbooks in library science on graduate and technician levels. Monographs and research studies in the area of library science and reference books in all areas.

LINKS BOOKS, 33 W. 60th St., New York NY 10023. Editors: Carol Fein and Jeffrey Friedman-Weiss. Publishes paperback originals. Published 15 titles last year. Query first with sample chapters. Enclose return postage.
Nonfiction: "We publish books we care about, books that will be sold in college bookstores and stores catering to other youth groups, including the counter-culture." Trade books on contemporary culture and society; practical and instructional books; photography and art books.

J.B. LIPPINCOTT CO., (General Division), E. Washington Square, Philadelphia PA 19105. General Adult Book Editor: Edward L. Burlingame. Publishes hardcover and paperback originals and reprints. Standard royalty schedule. Published 228 titles last year. Will send catalog on request. Reports in 3 to 4 weeks. Enclose return postage with ms.
General: Publishes general nonfiction; also history, biography, nature, sports, the arts, adult fiction.

J.B. LIPPINCOTT CO., (Juvenile Division), 521 5th Avenue, New York NY 10017. Editor-in-Chief, Books for Young Readers: Dorothy Briley. Publishes trade books for kindergarten through high school. Selected titles published simultaneously in paper and hardcover. Standard royalty schedule. Published 38 titles last year. Catalog sent on request. Reports in 8 to 10 weeks. Enclose return postage with ms.
Juveniles: Fiction and nonfiction. Current titles include *Of Love and Death and Other Journeys* (Holland); *Supersuits* (Cobb).

LITTLE, BROWN AND COMPANY, 34 Beacon St., Boston MA 02106. Editor-in-Chief: Roger Donald. Publishes hardcover and paperback originals and reprints. Offers royalty contract. Published 150 titles last year. "Contracts for nonfiction offered on basis of an outline and 3 or 4 sample chapters." Reports in 1 month. Enclose return postage.
General: "Fiction and general nonfiction book-length mss."
Juveniles: "All ages." Editor of Children's Books: John G. Keller.

LIVERIGHT PUBLISHING CORP., 500 Fifth Ave., New York NY 10036. Editorial Directors: Ned Arnold, Jean Naggar, Laurie Nevin Friedman. Publishes hardcover and paperback originals, reprints, and anthologies. "Payment is on a royalty basis." Published 30 titles last year. Will send a catalog to a writer on request. Manuscripts welcome. Contracts offered for good nonfiction material on the basis of an outline and several sample chapters. Reports in 60 days. Enclose return postage.
General: "Publishes good fiction and nonfiction over 60,000 words." Subjects for nonfiction include biography, autobiography, history, psychology, Americana, current events and public affairs. Especially wants "good fiction for 'New Writers Series'."

LIVING BOOKS, LTD., P.O. Box 593, Times Square Station, New York NY 10036. An affiliate of Diplomatic Press, Inc. Pays "the usual 10% of the published price in accordance with Author's Guild requirements." Advance varies, depending on author's reputation and nature of book. Send query first with outline and sample chapter to the Editor. Reports in 2 to 3 months. "Unsolicited mss are not returned, unless they are accompanied by S.A.S.E."
General: Publishes books in every field of human interest — adult fiction, history, biography, science, philosophy, the arts, religion, and general nonfiction. "List for fiction closed for the time being." Length: 65,000 to 125,000 words.

LONGMAN CANADA LTD., 55 Barber Greene Rd., Don Mills, Ont., Canada. Managing Editor: Alistair Hunter. Query on general nonfiction and science; completed mss preferred in all other categories. Do not need to include return postage. Does return mss and respond to queries.
Fiction: Publishes adult fiction. Fiction mss should run 80,000 words or more.
Nonfiction: History (Canadian preferred), biography (lives of Canadians preferred), popular science, general nonfiction.
Juveniles: Juveniles at the teenage level. Length: 50,000 words or more.
Textbooks: Textbooks on all levels.

ROBERT B. LUCE INC., 2000 N Street, N.W., Washington DC 20036. Offers standard 10%-12½%-15% royalty contract. Published 7 titles last year. Will send a catalog to a writer on request. Reports in 4 weeks. Enclose return postage.
General Fiction: "Publishes limited fictional works."
General Nonfiction: "Books dealing with current affairs: books of personal experience that are meaningful to general readers; how-to-do-it, self-help books that are authoritative and written for the popular audience. Books on controversial subjects. Mss should be 60,000 words and up; outline and sample chapters preferred initially." Current leading titles include *Cold in the Blue Ridge* (Innis). Dept. Editor: Joseph J. Binns.
History and Biography: "Mss should be 60,000 words and up; outline and sample chapters preferred initially." Current leading title is *White Flags of Surrender* (biography). Dept. Editor: Sarah B. Forman.
Public Affairs and Social Problems: "Query first with outline and sample chapters." Current titles include *The Bitter Harvest* (current affairs); *How Much for Health* (current affairs). Dept. Editor: Robert van Roijen.

McCLELLAND AND STEWART, LTD., 25 Hollinger Rd., Toronto 374, Ont., Canada. Royalties are standard, but often individually negotiated. Advances vary depending on author's reputation and nature of book. Published 100 titles last year. Will send catalog on request. Include with ms an outline plus brief history of writing credits. Send all mss to Editor-in-Chief. Reports in 5 to 8 weeks. Enclose S.A.E. and International Reply Coupons.
Fiction: Interested in Canadian writing of outstanding quality.
Nonfiction, Juveniles, and Poetry: General nonfiction, history, biography, the arts, sports, politics, poetry, secondary and college textboks in humanities. Juvenile nonfiction and fiction.

McCORMICK-MATHERS PUBLISHING CO., 450 W. 33rd St., New York NY 10001. Editor-in-Chief: Anthony J. Quaglia. Publishes paperback originals. Contract negotiated by flat fee. Published 50 titles last year. Will send catalog to writer on request. Will consider photocopied submissions. Submit outline and sample chapters. Reports as soon as possible. Enclose return postage.

Textbooks and Fiction: El-hi textbooks and action fiction within the el-hi age level from short stories to novellas; rural, suburban, city and inner city subject matter; school situations, inter-peer relationships, inter-family situations. Prefers third-person narrative without flashbacks. Value based in outlook, with strong emphasis on ethical good over ethical evil. "Our books are geared primarily to students with reading difficulties who have not profited from traditional reading instructions. We rewrite submitted material."

McGILL-QUEEN'S UNIVERSITY PRESS, 1020 Pine Ave. West., Montreal, Quebec, Canada, H3A 1A2. Editor: Miss Beverly Johnston. Publishes hardcover and paperback originals. "Standard royalty is 10% of net. Published 29 titles last year." Send outline. "If invited to submit work, send ms typed double-spaced throughout, with double-spaced notes at back of ms." Reporting time "depends on whether ms is to be read by specialists." Enclose International Reply Coupons for return postage.

General Nonfiction: "Books based on original scholarly research and serious nonfiction of general interest." Social sciences and humanities.

McGRAW-HILL BOOK COMPANY, 1221 Ave. of the Americas, New York NY 10020. Publishes hardcover and paperback originals, reprints, translations, and anthologies. Offers standard royalty contract: 10% to 5,000, 12.5% to 10,000, 15% thereafter. On textbooks, "royalties vary from 3% net to 15% list." Published 609 titles last year. Will send a catalog to a writer on request. Send outline and sample chapter. "Unsolicited mss rarely accepted. No poetry, mysteries or science fiction." Reports in 3 weeks. Enclose return postage.

General: Trade nonfiction and fiction. Dept. Editors: Fred Hills, General Fiction, General Nonfiction, Reference; Tyler Hicks, Technical and Scientific; Paul Schneider, Medical; Samuel Bossard, Religion and Philosophy; William Mogan, Business and Professional.

Juveniles: Editor-in-Chief, Junior Books: Eleanor Nichols.

College and University Textbooks: The College and University Division publishes college textbooks. "We aim for superior editorial content geared to course level and type of student. The writer must know the college curriculum and course structure. No 'relevance' readers and anthologies." Also publishes "scientific texts and reference books in medicine, nursing, the physical sciences, and mathematics. Material should be scientifically and factually accurate. Most, but not all, books should be designed for existing courses offered in various disciplines of study. Books should have superior presentations and be more up-to-date than existing textbooks." Dept. Editors: Joseph J. Brehm, Editor-in-Chief, Medicine and Psychiatry and Nursing; Bradford Bayne, Scientific, Mathematics, and Statistics textbooks.

Community College Textbooks: For Community College Division, wants material in the areas of "remedial/basic skills education, occupational education, technologies education, general/academic education in all media. The treatment must relate or conform to two-year college curriculums and course outlines specifically. The author must either be a teacher in a two-year college or an instructor in a business-industry training program. Clearly stated objectives, both macro and micro, must be an integral part of the ms." Dept. Editors: E. E. Byers, Editor-in-Chief, Business and Management; A. W. Lowe, Senior Editor, Electricity, Electronics, and Computer Science; R. Buchanan, Senior Editor, Engineering Technologies, Applied Math and Science; A. Cleverdon, Editor, Human Service Occupations; E. B. Fuchs, Editor, Basic Skills programs; G. O. Stone, Manager, General/Academic programs; P. Walker, Publisher, Professional Reference.

McGRAW-HILL RYERSON, LTD., 330 Progress Ave., Scarborough, Ontario, Canada M1P 2Z5. Publisher: Mr. Toivo Kiil. Publishes hardcover and paperback originals and reprints. Royalty schedule varies: 10% and more on list for trade titles; average advance is $1,000 for biographies. Published 32 titles last year. Will send a catalog to a writer on request. Query first with outline and sample chapter for nonfiction; send outline for fiction. Reports in 90 days. Enclose S.A.E. and International Reply Coupons.

General Fiction and Nonfiction: History, biography, art, general nonfiction, some fiction; mainly Canadian interest. Current titles include *The Book of Canadian Antiques* (Webster); *Something I've Been Meaning to Tell You* (Munro).

Biography: "Good market for book-length Canadian biographies." Length: 60,000 to 120,000 words.

Juveniles: Buys some illustrated juveniles.

MACMILLAN COMPANY OF CANADA, LTD., 70 Bond St., Toronto, Ont., Canada M5B 1X3. Trade Editors: D. M. Gibson, K.A. McVey. Published 25 titles last year. Payment by arrangement. Essential to query first. Unsolicited trade mss not accepted. Reports in 6 weeks. Enclose S.A.E. and International Reply Coupons.

General: Publishes Canadian books of all kinds. Biography, history, art, current affairs, juveniles, poetry and fiction.

Textbooks: Educational Editor: Gladys Neale.

Scientific and Technical: College, Medical, Nursing Editor: Virgil Duff.

MACMILLAN PUBLISHING COMPANY, INC., 866 Third Ave., New York NY 10022. Publishes hardcover and paperback originals and reprints. Published 26 paperback juveniles, 60 hardbound juveniles, 142 hardbound adult and 86 paperback adult titles last year. Send query letter before sending ms. Address all mss except juveniles to Trade Editorial Department; children's books to Children's Book Department. Will consider photocopied submissions. Enclose return postage.

Fiction and Nonfiction: Publishes adult fiction and nonfiction. Length: at least 75,000 words.

Juveniles: Children's books.

MACRAE SMITH COMPANY, 225 S. 15th St., Philadelphia PA 19102. Pays 10% of list price. Published 12 titles last year. Will send a catalog on request. Send outline and sample chapters or complete ms and letter reviewing relevant background and experience of author. Address mss to Ruth Allan Miner. Reports in 4 to 6 weeks. Enclose return postage.

General: "Adult trade books, fiction and nonfiction. Current issues and topical concerns, adventure, mysteries and gothics, history and science, biography."

Juveniles: For nonfiction books, interested in "biographies, history of world cultures, impact of the sciences on human affairs, cultural anthropology, scientific and medical discoveries, ecology, current social concerns and theory, peace research, international cooperation and world order, controversial issues, sports. Future-oriented subjects. For all ages, but prefer 8 to 12 and junior and senior high school." Also buys adventure stories, mysteries, history and science, biography, and girls' fiction. "We have found several of our best authors by reading manuscripts they submitted for themselves. What we want most now is good fiction for girls, middle-elementary age through high school. One word of caution: we look first at writing quality!" Length: 40,000 to 60,000 words.

MADRONA PRESS, INC., P.O. Box 3750, Austin TX 78764. Editor-in-Chief: Robert S. Weddle. Publishes hardcover and paperback originals. Offers standard minimum book contract of 10-12½-15%. "Author usually pays for artwork, unless publisher originates the notion of using art to begin with." No advance. Published 6 titles last year. Standard marketing methods with good coverage in the West and Southwest. Write for copy of guidelines for writers. Will consider photocopied submissions. Query first. Reports in 4 to 6 weeks. Enclose return postage.

Nonfiction: Material dealing in some way with the American West and Southwest. Focus on people, life styles, art, regional history, music; regional cookbooks. Art and music must be indigenous to the Southwest; recordings, photography, state of opera and ballet in the area, etc. No local (i.e., county or town) histories. No biographies of relatives. No autobiographies.

MANOR BOOKS, INC., 432 Park Ave., S., New York NY 10016. Editor-in-Chief: John S. Littell. Publishes hardcover and paperback originals and reprints. Offers standard minimum book contract on hardcover books; other contracts negotiated. Advance varies. Published 200 titles last year. Will send free catalog to writer on request. Query first to Joanmarie Kalter, Managing Editor, for nonfiction and niction. No unsolicited mss. Reports in 4 to 6 weeks. Enclose return postage.
Nonfiction and Fiction: For adults. Adult trade fiction. Biography, cookbooks, cooking and foods, history, humor, music, nature, politics, self-help and how-to, sociology, sports, hobbies, recreation and pets, and travel. Length: 55,000 to 70,000 words.

MASON/CHARTER PUBLISHERS, INC., 384 Fifth Ave., New York NY 10018. Executive Editor: Margaret B. Parkinson. Publishes hardcover and paperback originals and hardcover imports. Offers standard minimum book contract of 10-12½-15%. Published 30 titles last year. Will send free catalog to writer on request. Will consider photocopied submissions. Query first. Reports in 2 months. Enclose return postage.
General Trade: Fiction, mystery, biography, history, food topics, travel, political science, environment, poetry, hobbies, business, how-to, sports (mainly biography), etc. Recent titles include *P. G. Wodehouse: A Portrait of a Master* (Jasen) and *Pandora's Box* (Chastain), mystery/suspense about a heist of art masterpieces from the Metropolitan Museum of Art.

MEDICAL EXAMINATION PUBLISHING COMPANY, INC., 65-36 Fresh Meadow Lane, Flushing NY 11365. Royalty schedule is negotiable. Will send catalog on request. Send outlines to editor. Reports in 1 month. Enclose return postage.
Medical: Medical texts and medical review books; monographs and training material for the medical and paramedical professions.

MELMONT PUBLISHERS, 1224 W. Van Buren St., Chicago IL 60607. Managing Editor: Joan Downing. Enclose return postage with ms.
Juveniles: Publishes easy-to-read nonfiction for early grades.

ARTHUR MERIWETHER, INC., Box 457, 921 Curtiss St., Downers Grove IL 60515. Editor-in-Chief: Arthur L. Zapel, Jr. Publishes paperback originals. Royalty contract of 10%. Advance by individual negotiation. Published 11 titles last year. Marketed by direct mail. Will send free catalog to writer on request. Editorial guidelines also available. Will consider photocopied submissions. Query first. "Do not send ms until after query response from us." Reports in 1 month. Enclose return postage.
Education: Mss for educational use in schools and churches. Mss for business and staff training on subjects related to business communications and advertising. Religious, self-help and how-to, sociology, humor and books on economics are also published.
Drama: Plays on the same subjects as above.

CHARLES E. MERRILL PUBLISHING CO., a Bell & Howell Co., 1300 Alum Creek Dr., Columbus OH 43216. Publishes hardcover and paperback originals. Payment is on acceptance or on a royalty basis. "Our textbooks generally offer 6% at elementary school level; 8% at secondary school level; 10% to 15% at college level. Published 250 titles last year. Send brief outline and sample chapter. Reports in 4 to 12 weeks. Enclose return postage.
Textbooks: Education Division publishes texts, workbooks, instructional tapes, overhead projection transparencies and programmed materials for elementary and high schools in all subject areas, primarily language arts and literature, mathematics, science and social studies (no juvenile stories or novels). The College Division publishes texts and instructional tapes in all college areas, specializing in education, sociology, business and economics, engineering and technology, science, political science, speech and drama, health and physical education, career education. Editor-in-Chief, Educational Division: Ralph Hayashida; Editor, College Division: John Buterbaugh.

JULIAN MESSNER, Division of Simon & Schuster, Inc., 1 W. 39th St., New York NY 10018. Published 33 titles last year. Will send catalog on request. Query first with outline. Reports in 1 month. Enclose return postage.
Juveniles: Publishes only nonfiction books for young people. Nonfiction for elementary grades, or ages 8 to 12; Ms. Lee M. Hoffman, Executive Editor. Mss of 53,000 to 55,000 words for 12- to 15-year-olds; nonfiction, biographies, careers; Ms. Iris Rosoff, Assistant Editor.

MILITARY MARKETING SERVICES, INC., P.O. Box 4010, Arlington VA 22204. President: Mrs. Ann Crawford. Publishes originals. "Usually purchase books outright. Royalties are negotiable if outright purchase is not made. Advance is also negotiable." Published 1 title last year. Query first or submit complete ms. Enclose return postage.
Nonfiction: "Information-type books for military families. Books which show the military family, active or retired, how to save money are needed. Also, books explaining reservist and retiree benefits will be given special consideration. We're looking for more titles which will help make the military family's life easier and more enjoyable." Length: open.

MONTHLY REVIEW PRESS, 62 West 14th St., New York NY 10011. Director: Harry Braverman. Royalty schedule. Published 40 titles last year. Current catalog available on request. Send query letter, table of contents and two sample chapters; enclose return postage. Reports in 1 to 3 months.
Economics, History, and Politics: Publishes books on history, economics, political science, world events. Books should reflect or be compatible with the socialist point of view on world problems.

MOODY PRESS, 820 North LaSalle St., Chicago IL 60610. Editor: Leslie H. Stobbe. Publishes hardcover and paperback originals. Royalty schedule is usually 10% of the retail. No advance. Published 110 titles last year. Send query with outline and sample chapters. Reports within 3 months. Enclose return postage.
Religion: Publishes books that are definitely Christian in content. Christian education, Christian living, inspirational, theology, missions and missionaries, pastors' helps. Conservative theological position. Clothbound between 45,000 and 60,000 words.
Fiction: Adult; mostly paperback. Length: 25,000 to 40,000 words.
Juveniles: Fiction; mostly paperback. Length: 25,000 to 40,000 words.

MOREHOUSE-BARLOW COMPANY, 14 East 41st St., New York NY 10017. Editor: Margaret L. Sheriff. Hardbound and paperback originals and reprints. On royalty basis. "Advance depends entirely on author's reputation and nature of book." Published 15 titles last year. Send sample chapter and outline with query. Gives preliminary report in 4 to 6 weeks. Enclose return postage.
Nonfiction: Publishes nonfiction trade and textbooks, in religion and allied fields, for adults and children. Length: 20,000 to 25,000 words and up.

MORGAN & MORGAN, INC., 145 Palisade St., Dobbs Ferry NY 10522. Editor-in-Chief: Douglas O. Morgan. Publishes hardcover and paperback originals and reprints. Offers 10% of net sales. No advance. Published 15 titles last year. Will send free catalog to writer on request. Write for editorial guidelines sheet. Submit outline and sample chapters. Reports "immediately." Enclose S.A.E. and return postage.
Photography: Books on all phases of photography. "We want to see an outline on what the book is about; various chapter headings; and how this material will be covered in various chapters. Would like one chapter in its entirety so that we could better grasp the method of approach in writing and also would like to have writer's reasons why he feels this book would have a good sale potential. We feel that our books go into greater detail on the particular subject and reasons why the book is relevant to the person looking for help in that field. We're looking for mss dealing with the how-to side of photography aimed at the amateur market and the more serious amateur photographer." Length depends on book.

WILLIAM MORROW AND CO., 105 Madison Ave., New York NY 10016. Editor:

John C. Willey. Payment is on standard royalty basis. Published 175 titles last year. Query on all books. For nonfiction include outline and three sample chapters. For fiction send 50 pages or completed mss. Address to specific department. Reports in 4 weeks. Enclose return postage.
General: Publishes fiction, nonfiction, history, biography, arts, religion, poetry, how-to books, and cookbooks, all high-quality. Length: 50,000 to 100,000 words.
Juveniles: Juvenile Editor: Connie C. Epstein.

MOTT MEDIA, 342 Main St., Milford MI 48042. Publisher and Executive Editor: George Mott. Publishes hardcover and paperback originals and reprints. Straight royalty; no splitting of royalty on high discounts to the trade. Advance varies from $500 to $1,000. Published 1 title last year. Books are sold to bookstore trade and the Christian school market. Will consider photocopied submissions. Query first; include outline and sample chapters for textbooks and special series. Reports in 4 weeks. Enclose return postage.
Textbooks, Religion, and Reference: "We specialize in Christian educational and leisure reading books for preschool as well as Christian-oriented textbooks for elementary, secondary and college level students. We are also interested in some high interest leisure-time type of books on personalities who have exercised their faith or found answers to their problems in the practice of Christianity. If it is a textbook, the author should be an authority on his subject. Also, we desire a Christian emphasis when possible because our readers are interested in the connection between their faith and contemporary living or life styles. Books are always slanted toward the Christian school market and Christian readers in general. We would be interested in a children's Bible story series if we could find one with a unique approach; possibly relating Biblical incidents to contemporary life situations. We are planning a children's science series which gives the creationist viewpoint. Would also be interested in a series for young school children on famous personalities who have applied faith to overcome a difficult situation. We will not review any handwritten mss; all must be typed, double-spaced." Recent titles include *Why Johnny Can't Learn,* detailing what's wrong with our public education system; why it's not working and where it's headed.

MULTIMEDIA PUBLISHING CORP. (affiliates: Steinerbooks, Rudolf Steiner Publications, Biograf Books), 100 South Western Highway, Blauvelt NY 10913. Editor: Paul M. Allen. Publishes paperback originals and reprints. "We offer only 5% to 7% royalty; average advance, $300." Published 10 titles last year. Will send a catalog to a writer on request. Query first with outline and sample chapters for nonfiction. Will consider photocopied submissions. Reports on ms accepted for publication in 60 days. Returns rejected material in 3 weeks. Enclose return postage.
Nonfiction: "Spiritual sciences, occult, philosophical, metaphysical, E.S.P. These are for our Steiner books division only. Scholarly and serious nonfiction. How-to-do or make books using our patented format of Biograf Books. Examples: origami, breadbaking, calendar. We prefer not to see any more Tarot or religious books." Dept. Editor, Multimedia Materials and Self-Help: Beatrice Garber; Dept. Editor, Philosophy and Spiritual Sciences: Paul M. Allen.

NASH PUBLISHING CORPORATION, One Dupont St., Plainview NY 11803. Editor-in-Chief: Sylvia Cross. Hardcover and paperback originals and reprints. "Contract varies. We have given lower rates to authors of books that were very risky, or authors who were being published for the first time." Published 34 titles last year. Send query first to Ruth Gee for nonfiction; to Cynthia Swan for fiction. If query brings positive reply, may send outline and sample chapter. Reports within six to eight weeks. Enclose S.A.S.E. with sample.
General: Publishes mainly nonfiction: how-to, self-help, current issues, controversial subjects. Aim toward broad lay-readership; 80,000 to 100,000 words. Publishes no juveniles and very little fiction. Life assertive themes and controversial subject areas, but no pornography. Recent titles include *My Life With Brendan* (Behan), *Travel With Great Writers: An Informal Literary Guide to Europe* (Hector), *Hoffa: The Real Story* (Hoffa).

NATIONAL TEXTBOOK COMPANY, 8259 Niles Center Rd., Skokie IL 60076. Editorial Director: Leonard I. Fiddle. Publishes hardcover and paperback originals. Offers standard minimum book contract of 10-12½-15%. "Advances given only under special circumstances." Published 60 titles last year. Will send free catalog to writer on request. Query first. Will consider photocopied submissions. Enclose S.A.S.E.
Textbooks: "At this time, our chief emphasis is on specialized paperbacks for the so-called high school language arts elective program. Plus, we are interested in developing titles on subjects ranging from science fiction to the mystery story to poetry and the like. Also interested in paperbacks dealing with the film, theatre, mass media and photography. These paperbacks should be approximately 50,000 words long with appropriate diagrams, charts, etc., included. All should be approached as orientation books giving the students enough of a feeling for the subject to be able to decide whether to go further into it or rest content that he has become a better 'consumer' of whatever it is he has studied. The style should be light, without being breezy; informative without being overly technical; realistic in that even with areas stated, meaningful examples are given. Our books are up to date and written by people who demonstrate a real acquaintance and knowledge of high school students and the classroom situation." Length: 50,000 to 75,000 words.

THOMAS NELSON, INC., 30 E. 42nd St., New York NY 10017. Editor: Gloria Mosesson. Publishes hardcover and paperback originals, reprints, translations, and anthologies. Offers standard royalty contract. Advance varies. Published 50 titles last year. Will send a catalog to a writer on request. Send query with outline and sample chapter. Query letters for juveniles should include description of ms, length, subject matter, age group. Reports in 2 months. Enclose return postage and self-addressed envelope.
General Nonfiction: "Publishes general nonfiction, history, biography, science, philosophy, the arts, antique collectors' books."
Religion: Publishes Christian religious and inspirational books. Contact William Cannon, Religion Editor, 407 Seventh Ave. South, Nashville TN 37206.
Juveniles: "Junior books department publishes fiction and nonfiction for boys and girls 7 through 12 and for teenagers on just about every subject imaginable—treatment, writing, etc., matter most." Length: 15,000 to 50,000 words. "We do not publish juvenile picture books."

NELSON-HALL COMPANY, 325 West Jackson Blvd., Chicago IL 60606. Publisher: V. Peter Ferrara. Editor: Elbert P. Epler. Standard royalty schedule. Rarely offers an advance. Published 76 titles last year. Send query accompanied by outline and return postage. "Soundness of subject matter and its treatment more important than just 'good writing.'" Reports in about 3 weeks.
Social Sciences, Psychology, History, Biography, Health, and Applied Psychology: Publishes serious works in the behavioral sciences. Also more popular books on practical, applied psychology written by qualified writers; business subjects, employment and personnel, general self-improvement, techniques relating to memory efficiency, retirement, investment, hobbies, etc. Length: 50,000 to 100,000 words. Current titles include *American Way of Divorce* (Kessler), *How to Succeed in the Business of Finding a Job* (Taylor), *You and Your Child* (Moyer), *How to Be an Effective Group Leader* (Schul); *Generation in Revolt: A Social and Cultural Study of the Black South* (Heckel).

NEW AMERICAN LIBRARY (including Mentor Books and Signet Books), 1301 Avenue of the Americas, New York NY 10019. Editor-in-Chief: Elaine Geiger. Publishes paperback originals and reprints. Pays substantial advances with standard paperback royalties. Send complete ms to Angela Rinaldi, Managing Editor. Reports in about 4 weeks. Enclose return postage.
General Nonfiction and Fiction: Under the Signet imprint, publishes adult and young adult fiction. Interested in romantic novels, gothics, family sagas. Also interested in nonfiction: self-help, psychology, inspirational and topical subjects. Educational books under the Meridian and Mentor imprint. Length: 75,000 words minimum.

NOBLE AND NOBLE, PUBLISHERS, INC., 1 Dag Hammarskjold Plaza, New York NY 10017. Editor-in-Chief: Warren Cox. Royalty and advance varies. Published 149 titles last year. Prompt initial reply; subsequent replies may take several months. Enclose return postage with ms.

Textbooks: Elementary and secondary textbooks. Language arts and social studies are among the areas of interest.

NORTH RIVER PRESS, INC., Box 241, Croton-on-Hudson NY 10520. Publishes hardcover and paperback originals and hardcover reprints. Offers 10% of cash received on all copies sold and paid for. No advance. Published 3 titles last year. Will consider photocopied submissions. Submit outline and sample page or two. Reports in 3 weeks. Enclose S.A.E. and return postage.

Reference and History: Regional history, literature and lore. Special interest in Hudson Valley material. Reference material, especially psychiatric and psycho-analytic. No special approach. Also interested in politics. Current titles include *The Creative Expression* (Rosner and Abt), *Portrait of a Young Republic* (Millard), *An Informal Bicentennial History of Ossining, New York* (Oechsner).

NORTH STAR PRESS, P.O. Box 451, St. Cloud MN 56301. Editor: John N. Dwyer. Publishes hardcover originals. "New or unknown authors are offered a flat 10% for first printing. Advance is dependent on amount of funds author spent for art or photos, etc. Accepted authors will get advance only if their other books have been well-received." Published 4 titles last year. Will send a catalog to a writer on request. Query first "with outline or sample chapter in duplicate copy only—no original material on first inquiry." Reports in 2 weeks. Enclose return postage.

Americana: "Subject is middle western Americana; mainly nonfiction of historical interest to an adult. Style can be author's own, provided he can write complete and connected sentences. For out-of-doors, sports, etc., style is casual or folksy. Professional material must not contain professional jargon. We are open to camping specialty books or books on muzzle-loading guns used in middle western frontier—especially gun books which detail the gunmaker or his art by name and location." Dept. Editor, History and Sports: Jim Kain. Current titles include *Theater* (midwestern folk) and *Lumbering* (Wisconsin).

Juveniles: "Will read good, adapted historical material for children, especially if well-illustrated for youth."

NORTHLAND PRESS, P.O. Box N, Flagstaff AZ 86001. Editor: James K. Howard. "Query before sending outline, ms, or illustrative material." Published 18 titles last year. Enclose return postage.

Americana: "A small organization concentrating on fine books on western Americana, heavily illustrated, and priced, therefore, for the special, rather than the general, reader."

W.W. NORTON & COMPANY, INC., 55 Fifth Ave., New York NY 10003. Publishes hardcover originals. "Occasionally we offer a variation of the standard book contract, but almost never below the minimum." Published about 200 titles last year. "We service the general trade market audience and market through bookstores." Query with resume or outline for nonfiction; query, outline and several sample chapters for fiction. Reports in 4 weeks. Enclose return postage.

General Fiction and Nonfiction: Material in most areas: Mainstream, biography, economics, history, humor, psychiatry, music, nature, philosophy, politics, scientific, sociology, sports, hobbies, recreation, textbooks (for college only); travel. No cookbooks, medical, juvenile or religious books.

NOYES DATA CORPORATION (including Noyes Press), Noyes Bldg., Park Ridge NJ 07656. Publishes hardcover originals. Pays 10% royalty. Advance varies, depending on author's reputation and nature of book. Published 70 titles last year. Current catalog available on request. Query Editorial Department first. Reports in 1 to 2 weeks. Enclose return postage.

Nonfiction: "Art, classical studies, archaeology, history, other nonfiction. Material directed to the intelligent adult and the academic market."
Technical: Publishes practical industrial processing science; technical, economic books pertaining to chemistry, chemical engineering, food and biology, primarily those of interest to the business executive; books relating to international finance. Length: 50,000 to 250,000 words.

OCEANA PUBLICATIONS, INC., Dobbs Ferry NY 10522. President: Philip F. Cohen; Managing Editor: William W. Cowan; Legal Editor: Edwin S. Newman; "Docket Series" Editor: Julius Marke; Editor, Reprint Bulletin: Sam P. Williams. Pays a flat fee of $500 per ms; $250 on receipt of acceptable ms; $250 at date of publication. No advance. Published approximately 50 titles last year. Send outline and sample chapter. Reports in 60 days. Enclose return postage.
Nonfiction: "We publish 5 to 10 legal almanacs a year. Most of them deal with legal aspects of everyday living. The author should have legal training. The prospective author will find sample almanacs in most local libraries."

ODDO PUBLISHING, INC., P.O. Box 68, Beauregard Blvd., Fayetteville GA 30214. Managing Editor: Genevieve Oddo. Publishes hardcover and paperback originals. Scripts are usually purchased outright. "We judge all scripts independently." Royalty considered for special scripts only. Published 10 titles last year. Will send free catalog to writer on request. Send complete ms, typed clearly. Reports in 3 to 4 months. Return postage and envelope must be enclosed with mss.
Juveniles and Textbooks: Publishes language arts, workbooks in math, writing (English), photophonics, science (space and oceanography), and social studies for schools, libraries, and trade. Interested in children's supplementary readers in the areas of language arts, math, science, social studies, etc. Texts run from 1,500 to 5,000 words. Presently searching for mss carrying the positive mental attitude theme—how to improve oneself, without preaching; material on the American Indian (folklore and background). Ecology, space, oceanography, and pollution are subjects of interest. Books on patriotism. Mss must be easy to read, general, and not set to outdated themes. It must lend itself to full color illustration. No stories of grandmother long ago. No love angle, permissive language, or immoral words or statements. Current titles include *Little Indians ABC* (Lucero), *Safety on Wheels* (Boyer), *Gray Ghosts of Gotham* (Oetting).

ODYSSEY PRESS, A Division of The Bobbs-Merrill Company, Inc., 4300 West 62nd St., Indianapolis IN 46268. Publishes college texts. "No unsolicited mss at this time, but queries are acceptable."

OHARA PUBLICATIONS, INCORPORATED, 1845-51 W. Empire Ave., Burbank CA 91504. Editor: Gilbert L. Johnson. Publishes hardcover and paperback originals, reprints, and translations. Offers standard 10% royalty contract. 5% for first printing if advance is granted. Published 5 titles last year. Write for editorial guidelines sheet. Query first with outline and sample chapters. Will consider photocopied submissions. Reports in 2 to 4 weeks. Enclose return postage.
Nonfiction and Fiction: How-to and instructional manuals dealing specifically with the martial arts. Other material includes Oriental religion, philosophy and historical Samurai accounts. "Research our manuals and follow our basic format. Ohara is the world's largest publisher of martial arts books. Our books use better quality photos and the art layout is professionally handled. We do not want Oriental cookbooks and poetry. Interested in different styles of karate and kung-fu other than those already printed. Psychological, physiological and healthful aspects of the martial arts written by qualified authorities." Nonfiction Editor: John Corcoran. Fiction should relate to same subject matter as nonfiction. Fiction Editor: Richard Hennessey. Current titles include *The Sai, Karate Weapon of Self-Defense* (Demura), *Power Training in Kung-Fu and Karate* (Marchini and Fong), *The Bruce Lee Memorial, Weaponless Warriors* (Kim), *The Hapkido Korean Art of Self-Defense* (Han).
Juveniles: Nonfiction only. Deal specifically with the Orient. Illustrations necessary.

OHIO STATE UNIVERSITY PRESS, 2070 Neil Ave., Columbus OH 43210. Director: Weldon A. Kefauver. Payment on royalty basis. Published 20 titles last year. Query letter preferred with outline and sample chapters. Reports within 2 months. Ms held longer with author's permission. Enclose return postage.
Nonfiction: Publishes history, biography, science, philosophy, the arts, political science, law, literature, economics, education, sociology, anthropology, geography, and general scholarly nonfiction. No length limitations.

OLD TIME BOTTLE PUBLISHING COMPANY, 611 Lancaster Dr., Salem OR 97301. Editors: B.J. Blumenstein and Lynn Blumenstein. Publishes hardcover and paperback originals. Offers standard royalty contract with average $500 advance. Published 1 title last year. Send outline. Reports in 30 days. Enclose return postage.
Hobbies: "Generally new hobbies and any new approach to old hobbies such as treasure hunting, bottle collecting, and artifact collecting. Audience: general public, all ages. Approach is how to get started. Writing should be condensed, very informative, with simple, flowing manner. Step-by-step instructions with inspirational matter and purpose contained in foreword. Profusely illustrated with photos of high quality and identification of items. Average page count (book) 100 to 200 pages."

101 PRODUCTIONS, 834 Mission St., San Francisco CA 94103. Editor-in-Chief: Jacqueline Killeen. Publishes hardcover and paperback originals. Offers standard minimum book contract of 10-12½-15%. No advance. Published 5 titles last year. Will send free catalog to writer on request. Query first. Will consider photocopied submissions. Enclose return postage.
General Nonfiction: All nonfiction, mostly how-to; cookbooks, the home, gardening, outdoors, travel, sports, hobbies, recreation and pets. Heavy emphasis on graphics and illustrations. Most books are 192 pages.

OPEN COURT—LIBRARY PRESS INCORPORATED, Box 599, LaSalle IL 61301. Director: R. I. Weiss. Editor: Melvin J. Lasky. Offers standard royalty contract. Published 40 titles last year. Query first. Reports in 6 weeks. Enclose S.A.S.E.
General Nonfiction, Poetry, Drama, and Juveniles: "Dedicated to original works of quality and special public interest in biography, history, literary criticism, current affairs, and imaginative writing, and above all, to maintaining the authentic relationship between the author and his reader. Distinctly international in spirit, we are based both in LaSalle and London. We publish books of scholarship and general interest, including art books, cookbooks, history, humor and how-to books, poetry, and plays. Adult books for adults. Children's books for children. This is a publishing house run as a cultural enterprise, even as a literary handicraft, and not as an anonymous, assembly-line industry." Current titles include *Up Against Daley* (Mathewson); *Together: Famous Career Couples* (Alexander); *Cricket's Choice* (Fadiman/ Carus); *The Occult Establishment* (Webb).

ORBIS BOOKS, Maryknoll NY 10545. Editor: Philip Scharper. Publishes hardcover and paperback originals. Offers standard 10-12½-15% royalty contract; "standard advance, $500." Published about 20 titles last year. Query first with outline, sample chapters, and prospectus. Reports in 4 to 6 weeks. Enclose return postage.
Nonfiction: "Christian orientation in the problems of the developing nations. Transcultural understandings, mission theology and documentation."

OREGON STATE UNIVERSITY PRESS, P.O. Box 689, Corvallis OR 97330. Director: J.K. Munford. Hardcover and paperback originals and reprints. "Royalties vary." Published 6 titles last year. Will send a catalog to a writer on request. "Query before submitting ms." Reports in 2 months. Enclose return postage.
General Nonfiction: Wants "well-written mss of regional interest" on Pacific Northwest history, biography, and geography. Also "books on higher education for professional and lay audience." Recent titles include *Atlas of the Pacific Northwest* (5th ed.); *Hemingway in Our Time; The Biology of the Oceanic Pacific.*
Technical and Scientific: "Biological science for professional and advanced reader." Also geology, geography, higher education.

OUR SUNDAY VISITOR, INC., Noll Plaza, Huntington IN 46750. Editor-in-Chief: Albert J. Nevins, M.M. Publishes hardcover and paperback originals and reprints. Offers 10% of price received by publisher. Average advance is $100. Published 20 titles last year. Will send free catalog to writer on request. Query first, with outline and sample chapters for nonfiction, to Robert Quinn, Director Product Development. Reports in 2 to 3 months. Enclose return postage with S.A.E.
Religion: Textbooks for religious education; books on religious subjects, such as theology, history, philosophy, biography, ethics, prayer, reference, liturgical, general, self-help, etc. For adults, teenagers, youngsters; paperback, cloth bound, workbooks, coloring books. For a Catholic audience and general Christian markets, suited to the average adult reader. Should fill pocketbook size to about 196 plus pages. "We publish some similar and competing titles; some unique, as *The Catholic Almanac.* Subjects should be of general and current interest." Other catagories of books published are Americana, book trade, humor, juveniles, music, self-help and how-to, sociology. Current titles include *Chile: Allende and After* (Protopapas), *Charity, Morality, Sex and Young People* (Fox).

OXMOOR HOUSE (a division of The Progressive Farmer Co.), P.O. Box 2463, Birmingham AL 35202. Editorial Director: John Logue. Managing Editor: Mary Whitfield. Publishes hardcover and paperback originals. "Payment on royalty basis or fee." Published 17 titles last year. Address all inquiries to John Logue. Send outline and sample chapter. Reports in 10 days. Enclose return postage.
General Nonfiction: Publishes books of general interest to Southern readers—cookbooks, garden books, interior decorating, architecture, history travel, art, etc. Also publishes technical and nontechnical agricultural books. Their current leading titles include *Jericho: The South Beheld, Award Winning Quilts, A Catalogue of the South.*

P.A.R. INCORPORATED, Abbott Park Pl., Providence RI 02903. Editor-in-Chief: Barry M. Smith. Publishes paperback originals. Offers 10-12½% royalty contract. Advance varies from $300 to $500. Published 4 titles last year. Will send free catalog to writer on request. Query first. Reports in 1 to 4 weeks. Enclose return postage.
Textbooks: For business schools, junior or community colleges and adult continuing education programs. Books on developmental reading, adult basic studies, high school equivalency preparation, English grammar (linguistic), spelling, business math, typewriting, advanced shorthand dictation, speech, charm, advertising, public relations, secretarial procedures, clerical procedures, accounting. These are aimed at 15- to 16-week courses of study. Looking for innovative approaches to old subjects to make them more interesting. Recent titles include *Contemporary College Speech, Charm & Charisma,* and *Business Report Writing.*

PACIFIC BOOKS, PUBLISHERS, P.O. Box 558, Palo Alto CA 94302. Editor: Henry Ponleithner. Royalty schedule varies with book. No advance. Published 6 titles last year. Will send catalog on request. Send complete ms. Reports promptly. Enclose return postage with ms.
Nonfiction: General interest, professional, technical and scholarly nonfiction trade books. Specialties include western Americana and Hawaiiana.
Textbooks and Reference: Text and reference books; high school and college.

PAGURIAN PRESS LTD., Suite 603, 335 Bay St., Toronto, Ontario, Canada M5H 2R3. Editor: Dorothy Martins. Publishes hardcover and paperback originals and reprints. "All contracts vary. Usual advance is $500 to $1,500." Published 27 titles last year. Send outline and sample chapters for nonfiction. Will consider photocopied submissions. Reports in 1 month. Enclose S.A.E. and International Reply Coupons.
General Nonfiction: General interest subjects; for example, outdoor themes, hunting, fishing, etc.; biography, sports, crafts, business and finance, home economics. Current titles include *Brian McFarlane's Hockey Quiz, Complete Outdoorsman's Handbook, Where to Fish and Hunt in North America, Enjoying the Art of Canadian Cooking, Mastering the Art of Winning Tennis, Wilderness Survival, Year-Round Guide to Family Fun.*

PALADIN PRESS, Box 1307, Boulder CO 80302. Editor-in-Chief: Peder C. Lund. Publishes hardcover originals and hardcover and paperback reprints. Offers standard minimum book contract of 10-12½-15%. Published 15 titles last year. Will send free catalog to writer on request. Will consider photocopied submissions. Submit outline and sample chapters. Reports in 1 month. Enclose return postage.
Military: Books on weapons, survival, military science, guerrilla warfare. History, politics, sports, hobbies, recreation, technical.

PANETH PRESS LTD., P.O. Box 593, Times Square Station, New York NY 10036. Pays the usual 10% of the published price in accordance with Author's Guild requirements. Advance varies. Insists that first query letters with outlines and sample chapters be sent to the Editor. Reports in 2 to 3 months. Enclose return postage and label, "otherwise mss are not returned."
General: Publishes books in every field of human interest—adult fiction, history, biography, science, philosophy, the arts, religion and general nonfiction. Length: 65,000 to 125,000 words.

PANTHEON BOOKS, Random House, Inc., 201 E. 50th St., New York NY 10022. Managing Director: Andre Schiffrin. Published over 60 titles last year. Unable to read mss submitted without previous inquiry. Address queries to Dian G. Smith, Adult Editorial Department. Enclose return postage.
Fiction: Publishes fewer than 5 novels each year, including mysteries.
Nonfiction: Books mostly by academic authors. Emphasis on Asia, international politics, radical social theory, history, medicine, and law.
Juveniles: Publishes some juveniles. Address queries specifically to Juvenile Editorial Department.

PARENTS' MAGAZINE PRESS, 52 Vanderbilt Ave., New York NY 10017. Editor-in-Chief: Selma G. Lanes. Address queries and mss to Alvin Tresselt. Usual advance is $750 minimum, but this varies, depending on author's reputation and nature of book. Published 40 titles last year. Reports in 6 weeks. Enclose return postage with ms.
Juveniles: "Picture books, 500 to 1,500 words, for ages 4 to 8. Although there are no vocabulary restrictions, these stories must combine a high interest level with simplicity of style. It is, of course, essential that the material offer excellent possibilities for illustrations." Recent titles include *Handtalk* (Charlip), *Allumette* (Ungerer), *Cunningham's Rooster* (Rockwell).

PARKER PUBLISHING CO., West Nyack NY 10994. Publishes hardcover originals and paperback reprints. Offers 10% royalty; 5% mail order and book clubs. Published 90 titles last year. Will send catalog on request. Reports in 3 to 5 weeks. Enclose S.A.S.E.
Nonfiction: Publishes practical, self-help, how-to books. Subject areas include popular health, mystic and occult, inspiration, in-service teaching and education, secretarial, selling, personal and business self-improvement, money opportunities. Length: 65,000 words

PAULIST PRESS, 1865 Broadway, New York NY 10023. Publishes hardcover and paperback originals and reprints. Standard trade contract with basic royalty open to negotiation. Advance depends on length of ms. Published 50 titles last year. Send outline and sample chapter first to Editorial Department. Reports in 4 weeks. Enclose return postage.
Religion: Catholic and Protestant religious works, both popular and scholarly. Length: 30,000 words and up. "Photo books and multimedia materials, large amounts of contemporary religious education materials." Material tends to avant-garde; no homespun philosophy or pious rehashes.

PEGASUS, (A Division of The Bobbs-Merrill Co., Inc.), 4300 West 62nd Street, Indianapolis IN 46268. Publishes college texts. Biological sciences curriculum study series; traditions in philosophy series. "We are not interested in unsolicited mss at this time but queries are acceptable."

THE PENNSYLVANIA STATE UNIVERSITY PRESS, 215 Wagner Bldg., University Park PA 16802. "There are many variations offered on the standard royalty contract. Some authors are not given a royalty on the first 500 to 1,000 books. Others are given a 5-10-12½-15% contract. Advances are seldom given. Sometimes permission fees are paid and charged as advance royalties." Published 34 titles last year. Send outlines and sample chapters to Chris W. Kentera. Reports within 3 months. Enclose return postage.
Nonfiction: Publishes history, biography, science, philosophy, Americana, art, business, economics, library, medicine and psychiatry, music, nature, photography, politics, reference, religion, sociology, sports, hobbies, recreation, pets, technical, textboks, general and regional nonfiction, and art history. Length: 40,000 to 100,000 words. Current titles include *Custer and the Epic of Defeat* (Rosenberg), *Johann Strauss* (Gartenberg), *Roots of Russian Communism* (Lane).

THE PEQUOT PRESS, INC., Old Chester Road, Chester CT 06412. Publications Director: Sara Ingram. Publishes both hardbound books and several series of paperback monographs; originals and reprints. 7½-10-12½% royalty contract for casebound books; 5-7½% for paperback. Advances individually arranged. Send query with sample chapter. Published 20 titles last year. Current catalog available. Reports in two weeks. Enclose return postage.
Nonfiction: Publishes history, biography, special interest, and "how-to" books. Special field is genealogies, stories of towns from beginnings, interesting personalities in history of New England, New England historical sidelights, railways, maritime, New England arts and crafts, including antiques and architecture. Interested in Connecticut history, biography, the arts. "For book trade and elementary and high school markets." Length: open.

PEREGRINE SMITH, INC., 1877 E. Gentile St., Layton UT 84041. Editor-in-Chief: G. M. Smith. Publishes hardcover and paperback originals and reprints. Usually offers standard minimum book contract of 10-12½-15%, but variations differ according to the book and author. Will often tailor a contract to the needs of the project. Published 10 titles last year. Marketed through bookstores. Will send catalog to writer for 25¢. Will consider photocopied submissions. Query first, or submit outline and sample chapters. Follow *Chicago Style Manual.* Reports in 2 weeks to 2 months. Enclose return postage.
Architecture and History: Western American history, western American architecture, western American culture with particular emphasis on the state of California. Culture and history of Latter-Day Saints (Mormon) religion. "Our books are written for the generally intellectual audience, those interested in the arts and history. Many of the books are used for college texts. However, the style should not be stiff or overdone. It should be smooth, interesting reading." No poetry or fiction. Recent titles include *The Destruction of California Indians* (Heizer) and *Building With Nature: Architectural Roots of the San Francisco Bay Region Tradition* (Freudenheim and Sussman).

PETROCELLI/CHARTER, a division of Mason/Charter Publishers, Inc., 384 Fifth Ave., New York NY 10018. Executive Editor: Margaret B. Parkinson. Publishes hardcover and paperback originals and hardcover imports. Offers standard minimum book contract of 10-12½-15%. Published 30 titles last year. Will send free catalog to writer on request. Will consider photocopied submissions. Query first. Enclose return postage.
Scientific and Technical: Books on computer management, accounting, etc.

PFLAUM PUBLISHING, 2285 Arbor Blvd., Dayton OH 45439. Publishes paperback originals; some cloth. Published 17 titles last year. Royalties: "5% up; advance from $250 up." Will send a catalog to a writer on request. Send query with outline and sample chapter to John M. Heher. Reports in 4 weeks. Enclose return postage with ms.
General Education, Film, and Religion: "Books in the fields of guidance/mental health, personal and social development, cinema, religion (especially Catholic), religious education."

S.G. PHILLIPS, INC., 305 West 86th St., New York NY 10024. Editor: Sidney Phillips. Publishes hardcover originals. "Graduated royalty schedule varies where artists or collaborators share in preparation." Published 7 titles last year. Will send a catalog to a writer on request. "Query first; no unsolicited mss." Reports in 30 to 60 days. Enclose S.A.S.E.
General and Juveniles: "Fiction and nonfiction for children and young adults. Particular interests—contemporary fiction, mysteries, adventure, science fiction; nonfiction: biography, politics, urban problems, international affairs, anthropology, archaeology, geography. Length depends on age group." Recent titles include *Dark Dove* (Stewart); *The Metric System* (Ross).

PILOT BOOKS, 347 Fifth Ave., New York NY 10016. Publishes paperback originals. Offers standard royalty contract. Usual advance is $250, but this varies, depending on author's reputation and nature of book. Published 16 titles last year. Send outline. Reports in 4 weeks. Enclose return postage.
General Nonfiction, Reference, and Business: "Publishes financial, business, and personal guides, training manuals. Directories and books on moneymaking opportunities." Wants "clear, concise treatment of subject matter." Length: 12,000 to 20,000 words. Current leading titles include *A Chinese and Western Guide to Better Health and Longer Life* (Betty Yu-Lin Ho), *How to Make Money Selling at Flea Markets and Antique Fairs* (Harmon), *Return-on-Investment Concepts and Techniques for Profit Improvement* (Rachlin).

PINNACLE BOOKS, 275 Madison Ave., New York NY 10016. Editor: Andrew Ettinger. Publishes paperback originals and reprints. "Contracts and terms are standard and competitive." Published 210 titles last year. Will send brochure and requirements memo to a writer if S.A.S.E. is enclosed. "Will no longer accept unsolicited mss. Most books are assigned to known writers or developed through established agents. However, an intelligent, literate, and descriptive letter of query will often be given serious consideration." Enclose return postage with query.
General: "Books range from general nonfiction to commercial trade fiction in most popular categories. Pinnacle's list is aimed for wide popular appeal, with fast-moving, highly compelling escape reading, adventure, espionage, historical intrigue and romance, science fiction, western, popular sociological issues, topical nonfiction." Recent titles include *The James Dean Story* (Martinetti); *The Great Pyramid* (Valentine); *The Coming of the Horseclans* (Adams); *Dodge City Bombers* (Derrick); *The Complete Handbook for a Sexually Free Marriage* (Lobell).

PIONEER PRESS, P.O. Box 684-WD, Union City TN 38261. Publishes paperback originals and reprints. Pays flat fee up to $400 per ms, depending on length and content. Published 6 titles last year. Editorial guidelines available on request. No photocopied submissions. Submit complete ms. Reports in 30 days. Enclose return postage.
Americana: Guns and gun-related material (knives, Indian artifacts, cannons, etc.). Black powder, muzzle loading. No modern material. Books for gun collectors, dealers, shooters, etc. Length: 20,000 to 25,000 words. Pictures and illustrations essential. Recent titles include *Dixie Buckles* (Bridges), listing all of the American Tiffany buckles on the market today.

PIPER PUBLISHING, INC., 110 South Main St., Blue Earth MN 56013. Executive Editor: John M. Sullivan. Publishes hardcover and paperback originals. Standard minimum book contract "but we consider each publishing contract as an individual matter and make equitable variances for each author." Send outline or complete ms. Reports in 6 weeks. Enclose return postage.
General Nonfiction: Sports, history, politics, biography, cookbooks, and wine books.

PLATT & MUNK, 1055 Bronx River Ave., Bronx NY 10472. Editor: Leslie McGuire. Flat fee only, anywhere from $500 to $2,000, depending on size of book and its complexity. "We take on very few unsolicited mss and generally commission what we publish. All books aimed at Pre-K to Grade 6 market." Send ms or outline and sample chapter to Associate Editor. No art, except sample to Associate Editor. Reports in approximately 4 weeks. Enclose return envelope and postage.

Juveniles: Publishes juveniles, including picture books, fiction, nonfiction, biographies and photographic books; ages 2 to 12. Also publishes Peggy Cloth Books, washable cloth books and novelty books for children.

PLAYBOY PRESS, Division of Playboy Enterprises, Inc., 919 Michigan Ave., Chicago IL 60611. New York office: 747 Third Ave., New York NY 10017. Editorial Director (hardcover): Edward Kuhn, Jr.; Editorial Director (softcover): Mary Ann Stuart. Publishes hardcover and paperback originals and reprints. Royalty contract to be negotiated. Published 60 titles last year. Query first. Enclose return postage.

General: Fiction and nonfiction slanted to the adult male who reads *Playboy* magazine.

PLENUM PUBLISHING CORP., 227 W. 17th St., New York NY 10011. Imprints: Da Capo Press, Consultants Bureau, IFI/Plenum Data Corporation, Plenum Press. Publishes hardcover and paperback originals and reprints. Offers standard minimum book contract of 10-12½-15%. No advance. Published 450 titles last year. Query R.N. Ubell. Enclose return postage.

Nonfiction: Books on science, history, biography, art, music, and general trade.

POCKET BOOKS, 630 Fifth Ave., New York NY 10020. Paperback originals and reprints. Published 300 titles last year. Reports in one month. Submit through agent only. All unsolicited mss are returned unread. Enclose return postage.

General: History, biography, philosophy, inspirational, general nonfiction and adult fiction (mysteries, science fiction, gothics, westerns). Some biography, reference books, joke books, puzzles.

POET GALLERY PRESS, 224 W. 29th St., New York NY 10001. Editor: E.J. Pavlos. Publishes paperback originals. Offers standard 10-12½-15% royalty contract. Published 5 titles last year. Submit complete ms only. Enclose return postage with ms.

General: "We are a small specialty house, and we place our emphasis on publishing the works of young Americans currently living in Europe. We are interested in creative writing rather than commercial writing. We publish for writers who live overseas, who write and live, who produce writings from the self. Our books might turn out to be commercial, but that is a secondary consideration. We expect to emphasize poetry; however, our list will be concerned with all aspects of literature: the novel, plays, and cinema, as well as criticism." Recent titles include *Sarah*.

POPULAR LIBRARY, INC., 600 Third Ave., New York NY 10016. Editor-in-Chief: Patrick O'Connor. Publishes originals and reprints. Royalty contract to be negotiated. Published 242 titles last year. Query first. Enclose return postage.

General: Publishes adult general fiction and nonfiction.

BERN PORTER BOOKS, P.O. Box 209, Belfast ME 04915. Buys on outright purchase, 10% royalty, or combination, depending on value. Published 294 titles last year. Send complete ms. Enclose return postage with ms.

Fiction, Nonfiction, and Poetry: Looking for adult fiction and nonfiction including American vanguard expression—poetry, drama, experimental work. Science fiction, crime detection, love. Interested only in mss in complete, final version; 40,000 words and up. Highest possible literary quality demanded.

CLARKSON N. POTTER, INC., 419 Park Ave. S., New York NY 10016. Editor-in-Chief: Clarkson N. Potter. Senior Editor: Jane West. Production Editor: Diane Girling. Royalty schedule varies with each book. Published 17 titles last year. Query first. Reports in two weeks. Enclose return postage.

Nonfiction: General trade books, especially Americana, art, contemporary scene, cookbooks, cooking and foods, photography, politics, scientific, annotated literature also considered. "No fiction." Current titles include *Back Roads of New England*

(Thollander), *For the Sake of a Single Verse* (Rilke/Shahn), *Books of Firsts* (Robertson), *For Love of Her* (Dickinson/Stein).

PRENTICE-HALL, INC., Englewood Cliffs NJ 07632. Editor-in-Chief, Trade Division: John Grayson Kirk. Publishes hardcover and paperback originals and reprints. Offers standard 10-12½-15% royalty contract; advance usually $2,500 to $7,000. "A flat royalty is occasionally offered in the case of highly specialized hardcover series. A flat royalty is always offered on house paperbacks. Children's book contracts tend to average around 8% to 10% royalty rate. The advance depends on cost of artwork, but does not usually exceed anticipated first year royalties." Published 80 trade titles and 20 children's book titles last year. Will send a catalog to a writer on request. Submit outlines and sample chapters for nonfiction; submit complete ms for fiction. Will consider photocopied submissions. "Always keep 1 or more copies on hand in case original submission is lost in the mail." Reports in 4 to 6 weeks on trade books; reports in 2 to 4 weeks on juveniles. Enclose return postage with ms.
General: "All types of fiction and trade nonfiction, save poetry, drama, and westerns. Average acceptable length: 80,000 words. The writer should submit his work professionally and be prepared to participate to the extent required in the book's promotion." Publishes adult trade mainstream fiction, Americana, art, biography, business, cookbooks, history, humor, medicine and psychiatry, music, nature, philosophy, politics, reference, religion, science, self-help and how-to, sports, hobbies and recreation. Length: 80,000 to 90,000 words.
Juveniles: "Contemporary fiction for ages 8 and up; high interest, low reading level fiction and nonfiction, project books up to age 15. Style, outlook, and structure requirements vary with each ms. They are as much an integral part of the book as the subject matter itself. In general, writers should make their material as interesting, alive, and simple as possible. We are interested in very simple concept books for preschoolers (*not* alphabet books) about 500 to 1,000 words; books for ages 9 to 14 on one aspect of American history covering a wide time and geographical span. If a book is really good, it can usually survive the fact that the subject has been worked over. Because children's books are so expensive to produce and therefore expensive to buy, the trade market is limited. Libraries are the primary market. At this point, they seem to be showing a decided preference for books in which the child can participate—instructive books, involving books." Length: 15,000 words for teenage books; 5,000 to 15,000 for fiction and nonfiction, ages 7 to 12; Editor-in-Chief, Juvenile Books: Ellen E.M. Roberts.

PRINCE COMMUNICATIONS, INC., 99 Madison Ave., New York NY 10016. Editor-in-Chief: Harold Prince. Publishes hardcover and paperback originals. Offers Authors League contract; 5% maximum on mail order. Makes an advance of up to $1,000 depending on percentage of mail order royalties (higher royalties, lower advance). Published 4 titles last year. Marketed almost entirely by direct mail. "If we decide to work with writer, samples of our style will be made available." Will consider photocopied submissions. Query first. Reports in 2 to 4 weeks. Enclose return postage.
Health, Self-Help, Religion and Retirement: "Nonfiction (for the most part) in the fields of wealth, health, religion, human dignity and self-help. A specialty of the house is books in the field of retirement. Our books are sold to people who don't ordinarily read books. They want information that they can't easily and/or inexpensively get elsewhere. They want to put that information to use at once to get real results. No fancy writing. Just 1-2-3, step-by-step factual presentation. No gimmicks, tricks or misrepresentations. Our books are structured and written specifically for nonreaders. The prose is 8-year-old simple. The paragraphs seldom exceed 3 sentences. Polysyllables are unknown. Great pain is taken to make even the most abstruse subject understandable. There is no puff. We're planning a series of books showing how religion can solve everyday problems realistically. We're interested in publishing books on depression, recession, inflation, the loss of human dignity. We don't want to see anything on diet, nonsmoking, or get-rich-quick." Length: 20,000 to 60,000 words. Recently published titles include *Stories and Poems You*

Can Read to Your Grandchildren; Start Your Second Life Today: A Guide to Retirement; How to Get Rich Using Other People's Money.

PULSE-FINGER PRESS, Box 16697, Philadelphia PA 19139. Editor-in-Chief: Orion Roche. Publishes hardcover and paperback originals. Offers standard minimum book contract; less for poetry. Advance varies, depending on quality. "Not less than $100 for poetry; or $500 for fiction." Published 5 titles last year. Query first. "We consider unsolicited ms, but prefer to make our own contacts." Reports in 1 to 6 months. Enclose S.A.E. and return postage.
Fiction and Poetry: "We're interested in subjects of general concern with a focus on fiction and poetry. All types considered; tend to the contemporary-cum-avant-garde. No length requirements. Our only stipulation is quality, as we see it." Current titles include *Sistine Cartoons* (Phillips); *Bloodlines* (Phillips), books of poetry.

G.P. PUTNAM'S SONS, 200 Madison Ave., New York NY 10016. Editor-in-Chief: Harvey Ginsberg. Juvenile Editor-in-Chief: Charles Mercer. Publishes hardcover and paperback originals. Payment is on standard royalty basis. Published 252 titles last year. Well-known authors may submit outline and sample chapter. Lesser known authors should submit at least half the book for inspection. Reports in 2 to 4 weeks. Enclose return postage with ms.
Fiction: Publishes novels, 50,000 words and up, of all types.
Nonfiction: Nonfiction in history, biography, exploration, etc.
Juveniles: Juvenile fiction and nonfiction.

QUADRANGLE/THE NEW YORK TIMES BOOK CO., a subsidiary of the New York Times Co., 10 E. 53 St., New York NY 10022. Publishes hardcover and paperback originals and reprints. Royalty contract to be negotiated. Published 104 titles last year. Query first. Enclose return postage.
Nonfiction: "We are interested in generally serious nonfiction for the intelligent lay audience." Special emphasis on current affairs and information books, by recognized authorities.

RAINTREE EDITIONS, Advanced Learning Concepts, Inc., 211 W. Wisconsin Ave., Milwaukee WI 53203. Editor-in-Chief: Richard W. Weening. Publishes hardcover and paperback originals. Offers standard minimum book contract of 10-12½-15%. Advances range from $400 to $2,000. Published 8 titles last year. Will consider photocopied submissions. Submit outline and sample chapters or complete ms. Reports in 60 to 90 days. Enclose return postage.
Juveniles: "Individual or series of hardbound juvenile books for ages 5 to 9 and 9 to 12. Reality-oriented treatments of socially relevant themes that match the interest level and sophistication of the intended audience. Nonfictional how-to books, biographies, and other treatments that match interest and ability of intended audience. Books to aid children ages 5 to 12 in socio-emotional development. No poetry, no fantasy or fairy tales. Each ms should have a reality orientation. In a fictional narrative, this can be achieved by dealing with a socially relevant subject or theme of high personal interest to the intended audience. In a nonfiction book, the age, ability and interest level of the intended audience are key considerations. Tight, concise, journalistic writing with an adult interest level can be stimulating and thought-provoking. All books are screened by content area specialists and child development experts for authenticity, accuracy and relevance prior to publication. Where appropriate, each book is illustrated with color photography. No talking pigs or flying people; rather, a real extension of each child's real world experiences." Recently published books on how to play cards.

RAMPAGE PUBLISHERS, 7 West St., Suite 214, Danbury CT 06810. Editor-in-Chief: Robert Shure. Publishes paperback originals and reprints. Royalty contract of 10%. Published 4 titles last year. Marketed through college bookstores and metropolitan paperback shops. Will consider photocopied submissions. Query first or submit complete ms. Reports in 2 weeks. Enclose return postage.
Humor: Satire, wit, drollery (not simply jokes or cartoons) in any format (fiction

or nonfiction). Drawings may be used. No photographs. Light or humorous poetry also considered. Recent titles include *The Beard Book*.

RAND McNALLY, P.O. Box 7600, Chicago IL 60680. Trade Division and Education Division at this address. Variable royalty and advance schedule. Payment on royalty basis or outright, except for mass market books which are outright. Published 225 titles last year. Adult mss should be sent to Steven P. Sutton, Editor, Adult Books, Trade Division, but he should first be queried on the subjects of Americana, natural history, personal adventure, exploration and travel. Contracts on nonfiction are sometimes offered on the basis of an outline and sample chapter. Query Executive Editor, Education Division, for books of an educational nature. Reports in 6 to 8 weeks. Enclose return postage.
General Nonfiction: Publishes general nonfiction including travel, geography, adventure; all for the general reader.
Juveniles: Mass market books (Elf and Start-Right Elf). Picture book scripts, six years and under. Realistic stories, science, fantasy; not to exceed 600 words and must present varied illustration possibilities. Editor: Roselyn Bergman. Trade Books: Picture books for ages 3 to 8; fiction and nonfiction, ages 8 to 12; special interest books (no fiction) for young adults. Send picture book manuscripts for review. Query on longer mss. Editor: Dorothy Haas.
Textbooks: Education Division publishes texts, maps and related material for elementary, high schools and colleges in restricted fields.

RANDOM HOUSE, INC., 201 East 50th St., New York NY 10022. Also publishes Vintage Books. Publishes hardcover and paperback originals and reprints. Payment as per standard minimum book contracts. Query first. Enclose return postage.
Fiction and Nonfiction: Publishes fiction and nonfiction of the highest standards.
Poetry: Some poetry volumes.
Juveniles: Publishes a broad range of fiction and nonfiction for young readers, including Beginner Books, Step-up Books, Gateway Books, Landmark Books. Particularly interested in high-quality fiction for children.

RD COMMUNICATIONS, P.O. Box 42, Georgetown CT 06829. Editor-in-Chief: Richard Dunn. Publishes paperback originals. Straight book contract of 15%. Advance: $600. Published 10 titles last year. Marketed by direct mail and mail order advertising. No bookstore sales. Will send catalog to writer if professional in one of their fields of specialty. Editorial guidelines also available. Will consider photocopied submissions. Query first. Reports in 1 month. Enclose return postage.
Business, Economics and Technical: Technology, business, professional skills, education. Author should have working background in field in which he writes. Content must have immediate practical value to professionals in the field. Emphasis is on practical application rather than general discussion or theory. Recent titles include *The Coloring of Plastics: Theory and Practice, Basic Trouble-Shooting of Plastic Injection Molds, Reading Games Make Reading Fun.*

RED DUST, INC., 218 East 81st St., New York NY 10028. Editor: Joanna Gunderson. Publishes hardcover and paperback originals and translations. Specializes in quality work by new writers. Also publishes recordings. Books printed either simultaneously in hard and paper covers or in hardcover alone, in editions of 1,500 to 2,500. The author generally receives $300 on the signing of the contract, either outright (with 30% of the profits after the publisher's costs have been met) or as an advance against royalties (using the regular royalty schedule). Published 2 titles last year. Current catalog available on request. Query with sample chapter. Reports within a month. Enclose S.A.S.E.
Fiction: Novels and short stories.
Nonfiction and Poetry: Scholarly, art, art history, film and poetry (in book or record form).

REGAL BOOKS, Division of G/L Publications, 110 W. Broadway, Glendale CA 91204. Editor-in-Chief: David A. Stoop. Publishes paperback originals. 10% royalty contract. Will consider photocopied submissions. Query with outline and 2 or 3 sample chapters. Reports in 90 days. Enclose return postage.

Religion: All material is Christian in content. Christian education, Christian living; inspirational; theology, missionary and missions; church growth, family life, Bible study. Recent titles include *What the Bible Is All About* (Mears).

REGENTS PUBLISHING COMPANY, INC., Two Park Ave., New York NY 10016. Pays 10% to 15% royalty based on net sales. Usual advance is $500, but this varies, depending on author's reputation and nature of book. Published 48 titles last year. Prefers queries, outlines, sample chapters. Reports in 3 to 4 weeks. Enclose return postage.

Textbooks: Publishes foreign language texts, multimedia packages, English books for the foreign-born. Dept. Editors: Jacqueline Flamm, Editor of English as a Second Language Publications; Rachel Genero, Foreign Language Editor.

HENRY REGNERY CO., 180 N. Michigan Ave., Chicago IL 60601. Vice President, Editorial: Dominick Abel. Publishes hardcover and paperback originals, paperback reprints; juveniles. Offers standard 10-12½-15% royalty contract. Advance varies. Published about 75 titles last year. Query first with outline and sample chapters. Will consider photocopied submissions. Reports in 1 to 3 weeks. Enclose return postage.

General Nonfiction: Publishes general nonfiction; books on crafts, hobbies, sports, biography, entertainment, automotive repair, Americana, business, cookbooks, cooking, foods, history, medicine and psychiatry, nature, multimedia material, politics, self-help and how-to; adult education and text preparation materials. Length: open. Recent titles include *New Careers for Social Workers* (Richmond), *A Financial Guide for the Self-Employed* (Ellis), *Your Heart Is Stronger Than You Think* (Steincrohn).

RESTON PUBLISHING COMPANY (Prentice-Hall subsidary), P.O. Box 547, Reston VA 22090. President: Matthew I. Fox. Publishes hardcover and paperback originals. Offers standard minimum book contract of 10-12½-15%. Advance varies. "We are a wholly-owned subsidiary of Prentice-Hall, which has the most extensive marketing system in publishing." Will send free catalog to writer on request. Will consider photocopied submissions. Submit outline and sample chapters. Reports immediately. Enclose return postage.

Textbooks: "Primarily for the junior college and vocational/technical school market. Professionally oriented books for in-service practitioners and professionals. All material should be written to appeal to these markets in style and subject. We are able to attract the best experts in all phases of academic and professional life to write our books. But we are always seeking new material in all areas of publishing; any area that is represented by courses at any post-secondary level."

FLEMING H. REVELL COMPANY, Old Tappan NJ 07675. Editor-in-Chief: Dr. Frank S. Mead. Payment usually on royalty basis. Published 54 titles last year. Reports in a month to six weeks. Enclose return postage with ms.

Religion: Publishers of inspirational and religious books. Also books related to Sunday School and church work. Occasional biography and more general books that might appeal to the religious market. Length: usually 40,000 to 60,000 words.

THE REVISIONIST PRESS, PUBLISHERS, G.P.O. Box 2009, Brooklyn NY 11202. Editor-in-Chief: A. Ariadne, Jr. Publishes hardcover originals. Offers standard minimum book contract of 10-12½-15%. Published 16 titles last year. Query first with outline and sample chapters. Reports in 3 weeks. Enclose S.A.E. and return postage.

General Nonfiction: Doctoral dissertations in all areas of the humanities, literature and social sciences. Original works of merit. Planning the following series: English & American Literature, and Cinema, History, Sociology, Comparative Literature, and Philosophy.

REYMONT ASSOCIATES, 29 Reymont Ave., Rye NY 10580. Editor-in-Chief: D. J. Scherer. Publishes paperback originals. Offers standard minimum book contract of 10-12½-15%. Published 3 titles last year. Marketed direct to consumer by mail order. Will send free catalog to writer on request. Will consider photocopied submissions. Query first with outline. Reports in 4 weeks. Enclose return postage.
Finance, Travel and Hobbies: Must contain practical, how-to elements of family finance, travel, hobbies. Will also consider cookbooks; business, self-help, how-to, sports, hobbies and recreation mss. Length: 4,000 to 8,000 words. Recent titles include *How to Survive a Tax Audit.*

THE WARD RITCHIE PRESS, 474 S. Arroyo Parkway, Pasadena CA 91105. Editor-in-Chief: Shauna Bernacchi. Offers a standard 10-12½-15% royalty contract. Advance varies. Published 30 titles last year. Will send catalog to writer on request. Query first and submit outline and 2 chapters. Enclose S.A.E. with return postage.
Nonfiction and Fiction: Broad general interest. Americana (quality literature pertaining to any period and place in American history). Cookbooks (distinctive cookbooks only). Travel and history (short travel guidebooks which are fresh, imaginative, factual, and unique). Especially interested in guides to places close to or within major cities.
Juveniles: Few. Must be exceptionally unusual.

RONALD PRESS, 79 Madison Ave., New York NY 10016. Publishes hardcover originals. Royalty contract to be negotiated. Query first. Enclose return postage.
Reference and Textbooks: Publishes college textbooks. Also publishes reference books.

RICHARDS ROSEN PRESS, 29 E. 21st St., New York NY 10010. Editor: Ruth C. Rosen. Publishes hardcover originals. "Each project has a different royalty setup." Published 41 titles last year. Wants queries with outline and sample chapter. Reports within 3 weeks. Enclose return postage.
Nonfiction: "Our books are geared to the young adult audience whom we reach via school and public libraries. Most of the books we publish are related to guidance-career and personal adjustment." Also publishes material on the theatre, science, women, as well as journalism for schools. Interested in supplementary material for enrichment of school curriculum. Preferred length: 40,000 words.

ROUTLEDGE & KEGAN PAUL, LTD., 9 Park St., Boston MA 02108. Editorial Director: Brian Southam. Publishes hardcover and paperback originals and reprints. Offers standard 10-12½-15% royalty contract "on clothbound editions, if the books are not part of a series"; usual advance is $250 to $2,500. Published over 200 titles last year. Query first with outline and sample chapters. Submit complete ms "only after going through outline and sample chapters step." Returns rejected material in 1 to 2 months. Reports on ms accepted for publication in 1 to 6 months. Enclose return postage.
Nonfiction: "Academic, reference, and scholarly levels: English and European literary criticism, drama and theater, social sciences, philosophy and logic, psychology, parapsychology, oriental religions, mysticism, history, political science, education. Our books generally form a reputable series under the general editorship of distinguished academics in their fields. The approach should be similar to the styles adopted by Cambridge University Press, Harvard University Press, and others." Interested in material for Routledge Author Guides, the International Library of Sociology, Routledge Critics series, Birth of Modern Britain series, International Library of Social Policy, and the International Library of the Philosophy of Education. Dept. Editors: Norman Franklin, Chairman (sociology, philosophy, politics, history, economics); Brian Southam (education, literature); Peter Hopkins (social studies). Length: 30,000 to 250,000 words. Recent titles include *The Rosicrucian Enlightenment* (Yates); *The New Criminology* (Taylor, Walton and Young); *Ethics and Action* (Winch); *Pollution in the Air* (Scorer).

RUTGERS UNIVERSITY PRESS, 30 College Ave., New Brunswick NJ 08901. Pays approximately 10% royalty on most books. Published 28 titles last year. Catalog on request. Prefers queries. Final decision depends on time required to secure competent professional reading reports. Enclose return postage.

Nonfiction: Books with a New Jersey or regional aspect. Also scholarly books on history, science, biographies, philosophy, and the arts. Regional nonfiction must deal with mid-Atlantic region with emphasis on New Jersey. Length: 80,000 words and up. Recent titles include *The Little That Is All* (Ciardi); *The Ramapo Mountain People* (Cohen); *The Russian Dilemma* (Wesson); *Violence and Aggression in the History of Ideas* (Wiener and Fisher).

WILLIAM H. SADLIER, INC., 11 Park Pl., New York NY 10007. Director of Editorial: Herman J. Sweeney. Publishes hardcover and paperback originals. Offers 8% royalty contract for elementary textbooks; 10% for high school textbooks. Advance from $500 to $1,000. Published 135 titles last year. Submit outline and sample chapters to Editorial Department. Reports "as soon as possible." Enclose S.A.E. and return postage.

Textbooks: Elementary and secondary textbooks; all curriculum areas. Whole or significant part of school market should be identified, competition studied, proposal developed and submitted with representative sample. Interested in language arts and social studies. Business, economics, history, music, politics, religion, sociology.

ST. ANTHONY MESSENGER PRESS, 1615 Republic St., Cincinnati OH 45210. Editor-in-Chief: Rev. Jeremy Harrington, O.F.M. Publishes paperback originals. Offers 6% to 8% royalty contract. Usual advance is $500. Published 5 titles last year. Books are sold in bulk to groups (study clubs, high school or college classes). Will send free catalog to writer on request. Will consider photocopied submissions if they are not simultaneous submissions to other publishers. Query first or submit outline and sample chapters. Enclose return postage.

Religion: "We try to reach the Catholic market with topics near the heart of the ordinary Catholic's belief. We want to offer insight and inspiration and thus give people support in living a Christian life in a pluralistic society. We are not interested in an academic or abstract approach. Our emphasis is on the popular approach with examples, specifics, color, anecdotes." Length: 25,000 to 40,000 words. Recent titles include *The Commandments and the New Morality* which tells the spirit and real meaning of each of the Ten Commandments for today, in the light of recent Catholic moral thought.

ST. MARTIN'S PRESS, 175 Fifth Ave., New York NY 10010. Published 60 original titles last year; 275 foreign-originated titles. Query Editorial Secretary. Reports promptly. Enclose return postage.

General: Publishes general fiction and nonfiction; major interest in adult nonfiction, history, political science, popular science, biography, music and musicians, archaeology, gardening, boats and boating, scholarly, technical reference, etc.

Juveniles: Minor interest in juveniles.

Textbooks: College textbooks.

HOWARD W. SAMS & CO., INC., 4300 W. 62nd St., Indianapolis IN 46268. Manager, Book Division: C.P. Oliphant. Payment depends on quantity, quality, salability. Offers both royalty arrangements or outright purchase. Published 78 titles last year. Prefers queries, outlines, and sample chapters. Usually reports within 30 days. Enclose return postage.

Technical, Scientific, and How-To: "Publishes technical and scientific books for the electronics industry; Audel books for the homeowner, craftsman, and handyman; and books for the amateur radio field."

Textbooks: "Textbooks for industrial arts, technical, and vocational education."

PORTER SARGENT PUBLISHER, 11 Beacon St., Boston MA 02108. Publishes hardcover and paperback originals, reprints, translations, and anthologies. "Each contract is dealt with on an individual basis with the author." Published 4 titles last year. Will send a catalog to a writer on request. Send query with outline and sample chapter or complete ms. "It is helpful if label indicates it is a new, unsolicited ms, but it is not necessary." Enclose return postage.

General Nonfiction, Reference, Philosophy, and Textbooks: "Handbook Series and Special Education Series offer standard, definitive reference works in private education and writings and texts in special education. The Extending Horizons Series is an outspoken, unconventional series which presents topics of importance in contemporary affairs, viewpoints rarely offered to the reading public, methods and modes of social change, and the framework of alternative structures for the expansion of human awareness and well-being." Contact F. Porter Sargent. Current leading title: *And What Is to Be Undone* (Albert).

SCHIRMER BOOKS, Macmillan Publishing Co., 866 Third Ave., New York NY 10022. Editor-in-Chief: Ken Stuart. Publishes hardcover and paperback originals and paperback reprints. Offers standard minimum book contract of 10-12½-15%. Small advance. Published 30 titles last year. Will consider photocopied submissions. Query first, or submit outline and sample chapters or submit complete ms. Reports in several weeks. Enclose return postage.

Music: Books for college, trade and reference and music store markets. Textbooks on music history, music theory, music performance, music education. Books on musical celebrities, songbooks, method books, etc.

SCHOLASTIC BOOK SERVICES, 50 West 44th St., New York NY 10036. Includes Four Winds Press, See-Saw Book Club, Teen Age Book Club, Lucky Book Club, Campus Book Club, Arrow Book Club and Citation Press. Scholastic's standard contract for paperback rights provides for an advance against royalties which ranges, depending on the book's market potential, upward from $500. Paperback royalties start at 4% of the selling price. Scholastic's contracts are often made for both hard and softcover publications. Hardcover royalties begin at 10%. Query first. Enclose return postage.

Juveniles, Fiction, Teen and Young Adult, Science, and Education: "Fiction and nonfiction ranging from pre-school picture book level to adult. Subject for juvenile and young adult books should be limited to those acceptable to these audiences. See-Saw Book Club (grades kindergarten and 1) needs science picture books and easy-to-read books for end of first grade. Lucky Book Club (grades 2 and 3) wants science books and easy-to-read history, biography, mystery, adventure, sports books. Arrow Book Club (grades 4, 5, and 6) needs young science, mystery, humor, puzzle, how-to books and biographies at reader level. Also, nonfiction books on sports, biographies, simple how-to, etc. Books should not be babyish or oversimplified but should be subteen level in interest and vocabulary, and writing style should be direct. Teen Age Book Club (grades 7, 8, and 9) needs humor (cartoons, jokes); nonfiction about current interests of junior high readers: cars, hot rodding, movie and television personalitites, pro sports. Fiction about adolescent concerns and problems: school, friends, family, dating. Mystery and suspense novels at both juvenile and young adult levels (25,000 to 30,000 words). Campus Book Club (grades 10, 11, and 12) needs humor, superior contemporary fiction for older teenagers, dealing with young adult problems. Campus high school readers are quite sophisticated, so books should be written on a fairly adult level. Action Books needs fiction, about 10,000 words (ten 1,000-word chapters), aimed at junior-senior high school students who read at levels from grades 2 to 4. No writing down. Settings and characters should be easily identifiable to average teenagers (boys and girls), though we'd be happy to see science fiction that starts from a contemporary setting. Following the series' title, we'd like stories to move rapidly into action. Decision might be made on the basis of sample chapter and outline, but completed mss are preferred. Sprint Books wants fiction mss aimed at students ages 9 through 13 who read at the second grade level. Fast-moving plots with lots of action. Quality writing. No writing down. Mss of 3,000, 6,500 and 10,000 words are needed (divided into 10 chapters each). General lengths: A minimum of 32 pages for a picture book with a few words on each page. Books for young adult readers may range in length from 40,000 to 60,000 words. Middle grade books should be about 25,000 words."

SCHOLIUM INTERNATIONAL, INC., 130-30 31st Ave., Flushing NY 11354. Editor-in-Chief: Arthur L. Candido. Publishes hardcover and paperback originals. Standard minimum book contract of 12½%. Published 3 titles last year. Will send free catalog to writer on request. Will consider photocopied submissions. Query first. Reports in 2 weeks. Enclose return postage.

Science and Technology: Subjects covered are cryogenics, electronics, aviation, medicine, physics, etc. "We also publish books in other areas whenever it is felt the manuscript has good sales and reception potential. Contact us prior to sending ms, outlining subject, number of pages, and other pertinent information which would enable us to make a decision as to whether we would want to reveiw the ms." Recent titles include *Applications of Cryogenic Technology.*

CHARLES SCRIBNER'S SONS, 597 Fifth Ave., New York NY 10017. Director of Publishing: Jacek K. Galazka. Publishes hardcover originals and hardcover and paperback reprints. "Our contract terms, royalties and advances vary, depending on the nature of the project." Published 300 titles last year. Will send a catalog to a writer on request. Query first for nonfiction (juvenile and adult), adult fiction, and poetry; complete ms preferred for juvenile fiction, "but will consider partial ms and outline." Will consider photocopied submissions. Reports in 1 to 2 months on ms accepted for publication. Returns rejected adult material in 4 to 6 weeks; returns rejected juveniles in 3 to 4 weeks. Enclose return postage.

General: Publishes adult fiction and nonfiction, practical books, garden books, reference sets, cookbooks, history, science. Adult Trade Editors: Elinor Parker, Norman Kotker, Patricia Cristol, Elisabeth Aschermann, Connie Schrader and Laurie Graham. Science Editor: Kenneth Heuer.

Juveniles: "We publish books for children of all ages—pre-kindergarten up through high school age. We publish picture books, fiction, and nonfiction in all subjects. We have no special requirements in regard to special treatment or emphasis and length requirements. We're interested in books on any topical subject or theme, assuming we feel the material is exciting enough." Children's Book Editor: Lee Anna Deadrick.

SEABURY PRESS, 815 Second Ave., New York NY 10017. Editor-in-Chief, Clarion Books for Young People: James C. Giblin. Publishes hardcover originals. "Most new authors of our Clarion Books for Young People receive a 5% royalty on picture books, 10% on older age books. Average advance is $750 or $1,000, depending on the type of book." Published 25 titles last year. Send outline with sample chapter for nonfiction; complete ms for fiction. Enclose return postage.

Juveniles: Picture books for ages 5-8, 2,000 words or under. Fiction and nonfiction for ages 8-12, 20,000 to 30,000 words. Fiction and nonfiction for ages 12 and up, 30,000 words and up. Special stress is put on contemporary fiction and nonfiction in the social studies area—biography, history, natural sciences. "We have avoided straight how-it-works nonfiction and concentrated more on the humanistic and interpretive. For picture books, especially interested in fresh, amusing, and/or contemporary stories for ages 3 to 7. Currently overworked are animals who want to be something else and verse that doesn't read smoothly or effectively. If writers don't find the verse form comfortable, they'd be better off telling their stories in prose." Current titles include *That Crazy April* (Perl).

RICHARD SEAVER BOOKS, Viking Press, 625 Madison Ave., New York NY 10022. Editor: Richard Seaver. Publishes originals. "Royalties and advances for each book are negotiated separately." Published 22 titles last year. Queries only; no complete mss. Enclose return postage.

Fiction and Nonfiction: "Our main interest right now is in serious nonfiction, but in the past year we have been publishing more and more fiction. Fiction list includes William Burroughs, Eugene Ionesco, John Berger, Anne Steinhardt, Richard Gardner, and Daniel Stern." Recent titles include *The Hermit* (Ionesco); *The Adventures of Don Juan* (Gardner); *The Poor Mouth* (O'Brien); *The Look of Things* (Berger).

SHEED AND WARD, INC., 475 Fifth Ave., New York NY 10017. Editor-in-Chief:

James F. Andrews. Publishes hardcover and paperback originals. Offers standard royalty schedule. Advance negotiable. Published 16 titles last year. Will send free catalog to writer on request. Will consider photocopied submissions. Query first or submit outline and sample chapters to Kansas City office: 6700 Squibb Rd., Mission KS 66202. Reports in 7 weeks. Enclose S.A.S.E.

General Nonfiction: Political history and commentary, general interest, popular philosophical, theological, cartoon collections, how-to books in home interests, photography, textbooks. Books from 96 to 590 pages in length published within the past year. Recent titles include *The End of Intelligent Writing; Three Mobs; Inside Cuba.*

SHERBOURNE PRESS, 1640 S. LaCienega Blvd., Los Angeles CA 90035. Editor-in-Chief: Mr. Gil Porter. Publishes hardcover and paperback originals. Offers a standard royalty contract with varying advances. Published 20 titles last year. Prefers a query with sample chapter, outline or table of contents before submission. Reports in 3 weeks. Enclose return postage.

Nonfiction: Interested only in nonfiction titles with wide appeal; books that solve problems that many people encounter, but solve them in unique ways. "We want books that tell people how to make or manage their money, become healthier, happier, more fulfilled." "We are not afraid of sex-oriented nonfiction, but it must be very authoritative, yet written for the average couple to read and use." Books that have a strong feel for mail order promotion get a sympathetic hearing as Sherbourne can do major promotions this way.

SHOAL CREEK PUBLISHERS, INC., P.O. Box 9737, Austin TX 78766. Editor-in-Chief: W. L. Thompson. Publishes hardcover and paperback originals and reprints. Offers standard minimum book contract of 10-12½-15%. Published 6 titles last year. Will consider photocopied submissions if they are clear. Query first. Reports as soon as possible. Enclose return postage.

Nonfiction: Regional and western nonfiction, historical interest books; folklore, politics, biographies, collections, cookbooks, law, insurance, psychology. Americana, art, biography. Recent titles include *Talk of Texas* and *Texas Wild Flowers.*

SIGNPOST PUBLICATIONS, 16812 36 Avenue West, Lynnwood WA 98036. Editor-in-Chief: Larry Ferguson. Publishes hardcover and paperback originals. Offers standard minimum book contract of 10-12½-15%. Advance varies. Published 5 titles last year. Will send free catalog to writer on request. Query first. Enclose S.A.S.E.

Nonfiction: "Books on outdoor subjects. Limited to self-propelled wilderness activity. Also books of general interest to Northwesterners. History, natural science, related to the Pacific Northwest. Books should have strong environmental material for a general audience, where applicable. Our style of publishing does not lend itself easily to submissions. Usually we decide on a book and then find someone to write it." Recent titles include *Northwest Foraging, Backpacking With Babies.*

SILVER BURDETT, Subsidiary of Scott, Foresman Co., 250 James St., Morristown NJ 07960. Publishes hardcover and paperback originals. "Textbook rates only. El-Hi range." Published approximately 160 titles last year. Query first to Harrison Bell, Editor-in-Chief, Silver Burdett Division. Enclose S.A.S.E.

Education: Produces educational materials for preschoolers, elementary and high school students, and professional publications for teachers. Among materials produced: textbooks, teachers' materials, other print and non-print classroom materials including educational games, manipulatives, and audiovisual aids (silent and sound 16mm films and filmstrips, records, multimedia kits, overhead transparencies, tapes, etc.). Assigns projects to qualified writers on occasion. Writer must have understanding of school market and school learning materials.

SILVERMINE PUBLISHERS INCORPORATED, Comstock Hill, Silvermine, Norwalk CT 06850. Editor-in-Chief: William Wilson Atkin. Published 1 title last year. Will send a catalog to writer on request. Query first. Enclose S.A.S.E.

Nonfiction: Publishes general nonfiction, biography, and books dealing with fine arts and architecture. "We are not interested in name authors, but insist on good writing. Our books are designed to last (that is, they are not 1-season phenomena). Thus, a typical book over a period of 3 to 5 years may earn $3,000 to $6,000 royalties. It is our opinion that books that are solid text, unillustrated, are not salable any longer unless they are news or topical (which we are not interested in), fiction by established writers (which we are not interested in), or books on special subjects."

SIMON AND SCHUSTER, Trade Books Division of Simon and Schuster, Inc., 630 Fifth Ave., New York NY 10020. "If we accept a book for publication, business arrangements are worked out with the author or his agent and a contract is drawn up. The specific terms vary according to the type of book and other considerations. Royalty rates are more or less standard among publishers. Special arrangements are made for anthologies, translations and projects involving editorial research services." Published 256 titles last year. Catalog available on request. "All unsolicited mss will be returned unread. Only mss submitted by agents or recommended to us by friends or actively solicited by us will be considered. Our requirements are as follows: All mss submitted for consideration should be marked to the attention of the editorial department. Mystery novels should be so labeled in order that they may be sent to the proper editors without delay. It usually takes at least three weeks for the author to be notified of a decision—often longer. Sufficient postage for return by first-class registered mail, or instructions for return by express collect, in case of rejection, should be included. Mss must be typewritten, double-spaced, on one side of the sheet only. We suggest margins of about one inch all around and the standard 8½-by-11-inch typewriter paper." Prefers complete mss.
General: "Simon and Schuster publishes books of adult fiction, history, biography, science, philosophy, the arts and religion, running 50,000 words or more. We also publish poetry and juveniles. Our program does not, however, include school textbooks, extremely technical or highly specialized works, or, as a general rule, plays. Exceptions have been made, of course, for extraordinary mss of great distinction or significance."

SIMON & SCHUSTER OF CANADA LIMITED, 330 Steelcase Rd., Markham, Ontario, Canada. L3R 2M1. Editor: Paul A. Fulford. Publishes 24 titles a year. Royalties are standard at 6% on first 50,000 copies sold, 8% thereafter. Pays from $1,000 to $2,500 advance. Buys world rights. Prefers query with outline and sample chapters. Enclose S.A.E. and International Reply Coupons.
Nonfiction and Fiction: By Canadians only, but good enough for the worldwide English-speaking market. No books that appeal to segments of the reading public only. Recent titles include *The Last Canadian, The Happy Hairdresser, The Olympic Games.*

THE SMITH, 5 Beekman St., New York NY 10038. Publishes hardcover and paperback originals. The Smith is now owned by The Generalist Association, Inc., a non-profit organization, which gives grants to writers and awards publication. Grants are variable, averaging $500 for book projects. Published 6 titles last year. Will send catalog on request. Send query first for nonfiction; sample chapter preferred for fiction. Reports within six weeks. Enclose return postage.
Nonfiction and Fiction: No specific categories or requirements. Editor of Adult Fiction: Harry Smith. Nonfiction Editor: Sidney Bernard.

SOCCER ASSOCIATES, P.O. Box 634, New Rochelle NY 10802. Editor: Jeff Miller. Published 95 titles last year. Send finished book to Milton Miller. Enclose return postage.
Sports, Hobbies, and Recreation: Publishes sports, recreation, leisure time, and hobby books under Sport Shelf and Leisure Time Books imprints. Most titles are British and Australian although they do have a special service for authors who publish their own books and desire national and international distribution, promotion, and publicity.

SOUTHERN METHODIST UNIVERSITY PRESS, Dallas TX 75275. Director:

Allen Maxwell; Associate Director and Editor: Margaret L. Hartley. Payment is on royalty basis: 10% of list up to 2,500 copies; 12½% for 2,500-5,000 copies; 15% thereafter. No advance. Published 5 titles last year. Catalog available on request. Appreciates query letters, outlines and sample chapters. Reports tend to be slow for promising mss requiring outside reading by authorities. Enclose return postage.

Nonfiction: Regional and scholarly nonfiction. History, Americana, economics, banking, literature, and anthologies. Length: open. Recent titles include *Comanche Days* (Gilles); *The Making of an American* (Carrington); *The Bank Director* (Johnson); *Southern Methodist University: Founding and Early Years* (Thomas); *The Southwest Review Reader* (Hartley).

STACKPOLE BOOKS, Cameron and Kelker Sts., Harrisburg PA 17105. Executive Vice-President and Editorial Director: Clyde P. Peters. Standard royalties. Usual advance is $1,000, but this varies, depending on author's reputation and nature of book. Published 36 titles last year. Send query with sample chapter and outline to Neil McAleer, Managing Editor. Reports in less than one month. Enclose return postage.

Nonfiction: Major publisher of Americana, crafts, camping, hunting, fishing, recreation, history, firearms, and general nonfiction books on leisure-time activities for adults. Seeking new book-length mss that add new sales and content dimensions to these and related fields. New writers welcome. Length: 30,000 words minimum. Recent titles include *American Quilts, Quilting, and Patchwork; Building Early American Furniture; Looking for Gold: The Modern Prospector's Handbook.*

STANDARD PUBLISHING, 8121 Hamilton Ave., Cincinnati OH 45231. Product Planner: Shirley Beegle. Publishes paperback originals. Offers a cash payment or royalty depending upon length of book. Published 19 titles for children last year. "The majority of our books are sold through Christian bookstores." Will send a catalog to a writer on request. Query first for nonfiction; submit complete ms for fiction. Will not consider photocopied submissions. Reports in 2 to 3 months. Enclose return postage.

Juveniles: "The majority of our books are storybooks for children from 3 to 10. The material should be Bible-based or contain a definite Christian teaching. Also publish devotional books and puzzle books for children." Length: open. Recent titles include *Children's Favorite Bible Stories, A Child's Book of Manners, Seasons in God's World, Baby Jesus ABC Storybook.*

Nonfiction: Publishes some devotional books for adults. Bible story paperbacks; present-day with Christian teaching.

STATE HISTORICAL SOCIETY OF WISCONSIN PRESS, 816 State St., Madison WI 53706. Editor: Paul H. Hass. Publishes hardcover originals. Pays 10% of gross income. No advance. Published 6 titles last year. Send complete ms. (No corrasable bond, please.) Reports in eight weeks. Enclose return postage with ms.

History: Research and interpretation in history of the American Middle West—broadly construed as the Mississippi Valley. Must be thoroughly documented. 150,000 to 200,000 words of text, exclusive of footnotes and other back matter.

STECK-VAUGHN COMPANY, Box 2028, Austin TX 78767. Published 64 titles last year. "We've discontinued the publication of juveniles." Enclose return postage with ms.

Textbooks: "Elementary and secondary school textual and supplementary materials; adult education materials." Dept. Editor: Paul C. Craig, Vice-President, Editorial.

STEIN AND DAY, Scarborough House, Briarcliff Manor NY 10510. Offers standard royalty contract. Published about 100 titles last year. Not interested in unsolicited mss. Nonfiction, send outline or summary and sample chapter; fiction, send first chapter only. Enclose return postage.

General: Publishes general trade books; no juveniles or college. All types of nonfiction except technical. Quality fiction. Length: 75,000 to 100,000 words. Representative titles include: *The Understudy* (Kazan).

STORY HOUSE CORP. (SamHar Press), Charlotteville NY 12036. Editor: D. Steve Rahmas. Publishes paperback originals. Offers outright fee: "$150 upon completed and corrected final ms, and $150 after sale of 6,000 books. Fee includes research, proofreading, and lengthening or shortening of the text to conform with required length." Publishes about 100 titles a year. Write for copy of guidelines for writers. Query first; "do not begin writing until subject is confirmed. Subject is exclusive for 60 days. The right to assign the subject to another author is reserved if the work is not completed within 60 days if other arrangements have not been made. Please submit 3 or more subjects in order of preference." Enclose return postage.
Nonfiction: For "high school and college students," material is wanted for "Outstanding Personalities series (biographies), Events of Our Times series (study of single great events), Topics of Our Times (study of topics of special current interest), and Handcraft and Hobby series. In each of these series, the aim is creation of a basic research tool for assigned areas of interest. Work should be a concise description, but still interesting and intriguing. To be written in a free-flowing, interesting style, not a scholarly style. Must contain all basic facts about area of interest assigned, as indicated in information guidelines for prospective authors. No chapter or other subdivisions. For biography series, ms should be basic research tool for the assigned personality. Should cover information chronologically from birth to death or present. For the Events of Our Times series, each work should be devoted to only one single event, not to any movement or trend. The term 'event' is meant to include all occurrences leading to the event and all results flowing therefrom. For Handcraft and Hobby series, material should depict a craft or art by means of explanation and diagrams. For Topics of Our Times series, we are interested in any areas of interest that are currently of more than average interest to the common person, such as women's rights, ecology, population problem." Length: 9,500 to 10,500 words.

STRUCTURES PUBLISHING CO., P.O. Box 423, Farmington MI 48024. Editor: R. J. Lytle. Publishes hardcover and paperback originals. Offers standard 10-12½-15% royalty contract. Advance varies, depending on author's reputation and nature of book. Published 2 titles last year. Will send a catalog to a writer on request. Submit outline and sample chapters. Will consider photocopied submissions. Reports in 4 to 6 weeks. Enclose return postage.
Technical and How-To: Books related to building. Wants to expand Successful Series which include books published both for professionals and homeowners in paperback and hardcover. Current how-to titles include *Book of Successful Kitchens* (Galvin). Technical books are aimed at architects, builders and suppliers. Current titles include *Chemical Materials for Construction* (Maslow).

SUNSTONE PRESS, P.O. Box 2321, Santa Fe NM 87501. Editor-in-Chief: Jody Ellis. Publishes paperback originals; "sometimes hardcover originals." Offers 10% royalty contract. Advance varies. Published 13 titles last year. Will send a catalog to a writer on request. Query first. Reports in 1 month. Enclose return postage.
Nonfiction: How-to series craft books. Books on the Southwest, poetry. Length: open. Recent titles include *Fin de Fiesta, A Journey to Yucatan* (Scott).

SWEDENBORG FOUNDATION, 139 East 23rd St., New York NY 10010. Chairman, Editorial and Publications Committee: C. S. Priestnal. Publishes hardcover and paperback originals and reprints (limited to Swedenborgiana). Royalties negotiable. Published 5 titles last year. Catalog available on request. Query first. Will consider photocopied submissions. Reports in 1 month. Enclose return postage with query.
Nonfiction: The life and works of Emanuel Swedenborg. Studies of Swedenborg's scientific activities as precursors of modern developments. Studies of Swedenborg's contributions to the mainstream of religious thought. Also related history, science, philosophy, religion, parapsychology, sociology. "Objective and scholarly analysis. Our audience is ecumenical; serious students of all religions."

SYMPHONY PRESS, P.O. Box 515, Tenafly NJ 07670. Editor-in-Chief: Eric Weber. Publishes hardcover originals. Royalty of 5%. Advance varies from $2,000 to $3,000.

Published 5 titles last year. Will consider photocopied submissions. Submit complete ms. Reports in 2 weeks. Enclose return postage.

How-To: "Our how-to books are written with extreme simplicity and clarity. Any subject, but must have wide appeal to the general public and be written in a short, punchy, easy-to-read style." Length: 10,000 to 50,000 words. Recent titles include *How to Pick Up Girls* (Weber) and *How to Ask for a Raise and Get It!* (Bellonte).

SYRACUSE UNIVERSITY PRESS, 1011 E. Water St., Syracuse NY 13210. Associate Director and Editor: Arpena Mesrobian. The royalty schedule varies, but generally a royalty is paid on every title. Published 14 titles last year. Catalog available on request. Query first with outline or sample chapters. If the ms is not rejected outright, a decision may be expected in 3 to 4 months. Enclose return postage.

Nonfiction: Publishes nonfiction, scholarly books, including biography, regional (especially on New York State and Iroquois), technical, literary criticism, history, philosophy, politics, religion, and educational books. Approximate minimum length: 50,000 words. Current titles include *The Catskill Witch and Other Tales of the Hudson Valley* (McMurry); *Russian Literary Criticism: A Short History* (Stacy).

TAPE 'N TEXT, Williamsville Publishing Co., Inc., P.O. Box 237, 343 Countryside Lane, Williamsville NY 14221. Editor-in-Chief: William R. Parks. Publishes printed text closely coordinated with narration on cassette tape. Offers royalty contract of 5% minimum. Published 5 titles last year. Marketing currently limited to direct mail to schools and libraries. Will send free catalog to writer on request. Will consider photocopied submissions. Query first. Reports in 6 weeks. Enclose return postage.

Education and Training: "The kind of material we want from prospective authors is either a narration on tape with printed text which is very closely coordinated, *or* taped lectures or talks. Although we are now in mathematics, we have plans of going into religious education and, perhaps, other fields such as science, and English. We must have inquiries first before writers send in their material. We also request that writers consider that their educational background and experience are important factors. Authors should examine our existing Tape 'n Text titles so that they can follow this format for their development of material. It is important that the writer establish what his target audience is, i.e., level: elementary school, junior high school, high school, junior college, university, or the general trade market." Current titles include *Computer Mathematics: Computer Number Bases* (Parks).

TEACHERS COLLEGE PRESS, 1234 Amsterdam Ave., New York NY 10027. Publishes originals and reprints. Royalty schedule varies. No advance. Published 24 titles last year. Current catalog available on request. Send outline and sample chapter addressed to the Director. Enclose return postage.

Nonfiction: Publishes scholarly and professional books in education and allied subjects (psychology, sociology, social studies, etc.) as well as testing materials. Length: open.

TEXAS WESTERN PRESS, The University of Texas at El Paso, El Paso TX 79968. Director: E.H. Antone. Publishes hardcover and paperback originals. "We are a university press, not a commercial house; therefore, payment is in books and prestige more than money. Most of our books are sold to libraries, not to the general reading public." Published 10 titles last year. Will send a catalog to a writer on request. Query first. Will consider photocopied submissions. "Follow MLA Style Sheet." Reports in 1 to 3 months. Enclose return postage.

Nonfiction: "Scholarly books. Historic accounts of the Southwest (west Texas, southern New Mexico, and northern Mexico). Some literary works, occasional scientific titles. Our Southwestern Studies use mss of 20,000 words. Our hardback books range from 30,000 words up. The writer should use good exposition in his work. Most of our work requires documentation. We favor a scholarly, but not overly pedantic, style. We specialize in superior book design." Recent titles include *John F. Finerty Reports Mexico 1879* (Timmons) and *Sunward I've Climbed* (Craig).

THE THIRD PRESS, Joseph Okpaku Publishing Co., Inc., 444 Central Park West,

New York NY 10025. Editor-in-Chief: Grace Feliciano. Publishes hardcover and paperback originals and paperback reprints. Advance varies. Published 30 titles last year. Books marketed through trade promotions and direct mail. Will send free catalog to writer on request. Editorial guidelines also available. Will consider photocopied submissions. Query first or submit outline and sample chapters. Reports in 6 weeks. Enclose return postage.

Black Nonfiction and Drama: "We are a general trade book publishing house with a particularly impressive roster of Black literature; African, Afro-American and Caribbean writers. We also take a special interest in drama. All material must be written with originality and honesty. Being a small house, we are more willing to take a chance on the occasional trailblazer than the established house." Current titles include *The Misanthrope* (Harrison).

THREE CONTINENTS PRESS, 4201 Cathedral Ave., N.W., Washington DC 20016. Editor-in-Chief: Donald E. Herdeck. Publishes hardcover and paperback originals. Royalty contract of 10% of first $5,000 gross; 15% thereafter. Published 3 titles last year. Will send free catalog to writer on request. Will consider photocopied submissions. Query first with synopsis or outline and a sample chapter. Reports in 45 days. Enclose return postage.

Third World and History: Specializes in African and Caribbean literature and criticism, third world literature and history. Scholarly, well-prepared mss; creative writing. Fiction, poetry, criticism, history and translations of creative writing. "We search for books which will make clear the complexity and value of African literature and culture, including bilingual texts (African language/English translations) of previously unpublished authors from less well-known areas of Africa. We are always interested in genuine contributions to understanding African and Caribbean culture." Length: 50,000 words. Current titles include *Uahaba: The Hurtle to Blood River*, the first Zulu novel ever published in America.

TIDEWATER PUBLISHERS, Box 109, Cambridge MD 21613. Editor: Mary Jane Cornell. An imprint of Cornell Maritime Press, Inc. Publishes hardcover and paperback originals and reprints. Offers standard 10-12½-15% royalty contract. Published 4 titles last year. Will send a catalog to a writer on request. Query first with outline and sample chapters. Will not consider photocopied submissions. Reports in 2 to 3 weeks. Enclose return postage.

Nonfiction: "General nonfiction on Maryland and the Delmarva Peninsula." Recent titles include *Maryland State and Government; Shoremen: An Anthology of Eastern Shore Prose and Verse.*

TIME-LIFE BOOKS, Time & Life Building, New York NY 10020. Managing Editor: Jerry Korn. Publishes hardcover originals. "We have no minimum or maximum fee because our needs vary tremendously. Advance, as such, is not offered. Author is paid as he completes part of contracted work." Book distribution is primarily through mail order sale. Query first to Oliver Allen, Director of Editorial Planning. Enclose return postage.

Nonfiction: "General interest books. Most books tend to be heavily illustrated (by staff), with text written by assigned authors. We very rarely accept mss or book ideas submitted from outside our staff." Length: open. Recent titles include *The Individual* (first book in Human Behavior Series); *Novel Materials* (Art of Sewing Series); *The Expressmen* (Old West Series); *The Cascades* (American Wilderness Series); *The Celts* (Emergence of Man Series).

TIMES MIRROR MAGAZINES, INC., BOOK DIVISION, (Subsidiary of Times Mirror Company), 380 Madison Ave., New York NY 10017. Publishing books in the Popular Science and Outdoor Life fields. Editor: John W. Sill. Published 12 titles last year. Royalties and advance according to size and type of book. Wants outlines, sample chapters, author information. Enclose return postage.

How-To and Self-Help: Publishes books in Popular Science field: home building, repair and improvement, workshop, hand and power tools, automobile how-to. In the Outdoor Life field: hunting, especially big game and deer; fishing, camping, firearms. Small books to 30,000 words; large books to 150,000 words.

TRANSACTION BOOKS, Rutgers University, New Brunswick NJ 08903. Publisher: Irving Louis Horowitz; Executive Editor: Susan Ferris. Publishes hardcover and paperback originals and paperback reprints. "Contract depends on author's reputation and nature of his book. Advance is generally given only for anthologies, to cover, in part, permissions expenses." Published 22 titles last year. Will consider photocopied submissions. Conform to University of Chicago *Manual of Style.* Address submissions to Susan Ferris, Executive Editor. Reports in 3 months. Enclose return postage.

Social Sciences: "We publish in the social sciences; anthropology, sociology, psychology, political science, some social history, urban affairs. Books are generally hardcover and paperback originals, although sometimes we will publish a book in one edition only. We also publish paperback reprints and anthologies. Most of our books are by practicing social scientists, who generally are engaged in teaching and research. Our audience is also academic, mainly students or interested laymen, as well as fellow professionals. We plan to develop further our Third World Series and would like to continue expanding our urban affairs series." Length preferred: 150 to 500 ms pages.

TRANS-ANGLO BOOKS, P.O. Box 38, Corona del Mar CA 92625. Editorial Director: Spencer Crump. Royalty of 5%-10%. Published 4 titles last year. Catalog on request. Query required; do not send mss until requested. Reports in three weeks to one month. Enclose return postage.

Nonfiction: Publishes Americana, ecology, Western Americana, biography, and railroad books. "We are not interested in family histories or local history that lacks national appeal." Most books are 8½x11 hardcover with many photos supplementing a good text of 5,000 to 100,000 words. Recent titles include *Gold! And Where They Found It* (Western Americana); *Death Valley Scotty* (biography).

TREND HOUSE, P.O. Box 2350, Tampa FL 33601. Publishes hardcover and paperback originals. "We offer standard royalty arrangements and, occasionally, an advance, depending on the nature of the book and our interest in it." Published 8 titles last year. "Many of our books are sold through *Florida Trend Magazine* and *The South Magazine*, in addition to the usual means. Query, outline, or ms is acceptable." Will consider photocopied submissions. Reports in 2 to 3 weeks. Enclose return postage.

Nonfiction: "We publish books related to Florida in all fields. Books about Florida and southern real estate; business, estate planning and the South; condominiums, birds, retiring in Florida and figures about Florida, cooking, history of the South, famous men, and some Florida school textbooks. Looking for school material for use in southern public schools. No special length requirements. Also publish titles that are aimed at special markets, e.g., *300 Most Abused Drugs*, for law enforcement officers. Interested in seeing school and textbook materials for any individual state." Recent titles include *Confusion to the Enemy* (Griffith); *Florida Fossils* (Murray); *Guide to the Everglades* (Smith and Matusek).

TROUBADOR PRESS, INC., 126 Folsom St., San Francisco CA 94105. Editor-in-Chief: Malcolm Whyte. Publishes mostly paperback originals; some hardcover originals. "Royalties vary from 5% to 10%; also purchase whole mss outright. Advances from $200 to $1,000." Reports within 2 weeks. Published 13 titles last year. Distributed through book, gift, toy departments and stores, as well as museum stores and education markets. Will consider photocopied submissions. Query first with outline and/or sample illustrations. Address queries to Brenda Shahan. Reporting time varies. Enclose return postage.

General Nonfiction: "Entertainment, art, activity, nature, self-help, game and cookbooks for adults and children. Titles feature original art and handsome graphics. Primarily nonfiction. Always interested in adding to Puzzlebook line, as well as select (but not esoteric) craft and how-to ideas. Also interested in adding to cookbook line of alternative cooking, such as our *Sprouting* and *Yogurt* books. Interested in expanding on themes of 50 current titles. Maze Craze series and Wildlife series. Like books which can develop into a series." Current titles include *The Scrimshander*,

Papermovie Machines, Monster Gallery, Paper Airplanes, Dinosaur, Monster Movie Game, Sprouting.

TRUCHA PUBLICATIONS, INC., P.O. Box 5223, Lubbock TX 79417. Editor-in-Chief: Josie Mora. Publishes paperback originals. Offers standard minimum book contract of 10-12½-15%, but will generally work with author according to individual needs and situation. Published 6 titles last year. Will send free catalog to writer on request. Query first, or submit outline and sample chapters, or complete ms. Reports in 2 months. Enclose return postage.
Third World: "The thoughts, expressions, aspirations, and generally esthetic literary creations of oppressed peoples throughout the world, regardless of race, color, creed, nationality or sex. All genre of literature and varying in length. Special emphasis given to bilingual, bicultural literature. Must leave a feeling of hope and self-assertion in subject matter treated. Literature of despair not our forte, although due to the nature of our literature much suffering is necessarily expressed, but it is certainly not essential for publication. Do not wish to see mss by non-Third World persons jumping on the bandwagon of minorities." Length: open. Recent titles include *Chicano Counselor* and *The Black Sun*.

CHARLES E. TUTTLE CO., INC., Publishers & Booksellers, 26-30 S. Main St., Rutland VT 05701. Publishes originals and reprints. Pays $250 against 10% royalty. Advance varies. Published 34 titles last year. Current catalog available for 50¢. Send complete mss or queries accompanied by outlines or sample chapters to Charles E. Tuttle Co., Inc., Suido 1--Chome, 2-6, Bunkyo-Ku, Tokyo, Japan, where the editorial and printing offices are located. Reports in 4 to 6 weeks. Enclose return postage.
Nonfiction: Specializes in publishing books about Oriental art and culture as well as history, literature, cookery, sport and children's books which relate to Asia, Hawaiian Islands, Australia and the Pacific areas. Also interested in Americana, especially antique collecting, architecture, genealogy and Canadian. Not interested in travel, sociological or topical works even when in subject field. No interest in poetry and fiction except that of Oriental theme. Normal book length only.
Juveniles: Juvenile books are to be accompanied by illustrations.

TWAYNE PUBLISHERS, A division of G. K. Hall & Co., 70 Lincoln St., Boston MA 02111. Executive Editor: Thomas T. Beeler. Payment is on royalty basis. Published 123 titles last year. Query first. Reports in three weeks. Enclose return postage.
Nonfiction: Publishes scholarly books. Literary criticism and biography.

FREDERICK UNGAR PUBLISHING CO., INC., 250 Park Ave. S., New York NY 10003. Published 21 titles last year. Query first. Enclose S.A.S.E.
Nonfiction: "Scholarly books mainly in fields of literature and literary criticism. We do not encourage submission of mss by nonscholars." Mainly nonfiction literary, plus translations from European literature.

UNITED SYNAGOGUE BOOK SERVICE, 155 Fifth Ave., New York NY 10010. Hardcover and paperback originals. Royalty schedule: 10% of list price. No advance. Published 6 titles last year. Catalog on request. Send query, outline, sample chapter first. Address juveniles and history to Dr. Morton Siegel; biography, philosophy and adult religion to Rabbi Marvin Wiener. "Address general inquiries to George L. Levine, Director." Reports in one to eight weeks. Enclose return postage.
Religion: Publishes religious books only: textbooks, readers, Hebrew Language books, history, picture books. No length requirements.

UNITY PRESS, P.O. Box 1037, Santa Cruz CA 95061. Editor-in-Chief: Stephen Levine. Publishes hardcover and paperback originals. Offers standard minimum book contract of 10-12½-15%. Advance "depends; small though." Published 6 titles last year. Will consider photocopied submissions. Reports in 2 months. Query first. Enclose S.A.S.E.

Fiction and Nonfiction: Books of spiritual insight, biographies, poetry. Interest in the coming together of the planet family. Wildlife handling and care. Planet love. The search for the miraculous. "Planning additions to our Mindfulness Series (meditation books) and original science fiction collections. Only book-length mss."

UNIVERSITY OF ALABAMA PRESS, Drawer 2877, University AL 35486. Managing Editor: James Travis. Publishes hardcover originals. "Maximum royalty is 12½%; no advances made." Published 27 titles last year. Will send a catalog to a writer on request. Submit outlines and sample chapters. Will consider photocopied submissions, "although these are suspect." Reports in "about 6 months." Enclose return postage.
Nonfiction: "Scholarly nonfiction. Categories include biography, business, economics, history, philosophy, politics, religion, and sociology." Considers upon merit almost any subject of scholarly investigation, but specializes in linguistics and philology, political science and public administration, literary criticism and biography, philosophy, and scholarly history (especially southern). Also interested in biology, medicine, and agriculture.

UNIVERSITY OF CALIFORNIA PRESS, Berkeley CA 94720; Los Angeles CA 90024. Director: August Fruge. Los Angeles address is 60 Powell Library, Los Angeles CA 90024. Editor: Robert Y. Zachary. New York Office, Room 513, 50 E. 42 St., New York NY 10017. London Office IBEG, Ltd., 2-4 Brook St., London W1Y 1AA, England. Publishes hardcover and paperback originals and reprints. On books likely to more than return their costs, a standard royalty contract beginning at 10% is paid; on paperbacks it is less. Published 165 titles last year. Queries are always advisable, accompanied by outlines or sample material. Address to either Berkeley or Los Angeles address. Reports vary, depending on the subject. Enclose return postage.
Nonfiction: "It should be clear that most of our publications are hardcover nonfiction written by scholars." Publishes scholarly books including art, literary studies, social sciences, natural sciences and some high-level popularizations. No length preferences.
Fiction and Poetry: Publishes fiction and poetry only in translation. Usually in bilingual editions.

UNIVERSITY OF MASSACHUSETTS PRESS, Amherst MA 01002. Publishes original works and reprints. Typical royalties: none on first run; 10% of retail thereafter. Advances are rare. Published 18 titles last year. Address mss to the Editor. Initial reports in six to twelve weeks. Enclose return postage with ms.
Nonfiction and Poetry: Scholarly and esthetic merit, including history and political science, black studies, biography, science, poetry, art, and studies of regional interest. Current titles include: *Robert Frost: A Living Voice* (Cook); *Black Autobiography* (Butterfield); *Meyerhold: The Art of Conscious Theater* (Hoover); *Emily Dickinson and the Image of Home* (Mudge).

UNIVERSITY OF MINNESOTA PRESS, 2037 University Ave., S.E., Minneapolis MN 55455. Publishes hardcover and paperback. Royalties vary. Published 21 titles last year. Query letters to Director highly important. Mss should not be sent unless requested. Reports in three weeks to four months. Enclose return postage.
Nonfiction: Publishes scholarly nonfiction which has wide impact; interpretations for a more general audience; textbooks; regional books. No word length requirement, except that only book-length mss are acceptable. Representative titles: *Indian and Free* (Brill); *The Black Mind: A History of African Literature* (Dathorne).

UNIVERSITY OF NOTRE DAME PRESS, Notre Dame IN 46556. Editor: Ann Rice. Publishes hardcover and paperback originals and paperback reprints. Offers standard 10-12½-15% royalty contract; no advance. Published 16 titles last year. Will send a catalog to a writer on request. Query first. Will consider photocopied submissions. Reports in 2 to 3 months. Enclose return postage.
Nonfiction: "Scholarly books, serious nonfiction of general interest; book-length only. Especially in the areas of philosophy, theology, history, sociology, English literature

(Middle English period, and modern literature criticism in the area of relation of literature and theology), government, and international relations. Lately, especially Mexican-American studies. Also interested in books on the heritage of American beliefs and ideas suitable for junior college or high school students." Recent titles include *Chicano Revolt in a Texas Town* (Shockley); *Structural Fabulation: An Essay on Fiction of the Future* (Scholes).

UNIVERSITY OF OKLAHOMA PRESS, Norman OK 73069. Director: Edward A. Shaw; Editor: Mary Stith. Pays on royalty basis. Paperbacks, 5%; for some highly scholarly books with very limited markets, other arrangements are made other than the standard contract, but these vary with circumstances. No advance. Published 85 titles last year. Reports in 2 months. Query before sending ms. Enclose return postage.
Nonfiction: Publishes nonfiction books from 50,000 to 125,000 words in such fields as history, folklore, the American Indian, Western Americana, exploration and travel, farming, ranching, archaeology, anthropology, American literature; in fact, all of the fields of permanent interest which an American university press should cultivate.

UNIVERSITY OF UTAH PRESS, University of Utah, Building 513, Salt Lake City UT 84112. Director: Norma B. Mikkelsen. Publishes hardcover and paperback originals, reprints, and translations. Offers no royalty payment on first 500 copies sold; 10% on 501 to 2,000 copies sold; 12½% on 2,001 to 4,000 copies sold; 15% thereafter. No advance royalties. Published 8 titles last year. Will send a catalog to a writer on request. Query first with outline and sample chapter. "If extremely long ms, indicate number of typewritten pages in query." Reports in 2 to 4 months. Enclose return postage.
Nonfiction: Scholarly books on history, biographies, science, philosophy, religion, the arts, poetry, and general nonfiction. Length: author should specify word length in query. Recent titles include *Conversations With Frederick Manfred* (American literature); *To Utah With the Dragoons* (Western history, military history).

UNIVERSITY OF WISCONSIN PRESS, P.O. Box 1379, Madison WI 53701. Director: Thompson Webb, Jr. Editor: Joan M. Krager. Publishes hardcover and paperback originals, reprints, and translations. Offers standard royalty contract. No advance. Published 30 titles last year. Send complete ms. Follow Modern Language Association Style Sheet. Reports in 3 months. Enclose return postage with ms.
Nonfiction: Publishes general nonfiction based on scholarly research.

UNIVERSITY PRESS OF KANSAS, 366 Watson Library, Lawrence KS 66045. Editor-in-Chief: Yvonne Willingham. Publishes hardcover originals; paperbacks occasionally. "Royalties of 5% of retail until manufacturing costs recovered, 10% thereafter." No advance. Published 14 titles last year. "Our market is essentially libraries and scholars." Will send free catalog and editorial guidelines to writer on request. Query first or submit complete ms. Will consider photocopied submissions, "but must have original typed ms on good bond if we accept the title." Rejected material is returned within a few days; may hold material under consideration for 4 to 6 months. Enclose return postage.
Scholarly Nonfiction: History, philosophy, literature, religion, political science and so forth. Length is open. No special requirements, except writer must show competence, accuracy, and consistency in style and documentation. No dissertations. Current titles include *The Politics of Torch: The Allied Landings and the Algiers Putsch, 1942* (Funk), describes allied invasion and occupation of North Africa with stress on political rather than military considerations. Considers both Anglo-American and French interests. *The Presidency of George Washington* (McDonald), second volume in American Presidency Series.

THE UNIVERSITY PRESS OF KENTUCKY, Lexington KY 40506. Editor: Wm. Jerome Crouch. Hardcover and paperback originals and reprints. Pays royalties of 10% after first 1,000 copies. No advance. Published 25 titles last year. Current catalog

available on request. "Writers should query first, sending outline and describing their mss." Reports in approximately three months. Enclose return postage.
Nonfiction: Publishes general nonfiction including philosophy, biography, history, science and the arts. "This is the scholarly publishing arm of 13 Kentucky colleges and universities and its policy restricts it to the publishing of scholarly works, works which make some form of contribution to knowledge. Any mss submitted to us must receive a favorable evaluation from a scholar in field covered by the particular ms before it can be accepted for publication. The Press does not publish works of fiction, poetry, or drama as such." Length: approximately 30,000 words and up.

UNIVERSITY PRESS OF VIRGINIA, Box 3608, University Station, Charlottesville VA 22903. Publishes hardcover and paperback originals and reprints. "Royalty schedule varies with title, depending upon cost, potential sale, etc." No advance. Published 42 titles last year. Catalog on request. Send query letters to the Director. Reports in 8 weeks. Enclose return postage.
Nonfiction: History, bibliography, science, philosophy, the arts, religion, general nonfiction and monographs. Requires book-length mss.

THE VIKING PRESS, INC., PUBLISHERS, 625 Madison Ave., New York NY 10022. Royalties paid on all books. Published over 200 titles last year. Juvenile mss should be addressed to Viking Junior Books. Adult mss should be addressed to The Viking Press. Studio mss should be addressed to Viking Studio Books. Reports in 4 to 6 weeks. Enclose return postage with ms.
General: Publishes adult and Studio books (art, photography, etc.). Also publishes Viking Portable Library and Viking Critical Library.
Juveniles: Publishes juvenile books.

VULCAN BOOKS, Division of Trinity-One, Inc., P.O. Box 25616, Seattle WA 98125. Editor-in-Chief: Michael H. Gaven. Publishes hardcover and paperback originals and reprints. Offers standard minimum book contract, with quarterly royalty statements. "Advances offered only in special cases." Published 5 titles last year. "Our books are marketed by all major occult distributors and we sell them to practically every store in America dealing with our subject matter." Will send free catalog to writer on request. Submit outline and sample chapters for nonfiction; complete ms for fiction. Reports in 3 to 6 weeks. Enclose S.A.E. and return postage.
Astrology, Religion, and Metaphysics: Textboks and books for the student of astrology; no specific religious denomination whatsoever, but religious books that will appeal to all people of all the world; metaphysics. No mediumship, or messages from the other world will be considered. Top priority is material dealing with the interrelationship of man and nature written by qualified experts. "Author must be experienced in above fields, especially in astrology. Will immediately reject material that is called 'entertainment astrology'. We are searching for topics that need to be covered in the field of astrology: weather forecasting, minor aspects, mundane astrology, etc." Current titles include *Transits in Plain English* (Press and Ima Roberts), a text for the astrology student that deals with the transits of the planets and their effect in the horoscope; *Casanova's Book of Numbers and the Daily Horoscope* (Laskowski), the actual text that the lover Casanova used in his infamous intrigues in Europe.

WALKER AND CO., 720 Fifth Ave., New York NY 10019. Publishes hardcover originals. Offers standard 10-12½-15% royalty contract. Published over 100 titles last year. Query first. Send complete ms for juvenile picture books. Will consider photocopied submissions. Reports in 6 weeks. Enclose return postage.
Nonfiction: History, biography, science, business and economics, the arts, international affairs, military history, anthropology, archaeology, current affairs, psychology, crafts, gardening. Current titles include: *How to Buy Gold* (Green); *Easy Plants for Difficult Places* (Kramer); *Children of Cape Horn* (Swale); *Helping Children Overcome Learning Difficulties* (Rosner); *The Collapsing Universe* (Asimov).
Juveniles: "For nonfiction, we are interested in science books for young readers and, occasionally, in biography and nonfiction that is relevant or controversial. We

will consider nonfiction mostly for preschoolers through age 12. Length depends on the age group: anywhere from 2,000 words to 20,000 words. We are always open to many ideas for picture books for ages 3 to 8. Length for picture books: 1,500 to 4,000 words." Science Editor, Children's Books: Millicent E. Selsam; Associate Editor of Children's Books (fiction): Andrea Horyczun.

WARNER PAPERBACK LIBRARY, INC., 75 Rockefeller Plaza, New York NY 10019. Executive Editor: Bob Abel. Publishes paperback reprints and originals. Royalties vary. Competitive advances; one-half on signing; balance on acceptance. "No subsidy publishing, but will do premium publishing." Published 250 titles last year. Send query accompanied by outline and three sample chapters for both fiction and nonfiction. Reports in 1 to 2 months. Enclose return postage.
General: Publishes adult fiction and general nonfiction. Strong contemporary novels on controversial themes. The occult; humor. Send Gothic romances to Mrs. Kathy Malley. Length: 40,000 to 120,000 words; 65,000 to 110,000 for Gothics. Should have commercial, mass-audience appeal.

WATSON-GUPTILL PUBLICATIONS, One Astor Plaza, New York NY 10036. Publishes originals. Reprints foreign or out-of-print art instruction books. Pays, for originals, 10% of first 10,000; 12½% on next 5,000; 15% of selling price for all following 1,000's. Usual advance is $1,000, but average varies, depending on author's reputation and nature of book. Published 40 titles last year. Address queries (followed by outlines and sample chapters) to Diane C. Hines, Managing Editor. Reports on queries within 10 days. Enclose return postage.
Art: Publishes art instruction books. Interested only in books of a how-to-do-it nature in any field of painting, crafts, design, etc. Not interested in biographies of painters, art history books, aesthetic appreciation. Length: open.

WAYNE STATE UNIVERSITY PRESS, 5980 Cass Ave., Detroit MI 48202. Director: Bernard M. Goldman. Publishes hardcover originals and reprints. Royalty schedule standard, but separately negotiated for each book. No advance. Published 27 titles last year. Current catalog available on request. Send query accompanied by outline and complete ms. Address mss to the Director. Reports in 1 to 6 months. Enclose return postage.
Nonfiction: Publishes scholarly and nonfiction books including biographies, history, religion, science, and the arts. Length: 40,000 words and up.

WEBSTER DIVISION, McGraw-Hill Book Co., 1221 Ave. of the Americas, New York NY 10020. General Manager: Roger E. Egan. Editorial Director: John A. Rothermich. Royalties vary. "Our royalty schedules are those of the industry, and advances are not commonly given." Published 116 titles last year. Will consider photocopied submissions. Reports in 2 to 4 weeks. Always query. Enclose return postage.
Textbooks: Publishes school books, films, equipment and systems for elementary and secondary schools. Juveniles, history, science, the arts, mathematics. "Material is generally part of a series, system, or program done in connection with other writers, teachers, testing experts, etc. Material must be matched to the psychological age level, with reading achievement and other educational prerequisites in mind. Interested in a Basal Reading program and Career Education program for the elementary schools.

WESTERN ISLANDS, 4 Hill Rd., Belmont MA 02178. Royalty is usually straight 10% on cloth editions; 5% on paper editions. Published 4 titles last year. Query first. Reports in 1 month. Enclose return postage.
Nonfiction and Fiction: Specializes in books that have a conservative-political orientation: current events, essays, history, criticism, biography, memoirs, etc. No word length requirement. Current titles include *America's Steadfast Dream* (philosophy), *The Highest Virtue* (novel), *Cousin Mercedes and the White Russian* (autobiography), *Conspiracy Against God and Man* (history).

WESTERN PUBLISHING CO., INC., 1220 Mound Ave., Racine WI 53404. Publishes hardcover and paperback juvenile books only; originals and reprints. Mss purchased outright. Published 95 titles last year. Complete ms may be sent for picture books; query with outline and sample chapter on all mss over 1,000 words. Address mss and query letters for picture books to Miss Betty Ren Wright; query letters for novels, family, Family Funtime activity books to William Larson. Mss should be typed, double-spaced, with S.A.S.E. enclosed. Reports in two to five weeks.

Juveniles: Picture book lines include Whitman Tell-a-Tale books, Big Golden books, Family Funtime books, Little Golden books, Golden Play and Learn books, Golden Shape books, and Golden Touch and Feel books. Material should be concerned with familiar childhood experiences, early learning concepts, favorite subjects (animals, cars and trucks, play activities). Urban, suburban and rural settings welcome. Unless specifically indicated, books are planned to be read to children, but vocabulary should be simple enough for easy understanding and for young readers to handle themselves if they wish. "We are interested in a limited number of very simple beginning readers, preferably falling into the late first grade category. We are also looking for stories about animals, humorous stories, and stories that emphasize concepts important to preschool-primary learning. We have board books and cloth books for children two and under; most of our picture books are intended for ages 3 to 6. While we are definitely interested in stories that combine fun and learning, we see too many mss that are forced or uninteresting because the writer has tried too hard to make them 'educational.' Also, we see many stories that are about children without being for children. We would encourage writers to consider always whether the story is genuinely meaningful to children. We are also interested in seeing stories about little girls that enlarge upon the position of women in our society. It is easy to turn out a 'message' story, and we do not want to do that, but we would like to publish stories in which girls play a wide variety of roles." Length for picture books: 200 to 800 words. Also publishes novel-length hardcover books and story anthologies for ages 8-14. Length: 35,000 to 60,000 words. Should deal with subjects of genuine interest to pre-teens and early teens—mystery, adventure, and stories about high school activities.

WESTMINISTER PRESS, 902 Witherspoon Bldg., Philadelphia PA 19107. Editor, children's fiction and nonfiction books: Barbara Bates. "Royalty rate depends on type of book, proportion of illustration, expected sales, previous record of author. No longer give escalating royalties in standard contract. Advance varies, depending on author's reputation and nature of book and author's need and preference." Current catalog available on request. Published 18 titles last year. Query first with outline and sample chapter. Enclose return postage.

Juveniles: Fiction and nonfiction for children 9 years of age and up. No picture books, articles, gags, poetry, collections of stories. No mss over 40,000 words.

WEYBRIGHT AND TALLEY, 750 Third Ave., New York NY 10017. President: Truman M. Talley. Publishes hardcover originals and text paperbacks. Usually offers standard 10-12½-15% royalty contract; "there is no average advance—usually $2,000 on up, depending on many factors." Published 25 titles last year. Query first with outline and sample chapters. Will consider photocopied submissions "if clear." Reports in 1 to 2 weeks. Enclose return postage.

General Fiction: "One-third very selective fiction." Publishes mainstream fiction, historical novels, science fiction, and espionage.

General Nonfiction: "Two-thirds nonfiction." Publishes books on Wall Street, business, economics, history, Washington, politics, and is expanding its nature and environmental publishing. Length: 100,000 to 120,000 words. Recent titles include *The Go-Go Years* (Brooks), *The Benchwarmers* (Gouldan), *The Bankers* (Mayer).

WHITMORE PUBLISHING COMPANY, 35 Cricket Terrace, Ardmore PA 19003. Standard royalty contract, profit-sharing contract, or outright purchase. Published 6 titles last year. Send queries and sample chapters or poems to Blair A. Simon, Managing Editor. Reports in two to three weeks. Enclose return postage.

General Nonfiction: Publishing interest focused on books that will provide the reader with insight and techniques to manage his life more effectively. Interests include nutrition, education, community life, philosophy, self-improvement, family study and planning, career planning; explanations of significant science and technology not broadly understood.

WHITSTON PUBLISHING CO., INC., P.O. Box 322, Troy NY 12181. Editor: Stephen Goode. Publishes hardcover originals. Offers 10% royalty contract; "no advance. Our runs are almost never over 2,000." Published 15 titles last year. Will send a catalog to a writer on request. Query first. Reports "immediately." Enclose return postage.

Nonfiction: "We publish principally bibliographies, indexes, checklists, and the like, involving the humanities, social sciences, and in some instances those that are socio-medical. We have accepted bibliographies in card form, but generally prefer completed mss. Our audience is exclusively college and research libraries and larger public libraries reference and serials collections. Style and structure of each index or bibliography is unique to the book. Interested in unique indexes (original) and bibliographies and in cumulations of existing serial bibliographies, as in our *Bibliography of the Thoreau Society Bulletin Bibliographies*. A smaller emphasis is put on scholarly critical material, mostly essay collections by individuals or groups, involving modern letters."

WILDERNESS PRESS, 2440 Bancroft Way, Berkeley CA 94704. Editor: Thomas Winnett. Publishes paperback originals. "We offer 8% to authors who have not published before. Our average advance is $200." Published 6 titles last year. Query first. Will consider photocopied submissions. Reports in 2 weeks. Enclose return postage.

Nature: "We publish books about the outdoors. So far, almost all our books are trail guides for hikers and backpackers, but we will be publishing how-to books about the outdoors and personal adventures. The ms must be accurate. The author must research an area thoroughly in person. If he is writing a trail guide, he must walk all the trails in the area his book is about. The outlook must be strongly conservationist. The style must be appropriate for a highly literate audience." Recent titles include *The Pacific Crest Trail, Mt. Pinchot, Kern Peak* (outdoor recreation, self-powered); *Yosemite* (revised edition).

JOHN WILEY AND SONS, 605 Third Ave., New York NY 10016. Publishes hardcover and paperback originals. Royalty contract to be negotiated. Published 484 titles last year. Query first. Enclose return postage.

Technical and Textbooks: Publishes scientific works, business texts, research works, reference books and those in the social sciences and biomedical health areas. Publishes college textbooks.

WINCHESTER PRESS, 205 East 42nd St., New York 10017. Editor-in-Chief: Robert Elman. Publishes hardcover and paperback originals and reprints. Offers standard minimum book contract of 10-12½-15%. Average advance is $1,500 to $2,500 "for established authors." Published 30 titles last year. Will send free catalog to writer on request. Query first "if material is only marginally in our field." Submit outline and sample chapters for nonfiction "unless ms is already complete, in which case submit complete ms for nonfiction or fiction". Will not consider photocopied submissions. Reports within 3 months. "Material that is obviously unsuitable for our list is returned immediately; most other rejections within 30 days." Enclose S.A.E. and return postage.

Nonfiction: "Substantially all of our books deal with some aspect of the outdoors or outdoor recreation; wildlife or nature study, conservation, participant sports, hunting and fishing; hobbies related to outdoor recreation (decoy carving, game cookery, fly tying). In general, a strong how-to emphasis is preferred, and only book length mss are considered. We publish only a little fiction, and most of that is primarily humor. We try to get books that are unusually authoritative and well-written, and prefer books written by authors who are highly proficient and widely experienced in the fields they write about rather than research projects by professional writers. In general, we prefer not to see material dealing largely or wholly with foreign subjects or experiences." Length: 40,000 to 100,000 words.

WISCONSIN HOUSE BOOK PUBLISHERS, P.O. Box 2118, Madison WI 53701. Editor-in-Chief: Mark E. Lefebvre. Publishes hardcover and paperback originals and paperback reprints. Offers standard minimum book contract of 10-12½-15%. Published 6 titles last year. Will send free catalog to writer on request. Query first. Reports in 6 weeks. Enclose return postage.

Nonfiction and Fiction: Seeking quality book-length nonfiction and fiction. "Close consideration will be given to works with a regional atmosphere which address universal concerns. There is a belief here that one foot can be in the Midwest and another in the world at large. The writer should realize that Wisconsin House does not direct iteslf to a juvenile audience any more. Beyond that, any approach is acceptable from the traditional to the experimental. Our interest is in quality rather than quantity. It is well to note, too, that there are too many books growing out of family histories which obviously appeal to the writer, but do not achieve the necessary distance to create interest for others." Current titles include *A Woman of No Importance* (Crafton/Gard).

WOODBRIDGE PRESS PUBLISHING CO., P.O. Box 6189, Santa Barbara CA 93111. Editor-in-Chief: Howard B. Weeks. Publishes hardcover and paperback originals. Standard royalty contract. Rarely gives an advance. Published 4 titles last year. Books marketed by conventional methods. Query first. Will consider photocopied submissions. Returns rejected material immediately. Reports on material accepted for publication in 2 months. Enclose return postage with query.

General Nonfiction: "How-to books on personal health and well-being. Should offer the reader valuable new information or insights on anything from recreation to diet to mental health that will enable him to achieve greater personal fulfillment, with emphasis on that goal. Should minimize broad philosophy and maximize specific, useful information." Length: Books range from 96 to 300 pages. Also publishes cookbooks. Recent titles include *The Back to Eden Cookbook* (Kloss), *The Health Spas* (Yaller), *Hydroponic Gardening* (Bridwell).

THE WRITER, INC., 8 Arlington St., Boston MA 02116. Editor: A.S. Burack. Publishes hardcover originals. Standard royalty schedule. Advance varies. Published 6 titles last year. Catalog on request. Query first. Reports within three weeks. Enclose return postage.

Nonfiction: Books on writing for writers. Length: open.

WRITER'S DIGEST, 9933 Alliance Rd., Cincinnati OH 45242. Publishes hardcover and paperback originals. "Usual royalty contract is 10% of net. Books are sold in bookstores, by direct mail, and through regular advertising in *Writer's Digest* magazine." Send outline and sample chapters, or query; query followed by outline and sample chapters preferred. Reports in 8 weeks. Enclose S.A.S.E. or return postage with all correspondence.

Nonfiction: "Looking for down-to-earth how-to books offering practical advice to beginning and professional writers on the techniques of writing. Authors should be established, selling writers. Possible topics are writing genre type novels, religious articles, careers in writing, playwriting, case histories of books by 'big name' writers. Style should be conversational and anecdotal. Also interested in collections of interviews with writers, biographies of well-known writers, discussions of the current literary climate, and all other material relating to writers and writing." Leading titles include *Writing and Selling Nonfiction* (Hayes B. Jacobs); *Writing Popular Fiction* (Koontz); *The Greeting Card Writer's Handbook* (H. Joseph Chadwick); *The Creative Writer* (Aron Mathieu); and two hardcover annuals: *Writer's Market* (Adkins and Koester) and *Artist's Market* (Kirk Polking).

WWWWW/INFORMATION SERVICES, INC., 1595 Elmwood Ave., Rochester NY 14620. Editor-in-Chief: Robert A. Fowler. Publishes paperback originals. Offers standard minimum book contract of 10-12½-15%. Advance depends on book's potential. Published 1 title last year. Marketed through paperback distributors. Will send free catalog to writer on request. Will consider photocopied submissions. Query first. Reports quarterly. Enclose return postage.

How-To: Consumer/buyer how-to books such as how to buy a business, how to select a career, etc. Length: 60,000 to 70,000 words. Current titles include *Creative Winemaking* (Fowler/Rogers).

ZONDERVAN PUBLISHING HOUSE, 1415 Lake Drive S.E., Grand Rapids MI 49506. Editor-in-Chief: T. Alton Bryant. Publishes hardcover and paperback originals and reprints. Offers standard minimum book contract of 10-12½-15%. Advances paid only on assigned projects. Published 70 titles last year. Will send free catalog to writer on request. Query first with outline and sample chapters. Will consider photocopied submissions, "only if we are the only publisher considering at the time." Rejects in 3 to 4 weeks; reports in 6 to 8 weeks usually. Enclose return postage.
Religious Fiction and Nonfiction: For all ages. Material should be slanted to the conservative religious reader. Christian adult trade fiction, biography, book trade, business, cookbooks, cooking and foods, history, humor, medicine and psychiatry, nature, philosophy, plays, politics, reference, religion, scientific, self-help and how-to, sociology, sports, hobbies, recreation, pets, and textbooks. Conservative and biblical. Length: 12,000 to 100,000 words. Current titles include *The Literature of the Bible* (Ryken), a look at the Bible as literature, emphasizing its relevance for today's reader.

If this is 1977, this edition is out of date. See address in front of book to order latest edition. *Writer's Market* is published annually each fall.

SUBSIDY BOOK PUBLISHERS

If a writer is having a problem in getting a book published by a standard royalty book company, subsidy publishing is one alternative. A book manuscript submitted to a standard royalty book publishing company will either be rejected or accepted for publication. If a book manuscript is accepted for publication, the standard royalty book publisher will usually pay the author an advance on receipt of the signed contract and subsequently make royalty payments, based on the sale of the book.

However, many writers who have tried unsuccessfully to interest a standard royalty book publisher in their book may decide to pay to have the book published themselves.

How much does it cost? Here are some examples of estimates from subsidy publishers; but there are variations: 500 copies of a 48-page book of poetry, $1,700 to $2,000; 2,500 copies of a 96-page book, $3,100 to $4,000; 3,000 copies of a 176-page book, $4,500 to $5,000. The books are professionally printed, bound and may have an attractive dust jacket. While the subsidy book publishing contract agrees to pay 30 to 40% royalty to the author rather than the 10% offered by most standard book publishers, the problem is that the subsidy book publisher does not have book salesmen calling on bookstores to sell the book, is usually not able to get national review media to review the book, and can engage in only a certain amount of promotion and advertising. All of the subsidy publishers who advertise in *Writer's Digest* adhere to the advertising policies the magazine has established which require that they state specifically in their contract what they are offering and spell out to the writer exactly what he is getting for his payment. They will deliver everything that is promised in the contract. The following is a list of book publishers who specialize in subsidy publishing and who have agreed to abide by the *Writer's Digest* advertising policies.

Dorrance and Company, 1617 J. F. Kennedy Blvd., Philadelphia PA 19103.

Exposition Press, 900 S. Oyster Bay Rd., Hicksville NY 11801.

Mojave Books, 7040 Darby Ave., Reseda CA 91335.

Vantage Press, 516 W. 34th St., New York NY 10001.

William-Frederick Press, 55 East 86 Street, New York NY 10028.

MISCELLANEOUS FREELANCE MARKETS AND SERVICES

Audiovisual Markets

Because producers of "software"—the trade term for nonprint materials like records, filmstrips, tape cassettes, etc., as opposed to "hardware," which refers to the machines on which they are viewed or played, frequently have highly individualized editorial requirements, freelance writers are encouraged to seek firm assignments from audiovisual producers before writing or submitting finished scripts. A good query letter should outline the writer's credentials (as an educator, specialist in some subject, or professional scriptwriter), include a sample of his writing, and give details of his proposed script or series of scripts.

Many of the companies currently active in the audiovisual field are working with staff writers and do not actively seek freelance contributions. Those who are interested in staff positions will find a more complete list of audiovisual producers in the excellent Audiovisual Market Place *(published by R. R. Bowker).*

Software producers pay on a flat fee or royalty basis, depending on the company and the quality of the writer's material. The sponsored film production company, operating on a contract basis to produce audiovisuals for the government, business or private organizations, offers a flat fee payment, which varies according to the nature of the project and the writer's credentials. If a company produces and markets its own audiovisual products (usually to the elementary and secondary school and college markets), payment is most often according to a royalty contract with the writer, but a flat fee is sometimes paid. The flat fees vary widely, but royalty agreements usually approximate the ones offered for school texts. Based on the net money the publisher receives on sales, this is 3% to 5% for elementary and secondary school materials and 8% to 12% for college textbooks. A few producers offer an even higher percentage, some going as high as 18.75% for college materials.

ADVANCED LEARNING CONCEPTS, INC., 211 W. Wisconsin Ave., Milwaukee WI 53203. Editor-in-Chief: Richard W. Weening. For preschool, special education, elementary and high school in all content areas. Material is copyrighted. Query first for hardware kits. Submit outline and sample chapters for educational programs without learner verification data. Submit complete ms for complete educational programs with learner data. Will consider photocopied submissions. Enclose S.A.S.E. **Educational:** Hardware and software instructional systems, kits, games, texts, series of texts, criterion or norm-referenced texts. Educational materials must be based either on research or actual classroom experiences, preferably a combination of both. Each submission should include a clear explanation of instructional objectives, materials, and teaching procedure as well as any available data on classroom learner testing. "Educational programs subject to negotiated royalty rates."

AERO PRODUCTS RESEARCH, INC., 11201 Hindry Ave., Los Angeles CA 90045. Contact: J. Parr. Aviation education material for pilot training schools, private and

public schools from K through college. Copyrighted. Write for copy of guidelines for writers. "Writer would have to be qualified in specific project." Enclose S.A.S.E. for response to queries or return of submissions.
Education: "Developing and editing both technical and nontechnical material. Charts, silent filmstrips, models, multimedia kits, overhead transparencies, phonograph records, prerecorded tapes and cassettes, slides and study prints. Royalty arrangements are handled on an individual project basis."

ANIMATION ARTS ASSOCIATES, INC., 2225 Spring Garden St., Philadelphia PA 19130. Contact: Harry E. Ziegler, Jr. Copyrighted. For "government, industry, engineers, doctors, scientists, dentists, general public, military." Send "resume of credits for motion picture and filmstrip productions. The writer should have scriptwriting credits for training, sales promotion, public relations." Enclose S.A.S.E.
Business: Produces 3½-minute, 8mm and 16mm film loops; 16mm and 35mm motion pictures (ranging from 5 to 40 minutes), 2x2 or 4x5 slides and teaching machine programs for training, sales, industrial and public relations. Fee arrangements dependent on client's budget.

HAL MARC ARDEN AND COMPANY, Executive Offices: 240 Central Park South, New York NY 10019. Production Facility: 245 W. 55th St., New York NY 10019. President: Hal Marc Arden. Copyrighted. "Writer must have experience in writing for motion pictures. Scripts are not solicited, but we welcome resumes." Query first. Enclose S.A.S.E. for response to queries.
General: "Specialize in sponsored publications only: documentary, educational, public service." Produces silent and sound filmstrips, 16mm motion pictures, multimedia kits, phonograph records, prerecorded tapes and cassettes, and slides. "No royalties. Fee negotiated."

AUDIOTRONICS CORPORATION, 7428 Bellaire Ave., North Hollywood CA 91605. Address all correspondence to: Robert D. Siedle, Manager, Educational Systems. For preschool, elementary, junior high, high school, and adult education levels. Material is copyrighted. Buys all rights. Will send catalog to writer on request. Guidelines available. Writer should have college degree, preferably with teaching experience. Query first. Enclose S.A.S.E.
Education: Language arts, math, science, social studies, special education, bilingual education. Material criteria: supplementary (remedial or enrichment), universally acceptable, highly marketable, current, educationally sound. Producing prerecorded cassettes, filmstrips, and audiocard programs. Programs are organized into small, easily managed learning steps. Remedial and enrichment rather than basal. Royalty/fee arrangement: 5% to 10% dependent upon state of material supplied. Outright purchase via one payment handled on an individual basis. "We are constantly looking for new writers who are knowledgeable in the field of programmed instruction."

BARR FILMS, P.O. Box 7-C, Pasadena CA 91104. President: Donald Barr. For "classroom audience, grades K through secondary." Not copyrighted. Query first. "We are only marginally interested in outside scripts at this time, but will consider scripts that are of special interest to us. Send completed visual/dialog script." Enclose S.A.S.E. for return of submissions.
General: Produces 16mm motion pictures for "all curriculum areas. Supply visual treatment and proposed voice over, dialog, etc." Pay "negotiable; have paid $400 and up, depending on our interest."

BEAR FILMS, INC., 805 Smith St., Baldwin NY 11510. Contact: Frank Bear. For "elementary and secondary schools; some general adult." Copyrighted and not copyrighted material. Will assign projects to qualified writers. "Credentials according to project." Query first. Enclose S.A.S.E. for response to queries.
Education and General: Requirements "varied, according to subject matter and audience." Produces silent and sound filmstrips, 16mm motion pictures, multimedia kits, slides. "Fee according to project."

CHAMBA PRODUCTIONS, INC., 230 W. 105 St. (2A), New York NY 10025. President: St. Clair Bourne. For "general audiences, minority audiences. We make films for all levels (high school and adult). We prefer submission of film treatments first." Query first. Enclose S.A.S.E. for response to queries.
Education: "We make educational, motivational, and documentary films. However, I am beginning to branch out into feature-type films (story line, actors, etc.)." Produces 35mm motion pictures. Payment "negotiable"; minimum, $1,000.

COMMUNICATIONS/MEDIA PRODUCTIONS, c/o California Polytechnic State University, San Luis Obispo CA 93407. Director: Clyde Hostetter. For university and library audiences, including artists and art students, students in the various sciences, and researchers who need easy access to specialized subjects in which color is a key element. Buys all rights preferably, but can arrange for limited rights in case of color slides. Will send catalog to writer on request. Query first. "Nearly all production is handled through freelance contacts, with editorial supervision from this office. Credentials are the ability to do a professional job or to provide professional-quality photos." Enclose S.A.S.E.
Education: Sound filmstrips, multimedia kits, prerecorded tapes and cassettes, slides and color microfiche. "We are interested in producing audiovisual materials for college level use in areas where commercial producers feel the market is too 'thin' to be profitable. Of special interest to photographers and others with libraries of original slides is our recent entrance into the production of color microfiche for subjects in which color is a key element but where the intended audience may be limited. We also are producing tape-cassette reports on conferences and symposiums of significant educational value. All slides should be original horizontal 35mm format. Tape recordings should be 3¾ or 7½ ips, made on profesional equipment. In any case, persons should query first. In our new color microfiche operations, there is an opportunity for teachers or others with original slide collections of special educational value to work with us, even though they may not be experienced writers or av producers. We are not interested in slides which require complicated copyright clearance for their use by us. Payment subject to negotiation, but we prefer to make a flat payment rather than pay royalties. This arrangement is usually to the author's advantage, since we are a nonprofit organization without extensive marketing budget."

COMPRENETICS, INC., 9601 Wilshire Blvd., Suite #210, Beverly Hills CA 90210. Contact: Ira Englander. Target audience varies from entry-level hospital and health workers with minimal academic background to continued education programs for physicians and health professionals. Material is copyrighted. Query first. Enclose S.A.S.E.
Education and Medicine: Sound filmstrips, 16mm motion pictures, prerecorded tapes and cassettes. "Films are often programmed with response frames included. Subject areas are primarily in the health and medical field. We currently assign all of our writing responsibilities to outside personnel and intend to continue this arrangement in the future. Our in-house staff normally does subject matter research and content review which is provided for a writer. Writer is then required to provide us with rough outline or film treatment for approval. Due to a somewhat complex review procedure, writers are frequently required to modify through three or four drafts before final approval is granted. Payment is negotiable for each project." $1,000 to $2,500 per script.

CONCORDIA PUBLISHING HOUSE, PRODUCT DEVELOPMENT DIVISION, 3558 S. Jefferson Ave., St. Louis MO 63118. For preschool through adult; institutional and home use. Material is copyrighted. Will send a catalog to writer on request. Writer must have demonstrated skills in writing producible material for the audio and visual fields. Competence in the content area is necessary. Initial query is preferred in view of existing production commitments and necessity to maintain a satisfactory product mix. Enclose S.A.S.E.
Education and Religion: Silent and sound filmstrips, 16mm motion pictures, multimedia kits, overhead transparencies, phonograph records, prerecorded tapes and cassettes, 35mm slides and study prints. Content areas relate to the requirements

of religious and moral guidance instruction. Emphases may be curricular, quasi-curricular or enriching. Writing fees are negotiated in consideration of such factors as type of production, configuration, complexity of assignment, research required, field tests and production deadlines.

CONTEMPO COMMUNICATIONS, INC., 25 West 68th St., New York NY 10023. Contact: Joan Marshall. "Our audiences vary widely, from top management to consumers. We use topnotch freelance writers who are experienced in business communications, as well as related fields of TV, MP and theatre. Submit a detailed resume accompanied by a sample of your best work in each medium." Enclose S.A.S.E. for response to queries.
Business: "Our field is business communications in such areas as sales meetings, management conferences, sales promotion, public relations, new product introduction, sales training. We frequently use music and lyrics and comedy writing." Sound filmstrips, 16mm motion pictures, multimedia kits, phonograph records, prerecorded tapes and cassettes, and 35mm and super slides. "We work on a very high quality level and require strong creative concepts, as well as excellent writing skills. In-person contact imperative. Fees are paid on a per project basis and vary according to overall budget for the project."

CONTEMPORARY DRAMA SERVICE/ARTHUR MERIWETHER INC., Box 457, Downers Grove IL 60515. For high school students. Material is copyrighted. Will send catalog to writer for 50¢. "Prior professional experience is required. Query first. Background as an educator is often helpful." Enclose S.A.S.E.
Education: "We prefer items applying to speech, English, history, sociology and drama studies to be used as a supplement to regular curriculum materials." Filmstrips (silent and sound), motion pictures, multimedia kits, and prerecorded tapes and cassettes. Pays 5% to 10% royalty.
Religion: "Will consider filmstrip scripts that deal with subjects of contemporary religious importance for high school religious education groups. Liberal approach preferred. Professional quality only. Author is paid on a royalty basis."
Business: Business-oriented mss or scripts on marketing.

CREATIVE VISUALS, Division of Gamco Industries, Box 1911, Big Springs TX 79720. Contact: Stuart V. Forest. For K-12, with interests, needs and levels which would be applicable. Material is copyrighted. "Buys exclusivity to the material, covered under royalty contract." Will send a catalog to writer on request. Will send a copy of guidelines for writers. "We do assign many a-v projects outside. Our own editorial staff spends most of its time polishing such material to our own requirements. Authors generally are teachers or those closely associated with education, but others feeling they can serve the needs would not be excluded. Initial contact should contain only a general outline of the proposed material. A brief sample of the writing style, and an indication of the time required to complete project should also be included. Further correspondence and phone calls can firm up later details." Enclose S.A.S.E.
Education: Tapescripts for cassette tapes, filmstrip-cassettes, self-instruction materials, usually filmstrip-cassettes; overhead transparencies, study prints; and multimedia kits. Subject areas are all areas taught from K-12. Style varies with subject matter and medium used. Cassettes are preferred in dramatic skit form where applicable, or straight narrative if applicable. Visual material for filmstrips and transparencies should be photographic (provided by author) where necessary, or could be in form of adequate verbal descriptions for our artists. Back up visual material may be required for unusual subject matter, which would be rendered by our artists in such a way as to avoid copyright problems. We have our own format and will provide the necessary blanks to an author. We have a traditional slant, generally; we aren't missionaries trying to put across a particular point of view. Special emphasis within subjects will vary with subject and capability of author. Word length: reading level should correspond to subject matter. Where subject matter can have a wide application, language should be such that the youngest would understand and the older ones would not be offended by childishness." Royalty rates begin at 10% of net

sales, and after large volume will drop to 7% and will continue indefinitely at that level as long as the material is being sold.

DANREE PRODUCTIONS, 6065 Carlton Way, Hollywood CA 90028. For "primarily the viewer(s) who can stop the cassette (video or record) and repeat any portion they desire—or freeze frame and study, etc. We require first a basic subject matter contemplated with credentials proving ample knowledge of the subject and a manuscript or similar of a previous work of the writer." Enclose S.A.S.E.
Education: 16mm motion pictures designed for the home market, repetitive type viewing market. Emphasis on creative fun with the education a natural by-product. Payment varies according to project.

EMC CORP., 180 E. 6th St., St. Paul MN 55101. For kindergarten through grade 12. Material is copyrighted. Will send a catalog to writer on request. "Be able to write acceptable script." Query first. Enclose S.A.S.E.
Education: Charts, sound filmstrips, multimedia kits, educational fiction, social studies, sports, biographies, and phonograph records. "Usually an outline pertaining to the subject is first required. We usually purchase outright."

FAMILY FILMS/COUNTERPOINT FILMS, 5823 Santa Monica Blvd., Hollywood CA 90038. Contact: Paul R. Kidd, Director of Product Development. For all age levels from preschool through adult. Copyrighted. Will send a catalog to writer on request. Query first. "We don't encourage submission of mss. Majority projects are assigned and developed to our specifications. Writers may submit their credentials and experience. Some experience in writing film and filmstrip scripts is desired. A teaching credential or teaching experience valuable for our school materials. Active involvement in a mainstream church desirable for our religious projects."
Education and Religion: "Sound filmstrips, 16mm motion pictures and prerecorded tapes and cassettes for schools, universities, public libraries, and for interdenominational religious market. Motion pictures vary from 10 minutes to 30 to 40 minutes. Filmstrips about 50 to 60 frames with running time of 7 to 10 minutes. Emphasis on the human situation and person-to-person relationships. No royalty arrangements. Outright payment depends on project and available budget. As an example, usual filmstrip project requires 4 scripts, for which we pay $150 to $250 each."

GIRL SCOUTS OF THE U.S.A., 830 Third Ave., New York NY 10022. For girls and adults involved in the Girl Scout movement; the general public. Will send catalog to writer on request. Query first. All projects are generated within the organization, which is not seeking proposals, treatments, or manuscripts. Credentials for writer would depend on project. Enclose S.A.S.E.
General: All audiovisuals deal with some aspect of Girl Scout movement: program, training, administration, public relations, etc. Sound filmstrips, 16mm and 8mm motion pictures, multimedia kits, overhead transparencies, phonograph records, prerecorded tapes and cassettes, 35mm slides, and flip charts. "We work on fee basis only; the amount negotiable in terms of the assignment."

HANDEL FILM CORP., 8730 Sunset Blvd., West Hollywood CA 90069. Contact: Production Department. For variety of audiences, depending on film. Material becomes property of Handel Film Corp. if acquired. Submit only upon request. Do not send in unsolicited material. Query first. Enclose S.A.S.E.
Education and Documentary: 16mm motion pictures, approximately half-hour films for science, history and other areas. Payment is negotiable.

IMPERIAL INTERNATIONAL LEARNING CORPORATION, Box 548, Rt. 45 South, Kankakee IL 60901. Contact: Jim Hargrove, Director of Supplemental Programs. Buys considerable freelance material, but needs are extremely specialized. Will send free catalog to writer on request. Query first, stating background and professional writing experience. If possible, writers seeking assignments should include a sample of their work suitable for school-aged boys and girls, to be held on file. Enclose S.A.S.E. Reports within 8 to 10 weeks.

Education: Audiovisual learning systems targeted for students in kindergarten through high school, with special emphasis on the elementary school market. "The instructional formats we have worked with most successfully in recent years include cassette tape and tape-centered programs, sound filmstrips, and multimedia learning kits. Regardless of format, all instructional programs are closely associated with the el/hi curriculum, especially in the areas of reading, language arts, and math. Most of our freelance writers are also educators familiar with one or more of these curricula, or are experienced writers of av materials. We're also marketing a unique new learning system (under the tradename Small Talk) consisting of a miniature hand-held record player, called a Microphonograph, and small records about an inch and a half in diameter which are permanently affixed to printed pages, cards, and charts. Experienced writer/educators are invited to query regarding assignments for writing Small Talk programs to specifications provided by the publisher." Most interested in seeing the following materials in the following areas: language arts and reading, math, vocational and career education, early childhood, special education, and bilingual programs at the early elementary level. "Generally pay flat fee within 90 days after acceptance of ms or reprint contract."

INSGROUP, INC., One City Blvd. West, Orange CA 92668. For industrial, military (both enlisted and officer), public school (K through graduate level), police, nursing, and public administrators. Material is copyrighted. Criteria for writers are determined on a project by project basis. Query first, with resumes and be prepared to submit copies of previous efforts. Enclose S.A.S.E.
General: Charts, silent and sound filmstrips, multimedia kits, overhead transparencies, prerecorded tapes and cassettes, 35mm slides, study prints, teaching machine programs, and videotapes. Insgroup develops objective-based validated audiovisual instructional programs both for commercial customers and for publication by Insgroup. These programs cover the entire range of subject areas, styles, formats, etc. Most writing is on a fee basis. Royalties, when given, are 5% to 8%.

INSTRUCTIONAL DYNAMICS INCORPORATED, 450 E. Ohio St., Chicago IL 60611. For early learning through college level. Material is copyrighted. Will send catalog to writer on request. "Writer should have valid background and experience that parallels the specific assignment. Would like to have vita as first contact. We keep on file and activate as needs arise. We use a substantial group of outside talent to supplement our in-house staff." Enclose S.A.S.E.
Education: Silent filmstrips, sound filmstrips, multimedia kits, overhead transparencies, phonograph records, prerecorded tapes and cassettes, 2x2 slides, study prints and hard copy. "Requirements for these vary depending upon assignments from our clients. Payment depends on contractual arrangements with our client and also varies depending on medium or multimedia involved."

INSTRUCTOR CURRICULUM MATERIALS, 7 Bank St., Dansville NY 14437. Editor-in-Chief: Mrs. Ruth Ann Hayward. "U.S. and Canadian school supervisors, principals, and teachers purchase items in our line for instructional purposes." Buys all rights. Will send a catalog to a writer on request. Writer should have "experience in preparing materials for elementary students, including suitable teaching guides to accompany them, and demonstrate knowledge of the appropriate subject areas, or demonstrable ability for accurate and efficient research and documentation. Please query." Enclose S.A.S.E. for response to queries.
Education: "Elementary curriculum enrichment, all subject areas. Display material, copy, and illustration should match interest and reading skills of children in grades for which material is intended. Production is limited to printed matter: posters, charts, duplicating masters, resource handbooks, teaching guides." Length: 6,000 to 12,000 words. "Standard contract, but fees vary considerably, depending on type of project."

KEN-DEL PRODUCTIONS, INC., 111 Valley Rd., Richardson Park, Wilmington DE 19804. Contact: Ed Kennedy. For "elementary junior high, high school, and college level, as well as interested organizations and companies." Will assign projects to qualified writers. Query first. Enclose S.A.S.E. for response to queries.

General: Wants material for "topics of the present (technology, cities, traffic, transit, pollution, ecology, health, water, race, genetics, consumerism, fashions, communications, education, population control, waste, future sources of food, undeveloped sources of living, food, health, etc.); topics of the future; how-to series (everything for the housewife, farmer, banker, mechanic, on music, art, sports, reading, science, love, repair, sleep—on any subject)." Produces dioramas; sound filmstrips; 8mm, 16mm, and 35mm motion pictures; 16mm film loops; phonograph records; prerecorded tapes and cassettes; slides. Pays a flat fee.

LANSFORD PUBLISHING COMPANY, P.O. Box 8711, San Jose CA 95155. For "teachers in college and universities throughout the United States and Canada." Will send a catalog to a writer on request. "We are willing to assign audiovisual projects to qualified writers. We are always looking for new ideas to improve the effectiveness of the college teacher." Query first. Enclose S.A.S.E.

Education and Business: "The subject matter should deal with educational material that could be used in college and university classrooms. We also publish materials used in business by training directors in employee training sessions." Produces charts, dioramas, film loops, silent filmstrips, sound filmstrips, models, motion pictures, multimedia kits, overhead transparencies, prerecorded tapes and cassettes, slides, and study prints. "Payment varies with the subject."

LE ROY MOTION PICTURE PRODUCTION STUDIOS, 1208 E. Cliveden St., Philadelphia PA 19119. Contact: Charles Roy. For "general audiences: women, children, etc. Projects assigned. Resume required." Query first. Enclose S.A.S.E.

General: "We create and produce TV commercials and television programs and series. We create and produce documentary and theatrical motion pictures. Assignments might be on speculation or by negotiated contract. Payment varies with specific projects."

A. B. LeCRONE CO., 819 N.W. 92nd, Oklahoma City OK 73114. Contact: Bud LeCrone. For preschool through 6th grade elementary. Copyrighted. Will send catalog to writer on request. Query first. "Writer needs no special credentials; just produce excellent material." Enclose S.A.S.E. for response to queries.

Education: Educational recordings, teaching aids, activities, physical fitness, square dance, learning records; colors, shapes, ABC's, counting activities. 15 to 17 minutes on each side of record. "We negotiate payment. We have never paid less than $300 and have paid as much as $3,500, but this is not our base either way."

LYCEUM PRODUCTIONS, INC., P.O. Box 1226, Laguna Beach CA 92652. Contact: Patty Lincke. For grade levels from elementary school through college. Copyrighted. Rights purchased are subject to negotiation. Query first. No assignments are made. Enclose S.A.S.E.

Education: Produces sound filmstrips. "Most of our filmstrips provide curriculum support and enrichment in subject areas including natural science, ecology, science, social studies, language arts, art, history and citizenship. Many titles are interdisciplinary. Some titles span wide age groups while others may be more limited in scope. Whatever the concept of the filmstrip, it should stimulate the student to explore the subject more fully. Please submit an idea or an outline before sending a manuscript or transparencies. Completed material will only be considered if it has been requested upon the basis of a previous query. Our contracts provide for royalties based on sales with an advance upon acceptance. The possibilities for the unknown freelancer are difficult."

McGRAW-HILL FILMS/CONTEMPORARY FILMS, 1221 Avenue of the Americas, New York NY 10020. Contact: Edward J. Meell or Anne Schutzer. For elementary students, high school students; colleges, public libraries, government, business and industry. Buys all rights. Query first; "then if we notify you positively, send in material." Enclose S.A.S.E.

Education: "Social studies, science, language arts, career education, economics for elementary and high school market. Film loops (8mm), sound filmstrips, 16mm motion pictures, and prerecorded tapes and cassettes." Pays 5% to 20% depending on investment terms.

TOM MORRIS, INC., 621 Devon, Park Ridge IL 60068. Staff writer occasionally solicits outside talent for specific projects: brochures, slide shows, filmstrips, movies, news releases and feature articles, meetings. Send credentials. Enclose S.A.S.E.
General: Training, technical, promotional, motivational copy for industry, institution, religious organization. Prefers to work closely with local writers. Pays flat fee in line with client's budget.

MRC FILMS, INC., 71 W. 23rd St., New York NY 10010. Executive Producer: Larry Mollot. "Audience varies with subject matter, which is wide and diverse." Writer "should have an ability to visualize concepts and to express ideas clearly in words. Experience in motion picture or filmstrip script writing is desirable. Write us, giving some idea of background. Submit samples of writing. Wait for reply. We will always reply, one way or another. We are looking for new talent. No unsolicited material accepted. Work upon assignment only." Query first. Enclose S.A.S.E. for response to queries.
General: "Industrial, documentary, educational, and television films. Also, public relations, teaching, and motivational filmstrips. Some subjects are highly technical in the fields of aerospace and electronics. Others are on personal relationships, selling techniques, ecology, etc. A writer with an imaginative visual sense is important." Produces silent and sound filmstrips, 16mm motion pictures, prerecorded tapes, cassettes. "Fee depends on nature and length of job. Typical fees: $500 to $1,000 for script for 10-minute film; $1,000 to $1,400 for script for 20-minute film; $1,200 to $2,000 for script for 30-minute film. For narration writing only, the range is $200 to $500 for a 10-minute film; $400 to $800 for a 20-minute film; $500 to $1,000 for a 30-minute film. For script writing services by the day, fee is $60 to $100 per day."

NYSTROM, 3333 Elston Ave., Chicago IL 60618. For kindergarten through 12. Material is copyrighted. Will send catalog to writer on request. Required credentials depend on topics and subject matter and approach desired. Query first. Enclose S.A.S.E.
Education: Charts, sound filmstrips, models, multimedia kits, overhead transparencies, and realia. Social studies, earth and life sciences, career education, reading, and language arts. Payment varies with circumstances.

OUR SUNDAY VISITOR, INC., Audiovisual Department, Noll Plaza, Huntington IN 46750. Contact: John E. Covell. For students (K to 12), adult religious education groups, and teacher training. Copyrighted. Will send catalog to writer on request. Query first. "We are looking for well-developed total packages only. Programs should display up-to-date audiovisual technique and cohesiveness." Enclose S.A.S.E.
Education and Religion: "Broadly speaking, material should deal with religious education, including liturgy and daily Christian living, as well as structured catechesis. Must not conflict with sound Catholic doctrine. Should reflect modern trends in education. Word lengths may vary." Produces charts, sound filmstrips, overhead transparencies, phonograph records, prerecorded tapes and cassettes and 2x2 slides. Royalties vary from 5% to 10% of price received, depending on the product and its market. Fee arrangements also; for example, so many dollars per each 100, 500, or 1,000 sets or projects produced at time of production.

OXFORD FILMS, A Subsidiary of Paramount Pictures Corp., 1136 N. Las Palmas Ave., Los Angeles CA 90038. For general audiences. Material is copyrighted. Will send catalog to writer on request. Query first. Enclose S.A.S.E.
Education: 16mm motion pictures. "Because we are distributors as well as producers of educational films, much of our activity concerns post production work on films acquired and the marketing of these. For films which we produce, scripts are usually

written on assignment by staff or educational script writers known to us; educational films have special requirements to meet school curriculum requirements. Therefore, the opportunity for freelance writers here is limited, except for those living in the area, with the know-how for school scripts. However, if a writer has information on an unusual subject which could be of interest to schools, or a fresh approach to something which could fit into the less structured areas such as language arts or interpersonal relationships, it wouldn't hurt to query us (Art Evans, Vice President). Also we are beginning to consider the kind of films suitable for business sponsorship, and in some instances we sell to college, adult, church, health and vocational groups. Pay ranges from $500 to $1,000 for 10 to 20 minutes (pages) with rewrite fairly certain to be required."

PACE FILMS, INC., 411 E. 53rd St., New York NY 10022. Contact: Mr. R. Vanderbes. For "TV and theatrical audience in the U.S. and worldwide." Buys all rights. Writing assignments are handled through agencies, but independent queries or submissions are considered. Enclose S.A.S.E. for response.
General: "Documentaries and feature motion pictures for TV and theaters." Pays "Writers Guild of America minimums and up."

PFLAUM PUBLISHING, 2285 Arbor Blvd., Dayton OH 45439. School books and kits for first graders through adults. Royalty and advance negotiable. Will send a catalog to writer on request. Will assign projects to qualified writers if they have a proven track record. Query first. Enclose S.A.S.E.
Communications, Personal Development, and Social Sciences: Books, av kits on history, techniques, and social effects of media — cinema, television, print. Personal and social development materials. Social concerns. Contact: J. M. Heher.
Religion: Especially Catholic, religious education. Produces filmstrips, books (paper), and print materials. Contact: Rod Brownfield.

PLAYETTE CORPORATION, 301 E. Shore Rd., Great Neck NY 11023. Contact: Sidney A. Evans. For "all school levels, teachers, and libraries." Copyrighted. Writer must have "a complete and thorough knowledge of the subject with practical applied usage. Material must have been classroom tested before submission." Query first. Enclose S.A.S.E. for response to queries.
Education and Foreign Languages: Requirements "depend on subject selected." Charts, silent filmstrips, sound filmstrips, multimedia kits, overhead transparencies, phonograph records, prerecorded tapes and cassettes, slides, study prints, and foreign language training aids and games. "Payment for each subject on a separate basis."

PRODUCERS GROUP LTD., One IBM Plaza, Suite 2519, Chicago IL 60611. For general audiences. Material is copyrighted. "Make yourself known to us. We do, on some occasions, go outside for help. There is very little point in submitting scripts unless we have a specific project in hand. First, we get the assignment; then we go into creative work. We're probably not the best market for freelance submissions. Unsolicited mss are wasteful, inappropriate. We're too specialized. When and if writer has proven record, we match project to writer's skills, expertise. Originate most of our own creative material here. We prefer any writer to have at least a B.A., or equivalent experience. Must have a record in a-v writing, and hopefully, production. We require clean shooting script, with all visuals completely designated." Query first. Enclose S.A.S.E.
Education: Film loops and sound filmstrips, 8mm and 16mm motion pictures, and multimedia kits. Business-oriented multimedia shows, educational motion pictures, and talk demonstrations. Editorial requirements vary according to assignments. Usually aim toward higher levels of educational background for business communications; aim toward specific age groups for educational films, as required. Usual lengths are 20 minutes. Again, varied according to end use. Standard fee is 10% of gross production budget. No royalty arrangements under this schedule. Straight buyout.

PROFESSIONAL EDUCATION PRODUCTS, 4116 Farnam St., Omaha NE 68131.

Contact: Stanley L. Teutsch. For dental patients, children and adults. Copyrighted. Will send catalog to writer on request. Query first. Enclose S.A.S.E. for response to queries.

Education: "Patient education filmstrip and sound programs for the dental profession. Cover a variety of dental procedures, such as bridgework, etc. Also have preventive dentistry films on how to brush, floss, etc. Some films are slanted toward children, others on the adult level. Prerecorded tapes and cassettes. Our work is usually contracted out for a set fee, rather than paying royalties. Fees depend upon complexity of work."

Q-ED PRODUCTIONS, INC., P.O. Box 1608, Burbank CA 91507. For grade levels kindergarten through 12. Material is copyrighted. Buys all rights. Will send a catalog to writer on request. "We are interested in reviewing completed films or filmstrip packages (4 to 6 filmstrips in a set) for distribution on royalty basis or buy outright. Knowledge of the field and experience as writer of filmstrips and films for education required. Also demonstrated ability in research required." Query first. Send queries to Michael Halperin, Vice President/Production. Enclose S.A.S.E.

Education: Grade levels K-12. Interested in core curriculum materials. Historically strong in values. Materials should be inquiry oriented, open-ended, strong objectives (cognitive, affective, psycho-motor). Royalties open on original materials. Fees range from $450 for a 10-minute film or filmstrip.

RANDOM HOUSE, INC., School Division, 201 E. 50th St., Fifth Floor, New York NY 10022. Contact: Susan Tucker. For "elementary and junior high school students." Rights to be negotiated. "We are always interested in receiving resumes and project proposals, and will make every effort to respond within a reasonable length of time. Credentials should include experience in writing, experience in academic fields. Send one-page letter briefly describing the subject matter, grade level, point of view, scope of material, type of visuals the writer thinks should go with material, etc." Enclose S.A.S.E. for response.

Language Arts, Vocational Guidance, Science, and Social Studies: Requirements "vary. Subject matter includes English, social studies, guidance and vocational education, and science." Produces charts, sound filmstrips, multimedia kits, phonograph records, and prerecorded tapes and cassettes. Pay "varies."

REGENTS PUBLISHING COMPANY, INC., Two Park Ave., New York NY 10016. Contact: Julio I. Andujar, President. For foreign language students, in school and at home. Copyrighted. Will send catalog to writer on request. Query with description of material, table of contents and sample portions. Enclose S.A.S.E. for reply. No unsolicited mss. "It would be helpful if writer has done previous audiovisual work, has taught or is currently teaching."

Education: English as a second language. Spanish, French, German. Supplementary materials, cultural aspects of wide appeal in foreign language classes. Vocabulary within the range of foreign language students. Sound filmstrips, multimedia kits, phonograph records, prerecorded tapes and cassettes. Pays 6% of list price.

RHYTHMS PRODUCTIONS, Whitney Bldg., Box 34485, Los Angeles CA 90034. Contact: R.S. White. "Our audience is generally educational, with projects ranging from early childhood through adult markets." Copyrighted. Query first. "We need to know a writer's background and credits and to see samples of his work." Enclose S.A.S.E. for response to queries.

Education: Sound filmstrips, 16mm motion pictures, multimedia kits, phonograph records, prerecorded tapes and cassettes, and study prints. "Our firm specializes in creative productions, so though content is basic to the productions, a creative and imaginative approach is necessary." Usually pays $250 for filmstrip scripts.

RIDDLE VIDEO AND FILM PRODUCTIONS, INC., 507 Fifth Ave., New York NY 10017. President/Executive Producer: William Riddle. For "general public for television shows, young and old alike. Also for theater distribution." Material may be copyrighted or not copyrighted. Write for copy of guidelines for writers. Writer

"must be experienced and well-qualified in the subject in order to handle work assignments satisfactorily. We must see a sample of his or her work." Query first. Enclose S.A.S.E. for response to queries.
General: "Story boards and scripts are needed." Produces 8mm, 16mm and 35mm film loops; silent filmstrips; sound filmstrips; kinescopes; models; 8mm, 16mm, and 35mm motion pictures; multimedia kits; prerecorded tapes and cassettes; slides; study prints; videotape productions. Pays "standard going rates, with bonus on super work performed."

ROCKET PICTURES, INC., 1150 W. Olive Ave., Burbank CA 91506. Contact: Dick Westen. For cross section of all ages. Writer must have full knowledge of subject. Query first. Enclose S.A.S.E.
General: Silent and sound filmstrips, motion pictures, multimedia kits, phonograph records, prerecorded tapes and cassettes, and teaching machine programs. Sales, human relations, public relations, and selling; personal and management training are subjects of interest. Pays 5% to 10% of selling price; but payment varies, depending strictly on the assignment.

HOWARD M. SAMS & CO., INC., Education Division, 4300 W. 62nd St., Indianapolis IN 46268. Contact: John Obst, Managing Editor. Query first. Enclose S.A.S.E.
Education: Seeking scripts for "industrial arts and vocational/technical education subjects at the junior and senior high school and technical school levels." Payment by royalty arrangement.

WARREN SCHLOAT PRODUCTIONS, INC., 150 White Plains Rd., Tarrytown NY 10591. Contact Mrs. Barbara Martinsons. For K-14 and special education students. Copyrighted. Will send catalog to writer on request, "if warranted." Query first, "with proposal and possibly an outline." Enclose S.A.S.E.
Education and Language Arts: "Social studies, language arts, early childhood, science, math, career education, inservice. 8mm film loops, sound filmstrips, possibly models, and multimedia kits. Style should be stirring. Format exciting. Slant will vary." Length: 12 to 16 minutes for filmstrips. Pays $500 to $700 per script, or advance and royalty.

SNAPDRAGON PRODUCTIONS, 7785 S.W. 86th St., Miami FL 33143. Contact: Steven Cohen. Will assign projects to qualified writers. "We will have to see work." Query first. Enclose S.A.S.E. for response to queries.
General: Requirements "vary by job. Motion picture script format. Feature length." Pays "flat rate per script."

SPENCER PRODUCTIONS, INC., 507 5th Ave., New York NY 10017. Contact: Bruce Spencer. For high school students, college students, and adults. Occasionally uses freelance writers with considerable talent. Query first. Enclose S.A.S.E.
Satire: 16mm motion pictures, prerecorded tapes and cassettes. Satirical material only. Pay is negotiable.

BILL STOKES ASSOCIATES, 5642 Dyer St., Dallas TX 75206. Contact: Bill Stokes. Audience varies with projects undertaken; everyone from children to board chairmen. Rights purchased from author as payment for work performed. Writer must have experience in script writing, ability to visualize, good research habits, with recent reel or portfolio. Jobs are let on closed contract basis only. Query first. Enclose S.A.S.E.
General: Super 8mm, 16mm and 35mm film loops, sound filmstrips, 16mm and 35mm motion pictures, multimedia kits, phonograph records, prerecorded tapes and cassettes, and 35mm slides. All materials and requirements contingent upon clients' needs. "We produce sales meetings, industrial films, educational films, animated films, slide shows, filmstrips, multimedia programs, etc., covering a wide range of subjects and applications. Writer must be sufficiently acquainted with av and motion picture production formats to write within specific budget requirements." No royalties are paid. Contract basis only.

SUMMIT PICTURES INTERNATIONAL LTD., 1040 W. North Las Palmas Ave., Hollywood CA 90038. Contact: Martin Green. For general audience. Material is copyrighted. Occasionally uses freelance writers. Query first. Enclose S.A.S.E.
General: 16mm and 35mm motion pictures. Films, feature length, used for commercials, and industrial documentaries. Also television productions, musicals and variety shows. Payment is flexible, and negotiable.

TALCO PRODUCTIONS, 279 E. 44th St., New York NY 10017. President: Alan Lawrence. "We almost always assign scripts to freelance writers. In addition, we work with authors in developing ideas for television presentation. Generally, we like to review some of the writer's previous work in the medium." Query first, enclosing S.A.S.E. for reply.
General: "We produce television documentary and public relations/industrial presentations as well as educational programs (anthropology, archaeology, politics, labor, fashion, food, and art). Our areas of concentration are in TV documentary, educational and public relations programs for business and industry. We produce on quad and helical scan videotape, TV and radio cassette, 16 and 35mm film; also, sound filmstrips and slides. Monetary arrangements depend on the subject."

BOB THOMAS PRODUCTIONS, 23 Broad St., Bloomfield NJ 07003. President: Robert G. Thomas. Buys all rights. "Send material with introductory letter explaining ideas. Submit outline or rough draft for motion picture or business matter. If possible, we will contact the writer for further discussion." Enclose S.A.S.E.
Business, Education, and General: "We produce 3 types of material for 3 types of audiences: 8mm film loops in sports and pre-teen areas (educational); 8mm and 16mm motion pictures for business (educational, distributed by agencies); 35mm motion pictures for entertainment for a general audience (theater type). General subject matter may be of any style, any length. For the future, 35mm theatrical shorts for distribution." Payment "depends on agreements between both parties. On 8mm and 16mm matter, one fee arrangement. On 35mm shorts, percentage or fee."

UNITED METHODIST COMMUNICATIONS, 1525 McGavock St., Nashville TN 37203. Contact: Edgar A. Gossard, Director, Dept. Audiovisual Media. For children, from nursery age to 6th graders; youth, junior high to college age; young adults, middle adults, older adults, usually in church settings. Educational level for adults would range from high school graduate through college graduate. Copyrighted. "Normally, all rights purchased." Query first. "Writers should have professional experience in scripting for media. Background in Christian education and/or theology would be necessary for many projects, helpful for most, not required for some. Samples of previous work are most helpful to us in considering writers." Enclose S.A.S.E. for response to queries.
Education and Religion: "Subject areas are very broad, although much of our audiovisual production is done for use in church-school or Christian education settings. Interpersonal relationships, ethics, Bible study, church history, human growth and potential, theology, are some content areas in which we produce materials. Silent filmstrips, sound filmstrips, 16mm motion pictures, phonograph records, and prerecorded tapes and cassettes. All material written to specifications; requirements for scripts are transmitted with assignment. We are seldom, if ever, able to utilize unsolicited manuscripts. Projects vary from scripts for very short (3 to 4 minutes) recordings to scripts for 15- to 20-minute motion pictures. The bulk of the work is in 8- to 20-minute recordings and 70- to 80-frame filmstrips. Fees are paid on a per project basis. Minimum fees $50; maximum $1,500. No royalty arrangements."

VIDEO FILMS INC., 2761 E. Jefferson Ave., Detroit MI 48207. President: Clifford Hanna. For "adult, industrial audience." Send "resume of credentials with sample scripts." Query first. Enclose S.A.S.E. for response to queries.
Industry: Wants "shooting scripts." Produces silent filmstrips, 8mm and 16mm motion pictures, prerecorded tapes and cassettes, and slides. Payment "negotiable, usually $150 for proposal; $2,500 for script."

VISUAL TEACHING, 79 Pine Knob Terrace, Milford CT 06460. Contact: James A. Cunningham. For elementary through college level; most junior high level. Copyrighted. Will send a brochure to writer on request. Query first. "Writers should have a good knowledge and background in biology. We prefer to work with people that have developed a complete story of some aspect in nature accompanied by 2x2 color photos." Enclose S.A.S.E.

Science: "Texts to accompany 2x2 slide sets. 20 slides per set. Approximately 1,000 words. Prerecorded tapes and cassettes and slides. So far, all our topics have been nature and science. We would consider other topics if photographic materials were available or could be obtained. Our usual format is to use 20 2x2 color slides to teach some lesson in nature. The slides must be top quality and it is best that they all be taken by the same photographer. The descriptions are usually written on a general audience level since they are directed mainly toward teachers, not biologists. If writers furnish slides (their own), royalty may vary from 10% to 25%. If we buy the slides from other sources, we prefer to pay a straight fee for their descriptions."

VOCATIONAL EDUCATION PRODUCTIONS, c/o California Polytechnic State University, San Luis Obispo CA 93407. Contact: Steven LaMarine, Coordinator. For students who have an interest in occupational education, career education and the like. Copyrighted. Will send catalog to writer on request. "Because our program's scope is changing so rapidly, we would prefer to have writers, artists and photographers query us first. We are interested primarily in West Coast freelancers, but anything is possible. Credentials needed are simply the proven ability to produce professional work within a specified time-line. The writer must have a good visual sense, so that he thinks in terms of the total words-and-pictures impact of the material. An artist and/or photographer who can write well would probably be the ideal person to prepare our audiovisuals."

Education: "Most of our audiovisuals relate to occupational or vocational areas, slanted for use in an educational setting from grades 7 through college. There is a wide variety of requirements." Charts, sound filmstrips, multimedia kits, overhead transparencies, prerecorded tapes and cassettes, and 2x2 slides. "Payment would depend upon the type of material involved, but would usually be on a flat payment basis rather than royalties. We pay $100 to $500 for filmstrip scripts."

JERRY WARNER & ASSOCIATES, 31850 Village Center Rd., Westlake Village CA 91561. For business, government, schools, and television audiences. Copyright depending on client situation. "We buy full rights to writers' works for sponsored films. Writer must be a professional screenwriter or within the discipline of the special area of subject matter. Do not submit single copy material. Have material registered for datemark, or Writers Guild protection. We accept no responsibility of unsolicited mss." Will answer inquiries within the boundaries of production interest. Enclose S.A.S.E.

Business and General: Sound filmstrips, motion pictures, multimedia kits, and prerecorded tapes and cassettes. Sponsored business and government films; training, public information, public relations, sales promotion, educational, report films. Royalties are paid on proprietary films that writers take equity in rather than full fee, participations. "We read concepts for educational and documentary films and properties for feature films, but do not solicit scripts as a general rule. Fees vary and depend upon individual client or agency. We frequently pay from $50.00 to $75.00 per day for research periods and from $500.00 to $1,500.00 per reel of script. The wide variance is indicative of how each project has different scope and must be approached on the basis of talent requirement."

JACK WILLIAMSON MOTION PICTURE PRODUCTION, 426 31 St., Newport Beach CA 92660. "Our audiences are very critical." Buys all rights, but this is variable. "We've assigned very few scripts to freelance writers because we have found it difficult to discover capable ones with an understanding of our very exacting requirements. We're not looking for speculative properties, cute ideas or contest winners; we produce tools with which a customer can attain a well-defined goal. If the writer has to ask what format we use, he or she doesn't have the experience we need. If they wish to submit one script as a sample of their capabilities, we will look at it, return it within one week and contact those writers who interest us. The shorter the script, the better. If we weren't too busy to read lengthy scripts, we wouldn't be busy enough to hire you." Enclose S.A.S.E.

General: 16mm motion pictures. "We produce a broad range of non-theatrical films; educational, documentary, industrial; each sponsored by a company or organization. The film's style, slant, content and audience are dictated by the requirements of the sponsor. Most scripts pay the writer from $650 to $1,200 per ten minutes of picture, depending on their complexity and the amount of research required."

Authors' Agents

An agent must receive a certain amount in commissions each year to justify handling a writer's work. For this reason, many agents will take on only those new clients who have been recommended to them by editors or other professional writers. Such writers, these agents reason, are the most likely to achieve the minimum yearly sales figure that will enable the agent to make a profit (for example, an agent's commission would be $200 on a writer's $2,000 sales). Other agents are willing to read unsolicited mss from new writers, though some charge a reading fee—this pays for their time if a submission turns out to have little or no sales potential. Each agent's policy on new writers is given in the listings below.

It's generally a good idea for a new writer to market his material himself at first. Marketing experience is invaluable to a writer. It gives him direct contact with editors and producers, and he learns firsthand what they want and how close his work comes to their requirements.

Eventually, after he is successfully selling articles or fiction to quality and top-paying magazines; after he has sold a book; or after he has obtained several local productions of plays and/or publication by a play publisher; the writer may want an agent to handle his business. Some writers prefer to write full time, some like their marketing to be handled by a marketing specialist, some dislike seeing rejections, or have other reasons. Once the writer has established a "name," so that his work is in demand, an agent may also secure better contracts for him.

However, many successful professional writers continue to market their own material even after they've established a "name." Why? Because they prefer to keep the 10% of their gross income that an agent charges, they like personal contact with editors, they feel their writing stays closer to the market this way, or they have other personal reasons.

Writers are reminded that an agent cannot sell material that isn't right for today's market, or that is of low quality. All an agent can do is submit work he considers salable to those editors and producers whom he judges likely to be interested enough to buy it.

The television market is an exception to the general rule that a writer can act as his own agent. Television producers will not read unsolicited manuscripts for fear of possible charges of plagiarism; and all TV scripts are submitted through agents. Writers interested in finding a television agent should know that most successful television writers live in Los Angeles, where they can work directly with producers once their agents have sold their scripts or ideas.

ADAMS, RAY, AND ROSENBERG, 9220 Sunset Blvd., Suite 210, Los Angeles CA 90069. Agency Representatives: Sam Adams, Rick Ray, Lee Rosenberg. Established in 1963. Handles novels, nonfiction books, motion pictures (screenplays), plays, TV scripts plus services of writers, producers and directors. "Our firm functions primarily in the representation of creative individuals and material in the motion picture and television fields." 10% standard commission. New clients by referral. Not interested in unsolicited mss.

DOROTHY ALBERT, 162 W. 54th St., New York NY 10019. Established in 1959. Handles novels, motion pictures and TV scripts. Interested in TV pilot series, drama and comedy; original drama for motion pictures; and novels which are "well-plotted suspense; quality drama; adult fiction; human relations." 10% standard commission. New writer should send "letter of introduction, description of material, and resume of background." Enclose S.A.S.E. on all correspondence and submissions. The writer should have some foreknowledge of structure and endurance, whether it be motion pictures, TV or novels. No reading fee charged. Will not read unsolicited mss.

MAXWELL ALEY ASSOCIATES, 145 E. 35th St., New York NY 10016. Agency Representative: Mrs. Ruth Aley. Established in 1938. Handles magazine articles, nonfiction books, "top teenage fiction," and novels "if exceptional. I prefer books that have strong promotional possibilities bearing on current problems. The work should be totally professional and preferably of current interest." Recent sales for clients include *Race for Rose* (Kurzma). 10% standard commission. New clients "through recommendation from publishers or other authors." Will consider only mss of established writers that come with special professional recommendation. A writer preferably should have achieved $5,000 in sales and interest from major magazine or book publishers. Will read unsolicited queries or outlines accompanied by biographical data "if very professional." Enclose biography and S.A.S.E. for reply.

JOSEPH ANTHONY AGENCY, 530 Valley Road, Upper Montclair NJ 07043. Established in 1962. Specializes in books, motion pictures, short stories and plays. Charges reading fee of $20. Will work with a writer who wants to work hard. Enclose S.A.S.E. for return of submissions.

BILL BERGER ASSOCIATES, INC., 535 East 72nd St., New York NY 10021. Established in 1960. Specializes in books in all areas. Writer must have achieved minimum sales of $5,000 and must have been recommended. No reading fee. Will not read unsolicited mss.

LOIS BERMAN, W. B. Agency, Inc., 156 E. 52 St., New York NY 10022. Established in 1971. Handles magazine fiction, novels, motion pictures, and plays. "Most of our clients are playwrights, so most of the material I handle is dramatic in form. If, however, my clients choose to turn to narrative writing, I handle it, too. I now represent primarily young playwrights with workshop or off-Broadway credits." 10% standard commission. Will represent a writer whose "work is interesting to me. I am interested in quality material. The writer should have full-length theater work for initial consideration." Obtains new writers "from seeing productions and by referral." Will "sometimes" read unsolicited mss "on basis of letter outlining writing background." Enclose S.A.S.E. for reply to query and return of submissions.

BLOOM/MILLER ORGANIZATION (formerly Mel Bloom & Associates), 8693 Wilshire Blvd., Beverly Hills CA 90011. Established in 1966. Handles motion pictures and TV scripts; only completed screenplays or movies for television. No treatments, outlines, or scripts for episode shows. Send a motion picture script only. Will read unsolicited mss. 10% of gross sales. Obtains new clients by recommendation from others in the motion picture industry. Enclose S.A.S.E. with ms.

GEORGES BORCHARDT, INC., 145 E. 52nd St., New York NY 10022. Established in 1953. Specializes in novels and short stories of high literary quality and first-rate nonfiction. "Will represent new clients if recommended by someone whose judgment we trust." Will not read unsolicited mss.

AARON BOWMAN ENTERPRISES, 2813 Willow St., Granite City IL 62040. Contact: Aaron Bowman. Interested in new talent, especially in poetry, nonfiction and fiction book lengths 25,000 words and up. Charges $50 reading and critical analysis fee for TV scripts, $50 for short stories and articles to 6,000 words, $50 for poetry (100 poems maximum), and $100 for book mss. Reports in 4 weeks. "We either submit the work to editors, consider it for our own publications or react with detailed, constructive criticism, or advise otherwise. Reading-critique fee refunded upon sale or purchase. Upon sale, we contract 15% of royalties for placing ms. Enclose S.A.S.E."

CELINE BREVANNES, 28 Bauer Place, Westport CT 06880. Established in 1936. Specializes in children's books—mostly science from age 10 and up. Looks for quality of writing and subject matter. Charges reading fee. Will not read unsolicited mss. Enclose S.A.S.E. for reply to query.

ANITA HELEN BROOKS ASSOCIATES, 155 E. 55th St., New York NY 10022. Established in 1956. Specializes in fiction, nonfiction, mystery, books written by newspapermen and radio-TV executives and personalities; biographies, radio, TV scripts. 10% standard commission. No unsolicited mss. Query first. Enclose S.A.S.E.

BROOME AGENCY, INC., Box 3649, Sarasota FL 33578. 813-355-3036. Established in 1957. Directors: Sherwood and Mary Ann Broome. "We read unsolicited books, stories and articles (including teen material) of national or wider interest and handle on professional percentage basis under exclusive contract when work is acceptable to us. We charge fees based on time when author wishes us, by prior arrangement, to analyze, edit, revise, rewrite or collaborate. We handle all rights worldwide, but we must place material for publication before trying to sell TV or movie rights. No poems, young children's material, fillers, newspaper or trade magazine material or screen originals. Standard commission 10% on U.S. sales, 15% on Canadian sales, 20% on other foreign rights. We offer annual prizes of $1,250 for the best book manuscript of 50,000 words or more, and $750 for the best short story of 5,000 words or less. Enclose return postage." Recent sales for clients include *Where Have All the Woolly Mammoths Gone?* by Ted S. Frost, with Parker Publishing Co.

JAMES BROWN ASSOCIATES, INC., 22 E. 60th St., New York NY 10022. Established in 1949. Handles books primarily; handles stage plays for the writers it represents and sells short stories and articles, but does not work with writers devoting all of their time to articles and short stories. No poetry. Writer must be professional, but not necessarily published. 10% standard commission. "Writers should query us first with a statement, not a long description, of the book and the writer." Does not charge reading fee. Enclose S.A.S.E. for reply.

NED BROWN ASSOCIATED, 407 North Maple Dr., Beverly Hills CA 90210. Established in 1936. Handles nonfiction books, novels, motion pictures, and plays; also TV scripts and packages, but these "only by established writers." 10% standard commission. Works with writers who are earning at least $5,000 yearly from writing. Will work with new writer on occasion if highly recommended or if published by an established publisher. Will not read unsolicited mss.

SHIRLEY BURKE, 370 E. 76th St., Suite B-704, New York NY 10021. Established in 1948. Handles magazine fiction, novels, nonfiction books. Clients obtained through recommendation. Must have some writing experience. 10% standard commission. Will read unsolicited queries or outlines only. "Please inquire. Do not send mss without letter of inquiry." Enclose S.A.S.E. for return of outlines or reply to queries.

THE CAMBRIDGE COMPANY, 9000 Sunset Blvd., Suite 814, Los Angeles CA 90069. Agency Representatives: Lee Atkinson and Gloria Geale. Established in 1963.

Handles novels, nonfiction books, textbooks, motion pictures, and TV scripts. 10% standard commission. Will not read unsolicited mss. Will read unsolicited queries and outlines. Enclose S.A.S.E.

RUTH CANTOR, Room 1005, 156 Fifth Ave., New York NY 10010. Established in 1952. Handles "trade books, juvenile books, good fiction and nonfiction. I'm probably the best agent for children's books in the country. I prefer really good, solid novels and am allergic to potboilers. I am badly in need of really good nonfiction with broad market appeal. I no longer encourage picture books." Standard commission 10% for domestic sales, 20% for foreign sales. New clients through referrals, recommendations, and direct contact with writers. To be represented by this agent, a new writer "must have proven talent, which means that he has published at least something, or else that some responsible person (such as an editor, another writer, a teacher) recommends him to me. Even then, I will represent only such people as I think I can sell, but will give a promising writer a free reading and appraisal of his ms. A new writer should write me a letter, giving me a concise writing history and description of what he wishes to send me. Enclose return postage in stamps both with query letter and with ms."

CAPRICORN AGENCY, P.O. Box 8766, Phoenix AZ 85066. Contact: J. Steele. Established in 1974. Interested in novels, children's books, short stories, psychic phenomena. Standard 10% commission. Charges $5 to $25 reading fee for mss. New writers should query first. Enclose S.A.S.E.

COLTON, KINGSLEY, & ASSOCIATES, INC., 321 S. Beverly Dr., Beverly Hills CA 90212. Established in 1934. Specializes in TV, theater and motion pictures. Represents only recognized, established writers.

HAROLD CORNSWEET LITERARY AGENCY, P.O. Box 3093, Beverly Hills CA 90212. Established in 1950. Specializes in screenplay adaptations for motion pictures. 10% standard commission. Only talented writers need apply for literary representation. Ask for information card before submitting. Will read unsolicited mss. "We charge a nominal fee of $25 for each literary script submitted to us to read and evaluate for submission to studios, etc." Enclose S.A.S.E. for response to queries and return of submissions.

CREATIVE WRITERS AGENCY, 1127 S. Patrick Dr., Satellite Beach FL 32937. Contact: Mrs. Verda L. Veatch. Established in 1971. Handles novels, nonfiction books, textbooks, motion pictures, stage plays, and TV scripts. American film history, and American military history. Will take on new writers based on the merits of material submitted. Pay particular attention to formats recommended by *Writer's Market* and *Writer's Digest* for submission of material. Will criticize unsolicited mss for a fee of $7.50 (to 7,500 words), $15 (to 25,000 words), $25 (25,000 words and up; all plays). Offers complete administrative services for writers. 10% on book mss, 15% movies and plays. Recent sales for clients include *In the Devil's Triangle* (Jones). Enclose S.A.S.E. for return of submissions.

JOAN DAVES, 515 Madison Ave., New York NY 10022. Established in 1951. Handles magazine articles, magazine fiction, juvenile fiction, novels, nonfiction books. Negotiates dramatic, TV and film rights on behalf of clients, but does not handle original scripts. 10% standard commission on all domestic income. 20% commission on all foreign income. Advises writers to "query. Give details about background and professional achievement. Do not give plots of fiction in endless detail." Will read unsolicited queries and outlines. Will not read unsolicited mss. Enclose S.A.S.E.

ANITA DIAMANT, The Writers' Workshop, Inc., 51 E. 42 St., New York NY 10017. Established in 1917. Handles magazine articles and fiction, juvenile fiction, novels, motion pictures, and syndicated material. No juveniles for readers under 12 years. 10% domestic sales; 20% foreign sales. Potential clients must have at least 1 book published within past 2 years or magazine sales amounting to $2,000 within past year before representation by this agency. Obtains new clients on recommendation through Society of Authors' Representatives, publishers and other clients. Will read unsolicited queries and outlines. Always query first, giving history of ms and where it has been submitted already. Enclose S.A.S.E.

ECLECTIC HOUSE, 316 W. 90 St., Suite 4, New York, NY 10024. Contact: James J. Kery, Managing Director. Established in 1973. Handles material in the following nonfiction areas: art, military, crafts, popular psychology, performing and graphic arts, illustrated books, and any nonfiction book that has a broad, general appeal. Novels. 10% domestic sales; 20% foreign sales. New clients obtained through word of mouth and personal recommendations. Will read unsolicited queries and outlines, or complete mss. Enclose S.A.S.E.

FRIEDA FISHBEIN, 353 W. 57th St., New York NY 10019. Established in 1941. Handles novels, nonfiction books, children's books, motion pictures, plays, TV and radio scripts. Works on a 10% commission and an exclusive option for two years. Will read unsolicited mss and work with new writers. Reading fees vary, depending on whether ms is a play or a book. Enclose S.A.S.E. for return of submissions.

THE FOLEY AGENCY, 34 E. 38th St., New York NY 10016. Agency Representatives: Joan and Joseph Foley. Established in 1956. Handles novels and nonfiction books; limited amount of magazine material. 10% standard commission. Will not read unsolicited mss. Will read unsolicited queries (give all pertinent details) and outlines. Enclose S.A.S.E.

HAROLD FREEDMAN BRANDT & BRANDT DRAMATIC DEPT., INC., 101 Park Ave., New York NY 10017. Established in 1927. Specializes in theater. Reads some unsolicited mss, but inquire first. Enclose S.A.S.E. for reply to queries.

PEGGY LOIS FRENCH, 12645 Norwalk Blvd., Norwalk CA 90650. Established in 1952. Handles novels, juvenile books (for an older age group), and TV scripts and screenplays. Help with formats. Material must be high in quality. 10% standard commission. Will develop a writer with talent. "We are in need of good strong stories for both juvenile and adult. If a writer shows promise, I work with him until he makes a sale." Will read unsolicited mss. Charges $2 reading fee per 1,000 words (flat rate for longer mss) for unsolicited mss and new writers; none for professionals. Will read unsolicited queries and outlines. Enclose S.A.S.E.

JAY GARON-BROOKE ASSOC., INC., 415 Central Park West, New York NY 10025. Established in 1951. Handles novels, nonfiction books, textbooks, motion pictures, and stage plays. 10% standard commission. "Writer must be referred to us by an editor or one of our clients. We rarely accept a client who does not earn $10,000 a year. The writer should write to us, if established, and give his credits." Will not read unsolicited mss. Enclose S.A.S.E. for reply.

MAX GARTENBERG, 331 Madison Ave., New York NY 10017. Established in 1954. Handles novels and nonfiction books. 10% standard commission. Will not read unsolicited mss. "However, any writer, published or unpublished, who submits a grammatical, coherent letter describing what he has to sell will receive a reply if Mr. Gartenberg is interested." Enclose S.A.S.E. for reply.

IVAN GREEN AGENCY, 1900 Ave. of the Stars, Suite 1070, Los Angeles CA 90067. Established in 1954. Handles TV scripts, motion pictures, stage plays, novels, and nonfiction books. 10% standard commission. New clients through recommendations. Will not read unsolicited mss.

BLANCHE C. GREGORY, INC., 2 Tudor City Place, New York NY 10017. Established in 1950. Specializes in fiction (novels and stories) for the major national magazines and nonfiction books. Prefers an author who has already sold to a first-class market. Query first. Enclose S.A.S.E. for reply.

VANCE HALLOWAY, Box 518, Pearblossom CA 93553. Established in 1956. Handles novels and nonfiction books. Will read unsolicited queries, outlines. Enclose S.A.S.E. for return of submissions and reply to queries.

REECE HALSEY AGENCY, 8733 Sunset Blvd., Los Angeles CA 90069. Established in 1957. Handles novels, nonfiction books, and motion pictures. Handles novels, "after the subject matter has been discussed", and full screenplays, preferably contemporary. Recent sales for clients include *Lemmon* (Widener), *Supersecs* (Marchak-Hunter), *Mizmoon* (Soltysik). 10% standard commission. New clients through "referrals by other clients." Will not read unsolicited mss. Send "a query letter outlining the background of the writer." Enclose S.A.S.E. for response to query.

SHIRLEY HECTOR AGENCY, 29 West 46th St., New York NY 10036. Office in London also. "We request that a writer send us a brief account of what he has had published and a description of the work he wishes to submit. We do not encourage a writer to send us his ms unless he queries first." Enclose S.A.S.E. for response to query.

HEINLE AND HEINLE ENTERPRISES, 1095 Main St., Concord MA 01742. Established in 1973. Handles magazine articles, magazine fiction, juvenile articles, juvenile fiction, novels, and nonfiction books. Interested in identifying and developing authors whose main interest is in the New England scene, past, present, or future. History, novels, biography of New England figures, articles, short stories, almost any form of writing as long as it concerns New England places, people, or themes; food, sports, travel, sight-seeing, etc. 10% standard commission. Will consider reading unsolicited mss on basis of letter outlining writing background. Enclose S.A.S.E.

KURT HELLMER, 52 Vanderbilt Ave., New York NY 10017. Established in 1952. Handles novels, nonfiction books, textbooks, motion pictures, stage plays, and TV scripts. Recent sales for clients include *By the North Door* (Atkins); *Moment of Freedom* (Bjorneboe); *Acid Drop* (George). Standard commission 10% domestic, 20% foreign. New clients by "word of mouth, inquiries, and recommendations. A new writer must show promise." Will read unsolicited mss for a fee of $35 for books and $25 for plays. Query first. Enclose S.A.S.E. for response to queries and return of submissions.

DICK IRVING HYLAND ASSOCIATES, 8961 Sunset Blvd., Los Angeles CA 90069. Agency Representatives: Dick Hyland, Wende Hyland, Paula Stoppa. Established in 1951. Handles published novels for motion picture sale, plays, original screenplays, TV series. 10% standard commission. To be accepted, a writer "must be firmly established as a professional, or must win our respect after his material has been read, such material having been recommended by a respected professional or client of this office." Will not read unsolicited mss "unless recommended by a present client or a respected professional." Enclose S.A.S.E. for reply to queries.

GEORGE INGERSOLL AGENCY, 7167½ Sunset Blvd., Hollywood CA 90046. Established in 1949. Specializes in motion picture and television scripts. Will not read unsolicited mss.

KAHN, LIFELANDER & RHODES, 853 7th Ave., New York NY 10019. Contact: Barbara Rhodes. Established in 1968. Handles juvenile fiction, novels, nonfiction books, motion pictures, stage plays, and TV scripts. 10% standard commission. "We prefer published or produced writers on recommendation from professionals. We prefer a query letter." Will read unsolicited queries or outlines. Will read and criticize unsolicited mss for a fee of $15 (after query on suitability of material). Enclose S.A.S.E.

DANIEL P. KING, Literary Agent, 5125 N. Cumberland Blvd., Whitefish Bay WI 53217. Contact: Daniel P. King. Phone: 414-964-2903. Established in 1974. Handles magazine articles, fiction, novels, nonfiction books, textbooks, syndicated material and reprints of books originally published in the United Kingdom. Specializes in crime literature; mystery and detective short stories and novels, nonfiction articles and books dealing with crime, criminology, etc. Will consider general interest book-length mss. 10% commission. Majority of clients are members of The Crime Writers' Association (England). A preliminary letter giving information about the author and his proposed submission is essential before sending ms. Accepts new writers if work is of a marketable standard. No minimum sales volume required, although most clients are established British writers of mystery or nonfiction books on crime. Reading fee varies and is charged only to new and beginning writers, refundable upon sale of ms. Enclose S.A.S.E.

BERTHA KLAUSNER INTERNATIONAL LITERARY AGENCY, INC., 71 Park Ave., New York NY 10016. Established in 1938. Handles juvenile fiction books, novels, nonfiction books, textbooks, motion pictures, stage plays, and TV scripts. 10% standard commission. New clients accepted through recommendations. Will read unsolicited queries or outlines. A reading fee is charged for unsolicited mss. Will criticize unsolicited mss for a moderate fee. Query first. Enclose S.A.S.E.

LUCY KROLL AGENCY, 390 West End Ave., New York NY 10024. Established in 1950. Specializes in full-length plays, nonfiction and fiction. No unsolicited mss accepted; inquiries only, with S.A.S.E. for reply.

THE LANTZ OFFICE, INCORPORATED, 114 East 55th St., New York NY 10022. Contact: Robert Lantz. Established in 1973. Handles magazine articles, magazine fiction, novels, nonfiction books, motion pictures, stage plays and television scripts. List of clients is limited and new representations undertaken in exceptional circumstances only. Offers 10% commission. Recent sales for clients have been to Simon & Schuster, Random House, W. W. Norton, Bantam, Wm. Morrow, etc. New clients accepted by personal reference. Will not read unsolicited ms, but will read unsolicited queries or outlines. Does not charge a reading fee or a criticism fee. Enclose S.A.S.E.

LARSEN/POMADA LITERARY AGENTS, 1029 Jones St., San Francisco CA 94109. Contact: Michael Larsen or Elizabeth Pomada. Established in 1971. Handles juvenile fiction, novels, motion pictures, TV scripts, and juvenile and adult nonfiction. 10% standard commission. "We prefer to handle only completed books. New writer should mail finished book to the agency before meeting with us. We prefer to read an original, rather than a xeroxed copy, and it takes us 3 to 4 weeks to read things and then get back, by mail or phone, to the author." Recent sales for clients include: *I Shoulda Been Home Yesterday* (Harris) to Delacorte; *World Full of Strangers* (Freeman) to Bantan & Arbor House; and *BiCentennial Guide* (Lawlor) to Dell. Obtains new clients through personal recommendations, *Literary Market Place*, and yellow pages. Will read unsolicited mss. Charges unpublished writers a $25 reading fee. Enclose S.A.S.E.

LENNIGER LITERARY AGENCY, INC., 437 Fifth Ave., New York NY 10016. Established in 1923. Handles fiction and nonfiction books, stage plays, screenplays. 10% commission U.S. sales. Preliminary letter from prospective clients required. Enclose S.A.S.E. Recent sales include: *Bill Severn's Big Book of Magic* (Severn), *The House of Scorpio* (Wallace), and *I Tom Horn* (Henry).

PATRICIA LEWIS, 450 Seventh Ave., Room 602, New York NY 10001. Established in 1951. Handles juvenile fiction and nonfiction books. Specializes in "teenage fiction and nonfiction and general nonfiction; few novels." 10% standard commission. "Query first. Do not send material without okay from agent." Will read book-length unsolicited mss "only if writer has taken courses of study in writing or has been recommended by an editor or teacher." Enclose S.A.S.E. for reply to queries. Recent sales for clients include *Conquest of Mexico, An Amiable Journey, In Pursuit of Cortes* by Matthew J. Bruccoli, with Vanguard.

DONALD MacCAMPBELL, INC., 12 E. 41, New York NY 10017. Established in

1939. Handles novels and nonfiction books. 10% domestic, 15% Canada and Mexico, and 20% foreign. Mss by non-clients must be accompanied by return self-addressed, stamped envelope; ditto letters of inquiry which should always precede the mailing of material. Allow 10 days for consideration. Always submit a list of book credits, if any, with publication dates and titles. The agency welcomes telephone inquiries but will not accept collect calls from non-clients. There are no reading or criticism fees.

THE MANUSCRIPT AND BOOK SERVICE, 27 Chestnut St., Brookline MA 02146. Editor: Jean Poindexter Colby. Manager: Florence Buck. Established in 1952. Specializes in juveniles. Will read unsolicited mss for a fee of $20. "For this fee, a detailed report is given on the reasons the manuscript is or is not salable, and on ways to improve it." Enclose S.A.S.E.

BETTY MARKS, 51 E. 42 St., Suite 1406, New York NY 10017. Established in 1969. Handles magazine articles, magazine fiction, juvenile articles, juvenile fiction, novels, nonfiction books. Recent sales for clients include *City Notebook* (Phillips). 10% standard commission. Will represent new writer whose work is "of good quality in research, writing, and subject matter." Will read unsolicited queries and outlines. Will read unsolicited mss (maximum 100,000 words) for a fee of $75. Enclose S.A.S.E.

HAROLD MATSON COMPANY, INC., 22 East 40 St., New York NY 10016. Established in 1930. Specializes in any area in which a successful author's output can be exploited. Will represent a new writer if they are convinced of his potential possibilities. Does not read unsolicited mss; query first. No reading fee charged. Requires recommendation of an editor, writer, or professor. Enclose S.A.S.E. for response to queries.

SCOTT MEREDITH LITERARY AGENCY, INC., 845 Third Avenue, New York NY 10022. Established in 1941. Handles novels, nonfiction books, magazine articles, magazine fiction, juvenile books, textbooks, poetry collections, motion pictures, plays, TV scripts, columns and other material for syndication. Typical sales for clients include *Marilyn* (Mailer), *A Very Special Relationship* (Agnew), *Streets of Gold* (Hunter), *The Wall Street Gang* (Ney). Averages 600 to 700 sales yearly for new writers. 10% standard commission on American sales, 20% on all foreign sales. Charges a fee in working with writers who are not now selling regularly to major markets, and works on a commission basis with regularly selling writers. If a writer has sold to a major book publisher in the past year or has begun to make major national magazine or television sales with some regularity, "we drop fees and proceed on a straight commission basis." Booklet describing agency and terms available free on request. Will read unsolicited mss. Enclose S.A.S.E.

ROBERT P. MILLS LTD., 156 E. 52 St., New York NY 10022. Established in 1960. Specializes in general trade book publishing and general magazines; more emphasis on fiction than nonfiction. Recent sales for clients: *A Death With Dignity* by Lois Snow. 10% standard commission. A writer "must come to me recommended by a respected source or have established himself in some way as a professional writer; no minimum sales required, but I must have faith in the writer." Will not read unsolicited mss.

HOWARD MOOREPARK, 444 East 82nd St., New York NY 10028. Established in 1946. Handles magazine articles, magazine fiction, novels, nonfiction books. 10% standard commission; 19% overseas. New clients accepted through recommendations. Also will read unsolicited queries, outlines, and mss. Enclose S.A.S.E. for return of submissions and response to queries.

WILLIAM MORRIS AGENCY, INC., 1350 Avenue of the Americas, New York NY 10019. Contact: Literary Department. Established in 1898. Handles novels, and general trade nonfiction. 10% domestic sales; higher on foreign sales. "Will not read or handle short stories or articles for anyone not already a client. Will read unsolicited queries and outlines." Enclose S.A.S.E.

NATIONAL LAUGH ENTERPRISES, Box 835, Grand Central Station, New York NY 10017. Agency Representative: George Q. Lewis. Established in 1945. Will read unsolicited mss only if they are less than 10 pages in length. Will represent a writer "if he has great talent." Specializes in humor. Interested in the performing arts primarily: radio, TV, stage, off-Broadway, etc. 15% standard commission. Conducts "College of Comedy" for gagwriters and comedians in New York City, and guest teaches "The Art of Laughmaking" at varied schools in the Metropolitan New York area (including New Jersey) and does mini-courses in creative comedy. These courses provide a humor laboratory where skills and techniques are examined and tested, then channeled to members of Humor Exchange Network. Also invites membership in Humor Exchange Network, which sponsors Comedy Workshop activities in communities throughout the country. Also each month invites gagwriters to compete for Gagwriter-of-the-Month title, a showcase of 50 original jokes which is sent to prominent columnists and broadcasting executives to focus attention on new talented gagwriters. Enclose S.A.S.E. for return of submissions. Will answer questions about comedy and humor if sent with stamped, self-addressed envelope.

CHARLES NEIGHBORS, INC., 240 Waverly Place, New York NY 10014. Established in 1967. Handles magazine articles, juvenile fiction, novels, nonfiction books, motion pictures. Recent sales for clients include *Beginnings* (Juliusburger), *Andromeda Gun* (Boyd), and *Charley O* (Michelson). 10% standard commission. New writer must have "written and had published high quality material. I will, however, be willing to consider the work of unpublished writers on recommendation of existing clients or editors." Will also read unsolicited queries and outlines, if S.A.S.E. is enclosed.

B. K. NELSON LITERARY AGENCY, 210 E. 47 St., New York NY 10017. Established in 1968. Handles novels, nonfiction books, and motion pictures. 10% domestic, 20% foreign commission. Recent sales for clients include *Rape! One Victim's Story* (Follett), *She's a Cop, Isn't She?* (Dial), *Maneaters* (Drake), and *In Harmony With Nature* (Drake). New clients obtained through inquiries and other authors' recommendations. "Be honest with me. Be willing to work with the agency if rewrites are required." Will read unsolicited mss or unsolicited queries or outlines. Will read unsolicited mss for a fee of $35. Will criticize unsolicited mss for a fee of $35. Enclose S.A.S.E. for return of submissions.

NICHOLAS LITERARY AGENCY, 161 Madison Avenue, New York NY 10016. Agency Representative: Georgia C. Nicholas. Established in 1934. Handles novels and nonfiction books, motion pictures, stage plays, TV scripts, and radio scripts. "I handle the client first, mss second. If earning potential looks high, I'll even consider his poetry!" 10% standard commission. "Although I'm not seeking new clients, they come from market listing, personal recommendation, and Armed Forces Writers League for which I'm official representative. A new writer must have sincerity. Writers from minority backgrounds get special consideration and high priority. Will read unsolicited queries or outlines. We do not charge a reading fee, but we do assess a token handling fee if ms and client are accepted. $10 for a novel." Enclose S.A.S.E.

HAROLD OBER ASSOCIATES, INC., 40 E. 49 St., New York NY 10017. Handles magazine articles, magazine fiction, novels, nonfiction books. In business over 40 years. 10% standard commission, U.S. sales; 15%, British sales; 20%, translations. "Writer doesn't necessarily have to have been published before, but we must feel strongly about a person's potential before taking anyone new on." Will read unsolicited queries and outlines. Enclose S.A.S.E.

O'NEILL AND KRALIK LITERARY CONSULTANTS, P. O. Box 461, Birmingham MI 48012. Contact: Michael O'Neill or John Kralik. Established in 1973. Handles magazine fiction, novels, poetry, and book reviews. 10% standard commission. "We are actively seeking new writers from college campuses. Will read unsolicited mss and queries or outlines. We do not charge a reading fee or criticism fee." Enclose S.A.S.E.

DOROTHEA OPPENHEIMER, 866 United Nations Plaza, New York NY 10017. Established in 1959. Handles book-length adult fiction and nonfiction "of exceptional quality." 10% standard commission. "Not taking on new writers at present."

PARK AVENUE LITERARY AGENCY, 230 Park Ave., New York NY 10017. Agency Representative: Marie Wilkerson. Established in 1960. Handles nonfiction primarily; few novels, no plays or TV scripts. 10% standard commission. Query essential. Do not send material without okay from agent. Enclose S.A.S.E.

RAY PEEKNER LITERARY AGENCY, 2625 N. 36 St., Milwaukee WI 53210. Contact: Ray Puechner. Established in 1973. Associated with Larry Sternig Literary Agency. Not reading any unsolicited mss. Query first with S.A.S.E., listing previous credits. 10% on domestic sales, 15% on Canadian, and 20% on foreign. Interested in nonfiction book length projects, adult and juvenile. No poetry, plays, or juvenile picture books. Interested in category fiction (mystery, gothic, etc.) and quality fiction, booklength. Will handle shorter material only for clients also working in booklengths.

MARJORIE PETERS, PIERRE LONG, 5744 S. Harper, Chicago IL 60637. Established in 1953. Specializes in poetry and fiction. 10% standard commission. Works with new writers of caliber; no minimum sales requirement. Does not read unsolicited mss; query first. $50 reading fee charged for book-length mss of 200 pages or less; more for longer mss. For short stories, articles and essays of not more than 15 pages, double-spaced, poetry of not more than four pages double-spaced, and 15-minute TV plays, charges $25; more for longer plays. Enclose S.A.S.E. for response to queries.

ARTHUR PINE ASSOCIATES, INC., 1780 Broadway, New York NY 10019. Contact: Arthur Pine and Martin Pine. Established in 1968. Handles novels and nonfiction books. Writers must have some previously published in-depth magazine articles or books. 15% for overall literary and publicity services. Obtains new clients through recommendation from publishers and established authors. Will read or criticize unsolicited mss for a fee of $100. Enclose S.A.S.E.

PISCEAN PRODUCTIONS LITERARY AGENCY, 4576 11 Ave. North, St. Petersburg FL 33713. Contact: Tom or Mary Milner. Established in 1972. Handles magazine articles, novels, motion pictures, TV scripts, and syndicated material. Also 90-minute TV movies of the week. 10% standard commission. "We obtain new clients by word-of-mouth and market listing. Writers must follow a professional format. Will read unsolicited mss or unsolicited queries or outlines. We do not charge a reading fee. We do not charge a criticism fee." Enclose S.A.S.E.

SIDNEY PORCELAIN, Box J, Rocky Hill NJ 08553. Established in 1951. Handles magazine articles, magazine fiction, juvenile fiction, novels, nonfiction books, TV scripts. Recent sales for clients include *I Can Heal, So Can You; Walk Far Woman; Crystal Moment; Years Reflected.* 10% standard commission. New clients accepted by referrals. Will read unsolicited queries, outlines, and mss. Enclose S.A.S.E.

PORTER, GOULD, AND DIERKS AUTHORS' AGENTS, 1236 Sherman Ave., Evanston IL 60202. Successors to Max Siegel and Associates. Established in 1958. Handles magazine articles, magazine fiction, juvenile articles, juvenile fiction, novels, nonfiction books, textbooks, poetry, motion pictures, plays, TV scripts. "We are particularly interested in increasing our juvenile and textbook representation. These 2 areas have tended to handle their contracts without agents and are, as a result, subject to minimum contracts in royalty, rights, advances, and overseas edition income." Advises writers to "be explicit about publishing background, both in preparation and experience that relates to writing, and about all publishing success.

Make the first contact by mail. A serious writer should write." 10% standard commission. "We encourage new talent and work with it as aggressively as we do established writers. We prefer publishing experience, but the real test of a new writer is the quality of the ms offered." Will read unsolicited mss for a fee. Enclose S.A.S.E. for return of submissions or response to queries.

SUSAN ANN PROTTER, LITERARY AGENT, 156 E. 52 St., New York NY 10022. Established in 1971. Handles magazine articles, novels, and nonfiction books. 10% domestic sales and 20% foreign sales and translations. Recent sales for clients include: *Nutrition and Your Nerves* (Newbold); *Great Houses of Chicago* (Bruce). New clients obtained through referrals by editors and clients. Handles a wide variety of fiction and nonfiction books and handles magazine material only for established freelancers and clients who are working on books. Areas of interest are history, psychology, health, film, music, and photography. "Write an informative letter including short background, list published articles and books, and be specific about current projects." Will not read unsolicited mss, but will read queries. "Will read only materials submitted by persons recommended to me." Enclose S.A.S.E.

Q E D LITERARY AGENCY, 7032 Willis Ave., Van Nuys, Los Angeles CA 91405. President: Vincent J. Ryan. Established in 1966. Handles "scholarly or serious nonfiction; subject areas include philosophy, anthropology, theology, sociology, psychology, phenomenology, linguistics, ethnology, ethnomusicology, natural history, ecology, education, history, literature." Recent sales for clients include *The Story of the Universe: A History of Cosmology from the Earliest Times to the Present Day* (Grant) to Scribner's; *The People and the Faith of the Bible* (Chouraqui) to University of Massachusetts Press; and *Computerized Text Editing and Processing with Built-in Indexing* (Ryan and Dearing). 15% standard commission, descending with increasing sales volume. Authors should submit abstract or outline, table of contents, and possibly 1 or 2 chapters of ms. Do not send complete ms initially. Include information about page length of ms and number of tables and illustrations. Make submission on exclusive basis. If in process of writing, may submit ms piecemeal. Will read unsolicited queries or abstracts free of charge. Will read unsolicited ms for fee of $35. Will criticize unsolicited ms for fee of $100. About 15% of annual income is obtained from ms reading/criticism fees. Enclose S.A.S.E. for reply or return of submissions.

RAINES & RAINES, 244 Madison Ave., New York NY 10016. Contact: Joan Raines or Theron Raines. Established in 1961. Handles magazine articles and fiction, juvenile fiction, novels, nonfiction books, textbooks, poetry books, motion pictures, stage plays, TV scripts, radio scripts, and syndicated material. No specialties. 10% standard commission. Prospective clients must have published and be recommended. Will not read unsolicited mss. Does not charge a reading fee or a criticism fee. Enclose S.A.S.E.

ROBINSON LITERARY AGENCY, 29 Rankin Rd., Buffalo NY 14226. Contact: Mrs. Janet L. Robinson. Established in 1971. Handles novels, nonfiction books, and textbooks. 10% standard commission. Will read unsolicited queries or outlines. "Please send me a query letter with an outline." Enclose S.A.S.E.

LEAH SALISBURY, INC., 790 Madison Ave., New York NY 10021. Specializes in theatre. 10% standard commission. "Interested in writers of superior talent only." Reading fee is generally required for unpublished writers but returned if mss is accepted. Query first. Enclose S.A.S.E. for response to queries.

IRVING SALKOW AGENCY, 450 North Roxbury Dr., Beverly Hills CA 90210. Established in 1963. Handles motion pictures, plays, TV scripts. "The opportunities for writers in motion pictures and television are as strong as ever, if not a little more so, with the many pictures now being made for television exhibition." 10% standard commission. New writer must have "a willingness to write and demonstrate that, with written material in the form of scripts, treatments, or outlines intended for motion picture or television production." No interest in material in any form intended for The Established Episodic Series, where the writing is done on assignment. The producers of these do not consider unsolicited submissions for these series. Enclose S.A.S.E.

RITA SCOTT, INC., 25 Sutton Place South, New York NY 10022. Established in 1970. Handles magazine articles, novels, and nonfiction books. 10% standard commission. "New writers should contact me before sending their ms and give me a biography and some information regarding their work." Obtains new clients through editors and writers. Will read unsolicited queries or outlines. "Will read unsolicited mss only if preceded by a query as outlined above." Enclose S.A.S.E.

SELIGMANN & COLLIER, 280 Madison Ave., New York NY 10016. Agency Representatives: James Seligmann and Oscar Collier. Established in 1960. Handles novels and nonfiction books. Will consider work of new writers; no minimum sales volume required. Book projects and book mss only. Fantasy of interest but no science fiction. Recent sales for clients: *You Can Profit From a Monetary Crisis* by Harry Browne (Macmillan) and *The Gardener's Catalogue* by Harvey Rottenberg and Tom Riker (Morrow). Query first. Enclose S.A.S.E.

A. FREDERICK SHORR, INC., 1717 No. Highland Ave., Hollywood CA 90028. Agency Representative: A. Frederick Shorr. Established in 1971. Handles motion pictures and TV scripts. 10% standard commission. New clients through "referrals from other clients or friends." Will not read unsolicited mss.

H.E. SHUSTER AND COMPANY, 4930 Wynnefield Ave., Philadelphia PA 19131. Agency Representative: Harold Shuster. Established in 1961. Handles fiction and nonfiction books, magazine stories and articles, stage plays, television scripts and motion pictures. "Specializes in well-written, well-plotted, and well-characterized books." 10% standard commission on American sales, 15% on Canadian sales, 20% on foreign sales. No minimum sales required. "Will read unsolicited ms if writer has attained professional status, is recommended by an editor or author whose judgment we respect." No reading fee charged. Enclose S.A.S.E.

EVELYN SINGER LITERARY AGENCY, P.O. Box 163, Briarcliff Manor NY 10510. Established in 1951. Handles adult and juvenile novels and nonfiction books and magazine fiction and articles. Handles magazine material only in the form of subsidiary rights, or for clients represented in the past. Does not take on short material from new clients. Write, giving pertinent writing background and/or authority in the case of nonfiction. Do not phone. Briefly describe material you would like to send. Type queries; do not write in longhand. Will not read unsolicited mss. Will review contracts for $100 fee. This does not include any negotiation. A written evaluation of the contract will be made. Any resulting consultation will be prorated. 10% standard commission. Will work with writer who has earned $10,000 minimum from past sales. Reads book manuscripts (adult or juvenile, fiction or nonfiction) on recommendation of any professional writer or editor. Writer should contact by letter, giving his background and a description of work before sending ms. "Outline past publication history succinctly, include jackets if available, and describe briefly projects on hand. Do not phone." Will not read unsolicited mss. Enclose S.A.S.E. for response to query.

PHILIP G. SPITZER LITERARY AGENCY, 111-25 76th Ave., Forest Hills NY 11375. Established in 1969. Handles novels, nonfiction books, motion pictures; handles magazine articles and magazine fiction "when the writer is also working on book-length material." Recent sales for clients include *The Sensation* by Norman Keifetz (Atheneum) and *The Other Government: The Unseen Influence of Washington Lawyers* by Mark J. Green (Viking). 10% standard commission. Obtains new clients "primarily through recommendations of editors and established clients." Will read unsolicited queries or outlines. Enclose S.A.S.E. for response to queries.

C. M. STEPHAN, JR., 918 State St., Lancaster PA 17603. Established in 1971. Handles magazine fiction and novels. 10% standard commission. "Writing must display potential or be competitive. New clients obtained through advertising and editorial referral." Will read unsolicited mss for a fee of $10 for short stories, $25 for novels. Enclose S.A.S.E. for return of submissions.

LARRY STERNIG, 2407 N. 44th St., Milwaukee WI 53210. Established in 1953. Handles magazine articles, magazine fiction, juvenile articles, juvenile fiction, novels, nonfiction books. Recent sales for clients include *No Sight Without Stars* by Andre Norton (Atheneum); *The Wild Horse Killers* by Mel Ellis (Holt); *Tower of The Crow* by Dora Polk (McKay). 10% standard commission. Will represent a new writer "only if sent by some editor or valued client." Will not read unsolicited mss.

ELLEN STEVENSON & ASSOCIATES, P.O. Box 76973, Station S, Vancouver, British Columbia, Canada V5R 5T3. Contact: Ellen Stevenson. Established in 1973. 10% commission (Canadian and American), 15% (foreign). Handles magazine articles and fiction, juvenile fiction, novels, nonfiction books, textbooks, stage plays and TV scripts (Canadian). New clients obtained through newspaper ads and reputation from satisfied clients. Will handle new writers if they've studied and practiced the art of writing. Charges fees to beginners for reading and criticizing mss ($15 to $35). Straight commission basis for established writers. List credits. Enclose S.A.S.E.

GUNTHER STUHLMANN, 65 Irving Place, New York NY 10003. Established 1956. Specializes in book fiction and nonfiction. Also, quality juveniles for older age group. 10% standard commission in U.S. and Canada, 15% in Great Britain, 20% elsewhere. Previous sale to national market required. Query first. Enclose S.A.S.E.

TWIN PINES LITERARY AGENCY, 72 Truesdale Dr., Croton-On-Hudson NY 10520. Contact: Marty Lewis. Established in 1970. Magazine articles, fiction, juvenile articles and fiction, novels, nonfiction books, textbooks, motion pictures, stage plays, TV scripts, radio scripts, and syndicated material. "We specialize in motion picture, stage plays and TV scripts. New writers will have to pay reading fee depending on the material submitted. Established writers, no fee. Only requirement is that material be submitted in professional manner ready to be submitted to publishers. All material must be geared toward commercial market." Query first. Enclose S.A.S.E.

J.H. VAN DAELE, 225 E. 57th St., New York NY 10022. Agency Representative: Jacqueline H. Van Daele. Established in 1971. Handles nonfiction books. "I handle only psychiatrically oriented books, including all the behavioral sciences, aimed at the popular market." 10% standard commission. Obtains new clients "through recommendations." To be represented by this agency, a new writer "must be either an M.D. (psychiatrist) or a Ph.D. (psychologist). I only represent professional people. I will read outlines of potential mss only. I also create ideas for books for a higher percentage of commission." Enclose S.A.S.E.

W. B. AGENCY, INC., 156 E 52 St., New York NY 10022. Agency Representatives: Warren Bayless, Roberta Kent. Established in 1969. Specializes in fiction, nonfiction, film rights. "Author and materials must be recommended by competent editor, educator, writer, etc." Query first, Attention: Miss Kent. Enclose S.A.S.E. for response to query. Recent sales include *Raising the Only Child* (Kappelman); *The Money Harvest* (Thomas).

AUSTIN WAHL AGENCY, INC., 332 S. Michigan, Chicago IL 60604. Agency Representatives: Thomas Wahl, Paul Carson, Joel Rittley, Larry Dalicandro. Established in 1935. Handles motion pictures (theatrical and made-for-TV), TV scripts for series currently on the air, novels, nonfiction books (including educational, reference and technical), stage plays, short stories and articles; adult and juvenile material. Especially interested in novels which can arouse motion picture interest. 10% standard commission. New clients by referral and solicitation. Absolutely no unsolicited mss, but will read queries and brief outlines. Enclose S.A.S.E.

JAMES A. WARREN ASSOCIATES, 6257 Hazeltine, Suite 2, Van Nuys CA 91401. Contact James Warren or Barbara Thorburn. Established in 1969. Handles book-length fiction and nonfiction, textbooks, motion picture and TV scripts. No poetry or religious mss. "We are open-minded and willing to look at any good presentation, provided it is professional. Especially interested in previously published writers." 10% domestic, except 15% first sale; 20% foreign. "We are especially interested in good writing and tireless writers who are motivated toward continuing improvement and the building of a worthwhile oeuvre of published works. Equally interested in uncovering new talent; encouraging and working with it. Will read unsolicited queries and outlines. Although we are not a reading-fee agency and do not encourage that business, we will provide readings and critiques upon request for a fee of up to $100, but query first." Enclose S.A.S.E.

A. WATKINS INC., 77 Park Ave., New York NY 10016. Established in 1908. Specializes in all areas except juveniles and poetry. Enclose S.A.S.E.

WRITERS: FREE-LANCE, 426 Pennsylvania Ave., Fort Washington PA 19034. Director: Robert M. Cullers. Secures assignments for writers of all types who can produce the material needed by business, industry, science, technology, education, institutions and government. These assignments include advertising for print, broad-casting and direct mail, speeches, public relations, house organs, annual reports, audiovisual presentations, industrial films, business and educational books. Technical assignments include training manuals, instruction handbooks, control cataloging and all types of documentation. Writers are paid promptly on terms contracted in advance. No speculative writing is requested. Registration for assignments requires qualified writers to send detailed resumes, stressing their specializations. The Writers: Free-Lance network currently consists of over 2,500 writers in cities and towns across the United States, Canada and 50 countries overseas and can cover local writing and photographic assignments for commercial news events. Send resumes and samples which can be kept in writer's file. Enclose S.A.S.E.

MARY YOST ASSOCIATES, 141 E. 55 St., New York NY 10022. Established in 1968. Handles novels and nonfiction. Will not read unsolicited mss. Will read unsolicited queries and outlines. 10% commission on sales. Enclose S.A.S.E.

Contests and Awards

Unless otherwise noted, the following contests and awards are conducted annually. For information on irregular and "one shot" competitions, see the Writer's Market Column in Writer's Digest *magazine.*

Some of the listed contests and awards do not accept entries or nominations direct from writers. They are included because of their national or literary importance. When a competition accepts entries from publishers only, and the writer feels his work meets its requirements, he may wish to remind his publisher to enter his work.

To obtain specific deadline information, required entry blank, or further information, write directly to the address in the individual listing. Enclose a business-sized self-addressed, stamped envelope.

A.I.P.-U.S. STEEL FOUNDATION SCIENCE WRITING AWARD, Press Relations Division, American Institute of Physics, 335 E. 45 St., New York NY 10017. Awards $1,500, a certificate, and a symbolic device to stimulate and recognize distinguished writing that improves public understanding of physics and astronomy. Journalists must be professional writers whose work is aimed at the general public. Write for details and official entry form.

AAAS-WESTINGHOUSE SCIENCE WRITING AWARDS, Grayce A. Finger, 1515 Massachusetts Ave., N.W., Washington DC 20005. Awards three $1,000 prizes to recognize outstanding writing on the natural sciences, and their engineering and technological applications (excluding medicine), in newspapers and general circulation magazines.

HERBERT BAXTER ADAMS PRIZE, Committee Chairman, American Historical Association, 400 A St. S.E., Washington DC 20003. Awards $300 for an author's first book in the field of European history.

AMATEUR POETRY CONTEST, Poetry Press, Editor, Don Peek, Route 1, Box 96-AA, Pittsburg TX 75686. Prizes of $50, $25, and $10 will go to top 3 poems. Poems should be between 4 and 16 lines. Enclose S.A.S.E.

AMERICAN ACADEMY OF FAMILY PHYSICIANS JOURNALISM AWARDS, American Academy of Family Physicians, P.O. Box 8723, Wornall Station, Kansas City MO 64114. Awards a total of $2,000 to members of the press who write medical news and features clearly defining the family physician—his specialty, his interest in health education of the public, and his desire to help solve the medical manpower distribution problem.

AMERICAN DENTAL ASSOCIATION SCIENCE WRITERS AWARD, Science Writers Award Committee, 211 E. Chicago Ave., Chicago IL 60611. Awards $1,000 for best newspaper article and $1,000 for best magazine article which broadens and deepens public understanding of dental disease, dental treatment, or dental research. Write for entry rules.

AMERICAN OPTOMETRIC ASSOCIATION PUBLIC SERVICE AWARDS, Public Information Division, American Optometric Association, 7000 Chippewa St., St. Louis MO 63119. Awards $500 and bronze medallion plaque in each of five categories: Press (newspapers, feature syndicates, wire services), magazine, radio, television, and special recognition. To recognize outstanding print and broadcast news or features on the subject of vision as contributing to a better understanding of the importance of vision and its care; to honor writers of media presentations that focus public attention upon the significance and need for proper vision care and to create increased public and professional interest in programs for the care, improvement and preservation of vision. Published works must be accompanied by a completed official entry form.

AMERICAN OSTEOPATHIC JOURNALISM AWARDS, Journalism Awards Competition, American Osteopathic Association, 212 E. Ohio St., Chicago IL 60611. Awards three $250 prizes to recognize the growing corps of competent journalists who are reporting and interpreting the contributions of osteopathic medicine to the scientific community and the general public.

AMERICAN PSYCHOLOGICAL FOUNDATION NATIONAL MEDIA AWARDS, Mona Marie Wachtel, Public Information Officer, American Psychological Association, 1200 Seventeenth St., N.W., Washington DC 20036. Special citations in five categories (television/film, radio, magazine writing, newspaper reporting, books/monographs) to recognize and encourage outstanding, accurate reporting which increases the public's knowledge and understanding of psychology. A Grand Prix winner will be selected from the winners of the five categories and receive a $1,000 award.

ANIMAL LAW WRITING AWARD, Prof. Henry Mark Holzer, Chairman, Reviewing Committee, Society for Animal Rights, Inc., 400 East 51 St., New York NY 10022. Awards $300 to the author of an exceptionally meritorious published book or article in the field of animal law.

ASCAP-DEEMS TAYLOR AWARDS FOR WRITING ON MUSIC, American Society of Composers, Authors, and Publishers, One Lincoln Plaza, New York NY 10023. Awards four $500 prizes in two categories: best books and best newspaper or magazine articles covering music and/or its creators. Subject matter may be biographical or critical, reportorial or historical, nonfiction only; not an instructional textbook or work of fiction.

AVIATION/SPACE WRITERS ASSOCIATION WRITING AWARDS, Aviation/Space Writers Association, Cliffwood Rd., Chester NJ 07930. Awards $100 and engraved scroll for writing on aviation and space, in six categories: newspapers over 200,000 circulation, newspapers under 200,000 circulation, magazines, television and radio, photography, and nonfiction books.

BANCROFT PRIZES, Secretary, 311 Low, Columbia University, New York NY 10027. Awards three prizes of $4,000 for books in the categories of U.S. international relations, American diplomacy, and biography.

GEORGE LOUIS BEER PRIZE, Committee Chairman, American Historical Association, 400 A St., S.E., Washington DC 20003. Awards $300 for the best first book by a young scholar in the field of European international history since 1895.

STEPHEN VINCENT BENET NARRATIVE POETRY AWARDS, 52 Cranbury Rd., Box 350, Westport CT 06880. Awards $100 first prize, $50 second prize, three $20 third prizes, honorable and special mentions for original, unpublished narrative poems, to honor the poetic tradition of Stephen Vincent Benet.

CLAUDE BERNARD SCIENCE JOURNALISM AWARDS, National Society for Medical Research, Suite 103, 1330 Massachusetts Ave. N.W., Washington DC 20005. Awards $1,000 and a certificate to recognize responsible science reporting which has made a significant contribution to public understanding of basic research in the life sciences, including but not limited to experimental medicine. Articles or series of articles must have appeared in newspapers or magazines of general circulation.

BEST SPORTS STORIES AWARDS, Edward Ehre, 1315 Westport Ln., Sarasota FL 33580. Offers three story prizes of $250 each and two photo prizes of $100 each for sports stories and photos which have appeared in a magazine or newspaper. Story prizes awarded for the best news-coverage story, best news-feature story or column, and best magazine story. Photo prizes awarded for the best feature photo and best action photo.

ALBERT J. BEVERIDGE AWARD, Committee Chairman, American Historical Association, 400 A St., S.E., Washington DC 20003. Awards $5,000 for the best book published in English on American history of the U.S., Canada, and Latin America.

IRMA SIMONTON BLACK AWARD, Book Award Committee, Publications Division, Bank Street College of Education, 610 West 112th St., New York NY 10025. Awards a seal designed by Maurice Sendak and a scroll for an outstanding book published for young children.

HOWARD W. BLAKESLEE AWARDS, Chairman, Managing Committee, American Heart Association, 44 E. 23 St., New York NY 10010. Awards $500 honorarium and a citation to each winning entry, which may be a single article, broadcast, film, or book; a series; or no more than five unrelated pieces. Entries will be judged on the basis of their accuracy and significance, and on the skill and originality with which knowledge concerning the heart and circulatory system and advances in research or in the treatment, care and prevention of cardiovascular disease are translated for the public. Send for official entry blank and more details.

BOLLINGEN PRIZE IN POETRY, Yale University Library, New Haven CT 06520. Biennial award of $5,000 to an American poet whose published book of poetry represents the highest achievement in the field of American poetry.

BOOKS ABROAD/NEUSTADT INTERNATIONAL PRIZE FOR LITERATURE, Media Information Office, University Relations, The University of Oklahoma, 900 Asp Ave., Norman OK 73069. Biennial award of $10,000 to authors of drama, poetry, and fiction. Candidates are chosen by a jury of 12 internationally known writers.

BOWLING WRITING COMPETITION, American Bowling Congress, Public Relations, 5301 S. 76th St., Greendale WI 53129. $1,400 in gift certificate prizes divided equally between the top ten winners in the Feature and Editorial categories for previously published bowling writings. Top prize in each division is $200.

HEYWOOD BROUN AWARD, Broun Award Committee, Newspaper Guild (AFL-CIO, CLC), 1125 15th St., N.W., Washington DC 20005. Awards $1,000 and a citation for outstanding journalistic achievement in the spirit of Heywood Broun, who was distinguished by unceasing devotion to the public interest. All work in the public interest, including photos and cartoons, will receive consideration, particularly if it has helped right a wrong.

EMIL BROWN FUND PREVENTIVE LAW PRIZE AWARDS, Louis M. Brown, Administrator, University of Southern California Law Center, Los Angeles CA 90007. Awards $1,000 for a praiseworthy leading article or book, and $500 for student work in the field of Preventive Law published in a law review, Bar Journal or other professional publication.

BULTMAN AWARD, Chairman, Department of Drama, Loyola University, New Orleans LA 70118. Awards $100 for original, unpublished and unproduced plays under one hour in length, written by college students.

RUSSELL L. CECIL WRITING AWARDS IN ARTHRITIS, The Arthritis Foundation, 1212 Avenue of the Americas, New York NY 10036. Awards $1,000 in each of four categories (newspaper, magazine, radio, and television) to recognize and encourage the writing of news stories, articles and radio and television scripts on the subject of arthritis.

CHILDREN'S BOOK AWARD, Child Study Association of America/Wel-Met, 50 Madison Ave., New York NY 10010. Given to a book for children or young people which deals realistically with problems in their world. The book, published in the past calendar year, must offer an honest and courageous treatment of its theme.

CHRISTOPHER AWARDS, William J. Wilson, Associate Director, 12 E. 48th St., New York NY 10017. Awards bronze medallions for motion pictures (producer, director, writer), television (producer, director, writer), and books (author, editor, illustrator, photographer) to recognize individuals who have used their talents constructively, in the hope that they, and others, will continue to produce high quality works that reflect sound values.

COMMUNITY CHILDREN'S THEATRE OF KANSAS CITY MISSOURI PLAYWRITING FOR CHILDREN AWARD, Mrs. A. J. Sweeney, 2418 W. 71 Terr., Prairie Village KS 66208. Awards $500 for the best drama for children. Write for details. Enclose S.A.S.E.

ALBERT B. COREY PRIZE IN CANADIAN-AMERICAN RELATIONS, Office of the Executive Secretary, American Historical Association, 400 A St., S.E., Washington DC 20003. The Canadian Historical Association and American Historical Association jointly award $1,000 for the best book on the history of Canadian-United States relations, or on the history of both countries.

CLARENCE DAY AWARD, Staff Liaison, ALA Awards Committee, Mrs. Judith F. Krug, American Library Association, 50 E. Huron St., Chicago IL 60611. Awards $1,000, a citation, and a contemporary print to a librarian or another individual who has, through substantial published work such as a book, essay, or published lectures, promoted a love of reading. Such work is to have been published within the 5 calendar years preceding the presentation of the award. Donated by the Association of American Publishers. Write for more information. Enclose S.A.S.E.

DECORATIVE ARTS BOOK AWARD, L. M. Goodman, Coordinator, American Life Foundation and Study Institute, Watkins Glen NY 14891. Given to the author of a book in English which has most advanced the fields of antique collecting and decorative arts appreciation. Submission by publishers only.

THE DEVINS AWARD, University of Missouri Press, Columbia MO 65201. For poetry. Write for submission details.

DISCOVER NIAGARA INTERNATIONAL TRAVEL WRITING AWARD, P.O. Box 1111, Niagara Falls NY 14303. Awards $500 for the best article or series of articles on Niagara as an attraction and travel destination. The entry must have appeared in significant length in a magazine, newspaper, or other publication of general circulation.

JOHN H. DUNNING PRIZE IN AMERICAN HISTORY, Committee Chairman, American Historical Association, 400 A St. S.E., Washington DC 20003. Awards $300 biennially for an outstanding monograph in manuscript or in print on any subject relating to American history.

DUTTON ANIMAL BOOK AWARD, E. P. Dutton and Co., Inc., 201 Park Ave. S., New York NY 10003. Offers a guaranteed minimum $10,000 as an advance against earnings for an original book-length manuscript concerning a living creature (only Man and Plants are excluded as subjects); fiction or nonfiction.

EDUCATION WRITERS AWARD, Mrs. Dixie Lee, American Association of University Professors, Suite 500, One Dupont Circle, Washington DC 20036. Awards $500 and a citation to recognize outstanding interpretive reporting of issues in higher education, through newspapers, magazines, radio, television and films. Write for entry details. Enclose S.A.S.E.

EDUCATOR'S AWARD, Miss Catherine Rathman, Executive Secretary, Delta Kappa Gamma Society, P.O. Box 1589, Austin TX 78767. Awards $1,000 to recognize women and their contribution to education which may influence future directions in the profession. Previously published books may be in the fields of research, philosophy, or any other area of learning which is stimulating and creative.

EPILEPSY FOUNDATION OF AMERICA JOURNALISM AWARD, Epilepsy Foundation of America, 1828 L St. N.W., Suite 406, Washington DC 20036. Awards $500 to the writer of an article or series of articles about epilepsy published in a newspaper or magazine of general circulation or aired on television or radio.

EXPLICATOR PRIZE COMPETITION, *The Explicator,* Virginia Commonwealth University, 901 W. Franklin St., Richmond VA 23284. $200 and a bronze plaque for the best book of *explication de texte* published in the field of English or American literature during the calendar year. Write for submission details.

JOHN K. FAIRBANK PRIZE IN EAST ASIAN HISTORY, Committee Chairman, American Historical Association, 400 A St. S.E., Washington DC 20003. Awards $300 biennially for an outstanding book on the history of China proper, Vietnam, Chinese Central Asia, Manchuria, Mongolia, Korea, or Japan, since the year 1800.

CHARLES W. FOLLETT AWARD, Follett Publishing Co., 1010 W. Washington

Blvd., Chicago IL 60607. Awards $3,000 and royalties for an original manuscript (fiction or nonfiction) for children ages 9 to 12 or for readers 12 years old and older. 25,000 to 35,000 words if geared to the younger group; 40,000 to 60,000 words for ages 12 and older.

THE FORUM AWARD, Atomic Industrial Forum, Inc., Public Affairs and Information Program, 475 Park Ave. S., New York NY 10016. Awards $1,000 and a certificate for an article, series, program, book, or news report that best promotes public understanding of peaceful uses of nuclear energy. When a book, lengthy article or series is submitted, it will be necessary to submit at least five copies.

GEORGE FREEDLEY MEMORIAL AWARD, Dr. Robert M. Henderson, President, Theater Library Association, 111 Amsterdam Ave., New York NY 10023. Awards a plaque for the best published work in the field of theatre published in the United States. Only books related to live performance will be considered. They may be biography, history, criticism, and related fields.

FREEDOMS FOUNDATION AT VALLEY FORGE AWARDS, Awards Administration, Freedoms Foundation at Valley Forge, Valley Forge PA 19481. Awards honor medals, certificates and honor certificates for the most outstanding individual contribution supporting human dignity and the American credo, in fields of journalism, television and radio. Write for further details.

FRIENDS OF AMERICAN WRITERS AWARDS, Mrs. Robert Silver, 125 E. Kathleen Dr., Park Ridge IL 60068. Awards $1,000 for a published book with a midwestern locale or written by a native or resident author of the middle West. Books submitted by publishers only.

CHRISTIAN GAUSS AWARD, Phi Beta Kappa, 1811 Q St., N.W., Washington DC 20009. Awards $2,500 for a book of literary criticism or scholarship published in the United States. Books submitted by publishers only.

GOETHE HOUSE-P.E.N. TRANSLATION PRIZE, P.E.N. American Center, 156 Fifth Ave., New York NY 10010. Awards $500 for the best translation of a contemporary play from the German language, to honor the translator and to facilitate the production of a contemporary foreign play in the United States.

JOHN HANCOCK AWARDS FOR EXCELLENCE IN BUSINESS AND FINANCIAL JOURNALISM, Awards for Excellence, B-21, John Hancock Mutual Life Insurance Co., 200 Berkeley St., Boston MA 02117. Awards $1,000 in six categories to foster increased public knowledge of and interest in business and finance; to recognize editorial contributions to a better understanding of personal money management; to clarify the significance of political and social developments as they relate to the nation's economy; to stimulate discussion and thought by bringing together, in an academic environment, newsmakers, reporters, faculty, and students. Write for more details and official entry form.

CLARENCE H. HARING PRIZE, Committee Chairman, American Historical Association, 400 A St. S.E., Washington DC 20003. Awards $500 every five years to the Latin American who, in the opinion of the committee, has published the most outstanding book on Latin-American history during the preceding five years.

ERNEST HEMINGWAY FOUNDATION AWARD, P.E.N. American Center, 156 Fifth Ave., New York NY 10010. Awards $3,000 for the best first-published novel or first-published collection of short stories in the English language by an American author.

SIDNEY HILLMAN PRIZE AWARD, Sidney Hillman Foundation, Inc., 15 Union Square, New York NY 10003. Awards $500 for outstanding published contributions in nonfiction, fiction, radio and television dealing with themes relating to the ideals which Sidney Hillman held throughout his life. Such themes would include the protection of individual civil liberties, improved race relations, strengthened labor movement, advancement of social welfare, economic security, greater world understanding and related problems.

DON HOLLENBECK AWARD, Professor Richard Petrow, Chairman, Don Hollenbeck Award Competition, Department of Journalism and Mass Communications, Washington Square College of Arts and Sciences, New York University, 1021 Main Bldg., Washington Square, New York NY 10003. Awards $500 for the best newspaper article, magazine article, television or radio script, or book, evaluating the mass media or any particular publication or news organization.

HOUGHTON MIFFLIN LITERARY FELLOWSHIP, Houghton Mifflin Co., 2 Park St., Boston MA 02107. Awards $2,500 grant and $5,000 as an advance against royalties to help authors complete projects of outstanding literary merit. Candidates should submit at least 50 pages of the actual project (fiction or nonfiction), an informal description of its theme and intention, a brief biography, and examples of past work, published or unpublished.

THE HUMANITAS PRIZE, Executive Directors, The Human Family Institute, P.O. Box 861, Pacific Palisades CA 90272. Awards $10,000 for the thirty-minute teleplay, $15,000 for the sixty-minute teleplay, and $25,000 for the teleplay of ninety minutes or longer previously produced on national network commercial television, aired during prime time hours. To promote a greater appreciation of the dignity of the human person, to deepen contemporary man's understanding of himself, of his relationship to the human community, and to his Creator, to aid mankind's search for meaning, freedom and love; to liberate, enrich and unify the human family. Submission must be made by someone other than the writer of the produced play (for example, the program producer). Write for details and entry form.

INGAA-MISSOURI BUSINESS JOURNALISM AWARDS, Lyle E. Harris, Director, Neff Hall, School of Journalism, Colimbia MO 65201. Awards $1,000 in each of four categories to honor excellence in reporting and interpreting business, economic, trade and financial news. To encourage a greater public understanding of the American economic system through coverage of U.S. business in newspapers and magazines. Write for complete details and entry form.

IOWA SCHOOL OF LETTERS AWARD FOR SHORT FICTION, English-Philosophy Bldg., University of Iowa, Iowa City IA 52242. Awards $1,000 for a book-length collection of short fiction by a writer who has not yet published a volume of fiction.

JACKSONVILLE UNIVERSITY PLAYWRITING CONTEST, Davis Sikes, Director, College of Fine Arts, Jacksonville University, Jacksonville FL 32211. Awards $250 and premiere production of play, plus playwright's expenses in residence, for original one-act and full-length plays and musicals. Write for contest rules. Enclose S.A.S.E.

JEWISH BOOK COUNCIL AWARD FOR A BOOK OF JEWISH THOUGHT, Philip Goodman, National Jewish Welfare Board, 15 E. 26 St., New York NY 10010. Awards $500 and a citation to the author of a published book dealing with some aspect of Jewish thought, past or present, which combines knowledge, clarity of thought, and literary merit.

JEWISH BOOK COUNCIL AWARD FOR A BOOK ON THE NAZI HOLOCAUST, National Jewish Welfare Board, 15 E. 26 St., New York NY 10010. Awards $500 and a citation to the author of a published nonfiction book dealing with some aspects of the Nazi holocaust period. Books published in English, Yiddish, and Hebrew are acceptable.

JEWISH BOOK COUNCIL AWARD FOR BOOKS OF POETRY, Philip Goodman, National Jewish Welfare Board, 15 E. 26 St., New York NY 10010. Awards $500 and a citation to the author of a book of poetry of Jewish interest. Books published in English, Yiddish, and Hebrew are acceptable.

JEWISH BOOK COUNCIL JUVENILE AWARD, National Jewish Welfare Board, 15 E. 26 St., New York NY 10010. Awards $500 and a citation to the author of a published Jewish juvenile book.

JEWISH BOOK COUNCIL WILLIAM AND JANICE EPSTEIN FICTION AWARD, Philip Goodman, National Jewish Welfare Board, 15 E. 26 St., New York NY 10010. Awards $500 and a citation to the author of a published book of fiction of Jewish interest, either a novel or a collection of short stories, which combines high literary merit with an affirmative expression of Jewish values.

FRANK KELLEY MEMORIAL AWARD, American Association of Petroleum Landmen, P.O. Box 1984, Fort Worth TX 76101. Awards $250 and a plaque in appreciation for excellence in reporting oil and gas industry information to the general public. Previously published newspaper articles only.

JOHN T. KELLEY MEMORIAL AWARD FOR PLAYWRITING, Theatre East, 12457 Ventura Blvd., Studio City CA 91604. Awards $350 and full production of the selected work at Theatre East in Los Angeles CA. To be considered, a work must be unproduced and constitute a full evening in theatre.

THE ROBERT F. KENNEDY JOURNALISM AWARDS, Committee Chairman, 1035 30th St., N.W., Washington DC 20007. The awards honor journalists and broadcasters whose work has illuminated the problems of the disadvantaged in the United States. Write for complete details and entry form.

FLEDA KINNEMAN MEMORIAL PRIZE, Wauneta Hagelman, 5532 W. Monterosa, Phoenix AZ 85031. Awards $15, $10, and $5 for original poems for children. Send original and one copy. 28 line limit.

HAROLD MORTON LANDON TRANSLATION AWARD, The Academy of American Poets, 1078 Madison Ave., New York NY 10028. Awards $1,000 biennially to American poet for a published translation of poetry from any language into English. Translation may be a book-length poem, collection of poems, or a verse drama translated into verse.

JERRY LEWIS MDA WRITING AWARD, Horst S. Petzall, Director, Department of Public Health Education, Muscular Dystrophy Association, Inc., 810 Seventh Ave., New York NY 10019. Awards $1,000, $500, and $250, along with engraved medallions, to those writers whose works are considered most effective in stimulating public interest in the fight against muscular dystrophy and related diseases of the neuromuscular system. Previously published articles, feature stories, editorials or poetry, as well as commentaries, documentaries, dramas, or public-service announcements aired on radio or television, are eligible.

DAVID D. LLOYD PRIZE, Chairman of the Committee, Professor Thomas C. Blaisdell, Jr., Department of Political Science, 210 Barrows Hall, University of California, Berkeley CA 94720. Awards $1,000 biennially for the best published book on the period of the presidency of Harry S. Truman. Books must deal primarily and substantially with some aspect of the political, economic, and social development of the U.S., principally between April 12, 1945 and January 20, 1953, or of the public career of Harry S. Truman.

THE GERALD LOEB AWARDS, Graduate School of Management, UCLA, 405 Hilgard Ave., Los Angeles CA 90024. Awards $1,000 and a plaque for articles in newspapers and magazines, syndicated columns or editorials, radio and television programs. To further public understanding of business finance and the economy, to encourage high standards of responsibility, accuracy, clarity and insight in the writing and interpretation of news on investments and finance, and to reward writers and publications for distinguished business and financial journalism. Write for entry rules and required entry blank.

HARRY J. LOMAN FOUNDATION COMMUNICATIONS AWARD, P.O. Box 566, Media PA 19063. Awards $1,000 for the best written communication promoting better understanding of the economic and social functions of insurance. Eligible are editorials, articles or series published in a national business or financial publication directed toward the national business community, not primarily the insurance industry.

MAN IN HIS ENVIRONMENT BOOK AWARD, E. P. Dutton and Co., Inc., 201 Park Ave. S., New York NY 10003. Offers a guaranteed minimum $10,000 as an advance against earnings for an original single work of adult nonfiction submitted, dealing with the past, present or future of man in his environment, natural or man-made.

HOWARD R. MARRARO PRIZE IN ITALIAN HISTORY, Office of the Executive Secretary, American Historical Association, 400 A St. S.E., Washington DC 20003. Awards $500 for a book or article which treats Italian history in any epoch of Italian cultural history, or of Italian-American relations. Write for submission details.

JOHN MASEFIELD MEMORIAL AWARD, Poetry Society of America, 15 Gramercy Park S., New York NY 10003. Awards $500 for an unpublished narrative poem written in English, not exceeding 200 lines, in memory of the late Poet Laureate of England. Write for submission details.

EDWARD J. MEEMAN CONSERVATION AWARDS, Scripps-Howard Foundation, 200 Park Ave., New York NY 10017. Awards prizes totalling $10,000 to newspapermen and women on U.S. newspapers in recognition of outstanding work in the cause of conservation, including control of pollution, future technological developments, overpopulation, recycling, conservation of soil, forests, vegetation, wildlife, open space and scenery.

FREDERICK G. MELCHER BOOK AWARD, Doris Pullen, Director, 25 Beacon St., Boston MA 02108. Awards $1,000 and bronze medallion for a work published in America judged to be the most significant contribution to religious liberalism. Books submitted by publishers only.

FRANK LUTHER MOTT-KAPPA TAU ALPHA RESEARCH AWARD IN JOURNALISM, Dr. William H. Taft, Chief, Central Office KTA, School of Journalism, University of Missouri, Columbia MO 65201. Awards $200 and hand-lettered scroll for the best book published during the previous year.

NATIONAL ASSOCIATION OF BANK WOMEN AWARD FOR DISTINGUISHED JOURNALISM, Mary Margaret Carberry, Public Relations Director, 111 E. Wacker Dr., Chicago IL 60601. Awards $300 and a plaque for a by-lined interpretive article or related series of articles focusing on executive women in banking, their contributions to and place in the industry. Write for complete information and entry blanks.

NATIONAL ASSOCIATION OF REALTORS CREATIVE REPORTING CONTEST, Sue Davidson, Public Relations Department, 155 E. Superior St., Chicago IL 60611. Awards $200, $100, and $50 plus plaques for winning articles about local real estate problems involving real estate that also is a problem of national concern, consumer information, real estate as an investment, or real estate column on a continuing basis. Articles must have been published in newspapers and magazines going to the general public.

NATIONAL BOOK AWARDS, 1564 Broadway, Room 822, New York NY 10036. Awards $1,000 for literature written or translated by American citizens and published in the U.S. to honor outstanding creative writing by Americans and bring national attention to the literary arts and their contribution to the nation's cultural life. Categories include arts and letters, biography, contemporary affairs, children's books, fiction, history, poetry, philosophy and religion, the sciences, and translation. Will not accept submissions from authors.

THE NATIONAL FOUNDATION FOR HIGHWAY SAFETY AWARDS, P.O. Box 3059, Westville Station, New Haven CT 06515. Awards U.S. Savings Bond and plaques for specified themes relating to driving safety. Offered to editors, reporters, cartoonists, television and radio directors. Write for details and current contest theme.

NATIONAL HEADLINER AWARDS, Elaine Frayne, Secretary, National Head-liners Club, Convention Hall, Atlantic City NJ 08401. Awards the Headliner Medal for outstanding achievement in journalism. Open to all material published or broadcast during the year in newspapers, magazines, syndicates, radio and television, to recognize men and women who exemplify the responsibilities and traditions of the journalistic profession.

NATIONAL HISTORICAL SOCIETY BOOK PRIZE IN AMERICAN HISTORY, Board of Judges, Box 1831, Harrisburg PA 17105. Awards $1,000 for a first book published by an author, to encourage promising historians, young and old, in producing the sound but readable history that is so necessary for portraying our past to the general public.

NATIONAL INSTITUTE OF ARTS AND LETTERS AWARDS, Margaret M. Mills, Executive Director, National Institute of Arts and Letters, 633 W. 155 St., New York NY 10032. Annual awards include the Rosenthal Award ($2,000 for the best novel of the year which, though not a commercial success, is a literary achievement), the National Institute and American Academy Awards ($3,000 awarded to ten nonmembers to further their creative work), and Morton Dauwen Zabel Award ($2,000 to a poet, writer of fiction, or critic, in rotation). None of the awards may be applied for by individuals.

NATIONAL SOCIETY OF PROFESSIONAL ENGINEERS ANNUAL JOUR-NALISM AWARDS, Leonard J. Arzt, Director of Public Relations, National Society of Professional Engineers, 2029 K St. N.W., Washington DC 20006. Awards $500, $300, and $200 to newspaper writers who make the most significant contribution (article or series) to public knowledge and understanding about the role of engineers and creative technology in contemporary American life. Articles should deal with engineering subject matters as distinguished from science.

ALLAN NEVINS PRIZE, Professor Kenneth T. Jackson, Secretary-Treasurer, Society of American Historians, 706 Hamilton Hall, Columbia University, New York NY 10027. Awards $1,000 and publication of winning manuscript for the best written doctoral dissertation in the field of American history, dealing historically with American arts, literature, and science, as well as biographical studies of Americans in any walk of life.

CATHERINE L. O'BRIEN JOURNALISM AWARD, Room 1100, 110 E. 59 St., New York NY 10022. Awards $500, $300 and $200 to winners, plus journalism scholarships to students selected by winners. Award is provided for achievement in women's interest newspaper reporting to the individual writer who authors a newspaper story or series, which is of greatest interest and significance to the American woman. Write for entry blank.

OVERSEAS PRESS CLUB OF AMERICA NEWS AWARDS, Hotel Biltmore, 55 E. 43 St., New York NY 10017. Awards $500, $250, scrolls and medals, depending on classification of entry. Best reporting from abroad, best interpretation of foreign affairs, best radio documentary on foreign affairs, and other classifications. Write for required entry blank and complete details about classifications and awards.

P.E.N. TRANSLATION PRIZE, Chairman, Translation Committee, P.E.N. American Center, 156 Fifth Ave., New York NY 10010. Awards $1,000 for the best translation into English from any language published in the United States. Technical, scientific, or reference works are not eligible. Sponsored by the Book-of-the-Month Club.

FRANCIS PARKMAN PRIZE, Professor Kenneth T. Jackson, Secretary, Society of American Historians, 706 Hamilton Hall, Columbia University, New York NY 10027. Awards $500 and a bronze medal to recognize the author who best epitomizes the Society's purpose—the writing of history with literary distinction as well as sound scholarship. Books must deal with the colonial or national history of the United States. Books submitted by publishers only.

THE DREW PEARSON PRIZE FOR EXCELLENCE IN INVESTIGATIVE REPORTING, The Drew Pearson Foundation, 1156 15 St. N.W., Washington DC 20005. Awards $5,000 for significant investigative reporting by newspaper reporters, authors of books and magazine articles and journalists involved in radio and television.

PENNEY-MISSOURI MAGAZINE AWARDS, School of Journalism, University of Missouri-Columbia, Columbia MO 6520.. Awards $1,000 in each of the following categories: contemporary living, consumerism, health, personal life style, expanding opportunities, and excellence in smaller magazines. Write for complete details and required entry form.

PFIZER AWARD, c/o *Isis,* Editorial Office, Smithsonian Institution, Washington DC 20560. Awards $650 to an American scholar for the best published work related to the history of science.

EDGAR ALLAN POE AWARDS, Mystery Writers of America, Inc., 105 E. 19 St., New York NY 10003. Awards Edgar Allan Poe statuettes in each of nine categories: best mystery novel published in America, best first mystery novel by an American author, best fact crime book, best juvenile mystery, best paperback mystery, best mystery short story, best mystery motion picture, best television mystery, and best mystery book jacket.

THE POETRY CENTER DISCOVERY-THE NATION CONTEST, The Poetry Center of the 92nd St. YM-YWHA, 1395 Lexington Ave., New York NY 10028. Awards $50 to each of four winners, poets whose works have not yet been published in book form. Write for details.

GEORGE POLK MEMORIAL AWARDS, Professor Jacob H. Jaffe, Awards Curator, Department of Journalism, Long Island University, Brooklyn NY 11201. Awards bronze plaques and special citations to distinguished reporting, writing, editing, photography and production manifested through newspapers, magazines, books and radio/television. Works that express initiative, courage, perception and style, particularly in local, national and foreign coverage, community service and criticism.

PRIZE IN PHOTOGRAPHIC HISTORY, Prize Committee, Photographic Historical Society of New York, Box 1839, Radio City Station, New York NY 10019. Awards $100 to an individual who has written, edited, or produced an original work dealing with the history of photography. Books, magazine articles, monographs, slide sequences, television programs, radio programs, exhibitions, or motion pictures eligible.

PULITZER PRIZES, Secretary, Advisory Board on the Pulitzer Prizes, 702 Journalism, Columbia University, New York NY 10027. Awards $1,000 in categories of journalism, letters, and music for distinguished work by United States newspapers, and for distinguished achievement in literature.

PUTNAM AWARDS, G. P. Putnam's Sons, 200 Madison Ave., New York NY 10016. Awards $7,500 advance against royalties for outstanding fiction and nonfiction book manuscripts not less than 65,000 words.

ERNIE PYLE MEMORIAL AWARD, Scripps-Howard Foundation, 200 Park Ave., New York NY 10017. Awards $1,000 and a plaque for newspaper writing which exemplifies the style, warmth, and craftsmanship of Ernie Pyle.

REGINA MEDAL, Catholic Library Association, 461 W. Lancaster Ave., Haverford PA 19041. Awards a silver medal for the writing of good literature for children.

ST. LAWRENCE AWARD FOR FICTION, *Fiction International*, Department of English, St. Lawrence University, Canton NY 13617. Awards $1,000 to the author of an outstanding first collection of short fiction published by an American publisher during the current year. Editors, writers, agents, readers, and publishers are invited to suggest or submit eligible books.

ROBERT LIVINGSTON SCHUYLER PRIZE, Committee Chairman, American Historical Association, 400 A St. S.E., Washington DC 20003. Awards $500 every five years for recognition of the best work in the field of Modern British, British Imperial, and British Commonwealth history written by an American citizen.

SCIENCE IN SOCIETY JOURNALISM AWARDS, Administrative Secretary, National Association of Science Writers, Box H, Sea Cliff NY 11579. Awards $1,000 and an engraved medallion to recognize investigation and interpretive reporting about physical sciences and the life sciences and their impact for good and bad. Write for complete details and entry blank.

SERGEL DRAMA PRIZE, The Charles H. Sergel Drama Prize, The University of Chicago Theatre, 5706 S. University Ave., Chicago IL 60637. Awards $1,500 biennially for best original play, plus production of the play by The University of Chicago Theatre. Write for details and entry blank.

SIGMA DELTA CHI AWARDS IN JOURNALISM, 35 E. Wacker Dr., Suite 3108, Chicago IL 60601. Awards bronze medallions and plaques in sixteen categories for outstanding achievements in journalism during the calendar year. Write for details and required entry form.

THE SMOLAR AWARD, Council of Jewish Federations and Welfare Funds, Inc., 315 Park Ave. S., New York NY 10010. Awards a plaque to recognize outstanding journalists in North America whose work appears in English language newspapers substantially involved in the coverage of Jewish communal affairs and issues in the United States and Canada. Write for details and required entry form.

SOCIETY OF COLONIAL WARS AWARD, Awards Committee, 122 E. 58 St., New York NY 10022. Awards bronze medallion and citation to recognize contributions of outstanding excellence in the field of literature, drama, music or art relative to colonial Americana (1607-1775).

SPUR AWARDS, Western Writers of America, Inc., Nellie S. Yost, Secretary, 1505 West D St., North Platte NE 69101. Awards the Spur Award Trophy for the best western nonfiction book, western novel, western juvenile nonfiction book, western juvenile fiction book, western television script, motion picture script, and western short material. Write for current details and submission rules.

STANLEY DRAMA AWARD, Wagner College, Staten Island NY 10301. Awards $500 for an original full-length play or musical which has not been professionally produced or received tradebook publication. Consideration will also be given to a series of two or three thematically connected one-act plays. Write for applications.

THOMAS L. STOKES AWARD, The Washington Journalism Center, 2401 Virginia Ave. N.W., Washington DC 20037. Awards $1,000 and a citation for the best analysis, reporting or comment appearing in a daily newspaper on the general subject of development, use and conservation of energy and other natural resources in the public interest, and protection of the environment.

THE WALKER STONE AWARDS FOR EDITORIAL WRITING, Scripps-Howard Foundation, 200 Park Ave., New York NY 10017. Awards $1,000 and a certificate for first prize, and $500 honorable mention prize to newspaper men and women in the field of editorial writing, exemplifying general excellence, forcefulness of writing to a purpose, effectiveness as measured by results, and importance of the expression in the public interest.

JESSE STUART CONTEST, *Seven*, 115 South Hudson, Oklahoma City OK 73102. Awards $25, $15, $10, and $5 for the best unpublished poems in the Jesse Stuart tradition; any form or free verse; any length. Write for submission details.

CHARLES S. SYDNOR AWARD, Dr. Charles P. Roland, Committee Chairman, Department of History, University of Kentucky, Lexington KY 40506. Awards $500 biennially for an outstanding published book in the field of Southern history.

THEATRE ARTS CORPORATION PLAYWRITING CONTEST, Robert Garrison, President, 669 Canyon Rd., Santa Fe NM 87501. Awards $500 for original plays in each of five categories: straight plays, musicals, plays in verse, plays in mime and plays for children. The contest is supported by the National Endowment for the Arts in Washington DC.

THE PAUL TOBENKIN MEMORIAL AWARD, Graduate School of Journalism, Columbia University, New York NY 10027. Awards $250 and a certificate for outstanding achievement in the field of newspaper writing in the fight against racial and religious hatred, intolerance, discrimination and every form of bigotry.

UNITED STATES AWARD, International Poetry Forum's United States Award, University of Pittsburgh Press, Pittsburgh PA 15213. Awards $2,000 and publication of the winning manuscript by University of Pittsburgh Press. Entries must be original poetry in English and at least forty-eight typewritten pages.

UNITED STATES INDUSTRIAL COUNCIL EDITORIAL AWARDS COMPETITION, 918 Stahlman Bldg., Nashville TN 37201. Awards $250, $150, and $100 for the three editorials, published in a daily or weekly newspaper, which best interpret the spirit and goals of the free enterprise system in the United States and which describe and analyze the achievements of this system.

EDWARD LEWIS WALLANT BOOK AWARD, Dr. Lothar Kahn, Central Connecticut College, New Britain CT 06150. Awards $125 and citation for a creative work of fiction published during the current year which has significance for the American Jew.

WATUMULL PRIZE IN THE HISTORY OF INDIA, Committee Chairman, American Historical Association, 400 A St. S.E., Washington DC 20003. Awards $1,000 biennially for the best book originally published in the United States on any phase of the history of India.

W. D. WEATHERFORD AWARD, Thomas Parrish, Chairman of the Award Committee, Appalachian Center, CPO 2336, Berea KY 40403. Awards $500 and

$200 for published work that best illustrates the problems, personalities and unique qualities of the Appalachian South. Published works submitted may be fact, fiction, or poetry, any length, from magazine article or story length to book length.

WALT WHITMAN AWARD, The Academy of American Poets, 1078 Madison Ave., New York NY 10028. Award ensures publication of winning poet's first book of poems and carries a cash prize of $1,000. Entrants must be citizens of the U.S. who have not published a book of poetry, except in a limited, private, or subsidized small edition. The Award is supported by the Copernicus Society of America. Write for entry form.

WILMETTE CHILDREN'S THEATRE PLAYWRITING CONTEST, 7th and Laurel, Wilmette IL 60091. Awards $250 and $150 for the winning original plays, to encourage authors to increase the material available for production with child actors or with both child actors and adults.

THOMAS J. WILSON PRIZE, Harvard University Press, 79 Garden St., Cambridge MA 02138. Awards $500 to the author of a first book by a beginning author accepted by Harvard University Press and judged outstanding in content, style, and mode of presentation.

WOODROW WILSON BOOK AWARD, American Political Science Association, 1527 New Hampshire Ave., N.W., Washington DC 20036. Awards $1,000 and Woodrow Wilson Inaugural Medal for a prize-winning book which perpetuates the spirit of Woodrow Wilson's writing, to encourage significant research and reflection in the field of politics, government, and international relations.

LeROY WOLFE WRITING AWARDS, Cystic Fibrosis Foundation, 3379 Peachtree Rd. N.E., Atlanta GA 30326. Awards $1,000 in each of two categories: magazine and newspaper. To recognize outstanding writing of news and feature stories on cystic fibrosis and other children's lung-damaging diseases. Write for details and entry blank.

AUDREY WOOD AWARD IN PLAYWRITING, Kenneth Baker, Director of Theater, The American University, Washington DC 20016. Awards $500 and production of play for the best original (unproduced) script of any length.

CAPTAIN DONALD T. WRIGHT AWARD, Edmund C. Hasse, Assistant Professor, Journalism, Southern Illinois University at Edwardsville, Edwardsville IL 62025. Awards engraved bronze plaques to writers, photographers, producers and directors in the various mass media who have contributed significantly to public understanding and appreciation of our waterways resources. Published materials, whether a series of newspaper articles, photo essays, or books may be about river transportation, recreation, pollution, new inland and intercoastal waterways development.

WRITER'S DIGEST CREATIVE WRITING CONTEST. Write *Writer's Digest*, 9933 Alliance Rd., Cincinnati OH 45242. Awards 300 prizes worth over $10,000 (in cash value) for the best article, short story, and poetry entries. Deadline: midnight, May 31.
Nonfiction, Fiction, and Poetry: All entries must be original, unpublished, and not previously submitted to a *Writer's Digest* contest. Length: short story, 2,000 words maximum; article, 2,500 words maximum; poetry, 16 lines maximum. Entries must be typewritten, double-spaced, on 8½x11 paper with the name and address in the upper left corner. An entry form must accompany each entry. Each contestant is entitled to submit one entry in each category. All entries may be submitted elsewhere after they are sent to *Writer's Digest*. No acknowledgement will be made of receipt of mss. Mss will not be returned and enclosure of S.A.S.E. will disqualify the entry. Announcement of this contest is made yearly in the January through April issues of *Writer's Digest*.

WRITERS GUILD OF AMERICA WEST AWARDS, Allen Rivkin, Public Relations, Writers Guild of America West, 8955 Beverly Blvd., Los Angeles CA 90048. Awards plaques in screen, television, and radio categories for best written scripts.

WRITING CATEGORY AWARD, Academy Awards, Academy of Motion Pictures Arts and Sciences, 9038 Melrose Ave., Los Angeles CA 90069.

Gag and Humor Markets

Markets in this section include information about cartoonists who are looking for gags, as well as other markets for humorous material. Markets for cartoons may be found in Writer's Yearbook *and* Artist's Market. *Submissions to cartoonists should be made on 3x5 slips of paper. Briefly suggest the scene and add the gagline. For convenience in identifying the gag, include some identifying code number at the upper left-hand side of the gag slip. Your name and address should be typed on the reverse side of the gag slip in the upper left-hand corner.*

It should be noted that payment is not made for cartoon gags until the cartoonist has sold the cartoon and received his payment. Most of the listings for cartoonists indicate the number of gags they will consider as a single submission. The usual average is 10 to 20. Cartoonists usually return gags in 1 to 3 weeks. Individual listings cite the variations in reporting time, but cartoonists may want to keep ideas they've converted into cartoons for many years. They try to get them circulated everywhere, and in some cases, they may even resubmit them.

Originality is essential, but switching with a fresh idea is allowable. Allowances are made for coincidence since many gag men frequently come up with similar ideas. But submissions of "many that have been done before" will "turn off" the knowledgeable cartoonist and editor.

RAE AVENA, 36 Winslow Rd., Trumbull CT 06611. Cartoonist since 1965. Likes to see all types of gags. Has sold to *National Enquirer, New York Times,* and Pyramid Publications (paperbacks). "Gagwriters should send around 12 gags. Keep descriptions short." Pays 25% commission. Bought about 6 gags from gagwriters last year. Returns rejected material "as soon as possible—no more than 1 week later." Enclose S.A.S.E. for return of submissions.

NICHOLAS F. BOHN, 31373 Mound Rd., Apt. D, Bldg. 11, Warren MI 48092. Cartoonist since 1952. Interested in gags for cartoons, ideas for wrestling girl cartoon stories and horror stories; vampires and so on. Sold to *Humorama, California Supreme, Berlesk Publications,* Donald Bradford, a collector of cartoons, and others. Wants batches of 6 to 12 gags. Pays 25% commission, or $12.50 and up. Bought about 175 gags from gagwriters last year. Illustrates gags for writers at the rate of $2 per full (8½x11) page cartoon, and puts the writer's name on the drawing. No orders accepted for less than 5 cartoons. Is interested in ghosting a strip or single panel feature. Will send a sample cartoon to a gagwriter for $1. Returns rejected material immediately. Enclose S.A.S.E.

DOROTHY BOND ENTERPRISES, 2450 N. Washtenaw Ave., Chicago IL 60647. Syndicated cartoonist since 1944. "We carefully look at every submission. We want good, funny gags with a new slant and sell to top paying markets. Please, no pornography, no cannibal, monkey or elephant gags. Keep your gags brief. Submit on small, numbered cards, with self-addressed stamped envelope. If we sell your gag, we send you 40% of the sale price the same day we get the payment. If we reject your gag, we send it back to you within 3 days after receipt, without fail. You're important to us." Bought about 200 gags from freelancers last year. Unsold gags are returned within 3 months. Enclose S.A.S.E. for return of submissions.

BILL BOYNANSKY, 230 West 76 St., New York NY 10023. Cartoonist since 1936. Interested in general, sexy, girlie, family, children's and medical gags. Also general captionless gags. Will give full details to writer about trade and professional journal cartooning interests. "I will consider any and all new ideas but, please, save your old, old rejects! Currently doing a dog panel, syndicated, and would be grateful to see lots of funny ones with any or all kinds of dog situations. No rough stuff. Gags should be brief as possible, in wordage—I prefer to see 15 to 20 at one time and will not consider gags that have made the rounds. I am especially interested in seeing original ideas for comic strips, daily panel for syndication. Also, in humorous greeting card ideas. All material submitted to me must be original, professionally done or the writer is wasting his time. Please include age, occupation and list of sales in the past year. I never return unsold gags. All the gagwriter can expect is a check, in the event of a sale." Reports within 3 or 4 days; most of the time, the very same day. Pays 25% for regular gags; 35% for captionless. Bought between 200 and 300 gags last year. New York City writers contact by phone anytime after 2 P.M. at: 212-787-2520. Enclose S.A.S.E. for return of submissions.

JOE BUSCIGLIO, 420 W. North Bay, Tampa FL 33603. Cartoonist since 1943. Query first. State experience and if you are currently selling. General and family gags only. No sex. Pays 25% commission on sale. Currently selling to newspapers, trade journals, and house organs; also "ad" type art and some editorial panels. Will return promptly if material (gags) not adequate. Enclose S.A.S.E. No returns otherwise.

BOB CANNAVA, 33 Myrtlewood Lane, Willingboro NJ 08046. Cartoonist since 1971. Interested in general, family, medical trade gags. Sophisticated *New Yorker/ Cosmo* type. Also captionless sight gags; medical (from doctor's viewpoint) and general. Prefers to see 10 to 15 in a batch. Pays 25% commission. Returns same day in most cases, if material not suitable. May hold unsold gags up to 1 year. Bought approximately 50 gags last year from freelancers. Has sold to *National Enquirer, Medical Economics, Writer's Digest, Parade, Boys' Life.* Enclose S.A.S.E. for return of submissions.

COMEDY UNLIMITED, 343 Hearst Ave., San Francisco CA 94112. Contact: Jim Curtis. "We are always looking for original one-liners tailored especially for any of the following: radio announcers, public speakers, singers, comedians, magicians, or jugglers. We also buy fresh, new premise ideas for unique and creative standup comedy monologues as well as skits involving two or three people, plus clever and original sight gags, bits, and pieces of business. Since we build everything from night club acts to humorous corporate speeches, it would be advisable to send a S.A.S.E. and request a current projects list to find out exactly what we're most interested in buying during any given quarter. Keep in mind we are exclusively concerned with material intended for oral presentation." If S.A.S.E. is not enclosed with submission, all material will be destroyed after being considered, except items purchased. Pays $1 to $3 per line, on acceptance. Reports in 2 weeks.

EUGENE CRAIG, *Columbus Dispatch,* 34 S. Third St., Columbus OH 43215. Interested in batches of family gags, with accent on feminine foibles. "I want original cartoon gags—visual gags where part of the humor is in the drawing, not a one-liner with the humor in the words and the picture superfluous. No one-liners from TV." Submit any number of gags in a batch. Pays $3 each. Bought about 50 gags from gagwriters last year. Returns rejected material at once. Enclose S.A.S.E. for return of submissions.

A. CRAMER, 1909 Quentin Rd., Brooklyn NY 11229. Cartoonist since 1942. Wants family gags. Gags must have funny situations. Sells to the major markets. Prefers batches of 15 to 20. Pays 25% commission. Enclose S.A.S.E. for return of submissions.

CREATIVE CARTOON SERVICE, 3109 West Schubert Ave., Chicago IL 60647. Contact: Peter Vaszilson. Cartoonist since 1965. "Creative Cartoon Service is a cartoon agency that channels the work of over 42 cartoonists to major and minor markets. We are seeking gagwriters to assist our various cartoonists. Write us, stating qualifications." Pays 25% commission, "unless gagwriters can prove themselves otherwise." Enclose S.A.S.E. for return of submissions and response to queries.

DON CRESCI, 7 Jeanette St., Mocanaqua PA 18655. Cartoonist since 1965. Interested in general, medical, grocery slant (manager's viewpoint), offbeat, office, sophisticated, girlie slant, fishing, and golf gags, for use in all types of publications. Sold to *Medical Economics, Argosy, Saturday Evening Post, Progressive Grocer* and *Wall Street Journal.* Pays 30% commission. Returns rejected material same day received. Enclose S.A.S.E.

THOMAS W. DAVIE, 1407 S. Tyler, Tacoma WA 98405. Cartoonist since 1960. Interested in general gags, medicals, mild girlies, sports (hunting and fishing), business and travel gags. Gags should be typed on 3x5 slips. Prefers batches of 5 to 25. Sold to *Medical Economics, Sports Afield,* King Features, *Dugent, Chevron USA, Rotarian* and many others. 25% commission. Returns rejected material within 4 weeks. Enclose S.A.S.E.

GEORGE DOLE, P.O. Box 1396, Portland ME 04104. Cartoonist since 1952. Interested in "general situation gags." Has sold to *Playboy, Better Homes and Gardens, Argosy.* Pays 25% commission. Returns rejected material in 1 week. Enclose S.A.S.E. for return of submissions.

JAMES ESTES, 1916 Karen, Amarillo TX 79106. "Primarily interested in seeing good, funny material of a general nature. Most themes are acceptable, but the usual taboos apply. Submit on 3x5 cards or paper, 10 to 20 gags per submission; clear, concise ideas set down without excessive wordiness. Wholesome, family, general material wanted. I don't do sexy, girlie cartoons at all and it's a waste of gagwriters' postage to send that type gag." Has been selling cartoons for 3 years. Currently selling to *Changing Times, Reader's Digest, Medical Economics, Boys' Life, National Enquirer* and numerous others, including several farm magazines, horse and western magazines, medical and dental magazines. Returns rejected material as quickly as possible, usually in 2 to 3 days. Pays 25% of what cartoon sells for. Enclose S.A.S.E. for return of submissions.

MAL GORDON, 7 Elmwood St., Worcester MA 01602. Cartoonist since 1955. Interested in gags for cartoons for major or middle markets; no longer buying for minor house organs, trade journals, or consumers. "Gags must be good enough for at least $25 markets before I'll draw it up." 25% commission, when cartoon is sold. Sold to *Golf Digest, Writer's Digest, ADA News,* and *American Painting Contractor.* Reports in 10 days. Enclose S.A.S.E.

CHARLES HENDRICK, JR., Old Fort Ave., Kennebunkport ME 04046. Cartoonist since 1942. Interested in general and family gags. Main subjects are highway safety. No sex gags. Gagwriters are presently overworking the risque gags. Prefers batches of 6 to 10. Pays 35% commission. Returns unwanted material in a few days. May hold unsold gags up to 3 months. Bought 30 to 40 gags last year. Enclose S.A.S.E. for return of submission.

DAVID R. HOWELL, 675 10th St., Lebanon OR 97355. Seeks gags suitable for trade journals, in batches of 8 or more. Sold to *American Drycleaner, Horse & Rider, Easyriders Magazine, Salesman's Opportunity,* and *Cat Enterprises* (Sex on Sex). Also need medicals. Most gags should be visually funny. 25% commission, with raises up to 30%. Returns rejected gags same day as received. Will send sample cartoon to gagwriter for $1. Enclose S.A.S.E.

HUMOR HOUSE, Box F-178 Brightmoor Station, Detroit MI 48223. Interested in gags and cartoon roughs on the following themes: hospital-medical, banking, religious, students and teachers in elementary and secondary schools. Humor service for specialized publications and advertisers. Sold to over 50 medical publications last year. Pays $5 to $10 for gags, $15 to $20 for inked cartoon roughs within 2 weeks after acceptance. Buys all rights. Returns rejected material in 2 weeks. Enclose S.A.S.E.

LARRY "KAZ" KATZMAN, 101 Central Park West, Apt. 4B, New York NY 10023. Cartoonist since 1949. Wants only medical, nurse, hospital, drug store, and drug gags. "Mild sex is okay in a medical category." Uses hundreds of these per year for regular Nellie Nifty, R.N. feature and other medical and drug features. Any number per batch. Pays 25% commission plus bonus when gags are re-used in his Dell paperback collections. Enclose S.A.S.E. for return of submissions.

JEFF KEATE, 1322 Ensenada Dr., Orlando FL 32807. Cartoonist since 1936. Interested in general situation and timely gags, sports gags (all sports in season) for "Time Out" sports panel. "Be funny. No puns. No oldies. No old hat situations." Has sold all of the major publications over the past 30 years. Currently doing syndicated newspaper cartoon panels for Field Newspaper Syndicate. Pays 25% commission. Bought close to 200 gags from freelancers last year. Holds unsold gags for "approximately 2 years unless gagwriter requests gag back sooner." Returns rejected material immediately. Enclose S.A.S.E. for return of submissions.

REAMER KELLER, P.O. Box 3557, Lantana FL 33462. Cartoonist since 1935. Interested in general and medical gags. Seeks gags for daily doctor panel. Pays 25% commission. Returns rejected material in 1 month. May hold unsold gags for up to 1 year. Bought about 500 gags from freelancers last year. Sold to King Features, *McCall's, Better Homes and Gardens, Parade,* and *National Enquirer.* Enclose S.A.S.E. for return of submissions.

MILO KINN, 1413 S.W. Cambridge St., Seattle WA 98106. Cartoonist since 1942. Interested in medical gags, male slant, girly, captionless, adventure, and family gags. Wants anything that is funny. Sells trade journals, farm, medical, office, and general cartoons. Sold to *Medical Economics, Modern Medicine, Farm Wife News, Private Practice,* and *Wallace's Farmer.* Pays 25% commission. Enclose S.A.S.E. for return of submissions.

LAUGHS UNLIMITED, 106 W. 45 St., New York NY 10036. Contact: Art Paul. Cartoonist agent. "We've sold over 75,000 gags of all types to television, magazines, etc. We seek top cartoonists or ones who could make big sales with the right gags. We can supply the top gags if you have a great today style. Also, we can recaption your rejected cartoons. We sell cartoons in the U.S.A. and to foreign markets (the latter usually photostats of ones circulating here). We also buy cartoons and pay immediately if you need the money. We'll gamble on selling. Or we work on commission at 30% domestic, 50% foreign." Enclose S.A.S.E. for return of submissions.

C. W. LEGGETT, 4790 Lawrence Dr., Sacramento CA 95820. Cartoonist since 1966. Interested in general, family. Good animal gags are always welcome. Simplicity is of utmost importance. Pays 30% on all sales and reprints. Returns rejected material immediately. No specific time limit for holding unsold gags. Bought about 200 gags from freelancers last year. Sold to *Saturday Evening Post, Saturday Review/World,* King Features, and trade journals. Enclose S.A.S.E. for return of submissions.

LO LINKERT, 1333 Vivian Way, Port Coquitlam, B.C., Canada V3C 2T9. Cartoonist since 1957. Interested in clean, general, male, medical, family, office, outdoors gags; captionless ideas; greeting card ideas. "Make sure your stuff is funny. No spreads."

Wants "action gags—not two people saying something funny." Has sold to *National Enquirer, Parade, Macleans, Playgirl, Field and Stream,* and others. Prefers batches of 10 to 15 gags. Pays 25% commission. Returns rejected material in 1 week. Enclose S.A.E. and International Reply Coupons for return of submissions or 10¢ U.S. postage.

ART McCOURT, 3819 Dismount, Dallas TX 75211. Interested in general, family, medical, outdoors, kids, and farm gags. Sold 35 cartoons last year to *Chevron,* King Features, *Wallace's Farmer, Prairie Farmer, St. Anthony Messenger,* and others. Pays 25% on acceptance. Reports at once.

MASTERS AGENCY, P.O. Box 427, Capitola CA 95010. In business since 1967. Actively purchasing gags on banking, business, medical, religious, education, holidays (especially Christmas), outdoors, industrial safety themes. Pays to $7.50 for these. Gags for "Belvedere" ($5) panels. Will look at typers, but prefer scribbles or sketches, however crude, drawn on 3x5 gag slips. "It is our opinion that gagwriters would all greatly increase their sales average by this method. We also purchase cartoonists' inked roughs on the above subjects (at $15 each) and previously published clips (at $5 each)." Bought "many hundreds" of gags from freelancers last year. Returns rejected material in 2 weeks. Will send sample proofs on request. Enclose S.A.S.E. for return of submissions. George Crenshaw, Editorial Director.

RAY MORIN, 140 Hamilton Ave., Meriden CT 06450. Interested in general gags submitted on 3x5 slips. Has sold to King Features, *National Enquirer, Wall Street Journal, Saturday Evening Post,* and others. Will look at batches of 8 or 10 gags. Pays 25% commission. Returns rejected material in 2 weeks. Holds unsold gags "indefinitely." Enclose S.A.S.E. for return of submissions.

IRV PHILLIPS, 2807 East Sylvia St., Phoenix AZ 85032. Cartoonist since 1934. Interested in general, pantomime, and word gags. Submit on 3x5 cards. No limit to number of gags submitted. Pays 25% commission; $10 minimum on syndication. "A greater percentage to anyone who can produce a steady supply." Also looking for beginning gagwriters to work with beginning cartoonists from his classes at Phoenix College. Enclose S.A.S.E. for return of submissions.

DOM RINALDO, 29 Bay 20th St., Brooklyn NY 11214. Cartoonist since 1960. Interested in general, male, female, sexy, girlie, family, trade, professional, children's, adventure, sports, medical, science fiction, and all other types of gags. Mostly gags that the picture tells the joke as well as the gag. Gags should be on a 3x5 paper numbered for filing. Pays 25% for first 3 sold, and 40% thereafter. Pays 50% for any comic strip or feature cartoon. Returns rejected material same day as received. May hold unsold gags up to 6 months to a year. "I never give up on a gag until all markets are tried." Has sold to *Playgirl, Genesis, Gallery, National Star,* King Features, and a number of trade magazines. Enclose S.A.S.E. for return of submissions.

JOSEPH SERRANO, Box 42, Gloucester MA 01930. Cartoonist since 1950. Interested in sophisticated gags. Seasonal and social comment preferred. Has sold to most major and middle markets. Pays 25% commission. Enclose S.A.S.E. for return of submissions.

HARRY SEVERNS, 1623 Boyd, St. Joseph MO 64505. Interested in gags for telephone, medical, auto, farm, sports, and general family magazines. General gags should be current-topics-today type. Prefers batches of 12 to 15 gags. Pays 30% commission. Has sold to *Modern Medicine, Private Practice, Dakota Farmer* and *Telebriefs.* Enclose S.A.S.E. for return of submissions.

JOHN W. SIDE, 335 Wells St., Darlington WI 53530. Cartoonist since 1940. Interested in "small town, local happening gags with a general slant." Pays 25% commission. Will send a sample cartoon to a gagwriter for $1. Does not return unsold gags. Returns rejected material "immediately." Enclose S.A.S.E. for return of submissions.

PAUL SWAN, 2930 Randy Lane, Dallas TX 75234. Interested in medical, dental, fishing, flying, science, camping, safety, TV repair, farmers, antique collecting and office gags. Medicals and dentals from the doctor's viewpoint, office from the secretary's viewpoint. Doesn't need girlies or generals. Pays 25% commission quarterly. Bought 625 gags from gagwriters last year. Returns rejected material same day as received. May hold unsold gags for a year or so. Has sold to over 500 different markets, both foreign and domestic. Enclose S.A.S.E. for return of submissions.

BOB THAVES, P.O. Box 67, Manhattan Beach CA 90266. Cartoonist since 1950. Interested in gags "dealing with anything except raw sex. Also buy gags for syndicated (daily and Sunday) panel, 'Frank & Ernest.' Prefer offbeat gags (no standard, domestic scenes) for that, although almost any general gag will do." Will look at batches containing any number of gags. Pays 25% commission. Returns rejected material in 1 to 2 weeks. May hold unsold gags indefinitely. Enclose S.A.S.E. for return of submissions.

MARVIN TOWNSEND, 631 West 88th St., Kansas City MO 64114. Full time cartoonist since 1947. Interested in gags with a trade journal or business slant. "Religious and children gags also welcome. Caption or captionless. No general gags wanted. Don't waste postage sending worn-out gags or nonprofessional material." Sells to over 100 trade and business publications and church and school magazines. Prefers batches of 12 gags. Pays 25% commission. Enclose S.A.S.E. for return of submissions.

ART WINBURG, 21 McKinley Ave., Jamestown NY 14701. Cartoonist since 1936. Will look at all types of gags; general, house organs, trade journals, children's magazines. Gagwriter should "use variety, be original, and avoid old cliches." Would prefer not to see gags about "smoke signals, flying carpets, moon men, harems, or cannibals with some person in cooking pot." Has sold to *National Star, VFW Magazine, Highlights for Children.* Pays 25% commission, "sometimes 30%." Returns rejected material "usually within a week, sometimes same day as received." Will return unsold gags "on request. Always a possibility of eventually selling a cartoon." Enclose S.A.S.E. for return of submissions.

ANDY WYATT, 9418 N. Miami Ave., Miami Shores FL 33138. Cartoonist since 1960. Interested in general, topical, family, girly, and male slant gags. "I like visual gags, but any good gag is okay. There is always a better gag on the same old topic. Some of the funniest material comes from trying to top old cliches." Pays 25% commission. Bought "over 100" gags from gagwriters last year. Will send a sample cartoon to a gagwriter on request. Returns rejected material in "1 to 2 weeks if I definitely can't use; sometimes longer if I feel there's a possibility in the material." May hold unsold gags "until I sell, unless a writer specifies he wants gags back at a certain time." Enclose S.A.S.E. for return of submissions.

Government Information Sources

Information and statistics on just about any subject are provided by the administrative, judicial, and legislative offices of the United States government. Often a writer can locate a fact that has eluded his library research by writing a letter to the proper government agency and asking them to supply it or suggest where it might be available. The government offices in the following listings have indicated a willingness to assist writers with research in their areas of expertise. For a more comprehensive directory of government offices, see A Directory of Information Resources in the United States in the Federal Government. This is available from the U.S. Government Printing Office.

Most of the agencies listed here issue booklets about their operations. Copies of these are available (often at no cost) by request, from the individual agencies. The research done by these government offices is usually published in booklet or book form by the U.S. Government Printing Office. Details on getting copies of this material are given in the entry for that office.

ACTION, 806 Connecticut Ave. N.W., Washington DC 20525. Contact: Frank Matthews, Director. Federal agency for volunteer service, formed to coordinate federal volunteer programs in the United States and abroad. Provides writers with photos of project areas, volunteers and people with whom they work. Bibliographies of Peace Corps material are available, and writers may obtain biographies of personnel and contacts for additional information. Publishes feature stories, press releases, reports, brochures, fliers and program fact sheets.

ADMINISTRATIVE CONFERENCE OF THE UNITED STATES, 2120 L St. N.W., Suite 500, Washington DC 20037. Contact: Office of Chairman. Purposes are to identify the causes of inefficiency, delay and unfairness in administrative proceedings affecting private rights and to recommend improvements to the President, the agencies, the Congress and Courts. *Volume II* of the *Recommendations and Reports of the Administrative Conference of the U.S.*, published in June 1973, contains the official texts of the recommendations adopted by the Assembly, and may be obtained from Superintendent of Documents, U.S. Government Printing Office, Washington DC.

AGRICULTURAL MARKETING SERVICE, U.S. Department of Agriculture, Washington DC 20250. Contact: Director, Information Division. Responsible for market news, standardization and grading, commodity purchases, marketing agreements and orders, egg inspection, and specified regulatory programs. Provides various marketing services for nearly all agricultural commodities. Provides publications, photos, a catalog of available publications, and other assistance to writers.

AGRICULTURE, DEPARTMENT OF, Independence Ave. between 12th and 14th Sts. S.W., Washington DC 20250. Contact: Director of Communication. Directed by law to acquire and diffuse useful information on agricultural subjects in the most general and comprehensive sense. Performs functions relating to research, education, conservation, marketing, regulatory work, agricultural adjustment, surplus disposal, and rural development.

AIR FORCE, DEPARTMENT OF THE, The Pentagon, Washington DC 20330. Contact: Office of Information.

ARMY, DEPARTMENT OF THE, The Pentagon, Washington DC 20330. Contact: Public Information Officer.

CENSUS, BUREAU OF THE, U.S. Department of Commerce, Washington DC 20233. Contact: Public Information Officer. Conducts and reports results of censuses and surveys of U.S. population, housing, agriculture, business, manufacturing, mineral industries, construction, foreign trade and governments. Statistical information is available for each state, county, city, metropolitan area, and for portions of cities and metropolitan areas in the U.S. A special reference pamphlet to help librarians and library users quickly familiarize themselves with the many reports available from the Bureau of the Census is being provided by the Bureau. The pamphlet, *A Visual Aid for Quick Reference to Basic Census Bureau Publications*, may be obtained from the Subscriber Services Section (Publications), Social and Economic Statistics Administration, Washington DC 20233, for 10¢ per copy.

CENTRAL INTELLIGENCE AGENCY, Washington DC 20505. Contact: Assistant to the Director.

CIVIL SERVICE COMMISSION, 1900 E St. N.W., Washington DC 20415. Contact: Office of Public Affairs. Administers the civil service merit system and is responsible for competitive examinations for entry into Federal civil service. Library at central office of Commission in Washington DC is outstanding location for research. Material does not circulate.

COPYRIGHT OFFICE, Library of Congress, Washington DC 20559. Contact: Public Information Office. Registers claims to copyright and provides copyright searches, free circulars on copyright subjects, and other related services.

DEFENSE CIVIL PREPAREDNESS AGENCY, Information Services, Defense Civil Preparedness Agency, The Pentagon, Washington DC 20301. Contact: Vincent A. Otto, Assistant Director, Information Services. Purpose is to prepare the Nation to cope with the effects of attack and to help State and local governments plan and prepare to cope with natural disasters. An extensive file of disaster photos and movies regarding disasters and emergency preparedness available. Information and newsletters for the general public are available, many from State or local civil preparedness agencies, and also directly from above address.

DEFENSE, DEPARTMENT OF, The Pentagon, Washington DC 20301. Contact: Chief, Magazine and Book Branch, Office of the Assistant Secretary of Defense for Public Affairs. Assists magazine and book editors and writers in gathering information about the Department of Defense and its components.

DEFENSE SUPPLY AGENCY, Camron Station, Alexandria VA 22314. Contact: Chester C. Spurgeon, Special Assistant for Public Affairs. Provides supplies and services used in common by all the Military Services. Will provide writers with information on Defense Supply Agency areas of activity. *Introduction to the Defense Supply Agency* available upon request.

ECONOMIC ANALYSIS, BUREAU OF, U.S. Department of Commerce, Washington DC 20230. Contact: Public Information Officer. Provides basic economic measures of the national economy (such as gross national product), current analysis of economic situation and business outlook, and general economic research on the functioning of the economy.

ENERGY RESEARCH AND DEVELOPMENT ADMINISTRATION, Washington DC 20545. Contact: Office of Public Affairs.

ENVIRONMENTAL PROTECTION AGENCY, Washington DC 20460. Contact: Public Information Center (PM215). Available literature includes popular booklets and leaflets on water and air pollution, solid waste management, radiation and pesticides control, as well as noise abatement and control. 16mm color films on pollution control and photos of pollution problems available by contacting Communications Division of Office of Public Affairs at above address.

FARM CREDIT ADMINISTRATION, 490 L'Enfant Plaza S.W., Washington DC 20578. Contact: E. Carroll Arnold, Director of Information. Responsible for the supervision and coordination of activities of the farm credit system, which consists of federal land banks and federal land bank associations, federal intermediate credit banks and production credit associations, and banks for cooperatives. Writers should confine areas of questions to agricultural finance and farm credit.

FEDERAL JUDICIAL CENTER, Dolley Madison House, 1520 H St. N.W., Washington DC 20005. Contact: Mrs. Sue Welsh, Information Service. Purpose is to further the development and adoption of improved judicial administration in the courts of the United States. Information Service collection consists of books, articles, and periodicals in the field. Reference services and a few bibliographies are available. *The Third Branch*, free monthly newsletter of the federal courts, is also available. Information Service open to the public for research purposes and written requests, within the realm of jurisdiction, will be answered, with first priority to federal judicial personnel.

FEDERAL MEDIATION AND CONCILIATION SERVICE, Room 2317, Main Labor Bldg., 14th and Constitution Ave. N.W., Washington DC 20427. Contact: Norman Walker, Director of Information. Purpose is settlement and prevention of labor-management disputes. Collective bargaining is the general subject of programs. Brochures and annual reports are available.

FEDERAL POWER COMMISSION, 825 N. Capitol St. N.E., Washington DC 20426. Contact: William L. Webb, Director of Public Information. Regulation of interstate aspects of natural gas and electric power industries, and licensing of non-Federal hydroelectric power projects. FPC will provide, free of charge, lists of publications and special reports, and general information on regulatory activities. Media representatives may also receive, upon request, a complimentary copy of non-subscription items on the publications list.

FEDERAL TRADE COMMISSION, Sixth St. and Pennsylvania Ave. N.W., Washington DC 20580. Contact: Office of Public Information. The Commission is a law enforcement agency whose mission is to protect the public (consumers and businessmen) against abuses caused by unfair competition and unfair and deceptive business practices; to guide and counsel businessmen, consumers, and federal, state, and local officials, promoting understanding among them and encouraging voluntary compliance with trade laws; to develop and administer a nationwide consumer education program. Will assist a researcher with reprints, copies of speeches, or other documents pertinent to his subject. Most helpful when a writer's questions are specific rather than general. Publications available include *News Summary*, a weekly roundup of news stories emanating from the Commission.

FISH AND WILDLIFE SERVICE, Room 3240, Interior Bldg., Washington DC 20240. Contact: Office of Public Affairs.

FOOD AND DRUG ADMINISTRATION, Rockville MD 20852. Contact: Press Office. Purpose is to protect health of American consumers by insuring foods are safe, pure, and wholesome; that drugs are safe and effective; that cosmetics are harmless; that all these products are honestly and informatively labeled and packaged. Press releases are issued on all major actions of the agency and there are individual publications on its varied programs. Requests should indicate specific subject of interest.

FOREST SERVICE, U.S. Department of Agriculture, 12th and Independence Ave. S.W., Washington DC 20250. Contact: George Castillo, Office of Information, Room 3225, South Agriculture Bldg., Washington DC 20250. Responsible for management of 187 million acres of land in the national forest system; forestry research, and cooperation with state and private foresters. Works on multiple-use management programs, including forest recreation, timber management, range, watershed, wilderness, fire control, etc. Writers preparing material on specific subjects within the above areas may write the press officer.

GENERAL SERVICES ADMINISTRATION, 19th and F Sts. N.W., Washington DC 20405. Contact: Public Information Officer, (202) 343-4511.

INTERIOR, DEPARTMENT OF THE, Interior Bldg., Washington DC 20240. Contact: Director of Communications. The nation's principal conservation agency, with responsibilities for energy, water, fish, wildlife, mineral, land, park, and recreational resources, and Indian and territorial affairs. Requests for information should be directed to the office most concerned with specific subjects of interest. See listings for individual bureaus and agencies to locate the best source for information.

INTERSTATE COMMERCE COMMISSION, 12th and Constitution Ave., Washington DC 20423. Contact: Public Information Office. Has regulatory responsibility for interstate surface transportation by railroads, trucks, buses, barges, coastal shipping, oil pipe lines, express companies, freight forwarders, and transportation brokers. Jurisdiction includes rates, mergers, operating rights, and issuance of securities. Free list of publications available.

JUSTICE, DEPARTMENT OF, Constitution Ave. and 10th St. N.W., Washington DC 20530. Contact: Public Information Officer.

LABOR, UNITED STATES DEPARTMENT OF, 3rd and Constitution Ave. N.W., Washington DC 20210. Contact: Office of Information, Publications and Reports.

LAND MANAGEMENT, BUREAU OF, U.S. Department of the Interior. Washington DC 20240. Office of Public Affairs provides information and photos on the management of 451 million acres of National Resource Lands (Public Domain) mostly in 10 western states and Alaska; on forest, range, water, wildlife, and recreation resources; on resource uses including camping, hunting, fishing, hiking, rock-hounding, off-road vehicle use; and on primitive, historic, natural and scenic areas.

LIBRARY OF CONGRESS, Washington DC 20540. Serves as a research arm of Congress and as the national library of the U.S. Maintains reading rooms open to scholars for research on the premises. Provides bibliographic and reference information by mail only in cases where individuals have exhausted library resources of their own region. Such reference information should be sought from the General Reference and Bibliography Division. Free list of Library of Congress publications can be obtained from the Central Services Division. Photoduplicates of materials in the collections (not subject to copyrights or other restrictions) are available at set fees from the Photoduplication Service.

MANAGEMENT AND BUDGET, OFFICE OF, Old Executive Office Bldg., Washington DC 20503. Contact: Information Office.

NATIONAL ACADEMY OF SCIENCES, NATIONAL ACADEMY OF ENGINEERING, NATIONAL RESEARCH COUNCIL, INSTITUTE OF MEDICINE, 2101 Constitution Ave. N.W., Washington DC 20418. Contact: Public Information Officer. A private organization which acts as an official, but independent adviser to the Federal government in matters of science and technology. For writers on assignment, the Academies often can be helpful by identifying authorities in various scientific disciplines and sometimes by providing state-of-the-art reports on broad scientific and environmental subjects prepared by their committees.

NATIONAL AERONAUTICS AND SPACE ADMINISTRATION, Washington DC 20546. Contact: Public Information Office. Principal functions are to conduct research for the solution of problems of flight within and outside the earth's atmosphere and develop, construct, test, and operate aeronautical and space vehicles; conduct activities required for the exploration of space with manned and unmanned vehicles; arrange for most effective utilization of scientific and engineering resources of the United States with other nations engaged in aeronautical and space activities for peaceful purposes; provide for widest practicable and appropriate dissemination of information concerning NASA's activities and their results.

NATIONAL AIR AND SPACE MUSEUM, Smithsonian Institution, Washington DC 20560. Contact: Librarian, NASM. Purpose is to memorialize the national development of aviation and space flight; collect, preserve, and display aeronautical and space flight equipment of historical interest and significance; serve as a repository for scientific equipment and data pertaining to development of aviation and space flight; provide educational material for historical study of aviation and space flight. The Museum's Historical Library has books, drawings, photos, films, scrapbooks, and oral history tape records on all aspects of aviation and astronautics.

NATIONAL ARCHIVES AND RECORDS SERVICE, Pennsylvania Ave. at 8th St. N.W., Washington DC 20408. Contact: Public Information Officer. The National

Archives is the repository for permanently valuable, official records of the U.S. Government. All treaties, laws, proclamations, executive orders, and bills are retained. It is also authorized to accept private papers. Administering all presidential libraries from Herbert Hoover to Lyndon Johnson and 15 Federal Records centers across the nation, the National Archives was created to serve the government, scholars, writers, and students. Among its holdings are sound recordings, motion pictures, still pictures, and some artifacts.

NATIONAL CREDIT UNION ADMINISTRATION, Washington DC 20456. Contact: Herman Nickerson, Jr., Administrator. Has the regulatory responsibility to charter, supervise, examine, and insure up to $40,000 per individual shareholders' account some 13,000 Federal credit unions, and to provide such insurance to qualifying state-chartered credit unions requesting it. Reference information is available on request. Available free on request are *Credit Union Statistics* (monthly), occasional *Research Reports*, and certain other publications dealing with the credit union industry. Also free to individuals is the *NCUA Annual Report*. *NCUA Quarterly* is $2.25 a year from the Government Printing Office. Writers interested in the credit union story are offered assistance in developing their articles.

NATIONAL ENDOWMENT FOR THE ARTS, 2401 E St. N.W., Washington DC 20506. Contact: Office of Program Information. An independent agency of the federal government created to aid and encourage cultural resources in the U.S. through matching grants to nonprofit organizations and nonmatching grants to individuals of exceptional talent in the following areas: architecture and environmental arts, dance, education (does not include art history research projects which are handled through the National Endowment for the Humanities), expansion arts (community based, professionally directed arts programs), folk arts, literature, museums, music, public media (film, television, radio), theatre, visual arts, and special projects. Information brochures and latest annual report are available.

NATIONAL MARINE FISHERIES SERVICE, National Oceanic and Atmospheric Administration, Department of Commerce, Washington DC 20235. Contact: Public Affairs Office. Biological and technical research, market promotion programs, statistical facts on commercial fisheries, marine game fish, and economic studies are the responsibilities of this Service.

NATIONAL PARK SERVICE, Room 3043, Interior Bldg., Washington DC 20240. Contact: Office of Public Affairs, Charles C. Keely, Jr., Director. Provides information on more than 290 areas of National Park System which the Service administers. Information available includes park acreage and attendance statistics; data on camping, swimming, boating, mountain climbing, hiking, fishing, winter activities, wildlife research and management, history, archaeology, nature walks, and scenic features. Photos of many areas and activities are available. To obtain publications, contact Division of Public Inquiries, Room 1013, Interior Bldg.; to obtain photos, contact Branch of Still Photography, Room 8060, Interior Bldg.

NATIONAL TRANSPORTATION SAFETY BOARD, Washington DC 20591. Responsibility of this agency is the investigation and cause determination of transportation accidents and the initiation of corrective measures. Work is about 80% in the field of aviation; balance is in selected cases involving highways, railroad, pipeline, and marine accidents. Provides writers with accident reports, special studies involving transportation safety, and accident photos. Case history details of all cases available for review are in the Accident Inquiry Section of the Safety Board in Washington DC.

NATIONAL WEATHER SERVICE, National Oceanic and Atmospheric Administration, Department of Commerce, 8060 13th St., Silver Spring MD 20910. Contact: Public Affairs Officer. Reports the weather of the U.S. and its possessions, provides weather forecasts to the general public, and issues warnings against tornadoes, hurricanes, floods, and other weather hazards. Develops and furnishes specialized information which supports the needs of agricultural, aeronautical, maritime, space, and military operations. Some 300 Weather Service offices in cities across the land maintain close contact with the general public to ensure prompt and useful dissemination of weather information. Agency publications may be purchased from Superintendent of Documents, U.S. Government Printing Office, Washington DC 20402.

NUCLEAR REGULATORY COMMISSION, Washington DC 20555. Contact: Office of Public Affairs.

OCCUPATIONAL SAFETY AND HEALTH REVIEW COMMISSION, 1825 K St. N.W., Washington DC 20006. Contact: Linda Dodd, Director of Information. An independent agency of the executive branch of the government. Functions as a court by adjudicating contested cases under the Occupational Safety and Health Act of 1970. Operates under the mandates of the Freedom of Information Act. Its files are open to anyone who wishes to inspect them. Publishes press releases and a guide to *Rules of Procedure* written in laymen's language. Information available on written request.

OUTDOOR RECREATION, BUREAU OF, Department of the Interior, Washington DC 20240. Contact: Office of Communications. Serves as Federal coordinator of public and private outdoor recreation programs and activities; as administrator of the Land and Water Conservation Fund; as conveyor of Federal surplus properties to state and local governments for public recreation use. Provides information on national and statewide outdoor recreation planning; assistance available from other government and private sources; the L&WCF's Federal recreation land acquisition and state grant programs; Congressionally authorized resource studies for potential Federal recreation areas including national trails, wild and scenic rivers, lakeshores and seashores, Federal off-road vehicle regulations; Federal recreation area fee system; and sources of technical assistance, literature and research on outdoor recreation.

PATENT AND TRADEMARK OFFICE, U.S. Department of Commerce, Washington DC 20231. Contact: Public Information Officer. Administers the patent and trademark laws, examines applications, and grants patents when applicants are entitled to them under the law. Publishes and disseminates patent information, maintains search files of U.S. and foreign patents and a Patent Search Room for public use, and supplies copies of patents and official records to the public. Performs similar functions relating to trademarks.

RECLAMATION, BUREAU OF, Department of the Interior, Room 7640, Interior Bldg., Washington DC 20240. Contact: Information Officer. Provides information on Federal development of water and associated land resources in the 17 western states and Hawaii, including widespread recreational use of more than 100 reservoirs—fishing, water sports, boating, swimming; scenic tours and camping areas; sightseeing attractions at dams and related works; recreational development and plans on basin-wide pattern.

SECRET SERVICE, 1800 G St. N.W., Washington DC 20223. Contact: Office of Public Affairs.

SENATE, Senate Office Bldg., Washington DC 20510.

SOCIAL SECURITY ADMINISTRATION, 6401 Security Blvd., Baltimore MD 21235. Contact: Michael Naver, Press Officer. Administers the Federal retirement, survivors, and disability insurance programs and health insurance for the aged and certain severely disabled people (Medicare) and a program of supplemental security income for aged, blind, and disabled people. Publications on all social security programs are available free of charge from any social security office, or from the Office of Public Affairs, above address. Writers may also obtain statistical and historical information, news releases, photos, biographies of top SSA officials, and other information materials. Cannot provide information about any individual social security record or beneficiary. Under the law, all social security records are confidential.

SOIL CONSERVATION SERVICE, U.S. Department of Agriculture, Washington DC 20250. Contact: Hubert W. Kelley, Jr., Director, Information Division. Purpose is to help landowners and operators to use their land and water in the best possible manner. Assists local groups with flood, drought, excessive sedimentation, or other water problems. Main concerns are soil, water, plant, and wildlife conservation; flood prevention; better use of water by individuals and communities; improvement of rural communities through better use of natural resources. In addition to material of interest to the agricultural and outdoor media, also has work in urban and educational fields that offer article possibilities. Has an extensive b&w photo file. *Soil Conservation Service* magazine is not available for widespread distribution, but individual copies may be obtained on a limited basis. Puts out brochures containing technical information or providing information on aspects of SCS work. Individual copies are available.

SOUTHEASTERN POWER ADMINISTRATION, U.S. Department of the Interior, Samuel Elbert Bldg., Elberton GA 30635. Contact: Miss Mary George Bond, Chief, Division of Administrative Management. Responsible for transmission and disposition of electrical energy generated at reservoir projects under the control of the Corps of Engineers in the southeastern U.S., and for water resources development. Will answer inquiries from writers regarding the bureau.

SOUTHWESTERN POWER ADMINISTRATION, P.O. Drawer 1619, Tulsa OK 74101. Contact: Wanda M. Cantrell, Public Information Specialist. A bureau of the Department of the Interior, marketing agent for power and energy produced at 23 multi-purpose projects constructed and operated by U.S. Corps of Engineers. Specific requests for information are answered.

STANDARDS, NATIONAL BUREAU OF, U.S. Department of Commerce, Washington DC 20234. Contact: Chief, Office of Technical Information. The nation's central measurement laboratory, charged with maintaining and refining the standards and technology on which our measurement system is based. Covers the entire spectrum of the physical and engineering sciences. Provides the technical base for federal programs in environmental management, consumer protection, health, and other areas. Bureau publications are available through the U.S. Government Printing Office.

SUPREME COURT, No. 1 First St. N.E., Washington DC 20543. Contact: Barrett McGurn, Director of Public Information.

TENNESSEE VALLEY AUTHORITY, New Sprankle Bldg., Knoxville TN 37902. Contact: Director of Information. Regional resource development, including economic development, resource conservation and environmental protection, electric power production, waterway development, flood control, recreation, agriculture, forestry, fish and wildlife, and research relating to all these. Operates National Fertilizer Development Center. Provides reference information, publications, photos, on request. Publishes *TVA Press Handbook* for factual reference; *Tennessee Valley Perspective,* quarterly employee magazine (available on request).

TERRITORIAL AFFAIRS, OFFICE OF, C St. between 18th and 19th N.W., Washington DC 20240. Contact: Director of Territorial Affairs.

TRANSPORTATION, U.S. DEPARTMENT OF, 400 7th St. S.W., Washington DC 20590. Contact: Office of Public Affairs, S-80.

TREASURY DEPARTMENT, Room 2313, 15th St. and Pennsylvania Ave. N.W., Washington DC 20220. Contact: Public Information Office.

U.S. GEOLOGICAL SURVEY, Department of the Interior, National Center, Reston VA 22092. Contact: Information Officer. Principal Federal earth science agency charged with preparing accurate maps of the physical features of the country and providing basic scientific information essential to development of the Nation's land, mineral, energy, and water resources. Responsible for preparing national topographic map series; for assessing the quantity and quality of surface and ground-water resources; for supervising mining and oil and gas development on Federal and Indian lands; and for fundamental research in topography, hydrology, geology, geochemistry, geophysics and related sciences. Annually publishes over 6,000 maps, charts, professional papers, circulars, and special reports summarizing results of a wide variety of investigations. Maintains photo library and world's largest earth science library, and provides data centers on earthquakes, glaciers, water and mineral resources, and the availability of maps and aerial and space photography. Press releases, photo services, and nontechnical literature available to news media and other serious writers and editors.

U.S. GOVERNMENT PRINTING OFFICE, Superintendent of Documents, Washington DC 20402. More than 24,000 different books and pamphlets available from the Documents Sales Service, an activity of the Office of the Assistant Public Printer (Superintendent of Documents), at the above address. To keep abreast of Government publications and their selling price, write for the monthly Selected U.S. Government Publications list. Each month's issue lists and describes between 100 and 180 popular Government titles. There is no free distribution from the Superintendent of Documents.

U.S. INDIAN CLAIMS COMMISSION, 1730 K St. N.W., Room 640, Washington DC 20006. Contact: David H. Bigelow, Executive Director. Hears and determines pre-1951 claims against the U.S. by any Indian tribe, band, or other identifiable group of American Indians residing within the U.S. Very small size restricts services available, but will reply to written requests for information. *Annual Report* is available free on request. Sometimes able to suggest sources for additional information.

U.S. INTERNATIONAL TRADE COMMISSION, 8th and E Sts. N.W., Washington DC 20436. Contact: Kenneth R. Mason, Secretary. Purpose is to provide information for the President, the Congress and the public and to make determinations of fact pursuant to statute, particularly with respect to the impact of imports on domestic U.S. industries. Reference information is available in the Office of the Secretary, the Library, and the Law Library in the Washington office. Inquiries in person or in written form should be addressed to the Office of the Secretary. Publishes an *Annual Report* and an annual report on the *Operations of the Trade Agreements Program*, available on request.

VETERANS ADMINISTRATION, 810 Vermont Ave. N.W., Washington DC 20420. Contact: Information Service 063. Administers laws authorizing benefits principally for former members and certain dependents of former members of the Armed Forces. Major VA programs include education and training, compensation, pension, loan guaranty, and insurance. Two basic publications for veterans free from VA 27H, Washington DC 20420, are 20-67-1 for Vietnam veterans (*Benefits for Veterans and Servicemen with Service Since Jan. 31, 1955, and Their Dependents*) and 20-72-2 for other veterans (*Summary of Benefits for Veterans With Military Service Before Feb. 1, 1955, and Their Dependents*). A third basic Publication (VA 1S-1 Fact Sheet, *Federal Benefits for Veterans and Dependents*) may be purchased from the Superintendent of Documents, U.S. Government Printing Office in Washington DC 20402. The 1976 edition is 75¢. Specialized pamphlets describing individualized VA benefits are available free from VA 27H and a small booklet describing VA itself (9VA: What It Is, Was, and Does), is available from VA 063, both 810 Vermont Ave. N.W., Washington DC 20420.

WOMEN'S BUREAU, Employment Standards Administration, U.S. Department of Labor, Washington DC 20210. Contact: Chief, Information and Publications Division.

Greeting Card Publishers

Greeting card companies have specialized editorial needs, just as magazines and publishing houses do, so the successful greeting card writer must learn what kinds of cards each company buys. Many companies produce only a few kinds of cards; even big companies which produce all the standard kinds of cards may have staff writers to prepare some categories, so they may buy only a few kinds and ideas from freelance writers.

To submit conventional greeting card material, type or neatly print your verses on either 4x6 or 3x5 slips of paper or file cards. For humorous or studio card ideas, either use file cards or fold sheets of paper into card dummies about the size and shape of an actual card. Neatly print or type your idea on the dummy as it would appear on the finished card. Put your name and address on the back of each dummy or card, along with a code number of some type, such as 1, 2, 3, etc. The code number makes it easier for the editor to refer to your idea when writing to you, and also helps you in keeping records. Always keep a file card of each idea. On the back of each file card, keep a record of where and when the idea was submitted. Submit from 10 to 15 ideas at a time (this makes up a "batch"); be sure to include a stamped, self-addressed return envelope. Keep the file cards for each batch together until the ideas (those rejected) come back. For ideas you write that use attachments, try to get the actual attachment and put it on your dummy; if you cannot, suggest the attachment. For mechanical card ideas, you must make a workable mechanical dummy. Most companies will pay more for attachment and mechanical card ideas.

The listings below give the publishers' requirements for verse, gags, or other product ideas. Artwork requirements are also given for companies that are interested in buying a complete card from a greeting card specialist who can supply both art and idea.

Brief descriptions for the many types of greeting cards and terms used within the listings are as follows:

Contemporary card: upbeat greeting; studio card belonging to the present time; always rectangular in shape.

Conventional card: general card; formal or sentimental, usually verse or simple one-line prose.

Current needs list: see Market Letter.

Cute card: informal, gentle humor; slightly soft feminine-type card in which the text is closely tied to the illustration.

Everyday card: for occasions occurring every day of the year, such as birthdays and anniversaries.

Humorous card: card in which the sentiment is expressed humorously; text may be either verse or prose, but usually verse; illustrations usually tied closely to the text, and much of the humor is derived from the illustration itself; often illustrated with animals.

Informal card: see Cute card.

Inspirational card: slightly more poetic and religious sounding card within the conventional card line; purpose is to inspire, and is usually poetical and almost Biblical in nature.

Juvenile card: designed to be sent to children up to about age 12; text is usually written to be sent from adults.

Market letter: current needs list; list of categories and themes of ideas and kinds of cards an editor currently needs; some companies publish monthly market letters; others only when the need arises.

Mechanical: card that contains an action of some kind.

Novelty: refers to ideas that fall outside realm of greeting cards, but sent for the same occasion as greeting cards; usually boxed differently and sold at different prices from standard greeting card prices.

Other Product Lines: booklets, books, bumper stickers, buttons, calendars, figurines, games, invitations and announcements, mottoes, note papers, placemats, plaques, postcards, posters, puzzles, slogans, stationery, and wall hangings.

Pop-up: a mechanical action in which a form protrudes from the inside of the card when the card is opened.

Promotions: usually a series or group of cards (although not confined to cards) that have a common feature and are given special sales promotion.

Punch-outs: sections of a card, usually Juvenile, that are perforated so they can be easily removed.

Risque: card that jokes about sex.

Seasonal card: published for the several special days that are observed during the year; Christmas, Easter, Graduation, Halloween, etc.

Sensitivity card: beautiful, sensitive, personal greeting.

Soft line: gentle me-to-you message in greeting form.

Studio: contemporary cards using short, punchy gags in keeping with current humor vogues and trends; always rectangular in shape.

Topical: ideas or cards containing subjects that are currently the topic of discussion.

Visual gags: a gag in which most, if not all, the humor depends upon the drawing or series of drawings used in the card; similar to captionless cartoons.

Study the various types of cards available at your local card shops to see what's currently selling. Another excellent source for learning to write for the greeting card publishers is the complete handbook on writing and selling greeting cards—*The Greeting Card Writer's Handbook*, edited by H. Joseph Chadwick (*Writer's Digest*).

AMBERLEY GREETING CARD CO., P.O. Box 37902, Cincinnati OH 45222. Editor: Herb Crown. Buys all rights. Send for list of current needs. Submit ideas on regular 3x5 cards. "We always take a closer look if artwork (a rough sketch on a separate sheet of paper that shows how the card would appear) is submitted with the gag. It gives us a better idea of what the writer has in mind." Do not send conventional cards. Reports in 3 to 4 weeks. May hold ideas for approximately 2 weeks. Enclose S.A.S.E. for return of submissions.

Humorous, Studio and Promotions: Buys all kinds of studio and humorous everyday cards, "including relative and odd captions such as promotion, apology, etc. Birthday studio is still the best selling caption. We never get enough. We look for belly laugh humor, not cute. All types of risque are accepted. No ideas with attachments. We prefer short and snappy ideas. The shorter gags seem to sell best." Would prefer not to see "friendship titles, Easter, Mother's Day, and Father's Day ideas." Pays $10 to $25. Occasionally buys promotion ideas. Payment negotiable, "depending entirely upon our need, the quantity, and work involved."

Other Product Lines: Promotions, plaques, mottoes, postcards, buttons, and bumper stickers. "Humor is what we look for in other product lines." Pays $10 to $25 for mottoes and bumper stickers.

AMERICAN GREETINGS CORPORATION, 10500 American Rd., Cleveland OH 44144. Editorial Director: S. H. McGuire. Buys all greeting card rights. Pays on acceptance. Send seasonal material "any time." Submit on 3x5 cards. Do not send conventional verse, as "our staff handles all of that," and don't send juvenile book mss. Reports in 4 weeks. Enclose S.A.S.E.

Sensitivity, Humorous, and Promotions: Publishes all kinds of everyday cards. "We're billed as the Fresh Idea Company, and we're always interested in new, fresh approaches (yet salable) to anything we make ... or don't make. Idea people will do best here." Pay is $20 and up for humorous material. Buys greeting card promotion ideas, "especially humorous." Must be "something that looks, sounds, or feels different from the usual card in the racks. From a card manufacturer's viewpoint, it is something that will bring him plus business. We do not want to see reworks of other companies' promotions." Some recent promotions include Teddy Bears, Urchins, Soft Touch books. Payment open.

Studio: Send studio ideas to Jack Clements, Editor. Must be of professional quality. Not a large freelance market, mostly staff-written material, but does purchase a limited number of highly original studio ideas. "We do like to keep the door open for interesting, unusual material." Pay is $25 and up for studio ideas.

Other Product Lines: "Always in the market for new product ideas (figurines, puzzles, calendars, books, etc.). Also in the market for strong ideas for $1 and $2 greeting books. Generally have a 'from-me-to-you' message, i.e., missing you, love you, happy birthday, etc. Many of a friendship nature, paying a compliment to a friend or offering inspiration. Special books for holiday greetings. Copy should be simple and charming. Suggest study books available in department stores, etc. Rates vary with the idea, but normally run between $100 to $250." Send ideas to S. H. McGuire.

BARKER GREETING CARD CO., Rust Craft Park, Dedham MA 02026. Editorial Director: Stan Hurwitz. Buys all rights. Pays on acceptance. Send for periodical list of current needs. Buys Christmas, Halloween, Thanksgiving May through June; Mother's Day, Father's Day, Graduation, January through February; and Valentine's Day, St. Pat's, and Easter, September through October, although these seasonal schedules are subject to revision. Reports in 2 to 3 weeks. Enclose S.A.S.E.

Studio: Barker only wants material for studio cards. Birthday, (general, male, female), get well (general, hospital, accident), anniversary (general, non-wedding, wedding, husband, wife), and friendship (hello, miss you, some special categories). Some risque; some inexpensive mechanicals, at $1 (also attachments). No smut. Studios for all seasons (see above reading schedule). No more than 10 to 12 ideas per batch. Send no more than 2 or 3 batches at most per week. No rhyming verse. Only studio-type humor. Pays $25 minimum for studio ideas.

BRILLIANT ENTERPRISES, 117 W. Valerio St., Santa Barbara CA 93101. Editor: Ashleigh Brilliant. Buys all rights. Will send a catalog and sample set for $1. Submit seasonal material any time. "Submit words and art in black on 5½x3½ horizontal, thin white paper. Regular bond okay, but no card or cardboard." Does not want to see "topical references, subjects limited to American culture, or puns." Reports "usually in 10 days." Enclose S.A.S.E.

Other Product Lines: Postcards. "All our cards are everyday cards in the sense that they are not intended only for specific seasons, holidays, or occasions." Messages should be "of a highly original nature, emphasizing subtlety, simplicity, insight, wit, profundity, beauty, and felicity of expression. Accompanying art should be in the nature of oblique commentary or decoration rather than direct illustration. Messages should be of universal appeal, capable of being appreciated by all types of people and of being easily translated into other languages." Limit of 17 words per card. Pays $25 for "complete ready-to-print word and picture design."

COLORTYPE SERVICES OF LOS ANGELES, INC., 4374 E. La Palma Ave., Anaheim CA 92807. Reports in 4 to 6 weeks. Enclose S.A.S.E.

Sensitivity and Studio: Friendship and nature themes only. No everyday general cards. Body humor and risque. Brevity is important. Contemporary themes only. Payment negotiable, but conforms with established schedules.

CREATIVE PAPERS INC., 800 Park Ave., Keene NH 03431. Editor: J.G. Thorsen. Reports in 2 to 3 weeks. Enclose S.A.S.E.

Soft Line, Conventional, and Inspirational: Country look, inspirational and verses for animals in human situations. Pleasant humor, with a country look. No studio material. Payment varies but usually $10 to $25 for verse.

Other Product Lines: Promotions, posters, plaques, postcards, and calendars. Payment varies, but usually $10 minimum.

CUSTOM CARD OF CANADA LTD., 1239 Adanac St., Vancouver, B.C., Canada V6A 2C8. Editor: W.A. Richardson. Buys all rights. Reports within 3 weeks. Send for current needs list. Enclose S.A.E. and International Reply Coupons.

Studio: Birthday, get well, anniversary, thank you, congratulations, general friendship, etc. Publishes risque and non-risque studios only. Christmas, Valentine's, Easter, St. Patrick's Day, Mother's Day, Father's Day ideas read all year. Pays $25 for studio ideas or verse.
Other Product Lines: Promotions. Will look at any promotional idea in greeting cards.

DARCO, P.O. Box 5553, Cleveland OH 44101. Editor: Alan Romanoff. Buys all rights. Reports in 2 to 4 weeks. Enclose S.A.S.E.
Other Product Lines: Promotions, mottoes, plaques, postcards, and bumper stickers, and buttons. Short and snappy, generally 15 word limit for one-liners. Virtually, anything goes — humor, topical or otherwise; sentimental, seasonal, environmental, political. "Payment the same for all one-liners regardless of use, which we'll determine." Examples of one-liners: "I need help. I'm a parent!", "Thou shalt not pollute!", "Nobody's perfict" and "World's Greatest Golfer." Pays $2 to $5 for sensitivity and humorous ideas.

THE EVERGREEN PRESS (formerly Berliner & McGinnis), P.O, Box 4971, Walnut Creek CA 94596. Editor: Malcolm Nielsen. Buys all rights. Pays on publication. Write for specifications sheet. Submit Christmas material any time. "Initial offering may be in the rough. Will not publish risque or 'cute' art." Reports in 2 weeks. Enclose S.A.S.E.
Conventional, Inspirational, and Studio: Interested in submissions from artists. Publishes everyday cards in a "very specialized series using verse from Shakespeare, for example. Our major line is Christmas. We avoid the Christmas cliches and attempt to publish offbeat type of art. For Christmas cards, we do not want Santa Claus, Christmas trees, wreaths, poodle dogs or kittens. We don't want sentimental, coy or cloying types of art. For everyday greeting cards we are interested in series of cards with a common theme. We are not interested in single designs with no relation to each other. We can use either finished art which we will separate or can use the artist's separations. Our studio lines are a complete series with a central theme for the series. We do not try to compete in the broad studio line, but only with specialized series. We do not purchase verse alone, but only complete card ideas, including verse and art." Payment for art on "royalty basis, depending on the form in which it is submitted."
Other Product Lines: Bookplates, note papers, invitations, children's books, stationery. Payment negotiated.

D. FORER AND CO., 511 E. 72 St., New York NY 10021. Editor: Barbara Schaffer. Buys all rights. Pays on acceptance. Sometimes holds material up to 3 weeks. Enclose S.A.S.E.
Informal and Humorous: Anniversary, thank you, new home, birthday, get well, engagement, and general cards. A hint of risque. Cute humor. "We read all occasions all year round; Valentine, Christmas, Father's Day, Mother's Day. We prefer 3 to 4 line verse. Pay $15 for verse, $50 for humorous ideas."
Other Product Lines: Promotions, mottoes, postcards.

FRAN MAR GREETING CARDS, LTD., 630 S. Columbus Ave., Mt. Vernon NY 10550. Editor: Aglaia Solon. Buys all rights. Submit seasonal material (Valentine's Day, Mother's Day, Father's Day) any time. Reports in 2 to 10 days. Enclose S.A.S.E. for return of submissions.
Informal, Studio, and Humorous: All copy should be on the cute side. It should be short and whimsical, and not verse. It should appeal to the teen and college market primarily—no juvenile copy. "We're interested in entertaining, funny and/or whimsical ideas which suggest strong visual content." Publishes birthday, get well, anniversary, relative birthday, friendship cards, and special titles (engagement, travel, general, goodbye, etc.). "We have an image (Moppets) and try to maintain that image with appropriate copy. We do not use topical or dramatic copy. We rely on soft and sensitive copy. We prefer copy that does not rhyme—short prose of no more than 4 lines." Pays $15 to $25 for humorous and sensitivity ideas.

Other Product Lines: Plaques and posters. "Ideas for plaques should be short and strictly friendship." Pays $10 to $15 for plaque ideas. Also interested in novelty stationery.

GIBSON GREETING CARDS, INC., BUZZA, 2100 Section Rd., Cincinnati OH 45237. Material submitted to Gibson Greeting Cards, Inc., will be considered for both Gibson and Buzza greeting card divisions. Laurie Kohl, Editor, Everyday Lines; Vivian Kuhn, Editor, Seasonal Lines; Alice Davidson, Editor, Studio, Humorous Lines, Ancillary Products and Books; Jean Timberlake, Editor, Juvenile and Cute Lines, Promotions (seasonal and everyday promotions). Reports within 3 weeks. Enclose S.A.S.E.

Soft Line, Humorous, Studio, Conventional, Informal, and Juvenile: All everyday cards. General material. "We purchase more material for Studio and Humorous lines than any of the other lines. We seek ideas for all seasons. We do not purchase any inspirational material as we have Helen Steiner Rice on our staff. While we purchase material for all of our lines, we anticipate purchasing very little this year." Pays $50 for Studio ideas; $3 a line for verse; $25 for Humorous ideas; $20 for Cutes and "soft" type. Invitations and announcements also published.

Other Product Lines: Promotions and gift books. Children's stories, 400 words or less. Pays $40.

HALLMARK CARDS, INC., Contemporary Department, 25th & McGee, Kansas City MO 64141. Managing Editor: Kent DeVore. Buys all rights. "Needs lists are included with ideas returned. Seasonal ideas may be submitted any time during the year." Does not want to see finished artwork or poetic verse sentiments. Submit on 4x9 folded dummies or typed note cards. "Hallmark is currently reading all contemporary (studio) card ideas from the freelance market. We are unable to read other freelance submissions." Reports in 1 to 3 weeks. Enclose S.A.S.E. for return of submissions.

Studio: "Keep in mind Surprise, Structure, and Sendability. Surprise is very important. If the customer can guess the punch line, there's no reason for him to open the card. Reward him with a surprise inside. Structure is the actual composition of words. Keep your ideas casual. The cover should lead smoothly and progress logically into the punch line. Generally, the faster you can get to the punch line, the better. Sendability is the message factor, the me-to-you feeling. As greeting cards can be considered substitutions for letters, each card must have sendability. Funny jokes and clever word plays that lack sendability do not sell well. The average buyer is a woman, so avoid obviously masculine concepts. Remember Hallmark's tradition of quality and emphasis on good taste. Cards can be successful without being overly suggestive, too topical (energy crisis, for example), crude (bathroom humor, for example), etc. Your competition is in the card shop. You can't go wrong by studying what's already on the market. It's been said that a true artist is one who can recognize faults in his work, wipe his canvas clean, and start all over. Writing is an art. Don't be afraid to analyze your material and throw it out or redo it. Your ideas are the product Hallmark sells. Only the very best ideas, the ideas that appeal to the most and offend the least can be used. Finally, don't be discouraged by rejection letters. Study the ideas you get back and try to figure out why they couldn't become cards. Try to improve your next batch. We're *eager* to buy *usable* ideas." Pays $50 for studio ideas.

HAPPY THOUGHTS, INC., publishing Keep 'N Touch Greeting Cards, P.O. Box 337, Stoughton MA 02072. Editor: Rosalie Lapriore. Buys all rights. Will send a current needs list to writer if S.A.S.E. is enclosed with request. Submit seasonal material 6 to 8 months in advance. Reports in 1 month. Sometimes holds material for 2 months. Enclose S.A.S.E.

Studio, Humorous, Soft Line, and Sensitivity: Ideas most easily read when typed on 3x5 cards or roughed out in black and white on studio card size. Welcomes punch lines for sophisticated, humorous, contemporary greeting cards with or without artwork. Ideas must be original. All cards are clean humor. No off-color. Does not use any slam cards. Aims for sophisticated, offbeat, unusual cards that say something nice in a humorous way. Also has collegiate line. Pays $12 to $15 for ideas, $15 for art, and $25 and up for complete card.

LAKESHORE ARTISANS, INC., P.O. Box 160, Belgium WI 53004. Editor: Earl Sherwan. "Reproduction rights are not required, as we do not reproduce photos, only use them in preparation of our own original art. Photographers may price submissions individually for outright sale, in which case we want all rights. Pay on acceptance. Advance query is essential and should contain detailed description of material available. We will not necessarily respond to queries unless they evoke further interest on our part." Will furnish sample notes at 10¢ per sample. Reports in 2 weeks. Enclose S.A.S.E.

Photos: "Our product line is highly specialized, consisting of correspondence notes featuring dogs, cats, and wildlife in that order of current importance. We need sharp, extremely detailed, professional quality photos of dogs and cats for use in preparing original art. We do not reproduce the photos per se, but reproduce resulting art for both notes and for framing size prints. Expert knowledge of official conformation standards for these animals is a prerequisite. While candid shots are preferred, these must purposefully and obviously illustrate excellent conformation to the individual breed standard. In addition, expressions should be appealing, 'adorable.' 35mm color slides may show the entire animal, but the head is all important because most of our art involves only the head. 8x10 b&w prints must be head-only shots, unretouched. All subjects must be sharply delineated with no detail lost to shadow or background interference. Use of head only does not apply to wildlife shots which are desired only in the form of 35mm color slides. Mammals and birds preferably are in natural environmental situations and settings. Consumers use our notes for correspondence, everyday cards, and for greeting cards as well. Christmas card versions of the notes have been published in the past, but discontinued. We may consider reviving this idea if new and unusual treatments are suggested in query form." Pays $5 to $7.50 for material to be used and returned.

LOOART PRESS, INC., Box 2559, Colorado Springs CO 80901. Art Director: Joe Russo. Buys all rights and retains art. Write Art Director for detailed specifications. Submit material in March, June, September. Reports in 2 weeks. Enclose S.A.S.E.

Conventional, Inspirational, Humorous, and Other Product Lines: Christmas cards only. "Highly professional finished art, both gently humorous and general and/or religious interpretations of the Christmas theme." Pays $250 for art.

ALFRED MAINZER, INC., 39-33 29th St., Long Island City NY 11101. Editor: Arwed Baenisch. Buys all rights. Enclose S.A.S.E.

Conventional, Inspirational, Informal, and Juvenile: All types of cards and ideas. Traditional material. All seasonals and occasionals wanted. Payment for card ideas negotiated on individual basis only.

MARK I, 1700 W. Irving Park Rd., Chicago IL 60613. Editor: Alex H. Cohen. Buys all rights. Reports within 2 weeks. Enclose S.A.S.E. for return of submissions.

Soft Line, Sensitivity, Humorous, Studio: "We buy artwork as well as verse. The artwork being 'studio type.' The verse should fit the cards. Also interested in Christmas, (both sensitivity and studio) and Valentine's Day (sensitivity only). Verse should be short and direct, typewritten on one side of 3x5 card or submitted with a sketch." Pays $40 to $50 for studio artwork; $20 to $25 for verse; $20 to $25 for sensitivity ideas, and $125 to $150 for photographs.

MILLER DESIGNS, INC., 9 Ackerman Ave., Emerson NJ 07630. Editor: J. Schulman. Buys all rights. Submit seasonal ideas any time. Reports in 3 to 4 weeks. Enclose S.A.S.E.

Studio, Soft Line, Humorous, Conventional, Informal and Juvenile: Birthday, anniversary, get well, friendship, bon voyage, birth, as well as ideas for invitations and announcements. Mechanicals if possible, whimsical ideas, clever, witty, and humorous. Also buys Christmas, Easter, Valentine and Mother's Day. Prefer 1 line for front of card and no more than 2 lines for the inside. Pay is open.

NORCROSS INC., 950 Airport Rd., West Chester PA 19380. Attn: Nancy Lee Fuller. Will send seasonal schedule to writer on request. Reports within 3 weeks. Pays on acceptance. Enclose S.A.S.E.
Conventional, Inspirational, Informal, Soft Line, Humorous, Studio, and Juvenile: Seeks conversational verse; 2, 4, or 8 lines, for general or relative cards; contemporary prose, light and complimentary, for general and relative cards; studio, humor (all categories). Pays $1.50 to $3 per line for regular verse; $25 and up for humor and studio ideas. Submit copy on 3x5 cards (unless gag depends on illustration or dummy) with writer's name and address on each card and enclose S.A.S.E.

PANDA PRINTS, INC., 41 W. 25 St., New York NY 10010. Editor: F. Slavic. Buys all rights. Reports in 3 to 8 weeks. Enclose S.A.S.E. for return of submissions.
Humorous and Informal: Birthday, get well, anniversary, thank you, bon voyage, etc. Brief, literate, soft humor, invitations and announcements. Also wants ideas for Valentines. Pays $10 to $15 for verse. Pays $10 to $15 for humorous ideas.

PLASTIC LACE, INC., P.O. Box 2026, Salem MA 01970. Editor: I. T. Kutai. Buys all rights. Reports within 2 weeks. Enclose S.A.S.E.
Soft Line, Humorous, and Juvenile: Soft humor and friendship, youth oriented. Pencil sketches sufficient. Copy without illustration not to be presented, as "we are primarily interested in art work, illustration of lovable children, whimsical animals. Copy is secondary."
Other Product Lines: Posters, plaques and postcards. Size 4x6 and 7x9.

RUST CRAFT GREETING CARDS, INC., Rust Craft Rd., Dedham MA 02026. Editorial Director: Karen Middaugh. Submit studio ideas to Barker Greetings. Buys all rights. Pays on acceptance. Send for free list of current needs. Reports in 2 to 4 weeks. Enclose S.A.S.E.
Soft Line, Sensitivity, Humorous, Conventional, Inspirational, Informal, and Juvenile: All everyday lines, particularly illness and sympathy. "We always need good new birthday material, both general and for relatives. Fresh and original verse in all lengths having strong themes and/or design-sentiment tie-ins. Fresh, sophisticated humor, both prose and verse, in all lengths. Original sensitivity prose. We need fresh, new-sounding conventional verse sentiments for all lines, especially relative line units. Double relatives and masculine relatives are particularly difficult areas to find good material for. We seek ideas for all seasonals, particularly sentiments which capitalize strongly on the imagery connected with the season. Seasonal ideas read throughout the year, although our market letter informs the writer when needs for a particular season are strongest. Also buy ideas for invitations and announcements. Although we need verse, we prefer not to see very traditional material such as we already have in our files. Really corny humor is also unacceptable. No real length limits for greeting card verse, although 24 lines would probably be the practical limit for developing a long idea in a greeting card format." Pays $10 to $25 for verse, $10 to $15 for sensitivity ideas, $10 to $25 for humorous ideas.
Other Product Lines: Promotions, gift books, greeting books, and calendars. Pays $50 and up for books. Payment for other promotions will be negotiated.

SANGAMON COMPANY, Route 48 West, Taylorville IL 62568. Editor: Stella Bright. Buys all rights. Reports in 2 weeks. Enclose S.A.S.E.
Everyday and Humorous: Verse for "everyday" and all seasons; also cute and humorous gags. Payment depends on quality, usually $1.50 a line for verse, and up to $20 for gags. Length: 4 and 8 lines.

UNITED CARD COMPANY, 1101 Carnegie St., Rolling Meadows IL 60008. Editor: Mr. Edward Letwenko. Buys all right . Submission deadlines for seasonal material: December (St. Patrick's Day, Valentine's Day), July (Easter, Mother's Day, Father's Day, graduation), September (Halloween, Christmas). Does not buy artwork. Submit on 3x5 index card or dummy studio card. Reports in 3 to 4 weeks. Enclose S.A.S.E. for return of submissions.
Studio and Humorous: Birthday, get well, friendship, and anniversary. "We create

only humorous studio cards that include soft humor and risque. We keep a listing of all writers who contact us and send out specific bulletins when we are ready to buy seasonal material." Pays $25 for verse or humorous studio ideas.

VAGABOND CREATIONS, 2560 Lance Drive, Dayton OH 45409. Editor: George F. Stanley, Jr. Buys all rights. Submit seasonal material any time; "we try to plan ahead a great deal in advance." Submit on 3x5 cards. "We don't want artwork—only ideas." Reports within same week usually. May hold ideas 3 or 4 days. Enclose S.A.S.E. for return of submissions.

Soft Line and Studio: Publishes contemporary cards. Studio verse only; no slams, puns, or reference to age or aging. Emphasis should be placed on a strong surprise inside punch line instead of one that is predictable. Also prefers good use of double entendre. "Mildly risque." Purchases copy for Christmas, Valentine's and Graduation. Wants "1 short line on front of card and 1 short punch line on inside of card." Pays $10 "for beginners; up to $15 for regular contributors."

Other Product Lines: Interested in receiving copy for mottoes and humorous buttons. "On buttons we like double-entendre expressions—preferably short. We don't want the protest button or a specific person named. We pay $10 for each button idea." Mottoes should be written in the "first person" about situations at the job. about the job, confusion, modest bragging, drinking habits, etc. Pays $10 for mottoes.

VISUAL CREATIONS, 25 Hamilton Dr., Novato CA 94947. Editor: David Lieberstein. Buys all rights. Send for current needs list. Sometimes holds material for 3 to 6 weeks. Enclose S.A.S.E.

Inspirational, Informal, Soft Line and Sensitivity: Short, simple, sincere messages for birthday, anniversary, friendship, get well, travel. 1 line only. Buys all year. "We are also interested in ideas or art styles to develop a card line around." Pays $15 to $25 per verse. Original artwork for special card lines. Pays $50 per design and 2% royalty of gross sales.

WARNER PRESS PUBLISHERS, Fifth at Chestnut Sts., Anderson IN 46011. Greeting Card Editor: Dorothy Smith. Sometimes holds material up to 6 weeks. Pays on acceptance. Will read Christmas verses in November, Graduation verses in September, Everyday sentiments (friendship, birthday, get well, sympathy, baby birth, congratulations, etc.) in September. Enclose S.A.S.E.

Soft Line, Inspirational, and Religious: Birthday, get well, friendship, graduation, anniversary, wedding, sympathy, thinking of you, congratulations, and thank you, etc. Brief conventional greetings with a religious sentiment. Nothing lengthy, or poetic. Greeting cards must be religious, but not preachy or doctrinal, 4 to 6 lines in each verse. Suggest Scripture text for each sentiment. "We make no payment for Scripture suggestions." Each sentiment should be numbered, typed on separate sheets of paper and give author's complete name and address. "We're not interested in poetry — only greetings!" Pays $1 per line.

Play Producers

Producers of Broadway, Off-Broadway, and Off-Off-Broadway plays are listed below. Entries are also given for resident professional companies, amateur community theaters, and theater workshops in the United States. Non-paying theater workshops are included in this list because the experience and exposure offered by these outlets can introduce talented new playwrights and give them a better chance for commercial production of their plays.

ALLEY THEATRE, 615 Texas Ave., Houston TX 77002. A resident professional theatre; large stage seating 798; arena stage seating 296. Wants good plays, with no length restriction. Royalty arrangements vary. Send complete script. Enclose S.A.S.E. Reports in 6 to 8 weeks. Produces 6 to 8 plays a year.

APPLE HILL PLAYHOUSE, Box 60, Delmont PA 15626. Producer: Jack Zaharia. Plays produced in summer theatre, professional cast. Public audience, all ages; education varies. Looking for commercial comedies with small cast (maximum 10), 1 set or unit set. No political satire. Also 40-minute children's plays. Two-act or three-act plays. Pays $150 per week for main stage shows; $10 to $15 per performance for children's theatre. Query first with synopsis only. Enclose S.A.S.E. Usually reports in 3 to 4 weeks. Produces 10 plays a year.

BARTER THEATRE, Main St., Abingdon VA 24210. Producer: Rex Partington. Looks for good plays, particularly comedies. Two or three acts, preferably, but will consider good quality plays of shorter length. Pays 5% royalties. Send complete script only. Enclose S.A.S.E.

THE BOLTON HILL DINNER THEATRE, Doug Roberts, Producer, 1111 Park Ave., Baltimore MD 21201. Professional dinner theatre. Public audience, middle aged, who prefer comedy. No more than 10 characters in cast. Two-act, three-act, comedy and revue material. Payment is negotiable. Rarely copyrights plays. Send complete script only, with S.A.S.E. Produces about 10 plays a year.

GERT BUNCHEZ AND ASSOCIATES, INC., 7730 Carondelet, St. Louis MO 63105. Contact: Gert Bunchez, President. "We feel that the time is propitious for the return of stories to radio. It is our feeling that it is not necessary to 'bring back' old programs, and that there certainly should be contemporary talent to write mystery, detective, suspense, soap operas, etc. We syndicate radio properties to clients and stations. Requirements are plays with sustaining lead characters, 5 minutes to 30 minutes in length. Disclaimer letter must accompany scripts. Rates from $100 per script if acceptable for radio production and actually produced." Enclose S.A.S.E.

LAWRENCE CARRA, Great Lakes Shakespeare Festival, Carnegie-Mellon University, Pittsburgh PA 15213. For a public audience, paid admission, with preference toward classical theatre. Summer theatre with potential for Broadway; professional cast. Three-act or full-length plays. Open as to style, content and genre. Interested only in effective dramatic works. Buys class A rights. Not interested in plays with sex themes per se. Limitations in cast, approximately 20. Produces 5 plays per summer season. Payment is negotiable. Query first with synopsis only. Reports within 1 month. Enclose S.A.S.E. with query and synopsis.

THE CHANGING SCENE THEATER, 1527½ Champa St., Denver CO 80202. Year-round productions in theater space. Cast may be made up of both professional and amateur actors. For public audience; age varies, but mostly youthful, and interested in taking a chance on new and/or experimental works. No limit to subject matter or story themes. Emphasis is on the innovative. "Also, we require that the playwright be present for at least one performance of his work, if not for the entire rehearsal period. We have a small stage area, but are able to convert to round, semi-round, or environmental. Prefer to do plays with limited set and props." One-act, two-act, and three-act. Also interested in musicals. "We do not pay royalties, or sign contracts with playwrights. We function on a performance share basis of payment. Our theater seats 78, the first 35 seats go to the theater, the balance is divided among the participants in the production. The performance share process is based on the entire production run, and not determined by individual performances. We do not copyright our plays." Send complete script. Enclose S.A.S.E. Reporting time varies; usually several months. Produces approximately 10 to 15 new plays a year.

CHELSEA THEATER CENTER, 30 Lafayette Ave., Brooklyn NY 11217. Artistic Director: Robert Kalfin. Looking for full-length plays "that stretch the bounds of the theater in form and content. No limitations as to size of cast or physical production." Pays usually "$100 for an option to produce a play in workshop; $500 for a 6-month option for an off-Broadway production." Works 10 months in advance. Query first with synopsis. Enclose S.A.S.E. for reply to queries.

ALFRED CHRISTIE, 405 E. 54th St., New York NY 10022. "The theatre is a summer stock theatre and many of the people in the audience are on vacation, most are over age 30." Professional cast. Two-act or three-act plays. "We would like funny situation, contemporary farces or light comedies. Scripts that are sensational in theme, that can compete with today's frank and modern films are also possible. Also, we do children's shows. We like a well-written play with interesting switches or avant-garde scripts that are based on reality and make sense. We would expect the author to copyright the play but if the show moves on to other theatres or Broadway or to a film, etc., we would like a small percentage of the action. We want no family situation shows, no period plays involving many period costumes. We prefer small cast, single-set shows, but if a script is good we would do a larger cast and multiple set production." Produces 6 to 10 full productions and several children's plays yearly. Payment varies. A percentage or a flat fee is possible. "Does the author want to come and work with the people and on the play?" Send synopsis or complete script. "We like scripts by April of each year because we must arrange publicity, hire actors, etc." Enclose S.A.S.E. for return of submissions.

CLEVELAND PLAY HOUSE, 2040 East 86th St., Cleveland OH 44106. Director: Richard Oberlin. A professional, resident theater. Produces plays of "all types. We are interested primarily in full-length plays. One-acts are rarely used." Looks for special qualities in characterization and theme. "Our season of about 15 productions encompasses a wide range, from classics to current Broadway and Off-Broadway successes, plus new plays, to appeal to a wide interest range in our audience. We must keep in mind that the Play House is a family theater, supported by subscriptions and gifts. Blatant vulgarity and tastelessness would not be acceptable." Produces about 1 or 2 plays a year from freelancers. "Royalties are negotiated with individual authors or agents. In the case of new scripts, authors are usually in attendance during the rehearsal period and financial arrangements are made for this period." Send complete script to Robert Snook. Reports in 6 weeks. Enclose S.A.S.E. for return of submissions.

DAVID J. COGAN, 350 Fifth Ave., New York NY 10001. Produces three-act plays. Chiefly interested in contemporary topical material. Looks for special qualities of character development, comedy. Pays royalties on production; percentage of box office. Gives average advance of $2,500. Charges $10 reading fee. Send complete script. Reports in 1 to 2 months. Enclose S.A.S.E.

E.P. CONKLE WORKSHOP FOR PLAYWRIGHTS, University of Texas at Austin, College of Fine Arts, Austin TX 78712. Associate Directors: Webster Smalley, Chairman of Drama, and Frank Gagliano. "A summer project during which we produce 3 new scripts which are two- or three-act and full-length. Performances are for the general public. We also do new scripts on our major and experimental bills. Playwrights should be recommended by a recognized member of the educational theater, the professional theater, or by an agent. Playwrights are offered $1,000 fellowships to make it possible for them to be present for rehearsals and performances, which are held during June and the first 2 weeks of July. Financial arrangements for scripts on our major and experimental bills are worked out." Enclose S.A.S.E.

JEAN DALRYMPLE, 130 W. 56th St., New York NY 10019. Produces stage and television shows, Broadway, off-Broadway, summer theatre, regional theatre. For a general audience. Looking for warm, human subjects; humorous or dramatic plays. No anti-war plays; no "cause" plays. No sex plays, unless someone can find a new "angle." Small casts, few sets preferred because of economics. Any length considered, but not over-long (over 150 pages). Payment in royalties according to Dramatist Guild contract. Plays are first optioned for production on Dramtist Guild contract. Submit through agent only. Reports in 2 weeks. Enclose S.A.S.E. for return of submissions.

THE DRAMA SHELTER, 2020 North Halsted St., Chicago IL 60614. Darel Hale, Artistic Director. "All our shows are open to the public (currently our only source of income) with a serious interest in seeing serious drama (tragedy, comedy and what falls in between) done well. We're an all-year repertory theatre company, with 4 to 5 different plays presented each week. Our theatre is intimate; the cast, which practically lives at the theatre, professional. We prefer contemporary scripts which explore unusual facets of human relationships; in fact the play's humanity and the feeling it conveys to the audience are perhaps the most essential characteristics we look for in a new script. Perhaps, as has been said of Megan Terry, be a 'wrighter' instead of a 'writer'. We want plays that, through our intensive workshops, come alive; which means the writer, and what he/she writes is sensitive to both the comic and the tragic in life or society. We do a great variety of plays ranging from improvised skits, to off-off Broadway material, to Sartre, Cocteau, Williams, Albee. We like plays with action, movement, and certainly welcome any drama that explores multi-media approaches. No situation comedies, mysteries, or, in fact, any play which does not take the characters below the surface. We're also not currently set up to do musicals. Extremely involved sets are impossible for us, as are very large casts, as are those with too many scene changes unless they're simple. Payment is negotiated with the playwright, and usually a straight percentage of box office receipts. We buy only first rights; we hope that playwrights grow with us. We prefer consequently that the playwright is able to attend at least a percentage of rehearsals." Send complete script only. Reports within 4 weeks, although the actual production date will certainly vary. Produced at least 12 full productions, more if one-acts are counted, last year. Enclose S.A.S.E.

REV. DENNIS E. DWYER, 1110 W. Chenango Ave., Englewood CO 80110. Plays produced in Loretto Height College Center for the Performing Arts, Denver, with a high school age cast. For general, family audience. Emphasize good Christian morals and values, and plays in good taste only. Three-act plays and musicals. Payment negotiable. Query first with synopsis. Enclose S.A.S.E. Produces about 3 plays a year.

EARPLAY, Vilas Communication Hall, 821 University Ave., Madison WI 53706. A national project designed to produce radio drama for distribution to the public, non-commercial, radio stations in the United States. It's jointly sponsored by the University of Wisconsin-Extension, the Corporation for Public Broadcasting, and the National Endowment for the Arts. A new concept in radio drama for this country. An attempt to reawaken in playwrights and in listening audiences the interest and excitement in radio drama which has been dormant for so long. Produces plays written for the contemporary ear, and provides a writer's market modeled on that of the BBC in England where as many as 75 new dramatists are introduced every year on radio. Accepts scripts throughout the year. Interested in pieces with strong character treatment, bold, imaginative use of sound, and clear and compelling plot lines. Also considers pieces which are impressionistic in treatment or create purposeful ambiguity. An Earplay can be a sound essay or portrait, a verse drama, a poetic documentary, as well as the more conventional forms of radio theatre. Scripts purchased are produced at studios of WHA Radio in Madison, Wisconsin, and in other major studios throughout the country. Productions are performed by professional actors. All script purchase fees are based on estimated running time of the completed production. Usually pays $300 for 10 minutes, first rights; $150 for 10 minutes, previously published; $1,000 for 30 minutes, first rights; $500 for 30 minutes, previously published. Not interested in the following: drama aimed at children, religious drama, educational/instructional material, or occasional material written for holidays. Send S.A.S.E. for fact sheet to obtain complete submission details. It takes at least 2 to 3 months for a script to be given thorough consideration. Scripts received after June 1 may take somewhat longer. Enclose S.A.S.E. with all submissions and inquiries.

ZELDA FICHANDLER, c/o Arena Stage, 6th and M Sts., S.W., Washington DC 20024. Wants original plays preferably (but not necessarily) submitted through agents. "Plays with relevance to the human situation—which cover a multitude of dramatic approaches—are welcome here." Pays 5 percent of gross. Reports in 6 months. Enclose S.A.S.E.

FOLGER THEATRE GROUP, 201 E. Capitol St., Washington DC 20003. Produced in professional theatre, AEA Guest Artist Contract, for general public. All kinds of plays. "Since we produce 2 Shakespeare productions a season, we would rather not read Shakespearean adaptations or treatments." No limitations in cast, props; stage is small but flexible. Any length play. Payment negotiable. Send complete script or submit through agent. Enclose S.A.S.E. Reports "as soon as possible. We have a great many plays to read." Produces 2 new scripts a year, and various Shakespeares.

DR. KEITH FOWLER, Producing Director, Virginia Museum Theatre, Boulevard and Grove Ave., Richmond VA 23221. For public, well-educated, conservative, adventurous audiences. Professional repertory theatre. Looking for biography, experimental styles. Standard format of presentation. Light comedies, musicals. Two-act and three-act plays considered. Payment is negotiable. For a premiere, theatre requires share in future income. Produces one new script a year. Send complete script only. Reports in 3 to 5 months. Enclose S.A.S.E. for return of submissions.

ROY FRANKLYN, 29 W. 65th St., New York NY 10023. Produces two-act and three-act plays for "possibly off-Broadway, possibly summer theater, for commercial-type audiences." Interested in "good plays, small casts, simple sets." Buys subsidiary rights. Produces 2 plays a year "at most." Pays 5% of gross receipts. Query first with synopsis only. Reports in 3 weeks. Enclose S.A.S.E. for reply to queries.

JOSEPH N. FRENCH, Edison Institute, Dearborn MI 48121. Interested in two-act plays for "museum theater and semi-professional company." Audience is "middle-aged rural Americans." Wants "historical, patriotic plays. No depressing or downbeat themes; no anti-hero. Should have cast of 12 or less." Produces about 6 plays a year. Buys no rights. Pays $20 a performance. Send complete script only. Reports in 6 months. Enclose S.A.S.E.

GALWAY PRODUCTIONS, Suite 300, 1540 Broadway, New York NY 10036. Director: Paul Barry. Looks for controversial plays on the theme of the American Revolution. Pays standard Dramatists' Guild royalty percentage. Synopsis or full-length play. No one-acts. Enclose S.A.S.E.

THE GUTHRIE THEATER, David Ball, Vineland Pl., Minneapolis MN 55403. Professional repertory company for a general audience. Looking for all types of plays, especially those by the maverick playwright. New approaches, forms, and attitudes, as well as outstanding literary work. Any length. Payment arranged with each writer; professional theater rates. Authors retain copyrights. Send completed script only. Enclose S.A.S.E. Reporting time varies depending on the time of the year. Produces approximately 15 plays a year.

HARWICH JUNIOR THEATRE, Box 168, West Harwich MA 02671. Produces two-act and three-act plays; semiprofessional productions in winter theatre or summer children's theatre. Children's plays are 1½ hours in length; any size and age cast. Winter plays are full length with small casts. Drama, comedy, musicals, adaptations. Any structure which may be considered in play form. No happenings. Nothing controversial. Produces 13 plays a year; 6 children's plays and 7 adult. "We expect the playwright to obtain his own copyright." Pays an average of $10 to $15 per performance for children's plays; average of $15 to $20 for adult plays. Send complete script. Reports in March. Enclose S.A.S.E. for return of submissions.

HIGH TOR SUMMER THEATRE, Ashby West Rd., Fitchburg MA 01420. Produces three-act plays "performed during a summer season by professional and amateur performers in a resident company. Public audience of varying ages, education, and interests. Interested in all kinds of plays which might be suitable for our particular setup. No X-rated plays. Our theater is an arena stage, holding between 120 and 140 people. We sometimes perform end stage, i.e., three sides. Our repertoire is extremely varied." Produces about 8 plays a year. "Royalties are negotiable because of our nonprofit educational setup." Percentage offered will vary, according to author and nature of script. Send complete script only. Enclose S.A.S.E.

HONOLULU THEATRE FOR YOUTH, P.O. Box 3257, Honolulu HI 96801. Managing Director: Mrs. Lorraine Dove. Produces plays of "1 hour without intermission. Plays are produced in Honolulu in various theater buildings; also, an annual tour in theater buildings on Neighbor Islands, state of Hawaii. Casts are amateur with professional direction and production; adult actors, with children as needed. Plays are produced for school children, grades 2 through 12, individual plays directed to specific age groups; also public performances." Interested in "historical (especially American) plays, plays about Pacific countries and Pacific legends, and Asian legends and Asian history. Plays must have strong character with whom young people can identify, with stress on action rather than exposition, but not at the expense of reality (i.e., not slapstick). Plays should be reasonably simple technically and use primarily adult characters. Fairy tales (especially mod versions) are at the bottom of the priority list, as are elaborate musicals requiring large orchestras. Casts up to 15, preferably. Technical requirements should be reasonably simple, as sets have to be built at one place and trucked to the theater." Produces 6 plays a year. Royalty fee is based on number of performances. Query first with synopsis only. Reports in 1 to 2 months. Enclose S.A.S.E. for reply to queries.

WILLIAM E. HUNT, 801 West End Ave., New York NY 10025. Interested in reading scripts for stock production, off-Broadway and even Broadway production. "Small cast, youth-oriented, meaningful, technically adventuresome; serious, funny, far-out. Must be about people first, ideas second. No political or social tracts." Pays royalties on production. Off-Broadway, 5%; on Broadway, 5%, 7½% and 10%, based on gross. Reports in "a few weeks." Enclose S.A.S.E.

JON JORY, Producing Director, Actors Theatre of Louisville, 316 W. Main St., Louisville KY 40202. Actors Theatre of Louisville is a resident professional theatre operating under a L.O.R.T. contract for a 35-week season from September to June. Subscription audience of 16,000 from extremely diverse backgrounds. Plays with a strong story line, of highly theatrical structure. Not as interested in examinations of the American family or scripts without a sense of humor. Prefers plays with a cast of 12 or under. There are 2 theatres, one a 640 seat thrust and one, a 165 seat convertible arena or three-quarters. Multiple set shows are impossible here. One-act, two-act, and three-act plays considered. Payment is negotiated. Asks for financial participation in the play's future only when a work has been specifically commissioned. Send synopsis or complete script. Enclose S.A.S.E. Reports in 2 to 3 months. Produces 2 plays a year.

LAKEWOOD MUSICAL PLAYHOUSE, 277 W. 22nd St., New York NY 10011. Producer: Robert Buchanan. Produces two-act plays for "professional summer theater in Pennsylvania. The audience is varied; middle-aged. Interested in only musicals with any theme. Use whatever approach works. Have only done Broadway successes, but am somewhat secure enough now to do new shows." Produces 10 or 11 plays a year. Pays "about $500." Send synopsis or complete script. Enclose S.A.S.E.

DAVID LITT, 290 Southwood Circle, Syosset NY 11791. Semi-professional community theatre, for all ages, from 18 and up, middle class, suburban type with a year or two of college. Any kind of play that has a solid story line is acceptable. Playwright should have a balance between theme and structure. No "talky" plays. One set preferred. One-act, two-act, three-act. Payment depends on conditions, although royalty is usually Dramatists Guild contract minimum. Author must copyright his own play. Query first with synopsis. Enclose S.A.S.E. Reports in 3 months. Produces 5 plays a year.

LORETTO-HILTON REPERTORY THEATRE, 130 Edgar Rd., St. Louis MO 63119. Regional repertory theatre, professional equity company, for general public. Plays varied in themes. Interested in any play suitable for a subscription audience of over 13,000. Royalty payments negotiable; usually between 4% and 5% of gross. Send complete script. Enclose S.A.S.E. Reports within 4 months during the winter season; closed over the summer. Produces 5 plays a year, only one of them an original production.

THE MAGIC THEATRE, INC., 1615 Polk St., San Francisco CA 94109. Oldest experimental theatre in California; established in 1768. Director: John Lion. For public audience, generally college educated. General cross section of area with an interest in an alternative theatre. Plays produced in San Francisco, California; produced in the off-off-Broadway manner. Cast is part professional and part amateur. "The director of the Magic Theatre's concept leans toward Dada and Surrealist movements in the arts. Its main resident playwright is Michael McClure, well-known poet and playwright. For past 3 years has had Rockefeller funding for playwright-in-residence program. The playwright should have an avant-garde approach to his writing with a specific intellectual concept in mind or a specific theme of social relevance. We don't want to see scripts that would be television or 'B' movie oriented. Our productions are technically produced, very simply. One-act or two-act plays considered. Playwright usually copyrights own script. We pay 5% of gross, $100 advance." Produces 15 plays a year. Enclose S.A.S.E.

MANHATTAN THEATRE CLUB, Stephen Pascal, Literary Director, 321 E. 73 St., New York NY 10021. A three theatre, performing arts complex classified as off-off Broadway, using professional actors. "We have a large, diversified audience which includes a large number of season subscribers. We want plays about contemporary problems and people. No special requirements. No verse plays or historical dramas or large musicals. Very heavy set shows or multiple detailed sets are out. We prefer shows with casts not more than 10. No skits, but any other length is fine." Payment is negotiable. Query first with synopsis. Enclose S.A.S.E. Reports in 6 to 8 weeks. Produces 30 plays a year.

CHRISTIAN H. MOE, Theater Department, Southern Illinois University, Carbondale IL 62901. Plays will be performed in a university theater (either a 580-seat theater or an experimental theater which can seat 100 to 150). Cast will be non-equity. Audience is a public one drawn from a university community with disparate interests. Largest percentage is a student and faculty audience. Student age range is roughly from 16 to 25. Also a children's theatre audience ranging from pre-school to 13 years. No restriction on subject matter. "Since we do 3 to 4 children's plays each year, we are interested in children's theatre scripts as well as adult. We prefer full-length plays since we have many student one-acts, the best of which it is our first obligation to produce. Small cast plays are preferred. This applies to children's plays also. A limited budget prohibits lavish set or property demands." Two-act, three-act, and 50 to 60 minute children's plays. Payment is standard; no set figure. Normally pays $15 per performance for a children's play. Special arrangements made for plays that tour. Query first with synopsis. Enclose S.A.S.E. Usually reports in 3 months. Produces 18 plays a year.

DOUG MOODY MYSTIC SOUND STUDIO'S MYSTIC MUSIC CENTRE, Solar Records, 6277 Selma Ave., Hollywood CA 90028. For home entertainment, all ages. Works produced on phonograph albums and cassette tapes. "We are looking for works capable of being performed within one hour, non-visual. Can be musical. Can rely on sound effects to replace visual effects. Think about the medium!" Payment depending upon royalties to artists and musical copyright royalties. Buys phonograph and audio rights. Query first with synopsis only. Enclose S.A.S.E. for return of submissions.

OFFICE FOR ADVANCED DRAMA RESEARCH, 3526 Humboldt Ave. S., Minneapolis MN 55408. Director: Arthur H. Ballet. "The Office for Advanced Drama

Research, operating with a grant from the Rockefeller Foundation, the National Endowment for the Arts, the Mellon Foundation, and the Shubert Foundation, concentrates its entire attention on playwrights, who are invited to submit unproduced scripts for consideration. The Office each year reads hundreds of scripts; of these a number are selected and submitted to cooperating theatres for consideration. If a theatre agrees that rehearsal and production facilities should be made available to the playwright, the Office in essence underwrites limited facilities for the theatre and the playwright. For the most part these are professional or semiprofessional companies, but a limited number of educational and community theatres are included. The University of Minnesota, uniquely recognizing its responsibility to the art of the theatre as it long has recognized its responsibilities to the sciences, utilizes this facility for a laboratory where the artist can work his play, try a new idea, form, or style without great financial and personal risk as an artist. The O.A.D.R. is not dedicated to or limited to a particular kind of drama or theatre. The O.A.D.R. does not work with previously produced plays, with adaptations, or with musicals. The playwright agrees to make every effort to be available to the producing theatre before and during the rehearsal period, clearly understanding that the O.A.D.R. involvement is in behalf of the playwright and that that involvement presupposes substantial in-residence availability during the rehearsal period." For complete details of the terms and conditions of the program, write for brochure and enclose S.A.S.E.

OLD LOG THEATER, Box 250, Excelsior MN 55331. Producer: Don Stolz. Produces two-act and three-act plays for "a professional cast. Public audiences, usually adult. Interested in contemporary comedies. Small number of sets. Cast not too large." Produces about 14 plays a year. Payment by Dramatists Guild agreement. Send complete script only. Enclose S.A.S.E. for return of submissions.

OPERA VARIETY THEATER, 3944 Balboa St., San Francisco CA 94121. For "public audience of all ages, upper educational level. All types of interests. Plays produced in our theater. Professionals and non-professionals in cast. No special subjects, but plays must be suitable for family audience. Prefer musicals, but occasionally do plays. Must have some character interest; must have some plot interest. I'm not interested in social or other reforms, just entertainment. No vulgarities. No great emphasis on sex. No vulgar language or action. One-act, two-act, three-acts and skits considered. Payment is usually a percentage agreement. We don't copyright plays, unless in the case of foreign works that we translate ourselves." Produces 2 to 6 plays a year. Query first with synopsis only or send synopsis or complete script. Reports in 1 month. Enclose S.A.S.E. for return of submissions.

GUY PALMERTON, 210 W. 55 St., New York NY 10019. Plays produced in summer theater. Looking for high, fast comedy; farces; non-worry, non-political plays. No distasteful characters. Two-acts and three-acts. Comedy songs and parodies also. Enclose S.A.S.E.

JOSEPH PAPP, New York Shakespeare Festival Public Theater, 425 Lafayette St., New York NY 10003. "Interested in plays and musicals with contemporary relevance, but no restrictions as to style, historical period, traditional or experimental form, etc." Produces plays at the Public Theatre (housing six theatres), the Delacorte Theatre (Central Park) and at Lincoln Center (Beaumont and Newhouse Theatres). Pays according to standard play option and production agreements. Advance varies. Reports in 4 to 6 weeks. Enclose S.A.S.E.

POET'S REPERTORY THEATRE, Box 203, Brookhaven NY 11719. Both a tour program and a resident theater program. The tour program plays for any host organization, especially libraries, churches, public schools, colleges, arts conferences, private homes. Resident theater wing plays in four permanent locations twice each year, three performances per production per location. Audiences are both public and private, and are composed of all interests, intelligences, and educational levels. Shorter plays are wanted for tour program, 5 minutes to 55 minutes. Some longer plays for the resident theater program. No restriction on subject or theme. Small casts, preferably no more than 3 for the shorter plays to be toured (although 4 or 5 might get by), and 5 for the longer plays. Avoid extremes of age (no parts for children or the elderly); the play should be able to be cast with persons who are in the age range of 18 to 50. The play should not rely for its impact upon tricky lighting or scenery. No nudity, no on-stage sexual intercourse. One-act, two-act, three-act, or skits considered. "Royalty payments may range between $5 and $20 per performance for shorter plays; about $40 for longer plays. It should be stressed that we are in the context of the experimental and art theater movement and will only use material that is within that context." Send synopsis or complete script. Enclose S.A.S.E. Reports usually in 3 to 5 weeks. Produces about 12 plays a year.

REPERTORY THEATER OF AMERICA, P.O. Box 1296, Rockport TX 78382. Professional, national touring company. Most performances booked by colleges, universities, military bases, churches and community arts organizations. "Since we tour nationally, and perform to a wide variety of audiences, our material must be 'middle-of-the-road'. Experimental theater, or plays with questionable language or subject matter cannot be considered. Format is unimportant to us. We must have something that works on the stage, not the page. No absurd, experimental, oversexed stories, and no dialogue plagiarized from the walls of bus stop men's rooms." The cast is 2 men and 2 women. Props must be minimal. Special effects are out of the question except for simple sound cues. Two-act plays, no longer than 2 hours playing time. Usually pays between $10 and $15 per performance. A play is usually performed about 100 times a season. A very good script will get as many as 200 performances a year, and will be kept in the repertoire for several seasons. Query first with synopsis. Enclose S.A.S.E. Submissions received between October and January receive prompt reports. Those received during the spring and summer have a long wait. Produces between 3 and 4 plays a year.

STEFAN RUDNICKI, University of Rochester Drama Center, c/o Morey 411, University of Rochester, Rochester NY 14627. Plays produced for "summer theater, classroom, readers theater, and workshop productions (large and small scale). Casts will include students and professionals. For a university audience; some community orientation." Interested in "anything, but especially new translations of foreign works. Playwright in residence work possible. Avoid rigidness of thought or structure." Produces 15 plays a year; 8 to 10 are one-act plays. Pays "amateur royalty (a flat fee of $35 to $50 for the first performance and $15 to $35 for each subsequent performance, usually paid to author's agent)." Send synopsis or complete script. Reports in 2 months. Enclose S.A.S.E. for return of submissions.

ST. CLEMENTS, 423 W. 46 St., New York NY 10036. Plays will be produced at St. Clement's, an off-off Broadway theater; all productions are fully professional for public performances; audiences expect off-off Broadway to be somewhat experimental or innovative. One-act, two-act, or three-act plays. "Our productions are presented under the terms of the Equity Showcase Code. There are no royalties. It is a showcase for the playwrights." Send complete script or submit through agent. Enclose S.A.S.E. Reports in 3 to 6 months. Produces 4 or 5 major plays a year and 10 or 12 readings.

SCHOOL OF DRAMA-NORTH CAROLINA SCHOOL OF THE ARTS, P.O. Box 4657, Winston-Salem NC 27107. Plays will be performed in school; main stage or workshop theatre; student casts, possibly augmented by faculty. Community audience. Plays must have youthful casts, balance of male and female roles (best if more female). Any length acceptable. Payment: expenses of residency during rehearsals or standard royalties. Query first with synopsis. Enclose S.A.S.E. Takes several months to report (not enough readers to handle all the scripts received). Produces about 10 plays a year.

SCORPIO RISING THEATRE FOUNDATION, 426 N. Hoover St., Los Angeles CA 90004. For an audience of selected theatre buffs. "Scorpio Rising Theatre is an ensemble repertory theatre dedicated to the works of new playwrights. Looking for all kinds of plays, but prefer contemporary themes. The playwright should be familiar with the ensemble, preferably seeing some SRT productions. We don't want any situation comedies or Broadway type musicals. Simple cast, props, stage, etc. One-act, two-act, three-act, skits; prefer full lengths, but open to all." Also interested in developmental work with playwrights-in-residence. Buys amateur performance rights. Payment to be negotiated. Produces 12 plays a year. Send script to Alistair Hunter. Send complete script only. Reports in 1 to 2 months. Enclose S.A.S.E. for return of submissions.

SEATTLE REPERTORY THEATRE, P.O. Box B, Queen Anne Station, Seattle WA 98109. Plays will be produced on either main stage, or in second theatre, with professional casts in both cases. The second house performs younger, more avant-garde and special interest plays. Audience for main stage is middle class; high percentage of college graduates; ages ranging from teens to advanced middle age. Plays for second house, particularly, will involve novel forms of stage, experiments in style; particular interest in works that explore new ways to use language. In main house, more conventional plays with themes related to present time. Almost any format is acceptable providing the writing is of high quality. No limitations in cast, but prefers three-act plays. Payment depends on the plays; a guarantee against a percentage of the gross, usually starting at 4%. "When negotiating a new script, we retain a financial interest in subsequent productions of the play for a specified period of time." Send synopsis, with a dozen or so pages of script to give feeling of style, etc. Enclose S.A.S.E. Reports in about 3 months. Produces about 12 plays a year.

CHARLES STILWILL, Managing Director, Community Playhouse, Box 433, Waterloo IA 50704. Plays performed at Waterloo Community Playhouse with a volunteer cast. "We have 4,415 season tickets holders. Average attendance at main stage shows is 4,500; at studio shows 1,500. We try to fit the play to the theatre. We try to do a wide variety of plays." Looking for good plays with more roles for women than men. "Our public isn't going to accept nudity, too much sex, too much strong language. We don't have enough black actors to do all black shows. We have done plays with as few as 3 characters, and as many as 45. On the main stage we usually pay between $300 and $500. In our studio we usually pay between $100 and $200." Send synopsis or complete script. Enclose S.A.S.E. Reports negatively within 1 month, but acceptance takes a little longer because they try to fit a wanted script into the balanced season. Produces 7 plays a year: 1 musical, 3 comedies, 3 dramas.

TACONIC PROJECT, Box 10, Spencertown NY 12165. Workshop and fully staged new play series with professional company. For general public, with special interest in plays for young people on American subjects. Small cast, cabaret material. "Writer should see our company at work and be familiar with ensemble acting. No plays about war, discovery of sex, or screwed up people." Prefers casts of 4 to 6. One-act, two-act, three-act, cabaret material. Payment varies from no payment at all to a modest performance fee; $5 to $25, depending on length. Playwright retains copyright. Send complete script. Enclose S.A.S.E. Reports usually within 7 days. Produces 4 plays a season.

THEATRE AMERICANA, P.O. Box 245, Altadena CA 91001. Attn: Playreading Committee. In operation for 40 seasons. For public general audience. Local theatre. Showcase for unknowns in all phases of theater. Awards for best director, set designer, actors, as well as best play. Looking for plays with quality and originality. Any subject matter. Selections not made on the basis of any set structure, but if new forms are used, they must work successfully from an audience viewpoint. Two-act or three-act plays, 1½ to 2 hours playing time. Not interested in trite material; pornography for shock value unacceptable. Modern verbiage in a valid characterization not censored. Musicals should include piano arrangements. Plays with a Christmas theme or setting are welcomed. No royalties can be paid, but the 4 original plays produced each year are eligible to compete for the $300 C. Brooks

Fry Award. Authors copyright own plays. Send complete script only. Reporting time is "very slow. Read year-round. Plays retained until May, when 4 are selected for next season's production." Enclose S.A.S.E. for return of submissions.

THEATRE ARTS-UNIVERSITY THEATRE, A Theatre in Search of Playwrights Program, Virginia Polytechnic Institute and State University, Blacksburg VA 24061. Plays are produced as part of Theatre Arts-University Theatre major and studio seasons. Casts are students and occasionally guest or faculty artists. "We also recommend scripts to other producers — professional, stock, university and amateur community theatres, and generally operate as a kind of clearinghouse for new materials. Interested in plays and musicals for an adult audience, but will also read new children's scripts. Scripts should be inexpensively bound, not loose. Musicals should include score. Theatres are modern and well-equipped, so no restrictions." One-act, two-act, three-act, and musicals. Pays standard royalty rate: $50 for first performance, $25 for additional performances; negotiated rate for musicals. "We also provide transportation and expenses for playwright for a portion of rehearsal period in the event of a premiere." Send complete script and include playwright's resume, if available. Enclose S.A.S.E. Reports usually in 1 month. Produces 13 to 20 plays per season.

THEATRE RAPPORT, 8128 Gould Ave., Hollywood CA 90040. Artistic Director: Crane Jackson. Equity company. Produces plays of 1, 2, and 3 acts. Produces gutsy, relevant plays on highly artistic level and true subjects. No unjustified homosexuality, nudity or profanity; realistic acceptable. For a sophisticated, educated, non-fad, conservative (although venturesome) audience looking for something new and different. Not avant-garde, but a strong point of view is an asset. Approach must be unique. All plays must be West Coast premieres. Pays 20% of gross. Send complete script. Reports in 2 weeks. Enclose S.A.S.E. Produces 6 plays a year.

UNIVERSITY AND FESTIVAL THEATRE, W. E. Crocken, General Manager, 137 Arts Bldg., The Pennsylvania State University, University Park PA 16802. For general audience 18 to 60 years of age. Produced at either of the Pavilion of Playhouse Theatres located at University Park. University Theatre is an amateur/education program; the Festival Theatre is an equity/student theatre program offered during the summer. Any kind of play is considered. Usually does not copyright plays. For a straight play, pays between $25 and $50 per performance. Produces 12 to 16 plays a year. Send complete script only. Reports in 1 month. Enclose S.A.S.E.

UNIVERSITY THEATRES, Patricia McIlrath, Director, University of Missouri-Kansas City, Kansas City MO 64110. For the public. "The plays will be produced at the University Theatre by academic performers and professionals for the summer repertory. Will consider all types of dramas; however, no musicals. Under 20 in the cast; limited budget. All lengths are considered." Pays $50 and 5%. Produces 6 to 10 plays a year. Send complete script only. Reports in 1 month. Enclose S.A.S.E.

MAURICE WATSON, Brooklyn College, Department of Educational Service, Bedford Ave. and Ave. H, Brooklyn NY 11210. For general audience. Summer theatre, community theatre. The cast will be both professional and so-called amateur. Plays that are political in nature, social dramas, family dramas, contemporary issues. One-act plays are acceptable, but prefer two-act or three-act. "Sometimes copyright plays. I purchase the right to produce with an option for a movie." Pays $100; negotiation if the play moves to off-Broadway. Produces 2 to 4 plays a year. Send complete script or synopsis. Reports in 2 to 3 weeks. Enclose S.A.S.E. for return of submissions.

WAYSIDE THEATRE, c/o Gerald Slavet, Middletown VA 22645. Looks at original plays for small cast. Produces two-act and three-act plays; comedy, musicals, tragedy, drama and one-act children's plays. Pays royalties on production. Query first with synopsis. Reports "as soon as possible." Enclose S.A.S.E.

YALE REPERTORY THEATRE, Literary Manager, 222 York St., New Haven CT 06520. Resident professional theatre. For University-oriented audience, but with appeal to a larger community. No limitations of age or special interests, but emphasis on an audience with serious perceptual intelligence, receptive to experiment and innovation. No limitations on subject matter or theme; depth and intelligence of writer's approach are chief factors. No stylistic restrictions; no fakery, slickness, conventionality of expression, pseudo-light and pseudo-serious Broadway-style entertainment, etc. "We are generally limited to what the imagination can summon up on a small thrust stage with no flies and little wing space, but we have other stages available for projects with more ambitious physical requirements. Full-evening works preferred." Offers standard L.O.R.T. author contract. Copyright remains with author. "We retain limited residual rights and a small percentage of author's proceeds on subsequent sales of the work." Send synopsis or complete script. Enclose S.A.S.E. Reports in about 2 months. Produces 7 or 8 full professional productions a year, plus a variety of student full productions, workshops, and cabaret productions.

Play Publishers

Markets for the playwright's work are several: play publishers, whose names and addresses follow; play producers, listed in the Play Producers section; television producers, and motion picture poducers. Film producers, like television producers, will not look at scripts submitted directly by the writer. They must be submitted through recognized literary agents. A list of these appears in the Authors' Agents section.

Publications which do not primarily publish plays but occasionally may publish dramatic material in some form are listed in the Juvenile, Literary and "Little", and Theater, Movie, TV, and Entertainment categories in the Consumer Publications section. The playwright should also check the Book Publishers for additional play markets.

CONTEMPORARY DRAMA SERVICE, Box 457, Downers Grove IL 60515. Editor: Arthur L. Zapel, Jr. "Interested in one-act plays, documentary dramas, adaptations, and church liturgies. Subject matter should be of interest and concern to school-age audience, from junior high through college. Treatment of material should make classroom presentation easy. Current affairs and social dilemmas of special interest. Currently interested in women's lib, abortion, ecology. Plays must present both sides of issue. Presentations for religious holidays Christmas, and Easter accepted. Simple structure, not dependent on props and complicated staging. Novelty drama such as puppet-theater, skits, and monologues also considered. Particularly interested in good comedy material. We look most for unique style in staging ideas as well as action. We see drama as a means of communication through participation. Not interested in 3-act 'message plays' or traditional theater fare. We prefer realistic dialog written artfully. A 30-page script is maximum for us. Prefer about 6 in cast." Accepts over 20 plays a year from freelancers. Buys all rights. Pays 10% royalty "up to agreed amount." Send complete script with short synopsis and author's production notes. Reports in "about 1 month." Enclose S.A.S.E.

DODD, MEAD & COMPANY, 79 Madison Ave., New York NY 10016. Executive Editor: Allen T. Klots. Only interested in "playwrights after professional production, who promise to contribute to the literature of the theater." Royalty negotiated. Buys book rights only. Reports in about 4 weeks. Enclose S.A.S.E.

ELDRIDGE PUBLISHING COMPANY, P.O. Drawer 209, Franklin OH 45005. Editor: Kay Myerly. Wants good three-act and one-act plays. Publishes comedy, drama, high school plays, seasonal plays. Special day, church, and school entertainments for all ages and all occasions. Unusual plots, snappy dialog, good curtains. "All settings must be kept at a minimum. We do not accept anything on a controversial theme. Writers should bear in mind that short dialog is much better than a long, drawnout speech." Accepts 15 to 20 plays a year from freelancers. Payment on acceptance. "Payment varies with well-known authors and the type of script." Query first. Reports "as soon as possible; during our busy season it might take longer than 90 days." Enclose S.A.S.E. for reply to queries.

SAMUEL FRENCH, 25 W. 45th St., New York NY 10036. Willing at all times to read mss of books concerning the theater, as well as mss of plays. Wants plays that are "original, imaginative. Interested in character. No motion picture scenarios, verse plays, single-shot TV plays, Biblical plays, or children's plays on subjects already published." Accepts 10 to 15 mss a year from freelancers. No reading fee. In addition to publishing plays, also acts as agents in the placement of plays for Broadway production, and of program series for television production. Payment on royalty basis. Send complete script. Reports in 8 to 10 weeks. Enclose S.A.S.E. for return of submissions.

PERFORMANCE PUBLISHING, 978 N. McLean Blvd., Elgin IL 60120. Editor: Virginia Butler. Plays produced for stock, summer, college, high school, grade school, and community theatres. "We publish plays for all segments of the market. However, plays for and about young people tend to be more successful. For the non-Broadway market, plays for and about high school students are usually the most remunerative. We're looking for comedies, mysteries, dramas, farces, etc., with modern dialogue and theme. The writer should read a number of published plays before attempting to write one himself. Generally, a great deal more experience can be obtained by limiting oneself to the one-act market until one has had at least one work published. We don't want X-rated material." One-act, two-act, and three-act plays wanted. 50% high school, 15% children's theater, 35% college, community stock and church theater groups. "We offer royalty contract on industry standard terms. We usually copyright plays in the name of the author and in general acquire all publication and stage rights with exception of first-class professional rights, which remain the author's property, as do radio, film, TV, etc." Send synopsis or complete script. Enclose S.A.S.E. Reports in 3 weeks to 3 months. Publishes approximately 40 plays a year.

PIONEER DRAMA SERVICE, 2172 S. Colorado Blvd., Denver CO 80222. Editor and Publisher: Shubert Fendrich. "Our main needs now are for children's theater plays (plays that have been produced by adults for children), about an hour in length, and old-fashioned melodrama. We also buy a very few outstanding one-act plays. We are interested only in plays that have been successfully produced on the amateur or professional stage." Does not want to see "unproduced plays, one-acts with more than one set, plays which are largely male in cast." Accepts a maximum of 10 plays a year from freelancers. "We either select plays on a basis of outright purchase or pay a royalty of 10% of copy sales and 50% of production royalties and resale rights." Buys all rights. Reports in 1 to 2 months. Enclose S.A.S.E.

PLAYS, The Drama Magazine for Young People, 8 Arlington Street, Boston MA 02116. Associate Editor: Sylvia E. Kamerman. Publishes approximately 90 one-act plays each season. Interested in buying good plays to be performed by young people of all age groups—junior and senior high, middle grades, lower grades. In addition to comedies, farces, melodramas, skits, mysteries and dramas, can use plays for holidays and other special occasions, such as Bicentennial Book Week, National Education Week. Adaptations of classic stories and fables, historical plays, plays about other lands, puppet plays, plays for all-girl or all-boy cast, folk tales, fairy tales, creative dramatics, plays dramatizing factual information and on such concepts as good government, importance of voting, involvement and participation as citizens, and plays for conservation, ecology or human rights programs are needed. Prefers one scene; when more than one is necessary, changes should be simple. Mss should follow the general style of *Plays.* Stage directions should not be typed in capital letters or underlined. Every play ms should include: a list of characters, an indication of time, a description of setting; an "At Rise," describing what is taking place on stage as curtain rises; production notes, indicating the number of characters and the playing time, describing the costumes, properties, setting and special lighting effects, if any. Playwrights should not use incorrect grammar or dialect. Characters with physical defects, speech impediments should not be included. Desired lengths for mss are: Junior and Senior high—20 to 25 double-spaced ms pages (25 to 30 minutes playing time). Middle Grades—12 to 15 pages (15 to 20 minutes playing time). Lower Grades—6 to 10 pages (8 to 15 minutes playing time). Pays "good rates on acceptance." Annual $500 award for best play published. Reports in 3 to 4 weeks. Enclose S.A.S.E. for return of submissions.

Syndicates

Syndicates sell editorial copy to publishers on a commission basis, with the author receiving 40 to 60 percent of the gross proceeds. Some syndicates, however, pay the writer a salary or a minimum guarantee. Writers of top syndicated columns may earn $50,000 or more per year. The aspiring syndicate writer must first make sure his work won't be competing in an already flooded field. Second, he must select a syndicate which will properly promote his material. The larger syndicates, of course, usually have better promotional facilities. (A list of syndicates which includes all the titles of the columns and features they handle appears in the Editor and Publisher Syndicate Directory *($5) published at 850 Third Avenue, New York NY 10022.) It's best to query the syndicate editor first, enclosing a half-dozen sample columns or feature ideas and a stamped addressed envelope. Some writers self-syndicate their own material. The writer here earns 100% of the proceeds but also bears the expense of soliciting the clients, reproducing and mailing the features, billing, etc. See the chapter "How to Syndicate Your Own Column" in the* Writer's Digest *book,* The Creative Writer.

AMERICAN FEATURES SYNDICATE, 964 Third Ave., New York NY 10022. Editor: Robert Dehren. Copyrights material. Will consider photocopied submissions. Reporting time "varies." Enclose S.A.S.E. for return of submissions.
Nonfiction: Travel and true adventure. Buys single features and article series. Does not contract for columns. Length: 1,000 to 5,000 words. Pays $100 to $750. Usual outlets are newspapers and regional magazines, including some trade publications.

AMERICAN SYNDICATE, INC., P.O. Box 1000, Mid-City Station, Dayton OH 45402. Director: Albert (Hap) Cawood. Rights purchased vary with author and material. Will consider photocopied submissions. Reports in 2 weeks. Enclose S.A.S.E.
Nonfiction: News items and nonfiction. "We generally add one new column a year. Columns are contracted, but we are very picky and prefer to do our own hunting for talent in publications. Our talent already has a professional track record. We are not a general purpose syndicate but specialize in a select few columns and features. Must be brief, depending on type of feature. Pay 50% commission. We do not handle photos."

AP NEWSFEATURES, 50 Rockefeller Plaza, New York NY 10020. General Executive: Dan Perkes. Enclose S.A.S.E. for return of submissions.
Nonfiction and Photos: Buys article series or column ideas "dealing with areas of science, social issues that can be expanded into book form. Do not usually buy single features." Length: 600 to 1,000 words. Pays minimum $25.

ASSOCIATED CHURCH PRESS SYNDICATED FEATURES, 326 W. State St., Media PA 19063. Editor: Dennis E. Shoemaker. Rights purchased vary with author and material, but usually buys first rights. Buys 10 features a year. Will consider photocopied submissions. Query first. Reports in 2 weeks. Enclose S.A.S.E.

Nonfiction: Religious, global perspectives, third world, social justice, and ecumenical material. Single features. 2,500 words. Pays $100 to $150 direct payment to author or ½ of each sale, with minimum guarantee of $50. Pays $25 per each sale to ACP membership, split with author.

AUTHENTICATED NEWS INTERNATIONAL, ANI, 170 Fifth Avenue, New York NY 10010. Editor: Sidney Polinsky. Supplies material to national magazines, newspapers, and house organs in the United States and important countries abroad. Buys exclusive and non-exclusive rights. Reports in 3 months. Enclose S.A.S.E.
Nonfiction and Photos: Can use photo material in the following areas: hard news, photo features, ecology and the environment, science, medical, industry, education, human interest, the arts, city planning, and pertinent photo material from abroad. Prefers 8x10 b&w glossies, color transparencies (4x5 or 2¼x2¼, 35mm color). Where necessary, model releases required. Pays 50% royalty.

AUTO NEWS SYNDICATE, 8530 Canfield Dr., Dearborn Heights MI 48127. Editor: Don O'Reilly. Unsolicited material is acknowledged or returned within a few days, "but we cannot be responsible for loss." Enclose S.A.S.E.
Nonfiction and Photos: Syndicated articles, photos on automotive subjects and motor sports. Newspaper articles ("Dateline: Detroit" and "Inside Auto Racing"). Magazine articles. Radio broadcasts ("Inside Auto Racing"). 50% commission. No flat fees.

BUDDY BASCH FEATURE SYNDICATE, 771 West End Ave., New York NY 10025. Editor: Buddy Basch. Buys all rights. Will consider photocopied submissions. Query first or submit complete ms. Reports in 1 week to 10 days. Enclose S.A.S.E.
Nonfiction, Humor, Photos, and Fillers: News items, nonfiction, humor, photos, fillers, puzzles, and columns and features on travel and entertainment. "Mostly staff written at present. Query first."

BETTER WORLD EDITORIAL PRODUCTIONS, 809 F St., San Diego CA 92101. Editor: Fess Daniels. Rights purchased vary with author and material. Buys all rights on fillers, columns, regular features; first rights on articles, and second serial (reprint) rights. Buys about 50 articles and several hundred fillers a year, when available. Will consider photocopied submissions. Query first or submit complete ms. Reports in 1 week. Enclose S.A.S.E.
Nonfiction, Photos, and Fillers: Insights into environmental problems and solutions, exposes, etc. Features about new inventions, new products, a new approach to a national problem. "We are currently handling an article series on mass-transit, one on sickle cell anemia and one on alcoholism. We will consider subjects like drug addiction, race relations, ecology issues, politics, government, health, safety, education, and subjects with public impact by professionals in their respective fields. Feature length: 300 to 4,500 words. Column length: 300 to 400 words weekly. Photos are purchased with features. Payment for photos included in payment for feature. Features with photos will pay more. We buy fillers outright and pay 5c to 15c per word, on acceptance. When we decide to handle an article or other feature we will mail the writer a contract, stating our terms and the rate we will charge newspapers for the finished item, ready for publishing. We pay the writer 50% of that rate and mail him a check each month for that month's sales."

CANADA WIDE FEATURE SERVICE, 245 St. Jacques St., Montreal, Que. Canada H2Y 1M6. Stock photo agency. Photo Editor: Steve Pigeon. Supplies photographs "for editorial purposes, public relations advertisements, etc. Do not buy outright; accept on consignment."
Photos: Color transparencies of animals scenery, industry, sports, people in all situations (preferably with model release). Only top quality photography will be accepted. "We give 50% commission."

CANADIAN SCENE, Suite 305, 2 College St., Toronto, Ont., Canada. M5G 1K3. Editor: Miss Ruth Gordon. Query first. Submit seasonal material 3 months in advance.

Reports in 1 week. Pays on acceptance. Enclose S.A.E. and International Reply Coupons for reply to queries.

Nonfiction: "Canadian Scene is a voluntary information service. Its purpose is to provide written material to democratic, foreign language publications in Canada. The material is chosen with a view to directing readers to an understanding of Canadian political affairs, foreign relations, social customs, industrial progress, culture, history, and institutions. In a 700-word article, the writer can submit almost any subject on Canada, providing it leaves the newcomer with a better knowledge of Canada. It should be written in a simple, tightly knit, straightforward style." Length: 500 to 1,000 words. Pays 3¢ a word.

CHICAGO TRIBUNE-NEW YORK NEWS SYNDICATE, INC., 220 East 42nd St., New York NY 10017. Editor: Thomas B. Dorsey. Supplies material to Sunday supplements and newspapers in North America and abroad. Buys "worldwide rights, where possible; must have North American rights to be interested." Submit "at least 6 samples of any submission for continuing feature, plus statement of philosophy for column." Enclose S.A.S.E. for return of submissions.

Nonfiction, Photos, and Puzzles: "Political, women's, humor, sports, health, food, furnishings, fashion columns. We're looking for short, topical series on social, psychological, news-oriented subjects—6 to 12 parts, 7,500 to 15,000 words; topical and humor columns. Must be extremely well-written. No single features unless highly exclusive and topical." Buys article series. Contracts for columns. "Anything fresh and original is considered. Must be extremely well-written and provide a new idea or a very different approach to what's in field now. No bad carbon copies of columns already on market." Length: "whatever the writer is comfortable with and works for the subject." Pay "varies, depending on market. Usual 50-50 split on contractual material." Photos purchased with features. Wants "top grade b&w glossies and/or original color transparencies."

COLLEGE PRESS SERVICE, 1764 Gilpin St., Denver CO 80218. Rights purchased vary with author and material. Buys all rights, first rights, second serial (reprint) rights, but usually does not copyright material; articles published for one-time use by 380 subscriber papers now in 47 states; combined readership about 1.2 million. Buys 50 to 75 features a year from freelancers. Will consider photocopied submissions. Query first or submit complete ms. Reports in 4 to 6 weeks. Pays on publication. Enclose S.A.S.E. for return of submissions.

Nonfiction, Photos, Cartoons, and Fillers: News items, nonfiction, photos, political cartoons, comic strips (but no series strips), and filler graphics and sketches. "Features of a national angle that are of interest to a college audience. CPS covers events and activities on individual campuses; educational reform and campus trends; conferences and activities of national education and student groups; governmental activity and programs affecting higher education and students; alternative coverage of national and international affairs; news analysis, but no pure opinion articles. Buys single features. Short articles (up to 300 words) if based in a particular state or region should have a national angle. No pure opinion articles. Recent features have included articles on government regulation of student access to food stamps, student input into collective bargaining, exclusive coverage of the Kent State and Southern shootings trials, step-by-step coverage of the federal student file law controversy, and how to obtain scholarships and loans. We do not buy article series. Very seldom contract for columns. Features may range up to an ideal maximum of 1,200 words. Pay $5 to $25. We are nonprofit." Photos purchased with features. Captions required. Not fussy about size, but clarity important. Pays $1 to $15.

COLUMBIA FEATURES, INC., 36 West 44 St., New York NY 10036. Editor: William H. Thomas. Buys all rights and world rights, all media. Will consider photocopied submissions. Submit complete ms. Pays on a regular monthly basis for continuing column or contract. Reports in 2 to 4 weeks. Enclose S.A.S.E. for return of submissions.

Humor and Puzzles: Cartoons, comic strips, puzzles, and columns on a continuing basis. Features for special sections: family, home, women's, Sunday supplements. No single features, except series of 6 to 12 parts, about 750 to 1,000 words each article. Current features include "Antique Wise," question and answer column on antiques; "Under Twenty," for teenagers; "Cassini Carousel," gossip column; "Sex Information Service" feature, etc. Lengths vary according to features. Columns: 500 to 750 words. Pays 50% usually.

COMMUNITY AND SUBURBAN PRESS SERVICE, 100 E. Main St., Frankfort KY 40601. Managing Editor: Mike Bennett. Buys second serial (reprint) rights. Pays on acceptance. Enclose S.A.S.E. for return of submissions.
Humor and Photos: Cartoons, gag panels, human interest photos. 8x10 glossy photos purchased without features. Captions required. Pays $12.50 per cartoon.

CRISWELL PREDICTS NEWSPAPER SYNDICATE, 6620 Selma Avenue, TV-Bldg.-One, Hollywood CA 90028. Editor: Jeron King Criswell. Buys all rights. Will handle copyrighted material. Buys about 50 features a year from freelancers. Query first. Reports in 1 week. Enclose S.A.S.E. for reply to queries.
Nonfiction: Buys very specialized material dealing with predictions, past and present. Length: open. Pays 10¢ a word.

CRUX NEWS SERVICE, Shickshinny PA 18655. Editor: Thourot Pichel. Does not copyright material. Buys "very few" features a year from freelancers. Will consider photocopied submissions. Enclose S.A.S.E. for return of submissions.
Nonfiction: "History and political only." Buys single features. Does not buy article series or columns. Pays "nominal standard."

CURIOUS FACTS FEATURES, 514 Deerfield Road, Lebanon OH 45036. Editor: Donald Whitacre. Buys all rights. Pays on publication. Reports in 2 weeks. Enclose S.A.S.E.
Nonfiction: Uses "oddities" of all types including strange animals, strange laws, people, firsts, etc. Length: 50 to 100 words. Pays $10 to $15.

DIDATO ASSOCIATES, 280 Madison Ave., New York NY 10804. Rights purchased vary with author and material. Will consider photocopied submissions. Query first or submit complete ms. Pays on acceptance. Reports immediately. Enclose S.A.S.E.
Nonfiction: News items which have a behavior science or psychology angle. Must have solid research references by behavior scientists or related professionals. Single feature examples: your clothes tell your personality; study reveals sex attitudes of teenagers; depression linked up with job blahs; terrorists are suicidal personalities, survey shows. Length: 500 to 2,000 words. Pays negotiable rates. Especially needs news-related story ideas and leads in outline form of about 100 words; also with one or more research references. Pays $10 to $50 for leads. Currently handling behavior columns of various types and psychology quizzes.

DORN-FREDRICKS PUBLISHING CO., 35 East 35 St., Suite 7-H, New York NY 10016. Editor: Dona Davis Grant. Buys all rights, worldwide, foreign rights. Query first. Enclose S.A.S.E.
Nonfiction, Humor, Poetry, and Fillers: Gossip columns of worldwide interest; material for feminine markets; fashion, beauty, etc. Single features include: "Harvest Time of Life" (column), "Mighty Mixture" (column), "Famous Mothers," "Your Key to Courage," "How the West Was Won," "Crafts" and "Homemaker's New Ideas." Interested in humor columns of approximately 800 words. Famous personalities, and beauty. Column length: 800 words. Pays 3¢ a word minimum, depending on name value.

EDITORIAL CONSULTANT SERVICE, P.O. Box 120, Babylon NY 11702. Director: Art Ingoglia. Buys all rights. Pays on acceptance. Handles copyrighted material "on occasion." Query first. Reports in 2 to 3 weeks. Enclose S.A.S.E.
Nonfiction: Freelance material welcome for business press, newspapers, top magazines. Column ideas accepted for automotive column "Let's Talk About Your Car."

General features accepted after writer has been assigned by editor. Payment on percentage basis of 50%.

ENTERPRISE SCIENCE NEWS, 230 Park Ave., New York NY 10017. Editor: David Hendin. Buys all rights. Pays on acceptance. Query first. Reports in 2 to 4 weeks. Enclose S.A.S.E. for reply to queries.
Nonfiction: "We only buy from professional science-medical writers." Wants feature-type newspaper stories on scientific subjects of current interest. The science should be interesting and applicable to the reader. Must be clear, concise, accurate and objective. Stories with good art receive preference. Length: 700 to 1,200 words. Pays $30 to $500, "depnding on author, length and type of story, quality of writing, whether commissioned or not, etc."
Photos: Buys with features or with captions only. Color or b&w. Rates vary.

EZ INTERNATIONAL FEATURES, Apartado 540, Cuernavaca, Morelos, Mexico. Editor: Emil Zubryn. Rights purchased vary with author and material. Buys all rights or second serial (reprint) rights. Buys 24 to 50 features from freelancers a year. Query first or submit complete ms. Reports almost immediately. Enclose S.A.S.E.
Nonfiction, Fiction, Photos, and Humor: "Any published material that has wide universal appeal; readable, with photos for illustration. No run-of-the-mill, always something with hard impact, and exclusive, offbeat blockbusters. Buys single features if significant enough and with strong international interest; movie interviews, exposes, sensationalism, and hard impact. Always looking for series, signed celebrity stories and so-called blockbusters. No continuous features unless something absolutely fantastic with circulation building possibilities. Length: 750 minimum with photos to 5,000 words for singles; 3,000 words for 3-part series; 6,000 for 6-part series, etc. Pay 50% basis. Photos purchased with or without features, but must have major impact. Captions required. Especially interested in transparencies; pin-ups, nudes. Prefer 8x10 but will consider sharp 5x7, and transparencies in 4x5, although sharp 35mm okay. Photos handled on 50% basis."

FIELD NEWSPAPER SYNDICATE (formerly Publishers-Hall Syndicate), 401 N. Wabash Ave., Chicago, IL 60611. Editor: Richard Sherry. Supplies material to newspapers. Buys all rights. Reports in 3 to 4 weeks. Enclose S.A.S.E. for return of submissions.
Nonfiction: Article series "only on highly promotable topics by pros with top credentials." No single features. Contracts for columns. Syndicates columns such as Ann Landers, Sylvia Porter, Joseph Kraft, and Erma Bombeck. Interested in columns on "service, do-it-yourself, commentary." Length: 750 words maximum. Pay varies according to newspaper sales.

DAVE GOODWIN & ASSOCIATES, P.O. Box 54-6661, Surfside FL 33154. Editor: Dave Goodwin. Buys first rights. Will handle copyrighted material. Buys about 35 features a year from freelancers. No query required. Reports in 2 weeks. Enclose S.A.S.E. for return of submissions.
Nonfiction: "Money-saving information for consumers: how to save on home expenses; auto, medical, drug, insurance, boat, business items, etc." Buys single features "but prefer series." Buys column ideas. Material should be "brief, pithy, practical. We prefer meaty subject matter to lofty prose." Currently handling the following: Insurance for Consumers; Money Matters; Travel Log. Length: 50 to 500 words. Pays "50% on publication, or $3 per piece minimum and 10¢ per word maximum."

HARRIS & ASSOCIATES PUBLISHING DIVISION, 1661 E. 1220 North, Logan UT 84321. Rights purchased vary with author and material. May buy all rights or first rights. Does not purchase many mss per year since material must be in their special style. Pays on publication; sometimes earlier. Not necessary to query. Send sample or representative material. Reports in less than 30 days. Enclose S.A.S.E.
Nonfiction, Photos, and Humor: Material on driver safety and accident prevention. Humor for modern women (not women's lib); humor for sports page (golf is their

specialty). "We like to look at anything in our special interest areas. Will buy or contract for syndication. Everything must be short, terse, with humorous approach." Action, unposed, 8x10 b&w photos are purchased without features or on assignment. Captions are required. Pays 5¢ minimum per word and $15 minimum per photo.

HOLLYWOOD INFORMER SYNDICATE, P.O. Box 49957, Los Angeles CA 90049. Editor: John Austin. Buys first serial rights for one-time use. Handles copyrighted material. Usual outlets are Australia, England, Japan, Germany, U.S.A. Buys about 50 features a year from freelancers. Reports in 6 weeks. Enclose S.A.S.E.
Nonfiction and Photos: "Mainly 'show biz' oriented material, and offbeat human interest. New medical discoveries; personality features on new show business and TV faces, not written from 'clips.' Photojournalism pieces for Europe." Single feature length: 750 to 800 words. Also buys articles series such as photo features on exotic dancers for European magazines or offbeat series on famous murders. "Good market in Europe for photographers." Length: 4 to 6 parts, 1,500 words. Photos: 6x9 or 8x10 glossies. Captions required. Pays $20 to $150 and up for series.

HUMANIST FEATURES SYNDICATE, 3564 Clairemont Mesa Blvd., San Diego CA 92117. Editor: Ronald E. Hestand, Ph.D. Rights purchased vary with author and material. Buys first rights or second serial (reprint) rights. Reports in 6 weeks. Query first. Enclose S.A.S.E.
Nonfiction, Fillers and Cartoons: Humanistic, Atheistic, free-thinker, or rational based columns that emphasize man's ability to cope and live a better life without theistic superstitious beliefs. No religious material wanted. Recent and current columns include: The Humanist Viewpoint, Science for Youth, Swinging, Alcoholism, and Current Education Trends. Buys single features only if they have strong sales possibility. Article series vary with market, current sales. Feature length: 1,000 to 3,000 words. Column length: 500 to 1,000 words. 5x7 glossy photos purchased on assignment; captions required. Photo payment negotiable. Pays 75%, less expenses, for nonfiction; or as per sales contract.

IDEAL FEATURES, P.O. Box 1237-EG, Melbourne FL 32935. Editor: Harold Pallatz. Buys all rights. Buys up to 10 features a year. Will consider photocopied submissions. Query first. Reports in 2 to 4 weeks. Enclose S.A.S.E.
Nonfiction: Up to the minute information on health subjects, from a natural point of view (no medicines, chemicals or surgery). Personal stories (proof required) of ailments corrected in unusual manner or methods. Financial, how you make spare time income; short, concise, easy-to-read style. Include amounts (give figures) and other vital information. Now handling financial advice column and health columns. Column length: 100 to 500 words. Photos purchased with features; 5x7 or 8x10 glossies. Pays 5% to 25%, on publication.

INTERLUDE PRODUCTIONS, Box 157, Maplewood NJ 07040. Editor: Alan Caruba. Rights purchased vary with author and material. Buys first rights, second serial (reprint) rights, and other syndication rights. Pays on acceptance. Will consider photocopied submissions. Query first. Reports within 1 to 2 weeks. Enclose S.A.S.E.
Nonfiction: News items and nonfiction. "Interlude would welcome any weekly column ideas suitable for nationwide syndication. Currently we syndicate Bookviews, a book news and review column. Other materials include series dealing with wine and food news/commentary. Interlude will consider author interview articles of 500 to 1,000 words for distribution along with our Bookviews column. Payment will be 3¢ a word. Please make inquiry by letter first. Will buy articles series, but query first. Consider acquiring syndication rights to an article series, preferably dealing with cultural subjects, though by no means limited to that subject area. Interlude is fundamentally an in-house operation; however, we are open to good ideas for expansion in the handling of other columns. We would provide an equitable contract under such circumstances. Most likely asking the author to join us in the financing of the initial advertising and promotion of the column. The start-up costs are always the most critical. For columns, we believe no less than 300 and probably 500 words is the best length; though we are flexible depending on a subject. Features would

be 500 to 1,000 words or possibly more. Pay 50% following costs of production/mailing. Interlude does not accept photos at present."

INTERNATIONAL EDITORIAL SERVICES/NEWSWEEK, INC., 444 Madison Ave., New York NY 10022. Vice President: R.J. Melvin. Buys first rights or second serial (reprint) rights. Buys 50 to 100 features a year. Will consider photocopied submissions. Query first. Reports within 3 months. Enclose S.A.S.E.
Nonfiction and Photos: News items, backgrounders, personalities in the news. News-related features suitable for international syndication. Prefers approximately 1,200 words for features. Pays 50% on publication. Photos purchased with features. Pays $25 to $50 for b&w if purchased separately.

INTERPRESS OF LONDON AND NEW YORK, 400 Madison Ave., New York NY 10017. Editor: Jeffrey Blyth. Buys British and European rights mostly, but can handle world rights. Will consider photocopied submissions. Query first or submit complete ms. Pays on publication, or agreement of sale. Reports immediately or as soon as practicable. Enclose S.A.S.E.
Nonfiction and Photos: "Unusual stories and photos for British and European press. Picture stories, for example, on such 'Americana' as a five-year-old evangelist; the 800-pound 'con-man,' the nude-male calendar; tallest girl in the world; interviews with pop celebrities such as Yoko Ono, Bob Dylan, Sen. Kennedy, Valarie Perrine, Priscilla Presley, Bette Midler, Liza Minelli; cult subjects such as voodoo, college 'streaking,' anything amusing or offbeat. Extracts from books such as Earl Wilson's *Show Business Laid Bare*, inside-Hollywood type series ('Secrets of the Stuntmen,' 'My Life with Racquel Welch'). Real life adventure dramas ('Three Months in an Open Boat,' 'The Air Crash Cannibals of the Andes'). No length limits—short or long, but not too long. Payment varies; depending on whether material is original, or world rights. Pay top rates, up to several thousand dollars, for exclusive material. Photos purchased with or without features. Captions required. Standard size prints, suitable for radioing if necessary. Pay $50 to $100, but no limit on exclusive material."

KAMP STOOL FEATURES, Box 145, Meriden Rt., Cheyenne WY 82001. Editor: Joseph F. Prunty. Rights purchased vary with author and material. Buys second serial (reprint) rights, or all rights with photos. Buys 2 to 3 cartoons and about 40 photos a year. Reports in 30 days. Enclose S.A.S.E.
Cartoons and Photos: Modern rural cartoons. Cartoons on real estate, insurance, banking, and skiing. Cartoon series offered should be at least 1 year in duration. Pays 50%; authors' quote minimum guarantee. Payment made on acceptance by publication. Photos purchased without features; captions optional. 8x10 b&w. Nudes, complete or partial, for magazines. Also color photos. Pays $5 to $250. Rates vary with content and quality of material.

KING FEATURES SYNDICATE, 235 E. 45th St., New York NY 10017. Supplies material to newspapers. Submit new features and photos to Neal Freeman, Vice President and Editor. Enclose S.A.S.E. for return of submissions.
Nonfiction and Photos: "Topical nonfiction, 'service' material, leisure activities." Buys photo features and article series. Contracts for columns. Length: 500 to 750 words. Pays in commission percentage.

LOS ANGELES TIMES SYNDICATE, Times Mirror Square, Los Angeles CA 90053. Chief Editor: Patrick McHugh. Buys newspaper syndication rights. Reports in 2 weeks. Enclose S.A.S.E. for return of submissions.
Nonfiction: Buys columns. Interested in fresh and original features of a continuing nature. Syndicates the Art Buchwald, Joseph Alsop columns. Contract arrangements are made in payment for material.

McNAUGHT SYNDICATE, INC., 60 E. 42 St., New York NY 10017. Editor: Anne Rickey. Buys about 4 features a year from freelancers. Will consider photocopied submissions. Reports in 4 weeks. Enclose S.A.S.E. for return of submissions.
Nonfiction and Humor: Puzzles, cartoons, comic strips, political and medical columns.

Contracts for columns: Medical, astrology, political, career, inspirational, and humor. Length: 200 to 500 words. Payment is usually 50/50 after expenses. Pays $25 for cartoons for "Funny World." Newspapers are usual outlet for material.

MID CONTINENT FEATURE SYNDICATE, Box 1662, Pittsburgh PA 15230. Editorial Chairman: Charles L. Conover. Supplies material to "600 small and medium-sized daily newspapers." Buys North American rights. Pays on acceptance. Reports in 5 days. Enclose S.A.S.E. for return of submissions.

Nonfiction: Book reviews, serialized books, fashion series, urban redevelopment series, pollution control articles, memoirs, world movie (not Hollywood) material. Purchases single books for serialization; buys features in minimum six-article form in areas of current events, education, women's interest, cookbook materials. Wants "materials for syndicated columns being distributed: food, fashion, drama, business (2 columns), humor, book review (3 columns), Washington news, and special metals technical review. Our contracts with syndicated writers and artists call for the usual 50/50 division of net proceeds, after production and distribution expenses. Materials bought on a spot basis are on standard per word or per panel rates, depending on the stature of the writer or artist, and going from 5¢ a word upward."

NATIONAL CATHOLIC NEWS SERVICE, 1312 Massachusetts Ave., N.W., Washington DC 20005. Editor: A.E.P. Wall. "Individual judgments are made" as to copyrighting material. "We are served by a number of stringers as well as freelancers. We provide a daily service and have a fairly constant market. Inquiries are welcomed, but they should be both brief and precise. Too many inquiries are coy and/or vague. Will consider photocopied submissions." Reports in 2 to 3 weeks. Enclose S.A.S.E. for reply to queries.

Nonfiction: Short news and feature items of religious or social interest, particularly items with a Catholic thrust. Buys single features and articles series. Feature examples: Buddhists in Hawaii, religious life today in the Soviet Union, development of new teaching techniques in U.S. Catholic diocese; social-ethnic implications of the presidential election. Series examples: programs to provide alternatives to abortion for unwed pregnant women; changing attitudes toward activist programs among U.S. Protestants. Contracts for columns: "This is a highly competitive market and we are extremely selective. Our columns range from labor concerns to the liturgy." Length for single features: no minimum, maximum of 800 words. Article series: maximum of 3 parts, about 700 words each. Columns: open in length; generally, the shorter the better. Generally pays a maximum of 5¢ a word for news and feature copy. Buys book reviews at a rate of 3¢ a word for a maximum of 500 words. Does not buy *unsolicited* reviews, but welcomes queries. "We market primarily to more than 100 Catholic weekly newspapers. We also serve foreign Catholic agencies and U.S. Catholic weekly newspapers."

Photos: Purchased with or without features. Captions required. News and feature photos of interest to Catholic periodicals. "We operate a photo service that mails to clients four times a week." Pays from $5 to $15 for each photo, depending on quality and originality.

NATIONAL FEATURES SYNDICATE, 1001 National Press Bldg., Washington DC 20045. Editor: Fred Rosenblatt. Reports in 1 week or less. Pays on acceptance. Enclose S.A.S.E.

Nonfiction: Inside stories of politics and economics of health industry and no-fault and malpractice insurance. Buys singles as well as column ideas.

NATIONAL NEWSPAPER SYNDICATE, 20 N. Wacker Drive, Chicago IL 60606. Editor: John Hickey. Buys all rights. Reports in 3 weeks. Enclose S.A.S.E.

Nonfiction and Comic Strips: Buys only columns and comic strips on continuous basis, daily or weekly; no series or short run features. No general commentary; columns on specific subject areas only.

NEW YORK TODAY, INC., NEWS SERVICE, 850 7th Ave., PH C., New York NY 10019. Editor: Ray Wilson. Query first. Enclose S.A.S.E.

Nonfiction: Food, restaurants, entertainment, travel and astrology material for newspapers, radio, television and magazines. Authoritative stories on wine. "We buy something that fits into our scheme of things. Criswell Predicts, Ray Wilson on Broadway, Bob Dana on Wine and Food, and Travel by Hermes, are a few examples of columns we now handle." Length: 750 words. "We have no established rate of payment. We use writers on assignment basis only if our staff cannot cover. Other material is submitted for our approval through query. Then we contact the writer."

NEWS FLASH INTERNATIONAL INC., 508 Atlanta Ave., North Massapequa NY 11758. Editor: Jackson B. Pokress. Supplies material to Observer/Tribune newspapers and Champion sports publications. "Contact editor prior to submission to allow for space if article is newsworthy." Will consider photocopied submissions. Pays on publication. Enclose S.A.S.E. for reply to queries.
Nonfiction: "We have been supplying a weekly column on sports to many newspapers on Long Island as well as pictures and written material to publications in England and Canada. Payment for assignments is based on the article. It may vary. Payments vary from $20 for a feature of 800 words. Our sports stories feature in-depth reporting as well as book reviews on this subject. We are always in the market for good photos, sharp and clear, action photos of boxing, football and baseball. We cover all major league ball parks during the baseball and football seasons. We are accredited to the Mets, Yanks, Jets and Giants. During the winter we cover basketball and hockey and all sports events at the Nassau Coliseum."
Photos: Purchased on assignment; captions required. Uses "good quality 8x10 b&w glossies; good choice of angles and lenses." Pays $7.50 minimum for b&w photos.

NEWSPAPER ENTERPRISE ASSOCIATION, 230 Park Ave., New York NY 10017. Executive Editor: Robert J. Cochnar. Supplies material to "more than 600 daily newspapers." Buys world rights. Will handle copyrighted material. Buys 50 to 75 features a year from freelancers. Query first; send samples. Reports in 2 weeks. Enclose S.A.S.E. for reply to queries.
Nonfiction and Photos: "Science-oriented material; investigative reports; good ideas well-executed. We seldom purchase single features. We are interested in well-researched series on topics of particular interest to general audiences. We contract for columns and distribute material on practically all subjects. Do not want to see any Ann Landers type columns or humor columns." Length: 600 to 900 words. Pays $15 to $500. "We are launching a new service for Sunday newspapers and supplements and expect to purchase at least 12 nonfiction articles which should run about 1,500 to 2,500 words. For these, we expect to pay up to $2,500." 7x9 or 8x10 b&w glossies purchased with or without features; captions required.

NORTH AMERICAN NEWSPAPER ALLIANCE, 220 E. 42nd St., New York NY 10017. Executive Editor: Sidney Goldberg. Editor: Sheldon Engelmayer. Supplies material to leading U.S. and Canadian newspapers, also to South America, Europe, Asia and Africa. Buys newspaper syndication rights. Reports in 2 weeks. Enclose S.A.S.E. for return of submissions.
Nonfiction and Photos: In the market for background, interpretive and news features. The news element must be strong and purchases are generally made only from experienced, working newspapermen. Wants timely news features of national interest that do not duplicate press association coverage but add to it, interpret it, etc. Wants first-class nonfiction suitable for feature development. The story must be aimed at newspapers, must be self-explanatory, factual and well condensed. It must add measurably to the public's information or understanding of the subject, or be genuinely entertaining. Broad general interest is the key to success here. Rarely buys columns. Looking for good one-shots and good series of 2 to 7 articles. Where opinions are given, the author should advise, for publication, his qualifications to comment on specialized subjects. The news must be exclusive to be considered at all. Length: 800 words maximum. Rate varies depending on length and news value. Minimum rate $25, but will go considerably higher for promotable copy. Buys 8x10 glossy photos when needed to illustrate story. Pays $5 to $10.

NUMISMATIC INFORMATION SERVICE, Rossway Rd., Pleasant Valley NY 12569. Editor: Barbara White. Buys all rights and reprint rights. Reports in 1 week. Enclose S.A.S.E. for return of submissions.
Nonfiction: First-person articles concerning coins and coin collecting. In-depth studies of the technical aspects of numismatics. Background data on any field of coins, notes and related material. Buys single features as well as column ideas. Length: 500 words maximum. Pays $5 per column per week.

OCEANIC PRESS SERVICE, 4717 Laurel Canyon Blvd., North Hollywood CA 91607. Editor: J. Taylor. "We serve the entire free world and will only look at material which is of global interest from Finland to India. Material has to be published in the U.S.A. first and in one of the well-known magazines." Buys outright or pays 50/50 syndicate rate for serialization; 20% on foreign book and TV sales. Buys, if possible, U.S. second rights and world rights. Buys 300 to 400 features for reprint from freelancers each year. Query first. Reports in 1 month. Enclose S.A.S.E.
Nonfiction: Considers only published columns for foreign markets; ESP columns, Solve a Crime, 2-Minute Mystery, Test Yourself, illustrated tests, etc. Occasionally buys single features, if very outstanding and concern world known personalities.
Photos: Outdoors, sports, underwater picture stories; color transparencies (but not singles).
Fiction: Wants published books for serialization and syndication for U.S. and foreign markets. Prefers love novels, war books, science fiction, mysteries, psychological novels. Motion picture rights to published works only; paperback rights for abroad. Also TV screen plays.

PUNGENT PRAYER, 904 E. Main St., West Frankfort IL 62896. Editor: Rev. Phil E. Pierce. Supplies material to newspapers. "Copyright registration optional with author." Buys first, second or third reprint rights, if specified. Buys up to 50 features a year from freelancers. Will consider photocopied submissions. Reports in 3 weeks. Pays on publication. Enclose S.A.S.E. for return of submissions.
Nonfiction and Poetry: "Prayers and prayer stories only. Colorful prayers. Prayers that are different—salty, earthy, or humorous, with pathos or social concern, related to everyday life or life crises. Prayer-poems acceptable if colorful, especially those concerning church and patriotic holidays and major events. Colorful prayers and stories of answered prayers. No ordinary prayers. We welcome true stories of answered prayers with verification." Maximum length: 350 words or 40 lines. Pays $2 to $7.

REGISTER AND TRIBUNE SYNDICATE, 715 Locust St., Des Moines IA 50304. President: Dennis R. Allen. Supplies material to newspapers. Buys all rights. Buys about 10 features a year from freelancers. Reports in 4 to 6 weeks. Enclose S.A.S.E.
Nonfiction and Photos: Does not buy single features. Buys 6- to 12-article series "on current topics such as ecology and bicycles (safety and maintenance). We prefer not to see puzzles. Writers are overworking nostalgia features." Syndicates features like "The Family Circus," "The Better Half," "The Alumnae," Dr. Walter C. Alvarez, Dr. S. I. Hayakawa and others. Length: 50 to 1,000 words. Payment in royalty commission. 8x10 glossies purchased with features; captions optional.

RELIGIOUS NEWS SERVICE, 43 W. 57th St., New York NY 10019. Editor: Lillian R. Block. Supplies material to "secular press, religious press of all denominations, radio and TV stations." Enclose S.A.S.E. for return of submissions.
Nonfiction and Photos: "Good news stories on important newsworthy developments. Religious news." Will buy single features "if they have news pegs. Most of our article series are produced by our own staff." Length: 200 to 1,000 words. Pays 2¢ a word. Photos purchased with and without features and on assignment; captions required. Uses b&w glossies, preferably 8x10. Pays $5 minimum.

SAWYER PRESS, P.O. Box 46-578, Los Angeles CA 90046. Editor: E. Matlen. Buys all rights. Buys 50 cartoons a year. Will consider photocopied submissions. Submit complete cartoons only. Reports in 1 week. Enclose S.A.S.E.

Cartoons: Editorial cartoons suitable for college newspapers. Sophisticated social commentary. Pays 5% royalty.

BP SINGER FEATURES, INC., 3164 Tyler Ave., Anaheim CA 92801. Editor: Jane Sherrod. Rights purchased vary with author and material. Buys all rights, second serial (reprint) rights, and foreign reprint rights. Buys "very few originals a year. Many reprints. Hundreds of books." Query first. "We want tearsheets for reproduction." Returns rejected material within 3 weeks. Does not return accepted features. Reports sales only. Enclose S.A.S.E. for return of rejected material.
Nonfiction, Fiction, Photos, Puzzles, and Books: Reprints of good fiction from leading magazines, book reprints for foreign countries (doctor, nurse, Gothic, mystery novels). Only in book form. Contracts for illustrated puzzles. Does not want to see "crossword puzzles or articles on ecology, local events; no sex fiction." Photos purchased with features and on assignment; captions required. "Prefer 4x5 transparencies or jacket covers, greeting cards, posters of racing cars in action, romantic art, movie and TV stars." Payment negotiable; minimum $10.

SOCCER ASSOCIATES, P.O. Box 634, New Rochelle NY 10802. Editor: Irma Ganz Miller. Buys all rights. Query first. Reports at once. Enclose S.A.S.E.
Nonfiction and Photos: Buys very little. Currently syndicating "Soccer Shots" and special soccer coverage. Pays $25 to $100.

TEENAGE CORNER, INC., 4800 Ellinda Circle, N.W., Canton OH 44709. Editor: David J. Lavin. Buys no rights. Payment on publication. Reports in 1 month. Enclose S.A.S.E.
Nonfiction: Buys material on teenage problems and situations. Length: 300 to 500 words. Pays $5 to $10.

TRANSWORLD FEATURE SYNDICATE, INC., 141 E. 44th St., New York NY 10017. International Manager: Mary Taylor Schilling. North American Sales Manager: Elsa H. Zion. Supplies material to "magazine and newspaper publishers all over the world." Does not copyright material. Pays on publication. Reports "quarterly." Enclose S.A.S.E.
Nonfiction, Photos, and Illustrations: Wants "magazine features, pictures on personalities, and current events." Pays 40% to 50% commission. Photos purchased on assignment; captions required.

U-B NEWSPAPER SYNDICATE, 15155 Saticoy St., Van Nuys CA 91405. Editor: Steve Ellingson. Supplies material to "leading newspapers in all cities." Buys all rights. Will handle copyrighted material. Query first. Reports "immediately." Pays on publication. Enclose S.A.S.E. for reply to queries.
Nonfiction and Photos: Syndicates detailed do-it-yourself articles. Length: 200 to 400 words. Pays $100 to $500.

UNITED FEATURE SYNDICATE, 220 E. 42nd St., New York NY 10017. Managing Editor: Sidney Goldberg. Supplies material to newspapers throughout the world. Will handle copyrighted material. Buys 25 to 50 series per year, preferably 3 to 7 articles (world rights preferred). Buys first and/or second rights to book serializations. Query first with outline. Reports in 3 months. Enclose S.A.S.E. for reply to queries.
Nonfiction, Comic Strips and Puzzles: News, features, series, columns, comic strips, puzzles. Current columnists include Jack Anderson, Marquis Childs, Henry Taylor, Virginia Payette, Barbara Gibbons. Comic strips include Peanuts, Nancy, Tarzan. Rates negotiable for one-shot purchases. Standard syndication contracts are offered for columns and comic strips.

UNITED PRESS INTERNATIONAL (UPI), 220 E. 42nd St., New York NY 10017. Editor-in-Chief: H.L. Stevenson. "Features and columns are usually staff-written. We sometimes approach prominent personalities and authorities—such as a statesman or a doctor—to write for us. We do employ some freelance stringers, who supply us with local spot news. Professional writers interested in becoming stringers for UPI should query first."

U.S. NEWS SERVICE, Suite 862, National Press Building, Washington DC 20004. Bureau Chief: Walter Fisk. Buys all rights. May handle copyrighted material. May not return rejected material. Enclose S.A.S.E. for return of submissions.
Nonfiction, Humor, Fiction, Photos, Fillers, and Poetry: Buys single features and column ideas. Length varies. Payment varies. 8x10 single weight glossies purchased with features, without features, and on assignment. Captions required.

UNIVERSAL PRESS SYNDICATE, 475 Fifth Avenue, New York NY 10017. Editor: James F. Andrews. Buys syndication rights. Reports normally in 4 weeks. Submissions should be sent to Kansas City office: 6700 Squibb Rd., Mission KS 66202. Enclose S.A.S.E. for return of submissions.
Nonfiction: Looking for features—columns for daily and weekly newspapers. "Any material suitable for syndication in daily newspapers." Currently handling the following: Doonesbury by G.B. Trudeau, Garry Wills column, etc. Payment varies according to contract.

UNIVERSAL TRADE PRESS SYNDICATE, 37-20 Ferry Heights, Fair Lawn NJ 07410. Editor: Leon D. Gruberg. Buys first trade paper rights only. Query first. Enclose S.A.S.E. for reply to queries.
Nonfiction: Buys merchandising features in all fields; knitwear merchandising at the retail level; features on knitting mill operations. Length: 1,250 words. Pays 65%.

LEO WHITE PRODUCTIONS, INC., 168 Strasser Ave., Westwood MA 02090. Mary V. White, Editor. Will consider photocopied submissions. Buys a few cartoons a year. Reports promptly. Enclose S.A.S.E.
Cartoons, Comic Strips, and Puzzles: "We deal strictly in cartoons; especially if cartoons and puzzles combined. All contracts are standard. 50% syndicate contract."

DOUGLAS WHITING, LIMITED, 930 De Courcelle St., Montreal H4C 3C8, Que., Canada. Editor: D.P. Whiting. Supplies material to "all major dailies in Canada and many in the United States." Buys all newspaper rights. No query required. Reports in 4 to 6 weeks. Enclose S.A.E. and International Reply Coupons.
Nonfiction: Science panels, contest promotions, puzzle features and feature columns. "The freelancer should look for ideas and content that are unique. Too much of the sample material received by us is very similar to established syndicated features. Bear in mind, too, that we are a Canadian syndicate. Most of the material received is too American." Does not buy single features. Length: 150 to 250 words, daily columns; 700 to 1,000 words, weekly columns. "Usually author's share is 40% of net after production costs are deducted. Costs do not include our sales calls and promotion material."

WOMEN'S NEWS SERVICE (a division of North American Newspaper Alliance), 220 E. 42nd St., New York NY 10017. Editor: Sid Goldberg. Buys all rights. Will handle copyrighted material. Buys about 300 features a year from freelancers. No query required. Reports in 2 weeks. Enclose S.A.S.E. for return of submissions.
Nonfiction and Fillers: Buys background, interpretive and news features of interest to women. News element must be strong. Looking for good, sprightly news features that do not duplicate press association coverage, but add to it, interpret it, etc. Family problems, feminism, consumerism, female careers, abortion reform, women's rights, etc. Prefers single features. Rarely takes on a new column. Also looking for good series ideas. Make sure it has a news peg or relates to a current trend. Length: 300 to 1,500 words; 500 to 700 words, single features. Pays "$25 minimum, may go considerably higher for blockbusters, series." Also buys fillers (30 to 150 words) of interest to women. Pays $5 to $15.

WORLD-WIDE NEWS BUREAU, 309 Varick St., Jersey City NJ 07302. Editor: Arejas Vitkauskas. Enclose S.A.S.E. for return of submissions.

Nonfiction: "Our multiple writeups (separate, and in our weekly columns), start in greater New York publications, then go simultaneously all over the U.S.A. and all over the world where English is printed. News from authors, or literary agents, or publishers on books planned, or ready, or published. Anything from poetry and children's books, to space technology textbooks. We cover over eighty different trade fields."

ZODIAC NEWS SERVICE, 950 Howard St., San Francisco CA 94103. Editor: Jon Newhall. Supplies material to FM stations across the U.S. "We only require exclusive rights for 72 hours." Buys about 1,000 features a year from freelancers. "We purchase 3 each day. Please mail in material (typed) and include phone number for additional information." Will consider photocopied submissions. "If we accept an item for use, it is sent out within 48 hours." Pays on publication. Enclose S.A.S.E.

Nonfiction: "We want exclusive, short news stories suitable for radio reporting. Our audience is young, disenchanted with the establishment. All news stories must be national, not regional or local in interest. Features must be short. We have done radio features (150 to 200 words at most) on ecology problems such as Black Mesa and the Big Sky development, on war protests, on drugs, on rock musicals, on bizarre, offbeat human interest anecdotes and results of psychological studies." Does not buy article series or column features. Length: 200 words "at most, but the shorter, the better." Pays $10.

Writers' Clubs

The following clubs are local or regional, nonprofit social or professional groups. They are listed geographically by state, then club name within the state. Writers are requested to enclose a self-addressed stamped envelope when writing any club about membership, meeting times, or further information.

To obtain information on starting a writer's club, consult the booklet How To Start/Run a Writer's Club *(Writer's Digest, 50¢).*

Alabama

ALABAMA STATE POETRY SOCIETY, Riley Nicholas Kelly, President, Excel AL 36439.

CREATIVE WRITERS OF MONTGOMERY, Gary Earl Heath, Secretary, 3816 Governors Dr., #H-233, Montgomery AL 36111.

Arizona

AMERICAN POETRY LEAGUE, T. Mary Fowler, President, 10419 Audrey Dr., Sun City AZ 85351.

ARIZONA PRESS WOMEN, INC., Geraldine Paul, 8215 E. Devonshire Ave., Scottsdale AZ 85251.

INTERNATIONAL POETRY SOCIETY, Genevieve Sargent, P.O. Box 10592, Phoenix AZ 85060.

Arkansas

AUTHORS, COMPOSERS AND ARTISTS' SOCIETY, Peggy Vining, Counselor, 6817 Gingerbread Lane, Little Rock AR 72204.

NORTHWEST ARKANSAS BRANCH, NLAPW, Mrs. Virginia D. Sturm, Box 188, Sulphur Springs AR 72768.

POETS' ROUNDTABLE OF ARKANSAS, Roberta E. Allen, 6604 Kenwood Rd., Little Rock AR 72207.

California

ASPIRING WRITER'S CLUB, Gertrude Katz, P.O. Box 7042, Long Beach CA 90807.

CALIFORNIA WRITERS' CLUB, Dorothy Benson, Secretary, 2214 Derby St., Berkeley CA 94705.

CALIFORNIA WRITERS GUILD, Dorothy Marie Davis, Secretary, 2624 G North Lake Ave., Altadena CA 91001.

CHRISTIAN WRITERS' LEAGUE, Jean Hogan Dudley, 3700 Olds Rd., Oxnard CA 93030.

CUPERTINO WRITER'S WORKSHOP, Phyllis Taylor Pianka, 10117 N. Portal Ave., Cupertino CA 95014.

DALY CITY CREATIVE WRITERS' GROUP, Margaret O. Richardson, President, 243 Lakeshire Dr., Daly City CA 94015.

THE FICTIONAIRES, Armand Hanson, 10792 Harrogate, Santa Ana CA 92705.

FOUNTAIN VALLEY WRITERS WORKSHOP, Clara Schultz, 8815 Hummingbird Ave., Fountain Valley CA 92708.

GEORGE FREITAG WRITERS' SEMINAR, Jewell Swertfeger, Director, P.O. Box 814, Wrightwood CA 92397.

LOS ANGELES DEPARTMENT OF WATER & POWER WRITER'S CLUB, Syble Lagerquist, 3969 Barryknoll Dr., Los Angeles CA 90065.

LOS ESCRIBIENTES, Nora Collins, 107 Rancho Alipaz, 32371 Alipaz St., San Juan Capistrano CA 92675.

MOUNTAIN-VALLEY WRITERS, Pat Wolff, Secretary, 18140 Hawthorne, Bloomington CA 92316.

NORTHERN CALIFORNIA CARTOON & HUMOR ASSOCIATION, Walt Miller, Secretary, 609 29th Ave., San Mateo CA 94403.

RIVERSIDE WRITER'S CLUB, Mary L. Hughes, President, 5525 Jones St., Riverside CA 92505.

SAN DIEGO PROFESSIONAL WRITERS WORKSHOP, Chet Cunningham, 8431 Beaver Lake Dr., San Diego CA 92119.

SHOWCASE WRITERS CLUB, Larry Stillman, 7842 Barton Dr., Lemon Grove CA 92045.

SOUTHWEST MANUSCRIPTERS, R.E.B. Battles, 560 S. Helberta Ave., Redondo Beach CA 90277.

SPELLBINDER'S LITERARY GUILD, P.O. Box 10623, Santa Ana CA 92711.

SURFWRITERS, LaVada Weir, 905 Calle Miramar, Redondo Beach CA 90277.

TIERRA DEL SOL WRITERS CLUB, Valetta Smith, 9750 Ramo Court, Santee CA 92071.

WRITERS CLUB OF PASADENA, Willard C. Hyatt, 231 S. Hudson, No. 6, Pasadena CA 91101.

WRITERS' CLUB OF WHITTIER, INC., Marilyn Jensen, 10404 Payette Dr., Whittier CA 90603.

WRITERS' WORKSHOP WEST, Bob McGrath, 17909 San Gabriel Ave., Cerritos CA 90701.

Colorado

WE WRITE OF COLORADO, Hilda Sperandeo, 6680 Carr St., Arvada CO 80004.

Connecticut

CONNECTICUT WRITERS LEAGUE, Maryland Lincoln, P.O. Box 78, Farmington CT 06032.

District of Columbia

WASHINGTON AREA WRITERS, Deborah Ashby, 1232 17 St. N.W., Washington DC 20036.

Florida

WEST FLORIDA WRITERS GUILD, Beulah Springer, 408 Labree Rd., Warrington FL 32507.

Illinois

FRIENDS OF AMERICAN WRITERS, Mrs. Franklin Smith, President, 7744 W. Hortense Ave., Chicago IL 60631.

KANKAKEE AREA WRITERS GROUP, Daisy Cahan, Secretary, 1359 Blatt Blvd., Bradley IL 60915.

MONMOUTH WRITERS GROUP, Mavis M. Meadows, Box 187, Abingdon IL 61410.

OFF-CAMPUS WRITERS' WORKSHOP, Joella Cramblit, 4019 Brittany Rd., Northbrook IL 60062.

QUAD CITIES WRITERS' CLUB, David R. Collins, President, 3724 15th Ave., Moline IL 61265.

Indiana

POETS' STUDY CLUB OF TERRE HAUTE, Esther Alman, President, 826 S. Center St., Terre Haute IN 47807.

SOUTH BEND WRITER'S CLUB, Doris Nemeth, President, 2314 W. 6th St., Mishawaka IN 46544.

STORY-A-MONTH CLUB, Nancy Berwick, R.R. 2, Box 295, Mooresville IN 46158.

Iowa

JASPER COUNTY WRITERS, INC., Olin C. Bissell, 1320 N. 4th Ave. W., Newton IA 50208.

WRITERS' STUDIO, Haskell Sarver, President, 1120 State St., Bettendorf IA 52722.

Kansas

UNIVERSAL WRITERS GUILD, Robert W. Patrick, 1815 Walker Ave., Kansas City KS 66104.

WICHITA LINE WOMEN, Jacquelyn Terral Andrews, 2350 Alameda Pl., Wichita KS 67211.

Kentucky

KENTUCKY STATE POETRY SOCIETY, Betsy McGee, Membership Chairman, 7189 Tylersville Rd., West Chester OH 45069.

LOUISVILLE WRITERS CLUB, Beverly Giammara, 2205 Weber Ave., Louisville KY 40205.

Louisiana

RUSTON WRITERS CLUB, Dr. Rudolph Fichler, 125 Pine Crest, Ruston LA 71270.

SHREVEPORT WRITERS CLUB, R.D. Poe, Rt. 2, Box 336-B, Haughton LA 71037.

Maryland

WORDSMITHS: THE SSA CREATIVE WRITING GROUP, Robert Hale, Room 2-C-25 Operations Bldg., Social Security Administration, 6401 Security Blvd., Baltimore MD 21235.

WRITERS LEAGUE OF WASHINGTON, L.M. O'Connor, Corres. Secretary, P.O. Box 449, Silver Spring MD 20907.

Massachusetts

MANUSCRIPT CLUB OF BOSTON, Katherine Saunders, President, 76 Lincoln St., Norwood MA 02062.

PIONEER VALLEY SCRIPTORS, Merrie Hagopian, 116 Meadowbrook Rd. E., Longmeadow MA 01028.

Michigan

ANN ARBOR CHRISTIAN WRITERS CLUB, Lee F. Smith, 1839 Shirley Lane, Ann Arbor MI 48105.

ANN ARBOR WRITERS WORKSHOP, Mitzi Rachleff Crandall, 19 Heatheridge, Ann Arbor MI 48104.

CHRISTIAN SCRIBES, Elizabeth McFadden, Box 280, Gobles MI 49055.

DETROIT WOMEN WRITERS, Bettie Cannon, President, 2707 Comfort Dr., West Bloomfield MI 48033.

POETRY SOCIETY OF MICHIGAN, S. Geneva Page, President, 256 Burr St., Battle Creek MI 49015.

UPPER PENINSULA WRITERS, Prof. Harley Sachs, Humanities Department, Michigan Tech University, Houghton MI 49931.

Minnesota

A.A.U.W. WRITERS' WORKSHOP, Mary Timmons, 9125 Utica Ave., Bloomington MN 55437.

EASTSIDE FREELANCE WRITER'S CLUB, Marlys B. Oliver, 139 Birchwood Ave., White Bear Lake MN 55110.

MESABI WRITERS CLUB, Archie Hill, Mesabi Community College, Virginia MN 55792.

MINNEAPOLIS WRITER'S WORKSHOP INC., Louise N. Johnson, President, 545 Northeast Mill St., Minneapolis MN 55421.

MINNESOTA CHRISTIAN WRITERS GUILD, Ruth McKinney, President, 3420 Hennepin Ave. S., Minneapolis MN 55408.

Missouri

CARTHAGE WRITER'S GUILD, Jacqueline R. Potter, 608 W. Highland, Carthage MO 64836.

MISSOURI WRITERS' GUILD, Lawrence Maisak, President, 2616 S. River Rd., St. Charles MO 63301.

NATIONAL LEAGUE OF AMERICAN PEN WOMEN, ST. LOUIS BRANCH, G. H. Wofford, 4940 Magnolia Ave., St. Louis MO 63139.

OZARK CREATIVE WRITERS, INC., Lida W. Pyles, President, 1429 S. Maple, Carthage MO 64836.

ST. LOUIS WRITERS' GUILD, James H. Nash, 326 Luther Lane, St. Louis MO 63122.

WRITERS GUILD OF ST. CHARLES, Lilah Contine, Secretary, 3063 Ridgeview Dr., St. Charles MO 63301.

Nebraska

NEBRASKA WRITERS GUILD, Wayne C. Lee, Lamar NE 69035.

NORTHEAST NEBRASKA WRITERS, Mrs. Edwin A. Volk, Battle Creek NE 68715.

New Jersey

NEW JERSEY POETRY SOCIETY, INC., Howard Reeves, Vice President of Public Relations, P.O. Box 217, Wharton NJ 07885.

WRITERS' GROUP, R.C.L. ASSOCIATES, Rhea C. Levy, 1247 Magnolia Pl., Union NJ 07083.

WRITERS' WORKSHOP, Sylvia Dichner Weiss, Wynbrook W. J6, E. Windsor Township NJ 08520.

New Mexico

ROSWELL WRITERS GUILD, Lois Reader, 1104 Avenida Del Sumbre, Roswell NM 88201.

New York

ASSOCIATION OF PROFESSIONAL WOMEN WRITERS, Isabel K. Hobba, 6007 Lockport Rd., Niagara Falls NY 14305.

BROOKLYN CONTEST AND FILLER WRITING CLUB, Selma Glasser, 241 Dahill Rd., Brooklyn NY 11218.

BROOKLYN POETRY CIRCLE, Gabrielle Lederer, Secretary, 61 Pierrepont St., Brooklyn NY 11201.

NEW YORK POETRY FORUM, Dorothea Neale, Director, 221 E. 28 St., New York NY 10016.

North Carolina

CHARLOTTE WRITERS CLUB, Aline Thompson, 604 B Archdale Dr., Charlotte NC 28210.

MARTHA'S VINEYARD WRITERS WORKSHOP, Thomas Heffernan, Box F9, 1020 Peace St., Raleigh NC 27605.

Ohio

THE CINCINNATI WOMAN'S PRESS CLUB, Leona F. Westland, 9 Dick Ave., Hamilton OH 45013.

COLUMBUS WRITERS CLUB, Larry Hothem, P.O. 8280, Columbus OH 43201.

LUNCH-BUNCH, Norma Sundberg, R.D. 1, Mechanicsville Rd., Rock Creek OH 44084.

MANUSCRIPT CLUB OF AKRON, V.M. Preston, 394 Washington Ave., Barberton OH 44203.

MEDINA COUNTY WRITER'S CLUB, Carol J. Wilcos, 3219 Country Club Dr., Medina OH 44256.

VERSE WRITERS GUILD OF OHIO, Maurice E. Lowks, 2267 Edmonton Rd., Columbus OH 43229.

Oklahoma

OKLAHOMA WRITERS FEDERATION, Ernestine Gravley, 1225 Sherry Lane, Shawnee OK 74801.

STILLWATER WRITERS, Florence French, Corres. Secretary, 513 S. Knoblock, Stillwater OK 74074.

WRITERS' GROUP OF CUSHING, Mazie Cox Read, President, S. Kings Highway, Cushing OK 74023.

Oregon

MILE HIGH CREATIVE WRITERS CLUB, Shirley Sipp, Rt. 6, Box 700, Lakeview OR 97630.

WESTERN WORLD HAIKU SOCIETY, Lorraine Ellis Harr, Editor, *Dragonfly*, 4102 N.E. 130 Pl., Portland OR 97230.

WRITER'S WORKSHOP, Dorothy Francis, 114 Espey Rd., Grants Pass OR 97526.

Pennsylvania

DELAWARE VALLEY WRITERS, Barbara Ormsby, 402 Milmont Ave., Milmont Park PA 19033.

LEHIGH VALLEY WRITERS' GUILD, Margaret Cummings, President, 1035 N. Arch St., Allentown PA 18104.

NEW CASTLE POETRY SOCIETY, Allurah Leslie, 1001 Logan St., New Castle PA 16101.

POETRY AND WRITER'S GUILD, H. Bennett Bey, 4401 Centre Ave., Pittsburgh PA 15213.

THE SCRIBBLERS, Edith Blades, Director, 326 E. Moreland Ave., Hatboro PA 19040.

WILLIAMSPORT WRITERS FORUM, Dorothy Foresman, 431 Locust St., Williamsport PA 17701.

WRITERS' CLUB OF DELAWARE COUNTY, Mrs. John P. Looby, 7100 Llanfair Rd., Upper Darby PA 19082.

WRITERS WORKSHOP OF DELAWARE CO., Barbara Ormsby, 402 Milmont Ave., Milmont Park PA 19033.

Rhode Island

RHODE ISLAND WRITERS' GUILD, Muriel E. Eddy, President, 139 Colfax St., Providence RI 02905.

South Dakota

SIOUXLAND CREATIVE WRITERS' CLUB, Mrs. Larry Ells, 1905 S. Lake Ave., Sioux Falls SD 57105.

Texas

ABILENE WRITERS GUILD, Juanita Zachry, 502 E. N. 16th, Abilene TX 79601.

BEAUMONT CHAPTER OF THE POETRY SOCIETY OF TEXAS, Violette Newton, 3230 Ashwood Lane, Beaumont TX 77703.

FREELANCERS WRITERS' CLUB, Dorothy Prunty, 311 W. Archer St., Jacksboro TX 76056.

NATIONAL LEAGUE OF AMERICAN PEN WOMEN, SAN ANTONIO BRANCH, Dr. Stella Woodall, President, 3915 S.W. Military Dr., San Antonio TX 78211.

PASADENA WRITERS' CLUB, June Caesar, 2204 Cherry Lane, Pasadena TX 77502.

SOUTH PLAINS WRITERS ASSOCIATION, Nancy V. Cooley, 6012 Vernon, Lubbock TX 79412.

STELLA WOODALL POETRY SOCIETY, Dr. Stella Woodall, President, 3915 S.W. Military Dr., San Antonio TX 78211.

WRITERS OF THE PURPLE SAGE, Evelyn S. Sherritt, 1210 Ashland Dr., Richardson TX 75080.

Utah

SEVIER VALLEY CHAPTER OF UTAH LEAGUE OF WRITERS, Marilyn A. Henrie, 68 E. 2nd St., South, Richfield UT 84701.

Virginia

POETS TAPE EXCHANGE, Frances Brandon Neighbours, Director, 109 Twin Oak Dr., Lynchburg VA 24502.

Washington

GIG HARBOR WRITER'S DISCUSSION GROUP, J. Clayton Stewart, 612 N. Eye St., Tacoma WA 98403.

LEAGUE OF WESTERN WRITERS, Philip Lewis Arena, President, 5603 239th Pl. S.W., Mountlake Terrace WA 98043.

POETRY LEAGUE OF AMERICA, Philip Lewis Arena, Poetry Manager, 5603 239th Pl. S.W., Mountlake Terrace WA 98043.

QUILL 'N' QUERY, Joy Oravetz, 1296 S. Farragut, Coupeville WA 98239.

TACOMA WRITERS CLUB, Clydelle Smith, Secretary, 3806 E. 104th St., Tacoma WA 98406.

West Virginia

MORGANTOWN POETRY SOCIETY, Kimberly Dunham, Publicity Chairman, 673 Bellaire Dr., Morgantown WV 26505.

Wisconsin

GENEVA AREA WRITER'S CLUB, Mrs. Charles M. Butts, 1565 Orchard Lane, Lake Geneva WI 53147.

SHEBOYGAN COUNTY WRITERS CLUB, Marion Weber, 1929 N. 13 St., Sheboygan WI 53081.

THE UPLAND WRITERS, Mrs. Harry Johns, 213 W. Chapel, Dodgeville WI 53533.

WISCONSIN FELLOWSHIP OF POETS, Anne Stubbe, President, 905 S. 6th St., Wausau WI 54401.

Wyoming

WYOMING WRITERS ASSOCIATION, Mrs. Vandi Moore, Jelm WY 82063.

Canada

CANADIAN AUTHORS ASSOCIATION, 22 Yorkville Ave., Toronto, Ontario, Canada M4W 1L4.

Writers' Conferences

The following writers' conferences are usually held annually. Contact the conference direct for details about staff, workshops, manuscript criticism opportunities, fees, accommodations, length of conference and dates planned for the current year. Always enclose a self-addressed, stamped envelope when requesting any information.

Alabama

ALABAMA WRITERS' CONCLAVE, Raecile G. Davis, 5621 Sixth Ave. S., Birmingham AL 35212.

Arkansas

ARKANSAS WRITERS' CONFERENCE, Anna Nash Yarbrough, Director, 510 East St., Benton AR 72015.

California

CALIFORNIA WRITERS CONFERENCE, Dorothy Benson, 2214 Derby St., Berkeley CA 94705.

FOREST HOME SCHOOL OF CHRISTIAN WRITING, Wes Harty, Forest Home, Inc., Forest Falls CA 92339.

LA JOLLA WRITERS' CONFERENCE, University Extension, University of California, P.O. Box 109, La Jolla CA 92037.

LONG BEACH WRITERS CONFERENCE, Betty L. Roeckers, P.O. Box 5584, Fullerton CA 92635.

RENAISSANCE INTEGRATED WORKSHOP, P.O. Box 3094C, San Diego CA 92103.

SEMINAR FOR FREELANCE WRITERS, Gladys Cretan, 717 Barneson Ave., San Mateo CA 94402.

WRITERS CONFERENCE IN CHILDREN'S LITERATURE, P.O. Box 827, Laguna Beach CA 92652.

WRITERS' FORUM, Pasadena City College, Office of Continuing Education, 1570 E. Colorado Blvd., Pasadena CA 91106.

Colorado

PUBLICATIONS ADVISERS WORKSHOP, John W. Windhauser, Department of Technical Journalism, Colorado State University, Fort Collins CO 80523.

Connecticut

CONNECTICUT WRITERS LEAGUE NUTMEG CONFERENCE, P.O. Box 11454, Newington CT 06111.

SUFFIELD WRITER-READER CONFERENCE, Jeanne B. Krochalis, 51-2 Jacqueline Rd., Waltham MA 02154.

District of Columbia

GEORGETOWN UNIVERSITY WRITERS' CONFERENCE, Dr. Riley Hughes, School for Summer and Continuing Education, Georgetown University, Washington DC 20007.

WRITER'S CONFERENCE, Myra Sklarew, Director, The American University, Department of Literature, Washington DC 20016.

Florida

FLORIDA SUNCOAST WRITERS' CONFERENCE, Doris Enholm, University of South Florida, St. Petersburg Campus, 830 First St. S., St. Petersburg FL 33701.

FLORIDA WRITERS' CONFERENCE, W.M. "Bill" Scruggs, Jr., University of Florida, DOCE 805 Seagle Bldg., Gainesvilde FL 32601.

WRITERS' CONFERENCE, C. LaRue Boyd, Rollins College, Box 2729, Winter Park FL 32789.

Georgia

DIXIE COUNCIL OF AUTHORS & JOURNALISTS, INC., Mrs. Jos. E. Buffington, Executive Secretary, 393 S. Coconut Palm Blvd., Tavernier FL 33070.

Illinois

CHRISTIAN WRITERS INSTITUTE CONFERENCE AND WORKSHOP, Gundersen Drive and Schmale Rd., Wheaton IL 60187.

INTERNATIONAL BLACK WRITERS CONFERENCE, INC., Alice C. Browning, 4019 S. Vincennes Ave., Chicago IL 60653.

Indiana

MIDWEST WRITERS' WORKSHOP, Office of Continuing Education, Ball State University, 222 N. College Ave., Muncie IN 47306.

Kentucky

CREATIVE WRITING CONFERENCE, William Sutton, Eastern Kentucky University, Richmond KY 40475.

WRITING WORKSHOP FOR PEOPLE OVER 57, Council on Aging, University of Kentucky, Lexington KY 40506.

Maine

STATE OF MAINE WRITERS' CONFERENCE, Box 296, Ocean Park ME 04063.

Massachusetts

CAPE COD WRITERS' CONFERENCE, Box 111, West Hyannisport MA 02672.

Michigan

CLARION SF-WRITERS' WORKSHOP, Dr. Leonard N. Isaacs, Justin Morrill College, Michigan State University, E. Lansing MI 48824.

UPPER PENINSULA WRITERS CONFERENCE, Mrs. Leonard Harju, R. 1, Box 48, L'Anse MI 49946.

Minnesota

UPPER MIDWEST WRITERS' CONFERENCE, Margaret Thorbeck, Bemidji State College, Bemidji MN 56601.

Missouri

LENORE ANTHONY POETRY WORKSHOP, The American Poets Series of the Jewish Community Center, 8201 Holmes Rd., Kansas City MO 64131.

PARK COLLEGE-CROWN CENTER WRITERS CONFERENCE, Alice Lubin, Director, Park College-Crown Center School for Community Education, 2420 Pershing Rd., Kansas City MO 64108.

Nebraska

OMAHA WRITERS' CLUB SPRING CONFERENCE, Joann Deems, 4514 Hascall St., Omaha NE 68106.

New Hampshire

NEW ENGLAND CHRISTIAN WRITERS CONFERENCE, Alton Bay Bible Conference, Alton Bay NH 03810.

MILDRED I. REID WRITERS' COLONY, Contoocook NH 03229.

SEACOAST WRITERS CONFERENCE, Mrs. Samuel Crowell, Registrar, 160 Goodwin Rd., Eliot ME 03903.

New Jersey

COMEDY & HUMOR WORKSHOP COLLEGE OF COMEDY, George Q. Lewis, Director, National Association of Gagwriters, 74 Pullman Ave., Elberon NJ 07740.

FREE LANCE WRITING SEMINAR, Harriet S. Lefkowith, Coordinator, Women's Institute, Bergen Community College, 400 Paramus Rd., Paramus NJ 07652.

New York

CHRISTIAN WRITERS WORKSHOP, Don Booth, 6853 Webster Rd., Orchard Park NY 14127.

NATIONAL PLAYWRIGHTS CONFERENCE OF THE O'NEILL CENTER, 1860 Broadway, Suite 1012, New York NY 10023.

POETRY WORKSHOPS, The Poetry Center, YMHA, 1395 Lexington Ave., New York NY 10028.

ST. LAWRENCE UNIVERSITY WRITERS' CONFERENCE, Joe David Bellamy, St. Lawrence University, Canton NY 13617.

TECHNICAL WRITERS' INSTITUTE, Prof. Robert W. Elmer, Director, Rensselaer Polytechnic Institute, Troy NY 12181.

UNIVERSITY OF ROCHESTER WRITERS' WORKSHOP, Dean Robert Koch, Writers' Workshop, Harkness Hall 102, University of Rochester, Rochester NY 14627.

North Carolina

TAR HEEL WRITERS' ROUNDTABLE, Bernadette Hoyle, Director, P.O. Box 5393, Raleigh NC 27607.

Ohio

MANUSCRIPT CLUB OF AKRON'S ANNUAL WORKSHOP, Vivian M. Preston, Barberton Public Library, Barberton OH 44203.

MIAMI UNIVERSITY'S ANNUAL CREATIVE WRITING WORKSHOP, Milton White, Dept. of English, Miami University, Oxford OH 45056.

WRITER'S WORKSHOP, Jane Corbly, Director, Sinclair Community College, 444 W. Third St., Dayton OH 45402.

Oklahoma

OKLAHOMA WRITERS FEDERATION ANNUAL CONFERENCE, Ernestine Gravley, 1225 Sherry Lane, Shawnee OK 74801.

UNIVERSITY OF OKLAHOMA ANNUAL SHORT COURSE ON PROFESSIONAL WRITING, Leonard Logan, Oklahoma Center for Continuing Education, University of Oklahoma, 1700 Asp Ave., Norman OK 73069.

Oregon

HAYSTACK WRITERS' WORKSHOP, Sue Gordon, A-105, Oregon Division of Continuing Education, P.O. Box 1491, Portland OR 97207.

Pennsylvania

PHILADELPHIA WRITERS CONFERENCE, Emma S. Wood, Registrar, Box 834, Philadelphia PA 19105.

ST. DAVIDS CHRISTIAN WRITERS CONFERENCE, Edna Mast, Registrar, Route 2, Cochranville PA 19330.

Texas

ABILENE WRITERS GUILD CONFERENCE, Elva Morrison, 833 Briarwood, Abilene TX 79603.

PATRIOTIC POETRY SEMINAR, Dr. Stella Woodall, President, 3915 S.W. Military Dr., San Antonio TX 78211.

SOUTH TEXAS PRO-AM WRITERS' RALLY, Peggy Bradbury, 7010 Mark Dr., San Antonio TX 78218.

SOUTHWEST WRITERS' CONFERENCE, Sherman L. Pease, Director, 4800 Calhoun, Houston TX 77004.

TEXAS WRITERS ROUNDTABLE, Hill Country Arts Foundation, Box 176, Ingram TX 78025.

WRITERS CONFERENCE, Mrs. Edwin Low, 3302 Linda Lane, Canyon TX 79015.

Utah

WESTERN WRITERS' CONFERENCE, Conference and Institute Division, UMC 01, Utah State University, Logan UT 84322.

Virginia

CREATIVE WRITERS' DAY, Virginia Highlands Festival, Box 801, Abingdon VA 24210.

Washington

EASTERN WASHINGTON STATE COLLEGE SUMMER WRITING WORKSHOP, John Keeble or James J. McAuley, c/o Eastern Washington State College, Cheney WA 99004.

FORT WORDEN WRITERS' SYMPOSIUM IN CREATIVE PRINT, W.M. Ransom, Coordinator, Worden State Park, Port Townsend WA 98368.

PACIFIC NORTHWEST WRITERS CONFERENCE, Executive Secretary, 51 164th Ave., N.E., Bellevue WA 98008.

Canada

THE BANFF CENTRE, School of Fine Arts, P.O. Box 1020, Banff, Alberta TOL OCO Canada.

SUMMER WRITERS' WORKSHOP AT NEW COLLEGE, UNIVERSITY OF TORONTO, Gerald Lampert, Director, Suite 8, 165 Spadina Ave., Toronto, Canada M5T 2C4.

Mexico

INSTITUTO ALLENDE SUMMER WRITING CENTER PROGRAM, Admissions, Instituto Allende, Box B, San Miguel Allende, Guanajuato, Mexico.

FOREIGN

HOLIDAY WORKSHOP, Pauline Bloom, 20 Plaza St., Brooklyn NY 11238.

EUROPEAN HOLIDAY WRITERS' WORKSHOP, Pauline Bloom, 20 Plaza St., Brooklyn NY 11238.

COSTA RICA AND GUATEMALA HOLIDAY WRITERS' WORKSHOP, Pauline Bloom, 20 Plaza St., Brooklyn NY 11238.

Writers' Organizations

National organizations for writers listed here usually require that potential members have attained a professional status. Local or regional writers' clubs which are more social in nature are listed in the Writers' Clubs section. S.A.S.E. must be enclosed with all correspondence with these organizations.

ACADEMY OF AMERICAN POETS, 1078 Madison Ave., New York NY 10028. Established in 1934. President: Mrs. Hugh Bullock. Purpose of the Academy of American Poets is to encourage, stimulate, and foster the production of American poetry. Conducts poetry workshops and readings.

AMERICAN ACADEMY OF ARTS AND LETTERS, 633 W. 155th St., New York NY 10032. Established in 1904. Executive Director: Margaret M. Mills. An honor society of artists, writers, and composers created as a section of the National Institute of Arts and Letters, limited to 50 members chosen from the Institute.

AMERICAN AUTO RACING WRITERS AND BROADCASTERS ASSOCIA-TION, 922 N. Pass Ave., Burbank CA 91505. Established in 1955. Executive Secretary: Mr. Dusty Brandel. An organization of writers, broadcasters and photographers who cover auto racing throughout the U.S. Aims primarily to improve the relationship between the press and the promoters, sanctioning bodies, sponsors, and participants in the sport. Dues: $10 annually, full membership; $25 annually, associate membership.

THE AMERICAN GUILD OF AUTHORS AND COMPOSERS, 40 W. 57th St., New York NY 10019. Established in 1931. Executive Director: Lewis M. Bachman. President: Ervin Drake. This organization was formed to provide better royalty contracts from music publishers. AGAC collects royalties and audits for its members and charges 5% commission (but not exceeding $1,400 in 1 year). A regular member is a composer who has had at least 1 song published or recorded by a recognized company. Dues he pays are based on the size and activity of his catalog. Associate members are songwriters who have not yet published. Dues: $20 annually (associate members); $37.50 to $250 annually (members).

AMERICAN SOCIETY OF COMPOSERS, AUTHORS AND PUBLISHERS (ASCAP), 1 Lincoln Plaza, New York NY 10023. Director of Public Relations: Walter Wager. ASCAP licenses the right to perform in public for profit in the U.S. the copyrighted musical works of its 23,000 members and the members of affiliated societies in more than 30 countries. Any composer or lyricist of a copyrighted musical work may join if he or she has had at least 1 musical work regularly published. Associate membership is open to any writer who has had 1 work copyrighted. Annual dues: $10 for writers; $50 for publishers.

AMERICAN SOCIETY OF NEWSPAPER EDITORS, Box 551, 1350 Sullivan Trail, Easton PA 18042. Executive Secretary: Mr. Gene Giancarlo. Established in 1922. Serves as a medium for the exchange of ideas. Membership is limited to directing editors (managing editors, executive editors, associate editors, editors of editorial pages, etc.) of daily newspapers in the U.S. Dues: $125 annually.

AMERICAN TRANSLATORS ASSOCIATION, P.O. Box 129, Croton-on-Hudson NY 10520. Executive Secretary: Mrs. Rosemary Malia. Established in 1959 as a national professional society to advance the standards of translation and to promote the intellectual and material interest of translators and interpreters in the United States. Welcomes to membership all those who are interested in the field as well as translators and interpreters active in any branch of knowledge.

THE ARMED FORCES WRITERS LEAGUE, INC., George Washington Station, Alexandria VA 23305. Established in 1954. Executive Director: Col. Frank Martineau, SUAF Res. Founded as a mutual self-help organization for military writers needing technical assistance. Membership open to any U.S. citizen interested in the Armed Forces and the national defense of the U.S. Dues: $8 annually.

ASMP–THE SOCIETY OF PHOTOGRAPHERS IN COMMUNICATIONS, 60 E. 42nd St., New York NY 10017. (212) 661-6450. Executive Director: Arie Kopelman. Established to promote and further the interests of established workers in their profession. Publishes minimum rate standards and definition of rights; acts as a clearing house for photographic information on markets, rates, and business practices of magazines, advertising agencies, publishers and electronic media; works for copyright law revision; offers legal advice to members concerning questions of rights, ethics and payment. Membership categories include Sustaining, General, Associate, and Student.

THE ASSOCIATED BUSINESS WRITERS OF AMERICA, P.O. Box 135, Monmouth Junction NJ 08852. Executive Director: William R. Palmer. Members are skilled in one or more facets of business writing (advertising copy, public relations, ghost writing, books, reports, business and technical magazines, etc.). Members are full-time writers. Associates may hold other jobs. Does not place mss for its members. Dues: $40 annually; $10 initiation fee.

AUTHORS GUILD, 234 W. 44th St., New York NY 10036. Established in 1912. Executive Secretary: Peter Heggie. Basic functions and purposes are to act and speak with the collective power and voice of all American freelance writers in matters of joint professional and business concern; to keep informed on market tendencies and practices, and to keep its members informed; to advise members on individual professional and business problems as far as possible. Those eligible for membership include any author who shall have had a book published by a reputable American publisher within 7 years prior to his application; any author who shall have had 3 works (fiction or nonfiction) published by a magazine of general circulation, either national or local, within 18 months prior to application. Annual dues: $35.

AUTHORS LEAGUE OF AMERICA, INC., 234 West 44th St., New York NY 10036. Established in 1912. Executive Secretary: Mills Ten Eyck, Jr. The Authors League membership is restricted to authors and dramatists who are members of the Authors Guild, Inc., and the Dramatists Guild, Inc. Matters of joint concern to authors and dramatists, such as copyright and freedom of expression, are in the province of the League; other matters, such as contract terms and subsidiary rights, are in the province of the guilds.

AVIATION/SPACE WRITERS ASSOCIATION, Cliffwood Rd., Chester NJ 07930. Executive Secretary: William F. Keiser. Established in 1938. Founded to establish and maintain high standards of quality and veracity in gathering, writing, editing, and disseminating aeronautical information. The AWA numbers 930 members who work for newspapers, press services, TV, radio, or other media and specialize in writing about aviation or space. Dues: $10, initiation fee; $30, annual dues.

BOXING WRITERS ASSOCIATION, 6 Penn Plaza, New York NY 10001. Executive Secretary: Marvin Kohn. Established in 1922.

CONSTRUCTION WRITERS ASSOCIATION, 202 Homer Building, Washington DC 20005. Established in 1958. CWA offers its members a forum for the interchange of information, ideas and methods for improving the quality of reporting, editing and public relations in the construction field. It also provides contact between the membership and news-making officials in government, contracting firms, equipment manufacturers and distributors, consulting firms, and other construction trade and professional groups. Any person principally engaged in writing or editing material pertaining to the construction industry for any regularly published periodical of general circulation is eligible for membership. Any public information or public relations specialist who represents an organization or agency the existence of which depends in whole or in part on the construction industry is also eligible. Annual dues: $20.

COUNCIL FOR THE ADVANCEMENT OF SCIENCE WRITING, INC., Abbotts Bldg., Drexel University, Philadelphia PA 19104. President: Pierre C. Fraley. Purpose of the organization is to increase both the quality and quantity of the coverage of science, medicine and health, the environment, technology, social sciences, etc., in all the mass media. CASW is not a membership organization. The 20 members of the council actually make up the board of directors. The only other class of memberships are sustaining memberships at $1,000 a year.

DOG WRITERS' ASSOCIATION OF AMERICA, INC., 3 Blythewood Rd., Doylestown PA 18901. President: John T. Marvin. Secretary: Mrs. Sara Futh, Kinney Hill Rd., Washington Depot CT 06794. The association aims to promote and to encourage the exchange of ideas, methods and professional courtesies among its members. Membership is limited to salaried dog writers, editors and/or publishers of newspapers, magazines and books dealing with dogs. Annual dues: $10.

THE FOOTBALL WRITERS ASSOCIATION OF AMERICA, Box 1022, Edmond OK 73034. Secretary-Treasurer: Volney Meece. Membership is mainly sports writers on newspapers and magazines who cover college football, plus those in allied fields, chiefly college sports information directors. Dues: $5 annually.

GARDEN WRITERS ASSOCIATION OF AMERICA, INC., Gladys Reed Robinson, Membership Chairman, 680 Third Ave., Troy NY 12182. Dues: $7.50 annually.

INTERNATIONAL ASSOCIATION OF BUSINESS COMMUNICATORS, 870 Market St., Suite 469, San Francisco CA 94102. Executive Director: John N. Bailey. Established in 1970. Dedicated to the advancement of its members and to the advancement of the communication profession. Membership limited to those active in the field of the business of organizational communication.

MARIANIST WRITERS' GUILD, Marianist Community, University of Dayton, 300 College Park Ave., Dayton OH 45469. Executive Secretary: Louis J. Faerber, S.H., Ph.D. Established in 1947. Membership is limited to Marianists in America who have had at least 3 works published nationally since 1947.

MOTOR SPORTS PRESS ASSOCIATION, c/o Gordon H. Martin, 350 Liberty St., San Francisco CA 94114. Established for the advancement of editorial skills, ability and coverage of motor sports racing activities; for the interchange of ideas and information; to provide an authoritative platform, credentials and recognition to the motor sports press. To be a board member, one must be an editor or motor racing columnist or broadcaster for a newspaper, magazine, TV or radio station; bona fide motor sports journalists. Annual dues: $12.

MUSIC CRITICS ASSOCIATION, INC., c/o Richard D. Freed, Executive Secretary, 6201 Tuckerman Lane, Rockville MD 20852. President: Irving Lowens. The purposes of the Association are to act as an educational medium for the promotion of high standards of music criticism in the press in America, to hold meetings where self-criticism and exchange of ideas will promote educational opportunities, and to increase the general interest in music in the growing culture of the Americas. Membership is open to persons who regularly cover musical events in the U.S. and Canada. Annual dues: $15.

MYSTERY WRITERS OF AMERICA, INC., 105 E. 19th St., New York NY 10003. Established in 1944. Executive Secretary: Gloria Amoury. An organization dedicated to the proposition that the detective story is the noblest sport of man. Membership includes active members who have made at least one sale in mystery, crime, or suspense writing; associate members who are either novices in the mystery writing field or nonwriters allied to the field; editors, publishers, and affiliate members who are interested in mysteries. Annual dues: $30 for U.S. members; $8 for Canadian and overseas members.

THE NATIONAL ACADEMY OF TELEVISION ARTS AND SCIENCES, 291 South La Cienega Blvd., Beverly Hills CA 90211. President: Robert F. Lewine. A nonprofit membership organization of professionals working in the television industry. Active members must have worked actively and creatively in television for at least 2 years. Dues: $15 to $30 annually, according to chapter.

NATIONAL ASSOCIATION OF EDUCATIONAL BROADCASTERS, 1346 Connecticut Ave., N.W., Washington DC 20036. Established in 1925. President: William G. Harley. A professional society of individuals in educational telecommunications; composed of men and women who work in public broadcasting, instructional communications and allied fields. Annual dues: $35.

NATIONAL ASSOCIATION OF GAGWRITERS, 74 Pullman Ave., Elberon NJ 07740. Executive Director: George Q. Lewis. Members are primarily caption writers for cartoons and comedy writers for performers. Maintains a telephone comedy corps to answer questions from members and potential members. Call 201-229-9472 before noon. Dues: $25.

NATIONAL ASSOCIATION OF HOME WORKSHOP WRITERS, Richard Day, Membership Chairman, N.A.H.W.W., Palomar Mountain CA 92060.

NATIONAL ASSOCIATION OF SCIENCE WRITERS, INC., Box H, Sea Cliff NJ 11579. Established in 1934. Administrative Secretary: Rosemary Arctander. This organization was established to "foster the dissemination of accurate information regarding science through all media normally devoted to informing the public. In pursuit of this goal, NASW conducts a varied program to increase the flow of news from scientists, to improve the quality of its presentation, and to communicate its meaning and importance to the reading public. Anyone who is actively engaged in the dissemination of science information, and has two years or more experience in this field, is eligible to apply. There are several classes of membership. Active members must be principally engaged in reporting science through media that reach the public directly: newspapers, mass-circulation magazines, 'trade' books, radio, television and films. Associate members report science through special media: limited-circulation publications and announcements from organizations such as universities, research laboratories, foundations and science-oriented corporations. Affiliated membership is limited to those who have been active or associate members but are no longer primarily engaged in the reporting of science. Lifetime membership is extended to members after they have belonged to NASW for 25 years. Honorary membership is awarded by NASW to outstanding persons who have notably aided the objectives of the association." Annual dues: $25.

NATIONAL INSTITUTE OF ARTS AND LETTERS, 633 West 155th St., New York NY 10032. Established in 1898. Executive Director: Margaret M. Mills. Founded for the purpose of furthering literature and fine arts in the United States, the Institute has three departments: art, literature, and music. Membership is limited to 250 American citizens. In order to establish cultural ties with other countries, the Institute and the American Academy of Arts and Letters, a section of the Institute, elect 71 foreign artists, writers, and composers as honorary members.

NATIONAL LEAGUE OF AMERICAN PEN WOMEN, INC., 1300 17th St., N.W., Washington DC 20036. Established in 1897. "Professionally qualified women engaged in creating and promoting letters, art, and music" are eligible for membership. Women interested in membership must qualify professionally and be presented for membership and endorsed by two active members in good standing in the League. The League holds branch, state, and national meetings. Dues: Initiation fee $25. Annual branch dues plus $10 national dues. For further information, write to national president at address given above.

NATIONAL PRESS CLUB, National Press Bldg., 529 14th St. N.W., Washington DC 20004. Initiation fee: $25 to $125. Dues: $30 to $220 annually, depending on membership status.

NATIONAL TURF WRITERS ASSOCIATION, Willco Bldg., Suite 317, 6000 Executive Blvd., Rockville MD 20852. Secretary: Tony Chamblin. Membership limited to newspaper or magazine writers who regularly cover thoroughbred racing, sports editors of newspapers which regularly print thoroughbred racing news and results, and sports columnists who write columns on thoroughbred racing. Dues: $10 annually for regular membership; $20 annually, associate membership.

NATIONAL WRITERS CLUB, INC., 1365 Logan, Suite 100, Denver CO 80203. Established in 1937. Executive Director: Donald E. Bower. "Founded for the purpose of informing, aiding and protecting freelance writers worldwide. Associate membership is available to anyone seriously interested in writing. Qualifications for professional membership are publication of a book by a recognized book publisher; or sales of at least three stories or articles to national or regional magazines; or a television, stage, or motion picture play professionally produced." Annual dues: $17.50, associate membership; $22, professional membership.

NEWSPAPER FARM EDITORS OF AMERICA (NFEA), 4200 12th St., Des Moines IA 50313. Established in 1953. Executive Secretary: Glenn Cunningham. Writers employed by newspapers, farm editors and farm writers for national wire services are eligible for membership. Dues: $10 annually.

NEWSPAPER FOOD EDITORS AND WRITERS ASSOCIATION, Milwaukee Journal, Box 0227, Milwaukee WI 53201. Established in 1973. President: Peggy Daum. To encourage communication among journalists devoting a substantial portion of their working time to the furthering of public's knowledge of food; to uphold and foster professional ethical standards for such persons; to increase their knowledge about food and to encourage and promote a greater understanding among fellow journalists and those who manage news dissemination organizations. Dues: $25 annually.

OUTDOOR WRITERS ASSOCIATION OF AMERICA, INC., 4141 W. Bradley Rd., Milwaukee WI 53209. Established in 1927. Executive Director: Edwin W. Hanson. A nonprofit professional and educational organization comprised of newspaper and magazine writers, editors, photographers, broadcasters, artists, cinematographers, and lecturers engaged in the dissemination of information on outdoor sports such as hunting, boating, fishing, camping, etc., and on the conservation of natural resources. Its objectives are "providing a means of cross-communication among specialists in this field, promoting craft improvement, obtaining fair treatment from media, and increasing general public knowledge of the outdoors. Among other subjects, the membership deals extensively in current environmental issues." Requires that each member annually have published a specified quantity of paid material. Sponsorship by an active member of the OWAA is required for membership applicants. Dues: $25, initiation fee; $25, annual fee.

P.E.N., American Center, 156 Fifth Ave., New York NY 10010. Established in 1921. Executive Secretary: Kirsten Michalski. A world association of poets, playwrights, essayists, editors, and novelists, the purpose of P.E.N. is "to promote and maintain friendship and intellectual cooperation among men and women of letters in all countries, in the interests of literature, the exchange of ideas, freedom of expression, and good will." P.E.N. has 82 centers in Europe, Asia, Africa, Australia, and the Americas. "Membership is open to all qualified writers, translators, and editors who subscribe to the aims of International P.E.N." To qualify for membership, an applicant must have "acknowledged achievement in the literary field, which is generally interpreted as the publication by a recognized publisher of 2 books of literary merit. Membership is by invitation of the Admission Committee after nomination by a P.E.N. member."

PEN AND BRUSH CLUB, 16 E. 10th St., New York NY 10003. Established in 1893. President: Mrs. Harriet M. Hagerty. "The Pen and Brush Club is a club of professional women, writers, painters, graphic artists, sculptors, and craftsmen, with a resident membership limited to 350 active members in these fields. Exhibits are held in the galleries of the clubhouse by painters, sculptors, graphic artists, and craftsmen."

POETRY SOCIETY OF AMERICA, 15 Gramercy Park, S., New York NY 10003. Executive Secretary: Charles A. Wagner. The oldest and largest group working for an appreciation of poetry and for wider recognition of the work of living American poets, the Society has a membership of traditionalists and experimentalists. Dues: $18 annually.

RELIGION NEWSWRITERS ASSOCIATION, 1100 Broadway, Nashville TN 37202. Established in 1949. First Vice President: W. A. Reed. Officers and members of RNA comprise 300 reporters of religious and religious-related news in the United States and Canada.

SCIENCE FICTION WRITERS OF AMERICA, C. L. Grant, Executive Secretary, 44 Center Grove Rd. T-17, Dover NJ 07801. Membership is limited to established science fiction writers in the country. Purposes are to inform writers of matters of professional benefit, to serve as an intermediary in disputes of a professional nature, and to act as central clearing house for information on science fiction and science fiction writers. Dues: $12.50 annually.

SOCIETY OF AMERICAN SOCIAL SCRIBES, c/o The Plain Dealer, 1801 Superior Ave., Cleveland OH 44114. Secretary: Mary Strassmeyer. "The Society of American Social Scribes is a nonprofit organization dedicated to serving the interest of the reading public, to promote unbiased, objective reporting of social events and to promote journalistic freedom of movement. It endeavors to upgrade the professional integrity and skill of its members to work to increase the pleasures of the reading public, to support all legitimate efforts toward developing the education of its members, and to help its members offer greater service to their readers. Membership is limited to those regularly engaged as salaried society editors or devoting a substantial or regular part of their time to society coverage and the balance to other strictly editorial work. Society writers on daily newspapers with circulations of 200,000 or more and magazine writers and authors of books on the subject are also eligible for membership." Annual dues: $15.

SOCIETY OF AMERICAN TRAVEL WRITERS, 1120 Connecticut Ave., Suite 940, Washington DC 20036. Established in 1956. President: Carolyn Bennet Patterson. Dedicated to serving the interest of the traveling public, to promote international understanding and good will, and to further promote unbiased, objective reporting of information on travel topics. Active membership is limited "to those regularly engaged as salaried travel editors, writers, broadcasters, or photographers actively assigned to diversified travel coverage by a recognized medium or devoting a substantial or regular part of their time to such travel coverage to satisfy the Board of Directors; or to those who are employed as freelancers in any of the above areas with a sufficient steady volume of published work about travel to satisfy the Board. Associate membership is limited to persons regularly engaged in public relations or publicity within the travel industry to an extent that will satisfy the Board of Directors. All applicants must be sponsored by 2 active members with whom they are personally acquainted." Dues: $50 initiation fee for active members, $100 initiation fee for associate members; $35 annual dues for active members, $75 annual dues for associate members.

SOCIETY OF THE SILURIANS, INC., 103 Park Ave., New York NY 10017. Secretary: Barnett Bildersee. Established in 1924. Primarily a fraternal organization. Membership totals 700. Men and women are eligible for full membership if their history in the New York City media dates back 25 years, for associate membership after 15 years, whether or not they are still so engaged. Dues: $10 annually.

SOCIETY FOR TECHNICAL COMMUNICATION, 1010 Vermont Ave. N.W., Suite 421, Washington DC 20005. (202) 737-0035. Established in 1953. Executive Director: Curtis T. Youngblood. Dedicated to the advancement of the theory and practice of technical communication in all media, the STC aims primarily for the education, improvement, and advancement of its members. Dues: $20 annually.

SOCIETY OF CHILDREN'S BOOK WRITERS, P.O. Box 827, Laguna Beach CA 92652. Established in 1968. President: Stephen Mooser. "The Society is an organization for writers, editors, and others interested in and allied with the children's book field. Full membership is open to anyone who has published a children's story or book in the past 6 years. Associate membership is open to anyone with an interest in children's literature, whether or not they have published." Annual dues: $20.

SOCIETY OF MAGAZINE WRITERS, INC., 123 W. 43rd St., New York NY 10036. Established in 1948. President. Mrs. Terry Morris. Initiation fee: $25. Annual dues for residents of New York and environs: $60. Annual dues for those residing 200 or more miles from New York: $45. For further information, contact Mrs. Dorothea H. Lobsenz, Administrative Secretary.

SOCIETY OF PROFESSIONAL JOURNALISTS, SIGMA DELTA CHI, 35 E. Wacker Dr., Chicago IL 60601. Established in 1909. Executive Officer: Russell E. Hurst. Dedicated to the highest ideals in journalism. Membership extends horizontally to include persons engaged in the communication of fact and opinion by all media and vertically to include in its purposes and fellowship all ranks of journalists. Dues: $15 annually.

UNITED STATES HARNESS WRITERS' ASSOCIATION, INC., P.O. Box 10, Batavia NY 14020. Established in 1947. Executive Secretary: William F. Brown, Jr. 420 members. Involved in media coverage of harness racing and/or standardbred breeding. Dues: $25 annually.

WESTERN WRITERS OF AMERICA, INC., 1505 W. "D" St., North Platte NE 69101. Contact: Nellie Yost. Writers eligible for membership in this organization are not restricted in their residence, "so long as their work, whether it be fiction, history, adult, or juvenile, book-length or short material, movie or TV scripts, has the scene laid west of the Missouri River."

WOMEN IN COMMUNICATIONS, INC., National Headquarters, 8305-A Shoal Creek Blvd., Austin TX 78758. Established in 1909 as Theta Sigma Phi. President: Jo Ann Albers. A professional society for women in journalism and communications. Application fee: $32. Dues: $20 annually.

WRITERS GUILD OF AMERICA, Writers Guild of America, *East,* 22 W. 48th St., New York NY 10036. Writers Guild of America, *West,* 8955 Beverly Blvd., Los Angeles CA 90048. A labor organization representing all screen, television, and radio writers. Initiation fee: $200 (West), $300 (East). Dues: $12.50 per quarter (East), $10 per quarter (West), and 1% of gross earnings as a writer in WGA fields of jurisdiction.

If this is 1977, this edition is out of date. See address in front of book to order latest edition. *Writer's Market* is published annually each fall.

FOREIGN MARKETS

The following markets are willing to receive queries or original manuscripts from United States or Canadian writers. Some will consider material previously published in the United States or Canada, offered for first publication in their country. Bear in mind that the foreign editor, if not interested in your idea, may not reply to your query. It is wise to remember, too, that rights purchased (or acquired) are frequently negotiated on an individual basis.

Writers are advised to check their local post offices for the correct amount of postage necessary to airmail their mss or queries to these publishers. Details on the current "Printed Matter" rate (for book mss) are also available at your local post office.

Be sure to enclose International Postal Reply Coupons with submissions to foreign markets for safe return of your ms. Reporting times given by these foreign markets apply only to submissions which have enclosed sufficient reply coupons for an airmail reply. You can buy these coupons at your local post office. One of these coupons is exchangeable in any other country for a stamp or stamps representing the international postage on a single-rate surface-mailed letter. Details on the amount of return postage necessary from individual foreign countries to the U.S. for book mss, etc., is available from Director, Classification and Special Services Division, Bureau of Operations, Washington DC 20267.

Consumer Magazines

ADAM, 142 Clarence St., Sydney, N.S.W., Australia 2000. For a "general audience, but probably mainly men in the 18 to 35 group." Monthly. Circulation: 42,000. Rights negotiable. Buys 100 mss a year. Payment on publication. Will send a sample copy to a writer for 50¢. Reports "within a month." Enclose S.A.E. and International Reply Coupons for return of submissions.
Nonfiction and Fiction: Uses "action fiction, factual adventure, historical." Buys personal experience, humorous, and historical articles. Also buys mystery, science fiction, adventure, and humorous fiction. Nonfiction length: 2,000 to 3,500 words; Fiction length: 2,000 to 4,000 words. Payment negotiable.

AIRFIX MAGAZINE, PSL Publications Ltd., Bar Hill, Cambridge CB3 8EL, England. Editor: Bruce Quarrie. For plastic modelling enthusiasts, aviation and military nuts and historians, wargamers. Monthly. Buys UK and British Commonwealth rights. Buys 10 mss for an issue. Payment at end of month following publication. Query first or submit complete ms. Enclose S.A.E. and International Reply Coupons.
Nonfiction and Photos: "*Airfix* deals with all aspects of scale modelling, primarily based on plastic construction kits. It includes model conversion and 'scratch building' instruction articles alongside technical reference features on aircraft, tanks, ships, etc., their service history, colour schemes, armament, serial codes, etc., plus reviews of new kits and books of interest to modellers. Hard, factual information on any military or aviation subjects which can be reproduced in scale model form." Will consider the following material previously published in U.S. or Canada: "Any article dealing with aviation or military history, specific aircraft or vehicles, marking and camouflage schemes, unit serial codes, etc. The publication is basically directed at scale modellers and this should be borne in mind, but an article need not be specifically on modelling a piece of equipment. Should be readable English but note form is acceptable on unit code listings. Preferred length for a single article is 800 to 1,200 words plus illustrations, but ideas for series considered." Will consider the following unpublished material: "Anything on the Air Force, Army Air Force, Naval Air Force, Marine, and Army aircraft (including helicopters and hovercraft),

tanks, self-propelled guns, armoured cars, etc.; technical descriptions with scale drawings and photographs; service histories with photographs; marking scheme and camouflage descriptions with photographs and black and white line illustrations. Similarly for Canadian military forces. Main emphasis on WW2. Any style as long as grammatical. Length of single articles: approximately 800 to 1,200 words." Pays 7 pounds per published page "whether all text, all illustrations, or a combination of both. Average payment on an illustrated 800-word article would be approximately 12 pounds: on 1,000 words, 15 to 18 pounds; on 1,200 words, 18 to 24 pounds."

AMATEUR GARDENING, 189 High Holborn, London WE1V 7BA, England. Editor: Peter Wood, N.D.H. For keen British gardeners. Weekly magazine. Established in 1884. Circulation: 175,000. Copyrighted. Payment on publication. Will send free sample copy to writer on request. Query first. Enclose S.A.E. and International Reply Coupons.
Nonfiction: Specialist features on the science and practice of gardening for keen gardeners. Write-ups of outstanding gardeners. Readers have a good knowledge of gardening. Will consider material previously published in United States or Canada offered for first publication in England. Payment by arrangement.

AMATEUR PHOTOGRAPHER, Surrey House, 1 Throwley Way, Sutton, Surrey SM1 4QQ, England. Editor: R.H. Mason. Published weekly for amateur photographers. Established in 1884. Circulation: 90,000. Not copyrighted. Will send a sample copy to a writer for $2. Submit complete ms. Reports in 5 to 10 days. Include S.A.E. and International Reply Coupons.
Nonfiction and Photos: Buys "central photo features." Length: 1,000 to 3,000 words. Pays 7.50 pounds per page if accompanied by b&w photos, 10 pounds if accompanied by color photos.

AMATEUR WINEMAKER, South St., Andover, Hants, England. Editor: C. J. J. Berry. For persons from all walks of life interested in home winemaking and brewing. Monthly. Established in 1957. Circulation: 34,000. Payment on publication. Will send sample copy to writer for 50¢. Query first or submit complete ms. Enclose S.A.E. and International Reply Coupons.
Nonfiction and Photos: "Articles both for the beginner and for the more advanced hobbyist. Articles and photos to do with winemaking or home brewing, preferably of a good technical standard, or articles on allied subjects such as glassware, hops, commercial wines, bottling, etc." Will consider material previously published in United States or Canada, offered for first publication in England. Pays 4 pounds to 10 pounds.

AMBIT, 17 Priory Gardens, London N6 5QY, England. Editor: Martin Bax. For those interested in the arts. Quarterly. Established in 1959. Buys serial rights. Payment on publication. Reports in 3 months. Enclose S.A.E. and International Reply Coupons.
Nonfiction, Fiction, and Poetry: All critical material is commissioned. Query on feature articles. Also buys some original drawings, preferably line, some halftone. Buys short stories. Length: 5,000 words maximum. Buys some poetry. Payment in sterling, by arrangement; "about $2.50 a page."

THE ANGLO-WELSH REVIEW, Deffrobani, Maescelyn, Brecon, South Wales LD3 7NL. Editor: Roland Mathias. Established in 1949. 3 times a year. Circulation: 1,500. Not copyrighted. Will rarely consider material previously published in U.S. or Canada. Will send a copy to a writer for $1.50. Submit complete ms. Enclose S.A.E. and International Reply Coupons for return of submissions.
Nonfiction, Fiction, and Poetry: *AWR* exists to afford a platform for Welsh writers in English; also to outline and criticize the literary and cultural scene in Wales; and to review most, if not all, books about Wales or by Welsh authors. Its tone is generally academic. Interested in articles with a Welsh interest. Length: 1,500 to 4,500 words. Poems and stories also. Pays 2 pounds per page for prose; 1 pound to 25 pounds for poetry.

ANNABEL, D.C. Thomson & Co. Ltd., 80 Kingsway East, Dundee, Scotland. Editor: Mr. Scott Smith. For women. Established in 1966. Monthly. Circulation: 172,000. Will send free sample copy on request. Buys first British serial rights. Payment on acceptance. Will consider material previously published in U.S. or Canada offered for first publication in Britain. Submit complete ms. Enclose S.A.E. and International Reply Coupons.

Nonfiction: Wants personal experience stories, biographical articles of well-known personalities, articles on fashion, cookery, knitting. Interested in "good human stories simply told. There is wide coverage of the traditional subjects (fashion, beauty, etc.), but we seek to inform and entertain readers on a wide range of material slanted to the family woman." Length: 500 to 2,500 words. All payments are by mutual agreement between editor and writer with a minimum of $50.

Fiction: Emotional, romantic short stories; 1,000 to 3,000 words. Pays $50 minimum.
Fillers: Uses short humor and puzzles.

ART AND ARTISTS, Artillery Mansions, 75 Victoria St., London, SW1H OHZ. Editor: John George. For art dealers, students, artists interested in all aspects of fine art. Buys first rights. Buys 100 to 120 mss a year. Will send a free sample copy to a writer on request. Query first. Submit seasonal material 2 months in advance. Returns rejected material "as soon as possible." Enclose S.A.E. and International Reply Coupons for return of submissions.

Nonfiction and Photos: Subject matter is "international coverage of art world, avant-garde and traditional art movements as well as in-depth specialist features." Uses "art subjects, reviews of exhibitions, features on artists and art movements." Buys interviews, profiles, and think pieces. Length: 300 to 2,000 words. Buys photos with mss; payment is negotiable.

AUSTRALIAN HOME BEAUTIFUL, 61-73 Flinders Lane, Melbourne, Victoria, Australia. Editor: A.J. Hitchin. Published for homemakers. Payment by arrangement on acceptance, high by Australian standards "but finds much material unacceptable as being too U.S.-oriented." Reports promptly. Usually buys one-time Australian magazine rights only. Include S.A.E. and International Reply Coupons.

Nonfiction: Buys articles on decoration, room settings, gardens, do-it-yourself, etc.
Photos: Buys photo material—singles, series, illustrated articles, b&w and color.

AUSTRALIAN PHOTOGRAPHY, 381 Pitt St., Sydney, Australia 2001. Editor: James H. Coleman. Monthly magazine, 8¼x11. Established in 1950. Circulation: 16,000. Not copyrighted. Will send sample copy to writer for $1. Query first. Payment on publication. Enclose S.A.E. and International Reply Coupons.

Nonfiction and Photos: Reports on new or different techniques illustrated with appropriate photos. How-to-do-it articles. Similar characteristics to well-known U.S. magazines such as *Popular Photography*. Photos and scripts required, on photographic techniques. Will consider material previously published in U.S. or Canada, offered for first publication in Australia. Pays 10 to 25 Australian dollars per published page.

THE AUSTRALIAN SUNBATHER, P.O. Box 180, Nelson Bay, N.S.W., Australia 2315. Editor: Arthur E. Renforth. Australia's national nudist magazine. Quarterly. Established in 1950. Circulation: 12,000. Copyrighted. Payment on publication. Will send sample copy to writer for $1. Enclose S.A.E. and International Reply Coupons.
Nonfiction: Subjects on a nudist way of life. Health foods, personal experiences, naturists, experiences with local authorities, etc. Subjects on health and life in harmony with naturism. Short articles are preferred. Length: 500 to 1,000 words. Pays 1 Australian cent a word. B&w and color photos are used to illustrate articles. Will consider material previously published in United States or Canada offered for first publication in Australia.

BAPTIST TIMES, 4 Southampton Row, London WC1B, 4AB, England. Editor: Geoffrey R. Locks, M.J.I. For adults, total cross section in education and tastes. Established in 1865. Weekly. Circulation: 17,000. Not copyrighted. Payment on

publication. Will send free sample copy to writer on request. Usually reports in 12 weeks. Enclose S.A.E. and International Reply Coupons for return of submissions.
Nonfiction: Articles on church affairs. Length: 400 to 800 words. Pays 3 pounds to 8 pounds.

BLACKWOOD'S MAGAZINE, 32 Thistle St., Edinburgh EH2 1HA, U.K. Editor: Douglas Blackwood. *Blackwood's* is Britain's oldest monthly magazine. Its appeal is to intelligent people aged 40 and over. It is acknowledged as having one of the highest editorial standards in the world. Would-be contributors are asked to study the magazine. Monthly. Established in 1817. Circulation: 11,000. Material remains copyright of contributors. Payment on publication. Will send sample copy to writer for $1. Enclose S.A.E. and International Reply Coupons.
Nonfiction, Fiction, and Poetry: Buys "short stories, articles, poetry—all of a high standard. *Blackwood's* is unique." Buys personal experience and travel articles. Length: 3,000 to 9,000 words. Uses traditional, contemporary, and light verse. Payment is "according to merit. Basic rate: 8 pounds per 1,000 words for the first 3,000 words; 5 pounds per thousand thereafter."

BOOKS AND BOOKMEN, Artillery Mansions, 75 Victoria St., London, SW1H OHZ, England. Editor: Miss Cis Amaral. For "adults interested in literary subjects." Monthly. Buys first rights. Pays on publication. Will send a free sample copy to a writer on request. Query first. Submit seasonal material 2 months in advance. Reports "usually as soon as possible." Enclose S.A.E. and International Reply Coupons for return of submissions.
Nonfiction: Buys "reviews of books (fiction, biography, social studies, etc.)." Payment "by prior arrangement only."

BUSY BEES NEWS, PDSA House, South St., Dorking, Surrey, RH4 2LB, England. Editor: Robert Cookson. For children 4 to 12 years old, divided into 2 sections (4 to 6 years and 7 to 12 years). Monthly. Established in 1934. Circulation: 8,000. Not copyrighted, "but authors wishing to retain copyright may do so and it will be so noted in the magazine." Payment on acceptance. Will send free sample copy to writer on request. Submit complete ms. Enclose S.A.E. and International Reply Coupons for return of submissions.
Nonfiction, Fiction, Photos, and Poetry: Fact or fiction, realistic or fantasy, short stories about animals, life, welfare, preferably illustrated but not vital. Pet care and natural history features are also used. Length: 500 to 600 words. Serials with cliffhanger endings, with chapters of 500 to 600 words, not more than 12 chapters. Will consider material previously published in United States or Canada offered for first publication in England. Pays 1.50 pounds minimum for poetry; pays 2 pounds for average story; fee by negotiation.
Fillers: Puzzles, quizzes, jokes.

CAGE AND AVIARY BIRDS, Surrey House, Throwley Way, Sutton, Surrey, England. Editor: Walter J. Page. Newspaper for people interested in birds. Weekly. Established in 1902. Circulation: 48,000. Copyrighted. Payment on publication. Will send free sample copy to writer on request. Submit complete ms. Enclose S.A.E. and International Reply Coupons for return of submissions.
Nonfiction and Photos: Articles (based on personal experience) on keeping and breeding birds (canaries, parrotlike birds and exotic species). "We provide authoritative contributions on bird breeding, keeping and exhibiting. Also provide exhibitors with reports of competitions, shows, and meetings to give members of bird keepers' clubs an up-to-date news service." Length: 750 words minimum, but 1,000 to 2,000 words average preferred. Longer contributions frequently split and used over 2 or 3 issues. Pays 3 pounds to 4 pounds per 1,000 words minimum; features at higher rates by arrangement. Photos paid for at varying rates.

CATHOLIC FIRESIDE, 110 Coombe Lane, London, SW20 OAY, England. Editor: P. Charles Walker. Weekly magazine. Established in 1879. Copyrighted. Payment on publication. Will send sample copy to writer for 50¢. Study the magazine before

submitting. Submit complete ms. Enclose S.A.E. and International Reply Coupons.
Nonfiction, Fiction, and Photos: Articles, especially pictorial ones, with Christian interest. Nonfiction items should entertain as well as inform. Length: 2,000 words maximum. Stories up to 3,000 words. Fiction serials. Will consider material previously published in United States or Canada, offered for first publication in England. Pays 4 pounds to 50 pounds.

CHAPMAN, 118 Brankholm Brae, Hamilton, Lanarks, Scotland. Editor: Mrs. Joy Perrie. General arts magazine. Quarterly. Established in 1970. Circulation: 3,000. Copyrighted. Payment on publication "or later". Will send sample copy to writer for $1. Query first. Enclose S.A.E. and International Reply Coupons.
Nonfiction and Poetry: Literary and philosophical. A critique of current ideas and fashions. Partly academic style. Critical and philosophic. Any length up to 20,000 words. Will consider material previously published in United States or Canada, offered for first publication in Scotland. Payment is negotiable.

CLIMBER & RAMBLER, 16 Briarfield Rd., Worsley, Manchester M28 4GQ, England. Editor: Walt Unsworth. For anyone interested in mountains and mountain climbing (not skiing). Monthly. Established in 1963. Circulation: 15,000. Copyrighted. Payment on publication. Will send sample copy to writer for $1, if sent to Distribution Dept., 36 Tay St., Perth PH1 5TT, Scotland. Query first. Enclose S.A.E. and International Reply Coupons.
Nonfiction and Photos: World mountain climbing, illustrated by b&w photos. Personal adventure or practical details such as costs, transport, etc. No hack material wanted. Features may be technical or not, depending on subject. Readers have considerable knowledge of the sport. Will consider material previously published in United States or Canada offered for first publication in England. Length: 1,500 to 2,500 words. Pays 6 pounds to 10 pounds per 1,000 words; more for big names.

CONTEMPORARY REVIEW, 37 Union St., London, S.E.1., England. Editor: Rosalind Wade. For a "very intelligent lay audience; we have subscribers all over the world." Established in 1866. Monthly. Payment at end of month of publication. Query first. "Study journal; a query is desirable as to whether or not a particular subject has been covered recently. We are not interested in previously published material." Submit "topical material" 5 weeks in advance. Reports "within a week or so." Enclose S.A.E. and International Reply Coupons for reply to queries.
Nonfiction, Fiction, and Poetry: "We are completely 'independent' although 'liberal' in origin. We can provide a platform for a very wide range of ideas. Our circulation is greater in the U.S.A. than in England. Freshness of approach and some new and authoritative information is essential. Only material written with authority can be considered." Buys interviews, profiles, and personal experience articles on "the arts, history, home and international politics, domestic subjects, theology, etc." Occasionally buys "short stories and poems of the highest literary merit." Length: 1,500 to 3,000 words for articles; 4,000 words maximum for fiction. Pays 2 pounds 50 shillings per 1,000 words.

THE COUNTRYMAN, Sheep Street, Burford, Oxford, OX8 4LH, England. Editor: Crispin Gill. Quarterly. Established in 1927. Circulation: 68,000. Copyrighted. Will consider material offered for first time only. Will send sample copy to writer for 45 pence. Query first or submit complete ms. Enclose S.A.E. and International Reply Coupons.
Nonfiction: Rural life and interests, factual and down to earth. No townee sentimentalizing about the countryside. Length: 2,000 words maximum. Pays 12 pounds per 1,000 words minimum.

CRITICAL QUARTERLY, Department of English, The University, Manchester, England. Editors: C. B. Cox and A. E. Dyson. Journal of literary criticism and new poetry of highest standard. Established in 1959. Quarterly. Circulation: 5,000. Not copyrighted. Submit complete ms. Will send free sample copy to writer on request. Payment on publication. Enclose S.A.E. and International Reply Coupons.

Nonfiction and Poetry: English and American literature. Literary criticism and new poetry of highest standard. Payment by arrangement.

CRUSADE, 19 Draycott Place, London SW3 2SJ, England. Editor: John Capon. For Christians (interdenominational), all ages, fairly well educated, and thoughtful people. Monthly. Established in 1957. Circulation: 16,000. Not copyrighted. Payment on publication. Will send sample copy to writer for 47¢. Query first. Enclose S.A.E. and International Reply Coupons.
Nonfiction: Features on social, religious and international topics related to Christianity. People features. Christian topics on people, places and events from an Evangelical viewpoint. Also articles on people of interest to Christians. Contemporary issues of all sorts dealt with. Will consider material previously published in United States or Canada offered for first publication in England. Length: by prior agreement. Payment by arrangement.

DANCE AND DANCERS, Artillery Mansions, 75 Victoria St., London, SW1H OHZ, England. Editor: Peter Williams. For "dancers, students, dance lovers, interested in all aspects of dance in the theatre." Monthly. Buys first rights. Will send a free sample copy to a writer on request. Query first. "No unsolicited material should be sent." Reports "as soon as possible." Enclose S.A.E. and International Reply Coupons for reply to queries.
Nonfiction: Wants "in-depth coverage of current productions; special emphasis on new creations with experts reviewing production, dancing, and music; regular interviews with important personalities in every branch of the field." Payment negotiable.

DRIVE MAGAZINE, Fanum House, Basingstoke, Hants RG21 2EA, England. Editor: Anthony Peagam. Four-color glossy magazine sent free to all members of The Automobile Association. Quarterly. Established in 1967. Circulation: 5,222,000. Copyrighted. Payment on acceptance. Will send sample copy to writer for 20 pence. Query first. Enclose S.A.E. and International Reply Coupons.
Nonfiction: "Leisure, motoring, environment, and consumer protection within these areas. Undertake leading social and consumer research, but also aim to entertain. Will not consider material previously published, but fresh ideas based on published material okay." Length: 600 to 2,000 words. Pays 300 pounds maximum.

THE ECOLOGIST, 73 Molesworth St., Wadebridge, Cornwall, England. Editor: Edward Goldsmith. For people interested in ecology and related matters. Established in 1970. 10 issues a year. Circulation: 10,000. Will send free sample copy to writer on request. Pays on publication. Query first or submit complete ms. Enclose S.A.E. and International Reply Coupons.
Nonfiction: All subjects relating to ecology. Payment by arrangement.

ENCOUNTER, 59 St. Martin's Lane, London WC2N 4JS, England. Editors: Melvin J. Lasky and Anthony Thwaite. Monthly. Copyrighted. Established in 1953. Circulation: 20,000. Payment on publication. Will send sample copy to writer for $1.75. Submissions may be made directly by the author, "but intending contributors are strongly advised to study magazine first." Enclose S.A.E. and International Reply Coupons for return of submissions.
Nonfiction, Fiction, and Poetry: "Mainly interested in high quality short stories and poetry. Current affairs, literature and the arts. Average payment is 10 pounds per 1,000 words for prose."

ENVOI POETRY MAGAZINE, Lagan nam Bann, Ballachulish, Argyll, Scotland. Editor: J. C. Meredith Scott. Magazine, 6x8. Published 3 times a year. Established in 1957. Circulation: 1,000. Will send sample copy for $1. Query first or submit four mss. Enclose S.A.E. and International Reply Coupons for return of submissions or reply to queries.
Poetry: *Envoi* means poetry, brief; traditional not barred. "It's difficult to describe the inwardness of a poetry magazine. Poetry does not pay. The practicable thing

is to see poetry as a hobby. No poetry magazine could welcome the unending drain of a tiny minus multiplied by infinity! The ideal is to avoid, as much as is possible, the slide into being a vanity press." Payment small, but prompt.

FABULOUS 208, IPC Magazines, Tower House, 8-14 Southampton St., London WC2E 9QX, England. Editor: Betty Hale. Magazine aimed at young people, 13 to 16 years old. Weekly. Established in 1963. Circulation: 210,000. Copyrighted. Pays on acceptance. Will send sample copy to writer for International Reply Coupons. Enclose S.A.E. and International Reply Coupons.
Nonfiction and Fiction: Submit serial and feature ideas to The Editor. Submit short stories to The Fiction Editor. Ideal length for short stories is 2,000 words. "Stories should certainly not exceed this maximum. The majority of stories used are emotional, with strong romantic flavour. Main characters should be unmarried, modern young people. Plotting should be kept simple; a strong emotional theme expressed cleverly from a particular angle is much better than a complex story which involves a span of time and complicated relationships with which the author attempts to resolve successfully within 2,000 words – this rarely works out. By the same token stories should take place within a definite time-span, usually no longer than a month." No stories that deal with permissiveness, drugs, sudden death, or deformlty. Pays $50 to $70 for short stories. Will consider feature material of 1,500 words, dealing with particular aspects of the reader's life – emotional or practical. Occasional opening for quizzes on aspects of personality or the reader's life.

THE FIELD, 8 Stratton St., London, England, Editor: Wilson Stephens. Weekly. Sometimes buys first British serial rights only. Pays on publication. Include S.A.E. and International Reply Coupons.
Nonfiction: "Factual accounts on fishing, shooting, hunting, countryside, natural history." Minimum and maximum rates of payment are "at editor's discretion."

FILMS AND FILMING, Artillery Mansions, 75 Victoria St., London, SW1H, OHZ, England. Editor: Robin Bean. For "those with a serious interest in all aspects of films." Monthly. Buys all rights. Will send a sample copy to a writer on request. Query first. Reports "as soon as possible." Enclose S.A.E. and International Reply Coupons for reply to queries.
Nonfiction: Wants "in-depth coverage." Buys "reviews plus features on directors, actors, particular genre and picture spreads, sections on documentary, film music, animation." Payment negotiable.

THE FLOWER PATCH, 127 Tower Road South, Warmley, Bristol, England BS15 5BT. Editors: David and Anne Lazell. Published every 2 months. Established in 1972. Circulation: 1,000. Copyrighted. Payment on publication. Will send 2 copies to writer for $1. Query first or submit complete ms, but best to see magazine first. Enclose S.A.E. and International Reply Coupons.
Nonfiction and Photos: "Ours is a small, light-hearted nostalgia/literary/countryside magazine, using mainly old prints for illustrations, so articles usually fall in these areas: creative nostalgia, memories, crafts, etc.; literary styles pre-1939; gentle commentaries on pop culture, etc., today; countryside interests; also occasional mysticism piece." Will consider material previously published in United States or Canada, offered for first publication in England, "if suitable." Length: 1,000 to 1,800 words. Pays by arrangement, approximately $10 per 1,000 words.

GAMEKEEPER AND COUNTRYSIDE, "Corry's" Roestock Lane, Colney Heath, St. Albans, Herts ALA 0QW, England. Editor: Edward Askwith. Monthly. For shooters, landowners, anglers, farmers, gamekeepers, conservationists. Established in 1896. Circulation: 7,500. Not copyrighted. Will send free sample copy to writer on request. Payment is made on publication. Enclose S.A.E. and International Reply Coupons for return of submissions.
Nonfiction: "Authoritative, nonfiction, articles on field sports, natural history, shooting, guns, fly fishing, coarse fishing, keepering, conservation, gundogs, working dogs, and terriers; country life." Straightforward approach. "Material must be authori-

tative." Informational, how-to, personal experience, profile, humor, historical, think pieces, personal opinion, new product, and technical articles. Length: 1,000 to 2,000 words. Pays 5 to 9 pounds per 1,000 words.

GARDEN NEWS, 21 Church Walk, Peterborough, England PE1 2TW. Editor: Peter Peskett. A tabloid newspaper for amateur gardeners. Established in 1959. Weekly. Circulation: 132,000. Not copyrighted. Pays on publication. Will send free sample copy on request. Submit complete ms. Enclose S.A.E. and International Reply Coupons.
Nonfiction and Photos: "Our purpose is to inform our readers of latest gardening techniques and introduce them to new varieties, etc., and generally help them to become better gardeners. Cultural articles backed up by features and stories on individual gardeners. A short and chatty style. Stories together with photos (both b&w and color transparencies) about amateur gardeners with interesting and/or unusual stories to tell, and articles on any developments in commercial horticulture likely to be of interest to the amateur. Length: 200 to 1,000 words. Pay is 10 to 25 pounds per 1,000 words."

GAY WORLD MAGAZINE, 118 Windham Road, Bournemouth, Hampshire, England. Editor: Deric Robert James. For the homophile society. Quarterly. Established in 1965. Circulation: 2,500. Payment on publication. Will send free sample copy to writer on request. Submit complete ms. Enclose S.A.E. and International Reply Coupons for return of submissions.
Nonfiction and Fiction: Factual news bulletins on the homophile society; short stories, etc. All matters relating to the homophile society. Purpose is to give a service to gay people and provide them with up-to-date information on gay groups, etc. Length: 1,000 to 2,500 words. Will consider material previously published in United States or Canada offered for first publication in England. Payment by negotiation.

GEMS, 84 High Street, Broadstairs, Kent, England. Editor: Richard Lambert. For the British rockhound. Published every 2 months. Established in 1969. Payment on publication. Not copyrighted. Will send sample copy to writer for $1. Submit complete ms. Enclose S.A.E. and International Reply Coupons for return of submissions.
Nonfiction: Articles on gemology, mineralogy, lapidary, jewelery making and kindred crafts. Will consider material previously published in United States or Canada offered for first publication in England. Length: about 1,000 words. Pays 10 pounds.

THE GEOGRAPHICAL MAGAZINE, 128 Long Acre, London WC2E 9QH, England. Editor: Derek Weber. For the general reader. Monthly. Established in 1935. Circulation: 73,000. Copyrighted. Payment on publication. Will send free sample copy to writer on request. Query first. Enclose S.A.E. and International Reply Coupons.
Nonfiction: "*The Geographical Magazine* differs from its US counterpart in that most of its editorial material is produced by professional geographers. The purpose of the magazine is to interpret for the general reader the geographical approach to the understanding of the world. It is not a 'travel' magazine, but is concerned with people and places, and with people in their environment. The freelance requirement is restricted, but it does exist. A study is recommended." Authentic articles; informative, readable, well-illustrated, dealing with people and their environment in all parts of the world. Length: 1,500 to 2,000 words. Pays 20 pounds minimum per 1,000 words. Also interested in at least 6 photos for each 1,000 words submitted. Pays 8.40 pounds minimum for color; 3.15 pounds minimum for b&w photos.

GOLF INTERNATIONAL, 183/185 Askew Rd., London, W.12, England. Editor: John Ingham. Weekly. Established in 1969. Circulation: 20,000. Payment on publication. Will send sample copy to writer for $1. Enclose S.A.E. and International Reply Coupons for return of submissions.
Nonfiction: Any golf articles. Will consider material previously published in United

States or Canada offered for first publication in England. Length: 500 to 1,000 words. Pays $5 to $150.

GOLF MONTHLY, 113 St. Vincent St., Glasgow, Scotland. Editor: Percy Huggins. Monthly. Circulation: 41,500. Sample copy on request. Include S.A.E. and International Reply Coupons. Aimed at golfers. Buys all rights. Pays on publication.
Nonfiction: Can use nonfiction on golf topics and personalities, no word length limitations. Payment rates to be negotiated.
Photos: Purchased with mss or with captions only.
Fiction: About golf. Length: 2,500 words maximum.

GOOD HOUSEKEEPING, Chestergate House, Vauxhall Bridge Rd., London SW1V 1HF, England. Editor: Charlotte Lessing. A general interest women's magazine with the accent on service to the reader. Established in 1921. Monthly. Circulation: 285,000. Not copyrighted. Pays on publication. Submit complete ms. Enclose S.A.E. and International Reply Coupons.
Nonfiction and Fillers: Humorous or practical fillers (800 to 1,500 words), in a light-hearted style. Also personal experience stories of social or medical difficulties (around 1,500 words). All specialist features (cookery, fashion, design, etc.) written by staff writers. Payment varies.

HEMISPHERE, Box 826, Woden P.O., ACT 2606 Australia. Editor: Kenneth Russell Henderson. A goodwill publication of the Department of Education. Audience is mainly Asian, but the magazine circulates widely in Australian schools and universities, as well as in Asian ones. Monthly. Established in 1957. Circulation: 28,000. Copyrighted. Payment on acceptance. Will send free sample copy to writer on request. Query first. Enclose S.A.E. and International Reply Coupons.
Nonfiction and Fiction: Asian, Australian and occasionally African—science, history, city profiles, the arts, short stories, archaeology, human interest stories. Nothing remotely resembling propaganda. Main aim of the publication is to keep Colombo Plan students in touch when they return home, but it is also useful in informing scholars in one Asian country about the work of their colleagues elsewhere. Pays 50 Australian dollars per 1,000 words.

HERS, IPC Magazines, Ltd., 30-32 Southampton St. London, WC2E 9QX, England. Editor: Miss Katherine Walker. Address submissions to the American office: Philip Fleet, IPC Magazines, Ltd., 300 E. 42nd St., New York NY 10017. Established in 1965. For young, married women, low income group; a bit lonely, a bit uncertain. Magazine provides excitement, reassurance, through real life stories. Monthly. Circulation: 190,000. Rights purchased vary with author and material. Buys all rights; or first serial rights. Buys about 100 mss a year. Payment on acceptance. Will send a sample copy to a writer on request. Submit complete ms only through New York office of IPC Magazines, Ltd. Reports in 1 month. Enclose S.A.E. and International Reply Coupons for return of submissions.
Fiction: First-person narrator, confession-style stories, but not sensational or over-sexy. Narrator must face emotional problem with which any woman would sympathize; a problem arising out of her own immaturity. During story, faces it, works through it, grows up. Length: 2,000 words minimum. Payment according to merit of story: minimum about 10 pounds per thousand words.

HI-FI NEWS & RECORD REVIEW, Link House, Dingwall Ave., Croydon CR9 2TA, England. Editor: John Crabbe. Monthly. Established in 1956. Circulation: 62,000. Copyrighted "month of issue only, apart from equipment reviews, which are fully copyrighted." Will send sample copy to writer for 75 pence. Enclose S.A.E. and International Reply Coupons for return of submissions.
Nonfiction: Technical and musical aspects of hi-fi and records. Feature articles on any aspect. Emphasis on authoritative reviews and reports on hi-fi equipment, audio techniques and principles and all English classical record releases (and some pop). Pays 10 pounds to 25 pounds per 1,000 words. Will also consider material previously published in United States or Canada, offered for first publication in England.

THE INCORPORATED LINGUIST, The Institute of Linguists, 91 Newington Causeway, London S.E.1, England. Editor: D. Cook-Radmore. Journal of professional organization (The Institute of Linguists) dealing with use of language in all its aspects. Quarterly. Established in 1961. Circulation: 4,500. Copyrighted. Will send sample copy to writer for $2. Query first. Enclose S.A.E. and International Reply Coupons.
Nonfiction: Articles on languages and linguistics. Emphasis on practical rather than theoretical side. Will consider material previously published in United States or Canada offered for first publication in England. Length: 3,000 to 5,000 words. No payment.

INSIGHT MAGAZINE, 118 Windham Rd., Bournemouth, Hampshire BH1 4RD, England. Editor: Deric R. James. "Audience from all walks of life—professional people, retired people, artists, students, doctors, clergy, etc." Quarterly. Established in 1965. Circulation: 2,500. Buys first rights. Pay on publication. Will send a sample copy to a writer on request. Submit seasonal material 3 months in advance. Reports in 3 months. Submit complete ms only. Enclose S.A.E. and International Reply Coupons for return of submissions.
Nonfiction and Photos: "Any aspect of occultism, ceremonial magic, etc. The writer should always send a photo or sketch pertaining to his thesis. We also publish articles on black magic. No comparative and eastern religions material or paraphysical subjects, healing, etc." Buys personal experience articles, interviews, spot news, photo articles. Style in generalized terms, please. Will consider material previously published in United States or Canada, offered for first publication in England. Length: 1,000 words. Pays 50 pence to 2 pounds. Photos purchased with ms.

JEWISH TELEGRAPH, Levi House, Bury Old Rd., Manchester M8 6HB, England. Editor: Frank Harris. For family readership. Weekly. Established in 1950. Circulation: 10,000. Copyrighted. Will send free sample copy to writer on request. Payment on publication. Submit complete ms. Enclose S.A.E. and International Reply Coupons.
Nonfiction: Exclusive news and humorous and historical articles of Jewish interest. Payment by arrangement, usually 3 pounds minimum. Will also consider material previously published in United States or Canada, offered for first publication in England.

KENT LIFE, 109 Week St., Maidstone, Kent., England. Editor: Robert Songhurst. Magazine is aimed at county level (for example, nobility, gentry, and professional classes). Monthly. Established in 1962. Circulation: 14,000. Copyrighted. Payment on acceptance. Will send free sample copy to writer on request. Query first. Enclose S.A.E. and International Reply Coupons for reply to query.
Nonfiction: Partly social, partly cultural; remainder modern aspects of Kent, historical, and countryside, folklore, general articles. All material must have a strong link with Kent. Material can be topical or modern. Facts must be absolutely correct. Ideally, articles should be checked with source. Length: 1,000 to 1,200 words. Pays 2 pounds to 7.50 pounds.
Photos: "The majority of pictures are taken by staff photographers. However, I am always glad to consider unusual b&w pictures. Suggested subjects to avoid: Canterbury Cathedral, and Rochester and Dover Castles. Very fine buildings, but photographed to death." Buys photos with mss and occasionally with captions only. Pays 1 pound per picture.
Fiction and Poetry: "Must be connected with Kent. Avoid religion or race." Little fiction used. Length: 1,000 to 1,200 words for fiction; 20 to 30 lines for poetry. Pays 1 pound for poetry.

LIGHT HORSE, D. J. Murphy Publishers Ltd., 19 Charing Cross Rd., London WC2H OEY, England. Editor: Michael Williams. For an international, sophisticated audience. Monthly. Established in 1950. Circulation: 20,000. Copyrighted. Payment in month following publication. Will send free sample copy to writer on request. Submit complete ms. Enclose S.A.E. and International Reply Coupons.

Nonfiction: Any subject dealing with any aspect of equestrianism that is likely to be of interest to an international audience. Good writing essential. No fiction. Preferably with illustrations (b&w photos or drawings). Length: 750 to 1,600 words. One photo for an article of 750 words, 3 for 1,300 words, 2 for 1,600 words. Pays 8.50 pounds to 10.50 pounds per 1,000 words. Pays 2.50 pounds for each photo published.

LITTACK, 27 Brook Rd., Epping, Essex, England. Editor: William Oxley. A literary review whose prime concern is to find and publish good poetry for its readers. Biannually. Established in 1972. Circulation: 500. Not copyrighted. Payment on publication. Will send sample copy to writer for $2. Submit complete ms. Enclose S.A.E. and International Reply Coupons for return of submissions.

Nonfiction and Poetry: Poetry, literary criticism and related essays. Creates a new aesthetic for poetry which will enable the good to be defined, and at the same time, reassert the one eternal tradition underlying all the arts which, today, has become intolerably obscured by, inter alia, the propaganda for false values at all levels of thought. Such a new aesthetic, or rejuvenation of the old, cannot be achieved without a changing climate of thought; and this necessary change will not be brought about without first of all the destruction of the rotten, the pseudo, and the bad. Payment by negotiation.

LOOK AND LISTEN, Artillery Mansions, 75 Victoria St., London SW1H OHZ England. Editor: Robin Bean.

Nonfiction: General subject matter: "covers radio and TV."

LOOKEAST, Advertising and Media Consultants, Ltd., Thaniya Bldg., 62 Silom Rd., Bangkok, Thailand. Managing Director: Satish Sehgal. Mss should be directed to The Editor. A consumer travel magazine which is placed in almost all first-class hotel rooms in Thailand and Singapore. It is also circulated to some extent in Malaysia and India, and is sold on the newsstands of many Southeast Asian countries. It's written for the knowledgeable traveler, who is interested in Asia, wants hard facts but also wants to know something about the mood, people and culture of Asian countries. Monthly. Established in 1971. Circulation: 12,000. Copyrighted. Payment on publication. Will send sample copy to writer for $1 (seamail). Query first. Enclose S.A.E. and International Reply Coupons.

Nonfiction and Photos: "Travel articles concerning Asian region in its broad sense. Material can be personal in tone but must be up-to-date and absolutely accurate, as the magazine is read by people traveling now. We also use articles which concern other aspects of Asian region—culture, history, etc." Will consider material previously published in United States or Canada offered for first publication in Thailand. Length: 1,800 to 3,000 words. Pays $25 to $75. Photos are generally required for travel pieces; color slides, larger transparencies or b&w.

LOVING, P.O. Box 21, Tower House, 8/14 Southampton St., London WC2E, England. Editor: Alison Mackonochle. A weekly confession magazine for young working class readers (16 to 25 age group). Established in 1970. Circulation: 250,000. Payment on acceptance. Copyrighted. Submit complete ms (first installment only of serials, plus synopsis). Enclose S.A.E. and International Reply Coupons.

Fiction: First-person stories, mainly romantic interest tales. Stories may deal with problems confronting unmarried mothers, girls facing unwanted pregnancies, problems of living together, early married life, getting engaged, etc. Happy endings, or stories should end on hopeful note. No stories dealing with color question, homosexuality, drugs. Emphasis on strong emotional involvement. Will consider material previously published in United States or Canada offered for first publication in England. Length: 2,000 to 6,000 words. Pays 10 pounds per 1,000 words.

MEANJIN QUARTERLY, University of Melbourne, Parkville, Victoria 3052, Australia. Editor: J. H. Davidson. For an informed, but non-specialist, audience. Quarterly. Established in 1940. Circulation: 2,000. Not copyrighted. Payment on publication. Submit complete ms. Enclose S.A.E. and International Reply Coupons for return of submissions.

Nonfiction, Fiction, and Poetry: Short fiction, poetry; essays, articles, review-articles on contemporary literature and art, international affairs, socio-political subjects. Length: 4,000 words maximum. Pays $50 per 1,000 words. Pays $5 minimum for poetry.

MELODY MAKER, 24-34, Meymott St., London SE1 9LU, England. Editor: Ray Coleman. For music lovers. Weekly. Established in 1926. Circulation: 188,073. Copyrighted. Payment on publication. Will send free sample copy to writer on request. Submit complete ms. Enclose S.A.E. and International Reply Coupons.

Nonfiction: "Concert reviews; folk, rock, pop, jazz, country artists. Interviews with personalities. No set fees; we pay according to value of copy."

THE MODERN CHURCHMAN, Caynham Vicarage, Ludlow, Calop, England. Editor: W.H.C. Frend. For people interested in the study of religion. Established in 1911. Quarterly. Circulation: 1,500. Copyrighted. Will consider material previously published in U.S. or Canada offered for first publication in U.K. Will send a sample to a writer for $1. Query first or submit complete ms. Enclose S.A.E. and International Reply Coupons for return of submissions or reply to queries.

Nonfiction: Subjects relating to the history or philosophy of religion, discussed academically, with contemporary religious issues. Style: straightforward. Length: 4,000 words maximum. Pays 3.15 pounds.

MODERN LANGUAGES, Journal of the Modern Language Association, 3 Hamlea Close, Lee, London SE12 8EU, England. Editor: E. M. Batley. Quarterly journal, 6x9. Circulation: 4,000. Copyrighted. Will send sample copy to writer for $3. Requests for sample copies should be sent to: Modern Language Association, 35 Lewisham Way, London SE14 6PP, England. Submit complete transcript. Enclose S.A.E. and International Reply Coupons for return of submissions.

Nonfiction: Articles on modern languages (normally, French, German, Spanish, Italian and Russian), the teaching thereof, applied linguistics and general linguistic theory, literature and civilization pertaining to the above languages. Length: 3,500 to 4,000 words. No payment, except in copies.

MODERN MOTOR, 15 Boundary St., 3rd floor, Rushcutters Bay, Sydney, New South Wales, Australia 2011. Editor: John Crawford. For a motoring oriented audience, ages 13 through 70. Established in 1956. Monthly. Circulation: 70,000. Copyrighted. Buys full Australian rights. Payment on publication. Will send sample copy to writer on request (surface mail, unless payment for airmail included with request). Submit complete ms. Enclose S.A.E. and International Reply Coupons for reply to query.

Nonfiction: "Accent is on hard news. However, we are interested in hard-hitting features that show variety in motoring around the world. No travel articles. Our style is pure news—fast, race news, presentation, packed with fact and good info. We are not interested in flowery prose, but we welcome good 'color' writing." Informational and spot news. Length: 1,000 to 3,000 words. Pays $30 to $100 per 1,000 words. (May be increased substantially for world first news, or scoops.)

Photos: B&w 6x8 photos are purchased with or without accompanying mss and on assignment. Captions required. Pays A$5 each. Transparencies or good reflective art purchased for A$10 each. "We prefer photos with a high emphasis on action." **Fillers:** Newsbreaks and jokes. Length: 50 to 200 words. Pays A$5 to A$20.

THE MONTH, 114 Mount St., London W1Y 6AH, England. Editor: Michael J. Walsh. Primarily for Roman Catholics, educated readership in United Kingdom and abroad. Monthly. Established in 1864. Circulation: 4,500. Payment on publication. Will send sample copy to writer for $2.75. Query first or submit complete ms. Enclose S.A.E. and International Reply Coupons.

Nonfiction: Purpose is to examine anything of ethical interest in political affairs, and report on ecclesiastical matters. Style should be lively, and *English* English to be used. Ecclesiastical and political world affairs, some cultural articles of general interest. Length: 3,000 to 4,500 words. Pays up to 7.50 pounds per 1,000 words.

MOTHER MAGAZINE, 189 High Holborn, London W.C. 1, England. Editor: Catherine Munnion. For young mothers of preschool children who are very interested in their children's welfare and education. Monthly. Established in 1936. Circulation: 100,000. Rights purchased vary with author and material. May buy all rights. Payment on acceptance. Will send free sample copy to writer on request. Write for copy of guidelines for writers. Submit seasonal material 5 or 6 months in advance. Submit complete ms. Enclose S.A.E. and International Reply Coupons.
Nonfiction: Anything of interest to the parents of preschool children: medical, psychological, educational, general. Material should have intelligent, parent-to-parent approach, but must be very clear and straightforward. No gimmicks. Sound principles. "We are always interested in what is happening now, what today's parents and children need. Anything that looks at the questions in people's minds at the present time as they relate to parents and children. Christmas and summer material particularly welcome." Informational, how-to, personal experience, interview, profile, inspirational, humor and personal opinion. Length: 500 to 2,000 words. Pays about 17.50 pounds per 1,000 words.

MOTOR BOAT AND YACHTING, Dorset House, Stamford St., London SE1, England. Editor: Dick Hewitt. For people interested in motor boating, from large motor yachts in the luxury class to small boats with outboards. Established in 1904. Every two weeks. Circulation: 30,450. Copyrighted. Pays on publication. Query first or submit complete ms. Enclose S.A.E. and International Reply Coupons.
Nonfiction and Photos: Accounts of cruises; technical and informative features on boating subjects. Powerboat racing and inland waterway information. Length: 2,500 words maximum. Standard rate of payment is 12.50 pounds per 1,000 words. Photos purchased with accompanying mss or without mss. Captions required. B&w and color. Pays from 3.00 pounds to 10.00 pounds.

MUSIC AND MUSICIANS, Artillery Mansions, 75 Victoria St., London, SW1H OHZ, England, Editor: Michael Reynolds. For "professionals in the musical fields of publishing, performance, recording, instrument making, etc., and the general music public." Monthly. Buys first rights. Pays on publication. Will send a sample copy to a writer on request. Query first. Reports "as soon as possible." Enclose S.A.E. and International Reply Coupons for reply to queries.
Nonfiction and Photos: Uses "news features, musical extracts, and reviews. The publication covers a very wide musical field." Length: 600 to 2,000 words. Buys b&w glossy photos.

MY WEEKLY, 80 Kingsway East, Dundee, Scotland. Editor: Stewart D. Brown. For women everywhere. Established in 1910. Weekly. Payment on acceptance. Will send free sample copy to writer on request. Submit complete ms. Enclose S.A.E. and International Reply Coupons for return of submissions.
Nonfiction and Fiction: "We look for stories about ordinary people that are emotional, humorous, interesting. We are not interested in the controversial, the sensational or educational. Key word is entertaining." Will consider material previously published in United States or Canada offered for first publication in Scotland. Nonfiction length: 750 to 3,000 words. Payment by negotiation; usually 10 pounds minimum. Mystery, adventure, humorous, and romantic fiction. Fiction length: 1,000 to 5,000 words. Payment by negotiation; usually 12 pounds minimum.

THE NAUTICAL MAGAZINE, 52 Darnley St., Glasgow, G41 2SG, Scotland. Editor: R. Ingram-Brown. For "the seafaring profession." Monthly. Circulation: 3,500. Buys all rights. Pays on publication. Will send a sample copy to a writer on request. Enclose S.A.E. and International Reply Coupons for return of submissions.
Nonfiction: Articles of interest to merchant navy; astronomical; navigational. Length: 2,400 words. Pays 2 pounds per 500 words on publication.

THE NEW BEACON, Royal National Institute for the Blind, 224 Great Portland Street, London, W1N 6AA, England. Editor: Donald Bell. For "those interested in blind welfare." Monthly. Circulation: 3,700. Buys no rights. Pays on publication. Reports "immediately." Enclose S.A.E. and International Reply Coupons.
Nonfiction, Photos, and Poetry: Buys "authoritative articles on all aspects of blind welfare throughout the world and causes and prevention of blindness, news items (home and overseas)." Also buys "original material (prose and verse) by blind authors." Pays 2 pounds 10 pence per 1,000 words. Length: 900 to 5,000 words. Buys photos separately, "rarely" with articles. Payment negotiable.

NEW HUMANIST, 88 Islington High St., London N1 8EL, England. Editor: Nicolas Walter. *New Humanist* developed out of *Humanist*, which was the magazine for rational humanists. It is humanist in intention, but now appeals to a larger audience. Readership covers all ages and classes. Monthly. Established first in 1885 and again in 1972 (as *New Humanist*). Circulation: 7,000. Copyrighted. Payment on publication. Will send free sample copy to writer on request. Query first. Enclose S.A.E. and International Reply Coupons.
Nonfiction, Photos, and Poetry: Humanism, rationalism, philosophy, science, social science, arts, criticism, poetry (with a broad humanist base), current affairs, books, economics, matters of human concern generally; evils of religions and other dogmas. Articles need not be strictly humanist but rationalist in purpose. Articles tend to be of a fairish length (1,000 to 2,000 words), giving a more considered coverage to problems of the moment. A serious and concerned magazine, but not a specialist one. Will consider material previously published in United States or Canada offered for first publication in England. Length: 1,200 to 2,500 words. Pays 10 to 25 pounds per 1,000 words.

NEW POETRY, Box N110 Grosvenor Street Post Office, Sydney N.S.W., 2000 Australia. Editor: Robert Adamson. A journal for serious poetry writers and readers. Published quarterly. Established in 1952. Circulation: 1,000. Copyrighted. Payment on publication. Will send sample copy to writer for 1 Australian dollar. Enclose S.A.E. and International Reply Coupons for return of submissions.
Nonfiction and Poetry: Internationally relevant. Publishes contemporary poetry, critical articles, reviews, notes and comments. Open-ended policy, depending on quality of work. Will consider material previously published in United States or Canada offered for first publication in Australia. Pays $7.50 to $200.

OASIS MAGAZINE, 12 Stevenage Rd., London SW6 6ES, England. Editor: Ian Robinson. 3 times a year. Established in 1969. Circulation: 1,000. Not copyrighted. Payment only in copies. Will send sample copy to writer for $1.50. Enclose S.A.E. and International Reply Coupons for return of submission.
Nonfiction, Fiction, and Poetry: Will consider the following unpublished material: poetry, prose fiction, articles, criticism, essays, letters, reviews, and graphics. No maximum or minimum length; any structure, style, or approach. Only literary quality. Pays only in copies.

ORBIS, Hub Publications Ltd., Youlgrave, Bakewell, DE4 1UT, England. Editor: Robin Gregory. Quarterly. Established in 1969. Payment on publication. Will send sample copy to writer for $1. Submit complete ms. Enclose S.A.E. and International Reply Coupons for return of submissions.
Nonfiction: Payment is made for intelligent, readable articles about literature and literary figures, especially poetry and poets. No special length requirements. Small payment.

OSTRICH, 10 Greenhaugh Rd., Whitley Bay, Tyne and Wear NE25 9HF, England. Editor: Keith Armstrong. Quarterly. Established in 1971. Circulation: 500. Not copyrighted. Will send free sample copy to writer on request. Submit complete ms. Enclose S.A.E. and International Reply Coupons.
Nonfiction, Fiction, and Poetry: Poetry, short stories, general articles on the arts

and politics. Will consider material previously published in the United States or Canada offered for first publication in England. No payment.

OUTPOSTS, 72 Burwood Rd., Walton-on-Thames, Surrey, KT12 6AL, England. Editor: Howard Sergeant. *Outposts* is the oldest independent poetry magazine in the U.K. Quarterly. Established in 1944. Circulation: 1,500. Copyrighted. Will send sample copy to writer for 40¢. Payment on publication. Enclose S.A.E. and International Reply Coupons.
Poetry: Any subject acceptable provided it's not pornography. Complete freedom to poets for subject, style and form. Preferred length is 36 to 38 lines. Will consider poetry from any country in the world provided it is in English. Pays 1 pound per page.

OVER21 MAGAZINE, 5-7 Carnaby St., London, W.1, England. Editor: Audrey Slaughter. For career women (including marriage and motherhood as careers). Monthly. Established in 1972. Circulation: 128,000. Copyrighted. Payment on acceptance. Query first or submit complete ms. Enclose S.A.E. and International Reply Coupons.
Nonfiction and Fiction: Short, crisp articles, and strong short stories or serials for intelligent career women. No domesticity. Lively, modern features about relationships; the struggle to be working woman and wife; life styles; exclusive interviews with personalities; interesting viewpoints; crafts to make; chic do-it-yourselfery. Will consider material previously published in United States or Canada offered for first publication in England. Length: 3,000 words maximum. Pays minimum 15 pounds per page according to research involved, quality of author. Payment by negotiation.

PARENTS VOICE, National Society for Mentally Handicapped Children, Pembridge Hall, 17 Pembridge Square, London W2 4EP, England. Editor: Mrs. Christine E. P. Zwart. *Parents Voice* is the journal of the National Society for Mentally Handicapped Children, a consumer body for parents of handicapped children. Most copies go to parents of mentally handicapped children, and the rest go to professionals (for example, doctors, teachers, government officials) concerned with the mentally handicapped. Quarterly. Established in 1950. Circulation: 30,000. Copyrighted. Will send free sample copy to writer on request. Query first. Enclose S.A.E. and International Reply Coupons.
Nonfiction: "We aim to keep our readers informed of all new developments in the care of the retarded. Style is popular. We consider articles on any subject connected with the field of mental retardation; for example, anything from the personal experiences of the parent of the retarded child, to detailed papers on research into causes of mental handicap." Will consider material previously published in United States or Canada, offered for first publication in England. Length: 1,500 words maximum. No payment.

PLAYS AND PLAYERS, Artillery Mansions, 75 Victoria St., London, SW1H OHZ, England. Editor: Michael Coveney. For "the general theater-going public of all ages, students and professionals." Monthly. Buys first rights. Will send a sample copy to a writer on request. Writers are specifically requested not to submit unsolicited mss. Query first. Reports as soon as possible. Enclose S.A.E. and International Reply Coupons for reply to queries.
Nonfiction and Photos: Uses "reviews, feature reviews of new productions, plus features on directors, actors, etc., and regular complete text of play; also coverage of TV and radio drama plus regional, European, and New York newsletters." Wants in-depth coverage. Buys b&w glossy photos. Payment negotiable.

POETRY AUSTRALIA, 350 Lyons Rd., Five Dock, N.S.W., Australia 2046. Editor: Grace Perry. Poetry magazine for universities, schools and colleges; poets and writers. Quarterly. Established in 1964. Circulation: 2,000. Copyrighted. Will send sample copy for $2. Payment on publication. Submit complete ms. Enclose S.A.E. and International Reply Coupons for return of submissions.
Nonfiction and Poetry: Poetry contributors may need to read several issues to get

the "flavor," since some special issues may not present the whole picture. Pays $8 per page; $10 first time in print.

THE POLITICAL QUARTERLY, 48 Lanchester Rd., London, N6 4TA, England. Editors: William A. Robson and Bernard Crick. For "political scientists, politicians, officials, and general intelligent readers." Quarterly. Buys all rights. Pays on publication. Will send a sample copy to a writer for $2. Reports "usually within 4 weeks." Enclose International Reply Coupons for return of submissions.

Nonfiction: Wants "articles discussing political, social, or international questions or problems. The style must be appropriate for a highly educated audience, but we want lucidity, an absence of jargon, closely argued statements, rather than an abundance of footnotes. Study the periodical before submitting your article, and be sure that the length, style, and subject are appropriate." Length: 4,000 words. Pays 7.50 pounds.

PONY, D. J. Murphy Publishers Ltd., 19 Charing Cross Rd., London WC2H OEY, England. Editor: Michael Williams. An equestrian magazine for young readers. Monthly. Established in 1949. Circulation: 38,000. Copyrighted. Payment in month following publication. Will send free sample copy to writer on request. Submit complete ms. Enclose S.A.E. and International Reply Coupons.

Nonfiction, Fiction, and Photos: Short stories and/or articles on horse and pony subjects are normally sent to outside artists for illustration. Photos are preferred with nonfiction and paid for separately, usually at the rate of 2.50 pounds for each photo published. Articles and stories should interest readers between the ages of 9 and 18. Length: 750 to 1,600 words. Pays 6.50 pounds (when written by children), 10.50 pounds (middle rate), 12.50 pounds (top rate) per 1,000 words.

PRACTICAL MOTORIST, Fleetway House, Farringdon St., London EC4A 4AD, England. Editor: Harry Heywood. Do-it-yourself magazine for enthusiastic motorists. Monthly. Copyrighted. Payment on publication. Query first. Enclose S.A.E. and International Reply Coupons.

Nonfiction and Photos: Articles covering maintenance and repair from simple jobs like points setting to automatic gearbox overhauls. Step-by-step repair features supported by ample photos. Payment "purely on merit."

THE PSYCHOLOGIST MAGAZINE LTD., Denington Estate, Wellingborough, Northants, England. Editor: John Evans. For general readership. Monthly. Established in 1933. Circulation: 27,000. Copyrighted. Payment on publication. Will send free sample copy to writer on request. Submit complete ms. Enclose S.A.E. and International Reply Coupons for return of submissions.

Nonfiction: "Our theme is one of popular practical psychology as a means toward self-improvement and the overcoming of various problems and complexes. We want articles of an inspirational nature dealing with the application of sound practical psychology in dealing with human problems." Will consider material previously published in United States or Canada offered for first publication in England. Length: 1,500 words. Pays 5 pounds minimum.

PUNCH, 23 Tudor St., London EC4, England. Editor: William Davis. For quite young, more liberal type of businessman, well educated. Established in 1841. Weekly. Circulation: 100,000. Copyrighted. Payment at end of month of publication. "Will expect writer to be curious enough to buy or steal sample copy." Query first or submit complete ms. Enclose S.A.E. and International Reply Coupons.

Nonfiction and Fiction: "Topical humor, politics, fashionable but irritating subjects. Inside information. Anything that deflates pretension. Frivolous, stylish, informed unobscurantist, funny and about 1,200 words long, though we also print pieces of as little as 1,190. Brilliant humor on seasonal topics is always welcome, although almost impossible to find." Informational, personal experience, humor, expose, and book reviews. Humorous fiction. Length: "937 to about 1,425 words." Pays 20 to about 100 pounds.

Fillers: Filler Editor: David Taylor. "Unbelievable provincial cuttings." Length: open. Pays 1 pound.

QUADRANT, Daking House, Rawson Place, Sydney. Australia 2000. Editors: Peter Coleman and James McAuley. For "professionals, academics, students, and the general intelligent public." Established in 1956. Published every 2 months. Circulation: 4,000. Pays on publication. Not copyrighted. Will consider material previously published in U.S. or Canada offered for first publication in Australia. Will send a sample copy to a writer for A$1. Submit complete ms. Enclose S.A.E. and International Reply Coupons.
Nonfiction, Fiction, and Poetry: Literary criticism and articles on politics, history, social thought, the arts. In fact, on any topic whatsoever. Also buys short stories. Length: 2,000 to 6,000 words. Pays $30 to $60. Pays $10 for verse.

RACING PIGEON PICTORIAL, 19 Doughty St., London WC1N 2PT, England. Editor: Colin Osman. For hobby specialists all over the world. Monthly. Established in 1898. Circulation: 49,000. Copyrighted. Payment on publication. Will send sample copy to writer for $1. Query first. Enclose S.A.E. and International Reply Coupons.
Nonfiction and Photos: Factual items and human interest articles on pigeon racing and breeding. Expert in approach and vocabulary. Articles on local champions. Length: open. Payment by arrangement. Pays 5 pounds per page. Photos purchased with or without ms, or on assignment. 8x10 b&w or 2¼x2¼ color. Captions required. Photo Editor: Peter Turner. "All payment is by arrangement. Best paid work is commissioned from experts known to us."

RECORDS AND RECORDING, Artillery Mansions, 75 Victoria St., London, SW1H OHZ, England. Editor: Trevor Richardson. For "record collectors, music lovers, and professionals." Monthly. Buys first rights. Pays after publication. Will send a sample copy to a writer on request. Query first. "Unsolicited manuscripts should *not* be sent." Enclose S.A.E. and International Reply Coupons for reply to queries.
Nonfiction: Uses "material covering every aspect of classical music on record, plus rock, jazz, and folk and a substantial audio section; reviews and features on important artists in the field and events in the record world." Buys b&w glossy photos and color transparencies. Payment is negotiable.

ROD AND LINE, Butlaw Lodge, South Queensferry, West Lothian, Scotland. Editor: Michael Shepley. For persons interested in game fishing and sea angling. Monthly. Established in 1962. Circulation: 10,000. Not copyrighted. Payment on publication. Will send sample copy to writer for $1.50. Enclose S.A.E. and International Reply Coupons for return of submissions.
Nonfiction, Fillers, and Poetry: "Articles on salmon and trout, sea trout; all types of sea fishing with rod and line. Angling fiction acceptable. Occasionally short poems on angling are bought. Willing to consider any short fillers on angling matters." Length: 500 to 2,000 words. Pays 5 pounds to 15 pounds.
Photos: Purchased with or without ms. Captions required. Must be on angling subjects. 8x10 b&w glossies. Pays 1 pound 5 pence to 3 pounds. Color, minimum 2¼ square acceptable. Pays 6.50 pounds per transparency. All original material returned.

SEA ANGLER, East Midland Allied Press, Oundle Rd., Peterborough PE1 2TS, England. Editor: Peter Collins. For British sea fishermen (rod and line) from shore and boats. Monthly. Established in 1972. Circulation: 27,850. Not copyrighted. Payment on publication. Submit complete ms only. Enclose S.A.E. and International Reply Coupons for return of submissions.
Nonfiction and Photos: Interested in sea angling features, preferably illustrated, with tuitional theme. Will consider material previously published in United States or Canada offered for first publication in England. Length: 800 to 1,600 words. Pays 7.50 pounds to 20 pounds.

SEA SPRAY, P.O. Box 793, Auckland, New Zealand. Editor: David Pardon. New Zealand's largest selling yachting and powerboat magazine aimed at the pleasure craft market. Monthly. Established in 1947. Circulation: 14,200. Copyrighted. Payment on publication. Will send free sample copy to writer on request. Submit complete ms only. Enclose S.A.E. and International Reply Coupons for return of submissions.
Nonfiction and Photos: Articles on yacht and powerboat design, construction, maintenance, operation (pleasure craft only). New equipment, techniques relating to yacht and powerboat racing or cruising. Will consider material previously published in United States or Canada offered for first publication in New Zealand, "but at half normal payment rate." Length: 3,000 words maximum. Pays 20 New Zealand dollars per 1,000 words. Pays 2.50 New Zealand dollars for captioned b&w glossies. Size may vary with 8x6 a good average.

SEACRAFT, 142 Clarence St., Sydney, N.S.W., Australia 2000. Editor: Paul Hopkins. For "all interested in sailing, power boats, and boating in general." Monthly. Circulation: 19,000. Rights negotiable. Buys 150 mss a year. Pays on acceptance. Will send a sample copy to a writer for 70¢. Reports "within a month." Enclose S.A.E. and International Reply Coupons for return of submissions.
Nonfiction: Buys "technical and general articles on all forms of boating; also some factual cruising and sea adventure stories." Buys how-to and personal experience articles, profiles, and coverage of new boating products. Length: 1,500 to 3,000 words. Pays A$10 per 1,000 words "if up to standards. If an article is interesting but poorly written, payment is reduced."

SHE, Chestergate House, Vauxhall Bridge Rd., London, SW1V 1HF, England. Editor: Pamela Massingham. For lively, intelligent people, mostly women 18 to 35 years of age. Monthly. Established in 1955. Circulation: 300,000. Copyrighted. Payment on acceptance. Will send sample copy to writer for $1. Submit complete ms. Enclose S.A.E. and International Reply Coupons for return of submissions.
Nonfiction: All kinds of articles, very wide ranging interests, but no politics. Length: 500 to 2,500 words. Payment by arrangement.
Fiction: All kinds except romance and downbeat, depressing stories. Length: 1,000 to 2,500 words. Payment by arrangement.

SHIMANO WORLD, c/o Nova Advertising Inc., Tani Bldg. 2-54, Tsurigane-cho, Higashi-ku, Osaka 540, Japan. Publisher-Editor: Tatsuo Yamamoto. Editor: Gerald J. Lange. House publication of Shimano Industrial Co., Ltd., for the dealer, distributor, and traders to promote mutual understandings. Established in 1972. Quarterly. Circulation: 10,000. Copyrighted. Will send sample copy free to writer on request. Payment on publication. Query first. Enclose S.A.E. and International Reply Coupons.
Nonfiction and Photos: Anything related to bicycles; purchasing, sales, cycling, touring, remodeling, etc. Length: 1,500 to 2,000 words. Pays 7¢ to 10¢ per word. Buys color and b&w photos. Payment negotiable.

SPECTRE, 18 Cefn Rd., Mynachdy, Cardiff CF4 3HS, Great Britain. Editor: Jon M. Harvey. For fantasy/horror/supernatural enthusiasts, as well as folklorists. Established in 1975. Three times a year. Will consider material previously published in the U.S. or Canada if obscure enough in its first publication. Not copyrighted. Pays on publication. Will send sample copy to writer for $1. Submit complete ms. Enclose S.A.E. and International Reply Coupons.
Nonfiction, Fiction and Poetry: Publication has a bias toward fiction, although factual material (articles, criticism, etc.) also considered. Material desired on fantasy and folklore and fantasy-oriented science fiction. Length: 2,500 words minimum. Pays 1 pound (sterling) per 5 words for material over 1,000 words. This is the house publication of Spectre Press which deals in offtrail publications of fantasy and folklore material. Any material considered for *Spectre* will be considered as a general submission for Spectre Press. If it fits in with any project in process or is too long to fit into *Spectre,* it will probably find its way into a general Spectre Press publication.

SPORTS CAR WORLD, 142 Clarence St., Sydney, N.S.W., Australia 2000. Editor: Steve Cropley. For "sports car enthusiasts, generally in the 18 to 35 age group." Monthly. Established in 1956. Circulation: 18,500. Rights negotiable. Buys 150 mss a year. Pays on acceptance. Will send a sample copy to a writer for 40¢. Submit complete ms. Enclose S.A.E. and International Reply Coupons.
Nonfiction: Wants "factual material on sports and performance cars, car racing, and mechanics." Buys how-to articles, profiles, and coverage of new products in the car field. Length: 1,500 to 3,000 words. Payment by negotiation; usually 30 Australian dollars minimum.

STAMP COLLECTING, 42 Maiden Lane, London WC2E 7LL, England. Editor: Kenneth F. Chapman. Weekly. Established in 1913. Circulation: 25,000. Copyrighted. Payment on publication. Will send free sample copy to writer on request. Submit complete ms. Enclose S.A.E. and International Reply Coupons.
Nonfiction: Articles on any aspect of philately. This includes stamps, postal history, and air mails. Essentially a philatelic news magazine but carries serious articles on all philatelic topics and light-hearted material whenever obtainable. Length: 1,000 to 3,000 words. Pays 4 pounds per 1,000 words, up to 8 pounds in selected cases.

STAND, 58 Queens Rd., Newcastle on Tyne, NE2 2PR, England. Editors: Jon Silkin, Lorna Tracy, Ed Brunner, Robert Ober, Howard Fink, and Michael Wilding. Established in 1952. Quarterly. Circulation: 4,500. Copyrighted. Will send a sample copy to a writer for $1.25. Payment on publication. Submit complete ms. Enclose S.A.E. and International Reply Coupons.
Nonfiction, Fiction and Poetry: Poetry, fiction, criticism, translated work. Length: 10,000 words maximum for fiction. Pays 5 pounds per poem; 6 pounds per 1,000 words of prose.

THE STATESMAN, 260-C, Commercial Area, P.E.C.H.S., Karachi-29, Pakistan. Editor: Mohammed Owais. Weekly. Established in 1955. Circulation: 5,000. Copyrighted. Payment on publication. Will send free sample copy to writer on request. Submit complete ms only. Enclose S.A.E. and International Reply Coupons for return of submissions.
Nonfiction and Fiction: Short stories and articles on literature, international economic problems; special reports on events. Regular topics include international affairs, economic affairs, arts and letters, sports, films and, of course, book reviews. Pays 50 Pakistani rupees per 1,000 words.

STUDIES IN COMPARATIVE RELIGION, Pates Manor, Bedfont, Middlesex, TW14, 8JP, England. Editor: F. Clive-Ross. Quarterly. Established in 1941. Copyrighted. Payment on publication. Will send sample copy to writer for $3. Submit complete ms. Enclose S.A.E. and International Reply Coupons.
Nonfiction: Articles on religious and sacred subjects strictly from a traditional and Orthodox point of view. The journal is devoted to the sort of writings as expounded by Rene Guenon, A.K. Coomaraswamy and Frithjof Schuon. The journal does not cover so-called reformed religions. It is devoted to the perennial philosophy in its true sense, as the mystical aspect of a properly orthodox religion; for example, The Roman Catholic Church or Greek or Russian Orthodox Church, Islam, Buddhism, Judaism, Hinduism, Taoism, etc. The journal is not sympathetic to recent changes in the Catholic Church. Payment by arrangement.

SUNDAY MAIL, Campbell St., Bowen Hills, Brisbane, Queensland, 4006, Australia. Editor: H.G. Turner. Payment on acceptance. Established in 1916. Weekly. Circulation: 370,000. Will consider material previously published in U.S. or Canada offered for first publication in Australia. Sunday newspaper with offset color magazine insert. Will not consider photocopied submissions. Enclose S.A.E. and International Reply Coupons for return of submissions.
Nonfiction: Articles of general interest. This is a Sunday newspaper with a free color magazine. Length: about 1,200 words. Pays "on merit."

TEMPO, 295 Regent St., London W1A 1BR, England. Editor: David Drew. Independent journal of modern music. Quarterly. Established in 1939. Copyrighted. Payment on publication. Will send sample copy to writer for equivalent of 50 pence. Query first. Enclose S.A.E. and International Reply Coupons for reply to queries.
Nonfiction: Virtually anything in 20th century music, with music examples where necessary. Reviews, articles, phonographs, musical supplements; commentary on humorous aspects and specific rather than theoretical topics. Will consider material previously published in U.S. or Canada offered for first publication in England. Length: 6,000 words for articles. Payment is negotiable.

TIMES EDUCATIONAL SUPPLEMENT, New Printing House Square, London, WC1X 8EZ, England. Editor: Stuart Maclure. A weekly newspaper for teachers, administrators, policy-makers and interested laymen. Weekly. Established in 1910. Circulation: 113,000. Copyrighted. Payment on publication. Will send sample copy to writer for $9 (air freight to New York for both USA and Canada). Query first or submit complete ms. Enclose S.A.E. and International Reply Coupons.
Nonfiction: Articles on all aspects of education. Length: open. Pays 1.50 pounds to 2 pounds a hundred words and by arrangement.

TITBITS, 189 High Holborn, London, WC1V 7BA, England. Editor: George Anfield. Mid-market family publication. Weekly. Established in 1881. Circulation: 535,000. Copyrighted. Payment on publication. Will send free sample copy to writer on request. Submit complete ms. Enclose S.A.E. and International Reply Coupons.
Nonfiction and Photos: "Our prime object is to divert and entertain. Content is mainly light and the display is deliberately eye-catching. Human interest, crime, true-life adventure, exposes, showbiz. Must be factual, generally upbeat, tightly written, capable of good illustration." Will consider material previously published in United States or Canada, offered for first publication in England. Length: 400 to 2,500 words. Payment by arrangement.

TREES, 18 Lye Mead, Winford, Bristol BS18 8AU England. Editor: R. J. Gurney. Journal of The Men of the Trees, a society of tree lovers and conservationists. Published 3 times a year. Established in 1922. Circulation: 5,750. Not copyrighted. Will send sample copy to writer for 50¢. Payment on publication. Submit complete ms. Enclose S.A.E. and International Reply Coupons for return of submissions.
Nonfiction: Trees, nature subjects, conservation. Short articles, preferably illustrated. Will also consider material previously published in United States or Canada, offered for first publication in England. Length: 1,000 to 2,500 words. Pays "by arrangement, at valuation, generally 2 to 4 pounds per 1,000 words."
Photos: May be purchased with mss, with captions only. Subject matter should be "trees, or others if supporting text." Buys b&w glossy prints, 35mm color, and "larger color transparencies and prints." Pays 1.50 pounds for b&w, 5.25 pounds for color.
Fillers: Newsbreaks. Length: 100 to 150 words. No payment.

TROUT AND SALMON, 21 Church Walk, Peterborough, PE1 2TW, England. Editor: Jack Thorndike. Established in 1955. Monthly. Circulation: 38,360. Will send sample copy to writer on request. Will consider unpublished material offered for first time use. Submission of unpublished material may be made directly by the author. Query first. Enclose S.A.E. and International Reply Coupons.
Nonfiction: Will consider the following unpublished material: "Practical aspects of rod and line fishing with fly or lure for salmon, sea trout, brown and rainbow trout. Must not exceed 1,500 words." Pays minimum of 8.40 pounds per 1,000 words.

TV TIMES, Malta House, 630 George St., Sydney, N.S.W., Australia 2000. Editor: Christopher Day. TV magazine and program guide. Weekly. Circulation: 329,000. Buys Australian rights. Buys about 150 mss a year. Pays commissioned features on approval; submitted features on publication. Will send free sample copy to writer on request. Reports "almost immediately." Enclose S.A.E. and International Reply Coupons for return of submissions.

Nonfiction and Photos: Uses newsy stories and features about television series personalities; also features on trends in television and television series. "Thoughtful, penetrating profiles of TV performers. We are not a fan magazine in the accepted sense of the word." Length: 500 to 1,500 words. Payment negotiable; usually about $100. Color transparencies purchased with mss. Payment negotiable; about $25.

UN-COMMON SENSE, Woolacombe House, 141 Woolacombe Rd., Blackheath, London, S.E.3, England. Editor: Ronald Mallone. For intelligent readers interested in world peace, justice and purity of atmosphere. Monthly. Established in 1945. Circulation: 12,000. Copyrighted. Payment on publication. Will send sample copy to writer for 13 pence (surface mail). Submit complete ms. Enclose S.A.E. and International Reply Coupons for return of submissions.
Nonfiction, Fiction, and Poetry: Mainly articles, reports on politics and current affairs, reviews of the arts, poems, cricket and occasional stories. Articles of factual value on matters of international significance. Will consider material previously published in United States or Canada offered for first publication in England. Length: 600 to 2,000 words. Pays minimum of 1 pound per 500 words.

VOYAGER, 63 Shrewsbury Lane, Shooters Hill, London SE18 3JJ, England. Editor: Dennis Winston. *Voyager* is the free in-flight magazine for passengers of British Midland Airways, which has scheduled national and international flights within Europe and operates international and intercontinental charter flights. Published 3 times a year. Established in 1973. Circulation: 100,000. Copyrighted. Payment on publication. Will send sample copy to writer for $2. Submit complete ms. Enclose S.A.E. and International Reply Coupons for return of submissions.
Nonfiction: Entertaining, informative and amusing articles about tourism, business and facets of life in, particularly, France, Belgium, Holland, the United Kingdom, Denmark, Ireland, West Germany and Mediterranean holiday areas. Material should be generally upbeat, reasonably sophisticated, aimed at a middle to upper income and intelligence bracket. Will consider material previously published in United States or Canada, offered for first publication in England. Length: 1,000 to 3,000 words. Pays 20 pounds to 30 pounds sterling per 1,000 words, by agreement.
Photos: Purchased with or without accompanying mss; captions required. Payment depends on size, minimum $5 for b&w.
Fillers: Puzzles, all types. Maximum 100 words. Pays $10 to $20.

VTR/CCTV NEWS, c/o Nova Advertising Inc., Tani Bldg. 2-54, Tsurigane-cho, Higashi-ku, Osaka, 540 Japan. Editor: Tatsuo Yamamoto. House publication of Matsushita Electric Industrial Co., Ltd., VTR Department, for the dealers and concerned people to contribute to the development of VTR industries. Established in 1972. Every 2 weeks. Circulation: 3,000. Copyrighted. Will send free sample copy to writer on request. Buys no rights. Payment on publication. Query first. Reports immediately. Enclose S.A.E. and International Reply Coupons.
Nonfiction and Photos: Buys technical and interesting articles on all aspects of VTR/CCTV, concept of audiovisual methods. Length: 1,500 to 2,000 words. Pays from 5¢ to 10¢ per word. Buys b&w and color photos. Payment negotiable.

WHEELS, 142 Clarence St., Sydney, N.S.W. 2000, Australia. Editor: Peter Robinson. Monthly. Established in 1953. Circulation: 67,500. Copyrighted. Will send free sample copy to writer on request. Submit complete ms only. Enclose S.A.E. and International Reply Coupons for return of submissions.
Nonfiction: Uses "all types of motoring material." Buys how-to articles, profiles, and coverage of new products of motoring interest. Length: 1,500 to 3,000 words. Pays by negotiation; usually $30 to $75.

WILDLIFE (formerly *Animals*), 243 King's Rd., London SW3, England. Editor: Nigel Sitwell. For "all ages, social groups, fairly well-educated, unified by interest in wildlife and natural history." Monthly. Circulation: 35,000. Buys first rights. Payment on publication. Will send a free sample copy to a writer on request. Query first. Submit seasonal material 3 months in advance. Reports in 4 to 8 weeks. Enclose S.A.E. or International Reply Coupons.

Nonfiction and Photos: Reportage on all matters to do with wildlife, in any part of the world, from elephants to butterflies. Conservation, animal behavior, expeditions, personal experience preferred. Length: 1,500 to 3,500 words. Pays approximately $35 per thousand words. Will consider material previously published in United States or Canada, offered for first publication in England. Since much of the appeal lies in the illustrations, it is important that photos be of top quality. Color photos should be original transparencies and may be of any size. Good quality color prints acceptable, but only if color negative film stock is used. B&w photos should be glossy, and preferably half-plate size or larger. All photos will be returned. Pays $5 to $15 per each b&w photo; $30 per page for color; $60 for front cover and $50 for center spread.

WORKSHOP NEW POETRY, 2 Culham Ct., Granville Rd., London, N4 4JB, England. Editor: Norman Hidden. Established in 1967. Quarterly. Will consider unpublished material offered for first time use only. Query first. Will consider photocopied submissions. Enclose S.A.E. and International Reply Coupons.

Poetry: "A leading U.K. poetry magazine. Only the highest quality material will be considered." Length: "under 40 lines." Payment "by arrangement."

YORKSHIRE RIDINGS MAGAZINE, 33 Beverley Rd., Driffield, Yorkshire, England, Y025 7SD. Editor: Winston Halstead. For a mixed audience, but largely intelligent middle class. Established in 1964. Monthly. Circulation: 9,500. Not copyrighted. Pays on publication. Submit complete ms. Enclose S.A.E. and International Reply Coupons.

Nonfiction and Photos: "Almost all our material has a Yorkshire (country) flavor." Profile, humor, nostalgia, of approximately 1,000 to 1,500 words. Pays approximately 3 to 4 pounds per 1,000 words. Captioned photos are purchased with accompanying mss. Pays 75 pence for b&w; approximately 4 pounds for 2¼" color.

Trade, Technical, and Professional Journals

ACCOUNTANCY, City House, 56-66, Goswell Rd., London, E.C.1, England. Editor: Geoffrey Holmes. Monthly. Buys first serial rights. Pays on publication. Reports within 1 month. Submissions of previously published material may be made directly

by the author, through an agent or by the publisher or his representative. Enclose S.A.E. and International Reply Coupons for return of submissions or reply to query. Query first or submit complete ms.
Nonfiction: Articles on accountancy, tax, investment, management, and law. Length: 1,000 to 6,000 words. Pays 10 pounds to 30 pounds per 1,000 words.

ACCOUNTING & BUSINESS RESEARCH, 56-66 Goswell Rd., London, E.C.1, England. Editor: Walter Taplin. For "accountants, economists, businessmen interested in accounting research." Quarterly. Circulation: 3,000. Buys first rights. Buys 40 mss a year. Pays on publication. Will send a sample copy to a writer on request. Reports "by return mail." Enclose S.A.E. and International Reply Coupons for return of submissions.
Nonfiction: "Only high level professional articles of a research nature on accounting and finance." Length: 1,000 to 20,000 words. Pays 5 to 100 pounds.

ART & CRAFT IN EDUCATION, Montague House, Russell Sq., London, W.C.1, England. Editor: Henry Pluckrose. For "teachers in training; teachers of nursery, primary, secondary, and art school age levels; art school students, etc." Established in 1938. Monthly. Circulation: 20,000. Buys first rights. Buys 10 to 12 mss a year. Pays on publication. Submit seasonal material 3 months in advance. Reports "immediately." Enclose S.A.E. and International Reply Coupons for return of submissions.
Nonfiction: Any practical article on the arts or crafts using children between the ages of 6 and 13. Original and creative ideas most important. Also will consider material previously published in United States or Canada, offered for first publication in England. Length: 600 words average, with 3 b&w photos. Pays 5 pounds to 10 pounds.

BAKING INDUSTRIES JOURNAL, P.O.B. 109, Davis House, 69-77 High St., Croydon, CR9 1Q4, England. Editor: Kenn Grace. For the large-scale bakery industry. Monthly. Circulation: 2,500. Copyrighted. Pays on publication. Will send sample copy to American or Canadian writer for $1. Query first. Enclose S.A.E. and International Reply Coupons.
Nonfiction: Technical features on baking and allied subjects. Length: 1,000 to 3,000 words. Pays 10 pounds per 1,000 words.

THE BANKERS' MAGAZINE, 49-50 Great Marlborough St., London W1V 2BB, England. Editorial Director: Tim Rock. The oldest financial journal in the city of London. It has been relaunched by a division of the British Printing Corporation with the avowed purpose of being "the practical magazine for the practicing banker". Monthly. Established in 1844. Circulation: 11,000. Copyrighted. Payment on publication. Will send sample copy to writer for $1.50. Enclose S.A.E. and International Reply Coupons for return of submissions.
Nonfiction: Any articles submitted should be of direct interest to the branch manager who is actually in the field. Any subject relating directly to British banking or subjects of interest to British bank managers. Will consider material previously published in United States or Canada offered for first publication in England. Length: 1,500 to 2,000 words. Payment depends on length and quality of article.

BRITISH PRINTER, 30 Old Burlington St., London W1X 2AE, England. Editor: Michael Maddox. For commercial printers and printing technologists. Established in 1888. Monthly. Circulation: 10,300. Copyrighted. Pays on publication. Will consider material previously published in U.S. or Canada, offered for first publication in Europe. Submission of previously published material may be made directly by the author, through an agent, or by the publisher or his representative. Will consider unpublished material offered for first time use. Submission of unpublished material may be made directly by the author. Query first or submit complete ms. Enclose S.A.E. and International Reply Coupons for return of submissions or reply to queries.
Nonfiction: Will consider the following material previously published in U.S. or Canada: "The author should read *British Printer* and understand its purpose and

editorial style. He should also have a technical and, if possible, practical knowledge of printing or allied subjects. No PR promises and no long, boring historical pieces. BP is read by busy professionals." Pays 20 pounds per 1,000 words published. Will consider the following unpublished material: "Basically technical. All articles must be of direct, practical value to commercial printers and printing technologists."

BROADCAST, 111A Wardour St., London W1, England. Editor: Rod Allen. Professional weekly journal read by practitioners in broadcasting, including management, creative and programme executives, senior technicians, engineers as well as those in the advertising agency and television/radio commercial production and service industries. Weekly. Established in 1959. Circulation: 3,500. Copyrighted. Payment on publication. Will send sample copy to writer for 75¢ and International Reply Coupons for return. Query first. Enclose S.A.E. and International Reply Coupons.
Nonfiction: Features on items of professional interest to those engaged in broadcasting: programming, scheduling, engineering and broadcast advertising. Length immaterial, though news paragraphs not generally accepted. Will consider material previously published in United States or Canada, offered for first publication in England. All payment by individual negotiation.

CARPETS & TEXTILES, 40 Bowling Green Lane, London EC1R ONE, England. Editor: Jean Sheridan. For retailers in medium to top end of trade. Established in 1966. Circulation: 6,000. Copyrighted. Payment on publication. Will send free sample copy to writer on request. Query first. Enclose S.A.E. and International Reply Coupons.
Nonfiction and Photos: Aimed at helping the trade improve sales, distribution, promotion and display of carpets and textiles. Buys features and illustrations or photos of interest to those who sell or distribute carpets or textiles. Length: 500 to 2,000 words. Payment by arrangement.

THE CHRONICLE, 121 King Wm. St., Adelaide, South Australia 5001. Editor: J. B. McCarter. Rural agricultural weekly serving S.A. farming community. Weekly newspaper tabloid. Established in 1857. Circulation: 18,500. Not copyrighted. Payment on publication. Query first. Enclose S.A.E. and International Reply Coupons.
Nonfiction: Articles that will help readers achieve greater productivity and profitability in their farming enterprises by keeping them abreast of all relevant technical, practical and political, and marketing developments affecting them. Articles relating directly to agricultural industries in S.A.; beef cattle, pigs, sheep, pasture seeds, stock health, cereal production and marketing (wheat, barley, oats), oilseeds. Will consider material previously published in United States or Canada offered for first publication in Australia. Length: 1,500 words maximum. Pays 3 Australian to 6 Australian cents a line.

COFFEE INTERNATIONAL, Queensway House, 2 Queensway, Redhill, Surrey RH1 1QS, England. Editor: Richard V. Clark. Aimed at top management of companies who handle coffee in all stages from production to distribution. These include exporters, agents, shippers, insurance agents and bankers, machinery and plant manufacturers, processors, out-of-home distributors and the like. Established in 1974. Quarterly. Circulation: 6,000. Copyrighted. Pays on publication. Will send free sample copy on request. Query first. Enclose S.A.E. and International Reply Coupons.
Nonfiction: Articles of interest to people in the coffee industry. Payment negotiated.

CONCRETE, 52 Grosvenor Gardens, London SW1W OAQ, England. Editor: R. J. Barfoot. For civil engineers, architects, contractors, and all concerned in any way with concrete. Monthly. Established in 1968. Circulation: 12,000. Payment on publication. Will send free sample copy to writer on request. Submit complete ms. Enclose S.A.E. and International Reply Coupons.
Nonfiction and Photos: Covers all aspects of the English and International concrete and allied engineering construction industry, from photographic, technical and

humorous views. Wants interesting and unusual uses of concrete, new building projects, etc. Length: 500 to 2,000 words. Pays 5 pounds per 1,000 words.

THE CRIMINOLOGIST, P.O. Box No. 18. Bognor Regis, Sussex, U.K. For professionals and students interested in police affairs, criminology, forensic science, the law, penology, etc. Quarterly. Will send a sample copy to a writer for $1.70. Query first with outline. Enclose S.A.E. and International Reply Coupons.
Nonfiction and Photos: Considers articles of very high standards, authoritatively written and factually sound, informative and sober, and not in a popular or sensational style. All material must have attached list of references or sources (title of source, author or editor, town of publication, date, and, if a periodical, page number, issue number, and volume). Articles from police officials, experts, etc., are welcomed. Length: 2,000 to 5,000 words. Buys photos with mss. Payment negotiable.

DAIRY FARMER, Fenton House, Wharfedale Rd., Ipswich, IP1 4LG, Suffolk, England. Editor: David Shead. For commercial dairy farmers. *Dairy Farmer* is Britain's only independent journal devoted entirely to the specialist needs of the milk producer. Monthly. Established in 1929. Circulation: 14,000. Payment on publication. Will send free sample copy to writer on request. Query first or submit complete ms. Enclose S.A.E. and International Reply Coupons.
Nonfiction and Photos: New techniques, etc., of practical use to British dairy farmers. Length: 1,000 to 1,500 words. Pays 12 pounds per 1,000 words, or by special arrangement. "Illustrations required only to back up feature articles." Buys b&w glossies with mss; with captions only. Pays 1 to 25 pounds minimum, per photo, "maximum by negotiation."

DISPLAY INTERNATIONAL, 167 High Holborn, London, WC1V 6PH, England. Editor: Hazel Thompson. Monthly. Circulation: 19,000. Buys all rights. Will consider material previously published in U.S. or Canada, offered for first publication in Britain. Pays on publication. Will send a sample copy to a writer on request. Reports "as soon as possible." Enclose S.A.E. and International Reply Coupons for return of submissions.
Nonfiction and Photos: Buys news items and articles. Buys photos with mss and with captions only. Subjects should be "window displays, exhibition displays, new stores and shops (exterior and interior), shopping centres, all forms of visual merchandising and commercial presentation. Names of architects, display managers, and designers are desired." Length: 500 to 1,500 words. Payment negotiable, usually $24 to $85.
How To Break In: "We believe in emphasizing the 'personal' element in our industry. We should therefore be interested in hearing from writers who could contribute in-depth interviews with display managers or other personalities in the business."

ELECTRONIC COMPONENTS, 42-43 Gerrard St., London WIV FLP, England. Editorial Director: David Gibson. Published every 2 weeks. Circulation: 20,600. Copyrighted. Payment on publication. Will send free sample copy to writer if International Reply Coupons for postage are enclosed with request. Query first preferred. Enclose S.A.E. and International Reply Coupons.
Nonfiction and Photos: Articles in English, German, and French on electronics; the professional industry; products, services, news, companies. Emphasis on electronic components. Pays 10 pounds to 20 pounds per 1,000 words, including photos or illustrations.

ELECTRONICS AUSTRALIA, Box 163, Beaconsfield, NSW, Australia 2014. Editor: Mr. J. Rowe. Largest technical electronics magazine in Australia and New Zealand for students and hobbyists through radio amateurs and technicians to engineers and college lecturers. Monthly. Established in 1939. Circulation: 47,000. Copyrighted. Payment on publication. Will send sample copy to writer for $1. Submit complete ms. Enclose S.A.E. and International Reply Coupons for return of submissions.
Nonfiction: "We aim at high reader interest and technical accuracy. We try to help the reader understand why, but in a friendly, human way. Buy technical electronics

and electronics-orientated science features." Will consider material previously published in United States or Canada, offered for first publication in Australia. Length: about 1,000 to 2,000 words. Pays 15 Australian dollars to 25 Australian dollars per published page.

ENGINEERING, 28 Haymarket, London SW1Y 4SU, England. Acting Editor: A. H. Scott. The Design Council's magazine for engineers. Monthly. Established in 1866. Circulation: 20,000. Copyrighted. Payment on publication. Will send free sample copy to writer on request. Query first or submit complete ms. Enclose S.A.E. and International Reply Coupons.
Nonfiction: "Our aim is to improve standards of design, production, function and marketing. A horizontal journal to cross-fertilize all fields of engineering." Wants electrical or mechanical engineering articles, general or in-depth articles suitable for professional engineers. Prefers articles with design emphasis. Will consider material previously published in United States or Canada offered for first publication in England. Length: 5,000 words maximum. Pays an average of 18 pounds per 1,000 words.

FASHION WEEKLY, 40 Bowling Green Lane, London EC1R ONE, England. Editor: George Thomas White. Britain's weekly equivalent of the American *Women's Wear Daily* but also covers domestic textiles and drapes. Weekly tabloid glossy newspaper. Established in 1959. Circulation: 22,000. Copyrighted. Payment on publication. Will send free sample copy to writer on request. Query first. Enclose S.A.E. and International Reply Coupons.
Nonfiction: News and features about fashion and domestic textiles and drapes. Pays $1 a paragraph for news items; $5 per 100 words for features.

FLORIST TRADE MAGAZINE, (formerly *The Florist*), 120 Lower Ham Rd., Kingston upon Thames, Surrey, England. Editor: Jayne Foster. For professional retail florists and student florists. Monthly. Copyrighted. Payment on publication. Enclose S.A.E. and International Reply Coupons.
Nonfiction and Photos: "We must emphasize that this magazine is for professional retailers and that, other than the occasional humorous snippet (still on the subject of flowers and the use of) we want only accurate graphic accounts of professional use of flowers." Reports on and photos of floristry displays. Length: 500 to 1,500 words. Pays 10 pounds per 1,000 words.

FOOD MANUFACTURE, 30 Calderwood St., London SE18 6QH, England. Editor: Anthony Woollen. For "technical management in food manufacturing industry." Monthly. Circulation: 6,650. Buys first rights. Pays on publication. Will send a free sample copy to a writer on request. Query first with synopsis and suggestions. Reports "immediately." Enclose S.A.E. and International Reply Coupons.
Nonfiction: "Most articles are commissioned, but good freelance copy within our field is acceptable." Buys "review articles on technical developments in food processing; descriptions of new feed factories, processing machines, processes, and packaging techniques and materials. Brevity and readability are essential. Facts must be 100% accurate. We do not cover catering, distribution, or retailing." Buys how-to articles and coverage of new products and successful business operations. Length: 500 to 2,500 words. Pays about $30 per 1,000 words.
Photos: Buys original b&w photos. Pays $3.

FREIGHT MANAGEMENT, Dorset House, Stamford St., London SE1 9LU, England. Editor: Richard H. Willingham. Monthly. Established in 1966. Circulation: 20,000. Copyrighted. Payment on publication. Will send free sample copy to writer on request. Query first or submit complete ms. Enclose S.A.E. and International Reply Coupons.
Nonfiction: Articles dealing with physical distribution economics and management. Will consider material previously published in United States or Canada offered for first publication in England. Length: 2,000 words maximum. Pays 15 pounds to 20 pounds per 1,000 words printed.

GARDENERS CHRONICLE/HORTICULTURAL TRADE JOURNAL, Haymarket Publishing Ltd., Gillow House, 5 Winsley St., London W1A 2HG, England. For commercial growers of ornamental plants and those employed in public parks and gardens. Weekly. Established in 1841. Circulation: 11,000. Payment on publication. Copyrighted. Will send free sample copy to writer on request. Submit complete ms. Enclose S.A.E. and International Reply Coupons for return of submissions.
Nonfiction: "The magazine aims to provide its readers with knowledge of modern techniques of growing, management and finance. There is also a comprehensive news section. Our style is straightforward, not folksy. Interested in articles on commercial production of ornamental plants suitable for reading by practical horticulturists. Also interested in applied research and features on amenity horticulture—parks and public gardens (but not lists of plants). Will consider material previously published in United States or Canada, offered for first publication in England." Pays 15 pounds per 1,000 words.

GAS WORLD, 25 New Street Square, London EL4A 3JA, England. Editor: G. W. Battison. For senior engineers, marketers and management worldwide. Monthly. Established in 1864. Circulation: 3,300. Copyrighted. Payment on publication. Query first. Enclose S.A.E. and International Reply Coupons.
Nonfiction: Covers all aspects of natural gas—transmission and technology, marketing, management. Articles on major developments in gas transmission, involving new techniques. Length: open. Pays 10 pounds to 20 pounds per 1,000 words.

THE GROWER, 49 Doughty St., London, WC1N 2LP, England. Editor: John Bloom. For "commercial growers, seeds salesmen, and manufacturers of all equipment for commercial growers, markets men, universities, research stations, students, etc." Weekly. Circulation: 12,000. Will consider material previously published in the U.S. or Canada offered for first publication in U.K. Pays in "month following publication." Will send a sample copy to a writer for $2. Query first. Reports "as soon as possible." Enclose S.A.E. and International Reply Coupons.
Nonfiction, Photos, and Fillers: Buys "many mss, but mostly from experts in the field of horticulture." Uses "technical articles and news items of current research, marketing techniques, packaging, transport, weather, methods and culture of growing, etc." Articles should be "short, direct, simply written." Buys how-to and personal experience articles, interviews, spot news, photo features, and coverage of successful business operations, new products, and merchandising techniques. Also buys newsbreaks. Length: 1,500 words for articles; 500 words for news. Pays 20.50 pounds per 1,000 words. Buys b&w glossy photos with mss, with captions only. Payment by arrangement.

THE HOUSE BUILDER AND ESTATE DEVELOPER, 82 New Cavendish St., London W1M 8AD, England. Editor: Andrew Deg. Journal of the House-Builders Federation, the only trade association to represent exclusively British speculative house-builders and estate developers at government and at local authority levels. Monthly. Established in 1954. Circulation: 22,000. Copyrighted. Payment on publication. Will send free sample copy to writer on request. Query first. Enclose S.A.E. and International Reply Coupons.
Nonfiction: Anything on the design, construction and marketing of houses for sale; for example, residential housing as opposed to public authority housing estates. Will consider material previously published in United States or Canada offered for first publication in England. Length: 500 to 2,000 words preferred. Pays 5 pounds to 50 pounds.

INDUSTRIAL ADVERTISING AND MARKETING, Mercury House, Waterloo Rd., London SE1 8UL, England. Editor: Bill Price. Established in 1964. For industrial marketing men. Quarterly. Circulation: 1,500. Buys first U.K. rights. Payment on publication. Submit complete ms. Enclose S.A.E. and International Reply Coupons.
Nonfiction: Industrial advertising and marketing articles; case histories; principles, new ideas. In-depth style, no photos. Length: 2,000 to 4,000 words. Pays minimum of 15 pounds.

INDUSTRIAL DIAMOND REVIEW, 7 Rolls Buildings, Fetter Lane, London, EC4A 1HX, England. Editor: Paul Daniel. "For engineers in the metalworking, civil engineering, glass, ceramics, stoneworking, mining and electronics industries who have to grind, saw, and polish hard material at minimum cost. We want to show them how to do it with diamond tools." Established in 1941. Monthly. Circulation: 3,700. Not copyrighted. Payment on publication. Will consider unpublished material offered for first time use only. Will send a sample copy to a writer on request. Potential contributors should submit brief synopsis (400 words) of any lengthy article in first approach and not full ms. Enclose S.A.E. and International Reply Coupons.
Nonfiction: "Articles on industrial diamonds (basic and applied research), diamond tooling, machines for use with diamond tools, case histories on applications of diamond tooling." Length: 600 to 6,000 words. Pays 11 pounds per 1,000 words.
How To Break In: "We would welcome any article of a scientific or technical nature on the properties or use of diamond in any form. Workshop notes, hints on how to get maximum efficiency from industrial diamond tools, case histories, etc."

INDUSTRIAL FINISHING & SURFACE COATING, 157 Hagden Lane, Watford, Herts, WD1 8LW, England. Editor: J.B. Ward. For a "technical and management audience." Monthly. Circulation: 6,850. Not copyrighted. Pays on publication. Will send a sample copy to a writer on request. Submit seasonal material 1 month in advance. Reports in 2 weeks. Enclose S.A.E. and International Reply Coupons.
Nonfiction: "Technical articles which are end-use oriented. We do special coverage of marine wood finishing, marine coating, powder coating and plating on plastic." Length: 1,000 to 3,000 words. Pays $19 per 1,000 words.

INDUSTRIAL SAFETY, United Trade Press Ltd., 42 Gerrard St., London, W1V 7LP, England. Editor: Charles Micklewright. For "professional safety officers, factory inspectors, and other safety specialists. Also, management and manufacturers of protective clothing, equipment, and devices such as machine guards." Established in 1955. Monthly. Circulation: 10,000. Copyrighted. Will consider unpublished material offered for the first time only. Will send a sample copy to a writer on request. Query first. Enclose S.A.E. and International Reply Coupons.
Nonfiction and Photos: Occupational safety and health, at a level suitable for a readership of professional safety officers and factory inspectors and manufacturers of safety clothing and products. "Our object is to disseminate information on occupational health and safety, in the cause of improved safety and health at work." Length: 500 to 1,500 words. Usual rate of 10.50 pounds per 1,000 words. Pays 50 pence for photos.

INSURANCE BROKERS' MONTHLY, 9 Marcet St., Stourbridge, Worcs, England. Editor: Brian Susman. A professional journal for insurance brokers. Monthly. Established in 1950. Circulation: 8,000. Copyrighted. Payment 1 month after publication. Will send free sample copy to writer on request. Submit complete ms. Enclose S.A.E. and International Reply Coupons for return of submissions.
Nonfiction: "Articles of a technical or nontechnical character, but strictly about insurance and finance." Will consider material previously published in United States or Canada offered for first publication in England. Length: 1,500 to 3,000 words. Pays 5 pounds to 25 pounds per 1,000 words.

INTERNATIONAL HOTEL REVIEW, International Trade Publications Ltd., Queensway House, 2 Queensway, Redhill, Surrey RH1 1QS, England. Editor: Godfrey Blakeley. Mainly for managers of 4 to 5 star hotels worldwide; men who don't need teaching their jobs but who lack time to see new developments in context. Quarterly. Established in 1948. Circulation: 10,000. Not copyrighted. Payment on publication. Will send free sample copy to writer on request. Query first. Enclose S.A.E. and International Reply Coupons.
Nonfiction: "Our editorial purpose is to spark off ideas rather than give news. We want concise yet well-researched comment (in English or French) on trends in management on training, financing, tourism or equipping as they affect the hotel trade. Not acceptable are biographies, new hotel openings, equipment launches or

subjects with a parochial bias. Use concise writing style. Where possible, easy-flowing, educated style, yet never pompous. Half the readership does not have English as the mother tongue. Will consider material previously published in United States or Canada offered for first publication in England." Length: 400 to 2,000 words. Pays 10 pounds to 20 pounds per 1,000 words.

JOURNAL OF PARK AND RECREATION ADMINISTRATION, Lower Basildon, Reading, Berkshire R98 9NE, England. Managing Editor: Kenneth L. Morgan. For professional people, mostly members of Parks and Recreation. Monthly. Established in 1924. Circulation: 3,500. Not copyrighted. Payment on publication. Will send free sample copy to writer on request. Query first. Enclose S.A.E. and International Reply Coupons.
Nonfiction: Articles on parks, recreation, leisure, landscape design, horticulture. Will consider material previously published in United States or Canada offered for first publication in England. Length: 600 to 1,000 words. Pays 7 to 10 pounds, according to type and length of article.

LOCAL GOVERNMENT REVIEW, Little London, Chichester, Sussex, England. Editor: Barry Rose. Established in 1837. Weekly. Circulation: 2,000. Copyrighted. Will consider unpublished material for first time use only. Will send a sample copy to a writer on request. Query first or submit complete ms. Enclose S.A.E. and International Reply Coupons for return of submissions or reply to queries.
Nonfiction: "Deals with municipal law and with local government generally." Pays 10 pounds for 1,500 words.

MARKETING, Haymarket Publishing, Regent House, 54-62 Regent St., London W1A 4YJ, England. Editor: Michael Rines. Established in 1925. Monthly. Circulation: 20,000. Copyrighted. Will send sample copy to writer on request. Will consider unpublished material offered for first time use. Submission of unpublished material may be made directly by the author. Query first. Enclose S.A.E. and International Reply Coupons for reply to query or return of submission.
Nonfiction: Interested in unpublished "articles on marketing up to 3,000 words. Generally with a practical approach, or if there is a good story, or case of a firm's experience but only when written by an outsider other than a PR man." Pays up to 70 pounds.
How To Break In: "Write down-to-earth practical do-it-yourself style articles explaining how to carry out a novel or improved marketing technique. Or write controversial articles attacking bad marketing practices."

THE MASTER PHOTOGRAPHER, 1 and 2 Lincolns Inn Fields, London WC2, England. Editor: Derek Bradley. For professional photographers. Quarterly. Established in 1960. Circulation: 500. Copyrighted. Payment on publication. Will send sample copy to writer for 50¢. Submit complete ms. Enclose S.A.E. and International Reply Coupons.
Nonfiction: Articles on new techniques and equipment and improvements in business practice. Anything relating to the practice and business of professional photography. Will consider material previously published in United States or Canada offered for first publication in England. Pays $15 to $20 per 1,000 words.

MINE AND QUARRY, 42 Gray's Inn Rd., London WC1 X8LR, England. Editor: David Buntain. Journal for senior management at mines and quarries. Monthly. Established in 1924. Circulation: 5,500. Not copyrighted. Payment on publication. Will send free sample copy to writer on request. Submit complete ms. Enclose S.A.E. and International Reply Coupons for return of submissions.
Nonfiction: Articles of a practical nature dealing with mining and quarrying techniques. Emphasis on practical matters, aimed at reducing costs and increasing efficiency. Will consider material previously published in United States or Canada offered for first publication in England. Length: 2,000 words average. Pays 10 pounds per 1,000 words.

PIG FARMING, Fenton House, Wharfedale Road, Ipswich IP1 4LG, Suffolk, England. Editor: B. T. Hogley. For "pig producers of all ages all over the world." Five supplements a year: Pig Health, Pig Housing, Pig Management, Pig Feeding, Pig Breeding, National Pig Fair (held in Britain). Established in 1953. Monthly. Circulation: 17,800. Buys all rights. Buys 10 to 12 mss a year. Pays on publication. Will send a free sample copy to a writer on request, "if he can show he really knows something about pigs." Query first. Submit seasonal or special material 2 months in advance. Reports "immediately." Enclose S.A.E. and International Reply Coupons for reply to queries.

Nonfiction, Photos, and Fiction: Practical articles on all aspects of modern pig production. Also hints and tips about farm-made laborsaving devices, preferably with sketch or photos. Will consider material previously published in United States or Canada offered for first publication in England. Length: 1,000 to 2,000 words. Pays 12 pounds minimum per 1,000 words published. Pays 2 pounds each for b&w photos used.

POULTRY WORLD, Surrey House, Sutton, Surrey SM1 4QQ, England. Editor: John Farrant. Weekly. Established in 1874. Circulation: 12,000. Payment on publication. Will send free sample copy to writer on request. Submit complete ms. Enclose S.A.E. and International Reply Coupons.

Nonfiction: Covers the commercial poultry industry from breeding to marketing the products. Payment by negotiation.

PROFESSIONAL ADMINISTRATION, 388 Strand, London WC2R OLT, England. Editor: Michael Donovan. For members of the Institute of Chartered Secretaries. Monthly. Established in 1971. Circulation: 48,000. Copyrighted. Payment on publication. Will send free sample copy to writer on request. Query first. Enclose S.A.E. and International Reply Coupons.

Nonfiction: "Editorial consists of company tax and legal issues, administration aspects together with features concerned with such changes in overseas countries." Will consider material previously published in United States or Canada offered for first publication in England. Pays 20 pounds to 30 pounds per 1,000 words.

THE QUEEN'S HIGHWAY, 25 Lower Belgrave St., London SW1W OLS, England. Editor: Ian S. Menzies. Officially the house journal of the Asphalt and Coated Macadam Association, but accepted as a much more general interest magazine by some 5,000 highway engineers, central and local government, institutions, clubs, schools, etc. A special point of interest is that engineers will take this magazine home to be read by all their family. Published 2 times a year. Established in 1931. Circulation: 5,000. Copyrighted. Payment on acceptance. Will send free sample copy to writer on request. Query first. Enclose S.A.E. and International Reply Coupons.

Nonfiction and Photos: Technical subjects on flexible road construction, general subjects on highways (history, interrelation with environment, etc.), a small proportion of general nature articles. Illustrations essential with all mss. Will consider material previously published in United States or Canada offered for first publication in England. Length: 500 to 2,500 words. Pays 8 pounds per 1,000 words minimum.

REFRIGERATION AND AIR CONDITIONING, P.O. Box 109, Davis House, 69-77 High Street, Croydon, CR9 1QH, Surrey, England. Editor: T. A. O'Gorman. Monthly. Established in 1898 as *Cold Storage and Ice Trades Review*. Circulation: 5,000. Copyrighted. Payment on publication. Will send free sample copy to writer on request. Query first. Enclose S.A.E. and International Reply Coupons.

Nonfiction: "*Refrigeration and Air Conditioning* caters for the needs of the manufacturing, supply and contracting elements of the refrigeration and air conditioning industry, users, specifiers, researchers, government departments, etc. The editorial content includes commercial and technical news and features, presented in such a manner that the appeal can be made to all levels of readership. Contributors are welcomed from all over the world for the supply of commercial as well as technical news and feature articles. It is advisable to contact the editor before sending feature material or a regular supply of news. Certain material previously published in United States or Canada will be considered." Payment by arrangement.

SERVICE STATION, 178-202 Great Portland St., London W1N 6NH, England. Editor: Peter Noble. For people engaged in operating retail motor trade outlets; most are executives with buying influence. Established in 1925. Monthly. Circulation: 23,000. Not copyrighted. Will send sample copy to writer on request. Will consider material previously published in U.S. or Canada, offered for first publication in Great Britain. Submission of previously published material may be made directly by author, through an agent, or by the publisher or his representative. Will consider unpublished material offered for first time use. Submission of unpublished material may be made directly by the author. Query first. Enclose S.A.E. and International Reply Coupons for response to query.
Nonfiction: Will consider the following material previously published in U.S. or Canada: "Features and news of specific interest to British service station, garage, repair shop and tire shop operators. Preferably up to 1,500 words long. Emphasis on trade association and relevant political developments." Will consider the following unpublished material: Exclusive news stories about oil companies, motor manufacturers and North American trade associations. Pays by arrangement, but never less than 25 pounds per 1,000 words.

SHIP & BOAT INTERNATIONAL, Saracen's Head Buildings, 36-37 Cock Lane, London, EC1A 9BY, England. Editor: Kenneth D. Troup. Established in 1947. For "naval architects, shipbuilders, owners, consultants, engineers, equipment manufacturers." Monthly. Circulation: 6,000. Buys all rights. Buys 20 mss a year. Pays on publication. Will send a sample copy to a writer on request. Query first. Submit seasonal material 2 months in advance. Reports "immediately." Enclose S.A.E. and International Reply Coupons for reply to queries.
Nonfiction: Technical material regarding design and construction of commercial craft. Does not want to see "anything with a personal angle." Buys coverage of successful business operations and new products. Length: 500 to 1,500 words. Pays 14 to 20 pounds per 1,000 words.

SHOPFITTING INTERNATIONAL, Pembroke House, Wellesley Rd., Croydon CR9 2BX, Surrey, England. Editor: Martin Staheli. A trade newspaper for retailers with purchasing and specifying powers; property and premises managers, architects, designers, shopfitters, woodworking and metalworking equipment manufacturers; management and executive staffs in all retail trades and in most major commercial organizations which meet the public on their premises. Established in 1955. Monthly. Circulation: 18,000. Copyrighted. Pays on publication. Query or submit complete ms. Enclose S.A.E. and International Reply Coupons.
Nonfiction: News items and features on the fitting-out of shops, departmental stores, restaurants, hotels (public areas only), showrooms, offices, board rooms, bars, night clubs, theaters, banks, building societies; the materials and techniques used; the design brief for interior and exterior; use of sub-contractors, cost of job. Pays 15 pounds minimum to 30 pounds maximum.

SPECIAL EDUCATION: FORWARD TRENDS, Editorial address: 12 Hollycroft Ave., London NW3 7QL, England. Editor: Margaret Peter. Honorary Editors: R. Gulliford and S. Segal. Quarterly. Established in 1974. Circulation: 6,500. Copyright depends on whether article is commissioned or not. Payment on publication. Will send sample copy to writer on request. Submit complete ms. Enclose S.A.E. and International Reply Coupons for return of submissions.
Nonfiction: Articles on the education of all types of handicapped children. "The aim of this new journal of the National Council for Special Education is to provide articles on special education and handicapped children which will keep readers informed of practical and theoretical developments not only in education but in the many other aspects of the education and welfare of the handicapped. While we hope that articles will lead students and others to further related reading, their main function is to give readers an adequate introduction to a topic which they

may not have an opportunity to pursue further. References should therefore be selective and mainly easily accessible ones. It is important, therefore, that articles of a more technical nature (e.g., psychology, medical, research reviews) should, whenever possible, avoid unnecessary technicalities or ensure that necessary technical terms or expressions are made clear to nonspecialists by the context or by the provision of brief additional explanations or examples." Length: 750 to 3,750 words. Payment by arrangement.

TABLEWARE INTERNATIONAL, Queensway House, 2 Queensway, Redhill, Surrey, RM1 1QS, England. A multi-lingual international business journal for specialized retailers handling fine tableware (china, crockery, earthenware and cutlery) and buyers in prestige department stores handling these lines; for international importers and exporters; and for manufacturers of these products. Monthly. Established in 1877. Circulation: 5,500. Copyrighted. Payment on acceptance or on publication, "negotiated with authors." Will send sample copy to writer, "provided he convinces the editor he has substantial knowledge of the subject matter of the publication." Query first. Enclose S.A.E. and International Reply Coupons.
Nonfiction: "The editor usually requires that contributors of minor items, and always demands that contributors of full-scale feature articles, either are working within the industry or trade which the journal covers, have had substantial recent first-hand experience of working in that industry or trade, or are senior journalists working on a specialized journal serving that trade or industry. Wants news of trade developments affecting tableware products of international significance, including major appointments and personal news, and news of legislative changes affecting this trade. News of new products from manufacturers with international ambitions, restricted generally to luxury-class merchandise. Studies of buying trends, trading in tableware, reports on major exhibitions and analytical studies of trade, including commentaries on current events in the trade by big name buyers." News items (250 words) and articles (1,500 words). Pays minimum rates of $50 per 1,000 words, and pro rata. Higher rates can be negotiated for expert, analytical articles.

WORLD FISHING, Riverside House, Hough Street, Woolwich, London SE18, England. Editor: H. S. Noel. "We are serious minded, and read by people who have no romantic ideas about fishing—they do it for a living." Monthly. Established in 1952. Circulation: 7,500. Copyrighted. Payment on publication. Will send free sample copy to writer on request. Query first. Enclose S.A.E. and International Reply Coupons.
Nonfiction: "Articles that present new ideas, new pieces of equipment, new methods of fishing that pay off to people who fish for a living. Write as tightly as possible and stick to the facts. We want articles on all aspects of commercial fishing industry in Canada and United States, especially in case histories and development programmes of fishing companies; new vessels and why. Will consider material previously published in United States or Canada offered for first publication in England, if they have international implication." Length: up to 1,000 words if well illustrated, but shorter if no photos are available. Pays 15 pounds per 1,000 words for specialized knowledge. Pays 2 pounds per photo.

WORLD TOBACCO, 21 John Adam St., London WC2, England. Editor: Michael F. Barford. World's largest international tobacco journal; directed at management of tobacco manufacturing businesses and monopolies, and major distributors in 167 countries. Established in 1962. Quarterly. Circulation: 3,350. Buys all rights. Payment on or before publication. Query first with technical credentials in tobacco; firm assignment or "sorry, no" response usually immediate. Enclose S.A.E. and International Reply Coupons for reply to query.
Nonfiction and Photos: Standard diet is tobacco market analyses, articles on manufacturing technology, the "how" of distribution and marketing; strong preference for pieces about less sophisticated countries. Length: 1,200 to 1,500 words. Also uses notes (100 words plus photo) on new tobacco product brands from Latin America, Asia and Africa only. Pays 5¢ to 7½¢ per word. Buys b&w photos with mss or captions only.

Fillers: Buys material for three regular columns: New Brands and Packs; News, Views, Trends; Marketing Impact.

WORLD WOOD, Chaussee de Charleroi 123A, B-1060, Brussels, Belgium. Editor: Hugh R. Fraser. For professionals in the forest products industries and forestry around the world, excluding the U.S. and Canada. Owners, senior management, and production managers in the sectors: logging and forestry, sawmills, plywood plants, and particleboard (chipboard) plants. Monthly magazine; 40 (8x10) pages. Established in 1960. Circulation: 7,000. Buys all rights. Buys 12 mss a year. Payment on acceptance. Will send sample copy for $1.50. Reports "within 15 working days of receipt of material." Enclose S.A.E. and International Reply Coupons.
Nonfiction and Photos: Needs operational articles describing forest management techniques, logging operations and mills (as above) in the major producing countries of the world. Should be on-the-spot, technical material showing how an operation has been improved in efficiency, production, or safety. Needs trade names and equipment specifications. Authoritative news items and short news features on specific developments in the forest industries around the world, excluding North America. "Our readership is international. English is the second language of many readers. But a direct, uncomplicated style is required, strictly avoiding slang and colloquialisms of the day. We are not read in the fields of secondary conversion of wood, i.e., not in the fields of furniture manufacture or timber construction. Material must be authoritative, in describing industry operations or industry developments. Author need not be an expert, but must have expert sources of material." How-to, successful business operations. Length: 1,000 to 2,500 words. Pays minimum of $30 per published page. No additional payment for 8x10 b&w photos used with mss. Captions required.
Fillers: Short items of general industry news outside U.S.A. Length: 100 to 500 words. Pays $2.50 to $5.

THE WRITER, P.O. Box 52, Ashton Court, 1, Oxford Road, Aylesbury, Bucks, England. Editor: H. Johnson. For freelance writers. Monthly. Established in 1921. Copyrighted. Payment on publication. Will send sample copy to writer for 60¢. Submit complete ms. Enclose S.A.E. and International Reply Coupons for return of submissions.
Nonfiction: Advice on how to write and sell. Matters of interest to the freelance writer; informative; interviews with well-known writers, etc. Also will consider material previously published in United States or Canada, offered for first publication in England. Length: 1,200 words maximum. Pays 5 pounds per 1,000 words.

WRITING, 4 Union Place, Fowey, Cornwall, PL23 1BY, England. Editor: Sean Dorman. For authors and journalists. Biannually. Established in 1959. Circulation: 500. Copyright reserved to the author. Will send sample copy to writer for $1. Payment on publication. Submit complete ms. Enclose S.A.E. and International Reply Coupons.
Nonfiction and Poetry: Articles on authorship and journalism of 300 to 350 words. Poems of 8 to 24 lines. Besides the articles and poems, letters from readers, news from writers' circles. Literary style. Will consider material previously published in United States or Canada offered for first publication in England. Pays 2 pounds per poem or article.

Book Publishers

ADLARD COLES LTD., Granada Publishing, Frogmore, St. Albans, Hertfordshire AL2 2NF, England. Editor: Jeremy Howard-Williams. Established in 1964 as part of Granada Publishing. Publishes hardcover and paperback originals. Will consider material previously published in United States or Canada, "only if they had an outstanding sales record." Payment depends on the property. "We offer a 10% royalty with an adequate jump in royalty to 12½% and—on occasion—to 15%. Normal advances too." Published 12 books last year. Will send book catalog on request. Query first or submit outline and sample chapter. Enclose S.A.E. and International Reply Coupons.

Nonfiction: Granada Publishing is one of the larger publishing groups covering pretty well all areas in both paperback and hardback publishing. Adlard Coles Ltd. has a particularly fine record as the leading nautical publisher in the United Kingdom. Books on all aspects of sailing and allied nautical subjects. Particular interest in technical and technique books from the introductory level to the advanced level. Typical subjects would include cruising, racing, sail and powered boats, design and construction, technical aspects, naval architecture, etc. Length: 25,000 words minimum.

J.A. ALLEN & CO., LTD., 1 Lower Grosvenor Place, London, SW1W 0EL, England. Established in 1926. Publishes hardcover originals and reprints. Will consider material previously published in U.S. or Canada. Offers 10% royalty contract on previously unpublished books; offers 5% to 10% royalty on published retail price for material previously published in U.S. or Canada. Published 12 titles last year. Submission may be made by the author, his agent, or original publisher. Query first or submit complete ms for previously unpublished material. Enclose S.A.E. and International Reply Coupons for return of submissions.

Nonfiction: "Publications relating to the horse and equestrianism and allied activities such as racing and breeding, riding, schooling, driving, polo, snow jumping, etc."

AQUARIAN PUBLISHING CO. (LONDON) LTD., Denington Estate, Wellingborough, Northants NN8 2RQ, England. Editor-in-Chief: J. R. Hardaker. Established in 1968. Publishes hardcover and paperback originals and reprints. Will consider material previously published in U.S. or Canada offered for first publication in U.K. Offers 10% royalty contract for hardcover originals and 8% royalty contract for paperback originals. Will send a catalog to a writer on request. Submission may be made directly by author, his agent, or original publisher. Submit outline and sample chapters for nonfiction. Address communications to "The Editor." Enclose S.A.E. and International Reply Coupons with ms.

Nonfiction: "Publishers of books on astrology, magic, witchcraft, palmistry, and other occult subjects." Length: 15,000 to 60,000 words.

THE AQUILA PUBLISHING CO. LTD., Sculamus, Breakish, Isle of Skye, IV42 8QE, Scotland. Editors: J. C. R. Green and Michael Edwards. Publishes paperbacks, hardbacks, and pamphlets. Payment by negotiation, normally on royalty basis only. No advance. Query first, including 2 International Reply Coupons, before sending mss. Letters which indicate length and content of books will be more favorably considered.

Nonfiction and Poetry: "We publish books of poetry, or biographical and critical studies of writers. Always poetry or books about poetry or poets." Length: open.

HOWARD BAKER PRESS LIMITED, 27a Arterberry Rd., Wimbledon, London, S.W.20, England. Editor: W. Howard Baker. Publishes hardcover originals and reprints. Established in 1967. Usually offers an advance, plus 10% royalty. Will consider material previously published in the United States or Canada offered for first publication in England. Published 20 titles last year. Will send book catalog to writer on request. Submit outline and sample chapter. Enclose S.A.E. and International Reply Coupons.

General Nonfiction and Fiction: Political science, biography, sometimes leaning toward esoteric subjects. Mainly nonfiction. Length: 50,000 to 75,000 words.

CLIVE BINGLEY LIMITED, 16 Pembridge Rd., London, W11, England. Editor: John Buchanan. Established in 1965. Publishes paperback and hardcover originals. Offers standard 10% contract. Titles published last year: 20. Submit outline and sample chapter. Will send free catalog on request. Enclose S.A.E. and International Reply Coupons.

Nonfiction: Bibliography and library science; student textbooks and reference books. Any length considered. Mainly aimed at English-speaking countries worldwide. Books in the field of librarianship and information science and with an international appeal (not specifically for a home market).

BLADKOMPANIET A.S., Postboks 5249, Majorstua-Oslo 3, Norway. Editors: Claus Huitfeldt and Finn Arnesen. Publishes paperback and hardcover originals and reprints. Offers 7½% for reprints; quality paperback editions. Norwegian kroner 1,400 for reprints pocketbooks up to 20,000 copies. For 3,000 copies on royalty basis, whole fee for pocketbooks. Titles published last year: 50. Submit complete ms. Will consider photocopied submissions. Enclose S.A.E. and International Reply Coupons.
Western Fiction: Especially interested in Western fiction series about the same main character. Thrillers. General fiction. Dramatic and exciting fiction, openess towards sex, though no pornographic material is published. Popular literature. "We specialize in series. We are the largest selling house for pocket books in Norway and are extremely careful in selecting novels. Shorter lengths are also considered for a western magazine which we publish."

BOWKER PUBLISHING CO., LTD., Erasmus House, High St., Epping, Essex, England. Publishes paperback and hardcover originals. "We pay both fees and royalties, subject to negotiation in each case." Submit outline and sample chapter. Enclose S.A.E. and International Reply Coupons.
Nonfiction: Books on the book trade, librarianship, standard reference works, bibliographies, and work in the field of scholarly bibliography, documentation, and the information sciences. "We're the European partner of R. R. Bowker, New York. We specialize in international editions in the fields of librarianship, bibliography, the information sciences and book trade publishing."

BURKE PUBLISHING COMPANY LTD., 14 John St., London, WC1N 2EJ, England. Editor: Miss Naomi Galinski. Publishes hardcover and paperback originals. Established in 1934. Payment subject to negotiation; usually 5% of the published price. Published 40 titles last year, plus reprints and new editions. Will send book catalog to writer on request. Will consider material previously published in United States or Canada offered for first publication in England. Query first. Enclose S.A.E. and International Reply Coupons.
Juveniles: Books for young readers from preschool to school-leaving age. Books aimed at the educational and trade markets with international appeal. "We are a medium-sized privately owned publishing company, originally established in 1934. Our specialty is books for children, both in and out of school, fully illustrated in color and well produced."

BURKE'S PEERAGE LIMITED, 56 Walton St., London SW3 1RB, England. Editorial Director: Hugh Montgomery-Massingberd. Established in 1826. Publishes hardcover and paperback originals and reprints. "We usually purchase all the rights ourselves (but royalties can be negotiated in special circumstances)." Will send book catalog to writer on request. Published 2 titles last year, but "are now expanding our activities in the general field and this figure will soon increase considerably." Query first, submit outline and sample chapter or submit complete ms. Enclose S.A.E. and International Reply Coupons.
General Nonfiction and Reference: "We are chiefly famous for our series of Genealogical Reference Books (founded by the Burke family of heralds and genealogists in 1826), but we also publish general books on social history and allied subjects; and special books for the American market. Scholarly and popular works in the fields of social history, genealogy, heraldry, architecture, etc." Current titles include *Burke's Presidential Families of USA; Burke's Peerage and Baronetage; Burke's Guide to the Royal Family; The Records and Collections of the College of Army* (Sir Anthony Wagner).

BUSINESS BOOKS LTD., Mercury House, Waterloo Rd., London SE1 8UL, England. Editor: David Grossman. Payment by negotiation. Submit complete ms.

Will consider material previously published in United States or Canada offered for first publication in England. Enclose S.A.E. and International Reply Coupons for return of submissions.

Nonfiction: Books for managers and businessmen in all industries. Finance, marketing, management, work-management, etc. Length: 45,000 to 150,000 words.

CASSELL & CO. LTD., 35 Red Lion Square, London, W.C. 1, England. Editor: Kenneth Parker. Established in 1848. Publishes hardcover and paperback originals and reprints. Will consider material previously published in U.S. and Canada offered for first publication in British market. Royalty contract to be arranged. Published about 120 titles last year. Will send a catalog to a writer on request. Submission may be made by the author, his agent, or the original publisher.

General: "General books, memoirs, biographies, fiction, music, juvenile nonfiction, dictionaries, reference books, commercial, technical, etc. No verse, short stories, plays. We have a distinguished list of authors. Royalty terms vary from category to category."

CATHOLIC TRUTH SOCIETY, 39 Eccleston Square, London SW1V 1PD, England. Editor: David Murphy. Established in 1868. Publishes paperback originals and reprints. "We prefer to purchase copyright outright." Published 20 titles last year; and 50 or more reprints. Will consider material previously published in United States or Canada. Submit complete ms. Enclose S.A.E. and International Reply Coupons for return of submissions.

Religion: "The C.T.S. is a voluntary, charitable society whose objective is to share in the spreading of the gospel by means of the printed word. It has some 40,000 subscribing members and its aim is faithfully to present the authentic teaching of the Roman Catholic Church in a comprehensible and relevant way. Generally speaking, authors should try to restrict the area with which they deal to the smallest possible compass, and then treat it, at however profound a level, using commonplace language which does not presuppose readers of a Christian, let alone Catholic, background. No area of Catholic teaching, of Catholic practice or of religious interest falls outside the scope of the Society's objects, and it is always ready to consider new suggestions for the presentation of material which is designed to further them. We publish bibles and prayer books, as well as material for evangelization. Booklets for parents to read to their youngest children, children's story-readers, work books for use by children in schools, cartoon or comic strips directed toward younger people, material for high school pupils, material of interest to college students and teachers. Any material tending toward the spread of a better understanding of any aspect of Roman Catholic faith and practice, at every level from early childhood to postgraduate theology. Also consider material depending heavily on illustration." Length: 4,000 words maximum.

CAVEMAN PUBLICATIONS LTD., P.O. Box 1458, Dunedin, New Zealand. Editor: Trevor Reeves. Established in 1971. Publishes hardcover and paperback originals and reprints. Payment subject to negotiation. Published 12 titles last year. Will send book catalog to writer on request. Will consider material previously published in United States or Canada. Submit outline and sample chapter or submit complete ms. Enclose S.A.E. and International Reply Coupons.

Nonfiction: Publishes literary material essentially. No restrictions as to length, or style.

W. & R. CHAMBERS LTD., 11 Thistle St., Edinburgh EH2 1DG, Scotland. Chairman: A. S. Chambers; Managing Director: I. Gould. Publishes hardcover and paperback originals. Offers standard minimum book contract of 10-12½-15%. Some variation on the standard minimum book contract is offered on educational and children's books. Average depends on title. Does some subsidy publishing. Published 35 titles last year. Will consider photocopied submissions. Query first. Reports within 2 months. Enclose S.A.E. and International Reply Coupons.

Nonfiction, Juveniles, and Textbooks: Reference books, educational books, children's books, books of Scottish interest. History, multimedia material, reference, scientific, technical and textbooks. Planning series in mathematics, English language, children's series, picture books for schools. Length: open.

CROSBY LOCKWOOD STAPLES LTD., Granada Publishing, Frogmore, St. Albans, Hertfordshire, AL2 2NF, England. Editor: Oliver Freeman. Established in 1857 as Crosby Lockwood, Staples Press early 19th Century, and Crosby Lockwood Staples in 1972. Publishes hardcover and paperback originals. Offers 10% with a jump where appropriate to 12½% and—on occasion—a further rise to 15%. Normal advances. Published 22 titles last year. Will send book catalog to writer on request. Will consider material previously published in United States or Canada, "only if it has an outstanding sales record." Query first or submit outline and sample chapter. Enclose S.A.E. and International Reply Coupons.
Nonfiction: "Major subject areas are civil engineering, building and construction, surveying and quantity surveying, architecture, medicine, dentistry, nursing, psychology, psychiatry, and economics; agriculture and agricultural science. As far as levels go, we are most interested in importing professional and research material. We are unlikely to import college or technical text material."

DARTON LONGMAN & TODD LTD., 85 Gloucester Rd., London SW7 4SU, England. Established in 1959. Publishes hardcover and paperback originals. Payment is negotiable percentage of list price. Published 32 titles last year. Will send book catalog to writer on request. Will consider material previously published in United States or Canada. Submit outline and sample chapter. Enclose S.A.E. and International Reply Coupons.
General Nonfiction and Religion: "We're a small house, but the broad scope of our list has made us among the best known of the now comparatively few specialist religious publishers in England. Publishers of the *Jerusalem Bible*. Subjects are religion and theology and bible. Protestant and Catholic; ecumenical. Also consider general subjects: travel and tourism; history; biography; occult; 3rd world. Subject matter should be of interest to the world and not specifically North American background and audience." Length: 25,000 words minimum.

DAVID & CHARLES (HOLDINGS) LTD., South Devon House, Newton Abbot, Devonshire, TQ12 2BT, England. Editor: Mrs. Pamela M. Thomas. Publishes hardcover and paperback originals and hardcover reprints. "Contract varies according to book." Advance varies. Published 300 titles last year. Will send catalog to writer for 75¢. Will send author's guide to writer for 75¢. Query first. Usually reports in 1 month. Enclose S.A.E. and International Reply Coupons.
Nonfiction: "General nonfiction, including antiques and collecting, animals and natural history, geography, history, practical sports and open air books, gardening, cookery, crafts, large illustrated books, travel and topography. David & Charles books pay very careful attention to the quality of research and writing, and usually illustrations are regarded as an integral part of the work and not embellishments. Length varies according to the subject and market aimed at, but the firm has very precise views on the desirable length for most proposed books. David & Charles serves the whole English-speaking world. Many books originated in Britain are bought by United States publishers for publication under their own imprint. Other titles are distributed in the United States by David & Charles Inc. There is a Canadian subsidiary, Douglas, David & Charles in Vancouver, and strong agency arrangements in other Commonwealth countries. David & Charles runs the Readers Union group of book clubs. We have a saying: 'make your chalk chalk and your cheese cheese'. by which we mean that there may occasionally be room for a scissors and paste book as well as a scholarly one but there is no excuse to mix the two treatments. We like books that deal with their subject in the round without segments idiosyncratically missing, and we like to see only slight use made of the personal pronoun. Our philosophy is sketched out in our Author's Guide, sent to overseas inquirers on receipt of 75¢. We tend to be more thorough in our research especially but also pay more than usual attention to details like bibliographies and indexes."

DRUMMOND PRESS, 64 Murray Place, Stirling, Scotland FK8 2BX. Editor: John Birkbeck. Publishes paperback originals. Offers 10% contract. Royalty at end of each year on books sold. "Most books subsidy—we are a charity." Published 10 titles last year. Will send catalog and guidelines to authors on request. Query first. Enclose S.A.E. and International Reply Coupons.

Religion and Philosophy: "The books we publish are expressly religious. Tracts, sermons, pamphlets dealing with specific human problems, doctrine illustrations and quotations, anecdotes. Approach should be evangelical, but not fundamentalist. Use simple language, not calculated to confuse. Planning a series, A Devotional Diary of Scotland, writing by Scots abroad as well as in Britain. Science and religion are being overworked—a preponderance of this emanates from the USA. Some material submitted is well off the beat as to what we seek—indeed, some is in 'orbit' around some philosophical galaxy visited only by the author! Whew! I suppose such thoughts do come to some folk but why do they come couched in enigmatic guise and an abstruseness which challenges all heaven to decipher and admit failure at the end?" Current titles include *Saints and Sinners* which deals with the fellowship of faith; *God Within Us,* the work of the Holy Spirit.

PAUL ELEK (SCIENTIFIC BOOKS) LTD., 54-58 Caledonian Rd., London N1 9RN, England. Editor: Alan R. N. Rogers. Established in 1948. Publishes hardcover and paperback originals and reprints. Usually pays 10%. Published 15 titles last year. Will send book catalog to writer on request. Query first. Enclose S.A.E. and International Reply Coupons.

Nonfiction: All science books. "We publish science books in all categories from undergraduate texts to professional and trade monographs. We prefer illustrated books." Writers should bear in mind an international audience.

FEMINA BOOKS LTD., 1-A Montagu Mews North, London, W.1, England. Editor: Mrs. C. Whitaker. Established in 1966. Publishes hardcover and paperback originals and reprints. Will consider material previously published in U.S. or Canada offered for first publication in U.K. "Royalties usually start at 10%; an advance is paid against royalties." Published 3 titles last year. Will send a catalog to a writer on request. Submission may be made by the author, his agent, or the original publisher. Enclose S.A.E. and International Reply Coupons with ms.

Fiction and Nonfiction: "All books published by this company have to have a definite angle on women in general or a woman in particular." Length: 50,000 to 100,000 words.

G.T. FOULIS & CO., LTD., Sparkford, Yeovil, Somerset, England. Editor: Tim Parker. Established in 1926. Publishes hardcover and paperback originals and reprints. Will consider material previously published in U.S. or Canada offered for first publication in U.K. Payment for previously published material "always negotiable according to the book;" for unpublished books, offers "10% royalty on U.K. selling price of book." Published 20 titles last year. Will send a catalog to a writer on request. Submission may be made by the author, his agent, or original publisher. Submit complete ms for unpublished material. Enclose S.A.E. and International Reply Coupons with ms.

Nonfiction: "A small, well-established independent house specializing in motoring, aviation, general nonfiction, scientific and technical. Especially well-known for its traditionally strong motoring list. Interested in mss on motor sport, motor engineering, aviation, general adult nonfiction, biography. Length is immaterial to us."

LESLIE FREWIN PUBLISHERS LIMITED, 5 Goodwin's Court, St. Martin's Lane, London WC2N 4LL, England. Established in 1962. Publishes hardcover originals and reprints. Payment by negotiation. Published 30 titles last year. Will send book catalog to writer on request. Will consider material previously published in United States or Canada. Submit outline and sample chapter. Enclose S.A.E. and International Reply Coupons.

General Nonfiction: "We are considered to be one of the most vigorous and lively independent publishing houses in the UK. Close links with many other countries, co-productions, sales of rights, etc. Our list is wide-ranging from poetry to major books on contemporary themes. Books on virtually every subject except educational, scientific, or textbooks." Length: 80,000 to 120,000 words.

GENTRY BOOKS LIMITED, 85 Gloucester Road, London SW7, England. Established in 1971. Publishes paperback and hardcover originals. Titles published last year: 8. Will send free book catalog to writer on request. Offers 10% to 2,500, 12½% to 5,000, and 15% beyond. Will consider material previously published in the U.S. or Canada. Query first. Enclose S.A.E. and International Reply Coupons.
Nonfiction: Travel, man and machine, and general nonfiction. Books about people, sports, machines and aviation.

GOWER PRESS LIMITED, Epping, Essex CM16 4BU, England. Editor: R. J. Smith. Established in 1968. Publishes hardcover originals. Offers 10% royalty. Published 60 titles last year. Will send book catalog to writer on request. Will consider material previously published in United States or Canada. Query first or submit outline and sample chapter. Enclose S.A.E. and International Reply Coupons.
Nonfiction: "The leading European publisher of management books, a company owned by the Xerox Corporation. Books of an international nature in personnel, marketing, distribution, finance, materials handling, legal areas. Management subjects for executives in industry and commerce, with emphasis on practice. Manuscripts should be clearly structured, well-documented and 25,000 to 90,000 words long."

GEORGE G. HARRAP & CO., LTD., 182-4 High Holborn, London, W.C. 1, England. Editor: Kenneth Thomson. Established in 1902. Publishes hardcover and paperback originals and reprints. Will consider material previously published in U.S. or Canada offered for first publication in U.K. Royalty "negotiable, but usually not less than 10% of domestic published price." Published 120 titles last year. Submission may be made by the author, his agent, or original publisher. For unpublished material, query first for fiction; submit outline and sample chapters for nonfiction. "In certain instances, books are commissioned jointly by trade and educational editors." Enclose S.A.E. and International Reply Coupons.
General: "Full-length adult and juvenile fiction and nonfiction aimed at middle- to high-brow audience" wanted for previously published material. Length: 45,000 to 85,000 words.
Textbooks: "Leading modern language textbook publishing house in U.K., with world-famous dictionaries. 60% educational and college."

HART-DAVIS, MacGIBBON LTD., 3 Upper James St., Golden Square, London W1, England. Editor-in-Chief: Adrian Shire. Publishes hardcover originals and reprints. Usually offers standard minimum book contract of 10-12½-15%. Titles published last year: 60. Enclose S.A.E. and International Reply Coupons.
General Nonfiction and Fiction: General books for the non-specialist and leisure markets, particularly in the areas of biography, history, fiction and recreation. Mss of 50,000 words minimum, not too heavily illustrated. "We are aiming at the intelligent non-technical audience. Mss should be clearly written and not patronizing. Emphasis should be acceptable to a British or international audience. Interested in fiction, gardening, do-it-yourself, leisure skills, etc. Fiction covering crime, gothic, historical, show biz."

J. H. HAYNES & CO. LTD., Sparkford, Yeovil, Somerset, BA22 7JJ, England. Editor: Tim Parker. Established in 1958. Publishes hardcover and paperback originals and reprints. "Payment either by fee or 10% of net published price or a fee plus 10% of net receipts." Published 60 titles last year. Will send book catalog to writer on request. Will consider material previously published in United States or Canada. Submit outline and sample chapter or submit complete ms. Enclose S.A.E. and International Reply Coupons.
General Nonfiction: All motoring subjects with an emphasis on the technical side; for example, workshop manuals, tuning manuals, handbooks and similar. Also all

individual titles or ranges of books with a practical approach or common theme toward sports, hobbies and all leisure activities.

HOLLIS & CARTER, 9 Bow St., London WC2E 7AL, England. Editor: Guido Waldman. Established in 1943. Publishes hardcover and paperback originals. Titles published last year: 2. Will send free book catalog to writer on request. Offers an advance and fixed or sliding scale royalty. Query first or submit outline and sample chapter. Enclose S.A.E. and International Reply Coupons.
Nonfiction: Nautical books for the professional and amateur seaman. Recent titles include *Catamarans for Cruising* (Andrews); *Motor Boating: A Practical Handbook* (Wickham); and *The Physical Geography of the Oceans* (Cotter).

HUTCHINSON PUBLISHING GROUP LTD., 3 Fitzroy Square, London W1P 6JD, England. General Publishing Director: Francis Bennett. Publishes hardcover and paperback originals and reprints. "Generous royalties by negotiation." Published 400 titles last year. Will send book catalog to writer on request. Will consider material previously published in United States or Canada. Submit outline and sample chapter for nonfiction. Submit complete ms for fiction. Enclose S.A.E. and International Reply Coupons.
Nonfiction, Fiction, Educational, Poetry, and Juveniles: Belles-lettres, biography and memoirs, children's books (fiction, nonfiction, rewards, toy and picture books), current affairs, essays, fiction, general, history, humor, music, poetry, reference, and travel.

DERIC ROBERT JAMES, 118 Windham Rd., Bournemouth, Hampshire, England. Editor: Deric Robert James. Publishes paperback originals. Established in 1967. Published 4 books last year. Will send catalog to writer on request. Will consider unpublished material offered for first time publication. Submission of unpublished material may be made directly by the author. Query first, submit outline and sample chapters, or submit complete ms. Royalty payment by arrangement.
Nonfiction, Occult: "Only nonfiction general articles on all topics of occultism, especially cults and societies and ceremonial magic. Must be accompanied by photograph or sketch to illustrate same. Ceremonial magic and witchcraft. Not first hand accounts but general in style. Length: 10,000 words maximum."

KOTHARI PUBLICATIONS, Jute House, 12 India Exchange Place, Calcutta, 70000, India. Editor: Ing. H. Kothari. Send outline. Enclose International Reply Coupons.
Reference, Technical, Scientific, and Business and Professional: Publishes "mainly reference works."

JOHN LONG LTD., 3 Fitzroy Square, London, WIP 6JD, England. Editor: Gerald Austin. Established in 1898. Publishes hardcover originals. New titles published last year: 20. Will send book catalog to writer on request. Royalty arrangement by negotiation. Will consider material previously published in the U.S. or Canada. Enclose S.A.E. and International Reply Coupons.
Nonfiction and Fiction: General books on criminology, true crime and law. Detective novels and thrillers. Preferred length: 50,000 to 60,000 words.

LONGMAN GROUP LTD., Burnt Mill, Harlow, Essex, CM20 2JE, England. Managing Director: J.A.E. Higham (university and further education). Established in 1724. Publishes hardcover and paperback originals. "A royalty is offered based on British list price for global publications and local list price for local books priced only in currencies other than the pound sterling." Published over 500 titles last year. Will send book catalog to writer on request, "if subject interest is specified." Query first. Enclose S.A.E. and International Reply Coupons.
Textbooks: College and more advanced textbooks. "We're one of the largest British educational book publishers, using the Longman, Oliver and Boyd, and the Churchill Livingstone imprints. Longman Inc. is the American subsidiary of the group. Books on medicine, pure sciences, engineering, life sciences, business management, social sciences, humanities, at college and professional levels; both textbook and specialist use."

MACDONALD & EVANS, 8 John St., London, W.C. 1, England. Managing Director: G.B. Davis. Established in 1908. Publishes hardcover and paperback originals and reprints. Will consider material previously published in U.S. or Canada offered for first publication in U.K. Offers royalty payment according to title, author, market, and format. Offers from 7½% flat (paperback) to 10% to 12½% (hardcover). Published 70 titles last year. Will send a catalog to writer on request. Submission may be made by the author or the original publisher. Submit outline and sample chapters for unpublished material. Enclose S.A.E. and International Reply Coupons.
Textbooks: Commerce, management, professional studies; geography, geology; movement and movement notation; technical and scientific. Level: final years at high school, university, technical colleges. Length: 10,000 to 250,000 words. "Most titles are commissioned. Length would be stated in the contract."

MACDONALD AND JANE'S, Paulton House, 8 Shepherdess Walk, London N1, England. Editors: Penelope Hoare (general) and Sidney Jackson (military, naval, and aviation). Established in 1940. Publishes hardcover and paperback originals and reprints. Offers payment on sliding scale of royalties on the published price of the book. Published 200 titles last year. Will send catalog to writer on request. Will consider material previously published in United States or Canada. Submit outline and sample chapter or submit complete ms. Enclose S.A.E. and International Reply Coupons.
Nonfiction, Fiction, and Juveniles: History, biography, cinema books, cookery, children's, household affairs, sports, fiction, illustrated books, romances. Military, aviation, and naval. A middle-of-the-way general publisher with a specialist military list, and famous yearbooks. Books should be suitable for a United Kingdom and commonwealth market, suitable for trade sale through bookshops and libraries. Length: 70,000 to 100,000 words.

MARSHALL, MORGAN & SCOTT (PUBLICATIONS) LTD., 116 Baker St., London W1M 2BB, England. Editor: Miss Myrtle Powley. Established in 1806. Publishes hardcover and paperback originals and reprints. Offers 10% royalty for hardbacks; 5% or 7½% for paperbacks. Published 60 new titles last year. Will send book catalog to writer on request. Will consider material previously published in United States or Canada. Submit outline and sample chapter, or submit complete ms. Enclose S.A.E. and International Reply Coupons.
Religion: Theology, Christian apologetics, Christian biographies, devotional, inspirational. "We have three imprints: Marshall, Morgan & Scott (mainly evangelical emphasis); Oliphants (broader theological viewpoints); Lakeland (paperbacks). We have purchased the firm of Samuel Bagster & Sons Ltd., founded in 1794, publishers of bibles, concordances, etc." Will consider scholarly and devotional books.

THE MEDICI SOCIETY LTD., 34-42 Pentonville Rd., Islington, London N1, England. Publications Manager: D. H. McLean. Established in 1908. Publishes hardcover and paperback originals. Royalty arrangement is variable; 7% to 10%. Published 3 children's books and 1 artbook last year. Will send book catalog to writer on request. Will consider material previously published in United States or Canada. Submit outline and sample chapter. Enclose S.A.E. and International Reply Coupons.
Juveniles and Art: Picture stories for children ages 5 to 12; able to go into a book of 24 pages (usually with 12 pages of illustrations). Publishers of fine art reproductions, educational art books, children's books (mainly picture story books for primary children).

FREDERICK MULLER LIMITED, Victoria Works, Edgware Rd., London NW2 6LE, England. Editor: Paul Barnett. Publishes hardcover and paperback originals and hardcover reprints. Offers standard minimum book contract of 10-12½-15%, except on children's books, and sometimes adult books. Adult: flat 10%-12½%. Usually 10%-12½%-15%. Children's books: almost always 7½%-10%. Minimum advance on adult books is 200 pounds, rising well into four figures; minimum on juveniles is about 75 pounds. "We don't do subsidy publishing, but are always prepared to consider the opportunity. We don't consider publishing subsidy books that might damage our reputation." Published 75 titles last year. Will send free catalog to writer on request. Query first for adult nonfiction. Submit outline and sample chapters for juveniles. Enclose S.A.E. and International Reply Coupons.

Nonfiction: "Adult books: A general list that veers toward the academic. Special subjects are history, sociology and anthropology, biography, occult (serious, not mass market 'naked witch orgy' stuff), wildlife, philosophy; and, very occasionally, first rate true life adventure of the Papillon variety. No real parameters in approach or style of writing, except we have a strong dislike for bad popularization. Biography, history, nature, philosophy, scientific, self-help and how-to, sociology, technical and textbooks." Length: 20,000 words minimum.

Juveniles: "Children's books: A wide range of information books, for which we are particularly well known. We also publish fiction for older children and young adults, and our list in this category, though as yet still fairly small, is rapidly growing and excitingly so. In the case of fiction, it must be both imaginative and conscientious, as well as well written. In the case of nonfiction, the writing must be very clear and lucid, though we are one of the few publishers in this field who prefer nonfiction to be tackled imaginatively. In general, our children's books must never be patronizing." Length: 5,000 words minimum.

PHILLIMORE & CO. LTD., Shopwyke Hall, Chichester, Sussex, England. Editorial Director: Noel H. Osborne. Established in 1865. Publishes hardcover and paperback originals and reprints. Pays 10% royalty, "though since we specialize in books of limited appeal, sometimes requiring subsidy or grant-aid, we cannot always pay normal royalties." Published 70 titles last year. Will send book catalog to writer on request. Will consider material previously published in United States or Canada. Query first or submit outline and sample chapter. Enclose S.A.E. and International Reply Coupons.

Nonfiction: Books on British local and family history, geneaology, heraldry, archaeology, and architectural history; both primary source material and secondary works of original research. "We have a special reputation in Western Hemisphere with those interested in tracing their British origins in terms of ancestry, towns, buildings, etc. Books on general British antiquarian topics." Length: 25,000 to 500,000 words.

POPULAR DOGS PUBLISHING CO. LTD., 3 Fitzroy Square, London W1P 6JD, England. Editor: Gerald Austin. Established in 1922. Publishes paperback and hardcover originals and hardcover reprints. New titles published last year: 10. Royalty arrangement by negotiation. Will consider material previously published in U.S. or Canada. Will send book catalog to writer on request. Enclose S.A.E. and International Reply Coupons.

Nonfiction: Practical books on breeding, care, training, and general management of dogs.

RIDER AND COMPANY, Hutchinson Publishing Group, Ltd., 3 Fitzroy Square, London, W1P 6JD, England. Editor: Daniel Brostoff. Publishes hardcover and paperback originals and reprints. Offers 10% royalty contract. Published 6 books last year. Query first with outline and sample chapters. Enclose S.A.E. and International Reply Coupons.

Nonfiction: "Subjects: mediation, mysticism, Hinduism (including yoga), Buddhism, and other aspects of Oriental religion and philosophy. We aim to produce works of vigor and quality for 2 broad groups of people: absolute beginners in the quest for increased self-awareness who need some guidance in selecting the most suitable path, and advanced students who require critical commentaries and translations of original texts. In both cases, the writers need to be accomplished in a spiritual sense and have a masterly command of the subject matter. The ability to explain complex matters cogently and concisely is a prerequisite." Length: 50,000 to 90,000 words.

BARRY ROSE PUBLISHERS, Little London, Chichester, Sussex, England. Editor: Barry Rose. Publishes hardcover and paperback originals. Pays 10% "ordinarily," but if joint authorship, pays 12%. Advance negotiable. Published 50 books last year. Will send catalog to writer on request. Query first or submit outline and sample chapters. Will consider photocopied submissions. Reports in 6 weeks. Enclose S.A.E. and International Reply Coupons.
General Nonfiction: "We publish books on law and local government; sometimes legal history, memoirs, biographies, and legal and local government humor. Audience would be almost entirely professional lawyers, administrators, and treasurers. Always interested in short (14,000 words maximum) booklets describing various aspects of crime, punishment, law, and local government. Also publish longer length books."

SEVENSEAS PUBLISHING PTY., LTD., 5-7 Tory St., Wellington, New Zealand. Editor: Murdoch Riley. Publishes hardcover and paperback originals. Offers standard royalty contract; "have done subsidy publishing." Published 7 titles last year. Query first with outline and sample chapter. Reports "as soon as considered." Enclose International Reply Coupons for return postage. "We return mss by sea to overseas addresses unless postage for return mail is forwarded."
Fiction and Nonfiction: Publishes "books on the South Pacific, craft, music." Length: 10,000 words minimum; no maximum.

SHELDON PRESS, SPCK, Marylebone Rd., London N.W1, England. Editor: Darley Anderson. Established in 1973. Sheldon Press was originally established in 1922, but ceased to trade in 1945 except in a small number of education books. Publishes hardcover and paperback originals and reprints. Offers 7½% paperback; 10% rising hardback royalty. Advances split: half on signature, half on delivery of ms. Publishes 25 titles a year. Will send book catalog to writer on request. Will consider material previously published in United States or Canada. Submit outline and sample chapter or submit complete ms. Enclose S.A.E. and International Reply Coupons.
Nonfiction: Books on psychology (general and experimental), religion, social studies, politics (international), biography and memoirs. Length: 40,000 to 150,000 words.

SHEPPARD PRESS LIMITED, P.O. Box 42, 15 James St., London WC2E 8BX, England. Editor: T. R. Davies. Established in 1944. Publishes hardcover originals. Offers 10% royalty. Published 8 titles last year. Submit outline and sample chapter. Enclose S.A.E. and International Reply Coupons.
Nonfiction: Anything of direct interest to book collectors, librarians, and dealers in antiquarian, secondhand, rare and fine books; associated fields.

CHARLES SKILTON PUBLISHING GROUP, 90 The Broadway, London SW19, England. Editor: Leonard Holdsworth. Established in 1944. Publishes hardcover and paperback originals and reprints. "Payment generally as recommended by British Publishers' Association but often by individual agreement." Published 25 titles last year. Will send book catalog to writer on request. Will consider material previously published in United States or Canada. Query first. Enclose S.A.E. and International Reply Coupons.
General Nonfiction: Architecture, fine art, literary biography and literary research; illustrated books, cookery, and travel. Imprints are Albyn Press, Tallis Press, Polybooks, Fortune Press, and Luxor Press.

SOUVENIR PRESS, LTD., 43 Great Russell St., London, WC1, England. Executive Director: Ernest Hecht. Established in 1953. Publishes hardcover and paperback originals, reprints, translations, and anthologies. Offers standard royalty contract. Published 50 titles last year. Will send a catalog to a writer on request. Query first or submit outline and sample chapter. Enclose S.A.E. and International Reply Coupons.
General: Publishes books on all nonfiction subjects, both for general list and academic paperbacks. No limitation of subject matter or length of book. Has a reputation for best-sellers, especially of unusual books.

NEVILLE SPEARMAN LIMITED, 112 Whitfield St., London W.1, England. Editor: Neville Armstrong. Established in 1950. Publishes hardcover originals and reprints. Offers royalties starting at 10%, rising to 15%, plus an advance against royalties. Published 25 titles last year. Will send book catalog to writer on request. Will consider material previously published in United States or Canada. Query first or submit outline and sample chapter. Enclose S.A.E. and International Reply Coupons.
Nonfiction and Fiction: "We are specialist occult and metaphysical publishers and are also interested in controversial and unorthodox subjects. We have been called England's leading serious occult publishers, but we are not interested in spiritualism, per se." Length: 50,000 to 100,000 words.

SPHERE BOOKS LTD., 30-32 Gray's Inn Rd., London WC1X 8JL, England. Editor: Mr. Julian Shuckburgh. Established in 1966. Publishes paperback originals and reprints. Payment by arrangement. Published 200 titles last year. Will send book catalog to writer on request. Will consider material previously published in United States or Canada. Submit outline and sample chapter or submit complete ms. Enclose S.A.E. and International Reply Coupons.
General Nonfiction and Fiction: A leading British paperback publisher with a strong general fiction list and quality nonfiction imprints (Cardinal Books and Abacus Books). General and category fiction, biography, sociology, cookery, crafts, sports, health and medicine, history, archaeology, occult. Mass market readership. Length: 50,000 to 100,000 words.

PATRICK STEPHENS LIMITED, Bar Hill, Cambridge, CB3 8EL, England. Editor: Michael Gilliat. Established in 1967. Publishes hardcover originals and reprints. Offers 10% royalty; advance on royalty. Published 31 titles last year. Will send book catalog to writer on request. Will consider material previously published in United States or Canada. Query first. Enclose S.A.E. and International Reply Coupons.
Nonfiction: Subjects covered include aviation, militaria, model-making, motoring and motor racing, motorcycling, ships and the sea; art, photography, and wargaming. All books are illustrated, and contain 40,000 to 60,000 words. Current titles include *A Dictionary of Ships of the Royal Navy in the Second World War* (Young); *A Victorian Maritime Album* (Greenhill); *A Casebook of Military Mystery* (Brown); *Airfix Magazine Annual for Modellers 4* (Quarrie).

TEXTILE TRADE PRESS, 38 High St., New Mills, Stockport 5K12 4BR, England. Established in 1966. Publishes hardcover and paperback originals. "We are happy to consider any arrangement that is mutually beneficial to author and publisher. Write and see if we might be interested before risking ms and postage 'across the water.'" Published 3 titles last year. Will send catalog to writer on request. Enclose S.A.E. and International Reply Coupons with query.
Nonfiction: "Anything relating to textiles, fibres, marketing thereof, etc. Textile Trade Press concentrates entirely on technical and marketing mss concerning the textile industry in all its aspects. It is a small, specialized, and highly individualized organization." Length: 50,000 words minimum.

THAMES AND HUDSON LTD., 30-34 Bloomsbury St., London WC1B 3QP, England. Editorial Director: Stanley Baron. Address new projects to Jamie Camplin. Established in 1949. Publishes hardcover and paperback originals and occasionally hardcover and paperback reprints. Payment by negotiation. Published 150 titles last year. Will send book catalog to writer on request. Query first. Enclose S.A.E. and International Reply Coupons.
General Nonfiction: All nonfiction subjects; especially art, archaeology, history, biography, travel. For central market, intelligent layman. But academic and popular audience too. "We have an international reputation for illustrated books."

A. THOMAS & CO. LTD., Denington Estate, Wellingborough, Northants, England. Editor: J. R. Hardaker. Established in 1948. Publishes hardcover and paperback originals and reprints. Payment by negotiation. Published 5 titles last year. Will send book catalog to writer on request. Will consider material previously published in United States or Canada. Query first. Enclose S.A.E. and International Reply Coupons.

Nonfiction: "We specialize largely in inspirational books. Also practical psychology and self-improvement."

THORSONS PUBLISHERS LTD., Denington Estate, Wellingborough, Northants, NN8 2RQ England. Established in 1930. Publishes hardcover and paperback originals and reprints. Will consider material previously published in U.S. or Canada offered for first publication in England. Offers 10% royalty for hardcovers, 8% royalty for paperbacks. Submit outline and sample chapters. Enclose S.A.E. and International Reply Coupons.

General Nonfiction: Principally health books on such topics as nature cure, herbalism, dietetics, food supplements, etc. Yoga, occult, fringe medicine. Also publishes books on psychology, self-improvement, hypnotism, acupuncture and other fringe medicines. Activities center around the publishing of books advocating the benefits of healthy eating and living. Also an extensive occult list. Length: 15,000 to 60,000 words.

TRITON PUBLISHING CO. LTD., 1-A Montagu Mews North, London, W.1, England. Editor: Mrs. C. Whitaker. Established in 1963. Publishes hardcover originals and reprints. Will consider material previously published in U.S. or Canada offered for first publication in U.K. and British Commonwealth. "Royalties usually start at 10%; we offer an advance against royalties." Published 6 titles last year. Will send catalog on request. Enclose S.A.E. and International Reply Coupons with ms.

General: "General fiction of high quality and nonfiction of general interest (biographies, etc.). Length: 50,000 to 100,000 words."

TURNSTONE BOOKS, 37 Upper Addison Gardens, London, W14 8AJ, England. Editor: Alick Bartholomew. Publishes hardcover and paperback originals and reprints. Established in 1971. Offers standard British scale of royalties: 10% of list sliding to 15%. Publishes 20 books a year. Will send a catalog on request. Query first with outline and sample chapter. Follow Chicago *Manual of Style*. Enclose International Reply Coupons with query.

Nonfiction: "Popular, informative and practical books on philosophy, mysticism, parapsychology, prehistory and alternative therapies. British publisher of Jonathan Livingston Seagull, but don't send us novels. We are a small imprint publishing New Age themes. Emphasis on originality, integrity, and controversiality, with high standard of writing and international interest." Length: 60,000 to 85,000 words.

CHARLES E. TUTTLE CO., INC., Suido 1-Chome, 2-6, Bunkyo-ku, Tokyo, Japan. Editor: Florence Sakade. Publishes hardcover and paperback originals and reprints. Query first. Enclose S.A.E. and International Reply Coupons.

Nonfiction: Books on Japan with an emphasis on Asia. Chiefly interested in the Humanities. Not interested in politics, economics, biography, or technical material. Art, cookbooks, foreign language, nature, sports, hobbies, recreation, pets, and travel.

Syndicates

GRAHAM & HEATHER FISHER LTD., 29 Forest Drive, Keston, Kent, England BR2 6EE. "We place material in Britain, Europe and the British Commonwealth, selling it to top magazines in each country." Pays on acceptance for foreign reprint rights. Submit query with brief outline. "We prefer articles that have already sold in U.S. or Canada, but will also consider original material if subject is right." Enclose S.A.E. and International Reply Coupons for reply to query.

General Nonfiction: "Most of the magazines are aimed at women and it follows that so is the material we seek; celebrity interviews, stories of physical and emotional adventure involving women, articles dealing with women's emotional, sex and medical problems; in fact, almost any popular-type article which might appeal to the young marrieds or unmarrieds. But not articles about cooking, beauty, interior decoration, or other similar subjects which magazines prefer written by their own staffs." Length: one-shots, 1,000 to 4,000 words. Payment for these is 25 pounds to 50 pounds. Series, 3,000 to 3,500 words per part. Handles longer material on 50% basis.

HAMPTON PRESS FEATURES SYNDICATE, P.O.B. 114, Drummoyne, NSW 2047, Australia. Editor: R. Hall. Established in 1938. Places second serial rights. Places material in Australasia, Europe, England, South Africa, and Japan, etc. Will not consider photocopied submissions. Enclose S.A.E. and International Reply Coupons.
Nonfiction, Fiction, and Humor: Photo stories with universal appeal. Photos used with features or without features. Captions required. Minimum size 6x4. Cartoons. Also romance stories. Length: 1,500 to 4,000 words. Payment varies in all parts of the world.

MAHARAJA FEATURES PRIVATE LTD., 5/226 Sion Road East, Bombay-22, India. Editor: Mrs. Janaki Swamy. Supplies material to "major journals in Europe, British Commonwealth, India, and southeast Asia." Buys all rights. Query first— "summary advisable." Returns rejected material in 2 weeks "by surface mail." Enclose S.A.E. and International Reply Coupons for reply to queries.
Nonfiction: "Features of general interest, especially pertaining to India. It is essential that the features do not become dated or obsolete. We will buy single features on interesting places, monuments, historical events, and exotic subjects. Subjects like 'how rich were the maharajas' or 'they wanted to build another Taj Mahal.' Crisp style; exotic, interesting subjects." Length: 1,000 to 1,500 words. "Should be accompanied by 1 or 2 photos. Uses b&w glossies, color transparencies, color prints." Payment "depends on the articles—usually 50% commission or outright purchase."

Picture Sources

There are many sources of photographs which may have just the illustration you're looking for. Some of these libraries, museums, companies, and other organizations are included in the list which follows. Many offer free use of photos or charge only a modest fee. In addition, stock photo companies and agencies representing groups of photographers have photographs filed by subject on almost every conceivable topic. Fees for the one-time use of such photographs may vary from $25 for a b&w to several hundred dollars for the one-time reproduction of a color transparency. Obviously the freelance writer can't afford to deal with this latter group, but the editor does, and a few of these agencies are included in the following list for the convenience of editor-users of the *Writer's Market.*

Another editors' source for photography (stock or "to order") is the membership of ASMP — The Society of Photographers in Communications. Some members are included below, and a complete list appears in the ASMP Membership Directory, which gives the name, address, and specialties of over 700 professional photographers. It is available from ASMP, 60 East 42nd St., New York NY 10017.

Writers seeking further details from any of the sources below should be sure to enclose an S.A.S.E. with their inquiry.

Several of the photo agencies say they charge "ASMP rates." These are minimum fees set by ASMP as a basis for negotiation, and actual charges may be higher, depending on use. For a practical, complete guide to ASMP rates and policies, *Business Practices and Photography Guide* is available from ASMP for $5.

ASMP also sets minimum fees for photographers working on a day rate. These are outlined in the Membership Directory.

AAAASTOCK PHOTO, 154 E. Erie, Chicago IL 60611. Contact: David Maenza or David Honor. 33,0000 transparencies of over 300 subjects. "Excellent files on sports and entertainment." Transparencies ranging from 35mm to 4x5. One-time rights. Fee depends on use, circulation, etc. "We use the ASMP rate guide for price determination/scale."

AGENCY FOR INTERNATIONAL DEVELOPMENT, Office of Public Affairs, 21st and Virginia Ave., N.W., Washington DC 20523. Contact: Carl Purcell. Photographs on all phases of foreign assistance activity. Emphasis on increasing agricultural production and assisting in family planning, education and health programs in Latin America, Asia, Africa. Mostly b&w; some 35mm color. No fees, except when enlargements are required. Credit line required.

ALASKA PICTORIAL SERVICE, Box 6144, Anchorage AK 99502. Contact: Steve McCutcheon. 55,000 b&w, 65,000 color. "All subjects pertaining to Alaska from geomorphology to politics, from scenery to ethnical. We do not ship to individuals: only to recognized business firms, publishing houses, AV productions, governmental bodies, etc." B&w and color. Reproduction rights offered depend upon type of rights the publisher wishes or the advertising agency requires. Fees: minimum $35 b&w; minimum $125 color.

J. C. ALLEN AND SON, P.O. Box 2061, West Lafayette IN 47906. Contact: J. C. Allen or Chester Allen. 50,000 b&w negatives; 6,000 5x7 transparencies. "Specialize in agricultural illustrations made throughout the Corn Belt States; crops from soil preparation to harvest; livestock of all types. B&w prints are sold for one-time use unless special arrangements are made. Transparencies are usually rented but can be purchased. As long as customer attempts to be reasonable, we accept the rate established by a magazine or book publisher. Advertising use fees vary and are quoted after we know the details."

ALPHA PHOTOS ASSOCIATES, 251 Park Ave. S., New York NY 10010. Arnold M. Namm, Manager. One million photos in "almost every conceivable category." Offers "any rights client is willing to purchase. Pictures can even be bought for outright purchase if desired." Fees depend on use.

ALUMINUM COMPANY OF AMERICA, Alcoa Building, Pittsburgh PA 15219. Contact: Byron S. Campbell, Supervisor, Photographic Services. Many thousands of photos in "color and b&w on practically everything concerning aluminum — mining, refining, smelting, fabricating, products, uses, etc." Offers worldwide rights. No fees.

THE AMERICAN MUSEUM OF NATURAL HISTORY, Central Park West at 79th St., New York NY 10024. The Photography Department has a library of about 15,000 color transparencies and over 500,000 b&w negatives available for reproduction. Collection includes anthropology, archaeology, primitive art, botany, geology, mineralogy, paleontology, zoology, and some astronomy. Fees and other information will be supplied on request.

AMERICAN PETROLEUM INSTITUTE, 1801 K St., N.W., Washington DC 20006. Contact: Earl A. Ross, Manager, Press Relations. Photos pertaining to petroleum. B&w glossies. For non-commercial, non-advertising use only. Credit line required.

AMERICAN STOCK PHOTOS, 6842 Sunset Blvd., Hollywood CA 90028. Contact: Al Greene. Nearly 2 million photos. "All subjects: contemporary and historical. Mostly b&w; some color transparencies 4x5 or larger." Offers any rights desired. Only restrictions are limited to previous sales; i.e., 1 year calendar exclusive. Fees: "based on public exposure. $25 minimum."

AMERICAN TRUCKING ASSOCIATIONS, INC., 1616 P St., N.W., Washington DC 20036. Contact: Press Section, Public Relations Dept. B&w photographs of different types of trucks (twin trailers, auto carrier, livestock, etc.) and trucks in various situations (traffic, urban night, etc.). Limited number of color prints available for non-commercial use only. No fees but credit line and return of pictures required. (Pictures not available for advertising purposes.)

AMF INCORPORATED, 777 Westchester Ave., White Plains NY 10604. Contact: Ms. Cathy Rice. Photographs of AMF products being manufactured and being used. Many shots of sports equipment in use. B&w, color. No charge for b&w photos, but credit line and return of pictures required. Color originals can be viewed only at above offices and copy color prints or transparencies made to order and charged at cost.

ANIMALS ANIMALS, 161 E. 82nd St., New York NY 10028. Contact: Nancy Henderson. "Hundreds of thousands of pictures of animals from all over the world in their natural habitat in color and in b&w. Mammals, reptiles, amphibians, fish, birds, invertibrates, horses, dogs, cats, etc. One-time use, world rights, foreign language. Service fee of $25 if no sale is made — applicable only on lengthy requests. All uses, if unusual, are negotiable. We follow the ASMP guidelines."

APPEL COLOR PHOTOGRAPHY, Twin Lakes WI 53181. Contact: Thos. E. Appel. Exclusively color photography. Thousands of photos (4x5 transparencies); largest independent collection in the U.S. Stock nearly everything: general scenes, historicals, travel, points of interest, juveniles, human interest, outdoor sports, spectator sports, wildlife, girls, young adult activities, national parks, etc. Cover all the U.S., and some foreign. Reproduction rights; return required. Fees vary upon use and nature of publication.

ART REFERENCE BUREAU INC., Box 137, Ancram NY 12502. Contact: Donald R. Allen, President, or Janet L. Snow. Have "access to over a million subjects in

European locations. Painting, sculpture, graphics, architecture, archaeology, artifacts principally from European locations. B&w glossy photos may be purchased. Color transparencies supplied on 3-month loan only. We clear reproduction rights for any material supplied. Fees vary with the sources who supply material to us."

ASSOCIATED PICTURE SERVICE, Box 52881, Atlanta GA 30305. Phone: 404-948-2671. Manager: Buford C. Burch. Photos of nature, historical points, city-suburbs, major American cities, scenic views. 25,000 35mm only. Fees negotiable. Price list on request, in accordance with ASMP suggested price list.

ASSOCIATED PUBLISHERS, 1407 14th St., N.W., Washington DC 20005. Pictures of distinguished Negroes. Small pictures 1¾x2 up to wall size 19x24 posters, 50¢ to $3 each. Catalogue available.

ASSOCIATION OF AMERICAN RAILROADS NEWS SERVICE, American Railroads Building, 1920 L St., N.W., Washington DC 20036. Contact: J. Ronald Shumate. B&w glossies on railroad subjects. No fees. Credit line required.

AUSTRIAN INFORMATION SERVICE, 31 E. 69th St., New York NY 10021. Contact: Library Limited. B&w photos of Austria. No fees but credit line and return of pictures required.

AUTHENTICATED NEWS INTERNATIONAL, 170 Fifth Ave., New York NY 10010. Phone: 212-243-6995. Contact Managing Editor: Mr. Sidney Polinsky. Approximately 1½ million photos, b&w and color. Photo agency for all types of domestic and foreign news photos, stock photos on all subjects, including politics, pollution, geo-thermal and solar energy, etc. 50% commission on all photos sold; b&w and color. Credit line and return of photos required.

THE BANCROFT LIBRARY, University of California, Berkeley CA 94720. Contact: Curator of Pictorial Collections. Portraits, photographs, original paintings and drawings, prints and other materials illustrating the history of California, western North America, Mexico. Researchers must consult card indexes and book catalogs to the collection. The Library cannot make selections. Photographic reference copies are available for purchase; negatives and transparencies on a loan basis only. "Commercial users of our pictorial resources are asked to make a donation equivalent to the per-unit prices charged by commercial picture outlets for similar materials." Credit line required.

BILLY E. BARNES, 313 Severin St., Chapel Hill NC 27514. Phone: 919-942-6350. 50,000 photos of civil rights activities, small-town scenes, nature, poverty, farms. Spans the period 1960 to present; 10,000 color, 40,000 b&w. Also photos of family situations, school situations, children, industrials, graffiti, industrial training, and health care. No photos released for advertising use. Offers one-time use. $40 per b&w, $75 per color photo for profit publications; 50% discount offered for nonprofit publications.

BBM ASSOCIATES, 741 Addison Street, Berkeley CA 94710. Contact: Elihu Blotnick. 300,000 "b&w and color pictures ranging over all subject areas; emphasis on the San Francisco Bay area with a little bit of everything from the rest of the world. Specialties: ecology, ethnic, children, nature, political, and radical photography." One-time North American usage. Subsequent fees for additional reproduction. Fees: "Standard ASMP with consideration for certain budget problems."

BECKWITH STUDIOS, 81 Columbia Hghts., Brooklyn NY 11201. Contact: E. S. Beckwith. General illustrative material; travel, people, scenes, etc. B&w and color. Does a great deal of textbook work; some trade book. Also works on assignment, shooting specifically what is needed. Standard fees; will work within client's budget. One-use rights; will negotiate other rights on request. Written request required, stating potential use, material desired, length of time to be held.

RICHARD BELLAK — PHOTOGRAPHER, 127 Remsen St., Brooklyn NY 11201. Phone: 212-858-2417. Contact: Richard Bellak. About 10,000 photos on a wide variety of people-oriented subjects including migrant workers, Appalachia, children, elderly people, blacks in rural Alabama, youth scenes, third world people. B&w and color. Usually offers one-time, non-exclusive reproduction rights. Minimum fee for b&w is usually $50; $100 minimum for color. Unused photos may not be held longer than 10 days. All photos must be returned undamaged.

BLACK STAR, 450 Park Ave. S., New York NY 10016. Phone: 212-679-3288. President: Howard Chapnick; Executive Vice-President: Benjamin J. Chapnick. Represents 120 photographers for assignment work. Color and b&w photos of all subjects. Two million photos in collection. One-time use or negotiations for other extended rights. $50 minimum per b&w, $150 minimum per color. Assignment rates quoted on request.

BLACKSTONE-SHELBURNE NEW YORK, INC., 3 W. 30 St., New York NY 10001. Phone: 212-736-9100. Manager: David Jacobs. 180,000 sets of negatives. Photos (portraits) of personalities, businessmen, dignitaries.

DR. BLOCK COLOR PRODUCTIONS, 1309 N. Genesee Ave., Hollywood CA 90046. Contact: Mrs. Fred Block. 3,300 color slides, 2x2. "Large collection in the art field. We have sold reproduction rights to publishers for prints in book publications." Credit line requested. Fee: "about $60 for single slide for reproduction." Requests return of originals. Request sheet available of detailed list of photos and prices.

THE BOSTONIAN SOCIETY, Old State House, 206 Washington St., Boston MA 02109. Contact: Mrs. Ropes Cabot, Curator. Large collection of pictures and negatives of Boston and Boston people and events. B&w and color. Color reproduction to be arranged. One-time reproduction fee $25, first item used; subsequent items by negotiation. Credit line required.

BOY SCOUTS OF AMERICA, P.O. Box 521, North Brunswick NJ 08902. Contact: George A. Corrado, Art Director. Photographs of Cubs, Scouts, Explorers, and adult leaders. Fees: $5 for b&w; $10 for color. Credit line required. Return of pictures required.

PHILIP BRODATZ, 100 Edgewater Drive, Coral Gables FL 33133. B&w and color pictures of nature, trees, scenics in USA and Caribbean Islands; clouds, water. "Textures" of many kinds. Rights offered for use in books or advertising. Fees depend on use — "whether for book illustration or advertising and one-time use or repeated use. From $25 up."

BROOKLYN PUBLIC LIBRARY, Grand Army Plaza, Brooklyn NY 11238. Contact: Elizabeth L. White, Brooklyn Librarian. The History Division's Brooklyn Collection contains about 2,300 b&w photos of Brooklyn buildings and neighborhoods. Also has photograph file of the Brooklyn Daily Eagle, covering photographs used from c. 1905 to 1955; it contains thousands of prints of national as well as local news subjects. Some of these are wire service photos and many have been retouched. The photographs cannot be loaned, but arrangements can be made for their reproduction; the costs are $4.50 for each print from a negative and $6 for each print from a positive. Permission to use the wire service photos must be obtained from that service. There is no other charge or rental fee for use of these photos, but a credit line to the Brooklyn Public Library is requested.

BUFFALO AND ERIE COUNTY HISTORICAL SOCIETY, 25 Nottingham Court, Buffalo NY 14216. Contact: Richard M. Hurst, Chief of Resources. Photographs of western New York, Niagara frontier in b&w. One-time reproduction fee: $19. Credit line required.

BUREAU OF TRAVEL DEVELOPMENT, DELAWARE STATE VISITORS SERVICE, State of Delaware, 45 The Green, Dover DE 19901. Contact: Donald Mathewson, Tourism Coordinator. 2,000 photos. "Historic buildings and sites. Indoor-outdoor photos of museums. Camping, boating, fishing, and beach scenes. Auto, flat and harness racing. State park nature scenes. Historic churches, monuments, etc." B&w and color. Rights offered unlimited, except credit line required in some cases. No fees charged. "Released on a loan only basis. Must be returned after use."

GUY BURGESS, PHOTOGRAPHER, 202 Old Broadmoor Road, Colorado Springs CO 80906. Contact: Guy Burgess. 1,800 5x7 color transparencies of garden scenes, plant portraits. One-time use. Fees: $100 to $250. Return required.

CALIFORNIA STATE LIBRARY, Library and Courts Bldg., P.O. Box 2037, Sacramento CA 95809. Contact: Kenneth I. Pettitt, California Section Head Librarian. California historical pictures, portraits of Californians (mostly early residents) in b&w only. "Photocopies of specific pictures may be ordered by mail. Selection should be done at the library by the researcher. Names of private researchers, who work on a fee basis, are available. Fees for photocopies vary according to type and size of print. Library retains negatives. Credit line required."

CAMERA CLIX, INC., 404 Park Ave. S., New York NY 10016. Phone: 212-684-3526. Manager: Dorean Davis. Photos of children, animals, historic points, major American cities, scenics, art reproductions, girls, and family life. Large format color transparencies. Rights offered are negotiable. Fees depend on type of rights purchased.

CAMERA HAWAII, INC., 206 Koula Street, Honolulu HI 96813. Contact: Photo Librarian. Estimated over 50,000 color and b&w pictures of Hawaii; cross section of all islands, scenics, travel, aerial and general. Also selection of photos from New Zealand, Sydney, Bali, Manila, Taiwan, Hong Kong, Korea, Tokyo and parts of Japan, Guam: minor file of other areas such as Tahiti, West Coast; Washington, New York, Boston area; Quebec, Niagara Falls; spring flowers in Washington, Capitol, New York scenes and others. Usually offers one-time rights, but subject to negotiation according to needs. Fees dependent upon usage and rights required. Minimums generally in line with ASMP standards.

CAMERA M D STUDIOS INC., Library Division, 122 E. 76 St., New York NY 10021. Phone: 212-628-4331. Manager: Carroll H. Weiss. 100,000 photos of the medical and natural sciences. Offers all rights. ASMP rates.

CAMERIQUE STOCK PHOTOS, P.O. Box 175, Blue Bell PA 19422. Contact: Orville Johnson. B&w photos and color transparencies on a variety of subject matter. Selection can be sent on ten-day approval. One-time reproduction fee varies with importance of use, media, circulation, etc. Fee quoted on receipt of this information. Credit line required. Return of pictures required in 10 days, unless extended.

WOODFIN CAMP AND ASSOCIATES, 50 Rockefeller Plaza, New York NY 10020. Contact: Midge Keator or Woodfin Camp. Over 100,000 photos representing general geographic coverage of most countries in the world, with particular emphasis on India, Africa, Russia, Western Europe, South America, Southeast Asia, and the U.S. B&w and color. Fees depend on usage, beginning at $50 per b&w; $150 for color. Usually offers one-time, non-exclusive North American rights. Since most photos were produced from reportage assignments, there are no model releases for the subjects. Requests must be as specific as possible regarding the type of photo needed and its intended use, and rights required.

CANADA WIDE FEATURE SERVICE LTD., 231 rue St.-Jacques, Montreal, Canada H2Y 1M6. Phone: 514-282-2434. Photo Sales Manager: Steve Pigeon. Editorial and advertising photos of all subjects.

CANADIAN & SASKATCHEWAN SCENICS, 4358 Castle Road, Regina, Saskatchewan, Canada S4S 4W3. Contact: Ken Patterson. Approximately 2,000 pictures of "agricultural scenes, animals, cattle and horses, cities, dog sleighs, farm scenes, fishing, historic views, hunting, Indians, mining, oil wells, provincial and national parks, scenic views, seeding & harvesting, snowmobiles, ranching, rivers and lakes, wild flowers, plants & nature close-ups. Photos are 90% color (2¼); some 4x5 color." Offers "mainly one-time publication rights, at times exclusive rights." Fee: varies; $20 to $50 for one-time use. "Fee is negotiable depending upon use made of photo."

CANADIAN CONSULATE GENERAL, 1251 Avenue of the Americas, New York NY 10020. (Territory comprises Connecticut, New Jersey, and New York State only.) Contact: Photo Librarian. 8x10 b&w glossies and 35mm color transparencies of Canadian scenes and the people of Canada are available, gratis, on a loan basis from the Canadian Consulate General at the above address. Credit line required. Return of pictures requested.

CANADIAN PACIFIC, Windsor Stn., Montreal, P.Q., H3C 3E4. Contact: F. E. Stelfox. Photographs on all Canadian subjects: scenic, industrial, etc. Also, some foreign scenics. B&w and color. No fees but credit line required.

CANADIAN PRESS, 50 Rockefeller Plaza, New York NY 10020. Phone: 212-247-6371. 600,000 photos of current and historic Canadian personalities and life; mostly b&w. Canadian agents for Wide World Photos, Inc. Offers one-time rights. Charges $20 to $35 for b&w, depending on publication's circulation.

CAPITAL PUBLISHING COMPANY, Box 1783, Rockville MD 20050. Contact: John Phillips, Editor. Color transparencies and b&w prints of Washington landmarks. "We will sell any and all rights, and will provide any specified sizes. Our rates which reflect the rights being sold and the quality of the photos, generally range between $10 and $25." Credit line requested.

HARVEY CAPLIN'S PHOTOGRAPHIC LIBRARY OF THE SOUTHWEST, 5132 Bates Court or P.O. Box 10393, Alameda NM 87114. Contact: Harvey Caplin. 45,000 b&w, 15,000 color pictures "of Southwestern subjects such as cattle, sheep, Indians, scenics, national parks and monuments, state parks, mountains, recreation, cowboys." Offers one-time use or outright purchase if necessary. Fees are "whenever possible, the established rates of the publication or organization with which I am dealing, a minimum of $25 local, $50 national fee for one-time b&w use and $50 local, $100 national for one-time color use."

WILLIAM CARTER, PHOTOGRAPHER AND WRITER, 2430 Ross Rd., Palo Alto CA 94303. Phone: 415-321-3594. Contact: William Carter. About 30,000 photos on a variety of worldwide subjects, particularly U.S. Middle West, western ghost towns, children, show horses, Middle East, special subjects. Fees negotiable.

WALTER CHANDOHA, RFD, Annandale NJ 08801. Contact: Walter Chandoha. 100,000 color and b&w pictures of "cats, dogs, horses and other animals. Nature subjects, weather situations, trees and leaves, flowers (wild, domestic, tropical); growing vegetables and fruits; sunsets, clouds, sky and scenics; water, conservation." Offers non-exclusive, limited exclusive, exclusive rights and outright purchase. Fees: Minimum $50 for b&w, minimum $150 for color and up to $2,500 depending on use. "We do not deal with authors direct; we prefer to work with their publishers."

THE CHASE MANHATTAN BANK MONEY MUSEUM, 1254 Avenue of the Americas, New York NY 10020. Contact: Gene Hessler, Curator. Photographs of coins and currency (ancient, modern); primitive money; Indian currency. B&w only. No charge for photos but requires credit line.

CHICAGO HISTORICAL SOCIETY, Dept. of Prints, Photographs, and Broadsides, North Ave. at Clark St., Chicago IL 60614. Contact: John S. Tris, Curator of Prints. Does not sell prints but charges a fee for the service of copying any of the 350,000 pieces in its collecton of American and Chicago history. Selection should be made on the premises; by appointment only. Specific pieces may be ordered by mail. No reproduction fee. On-page credit line mandatory.

CINCINNATI HISTORICAL SOCIETY, Eden Park, Cincinnati OH 45202. Contact: Ms. Carmeletta Malora, Picture Librarian. Over 750,000 photos and slides of Cincinnati and Cincinnati-related material; general pictures on subjects such as World War I, urban decay, Ohio River transportation. B&w and color slides. One-time use, with fee for commercial use.

JOE CLARK, HBSS, PHOTOGRAPHY, 8775 West 9 Mile Rd., Oak Park MI 48237. Contact: Joe Clark. Over 10,000 pictures of "scenes and people in Michigan, Tennessee, Detroit, down South, Panama, Scotland — various states in U.S.; miscellaneous; people, pets, children, landscapes." One-time use or as agreed. Fees "depend on use."

BRUCE COLEMAN INCORPORATED, 15 E. 36th St., New York NY 10016. Phone: 212-683-5227. Contact: Norman Owen Tomalin. Maintaining a comprehensive library of over 200,000 top quality color transparencies on all subjects other than news. All rights available. A.S.M.P. rates.

COLLEGE NEWSPHOTO ALLIANCE, 342 Madison Ave., New York NY 10017. Phone: 212-697-1136. Manager: Ted Feder. 100,000 b&w photos and color transparencies of college life including political activity, people, current economic and social trends, urban and rural subjects, ecology. Offers one-time to world rights. Fees depend on the reproduction rights and size of reproduction on the page; average $50 for b&w, $100 to $125 for color.

COMPSCO PUBLISHING CO., 663 Fifth Ave., New York NY 10022. Phone: 201-962-4114 or 212-PL7-6454. Contact: Ernst A. Jahn. 40,000 photographs on travel, buildings, scenery, people, workmen, railways, roads in Mexico, Central America, South America, USA, Holland, Germany, Easter Islands, Tahiti, South Africa, Tunisia, Jamaica, Finland, Russia, Middle East Arab World, Robinson Crusoe Islands, Galapagos Islands, San Blas Islands, Windward Islands, Grenadine Islands, Greece, and Rhodos Islands. 35mm b&w, color. One-time rights. $5 holding fee after 30 days. One-time reproduction fee: $100 for color; $25 for b&w. Credit line and return of pictures required.

CONSOLIDATED EDISON COMPANY OF NEW YORK, INC., 4 Irving Place, New York NY 10003. Contact: William O. Farley, Director, Public Information. Single copies of prints available on electric, gas, steam generation and distribution facilities. No fees.

JERRY COOKE INC., 161 E. 82 St., New York NY 10028. Phone: 212-288-2045. Manager: Nancy Henderson. B&w and color photos of children, scenic views, sports, travel, foreign countries, including China. Rights and fees negotiable.

CULVER PICTURES, INC., 660 First Ave., New York NY 10016. Contact: R. B. Jackson. "Widely known in historical field, with over 7 million b&w photos, old prints, engravings, posters, paintings, movie stills covering every imaginable subject. We like to work with writers but cannot send material until acceptance of article or story by magazine or publisher is final. We have found that we cannot tie up pictures on speculative ventures." One-time reproduction fee varies; $25 to $300 (for cover use). Credit line and return of pictures required.

DANDELET INTERLINKS, 126 Redwood Rd., San Anselmo CA 94960. Phone: 415-456-1260. Contact: Lucile Dandelet. West Coast stock selection and worldwide assignments. B&w and color. Charges for selection and overlong holding fees.

One-time reproduction fee depends on use and rights bought. Assignment rates per ASMP. Credit line and return of pictures required.

ALFRED DE BAT PHOTOGRAPHY, 4629 N. Dover Street, Chicago IL 60640. Contact: Alfred DeBat. 30,000 pictures of "foreign travel, U.S. travel, Chicago area scenes and activities. Mainly color — some b&w." Offers world, North American, first, one-time, and stock rights. Charges standard ASMP rates.

DE WYS INC., 60 E. 42nd St., New York NY 10017. Contact: Leo de Wys. 325,000 photos on Africa and Asia, Latin America and Europe. Collections on many primitive tribes, nomads, etc., such as Bororos in Niger, Dyaks in Borneo, Danis in West New Guinea, Campa Indians in Peru. Unusual travel photos in the U.S.A. and Europe, human interest. B&w and color transparencies only. One-time rights. Fees: $25 and up for b&w; $50 and up for color transparencies, depending on use.

DR. E. R. DEGGINGER, APSA, P.O. Box 186, Convent NJ 07961. Contact: E. R. Degginger. About 80,000 color transparencies on wide range of subject matter including pictorial and nature photography: scenics, travel, industry, science, abstracts, sports, all facets of the natural world. 35mm color. Rights to be negotiated. Charges $125 for one-time usage; covers are higher.

VIVIENNE DELLA GROTTA, 154 Hot Springs Road, Santa Barbara CA 93108. 25,000 color transparencies, 25,000 b&w photos of human interest, scenic and travel. "My specialties are babies, children, teens and pre-teens." Generally offers one-time reproduction rights unless on special arrangement. Fees: ASMP minimums.

DESIGN PHOTOGRAPHERS INTERNATIONAL, INC., 521 Madison Avenue, New York NY 10022. Phone: 212-752-3930. Contact: Alfred W. Forsyth. "Over 1½ million pictures. Comprehensive contemporary collection of worldwide subjects in color and b&w." Offers one-time reproduction rights "unless other specific terms are agreed upon and additional fee is paid for said additional rights." Fees vary "depending on media and specific use."

A. DEVANEY, INC., 40 E. 49th St., New York NY 10017. Contact: John Satterthwaite. Types of photos available: scenics, seasonal, U.S. and foreign cities, industrials, farming, human interest, religious, etc. "Our preference is to deal with editors or publishers and not with the freelance writers unless they have authorization from the editor or publisher." B&w, color. Holding fee after 15 days. One-time reproduction fee: $15 to $2,500 according to use. Credit line required for editorial use only. Return of pictures required for those not purchased.

DIVISION OF MICHIGAN HISTORY, Department of State, 3423 N. Logan St., Lansing MI 48918. Contact: David J. Olson, State Archivist. Files of original and reproduction prints and negatives accumulated over a period of time and depicting all phases of the Michigan scene. Approximately 100,000 photo items in the collection. The cost of an individual print varies according to the size and finish of the print desired. In those cases where the Division of Michigan History does not have a negative, an additional charge is made for a copy negative, which remains in the collections of the Division of Michigan History. In advance of placing any order, there is a charge of $1 as a service fee, payable to the State of Michigan. Checks and money orders are to made payable to the State of Michigan. The service fee paid is solely for the cost of handling the order, and does not include the right to further reproduction or publication. If the Commission grants the right to production, the credit line "From the collections of the Michigan Historical Commission" is requested; and, when used in publication, two copies of the article, publication or book are requested for inclusion in the Division's research library.

IRVING DOLIN PHOTOGRAPHY, 124 Ludlow St., New York NY 10002. Contact: Irving Dolin. Several thousand pictures. "All types of auto racing, in b&w and color.

Racing drivers. Files date from 1948. Most is 35mm." Prefers to sell one-time rights; depends upon fee paid. Minimum b&w fee is $35 for one-time editorial use.

DONDERO PHOTOGRAPHY, P.O. Box 1006, Park Lane Centre, Reno NV 89504. Contact: Donald Dondero. "Thousands of color and b&w pictures of all western activity in the four seasons; celebrities, mainly entertainment; gambling; legalized prostitution — mood — unidentifiable subjects." Offers one-time rights on stock pictures; exclusive rights when shooting on assignment. Fees: "one-time publication rights for area publications and small newspapers, $10 for b&w, $25 for color; standard space rates for national publications."

DRAKE WELL MUSEUM, Titusville PA 16354. Contact: Alan W. Perkins, Curator. Photographs available on oil history, with special emphasis on period before 1900, beginning in 1860. Library contains some 5,000 prints and negatives. "As most users of our collection are writing articles of scholarly interest, we try to keep the price of prints as low as possible, taking into consideration the amount of work required to provide the desired photographic material." Outright purchase price varies, usually $2 to $5 per print. Credit line required.

EASTFOTO AGENCY, 25 W. 43 St., New York NY 10036. Phone: 212-279-8846. Manager: Leah Siegel. 900,000 color and b&w photos on all aspects of life in E. Europe, China, Vietnam, etc. Industrial, political, historical, entertainment, news photos. Offers one-time rights, North American, world in English, world rights in translation. Fees vary according to usage. Minimum of $35 for one-time use of b&w photos; $125 for color.

EDITORIAL PHOTOCOLOR ARCHIVES, 342 Madison Ave., New York NY 10017. Phone: 212-697-1136. B&w photos; color transparencies: 35mm, 2¼x2¼ formats. Subjects include foreign countries and cultures, ecology, children, works of art, family life, human activities, nature. Fees vary depending on use. Generally the b&w fee is $50 and color is $100 to $125.

NIKI EKSTROM, 417 E. 75th St., New York NY 10021. Phone: 212-744-2972. Contact: Niki Ekstrom. Over 10,000 photos of writers, artists, dancers, musicians, as well as travel subjects, natural history, history of the ballet, and still life. B&w and color. Usually offers one-time rights. Fees charged follow American Society of Magazine Photographers' recommendations.

ENTHEOS/NORTHWEST, Bainbridge Island WA 98110. Contact: Steven C. Wilson. 100,000 photos in collection, "all 35mm color and 16mm color movie footage. Western U.S. and Canada, Alaska, the arctic; nature, animals, plants, man." Rights to be negotiated with each purchase; varies from exclusive to one-time educational book rights. Fees: $100 minimum per photo for one-time book rights.

EUROPEAN ART COLOR SLIDES, Peter Adelberg, Inc., 120 W. 70th St., New York NY 10023. Contact: Peter Adelberg. About 6,000 titles. "Archives of original color transparencies photographed on-the-spot from the original art object in museums, cathedrals, palaces, etc. Prehistoric to contemporary art; all media. Transparencies instantly available from New York office." Charges selection and holding fees. One-time reproduction fee varies from $55 and up for b&w to $125 and up for color. Credit line and return of pictures required.

FIELD MUSEUM OF NATURAL HISTORY, Roosevelt Rd. at Lake Shore Dr., Chicago IL 60605. No catalogue of photos available so it is necessary in ordering photos either to inspect the Museum albums or to write, giving precise specifications of what's wanted. Prices and requirements for permission to reproduce available on request. Write to Division of Publications.

FLORIDA CYPRESS GARDENS, INC., P.O. Box 1, Cypress Gardens FL 33880. Contact: Bert Lacey, Director of Public Relations. Photos of flowers, plants, scenics, boating, water skiing, fishing, camping, pretty girls. One-time reproduction fees; $300 without credit line or no charge with credit line. Return of pictures required. Cypress Gardens also has a staff of photographers that can take pictures in above categories. Prices available on request.

FLORIDA NEWS BUREAU, 107 W. Gaines St., Tallahassee FL 32304. Contact: Photo Librarian. Photographs on all areas and phases of Florida; b&w available to freelancers, b&w and color transparencies to publications. "To receive the greatest value for the tax money that supports our operation, we apply the following guidelines in filling photographic requests: 1) requests direct from publications get first priority; 2) requests from freelancers who have established a record of cooperation with us (tearsheets, credit lines and other acknowledgments) receive second priority; and 3) requests from unknown freelancers are handled on a 'time available' basis. A freelancer who has not worked with us previously should allow plenty of time on photo requests." No fees but credit line and return of transparencies required.

FORD FOUNDATION PHOTO LIBRARY, 320 E. 43 St., New York NY 10017. Phone: 212-573-5000. Over 10,000 in contact sheets. Primarily b&w. All related to projects supported by the Foundation: agricultural research, family planning, reproductive biology, public and higher education, community development. Use restricted to bona fide publications; photos must be for use in context of project. No fees; only print costs.

HARRISON FORMAN WORLD PHOTOS, 555 Fifth Ave., New York NY 10017. Contact: Harrison Forman. "Over 300,000 selected Kodachromes on countries throughout the world and numerous subjects, such as religions of the world, dances, children, recreation, native rituals, imports and exports, rivers, jungles, etc. Photos of China; light and heavy industries, art and architecture, consumer products, education, acupuncture, children, communes, transportation, irrigation projects, cities, towns, villages, and many more. Rates vary greatly, depending on editorial use, publication, repro rights offered. Our rates are in conformance with standards of ASMP."

FOTOS INTERNATIONAL, 130 West 42nd Street, New York NY 10036. Contact: Baer M. Frimer. B&w and color transparencies "covering the entertainment field in all its phases—motion pictures (international); television, radio, stage." One-time reproduction rights. Fee: $25 minimum.

FOUR BY FIVE, INC., 342 Madison Ave., New York NY 10017. Phone: 212-697-8282. Manager: Bill Beermann. Photos of people, scenics, travel, and concept. All four color catalogs available. Fees depend on usage and exposure.

FRANKLIN PHOTO AGENCY, 39 Woodcrest Ave., Hudson NH 03051. Photographs available of flowers, gardens, trees, plants, wildflowers, etc.; foreign countries; interiors and exteriors of homes, scenics (all seasons), antique cars, insects and small animals, dogs (all breeds), fish pictures, horses (all breeds), fishing and hunting scenes, some sports. Mostly 4x5 color. One-time reproduction and rental fees vary according to use and quantities printed, etc. Not less than $50 minimum. Credit line requested and return of pictures required.

FREE LIBRARY OF PHILADELPHIA, Print and Picture Department, Logan Square, Philadelphia PA 19103. Contact: Robert F. Looney. Photographs available on a wide range of subjects. Original prints: historical and fine arts. Also clippings, plates, news photos. Specialties: portrait collection (300,000 items), Philadelphia history (9,000 items), Napoleonica (3,400 items), fine prints (1,000 items). "Unfortunately we cannot send out samples of literature or groups of pictures from which selections may be made." Photocopies: $3.50 each. Credit line required for original material only.

FREELANCE PHOTOGRAPHERS GUILD, 251 Park Ave. S., New York NY 10010. Contact: Gary Elsner. Photos of all countries, U.S.A., and major cities, human interest, subjects from accidents to zoot suits. 5,000,000 b&w, color photos. Reproduction fee depends on usage.

FREEPORT MINERALS COMPANY, 161 E. 42nd St., New York NY 10017. Contact: E.C.K. Read, PR Division. Color and b&w photos of sulphur, kavlin, copper, potash, phosphates, nickel-cobalt operations. Usually no restrictions on rights offered. No fees charged.

FREER GALLERY OF ART, Smithsonian Institution, Washington DC 20560. Contact: Mrs. Willa R. Moore. Photographs of Near and Far Eastern paintings, bronzes, porcelains, wood and stone sculptures, jades, and some Whistler paintings. B&w photos and Ektachromes. $1.50 for 8x10 photos, $50 for 8x10 Ektachromes. Request to reproduce must be made in writing to the Director.

LAWRENCE FRIED PHOTOGRAPHY LTD., 330 East 49th St., Studio 1A, New York NY 10017. Contact: Lawrence Fried or Winkie Donovan. "500,000 subjects, ranging from travel throughout the world, international and domestic political figures, society, theatre (stage and film), sports, editorial and commercial illustration, military, medical, personalities in b&w and color." Rights offered flexible, "depending on negotiation in each individual case." Fees: minimum b&w, $50; minimum color, $125.

EWING GALLOWAY, 420 Lexington Ave., New York NY 10017. Photo agency offering all types, both b&w and color. Prices are based on how and where a photo will be used.

GENERAL PRESS FEATURES, 130 W. 57 St., New York NY 10019. Phone: 212-265-6842. Manager: Gabriel D. Hackett. Still photo archives, written and illustrated features. Photos of all subjects; lists available. Over 100,000 photos: historic and documentary, social changes (U.S. and Europe), music, fine arts, artists, Americana; pictorials (U.S. and France, Switzerland). Towns, landscapes, politicians, statesmen, celebrities. Both color and b&w. Rights offered open to negotiation. Fees are ASMP minimum code rates. Discount on larger orders.

A. JOHN GERACI, 279 E. Northfield Rd., Livingston NJ 07039. Contact: A. John Geraci. 100,000 b&w and color pictures of general subjects — "medical, scenic, sports, still life, people, creative." One-time rights offered. Fees: ASMP minimum and above; "depends on use and medium."

GLOBE PHOTOS, 404 Park Ave. S., New York NY 10016. Phone: 212-689-1340. Sales Manager: Elliot Stern. 10,000,000 photos of all subjects. B&w and color. Offers first rights, all rights, second rights; depends on the price. $35 minimum for b&w. $100 minimum for color.

GOVERNMENT OF SASKATCHEWAN, Photographic/Art Division, Room 3, Legislative Building, Regina, Saskatchewan, Canada. Contact: Ray W. Christensen. A large variety of photographs of all aspects of life in Saskatchewan available as prints in black and white and color, available to publishers only; supplies photos directly to publications, but not to freelance writers. Credit line required.

PETER GOWLAND, 609 Hightree Road, Santa Monica CA 90402. Contact: Peter Gowland, Alice Gowland, or Mary Lee Gowland. Over 3,000 photos catalogued and over 100,000 photos in total collection. "Beautiful women — heads, full-lengths, bathing suits, some nudes — in both b&w and color." Non-exclusive rights offered. Fees: b&w, $30 per picture for circulation under 100,000, $60 per picture for circulation over 100,000; color, $75 to $500 depending on use.

THE GRANGER COLLECTION, 1841 Broadway, New York NY 10023. Contact: William Glover, Director. A general historical picture archives encompassing the people, places, things, and events of the past in b&w prints and color transparencies. Free descriptive illustrated folder available on request. Holding fee varies and one-time reproduction fee depends on use, but minimum fee is $15. Credit line and return of pictures required.

GREATER PROVIDENCE CHAMBER OF COMMERCE, 10 Dorrance St., Providence RI 02903. Contact: William S. Northup, Vice President, Communications. Photos of Providence in b&w; limited 35mm color slides. Credit line and return of photos required.

HAROLD V. GREEN, 570 St. John's Blvd., Pointe Claire, Quebec, Canada. Contact: H. Green. Approximately 20,000 photos. "Wide spectrum of natural history and general biology photos. Also botanical and some zoological photomicrographs. Mainly 35mm color." One-time reproduction rights usually; other rights by agreement. Fees: $50 to $150, color; $25 to $75, b&w.

AL GREENE & ASSOCIATES, 1333 S. Hope St., Los Angeles CA 90015. "100,000 scenics and points of interest around the world. Mostly color on scenics and farming, otherwise b&w." Offers normal one-time reproduction rights, exclusive rights available at additional charge. Fees: $25 minimum.

ARTHUR GRIFFIN, 22 Euclid Ave., Winchester MA 01890. Phone: 617-729-2690. 50,000 color photos of New England and other states; Orient, Canada and South America; mostly scenics. Majority are 4x5 transparencies. Offers first rights. ASMP rates.

JUDSON B. HALL, PHOTOGRAPHER, R.F.D. 3, Putney VT 05346. Contact: Judson B. Hall. "Approximately 10,000 b&w pictures of Marlboro Music Festival— Rudolf Serkin, Alexander Schneider, Pablo Casals and others. Feature material on sugaring, lumbering, education, skiing, animals, seasons, Vermontiana, Sweden in 1963, Kiruna, Vasteras, Stockholm; color photos of Europe, Marlboro, Vermont scenes." Rights negotiable according to ASMP. Fees: b&w stock $35 minimum; color editorial, $100 minimum.

HARRIS & EWING, 1304 G St. N.W., Washington DC 20005. Phone: 202-NA8-8700. Over 1,000 photos of famous personalities; Presidents from 1905 to date; Supreme Court justices and other personalities of the past. Offers worldwide rights. Charges $75 minimum for one-time publication rights.

HAWAII VISITORS BUREAU, 2270 Kalakaua Ave., Honolulu HI 96815. Contact: Photo Librarian. Photographs in b&w, 35mm, and 2¼x2¼ color available on evidence of firm assignment. B&w no charge; color on loan. Credit line and return of color required.

HEDRICH-BLESSING, LTD., 450 E. Ohio St., Chicago IL 60611. Contact: Peggy Huffman. Photographs in b&w and color (all 8x10) of residential interiors and exteriors, commercial buildings, interiors and exteriors; scenics of mountains, lakes, woods, etc., mostly without people. City views, especially Chicago. One-time reproduction fees for editorial use: color, $75 to $125; b&w, $25 to $35. Credit line frequently required. Return of pictures required for color.

HEILPERN PHOTOGRAPHERS INC., Box 266, Blue Hills Station, 151 Homestead Ave., Hartford CT 06112. Contact: George S. Heilpern. Approximately 25,000 aerial photographs, mostly b&w, "of every type of subject, from close-ups of modern buildings and highway intersections to over-all views of cities." One-time reproduction rights. $40 for 7x7 contact print, $8.55 for two 8x10 enlargements of whole negatives or any portion.

KEN HEYMAN, 64 E. 55th St., New York NY 10022. Contact: Natalie Smith or Ken Heyman. "Over 15,000 b&w and color photos of family types—50 countries around the world; general emphasis on people. Also USA in categories; art, America, education, medicine, research, work, industry, American people, cities, poverty—rural and urban; agriculture, youth, military, space, sports; some personalities." Generally offers one-time, non-exclusive North American (or world) rights. Fees: b&w, $50 minimum; color, "proportionately higher."

HISTORICAL PICTURES SERVICE INC., 17 N. State St., Room 1700, Chicago IL 60602. Contact: James I. Nicholas. Approximately 3,500,000 b&w photos, photocopies, and photostats of engravings, drawings, photos, paintings, cartoons, caricatures, and maps, covering all important persons, places, things and events. Pictures sent on 60-day approval. One-time, North American, world rights, or multiple use. One-time reproduction fee: $30 average, but varies with use. Credit line and return of pictures required.

MEL HORST PHOTOGRAPHY, 441 Mt. Sidney Rd., Witmer PA 17585. "Specializes in stock photos portraying historic, quaint, scenic, Pennsylvania Dutch, and artifacts of rustic and rural Americana." B&w, color. "Charges for use of our pictures depend on how they are used. All photos are sold for non-exclusive use. All photos are available on 10 days approval. Write for free copy of current catalog. A $15 service charge is billed to every approval request" and deducted from the order.

THE LEONARD V. HUBER COLLECTION, at The Historic New Orleans Collection, 533 Royal St., New Orleans LA 70130. Contact: Research Department. About 10,000 b&w photos, engravings, lithographs of New Orleans architecture, cemeteries, customs, people, the Mardi Gras, Mississippi River steamboating and life along the river (chiefly 19th century). Charges: reproduction privilege fee of $20 per item used.

IDAHO STATE HISTORICAL SOCIETY, 610 North Julia Davis Drive, Boise ID 83706. Contact: James H. Davis. 60,000 photos. "Primarily Idaho people, scenes, buildings, farms, mines, logging industry, and Indians." B&w; "only a very few color." Offers unrestricted rights on almost all photographs. Fees: $2 to $7.95 for glossies.

THE IMAGE BANK, 88 Vanderbilt Ave., The Penthouse, New York NY 10017. Phone: 212-371-3636. Director of Photography: Lawrence Fried. High quality, color transparencies for use in advertising and publishing. About 100,000 transparencies in color only.

INFORMATION CANADA PHOTOTHEQUE, 440 Coventry Road, Ottawa, Ontario, Canada K1A OT1. Contact: Richard Sexton or C. McDonald, Photo Librarian. About 300,000 b&w photos and color transparencies "illustrating the social, economic and cultural aspects of Canada." Photos purchased for one-time use only. Pictures can be purchased for editorial and commercial use. Approval fee of $1.25. Fees vary according to the purpose for which the photos are required.

INTERNATIONAL MUSEUM OF PHOTOGRAPHY, George Eastman House, 900 East Ave., Rochester NY 14607. Contact: Martha Jenks. Collection spans the history of photography — 1839 to present day. Open to qualified researchers 1:30 to 5, Tuesdays through Fridays, or a research service is available at $7.50 an hour. Work is listed by photographer and subject. "Rates determined by circulation." Fee: $15, one-time reproduction.

INTERPRESS OF LONDON & NEW YORK, 400 Madison Ave., New York NY 10017. Phone: 212-832-2839. Manager: Jeffrey Blyth. Photos of personalities; specializing in photojournalism. Topical or unusual picture stories.

LOU JACOBS, JR., 13058 Bloomfield St., Studio City CA 91604. Contact: Lou Jacobs, Jr. About 25,000 b&w negatives and 5,000 color slides. "All manner of subjects from animals to industry, human interest to motion picture personalities, action, children, scenic material from national parks and various states." Offers first rights on previously unpublished material; one-time reproduction rights on the remainder, except for exclusive rights by agreement. Fees: b&w minimum $50 each up to five, and $40 each for five or more; color is $150 each for one to five and $125 each for more than five.

ERNST A. JAHN, 18 Blackrock Terrace, Ringwood NJ 07456. Contact: Ernst A. Jahn. 40,000 transparencies and b&w photos of subjects ranging from scenery, people at work, buildings, highways, from all Latin America, Caribbean Islands, Finland, Russia, South Africa, Middle East countries of Arab World, Tunisia, Western Europe, Galapagos Islands,. Tahiti, Easter Islands, Juan Fernandez Island, San Blas Islands and United States. Offers one-time reproduction rights. Other reproduction rights to be negotiated. Fee: b&w (one-time rights), $25; color transparency (one-time rights), $100. One copy of printed picture is required with credit line. Return required.

JUDGE STUDIO, 610 Wood St., Pittsburgh PA 15222. "500 to 1,000 old city views of Pittsburgh and air views; industrial, coal towns, bridges; all b&w prints." Offers one-time reproduction rights. $50 fee charged for one-time.

VINCENT JULIANO STUDIOS, INC., 24 E. 22nd St., New York NY 10010. "About 10,000 color and b&w photos of industry, France, Italy, Spain and other countries." Offers one-time use. Fees: color, $200 to $500; b&w, $150 to $200.

CURT W. KALDOR, 603 Grandview Dr. S., San Francisco CA 94080. Phone: 415-583-8704. Several thousand photos of scenic views and city-suburbs; street scenes, aircraft, people, architectural, railroads, shipping and boating, redwoods and timbering, and others. Offers all types of rights up through complete purchase. Charges a flat fee for purchase of reproduction rights. That fee is based on type of usage.

CLEMENS KALISCHER, Main St., Stockbridge MA 01262. Contact: Clemens Kalischer. "About 250,000 b&w and color pictures of general subjects; educational, N.E., architecture, personalities, the arts, western Europe, India, music, abstractions, religion." Offers one-time publication rights generally. Fees, depending on use: $35 to $75, b&w; $75 to $150, color.

KANSAS STATE HISTORICAL SOCIETY, 120 W. Tenth St., Topeka KS 66612. Contact: Robert W. Richmond, State Archivist. Photographs available of Indians, the American West, Kansas and Kansans generally. B&w, all sizes; 35mm and 4x5 color transparencies when feasible. Print fees: 4x5, 65c; 5x7, $1.25; 8x10, $2.50. Minimum order $1. $1 copy fee if new negative is required. Credit line required.

KENTUCKY DEPARTMENT OF PUBLIC INFORMATION, Advertising and Travel Promotion, Capitol Annex, Frankfort KY 40601. Contact: W. L. Knight, Director. B&w and color photos of scenic, historic; parks, recreation, events. No fees, but credit line and return of pictures required. General information and editorial material available on most areas.

KEYSTONE PRESS AGENCY, INC., 170 Fifth Ave., New York NY 10010. Contact: Walter Schrenck-Szill, Managing Editor. Singles and feature sets of news, political, scientific, business, human interest, animals, inventions, education, recreation, underwater, scenics, explorers, personalities, odds, pop and hippies, art, pretty girls, medical, sports, and many more. B&w and color. Pictures must be returned within two weeks; longer period for free holding must be negotiated. One-time reproduction fee for b&w, $35 minimum. Credit line and return of pictures required.

ERWIN KRAMER PHOTOGRAPHY, INC., 18-50 211th St., Bayside NY 11360. Phone: 212-224-1758 or 212-532-9095. Contact: Joan Kramer or Erwin Kramer. Over

100,000 photos including abstracts, boats, children, ethnic groups, fisheye shots, nature, people shots, scenics, teenagers, winter scenes and zoos. B&w (8x10) and color (35mm). Rights negotiable. Fees are based on budget available and photo use.

JAMES W. LA TOURRETTE, PHOTOGRAPHER, 170 N. E. 170th St., North Miami Beach FL 33162. Contact: Mr. James W. LaTourrette. About 4,000 b&w and color pictures. "2¼ and 35mm underwater color transparencies of the waters in the Florida Keys and Bahama Islands. Some 4x5 color scenics. Motor sports events; boat races, sports car races; scenics, eastern U.S., West Coast, Everglades wildlife and plants." Offers one-time rights. Fees: b&w 8x10 prints, $15 to $25; color transparencies, $25 to $50. "Color to be returned after use."

HAROLD M. LAMBERT STUDIOS, INC., 2801 W. Cheltenham Ave., Philadelphia PA 19150. Contact: R. W. Lambert. Complete photo service has over a half-million b&w photos on hand to cover all subjects from babies to skydiving, plus 50,000 color transparencies covering same subjects. Rental fee varies. "Average rates: $10 editorial use with credit line; $25 minimum promotional rate."

LAS VEGAS NEWS BUREAU, Convention Center, Las Vegas NV 89109. Contact: Don Payne, Manager. B&w, color, both stills and 16mm, available from files or shot on assignment for accredited writers with bona fide assignments. Return of color required.

LENSTOUR PHOTO SERVICE, 5301 Laurel Canyon Blvd., North Hollywood CA 91607. Contact: Eric C. Ergenbright. About 250,000 photos. "We deal mainly in color, and our basic subject matter is travel-oriented. But we do have more general categories such as water, mountains." Rights offered are "flexible; multiple-use or exclusive use." Fees: "depend entirely on use, but are in line with West Coast prices."

FRED LEWIS, 175 West 93rd St., New York NY 10025. Phone: 212-749-6848. Contact: Fred Lewis. Over 3,000 scenics, animals, night photography, travel, experimental, etc. Color transparencies; 2¼ and 35mm. Offers one-time rights and full rights. Fees range from $100 to $2,000, depending on use.

FREDERIC LEWIS, INC., 35 E. 35th St., New York NY 10016. Contact: Irwin Perton. More than 1 million b&w and color photos of "people, places, things, events, historical subjects." Offers "whatever rights are required by user." Fees: b&w, $35 to $125; color, $100 to $200.

LIAISON PHOTO AGENCY, 150 E. 58th St., New York NY 10022. Contact: Rosa Francisco. Approximately 500,000 b&w and color photos on general subjects: "political, television, movie personalities, animals, children, sports, fashion, political events in countries around the world, human interest stories, nature pictures." Domestic and foreign and sometimes world rights offered. "Fee depends on nature of material and the publication."

LICK OBSERVATORY, University of California, Santa Cruz CA 95064. Contact: Administrative Office. Users of astronomical photographs should make their selections from the standard list in the current catalogue of Astronomical Photographs available as slides or prints from negatives obtained at Lick Observatory, since it is not possible to supply views of other objects or special sizes. B&w, 2x2, 8x10, and 14x7. Color, 2x2. Catalogues are free upon written request. Purchasers are reminded that permission for use of Lick Observatory photographs for reproduction or commercial purposes must be obtained in writing from the Director of the Observatory. Fee: 55c to $4 for b&w; $1.10 for 2x2 color.

LIGHTFOOT COLLECTION, P. O. Box 554, Greenport NY 11944. Contact: Frederick Lightfoot. Over 30,000 photos on Americana (1854 to 1920); city, town, village and country scenes. Architecture, transportation, industrial, culture, famous people, wars, agriculture, mining, fisheries, as well as foreign photos. Fees depend on proposed use and quantity of pictures desired. Base price of $15 for one use; $5 for repeat use by same purchaser, and no charge for repeat use in later editions of original publication.

LINCOLN FARM TEEN CAMP, Ardsley NY 10502. Contact: Harold Loren. 4,000 8x10's in b&w of teenagers in work, recreation and social activities. Borrower to pay processing costs and postage and furnish examination copy of final use. Credit line and return of pictures required.

LINCOLN PICTURE STUDIO, 225 Lookout Dr., Dayton OH 45419. Contact: Lloyd Ostendorf. Photographs in b&w, Civil War era, 1850-1870; photographs of American scenes, people, places; special collection of photographs of Abraham Lincoln, his family, friends and notables of his day. Selecting photographs for an author or publisher is often done with only a small fee for cost of prints and mailing. The reproduction fee ($35 to $50 each) is payable when user holds them for reproduction and publication. Credit line and return of photos required.

THE LONG ISLAND HISTORICAL SOCIETY, 128 Pierrepont St., Brooklyn NY 11201. Contact: James Hurley, Executive Director. Photographs in b&w on a wide variety of subjects concerning history of Long Island. All negatives retained by the Society. Credit line required.

LOUISIANA STATE LIBRARY, P. O. Box 131, Baton Rouge LA 70821. Contact: Mrs. Harriet Callahan. This is a collection pertaining to the state of Louisiana and persons prominent in Louisiana history. Most of the photographs are b&w. It does contain color pictures during the past 5 years. This is a non-circulating, historical collection. Credit line and return of pictures required.

THOMAS LOWES PHOTOGRAPHER, 491 Delaware Ave., Buffalo NY 14202. Phone: 716-883-2650. Contact: Thomas D. Lowes. Collection of over 50,000 photos including Americana, boating, construction, experimental, farming, hippies, industrials, London, general office scenes, psychedelic, seascapes, tropical scenes, waterfronts, weather. Color transparencies; 35mm. Fees depend on reproduction rights client is interested in purchasing.

EUGENE LUTTENBERG, 26-19 141 St., Flushing NY 11354. "Large library of stock photos for the trade, including students on college campus, protest, demonstrations, textbook subjects, others. Willing to work within budgets of writers in and out of town." Fee: b&w for one-time use, $15; color for one-time use, $50.

BURTON McNEELY PHOTOGRAPHY, P.O. Box 338, Land o' Lakes Fl 33539. Contact: Burton McNeely. "About 10,000 color only: recreation, travel, romance, girls, underwater, and leisure time activities." Offers any and all rights. "Fees are based on the use of the photos, such as circulation of magazine or type of book. Minimum one-time rate for any published use is $125."

MAC'S FOTO SERVICE, 217 E. Fourth Ave., Anchorage AK 99501. Phone: 907-272-6224. 550 35mm Kodachrome slides of Alaska.

MAGNUM, 15 W. 46th St., New York NY 10036. Gerald Rosencrantz, Director. Over 1,000,000 photos. Photojournalistic reportage, documentary photography, feature and travel coverage; mainly from the thirties. B&w and color. Standard American Society of Magazine Photographers fees.

THE MAYTAG COMPANY, 403 W. Fourth St., N., Newton IA 50208. Contact: Ronald L. Froehlich, Manager, Public Information. Photos of home laundry settings; kitchens; anything in area of laundry appliances, laundering, kitchen appliances, use of dishwashers, disposers; laundering procedures. Also available are industrial shots, in-factory assembly line photos. Both b&w and color (laundry and kitchen settings), transparencies, slides. Credit line and return of color transparencies required.

MEMORY SHOP, 109 E. 12th St., New York NY 10003. Contact: Mark Ricci. "Four million photos. Specializing in movie memorabilia." Offers one-time repro rights. Fees: $5 to $15.

LOUIS MERCIER, 342 Madison Ave., New York NY 10017. Stock photographs; color scenics USA and worldwide; personalities, fashion, food, industry, and the arts. Fees: $35 minimum for b&w; $100 for color depending on use.

MERCURY ARCHIVES, 1574 Crossroads of the World, Hollywood CA 90028. Over a million photos. "Woodcuts and engravings on all subjects; pre-1900. We operate as a stock photo rental service." Full rights offered. Fees: $25 per picture on a one-time and one-use basis. Research/service fee charged when pictures not used for reproduction.

THE METROPOLITAN MUSEUM OF ART, Fifth Ave., at 82nd St., New York NY 10028. Contact: Photograph and Slide Library. History of art from ancient times to the present. B&w photos: 4x5 and 8x10 for sale; color transparencies: mostly 8x10, rental, for purposes of publication only. These cover only paintings and other objects in the Museum's collections. Research must be done by user. Copy photo price schedule available. Fee: $2.50 to $5 per 8x10 photo. Credit line required. Return required on color transparencies only; photographs made to special order are sold outright with one-time reproduction rights included.

MIAMI SEAQUARIUM, 30 Rickenbacker Causeway, Miami FL 33149. Contact: Zoe Todd. Photos in b&w and color of the Seaquarium and a variety of sea creatures. The Miami Seaquarium makes photographs available to all writers and editors free of charge, providing either the Seaquarium is given a credit line ("Miami Seaquarium Photo"), or the Seaquarium is mentioned in the caption. Return required for color only.

MINISTRY OF INDUSTRY AND TOURISM, Hearst Block, Parliament Bldgs., Toronto, Ontario, Canada. Contact: Robert Muckleston. "About 40,000 color transparencies and b&w photos of outdoors and travel, fishing, hunting, boating, camping. To be used for travel articles only. Would appreciate a credit line." No fee.

MINNESOTA HISTORICAL SOCIETY, St. Paul MN 55101. Contact: Bonnie Wilson, Reference Librarian, Audio-Visual Library. Emphasis on Minnesota subjects, especially Indians, pioneers, lumbering, mining, agriculture, transportation, recreation, and social life. Approximately 150,000 b&w photos and prints of all types. "A search will be made for requested subjects." Fee: 25¢, photoduplicates; $2, 8x10 glossy photos ($4 if negative has to be made). Reproduction use fee charged for commercial use. Credit line required.

MISSISSIPPI DEPARTMENT OF ARCHIVES AND HISTORY, P.O. Box 571, Jackson MS 39205. Contact: Director, Archives and Library Division. Photos, Civil War prints from *Harper's Weekly* and Frank Leslie's *Weekly* (some hand-colored); prominent Mississippians; historic spots and other Mississippi scenes; historic buildings and antebellum mansions; Mississippi River and steamboats. A search will be made through readily available sources, but staff is too small to undertake extensive research. Charge: $2.50 for positive photostat. Cannot make glossies, but will make available to local photographers for copying. Credit line required.

MISSOURI HISTORICAL SOCIETY, Jefferson Memorial Bldg., St. Louis MO 63112. Contact: Miss Gail R. Guidry, Curator, Pictorial History Gallery. B&w photocopies and color transparencies of Missouri and Western life. Fee for photocopies and reproduction fees will be quoted upon request for specific item, and information as to how picture is to be used and by whom. Research fee may be incurred if unusual amount of staff time is required to fill order. Negatives become property of Society. No slides permitted. Charges one-time reproduction fee. Credit line required.

GEORGE A. MOFFITT, COLLECTION, 306 W. 94th St., New York NY 10025. Contact: George A. Moffitt. Photos of pre-war American and Continental standard and custom cars of the movies with stars that owned them; cars shown with public figures of the past; custom body builders' renderings; antique cars of early American production; racing car scenes, b&w and color; also post-war photos of American and Continental production. One-time reproduction fee for editorial use: $25, b&w; $75, color.

MONTANA DEPARTMENT OF HIGHWAYS, Montana Travel Promotion Unit, Helena MT 59601. Contact: Josephine Brooker, Director. Scenic, historic, recreational, official (state seal, flag, etc.) photos in 8x10 glossy b&w and 35mm. 2¼ square, 4x5 color transparencies. Writer receives a memo invoice with shipment of photos. If photos are returned within reasonable time, in same condition, invoice is canceled. Credit line required. Return of pictures required for color only. Editorial material also available.

MONTGOMERY PICTURES, Box 722, Las Vegas NM 87701. Contact: C.M. Montgomery. "6,000 4x5 color transparencies and 10,000 35mm color transparencies of animals, birds, reptiles, flora, scenics, state and national parks, ghost towns, historic, Indian and petroglyphs." One-time reproduction rights in one country preferred; all other rights by negotiation. Fees: "ASMP rates, where applicable. Otherwise, the publisher's current rates; but not less than $25 per transparency."

THE MUSEUM OF MODERN ART, Film Stills Archive, 11 W. 53rd St., New York NY 10019. Contact: Mrs. Mary Corliss. Approximately 3,000,000 b&w stills on foreign and American productions, film personalities, and directors. Duplicates of original stills are sold at a cost of $5 per still. Credit line required.

MUSEUM OF NAVAHO CEREMONIAL ART, INC., P.O. Box 5153, 704 Camino Lejo, Santa Fe NM 87501. Contact: Director. Photos available in b&w and color. "A few years ago a new administration at this museum took over a photographic collection which was uncatalogued and unlabeled for the most part. Time has not yet permitted us to get this collection into readily usable order. Within due time we shall appreciate more attention given to our collection and offerings." Copy prints, $1 to $15. One-time reproduction fee: $25, b&w; $75, color. Credit line required.

MUSEUM OF NEW MEXICO, P. O. Box 2087, Santa Fe NM 87501. Contact: Photo Archives. 70,000 photos available: archaeology, anthropology, railroads, Southwestern Americana, Southwestern Indians. Some 19th Century foreign holdings including Oceania, Japan, Middle East. Copy prints $2 and up. Reproduction/publication fees and credit lines required. Catalogs and photographer indexes available.

MUSEUM OF SCIENCE, Science Park, Boston MA 02114. Contact: Bradford Washburn. Contact prints of Alaskan and Alpine mountains and glaciers. All b&w. Copy prints, $5 and up. One-time reproduction fee $30. Credit line required.

MUSEUM OF THE AMERICAN INDIAN, Broadway at 155th St., New York NY 10032. Contact: Carmelo Guadagno. The Photographic Archives of the Museum include negatives, b&w prints, and color transparencies from Indian cultures throughout the Western hemisphere. The various categories present a selection of everyday customs, ceremonial paraphernalia, costumes and accessories, dwellings and physical types from a majority of areas. B&w photos, 35mm and 4x5 color transparencies. 3,500 Kodachrome slides; list available. Send stamp. One-time editorial reproduction fee is $10 for b&w and $25 for color. Credit line required. Folder of information available; send stamp.

MUSEUM OF THE CITY OF NEW YORK, 1220 Fifth Ave., New York NY 10029. Contact: Photo Library. Photographs on New York City historical, geographical, and social material; portraits, antiques, etc., which are in the Museum's collection. Also Currier & Ives prints. Two best-known collections are the Jacob A. Riis pictures of the Lower East Side slums and the Byron photos. Sells b&w prints outright. Color transparencies sent on 3 months' rental and must be returned. $3 per 8x10 glossy print from available negatives; plus $10 for permission to reproduce in a book or magazine. Write for prices on new photo and color transparencies. Material may not be taken out "on approval" or for selection. Credit line required.

THE MUSICAL MUSEUM, Deansboro NY 13328. Contact: Arthur H. Sanders. An extensive collection of musical antiques, mostly restored, refinished, etc., including melodeons, organs, nickelodeons, music boxes, zithers, harpsichords, etc. "We are limited with photographic equipment and manpower. If we have a suitable photo, we would be happy to sell it, but probably writer would prefer to have a photo taken — with or without color, with or without other items, etc., and we will work with him in this case." Credit line required. Office open from 10 A.M. to 5 P.M. daily.

HANS NAMUTH, LTD., 157 West 54th St., New York NY 10019. Contact: Hans Namuth. "About 5,000 b&w and color photos of people (American artists); architecture (modern houses)." One-time U.S. reproduction rights offered. Fees: b&w, $50 minimum; color, $125 minimum.

NATIONAL AIR AND SPACE MUSEUM, Smithsonian Institution, Washington DC 20560. Contact: Catherine D. Scott, Librarian. 900,000 photos. Aviation and space; both b&w and color. Fees: $2.50 per 8x10 b&w glossy or matte. Color, $10. Credit must be given to NASM. Checks are made payable to the Smithsonian Institution.

NATIONAL ARCHIVES AND RECORDS SERVICE, 8th and Pennsylvania Avenue, N.W., Washington DC 20408. Contact: James W. Moore, Director, Audiovisual Archives Division, or William Leany, Archivist, Audiovisual Archives Division. Over five million "b&w, color, posters, photographs of art works, and original art works, dating from the 18th century to the present. In addition to documenting activities of some 125 federal agencies, they illustrate the social, economic, cultural, political, and diplomatic history of America from the earliest colonial times to the present, and many aspects of life in other parts of the world. Included are several large collections such as the Mathew Brady Civil War photographs, the picture files of the Paris branch of the *New York Times,* 1900 to 1950, and the Heinrich Hoffmann files illustrating activities of the Nazi party in Germany, 1923 to 1945. Many of our photos are in the public domain and may be freely reproduced. Others are subject to copyright and/or other restrictions imposed by the agency of transfer or donor, and user must negotiate release with the owner of rights to these items." Fees: $3 per 8x10 print; $5.80 per 4x5 color transparency; $1.20 per 2x2 slide.

NATIONAL AUDUBON SOCIETY, Photo Section, 950 Third Ave., New York NY 10022. Contact: Sam Dasher. B&w and color photos available of animals, marine life, plant life, insects, conservation, pollution, ecology, scenics, weather microphotos. Modest fee for making selection. Also charges holding fee. One-time reproduction fee depends on usage. Credit line and return of pictures required.

NATIONAL CATHOLIC NEWS SERVICE, 1312 Massachusetts Ave. N. W., Washington DC 20005. Phone: 202-659-6722. Contact: A.E.P. Wall, Director and Editor-in-Chief; Thomas N. Lorsung, Photo Editor. Collection covers the religious, social and cultural life of the Third World. Offers one-time publication rights. Fees depend on usage and begin at $7.50 for b&w. No color.

NATIONAL COAL ASSOCIATION, 1130 17th St. N.W., Washington DC 20036. Contact: Herbert Foster. 2,000 photos, "mostly b&w shots of bituminous coal production, transportation and use, and reclamation of mined land. Some color transparencies of coal production, many showing land reclamation. Most are modern — no historical pix." Allows free editorial use. No fees. "Credit line to NCA."

NATIONAL GALLERY OF ART, Washington DC 20565. Contact: Kathleen Ewing, Photographic Services. Photographs available of all objects in the Gallery's collections, from medieval to present times, except drawings, etchings, and engravings, and renderings of American folk-art objects. B&w glossy prints. For photographs of drawings, etchings, etc., contact Department of Graphic Arts, Mr. Fred Cain; for renderings of American folk-art objects, contact Index of American Design, Dr. Grose Evans, Curator. For color transparencies or Kodachromes, contact Katherine Warrick, Director of Public Information. "A modest charge is made for these services; please write for further information." Credit line and return of pictures required following their use in reproduction processes. Permission for reproduction is granted in writing for each specific item. Permission is not granted for advertising purposes.

NATIONAL LIBRARY OF MEDICINE, 860 Rockville Pike, Bethesda MD 20014. Contact: Chief, History of Medicine Division. Photographs available on the history of medicine (portraits, institutions, scenes), not related to current personalities, events, or medical science. B&w. Copy prints: 8x10, $2 and up. Credit line required. Prices vary according to service provided, and are subject to change without notice. No pictures sent out on approval.

NATIONAL PHOTOGRAPHY COLLECTION, Public Archives of Canada, 395 Wellington St., Ottawa, Canada K1A ON3. Contact: Reference Officers. 3,500,000 photos, "all Canadian historical subjects: documenting the political, economic, industrial, military, social and cultural life of Canada from 1850 to the present, with a concentration on material prior to 1950. B&w negatives and prints; color transparencies. On unrestricted or non-copyright material, reproduction rights are normally granted upon request after examination of a statement of purpose, or legitimate use in publication, film or television production, exhibition or research." Fees: b&w 8x10 print, $2.75.

NEBRASKA STATE HISTORICAL SOCIETY, 1500 R St., Lincoln NE 68508. Contact: Marvin F. Kivett, Director. Photographs available of historical subjects pertaining to Nebraska and trans-Missouri west; agriculture; steamboats; Indians. B&w 8x10 glossy prints $2. Credit line required.

NEIKRUG GALLERIES, INC., 224 E. 68th St., New York NY 10021. Contact: Mrs. Marjorie Neikrug. Collection of several hundred contemporary and antique photos. B&w and color. Offered for one-time use at fee varying with size of reproduction, whether color or b&w.

NEVILLE PUBLIC MUSEUM, 129 S. Jefferson, Green Bay WI 54301. Contact: James L. Quinn, Director. Historical photographs available pertinent to northeastern Wisconsin, especially Green Bay area in b&w and some contemporary color. Photos available at cost only for educational purposes. Museum credit line required.

THE NEW JERSEY HISTORICAL SOCIETY, 230 Broadway, Newark NJ 07104. Contact: Howard W. Wiseman, Curator. Photos available of historical houses, buildings, streets, etc., filed by the name of the town (must know the name of town; not filed by subject matter). Charge for making selection: $1.25. One-time reproduction fee $10 each. Credit line required.

THE NEW YORK BOTANICAL GARDEN LIBRARY, Bronx Park, New York NY 10458. Contact: Mr. Charles R. Long, Administrative Librarian or Ms. Helen Schlanger, Photo Librarian. "Collection being reorganized. Limited access." B&w

photos (original and copy), glass negatives, film negatives, clippings, postcards, old prints, original drawings and paintings. Subjects: botany, horticulture; portraits of botanists and horticulturists; pictures from seed catalogues. One-time reproduction fee $35 per print for original b&w photos, $100 for original 35mm color. Credit line required.

NEW YORK CONVENTION AND VISITORS BUREAU, 90 E. 42nd St., New York NY 10017. Contact: John P. MacBean. B&w glossies of New York City visitor-interest sights. No factories, industrial sites, etc. Only city sights; no N.Y. State photos. No fees, but credit line requested.

THE NEW YORK HISTORICAL SOCIETY, 170 Central Park W., New York NY 10024. Phone: 212-TR3-3400. Contact: Print Room. About 20,000 photos primarily New York City and state; some other American locations; portraits, city views, buildings, daguerreotypes; mostly 1850 to 1920, some later photos. B&w. Almost unrestricted use upon payment of reproduction fee. Fee varies with size of photo desired, whether or not already have a negative, etc.

NEW ZEALAND EMBASSY, 19 Observatory Circle N.W., Washington DC 20008. Contact: Information Officer. A limited number of photos and color slides of a general nature about New Zealand. No fees, but credit line and return of pictures requested.

NEWARK MUSEUM, 49 Washington St., Newark NJ 07101. Contact: Public Relations Office. Photos available on American art (18th, 19th and 20th centuries; painting and sculpture); Oriental art (especially Tibet, Japan, and India); decorative arts (furniture, jewelry, costumes). 8x10 b&w photos. Fee: $2 for copy prints; $10, one-time reproduction fee. 4x5 transparencies. $60 sale or $35 for 3-month rental, including reproduction fee. Credit line required.

NEWSWEEK BOOKS, 444 Madison Ave., New York NY 10022. Contact: Laurie Winfrey. Collection of about 8,000 photos on art of all kinds, architecture, American and world history. B&w and color. Offers reproduction rights for one-time, non-exclusive use. Charges $35 to $50 for b&w; up to $150 for color.

NORTH CAROLINA DIVISION OF ARCHIVES AND HISTORY, 109 East Jones Street, Raleigh NC 27611. Contact: Photographic Unit. Approximately 250,000 photos and 5,000 color slides. "The subjects of all our graphic collections primarily are related to N.C. history or to national or world history which has some effect on North Carolina. Currently, we are in the process of compiling an extensive collection of photographs of historic buildings and places in this state as a part of the National Register project of the National Park Service." Photographs, lithographs, drawings, paintings, and other graphic representations: b&w and color negatives. "Where restricted and non-copyrighted materials are concerned, our photographs may be reproduced simply by (1) paying the nominal purchase price for a print or negative and (2) giving the following credit line: North Carolina Division of Archives and History." Fees: $3.50 to $8.00 for b&w; 35mm color "usually between 75¢ and $4, depending on size of an order, etc. Schools, students, state agencies, and nonprofit educational institutions may receive b&w prints at $2.00 each, except for the 16x20 size which is $5.00; 50¢ each for 35mm duplicate transparencies."

NORTH CAROLINA MUSEUM OF ART, Raleigh NC 27611. Contact: Head, Collections Research and Publications Branch. 8x10 b&w glossies; 2x2 color slides; 4x5 color transparencies on permanent collections. Fees: $1.50 for glossies; 75¢ for original slides; 50¢ for duplicate slides; $35 for transparencies. Permission to publish is required.

NOTMAN PHOTOGRAPHIC ARCHIVES, McCord Museum, 690 Sherbrooke St., W., Montreal, Quebec, Canada. Contact: Stanley Triggs. 400,000 photos. "Portraits, landscapes, city views, street scenes, lumbering, railroad construction, trains, Indians, fishing, etc." Offers one-time publication rights. Fees: $15 for most publications. "Photographs on loan only — to be returned after use."

OREGON HISTORICAL SOCIETY, 1230 S.W. Park Ave., Portland OR 97205. Contact: Richard H. Engeman, Photographs Librarian. Several hundreds of thousands — 300,000 catalogued photos. "All subjects in geographical range: Pacific Northwest (Oregon, Washington, Idaho, British Columbia), Alaska, North Pacific. Most b&w prints and negatives; also color transparencies and negatives, engravings, lantern slides (color and b&w), etc. Virtually all material is available for publication; credit line required." Fees: $2.50 usual for magazine publication, in addition to processing charges.

ORGANIZATION OF AMERICAN STATES, Central Photographic Collection, Columbus Memorial Library, Washington DC 20006. Contact: Carl L. Headen, Photograph Librarian. Prints of Latin America, Barbados, Jamaica, Trinidad, and Tobago. "Prints cover agriculture, antiquities, art, cities and towns, education, history, industry, minerals, native types, natural history, portraits, public welfare, recreation, topography, and transportation." B&w prints. No fees. Credit line required. Return of pictures required.

OUTDOOR PHOTOGRAPHERS LEAGUE, 4486 Point Loma Ave., San Diego CA 92107. Contact: Ormal I. Sprungman, Manager. B&w and color transparencies on hunting, fishing, camping, boating, trailering, natural history; plant, animal, bird and fish life; ecology subjects. Standard fee varies with use. Credit line requested. Return of transparencies after use required.

PACIFIC RESOURCES INC., Aerial Photographic Division, Oakland Airport Bldg., L 643, P. O. Box 2416, Airport Station, Oakland CA 94614. Contact: Jack E. Logan. Aerial photographs of western U.S. only. B&w, color. Outright purchase price: b&w 8x10, $50; color transparency, $100. One-time reproduction fee: b&w, $25; color, $50. Credit line and return of pictures required.

PAN AMERICAN AIRWAYS, Pan Am Bldg., New York NY 10017. Attn: Photo Library. Contact: Ruth Keary, Manager-Film. Photos of Pan Am equipment (airplanes, etc.). B&w and color. Photos supplied for use within travel context. Charges reproduction fee (lab costs) to supply duplicates, whether b&w or color. Fee varies depending upon what is required.

PEABODY MUSEUM OF SALEM, East India Square, Salem MA 01970. Contact: Curators of the various departments. Photographs available: principally maritime history and ethnology of non-European peoples. B&w and color. 250,000 negatives on file. Credit line required. Send for free price list and descriptive brochure.

PENGUIN PHOTO, 663 Fifth Ave., New York NY 10022. Contact: Mrs. Ena Fielden. Over 50,000 photos in b&w and color. Accent is on the field of entertainment: film, stage, music, dance, radio, and TV. "Photos are for strictly editorial use only." $15 to $150 up for b&w, depending on use and layout. Color minimum is $75 and up. "Photos are on loan from collection and must be returned after use in condition as submitted."

ROBERT PERRON, 104 E. 40th St., New York NY 10016. Phone: 212-661-8796. Photos of nature, coastal scenes, architecture. About 10,000 in collection. Offers one-time rights. Fees: $50 for b&w, $150 for color, editorial.

PHILADELPHIA MUSEUM OF ART, Photographic Department, P. O. Box 7646, Philadelphia PA 19101. Contact: Alfred J. Wyatt, Director of Photographic Services. 250,000 photos and color transparencies. "Paintings, prints, furniture, silver, sculpture, ceramics, arms and armor, coffers, jades, glass, metal objects, ivory objects, textiles, tapestries, costumes, period rooms; photos of works of art in our museum." 8x10 b&w and 5x7 color transparencies. "World rights of reproduction will be granted if the publication is educational in nature. Reproduction fees will be waived and we will request instead that two copies of the book be sent to us upon publication. Commercial reproduction fees are charged for use of material on covers of books and magazines." Fees: $1.50 for 8x10 b&w; $50 and up for color.

PHOTO MEDIA, LTD., 5 West 20th St., New York NY 10011. Contact: W. Walter Hayum or Mitchell Harte. "In excess of 100,000 color photos. Human interest, paperbacks, advertising, children, couples, mood, nature, landscapes, record covers." One-time repro rights offered. Fee: "domestic charge minimum $150, but fee depends on rights, use, and picture."

PHOTO RESEARCHERS, INC., AND RAPHO DIVISION, 60 E. 56 St., New York NY 10022. Phone: 212-758-3420. Photo Researchers Manager, Jane S. Kinne; Rapho Division Manager, Mrs. Suzanne Goldstein. Worldwide geographical coverage including aerials, prominent personalities; contemporary American scene (political, economic, social, educational and family life). Topical subjects: population explosion, ecology, drugs, old age, law and order, energy crisis, poverty, consumerism, medicine, encounter and liberation movements; camera studies; abstracts and geometrics. Offers USA, North American, English language and world reproduction rights. Fees begin at $50 for b&w; at $125 for color.

PHOTO TRENDS, 1472 Broadway, New York NY 10036. Contact: R. Eugene Keesee. "About 300,000 b&w and color (mostly 35mm) photos. Subjects: children, education, scientific subjects such as photomicrographs, people in places around the world, scenics around the world, wonders and disasters occurring on planet Earth." For editorial, offers "usually North American rights only. World rights available for 95% of the materials." Fees: "pretty much ASMP rates."

PHOTO WORLD, 251 Park Ave. S., New York NY 10010. Phone: 212-777-4214. Manager: Arnold M. Namm. Photos of personalities, history, World War II, and all other subjects; some specialties. 1,000,000 photos in collection. Rights offered negotiable. Fees depend on reproduction rights.

PHOTOGRAPHY COLLECTION, Special Collections Division, University of Washington Libraries, Seattle WA 98195. Contact: Curator of Photography. Collection of 200,000 images devoted to history of photography in Pacific Northwest and Alaska from 1860-1920. Most early photographers of the two regions are represented, including Eric A. Hegg (Gold Rush), Wilhelm Hester (Maritime), and George T. Emmons (Anthropology). Special topical assemblies maintained for localities, industries and occupations of Washington Territory and State, for Seattle history, for Indian peoples and totem culture, for ships, whaling and for regional architects and architecture. No printed catalog available; will provide xeroxes of selected views (at 10¢ each) upon receipt of specific statements of needs. No use fees are charged. Picture credits required for publication and television uses.

PHOTOGRAPHY FOR INDUSTRY (PFI), 850 Seventh Ave., New York NY 10019. Contact: Charles E. Rotkin. Over 100,000 photos, color and b&w. Maintains library of creative photography for Annual Reports and prestige publications, industrial stock color, and low-level aerial photographs (Europe, U.S. and Asia), and is available for magazine, advertising, and industrial photography on location; special aerial assignments, domestic and foreign. Offers any rights desired, except all rights. Fees charged equivalent to ASMP rates for one-time use.

PHOTO-LAB, 426 Gravier St., New Orleans LA 70130. Phone: 504-523-3881. Manager: Marcus Streng. 5,000 color transparencies and b&w scenics of South Europe, North Africa; some Far East, Midwest; animals. Offers one-time rights. Fees: $50 per transparency, $35 per b&w print.

PHOTOPHILE, 2311 Kettner Blvd., San Diego CA 92101. Contact: Gordon Menzie. Supplies creative, color transparencies for advertising, textbook, magazine and other publications. Photophile maintains current files on a wide range of subject matter: topical southwestern U.S. and Mexican stock, Europe, underwater life, human interest situations, Africa, and the Far East. $85 minimum transaction fee. Prices vary according to reproduction size, publication distribution, size of run, and purchase of rights. Transparencies may be held for 30 days. Extension time may be requested. Penalty fee of $1 per day per picture for failure to return consigned transparencies, or $500 for loss or damage.

PHOTOVILLAGE, 117 Waverly Place, #5E, New York NY 10011. Phone: 212-260-6051. Contact: Geoffrey R. Gove. Collection of over 50,000 photos, primarily geographic coverage, as well as Americana, ecology, sports, special events, cover graphics, personalities. B&w and color. Offers non-exclusive reproduction rights. Minimum fee of $50 for b&w; $150 minimum for color. Will shoot to order for $150 minimum purchase.

PHOTOWORLD, Division of FPG, 251 Park Ave. S., New York NY 10010. Contact: Fran Black. 3 million b&w photos dating back to the late 1800's. Historical, human interest, sports, and personalities. One-time reproduction rights unless client specifies otherwise. Price depends entirely upon use.

PICTORIAL PARADE, INC., 130 W. 42 St., New York NY 10036. Phone: 212-695-0353. Manager: Baer M. Frimer. Photos of all subjects.

PICTUREMAKERS, INC., 1 Paul Dr., Succasunna NJ 07876. Phone: 201-584-3000. President: Bill Stahl. Photos of all subjects.

ENOCH PRATT FREE LIBRARY, 400 Cathedral St., Baltimore MD 21201. Contact: Maryland Department. B&w 8x10 glossies of Maryland and Baltimore: persons, scenes, buildings, monuments. "Copy prints at nominal fees." Credit line required.

PUBLIC ARCHIVES OF CANADA, 395 Wellington St., Ottawa 4, Ont., Canada. Contact: Georges Delisle, Chief, Picture Division. Photos available on Canadiana: historical views, events; portraits. B&w and color. Print fee, minimum charge $2.75. Credit line required.

QUEENS BOROUGH PUBLIC LIBRARY, Long Island Division, 89-11 Merrick Blvd., Jamaica NY 11432. Contact: Davis Erhardt. B&w original photos, glass negatives, clippings, postcards, old prints. Subjects: Long Island history, all phases. Print fees charged; no reproduction fees. Credit line required.

REFLEX PHOTOS INC., 186 Fifth Ave., New York NY 10010. Phone: 212-691-1505. Manager: Lawrence Woods. 6,000 photos. Life in b&w and color. Offers one-time rights, first rights, exclusive rights, translation rights, distribution rights and promotion rights. Service charge, holding fee, losses and damage protection negotiable.

RELIGIOUS NEWS SERVICE, 43 W. 57th St., New York NY 10019. Contact: David B. Sommer, Photo Editor. Over 200,000 items on file. "Religious and secular topics. Largest collection of religious personalities in world. Also fine selection of scenics, human interest, artwork, seasonals, social issues, history, cartoons, etc. RNS can be called on for almost all photo needs, not just religious topics." B&w only. Offers one-time rights. Fees: $12.50 to $15.00.

REMINGTON ART MUSEUM, 303 Washington St., Ogdensburg NY 13669. Contact: Mildred B. Dillenbeck, Curator. Photos of Frederic Remington paintings, watercolors, drawings, and bronzes. B&w prints and color transparencies available. The largest and most complete collection of works by Remington. Charges rental and one-time reproduction fee. "$6 photographer's fee for b&w; $35 photographer's fee for color." Credit line and return of pictures required.

RHODE ISLAND DEPARTMENT OF ECONOMIC DEVELOPMENT, Tourist Promotion Division, One Weybosset Hill, Providence RI 02903. Contact: Leonard J. Panaggio, Assistant Director. 2,500 to 5,000 photos. Subjects deal primarily with those used in the promotion of tourism and the state of Rhode Island. 8x10 b&w photos, 35mm color transparencies. Color transparencies must be returned. Any pictures or color transparencies can be used for editorial purposes. Any and all of material is available.

RICHARDS COMMERCIAL PHOTO SERVICE, 734 Pacific Ave., Tacoma WA 98402. Contact: Mr. Ed Richards. "Thousands of b&w and color photos of children, people, animals, farms, forests, all types of industry." Rights offered: "any required." Fees: $25 minimum.

H. ARMSTRONG ROBERTS, 4203 Locust St., Philadelphia PA 19104. Phone: 215-386-6300. 420 Lexington Ave., Room 509, New York NY 10017. Phone: 212-532-6076. Tina Veiga, Manager. 203 N. Wabash Ave., Room 819, Chicago Il 60601. Phone: 312-726-0880. Howard Cox, Manager. Over one-half million stock photographs of all subjects in color and b&w. Also historical file. Catalog and/or 10-day fee approval submissions available. Research and holding fees not generally charged. Reproduction fees vary according to nature and extent of media.

SAN FRANCISCO MARITIME MUSEUM, Foot of Polk St., San Francisco CA 94109. Contact: Mrs. Matilda Dring or Mrs. Danee McFarr. Photos of West Coast shipping, deep-water sail, steamships, etc. Mostly b&w, some color (contemporary ships). Print fee: $2.50 (8x10 glossy). Textbooks repro fee is $7.50. Credit line required.

SANFORD PHOTO ASSOCIATES, 219 Turnpike Road, Manchester NH 03104. Contact: Miss Gene Tobias, Freelance Photography Coordinator. Over 50,000 photos in collection. "Color (primarily 4x5 transparencies), 35mm, 2¼, some 8x10 transparencies; color negatives — mostly New England scenics and varied all-occasion type photographs. B&w 8x10 scenics and miscellaneous subjects. Our files in both b&w and color cover a wide range of subjects: flowers, children, animals, houses, industry, pollution, soft focus, some other areas in U.S. and many foreign countries. Usually one-time reproduction rights, but more specifically this would depend on whatever the use." Fees: (minimum for one-time reproduction use) 8x10 b&w, $35; color, $125.

SCALA FINE ARTS PUBLISHERS, INC., 28 W. 44th St., New York NY 10036. Contact: Ann Byford, Assistant Manager. Photos of art objects. "Chronologically, the range is from the caveman to the present; geographically, we cover all Europe, the Near East, and India with a specialty collection from Japan and a small selection of Mayan and Incan objects." Photos available of "paintings, sculpture, architecture, tapestry, pottery, manuscript illumination, and a wide variety of other art styles." Has archive of scientific subjects; "the main topics covered include botany, zoology, geography, geology, biology, medicine, marine life (with special emphasis on underwater), and a wide range of photographs of farming, industry, living conditions, etc., around the world. We represent the famous Alinari collection in the United States. These b&w photographs for rental include objects of art from Greece, Italy, Germany, France, and numerous other countries." B&w photos; color transparencies, 35mm to 8x10. Fee: "varies according to the usage. We will submit photos on approval."

EARL SCOTT PHOTOGRAPHY, 4169 W. 2nd St., Los Angeles CA 90004. Contact: Earl Scott. About 2,000 photos. "Places and scenes of the west; poster and greeting card art; flowers, cattle, horses, ocean; semi-abstract, design, mood. All 35mm Kodachrome." Offers exclusive, first or limited rights depending on use and price. Fees "depend entirely on use."

SY SEIDMAN COLLECTION OF AMERICANA, 4 W. 22nd St., New York NY 10010. Contact: Sy Seidman. "The Americana Collection of Sy Seidman deals mainly with social events which have some relation to industry, business, labor. The Collection offers a novel approach to pictorial history." Offers one-time reproduction rights. Fees: $50 for b&w; $150 for color ("average size usage").

SEKAI BUNKA PHOTO, 501 Fifth Ave., Room 2102, New York NY 10017. Phone: 212-490-2180. Manager: Barbara Jurin Reid. Over 100,000 color and b&w photos of Japan and the Far East for usage in New York branch, including modern scenes, historical art treasures, temples/shrines, architecture, costume, manners, etc. Expanding to similar coverage, especially of people and their life styles in the United States (including calendar pin-ups) for usage in Tokyo office branch. B&w are quality 5x7 or larger glossy and color are usually 2¼, 4x5 or larger. Usually offers one-time rights, non-exclusive usage, although other rights are negotiable. No research or holding fees on routine assignments. Discounts from basic prices for quantity use in same work. Basic price minimums (generally $50 for b&w and $75 for color) vary depending upon usage, quantity; other factors depending upon final fee negotiations. Available for special assignments in Japan and Far East.

THE SHAKER MUSEUM, Shaker Museum Rd., Old Chatham NY 12136. Contact: Robert F. W. Meader, Director. Photographs of Shaker buildings and members; museum galleries; some furniture and other artifacts; B&w only. Charge for making selection $1. Print fees: for first requested copy if not in files, $10, including one 8x10 print; second prints, or if from negative in files, $5. Negative of any requested copy stays in files. Billed by photographer. Credit line required.

ANN ZANE SHANKS, 201 B East 82nd St., New York NY 10028. Contact: Ann Zane Shanks. "About 5,000 items. Stock picture file, color and b&w of people — from the very young to the very old. Celebrities, scenes, hospitals, travel, and interracial activities." Offers one-time rights only. Fees: $35 minimum, b&w; $125 minimum, color. Credit line requested.

RAY SHAW, Studio 5B, 255 W. 90th St., New York NY 10024. Contact: Ray Shaw. "Has stock photographs of Algeria, Denmark, England, Iceland, India, Iran, Morocco, Switzerland, Tunisia, Turkey, U.S.A., American Indians, etc. 75,000 b&w stock photos; 60,000 color."

SHOSTAL ASSOCIATES, INC., 60 East 42nd St., New York NY 10017. Extensive all-color file on every subject of general interest, contemporary and traditional, as well as complete geographical coverage of all countries of the world. Offers any reproduction rights desired. Fees depend on rights purchased.

SICKLES PHOTO-REPORTING SERVICE, P. O. Box 98, 410 Ridgewood Rd., Maplewood NJ 07040. Contact: Gus Sickles, Jr. About 25,000 photos of business, industry, agriculture, retailing distribution. Offers various rights. Fees: ASMP rates or state what you can afford to pay for each job. "Basically we are an assignment service."

SISTO ARCHIVES, 3531 South Elmwood Avenue, Berwyn IL 60402. Contact: John A. Sisto. Over 3 million "historical photos and old prints, over four thousands subject categories." B&w and color available. "The photographs may be reproduced in the manner specified on our invoice. They may not be syndicated, rented, loaned, or re-used in any manner without special permission." Fees: "minimum $25, maximum $500."

SKYVIEWS SURVEY INC., 50 Swalm St., Westbury NY 11590. Phone: 516-333-3600. Over 100,000 photos of aerial subjects in northeast region of United States. B&w and color. Catalogued geographically and by subject. Publication use rights varies from single use in local advertising to national advertising. Fees range from $37.50 to $200 and over.

BRADLEY SMITH PHOTOGRAPHY, 2871 Inverness Dr., LaJolla CA 92037. Phone: 714-453-7010. Manager: Sharon Weldy. Photos of all subjects. Color and b&w; 35mm and 4x5 and larger. Folkways and scenics (Japan, Spain, Mexico, United States, West Indies, India); Paintings of the world (all periods, prehistoric to modern; Spanish, French, Mexican, Japanese, Chinese); Arts and crafts of the United States. Offers all rights. All rates as outlined in the ASMP *Business Practices and Photography Guide.*

DICK SMITH PHOTOGRAPHY, P. O. Box X, North Conway NH 03860. Contact: Dick Smith. "10,000 b&w and 5,000 4x5 color transparencies. Scenics, tourist attractions, geologic and geographic features, farming, animals, lakes, mountains, snow scenes, historic sites, churches, covered bridges, flowers and gardens, aerials, Atlantic coast, skiing, fishing, camping, national parks. These are mostly of New England, but I do have some of the South and West." Offers usually one-time rights for the specific use. Fees: minimum b&w $35, minimum color $100.

SOPHIA SMITH COLLECTION, Women's History Archive, Smith College, Northampton MA 01060. Contact: Mary-Elizabeth Murdock, Ph.D., Director. About 5,000 photos emphasizing women's history and general subjects; abolition and slavery, American Indians, outstanding men and women, countries (culture, scenes), U.S. military history, social reform, suffrage, women's rights. Mainly b&w or sepia. Offers U.S. rights, one-time use only. Print fee based on cost of reproduction of print plus intended use. *Picture Catalog* including fee schedule available for $6 postpaid.

SMITHSONIAN INSTITUTION, National Anthropological Archives, Washington DC 20560. There are approximately 50,000 b&w negatives pertaining to the more than 350 Indian tribes of North America in this collection. Most of the photographs were taken between 1860 and 1900. Collections include about 14,000 photographs of anthropological subjects throughout the world. Print fees: 8x10, $1.50 plus mailing charges; advance payment required. Credit line required.

SOCCER ASSOCIATES, 2 Holly Drive, New Rochelle NY 10801. Contact: Miss Ganz. More than 5,000 b&w photos on soccer only. Rights offered vary. Fee varies with usage.

HOWARD SOCHUREK, INC., 680 Fifth Ave., Suite 2305, New York NY 10019. Contact: Howard Sochurek. 250,000 b&w and color. "Science, travel, high technology, social concern, industrial, journalistic subjects, personalities." Fees: $50 and up, b&w; $150 and up, color.

SOIL CONSERVATION SERVICE, U.S. Department of Agriculture, Washington DC 20250. Contact: Chief, Audio-Visual Branch, Information Division. Approximately 10,000 b&w photographs covering a wide range of soil and water conservation practices, rural and suburban land, etc. No fees, but credit line requested.

SOUTH DAKOTA STATE HISTORICAL SOCIETY, Soldiers Memorial, Pierre SD 57501. Contact: Mrs. Bonnie Gardner. Photos of Indians, especially Sioux, frontiersmen, life in Dakota Territory, early mines and mining, various other frontier subjects. B&w glossy, matte. Fees: $2 for 5x7; $4 for 8x10. Credit line required.

SOVFOTO/EASTFOTO, 25 W. 43rd St., New York NY 10036. Contact: Leah Siegel. Over 900,000 photos. Photographic coverage from the Soviet Union, China and all socialist countries. B&w and color. Fees vary, depending on use. Minimum charge for b&w photos is $35 for one-time use. Minimum fee for color is $125.

HUGH SPENCER, 3711 El Ricon Way, Sacramento CA 95825. Contact: Hugh Spencer. 5,000 b&w, 3,500 35mm color. Plant and animals, biological sciences, birds, mammals, insects, reptiles, amphibians, marine life; ferns, wild flowers, trees, mosses, lichens, fungi, etc. Photomicrographs of plant tissues, sections, algae, protozoa. Offers non-exclusive rights on all subjects. Fees: "$20 to $25 for b&w; $75 to $100 for color, or will negotiate."

BOB AND IRA SPRING, 18819 Olympic View Drive, Edmonds WA 98020. Contact: Mr. Ira Spring. "40,000 color transparencies and 40,000 b&w outdoor scenes of the Pacific Northwest, Canada, Alaska, and a comprehensive collection (including industry, homes, schools, scenics) of Japan and Scandinavian countries." Offers one-time use or outright sale. Fees are "negotiable."

TOM STACK & ASSOCIATES, 2508 Timber Lane, Lindenhurst IL 60046. Contact: Tom or Irene Stack. Over 500,000 color transparencies and 100,000 b&w prints of "wildlife from around the world, flowers and plants, insects, children, people, boating and marine, scenics, farm and country, seasonal subjects, girls and nudes, romantic couples, foreign countries and foreign geographical locales, sports and hobbies, underwater, medical, churches, clouds, aerials, abstract and arty photos, demonstrations and peace marches." Offers one-time, first time or exclusive rights. Fees: $75 to $125 for one-time color use, general purposes; $15 to $35 for one-time b&w use, general purposes.

STATEN ISLAND HISTORICAL SOCIETY, 302 Center Street, Staten Island NY 10306. Contact: Mr. Raymond Fingado. 10,000 photos, "mostly Staten Island scenes, houses, landscapes. However, we own the famed Alice Austen Collection — excellent shots of New York City street scenes circa 1895 to 1910, waterfront scenes of old sailing ships, Quarantine Station, famous old steamships, immigrants, life of the society set on Staten Island." Primarily b&w. "Usually one-time publication rights for each picture." Fees are "flexible, but generally average $25 per plate — sometimes, but rarely lower and sometimes higher. Negotiated according to the nature of the project."

STEAMSHIP HISTORICAL SOCIETY OF AMERICA, 414 Pelton Ave., Staten Island NY 10310. Contact: Mrs. Alice S. Wilson, Secretary. Over 10,000 pictures of ships: ocean, coastal, rivers, etc. B&w. Charge for making selection if request includes research, $5 an hour. Contact prints, 50¢ and up. One-time reproduction fee, $5 for commercial use. "We do not have our own photographic lab and cannot handle requests from periodicals with instant deadlines. Normal service 4 to 6 weeks." Credit line required.

FRED C. STEBBINS, 2643 Maryland Ave., Topeka KS 66605. Contact: Fred or Jeanne Stebbins. 400 to 500 photos; b&w and transparencies, 2¼x2½ and 35mm. Outdoors, Kansas scenes, Midwest scenes. Offers all rights or outright sale. Fees: $25 b&w 8x10 print, $50 color transparency.

STOCK, BOSTON, INC. 739 Boylston St., Boston MA 02116. Contact: Mike Mazzaschi. Over 100,000 photos on all subjects. Edited stock. Foreign and domestic. B&w and color. All rights available; one-time use normally. Fees for reproduction vary by use. Credit line and return of photographs required.

STOCKPILE, 150 West End Ave., New York NY 10023. Contact: Miss E. L. Eade. 10,000 photos. "Scenic, religious, personalities, sports, children, snowscapes, waterscapes, coral reefs, fishing, frost pictures. craters, mountains, skiing, photos all around the world." $15 service charge, which is deductible from purchase price. "Pictures may not be held for more than 14 days after submission unless written consent is given. There is a holding charge of $25 for each week held over the period." Outright sales and one-time rights offered. Fees: b&w, $25 minimum, depending on usage. Color: frontispiece and unit openers, $150 each; for textbooks, ½ page or less, $125; for textbooks, over ½ page, $150-$175. "Photos can also be purchased outright." Credit line and return of pictures required unless purchased as an outright sale.

SUFFOLK MUSEUM AND CARRIAGE HOUSE, Stony Brook Long Island NY 11790. Contact: Librarian. Print fee: $5 for 8x10 glossy. Transparency rental: $35 for 2 months. One-time reproduction fees: $10, books; $20, commercial or advertising. Credit line required.

SWEDISH INFORMATION SERVICE, 825 Third Ave., New York NY 10022. Phone: 212-PL1-5900. Information Officer: Eva von Usslar. Photos of all Swedish subjects except tourism. About 20,000 photos; mostly b&w, some color. Free reproduction.

SWISS NATIONAL TOURIST OFFICE, 608 Fifth Ave., New York NY 10020. Contact: Walter Bruderer, Public Relations Director. No fees, but credit line and return of pictures required.

SYGMA, 322 W. 72 St., New York NY 10023. Phone: 212-595-0077. Manager: E. Laffont. 80,000 photos of international news subjects, political, social, worldwide, movies. Offers United States rights. $50 for b&w, $250 for color.

MAX THARPE PHOTO LIBRARY, Box 1508, Statesville NC 28677. Contact: Max Tharpe. "10,000 photos plus 20,000 negatives of general subjects. Human interest, children, teenagers, candid, scenic, mountains; sea pictures with mood and feeling, sensitive from real life. Some Appalachian children. B&w and color, aimed mainly for use in Christian publications." Usually one-time rights offered. Fee varies.

THEATRE COLLECTION, New York Public Library, 111 Amsterdam Ave., New York NY 10023. Theatre production shots, cinema stills, portraits of theatre personnel; circus, radio, television. This is a research collection and no material is available on loan. Only reproduction through New York Public Library Photographic Service. Print fees on request. Credit line required.

THIGPEN PHOTOGRAPHY, P.O. Box 9242, 1442 South Beltline, Mobile AL 36609. Contact: Roy M. or Virginia Galt Thigpen. About 3,000 stock photos; 1½ million job negatives. "Aerial views, architectural, historic, iron-lace, marine and yachting, sports, fishing, hunting; sea-life 'Jubilee' (exclusive coverage of this unusual phenomenon)." Rights offered "negotiable." Fees: "dependent on use."

TIME-LIFE PICTURE AGENCY, Time-Life Bldg., Rockefeller Center, Room 2858, New York NY 10020. Phone: 212-556-4800. Sales Manager: Hannah Bruce. 18 million photos of all subjects.

LESTER TINKER PHOTOGRAPHY, Route 3, Box 290, Durango CO 81301. Contact: Lester Tinker. "B&w and color photos of scenes of the west. Good selection of Rocky Mountain wildflower photos and various historic areas." Fees: $25 minimum for b&w; $100 minimum for color. Credit line requested. Except in cases of outright purchase, all transparencies must be returned.

TRANS WORLD AIRLINES, 605 Third Ave., New York NY 10016. Contact: Rose Scotti. 4,000 photos. "Jet aircraft operated by TWA — in-flight, on ground, interiors with passengers, interior and exterior terminal activities, ticket offices, all other airline activities. Scenics of most all countries served by TWA across the United States and around the world. Photos of famous personalities arriving/departing via TWA circa 1950 to 1965. Historic commercial aircraft and early airline operations." All picture requests must be submitted in writing and provide the following information: "Subject matter — be specific; specify color or b&w; specify vertical or horizontal. If you are requesting airplane pictures, specify: right-to-left, left-to-right, takeoff or landing, on ground or in the air, type of plane, if possible. Most important: Describe as best you can your subject matter to us. The more we know, the better we can help you. If we have a good grasp of your subject, we can often provide pictures that best help you illustrate it. Photos free for editorial use only. There is no charge. A credit line must be given for each picture used if TWA's name or logotype is not a logical element of the picture. Color is available on a loan basis only."

TRANSWORLD FEATURE SYNDICATE, 141 E. 44 St., New York NY 10017. Phone: 212-YU6-1505. Manager: Mary Taylor Schilling. Photos of children, special events, beauty heads, personalities, photojournalism.

TRANS-WORLD NEWS SERVICE, Box 2801, Washington DC 20013. Phone: 202-638-5568. Bureau Chief: G. Richard Ward. Director of Photography: Paul Malec. 18,000 photos of all subjects. B&w and color. Maintains considerable background motion picture footage on the Washington area as well as travel footage on a worldwide basis. One-time rights only, except on custom photos. Fee varies from $5 to $100 depending on subject and usage.

UNDERWOOD & UNDERWOOD NEWS PHOTOS INC., 3 W. 46th St., New York NY 10036. Phone: 212-JU6-5910. Manager: Milton Davidson. 5 million photos of all subjects and personalities. B&w and color. Charges for making selection and holding.

UNION PACIFIC RAILROAD, 1416 Dodge Street, Omaha NE 68179. Contact: Mr. Barry B. Combs, Director of Public Relations. 15,000 color transparencies and many b&w's on national parks and monuments, cities and regions covered by the railroad. Also photos on railroad equipment and operations, and western agriculture and industry. No fees, but credit line required.

UNITED NATIONS, UN Plaza and 42 St., New York NY 10017. Contact: Marvin Weill, Distribution Officer. More than 125,000 selected negatives on the work of the United Nations and its Specialized Agencies throughout the world. In addition to meeting coverage, illustrations primarily represent the work of the United Nations in economic and social development and human rights throughout the world. B&w and color. May not be used for advertising purposes and must be used in a United Nations context. B&w photos, if credited to the United Nations, are currently available for reproduction free of charge, although it is expected one will be instituted in the near future. There is a non-refundable service fee of $5 per color transparency. Type C prints (8x10) available for $15 each. In addition, there is a fee of $25 for each color photograph published. Unused transparencies must be returned, in usable condition, within 30 days.

UNITED PRESS INTERNATIONAL (Compix Division), 220 E. 42 St., New York NY 10017. Contact: Library Photo Sales Manager. Over 5 million negatives plus b&w print file of 2 million, plus a color transparency file of over 100,000. "Period covered (various collections) from Civil War to present time. Worldwide newsphotos, personalities, human interest and features. Photo Library contains the combined files of Acme, Newspictures, International News photos and United Press Rau Collection." B&w and color. Rights offered for editorial, advertising, and private use. "Fees range upward from a minimum of $35, depending on usage."

U.S. AIR FORCE CENTRAL STILL PHOTO DEPOSITORY (AAVA) (MAC), 1221 South Fern Street, Arlington VA 22202. Approximately 300,000 exposures with a corresponding visual print file for research use. "The collection consists of b&w and color still photos, negatives and transparencies depicting the history and progress of the U.S. Air Force. This coverage includes equipment, aircraft, personnel, missiles, officer portraits, unit insignia, etc." Fees: 75¢ to $6.50 for b&w; $1 to $17.50 for color.

U.S. COAST GUARD, Public Information Office, Governors Island, New York NY 10004. Contact: Public Information Officer. Primarily b&w photos available. Subjects: U.S. Coast Guard, search and rescue, marine safety, aids to navigation, recreational boating, bridge construction work, oil pollution abatement, lighthouses, etc. Generally no charge to qualified sources for publication. Modest charges for personal collections, etc. Credit line required.

U.S. COAST GUARD HEADQUARTERS, 400 7th St., S.W., Room 8315, Washington DC 20590. Contact: Chief, Public Information Division. 100,000 photos of "vessels, light stations, other shore stations, rescues, Alaskan Patrols, Arctic, Antarctic, boating safety, and various others illustrating the multi-roles of the Coast Guard. Mostly 8x10 b&w glossies are available; some 35mm color transparency slides. Generally no fee when photos are to be used for publication. There is a fee of $1 for each 8x10 b&w glossy for mere personal use. Color is not available for personal use. If for publication, the Coast Guard credit line must be used. The number of photos selected must be kept within reason. Photos not used are requested to be returned."

U.S. DEPARTMENT OF AGRICULTURE, Photography Division, Office of Information, Washington DC 20250. Contact: Chief, Photography Division. 500,000 or more photos; some very technical, others general. B&w and color (mostly 35mm color) on agricultural subjects. Print fee: $2.70 per 8x10, 30¢ for duplicate 35mm color. Credit line requested. "Slide sets and filmstrips ($13 and up) available on Department programs."

U.S. DEPARTMENT OF THE INTERIOR, Bureau of Reclamation, Room 7444, C St. between 18th and 19th Sts., N.W., Washington DC 20240. Contact: Commissioner, Att'n Code 910. B&w and 35mm color photos available on water-oriented recreation, municipal and industrial water supply, irrigation, agriculture, public works construction, processing of agricultural products, Western cities and scenery, hunting, fishing, camping, boating in the western U.S. Staff is too limited to permit search for supplying requests for speculative inquiries. However, we are able to respond to requests from publications and from freelancers with assignments for articles. No fees, but credit line requested and return of color pictures required.

UNIVERSITY MUSEUM, 33rd and Spruce Sts., Philadelphia PA 19104. Contact: Caroline Gordon Dosker, Assistant Registrar for Photographs. Photos on archaeological and ethnological subjects. Print fee $7.50. One-time reproduction fee: $10 for textbooks, $20 for commercial. Credit line required.

UTAH STATE HISTORICAL SOCIETY, 603 E. South Temple, Salt Lake City UT 84102. Contact: Mrs. Margaret D. Lester. B&w historic photos on everything pertaining to Utah and Mormon history; industry, architecture, biography, Indians, drama and theater, athletics, musical bands, orchestras, etc. Photos are made to order; allow 10 days to two weeks for delivery. Photos are not sent on approval; they may not be returned once they are made. Print fees: 5x7 glossy prints, $1.75; 8x10, $2.25, etc. Credit line required.

VAN CLEVE PHOTOGRAPHY, INC., P.O. Box 1366, Evanston IL 60204. Contact: Barbara Van Cleve or Linda Brown. Approximately 2½ million photos of all subjects from around the world in color and b&w. "Our color ranges from 35mm transparencies up to 8x10 color transparencies. B&w photographs are 8x10. Generally we market one-time reproduction rights." Fees: minimum $25 for b&w used editorially; minimum $50 for color used editorially.

JOHN WARHAM, Zoology Dept., University of Canterbury, Private Bag, Christchurch, New Zealand. "About 30,000 color (35mm to 5x4) and b&w photos of natural history subjects: birds, mammals, insects from Australia, New Zealand, the Subantarctic and Antarctic and U.K." Normally one-time, non-exclusive rights offered. Fees: $25 b&w, $100 plus for color.

WASHINGTON STATE HISTORICAL SOCIETY, 315 N. Stadium Way, Tacoma WA 98403. Contact: Frank Green, Librarian. 75,000 photos — "general Pacific Northwest history and scenic views; lumbering, fishing, railroads, Indians." B&w

and a large collection of glass plate negatives. Fees: $1 to $3.50; reproduction fee for purposes of publication, $25 per print. Credit line is required.

ALEX WASINSKI STUDIOS, 16 W. 22nd St., New York NY 10010. Contact: Alex Wasinski. Collection of about 1,800 scenics, cityscapes (day and night), TV and film personalities; fashion, food, moody landscapes, boats, etc. B&w and color. One-time reproduction rights. Fees for b&w begin at $200; at $250 for color. Maximum is usually $500 for 4x5 color slides.

ROBERT WEINSTEIN HISTORIC PHOTO COLLECTION, 1253 S. Stanley Ave., Los Angeles CA 90019. Contact: Robert Weinstein. Photos available on maritime (sailing vessels largely) and western Americana, late 19th century. B&w. Fees subject to mutual agreement; dependent on use.

WEST VIRGINIA DEPARTMENT OF COMMERCE, State Capitol, Charleston WV 25305. Contact: Barbara Beury McCallum. Photos on West Virginia subjects in 8x10 b&w glossy prints, color in 35mm. Also offers free information on West Virginia attractions and facilities. No fees, but credit line desired and return of color pictures required.

WESTERN HISTORY DEPARTMENT, Denver Public Library, 1357 Broadway, Denver CO 80203. Contact: Mrs. Eleanor M. Gehres, Western History Department. B&w photos on the social, economic, political, and historical developments of the U.S. west of the Mississippi River, especially the Rocky Mountain states. Large holdings of Indians, railroads, towns, outlaws, irrigation, livestock, and forts. "The Department is continually adding to the collection, increasing the holdings by several thousand annually." Prints are not available to lend for consideration purposes. The Department is willing to furnish short descriptive lists or make selections on the subjects needed. About 275,000 items in the collection. Print fees: $3.50 for 4x5 b&w; $4.50 for 8x10 b&w; $8 for 35mm color; $20 for 4x5 color. Postage and packaging are extra.

WHALING MUSEUM, 18 Johnny Cake Hill, New Bedford MA 02740. Contact: Richard C. Kugler, Director. This museum adheres to the fee schedules recommended by the Association of Art Museum Directors. Permission to reproduce Whaling Museum material will only be granted publications protected by copyright. Such copyright, where it applies to Museum material, is understood to be waived in favor of the Whaling Museum. Credit line and return of pictures required.

KEN WHITMIRE ASSOCIATES PROFESSIONAL PHOTOGRAPHY, 306 West Walnut, Yakima WA 98902. Contact: Ken Whitmire or Jharv Kasinger. Approximately 10,000 in collection. "Cascade Mountain scenes, trail riding, scenic, Mt. Rainier, Mt. Adams, fruit industry, general farming, seacoast scenes, aerial scenes, skiing, swimming, recreation, and many other photos of the Pacific Northwest. Transparencies, color negatives, and monotone negatives." Offers one-time use rights, or anything that is pre-negotiated. Fees: minimum $50 color transparencies. Return required.

WHITNEY MUSEUM OF AMERICAN ART, 945 Madison Ave., New York NY 10021. Contact: Rights and Permissions. Color transparencies. Rentals: $50 per 3 months; $10 per month thereafter. B&w photographs are also available for reproduction and reference purposes. Credit line and return of ektachromes required.

WIDE WORLD PHOTOS, INC., 50 Rockefeller Plaza, New York NY 10020. Contact: On Approval Section. About 50 million photos. "All subjects in b&w, thousands of them in color. Wide World Photos is a subsidiary of The Associated Press." Offers national, North American, and world rights. Fees start at $35.

MARGARET WILLIAMSON, 345 East 61st St., New York NY 10021. Collection of about 10,000 photos on European travel, as well as worldwide sports. B&w and color. Charges fee of $25 for one-time use of b&w; $50 for one-time use of color.

THE HENRY FRANCIS DU PONT WINTERTHUR MUSEUM, Wintherthur DE 19735. Contact: Ms. Karol A. Schmiegel, Assistant Registrar. B&w photos and color transparencies of furniture, silver, ceramics, prints, paintings, textiles, and other decorative art objects made or used in America from 1640 to 1840. Selection of photos should be made from Winterthur publications or from photo files in Registrar's Office at the Museum. Fee: $10 for b&w print; charge includes print and one-time use. Credit line required.

WOLFE WORLDWIDE FILMS, 1657 Sawtelle Blvd., Los Angeles CA 90025. Contact: Larry Benton. About 11,000 35mm color slides, "basically travel, covering what the tourist sees." Offers non-exclusive worldwide rights. Fees vary, but are dependent upon quantity used, ranging from $25 for one slide down to $5 for a large quantity for reproduction.

GERALD WOLFSOHN PHOTOGRAPHY, 9554 S. W. 82nd St., Miami FL 33173. "Slide file of western landscapes, New York scenes, South Florida scenes, Key West, gulls, and other subjects. Specialized forensic photography on request." Fees: $50 for one-time use. Credit line required.

WOLLIN STUDIOS, 151 E. Gorham St., Madison WI 53703. Contact: William Wollin. Thousands of color and b&w photos of Wisconsin buildings, activities, scenes. Rights offered: "Any desired, single to exclusive." Fees: $20 and up for b&w, $50 and up for color.

WYOMING STATE ARCHIVES AND HISTORICAL DEPARTMENT, State Office Bldg., Cheyenne WY 82001. Contact: Photographic Section. Photos on all subjects pertaining to Wyoming (towns, persons, railroads, ranches, cattle, etc.). These are all b&w glossy prints. Color prints are limited to the State and Territorial seals. Fees: $2 to $3, b&w glossy prints; $2, 35mm color slides; $4 to $8, photographs of state or territorial seal. "Special request priced according to size and work involved." Credit line required each time a photograph is used. Prices subject to change.

KATHERINE YOUNG AGENCY, 140 E. 40th St., New York NY 10016. Contact: Katherine Young. Over 20,000 general world coverage photos plus historic landmarks, architecture, scenics, people, children and family situations, monuments, American Indians; animals, flowers, churches and temples. Some historic prints of personalities as well as portraits of famous people. Offers U.S., North American and world rights; one-time use with further option. Standard American Society of Magazine Photographers fees. Special arrangements negotiable.

A Glossary of Publishing Terms

(and other expressions used in this directory).

All rights—author gives the publisher complete rights for any use of his material and forfeits any further use of that same material by himself.

Alternative culture—the life styles, politics, literature, etc., of those persons with cultural values different from the current "establishment."

Assignment—editor asks a writer to do a specific article for which he usually names a price for the completed manuscript.

B&w—abbreviation for black and white photograph.

Beat—a specific subject area regularly covered by a reporter, such as the police department or education or the environment. It can also mean a scoop on some news item.

Bimonthly—every two months. See also semimonthly.

Biweekly—every two weeks.

Blue-pencilling—editing a manuscript.

Caption—originally a title or headline over a picture but now a description of the subject matter of a photograph, including names of people where appropriate. Also called cutline.

Chapbook—a small booklet, usually paperback, of poetry, ballads or tales.

Chicago Manual of Style—a format for the typing of manuscripts as established by the University of Chicago Press (Chicago, 60637, revised 12th edition, $10).

Clean copy—free of errors, cross-outs, wrinkles, smudges.

Clippings—of news items of possible interest to trade magazine editors.

Column inch—all the type contained in one inch of a newspaper column.

Comp copy—means complimentary copy.

Contributors' copies—copies of the issues of a magazine in which an author's work appears.

Copy—manuscript material is often called copy by an editor before it is set in type.

Copy editing—editing the manuscript for grammar, punctuation and printing style as opposed to subject content.

Copyright under the present law is for 28 years with one renewal for 28 years. Since 1962, Congress has been considering revising the Copyright Law and has been automatically extending any copyrights which might have expired since 1962.

Correspondent—writer away from the home office of a newspaper or magazine who regularly provides it with copy.

Epigram—a short, witty, sometimes paradoxical saying.

Erotica—usually fiction that is sexually oriented; although it could also be art on the same theme.

Fair use—a provision of the Copyright Law that says short passages from copyrighted material may be used without infringing on the owner's rights. There are no set number of words. A good rule of thumb: "Does my use of this copyrighted material impair the market value of the original?"

Feature—an article, usually with human interest, giving the reader background information on the news. Also used by magazines to indicate a lead article or distinctive department.

Filler—a short item used by an editor to "fill" out a newspaper column or a page in a magazine. It could be a timeless news item, a joke, an anecdote, some light verse or short humor, a puzzle, etc.

First North American serial rights—the right to first publish an article, story or poem in a copyrighted newspaper or magazine in the U.S. or Canada.

Flesch formula—developed by Rudolf Flesch, attempts to determine by a mathematical formula the "readability" of writing. Its theory is based on a "write-as-you-talk" idea and the formula measures the number of syllables in a 100-word passage of writing, the number of words per sentence and the percentage of "personal" words, such as personal pronouns, names of people, spoken dialogue, etc. See Rudolf Flesch's *The Art of Readable Writing*, for more details.

Format—the shape, size and general makeup of a publication; that is, for example, 8½x11" offset printed glossy publication. May sometimes also be used to apply to the general plan of organization of an article as preferred by an editor.

Formula story—familiar theme treated in a predictable plot structure—such as boy meets girl, boy loses girl, boy gets girl.

Gagline—the caption for a cartoon, or the cover teaser line and the punchline on the inside of a studio greeting card.

Ghostwriter—a writer who puts into literary form, an article, speech, story or book based on another person's ideas or knowledge.

Glossy—a black and white photograph with a shiny surface as opposed to one with a non-shiny matte finish.

Gothic novel—one in which the central character is usually a beautiful young girl, the setting is an old mansion or castle; there is a handsome hero and a real menace, either natural or supernatural.

Honorarium—a token payment. It may be a very small amount of money, or simply a byline and copies of the publication in which your material appears.

Horizontal publication—usually a trade magazine, published for readers in a specific job function in a variety of industries. For example, *Purchasing Magazine*. (See also vertical publication.)

House organ—a company publication: internal—for employees only; external for customers, stockholders, etc., or a combination publication to serve both purposes.

Illustrations—may be photographs, old engravings, artwork. Usually paid for separately from the manuscript. See also "package sale."

Imagery—poetry that lends itself to visualization.

International Postal Reply Coupons—can be purchased at your local post office and enclosed with your letter or manuscript to a foreign publisher to cover his postage cost when replying.

Invasion of privacy—cause for suits against some writers who have written about persons (even though truthfully) without their consent.

Kill fee—a portion of the agreed-on price for a complete article that was assigned but which was subsequently cancelled.

Libel—a false accusation; or any published statement or presentation that tends to expose another to public contempt, ridicule, etc. Defenses are truth; fair comment on a matter of public interest; and privileged communication—such as a report of legal proceedings or a client's communication to his lawyer.

Little magazines—publications of limited circulation, usually on literary or political subject matter.

MLA Style Sheet—a format for the typing of manuscripts established by the Modern Language Association (62 Fifth Ave., New York NY 10011, 2nd edition $1.25).

Model release—a paper signed by the subject of a photograph (or his guardian, if a juvenile) giving the photographer permission to use the photograph, editorially or for advertising purposes or for some specific purpose as stated.

Ms—abbreviation for manuscript.

Mss—abbreviation for more than one manuscript.

Multiple submissions—some editors of non-overlapping circulation magazines, such as religious publications, are willing to look at manuscripts which have also been submitted to other editors at the same time. See individual listings for which editors these are. No multiple submissions should be made to larger markets paying good prices for original material, unless it is a query on a highly topical article requiring an immediate response and that fact is so stated in your letter.

Newsbreak—a newsworthy event or item. For example, a clipping about the opening of a new shoe store in a town might be a newsbreak of interest to a trade journal in the shoe industry. Some editors also use the word to mean funny typographical errors.

Novelette—a short novel, or a long short story; 7,000 to 15,000 words approximately.

Offprint—reprints of a published article, story, poem.

Offset—type of printing in which copy and illustrations are photographed and plates made, from which printing is done; as opposed to letterpress printing directly from type metal and engravings of illustrations.

On assignment—the editor asks you to do a specific article for which he pays an agreed-on rate.

On speculation—the editor is willing to look at an article or story manuscript but does not promise to buy it, until he reads it.

One-time rights—is a phrase used by some publications, especially newspapers, to indicate that after they use the story, the writer is free to resell it elsewhere, outside their circulation area, after they've published it. It is not the same as "first rights" since they may be buying one-time rights to a story that has already appeared in some other publication outside their area.

Outline—of a book is usually a one-page summary of its contents; often in the form of chapter headings with a descriptive sentence or two under each one to show the scope of the book.

Package sale—the editor wants to buy manuscript and photos as a "package" and pay for them in one check.

Page rate—some magazines pay for material at a fixed rate per published page, rather than so much per word.

Payment on acceptance—the editor sends you a check for your article, story or poem as soon as he reads it and decides to publish it.

Payment on publication—the editor decides to buy your material but doesn't send you a check until he publishes it.

Pen name—the use of a name other than your legal name on articles, stories, or books where you wish to remain anonymous. Simply notify your post office and bank that you are using the name so that you'll properly receive mail and/or checks in that name.

Photo story—a feature in which the emphasis is on the photographs rather than any accompanying written material.

Photocopied submissions—are acceptable to some editors instead of the author's sending his original manuscript. See also multiple submissions.

Piracy—infringement of copyright.

Pix—an abbreviation for the plural of photo.

Plagiarism—passing off as one's own, the expression of ideas, words of another.

Primary sources—of research are original letters and documents, as opposed to published articles, books, etc.

Pseudonym—see pen name.

Public domain—material which was either never copyrighted or whose copyright term has run out.

Publication not copyrighted—publication of an author's work in such a publication places it in the public domain, and it cannot subsequently be copyrighted. Poets especially should watch this point if they hope to republish their work elsewhere.

Qualified freelancer—a professional writer who has published work in the specific field in which the editor is seeking material.

Query—a letter of inquiry to an editor eliciting his interest in an article you want to write.

Reporting times—the number of days, weeks, etc., it takes an editor to report back to the author on his query or manuscript.

Reprint rights—the right to reprint an article, story, poem that originally appeared in another publication.

Retention rights—you agree to let a magazine hold your article or story or poem for a length of time to see if they can find space to publish it. Since this keeps you from selling it elsewhere (and they might subsequently decide to return it), we don't advocate this practice.

Round-up article—comments from, or interviews with, a number of celebrities or experts on a single theme.

Royalties, standard hardcover book—10% of the retail price on the first 5,000 copies sold; 12½% on the next 5,000 and 15% thereafter.

Royalties, standard mass paperback book—4 to 8% of the retail price on the first 150,000 copies sold.

Runover—the copy in the back of a magazine continued from a story or article featured in the main editorial section.

S.A.E.—self-addressed envelope.

S.A.S.E.—self-addressed, stamped envelope.

Sample copies—will be sent free to writers by some editors; others require sample copy price and/or postage. See individual listings.

Second serial rights—publication in a newspaper or magazine after the material has already appeared elsewhere. Usually used to refer to the sale of a part of a book to a newspaper or magazine after the book has been published, whether or not there was any first serial publication.

Semimonthly—twice a month.

Semiweekly—twice a week.

Serial—published periodically, such as a newspaper or magazine.

Shelter books—magazines that concentrate on home decoration.

Short-short story—is usually from 500 to 2,000 words.

Short story—averages 2,000 to 3,500 words.

Simultaneous submissions—submissions of the same article, story or poem to smaller magazines with non-competing circulations and whose editors have agreed to accept same.

Slant—the approach of a story or article so as to appeal to the readers of a specific magazine. Does, for example, this magazine always like stories with an upbeat ending? Or that one like articles aimed only at the blue-collar worker?

Slanted—written in such a way to appeal to a particular group of readers.

Slides—usually called transparencies by editors looking for color photographs.

Special 4th class rate—manuscripts—can be used by writers submitting articles, stories, books to publishers. Rate is 18¢ for first pound, 8¢ each additional pound with an extra 10¢ if first class letter is enclosed. (These are rates for mailing in U.S. Consult Post Office for Special Foreign Rates.) Be sure to add "Return Postage Guaranteed" on your outside envelope; otherwise Post Office is not obliged to return to you if for some reason package is undeliverable.

Speculation—the editor agrees to look at the author's manuscript but doesn't promise to buy it until he reads it.

Stringer—a writer who submits material to a magazine or newspaper from a specific geographical location.

Style—the way in which something is written—short, punchy sentences or flowing, narrative description or heavy use of quotes or dialogue.

Subsidiary rights—all those rights, other than book publishing rights included in a book contract—such as paperback, book club, movie rights, etc.

Subsidy publisher—a book publisher who charges the author for the cost to typeset and print his book, the jacket, etc., as opposed to a royalty publisher which pays the author.

Syndication rights—a book publisher may sell the rights to a newspaper syndicate to print a book in installments in one or more newspapers.

Tabloids—newspaper format publication on about half the size of the regular newspaper page. A group of publications in this format on major newsstands, such as *National Enquirer*.

Tagline—an editorial comment on a filler, such as those in *The New Yorker*. In some contexts, it is also used to mean a descriptive phrase associated with a certain person, such as newscaster John Cameron Swayze's "Glad we could get together ..."

Tearsheet—pages from a magazine or newspaper containing your printed story or article or poem.

Think piece—a magazine article that has an intellectual, philosophical, provocative approach to its subject.

Third world—usually refers to the undeveloped countries of Asia and Africa, but used by some to mean underprivileged or underdeveloped minorities anywhere in the world.

Thirty—usually shown as -30- means "the end" on newspaper copy. It is a remainder from the days when newspaper telegraphers used it as a symbol for the end of a story transmission.

Topical—very timely, of current news interest.

Transparencies—positive color slides; not color prints.

Uncopyrighted publication—such as most newspapers or small poetry and literary magazines. Publication of an author's work in such publications puts it in the public domain.

Unsolicited manuscripts—a story or article or poem or book that an editor did not specifically ask to see, as opposed to one he did write the author and ask for.

Vanguard—in the forefront.

Vanity publisher—same as subsidy publisher. One who publishes books for an author who pays the production cost himself.

Vertical publication—a publication for all the people in a variety of job functions within the same industry, such as *Aviation Week and Space Technology* or *Hospitals*.

Vignette—a brief scene offering the reader a flash of illumination about a character as opposed to a more formal story with a beginning, middle and end.

INDEX